The

Bessie Parmet Kannerstein '32

Memorial Fund

Established by

MR. JOSEPH PARMET

for the purchase of

REFERENCE BOOKS

for the

CEDAR CREST COLLEGE

LIBRARY

Encyclopedia of World Literature in the 20th Century

Encyclopedia of
World Literature
in the 20th
Century

VOLUME 4: S–Z
Indexes

ST. JAMES PRESS

Steven R. Serafin, *General Editor*

Laura Standley Berger, *Project Coordinator*

Joann Cerrito, Dave Collins, Nicolet V. Elert,
Miranda Ferrara, Kristin Hart, Margaret Mazurkiewicz, Michael J. Tyrkus
St. James Press Staff

Peter M. Gareffa, *Managing Editor, St. James Press*

Mary Beth Trimper, *Production Director*
Deborah Milliken, *Production Assistant*

Cynthia Baldwin, *Product Design Manager*
Eric Johnson, *Art Director*
Pamela A. Reed, *Photography Coordinator*
Randy Bassett, *Image Database Supervisor*
Robert Duncan, Mike Logusz, *Imaging Specialists*

Susan Trosky, *Permissions Manager*
Kelly A. Quin, *Permissons Associate*

Encyclopedia of World Literature / Steven R. Serafin, general editor. — 3rd ed.
　　　　p.　　　　cm.
　　　　Includes bibliographical references and index.
　　　　Contents: v. 1. A-D — v. 2. E-K — v. 3. L-R — v. 4. S-Z and indexes
　　　　ISBN 1-55862-373-6 (set). — ISBN 1-55862-374-4 (v. 1). — ISBN 1-55862-375-2 (v. 2). — ISBN 1-55862-376-0 (v. 3). — ISBN 1-55862-377-9 (v. 4).
　　　　1. Literature, Modern—20th century—Bio-bibliography.
　　　　2. Literature, Modern—20th century—Encyclopedias　I. Serafin, Steven.
　　　　PN771.E5　1998
　　　　803—dc21　　　　　　　　　　　　　　　　　　　　　　　　　　　　　　　98-40374
　　　CIP

Printed in the United States of America
St. James Press is an imprint of Gale

10 9 8 7 6 5 4 3 2

BOARD OF ADVISORS

v

PERIODICALS USED

A&E	Anglistik & Englischunterricht	*AL*	American Literature
AAS	Asian and African Studies		Alaluz: Revista de Poesia, Narracion y Ensayo
AAW	Afro-Asian Writing	*AL&C*	African Languages & Cultures
ABnG	Amsterdamer Beiträe zur Neueren Germanistik	*ALEC*	Anales de la Literatura Española Contemporánea
ACLALSB	ACLALS Bulletin	*ALHis*	Anales de Literatura Hispanoamericana
	Actualidades: Consejo Nacional de la Cultura, Centro de Estudios Latinoamericanos "Romulo Gallegos"/Caracas, Venezuela	*ALR*	American Literary Realism, 1870-1910
		ALS	Australian Literary Studies
ADP	Arbeiten zur deutschen Philologie	*ALT*	African Literature Today
	Africa: Rivista Trimestrale di Studi e Documentazione	*AmerD*	American Drama
AfricaL	Africa: Journal of the International African Institute/Revue de l'Institut Africain International	*AmerP*	American Poetry
		AmerT	American Theatre
AfricaR	Africa Report	*AmLH*	American Literary History
AfrLJ	African Journal	*AmRev*	Americas Review
AfrLS	African Language Studies	*AN*	Acta Neophilologica
AfrSR	African Studies Review	*ANP*	Anales de la Narrative Española Contemporánea
AGald	Anales Galdosianos		
AGR	American-German Review	*AnUs*	Annual of Urdu Studies
AHR	Afro-Hispanic Review	*ANZSC*	Australian and New Zealand Studies in Canada
AICRJ	American Indian Culture and Research Journal	*APR*	American Poetry Review
AIPHOS	Annuaire de l'Institut de Philologie et d'Histoire Orientales et Slaves	*AQ*	American Quarterly
		AR	Antioch Review
AIQ	American Indian Quarterly		Arabica: Revue d'Études Arabes
AJFS	Australian Journal of French Studies	*ARD*	African Research and Documentation
AJPh	American Journal of Philology	*ArielE*	Ariel: A Review of International English Literature
AJS	American Journal of Semiotics		

ArielK	Ariel
ArO	Archív Orientální: Quarterly Journal of African, Asian, and Latin-American Studies
ArQ	Arizona Quarterly
ASch	American Scholar
ASEER	American Slavic and East European Review
	Asemka: A Literary Journal of the University of Cape Coast
ASPAC	Asian Pacific Quarterly of Cultural and Social Affairs Quarterly
ASQ	Arab Studies Quarterly
ASR	American Scandinavian Review
	Atenea: Revista de Ciencia, Arte y Literatura de la Universidad de Concepción
AUB-LLR	Analele Universității, București, Limbă și Litereră Română
AUC	Anales de la Universidad de Chile
AUMLA	AUMLA: Journal of the Australasian Universities Language and Literature Association—A Journal of Literary Criticism and Linguistics
AWR	Anglo-Welsh Review
BA	Books Abroad
BAALE	Bulletin of the Association for African Literature in English
BAC	Boletín de la Academia Colombiana
BALF	Black American Literature Forum
BalSt	Balkan Studies
BB	Bulletin of Bibliography
BeneN	Bete Noire

BEPIF	Bulletin des Etudes Portugaises et Brésiliennes
BF	Books from Finland
BHe	Baltische Hefte
BHS	Bulletin of Hispanic Studies
BlackI	Black Images: A Critical Quarterly on Black Arts and Culture
BMMLA	Bulletin of the Midwest Modern Language Association
BO	Black Orpheus
Boundary	Boundary 2: A Journal of Postmodern Literature and Culture
BRMMLA	Rocky Mountain Review of Language and Literature
BRP	Beiträge zur Romanischen Philologie
BR/RB	Bilingual Review/La Revista Bilingüe
BSIS	Bulletin of the Society for Italian Studies
BSS	Bulletin of Spanish Studies
BSUF	Ball State University Forum
BUJ	Boston University Journal
BuR	Bucknell Review
BW	Black World
CA	Cuadernos Americanos
CALC	Cahiers Algériens de Littérature Comparée
	Callaloo: A Black South Journal of Arts and Letters
CalSS	California Slavic Studies
CanL	Canadian Literature
CARHS	Canadian-American Review of Hungarian Studies
CarQ	Caribbean Quarterly

CasaA	Casa de las Américas	*CJItS*	Canadian Journal of Italian Studies
CAsJ	Central Asiatic Journal	*CL*	Comparative Literature
CASS	Canadian-American Slavic Studies	*CLAJ*	College Language Association Journal
CatR	Catalan Review	*CLAQ*	Children's Literature Association Quarterly
CBAA	Current Bibliography on African Affairs		
CBC	Cesare Barbieri Courier	*CLC*	Columbia Library Columns
CCrit	Comparative Criticism	*CLEAR*	Chinese Literature: Essays, Articles, Reviews
CCur	Cross Currents: A Yearbook of Central European Culture	*CLQ*	Colby Library Quarterly
		CLS	Comparative Literature Studies
CE	College English	*CML*	Classical and Modern Literature
CE&S	Commonwealth Essays and Studies	*CMo*	Creative Moment
CEA	CEA Critic	*CMRS*	Cashiers du Monde Russe et Soviétique
CEAfr	Cahiers d'Études Africaines	*CNIE*	Commonwealth Novel in English
CelfanR	Revue Celfan/Celfan Review	*CNLR*	CNL/Quarterly World Report
CentR	Centennial Review	*CollG*	Colloquia Germanica
CFM	Canadian Fiction Magazine	*Colóquio*	Colóquio/Letras
CFR	Canadian Fiction Review	*ColQ*	Colorado Quarterly
CFrC	Contemporary French Civilization	*CompD*	Comparative Drama
CH	Crítica Hispánica	*ComQ*	Commonwealth Quarterly
CHA	Cuadernos Hispanoamericanos		Confluencia: Revista Hispánica de Cultura y Literatura
	Chasqui: Revista de Literatura Latinoamericana	*ConL*	Contemporary Literature
ChicL	Chicano Literature	*ContempR*	Contemporary Review
ChinL	Chinese Literature	*CP*	Concerning Poetry
ChiR	Chicago Review	*CQ*	Cambridge Quarterly
CJAS	Canadian Journal of African Studies	*CR*	Critical Review
CJLACS	Canadian Journal of Latin American and Caribbean Studies	*CRCL*	Canadian Review of Comparative Literature
CJIS	Canadian Journal of Irish Studies		

CREL	Cahiers Roumains d'Études Littéraires: Revue Trimestrielle de Critique, d'Esthétique et d'Histoire Littéraires
CRevAS	Canadian Review of American Studies
Crit	Critique: Studies in Modern Fiction
CritI	Critical Inquiry
	Critique: Revue Générale des Publications Françaises et Étrangères
CritQ	Critical Quarterly
CS	Cahiers du Sud
CSP	Canadian Slavonic Papers
CSR	Christian Scholar's Review
CSS	Canadian Slavic Studies
CTR	Canadian Theatre Review
CV II	Contemporary Verse II
Dada	Dada/Surrealism
DASDJ	Deutsche Akademie für Sprache und Dichtung, Darmstadt, Jahrbuch
DeltaES	Delta: Revue du Centre d'Études et de Recherche sur les Écrivains du Sud aux États-Unis
	Diacritics: A Review of Contemporary Criticism
	Dimension: Contemporary German Arts and Letters
DLB	Dictionary of Literary Biography
DLit	Discurso Literario: Revista de Temas Hispánicos
DQ	Denver Quarterly
DQR	Dutch Quarterly Review of Anglo-American Letters
DR	Dalhousie Review

DSt	Deutsche Studien
DU	Der Deutschunterricht: Beiträge zu Seiner Praxis und Wissenschaftlichen Grundlegung
DUJ	Durham University Journal
DUR	Dublin University Review
DutchS	Dutch Studies
DVLJ	Deutsche Vierteljahrsschrift für Literaturwissenschaft und Geistesgeschichte
EA	Études Anglaises
	Eco: Revista de la Cultura de Occidente
ECr	L'Esprit Créateur
ECW	Essays on Canadian Writing
	Edebiyat: A Journal of Middle Eastern Literatures
EF	Études Françaises
EG	Études Germaniques
EI	Études Irlandaises
EinA	English in Africa
Éire	Éire-Ireland: A Journal of Irish Studies
EJ	English Journal
ELH	English Literary History (formerly Journal of English Literary History)
ELit	Études Littéraires
ELT	English Literature in Transition
ELWIU	Essays in Literature
	English: The Journal of the English Association
Ensayistas	Los Ensayistas: Georgia Series on Hispanic Thought

ES	English Studies
ESA	English Studies in Africa
ESC	English Studies in Canada
	Escritura: Revista de Teoría y Crítica Literarias
ETJ	Educational Theatre Journal
ETR	East Turkic Review
Evergreen	Evergreen Review
ExTL	Explicación de Textos Literarios
FE	France-Eurafrique
FI	Forum Italicum
FLS	French Literature Series
FMLS	Forum for Modern Language Studies
	Folio: Essays on Foreign Languages and Literatures
FR	French Review
FS	French Studies
Francofonia	Studi e Ricerche Sulle Letterature di Lingua Francese
FrF	French Forum
	Frontiers: A Journal of Women Studies
FSt	Feminist Studies
GaR	Georgia Review
GerSR	German Studies Review
GettR	Gettysburg Review
GL&L	German Life and Letters
GN	Germanic Notes
GQ	German Quarterly
GR	Germanic Review

GRM	Germanisch-Romanische Monatsschrift
GSlav	Germano-Slavica: A Canadian Journal of Germanic and Slavic Comparative Studies
HAHR	Hispanic American Historical Review
HAR	Hebrew Annual Review
HC	Hollins Critic
HisJ	Hispanic Journal
Hispam	Hispamérica: Revista de Literatura
	Hispania: A Journal Devoted to the Interests of the Teaching of Spanish and Portuguese
Hispano	Hispanófila
HJAS	Harvard Journal of Asiatic Studies
	Horizontes: Revista de la Universidad Católica de Puerto Rico
HR	Hispanic Review
HSL	University of Hartford Studies in Literature
HSS	Harvard Slavic Studies
HudR	Hudson Review
HungQ	Hungarian Quarterly
I&FR	Indian & Foreign Review
I&L	Ideologies and Literature
Ibero	Iberoromania
	IBLA: Revue de l'Institut des Belles Lettres Arabes
IBSB	International P.E.N. Bulletin of Selected Books
IC	Islamic Culture
IFR	International Fiction Review
IFRev	International Folklore Review

IJMES	International Journal of Middle East Studies	*JARCE*	Journal of the American Research Center in Egypt
IJSLP	International Journal of Slavic Linguistics and Poetics	*JASO*	Journal of the Anthropological Society of Oxford
	Imagine: International Chicano Poetry Journal	*JASt*	Journal of Asian Studies
IndL	Indian Literature	*JATJ*	Journal of the Association of Teachers of Japanese
IndSch	Indian Scholar	*JBalS*	Journal of Baltic Studies
	Inti: Revista de Literatura Hispánica	*JBlS*	Journal of Black Studies
IonC	Index on Censorship	*JBRS*	Journal of the Burma Research Society
IowaR	Iowa Review	*JByelS*	Journal of Byelorussian Studies
IQ	Italian Quarterly	*JCF*	Journal of Canadian Fiction
IranS	Iranian Studies: Journal of the Society for Iranian Studies	*JCH*	Journal of Contemporary History
IRLI	Italianistica: Rivista di Letteratura Italiana	*JCL*	Journal of Commonwealth Literature
IS	Italian Studies	*JCLTA*	Journal of the Chinese Language Teachers Association
ItalAm	Italian Americana	*JCS*	Journal of Croatian Studies
Italianist	The Italianist: Journal of the Department of Italian Studies, University of Reading	*JCSR*	Journal of Canadian Studies/Revue d'Études Canadiennes
ItC	Italian Culture	*JCSt*	Journal of Caribbean Studies
IUR	Irish University Review: A Journal of Irish Studies	*JEGP*	Journal of English and Germanic Philology
IWT	Indian Writing Today	*JES*	Journal of European Studies
JAAC	Journal of Aesthetics and Art Criticism	*JEthS*	Journal of Ethnic Studies
JAC	Journal of American Culture	*JFCS*	Journal of Feminist Cultural Studies
JAOS	Journal of the American Oriental Society	*JGE*	Journal of General Education
JapQ	Japan Quarterly	*JHD*	Journal of the Hellenic Diaspora
JAPS	Journal of the American Portuguese Society	*JHI*	Journal of History of Ideas
		JIAS	Journal of Inter-American Studies
		JIL	Journal of Irish Literature
JArabL	Journal of Arabic Literature	*JIWE*	Journal of Indian Writing in English

JJS	Journal of Japanese Studies		*L&P*	Literature and Psychology
JLSTL	Journal of Literary Studies		*LAAW*	Lotus: Afro-Asian Writing
JMAF	Journal of Modern African Studies		*LALR*	Latin American Literary Review
JNALA	Journal of the New African Literature and the Arts			Landfall: A New Zealand Quarterly
JNT	Journal of Narrative Technique		*Lang&S*	Language and Style
JNZL	Journal of New Zealand Literature		*LangF*	Language Forum
JOL	Journal of Oriental Literature		*LangQ*	USF Language Quarterly
JPalS	Journal of Palestinian Studies		*LARR*	Latin America Research Review
JPC	Journal of Popular Culture		*LATR*	Latin American Theatre Review
JPrag	Journal of Pragmatics		*LBR*	Luso-Brazilian Review
JRS	Journal of Russian Studies		*LCUT*	Library Chronicle of the University of Texas
JSoAL	Journal of South Asian Literature		*LE&W*	Literature East and West
JSS	Journal of Semitic Studies		*LHY*	Literary Half-Yearly
JSSB	Journal of the Siam Society		*LitG*	Literary Griot
JSSE	Journal of the Short Story in English		*LitR*	Literary Review
JSSTC	Journal of Spanish Studies: Twentieth Century			Lituanus: Baltic States Quarterly of Arts & Sciences
JTamS	Journal of Tamil Studies		*LJ*	Library Journal
JUkGS	Journal of Ukrainian Graduate Studies		*LJGG*	Literaturwissenschaftliches Jahrbuch im Auftrage der Görres-Gesellschaft
JUkS	Journal of Ukrainian Studies			
JWIL	Journal of West Indian Literature		*LM*	London Magazine
KanQ	Kansas Quarterly		*LOS*	Literary Onomastics Studies
KFLQ	Kentucky Foreign Language Quarterly		*LPer*	Literature in Performance: A Journal of Literary and Performing Art
KFQ	Keystone Folklore			
	Kiabàrà: Journal of the Humanities		*LQ*	Literary Quarterly
KR	Kenyon Review		*LuK*	Literatur und Kritik
KRQ	Romance Quarterly (formerly Kentucky Romance Quarterly)		*LWU*	Literatur in Wissenschaft und Unterricht
			MAL	Modern Austrian Literature

MAPS	Memoirs of the American Philosophical Society		*MLS*	Modern Language Studies
MarkhamR	Markham Review		*MMisc*	Midwestern Miscellany
MAWAR	MAWA Review		*MN*	Monumenta Nipponica
MBL	Modern Black Literature		*ModA*	Modern Age
MCL	Modern Chinese Literature			Monatshefte: Für Deutschen Unterricht, Deutsche Sprache und Literatur
MD	Modern Drama			Mosaic: A Journal for the Interdisciplinary Study of Literature
MEF	Middle Eastern Forum			
MEJ	Middle East Journal		*MP*	Modern Philology: A Journal Devoted to Research in Medieval and Modern Literature
MelbSS	Melbourne Slavonic & East European Studies (formerly Melbourne Slavonic Studies)		*MPS*	Modern Poetry Studies
	Merkur: Deutsche Zeitschrift für europäisches Denken		*MQ*	Midwest Quarterly: A Journal of Contemporary Thought
MES	Middle Eastern Studies		*MQR*	Michigan Quarterly Review
MFS	Modern Fiction Studies		*MR*	Massachusetts Review: A Quarterly of Literature, the Arts and Public Affairs
MGS	Michigan Germanic Studies		*MRRM*	Monographic Review/Revista Monográfica
MHL	Modern Hebrew Literature		*MSFO*	Mémoires de la Société Finno-Ougrienne
MHRev	Malahat Review		*MSpr*	Moderna Språk
MichA	Michigan Academician: Papers of the Michigan Academy of Science, Arts, and Letters		*MuK*	Maske und Kothurn
			MV	Minority Voices: An Interdisciplinary Journal of Literature and the Arts
MinnR	Minnesota Review		*MW*	Muslim World
MissQ	Mississippi Quarterly		*NAR*	North American Review
ML	Modern Languages		*NConL*	Notes on Contemporary Literature
MLF	Modern Language Forum		*NDEJ*	Notre Dame English Journal
MLJ	Modern Language Journal		*NDH*	Neue Deutsche Hefte
MLN	Modern Language Notes		*NDL*	Neue Deutsche Literatur
MLQ	Modern Language Quarterly			Neohelicon: Acta Comparationis Litterarum Universarum
MLR	Modern Language Review			

Neophil	Neophilologus
NEQ	New England Quarterly
NER	New England Review and Bread Loaf Quarterly
NewA	New African
NewC	New Criterion
NewL	New Letters: A Magazine of Fine Writing
NewR	New Republic
NewS	New Scholar
NFS	Nottingham French Studies
NGC	New German Critique: An Interdisciplinary Journal of German Studies
NGS	New German Studies
NHQ	New Hungarian Quarterly
NL	Nouvelles Littéraires
NLH	New Literary History: A Journal of Theory and Interpretation
NLitsR	New Literatures Review
NMAL	Notes on Modern American Literature
NME	New Middle East
NMQ	New Mexico Quarterly
NorS	Northern Studies
NorthwestR	Northwest Review
	Novel: A Forum on Fiction
NR	New Republic
NRF	Nouvelle Revue Française
NRs	Neue Rundschau
NS	New Statesman

NTQ	New Theatre Quarterly
NWR	Northwest Review
NYHT	New York Herald Tribune
NYHTBR	New York Herald Tribune Books Review
NYLF	New York Literary Forum
NYRB	New York Review of Books
NYT	New York Times
NYTBR	New York Times Book Review
NYTMag	New York Times Magazine
NZSJ	New Zealand Slavonic Journal
O&C	Œuvres & Critiques
	Obsidian II: Black Literature in Review
ÖGL	Österreich in Geschichte und Literatur
OJES	Osmania Journal of English Studies
OL	Orbis Litterarum
OLR	Oxford Literary Review
OnsE	One Erfdeel: Algemeen-Nederlands Tweemaandelijks Cultureel Tijdschrift
OntarioR	Ontario Review
OSP	Oxford Slavonic Papers
P&R	Philosophy and Rhetoric
PA	Présence Africaine
PAJ	Pan-African Journal
PakR	Pakistan Review
	Paragraph: The Journal of the Modern Critical Theory Group
	Parnassus: Poetry in Review
PCL	Perspectives on Contemporary Literature

PCLS	Proceedings of the Comparative Literature Symposium	*PSMLAB*	Pennsylvania State Modern Language Association Bulletin
PCP	Pacific Coast Philology	*PStud*	Portuguese Studies
PEGS	Publications of the English Goethe Society	*QI*	Quaderni d'Italianistica
PFr	Présence Francophone: Revue internationale de langue et de littérature	*QIA*	Quaderni Ibero-Americani
	Plaza: Revista de Literatura	*QL*	La Quinzaine Littéraire
PLL	Papers on Language and Literature	*QQ*	Queen's Quarterly
	Ploughshares	*QRFS*	Quarterly Review of Film Studies
	Plural: Revista Cultural de Excelsior	*QRL*	Quarterly Review of Literature
	PMLA: Publications of the Modern Language Association of America		Quimera: Revista de Literatura
PoetryR	Poetry Review	*RaJAH*	Rackham Journal of the Arts and Humanities
PolP	Polish Perspectives	*RAL*	Research in Africa Literatures
PolR	Polish Review	*RALS*	Resources for American Literary Study
POMPA	Publications of the Mississippi Philological Association	*RCB*	Revista de Cultura Brasileña
PoT	Poetics Today	*RCEH*	Revista Canadiense de Estudios Hispánicos
PPNCFL	Proceedings of the Pacific Northwest Conference on Foreign Languages	*RCF*	Review of Contemporary Fiction
PQ	Philological Quarterly	*RChL*	Revista Chilena de Literatura
PQM	Pacific Quarterly (Moana)	*RCL*	Revue de Littérature Comparée
PR	Partisan Review	*RCLL*	Revista de Crítica Literaria Latinoamericana
PRev	Poetry Review	*RC-R*	Revista Chicano-Riqueña
	Prismal/Cabral: Revista de Literatura Hispánica/Caderno Afro-Brasileiro Asiático Lusitano	*RCSCSPL*	Russian, Croatian and Serbian, Czech and Slovak, Polish Literature
PRL	Puerto Rican Literature	*REH*	Revista de Estadios Hispánicos
PrS	Prairie Schooner	*RELC*	RELC Journal
PSA	Papeles de Son Armandans		Renascence: Essays on Value in Literature
			Renditions: A Chinese-English Translation Magazine
PSM	Philippine Studies	*RevB*	Revista Bilingüe

RevI	Revista/Review Interamericana		*RRWC*	Renaissance and Renascences in Western Literature
	Review: Latin American Literature and Arts		*RS*	Research Studies
RG	Revue Générale		*RSI*	Revista Storica Italiani
RH	Revue Hebdomaire		*RUO*	Revue de l'Université d'Ottawa
RHL	Revue d'Histoire Littéraire de la France		*RUS*	Rice University Studies
RHLQCF	Revue d'Histoire Littéraire du Québec et du Canada Français		*RusL*	Russian Literature
			RusR	Russian Review
RHM	Revista Hispánica Moderna		*SAB*	South Atlantic Bulletin
RI	Revista Iberoamericana		*SAD*	Studies in American Drama
RIB	Revista Interamericana de Bibliografía/ Inter-American Review of Bibliography		*SAF*	Studies in American Fiction
			SAIL	Studies in American Indian Literature
RLA	Romance Language Annual		*SAJL*	Studies in American Jewish Literature
RLC	Revue de Littérature Comparée		*SAQ*	South Atlantic Quarterly
RLJ	Russian Language Journal		*SatR*	Saturday Review
RLI	Rassegna della Letteratura Italiana		*SBL*	Studies in Black Literature
RLMC	Rivista di Letterature Moderne e Comparate		*SBR*	Swedish Book Review
			Scan	Scandinavica
RLT	Russian Literature Triquarterly		*ScanR*	Scandinavian Review
RLV	Revue des Langues Vivantes		*SCB*	South Central Bulletin
RMS	Renaissance & Modern Studies		*SchM*	Schweizer Monatshefte
RNL	Review of National Literatures		*SCL*	Studies in Canadian Literature
RO	Revista de Occidente		*ScotIR*	Scottish International Review
ROMM	Revue de l'Occident Musulman et de la Méditerranée		*ScotR*	Scottish Review
			SCR	South Carolina Review
RomN	Romance Notes		*SDR*	South Dakota Review
RoR	Romanian Review		*SEACS*	South East Asian Cultural Studies
RPh	Romance Philology			
RR	Romanic Review		*SEEA*	Slavic and East European Arts

SEEJ	Slavic and East European Journal		*SSF*	Studies in Short Fiction
SEER	Slavonic and East European Review		*SSl*	Scando-Slavica
SFC	Science Fiction Chronicle		*SSL*	Studies in Scottish Literature
SFR	Stanford French Review		*SSLit*	Soviet Studies in Literature
SHEH	Stanford Honors Essays in the Humanities		*SSMLN*	Society for the Study of Midwestern Literature Newsletter
SHR	Southern Humanities Review		*SSR*	Scottish Slavonic Review
Siglo	Siglo XX/20th Century		*StBL*	Studies in Black Literature
	Signs: Journal of Women in Culture and Society		*StIsl*	Studia Islamica
SlavonicR	Slavonic Review		*StTCL*	Studies in Twentieth Century Literature
SlavR	Slavic Review			Studies: An Irish Quarterly Review
SLitI	Studies in the Literary Imagination			SubStance: A Review of Theory and Literary Criticism
SLJ	Southern Literary Journal		*SuF*	Sinn und Form
	Slovo: Časopis Staroslavenskog Zavoda u Zagrebu		*Sur*	Revista Sur
SlovLit	Slovenská Literatúra: Revue Pre Literárnu Vedu		*SUS*	Susquehanna University Studies
SlovS	Slovene Studies		*SWR*	Southwest Review
SNNTS	Studies in the Novel		*SXX*	Secolul XX
SoQ	Southern Quarterly			Symposium: A Quarterly Journal in Modern Foreign Literatures
SoR	Southern Review (Baton Rouge, LA)		*T&K*	Text & Kontext
SoRA	Southern Review (Adelaide, Australia)		*TA*	Theatre Annual
	Southerly: A Review of Australian Literature		*TAH*	The American Hispanist
SovL	Soviet Literature		*TamR*	Tamarack Review
SPFA	Bulletin de la Société des Professeurs Français en Amérique		*TC*	Twentieth Century
SPHQ	Swedish Pioneer Historical Quarterly		*TCL*	Twentieth Century Literature
SR	Sewanee Review		*TCrit*	Texto Crítico
			TDR	Tulane Drama Review/The Drama Review
SS	Scandinavian Studies		*TheatreQ*	Theatre Quarterly

	Theoria: A Journal of Studies in the Arts, Humanities and Social Sciences	*VLang*	Visible Language
TJ	Theatre Journal	*VQR*	Virginia Quarterly Review
TkR	Tamkang Review	*W&L*	Women & Literature
TLS	[London] Times Literary Supplement	*WAJML*	West African Journal of Modern Languages
TM	Temps Modernes	*WAL*	Western American Literature
TQ	Texas Quarterly	*WascanaR*	Wascana Review
Transatlantic	Transatlantic Review	*WB*	Weimarer Beiträge
TRev	Translation Review	*WCR*	West Coast Review
TriQ	TriQuarterly		Westerly: A Quarterly Review
TSAR	Toronto South Asian Review	*WHR*	Western Humanities Review
TSLL	Texas Studies in Literature and Language	*WI*	Die Welt dea Islams
TSWL	Tulsa Studies in Women's Literature	*WIRS*	Western Illinois Regional Studies
TuK	Text + Kritik: Zeitschrift für Literatur	*WLT*	World Literature Today
TWQ	Third World Quarterly	*WLWE*	World Literature Written in English
TxSE	Texas Studies in English	*WR*	Western Review
UDQ	Denver Quarterly	*WS*	Women's Studies: An Interdisciplinary Journal
UDR	University of Dayton Review	*WSCL*	Wisconsin Studies in Contemporary Literature
UES	Unisa English Studies		
UHSL	University of Hartford Studies in Literature	*WSJ*	Wiener Slavistisches Jahrbuch
UkrR	Ukrainian Review: A Quarterly Magazine Devoted to the Study of the Ukraine	*WSl*	Die Welt der Slaven
		WSlA	Wiener Slawistischer Almanach
UQ	Ukrainian Quarterly: Journal of East European and Asian Affairs	*WVUPP*	West Virginia University Philological Papers
UR	University Review	*WZ*	Wort in de Zeit
UTQ	University of Toronto Quarterly	*WZUG*	Wissenschaftliche Zeitschrift der Ernst Moritz Arndt-Universität Greifswald
UWR	University of Windsor Review (Windsor, Ontario)		
V&I	Voix et Images: Littérature Québécoise	*YCC*	Yearbook of Comparative Criticism

YCGL	Yearbook of Comparative and General Literature	*Y/T*	Yale/Thestre
YES	Yearbook of English Studies	*ZAA*	Zeitschrift für Anglistik und Amerikanistik
YFS	Yale French Studies	*ZS*	Zeitschrift für Slawistik
YItS	Yale Italian Studies	*ZSP*	Zeitschrift für Slavische Philologie
YR	Yale Review		

ACKNOWLEDGMENTS

For permission to reproduce the illustrations in this edition of the *Encyclopedia of World Literature in the 20th Century,* the publisher is indebted to the following:

Abe, Kōbō, photograph by Jerry Bauer. © Jerry Bauer. Reproduced by permission.—Achebe, Chinua, photograph. AP/Wide World Photos. Reproduced by permission.—Adams, Henry S., photograph. AP/Wide World Photos. Reproduced by permission.—Adorno, Theodore W., photograph. Archive Photos, Inc. Reproduced by permission.—Agee, James, photograph. The Library of Congress.—Akhmatova, Anna Andreevna, photograph. The Library of Congress.—Albee, Edward, photograph. The Library of Congress.—Alegría, Fernando, photograph. Arte Publico Press Archives, University of Houston. Reproduced by permission.—Aleixandre, Vicente, photograph. AP/Wide World Photos. Reproduced by permission.—Algren, Nelson, photograph. The Library of Congress.—Allende, Isabel, photograph. AP/Wide World Photos. Reproduced by permission.—Amado, Jorge, photograph. AP/Wide World Photos. Reproduced by permission.—Amichai, Yehuda, photograph by John Reeves. Reproduced by permission.—Amis, Kingsley, photograph. AP/Wide World Photos. Reproduced by permission.—Anderson, Sherwood, photograph. Archive Photos, Inc. Reproduced by permission.—Angelou, Maya, photograph. AP/Wide World Photos. Reproduced by permission.—Anouilh, Jean, photograph. AP/Wide World Photos. Reproduced by permission.—Aragon, Louis, photograph. The Library of Congress.—Ashbery, John, photograph. AP/Wide World Photos. Reproduced by permission.—Atwood, Margaret, photograph. The Library of Congress.—Auchincloss, Louis, photograph by Jerry Bauer. © Jerry Bauer. Reproduced by permission.—Auden, W. H., photograph. Corbis-Bettmann. Reproduced by permission.—Audiberti, Jacques, photograph. AP/Wide World Photos. Reproduced by permission.—Azuela, Mariano, photograph. The Library of Congress.—Baraka, Imamu Amiri (LeRoi Jones), photograph. Corbis-Bettmann. Reproduced by permission.—Barnes, Djuna, photograph. UPI/Corbis-Bettman. Reproduced by permission.—Baroja, Pìo, photograph. AP/Wide World Photos. Reproduced by permission.—Barrie, Sir James M., photograph. AP/Wide World Photos. Reproduced by permission.—Barth, John, photograph. AP/Wide World Photos. Reproduced by permission.—Barthelme, Donald, photograph by Jerry Bauer. © Jerry Bauer. Reproduced by permission.—Bates, H. E., photograph. Mark Gerson Photography. Reproduced by permission.—Beattie, Anne, photograph by Jerry Bauer. © Jerry Bauer. Reproduced by permission.—Beckett, Samuel, photograph. Archive Photos, Inc. Reproduced by permission.—Behan, Brendan, photograph. AP/Wide World Photos. Reproduced by permission.—Bellow, Saul, photograph. Archive Photos, Inc. Reproduced by permission.—Benét, Stephen Vincent, photograph by Pirie MacDonald. The Library of Congress.—Bergson, Henri, photograph. The Library of Congress.—Berryman, John, photograph. AP/Wide World Photos. Reproduced by permission.—Betjeman, Sir John, photograph. Archive Photos, Inc. Reproduced by permission.—Bialik, Hayyim N., photograph. The Library of Congress.—Bierce, Ambrose, photograph. Corbis-Bettmann. Reproduced by permission.—Bishop, Elizabeth, photograph. AP/Wide World Photos. Reproduced by permission.—Blaise, Marie Claire, photograph by John Reeves. Reproduced by permission.—Blasco Ibáñez, Vicente, photograph. AP/Wide World Photos. Reproduced by permission.—Bloom, Harold, photograph by Jerry Bauer. © Jerry Bauer. Reproduced by permission.—Böll, Heinrich, photograph. Archive Photos, Inc. Reproduced by permission.—Borges, Jorge Luis, photograph. The Library of Congress.—Bowen, Elizabeth, photograph. The Library of Congress.—Breton, André, photograph. Archive Photos, Inc./AFP. Reproduced by permission.—Brookner, Anita, photograph by Jerry Bauer. © Jerry Bauer. Reproduced by permission.—Brooks, Gwendolyn, photograph. The Library of Congress.—Brutus, Dennis, photograph. AP/Wide World Photos. Reproduced by permission.—Buber, Martin, photograph. The Library of Congress.—Bullins, Ed, photograph by Marva Rae. Helen Merrill Ltd. Reproduced by permission of the photographer.—Bunting, Basil, photograph by Thomas Victor. Copyright © 1986 by Thomas Victor. All rights reserved. Reproduced by permission of the Estate of Thomas Victor.—Burgess, Anthony, photograph. AP/Wide World Photos. Reproduced by permission.—Burke, Kenneth, photograph. The Library of Congress.—Burroughs, William S., photograph. AP/Wide World Photos. Reproduced by permission.—Caldwell, Erskine, photograph. The Library of Congress.—Čapek, Karel, photograph. AP/Wide World Photos. Reproduced by permission.—Capote, Truman, photograph. The Library of Congress.—Cardenal, Ernesto, photograph by Lou Dematteis. Reuters/Corbis-Bettmann. Reproduced by permission.—Carpentier, Alejo, photograph. Archive Photos, Inc. Reproduced by permission.—Carver, Raymond, photograph. Archive Photos, Inc. Reproduced by permission.—Cather, Willa, photograph by Carl Van Vechten. The Library of Congress.—Cela, Camilo José, photograph by Jerry Bauer. © Jerry Bauer. Reproduced by permission.—Celine, Louis F., photograph. Archive Photos, Inc. Reproduced by permission.—Chandler, Raymond, photograph. The Library of Congress.—Cheever, John, photograph. The Library of Congress.—Chekov, Anton, photograph. International Portrait

Gallery/Library of Congress.—Chesterton, G. K., photograph. Archive Photos, Inc. Reproduced by permission.—Claudel, Paul, photograph. The Library of Congress.—Cocteau, Jean, photograph. AP/Wide World Photos. Reproduced by permission.—Cortázar, Julio, photograph. AP/Wide World Photos. Reproduced by permission.—Coward, Sir Noel (Peirce), photograph. AP/Wide World Photos, Inc. Reproduced by permission.—Crane, Hart, photograph by Walker Evans. The Library of Congress.—cummings, e. e., photograph. The Library of Congress.—Day Lewis, Cecil, photograph. Archive Photos, Inc. Reproduced by permission.—de Beauvoir, Simone, photograph. AP/Wide World Photos. Reproduced by permission.—de la Mare, Walter, photograph. The Library of Congress.—Derrida, Jacques, photograph. Archive Photos, Inc. Reproduced by permission.—Dickey, James, photograph. AP/Wide World Photos. Reproduced by permission.—Didion, Joan, photograph by Jerry Bauer. © Jerry Bauer. Reproduced by permission.—Doctorow, E. L., photograph by Horst Tappe. Archive Photos, Inc. Reproduced by permission.—Doolittle, Hilda, photograph. The Library of Congress.—Dos Passos, John, photograph. The Library of Congress.—Drabble, Margaret, photograph. AP/Wide World Photos. Reproduced by permission.—Dreiser, Theodore, photograph by Pirie MacDonald. The Library of Congress.—DuBois, W. E. B., photograph. The Library of Congress.—Ehrenburg, Ilya Grigoryevich, photograph. The Library of Congress.—Eliot, T. S., photograph. The Library of Congress.—Ellison, Ralph, photograph. AP/Wide World Photos. Reproduced by permission.—Elytis, Odysseus, photograph. AP/Wide World Photos. Reproduced by permission.—Farrell, James T., photograph. The Library of Congress.—Faulkner, William, photograph by Carl Van Vechten. The Library of Congress.—Fitzgerald, F. Scott, photograph by Carl Van Vechten. The Library of Congress.—Fo, Dario, photograph. © Jerry Bauer. Reproduced by permission.—Forster, E. M., photograph. Archive Photos, Inc. Reproduced by permission.—France, Anatole, photograph. The Library of Congress.—Freire, Romulo Gallegos, photograph. The Library of Congress.—Freud, Sigmund, photograph. The Library of Congress.—Frost, Robert, photograph. The Library of Congress.—Fuentes, Carlos, photograph. AP/Wide World Photos. Reproduced by permission.—Furphy, Joseph, photograph. The Library of Congress.—Gaines, Ernest, photograph. AP/Wide World Photos. Reproduced with permission.—Gaitán Durán, Jorge, photograph. The Library of Congress.—García Lorca, Federico, photograph. Archive Photos/Popperfoto. Reproduced by permission.—García Márquez, Gabriel, 1982, photograph. AP/Wide World Photos. Reproduced by permission.—Gass, William, photograph by Miriam Berkley. © Miriam Berkley. Reproduced by permission.—Genet, Jean, photograph. Archive Photos, Inc. Reproduced by permission.—Gibran, Kahlil, photograph. UPI/Corbis-Bettman. Reproduced by permission.—Gide, André, photograph. UPI/Corbis-Bettman. Reproduced by permission.—Glissant, Edouard, photograph. AP/Wide World Photos. Reproduced by permission.—Golding, William, photograph by Caroline Forbes. The Library of Congress.—Gordimer, Nadine, photograph. AP/Wide World Photos. Reproduced by permission.—Gordon, Caroline, photograph. The Library of Congress.—Gorky, Maxim, photograph. The Library of Congress.—Grass, Günter, photograph by Fred Stein. The Library of Congress.—Graves, Robert, photograph. AP/Wide World Photos, Inc. Reproduced by permission.—Greene, Graham, photograph. AP/Wide World Photos, Inc. Reproduced by permission.—Hammett, Samuel D., photograph. The Library of Congress.—Hamsun, Knut, photograph. The Library of Congress.—Handke, Peter, photograph by Jerry Bauer. © Jerry Bauer. Reproduced by permission.—Hansberry, Lorraine V., photograph. The Library of Congress.—Hardy, Thomas, photograph. Archive Photos, Inc. Reproduced by permission.—Hauptmann, Gerhart, photograph. The Library of Congress.—Head, Bessie, photograph. Reproduced by the kind permission of the Estate of Bessie Head.—Hellman, Lillian, photograph. AP/Wide World Photos. Reproduced by permission.—Hemingway, Ernest, photograph. Archive Photos, Inc. Reproduced by permission.—Housman, A. E., photograph. Archive Photos, Inc. Reproduced by permission.—Hughes, James Langston, photograph by Carl Van Vechten. The Library of Congress.—Hughes, Ted, photograph by Mark Gerson. Mark Gerson Photography. Reproduced by permission.—Hurston, Zora Neale, photograph. AP/Wide World Photos. Reproduced by permission.—Inge, William R., photograph. The Library of Congress.—Ionesco, Eugéne, photograph. The Library of Congress.—Irving, John, photograph. AP/Wide World Photos. Reproduced by permission.—Isherwood, Christopher, photograph. Archive Photos, Inc. Reproduced by permission.—James, Henry, photograph. The Library of Congress.—Jarry, Alfred, drawing by F. A. Cazalz, 1897, photograph. Corbis-Bettmann. Reproduced by permission.—Jeffers, Robinson, photograph. The Library of Congress.—Jiménez, Juan Ramón, photograph. AP/Wide World Photos. Reproduced by permission.—Johonson, James Weldon, photograph. The Library of Congress.—Jones, James, photograph. Corbis-Bettmann. Reproduced by permission.—Joyce, James (Ulysses), photograph. The Library of Congress.—Jung, Carl, photograph. The Library of Congress.—Jünger, Ernst, photograph. Archive Photos/Camera Press. Reproduced by permission.—Kafka, Franz, photograph. AP/Wide World Photos. Reproduced by permission.—Kawabata Yasunari, photograph. AP/Wide World Photos. Reproduced by permission.—Kerouac, Jack, photograph. Archive Photos. Reproduced by permission.—Killens, John O., photograph by Carl Van Vechten. The Library of Congress.—Kristeva, Julia, photograph by Jerry Bauer. © Jerry Bauer. Reproduced by permission.—Kumin, Maxine, photograph. AP/Wide World Photos. Reproduced by permission.—Kundera, Milan, photograph. Archive Photos.

Reproduced by permission.—Lagerkvist, Pär F., photograph. The Library of Congress.—Lawrence, D(avid) H(erbert), photograph. AP/Wide World Photos. Reproduced by permission.—Lessing, Doris, photograph by Jerry Bauer. © Jerry Bauer. Reproduced by permission.—Levi, Carlos, photograph. Archive Photos, Inc. Reproduced by permission.—Levi, Primo, photograph. The Library of Congress.—Lewis, Sinclair, photograph. The Library of Congress.—Lindsay, Vachel, photograph. Corbis-Bettmann. Reproduced by permission.—London, Jack, photograph. The Library of Congress.—Lowell, Amy, photograph. UPI/Corbis-Bettman. Reproduced by permission.—Lowell, Robert, photograph. The Library of Congress.—Lukács, György, photograph. Hulton-Deutsch/Corbis-Bettmann. Reproduced by permission.—Macleish, Archibald, photograph. The Library of Congress.—MacLennan, Hugh, photograph. AP/Wide World Photos. Reproduced by permission.—Maeterlinck, Maurice, photograph. The Library of Congress.—Mailer, Norman, photograph by Carl Van Vechten. The Library of Congress.—Malamud, Bernard, photograph. The Library of Congress.—Mamet, David, photograph by Brigitte Lacombe. Grove/Atlantic, Inc. Reproduced by permission.—Mann, Luiz Heinrich, photograph. The Library of Congress.—Mann, Thomas, photograph. The Library of Congress.—Mansfield, Katherine, photograph. Corbis-Bettmann. Reproduced by permission.—Marcel, Gabriel, photograph. Archive Photos, Inc. Reproduced by permission.—Marquand, John, photograph. Archive Photos, Inc. Reproduced by permission.—Masefield, John, photograph. The Library of Congress.—Maugham, W. Somerset, photograph by Carl Van Vechten. The Library of Congress.—Mauriac, François, photograph. The Library of Congress.—McCarthy, Mary, photograph. The Library of Congress.—McCullers, Carson, photograph. AP/Wide World Photos. Reproduced by permission.—McKay, Claude, photograph. The Library of Congress.—Mencken, Henry Louis, photograph. The Library of Congress.—Merrill, James, photograph. AP/Wide World Photos. Reproduced by permission.—Millay, Edna St. Vincent, photograph. The Library of Congress.—Miller, Arthur, photograph. Archive Photos, Inc. Reproduced by permission.—Miller, Henry, photograph. The Library of Congress.—Milosz, Czeslaw, photograph by Jerry Bauer. © Jerry Bauer. Reproduced by permission.—Mishima, Yukio, photograph. AP/Wide World Photos. Reproduced by permission.—Mistral, Gabriela, photograph. The Library of Congress.—Momaday, N. Scott, photograph. AP/Wide World Photos. Reproduced by permission.—Moore, Marianne, photograph. The Library of Congress.—Moravia, Alberto, photograph. The Library of Congress.—Morrison, Toni, photograph. AP/Wide World Photos. Reproduced by permission.—Mukherjee, Bharati, photograph. AP/Wide World Photos. Reproduced by permission.—Nabokov, Vladimir, photograph. AP/Wide World Photos. Reproduced by permission.—Naipaul, V. S., photograph. AP/Wide World Photos. Reproduced by permission.—Narayan, R. K., photograph. The Library of Congress.—Nemerov, Howard, photograph by Margaret Nemerov. Reproduced with permission.—Neruda, Pablo, photograph by Jerry Bauer. © Jerry Bauer. Reproduced by permission.—Nin, Anaïs, photograph. The Library of Congress.—O'Casey, Sean, photograph. The Library of Congress.—O'Connor, Flannery, photograph. Corbis-Bettmann. Reproduced by permission.—O'Hara, Frank, photograph. AP/Wide World Photos. Reproduced by permission.—O'Hara, John, photograph. The Library of Congress.—O'Neill, Eugene G., photograph. The Library of Congress.—Oates, Joyce Carol, photograph. UPI/Corbis-Bettmann. Reproduced by permission.—Odets, Clifford, photograph. AP/Wide World Photos, Inc. Reproduced by permission.—Ōe Kenzaburō, photograph. Reuters/Kyodo/Archive Photos. Reproduced by permission.—Ortega y Gasset, José, photograph. AP/Wide World Photos. Reproduced by permission.—Orwell, George, photograph. AP/Wide World Photos. Reproduced by permission.—Osborne, John, photograph. AP/Wide World Photos. Reproduced by permission.—Ozick, Cynthia, photograph. Corbis-Bettmann. Reproduced by permission.—Parra, Nicanor, photograph by Miriam Berkley. © Miriam Berkley. Reproduced by permission.—Pasolini, Pier Paolo, photograph. AP/Wide World Photos, Inc. Reproduced by permission.—Paton, Alan, photograph. The Library of Congress.—Pavlović, Miodrag, photograph by John Reeves. Reproduced by permission.—Paz, Octavio, photograph. AP/Wide World Photos. Reproduced by permission.—Percy, Walker, photograph by Jerry Bauer. © Jerry Bauer. Reproduced by permission.—Pérez Galdós, Benito, photograph. The Library of Congress.—Perse, Saint John, photograph. AP/Wide World Photos. Reproduced by permission.—Pietri, Dr. Arturo Uslar, photograph. AP/Wide World Photos. Reproduced by permission.—Pinter, Harold, photograph. AP/Wide World Photos. Reproduced by permission.—Pirandello, Luigi, photograph. AP/Wide World Photos. Reproduced by permission.—Plath, Sylvia, photograph. Corbis-Bettmann. Reproduced by permission.—Porter, Katherine Anne, photograph. Archive Photos, Inc. Reproduced by permission.—Pound, Ezra, photograph. The Library of Congress.—Pritchett, V. S., photograph by Jerry Bauer. © Jerry Bauer. Reproduced by permission.—Proust, Marcel, photograph. The Library of Congress.—Puig, Manuel, photograph by Jerry Bauer. © Jerry Bauer. Reproduced by permission.—Purdy, James, photograph. The Library of Congress.—Pynchon, Thomas R., photograph. UPI/Corbis-Bettmann. Reproduced by permission.—Quasimodo, Salvatore, photograph. Corbis-Bettmann. Reproduced by permission.—Remarque, Erich M., photograph. The Library of Congress.—Renault, Mary, photograph. AP/Wide World Photos. Reproduced by permission.—Rexroth, Kenneth, photograph. AP/Wide World Photos. Reproduced by permission.—Rice, Elmer, photograph. AP/Wide World Photos.

Reproduced by permission.—Rich, Adrienne, photograph. AP/Wide World Photos. Reproduced by permission.—Richler, Mordecai, photograph by John Reeves. Reproduced by permission.—Robbe-Grillet, Alain, photograph by Jerry Bauer. © Jerry Bauer. Reproduced by permission.—Robinson, Edwin Arlington, photograph. AP/Wide World Photos. Reproduced by permission.—Roethke, Theodore, photograph by Imogen Cunningham. AP/Wide World Photos, Inc. Reproduced by permission.—Roth, Philip, photograph. Corbis-Bettmann. Reproduced by permission.—Rukeyser, Muriel, photograph. AP/Wide World Photos. Reproduced by permission.—Rulfo, Juan, photograph. AP/Wide World Photos. Reproduced by permission.—Rushdie, Salman, photograph. Archive Photos, Inc. Reproduced by permission.—Russell, George William, photograph. The Library of Congress.—Salinger, J. D., photograph. AP/Wide World Photos, Inc. Reproduced by permission.—Sandburg, Carl, photograph. The Library of Congress.—Santayana, George, photograph. The Library of Congress.—Saroyan, William, photograph. The Library of Congress.—Sarraute, Nathalie, photograph. AP/Wide World Photos. Reproduced by permission.—Sarton, May, photograph. UPI/Corbis-Bettmann. Reproduced by permission.—Sassoon, Siegfried, photograph. The Library of Congress.—Schnitzler, Arthur, photograph. Archive Photos, Inc. Reproduced by permission.—Sexton, Anne, photograph. AP/Wide World Photos. Reproduced by permission.—Shaw, George Bernard, photograph. The Library of Congress.—Shepard, Sam, photograph. Archive Photos, Inc. Reproduced by permission.—Simenon, Georges, photograph. AP/Wide World Photos, Inc. Reproduced by permission.—Sinclair, Upton, photograph. AP/Wide World Photos, Inc. Reproduced by permission.—Singer, Isaac Bashevis, photograph. UPI/Corbis-Bettmann. Reproduced by permission.—Sitwell, Edith, photograph. UPI/Corbis-Bettman. Reproduced by permission.—Škvorecký, Josef, photograph by John Reeves. Reproduced by permission.—Snow, Charles Percy, photograph. Corbis-Bettmann. Reproduced by permission.—Snyder, Gary, photograph. AP/Wide World Photos. Reproduced by permission.—Sontag, Susan, photograph. AP/Wide World Photos. Reproduced by permission.—Soto, Pedro Juan, photograph. Arte Publico Press Archives, University of Houston. Reproduced by permission.—Soyinka, Wole, photograph. Archive Photos/Trappe. Reproduced by permission.—Spark, Muriel, photograph. AP/Wide World Photos. Reproduced by permission.—Stein, Gertrude, photograph by Carl Van Vechten. The Library of Congress.—Steinbeck, John, photograph. Archive Photos, Inc. Reproduced by permission.—Stevens, Wallace, photograph. The Library of Congress.—Strachey, Lytton, photograph by E. O. Hoppe. Corbis-Bettmann. Reproduced by permission.—Strand, Mark, photograph. The Library of Congress.—Szymborska, Wislawa, photograph. AP/Wide World Photos. Reproduced by permission.—Tate, Allen, photograph. UPI/Corbis-Bettman. Reproduced by permission.—Thomas, Dylan, photograph. AP/Wide World Photos. Reproduced by permission.—Thurber, James, photograph. AP/Wide World Photos. Reproduced by permission.—Tolkien, J. R. R., photograph. AP/Wide World Photos. Reproduced by permission.—Tremblay, Michel, photograph by Yves Renaud. Agence Goodwin. Reproduced by permission of the photographer.—Trevor, William, photograph by Kristin Morrison. Mark Gerson Photography. Reproduced by permission.—Tyler, Anne, photograph. AP/Wide World Photos. Reproduced by permission.—Unamuno, Miguel de, photograph. Corbis-Bettmann. Reproduced by permission.—Undset, Sigrid, photograph. AP/Wide World Photos. Reproduced by permission.—Updike, John, photograph. AP/Wide World Photos. Reproduced by permission.—Valéry, Paul, photograph. Archive Photos, Inc. Reproduced by permission.—Vargas Llosa, Mario, photograph. AP/Wide World Photos. Reproduced by permission.—Vidal, Gore, photograph. AP/Wide World Photos. Reproduced by permission.—Villa, José Garcia, photograph. AP/Wide World Photos. Reproduced by permission.—Vonnegut, Kurt, Jr., photograph. Archive Photos/Saga 1991 Frank Capri. Reproduced by permission.—Walcott, Derek, photograph by Jerry Bauer. © Jerry Bauer. Reproduced by permission.—Walker, Alice, photograph. Archive Photos, Inc. Reproduced by permission.—Warren, Robert Penn, photograph. The Library of Congress.—Wassermann, Jakob, photograph. Archive Photos, Inc. Reproduced by permission.—Waugh, Evelyn, photograph. Mark Gerson Photography. Reproduced by permission.—Wedekind, Frank, photograph. Hulton-Deutsch Collection/Corbis-Bettmann. Reproduced by permission.—Weiss, Peter, photograph. AP/Wide World Photos. Reproduced by permission.—Weldon, Fay, photograph. AP/Wide World Photos. Reproduced by permission.—Wells, H. G., photograph. The Library of Congress.—Welty, Eudora, photograph. AP/Wide World Photos. Reproduced by permission.—Wesker, Arnold, photograph. UPI/Corbis-Bettman. Reproduced by permission.—Wharton, Edith, photograph. AP/Wide World Photos. Reproduced by permission.—White, E. B., photograph. AP/Wide World Photos. Reproduced by permission.—White, Patrick, photograph. AP/Wide World Photos. Reproduced by permission.—Wiesel, Elie, photograph by Nancy Rica Schiff. Archive Photos, Inc. Reproduced by permission.—Wilbur, Richard, photograph. AP/Wide World Photos. Reproduced by permission.—Wilder, Thornton, photograph by Carl Van Vechten. The Library of Congress.—Williams, Tennessee, photograph. AP/Wide World Photos. Reproduced by permission.—Wilson, August, photograph. AP/Wide World Photos. Reproduced by permission.—Wodehouse, P. G., photograph. AP/Wide World Photos. Reproduced by permission.—Wolfe, Thomas, photograph by Carl Van Vechten. The Library of Congress.—Wolfe, Tom, photograph. AP/Wide World Photos. Reproduced by permission.—Woolf, Virginia, photograph. AP/Wide World Photos. Reproduced by permission.—Wright, James, photograph by Ted Wright. Reproduced by permission of the Estate of James Wright.—Wright, Richard, photograph by Carl Van Vechten. The Library of Congress.—Yeats, William Butler, photograph. The Library of Congress.—Yourcenar, Marguerite, photograph. AP/Wide World Photos. Reproduced by permission.

INTRODUCTION

This four-volume third edition of the *Encyclopedia of World Literature in the 20th Century* is designed as a comprehensive survey of significant literary activity of international scope and proportion extending from the beginning of the century to the present. The breadth and complexity of this activity demands progressive study, analysis, and evaluation, and the *Encyclopedia* serves as an inclusive and authoritative guide for this purpose. Responsive to the needs of scholarly and general readers alike, the *Encyclopedia* provides in a reference work of singular importance the most extensive treatment of information necessary to the assessment and appreciation of the growth and development of modern world literature.

The twentieth century represents a period of extraordinary literary productivity and proliferation realized within the framework of unprecedented historical transformation and challenge. The decades preceding the publication of the *Encyclopedia* have produced global transition, dominated by the impact of social and political upheaval and the redefinition of national boundaries and identities. We have witnessed events that have altered the shape of the world in which we live and the terms by which we discuss literature. Although the sociopolitical as well as cultural ramifications of these alterations have yet to fully realize themselves and be understood, we have made every effort to incorporate these developments within the context of the *Encyclopedia,* thus enhancing the reader's perception of the relationship between literature and society.

This edition is a collaborative effort to cover, in more than 2,300 article entries in four volumes, the major aspects of world literature in the twentieth century. To this end, nearly all the literatures of the world with claim to a substantial productivity within the century are discussed in survey articles. Likewise, in their relationship to the literature of the century, literary movements of consequence (e.g., expressionism, futurism, surrealism) are covered in separate topical articles, as are movements in ideas (e.g., existentialism, historicism, postmodernism). The core of the *Encyclopedia* consists of separate articles on major and representative writers incorporating salient biographical information and critical analysis of the writer's major themes and works.

Bases of Selection: The selection of individual entries represents extensive assessment and evaluation of critical recognition earned from the international literary community as well as endorsement as figures of substantial literary importance from specialists of representative national literatures. In order to fulfill its purpose as a reference work, the *Encyclopedia* attempts to be as comprehensive as possible within the limitations imposed by the span of the edition. It is also important to maintain the international scope of the *Encyclopedia.* Thus, many authors—American, British, European—who are well known to English-speaking readers do not receive individual entries but are instead treated within the survey articles of national literatures. Many of the authors receiving individual entries are from less familiar literatures who have limited exposure to English-speaking readers, and a significant number to date have not been translated into English or have not generated criticism in English of scholarly merit. For these authors, the *Encyclopedia* serves as the primary source of reference to English-speaking readers.

Omissions: Despite the scope and magnitude of the *Encyclopedia,* it is inevitable that an appreciable number of writers have been omitted. In works of this kind, with claims of a wide coverage, the inclusion of some writers as against others is of course subject to debate. Regrettably, it was not always possible to identify a specialist of sufficient expertise to prepare individual author entries or to compile and research a national literature. As a result, there is unfortunately at times insufficient coverage of writers deserving of inclusion from relatively obscure or isolated literatures.

Entries: Organization and Data—Individual author entries have been arranged into four parts: a headnote containing vital statistics; a body that includes biographical information and a critical assessment of the author's achievement; a section titled *Further Works* containing publications not mentioned in the body of the article; and a final section titled *Bibliography* comprising selective bibliographical material concerning the author and his or her work. A list of periodicals and their abbreviations cited will be found at the front of Volume 1, and an index to the entries will be included at the end of Volume 4. In a very few of the headnotes the statistics are incomplete, owing to the difficulty of obtaining conclusive confirmation from accessible, reliable sources.

Works featured in the body of the article, as well as in the *Further Works* section, carry their full title and, wherever possible, their original year of publication. In the case of authors writing in languages other than English, titles of published English translations are cited in parentheses, along with their original publication dates. Where several translations of a non-English work have been made under the same title in English, only the publication date of the earliest translation is given. With those works that have been translated under more than one English title, we have tried to feature the titles of all such translations. For non-English works that have not been translated into English, original titles will appear followed by the year of publication and the title's literal translation in parentheses.

Cross References and Pseudonyms: Extensive cross-references to other authors, literatures, and movements appear wherever appropriate in the texts of articles. Where a writer with an individual entry is referred to in another entry, at the first mention his or her last name appears in small capital letters. Likewise, where a movement with a separate entry is referred to in another entry, at the first mention the topic appears in small capital letters. The survey articles on national literatures are cross-referenced by language so that the reader will be directed to the appropriate national literature or literatures (e.g., under Bengali Literature will be found "See Bangladeshi Literature and Indian Literature").

Authors known primarily by their *non de plume* will be listed under their pseudonym (e.g., Blixen under *Dinesen,* Gorenko under *Akhmatova,* Hadjiandreas under *Tsirkas*). For the convenience of readers certain of these names have been cross-referenced, but the abiding principle in this regard has been to avoid overelaboration.

Transliterated and Romanized Languages: As an international reference work, the *Encyclopedia* attempts to be as consistent as possible with the transliteration and romanization of non-English names, most notably those in Arabic, Chinese, Japanese, and Russian. In Arabic, prefixes that are part of the surname will be retained when the surname is used for alphabetizing (e.g., 'Abd al-Hamīd ibn Hadūga under *Ibn Hadūga*). In Chinese practice, the family name comes before the given name, which usually has two elements. The family name and the first element of the given name are capitalized, and the given name is hyphenated (e.g., Kao Hsiao-sheng). Chinese names wherever necessary are cross-referenced in the index by their updated romanization (e.g., Gao Xiaosheng. *See* Kao Hsiao-sheng). In Japanese practice, the family name also comes before the given name (e.g., Ōe Kenzaburō rather than Kenzaburō Ōe). While there are many systems for transliterating Russian names, the phonetic method adopted was considered the most appropriate for a general reader, and the most easily recognizable from the viewpoint of common usage (e.g., see *Gorky,* not Gorki, Gorkii, or Gor'kiy).

Quotations: To some entries, primarily authors of international repute, the *Encyclopedia* appends a selection of critical excerpts to further enhance the reader's understanding and perception of the author's productivity and contribution to world literature. The excerpts are cited by author, source, year of publication, and page number(s).

The Contributors: These have been drawn from a wide sphere of literary authorities, both from the United States and abroad, most often based on the recommendation of the advisers in national literatures. The name of the contributor appears at the end of each article in the *Encyclopedia.*

The general editor wishes to express his appreciation, first, to the hundreds of individuals whose contributions have helped to make the *Encyclopedia* a reference work of distinction. He is most indebted to those individuals listed in the board of advisers, whose generosity of time and expertise provided proportion, balance, and consistency in the preparation of the edition. He also expresses his appreciation to Peter M. Gareffa, managing editor of St. James Press, and Laura Berger, senior editor.

Assisting the general editor, Madeline D. Murray was the senior editor and production coordinator of the *Encyclopedia.* Production editors were Sonya Collins, Victoria Eng, and Matthew Miller. Technical assistance was provided by Enercida Guererro, Ana Angelillo, and Harlan Cayetano. Editorial assistance was provided by Carina Garcia, Bonnie MacSaveny, Denise Galang, Sean O'Hanlon, Chriscita Corbin, Rachel Shook, Michelle Gonzalez, Christine Cifra, Anna Degrezia, Francesca Fiore, Rebecca Lawson, Jill Bauer, Lisa Butler, Michelle Cutler, Julie Miele, Anna Gross, Karma Cloud, Nancy Moore, Joseph Weissman, Rose Sung, Jason Berner, and Greta Wagle.

STEVEN R. SERAFIN
HUNTER COLLEGE OF THE CITY UNIVERSITY OF NEW YORK

S

SÁ-CARNEIRO, Mário de

Portuguese poet, short-story writer, and novelist, b. 19 May 1890, Lisbon; d. 26 April 1916, Paris, France

From a well-to-do family, S.-C., while still an adolescent, collaborated on a play, *Amizade* (pub. 1912; friendship), with a classmate who was soon to take his own life. In 1911 he enrolled at the Coimbra University law school but did not attend classes. The next year he followed the same procedure at the Sorbonne in Paris. During his lifetime he published two collections of short narratives, *Princípio* (1914; beginning) and *Céu em fogo* (1915; the heavens ablaze); one novel, *A confissão de Lúcio* (1914; Lúcio's confession); and a volume of verse, *Dispersão* (1914; dispersal). Except for occasional trips to Lisbon, he remained in Paris from 1912 until his suicide in 1916.

In 1915 S.-C. and his friend Fernando PESSOA edited the second number of *Orpheu*, the magazine that introduced MODERNISM to Portugal. They prepared a third issue but were unable to finance its publication. During his stay in Paris S.-C. was in a state of increasing mental instability. He discussed his problems in his letters to his friend, published in *Cartas a Fernando Pessoa* (2 vols., 1958–59; letters to Fernando Perssoa). During these years Pessoa was his only intimate friend, and S.-C. depended on him for moral and occasional financial support. Pessoa, although only two years his senior, was also his literary mentor. In return, Pessoa learned from S.-C. about Parisian literary life and through him was first brought into touch with CUBISM and FUTURISM. The two men and José Almada-Negreiros (1893–1970), a painter and writer, were the leading figures of Portuguese modernism.

S.-C. wrote almost all his poetry between 1912 and 1916, moving from SYMBOLISM to modernism. The influence of Rimbaud and Mallarmé is evident in the abstract imagery and oneiric symbols of *Dispersão*. Among the Portuguese symbolists, Camilo Pessanha (1867–1926) is probably closest to him in his poetic achievement, his narcisism, and his extreme sensitivity. Although Pessanha did not commit suicide, he did destroy himself through his addiction to drugs. S.-C. had been introduced to Pessanha's work by Pessoa; the influence of Pessoa's *paùlismo* (postsymbolism), with its confusion of subjectivity and objectivity, its vagueness, and its surprising associations of ideas, and of the same writer's *interseccionismo* (a form of futurism), with its juxtaposition of present and past, and present and distant, are to be seen in many of the poems of S.-C.'s posthumously published *Indícios de oiro* (1937; traces of gold).

The themes of suicide, incest, and loss of personal identity and the scenes of sexual promiscuity and deviance in S.-C.'s fiction recall the French Decadents. In both his fiction and poetry he is concerned with dream states and the subconscious, and he betrays in these concerns his schizoid personality, his constant anxiety, his alienation, and especially his abysmally low self-image, with its resultant identity diffusion. One example is in the sonnet "Aqueloutro" (that other one) in *Últimos poemas* (last poems), published in the posthumous collection *Poesias* (1946; poems). Speaking directly to his readers, he calls himself a presumptuous fool and a fat sphinx. Another example is in the prose narrative "Eu-próprio o *outro*" (I myself the other) in *Céu em fogo*, in which he creates a persona who has two individual existences.

S.-C. is one of the two great poets of the Portuguese modernist period, and with Pessoa and Pessanha one of the greatest poets of the century. He published only fifty-one poems, but he deserves such high regard because of his originality and intensity and his creative, experimental use of language and imagery, which develops through the abstraction and vagueness of the early poems to the vivid symbols and personal, colloquial style of his self-destructive last poems, where he belittles himself and calls for ridicule and merriment at his death.

FURTHER WORKS: *Obras completas* (5 vols., 1945–59)

BIBLIOGRAPHY: Houwens Post, H., "M. de S.-C.: Premier poète surréaliste portugais (1890–1916)," *Neophil*, 49 (1965): 301–6; Megenney, W. W., "This World and Beyond: M. de S.-C.'s Struggle for Perfection," *Hispania*, 59 (1976): 258–67

—RAYMOND S. SAYERS

SAARIKOSKI, Pentti

Finnish poet, b. 2 Sept. 1937, Impilahti; d. 24 Aug. 1983, Joensuu

S. studied classical literature at Helsinki University. He wrote for a student newspaper and from 1958 to 1960 was a columnist for the Helsinki daily *Uusi Suomi*, using the pseudonym "Nenä." His satirical sketches gained him an early reputation as an enfant terrible. In 1975 he moved to Göteborg, Sweden, where he lived until shortly before his death.

Critics have divided his career into three periods. From his "Greek" period (1958–61) are the collections *Runoja* (1958; poems), *Toisia runoja* (1958; other poems), and *Runot ja Hipponaksin runot* (1959; poems and Hipponax's poems). The short poems in these volumes are notable for their subtle imagery and their feeling.

Between 1961 and 1970 S. was engaged in literary experimentation and political activity as a communist of independent leanings. *Mitä Tapahtuu todella?* (1962; what is really happening?), *Ääneen* (1966; aloud), and *Katselen Stalinin pään yli ulos* (1969; I look out over Stalin's head) are unusual in form, outspoken, and often satirical. These prose poems are characterized by complex imagery, an aphoristic colloquial style, a free association reminiscent of SURREALISM, and an erudition recalling Ezra POUND and T. S. ELIOT.

After 1970 S.'s work showed a resurgence of the Greek influence. He became deeply preoccupied with contemporary science and the hazards of the nuclear age. The brief pieces in *Onnen aika* (1971; happy time) are suggestive of classical Greek poetry as well as of Japanese verse. Their simplicity and relative cheerfulness contrast with the somber tone and obscure style of the collection *Alue* (1975; territory). *Ihmisen ääni* (1976; human voice) is in prose, much of it confessional in nature. The uncertainty of the modern age is also the theme of the collection *Tanssilattia vuorella* (1977; dance floor on the mountain); the disenchantment is, however, relieved by wry humor. In this volume such mytho-logical figures as Sisyphus, Ulysses, and Hercules appear in present-day political situations.

In the essay "Minun runoni ja minun aatteeni" (1978; my poems and my beliefs) S. expresses hope that knowledge will win out over brute power, announces a new work to be called *Tanssiinkutsu* (invitation to the dance), and takes exception to the opinion of one critic that his political phase is over. *Tanssiinkutsu* (pub. 1980) is a collection of short pieces of free verse, ringing the same notes of melancholy and irony as *Tanssilattia vuorella*.

S. was not successful as a novelist. Yet fictional works like the "collage novel" *Ovat muistojemme lehdet kuolleet* (1964; our leaves of memory are dead), *Aika Prahassa* (1967; while in Prague), and *Kirje vaimolleni* (1968; letter to my wife) do have autobiographical interest. The last reflects a sojourn in London and Dublin. *Asiaa tai ei* (1980; matter or not) is a sort of diary reporting on his life in Sweden. He indicates that he had left Finland because he was weary of the Helsinki literary scene. His thoughts on the art of translation are of particular interest.

S.'s numerous translations include writers of antiquity like Xenophon and Aristotle, and such moderns as J. D. SALINGER and Henry MILLER. It is significant that he translated both Homer's *Odyssey* and James JOYCE's *Ulysses*.

FURTHER WORKS: *Nenän pakinoita* (1960); *Maailmassa* (1961); *Kuljen missä kuljen* (1965); *Punaiset liput* (1966); *En soisi sen päättyvän* (1968); *Eino Leino: Legenda jo eläessään* (1974); *Ja meille jää kiireetön ilta* (1975, with Mia Berner); *Euroopan reuna: Kineettinen kuva* (1982). **FURTHER WORKS IN ENGLISH:** *Helsinki: Selected Poems* (1967)

BIBLIOGRAPHY: Ahokas, J., *A History of Finnish Literature* (1973): 363–64, 381–82; Dauenhauer, R., in Dauenhauer, R., and P. Binham, eds., *Snow in May* (1978): 74-75, 384-85; Simonsuuri, K., "Myth and Material in the Poetry of P. S. since 1958," *WLT*, 54 (1980): 41–46

—REINO VIRTANEN

SABA, Umberto

(pseud. of Umberto Poli) Italian poet, b. 9 March 1883, Trieste (then in Austro-Hungarian Empire); d. 25 Aug. 1957, Gorizia

S.'s mother was Jewish; his father deserted her before the boy's birth. Largely self-educated, at twenty S. enlisted for several years in an infantry regiment. When Trieste became part of Italy after World War I, S. established the antiquarian book shop that was to occupy him off and on for the rest of his life. During World War II, because of Italian racial laws, S. went to Paris, but he later returned to live secretly in Rome and Florence. After the liberation, he resettled in Trieste. In the last decade of his life he was awarded several literary prizes and honors, including the coveted Viarreggio Prize (1946).

Perhaps more than any other 20th-c. poet, S. succeeded in achieving the tone as well as the edge and subtlety of modern poetry without discarding conventional forms and meters. His language is for the most part conventional, even in poems where the pulse of modernity beats most strongly. But unlike Giuseppe UNGARETTI, Salvatore QUASIMODO, or Eugenio MONTALE, S. was

an extremely uneven poet, and his reputation is based on a comparatively small portion of his total output. S.'s artistic maturi-ty was the result of gradual development and experimentation rather than something that was inborn and present almost from the very outset.

Literary influences and poetic theories play an insignificant role in S.'s mature poetry, a fact that may account for the simplicity and naturalness of his style. His early poetry, however, is full of echoes of Giacomo Leopardi (1798–1837) and displays the worst weak-nesses of derivative verse. In addition, his choice of themes often betrayed him into sentimentality; and because his style is perilously close to the rhythms of prose, he did not always avoid the pitfall of writing versified prose.

In *Casa e campagna* (written 1909–10; home and countryside), first published as part of the collection *Il canzoniere* (1921; the songbook), S. achieved a masterly ease and naturalness, and a happy union between prose and poetic cadences. *Trieste e una donna* (written 1910–12; Trieste and a woman), also published in *Il canzoniere* of 1921, is the supreme illustration of what Montale called "pure feeling, comparable to music." The lyric poems in it show a poetic and linguistic maturity guided by a stricter architec-tonic compactness. Topographical realism combined with an im-pressive degree of lyric intensity gives the verse its hard, crystalline timbre. These poems also evidence a more complex synthesis between S.'s own life and feelings and his attitude toward Trieste. In *Autobiografia* (1924; autobiography), too, there is a striking consistency of lyric tone as he deals with what Robert Browning called "incidents in the development of the soul".

In *Parole* (1934; words) and *Ultime cose* (1944; last things) S. sounded an altogether new note. Verbal diffuseness gave way to a quintessential laconism without leading to the sort of obscurity associated with HERMETICISM. Concentration and economy both at the verbal level and at that of the organization of thought and feeling are complemented by an inner moral ripening. Poetic images and terms of moral and psychological reference change significantly and point up both the underlying symbolism of the familiar and the poet's awareness of things previously ignored. Painful and joyous youthful memories revive and show him the present in a new light and himself in a different perspective.

Mediterrance (1946; Mediterranean poems) contains two of S.'s best-known poems: "Ebbri canti" (drunken songs) and "Ulisse" (Ulysses). However, *Uccelli* (1950; birds) and *Quasi un racconto* (1951; almost a tale), S.'s last two volumes published in his lifetime, register a notable decline in poetic powers.

S.'s contribution to 20th-c. Italian poetry is both substantial and original. Like Ungaretti and Guido GOZZANO, he helped emanci-pate the language of poetry from both Giosuè Carducci's (1835–1907) academic pastoralism and Gabriele D'ANNUNZIO'S rhetoric. For a long time, the very originality and revolutionary character of his innovations prevented recognition of him as a major poet.

FURTHER WORKS: *Poesie* (1911); *Coi miei occhi* (1912); *Cose leggere e vaganti* (1920); *La serena disperazione* (1920); *L'amorosa spina* (1921); *Preludio e canzonette* (1922); *Figure e canti* (1928); *Preludio e fughe* (1928); *Tre composizioni* (1933); *Ammonizione, ed altre poesie* (1909–1910) (1933); *Il canzoniere 1900–1945* (1945); *Scorciatoie e raccontini* (1946); *Il canzoniere 1900–1947* (1948; new ed., 1951); *Storia e cronistoria del Canzoniere* (1948); *Tutte le opere* (8 vols., 1949–59); *Ricordi-racconit* (1910–1947) (1956); *Epigrafe: Ultime prose* (1959); *Il canzoniere* (1961);

Lettere a un'amica (1961); *Antologia del Canzoniere* (1963); *Prose* (1964); *Il vechio e il giovane: Carteggio 1930–1957* (1965); *S., Svevo, Comisso: Lettere inedite* (1969); *L'adolescenza del Canzoniere e undici lettere* (1975); *Amicizia: Storia di un vecchio poeta e un giovane canarino* (1976); *Ernesto* (1978); *Lettere a un amico vescovo* (1980). FURTHER WORKS IN ENGLISH: *The Promised Land, and Other Poems: An Anthology of Four Contemporary Italian Poets: U. S., Giuseppe Ungaretti, Eugenio Montale, Salvatore Quasimodo* (1957, bilingual)

BIBLIOGRAPHY: Pacifici, S., *A Guide to Contemporary Italian Literature* (1962): 161–67; Bergin, T. G., "S. and His Canzoniere", *BA* (1968): 503–8; Singh, G., "The Poetry of U. S.," *IS*, 23 (1968): 114–37; Cary, J., *Three Modern Italian Poets: S., Ungaretti, Montale* (1969): 31–133; Donadoni, E., *A History of Italian Literature* (1969), Vol. 2: 624–25; Wilkins, E. H., *A History of Italian Literature*, rev. ed. (1974): 510–12

—G. SINGH

SÁBATO, Ernesto

Argentine novelist and essayist, b. 24 June 1911, Rojas

Although his early interests were painting and literature, S. studied science and received a degree in physics from the University of La Plata in 1937. In his youth he worked actively with the anarchists. Later he joined the Communist Party. In 1934 he was a delegate to a congress, held in Brussels and directed by Henri BARBUSSE, the purpose of which was to openly oppose war and fascism. Soon thereafter S. broke with the Party. In 1938 he was awarded research scholarships at the Curie Institute in Paris and at the Massachusetts Institute of Technology in the U.S. In Paris he became acquainted with SURREALISM, and his literary interests were stimulated. Upon his return to Argentina in 1940, S. taught physics at the University of La Plata. His first essays, published in periodicals and newspapers, immediately attracted the attention of critics. In 1944 he decided to devote himself to a literary career.

S.'s essayistic works, from *Uno y el universo* (1945; a self and the universe) to *El escritor y sus fantasmas* (1963; the writer and his ghosts), present a chaotic vision of the world, influenced by European writers, mainly Dostoevsky and Jean-Paul SARTRE. Using a confessional technique, he examines some of the significant contemporary themes: solitude and lack of communication, art and life, reality and imagination, sex and eroticism. *Hombres y engranajes* (1951; men and gears) focuses on man's frustration in a technological society. For S., art is the sole means for regaining the lost unity with the world. Other, short, essays reflect S.'s political position: he opposed both Perón and the subsequent revolutionary government of 1955. Some of these political essays were collected in *El caso S.* (1956; the S. case) and *Claves políticas* (1971; political clues).

Fiction has been S.'s chief genre. After a first attempt in "La fuente muda" (the silent fountain)—a work never completed—he wrote *El túnel* (1948; *The Outsider*, 1950), which brought him international recognition and was praised by Albert CAMUS and Graham GREENE, among others. The novel revolves around a convicted murderer, the painter Pablo Castel, who narrates why

and how he killed his mistress. The plot is only a means for his self-analysis, in which he is obsessed with his inability to communicate his jealousy, solitude, contradictions, and doubts. It is the story of a man whose loneliness is so total that he cannot unburden himself to anybody, not even to his beloved. He lives in agony because of his feeling of living in a tunnel closed at both ends.

S.'s second novel, *Sobre héroes y tumbas* (1961; *On Heroes and Tombs*, 1981), has been translated into many languages. Epic in scope, this ambitious, uneven work juxtaposes a variety of narrative techniques that convey the structure of a classical sonata, with four parts and four characters trapped in their tragic fate. Among these, Alexandra emerges as the protagonist. Her incestuous relations with her father lead her to kill him and then lock herself in their house and set it on fire. By means of a labyrinthine plot, S. reiterates the existential themes of *El túnel*—love, alienation, and death—and includes discussions of philosophical and theological questions. Tradition and history are recurring presences in Argentine life as depicted in the novel. The author portrays the various strata of Buenos Aires society, emphasizing the social and psychological implications of man's banishment in the big city. S. seeks to reveal the contradiction of Argentine culture, which he characterizes as at the same time barbaric and bourgeois.

Abbadón el exterminador (1974; *The Angel of Darkness*, 1991), which won the Prize for Best Foreign Book in France, is the culmination of his narrative production. The novel takes its title from the name of the biblical angel of vengeance. Abbadón is the symbolic figure of evil, bearing an apocalyptic vision that announces the destruction of the universe. Characters and places from S.'s previous works reappear. S. himself is presented as a protagonist who poses metaphysical questions about life. The novel combines autobiography, essay, fiction, science, and poetry. The dominant essayistic approach, however, and the discursive language and rationalistic attitude of the characters, keep S. from fully achieving the ambitious goal he had set himself.

S. is, by temperament, a tortured, rebellious writer. His work is polemical, and his style vigorous, with touches of humor and keen sarcasm. His fiction—a chaotic quest for a radical new meaning for man—has won him a place among the most prestigious practitioners of the new Latin American novel.

FURTHER WORKS: *Heterodoxia* (1953); *El otro rostro del peronismo* (1956); *Tango, canción de Buenos Aires* (1962); *Tango: Discusión y clave* (1963); *Tres aproximaciones a la literatura de nuestro tiempo: Robbe-Grillet, Borges, Sartre* (1968); *La convulsión política y social de nuestro tiempo* (1969); *Itinerario* (1969); *La cultura en la encrucijada nacional* (1973); *Diálogos* (1976, with Jorge Luis Borges); *Apologías y rechazos* (1979). FURTHER WORKS IN ENGLISH: *The Dark of the Sun: Selected Poems* (1994)

BIBLIOGRAPHY: Oberhelman, H. D., *E. S.* (1970); Wainerman, L., *S. y el misterio de los ciegos* (1971); Cerosimo, E., "*Sobre héroes y tumbas*": *De los caracteres a la metafísica* (1972); Catania, G., S. *entre la idea y la sangre* (1973); Montenegro, N., "The Structural and Thematic Elements in *Abbadón el exterminador*," *LALR*, 12 (1978): 38–56; Bacarisse, S., "*Abbadón el exterminador*: S.'s Gnostic Eschatology," *FMLS*, 15 (1979): 184–205; Polakovic, E., *La clave para la obra de E. S.* (1981); Coover, R., on *On Heroes and Tombs*, *NYTBR*, (26 July 1981): 1, 25

—ZUNILDA GERTEL

SABINES, Jaime

Mexican poet, b. 25 Mar. 1926, Tuxtla Gutiérrez, Chiapas

S. was born and has spent most of his life in Chiapas. He studied medicine and literature as a young man in Mexico City during the late 1940s and early 1950s. During that time, S. became involved with the so-called "América" group, which included such future literary figures as Emilio CARBALLIDO and Rosario CASTELLANOS. But S. has steadfastly refused to live amidst or participate in the tumultuous and heady literary circles of the capital on a long-term basis, preferring instead the provincial Chiapas. Moreover, even though he enjoys considerable stature in Mexican letters, S. has chosen to make his living in the business world and not that of academia.

In spite of the fact that S. and his poetry have been critically acclaimed, the poet openly disavows poetic convention and technique. The result has been that S. has also produced some poetry of uneven quality. Most critics point to the obvious lack of trajectory or development throughout some thirty years of poetry, suggesting, therefore, a surprising lack of growth or maturation. Nevertheless, S. has received a wide variety of literary awards, including the Chiapas Prize (1960), the Xavier Villaurrutia Award (1972), and the National Prize for Literature (1983).

S. established himself in the 1950s as a major poet by producing four collections. The first, *Horal* (1950; horal), revealed a number of elements and preoccupations that S. would treat in his subsequent poetry: death, alienation, despair, and fear, all presented with shocking intensity. It was a highly lyrical poetry of transcendental inspiration. *La señal* (1951; the sign) continued in the vein of *Horal*, emphasizing death as the one constant of life. S. revealed deeper and darker shadows underscoring a suffocating reality marked by the marginal time or mortality. Additionally, it was a poetry of bitterness and fear.

Perhaps S.'s most provocative work came in 1956 with *Tarumba* (tarumba), a kind of confessional-testimonial cry that is at once violent, sordid, and aggressive. It smacked of self-indulgence and self-preoccupation, but it caught the attention of writers and critics alike, many of whom were intrigued by its experimental nature. In the broadest sense, the work represents the author's intense reaction to his natural state. *Tarumba*, with its cynicism, clamoring, and disdain has helped support an image of S. as a counterhero of sorts, somewhat akin to the beat poets of the 1950s and 1960s in the U.S.

During the 1960s, S. published several collections of poetry and began experimenting with poetic prose, a literary form that he would continue to cultivate. Of particular interest is *Diario semanario y poemas en prosa* (1961; weekly diary and poetry in prose). Using a wide range of everyday topics, S. embarked on a lyrical investigation of the ordinary, in prose, that reflects his already established poetic view as poet. *Diario semanario* exhibits a socially conscious poet who, for the first time in his literature, espouses what might be considered an emerging ideological position.

Yuria (yuria), written in 1967, is a collection of twenty-six poems, thirteen of which were written in poetic prose. It has been judged by critics as extremely irregular in quality. Perhaps its most noteworthy feature is its political orientation relative to its defense of the Cuban revolution, coupled with a distinct anti-American point of view. *Maltiempo* (1972; bad times), S.'s last collection of published works, was also received with widely differing critical evaluations. It is laced with pessimism and despair, suggesting a futility of life. Some critics see in *Maltiempo* S.'s emerging view

that poetry is no longer an efficacious manner in which to confront or examine the world.

Nuevo recuento de poemas (1977; new recompilation of poems) was a collection of all of S.'s poetry in one volume—a major testament to the poet's breadth and importance as an artist. Since *Nuevo recuento* S. has not continued to produce published poetry. Some critics suggest that S. has lost faith in poetry and no longer chooses to write.

Only time will tell whether S. will break his self-imposed poetic silence, but it is certain that S. occupies a major position in 20th-c. Mexican poetry. Both his poetry and poetic prose have earned the author recognition as an outstanding artist.

FURTHER WORKS: *Adán y Eva* (1952); *En mis labios te sé* (1961); *Recuento de poemas* (1962); *Dos poemas=Two poems* (1967); *Poemas sueltos* (1981); *Crónicas del volcán* (1988)

BIBLIOGRAPHY: Durán, M., "J. S. and Mario Antonio Montes de Oca: A Study in Contrast," *Mundus Artium*, 3, 2 (1970): 44–55; Dietrick, C. P., "Breaking Myth, Making Myth: 'Así es' by J. S.," *Chasqui*, 4, 1 (1974): 34–49; Mansour, M., "J. S.: Malestares y desconciertos," *Plural*, 12, 4 (1983): 38–45; Mansour, M., "Estructuras rítmicas y ritmo semántico en la poesía: Un poema de J. S.," *TCrit*, 10, 29 (1984): 159–72; Hurtado, E., "J. S.: el inútil milagro del misterio," *México en el Arte*, 14 (1986): 125–26; *La poesía en el corazón del hombre: J. S. en sus sesenta años* (1987); Armenjol, A., "El experimento de J. S.: estudio de *Turumba*," *Plural*, 17, 199 (1988): 25–35

—SAM L. SLICK

SACHS, Nelly

German poet, b. 10 Dec. 1891, Berlin; d. 12 May 1970, Stockholm, Sweden

Widely regarded as the most powerful poetic voice in the German language commenting on the Nazi Holocaust, S. grew up in Berlin as the only child of a well-to-do industrialist. Her education was in large part a private one, and the artistic home environment of her assimilated Jewish family instilled in the child a love of literature and a desire to become a dancer. At the age of seventeen she began to write, producing mostly atmospheric, slightly melancholy, neoromantic poetry in traditional, rhymed forms, including some sonnets, but also puppet plays with a fairytale flavor. In 1921 she published a volume entitled *Legenden und Erzählungen* (legends and tales). Reflecting the author's interest in the common roots of Judaism and Christianity, some of these early stories are Christological. In succeeding years S. became absorbed in both German and Jewish mysticism, particularly the writings of Jakob Böhme (1575–1624), the Zohar (the cabalistic "Book of Splendor"), and the lore and literature of Hasidism. Her verse appeared in various newspapers and between 1933 and 1938 in Jewish journals. (She later rejected her early work and declined to have it reissued.) In the 1930s S. was caught up in the tragedy of German Jewry, watching friends and relatives being carried off to their doom. In 1940 she and her mother were able to escape to Sweden through the good offices of a German lady who had befriended them, Gudrun Harlan Dähnert, of Prince Eugene of the Swedish Royal Court, and of the writer Selma

Lagerlöf (1858–1940), with whom her admirer S. had corresponded for many years.

While living in Stockholm and caring for her ailing mother (who died in 1950), S. resumed writing in 1943 in a state of great agitation. "Death gave me my language. . . My metaphors are my wounds," she once said, and her statement "Writing is my mute outcry; I only wrote because I had to free myself" stamps her as a soul sister of Franz KAFKA. With volume after volume of searingly accusatory yet ultimately conciliatory poetry she disproved Theodor W. ADORNO'S dictum that after Auschwitz poetry could no longer be written. S. eventually achieved such competence in the Swedish language that she was able to publish several highly praised volumes of translations from such poets as Gunnar EKELÖF, Erik LINDEGREN, and Johannes Edfelt (b. 1904).

Her seventieth birthday was marked by the publication of her collected poetry under the title *Fahrt ins Staublose* (1961; journey into a dustless realm). Following years of isolation and obscurity, S. found an increasing international readership. The culmination of several honors—including the Droste-Hülshoff Prize and the Peace Prize of the German Book Trade, both received in her native country—was the Nobel Prize for literature (for "her works of forgiveness, of deliverance, of peace"), which she shared in 1966 with S. Y. AGNON—"Agnon," she said, "represents the State of Israel. I represent the tragedy of the Jewish people." There have been several homage volumes dedicated to her, including two entitled N. S. *zu Ehren* (1961, 1966; in honor of N. S.), and *Das Buch der N. S.* (1968; the book of N. S.). Beset by physical ailments and nervous breakdowns over a period of many years, S. finally succumbed to cancer.

The richly allusive verse play *Eli: Ein Mysterienspiel vom Leiden Israels* (1951; *Eli: A Mystery Play of the Sufferings of Israel*, 1967), written in 1943 and years later presented on the stage, as a radio play, and as an opera, may be regarded as the fountainhead of S.'s subsequent work. In seventeen loosely connected scenes the tragedy of an eight-year-old shepherd boy in a Polish village during the war is presented through flashbacks interwoven with the legend of the "Lamed Vovniks," the Thirty-six Just Men, those who support the "invisible universe." Recurring images in S.'s poetry are stars, dust, sand (symbolizing the past and the passing of time), and the butterfly (signifying transcendence and re-creation). The motif of flight and pursuit and the symbol of the hunter and his quarry are at the center of her thought, and for their expression she favored the cyclic form, particularly in the collection *In den Wohnungen des Todes* (written 1944–45, pub. 1947; in the habitations of death). *Sternverdunkelung* (1949; eclipse of the stars), contains poems expressing an unquenchable faith in the indestructibility of the Jewish people and the significance of their mission. The extended sequence *Glühende Rätsel* (1963–66; glowing enigmas) consists of curiously compressed, elliptic, abstract, and hortatory poems. *Zeichen im Sand* (1962; signs in the sand), S.'s collected dramatic works, comprises fourteen dramas—short experimental and ritualistic plays, dramatic happenings, and "scenic studies." Reality coalesces with vision, and the word spills over into music, pantomime, and the dance.

Through her painfully beautiful allegorical and metaphorical variations on her basic theme, the Holocaust, hauntingly expressed in free verse employing an ecstatic, imagistic, hymnal language, S. planted "lilies on the equator of anguish" and lifted the sufferings of her people onto a cosmic plane. Hans Magnus ENZENSBERGER has called her work "the only poetic testimony that can hold its own next to the speechless horror of documentary reports," and the German-Jewish critic Kurt Pinthus (1886–1975) has described it as "the presumably final expression in the German language of the ancestral sequence of six thousand years that began with the psalmists and the prophets."

FURTHER WORKS: *Und niemand weiß weiter* (1957); *Flucht und Verwandlung* (1959); *Späte Gedichte* (1965); *Die Suchende* (1966); *Teile dich Nacht* (1971); *Briefe der N. S.* (1984). FURTHER WORKS IN ENGLISH: *O the Chimneys* (1967); *The Seeker and Other Poems* (1970)

BIBLIOGRAPHY: Zohn, H., "N. S.: Catharsis and Purification," *Congress Bi-weekly*, (17 Nov. 1966): 18–20; Syrkin, M., "N. S.: Poet of the Holocaust," *Midstream*, (Mar. 1967): 13–23; Bronsen, D., "The Dead among the Living: N. S.'s *Eli*," *Judaism*, 16, 1 (1967): 120–28; Bauke, J. P., "N. S.: Poet of the Holocaust," *Jewish Heritage*, 10, 4 (1968): 34–37; Kersten, P., N. S. (1969); Blomster, W. V., "A Theosophy of the Creative World: The Zohar Cycle of N. S.", GR, 44 (1969): 211–17; Bezzel-Dischner, G., *Poetik des modernen Gedichts: Zur Lyrik von N. S.* (1970); Berendsohn, W. A., N. S. (1974); Dodds, D., "The Process of Renewal in N. S.'s *Eli*," GQ, 49 (1976): 50–58; Bahr, E., N. S. (1980); Dinesen, R., N. S. (1992); Kessler, M., et al., eds., N. S. Neue Interpretationen (1994)

—HARRY ZOHN

al-SA'DĀWĪ, Nawāl

Egyptian novelist and short-story writer, b. 1931, Kafr al-Tahla

From a village in Lower Egypt's Delta, S. began writing stories as a child, a predilection she resumed while a medical student at Cairo University. Graduating in 1955, she worked in public-sector medicine, becoming director general of health education and editor of a health journal in the Ministry of Health. She began publishing fiction in the late 1950s; her first book was the short-story collection, *Ta'allamtu al-hubb* (n.d.; I Learned Love), followed shortly thereafter by more short stories and her first novel, *Mudhakkirāt tabība* (1957; *Memoirs of a Woman Doctor*, 1989). She went on to become a prolific novelist and short-story writer, widely translated across the globe. Perhaps her best-known novel remains *Imra'a 'inda nuqtat al-sifr* (1975; *Woman at Point Zero*, 1983). Her fiction explores gender politics in Arab, majority-Muslim societies, tackling the interplay of economically, politically, and religiously shaped modes of class and gender oppression, as in *Mawt al-rajul al-wahīd 'alā al-ard* (1976; *God Dies by the Nile*, 1985); *Ughniyat al-atfāl al-dā'iriyya* (1978; *The Circling Song*, 1989); *Suqūt al-Imām* (1987; *The Fall of the Imam*, 1988); *Jannāt wa-Iblīs* (1992; *The Innocence of the Devil*, 1994); *al-Hubb fizaman al-naft* (1993; Love in the Era of Oil). She has also published a memoir of imprisonment under Sadat entitled *Mudhakkir ātī fī sijn al-nisā'* (1983; *Memoirs from the Women's Prison*, 1986); a descriptive memoiristic travel account, *Rihlātī fī al-'alam* (1987; *My Travels around the World*, 1991); and two plays, the most well-known of which is *Isīz* (1986; Isis).

S.'s fame in the Arab world stems primarily from her nonfictional writing; the fearless and iconoclastic *al-Mar'a wa'l-jins* (1970; Woman and Sex) was the partial or whole cause of her dismissal from the Ministry of Health in 1972, and it was followed by other works that explore the politics of sexuality on the experiential and empirical basis provided by her work as a psychiatrist. After her dismissal from the Ministry, she worked on issues of gender and neurosis at Ain Shams University in Cairo and had a private practice. She first came to the attention of feminists in the West with an English-language summation of some of these nonfictional writings, *The Hidden Face of Eve: Women in the Arab World* (1980), and since that time she has become a familiar figure on international feminist circuits. She worked as a UN advisor for programs on women in Africa and the Middle East (1979-80). She founded the Arab Women Solidarity Association (AWSA) in 1982, which was dissolved by the government in 1991 and since has been involved in court challenges to that decree, as she outlines in *Ma'raka jadīda da fī qadiyat al-mar'a* (1992; A New Struggle in the Women's Cause). A collection of her speeches and occasional writings has appeared as *The N. al-S. Reader* (1997).

S. has been controversial not only for her criticism of gender- and class-based oppression in Third World societies but also as a fiction writer in the limelight. Respect for her courage as an activist has not always been matched by admiration for her fictional writing, which has often been attacked among critics in the Arab world and in the West as repetitive in theme and language, programmatic, and superficial in characterization. On the other hand, her oeuvre has been analyzed in detail as a radical and artistically powerful rewriting of received textual and social practices in contemporary Egypt. Whatever one's opinion, her presence and her works are difficult to ignore.

FURTHER WORKS: *'An al-mar'a* (1988)

BIBLIOGRAPHY: Malti-Douglas, F., *Woman's Body, Woman's Word: Gender and Discourse in Arabo-Islamic Writing* (1991); Malti-Douglas, F., *Men, Women, and God(s): N. al-S. and Arab Feminist Poetics* (1995)

—MARILYN BOOTH

SADOVEANU, Mihail

Romanian short-story writer and novelist, b. 5 Nov. 1880, Paşcani; d. 19 Oct. 1961, Bucharest

S. was from Moldavia, and the regional background is important to his works. Although from an intellectual family, he did not complete his university studies but instead established himself quickly as a writer. In a single year, 1904, he published three volumes of short stories—*Povestiri* (tales), *Dureri înnăbuşite* (stifled woes), and *Crîsma lui Mos Precu, si alte povestiri* (Old Precu's pub, and other tales)—and a novel, *Şoimii* (the Soimis). His productivity remained high; he contributed to countless literary magazines and was the editor of a number of literary periodicals. Although he did not consider himself a dramatist, he wrote some plays between 1910 and 1919, when he was director of the National Theater in Iaşi—for example, *Zile vesele după război* (happy days after the war) and *De ziua mamei* (on mother's day)—all unpublished.

In his early works, S. penetrates the souls of primitive men. His characters are taciturn, passive people. A single act drains all their vitality, and they relapse into their initial savagery and silence. One

of S.'s preferred subjects is the peasant's confrontation of modern civilization. The civilized world appears absurd or decadent, and the traditional way of life is always favored.

A number of S.'s works, for example, *Floare ofilită* (1906; a withered flower) and *Însemnările lui Neculai Manea* (1907; the notes of Neculai Manea), describe the barren lives of petty bureaucrats and frustrated intellectuals in provincial towns. The main character in the novel *Apa mortilor* (1911; the water of the dead) is a Madame Bovary type, whose accumulated dissatisfaction leads to regression: she abandons family life and retires to the countryside. The village acts as a haven for those who cannot adapt to modern life. S. excelled in describing nature and in portraying characters in total communication with it.

With *Soimii, Neamul Soimărestilor* (1915; Şoimaru's kin), *Zodia Cancerului; sau, Vremea Ducăi Vodă* (1929; *Under the Sign of the Crab*, 1963), *Nunta domniţei Ruxandra* (1932; Princess Ruxandra's wedding), *Fratii Jderi* (3 vols., 1935–42; the Jder brothers), and *Nicoară Potcoavă* (1952; *Nicoară Potcoavă* 1963), S. developed the Romanian historical novel. Lacking epic invention, these works are strong in their creation of the atmosphere of a specific epoch.

S.'s most important work is the novel *Baltagul* (1930; *The Hatchet*, 1965). Inspired by the epic ballad *Miorita* (Mioriţa), a masterpiece of Romanian folklore, the story has the quality of a peasant detective novel: intelligent and determined, Vitoria Lipan discovers and punishes her husband's murderers.

S. used colorful language with archaic inflections, influenced by 17th- and 18th-c. written Romanian—a language that is sui generis and cannot be assigned to any particular region or period.

After the establishment of the Communist regime, S. became a spokesman for the new system. He tried to convince his readers that the Soviet Union was Romania's best friend in *Lumina vine de la răsărit* (1945; light comes from the east); that even before the existence of Russia or Romania, the Cossacks acted fraternally toward the Moldavians in *Nicoară Potcoavă*; and that the collectivization of agriculture in Romania was an option that the farmers elected in *Mitrea Cocor* (1949; *Mitrea Cocor*, 1953). For these works, the regime rewarded him with high official positions and prizes.

FURTHER WORKS: *Comoara dorobanţului* (1905); *Povestiri din război* (1905); *Povestiri de sărbători* (1906); *Mormîntul unui copil* (1906); *Amintirile căprarului Gheorghiţă* (1906); *Vremuri de bejenie* (1907); *La noi la Viisoara* (1907); *O istorie de demult* (1908); *Duduia Margareta* (1908); *Haia Sanis* (1908); *Oameni şi locuri* (1908); *Cîntecul amintirii* (1909); *Povestiri de sară* (1910); *Un instigator* (1912); *Bordeienii, şi alte povestiri* (1912; *The Mud-Hut Dwellers*, 1964); *Foi de toamnă* (1916); *44 de zile în Bulgaria* (1916); *File însîngerate* (1917); *Frunze în furtună* (1920); *Cocostîrcul albastru* (1921); *Strada Lăpusneanu* (1921); *Pildele lui Cuconu Vichentie* (1922); *Neagra Sarului* (1922); *Nuvele şi schite* (1922); *Ti-aduci aminte* (1922); *Oameni din lună* (1923); *Venea o moară pe Siret* (1925; *The Mill That Came with the Floods*, 1963); *Tara de dincolo de negură* (1926); *Dumbrava minunată* (1926); *Împărăţia apelor* (1928); *Demonul tinereţii* (1928); *Hanul-Ancuţei* (1928; *Ancuţas Inn*, 1962); *Olanda: Note de călătorie* (1928); *O întîmplare ciudată* (1929); *Măria-Sa puiul pădurii* (1931); *Uvar* (1932); *Trenul fantomă* (1932); *Creanga de aur* (1933); *Locul unde nu s-a întîmplat nimic; sau, Tîrg moldovenesc din 1890* (1933); *Soarele în bal a; sau, Aventurile sahului* (1933); *Viaţa lui Stefan cel Mare* (1934); *Noptile de Sînziene* (1934); *Cele mai vechi amintiri* (1935);

Pastele bla jinilor (1935); *Cazul Eugenitei Costea* (1936); *Istorisiri de vînătoare* (1937); *Valea Frumoasei* (1938); *Ochi de urs* (1938); *Culegere de povestiri* (1939); *Vechime* (1940); *Divanul persian* (1940); *Opere* (4 vols., 1940–45); *Ostrovul lupilor* (1941); *Povestile de la Bradu-Strîmb* (1943); *Anii de ucenicie* (1944); *Caleidoscop* (1946); *Fantezii răsăritene* (1946); *Păuna mică* (1948); *Focuri în ceață* (1948); *Poezia cimiliturilor* (1949); *Povestiri* (1950); *Povestiri din trecut* (1950); *Despre marele povestitor Ion Creangă* (1951); *Lupta pentru pace* (1951); *Nada florilor-Amintirile unui pescar cu undita* (1951); *Clont de fier* (1951); *Cîntece bătrîneşti* (1951); *Opere alese* (4 vols., 1952): *Aventuri în lunca Dunării* (1954); *Muncitori şi păstori* (1954); *Istorisiri vechi si noi* (1954); *Evocări* (1954); *Opere* (22 vols., 1954–73); *Corespondenta debutului, 1894–1904* (1977). **FURTHER WORKS IN ENGLISH:** *Evening Tales* (1962); *Tales of War* (1962)

BIBLIOGRAPHY: Ciopraga, C., *M. S.* (1966); Paleologu, A., *"The Golden Bough in S.'s Golden Bough, CREL,* No. 4 (1977): 68–79; Paleologu, A., "The Murdered God: A Central Theme in S.'s Work," *CREL,* No. 4 (1979): 26–35; Brezianu, A., "The Unknown Gate': *Ochi de Urs* by M. S. and *The Bear* by William Faulkner: A Parallel," *Synthesis,* 7 (1980): 123–30

—CONSTANTIN ERETESCU

SA'EDI, Gholam-Hossein

(pseud.: Gowhar Morad) Iranian dramatist, short-story writer, screenwriter, and novelist; b. 1935, Tabriz; d. 24 Nov. 1985, Paris, France

S. was born to the poverty-stricken family of a tailor apprentice turned civil servant. He spent his childhood in Tabriz, where he received his secondary education. From the time he learned to read, he was a lover of literature. Even when he was in medical school in Tabriz and Tehran, he said that for every medical book he read, he read ten novels. Writing became second nature, first for newspapers and then his own fiction and nonfiction. By the time he died one month short of his fiftieth birthday, he had more than forty works to his credit.

S. was an engaging writer committed to the improvement of the lot of the poor and downtrodden. His commitment to destitute people led him to open a doctor's office in the poor section of Tehran, where he offered psychiatric consultations free of charge. S. also became an amateur anthropologist who traveled around the country studying the living conditions of people in rural areas and writing about their experiences. He was arrested several times for these sociopolitical activities and in 1974–1975 spent eleven months in prison.

S.'s visit to the U.S. in 1978 under the auspices of a group of American writers and publishers turned into a crusade for freedom of expression in Iran, and was well-reflected in three articles in the *New York Times* and one in the *Washington Post.* S.'s desire for freedom of expression made him settle in France during the revolutionary upheaval in Iran. Heartbroken and far from home, he died in exile in Paris.

S. must be considered the leading dramatist of Iran. His plays, marked by political symbolism and allegory, combine elements of the traditional Iranian performing arts, Western classical drama, and the THEATER OF THE ABSURD. Though S.'s plays are set predominantly in Iranian locales, they transcend national and artistic boundaries as they join the universal battle against tyranny, oppression, alienation, poverty, suffering, and ignorance. Even when S. objects to the blind copying of the Western life-style by Iranians, it has a universal dimension. He sees national customs, traditions, and ways of life as complementing other people and nations rather than creating separation.

S. began his career as a dramatist in 1957 with the publication in literary magazines of three short one-act plays. This was followed by a collection of one-act plays under the title *Panj namayeshnameh az enqelab-e mashrutiyyat* (1966; five plays from the constitutional revolution). These one-act plays should be regarded as studies that S. wrote to test his skills in play writing fundamentals such as unity of time and action. The action in these plays takes place in his native Azerbaijan during the constitutional movement from 1905 until the coup by Reza Khan, later Reza Shah. Social and national issues underline the action of the plays. In his next collection of one-act plays, *Khaneh rowshani* (1967; housewarming), S. brings in complex psychological problems that no doubt were drawn from his psychiatric practice. Some of the plays from the first and second collections were well received by television viewers. Symbolism and allegory play an important role in S.'s writing and go hand in hand with the stark realism. However, in his *Dah lal bazi* (1963; ten pantomimes) S. departs from a realistic portrayal and plunges into a surrealistic world bordering on the absurd.

S.'s first full-length play was *Karbafakha dan sangar* (1960; *Workaholics in the Trenches,* 1989). The play, which deals with the ecological dangers to the shores of the Persian Gulf posed by development of a sulfur mine and processing plant, probably would have fared well in the Western world today. Against this background, the play tells the story of a young, newly married engineer and his wife. It is a strong commentary on how rapid industrialization in a traditional society uproots individuals and groups of people. *Club be Dastha-ye Varazil* (1965; the stick wielders of Varazil) is a highly symbolic play, in which the fields of poor villagers are being destroyed by wild boars. However, it is the hunters invited to take care of the boars who pose the greater threat to the villagers' meager wealth. It is easier for the villagers to cope with the hardship represented by boars than by their "liberators." Another community unable to fend off danger is portrayed in the play *A-ye bi Kolah, A-ye ba Kolah* (1967; *O Fool, O Fooled,* 1987). In *Mah-e Asal* (1978; *Honeymoon,* 1989), the last play he wrote in Iran before emigrating to Paris, he portrays the life of an individual in a police state. It is a strong condemnation of the Iran of the 1970s. S.'s last plays, written in exile and published posthumously, are *Pardedaran-e a'ineh afruz* (1986; the mirror-polishing storytellers) and *Otello dar sarzamin-e ajayeb* (1986; Othello in wonderland). Both are sardonic attacks on the Islamic Republic of Iran's enforcement of behavior patterns acceptable to the new, revolutionary standards as well as the war with Iraq, in which young men die only to bring anguish to their families.

S.'s screenplays are as powerful as his plays, and several movies based on his screenplays received international awards. *Gav* (the cow) won the 1971 Venice Film Festival Award, and *Dayere-ye Mina* (the cycle) earned an award at the 1977 International Paris Film Festival. The screenplays are based on S.'s short stories. He has six stories to his credit: "Shabneshini ba Shokuh" (1960; the splendid evening party), "Azadaran-e bayal" (1964; the mourners of bayal), "Dandil" (1966; "Dandil," 1981), "Vahemenha-ye bi namo neshan" (1967; vague misgivings), "Tars-o larz" (1968;

fear and trembling), and "Gur-o gahvareh" (1972; the grave and the cradle).

In both his dramas and short stories, S. is interested in the common human being's daily struggles, fears, hopes, and sorrows. The stories are like vignettes of Iranian life with real people and their national and religious customs, full of human irony and political metaphor. As a dramatist S. was influenced by Samuel BECKETT, Eugène LONESCO, and the Theater of the Absurd.

S.'s novel is entitled *Tup* (1967; the cannon). The few issues of S.'s magazine *Alefba*, which he tried to continue in France, are further monuments to his genius and versatility.

FURTHER WORKS: *Kalate-ye gol* (1961); *Behtarin baba-ye donia* (1965); *Dikteh va zaviyeh* (1968); *Parvarbandan* (1969); *Janeshin* (1970); *Vay bar maghlub* (1970); *Aqebat-e qalam-e farsai* (1975); *In dar on dar* (1975). FURTHER WORKS IN ENGLISH: *Dandil: Stories from Iranian Life* (1981)

BIBLIOGRAPHY: Hillmann, M. C., ed., *LE&W*, 20 (1976): 144–47; Southgate, M. S., *Modern Persian Short Stories* (1980): 180–201; Javadi, H., Introduction to *Dandil: Stories from Iranian Life* (1981): vii–xiii; Jabbari, A., and R. Olson, eds., *Iran: Essays on a Revolution in the Making* (1981): 130–33; Kapuscinski, G., *Modern Persian Drama* (1987): xiii–xvii: 101–73; Ghanoonparvar, M. R., and J. Green, *Iranian Drama* (1989): xxi–xxii: 1–132; Hillmann, M. C., *Iranian Culture: A Persianist View* (1990): 111–18

—PETER J. CHELKOWSKI

SAGAN, Françoise

(pseud. of Françoise Quoirez) French novelist and dramatist, b. 21 June 1935, Cajarc

Born into a well-to-do family (her father was an industrialist), S. lived in Paris from 1935 to 1939. With the outbreak of World War II, the family moved to the provinces, living mainly in Lyon. After the liberation of France in 1945, S. returned to Paris. In 1952 she enrolled at the Sorbonne, but in July 1953 failed the examinations that would have permitted her to pursue her studies toward a higher academic degree.

Gently chided by her mother for her failure, S., then eighteen years old, spent several weeks during the summer writing her first novel, *Bonjour tristesse* (1954; *Bonjour Tristesse*, 1955). The novel was an immense commercial success. The extravagant publicity that surrounded the young writer, transforming her into the spokeswoman of a generation of bored and jaded teenage girls, made S.'s name famous overnight. (Her pseudonym is derived from the fictional Princess of Sagan in Marcel PROUST's *Remembrance of Things Past*.)

Like all of S.'s subsequent fiction, *Bonjour tristesse* is short. The narrator, who is a seventeen-year-old girl, her father, and his current, rather vulgar mistress, are spending the summer in a rented villa on the Mediterranean coast. When an elegant former mistress arrives for an extended stay, the two older women engage in a covert struggle for the man's affections. In addition, the narrator begins a liaison with a young man who lives in the neighboring villa. The shifting relationships are ultimately resolved by an automobile accident in which the father's former mistress dies (actually she committed suicide) and by the approach of autumn, marking, as it does, a return to Paris and the termination of the summer's bittersweet idyll.

The plots of S.'s novels are invariably thin, the characters sketchy. Still, her fiction clearly belongs in the venerable tradition of the French psychological novel. S.'s restrained prose, dry and austere, recalls that of the great classical French writers. Within the coordinates of a classical form, however, S. expresses an amoralism, a precocious weariness with the world that many of her readers find modern and comfortingly fashionable. Strongly influenced by the early works of Jean-Paul SARTRE and Simone de BEAUVOIR, she creates characters whose lives are marked by loneliness, by an acute sense of the passage of time, and especially by boredom. Their principal occupation is the pursuit of pleasure, and they view each other mainly as instruments to bring them enjoyment. But they are continually disappointed by the ephemerality and vanity of all pleasure, of all human relationships. Eschewing grandiloquence of any kind, S. presents a view of reality that is fundamentally harsh and uncompromising.

Succeeding novels are variations of the themes enunciated in *Bonjour tristesse*. S.'s fiction has remained confined within the boundaries of the tiny world evoked in that first novel. Her characters, although they tend to be somewhat older in her more recent fiction, are virtually interchangeable from one book to another. Taken together, her novels express a certain state of mind, a certain mood, a certain sense of malaise and bewilderment that accurately characterize the life of one segment of western European society from the 1950s to the mid-1970s.

One of S.'s most interesting works is *Des bleus à l'âme* (1972; *Scars on the Soul*, 1974), a book that is part essay, part autobiography, and part novel. Here she comments with lucidity and irony on her own life, her fictional world, and on the charmingly fanciful novella that is woven into the fabric of the book.

Also the author of several delightfully stylish plays, S. has shown considerable talent in writing dialogue that is witty and entertaining.

FURTHER WORKS: *Un certain sourire* (1956; *A Certain Smile*, (1956); *Dans un mois, dans un an* (1957; *Those without Shadows*, 1957); *Aimez-vous Brahms?* (1959; *Aimez-Vous Brahms?*, 1960); *Château en Suède* (1960); *Le gigolo* (1960); *Les merveilleux nuages* (1961; *The Wonderful Clouds*, 1962); *Les violons parfois* (1962); *La robe mauve de Valentine* (1963); *Landru* (1963); *Toxique* (1964; *Toxique*, 1964); *Bonheur, impair et passe* (1964); *La chamade* (1965; *La Chamade*, 1966); *Le cheval évanoui, suivi de L'écharde* (1966); *Le garde du cœur* (1968; *The Heart-Keeper*, 1968); *Un peu de soleil dans l'eau froide* (1969; *A Few Hours of Sunlight*, 1971); *Un piano dans l'herbe* (1970); *Il est des parfums* . . . . . . (1973); *Un profil perdu* (1974; *Lost Profile*, 1977); *Réponses 1954–1974* (1974; *Nightbird: Conversations with F. S.,*, 1980); *Brigitte Bardot* (1975; *Brigitte Bardot*, 1976); *Des yeux de soie* (1975; *Silken Eyes*, 1977); *Le lit défait* (1977; *The Unmade Bed*, 1978); *Le sang doré des Borgia* (1977); *Il fait beau jour et nuit* (1979); *Le chien couchant* (1980; *Salad Days*, 1984); *La femme fardée* (1981; *The Painted Lady*, 1983); *Musiques de scènes* (1981; *Incidental Music*, 1983); *Un orage immobile* (1983; *The Still Storm*, 1986); *Avec mon meilleur souvenir* (1984; *With Fondest Regards*, 1985); *De guerre lasse* (1985; *Engagements of the Heart*, 1987); *Sand et Musset: lettres d'amour* (1985); *Un sang d'aquarelle* (1987; *Painting in Blood*, 1988); *Sara Bernhardt: le rire incassalbe*

(1987; *Dear Sarah Bernhardt*, 1988); *La sentinelle de Paris* (1988); *La laisse* (1989); *Les faux-fuyants* (1991; *Evasion*, 1993); *Répliques* (1992); *Et toute ma sympathie* (1993); *Un chagrin de passage* (1994; *A Fleeting Sorrow*, 1995); *Le miroir égaré* (1996)

BIBLIOGRAPHY: Hourdin, G., *Le cas F. S.* (1958); Mourgue, G., *F. S.* (1958); Cismaru, A., "S.'s Theory of Complicity," *DR*, 45 (1966): 457–69; Vandromme, P., *F. S.; ou, L'élégance de survivre* (1977); Garis, L., "S: Encore Tristesse," *NYTMag*, (16 Nov. 1980): 64–80; Poirot-Delpech, B., *Bonjour S.* (1985); Miller, J., *F. S.* (1988); Lamy, J., *S.* (1988)

—ROBERT D. COTTRELL

SAINT-EXUPÉRY, Antoine de

French novelist, journalist, and philosopher, b. 29 June 1900, Lyon; d. 31 July 1944, near Corsica

S.-E.'s mother, of Provençal ancestry, was the Baroness de Fonscolombe. His father, Count Jean Marie de Saint-Exupéry, of an old Limousin family, died four years after the birth of Antoine. The youngest of five children, S.-E. had a happy childhood under the tutelage of his gentle and charming mother. After failing in his examination for naval school, he took military training in Strasbourg, then at a flying school in Rabat, Morocco, where he obtained his pilot's license and a commission as second lieutenant. Unhappy as a truck salesman in Paris, he became mail pilot for the Latécoère line from Toulouse to Dakar, Senegal, then chief of the Cape Juby airport. Returning to France with the manuscript of his first novel, *Courrier Sud* (1929; *Southern Mail*, 1933), he was sent to South America as director of Aeroposta Argentina. He came back to France in 1931 with the manuscript of *Vol de nuit* (1931; *Night Flight*, 1932). After Aeroposta failed, S.-E. spent several years as a test pilot. In 1935, competing for a prize for fastest flight from Paris to Saigon, he crashed in the Libyan desert. After newspaper assignments covering Russia and the Spanish Civil War, S.-E. attempted to fly from Canada to the tip of South America; he sustained serious injuries when he crashed on a takeoff in Guatemala. At the outbreak of World War II he enlisted as a combat pilot, and when France fell he went into exile in New York. After the American invasion of North Africa, S.-E. rejoined his squadron, flew eight dangerous missions, and was shot down and killed over the Mediterranean while returning to his Corsica base.

S.-E.'s first complete novel, *Courrier Sud*, is a not entirely successful attempt to bind together his own unhappy love story and his adventurous life as an aviator in North Africa. *Vol de nuit*, which won the Fémina Prize and was filmed with an all-star cast, is a superior novel. In the character of Rivière, director of a South American airline, we see allegiance to a cause greater than any individual: the triumph of an idea. The success of this novel is due not only to its philosophical grandeur but also to its pictorial beauty and its tense and dramatic story of the aviator's struggle with the storm.

Terre des hommes (1939; *Wind, Sand and Stars*, 1939), awarded the Grand Prize for the Novel of the French Academy, is not so much a novel as a series of character studies, vivid travelogues, philosophic reflections, and epic adventures. It would be difficult to surpass the quiet dignity with which Mermoz meets his final rendezvous with destiny over the South Pacific, while the fantastic saga of Guillaumet dragging himself day after day over the icy crags of the Andes shows the triumph of the indomitable human spirit. The crowning episode of the book, a plane crash followed by a long march of two parched and staggering men through the Libyan desert, ranks with the great adventure tales of all time.

Ostensibly, *Pilote de guerre* (1942; *Flight to Arras*, 1942) retells the reconnaissance flight of S.-E. as he skimmed low over flaming Arras. Flashes of poetic description of the strange and savage beauty of war contrast with his lyric portrayal of the unadorned beauty found in the humble household things of his Orconte billet. Here also we find the thoughtful musings of a moralist and philosopher as S.-E. takes up the defense of France against foreign critics.

Le petit prince (1943; *The Little Prince*, 1943), unique among all his writings, is a delicate and ethereal fairy tale; it is apparently addressed to children, but its philosophical overtones as a parable will be understood only by adults. Because of its poetic grace, freshness of imagery, whimsical fantasy, delicate irony, and warm tenderness it is likely to join that select company of books that have endeared themselves to children and grown-ups alike.

Lettre à un otage (1944; *Letter to a Hostage*, 1950) is one of the most exquisite of S.-E. works. The hostage to whom this letter is addressed is his dear friend Léon Werth, whose life is in jeopardy because he is old, because he is ill, and above all because he is a Jew. The central episode recounts the happy hours S.-E. and Werth spent together on the terrace of a little inn over the Saône. It is characteristic of S.-E. that in the conclusion he should give a universal significance to a purely personal anecdote.

The vast *Citadelle* (1948; *The Wisdom of the Sands*, 1950), assembled from the notes left by S.-E., is laid in the Sahara. The title *Citadelle* may be understood first as the empire of traditions, rituals, and patriotic fervor with which the Berber prince binds its citizens together, and second as the city of the spirit to be founded in each individual heart. With its biblical rhetoric, *Citadelle* lacks the dramatic power of the earlier volumes, but it is a treasure house of observations on all the great problems of human life and destiny, reminiscent of Pascal.

Every year new biographies and essays prove that the popularity and influence of S.-E. show no signs of diminishing. The critic Henri Peyre is probably correct in his judgment that although S.-E. will not rank among the giants of the French novel, he is destined for immortality as thinker and philosopher. Unlike those of most writers, his books grew out of actual, not vicarious, participation. The final form in which this theme of participation is expressed is the role of "exchange" or creative impulse-exchanging oneself for something nobler and more precious-closely allied to the feeling for immortality. The essential unity of S.-E.'s life and philosophical message to our times is this joy of participation, of sharing and sacrifice for others, inbued with a faith in the triumph of the human spirit.

FURTHER WORKS: *L'aviateur* (1926); *Lettres de jeunesse* (1953); *Lettres à l'amie inventée* (1953); *Lettres à sa mère* (1955); *Un sens à la vie* (1956; *A Sense of Life*, 1966)

BIBLIOGRAPHY: Anet, D., *A. de S.-E.* (1946); Chevrier, P., *A. de S.-E.* (1949); Pelissier, G., *Les cinq visages de S.-E.* (1951); Smith, M., *Knight of the Air: The Life and Works of A. de S.-E.* (1956); Estang, L., *S.-E. par luimême* (1956); François, C., *L'esthétique de S.-E.* (1957); Crane, H. E., *L'humanisme dans l'oeuvre de S.-E.*

(1957); Migéo, M., *S.-E.* (1958); Albérès, R., *S.-E.* (1961); Cate, C., *S.-E.: His Life and Times* (1970); Robinson, J. D., *A. de S.-E.* (1984)

—MAXWELL A. SMITH

SAINT-JOHN PERSE

(pseud. of Alexis Saint-Léger Léger) French poet, b. 31 May 1887, Saint-Léger-les-Feuilles, Guadeloupe; d. 20 Sept. 1975, Giens

S.-J. P. drew upon an extraordinarily varied experience: childhood years in and around the tropical island of Guadeloupe; adolescence in Pau, France; formal training at the University of Bordeaux, where he received a degree in law (1910) but also studied philosophy, classics, anthropology, and science. His first poems date from this period. In 1916, having entered the Foreign Service, S.-J. P. embarked for a tour of duty in China and remained there through 1921. Recalled to France, he rose steadily in the diplomatic ranks, eventually serving as Secretary General for Foreign Affairs. In private, he pursued his poet's calling but did not publish. At the capitulation of France in 1940, S.-J. P., a confirmed anti-Nazi, was dismissed from government service; half a dozen of his unpublished manuscripts were confiscated by the Germans and presumably lost. Taking refuge in the U.S., he settled in Washington, D.C., and soon resumed writing. Two important events marked the poet's late years: his receiving the Nobel Prize for literature (1960) and his decision to return permanently to France (1967).

The poems of the early Éloges (1911, rev. ed., 1925; *Éloges, and Other Poems,* 1944) celebrate S.-J. P.'s Antillian childhood, the people and events of the West Indies, a way of life centered in the patriarchal family, and especially nature—lush tropical vegetation, volcanic landscapes, the sea, experienced by the poet as light and as movement. In "Images à Crusoé" ("Pictures for Crusoe"), written when S.-J. P. was seventeen, childhood assumes the form of a retrospective, dreamlike vision, conveyed indirectly through the persona of the aging Robinson Crusoe. By contrast, the overtly autobiographical "Pour fêter une enfance" ("To Celebrate a Childhood") and "Éloges" ("Éloges") re-create impressions as they were first experienced, bringing into relief a world of wonder seen through the child's sensibility: pungent tastes, strange, monstrous creatures, forms and objects that blend one with the other or acquire human features. Within this fluid universe of sensuously felt harmonies and connections, of a near instinctive connivance between man and nature, childhood is not so much remembered as made present by means of eulogistic, hieratic language.

Anabase (1924; *Anabasis,* 1930) and *Amitié du prince* (1924; part of 2nd ed. of *Éloges,* 1925; "Friendship of the Prince," in *Éloges, and Other Poems,* 1944), two of the three known poems from the diplomatic period, initiate S.-J. P.'s mature idiom, characterized by elegance in diction, stylization, extreme compression, the consistent use of the verset (a stanza form with long, irregular lines derived from biblical passages), recurrent elliptical images, and a thematic shift from fascination with the forces of nature to a concern for human action. *Anabase* conceives action both as external action among men and as inward striving. A sustained but rhapsodical narrative overlaid with metaphors, it suggests, by means of loosely connected images, a military expedition recounted by a nomad leader. On the symbolic level, reaching out beyond the accidents of action, beyond time and beyond geography, the

Saint-John Perse

poet strives to present a mythic vision of the potentialities and achievements of the human spirit. He highlights the force of dreams, the will to transcendence, the drive to control the external world, and also the conflict between fidelity to the past and the forward pull of history. An austere work of great strength and beauty, a questing, haunting, often enigmatic hymn, *Anabase* has been hailed by many as S.-J. P.'s masterpiece.

In the oscillation between private concerns and collective action, S.-J. P.'s poems written in exile represent a return to the former mode. They draw their substance from the author's wartime experiences and signal a darkening tonality, which ranges from gentle lamentation to invective to urgent expressions of profound anguish. *Exil* (1942; "Exile," in *Exile, and Other Poems*), the earliest of the American poems, is the least personal. It relies on elemental images—images of barren sand and desolate beaches—to raise the poet's private feelings to the level of universal statement and identifies exile as man's ever-present condition rather than one of political circumstance. At the same time, in a characteristic attempt to draw vitality from negative experiences, S.-J. P. transmutes the exile's solitude into a ritual of purification. A similar progression surfaces in *Pluies* (1944; "Rains," in *Exile, and Other Poems*, 1949), a turbulent poem taking its rhythms and symbolism from the opening image of a torrential rainstorm. By contrast, *Poème à l'étrangère* (1943; "Poem to a Foreign Lady," in *Exile, and Other Poems*, 1949) and *Neiges* (1945; "Snows," in *Exile, and Other Poems*, 1949) are muted, tender. They usher in a period of reconciliation, mediated by two female figures, the sorrow-laden solitary of *Poème à l'étrangère* and, in *Neiges*, the poet's mother. A beautifully evocative poem, *Neiges* has the picturesque concreteness of things seen as well as a rich symbolic resonance deriving from the author's skillful association of snow with the concept and the emotion of absence.

Vents (1946; *Winds*, 1953) and *Amers* (1957; *Seamarks*, 1958) take up the dominant motifs of S.-J. P.'s previous works, building them into a monumental, many-layered summa—both a meditation on man's destiny and a cosmology. *Vents*, his longest and most ambitious undertaking, brings together two kinds of movement, that of nature's forces exemplified by the winds and that of human action. With a rare command of history and an eye for the characteristic detail, S.-J. P. sets before the reader a vast array of representative human figures: pioneers, poets, conquistadors, scientists. He takes us through immense panoramas of human activities, conquests, experiments, ceremonies, and rituals, creating not mirror reflections of history but a poetic image, a metaphor of movement that expresses man's drive westward to the New World, across the North American plains, and toward the summits of 20th-c. achievements, interpreted dialectically in the light of S.-J. P.'s horror at man's power to destroy as well as his abiding faith in the creative human energies. *Amers* extends the idea of human advance in *Vents*, taking it past the barrier separating the temporal and the transcendent. It represents S.-J. P.'s most sustained attempt to give voice to man's spirituality and culminates in a grandiose image of men and women descending in a ritualistic procession to salute the sea, identified by the poet as Universal Being. After *Vents and Amers, Chronique* (1960; *Chronique*, 1961) and *Oiseaux* (1962; *Birds*, 1966) are poems of serenity, expressing in a more quiet, reflective way the poet's intuition of time, eternity, and human creativity.

S.-J. P. is a poet's poet, complex, rhetorical, self-conscious, a superb stylist with a gift for highly wrought verbal textures and dazzling imagery, an artisan choosing his words with great care, and a learned writer inclined toward the oblique and the encyclopedic reference. Despite the emphasis on formal perfection, his poetry maintains a steady gaze on the world, searching out a wide temporal and spatial range of human experience for man's most constant features. It originates in the desire to understand, to establish relationships, to organize. It finds its most natural mode of expression in myths, in metaphors sustained by an imagination both factual and archetypal, and especially in symbols that set up allusive analogies and multiple associations and uncover, beneath the palpable, spiritual phenomena. Writing out of a deep sense of responsibility, S.-J. P. held that poetry is a way of life and a means to live better: it holds up a mirror to the human condition and by celebrating transcendence restores man to his original unity. The strength of S.-J. P.'s poetry lies in its sumptuous, solemn beauty and the power to ascribe eternal meaning to all that appears ephemeral.

FURTHER WORKS: *Éloges*, 3rd ed. (1948); *Poésie: Allocution au banquet Nobel du 10 décembre 1960* (1961; *On Poetry*, 1961); *Pour Dante* (1965; "*Dante,*" in *Two Addresses*, 1966); *Collected Poems* (1971, bilingual; new ed., 1982); (*Œuvres complètes* (1972); *Chant pour un équinoxe* (1975; *Song for an Equinox,* 1977). FURTHER WORKS IN ENGLISH: *Letters* (1979)

BIBLIOGRAPHY: Caillois, R., *Poétique de S.-J. P.* (1954); Paulhan, J., ed. *Honneur à S.-J. P.* (1965); Poggioli, R., *The Spirit of the Letter* (1965): 229–53; Knodel, A., *S. -J. P.: A Study of His Poetry* (1966); Weinberg, B., *The Limits of Symbolism* (1966): 365–419; Galand, R., *S. -J. P.* (1972); Fournier, C., *Les thèmesédeniques*

dans l'œuvre de S.-J. P. (1976); Caduc, E., *S. -J. P.: Connaissance et création* (1977); Little, R., "The World and the Word in S.-J. P.," in R. Cardinal, ed. *Sensibility and Creation: Studies in Twentieth Century French Literature* (1977): 122–35; Nasta, D. I., *S.-J. P. et la déouverte de l'être* (1980)

—VIKTORIA SKRUPSKELIS

SAINZ, Gustavo

Mexican novelist, critic, and journalist, b. 13 July 1940, Mexico City

After studying philosophy and literature at Mexico's National University, S. began his career as a journalist, critic, and writer of fiction. In 1968 he received a Rockefeller grant to participate in the International Writing Program at the University of Iowa. He has been editor of *Siete*, a cultural journal, director of literature at the Institute of Fine Arts, a cultural agency of the Mexican government, and, most recently, professor of Spanish American literature at the University of New Mexico.

S.'s first novel, *Gazapo* (1965; *Gazapo*, 1968), made him a leader of "The Wave," a movement of young, irreverent Mexican writers whose works reflect the attitudes of rebellious youth. The protagonist is a teenager named Menelao who has left home after a quarrel with his stepmother. During his own mother's absence from the Mexican capital he and his friends meet in her apartment, where they can freely express their frustrations and fantasies. The novel consists of a montage of real and imagined episodes, often erotic, which take the forms of tape recordings, telephone conversations, letters and diaries. Deftly manipulated, these devices freeze moments of time, capturing the immediacy of events as well as the humor and spontaneity of adolescent behavior. Important also is the devastating indictment of social institutions for their failure to achieve their purpose in today's world. S.'s original interpretation of the turbulent maturation process makes *Gazapo* a landmark in recent Mexican fiction.

Whereas S.'s first novel exudes a comic air of youthful exuberance, *Obsesivos días circulares* (1969; rev. ed., 1979; obsessive circular days) emerges as a complex metanovel about the narrator-protagonist's struggles to create a work of art from the recalcitrant raw materials of language and the overwhelming reality he confronts. A paranoiac, introspective intellectual, Terencio works as a caretaker in the girls' school owned by a powerful underworld figure. The loosely organized plot is generated by Terencio's terror of physical violence, his erotic fantasies, and his sophisticated literary tastes, which provide a refuge of stability in his life. In the final pages the language of his manuscript becomes yet another manifestation of the chaos threatening him.

The protagonist of *La princesa del Palacio de Hierro* (1974; *The Princess of the Iron Palace*, 1987) is a shallow, upper-middle-class woman who describes the frenetic escapades of her youth in a hedonistic society of conspicuous consumers. At first her compulsive monologue conveys a carefree, effervescent quality, but as her disillusion grows, her flow of words becomes little more than a vain attempt to fill the void in her meaningless existence. *Compadre Lobo* (1978; friend Lobo) is replete with scenes of gratuitous cruelty and violence that the author implies owe their origin to the Aztec rituals of human sacrifice. Thus, the artist-protagonist, Lobo ("wolf"), is strangely drawn to death, and his bohemian friends engage in endless sprees, brawls, and sexual orgies. Dramatic tension is heightened, moreover, through the subtle contrast between two basic styles: the vernacular used in the dialogues and the sparse, cultivated idiom of the narrator, a writer friend of Lobo.

In his subsequent novels, including *Fantasmas aztecas* (1982; Aztec Phantoms), *Muchacho en llamas* (1988; Boy in Flames), and *A la salud de las serpiente* (1991; To the Serpent's Health), S. utilizes metafiction, history, and myth to explain present-day Mexican culture.

S. has evolved from an exponent of the student-protest generation of the 1960s to one of Mexico's most highly esteemed men of letters. Although he focuses on life in the sprawling metropolis of his birth, his aesthetic ideals and experimentation with literary forms have expanded the dimensions of his fiction beyond the borders of his native land.

FURTHER WORKS: *G. S.* (autobiography, 1966); *Fantasmas aztecas* (1982)

BIBLIOGRAPHY: Langford, W. M., *The Mexican Novel Comes of Age* (1971): 203–4; Gyurko, L. A., "Reality and Fantasy in Gazapo," *REH*, 8 (1974): 117–46; Brushwood, J. S., *The Spanish American Novel* (1975): 269–74, 315; Foster, D. W., and V. R. Foster, eds., *Modern Latin American Literature* (1975), Vol. 2: 318-23; Decker, D., "The Circles and Obsessions of G. S.," *Review*, 18 (1976): 44–47; Durán, M., "¿Quién le teme a G. S.?," *Inti*, 3 (1976): 7–19; Hancock, J., "The Narrator and His Craft: Artistic Impulse and Authorial Presence in G. S.'s *Compadre Lobo*" CH, 4, 2 (1982): 149–55

—GEORGE R. MCMURRAY

SALACROU, Armand

French dramatist, b. 9 Aug. 1899, Rouen

S. grew up in Le Havre, and as a boy he was rebellious against religious and political institutions. After first studying medicine in Paris, he worked for the Communist newspaper *L'humanité*. S. was involved for a time with both the Communist Party and the SURREALIST movement. In 1949 he was elected to the Goncourt Academy.

S.'s first plays were not successful, but he was encouraged to continue writing for the theater by the directors Lugné-Poe and Charles Dullin. The most interesting of these early plays is *Le pont de l'Europe* (1925; the bridge of Europe), in which S. raises the philosophical problem of choice: a man, by choosing one thing or belief, excludes all the rest, but if he does not choose, he denies the very conditions of existence and action.

Atlas-Hôtel (Atlas Hotel), produced by Dullin in 1931, was the first of a long series of successes. Its hero has compromised a career as a serious writer to become a financial success. He feels a hopeless nostalgia for lost purity in later meeting his former wife, whom he has abandoned, and her present husband, who has retained something of his childlike purity.

In *L'inconnue d'Arras* (the unknown woman of Arras), directed by Lugné-Poe in 1935, Ulysse, the principal character, shoots himself at the beginning of the play because of his wife's infidelity. Using the cinematic technique of the flashback, S. allows Ulysse,

between his pistol shot and his death, to relive his life. At the core of these scenes is a barely remembered encounter with an unknown woman for whom he felt a deep sense of pity. The memory stirs an awareness of life's possibilities. Ulysse regrets his action, but the bullet is already on its way.

The hero of *La terre est ronde* (1937; *The World Is Round*, 1967) is the 15th-c. Florentine reformer Savonarola. With Nazi Germany casting its shadow over Europe, the first audiences interpreted the play as a commentary on fascism and tyranny. But the real meaning lies deeper, involving the universal struggle between the flesh and the spirit, between the relative and the absolute.

S.'s best play since World War II, *Les nuits de la colère* (1946; nights of anger), deals with the moral dilemmas of the Resistance: a man opposed to violence betrays a friend wanted by the Nazis in order to protect his family, but then is killed by other members of the Resistance.

Boulevard Durand (1961; Boulevard Durand) recounts the story of Jules Durand, a strike leader who was condemned to death in 1910 but was later released, and who eventually went mad. S. thus condemns, as he says, "bourgeois" justice, by insisting on the conflict between working-class and middle-class values.

S.'s plays are extremely well constructed, and the earlier ones are now considered by many to foreshadow the philosophical theater of Jean-Paul SARTRE and Albert CAMUS. S.'s entire oeuvre is a meditation on human fate, especially the problem of evil and the suffering of innocent people. He is unable to reconcile belief in the existence of God with a universe dominated by injustice. S.'s essential solitude is confirmed in his two volumes of autobiography, collectively titled *Dans la salle des pas perdus* (in the waiting room): *C'était écrit* (1974; it was written) and *Les amours* (1976; loves).

FURTHER WORKS: *Le casseur d'assiettes* (1922); *La boule de verre* (1924); *Magasin d'accessoires* (1925); *Tour à terre* (1925); *Histoire de cirque* (1925; *A Circus Story*, 1964); *Trente tombes de Judas* (1926); *Patchouli* (1930); *La vie en rose* (1931); *Une femme libre* (1934); *Les frénétiques* (1935); *Un homme comme les autres* (1936); *Histoire de rire* (1939; *When the Music Stops*, 1967); *La Marguerite* (1944; *Marguerite*, 1967); *Les fiancés du Havre* (1944); *Le soldat et la sorcière* (1945); *L'archipel Lenoir* (1947); *Poof* (1950); *Pourquoi pas moi?* (1950); *Dieu le savait!* (1950); *Sens interdit* (1953); *Les invités du bon Dieu* (1953); *Le miroir* (1956); *Une femme trop honnête* (1956); *Les idées de la nuit* (1960); *Comme les chardons* (1964); *Impromptu délibéré* (1966); *La rue noire* (1967); *Le manteau d'Arlequin* (1967)

BIBLIOGRAPHY: Van den Esch, J., *A. S.* (1947); Chiesa, I., *Théâtre de S.* (1949); Mignon, P.-L., *S.* (1960); Silenieks, J., *Themes and Dramatic Forms in the Plays of A. S.* (1967); Franco, F., *di, Le théâtre de S.* (1970); Bébon, P., *S.*, (1971)

—CHARLES G. HILL

SALAMA, Hannu

Finnish novelist and short-story writer, b. 10 June 1936, Kouvola

The detachment that characterizes S.'s attitude toward society springs from two sources: his keen intellect and his personal experiences, including the fear of hereditary schizophrenia. S. prepared for a literary career through his extensive reading of EXISTENTIALIST writers such as Jean-Paul SARTRE and Albert CAMUS, and he had already established a reputation when he published *Juhannustanssit* (1964; Midsummer dance), a novel that provoked a storm of reaction, ending in nothing less than the conviction of S. on the antiquated grounds of blasphemy, although the president of Finland later nullified the suspended sentence. The central event of the novel is a pagan Mid-summer ritual planned by a young people's collective, which ends in disaster. The novel exposes the superficiality of the values of the upper class.

The trial tormented S. He felt that the bourgeoisie had persecuted him, and he became further alienated from organized society. Thus, his next major novel, *Minä, Olli ja Orvokki* (1967; I, Olli, and Orvokki), is set in a bohemian environment. The characters, including the narrator, have broken all relations with society. As the action of the novel progresses, they become isolated from each other as well. Thus, the theme is the tragic dilemma of individual freedom.

S. further developed his "between opposites" position with his best novel, *Siinä näkijä missä tekijä* (1972; where there is a doer, there is one who sees)—the title is a Finnish proverb. Criticism now came from the extreme left, the so-called Stalinist wing of the Finnish Communist Party. The prize-winning novel deals with the communist resistance movement against Finland's alliance with Germany during World War II. S. gives a social, political, and cultural account of the Finnish worker between 1918 (the year of the Finnish civil war) and 1944, with retrospective glimpses from the author's own time. He accomplishes this demanding undertaking by using several narrators in addition to the chief one, and by using dialogue, monologue, and straight narration to provide multiple perspectives. This complex work is simultaneously a psychological, a social, and a political novel.

S. has also published several collections of short fiction, which include some of the best stories in Finnish literature. His relentless scrutiny of social, economic, political, even cultural-anthropological problems reflects the major commitment in his life: a basically existentialist outlook combined with an unyielding sense of responsibility for the human condition. S. subscribes to the thesis that it is the writer's duty to give voice to human cries, to accept guilt for them, to disclose reality on its essential levels. This responsibility is the overriding factor in *Vuosi elämästäni* (1979; a year of my life), a series of diary notes and personal comments on the current state of affairs of mankind. S. can be characterized as a prophet of a radical kind: he is an uncompromising critic of society, a bold renewer of the realistic novel, and a champion of individualism.

FURTHER WORKS: *Se tavallinen tarina* (1961); *Lomapäivä* (1962); *Puu balladin haudalla* (1963); *Kenttäläinen käy talossa* (1967); *Joulukuun kuudes* (1968); *Kesäleski* (1969); *Tapausten kulku* (1969); *Lokakuun päiviä* (1971); *Villanpehmee, taskulämmin* (1971); *Runot* (1975); *Pentti Saarikoski* (1975); *Kosti Herhiläisen perunkirjoitus* (1976); *Kolera on raju bändi* (1977); *Ihmisen ääni* (1978); *Kolme sukupolvea* (1978)

BIBLIOGRAPHY: Ahokas, J. A., *A History of Finnish Literature* (1973): 382–83; Tarkka, P., "H. S.: A Writer between the Social Classes," *WLT*, 54 (1980): 28–32

—K. BÖRJE VÄHÄMÄKI

ŠALAMUN, Tomaž

Slovene poet, b. 4 July 1941, Zagreb

After graduating with a degree in art history at the Faculty of Philosophy in Ljubljana, Š. worked as a curator of the Modern Gallery in Ljubljana, taught at the Academy of Fine Arts in Ljubljana, and worked as a professional artist. From 1968 to 1970 he was a member of the group *Grupa OHO*, and exhibited in Zagreb, Ljubljana, Novi Sad, Beograd, and New York.

In 1966 Š. published his first collection of poems, *Poker* (Poker), which is considered to have paved the way for Slovene modernist poetry in the second half of the 20th c. Strongly influenced by major European language experimentalists, especially Velimir Hlebnikov, Š. has shown new possibilities for the Slovene language. His poetics is based on word-play, neologisms, and various lexical and stylistic excesses. The lyrical subject is constituted by means of language. Š. uses the experience of language to create a characteristic mythological space, which he later enriches in contacts with other cultures and authorial practices. Š. used poetic experiences in his painting as well: he would pronounce an object that he found a sculpture and transfer it into the space of art, emphasizing the act of choice and the context of import. In this way works of art become similar to the "poker" of animating things and phenomena in poetry.

At the beginning of the 1970s, during a study period in the U.S., Š. internalized certain procedures and perceptions of American poetry, especially that of Walt Whitman, which gave his poetic style a new impulse: the world ceased to be an object that he learned by listing, observing, and copying, and became a live organism that had to be observed in its continuous change. The realization of the total inclusion into an endless live organism appeared in a highly esteemed collection of poetry *Balada za Metko Krašovec* (1981; A Ballad for Metka Krašovec), where the lyrical subject constantly questions the invisible boundaries between poetic and everyday reality. Experiences that emerge in this process shape the text as the only reality of life. Identity is universal.

The collection *Maske* (1988; Masks), the most important of Š.'s work after *Poker*, appeared as a realized metaphor of one of Š.'s most obsessive themes. The mask represents a pseudo-real world that can be concealed, exposed, or altered. The mask is a secret. It is always there where the poet is, because it is the only firm foothold in the endless passing of things and conditions. The mask is the beginning and the end, the point at which the possibility of writing as linguistic experiment is taken to the extreme. Š.'s poems in this collection are to a large extent a break with his previous life and artistic practice, his ironic self-magnification, his attacks at national values and institutions. This, as critics have pointed out, is also the end of the poet's elegant cosmopolitanism, because he has exhausted the motive of homelessness as a certain kind of correlative of the endless exploration of the world.

Š.'s poetry is built on the principle of paradox. Even the lines are often mutually contradicting. Paradoxes are the boundaries of the poet's world. They bring in the feeling of discord, discomfort, and relativity. They initiate the wish for new conquests of the world as text and the text as the world.

FURTHER WORKS: *Namen pelerine* (1968); *Romanje za Maruško* (1971); *Bela Itaka* (1971); *Amerika* (1972); *Ein Stengel Petersilie in Smoking* (1972); *Arena* (1973); *Sokol* (1974); *Imre* (1975);

Druidi (1975); *Turbine* (1975); *Praznik* (1976); *Zvezde* (1977); *Metoda, Angela* (1978); *Pesmi* (with N. Grafenauer, 1979); *Zgodovina svetlobe je oranžna* (1979); *Pesmi*(1980); *Živa rana, živi sok*(1988); *Painted Desert: Poems* (1991). FURTHER WORKS IN ENGLISH: *Selected Poems* (1989)

BIBLIOGRAPHY: Makoviæ, Z., "Amerika ubija metafiziku," *Quorum*, 5-6 (1989): 3-12; Debeljak, A., "Temelji literarne hagiografije," *Quorum*, 5-6 (1989): 18-21; Kermauner, T., "Pjesma u maskama," *Quorum*, 5-6 (1989): 22-30; Hass, R., "T. Š.," *Quorum*, 5-6 (1989): 31-38; Brejc, T., "T. Š. i Julian Schnabel," *Quorum*, 5-6 (1989): 39-44; Zabel, I., "Uloga igre u djelu grupe OHO" in Benčič, Ž., and A. Flaker, eds., *Ludizam* (1996): 355-61

—IRENA LUKSIC

SALARRUÉ

(pseud. of Salvador Salazar Arrué) Salvadoran novelist, short-story writer, and poet, b. 22 Oct. 1899, Sonsonate; d. Nov. 1975, El Salvador

One of the few Central American writers from the first half of the 20th c. who is mentioned in many of the classic histories of Latin American literature and included in numerous anthologies of the Latin American short story, S. was an acknowledged master of this genre. Born in a small town in rural El Salvador in a region with a strong indigenous presence, in 1917 he received a grant from the Salvadoran government that allowed him to study at the Corcoran Academy in Washington, D.C. Upon returning to El Salvador he worked as a writer and illustrator for various literary journals. S. devoted his life to writing, painting, and the study of theosophy. He spent most of his life in El Salvador, except for the periods from 1919 to 1921 in Washington, D.C. and again from 1946 to 1951 when he served as cultural attaché at the Salvadoran Embassy and lived in New York and Washington, D.C.

S. is best known for his collection of stories about Salvadoran *campesinos*, *Cuentos de barro* (1933; Stories of Clay). In these stories he re-creates with realism and compassion the rural Salvadoran world he knew and loved. These stories figure significantly in the development of costumbrismo in Central America and are justifiably praised for their skillful portrayal of the indigenous population of El Salvador. Yet while these stories certainly are part of the at once beloved and maligned tradition of costumbrismo literature so popular in Central America at the turn of the century, they do not, as is often the case with this genre, paint an innocent picture of rural simplicity, but rather face clearly the reality of a people long oppressed by a system that favors another class and ethnicity. S. has been praised in Central America not only for his mastery of the short story, but also for his humanity. Salvadoran writer Manlio ARGUETA described him, in his poem entitled "Salarrué," as "Teacher of tenderness / in a country of war." Besides his ability to deal tenderly with his characters, even in their violence and vengeance, what makes these stories so appealing is the attention paid by the author to the language spoken by the people of a specific ethnicity in a specific geographic space. The non-Salvadoran reader must make reference to the glossary invariably included in his books to appreciate the vernacular used in all his rural stories.

It would be impossible to describe or deeply comprehend the work of S. without reference to theosophy, an eclectic system of belief that strives for a synthesis, through reason and intuition, of the essential truths of religion, science, and philosophy, with an ethics of universal brotherhood and social responsibility. Among the esoteric principles of theosophy are the belief in astral spheres within which one moves by desire and will, and the essential unity of all life. S., like many other writers, educators, and politicians of Central America during the late 19th and early 20th cs., was drawn to this vision of a universe guided by the dynamic interplay of the seemingly contradictory and opposing forces of masculine and feminine, yin and yang, light and dark, good and evil. He remained faithful throughout his life to his quest for an ever more profound comprehension of the nature of the universe. This spiritual quest permeates his entire oeuvre, both his writing and his painting, at times explicitly, at times as an implicit world view.

In his first published work, a short novel based on the legend of the Black Christ, S. explores a theme that will continue to intrigue him until the end of his life: the nature of good and evil. In *El cristo negro* (1926; The Black Christ) he reverses the expected manifestations of good and evil to lead the reader to a questioning of accepted notions of goodness and saintliness. In later collections of short stories he returns to this theme, positing evil as an attribute of God, the infant Jesus as the Devil, saints as sinners, and sinners as saints.

His second major work, *O' Yarkandal* (1929; O' Yarkandal), is a collection of stories that defy classification, but that resemble legends, fairy tales, creation myths, and archetypal dream scenes. They reflect his interest in multiple spheres of consciousness and demonstrate his penchant for fantasy. He himself illustrated the book with paintings that reproduce visually a "remote empire" where one encounters cities of winged men, islands adrift in unknown seas, strange perfumes, and gardens perennially in bloom—where the first man and woman were born from the egg of a bird known as Alm-a (Soul). *O' Yarkandal* is a book of pure creation and experimentation for which S. has invented even a language, bilsac, the fabrication of which he describes in the prologue as having been a euphonic and euphoric experience. His sensual delight in language, whether the idiosyncratic speech of rural Salvadorans or the invented speech of the inhabitants of his imagination, is one of the characteristic of S.'s prose that makes it identifiable and memorable.

S.'s enjoyment of language combines in a unique way with his sense of fantasy and humor in *Cuentos de cipotes* (1961; Kid's Stories)—stories that are not for children, he explains in the prologue, but by children, more specifically, by the child in him. They are the stories children tell each other or tell adults, although adults never listen. They are small stories that speak like kids, full of mispronunciations, malapropisms, riddles, rhymes and invented language. They are silly, ingenuous, wise, and candid. The first edition was illustrated by his wife, Zelie Lardé, while the second edition was illustrated by his daughter, Maya. Like everything he wrote, these stories are influenced by his fascination with the essential unity of all planes of existence, in this case the child that lives in the adult and that coexists with the maturity of the child, the wisdom of nonsense and the foolishness of being serious.

S. also wrote stories some critics have called his cosmopolitan ones, but that might also be described as urban-esoteric. Drawing on his experiences during his residence in New York and Washington, D.C., these places and the kinds of people he met there appear in tales that explore such phenomena as astral travel, reincarnation, and, again, the nature of good and evil. Sophisticated settings form the background for esoteric mind games in a world of international travel, archeological digs, and elegant mansions on Riverside Drive.

S. was a bohemian, an eccentric, an artist, and a theosophist, a Central American writer who sometimes went to cocktail parties with ambassadors and sometimes was so poor he traded his paintings for art supplies. He was a writer with his feet firmly planted in his homeland and his head in the clouds. For all his eccentricity, he was an active and influential figure in Salvadoran and Central American art and literature. Critical commentary has tended to focus on his telluric, socially realistic stories. But the nature of S.'s vision has not yet been adequately described. His body of work is diverse and original. From numerous points in the universe he begins his stories, stories that inevitably end up in the same place: face to face with the mystery.

FURTHER WORKS: *El señor de la burbuja* (1927); *Remon tando el Uluán* (1932); *Eso y más* (1940); *Trasmallo* (1954); *La espada y otras narraciones* (1960); *Ingrimo* (1970); *La sed de Sling Bader* (1971); *Catleya luna* (1974); *Mundo nomasito* (1975)

BIBLIOGRAPHY: Ramírez, S., Prologue to *"El ángel del espejo" y otros relatos* (1977): ix-xxv; Acevedo, R., *La novela centroamericana* (1982): 153-81; Acevedo, R., "Lo fantástico y lo maravilloso en *O' Yarkandal* de S.," in Oyarzun, K., ed., *The Latin American Short Story* (1989): 3-14

—JANET N. GOLD

SALAZAR BONDY, Sebastián

Peruvian dramatist, b. 1924, Lima; d. 4 July 1965, Lima

S. B. was one of the most successful and prolific 20th-c. Peruvian authors. His writings spanned the spectrum from drama and essay to poetry and prose fiction. A graduate of the University of San Marcos, he traveled widely abroad and worked for many years as a journalist and drama critic. From 1948 to 1950 he lived in Buenos Aires as a correspondent for *La Nación*. He received a scholarship from the French government enabling him to study at the National Conservatory of Dramatic Arts in Paris. In 1953, shortly after his return to Peru, he founded the Club de Teatro de Lima, an important theater group that staged foreign as well as local plays and became a major factor in the revitalization of Peruvian drama.

S. B. was the leading dramatist in his country during the first half of the 20th c. Productions of his plays had successful runs not only in Lima but also in Buenos Aires and other South American cities. Ranging from serious drama to comedy and including full-length as well as one-act pieces, his theatrical works made good use of dialogue while conveying irony and humor and allowing readers and spectators glimpses of the characters' psychological makeup. S. B.'s first play, the satirical farce *Amor, gran laberinto* (perf. 1946, pub. 1948; love, great labyrinth), won the national theater prize in 1947, an award he received again in 1952 for the historical drama *Rodil* (1952; Rodil). His two best plays were the three-act tragedy *No hay isla feliz* (1954; there is no happy island), a social drama on the theme of frustration that portrayed the spiritual downfall of a middle-class family, and *El fabricante de deudas* (perf. 1962, pub. 1964; the debt maker), a lighter work in two acts inspired by Balzac's *Le faiseur* and employing the Brechtian technique of allowing the characters to speak directly to the

audience. In 1965 he won a third national theater prize (given posthumously) for the one-act drama *El rabdomante* (1965; the diviner), his final play. He also coauthored, with César Miró Quesada (b. 1907), a modern version of the Quechua drama *Ollantay* (1953; Ollantay) and collaborated on *La escuela de los chismes* (1965), an adaptation of a classic 18th-c. work, Sheridan's *The School for Scandal*.

Although S. B. made his most important contributions in the field of drama, his initial publication was a volume of poetry, *Rótulo de la esfinge* (1943; sign of the sphinx), produced in collaboration with Antenor Samaniego (b. 1919). Numerous collections followed, and he maintained an active interest in the genre throughout the remainder of his life. At the time of his death in 1965, he was working on yet another book of verse. *El tacto de la araña* (1966; the spider's touch).

In addition to the drama and poetry S. B. also penned numerous journalistic pieces. In these nonfiction writings he was concerned with social problems relating to the indigenous population and was highly critical of Peru's social structure, especially the Lima aristocracy. His polemical book-length essay *Lima, la horrible* (1964; Lima the horrible) challenged the nostalgic, picturesque evocation of life during the Viceroyalty in Ricardo Palma's (1833–1919) famous *Tradiciones peruanas* (Peruvian traditions). According to S. B.'s revisionist X-ray of the city, the portrait of society contained in the *Tradiciones peruanas* was incomplete and therefore false, because Palma, despite his incisive social and political satire, failed to denounce the exploitation of the country's indigenous citizens.

As a short-story writer S. B. examined philosophical questions as well as contemporary problems of urban life. The stories in *Náufragos y sobrevivientes* (1954; shipwrecked souls and survivors), written in an existentialist vein, dealt with distorted values, hypocrisy, and corruption. Another prose work, *Pobre gente de París* (1958; poor people of Paris), was composed of vignettes about young Latin Americans living in France and their common feeling of uprootedness. A posthumous novel, *Alférez Arce, Teniente Arce, Capitán Arce* (1969; Ensign Arce, Lieutenant Arce, Captain Arce), departed from the traditional linear format by employing multiple narrative perspectives and flashbacks.

S. B. was one of a group of Peruvians who in the 1950s began to write about the city, focusing on social and political problems and incorporating universal themes along with technical advances. Appearing on the literary scene at a time when support and interest were low, S. B. led a resurgence in the arts in his country. Perhaps the most revealing indication of S. B.'s significance can be seen in the influence he exerted on authors of his and the succeeding generation. The universally acclaimed Peruvian novelist Mario Vargas LLOSA acknowledged his intellectual debt and paid homage to his fellow countryman by writing a prologue to S. B.'s *Obras* (3 vols., 1967; complete works) and by dedicating a book, the short novel *Los cachorros* (1967; *The Cubs*, 1979), to S. B.'s memory.

FURTHER WORKS: *Bahía del dolor, Sinfonia del alma y Tránsito a la muerte* (1944, with Antenor Samaniego); *Voz desde la vigilia* (1944); *Cuaderno de la persona oscura* (1946); *Poesía contemporánea del Perú* (1946); *Máscara del que duerme* (1949); *Tres confesiones* (1950); *Pantomimas* (1950); *Los ojos del pródigo* (1951); *Algo que quiere morir* (1956); *Antología general de la poesía peruana* (1957); *Seis juguetes* (1958); *Dos viejas van por la calle* (1959); *Conducta sentimental* (1960); *Teatro* (1961); *Confidencia en alta voz* (1964); *Poesía quechua* (1964)

BIBLIOGRAPHY: Monguió, L., *La poesía postmodernista peruana* (1954): 180–81: 232–33; Hesse Murga, J. H., Prologue to *Teatro peruano contemporáneo*, 2nd ed. (1963): 21–24; Powell, O. B., untitled article on S. B., *Americas*, (October 1965): 39; Aldrich, E. M., Jr., *The Modern Short Story in Peru* (1966): 147–49; Jones, W. K., *Behind Spanish American Footlights* (1966): 269–71; Gómez Gil, O., *Historia crítica de la literature hispanoamericana* (1968): 730–31; Franco, J., *The Modern Culture of Latin America: Society and the Artist*, rev. ed. (1970): 225–38; Morris, R. J., *The Contemporary Peruvian Theatre* (1977): 28–40; McMurray, G. R., *Spanish American Writing since 1941: A Critical Survey* (1987): 118–19: 292–95

—MELVIN S. ARRINGTON, JR.

ŠALDA, František Xaver

Czechoslovak critic, essayist, poet, novelist, and dramatist (writing in Czech), b. 22 Dec. 1867, Liberec; d. 4 April 1937, Prague

Š studied law in Prague. After 1892 he was a frequent contributor to literary journals and the standard Czech encyclopedia. His first collection of essays was called, characteristically, *Boje o zítřek* (1905; battles for tomorrow). For a time (1901–10) he edited *Volné směry,* the main Czech art magazine. In 1916 Š became a docent and in 1919 a professor of Western literatures at the Charles University in Prague. In 1928 he founded a monthly review, Šaldův zápisník (Š.'s notebook), which he wrote from cover to cover until his death.

Š. completely reformed Czech criticism, which up to his time had been either provincial or professorial. His first important article, "Synthetism v novém umění" (1892; synthetism in new art), was an account of symbolist aesthetics and poetics drawn mainly from French sources. This and many other essays soon put Š. into the forefront of the new generation of the 1890s, which rejected the Parnassian and folkloric literature of the 19th c. and exalted new poets—symbolists such as Otokar BŘEZINA and Antonín Sova (1864–1928), and realists such as Josef Svatopluk MACHAR.

With the years, Š. outgrew his original symbolist creed, which had been somewhat incongruously combined with an interest in "scientific" criticism. He developed a clearly articulated, fiercely defended view of literature that allowed him to judge the whole Czech literary past and present. Besides this, Š. made frequent excursions into foreign literatures, particularly French and German.

The collection *Duše a dílo* (1913; soul and work) contains essays on the problem of romanticism from Rousseau to the early Flaubert; it centers on the Czech romantic poet K. H. Mácha (1810–1836). Later Š. wrote commentaries on Shakespeare and Dante and a short book on Rimbaud, *J. A. Rimbaud, božský rošťák* (1930; J. A. Rimbaud, the divine tramp). But his main work was devoted to commentary on the Czech literary scene.

After World War I Š. became a fervent defender of the avant-garde movements, such as proletarian poetry and poetism, although he always avoided an ideological commitment, rejecting both Marxism and Roman Catholicism. In literary theory, Š., late in life, claimed to be a "structuralist"—that is, he defended the unity of form and content, suspicious of both didacticism and naturalism. He rejected both impressionistic and dogmatic criticism and cultivated an art of characterization and portraiture that might remind one of Sainte-Beuve (1804–1869) in its breadth and evocative

power, if Š had not been so deeply engaged in the polemics of the time. With all his wide historical knowledge he remained a militant critic: praising, exhorting, chastising, never shirking the main duty of the critic of judging, and judging from his center of his personality, an attitude, he felt, that guarantees a final justice and the only objectivity man can reach.

Especially from the time when he founded several journals, all of them short-lived, Š. moved more and more into a general criticism of civilization. He became a great public figure, comparable only to Thomas G. Masaryk (1850–1937), the great Czech statesman and philosopher. His last essays, often phrased with poetic power or polemical harshness, examine almost every topic of the times: art, religion, and politics, as well as literature. But the fervor of a commitment to great poetry as a source of insight and as a preservative of the belief in the reality and value of the individual always remained central.

Compared to Š.'s work in criticism, his many attempts at writing fiction, for example, the novel *Loutky i děllńci boži* (2 vols., 1917; puppets and laborers of God); plays, such as *Tažení proti smrti* (1926; the expedition against death); and lyrical poetry, for instance, the collection *Strom bolesti* (1920; the tree of pain) are considered relatively unsuccessful.

Š. was not only the greatest Czech critic. Wide-ranging, open to all the winds of doctrine from the West, with a passionate personal core, he also became the conscience of his nation between the two world wars.

FURTHER WORKS: *Moderní literatura česká* (1909); *Život ironický a jiné povídky* (1912); *Umění a náboženství* (1914); *In memoriam R. Svobodové* (1920); *Zástupové* (1921); *Dítě* (1923); *Antonín Sova* (1924); *Juvenilie* (1925); *Pokušení Pascalovo* (1928); *O nejmladší poesii české* (1928); *Krásná literatura česká v prvním desetiletí republiky* (1930); *Mladé zápasy* (1934); *Dřevoryty staré i nové* (1935); *Časové a nadčasové* (1936); *Mácha snivec i buřič* (1936); *Studie literárně historické a kritické* (1937); *Kritické glossy k nové poesii české* (1939); *Tajemství zraku* (1940); *Medailony* (1941); *Soubor díla* (20 vols., 1948–1963); *F. X. Š.-Antonín Sova: Dopisy* (1967)

BIBLIOGRAPHY: Wellek,, R., "Modern Czech Literary Criticism and Literary Scholarship," *HSS*, 2 (1954): 343–58 (rpt. in Wellek, R., *Essays on Czech Literature* [1963]): 179–93; Bielefeldt, S., *Die čechische Moderne im Frühwerk Š.s* (1975); Novák, A., *Czech Literature* (1976): 256–60

—RENÉ WELLEK

SALINAS, Pedro

Spanish poet, b. 27 Nov. 1891, Madrid; d. 4 Dec. 1951, Boston, Mass., U.S.A.

S., whose parents owned a small shop in Madrid, attended the University of Madrid, graduating in 1913 with a degree in romance philology. He accepted a position as a lecturer in Spanish at the Sorbonne in 1914 and, after receiving his doctorate, became a professor at the University of Seville (1918–26). From 1928 to 1936 he was at the Center for Historical Research in Madrid. A liberal Republican, although not politically active, he went to Wellesley College in Massachusetts in 1936 for a visiting position, but the appointment turned into a permanent one. In 1940 he became professor of Hispanic literature at Johns Hopkins, where he remained until his death.

S.'s early poetry gives the impression of still-life painting and shows the direct influence of Juan Ramón JIMÉNEZ. Abstract and conceptual, the poetry nonetheless fits S.'s overall definition of his creation as an "adventure toward the absolute." His first collection, *Presagios* (1923; presages), deals with landscapes and love. Youthful and joyous in his pursuit of the infinite and happiness, he acknowledges, with a kind of intellectual irony, that the search for perfection may be an illusion. His is a concrete universe of land and water, a nature that reflects his love of life but also implies his first inkling of nothingness. The outer world proves to be deceitful, for he wants form and not shadow, substance and not illusion. Since external reality is illusory, he turns for love and clarity to an inner world, less frustrating to his deep desires.

In *Seguro azar* (1929; sure chance) S. revisits the material world, the technical universe of modern inventions and futuristic possibilities. Maintaining his delicate and musical style, he continues to develop his notion of an alluring yet unfulfilling reality. *Fábula y signo* (1931; fable and sign) shows his growing awareness of the absolute as he confronts both reality and myth. Reality still appears as a world in flux, a world of change and renewal. Unable to achieve happiness, S., torn between poetic reality and objective certainty, tries to define the nature of an elusive love.

His masterpiece, *La voz a ti debida* (1933; *My Voice Because of You*, 1976), whose title is based on a line from an eclogue of Garcilaso de la Vega (1503–1536), is the first volume of a poetic trilogy. S. describes the genesis of love—the only reality—in its painful and pleasant aspects. Exalted at first by love's presence, for him an affirmation of a perfect state, S. soon suffers the sorrows of doubt and separation. He wonders at the ineffable beauty of his beloved, sensual and yet almost mystical. He exists outside time and space through the power of love, and he sees his beloved as a metaphysical reality but also as human, vivid, and eternal. She helps give form to his poetic thought and aids in his search to define his true identity. S. half glimpses, through his innocent exposure to love, a paradise lost but, he hopes, to be rediscovered as the justification for human existence. The poem becomes a paean to her existence, and she in turn shows him an inner world of dreams, a new paradise where perfect love is shared. This harmony, impossible to maintain except through memory, which eternalizes the moment, must yield to reality, for only in a world where love implies infinity may one possess the beloved in an eternal glory of fulfilled desire.

Razón de amor (1936; love's reason), the second volume of the love trilogy—the third, *Largo lamento* (1971; long lament), was not published in S.'s lifetime—continues the search for happiness but in a chaotic world of existential anguish, where one may lose not only joy but life itself. Again the poet must seek happiness in an inner world as he continues the amatory dialogue of his previous volume. But here S. stresses more the transitory nature of the world and man's relationship to the universe and to his fellow man. His desire for love, perfect union, and salvation, in a life that may be a nebulous dream, may come only through a meaningful sacrifice.

In *El contemplado* (1946; *Sea of San Juan: A Contemplation*, 1950) S. engages in a colloquy with the sea, which fascinates him. The poem praises nature's creativity and condemns modern city life. Refined, subtle, intellectual, but intensely human, this almost mystical work celebrates a union with nature, the play of shadow with light triumphant, the harmony and perfection of sea, clouds, and beaches, part of a cosmos in which the sea of life, permanent in its beauty, offers the poet solace and salvation.

S.'s most anguished collection, *Todo más claro, y otros poemas* (1949; everything clearer, and other poems), shows us a poet overcome by the materialism of a modern world that man seems determined to destroy. S. pleads for the restoration of idealism in a loveless and mechanistic universe. He condemns war but extols poetry as a vehicle for the preservation of permanent values. To find salvation S. renounces the physical for the spiritual. *Cero* (1944; *Zero*, 1947), later included as part of *Todo más claro*, proclaims that man's work becomes zero when the world explodes and disappears. The "man on the shore," an observer, sees the march toward nothingness with dark foreboding, because chance and not logic seems to rule men's lives. Even if man is without leisure, poetry, which offers clarity in the darkness, may help save him from a loveless shadow world where he sorts through debris and ruins for the rubble of destroyed time.

In addition to his poetry S. wrote a number of prose works: he published several studies on Spanish literature and also wrote fourteen plays, for him an extension of his poetry—imaginative interplays of illusion and reality. He also published some short stories and one novel, *La bomba increíble* (1950; the incredible bomb), which he labeled "a conversation." In it he discusses his love for mankind and the menace he finds in the technology of the modern world.

S. has been called Neoplatonic, mystic, pantheistic, and metaphysical. In his poetry he longs to express the fullness of life and existence, rejecting the limits reality places on the poet in favor of an interplay of inner and outer reality, light and darkness. S. combines evanescent sensations with profound emotions to create, in the words of Federico de Onís, a "verse unique in its precise delicacy . . . richness of images and . . . lyric beauty." His central concern was the meaning of reality in a modern materialistic world he viewed with suspicion and whose masks he attempted to penetrate. He believed that a more significant reality lay in an inner spiritual world, beyond tragic solitude and limitations, and that it more cogently expressed the concept of charity and belief in humanity.

FURTHER WORKS: *Víspera del gozo* (1926; *Prelude to Pleasure*, 1993); *Error de cálculo* (1938); *En busca de Juana de Asbaje* (1940); *Reality and the Poet in Spanish Poetry* (1940; Sp. tr., *La realidad y el poeta*, 1976); *Literatura española, siglo XX* (1941); *Poesía junta* (1942); *Aprecio y defensa del lenguaje* (1944); *Jorge Manrique; o, Tradición y originalidad* (1947); *El defensor* (1948); *La poesía de Rubén Darío* (1948); *El desnudo impecable, y otras narraciones* (1951); *Teatro* (1952); *Poemas escogidos* (1953); *Confianza* (1955); *Poesías completas* (1955); *Teatro completa* (1957); *Volverse sombra, y otros poemas* (1957); *Dueño de ti mismo* (1958); *Ensayos de literatura hispánica* (1958); *Amor, mundo en peligro* (1958); *La responsabilidad del escritor* (1961); *Poesías completas* (1961); *Poesías completas* (1971); *Narrativa completa* (1976); *Teatro* (1979); *Poesías completas* (1981). FURTHER WORKS IN ENGLISH: *Lost Angel, and Other Poems* (1938); *Truth of Two, and Other Poems* (1940); *To Live in Pronouns* (1974)

BIBLIOGRAPHY: Spitzer, L., "El conceptismo interior de P. S.," *RHM*, 7 (1941): 33–69; special S. issue, *Hispania*, 35, 2 (1952); Arellano, D. Ramírez de, *Caminos de la creación poética en P. S.* (1956); Feldbaum, J., "El trasmundo de la obra poética de P. S.,"

RHM, 20 (1956): 12–34; Deibe, C. Feal, *La poesía de P. S.* (1965); Marichal, J., "P. S.: La voz a la confidencia debida," *RO*, 26 (1965): 154–70; Palley, J., *La luz no usada: La poesía de P. S.* (1966); Viva, O. Costa, *P. S. frente a la realidad* (1969); Zubizarretta, A. de., *P. S.: El diálogo creador* (1969); Crispin, J., *P. S.* (1974); Havard, R. G., "The Reality of Words in the Poetry of P. S.," *BHS*, 51 (1974): 28–47; Stixrude, D., *The Early Poetry of P. S.* (1975); Orringer, S. L., *P. S.'s Theatre of Self-Authentication* (1995)

—KESSEL SCHWARTZ

SALINGER, J(erome) D(avid)

American novelist and short-story writer, b. 1 Jan. 1916, New York, N.Y.

Because of the way he has chosen to preserve his privacy (since 1953 he has spent most of his time in seclusion in New Hampshire), not a great deal is known about S.'s personal life. He attended schools in Manhattan, where he was something of a problem student, and eventually graduated from Valley Forge Military Academy in Pennsylvania. After briefly attending New York University and Ursinus College in Pennsylvania, and after an equally brief try as an apprentice in his father's import meat business, S. signed up for Whit Burnett's (1899–1973) course in short-story writing at Columbia University. He published his first story in Burnett's *Story* magazine in 1940. Throughout the 1940s (even while he was serving in the U.S. Army in Europe as a counterintelligence officer), S.'s work appeared in *Collier's, Esquire, The Saturday Evening Post*, and *The New Yorker*. Following the immense success of *The Catcher in the Rye* (1951), S. became more reclusive, maintaining long periods of silence that led his readers to wonder whether he had stopped writing altogether.

S. has been charged—because of his essential optimism, because of his refusal to be as grimly EXISTENTIALIST as Jean-Paul SARTRE—or as bleak as Samuel BECKETT—of retreating into mysticism. Yet in reality, the movement of his work suggests a kind of pilgrim's progress, a journey from the melancholia of his early stories, through the trauma of *The Catcher in the Rye* and *Nine Stories* (1953), to the moments of revelation in *Franny and Zooey* (1961) and the two novellas in the volume *Raise High the Roof Beam, Carpenters* and *Seymour: An Introduction* (1963). Again and again, S. writes on the relationship of man to God—or, to state it more subtly and accurately, man's relationship to the *lack* of God and how that sense of emptiness may be treated and perhaps alleviated through a sometimes bizarre combination of Buddhist and Christian attitudes. At the same time, S.'s humor, often wry, often understated, but never bitter, is there, a humor that directs us away from the tragic and toward the comic: poignancy turns into hopefulness, and the objective is enlightenment, not despair.

The Catcher in the Rye remains S.'s most famous, and certainly most controversial work. It appeared at a sober and realistic time, a period of general disenchantment with ideologies, with schemes for the salvation of the world. S.'s novel, like the decade for which it has become emblematic, begins with the words, "If you really want to hear about it," words that imply a full, sickening realization that something has happened that perhaps most readers would not want to know about. What we find out about directly in the novel is, of course, what happens to S.'s adolescent narrator, Holden Caulfield, as he drops out of prep school and returns to New York City; but we

J. D. Salinger

also find out what has happened generally to human ideas on some simple and ultimate questions in the years following World War II. Is it still possible to reconcile self and society? Is it any longer possible to separate the authentic from the phony? What beliefs are essential for survival? What is the role of language in understanding the nature of our reality? Is it possible to create value and endow the universe with meaning? That S. deals with these questions in one way or another points to a problem with *The Catcher in the Rye* that has often been ignored or not taken seriously—that the climate of ideas surrounding the novel is dense, and that the book is not just the extended and anguished complaint of a wise-guy hero whose main trouble is that he does not want to grow up.

S.'s use of language is one of his most distinctive qualities. If we look at Holden's speech all by itself, it is crude, profane, and obscene. But if we look at its relationship to the overall effect of the novel, another conclusion emerges—that no other language would be suitable. Holden's swearing is so habitual and so unconsciously ritualistic that it contributes to, rather than diminishes, the theme of innocence that runs through the novel.

In the real and relevant idiom of Holden, S. caught and dissected modern society through a symbolic structure of language, motif, and episode that is as masterful as anything in contemporary literature. *The Catcher in the Rye* is a novel that fights obscenity with an amazing mixture of vulgarity and existential anguish, and it does this through a style that moves the narrative effortlessly along on a colloquial surface that suddenly parts to reveal the terror and beauty of the spiritual drama that Holden enacts.

All phases of S.'s career must be taken into account in assessing his career, and *Nine Stories* certainly deserves a place alongside *The Catcher in the Rye* as S.'s most satisfying work. With *Nine Stories* S. established a reputation that puts him easily in the class of John CHEEVER, John UPDIKE, and James PURDY as a writer of short stories. It is in *Nine Stories* that the influence of Oriental thought can be seen most clearly in S. The secret of balancing form with emptiness and in knowing when one has said enough is behind the art of the modern short story. This secret is also apparently behind S.'s interest in the art forms of Zen Buddhism, with its emphasis on an idea that must be at the center of every good short story: one showing is worth a hundred sayings. The short-story writer, like the Zen artist, must work to convey the impression of unhesitating spontaneity, realizing that a single stroke is enough to give away character, and avoiding filling in the essential empty spaces with explanations, second thoughts, and intellectual commentary. S. brought these principles together in *Nine Stories*, a collection of some of his finest writing and a startling blend of West and East in its aesthetic assumptions.

S.'s later work is another matter, however. It turned more and more inward, until in parts of the last two books it becomes such a commentary on itself that it becomes difficult to believe that here is a writer who was once a best-selling novelist, his most famous work a Book-of-the-Month-Club selection. But S.'s later work can be seen as part of a development in American fiction that has been going on ever since the conservative stability of form that had long dominated American writing was challenged by a growing awareness of the artistry, not only of James JOYCE and Franz KAFKA, but also of more exotic talents such as Herman HESSE, Alain ROBBE-GRILLET, Julio CORTÁZAR, and Jorge Luis BORGES. Another important point is that S.'s development is not unlike that of Kurt VONNEGUT and other writers of his generation in that S. moves steadily away from old-fashioned techniques. Like Vonnegut, S. seems to have resolved to avoid ordinary storytelling in favor of a kind of writing that, through its observations on the process by which it was created, and through the conceptualizing frame of the fictional Glass family upon which S.'s later books focus, shows us one way of combating the obscenity of modern life and adapting to a chaotic, but ultimately benign, universe.

S.'s work shows a surprising growth and increasing sophistication. In the process of change, S. has become, at points in his performance, both a stylist whose comic mastery of the language approaches that of Mark Twain and a writer of considerable religious vision whose books themselves remain in the mind as incarnations of spirit long after they are put down.

BIBLIOGRAPHY: Gwynn, F. L. and Blotner, J. L., *The Fiction of J. D. S.* (1958); Grunwald, H. A., ed., *S.: A Critical and Personal Portrait* (1962); French, W., *J. D. S.* (1963); Laser, M., and N. Fruman, eds., *Studies in J. D. S.* (1963); Marsden, M. M., ed., *If You Really Want to Know: A Catcher Casebook* (1963); special S. issue, *WSCL*, 9, 1 (1963); Miller, J. E., *J. D. S.* (1965); special S. issue, *MFS*, 12, 4 (1966); Hamilton, K., *J. D. S.: A Critical Essay* (1967); Schulz, M. F., "Epilogue to *Seymour: An Introduction*: S. and the Crisis of Consciousness," *SSF*, 5 (1968): 128–38; Bryan, J. E., "The Psychological Structure of *The Catcher in the Rye*", *PMLA*, 89 (1974): 1065–74; Lundquist, J., *J. D. S.* (1979); Hamilton, I., *In Search of J. D. S.* (1988); Wenke, J. P., *J. D. S.: A Study of the Short Fiction* (1991)

—JAMES LUNDQUIST

SALKEY, Andrew

Jamaican poet, novelist, essayist, critic, and writer of children's books, b. 30 Jan. 1928, Colon, Panama; d. 28 Apr. 1995, Amherst, Massachusetts, U.S.A.

Though S. was born in Panama, he was reared in Jamaica. His writing career began with poems in the *Daily Gleaner*. He left for England in 1952, where he obtained a B.A. and an M.A. from the University of London. S. was a prime mover of and an active participant in Caribbean literature of the 1950s and 1960s, encouraging and promoting writers such as Sam SELVON, V. S. NAIPAUL, and Wilson HARRIS; his fourteen-page evaluation of Harris's *Palace of the Peacock* persuaded Faber & Faber to publish the mysterious, metaphysical novelist. He taught for two decades at Hampshire College, where, at the time of his death, he was professor of writing.

S.'s writing explores the impact of colonialism and neocolonialism, seeking local and worldwide strategies and frequently playing the role of trickster to break through barriers in the minds of his readers and listeners, as in his modern stories about the spider who came to Jamaica with the kidnaped Africans, *Anancy's Score* (1973) and *Anancy, Traveller* (1992). He does not so much write about tricksters as create trickster texts. His first novel, *A Quality of Violence* (1959), was praised by critics, few of whom realized that the hills in the novel are based on those of the country in which his mother was born, Haiti—mother is teacher in much of his work—and that the novel sways our feelings one way and then the other to make us uncover implanted patterns of perception. *The Adventures of Catullus Kelly* (1969) presents what turns out to be the fantasy world of the neocolonized black male in order to remove the mask of self-deception and track colonialism back to its Roman roots and forward to its modern flowering. Recognizing that colonialism was always prefaced and followed by travelogues, S. wrote crisp countertravelogues, *Havana Journal* (1971) and *Georgetown Journal* (1972), to make his readers see.

S. made a promise to the widow of Victor Jara that he would write a poem to Chile every year until democracy returned. "Chile" in *In the Hills Where Her Dreams Live* traces the ongoing struggle between despotism and freedom in the country from early independence to the murder of President Salvador Allende; the volume received the 1979 Casa de Las Americas Prize. His last poem to Jara was posthumously placed on the web by the *Boston Review* (1998). In his epic poem *Jamaica* (1973), history is to be found by the people from within, from Caribbea.

S. received the Deutscher Kinderbuchpreis in 1967 for his first novel for children, *Hurricane* (1964). Nine other novels followed. The protagonist of *Danny Jones* (1980) was born in London of an English mother and a West Indian father; the father learns from his son that the Mother Country can be racist while the son learns from his father that not only race but also structures and strategy are important. In *Joey Tyson* the protagonist's family faces the crisis brought about by the Jamaican government's ban on a radical thinker and activist like Walter Rodney. The early novels dealt with natural disasters, the later ones with man-made political crises.

S. is known as the dynamo of modern Caribbean writing, having edited anthologies such as *West Indian Stories* (1960), *Caribbean Prose* (1967), *Island Voices* (1970), *Breaklight* (1972), *Writing in Cuba since the Revolution* (1977), and *Caribbean Folk Tales and Legends* (1980). Although he has received numerous awards, including the Thomas Helmore Poetry Prize (1955), the John

Simon Guggenheim Award (1960), and the Sri Chinmoy Poetry Award (1977), the skill and range of his writing are only just receiving serious attention by scholars. Few of his radio plays broadcast by the BBC are in print, but his work continues to emerge: Bogle-L'Ouverture Press is publishing *In the Border Country and Other Stories* featuring the sempiternal Anancy.

FURTHER WORKS: *The Late Emancipation of Jerry Stover* (1968); *Jonah Simpson* (1969); *Come Home, Malcolm Heartland* (1976); *Away* (1980); *The One* (1985)

BIBLIOGRAPHY: Birbalsingh, F., *Frontiers of Caribbean Literature in English* (1996): 29-41; Nazareth, P., *In the Trickster Tradition: The Novels of A. S., Francis Ebejer and Ishmael Reed* (1994): 15-94

—PETER NAZARETH

SALLAH, Tijan M.

Gambian poet, short-story writer, and essayist, b. 6 Mar. 1958, Serekunde

Of Wolof-speaking parents, S. was first educated in elementary and Koranic schools before leaving in 1970 for St. Augustine's High School, run by fathers of the Holy Ghost Order in Gambia. After high school graduation in 1975, he left for the U.S. He spent a brief orientation at Rabun Gap Nacoochee High School in Georgia before leaving for Berea College, where he received a B.S. in business management and a B.A. in economics in 1982. In 1987 he received a Ph.D. in economics from Virginia Polytechnic Institute. He taught economics at Virginia Polytechnic Institute, Kutztown University, and North Carolina A&T University at Greensboro. In addition, he has served in various capacities as an economist for the World Bank, covering countries in Asia, West Africa, and the Middle East. Presently, he serves as senior economist for the World Bank in Washington D.C.

S.'s career as an economist has had no negative effect on his remarkable engagements as a writer. He is best known as a poet, a calling that appears to have deep roots in the Gambian Koranic schools where part of the religious discipline of young people is the recitation of poetic verses. That foundation also took a boost from one of his English teachers at St. Augustine's, Reverend Father Gough, who recognized S.'s talent and encouraged him to write poetry, with a prophetic declaration that he would one day become famous. At Berea he won the Francis S. Hutchins Award in Literature. His critical essays, short stories, and poems have appeared in numerous publications such as *Présence Africaine*, *Callaloo, Okike, West Africa, Poet, Kentucky Review, Poetry Africa*, and *Appalachian Heritage*. S. has published a book in anthropology, *Wolof* (1996), edited a poetry collection, *New Poets of West Africa* (1995), and published three books of his poetry— *When Africa Was a Woman* (1980), *Kora Land* (1989), and *Dreams of Dusty Roads* (1993)—and a collection of short stories, *Before the New Earth* (1988) .

S. admits the influence of Chinua ACHEBE, Lépold Sédar SENGHOR and the NÉGRITUDE poets on his thought and craft in his formative years. Those influences constitute the cultural and political fulcrum of his first book, *When Africa Was a Woman*. The title poem explores the image of Africa as a woman abused by sundry aspects of imperialism. It is a predictable collection in harmony with the political gambit of most sensitive writers of modern Africa, with potshots at the Tarzanic and other demeaning images foisted on Africa by colonialism. *Before the New Earth*, his collection of short stories, and *Kora Land* concentrate on a somewhat realistic representation or depiction of Gambia, its land, the people and their ways, impulses, and consciousness. As explained by S., there was no longer need for an art engaged in "grandstanding." Whether it is prose or poetry, his work is an art of life or lived experience which approaches humanity tenderly, frankly, and humorously, based on transparent particularities.

Dreams of Dusty Roads is an engaging text executed in a simplicity that is both charming and unsettling because of numerous ironic twists and turns in the character of the ideas and the vehicular images. The collection is a symbolic journey in which the poet metaphorically drives the reader through his life from Africa to America. Nostalgia mounts at every human road sign as the poet contemplates our differences as human beings in different national or cultural spaces. The whole journey appears to initiate and proceed horizontally with periodic vertical dips into the poet's passionate and humane consciousness.

One of his representative poems from *Dreams of Dusty Roads* is "Love," where the poet revises and culturally domesticates the old English theme of love unrequited: "You see, it seems / Time trims the genuine / Out of love / If the two bean-lobes / Of love / Are not careful." The economy of that line is the general character of S.'s work, whether the theme from his wide ranging concerns is damnation or salvation, whether the subject is politicians or plain folk, the unsullied and primordial or the glitzy shallows of the Western world. His sensitivities do not run away with his craft. "The fully integrated person," declared S. in an interview, "and the fully integrated society, must be able to merge the head with the heart." This is true about society as it is about S. and his work.

BIBLIOGRAPHY: Garren, S. B., "Exile and Return: The Poetry and Fiction of T. S.," *Wasafiri*, 15 (Spring 1992): 9-14

—CHIMALUM NWANKWO

SALTER, Mary Jo

American poet, b. 15 Aug. 1954, Grand Rapids, Michigan

Since many of her poems invoke the nuanced perceptions of an American living abroad, S. has been characterized as a writer of travel poetry, a task for which she is well qualified. Born in Grand Rapids, Michigan, S. was reared in Detroit and Baltimore. She received her B.A. from Harvard in 1976 and her M.A. from Cambridge with first-class honors in 1978. Since then, she has lived in France, Italy, Japan, and Iceland, having made most of her travels with husband and poet Brad Leithauser (b. 1953), whom she married in 1980. S. is also known for her command of poetic forms, both traditional and experimental.

The rhetorical situation of the title poem in S.'s first book of poems, *Henry Purcell in Japan* (1985), has characterized much of her oeuvre. The poem dramatizes the tension between a sense of the familiar and of the unfamiliar, as the speaker comes upon a Japanese funeral, and experiences a Westerner's sense of mystification at how death is perceived differently in the East. S. uses music in this instance to delineate the two cultures, contrasting the silent beauty of written Japanese characters with a choir she later hears singing the music of Henry Purcell. Whereas the Japanese letters bespeak a silent resignation to mortality, Purcell's music typifies the Western penchant for "harmonies layered against the cold" of death and loss. Although this poem is written in free verse, many of the poems in her first collection are composed in carefully rendered forms, using rhyme and meter flexibly but dramatically. "Shisendo," for example, makes skillful use of blank verse in describing a pilgrimage to the Hall of the Hermit-Poets. The poem is rich in visual detail and invokes a sense of mystery at the human attempt to memorialize poetry through visual artifice.

S.'s father was an advertising executive, and has yet to figure prominently in her work. By contrast, her mother was a painter, and appears in many poems, most notably in the title poem of S.'s second volume, *Unfinished Painting* (1989). The title poem shows S.'s characteristic impulse toward ekphrasis, or creating art that responds explicitly to another piece of art. The speaker describes the painting of a mother who has tried to paint her son, but who has been called away from her art by the demands of real life: "It seems that bringing / the real boy up had taken time / away from painting him." Its very incompleteness embodies the fact the mother's art has been sacrificed, forming a pointed commentary on the female artist's predicament. The poem also displays S.'s formal flexibility and skill, consisting of five-line stanzas, the first four of which are tetrameter, followed by a trimeter. This metrical abbreviation in the last line may rhetorically underline the poem's reflection on incompleteness. Moreover, the rhythmically "unfinished" last line rhymes at random with one of the preceding lines, giving the poem additional aural subtlety.

Although *Unfinished Painting* is dedicated to S.'s biological mother, it also acknowledges at least one poetic mother. The book contains two poems about Emily Dickinson, as well as one about S.'s daughter, also named Emily. "Reading Room" is set in the Williston Memorial Library at Mount Holyoke College, where Dickinson matriculated and where S. has taught periodically since 1984. *Unfinished Painting* won the 1988 Lamont Poetry Prize of the Academy of American Poets.

Iceland forms the backdrop for a series of poems in S.'s third collection, *Sunday Skaters* (1994). The title poem begins by noting that "These days / the sky composes promises / and rips them to pieces," briskly using the pathetic fallacy to set an elegiac tone, which S. uses in many other poems. The poem proceeds to describe a frozen pond in the distance where children and adults skate on a Sunday afternoon in March. Halfway through, the poem takes an unexpected psychological turn as the speaker describes a small boy's face as "Stock still at the clock's center, / the pin that everything hinges on," which leads her to exclaim "It's all / about time, about time!" The skaters them become an index for the passage of time, as they inscribe lines in the ice that will surely melt.

Sunday Skaters also contains work of a more personal nature, including poems to her daughters Emily and Hilary. One of the more moving poems in the book, "Poppies," characteristically begins by describing a Renoir painting, but spirals back in time to describe a scene of childhood illness and a flickering black and white television movie, both of which form a backdrop for recounting the terror of abandonment at the premature loss of the poet's mother.

While some critics have implied that S.'s impulse toward formal verse can limit her poetic range, others find that her commitment to rhyme and meter adds acoustic incisiveness to her voice, which speaks with remarkable confidence. As Judith Hall has observed, a "reader, relaxing in the unflinching authority of her voice, may forget how rare it is in American poetry for a woman to claim this power." *Sunday Skaters* also pays homage to Robert FROST in "Frost at Midnight," a masterful blank verse meditation on the more telling episodes of Frost's life. Coleridge's poem of the same title, with its abstruse musings on the strange fabric of childhood memory, forms the perfect fulcrum. S. has a particular affinity with Frost, having returned from Japan in 1981 to serve as poet-in-residence at Robert Frost Place.

S.'s other honors have included the Discovery Prize from *The Nation* (1983), a fellowship from the National Endowment of the Arts (1984-84), a fellowship from the Ingram-Merrill Foundation (1989), the Witter Bynner Foundation Poetry Prize (1989), the Peter B. Lavan Award from the Academy of American Poets (1990), and a Guggenheim Fellowship (1993).

S. served as poetry editor for the *New Republic* from 1992 to 1995, and has served as an editor for *The Norton Anthology of Poetry* (1996). Her latest poems appear in *Poetry*, *Ploughshares*, and the *Yale Review*, exhibiting S.'s typical formal sophistication and psychological acuity. As they confront various species of human darkness, S.'s poems continue to exhibit uncommon sweetness and light.

FURTHER WORKS: *The Moon Comes Home* (1989)

BIBLIOGRAPHY: Lehman, D., "The Not So New Formalism," *MQR*, 29 (Winter 1990): 140-44

—R. A. BENTHALL

SAMARAKIS, Andonis

Greek short-story writer and novelist, b. 16 Aug. 1919, Athens

S. holds a law degree from the University of Athens. Between 1935 and 1963 he worked for the Greek Ministry of Labor while also traveling extensively for the United Nations as an adviser on labor and social problems in Africa, Brazil, and elsewhere. Since 1963 he has devoted himself to writing, while also speaking throughout Greece on behalf of humanitarian causes and continuing to travel widely.

Modern Greece's most widely translated writer after Nikos KAZANTZAKIS, S. has written three collections of short stories and two novels since 1954. His novel *To lathos* (1965; *The Flaw*, 1969) has been translated into almost thirty languages and filmed in French as *La faille* (1975). Popular at home and abroad, S. has been described as a Greek KAFKA.

S. writes about common people who could be from any highly urbanized society in which the boredom of contemporary life alternates with the increasing threat of totalitarian political systems. His protagonists, often lonely middle-aged men, typically begin as frustrated victims and end as individuals who take a personal and thus often political stand in their own modest, antiheroic ways. Considering himself a "nonwriter," S. conveys his vision in simple, direct, and honest prose, which is accessible to a large audience. His short-story collection *Arnoumai* (1961; I refuse) suggests the personal protest his characters finally wage.

To lathos, the novel that won many awards, including the French Grand Prize for Detective Literature, concerns a man in an unidentified country arrested and questioned by agents of a totalitarian government. Using detective-fiction elements for a modern political fable with the skill of Graham GREENE, S. follows the suspect's escape and final impassioned protest as the police close in. S.'s deceptively simple style traps the reader in an almost cinematic montage of flashbacks and switches in points of view that approximate the confusion felt by the protagonist.

The satirical power of S.'s writing is clear in all his stories, but particularly in his longest one, "To diavatirio" (1973; "The Passport", 1979), a tale that grew out of S.'s own experiences with the Greek military junta (1967–74). Here, as in many of his other stories, someone is arrested on absurd charges (an offending remark in a poem about soccer written when he was a child) and handled by an anonymous totalitarian bureaucratic branch known by an acronym, in this case, SCED (Section for Citizens' Emotional Decontamination). Beyond satire, however, is a sense of irony and sympathy for his commonman antiheroes. The sympathetic narrator of the story "E teleftaia simmetohe" (1976; "The Last Participation", 1977), for instance, turns out to be the corpse of the father of a young student arrested for protesting against the military government. Even from the open grave, S.'s protagonist calls out in support of his son's actions.

S. has continued to transcend his own experience and particular culture in order to create more universal tales. His stories have been made into television films in various countries, including Canada and Japan.

FURTHER WORKS: *Zhitetai elpis* (1954); *Sima kindinou* (1959); *To diavatirio* (1959; The Passport, 1981); *I kontra* (1992)

BIBLIOGRAPHY: Hemmings, J., on *The Flaw, Listener* (3 July 1969); 24; Jordan, C., on *The Flaw, New Statesman* (4 July 1969): 21; Sokolov, R. A., on *The Flaw, NYTBR* (5 Oct. 1969): 55; Friar, K., on *The Flaw, SatR*, (3 Jan. 1970): 82; Jaheil, E., "The Cinematic World of A. S.," *The Charioteer*, No. 13 (1971): 12–23; Horton, A., " *The Athenian* (Feb. 1975): 18–21; Horton, A., "The Craft and Reality of A. S.'s 'The Passport'" *JHD*, 6, 3 (1979): 65–73

—ANDREW HORTON

SÁNCHEZ, Florencio

Uruguayan dramatist, b. 17 Jan. 1875, Montevideo; d. 7 Nov. 1910, Milan, Italy

A chronic victim of poverty, and disillusioned with politics by the bitter Uruguayan revolution of 1896, S. abandoned traditional political parties and became active in anarchist circles. He had first gone to Buenos Aires in 1892 to look for work; after traveling back and forth between Argentina and Uruguay during the next few years, in 1898 he settled in Buenos Aires. He wrote for newspapers and composed his plays in cafés. Self-taught as a dramatist, S. was not the casual bohemian of legend: his plays demonstrate the seriousness of his craft. His first success came with *M'hijo el dotor* (1903; *My Son the Lawyer*, 1961), in 1903. Only a few years later, while in Milan studying Italian theater on a fellowship, he died of tuberculosis.

S.'s work consists of twenty extant plays; he is known to have written two others, which have been lost. The most important full-length plays are *M'hijo el dotor, La gringa* (1904; *The Foreign Girl*, 1942; later tr., *The Immigrant Girl*, 1961), and *Barranca*

abajo (1905; *Down the Gully*, 1961). In *M'hijo el dotor* he depicts the corruption of the city infecting rural life. *La gringa* presents the conflict between the old rural land system and the austere customs of the Italian immigrants. Old Cantalicio loses everything because he has not paid his debts to the immigrant, but S. provides an atypical happy ending and points out the road to the future: the wedding between members of the second generation of the two contending families. These plays are not exclusively denunciations of injustice, however; they show the conflict between two ways of understanding life, between two moralities, between the love for tradition and the need for change. This is the theme of S.'s most polished work, *Barranca abajo*, which dramatizes the slow stripping away of everything important to old Don Zoilo: he loses money, land, family. The final scene of Zoilo's suicide is almost mute, and has a tragic dignity.

S. also wrote of the metropolis, particularly in works using the structure of the *sainete*, a short melodramatic form with music and dance. *El pasado* (1906; the past) and *Nuestros hijos* (1907; *Our Children*, 1961) attack the hypocrisy of urban morality; *Canillita* (1904; *The Newspaper Boy*, 1961) is a compassionate portrait of a street child. *El desalojo* (1906; *Evicted*, 1961) shows the desperate life of the urban poor, who have no recourse of any kind; *La tigra* (1907; *The Tigress*, 1961) is a sensitive portrait of an aging prostitute. In all these plays S. transcended the limitations of the *sainete* form and created real masterpieces, tragedies in miniature.

There is a basic unity to S.'s work. His purpose was didactic: he wanted to show economic misery, social abuses, and the deplorable moral state he found all about him. But there is also a message of love and of understanding. Essentially a moralizing observer, S. stumbled at times in the psychology of his creations, and at times he exaggerated, but at his best he created living people. The larger and better part of S.'s theater is frankly naturalistic and socialistic. Italian naturalism, especially through the work of the actor Ermete Zacconi, the productions of André Antoine's Théâatre Libre in Paris, and the technique of Ibsen influenced his work strongly. But S. was not a mere imitator; he created vigorously local dramas, and his originality is evident in the authentic speech of his characters and the images they use.

S. is the most important of the playwrights who gave to the rural theater of Argentina and Uruguay the seriousness and solidity that transformed it from embittered individualism, the cult of bravery, xenophobia, and the hatred of authority, into a movement that would dominate the stage for decades. S.'s theater suffers at times from pseudo philosophical vagueness. But at his best he offers a message of tolerance and compassion.

FURTHER WORKS: *Puertas adentro* (1897); *Cédulas de San Juan* (1904; *Midsummer Day Parents*, 1961); *La pobre gente* (1904); *Mano santa* (1905; *The Healing Hand*, 1961); *En familia* (1905; *The Family Circle*, 1961); *Los muertos* (1905); *El conventillo* (1906); *Los curdas* (1907); *Moneda falsa* (1907; *Phony Money*, 1961); *El cacique Pichuleo* (1907); *Nuestro hijos* (1907; *Our Children*, 1961); *Los derechos de la salud* (1907); *Marta Gruni* (1908); *Un buen negocio* (1909); *Teatro* (1967). FURTHER WORKS IN ENGLISH: *Representative Plays of F. S.* (1961)

BIBLIOGRAPHY: Richardson, R., *F. S. and the Argentine Theater* (1933); Freire, T. J., *Ubicación de F. S. en la literatura teatral* (1961); Cruz, J., *Genio y figura de F. S.* (1966); Lafforgue, J., *F. S.* (1967); Costa, R. de, "The Dramaturgy of F. S." *LATR*, 7, 2 (1974): 25–37; Foster, D. W., and V. R. Foster, eds., *Modern Latin*

American Literature (1975), Vol. 2: 327-38; Rojas, S., "El criollo viejo en la trilogía rural de F. S.", *LATR*, 14, 1 (1980): 5–13

—FRANK DAUSTER

SÁNCHEZ, Luis Rafael

Pureto Rican novelist, short-story writer, dramatist, and essayist, b. 17 Nov. 1936, Humacao

S. was born in a small Puerto Rican city, far from the capital, on the southern portion of the island, not far from the sea, and as a child he lived in the rather small quarters of a public-housing development. He completed a doctorate, and became a professor of literature, eventually joining the faculty at the University of Puerto Rico. His teaching career has been quite distinguished, and S. has often participated in international university conferences and literary symposia. He has recently accepted a teaching appointment at the City College in New York.

S. started his career as a dramatist with the publication of a few plays that have been performed in Puerto Rico since the late 1950s. These early works announced his talent but did not achieve the status of *La pasión según Antígona Pérez* (1968; the passion according to Antígona Pérez), a vigorous text that examines an archetypal Latin American dictatorship, and focuses on the unnecessary suffering of young people against a backdrop of false pretenses and indifference. Although indeed remarkable, the play does not approximate the impact of a previous work that reveals S.'s exceptional talent: his first collection of short stories, *En cuerpo de camisa* (1966; in shirt sleeves). The fifteen stories that comprise this volume—four have been added since the first edition—although seemingly unrelated, have in common a profound interest in people, especially the ones suffering from the incomprehension of others, the marginal, the weak, and the destitute.

S.'s style is rich in vernacular expressions and quite successfully explores the poetry of everyday language. In that sense it has been said that some, if not most, of his work has been written in "Puerto Rican," and although that is a fair assessment of one aspect of his writing, it is not all. The language of his characters accurately reflects their predicaments, and becomes an allusion to social stratification. The orality of S.'s style tends to open the text, rather than confine it to a specific region.

In addition to his teaching and multiple contributions in periodical publications, S. wrote a few more stage productions, and ten years after the publication of *En Cuerpo de camisa* he published his first novel, *La guaracha del Macho Camacho* (1976; *Macho Camacho's Beat*, 1982). This text has enjoyed a great deal of critical attention, and it is by far the best known of S.'s works to date. S.'s poignant criticism of the manipulation of people's minds by the mass media, his vehement attack on political corruption, social discrimination, and sexual exploitation, make *La guaracha del Macho Camacho* a formidable document. Reality, however, is enhanced—and at the same time subtly subdued—by S.'s sense of humor and the incomparable richness of his imagery. S.'s exuberant narration betrays a certain bitterness about reality in Puerto Rico and the rest of "America the invaded." The characters are archetypal, and the situations are sufficiently distorted to become a parody of some elusive reality. It has been repeated that "nothing happens" in the novel. Nothing happens, except everything.

S.'s second novel. *La importancia de llamarse Daniel Santos* (1988; the importance of being called Daniel Santos), is a celebration of the language, the culture, and the peoples of Spanish-speaking America. An impressive inventory of popular culture, intertwined with nearly obsessive intertextual references to the most notable writings of the history of Western literature (Shakespeare, Kafka, Tennessee Williams, Borges, Sor Juana, Proust, Carpentier, Neruda, and Baudelaire, among a host of others), *La importancia de llamarse Daniel Santos* is a most enjoyable text. Daniel Santos, a popular singer, incarnates the multifaceted spirit of very dissimilar societies that in spite of their differences share language, misery, and an unquenchable desire for living. The text, again, is chaotic, repetitive—S. is particularly fond of the use of *anaphora*—and written with a particular flare for vernacular expressions that transcend the Puerto Rican dialect. There is a very reverent, and skillful, blending of very diverse linguistic manifestations, from the highly cultivated to the very foul, that enhances the carefully structured prose of a writer who knows exactly what he wants to say and exactly how he wants to say it.

FURTHER WORKS: *La espera* (1959); *Sol 13, Interior* (1961); *Farsa del amor compradito, o casi el alma* (1966); *Quíntuples* (1985); *La guagua aérea* (1994)

BIBLIOGRAPHY: Rodríguez, M. C., "Poor-Black, Rich-White: Women in *La guaracha del Macho Camacho*," *Studies in Afro-Hispanic Literature*: 2–3 (1978–1979): 244–54; Castro, R. García, "*La guaracha del Macho Camacho* de L. R. S. y 'que sepa abrir la puerta para ir a jugar' de Julio Cortázar," *Chasqui*, 9 (Feb.-May 1980): 71–74; Silva, L. Santos, "*La pasión según Antígona Pérez*: La mujer como reafirmadora de la dignidad politica," *Revl*, 11, 3 (Fall 1981): 438–43; Guinnes, G., "*La guaracha* in English: Traduttore traditore," *REH*, 8 (1981): 107–22; Agura, H. C. and Englebert, J. A., "L. R. S. Speaks about *Macho Camacho's Beat*," *Review*, 28 (1981): 39–41; Zalacain, D., "*La Antígona* de S.: Recreación p uertorriqueña del mito," *ExTL*, 9, 2 (1981): 111–18; Colón Zayas, E. R., *El teatro de L. R. S.* (1985); Gelpi, J., "Lacuentística antipatriarcal de L. R. S.," *Hispam*, 15, 43 (April 1986): 113–20

—HORACIO XAUBET

SANCHEZ, Sonia

American poet, short-story writer, and essayist, b. Sept. 9. 1934, Birmingham, Alabama

Born Wilsonia Driver, S. is the daughter of Wilson L. Driver, a teacher/musician and griot, whose influence has found its way into her writing. Her mother having died one year after her birth, S. and her sister were raised in Harlem, where they moved when S. was nine years old. Residing in Harlem provided the foundation for developing her writing and artistic ability and planted the seeds for the activism that characterizes her writing career. S. couples her career as a poet with that of teacher and activist, having been one of the founders of the black studies program at San Francisco State College. Her activism subsequently forwarded a movement that sparked the implementation of black studies programs throughout the country in the 1960s. Major influences on her writing as a result of her participation in black studies include W. E. B. DUBOIS, Marcus Garvey, and Paul Robeson.

One of the original Broadside poets who emerged during the Black Arts movement in the 1960s, S. published her first book of poetry, *Home Coming*, in 1969 with Broadside Press, the publishing company founded by Dudley Randall (b. 1914). Filled with anger, sarcasm, and wit, the book protests loudly against the racist attitudes S. undoubtedly witnessed growing up in the Deep South and asserts revolutionary themes through incisive language. A master of satire, she presents a direct, searing indictment of America's exploitation of blacks during the Vietnam War in "The Final Solution" and plays on the well-known inscription from its most famous symbols of freedom, the Statue of Liberty: "give us your hungry / illiterates / dropouts." Similarly, in "Small Comment," she attacks the moral emptiness of white Americans for subjecting blacks to human degradation.

Themes attacking the effects of racial oppression and the dominance of Western politics also pervade her later poetry collections. One of the common themes she expounds is the use of drugs, a major destructive force of racism. In "Blk Lovers" she decries the harmful effects of drugs on blacks in love relationships. In "homecoming" she looks at heroin as a form of genocide for inner-city blacks. Similarly, several of her poems in *homegirls and handgrenades* (1984) examine the deleterious and constraining effects of drugs on bright, articulate urban youth. With irony and biting wit, "Norma," "After Saturday Nite Comes Sunday," and "Bubba" provide this heretofore unexamined perspective on how drug use affects this segment of the black population.

Though she typically treats racism and political topics, S. displays versatility in that she expands her range and scope of topics. One of her early works displaying the breadth of her topics includes the collection *We a BadddDD People* (1970), where she examines a diversity of subjects including loneliness and suicide and black male-female relationships, including hers with Etheridge Knight (1931-1991), to whom she was married at that time. In another collection, *I've Been a Woman* (1985), she presents some of her best previously published works, exemplifying topics, such as the assassination of Malcolm X, a quest for the self, and the relationship between art and cultural politics. Considered one of her most forceful poetry collections, *Under a Soprano Sky* (1987) continues to exhibit S.'s flexibility at her craft. In her typical style she examines a socially relevant, but personal theme, when she writes of her brother's death from AIDS in "a poem for my brother"; however, her use of form in the poem represents a departure from her traditional short, crisp, sarcastic style. Divided into six sections, with each one analyzing a dimension of her brother's death, the poem abundantly uses images of nature. Told in her brother's voice, the poem, grounded in the African ancestral worldview, helped to awaken many to admit the truth to others about their own relatives who had died of this disease. In addition, her haikus, tankas, sonkus, and blues poems in this collection represent her mastery of short verse forms.

As part of the Black Aesthetic movement of the 1960s, S. sought to spiritually liberate African-Americans. Her book *A Blues Book for Blue Black Magical Women* (1973) issues a call to African-Americans, especially women, to acquire self-knowledge as a major step towards their liberation. Part autobiographical, the book describes S.'s own spiritual and psychological quest, including her transition in the Nation of Islam. She uses her own experience as a model for nation building within the African-American community: its members must become self-determined individuals who are knowledgeable of their historical past before they can ready themselves for the future .

S.' s poems are characteristic of the energetic style with which S. renders them during an oral presentation. They often reflect the dialect of African-Americans and use white space, punctuation, lack of capitalization, and abbreviated spellings of words to emphasize her unconventionality and to heighten the radicalism of her art.

S.'s writing has progressed through wide collections of poems, plays, short stories, essays, and children's books. Throughout this evolutionary journey, S. has managed to successfully wed politics and art, rendering her finely crafted poems with sensitivity and beauty. Whether writing about the villages and towns of Africa or the ghettos and cities of America, she continues to captivate readers with her fresh style of poetry.

FURTHER WORKS: *We Be Word Sorcerers* (1973); *Sound Investment* (1980); *Wounded in the House of a Friend* (1995); *Does Your House Have Lions?* (1997); *Like the Singing Coming Off the Drums* (1998)

BIBLIOGRAPHY: Barksdale, R. K., and K. Kinnamon, eds. *Black Writers of America* (1972): 804-11; Kent, G. E., "Notes on the 1974 Black Literary Scene," *Phylon*, 36 (June 1975): 182-203; Joyce, J. A., *Warriors, Conjurers, and Priests* (1994):173-97

—LENA AMPADU

SÁNCHEZ FERLOSIO, Rafael

Spanish novelist, b. 4 Dec. 1927, Rome, Italy

S. F. was born in Rome, where his father, Rafael Sánchez Mazas (1894–1966), a lawyer who was himself a writer, was the Spanish consul at the time. S. F. was encouraged by his father to pursue a literary career. However, after publishing a number of books, which at the time were unusual in contemporary Spanish writing, he shifted his creative interests almost completely to linguistic and scientific studies.

Industrias y andanzas de Alfanhuí (1951; *The Projects and Wanderings of Alfanhuí*, 1975) is a highly inventive picaresque work in which reality and fantasy are interwoven. Its thirteen episodes, in fact complete short stories in themselves, relate the extraordinary adventures of young Alfanhuí, a latter-day Lazarillo de Tormes who travels throughout Castile performing bizarre tasks and serving unusual masters. Somewhat a dreamer, Alfanhuí lives in an atmosphere of magic reminiscent of Oriental tales, Lewis Carroll's Alice in Wonderland, and the SURREALIST stories of Jules SUPERVIELLE. S. F.'s rich, sober Spanish adds a rural flavor to a highly sophisticated framework. The book is a journey into fantasy, controlled by the use of concrete, realistic detail.

El Jarama (1956; *The One Day of the Week*, 1962) won the 1955 Nadal Prize for manuscripts. It was also awarded the Critics' Prize of 1956. *El Jarama* is an extraordinarily perceptive slice of life, and its objective technique opened a new path for the contemporary Spanish novel. Although the book's realism is photographic in precision, by focusing on details S. F. achieves a poetic intensity that verges on the super-realistic. Dwarfed against a landscape that is continually changing as the day wanes, a group of urban clerks spend a lazy summer Sunday picnicking on the banks of the Jarama

River. Our knowledge of them is confined to the present, and as we watch their interaction we participate in the grayness of lives drained of individuality and introspection. S. F.'s achievement is to make them psychologically interesting without resorting to sharp contrasts or speeding up the slow tempo of the narration. The book might be intended to depict the traditional Spanish stoicism as remolded by the conditions of the modern affluent society.

Alfanhuí, y otros cuentos (1961; Alfanhuí, and other tales) includes the previously published adventures of Alfanhuí plus two short stories written in 1956: "Y el corazón caliente" (and the warm heart) and "Dientes, pólvora, Febrero" ("Teeth, Gunpowder, February," 1965). The first, closely linked in technique with *Alfanhuí* and in a way with *El Jarama*, deals with a man's odd behavior when he is subjected to the extremes of nature. The second, narrated, like the first, in a conversational matter-of-fact tone, recounts a few hours in a February day when some villagers set out to hunt a marauding she-wolf.

Because S. F. in his two main works, two unquestionable masterpieces, employs two completely different literary approaches and because he has several works in manuscript that he has refused to publish so far, his place in contemporary Spanish letters cannot yet be accurately ascertained. It is indisputable, however, that he has shown most eloquently what can be done with language at the two extremes of realism and fantasy.

FURTHER WORKS: *El huésped de las nieves* (1963); *Las semanas del jardín: Semana primera* (1974); *Las semanas del jardín: Semana segunda* (1975)

BIBLIOGRAPHY: Castellet, J. M., "Notas parauna iniciación a la lectura del *Jarama*," PSA, 1 (1956), 205–17; Alborg, J. L., *Hora actual de la novella española* (1958), Vol. I: 305–20; Nora, E. G. de, *La novela española contemporánea* (1962), Vol. 2: 299-305; Villanueva, D., *"El Jarama" de S. F.: Suestructura y significado* (1973); Risco, A., "Una relectura de *El Jarama* de S. F.," CHA, 288 (1974): 700–711; Danald, R., Introduction to *The Projects and Wanderings of Alfanhuí* (1975): 1–28; Durante, I. Soldevila, *La novela desde 1936* (1980): 228–32

—ALBERT M. FORCADAS

SANDBURG, Carl

American poet, biographer, historian, children's book writer, and journalist, b. 6 Jan. 1878, Galesburg, Ill.; d. 22 July 1967, Flat Rock, N.C.

S. was born into a working-class Swedish-immigrant family. He worked at a variety of jobs, and at seventeen he "rode the rails" west to Kansas. During the Spanish-American War he served in Puerto Rico. Upon his return he enrolled at Lombard College in Galesburg. Just short of receiving his degree, S. moved to Wisconsin, where his growing proletarian sympathies and political radicalism found an outlet in the Social-Democratic Party. While working at journalism, he agitated and wrote for the party, and in 1908 was involved in the presidential campaign of Eugene V. Debs. In 1910 he was appointed private secretary to the Socialist mayor of Milwaukee. In Wisconsin he met and in 1908 married a schoolteacher and fellow socialist, Lilian Steichen (whom S. called

Paula), sister of the photographer Edward Steichen, who became S.'s lifelong friend. The family moved to a suburb of Chicago in 1913, and he worked for several newspapers, particularly the Chicago *Daily News*, until 1932.

S.'s first significant successes as a poet came with publication in 1914 of several poems in Harriet Monroe's (1860–1936) *Poetry: A Magazine of Verse* and with his first important books, *Chicago Poems* (1916), which contains the famous "Chicago" and "Fog," and *Cornhuskers* (1918). In 1928 the family moved to Harbert, Michigan, nestled in the dunes S. loved. In 1943, seeking a milder climate and more room in which to raise their prize goats, they moved again, to Connemara, a farm in Flat Rock, North Carolina, where he lived the rest of his life.

S.'s prose writings are more varied than his poetry. *The Chicago Race Riots* (1919) is a collection of exemplary pieces of reportage. His volumes of poetic stories for children, beginning with the best of them, *Rootabaga Stories* (1922), are charming and delightful. His writings on Lincoln are as important to his reputation as is his poetry. *Abraham Lincoln: The Prairie Years* (2 vols., 1926) established S.'s significance as a biographer of the President, and *Abraham Lincoln: The War Years* (4 vols., 1939) won the 1940 Pulitzer Prize for history. S. provided Americans with a picture of Lincoln as a complex, brooding, tragic figure, but as a man of the people nevertheless. The scholarship of the biographies is sound on the whole, but their major contribution lies in their myth-making, lyrical qualities. S.'s autobiography of his youthful years, *Always the Young Strangers* (1953) is evocative, but not as powerful as his biographies, and his only novel, *Remembrance Rock* (1948), has not received very wide critical acclaim.

The direction of S.'s poetic concerns was established from his very first volumes. He was interested in the spoken language of the American people, in particular in the speech of midwesterners, of immigrants, and of ethnic minorities. The locale of his verse is most often the Midwest, but not, as was the case with his contemporary Edgar Lee MASTERS, the small town. S.'s focus is on the big city, industrialized and peopled by a vigorous but often dispossessed proletariat, the "city of the big shoulders," the "hog butcher to the nation."

In *The People, Yes* (1936), probably S.'s most popular single book, his interest in folk speech and folk expression became even more clearly a feature of his poetry. If one considers this book-length poem together with S.'s collections of folk songs, *The American Songbag* (1927) and *New American Songbag* (1950), and thinks of him on the lecture platform, singing songs from these volumes while accompanying himself on the guitar, the folk roots of his poetry are evident. *The People, Yes* also gives ample evidence of S.'s epigrammatic skill and felicitous phrasing; some critics, however, complained about the poem's inchoateness. The best overview of S.'s poetry during his most productive years can be obtained from his *Collected Poems* (1950), which won a Pulitzer Prize. In this collection the extent of his innovative, democratic ideas can be seen.

The poet Randall JARRELL wrote that S. "is probably at his best in the slight pieces like 'Grass' or 'Losers,' or in such folkish inventions as 'tell me why a hearse horse snickers/hauling a lawyer's bones.'" Such an impression, however, is considerably corrected when one examines the total corpus of his work, as found in *Complete Poems Revised and Expanded* (1970). This book supports claims of his champions that, among other things, S. developed free verse, based on French *vers libre* and short Oriental forms, so that it became acceptable in American poetry. They also argue that he had a much firmer sense of structure than is apparent when one reads only his best-known poems.

There is little doubt that S. has won a permanent place in the history of 20th-c. American poetry. He played a significant role in the important developments in poetry that took place during the first two decades of the century, and he was a central figure in the "Chicago Renaissance." His work has not been as influential as that of such of his contemporaries as T. S. ELIOT, Wallace STEVENS, William Carlos WILLIAMS, and Robert FROST, in part because it is not as challenging as theirs, either intellectually or formally.

His emphasis on and exploration of the particulars of the American experience associate him rather with Hart CRANE and Robinson JEFFERS. S.'s work follows in the tradition in American poetry established by Walt Whitman, but does not move much beyond it, except in its extensive inclusion of folk materials. His reputation as a poet stems from his integrity, his lifelong, uncompromising devotion to the needs of the least powerful, and his mythic and hopeful evocation of a democratic people in all its complexity.

FURTHER WORKS: *In Reckless Ecstasy* (1904); *The Plaint of a Rose* (1905?); *Incidentals* (1905); *Smoke and Steel* (1920); *Slabs of the Sunburnt West* (1922); *Rootabaga Pigeons* (1923); *Selected Poems of C. S.* (1926); *Good Morning, America* (1928); *Abe Lincoln Grows Up* (1928); *Steichen the Photographer* (1929); *Early Moon* (1930); *Potato Face* (1930); *Mary Lincoln: Wife and Widow* (1932, with Paul M. Angle); *Lincoln and Whitman Miscellany* (1938); *Bronze Wood* (1941); *Storm over the Land* (1942); *Home Front Memo* (1943); *The Photographs of Abraham Lincoln* (1944, with Frederick Hill Meserve); *Poems of the Midwest* (1946); *Lincoln Collector: The Story of Oliver R. Barrett's Great Private Collection* (1949); *The Sandburg Range* (1957); *Address before a Joint Session of Congress, February 12, 1959* (1959); *Wind Song* (1960); *Harvest Poems, 1910–1960* (1960); *Six New Poems and a Parable* (1961); *Honey and Salt* (1963); *The Letters of C. S.* (1968); *Ever the Winds of Chance* (1983); *Arithmetic* (1993); *Billy Sunday and Other Poems* (1993)

BIBLIOGRAPHY: Allen, G. W., "C. S.: Fire and Smoke," *SAQ*, 59 (1960): 515–31; Golden, H., *C. S.* (1961); Doren, M. Van, *C. S.* (1969); Callahan, N., *C. S.: The Lincoln of Our Literature* (1970); Flanagan, J. T., "C. S., Lyric Poet," *MidAmerica*, 4 (1977): 89–100; Rubin, L. D., Jr., "Not to Forget C. S. . . .," *SR*, 85 (1977): 181–89; Stern, F. C., "C. S. as Poet: An Evaluation," *MMisc*, 5 (1977): 1–11; Crowder, R. H., "The Influence of C. S. on Modern Poetry," *WIRS*, 1 (1978): 45–64; Hoffman, D., "'Moonlight dries no mittens': C. S. Reconsidered," *GaR*, 32 (1978): 390–407; Duffey, B., "C. S. and the Undetermined Land," *CentR*, 23 (1979): 295–303; Niven, P., *C. S.: A Biography* (1991); Yannella, P., *The Other C. S.* (1996)

—FREDERICK C. STERN

SANDEL, Cora

(pseud. of Sara Fabricius) Norwegian novelist and short-story writer, b. 20 Dec. 1880, Oslo; d. 3 Apr. 1974, Uppsala, Sweden

S. is one of 20th-c. Norway's most admired novelists and short-story writers. She was born in Oslo, and her family moved to the

Carl Sandburg

northern city of Trømso when she was twelve, a difficult move for the child who resented the provincialism of the smaller city as well as its cold climate and long periods of winter darkness. Aspiring to be a painter, S. moved to France in 1905 and for the next fifteen years struggled to scrape together a living while pursuing her artistic ambitions. In part she supported herself by writing articles for Norwegian newspapers and in this way began to develop her writing talent. Also during these years in France, she got married and divorced. In 1920 S. moved to Sweden, where she resided for the rest of her life.

S.'s major work is a trilogy of novels about her fictional alter ego, Alberte, the first volume of which was published when she was forty-six: *Alberte og Jakob* (1926; *Alberte and Jacob*, 1962). It tells the story of Alberte's childhood in her northern city above the polar circle. Through careful selection of sensuous detail S. vividly communicates Alberte's dread at the harsh climate, her family's near-poverty, and the awful respectability of the town's middle-class ladies with their "oil cloth sofas and porcelain dogs." As the first volume ends, Alberte half-heartedly attempts to commit suicide and then recovers her will to live. Volume two, *Alberte og friheten* (1931; *Alberte and Freedom*, 1963), relates the story of Alberte in Paris, where she ekes out a living by working as a model—lonely, almost morbidly sensitive, but with a toughness in her that ultimately saves her. The final volume, *Bare Alberte* (1939; *Alberte Alone*, 1966), chronicles Alberte's final, painful steps in becoming an artist. She returns to Norway and finally writes a novel very much like the Alberte trilogy.

S.'s other books include the novels *Kranes konditori* (1945; *Krane's Sweetshop*, 1968) and *Kjøp ikke Dondi* (1958; *The Leech*, 1960), also the following collections of short stories: *En blå sofa* (1927; a blue sofa), *Carmen og Maja* (1932; Carmen and Maja), *Mange takk, doktor* (1935; many thanks, Doctor), *Dyr jeg har kjent* (1945; animals I have known), *Figurer på mørk bunn* (1949; figures against a dark background), and *Vårt vanskelige liv* (1960; our difficult life). In these works S. turns her attention to struggles similar to those in the Alberte books, to portraits of children, dreamers, trapped housewives, passionate and inept people who struggle to maintain themselves against the forces of small-mindedness and bigotry.

Occasionally S. depicts her characters' struggles with the cold but angry objectivity of the outsider, as in the remarkable and chilling short story "Kunsten å myrde" (the art of murder).

FURTHER WORKS: *Selected Short Stories* (1985); *The Silken Thread, Stories and Sketches* (1987).

—WILLIAM E. MISHLER

SANDEMOSE, Aksel

Norwegian novelist and essayist (also writing in Danish), b. 19 March 1899, Nykøbing, Denmark; d. 5 Aug. 1965, Copenhagen, Denmark

S. grew up in Jante, Denmark, left school at fourteen and went to sea, attended a seminary for one year, and worked intermittently as a farmhand, office clerk, teacher, and journalist. His voyages took him to Canada and the West Indies. *Klabavtermanden* (1927; the shackled man) and *Ross Dane* (1928; Ross Dane) established his reputation and won him a Danish stipend.

To satisfy a long-cherished dream of living in the land of his mother's ancestry, and encouraged by the enthusiastic reviews he received from the prominent novelist and critic Sigurd HOEL in the Oslo *Arbeiderbladet*, S. moved to Norway in 1929. Soon after he started to write in Norwegian, and all his work after 1931 appeared in that language. In the early 1930s, through articles in the Norwegian press, S. exposed the growth of Nazism in Germany and warned readers of its likely spread northward. He foresaw that an organization born out of evil was breeding a kind of mass psychology in Germany that could easily develop anywhere anytime.

S. remained in Norway until 1941, when his involvement in the resistance movement forced him to escape to Sweden. When he returned after the war, he settled with his family on a farm, Kjørkelvik, near Risør. From 1951 to 1955 he published *Årstidende*, a quarterly made up exclusively of his own writings. In 1952, in recognition of his merit as a literary artist, the Norwegian government awarded him a lifelong pension.

Four novels—*En sjømann går iland* (1931; a sailor goes ashore), *En flyktning krysser sit spor* (1933; *A Fugitive Crosses His Tracks*, 1936), *Der stod en benk i haven* (1937; a bench stood in the garden), and *Brudulje* (1938, noisy confusion)—all concern Espen Arnakke's striking out against the tyrannical conformity of his childhood environment. An impulsive seventeen-year-old sailor, rebellious to the point of murdering a rival, becomes an anxiety-ridden runaway in search of explanations for his own irrational act.

Espen is the fictionalization of the youthful S., his growing up reflecting S.'s life in Jante, where he absorbed demoralizing and crushing commandments, from whose effects he suffered the rest of his life. This Arnakke quartet, however, is not a mere tabulation of indictments against small towns, conventional mores, or the disciplined life. It is a bill of rights for all men to have dreams, test values, and live in terms of their own problems.

The critic Philip Houm said that *Det svundne er en drøm* (1946; the past is a dream), which was first published in Swedish in 1944, is "a hundred percent S.," the finest account of the day of the German invasion of Norway (April 9, 1940), and a genuine testimony to the indomitable fiber of the Norwegian people.

Varulven (1958; *The Werewolf*, 1966) is the poignant story of the struggle of two men and a woman against the same Jante intolerance symbolized by the werewolf. The three stand up heroically to the inhibitions bred by their past and to the judgments of their fellow men, but in the end they are indeed battle-scarred. Whether they are also vindicated is left to the reader's determination.

One can detect the influence on S. of Sigmund FREUD and see similarities in style and substance to writers such as Sinclair LEWIS, William FAULKNER, Ernest HEMINGWAY, August STRINDBERG, James JOYCE, and D. H. LAWRENCE. Nevertheless, S.'s views and methods are highly individual, and his approach is interestingly original. In his psychological probing he has been compared to an archeologist scrutinizing artifacts laid bare by excavation and trying to fit the shards together into a once operative whole. In spite of loosely constructed plots and philosophical digressions, S.'s exciting handling of narration and vividly introspective characterization create suspense, stimulate speculation, and invite fresh insights. Purposeful obscurity adds mystery. Finally, his language is rich and poetic, bold and explicit.

S. ranks among the most articulate enemies of sophistry, prudery, and parochialism in the adjustment-oriented society of the 20th c. and among the most ardent advocates of self-examination and environmental analysis as man's only means of liberation and fulfillment. He never loses sight of the clash between mind and spirit, the individual and the group, reason and emotion. The inevitable question—whether any point of resolution exists at which these contenders can meet on equal terms—remains unanswered.

FURTHER WORKS: *Fortællinger fra Labrador* (1923); *Storme ved jævndøgn* (1924); *Ungdomssynd* (1924); *Mænd fra Atlanten* (1924); *Vi pynter oss med horn* (1936; *Horns for Our Adornment*, 1938); *S. forteller* (1937); *Fortellinger fra andre tider* (1940); *Tjærehandleren* (1945); *Alice Atkinson og hennes elskere* (1949); *En palmegrønn øy* (1950); *Reisen til Kjørkelvik* (1954); *Mureneø rundt Jeriko* (1960); *Felicias bryllup* (1961); *Mytteriet på barken Zuidersee* (1963); *Dans, dans, Roselill* (1965); *Verker i utvalg* (8 vols., 1965–1966); *Dikteren og temaet* (1973); *Brev fra Kjørkelvik* (1974); *Bakom står hin Onde og hoster så smått* (1976)

BIBLIOGRAPHY: Kronenberger, L., on *A Fugitive Crosses His Tracks*, *NYTBR*, 12 July 1936, 1; Jarrett, O., on *A Fugitive Crosses His Tracks*, *SatR*, 18 July 1936, 11; Guterman, N., on *A Fugitive Crosses His Tracks*, *New Republic*, 26 Aug. 1936, 80; Kronenberger, L., on *Horns for Our Academy*, *NYTBR*, 25 Sept. 1938, 26; Naess, H., Introduction to *The Werewolf* (1966): vii–xiv; Rossel, S. H., *A History of Scandinavian Literature, 1870–1980* (1982): 190–92.

—AMANDA LANGEMO

SANGUINETI, Edoardo

Italian novelist, poet, critic, and dramatist, b. 9 Dec. 1930, Genoa

Educated at the University of Turin, where he earned a degree with a thesis on Dante, S. displayed great maturity and originality in his early experiments with language. In spite of negative critical responses to his first poetic attempts, S. rigorously followed his inclination with impressive creative results. By 1951 his verse was already marked by what were to become the essential elements of his poetics: mythological images, oneirism, Marxism, psychoanalysis, eroticism, and linguistic innovations. In the 1960s, S. achieved notoriety as one of the major exponents of the avant-garde movement called Group 63 and as a contributor to *I novissimi* (1961; the newest), a collective volume by a group of poets whose common interest was to denounce worn-out literary institutions and to propose new forms. At present, S. is a professor of Italian at the University of Genoa and an active member of the Italian Communist Party.

As a novelist, both in *Capriccio italiano* (1963; Italian whimsy) and in *Il giuoco dell'oca* (1967; the goose game), S. dismantles the traditional narrative structure and sequence and replaces them with the unstructured and asequential paradigms of the "oneiric fabula" and "cabalistic" writings. *Capriccio italiano* is the account of the narrator's nightmare at the vigil of his wife's delivery of a child. As the anxieties and fears of the present expand and fuse with the anxieties and fears of the past, slowly but steadily the origin of the nightmare comes to the surface (the "accidental" conception of the child, the parents' initial rejection of it, and their fear of punishment for that rejection) and brings about its own resolution (with the birth of the child). *Il giuoco delloca* is, according to the writer's instructions, a game consisting of one hundred eleven "houses" (spaces) to be played with two dice numbered one through six. The "story" is the description of the one hundred eleven imaginary hallucinatory pictures; the "structure" is the precarious, self-effacing, ever-changing structure of the dream; the "pot" is the reader's reward for having met the challenge of reading the novel to the "end."

As a poet, S. deliberately and consistently celebrates the "poetics of disorder." The titles of his collections are often running neologisms. S.'s shock approach to language, which engenders a parodic disfigurement of language, is both the expression of the writer's fury at the exhausted linguistic model available to him, and his means of freeing it from the automatisms that shackle it.

S.'s concern with language, his attempt to create new temporal and spatial dimensions by forgoing grammatical and syntactical rules, his struggle to invest words with new life, is also the basis of his dramatic works: *K* (1962; K), *Passaggio* (1963; passage), *Traumdeutung* (1966; German: the interpretation of dreams), *Protocolli* (1962; protocol). Collected as *Teatro* (1969; theater), these plays, along with *Storie naturali* (1971; natural histories), can be considered dramatizations of the "poetics of disorder."

As a critic, S. has written on Dante, on modern Italian literature, and on language and ideology. He has also edited a controversial anthology of modern poetry, *Poesia italiana del novecento* (1970; Italian poetry of the twentieth century), in which he openly subverts long-accepted values.

Versatile, prolific, and controversial, S. has proven to be, and will undoubtedly remain, one of the more important Italian writers of the 20th c.

FURTHER WORKS: *Laborintus* (1956); *Opus metricum* (1960); *Triperuno* (1960); *Interpretazione di Malebolge* (1961); *Tra liberty e crepuscolarismo* (1961); *Tre studi danteschi* (1961); *K, e altre cose* (1962); *Alberto Moravia* (1962); *Ideologia e linguaggio* (1965); *Il realismo di Dante* (1966); *Guido Gozzano, indagini e letture* (1966); *Wirrwarr* (1972); *Laborintus II* (1972); *Catamerone 1951–1971* (1974); *Stracciafoglio: Poesie 1977–1979* (1980)

BIBLIOGRAPHY: Musumeci, A., "S.: The Revolution of the Word," *PCL*, 2 (1976): 47–59; Alexander, G., "Poetry and Politics: S. and the Novissimi," in Trambaiolo, S., and N. Bewbigin, eds., *Altro Polo: A Volume of Italian Studies* (1980): 193-214

—MARIOLINA SALVATORI

SANSKRIT LITERATURE
See Indian Literature

SANSOM, William

English short-story writer, novelist, essayist, and biographer, b. 18 Jan. 1912, London; d. 20 April 1976, London

S. received a middle-class education at Uppingham School; in his youth he traveled on the Continent, where he prepared for a banking career. While working in a London bank, he started writing cabaret music. He turned to writing copy for an advertising agency but continued composing jazz and often worked evenings in a nightclub. Later S. worked briefly as a film scriptwriter, and throughout his career he accepted lucrative writing assignments for travel magazines.

S. began publishing stories during World War II, and his first collection, *Fireman Flower, and Other Stories* (1944), reflected his experiences as a firefighter during the London Blitz. Critics at once noted resemblances to Franz KAFKA in theme and manner. "In the Maze" and "The Long Sheet" in this volume and similar stories in later volumes seemed to place S. in a surrealistic landscape somewhere between Edgar Allan POE and Jorge Luis BORGES. Sometimes the metaphysical burden of an irrational universe threatened the flimsy structure of his pieces, but there was also a perceptible movement away from allegory toward a comedic and more appealing variety of idiosyncratic viewpoints, incarnated in delightfully realized characters like the cleaning woman in "The Cleaner's Story," in the collection *Three* (1946), and the vertiginous bachelor in the novella *The Equilibriad* (1948).

The comedy continued in S.'s first novel, *The Body* (1949), in which a middle-aged barber, transformed by jealousy into a farcical Othello, stalks his wife and her supposed lover through pages booby-trapped with Dickensian devices. In succeeding novels of varying degrees of seriousness, S. created a procession of quite ordinary people made somehow interesting for their neurotic or obsessional behavior: the compulsive liar Eve in *The Face of Innocence* (1951), the masochistic heroine of *A Bed of Roses* (1954), the voyeuristic hero of *The Loving Eye* (1956). What might pass for romantic comedy, however, is often stained with dark instances of gratuitous cruelty, or even physical brutality. And it is surprising how often the protagonist, as in *The Cautious Heart* (1958), toys with a startlingly real urge to kill a rival in love. Incidents in *The Last Hours of Sandra Lee* (1961; reissued as *The Wild Affair* 1964) and in *Goodbye* (1966) jangle with the generally light tone that conditions the reader.

Although S.'s novels are rarely entirely satisfying, he has shown himself to be a master of short forms. Some volumes of short fiction, notably *South: Aspects and Images from Corsica, Italy and Southern France* (1948), *The Passionate North* (1950), and *A Touch of the Sun* (1952), feature a unique form of travel sketch, "hybrid things," S. called them, fiction grafted onto "true things against a background of known places."

In all his fiction, S.'s prevailing strength is his ability to convey sensations, speech rhythms, and pictures, although this genuine word power may finally seem wasted on the subject at hand.

FURTHER WORKS: *Jim Braidy: The Story of Britain's Firemen* (1943, with James Gordon and Stephen Spender); *Westminster at War* (1947); *Something Terrible, Something Lovely* (1948); *Pleasures Strange and Simple* (1953); *It Was Really Charlie's Castle* (1953); *The Light That Went Out* (1953); *Lord Love Us* (1954); *A Contest of Ladies* (1956); *Among the Dahlias, and Other Stories* (1957); *The Icicle and the Sun* (1958); *Blue Skies, Brown Studies* (1961); *The Stories of W. S.* (1963); *Away to It All* (1964); *The Ulcerated Milkman* (1966); *Grand Tour Today* (1968); *Christmas* (1968; Am., *A Book of Christmas*); *The Vertical Ladder, and Other Stories* (1969); *Hans Feet in Love* (1971); *The Birth of a Story* (1972); *The Marmalade Bird* (1973); *Proust and His World* (1973); *Skimpy* (1974); *A Young Wife's Tale* (1974); *Victorian Life in Photographs* (1974)

BIBLIOGRAPHY: Nemerov, H., "S.'s Fictions," *KR*, 17 (1955): 130–35; Bowen, E., Introduction to *The Stories of W. S.* (1963): 7–12; Burgess, A., *The Novel Now* (1967): 109–12; Neumeyer, P. F., "Franz Kafka and W. S.," *WSCL*, 7 (1966): 76–84; Michel-Michot, P., *W. S.: A Critical Assessment* (1971); Karl, F., *A Reader's Guide to the Contemporary English Novel* (1972): 283–85; Chalpin, L., *W. S.* (1980)

—CARL D. BENNETT

SANTAYANA, George

American philosopher, critic, essayist, novelist, and poet, b. 16 Dec. 1863, Madrid, Spain; d. 26 Sept. 1952, Rome, Italy

Descended from an old Spanish family established in Avila, S. was brought to Boston at the age of nine to be raised with the children of his mother's first marriage. Although he learned English and made it his literary language, attended Boston Latin School, and studied and later taught philosophy at Harvard, he never became an American citizen, never adopted American values, and took his place in the national letters and thought because of his caustic, ironic reactions to American culture rather than his involvement with it. After college he studied Greek philosophy in Berlin, wrote a dissertation at Harvard on a minor German thinker, and began a distinguished academic career. At the university he was the colleague (and former pupil) of William James (1842–1910) and the eloquent teacher of Gertrude STEIN, T. S. ELIOT, and

Walter Lippmann (1889–1974). In 1912 S. gave up tenure and departed for Europe and the life of the "wandering scholar" he worked in England and Spain and later settled in Rome, where he took refuge during his last years with the Blue Sisters, an English Catholic order. S.'s three-volume autobiography, consisting of *Persons and Places: The Background of My Life* (1944), *The Middle Span* (1945), and *My Host the World* (1953), gives great color to these events and to his friendships and ideas.

The attitudes and ideas of S.'s work resist categorizing: as a thinker he brought both reason and reverence for tradition to bear on philosophical problems. Skepticism and an intense personal faith in ideas seem to coexist in his books. While rejecting supernaturalism, absolutes of all kinds, and the "fanaticism" of Christian doctrine and German idealism, he is profoundly involved with man's spiritual development. Ideals, he argues, are not disconsonant with our animal nature. This "naturalism" has its roots in the classical world, in 19th-c. scientific discovery, and in an experiential as opposed to a theoretical sense of the physical world. He insists that "the loftiest edifices have the deepest foundations": such an idea is cognate with FREUD'S biological realism, but it includes S.'s very classical notion that man's goal is the pursuit of perfection and the search for "essences." While beginning as a creature, man uses intuition and sense experience to move toward a life of contemplation. S. deposited these ideas throughout works that reflect his complex commitment to artistic beauty and reason. He wrote philosophical discourses, "soliloquies" and "dialogues" that are presented in a figurative, highly poetic language, as well as a novel, poems, and literary essays that are replete with doctrine and argument.

Never comfortable as an academic philosopher and claiming no system or original ideas, S. found pleasure "in expression, in reflection, in irony." Yet he acquiesced to his professional position by writing *The Sense of Beauty* (1896), a highly analytic work dealing with the interrelationships between form and substance and questions of taste and sensuous effects. The great work of his early years, *The Life of Reason* (5 vols., 1905–6; rev. ed., 1954), is a study of the phases of human progress. S.'s principal concept is that all ideals have a natural basis. The work is a charting of man's harmonious rational adjustments to his environment and to the past.

S.'s second mammoth work is the four-volume *The Realms of Being*, comprising *The Realm of Essence* (1927), *The Realm of Matter* (1930), *The Realm of Truth* (1937), and *The Realm of Spirit* (1940). It is at once a theory of knowledge and a geography of mental life. This work describes categories of being and the ways they play a part in human life: essence, which is the realm of timeless, universal forms that can be intuited; matter, which S. believes to be unstable and which man's mind can transcend; truth, which is a summation of all propositions about matter; and spirit, which is the realm of beauty, the arts, and transcendent ideals. S.'s view of the human situation—ideal yearning having its origins in animal life—is, in his own words, "not new and not mine." It is a synthesis of Platonism, Aristotelianism, and his own naturalism. S.'s ideas about mind, art, and ideals are also wittily presented in *Dialogues in Limbo* (1926; enlarged ed., 1948).

S.'s literary essays and imaginative writings are often addressed to the pursuit of essences and are concerned with social, temperamental, and cultural obstacles. *Interpretations of Poetry and Religion* (1900) contains an essay on the "poetry of barbarism": in devastating, witty prose, Santayana attacks Whitman and Browning, two poets immersed in pure sensation and the "spontaneous

Me." S. argues that such "vagrancy" ignores meaning while pursuing momentary thrills. In *Three Philosophical Poets* (1910) S. presents critiques of Lucretius, Dante, and Goethe: the poets are subtly contrasted with regard to richness of experience and wholeness of vision. S. ends the essay by arguing that each of the three falls short of the ideal of rational art, an art including a comprehensive view of matter and spirit. S.'s individual essays are sometimes less demanding about the obligations of writers: his essay on Dickens in *Soliloquies in England* (1922) is a warm celebration of an artist's devotion to the physical world.

But in exploring the American scene, S. is again acerbic. *The Last Puritan* (1935), a novel written over twenty years, is about attenuated Calvinism and the tragic fate of a sincere and intelligent man struggling against Boston gentility. A novel of ideas, the book is S.'s direct and passionate attack on the provincial mind. America is the locale of what S. called "an unintelligible, sanctimonious, and often disingenuous Protestantism." Earlier, S. had written of this obstructive mentality in *The Genteel Tradition at Bay* (1931), a somewhat subtler attack on contemporary puritanism and a call for a larger, less moralistic view of culture.

S.'s reputation is in eclipse: the irony of his work, his unorthodox love of Catholic tradition, his distrust of democratic culture, and his general skepticism set him at a distance from post-World War II currents in philosophy and literature. His nuanced prose is difficult to paraphrase and immune to popularization. Yet his presence has been apparent in the work of America's other great skeptical idealist, Edmund WILSON, as well as in the academic world.

FURTHER WORKS: *Sonnets and Other Verses* (1894; enl. ed., 1896); *Lucifer* (1899; rev. ed., 1924); *A Hermit of Carmel and Other Poems* (1901); *Egotism in German Philosophy* (1916; rev. ed., 1940); *Essays in Critical Realism* (1920, with others); *Little Essays* (1920); *Character and Opinion in the United States, with Reminiscences of William James and Josiah Royce and Academic Life in America* (1920); *Scepticism and Animal Faith: Introduction to a System of Philosophy* (1923); *Poems* (1923); *Platonism and the Spiritual Life* (1927); *Some Turns of Thought in Modern Philosophy* (1933); *Obiter Scripta* (1936); *The Philosophy of S.* (1936; 2nd ed., 1953); *The Works of G. S.* (14 vols., 1936–1937); *The Idea of Christ in the Gospels; or, God in Man: A Critical Essay* (1946); *Atoms of Thought* (1950); *Dominations and Powers: Reflections on Liberty, Society and Government* (1951); *The Poet's Testament: Poems and Two Plays* (1953); *Letters* (1955); *Essays in Literary Criticism* (1956); *The Idler and His Works, and Other Essays* (1957); *Animal Faith and Spiritual Life* (1967); *G. S.'s America: Essays on Literature and Culture* (1967); *The Birth of Reason and Other Essays* (1968); *Selected Critical Writings* (1968); *Physical Order and Moral Liberty: Previously Unpublished Essays of G. S.* (1969)

BIBLIOGRAPHY: Howgate, G. W., *G. S.* (1938); Wilson, E., *Europe without Baedeker* (1947): 41–55; Schilpp, P. A., ed., *The Philosophy of G. S.*, 2nd ed. (1951); Edman, I., Introduction to *The Philosophy of S.*, 2nd ed. (1953): xi–lvi; Lamont, C., ed., *Dialogue with S.* (1958); Cory, D., *S.—the Late Years: A Portrait with Letters* (1963); Ashmore, J., *S., Art, and Aesthetics* (1966); Arnett, W. E., *G. S.* (1968); Price, K., ed., *Critical Essays on G. S.*, (1991); Carter, D., *G. S.* (1992)

—DAVID CASTRONOVO

George Santayana

SANTOS, Bienvenido N.

Philippine novelist, short-story writer, and poet (writing in English), b. 22 Mar. 1911, Manila, Philippines, d. 17 Feb. 1997, Brasilia

An outstanding "practice teacher" with a B.S. in education from the University of the Philippines, S. was sent abroad in 1941 for graduate courses at several American universities. When World War II broke out, his embassy asked him to lecture throughout the country on the merits of his people. The fact that he had left his own wife and children behind helped him sympathize with homesick Pinoys (overseas Filipinos) wherever he went. After the war he became president of Legaspi College and, later, of the University of Nueva Caceres, both in the rural Albay peninsula of Luzon. He returned to the U.S. on a Rockefeller grant (1958–1960), then extended his stay one year on a Guggenheim fellowship while he taught at the University of Iowa. From 1961 to 1972, he alternated teaching writing between Luzon and Iowa until martial law under President Ferdinand Marcos convinced him, in 1976, to become an American citizen. From 1973 to 1982 he served as writer-in-residence at Wichita State University in Kansas. In 1981, his collected stories, *Scent of Apples* (1980), won an American Book Award. Since then he has alternated between his homeland and his adopted country.

Compelled by circumstance to spend much of his life abroad, S. developed close ties with several generations of Filipinos in America. "Old-timers" particularly, those originally confined to bent-labor in California fields or to lonely lives in urban slums, he considered his fellow exiles. His first series of short stories, *You Lovely People* (1955), portrayed them with compassion but also with admiration for their courage in the face of economic and psychological adversity. With controlled sentiment, however, he ended that collection with the tale of Filipino returnees to an unrecognizable land so devastated by war that some immediately reemigrated. The best of those stories reappeared in *Scent of Apples*, along with selections from two interim volumes. *Brother. My Brother* (1960) and *The Day the Dancers Came* (1967). The title story in the latter group epitomizes the generation gap and cultural barriers between Filipinos abroad, when two "old-timers" become painfully invisible in the eyes of a visiting troupe of young, college-educated *bayanihan* dancers. The ideal of traditional *bayanihan* (togetherness) is recaptured in both *Brother. My Brother* and *Dwell in the Wilderness* (1985), largely unsophisticated stories of the Philippines before the war when the underclass occasionally pursued dreams away from their peasant origins but felt disgraced unless they revisited their parents in humble gratitude. Having often suffered rejection by others, they cannot in turn deny the embrace of their ordinary ancestors.

This same motif of memory as measurement of one's concern for others recurs in S.'s novels. In *Villa Magdalena* (1965) Fred Medallada, born poor but wed to the Conde leather fortunes, is nearly permanently corrupted by his passion for self-advancement. *The Volcano* (1965) dramatizes the rise and decline of relations between American missionaries and Filipino peasants between 1928 and 1958. During those years once gentle people, turned violent by their war experiences, reject those who had wished them well. The loss is irreparable. In *The Praying Man* (1982) the central character is a corrupt bureaucrat who, remembering sacred loyalties from his past in Manila's slums, finally makes peace with his conscience; Solomon King in *The Man Who (Thought He) Looked Like Robert Taylor* (1983) is a Pinoy who, after thirty years in the U.S., retires as an overseer in the stockyards and travels in search of friends, only to wonder if in his self-engrossment he ever did develop any real friendships; David Tolosa, narrator of *What the Hell For You Left Your Heart in San Francisco* (1987), is an intellectual and a writer, who discovers that nouveau riche Filipino professionals, potential sponsors of a magazine for their overseas countrymen, are too shallow culturally to keep their promises.

No Filipino has been more faithful in portraying the temptations faced by his compatriots abroad. Although all of these novels suffer from inconsistencies in character development and from dramatic lags, they share with the short stories of S. a genuine sense of Philippine ideals worth commemorating even as they erode.

FURTHER WORKS: *The Wounded Stag, 50 Poems* (1956); *Distances: In Time, Selected Poems* (1983)

BIBLIOGRAPHY: Bernad, M. A., *Bamboo and the Greenwood Tree* (1961): 33–41; Casper, L., *New Writing from the Philippines* (1966): 125–33; Manuud, A. G., ed., *Brown Heritage* (1967): 714–21; Galdon, J. A. ed., *Philippine Fiction* (1972): 101–12; Alegre, E. N. and D. G. Fernandez, *The Writer and His Milieu* (1984): 217–58; Casper, L., *Firewalkers* (1987): 21–34; Abad, G. H. and E. Z. Manlapaz, eds., *Man of Earth* (1989): 176–82

—LEONARD CASPER

SÃO TOMÉ AND PRÍNCIPE LITERATURE

Around the year 1471 Portuguese navigators chanced on two small, uninhabited islands in the Gulf of Guinea. The larger of the equatorial islands was called, with the proper religious zeal, São Tomé (Saint Thomas) and the smaller was called, with all due devotion to the Portuguese royal family, Príncipe (prince). Over the centuries cultural and not a little biological mixing among African slaves and their descendants and Portuguese landowners, administrators, and convicts resulted in a creolization akin to that which occurred on the Cape Verde archipelago. Unlike this process in Cape Verde, however, creolization in São Tomé and Príncipe was undercut by a flourishing plantation economy nurtured by an abusive system of contract labor that for decades after the abolition of slavery brought thousands of black workers from the African continent and Cape Verde.

Despite the lack of a comparable base for the formation of an intellectual elite, by the late 19th c. São Tomé and Príncipe, like Cape Verde, did boast a small black and mestizo (mixed-race) landowning class. From the ranks of this group emerged a tiny number of writers, the first noteworthy one being Caetano da Costa Alegre (1864-1890). Born into a relatively well-to-do black family, he was sent as a boy to study in Portugal, where he lived most of his short life and where he wrote the ninety-six love poems, some of them racially self-conscious, posthumously published by friends in the volume *Versos* (1916; verses).

Nearly a half century would elapse after Alegre's death before another writer of high caliber would appear on the scene; and again the scene was Portugal. Francisco José Tenreiro (1921-1963), the son of a black mother and a white father, also spent most of his life in Portugal, where he rose to prominence as a professor, a geographer, a deputy to the Portuguese National Assembly, and a poet. Together with the Angolan writer Mário de Andrade (b. 1928), Tenreiro compiled the first anthology of black poetry in Portuguese, published in 1953. And although Tenreiro came to be recognized as the foremost poet of Portuguese-language NEGRITUDE, he also wrote nostalgic and implicitly anticolonialist verse about the island of his birth.

The literature of São Tomé and Príncipe was, in effect, born in Portugal. But Alda Espírito Santo (b. 1926) became the central figure in what can be termed the beginnings of a home-grown literature. Except for a brief period in Lisbon, she has spent most of her life teaching grammar school on her native island of São Tomé. Her forceful, declamatory poems, brought together in *E' nosso o solo sagrado da terra* (1978; the sacred soil of the land is ours), lay defiant claim to the obscure, long exploited, but beautiful and potentially bountiful islands.

When independence was won in 1975, Alda Espírito Santo became the Minister of Education and Culture of the Democratic Republic of São Tomé Príncipe, and, not surprisingly, her writing virtually came to a halt under the pressure of official duties. Nevertheless, her works, like those of Tenreiro, Tomás Medeiros (b. 1931), and, from Príncipe, Marcelo Veiga (1892–1976) and Maria Manuela Margarido (b. 1925), serve as models for a literature to come.

In 1987, under the leadership of Alda Espírito Santo, the National Union of Writers and Artists of São Tomé and Príncipe (UNEAS) came into being. By the early 1990s the UNEAS had nearly sixty members, a respectable number for a nation with fewer than 150,000 inhabitants.

Beginning in the mid-1980s, Frederico Gustavo dos Anjos (b. 1954) has been a moving force behind the islands' postcolonial literary movement. Anjos compiled the islands' first postcolonial anthology of poetry with the title *A descoberta das descobertas ou as descobertas da descoberta* (1984; the discovery of the discoveries or the discoveries of the discovery). In contrast to its long title the anthology has only forty pages containing ten poems by six poets, including Anjos. Its modest dimensions notwithstanding, this anthology helped launch São Tomé and Príncipe's postcolonial poetry movement.

In that same year Anjos also published his *Bandeira para um cadáver* (1984; a banner to cover a cadaver), a very short story, but one of the country's first works of fiction written and published in the postcolonial era. Oddly enough, a little-known novel, *Tonga Sofia* (1981; Tonga Sofia), by Sacramento Neto (dates n.a.), a rather obscure author, preceded Anjos's short story. Neto followed this novel with one entitled *Milongo* (1985; Milongo). It is however *Rosa do Ribouque e outros contos* (1985; Rosa from Ribouque and other stories) by Albertino Bragança (b. 1942) that qualifies to date as the islands' most substantial postcolonial and best-known work of fiction. Also in 1985 Manu Berreto (dates n.a.) published his *Sam Gentí!* (1995; Sam Gentí!), which, according to the author, is a true story that should be read as a report.

In the 1990s Francisco Costa Alegre's (b. 1954) *Cinzas do Madala* (1993; Madala's ashes) stands out as one of São Tomé and Príncipe's most compelling collections of poetry. Perhaps the poet's protracted stay in Portugal and the U.S. (he has lived and gone to school in New York City) have contributed to his cosmopolitanism and what seems to be a kind of dialogue with Africa, Europe, and America. Ironically, the tiny, isolated, two-island Republic of São Tomé and Príncipe has produced a universalist literature.

BIBLIOGRAPHY: Moser, G. M., "The Social and Regional Diversity of African Literature in the Portuguese Language," *Essays in Portuguese-African Literature* (1969): 15-29; Preto-Rodas, R., *Negritude as a Theme in the Poetry of the Portuguese-Speaking World* (1970): 32-54; Ortega, N., "The Motherland in the Modern Poetry of São Tomé e Príncipe," *WLT*, 53(1979): 53-56; Hamilton, R. G., "Portuguese-Language Literature," in Owomoyela, O., ed., *A History of Twentieth-Century African Literatures* (1993): 240-84

—RUSSELL G. HAMILTON

SARAMAGO, José

Portuguese novelist and short-story writer, b. 16 Nov. 1922, Azinhaga, Golegã

S.'s novels view the Portuguese existence within an artistic framework that seamlessly melds myth, history, and fiction. Raised in the Alentejo province, S. wrote fiction before the 1970s, but he was primarily a journalist. His membership in the illegal Communist Party led to repeated difficulties with the Salazar-Caetano dictatorship. After the 1974 revolution, he abandoned journalism. In recent years, he has become Portugal's most widely read modern novelist both at home and abroad. In 1998 S. was awarded the Nobel Prize for Literature.

S. recreates significant moments of Iberian peninsular history from a Portuguese point of reference. National events are highlighted within the context of European existence, which was once quite foreign to Portuguese writers. His inspiration is purely peninsular, however. Social-class relationships—the relations between the nobility and the popular classes, between maids and guests in a hotel—and questions of ideology and the abuse of power are subtly debated with lyricism and humor.

Levantado do chão (1980; raised from the ground) is a three-generation saga of a poor sharecropper family from the post-World War I period through 25 April 1974, the date of the Portuguese revolution. The still prevailing medieval Portuguese mentality and organization of latifundia are evoked to explain the centuries-old disgrace of generations of a family. This portrait includes popular, fantastic elements of the rural existence—werewolves, talkative angels, and the dead actively participating in the lives of the living. The story is presented through mixed forms of monologue and dialogue. *Memorial do convento* (1982; *Baltazar and Blimunda*, 1987) is a complex memoir-chronicle of the sociopolitical, religious, and mystical fates of all strata of Portuguese life set during the 18th-c. construction of the Mafra Convent by King John V. The novel delightfully wavers at the point where reality collides head-on with fantasy, and the description of 18th-c. life may be seen as a symbolic discussion of the Portuguese present. In *O ano da morte de Ricardo Reis* (1984; *The Year of the Death of Ricardo Reis*, 1991) S. brings to fictional life Ricardo Reis, a heteronym of the illustrious Portuguese poet Fernando Pessoa (1888–1935), who supposedly returns to Portugal from Brazil upon learning of Pessoa's death. It is Portugal of the fascist 1930s, the years of the onset of the Spanish Civil War, and the rise of Hitler. Mussolini, Franco, and Salazar. S.'s melding of history, fiction, myth, and poetry once again produces a profoundly moving tale of the Portuguese and Iberian existence of the time.

In *A jangada de pedra* (1988; *The Stone Raft*, 1995) the Iberian Peninsula mysteriously separates from the rest of Europe owing to a crack in the Pyrenees—a symbolic story of Portugal's (and Spain's) centuries of exclusion from Europe and the recent integration into the European Economic Community and a new society. In *História do cêrco de Lisboa* (1989; history of the siege of Lisbon) S. skillfully interweaves the past with the present through two love stories: one medieval and one modern. The medieval story, of Moorish-Christian passion, and the modern tale are set against the backdrop of Lisbon of the past and the present.

S.'s panoramic and sweeping characterization of the Portuguese and peninsular existence has struck a chord not only among his compatriots in Portugal, but also in Spain and beyond. His fiction is not only a continual dialogue with the Portuguese character and the nation's history but also a revelation of basic human desires and fantasies.

FURTHER WORKS: *Os poemas possíveis* (1966); *Provàvelmente alegria* (1970); *Deste mundo e do outro* (1971); *A bagagem do viajante* (1973); *As opiniões que o DL teve* (1974); *O ano de 1993* (1975); *Os apontamentos* (1977); *Objecto quase* (1978); *Poética dos cinco sentidos. O ouvido* (1979); *A noite* (1979); *Que farei com este livro* (1980); *Viagem a Portugal* (1981); *O evangelho segundo Jesus Cristo* (1991); *In nomine Dei* (1993); *Ensaio sobre a cegueira* (1995)

BIBLIOGRAPHY: Howe, I., on *Baltasar and Blimunda*, *NYTBR* (1 Nov. 1987):, 1; Goodman, W., on *Baltasar and Blimundax*, *NYT* (5

Dec. 1987): A12; Daniel, M. L., "Ebb and Flow: Place As Pretext in the Novels of J. S.," *LBR*, 27, 2 (Winter 1990): 25–40; Mitgang, H., on *The Year of the Death of Ricardo Reis, NYT* (30 Apr. 1991): C17

—IRWIN STERN

SARDUY, Severo

Cuban novelist and literary theorist, b. 25 Feb. 1937, Camagüey; d. 8 June 1993, Paris

After finishing secondary school in Camagüey in 1955, S. moved to Havana, where he involved himself in literary and artistic circles. In 1960 he received a grant from the Castro government to study art criticism in Europe. He never returned to Cuba, taking up residence in Paris, where he was a significant contributor to avant-garde literary and linguistic theory. His ideas were based on the semiotics of Roland BARTHES, Jacques Derrida (b. 1930), and the group associated with the journal *Tel Quel*.

S.'s ideas may be found in two books of essays, *Escrito sobre un cuerpo* (1969; written on a body) and *Barroco* (1974; baroque). Essentially, he resisted the view that literature is an imitation of reality in the classical Aristotelian sense. Instead, he saw it as self-referential, tautological, a purely linguistic phenomenon in which the message, if indeed one can speak of a message, is the medium of language itself. S. was also interested in the relationship between baroque and neobaroque style and modern astrophysical theories about the nature of the cosmos. He was especially fascinated by the possibility of nothingness at the center of the universe. The idea of cosmic phenomena in a process of infinite and constant transformation, with a void at the center, is analogous to S.'s concept of narrative; his novels are made up of characters who are forever "changing skin," of frustrated action leading nowhere, and of shifting verbal styles and tones.

S. is known primarily for the novels *Gestos* (1963; gestures), *De donde son los cantantes* (1967; *From Cuba with a Song*, 1972), and *Cobra* (1972; *Cobra*, 1975). *Gestos* owes a great deal to Alain ROBBE-GRILLET and the French New NOVEL. The scene is Havana during the last days of Batista. As in a fragmented documentary film where surface imagery is the essence, the reader witnesses a theatrical rehearsal, a political rally, a religious procession, police terrorism, and a bomb explosion, and follows an anonymous black nightclub singer as she plants a terrorist bomb in the city's electric power plant. The plot is obscured by the often abstractly described atmosphere, and the subjective elements of the protagonist are minimized as she is viewed primarily as one object among many.

De donde son los cantantes is even more experimental and stylistically dehumanized. A dizzying verbal kaleidoscope in the manner of James JOYCE, it deals with Cuban reality in three cultural modes: Chinese, African, Spanish. In addition, it burlesques three typically Cuban themes: eroticism, political power, and messianic religion. Three "characters," Auxilio, Socorro (females), and Mortal Pérez (male), who are not characters in any traditional sense, are made to play numerous roles in an ever-shifting series of comic charades created by the narrator. Although some critics have tried to read it as a Cuban allegory, it seems more appropriate to view it as an exercise in exuberant verbal humor.

The most chaotic of S.'s novels is *Cobra*, a title that according to the author has multiple meanings. Similar in structure and style to *De donde son los cantantes*, it has nothing to do with Cuban reality. Instead, S. turns his attention to something akin to the Japanese Bunraku puppet theater, the international drug culture, transsexuality and transvestism, Oriental mysticism, and erotic rituals. None of the motifs are explored *per se* but are used as transformational signs in a hallucinatory, made-up world. The main "character," Cobra, is a pretext for a series of metamorphoses—she changes from doll, to woman, to her own double, to man, among other things. A thematic constant that might possibly bring order to the chaos is the play of opposites—Oriental-Occidental, yin-yang, male-female, illusion-reality, and so forth.

S. is not a popular writer. He demands unusual reader participation. Whether he will become a part of the literary mainstream or be looked upon as an interesting experimenter remains to be seen.

FURTHER WORKS: *Sobre la playa* (1971); *Big bang* (1974); *La caída* (1974); *Relato* (1974); *Los matadores de hormigas* (1976); *Maitreya* (1977); *Colibrí* (1984); *El Cristo de la rue Jacob* (1987)

BIBLIOGRAPHY: Christ, R., "Emergency Essay," *Review* (1972): 33–36; Johndraw, D., "Total Reality in S.'s Search for *lo cubano*," *RomN*, 13 (1972): 445-52; special S. section *Review*, No. 13 (1974): 5–44; Levine, S., "Jorge Luis Borges and S. S.: Two Writers of the Neo-Baroque," *LALR*, 2, 4 (1974): 22-37; Weiss, J., "On the Trail of the (Un)holy Serpent: *Cobra*, by S. S.," *JSSTC*, 5, 1 (1977): 57–69; Johnston, C., "Irony and the Double in Short Fiction by Julio Cortázar and S. S.," *JSSTC*, 5, 2 (1977): 111–22; Santi, E., "Textual Politics: S. S.," *LALR*, 8, 16 (1980): 152–60; González Echevarría, R., *La ruta de S. S.* (1987); Perez, R., *S. S. and the Religion of the Text* (1988)

—ROBERT H. SCOTT

SARGESON, Frank

(born Norris Frank Davey) New Zealand short-story writer and novelist, b. 23 March 1903, Hamilton; d. 2 March 1982, Auckland

S. grew up in the provincial town of Hamilton, completed his studies there and in Auckland, and was admitted as a solicitor (although he never practiced) in 1926. He spent two years in England and Europe, returning to New Zealand in 1928. He then worked at a variety of jobs and eventually settled in Takapuna, near Auckland, in 1933.

S.'s commitment to writing as a full-time occupation began in the mid-1930s, when New Zealand was in the depths of economic depression. His first sketches, published in the radical periodical *Tomorrow* beginning in 1935, indicate the form his stories were often to take during the next ten years: he uses the device of a tale or yarn told about, or often by, a character who typically is a lonely, isolated, itinerant New Zealand male, simple and awkward in his puritanical society, semiarticulate, questing for the company of the "mate who won't let him down."

S. published about forty stories through 1954. They appeared in local periodicals and in small collections, chiefly *Conversation with My Uncle, and Other Sketches* (1936), *A Man and His Wife* (1940), and *That Summer, and Other Stories* (1946). His "The Making of a New Zealander" was a cowinner of the first prize in the short-story division of the country's Centennial Literary Competitions in 1940. He also wrote a novel, *I Saw in My Dream* (1949), whose first section had been published earlier as *When the Wind Blows* (1945). By the end of the 1940s S. had created a significant local fiction where none had really existed before, and had helped foster a climate favorable to younger short-story writers.

During the 1960s S. experienced a remarkable new burst of literary energy. Two plays, *A Time for Sowing* and *The Cradle and the Egg*, were published in 1965 under the collective title *Wrestling with the Angel*. He also wrote new short stories, centered on wry middle-class characters—more articulate but no less isolated or puritanically constrained than the protagonists of his earlier fiction. His three novels from the 1960s, *Memoirs of a Peon* (1965), *The Hangover* (1967), and *Joy of the Worm* (1969), are dark comedies of high local reputation. Each explores puritanism and its effects upon sexuality in New Zealand society. The first is a chronicle of a modern-day Casanova, the second a horror story of adolescent neurosis set in academic and bohemian circles of Auckland, and the third a tale of comically erotic competitiveness between father and son.

S. continued to be highly productive in the 1970s. In addition to the story collection *Man of England Now* (1972), which contains the previously published novella *I for One* (1956), S. published two new short novels, *Sunset Village* (1976), a comic whodunit set in a geriatric housing project, and *En Route* (1979), an erotic comedy about elderly "liberated" women. His three volumes of memoirs, *Once Is Enough* (1973), *More Than Enough* (1975), and *Never Enough!* (1977)—reprinted together under the title *Sargeson* (1981)—are valuable both as examples of the art of autobiography and as descriptions of the world of the writer and his art, and their place in early and middle 20th-c. New Zealand.

S. is, after Katherine MANSFIELD, New Zealand's most important short-story writer, a major novelist, and the first writer of fiction to capture with complete accuracy the nuances of the New Zealand vernacular and the society from which it comes.

FURTHER WORKS: *Collected Stories* (1964); *The Stories of F. S.* (1973; expanded ed., 1982)

BIBLIOGRAPHY: Pearson, B., Introduction to *Collected Stories 1935–1963* (1964): 7–19; Rhodes, H. W., *F. S.* (1969); Copland, R. A., *F. S.* (1976); McEldowney, D., *F. S. in His Time* (1976); Copland, R. A., "F. S.: *Memoirs of a Peon*," in C. Hankin, ed., *Critical Essays on the New Zealand Novel* (1976): 128–39; special S. issue, *Islands*, 6, 3 (1978); King, B., *The New English Literatures: Cultural Nationalism in a Changing World* (1980): 140–56

—W. S. BROUGHTON

SAROYAN, William

American short-story writer, novelist, dramatist, memoirist, and essayist, b. 31 Aug. 1908, Fresno, Cal.; d. 18 May 1981, Fresno, Cal.

S. was the son of an Armenian-American small vineyard owner who had previously been a Presbyterian minister. As a result of his father's early death, S. was forced to spend his early years in an orphanage in Alameda. When he was seven he returned with his mother to Fresno, where he went only as far as the ninth grade. After leaving school he took one job after another in rapid succession until becoming the local manager of the Postal Telegraph office in San Francisco. *The Overland Monthly* published a

William Saroyan

few of his short articles, and then, in 1933, *Hairenik*, an Armenian magazine, published his first short story written under the pseudonym of Sirak Goryan.

S. gained national prominence in 1934 with "The Daring Young Man on the Flying Trapeze," a story of an impoverished young writer in a Depression-ridden society. Its enormously effective title soon became a widely accepted sobriquet for the author himself as his writings began to appear in increasing number in leading periodicals and were reprinted in successive volumes—seven by the end of the decade. It appeared that he could perform with the greatest of ease; actually, however, he was working tirelessly to perfect a prose style that was swift, lean, and seemingly spontaneous in its colloquial freshness. He kept himself at the center of this fiction, whether it was drawn from his boyhood among the Armenian-American fruit growers of the San Joaquin Valley or from his struggles as a young writer in San Francisco. His successive collections of individual pieces moved steadily toward the form of the story cycle; the best of them is *My Name Is Aram* (1940), stories unified by their valley setting and by a pervasive lyricism in their treatment of the rival claims of the poetic and the practical.

S.'s fiction with a San Francisco setting sometimes resembles that of the naturalists who dominated the period, but it differs markedly in its underlying faith in the inviolability of the individual. S.'s assumption of the priority of heritage over environment in the makeup of character was undoubtedly instinctive to one who had grown up among people whose customs, values, and language were brought to this country from the land of their birth. The ineffable sadness of these uprooted immigrants and their unshakable conviction of the preciousness of life were important in the formation of the young writer, and, blended with his own ebullience of spirit, make up the inimitable quality of imagination that has become known as "Saroyanesque."

S.'s drama is also drawn from deeply personal sources. He was the first American playwright to disregard the conventional idea of conflict as essential to drama and to create a theater of mood. One of his best gifts to the American stage is the character who embodies the bittersweet loneliness of the foreign born American, regardless of national origin. *My Heart's in the Highlands* (1939) and *The Time of Your Life* (1939), which was offered the Pulitzer Prize (although S. declined it), are his most notable plays.

Returning to fiction at the outbreak of World War II, S. began to cultivate longer forms. *The Human Comedy* (1943), essentially a story cycle with a slight gesture toward narrative form, was enormously popular during the war and was made into a successful film. In the title novella of *The Assyrian, and Other Stories* (1950) and in *The Laughing Matter* (1953) S. experimented with allegorical effects within the framework of realistic fiction. Both have clearly autobiographical content.

In 1952 S. published the first of several book-length memoirs, *The Bicycle Rider in Beverly Hills*. With the passing years he continued to be astonishingly prolific, publishing at the rate of about one book a year. The best of these is *Sons Come and Go, Mothers Hang In Forever* (1976), because it is freer of the unevenness that is inevitable for one disinclined to edit or rewrite his own work. The underlying impulse of this writing is an irrepressible sense of self and his own remembered past, remote or recent.

S.'s creativity was strongest when closest to memory. Thus, his work diminishes the customary distinction between fiction and autobiography. In his fiction the narrative point of view is invariably his own sensibility, sometimes slightly disguised; and in his memoirs recollection is so shaped by fancy and narrative skill that what is remembered and what is imagined merge into one creative act. Moreover, in reflecting a highly idiosyncratic responsiveness, both tend toward the more private form of the familiar essay. Whether presented as fiction, autobiography, or drama, his writing has the flavor of an open letter to the world. It is this essayistic quality, essentially lyrical in tone, that is the most identifiable element in S.'s writing.

FURTHER WORKS: *Inhale and Exhale* (1936); *Three Times Three* (1936); *Little Children* (1937); *Love, Here Is My Hat and Other Short Romances* (1938); *The Trouble with Tigers* (1938); *Peace, It's Wonderful* (1939); *Three Plays: My Heart's in the Highlands; The Time of Your Life; Love's Old Sweet Song* (1940); *Three Plays: The Beautiful People; Sweeney in the Trees; Across the Board on Tomorrow Morning* (1941); *S.'s Fables* (1941); *Razzle-Dazzle* (1942); *Get Away Old Man* (1944); *Dear Baby* (1944); *The Adventures of Wesley Jackson* (1946); *Jim Dandy: Fat Man in a Famine* (1947); *The S. Special* (1948); *Don't Go Away Mad and Other Plays* (1949); *Twin Adventures* (1950); *Rock Wagram* (1951); *Tracy's Tiger* (1951); *Mama, I Love You* (1956); *The Whole Voyald and Other Stories* (1956); *Papa, You're Crazy* (1957); *The Cave Dwellers* (1958); *A W. S. Reader* (1958); *Here Comes/There Goes/You Know Who* (1961); *Boys and Girls Together* (1963); *Not Dying* (1963); *One Day in the Afternoon of the World* (1964); *After Thirty Years: The Daring Young Man on the Flying Trapeze* (1964); *Short Drive, Sweet Chariot* (1966); *Lily Dafon* (1966); *Look at Us; Let's*

See; Here We Are; Look Hard, Speak Soft (1967); *I Used to Believe I Had Forever, Now I'm Not So Sure* (1968); *Letters from 74 rue Taibout* (1969); *Making Money, and 19 Other Very Short Plays* (1969); *Days of Life and Death and Escape to the Moon* (1970); *Places Where I've Done Time* (1973); *The Tooth and My Father* (1974); *Chance Meetings: A Memoir* (1978); *Obituaries* (1979); *Births* (1983); *My Name Is S.: A Collection* (1983); *An Armenian Trilogy* (1986); *Madness in the Family* (1988); *Warsaw Visitor; Tales from the Vienna Streets* (1991)

BIBLIOGRAPHY: Floan, H. R., *W. S.* (1966); Angoff, C., "W. S.: Some Footnotes," in Angoff, C., ed., *The Tone of the Twenties, and Other Essays* (1967): 203–8; Justus, H. H., ldquo:W. S. and the Theatre of Transformation," in ed.,*The Thirties: Fiction, Poetry, Drama* (1967): 211–19; Shinn, T. J., "W. S., Romantic Existentialist," *MD*, 15 (1972): 185–94; Rhoads, K. W., "Joe as Christ-type in S.'s *The Time of Your Life,*" *ELWIU*, 3 (1976): 227–43; Keyishian, H., "Michael Arlen and W. S.: Armenian Ethnicity and the Writer," in Rosa, A., ed., *The Old Century and the New: Essays in Honor of Charles Angoff* (1978): 192–207; Calonne, D. S., *W. S.: My Real Work Is Being* (1983); Foster, E. H., *W. S.: A Study of the Short Fiction* (1991); Keyishan, H., ed., *Critical Essays in W. S.* (1995); Balakian, N., *The World of W. S.* (1998)

—HOWARD R. FLOAN

SARRAUTE, Nathalie

(née Tcherniak) French novelist, critic, and dramatist, b. 18 July 1900, Ivanovo Voznesensk (now Ivanovo), Russia

S.'s parents were divorced when she was two, and her mother took her to Geneva and then to Paris; she also spent some time with her father in Russia. When she was six, her mother took her back to Russia, but at the age of eight she returned to Paris to live with her father, who had by then settled there. She went to school in France and then studied English literature at the Sorbonne, history at Oxford, and sociology at the University of Berlin; enrolled at the University of Paris law school, she married a fellow law student in 1925. After being admitted to the bar, she practiced law until 1940. During the Nazi occupation of France S., who is Jewish, had to hide from the German police by posing as the governess of her own three daughters.

Tropismes (1939; *Tropisms*, 1963), her first book, was begun in 1932. It is composed of twenty-four brief pieces, difficult to classify by any traditional genre. They are "micro-dramas" (her own term), without specific mention of time or place, presenting nameless people caught up in the web of their interdependence. The only unifying principle that she was to use in all her novels is the concept of "tropisms," which she describes as the "things that are not said and the movements that cross the consciousness very rapidly; they are the basis of most of our life and our relations with others—everything that happens within us which is not spoken by the interior monologue and which is transmitted by sensations."

In her next book, *Portrait d'un inconnu* (1948; *Portrait of a Man Unknown*, 1958), S. borrowed from Balzac's *Eugénie Grandet* the theme of the relationship of a miserly father and his daughter in order to counter the 19th-c. idea of firmly delineated characters. She breaks so radically with conventional fiction in her handling of characterization and plot, chronology and milieu, point of view and dialogue, that Jean-Paul SARTRE, in the preface he wrote for it, coined the term "antinovel" to designate the new form.

The conventionally well-defined character is also the literary victim of her third book, *Martereau* (1953; *Martereau*, 1958). How to interpret Martereau as a character is the central theme of this novel. Is he the honest, conventional, solid, well-balanced, practical man he appears to be in the eyes of a hypersensitive narrator, only too anxious to admire and idealize a person totally unlike himself? Suspicion has a corroding effect, and by the end of the novel a totally disintegrated Martereau has become a part of the narrator's tropistic universe. Uncertainty as to his true nature prevails, and Martereau has lost his wax-doll solidity as well as the hammerlike hardness that the narrator had first found so reassuring in him.

In *Le planétarium* (1959; *The Planetarium*, 1960) the narrator has been eliminated. The novel can be read as a parable of the creative process. It is also an ironic comedy of manners introducing what S. calls "subconversation," a new way of communicating tropisms. The spoken words of the dialogue appear as the surfacing of subterranean movements evoked through poetic metaphors. There is usually a great disparity of tone between the undercurrents and the surface conversation. Time is thus considerably extended, and a whole chapter may be devoted to a single conversation filled with dramatic movements of great violence and intensity.

A series of essays collected as *L'ère du soupçon* (1956; *The Age of Suspicion*, 1963) explains and justifies what S. does in her own novels while analyzing the methods used by other novelists with whom she has affinities, such as Marcel PROUST, James JOYCE, Virginia WOOLF, Ivy COMPTON-BURNETT, and Dostoevsky.

In later novels like *Les fruits d'or* (1963; *The Golden Fruits*, (1964), *Entre la vie et la mort* (1968; *Between Life and Death*, 1969), *Vous les entendez?* (1972; *Do You Hear Them?*, 1973), S. dispenses entirely with signs for recognizing characters. In "*disent les imbéciles*" (1976; "*fools say*," 1977) the characters are virtually interchangeable and there is no story line. *L'usage de la parole* (1980; *The Use of Speech*, 1983), composed of brief pieces, marks a return to the form of *Tropismes*. *Enfance* (1983; childhood), however, is autobiographical.

Since 1964 S. has also written radio and stage plays, in which she succeeds in integrating subconversation into conversation. Her dialogue is commonplace and banal, the characters functions almost anonymously, the hidden powers of language and silence are revealed, and language is in fact the main center of interest. As in the novels, tropisms constitute the core of dramatic action.

S.'s early works were precursors of the NEW NOVEL in France. However, her place in fiction is really in the great tradition of Dostoevsky, Proust, Joyce, and Henry JAMES as inventor and theoretician of a new form of psychological novel.

FURTHER WORKS: *Théâtre: Elle est là C'est beau; Isma; Le mensonge; Le silence* (1978; *Collected Plays: She Is There; It's Beautiful; Izzum; The Lie; Silence*, 1981); *Pour un oui ou pour un non* (1982)

BIBLIOGRAPHY: Cranaki, M., and Y. Belaval, *N. S.* (1965); Temple, R. Z, *N. S.* (1968); Zants, E., *The Aesthetics of the New Novel in France* (1968), passim; Fleming, J. A., "The Imagery of Tropisms in the Novels of N. S.," in Frohock, W. M., ed., *Image and Theme: Studies in Modern French Fiction* (1969): 74–98; Mercier, V., *The New Novel from Queneau to Pinget* (1971): 104–64; TisonBraun, M., *N. S.; ou. La recherche de l'authenticité* (1971); Roudiez, L. S.,

Nathalie Sarraute

French Fiction Today (1972): 28–54; Besser, G. R., *N. S.* (1979); Minogue, V., *N. S.: The War of the Words* (1981); Watson-Williams, H., *The Novels of N. S.: Towards an Aesthetic* (1981)

—FREDERIC J. GROVER

SARTON, May

American; poet, novelist, and memoirist, b. 3 May 1912, Wondelgem, Belgium; d. 16 July 1995, York, Maine

Daughter of two gifted parents—George Sarton, a world-renowned Harvard professor of the history of science, and Mabel Elwes, an artist and designer—S. grew up in Cambridge, Massachusetts. After high school she acted for two years with Eva Le Gallienne's Civic Repertory Theatre Company, then worked in her own theater company for the next four. After publishing her first book of poems, *Encounter in April* (1937), she totally committed herself to writing.

S.'s life is recorded in three excellent memoirs. *I Knew a Phoenix* (1959) details the first twenty-six years of her life, in Belgium and in Cambridge; *Plant Dreaming Deep* (1968) begins when she is forty-five and living in New Hampshire; *A World of Light* (1976) fills in the biographical gap through a series of twelve insightful portraits of those who created what she terms the "pivotal

May Sarton

tensions" of her life, including her father, her mother, Elizabeth BOWEN, and Louise BOGAN. To balance these memoirs, which are deliberate reshapings of her experience, S. has also written several journals. *Journal of a Solitude* (1973) is a year-long record of her exploring both the growth of a poet's mind and the complexities of solitude. *The House by the Sea* (1977) continues this solitary journey into the self, with the attendant pain of watching Judy, her Cambridge companion of thirty years, deteriorate into uncomprehending senility. *Recovering: A Journal* (1980), true to its title, details S.'s own descent into hell, as she tries to resurrect her life from the despair stemming from physical illness, a searing personal relationship, and a devastating review of her novel *A Reckoning* (1978).

These memoirs and journals parallel the milieu and themes of S.'s other creative work. Her world is an admittedly rarefied one where few have to worry seriously about money, where culture is assumed, where time and energy can be devoted to developing profound and complex relationships. In this world of both her life and art she reveals her own preoccupation with the attempt to feel and communicate love, the struggles of people to achieve personal and communal harmony through friendships even while understanding the creative power of solitude, and the need to accept aging and death as cyclical necessities.

These themes dominate both her poetry and her prose. Her poetry is traditional, with a consistent preference for strict metrical forms. But she is extremely eclectic in her structures, which range from the discipline of the sonnet to blank and free verse. The breadth and excellence of her work is best exemplified in her twenty-sonnet sequence "Divorce of Lovers" in *Cloud, Stone, Sun, Vine* (1961), in which she details the bitter end of a long love affair; in another sequence, "Autumn Sonnets" in *A Durable Fire* (1972); and in such fine poems as "My Sisters, O My Sisters" in *The Lion and the Rose* (1948), which is on poets and poetry, and "Gestalt at Sixty" in *A Durable Fire*, where she turns the heroic mode of Tennyson's "Ulysses" into an intensely personal statement on solitude. S. views poetry as a way of life that in itself sets the poet apart and requires of her tremendous personal intensity and a dedication to technical perfection.

Although she considers herself primarily a poet, S. is best known for her novels, all of which emphasize the intricacies of mature human relationships. While occasionally lapsing into sentimentality, and more often exhibiting a reluctance to portray the violence of human nature, she nonetheless captures the refined subtleties of warring and loving interactions. Generally agreed to be her best novels are *Faithful Are the Wounds* (1955), the story of the suicide of a Harvard professor after being hounded for his political commitments; *The Small Room* (1961), a novelette set in a private women's college, exploring the price one pays for excellence; *Mrs. Stevens Hears the Mermaids Singing* (1965), a daring novel about the sources and characteristics of poetic inspiration; *Kinds of Love* (1970), the story of an older woman and her sick husband who come to a renewal of their love and an understanding of the debilitating years to come; *As We Are Now* (1973), one of the few realistic fictional accounts of what it means to the human psyche to be in a nursing home; and *A Reckoning*, the sensitive story of a woman dying of cancer and determined to do it on her own terms.

S.'s reputation could undoubtedly rest comfortably on *Mrs. Stevens Hears the Mermaids Singing* and *As We Are Now*. In the first, S. Proclaims that her Muse is always feminine, and that women move and shake her, although she is "nourished by men." In *As We Are Now* S. carries forward her belief that "true feeling justifies, whatever it may cost," but graphically illustrates how devastating this commitment can be in the nursing-home prisons where society relegates the aged to lives of loneliness, dehumanization, and despair.

All of S.'s best works assault the complex barriers that separate people, arguing always that developing creative friendships is the goal of the examined life.

FURTHER WORKS: *The Single Hound* (1938); *Inner Landscape* (1939); *The Bridge of Years* (1946); *Shadow of a Man* (1950); *The Leaves of the Tree* (1950); *A Shower of Summer Days* (1952); *The Land of Silence* (1953); *The Birth of a Grandfather* (1957); *The Fur Person* (1957); *In Time Like Air* (1958); *Joanna and Ulysses* (1963); *Miss Pickthorn and Mr. Hare* (1966); *A Private Mythology* (1966); *As Does New Hampshire* (1967); *The Poet and the Donkey* (1969); *A Grain of Mustard Seed* (1971); *Collected Poems, 1930–1973* (1974); *Crucial Conversations* (1975); *A Walk through the Woods* (1976); *Selected Poems* (1978); *Halfway to Silence: New Poems* (1980); *Writings on Writing* (1980); *Anger* (1982); *M. S.: A Self-Portrait* (1982); *Letters from Maine: New Poems* (1984); *The Magnificent Spinster* (1985); *The Silence Now: New and Uncollected Poems* (1988); *The Education of Harriet Hatfield* (1989); *S. Selected: An Anthology of the Journals, Novels, and Poems of M. S.* (1991); *Coming into Eighty: New Poems* (1994)

BIBLIOGRAPHY: Sibley, A., *M. S.* (1972); Blouin, L., *M. S.: A Bibliography* (1978); Shelley, D., "A Conversation with M. S.,"

W&L, 7, 2 (1979): 33–41; Springer, M., "As We Shall Be: M. S. and Aging," *Frontiers*, 5 (1979): 46–49; Woodward, K., "M. S. and Fictions of Old Age," in Todd, J., ed., *Women and Literature: Gender and Literary Voice* (1980): 108–127; Hunting, C., ed., *M. S.: Woman and Poet* (1982); Simpson, M., and M. Wheelock, *World of Light: A Portrait of M. S.* (1982); Peters, M., *M. S.: A Biography* (1997)

—MARLENE SPRINGER

SARTRE, Jean-Paul

French philosopher, dramatist, novelist, and essayist, b. 21 June 1905, Paris; d. 15 April 1980, Paris

The greatest influence on S.'s boyhood was his Alsatian grandfather, Charles Schweitzer (an uncle of Albert Schweitzer), with whom S. and his mother lived in Paris after his father's early death. When S.'s mother remarried in 1917, the family moved to La Rochelle. He later studied in Paris lycées and at the École Normale Superieure, where in 1929 he met Simone de BEAUVOIR, with whom he formed a lifelong liaison.

After teaching philosophy in Le Havre (1931–33), S. went to Berlin (1933–34) to study the writings of the German philosophers Edmund Husserl (1859–1938) and Martin Heidegger (1889–1976). From 1934 to 1939 S. taught in various secondary schools. Mobilized in September 1939, he was taken prisoner by the Germans in June 1940 and escaped in March 1941. Returning to Paris, he continued to teach until 1944 and founded the literary review *Les temps modernes* in 1945.

By that time, S.'s EXISTENTIALISM had won worldwide acclaim, especially among the young. Active in the Resistance during the German occupation, S. was from then on "committed to his time," first in insisting that literature be *engagée* (committed) in his manifesto for *Les temps modernes*, and later by taking strong stands against French policies in Indo-China and Algeria, the Russian invasions of Hungary and Czechoslovakia, and the American involvement in Vietnam. He was awarded, but refused, the Nobel Prize for literature in 1964 and presided at the International Tribunal against War Crimes in Vietnam, organized by Bertrand Russell and held in Sweden in 1967. S.'s political activity became increasingly militant during the 1970s until it was seriously curtailed, as was his writing, by failing eyesight in 1975.

S.'s largely autobiographical first novel, *La nausée* (1938; *Nausea*, 1949), shows the influence of Husserl's phenomenology and Heidegger's existential philosophy. It describes Roquentin's growing awareness of the purposelessness of the physical world and of his own existence, his discovery of the obscene overabundance of the world around him. Roquentin's perception of his own gratuitousness and solitude induces several experiences of psychological nausea, but he is unable to use this revelation effectively.

The stories in *Le mur* (1939; *The Wall, and Other Stories*, 1948) are studies of "bad faith," or inauthenticity, of people unwilling to recognize that the absurdity of life imposes on them complete responsibility for what they do and what they become. All the characters take refuge in some value outside of their own consciousness.

In his first play, *Les mouches* (1943; *The Flies*, 1947), S. was able to encourage resistance under the very noses of the German occupiers by selecting ancient Argos as the scene of his dramatic action. Here S.'s emphasis is on commitment and responsibility to others as well as to oneself. After the murder of Agamemnon by his wife Clytemnestra and her lover Aegisthus, the people of Argos are visited by a plague of flies—S.'s version of the Furies—a symbol of their guilty torments over their complicity in the king's death. Freely taking upon himself responsibility for avenging his father, Orestes kills the murderers, thus freeing the people of the city from the burden of guilt that has kept them in submission to both Zeus and the usurpers of Agamemnon's throne. Abandoned by his sister Electra, he assumes total responsibility for his act, without guilt, and leaves, pursued by the flies.

S.'s second play, *Huis clos* (1944; *No Exit*, 1947), is a powerfully concentrated drama of some of the tenets of existentialism. Choosing a contemporary notion of hell as his setting, he analyzes the bad faith of a trio—a traitor, a lesbian, and a nymphomaniac—who after their deaths are forced to "live" their inauthenticity throughout eternity. Confined to a small, ugly room beyond which they fear to venture, they attempt to justify their behavior on earth while they tensely await their torturers. Gradually they come to realize that each will be tortured by the other two, who will not permit the third to "live" his or her bad faith, and who will define him or her in their terms.

S.'s earlier ontological study *L'etre et le néant* (1943; *Being and Nothingness*, 1956) had presented the philosophical basis for these literary works. "Being" is the objective world of things (being-in-itself), which exists independently of human consciousness. The discovery of this undifferentiated matter produced Roquentin's nausea. But consciousness, which S. calls "being-for-itself," must be consciousness of something to the exclusion of all else. This "else" becomes S.'s "nothingness" in relation to our consciousness.

In other words, man must detach himself from things to give them meaning. The fact that neither the objective world nor human existence has any meaning in itself constitutes the freedom given everyone to "become," since he "is" nothing. Only one who chooses to assume the responsibility of acting in a particular situation, like Orestes, makes effective use of his freedom. Most people prefer to "be" what someone else (like the others in *Huis clos*) has chosen for them and are therefore merely "things."

This concept is the essence of the phrase "existence precedes essence" from *L'existentialisme est un humanisme* (1946; *Existentialism*, 1947), that is, that man "exists" first, then makes an authentic, "free" choice, *en situation*, thereby defining himself by *his* act.

S. explored these ideas in a trilogy of novels collectively titled *Les chemins de la liberté* (*The Roads to Freedom*). *L'age de raison* (1945; *The Age of Reason*, 1947) describes the paralysis of French intellectuals in the 1930s: Mathieu Delarue, a young philosophy professor, is unable to assume his responsibility either to his pregnant mistress or to the Spanish Loyalists' struggle against Franco, which he supports. In *Le sursis* (1945; *The Reprieve*, 1947), S. focuses on the appeasement pact negotiated with Hitler in 1938 by the leaders of England and France. The action, which covers less than a week, moves without transition—often in the middle of a sentence—among several groups of characters in various parts of the world. The close integration of the private concerns of the protagonists with the public concerns of world leaders shows S.'s belief that everyone was equally responsible for the pact. In *La mort dans l'âme* (1949; *Troubled Sleep*, 1951), Mathieu finally redeems all his weaknesses and frees himself from the past by making the positive gesture of firing on the advancing German troops in 1940 just before he is presumably killed by them.

S.'s plans for a fourth volume to be entitled *La dernière chance* (the last chance) were later abandoned.

In *Baudelaire* (1947; *Baudelaire*, 1949), a long essay in existential psychoanalysis, S. attempts to show that the poet, despite his creative genius, chose to accept the definition of himself imposed by the world around him. S.'s own view of the relationship between the writer, his work, and society is outlined in *Qu'est-ce que la littérature?* (1947; *What Is Literature?*, 1949; repub. as *Literature and Existentialism*, 1962). This important text was later published in *Situations II* (1948; situations II), the second volume of a series of ten, collecting literary, philosophical and political essays. For S., literature must be totally involved with the problems of the writer's own time, and writing is one form of commitment in the practical world.

The play *Les mains sales* (1948; *Dirty Hands*, 1949) stresses the practical necessity for commitment even though the choice is ambiguous. Hoederer, a communist leader, chooses in this play to dirty his hands in political action despite his disagreement on some points with the Party's policies. Hugo, the young bourgeois intellectual, on the other hand, is unwilling to make a commitment that may compromise the principles of the Party he has adopted.

In *Le diable et le bon Dieu* (1951; *The Devil and the Good Lord*, 1960), a drama set in Reformation Germany, the problem of commitment reaches an impasse. Although Goetz, a man of action, finds that it is impossible to do either absolute evil or absolute good, he is finally persuaded to take practical action in the peasants' revolt. However, Heinrich, a man of the Church, is unable to choose either the Church, which has abandoned the poor, or the poor, who have abandoned the Church. The play reveals S.'s developing reservations about the individual's freedom to act in the face of circumstances he cannot control.

S.'s last important play was *Les séquestrés d'Altona* (1960; *The Condemned of Altona*, 1961), in which Franz, unable to find "law" in his father or in the postwar society of Germany, retreats into madness rather than assume the responsibility for his war crimes. But S. is really concerned here with the ambiguous problem of guilt for French atrocities in Algeria, which was his primary preoccupation in the late 1950s, and with the more general problem of the individual's entanglements with history and collective political policy.

The difficulty of effective independent action had been anticipated by S.'s own abortive attempt to form a non-communist leftist political party in 1948. This effort led to his gradual movement toward a reconciliation between existentialism and Marxism and to his uncomfortable collaboration with the French Communist Party as the only hope of bettering the lot of the working classes. The publication of Albert CAMUS's *The Rebel* in 1951 caused a break between the two friends over S.'s tendency to act too exclusively (for Camus) in the immediate historical context, to the exclusion of moral principles.

This evolution in S.'s thought is also evident in his long essay *Saint Genet: Comédien et martyr* (1952; *Saint Genet: Actor and Martyr*, 1963), a brilliant analysis of Jean GENET'S novels and plays. S. sees Genet as conditioned by society to be a criminal, totally accepting this conditioning to evil, but nonetheless making himself a poet within the limits or the framework established. Just as S. did not condemn the characters of *Le disable et le bon Dieu* as he had those of *Huis clos*, he does not condemn Genet as he had Baudelaire, but rather praises him for taking "certain routes which were not initially given."

Questions de méthode (1957; *Search for a Method*, 1963) was S.'s first public statement of his attempt to reconcile existentialism

and Marxism. *Critique de la raison dialectique, I: Théorie des ensembles pratiques* (1960; *Critique of Dialectical Reason, I: Theory of Practical Ensembles*, 1976), in which *Questions de méthode* was reprinted as a preface, attempts to establish a philosophical basis for this reconciliation between an essentially psychological orientation and the historical and sociological perspectives of Marxism. It marks the term of the evolution of his thought from *L'être et le néant*, *Les mouches*, and *Baudelaire*, all of which insist on total individual responsibility, through *Saint Genet et Le disable et le bon Dieu*, which recognize the two factors of individual freedom and social conditioning, to an attempt to forge a new collective human ethic based on the dialectical interaction of existentialist and Marxist philosophies. A projected second volume, to treat concrete historical examples, never appeared.

S.'s autobiography *Les mots* (1964; *The Words*, 1964) satirized the conscious and unconscious bad faith of his own childhood and affirmed that his previous desire, as a bourgeois intellectual, to achieve salvation through writing had been almost entirely replaced by his current involvement with social and political causes. It is a self-analysis comparable to *Baudelaire* and *Saint Genet*; it shows on a personal level the philosophical evolution evident in *Critique de la raison dialectique*.

L'idiot de la famille: Gustave Flaubert de 1821 à 1857 (3 vols., 1971–72; Vol. I tr. as *The Family Idiot: Gustave Flaubert, 1821–1857, Vol I*, 1981), S.'s monumental study of Gustave Flaubert, had been fifteen years in the making. S. had been preoccupied with Flaubert since childhood and had used him in the 1940s to exemplify the bourgeois writer whose conception of literature and view of society were the exact opposite of his own. Here, with considerable empathy, he uses the huge amount of material available to show in the first two volumes how Flaubert lived his neurotic experience, choosing to become the person his family and society determined him to be. The third volume relates this "lived experience" to the collective experience of the society in which Flaubert lived. An analysis of *Madame Bovary* in this light, which was to constitute a fourth volume, was never completed.

This Flaubert study is a practical application and further development of the interaction of individual and collective values presented in *Critique de la raison dialectique*. It places greater emphasis than *Saint Genet* on the historical conditioning or "totalization" of individual action, and like the *Critique* marks a term in the evolution of S.'s philosophy from its phenomenological beginnings to his later belief in the almost total conditioning of the individual by society.

Through the variety and pertinence of his literary and philosophical writings, S. was probably the single most important figure in mid-20th-c. French literature. He captured the sense of despair during the German occupation, yet insisted on man's freedom to go beyond despair in creative action.

The active conscience of an entire generation, S. played a leading role in the political, social, and intellectual life of his country and the world, lending his prestigious name to the support of many oppressed writers and taking vigorous stands on a variety of unpopular causes.

Despite his tremendous influence during the years following World War II, S. always discouraged "disciples," since he considered everyone's relationship between the "lived" experience and his social conditioning to be different. In later years S.'s influence on the young was less pronounced, but his remarkable lucidity allowed his philosophical position to develop in the light of his own experience and the changing demands of the world in which he lived. His fundamental independence and refusal to be bound by the past allowed him to continue to express himself openly regardless of the opinion of others or the effect of his statements on his personal position.

FURTHER WORKS: *L'imagination: Étude critique* (1936; *Imagination: A Psychological Critique*, 1962); *La transcendance de l'égo: Esquisse d'une description phénoménologique* (1937; *The Transcendence of the Ego*, 1957); *Esquisse d'une théorie des émotions* (1939; *The Emotions: Outline of a Theory*, 1948); *L'imaginaire: Psychologie phénoménologique de l'imagination* (1940; *The Psychology of Imagination*, 1948); *Réflexions sur la question juive* (1946; *Anti-Semite and Jew*, 1948); *Morts sans sépulture* (1946; *The Victors*, 1949); *La putain respectueuse* (1946; *The Respectful Prostitute*, 1949); *Les jeux sont faits* (1947; *The Chips Are Down*, 1948); *Situations I* (1947); *Théâtre* (1947); *L'engrenage* (1948; *In the Mesh*, 1954); *Entretiens sur la politiqué* (1949); *Situations III* (1949); *L'affaire Henri Martin: Commentaire* (1953); *Kean; ou, Désordre et génie* (1954; *Kean; or, Disorder and Genius*, 1954); *Nekrassov* (1956; *Nekrassov*, 1956); *Ouragan sur le sucre* (1960; *S. on Cuba*, 1961); *Bariona: ou, Le fils du tonnerre* (1962; *Bariona; or. The Son of Thunder*, 1970); *Théâtre* (1962); *Situations IV: Portraits* (1964; *Situations*, 1965); *Situations V: Colonialisme et néo-colonialisme* (1964); *Situations VI: Problèmes du marxisme 1* (1964; *The Communists and Peace*, 1968); *Les Troyennes* (1965; *The Trojan Women*, 1967); (*Œuvres romanesques* (5 vols., 1965); *Situations VII: Problèmes du marxisme 2* (1965; *The Ghost of Stalin*, 1968); *Que peut la littérature?* (1965); *Situations VIII: Autour de 1968* (1972); *Situations IX: Mélanges* (1972); *Un théâtre de situations* (1973; *S. on Théater*, 1976); *Situations X* (1976; *Life/Situations: Essays Written and Spoken*, (1977); *Œuvres romanesques* (1981); *Les carnets de la drôle de guerre* (1983). **FURTHER WORKS IN ENGLISH:** *Literary and Philosophical Essays* (1955); *Essays in Aesthetics* (1963); *The Philosophy of Existentialism* (1965); *The Philosophy of J.-P. S.* (1965); *Of Human Freedom* (1967); *Politics and Literature* (1973); *The Writings of J.-P. S.*, Vol. 2: *Selected Prose* (1974); *Between Existentialism and Marxism* (1974)

BIBLIOGRAPHY: Jeanson, F., *Le problème moral et la pensée de S.* (1947); Jeanson, F., *S. par lui-même* (1955); Jameson, F., *S.: The Origins of a Style* (1961); Barnes, H., *An Existentialist Ethics* (1967); Manser, A. R., *S.: A Philosophical Study* (1967); McCall, D., *The Theater of J.-P. S.* (1967); Prince, G. J., *Métaphysique et technique dans l'œuvre romanesque de S.* (1968); Bauer, G. H., *S. and the Artist* (1969); Thody, P., *S.: A Biographical Introduction* (1971); Grene, M., *S.* (1973); Contat, M., and M. Rybalka, *The Writings of J.-P. S.* (2 vols., 1974); Aron, R., *History and the Dialectic of Violence* (1975); Chiodi, P., *S. and Marxism* (1976); Craib, I., *Existentialism and Sociology: A Study of J.-P. S.* (1976); Halpern, J., *Critical Fictions: The Literary Criticism of J.-P. S.* (1976); Lawler, J., *The Existentialist Marxism of J.-P. S.* (1976); Caws, P., *S.* (1979); Collins, D., *S. as Biographer* (1980); Barnes, H. E., *S. and Flaubert* (1981); Hill, C., *J. P. S.: Freedom and Commitment* (1992); Thody, P. M., *J. P. S.* (1992)

—CHARLES G. HILL

Any worthwhile thought implies that it will be surpassed, and one cannot go beyond the thought without at least partially refusing to accept it. But not to accept is not necessarily to refute. There are degrees of refusal, from simply insisting on preserving one's own freedom of judgment to wishing to combat one thought with another. S. gives us a means of understanding human reality that is fully satisfying. One can't deny that this method opens up dangerous perspectives; the moral undertaking that everyone is called upon to engage in on his own responsibility is—as Plato suggested—a "fine risk." And it is doubtless impossible to run such a risk without committing others, to some degree, to the consequences of an adventure which cannot remain strictly personal.

Francis Jeanson, *Le problème moral et la pensée de S.* (1947), p. 293

After the special case of *Nausea* the later novels have to be a beginning again, in a formal void. The idea of freedom which they seem to deal with and which is present in their titles does not stand in the same relationship to their contents as did the idea of existence in the earlier work. It tends to imply in spite of itself an opposite, a condition of not being free, which lends it a didactic movement and threatens to turn the earlier discovery which was not a discovery of anything new into a real revelation, a real moment of truth or of the appearance of an "idea"; and because these works are a series of dramas rather than that of a single individual, the problem of freedom threatens to reduce itself to the preoccupation of a single character, no more privileged than the quite different preoccupations of the others. And just as the shape of the idea in *Nausea* seemed to dictate its form, so here each novel, the evocation of a historical moment of distinct quality, crystallizes into a form different from each of the others: the progressive dramatic organization of *The Age of Reason*, the formal innovation of *The Reprieve*, and the chaos and loose ends of *Death in the Soul* that finally resolve themselves into a simple linear narrative in the story of the prison camp.

The Reprieve is a kind of great reaching out for everything, an expansion of the novel's ambitions until they seem to reach the point of an equivalence between the work of art and the world itself: everything in Europe at this moment in time is supposed to leave its traces here, for the moment of crisis is not only related to those actors directly concerned with it but also profoundly influenced by all the personal dramas that deliberately ignore the danger of war and pursue themselves in indifference to it. Just as the great catalogues of the individual events of a life, or the things that happen in peace time, fill in the abstract words Life and Peace, so *The Reprieve* is the working out in solid details of the abstract vision Mathieu had of an unimaginable world full of autonomous consciousnesses.

Frederic Jameson, *S.: The Origins of a Style* (1961), pp. 186–87

Because S. does not describe any situation from an absolute perspective, he rejects the concept of the omniscient novelist and adopts in all his novels the characters' points of view, which are "in situation," relative, changing. And in presenting his universe from various vantage points, he moves constantly from the exterior to the interior, from the objective to the subjective, thus emphasizing the alienation of the self inherent in the consciousness and instability of that universe. In order not to vitiate the duration and therefore the freedom of his characters, he does not cut off their conversations but presents them in their babbling and revealing entirety. S. substitutes for the traditional causal relationships aesthetic ones based on fictional combinations, in order to emphasize the contingency of events and to preserve the essential freedom of the characters.

> Gérald Joseph Prince, *Métaphysique et technique dans l'œuvre romanesque de S.* (1968), pp. 137–38

The connecting link between commitment and authenticity is freedom. The authentic man is one who has a right appreciation of his own freedom, and hence respects that of others. Similarly, the committed writer understands the way in which freedom is involved in writing a novel, and hence respects the freedom that is required to read it. S.'s changing view of the nature of freedom explains here, just as it does in the case of his ethics, the changes in his judgment of particular works; the principle of that judgment remains the same. . . . If the conclusion of a novel is given before the author starts, then there can be no room for genuine freedom; the reader is in some way tricked. I think that the same reasoning lies at the basis of S.'s controversial assertion that "No one would imagine for a moment that it is possible to write a good novel in praise of anti-Semitism." Unfortunately such an example involves our emotional sympathies, or else makes us want to say that there is no reason why such a novel should not be written. S., however, wants to argue for this as a matter of general principle: "Thus whether he be an essayist, a pamphleteer, a satirist or a novelist, whether he deals with only the passions of an individual or attacks the whole of society, the writer, a free man talking to free men, has one single subject: freedom."

> Anthony R. Manser, *S.: A Philosophical Study* (1967), p. 253

The view that S. the imaginative writer is much better than S. the philosopher . . . is only partly true [, as] can be seen in *L'imaginaire* or part IV, chapter I of *L'être et le néant*. This is philosophical writing at the highest level, and the same thing is true of sections of *La critique de la raison dialectique*. Moreover, there is one passage here that is peculiarly appropriate to the effect which S.'s work has on some of his more hostile critics. When I hear a political broadcast with which I disagree, argues S., I am annoyed less by its actual contents—for I, after all, know how to refute this pernicious nonsense—than

by the effect which I realize it might have on an uncommitted but easily influenced listener. The censors and moral theologians who placed S.'s work on the Index were acting in accordance with this analysis, and the more violent the insults directed against him the greater the implicit acknowledgment of S.'s persuasiveness as a writer.

> Philip Thody, *S.: A Biographical Introduction* (1971), p. 139

Of all the "existentialists" it is perhaps S. more than any other who stands out as being relevant to sociology. His early work is self-evidently of some concern to the sociology of interpersonal relationships that has developed so rapidly over recent years, and his later work deals with the type of social formations that have been that province of traditional sociology; his later work is also an attempt to "found" Marxism, to provide Marxist concepts with the roots that have been lacking hitherto, and insofar as he succeeds S. offers us a Marxism which is open and developing, which can take account of the work of non-Marxists and which promises a compensation for sociology's general neglect of Marx.

> Ian Craib, *Existentialism and Sociology: A Study of J.-P. S.* (1976), p. 11

[In *L'idiot de la famille* S.] no longer seems so concerned with the self he sought to define, nor with the childhood he once rejected; he is willing to let the self be invented through another.

Through empathy he reaches for a new prose form, which he perceives as a negation and reconstruction of his previous work. His early critical essays are, relatively, rigid constructs, unchangeable and set, once conceived. They imply little openness to facts or willingness to change, to retotalize, interpretation through the addition of new facts. The new form of S.'s criticism is based on the rejection of criticism as a closed construct. He aims, then, at a comprehensively ordered form through a continually changing point of view, through the disorder of words and the disorder of the self; he creates a form both tighter and looser than his early works, truly a critical fiction that expresses two opposing directions of S.'s project. On the one hand, S. has never ceased striving to make himself into a steely, silent, and manly hero of literature and philosophy; on the other, he is always drawn back to art to make of himself a complete and integrated creator.

> Joseph Halpern, *Critical Fictions: The Literary Criticism of J.-P. S.* (1976), pp. 164–65

The inscription at the end of the Sartrian corpus is, as was to be expected, "to be continued." But as S. himself has said of his last unfinished work [*L'idiot de la famille*], the fact that he will never finish it "does not make me so unhappy, because I think I said the most important things in the first three volumes. Someone else could write the fourth on the basis of the three I have written." Anyone, that is to say, can read *Madame Bovary* as well as S. could have read it, on condition of doing or at any rate following the kind of work that S. has done. This in the end is the hallmark not only of his reading but of his philosophy: it is accessible to everyone. By this I do not mean that what may be called "the philosophy of J.-P. S." is accessible to everyone or even anyone without effort; I mean that philosophy, for him, is accessible to everyone, it is not the province of a professional elite but an engagement with a condition which is common to all.

Peter Caws, *S.* (1979), pp. 197–98

SARVIG, Ole

Danish poet and novelist, b. 27 Nov. 1921, Copenhagen; d. 4 Dec. 1981, Copenhagen

After passing his matriculation examination in 1940, S. studied art history. During World War II he held various jobs in Copenhagen and North Zealand. From 1946 on he worked as an art critic and translator. He traveled extensively in Europe between 1947 and 1950, lived in Spain from 1954 to 1962, and received numerous literary awards. He became a member of the Danish Academy in 1972.

S.'s major poetic work—and the major Danish lyrical achievement of the 1940s—consists of a cycle of poems in five volumes, the most important being *Grfønne digte* (1943; green poems), *Jeghuset* (1948; the house of self), and *Menneske* (1948; man). Using a modern, metaphorical language related to abstract art, S. created a coherent analysis of 20th-c. man's insecurities and anxieties in a world lacking fixed moral and ethical standards. The cycle concludes with the triumph over loneliness and darkness through love for a woman and for God.

Transcending this state of existential anxiety is also a main theme in S.'s novels. In *Stenrosen* (1955; the stone rose) the situation of man facing the void is expressed symbolically through the setting—the ruins of Berlin after World War II. *De sovende* (1958; the sleepers) and *Havet under mit vindue* (1960; the sea under my window) take the form of detective stories. Like Graham GREENE, S. uses this genre to investigate the misery and wickedness of man: to solve the crime means to comprehend the evil and destructive forces—and possibly to overcome them. S.'s novels became increasingly symbolic and religious, with external reality fragmented. In *Limbo* (1963; limbo) he completely abandons the traditional novel structure in favor of a lyrical STREAM-OF-CONSCIOUSNESS technique to describe the mind of a widow longing for her beloved husband. The title refers to the woman's state—her current darkness and the light of redemption through death. The redemption theme leads to a magnificent vision of eternal love.

Elements of the detective story, although without metaphysical overtones, can be found again in S.'s satire on Danish provincial life, *Glem ikke* (1972; don't forget). S.'s most significant work of fiction, *De rejsende* (1978; the travelers)—conceived of as the first volume of a novel cycle, a plan cut short by S.'s death—continues the main theme of his work: the threatened individual in contemporary society. On the surface, it tells of a middle-aged Danish-American's attempts to settle accounts with the myths and traumatic experiences of his childhood. On a more profound level the novel deals with the problems of finding oneself, one's lost identity. Through the novel emerges S.'s view of life as a journey marked by agony and fear, a path man has to follow to achieve redemption—the identification with the mystery of human and divine love. This theme pervades his works from the earliest to the latest collections of poetry, *Forstadsdigte* (1974; suburban poems) and *Salmer* (1981; hymns). *Salmer* contains religious texts, speculations and meditations about Christ as the redeemer of man's suffering.

Throughout his career S. analyzed the problems of modern man in a fragmented and materialistic world. His attempt to deal with this grave crisis, to avert an impending catastrophe, drew him both into his inner self and also outward toward the divine. He was the most important exponent of the metaphysical trend in Danish literature after World War II, which went beyond any psychological or social explanation of mankind.

FURTHER WORKS: *Mangfoldighed* (1945); *Legende* (1946); *Edward Munchs grafik* (1948; *The Graphic Works of Edvard Munch*, 1980); *Tre elegier* (1948); *Krisens billedbog* (1950); *Midtvejs i det 20. århundrede* (1950); *Nattevagten* (1951); *Minkærlighed* (1952); *Evangeliernes billeder* (1953); *Glimt* (1956); *Den sene dag* (1962); *Palle Nielsen* (1966); *Efterskrift* (1966); *Stedet, som ikke er* (1966); *I forstaden* (1967); *Poèmes germes/Spirende digte* (1967); *Kaspariana* (1967); *Tre Skude—en krone* (1968); *Stemmer; I mørket* (1970); *Zoo-rim* (1970); *I lampen* (1974); *Jantzens sommer* (1974); *Sejlads* (1974); *Igår—om lidt* (1976); *Jydske essays* (1976); *Hør jordens råb* (1982); *Jeg synger til jer* (1982). FURTHER WORKS IN ENGLISH: *Late Day* (1976)

BIBLIOGRAPHY: Rossel, S. H., "Crisis and Redemption: An Introduction to Danish Writer O. S.," *WLT*, 53 (1979): 606–9

—SVEN H. ROSSEL

SASSOON, Siegfried

English poet and memoirist, b. 8 Sept. 1886, Weirleigh; d. 2 Sept. 1967, Heytesbury

S. was born into a distinguished and wealthy Anglo-Jewish family with an artistic bent. He studied at Clare College, Cambridge; poetry and the sports of an English gentleman were the preoccupations of his youth.

S.'s acute powers of observation are evident in all his literary endeavors, although the objects of those works changed. Before World War I, a number of privately printed volumes of his poetry appeared, some of which were published anonymously and others under various pseudonyms. These contain mostly lyrical poems that evidence what S. called a "vaguely instinctive nature worship." They seem an anodyne to what he termed the "bewilderments and inconsistencies of existence."

With his participation in the war, the country gentleman's pleasure in pastoral scenes gave way to indignation at the hideous ravages of modern battle. His first-hand experiences stirred an

Siegfried Sassoon

acidic response that was expressed in an unflinching view of war's carnage. *The Old Huntsman, and Other Poems* (1917), *Counterattack, and Other Poems* (1917), *Picture-Show* (1919), and *The War Poems* (1919) dashed the romantic prospects of war, proffering instead the senseless loss and the mindless support for adventure by spectator civilians and self-interested generals alike. His fierce objections to the war, his refusal to serve again after being wounded, were circumvented by military authorities, and he was sent back to France, where he was wounded a second time. Still, his courage and defiant independence live in the war poems. All S.'s subsequent poetry is measured against them, a fact that unfortunately restricts an appreciation of his range.

After the war his focus of observation changed again. The satirical poems of this period were ironic descriptions of man in society, containing some shrewd social commentary. In *Satirical Poems* (1926; enlarged ed., 1933) incongruities in human behavior, custom, and intellectual pursuits are exposed and taken to task, although the savage tone of the war poetry is lacking. S. said he attempted a "laconic, legato tone of voice, and endeavoured to be mellow, sophisticated, and mildly sardonic."

S. the acute observer also turned his vision to his inner self, to the "problem which concerned me most"—whether or not he had a soul. Volumes of poetry like *The Heart's Journey* (1927), *Rhymed Ruminations* (1939), *Common Chords* (1950), *Sequences* (1956), and *The Path to Peace* (1960) present a lucid if not modest pilgrimage of the soul akin in feeling to the verse of the Metaphysical poet Henry Vaughn (1622–1695).

Between 1928 and 1945 S. composed six volumes of memoirs. The most widely read of his prose works is the elegant and carefully wrought *Memoirs of a Fox-Hunting Man* (1928). This work, along with *Memoirs of an Infantry Officer* (1930) and *Sherston's Progress* (1936), was republished as *The Complete Memoirs of George Sherston* (1937); Sherston is the persona S. uses in these books. S.'s Arden-like return to England before the war had wide appeal. The idyllic nostalgia and subtle humor are nicely balanced with the development of the protagonist through the double-vision narrator, analogous to Joseph CONRAD'S Marlow in "Youth." S.'s last three memoirs—*The Old Century and Seven More Years* (1938), dedicated to Max Beerbohm, *The Weald of Youth* (1942), and *Siegfried's Journey 1916–1920* (1945)—which work their way through the war, have received less critical acclaim, perhaps unfairly, because they lack the continuity that marks the earlier trilogy.

S.'s range of vision makes him deserving of close attention and further exploration.

FURTHER WORKS: *Poems* (1906); *Orpheus in Diloeryum* (1908); *Sonnets* (1909); *Sonnets and Verses* (1909); *Twelve Sonnets* (1911); *Poems* (1911); *An Ode for Music* (1912); *Hyacinth: An Idyll* (1912); *Melodies* (1912); *The Daffodil Murderer* (1913); *Discoveries* (1915); *Morning-Glory* (1916); *The Redeemer* (1916); *To Any Dead Officer* (1917); *Four Poems* (1918); *A Literary Editor for the New London Daily Newspaper* (1919); *Lines Written in the Reform Club* (1921); *Recreations* (1923); *Lingual Exercises for Advanced Vocabularians* (1925); *Selected Poems* (1925); *The Augustan Book of Modern Poetry* (1926); *Poems* (1931); *The Road to Ruin* (1933); *Vigils* (1934); *Poems Newly Selected 1916–1935* (1940); *Collected Poems* (1947); *Meredith* (1948); *Emblems of Experience* (1951); *The Tasking* (1954); *An Adjustment* (1955); *Poems* (1958); *Lenten Illuminations, Sight Sufficient* (1958); *Collected Poems 1908–1956* (1961); *An Octave: 8 September 1966* (1966); *Letters to a Critic* (1976); *S. S., Diaries: 1915–1918* (1983); *S. S.'s Long Journey: Selections from the Sherston Memoirs* (1983)

BIBLIOGRAPHY: Keynes, G., *A Bibliography of S. S.* (1962); Johnston, J. H., *English Poetry of the First World War* (1964): 71–112; Parsons, I. M. ed., Introduction to *Men Who March Away: Poems of the First World War* (1965): 13–28; Thorpe, M., *S. S.: A Critical Study* (1967); Corrigan, D. F. ed., *S. S.: Poet's Pilgrimage* (1973); Martin, W. R., "Bugles, Trumpets, and Drums: English Poetry and Wars," *Mosaic*, 13 (1979): 31–48; Lohf, K. A., "Friends among the Soldier Poets," *CLC*, 30 (1980): 3–18

—ROBERT LANGENFELD

SASTRE, Alfonso

Spanish dramatist, critic, and essayist, b. 20 Feb. 1926, Madrid

Born into a progressive family of the professional class, S. experienced the Spanish Civil War as a child. He studied philosophy at the universities of Madrid and Murcia. Involved from adolescence in experimental, "revolutionary" theater, his noncommercial successes date from 1946, but commercial production for two thirds of his plays was prohibited under Franco. S.'s politically motivated manifestos and implicit calls for revolution resulted in repeated imprisonment, fines, and extreme censorship. When Admiral Carrero Blanco was assassinated shortly before

Franco's death, S. and his wife suffered lengthy imprisonment as suspects, which provoked international protest.

S. dramatizes social struggles (contemporary or historical), war, strikes, anarchism, terrorism, economic exploitation, conspiracy, revenge, crimes of violence, and miscarriages of justice. His "theater of social agitation" indicts the established social and political orders without overt propagandizing. S.'s main preoccupation is injustice. Revolution, while not a panacea, is the only remedy suggested. A favorite format utilizes the investigation and reenactment of a crime.

In S.'s drama life is portrayed as inherently tragic; such an outlook is part of S.'s attempt to combat what he perceives as Spanish theater's lack of "real"—that is, social—tragedy. S.'s focus is usually collective, and his most characteristic works utilize not individual heroes but stereotypes or generic figures symbolic of social groups or ideologies. Socialists and communists are often his protagonists or spokesmen. His literary theory and criticism as outlined in *Drama y sociedad* (1956; drama and society) and *Anatomía del realismo* (1965; anatomy of realism) show significant Marxist input, and several plays evince a dialectical interpretation of history. EXISTENTIALIST themes and influences are also present.

Escuadra hacia la muerte (1953; *The Condemned Squad*, 1961) is S.'s best-known work outside Spain. The setting is an isolated outpost during a third world war. A squad including five soldiers and an officer patrol a forested no-man's-land. The leader is murdered, and each of the soldiers faces his responsibility in his own way. Denouncing the absurdity of war, S. handles the action so objectively that the play has also been interpreted as pro-militaristic. Franco's censors banned the play after initial performances.

S.'s most characteristic dramas involve aspects of revolution. *Tierra roja* (1954; red earth), a dramatization of miners' strikes and bloody reprisal, depicts the slow but inexorable development of social consciousness across three generations. *El pan de todos* (1957; every man's bread) adapts the myth of Orestes and Clytemnestra to the modern context: a fanatically idealistic communist denounces his own mother and commits suicide, unable to live with his guilt. In *Muerte en el barrio* (1961; death in the neighborhood) S. employs a police investigation to re-create the execution of a socially irresponsible doctor by patrons of a local bar. The revolutionary theme is played down in *Guillermo Tell tiene los ojos tristes* (1955; *Sad Are the Eyes of William Tell*, 1970) as S. emphasizes the tragic loneliness of the archetypal rebellious hero.

The issue of academic freedom as understood in the U.S. had no direct complement in Francoist Spain, but questions of intellectual liberty nonetheless concern S. in his works on Miguel Servet. This Renaissance Catalan physician symbolizes the integrity of inquiry. Servet fled to Switzerland to escape the Spanish Inquisition but fell into the hands of John Calvin, who had him burned at the stake. With his drama on Servet censored, S. published a lengthy biography, *Flores rojas para Miguel Servet* (1964; red flowers for Miguel Servet) and the expurgated script, *La sangre y la ceniza* (1965; blood and ashes). The play was not performed until after the death of Franco; the definitive edition is found in *M. S. V.; o, La sangre y la ceniza/Crónicas romanas* (1979; M. S. V.; or, blood and ashes/Roman chronicles), a volume containing two works—the second, *Crónicas romanas*, also long prohibited, dates from 1968.

S. has also made excursions into poetry and fiction. His poetry includes *Baladas de Carabanchel, y otros poems celulares* (1976; Carabanchel ballads, and other cellular poems), a defiant declaration of love for communism during his confinement in Madrid's

Carabanchel prison. While interesting sociologically, it is very bad poetry. Other collections, *El español al alcance de todos* (1978; Spanish in the reach of all) and *T. B. O.* (1978; T. B. O.) would be more aptly classed as linguistic observations. Dialects, slang, underworld jargon, argot, and forms of expression peculiar to slum dwellers, gypsies, and convicts interest S., who employs a mixture of novel and essay to explore these sublanguages in *lumpen, marginación y jerigonça* (1980; lumpen, marginality, and jargon). Ostensibly a picaresque novel whose protagonist is S. himself, this work contains little fiction, combining autobiographical elements with extensive digressions on literary theory. An earlier narrative volume, *Las noches lúgubres* (1946; lugubrious nights), best described as neogothic tales, initiated a parodic or metaliterary vein that surfaced again in *lumpen, marginación y jerigonça*.

While S. attempts to transcend simple naturalism, his works are usually grounded in it technically or thematically. Presentation is normally direct, linear, and uncomplicated, although experiments with time and relativity are essayed in some plays. Impact derives mainly from S.'s instinct for inherently dramatic situations, erupting in violence and revolutionary fervor.

FURTHER WORKS: *Uranio 235* (1946); *Cargamento de sueñs* (1946); *Ha sonado la muerte* (1946, with Medardo Fraile); *Comedia sonámbula* (1947, with Medardo Fraile); *Prólogo patético* (1950); *Pathetic Prologue* (1968); *El cubo de basura* (1951); *La mordaza* (1954); *La sangre de Dios* (1955); *El cuervo* (1957); *Ana Kleiber* (1957; *Anna Kleiber*, 1962); *El paralelo 38* (1958); *Asalto nocturno* (1959); *Teatro I* (1960); *La cornada* (1960; *Death Thrust*, 1967); *En la red* (1961); *Oficio de tinieblas* (1962); *Cuatro dramas de la revolución* (1963); *Historia de una muñeca abandonada* (1964); *La taberna fantástica* (1966); *El banquete* (1967); *La revolución y la crítica de la cultura* (1970)

BIBLIOGRAPHY: Woolsey, W., "Man's Tryst with Death as an Element of S.'s Dramatic Art," *SCB*, No. 29 (1969): 150–52; Anderson, F., "S. on Brecht: The Dialectics of Revolutionary Theater," *CompD*, 3 (1969–70): 282–96; Moore, J. A., "S.—Dramatist and Critic," *SAB*, 3, 35 (1970): 22–28; Anderson, F., *A. S.* (1971); Vogely, N., "A. S. on A. S.," *Hispania*, 64 (1981): 459–65; Harper, S., "The Function and Meaning of Dramatic Symbol in *Guillermo Tell tiene los ojos tristes*," *Estreno*, 9, 1 (1983): 11–14

—ROBERT LANGENFELD

SĀYIGH, Tawfīq

Palestinian poet and critic (writing in Arabic and English), b. 14 Dec. 1923, Khirba, Syria; d. 3 Jan. 1971, Berkeley, Calif., U.S.A.

Although S. was born in Syria, he and his family were citizens of the British Mandate of Palestine, and S. grew up on the shore of the Sea of Galilee, in the town of Tiberias. After the establishment of Israel in 1948, the family fled to Beirut, where S. had obtained his B.A. degree from the American University in Beirut in 1946. Later in life, S. was haunted by this trauma, and his poetry constantly returns to the themes of exile and the search for identity.

S. was the son of a Protestant minister, and from his earliest days he was surrounded by an environment saturated in the Scriptures. Thus it is not surprising to find much biblical quotation and imagery in his poetry. Although he rejected conventional religiosity in later life, the Bible, and especially the figure of Christ in the New Testament, never lost its hold on his imagination.

In 1951 S. obtained a Rockefeller Foundation grant to study in the U.S., first at Harvard, and later at the University of Indiana (1952). In 1953–1954 he studied at Oxford and Cambridge, under the auspices of the British Council. S. stayed in England for about a decade after finishing his studies, teaching at Cambridge and the University of London.

In 1961 S. agreed to serve as editor of an Arabic literary and cultural magazine, eventually entitled *Hiwār*, which was funded by an organization called the Committee for Cultural Freedom. This committee was exposed in 1966 as a CIA front organization. In the ensuing scandal. S.'s reputation was savagely attacked. Though S. steadfastly maintained that he had no knowledge of the committee's source of funding, and would not have accepted its support if he had known, in the politically charged atmosphere of the Middle East at the time such denials carried little weight. Thus, S. felt obliged to leave Beirut when he was offered the opportunity to spend a year lecturing at a number of U.S. universities, culminating in his appointment as a lecturer in Near Eastern languages and comparative literature at the University of California, Berkeley, in 1968. He died suddenly there, of a heart attack, in 1971.

From the first, English syntax and idiomatic structure had a strong stylistic influence on S.'s poetry. In fact, one of his early successes, "Sermon on the Mount" (1952), was initially composed in English and only later recast in Arabic. Ironically, this English influence has meant that S.'s poetry often reads more naturally in translation than in the original Arabic. It also explains some of the resistance shown by critics to S.'s poetry, which was reinforced by his thoroughgoing assimilation of a variety of trends in Anglo-American MODERNISM during his studies in the U.S. and England. It is not without significance that all three of his collections of poetry, *Thalāthūn Qasīdah* (1954; thirty poems), *Al-Qasīdah K* (1960; the K poem), and *Mu'allaqat T. S.* (1963; the mu'allaqah [ode] of T. S.), were published during his sojourn abroad when he was actively engaged in assimilating modernist poetics.

S.'s later poetry resembles far more the postwar work of poets like William Carlos WILLIAMS and his objectivist followers than the more formalized metrics and rhymes found in the poetry of the Arab "Free-Verse Movement" with which S. is usually associated. For example, his well-known work "Bid' at as'ilah li-atrahhā alā alkarkadān" (1963; some questions I would ask the unicorn) reflects the influence of Williams's long poem *Paterson* both formally and thematically, especially in its exploration of the dynamics of male and female identity.

This concern with the male-female relationship, often expressed in highly charged erotic imagery, becomes more central to S.'s work in the late 1950s and early 1960s. It frequently fuses with the themes of exile and alienation. Like many Palestinian poets, S. often represented his lost homeland in the form of an unobtainable human beloved, an identification facilitated by the fact that the word "land" in Arabic is of feminine gender. For S. personally, the loss and despair he felt at becoming a stateless person was paralleled by the sufferings he endured during a long and painful love affair he had with an Englishwoman, Kay Shaw. This affair forms the main focus of his second collection of poetry, *Al-Qasīdah K*, and "K" continues to appear, in various forms, in his poetry throughout the remainder of his life.

In a very real sense, S.'s poetry was far in advance of its time. Whether it will fall in the center or more toward the margins in the eventual writing of the history of contemporary Arabic poetry, his work will continue to be of interest to literary historians as marking one limit of the Westernizing tendency in modern Arabic poetry.

FURTHER WORKS: *Adwā jadīdahalā Jubrān* (1966)

BIBLIOGRAPHY: Boullata, I. J., "The Beleaguered Unicorn: A Study of S.," *JArabL*, 4 (1973): 69–93; Khouri, M. A., "The Paradise Lost in S.'s Poetry," *Studies in Contemporary Arabic Poetry and Criticism* (1987): 139–47; Allen, R., ed., *Modern Arabic Literature* (1987): 275–79

—TERRI DE YOUNG

al-SAYYĀB, Badr Shākir

Iraqi poet, b. 1926, Jaykūr; d. 24 Dec. 1964, al-Kuwait, Kuwait

After graduating from the Teachers' Training College in Baghdad in 1948, S. worked very briefly as a schoolteacher, then primarily in the Iraqi civil service and also as a freelance journalist. In his youth (until 1954) he was a communist, and later became an Arab nationalist. Because of his political activities, he was frequently arrested and dismissed from jobs, both under the monarchy and later under the republic, when Iraq was in turmoil amid rival political programs and conflicting national and international ideologies. Between 1961 and 1964 he suffered from a degenerative disease of the nervous system, which gradually paralyzed him. In vain he sought a cure in Baghdad, Beirut, London, Paris, Basra (Iraq), and Kuwait—where he finally died. Buried inconspicuously in his homeland, he was honored in 1971 by the Iraqi Ba'th government, which erected a statue of him in Basra.

S.'s first collection, *Azhār dhābila* (1947; faded flowers), like much of the period's poetry, dwelt on emotions of romantic love, mostly unrequited. In one poem he experimented with form by discarding the traditional verse of six or eight feet per line and adopting the single foot as the metrical unit, using as many feet per line as thought required. Later called "free verse" as it spread first in Iraq and then in the rest of the Arab world, this form was better used in his second collection, *Asātīr* (1950; legends), in which the new rhythm is heightened by unconventional imagery, attention to detail, and language that helps evoke atmosphere and fuse things perceived with things remembered.

Although S. wrote socially and politically committed poems, only a few were published in his early collections and in Iraqi newspapers; the rest he recited at mass meetings. As he developed subtle and indirect methods of expression in the 1950s, he published poems that expressed the anguish of the Arab people, their hopes for change, and their vision of a new life in their struggle for freedom from not only external domination but also internal exploitation and repression. His own feelings were so engrossed in Arab society's predicament that it is hardly possible to disentangle the personal from the social in them.

S.'s works of the 1950s are gathered in *Unshūdat al-matar* (1960; the song of rain), in which his poetic genius is fully evident. Using the Arab literary tradition with rare sensitivity and depth, he introduced new rhythms and innovative ideas, which pulled the Arabic language daringly into modernity, at the same time portraying an Arab nation in travail and giving its hopes the most poignant contemporary expression. Images from Arab folklore, literary allusions full of rich associations, references to little things of daily life or places and events, even words from colloquial everyday speech—all were given symbolic dimensions. When he came upon myths—especially of suffering, death, and resurrection—as a framework for his poetic outpourings, S. achieved his best representations of his vision.

Although his ebullient spirit was gradually crushed by his growing paralysis in the 1960s, S. continued to publish poetry in an amazing abundance, as if to cling through it to life, but his poems became more personal and of uneven quality. Occasionally they offer terrifying insights of despair or resigned acceptance of death mellowed by sweet reminiscences of childhood and fleeting happiness. His greatness rests in the fact that, creating a new idiom and new rhythms, he captured for modern Arabs their painful and hopeful moments of transition.

FURTHER WORKS: *'Uyūn Elsa aw al-hubb wa al-harb* (1951; tr. of Louis Aragon's *Les yeux d'Elsa*); *Fajr al-salām* (n.d. [1951]); *Haffār al-qubūr* (1952); *Al-Asliha wa al-atfāl* (1954); *Al-Mūmis al-'amyā'* (1954); *Qasā'id mukhtāra min al-shi'r al-'alamī al-hadīth* (n.d. [1955]); *Al-Ma'bad al-gharīq* (1962); *Manzil al-aqnān* (1963); *Azhār wa asātīr* (1963); *Shanāshīl ibnat al-Chalabī* (1964); *Iqbāl* (1965); *Qasā'id* (1967); *Qīthārat al-rīh* (1971); *A'āsīr* (1972); *Dīwān B. S. al-S.* (2 vols., 1971–1974); *Rasā'il al-S.* (1975)

BIBLIOGRAPHY: El-Azma, N., "The Tammuzi Movement and the Influence of T. S. Eliot on B. S. al-S.," *JAOS*, 88 (1968): 671–78; Boullata, I. J., "B. S. al-S.: A Life of Vision and Agony," *MEF*, 46 (1970): 73–80; Boullata, I. J., "B. S. al-S. and the Free Verse Movement," *IJMES*, 1 (1970): 248–58; Boullata, I. J., "The Poetic Technique of B. S. al-S.," *JArabL*, 2 (1971): 104–15; Loya, A., "Al-S. and the Influence of T. S. Eliot," *MW*, 61 (1971): 187–201; 'Abd al-Halīm, M. A. S., "Al-S.: A Study of His Poetry," in R. C. Ostle, ed. *Studies in Modern Arabic Literature* (1975): 69–85; Badawi, M. M., *A Critical Introduction to Modern Arabic Poetry* (1975): 250–58

—ISSA J. BOULLATA

SBARBARO, Camillo

Italian poet and translator, b. 12 Jan. 1888, Santa Maria Ligure; d. 31 Oct. 1967, Savona

S. was never a professional or full-time man of letters. Following service in World War I, he spent many years in Genoa as a teacher of Greek and Latin and as a translator from French and ancient Greek. He also gained an international reputation among botanists as a specialist in lichens. He cherished his apartness, and it is this intensely lived solitude and an acute sense of sterile estrangement that inform the content of his poetic production, which, although scanty, is so probing in utterance and emblematic characterization as to make it one of the most authentic expressions of the crisis (existential and sociocultural) that marked the Italian intelligentsia even in the early years of the 20th c.

In this respect, S.'s most important work is the slim volume of poems *Pianissimo* (1914; pianissimo), whose very title bespeaks an antiheroic attitude, opposite that of Gabriel D'ANNUNZIO—an

attitude that had already been adopted by the Crepuscolari poets. But S. differs significantly from these poets because of the absence in his verse of indulgence in a sentimentalizing self-irony. Stylistically, too, he is different: his creation of a nonrhetorical, nonmelodious manner gives the impression of the essentiality of prose while remaining true verse, again without a sense of self-consciousness.

S.'s portrayal of himself as a protagonist incapable of "living" or responding to life is close to the depiction of the alienated types, immobilized in a passive despair, to be found in the fiction of Italo SVEVO, Federigo TOZZI, and Luigi PIRANDELLO. However, S.'s poetry also contains a reaching out for human affections and a sense of the persistence of the beauty of nature. In all of this, the great presence behind S. is Giacomo Leopardi (1798–1837).

Some of S.'s most convincing moments occur in connection with the themes of familial relationships (his father and sister), the yearning for purity, and the momentary hope of love as a saving grace. But these moments are played against the representation of himself as an apathetic protagonist caught up in an endless round of impurity, immobility, and accursedness in the city.

S. expressed many of the same themes in the lyrical prose of the quasi-diaristic *Trucioli* (1920; expanded ed., 1948; shavings). His emblematic manner and some of his thematic material—especially the vision of dismayed man imprisoned within a morally and socially confining contemporary reality—recall and, indeed, may have influenced the early poetry of his great fellow Ligurian, Eugenio MONTALE.

FURTHER WORKS: *Resine* (1911); *Liquidazione* (1928); *Rimanenze* (1955; expanded ed., 1956); *Fuochi fatui* (1956; expanded ed., 1958); *Primizie* (1958); *Scampoli* (1960); *Poesie* (1961)

BIBLIOGRAPHY: Perella, N. J., *Midday in Italian Literature: Variations on an Archetypal Theme* (1979): 309–10; Corrado, F., "Indifference in C. S.'s *Pianissimo*," *CJItS*, 2 (1978–1979): 92–104

—NICOLAS J. PERELLA

SCHADE, Jens August

Danish poet, novelist, and dramatist, b. 10 Jan. 1903, Skive; d. 20 Nov. 1978, Copenhagen

S. grew up in a provincial middle-class milieu, which he rebelled against throughout his life. Following his matriculation examination in 1921 he studied economics for one year at the University of Copenhagen. Thereafter he lived a bohemian life and wrote.

S.'s first poetry collection, *den levende violin* (1926; the living violin), aroused great interest because of its innovative and surprising form and content: in a colloquial, deliberately naïve style—mainly unrhymed prose poetry—he conveys his strictly subjective experiences of the cosmic coherence in nature and the universe, which are made possible through the expansive miracle of love. After the autobiographical epic poem *Sjov i Danmark* (1928; fun in Denmark [Sjov is also the name of the hero]), a satire on the bourgeois society of the interwar period, S. resumed his worship of eroticism as the means for man to experience timelessness. This eroticism unites the physical aspects of love, depicted with bold naturalism, and the spiritual ones. S.'s all-embracing philosophy is given its most succinct expression in *Hjerte-bogen* (1930; the heart-book); *Jordens ansigt* (1932; the face of the earth), which shows the strong influence of Walt Whitman; and *Kærlighed og kildevand* (1936; love in a cottage). In *Kællingedigte* (1944; hag poems), however, a predilection for vulgarity overshadows the poetic flight and linguistic imagination.

S.'s fiction, which has a fine lyrical quality, lacks coherent structure, resulting in a series of sketchy, almost fairy-tale-like texts. Typical titles such as *Den himmelske elskov på jorden* (1931; heavenly love on earth) and *Kærlighedens symfoni* (1942; symphony of love) indicate the thematic scope. S.'s major prose work is *Mennesker mødes og sød musik opstår i hjertet* (1944; people meet, and sweet music fills the heart), a *succès de scandale* for which S. was accused of writing pornography. Time and space are suspended in dreamlike erotic fantasies; the characters are transformed or doubled as an effect of their subconscious minds being activated.

Themes derived from psychoanalysis and FREUD also dominate S.'s experimental dramas, *Myggestikket* (1931; the mosquito bite), *Marsk Stig* (1934; Marsk Stig), and *Hos Skøgen Phyllis* (1957; with the whore Phyllis). But it is chiefly as a lyrical poet that S. made a place for himself in literature. His poetic powers did not diminish over the years. In his later collections—the major works being *S.s nøjsang* (1958; S.'s song of songs) and *Overjordisk* (1973; supernatural)—he proved himself the most significant Danish representative of SURREALISM and of a sexual vitalism inspired by D. H. LAWRENCE. With intense feeling S. sings the praise of woman and nature as expressions of a mysterious unity that can be realized in love. The acceptance of this love liberates man and ultimately elevates him to a level of purity and eternity.

FURTHER WORKS: *En mærkelig often på jorden* (1933); *En forårsaften* (1935); *En eneste stor hemmelighed* (1937); *Kommodetyven* (1939); *Jeg er tosset efter dig* (1945); *Hvor hjertet hører til, holder forstanden aldrig op* (1949); *Jordens største lykke* (1949); *Til en uartig pige* (1949); *Helvede opløser sig* (1953); *Der er kærlighed i luften* (1954); *Udvalgte digte* (1962); *S.-bogen* (1963); *S.-symfonier* (1963); *Sjov i verden* (1965); *En kærlighedshistorie fra provinsen* (1967); *S.'s erotiske univers* (1967); *Den ukendte J. A. S.* (1967); *Danmarksrejse* (1970); *Besøg på Danmarks Limfjord* (1974). FURTHER WORKS IN ENGLISH: *Selected Poems* (1985)

BIBLIOGRAPHY: Mitchell, P. M., *A History of Danish Literature* (1957): 238–39

—SVEN H. ROSSEL

SCHALLÜCK, Paul

West German novelist, essayist, poet, and television and radio dramatist, b. 17 June 1922, Warendorf; d. 29 Feb. 1976, Cologne

The son of a Russian mother from Siberia and a German father, S. originally intended to become a Catholic missionary, but the experience of captivity during World War II caused him to alter his plans. That experience, coupled with the discovery of French partisans' humanity toward their prisoner, made him decide to become active in the postwar rapprochement between France and Germany. He subsequently became vocal in all groups that pleaded for understanding between nations, especially between East and West, and at the end of his life was editor-in-chief of *Dokumente*, a Catholic journal devoted to the cooperation between nations.

After the war he studied widely in the humanities. Joining the writers known as Group 47, he started writing radio and television plays, essays, novels, and occasional small volumes of poetry. Having a sensitive ear for the subtleties of language, he campaigned against the increasing sensationalism in the press and the many inroads made by vulgarity and lax writing in German public life.

S.'s reputation was established with his first novel, *Wenn man aufhören könnte zu lügen* (1951; if one could stop lying), which deals with the problem of postwar youth, torn between cynical hedonism and the need to establish new values. In subsequent novels S. experimented with narratives projected against kaleidoscopic backgrounds of a society in transition. *Ankunft null Uhr zwölf* (1953; arrival 12:12 A.M.) makes use of flashbacks, dialogue, and STREAM-OF-CONSCIOUSNESS to create a simultaneous portrait of several members of a family. *Die unsichtbare Pforte* (1954; the invisible door) is a far more tightly knit account of the Kafkaesque intricacies of a drug addict's cure.

Engelbert Reineke: Die vergessene Schuld (1959; Engelbert Reineke: the forgotten guilt) forcefully depicts the efforts of a young teacher, who returned to his home town after the war, to come to terms with his unassimilated past by exploring the motives of his guilty or indifferent colleagues who remained at home. A volume of short stories, *Lakrizza* (1966; *Lakrizza*, 1969), shows S.'s mastery of this genre in satirical yet warm-hearted sketches that give evidence of a keen sense of humor.

In *Don Quichotte in Köln* (Book 1, 1967; Don Quixote in Cologne), S.'s most ambitious work, which remained uncontinued at his death, he interweaves the text with dramatic and lyrical episodes. The result is an unorthodox, psychologically and intellectually stimulating tale of a sensitive and confused modern knight-errant on his quest for truth. Bigotry and mindless success hunting are the main targets of S.'s biting humor.

The essays in *Zum Beispiel* (1962; for example) are outstanding illustrations of S.'s concern for real democracy, for peace and mutual respect among people of different religions and races. The incisive essayist insists, just as strongly as does the novelist, that his countrymen must overcome the unresolved past of the Nazi era—a theme most successfully presented in the novel *Engelbert Reineke*—by struggling to understand the present so that his contemporaries, a generation marked by the death and destruction of the war, can successfully shape the future. Consistently, S. insisted in his writings on the necessity for reconciliation between Jews and Germans. He participated in panels and served on executive boards concerned with German-Jewish cooperation and became one of the few postwar German writers to be invited to Israel, a country often described in his poetry.

S.'s stature as a writer is growing, as witnessed by the edition of his complete literary works and the many testimonials at the time of his death, which was due in part to wartime injuries. He was also one of the relatively few intellectuals genuinely interested in mass education and was frequently called on by trade unions to speak on matters of cultural and political concern.

FURTHER WORKS: *Weiße Fahnen im April* (1955); *Q 3 und die Hohe Straße* (1956); *Hand und Name* (1962); *Abschied von Bremen* (1965); *Die Hand* (1966); *Nachts im Kloster* (1966); *Auf eigenen Füßen* (1966); *Orden* (1967); *Heimat, Satire und Pferdeäpfel* (1967); *Gesichter* (1968); *Karlsbader Ponys* (1968); *Als ich fünfzehn war* (1969); *Die Sprache der Gesetze* (1969); *. . .bis daß der Tod each scheidet* (1970); *Bekenntnisse eines Nestbeschmutzers* (1970); *Hierzulande und anderswo* (1974); *Countdown zum Paradies: Oratorium* (1976); *Dein Bier und mein Bier: Monolog und Briefe* (1976); *Gesamtwerk* (1977)

BIBLIOGRAPHY: Andrews, R. C., "The German School-Story: Some Observations on P. S. and Thomas Valentin," *GL&L*, 23 (1969): 103–12; Domandi, A. K., ed., *Modern German Literature* (1972), Vol. 2: 231-32; Krohn, P. C., "P. S.," in Böttcher, K., ed., *Lexikon deutschsprachiger Schriftsteller* (1974), Vol. II: 254–55; Böll, H., "Gedenkwort für P. S.," *DASDJ* (1976): 177–78; Wintzen, R., "P. S.," *Dokumente*, 23, 2 (1976): 89–93; Reding, J., "P. S.," *Dokumente*, 23, 2 (1976): 93–94; Erné, N., "P. S.," in Kunisch, H., ed., *Handbuch der deutschen Gegenwartsliteratur* (1981): 431–32

—KONRAD BIEBER

SCHENDEL, Arthur van

Dutch novelist and short-story writer, b. 5 March 1874, Batavia, Dutch East Indies (now Djakarta, Indonesia); d. 11 Sept. 1946, Amsterdam

Born in the Dutch East Indies, S. grew up in Amsterdam and spent two years studying and teaching in England. He returned to Holland for some time but in 1921 moved to Italy, where he spent most of the rest of his life; he returned to Amsterdam shortly before his death.

S. began his literary career with *Drogon* (1896; Drogon), a historical novel set in the Middle Ages. Similar in style were *Een zwerver verliefd* (1904; a vagabond in love) and *Een zwerver verdwaald* (1907; a vagabond astray). These early works were a late romantic reaction against the then prevailing realism and naturalism. Set for the most part in Italy and in a colorful and distant past, they are animated by the sense of dreamy longing that impels their central characters.

After moving to Italy, S.'s work took a different turn: *Angiolino en de lente* (1923; Angiolino and the spring) is a more substantial novel with an Italian setting. Nevertheless, all these earlier works seem preliminary to the more important novels S. was able to write about his native land once he had sufficiently distanced himself from it.

Het fregatschip Johanna Maria (1930; *The Johanna Maria*, 1935) marks the beginning of a series of impressive novels set in 19th-c. Holland. In these works S. evokes a somber and shadowy world in which a central character assumes a self-imposed burden that becomes at the same time his ideal and his obsession. The result is a densely structured universe where an implacable fate stalks the protagonist but does not quite deprive him of his triumph before he falls. Finely realized physical detail and carefully observed characterization give these novels a quality that seems very typically Dutch and made S. one of the most popular and beloved Dutch novelists of his time.

Het fregatschip Johanna Maria takes place entirely on one of the last wooden sailing ships; the central character is the sailmaker whose ambition is to own the boat on which he comes to spend his life. It was followed by *Jan Compagnie* (1932; *John Company*, 1983), a historical novel about the early days of the East Indies trade, but the series of more realistic "Holland" novels continued with *De waterman* (1933; *The Waterman*, 1963), the story of a man whose life's work has to do with the dikes and canals where he feels more at home than in the social world with which he makes an uncertain peace. The culmination of this series is *Een Hollandsch drama* (1935; *The House in Haarlem*, 1940), a dark and moving story of a shopkeeper struggling to preserve his sense of honor by assuming a crushing lifelong financial burden, and his failure to save his weak-willed nephew from his conviction that he is doomed to a life of sin and degradation.

With *De grauwe vogels* (1937; *Grey Birds*, 1939) S. began to move away from this kind of work. The last of his generally admired novels, *De wereld een dansfeest* (1938; the world a feast of dancing), focuses on the love between two dancers and is noteworthy for its carefully woven musical prose. But in his later work, a further group of novels that ends with the posthumously published *Het oude huis* (1946; the old house), the distance between himself and his material that S. always seems to need becomes too great; the characters are no longer seen from within as in his best fiction, and the operations of fate become too smooth in their inevitability.

S. was also an accomplished master of the short story throughout his career. At the end of his life he published a long poem in blank verse, *De Nederlanden* (1945; the Netherlands). Among his miscellaneous work of other kinds, a posthumously assembled volume of autobiographical writings, *Her denkingen* (1950; commemorations), has a special interest.

S. has generally been regarded as a fine craftsman rather than as one of the great Dutch novelists. He is a superb storyteller, and the rapidity and purity of his narrative line, uninterrupted by digressions of reflections, is one of his great strengths. He is noteworthy for the convincing accuracy of the psychology of his characters rather than for their psychological complexity. The reader is never told what makes them do what they do, but he believes in them completely. These qualities, combined with the brooding sense of an inscrutable fate, make S. an extremely satisfying novelist to read, and give a very individual strength to a career whose best work seems typical, in an exemplary way, of its time and place.

FURTHER WORKS: *De schoone jacht* (1908); *Shakespeare* (1910); *De berg van droomen* (1913); *De mensch van Nazareth* (1916); *Verhalen* (1917); *Pandorra* (1919); *Tristan en Isolde* (1920); *Der lifede bloesems* (1921); *Rose Angélique* (1922); *Blanke gestalten* (1923); *Oude italiaansche steden* (1924); *Verdichtsel van zomerdagen* (1925); *Verlaine* (1927); *Merona, een edelman* (1927); *Fratilamur* (1928); *Florentijnsche verhalen* (1929); *Een eiland in der Zuidzee* (1931); *Bijbelsche verhalen* (1932); *Herinneringen van een dommen jongen* (1934); *De rijke man* (1936); *De zomerreis* (1937); *Nachtgedaanten* (1938); *De zomerreis* (1938); *Le dessin de Lombardie* (1938); *De zeven tuinen* (1939); *Anders eneender* (1939); *Mijnheer Oberon en mevrouw* (1940); *De menschenhater* (1941); *De fat, de nimfen en de nuf* (1941); *De wedergeboorte van Bedelman* (1942); *Een spel der Natuur* (1942); *Sparsa* (1944); *Menschen en honden* (1947); *Voorbijgaande schaduwen* (1948); *Een zindelijke wereld* (1950); *De pleiziervaart* (1951); *Verzameld werk* (8 vols., 1976–1978)

BIBLIOGRAPHY: Flaxman, S., "Nationalism and Cosmopolitanism in Modern Dutch Literature," in F. Jost, ed.*Proceedings of the IVth Congress of the International Comparative Literature Association* (1966), Vol. I: 511–19; Mooij, J. J., "On Literature and the Reader's Beliefs: With Special Reference to *De waterman* by A. van S.," in F. van Ingen, et al., eds., *Dichter und Leser: Studien zur Literatur* (1972): 143–50; Meijer, R. P., *Literature of the Low Countries*, new ed. (1978): 289–94

—FRED J. NICHOLS

SCHMIDT, Arno

West German novelist, short-story writer, and essayist, b. 18 Jan. 1914, Hamburg; d. 3 June 1979, Bargfeld/Celle

After an apparently unhappy childhood, S. was prevented from completing his university education as a result of political pressures, and served from 1940 to 1945 in the German army. Released from British captivity in 1945, he worked for two years as a translator and then concentrated on his own writing. His last twenty-one years were spent in aggressively guarded isolation in a small village on the Lüneburger Heide in Lower Saxony.

The motifs of catastrophe, flight, and the search for a redemptive idyll are constant themes in S.'s work. Society is rotten through and through, God is malignant—*Leviathan* (1949; Leviathan)—or else nonexistent—*Nobodaddy's Kinder* (1963; Nobodaddy's children), a republication as a trilogy of *Leviathan, Brand's Haide: Zwei Erzählungen* (1951; Brand's heath; two stories), and the novel *Aus dem Leben eines Faun* (1953; *Scenes from the Life of a Faun*, 1983). S.'s autobiographically colored early protagonists savagely reject conformism and nonconformism alike, but especially all those who subscribe to any comforting system of belief. The S. persona of *Das steinerne Herz* (1956; *Heart of Stone*, 1997) typically flees what he sees as a contemptible and chaotic society for the surrogate orderliness of historical statistics and the world of books and literary tradition. All that prevents these early works from sliding into hopeless cynicism is S.'s consistent balancing of the bleakest pessimism with a wry humor, however black.

The action in S.'s stories is always far less important than the attempt to evoke adequately the discontinuity and insecurity of modern life, and this attempt is reflected in progressively bolder and more disturbing formal experimentation. *Das steinerne Herz*, for example, consists of a series of paragraphs representing snapshotlike illuminations of the story line, with very little connecting material to ease the reader's task, already made difficult by aggressively idiosyncratic spelling, syntax, and punctuation as well as by a scatological and irreverent vocabulary, which at one point provoked a legal action against him for both sacrilege and pornography.

The novel *Die Gelehrtenrepublik* (1957; *The Egghead Republic*, 1979) again deals with the rejection of reality for escape into fantasy. The novel *Kaff, auch Mare Crisium* (1960; one-horse town, alias Mare Crisium), seen by some as S.'s masterpiece, turns the same theme yet again into a structural principle, represented by the graphic arrangement on the page: the fictive reality of the narrator's visit to a relative in a "one-horse town" in 1960 occupies the left-hand side of the page, while his fantasy, a lunar utopia set in 1980, relativizes that reality in the right-hand column.

The formal experimentation of *Kaff*, together with S.'s study of JOYCE and FREUD, prepared the way for the massive *Zettel's Traum* (1970; Zettel's dream), his largest achievement and something of a German answer to *Finnegans Wake*. The very title suggests the complexity of its multilingual punning and wordplay: *Traum* is "dream," *Zettel* means "index card" (S. collected material for the book on 130,000 cards), as well as being the name of Bottom the Weaver in the standard German translation of Shakespeare's *A Midsummer Night's Dream*. English "bottom" gives German *Po* ("buttocks"), which refers punningly both to Poe (Edgar Allan) and the latter's alleged sexual proclivities, the psychoanalytical investigation of which is the main concern of the work. The bewildered reader now has three columns on the page to contend with, often simultaneously, as well as an almost total abandonment of traditional spelling in favor of distorted phonetic versions allegedly revealing the subliminal erotic obsessions camouflaged behind socially acceptable discourse.

The structural and textural complexity persists, although less obstreperously, in *Die Schule der Atheisten* (1972; the school for atheists) and *Abend mit Goldrand* (1975; *Evening Edged in Gold*, 1980), both generic hybrids of drama and novel, and both eagerly seized upon by the S. cult, which grew up in the wake of *Zettel's Traum*. Both content and language continue to shock the traditionally minded, but there is some indication that the "savage indignation" of both the protagonists and their creator was at last mellowing.

S. is an irritation, a rogue elephant of recent German literature, and an assessment of his importance continues to be difficult. He can justly be accused of solipsistic arrogance, gratuitous complexity, miserable puns, extravagant subjectivism, and fatuously exaggerated psychologism. He has also been called the most important German writer of our time. Whatever the final reckoning, however, his structural innovations, his challenging handling of language and literary mechanics, and not least his incisive deployment of a sense of humor comparable to that of Jonathan Swift or Samuel BECKETT undoubtedly represent a real and solid contribution to 20th-c. literature.

FURTHER WORKS: *Die Umsiedler* (1953); *Kosmas; oder, Vom Berge des Nordens* (1955); *Dya na Sore* (1958); *Fouqué und einige seiner Zeitgenossen* (1958); *Rosen & Porree* (1959); *Belphegor: Nachrichten von Büchern und Menschen* (1961); *Sitara und der Weg dorthin* (1963); *Tina; order, Die Unsterblichkeit* (1964); *Kühe in Halbtratuer* (1964); *Die Ritter vom Geist* (1965); *Trommler beim Zaren* (1966); *Der Triton mit dem Sonnenschirm* (1969); *Julia; oder, Die Gemälde* (1983). FURTHER WORKS IN ENGLISH: *The Collected Stories of A. S.* (1996)

BIBLIOGRAPHY: special S. issue, *TuK*, No. 20 (1968; 2nd ed., 1971); Moller, H. B., "Perception Word-Play,and the Printed Page: A. S. and His Poe Novel," *BA*, 45 (1971): 25–30; on *Die Schule der Atheisten, TLS* (21 July 1972): 843–44; Prawer, S., "'Bless Thee! Thou Art Translated!': Typographical Parallelism, Word-Play and Literary Allusion in A. S.'s *Zettel's Traum*," in Robson-Scott, W. D., ed., *Essays in German and Dutch Literature* (1973): 156–91; Ott, E. P., "Tradition and Innovation: An Introduction to the Prose Theory and Practice of A. S.," *GQ* 51(1978): 19–38; Prawer, S., *Evening Edged with Gold TLS* (5 Sept. 1980): 949–50; Pross, W., *A. S.* (1980); Minden, M. R., *A. S.: A Critical Study of His Prose* (1982)

—PATRICK O'NEILL

SCHNITZLER, Arthur

Austrian novelist, dramatist, short-story writer, and essayist, b. 15 May 1862, Vienna; d. 21 Oct. 1931, Vienna

Son of a renowned laryngologist and university professor, S. studied medicine at his father's wish and started to practice, but he soon became disillusioned with the medical establishment of his day. He also felt that he had chosen the wrong specialty, laryngology; his real medical interest lay in psychiatry. He finally gave up his practice altogether to devote himself to his writing, which had been his other lively interest almost since his childhood, when he wrote his first play. Along with Hermann BAHR, Hugo von HOFMANNSTHAL, and Richard BEER-HOFMANN he was a member of the Young Vienna group.

Concurrently with Sigmund FREUD and Josef Breuer, S. discovered the significance of the unconscious and of the subconscious, the significance of instinctive life. In a congratulatory letter on the occasion of S.'s sixtieth birthday in 1922, Freud wrote: "I think I have avoided you from a kind of reluctance to meet my double. . . . Whenever I get deeply absorbed in your beautiful creations, I invariably seem to find beneath their poetic surface the very presuppositions, interests, and conclusions which I know to be my own. . . . So I have formed the impression that you know through intuition—or rather from detailed self-observation—everything that I have discovered by laborious work on other people."

S.'s early literary reputation was largely gained through his plays, such as *Anatol* (1893; *Anatol A Sequence of Dialogues*, 1911), *Liebelei* (1896; *Light-o'-Love*, 1912; later tr., *The Game of Love*, 1967), and *Reigen* (1900; *Hands Around: A Roundelay in Ten Dialogues*, 1929; later trs., *Round Dance*, 1949, *La Ronde*, 1959). Primarily, he explored the relationship between the sexes in his dramas in a manner daring and extremely unusual for his time. *Anatol* is a series of short dialogues, for which Hugo von Hofmannsthal wrote a preface under the pseudonym Loris. This early work is about love affairs of a frivolous, melancholy, and, in the final analysis, irresponsible young man. In *Liebelei* S. depicts the playful sentiment of Fritz, the well-born young protagonist who cannot achieve a genuine relationship in his affair with Christine, whose love is true and self-sacrificing. The love game ends tragically when Fritz is killed in a duel with the husband of another woman; and the end of the play implies that Christine, too, dies. In the ten scenes of *Reigen* S. again explores sexual hypocrisy and infidelity in a series of dialogues between sexual partners—a round dance that encompasses almost all levels of society.

Attacking long-standing but outworn customs was a task S. set for himself throughout his work. In the novella *Leutnant Gustl* (1901; *None but the Brave*, 1926) he combined psychological analysis with social criticism, exposing the threadbareness of the lieutenant's concept of honor and the hollowness of military convention. In the checkroom after a concert young Gustl has been insulted by another man and so sees his honor damaged. Because the insulter, a master baker, is not qualified to give satisfaction to an officer, Gustl must, according to the military code of honor, shoot himself. The confused thoughts going through his head during the following night, most of all his ineluctable suicide, are recorded in STREAM-OF-CONSCIOUSNESS technique. They show his class conceit and his conventional prejudices, and also demonstrate that what he thinks of himself means nothing to him, but what he is in the eyes of others means everything. An unexpected accident—the master baker has died during the night—and also the fact that the

Arthur Schnitzler

insult had not been witnessed by anybody combine to save his life, which he now can continue in undiminished honor. He has not gained any insight into his own vacuousness; what is illustrated is rather the bankruptcy of a mind devoid of any substance.

In *Fräulein Else* (1924; *Fräulein Else*, 1925), one of S.'s most celebrated novellas, he depicts certain decadent elements of Viennese society. Else, a lawyer's daughter sojourning in the country, is implored by her mother to ward off her father's ruin: the father has embezzled trust money and lost it speculating on the stock market. The art dealer von Dorsday, staying in the same hotel, declares his willingness to extend financial help to her father on condition that she show herself to him in the nude. This frivolous demand brings Else into a grave moral conflict, expressed in various subtle nuances of despair in an interior monologue. Living up to a daughter's duty, she yields to this demand but then commits suicide by taking poison.

As a Jew, S. felt throughout his life the pervasive hostility of many Austrian journalists and writers. Their distortion of his work and their denunciations proved so effective that a stereotype of the writer was soon created, which pictured him as a frivolous erotomaniac and an atheistic relativist who denied stable values. The opposite, in fact, is true. The deeply ethical note in his work can hardly be overlooked. In his novel *Der Weg ins Freie* (1908; *The Road to the Open*, 1923) S. for the first time dealt with the problem of anti-Semitism, which became the central theme of his play *Professor Bernhardi* (1912; *Professor Bernhardi*, 1928). Here he explores the delicate question of whether the final hours of a dying person, unaware that she is close to death, should be disturbed by the last rites a priest is about to administer. A decision against such rites is made by the Jewish clinic director, who acts according to his conscience. The incident is distorted into interference with religion. Professor Bernhardi is suspended from his position, accused of having hastened the patient's death, and sentenced to jail.

The unmasking of erotic adventurism as an unauthentic life style, one of S.'s major themes in his early works, is taken up again in one of his most beautiful later novellas, *Casanovas Heimfahrt* (1918; *Casanova's Homecoming*, 1922). It presents the splendor and misery of the adventurer with rare power. He is exposed as the great egoist who never gives of himself, who never truly loves. He ends in despair and moral collapse. His had been an attitude opposed to life. The willingness to sacrifice oneself, to restrain one's self-centeredness, is the only reliable basis for human community.

Although S. was open to the various literary currents of his time, his complexity resists easy classification. With his physician's sensibility, he had a horror of the power of death and transitoriness. What he created again and again is the recognition of the unfathomably enigmatic character of life behind the pseudocertainty of convention and reality. He saw in the many-colored fullness of life only a pleasing appearance spread over the abyss of death. What mattered to S. were the enduring mythical components of human existence, that is, love, play, and death, in which he finds the "sense of soul of all things earthly."

S. was not religious in the usual sense of the word, and he remained highly skeptical about organized religion. Yet the chaotic diversity of life and the cryptic nature of fate and its inscrutability filled him with wonder, with awe, with an almost religious feeling.

S. hated politics and was not connected with any party, but he raised his voice as an individual in support of ethical principles and against the corruption of political parties, the fickleness of public opinion, and society's pervasive materialism. Despite his skepticism, and even though such concepts as patriotism, eternal love, and the constancy of emotions were revealed under his penetrating eye often to be the stirrings of selfishness or were unmasked as self-deception, S. had faith in the possibilities of the human condition and hope that life could be made worthwhile.

As a man of letters, S.'s importance is his introduction of the psychological play into modern drama. His dramatic work focuses mainly on the relationship between the sexes, but his significance transcends this narrow categorization. He not only was one of the great literary figures of his time, a writer of technical virtuosity and innovative ingenuity; he also introduced the interior monologue to German literature long before James JOYCE and Virginia WOOLF brought that mode to English writing.

S.'s great contemporaries paid the highest tribute to his achievements. Thomas MANN, for one, praised "his virile knowledge of people and the world, the fascination of the problems he poses, the graceful purity of his style . . . and best of all, the personal charm that emerges from everything he has created." Frank WEDEKIND called him a German classic: "No one deserves the name of master more than he does." Heinrich MANN and Hugo von Hofmannsthal admired his witty sophistication, delicate irony, and subtlety of style, as did many others.

S.'s work also gives a matchless cultural-historical picture of the era of Emperor Franz Josef's reign in Austria. An entire epoch takes form in his stories and plays. He presents a classic portrait of the turn-of-the-century Vienna, the monarchy's still glamorous capital which he knew so well and which came to an end in 1914 with World War I. Even though the world he captured with such charm and refinement has long since disappeared, S.'s characters are still very much alive, and his work still speaks to us today.

FURTHER WORKS: *Sterben* (1894; *Dying*, 1977); *Freiwild* (1898; *Free Game*, 1913); *Die Frau des Weisen: Novelletten* (1898); *Der grüne Kakadu* (1899; *The Green Cockatoo*, 1913); *Das Vermächtnis* (1899; *The Legacy*, 1911); *Der grüne Kakadu; Paracelsus; Die Gefährtin: Drei Einaker* (1899); *Frau Bertha Garlan* (1901; *Bertha Garlan*, 1913); *Der Schleier der Beatrice* (1901); *Lebendige Stunden: Vier Einakter* (1902); *Der tapfere Cassian: Puppenspiel in einem Akt* (1904; *Gallant Cassian: A Puppet Play in One Act*, 1921); *Der einsame Weg* (1904; *The Lonely Way*, 1904); *Die griechische Tänzerin: Novellen* (1905); *Der Ruf des Lebens* (1906); *Marionetten: Drei Einakter* (1906); *Zwischenspiel* (1907; *Intermezzo*, 1915); *Dämmerseelen: Novellen* (1907); *Komtesse Mizzi; oder, Der Familientag* (written 1907. pub. 1908; *Countess Mizzie; or, The Family Reunion*, 1907); *Der junge Medardus* (1910); *Das weite Land* (1911; *The Vast Domain*, 1923; Eng. version, *Undiscovered Country*, by Tom Stoppard, 1980); *Masken und Wunder: Novellen* (1912); *Frau Beate und ihr Sohn* (1913; *Beatrice*, 1926); *Die griechische Tänzerin, und andere Novellen* (1914); *Komödie der Worte: Drei Einakter* (1915); *Fink und Fliederbusch* (1917); *Doktor Gräsler, Badearzt* (1917; *Dr. Graesler*, 1923); *Die Schwestern; oder, Casanova in Spa* (1919); *Die dreifache Warnung: Novellen* (1924); *Komödie der Verführung* (1924); *Die Frau des Richters* (1925); *Traumnovelle* (1925; *Rhapsody: A Dream Novel*, 1927); *Der Gang zum Weiher* (1926); *Spiel im Morgengrauen* (1926; *Daybreak*, 1927); *Buch der Sprüche und Bedenken: Aphorismen und Fragmente* (1927); *Der Geist im Wort und der Geist in der Tat* (1927; *The Mind in Words and Actions*, 1972); *Therese: Chronik eines Frauenlebens* (1928; *Theresa: The Chronicle of a Woman's Life*, 1928); *Im Spiel der Sommerlüfte* (1930); *Flucht in die Finsternis* (1931; *Flight into Darkness*, 1931); *Traum und Schicksal: Sieben Novellen* (1931); *Die kleine Komödie: Frühe Novellen* (1932); *Abenteurernovelle* (1937); *Über Krieg und Frieden* (1939); *Flucht in die Finsternis, und andere Erzählungen* (1939); *Ausgewählte Erzählungen* (1950); *Der Briefwechsel A. S.-Otto Brahm*, 1953; enlarged ed., 1975); *Meisterdramen* (1955); *Georg Brandes und A. S.: Ein Briefwechsel* (1956); *Große Szene* (1959); *Die erzählenden Schriften* (2 vols., 1961); *Die dramatischen Werke* (2 vols., 1962); *Hugo von Hofmannsthal-A. S. Briefwechsel* (1964); *Erzählungen* (1965); *Spiel im Morgengrauen, und acht andere Erzählungen* (1965); *Das Wort: Tragikomödie in fünf Akten: Fragment* (1966); *Aphorismen und Betrachtungen* (1967); *Jugend in Wien: Eine Autobiographie* (1968; *My Youth in Vienna*, 1970); *Meistererzählungen* (1969); *Frühe Gedichte* (1969); *Zug der Schatten: Drama in neun Bildern* (*unvollendet*) (1970); *A. S.-Olga Waissnix: Liebe, die starb vor der Zeit: Ein Briefwechsel* (1970); *Der Briefwechsel A. S.s mit Max Reinhardt und dessen Mitarbeitern* (1971); *The Correspondence of A. S. and Raoul Auernheimer, with Raoul Auernheimer's Aphorisms* [in German] (1972); *Dilly: Geschichte einer Liebe in Briefen, Bildern und Dokumenten: Adele Sandrock und A. S.* (1975); *Hugo von Hofmannsthal: Charakteristik aus den Tagebüchern* (1975); *Ritterlichkeit: Fragment aus dem Nachlaß* (1975); *Entworfenes und Verworfenes* (1977); *The Letters of A. S. to Hermann Bahr* [in German] (1978); *A. S.: Sein Leben, sein Werk, seine Zeit* (1981); *A. S.s Tagebuch 1909–1912* (1981); *Briefe 1875–1912* (1981). FURTHER WORKS IN ENGLISH: *Living*

Hours: Four One-Act Plays (1913); *Viennese Idylls* (1913); *The Green Cockatoo and Other Plays* (1913); *Anatol; Living Hours; The Green Cockatoo* (1917); *Comedies of Words and Other Plays* (1917); *The Shepherd's Pipe and Other Stories* (1922); *Beatrice and Other Stories* (1926); *Little Novels* (1929); *Viennese Novelettes* (1931); *Reigen, The Affairs of Anatol and Other Plays* (1933); *Some Day Peace Will Return: Notes on War and Peace* (1972); *Vienna 1900: Games with Love and Death* (1974); *The Little Comedy and Other Stories* (1977); *A. S.: Plays and Stories* (1983); *The Round Dance; Anatol; Love Games* (1983); *Three Late Plays* (1992); *Professor Bernhardi and Other Plays* (1993); *Paracelsus and Other One-Act Plays* (1995)

BIBLIOGRAPHY: Liptzin, S., *A. S.* (1932); Bithell, J., *Modern German Literature 1880–1950* (1959): 229–37; Garten, H. F., *Modern German Drama* (1959): 55–63; Hill, C., "The Stature of A. S.," *MD* 4 (1961): 80–91; *Journal of the International A. S. Research Association* (1962 ff.); Politzer, H., "A. S.: Poetry of Psychology," *MLN* 78 (1963): 353–72; Reichert, H. W., and H. Salinger, eds., *Studies in A. S.* (1963); Garland, H. B., "A. S.," in Natan, A., ed. *German Men of Letters*, Vol. II (1963): 55–75; Swales, M., *A. S.: A Critical Study* (1971); Urbach, R., *"A. S.,* (1973); Williams, C. E., *The Broken Eagle: The Politics of Austrian Literature from Empire to Anschluss* (1974): 45–59; special S. issue, *MAL*, 10: 3–4 (1977); Roberts, A. C., *A. S. and Politics* (1989); Thompson, B., *S.'s Vienna: Image of a Society* (1990); Wisely, A. C., *A. S. and the Discourse of Honor and Dueling* (1996)

—FREDERICK UNGAR

SCHREINER, Olive

South African novelist (writing in English), b. 24 March 1855, Wittebergen; d. 10 Dec. 1920, Wynberg

The daughter of missionary parents, S. spent her early years on isolated mission stations, receiving no formal education. She became a governess on Eastern Cape farms (1871–80), where she read the works of Charles Darwin, Herbert Spencer, John Stuart Mill, and Ralph Waldo Emerson. They confirmed her instinctive tendency to reject formalized Christianity for an intuitive perception of spiritual truth, an adherence to individual rights, and a belief in evolutionary progress. From 1881 to 1889 S. lived in England, meeting such members of early socialist groups as Edward Carpenter (1844–1929) and sexologist Havelock Ellis (1859–1939), and traveling in Europe. After her return to South Africa her energies were taken up mainly in polemical journalism and other nonfiction writing, crusading against Cecil Rhodes and British expansionism in Africa, expressing the South African outlook during the Boer War (1899–1902), and developing her view of women's problems and rights. Although she married a liberal South African farmer, S. C. Cronwright, in 1894, she spent the last seven years of her life alone in England before returning to South Africa to die.

S.'s main achievement as a novelist is *The Story of an African Farm* (1883), first published under the pseudonym Ralph Iron. It is a landmark work in South African fiction because of its powerful imaginative use of the landscape of the Great Karoo, an arid interior plateau of South Africa sparsely populated by farmers, and its exploration of spiritual conflict in its young protagonists, Lyndall and Waldo. The novel aroused controversy in England because of Lyndall's championship of women's rights and rejection of conventional marriage, and also because of Waldo's rejection of orthodox Christian belief. S.'s second published novel, *Trooper Peter Halket of Mashonaland* (1897), directed at Rhodes and his policies, is a satirical allegory in which a young trooper is confronted by Jesus Christ as a nighttime visitant. Her most ambitious work, the posthumously published *From Man to Man* (1926), never completed, focuses on the contrasted lives of two sisters who struggle in different ways against social norms and sexual hypocrisy. *Undine* (1929) is a posthumously published juvenile work, combining realistic scenes of the Kimberley diamond fields with a fairytale English setting.

Shorter fictions by S. include allegories in the form of dream visions, a few short tales for children, and autobiographical stories exalting the need for the renunciation of possessive sexual love. "Eighteen-Ninety-nine" (pub. 1923), generally considered her best short story, is a celebration of Afrikaner endurance that links the Afrikaner with the cyclical fertility of the land.

All of S.'s fiction is concerned with the centrality of childhood experience in shaping later life and with the difficulty of maintaining ideals or individual integrity in a corrupt or hostile environment. Her vision is one of suffering and of struggle toward a glimpse of universal harmony. The 19th-c. belief in progress is tempered by her early experience of hardship, by the asthmatic illness that troubled her from adolescence onward, and by an awareness of painful conflict in sexual relationships. Her fiction speaks didactically to contemporary issues, such as socialism, feminism, imperialism, and racism; but, in a carefully structured blend of realism and allegory, it situates these causes in a cosmic framework. She spans concrete local detail and dream landscapes, social protest and philosophical meditation, with enormous confidence and power.

S.'s belief in individual rights remained a central tenet of her polemical writing. Her political pamphlets included *Closer Union* (1909), which advocates a form of federal government to protect the individual features of the provinces as South Africa moved toward unification. Her concern with women's rights resulted in an influential and ardent work, *Woman and Labour* (1911), which proclaimed a woman's need to escape parasitic dependence and her right to choose any occupation. *Thoughts on South Africa* (1923) is a lucid study of the country's features and problems, revealing a strong grasp of their historical and geographical causes.

Despite S.'s belief in the organic unity of art, she always stressed that art should be of assistance to others. She believed in a shared human nature and condition, and felt that the passionate exploration of basic problems, especially discord in male-female relationships, would show other women that they were not suffering alone. She is honored by later generations of South African writers for making the local landscape vivid and viable in *The Story of an African Farm*. Many of her statements on the South African "race problem" are now seen as prophetic and ahead of her time. Her compassion and eloquence in speaking out for women have made her a symbolic founding mother of the feminist movement of recent decades.

FURTHER WORKS: *Dreams* (1890); *Dream Life and Real Life* (1893); *The Political Situation* (1895, with S. C. Cronwright-Schreiner); *An English-South African's View of the Situation*

(1899); *Stories, Dreams and Allegories* (1923); *The Letters of O. S.* (1924); *An O. S. Reader* (1987)

BIBLIOGRAPHY: Lessing, D., Afterword to *The Story of an African Farm* (1968): 273–90; Jacobson, D., "O. S.: A South African Writer," *London* (Feb. 1971): 5–21; Berkman, J. A., *O. S.: Feminism on the Frontier* (1979); Gray, S., *Southern African Literature: An Introduction* (1979); 133–59; First, R., and A. Scott, *O. S.* (1980); Clayton, C., ed., *O. S.* (1983); Berkman, J., *The Healing Imagination of O. S.* (1989); Clayton, C., *O. S.* (1997)

—CHERRY CLAYTON

SCHULZ, Bruno

Polish short-story writer, b. 12 July 1892, Drohobycz (now Drogobych, Ukraine); d. 19 Nov. 1942, Drohobycz

S., the son of a Jewish textile merchant, was born into a typical *shtetl* milieu. A self-taught draftsman, he made his living as an art instructor in a local school and lived as a recluse. S. did not begin his literary career until age forty, writing only in Polish (although he knew both Yiddish and German and had translated KAFKA's *The Trial*). Many of his early stories had their genesis in letters written to a woman acquaintance. These stories, along with others he had written, were later published at the urging of the Polish novelist Zofia NALKOWSKA; this first collection, *Sklepy cynamonowe* (1934; *The Street of Crocodiles*, 1963), was honored by the Polish Academy of Letters and lifted its author into the front ranks of the Polish avant-garde. His modest oeuvre includes, besides two collections of stories, an unfinished novel, literary criticism, and a body of correspondence with such Polish avant-gardists as Witold GOMBROWICZ and Stanislaw Ignacy WITKIEWICZ. His brief career ended abruptly when he was gunned down in the street by a Gestapo officer during the Nazi occupation.

S.'s native Drohobycz, his Jewishness, his career in art, and his isolation were the major shaping factors of his work. Set primarily in the Jewish quarter of town, his stories center around the author's family, notably the father, although the treatment is less autobiographical and ethnographic than mythic. The biblical names of S.'s adolescent narrator, Józef, and of the narrator's father, Jakub, indicate the characters' archetypal and mythic resonances. The prominence of the father-figure, together with S.'s taste for the fantastic, have tempted critics to compare him to Kafka, although S.'s metaphysical obsessions lack the dimension of psychological guilt found in Kafka. For at the heart of S.'s work is an obsession with being, in all its bewildering diversity, and nothingness, evoked in numerous nocturnal landscapes. The reconstruction of a mythic family, furthermore, led the author to be fixated upon the past: memory, Proustian in its obsessiveness, and childhood are the dominant motifs of all his fiction.

The father-figure, symbolizing a traditional, patriarchal way of life—the world of "cinnamon shops" (the literal meaning of *Sklepy cynamonowe*)—is set off against an age of encroaching vulgarity, sham, and mindless materialism, epitomized by "the street of crocodiles." The women characters are often identified with the forces of destructive energy and benign indifference—for example, the servant girl Adela and the narrator's mother—while the

male characters are associated with the solitary life of the mind and imagination. (A submerged sexuality, often with masochistic and homoerotic overtones, lurks beneath many of the stories.) In the concluding stories of S.'s second collection, *Sanatorium pod Klepsydrą* (1937; *The Sanatorium under the Sign of the Hourglass*, 1978), the father's demise connotes the passage of an order threatened by mendacity and incipient barbarism.

The elevation of Drohobycz and the particulars of childhood to the mythic is accomplished almost entirely through style. S.'s stories are highly unconventional in form, lacking in most of the traditional devices of narrative. In this, as well as in other respects, he recalls his Russian contemporary Isaak BABEL. Weak in plot and incident, reckless with chronology, and veering constantly into the phantasmagoric, his stories are hallucinatory evocations of states preceding the rational cognition of the adult mind, and are paganlike in their primitivism. Not content with lyrical descriptions of nature, S. used language to animate the world about him and to reveal the latent possibilities within nature for endless transmutation. As such, his stories resemble prose poems, and are perhaps unique in their accretion of metaphor, simile, and plenitude of sensuous imagery.

S.'s "rediscovery" in Poland in the late 1950s was a major literary event. He belongs to that triumvirate of writers—the others are Witkiewicz and Gombrowicz—credited with having raised Polish literature between the wars to European standards. In Poland he is recognized as the finest prose stylist this century has produced.

FURTHER WORKS: *Proza* (1964); *Księga listów* (1975). FURTHER WORKS IN ENGLISH: *The Complete Fiction of B. S.* (1989)

BIBLIOGRAPHY: Wieniewska, C., Introduction to *The Street of Crocodiles* (1963): 7–10; Milosz, C., *The History of Polish Literature* (1969): 429–30; Ficowski, J., Introduction to *The Street of Crocodiles* (Penguin ed. 1977): 9–22; Ozick, C., on *The Street of Crocodiles NYTBR* (13 Feb. 1977): 4; Wieniewska, C., Introduction to *Sanatorium under the Sign of the Hourglass* (1978): ix–xi; Bayley, J., on *Sanatorium under the Sign of the Hourglass, NYRB* (20 July 1978): 35–36; Updike, J., on *Sanatorium under the Sign of the Hourglass, NYTBR* (9 Sept. 1979): 36–39

—LOUIS IRIBARNE

SCHUTZ, David

Israeli novelist and short-story writer, b. 5 Aug. 1941, Berlin, Germany

S. arrived in Palestine on the eve of Israeli independence in 1948, and later studied history at the Hebrew University, Jerusalem. His first published work, a novel, *Haesev vehahol* (1979; the grass and the sand), went into four editions. Since then he has produced a collection of short stories, *Hahizdamnut haaharonah* (1980; the last chance), and three additional novels: *Ad olam ahakeh* (1987; I shall wait forever), *Shoshan lavan shoshan adom* (1988; white rose, red rose), and *Avishag* (1989; Avishag).

Although the narratives are set within the social reality of contemporary Israel, they also treat the past through the present. Many of the principal protagonists are immigrants and survivors; a main theme of S.'s work is the encounter between past and present, between outsider and insider. Another constant theme is the slippery face of reality, particularly female reality. A question posed throughout the S. opus is: Who is this woman—is she the person she seems to be, is there a further reality behind the one that immediately presents itself?

Whether third-or first-person narrator, it is the male who observes, who loves, and who loses the love, either in reality or in imagination. *Ad olam ahakeh* opens with the observation that Peretz, out walking with his daughter, "was already convinced that his wife was unfaithful." *Shoshan lavan shoshan adom* starts with "By chance I met Lily and by chance I lost her." And *Avishag* is really a novel in celebration of the eponymous heroine and in search of her. Here, the narrator tells us from his seemingly comfortable family situation how he is tortured by the floating identity of his wife. He is seen both in the first person, through his own narrative, and in the third, as the uncertain, dependent Amos, hanging onto the good will of his dominating father-in-law. That other man seems to serve as a model for all that Amos aspires to be, in his learning, in his confidence and competence, and in his material success. Avishag's father and her husband represent past and present, together with their alternative claims.

Obsessive love is a linking theme of the novels. The title of *Ad olam ahakeh* indicates this posture. The social realism of the narrative is always partially undermined by the awareness that reality is a composite of disparate elements. The future, as contained by the daughter, is also full of ambiguity, as he notes how different she is from him and how awkward are his efforts to approach her.

Shoshan lavan shoshan adom explicitly delves into the past, and takes as its point of departure those early days in April 1948 when the narrator (seemingly based on the author's own biography) found himself in Israel just before independence. His contact with Lily as a child is both physical and "unreal," as she can be transformed from a concrete creature of flesh and blood into "a princess of the night," "like a picture from a story book." An air of melancholy hovers over S.'s open narratives.

FURTHER WORKS: *Avishag* (1990).

—LEON I. YUDKIN

SCHUYLER, James

American poet, b. 9 Nov. 1923, Chicago, Illinois; d. 12 Apr. 1991, New York, New York

S. was reared in and around Chicago, Washington, D.C., and Buffalo, New York. After attending Bethany College in West Virginia, he joined the navy and served in the North Atlantic during World War II; the discovery of his homosexuality resulted in his discharge. After the war S. lived mainly in New York City, working in bookstores and museums and writing art reviews. On several occasions he entered psychiatric hospitals; his convalescence at the home of Fairfield Porter after a 1961 breakdown led to a twelve-year stay with the painter and his family. From 1979 until his death he lived at New York's Chelsea Hotel, supported by artist grants and prize money.

S. is usually associated with the poets Frank O'HARA, Kenneth Koch (b. 1925), and John ASHBERY; the four have been dubbed the New York School of Poets, though all of them were ambivalent about that label. S. was greatly influenced by (and influenced) the other members of this coterie. His early work, like theirs, is largely impersonal, and shows a fondness for collage and SURREALISM. In the 1970s, however, his work became more direct and autobiographical.

Intimidated early on by the traditional craftsmanship of W.H. AUDEN, for whom he worked briefly as a typist, S. almost always wrote free verse. He developed two trademark styles. One is a "skinny" poem having at most three or four words per line, and sometimes only one; the most extreme example is "Buttered Greens." The other is a long poem written in long lines, a form he was inspired to attempt after reading Walt Whitman. Two meditations in this latter mode are the title poems of his collections *The Crystal Lithium* (1972) and *Hymn to Life* (1974).

S.'s long line becomes even longer in his masterpiece, the sixty-page title work of his Pulitzer Prize-winning collection *The Morning of the Poem* (1980). The poem is addressed to his friend, the painter Darragh Park, and is part letter and part diary. S. oscillates between the distant past and the present: he recalls scenes from his boyhood, his discovery of James JOYCE's *Ulysses*, and several former lovers, but alternates these memories with vivid evocations of daily life in the present. In addition to this STREAM-OF-CONSCIOUSNESS narrative, "The Morning of the Poem" also features self-contained lyrics set off by short lines. The poem's trail of associations can sometimes seem random, but commentators have pointed out a number of symmetries and other unifying principles.

For most of his creative life S. lived in New York City, yet he is a poet of nature. Many of his poems are about the weather, sunrise, sunset, or simply the quality of natural light on any given day. His poems are full of flowers, all named precisely: one does not find a mere rose in S.'s work, but a Georg Arends, or a Gloire de Dijon, or a Variegata di Bologna. This is typical of a larger characteristic of S.'s poetry, his Adamic insistence on giving each thing its proper name.

Although S. is best known for his poems, his first publications were short stories. His prose fiction includes three novels: *Alfred and Guinevere* (1958); his collaboration with John Ashbery, *A Nest of Ninnies* (1969); and *What's for Dinner?* (1978). But his major prose work is probably the diary he kept for twenty-four years, excerpts of which appeared in print during his lifetime. The whole was edited after his death by Nathan Kernan, and published as *The Diary of J. S.* (1997).

S.'s future reputation is hard to predict. Other poets have praised him highly, comparing his poetry to that of Walt Whitman and Elizabeth BISHOP; academic critics, on the other hand, have been slow to consider his work. Regardless, S.'s love of beauty and truth, his careful attention to nature, and his ability to convey without sentimentality a sense of life's preciousness guarantee that he will always have his readers.

FURTHER WORKS: *Freely Espousing* (1969); *The Home Book: Prose and Poems 1951-1970* (1977); *A Few Days* (1985); *Selected Poems* (1988); *Collected Poems* (1993)

BIBLIOGRAPHY: Moss, H., "J. S.: Whatever Is Moving," *APR*, 10, 3 (1981): 14-16; Whedon, T., "Occasions for Morning," *APR*, 18, 6 (1989): 9-15; special S. issue, *DQ*, 24, 4 (1990); Little, C., "An Interview with J. S.," *Agni*, 37 (1993): 152-82; Ward, G., *Statutes of Liberty: The New York School of Poets* (1993): 10-35

—ROBERT WEST

SCHWARTZ, Delmore

American poet, short-story writer, and critic, b. 8 Dec. 1913, Brooklyn, N.Y.; d. 11 July 1966, New York, N.Y.

S. grew up in Brooklyn and studied philosophy at the University of Wisconsin, New York University, and Harvard. From 1940 to 1947 he taught English at Harvard. He served on the editorial board of *Partisan Review* (1943–55), was poetry editor of *The New Republic* (1955–57), and was *Kenyon Review* Fellow in 1957. S. taught and lectured at various American universities and received awards from *Poetry* magazine and from the National Institute of Arts and Letters. In 1966, alone and plagued by manic-depression, S. died of a heart attack in a Manhattan hotel.

S.'s first book, *In Dreams Begin Responsibilities* (1938), is a miscellany of short fiction, poetry, a modern adaptation of Shakespeare's *Coriolanus*, and a rather feeble drama, *Dr. Bergen's Belief*. The outstanding title story is a graphic dream of a single afternoon about the courtship of a couple as witnessed by their son in a movie theater. It reflects S.'s own agony and insecurity in regard to his mother and father. Two of the poems in this volume were singled out for praise: "In the Naked Bed, in Plato's Cave," a vivid account of sleeplessness caused by fatigue brought on by contemplation of history and the inexorable passing of time; and "The Heavy Bear Who Goes with Me," a powerful representation of male sexuality.

S.'s long autobiographical poem *Genesis, Book I* (1943) only partially confirmed his earlier promise. Portions capture the brilliant wit and irony of his earlier verse, but the entire poem is too inflated. S. contemplated additional volumes of Genesis, but he never completed them. *Vaudeville for a Princess, and Other Poems* (1950) is a collection of prose sketches and lyrics, with emphasis on the sonnet form. With the exception of "Starlight Like Intuition Pierced the Twelve" and a few other poems, this book is undistinguished.

S. received the Bollingen Poetry Prize and the Shelley Memorial Award for *Summer Knowledge: New and Selected Poems, 1938–1958* (1959). Of the new poems, however, only the series of dramatic monologues by biblical characters and "Seurat's Sunday Afternoon along the Seine" are outstanding—meditative and eloquent.

S.'s verse is extremely allusive. He was much influenced by Plato, Shakespeare, and Rimbaud, whose *A Season in Hell* he translated (1940), as well as by T. S. ELIOT and James JOYCE. His favorite theme is what he calls "the wound of consciousness," which involves the ego, a sense of guilt and alienation operating within a consciousness of his Jewish background, and a troubled awareness of the vastness and weight of history and time. In his concern for self-identity he emphasizes the role of the poet in the modern world.

S. also published two volumes of stories, *The World Is a Wedding* (1948) and *Successful Love, and Other Stories* (1961). The first contains sensitive depictions of middle-class American Jewish life during the 1930s. In the second volume, however, the quality was diminished because he wrote about a wider social milieu—for example, suburban families—with which he could not identify.

S.'s criticism, which appeared chiefly in periodicals, ranged widely, including essays on Marianne MOORE, Eliot, and Ring Lardner (1885–1933). Sound and reliable, his criticism is buttressed by a phenomenal knowledge not only of individual writers but also of cultural traditions and the trends of his own time.

S. was an extremely gifted poet. Yet his personal problems during the last twenty years of his life hampered his artistic development considerably and led to his tragic isolation and creative decline.

FURTHER WORKS: *Shenandoah* (1941); *The Imitation of Life* (1943); *Selected Essays* (1970); *Last and Lost Poems* (1979); *The Ego is Always at the Wheel: Bagatelles* (1986)

BIBLIOGRAPHY: Rahv, P., "D. S.: The Paradox of Precocity," *NYRB*, 20 (May 1971): 19–22; McDougall, R., *D. S.* (1974); Atlas, J., *D. S.: The Life of an American Poet* (1977); Howe, I., "D. S.: An Appreciation," *Celebrations and Attacks: Thirty Years of Literary and Cultural Commentary* (1979): 183–88; Van Doren, M., "Music of a Mind: On D. S.," *The Essays of Mark Van Doren (1924–1972)* (1980): 152–54; Barrett, W., *The Truants: Adventures among the Intellectuals* (1982): 209–40 and passim

—B. BERNARD COHEN

SCHWARZ-BART, Simone

Guadeloupean novelist and dramatist, b. 8 Jan. 1938, Saintes, France

S. is one of the francophone Caribbean's best-known writers. Born in France, she moved at a very early age to Guadeloupe where she lived and attended school until 1958, when she left for Paris to prepare for the baccalaureate exam and study law. There she met and married novelist Andre Schwarz-Bart (b. 1928) who won the Gomcoun Prize for *Le dernier des justes* (1959; *The Last of the Just*, 1960). They would collaborate on *Un plat de porc aux bananes vertes* (1967; a plate of pork with green bananas) and *Hommage à la femme noire* (1988; homage to the black woman). She also studied at the universities of Dakar in Senegal and Lausanne in Switzerland. S. presently resides in Guadeloupe.

S.'s literary universe is the Caribbean. Her first two novels have women narrators who tell their life story. In *Un plat de porc aux bananes vertes* an old woman in a Parisian nursing home reflects on her past in Martinique. In *Pluie et vent sur Télumée Miracle* (1972; *The Bridge of Beyond*, 1974), S.'s first non-collaborative novel, the protagonist relates not only her life, but that of her mother and grandmother. This combination biography/autobiography of three generations of strong, courageous, rural women who triumph over adversity is recounted by the narrator while she stands in her garden. S. emphasizes the importance of women's oral culture and how mutual support, role models, and the transmission of knowledge to the young are essential to their survival. *Pluie et vent sur Télumée Miracle* is S.'s most widely read and studied work.

Ti-Jean l'Horizon (1979; *Between Two Worlds*, 1981) is based on a popular oral story. In this version Ti-Jean, attracted to a mythical Africa, leaves Guadeloupe in search of his identity. During his journey, which includes a visit to France, he undergoes several tests. Upon returning to Guadeloupe he realizes that his identity is to be found at home. In this novel S. transforms the Western literary identity quest into a traditional African and Caribbean initiation tale.

Ton beau capitaine (1987; *Your Handsome Captain*, 1988), her only published play, was inspired by her Haitian gardener who communicated with his wife in Haiti by way of audiocassettes. Set in a one-room shack in Guadeloupe, Wilnor, an agricultural worker, listens to the latest cassette sent by his wife in Haiti and records a response. The play explores the effects of separation on a couple, which is made even more poignant as Marie-Ange never appears on stage. The play, which has been performed on three continents, has broader meaning as it also exposes the plight of migrant workers who leave their native land only to suffer loneliness, economic hardship, and discrimination. On another level it condemns the original displacement and forced exile of Africans due to the slave trade.

While S.'s writing has evolved over the past twenty years, certain themes recur: the long-term effects of slavery, the island isolated from the rest of the world, exile and alienation in a foreign land, and the search for identity and stability—in short, the Caribbean landscape, cultural heritage, and experience. In addition, she is probably best known for her fully developed female characters. S.'s works do not fit into traditionally defined genre categories. For example, *Ton beau capitaine* includes songs, dance, and music, while her novels incorporate proverbs, MAGIC REALISM, and the Creole language in an attempt to recreate the oral tradition. By privileging speech, S. places herself in the long line of oral storytellers.

BIBLIOGRAPHY: Scharfman, R., "Mirroring and Mothering in S.'s *Pluie et vent sur Télumée Miracle* and Jean Rhys's *Wide Sargasso Sea*," YFS, 62 (1982): 88–106; Bernabé, J., "Le travail de l'écriture chez S.," *PA*: 121–22 (1982): 166–79; Cailler, B., "Ti-Jean l'Horizon de S. ou la leçon du royaume des morts," *SFR*, 6 (1982): 283–97; Ormerod, B., "The Boat and the Tree: S.'s *The Bridge of Beyond*," *Introduction to the French Caribbean Novel* (1985): 108–31; Toureh, F., *L'imaginaire dans l'œuvre de S.* (1986); Smyley-Wallace, K., "The Female and the Self in S.'s *Pluie et vent sur Télumée Miracle*," *FR*, 59 (Feb. 1986): 428–36; Busia, A., "This Gift of Metaphor: Symbolic Strategies and the Triumph of Survival in S.'s *The Bridge of Beyond*," in Davies, C. B., and Fido E. S., *Out of the Kumbla: Caribbean Women and Literature* (1990): 289–301; Larrier, R., "The Poetics of Ex-île S.'s *Ton beau capitaine*," *WLT*, 64, 1 (Winter 1990): 57–59

—RENÉE LARRIER

SCIASCIA, Leonardo

Italian novelist, short-story writer, dramatist, essayist, and journalist, b. 8 Jan. 1921, Racalmuto; d. 20 Nov. 1989, Palermo

Luigi Barzini (b. 1908) said of S. that he "has one advantage many Italians envy him for. He is Sicilian." For almost ten years S. was an elementary-school teacher in his native town in the province of Agrigento; there he was directly exposed to the problems of his pupils and their families—miners of sulphur and salt, farmers—who were victims of centuries of poverty. During these years S. wrote two small books: *Favole della dittatura* (1950; fables of dictatorship) and *La Sicilia, il suo cuore* (1952; Sicily, its heart). The fables of the first volume attack Fascism, and the poems of the second deal with the children of the poor in field and school. These little-known books indicate S.'s early socio-political consciousness, prominent in his later works.

It was only with "Cronache scolastiche" (1955; school chronicles)—first published in the journal *Nuovi argomenti*—a long

account based on his experiences as an elementary school teacher in Racalmuto in which he exposes the debased life of his pupils and their families, that S. became widely known to the general public. He was then asked by the prestigious publisher Laterza to write a full-length book about his birthplace. The result was *Le parrocchie di Regalpetra* (1956; *Salt in the Wound*, 1969), which contains "Cronache scolastiche" as well as other stories documenting the humiliating conditions of his people from the Middle Ages to the Fascist era and through the rise of democracy—their abuse by landlords, politicians, and, of course, the Mafia. These stories, as well as the many essays contained in *Pirandello e la Sicilia* (1961; Pirandello and Sicily) and *La corda pazza* (1970; the crazy string) give a highly accurate picture of Sicily, its people, and its writers, and are of paramount importance in understanding S.'s artistic world and the major themes of his later works.

Sicily, where for centuries injustice and crime, poverty and plague, oppression and abuse have been the people's lot, is S.'s constant theme and preoccupation. With the sun-baked Sicilian landscape as background, S. portrays the victims and the oppressors of the past, as in *Morte dell'inquisitore* (1964; "The Death of the Inquisitor," in *Salt in the Wound*, 1969), a historical novella about a victim of the Inquisition; and of the present, as in *La scomparsa di Majorana* (1975; the disappearance of Majorana). S.'s writings are always in some sense historical, even when, as in *Il giorno della civetta* (1961; *Mafia Vendetta*, 1964) and *A ciascuno il suo* (1966; *A Man's Blessing*, 1968), they take the form of a detective story. This is true as well of his dramas, such as *L'onorevole* (1965; the honorable one) and *I mafiosi* (1972; the Mafia men).

S.'s primary model is the Alessandro Manzoni (1785–1873) of *The Column of Infamy*, a historical treatise in which the "moralist" (as S. calls his master and himself) forcefully condemns the injustice of the Milanese judges who in 1630 sentenced to be tortured innocent men accused of being spreaders of the plague. Sifting the complex and varied history of his Sicilians—victims of man and nature—S. searches in the wounds of the past for a cure to present evils. Because he is able to universalize both the oppressors and the victims, giving them an importance that transcends the particular, it is possible for him to render a portrait of man appropriate to all times, all societies. Although his books are an implicit condemnation of the Italian upper class, they all carry a message of redemption. In the very last words of *Morte dell'inquisitore*, S. points out that he has written Fra Diego's story because he "was a man, who held aloft the dignity of man."

Some critics have called S. an "Enlightenment writer," and they consider his works "philosophical stories." S. himself notes that as a child he was given the works of Denis Diderot before he had even read *Pinocchio*. "I believe in human reason, and in the liberty and justice it engenders."

S. describes himself as a "very impure writer," because his stories are always intertwined with criticism, and a "pamphleteer," because there is no work in which he does not denounce some form of injustice. As a writer and a Sicilian he believes that "a slash of the pen . . . like a slash of the sword, is enough to right a wrong or rout injustice and exploitation."

Recent evidence of this attitude is *Nero sunero* (1979; black on black), a ten-year diary of private, literary, and political "meditation" and polemic about the evils that plague Italy. S. states that this book contains all his books written since 1969 and that its title is a parodistic answer to those who accuse him of pessimism: it means "black writing on the black page of reality." In 1979 S. was elected to the Chamber of Deputies as a member of the Radical Party. He has stated, "I made a politics by writing, and at a certain point I wanted to make a politics in order to write." His *L'affaire Moro* (1978; *The Moro Affair*, 1987) is a logical consequence of this double concern.

S.'s style is precise and vivid, condensed, yet rich and colorful in its use of foreign and dialect words and idioms. His primary mode is satire, because, he says, it is for him like "Gogol's mirror, which enables him to see the crooked nose of society."

Certainly one of the major contemporary Italian writers, S.— like other Sicilian writers such as Giovanni VERGA, Luigi PIRAN-DELLO, Vitaliano BRANCATI, Elio VITTORINI, and Giuseppe Tomasi di LAMPEDUSA—has portrayed the people of his "exasperated and tragic Eden" in such a way that men everywhere can identify with their search for self-hood and dignity.

FURTHER WORKS: *Pirandello e il pirandellismo* (1953); *Gli zii di Sicilia* (1958); *Il consiglio d'Egitto* (1963; *The Council of Egypt*, 1966); *Feste religiose in Sicilia* (1965); *Recitazione della controversia liparitana dedicata a A. D.* (1969); *Atti relativi alla morte di Raymond Roussel* (1971); *Il contesto* (1971; *Equal Danger*, 1974, 1984); *Il mare color del vino* (1973); *Todo modo* (1974; *One Way or Another*, 1977); *I pugnalatori* (1976); *Candido; ovvero, Un sogno fatto in Sicilia* (1977; *Candido; or, A Dream Dreamed in Sicily*, 1979); *La Sicilia come metafora* (1979); *Dalle parti degli infedeli* (1979); *La Sicilia mito di acque* (1981); *Il teatro della memoria* (1981); *Kermesse* (1982); *Conversazione in una stanza chiusa* (1982, with Davide Lajolo); *La sentenza memorabile* (1982); *Cruciverba* (1983). FURTHER WORKS IN ENGLISH: *The Wine Dark Sea* (1985); *Sicilian Uncles* (1986); *Open Doors and Three Novellas* (1992); *Sicily as a Metaphor* (1994)

BIBLIOGRAPHY: Biasin, G. -P., "The Sicily of Verga and S.," *IQ*, 9 (1965): 3–22; West, A., "Games That Are Played for Keeps," *New Yorker* (19 March 1966): 206–8; Barzini, L., "Dangerous Acquaintances," *NYRB* (9 Oct. 1969): 36–44; Bonnet, J., et al, eds., special S. issue, *L'arc*, No. 77 (1979); Vidal, G.,, "On the Assassins' Trail," *NYRB* (25 Oct. 1979): 17–23; McCarthy, P., "The Spirit of Contradictions," *TLS* (2 May 1980), 490; Jackson, G., *L. S., 1956–1976: A Thematic and Structural Study* (1981)

—M. RICCIARDELLI

SCLIAR, Moacyr

Brazilian novelist and short-story writer, b. 23 Mar. 1937, Porto Alegre

S. has attracted international recognition as one of the foremost Jewish writers of Latin America. The unusual fact that he has ten paperback books published in the U.S. in English translation has made him one of the most widely reviewed contemporary Brazilian writers in the American press. In Brazil he has been recognized with numerous literary prizes. S. grew up in Porto Alegre, the capital of the southern Brazilian state of Rio Geande do Sul. His father was a businessman who had emigrated to Brazil from eastern Europe. From early childhood, S. desired to become a fiction writer. This calling has been nourished by the experiences of a full professional life as a public-health physician in Porto Alegre. Perhaps because of what he has seen as a doctor, the characters and situations in his narratives are often macabre or grotesque. The ugly is, however, treated with irony, wit, and humor, a lightness of touch that lends charm and childlike innocence to his fiction. Indeed, S. is also a noted writer of children's literature, as well as the author of essays and commentaries on contemporary Brazil and public-health issues. S. offers a unique view of the realities of the Brazilian middle class through the various lenses of physician, member of the small Brazilian Jewish minority, and fabulist.

The universal themes of S.'s fiction are love, disease, death, and regeneration. Woven into this tapestry are the special concerns of a Jewish people exiled in a complex, multicultural society. The bestiary is a primary leitmotiv of the narratives; humans behave like animals, and animals have an angelic, transforming energy. The first book of S.'s long bibliography is the volume of short stories entitled *O carnaval dos animais* (1968; *The Carnival of the Animals*, 1985). Subsequent works that have been singled out as among his best are *O centauro no jardim* (1980; *The Centaur in the Garden*, 1985) and *A estranha nação de Rafael Mendes* (1983; *The Strange Nation of Rafael Mendes*, 1988).

O centauro no jardim is a picaresque fable that illustrates the human difficulty in accepting those not of one's own kind. This is the story of a young Jew who was born a centaur. It traces his early childhood exile because of his deformity, his flight from home, his encounter and marriage with a female centaur, their plastic surgery to remove their equine features, and their life as an almost human couple. Their flaw is that of eternal longing for the life of the centaur, and the inability of both "species" to fully accept the other. *A estranha nação de Rafael Mendes* creates the endearing character of the Brazilian Jewish yuppie, whose existential angst is occasioned by numerous family and professional problems. Mendes strikes a Faustian deal with a cunning old genealogist, who sells him his family history. This novel makes a universal statement on the drama of being different, while offering a vivid portrait of the tensions and beauties of Brazil's unique cultural mix, its blends of Catholic and Candomblé, native Brazilian Indian and European, Eastern and Western elements.

The quality of S.'s writing has invoked comparisons to writers such as La Fontaine, Voltaire, Melville, Isaac Bashevis SINGER, Jorge Luis BORGES, and Gabriel GARCÍA MÁRQUEZ. Like other Latin American writers of his generation, S. crafts stories by linking and multiplying words, images, plots, subplots, and narrative points of view into a patterned whole. His trademark is a tender humor that keeps his narratives from becoming cerebral puzzles or stark statements of defeat. While his heroes may fail, they are treated with compassion. They are all travelers, and their destination, it is important to note, is always Jerusalem.

FURTHER WORKS: *A guerra no Bom Fim* (1972); *O exército de um homem só* (1973; *The One-Man Army*, 1986); *Os deuses de Raquel* (1975; *The Gods of Raquel*, 1986); *Os mistérios de Porto Alegre* (1976); *A balada do falso messias* (1976; *The Ballad of the False Messiah*, 1987); *O ciclo das águas* (1977); *Mães de cães danados* (1977); *Os voluntários* (1979; *The Volunteers*, 1988); *Doutor miragem* (1979); *Cavalos e obeliscos* (1981); *Max e os felinos* (1981; *Max and the Cats*, 1989); *Memórias de um aprendiz de escritor* (1984); *A massagista japonesa* (1984); *O olho enigmático* (1986; *The Enigmatic Eye*, 1989); *O tio que flutuava* (1988); *No caminho dos sonhos* (1988); *Os cavalos da república* (1989); *Um país chamado infância* (1989); *Pra você eu conto* (1991)

BIBLIOGRAPHY: Lowe, E., *The City in Brazilian Literature* (1982), 10, 19, 192, 204; Lindstrom, N., "Oracular Jewish Tradition in Two Works by M. S.," *LBR*, 12, 2 (Winter 1984): 23–33; Franco, J., on *The Strange Nation of Rafael Mendes, NYTBR*, 30 June 1985: 12; Vieira, N., "Judaic Fiction in Brazil: To Be or Not To Be," *LALR*, 14, 28 (July–Dec 1986): 31–45; Jackson, K. D., "*The One-Man Army*," *WLT*, 61, 2 (Spring 1987): 261–62; Donovan, L., "S.'s Mendes Differs from Usual Magic Realism," *Miami Herald*, 1 May 1988; Day, D., "The Beast in Us," *NYTBR*, 4 May 1986: 34; Stavans, I., on *The Strange Nation of Rafael Mendes, Review*, 39 (Jan.–June 1988): 63; Stern, I., *Dictionary of Brazilian Literature* (1988): 313–14

—ELIZABETH LOWE

SCOTT, Dennis

Jamaican poet and dramatist, b. 16 Dec. 1939, Kingston; d. 21 Feb. 1991, New Haven, Connecticut, U.S.A.

Born to a middle-class family, S. attended the prestigious Jamaica College and then the University College of the West Indies where he began a degree in English that he would complete several years later after a period of high school teaching in Trinidad and Jamaica. S.'s professional theater experience began as a dancer for the National Dance Theatre Company of Jamaica. He would go on to become one of the most respected directors in Caribbean theater and the director of the Theater Department at the Cultural Training Center in Jamaica. S. moved to the U.S., where he pursued graduate studies to become a professor of directing at the Yale School of Drama.

With only three collections of poetry, two published plays, and a handful of produced plays to his name, S. would seem unlikely to be regarded as an important figure in West Indian literature. However, his play *An Echo in the Bone*, remains one of the most important treatments of the history of the West Indies, replete with themes of identity, sexuality, slavery, memory, and racial politics, not to mention the complexity of the colonial experience. It falls within the same category of importance as Derek WALCOTT's *Dream on Monkey Mountain*, Michael Gilke's *Couvade and Errol*, and Johns Moon's *On a Rainbow Shawl* in terms of important Caribbean plays. *An Echo in the Bone* is thematically similar to S.'s poetry in that it combines a political awareness with a remarkable lyrical intensity—a combination that represents a shift away from the detachment of modernism to the more passionate and sometimes more complex spirit of modern American verse of the 1950s and 1960s, including the work of such poets as Amiri BARAKA and Gwendolyn BROOKS. But S.'s writing stands on its own, as it is fed not so much by the blues as by a powerful reggae aesthetic that emerged in the West Indies in the 1970s. Yet, while there is a strong awareness of political realities, S.'s play is unwilling to settle for pat answers. There is no question that slavery is a problem to S., but S. complicates the slave dynamic by somehow humanizing the white slave owner who has an affair with a black servant. The play—centered on a nine-night ceremony in which the spirits of the dead are prone to enter the celebrants and bring about some kind of revelation of human importance—becomes a fascinating study of the use of ritual in drama. The nine-night ritual, derived from West Africa, constitutes a strong ideological articulation by S., who would see in that powerful connection to the past a way toward an understanding of the present.

S.'s poetry is equally adept at simultaneously exploring the personal, the lyrical, and the political. S.'s poetic line is a tightly-wound elastic band that contains a complex of images that explode into multiple meanings when properly organized. S. is fascinated by the bird as an image and with flight. He is also interested in the use of the language and idiom derived from the streets of Kingston to feed his poetry with a metaphysical intensity that is enviable. In this S. is sometimes embarking on a postmodernist excursion that places him far beyond the work of someone like Derek Walcott, who remains, sometimes to a fault, deeply enshrined in the Western ideologies of beauty and symmetry. S.'s willingness to draw on Rastafarianism, reggae, and the surreal madness of 1970s and 1980s Jamaica—complete with the twisted innovations of the dub music scene and the foregrounding of political ideologies even among the least educated of the population—all lead to the generation of poems that are complex and filled with the layered discourse of the urban setting.

This quality is tellingly revealed in S.'s play *Dog*, which, like *An Echo in the Bone*, would have a significant influence of the experimental dramas that would emerge in the Caribbean during the late 1970s and early 1980s. S. would employ an absurdist, Beckett-like technique of modern drama in a theatrical environment that was more comfortable with social realist and naturalist dramas. *Dog* is a grand allegory that examines class and race dynamics in Jamaican society. The work is set in contemporary Jamaica, to the extent that some of the events that are dealt with had immediate resonance in the society when it was staged. The themes of flight, of interclass warfare, of Rastafarianism, and of the hope of some kind of spiritual redemption all proved important to the Jamaicans at the time. *Dog* would be staged throughout the Caribbean and the influence of that work on other Caribbean dramatists is immeasurable.

S.'s final collection of poems, *Strategies*, appeared in 1989. This collection is filled with profoundly personal poems—particularly a cycle of letter poems to his son—that are lyrical and held together by a strong exploration of the bird-image that appeared in much of his earlier work. In S.'s poetry at this stage, one can sense a stronger indebtedness to the confessional poets of America, yet there is always a tension—the tension between the confessional mode and a social and political consciousness. It is this tension that marks S. as a distinctive poetic voice in Caribbean writing. S.'s work has always sought to find ways to extend the use of the Jamaican language in verse. His poems represent some of the most interesting examples of the continuum of West Indian language—the use of puns, allusions, proverbs, and other idiomatic expression and the games with syntax are all tackled by him in his writing.

FURTHER WORKS: *Terminus: A Play in One Act* (1966); *Uncle Time* (1973); *The Fantasy of Sir Gawain and the Green Knight* (1978); *Dreadwalk* (1982)

BIBLIOGRAPHY: McNeill, A., "D. S., Maker: Part 1, "Journeys,'" *Jamaica Journal*, 5 (1971): 49-52; Brown, S., "New Poetry from Jamaica," *New Voices*, 5 (1975): 48-50; Brown, L. W., *West Indian Poetry* (1978): 168-71; Omotoso, K., *The Theatrical Into Theatre: A Study of the Drama and Theatre of the English-Speaking Caribbean* (1982): 94-95; Smith, I. D., "The Poetics of Self: D. S.'s Dangerous Style," *CarQ*, 30 (1984): 23-32; Jonas, J., "The Carnivalesque World of D. S.'s *Strategies*," *Kyk-over-al*, 42 (1991):

69-70; Dawes, K., "Politics and Violence in D. S.'s *Dog*: A Study in Political Pessimism," *JWIL*, 6 (1994): 17-31; Gainor, E. J., ed., *Imperialism and Theatre: Essays on World Theatre, Drama and Performance* (1995)

—KWAME DAWES

SCOTT, Paul

English novelist, b. 25 Mar. 1920, London; d. 1 Mar. 1978, London

S., best known for the widely acclaimed work *The Raj Quartet*, was born in suburban North London, where he would continue to reside throughout most of his life. S.'s father was a commercial artist, his mother a former shop clerk with working-class roots. At sixteen, following his mother's wishes. S. left London's Winchmore Hill Collegiate School to train for a career in accountancy.

S. served as a supply officer during World War II; his duties took him to Malaysia, Burma, and India during the final phase of the British Empire. After the war, S. worked as a secretary at a small publishing firm; in 1950 he became a literary agent, and—by writing in his spare time—managed to publish a string of novels, including *Johnnie Sahib* (1952), *The Alien Sky* (1953), and *The Mark of the Warrior* (1958). All of these solid but rather undistinguished works deal in some way with British military figures on duty in foreign lands. In *A Male Child* (1956) S. effectively depicts the grim atmosphere of postwar Britain, but again centers on characters who spent the war years in Asian locales.

After *The Chinese Love Pavilion* (1960), the most deftly plotted and lushly written of his earlier novels, S. began writing fiction full-time. The fruits of his more focused attention soon began to show. Although *The Bender* (1963) is muddled and dull, both *The Birds of Paradise* (1962), a particularly fine novel, and *The Corrida at San Feliu* (1964), one of the more innovative English fictions of the 1960s, present characters of increasing intricacy while employing ever more sophisticated narrative techniques.

In 1964 S. revisited India and began to plan his next series of novels, including *The Jewel in the Crown* (1966), which revolves around the rape of a young Englishwoman during the closing years of English rule. In this novel—the first in what would become known as *The Raj Quartet*—S. reveals himself to be an absolute master of his craft, creating characters of considerable depth while using an abundance of historical material in a manner that is both imaginative and scrupulous.

In *The Day of the Scorpion* (1968), *The Towers of Silence* (1971), and *A Division of the Spoils* (1975), S. continues the story he began in *The Jewel in the Crown*, linking the series largely through the figure of Ronald Merrick, the tormented, sadistic British police official who emerges as one of the most complexly drawn and memorable figures in postwar fiction.

Some, including the novelist Salman RUSHDIE, have criticized *The Raj Quartet* for perpetuating, perhaps unintentionally, a series of racial stereotypes and colonialist assumptions. It is true that S. does not demonize the British in these novels; and yet, as other critics have pointed out, S. successfully avoids prejudice, condescension, and sentimentality in his depiction of Indian life. And he repeatedly makes clear, through Merrick, that he has no sympathy for the practice of rule by force and intimidation that is inevitably a part of any colonialist enterprise.

S.'s best single novel is, arguably, his last, *Staying On* (1977). Connected loosely to *The Raj Quartet*, it focuses on two elderly Britishers—Tusker Smalley and his wife Lucy—who first appear, briefly, in *The Day of the Scorpion*. Here, the two are determined to live as long as possible in their Indian home, despite the fact that national independence has hastened the departure of most of their fellow countrymen. This brilliantly structured novel is informed by a rich comic sensibility that is, regrettably, rarely displayed in his earlier fiction.

Although *Staying On* won Britain's prestigious Booker Prize (1977), the great increase in critical and popular acclaim for S.'s work undoubtedly owes most to the enormous success of the superb adaptation, for television, of *The Raj Quartet* (called *The Jewel in the Crown*), which features strong performances by a large cast of accomplished actors led by Dame Peggy Ashcroft.

As a growing number of critics and scholars have begun to suggest, *The Raj Quartet*—and many of S.'s other novels—will continue to survive on the strength of their own merit. S. was one of his generation's finest novelists, a gifted and disciplined artist who consistently offered humane portraits of men and women alive in turbulent times.

FURTHER WORKS: *I Gerontius: A Trilogy* (1941); *After the Funeral* (1979); *My Appointment with the Muse: Essays, 1961–75* (1986)

BIBLIOGRAPHY: Weinbaum, F. S., "P. S.'s India: *The Raj Quartet*," *Crit*, 20, 1 (1979): 100–10; Swinden, P., *P. S.: Images of India* (1980); Rao, K. B., *P. S.* (1980); Tedesco, J., and J. Popham, *Introducing The Raj Quartet* (1985); Rubin, D., *After the Raj: British Novels of India since 1947* (1986): 103–56; Spurling, H., *P. S.: A Life of the Author of The Raj Quartet* (1990); Moore, R., *P. S.'s Raj* (1990); Rushdie, S., "Outside the Whale," *Imaginary Homelands* (1991): 87–101

—BRIAN MURRAY

SCOTTISH LITERATURE

To insist upon a national character for Scottish literature is to fashion myth—a myth, nevertheless, that Scotsmen, particularly, regard seriously. Thus, the character is given as at the same time sentimental and dour, as bibulous and teetotal, as Calvinistic and democratic, as humane and miserly, as violent and shy, as anticosmopolitan and friendly: in short, as anomalous and paradoxical. Behind most of this anomaly and paradox, however, are such real opposites as the cultural outlook of the Highlands and of the Lowlands, Scots (the vernacular speech of Scotland) and Gaelic, Lallans (the historic speech of Lowland Scotland) and English, local attachment and preoccupation with exile. If 20th-c. Scottish literature is to be thought of as the creation of any writer who declares his nationality Scots, one must then consider works in Gaelic and English as well as in the Scots dialects.

Late 19th-c. Scottish writers had concentrated on the sentimental treacle of the Kailyard school, parochial satire, bothie (rustic, farmhand) humor, and whaup-and-heather (derring-do) romance. This approach continued into the early 20th c. with such poems as "Hamewith" (1900) by Charles Murray (1864–1941) and "Shy

Geordie" (c. 1922) by Helen B. Cruickshank (1886–1975). It is to be found, moreover, in James M. BARRIE and, with increasing skill, in the works of J. Logie Robertson (1846–1922), R. B. Cunninghame Graham (1852–1936), and John Buchan (1875–1940).

Early objection to these accents upon the tender and the homespun is evident in the grimness of Robert Louis Stevenson's (1850–1894) novel *Weir of Hermiston* (1896) and in the precise language of such poems as his "Epistle to Charles Baxter" (1875). Later and stronger reaction came with George Douglas Brown (1869–1902) in the novel *The House with the Green Shutters* (1901), an uncompromising study of Scottish brutality and decadence. Other reactions have been the translations of German ballads by Sir Alexander Gray (1882–1968), the lyricism and graceful simplicity of the verse of Violet Jacob (1863–1946), and the superior poetry of Marion Angus (1866–1946). On a longer scale, the sense of national identity that Scotland developed during World War I hastened the rejection of Kailyard tradition and quickened the first impulses of the Scottish renaissance. The war years heightened proletarian revolt against industrialism and weakened the conviction that in order to deal with the most basic human problems a Scotsman must use English.

The dominant feature of Scottish literature in the 20th c. has been the Scottish renaissance, the post–World War I movement born of reaction under the commanding spirit of Hugh MACDIARMID'S motto "Back to Dunbar." MacDiarmid, seeking a personal base from which to move forward in the 1920s, grandly conceived of a national regeneration, which was to begin with literature. His tough, masculine poem *A Drunk Man Looks at the Thistle* (1926) and his anthologies of current Scottish poetry encouraged others to treat serious and modern themes in an eclectic Scots that revived both dictionary usages and borrowed dialect idioms. Further experiments of this "mad Gael" came in the 1930s and thereafter, published in the magazine he edited, *Voice of Scotland* (1938–39, 1945–49, 1955–58).

Others were won over to the theme of revolt against the accepted order and to the medium—synthetic Scots. High success is to be read in such "lemanrie" (love poetry) as *Under the Eildon Tree* (1948; rev. ed., 1954) by Sydney Goodsir SMITH, "Letter to Hugh MacDiarmid" (1950) by Douglas Young (1913–1973), "Embro to the Ploy" (1952) by Robert Garioch (b. 1909), "The Tryst" (1948) by William SOUTAR, and "Orpheus" (1963) by Tom Scott (b. 1918).

Further impetus to the Scottish renaissance was given by the criticism of David Daiches (b. 1912), by the founding of the Saltire Society in 1936 and the launching of its quarterly, the *Saltire Review* in 1954, for the preservation, encouragement, and development of Scottish art, literature, and music. Poets like Goodsir Smith remained constant to the ideal of a synthetic Scots, fashioned from the language of 16th-c. *makars* (poets) and from local dialects with modern jargon. MacDiarmid, however, also championed Gaelic in his search for the true spirit of Scotland.

Gaelic writers, of course, had already been utilizing the qualities for which Gaelic is known: richness of sound from rhyme, assonance, and alliteration; traditional intricacies of syllabic meter; and sharp clarity. The finest modern examples of these qualities may be found in the poems *Dàin do Eimhir* (1943; *Songs to Eimhir*, 1971) by Somhairle Maclean (b. 1911) and *Fuaran Sléibh* (1948; mountain spring) by George Campbell Hay (b. 1915). Even when Hay writes in English, as in "The Kerry Shore" or "The Old Fisherman" in *Wind on Loch Fyne* (1948), his voice is that of the Gael. A similar voice speaks in some of the English poetry of

Norman MACCAIG and Joseph Macleod (b. 1903). More recently, Fionn MacColla (b. 1900), Derick Thomson (b. 1921), and Iain Crichton Smith (b. 1928) have contributed to the Gaelic revival.

From its start, the Scottish renaissance was countered by disparate influences. Public apathy was manifested in the poor reception given the *New Scottish Dictionary* (1935–76) and in the failure of both the *Saltire Review* in 1960 and of the *New Saltire Review* in 1964. What is more, English was the principal language in the schools, and London dominated the publishing market and the influential literary circles. Again, the purely regional concerns of much Scottish literature confronted a formidable challenge in the attitudes of those writers whose experience included World War II and its aftermath of nuclear weapons, space exploration, and student protest; such has been the challenge of David Craig (b. 1932), Alastair Mackie (b. 1925), and Robin Fulton (b. 1937), who shared the last *New Saltire Review* Poetry Prize in 1963.

MacDiarmid could not have had a more redoubtable opponent than Edwin MUIR, the first great metaphysical poet of Scotland, the finest critical intelligence, and the chief advocate of the Anglo-Scot position. Today the reputation of no other Scots poet rises more dramatically, worldwide, than Muir's. In his lectures *Scott and Scotland* (1936), Muir repudiated the Scottish renaissance, arguing that because a writer in Scots lacked an organic community, a major literary tradition, a unified diction, and a livelihood, he must therefore accept English as his medium and absorb English tradition. The measure of Muir's own accomplishments in poetry—*The Labyrinth* (1949), *One Foot in Eden* (1956)—as much as his critical persuasion—*The Estate of Poetry* (1962)—influenced others. MacCaig in *The Sinai Sort* (1957) and W. S. Graham (b. 1918) in *The Nightfishing* (1955) gave further proof that excellent poetry could be written in English by Scotsmen, and such poets as Lewis Spence (1874–1955) had already become increasingly impatient with the spirit of the renaissance.

One of the last to leave the movement was Maurice Lindsay (b. 1918), who had lent the renaissance a strong hand through his periodical *Poetry Scotland* (1944–49) and his anthology *Modern Scottish Poetry* (1946; 3rd ed., 1978). Lindsay prefaced his *Snow Warning, and Other Poems* (1962) with an assertion that English must be the dominant language of Scottish literature, only partly because television, through its wide dissemination of English-language programs, was drastically reducing opportunities for use of the Scots tongue. This tongue, Lindsay noted, had become little more than a local dialect and had scarcely at all been used in any literary work of significance for the contemporary reader. Lindsay, therefore, chose English for his new poems, and Liz Lochhead (b. 1948), Giles Gordon (b. 1940), and Douglas Dunn (b. 1942), several of the most promising younger poets today, also write in English.

Discontent with the use of the Scots tongues extends to the compilation of anthologies. Thus, in 1954 an anti-Lallans group led by W. Price Turner (b. 1927), editor of *The Poet* (1952–57), published *Eleven Scottish Poets*, a volume dedicated to Muir and including only works in English. In 1959 MacCaig's anthology of modern Scottish poetry, *Honour'd Shade*, printed poems by twenty-seven contributors. Two-thirds of the seventy-eight pieces are in English. Protesting the views of the nationalistic "Rose Street" establishment (the reference is to the Abbotsford, a pub on Rose Street in Edinburgh, which the literati frequented) propounded in this volume, seven "non-Abbotsford" poets (who regarded Sir Walter Scott's poetry as an unhappy influence) recorded their poems on tape as *Dishonour'd Shade* (1960). In this way younger poets like Ian Hamilton Finlay (b. 1925) and Tom Buchan (b. 1931) presented their new ideas. Finlay later joined Jessie McGuffie in founding the Wild Hawthorn Press to print such poetic broadsheets as *Poor, Old, Tired Horse* (1961–67), an attack upon MacDiarmid.

The Scottish renaissance extended beyond poetry, even though it failed to develop anything like a common prose idiom. Undoubtedly, during the first quarter of the 20th c. drama was the sickly child. Not a single Scottish playhouse existed in the early 1930s, and in 1939 only the Perth Repertory functioned as a fully professional, native enterprise. Vital advances occurred, however, in the 1940s: first in the establishment of the Glasgow Unity Theatre (1941), then in the Glasgow Citizens Theatre (1943) and the College of Drama (1950), with a bilingual system of training. The last two were incomparable legacies from James BRIDIE. In addition, the International Arts Festival established in Edinburgh in 1948 offered new opportunities to Scots playwrights and actors, as did the opening in Edinburgh of the Gateway Theatre in 1950 and the Traverse Theatre in 1963.

Bridie's reputation was made in London with some forty-two plays directed primarily toward an English audience, such as *The Anatomist* (1930) and *Susannah and the Elders* (1937). The last plays, however, like the moralities *The Baikie Charivari* (1951) and *The Queen's Comedy* (1950), were staged at home in Glasgow. Other dramatists have also left their mark. The playwright John Brandane (pseud. of Dr. John MacIntyre, 1869–1947) is remembered for *The Glen Is Mine* (1925), depicting conflict in Highland life. *Jamie the Saxt* (1937) by Robert MacLellan (b. 1907) and *The Lass wi' the Muckle Mou* (1950) by Alexander Reid (b. 1914) are light-hearted Scottish comedies written in Doric (rustic Scots). Promising material appeared in the experimental dramas of Neil M. Gunn (1891–1974), who turned to drama for such notable achievement as *The Ancient Fire* (1929); of Robert Kemp (b. 1908); and of Alexander Scott (b. 1920). Eric Linklater (1899–1974) occasionally turned from novels to sharply pointed satiric comedy like *Love in Albania* (1949); and Sydney Goodsir Smith turned to verse tragedy in *The Wallace* (1960), after having written his unpublished comedy *Colickie Meg*.

Three Scottish-born novelists gained wide popular favor in London: Compton Mackenzie (1883–1972) with *Carnival* (1912) and *Whisky Galore* (1947); John Buchan with *The Thirty-nine Steps* (1915) and *Witch Wood* (1927); Linklater with *White-Maa's Saga* (1929) and *Juan in America* (1931). Life in western Scotland has been treated in the fiction of such writers as J. MacDougal Hay (1881–1919), known for his *Gillespie* (1914); Alexander McArthur (1901–1947), known for his *No Mean City* (1935); and George Blake (1893–1940), known for his *The Valiant Heart* (1940). Western Scotland figures prominently in the work of three other novelists whose fiction is even more highly regarded: Neil Munro (1864–1930), Neil Gunn, and Fionn MacColla. In *The New Road* (1914), Munro as Stevenson of the Highlands wrote the finest historical romance published between Stevenson's work and Naomi Mitchison's (b. 1897) *The Bull Calves* (1947). Gunn wrote searchingly and beautifully of the crofting and fishing communities in Caithness and Sutherland. His *Sun Circle* (1933), *Butcher's Broom* (1934), and *Highland River* (1937) are high points of modern Scottish fiction. He is seconded in his concern for the Gael by MacColla, who, in *The Albannach* (1932), angrily protests the wastage of men and land in the Highlands.

Certainly the most impressive extended work of fiction is the trilogy *A Scots Quair—Sunset Song* (1932), *Cloud Howe* (1933), and *Grey Granite* (1934)—by Lewis Grassic Gibbon (pseud. of

James Leslie Mitchell, 1901–1935). Gibbon's theme that nothing endures but the land is stated dramatically through Chris Guthrie, a crofter's daughter born to live out her life on the northeast coast below Aberdeen. Gibbon's Scots, used for narrative as well as dialogue, has been cited by critics as the most promising attempt yet made toward the creation of a modern Scots prose. Another remarkable work is Sydney Goodsir Smith's *Carotid Cornucopius* in the revised and enlarged edition of 1964. A complex wordplay on Edinburgh's modern "roarin' Willies" (the phrase, from a song by Robert Burns, refers to the bibulous literati of the city), this novel was greeted by MacDiarmid as "the very quintessence of Scottishness." Less ardent patriots may prefer the truths of Scottishness in the diaries of William Soutar or in such impressive autobiographies as John Buchan's *Memory Hold-the-Door* (1940), Compton Mackenzie's *My Life and Times* (10 vols., 1963–1971), and Edwin Muir's *An Autobiography* (1954).

Today the literature of Scotland can be described neither as a "cultural ruin" (Ian Hamnett) nor as the rich harvest forecast by Gunn in the 1930s. Since 1966 the University of Edinburgh Press has been publishing an impressive annual anthology titled *Scottish Poetry*. Series devoted to Scottish writing have been initiated by both Scottish and English publishers. Among the new faces, however, one sees no single unified movement but rather a general agreement that Scots men and women choose to write about "anything that comes up their backs" and in whatever manner inspires them. The famous Scottish historian William Robertson (1721–1793) anticipated that, as a result of Scotland's union with England in 1707, English would eventually dominate almost to the exclusion of Scots. Now is the day of this "almost." Yet Scots hangs on with amazing tenacity and capacity, as volumes like Tom Scott's *The Ship, and Ither Poems* (1962), Sydney Goodsir Smith's *Collected Poems* (1975), and Robert Garioch's *Selected Poems 1943–1974* (1975) attest. Outside the vernacular, Norman MacCaig has moved from "apocalypticism" to the stature of a Muir or MacDiarmid. His later volumes, like *Rings on a Tree* (1968) and *A Man in My Position* (1969), present beautifully structured pieces, full of dramatic phrases, brilliant details, and intense feeling for nature, with rich imagery from everyday experience of Edinburgh and the western Highlands.

New and old novelists continue to draw from Scottish materials. Clifford Hanley (b. 1922) offers a jolly dollop of nostalgia for Glasgow tenements in his *Dancing in the Streets* (1958) and jesting upon the modern theater in *The Redhaired Bitch* (1969). Ten of Robin Jenkins's (b. 1912) novels are set in Scotland; moreover, when the setting is not Scotland, the protagonist is likely to be a Scotsman like Ronald McDonald of *The Expatriates* (1971). Muriel SPARK and James Kennaway (1928–1968) are thought to have lost contact with contemporary Scottish environment. Kennaway's *Some Gorgeous Accident* (1967) has no Scottish element; but four of his other novels reveal an active Scottish memory, especially *Tunes of Glory* (1956), with its hero, ex-piper Jock Sinclair. *The Prime of Miss Jean Brodie* (1961) suggests that Spark, like Kennaway, has done her finest work in an explicitly Scottish novel. Her other novels are sparse in obviously Scottish elements; yet in reading any one of them, a person would be wise to recall that this author, the most widely praised living novelist of Scottish birth, identifies her exile from Edinburgh as the key to her life.

New vitality, renewal of Scottish situations and motifs, experimentation, and nationalistic tones mark those novels of the more recent generation, such as Allan Sharp's (b. 1934) *A Green Tree in Gedde* (1965), William McIlvanney's (b. 1936) *Docherty* (1975), and Elspeth Davie's (dates n.a.) *Creating a Scene* (1971). Like many another Scot in a long line, Elspeth Davie writes excellent short stories as well as novels (for example, *The Spark, and Other Stories*, 1968). Indeed, such a volume as *Modern Scottish Short Stories* (1978) includes the work of twenty-nine authors who represent contemporary Scottish fiction at its very best in their vigor and imagination: the novelists Davie, Gunn, Spark, Kennaway, Linklater, and Jenkins, the poets George Mackay Brown (b. 1927), Giles Gordon, Iain Crichton Smith, and Douglas Dunn. Together they stand on the common ground of love for, and understanding of, Scotland herself, various though their subjects and voices may be.

Scottish Literature since 1980

The 1980s marked a boom in modern Scottish fiction with an urge for new work and a growing opportunity to be published. Two distinct tendencies are obvious: sentimentalism and realism. One major shift is apparent: that from rural to urban subject matter. Some thirty-three Scottish novels were published from 1978 to 1981; first place goes to Alasdair Gray's (b. 1934) *Lanark* (1981), which Douglas Clifford praises as "a magnificent surrealist satire on the West of Scotland." Other novelists contending for recognition were Robert Jamieson with *Thin Wealth* (1986), continuing the promise of his first novel *Soor Hearts* (1983), and Ian Rankin (b. 1960) with his admirably deft and intense first novel *The Flood* (1986). Probably nobody strove more convincingly during this period than William McIlvanney (b. 1936). His *The Big Man* (1985), like his third and best-known novel *Docherty* (1975), concentrates on the working class; but, unlike *Docherty*, it turns to English, not Scots, for the dialogue.

The novelist Stuart Hood (dates n.a.) emerged in 1986 as a very skilled writer with publication of his second novel, *A Storm from Paradise*, which won the Scottish Book of the Year Prize. A competitor with Hood was Iain BANKS who published his psychosurreal mystery on the Fourth Railway Bridge, *The Bridge*, in 1986. Neither Ronald Frame's (b. 1953) *A Woman of Judah*, an all-the-way English novel by a Scotsman, nor William Boyd's (b. 1952) *The New Confession* was so successful in 1987 as John Burrowes's (dates n.a.) Glaswegian *Incomers*, although the affectingly mythic fourth novel of Dominic Cooper (b. 1944), *The Horn Fellow*, came near. Closing out this decade were the republication of Fred Urquhart's (b. 1912) *Time Well Knit* (1988), and the powerfully elegiac *The Sound of the Sea* (1989) by the poet-dramatist Colin MacKay (b. 1944).

The short story as well as the novel flourished during the period 1975–1990; indeed, Scotsmen believe that Scotland all but invented the modern short story. That these stories are excellent can be read from *Modern Scottish Short Stories* (1978), which includes the work of twenty-nine authors representing contemporary Scottish fiction at its very best in their vigor and imagination and in their common love for and understanding of Scotland, various though their subjects and voices may be. Here again are the novelists Muriel SPARK, James Kennaway (1928–1968), Eric Linklater (1899–1974), and Robin Jenkins (b. 1912); here again the poets George Mackay Brown (b. 1921), Giles Gordon (b. 1940), and Iain Crichton Smith (b. 1928).

Each passing year marks new successes, like the award-winning ones of Jackson Webb (b. 1940) and the 1980 *Prosepiece*, a volume of Carl Macdougall's (dates n.a.) short stories. Between 1980 and 1985, the reader had the stories of Ian Stephen's (b. 1955) *Living at the Edge* (1982) and those of Alasdair Gray's *Unlikely Stories, Mostly* (1983). Thriving, the short story lost no force as manifested in the collection *I Can Sing, Dance, Rollerskate, and Other Stories by Scottish Writers* (1988), the work of eighteen authors, generally born in the 1950s. The poet Douglas Dunn (b. 1942) turned his powers of clinical observation to the short story, publishing his *Secret Villages* in 1986. Two years later, Irish-born Bernard MacLaverty (b. 1942) won a National Cash Register Award with his collection *The Great Profundo* (1988); and the following year, William McIlvanney published his first collection, *Walking Wounded* (1989), a volume loaded with this author's consistently intelligent observation and strong sense of character.

John Linklater's edition of short stories, *The Red Hog of Colima* (1989), presents mainly new writers like Ken Ross (b. 1941), as does Collin's *A Roomful of Birds* (1990). The outstanding short-story writer Fred Urquhart displays his technical mastery of both Scots and English in two volumes of his own short stories, both published in 1980: *A Diver in China Seas* and *Proud Lady in a Cage*. Urquhart's collected stories *Full Scors* (1990) would support this judgment.

Some would argue that today the literature of Scotland may be described neither as "a cultural ruin" nor as "the rich harvest" forecast by Gunn in the 1930s; but never before has the Scots writer been offered at home more hope to be published, insufficient though the encouragement still appears to a few. Duncan Glen's (b. 1933) periodical *Akros* had life from 1965 to 1983. Since 1966, the University of Edinburgh Press has been publishing an impressive annual called *Scottish Poetry*. In 1969 Southside, a new Scottish imprint, announced its first publication as Sydney Goodsir SMITH's *Fifteen Poems and a Play*; a year later the literary magazine *Chapman* first appeared, and in 1970 Calder and Boyars published *Contemporary Scottish Verse*, edited by Norman MACCAIG and Alexander Scott (b. 1920), as the first volume of the Scottish Library; and in 1972 Routledge & Keagan Paul published *The MacDiarmid Reader* as the first volume of the Scottish Series. Thomas Crawford at Aberdeen University became in 1974 the first editor of *The Scottish Literary Journal*, published by the Association for Scottish Literary Studies.

Tessa Ransford (b. 1938) founded "The School of Poets" in 1981, a time when the Hawthornden International Retreat for Writers was going strong. *Orbis* had its issue of Scottish poetry in 1985, the same year Peter Kravitz dropped "New" from *The New Edinburgh Review* and gave that literary magazine another motto: "To gather all the rays of culture into one whole." A year later, *New Writing Scotland* began to be published with Alexander Scott and James Hutchinson as editors; its intent has been to become "a showcase for new writers." *Lines Review* celebrated its one-hundredth number in 1987, and in January 1991 entered its thirty-ninth year. Today the phenomenon of the corporate sponsor behind such endeavors as the United Biscuit £5,000 check or, in 1987, the first McVitie Prize for Scottish Writer of the Year is as accepted as the Edinburgh Book Festival with its 1.6 miles of shelved books in its fourth year of 1989, a year that showed a 100 percent increase in ticket sales.

Among women writers, Spark has published more than seventeen novels since 1957, including *Symposium* (1990), a "rich brew" about original sin, a fit subject for this Catholic expatriate novelist. Along the way of her career, she has turned from the novel to write a play, a children's book, poetry, criticism, and biography. Janet Caird (b. 1913) composes flowing free verse, but also traditional verse like her lovely "Black Night" (1987) in cinquains, opening "I could not sleep for sorrow"; in addition, as a prose writer, she has short stories, a children's book, and six novels to her credit. The homely muse of Helen B. Cruickshank (1886–1975) found its voice in Hugh MACDIARMID'S editions of *Northern Lights* (1920–1922). Marion Angus (1866–1946), rooted like Cruickshank in the northeast, achieved technical mastery for the poetry of her *The Lilt and Other Poems* (1922). Anne Stevenson (b. 1933) had published seven volumes before Oxford published her *Selected Poems, 1956–1986* (1987), whereas Agnes C. Carnegie (d. 1984) was not heard until 1985 when the Aberdeen University Press posthumously published a selection from her poetry entitled *The Timeless Flow*.

The great efflorescence of women's writing in Scotland that leads to the 21st c. cannot be missed; faces of women seem everywhere. For Anne Born (b. 1924) it is translating *Spring Tide* (1990) from the Danish of Pia TAFDRUP and, thus, extending the line from Willa Muir's (b. 1890) great translations of Kafka and Asch; for Tessa Ransford it is writing six volumes of poems, often metaphysical and religious, and then taking on (1989) the editing of *Lines*. Other Scots women like Judith Weir (b. 1954) have looked to music and the writing of a libretto for Scottish opera, such as her *The Vanishing Bridegroom* (1990), or like Mary Gladstone (dates n.a.) have written or adapted plays. Liz Lochhead (b. 1947) has published several volumes of poetry, none better than her first, *Memo for Spring* (1972). Her witty, natural, alert muse delights in sexual scenarios and aspects of womankind. Working usually in English, Lochhead has been turning more and more to composition of plays and revues. She has translated *Tartuffe* successfully into Scots and published in 1985 her *True Confessions and New Clichés*, hilariously satirical dramatic monologues, sketches, and reviews for live performance on the stage.

Numbers of other Scotswomen today favor writing novels or poems or both. First novels have come from Elizabeth Sutherland (b. 1926), *The Weeping Tree* (1980), and from Agnes Owens (b. 1926), *Gentlemen of the West* (1984). Canongate reprinted Nan Shepherd's (b. 1893) *The Quarry Wood* (1928) in 1987, and Faber and Faber reissued Emma TENNANT'S *The Bad Sister* (1978) in 1989. Tennant's *Two Women of London: The Strange Case of Ms Jekyll and Mrs. Hyde* (1989) alludes to Hogg's *Justified Sinner* and is Scottish through and through. Joan Lingard (b. 1932) worked the theme of Edinburgh's respectability into her *The Prevailing Wind* (1964); she has nine other novels and eighteen books for young people, which won her a coveted West German award for children's literature in 1987. Rosalind Brackenbury's (b. 1942) ninth novel, *Taxus* (1988), is a fine example of how Scotland can evoke poetry in a Scotswoman; again, love of Scotland is written deeply into Margaret Elphinstone's (b. 1948) *A Sparrow's Flight* (1990). Most recently, more than two-thirds of Scottish short stories have been written by women like Moira Burgess (b. 1936), editor with Hamish Whyte of *Scottish Short Stories* (1985).

Frequently, the latest women poets got their start in *Lines*; for example, almost one-third of the poets published in the September 1989 issue are women. Such are Anne Turner (b. 1925) and Valerie Thornton (b. 1954). Having found encouragement, such poets go on to a volume of their own; so it has been with Elizabeth Jennings (b. 1926) and Gail Fox (b. 1943).

Three of the best known women poets writing today are Val Warner (b. 1946), Valerie Gillies (b. 1948), and Sheena Blackhall (b. 1947). Warner's *Before Lunch* (1986), published thirteen years after her first volume, displays a wide knowledge of languages. Gillies has published three volumes of clear, cool, sharp, poems as

well as other books, radio scripts, and reviews. Blackhall has become an accomplished singer. An early volume *The Cyard's Kist* (1986) reveals the influence of ballad and folksong; the poetry of *The Spark O' the Land* (1987), *Hame-Drauchtit* (1988), and *The Nor'East Neuk* (1989) is composed refreshingly and naturally in Scots, the mastery of which is apparent elsewhere in Blackhall's collection of short stories entitled *A Nippick o' Nor'East Tales* (1989).

Scots writers, men and women, with their evergrowing output of new titles, make it seem as though a literary renaissance will mark the 1990s North o' the Tweed. Among the ranks, one sees no unified movement but rather a general agreement that Scots men and women choose to write about "anything that comes up their backs and in whatever manner inspires them."

Variety can be an index of vitality. Scotland's contemporary poets certainly include disparate accents: the Freudian tones of Robert Duncan (1919–1988), the surrealism of Tom Leonard (b. 1944), the symbolism of G. F. Dutton (b. 1924), the pastoralism of Margaret Gillies Brown (b. 1929), the visual primer of Ian Hamilton Finlay (b. 1925), the free verse of Tom Scott (1918-1995), the "instamatic" poems of Edwin Morgan (b. 1920), the delightful rhymes of John Mole's (b. 1941) children's verses, the black humor of George Macbeth, the Orientalism of Ron Butler (b. 1949), the light verse of Gavin Ewart (1916-1995), the performance poetry of Brian McCabe (b. 1951), and the poetry of Andrew Greig (b. 1951) on radio.

This vitality has no geographical bounds in Scotland. Expatriates apart, in such far places as Australia and Nigeria, Canada and San Francisco, Scots writers at home compose in every corner of the old kingdom. From the Burns Country come the scatological excursions of William S. Graham (b. 1948) and the consistently good poems of the Celtic scholar-poet William Neill (b. 1922) in eight collections—Gaelic, Scots, and English–the latest being *Making Tracks* (1988).

In the demotic speech of Glasgow invigorated by Irish and other foreign elements are Alan Hayton's (b. 1967) *Far Cry from 1945* (1988), Frank Kuppner's (b. 1951) poetry in four books (1984–1989), William Montgomarie's (b. 1934) *From Time to Time* (1985) with its scholarly free verse, and Tom Leonard's "A Priest came on at Merkland Street." Maurice Lindsay (b. 1918) and Edwin Morgan are sons of Glasgow; so is Robert Crawford (b. 1959), a writer of ever-increasing stature. Glasgow University professor, coeditor of *Verse*, critic on Eliot or Kuppner, short-story writer in *Sterts and Stobies* (1985), and poet in *A Scottish Assembly* (1990), Crawford expresses his love for Glasgow and Scotland. His prize-winning verses are *pang'd fu'o'* interest in innovation, biting wit, and delightful humor.

Across from Glasgow, in Edinburgh, Stewart Conn (b. 1936), Alan Bold (b. 1943), and Alastair Fowler (b. 1930) take places in volumes of contemporary Scottish verse, as James Meek (b. 1962) puts Edinburgh at the heart of his first novel *McFarlane Boils the Sea* (1989), as Rayne Mackinnon (b. 1937) makes an Edinburgh hospital the base of his first volume of poems, *Northern Elegies* (1986), and as Hugh McMillan (b. 1955) fills his first book of poetry, *Triumph of the Air* (1990), with the residents, pubs, and public places of Auld Reekie.

Above Edinburgh, in the east neuk o' Fife, are the four poets John Brewster (b. 1957), William Hershaw (b. 1957), Henry Holton (b. 1949), and Tom Hubbard (dates n.a.) composing verses on the Fife environment and community to be found in their *Four Fife Poets: Fower Brigs to a Kinrik* (1988). Nourished by Fife is also the poet and short-story writer Christopher Rush (b. 1944).

Sharing the northeast with Sheena Blackhall is the Aberdeen psychiatrist Ken Norrice (b. 1924) whose self-questioning punctuates the themes of sterility, escape, and maternity, most notably in *When Truth Is Known* (1989). Norrice's fellow poet David Morrison (b. 1941), vividly Scottish, offers poems that center on Caithness and isolation. The anthology *Ten Northeast Poets* (1985) represents older poetry of 1900–1950; the anthology *Moments in A Glass House* (1988) offers the verses of five young poets, serious and otherwise unpublished.

Far out to sea in the Shetlands, William J. Tait (b. 1918) recovers forty years of his poetry in *A Day between Weathers: Collected Poems 1938–1978* (1980), written in Scots, English, and Shetland speech. South in the Orkneys, George Mackay Brown has written Orcadian novels like *The Golden Bird* (1987) and short stories spoken of as "prose poems" like those in *The Masked Fisherman* (1990). Tait's *The Wreck of the Archangel* (1990) is excellent poetry with kennings, compounds, and archaisms, fine use of alliteration, and deep religious conviction.

The most illustrious island voice belongs to Iain Crichton Smith from the Hebridean Isle of Lewis. In a way, all of the more than fifty volumes by Smith may be said to be rooted in Lewis; for example, he tells the story of his life in the fifty-nine autobiographical poems of *A Life* (1986). A previous volume, *Selected Poems, 1955–1980* (1982), is Robert Fulton's choice of superlative poems from Smith's five earlier books of poetry; *The Village and Other Poems* (1989) shows the continuing development of a major poet and the luminosity of his art. Subtle, gentle, original, complex—a poem by Smith is the statement of a true island poet. Much of Smith's recent work is a turning from the poem to the novel, such as *In the Middle of the Wood* (1987), to the short story (*Selected Stories*, 1990), to the essay replete with loyalty and allegiance to Lewis (*Towards the Human*, 1987), to translation from Gaelic into English (Duncan Ban MacIntyre's *Ben Dorain*, repub. 1988), and to editing (*Twelve More Modern Scots Poets*, 1987).

Today Gaelic, Scots, and English serve Scottish literature. Thus Iain Smith will compose in Gaelic and then make his own translation into English. The diction of Duncan Glen is genuinely, everyday Scots diction (e.g., the poems in *Tales To Be Told*, 1988), and the poems in Raymond Vettese's (b. 1950) *The Richt Noise and Ither Poems* (1988) support that poet's belief that Scots is "the richt noise tae hurl at the storm's rattle."

Scots got one of its strongest boosts in 1984 when William Laughton Lorimer published his mind-boggling *The New Testament in Scots*, a volume Billy Kay called "the most important single book published in Scotland since World War II." Obviously it is likely to remain a major influence on the majority of Scottish writers far into the 21st c. Another big boost was given to Scots in 1990 with the publication of Isabail Macleod's *The Scots Thesaurus*. Even without such upliftings, Scottish writers are not likely to renounce Scots just as long as any one of them gives ear to the utter beauty of lines like these, from William SOUTAR'S "The Tryst" (1988): "A' thru the nicht we spak nae word, / Nor sinder'd bane frae bane, / A' thru the nicht I heard her hert, / Gane soundin' wi' my ain."

BIBLIOGRAPHY: Wittig, K., *The Scottish Tradition in Literature* (1958); MagCaig, N. and A. Scott, eds., Introduction to *Contemporary Scottish Verse* (1970): 5-22; Garioch, R., *Made in Scotland* (1974); Lindsay, M., *Modern Scottish Poetry* (1976); Lindsay, M., *History of Scottish Literature* (1977); Wilson, N., ed., *Scottish Writing and Writers* (1977); Hart, F. R., *The Scottish Novel* (1978);

Urquhart, F., Introduction to F. Urquhart and G. Gordon, eds., *Modern Scottish Short Stories* (1978): vi-x; Lindsay, M., ed. *As I Remember: Ten Scottish Authors Recall How Writing Began for Them* (1979); Aitken, W. R., *Scottish Literature in English and Scots* (1982); Daiches, D., *Literature and Gentility in Scotland* (1982); Royle, T., *The Macmillan Companion to Scottish Literature* (1983); Thomson, D. S., *The Companion to Gaelic Scotland* (1983); Bold, A., *Modern Scottish Literature* (1983); Watson, R., *The Literature of Scotland* (1984); Scott, A., *Voices of Our Kind*, 3rd ed. (1987); Craig, C., *The History of Scottish Literature* (1988), Vol. 4; Gardner-Medwin, A., and J. H. Williams, *A Day Estivall* (1990); Macleod, I., *The Scots Thesaurus* (1990)

—ROBERT D. THORNTON

SEBBAR, Leïla

Algerian novelist, short-story writer, and essayist, b. 19 Nov. 1941, Aflou

S. is the daughter of an Algerian father and French mother. During her childhood in Algeria she witnessed the nation's war of independence, and moved to France at the age of seventeen. She pursued her university studies in Aix-en-Provence and then Paris, where she has lived since 1963. In addition to writing novels and stories, S. contributed to the newspaper *Sans Frontière*, which was created primarily for immigrant readers.

S. was one of the first women to write about the lives of North African immigrants in France. Belonging simultaneously to two cultures, S. writes from the perspective of both insider and outsider when probing the French and Algerian communities that figure in her novels. Positioning herself as a woman in geographical and psychological exile, she writes of the various difficulties encountered by "crossbreeds" who are torn between warring nations. S. uses fiction to understand experiences of being uprooted and displaced, which she elaborates upon in a collection of correspondences with Canadian author Nancy Huston (b. 1953) entitled *Lettres parisiennes. Autopsie de l'exil* (1986; Parisian letters. Autopsy of Exile).

S. is especially interested in the fragmentation of the second generation of Magrebian immigrants born and raised in France, known as the Beurs. Her most well-known novel, *Shérazade, 17 ans, brune, frisée, les yeux verts* (1992; *Shérazade: Missing, aged 17, dark curly hair, green eyes*, 1991), depicts a young Beur runaway named Shérazade who spends much of her time viewing French paintings of North African women. Through Shérazade, S. critiques this Orientalist art, which distorts Eastern cultures to suit the fantasies of French men wanting to see beyond the veils of Muslim women in European colonies. The novel stages a reversal of power in which Shérazade speaks against representations of women from her culture and refuses to become an object for photographers who find her exotic. Like the princess-narrator in the *Arabian Nights* after whom Shérazade is named, S. employs the power of representing to express her own interpretations of characters and events. The sequels to the novel, *Les carnets de Shérazade* (1985; the notebooks of Shérazade) and *Le fou de Shérazade* (1991; Sherazade's fool), similarly express women's versions of their own culture, thus appropriating the power of expression and representation which was formerly reserved for the French.

S. often employs the technique of literary montage, portraying the thoughts and experiences of diverse characters that are woven together in complex patterns. She prefers an "indirect libre" style which moves from the descriptive exterior to characters' inner thoughts, concentrating on psychology rather than events. S.'s settings are usually French suburbs inhabited by immigrant families, places that are also explored in the novels of Cameroonian Calixthe BEYALA. In *Les carnets de Shérazade* S. draws connections between experiences of urban and rural exiles, as Shérazade is joined by a Magrebian woman running from farm life and the restrictions placed upon her by her family.

Although S. emigrated from Algeria to France, her protagonists often dream of escaping marginalization by fleeing to Algeria, Morocco, or Tunisia. While the richness and complexities of the traditions found in cultures of the Magreb are given a deep appreciation, they are also often critiqued for their treatment of women, whose experiences of confinement and domination by paternal authorities lead them to self-exile. Always concerned with the vast diversity of immigrants' lives, S. published a collection of short stories by a variety of authors entitled *Une enfance algérienne* (1997; An Algerian Childhood). In a world where Western misrepresentations of Muslims often engender ignorance and animosity, S.'s thoughtful counter-representations offer an important corrective as well as fascinating reading.

FURTHER WORKS: *On tue les petites filles* (1978); *Le pédophile et la maman* (1980); *Fatima ou les Algériennes au square* (1981); *Des femmes dans la maison* (1981); *Le Chinois vert d'Afrique* (1984); *Parle mon fils, parleà ta mère* (1984); *J. H. cherche âme soeur* (1987); *La négresse et l'enfant* (1990); *La jeune fille au balcon* (1996)

BIBLIOGRAPHY: DuPlessis, N., "L. S., Voice of Exile," *WLT*, 23 (Spring 1989): 415-17; Bruner, C., "La négresse à l'enfant," *WLT*, 65 (Spring 1991): 347-48; Mortimer, M., "On the Road: L. S.'s Fugitive Heroines," *RAL*, 23, 2 (1992): 195-202; Woodhull, W., "Exile," *YFS*, 82 (1993): 82-89; Woodhull, W., *Transfigurations of the Magreb* (1993): 102-33

—ELLIE HIGGINS

SEEBERG, Peter

Danish novelist and short-story writer, b. 22 June 1925, Skrydstrup

S. received his M.A. in Danish and comparative literary history from the University of Copenhagen in 1950. During the 1950s he worked for the National Museum in Copenhagen, the Hanseatic Museum in Bergen, and the Historical Museum in Ålborg before becoming the assistant curator at the Diocesan Museum in Viborg in 1960. S. participated in Danish archaeological expeditions to Kuwait in 1960 and 1961–62 and in the Jens Munk commemorative expedition to the Churchill River in Canada in 1964. In 1977 he received the Prize of the Danish Academy.

S.'s novels and short stories all deal with existential and ontological problems. Absurdity and discontinuity are the major characteristics of contemporary life, with alienation and loss of identity as the resultant condition of modern man. S.'s neutral, matter-of-fact tone keeps the reader at a reflective distance, and the accurate accounts are scaled down to underscore the few but basic

EXISTENTIALIST themes. The sparse yet exact descriptive details serve to intensify and augment the realistic images, until they become symbolic.

The novel *Bipersonerne* (1956; the secondary characters) takes place in a German work camp during World War II, whose slave-laborers are participating in the making of Nazi propaganda films. The Dane, Sim, is an outsider, who voluntarily joins the camp in order to seek reality in the midst of events. However, the barren, routine life in the camp while Germany is being bombed is as meaningless as the planned propaganda films, which never materialize.

Powerlessness and unreality are further illustrated in *Fugls føde* (1957; bird's scrapings), in which a nihilistic writer lives in an unfinished house surrounded by scaffolding in an anonymous suburb. The almost arrogantly self-abasing protagonist never succeeds in writing a single line of "something that is real," even when an acquaintance offers him a large sum of money for doing so. Here the identity crisis is the outcome of the self-perpetuating reflectiveness—supposedly a typical writer's problem—which hinders an immediate or "real" participation in life.

The short stories in *Eftersøgningen* (1962; the search) each focus on one problem, one characteristic, or one attitude. Through this isolation of subjects from larger contexts and the concentration on one question, S. creates a sense of absurdity. In the title story a man who has become involved in a search intensifies his efforts when the search clearly has become purposeless. Not the goal but the search itself has become important. In "Hullet" (the hole) the diggers do not know why they have been employed to dig a hole, nor how big it should be. There is much humor in the description of their various reactions to this meaningless task. There are no inherent meanings, only different attitudes; and if any values are to be found in this nihilistic universe, it is within a certain attitude. The main character in "Patienten" ("The Patient," 1973) has limb after limb amputated until nothing is left of the original person. His identity is affirmed, however, because his wife declares that she still loves him for what he is.

In the novel *Hyrder* (1970; shepherds) the protagonist, after an automobile accident, exists only as a body without consciousness. His "existence," however, continues indirectly, expressed through various symbols but cut off from direct communication with others. Thus separated from the other characters, he is gradually transformed, into a "thing," and the reification process has become complete.

S.'s grim understanding of crises of identity has not hampered his own productivity and effectiveness. Besides being an innovative and respected museum curator and adapter of literary works for other media, he holds a firm position in contemporary literature as a productive modernist writer of significant originality.

FURTHER WORKS: *Jens Munks Minde-Ekspedition* (1965, with Thorkild Hansen); *Ferai* (1970); *Dinosaurusens sene eftermiddag* (1974); *Erobringen af Fyn* (1975); *Argumenter for benåding* (1976); *Efter middagssluren* (1976); *En lille museborg tilligemed en historie om en mus* (1977); *Påselve dagen* (1978); *Ved havet* (1978); *Hovedrengøring* (1979); *Om fjorten dage* (1981)

BIBLIOGRAPHY: Mitchell, P. M., *A History of Danish Literature*, 2nd ed. (1971): 316; Borum, P., *Danish Literature* (1979): 101–2; Rossel, S. H., *A History of Scandinavian Literature 1870–1980* (1982): 326–28

—CHARLOTTE SCHIANDER GRAY

SEFERIS, George

(pseud. of Yorghos Seferiadhis) Greek poet, essayist, and critic, b. 29 Feb. 1900, Smyrna, Ottoman Empire (now Izmir, Turkey); d. 20 Sept. 1971, Athens

From Athens, where his family moved in 1914, S. went to Paris, where he reluctantly studied law at the Sorbonne (1918–24) while writing verse and familiarizing himself with contemporary French poetry. During the 1922 Asia Minor disaster, Smyrna, his native city, was retaken by the Turks and its Greek population displaced; this loss gave S. a sense of permanent exile, a feeling later reinforced by his itinerant career as a diplomat. Upon graduation from the Sorbonne he entered the Greek diplomatic service, serving first at the Ministry of Foreign Affairs. In 1931 he was appointed Greek vice-consul in London; it was during his tour of duty there that he discovered the poetry of T. S. ELIOT, whose style greatly influenced him and whose *The Waste Land* he later translated (1936). S. subsequently served as consul in Koritsa, Albania (1936–38), and as a press officer in Athens (1939). He married in 1941, and after the German invasion served with the Greek government-in-exile in Egypt, South Africa, and Italy. Soon after the liberation he returned to Greece and held a number of diplomatic posts, including ambassador to Great Britain (1957–62). He received numerous honorary degrees and awards, including the Nobel Prize for literature in 1963.

S.'s two early poetry collections, *Strofi* (1931, *Turning Point*, 1967) and *I sterna* (1932, *The Cistern*, 1967), springing from his deep acquaintance with SYMBOLISM, particularly the poetry of Mallarmé and VALÉRY, contained considerable technical experimentation together with a masterful use of colloquial Greek and other elements drawn from early Greek poetry, folk songs, and ballads. The poems are the best Greek specimens of *poésie pure*, especially "Erotikos loghos" (1930; "Erotikos Logos," 1967), with its compact lyrical beauty and power.

These collections, while marking the closing of the symbolist period in Greek poetry, were a prelude to the era of modernism, marked by the publication of S.'s *Mythistorima* (1935; *Mythistorema*, 1960), in which, leaving lyricism behind, he assimilated what he learned from CAVAFY, ELIOT, and Ezra POUND as well as from the ancient Greek dramatists and poets, who were perpetually to enrich his tragic sense of life. In *Mythistorima* S. attained a maturity and an originality of style that was to be remarkably his own and has been greatly influential on the development of modern Greek verse. Besides the poems in *Mythistorima*, those that achieved the widest popularity and are landmarks of S.'s middle period are "Santorini" (1935; "Santorini," 1960), "Me ton tropo tou G. S." (1936; "In the Manner of G. S.," 1960), "vasilias this Asinis" (1940; "The King of Asine," 1960), and "Telefteos stathmos" (1944; "Last Stop," 1960).

Highly conscious of the "language problem"—the conflicts over the use of the demotic or *katharevousa* (modern classical)—S. chose to perfect the vernacular, the language spoken by literate Greeks, denuding it of its burden of ornaments and writing a natural, proselike verse, predominantly dramatic, tragic in essence, compact and highly suggestive in its apparent simplicity and directness. With this language he was able to express a deep and painful mythical-historical awareness of the modern Greek consciousness. Contemporary personal and historical experience is deepened and enriched through reference to classical myth. The result is a personal mythology projected through image, symbol, and metaphor, in which the present is always bending under the weight of past memories. The Greek landscape and seascape, the barren soil, the mountains, the islands, the rocks, the ruins, the mutilated statues, the empty cisterns, and the wrecks of ships—all are carriers and reminders of a long historical experience uniting the living with the dead.

"Wherever I travel," S. wrote, "Greece wounds me." The poet's persona is a modern embodiment of the wandering Ulysses. The Ulyssean identity was further developed in his poetry in the persona of Stratis Thalassinos (Strates the sailor) in three collections: *Imerologhio katastromatos A'* (1940; *Logbook 1*, 1967), *Imerologhio katastromatos B'* (1944; *Logbook 2*, 1967), and *Imerologhio katastromatos C'* (1965; *Logbook 3*, 1967). The first was written mostly in Koritsa, Albania, when he was desperately lonely, during the time that ominous war clouds were gathering. The second deals with the poet's experience as an exile in South Africa and in Italy while waiting for the return that does not promise to give solace. The third is devoted to Cyprus—its ancient and eternal Greekness and its struggle for liberation.

S.'s long poem *Kihli* (1947; *Thrush*, 1967), composed on the island of Poros, is his Greek equivalent of Eliot's *Four Quartets*, whose influence it clearly evinces. The poet's incurable nostalgia and metaphysical anxiety are expressed through references to the *Odyssey* and to the deaths of Socrates, Oedipus, and Antigone. The three parts of the poem reflect the poet's anxious search for the meaning of life, for a sense of justice, and for proof of the immortality of the soul. The search culminates in the image of "light, angelic and black"—the Greek light in its apparently antithetical, spiritual and mystical essence.

S.'s volume of essays *Dhokimes* (1944; expanded ed., 1962; partial tr., *On the Greek Style: Selected Essays in Poetry and Hellenism*, 1966) is, in terms of language and critical perception, regarded as the best volume of literary criticism in contemporary Greek letters. It is also a primary source for a better understanding of S.'s own mind and work.

FURTHER WORKS: *Ghymnopedhia* (1935; *Ghymnopedhia*, 1967); *Tetradhio ghymnasmaton* (1940; *Book of Exercises*, 1967); *Tria kryfa piimata* (1966; *Three Secret Poems*, 1969). FURTHER WORKS IN ENGLISH: *Six Poems from the Greek of Sikelianos and S.* (1946); *The King of Asine and Other Poems* (1948); *Poems* (1960); *Collected Poems 1924–1955* (1967, bilingual); *Collected Poems 1924-1970* (1975, bilingual)

BIBLIOGRAPHY: Sherrard, P., *The Marble Threshing Floor* (1956): 185–231; Keeley, E., "T. S. Eliot and the Poetry of G. S.," *CL*, 8 (1956): 214–26; Friar, K., "G. S.: The Greek Poet Who Won the Nobel Prize," *SatR* (30 Nov. 1963): 16–20; Keeley, E., "S.'s Elpenor, 'A Man of Fortune,'" *KR*, 28 (1966): 378–90; Decavalles, A., "Greekness and Exile," *Spirit* (Sept. 1968): 111–15; Levi, P., "S.'s Tone of Voice," in Bien, P., ed. and Keeley, E., ed., *Modern Greek Writers* (1972): 172–89; Friar, K., *Modern Greek Poetry* (1973): 66–72, 740–47; Thaniel, G., "G. S.'s 'Thrush': A Modern Descent," *CRCL* (1977): 89–102; Capri-Karka, C., *Love and the Symbolic Journey in the Poetry of Cavafy, Eliot and S.* (1982): 155–350; Tsatsos, J., *My Brother G. S.* (1982); Beaton, R., *G. S.* (1991)

—ANDONIS DECAVALLES

ŠEGEDIN, Petar

Croatian novelist, short-story writer, and essayist, b. 8 Aug. 1908, Žrnovo, Korèula

Š. attended Teacher's College in Dubrovnik and graduated from the Pedagogical Academy and the Faculty of Philosophy in Zagreb. As a primary school teacher he worked in Kula, Norinska, and Račište (1928-31), and as a secondary school teacher in Korčula (1933-37), and later in Zagreb. His first literary appearance was in the literary journal *Pečat* (1939), edited by Miroslav KRLEŽA. As a left-wing intellectual he had an important position in the cultural life in Croatia after World War II: he was the secretary of the cultural association *Matica hrvatska* (1946-47) and the president of the Croatian Writer's Association. From 1956 to 1960 he was attaché of cultural affairs in the Yugoslav embassy in Paris. After returning to Zagreb, he was active as a freelance artist.

Š's novels *Djeca božja* (1946; God's Children) and *Osamljenici* (1947; The Lonely People) marked an important poetic declension from the predominant literary aesthetics of the period. Š.'s prose was attacked by the dogmatic criticism, but it succeeded in consolidating the existentialist model. The focus was on individual human fates—depicted both from the psychological and the phenomenological point of view. Anxiety, alienation, and loneliness, under which Š.'s characters suffer, were primarily conditioned by the fear from manipulation and repression by the authorities. Although an explicit individualist and a rare lyrical poet of early post-World War II literature, Š.—as an intellectual—felt a need to speak in public about all topical literary and social issues. As early as 1949 he was one of the first to oppose publicly the dogmatism and exclusiveness of SOCIAL REALISM. At the Yugoslav Writer's Conference he openly pleaded for artistic and literary freedom. His subjective experience of the world is reflected in his travelogues, short stories, and essays: *Na putu* (1953; On The Road), *Mrtvo more* (1953; Dead Sea), *Eseji* (1956; Essays), *Na istom putu* (1963; On The Same Road), and *Orfej u maloj bašti* (1964; Orpheus in a Small Garden). In 1964 he was awarded the prestigious Ivan Goran Kovačić Prize for his distinctive prose. His collections of short stories, *Sveti vrag* (1966; The Holy Devil), *Crni smiješak* (1969; The Black Smile), *Izvještaj iz pokrajine* (1969; A Report from the Province), and *Riječ o riječi* (1969; A Word on the Word), preceded his collection of essays *Svi smo odgovorni* (1971; We Are All Responsible), in which he rejects the possibility of realizing the individual freedom within the collective lack of freedom. Having renounced an isolated literary activity in dramatic social circumstances, Š. found himself on the list of proscribed authors—because of his public stands during the "Croatian Spring" of 1971, when Croatian communists—supported by a huge national movement—made an attempt to oppose the Yugoslav political and cultural unitarism. As a result, his works were not allowed to be published for nearly a decade.

After living several years abroad, Š. returned and the prohibition on publication was lifted. His literary comeback includes a number of books of essays, short stories, and memoirs: *Getsemanski vrtovi* (1981; The Gardens of Gethsemane), *Tišina* (1982; Silence); *Vjetar* (1986; The Wind); *Licem u lice* (1987; Face to Face); *Krug što skamenjuje* (1988; A Petrifying Circle), *Pričanje* (1991; Storytelling); *Izdajnik* (1993; The Traitor), *Franfurtski dnevnik* (1993; The Frankfurt Diary), and *Novele* (1996; Stories). In the life of this prolific writer the act of political protest has always been an expression of his personal conscience and an intellectual and moral

obligation. This is especially true of Š.'s activity at the beginning of the aggression war against Croatia in 1991, as he dared—in hopeless circumstances—to unmask the "Eastern barbaric genius" from the psychological point of view. In the aftermath of World War II he was the first Croatian writer to employ a postmodern literary style. Searching for a harmonious relation between existence and aesthetics, he used his rich artistic skills in the psychoanalysis of human traumas, degeneration and perversion, and the secrets of human soul, in which the external events are reflected and deformed. Š.'s lonely characters live in their introverted thoughts and rich reminiscences. However, the interweaving of their consciousness and their subconsciousness gives them no impulse for action but only reflects a situation in which they are looking for the sense of their existence.

BIBLIOGRAPHY: Vaupotić, M., *Hrvatska suvremena književnost*: *Contemporary Croatian Literature* (1966): 114-16; Šicel, M., *Hrvatska književnost* (1982): 191-92; Frangeš, I., *Povijest hrvatske književnosti* (1987): 364-68; Milanja, C., *Hrvatski roman 1945-1990* (1996): 43-53; Jelčić, D., *Povijest hrvatske književnosti* (1997): 296-97

—DUBRAVA SESAR

SEGHERS, Anna

(pseud. of Netty Reiling Radvanyi) German novelist and short-story writer, b. 19 Nov. 1900, Mainz; d. 1 June 1983, East Berlin (now Berlin)

Influenced by her father, an antique dealer and art expert, S. exhibited an early interest in art. After studying philology, history, art history, and Sinology in Cologne and Heidelberg, she received her doctorate in 1924 for a dissertation on Rembrandt. In 1928 she joined the German Communist Party and the Union of Proletarian and Revolutionary Writers.

S.'s literary and political activities caused her arrest and led to her flight to Paris in 1933. In 1940 she was forced to flee again, first to southern France, then to Mexico. After the war she settled in East Berlin. In 1950 she was elected president of the German Writers' Union and later pursued a variety of literary responsibilities in the German Democratic Republic.

In her first major book, *Aufstand der Fischer von St. Barbara* (1928; *The Revolt of the Fishermen*, 1929), S. created a work marked by an almost painful precision and objectivity. The strict attention to detail is both an outgrowth of her art studies and a response to stimuli from the Neue Sachlichkeit (new factualism) that replaced EXPRESSIONISM. There is no attempt at polemic. Figures and milieu speak for themselves in a realistic portrayal of the common man within his world. Against a background of hunger, exploitation, and an abortive strike, S. develops the theme of revolution as a symbol for the transformation of the working class and the generation of a new, socially conscious individual.

Excepting *Der Ausflug der toten Mädchen* (1946; the excursion of the dead girls) and *Die Überfahrt* (1971; the crossing), which draw material from her youth, her life in exile, and her later travels, there is little of the autobiographical in S.'s work. Rather, she relies for substance on impressions of everyday life, focusing on current themes and stressing the dignity and inherent worth of the individual.

Earlier writers made a strong impression on S. The influence of Dostoevsky is apparent in "Grubetsch" (Grubetsch) and "Die Ziegler" (the Zieglers), both of which appeared in *Auf dem Wege zur amerikanischen Botschaft, und andere Erzählungen* (1930; on the way to the American embassy, and other stories). Both stories are permeated by a feeling of alienation and the hopelessness of bourgeois existence. Other writings reflect her interest in Gotthold Ephraim Lessing, Heinrich von Kleist, Georg Büchner, and Lev Tolstoy.

S. wrote her most significant books while in exile. In them she challenged the German nation to practice introspection, presenting man's moral and ethical attitudes as a function of social conditions. Of primary concern to her is the possibility for change in man as a result of the social process. In her best-known work, *Das siebte Kreuz* (1942; *The Seventh Cross*, 1942), these factors are intertwined with a mastery that she had not achieved in her previous novels.

Based on firsthand knowledge and pertinent eyewitness reports of Nazi terror, *Das siebte Kreuz* is a character sketch of an entire people. Of seven men who escape a Nazi concentration camp, only one survives. Woven into the narration of the survivor's flight across Germany is the picture of people going about their everyday lives. By contrasting mundane affairs and fears with the drama of the escape, S. underscores the potential of extraordinary situations for motivating heroic actions. Her narrative method is a combination of novella technique, in which all aspects of the story enhance the depiction of a single unusual event, and a deliberate bundling together of parallel threads of plot to create a novel of many facets. The latter tendency is characteristic of S.'s style in all her subsequent major literary endeavors.

In *Die Toten bleiben jung* (1949; *The Dead Stay Young*, 1950), which braids together the stories of individuals associated with a martyred communist, the handling of the many narratives is cumbersome and makes the novel difficult to read. Nonetheless, the illumination of society generated by an intense penetration of social strata, a complete psychological portrayal of even the most negative figures, and an accurate revelation of both internal and external realities, outweighs in import the stylistic weaknesses of the work. Unfortunately, that cannot be said of *Die Entscheidung* (1959; the decision) and *Das Vertrauen* (1968; trust), which bog down in trivial complexity.

The most interesting of S.'s late fiction deviates markedly from mainstream tendencies in East German literature. "Sagen von Unirdischen" (tales of extraterrestrials), from the volume *Sonderbare Begegnungen* (1972; peculiar encounters), is an artistically successful science fiction story. The novella *Steinzeit* (1975; stone age) powerfully portrays the psychological and physical self-destruction of an American Vietnam veteran.

S. was an indisputable master of the portrayal of individual reality. Because her characters and their world are real, they are timelessly relevant. That fact alone made her the First Lady of East German literature.

FURTHER WORKS: *Die Gefährten* (1932); *Der Kopflohn* (1933; *A Price on His Head*, 1961); *Der Weg durch den Februar* (1935); *Ernst Thaelmann: What He Stands For* (1935); *Die Rettung* (1937); *Transit* (1944; *Transit Visa*, 1945); *Das Ende* (1948); *Die Hochzeit von Haiti; Wiedereinführung der Sklaverei in Guadeloupe: Zwei Novellen* (1948); *Sowjetmenschen* (1948); *Die Rückkehr* (1949); *Crisanta* (1950); *Friedensgeschichten* (1950); *Die Linie* (1950); *Die Kinder* (1951); *Der Mann und sein Name* (1952); *Der erste Schritt* (1952); *Frieden der Welt: Ansprachen und Aufsätze*

1947–1953 (1953); *Brot und Salz* (1958); *Das Licht auf dem Galgen* (1961); *Über Tolstoi; Über Dostojewskij: Essays* (1963); *Die Kraft der Schwachen* (1965); *Geschichten von heute und gestern* (1966); *Das wirkliche Blau* (1967; *Benito's Blue*, 1973); *Glauben an Irdisches* (1969); *Briefe an Leser* (1970); *Über Kunstwerk und Wirklichkeit* (4 vols., 1970–1978); *Wilkommen Zukunft!* (1975); *Steinzeit; Wiederbegegnung* (1978); *Die Macht der Worte* (1979); *Woher sie kommen, wohin sie gehen: Essays aus vier Jahrzehnten* (1980); *Drei Frauen aus Haiti* (1980); *Aufsätze, Ansprachen, Essays 1927–1953, 1954–1979* (2 vols., 1980); *Was ein Volk denkt und fühlt, spricht sein Schriftsteller aus* (1982); *Gewöhnliches und gefährliches Leben: Ein Briefwechsel aus der Zeit des Exils* (1986); *Der gerechte Richter* (1990); *Der letzte Mann der Höhle* (1994). FURTHER WORKS IN ENGLISH: *Benito's Blue and Nine Other Stories* (1973)

BIBLIOGRAPHY: Andrews, R. C., "An East German Novelist: A. S.," *GL&L*, 8 (1955): 121–29; Albrecht, F., *Die Erzählerin A. S.* (1965); Triesch, M., "Martyrdom and Everlasting Life: Two Stories by A. S.," *SSF*, 3 (1966): 236–45; Huebener, T., *The Literature of East Germany* (1970): 66–78; Szepe, H., "The Problem of Identity in A. S.'s *Transit,*" *OL*, 27 (1972): 145–52; Sauer, K., *A. S.* (1978); Bangerter, L. A., *The Bourgeois Proletarian: A Study of A. S.* (1980); Brandes, U., *A. S.* (1992); Schrade, A., *A. S.* (1993); Stephan, A., *A. S. im Exil* (1993); Zehl Romero, C., *A. S.* (1993); Wagner, F., et al., eds., *A. S.* (1994)

—LOWELL A. BANGERTER

SEIFERT, Jaroslav

Czechoslovak poet (writing in Czech), b. 23 Sept. 1901, Prague; d. 1 Jan. 1986, Prague

S. was born into a poor family and grew up in Žižkov, a working-class suburb of Prague. As he was later to recall it, his childhood was spent in two dissonant and mutually exclusive worlds: with his devout Catholic mother he would attend the seasonal rituals in splendid baroque churches; but on his own he would take to the streets to overhear the bawdy songs and the profane talk emanating from the neighborhood taverns.

S.'s first volume of poetry, *Město v slzách* (1921; city in tears), in which he unfurled the banner of proletarian messianism, was dubbed by the leading aesthetic critic, F. X. ŠALDA, "a cry of hungering after the joys of life." In it the young poet looks back in anger at the human waste of the great "bourgeois" war (World War I) and urges proletarian revolt. The large breathing rhythm of the free verse reflects the inspiration of the leading Czech socialist poet, Stanislav Kostka Neumann (1875–1947), to whom the book is dedicated.

In 1923 S. made his first journey to Paris and fell under the spell of the city and its poets. He translated works of Guillaume APOLLINAIRE, who served as his bridge to Czech "poetism." Together with a fellow-proletarian Czech poet, Jiří WOLKER, S. saw the program of poetism—with its emphasis on joy, innocent sensuality, and play—as a necessary antidote to bourgeois hypocrisy and as a healthy reaction to the horrors of World War I.

S.'s second volume of poems, *Samá láska* (1923; all love), marks his transition into the realm of private experience. In the opening poem he invokes his "modern Muse," who, like her

FUTURIST sister, frequents the cinema and the circus but whose songs are no less holy for being sung to the music of an electric lyre. His third collection, *Na vlnách TSF* (1925; on the waves of the TSF [i.e., French radio]; repub. as *Svatební cesta*, 1938; the wedding trip), comes closest to fulfilling the norms of poetism, with exotic and playful imagery and a touch of frivolity.

In 1925 S. made the obligatory pilgrimage to the U.S.S.R. The visit yielded a book of poems, *Slavík zpívá špatně* (1926; the nightingale sings badly), in which the verse is more traditional than his earlier poetry, with a short-lined, rhymed stanza predominating. Yet the poems are full of surprising auditory and visual effects. In spite of his ideologically correct references to Europe as the "ruined chessboard," as well as a fine poem on the death of Lenin, S.'s vignettes of Soviet life did not gain him much favor among the Communists, since his re-creation of picturesque, old-fashioned sights, such as gilt cupolas of old churches and improvised private markets, was considered reactionary.

In 1929 S. was among those who refused to follow Klement Gottwald's Moscow-inspired line of systematic opposition to the legitimacy of the Czechoslovak Republic. As a result, he was expelled from the Communist Party. He joined the Social Democrats, who advocated the advancement of the workers' cause within the framework of parliamentary democracy.

S.'s poetic maturity began with the cycle of poems *Poštovní holub* (1929; the carrier pigeon). During the ensuing decade he developed and refined his lyric voice, drawing on the experiences of everyday life and occasionally making use of the great commonplaces of the Czech poetic tradition, such as the evocation of a quasi-mythical mother figure. But his balladic nostalgia for a lost childhood is always seasoned with a pungent, almost Horatian sensuality.

The national catastrophe at Munich (1938) and the Nazi occupation that followed brought out S.'s deep patriotism. Several cycles of poems, published after the war under the collective title *Přilba hlíny* (1945; a helmet of earth), established him as a national poet. He identified himself fully with the people's grief, sense of bitter betrayal, and hope for survival, but he expressed these themes and moods in images and symbols that are never hackneyed or abstract. Particularly memorable are the poems that evoke the four days in May 1945 when the people of Prague rose against the remnants of the occupying Nazi army. In them S. pits the brief violence and the eerie excitement of improvised barricades against the startling beauty of the lilacs, the acacias, and the chestnuts in bloom.

From 1945 to 1949 S. was prominent as the editor of the Trade Union daily *Práce*. But he never enjoyed the confidence and the patronage of the Communist Party; and in 1950, after publishing a poem mourning the death of his friend, the Communist poet Frantisek HALAS, he was attacked by a Party critic for sinking into subjectivism. His new poetry was shunned by the press, even while his collected works were being published. In 1969, a year after the Soviet invasion, he was elected to the post of President of the still defiant Union of Czechoslovak Writers. Subsequently, when the policy of "normalization" went into effect, he was ousted.

Morový sloup (1977; *The Plague Column*, 1979) was denied publication in Czechoslovakia and had to be published abroad. The collection was a new departure for S. The sparse, unassuming, almost prosaic poems are vibrant with the pathos of beginnings and endings, as the last survivor of a spectacular generation of poets resurrects the past, under the light touch of the wings of the approaching angel of death.

In 1981 S.'s autobiography *Všecky krásy světa* (*All the Beauty of the World*, 1991) appeared abroad, in two émigré publications. Rich in evocative anecdotes and individualized portraits, this memoir lovingly recreates the spirit of the Czech avant-garde between the two World Wars and during the Nazi occupation. The wide resonance of this cultural testament led to the Nobel Prize for literature in October of 1984. In singling out S., the first Czech or Slovak writer to be so honored, the Nobel Committee praised his poetry for "conjuring up another world than that of tyranny and desolation—a world that exists both here and now . . . one that exists in our dreams and our will and our art."

Too old and ill to travel, S. welcomed the news from his hospital bed. In the brief spell of time remaining to him, he could still savor the flurry of translations of his prose and poetry that followed. S.'s funeral was a national event, an outpouring of memory and hope presaging the festive days of the Velvet Revolution.

FURTHER WORKS: *Revoluční sborník Devětsil* (1922); *Jablko s klína* (1933); *Ruce Venušiny* (1936); *Zpíváno do rotačky* (1936); *Jaro, sbohem* (1937); *Basníku Karlu Tomanovi* (1937); *Osm dní* (1937); *Zhasněte světla* (1938); *Světlem oděná, Praha 1940* (1942); *Kamenný most* (1944); *Ruka a plamen* (1948); *Dokud nám neprší na rakev* (1948); *Šel malíř chudě do světa* (1949); *Pozdrav Františkovi Halasovi* (1949); *S obláčky hroznu* (1949); *Romance o Králi Václavu IV* (1949); *Píseň o Viktorce* (1950); *Petřín* (1951); *Romance o mládí a o víně* (1954); *Maminka* (1954); *Dílo* (7 vols., 1954–1968); *Koulelo se, koulelo* (1955); *Mozart v Praze* (1956); *Chlapec a hvězdy* (1956); *Koncert na ostrově* (1965); *Dva světy* (1966); *Prsten Třeboňské Madoně* (1966); *Halleyova kometa* (1967); *Odlévání zvonů* (1967; *The Casting of the Bells*, 1983); *Zpěvy o Praze* (1968); *Deštník z Piccadilly* (1979; *An Umbrella from Piccadilly*, 1983); *Všecky krásy světa* (1981). **FURTHER WORKS IN ENGLISH:** *Eight Days, an Elegy for T. G. M.* (1985); *Mozart in Prague* (1985); *The Selected Poetry of J. S.* (1986); *Dressed in Light* (1992)

BIBLIOGRAPHY: French, A., *The Poets of Prague: Czech Poetry between the Wars* (1969): 91–94, 113–16; Mihailovich, V. D., et al., eds., *Modern Slavic Literatures* (1976), Vol. 2: 188-92; Novák, A., *Czech Literature* (1976): 322–44; Parrott, C., Introduction to *J. S., The Plague Column* (1979): 9–19

—MARIA NĚMCOVÁ BANERJEE

SELIMOVIĆ, Meša

Yugoslav novelist and short-story writer (writing in Serbian), b. 26 April 1910, Tuzla; d. 11 July 1982, Belgrade

S. graduated from the University of Belgrade in 1933 and until 1941 taught literature at Tuzla High School in his native Bosnia. During World War II he joined Tito's partisan forces but became disillusioned with the postwar communist regime and was expelled from the Party in 1947. Until 1961, when he was appointed editor-in-chief of Svjetlost Publishers in Sarajevo, S. held several short-term jobs and was unemployed for a while. He settled in Belgrade, won several prestigious literary awards, and was a member of both the Serbian and Bosnian/Herzegovinian Academies of Arts and Sciences.

During the first two decades after the war S. produced a small number of short stories and two novels, *Tišine* (1961; new version 1965; silences) and *Magla i mjesečina* (1965; fog and moonlight). These early works, inspired by the war, stand far above most of Yugoslav World War II literature. S. analyzes moods and attitudes of men in war and the difficulties of adjustment to the totally changed conditions of peacetime.

S.'s masterpieces, *Derviš i smrt* (1966; the dervish and death), and another excellent novel, *Tvrdjava* (1970; fortress), firmly established him as one of the most distinguished writers in Yugoslavia. These two works are set in Islamic Bosnia, in the rather distant past, a setting that allows S. virtually unlimited freedom of expression. The dervish, Ahmed Nurudin, has for years lived the secluded and protected life of a servant of God, enjoying quiet meditation and prayer. Suddenly, he is struck by a personal tragedy: the authorities imprison, try, and brutally execute Ahmed's brother for a crime he did not commit. His deep resentment of injustice and an intense desire to punish his brother's murderers compel Ahmed to become actively involved in life. With the same passion with which he once espoused the love of God, he now hates his enemies and strives to gain power in order to carry out his revenge. Intelligent and determined to succeed, Ahmed achieves his goal but soon meets a tragic end, having found himself hopelessly entrapped in the very same power structure that helped him destroy his enemies.

Ahmet Sabo, the protagonist of *Tvrdjava*, is a poet and, like the dervish, a man of principles and high integrity. He knows that he is different from the people among whom he must live, suffers because of that, yet realizes that he cannot give up his views and ethical norms in order to gain their acceptance. Gradually, he encloses himself in an invisible fortress of loneliness. When this loneliness becomes unbearable and threatens to destroy him, he moves to a fortress of love. His original belief that life is worth living is now restored, and once again he feels fit to accept its challenges.

S.'s allegorical novel *Ostrvo* (1974; the island) also focuses on the problem of alienation and loneliness, but from a different angle. An older couple, Katarina and Ivan, are weary of living on the drab periphery of life, from which they expected much but have received very little. Following an old dream, they retreat to a faraway deserted island in search of beauty and happiness. They soon discover how devastating isolation can be for a human being. S.'s message is unambiguous: human beings are social animals. Only confronting life brings true satisfaction and fulfillment.

Well-constructed, bursting with internal tension, yet written in a calm and elegant style, S.'s fiction contains a treasury of clear, well-formulated thought, forged through the author's own painful and tragic experiences and concerned with the dilemmas and problems that have tormented men of intellect in all times and all epochs. Often compared with Ivo ANDRIC, S. is today the leading writer from Bosnia and one of the best, most honest, and most universal novelists in contemporary Yugoslavia.

FURTHER WORKS: *Uvrijedjeni čovjek* (1947); *Prva četa* (1950); *Tudja zemlja* (1962); *Za i protiv Vuka* (1967); *Djevojka crvene kose* (1970); *Sjećanja* (1976); *Pisci, mišljenja i razgovori* (1977); *Sabrana dela* (9 vols., 1979)

BIBLIOGRAPHY: Trumić-Kisić, M., "An Interview with M. S.," *Review* (Belgrade), 3 (1971): 30–31; Butler, T. J., "Literary Style and Poetic Function in M. S.'s *The Dervish and Death*," *SEER*, 52 (1974): 533–47; Eekman, T., *Thirty Years of Yugoslav Literature (1945–1975)* (1978): 104–10

—BILJANA ŠLJIVIĆ-ŠIMŠIĆ

SELVON, Samuel

Trinidadian novelist and short-story writer, b. 20 May 1923, Trinidad; d. 16 April 1994

S. began to write poetry and fiction after graduating from Naparima College in 1938. He continued writing while he worked as a wireless operator for the Royal Navy Reserve during World War II. When the war ended S. turned to journalism and became the fiction editor of the literary magazine of the *Trinidad Guardian*. But like so many promising West Indian writers, S. was forced to leave home if he wished to have his work reach an international audience. In 1950 he set out for England, but the journey was also an escape from the complacency and easy rhythms of Trinidad to which he found himself increasingly drawn. It was S.'s good fortune to live in London's Balmoral Hostel where he met several displaced West Indians, Africans, and Indians. These expatriate colonials inspired the creation of many of the ebullient characters of S.'s "London fiction." While he worked at a variety of jobs, S. contributed fiction to journals and newspapers, and his first novel, *A Brighter Sun*, was published in 1952. Nine additional novels, numerous short stories, articles, radio plays, television and film scripts followed. After living in England for some twenty-eight years, S. emigrated to Calgary, Canada.

S.'s *A Brighter Sun* is a historically important novel in the development of West Indian fiction because the young hero's quest for self-awareness and wholeness in a colonial, pluralistic, and racially divisive society is a significant theme. The novel is a sensitive exploration of the growth of the callow Tiger from childish naïveté and ignorance to adult responsibility. Tiger's quest for maturity and self-knowledge is continued and consolidated in *Turn Again Tiger* (1958), which has some important links with *Those Who Eat the Cascadura* (1972). Both novels examine the individual's search for integrity in a society psychologically crippled by years of an effete colonialism. Sans Souci, the isolated and idyllic setting of *Those Who Eat the Cascadura*, is a microcosm of preindependent, colonial Trinidad complete with the three-tiered racial hierarchy and its antagonisms and divisiveness. The theme of individual integrity is crucial in this novel, and it emerges rather subtly in the female protagonist's relationship with an Englishman visiting Sans Souci. In *Turn Again Tiger* the hero's hunger for self-possession is dramatically conveyed in his violent sexual encounter with the white Doreen. The revenge motive, a feature of the black-male/white-female syndrome often explored in West Indian fiction, is rather prominent in the encounter.

Scholars have neglected S.'s *I Hear Thunder* (1963) and *An Island Is a World* (1955) in favor of his less ponderous, more satirical, and humorous fiction. However, these novels reveal S.'s meditative and philosophical side, and, furthermore, they call up a finely focused and particularly accurate picture of Trinidad society in the 1940s and 1950s. The characters are complex and fully embodied, and some of S.'s best female portraits appear in these two novels.

In his brilliant "London fiction" S. explores the harassed and sometimes bizarre lives of West Indians trying to survive in the hostile "Mother Country." The world of these novels, *The Lonely Londoners* (1956), *The Housing Lark* (1965), *Moses Ascending* (1975), and *Moses Migrating* (1983), is ferociously masculine. S.'s expatriates maintain a cohesive male community closed to women, most of whom are regarded as nuisances. More pertinently, S.'s West Indians have a psychological need to form a colony with a governor-leader if they are to survive in London. That governor is Moses, the charismatic Trinidadian in whose basement room "the boys" assemble each Sunday morning for sustenance.

S. is one of the brilliant writers who contributed to the remarkable development of a vibrant West Indian literature in the 1950s and 1960s. Increasingly scholars from several countries are discovering and elucidating the value of this contribution.

His pioneering work in the use of Trinidadian dialect, his incomparable gift for dialogue and pungent satire, and his sensitive treatment of alienated West Indians guarantee his place in the history of West Indian literature.

FURTHER WORKS: *Ways of Sunlight* (1957); *Carnival in Trinidad* (1964); *Lost Property* (1965); *A Cruise in the Caribbean* (1966); *Perchance To Dream* (1966); *Rain Stop Play* (1967); *Highway in the Sun* (1967); *A Drink of Water* (1968); *You Right in the Smoke* (1968); *El Dorado, West One* (1969); *Bringing in the Sheaves* (1969); *The Plains of Caroni* (1970); *Mary, Mary Shut Your Gate* (1971); *Voyage to Trinidad* (1971); *Cry Baby Brackley* (1972); *Water for Veronica* (1972); *The Harvest in the Wilderness* (1972); *Anansi the Spider Man* (1974); *Milk in the Coffee* (1975); *Zeppi's Machine* (1977); *Pressure* (1978); *Foreday Morning; Selected Prose* 1946–1986 (1989)

BIBLIOGRAPHY: Brathwaite, E., "Sir Galahad and the Islands," *Bim*, 7 (1957): 8–16; Ramchand, K., *An Introduction to the Study of West Indian Literature* (1976): 58–72; Nazareth, P., "The Clown in the Slave Ship," *CarQ*, 23: 2–3 (1977): 24–29; Rohlehr, G., "S.S. and the Language of the People," in Baugh, E., ed., *Critics on Caribbean Literature* (1978): 153–61; Fabre, M., "S. S.," in King, B., ed., *West Indian Literature* (1979): 111–25; Baugh, E., "Friday in Crusoe's City: The Question of Language in Two West Indian Novels of Exile," *ACLALSB*, 3 (1980): 1–12; Barratt, H., "Dialect, Maturity, and the Land in S. S.'s *A Brighter Sun:* A Reply," *ESC*, 7, 3 (1981): 329–37; Ramchand, K., "Song of Innocence, Song of Experience: S. S.'s *The Lonely Londoners* As a Literary Work," *WLWE*, 21, 3 (1982): 644–54; Barratt, H., "Individual Integrity in S.'s *Turn Again Tiger* and *Those Who Eat the Cascadura,*" *Toronto South Asian Review*, 5, 1 (1986): 153–59; Nasta, S., ed., *Critical Perspectives on S. S.* (1988)

—HAROLD BARRATT

SEMBÈNE Ousmane

Senegalese novelist and filmmaker (writing in French), b. 8 Jan. 1923, Ziguinchor

S. never received a formal education. At the age of fifteen he enlisted in the French army and fought in Italy and Germany in World War II. He returned to Senegal in 1947 and participated in the Dakar-Niger railroad workers' strike. He then spent ten years in Marseille, where he became the leader of the longshoremen's union.

S.'s first novel, *Le docker noir* (1956; the black dock worker), depicts the betrayal suffered by an African writer whose novel is published under false pretenses, as well as the betrayal suffered by African workers who lead a wretched existence in Marseille. His second novel, the lyrical *Oh pays, mon beau peuple* (1957; oh country, my beautiful people), presents as its hero an enlightened self-made man who seeks to liberate his countrymen much in the manner of Manuel, the self-sacrificing hero of the Haitian writer Jacques ROUMAIN's masterpiece *Masters of the Dew*.

S.'s style continued to improve, and his third novel, *Les bouts de bois de Dieu* (1960; *God's Bits of Wood*, 1962), was well received by the critics. A sprawling fresco dealing with the Dakar-Niger railroad strike in 1947, *Les bouts de bois de Dieu* is set in three main towns along the railroad: Dakar, Thiès, and Bamako. In each town S. focuses on a particular family's hardships arising from the strike. In each case the workers and their loved ones must choose between continued struggle and surrender.

The structure of *Les bouts de bois de Dieu* has been compared with that of *Man's Fate* by André MALRAUX. Indeed, Tiémoko, the leader of the unit in charge of punishing strikebreakers, studies the Malraux novel to learn how to deal with those who desert the workers' cause. The two novels differ, however, in that S. favors nonviolent resistance over violence. This novel, unlike the works of Léopold Sédar SENGHOR and Camara LAYE, was not written for the African elite; S. speaks to the workers as one of them.

S.'s desire to touch the common people in Senegal, who can neither read nor write, and who speak Wolof, not French, led him to turn to film making in the early 1960s. His heartbreaking film *La noire de . . .* (1966; the black girl of . . .), adapted from his story of the same name in the collection *Voltaïque* (1962; *Tribal Scars, and Other Stories*, 1975), was based on an actual event reported in the newspaper *Nice-matin* in 1958: the suicide of a young Senegalese servant who, while vacationing with her boss's family on the Riviera, suffered from homesickness and from the insensitivity of her European masters.

When S. turned his short novel *Le mandat* (*The Money-Order*)—published in *Véhi-Ciosane ou Blanche-Genèse, suivi du Mandat* (1965; *The Money-Order, with White Genesis*, 1972)—into a film in 1969, he produced two versions, one in French for European audiences, and one in Wolof. Thus, both French and Senegalese were able to appreciate the comedy and the pathos of this film, depicting the frustrations encountered by a poor, unemployed African who tries desperately to cash a money order sent to him by his nephew in Paris.

In recent years, S.'s works have become increasingly bitter and exclusively African-oriented. The novel *Xala* (1973; *Xala*, 1976), which S. adapted into a film of the same name (1974), starts in a humorous, almost farcical vein when the pompous protagonist El Hadji Beye is mysteriously afflicted with a curse of impotence (or *xala*) on the night of his wedding to a third bride. *Xala* is a parable of a wealthy, conceited, and basically foolish businessman's downfall. Here, as in his earlier story "Ses trois jours" (her three days) from the collection *Voltaïque*, S. attacks polygamy, vividly depicting the plight of older wives whose husbands acquire younger, more desirable brides. Yet the tone in *Xala* becomes unexpectedly harsh and distressing, as punishments are heaped upon El Hadji, whose manhood can only be restored after he has lost all material possessions, including his bride, and after he has been publicly humiliated for having exploited his fellow Africans in earlier selfish business dealings.

The "father of the African film," S. now devotes his talents to film making. *Ceddo* (1977; common people), which presents the taboo subject of African cooperation in supplying slaves to be sent to the western hemisphere in the 17th c., was banned in Senegal. S.'s open hostility and bitterness toward foreigners, religious leaders, and the African bourgeoisie pitted him against then-president Senghor. Deeply committed to spreading socialism and trade unionism in Africa, S. shows in his films and his novels that excessive reverence for authority, whether bureaucratic or traditional, can only impede the progress necessary to build a modern and totally independent Africa.

FURTHER WORKS: *L'harmattan* (1964); *Le dernier de l'empire* (2 vols., 1981; *The Last of the Empire*, 1983). FURTHER WORKS IN ENGLISH: *Niiwam and Taaw* (1992); *O. S.: Dialogues with Critics and Writers* (1993)

BIBLIOGRAPHY: Beier, U., on *O pays, mon beau peuple, BO* (Nov. 1959): 56–57; Brench, A. C., *The Novelists' Inheritance in French Africa* (1967): 109–19; Ortava, J., "Les femmes dans l'œuvre littéraire d'O. S.," *PA*, No. 3 (1969): 69–77; Vieyra, P. S., *S. O. cinéaste* (1973); Achiriga, J. J., *La révolte des romanciers noirs de langue française* (1973); Minyono-Nkondo, M.-F., *Comprendre "Les bouts de bois de Dieu" de S. O.* (1979); Bestman, M. T., *S. O. et l'esthétique du roman négro-africain* (1981)

—DEBRA POPKIN

SENA, Jorge de

Portuguese poet, critic, essayist, translator, dramatist, short-story writer, and novelist, b. 2 Nov. 1919, Lisbon; d. 4 April 1978, Santa Barbara, Cal., U.S.A.

S. earned a degree in civil engineering in Oporto in 1944 and worked as an engineer until 1959. He then left for Brazil, where he began his teaching career and received a Ph. D. in literature from the University of São Paulo (1964). He also became a Brazilian citizen. From 1965 until his death S. lived in the U. S., teaching first at the University of Wisconsin and then at the University of California, Santa Barbara.

S. was a remarkable poet who combined MODERNIST tendencies with echoes of classical Portuguese poetry. His first volume, *Perseguição* (1942; persecution), explores a variety of forms, employing SURREALIST and modernist techniques. Subsequent books—*Coroa da terra* (1946; crown of the earth), *Pedra filosofal* (1950; philosopher's stone), and *As evidências* (1955; the evidence)—represent an allegorical spiritual journey in which S. pursues truth. In *Metamorfoses* (1963; metamorphoses) he relates his experiences and impressions of the visual arts. And in *Arte de musica* (1968; art of music) he does the same for music.

S. also wrote several serious plays and farces on historical and classical themes; they are surrealistic and heavily tinged with irony. *O indesejado* (1949; the undesirable), for example, is a verse tragedy dealing with the Portuguese political crisis of 1580 and the legend of King Sebastian.

With the appearance of the collection of stories *Andanças do demónio* (1960; exploits of the devil), which was followed by

Novas andanças do demónio (1966; new exploits of the devil), S. established himself as a writer of fiction. These tales, medieval and moral in tone, explore the theme of good versus evil. Another collection of stories, *Os grãocapitães* (1976; the great captains), set during the period 1930–50, presents a series of characters—captains of the army and the navy, soldiers, bureaucrats—who are servants all of a mythical terrorist regime, reflecting the situation in Spain after the civil war. S.'s only novel, *Sinais de fogo* (1979; fire signals), continues and expands the theme of the effect of the Spanish Civil War on the Portuguese.

It was as a literary critic and translator that S. excelled, writing extensively on the poetry and culture of his nation. Having been educated as an engineer, S. applied the scientific qualities of analysis, precision, and meticulousness to literary criticism. *Os sonetos de Camões e o soneto quinhentista peninsular* (1969; the sonnets of Camões and the peninsular sonnets of the sixteenth century) studies the structure of the sonnets of Camões (1524–1580), author of the *Lusiad*, collating them with other versions, thereby establishing their authorship.

S. is also credited with being the first to write a history of English literature in Portuguese: *A literatura inglesa* (1963; English literature). He translated numerous works by English, American, and French writers.

S. achieved worldwide fame through his individualistic approaches to literature. He was bold in his style, his language, and his sociopolitical themes, and innovative in applying the rigorous requirements of modern criticism to Portuguese literature.

FURTHER WORKS: *Fernando Pessoa: Páginas de doutrina estética* (1947); *Amparo de mãe* (1951); *Ulisseia adúltera* (1952); *Dez ensaios sobre literature portuguesa* (1958); *Líricas portuguesas* (1958); *Fidelidade* (1958); *Da poesia portuguesa* (1959); *Ensaio de uma tipologia literária* (1960); *A estrutura de "Os Lusíadas"* (1961); *O poeta é um fingidor* (1961); *O reino da estupidez I* (1961); *Postscriptum* (1961); *Maravilhas da novela inglesa* (1963); *Sobre o realismo de Shakespeare* (1964); *Edith Sitwell e T. S. Eliot* (1965); *Manierismo e barroquismo na poesia portuguesa dos séculos XVI e XVII* (1965); *Teixeira de Pascoaes: Poesia* (1965); *Uma canção de Camões* (1966); *Estudos de história e de cultura* (1967); *Peregrinatio ad loca infecta* (1969); *Exorcismos* (1972); *Camões dirige-se aos seus contemporâneos* (1973); *Dialécticas da literatura* (1973); *Conheço o sal . . . e outros poemas* (1974); *Francisco de la Torre e D. João de Almeida* (1974); *Maquiavel, e outros estudos* (1974); *Poemas ingleses de Fernando Pessoa* (1974); *O físico prodigioso* (1977); *Sobre esta praia* (1977; *Over This Shore*, 1979); *Sobre Régio, Casais, a "Presença" e outros afins* (1977); *Dialécticas aplicadas da literatura* (1978); *O reino da estupidez II* (1978); *Quarenta anos de servidão* (1979); *Seqüências* (1980); *Trinta anos de Camões: Estudos camonianos e correlates* (1980). FURTHER WORKS IN ENGLISH: *In Crete, with the Minotaur and Other Poems* (1980); *The Poetry of J. de S.: A Bilingual Selection* (1980); *England Revisited* (1986); *By the Rivers of Babylon and Other Stories* (1989)

BIBLIOGRAPHY: Williams, F. G., "Prodigious Exorcist: An Introduction to the Poetry of J. de S.," *WLT*, 53 (1979): 9–15; Sharrer, H. L., and F. G. Williams, eds., *Studies on J. de S.* (1980); Martins, W., on *Seqüências, WLT*, 55, 2 (1981): 290; Müller-Bergh, K., on *The Poetry of J. de S., WLT*, 56, 2 (1982): 316–17

—RENÉ CONCEPCIÓN

SÉNAC, Jean

French-Algerian poet, b. 29 Nov. 1926, Béni-Saf (near Oran), d. 29 or 30 Aug. 1973, Algiers

The illegitimate son of Jeanne Coma, a poor woman of Spanish descent, S. received his name from his stepfather, Edmond Sénac, who recognized him when he was five years old. He was brought up in a devout Catholic manner, which only heightened his homosexual crisis as an adolescent. S. began publishing in his teens and winning prizes for his artwork. He taught before serving in the military during World War II. After the war, S. became very active in Algerian literary and artistic circles. In addition to publishing in numerous periodicals, he worked as a producer for Radio-Algiers and founded two extraordinary, albeit short-lived, literary reviews *Soleil* (1950) and *Terrasses* (1953). S. resided in Paris during the Algerian war of liberation, where he supported the Algerian Liberation Front (FLN). His positions in favor of Algerian independence led to a bitter polemic with his mentor Albert CAMUS. In 1962 S. returned to Algeria where he worked for the Ministry of National Education, founded the Galery 54 with the painter Khadda, and served as secretary-general of the Union of Algerian Writers from 1963 to 1967. S. worked for Radio-Algiers until 1972, when his program was prohibited by the Boumedienne government. Brutally assassinated during the night of August 29-30 1973, the circumstances surrounding his death still remain a mystery.

Many French and Algerian intellectuals hail S. as the leading Algerian poet of French expression. The Algerian writer Rachid BOUDJEDRA claims that many writers who came of age in independent Algeria owe everything to S., "the Algerian, the *pied-noir*. . . the greatest poet of the Maghreb." S.'s rich network of acquaintances and audacious cultural politics put him at the forefront of French-Algerian cultural life from the 1950s to the 1970s. He played a major role in making a new generation of Algerian poets heard in postindependence Algeria, several of whom—Tahar DJAOUT and Youcef Sebti (dates n.a.)—would be assassinated in the Algerian civil war of the 1990s.

S. authored more than fifteen volumes of poetry and prose, and edited several anthologies of Algerian poetry such as *Anthologie de la nouvelle poésie algérienne* (1971; Anthology of the New Algerian Poetry). His first collection of poetry, *Poèmes* (Poems), prefaced by René CHAR, was published by Gallimard in 1954. His poetry is characterized by a tension between a mystical vein and a sexual awakening. The poetic manifesto *Le soleil sous les armes* (1957; The Sun at War) and the poetry collection *Matinale de mon peuple* (1961; The Morning of My People) bring together a poetic and a political revolution. With *Citoyens de beauté* (1967; Citizens of Beauty) the divergence between a personal form of liberation and a collective revolution becomes pronounced. S. feels like a foreigner in Algeria. Although S. initially defined the Algerian writer as any writer opting for the Algerian nation, as the years went by, it became clear that there was no place for him as a gay French-Algerian poet in a socialist state founded on Arabo-Muslim principles. A bold affirmation of desire informs *Avant-corps précédé de Poèmes iliaques et suivi de Diwân du Noûn* (1968; Avant-Corps Preceded by Ilian Poems and Followed by Diwân of the Noûn) and *Les désordres* (1972; The Disorders) at the same time that a profound sense of alienation sets in. The latter becomes particularly pronounced in *Dérisions et vertiges* (1983; Derisions and Vertigos) and *Le mythe du sperme—Méditerranée* (1984; The Myth of the Sperm—Mediterranean), which were

published posthumously. S.'s subversive poetics of the body represents a from of resistance to those manifestations of nationalism, fundamentalism, and terrorism that deny a person his/her language, culture, identity, and life.

S. always felt stigmatized by his bastard origins which are at the root of his poetic identity as a *poète maudit*. His writing, like that of the Camus, is marked by the search for a father which also converges with the search for a fatherland. This theme, already present in his earlier poetry, is the subject of his only novel, *Ebauche du père: pour en finir avec l'enfance* (1989; Sketches of the Father: To Be Done with Childhood), published posthumously.

Like Camus and other *pied-noir* writers, S. was deeply marked by the experience of trying to reconcile two opposed cultures. He never ceased to believe that a reconciliation was not only possible but desirable. His lifelong struggle for a cultural politics that transcended restrictive ethnic and religious (Arabo-Muslim) determinations finally cost him his life under the Boumedienne regime in 1973, whereby he became one of the first martyrs of a terrorist fundamentalism that has taken thousands of lives during the last decade. S.'s trajectory as a gay, *pied-noir* writer at the cultural forefront of an emergent nation gives us a unique perspective for analyzing the linguistic, ethnic, religious, and sexual differences at work in nation building and the formation of national identity.

FURTHER WORKS: *Aux héros purs* (1962); *Le torrent de baïn* (1962); *Le diwân du môle* (1962); *La rose et l'ortie* (1964); *Journal Alger suivi de les leçons d'Edgard* (1983); *A corpoème, les désordres* (1981); *Poèmes* (1986)

BIBLIOGRAPHY: Déjeux, J., *Littérature maghrébine de langue française* (1973); Déjeux, J., et al., *J. S. Vivant* (1981); Bencheikh, J.-E., *L'homme-poème: J. S.* (1983); Péroncel-Hugoz, J. P., *Assassinat d'un poète* (1983); Belamri, R., *J. S.: Entre désir et douleur* (1989)

—DANIELLE MARX-SCOURAS

SENDER, Ramón J.

Spanish novelist, short-story writer, and essayist, b. 3 Feb. 1901, Chalamera de Cinca; d. 16 Jan. 1982, San Diego, Cal., U.S.A.

The son of small-farm owners, S. graduated from the Institute of Teruel in southern Aragon in 1918. In 1927 he was briefly imprisoned in Madrid for revolutionary activities against the Primo de Rivera dictatorship. During the civil war he served as an officer with the Loyalist forces, escaping to France in December 1938. In March 1939 he emigrated to Mexico, and from there he entered the U.S. on a Guggenheim fellowship in 1942. In 1946 S. became an American citizen. He taught Spanish literature at the University of New Mexico from 1947 until 1963 and at the University of Southern California from 1965 until his retirement in 1971. He lived in San Diego until his death.

In 1930, while on the editorial staff of *El sol* in Madrid, S. published his first novel, *Imán* (*Pro Patria*, 1935), based on his experiences as a soldier in Morocco, 1923–24. A greater success abroad than in Spain, *Imán* was translated into ten languages.

Before the outbreak of the civil war in 1936, S. published six other novels, most noteworthy of which is *Mr. Witt en el cantón*

(1936; *Mr. Witt among the Rebels*, 1938), a historical novel set in 1873, during the short-lived First Spanish Republic. For this work S. received Spain's highest literary award, the National Literature Prize.

A short novel, first published as *Mosén Millán* (1953; Mosén Millán) and later as *Réquiem por un campesino español* (1960; *Requiem for a Spanish Peasant*, 1960), is perhaps S.'s masterpiece. While waiting to say requiem mass on the first anniversary of the execution by Falangist gunmen of Paco, a villager who had worked for social reform, Mosén Millán, an Aragonese village priest, recalls in memory flashbacks the life and death of Paco, whose fate subtly comes to symbolize that of the Spanish people during the civil war.

S. regarded *La esfera* (1947; *The Sphere*, 1949), a work he first issued in a much shorter version under a different title, *Proverbio de la muerte* (1939; proverb of death), and which he continued to recast until its definitive edition in 1969, as his most serious and philosophical novel. In it he sought to novelize his view that apparent opposites such as love and hate, life and death, are in ultimate reality spheroids, that is, merely opposite "hemispheres" of final, single "spheres." Most critical opinion agrees that the narrative elements of *La esfera* are insufficiently integrated into the book's excessive cargo of lyrical-metaphysical and symbolic meanings to allow it full artistic unity.

The story of a Spanish gardener's intimate quest for the absolute ideal—an enduring theme in S.'s work—set against the background of civil war in Madrid, is the basis of one of S.'s most perfectly structured novels, *El rey y la reina* (1949; *The King and the Queen*, 1948). In *Crónica del alba* (1966; chronicle of dawn), a monumental three-volume, nine-part, highly autobiographical novel, S. returned in time to his childhood and youth in old Aragon to rediscover and examine the sources of his life-long idealism. The first four parts of the completed cycle had originally appeared as separate novels—*Crónica del alba* (1942; *Chronicle of Dawn*, 1944), *Hipogrifo violento* (1954; *The Violent Griffin*, 1958), *La Quinta Julieta* (1957; *The Villa Julieta*, 1958), and *El mancebo y los héroes* (1960; the youth and the heroes). Under the title *Before Noon*, Volume I (the first three parts) was issued in English translation in 1958.

The novel *En la vida de Ignacio Morel* (1969; in the life of Ignacio Morel) won Spain's Planeta Prize. *El fugitivo* (1972; the fugitive), written in an allegorical vein, is one of S.'s better recent novels; in it reality and fantasy are interwoven while the action moves on multiple levels.

Although Spain, in one form or another, is a constant in S.'s work, a substantial portion of his production portrays life in the New World, especially in the American Southwest and Mexico. Of special literary merit are some of the short narratives of *Novelas ejemplares de Cíbola* (1961; *Tales of Cibola*, 1964), some of which are set in Cíbola, the conquistadors' name for the American Southwest. *El alarido de Yaurí* (1977; the howl of Yaurí) is noteworthy for its vivid and poetic recreation of life in the Peruvian Andes. A Caribbean penal island off the coast of Mexico provides the setting for one of S.'s finest earlier novels, *Epitalarnio del prieto Trinidad* (1942; *Dark Wedding*, 1943).

The author of over sixty novels, numerous collections of short stories and books of essays and journalistic articles, a number of dramatic pieces, and two thick volumes of poetry (which has aroused little critical interest), S. also published more than eight hundred articles in his literary column, "Los libros y los días," syndicated in Spanish-language newspapers throughout the western hemisphere beginning in January 1953. Regarded by many

critics as the greatest of contemporary Spanish novelists, S. revealed in his work and abiding faith in man, an implicit but uncompromising protest against social injustice, rare capacity for infusing realistic narrative with a lyrical sense and a metaphysical dimension, and great talent for impregnating ordinary reality with the mysterious and the marvelous. Characteristically, his style is that of ordinary speech, unaffected, direct, lucid. His satire and humor are highly noteworthy. He was a writer of substance rather than a polished stylist, but his style is nevertheless distinctive and authentic. Although uneven in quality, his vast literary output, which was sustained through more than five decades, assures him a permanent place in Hispanic literature.

FURTHER WORKS: *El problema religioso en México* (1928); *El Verbo se hizo sexo* (1931); *O. P.* (1931); *Siete domingos rojos* (1932; *Seven Red Sundays*, 1936); *Viaje a la aldea del crimen* (1934); *La noche de las cien cabezas* (1934); *Madrid-Moscú* (1934); *Contraataque* (1938; *Counterattack in Spain*, 1937); *El lugar del hombre* (1939; *A Man's Place*, 1940); *Hernán Cortés* (1940); *Mexicayotl* (1940); *El verdugo afable* (1952; *The Affable Hangman*, 1954); *Unamuno, Baroja, Valle-Inclán, y Santayana* (1955); *Bizancio* (1956); *Los cinco libros de Ariadna* (1957); *El diantre* (1958); *Los laureles de Anselmo* (1958); *Las imágenes migratorias* (1960); *La llave* (1960); *Examen de ingenios, los noventayochos* (1961); *La tesis de Nancy* (1962); *La luna de los perros* (1962); *Carolus Rex* (1963); *Los Tontos de la Concepción* (1963); *La aventura equinoccial de Lope de Aguirre* (1964); *Jubileo en el Zócalo* (1964); *Valle-Inclán y la dificultad de la tragedia* (1965); *El bandido adolescente* (1965); *Cabrerizas Altas* (1966); *Tres novelas teresianas* (1967); *Ensayos sobre el infringimiento cristiano* (1967); *Las gallinas de Cervantes, y otras narraciones parabólicas* (1967); *Las criaturas saturnianas* (1968); *Don Juan en la mancebia* (1968); *El extraño señor Photynos, y otras novelas americanas* (1968); *Nocturno de los 14* (1969); *Tres ejemplos de amor y una teoria* (1969); *Novelas del otro jueves* (1969); *Ensayos del otro mundo* (1970); *Tanit* (1970); *Relatos fronterizos* (1970); *Zu, el ángel anfibio* (1970); *La antesala* (1971); *Túpac Amaru* (1973); *Una virgen llama a tu puerta* (1973); *Nancy, doctora en gitanerí* (1974); *Libro armilar de poesía y memorias bisiestas* (1974); *La mesa de las tres moiras* (1974); *Nancy y el Bato loco* (1974); *Cronus y la señora conrabo* (1974); *Las tres sorores* (1974); *El futuro comenzó ayer* (1975); *Arlene y la gaya ciencia* (1976); *La efemérides* (1976); *El pez de oro* (1976); *El mechudo y la llorona* (1977); *Gloria y vejamen de Nancy* (1977); *Adela y yo* (1978); *El Superviviente* (1978); *Solanar y lucernario aragonés* (1978); *La mirada inmóvil* (1979); *Epílogo a Nancy* (1979); *Por qué se suicidan las ballenas* (1979); *Ver o no ver* (1980); *Saga de los suburbios* (1980); *Luz zodiacal en el parque* (1980); *Una hoguera en la noche* (1980); *La muñeca en la vitrina* (1980); *Monte Odina* (1980); *Ramú y los animales propicios* (1980); *Segundo solanar y lucernario* (1981); *Chandrío en la plaza de las cortes* (1981); *El Oso Malayo* (1981); *Orestíada de los pingüinos* (1981); *La cisterna de Chichén-Itzá* (1981); *El jinete y la yegua nocturna* (1982); *Album de radiografías secretas* (1982)

BIBLIOGRAPHY: King, C. L., "S.'s 'Spherical' Philosophy," *PMLA*, 69 (1954): 993–99; Rivas, J., *El escritor y su senda: Estudio crítico-literario sobre R. J. S.* (1967); Carrasquer, F., *"Imán" y la novela histórica de S.* (1970); Peñuelas, M. C., *Conversaciones con R. J. S.* (1970); King, C. L., "R. J. S.: Don Quixote Rides Again," *American Book Collector* March 1970–April 1970: 16–22; Palley,

J., *"The Sphere Revisited," Symposium* 25 (1971): 171–79; Peñuelas, M. C., *La obra narrativa de R. J. S.* (1971); King, C. L., *R. J. S.* (1974); de Watts, L. C., *Veintiún días con S. en España* (1976); King, C. L., *R. J. S.: An Annotated Bibliography, 1928–1974* (1976); Nonoyama, M., *El anarquismo en las obras de R. J. S.* (1979); Collard, P., *R. J. S. en los años 1930–1936: Sus ideas sobre la relación entre literatura y sociedad* (1980); Mainer, J.-C., ed., *R. J. S.: In Memoriam* (1983)

—CHARLES L. KING

SENEGALESE LITERATURE

There are literatures in the various African languages spoken in Senegal, notably Wolof, Tukolor, Peul, Serere, and Malinké. Since these literatures have been mostly oral, we have little evidence of their history save what can be surmised from songs and chronicles transcribed in Arabic or European script, and from those traces of tradition that remain in the oral African-language literatures today or in Francophone writing based on traditional forms, such as the poems and stories of Birago DIOP.

In the 19th c. there was an Islamic revival led by al-Hajj Umar ibn Saïd Tall (1794–1864), which led to considerable composition in Arabic, with most of the texts of a theological or philosophical nature and some of them composed in verse. At this time, Islam spread dramatically in Senegal and elsewhere in West Africa and became interfused with the traditional culture. The African and Francophone literatures alike to this day show the Islamic influence. In addition, secular writings in Arabic as well as in native languages have often sung the praise of folk heroes like Lat-Dior.

Today there is a revitalized interest in the oral literatures, and television and other media are helping to disseminate and preserve these art forms. Some contemporary writers have also produced written work in autochthonous languages as well as in French. For example, Cheikh A. NDAO's first book of verse, *Kaïrée* (1962; Kaïrée), contains poems in French, English, and Wolof; and Assane Diallo (b. c. 1940), who has written poems in French, has also published a book of poems in his native Peul, *Leyd'am* (1967; my land).

Internationally, and in the narrowest sense of what is meant by "literature," the most significant writing in 20th-c. Senegal is in French. The country enjoys a special position in the Francophone community because of its historical links with France and the special status its people were granted under new policies adopted after the French Revolution of 1789. Educational, economic, and cultural ties with France have remained very strong.

Senegalese writing, as well as politics, has been dominated by one person—Léopold Sédar SENGHOR. As a founding father of the nation, a major poet, and perhaps the leading African intellectual of the last thirty years, Senghor has inspired several generations of African writers and thinkers. His stance on behalf of black culture—crystallized in NÉGRITUDE, of which he was a prime mover—has given rise to much debate but has seldom been disregarded. His romantic ethnomystical image of the black man and his defense of an even-handed dialogue with Europe have drawn both praise and criticism; some hail his role as a decolonizer, while others take him to task for being too narrowly restricted to the

African, ignoring oppressed peoples of other colors. Whatever one's views on Senghor's philosophy and politics, he looms as an intellectual and political giant in Senegalese and African culture.

Fiction

African fiction is often autobiographical or else closely based on the oral tradition of the tale and its component, the proverb. A link between traditional African-language literature and the young but vital Francophone literature is found in the work of Birago Diop. In his two important collections, *Les contes d'Amadou Koumba* (1947; tales of Amadou Koumba) and *Les nouveaux contes d'Amadou Koumba* (1958; new tales of Amadou Koumba), Diop combines faithfully retold versions of fables he had heard as a youth from the *griot*, or wise-man storyteller, with personal creations based on the old models.

Early novels include *Les trois volontés de Malic* (1920; the three wishes of Malic) by Ahmadou Mapaté Diagne (ca. 1890–19??), which may be the first novel written in French by a black African; *Le reprouvé: Roman d'une Sénégalaise* (1925; the outcast: a novel about a Senegalese girl) by Birago Diop's brother Massyla Diop (c. 1886–1932); *Force-bonté* (1926; good will) by Bakary Diallo (1892–1978); and Ousmane Socé Diop's (b. 1911) novel *Karim: Roman sénégalais* (1935; Karim: a Senegalese novel).

The foremost contemporary novelist is Ousmane SEMBÈNE, whose films—often based on his novels and stories—have brought him international recognition. Unlike most African novelists, who base their styles and subject matter on traditional and proverbial forms, Sembène has adopted a technique not unlike André MALRAUX's, one in which social commentary and psychological portrayal of characters prevail. Furthermore, whereas most African novels tend to be episodic, Sembène's have a larger sweep one tends to associate with European novels. The best of them—for example, *Les bouts de bois de Dieu* (1960; *God's Bits of Wood*, 1962) and *L'harmattan* (1964; the harmattan [a wind from the desert])—address themselves to crucial issues, specifically the 1947 strike on the Dakar-Niger railroad and the historic 1958 French Federation referendum.

Although he has written only one book, Cheikh Hamidou Kane (b. 1928) managed, with *L'aventure ambiguë* (1961; *Ambiguous Adventure*, 1963), to address in a most concise manner the fundamental problems of colonization and decolonization. This novel has been translated into many languages and has been the focus of much critical analysis. Although discursive and slim of plot, it brilliantly presents the dilemma facing the young protagonist and his community: to struggle to preserve traditional African and Islamic values, or to embrace the new ways imported by colonialism.

Another novel of note, *La plaie* (1967; *The Wound*, 1973) by the poet Malick Fall (1920–1978), is a sardonic tale of a man with a wound that will not heal whose quest for relief and a permanent cure from his ills, paralleled as it is by a search for moral fulfillment, invites manifold and mythic interpretation.

Two woman novelists—a relative rarity in Francophone Africa—have recently attracted considerable critical scrutiny, as much for the social problems they highlight as for their intrinsic literary merit. Mariama Bâ (1929–1981) was awarded the 1980 Noma Prize for her novel *Une si longue lettre* (1979; such a long letter), which focuses on the role women are called upon to play in a changing African society. Aminata SOW FALL has published several novels. Her *La grève des Bàttu; ou, Les déchets humains* (1979;

The Beggars' Strike; or, The Dregs of Society, 1981) tells of a beggars' strike after an official has tried to restrict downtown begging. This strike wreaks havoc with the almsgiving that is required by local custom.

There is, on the part of many African fiction writers, as well as dramatists, a penchant for satirical treatment of the constraints on today's citizens and the corruption they encounter. The African sense of humor, linked as it often is to a moral lesson, often expresses itself in caricature and lampoon, as in the traditional trickster tales and such modern political satires as Sembène's *Xala* (1973; *Xala*, 1976) and *Le mandat* (1965; *The Money-Order*, 1972).

Poetry

Léopold Sédar Senghor and David Diop (1927–1960) have dominated Senegalese poetry in French. Senghor has produced a significant corpus of poetry despite the many obligations of his high office. His work tends to the long line, or biblical *verset*, and he has acknowledged his debt to Paul CLAUDEL, SAINT-JOHN PERSE and Walt Whitman. However, Senghor has brought to the long line two elements with which he has enriched its imagery: a rhythm based on African metrical conventions, and images of such Senegalese landscapes as the coast south of Dakar. His poems are humanistic, optimistic, and enthusiastic. For example, "Congo" (1956; "Congo," 1964) sings the poet's love of Africa and his vision of a dawning era of hope and fulfillment: "But the canoe will be born anew in the slackwater lilies/And will glide over the sweetness of the bamboo in the transparent morning of the world." Such poems as "Nuit de Sine" (1945; "Night of Sine," 1963), "Femme noire" (1945; "Black Woman," 1964), and "Prière aux masques" (1945; "Prayer to Masks," 1963) are often cited as typifying in literature the spirit of Senghor's rhapsodic version of Négritude.

David Diop was born in Bordeaux to a Senegalese father and a Cameroonian mother, but his fate has been intimately linked with Senegal, which he came to consider his homeland and off whose coast he died in a plane crash. The work he left behind is limited in quantity (twenty-two poems) and not outstanding in execution (he was not yet an experienced writer), but Diop has achieved almost legendary status in the eyes of those who consider him to be the poetic standardbearer of African nationalism and liberation of oppressed classes. He published only one slim collection of poems, *Coups de pilon* (1956; *Hammer Blows*, 1973), but he had already acquired a following based on five poems published by Senghor in the latter's important *Anthologie de la nouvelle poésie nègre et malgache de langue française* (1948; anthology of the new black and Malagasy poetry in French). Diop's work celebrates the natural beauties of Africa and Africans, while it scathingly condemns the arrogance of colonialism.

Several other poets warrant mention as exponents, in one way or another, of Négritude. Birago Diop's beautiful "animistic" poems in *Leurres et lueurs* (1960; lures and glimmers) are poetic counterparts to his tales. Lamine Diakhaté (b. 1928) reveals in his poetry, for example, *Primordial du sixième jour* (1963; prime order of the sixth day), the same political concerns he expresses in his fiction, as in the novel *Chalys d'Harlem* (1978; Chalys of Harlem). Ousmane Socé Diop's *Rythmes du khalam* (1962; rhythms of the khalam [a guitarlike instrument]) and Lamine Niang's (dates n.a.) *Négristique* (1968; negristics) are lyrical paeans to, and veritable rediscoveries of, African history.

Drama

Drama in the European sense of staged performances of original works designed for the theater has been slow to develop and is rather limited in scope, as in the rest of black Africa. It is not surprising that such should be the case, since African "dramas" in the form of traditional dances, choral song fests, tales told aloud, and mime have wide popularity and consequently render formal staging somewhat alien to the African spirit. Senegal is no exception, and a typical evening's fare at the Daniel Sorano Theater in Dakar consists of a staged adaptation of a tale by Birago Diop and a formalized version of a village *khawaré* (variety show). Even when there is a play proper, it is often poetic in nature, choral in structure. It is difficult to determine, for example, if Senghor's *Chaka* (1956; *Chaka*, 1964) is a poem or play, and many of the epic-historical plays, such as *L'exil d'Albouri* (1967; Albouri's exile) and *Le fils d'Almamy* (1973; Almamy's son) by Cheikh A. NDAO, and *Les Amazoulous* (1972; the Amazulus) by the poet Abdou Anta Ka (dates n.a.), are just as suited to dramatic reading as to full-scale staging.

The Essay

The historical studies of Cheikh Anta Diop (b. 1923), whose thesis posits a preponderant African input in modern world civilization through the intermediary of ancient Sudanese-Nilotic cultures, have brought their author considerable fame, especially in the U.S., where his books are often required reading in courses on African history and culture.

Alioune Diop (1910–1980) made his mark on African cultural affairs as a thinker and as a founder and editor of *Présence africaine*, the pioneering journal and publishing enterprise founded in Paris in 1947.

The Senegalese essay, like poetry, is dominated by Senghor. His academic and presidential speeches, reviews, commemorations, articles, prefaces, and interviews fill many books, the most pertinent to literary and aesthetic theory being collected in *Liberté I: Négritude et humanisme* (1964; Liberty I: Négritude and Humanism) and *Liberté III: Négritude et civilisation de l'universel* (1977; Liberty III: Négritude and the Civilization of the Universal).

Senghor's broad knowledge—which spans African literature and philology, Greek philosophy, modern European literature, and many other domains—abetted by his self-discipline and tremendous stamina, has permitted him to continue to write on the humanities while producing an equally impressive body of political essays, notably those collected in *Liberté II: Nation et voie africaine du socialisme* (1971; liberty II: nationhood and African socialism), in which he explains and defends his party's particular brand of socialism as applied to African needs and hopes.

For years, critics spoke of such entities as West African literature, lumping writers from Senegal with those from other Francophone countries in the region. Indeed, the presence in Dakar of exiled Guinean novelist Camara LAYE during the last fifteen years of his life had an undeniable impact on Senegalese culture. However, a growing critical acumen among African critics has recently pointed toward a rejection of regional generalization and toward a higher valuation of both national and individual identities. This is true, of course, of all African countries. As in other countries, indicators suggest an ongoing Senegalese Francophone literature for years to come, even as expression continues to be encouraged in African languages and writers lean more and more to such traditional literary components as the proverb and the aphorism.

BIBLIOGRAPHY: Pageard, R., *Littérature négro-africaine* (1966), passim; Jahn, J., *Neo-African Literature: A History of Black Writing* (1968), passim; Michelman, F., "The Beginnings of French-African Fiction," *RAL*, 2, 1 (1971): 5–17; Kesteloot, L., *Black Writers in French: A Literary History of Negritude* (1974), passim; Blair, D. S., *African Literature in French* (1976), passim; Case, F. I., "The Socio-Cultural Functions of Women in the Senegalese Novel," *Cultures et développement*, 9 (1977): 601–29; Dorsinville, R., "Littérature sénégalaise d'expression française," *Éthiopiques*, 15 (1978): 41–51; Wauthier, C., *The Literature and Thought of Modern Africa*, 2nd rev. ed. (1979), passim; Gérard, A. S., and J. Laurent, "Sembène's Progeny: A New Trend in the Senegalese Novel," *StTCL*, 4, 1 (1980): 133–45; Sahel, A. P., "Calliope au Sénégal," *Éthiopiques*, 22 (1980): 65–80; Gérard, A. S., *African Language Literatures* (1981): 40–45, 57–58, 71–74; "Literature and Civilization of Black Francophone Africa," special issue, *FR*, 55, 6 (1982)

—ERIC SELLIN

SENGHOR, Léopold Sédar

Senegalese poet and essayist (writing in French), b. 9 Oct. 1906, Joal

After receiving his early education in Senegal, S. went to Paris in 1928, where he attended the Lycée Louis-le-Grand and the Sorbonne. During his time in France, S. met other black students from Africa and the Caribbean, and together they began to formulate the principles of NEGRITUDE. After World War II, having spent about sixteen years in France, S. returned to Senegal to begin a distinguished and influential career as a writer and politician, which was to bring him international recognition. He very quickly assumed the political leadership of Senegal and played a major role in the decolonization of the French African colonies. In 1960 he became the first president of independent Senegal; he held this position without interruption until his retirement in 1980.

S.'s first volume of poetry, *Chants d'ombre* (1945; songs of shadow) revealed the style and themes that were to remain characteristic of his work: the long, biblical line and the celebration of the African past and cultural values. While it is obvious that at least some of these first poems were written before the war, the majority, if not all, of the poems in his next volume, *Hosties noires* (1948; black victims) were inspired by S.'s experience of the war in Europe, particularly as a conscripted soldier in the French army and then as a prisoner-of-war in Germany. He notes with perception but entirely without bitterness the racism to which the black conscripts were subjected by the white soldiers. In the same year, S. published his *Anthologie de la nouvelle poésie nègre et malgache de langue française* (1948; anthology of the new black and Malagasy poetry in French), which, with its famous preface by Jean-Paul SARTRE, has acquired an historical importance in the development of modern black writing in French.

Éthiopiques (1956; Ethiopics) is probably S.'s most significant collection and contains some of his best-known poems. Written at the height of his powers as a poet and at a time when his political career was at its most successful, the poetry in this volume has a striking quality of self-assurance, celebrating not only the well-established themes of Negritude but also the poet's own very personal preoccupation with leadership.

Although his subsequent collections have received less attention than these early ones, they show no diminution in the poet's command of his medium. *Nocturnes* (1961; *Nocturnes*, 1969) incorporates a number of love poems previously published in *Chants pour Naëtt* (1949; songs for Naëtt) and a series of new elegies, somewhat reminiscent of Paul CLAUDEL's odes, on the subject of poetry and the creative imagination. He later returned to the love poem with *Lettres d'hivernage* (1972; letters from the wet season), and then to the elegy, with *Élégies majeures* (1979; major elegies).

The themes of S.'s poetry derive very largely from his belief in the importance of justifying African culture in the face of colonialism. As he has felt the success of his enterprise becoming more and more evident, he has increasingly emphasized the need for reconciliation and the fact of interdependence. Indeed, S.'s poetry gains its vitality not so much from the themes based on intellectual principles as from those themes that are important to him personally at a deep emotional level. Reconciliation is one of these, and it expresses itself in much of his poetry as a tension between his love of Africa and his love of Europe. S. is a man of considerable breadth of culture; he therefore finds it extremely difficult to make absolute choices in this area.

Alongside his poetry, S. has published a considerable number of both shorter and book-length works on literary, cultural, and political subjects. The majority of these have been collected in three volumes under the general title of *Liberté*, numbered from I to III (1964, 1971, 1977; liberty). More recently, he has published a survey of his whole career in the form of a series of interviews with a journalist, under the title *La poésie de l'action* (1980; the poetry of action).

Although his style has had virtually no imitators, and although Négritude, which romanticized Africa, is often strongly criticized by the younger generation of black intellectuals, S.'s influence as a poet and thinker, particularly in the period from the late 1940s until 1960, has been very great indeed. In spite of a certain artificiality in the deliberately cultivated rhetoric of his poetry, which many readers now find unattractive, there can be no denying the rich and perceptive imagination that has generated the powerful, often sensuous, imagery and rhythms of his poetry, or his skillful command of the French language as a creative medium.

FURTHER WORKS: *Nation et voie africaine du socialisme* (1961; *On African Socialism*, 1964); *Pierre Teilhard de Chardin et la politique africaine* (1962); *Poèmes* (1964; enlarged ed., 1973); *Les fondements de l'africanité; ou, Négritude et arabité* (1967; *The Foundations of "Africanité"; or, "Négritude" and "Arabité,"* 1971); *Élégie des alizés* (1968); *La parole chez Paul Claudel et chez les négro-africains* (1973); *Paroles* (1975). FURTHER WORKS IN ENGLISH: *Selected Poems* (1964); *Prose and Poetry* (1965)

BIBLIOGRAPHY: Markovitz, I., *S. and the Politics of Negritude* (1969); Hymans, J., *L. S. S.: An Intellectual Biography* (1971); Bâ, S., *The Concept of Negritude in the Poetry of L. S. S.* (1973); Mezu, S., *The Poetry of L. S. S.* (1973); Reed, J., "L. S. S.," in King, B. and Ogungbesan, K., eds., *A Celebration of Black and African Writing* (1975): 102–11; *Hommage à L. S. S.: Homme de culture* (1976); Irele, A., Introduction to L. S. S., *Selected Poems* (1977): 1–37; Peters, J., *A Dance of Masks: S., Achebe, Soyinka* (1978): 15–89; Little, R., "'Je danse, donc jesuis': The Rhythm of L. S. S.'s Two

Cultures," in Bishop, M., ed., *The Language of Poetry: Crisis and Solution* (1980): 161–76; Moore, G., *Twelve African Writers* (1980): 16–38; Mbabuike, M., *Notes on the Poems of L. S.* (1989); Vaillant, J. G., *Black, French and African: A Life of L. S.* (1990)

—CLIVE WAKE

SENIOR, Olive

Jamaican short-story writer, b. 1941, Troy, Jamaica

S. spent her childhood in Jamaica traveling between her farming parents and well-off urban relatives, a routine that would become an important motif in her short stories. Her goal was to be a journalist, and she became an apprentice at Jamaica's *Daily Gleaner* and later earned a degree in journalism at Carleton University in Ottawa. She has edited West Indian journals and written about the role of women in the West Indies; however, she made her mark in the short story when *Summer Lightning and Other Stories* (1986) won the 1987 Commonwealth Writer's Prize.

In S.'s fiction stress falls on the child's problematic relationship with adults who have either alienated him, or kept him confined to a severely circumscribed role. S.'s children are often discards in search of a supportive adult, usually a mentor or parent-surrogate with whom they establish an ambivalent, psychologically dependent relationship. This ambivalence is noticeable in "Bright Thursdays" in which the illegitimate Laura is tensely poised between Miss Myrtle, the mother who tries to "whiten" her to make her acceptable to Jamaican society, and her well-to-do grandparents who force her into an artificially mannered world. S.'s young boy of "Summer Lightning" is wrenched out of his familiar world and dispatched to his aunt's and uncle's uncomfortable home where he retreats to a symbolically charged garden room only to have this Edenic refuge violated by a pedophile.

The bonding of displaced child and rejected or scorned adult who is receptive to the child's awakening sensibilities is a recurring motif in S.'s fiction. It appears again in her collection of stories, *Discerner of Hearts* (1995). In the story "Zig-Zag" the vicissitudes and hardships of her family's servant, whose blackness and poverty banish her to the bottom of the Jamaican social and racial hierarchy, force the child Sadie to confront the prime stuff of life, and she notices in the servant an integrity she cannot discern in her own starchy family.

Some of S.'s children remind one of the imaginative youngsters of Michael ANTHONY's fiction. For instance, the boy of "Summer Lightning" resembles Dolphus of Anthony's *The Games Were Coming* (1963). Discarded to the periphery of the adult world, the boy withdraws into a private world of imaginative richness where he tends to deal metaphorically with the problems plaguing him. For instance, he imagines the doors of his mind opening one after another as if he were living within a slowly opening flower. In "Love Orange" the child conceives of love in terms of orange segments, each segment fixed and finite. It is her way of coming to terms with the deficiencies of human love.

Many of S.'s recurring themes appear in "Ballad," and they are largely conveyed through a young girl's shifting consciousness. In this story S. depicts a Jamaican society crippled by its obsession with race and color, and Lenora, whose blackness is a decided handicap, is warned not to set high goals for herself. Set aside and unloved, Laura turns to Miss Rilla, a woman of dubious reputation who befriends her. This is an important syndrome in S.'s fiction: the parent-surrogate is herself a moral outcast of the community. Self-righteous Christianity that breeds intolerance and cruelty is also a pervasive theme in S.'s fiction and is particularly noticeable in "Ballad" and the title story of *Arrival of the Snakewoman and Other Stories* (1989). While Lenora's father's relationship with her stepmother is tense and violent, Miss Rilla, condemned as a profligate and unworthy of Lenora's friendship, is united with her lover in a stable and loving bond. Laura notices in the claustrophobic community the discrepancy between the espousing of Christianity and the practice of a condemning, intolerant fundamentalism. In the small, isolated Jamaican communities such as Mount Rose, the setting of "Arrival of the Snakewoman," the rejected adults to whom children turn for succor function largely as Chiron figures and corrective counterpoints to a world of sham respectability, empty values, and petty racism, all of which the children eventually reject.

The exploration of the child's fragile world and growing sensibilities seems particularly congenial to S.'s artistic temperament. Her fiction shows a compassionate understanding of the legacy of the abused and often abandoned West Indian child, and she uses the child's innocent eye and resourceful imagination as the vehicles to explore the vicissitudes of both the child and the adult world. At the end of their exploration S.'s children have a better understanding not only of the adult world, but of the self, and their psychological dependence on parent-surrogates is gradually replaced by a growing identity and a better understanding of human interdependence.

FURTHER WORKS: *The Message is Change: A Perspective on the 1972 General Elections* (1972); *One Upon a Time in Jamaica* (1977); *A-Z of Jamaican Heritage* (1983); *Talking of Trees* (1985); *Working Miracles: Women's Lives in the English-speaking Caribbean* (1991); *Gardening in the Tropics* (1994)

BIBLIOGRAPHY: Gersche, L., "Caribbean Childhoods," *TWQ*, 10 (April 1988): 995-98; O'Callaghan, E., "Feminist Consciousness: European/American Theory, Jamaican Stories," *JCS*, 6 (Spring 1988): 143-62; Pollard, V., "An Introduction to the Poetry and Fiction of O. S.," *Callaloo*, 11 (Summer 1988): 540-46; James, L., "The Other Side of the Mirror: The Short Stories of Jean Rhys and O. S.," in Bardolph, J., ed., *Short Fiction in the New Literatures in English* (1989): 89-94; Louvel, L., "'Summer Lightning': A Reading of O. S.'s Short Story," *CE&S*, 13 (Spring 1991): 42-48; Gafoor, A., "The Image of the Indo-Caribbean Woman in O. S.'s 'The Arrival of the Snakewoman,'" *Callaloo*, 16 (Winter 1993): 34-43; Patteson, R., "The Fiction of O. S.: Traditional Society and the Wider World," *Ariel*, 24 (January 1993): 13-33

—HAROLD BARRATT

SERBIAN LITERATURE

See under Yugoslav Literature

SERENI, Vittorio

Italian poet and prose writer, b. 2 July 1913, Luino; d. 10 Feb. 1983, Milan

S. is the most complex poet, and perhaps the best, of his generation. From his native town, Luino, a continuous point of reference for the poet, S. followed his family to Brescia and to Milan in 1933, where he studied at the university. He was strongly influenced by Antonio Banfi's (1886–1957) teaching on the importance of a phenomenological approach to reality, and with a group of Banfi disciples he cofounded and coedited the literary magazine *Corrente*, suppressed in 1940 by fascist authorities. In World War II, as an army lieutenant, S. served in Greece and Sicily. Captured by the Allies, he spent two years in a prison camp in Algeria. At the end of the war, after a few years of teaching, he joined the industrial sector, working first for the Pirelli company and later for the Mondadori publishing house. He has been awarded several prestigious prizes for poetry, including the Montefeltro Prize (1965), the Bagutta Prize (1981), and the Viareggio Prize (1982).

The prewar crisis, the experience of war and prison camp, and the exposure to the industrial world form the basis of S.'s poetic itinerary. Fully aware of the then-dominant tradition of the hermeticist school and its pursuit of pure poetry, S. distanced himself from it, opting for a poetry that springs from the poet's relationship with objects and with life's events. This is evident even in his first collection of poems entitled *Frontiera* (1941; *Frontier*, 1990). The title is a reference to the actual boundary between fascist Italy and Switzerland and to the political boundary between fascist Italy and free European countries. The main feature of this early poetry is the delineation of an intimate and private world undermined by the presage of the war and disasters. Luino's stormy lake, the fog, and the changing of seasons are a part of the landscape and also signs of an alarming future.

The second collection of poems, *Diario d'Algeria* (1947; *Algerian Diary*, 1990), ripens along the lines of S.'s ordeal with war and prison camp. The tone is darker than in *Frontiera*, the language more intense and essential. S's identification with European civilization comes to grips with the reality of a divided Europe, and the poet finds himself unwillingly on the side of the oppressor. In a sense the wandering of Lieutenant Sereni through Europe is an initiation into life, but it paradoxically lands him in a prison camp where he remains impotent and totally idle. Beyond its autobiographical vicissitudes, *Diario d'Algeria* is the drama of a generation caught in a war it didn't fully understand, then defeated, confined, and limited to watching the unfolding of history. At the same time, the exemplary experience is an allegory of life as imprisonment.

Gli strumenti umani (1966; *The Human Implements*, 1990) appeared twenty years later. Once more by measuring his personal experience with the problems of his times, S. faces the upheaval of the Italian industrial boom, the rejection of the democratic values espoused by the antifascist resistance, and the political disarray of its present alienating industrial society. Such an implacable environment estranges the poet who feels as impotent as he had felt when he was a prisoner of war. A sense of perplexity, a lack of guidelines, and unanswerable questions are his perimeters. S.'s search for a language that would adequately represent the transformations of this historical reality produces a lyric language capable of handling colloquial forms of the dominant entrepreneurial class and, at times, anger and hate at the betrayal of democratic ideals.

In his last collection, *Stella variabile* (1981; *Variable Star*, 1990), S. still faces the issues of his day. However, the negativity of contemporary reality is more pervasive, and his feelings of alienation toward such an absurd society throw him into a state of nihilism. The poetic self is exploded into pieces, reduced to a sense of nothingness. Life is like a race from tunnel to tunnel with brightness appearing only momentarily in between tunnels of emptiness. However, his belief in poetry, though questioned, remains strongly committed. Moments of brightness are those moments in which poetry has the power to denounce and unmask hypocrisy, trickery, hate, and exploitation.

Special mention must be made of his prose works: *Gli immediati dintorni* (1962; the immediate surroundings), a literary diary, and *L'opzione e allegati* (1964; the option); they are closely related to his poetry and shed clarity on it. It was S.'s conviction that writing is an essential act of existing, and that his greatness as a poet would be measured by how well he had succeeded in mirroring the human condition. Without doubt he has remained faithful to his beliefs, and as time passes, it is evident that S. is one of the few great Italian poets of the century.

FURTHER WORKS: *Poesie* (1942); *Frammenti di una sconfitta. Diario bolognese* (1954); *La guerra girata altrove* (1969); *Ventisei* (1970); *Letture preliminari* (1973); *Il sabato tedesco* (1980); *Gli immediati dintorni primi e secondi* (1983); *Senza l'onore delle armi* (1986); *Tutte le poesie* (1986). FURTHER WORKS IN ENGLISH: *Selected Poems of V. S.* (1990)

BIBLIOGRAPHY: Fortini, F., "S.," in R. Trevelyan, ed., *Italian Writing Today* (1967): 152–54; Dego, G., "A Poet of Frontiers," *LM* (October 1969): 38; Merry, B., "The Poetry of V. S.," *IS*, 29 (1974): 88–102; Perryman, M., and P. Robinson, Introduction to *Selected Poems of V. S.* (1990): 11–27

—ROSARIO FERRERI

SETH, Vikram

Indian poet, travel writer, and novelist, b. 20 June 1952, Calcutta

S. grew up in Calcutta where his father was in business and his mother a judge. Typical of this social class in India, S. went abroad to study, receiving his undergraduate degree at Oxford and his master's degree at Stanford University. He also studied at Nanjing University, China, and is fluent in Chinese. He lives in Delhi but spends part of his time abroad.

His first publication was a collection of poems, *Mappings* (1980), published by Calcutta's Writers Workshop, a small publishing house that has helped send several Indian writers on their way to international recognition. In 1983 his travel book, *From Heaven Lake: Travels Through Sinkiang and Tibet*, was published in England, then internationally in 1987. Widely praised, it covers S.'s hitchhiking trip from Eastern China through Tibet and Nepal to Delhi. One of the book's charms lies in S.'s self-deprecating humor as he faces the difficulties of such rigorous travel, the unfamiliar civilizations, and an assortment of fascinating people. Never a critical or finicky tourist, S. fully accepts cultural differences and leads his reader to do the same.

S.'s verse novel, *The Golden Gate* (1986), received acclaim from critics in a time when poetry usually gains little attention. Praised equally for its form and its content, the narrative poem was patterned after Aleksander Pushkin's *Eugene Onegin*. It contains some six hundred sonnets of iambic tetrameter, which are marked by an artless simplicity, perfect diction, wit, and personal reflection. Through this medium S. introduces a group of young professionals in San Francisco during the 1980s, and recounts their struggles for success and personal fulfillment. The fully developed characters—including an advertising executive, a lawyer, an activist, a computer expert, and a sculptor and drummer—typify San Francisco society as they make their way through singles bars, apartments, parks, and cafes; for that matter, the group could live in any large American city. In an intriguing digression set during an antinuclear demonstration, S. examines the fears inherent to the nuclear age. One critic noted that the reader tends to forget the structural dexterity of this tour de force and focuses attention instead on the characters' lives.

Making an abrupt change in subject matter and form, S. turned to prose fiction with a vengeance in his next publication, *A Suitable Boy* (1993). This novel of 1,349 pages brings to mind the Victorian and 19th-c. Russian novelists. Set in India during the 1950s shortly after independence from Great Britain, the narrative follows a widowed mother's search for "a suitable boy" for her daughter to marry. The memorable mother, Mrs. Rupa Mehra, moves from one part of India to another in her quest, and along the way interacts with a wide assortment of characters, some family, some casual acquaintances. Other families are introduced along with their idiosyncrasies.

The action in *A Suitable Boy* takes place on a well-painted tapestry that brings to life the dusty streets, academia, slums, fine houses and the sophisticated life within, commerce and industry, religious rites, marriage, and a thousand other parts that make up India. Likewise, the historical background and the public concerns of the time are rendered with exactitude. The process of storytelling also plays a role through one of the characters who is attempting to write a novel about India. Yet the engaging characters dominate. Unlike many contemporary Indian novels, *A Suitable Boy* does not dwell on social problems, poverty, and injustice, but simply tells the stories of ordinary Indians going about their daily lives. At the end, once "a suitable boy" has been found, the characters have not changed much and will likely continue in the same patterns—just as Mrs. Mehra sets out again, this time to find "a suitable girl" for her son.

S. belongs to a new generation of Indian writers in English, who are more international than they are either Eastern or Western. Having experienced various cultures and having learned to make his way at ease through them provides S. with a broad insight into the human condition. This knowledge, along with his ability to use language skillfully whether in poetry or prose, certainly foretells more books like *The Golden Gate* and *A Suitable Boy*, or perhaps something entirely different.

FURTHER WORKS: *The Humble Administrator's Garden* (1985); *All You Who Sleep Tonight* (1990)

BIBLIOGRAPHY: King, B., "Postmodernism and Neo-Formalist Poetry: S., Steele, and Strong Measures," *SoR*, 23 (Winter 1987): 224-31; Gupta, S., " *The Golden Gate*: The First Indian Novel in Verse," in Kirpal, V., ed., *The New Indian Novel in English* (1990): 91-100; Desai, A., "Sitting Pretty," *NYRB*, 27 May 1993: 22-26

—ROBERT ROSS

SEVAG, Barouyr

(pseud. of Barouyr Raphael Ghazarian) Armenian poet and literary historian, b. 26 Jan. 1924, Chanakhchi (now Sovedashen); d. 17 June 1971, Erevan

S. graduated from Erevan State University in 1945 and did graduate work in ancient and medieval Armenian literature at the Abeghian Institute of Literature. His doctoral dissertation, *Sayat-Nova* (pub. 1969; Sayat-Nova), is an analysis of the work of the famous poet-minstrel (1712–1795). In 1968 S. was elected to the Soviet Armenian parliament. His two careers complemented and sustained each other, with politics adding a special piquancy and interest to his poems.

After Egishe CHARENTS, S. is singled out most frequently as the outstanding Soviet Armenian poet. Although the poems of his contemporary, Gevorg Emin (b. 1919), are more often translated, because of Emin's original and striking images, S.'s poetry, with its lyricism, wit, and irony, is accessible on many levels.

In his first two books of poetry, *Anmahneruh hramayoum en* (1948; the immortals are in command) and *Seero janabar* (1954; love's road), S. examines the postwar era and shows concern for mechanization and nuclear proliferation in verse using scientific and political imagery. In *Noreetz kez hed* (1957; with you again) his emotionalism and dizzying rhetorical excesses are softened and brought under control. His witty style, replete with puns and layered meanings, has matured.

Prizes and honors followed the publication of *Anlerelee zankagadoun* (1959; the belltower that would not stop ringing), dedicated to the musician-monk Komitas, who had lost his sanity during the 1915 Turkish massacre of Armenians. Until that time Komitas had been compiling all of Armenia's folk music and arranging it for concert presentations. S.'s poem is not only a celebration of Komitas's creativity; it is also a speculation on the mysteries of creation and a contemplation of good and evil. *Martuh apee mech* (1963; man in the palm of the hand), politically controversial, scrutinizes the individual and castigates hypocrisy and fraud.

Eratsayn badarak (1965; Mass for three voices), published on the fiftieth anniversary of the Turkish massacre, is another angry treatment of the subject of victimization. Its style is similar to the torrential rhythms S. had used in *Ev ayr mee Mashdots anoon* (1962; a man named Mashdots).

S.'s last volume, *Eghetsee louys* (1969; let there be light), an examination of modern man's predicaments, firmly established him as the leading poet of his generation. Two years later he and his wife died in an automobile accident, and his readers learned the news with horror and a sense of being robbed of the wisest writer of their time.

FURTHER WORKS: *Anhashd mdermoutioun* (1953); *Erp mertsoom eh ampoghch erkiruh* (1961).

—DIANA DER HOVANESSIAN AND MARZBED MARGOSSIAN

Anne Sexton

SEXTON, Anne

(born Anne Gray Harvey) American poet, b. 9 Nov. 1928, Newton, Mass.; d. 4 Oct. 1974, Weston, Mass.

Raised in a well-to-do Massachusetts family, S. was educated in various Massachusetts public and boarding schools, and after graduation she worked as a bookstore clerk and fashion model while her husband served in the Korean War. Aside from a few poems published in her high-school yearbook, S. did not truly begin writing poetry until 1956, after the birth of her second child. At that time, S. was receiving regular psychiatric treatment, and one of her doctors encouraged S. to try writing as a form of therapy. Some four years later, the "results" of this therapy were published in the collection *To Bedlam and Part Way Back* (1960), which was nominated for the National Book Award. Although this collection received mixed reviews—some readers were disturbed by the confessional and extremely personal nature of the poems—it quickly established S. as an important American poet. Her second collection, *All My Pretty Ones* (1962), received the Levinson Prize from *Poetry* magazine.

Despite the fact that her literary career spanned less than twenty years and was cut short by suicide, S. is recognized as one of the premier poets of her generation. Her work is popularly classified as "confessional poetry." In this type of poetry there are no "rules" as to appropriateness of subject matter; highly personal, sometimes embarrassing, topics become grist for the poetic mill. S. wrote about such previously "taboo" topics as sex, abortion, and her own psychiatric problems and subsequent treatment. Her depiction of intimate and often depressing subjects in a clear and honest style, combined with a celebrity status earned by frequent readings of her own work, made S. a popular public figure as well as an accomplished literary artist.

Live or Die (1966) is S.'s best-known and most highly acclaimed collection. In this work S. continues to employ such familiar themes as death, madness, and depression; a number of the poems, including "Wanting To Die," "Suicide Note" and "Sylvia's Death," display S.'s fascination with suicide, and perhaps foreshadow her own tragic end. In *Live or Die* S. displays the fully developed poetic voice that would make her, along with Sylvia PLATH and Adrienne RICH, one of the most influential female poets of her era. In 1967 she received both the Shelley Award from the American Society of Poetry and the Pulitzer Prize for this book, and in 1968 S. received an honorary Phi Beta Kappa from Harvard University.

Later poetry collections include *Love Poems* (1969), *Transformations* (1971)-an extremely popular collection in which S. retells a number of Grimm's fairy tales-*The Books of Folly* (1972), and *The Death Notebooks* (1974). Two more collections, *The Awful Rowing toward God* (1975) and 45 *Mercy Street* (1976), were published posthumously. In addition to poetry, S. also wrote *Mercy Street* (1969), a play that enjoyed a successful off-Broadway run. S. collaborated with Maxine KUMIN on a number of children's books: *Eggs of Things* (1963), *More Eggs of Things* (1964), *Joey and the Birthday Present* (1971), and *The Wizard's Tears* (1975).

Afraid that she was losing her creativity, S. committed suicide by carbon-monoxide poisoning in 1974, shortly before her forty-sixth birthday. In her brief literary career, S. produced a significant body of work that makes her one of the most significant poets of the late 20th c.

FURTHER WORKS: *Poems* (1968, with Thomas Kinsella and Douglas Livingstone); *A. S.: A Self-Portrait in Letters* (1977); *Words for Dr. Y.: Uncollected Poems with Three Stories* (1978); *The Complete Poems* (1981); *No Evil Star: Selected Interviews, Essays and Prose* (1985); *Selected Poems of A. S.* (1988)

BIBLIOGRAPHY: Northouse, C., and Walsh, T. P., eds., *Sylvia Plath and A. S.: A Reference Guide* (1974); McClatchy, J. D., ed. *A. S.: The Artist and Her Critics* (1978); Middlebrook, D. W., "'I Tapped My Own Head': The Apprenticeship of A. S.," in Middlebrook, D. W., and Yalom, M., eds., *Coming to Light: American Women Poets in the Twentieth Century* (1985); George, D. H., "How We Danced: A. S. on Fathers and Daughters," *WS*, 12, 2 (1986): 179–202; George, D. H., *Oedipus Anne: The Poetry of A. S.* (1987); George, D. H., "The Poetic Heroism of A. S.," *L&P* 33: 3–4 (1987): 76–88; Bixler, F., ed., *Original Essays on the Poetry of A. S.*(1988); Colburn, S. E., ed. *A. S.: Telling the Tale* (1988); George, D. H., ed. *S. Selected Criticism* (1988); Morton, R. E., *A. S.'s Poetry of Redemption: The Chronology of a Pilgrimage* (1988); Hall, C. K. B., *A. S* (1989); Wagner-Martin, L., ed. *Critical Essays on A. S.* (1989); Middlebrook, D. W., *A. S.: A Biography* (1991); Gray, L., *Searching For Mercy Street* (1994)

—JASON BERNER

al-SHĀBBĪ, Abū al-Qāsim

Tunisian poet, b. 24 Feb. or 3 Mar. 1909, Tozeur; d. 9 Oct. 1934, Tozeur

S. was born in Tozeur in southwestern Tunisia, a lush oasis where he spent an enchanting childhood. This joyous and carefree childhood, a recurrent theme in his poetry, contrasts with his unhappy adolescence, marred by depression, loneliness, and illness. After he attended the Koranic school in his native town, S. moved to Tunis, where he enrolled at Al-Zeituna University. Despite his frail health, S. led a life effervescent with intellectual and political activities. While still a student at the university at Al-Zeituna, S. penned numerous literary and political articles and manifestos in the journals of the 1930s and delivered lectures where he expounded his ars poetica as well as his political views. He succumbed to consumption at the age of twenty-five.

S. is Tunisia's national poet. His patriotic verse found its way not only into his country's national anthem but also into the hearts of many generations of schoolchildren in the Arab world. But beyond the nationalistic appeal of his poetry, S. remains for many the poet of youth, of dreams, and of romantic love. His verbal inventiveness and audacious imagery rank him as one of the best poets in contemporary Arabic literature. His untimely death and unfinished work have, for generations, fostered among students and critics a Rimbaud-type myth—of the radical social rebel and of the prophetic poet. His only book of poems. *Aghānī al-hayāt* (hymns to life), was published posthumously in Cairo in 1954. His diary and correspondence—an invaluable source of bio-bibliographical information as well as an important social document on the period—were published in Tunis in 1965.

S. owes his patriotic and nationalistic credentials and reputation to a relatively small number of poems where he vehemently assails the colonial order and its oppressive policies, and where he castigates, with equal energy, his compatriots for their lethargy, childishness, and backwardness. More important, as one of the leaders of the literary and intellectual renaissance or *Nahdah* movement in Tunisia, S. strove to forge a new and modern Arab cultural identity and sensibility that would be locally inspired as well as expressive of contemporary reality and preoccupations. These new aesthetic and intellectual orientations are expounded particularly in his famous lecture *Al-Khāyal al-shi'rī 'inda al-'Arab* (1929; the poetic imagination of the Arabs). In this lecture he vigorously attacks contemporaries who dwell on the past glories of Arabic classical literature and who, for lack of imagination, continue a sterile poetic and rhetorical tradition that can no longer accommodate a modern sensitivity and concerns. His active advocacy of *Tajdīd* or modernism, as a catalyst of social, political, and cultural change as well as a means of disenfranchisement from the vestiges of a suffocating past, is not, however, without contradictions.

Ironically, S.'s own poetry is hardly demonstrative of the aesthetic and original ideas and spirit he set forth in his lectures. His poetry adheres, except for a few promising but unconvincing attempts, to the metrical and rhetorical canons of the traditional *qasīda* as established by the classical and postclassical poets of long ago. However, his innovation is discernable in other aspects of his language; in the poems of *Aghānī al-hayāt*, S. eschews stock imagery and clichés and favors an individualistic, if not intimist, tone. A sense of tragic loss, especially of innocence, pervades the dominant themes of his poetic inspiration: love, death, and freedom. Some of S.'s poems hark back, via the poets of Al-Mahjar

(Arab poets who emigrated to the Americas in the late 19th and early 20th cs.) to the European romantics whose angst and morbid imagination as well as suffusive language have struck a congenial cord with many Arab poets of the period.

Above all, S. remains the symbol of a whole generation of writers, poets, and intellectuals caught, as he was, in the bind between tradition and modernity, identity and difference. Although he remains Tunisia's best-known poet, whose poetry is still relished by the general public and especially the young, S. is, paradoxically, a lone and orphan voice as he neither inspired disciples nor initiated any recognizable literary or aesthetic following.

BIBLIOGRAPHY: Zmerli, S., *Figures tunisiennes: les contemporains et les autres* (1972), passim; Baccar, T., and S. Garmadi, eds., *Écrivains de Tunisie* (1981): 11–54; Allen, R., ed., *Modern Arabic Literature* (1987): 289–93

—HÉDI ABDEL-JAOUAD

SHABTAI, Yaakov

Israeli novelist, short-story writer, and dramatist, b. 8 Mar. 1934, Tel Aviv; d. 4 Aug. 1981, Tel Aviv

S. began his literary work mainly as a playwright, although he also wrote stories in the early period. *Hadod peretz mamriy* (1972; Uncle Peretz takes off) is a collection of thirteen stories of the first stage of his work. His first novel (the only one that he himself completed for publication) was *Zikhron dvarim* (1977; *Past Continuous*, 1983); his posthumous novel, *Sof davar* (1984; *Past Perfect*, 1987), acquired its title at his own suggestion, and, although it was edited and brought to publication by his widow, Edna Shabtai, together with Dan Miron, no word was added to the original manuscript. Only existing alternatives were selected by the editors.

S.'s work is the product of a short life and a writing career of some fifteen years. The early works are lyrical, exuberant, and humorous, although, as throughout the S. opus, the theme of death predominates. The setting is very firmly the Israel of the 1960s, especially Tel Aviv, but it is an Israel that although located in the present is a very conspicuous witness to the shadow, the decay, and the death of the past. Over the existent secular society hovers another presence, that of the old world. The actuality of this world can become metaphor too, as in the story "Histalqut" (passing away). In *Hadod peretz mamriy*, which describes the death of the narrator's grandmother, and the manner in which the family increasingly rejects the traditional way of life that had been accepted under her influence. *Zikhron dvarim* was a new departure in narrative, not only for the author but for Israeli prose, marking a radical departure that is still very much a major influence in current Israeli fiction. The title is ambiguous, associating the senses of "protocol," a record of events, with memory. The typographical innovation that the author introduces is that the whole novel has no paragraph and chapter divisions, although it consists of 275 pages in the Hebrew edition (the English translation abandons this apparently difficult device).

S.'s final work yet again marked a new departure. This time, there are four sections in the novel, and they are all presented differently, although they all relate to one character, Meir. The first section adopts the flowing technique of the earlier novel, its tone, its preoccupation (with death), and its approach, although it abandons the use of the single paragraph. The second section moves at a slower pace and gives graver consideration to the actuality of death, in this case, the death of Meir's mother. The third section focuses on Meir's own attempt at self-renewal, here exemplified by a trip that he takes alone to Amsterdam and London. It is in Europe, away from his home, that he discovers how sick he is. The crisis occurs in Foyle's Book Shop in London, which follows a series of minor disappointments that, for him, are full of foreboding. Meir senses loss of control, and from here on he subjects his mind and faculties to close scrutiny to detect signs of abnormality. The last section, back in Tel Aviv, brings the narrative to a climax and conclusion, with a mixture of NATURALISM and SURREALISM.

S.'s fiction is marked by scrupulous, precise observation of consciousness, by attention to detail in full-blooded and appropriate narrative. The experimental nature of the prose derives from the pressure to push writing beyond the confines of the naturalistic and toward a grasp of the essential elements of life.

BIBLIOGRAPHY: Yudkin, L. I., 1948 and After Aspects of Israeli Fiction (1984): 112–16; Yudkin, L. I., "Transmission of Reality in the Fiction of Y. S." Jewish Book Annual (1990–1991): 132–47

—LEON I. YUDKIN

SHAFFER, Peter

English dramatist, critic, and novelist, b. 15 May 1926, Liverpool

Son of a realtor, S. received his education at St. Paul's School, London, and Trinity College, Cambridge. Before entering Cambridge, S. was conscripted and from 1944 to 1947 worked in coal mines to satisfy his national service. He lived in New York for three years, working in the Public Library (1951–54), then returned to London, where he was employed by the music publisher Boosey and Hawkes (1954–55). S. and his twin brother, Anthony, also a playwright, co-authored three novels, published in the early 1950s, under the joint pseudonym Peter Anthony. By 1955 S. was devoting all his time to writing, and in 1958 his first play, Five Finger Exercise, was produced in London's West End. He also served as literary critic for Truth (1956–57) and music critic for Time and Tide (1961–62).

Of all S.'s plays, Equus (perf. 1973, pub. 1974) and Amadeus (1980) have received the greatest attention in England and the U.S. With its style and technique derived from Bertolt BRECHT, Equus uses narrative and episodic reenactment to piece together the psychological puzzle of a teenage boy's blinding of six horses. The psychiatrist Martin Dysart's intellectual manipulation of the youth, Alan Strang, succeeds in eliciting both confession and cause, but so also does it reveal a Dionysian vision of life that Dysart can only envy and emulate in dream.

Amadeus uses similar theatrical techniques to dramatize the professional conflict between two 18th-c. composers: the commercially successful Antonio Salieri and, as he is portrayed here, the ill-mannered and ill-tempered musical genius Mozart. Salieri's simultaneous admiration and jealousy create an intense personal conflict as well, as does his growing belief that God has reneged on the Faustian bargain that assured Salieri fame but denied him the genius of his nemesis.

An earlier play which has not enjoyed the popularity of the two more recent ones but which is undoubtedly S.'s most ambitious is The Royal Hunt of the Sun (1964), a spectacle of epic proportions (probably suggested by a scenario for a projected work by Antonin ARTAUD, dramatizing the 16th-c. Spanish conquest of Peru. Five Finger Exercise, a domestic drama in the 19th-c. style, and Black Comedy (perf. 1965, pub. 1967), a modern farce, attest to the playwright's versatile craftsmanship.

When S. came to the British stage in the late 1950s, he was among the generation of playwrights writing in the wake of a renewed enthusiasm for drama, occasioned by John OSBORNE's Look Back in Anger (1956). Although S. remains less angry a social critic than his contemporaries, he has developed into an insightful psychological dramatist, whose sure sense of plotting and shrewd sense of conflict have earned him a respected place among contemporary dramatists.

FURTHER WORKS: How Doth the Little Crocodile? (1951, with Anthony Shaffer, under joint pseud. Peter Anthony); Woman in the Wardrobe (1952, with Anthony Shaffer, as Peter Anthony); Withered Murder (1955, with Anthony Shaffer, as Peter Anthony); The Prodigal Father (perf. 1955); The Salt Land (perf. 1955); Balance of Terror (perf. 1957); The Private Ear [and] The Public Eye (1962); The Merry Roosters Panto (perf. 1963); A Warning Game (perf. 1967); White Lies (Am. title, 1967; Br., The White Liars, 1968); It's About Cinderella (perf. 1969); The Public Eye (screenplay, 1972); The Battle of Shrivings (perf. 1970, pub. as Shrivings, 1974); The Collected Plays of P. S. (1982); Lettice and Lovage (1988)

BIBLIOGRAPHY: Taylor, J., P. S. (1974); Barnish, V., Notes on P. S.'s "The Royal Hunt of the Sun" (1975); Stacy, J., "The Sun and the Horse: P. S.'s Search for Worship," ETJ, 28 (1976): 325–37; Kerensky, O., The New British Drama: Fourteen Playwrights since Osborne and Pinter (1977): 31–58; Dean, J., "P. S.'s Recurrent Character Type," MD, 21 (1978): 297–307; Klein, D., P. S. (1979); Gianakaris, C. J., "A Playwright Looks at Mozart: P. S.'s Amadeus," CompD, 15, 1 (1981): 37–53; Plunka, G., P. S.: Roles, Rites, and Rituals in the Theatre (1988)

—JUNE SCHLUETER

SHAHNON Ahmad

Malaysian novelist and short-story writer (writing in Malay), b. 13 Jan. 1933, Sik

S. was born in a village in the state of Kedah. After attending secondary school in Alor Setar (1947–53), he began a career as a schoolteacher in 1954, and except for a stint as an army officer (1955–56), he continued to teach until he went to Australia in 1968 for university study. He received his B.A. in 1971. He later earned an M.A. (1975) from the University of Science in Penang, where he is currently a professor of Malay literature. Although an academician now, S., who began writing in 1956, continues to publish novels and short stories as well as essays and criticism.

Above all, S. is a fighter. His essays and literary works always contain a note of protest and defiance at the order of things. The twist of fate, irony, and pathos are the hallmarks of his short stories, but at the same time he believes that literature should have a social function. His novels in particular are realistic and deal with sensitive issues.

Although S.'s early short stories, collected in *Anjing-anjing* (1964; dogs) and *Debu merah* (1965; red dust), are superior to most Malaysian short fiction, it was not until he began publishing novels that he was acclaimed as the master of modern Malay prose. His first novel, *Rentong* (1965; burned to ashes), deals with Malaysia's unfortunate rural population. Having come from a peasant village himself, S. showed his sympathy for these people, who are ill-equipped to deal with natural disasters and social change.

Ranjau sepanjang jalan (1966; *No Harvest but a Thorn*, 1972) also concerns the extreme difficulty of the peasants' lives, detailing not only their struggle with the physical environment but their relationships with one another and their belief in the supernatural. Man's relationship with his fellow men is also the subject of the novels *Protes* (1967; protest), *Menteri* (1967; the minister), and *Perdana* (1969; premier). *Protes* is largely an argument between the main characters about religious subjects; *Menteri* is a satirical treatment of political and bureaucratic corruption; and *Perdana* deals with the political events of the period of the struggle for independence. All three novels illustrate S.'s contention that weakness is found among urban dwellers and the educated middle class as well as the peasantry.

Srengenge (1973; *Srengenge*, 1980), which won an important literary prize in Malaysia, is more symbolic than S.'s earlier fiction. The hill of the title is believed to be possessed by a powerful evil spirit. By showing how the people who live around the hill react to this spirit, S. examines man in relation to religion and the supernatural. Religious themes have been the primary focus of S.'s recent writings.

FURTHER WORKS: *Terdedah* (1965); *Sampah* (1974); *Kemelut* (1977); *Selasai sudah* (1977); *Seluang menolak Baung* (1978); *Penglibatan dalam puisi* (1978); *Gubahan novel* (1979); *Kesusasteraan dan etika Islam* (1981). FURTHER WORKS IN ENGLISH: *The Third Notch, and Other Stories* (1980)

BIBLIOGRAPHY: Osman, Mohd. Taib bin, "Modern Malay Literature: A Reflection of a Changing Society and Culture," *ASPAC Quarterly*, 5, 3 (1973): 23–37; Johns, A. H., on *No Harvest but a Thorn, Hemisphere*, (September 1973): 40–41; Fernando, L., Introduction to *The Third Notch, and Other Stories* (1981): i–xiv; Nazareth, P., On *The Third Notch, and Other Stories, WLT*, 56 (1982): 408

—MOHD. TAIB BIN OSMAN

SHAPIRO, Karl

American poet, critic, and editor, b. 10 Nov. 1913, Baltimore, Md.

Prior to serving in the U.S. Army (1941–45), S. attended the University of Virginia, Johns Hopkins University, and Pratt Library School in Baltimore. Following his military service, S. taught as regular faculty member or visiting professor at several universities. He edited *Poetry* (1950–56), *Newberry Library Bulletin* (1953–55), and *Prairie Schooner* (1956–66), as well as serving as consultant in poetry to the Library of Congress (1946–47).

Person, Place and Thing (1942), S.'s first mature collection of verse, published while he was on active military duty in the South Pacific, included poems that are technically proficient and reveal his personalism and willingness to confront the world as it is, themes that were to develop into greater emphasis on S.'s Jewishness and on social criticism. With the publication of *V-Letter, and Other Poems* (1944), which won the 1945 Pulitzer Prize, S. consolidated his position in American verse at the moment as a social critic in the manner of W. H. AUDEN. Such poems as "University," "Washington Cathedral," "Auto Wreck," and "Drug Store," which S. included in *Poems, 1940–1953* (1953), struck readers as strikingly original. They are realistic, detailed, and assertive only about factual matters. After a long period in which nothing new appeared in the poetry he wrote, S. published *The Bourgeois Poet* (1964), which in both its prose poems and themes revealed a sharp change in direction. This volume tacitly acknowledges the fundamentally romantic basis of the theory of literature, which had been taking shape in his criticism.

In his *Essay on Rime* (1945), also written in the South Pacific, S. initiated an attack on modern intellectualist poetry and New Criticism, which he intensified in subsequent critical essays. *His Beyond Criticism* (1953; repub. as *A Primer for Poets*, 1965) continued the attack on modernist poets and critics, especially on YEATS, POUND, and ELIOT, who, ironically, had influenced the generally "new critical" forms of his own early verse. Between this volume and *In Defense of Ignorance* (1960), S. found in Walt Whitman, as he announced in his essay "The First White Aboriginal" (1957), a model, a resource to counter the "negativity of modern intellectual life." S. saw William Carlos WILLIAMS, Henry MILLER, D. H. LAWRENCE, and Dylan THOMAS aligned with Whitman in favor of feeling and experience, and opposed to desiccated modernism, as he perceived it. S. also acknowledged the positive influences of the psychoanalyst Wilhelm Reich, of JUNG, and of the Zen Buddhism movement in general.

Most critical readers are inclined to see two of S.'s volumes of verse, *Poems of a Jew* (1958) and *White-Haired Lover* (1968), as idiosyncratic reflections of his rejection of the intellectualism of the "Trio," as he called Yeats, Pound, and Eliot, and of his enthusiasm for the experience-based work of William Carlos Williams and Henry Miller. Except for the topical interest of his World War II poems and the unexpected formal attributes of *The Bourgeois Poet*, S.'s verse will probably slip into obscurity. Ironically the poems most likely to survive—"Auto Wreck," "University," and "Elegy for a Dead Soldier"—embody both his celebrated personalism and elements of the kind of formalistic verse against which he has warred. In criticism, he will be remembered for his vigorous and individualistic challenge of the modernists.

FURTHER WORKS: *Poems* (1935); *Five Young Poets* (contributor, 1941); *The Place of Love* (1942); *Trial of a Poet, and Other Poems* (1947); *English Prosody and Modern Poetry* (1947); *Poets at Work* (contributor, 1948); *A Bibliography of Modern Prosody* (1948); *The Tenor* (opera, 1956); *The House* (1957); *Start with the Sun: Studies in Cosmic Poetry* (1960, with James Miller, Jr., and Bernice Slote); *The Writer's Experience* (1964, with Ralph Ellison); *A Prosody Handbook* (1965; with Robert Beum); *Randall Jarrell* (1967); *To Abolish Children, and Other Essays* (1968); *Selected Poems* (1968); *Edsel* (1971); *The Poetry Wreck* (1975); *Adult Bookstore* (1976); *Collected Poems, 1940–1978* (1978); *Love and War, Art and God: The Poems of K. S.* (1984); *New and Selected*

Poems 1940-1986 (1987); *Poet: An Autobiography in Three Parts* (1988); *Reports of My Death* (1990)

BIBLIOGRAPHY: Daiches, D., "The Poetry of K. S.," *Poetry*, 66 (1945): 266–73; Fussell, E., "K. S.: The Paradox of Prose and Poetry," *WR*, 18 (1954): 224–44; Rosenthal, M. L., *The Modern Poets: A Critical Introduction* (1960): 245, 248–50; Stepanchev, S., *American Poetry since 1945: A Critical Survey* (1965): 53–68; Waggoner, H. H., *American Poets from the Puritans to the Present* (1968): 585–96; Malkoff, K., "The Self in the Modern World: K. S.'s Jewish Poems" in Malin, I., ed., *Contemporary American-Jewish Literature* (1973): 213–28; Reino, J., *K. S.* (1981)

—ARTHUR B. COFFIN

SHAW, George Bernard

Anglo-Irish dramatist, essayist, critic, and novelist, b. 26 July 1856, Dublin; d. 2 Nov. 1950, Ayot St. Lawrence, England

Born into a middle-class Irish Protestant family, S. spent his childhood with few material advantages. His father was a heavy drinker of little accomplishment, but his mother was a woman of some musical talent whom S. later described as a "Bohemian anarchist with lady-like instincts." She largely supported the family by giving singing lessons. S. received his early schooling in

George Bernard Shaw

Dublin and in 1871 began work for a Dublin estate agent, earning a mere pittance. In 1871 also he first saw Henry Irving act and became interested in the theater.

In 1876 S. moved to England, where he lived for the remainder of his life. In London he worked for the Edison Telephone Co. and undertook a program of self-education, reading extensively at the British Museum and availing himself of the city's cultural life. At the British Museum S. first became familiar with Karl Marx's *Das Kapital*, a work that guided him to the socialist philosophy articulated in almost all his writings.

In September 1882 S. heard the American economist Henry George speak in advocacy of the single tax (based upon land value) as the solution to social injustice and was deeply impressed with the socialist viewpoint. In 1884 he joined the Fabian Society, a small group of intellectual socialists whose approach to social reform was one of gradual and continual progress through education, rather than through the revolutionary upheavals advocated by Marx. In his writing and his extensive public speaking, S. became the principal spokesman for the Fabian Society from 1886 on.

In the 1880s S. became familiar with the plays of Henrik Ibsen, a dramatist he was repeatedly to champion, notably in *The Quintessence of Ibsenism* (1891). S.'s early plays were strongly influenced by Ibsen's iconoclastic social dramas. Other major influences, S. himself later claimed, were Shakespeare, Mozart, and Wagner.

Also in the 1880s S. became a journalist-critic, a career that brought little remuneration but considerable renown. He began in 1885 as a book reviewer for the *Pall Mall Gazette*; in the following year he became as well art critic for *The World*. From 1888 to 1890 he wrote music reviews for *The Star* under the pseudonym Corno di Bassetto, and from 1890 to 1894 his music reviews were published in *The World*, where he signed himself "G. B. S." His reputation as a brilliant critic of all the arts was assured when he wrote drama criticism for *Saturday Review*, from 1895 to 1898.

Aside from journalism, S.'s earliest literary efforts were in the field of fiction. By 1883 he had written five novels, all unpublished. None of these is considered today a significant item in the Shavian canon; it was as a dramatist that he found both publishers and readers. His first collection of plays, the two-volume *Plays, Pleasant and Unpleasant* (1898), earned considerable critical attention. It was quickly followed by *Three Plays for Puritans* (1900). S. remained principally a playwright throughout his career, producing some sixty plays and playlets, almost all accompanied by lengthy prefaces, essays, and other appendixes. He was awarded the Nobel Prize for literature in 1925.

S.'s literary reputation reached its zenith in the first three decades of the 20th c., when the best of his plays were produced. He also earned a reputation for personal eccentricity. He married Charlotte Payne-Townshend in 1898, but it has been suggested that the relationship was platonic. His Fabian views were considered, at the least, unorthodox, and he was as well a vegetarian, a teetotaler, and a vociferous foe of tobacco. He mingled with atheists and was frequently associated with their causes, although he denied his own atheism. When quizzed on religion, he proclaimed himself a Creative Evolutionist, one influenced by Henri BERGSON's philosophy of the freedom of the human will. This faith is reflected in many of his plays, notably *Man and Superman* (written 1902, perf. 1905) and *Back to Methuselah* (written 1918–20, perf. 1922). The revolutionist hero of the former play, John Tanner, champions the indestructible power of the Life Force, S.'s rendering of Bergson's *élan vital*.

S.'s career as a dramatist may be divided into three periods. The first is represented by the ten early plays published in the three volumes cited above. The second encompasses his mature work, the plays produced between 1905 and 1923 and best known today. In his final period, from roughly 1925 on, S. produced little of interest for the contemporary reader or theatergoer.

S.'s avowed purpose in writing the seven plays published as *Plays, Pleasant and Unpleasant* was to launch a "general onslaught of idealism," attacking social institutions, Victorian ideals of goodness, and the stifling effects of "duty" on human conduct. Despite their unorthodox content, the plays are conventional in form and structure, drawing upon the features of the "well-made plays" of Eugène Scribe (1791–1861), Victorien Sardou (1831–1908), and Émile Augier (1820–1889). They are within the mainstream of late-19th-c. naturalism and exemplify such popular genres as the problem play, domestic drama, romantic drama, farcical comedy, and melodrama. Each play advances S.'s socialist viewpoint and is essentially an argument or demonstration focusing on some current social or political problem.

S. called his three "unpleasant" plays "dramatic pictures of middle class society from the point of view of a Socialist who regards the basis of that society as thoroughly rotten economically and morally," claiming that "their dramatic power is used to force the spectator to face unpleasant facts." The plays are *Widowers' Houses* (1892), an indictment of slum housing and of the system that allows capitalists to profit from it; *The Philanderer* (written 1893, perf. 1905), an autobiographical melodrama that debunks romantic love and exposes marriage as a useless institution perpetuated by capitalist ideals; and *Mrs. Warren's Profession* (written 1894, perf. 1905), a domestic drama that is the best of the three.

Mrs. Warren's Profession depicts a woman who has risen from poverty to a position of wealth (if not class) through prostitution and, finally, through management of a successful chain of brothels. Mrs. Warren is drawn as a woman of strong character who is forced through economic necessity alone into a life of prostitution. She is pitted against her daughter Vivie, S.'s portrait of the New Woman, who earns her living through the use of her intellect and deplores her mother's "profession." S.'s purpose in this play, widely misunderstood, was to expose the inequity of the underpayment of women laborers and their treatment as second-class citizens. S. deplored the sentimental attitudes and self-righteous moralizing that kept society from dealing with problems like prostitution, poverty, and economic exploitation. Unfortunately, many of his readers objected to being confronted with their own complicity in Mrs. Warren's fate, and the play was suppressed for a number of years.

The four "pleasant" plays are more subtle in their indictment of ideals and institutions. S.'s method in the "unpleasant" plays had been to preach; his technique here was to instruct by entertaining. All four plays are comedies whose central characters, although quite sympathetic, are made to appear ridiculous because they act according to commonly accepted codes of behavior.

Best of the four are *Arms and the Man* (1894) and *Candida* (written 1895, perf. 1897). *Arms and the Man*, S.'s first popular success, is a satire on romantic views of love and militaristic heroism. Its idealistic heroine, Raina, at first enamored of the dashing aristocratic officer Sergius, learns from the pragmatic Swiss soldier Bluntschli, who carries chocolates instead of bullets, what love and war are really all about. She ultimately marries him rather than Sergius. Despite its popularity, *Arms and the Man* is not among S.'s best plays. He himself later referred to it as "flimsy" and "fantastic."

Candida, a more satisfactory comedy, is cast in the vein of domestic naturalism. S. examines here the real nature of domesticity, as opposed to sentimental ideals about the "sanctity" of marriage and home. A weak, sensitive young poet intrudes into the home of a self-confident Christian socialist preacher, claiming that his poetic idealization of the clergyman's wife, Candida, makes him worthy of taking the woman from her home and family. The preacher learns that it is not his strength but his weakness that keeps his home together—that the poet is the stronger of the two, for he can live without love. *Candida* remains a touching and delightful comedy, one in which S. lost no opportunity to advance the socialist doctrine.

The remaining two "pleasant" plays are *You Never Can Tell* (written 1896, perf. 1899), a farcical satire on pseudoprogressive idealism, and *The Man of Destiny* (written 1895, perf. 1897), a one-act comedy about Napoleon that S. wrote expressly as a popular West End vehicle for Richard Mansfield and Ellen Terry. The author himself dismissed it as a "trifle."

The *Three Plays for Puritans* are *The Devil's Disciple* (1897), *Caesar and Cleopatra* (written 1898, perf. 1901), and *Captain Brassbound's Conversion* (written 1899, perf. 1900). They represent a departure from S.'s earlier naturalistic, domestic plays, for all three are historical melodramas with protagonists of heroic proportions. Aimed at the popular audience, they are set in exotic times and places, concerned with violent actions, and mounted within militaristic frameworks.

The Devil's Disciple, set in the American Revolutionary period, has as its protagonist Dick Dudgeon, a self-serving profligate who responds to his better nature by offering up his own life to save that of the town clergyman, Anthony Anderson. It is one of S.'s most frequently performed plays, and its character of General Burgoyne is a comedic gem.

In *Caesar and Cleopatra* S. attempted to create a stage hero of Shakespearean proportions. He stated that he believed Caesar to be the "greatest man that ever lived," and his dramatization of the Roman conveys his admiration. The play successfully blends serious actions and farcical episodes. Moreover, it advances S.'s didactic viewpoints through the attitudes and actions of its characters, so that the work, despite a considerable amount of Shavian discussion, never seems preachy. The play's principal flaw is its episodic and rambling structure.

Captain Brassbound's Conversion, not nearly so successful a play as the other two, attempts to create in a female protagonist the same sort of heroic magnitude as that represented in the Caesar play. Its captivating heroine, Lady Cicely Waynflete, is S.'s version of ideal British womanhood. Unfortunately, much of the play is slow-moving and inconsistent in style.

From S.'s mature, middle period, at least half a dozen plays, popular even today, are considered modern masterpieces. One of the best is *Man and Superman*, a philosophical comedy of manners that sets forth S.'s views on love, marriage, and sexuality. S. managed to defy preexisting notions of dramatic structure by combining two separate plays within one work. Farcical comedy is mixed with an interval of profound philosophizing.

The main plot depicts John Tanner, a self-proclaimed revolutionist, as he attempts to escape marriage to Ann Whitefield. S.'s thesis is that the male is the biological victim of the female, whose sole mission it is to pursue and entrap a father for her children. In Tanner, S. created a delightful hero who is spokesman for the playwright's own serious considerations on economic and moral reform. He is, at the same time, as ridiculously comic as a Molière hero. Tanner's fatuous revolutionary zeal endears him to us, allowing us to contemplate S.'s radical views without being repelled by them. Tanner refers frequently to his own book, "The Revolutionist's Handbook," which S. happily appended, in toto, to the text of the play itself. It is a virtual manifesto of socialist reform and an entertaining denunciation of bourgeois capitalist society.

The second plot is the third-act dream sequence often referred to as "Don Juan in Hell," a Platonic dialogue without overt stage action of any kind. Through its mythic antagonists Don Juan and the Devil, S. voiced his views on salvation, man's destructive impulse, and the relationship of male and female. Despite its lack of dramatic action, its play of ideas is compelling. It is surely among S.'s most profound writings.

In *Major Barbara* (1905) S. satirized sentimental and misguided liberalism in the figure of a Salvation Army worker, Barbara Under-shaft. Her father is a capitalist munitions manufacturer and therefore her ideological adversary. Her mother is Lady Britomart, who, while staunchly defending humanitarian ideals, reveals herself as spokesperson for the very aristocracy that prevents such ideals from being realized. The comedy has been acclaimed for its intellectual and philosophical insights, but its verbal debates and its emphasis upon ideas impede its theatrical effectiveness.

The Doctor's Dilemma (1906), which S. labeled a tragedy, is a problem play no less rich in ideas but one in which philosophy does not overshadow character interaction. In this domestic drama, the broad sociopolitical statements of S.'s earlier comedies give way to concerns with marriage, parenting, and medicine. Its derisive commentary on the medical profession is in the tradition of Molière's numerous "doctor" plays. Unfortunately, its unity— hence, its theatrical viability—is marred by a final act that, although appropriate to the thematic resolution of the play, seems anticlimactic.

One of S.'s most popular plays, thanks to subsequent motion-picture and musical-theater adaptations, is *Pygmalion* (1913), a comedy that the author thought little of and referred to as a "pot-boiler." Nevertheless, it is a delightful "Cinderella" play in which a common flower girl is transformed into a grand lady. S. drew upon the Ovidian myth of Pygmalion and Galatea for his theme, but his protagonist is a professor of phonetics whose relationship to his protégée and pupil is singularly unromantic. The comedy's chief flaw is its inconclusive, or at least unsatisfying, ending, which relegates the ultimate fate of the flower girl to a prose postscript. The character of Doolittle, a philosophizing dustman who acquires sudden wealth, is one of S.'s happiest creations.

In *Heartbreak House* (written 1913–16, perf. 1920), subtitled "A Fantasia in the Russian Manner on English Themes," S.'s avowed purpose was to imitate the style of Anton CHEKHOV. His success was considerable. This tragicomedy, S.'s own favorite of all his plays, is the most poetic and symbolic of his works. Almost dreamlike at times, it is concerned with the disillusionment and despair generated in upper-class Britons by World War I. Its tone alternates between broad farce and lyrical melancholy; it includes the deaths of two of its characters in its last-act air raid.

The most monumental of S.'s dramas is *Back to Methuselah*, a work composed of five separate plays and subtitled "A Metabiological Pentateuch." The first play is set in the time of Adam and Eve; the final part takes place in A.D. 31,920. S.'s purpose was to chronicle the evolution of mankind, not only to the present but beyond, and to explore the nature of evil while setting forth his vision of an eventual utopia. *Back to Methuselah* is perhaps the least popular of S.'s major plays. Its length alone causes difficulties in staging, and the complex ideas expressed in the texts are a challenge to the patience of the reader or playgoer. The three central parts especially are marred by poor characterization and excessive (even for S.) discussions and arguments.

The last of S.'s major plays, and the one that some consider his greatest, was *Saint Joan* (1923). It approaches the tragic realm in its recounting of the rise and fall of France's famed saint. S. had read virtually every work on Joan from Shakespeare on, and his purpose was to strip the historical figure of the romance and melodrama bestowed upon her by his predecessors. His Joan is neither saintly heroine nor hapless martyr. Rather, she is a stubborn, single-minded, aggressive, and sexless young woman of great spirit who runs afoul of ecclesiastical authority. Although the play has moments of comic appeal, its central action is profoundly serious. Its potentially tragic effect is mitigated, however, by an epilogue that briefly resurrects Joan in a dream sequence so that she can learn of her 20th-c. beatification and canonization. (Joan was declared a saint in 1920.)

Saint Joan is a powerful and affecting drama. S. lifted the play above the realm of melodrama by endowing Joan's judges with sympathy and understanding. We cannot dismiss them as mere stage villains, championing the heroine as misunderstood and persecuted. The play is filled with fascinating and persuasive dialogues that advance the position of the Church. The figure of Bishop Cauchon is one of S.'s most complex character creations.

The final dozen or so of S.'s plays, performed between 1926 and 1950, evidence a decline in the dramatist's powers. Among them, *The Apple Cart* (1929) and *Too True to Be Good* (written 1931, perf. 1932) might interest the contemporary reader. The former is a futuristic "political extravaganza" in a cartoonlike form; the latter is an allegorical dream play on the state of the world according to S., with characters like the Patient, the Monster, the Burglar, and so on.

S. has been called the greatest dramatist writing in English since Shakespeare. He himself frankly proclaimed his dramaturgy, based upon his particular vision of the drama as a vehicle for ideas, not simply a stimulus for emotions, as superior to the Bard's. This is not to say S.'s plays are heartless; they teem with feeling—feeling expressed by characters who spring to life with the urgency of their convictions. As a dramatic prose stylist, S. was a master at the lucid expression of complex ideas with pungency and wit.

S.'s contributions to 20th-c. thought and expression were considerable, in bulk as well as substance. His collected plays, essays, letters, and criticisms fill many volumes. As a propagandist for the socialist cause, through his work in the Fabian Society and his lecturing and writing, he helped to achieve the eventual acceptance of socialist ideas in Britain and elsewhere. His rejection of easy sentiment and melodramatic oversimplification in his plays brought back seriousness to English drama. The Shavian canon paved the way for a drama that could focus on social issues rather than on fictionalized domestic and sexual intrigues, its topics throughout most of the 19th c.

FURTHER WORKS: *My Dear Dorothea* (1878); *Cashel Byron's Profession* (1886); *An Unsocial Socialist* (1887); *Fabian Essays in Socialism* (1889); *The Perfect Wagnerite* (1898); *Love among the Artists* (1900); *The Admirable Bashville* (1902); *John Bull's Other Island* (1904); *The Commonsense of Municipal Trading* (1904); *How He Lied to Her Husband* (1904); *The Irrational Knot* (1905);

Passion, Poison, and Petrifaction; or, The Fatal Gazogene (1905); *Dramatic Opinions and Essays* (1906); *Getting Married* (1908); *The Sanity of Art* (1908); *The Fascinating Foundling* (1909); *Press Cuttings* (1909); *The Shewing-Up of Blanco Posnet* (1909); *Socialism and Superior Brains* (1909); *Misalliance* (1910); *The Dark Lady of the Sonnets* (1910); *Fanny's First Play* (1911); *Overruled* (1912); *Great Catherine* (1913); *Androcles and the Lion* (1913); *Commonsense about the War* (1914); *The Music-Cure* (1914); *The Inca of Perusalem* (1916); *Augustus Does His Bit* (1917); *O'Flaherty V. C.* (1917); *Annajanska, the Bolshevik Empress* (1918); *Peace Conference Hints* (1919); *Imprisonment* (1925); *The Glimpse of Reality* (1927); *Letters from G. B. S. to Miss Alma Murray* (1927); *The Intelligent Woman's Guide to Socialism and Capitalism* (1928); *Ellen Terry and B. S.: A Correspondence* (1930); *Immaturity* (1930); *Major Critical Essays* (1930); *What I Really Wrote about the War* (1930); *Complete Works* (38 vols., 1931–1950); *Doctors' Delusions, Crude Criminology, Sham Education* (1931); *Music in London, 1890–94* (1931); *Pen Portraits and Reviews* (1931); *Our Theatres in the Nineties* (1931); *The Adventures of the Black Girl in Her Search for God* (1932); *Essays in Fabian Socialism* (1932); *Short Stories, Scraps & Shavings* (1932); *On the Rocks* (1933); *The Six of Calais* (1934); *Village Wooing* (1934); *The Simpleton of the Unexpected Isles* (1935); *The Millionairess* (1936); *The King. the Constitution, and the Lady* (1936); *Cymbeline Refinished* (1937); *London Music in 1888–89* (1937); *Geneva* (1938); *"In Good King Charles's Golden Days"* (1939); *S. Gives Himself Away* (1939); *Everybody's Political What's What* (1944); *Buoyant Billions* (1948); *Shakes versus Shav* (1949); *Sixteen Self-Sketches* (1949); *Far-fetched Fables* (1950); *Why She Would Not* (1950); *B. S. and Mrs. Patrick Campbell. Their Correspondence* (1952); *Advice to a Young Critic* (1955); *Letters to Granville-Barker* (1956); *B. S.: Platform and Pulpit: Previously Uncollected Speeches* (1961); *Collected Letters* (2 vols., 1965, 1972); *B. S.'s Nondramatic Literary Criticism* (1972); *Complete Plays with Their Prefaces* (1975); *The Collected Screenplays of B. S.* (1980); *S.'s Music: The Complete Musical Criticism* (3 vols., 1981); *B. S.'s "Arms and the Man": A Composite Production Book* (1981); *B. S. and Alfred Douglas: A Correspondence* (1982); *The Playwright and the Pirate: B. S. and Frank Harris, a Correspondence* (1983); *Agitations: S.'s Letters to the Press, 1875–1950* (1984); *B. S.'s Book Reviews* (1991); *The Complete Prefaces* (1993); *The Drama Observed* (1993); *Unpublished S.* (1996)

BIBLIOGRAPHY: Henderson, A., *B. S.: Playboy and Prophet* (1932); Pearson, H., *G. B. S.: A Full-Length Portrait* (1942; enlarged ed., with a Postscript, 1950); Winsten, S., ed., *G. B. S. 90* (1946); Bentley, E., *B. S.* (1947); Irvine, W., *The Universe of G. B. S.* (1949); Fuller, E., *G. B. S.* (1950); Ward, A. C., *B. S.* (1951); Ohmann, R. M., *S.: The Style and the Man* (1962); Weintraub, S., *Private S. and Public S.* (1963); Meisel, M., *S. and the Nineteenth-Century Theatre* (1963); Woodbridge, H. E., *G. B. S.: Creative Artist* (1963); Watson, B. B., *A Shavian Guide to the Intelligent Woman* (1964); Brown, I., *S. in His Time* (1965); Kaufmann, R. J., ed. *G. B. S.: A Collection of Critical Essays* (1965); Smith, J. P., *The Unrepentant Pilgrim: A Study of the Development of B. S.* (1965); Carpenter, C. A., *B. S. and the Art of Destroying Ideals* (1969); Crompton, L., *S. the Dramatist* (1969); Wilson, C., *B. S.: A Reassessment* (1969); Rosenblood, N., ed., *S.: Seven Critical Essays* (1971); Weintraub, S., *Journey to Heartbreak: The Crucible Years of B. S., 1914–1918* (1971); Morgan, M. M., *The Shavian Playground* (1972); Berst, C. A., *B. S. and the Art of Drama* (1973); Dukore, B. F., *B. S.: Playwright* (1973); Valency, M., *The Cart and the Trumpet* (1973); Weintraub, R., ed., *Fabian Feminist: B. S. and Women* (1977); Whitman, R. F., *S. and the Play of Ideas* (1977); Hill, E. C., *G. B. S.* (1978); Holroyd, M., ed., *The Genius of S.: A Symposium* (1979); Silver, A., *B. S.: The Darker Side* (1982); Smith, W. S., *Bishop of Everywhere: B. S. and the Life Force* (1982); Gordon, D. J., *B. S. and the Comic Sublime* (1990); Davis, T., *G. B. S. and the Socialist Theatre* (1994)

—JACK A. VAUGHN

The brain of B. S. was like a wedge in the literal sense. Its sharpest end was always in front; and it split our society from end to end the moment it had entrance at all. As I have said he was long unheard of; but he had not the tragedy of many authors, who were heard of long before they were heard. When you had read any S. you read all S. When you had seen one of his plays you waited for more. And when he brought them out in volume form, you did what is repugnant to any literary man—you bought a book.

The dramatic volume with which S. dazzled the public was called *Plays, Pleasant and Unpleasant*. I think the most striking and typical thing about it was that he did not know very clearly which plays were unpleasant and which were pleasant. "Pleasant" is a word which is almost unmeaning to B. S. Except, as I suppose, in music (where I cannot follow him), relish and receptivity are things that simply do not appear. He was the best of tongues and the worst of palates. With the possible exception of *Mrs. Warren's Profession* (which was at least unpleasant in the sense of being forbidden) I can see no particular reason why any of the seven plays should be held specially to please or displease. First in fame and contemporary importance came the reprint of *Arms and the Man*, of which I have already spoken. Over all the rest towered unquestionably the two figures of Mrs. Warren and of Candida. They were neither of them really unpleasant except as all truth is unpleasant. But they did represent the author's normal preference and his principal fear; and those two sculptured giantesses largely upheld his fame.

G. K. Chesterton, *G. B. S.* (1909), pp. 115–16

In all Mr. S.'s work in the arts, critical and creative, a part is . . . played by the irrelevant motive. Never very far from the centre of his mind are "all the detestable fruits of inequality of condition." In this life there are secular hardships and anomalies enough for correction, God knows; but the artist, *qua* artist, does not find, I suppose, the fruits of inequality of condition detestable. For him they rather add to the fun of the human spectacle. But Mr. S. is out to alter all that. What Mr. S. wants, more than anything else, is to change our ideas; and art is a weapon in the *chambardement général*. He condescends to the fun of the human spectacle, not for its own sake, but to point a moral. Just as the persons of his drama are logical abstractions to whom, to aid in their acceptance, a surface humanity is added, so is his drama itself a secondary image of his picture of the world. He sees men as ideas walking. He sees art as a conflict of ideas. A thousand lovable, intimate, humorous, ridiculous, recognizable traits he sees, and he makes a pastiche of them for his purposes. They do not result in the comic vision. (Impossible, when the whole stretch of his work is remembered, to say that they result in that!) They do not result in the tragic vision. "The very same thing, don't you see," says Tolstoy in *Anna Karenina*, "may be looked at tragically, and turned into misery, or it may be looked at simply and even humorously." Impossible to assert that Mr. S. has turned things into misery. All the time one remembers Trefusis, that hero of his early novel [*An Unsocial Socialist*], whose "sympathies were kept awake and his indignation maintained at an exhilarating pitch by the sufferings of the poor." Mr. S.'s vision is so composed of mind and heart that it has maintained his indignation "at an exhilarating pitch." It is the publicist's vision.

> P. P. Howe, *B. S.: A Critical Study* (1915), pp. 160–62

S. identifies the modern drama with the type of play in which he excels. His first business is the exposure of current morality, with the implication that it would be wise and sensible to scrap it and resort to another kind. "People have told me that my plays have made them alter their whole view of life. This is probably an exaggeration; possibly an illusion. They do not say this of Shakespear and Moliére. But with every disposition to do so, I do not on that account think myself greater than Shakespear or Molière."

S. . . . declares with delightful dogmatism that people do not go to the theatre to be amused. A great proportion, I contend, go to the theatre for no other purpose. It is quite true that they want to have a new light thrown upon their own lives and the lives of those around them; but they could often dispense with argument and discussion in favor of action: things actually happening. S. writes plays in which people argue things out, vehemently and boisterously; and then act or remain immobile as the result of their conclusions. S.'s plays are not always sound, psychologically, since people's deeper motives are often not guided by reason at all, but by impulses which arise from the depths of the subconscious.

S. is one of those strange beings for whom the working of the intellect is a theme of passionate interest. In *Back to Methuselah* intellect figures as a passion capable of giving a more lasting enjoyment than any other passion. S.'s plays show the excited cerebration of a number of people in combination; and the particular sort of mental stimulus which comes from the cut and thrust of dialectic and discussion fortifies and deepens the emotive appeal of the classic drama.

> Archibald Henderson, *B. S.: Playboy and Prophet* (1932), pp. 602–3

The principal pattern which recurs in B. S.—aside from the duel between male and female, which seems to me of much less importance—is the polar opposition between the type of the saint and the type of the successful practical man. This conflict, when it is present in his other writing, has a blurring, a demoralizing effect . . . but it is the principle of life of his plays. We find it in its clearest presentation in the opposition between Father Keegan and Tom Broadbent in *John Bull's Other Island* and between Major Barbara and Undershaft—where the moral scales are pretty evenly weighted and where the actual predominance of the practical man, far from carrying ominous implications, produces a certain effect of reassurance: this was apparently the period—when B. S. had outgrown his early battles and struggles and before the war had come to disturb him—of his most comfortable and self-confident exercise of powers which had fully matured. But these opposites have also a tendency to dissociate themselves from one another and to feature themselves sometimes, not correlatively, but alternately in successive plays. In *The Devil's Disciple* and *The Shewing-up of Blanco Posnet*, the heroes are dashing fellows who have melodramatic flashes of saintliness; their opponents are made comic or base. *Caesar and Cleopatra* is a play that glorifies the practical man; *Androcles and the Lion* is a play that glorifies the saint. So is *Saint Joan*, with the difference that here the worldly antagonists of the saint are presented as intelligent and effective.

Certainly it is this theme of the saint and the world which has inspired those scenes of S.'s plays which are most moving and most real on the stage—which are able to shock us for the moment, as even the "Life Force" passages hardly do, out of the amiable and objective attention which has been induced by the bright play of the intelligence. [1938]

> Edmund Wilson, *The Triple Thinkers*, rev. ed. (1948), pp. 184–86

If S.'s plays are in the first place the meeting-ground of vitality and artificial system and in the second of male and female they are in the third place an arena for the problem of human ideals and their relation to practice. His characters may be ranged on a scale of mind, ideas, aspirations, beliefs and on a scale of action, practicality, effectiveness. At one extreme there are men of mind who make as little contact with the world of action as possible. Such are most of S.'s artists. At the other extreme are men of action who lack all speculative interests and ideal impulses. Such are S.'s professional men: soldiers, politicians, doctors. At a little distance from the one extreme are the men of mind who are interested in this world even if they can do nothing about it. Such, in their different ways, are Tanner, Cusins, Keegan, Shotover, and Magnus. At a little distance from the other extreme are certain practical men with a deep intellectual interest in the meaning of action. Such are the businessmen Undershaft and Tarleton, the soldiers Napoleon and Caesar.

The conversations which all these men, of mind or of action, have with each other have, perhaps, more nervous energy, a more galvanic rhythm, than any other disquisitory passages in all S. For they are all pushing, probing towards the solution of the problem of morals in action. They are all part of the search for the philosopher-king. Keegan talks with the politician Broadbent, Shotover with the businessman Mangan, Magnus with his cabinet. Most strikingly, perhaps, Undershaft talks with his Professor Cusins. They are agreed that there is no hope until the millionaires are professors of Greek and the professors of Greek are millionaires.

Eric Bentley, *B. S.* (1947), pp. 158–59

[S.] has been a great fighting pamphleteer and journalist, who has left a deep imprint upon his time. This is the consciously thinking S., who is very definitely "of an age"; the S. of the future, and perhaps "for all time," is the imaginative and intuitive creator of ten or a dozen great plays and of scores of unforgettable characters. As we have seen, the "division and estrangement" between the crusading philosopher-reformer and the dramatic prose-poet has extended into the plays, some of which are scarcely more than dramatized pamphlets, while others in which the poet has had a larger share are more or less crippled by his struggle with the pamphleteer. But the division is not complete. When the poet is in full command, as in *Caesar and Cleopatra* and *Saint Joan*, he has triumphantly fused the intellectual material with the imaginative into superb dramatic form. Something like this happened in *Mrs. Warren's Profession*, in all the *Pleasant Plays* and the *Plays for Puritans*, in *Man and Superman, Androcles and the Lion. Pygmalion. Heartbreak House, Good King Charles*, and in the best of the one-act pieces. In another group of plays, including the early prentice efforts, the series from *John Bull's Other Island* through *Misalliance*, and *The Apple Cart*, the dramatic poet is at work in uneasy partnership with the philosopher-reformer; here the result is a sequence of interesting and distinguished plays marred by more or less serious flaws and imperfections. In *Back to Methuselah* and most of the plays since *The Apple Cart*, the didactic purpose operates with much less than the old intellectual vigor, and the imagination only flickers rather palely here and there. But S.'s genius must not be judged by these. It is useless to speculate on what he might have accomplished if he had been content to be a dramatist only, but it is certain that he could not have been the author of some of the plays by which he will be remembered. His success in revitalizing English drama is due in part to the invigorating current of ideas which he brought into it. In far larger part, of course, it is due to his mastery of character, of dramatic situation, and of brilliant and flexible dialogue.

Homer E. Woodbridge, *G. B. S.: Creative Artist* (1963), pp. 163–64

Is S. dated? The answer is yes, as every classic is dated. The specific personalities and political crises that moved him to write are now part of history, as Plato's and Aristophanes' debaters and statesmen are. The images of his plays belong to an eternal world, as his ideas on government, economics, sex, psychology, logic, and art, now seen apart from the novel and amusing expression he gave them, form part of a perennial philosophy which we can call "Shavian." But there is still a third aspect of the question. One might perhaps hope that the particular social outrages S. wrote about in his "problem" plays might by now be things of the past. Nothing could be more gratifying than to pronounce S. hopelessly out of date in such matters. Unfortunately, I cannot see that this is so. To take two clear-cut examples: the demoralization of men by poverty is still the world's first problem, and our national system of criminology is still outrageously perverse in its intentions and pernicious in its results.

Louis Crompton, *S. the Dramatist* (1969), p. vii1

In his plays [S.] created perhaps the most fascinating gallery of women in modern drama, female characters who usually prove more interesting and more vital than his male characters. His impatience with female stereotypes, although he used them where dramatically valid—and sometimes subconsciously in spite of himself—is everywhere in his writings. In *The Apple Cart*, Orinthia as royal mistress is no longer a sexual vessel but, in effect, a government employee whose "relationship" to the king satisfies the vestigial and vicarious machismo of the populace. In *Heartbreak House*, the husband, not the wife, is kept. In *Pygmalion*, the cockney flower girl is a human being clever enough to rise by her ability, and, if she chooses, to support a husband rather than fulfill her stereotypic destiny of seeking social and financial security through the prudent bartering of herself in marriage, as her male sponsors Pickering and Higgins recommend. As for romance between Eliza and Higgins, S. rejected, from *Pygmalion's* original performance to its being made into a film, any suggestion that there could be a romantic attachment between the "middle-aged bully" and the now beautiful, young flower girl. In *Getting Married*, "Leo" Hotchkiss is not the victim of a mistress-seeking husband; she herself desires a legal, everyday husband and a "Sunday husband" for variety. . . .

Other plays evoke even more outrageous reversals of traditional female subservience. In the fantasy *The Simpleton of the Unexpected Isles*, a communal—yet matriarchal—group of six persons of mixed races and sexes produces four futuristic offspring. Earlier Shavian women are less unconventional in their rejection of marriage. Lavinia in *Androcles and the Lion* spurns a husband because she has more important work to do, while the former Major Barbara of the Salvation Army embraces marriage and a husband because only in marriage can she inherit the power to do her work. Cleopatra in *Caesar and Cleopatra* is no seductive sex-kitten. Rather she is an innocent child whom Caesar regards as a future ruler to be trained in politics and governing. Saint Joan leads an army not because she is a woman, or even in spite of that womanhood, but because she has the instincts and the capacity for leadership.

Rodelle Weintraub, Introduction to Rodelle
Weintraub, ed., *Fabian Feminist: B. S. and
Women* (1977), pp. 8–9

al-SHAYKH, Hanān

Lebanese novelist, b. 1945, Beirut

S. was brought up in Ras al-Naba, a very conservative, unfashionable sector of Beirut. She first attended the local Muslim girls' primary school and then the more sophisticated Ahliya School. While still at school, she contributed articles to newspapers like *al-Nahār*. In 1963 she went to Cairo to study at the American College for Girls. During the four years she lived in Egypt, she wrote her first novel, *Intihār rajul mayyit* (1967; suicide of a dead man). In 1967 she returned to Beirut to resume journalism. But she did not stay long. Subsequently she has lived in the Arabian Peninsula, where she wrote *Faras al-shaitān* (1971; praying mantis), and in London, where she published two more novels: *Hikāyat Zahrah* (1980; *The Story of Zahra*, 1987) and *Misk al-ghazāl* (1989; *Women of Sand and Myrrh*, 1990), as well as a collection of short stories, *Wardat al-sahrā* (1982; the desert rose).

S. first came to international attention with the publication of *Hikāyat Zahrah*. Lebanese critics condemned its overt expression of sexuality, unprecedented for a woman. Many tried to dismiss the novel as artless. But this ploy for the suppression of women's writings failed; in 1986, the novel was translated into French under the title *L'histoire de Zahra*, and the following year it came out in English. European accolades found their echo at home, so that when *Misk al-ghazāl* was published, its sensationalist language and subject matter were not universally attacked. Indeed, some Arab critics in the West hailed it as a great novel.

Whereas her earlier works are more autobiographical in nature, *Hikāyat Zahrah* conveys little if anything of the author's life. It tells the story of a pathetic middle-aged woman who finds in the Lebanese Civil War an opportunity to escape the oppression and physical exploitation that had until then been her lot. After a brief sojourn in Africa, where she had stayed with her lecherous uncle and had to marry one of his undesirable associates, she returns to a Beirut at war with itself. Chaos transforms her and gives her a courage she had never before experienced. She initiates an affair with a sniper, which culminates in a pregnancy that she wants, but which he ends by killing her.

Misk al-ghazāl is more sexually explicit in its language than *Hikāyat Zahrah* and more critical of social mores. Set primarily in an expatriate community in an anonymous desert country, *Misk al-ghazāl* tells the story of four women, each from her own perspective. Two of the women are Arabs from the country in question, one is Lebanese, and the fourth is American. Each woman is seeking to fulfill herself in a context that militates against women's self-assertion. Each woman chooses a different path that is ultimately self-destructive. The novel allows for few successful feminist options.

Although S. has become known as a novelist, her short stories are powerful and well crafted. They criticize patriarchal notions of how Arab women should behave, but they also praise Arab cultures that adhere to a premodern way of life and to traditions that give women a measure of power to negotiate their own realities.

BIBLIOGRAPHY: Cooke, M., *War's Other Voices: Women Writers on the Lebanese Civil War* (1988): 50–60; Larson, C. R., "The Fiction of H. al-S., Reluctant Feminist," *WLT*, 65, 1 (Winter 1991): 14–17

—MIRIAM COOKE

SHEPARD, Sam

(born Sam Shepard Rogers, Jr.) American dramatist, b. 5 Nov. 1943, Fort Sheridan, Ill.

S.'s youth covered the American continent as thoroughly as his plays capture the American spirit. Following his army-officer father, the family moved from base to base. S. finished high school in California and arrived in New York in 1963, where, dropping the name Rogers, he worked as an actor and rock musician. He has acted in several films. Probably the most prolific American playwright since Eugene O'NEILL, S. has seen more than three dozen of his plays produced in the past two decades. And he has consistently won praise and awards, including the Pulitzer Prize for *Buried Child* (1979).

So far, S.'s plays fall into three distinct phases. His earliest plays are freewheeling excursions, which start out in the mundane world and take flight through dreamlike torrents of language and images. Plays like *Icarus's Mother* (1966) burst with ferocious energy into monologues of memory and intense physical sensations.

In his second phase S. continued to stress the verbal riffs and haunting images of split identity. Now, however, these jazz riffs and images of a lost self are firmly anchored in pop-culture plots, myths, American legends, and tall tales. Characters hurl words like weapons, wounding with S.'s heightened version of American English, a language culled from slang, rock music and all its sources, action comics, punk talk, dime novels, and B-movies. *The Tooth of Crime* (1972), for example, explodes with what S. calls "visual music" as well as with kinetic language characterized by sudden leaps from jargon to incantation, from lyricism to pop lyrics.

In plays written during this second phase, an emphasis is placed on shifting identities, no longer in a general sense, but quite specifically on artists or mythical figures who lose their way, lose touch with what Cody in *Geography of a Horse Dreamer* (1974) calls the magic "space inside where the dream comes." In *Angel City* (1976), for example, a writer who agrees to script a blockbuster disaster-horror movie discovers that "the ambition behind the urge to create is no different from any other ambition. To kill. To win. To get on top." And *Seduced* (1976) depicts an aged Howard Hughes-like recluse, destroyed by power, who can only escape from his demons through verbal reveries of soaring.

S.'s third phase of playwriting coincided with his move back to California and to his association since 1975 with San Francisco's Magic Theater. There S. has found a home conducive to plays that, more and more, explore character rather than isolated images, the nexus of the family rather than heroic myths. *The Curse of the Starving Class* (1978), for example, is a zany comedy revolving around Wesley, a sympathetic young man who tries to belong in a family of idiosyncratic misfits. The play also has a darker side: the old family tale conjures up the clawing animal hunger, and S. gives terrifying meaning to being bound together by blood.

Buried Child is about yet another family of "hopers" tied to the land, each other's secrets, and a dream gone sour. This play takes the shape of a homecoming. No one in this mutilated family ever recognizes Vince, and none bears even the "slightest resemblance" to the faces in the idyllic family portrait he described to his girlfriend on the way home. Even the fertility of the land has gone awry, producing a sudden bumper crop of corn and carrots that no one has planted and giving forth the buried baby who is part of Vince's heritage. Finally, the disillusioning pilgrimage takes Vince back to a primal vision of his legacy—to a family identity he recognizes revealed in his own haunted image.

True West (1980) focuses again on the integrity of the land beneath suburban developments and on the strangling yoke of the family. But now, S. merges these concerns with his earlier concern about the creative artist—that is, the escape artist—and his place in a modern mythology. Two brothers, one a screenwriter and the other a petty thief just back from the desert, turn their mother's suburban California kitchen into a primal arena where they square off in a showdown of identities. While entertaining us with funny dialogue about formula movie westerns and suburban paradises, *True West* cuts like a knife to the truth at the heart of hackneyed chase plots, to the fear felt by brothers, each scared of the other's dark impulses, each wary of the part of himself he sees behind his brother's eyes.

In *The Curse of the Starving Class, Buried Child*, and *True West* S. explores frontiers of identity in families and shows us characters devoured by false visions of escape and by false pretty memories of home. In stark, yet often hilarious family squabbles, such mundane stuff as refrigerators, vegetable gardens, and toasters take on a poetry of the theater, a concrete physical poetry that expresses through everyday objects the yearnings, the forbidden impulses, and the deadly struggles beneath the surface of civilization.

FURTHER WORKS: *Cowboys* (1964); *The Rock Garden* (1964); *Up to Thursday* (1964); *Dog* (1964); *Rocking Chair* (1964); *4-H Club* (1964); *Fourteen Hundred Thousand* (1966); *Chicago* (1966); *Red Cross* (1966); *Forensic and the Navigators* (1967); *Melodrama Play* (1967); *Cowboys #2* (1967); *Me and My Brother* (screenplay, 1967, with Robert Frank); *Five Plays* (1967); *La Turista* (1968); *Zabriskie Point* (screenplay, 1968, with others); *The Holy Ghostly* (1969); *Operation Sidewinder* (1970); *Shaved Splits* (1970); *The Unseen Hand* (1970); *Ringaleevio* (screenplay, 1971, with Murray Mednick); *Mad Dog Blues* (1971); *Back Bog Beast Bait* (1971); *Cowboy Mouth* (1971, with Patti Smith); *Hawk Moon* (1972); *Mad Dog Blues, and Other Plays* (1972); *The Unseen Hand, and Other Plays* (1972); *Killer's Head* (1975); *Suicide in B* (1976); *Angel City, Curse of the Starving Class, and Other Plays* (1976); *Rolling Thunder Logbook* (1977); *Tongues* (1978–79, with Joseph Chaikin); *Buried Child; Seduced; Suicide in B* (1979); *Seven Plays* (1981); *Fool for Love* (1983); *Motel Chronicles* (1983); *The Unseen Hand and Other Plays* (1986); *A Lie of the Mind: A Play in Three Acts* (1987); *States of Shock* (1992); *Cruising Paradise* (1996)

BIBLIOGRAPHY: Schechner, R., "S. S.," in Vinson, J., ed., *Contemporary Dramatists* (1973): 696–99; Hughes, C., *American Playwrights, 1945–75* (1976): 72–80; Rosen, C., "S. S.'s *Angel City*: A

Sam Shepard

Movie for the Stage," *MD*, 22 (1979): 39–46; Wetzsteon, R., "The Genius of S. S.," *New York* (24 Nov. 1980): 20–25; Coe, R., "The Saga of S. S.," *NYTMag* (23 Nov. 1980): 56–59: 118–24; Marranca, B., ed., *American Dreams: The Imagination of S. S.* (1981); Gilman, R., Introduction to S. S., *Seven Plays* (1981): ix–xxv; Cohn, R., *New American Dramatists 1960–1980* (1982): 171–86; Tucker, M., *S. S.* (1992); Wade, L., *S. S. and the American Theatre*; Bottoms, S., *The Theatre of S. S.*

—CAROL ROSEN

SHEVCHUK, Valery

Ukrainian novelist, translator, literary historian, critic, and editor, b. 20 Aug. 1939, Zhytomyr

S. was born into a family of blue-collar workers. Upon completing secondary schooling in 1956, he received an additional year of technical training and found employment in the construction industry. In 1958 he enrolled at the Kiev University, from where he graduated in 1963 with a degree in history and archival sciences. S. worked briefly as a reporter for the newspaper *Moloda Hvardiya*, and served from 1963 to 1965 in the Soviet army in the Murmansk region. Upon discharge from the army, S. returned to Kiev, where he managed to obtain employment as a museum specialist. He lost his position in 1966, after the arrest of his brother, Anatoly, and took up writing as a full-time profession. S. is a member of the Union of Writers and a member of the International P.E.N. Club.

During the Thaw of the 1960s, S. made a name for himself with the publication of the collections of short stories *Sered tyzhnya* (1967; during the week) and *Vechir svyatoyi oseni* (1969; night of the sacred autumn), of which the miniature "Miy batko nadumav sadyty sad" ("My Father Decided to Plant Orchards," 1973), a beautifully gentle autobiographical tale of life and a father-son relationship, is a masterpiece of short prose. At that time he also published a collection of novels dealing with life in contemporary Ukraine, *Naberezhna, 12. Seredokhrestya* (1968; 12 Riverside, the crossroads), for which he was taken to task by Soviet critics and officially excluded from Ukraine's literary life until 1979. His superb translation of a collection of poems by Ukraine's premier philosopher, Hryhory Skovoroda (1722–1794), entitled *Sad pisen* (1968; repub. 1972, 1980, 1983; orchard of songs), initiated a new phase in his activity. S. eventually established himself as a translator par excellence of Ukrainian baroque literature and of Polish poetry of the 17th and 18th cs.

S. broke his enforced silence in 1979 with the publication of his collection of novels entitled *Kryk pivnya na svitanku* (the cry of the cock at dawn), and in the 1980s his works began to appear regularly. A new collection of short stories, *Dolyna dzherel* (1981; valley of springs), featuring themes from lives of Ukrainian artists, was followed by a series of historical novels set in the 12th to 19th cs., in which fact and fiction, closely interwoven, provide an evolving portrait of the Ukrainian intellectual and his role in Ukraine's historical process. They include *Na poli smyrennomu* (1983; *The Meek Shall Inherit*, 1989), set in the days of Kievan Rus', and *Try lystky za viknom* (1986; three leaves outside the window), for which he was awarded the prestigious Shevchenko Prize for 1989. Of special significance among his recent publications are the novel *Dzygar odvichny* (1990; the eternal clock), a chronicle of contemporary family life presented from the perspective of a child, and the powerful short story *Ya duzhe khochu podyvytys* (1991; I very much like to see), written in 1962 in the form of the memoir of a dead man, about the horror of death, revolution, war, and life in a totalitarian system.

S.'s imaginative prose is informed by MAGIC REALISM, in which the elements of Ukraine's legends and mythology are interwoven with subtle psychological probings into the human soul. His is a *littérature désengagée*, nonpolitical and deideologized, focused on the human being's role in life and the history of the nation. In works that have a contemporary setting, S. seeks to eschew moral values and ethical norms for a society that has lost its spiritual absolutes. In this quest, the author journeys into Ukraine's historical past and into his own soul. His mission is to acquaint his reader with the complexities, enigmas, and mysteries of Ukrainian culture, a great part of which, according to him, has been forgotten or lost over the centuries. His ultimate goal is to rediscover and to redefine this culture in the light of objective truth, and to see himself and his contemporaries as its product.

S.'s work as compiler and editor of literary collections is of special significance for Ukraine's cultural renaissance of the 1980s and 1990s. Deftly combining literary scholarship with artistic taste and intuition, he has edited or coedited a number of anthologies of Ukrainian poetry, among them *Apollonova lyutnya: Kyyivski poety XVII–XVIII st.* (1982; Apollonian lute: Kievan poets of 17th-18th cs.), *Antolohiya ukrayinskoyi poeziyi. Ukrayinska dozhovtneva poeziya. Poeziya XI–XVIII st.* (1984; an anthology of Ukrainian

poetry: Ukrainian pre-October poetry. Poetry of the 11th-18th cs.). *Pismi Kupidona. Lyubovna poeziya na Ukrayini v XVI poch. XIX st.* (1984; the songs of Cupid: love poetry in Ukraine from the 16th c. to the beginning of the 19th c.), and an anthology of Ukrainian heroic poetry in two volumes entitled *Marsove pole* (1988–1989; the field of Mars). He has also edited the works of a number of Ukrainian classical authors, and written several full-length studies on Ukrainian literature and culture.

Selected works of S. have been translated into more than twenty languages. Most recently, some of his works have been dramatized and performed in Ukrainian theaters, and his popularity, both in Ukraine and outside its borders, is steadily increasing.

FURTHER WORKS: *Dim na hori* (1983); *Malenke vechirnye intermetstso* (1984); *Kamyana luna* (1987); *Myslenne derevo* (1989); *Ptakhy z nevydymoho ostrova* (1989); *Vybrani tvory* (1989); *Panna kvitiv* (1990)

BIBLIOGRAPHY: Luckyj, G. S. N., *Modern Ukrainian Short Stories* (1973): 226; Bilenko, A., "V. S.: *The Ferryman*," *Ukraine*, 3 (March 1987): 34–37; Pavlyshyn, M., "Mythological, Religious, and Philosophical Topoi in the Prose of V. S.," *SlavR*, 50 (1991): 905–13

—LEONID RUDNYTZKY

SHIGA Naoya

Japanese short-story writer and novelist, b. 20 Feb. 1883, Ishimaki; d. 21 Oct. 1971, Tokyo

S. was raised in a family that had prospered during the Meiji Restoration. Indeed, it was his father's wealth and social standing that made it possible for S. to attend the exclusive Peers' School, where he first became involved in literature. It was also this family wealth that allowed him the leisure to pursue his artistic interests and his association with other artists in the White Birch group.

S.'s writing career passed through various stages. He began writing at a time when the Japanese variant of naturalism was at its peak, and his early works tend to focus on the extreme conditions of insanity and suicide. He quickly outgrew this period of experimentation, however, and concentrated on works that emphasized psychological development. Many of his early stories deal with family situations, and a significant number of them resulted from his seventeen-year estrangement from his father. Although willing to live on his father's money, S. felt that his father was vulgar, philistine, grasping, and insensitive. Independence as an individual and as an artist is one of the chief characteristics of S. This was so much the case that he defined morality in terms of freedom, saying in one of his works: "My likes and dislikes are the basis of my personal sense of good and evil." This independence kept him aloof from every sort of literary or political ideology and dogma. Thus, although S. was a founding member and a leader of the White Birch group, it was such a diverse collection of artists and scholars that he always felt free to pursue his own artistic directions without inhibition.

During the middle years of his career S. attempted to capture the tranquillity of nature and of men who are able to live harmoniously with nature and with their fellow man. Typical of these works is the story "Kinosaki nite" (1917; "At Kinosaki," 1956), a lyrical reflection on death in which the narrator learns to come to terms with his own inevitable end as he encounters death in nature. Since death cannot be avoided, it must be accepted with tranquillity.

Another representative story of this period is "Takibi" (1920; "The Bonfire," 1975). Here the need for dramatic conflict and resolution gives way to an evocation of shared emotions. Again, the story is a lyric about man immersed in nature. Although some have condemned it for being meandering and pointless, it is vintage S. His intention was to evoke a mood, to express the tranquillity of mind and harmony with nature he had always sought. While it is true that he violates most Western concepts of acceptable literary form—there is no organized plot, no dramatic conflict, no climax and resolution, and no characterization—nevertheless, the story has its own integrity and great beauty, and it has been extravagantly admired by Japanese writers and readers alike.

S.'s best-known work and his only novel is *An'ya kōro* (1937; *A Dark Night's Passing*, 1976). Here he brings the two basic strands of his work together. On the one hand, he depicts difficult family relationships; on the other, he uses loose structure to evoke emotions and the final harmonious unity with nature. His concern, S. said, was not so much with what happened as with what it felt like when it happened.

After the mid-1930s S. continued to write works of great skill and carefully polished style, but few of them achieved the intensity of his earlier creations. Still, a few works stand out, such as "Haiiro no tsuki" (1945; "The Ashen Moon," 1977), a brilliant evocation of Japan immediately after World War II.

Not widely known outside Japan, S. is considered one of the finest Japanese writers of the 20th c. He is called "the god of fiction," and was greatly admired by such diverse authors as AKUTAGAWA Ryūnosuke and Kobayashi Takiji (1903–1933), both of whom sought to use S.'s work as models for their own writing.

FURTHER WORKS: *S. N. zenshū* (14 vols., 1973–1974). FURTHER WORKS IN ENGLISH: *The Paper Door and Other Stories* (1987)

BIBLIOGRAPHY: Mathy, F., *S. N.* (1974); Kohl, S. W., et al., *The White Birch Society (Shirakabaha): Some Sketches and Portraits* (1975): 28–41; Kohl, S. W., "S. N. and the Literature of Experience," *MN*, 32 (1977): 211–24; Sibley, W. F., *The S. Hero* (1979)

—STEPHEN W. KOHL

SHIMAZAKI Tōson

Japanese poet, novelist, short-story writer, dramatist, and essayist, b. 25 March 1872, Magome; d. 22 Aug. 1943, Higashi-Koiso

Born into a prominent family living in a remote mountain village, S. was sent to Tokyo to study in 1886. In 1887 he entered a Protestant missionary academy and was baptized. Upon graduation he began teaching, translating, and writing poetry, plays, and book reviews. His highly romantic poetry kept the rhythms of traditional verse while bringing in fresh ardor and passion. After winning acceptance, he published the first collection of his verse, *Wakana-shū* (1897; young leaves), which earned him lasting fame as the first important poet of modern Japan.

During the first decade of the 20th c. S. turned to fiction, which became his preferred genre. *Hakai* (1906; *The Broken Commandment*, 1974), his most widely known work, deals openly with the social problems of members of the outcast minority group known as Eta; consequently, S. had to publish the novel at his own expense. Indeed, the Japanese are still reluctant to discuss the position of these "base people," who traditionally worked as scavengers, tanners, and executioners, and who were prohibited from mingling with ordinary citizens. The hero of the novel, Ushimatsu, is one of the earliest characters in modern Japanese fiction who conveys a sense of deeply lived personal experience. *Hakai* may be thought of as the first novel of the inner life in 20th c. Japanese literature.

During this period the trend toward naturalism was growing stronger in Japan; S., along with authors such as Tayama Katai (1871–1930), added impetus to the movement. S.'s next two novels mark the apex of Japanese naturalism. *Haru* (1908; spring), an autobiographical account, foreshadowed his mature style. *Ie* (1911; *The Family*, 1976), his best naturalistic work, is a chronicle of a household that is paradoxically destroyed by the desire to save it.

Shinsei (1919; a new life) tells the story of a man (in reality, S. himself) who, having lost his wife, takes up with a niece. She becomes pregnant, and he, fearing a scandal, flees to France. But his wartime experiences lead him to reflect on where he really belongs, and in the end he recognizes his responsibilities as a father and returns. By publicly confessing his secret, the protagonist hopes to begin a new life. Although often criticized for disregarding accepted standards of respectability, the novel nevertheless skillfully exploited the change in literary fashion, which was now concerned with a protagonist's spiritual growth.

S.'s last and most ambitious novel, *Yoakemai* (serial pub., 1929–35; before the dawn), impresses the patient reader with its grandeur, restraint, and genuine sense of tragedy. Set in the author's native village, Magome, the story opens in the 1850s, during the waning years of the Tokugawa period (1600–1868). The hero, Aoyama Hanzō, is modeled on S.'s father. Sympathetic to the movement to revive national institutions, he becomes actively involved in political affairs. But as village headman, as the community's wholesale merchant, and as keeper of the inn designated for travelers on official business, he finds himself trapped between the farmers and the samurai. Although his own party, favoring restoration of the power of the emperor (Meiji restoration, 1868), prevails, he is unable to cope with the rapid changes; he turns to drink, incurs large debts, and eventually goes insane. He is placed in a makeshift cell behind his house, where he dies, "without ever seeing the sun again." Nowhere in modern Japanese fiction does one find a more compelling account of the process of transformation from the old to the new.

The central theme is S.'s writing—how a new Japan after the Meiji restoration grew out of the decay of the old, but only at a cost of grievous personal suffering and loss—is made poignant by the autobiographical and historical material that illustrates and documents his theme. Yet another theme that runs throughout S.'s writings involves the new ideal of individualism, which entered Japan from the West at the beginning of the 20th c., with all of its humanistic and positive implications.

FURTHER WORKS: *Natsugusa* (1898); *Hitohabune* (1898); *Rakubai-shū* (1901); *T. shishū* (1904); *Ryokuyō-shū* (1907); *Shin-katamachi yori* (1909); *T. shū* (1909); *Chikuma-gawa no suketchi* (1911;

Chikuma River Sketches, 1991); *Shokugo* (1912); *Bifū* (1913); *Sakura no mi no jukusuru toki* (1919); *Furusato* (1920); *T. zenshū* (12 vols., 1922); *Osana monogatari* (1924); *Haru o machitsutsu* (1932); *Tōhō no mon* (1943); *T. zenshū* (18 vols., 1966–1971)

BIBLIOGRAPHY: Shinkōkai, Kokusai Bunka, ed., *Introduction to Contemporary Japanese Literature* (1939): 300–311; Roggendorf, J., "S. T.: A Maker of the Modern Japanese Novel," *MN*, 7 (1951): 40–46; McClellan, E., *Two Japanese Novelists: Sōseki and Tōson* (1969); Morita, J. R., "S. T.'s Four Collections of Poems," *MN*, 25 (1970): 325–69; Yamanouchi, H., *The Search for Authenticity in Modern Japanese Literature* (1978): 20–39; Walker, J. A., *The Japanese Novel of the Meiji Period and the Ideal of Individualism* (1979), passim

—LEON M. ZOLBROD

SHINA LITERATURE

See Pakistani Literature

SHOLOKHOV, Mikhail

Russian novelist, b. 24 May 1905, Kruzhilin; d. 21 February 1984, Veshenskaya

Born in the Don Cossack Military Region, the author of the greatest novel about the Cossacks is not a Cossack by origin. His father was a Russian of the lower middle class and his illiterate mother came from Ukrainian peasant stock. His formal education ended in 1918 when the civil war engulfed the Upper Don region. For the greater part of the war S. lived in or near the battle zone. After the Bolshevik victory he served in food-requisitioning and punitive detachments, taking part in the fighting against anti-Bolshevik guerrillas. Much of what he saw in the 1918–22 period was reflected in his works. An inveterate fisherman and hunter, S. has lived almost all his life in the Don countryside, in the village of Vyoshenskaya. During the 1933 famine he saved thousands of lives by persuading Stalin to send grain to the Upper Don region. Stalin followed S.'s literary career, influenced publication of his works, and decided against liquidating him during the purges. A Communist Party member since 1932, S. is the most celebrated figure of the Soviet literary establishment. He is a member of the Party's Central Committee, a Hero of Socialist Labor, and a recipient of the Stalin and Lenin Prizes for literature. By 1980 almost seventy-nine million copies of his works had been printed in the Soviet Union in eighty-four languages. No new literary work of his has appeared since 1969.

Between 1923 and 1927 S. published about thirty short stories in various periodicals and in the collections *Donskie rasskazy* (1926; *Tales of the Don*, 1962) and *Lazorevaya step* (1926; tulip steppe, included in *Tales of the Don*). Their dominant theme is the bitter political strife within a village or a family during the civil war and the early 1920s. S.'s sympathies are on the Soviet side. The stories demonstrate his rapid development from an imitative apprentice into an original writer with a keen eye for detail, a skill in using the racy Cossack dialect, an earthy sense of humor, and a

penchant for dramatic situations. S.'s sketches written during World War II and the wartime story "Nauka nenavisti" (1942; *The Science of Hatred*, 1943) are essentially agitational. Propaganda for Soviet patriotism and the theme of personal grief blend in the story "Sudba cheloveka" (1957; "The Fate of a Man," 1959), which is narrated by its protagonist.

S.'s major work is the epic novel *Tikhy Don* (4 vols., 1928–40; abridged tr., *The Silent Don*, 1942; I, *And Quiet Flows the Don*, 1934; II, *The Don Flows Home to the Sea*, 1941). Set in 1912–22, the novel presents a broad picture of the Don Cossacks' life in the time of peace and during the fateful years of war and revolution. S. views man primarily as a part of nature, with love, procreation, and perpetual renewal being the very essence of existence. Emotions and actions are often related to processes occurring in nature, which is depicted with striking vividness and keen attention to details of shape, color, sound, and smell. The novel features a passionate and tragic love story illustrating the author's idea that almost every true love ends in forced separation or loss. Characters are full-blooded individuals, and historical events are portrayed with considerable objectivity. The novel abounds in tense situations arising from personal or sociopolitical confrontations. The dialogue between Cossack characters is superb, and S. liberally employs dialecticisms and the imagery of Cossack folk poetry in his own narrative.

In its prolific use of color, figures of speech, and certain syntactical constructions the novel's style reveals a kinship with the Soviet ornamental prose of the 1920s. The plot unfolds smoothly, except in Volume II, which is too fragmentary and overpopulated with episodic characters. In 1965 S. was awarded the Nobel Prize for literature, primarily for *Tikhy Don*. Rumors have circulated since 1928 that he could not have written all or part of the novel because of his young age or pro-Soviet orientation: the work is politically objective, describing atrocities on both sides. In the 1970s his authorship was questioned in print by Aleksandr SOLZHENITSYN and Roy Medvedev (b. 1925), but neither presented any convincing evidence for plagiarism. Throughout the years Soviet censors made numerous deletions in *Tikhy Don*, chiefly in unflattering descriptions of the Reds. Some 250 deletions remain unrestored to this day.

S.'s second novel, *Podnyataya tselina* (2 vols., 1932, 1960; I, *Seeds of Tomorrow*, 1935; II, *Harvest on the Don*, 1961), deals with the collectivization of agriculture in the Don region, involving a political struggle between local Communists and former White Army officers. In Volume I dramatic scenes alternate with comic episodes, which provide relief from tension and suspense. Volume II covers only the summer of 1930, and the story of collectivization remains unfinished. The reader learns nothing about the terrorism and famine of 1932–33. Dramatic episodes in Volume II are few; it is filled with static material, notably with various tales narrated by the characters and with comic episodes presented by the author in the form of anecdotes. *Podnyataya tselina* lacks the objectivity and artistic power of *Tikhy Don*, bespeaking S.'s growing adherence to the Communist Party line and a certain exhaustion of his creativity. This is even truer of *Oni srazhalis za rodinu* (serially, 1943–69; *They Fought for Their Country*, serially, 1959–69), an unfinished novel conceived as a trilogy about World War II. Its published portions depict fighting in the Don region and provide flashbacks into the characters' prewar lives.

In most of his speeches and journalistic writings S. faithfully follows the official policy of the day. Some of his attacks on Western leaders and dissident Soviet writers are singularly vicious.

S.'s claim to an enduring place in world literature rests on *Tikhy Don*. A kind of Cossack *War and Peace*, it recreates graphically the historical atmosphere and offers an original and sensitive treatment of the eternal themes of love, death, and humanity.

FURTHER WORKS: *Slovo o Rodine* (1951); *Sobranie sochineny* (2 eds., each 8 vols., (1956–1960); *Sobranie sochineny* (8 vols., 1962); *Slovo o Rodine: Rasskazy, ocherki, stati* (1965); *Sobranie sochineny* (1965 ff.); *Po veleniyu dushi: Stati, ocherki, vystupleniya, dokumenty* (1970); *Sobranie sochineny* (8 vols., 1975); *Rossiya v serdtse: Sbornik rasskazov, ocherkov, publitsistiki* (1975); *Sobranie sochineny* (8 vols., 1980); *Slovo o Rodine* (1980). FURTHER WORKS IN ENGLISH: *One Man's Destiny, and Other Stories, Articles, and Sketches, 1923–1963* (1967); *At the Bidding of the Heart: Essays, Sketches, Speeches, Papers* (1973)

BIBLIOGRAPHY: Simmons, E., *Russian Fiction and Soviet Ideology: Introduction to Fedin, Leonov, and S.* (1958): 163–252; Muchnic, H., *From Gorky to Pasternak: Six Writers in Soviet Russia* (1961): 304–40; Stewart, D., *M. S.: A Critical Introduction* (1967); Bearne, C., *S.* (1969); Klimenko, M., *The World of Young S.: Vision of Violence* (1972); Yakimenko, L., *S.: A Critical Appreciation* (1973); Medvedev, R., *Problems in the Literary Biography of M. S.* (1977); Ermolaev, H., *M. S. and His Art* (1982)

—HERMAN ERMOLAEV

SHONA LITERATURE
See Under Zimbabwean Literature

SHTEYNBARG, Eliezer

Yiddish fabulist, poet, dramatist, and writer of children's stories, b. 1880, Lipkany, Russian Empire (now in Moldavia); d. 28 March 1932, Cernăuţ Romania (now Chernovtsy, Ukraine)

S. received a thorough Jewish education and studied European literature and philosophy on his own. He became a teacher and was soon known in his hometown for his beautiful children's stories and plays, and above all for his fables. In 1919 he was moved to Cernăuţi, where he assumed a leading position in Yiddish cultural life. He lectured and edited the periodical *Kultur* and a series of brochures called *An entfer di gegner fun yidish* (a reply to the opponents of Yiddish); he also wrote for the newspapers *Dos naye lebn* and *Di frayhayt*. He was instrumental in creating a children's theater and wrote and directed several musical plays and dramas based on legends and biblical themes: *Di gliklekhe* (pub. 1950; the happy ones), *Reb Khananie Ben Doyse* (1931; Reb Khananie Ben Doyse); *Di Bove mayse* (1920; the Buovo tale); and *Yosef Moykher Shabes* (1920; Yosef Moyker Shabes). In the late 1920s S. was invited to become headmaster of a Yiddish day school in Rio de Janeiro. After two years he returned to Cernăuţi. Having completed his collection of fables, S. underwent surgery and died soon after.

S. was an innovator in the genre of the fable in both style and subject matter. Displaying great virtuosity and linguistic skill, he elevated the Yiddish fable to the highest artistic level. He found his personages not merely among the traditional beasts, birds, and vegetation but also in the realm of abstract and inanimate objects. Through this cast of characters, he voiced his skeptical view of the human condition. Entangled in a vicious circle, the oppressed and the oppressor seem to bear the same guilt. His *Weltschmerz* is sometimes presented in a lyrical tone. The fool and the hypocrite are dealt with without pity. Irony and humor generally prevail and the persona's tongue-in-cheek comments, perfectly interwoven into the texture of the whole, add an impish vividness.

S. was a master of language, creating neologisms, reshaping proverbs, and drawing from the rich folk idiom and the Talmud. His abundant use of diminutives is itself worthy of special study. He had a distinctive manner of rhyming long lines with short ones and used very specific rhythms. His fables are collected in *Mesholim* (1932; fables), illustrated by Arthur Kolnik and reissued five times in different editions, and in *Mesholim II* (1956; tales II).

S. was also a talented writer of children's books. His Hebrew *Alfon* (1920; primer) and Yiddish *Alef Beys* (1921; ABC) are minor masterpieces. S. also wrote plays, essays, and poetry and made translations from the Hebrew of Chayim Nachman BIALIK.

Mayselekh (1936; tales) is a collection of fairy tales wrought out of proverbs, idioms, and bits of legends. It is partly in verse, and the heroes are animals, birds, and letters of the alphabet. Written in a seemingly childish voice, the tales are full of hidden meaning and symbolism, trying to uncover the mystery of the universe and the man-made world. Adding to its magic are the 109 illustrations by Arthur Kolnik.

S. is the foremost master of fables in Yiddish. They were recited by heart long before his first collections appeared in print. Because of his erudition, his talent, and his personality, he was widely loved and venerated, and he became a cult figure during his lifetime.

FURTHER WORKS: *Vi azoy di feygelekh hobn gelernt khumesh* (1923); *Durkh di briln* (1928); *Tsen mesholim* (1970)

BIBLIOGRAPHY: Robak, A. A., *The Story of Yiddish Literature* (1940): 328–29, 350; Dobzynski, C., ed., *Le miroir d'un peuple: Anthologie de la poésie yidich 1870–1970* (1971): 84; Liptzin, S., *A History of Yiddish Literature* (1972): 189, 227–29

—BELLA SCHAECHTER-GOTTESMAN

SHUA, Ana María

Argentine novelist, short-story writer, poet, screenwriter, and dramatist, b. 22 Apr. 1951, Buenos Aires

S.'s literary career began at the age of sixteen when she received an award from the National Foundation for the Arts for the poem "El sol y yo" (1967; The Sun and I). Since then, she has won the International Narrative Prize, the International Prize for short story from Puebla, México, and first prize from *Don* magazine for erotic short story. S. has had several of her works translated into German, Portuguese, Italian, and English.

After completing a degree in literature at the University of Buenos Aires, S. worked as a copywriter, journalist, and scriptwriter. S.'s works converge on the intimate as she is a keen observer of the individual as well as the strife and complexities within contemporary Argentine society. As such S.'s fiction takes on a testimonial quality where the limits between invention and authenticity are not easily nor clearly delineated. In the novel *El libro de los recuerdos* (1994; The Book of Memories) she depicts the immigration, acculturation, and incorporation of an Eastern European Jewish family into Argentine society over three generations. While fictional, the events, characters, and reality of the immigrant situation are drawn from S.'s own family history.

Although her style is eclectic and constantly evolving, there are two constants interwoven throughout her fiction. They are the use of humor and irony to debunk and expose cultural foibles—the fact that many of her protagonists are identified as a minority—and the exploration of the lives of Argentine-acculturated Jews. These factors constitute the groundwork for her recurring chronicle of modern urban society in the metropolis of Buenos Aires. *Los amores de Laurita* (1984; Laura's Loves) also contains as a subtext the Argentine-Jewish experience. Laura, the protagonist, recounts her young life through remembrances of the men with whom she has had relationships over the years. Thus, this novel also chronicles cultural and historic events as Laura matures and comes of age in the 1960s and 1970s. *El marido Argentino Promedio* (1991; The Average Argentine Husband) mimics the ever popular contemporary self-help books as it wryly proffers advise on spousal habits and training in the opening section. Later sections examine immigration—the grandparents who came from Europe for freedom and the irony of the new expatriates who leave to find freedom in the 1970s.

While her writings seem disparate and to incorporate abundant subjects, at the core is an interest in portraying contemporary society as a paradoxical and complex structure. At times society opposes the individual's needs, as in *Soy paciente* (1980; *Patient*, 1997), where a young man is caught in the bureaucracy of a hospital and he learns to suffer "patiently" the absurdities of a health-care system that dehumanizes. In *La muerte como efecto secundario* (1997; Death as a Secondary Effect) S. again questions the possibilities the future holds as presented through a father-son relationship in a not too distant future where geriatric patients are warehoused in private institutions for economic gain.

In spite of her biting wit and her perspicacious and probing chronicling of cosmopolitan life, S.'s writings do not overtly censure nor criticize the politics and recent events in her homeland. Repeatedly, the characters that inhabit S.'s novels and stories seem to capitulate to the forces of social order externally but internally resist conformity such as Laura, protagonist of *Los amores de Laurita*.

Many of S.'s short stories are micro stories that deal with societal norms, principles, and conduct, as in *El marido argentino promedio* and *Casa de geishas* (1992; Geisha House). Time and again, S. challenges the status quo through her use of irony and humor. We laugh at our imperfections and the futility of our attempts to attain an ideal as depicted in the section on the feminine condition in *El marido argentino promedio*.

Satire and black humor is the preferred medium utilized by S. to demonstrate the disparity between "fact and fiction" in quotidian events. Her prose writings attempts to reconcile a personal perception of reality and the idealization of that same perception. S. is above all else a contemporary Scherazade. Her priority as an author is to be an effective storyteller, a weaver of anecdotes. Her narratives are entertaining and her perspicacity and ability to observe, to comment and to compel us to react to how she perceives her world are what make her an exceptional commentator on modern society. Although she maintains certain constants, her style changes with each work.

FURTHER WORKS: *Los días de la pesca* (1981); *La sueñera* (1984); *Viajando se conoce gente* (1988); *Risas y emociones de la cocina judía* (1993); *El pueblo de los tontos* (1995)

BIBLIOGRAPHY: Pollack, B., "A. M. S.," *Hispam*, 23 (1994): 45-54; Leonard, K., ed., *Cruel Fictions, Cruel Realities: Short Stories by Latin American Women Writers* (1997)

—BETH POLLACK

SHUKSHIN, Vasily Makarovich

Russian short-story writer, screenwriter, and novelist, b. 25 July 1929, Srostki, Altai; d. 2 Oct. 1974, Stanitsa kletskaya, Volgograd Region

The year of S.'s birth coincided with the forced collectivization of peasant farmers in the U.S.S.R., a fact not lost on S.'s literary biography. The massive destruction of entire villages and the uprooting of families through inclusion into collective farms (kolkhozy) or migration into the cities haunt the histories of S.'s characters. Born in a small rural village, S. finished seven years of school, worked at his local kolkhoz, then at odd jobs in central Russian cities, before serving in the Soviet navy from 1949 to 1952. Finishing high school by correspondence, S. taught evening school in Srostki before entering the All-Union Institute of Cinematography in Moscow in 1954, where he studied directing with M. I. Romm. He began writing as part of his film training and published his first collection of short stories, *Selskie zhiteli* (1963; country folk), two years after graduating. His first full-length film, *Zhivyot takoy paren* (1964; there lives this guy), won the Golden Lion of Saint Mark Award at the 16th Venice Film Festival. His second film, *Vash syn i brat* (1965; your son and brother), followed a year later and was awarded the Vasilev Brothers State Prize of the Russian Republic (RSFSR). Both films drew on S.'s short stories for their scripts. In 1965 S.'s first novel, *Lyubaviny* (the Lyubavins), was also published, whose sequel was posthumously discovered and brought out in 1987.

S.'s early stories introduce characters who normally hail from the country, particularly his own Altai region of Siberia. These characters are fiercely independent, simple people: drivers, mechanics, carpenters, librarians. Suspicious of the big city, they are prickly, uncompromising people whose moral discoveries often stem from the offenses and injustices they suffer at the hands of their spouses, neighbors, or friends. Description is spare. Plots are advanced primarily through character dialogues colored by local dialects and conversational turns of speech. The cinematic style of S.'s stories lends freshness and immediacy. Many stories are ironic or slightly humorous.

In tone and theme, *Lyubaviny* strikes a more somber note. Set in the 1920s on the eve of collectivization, it depicts an Altai village where Soviet reforms have yet to penetrate. Yegor Lyubavin is the first of the more elemental characters in S.'s prose who rebel against authority and seek some sort of higher transcendence. This spiritual deliverance—the search for *volya* (liberty or freedom) or a "holiday of the soul"—is a recurring theme in S.'s mature prose and figures in the title of S.'s second novel, *Ya prishel dat vam volyu* (1971; I have come to give you freedom). The latter is a treatment of Stenka Razin, the leader of a peasant rebellion against

Czar Aleksey in 1670. S. admired Razin's intensely felt craving for immediate and complete justice, a trait shared by many of S.'s characters.

S.'s stories written in the mid-1960s and later are more complex thematically. Although neither collectivization nor World War II are treated directly by S., the uprooting of millions of Russians finds its reflection in the lives S. describes. These heroes of his mature works often cannot find a place for themselves. In seeking physical roots and spiritual transcendence, they become transient truth seekers who, through a combination of naïveté, misdirected passion, restlessness, rootlessness, or impulsiveness, clash with falsehood, complacency, and pettiness. In collections such as *Tam, vdali* (1968; there, in the distance), *Zemlyaki* (1970; men of one soil), *Kharaktery* (1973; types), and *Besedy pri yasnoy lune* (1974; conversations under a clear moon), S.'s protagonists suffer when their visions of spiritual release—often as vague and boundless as their native Siberian landscapes—are clouded by petty bureaucrats, antagonistic colleagues, unsympathetic women, or the finality of death. S.'s characters often are depicted in transition, either moving from the country to the city or adapting to a changing countryside that is absorbing city culture and values. *Kalina krasnaya* (1974; *Snowball Berry Red*, 1979) treats all of these themes in its depiction of a recidivist thief's failed attempt to give up his former gang of urban criminals and reclaim the folk heritage of his rural childhood. The hero's rootlessness is seen as the cause for his life of crime. Controversial in its atypical themes and almost killed by censorship, the film—and through it, the novella—was nevertheless an incredible national success, for which S. was posthumously awarded the Lnin Prize in 1976.

S.'s later works are also pervaded by an urgent existential questioning, and it is his exploration of existential themes that makes him a more universally interesting and important author. S. resisted being labeled a writer of "village" or "country prose," insisting his interests lay primarily with humanity. How people are born, marry, and die is his self-professed interest as a writer. As if testifying to this fact, the titles of over half of his stories refer, through epithets, names, or quoted speech, directly to people. Moreover, the "eccentrics," "cranks," "strange people," and "scandal-mongers"—highlighted by critics as favorite subjects for S.—are really not country "types" or urban misfits so much as they are recognizable, even typical, representatives of the human race. Reflections on death and the purpose of life also inform S.'s later stories.

Today, S. is rightfully credited with revitalizing the short-story form in the former Soviet Union. His anecdotal, powerfully economic authorial voice, and the wonderfully understated quality of his prose, have earned S. a distinct place in Soviet literary history.

FURTHER WORKS: *Brat moy* (1975); *lzbrannye proizvedeniya v dvukh tomakh* (1975); *Kinopovesti* (1975; rev. ed., 1988); *Rasskazy* (1975); *Osemyu* (1976); *Do tretikh petukhov* (1976); *Okhota zhit* (1977); *Nrastvennost est pravda* (1979); *Voprosy samomu sebe* (1981); *Rasskazy* (1984); *Sobramie sochineniy v tryokh tomakh* (1984); *Mgnoveniya zhizni* (1989); *Stories from a Siberian Village* (1996). FURTHER WORKS IN ENGLISH: *I Want to Live* (1973); *Snowball Berry Red, and Other Stories* (1979); *Roubles in Words, Kopeks in Figures* (1985)

BIBLIOGRAPHY: Baklanov, G., et al., "Reality and the Writer's Vision: Round Table Discussion," *SovL*, 9, 330 (Sept. 1975): 123–38; Fleming, S. le, "V. S.-A Contemporary Scythian," in Freeborn, R., R. R. Milner-Gullard, and C. A. Ward, eds., *Russian and Slavic Literature* (1976): 449–66; Dunlop, J. B., "The Search for Peace," *TLS* (30 June 1978): 739–40; Heller, M., "V. S.: In Search of Freedom," *Snowball Berry Red, and Other Stories* (1979): 213–33; Hosking, G., *Beyond Socialist Realism* (1980): 162–79; Mann, R., "St. George in V. S.'s 'Kalina krasnaya,'" *SEEJ*, 28 (1984): 445–54; Ignashev, D. N, "V. S.'s *Srezal* and the Question of Transition," *SEER*, 66, 3 (July 1988): 337–56; Ignashev, D. N., "The Art of V. S.: *Volya* through Song," *SEEJ*, 32, 3 (Fall 1988): 415–27; Christian, N., "Manifestations of the Eccentric in the Works of V. S.," *SEER*, 75, 2 (1997)

—JOHN R. GIVENS

SIBURAPHA

(pseud. of Kulap Saipradit) Thai novelist, essayist, and journalist, b. 31 March 1905, Bangkok; d. 16 June 1974, Beijing, China

Despite a modest family background S. attended the prestigious Thepsirin School in Bangkok, where his interest in writing was awakened. On leaving school he worked as a journalist while contributing fiction to various magazines. In 1928 he launched the short-lived but popular *Suphapburut* magazine, which established his reputation in journalistic and literary circles. For the next decade he held senior editorial posts on most of the major Bangkok dailies; disillusioned, however, by the failure of the 1932 revolution to institute genuine reform, S. became more outspoken in his views on social injustice and censorship, which led him increasingly into conflict with the government of Field Marshal Phibun Songkhram.

In 1947 S. went to Australia on a study trip; when he returned the following year, he became more active in his opposition to the ruling military régime. His criticisms were expressed both in newspaper articles and in short stories while he also became a prominent figure in the Thai branch of the worldwide Peace Movement set up to oppose the war in Korea. He was eventually arrested in 1952 as part of a broad military clamp-down on those suspected of communist sympathies. He was sentenced to thirteen years imprisonment but released in 1957 in an amnesty. He made trips to Moscow and Beijing, but, while in the latter, decided to seek asylum when he learned that Field Marshal Sarit Thanarat had seized power in a military coup in 1958. S. never returned to Thailand and died in exile in 1974.

S. achieved rapid popularity as a romantic novelist in the late 1920s when the Thai novel was beginning to develop its own identity. Many of his early novels were serialized in his own *Suphapburut* magazine. Works of this period such as *Luk phuchai* (1928; a real man), *Prap phayot* (1928; taming a shrew), *Hua chai pratthana* (1928; the heart's desire), *Lok sanniwat* (1928; life's destiny), *Man manut* (1928; the evil one), and *Phachon bap* (1929; encounter with sin) are characterized by complex plots that depend on improbable coincidences for their satisfactory resolution. There is evidence of S.'s concern with social injustice, especially in *Luk phuchai* and *Lok sanniwat*, but it does not constitute a major theme in his early works.

Throughout the 1930s S.'s fictional output was small, although it included two of his best-known novels, *Songkhram chiwit* (1932; the war of life) and *Khang lang phap* (1937; *Behind the Painting,*

1990). The former was a major departure from his early work and reflected a more mature appreciation of the role and responsibility of the writer. Influenced by Dostoevsky's *Poor Folk* (1846) and likewise written in an epistolary style, it is often described by Thai critics as a "humanitarian" novel; in fact, the novel is an outspoken attack on aspects of Thai society, the letters describing the miseries of poverty, the selfishness and vanity of the rich, religious hypocrisy, government corruption, inadequate medical facilities, and the lack of freedom of speech. By contrast, *Khang lang phap*, set partly in Japan, is a confessional novel about a young man's infatuation with an older married woman and his subsequent awakening, after the death of her husband, to the frailty of his own romantic feelings. With its subtle undercurrent of frustrated sexuality and its attempt to deal with emotions in an honest way, it is considered by most Thais to be not only S.'s most stylistically accomplished work but also one of the best-written novels in Thai. *Khang lang phap* has been reprinted more than a dozen times, made into a film (directed by Piak Poster), studied in schools, and translated into Chinese, Japanese, and English.

In the decade that followed the appearance of *Khang lang phap* S.'s fictional output was minimal. On his return from Australia in 1948, however, he once again began to write prolifically. His nonfiction of the period included a series of articles on Marxism, and translations from Maxim GORKY and Anton CHEKHOV. Short stories such as "Khon phuak nan" (1950; "Those Kind of People," 1990), "Kho raeng noi thoe" (1950; "Lend us a Hand," 1990), and "Khao tu'n" (1952; "The Awakening," 1990), and the short novel, *Chon kwa rao cha phop kan ik* (1950; *Until We Meet Again*, 1995), were blunt and uncompromising in their portrayal of social injustice and reflected S.'s politically committed view of literature. More ambitious in conception was *Lae pai khang na* (2 vols., 1955, 1957; look forward), conceived as a trilogy, but of which only the first two volumes appeared; in this work S. set out to provide a panoramic view of Thai history from the end of the absolute monarchy in 1932, through the experiences of a young boy studying and later working in Bangkok.

Throughout the 1960s S.'s links with communism made his name taboo in Thailand. In the liberal political climate of the 1970s, however, he was rediscovered and energetically promoted as a major figure in the struggle for social justice within Thailand. His later fiction was highly praised by progressive critics and became a model for many young writers in the 1970s. Conservative critics, though, regarded it as lacking literary merit but saw S.'s early novels as important in the development of the Thai novel. As a result of Thailand's stability in the 1980s S. is no longer regarded as a "dangerous" writer, and recent evaluations of his work acknowledge the significance of both his early "romantic" work and his later "political" writing in the development of Thai fiction.

FURTHER WORKS: *Amnat chai* (1930); *Saen rak saen khaen* (1930); *Tham ngan tham ngoen* (1934); *Phu thi ma chak lok borisut* (1934); *Phu'an tang phet* (1934); *Tai hon raek* (1934); *Thaeng thong* (1935); *Khang khu'n khang raem* (1935); *Kon taeng ngan* (1937); *Nop* (1938); *Sing thi chiwit tongkan* (1939); *Sunthari* (1942); *Kae thi phlat fung* (1949); *Nak bun chak chantan* (1949); *Mahaburut khong chantima* (1949); *Khao lu'ak lambarene nai sayam* (1949); *Kham khan rap* (1950); *Ai nu long thang* (1950); *Prakai mai nai duangta khong khao* (1951)

BIBLIOGRAPHY: Batson, B., "K. S. and the 'War of Lifersquo;" *JSSB*, 69 (1981): 58–73; Smyth, D. A., "The Later Short Stories of S.," in Davidson, J. H. C. S., ed., *Lai Sü Thai: Essays in Honour of E. H. S. Simmonds* (1987): 98–115; Smyth, D. A., Introduction to *Behind the Painting and Other Stories* (1990): 1–44; Barmé, S., *Kulap in O3* (1995)

—DAVID A. SMYTH

SIDAORÜANG

(pseud. of Wanna Thappananon) Thai short-story writer and novelist, b. 14 Dec. 1943, Phitsanulok

S. was born in 1943 in Phitsanulok province, central Thailand, the third of ten children. Her father worked on the railway and her mother as a market vendor. At the age of twelve her formal schooling came to a premature end when her mother sent her away to Bangkok to work as a maid. She subsequently spent many years working in a variety of menial jobs that included factory work, selling food in the market and waitressing. Following a chance meeting with the prominent writer, editor, and intellectual, Suchat Sawatsi, later to become her husband, S. began to broaden her own reading and to try her hand at writing. Although she has since written four novels, it is as a short-story writer that she is best known.

S.'s early stories were influenced by the socialist-inspired "literature for life" movement of the early 1970s. She drew on personal experience as a low-paid worker in "Kaew yot diaw" (1975; "A Drop of Glass," 1994), to portray labor unrest in a glass factory. The prize-winning "Khon dai ya" (1979; "The Grasscuter," 1984), and "Mu'" (1976; "The Hand," 1994), narrated by a maimed ex-factory worker who scavenges among rubbish heaps in search of plastic bags for recycling, both highlight the pitiful existence of workers eking out a living on the margins of society. "Chai pha luang" (1975; "The Edge of the Yellow Robe," 1981), which deals with corruption within the monkhood, and "Mu't laeo sawang" (1980; "Light After Dark," 1994), a sympathetic portrayal of the life of a prostitute, are typical in theme and treatment of many of the kind of stories being written by serious writers during the 1970s.

S.'s more recent work has moved away from the documentary fiction of the 1970s to explore themes of family, motherhood, sexual inequality, female identity, and domestic betrayal. "Matsi" (1985; "Matsi," 1996), with its deliberate subversion of a well-known Buddhist jataka tale, deals with a young woman who abandons her child, while "Sida dap fai" (1984; "Sida Extinguishes the Flames," 1998), is one of a series of stories that humorously portray gender conflict in urban middle-class families.

S. has won a number of literary prizes in Thailand and several works have been translated into English and other foreign languages. Although her work has a more limited readership than that of many of her female contemporaries, she nevertheless remains one of Thailand's best-known women writers, respected for her integrity and originality.

FURTHER WORKS: *Kaew yot diaw* (1983); *Bat prachachon* (1984); *Noen mafu'ang* (1987); *Chao ka wa oei* (1988); *Dek bin dai* (1989); *Phap luang ta* (1989); *Mae salu* (1993); *Lakhon haeng lok* (1994); *Lakhon haeng rak: lao ru'ang nangsu'* (1996); *Mak* (1997)

BIBLIOGRAPHY: Anderson, B. R. O'G., and Ruchira Mendiones, *In the Mirror: Literature and Politics in Siam in the American Era*

(1985); Harrison, R. V., *A Drop of Glass and Other Stories* (1994); Harrison, R. V., "Birth, Death and Identity in the Writing of S.," in Manas Chitakasem, ed., *Thai Literary Traditions* (1995): 87-117; Kepner, S. F., *The Lioness in Bloom: Modern Thai Fiction about Women* (1996)

—DAVID A. SMYTH

SIENKIEWICZ, Henryk

Polish novelist, short-story writer, and essayist, b. 5 May 1846, Wola Okrzejska; d. 11 Nov. 1916, Vevey, Switzerland

S. was born into a landowning family whose patriotic traditions were reflected in his novels. He began to write short stories and newspaper columns while a student at Warsaw University. The years 1876–79 he spent in the U.S. as a correspondent for the Warsaw daily *Gazeta polska*. In 1879 he became editor of the conservative newspaper *Slowo*, where he published many of his novels in installments. In the last decade of his life S. wrote political and social essays.

Critics usually divide S.'s work into two periods: the "positivist" one, in which he wrote short stories with a social message; and the "conservative" one, in which he produced historical novels and novels of manners. In early stories like "Szkice węglem" (1877; "Charcoal Sketches," 1897), "Janko muzykant" (1879; "Yanko the Musician," 1893), and "Za chlebem" (1880; "For Daily Bread," 1897), S. presents peasants and members of the lower class overburdened with poverty, social injustice, national discrimination, and other assorted evils. They invariably lack good judgment and come to a tragic end. The narrator of these stories has usually been viewed by critics as a humanitarian and compassionate person; however, he also patronizes his characters and indirectly invites the reader to join him in this attitude.

S.'s best works are his historical novels. The most popular, *Trylogia (The Trilogy)*, consists of *Ogniem i mieczem* (4 vols., 1884; *With Fire and Sword*, 1890), *Potop* (6 vols., 1886; *The Deluge*, 1891), and *Pan Wolody-jowski* (3 vols., 1887–88; *Pan Michael*, 1893). It covers the period 1648–72 in Polish history, when Poland was fighting Muscovites, Turks, Tartars, and Swedes, as well as rebellious Cossacks. S.'s successful rendering of the language and customs of those turbulent times far surpassed the romantic novelists' stylized accounts of past epochs.

Quo vadis? (3 vols., 1896; *Quo Vadis?*, 1896) is artistically less successful, but it became an international best seller, and it was largely due to this novel that S. received the Nobel Prize for literature in 1906. It deals with the persecution of Christians in the first century. The historical detail is accurate, but *Quo Vadis?* lacks the fiery temper of *Trylogia* and of *Krzyżacy* (4 vols., 1897–1900; *The Knights of the Cross*, 1900), a historical novel of the Middle Ages that presents the conflict between the Poles and the Teutonic Knights, who under the pretext of converting the pagans to Christianity raided the long-Christianized Polish kingdom.

Prusse et Pologne: Enquête internationale organisée par H. S. (1907; Prussia and Poland: international inquiry organized by H. S.), edited and co-authored by S., is a polyglot volume (not published in Polish) that best represents the political and social concerns of S.'s later years. In it he wrote passionately about the Prussian government's policy of expropriating Polish landholders in Prussian-occupied Poland, and he enlisted several dozen European intellectuals in support of his cause.

Among S.'s late novels, *W pustyni i w puszczy* (1912; *In Desert and Wilderness*, 1912) achieved great popularity. This book for children deals with a Polish boy and an English girl whose fathers work in Africa and who are kidnapped by the Bedouin insurgents in the 1881–84 uprising against the British. The children manage to escape, and they wander for weeks in the deserts of Africa before being rescued. S.'s own travels in Africa in the years 1890–91 gave a measure of authenticity to this tale of gallantry, brutality and adventure.

In some ways, S. is a Catholic writer first and a Polish writer second. His novels usually incorporate a Catholic message. For instance, *Rodzina Polanieckich* (1893; *Children of the Soil*, 1895) depicts a marriage in conventional Warsaw society. On another level, its theme is a contest between vanity and the obligations of family life. S.'s novels are often built around the idea that suffering can heal one's pride and dissolve hatred of the enemy. The fates of Jurand of Spychów in *Krzyżacy*, Kmicic in *Potop*, and Vinicius in *Quo vadis?* are all variations on this theme.

Polish critics have reproached S. for his lack of formal originality and philosophical depth. It is true that his men and women do not experience the anxieties of the modern self-searching heroes. His accomplishments, however, outweigh his shortcomings. S. knew how to tell a good story. He displayed a remarkable artistic intuition in his choice of the Baroque period as the setting for *Trylogia*. He felt, as did Witold GOMBROWICZ many years later, that the Polish tradition derived from the exuberance of the Polish Baroque rather than from the moroseness of Polish romanticism. These qualities, in addition to his strongly Catholic world view, account for his popularity in largely Catholic Poland. His influence on the Polish reading public can hardly be overestimated. What his novels have said about life in general and Poland in particular has become part of Polish popular culture.

FURTHER WORKS: *Humoreski z teki Worszyłły* (1872); *Na marne* (1872; *In Vain*, 1899); *Stary sługa* (1875); *Hania* (1876; *Hania*, 1898); *Listy Litwosa z podróży do Ameryki* (1876–1878; *Portrait of America*, 1959); *Selim Mirza* (1877); *Za chlebem* (1880; *After Bread*, 1897); *Pisma* (38 vols., 1880–1917); *Na jedną kartę* (1881; *On a Single Card*, 1898); *Bartek Zwycięzca* (1882; *The Fate of a Soldier*, 1898); *Bez dogmatu* (1891; *Without Dogma*, 1892); *Listy z Afryki* (2 vols., 1892); *Pójdźmy za Nim!* (1893; *Let Us Follow Him*, 1897); *Na jasnym brzegu* (1897; *On the Bright Shore*, 1898); *Pisma H. S.* (81 vols., 1899–1906); *Na polu chwały* (1906; *On the Field of Glory*, 1906); *Wiry* (1910; *Whirlpools*, 1910); *Legiony* (1918); *Pisma* (46 vols., 1929–1939). FURTHER WORKS IN ENGLISH: *Yanko the Musician and Other Stories* (1893); *Lillian Morris and Other Stories* (1894); *Let Us Follow Him, and Other Stories* (1897); *Hania* (1897); *For Daily Bread and Other Stories* (1898); *Sielanka: A Forest Picture and Other Stories* (1898); *So Runs the World* (1898); *Life and Death and Other Legends and Stories* (1904); *Tales* (1931)

BIBLIOGRAPHY: Gosse, E., "H. S.", *Living Age* (22 May 1897): 517–27; Lednicki, W., *H. S.: A Retrospective Synthesis* (1960); Giergielewicz, M., *H. S.* (1968); Welsh, D. J., *S.'s "Trilogy": A Study in Novelistic Techniques* (1971); Thompson, E. M., "H. S. and Aleksei K. Tolstoy: A Creative Borrowing", *PolR*, 17 (1972): 52–66; Welsh, D. J., "Two Contemporary Novels of H. S.: A Reappraisal," *SEEJ*, 16 (1972): 307–12; Krzyżanowski, J., "The

Polish-Californian Background of H. S.'s Burlesque 'A Comedy of Errors,'" in Erlich, V., et al., eds., *For Wiktor Weintraub: Essays in Polish Literature* (1975): 251–56

—EWA M. THOMPSON

SIERRA LEONEAN LITERATURE

Sierra Leone, a British colony from 1808 to 1961, was used to resettle freed slaves. The political writings, mainly pamphlets, of James Africanus Horton (1835–1883), a local doctor, is the only literary work from the 19th c. that remains of interest today. He vigorously argued for self-government in Africa. After Horton there was a period of nearly a hundred years before a vigorous Sierra Leonean literature developed. Political circumstances were not advantageous but cannot totally explain this puzzling gap.

Contemporary literature began in the late 1950s, with the publication of several competent, if somewhat unimaginative, books written by professional men during their leisure hours. Robert Cole's (b. 1907) autobiographical novel *Kossah Town Boy* (1960), was admired for its enthusiastic and innocent portrayal of village life, but it is little read now. The Gambian-born William Conton (b. 1925) lived long enough in Sierra Leone for his pioneering novel *The African* (1960) to be considered part of the new literature of his adopted country. John Akar's (b. 1927) *Valley without Echo* (1954) was the first African play to be produced in Britain. Dr. Raymond Sarif Easmon (b. 1913) wrote two somewhat formal, artificial plays: the domestic comedy *Dear Parent and Ogre* (1964), and the more satirical *The New Patriots* (1965). Although the characters are African, the general tone and spirit of the plays seems redolent of typically British popular fare.

Dr. Davidson Nicol (b. 1924) wrote one volume of short stories, *The Truly Married Woman* (1965). He is best remembered for a regularly anthologized poem, "The Meaning of Africa" (1959), which received both sympathetic and antagonistic responses, because of its expression of the mixed feelings of the elite toward African culture. An unquestioning acceptance of British values and styles was typical of much writing in the 1960s.

For ten years following this lively beginning there was little publication. Probably because of increasingly restrictive government policies, writers had to leave the country; it is significant that the three most promising younger Sierra Leonean writers composed their main works abroad. Lemuel Johnson's (b. 1940) *Highlife for Caliban* (1975) and Syl CHEYNEY-COKER's *Concerto for an Exile* (1973), both collections of poetry, were written in the United States. These two writers share a highly sophisticated and experimental language that owes much to their knowledge of poetic techniques from the rest of the English-speaking world. In theme, they share an angry, embittered disillusion with present-day conditions in Africa—the heavy pressures of external economic forces and the oppressive internal policies of various governments. Their difference is primarily in tone. Johnson uses sardonic wit and penetrating sarcasm. Cheyney-Coker writes with a far more direct anger; dismay burns in his lines.

Yulisa Amadu Maddy (b. 1936) has produced a variety of works. His first volume of verse was published in Denmark and his plays, published in *Obasai, and Other Plays* (1971), were broadcast over European radio services. His first novel indicates much by its very title: *No Past No Present No Future* (1973), although the

disintegration suffered by the main characters actually occurs after they arrive in Britain.

Censorship imposed by the government is likely to inhibit the development of Sierra Leonean literature at home, at least as concerns writing in English by the sophisticated elite. But Creole English (Krio), widely spoken in Sierra Leone, is the language of the vigorous, popular street-theater groups and is also printed. Thomas Decker's (1916) Krio poetry is widely known, and he has translated Shakespeare's *Julius Caesar* into Krio (1964). There is a great local vitality in such work, and its potential cannot yet be measured.

BIBLIOGRAPHY: Fyfe, C., and E. Jones, eds., *Freetown: A Symposium* (1968); Cartey, W., *Whispers from a Continent* (1969): 20–23; Olney, J., *Tell Me Africa* (1973): 37–55; Dathorne, O. R., *The Black Mind* (1974), passim; Palmer, E., "The Development of Sierra Leone Writing," in King, B., and Ogungbesan, K., eds., *A Celebration of Black and African Writing* (1975): 245–57; Gérard, A. S., *African Language Literatures* (1981): 243–46, 259–60

—JOHN POVEY

SIGURDSSON, Ólafur Jóhann

Icelandic novelist, short-story writer, and poet, b. 26 Sept. 1918, Álftanes; d. 30 July 1988, Reykjavík

Son of a poor farmer, S. decided at an early age to become a writer and moved to Reykjavík, where—apart from brief periods of study in Copenhagen and New York—he resided until his death. S.'s first publications were short stories for children, written during his teens. His first novel, *Skuggarnir af bænum* (shadows of the farmhouse) appeared in 1936.

During the 1940s S. published three collections of short stories, while working on *Fjallið og draumurinn* (1945; the mountain and the dream), his first major work, and its sequel, *Vorköld jörð* (1951; spring-chilled earth). These two novels, set in the final phase of Icelandic peasant society, which in the 20th c. has given way to urbanization and partial industrialization, describe the childhood, youth, and marriage of a country girl in the early decades of this century. Society is bitterly criticized, and the harsh conditions of rural life depicted. Yet even in these stark surroundings some of the characters display a striking fineness and integrity, rooted in traditional culture.

The setting for S.'s later novels is the period from the start of World War II to the present. In them the values and culture of the old society are depicted as losing ground to moral and spiritual decay, although the cultural pessimism dominating these works is mitigated by humor and a lyrical worship of nature.

S. is a master of subdued prose, and his fine qualities as a writer of fiction are probably best seen in his shorter fiction, especially in the novellas *Litbrigði jarðarinnar* (1947; *The Changing Earth*, 1980) and *Bréf séra Böðvars* (1965; letter from Reverend Böðvar). The former is the story of a young man's first love and disillusionment, told simply and straightforwardly with the accompaniment of nature symbolism; the latter recounts the last hours in the life of an old man, hours in which he finally faces, and succumbs to, the realization of a failed life. The values of the cultivated and aesthetically minded protagonist are contrasted with the vigor and coarse vulgarity of a younger generation. S.'s message is that refusal to face the harsh facts of life neither removes them nor protects one's values against them.

In more recent years the lyrical element, always present in S.'s prose, has asserted itself to the full in several volumes of poetry. Combining traditional poetic forms with unmistakably modern diction, S. evokes, more successfully than ever, the life-giving force of nature and the value of a simple life in harmony with nature. Although the poet views contemporary society with a pessimism verging on despair, his poems nevertheless contain powerful symbols of hope and faith in life.

S. is one of comtemporary Iceland's leading authors. Many of his short stories have been translated into a number of languages. In 1976 he won the Nordic Council's Annual Award for Literature.

FURTHER WORKS: *Við Álftavatn* (1934); *Um sumarkvöld* (1935); *Liggur vegurinn pangað?* (1940); *Kvistir í altarinu* (1942); *Teningar í tafli* (1945); *Speglar og fiðrildi* (1947); *Nokkrar vísur um veðrið og fleira* (1952); *Gangvirkið* (1955); *Á vegamótum* (1955); *Spói* (1962); *Leynt og ljóst* (1965); *Glerbrotið* (1970); *Hreiðrið* (1972); *Seint á ferð* (1972); *Að laufferjum* (1972); *Að brunnum* (1974); *Seiður og hélog* (1977); *Virki og vötn* (1978). FURTHER WORKS IN ENGLISH: *The Stars of Constantinople* (1992)

BIBLIOGRAPHY: Einarsson, S., *A History of Icelandic Literature* (1957): 326–27; Gustavs, O., "Nachbemerkung", in Ó. J. S., *Farbenspiel der Erde; Pastor Bödvars Brief* (1978): 175–83

—VÉSTEINN ÓLASON

SIGURJÓNSSON, Jóhann

Icelandic dramatist and poet (also writing in Danish), b. 19 June 1880, Laxamýri, Aðaldal; d. 30 Aug. 1919, Copenhagen, Denmark

S. grew up on a prosperous farm in northern Iceland. He studied for a time to become a veterinarian but turned instead to playwrighting. Because at that time there was no professional theater in Iceland, S. wrote in Danish as well as in Icelandic. He became a pioneer in a phenomenon peculiar to Icelandic literature at the beginning of the century: a group of Icelandic poets and writers who moved to Denmark, wrote in Danish, and for a while became important also for Danish literature. They were encouraged by the success of S., the first Icelandic writer in modern times to gain international fame.

After two plays that have been termed "interesting dramatic failures," S. had a triumph with *Fjalla-Eyvindur* (Danish title: *Bjærg-Ejvind og hans Hustru*, 1911; *Eyvind of the Hills*, 1916). Based on a popular Icelandic folktale, the play has a typical neoromantic theme of passionate love and a free life, where ordinary morality is defied. Halla, a young widow, gives up everything and flees with the outlaw Eyvind to the mountains. In the climactic scene, after a fight with him and with starvation near, she goes off to die in a snowstorm. The play is set against a majestic natural background of glaciers and waterfalls.

Neoromantic and Nietzschean influences can be seen even more clearly in his fourth and greatest play, *Galdra-Loftur* (Danish title: *Ønsket*, 1915; *Loftur*, 1939; later tr., *The Wish*, 1967), also based on a well-known Icelandic folktale, about the legendary figure of a student at the Cathedral School who sells his soul to the devil for power. But the play is not in any way a mere repetition of the Faust story. It grows out of a simple tale of sorcery and the devil's final claim into a revelation of a strange paradox of human nature, which leads to insanity and destruction. The hero is an extremely ambitious young man who wants fame and power, and who is known to seek knowledge even in obscure secret books of sorcery. When he learns that he has made a servant girl pregnant and realizes that this will terminate his hopes of attaining high social status, he decides to test his terrible knowledge by trying to kill the girl by sorcery, thereby removing the obstacle to his rise. But he must bind himself to the devil, and to free himself he tries to become greater than the devil and tame the master of darkness. If he then used evil only to do good, he would in fact have eliminated both good and evil. This is the paradox that breaks him. Although the theme is based on sorcery, everything can be explained rationally: the girl commits suicide, and the hero slowly becomes insane.

With *Galdra-Loftur* S. became the greatest Icelandic playwright of his time, but he was also the major Icelandic poet of the neoromantic and SYMBOLIST period. He published only a few poems in Icelandic in periodicals, and a slim volume of poetry in Danish was published posthumously under the title *Smådigte* (1920; short poems), yet he was perhaps the most important innovator in modern Icelandic poetry. He eliminated all traces of narration from his poems and instead based them on dense imagery and symbolism. In his great visionary poem "Sorg" (written 1905–10, pub. 1927; sorrow) he even turned to free form and compression of language, which probably makes it the first MODERNIST poem in Icelandic.

FURTHER WORKS: *Dr. Rung* (1905); *Bóndinn á Hrauni* (1908, *The Hraun Farm*, 1916); *Mörður Valgarðsson* (Danish title: *Løgneren*, 1917); *Rit* (2 vols., 1940–1942); *Bréf til bróður* (1968)

BIBLIOGRAPHY: Hermannsson, H., *Icelandic Authors of To-day* (1913): 48–49; Leach, H. G., "Eyvind of the Hills/Outlaws," *ASR* 4 (1916): 346–54; Magoun, F. P., Jr., "J. S.'s *Fjalla-Eyvindur*: Source, Chronology and Geography," *PMLA* 61 (1946): 269–92; Toldberg, H., *J. S.* (1965)

—NJÖRDUR P. NJARDVÍK

SIKELIANOS, Angelos

Greek poet and dramatist, b. 15 March 1884, Levkas; d. 19 July 1951, Athens

The youngest of seven children, S., after completing his schooling on the Ionian island of Levkas, moved to Athens to study law at the university. Instead, however, he became active in the New Stage, the experimental theater of Constantine Christomanos (1867–1911). S.'s sister Penelope married Raymond Duncan, brother of Isadora Duncan; it was at his sister's home that S. met the wealthy New Yorker Eva Palmer, whom he followed to the U.S. and married in 1907. They traveled together in Europe in 1911–12, and in 1912 he served as a soldier in Epirus during the struggle against

Ottoman rule. He became a close friend of Nikos KAZANTZAKIS, with whom in 1914–15 he toured Mount Athos and other classical and Byzantine sites in Greece. Eva Palmer was to devote herself and her fortune to the realization of her husband's "Delphic Idea"–turning the ancient site of Delphi into an international cultural and spiritual center, which would promote freedom and international brotherhood. The results of her efforts were the two Delphic Festivals of 1927 and 1930, which consisted of highly successful performances of ancient drama and dance, concerts, athletic competitions, and folk-art exhibits. Her money exhausted, Eva returned to America in 1933, and they later divorced. S. married again, in 1940. He supported the resistance during the Nazi occupation of Greece. In 1947 he was elected president of the Society of Greek Writers and in 1951, the year of his death, was nominated for membership in the Academy of Athens.

An extraordinarily gifted man, a genuine visionary, and a legend in his time, S. is one of the major figures of modern Greek poetry. His first major poetic work, which immediately established his reputation, was the long autobiographical poem *Alafroiskiotos* (1909; the visionary), composed in fifteen days in the Libyan desert. It reflects the poet's youth and early manhood on his native island, and his sensuous as well as intellectual contact with the world of nature. In this poem S. expresses a youthful, impulsive delight in the body's contact with every living thing.

This youthful exuberance, already tinged with a mythopoeic coloring, developed into deeper spiritual concerns, into a search for the primordial, original unity of life before it was divided by time into multiplicity. That division makes necessary within the poet himself a reconciliation of all conflicts through a spiritual vision inspired mostly by ancient wisdom, which S. found still surviving in the Greek folk tradition. This theme dominates his *Prologhos sti zoi* (prologue to life), consisting of five parts: *I sinidhisi tis yis mou* (1915; the consciousness of my earth), *I sinidhisi tis fylis mou* (1915; the consciousness of my race), *I sinidhisi tis yinekas* (1916; the consciousness of woman), *I sinidhisi tis pistis* (1917; the consciousness of faith), and *I sinidhisi tis prosopikis dhimiouryias* (1947; the consciousness of personal creativity). The long sequence registers the stages in the poet's efforts to recover man's Dionysiac side–original yet universal, physical yet spiritual, human yet divine—as it is expressed in the pre-Socratic, Orphic, Pythagorean, Eleusinian, and Oriental cults and traditions. The sequence contains lyrical poems and hymns as parts of its larger units.

The death of S.'s sister Penelope in 1914 inspired one of his best poems, *Mitir Theou* (1917; final version, 1944; Mother of God), in which the painful consciousness of death becomes dominant and is then associated with the Virgin Mary, symbolic of Mother Earth and of the eternal feminine. The poems of the later *Akritika* (1942; *Akritan Songs*, 1944) celebrate the heroic spirit of Greece on the Albanian front in 1941, and express the poet's sympathy for the socialist cause and for the resistance to fascist and autocratic forces.

S.'s Delphic idea had already given birth to his first dramatic work, *O dhithyramvos tou rodhou* (1932; *The Dithyramb of the Rose*, 1939). During the war and postwar years, in the last decade of his life, S. concentrated on drama and wrote his five tragedies: *O Dhedhalos stin Kriti* (1943; Daedalus in Crete), *Sivilla* (1944; the sibyl), *O Hristos sti Romi* (1946; Christ in Rome), *O thanatos tou Dhiyieni* (1947; the death of Digenes), and *Asklipios* (1954; Asklepios). All of them are more powerful lyrically than dramatically in voicing the Greek spirit's battle for freedom, truth, and the dignity of man.

The essence of S.'s poetry is visionary, while its power is mostly lyrical, of a Dionysiac nature, ecstatically rising to solemn, hieratic grandeur, yet not totally escaping obscurity in its complex metaphysics. His subtly intellectual plays are more suited to reading than performance. His popularity rests mainly on his shorter poems. S. is credited with having achieved a masterful synthesis of the elements of the Greek tradition, ranging from early mythology to Orthodox Christianity.

FURTHER WORKS: *Stihi* (1921); *Dhelfikos loghos* (1927; *The Delphic Word*, 1928); *Antidhoro* (1943); *Lyrikos vios* (3 vols., 1946–1947); *Thymeli* (3 vols., 1950–1954); *Ghrammata tou A. S.* (1954); *Apanta* (14 vols., 1965–1980); *Ghrammata stin Anna* (1980). FURTHER WORKS IN ENGLISH: *Six Poems from the Greek of S. and Seferis* (1946); *Selected Poems* (1979)

BIBLIOGRAPHY: Liddell, R., "The Poetry of A. S.," *Penguin New Writing*, No. 39 (1950): 72–83; Demaras, C. T., "A. S.," *Hermes*, August 1951–September 1951: 174–75; Sherrard, P., *The Marble Threshing Floor* (1956): 125–83; Seferis, G., *On the Greek Style* (1966): 15–21; Friar, K., *Modern Greek Poetry* (1973): 27–31, 747–52; Politis, L., *A History of Modern Greek Literature* (1975): 193–200; Keeley, E., "A. S.: The Sublime Voice," *OntarioR*, 11 (1979–1980): 73–81

—ANDONIS DECAVALLES

SILKO, Leslie Marmon

American poet and novelist, b. 5 Mar. 1948, Albuquerque, New Mexico

S. is one of the most distinguished Native American writers of the late 20th c. Of Laguna Pueblo, Plains Indian, Mexican, and Anglo-American descent, S. was raised in west-central New Mexico on the Laguna Pueblo Reservation. While she attended the schools administered by the Bureau of Indian Affairs, it was S.'s family, and especially her great-grandmother, who educated her in the traditions and legends of Laguna culture. S. graduated magna cum laude from the University of New Mexico in 1969, and has taught at a number of universities and colleges in the Southwest.

Many of the overarching themes that run through the body of S.'s work can be illustrated by her masterful first novel, *Ceremony* (1977). Blending contemporary narrative with free-verse poetry and traditional Laguna Pueblo legends and stories, S. tells the story of a World War II veteran who, crushed by his wartime experiences, returns to the reservation in need of emotional and spiritual healing. Like many of S.'s characters, Tayo is of mixed Anglo and Laguna descent, and learns that the moral strength and spiritual resolution he searches for has always been available in the traditional stories, legends, and ceremonies of Laguna culture. Most importantly, Tayo learns that it is his people's enduring connection to the American landscape and the natural world around them that offers the antidote to the spiritually poisonous effects of the white world. In his guilt and despair over his actions during the war (and his ultimate survival of it), Tayo comes to believe that he is at fault for the deaths of his cousin, Rocky, and his uncle, Josiah. It is only through the ceremonies given him by old Betonie, a Navajo medicine man, and his encounters with Ts'eh, a reincarnation of the Mother who also created the land (Spiderwoman), that Tayo eventually is able to find healing and balance.

S.'s *Storyteller* (1981) is a multigeneric effort which integrates poetry, short stories, legend, historical fact, photography, and autobiography. Included in *Storyteller* is the short story "Yellow Woman," S.'s modern retelling of a traditional abduction narrative in which a young woman is abducted and seduced by a ka'tsina, a mountain spirit. In S.'s version of the Yellow Woman story, the unnamed female narrator eventually comes to realize that the story of her affair with a cattle rustler is in fact a reenactment of the ancient legend, confirming and strengthening her connection to the traditions and stories of her people. As in much of her work, in "Yellow Woman" S. suggests that narrative offers a more morally and spiritually meaningful reality than objective reality—that true identity is available only through the fusion of tradition, community, and individual available in storytelling.

Critics have called S.'s novel *Almanac of the Dead*, published in 1992, an apocalyptic work. The novel foretells the Native Americans' ultimate reclamation of their ancestral lands after the self-destructive elements of contemporary white civilization (moral and spiritual weakness, crime, drug addiction, sexual depravity, and the abuse of the environment) finally bring about its destruction. Not surprisingly, S.'s depiction of white people in this novel has not sat well with some critics, yet most reviewers find the work a cogent and timely critique of Anglo-America.

FURTHER WORKS: *Laguna Woman: Poems* (1974); *The Delicacy and Strength of Lace: Letters between L. M. S. & James Wright* (1985); *Yellow Woman* (1993); *Sacred Water: Narratives and Pictures* (1994); *Yellow Woman and a Beauty of the Spirit : Essays on Native American Life Today* (1996)

BIBLIOGRAPHY: Seyersted, P., *L. M. S.* (1980); Gunn Allen, P., "The Feminine Landscape of L. M. S.'s 'Ceremony,'" *Studies in American Literature: Critical Essays and Course Designs* (1983): 127-133; Hirsch, B., "'The Telling Which Continues': Oral Tradition and the Written Word in L. M. S.'s 'Storyteller,'" *AIQ*, 12, 1 (1988): 1-28; Danielson, L., "Storyteller: 'Grandmother Spider's Web,'" *Journal of the Southwest*, 30, 3 (1988): 325-55; Ruppert, J. "The Reader's Lessons in 'Ceremony,'" *ArQ*, 44, 1 (1988): 78-85; Salyer, G., *L. M. S.* (1997); Jaskoski, H., *L. M. S.: A Study of the Short Fiction* (1998)

—MARSHA WATSON

SILLANPÄÄ, Frans Eemil

Finnish novelist, short-story writer, and memoirist, b. 16 Sept. 1888, Hämeenkyrö; d. 3 June 1964, Helsinki

S.'s first-hand knowledge of rural life as the son of an impoverished day-laborer was augmented by schooling in the natural sciences. In particular, the monistic theories of the German scientists Ernst Haeckel (1834–1919) and Wilhelm Ostwald (1853–1932), which explained the unity of all nature in terms of physical laws, influenced S.'s world view. He saw man as a small but integral part of the natural universe. In its cosmic omnipotence, the sun, source of all energy, frequently observes the successes and failures of S.'s frail humans.

S.'s first novel was significantly called *Elämä ja aurinko* (1916; life and the sun). Many stylistic traits that would become characteristic of S.'s strong fiction of the 1930s are present in his debut novel, only in a less polished form: here the nature metaphors are overdone, and the narrator's comments are at times too obtrusive. *Hurskas Kurjuus* (1919; *Meek Heritage*, 1938), his second novel, bears the imprint of a mature artist. It is a classic depiction of a highly controversial event, the 1918 Finnish civil war. Its boldness lies in its refusal to take sides and to glorify the victorious Whites. Instead, S. focuses on the protagonist, a passive and rather repugnant poor sharecropper whose declining fortunes are traced from his birth to his violent death as a guiltless victim of the cruel war. Beneath the thick crust of dirt, inertia, and ugliness lies the very essence of humanity with which the reader is made to identify and empathize.

S.'s paradoxical belief in man's insignificance in the universe and in man's simultaneous impact on and responsibility within his own immediate environment led him to regard the farmer, rooted in the soil and entrusted with inherited land, as an ideal hero. In S.'s view, either ignoring material concerns or, conversely, single-mindedly worshiping material values exacts a price from the individual. *Nuorena nukkunut* (1931; *The Maid Silja*, 1933), his most popular novel, depicts the loss of a farm and the extinction of a family. The father, a man of honorable character, attuned to his natural instincts but overlooking the welfare of the estate, errs in marrying a servant girl. After the forced sale of the farm, the father's sole legacy to his beneficiary is his nobility of mind. As the daughter's fortunes ebb, this legacy, her inner beauty, intensifies. The girl dies young and blissful, at the height of a sunny summer. With the inherited land gone, she, the last of her line, is free to leave and, through death, be reunited with the land, her father, and the lover of her dreams.

In *Miehen tie* (1932; the way of a man) S. again presents an ideal hero. At the end of a lengthy period of youthful quests and mistakes, the protagonist finds his rightful place as a tiller of the soil and marries the woman he desires. Together the two will live in harmony with nature and replenish the earth. From *Nuorena nukkunut*, with its mystic romanticism reminiscent of Maurice MAETERLINCK, S. here moved closer to a sensualism akin to that of D. H. LAWRENCE.

When in 1939, on the eve of the Finnish Winter War, S. was awarded the Nobel Prize for literature, he was already past his creative prime. The lyrical novel *Ihmiset suviyössä* (1934; *People in the Summer Night*, 1966), highly acclaimed by critics, had already had a tone of nostalgia and resignation. The narrator adopts the attitude of an uninvolved observer in presenting the many happenings of a summer weekend. New life is born, old life dies; young love blossoms, while another man is slain in his prime. Everything, however, adds valuable strands to nature's inextricable web.

S. wrote many short stories in the 1920s. Many of them are openly autobiographical and replete with an intriguing blend of sentimental lyricism and biological realism: S. regarded man as a species of animal subject to natural laws. After 1945 he fell silent as a writer of fiction and devoted his remaining years to his memoirs.

S., Finland's only Nobel laureate, is still regarded as a writer of international stature. Like his Scandinavian colleagues, the Swedish poet E. A. Karlfeldt (1864–1931) and the Norwegian novelist Knut HAMSUN, both of whom S. greatly admired, he idealized rural life and depicted an agrarian society that belongs irrevocably to the past. Today's ecology-minded reader finds S.'s works refreshingly alive and can understand his concept of man as a part of nature, fundamentally dependent on and ultimately accountable to Mother Earth.

FURTHER WORKS: *Ihmislapsia elämän saatossa* (1917); *Rakas isänmaani* (1919); *Hiltu ja Ragnar* (1923); *Enkelten suojatit* (1923); *Maan tasalta* (1924); *Omistani ja omilleni* (1924); *Töllinmäki* (1925); *Rippi* (1928); *Kiitos hetkistä Herra . . .* (1930); *Kootut teokset* (12 vols., 1932–1948); *Virran pohjalta* (1933); *Viidestoista* (1936); *Elokuu* (1941); *Muistoja painotuotteista* (1943); *Ihmiselon ihanuus ja kurjuus* (1945); *Erään elämän satoa* (1947); *Poika eli elämäänsä* (1953); *Kerron ja kuvailen* (1954); *Valitut teokset* (1954); *Päivä korkeimmillaan* (1956); *Ajatelmia ja luonnehdintoja* (1960); *Novellit* (1961); *Valitut teokset* (1969); *Piika ja muita kertomuksia* (1978)

BIBLIOGRAPHY: Beck, R., "S.—Finland's Winner of the Nobel Prize," *Poet Lore*, 46 (1940): 358–63; Rothery, A., "Novels from Finland, *VQR*, 16 (1940): 296–99; Viljanen, L., "S.," *ASR*, 28 (1940): 49–53; Laurila, A., "F. E. S.," *ASR* 53 (1965): 284–87; Ahokas, J. A., *A History of Finnish Literature* (1973): 217–28; Tarkka, P., "The Nobel Pursuit," *BF*, 14 (1980): 13–16; Rossel, S. H., *A History of Scandinavian Literature, 1870–1980* (1982): 235–36

—VIRPI ZUCK

SILLITOE, Alan

English novelist, short-story writer, and poet, b. 4 March 1928, Nottingham

Leaving school at fourteen to work in a bicycle factory, S. early became the most authentic chronicler of working-class life that England has produced. Since the appearance of *Saturday Night and Sunday Morning* (1958), he has published numerous volumes of fiction, most of which attempt to define the moral identity and aspirations of a man of his origin. He is also a minor poet of some range.

Saturday Night and Sunday Morning and the short-story collection *The Loneliness of the Long-Distance Runner* (1959), his two earliest works of fiction, continue to be the most impressive of his oeuvre. They depict the formation of the young workingman in a slum world, where there is never enough money, where education is gained in the street, factory, and pub, and where the ultimate product of all this is a kind of persistent rage. The beer mug that Arthur Seaton in *Saturday Night and Sunday Morning* hurls through an undertaker's window "synthesized all the anarchism within him," an attitude echoed by his remark that "I've never queued in my life."

The various protagonists of S.'s fiction are generally young men of this stamp. They are amoral, dominated by an egotistical indifference to social rules, initially seeking only survival and such sensual gratification as they can get along the way. This attitude is summed up in Seaton's remark, "Whatever I do is right, and what people do to me is right."

When the novels are confined within these moral and psychological limits they are brilliant and absolutely convincing both in

language and depiction of character. This early mastery, however, has not been sustained. S.'s characters in later works have become more complex as they have sought a target for their rage and have tried to define themselves in the world beyond the Nottingham slums. Without formal education, they become readers, and in a frenzy of self-education look for purpose and meaning outside themselves, thereby losing the compact body of their being. To a considerable extent, meaning came for a time to be embodied in a diffuse anarchism, an espousal of violence for its own sake, especially as it constitutes retaliation against the snobbish masters, or servants, of the establishment. Unfortunately, when his characters began to think and the novels ranged beyond the lower-class environment, S.'s works lost their authenticity.

A case in point is the autobiographical *Raw Material* (1972), which brilliantly shows the genesis of rage in the lives of the writer's grandparents. But then it diverges into a trite and largely irrelevant diatribe against World War I, seeing it as a conspiracy to keep the working class down.

A question of increasing importance raised in S.'s later fiction is what happens to the raging young man. It is variously answered. In *The Death of William Posters* (1965) and in *A Tree on Fire* (1967) Frank Dawlish becomes a mercenary in the Algerians' struggle for independence—for no good reason except that violence is there. In *A Start in Life* (1971) Michael Cullen, after melodramatic adventures as sexual athlete and criminal, suddenly turns into a Candide, cultivating his garden in the unused premises of a former rural railroad station. He is bemused, however, by a prophecy that he will go wild again at thirty-five. Some of S.'s latest and finest work has turned toward analysis of psychological states. The story "Mimic," in *Men, Women and Children* (1973), shows a harrowing descent into madness, a theme that is echoed in the novel *The Storyteller* (1979). *The Widower's Son* (1976) gives hope that S. has joined the mainstream with its study of how an undeveloped heart distorts all relationships.

In showing what it is like for Englishmen to grow up poor with barriers all around them, S. is unmatched. There is now evidence that he will be able to extend his range effectively.

FURTHER WORKS: *Without Beer or Bread* (1957); *The Rats, and Other Poems* (1960); *The General* (1960); *Key to the Door* (1961); *The Ragman's Daughter* (1963); *A Falling Out of Love and Other Poems* (1964); *The Road to Volgograd* (1964); *The City Adventures of Marmalade Jim* (1967); *Guzman, Go Home* (1968); *Shaman and Other Poems* (1968); *A S. Selection* (1968); *Love in the Environs of Voronezh* (1968); *This Foreign Field* (1970); *Travels in Nihilon* (1971); *Poems* (1971); *Raw Material* (1972); *The Flame of Life* (1974); *Mountains and Caverns* (1975); *Three Plays* (1978); *Snow on the North Side of Lucifer* (1979); *The Second Chance, and Other Stories* (1981); *Her Victory* (1982); *The Lost Flying Boat* (1983); *Out of the Whirlpool* (1988); *Collected Stories* (1995); *Life without Armour* (1995)

BIBLIOGRAPHY: Gindin, J., "A. S.'s Jungle," *TSLL*, 4 (1962): 35–48; Kermode, F., on *The Death of William Posters, New Statesman* (14 May 1965): 765–66; Penner, A. R., *A. S.* (1972); Craig, D., *The Real Foundations: Literature and Social Change* (1973): 270–85; Lee, J. W., "Myths of Identity: A. S.'s *The Death of William Posters; A Tree on Fire* (1965, 1967)," in Morris, R. K., ed., *Old Lines, New Forces* (1976): 120–30; Roskies, D. M., "A. S.'s Anti-Pastoral," *JNT*, 10 (1977): 170–85; Atherton, S. S.,

A. S.: A Critical Assessment (1979); Hitchcock, P., *Working-Class Fiction in Theory and Action: A Reading of A. S.* (1989)

—GEORGE J. BECKER

SILONE, Ignazio

(pseud. of Secondo Tranquilli) Italian novelist, essayist, and dramatist, b. 1 May 1900, Pescina dei Marsi; d. 22 Aug. 1978, Geneva, Switzerland

S.'s father was a small landowner in the province of Aquila in the Abruzzi; his mother, a weaver, introduced her child to evangelical Christianity. Both parents died in an earthquake in 1915. Of his boyhood friends, the children of poor peasants, S. said, "They were my university"—an attitude also expressed by the character Rocco De Donatis in S.'s *Una manciata di more* (1952; *A Handful of Blackberries*, 1953): "The choice of the poor as companions remains the most important act in my life."

In 1917, after sending to the socialist newspaper *Avanti!* three articles critical of the misappropriation of funds for disaster relief in his village, S. found himself regional secretary of the Abruzzi Farmworkers' League in Avezzano. In the same year he was prosecuted for leading a violent demonstration against Italy's participation in World War I and was sent to prison. Released soon after, he went to Rome, where he became secretary of the Socialist Youth League and editor of the weekly *L'avanguardia*.

In 1921 S. was one of the founders of the Italian Communist Party. In the years following he changed his name and went underground to escape Fascist persecution. On behalf of the Party, he traveled to Germany, Spain, and France. As Secretary of the Central Committee of the Italian Communist Party, he participated in the activities of the Comintern in Moscow.

From Russia he went to Switzerland in 1929 as a political exile. Because he was not able to publish in Italy during the ensuing period, his writings of the 1930s and early 1940s were published first in German translation in Zurich and only later in Italian outside Italy. After the war they all appeared in Italy. In 1930 he wrote his first novel, *Fontamara* (Ger. tr., 1933; It., 1934; *Fontamara*, 1934; new tr., 1960). In 1931, because of the brutal practices of Stalin, S. left the Party. The publication of the German translation of *Fontamara* brought him international success, and his two other novels written in exile were equally well received: *Pane e vino* (Ger. tr., 1937; It., 1937; rev. as *Vino e pane*, 1955; *Bread and Wine*, 1937; new tr., 1962) and *Il seme sotto la neve* (Ger. tr., 1941; It., 1942; rev. ed., 1961; *The Seed Beneath the Snow*, 1942; new tr., 1965).

In 1944 S. reentered Italy. He was an active socialist until 1949 when, having become bitterly disappointed, he declared himself "a Christian without a church and a socialist without a party." He founded the International Committee on Cultural Freedom and devoted himself to his writing for the rest of his life. Like Rocco De Donatis, S. failed in the world of politics because "he expect[ed] from secular life the absolutism he could have found only in a monastery."

Uscita di sicurezza (1965; *Emergency Exit*, 1968) is a collection of autobiographical pieces reviewing S.'s spiritual development: a boyhood inspired by his father's humane concerns, an adolescence during which he read Tolstoy's story "Polikushka" to the illiterate farmers of the village, a conversion in early manhood to the revolutionary tactics of Communism, his break with the Party and his disillusionment with politics, his belief (finally) that the solution to any kind of problem—economic, social, political, or ideological—must serve humanitarian values.

Writing offered S. the outlet for his "absolute need to be a witness," to participate in the history of mankind. His primary concern was the dignity of every human being, especially those forever excluded from history who have always borne its burden in poverty and misery, without group or individual rights. S. knew these people could be found all over the world, but he depicted those he was familiar with from boyhood, the *cafoni*, the very small landowners and peasants of his native region. *Fontamara* presents their mute resignation. The *cafoni* had been subjected to exploitation for so long that they considered it as unavoidable as natural calamities: floods, droughts, and earthquakes. There is a choral feeling to the narration and a lack of deep psychological analysis of individual figures. The exploiters—large landowners, lawyers, priests—abetted by the Fascists, are presented in a broad, folklorically grotesque manner. At the end of *Fontamara* a glimmer of a sense of self-worth emerges from the pitiful, inchoate chorus, and a desire for dignity is embodied in Berardo Viola, who sacrifices himself so that a revolutionary leader can escape the Fascist police and return to Fontamara. The title of the newly born clandestine newspaper of the *cafoni, Che fare?* (what is to be done?), reveals their changed status. Although physically crushed by the brutality of the Black Shirts, the *cafoni* at the end claim our respect rather than our pity.

In S.'s next three novels, *Pane e vino, Il seme sotto la neve*, and *Una manciata di more*, the major figures, although still paradigmatic and representative, are psychologically more individualized. Although S. continued to be interested in the fate of the *cafoni*, he shifted the focus and enlarged the scope of his fiction. The autobiographical element is evident in the conflict between conscience and discipline in his protagonists when they renounce the Communist Party; Pietro Spina in *Pane e vino* and *Il seme sotto la neve*, for example, his most autobiographical creation, achieves a heightened sense of freedom that neither theory nor authority can hamper. S.'s characters strive for a primitively evangelical society based not on justice but on friendship and *caritas*; the fictive expression of their desire to communicate is their telling others anecdotes, fables, stories, allegories, and the events of their lives.

In *Il segreto di Luca* (1956; *The Secret of Luca*, 1958) S. seems to put aside his political concerns to recount a lofty and chaste tale of love, but his use of detective-story techniques reveals his strong need to bear witness. Andrea Cipriani neglects his political work to find out why his father's friend Luca, with the acquiescence of the entire village, allowed himself to be sent to prison for murder. In his search Cipriani not only discovers Luca's secret but also exposes the stifling ambience that clouds every aspect of life in the village and precludes any possibility of self-realization and sincere relationship. This is the only novel in which S. relegates politics to the background.

L'avventura d'un povero cristiano (1968; *The Story of a Humble Christian*, 1970), a play with a long novelistic introduction, reflects S.'s final conversion from political ideologies to the power of charity. It recounts the famous story of the pious monk from the Abruzzi, Pietro di Murrone (1215–1296), who, having been elected Pope in 1294, reigning as Celestine V, abdicated after five months because he found it impossible to reconcile his evangelical anarchism with the temporal power of the organized church (he was later canonized).

All of S.'s books, with the exception of *Il segreto di Luca*, revolve around two complementary themes. On one hand, there is the struggle of the beleaguered class for its well-being, its human rights, its moral and civil liberties. On the other, S.'s protagonists, representing the conscience of that class, are often in opposition to those organizations (Party or Church) that want to realize the aspirations of unrealized human beings. These personae find themselves tragically torn between the absolute and the historical, and this conflict provides his works with an underlying spiritual tension and elevates them from the political to the aesthetic plane. Although they all end badly for the protagonists—in flight, imprisonment, death, suicide, self-sacrifice—the endings are not despairing. Rather, they communicate the conviction that life without dignity and moral freedom is not worth living.

FURTHER WORKS: *Der Faschismus* (1934; pub. only in Ger. tr.); *La scuola dei dittatori* (Ger. tr., 1938; It., 1962; *The School for Dictators*, 1938); *The Living Thoughts of Mazzini Presented by I. S.* (1938; pub. only in Eng. tr.); *Ed egli si nascose* (1944; *And He Hid Himself*, 1945); *La volpe e le camelie* (1960; *The Fox and the Camellias*, 1961); *Severina* (1982). FURTHER WORKS IN ENGLISH: *Mr. Aristotle* (1935)

BIBLIOGRAPHY: Scott, N., *Rehearsals of Discompose: Alienation and Reconciliation in Modern Literature* (1952): 66–111; Howe, I., *Politics and the Novel* (1957): 203–34; Lewis, R. W. B., *The Picaresque Saint: Representative Figures in Contemporary Fiction* (1958): 109–78; Krieger, M., *The Tragic Vision: Variations on a Theme in Literary Interpretation* (1960): 72–85; Heiney, D., *America in Modern Italian Literature* (1964): 114–25; Mueller, W. R., *The Prophetic Voice in Modern Fiction* (1966): 159–86; Brown, R. M., "I. S. and the Pseudonyms of God," in H. J. Mooney and T. F. Staley, eds. *The Shapeless God* (1968): 19–40; Camus, A., "On I. S.'s *Bread and Wine*," *Lyrical and Critical Essays* (1968): 207–9; Rühle, J., *Literature and Revolution: A Critical Study of the Writer and Communism in the Twentieth Century* (1969): 367–85; Caserta, E. G., "The Meaning of Christianity in the Novels of S.," *IQ*: 62–63 (1972): 19–40; Gatt-Rutter, J., *Writers and Politics in Modern Italy* (1978): 29–33

—EMANUELE LICASTRO

SIMENON, Georges

Belgian novelist (writing in French), b. 13 Feb. 1903, Liège; d. 4 Sept. 1989, Lausanne, Switzerland

Forced by his father's ill health to abandon his studies before he was sixteen, S. became a reporter and humor columnist for the *Gazette de Liège*. He published his first novel when he was seventeen. In December 1922 he went to Paris to build a career as a fiction writer. He began by putting himself through an apprenticeship in which he published a staggering number of short stories and popular novels under almost two dozen different pen names. The first novel he published under his own name was *Pietr-le-Letton* (1931; *The Strange Case of Peter the Lett*, 1933); it was followed over the next forty-one years by more than two hundred titles, nearly all of them short novels. Since S. announced his retirement from writing in 1972, he published only nonfiction of an autobiographical sort.

S. could be said to have had two careers as a writer, one as author of "Maigrets," a series of some eighty novels and short-story collections about Chief Inspector Maigret of the Paris police, and a second as author of 115 short, intense psychological novels generally referred to as "Simenons." Although he has been extraordinarily successful in both careers—so much so that his books have been translated into dozens of languages and published and republished innumerable times—in the U.S. the popularity of his Maigrets seems to have prevented recognition of the high quality of his Simenons.

That popularity is well deserved. The Maigrets focus with unfailing intelligence and compassion on the circumstances and stresses that compel one person to murder another rather than on a dreary succession of clues and plots; they are written in a spare, undecorated style; and they move through their narrative sequences quickly and surely. Although they are customarily segregated in the "mysteries" section of bookstores and libraries, the Maigrets are best described, as S. has described them, as sketches, comparable to the sort of things a painter does for his pleasure or for preliminary studies, and they have won the respect of writers who are seriously involved with the craft of fiction. Good examples are *Maigret au Picratt's* (1951; *Inspector Maigret and the Strangled Stripper*, 1954), with its rendition of the ambience of a sleazy nightclub; *Maigret s'amuse* (1957; *Maigret's Little Joke*, 1957), with its artful inversion of customary methods (Maigret solves a case while he is on vacation by following newspaper accounts and mailing suggestions on anonymous postcards like a typical crank); and *L'ami d'enfance de Maigret* (1968; *Maigret's Boyhood Friend*, 1970), with its sustained comedy focusing on the complex feelings a mature man must have when he has to deal fairly and accurately with someone he knew as a schoolboy thirty years earlier.

A few months after the publication of the first of the Maigrets S. took up his career as a writer of Simenons with the publication of *Le relais d'Alsace* (1931; *The Man from Everywhere*, 1941). Although he thought of himself as moving cautiously through a series of journeyman books, which he dubbed "semi-literature," by the mid-1930s Ernest HEMINGWAY was reading his novels with pleasure and André GIDE was not only reading them but making copious notes in the margins. By the late 1930s S. had arrived at something approaching full command of his own distinctive form with novels such as *L'homme qui regardait passer les trains* (1938; *The Man Who Watched the Trains Go By*, 1942) and *Chez Krull* (1939; *Chez Krull*, 1955).

All of the Simenons are short, with the single exception of *Pedigree* (1948; *Pedigree*, 1962), a long, naturalistic, and highly autobiographical novel. After a doctor misread an x-ray and told him he had less than two years to live, he wrote this book so that his young son would be able to know about his father when he grew up. Almost all the Simenons involve acts of violence—although in *Les anneaux du Bicêtre* (1963; *The Bells of Bicêtre*, 1963) the "violence" is a severe heart attack—because they are concerned with people who are driven to their limits. Set in many different countries and dealing with characters in all walks of life, they all—without exception—compel the reader to join the writer in recognizing that the other man is like himself, even when the other man is a sexually twisted murderer, as he is in *La neige était sale* (1948; *The Snow Was Black*, 1950).

It has been customary to speak of S. as a tragic writer, for there is much grim suffering in the world of the Simenons—for example, *Les frères Rico* (1952; *The Brothers Rico*, 1954), *Le petit homme d'Arkhangelsk* (1956; *The Little Man from Archangel*, 1957), and *La chambre bleue* (1964; *The Blue Room*, 1965). Yet S. describes himself in *Quand j'étais vieux* (1970; *When I Was Old*, 1971) as happy, as well as optimistic about man. One can see that joy in life and fundamental optimism most plainly in *Le petit saint* (1965; *The Little Saint*, 1966), a novel that S. considered a breakthrough for him; its artist-hero is indeed "a perfectly serene character in immediate contact with nature and life." But joy and serenity can also be found in such earlier works as *Trois chambres à Manhattan* (1946; *Three Beds in Manhattan*, 1964), *Les Mémoires de Maigret* (1950; *Maigret's Memoirs*, 1963) and *Le président* (1958; *The Premier*, 1961).

S. never wrote the "big" novel that many critics demanded of him, but his "small" novels—taken collectively, or even in any sizable part—constitute a mosaic of great power and interest. They give us a mature, lucid perception of what the great forces—sex, money, alcohol, society, and culture—do in and to the lives of men and women.

FURTHER WORKS: *45° à l'ombre* (1936; *Aboard the Aquitaine*, 1979); *Les sœurs Lacroix* (1938; *Poisoned Relations*, 1950); *Bergelon* (1941; *The Delivery*, 1981); *Le fond de la bouteille* (1949; *The Bottom of the Bottle*, 1954); *Maigret et la vielle dame* (1950; *Maigret and the Old Lady*, 1958); *Le Grand Bob* (1954; *Big Bob*, 1969); *L'horloger d'Everton* (1954; *The Watchmaker of Everton*, 1955); *Les complices* (1955; *The Accomplices*, 1964); *Dimanche* (1958; *Sunday*, 1960); *Le veuf* (1959; *The Widower*, 1961); *L'ours en peluche* (1960; *Teddy Bear*, 1972); *Le train* (1961; *The Train*, 1964); *La mort d'Auguste* (1966; *The Old Man Dies*, 1968); *Le chat* (1967; *The Cat*, 1967); *Maigret à Vichy* (1968; *Maigret in Vichy*, 1969); *Maigret et le marchand de vin* (1970; *Maigret and the Wine Merchant*, 1971); *Le riche homme* (1970; *The Rich Man*, 1971); *Les innocents* (1972; *The Innocents*, 1973); *Lettre à ma mère* (1974; *Letter to My Mother*, 1976); *Mémoires intimes; Le livre de Marie-Jo* (1981). FURTHER WORKS IN ENGLISH: *Justice* (1985); *The Outlaw* (1986); *The Rules of the Game* (1988)

BIBLIOGRAPHY: Galligan, E., "S.'s Mosaic of Small Novels," *SAQ*, 56 (1967): 534–43; Raymond, J., *S. in Court* (1968); special S. issue, *Adam*, 34: 328–330 (1969); Fallois, B. de, *S.*, rev. ed. (1971); Lacassin, F., and G. Sigaux, *S.* (1973); Becker, L., *G. S.* (1977); Eskin, S., *S., a Critical Biography* (1987)

—EDWARD L. GALLIGAN

SIMON, Claude

French novelist, b. 10 Oct. 1913, Tananarive, Madagascar

Son of an army officer, S. spent his early childhood at Perpignan in the eastern Pyrenees. His father was killed during World War I. Between the ages of seven and sixteen he attended the Collège Stanislas in Paris, then studied painting with André Lhôte. In the 1930s he fought on the Republican side in the Spanish Civil War; at

Georges Simenon

the outbreak of World War II he was drafted into the cavalry. In May 1940 he became a prisoner of war in Germany but escaped in November of the same year. He lived in Perpignan until 1944, when he returned to Paris. Since then he has lived alternately in Salses, a small village near Perpignan, and in Paris.

Since 1945 S. has published more than fifteen novels, several of which have been critically acclaimed as major contributions to contemporary French fiction. His evolution as a novelist has been relatively clear-cut, as the artist gradually and painfully attempted to liberate himself from an obsession with the archetypal problems of human existence, those unresolvable questions of time, space, nature, war, and love. The passion to know and understand was replaced by a desire to investigate the generative potential of language.

Although frequently associated with the NEW NOVEL, S.'s works are never just linguistic puzzles or intellectual exercises; they are rooted in a pulsating, physical world. Indeed, as he moves away from the archetypal images of the human condition, S.'s novels come closer and closer to the immediate experiences of daily life. A trip to a writers' congress in Latin America is the source of the airplane perspective that dominates much of *Les corps conducteurs* (1971; *Conducting Bodies*, 1974), memories of his childhood village provide the unity in *Triptyque* (1973; *Triptych*, 1976), the demolition of a Paris apartment offers the focus in *Leçon de choses* (1975; *The World about Us*, 1983). Increasingly, S.'s works bear witness to an exceptional appreciation of nature and the ordinary objects of the world: grass, wildflowers in the field, the ripples of stream water, the collage effect provided by a wall of Parisian graffiti. Perhaps more fully than any other contemporary novelist S. has explored the relationship between literature and painting.

While the emphasis on visual perception dominating S.'s later works suggests photographic objectivity, his descriptions remain the product of a personal vision rather than images arbitrarily recorded on a camera lens. In fact, the basic source of inspiration for S.'s fiction is his own family history—ancestors known through documents, paintings, and various memorabilia handed down from the past—as well as his personal experiences of war, love, and death relived in memory. It is fair to say that S.'s novels are attempts to tell and retell one basic story in many different ways.

S.'s oeuvre is generally broken down into three periods. The books written prior to *Le vent* (1957; *The Wind*, 1959), while unimportant as works of art, are the foundation upon which his later aesthetic philosophy was built. These novels are the products of an artist searching for appropriate themes and a personal style, and they bear witness to S.'s disillusionment with the novel of political involvement and his rejection of any faith in progress. The period from the publication of *L'herbe* (1959; *The Grass*, 1960) through *La bataille de Pharsale* (1969; *The Battle of Pharsalus*, 1971) is often considered to have been S.'s most creative phase. *La route des Flandres* (1960; *The Flanders Road*, 1961) and *Histoire* (1967; *Histoire*, 1967) provide a textual and thematic richness that may be unmatched in 20th-c. literature except in the works of Marcel PROUST and James JOYCE. The subtlety and complexity of the imagery convey an extraordinary sensitivity to the profound pain and joy of the human experience. At the same time the novel form becomes gradually more and more experimental.

Above all, S. does not believe in the artist's ability to see beyond or behind apparent reality. He appears to tell us that since the human experience is basically uniform regardless of time and place, it is only through language that the writer can hope to become a breaker of new paths. In *Orion aveugle* (1970; Orion blinded) he compares himself as a writer to the mythical giant who moves in fumbling fashion in the direction where the source of light appears to be located. Since the artist has no special insights into the future of the world or the novel, his only recourse is to advance and learn through exploration and experimentation with words. While this experimentation undoubtedly is significant in all of S.'s novels, it becomes most aggressive in works such as *Triptyque* and *Leçon de choses*, which gained him a significant place among the avantgarde in France in the 1970s. A critic might say that S.'s quest for newness was too heavily influenced by STRUCTURALIST and deconstructionist trends in Paris in the 1970s, and that in the process he sacrificed his authentic artistic world as reflected in works like *La route des Flandres* and *Histoire*. A thorough, progressive reading of his novels, however, makes it obvious that his artistic evolution has been autonomous, built upon internal necessity and personal quest rather than influenced by any contemporary, external influence. *Les Géorgiques* (1981; Georgics) successfully reintegrates a highly personal vision of the past into an experimental form, thus providing a kind of umbrella encompassing his total work.

While S. has never achieved the popular acclaim of Alain ROBBE-GRILLET or Michel BUTOR, critics consider his work to be one of the most original and significant to have emerged in France since World War II. It is no exaggeration to claim that with its ever-changing focus and techniques, it reflects the history of the French novel in the 20th c. While the influences of William FAULKNER,

Proust, and Joyce have undoubtedly been great, S.'s works basically reflect an intensely personal quest. A disciple of the great modernist novelists of the early part of the century, he is exploring in their wake the possibilities of the novel. In 1985, S. won the Nobel Prize for Literature.

FURTHER WORKS: *Le tricheur* (1945); *La corde raide* (1947); *Gulliver* (1952); *Le sacre de printemps* (1954); *Le palace* (1962; *The Palace*, 1963); *Femmes* (1966, notes for paintings by Joan Miró)

BIBLIOGRAPHY: Sturrock, J., *The French New Novel* (1969): 43–103; Roudiez, L. S., *French Fiction Today* (1972): 152–82; Séguier, M., ed., *Entretiens: C. S.* (1972); Ricardou, J., ed., *C. S.*, Colloque de Cerisy (1975); Fletcher, J., *C. S. and Fiction Now* (1975); Jiménez-Fajardo, S., *C. S.* (1975); Loubère, J. A. E., *The Novels of C. S.* (1975); Roubichou, G., *Lecture de "L'herbe" de C. S.* (1976); Gould, K., *C. S.'s Mythic Muse* (1979); Sykes, S. W., *Les romans de C. S.* (1979); Birn, R., and K. Gould, eds., *Orion Blinded: Essays on C. S.* (1981); Britton, C., *C. S.: Writing the Visible* (1987); Sarkonak, R. W., *Understanding C. S.* (1989)

—RANDI BIRN

SIMONOV, Konstantin Mikhaylovich

Russian novelist, dramatist, poet, and journalist, b. 28 Nov. 1915, Petrograd (now St. Petersburg); d. 29 Aug. 1979, Moscow

From a proletarian family, S. began his literary career with poems published in his factory's wall newspaper when he was a teenaged lathe operator in Moscow. In 1934 he entered the Gorky Literary Institute, graduating in 1938. He then went to the Far East as a correspondent, where he covered the battle of Khalkin Gol during the undeclared war between the U.S.S.R. and Japan. During World War II he reported on battles from Stalingrad to Berlin. The popular poetry, war fiction, and journalism he published at that time laid the foundations for his wide, and until recently undiminished, appeal to average Soviet readers. After the war he was co-opted into the Communist Party and the cultural establishment. He received many official awards, including four Stalin Prizes, and was an active cold-war propagandist, especially during Stalin's lifetime. He wrote plays that were highly successful on the Soviet stage and completed a cycle of four war novels: *Dni i nochi* (1943–44; *Days and Nights*, 1945), *Tovarishchi po oruzhiyu* (1952; comrades in arms), *Zhivye i myortvye* (1960; *The Living and the Dead*, 1962), and *Soldatami ne rozhdayutsya* (1964; we are not born soldiers). After Stalin's death S. advocated more liberal literary views, and during his editorship of the prestigious journal *Novy mir* (1954–57) he spoke out against "fabrications" in Soviet novels and in favor of revising the restrictive rules of SOCIALIST REALISM.

S. achieved instant fame with the publication of his wartime poem "Zhdi menya" (1944; "Wait for Me," 1945), about a soldier at the front who pleads with his faraway sweetheart to wait faithfully for his return. The poem's sentimental, poignant tone—a notable feature of S.'s poetry—added greatly to its popular appeal. It was adapted for the stage under the same title in 1942. Even when his poetry deals with patriotic and war themes, it often touches on intimate human feelings and concerns. S.'s poetry is easy to understand, technically polished, and faithful to the classical traditions of Russian prosody. But it is somewhat monotonous and lacks true originality.

S.'s fiction is far superior. Marc Slonim has justly called *Dni i nochi* an "impressive panorama of military events." The writer's vivid descriptions of the relentless, house-to-house struggle for Stalingrad has the stamp of authenticity. Description of the action is skillfully blended with renderings of the thoughts and feelings of typical Russian soldiers.

In *Tovarishchi po oruzhiyu* S. describes the Russo-Japanese conflict of 1938–39. He himself later admitted the weaknesses of this novel. It does, however, have some of the qualities of his other novels: an interesting, well-constructed plot, a mastery of detail, a skill in describing people, and the power to win and hold the reader's attention.

The milder political climate of the "thaw" after 1953 allowed S., in *Zhivye i myortvye* and *Soldatami ne rozhdayutsya*, to be more open and truthful about the Red Army's disastrous situation early in the war. In both novels the hero is an officer who experienced the ordeal of a concentration camp, was rehabilitated, and was then compelled to fight for his country under an assumed name.

S. was not a very gifted playwright. His best-known plays, *Russky vopros* (1946; *The Russian Question*, 1947) and *Chuzhaya ten* (1949; the foreign shadow), mere cold-war propaganda, blatantly embellish Soviet realities and glorify the system.

S.'s collections of essays and impressions about war, writers, and books, such as *Segodnya i davno* (1976; today and long ago) and *V odnoy gazete* (1979; in one newspaper), reveal his high regard for integrity and loyalty to one's convictions. This attitude is evident in his own relationship with the controversial Alexandr TVARDOVSKY, his predecessor as well as successor as editor of *Novy mir*. In S.'s essayistic works he blends keen observation and a concise, understated style with the devices of a short-story writer.

Although not an unusually distinguished or original writer, S. was a notable exponent of what Vera Dunham has called "middle-class values in Soviet fiction"—perhaps the only road still open to Soviet writers after the important modernist tendencies in Russian literature were suppressed in the late 1920s and 1930s. During the thaw of the Khrushchev era, in creating characters of independent spirit like Kondrashov in the novella *Dym otechestva* (1956; smoke of the fatherland), he helped to broaden the outlook and humanize the responses of many average Soviet readers.

FURTHER WORKS: *Pavel Chyorny: Poema* (1938); *Istoria odnoy lyubvi* (1940); *Paren iz nashego goroda* (1941); *Russkie lyudi* (1942; *The Russians*, 1944); *Ot Chyornogo do Barentsova morya* (1942; *From the Black to the Barents Sea*, n.d.); *Tak i budet* (1944; *The Whole World Over* [adaptation], 1947); *Pod kashtanami Pragi* (1945; *Beneath the Chestnuts of Prague*, 1946); *Druzya i vragi: Kniga stikhov* (1948; *Friends and Foes: A Book of Poems*, 1951); *Ot nashego voennogo korrespondenta* (1948); *Srazhayushchysya Kitai* (1950; *The Fighting China*, 1950); *Dobroe imya* (1953); *Piesy* (1954); *Na literaturnye temy: Statyi 1937–1955* (1956); *Norvezhsky dnevnik* (1956); *Lyudi s kharakterom* (1958); *Chetvyorty: Drama* (1962); *Yuzhnye povesti* (1963); *Iz zapisok Lopatina* (1965); *Kazhdyi den—dlinny: Iz voennykh dnevnikov 1941–1945 godov* (1965); *Sobranie sochineny* (6 vols., 1966–1970); *Ostayus zhurnalistom: Putevye ocherki, zametki, reportazhi, pisma 1958– 1967* (1968); *Daleko na vostoke: Khalkingolskie zapisi* (1969); *Razgovor s tovarishchami* (1970); *Poslednee leto* (1971); *Tridtsat*

shestoy—semdesyat pervy: Stikhotvorenia i poemy (1972); *Dvadtsat dney bez voyny (Iz zapisok Lopatina)* (1973); *Ot Khalkingola do Berlina* (1973); *Nezadolgo do tishiny: Zapiski 1945 g. mart-apr-may* (1974); *Druzyam na pamyat: Stikhi* (1975); *Povesti i rasskazy* (1978); *Iz tryokh tetradey: Stikhi, poemy* (1979). FURTHER WORKS IN ENGLISH: *On the Petsamo Road: Notes of a War Correspondent* (1942); *No Quarter* (1943)

BIBLIOGRAPHY: Slonim, M., *Soviet Russian Literature: Writers and Problems, 1917–1967* (1967): 271–75 and passim; Struve, G., *Russian Literature under Lenin and Stalin 1917–1953* (1971): 312–18, 323–27, and passim; Dunham, V. S., *In Stalin's Time: Middleclass Values in Soviet Fiction* (1976): 121–24 and passim; Segel, H. B., *Twentieth Century Russian Drama* (1979): 308–11, 322–27, and passim

—VICTORIA A. BABENKO-WOODBURY

SIMPSON, Mona

American novelist, b. 14 June 1957, Green Bay, Wisconsin

S. has worked as a senior editor at the *Paris Review* and as a novelist, and has published three novels since 1987. In her fiction S. has written of absent fathers, searching daughters, and irresponsible mothers, and has done so in a finely crafted style. While praised for her exact and affecting language, and for articulating the desire that drives the young women at the center of these stories, she has been criticized for the formal constraints and thematic limits her subject has placed on them.

Anywhere But Here (1987) is almost entirely narrated by Ann Stevenson, twelve-year-old daughter of Adele. Adele is twice-divorced and not entirely stable, and when she decides to take her daughter from Wisconsin to California, where she plans to make Ann a child star or to meet a wealthy husband, the novel sets off with them on a journey marked by a string of broken promises and roadside abandonments. Over the course of the trip, Ann struggles to find a way to relate to both the mother she loves and the mother who leaves her standing on the side of the road in the middle of nowhere. We see Adele, then, entirely through Ann's eyes; the picture that results is one of a fascinating but inexplicable woman—a woman whose inexplicability is the very source of her fascination.

In *The Lost Father* (1992) Ann reappears as Mayan Amneh Stevenson, adopting the name given her by her "lost" Egyptian father. What is an interest in the first novel becomes an obsession, ruining her life and taking over the novel. Mayan's father is even more unknown than her mother in *Anywhere But Here*, but he is not present as Adele was in the first novel, and Mayan's search for him is obsessive in a way that Ann's quest in the first novel was not. And because the man Mayan's search eventually finds seems not to have been worth the effort, her obsession may have less power for readers than her earlier struggle with her mother.

With her third novel, *A Regular Guy* (1996), S. again covers similar ground, but takes a different path. Here, she brings us closer to the father by allowing him a greater presence in the novel, but she distances us from the daughter by writing the novel in the third person. Her account of Tom Owens, wildly successful Northern California entrepreneur, is focalized mostly through his illegitimate daughter Jane, and includes a mother who is less than practical. What might have been gained by spending more time with this novel's "lost" father is squandered by a distance both from him and from the registering intelligence of the one character, Jane, whom his half-absence is supposed to most affect. In setting Jane and her mother up in a bungalow near him but keeping his distance, Owens places them as close as he has to without having to get to know them, and so sympathize with them. Readers might be forgiven for feeling as if S. has done the same to them. However, as with *Anywhere But Here* and *The Lost Father*, *A Regular Guy* offers the pleasures of S.'s language. S. is most appreciated for the clarity and beauty of her words; while critics differ over her subject matter and her handling and rehandling of it, they agree in their praise of the grace of her language, the realistic immediacy of her cross-country journeys, and the emotional realism of her fictional situations.

BIBLIOGRAPHY: Heller, D. A., "Shifting Gears: Transmission and Flight in M. S.'s *Anywhere But Here*," *UHLS*, 21 (1989): 37-44; Morse, D. D., "The Difficult Journey Home: M. S.'s *Anywhere But Here*," in Pearlman, M., ed., *Mother Puzzles: Daughters and Mothers in Contemporary American Literature* (1989): 67-75

—SAM COHEN

SINCLAIR, May

English novelist, short-story writer, essayist, and poet, b. 24 Aug. 1863, Rock Ferry; d. 14 Nov. 1946, Bierton

S. was the daughter of a Liverpool shipowner who went bankrupt when S. was about seven. Although she became a scholar, she was almost completely self-taught and had only one year of formal education. The principal of Cheltenham Ladies College, which S. attended in 1881–82, encouraged her to pursue metaphysical issues. S.'s interest in women's roles in society led her to participate in the suffrage movement and to write a pamphlet for the Women Writers Suffrage League entitled *Feminism* (1912). Preoccupied with self-transcendence as well as with the integrity and full development of the individual, S. read mystical and psychoanalytical literature. In 1913 she was one of the founders of the Medico-Psychological Clinic of London. During World War I she spent a brief time in Belgium as part of an ambulance corps. Elected a member of the select Aristotelean Society in 1917, S. showed her commitment to philosophy in *A Defence of Idealism* (1917) and *The New Idealism* (1922), as well as in various essays.

These interests also govern her fiction. *The Divine Fire* (1904), which won her the most popularity during her lifetime, is not, however, her best novel. It subordinates believable characters to philosophical ideas and direct statement to florid prose. Interested in the effects of heredity and environment, S. wrote the naturalistic novella *Superseded* (1901). More succinct and direct than *The Divine Fire*, it is related to a number of S.'s other novels that explore factors that prevent people from realizing their full potential. Among these are *The Helpmate* (1907), *The Judgment of Eve* (1907), *Kitty Tailleur* (1908; Am., *The Immortal Moment: The Story of Kitty Tailleur*), and *The Combined Maze* (1913). The institutions of marriage and the family, idealized by the Victorians, as well as the stereotypes of women as spiritual, asexual, and at the same time purely reproductive are revealed as destructive to both sexes. In *The Creators* (1910) S. combined her examination of domestic life and women's roles with an exploration of the difficulties of women artists.

In her best work S. shifted the emphasis from heredity and environment to their effects upon the individual consciousness. This interest, growing out of her reading of certain older literary contemporaries like Henry JAMES and Thomas HARDY and predecessors like Charlotte, Emily, and Anne Brontë, as well as psychoanalytical writers, led her to a variety of experiments. S. sometimes used supernatural phenomena to suggest her characters' mental states. Often she filtered the repressions and inadequacies of her characters through the minds of peripheral characters. She also recreated in her novels the effects of restricted lives on people's states of mind and behavior. *The Three Sisters* (1914), inspired by the lives of the Brontë sisters, is a good example.

Most effective, however, is *Mary Olivier, a Life* (1919), an autobiographical *Bildungsroman* influenced in part by Dorothy Richardson (1873–1957) and the method of her long multivolume work, *Pilgrimage* (1915–38). In an essay on Richardson's work, "The Novels of Dorothy Richardson" (1918), S. was the first to apply to literature William James's (1842–1910) metaphor, STREAM OF CONSCIOUSNESS. Her defense of the IMAGISTS and other avant-garde poets, reflected in her essays and in the novel *The Tree of Heaven* (1917), is also in the background of the experiment in *Mary Olivier*. This novel, like imagist poetry, embodies a desire to present reality directly. Its main character struggles to develop her potential in the face of numerous impediments and is more successful in her struggle than is the main character in *Life and Death of Harriett Frean* (1922), another experiment with stream-of-consciousness writing.

S. was a prolific writer. Varying in quality, her output reflects the intellectual, artistic, and social interests of her times. Her best works, however, are in their own right effective renditions of the inner lives of her characters, particularly of women trying to deal with the discrepancies between restrictive social roles and intellectual or creative potential.

FURTHER WORKS: *Nakiketas, and Other Poems* (1886); *Essays in Verse* (1892); *Audrey Craven* (1897); *Mr. and Mrs. Nevill Tyson* (1898; Am., *The Tysons*); *Two Sides of a Question* (1901); *The Flaw in the Crystal* (1912); *The Three Brontës* (1912); *The Judgement of Eve and Other Stories* (1914); *The Return of the Prodigal and Other Stories* (1914); *Tasker Jevons: The Real Story* (1916; Am., *The Belfry*); *The Romantic* (1920); *Mr. Waddington of Wyck* (1921); *Anne Severn and the Fieldings* (1922); *Uncanny Stories* (1923); *A Cure of Souls* (1924); *The Dark Night: A Novel in Verse* (1924); *Arnold Waterlow, a Life* (1924); *The Rector of Wyck* (1925); *Far End* (1926); *The Allinghams* (1927); *History of Anthony Waring* (1927); *Tales Told by Simpson* (1930); *The Intercessor and Other Stories* (1931)

BIBLIOGRAPHY: Brewster, D., and A. Birrell, *Dead Reckonings in Fiction* (1924): 176–228; Boll, T. E. M., *Miss M. S., Novelist: A Biographical and Critical Introduction* (1973); Robb, K. A., "M. S.: An Annotated Bibliography of Writings about Her," *ELT*, 16, 3 (1973): 177–231; Kaplan, S., *Feminine Consciousness in the Modern British Novel* (1975): 47–75; Zegger, H. D., *M. S.* (1976); Gillespie, D. F., "M. S. and the Stream of Consciousness: Metaphors and Metaphysics," *ELT*, 21, 2 (1978): 134–42; Neff, R. K.,

"'New Mysticism' in the Writings of M. S. and T. S. Eliot," *TCL*, 26 (1980): 82–108

—DIANE FILBY GILLESPIE

SINCLAIR, Upton

American novelist, social critic, essayist, journalist, and dramatist, b. 20 Sept. 1878, Baltimore, Md.; d. 25 Nov. 1968, Bound Brook, N.J.

Born into a once-aristocratic family in Baltimore, S. had a childhood that provided an intense context for a lifetime of resistance to the disparities of income levels between social classes and to individual disasters caused by irrational behavior—as personified in a frustrated father who escaped the pressures of commercialism through whiskey. Existing in a series of infested apartments, S. studied in the streets; the family moved to New York City, where he eventually passed through the eight elementary grades in two years. He then entered the College of the City of New York at fourteen years of age.

S. learned early to support himself by writing ethnic jokes and hack fiction for popular magazines. His adolescent writing is of no interest today, but it taught him a systematic and disciplined approach to self-assigned topics, thus providing a foundation for a lifetime of astounding productivity. In 1897 he enrolled at Columbia University, determined to succeed "in the genius business" while churning out one novelette per week.

Although S. absorbed little from Columbia's classrooms, he read so voraciously that he later felt qualified to comment on practically every Western writer of significance between Homer and Jack London, as in *Mammonart* (1925). In S.'s judgment, his academic training failed him completely because it did not even introduce him to what he discovered in 1902 to be the educational key to the coming century—democratic socialism. An unhappy first marriage led to the writing of *Springtime and Harvest* (1901; repub. as *King Midas*), a tale of penniless lovers that reflects only half of S.'s later formula: it contained the mandatory personal experience but lacked the socialist theory within which personal struggle becomes a rational movement toward social goals.

By 1904, S. was moving toward a realistic fiction in which historical facts were focused through an ideological lens. Having become a regular reader of the *Appeal to Reason*, a socialist-populist weekly, he began to write for it, doing a series called *The Jungle* depicting modern wage slavery in a typical industry, the meatpacking plants of Chicago. In S.'s depiction of Packingtown, Lithuanian immigrants are reduced to lard in order to grease the wheels of American capitalism. *The Jungle* was rejected by five publishers, but in 1906, when it was finally published as a book, S. quickly established himself as a leader within the group of writers that Theodore Roosevelt labeled "muckrakers." In the novel, Jurgis Rudkis discovers that the American Dream—work hard and achieve individual success—is systematically stifled. Instead, the law of an industrialized jungle leads to the survival of those with no remaining moral scruples. The book was a resounding success in that it gave concrete literary life to an abstract concept and led directly to beneficial social change—the implementation of the Pure Food and Drug Act in 1906. It did not, however, achieve S.'s larger goal—to

Upton Sinclair

bring democracy to industry. It did, however, provide a financial base and a national reputation that enabled S. to keep trying.

And this he did. S.'s *Autobiography* (1962) contains a photograph of the author, age eighty-four, standing beside a stack of his books that rises higher than he can reach. The breadth of his concerns is demonstrated by mere itemization: medicine—*Good Health and How We Won It* (1909), *The Fasting Cure* (1911); business—*The Flivver King* (1937), *Money Writes* (1927); education— *The Goose-step* (1923), *The Goslings* (1924); religion—*The Profits of Religion* (1918), *What God Means to Me* (1936), *A Personal Jesus* (1952); Prohibition—*The Wet Parade* (1931); alcoholism—*The Cup of Fury* (1956); philosophy—*The Book of Life* (2 vols., 1921–22); psychology—*Mental Radio* (1930); and journalism—*The Brass Check* (1920). This list is not complete. Nor does it reflect the fact that the primary work of this writer was in fiction.

While his vision was broad, S.'s concentration was quite intense. In each of these works, as well as in countless letters, essays, and public statements, S. offered the same solution. The Reformation had brought about equality before God; the American and French revolutions had brought about political equality; the stage was set for a third step toward human dignity—economic equality.

Ever the salesman, S. tried various packages for his ideals. He financed Helicon Hall in Englewood, New Jersey, a communal effort to create a miniature utopia, which literally turned to ashes in 1907. He tried experiments in parapsychology. He produced and published radical dramas. He ran for governor of California in

1934. His greatest effectiveness, however, was as the creator of fictional characters who convincingly carried the message that one could function pragmatically in the real world while bringing gradual change toward democratic societies. These idealistic liberal protagonists agonize over the apparent differences between the American Dream and daily reality, helping to correct mismanagement from below, without resort to revolutionary violence.

In *King Coal* (1917) a mine that catches fire is sealed because the owners calculate the consequent loss of human resources to be more easily replaced than the coal that would burn if the fire (and the men) were not suffocated. In response, Hal Warner organizes a union, keeping his work secret until the United Mine Workers have organized the surrounding camps.

In *Jimmie Higgins* (1919) S. portrays the dilemma of American leftists who felt temporarily obliged to support the ruling classes of England and France in their war against an imperialistic Kaiser. S. withdrew from the Socialist Party in order to respond to President Wilson's request for undivided loyalty until the world was once again safe enough for democratic experimentation. He later regretted his public position, but he essentially repeated his response during World War II and the Cold War, suspending his outspoken social criticism "for the duration."

Oil! (1927) is often considered S.'s most effective writing, judged by literary criteria, in that with Bunny Ross, S. achieves a truly complex character. In fact, Bunny is still a stereotype, but of a complex person—the American liberal who sees many of his cherished values set in opposition to the ultimate value of pragmatism. Bunny realizes that his father, a self-made success, knows how to run a business effectively. He is also mightily impressed by the rhetoric of Paul, the spokesman of a "Bolshevik bunch." His goal: to get the two opposing forces, both of whom he loves, to work together.

In his next major work, *Boston* (1928), S. has his liberal protagonist caught again between conservatives and radicals. Reflecting the pervasive dismay felt by American liberals at the arrest of Sacco and Vanzetti in 1920, Cornelia Thornwell rejects, out of principle, her chance to have the case dropped by the strategic placement of an affordable fifty thousand dollars. She is then stunned to discover that the leading purveyors of New England culture—governors, the president of Harvard—are willing to allow the execution of two anarchists in the face of more than reasonable doubt of their actual guilt.

Having spent the 1930s in various experiments with telepathy, making movies with Sergey Eisenstein, and running for political office, S. returned to fiction in the 1940s—producing over four million words in his Lanny Budd series of novels, beginning with *World's End* (1940). A plot synopsis of these annual installments would necessarily summarize the history of the world between World War I and the Korean War. Suffice it to say that Lanny is in attendance at most events of significance, and that he does his best to move history in the directions desired by American liberals.

The elderly S. now had to substitute correspondence for personal experience and research. So he wrote to Albert Einstein and Robert Oppenheimer about the development of the atomic bomb, and to diplomats, editors, musicians, politicians, laborers—all in an effort to provide indisputably accurate details within historical novels that could then convincingly carry the important social message of the narrative.

Still one of the most widely translated and read of all American authors, S. earned the respect and friendship of many of the most revered writers of his time, making the reading of his letters as interesting as his literature. His currently low status in American literary circles reflects a general rejection of literature that has social change rather than aesthetic effectiveness as its primary goal. For S., this was a conscious stance, in line, he thought, with countless writers before him who were interested in changing the world in which they found themselves.

FURTHER WORKS: *The Journal of Arthur Stirling* (1903); *Prince Hagen* (1903); *Manassas* (1904); *A Captain of Industry* (1906); *The Industrial Republic* (1907); *The Overman* (1907); *The Metropolis* (1908); *The Moneychangers* (1908); *Prince Hagen* (play, 1909); *Samuel the Seeker* (1910); *Love's Pilgrimage* (1911); *Plays of Protest* (1912); *Sylvia* (1913); *Damaged Goods* (1913); *Sylvia's Marriage* (1914); *100%: The Story of a Patriot* (1920); *Mind and Body* (1921); *They Call Me Carpenter* (1922); *Love and Society* (1922); *Hell* (1923); *The Pot Boiler* (1924); *The Millennium* (1924); *Singing Jailbirds* (1924); *Bill Porter* (1925); *Letters to Judd* (1926); *Mountain City* (1930); *Roman Holiday* (1931); *American Outpost* (1932); *U. S. Presents William Fox* (1933); *I, Governor of California and How I Ended Poverty* (1933); *The Way Out* (1933); *An U. S. Anthology* (1934); *The EPIC Plan for California* (1934); *I, Candidate for Governor: and How I Got Licked* (1935); *Depression Island* (1935); *Wally for Queen* (1936); *Co-op* (1936); *The Gnomobile* (1936); *No Pasaran!* (1937); *Little Steel* (1938); *Terror in Russia* (1938); *Our Lady* (1938); *Expect No Peace* (1939); *Marie Antoinette* (1939); *Between Two Worlds* (1941); *Dragon's Teeth* (1942); *Wide Is the Gate* (1943); *Presidential Agent* (1944); *Dragon Harvest* (1945); *A World to Win* (1946); *Presidential Mission* (1947); *One Clear Call* (1948); *A Giant's Strength* (1948); *O Shepherd, Speak!* (1949); *Another Pamela* (1950); *The Enemy Had It Too* (1950); *The Return of Lanny Budd* (1953); *What Didymus Did* (Br., 1954; Am., *It Happened to Didymus*, 1958); *Theirs Be the Guilt* (1959); *My Lifetime in Letters* (1960); *Affectionately Eve* (1961); *Sergei Eisenstein and U. S.: The Making and Unmaking of "Que Viva Mexico!"* (1970)

BIBLIOGRAPHY: Dell, F., *U. S.* (1927); Harte, J., *This Is U. S.* (1938); Hicks, G., "The Survival of U. S.," *CE*, 4 (1943): 213–20; Koerner, J., "The Last of the Muckrake Men," *SAQ*, 55 (1956): 221–32; Swados, H., "The World of U. S.," *Atlantic* (Dec. 1961): 96–102; Gottesman, R., *U. S.: An Annotated Checklist* (1973); Yoder, J., *U. S.* (1975); Harris, L., *U. S.: American Rebel* (1975); Bloodworth, W., *U. S.* (1977); Mookerjee, R. N., *Art for Social Justice: The Major Novels of U. S.* (1988)

—JONATHAN A. YODER

SINDHI LITERATURE

See Indian and Pakistani Literature

SINGAPORE LITERATURE

Singapore is an island republic, independent since August 9, 1965. It is a multiracial and multilingual city-state, and its literature is written in the four official languages of the country: Chinese, Malay, Tamil, and English. Strictly speaking, only literature produced after 1965 can be regarded as Singapore literature; most works written before 1965 belong to Malaysian (or Malayan) literature. Nevertheless, some pre-1965 writing may be regarded as Singapore literature, by virtue of the authors' Singapore residence or subsequent citizenship.

Before 1965 it is difficult to isolate a specifically Singapore literature. But the period of 1945 to 1957 saw a blossoming of Singapore writing in Chinese and Malay. The main theme of Chinese works was the suffering of the poor and the struggle against the British colonial government. Miao Xiu (1920-1980), a prolific novelist and short-story writer, depicts the love between a gangster and his prostitute-mistress in *Hsin Chia Po wu ting hsia* (1962; Under the Roofs of Singapore). Xie Ke (b. 1931), in the collection of poems *Wu Yueh* (1955; The Month of May), delineates the students' and workers' agitation and struggle against the colonial govenment.

There were, however, those who preferred to write on personal themes. One example is the poet Xhou Can (b. 1934), author of *Hai ize te meng* (1953; A Child's Dream). Yao Zi, also known as Hauang Huai (pseuds. of Zheng Meng Zhou, 1920-1982), a master storyteller, published many novels and short stories marked by detailed descriptions of sex; as a consequence, his writings are regarded by some as pornographic.

The Malay writers who thronged to Singapore because of the Emergency (1948-60)—a period of communist insurrection during which the colonial government curtailed freedoms—also took as their main theme the injustices suffered by the urban poor, fishermen, and villagers. They formed an association, Asas '50, to fight for equality. Suratman Markasan (b. 1930), in his short stories and in the novel *Tak ada jalan keluar* (1962; *Conflict*, 1982), captured the spirit of the age.

The few Malay witers who remained in Singapore following the exodus to Kuala Lumpur after Malaya's declaration of independence on August 31, 1957 are not typical of the Malay writers of the period. Harun Aminurrashid (1907-1986) has published nearly twenty historical novels glorifying the heroic deeds of the Malays of generations past, the most famous being *Panglima Awang* (1958; *A Malay among the Portuguese*, 1961).

Masuri S. N. (b. 1927) has published three collections of poems, in which he philosophizes on the meaning of life, morality, and peace. Noor S. I. (pseud. of Ismail bin Haji Omar, 1933-1990) is the forerunner of symbolic poetry in Malay. His poems are difficult to understand, but they have a sonorousness not often found in Malay verse. His most famous work is *Rakaman roh* (1963; Etchings of the Soul).

During this period poetry in English began to emerge. Most of the works were imitative and based on models learned at school that did not reflect the spirit of the age. But among the poets writing at that time was Edwin Thumboo (b. 1933), who was an important influence on other poets.

The Tamil writers focused on the social problems of their own community. N. Palanivelu (b. 1908) attacked meaningless traditional practices in his short stories, while P. Krishnan (b. 1932) dealt with the problems of intermarriage. The most popular subjects, however, were love and passion.

A distinct Singapore identity is manifested in nearly all postindependence writing. Writers, especially those in Chinese and Tamil, began to praise Singapore's efforts at nation building, as well as the country's beauty. Malay writers tend to be nostalgic and express anxiety about the future of the Malay community in fast-changing Singapore. Among the works of new writers, particularly promising are Abdul Ghani Hamid's (b. 1933) landscape poems,

Muhammad Latiff Muhammad's (b. 1950) social poems, and Mohammad Fuad Salim's (b. 1939) short stories. Isa Kamari (b. 1960) is noteworthy among younger writers with his collections of poetry *Sumur usia* (1933; The Ancient Well) and short stories *Sketsa minda* (1994; Sketches of the Mind).

The pre-1965 Chinese writers, with the exception of Yao Zi, continued to publish after independence. Among the many new writers, Mu Ling-Nu (pseud. of Tan Siew Hian, b. 1943), who is better known as an artist, and Wong Yoon Wah (b. 1941). Mu and Wong have introduced Western techniques into poetry, especially symbolism—Mu in *Chu jen* (1968; The Giant) and Wong in *Hsiang chiao shu* (1980; Rubber Trees). Also noteworthy for the expression of the feminine sensibility in her poetry is Dan Ying (b. 1943), as exemplified in the volume *Fa shang de sui yue* (1993; The Aging Hair). Perhaps the major achievement in this period was the publication of the narrative poem *Wu se te hung* (1977; The Colorless Rainbow) by Liu Pei An (b. 1903), which describes the checkered career of an immigrant from China. Among the younger writers of prose the most prominent is Xi Ni Er (b. 1957), whose *Sheng ming li nan yi cheng shou de zhong* (1994; The Unbearable Heaviness of Being) is remarkable for its attempt to weave philosophical ideas in fiction. In literary criticism, Fang Xiu's (b. 1921) and Wong Meng Voon's (b. 1937) essays have contributed greatly to an understanding of Chinese writing both in Singapore and Malaysia.

Many Tamil poets praise Singapore's success in building an independent nation, for example, K. Perumal (1921-1979) in *Singapore paadalkal* (1979; Songs of Singapore). In novels and short stories Tamil writers deal with the problems of national identity, multiracialism, and marriage between Indian men and Chinese women. Prominent among these writers are S. V. Shanmugam (b. 1933), P. Krishnan and Ma Illangkannan (pseud. of M. Balakrishnan, b. 1938). The future of Tamil writing in Singapore does not appear to be bright. Most literary works are published in India and do not sell more than three hundred copies locally. Nevertheless, there have been some notable recent writers, even if the readership is diminishing, such as the writer of fiction Rama Kannabiran (b. 1943) and the poets Paranan (pseud. of C. Veloo, b. 1944) and Elangovan (b. 1957). Apart from being perhaps the foremost poet writing in Tamil in the late 20th c., Elangovan is also a highly respected cultural spokesman for Tamil literature in Singapore.

The 1970s witnessed the flowering of writing in English. Many anthologies of short stories and individual collections were published. One of the best short-story writers in English is Catherine Lim (b. 1942). In *Little Ironies* (1978) she captures the fast changes in Singapore, especially the conflict between Western-educated children and their elders. Among many autobiographical novels, the most notable has been Tan Kok Seng's (b. 1936) *Son of Singapore* (3 vols., 1972-75). This trilogy tells the success story of a coolie. Goh Poh Seng (b. 1936) has written several novels. In *The Immolation* (1977), set in South Vietnam, he writes about the disillusionment of a young student, returned from Europe, with war and revolution in his country. Goh's poems—as in *Lines from Batu Feringgi* (1972) and *Eyewitness* (1976)—are records of his love for nature and his distaste for modern life.

Fiction in English continued to grow in the 1980s and 1990s, with works such as Christine Lim Suchen's (b. 1948) *Rice Bowl* (1984); Gopal Baratham's (b. 1935) *Figments of Experience* (1981) and *A Candle or the Sun* (1991); Claire Tham's (b. 1967) *Facist Rock: Stories of Rebellion* (1990); and Philip Jeyaretnam's (b. 1944) *First Loves* (1987) and *Abraham's Promise* (1994). Interest in Jeyaretnam's work has an extra-literary dimension, as he is the son of the opposition leader, J. B. Jeyaretnam; it is in fact widely believed that *Abraham's Promise* makes veiled references to the problems faced by his father in the political sphere. Also prominent in Singapore fiction of the 1990s are the novels on the Eurasian community in Singapore, such as Wilfred Hamilton-Shimmen's (b. 1940) *Seasons of Darkness: A Story of Singapore* (1993), and the tetralogy by Rex Shelly (b. 1930), the most famous of which is the first volume, *The Shrimp People* (1991).

The 1980s and 1990s also saw the flowering of drama, with works such as Robert Yeo's *One Year Back Home* (1990) and Stella Kon's (b. 1944) *Emily of Emerald Hill* (1989), which is a monodrama requiring only a single actress for its performance. One of the most prominent dramatists is Kuo Pao Kun (b. 1939) who writes plays in both English and Chinese. He has also experimented with plays that require several languages, such as *Mama Looking for Her Cat,* which is published in the volume *The Coffin is Too Big For the Hole—And Other Plays* (1990). Among the younger playwrights, the most promising is Haresh Sharma (b. 1965), as seen in his *Still Building* (1994). Kuo and Sharma are intimately connected to drama as theater; as such, their plays should not only be judged in relation to their published works.

Before the rise of fiction and drama in the last decades of the 20th c., literature in the English language was dominated by poetry, with Edwin Thumboo being its most notable practitioner. In collections such as *Gods Can Die* (1977) and *Ulysses by the Merlion* (1979), he has gone beyond his earlier exploration of self, as in the privately-published collection, *Rib of Earth* (1956). However, his later poems, as found in his latest volume of poetry, *A Third Map: New and Selected Poems* (1993) are not of the same quality as his earlier poems, some of which are printed again in the volume. In the development of his poetry over the years, Thumboo increasingly adopts a public voice, and has tried to depict the social reactions to the events taking place in Singapore. Another poet who has a preoccupation with social concerns is Robert Yeo (b. 1940), whose collection of poems *and napalm does not help* (1977) has a strong Singapore flavor. As an antithesis to Thumboo, Lee Tzu Pheng (b. 1946) has cultivated an increasingly private voice over the years. This development can be seen when one contrasts Lee's first volume *Prospect of a Drowning* (1980) with a later volume such as *The Brink of an Amen* (1991).

Perhaps the finest poet writing in English is Arthur Yap (b. 1943). Like the Chinese language poet Mu Ling-Nu, Yap is also a painter, although unlike Mu (who, as a painter, is better known by his real name Tan Siew Hian) his poetry has not been eclipsed by his work in the visual arts in later years. Yap's poems, as seen in the collections *Commonplace* (1977), *Down the Line* (1980), and *Man Snake Apple & Other Poems* (1966), are noted for their experiments with linguistic and poetic possibilities. Among the younger poets, the finest is perhaps Boey Kim Cheng (b. 1965), whose works, as collected in *Somewhere-Bound* (1989) and *Another Place*, are a depiction of a physical and spiritual wanderlust.

Written literature in Singapore today faces several challenges. A major challenge is linguistic. Today, English is used in all schools in Singapore. In the future it is likely that English will become the dominant literary language, thus posing a problem for literature written in the other languages of Singapore.

BIBLIOGRAPHY: Yap, A., *A Brief Critical Survey of Prose Writings in Singapore and Malaysia* (1971); Singh, K., "Singapore and Malaysian Literature in English," *SoRA*, 10 (1977): 287-99; Wong M. V., Introduction to *Anthology of Singapore Chinese Literature* (1983): ix-xvi; Thumboo, E., ed., *The Fiction of Singapore* (1990); Talib, I. S., "The Development of Singaporean Literature in English," *JMMD*, 15 (1994): 419-429; Talib, I. S., "Singapore Literature in English," in Foley, J. A., et al., eds., *English in New Cultural Contexts: Reflections from Singapore* (1988): 270-86

—ISMAIL S. TALIB

SINGER, Isaac Bashevis

American novelist, short-story writer, essayist, and children's book writer (writing in Yiddish), b. 21 Nov. 1904, Leoncin, Poland; d. 24 July 1991, Miami, Fla.

S.'s family moved to Radzymin soon after his birth, which was on November 21, 1904, not, as was previously believed, on July 14. His earliest influence was his upbringing as the son of a Hasidic rabbi. As a result of his father's cabalistic mysticism and interest in the occult, his mother's rationalism, and his older brother's bohemianism, S.'s experience encompassed two worlds: the traditional Jewish religious existence and the secular modernist explosion of the 19th c., the Haskalah (Enlightenment). S. received a religious education both in the urban environment of Warsaw and in the rural *shtetl* (Jewish village) community of Bilgoray. In 1920 he enrolled in a Warsaw rabbinical seminary, but withdrew after one year.

S.'s older brother, Israel Joshua SINGER, served as his primary literary mentor. From 1923 to 1935, S. worked as a translator and proofreader for a Yiddish newspaper in Warsaw, where he associated with his brother's circle of writers at the Yiddish P.E.N. club. Under his brother's influence, S. decided to write in Yiddish rather than in Hebrew and became familiar with such authors as Dostoevsky, Gogol, Poe, E. T. A. Hoffmann, and Knut HAMSUN. S. joined his brother in the U.S. in 1935. He worked in New York as a free-lance writer for the Jewish daily *Forward*.

The question of whether S. is an American or Yiddish author deserves some consideration. All of his work is composed and published in Yiddish and then translated into English. But the Yiddish-language audience, accustomed to warm sentiment and social commitment in literature, was puzzled by S.'s emphasis on magic, sexuality, passion, and asceticism. Increasingly, as his translated work became popular in English, S. has encouraged the idea that his English translations are primary texts. S. supervises the translation of his texts, opting in many cases to work with "translators" who do not know Yiddish. Further, he chooses not to list the original Yiddish publication dates of his work when translated into English: "When you read a collection of short stories of mine one story might have been written twenty years ago and the other, four weeks ago." As a result, his status as a Yiddish or American writer is secondary to his own sense of himself: "A real writer creates his own tradition."

S.'s entire creative sensibility has been forged by his experience of literary and cultural exile. The theme of exile—from religion, culture, region, morality, God—is crucial in his fiction. For S., exile is a means of affirming contrasts and contradictions. He explores the ambivalence between hedonism and asceticism, between physical passion and religious devotion. The world is depicted as a realm of demons and nightmares run rampant, through which one may proceed only by embracing religious and cultural traditions. These traditions, although outdated, are nonetheless essential.

S.'s first novel, *Shoten an Goray* (1935; *Satan in Goray*, 1943), describes a 17th-c. Polish *shtetl* whose population has been decimated by Cossack raiders. S. views the external crisis and tragedy as secondary to his primary concern: the inner crisis of despair and lack of religious faith. What later became S.'s mature gifts are in evidence in his evocation of a village from a bygone era through specific worldly details and procedures. Lulled into a deceptive sense of security after the program, the village is lured by the devil into the heretical arms of the disciples of Sabbatai Zevi, the false Messiah. But despite the stark images, the powerful materials, the creative conjuring of grotesque and demonic scenes, the novel is uncertainly conceived and constructed. S. juggles his characters to no satisfying result: for instance, the appalling anguish inflicted upon the female protagonist is essentially a mere reiteration of the town's suffering; the fictional crisis is terminated by the author's urging to cling to the strait and narrow path of religious observation and ritual.

S. wrote three historical novels: *The Family Moskat* (1950), *The Manor* (1967), and *The Estate* (1969). All of them attest to the powerful influence of I. J. Singer. Although the milieu and texture of Jewish life in Poland during the last two centuries are presented convincingly, the breadth of fictional scope weakens the characterization. S. lacks the power of social and political observation of his brother; his is an art of close focus and intensive particulars displayed within a generalized historical context.

S.'s best novels contrast the individual instincts of one central character against the constrictive forces of society. S. is interested in the "really passionate man [who] does not belong. He's either a criminal, or he's crazy, or he's an outcast." Yasha Mazur, the protagonist of S.'s brilliant novel *The Magician of Lublin* (1960), possesses all of these qualities in varying degrees. The magic is embodied by Yasha's walking a tightrope between his instinctual gratification and his spiritual fulfillment. Half-assimilated into the Gentile world of urban and rural Poland, the magician struggles to balance a variety of mistresses and conflicting commitments until his world comes toppling down upon him. The antidote to hedonism is asceticism: the lusty magician has himself walled up and becomes a penitent. In this controlled and eloquent work, the existential dilemma of the failed magician becomes an exemplum for the human condition.

The Slave (1962), set in the 17th c., is a poignant and moving novel of religious commitment and devotion. Jacob, a Jewish slave to Polish peasants, falls in love with a Polish girl and, despite Jewish and Gentile opposition, is able to retain his faith. The individual's bond with God is held to be supreme, transcending society; hence, each person's interpretation of the holy law is an act of creation in the highest sense—something that approaches the divine.

S.'s masterpiece, *Enemies: A Love Story* (1972), expands upon his earlier notion of marginality. The Holocaust is not simply a historical tragedy; it has also become a state of mind. The brutality of the death camps may be found in the war between the sexes, in the basic structure of society, even in the relation between man and God. The life of every human being is determined by inescapable passions and desires. Herman Broder, the protagonist, is a modernized magician of Lublin transported to New York. His cynical nihilism leads him to three simultaneous marriages; when his multiple marriages and other deceits are exposed, he repeats his

Isaac Bashevis Singer

response to the Nazis—he hides. In a state of permanent estrangement, S. argues, one can only hide: from the indignity of existence, and from God Himself.

S. first achieved recognition through his short stories and he continues to write prolifically in that form. They are collected in *Gimpel the Fool* (1957), *The Spinoza of Market Street* (1961), *Short Friday* (1964), *The Seance* (1968), *A Friend of Kafka* (1970), *A Crown of Feathers* (1973), *Passions* (1975), and *Old Love* (1979). At his best—in his early stories about Polish *shtetl* life and in his initial stories about eastern European Jews in America—he achieves an intensity and profundity of emotional range that have few parallels in modern literature. But increasingly S. has tended to write superficially, focusing either on vignettes related to an autobiographical author-figure, or on the vicissitudes accompanying the life of an esteemed author resembling S. himself.

S. has been drawn repeatedly to compose his autobiography. *In My Father's Court* (1966), *A Little Boy in Search of God* (1976), *A Young Man in Search of Love* (1978), and *Lost in America* (1981) all mirror S.'s fascination with rendering the absorbing events of his life story. Appropriately, his creative impulses have dominated his inclination toward accuracy so that he considers the most recent three works as "no more than fiction set against a background of truth." In them he outlines his intellectual and philosophical development highlighted with ironic anecdotes illustrating his view that "life itself is a permanent crisis."

S. has been a prolific author of children's books. Children, he has written, "still believe in God, the family, angels, devils, and witches." His children's version of his early memoirs, *A Day of Pleasure* (1969), received a National Book Award, and *Zlateh the Goat, and Other Stories* (1966) was the recipient of the Newbery Honor Award.

S. has written that "the writer tries to reflect life according to his own vision." For his special literary vision, he was awarded the Nobel Prize in 1978. Spanning the Old World and the New, presenting paradoxes of faith, passion, desire, and love, affirming the interrelationship of the sacred and the secular, merging the traditional with the contemporary, S.'s works are unique: he has succeeded, in his own words, in "creat[ing] his own tradition."

FURTHER WORKS: *The Fearsome Inn* (1967); *Mazel and Shlimazel; or, The Milk of a Lioness* (1967); *When Shlemiel Went to Warsaw and Other Stories* (1969); *Elijah the Slave* (1970); *Joseph and Koza; or, The Sacrifice to the Vistula* (1970); *Alone in the Wild Forest* (1971); *The Topsy-Turvy Emperor of China* (1971); *The Wicked City* (1972); *The Fools of Chelm and Their History* (1973); *Why Noah Chose the Dove* (1974); *A Tale of Three Wishes* (1976); *Naftali the Storyteller and His Horse, Sus and Other Stories* (1976); *Shosha* (1978); *Eight Hannukah Stories* (1979); *Nobel Lecture* (1979); *Reaches of Heaven: A Story of the Life of the Baal Shem Tov* (1980); *The Collected Stories of I. B. S.* (1982); *The Penitent* (1983); *Love and Exile* (1984); *Gifts* (1985); *The Image and Other Stories* (1985); *The Death of Methuseleh and Other Stories* (1988); *The King of the Fields* (1988); *Scum* (1991); *The Certificate,* (1992); *Meshugah* (1994); *Shadows on the Hudson* (1998)

BIBLIOGRAPHY: Howe, I., "Demonic Fiction of a Yiddish 'Modernist'" (1960), in Kostelanetz, R., ed., *On Contemporary Literature* (1969): 579–85; Hyman, S. E., "The Yiddish Hawthorne" (1962), in Kostelanetz, R., ed., *On Contemporary Literature* (1969): 586–90; Buchen, I., *I. B. S. and the Eternal Past* (1968); Malin, I., ed., *Critical Views of I. B. S.* (1969); Schulz, M., *Radical Sophistication* (1969): 13–23; Siegel, B., *I. B. S.* (1969); Rosenblatt, P., and G. Koppel, *A Certain Bridge: I. B. S. on Literature and Life* (1971); H., Gass. W., *Fiction and the Figures of Life* (1972): 140–53; Pondrom, C. N., "I. B. S.: An Interview," in Dembo, L. S. and Pondrom, C. N., eds., *The Contemporary Writer* (1972): 61–112; Kazin, A., *Bright Book of Life* (1973): 157–62; Burgin, R., "I. B. S. Talks . . . about Everything," *NYTMag* (26 Nov. 1978): 24–48; Burgin, R., "I. B. S.'s Universe," *NYTMag* (3 Dec. 1978): 38–52; Kresh, P., *I. B. S.: The Magician of West 86th Street* (1979); Alexander, E., *I. B. S.* (1980); Farrell, G., ed., *Critical Essays on I. B. S.* (1996); Hadda, J., *I. B. S.: A Life* (1997)

—GEOFFREY GREEN

It is hardly a secret that in the Yiddish literary world S. is regarded with a certain suspicion or at least reserve. His powers of evocation, his resources as a stylist are acknowledged, yet many Yiddish literary people, including serious ones, seem to be uneasy about him. One reason is that "modernism"—which, as these people regard S., means a heavy stress upon sexuality, a concern for the irrational, expressionist distortions of character, and an apparent indifference to the more conventional aspects of Jewish life—has never won so strong a hold in Yiddish writing as it has in most Western literatures. For the Yiddish writers, "modernism" has often been a mere adornment of manner upon a subject inescapably traditional, or a means of intensifying a sense of estrangement from collective values to which they nevertheless remain bound.

. . . S.'s moral outlook, which seems to move equally toward the sensational and the ascetic, and his assumption that in fiction grotesquerie can be made to serve almost as a mode of knowledge, are hardly traits calculated to put Yiddish readers at their ease.

Irving Howe, "Demonic Fiction of a Yiddish 'Modernist'" (1960), in Richard Kostelanetz, ed., *On Contemporary Literature* (1969), pp. 580–81

If Sholom Aleichem is the Yiddish Mark Twain, S. is the Yiddish Hawthorne. . . S. writes what Hawthorne called "romances" rather than novels, and moral fables and allegories rather than short stories. I cannot imagine anyone since Hawthorne writing such a tale as "The Gentleman from Cracow" in *Gimpel the Fool*, in which a generous stranger who corrupts and destroys the little town of Frampol is revealed to be Ketev Mriri, Chief of the Devils. . .

. . . S.'s subject is *shtetl* (Jewish village) life in Poland, sometimes in the 17th and sometimes in the late 19th century, and he brings it into being so powerfully that reading his books one soon comes to believe that our world is a fantastic vision.

S.'s style, like that of Hawthorne and Melville, is often rhetorical and flamboyant, but there is not an ounce of fat on his prose. His characters sometimes bandy proverbs wittily, like West Africans, and like them he is sometimes folksy and proverbial. S.'s most characteristic style is one of sophisticated ironic juxtaposition. . .

Except for a lady who lives in my house, S. seems to be the only writer in America who believes in the real existence of Satan.

Stanley Edgar Hyman, "The Yiddish Hawthorne" (1962), in Richard Kostelanetz, ed., *On Contemporary Literature* (1969), pp. 586–87

S.'s works tend to resist classification. They are simultaneously supernatural and rational, strange and familiar. To be sure, his works often lean toward one or the other pole and thus support the notion that they are basically of two types: the demonic and the historical. But that initial clarity has to be hedged, for what ties both types together is not mode but scale. S. is preoccupied with excess—with those who seek 100 percent. Controlled and counseled by contraries, he constitutionally resists extremes. In the demonic novels and short stories, the excesses are cosmic and messianic and emerge out of man's relation with God. In the historical works, the excesses are individual and communal and grow out of man's relation with his fellowman. But far from being mutually exclusive, the modes are transmutations of each other. Thus, in the historical works the demonic appears as the sceptical; in the demonic pieces the historical is heightened to the messianic. What eases S.'s transmigrations from one mode and world to another is his notion that between the holy and the unclean, between the supernatural and human, there exists a secret partnership.

Irving Buchen, *I. B. S. and the Eternal Past*
(1968), p. 12

S.'s is a twentieth-century sensibility attempting an imaginative re-creation of the social and religious milieu of Polish Jewry of the previous three centuries. The unique—and now vanished—circumstances of this society confront S.'s historical consciousness with special irrefrangibility. Tolstoy could revert in *War and Peace* to the time of the Napoleonic invasions without risking intellectual dislocation, for his society still assented essentially to the assumptions of his grandfather. Tension of a profound philosophical order, however, affects the moral pattern of S.'s stories as a result of the radically different *Zeitgeists* of the author and of his dramatis personae. One of the central paradoxes of S.'s fictional world is that even as he pays loving tribute to the value system of a back-country Jewry—dirty, ignorant, but firm in a simplistic faith in what Dr. Yaretsky in "The Shadow of a Crib" calls "a seeing universe, rather than a blind one"—S. questions such a world picture with the narrative structures he composes for them. His rabbis and pious matrons may think and act in unquestioning accord with a Jewish cosmic vision, but their lives present the absurd pattern familiar to the modern sensibility.

Max F. Schulz, *Radical Sophistication* (1969),
pp. 13–14

The whole of S.'s fiction possesses this magnificent ontological equality (fables, fantasies, and fairy tales are therefore never out of place); it has exactly the material solidity it claims for everything, since everything is open, and in space. The sensational, the extreme and extraordinary, the violent, saintly, severe and the cruel, the divine, the human, the diabolical: all are mastered by his method, placed in a line on the same plane; ritual acts and uncontrollable savagery, marriage and murder, prayers and pogroms; for they are all acts, acts like tangible objects resting in the world. After all, the flower and the phallus both exist, so do stones in a wall, or passions in a person. This gives S. an important freedom. If, on the one hand, facts are everything, on the other, everything can be factual. No mind and body problem here, no links to be forged between percept and object, or bridges to be built between nature and the unnatural, thought, dream, and thing. Whatever is, is matter in ritual motion. An intense sense of reality in the reader is the initial advantage. No one quite believes in any inner spirit but his own.

William H. Gass, *Fiction and the Figures of Life*
(1972), p. 143

S. represents the transformation of all Jewish history into fiction, fable, story. He accepts it for his own purposes. He is a skeptic who is hypnotized by the world he grew up in. No one else in modern Jewish writing stems so completely from the orthodox and even mystical East European tradition. No one else has turned "*the tradition*" into the freedom of fiction, the subtlety and mischievousness and truthfulness of storytelling. S., totally a fiction writer but summing up the East European Yiddish tradition in his detached, fatalistic, plainspoken way, represents a peculiar effortlessness in the writing of "Jewish fiction," when compared with the storminess of Bellow and Mailer. That is because S. shares the orthodox point of view without its belief, and he meticulously describes, without sentimentalizing any Jew whatever, a way of life which was murdered with the millions who lived it. The demons and spirits so prominent in S.'s East European narratives have in his "American" ones become necessary to the survivors.

Alfred Kazin, *Bright Book of Life* (1973), p. 157

Behind the tenement walls there lurks a Jewish underworld, a subcity of thieves and criminals; and beneath that, the dark unmapped terrain of Gehenna itself. Only the few who fast enough and pray enough, who are strong enough to withdraw from all that is worldly, attain that peculiar paradise in which the reward for piety is an eternity of study in a celestial university where angels make music and a man's wife is privileged to serve until the end of time as his footstool. Even so, every inch of S.'s world, from the prehistoric mountains of *The Slave* to the cafeterias of New York's Lower East Side, where decaying journalists lament old failures over their tea and rice pudding, is pulsing with life, with suspense, with the twinkle of mischief that age cannot extinguish from this author's eyes. It is a world so persuasively constructed that within its confines even the unreal seems real, the cushions on chairs still warm from the recent press of living bodies, the air breathable, the rain moist, the ice cold enough to freeze the reader's flesh.

Paul Kresh, *I. B. S.: The Magician of West 86th
Street* (1979), p. 5

SINGER, I(srael) J(oshua)

Yiddish novelist, short-story writer, dramatist, memoirist, and essayist, b. 30 Nov. 1893, Bilgoray, Poland; d. 10 Feb. 1944, New York, N.Y., U.S.A.

S., the son and grandson of rabbis, began his literary career during World War I after he had moved to Warsaw and broken out of the confines of the Hasidic life he had been born into. S. had received intensive religious training, but he supplemented this education with a secular one. He began to contribute stories to Yiddish publications while supporting himself in whatever way he could. Excited by the Russian Revolution, he moved to Kiev in 1918 and then to Moscow, at the time a Yiddish literary center, but he returned to Warsaw in 1921, having become disillusioned with Bolshevism. In addition to writing for and editing various literary journals, S. became a foreign correspondent for the New York newspaper *Forverts* in 1923. In 1933 he emigrated to the U.S., settling in New York.

Although Poland serves as the major background for S.'s works, it is not eastern Europe itself that concerns him. It is, rather, the harsh historical changes that have taken place and the way they have affected social relationships and the individual will that serve as the focus of his concentration.

In every sense a "modern" Yiddish writer, that is, one not interested in sentimentalizing *shtetl* life as did most of the Yiddish novelists before him, S. views his panorama with aesthetic distance, with deliberate detachment. His early stories are almost unrelentingly severe. In "Perl" (pearls) in *Perl, un andere dertseylungen* (1922; pearls, and other stories), for example, S. vividly portrays an aged, miserly, hypochondriacal merchantlandlord. The miserable decadence of his life is matched by the authentic, horrible poverty of those around him. Another story in the volume, "Altshtot" (old city), presents an even more loathsome main character, a neurotic sadist. Other principal figures in his early stories include murderers, swindlers, apostates, and pogromists.

S.'s novels display the same lack of sentimentality as his stories. *Shtol un ayzn* (1927; *Blood Harvest*, 1935), based on the author's own sorrowful experiences of laboring for the Germans in World War I, tells of constant strife, hardship, and disillusionment. As always, he portrays Jews not only as the primary victims of war and revolution but also as deficient beings in themselves. S. the realist coolly observes his characters' petty struggles and vain hopes, while he sees their world shattering about them. It is the artist's vision, his ability to penetrate the sham and illusory, that is so illuminating.

In *Yoshe Kalb* (1932; *The Sinner*, 1933; repub. as *Yoshe Kalb*, 1965) this technique is even more apparent. While seventy rabbis and whole communities argue over whether the protagonist is a saint or a sinner, a simpleton or a learned Cabalist, S. underlines the state Hasidism had reached by the late 19th c., when it had changed from an ecstatic religious sect to a motley assortment of cliques.

S.'s narrative style found its best outlet in the spacious "family novel." *Di brider Ashkenazi* (1936; *The Brothers Ashkenazi*, 1936) was a great popular and critical success. S. here skillfully weaves together the story of three generations in Łódź as they are affected by industrialization, war, the German occupation, programs, revolution, the labor movement and its bloody strikes, and ever-increasing anti-Semitism. The events described are horrible, yet the grimness is somewhat mitigated this time by the introduction of a few positive, although minor, characters who are genuinely altruistic, and by fuller treatment of the main characters, who are no longer as one-sidedly negative as they were in earlier works. Good intentions of the individual, however, are always canceled out by uncontrollable historical events. This novel is considered to be among the finest in all Yiddish literature.

Khaver Nakhman (1938; *East of Eden*, 1939), an indictment of communism, and *Di mishpokhe Karnovsky* (1943; *The Family Carnovsky*, 1943), treating the Hitler era, are other large family novels. These are literarily less successful than *Di brider Ashkenazi*, primarily because S.'s usual detachment breaks down here. The writer's sorrowful disappointment with the panacea of Bolshevism and the infinite pain caused by the Holocaust could no longer allow him to remain an objective observer of events. S.'s technical skills in handling the many motifs and characters, however, remain intact.

S. wrote a few original plays, but it was the dramatization of his novels, particularly of the extremely popular *Yoshe Kalb* by Maurice Schwartz's Yiddish Art Theater in 1932, that met with the greatest success. His early memoirs, *Fun a velt vos iz nishto mer* (1946; *Of a World That Is No More*, 1970) are among the finest in any language, and are a particularly engaging testament to Polish-Jewish life before its destruction.

Because of his ability to treat events with biting realism, because of his vision, his ability to permeate outward appearances, and, not least, because of his lucid narrative style, S. is one of the greatest Yiddish writers. Indeed, many eminent Yiddish literary critics acclaim him to be at least as great a writer as his younger brother, Nobel laureate Isaac Bashevis SINGER.

FURTHER WORKS: *Erdvey* (1922); *Leymgrubn* (1924); *Oyf fremder erd* (1925); *Nay-Rusland* (1928); *Friling, un andere dertseylungen* (1937); *Vili* (1948); *Dertseylungen* (1949); *Oysgeklibene shriftn* (1975). FURTHER WORKS IN ENGLISH: *The River Breaks Up: A Volume of Stories* (1938)

BIBLIOGRAPHY: Roback, A. A., *The Story of Yiddish Literature* (1940): 305–8; Singer, I. B., *In My Father's Court* (1962), passim; Singer, I. B., Introduction to *Yoshe Kalb* (1965): v–x; Howe, I., "The Other S.," *Commentary* (March 1966): 78–82; Madison, C., *Yiddish Literature: Its Scope and Major Writers* (1968): 449–78; Ravitch, M., "I. J. S.," in Steinbach, A. A., ed., *Jewish Book Annual*, 26 (1968): 121–23; Liptzin, S., *The Maturing of Yiddish Literature* (1970): 160–64; Siegel, B., "The Brothers S.: More Similarities than Differences," *ConL*, 22 (1981): 42–47; Sinclair, C., *The Brothers Singer* (1983); Norich, A., *The Homeless Imagination in the Fiction of I. J. S.* (1991)

—HANNAH BERLINER FISCHTHAL

SINGH, Khushwant

Indian novelist, short-story writer, translator, editor, and historian (writing in English), b. 2 Feb. 1915, Hadali

S.'s early years in West Punjab are richly recorded in his novel of Sikh family life, *I Shall Not Hear the Nightingale* (1959). He attended public schools in Lahore and Delhi and took degrees from St. Stephen's College, Delhi (1934) and King's College, London (1936). Called to the bar at the Inner Temple, he practiced law at the Punjab High Court and taught jurisprudence at the Law College in Lahore (1939–47). At independence, he began a stint as press attaché with the Indian foreign service in Toronto and London. From 1954 to 1956 S. served on the communications staff of UNESCO in Paris, and from 1956 to 1958 he edited *Yejna*, an Indian government publication. His *A History of the Sikhs* (2 vols., 1963–66) was completed during a period of travel, teaching, and research at various American universities. S. was chief editor of *The Illustrated Weekly of India* from 1969 until his retirement in 1978.

S. is well known as a writer of short stories, many of which have been anthologized and collected, his first collection being *The Mark of Vishnu, and Other Stories* (1950; expanded ed., *The Voice of God, and Other Stories*, 1957). S.'s writing is fundamentally comic, with laughter used as a social corrective: pompous, opinionated Indians are butts of his satire. He delights in puncturing the pretentious with bawdy humor typical of the Punjabi. S.'s plots, however, tend to be flimsy, often resolved by improbable coincidences.

Similar criticism must be made of his novels, which deal with independence and partition. *Mano Majra* (1956; retitled *Train to Pakistan*) is a stark, realistic novel of religious tension in a Punjabi village. As Muslims flee to Pakistan and communal atrocities multiply, a Sikh dacoit (bandit) sacrifices his life to save his Muslim sweetheart. *I Shall Not Hear the Nightingale* chronicles acts of violence by a young Sikh whose father is trusted by British authorities.

S. has dedicated himself to conveying the story of the Sikhs and has succeeded remarkably in his accurate and readable histories, which remain a major contribution to the world of letters.

As Sikh history has evolved with the events of Operation Bluestar and the struggle for political control in Haryana and Punjab, S. has continued to serve as a rational spokesman for his people. His delightful and intelligent essays, printed originally as columns in Indian magazines and newspapers, have been collected and edited in recent years by Rohini Singh. These constitute a set of memoirs, unrivaled in modern India, by a perceptive interpreter of Delhi, as well as of the Indian and British literary scenes. S. also makes forays into Islam and Hinduism, modeling openness and tolerance sorely needed in today's India.

FURTHER WORKS: *The Sikhs* (1952); *Japji: The Sikh Morning Prayer* (1954); *The Unending Trail* (1957); *The Sikhs Today: Their Religion, History, Culture, Customs and Way of Life* (1959; rev. ed., 1964); *Ranjit Singh, Maharajah of the Punjab, 1780–1839* (1962); *Fall of the Kingdom of the Punjab* (1962); *Sunset of the Sikh Empire* (1959, with Sita Ram Kohli); *Ghadar, 1919: India's First Armed Revolution* (1966, with Satindra Singh); *Homage to Guru Govind Singh* (1966, with Suneet Veer Singh); *A Bridge for the Sahib and Other Stories* (1967); *Shri Ram: A Biography* (1968, with Arun Joshi); *Hymns of Nanak the Guru* (1968); *Black Jasmine* (1971); *K. S.'s View of India* (1975); *K. S.'s India without Humbug* (1977); *Around the World with K. S.* (1978); *Indira Gandhi Returns* (1979); *Delhi: A Portrait* (1983); *Tragedy of Punjab: Operation Bluestar and After* (1984, with Kuldip Nayar); *Ranjit Singh: Maharajah of the Punjab* (1986); *Collected Short Stories of K. S.* (1991); *India: An Introduction* (1990); *Delhi* (1991); *Need for a New Religion in India* (1991); *My Bleeding Punjab* (1992); *Sex, Scotch and Scholarship* (1993); *From Mind to Super-Mind: A Commentary on the Bhagavad Gita* (1996); *Women and Men in My Life* (1996)

BIBLIOGRAPHY: Singh, R., *K. S.'s India* (1969); Coppola, C., "Interview with K. S.," *Mahfil*, 5 (1969): 27–42; Kulsreshstha, C., "K. S.'s Fiction: A Critique," *IWT*, 11 (1970): 19–26; Tarinayya, M., "Two Novels," *IndL*, 13 (1970): 113–21; Shahane, V. A., *K. S.* (1972); Shahane, V. A., "K. S.'s *Train to Pakistan*: A Study in Contemporary Realism," in Mohan, R., ed., *Indian Writing in English* (1978): 65–79; Singh, R., *Man Called K. S.* (1996)

—JANET POWERS GEMMILL

SINHALA LITERATURE

See under Sri Lankan Literature

SINYAVSKY, Andrey Donatovich

(pseud.: Abram Terts) Russian novelist, short-story writer, critic, and essayist, b. 8 Oct. 1925, Moscow; d. 25 Feb. 1997, near Paris, France

After graduation from Moscow University in 1952 S. did research at the Gorky Institute of World Literature in Moscow. His reviews in the relatively liberal journal *Novy mir* attracted attention from 1959 to 1965. In 1960 he coauthored a brief, illustrated book on Picasso and then collaborated with A. Menshutin (dates n.a.) on an admirable study of early Soviet poetry, *Poezia pervykh let revolyutsii, 1917–1920* (1964; poetry in the first years of the revolution, 1917–1920). His introduction to an expanded Soviet edition of the poems of Boris PASTERNAK appeared in 1965.

In September 1965 S. was arrested, together with the Jewish writer Yuly Daniel (b. 1925), tried, and sentenced to seven years' hard labor for alleged anti-Soviet writings, published abroad under the pseudonym of Abram Terts. Released in 1971, S. was allowed in August 1973 to emigrate to France, where he lived until his death in 1997.

Works ascribed to Terts have appeared only in the West, both in the original Russian and in translation. The first, "Chto takoe sotsialistichesky realizm," initially published in Russian in *Fantastichesky mir Abrama Tertsa* (1967; the fantastic world of Abram Terts), was published in English as *On Socialist Realism* (1960). This trenchantly witty long essay expresses misgivings about the teleological nature of SOCIALIST REALISM and affirms S.'s belief in phantasmagoric art.

Sud idyot (1960; *The Trial Begins*, 1960) is a novel exemplifying this credo, commingling the realistic and the fantastic, scrutinizing ends and means in a communist context, evoking a nightmare vision of Moscow before and after Stalin's death and foreshadowing uncannily S.'s later arrest and imprisonment.

Fantasticheskie povesti (1961; *Fantastic Stories*, 1963) consists of five tales. Common to all are grotesquerie, a penchant for the erotic, and a dark and disturbing laughter. Usually grouped with these is "Pkhents" (1967; "Pkhentz," 1968), in which the narrator, a cactuslike creature from another planet, pretends to be a hunchback so as to avoid human contact and keep his true nature secret. In his isolation and disgust with humanity it is tempting to see the hyperbolically rendered plight of S. himself. The title of the story is a name sacred to the inhabitants of the planet from which the narrator hails. The style and psychology of these stories recall Gogol and Dostoevsky. Time, action, and personality are continually blurred in a manner reminiscent of such early 20th-c. writers as Andrey BELY and Yevgeny ZAMYATIN.

S.'s longest novel, *Lyubimov* (1964; *The Makepeace Experiment*, 1965), tells of a bicycle mechanic whose hypnotic powers bring about revolution in a remote town. As is the case with many of S.'s works, it is narrated in the first person, although, bizarrely, by two people with the same surname—one alive, the other dead. Its satirical form (for example, comic footnotes) derives from Mikhail Saltykov-Shchedrin's (1826–1889) *The History of a Town* (1870), but atmosphere and setting belong unmistakably to modern Russia, offering scope for political interpretation.

Mysli vrasplokh (1966; *Unguarded Thoughts*, 1972) is a booklet of philosophical reflections. Despite the cogitative references to sex, typical of S., his tendency is to glorify the soul and disparage the body. On the surface, the work suggests a deeply religious man who is yet sufficiently world-weary to find death attractive—although S.'s irony must be taken into account. His thoughts are dispensed less cavalierly than the seeming randomness and abrupt transitions might indicate, but are, rather, arranged with a view to artistic effect.

After his emigration, S. published mostly nonfiction. *Golos iz khora* (1973; *A Voice from the Chorus*, 1976), based on S.'s prison letters to his wife, deals extensively with aesthetic matters and underlines his religious faith. Two impressionistic works of literary criticism, both written in prison, are *Progulki s Pushkinym* (1975; strolling with Pushkin) and *V teni Gogolya* (1975; in the shadow of Gogol). *Kroshka Tsores* (1980; little Tsores), a work of fiction, is a largely phantasmagoric treatment of neurosis and alienation, dedicated to E. T. A. Hoffmann.

Although the influence of earlier Russian writers can be felt in his fiction, S. commands a distinctive, often enigmatic voice. He displays an immense stylistic virtuosity, revealing one of the strangest and most powerful talents to have emerged in recent decades from the Soviet Union.

BIBLIOGRAPHY: Field, A., "Abram Tertz's Ordeal by Mirror," Preface to *Mysli vrasplokh* (1966): 7–42; Labedz, L., and Hayward, M., *On Trial: The Case of S. (Tertz) and Daniel (Arzhak)* (1967); Mihajlov, M., *Russian Themes* (1968): 3–77; Brown, D., "The Art of A. S.," *SlavR*, 29 (1970): 663–81; Dalton, M., *A. S. and Julii Daniel: Two Soviet "Heretical" Writers* (1973); Lourie, R., *Letters to the Future: An Approach to S.-Tertz* (1975); Leatherbarrow, W., "The Sense of Purpose and Socialist Realism in Tertz's *The Trial Begins*," *FMLS*, 11 (1975): 268–79

—RICHARD HALLETT

SITWELL, Edith

English poet, essayist, and biographer, b. 7 Sept. 1887, Scarborough; d. 9 Dec. 1964, London

The daughter of Sir George and Lady Ida S., along with her younger brothers Osbert (1892–1969) and Sacheverell (b. 1897)—the siblings later became a famous literary trio—S. grew up in an ambience of wealth and leisure. She was educated at home and spent much of her early life, until she was twenty-six, at Renishaw Hall, the family seat in Derbyshire. From this period came important influences on S.'s poetry: her father's passion for landscape gardening, her interest in music, and her introduction to the French SYMBOLISTS by her gifted governess, Helen Rootham.

S. published her first poem in 1913 and came to London in 1914 to pursue a career as a poet. Within a year she published her first volume of poetry, *The Mother* (1915), and began to take an increasingly active role in London literary circles. Her abiding flair for public controversy (which she shared with Osbert) began in those years when she edited *Wheels* (1916–21), a yearly anthology of new poetry designed to combat the conservative Georgian poetry of that era. As an editor, she had the distinction of recognizing Wilfred OWEN's talent, and in 1919, in *Wheels*, was the first to publish his work.

The greatest accomplishment of S.'s early years—and perhaps of her whole career—was *Façade* (1922), a suite of challenging and witty poems recited to music specially composed by William Walton, an Oxford friend of Sacheverell's. *Façade* was designed by S. (and produced in collaboration with her brothers) as an abstract and difficult exercise in sound, to rescue English poetry from what she called the "verbal deadness" of the preceding era. *Façade* was an important weapon in what Evelyn WAUGH called S.'s "war on dullness."

After a prolific output of innovative poetry during the 1920s, culminating in *Gold Coast Customs* (1929), a Juvenalian satire on contemporary mores, S. wrote little poetry during the 1930s, but, in financial need, produced a considerable amount of prose, including a critical study, *Alexander Pope* (1930); a biography, *Victoria of England* (1934); and a novel (based on the life of Jonathan Swift), *I Live under a Black Sun* (1937).

The outbreak of World War II turned S. back to poetry and to a more discursive technique celebrating the possibilities of endurance in the midst of terror. This style of eloquent symbolism, rooted in religious faith, embodied natural images such as sun and shadow, in contrast to the more esoteric symbolism of her early poetry, which derived from the commedia dell'arte, the Russian ballet of Serge Diaghilev, and the French symbolists. The poems of *Street Songs* (1942), *Green Song* (1944), and *Song of the Cold* (1945), with their involvement with common concerns, gave her a wider fame than her more hermetic early work. The critic Kenneth Clark expressed the opinion of many in calling S.'s poetry of the 1940s the "greatest poems of the war." This heightened reputation led in 1948 to the first of several triumphant reading tours of the U.S. Consistent with the increasingly religious nature of her later poetry, she became a Roman Catholic in 1955.

The Royal Society of Literature gave S. its medal for poetry in 1934, largely through the insistence of W. B. YEATS, who praised her poetry; in 1944, the Society made her one of its Fellows. She was also awarded several honorary degrees, and in 1954 she was made a Dame Grand Cross of the Order of the British Empire. Recent critical studies assess her as a minor but important poet who contributed to, encouraged, and rigorously defended the modernist movement.

FURTHER WORKS: *Twentieth Century Harlequinade* (1916, with S. Osbert); *Clowns' Houses* (1918); *The Wooden Pegasus* (1920); *Bucolic Comedies* (1923); *Poor Young People* (1925, with S. Osbert and S. Sacheverell); *Troy Park* (1925); *Poetry and Criticism* (1925); *E. S.: Poems* (1926); *Elegy of Dead Fashion* (1926); *Rustic Elegies* (1927); *Five Poems* (1928); *Popular Song* (1928); *Collected Poems* (1930); *Jane Barston, 1719–1746* (1931); *Bath* (1932); *The English Eccentrics* (1933); *Five Variations on a Theme* (1933); *Aspects of Modern Poetry* (1934); *Selected Poems* (1936); *Trio* (1938, with S. Osbert and S Sacheverell); *Poems New and Old* (1940); *English Women* (1942); *A Poet's Notebook* (1943); *Fanfare for Elizabeth* (1946); *The Shadow of Cain* (1947); *A Notebook on William Shakespeare* (1948); *The Canticle of the Rose: Selected Poems 1920–1947* (1949); *Poor Men's Music* (1950); *Façade and Other Poems* (1950); *Selected Poems* (1952); *Gardeners and Astronomers* (1953); *Collected Poems* (1954); *The Pocket Poems: E. S.* (1960); *The Queens and the Hive* (1962); *The Outcasts* (1962); *Music and Ceremonies* (1963); *Taken Care Of: An Autobiography* (1965); *Selected Poems* (1965); *Selected Letters 1919–1964* (1970); *E. S.: Fire of the Mind* (1976)

BIBLIOGRAPHY: Villa, J. G., ed., *A Celebration for E. S.* (1948); Salter, E., *The Last Years of a Rebel: A Memoir of E. S.* (1967); Brophy, J., *E. S.: The Symbolist Order* (1968); Lehmann, J., *A Nest of Tigers* (1968); Pearson, J., *The Sitwells* (1980); Glendining, V., *E. S.: A Unicorn among Lions* (1981); Elborn, G., *E. S.: A Biography* (1981)

—JAMES D. BROPHY

Edith Sitwell

SKALBE, Kārlis

Latvian poet and fairy-tale writer, b. 7 Nov. 1879, Vecpiebalga; d. 15 April 1945, Stockholm, Sweden

The son of a smith, S. became a major Latvian poet and a notable contributory force in the realization of Latvian independence. Even in his early volumes of verse, *Cietumnieka sapni* (1902; a prisoner's dreams) and *Kad ābeles zied* (1904; when apple trees blossom), he protested against oppression and injustice. In his modern fairy tale, *Kā es braucu Ziemelmeitas lūkoties* (1904; how I traveled to see the princess of the North Pole), he protested against shallow social values. An active participant in the abortive 1905 revolution against Russian autocracy, he had to go into exile. After a few years in Norway he returned and was imprisoned. His melancholy mood during these years is evident in the titles of his collections of this period: *Zemes dūmos* (1906; in the earth's smoke), *Velu laikā* (1907; in the season of the spirits of the dead), and *Emigranta dziesmas* (1909; songs of an exile).

During World War I S. was a war correspondent with the Latvian Riflemen fighting a German invasion of Latvia. It was then he developed his individual style of short poetic notes—*Mazās piezīmes* (serially, 1917–20; in book form, 1920; brief observations)—which he continued to employ in the postwar years.

S.'s influence on Latvian cultural and political life was considerable. His collection of epic poems, *Daugavas vilni* (1918; waves of the river Daugava), with rhythms echoing the river's waves, expresses the nation's feelings in the course of attaining its hard-won independence. S. became a member of the Latvian parliament, but at the end of World War II, with the Soviet takeover, he again went into exile, to Sweden, where he soon died.

S. was influenced by SYMBOLISM, but his poetry developed toward greater simplicity and poetic concentration akin to that of the Latvian folk song. Without imitating its form, S. achieved a similar concreteness of images and economy of expression. In the collections *Sirds un saule* (1911; heart and sun), *Sapni un teikas* (1912; dreams and legends), *Zāles dvaša* (1931; breath of grass), and *Klusuma melodijas* (1941; melodies of silence), his poetry is suffused with peace and serenity always gravitating to ethical values.

S. also established the genre of the modern Latvian fairy tale. He used motifs from Latvian as well as other folktales, and these stories are dominated by the same ethical principles as Latvian folklore, where good triumphs over evil. S. was devoted to small things and humble people: the title of his first collection of fairy tales, *Pazemīgās dvēseles* (1911; humble souls), is characteristic. In later collections, *Ziemas pasakas* (1912; winter tales), *Pasaka par vecāko dēlu* (1924; the tale of the eldest son), *Manu bērnības dienu mēnesis* (1926; a month in my childhood), *Mulka laime*

(1933; the fool's luck), and *Garā pupa* (1933; the long beanstalk), he achieved a vividness and exactitude of images unsurpassed in Latvian. His tales resemble those of Hans Christian Andersen in their form and literary excellence, although S. placed more emphasis on the expressiveness of each single sentence. A fine example is the well known "Kakīša dzirnavas" (1931; "Pussy's Water Mill," 1952).

S.'s poetry is characterized by great subtlety and conciseness, and in all his work he expressed a strong belief in humanitarian ideals and made a stand against authoritarian power. The thematic range of S.'s work is not wide; his writings remain within the limits of personified, spiritualized nature and the world of the peasant. Yet he was able to capture delicate nuances of emotion in simple words. The specific ethos of the Latvian nation may well have found its definitive expression in his work.

FURTHER WORKS: *Sarkangalvīte un citas pasakas* (1913); *Pēclaikā* (1923); *Kopoti raksti* (5 vols., 1922–1923); *Kopoti raksti* (6 vols., 1952–1955)

BIBLIOGRAPHY: Baumanis, A., ed., *Latvian Poetry* (1946): 38–39; Andrups, J., and V. Kalve, *Latvian Literature* (1954): 132–33; Matthews, W. K., ed., *A Century of Latvian Poetry* (1957): 9; Scholz, F., "K. S. (1879–1945): Ein lettischer und ein europäischer Dichter," *JBalS*, 10 (1979): 205–17

—JĀNIS ANDRUPS

SKÁRMETA, Antonio

Chilean novelist and short-story writer, b. 7 Nov. 1940, Antofagasta

After President Salvador Allende's socialist regime was overthrown by a military coup in September 1973, many Chilean writers took refuge abroad; among these, S. is perhaps the best known. The grandson of Yugoslavian immigrants who arrived in Chile in the late 19th c., S. graduated from the University of Chile with a degree in philosophy. With the aid of a Fulbright scholarship he completed his M.A. in Spanish literature at Columbia University and then returned to Chile to teach at his alma mater and work as a journalist. He lived in Buenos Aires from 1973 until 1975, after which he spent more than a decade in West Berlin, where he directed films and held a professorial post at the German Academy of Cinematography. In 1989 he returned to Chile.

S.'s first book, a collection of short fiction entitled *El entusiasmo* (1967; enthusiasm), depicts the vitality and spontaneity of youth on the thresh-hold of adulthood. *Desnudo en el tejado* (1969; naked on the roof), S.'s second collection, initiates the author's preoccupation with social and political issues, for which he is well known today. Although not political in its subject matter, the best tale of this collection is "El ciclista del San Cristóbal" (the bicyclist of San Cristóbal), which is narrated by a young bicyclist before, during, and after a race. What determines the excellence of this story is its celebration of two victories, one sporting and the other spiritual. Thus the narrator not only wins the race, but also, through love and will power, effects the resurrection of his dying mother. Other virtues of this story are S.'s adept manipulation of the interior monologue and colloquial language, by which he brings the reader into direct contact with the emotions gushing from the mind of the bicyclist.

A fine example of S.'s politically inspired short fiction is "La llamada" (the telephone call), which appeared in his collection *Novios y solitarios* (1975; fiancés and lonely beings). This brief sketch portrays a professor of literature who has recently been intimidated by the police, perhaps because of something he said in the classroom; as he leaves the institution where he is employed, he is again accosted by two policemen, one formerly his student. An unnerving conversation ensues, after which the professor enters a café to make a telephone call. But upon seeing a man sitting nearby reading a newspaper, he changes his mind and leaves. S.'s technique is reminiscent of Ernest HEMINGWAY's, consisting of dialogue and unadorned narration, obliging the reader to discover possible cause-and-effect relationships from the limited material presented. "La llamada" depicts the terror and paranoia felt by Chileans, who prior to 1973 had taken democracy and freedom of speech for granted.

S.'s first novel, *Soñé que la nieve ardía* (1975; I Dreamt the Snow Was Burning, 1985), is a moving dramatization of events during and immediately following the Allende regime. The protagonist is a young, ambitious soccer player, Arturo, who comes from the backwaters of Chile to Santiago determined to make his fortune in a professional sports career. His materialistic, bourgeois agenda soon clashes with the values of idealistic Marxists sharing his boarding house. Revolutionary in its negation of classical syntax, the experimental style of this novel captures the intensity of a crucial period in recent Chilean history. S.'s next novel, *No pasó nada* (1980; nothing happened) stems directly from S.'s exile in West Germany. A bildungsroman, its subject matter is the rite of passage to manhood of a fourteen-year-old son of Chilean exiles in West Berlin. As in most of S.'s works, language plays an important role; in this case it reveals the protagonist's psychological adjustment to his new environment as he assimilates German slang and the vocabulary of sports, food, and pop art. As a story of exiles suddenly thrust into an unfamiliar environment, *No pasó nada* is both timely and universal. S.'s commitment to the socialist cause is nowhere more evident than in *La insurrección* (1982; The Insurrection, 1983), about the Sandinistas' revolt against Anastasio Somoza's dictatorial regime in Nicaragua. Described in epic form, the action takes place in the city of León, where the two leading characters become leaders in the movement, which triumphs on 19 July 1979. The use of many narrative voices in the text seems particularly appropriate because this technique, like the array of characters, expresses the collective will of Nicaragua in crisis.

S.'s most successful novel to date is *Ardiente paciencia* (1985; *Burning Patience*, 1987), the protagonists of which are the poet Pablo NERUDA and Mario Jiménez, a seventeen-year-old fisherman's son who becomes Neruda's mailman and intimate friend. The novel's time frame covers the period between 1969 and 1973, that is, from the year before the election of Salvador Allende to less than a month after the military coup and Neruda's death. The most important theme is the power of poetry. *Ardiente paciencia* is a tragicomical tribute to Latin America's greatest poet, but it is also replete with passages reminiscent of Gabriel GARCÍA MÁRQUEZ's *Cien años de soledad* (1967; *One Hundred Years of Solitude*, 1970). Characterized by parody, irony, and the masterful use of metaphor, S.'s style in this novel is worthy of the highest praise.

Match Ball (1989; set point) marks a new direction in S.'s oeuvre because of its total lack of political commitment. Laced with irony and black humor, this novel is narrated by a middle-aged American antihero, who is married to a wealthy, aristocratic German woman. While successfully practicing medicine in West Berlin he falls madly in love with a fifteen-year-old tennis champion, for whom he sacrifices marriage and professional reputation. Perhaps the most entertaining of S.'s novels, *Match Ball* emerges as a satire of the pleasure-seeking, cosmopolitan jet set, a satire enhanced by a sprinkling of erotic scenes, foreign words, and references to other literary works.

In both his novels and short stories S. has demonstrated a remarkable sensitivity to today's political climate. More important, however, are his mastery of poetic style, his insightful understanding of youth, and his subtle sense of humor. It is hardly surprising that he has become one of Spanish America's most admired and popular writers.

FURTHER WORKS: *El ciclista del San Cristóbal* (1971); *Tiro libre* (1973)

BIBLIOGRAPHY: Lyon, T., on *La insurrección*, WLT, 57, 3 (Summer 1983): 433; McMurray, G. R., "The Spanish American Short Story from Quiroga to Borges," in M. S. Peden, ed., *The Latin American Short Story: A Critical History* (1983): 131–32; Silva Cáceres, R., ed., *Del cuerpo a las palabras: La narrativa de A. S.* (1983); Rojo, G., "Explicacion de A. S.," *Hispam*, 13, 37 (April 1984): 65–72; Benavides, R. F., on *Soñé que la nieve ardía*, WLT, 58, 4 (Autumn 1984): 577; Filer, M. E., on *Ardiente paciencia*, WLT, 60, 3 (Summer 1986): 450; Rojo, G. and C. Steele, *Ritos de iniciación: Tres novelas cortas de Hispanoamérica* (1986): 65–75; McMurray, G. R., *Spanish American Writing since 1941* (1987): 138–40; Bannura-Spriga, M. G., "El juego y el deseo en la obra de A. S.," *Inti*: 24–25 (Fall-Spring 1986–1987): 155–61; Rodríguez,

F. M., "A. S.: De *El entusiasmo a La insurrección*," *Atenea: Revista de Ciencia, Arte y Literatura de la Universidad de Concepción*, 455 (1987): 175–78; Rodríguez Hernández, R., "Nueva novela histórica hispanoamericana: *La insurrección y Un día en la vida*," *TCrit*, 13: 36–37 (1987): 153–63; Cortínez, V., "Polifonía: Isabel Allende y A. S.," *Plaza: Revista de Literatura*: 14–15 (Spring-Fall 1988): 73–80; Blanc, M., "A. S.: Cuentos y novelas," *Chasqui*, 13, 2 (November 1989): 64–78; Tittler, J., "Toward a Revolutionary Writing: A. S.'s *La insurrección*," in D. Bevan, ed., *Literature and Revolution* (1989): 97–105

—GEORGE R. MCMURRAY

ŠKVORECKÝ, Josef

Czechoslovak novelist, short-story writer, poet, essayist, translator, and screenwriter (writing in Czech and English), b. 27 Sept. 1924, Náchod

Josef Škvorecký

Š. studied English and philosophy at Charles University in Prague. He became an editor of the review of foreign literatures *Světová literatura*. In 1969, after the reform movement had been suppressed by Soviet arms, Š. left Czechoslovakia. He now lives in Canada in retirement. Until recently, he taught English and American literature at the University of Toronto. Between 1971 and 1993 Š. and his wife, writer Zdena Salivarová (b. 1933), ran 68 Publishers Corp., a Czech-language publishing house in Canada, which brought out some two hundred and thirty original works, banned in Czechoslovakia until 1989. Š.'s publishing venture was of major importance for the preservation of an authentic literary tradition during the two decades of totalitarianism following the Russian-led invasion in 1968.

Š. first became known in the mid–1950s for his essays on modern American writers and for his translations into Czech of Ernest HEMINGWAY, William FAULKNER, Ray Bradbury (b. 1920), and others. His first novel, *Zbabělci* (written 1948, pub. 1958; *The Cowards*, 1970), was banned two weeks after publication. Based undoubtedly on personal experience, it combines a record of a young man's mostly imaginary love exploits with an account of the tragicomic events in a small Bohemian town during a week in May 1945. Both conservatives and communists are already jockeying for political positions in the new era that the end of the war promises to bring. With this irreverent presentation of the nation's recent history, Š. not only aroused the anger of official Communist ideologists but also alienated some people in his home town. Š.'s main offense was to have ignored the tenets of SOCIALIST REALISM. Instead, he offered slang, a lot of talk about American jazz, and a suggestion of sex—all forbidden subjects.

In the ensuing propaganda campaign and purge Š. was one of the few people in any way connected with the publication of *Zbabělci* who did not lose his job, although he was removed as deputy editor-in-chief of *Světová literatura* and demoted to his old post as book editor, and for almost five years was in official disfavor. It was not until 1963, when the political climate had become less severe, that he was allowed to publish again. In *Legenda Emöke* (1963; *The Emöke Legend*, 1979) the nostalgia, sensitivity, and irony that characterize all of his work are perhaps brought to their height. It is the story of a budding love between a city cynic and a young widow from Slovakia, psychologically wounded by her first marriage. Their shy relationship is frustrated

by the brutal intrigue of a mediocre and egotistic man. In this figure, almost a caricature, Š. bitterly attacks everything philistine and despicable that the new Communist state has bred.

In two collections of short stories Š. focused on subjects that can be traced through most of his fiction. The overall theme of *Sedmiramenný svícen* (1964; the seven-branched candelabra) is the tragic fate of the Jews of Czechoslovakia under the Nazi occupation. *Babylónský příběh* (1967; the Babylonian story) contains the long story "Bassaxofon" ("The Bass Saxophone," 1979), which proclaims Š.'s lifelong love of jazz.

The translating of American detective fiction led him to write a series of essays, collected in *Nápady čtenáře detektivek* (1965; reflections of a detective-story reader), examining the origins and rules of the genre, as well as the work of its chief exponents. Some of Š.'s own detective stories have been made into successful films. He used a thrillerlike plot in *Lvíče* (1969; *Miss Silver's Past*, 1975), which satirizes life in a state publishing house in Prague.

Drawing once again on his own experience, this time in the Czechoslovak army in the 1950s, Š., before he left Czechoslovakia, wrote the satirical novel *Tankový prapor* (1971; *Republic of Whores*, 1993). Its publication in Czechoslovakia was prevented by the change in the political climate that followed the Soviet invasion in 1968.

Mirákl (1972; *The Miracle Game*, 1991), published, like all of his postemigration works, in Canada, draws a sometimes comic, sometimes sad picture of the rise and fall of the reform movement in Czechoslovakia. It is a roman à clef with a quasi-detective-story plot, and well-known public figures are only lightly disguised in it. The communist system is depicted by Š. as one that did away with the need for charity, but at the same time as one that destroyed the charity of the heart.

In exile Š. has remained prolific. The number of translations of his works and his reputation in the West have been growing. He was awarded the Neustadt International Prize for Literature in 1980.

Š.'s most important book of his emigration period is *Příběh inženýra lidských duší* (1977; *An Engineer of Human Souls*, 1983), a complex novel that interweaves several story lines in narrative and epistolary forms, occurring at different times and places. They are connected by Š.'s customary alter ego, Danny Smiřický, now a university professor in Toronto, who tries to convey to his students his experience of totalitarianism by elucidating from this point of view the message contained in masterworks of English and American literature. The different planes of the novel encompass hilarious satire as well as tragedy; of particular interest are scenes from the life of Czech émigrés in Canada.

Published in 1984, *Scherzo capriccioso* (*Dvorak in Love*, 1986), is a novel about Czech composer Antonín Dvořák's stay in America. The work pays homage to the mysterious essence of the creative genius, which occasionally manifests itself in man, dealing also with the themes of love and death and producing a complex picture of 19th-c. U.S. and Bohemia. *Nevěsta z Texasu* (1992; *A Bride from Texas*) is an account of the fortunes of Czechs in the American Civil War.

Over the years since he left Czechoslovakia, Š. has made a valuable contribution to the cultural life of Canada. In Czechoslovakia his popularity diminished little in the two decades during which he was officially a non-person; Š.'s new books, brought from the West, continued to be read there clandestinely. After the fall of communism, a feature film was made of Š.'s satirical novel *Tankový prapor* in Prague, while his collection of nostalgic short stories *Prima sezóna* (1975; *The Swell Season*, 1982), set in a small Czech town during the war and dealing with a young man's attempts to court girls, became a highly successful TV series.

Š. was one of the main intellectual personalities of Czech exile and on many occasions the spokesman for his fellow writers silenced at home.

FURTHER WORKS: *Ze života lepší společnosti* (1965); *Smutek poručíka Borůvky* (1966; *The Mournful Demeanor of Lieutenant Boruvka*, 1973); *Konec nylonového věku* (1967); *O nich—o nás* (1968); *Farářův konec* (1969, with Evald Schorm); *Hořkej svět* (1969); *All the Bright Young Men and Women* (1971); *Hříchy pro pátera Knoxe* (1973); *Prima sezóna* (1975; *The Swell Season*, 1982); *Konec poručíka Borůvky* (1975); *Samožerbuch* (1977; with Zdena Salivarová); *Na brigádě* (1979, with Antonín Brousek); *Nezoufejte* (1979); *Velká povídka o Americe* (1980); *Bůh do domu* (1980); *Dívka z Chicaga* (1980); *Návrat poručíka Borůvky* (1981); *Jiří Menzel and the History of the Closely Watched Trains* (1982); *Scherzo capriccioso* (1983). FURTHER WORKS IN ENGLISH: *Talking Moscow Blues* (1988); *The End of Lieutenant Borůvka* (1989); *The Return of Lieutenant Borůvka* (1990); *Sins for Father Knox* (1990)

BIBLIOGRAPHY: Kohák, E. V., on *The Cowards, Dissent*, 17 (1970): 543–56; Ascherson, N., on *The Cowards, NYRB* (19 Nov. 1970), 45; Liehm, A. J., *The Politics of Culture* (1972): 153–80; Mihailovich, V. D., et al., eds., *Modern Slavic Literatures* (1976), Vol. II: 192–98; special Š. issue *WLT*, 54, 5 (1980); Pletánek, V., "The Language and Style of Š.'s *The Cowards*," *CSP*, 23 (1981): 384–93; French, A., *Czech Writers and Politics, 1945–1969* (1982): 129–32 and passim; ; Kalish, J., *J. Š.: A Checklist* (1986); Trensky, P. I., *The Fiction of J. Š.* (1991)

—IGOR HÁJEK

SLAUERHOFF, Jan Jacob

Dutch novelist and poet, b. 15 Sept. 1898, Leeuwarden; d. 5 Oct. 1936, Hilversum

From his graduation from medical school in Amsterdam in 1923 almost until his death, S. worked as a ship's physician, in which capacity he visited the Dutch East Indies, China, Japan, the West Indies, South America, and South Africa. He also traveled extensively in France and Spain, and for a brief period practiced medicine in Tangier. His adventurous career, while providing the inspiration for much of his writing, was itself a manifestation of his essentially romantic yearning for another world. An incurable and ultimately fatal disease contributed to his feeling of being an outsider in his time and society.

S. published his prolific lyric work in the leading literary journals, beginning with his 1921 debut in *Het getij*, which was then the focal point of a radical renewal in Dutch poetry. But his verse did not meet with unqualified acceptance by literary critics, some of whom objected to its often careless execution. Others, however, applauded the informality of S.'s poetic diction, which was consistent with the emphasis on ethics rather than aesthetics, propounded by the journal *Forum*. The spokesman for this view, Edgar du PERRON, was instrumental in winning wide recognition for S. Actually, S. felt more affinity with the "poètes maudits" like Trist an Corbière (1845–1875) than with any contemporary writers.

In several novels and short stories S. assumed the same creative stance and showed the same preference for exotic settings as in his poetry. The novels *Het verboden rijk* (1932; the forbidden realm) and *Het leven opaarde* (1934; life on earth) deal with the identity crises and existential despair of a ship's officer who in many respects is S.'s alter ego. In *Het verboden rijk*, the hero is mysteriously drawn to Macao, where he becomes aware of a profound affinity with the 16th-c. Portuguese poet Luís Vaz de Camões (1524?–1580), which ultimately leads to the extinction of all sense of self. *Het leven op aarde* is set in China, where the protagonist finally finds the longed-for oblivion in opium. A third work in this series was projected but never written; however, a short novel, *De opstand van Guadalajara* (1937; the uprising of Guadalajara), also deals with an outsider who seeks refuge from his own society in an exotic land.

Flawed though S.'s work may be, in its technical weaknesses no less than in the overly sentimental Weltschmerz it expresses, an unmistakable element of genuine feeling makes it stand out from most Dutch writing of the 1920s and 1930s. S.'s fascination with faraway places provides welcome relief from the generally restricted thematic range of Dutch literature.

FURTHER WORKS: *Archipel* (1923); *Clair obscur* (1927); *Oost-Azië* (1928, under pseud. John Ravenswood); *Fleurs de Marécage* (1928); *Eldorado* (1928); *Saturnus* (1930); *Yoeng poe Tsjoeng* (1930); *Serenade* (1930); *Schuim en asch* (1930); *Het lente-eiland* (1930); *Jan Pietersz. Coen* (1931); *Soleares* (1933); *Een eerlijk zeemansgraf* (1936); *Verzamelde werken* (8 vols., 1940–1958); *Dagboek* (1957); *De laatste reis van de Nyborg; Het eind van het lied* (1958); *Verzamelde gedichten* (1961); *Ster* (1973); *Een bezoek aan Makallah* (1975)

BIBLIOGRAPHY: Meijer, R. P., *Literature of the Low Countries*, new ed. (1978): 329–32

—EGBERT KRISPYN

SLAVEYKOV, Pencho

Bulgarian poet and critic, b. 27 April 1866, Tryavna; d. 28 May 1912, Como Brunate, Italy

S. was the youngest son of Petko Rachov S. (1827–1895), who was a pioneer journalist and poet, and doyen of the Bulgarian National Revival. In 1882 S. had an accident that left him lame, yet (as with the heroes of his poems), this misfortune seemed to strengthen his character and sharpen his mind. He studied philosophy and aesthetics in Leipzig from 1892 to 1898. While preparing his thesis on Heine and Russia, he contributed satires on the dictatorial regime of Stefan Stambolov to the Sofia literary monthly *Misul*, edited by his friend Dr. Krustyo Krustev (1866–1919).

Back in Sofia, S. became assistant director and finally director of the National Library; he took a year's leave to direct the National Theater (1908–9). Despite being nominated for a Nobel Prize, he was dismissed in June 1911 by the minister of education for attacking the unprogressive character of the Slav Congress held in Sofia in 1910. This treatment embittered him and probably hastened his death; he retired abroad with his devoted friend, the poetess Mara Belcheva (1868–1937).

S.'s early work includes the lyrics in *Momini sulzi* (1888; maidens' tears), influenced by Heine's *Book of Songs*, and the translations he did with Aleko Konstantinov (1863–1897) from the Russian, notably of Lermontov's *Demon*. With his *Epicheski pesni* (2 vols., 1896–98; rev. in 1 vol., 1970; epic songs), the second volume of which bears the title *Blyanove* (daydreams), S. became central figure of the *Misul* circle, a leading literary mentor and patron of young writers, notably Peyo YAVOROV and Petko Todorov (1879–1916). His preface to Yavorov's *Stikhotvorenia* (1904; verses) was an attack on Ivan Vazov's (1850–1921) preface to a book of poems of the same title (1903) by Kiril Khristov (1875–1944); here and in his essays and reviews S. eloquently defended the freedom and integrity of the creative personality. In a literature before then (and mostly since) heavily committed to religious, national, or sociopolitical causes, S. was a rebel of unusual stature. Advocating a new "individualism," he joined Krustev in condemning tendentiousness and topicality.

With Krustev, too, S. first challenged the laureateship of Vazov. In contrast to Vazov's patriots' gallery in his poetic cycle "Epopeya na zabravenite" (1881; epic of the forgotten), S. ranged beyond Bulgarian history and lore (though he included them) in his similarly titled *Epicheski pesni*. Reflecting perhaps his own strong sense of life's struggles, he chose among his epic subjects Prometheus, the 4th-c. B.C. Greek hetaera Phryne, Beethoven, Shelley, the poet Nikolaus Lenau (1802–1850), aiming to identify in them genius at the very peak of spiritual and artistic achievement. Accused of irrelevant "Europeanism," S. offered these ideal

portrayals as models for a renascence to follow the then-recent national liberation, "to extricate the man in the Bulgarian."

S. drew inspiration both from Nietzschean superman idealism and from the humanism of Heine and the 19th-c. Russian novelists. They had "sought out the man in the beast"—the very antithesis of Zola's naturalism, which S. found repugnant. Moods of elation and despair reflecting S.'s high ideals and fury at *fasulkovtski* (the philistines of contemporary society) mark his later lyrics in *Sun za shtastie* (1907; a dream of happiness) and particularly *Na ostrova na blazhenite* (1910; on the isles of the blessed), a largely autobiographical anthology of imagined poets who represent facets of his own muse. S.'s magnum opus, a national epic on the abortive anti-Turkish uprising of 1876, *Kurvava pesen* (Vol. I, 1913; a song of blood), was never completed.

S. never enjoyed Vazov's popularity, nor did he seek it; he rated public taste low. Criticized as a "cerebral" poet, he could write lighthearted vignettes of the countryside as well as profound testaments like "Psalom na poeta" (1904; the poet's psalm). He introduced philosophical themes into Bulgarian poetry, practicing no less than preaching new literary ideals.

Despite his chronic physical and mental anguish, S. labored devotedly to enhance Bulgarian literature's standing by collecting folksongs, providing the material for Henry Baerlein's selection of Bulgarian folk songs in translation, *The Shade of the Balkans* (1904), published in London, and translating from German and, through it, from other literatures as well.

FURTHER WORKS: *Nemski poeti* (1911); *Subrani suchineniya* (8 vols., 1958–1959)

BIBLIOGRAPHY: Pinto, V., ed., Introduction to *Bulgarian Prose and Verse* (1957): xxviii–xxix; Moser, C. A., *A History of Bulgarian Literature, 865–1944* (1972): 128–34

—VIVIAN PINTO

SŁONIMSKI, Antoni

Polish poet, dramatist, novelist, satirist, and critic, b. 15 Oct. 1895, Warsaw; d. 4 July 1976, Warsaw

Born into a prominent Warsaw family, S. studied art in Warsaw and Munich before finding his vocation as a writer. He made his formal literary debut with the publication of a volume of neoclassical sonnets, *Sonety* (1918; sonnets). In the same year he collaborated in the organization of the lively literary café, Pikador. The Pikador writers (known as the Skamander poets after their literary journal was founded in 1920) were perhaps the most popular literary grouping in Poland in the 1920s and 1930s. S. contributed a number of witty topical satirical sketches to the Pikador/Skamander repertoire, some of these written in collaboration with his lifelong friend, Julian TUWIM. During the inter-war years S. also served as critic for several Warsaw newspapers, contributing a weekly feuilleton of trenchant social and political commentary to *Wiadomości literackie* from 1927 through 1939. Selected columns were reprinted as *Kroniki tygodniowe 1927–1939* (1956; weekly chronicles 1927–1939).

S. fled Poland after the German invasion in September 1939 and spent the war years in Paris and London. His patriotic poems of this period, most notably the volume *Alarm* (1940; alarm), which went through at least six editions, and the long narrative poem about the Warsaw of his youth, *Popiół i wiatr* (1942; ashes and wind), were extraordinarily popular. S. worked for UNESCO from 1946 through 1948, resigning to serve as Poland's cultural representative in London. He returned to Warsaw in 1951 where, until his death in 1976, his was one of the most consistently brave and enlightened voices in the politically charged atmosphere of communist Poland.

For much of his life S. was an energetic traveler. His poems of the 1920s are suffused with the adventure of travel. During the 1930s historical events introduced catastrophic presentiments into S.'s always politically sensitive verse. His poems from these years, like his feuilletons, comedies, and the novel *Dwa kónca świata* (1937; two ends of the world) portray a world in imminent danger of collapse. The poems of the war years are marked by poignant nostalgia for the lost country and beliefs of his youth. In the post war years S. often addressed the question of the compatibility of scientific and technical progress with humane civilization.

In all the genres in which he wrote S. most characteristically posed as a somewhat detached observer, offering urbane or scathing commentary on the follies of modern society. His rational humanism was a steadying note during the turbulent decades in which he produced his work.

FURTHER WORKS: *Facecje republikańskie* (1919, with Jan Lechoń); *Harmonia: Wieniec sonetów* (1919); *Parada* (1920); *Pierwsza szopka warszawska* (1922; with Julian Tuwim and Jan Lechoń); *Teatr w więzieniu* (1922); *Czy chcesz być dowcipny: Straszliwe opowieści "na wesoło"* (1923, under pseud. Antoni Bączek, with Magdalena Samozwaniec); *Dialog o miłości ojczyzny między Josephem a Stefanem* (1923); *Godzina poezji* (1923); *Droga na wschód* (1924); *Torpeda czasu: Powieść fantastyczna* (1924); *Pod zwrotnikami: Dziennik okrętowy* (1925); *Z dalekiej podróży: Poezje* (1926); *Wieża Babel: Dramat w 3 aktach* (1927); *O dzieciach, wariatach i grafomanach* (1927); *Polityczna szopka "Cyrulika Warszawskiego"* (1927, with Marian Hemar, Jan Lechoń and Julian Tuwim); *Oko w oko: Poemat* (1928); *Król Amanullach, czarny władca* (1928); *Murzyn warszawski: Komedia w 3 aktach* (perf. 1928, pub. 1935); *Mętne łby* (1929); *Szopka polityczna 1930* (1930, with Marian Hemar, Jan Lechoń and Julian Tuwim); *Lekarz bezdomny: Komedia w 3 aktach* (1930); *Moje walki nad bzdurą* (1932); *Moja podróż do Rossji* (1932); *Rodzina: Komedia w 3 aktach* (1933); *Heretyk na ambonie* (1934); *Okno bez krat: Poezje* (1935); *W beczce przez Niagarę* (1936); *Wiek Klęski: Wiersze z lat 1939–1945* (1945); *Wspomnienia warszawskie: Szkice literackie* (1957); *Liryki* (1958); *W oparach absurdu* (1958, with Julian Tuwim); *Artykuły pierwszej potrzeby: Notatki i uwagi 1951–1958* (1959); *Nowe wiersze* (1959); *Rozmowa z gwiazdą: Poezje z lat 1919–1961* (1961); *Załatwione odmownie* (1962); *Wiersze 1958–1963* (1963); *Poezje zebrane* (1964); *Jawa i mrzonka: Spowiedź emigranta: Jak to było naprawdę* (1966); *Jedna strona medalu: Felietony i artykuły z lat 1918–1968* (1971); *Obecność: Felietony z lat 1971–1972* (1973); *138 wierszy* (1973); *Wiersze* (1974); *Alfabet wspomnień* (1975)

BIBLIOGRAPHY: Miłosz, C., *The History of Polish Literature* (1969): 393–95; Mihailovich, V. D., et al., eds., *Modern Slavic Literatures* (1976), Vol. 2: 399-401

—MADELINE G. LEVINE

SLOVAK LITERATURE

The literary history of the Slovaks is closely connected with that of the Czechs, both because of the great similarities between their languages and because of their common political history. From the 15th c., Czech was used, along with Latin, as the literary language of the Slovaks; seldom do we find a literary work in Slovak before the beginning of the 19th c. But since the 1840s, Slovak has been used almost exclusively as the literary medium in Slovakia.

Throughout the 19th c. and until the end of World War I Slovak literature was primarily an instrument in the struggle for national survival against ever-increasing oppression by the kingdom of Hungary, of which Slovakia was a part until 1918. The first concern of the Slovak writers was with fighting for the right of the people to use the Slovak language in schools and in public life and with helping to develop national consciousness.

The literary scene in the 1880s and 1890s was dominated by Svetozár Hurban Vajanský (1847–1916), a journalist and literary critic, writer of romantic poetry, and author of several novels in which the influence of Russian realists was discernible. Like Ján Kollár (1973–1852) and other earlier Czech and Slovak pan-Slavists he believed in Russia as a liberator of all the oppressed Slavic peoples.

Some younger Slovak intellectuals, dissatisfied with the conservative ideas and political passivity of Vajanský and his followers, and seeking closer cooperation with the Czechs, founded the monthly *Hlas* in 1898. In literature the so-called *hlasisti* rejected romanticism and sought to promote realism, stressing at the same time the social function of literature.

Both romanticism and realism appear in the poetry of Pavol Országh Hviezdoslav (1849–1921), whose epic-lyric poems, such as *Hájnikova žena* (1886; the forester's wife), as well as his antiwar poems in *Krvavé sonety* (1919; *Bloody Sonnets*, 1950) are among the most popular Slovak books. The short stories and novels of Martin KUKUČÍN, however, are dominated by realistic elements.

Among Kukučín's followers was Jozef Gregor-Tajovský (1874–1940), who, like his mentor, dealt in his stories with the life of Slovak villagers; he was also an accomplished playwright. Themes taken from village life also appear in the works of Timrava (pseud. of Božena Slančcíková, 1867–1951). In her almost NATURALISTIC stories she often used the colloquial language of her peasant protagonists. Another writer with naturalist tendencies was Jégé (pseud. of Ladislav Nádaši, 1866–1940). His bet-known novel, *Adam Šsangala* (1923; Adam Šangala) is set during the Counter-Reformation. Jégé also wrote several comedies satirizing the petty doings of small-town people. The short stories and novels of Kristína Royová (1867–1937), imbued with moral and religious preoccupations, were avidly read at home and widely translated abroad, although many of them lack artistic value.

The most popular Slovak playwright of the pre-World War I period was Ferko Urbánek (1859–1934), author of some fifty plays, all of them patriotic and didactic, generally shallow and excessively sentimental.

The generation of intellectuals grouped around the journals *Sborík slovenskej mládeže* (founded 1909) and *Prúdy* (1909–1914) produced a literary school influenced by SYMBOLISM and known as Slovak MODERNISM. The most representative members of this school are the poet Ivan KRASKO, Janko Jesenský (1874–1945), and Martin Rázus (1888–1937). Jesenský wrote subjective poetry before publishing his best-known work, the two-volume novel

Demokrati (1934–37; the democrats), in which he satirized the bureaucracy of the young republic. Rázus was the author of fiery and tendentious patriotic, social, and political verse; one of his best-known collections is *Z tichých i búrnych chvíl* (1919; from times quiet and stormy), which he wrote as a protest against the cruelties of World War I. Rázus also published several novels, notably the four-volume *Svety* (1929; the words), portraying the contemporary countryside and political milieu. Another representative of the modernists was Vladimír Roy (1885–1935), the author of melancholy and dreamy verse, and an accomplished translator of English, French, and German poetry.

After the establishment of the republic of Czechoslovakia in 1918, a spectacular cultural expansion took place in Slovakia. In the 1920s and 1930s every major literary movement of the time was represented among the increasingly numerous Slovak writers. Several of the older writers, whose reputations had been established prior to 1918, continued publishing after the liberation.

In the postwar years a new group of writers emerged. The prose writers of this "middle" generation included Jozef Cíger-Hronský (1896–1960), the author of several books for children and of such important novels as *Pisár Gráč* (1933; the scribe Gráč) and *Andreas Bur Majster* (1947; Master Andreas Bur), written in lyrical prose.

The best-known poets of the 1920s and 1930s were Ján Smrek (pseud. of Ján Čietek, b. 1899) and Emil Boleslav Lukáč (1900–1979), both also active as editors of literary magazines. Smrek wrote patriotic verse and love poems notable for their vitality. Lukáč's symbolic, meditative, and patriotic verse is rather sad and pessimistic in tone.

During this period several younger writers wrote poetry inspired by their Roman Catholic faith. Noteworthy among them are Andrej Žarnov (pseud. of František Šubík, b. 1903) and Rudolf Dilong (b. 1905). Žarnov published patriotic and meditative poems, while the Franciscan priest Rudolf Dilong, the most prolific among contemporary Slovak poets, writes ruralistic, religious, and patriotic verse. Both Žarnov and Dilong live in exile in the U.S.

Milo Urban (b. 1904), another writer influenced by Catholicism, is the author of the trilogy *Živý bič* (1927; the living scourge), *Hmly na úsvite* (1930; the fog at dawn), and *V osídlach* (1940; in the trap). In *Živý bič*, one of the most significant and widely read Slovak novels of the interwar period, Urban dramatically portrays the life of a Slovak village during World War I; the other two works describe the country side in the 1920s and 1930s.

In the early 1920s a group of young Marxist intellectuals became associated with the periodical *DAV* (1924–37). The most prominent members of this group are the poet Ladislav NOVOMESKÝ, who wrote largely proletarian but occasionally lyric and meditative poetry, and the Czech-born Peter JILEMNICKÝ, author of numerous best-selling socially conscious novels.

The leading Slovak playwright in the interwar period was Ivan Stodola (1888–1977), whose realistic plays satirize the shortcomings and vices of individuals as well as society. Some of Stodola's more successful plays are *Jožko Púčik a jeho kariéra* (1931; Joe Púčik and his career) and *Kráľ Svätopluk* (1931; King Svatopluk).

During the first three years after World War II Czechoslovakia was ruled by a coalition government, and both Czech and Slovak literature displayed a certain freedom, as indicated by the saying of the time: "Everything is allowed except the criticism of the Russians." The most interesting poets of this period were Rudolf Fábry (b. 1915) and Vladimír Reisel (b. 1919), both strikingly influenced by SURREALISM. The first book of the Slovak *nadrealisti*,

Fábry's *Uťaté ruky* (the severed hands), had been published as early as 1935, and his *Vodné hodiny, piesočné hodiny* (the waterclock, the hourglass) soon followed in 1938. But the movement did not develop fully until after 1945 with the publication of another book by Fábry, *Já je niekto iný* (1946; I is somebody else).

The theoretician of surrealism was Vladimír Reisel, a writer of great poetic imagination who published literary essays and several volumes of poems. A large selection of his love poems came out in 1979 under the title *Premeny milovania* (the metamorphoses of loving).

Among Slovak poets after the Communist takeover, permanent places belong to Ján Kostra (1910–1975) and Valentín Beniak (1894–1973), although their human experience and literary history are dissimilar. Kostra, the author of eighteen volumes of poems, whom the Communist regime rewarded in many ways, including the bestowal of the all-important title of "National Artist," wrote exquisite love poems, social and humanistic poetry, but also shallow and ingratiating political verse during the Stalinist period. The themes that Valentín Beniak handles best are love of nature, of a woman, and of his family and country, and religious motifs. After the war, he was not allowed to publish and it was not until 1966 that a selection of his religious and patriotic poems, some of them truly charming, others profound, was issued under the title *Reťaz: z básnickej tvorby* (the chain: selection from poetic works). In the 1970s two slender volumes of Beniak's verse were also published.

Better-known prose writers are Ladislav MŇAČKO; František Hečko (1905–1960), author of the best-sellers *Červené víno* (1948; the red wine) and *Drevaná dedina* (1951; the wooden village); and Dominik Tatarka (b. 1913), noted for his wartime novel *Farská republika* (1948; the priests' republic). In drama the works by Peter KARVAŠ and Štefan Králik (b. 1909) were received with considerable attention. Králik wrote a dozen plays, most mature among them being *Svätá Barbara* (1953; Saint Barbara), dealing with the plight of coal miners during World War I.

The Soviet invasion of Czechoslovakia in 1968 had a devastating effect on Slovak literature and on cultural life in general. Some forty writers were expelled from the Society of Slovak Writers, with the result that they not only cannot publish, but they themselves became "nonpersons" in public life. A few of them had their manuscripts circulated in typewritten form in *Edice Petlice* (the Padlock edition), the Czechoslovak equivalent of Russian *samizdat*. Several writers fled the country shortly after the invasion, among them Ladislav Mňačko, Jaroslava Blažková (b. 1933), who has written excellent short stories about contemporary youth, and Ladislav Grosman (b. 1921).

BIBLIOGRAPHY: Mráz, A., *Die Literatur der Slowaken* (1943); Otruba, M., and Pešat, Z., eds., Introduction to *The Linden Tree: An Anthology of Czech and Slovak Literature, 1890–1960* (1962): 13–21; Noge, J., *An Outline of Slovakian Literature* (1968); Kirschbaum, J. M., *Slovak Language and Literautre: Essays* (1975); Strmen, K., "Slovak Literature: A Brief History," in A. Cincura, ed., *An Anthology of Slovak Literature* (1976): xix–liv

—RUDOLF STERN

Slovak Literature since World War II

In the early 1950s the first wave of *schematism*, the simplified model of the SOCIALIST REALISM of the late 1920s and 1930s, dominated Slovak literature, as illustrated in Alfoz BEDNÀR's novel *Sklený vrch* (1954; The Glass Mountain) and as well in Milan Rùfus's (b. 1928) *Až dozrieme* (1956; When We Mature) and Miroslav Vàlek's (1927-1990) *Dotyky* (1959; The Touches), both collections of poetry.

Among the writers active before the Communist takeover in 1948 only a few continued to be productive, namely the novelist and essayist Dominik Tatarka, awarded the Jaroslav Seifert Prize (1986), with his short novel *Prútené kreslá* (1963; The Wicker Chairs), *Písačky* (1979; Scriblings), and *Navrávačky* (1988, Recordings) published in *samizdat* and abroad; younger surrealists Ivan Kupec (b. 1922) and Albert Marenčin (b. 1922); and the playwright Peter Karvaš.

With exceptions of Alfonz Bednár, namely his novels *Hromový zub* (1964; The Thunder Tooth) and *Deravý dukát* (wr. ca. 1972, pub. 1992; Perforated Coin) and novellas in *Hodiny a minúty* (1956; Hours and Minutes), Rudolf Jašík (1919-1960) with his novel *Námestie svätej Alžbety* (1958; Saint Elisabeth's Square), and Ladislav ťažký (b. 1924) with his novels *Amenmária. Samí dobrí vojaci* (1964; Amenmaria. Only Good Soldiers) and *Kŕdeľ divých Adamov* (1965; The Herd of Wild Adams), the development of prose was fostered by younger writers appearing since the early 1960s. The most important include best-selling Rudolf Sloboda (1938-1995), lyrical prose writer depicting village life, Vincent Šikula (b. 1936), existentialist and l'art-pour-l'artist Ján Johanides (b. 1934), postmodernists Pavel Vilikovský (b. 1941) and Pavel Hrúz (b. 1941), and traditionalists Ladislav Ballek (b. 1941) and Peter Jaroš (b. 1940). Dušan Dušek (b. 1946) and Dušan Mitana (b. 1946) are among the most accomplished short-story writers.

The most important contemporary poets are Milan Rúfus with his collections *Zvony* (1968; The Bells) and *Stôl chudobných* (1972; The Table of the Poor) and Miroslav Válek with *Príťažlivosť* (1961; The Attraction), *Nepokoj* (1963; The Restlessness), and *Milovanie v husej koži* (1965; Love-Making in the Goose Skin). Rúfus follows the line of Krasko-Novomeský's symbolisn and stresses the fundamental values of Christianity and archetypal peasants' life. Válek, who served as a member of Communist Politburo in the 1970s and 1980s, absorbed as the translator both modern Western and Slavic poetry, and developed a very skeptical, even cruel approach to man and mankind. In 1956 the manifesto of the *concretists* (or the so-called Trnava group) appeared, and since then Ľubomír Feldek (b. 1936), Ján Stacho (1936-1995), Ján Ondruš (b. 1932), and Jozef Mihalkovič (b. 1935) have dominated the scene, stressing both ethical and aesthetic values. Philosophically oriented Ján Buzássy (b. 1935), minimalist Štefan Strážay (b. 1940), and ruralist Štefan Moravčík (b. 1943) are also hugely appreciated. In the mid-1960s Ivan Štrpka (b. 1944), Ivan Laučík (b. 1944), and Peter Repka (b. 1944) entered Slovak poetry as the group *Osamelí bežci* (The Lonely Runners), and presented unconventional verses in which the influences of DADAISM and the beat generation are present.

Since theaters were firmly controlled by government censorship, only a few playwrights achieved artistic recognition, namely Stanislav Štepka (b. 1944) with his *Radošinské naivné divadlo* (The Naive Theater of Radošina), Milan Lasica (b. 1940), Július Satinský (b. 1941), and Karol Horák (b. 1943).

The generation that emerged during *perestroika,* which later called itself the barbaric generation, closely connected with extreme streams of pop-music, but only a few of them have demonstrated extraordinary literary qualities, notably poet and playwright

Viliam Klimáček (b. 1958) and poet Taťjana Lehenová (b. 1961), or achieved popular success like novelist Peter Pišťanek (b. 1960).

—BRAŇO HOCHEL

Hungarian Literature in Slovakia

Amid the political and social upheavals that have shaken central and eastern Europe since World War I, Hungarian literature in Slovakia, formerly northern Hungary, evolved along three occasionally overlapping ideological lines. Some poets and writers congregating in various literary circles, such as the Kazinczy Kör, sought to preserve national Hungarian traditions while experimenting with avantgarde poetic and dramatic forms. The influence of ADY and other SYMBOLISTS is clearly discernible in the poems of the priest-poet László Mécs (b. 1895)—*Hajnali harangszó* (1923; bells at dawn); *Rabszogák énekelnek* (1925; slaves sing)—which reflect a deep social consciousness inspired by Christian compassion. His contemporary, László Ölvedi (1903–1931) used allegorical forms to express a militant commitment to the preservation of the Hungarian minorities' cultural identity, as in *A bányász éneke* (1923; the song of the miner). The ideological orientation of another group reflected their growing concern over problems created by the emergence of extreme-rightist trends. The most prominent representative of that group, Dezső Győry (b. 1900), used a variety of literary forms—poems, essays, and later, novels—to promote a world view inspired by humanism, pacifism, and the respect for moral truth. A similar tone is struck in the short stories of Viktor Egri (b. 1898), whose later plays, such as *A Gedeon ház* (1936; the Gedeon house) and *Közös út* (1951; common road) provide a realistic insight into the social and psychological problems of the Slovak-Hungarian villages. Social protest couched in witty, satirical form is the hallmark of Dezső Vozáry's (b. 1904) Villonesque poetry.

The arrival of Hungarian émigrés in Czechoslovakia, seeking refuge after the collapse of Béla Kun's Communist regime (1919), added strong stimulus to the emergence of literary trends of markedly socialist orientation. Among the poets who sought to express Marxist commitment in expressionist forms, Imre Forbáth (1898–1967) attracted considerable attention. The social problems of the peasantry provide the main theme for József Sellyei's (1909–1941) well-constructed novels and short stories. Béla Szabó's (b. 1906) best novel, *A család kedvence* (1957; the favorite of the family) re-creates the suffocating atmosphere of the Nazi era. Protest against racism along with polemical advocacy of so-called "socialist culture" is the hallmark of Zoltán Fábry's (b. 1897) critical oeuvre.

In recent decades, Tibor Babi's (b. 1925) poetry, Béla Lovicsek's (b. 1923) realistic novels, and Teréz Dávid's (b. 1906) psychological plays testified to the continuing vitality of Hungarian literature in Slovakia.

—ANN DEMAITRE

SLOVENE LITERATURE

In the late 19th c. Slovene literature was dominated by three significant currents: naturalism, professed by young writers gathered around the magazine *Vesna* (1892-94); Catholicism, the representatives of which demanded that national literature be based on Christian foundations because they regarded the Christian worldview as the bearer of true beauty; and liberalism, advocating the artistic right to aesthetic subjectivism.

The literature of *moderna*, the modernist period extending from 1895 to the end of World War I, inspired by the intellectual turbulence of Vienna, found its representatives in Slovene literature in Dragotin Kette (1876-1899), Josip Murn-Aleksandrov (1879-1901), Ivan CANKAR, and Oton ŽUPANČIČ . The breakthrough of MODERNISM was marked by two publications in 1899: Cankar's *Erotika* (Erotica) and Župančič's *Čaša Opojnosti* (A Cup of Ecstacy), which introduced SYMBOLISM and poetic impressionism into Slovene literature. Kette is primarily a light-hearted poet of love, reflection, and nature, leaning towards "folk" expression, whereas the poetry of Murn-Aleksandrov reaches to nature for its motives, mostly to evoke dark and complex moods, as in *Pesmi in Romance* (1903; Poems and Romances). At the same time the circle around the magazine *Dom in Svet* promoted realism. Fran S. Finžgar (1871-1962) concentrated his epic talent on village life in prose and drama, notably with his historic novel *Pod Svodobnim Soncem* (1906-7; Under a Free Sun), which was in critical opinion intended to complement the epic of Slovene thought and history. Fran Ksaver Meško (1874-1964) wrote realistic and symbolist poetic sketches.

After World War I literary currents developed simultaneously in several directions. On one side were the followers of *moderna*, influenced by the techniques of symbolism and impressionism. Alojz Gradnik (1882-1967) in his powerful love poetry fluctuates between *eros* and *thanatos* and man's tragic dislocation with nature, illustrated in *Padajoče Zvezde* (1916; Falling Stars). Revolutionary moods appear in poems by Fran Albreht (1889-1963). Igo Gruden (1893-1948) developed from a poet full of vitality, zest for life, and revolutionary national spirit to one depicting the crisis of the European consciousness in the Nazi era.

Toward the end of *moderna*, many writers began to intensively search for new modes of expression. In his travelogue *S Puta* (1913; From a Journey) Izidor Cankar (1886-1958) turned to psychological prose in the spirit of modern Dostojevskian intellectualism, and this mode of philosophical narrative soon became established as a significant element of modern Slovene literature. Vladimir Levstik (1886-1957) depicted in his best work, the war novel *Gadje Gnezdo* (1918; Snake Nest), the psychology of the Slovene national being, synthesizing in a specific way the national and the cosmopolitan spirit. Ivan Pregelj (1883-1960) explores the dilemma of the relationship between the physical and the spiritual. In his historic novels he paints the rebellious nature of the people of the Tolmine area, with accent on the psychology of the mass, as in *Tolminci* (1916; The People of Tolmin), and of the individual, as in *Štefan Golja i Njegovi* (1919; Štefan Golja and His Fellows).

The most fruitful of the more recent writers, France Bevk (1890-1970), used the analytical method to explore hidden corners in the psychology of the people in the mountains of Primorje, and introduced into Slovene literature the everyday life of the common man. The initial preoccupation of Juš Kozak (1892-1964), who portrayed the passing of old Ljubljana, was to approach complex passions by almost naturalist methods. Later he became increasingly troubled by the destiny of European culture and the ultimate meaning of human existence. Other representatives of the psychological approach are Ferdo Kozak (1894-1957), Vladimir Bartol (1903-1967), and Bogomir Magajna (1904-1964).

Futurism and expressionism in prose contested the validity of impressionism and neoromanticism. Vague desires and the atmosphere of beauty were repressed by vociferous rhetoric and harsh metaphor, saturated with protest against the decay of social and moral values of society, illustrated by such writers as France Bevk, visionary Miran Jarc (1900-1942), and Anton Podbevšek (b. 1898), who successfully experimented with forms of visual poetry. Socially engaged and revolutionary expressionists include Mile Klopčič (b. 1905), with his collections of poems *Plamteči Okovi* (1924; Flaming Chains), dedicated to Lenin, and *Preposte Pesmi* (1934; Simple Poems), Tone Seliškar (1900-1969), and Srečko Kosovel (1904-1926). Together with the painter Avgust Černigoj, Kosovel edited the magazine *Konstruktor* (1925) and conducted poetic experiments in the manner of constructionalist poetics. The main representative of Catholic expressionism is Anton Vodnik (1901-1965), whose poems are predominantly based on the theme of love, notably with the collection entitled *Žalostne Roke* (1922; Sad Hands). Another expressionist was Slavko Grum (1901-1949), with the plays *Trudni Zastori* (1924; Heavy Curtains), *Upornik* (1926; Rebel), and *Dogodek v Mestu Gogi* (1930; What Happened in the Town of Goga).

In the 1930s a new generation of writers took Slovene literature into artistically more moderate waters. They gathered mostly round the magazine *Sodobnost* (1933-41), founded by Josip Vidmar (1895-1991), the leading critic of the generation, Ferdo Kozak, Stanko Leben, and Fran Albreht (dates n.a.). These writers shared a common Marxist ideology. They depicted and professed things important to the common man, a desire for freedom and connection with land. The most important representatives of this socially engaged literature are Miško Kranjec (b. 1908), the voice of the proletarianized village, illustrated in *Poves o dobrih ljudeh* (1940; A Story of Good People); Lovro Kuhar (1893-1950), who wrote under the pseudonym of Prežihov Voranc; Ciril Kosmač (b. 1910), whose novels from the interwar period mostly deal with national issues; Anton Ingolič (b. 1907); Ivan Potrč (b. 1913), as the most convincing representative of "village" fiction; and Bratko Kreft (1905-1997), who mostly presented current ethical problems of the society in dramas of historical content, as in *Celjski Grofje* (1932; The Counts of Celje).

At the onset of World War II most writers joined Osvodobilna Fronta (the Liberation Front). Most distinguished among numerous anonymous and known partisan poets are Matej Bor (pseud. of Vladimir Pavšič, b. 1913), with partisan songs and moving ballads, illustrated in his collection of poems entitled *Previharimo Viharje* (1942; Let Us Outstorm the Storms); Karel Destovnik Kajuh (1922-1944), with sentimental poetry in the traditional manner; and Jože Udovič (b. 1912), with a manifest tendency toward the grotesque. The postwar literature for the most part retained the spirit and stylistic divisions of the interwar period, but also a new generation of writers appeared who sought their models and inspiration in global intellectual movements and phenomena. At the beginning of the 1950s Slovene literature was influenced by the writers of the lost generation, especially the fiction of Ernest HEMINGWAY, and by contemporary American dramaists such as Eugene O'NEILL, Arthur MILLER, and Tennessee WILLIAMS, as well as French and German existential philosophy. However, authors such as Prežihov Voranc, Miško Kranjec, Anton Ingolič, Juš Kozak, Edvard Kocbek, and Vladimir Kralj (dates n.a.) remained true to the realistic and sociorealistic method. The STREAM-OF-CONSCIOUSNESS novel, with its precise exploration of the psychological world, is represented by Matej Bor, Ciril Kosmač (b.

1925), and Beno Zupančič (dates n.a.), notably in *Sedmina* (1925; One Seventh), as well as by writers from Trieste—Boris Pahor (b. 1913) and Alojz Rebula (b. 1924). Psychoanalytic prose was written by Andrej Hieng (b. 1925), Lojze Kovačič (b. 1928), and—in its most extreme form—by Peter Božič (dates n.a.). The most significant poets include Jože Udovič, Matej Bor, whose poetry expresses his concern for man's destiny in the atomic age, and Cene Vipotnik (b. 1914). New tendencies in poetry were formulated by the magazines *Besed* and *Revija 57*, and their practical application were realized in Dane Zajc's *Pož gana Trava* (1958; Burned Grass), Vene Taufer's *Svinčene Zvezde* (1958; Lead Stars), and Gregor Strniša's (dates n.a.) *Mozaici* (1959; Mosaics).

Ideologically and aesthetically, the poets of the 1960s and the first half of the 1970s were, in spite of individual differences or even contrasts, quite uniform. By the middle of the 1970s three major tendencies crystallized: the traditional current, based on the romantic discrepancy between ideals and reality and often connected with the old duality of the town and the village, illustrated by Tone Kuntner and France Vurnik; a current based on the belief in universal human values and the special mission of poetry, illustrated by Marko Kravos, Janez Premk and, partly, Andrej Medved; and a current that insisted on absurd activity as man's only possible course of action, employing the use of philosophical language, illustrated by Braco Rotar and Vladimir Gajšek, or metaphoric expression, illustrated by Jože Snoj, Valentin Cundrič, Evald Fisar, and Franček Rudolf (dates n.a.).

The most distinctive poets of this period are Ivan Minatti (b. 1927), a poet obsessed with the question of discord between man and the world, notably in *Pesmi* (1971; Poems), Ciril Zlobec (b. 1925), the author of *Pesmi Jeze in Ljubezni* (1968; Poems of Love and Hate), Janez Menart (b. 1929), who sought concord between the subject and reality, notably in *Bela Pravljica* (1963; A White Tale), Kajetan Kovič (b. 1931), also preoccupied with the relationship between man and reality, as in *Ogenjvoda* (1965; Firewater), Dane Zajc (b. 1929), the author of *Ubijavci Kač* (1968; Snake Killers), and Gregor Strniša, a hermetic existentialist, the author of *Zvezde* (1965; Stars). Formal poetic experiments are characteristic of Veno Taufer (b. 1933), Franci Zagoričnik (1933-1997), and Tomaš Šalamun (b. 1941).

The most significant prose writers of the 1970s include Pavle Zidar (pseud.of Zdravko Slamnik, b. 1932), fascinated by the phenomenon of corporeality and transitoriness, notably in *Dim Ki Diši Po Sestri Juli* (1970; Smoke with the Scent of Sister Jula), and Rudi Šeligo (b. 1935), the founder of the Slovenian variant of the *roman nouveau* with *Ali Naj Te z Listjem Posujem* (1971; Should I Cover You with Leaves). During this same period the most important dramatist to emerge was Dominik Smole (b. 1929), whose plays captured the existential condition of postwar Slovenia.

In the 1980s the poets of "language experience," notably Franci Zagoričnik and Tomaš Šalamun, came into the foreground and produced their most mature work. Noteworthy collections include Zagoričnik's *Sveder* (1983; A Drill) and Šalamun's *Balada za Metko Krašovec* (1981; A Ballad for Metka Krašovec). Among the younger generation of writers, Aleš Debeljak's (b. 1961) *Slovar Tišine* (1987; A Dictionary of Silence) represents the most significant poetic achievement of the second half of the decade. The postmodern sensibility left a powerful trace in drama as well, illustrated in Dušan Jovanovič's (b. 1939) *Karamazovi* (1981; The Karamazovs). Experimental literature discretely turned to social engagement in the 1990s, retaining its formal aestheticism and

freedom, notably in Franci Zagoričnik's collection of poems entitled *Slovenski Gambit* (1994; The Slovene Gambit).

BIBLIOGRAPHY: Kadić, A., *Modern Yugoslav Literature: An Anthology with Biographical Sketches* (1956); Predan, V., *Od premiere do premiere* (1966); Zadravec, F., *Zgodovina slovenskega slovstva II. Ekspresionizem in socialni realizem* (1972); Pogaènik-Franc Zadravec, J., *Istorija slovenačke knjiž evnosti* (1973); Rogel, C. R., and Orton, L. D., eds., *Reader's Guide to Slovenia* (1992); Debeljak, A., *Twilight of the Idols: Recollections of a Lost Yugoslavia* (1994); *The Veiled Landscape: Slovenian Women Writing* (1995); *At Three and a Half Past Midnight: Anthology of Young Slovene Poetry, Fiction and Nonfiction* (1996)

—IRENA LUKŠIĆ

SMILEY, Jane

American novelist, short-story writer, and essayist, b. 26 Sept. 1949, Los Angeles, California

S. was educated at Vassar (B.A., 1971) and the University of Iowa (M.A., 1975; M.F.A., 1976; Ph.D., 1978). Honors and awards include a Fulbright Fellowship (1976-77); grants from the National Endowment for the Arts (1978, 1987); Friends of American Writers Prize (1981); O. Henry Awards (1982, 1985, 1988); and the Midland Authors Award (1992). Published in 1991, S.'s novel *A Thousand Acres* in that same year won the Heartland Award, the National Book Critics Circle Award, and the Pulitzer Prize. S. is also a fellow of the American Academy of Arts and Sciences.

S.'s work crosses several genres. Although best known for her novels, she is also a noted writer of short stories and novellas. *The Age of Grief* (1987) is a collection of short stories and one novella. Other of S.'s short stories appear in anthologies and as well in *Redbook, Atlantic, Mademoiselle, Fiction*, and *TriQuarterly*. *Ordinary Love* and *Good Will*, two novellas, were published together in 1989.

S.'s best-known novels are *The Greenlanders* (1988), *A Thousand Acres*, and *Moo* (1995). *The Greenlanders*, an historical novel set in Greenland during the 14th c., is based on Norse sagas as well as colonial history. *A Thousand Acres*, S.'s most successful novel, is a modern retelling of *King Lear* set in Iowa during the farm crisis of the 1980s. A satiric look at academic life at a Midwestern university, *Moo*, written while S. was a professor of English at Iowa State University, pokes fun at everything from an experimental pig project to the provost's secretary. *The All-True Travels and Adventures of Lidie Newton* (1998), an historical novel concerning the issue of slavery, is set in Illinois, Missouri, and Kansas just prior to the Civil War.

While S.'s subjects cover a wide gamut, her works contain recurring themes, the most common of which are troubled family relationships, marriage, betrayal, aging, and death. With S.'s strong skill as a storyteller, each narrative unfolds with characters whose stories are timeless in theme but intricately connected to the complexities of contemporary life. Sometimes the narrative focus is male; sometimes female; sometimes a variety of viewpoints. Regardless of the technique, S. realistically probes into human motivations and interactions. She portrays painful topics—incest, infidelity, tragic deaths, fractured marriages, cancer, and financial problems. Stories are carefully constructed with multiple subplots and complex characters. Many works deal with ties to the land, such as *The Greenlanders* and *A Thousand Acres*, where the land itself becomes a major character.

Critics have generally considered S.'s work to be powerful—skillfully drawing readers into stories that are sometimes almost too painful to read. They recognize her ability to delineate realistic lives, particularly of women, exploring in full dimensions the roles that women play. S.'s characters are realistic more often than sympathetic, and she generally explores multiple generations of a family, thus giving characters further depth and complexity. A character is often examined in the context of his or her family, showing the family as the conduit between the person and society. Some reviewers denounced *A Thousand Acres* as too close to Shakespeare's work, thus lacking originality or sufficient depth to be represented as a modern farm novel. *Moo* received mixed reviews, some critics feeling that it tried to cover too many areas and that it lacked sufficient bite. Occasionally, critics find S.'s work to be lengthy, depressing, and detail-heavy, but most readers and critics applaud the reality of her characters and plots as she explores the human condition through the full ranges of age, class, and geography. Her focus on the diverse elements of our society reflects S.'s blend of scholarship in researching her ideas and storytelling in presenting them. S.'s works encourage a reader to think rather than simply react.

S.'s career has been prolific and multidimensional. She has a keen eye for a story in both traditional and nontraditional subject matter, a talent that will keep her future work fresh as readers and critics will be unable to predict around what topics her future works will be created.

FURTHER WORKS: *Barn Blind* (1980); *At Paradise Gate* (1981); *Duplicate Keys* (1984); *Catskill Crafts: Artisans of the Catskill Mountains* (1987)

BIBLIOGRAPHY: Graeber, L., "The Problem is Power," *NYTBR*, 5 November 1989: 45; Pearlman, M., *Listen to Their Voices: 20 Interviews with Women Who Write* (1993): 99-111; Leslie, M., "Incest, Incorporation, and 'King Lear' in J. S.'s 'A Thousand Acres,'" *CE*, 60 (Jan. 1998): 31-50

—REBECCA FARBER

SMITH, Lee

American novelist and short-story writer, b. 1 Nov. 1944, Grundy, Virginia

S. was reared in Grundy, a small community in the coal mining region of the Appalachian mountains of southwestern Virginia. While her family was comfortably middle class, she became sensitive to the struggles with poverty around her. From early childhood S. wanted to be a writer and pursued this dream by attending Hollins College where she and classmate Annie Dillard (b. 1945) studied under Louis Rubin. Her senior creative writing project resulted in her first novel, *The Last Day the Dogbushes Bloomed* (1968). In addition to pursuing her own successful writing career, S. has taught creative writing, most recently at North Carolina State University.

S.'s early novels are notable as apprentice pieces in which she was perfecting her control of narrative voice and groping for her

subject matter. The first two novels are first-person coming of age stories in which the young heroines begin to grasp the difficulties of becoming adult women in the contemporary South. Her third novel, *Fancy Strut* (1973), shifts to multiple third-person points of view and showcases S.'s comedic talents in her satire of the efforts of a small Southern town to stage a sesquicentennial celebration. Because the early novels were not commercial successes, publishers were reluctant to consider other novels, so for several years S. focused on short fiction, publishing in little magazines and in popular periodicals. She has continued to write both short and long fiction, collecting three volumes of short stories to date.

S.'s fourth novel, *Black Mountain Breakdown* (1981), heralded her emergence as a significant voice in contemporary Southern American letters. For the first time, S. engaged her native material by setting her story in Black Rock, a small town very like her home town of Grundy. This coming of age story shows S.'s greater maturity as the novel transcends the limitations of that genre by not only probing Crystal Spangler's coming of age, but also by fully imagining the community from which she emerges.

S.'s reputation was firmly established with the publication of *Oral History* (1983), which many critics still regard as her finest work. The complicated oral history of the Cantrell family exhibits S.'s mastery of narrative voice and multiple points of view as well as displaying her careful research into and integration of the history and folklore of the Appalachian mountain region. As the readers follow all of the different narrators' versions of the Cantrell history, they come to realize that the truth lies not in any one teller's version of the story but somewhere among them all. S.'s other best-known novel is *Fair and Tender Ladies* (1988), which incorporates a range of Appalachian history and folkways into the life of Ivy Rowe. This novel's epistolary narrative strategy allows Ivy to wrestle with the conflict between her desire to become a writer and the harsh limitations imposed by her personal life. At the novel's end, she despairs that she never has become a writer, but the reader knows differently. Destroying her letters, Ivy recognizes that the act of writing them has given shape and meaning to her life. The power of this ending as well as the beautiful lyric quality that Ivy's voice has acquired cause many to rate this as S.'s best novel.

S.'s dominant themes are those of self-identity, especially for women born and reared in the constricting confines of small Southern communities, of the individual's place within a family and/or a community, of the individual's search for spiritual values, and of the loss of traditional values under the onslaught of modern commercialism. The latter two themes have emerged most strongly in *The Devil's Dream* (1992) and *Saving Grace* (1995). S.'s penchant for careful research is evident in both of these novels as she explores the history of the country music industry and the revival of extreme, fundamentalist religion. *The Devil's Dream* is another family saga, tracing the rise to fame and fortune of a country music family who turn a love for traditional bluegrass music into commercial Opryland success. As members of various generations of the Bailey family tell their stories, the readers see the values in and of their traditional music being corrupted by the trappings and violence of modern life. *Saving Grace* is the life story of Florida Grace Shepherd, daughter of a snake-handling preacher in western North Carolina. Grace's efforts to become a dutiful daughter, wife, and mother fail in conflict with the urges of the flesh. The flesh also fails, and Grace retreats to her childhood home, emerging with renewed faith in her mother's version of her father's religion.

With the further depth that her exploration of spiritual values has added to her continued mastery of the voices, history, and folk traditions of her Appalachian mountain home, S. is becoming one of the most important voices from the contemporary South. Like the best of all regional literature, S.'s fiction, through the specificity of her presentation of people and places, allows readers to understand the universal issues that her themes raise. S. not only informs readers about Appalachian history, folklore, and contemporary reality, she also enables them to see that the people of Appalachia share struggles that affect all humanity.

FURTHER WORKS: *Something in the Wind* (1971); *Cakewalk* (1981); *Family Linen* (1985); *Me and My Baby View the Eclipse* (1990); *The Christmas Letters: A Novella* (1996); *News of the Spirit* (1997)

BIBLIOGRAPHY: MacKethan, L. H., "Artists and Beauticians: Balance in L. S.'s Fiction," *SLJ*, 15 (Fall 1982): 3-14; Jones, A. G., "The World of L. S.," *SoQ*, 22 (Fall 1983): 115-39; special S. issue, *Iron Mountain Review*, 3 (1986); special S. section, *SoQ*, 28 (Winter 1990): 5-34; Buchanan, H. C., "L. S.: The Storyteller's Voice," in Inge, T. B., ed., *Southern Women Writers: The New Generation* (1990): 324-45; Smith, V. A., "On Regionalism, Women's Writing, and Writing as a Woman: A Conversation with L. S.," *SoR*, 26 (Autumn 1990): 784-95; Hill, D. C., *L. S.* (1992); Smith, R., *Gender Dynamics in the Fiction of L. S.* (1997); Parrish, N. C., *L. S., Annie Dillard and the Hollins Group: A Genesis of Writers* (1998)

—HARRIETTE C. BUCHANAN

SMITH, Pauline

South African short-story writer and novelist (writing in English), b. 2 April 1882, Oudtshoorn; d. 29 Jan. 1959, Broadstone, England

S. spent her childhood in the Little Karoo region, just south of Olive SCHREINER's Great Karoo. She completed her formal education in England and spent the rest of her life quietly in Dorset, returning on several occasions to South Africa to gather material for her fiction.

During her adolescence and twenties S. began the stories about her childhood that later became the children's stories *Platkops Children* (1935). She also published in Aberdeen newspapers a set of sketches and poems about Scottish life. The period of her friendship with Arnold BENNETT from 1909 to 1931 coincided with her major literary activity, in which she published twelve short stories (a thirteenth, undated, was published posthumously), several sketches based on her South African journals, a one-act play, and a novel called *The Beadle* (1926). That she was unable to finish the novel she worked on for the rest of her life was probably due to growing despair at the political climate in Europe and South Africa and to chronic ill health, which worsened during the war years.

The stories collected in *The Little Karoo* (1925; expanded ed., 1930) deal with relations between rich and poor, God and man, farmer and *bywoner* (sharecropper), man and woman; the atmosphere of poverty and dependency is partially alleviated by love and forgiveness, generally embodied in women. The comment is often

harsh: in "The Sisters" a young girl's sacrifice to a rich farmer to pay off her father's mortgage is represented by the image of blood flowing in the place of water through her father's lands.

S. was the first South African English writer to focus on the Afrikaner rural proletariat. The sympathetic attitude taken in *The Little Karoo*, which constituted a significant revision of the predominant British anti-Boer attitude, is balanced by a depreciation of patriarchy: men, victims of drought, poverty, and encroaching industrialism, in turn victimize their dependents. In *The Beadle*, however, S. presents the community as feudal, in tones more nostalgic than corrective. While she provides a critique of the destructive tendencies that fester in this isolated, suspicious, and intensely religious community, her celebration of innocence, embodied both in the heroine and in the organic community, places the novel in the idyllic mode and softens her polemic.

While S.'s reputation will depend partly on the evaluation of her liberal perspective, her technical achievements secure her a prominent place in South African literature: she is distinguished particularly for her thematically significant blending of the rhythms of Afrikaans speech and Old Testament prose, her control of narrative distance, the use of structural features that recall the classic folktale, and the balance and limpidity of her prose. She will be remembered above all as South Africa's first successful regional writer, who depicted a community and a landscape in such a way that they appear at once familiar and strange.

FURTHER WORKS: *A. B. ". . . a minor marginal note"* (1933); *South African Journal, 1913–1914* (1983); *Stories, Diaries and Other Unpublished or Out-of-Print Work* (1983)

BIBLIOGRAPHY: Haresnape, G., *P. S.* (1969); Beeton, R., "P. S. and South African Literature in English," *UES*, 11, 1 (1973): 35–50; Ravenscroft, A., "P. S.," in K. Parker, ed., *The South African Novel in English* (1978): 46–56; Christie, S., et al., *Perspectives on South African Fiction* (1980): 57–69; Marquard, J., "P. S. and Her Beadle: Chosen or Fallen?" *English Academy Review* (1981): 16–25; Driver, D., ed., *P. S.* (1983); Gardiner, M., "Critical Responses and the Fiction of P. S.," *Theoria*, 60 (1983): 1–12

—DOROTHY DRIVER

SMITH, Stevie

(born Florence Margaret Smith) English poet and novelist, b. 20 Sept. 1902, Hull; d. 7 March 1971, London

S. lived for sixty-four years in the same house on Avondale Road in Palmers Green, North London. She was educated at Palmers Green High School and the North London Collegiate School for Girls, and worked as a private secretary to magazine publishers until her retirement in 1953. Small (she was nicknamed "Stevie" after a famous jockey of the day) and somewhat sickly, S. lived for almost all of her life with her beloved "Lion Aunt." In the 1950s and 1960s she became well known for her accomplished poetry readings and was given the Chomondeley Award in 1966 and the Queen's Gold Medal for Poetry in 1969. *Stevie*, a film based on her writings starring Glenda Jackson, was released in 1981.

S. wrote three clever novels— *Novel on Yellow Paper* (1936), *Over the Frontier* (1938), and *The Holiday* (1949)—but unquestionably her most important work was her poetry. Her posthumous *Collected Poems* (1975) brings together eight previous volumes of poetry. All of S.'s work is characterized by her lively sensibility and sprightly, unpredictable wit. The most idiosyncratic and perhaps even improbable of poets, her books are distinguished by their synthesis of a jaunty or "comical" formal means and an otherwise dark thematic concern. The singsong rhythms, obvious full rhymes, and epigrammatic brevity of her work are reminiscent of a comic poet like the American Ogden Nash (1902–1971), and yet in her fierce, sardonic honesty and compelling, near-obsessive concern with death she is closer to Emily Dickinson.

This apparent disjunction between surface and content often gives an eerie, lucid, cheerfully gruesome tone to her writings. For example, S.'s preoccupation with the grim comicality of human suffering is best expressed in her most famous and unforgettable image: the flailing swimmer whose desperate attempt not to drown is mistaken for distant waving by those on shore. The swimmer in "Not Waving but Drowning" (1957) may also stand as the central emblem of a poetry whose playful surface is underlined by an unwavering concern with human isolation and desperation.

S. "embroidered" most of her books with her own small and saucy drawings. These drawings—some of which have been collected in the sketch book *Some Are More Human than Others* (1958)—emphasize the charming and *faux-naïf* quality of her work. This quality is deepened, however, by her ongoing preoccupation with what is always her first and final subject: death. Sometimes in her poems death is personified as a shrouded stranger sitting in a boat ("The River Deben," 1937), sometimes as a delicate child who is "very gay" ("The Deathly Child," 1938). Often there is the suggestion that one must live one's life and endure in order to earn one's own death ("Study to Deserve Death," 1938). If S.'s poems show a high spirited and buoyant attraction to life, this is always balanced by a kind of secret longing for and commitment to death. "Come Death (1)" (1938) explicitly asks; "Why should man more fear Death than fear to live?" If death sometimes appears as a stranger who may summon us at any time (as in "Proud Death with Swelling Port," 1938), more often it appears as a god who may himself be earnestly summoned (as in "Exeat," 1966). This theme is most poignantly and beautifully expressed in S.'s final poem, "Come Death (2)" (1972): "Ah me, sweet Death, you are the only god/Who comes as a servant when he is called, you know,/Listen then to this sound I make, it is sharp,/Come death. Do not be slow." Always in S.'s work death is treated as a last exciting mystery, an end and a remedy to life.

S. was the most independent poet of her generation, and no other writer is quite like her. There can be little doubt that her highly original work considerably brightens the landscape of 20th-c. English poetry.

FURTHER WORKS: *A Good Time Was Had by All* (1937); *Tender Only to One* (1938); *Mother, What Is Man?* (1942); *Harold's Leap* (1950); *Not Waving but Drowning* (1957); *Selected Poems* (1962); *The Frog Prince* (1966); *The Best Beast* (1969); *Scorpion* (1972); *Me Again: The Uncollected Writings of S. S., Illustrated by Herself* (1981); *S. S.: A Selection* (1983)

BIBLIOGRAPHY: Dick, K., *Ivy and Stevie: Ivy Compton-Burnett and Stevie Smith: Conversations and Reflections* (1971): 33–66;

Bedient, C., *Eight Contemporary Poets* (1974): 139–58; Bromwich, D., "Waving and Drowning," *Poetry*, 129 (1976): 172–76; Helmling, S., "Delivered for a Time from Silence," *Parnassus*, 6, 1 (1977): 314–30; Wade, S., "S. S. and the Untruth of Myth," *Agenda*, 15, 2 (1977): 102–6; Simon, J., "The Poems of S. S.," *Canto*, 1, 1 (1977): 181–98; Storey, M., "Why S. S. Matters," *CritQ*, 21, 2 (1979): 41–55

—EDWARD HIRSCH

SMITH, Sydney Goodsir

Scottish poet, dramatist, and critic, b. 25 Oct. 1915, Wellington, New Zealand; d. 15 Jan. 1975, Edinburgh

Although born in New Zealand and educated at English schools and Oxford University, S. identified strongly with his Scottish ancestry when he came to live in Scotland in his late teens, and he settled permanently in Edinburgh in 1942. He acquired a deep knowledge of Scots vernacular literature, became a committed left-wing Scottish nationalist, and chose to write all but his earliest poetry in Scots, the language of Lowland Scotland, as distinct from the Gaelic of the Highlands. The crucial influence on S. was Hugh MACDIARMID, who had shown that Scots could be revived as a medium for modern poetry of outstanding quality.

Some of S.'s early poetry, especially in *Skail Wind* (1941), shows the strain imposed on his technical resources by writing in a literary language the relationship of which to actual speech idioms he had not yet mastered. But he rapidly developed a remarkable ear for rhythms and sound effects in Scots, and he had notable success in the musical phrasing of his simple, direct, but distinctively memorable lyrics.

From *The Deevil's Waltz* (1946) onward he evolved for himself a characteristic style in which elements drawn from the repertoire of various Scots poets of the 15th and 16th cs., when Scots flourished as a national literary language, were counterpointed against the living speech of contemporary Edinburgh, where the vernacular survived most strongly in the less respectable pubs and purlieus of a superficially Anglicized city. S., in common with other Scottish poets like MacDiarmid, Robert Garioch (1909–1981), and Norman MACCAIG, brought a lively sense of humor to his poetry, and he combined this with a strong strain of romantic irony. If "freedom and whisky gang the-gither," and he celebrated Love and Liberty with Burns, it was with Byron that he recovered from the hangover. Explicitly political poems in which commitment leaves no room for humor or irony, and not much for his particular talents, are largely confined to his early work.

Alongside the direct, intense lyric, S. developed longer, loosely knit forms of poems in which the exuberance of having "language at large" was cunningly controlled by the cadenced patterns of his syntax. His most sustained work in this style is to be found in *Under the Eildon Tree* (1948; rev. ed., 1954), a set of twenty-four elegies exploring the ramifications of erotic experience in a context that is simultaneously the shabby Edinburgh of contemporary reality and a romantic landscape peopled with legendary figures from the past. Another poem in his extended, more flexible style, "The Grace of God and the Meth-Drinker," is perhaps the most striking success in *Figs and Thistles* (1959), a collection that also contains his fine translation into Scots under the title "The Twal," of Alexandr BLOK'S revolutionary Russian poem "The Twelve." Shorter poems showing welcome signs of a strengthening of his imagery alongside the always more impressive power of his rhythmic sense are mostly found in *So Late into the Night* (1952).

S. wrote verse for radio (for example, *The Vision of the Prodigal Son*, 1960) and television (*Kynd Kittock's Land*, 1965), as well as a stage play, *The Wallace* (1960), which achieved a popular success when performed at the Edinburgh Festival not easily envisaged from the bare text on the printed page. *Carotid Cornucopius* (1947; rev. and expanded ed., 1964) is an outrageously funny tour de force of Scots prose, bringing together Sir Thomas Urquhart, the 17th-c. Scottish translator of Rabelais, and the JOYCE of *Finnegans Wake*. This book has the unusual distinction of being a modernist work that actually achieves its object of making the reader laugh out loud, and to such an extent that he is in some danger of sharing the fate of Urquhart, who is reported to have died laughing.

S. made light of his substantial critical scholarship, which was put to use all too briefly in such projects as the collection of essays *Robert Fergusson, 1750–1774* (1952), about his Edinburgh predecessor and inspirer of Robert Burns, as of S. himself; *A Short Introduction to Scottish Literature* (1951); and his selection from the work of the translator of Vergil, Gavin Douglas (1475?–1522), a master in the poet's craft of rhetoric. His own *Collected Poems* (1975) contains work that, allied to the prose of *Carotid Cornucopius*, makes a valuable and distinctive contribution to the living tradition of literature in Scots, which continues to survive, however improbably, the massive presence of English in Scotland.

FURTHER WORKS: *The Wanderer, and Other Poems* (1943); *Selected Poems* (1947); *The Aipple and the Hazel* (1951); *Cokkils* (1953); *Orpheus and Eurydice* (1955); *Omens* (1955); *Fifteen Poems and a Play* (1969); *Gowdspink in Reekie* (1974)

BIBLIOGRAPHY: MacCaig, N., "The Poetry of S.," *Saltire Review*, 1 (1954): 14–19; MacDiarmid, H., *S. G. S.* (1963); special S. section, *Akros*, 4, 10 (1969): 17–51; Crawford, T., "The Poetry of S.," *SSL*, 7 (1969–1970): 40–59; Gold, E., *S. G. S.'s "Under the Eildon Tree"* (1975); Garioch, R., et al., *For S. G. S.* (1975); Buthlay, K., "Makar Macironical," *Akros*, 11, 31 (1976): 46–56

—KENNETH BUTHLAY

SMITHYMAN, Kendrick

New Zealand poet, b. 9 Oct. 1922, Te Kopuru; d. 28 Dec. 1995, Auckland

S.'s first major collection, *The Blind Mountain* (1950), manifests the complex phrasing and sometimes disorientating linguistic and narrative maneuvers that characterize his mature work. Even at this stage, S. eschews the romantic, self-assured voice, preferring a more ruminative and tentative one. Two important collections, *The Seal in a Dolphin Pool* (1975) and *Dwarf with a Billiard Cue* (1978), reflect the emergence of a more affable, colloquial tone, although without compromising the rigorous forms and serious purpose of the work.

S. prioritizes "irony, wit, baroque and complex structures, verbal play," basing the poems on "an active body of information" rather than the self-authenticating, nationalistic tendencies that dominated New Zealand literature from the 1930s through the 1960s. His poems also steer a wide course around the confessional genre, even when dealing with the events and personalities that shaped his own life, as in *Auto/Biographies* (1992).

A mixture of internationalist and ardently regionalist concerns gives S.'s work its idiosyncratic flavor and its broad sphere of reference. His most accomplished collection of short poems, *Stories about Wooden Keyboards* (1985), uses such characters as the Polish pianist in the title poem to embody the plight of the individual adrift in the human landscape of the 20th c. S.'s use of narratives is often allegorical but seldom in a conclusive way—the poems are open-ended and suggestive rather than definitive or moralistic.

Initially influenced by Wallace STEVENS, S.'s work reflects a commitment to MODERNISM and experimentalism unparalleled in New Zealand literature. At once compressed yet discursive, prosaic yet refined, S.'s poetry parallels that of English poet Basil BUNTING or American poet Louis ZUKOFSKY. Critics have struggled with his deliberately distorted syntax and his "creative constructing of surface structures which appear to be deviant or ill-formed." The 1989 publication of S.'s *Selected Poems*, edited by Peter Simpson, went some way to making his work accessible to a wider audience, offering a well-orchestrated, albeit less than definitive, selection, spanning S.'s career until 1987.

Published posthumously in 1997, *Atua Wera* is a 261-page epic poem based around the Hokianga Harbour (near the poet's birthplace in Northland). Using oral and written sources, S.'s imaginative reconstruction of events surrounding the 19th-c. Maori prophet Papahurihia (also known as Te Atua Wera, or "the fiery god") imparts both a sense of the impenetrability of history and the need to connect with, and understand, the history of Maori-Pakeha (European) relations. Avoiding the compression and contorted syntax of his shorter works, it shows the expansive, discursive mind and voice of the poet in full flight. S.'s greatest single achievement, *Atua Wera* presents a more fully formed world than the allusive, open-ended peregrinations of his shorter poems. It shares with all S.'s poetry an obsession with place and the layering of human histories onto the landscape. Such important earlier poem sequences as "An Ordinary Day beyond Kaitaia" (1972), "Tomarata" (1975), and "Reading the Maps, an Academic Exercise" (1985) anticipate S.'s epic.

Atua Wera and such accomplished poems as those mentioned above ensure S.'s status as a major New Zealand poet. He will be remembered as a poet of the out-of-the-way location, the oblique angle, the arcane and surprising research. His best poems trace the trajectory of words and meanings, sounds and echoes shuttling between the physical world and the mind of the poet. "If we live we stand in language," S. wrote. The finely crafted yet thorny structures of the poems house one of New Zealand literature's most distinctive intellects.

FURTHER WORKS: *Seven Sonnets* (1947); *Inheritance* (1962); *A Way of Saying: A Study of New Zealand Poetry* (1965); *Flying to Palmerston* (1968); *Earthquake Weather* (1972); *Are You Going to the Pictures?* (1987)

BIBLIOGRAPHY: Geraets, J., "K. S. and Brash's *Landfall*," *Landfall*, 40, 4 (1986); Berry, R., "Hard Yakker: K. S.'s Colorless Green

Ideas," *Landfall*, 42, 4 (1988): 388-402; Jackson, M., "Interview with K. S.," *Landfall*, 42, 4 (1988): 403-20; Edmond, M., "Divagations: K. S.'s Poetry," *Landfall*, 42, 4 (1988): 447-56; O'Brien, G., "A Journey around K. S.'s *Atua Wera*," *Landfall*, 5, 2 (1997): 306-21

—GREGORY O'BRIEN

SNOW, C(harles) P(ercy)

English novelist and essayist, b. 15 Oct. 1905, Leicester; d. 1 July 1980, London

S., born poor, studied chemistry at a local college and won a graduate scholarship for research in physics at Cambridge. There he received a doctorate and remained as a research fellow and college administrator through the 1930s, meanwhile beginning his "ultimate vocation" as a writer. During World War II he recruited scientists for military projects, after the war remaining in the civil service, until 1959. In 1950 he married Pamela Hansford Johnson (1912–1981), herself a distinguished novelist. In 1964 he became Lord S., and served for two years in Harold Wilson's Labour cabinet as Parliamentary Secretary to the Ministry of Technology. In his later years he often addressed public issues, sometimes controversially, as when his *The Two Cultures and the Scientific Revolution* (1959) provoked caustic rebuttal by the distinguished literary critic F. R. LEAVIS.

From 1935 until 1970, during what might seem an all-engrossing public and scientific career, S. wrote an eleven-volume sequence of novels, collectively titled *Strangers and Brothers*. Its narrator, Lewis Eliot, whose life in many ways echoes S.'s (but whose personality is far blander), describes the ascent of a young man through the layers of English society and the halls of English power. Some of the novels—*Time of Hope* (1949), *Homecomings* (1956), and *Last Things* (1970)—center on Eliot's life; *George Passant* (originally titled *Strangers and Brothers*, 1940) on a provincial solicitor and romantic radical; *The Conscience of the Rich* (1958) on a wealthy Jewish family split by the younger generation's radicalism; *The Light and the Dark* (1947) on a brilliant scholar momentarily attracted to fascism; *The New Men* (1954) on the development and the politics of the atomic bomb (in which S. had played a part); *Corridors of Power* (1964) on the parliamentary politics of disarmament; and *The Sleep of Reason* (1968) on the social and moral implications of a horrible crime. *The Light and the Dark, The Masters* (1951)—probably S.'s best novel—and *The Affair* (1960) concern the politics of a Cambridge college, and serve as microcosms of political processes examined in other novels. These novels make a central point: power dominates human relations, whether in marriages, families, small societies, or those larger groups we more naturally see as being political. The view is not a cynical one: love, friendship, knowledge, and moral concern ameliorate the struggles for power but do not diminish the strength of the urge to gain power; it is part of S.'s realism to trace dispassionately the working of these forces.

S. wrote unashamedly in the realistic mode; indeed, he attempted to revive the subjects and conventions of 19th-c. REALISM, in both their English and their Continental strands, setting them against what he regarded as the often ethically negative and

C. P. Snow

socially unreconstructive canons of modernist fiction. As novelist, critic, and cultural commentator he aimed at reconnecting fiction with social, public, and moral issues, an aim reflected in his lucid, simple, and, to some readers, pedestrian manner of writing, his relative lack of interest in the deeply buried inner lives of his characters, his willingness to bring ideas into his novels, and his championing of such writers as Balzac, Pérez GALDÓS, Tolstoy, and Trollope.

Many modern critics follow Leavis in dismissing his work as artistically barren and morally misguided, his style as wooden, his characters cardboard, his ideas stale. Others, including Lionel TRILLING, George STEINER, and Alfred Kazin (b. 1915) have taken S. on his own terms, finding the novels at least an interesting attempt to revive an important and still useful tradition. His work will probably never be awarded a place like that reserved for the writers he most admired—Tolstoy, Trollope, Balzac, and PROUST—but if, as S. predicted in his critical study *The Realists* (1978), a time comes when realistic fiction is once again valued, readers may find his work interesting, not just as social history, but as a thoroughly drawn if in some ways limited picture of reality, sketched on a broad and inclusive canvas.

FURTHER WORKS: *Death under Sail* (1932; rev. ed., 1959); *New Lives for Old* (1933); *The Search* (1934; rev. ed., 1958); *Variety of Men* (1967); *Public Affairs* (1971); *The Malcontents* (1972); *In Their Wisdom* (1974); *Trollope: His Life and Art* (1975); *A Coat of Varnish* (1979); *The Physicists* (1981)

BIBLIOGRAPHY: Leavis, F. R., *Two Cultures? The Significance of C. P. S.* (1962); Davis, R. G., *C. P. S.* (1965); Trilling, L., "Science, Literature, and Culture: A Comment on the S.-Leavis Controversy" (1965); *Beyond Culture*, rev. ed. (1977): 126–54; Steiner, G., on *Sleep of Reason, New Yorker*, (12 July 1969): 89; Curtis, H. C., *After the Trauma: Representative British Novelists since 1920* (1970): 168–90; Cooper, W., *C. P. S.*, rev. ed. (1971); Boytinck, P., *C. P. S.: A Reference Guide* (1980); Snow, P., *Stranger and Brother* (1983)

—RICHARD A. JOHNSON

SNYDER, Gary

American poet and essayist, b. 8 May 1930, San Francisco, Cal.

S. is a poet often identified with the San Francisco Renaissance of the 1950s and with the ecology movement that began in the 1960s and continues today. Born in San Francisco, he moved to Portland, Oregon, attended Reed College, studied anthropology, and briefly attended graduate school. But in 1956, after working as a logger and forest ranger in the Pacific Northwest, he went to Japan where he lived for over a decade, eventually becoming a practicing Buddhist. He returned to the U.S. in 1968 and now lives in the foothills of the Sierra Nevada range in California; he recently joined the faculty at the University of California, Davis.

Gary Snyder

S.'s poetry was deeply marked from the first by his interest in hiking and the closely observed—even intensely worshiped—processes and values of nature. As for poetic form, S. has claimed that the rhythms of his physical work determine the rhythms of his line. In *Myths and Texts* (1960; rev. ed., 1978) he demonstrated this claim in tightly constructed, meditative lyrics in a sequence that drew on imagism and Zen philosophy.

In *The Back Country* (1968) and *Regarding Wave* (1970) he began to move beyond imagism and its extension into objectivism by exploring more deeply the metaphoric basis of the common and mythic patterns of life and consciousness. He accomplished this largely by intensifying his commitment to a precise and even austere use of language and rhythm. His essays in *Earth House Hold* (1969) did a great deal to articulate the ecological consciousness that formed a valuable part of the social activism of the time. These essays are remarkably consonant with his poetry, and demonstrate a focus of intellect and feeling, combined with a social awareness and political commitment that set his work apart from the confessional and academic writing of many of his contemporaries. In 1977, he published another book of essays, *The Old Ways*, followed by a collection of interviews and talks, *The Real Work* (1980). *The Practice of the Wild* (1990) is the latest collection of S.'s prose, and continues his discussion of the crucial ethical and political issues associated with ecology and its critique of industrial capitalism.

In the poems of *Turtle Island* (1974), awarded the Pulitzer Prize, S. extended his explorations into myth and metaphor, invoking both the ancient fables of pre-Columbian America and the prophetic tradition and shamanistic practices more frequently found in the writings of anthropologists and students of comparative religion. After a decade in which S. published little, there appeared two more volumes of poetry, *Axe Handles* (1983) and *Left Out in the Rain* (1986). The latter volume contained poems from as far back as the earliest volumes and showed how consistent are S.'s concerns and how patient he is as a reviser and polisher of his work.

S.'s work has been widely appreciated and continues to influence poets, but also students of ecology. Often seen by some as no more than a "beatnik," S. has carved for himself a steady path from the imagism and bohemianism of his early work through to a more articulated and even cosmic view of modern experience. He is part of that culture of modernism which calls into question the very valuation of culture itself. His use of "primitive" values, and his suggestion that a life that is separated from natural rhythms and a respect for the biosphere is not worthy of human effort, makes him considerably bolder than many lyric poets.

FURTHER WORKS: *Riprap and Cold Mountain Poems* (1959; rev. ed. 1965); *Six Sections from Mountains and Rivers without End* (1970; rev. ed. 1977); *He Who Hunted Birds in His Father's Village* (1979)

BIBLIOGRAPHY: Parkinson, T., "The Poetry of G. S.," *SoR*, 4 (Summer 1968): 616–32; Altieri, C., "G. S.'s *Turtle Island*: Reconciling the Roles of Seer and Prophet," *Boundary 2*, 4 (1976); Steuding, B., *G. S.* (1976); Kern, R., "Clearing the Ground: G. S. and the Modernist Imperative," *Criticism*, 19 (Spring 1977): 158–77; Molesworth, C., *G. S.'s Vision: Poetry and the Real Work* (1983); Murphy, P. D., *Critical Essays on G. S.* (1990)

—CHARLES MOLESWORTH

SOBIR, Bozor

(also spelled Sobirov) Tajik poet and critic, b. 20 Oct. 1938, Faizabad

S. was born to a rural family of southern Tajikistan. As an orphan, his early life was fraught with difficulties. Nevertheless, he graduated from Tajikistan University in 1962 with a degree in Tajik language and literature. Subsequently, he worked with the media and, between 1975 and 1979, served as the editor of *Sado-i Sharq*, *Ma'orif ve Madaniyyat*, and *'Idolat*. His rustic background, youthful travails, and love of mother and homeland have impacted his work tremendously.

S. began publishing his poetry in the 1960s. His collections include *Payvand* (1972; Connection), *Otashbarg* (1974; Fire in the Leaves), *Gul-i Khor* (1978; The Thorn Flower), *Mizhgon-i Shab* (1981; The Night's Eyelids), *Aftobnihol* (1982; Aftabnihal), and *Ba Chishidan, Ba Chamidan* (1987; In Taste and Act). S.'s lyric poetry is generally sentimental, but at times can be psychological or dramatic. His social themes, which view the subject from historical, humanitarian, and philosophical perspectives, are developed with extreme care.

Tajikistan's rustic scene forms the backdrop to his early works. "Mo Kudakon Budim" (1984; We Were Children), "Kudakiam Hanuz Giryon Ast" (1984; My Childhood Still Weeps), "Kudaki Ku?" (1984; Where Is Childhood?), and "Bachcheho-i Dihoti" (1984; Village Children) hark back to the poet's formative years, while "Zan-i Tojik ve Pakhta" (1989; Tajik Women and Cotton) describes the tragic situation of working women. He also has written elegies for and dedication poems to almost all the major poets, learned men, and revolutionary figures of Tajikistan and Central Asia, among them Abu Abdullah Rudaki (858-941), Abu Ali Ibn-i Sina (980-1037), Vosse (1847-1888), Abu al-Qasim Lahuti (1887-1957), and Sadriddin AINI.

Unlike the majority of his peers, S. did not praise the Soviet system and its contributions to Tajikistan. In fact, he is the only Tajik poet to rise against Communist aggression during the heyday of the Party and survive. As a social critic, he faced issues frankly; his criticism was strong and unrelenting. For instance, in *Sahna* (1984; The Stage), he criticized all levels of Soviet society except the working classes. In "Pas az Mo" (1970s; After Us), apparently, he crossed the line; he was subjected to the most vociferous criticism by his peers. In 1978 he went even further and, in an assembly at the Writers Union of Tajikistan, criticized Soviet activities in Afghanistan.

Between 1990 and 1992, when Tajikistan experienced its darkest days, S. served as the voice of the opposition. His poignant poetry reflects the turbulent days when Tajiks sought to cast off their Soviet yoke and reestablish their traditional Islamic identity. In this context S. took on not only the issues of Sovietization and Russification, but the more delicate issues of Uzbekization and Pan-Turkism. During the demonstrations and vigils held at the Shahidan Square, he openly incited the public to support the opposition rather than the constitutional government. On March 26, 1993 he was imprisoned for his anti-Uzbek remarks and remained in custody for over a year. Pardoned by the president, he traveled to the U.S. and lectured on the situation in Tajikistan, especially on the conflict that pitted the Muslim south against the Communist north.

S.'s "Tiflis" (n.d.; Tiblisi), while detailing Soviet atrocities in the capital of Soviet Georgia, indirectly reflects the Soviets' use of the city of Khujand (former Leninabad), Tajikistan's main northern city, as an instrument of division and regionalism. His "Bukhoro" (1984; Bukhara), "Divor-i Bukhoro" (1984; The Wall of Bukhara), and "Ahmad Donish" (n.d.; Ahmad Donish) similarly expose the Soviets' suppression of the major cultural centers of the Tajiks. The latter poem, in the course of exposing the fraudulent claim of the Soviets regarding equality, brotherhood, camaraderie, and internationalism, underscores the paucity of the symbols of traditional life.

S. uses both the traditional meters and the new interpretations of the classical devices. In either case, however, following the advice of Muslih al-Din Sa'di (1213-1292), and the example of Nima Yushij (1895-1960), he allows the content to take precedence over the form of the composition. Consequently, he is known more for his patriotism and stance against Communist aggression than for either his poetic style or introduction of innovative methods into Tajik literature. None of S.'s contemporaries has left a legacy as varied, profound, and poignant about the social scene in Tajikistan of the 1990s as has S. In fact, often he was the only poet to be seen on the streets of Dushanbe—all others, even those who had not criticized the system, having fled the capital.

One could easily argue that S.'s rustic background and youthful difficulties as well as his love for his mother and for his homeland form the major foci of his poetic endeavor. S.'s lyric poetry, centered on his personal sentiments, deals with romantic themes in the tradition of the Tajiks. Later on, his world view changes, although not the intensity of his conviction. In fact, patriotism and nationalism dominate the latter part of his poetic career.

FURTHER WORKS: *Chashm-i Safidor* (1991)

BIBLIOGRAPHY: Abdumannonov, A., "B. S.," *Ensaiklopidio-i Soveti-i Tojik* (1978), Vol. 1: 288-89; *Ensaiklopedio-i Adabiyyot va San'at-i Tojik* (1988), Vol. 1: 288-89; Mirzozoda, Kh., *Adabiyyot-i Soveti-i Tojik* (1990): 225; Kenjaev, S., *Tabaddulot-i Tojikiston* (1993), Vol. 1: 168, 234; Musalmanian Qabodoani, R., "Sha'iri Yak Ruya ve Yak Zabona," *Kayhon Farhangi*, 103 (1994): 15-21

—IRAJ BASHIRI

SŎ Chŏng-ju

South Korean poet and essayist, b. 18 May 1915, Koch'ang

As a youth, S. went through a period of aimless wandering until he entered a monastery to study Buddhism. He continued his studies at the Central Buddhist College (now Tongguk University) and then again led the life of a vagabond in southern Manchuria during the dark days of the Japanese occupation. After the liberation (1945), he worked for newspapers and taught at high schools and universities. Currently, he is a professor of literature at Tongguk University. In addition to his volumes of poetry, which have earned him the Freedom Literature Award (1955) and the Korean Academy of Arts Award (1967), he has written literary criticism.

S. has been dubbed the Korean Baudelaire. His early poetry in *Hwasa* (1938; the flower snake), was characterized by sensuality and diabolism in a specifically Korean setting. With *Kwich'okto* (1948; the cuckoo) S. returned to broader East Asian themes and emotions, seeking eternal life and championing poetry for life's sake as opposed to art's sake. In *Silla ch'o* (1961; Silla sketches) he presented a vision of an idealized Silla (an ancient Korean kingdom) in which man and nature were one. S. forged the themes of Buddhist tales and legends into new entities with a sure touch. He has continually presented a view of life imbued with a dark, mysterious stillness, akin to the feeling associated with Zen meditation, and enhanced by skillful use of Buddhist metaphors, as in *Tongch'ŏn* (1968; winter sky). His most recent works show him delving into native shamanism to transform intractably unpoetic elements into works of art.

S. is credited with exploring the hidden resources of the Korean language, from sensual ecstasy to spiritual quest, from haunting lyricism to colloquial earthiness. Some consider S. the most "Korean" of contemporary poets. Yet he appears to have remained untouched by historical forces, even though he attempted suicide during the Korean War.

FURTHER WORKS: *S. C. sisŏn* (1956); *S. C. munhak chŏnjip* (5 vols., 1972); *Chilmajae sinhwa* (1975); *Ttŏdori ŭi si* (1976)

BIBLIOGRAPHY: Tong-gyu Hwang, Critical Introduction to *Selections from S. C.* (1981): 221–44; Kim, U., Foreword to "S. C." [translations], *Quarterly Journal of Literature*, 22 (1981): 7–12

—PETER H. LEE

SOCIALIST REALISM

Socialist Realism was introduced as the official artistic and literary doctrine of the Soviet Union at the First All-Union Congress of Soviet Writers in 1934. It was developed as a reaction against certain avant-garde and Marxist concepts of art that had flourished in the 1920s, such as proletarian literature and Alexander Konstantinovich Voronsky's (1884–1943) theory of realism; Voronsky saw art and literature as means to a direct understanding of reality. Essentially, the promulgation of Socialist Realism marked both the end of the relatively free creative atmosphere and an increasing bureaucratization of the country's ideological superstructure.

It would be wrong, however, to believe that Socialist Realism is a cluster of administrative orders given by the Party or government. One among several possible Marxist theories of art, it evolved by adjusting itself to the needs of a historical situation where the Party seized power and aimed at achieving stabilization and gaining control of intellectual and creative activity in the new state. While proletarian art was based on the principle of *class* solidarity between artists and workers, Socialist Realism promoted the idea of the artist's loyalty to the socialist *state* built by the working class, peasants, and intelligentsia, and leading to a classless society.

The official introduction of the doctrine was preceded by an intensive campaign for its explanation and acceptance. It has been maintained for some time that Stalin invented the term. While he called on writers to be the "engineers of human souls", there is no evidence that he made up the term. It was probably coined by a collective effort of Party-minded critics in the early 1930s. At any rate, the term appeared for the first time in the Soviet press in 1932.

The driving force behind the imposition of Socialist Realism in the Soviet Union was Maxim GORKY. At the First All-Union Congress of Soviet Writers he was the only writer to deliver a major speech about the future development of Soviet literature. The remaining three speakers were professional politicians: Karl Radek (1885–1939), Nikolay Bukharin (1888–1938), and Andrey Zhdanov (1896–1948); the first two were shot in the purges, while Zhdanov became an official spokesman of Soviet aesthetics during the worst years of Stalinist terror.

Gorky's novel *Mat* (1907; *Mother*, 1907) is considered the first example of Socialist Realism in literature. In his theoretical statements Gorky stressed that Socialist Realism is the inheritor of the best traditions of world culture and should reflect not only people's preoccupations with reality, their worries or doubts, but also their joys and hopes. As one means of working toward this goal, Socialist Realism should make use of folklore.

By and large, however, the first attempts to define the essence of Socialist Realism were marked by a great deal of confusion. Was the new program to be treated as a literary movement, as a style, or as a poetics? During early discussions all these questions were asked, but no clear answer emerged. Some critics, such as Isak Nusinov (1889–1950), understood Socialist Realism as an entirely new aesthetic phenomenon, opposed to the literary trends of the past, including the realism of Tolstoy and Dostoevsky, whom he called representatives of bourgeois and feudal art. This position was in clear contradiction to Gorky's views. Another critic, P. Rozhkov (dates n.a.), presented Socialist Realism as a manifestation of dialectical materialism in art and literature.

At the First All-Union Congress Socialist Realism was defined as a *method* aimed at giving a truthful reflection of reality in its constant revolutionary development. At the same time, the educational role of art in general and of literature in particular was emphasized. The word "method", meaning "system", "orderliness", or "way of doing something", implies a normative understanding of the creative process and the writer's role in it. Consequently, one may say that Socialist Realism is the only normative program of art and literature developed in the 20th c. This normative character is discernible in both the artistic origins of the doctrine and the ideological core that constitutes the method.

The literary roots of Socialist Realism can be traced back to some works of the 1920s that immediately preceded the rise of the doctrine—for example, Dmitry Furmanov's (1891–1926) *Chapaev* (1923; *Chapayeve*, 1935), Fyodor GLADKOV's *Tsement* (1925; *Cement*, 1929), Konstantin Trenyov's (1878–1945) drama *Lyubov Yarovaya* (1926; *Lyubov Yarovaya*, 1946), Vladimir MAYAKOVSKY's poem *Vladimir Ilyich Lenin* (1924; "Vladimir Ilyich Lenin", 1939)—and, generally speaking, the tradition of realism. The literary seeds of Socialist Realism can also be found in the theoretical statements made by such 19th-c. radical critics as Vissarion Belinsky (1811–1848), Nikolay Chernyshevsky (1828–1889), and Nikolay Dobrolyubov (1836–1861). They formulated the idea of art as social commitment, demanded that literature depict reality "as it should be", and introduced the notion of the "positive hero".

The philosophical and ideological sources of Socialist Realism are two basic theses: (1) Marx's eleventh thesis on the philosopher Ludwig Feuerbach (1804–1872), stating that "philosophers have only interpreted the world, in various ways; the point, however, is to change it"; (2) Lenin's theory of reflection, which is considered to be the "soul of the materialist theory of cognition." Marx's thesis implies that a writer ought to have an *active* and positive relation to reality; that is, he cannot limit himself to a passive description of the world. As one Soviet critic has indicated, the central question of Socialist Realism is how to change social reality. The task of literature, therefore, is to promote the principle of "life as it should be". On the other hand, the sobering demand of Lenin's thesis calls for an objective presentation of reality and thus promotes the principle of describing "life as it is".

If analyzed in terms of literary terminology, the above contradiction corresponds to the well-known differentiation between (revolutionary) romanticism and realism. Despite assurances by Soviet critics that there is no contradiction between these two principles as combined in one literary method, this split is visible at all evolutionary stages of Socialist Realism. The call for revolutionary romanticism or description of "reality as it should be", which prevailed in the Stalinist period of Socialist Realism, produced schematic works with heroes that had little in common with reality. In the late 1940s this practice led to the rise of what was called the literature of "conflictlessness" and the "embellishment" of reality, in which a pastoral presentation of Soviet life and its people was considered to be imperative. This type of literary craftsmanship was based on extreme subjectivity of vision. This subjectivity, however, was ideologically motivated; that is, it was entirely determined by the Marxist world outlook. The fully developed doctrine of Socialist Realism found its most "classic" examples in the works of such writers as Mikhail SHOLOKHOV, Alexey TOLSTOY, Alexandr FADEEV, Boris Polevoy (pseud. of Boris Kampov, b. 1908), and Pyotr Pavlenko (1899–1951).

The post-Stalinist relaxation and the "thaw" in the mid-1950s allowed some writers to approach Soviet society from a more objective vantage point. This attitude dampened the ideological factor in favor of the principle of reflecting "reality as it is." Some writers of this bent, however, were accused of revisionism or reprimanded for their lack of ideological purity; consequently, some of them, for example, Aleksandr SOLZHENITSYN, were branded enemies of the people. In other words, this stream within official Soviet literature helped the rise of dissident literature.

To prevent ideological deviations and to preserve the "correctness" of the creative process, Socialist Realism envisages six precepts that constitute the very core of its method. These are (1) *partynost* (partisanship); (2) *narodnost* (a term difficult to translate; possible English equivalents are "peopleness" or "nationality"); (3) typicality; (4) the positive hero; (5) historicism; (6) revolutionary romanticism.

The most important component of the Socialist Realist creative method is *partynost*, which demands of writers a complete and unquestioning obedience to the Party's directives. It is a sort of safety valve to prevent revisionism by writers, because it implies not only artistic fidelity to Marxist philosophy but also support for the tactical swings in Party policy. *Narodnost* aims at two objectives: first, a work of art must communicate to readers some important messages concerning the life of the people and the nation as a whole; second, it must be communicative and understandable to the masses. Thus, it promotes realism as the fundamental principle of artistic (literary) creativity. *Typicality* calls for a presentation of typical characters in typical social circumstances. The interpretation of this concept, however, has always been a contentious issue. The notion of the *positive hero* tempers to some extent the category of typicality in that it encourages writers to create characters who could serve as models of political, social, and moral behavior or could project the "man of the future." *Historicism* means that writers should set their heroes in a definite historical context and avoid their presentation in a timeless vacuum. Characters ought to have historically identifiable features and not be bearers of universal values. Finally, *revolutionary romanticism*, with its vision of the future as it should be, in most cases is understood as a feature that should be part of every realistic work of

art. Some Soviet critics, however, are inclined to separate it entirely from the concept of Socialist Realism and suggest that one should recognize within Soviet literature the existence of a romantic trend.

The above rules account for the normative nature of Socialist Realism, since they try to regulate the ideological stand and the artistic practice of writers.

Conceived in Soviet Russia, Socialist Realism was imposed on non-Russian Soviet literatures and had some followers in the West, for example, Louis ARAGON, Bertolt BRECHT, and Martin Andersen NEXØ.

Aragon was one of the most ardent advocates of Socialist Realism in France. In *Pour un réalisme socialiste* (1935; for socialist realism) he denounced his ties with SURREALISM and expressed support for a literature that would serve to implement the ideals of socialist revolution as practiced in the Soviet Union. According to Aragon, Socialist Realism was the method that assured writers of the opportunity to exercise a direct and practical impact on the course of social and political events in the world. The most typical Socialist Realist writer in France, however, was André Stil (b. 1921), who received the Stalin Prize for his novel *Le premier choc* (2 vols., 1951–53; *The First Clash*, 2 vols., 1954).

Similarly, in Denmark, Nexø formulated and practiced a very militant version of Socialist Realism, which he considered to be a weapon in the struggle against fascism. The strict application of this method in some of his later novels, for example, *Morten hin røde* (3 vols., 1945–57; Morten the red), made them less effective than his masterful earlier works.

Brecht, although subscribing to some aspects of Socialist Realism, refused to follow the Soviet model closely, but rather defended the need for artistic experimentation and for the integrity of literature, which should not be identified with ideology.

In the English-speaking world Socialist Realism found favor especially with the English essayist and literary critic Ralph Fox (1900–1937) and the American novelist Howard Fast (b. 1914). Fox saw in Socialist Realism a chance for the revival of the traditional hero, who would embody the new ideas of Marxism. Fast, in the novels *Freedom Road* (1944) and *Spartacus* (1952), employed Socialist Realist methods. But he denounced both Communism and Socialist Realism after Khrushchev's revelations at the Twentieth Congress in 1956.

After World War II Socialist Realism was forcefully imposed on the Soviet-bloc countries of eastern Europe. Such writers as the Bulgarian Georgi Karaslavov (b. 1904) and the Czechs Marie Pujmanová (1893–1958) and Marie Majerová illustrate the doctrine. Some writers, however, managed to offset its detrimental impact by creating a more independent concept of socialist art. For example, Miroslav KRLEŽA, Oskar DAVIČO, and Mihailo LALIĆ in Yugoslavia, Kazimierz BRANDYS and Jerzy ANDRZEJEWSKI in Poland, Milan KUNDERA and Josef ŠKVORECKÝ in Czechoslovakia, and Yordan Radichkov (b. 1929) in Bulgaria either resisted the main ideas of Socialist Realism or made significant contributions to overcome its rigid, dogmatic demands and thus showed the way out of the existing stalemate. Some of them (Škvorecký, Kundera) had to pay for their opposition by being forced into exile.

BIBLIOGRAPHY: Sinyavsky, A., *On Socialist Realism* (1960); Ermolaev, E., *Soviet Literary Theories, 1917–1934: The Genesis of Socialist Realism* (1963); Lukács, G., *Realism in Our Time: Literature and the Class Struggle* (1964); Struve, G., *Russian Literature under Lenin and Stalin, 1917–1953* (1971); James, C. V., *Soviet Socialist Realism: Origins and Theory* (1973); Le

Roy, G. C. and U. Beitz, eds., *Preserve and Create: Essays in Marxist Literary Criticism* (1973); Możejko, E., *Der sozialistische Realismus: Theorie, Entwicklung und Versagen einer Literaturmethode* (1977); Ovcharenko, A., *Socialist Realism and the Modern Literary Process* (1978); Clark, C., *The Soviet Novel: History as Ritual* (1981)

—EDWARD MOŻEJKO

SOCIETY AND LITERATURE

Literature in this century has been concerned above all with a renewed attempt to answer the question "what is man?" in terms that are usually Freudian and often verge on the solipsistic. Yet because of its heritage it cannot escape entirely from considering man as a social being even when it turns away with some violence from the goals and assumptions of a preceding age. Whereas the writers of the romantic generation of the early 19th c. engaged in much the same kind of inquiry, were inclined to see man as essence, not existence, as abstraction, not concrete, mutable entity, and thus were able to remove him from his social milieu or to present it also in general and abstract terms, writers of our day are more empirical than philosophical and feel that some filiations with external reality must be given the persona. It may be said, in short, that the prevailingly realistic mode of the last part of the 19th c. acted as a bridge between these two major explorations of the human psyche, that we have come back to the romantic quest better equipped in knowledge and with a sense of the importance of the social matrix that did not exist before.

The general scientism of the latter part of the 19th c., positivistic in temper, inductive and experimental in method, had for a time an overwhelming influence on literary endeavors. It was not merely that writers sought to explore society in all its manifestations, but that they became convinced that they were servants of truth, that their "experiments" à la Émile Zola had the same fundamental utility as the laboratory findings of a Pasteur. They were disenchanted with the invented personalities that appeared in the works of their predecessors, they had doubts about the possibility of reliable access to the mind, and they were intoxicated by the broad vistas of external social depiction that suddenly opened up before them. Thus they gave primacy to that which they could observe in the world around them, often in the process adopting a kind of epiphenomenalism by which they reduced mental states to ineffective shadows accompanying the material causal process. Although the impulsion of this literary scientism showed a decided slackening by the turn of the century (particularly in Europe; the United States and other provincial areas were at least a generation behind), it has never disappeared. It has continued to produce works in the traditional social framework of the realist-naturalists and has at the same time helped to shape the literature called psychological, giving it a social reference and density that the romantics were not equipped to bring to it.

To many writers after the turn of the century these inherited social preoccupations were an albatross around the neck, something that they felt they must throw off at any cost if they were to develop in their proper bent. They sought to repudiate Zola and all his pomps, in the fashion of Marcel PROUST at the end of *Le temps retrouvé* (1927; *The Past Recaptured*, 1932), asserting in concert with Dostoevsky, although with a different emphasis, that they practiced a "higher realism," that truth was not to be found on the surface of things. In particular they repudiated the basic realist assumption that truth was objective, inherent in the data of perception, accessible to all on nearly equal terms. Influenced by the new psychology and the new physics, they shifted their emphasis from the perceived object to the perceiving mind and made their capital of the myriad possibilities, the myriad patterns of individual perception. Society as a thing in itself, mappable and analyzable, capable of dissection like a corpse upon a table, was dissolved into multiple fluctuating perceptions, to a very real extent into a country of the mind, or of many minds.

Yet quietly the inherited realistic conceptions continued to exert their pull, to topple the exuberant antisocial hyperbole of the SURREALISTS, for example, to provide a constant reminder that the new object of literary cultism, psychological man, was also social man. Zola's reputation, which had been the barometer of the fortunes of the naturalist doctrine and had subsided to insignificance with the dominance of the poetic, the symbolic, and the psychological way of writing, began to rise again after World War I. There was guarded admission that the realists had a point in their insistence on society as a subject for literature. A populist school arose in France, a NEOREALIST group in Portugal; and after World War II a group of practicing realists emerged in Italy. Meanwhile, in the Soviet Union writers found it advisable to conform to the dictates of SOCIALIST REALISM. Even if it is doubtful that realism as a doctrine will ever hold sway again, it is evident that in the 20th c. it exerts a steady influence on literature and acts as a brake on writing that would remove man from his habitat.

To be sure, the authentic voice of poetry in our age is ruminative, self-probing, self-revelatory. Always teetering on the precipice of the uniquely private system of reference, it does attempt to draw away from the public world of social data or it filters them through the sieve of association to the point where they lose objective importance. But not entirely. Poets like Rainer Maria RILKE, Federico GARCÍA LORCA, W. B. YEATS, W. H. AUDEN, and Ezra POUND will suddenly reveal the grounding of the private experience in the public condition or event. William Carlos WILLIAMS will write a long poem, *Paterson* (1946–58), one of the major themes of which is "Outside outside myself there is a world," which has the power to inform thoughts concretely. In another way, too, poets find that they cannot ignore society, as the young Russians attest in their increasingly open attack on rigid and restrictive social attitudes. And, of course, the poetry that sprang from two world wars must, even in its anguished rejection of war, still incorporate the distant rumble of the guns.

With this partial qualification made for poetry, we must recognize that 20th-c. literature cannot avoid placing man in his setting, that it adopts a practical Thomism in accepting the fact that at least most of what exists in the mind must previously have existed outside it, and that it accepts for better or worse that social forms are dominant in the shaping of a human being. However, writers today are much less interested in the representative, average man than were their predecessors. They are not epiphenomenalists either, but phenomenalists. What man makes of the world via perception is more important than what it may be in itself, if indeed it is anything in itself. In other words, there is a shift away from the realist view that man is essentially subject to his environment and a kind of fixture in it to the view that social data are merely the raw material to be fed into the hopper of the mind from which will issue, not something rich and strange, in the spirit of the romantics, but something rich and substantial in its contribution to an understanding of the human condition.

From this standpoint it is no accident that the bildungsroman should have become a major genre of the age. It is, naturally, most frequently a bildungsroman of the mind: what a man learns *from* his inescapable involvement in society, not what he learns *about* society, is the important thing. To a considerable extent what a man must learn is that there are no solutions to social problems, which he can only endure; therefore he must come to know himself, for only in that way can he live with the unresolved and the paradoxical, anesthetizing himself to the goring horns of the dilemma of his life. Since value systems are no longer achieved by putting a coin in the appropriately designated slot of tradition, the hero of the quest has to make them up as he goes, not out of whole cloth, but in full awareness of the patchwork nature of the society in which he lives.

This is to put the most optimistic tone to the process. It is what is achieved by Robert Jordan in Ernest HEMINGWAY's *For Whom the Bell Tolls* (1940), by Jack Burden in Robert Penn WARREN's *All the King's Men* (1946), perhaps by Lewis Eliot in the novels of C. P. SNOW. The provenance of titles is significant: such an unbeleaguered achievement of insight is less frequent outside the Anglo-American literary tradition. Beyond this zone of partial comfort we confront the no-man's-land of EXISTENTIALISM, a pessimistic obverse of statements like the above, exhorting men to make the best of what is, by common agreement, the worst. Since the time of Kierkegaard, religious existentialism has had a growing influence in the West, but on the whole it is its secular counterpart that manifests itself in contemporary literature. It is significant that the novels of Franz KAFKA, which seem to yield most by a religious and/or Freudian reading, are seized upon by the common reader as reflecting the dilemma of the social man. Even without the metaphor of arrest and trial, which is certainly an invitation to such an interpretation, readers would no doubt seize upon a central concept that reflects the capricious and impersonal working of institutions, since their own existential predicament is not highfalutin or abstract, but is seen most clearly in terms of their daily life in society, subject as they are to being parts of the machine and to decisions by the supermachine.

This is one of the major points where the literature of self-analysis is thrown back into the broad stream of literature about society. Existentialist thought does not allow man to withdraw from society, since that is impossible, in order to loaf and invite his soul. And the reason this is impossible is the same reason that has caused the popularity of this doctrine—a galling awareness of the adverse conditions of life. Jean-Paul SARTRE bridged the two kinds of literature effectively in his categorical imperative "choose thyself," which has its foundation both in a sense of the social barriers to authentic being and in psychological fracture or incapacity. The Sartrean protagonist is physically hemmed in on every side by institutions and social attitudes that function less absurdly than ineluctably. His act of choosing, his attempt at authenticity, must be made in full awareness of his act's being a wager in which the cards are stacked against him.

Finally, in this spectrum of the possibilities of self-knowledge open to the social man, we go beyond existentialism to the existential monster, whose being is less an act of knowing than a sly revenge on the tyrannical forces that mutilate him. His act is to choose a grotesque, perverted, and ultimately (by repetition) banal self in the manner of Samuel BECKETT, Jean GENET, and Henry MILLER. This is less a choice of self than a retreat into the porcupine ball of an authorially contrived *Ur*-self, a recoil into a fetal id position from which to make an ultimate, despairing, defensive self-assertion. To the reader who is not hypnotized by doctrine, such postures in time come to seem frenetically inauthentic, although their purpose of arousing nausea toward current social values by means of a shower of ordure is clear enough.

These existentialist and subexistentialist attitudes are frequently referred to under the general rubric of "alienation," the contemporary idiom for angst or even *Weltschmerz*. Although alienation is frequently offered as a kind of absolute, it is a relative term, for it necessitates referent, that from which man is alienated. He may, to be sure, be alienated from himself or, in traditional religious terms, from God; but the usual form in our literature is the human being alienated from society. This common adolescent phenomenon becomes alarming when it is prolonged into maturity, when it becomes the gestalt of middle age. Partly it is a delayed reaction to disillusionment over the promises of rationalism and optimism; partly it is the result of shock from the lurid events of the 20th c., although the most vocal exponents of alienation have usually suffered those shocks only at second hand. In its basis it is born merely of frustration, of a sense of inadequacy in a world that is too mechanical and too complex to regard the individual. There has been a good deal of rushing about during the 20th c. for a formula, a doctrine, that would provide the basis for a manageable and predictable society, that would set up values both immutable and man-directed. The failure of these frenetic quests has merely compounded the sense of alienation from which they arise.

It is to be concluded that even that body of writing that is not by definition social, that is in revolt against the conceptions and the literary practices of the 19th c., must be seen to be conditioned by society and societal problems. Beyond it lies that body of literature that is a direct continuation of the social representation dominant in the earlier period, that takes for granted the primacy of social subjects for literature and seeks to present man's condition in those terms. Certain important modifications of view are to be noted, however. Most important is a sense of society as process rather than fixed tableau, as becoming rather than being, as dynamic rather than static. This is an inevitable result of close observation of modern life. It is a condition that was only vaguely discernible when Zola wrote the Rougon-Macquart cycle, although he did capitalize on it in *Germinal* (1885; *Germinal*, 1895).

This change in turn entails important modifications of the sense of causality that underlies society. A strict materialistic determinism no longer suffices, except in that intellectual climate where it is a basic article of faith; in its place there is both a reliance on interaction and an allowance for the random event, intolerable as the latter concept is to any tightly rational system. Brilliant as Thomas MANN's *Der Zauberberg* (1924; *The Magic Mountain*, 1927) is in its analysis of the process of breakdown and resynthesis of social forms, it does in a way rest on a simplified and old-fashioned base in the symmetry and inevitability of social patterns that it hypothesizes. It states that when a social complex (institutions and values) ceases to meet human needs adequately, it is undermined by the pull of those elements that are lacking and is moved to a position that incorporates them. As Mann conceived of it, the formal elements of the bourgeois culture of western Europe tend ultimately to squeeze out life-giving content. The individual and his society out of inner necessity move toward the latter and eventually create a new complex where needs for order and vital being are in balance. By this argument Germany became the land of the middle, the geographical and cultural locus of the new synthesis that would harmonize East and West. Satisfying as this structure is as hypothesis, the failure of actuality to conform to it may derive from the restrictive causal pattern on which it rests.

The third shift away from traditional conceptions has already been dealt with. The individual human being has been raised to a level of greater importance than those conceptions accorded him. People do not exist in society merely as objects for the steamroller of impersonal social force to run over and crush. Rather they exist in the midst of exterior social forces as dynamic beings, fighting back significantly if not efficaciously instead of inertly allowing themselves to be destroyed. It is a David-against-Goliath struggle, with David losing—or at least not winning; but man as hero has been reinstated to a degree, even though the naïve and shocked idealist may speak of him as antihero. This is the importance of James JOYCE's Leopold Bloom. In its social dimensions Ulysses (1922) is an unsparing demonstration of the inertia of Dublin life at the turn of the century. The background figures have been ground down to immobile stumps. A promising creative personality, Stephen Dedalus, is frustrated by the social attitudes that rule over him from the past (although some of the blame for his failure is shown to lie within him). But the Everyman of the novel, Leopold Bloom, who is crushed many times a day, whose creative capacities are abortive, nonetheless bounces back, carries on a running fight with his society, refusing to be crushed, looking hopefully to the future, insisting that man is more than a speck of dust in interstellar space or more than a black dot in a white space at the bottom of a page.

For purposes of convenience we may designate two types of social depiction in the literature of our time. These are social chronicle and social parable, the primary distinction between them being the degree of literalness of representation that they offer.

Social Chronicle

It is in this area that the direct inheritance from 19th-c. realism makes itself most strongly felt. The powerful examples of Zola, Lev Tolstoy, Benito PÉREZ GALDÓS, even of Balzac and Stendhal, are undeniably present to the 20th-c. writer even when he feels he must repudiate them as being old-fashioned. With a few exceptions the social chronicles of today do not have the compelling power or novelty of their prototypes, but they still flourish as a conventional (and prolix) way of fiction. Such works are responsive to a compulsion to tell what life is like in a given time and place, not least in those areas without a previous literary history where current inventory seems of immediate importance. This desire to set down the truth is no doubt closely allied to a rising social and political consciousness in developing areas, which wishes to set the record of social conditions straight so that something can be done about them, proving once more that since Zola, social action and social depiction have been linked together in the popular mind.

On a more sophisticated level the 20th c. has provided a host of panoramic novels on a large scale. There come to mind the social chronicles of modern Brazil, Camilio José CELA's La colmena (1951; The Hive, 1953), set in modern Madrid, or John DOS PASSOS's trilogy U.S.A. (1930–36). The most notable example is Jules ROMAINS's Les hommes de bonne volonté (1932–46; Men of Good Will, 14 vols., 1933–46), which in twenty-seven volumes attempts to give an overview of French and European life from 1908 to 1933, playing down, though not ignoring, salient historical events in the interest of giving the "feel" of the period. The novel is straight empiricism, raising the question as to what were the major

causal forces in the development of the period, but containing an inherent irony in that the men of good will whom the work traces are found to be helpless against the downhill rush of events that culminates in Hitler's rise to power in 1933. There are certain to be more works like this, for the genre is capable of infinite variation. Potentially, what Romains did for Paris and France can be done for Belgrade and Bombay, for Johannesburg and Djakarta, and moreover can be reattempted for random time spans for generations to come. Such chronicles adhere to the slice-of-life, average-man convention. They make capital, not of exciting events, but of what life is like in its mediocre, unheroic continuity and repetition. They do, however, depend on a sense of historical process, first exhibited by Tolstoy in War and Peace. They depend also on an acute awareness of social change: the attempt to seize on the significant pattern of an era would make no sense in a society of fixed social values and observances.

A limited derivative from this broad genre is the depiction of institutions in the specific sense of the term. The relationship is much like that of the individual Zola novel to the total sweep of the Rougon-Macquart cycle, although usually without the continuing matrix of the roman-fleuve. Here the emphasis is often informational: what it is like to make one's living in a steel foundry or coal mine, as a stevedore or laboratory technician; what the interplay of forces, human and material, is in factory, department store, hospital, or university, not to mention big government. Such works no doubt serve a useful function in a world of compartmentalized experience, where it is rarely possible for a single individual to have close experience of more than three or four institutional worlds. From one standpoint this kind of writing was the forte of Sinclair LEWIS, with the obvious added dimension of satire. It is a genre that is factually revealing of transient data but that with predictable regularity bogs down in those data, which are by the nature of vocational and institutional process highly transitory and as a result incapable of much illumination. An exception of some importance is Winifred Holtby's (1898–1935) novel South Riding (1936), which shows the working of local government in Yorkshire. This form becomes more sophisticated when it provides a background for psychological growth, as in Meyer Levin's (1905–1981) Citizens (1940), where the events of a strike are no more important than the protagonists' response to them.

The essence of the kind of chronicle just described is the humdrum, nonexceptional train of life which it depicts. What the 20th c. has provided in plenty is the exceptional social event, the public catastrophe, jarring to moral conviction and literary convention alike. To such events writers of the last sixty-odd years have been drawn with inescapable fascination. This has been the era of the war novel, not war seen as an arena for private heroism or despair, but war in its broad social sweep, as impersonal machine that mows down men and nations and engulfs social landmarks. The protagonist may be multiple and faceless. Whoever he is, what happens to him is less poignant in itself than in the insistent sense of general suffering and waste that the account provides. Emphasis in this genre has varied over the years: Henri BARBUSSE's pioneer work Le feu: Journal d'une escouade (1916; Under Fire: The Story of a Squad, 1917) is more personal and lyrical than Jules Romains's Verdun (1938; Verdun, 1939). Erich Maria REMARQUE's Im West-ern nichts Neues (1929; All Quiet on the Western Front, 1929) is narrower in focus than Arnold ZWEIG's tetralogy of war novels, of which Der Streit um den Sergeanten Grischa (1927; The Case of Sergeant Grischa, 1928) is removed from the scene of active fighting and seeks to show the general demoralization produced by the military machine of the necessary safeguards of civilian life. James JONES's *The Thin Red Line* (1962) and Theodor Plievier's (1892–1955) trilogy *Stalingrad* (1945; *Stalingrad*, 1948), *Moskau* (1952; *Moscow*, 1953), and *Berlin* (1954; *Berlin*, 1956) are masterpieces of the impersonal ballet of military action. Whereas the works emanating from experience of World War I had a tendency to outrage and anger, this is less true of those about World War II. Certainly such writing is not complacent about war, but it seems to imply that a full and honest account is more compelling than any amount of special pleading.

Not only has this century been a time of war; it has also been an age of revolution, of revolutions that have produced vast social changes at dramatic cost. These have inevitably cried out for chronicles, if only in justification of the triumphant regime. Mikhail SHOLOKHOV, Nobel laureate in 1965, received that prize primarily for his *Tikhy Don* (4 vols., 1928–40; *And Quiet Flows the Don*, 1934; *The Don Flows Home to the Sea*, 1941), which portrayed world war, revolution, and civil war from the vantage point of the Don Cossacks. Something of the same effort was made by Alexey TOLSTOY in *Khozhdenie po mukam* (1922–41; *Road to Calvary*, 1946) and by Konstantin Alexandrovich FEDIN in *Goroda i gody* (1924; *Cities and Years*, 1962), although the latter is notable in that it does not adhere to the Tolstoyan saga of war and peace but attempts by a mosaic of symbolic actions to convey the dislocating effects of a social convulsion. In Germany, Heinrich BÖLL and Günter GRASS have used this type of symbolic structure for an analysis of the descent of Germany into the abyss under the Nazi regime, a path that had been marked out by Thomas Mann in *Doktor Faustus* (1947; *Doctor Faustus*, 1948). Heimito von DODERER charted crucial events of breakdown in Austria in his leisurely novel *Die Dämonen* (1956; *The Demons*, 1961). For the Spanish Civil War there is the sweeping chronicle composed by José María GIRONELLA, of which two volumes, *Los cipreses creen en Dios* (1953; *The Cypresses Believe in God*, 1955) and *Un millón de muertos* (1961; *One Million Dead*, 1963), deal with the war.

The development of Gironella's three-part chronicle—the third volume, *Ha estallado la paz* (1966; *Peace after War*, 1969), deals with the aftermath of the war—is especially interesting in that it begins with a narrow circle of personal experience in separatist Catalonia and then gradually widens to take in the whole of Spain as the avalanche of the disaster spreads. For Italy under the domination of Mussolini there were the works of Ignazio SILONE written in exile, especially his *Fontamara* (1934; *Fontamara*, 1934) and *Pane e vino* (1937; *Bread and Wine*, 1937). It is significant that after the fall of the regime Silone rewrote the former in less reportorial terms, in tacit recognition of the limitations of the strictly chronicle account.

There have also been accounts of more special situations during these eight decades of misery and loss. The ravages of anti-Semitism in prewar Europe, the calculated effort at extermination of the Jewish people, the painful building of a new Jerusalem have been extensively documented. Of equal scope is the literature arising from the great economic depression of the 1920s and 1930s. *Kleiner Mann, was nun?* (1932; *Little Man, What Now?*, 1933), a novel by Hans Fallada (pseud. of Rudolf Ditzen, 1893–1947) dealing with the plight of the white-collar class in Berlin, is a well-known example. Works of this sort written in the U.S. and England have tended to become special pleading, an attempt to advocate basic, even revolutionary reforms in the economic system by

recounting the plight of people living under that system. This particular outburst was preceded in the U.S. at the turn of the century by an unusual phenomenon, the muckraking movement, by which a group of magazine writers and writers of fiction delved into the various ways in which malefactors of great wealth acquired their riches and abused their privileges, to the danger of the fundamental institutions of the country. This was the first instance of reporter turned man of letters, although it soon fizzled off into sensationalism.

Because of this widespread effort at chronicling the events of the time it is easy to see that virtually no aspect of the history of this century, in Europe and America at least, has been left untouched. The popular success of this kind of writing has led to an extension retrospectively into the social history of the past, particularly in industrial countries where the ravages of the recent changes provided dramatic materials. American writers have also tried retrospectively to re-create the experience of life on the frontier and to treat the Civil War in fictional terms as social phenomenon. Historical fiction of documentary nature is less prevalent on the continent, although Giuseppe Tomasi di LAMPEDUSA's *Il gattopardo* (1958; *The Leopard* 1960) is an important exception.

A new genre of considerable importance that is very largely the product of this century is reportage. This need not be social in subject matter, for it often is a form of biography, but in practice it is usually an account of a social situation. It differs from the traditional parliamentary report or sociological treatise in that it is directed at a mass audience and seeks to involve readers in a way that straight analysis cannot do. In part this genre is made possible by the rapidity of communication of our era. This development depends on a reading public with a taste for fact that newspapers and news services have created by their worldwide networks of reporters, although it must be observed that reportage demands a skill and objectivity not always available to the reporter on the spot. Such writing embraces the great general human catastrophes—fire, flood, famine, drought, and earthquake—but it can also be evoked by much more particular events, provided they have a broad human (that is, social) relevance. What it depends on for effect is an eye for significant detail and a disposition to let the facts speak for themselves. The classic instance is John Hersey's (b. 1914) *Hiroshima* (1946). More recently in the U.S. a somewhat exaggerated furor was caused by Truman CAPOTE's *In Cold Blood* (1966), which he called a "nonfiction novel." While the label is more arresting than meaningful, it does attest to a tendency of modern fiction to rely on and move toward the actual in its depictions. What is more important about the Capote book is that it sits squarely astride the two major interests of contemporary writing: it attempts to make sense of the aberrant personalities that committed a horrible and senseless crime, and it attempts to see that crime not as an isolated and sensational event but in a social perspective.

Social Parable

Robert FROST, in the midst of the spate of Depression writing in the U.S., made an important distinction between the literature of griefs and the literature of grievances: the former, he said, dealt with the constants of the human condition; the latter was concerned with limited and transitory situations, and although it produced detailed and often poignant pictures of suffering, they were of too local and passionate a nature. This distinction has some relevance in drawing a line between social chronicle and social parable. To avoid the limiting effects of overminute documentation, many writers have turned their backs on social history and have sought out another path, that which will lead to illumination of social situations without dulling them with detail. Here the literary work aims at a general, not a specific, statement; the attachment to specific setting or situation is less fully delineated, such elements being purged of the local and being raised to the universal. Sometimes to its loss, it aims to avoid the emotional involvement that comes from the situation seen too near at hand. Immediacy of experience does have its dangers in literature, as can be seen by the passion aroused after several decades by any literary treatment of the Spanish Civil War. It is this kind of partisan readership that the social parable tries to avoid. It provides imaginative constructions that are tantalizingly similar to real historical situations but are not facsimiles of them. With a much more immediate social reference than most great works of the past, such writing nonetheless is engaged in the same process as that which made of the Seven against Thebes more than a local conflict or raised the failure of Richard II to a parable on kingship.

A popular form, and one close to chronicle, is the historical reconstruction that emphasizes its parallel to a contemporary situation at the cost of historical exactness. Such a device is both necessary and effective under an authoritarian regime: witness the impact of Jean ANOUILH's *Antigone* (1944; *Antigone*, 1946) in Paris during the German occupation. It is one that is used with a more general reference by Albert CAMUS in *Caligula* (1944; *Caligula*, 1947) and Friedrich DÜRRENMATT in *Romulus der Große* (1956; *Romulus the Great*, 1956). So widespread are the biographical and historical studies in semifictional guise of the decline of the Roman Empire and the fragmented society of the Middle Ages that they seem to reflect a preoccupation with the fate of contemporary society.

Still another variant is the pseudohistory of future events, a forward projection of outcomes inherent in current social tendencies. Sinclair Lewis's *It Can't Happen Here* (1935) is a well-known instance; George ORWELL's *1984* (1949) is another. This form is rather transparent in its polemic purpose but is effective up to a point. Sometimes called the inverted utopia, it is a natural vehicle in a pessimistic age, when social disaster seems more likely than the achievement of an ideal state. It is to be observed, moreover, that this century has not been prolific of true utopias, the last impressive blueprint of an ideal future being H. G. WELLS's *A Modern Utopia* (1905). B. F. Skinner's (1904–1990) *Walden Two* (1948), some four decades later, offers a challenging and controversial formula for the "behavioral engineering" necessary as a precondition to the establishment of a utopia.

An important subgenre, almost entirely of this century, is the science-fiction story, which, when it goes beyond mere adventure, readily takes on the mantle of social parable. Habitable stars millions of light years away from Terra have an uncanny likeness to our planet and provide a ready environment in which to reenact Terran errors or to make a fresh start on new principles in an effort to avoid those errors. Such stories, which manipulate time as well as space, sometimes pick a critical juncture in the operation of historical causality and project forward on the road not taken. More important than the utopian overtones of this genre is the general reflection it provides of social anxieties in the contemporary world. A somewhat monotonous preoccupation is the danger of annihilation by nuclear weapons and the necessity of saving a remnant of humanity for a new start somewhere out in space. Another anxiety is the pressure of population; a third is the general tyranny of an automated society. Both these last conditions are seen as forcing man out into space in order to reestablish the old, simple, human-centered way of life.

Interesting and voluminous as science fiction is, it cannot thus far be considered of major literary importance, but it does provide a useful oblique reflection of the temper and attitudes of the Age of Anxiety. Of more enduring value is the strict social parable, which provides a fictive microcosm as a mirror to the real world. The plays of Bertolt BRECHT often fall into this category, although with an obvious doctrinal slant. William GOLDING's *Lord of the Flies* (1954) is an unusually powerful parable of the havoc wrought by original sin, that is, human imperfection, in attempts at social harmony. Of utmost relevance are the works of William FAULKNER, which at one and the same time are a syncopated social history of a specific region and a universal parable of human endeavor, thus generalizing from the fall of the Old South to the fall of man. Similar, although more limited in scope, is Camus's *La peste* (1947; *The Plague*, 1948), which takes a very local situation in Oran as a springboard for broad implications about the human condition. In both Faulkner's and Camus's cases the place is real, the events are largely imaginary, and the human responses are both realistic and archetypal. By its very extent, Faulkner's work is the more elaborate parable, but the significant thing is that fictive works of this kind are always massively rooted in actuality; or rather, by pervasive reference they summon up that actuality to buttress the imaginary action.

Beyond social chronicle and social parable there has continued to exist the traditional area of social satire, running a gamut from comedy of manners to bitter social polemic. Although literature in this century has made no significant innovations in this realm, it is notable for the wide range of subjects it treats. In every country there are incongruities of statement and behavior that provide ready targets. Mossbacks and angry young men, bureaucrats and starry-eyed idealists, do-gooders and do-nothings, men in grayflannel suits and discontented youth in blue jeans have been ticked off in virtually every language. No situation is too poignant or too ominous to escape the flick of satire or the rough and tumble of burlesque. If, for example, we cannot neutralize the bomb, we can learn to live with it, as many a thriller devoted to atomic crisis has shown. Ephemeral as most of these works are, they provide indication of a healthy skepticism and of the readiness of literature to make use of all social subjects.

It is easy to forget in a period of relatively free expression that there is another aspect to the relation of literature and society: to what extend does society exert a formal pressure on literature, determining what paths it shall venture upon, what paths it shall avoid? Certainly in terms of positive encouragement there is little evidence of influence. The academies, where they exist, seem to have no power except, perhaps, to excite rebellion against convention, as if that were ever necessary, and it is doubtful that the great literary prizes do more than bring to notice works of varying degrees of merit. Similarly, the educational establishment, in those countries where contemporary literature is taught, may help to provide a reading public but is ineffectual in determining what writers shall provide for that public. Even in the U.S., where the university is increasingly a patron of the arts, there is no discernible influence on the course of literature from that source except for the ephemeral faddism that is as indigenous to the classroom as to the Left Bank café.

There is, to be sure, the negative power of censorship that attempts to coerce thought and art into approved channels. Psychological literature most commonly comes up against censorship concerned with faith and morals, social literature with that involving political and economic doctrine; but in practice the two types of censorship are not that easily separable. Political authority, finding a book dangerous on doctrinal grounds, may prefer to ban it on moral grounds; thus, we have frequently seen books labeled "decadent" and "obscene" when the real charge against them was political and economic heterodoxy. Each of the authoritarian regimes during this century has implemented a severe censorship as a matter of course. Such curbs certainly prevent publication within the country, but they are not successful in preventing a manuscript's being smuggled out or the published copy's being smuggled in. Neither do they prevent clandestine circulation of illicit foreign books. Nonetheless, such coercion can be said to have a considerable effect either in drying up literary activity altogether or in forcing it into approved channels. It took nearly fifty years for Soviet writers to rebel against the restrictions of Socialist Realism, and that battle is by no means won.

In the democratic countries at least, the relationship of literature to society is one of free use of the materials that social life provides. The very terms of reference of contemporary life, the rapidity of communication by which readers become aware of events in the social environment, the provision of a way of thinking about society by the social sciences, and indeed a general disposition to seek out the lines of causality in the data of experience—all these forces have caused the literature of this century to shun for the most part isolation in a dream world of the imagination and to make greater use of the data of social experience than has ever been the case before.

BIBLIOGRAPHY: Trotsky, L., *Literature and Revolution* (1925); Guérard, A., *Literature and Society* (1935); Plekhanov, G., *Art and Society* (1936); Read, H., *Art and Society* (1937); Frye, N., *The Critical Path: An Essay on the Social Context of Literary Criticism* (1971); Green, M., *Cities of Light and Sons of the Morning: A Cultural Psychology for an Age of Revolution* (1972); Bradbury, M., *The Social Context of Modern Literature* (1974); Craig, D., *The Real Foundations: Literature and Social Change* (1974); Heilman, R. B., *The Ways of the World: Comedy and Society* (1978); Kernan, A. B., *The Imaginary Library: An Essay on Literature and Society* (1982)

—GEORGE J. BECKER

SÖDERBERG, Hjalmar

Swedish novelist, short-story writer, dramatist, and critic, b. 2 July 1869, Stockholm; d. 14 Oct. 1941, Copenhagen, Denmark.

S. grew up in a materially comfortable and emotionally secure middle-class Stockholm family. As a schoolboy, however, he was teased and humiliated for his physical weakness; a deeply felt sympathy for the plight of the outsider runs through his literary production. After his matriculation examination in 1888, S. briefly became a minor bureaucrat, then turned to journalism, through which he soon won recognition as a perceptive literary critic. His

reputation as a writer of fiction was secured by short stories published in the 1890s, in particular those collected in *Historietter* (1898; little stories). From 1917 until his death he lived in Copenhagen.

S.'s first novel, *Förvillelser* (1895; aberrations), created something of a scandal because the erotic escapades of the main character were not presented in a moralizing light. It is, nevertheless, an accurate document of the times, a reflection of prevailing class attitudes in sexual matters. The novel displays several features typical of S.'s more mature works: the character of the dandy who spends much of his time in restaurants and cafés, watching the passers-by and discussing matters of deep philosophical import with like-minded friends; the anchoring in the Stockholm milieu; and a graceful, flexible prose style. These attributes are further developed in the pieces in *Historietter*, several of which also have a symbolic resonance lacking in the novel. In these minor masterpieces—anecdotes or vignettes rather than true short stories—a pose of ironic skepticism only partly disguises the underlying tone of pessimism and anguish.

The autobiographical opening portion of the novel *Martin Bircks ungdom* (1901; *Martin Birck's Youth*, 1930) centers on the loss of traditional faith and the development of a deterministic philosophy. Paralyzed by his own growing perception of the meaninglessness of life, Martin Birck becomes a passive observer, capable of speculation but not action. Although a love affair offers some consolation and hope, the relationship is stymied by practical and conventional considerations: the couple cannot afford to marry and must meet in secret to protect her reputation.

Doktor Glas (1905; *Doctor Glas*, 1963) initially aroused indignation among conservatives, who viewed the novel solely as a polemic against unquestioning acceptance of a husband's "marital rights" and in favor of ethical murder: the title character poisons the odious pastor Gregorius so that his young wife may join the man she loves. But this external action is secondary to S.'s psychological character study of Glas, an analysis that in many respects prefigures FREUD.

The impossibility of mutual, enduring love is the theme of both the drama *Gertrud* (1906; Gertrud) and the novel *Den allvarsamma leken* (1912; the serious game); their common source was a tempestuous affair that for S. ended bitterly. Gertrud herself represents the demand that love be the all-important primary focus of life, a demand that remains unsatisfied; the relationship between Arvid Stjärnblom and Lydia Stille in *Den allvarsamma leken* is a series of thrusts and parries that does not lead to permanent happiness, despite the fact that each loves the other deeply.

Creating a fictional framework was never easy for S.; in his last decades, he gradually dropped the fictional mask altogether. His antipathy toward traditional, institutionalized Judeo-Christianity is manifested in the religious-historical interpretations *Jahves eld* (1918; Jehovah's fire), *Jesus Barabbas* (1928; Jesus Barabbas), and *Den förvandlade Messias* (1932; the transformed Messiah). Toward the end of his life S. once more played an active role in contemporary political debate through his outspoken opposition to fascism.

S.'s literary roots lie in two quite divergent traditions: the political, social, and religious radicalism of the 1880s and the disillusioned pessimism of fin-de-siècle decadence. His works focus on thoughts, feelings, and moods, not on action or plot. He is justly famous for his impressionistic, evocative portrayal of turn-of-the-century Stockholm, the setting of virtually all his fiction. S.'s prose style—simple, unadorned, clear, controlled, with a relatively small vocabulary and an omnipresent undercurrent of melancholy irony—was a profound influence both on his contemporaries and on later generations of Scandinavian writers.

FURTHER WORKS: *Främlingarna* (1903); *Det mörknar öfver vägen* (1907); *Valda sidor* (1908); *Hjärtats oro* (1909); *Aftonstjärnan* (1912); *Den talangfulla draken* (1913); *Mittår* (1913); *Preludier* (1919); *Skrifter* (10 vols., 1919–1921); *Forntid och saga* (1921); *Samtidsnoveller* (1921); *Vers och varia* (1921); *Ödestimmen* (1922); *Resan till Rom* (1929); *Sista boken* (1942); *Samlade verk* (10 vols., 1943); *Makten, visheten och kvinnan* (1946); *Vänner emellan* (1948, with C. G. Laurin); *Aforismer och maximer* (1969); *Skrifter* (2 vols., 1969); *Kära Hjalle, Kära Bo: Bo Bergmans och H. S.s brevväxling 1891–1941* (1969). FURTHER WORKS IN ENGLISH: *The Chimney-Sweeper's Wife* (1923); *Selected Short Stories* (1935)

BIBLIOGRAPHY: Björkman, E., *Is There Anything New under the Sun?* (1911): 203–15; Stork, C. W., Preface to *Martin Birck's Youth* (1930): vii–xvi; Söderberg, E., " H. S.", *ASR*, 24 (1941): 334–37; Gustafson, A., *A History of Swedish Literature* (1961): 356–58; Geddes, T., *H. S.: "Doktor Glas"* (1975); Lofmark, C., *H. S.: "Historietter"* (1977); Hedberg, J., "A Coincidence according to the Gospel of St. James?" *MSpr*, 72 (1978): 1–11; Merrill, R., "Ethical Murder and *Doctor Glas*," *Mosaic*, 12, 4 (1979): 47–59; Warme, L. G., ed., *A History of Swedish Literature* (1996): 292-95

—ROCHELLE WRIGHT

SÖDERGRAN, Edith

Finnish poet (writing in Swedish), b. 4 April 1892, St. Petersburg (now Leningrad), Russia; d. 24 June 1923, Raivola (now Rodzino, Russia)

The daughter of Finland-Swedish parents, S. was educated at a German school in St. Petersburg. Most of her schoolgirl verse, reminiscent of Heine, was written in the German she had acquired in the classroom, the language also spoken in the tuberculosis sanatorium at Davos, Switzerland, where she was twice a patient (1912–13 and 1913–14). Save for her several sojourns in a sanatorium at Nummela in Finland (1909–11), she never lived in a milieu where Swedish was substantially represented. On the eve of World War I S. and her mother settled permanently in the family's summer home at Raivola on the Karelian Isthmus, among a population partly Finnish, partly Russian; her mother (who herself had been born in St. Petersburg) remained the principal person with whom she spoke Swedish.

In her isolation S. dreamed of taking Finland's literary world by storm. She made several short visits to Helsinki in 1915 and 1916, where she showed her manuscripts to the poet Arvid Mörne (1876–1946) and the critic Gunnar Castrén (1878–1959); a chance meeting with the philologist Hugo Bergroth (1866–1937) is thought to have persuaded her to abandon German for Swedish as a vehicle of lyric expression. Yet, save for two authors from the first half of the 19th c.—C. J. L. Almqvist (1793–1866), with his novel, *Drottningens juvelsmycke* (1833; the queen's jewelry) and its androgynous main figure, Tintomara, and J. L. Runeberg (1804–1877), with his epigrammatic lyrics—literature in Swedish interested her very

little, a blessing in disguise if one considers the extreme conservatism of Swedish and Finland-Swedish prosody in her day. Instead, she was drawn to the German EXPRESSIONISTS Else Lasker-Schüler (1869–1945) and Alfred Mombert (1872–1942) and the exoticist Max Dauthendey (1867–1918), to Victor Hugo's *Les Misérables* and to Rudyard KIPLING's *Jungle Book*, and to such disparate poets as Walt Whitman, Maurice MAETERLINCK, and the Russians Konstantin BALMONT and Igor Severyanin (1887–1941).

An unhappy love affair may have been the direct inspiration of much of the poetry of her first collection, *Dikter* (1916; poems), the critical reception of which ranged from puzzled admiration to ridicule; a final clumsy attempt to enter the Finland-Swedish literary circles of Helsinki, in September 1917, ended in a flight to Raivola. Then, the October Revolution wiped out the family's Russian savings, and extreme poverty was added to illness and loneliness. After a period of severe depression, her reading of Nietzsche and the events of the Finnish civil war (January-May 1918) put S. into a state of febrile excitement, during which she wrote *Septemberlyran* (1918; the September lyre). Its appearance gave rise to a journalistic debate that cast doubts—first in jest and then in earnest—on her sanity. However, an enthusiastic review by a young critic and novelist, Hagar Olsson (1893–1978), led to a close friendship between the two women. A standard-bearer of MODERNISM, Olsson encouraged the composition of *Rosenaltaret* (1919; the rose altar), with its aggressive cult of beauty, its love poems to the newly found "sister," its hymn to Dionysus, and its remarkable portrait ("Scherzo") of the poet as a dancer on a tightrope. The collection was followed by the sheaf of aphorisms, *Brokiga iakttagelser* (1919; varied observations), and the cosmic-prophetic poems of *Framtidens skugga* (1920; the future's shadow), which bespeaks S.'s ecstatic eroticism and her fear of death.

A sudden conversion to the anthroposophy of Rudolf Steiner (1861–1925) and then to a primitive and personal Christianity led S. to abandon the writing of poetry, and she returned to it only near the end of her life; in the bilingual (Finnish and Swedish) journal *Ultra*, one of whose editors was Olsson, she was paid homage as the pioneer of Finnish modernism. After her death, the poet Elmer DIKTONIUS assembled and issued her uncollected verse (from 1915 on) as *Landet som icke är* (1925; the land which is not), the title of a poem written on her deathbed.

In the 1930s Raivola became a place of pilgrimage for aspiring lyricists: S. was revered by younger contemporaries with styles of their own—for example, Gunnar EKELÖF and the Finnish poet Uno Kailas (1901–1933)—and imitated by weaker talents. Her example was of central importance in liberating Nordic verse from the confines of rhyme, regular rhythm, and traditional imagery.

The work of S. is unmistakable in its intensity, its variously desperate and childlike humor, and its almost gauche frankness. Her curiously innocent and unrequited sexuality, her sometimes pathetic narcissism, her persistent attempts to achieve a union with nature, her passion for beauty, and her terror of nonexistence, are all facets of an honest and defenseless personality. Her simple directness, enlivened by her genius for the unexpected in language, is seen to best advantage when S. is overwhelmed by forces outside herself, as in *Septemberlyran*, *Rosenaltaret*, and the concluding poems of the posthumous collection.

FURTHER WORKS: *Min lyra* (1929); *E. S.s dikter* (1940; *The Collected Poems of E. S.*, 1980); *Triumf att finnas till* (1948); *Samlade dikter* (1949); *Ediths brev: Brev från E. S. till Hagar*

Olsson (1955); *E. S.s dikter 1907–1909* (2 vols., 1961). **FURTHER WORKS IN ENGLISH:** *We Women: Selected Poems* (1977); *Love & Solitude: Selected Poems 1916–1923* (1981); *Poems* (1983)

BIBLIOGRAPHY: Schoolfield, G. C., "E. S.'s 'Wallenstein-profil,'" in Bayerschmidt, C. F., and Friis, E., eds., *Scandinavian Studies: Essays Presented to Henry Goddard Leach* (1965): 278–92; de Fages, L., *E. S.* (1970); Boyer, R., "Les structures de l'imaginaire chez E. S.," *EG*, 26 (1971): 526–49; Espmark, K., "The Translation of the Soul: A Principal Feature in Finland-Swedish Modernism," *Scan*, 15 (1976): 5–27; Hird, G., "E. S.: A Pioneer of Finland-Swedish Modernism," *BF*, 12 (1978): 5–7; Mossberg, C. L., "I'll Bake Cathedrals: An Introduction to the Poetry of E. S.," *Folio*, 11 (1978): 116–26; Schoolfield, G. C., *E. S.: Modernist Poet in Finland* (1984); Warme, L. G., *A History of Swedish Literature* (1996): 335-39

—GEORGE C. SCHOOLFIELD

SOGA LITERATURE

See Ugandan Literature

SOKOLOV, Sasha

Russian novelist, essayist, and poet, b. 6 Nov. 1943, Ottawa, Canada

S. is the premier avant-garde stylist to appear in Russian literature during the 1970s and 1980s. Born in Canada, where his father (in reality a spy) was stationed as a military diplomat, S. returned to Moscow in 1946. After an unsuccessful period in a military foreign-language training institute, an undetected attempt at defection, and short stays in jail and a mental hospital, S. was a member of the short-lived modernist literary group SMOG, which was broken up by the KGB in the mid 1960s. During and after attending Moscow University, S. worked as a journalist in the provincial and Moscow press, before becoming a game warden so that he would have time to write. Completing his first novel in 1973, S. sent it abroad and began his long campaign to emigrate. S.'s arrival in the U.S. in 1976 was heralded by Vladimir NABOKOV's rare praise for the young writer's work. For the next twelve years S. lived in the U.S. and Canada while gaining a reputation as a brilliant, if difficult, writer. In 1988 S. returned to Europe; first to Greece, and then, with the flowering of glasnost, to the U.S.S.R., where he was effusively welcomed as a major literary figure. S. returned to his native Canada in 1990.

Shkola dlia durakov (1976; *A School for Fools*, (1977) grows out of S.'s childhood encounters with Soviet educational institutions and the dreary duplicity of daily Soviet life. These experiences are depicted through the innocent eyes of the schizophrenic narrator, a student at a "special" school, who sees himself as two people. Much of the dialogue-free novel is in the form of exchanges between the boy's two competing personalities. There is no plot, and the narrative consists of a small number of scenes that recur in evolving variants. These center upon his attempts to understand the fundamental human experiences of love, sex, and death. The novel's central conflict is between the forces that oppress the boy: the misanthropic father, who is a public prosecutor, the psychiatrist and the hospital, and certain of the officials of the school for fools and those that promise freedom of person and imagination. Characters representing the latter are identified with nature and the liberating force of the wind. The narrative, which has no time line, progresses by a complex pattern of phonetic associations and recurrent images. The language is intensely poetic, full of wit and invention. Widely admired and much translated abroad, *Shkola dlia durakov* became an underground classic in the U.S.S.R. Finally published there thirteen years after its appearance in the West, it received an award as one of the best works published in 1989. It remains S.'s most popular work.

Mezhdu sobakoi i volkom (1980; between dog and wolf) differs radically in setting and complexity from S.'s first novel, which was set among the urban professional classes. S.'s duties as a game warden took him into the deep provinces of the upper Volga, a primitive timeless land of hunters and fishermen where his predecessor had died under mysterious circumstances. This provided the setting and central event of his second novel. Its title phrase "between dog and wolf" is an idiom meaning "twilight," that time of day when the shepherd cannot distinguish between his dog that guards his flock and the marauding wolf. All things blur indistinguishably: dog and wolf; day and night; life and death; reality and fantasy. In a broader sense the meaning of the title is "ambiguity," perhaps the key word in characterizing S.'s oeuvre. Groups of chapters are separated by sections of whimsical poetry that, in passing, provide glimpses of the real state of affairs. The book is a structural and stylistic tour de force, which has proved untranslatable. The novel has garnered much critical acclaim, but few readers. Nonetheless, the underground Leningrad literary journal *Chasy* awarded it its 1981 Andrey Bely Prize—an award especially appropriate since BELY's masterpiece, *Peterburg* (1916, rev. ed., 1922; *Petersburg*, 1959, 1978) was one of the foundation works of literary MODERNISM.

Palisandriia (1985; *Astrophobia*, 1989) is an abrupt departure from the earlier, more involute novels. It is, in part, S.'s attempt to reach a wider audience. *Palisandriia* (the epic of Palisander) is a comic picaresque work with all the attributes of the mock epic: a hero of national importance, an extended journey, great obstacles surmounted, supernatural participation, and a baroquely ceremonious style. The book is also elegantly and perversely erotic. In a deliberate inversion of Nabokov's *Lolita* (1955), the very youthful Palisander is drawn to elderly women. Most of all, *Palisandriia* is a lampoon of several commercial genres: the juicy, name-dropping memoir, the political espionage thriller, the futurological fantasy, and the pornographic novel. *Palisandriia* is parody raised to the level of high art.

The heterogeneity of content and setting in S.'s novels is striking, but from a formal viewpoint, they are united by their obsession with language and by their tendency to dislocate the reader's consciousness and expectations. Time is not linear, but circumambient. Memories may be of the future as well as the past. The individual is not necessarily restricted to one gender; nor is incest to be avoided. Even the distinction between the living and the dead is blurred. S.'s novels contain no real plots; no temporal continuity, and little dialogue. Intended for sophisticated readers, they are elegant poetic structures, both disconcertingly elliptical and highly allusive. S. has discussed some of these matters in a series of essays initially delivered as lectures. No less than his novels, the essays are works of art, but in miniature.

S.'s highly stylized writing and his indifference to political and social concerns set him at odds with the realism that has dominated Russian prose in the 19th and 20th cs. He sees his goal as raising the level of Russian prose to that of poetry of the very highest order.

BIBLIOGRAPHY: Johnson, D. B., "A Structural Analysis of S. S.'s *School for Fools*: A Paradigmatic Novel," in H. Birnbaum and T. Eekman, eds., *Fiction and Drama in Eastern and South-eastern Europe: Evolution and Experiment in the Postwar Period* (1980): 207–37; Matich, O., "S. S.'s *Palisandriia*: History and Myth," *RusR*, 45 (1986): 415–26; Johnson, D. B., "S. S.'s *Palisandriia*," *SEEJ*, 30, 3 (Fall 1986): 389–403; Johnson, D. B., "S. S.'s Twilight Cosmos: Themes and Motifs," *SlavR*, 45, 4 (1986): 639–49; special S. issue, *CASS*, 21: 3–4 (1987); Simmons, C., "Incarnations of the Hero Archetype in *School for Fools*," in A. Mandelker and R. Reeder, eds., *The Supernatural in Slavic and Baltic Literature: Essays in Honor of Victor Terras* (1988): 275–89; Johnson, D. B., "S. S.: The New Russian Avant-Garde," *Crit*, 30, 3 (Spring 1989): 163–78; Johnson, D. B., "The Galoshes Manifesto: A Motif in the Novels of S. S.," *OSP*, 22 (1989): 155–79; McMillin, A., "Aberration or the Future: The Avant-Garde Novels of S. S.," in A. McMillin, ed., *From Pushkin to Palisandriia: Essays on the Russian Novel in Honor of Richard Freeborn* (1990): 229–43

—D. BARTON JOHNSON

SOLARES, Ignacio

Mexican novelist and short-story writer, b. 15 Jan. 1945, Ciudad Juárez

S. has spent his professional life in Mexico City, where he works as a journalist and professor of literature at the National University of Mexico. From 1966 until 1976 he directed the cultural section of *Excélsior*, one of Mexico's leading newspapers. More recently he has edited several journals including *Revista de Revistas, Plural, Quimera*, and *Hoy*. Like many of Mexico's bestknown men of letters, S. launched his career with the aid of a grant from the *Centro Mexicano de Escritores*, a workshop for aspiring young writers.

S.'s first novel, *Puerta del cielo* (1976; door to heaven), typifies his oeuvre. Its style is direct and readily accessible to most readers, its setting (Mexico City) and much of its action appear to be realistic, and its episodes bordering on the surreal or fantastic set it apart from the mainstream of Mexican fiction. The protagonist, a sixteen-year-old boy named Luis, is torn between religious fervor and sexual impulses that cause him intense feelings of anguish and guilt. The two narrative voices, that of the protagonist and that of the omniscient author, underscore the conflict between the natural desires of youth and an oppressive social environment. But it is the realistic presentation of Luis's religious hallucinations, and the fading thereof when he marries, that suggest the author's pessimistic view of the human.

In *Anónimo* (1979; the anonymous note) the two protagonists emerge as psychological doubles, each complementing the other. Raúl Estrada, a middleaged journalist and one of the two first-person narrators, awakens one night finding himself in the body of another man, Rubén Rentería. The story ends when the two protagonists fuse into a single identity bearing the name of Raúl Rentería. Though utterly fantastic, *Anónimo* is told in a straightforward manner both convincing and at times amusing to the reader. Its open ending creates the possibility of either a psychological or a metaphysical interpretation.

S.'s next novel, *El árbol del deseo* (1980; the wish tree) has been called the most intense and disturbing of his works. A psychological study of fear, it portrays a ten-year-old girl who, having been sexually abused by her father, flees from her home in terror, taking along her four-year-old brother. The novel is narrated by an objective, casual observer of surface reality, a strategy that stimulates the reader's imagination. The girl's adventures, one suspects, are more dream than reality, her nightmarish images of the city representing a fear-induced metaphor of pervasive evil and hopelessness.

S.'s fascination with Mexico City, both its past and its present, is nowhere as evident as in his most complex novel, *Casas de encantamiento* (1987; houses of enchantment). The plot derives from two principal narrative sources: the diary of a recently deceased journalist and the comments made by his friend as he reads the diary. An ingenious melange of science and self-conscious fiction, the novel not only depicts S.'s efforts to recreate the Mexican capital of four decades ago, but also includes within its text one of his stories, "La ciudad" (1975; the city). The fusion of dream and reality, together with temporal displacements and adroit use of different narrative perspectives, makes this work a significant achievement in literary technique.

S.'s best work to date is *Madero, el otro* (1989; Madero, the other), which combines elements of psychological and historical novels to paint a compelling portrait of Francisco Madero, the leader of the Mexican Revolution of 1910. In addition to the carefully researched historical events informing the plot, S. uses the second-person narrative voice to address "the other Madero" and thus delineate the dual nature of one of Mexico's most complex public figures. A spiritualist who sought to communicate with the dead, Madero was, on the one hand, a mystic and pacifist, and, on the other, a politician and revolutionary. This dichotomy in his psyche emerges not only from the narrative point of view, but also from the tragic turn of events when he fails to deal decisively with his enemies. S. admits that he invented scenes and dialogues and that in some instances he had to choose between conflicting versions of events. The end result of his endeavor is nevertheless a moving work of fiction with a ring of truth and a texture enhanced by the density of human experience.

El gran elector (1993; the great elector) is another fine novel about Madero and how his revolution was betrayed by subsequent presidents. S. emerges as one of contemporary Mexico's most talented novelists. His ability to capture the interest of his readers is one of his major assets, a feat he accomplishes by first representing a real, everyday situation and then effecting a smooth transition into the realm of the unreal. Although Mexico, its past, and its capital provide a familiar backdrop for his plots, his novels are also informed by the dreams, fears, and abnormal behavior of his protagonists. As critic Alfonso González states, S.'s works have the simplicity of a fairy tale and the complexity of a metaphysical treatise.

FURTHER WORKS: *El hombre habitado* (1975); *El problema es el otro* (1978); *Delirium tremens* (1979); *La fórmula de la inmortalidad* (1982); *Serafín* (1985)

BIBLIOGRAPHY: Beaupied, A. M., "La teoría de lo fantástico de Todorov en *Anónimo* de I. S.," *Chasqui*, 9: 2–3, (Feb.–March 1980): 59–64; Brushwood, J. S., "La realidad y la fantasía: Las novelas de I. S.," *La Semana de Bellas Artes*, 143 (27 Aug. 1980): 10–12; Ortega, M., "La 'Cristina' de S.," *El Machete*, 10 (Feb. 1981): 58; Brushwood, J. S., *La novela hispanoamericana del siglo XX* (1984): 344–46; Torres, V. F., on *Serafín*, "Sábado," supplement to *Uno Más Uno*, 14 Dec. 1985: 12; Brushwood, J. S., "Narrating Parapsychology: The Novels of I. S.," *Chasqui*, 18, 2 (Nov. 1989): 12–17; Prieto, F., on *Madero, el otro, Proceso*, 11 Dec. 1989: 56; Torres, V. F., "I. S.: Conocer al diablo para creer en Dios," *Narradores mexicanos de fin de siglo* (1989): 9–38; Brushwood, J. S., "Casas de encantamiento," *Chasqui*, 19, 1 (May 1990): 121–22; González, A., "I. S.: Fear and Fantasy as Reality," *Euphoria and Crisis: Essays on the Contemporary Mexican Novel* (1990): 44–51

—GEORGE R. MCMURRAY

SOLDATI, Mario

Italian novelist, short-story writer, critic, and journalist, b. 17 Nov. 1906, Turin

S.'s education by the Jesuits during his teens remained pivotal to his spiritual development. He decided against entering the priesthood and then studied literature and philosophy at the University of Turin, art history in Rome, and for two years (1929–31) he held a fellowship at Columbia University in New York. From this last experience came the volume *America primo amore* (1935; America first love) a collection of vignettes on various aspects of life in the U.S. Although he traveled widely, S. resided in Rome from the 1930s to 1960, during which time he directed or codirected about forty films, most of them undistinguished. Since the 1960s he has lived in Milan.

Salmace (1929; Salmace), a collection of short stories, depicts, moralistically and satirically, the casuistry of the upper middle class and aristocracy in Turin. S.'s language became lighter and more relaxed in later short-story collections—*L'amico gesuita* (1943; the Jesuit friend), *44 novelle per l'estate* (1979; 44 short stories for summer)—and in the novellas *La verità sul caso Motta* (1941; the truth about the Motta case) and *A cena col commendatore* (1950; *Dinner with the Commendatore*, 1953). This last is unforgettable for its mixture of oneiric and realistic elements in a detective story.

Le lettere da Capri (1954; *The Capri Letters*, 1956) recounts the story of an American couple who lead split lives: one properly middle class, the other instinctual and passionate with their Italian lovers.

S.'s most appealing work is the short novel *Il vero Silvestri* (1957; *The Real Silvestri*, 1961), an unresolved inquiry into the psyche of Silvestri, who may be an honest man or a blackmailer. In felicitous prose S. explores the impossibility of resolving the ambiguities of the human soul.

The protagonists of *La busta arancione* (1966; *The Orange Envelope*, 1969) and *Le due città* (1964; *The Malacca Cane*, 1973) are not true to themselves: one loses his love because of his prudish mother's intervention; the other renounces love and marries for money.

S.'s most effective works search for the self that existed before familial and social distortions set in.

FURTHER WORKS: *Pilato* (1924); *Ventiquattro ore in uno studio cinematografico* (1935); *Fuga in Italia* (1947); *L'accalappiacani* (1953); *La confessione* (1955; *The Confession*, 1958); *La messa dei villeggianti* (1959); *I racconti (1927–1947)* (1960); *Canzonette e viaggio televisivo* (1962); *Storie di spettri* (1962); *I racconti del maresciallo* (1967); *Fuori* (1968); *Vino al vino* (1969); *I disperati del benessere* (1970); *L'attore* (1970); *55 novelle per l'inverno* (1971); *Da spettatore* (1973); *Un prato di papaveri* (1973); *Lo smeraldo* (1974; *The Emerald*, 1977); *Lo specchio inclinato* (1975); *Vino al vino, 3°* (1976); *La sposa americana* (1977); *Addio diletta Amelia* (1979); *L'incendio* (1981)

BIBLIOGRAPHY: Pacifici, S., *A Guide to Contemporary Italian Literature* (1962): 298–302; Heiney, D., *America in Modern Italian Literature* (1964): 187–201; Lawton, A., on *The Emerald*, *ItalAm*, 4 (1978): 138–40

—EMANUELE LICASTRO

SOLLERS, Philippe

French critic, novelist, and essayist, b. 28 Nov. 1936, Bordeaux

After completing his secondary education in metropolitan Bordeaux, S. studied with Jesuits in Versailles. At age twenty-two, after the publication of his first two works, S. was acclaimed as a promising young writer of fiction. He later became the primary organizing force for the *Tel Quel* group, a literary avant-garde circle whose doctrines often appear in *Tel Quel*, a Paris-based journal founded by S. and others in 1960. S. has guided the journal from its early association with the NEW NOVEL through a leftist, dogmatic, and avant-garde ideology developed during the late 1960s. His own creative and critical works parallel the development of the *Tel Quel* identity. In 1968 he married the writer Julia Kristeva (b. 1941), who has injected into S.'s work and that of *Tel Quel* the influences of semiotics and feminist thought. In 1983 he began editing the journal *L'infini*.

His early story, "Le défi" (1957; the challenge), received the Fénéon Prize, and his first novel, *Une curieuse solitude* (1958; *A Strange Solitude*, 1959) was praised by Louis ARAGON and François MAURIAC. Both of these narratives are conventional in form. "Le défi" is an adolescent's account of his seduction of a girl and his subsequent repudiation of her. S.'s first novel is in the form of a diary of a twenty-year-old man who once had an affair with an older Spanish maid and now reflects upon those moments of lost splendor.

S. soon abandoned traditional narrative form and, under the influence of the New Novel, wrote *Le parc* (1961; *The Park*, 1969) and *Drame* (1965; drama), which experiment with multiple narrative voices while eschewing temporal sequence, character development, and recognizable plot. In *Nombres* (1968; numbers), narrative experiment results in an alternation among four specific voices, identified as roman numerals I to IV, which do not communicate a specific, developed content. *Lois* (1972; laws) and *H* (1973; h) go even further in the fragmentation of traditional narrative form. They entail a gathering of different voices from various historical periods to speak about the underlying assumptions that constitute culture. S. has also been writing a fictional work called *Paradis* (paradise) that has been appearing sporadically in *Tel Quel* since 1974. Volume I of *Paradis* was published in book form in 1981, and additional volumes are in the offing.

S.'s literary criticism is probably his most significant work. He has written many articles for *Tel Quel*, presenting literary figures such as Dante, the Marquis de Sade, Georges BATAILLE, James JOYCE, and many others in light of "modern reading." His *Logiques* (1968; logics) brought together many of these essays and appeared in the same year as did *Nombres* and *Théorie d'ensemble* (1968; a holistic theory), thus establishing S. as a major French writer developing the ideology of the *Tel Quel* group. In *L'écriture et l'expérience des limites* (1971; *Writing and the Experience of Limits*, 1983) S. provided theoretical unity to the themes he developed in *Logiques* and proposed that literary criticism was a means of discovering new insights leading to a cultural revolution. In *Vision à New York* (1981; a vision in New York), a collection of interviews with S. conducted by David Hayman, S. discusses his personal history and its connections to the evolution of his literary work.

S.'s literary criticism seems to have had the most impact upon the literary scene in France and elsewhere. His "fiction" is either too imitative of the New Novel or too specialized for most readers. His creative writing does, however, have value for its focus upon the problems of reading revealed by his concern for the cultural implications of the act of organizing a story and narrating it.

FURTHER WORKS: *L'intermédiaire* (1963); *Francis Ponge; ou, La raison à plus haut prix* (1963); *Entretien avec Francis Ponge* (1970); *Sur le matérialisme* (1974); *Femmes* (1983)

BIBLIOGRAPHY: Heath, S., *The Nouveau Roman* (1972): 179–242; Roudiez, L., *French Fiction Today* (1972): 341–68; "Rejoycing on the Left," *TLS*, (22 September 1972): 1088; Caws, M. A., "*Tel Quel*: Text and Revolution," *Diacritics*, 3, 1 (1973): 2–8; Champagne, R. A., "The Evolving Art of Literary Criticism: Reading the Texts of P. S.," *FLS*, 4 (1977): 187–96; Kritzman, L., "The Changing Political Ideology of *Tel Quel*," *CFC*, 2 (1978): 405–21; Kafelanos, E., "P. S.'s *Nombres*: Structure and Sources," *ConL*, 19 (1978): 320–35

—ROLAND A. CHAMPAGNE

SOLOGUB, Fyodor

(pseud. of Fyodor Kuzmich Teternikov) Russian poet, novelist, short-story writer, and dramatist, b. 1 March 1863, St. Petersburg; d. 5 Dec. 1927, Leningrad

Son of a tailor and a domestic servant, both of peasant origin, S. was educated at the St. Petersburg Teachers' Institute. A high-school teacher and inspector of schools for twenty-five years, he taught first in the provinces before settling permanently in St. Petersburg.

S. published the first of his poems in 1884, but only gained widespread recognition with the appearance of *Stikhi* (1896; poems), *Teni: Rasskazy i stikhi* (1896; shadows: stories and poems),

and the novel *Tyazhyolye sny* (1896; *Bad Dreams*, 1978). A prominent representative of the first generation of Russian SYMBOLISTS and the exemplification of Decadence, S. reveals in his many collections of verse, including the renowned *Plamenny krug* (1908; circle of fire), his extreme subjectivism, world-weariness, revulsion to life, and aesthetic eroticism.

The form of S.'s verse remains traditional and is distinguished by classical clarity, succinctness of expression, and a restraint that borders on aloofness. Central to all his works is his dualistic *Weltanschauung*. Close to Manichaeism in his rejection of the world dominated by evil, injustice, cruelty, and ugliness, S. advocated the transcendence of this life to enter a realm of harmony, peace, and beauty, created in imagination and art by one's creative will. S. takes from Cervantes's *Don Quixote* the dual image of Dulcinea-Aldonsa, which he employs as his most frequently recurring symbol to reveal the striving of beauty hidden in ugly reality to emerge and to gain recognition.

S.'s first novel, *Tyazhyolye sny*, set in the provincial school milieu well known to him, contains many of the elements and themes of his later prose works, but is marred by over-philosophizing and an excessive number of subplots. His second novel, *Melky bes* (1907; *The Little Demon*, 1916; later tr., *The Petty Demon*, 1983), acclaimed his masterpiece, demonstrates the skillfully subtle blending of reality and the fantastic that is characteristic of S.'s prose. Also set in a provincial Russian town, the repository of all that is mediocre and vile, this tale of the incarnation of *poshlost* (mediocrity, vulgarity), the ambitious teacher Peredonov who cannot rise above the filth and ugliness of everyday reality and who is ultimately overwhelmed by it as his paranoia increases, is among the most condemnatory portrayals of provincial life to be found in Russian literature and provided a new term for the syndrome: *Peredonovshchina* (Peredonovism). Contrasted to the sordid, destructive world of Peredonov is the idyll of Lyudmila and the schoolboy Sasha, as the young woman seeks to create an enclave of beauty and harmony untrammeled by the vileness of the reality about her. Because of its erotic overtones, for a healthy sensuality is an attribute of S.'s world of beauty, the Sasha-Lyudmila episode has frequently been misunderstood and regarded as perverse.

S. more explicitly reveals his concept that the individual creative will must constantly strive to create an ideal world, its own legend, which is always in the process of creation, in his three-part *Tvorimaya legenda* (*The Created Legend*): *Tvorimaya legenda* (1907; repub. as *Kapli krovi*, 1908; *The Created Legend*, 1916; new tr., *Drops of Blood*, 1979); *Koroleva Ortruda* (1909; *Queen Ortruda*, 1979); and *Dym i pepel* (1914; *Smoke and Ashes*, 1979). Although less successful here than in *Melky bes* in its blending of fantasy, science fiction, and the sordid reality of Russia and its Black Hundreds (an organization of reactionary anti-Semitic groups) on the eve of the revolution of 1905, *Tvorimaya legenda* reveals more clearly S.'s pessimism regarding the accomplishment of reform in Russia.

S. set forth his theories of the drama in the essay *Teatr odnoy voli* (1908; theater of one will). All those involved in a theatrical production, audience no less than author, director, and actors, unite into a single will in order to participate, as it were, in the reenactment of a religious mystery. These theories coincided with the symbolist *uslovny* ("conditional") theater of the great director Vsevolod Meyerhold (1874–1942). Unlike many contemporary symbolist plays, the majority of S.'s were staged and seriously discussed in the press. The theater gave him an opportunity to present his favorite philosophical views in a more direct, graphic form than in his fiction and poetry. Whether based on mythological or folkloric subjects, like *Pobeda smerti* (1908; *The Triumph of Death*, 1916), *Dar mudrykh pchyol* (1918; gift of the wise bees), and *Nochnye plyaski* (1908; nocturnal dances), or having a modern setting, like *Lyubvi* (1907; loves) and *Zalozhniki zhizni* (1912; hostages of life), S.'s plays develop the eternal themes of death and love, and the transfiguration of life through beauty and the revelations of art.

Although the quality of his fiction is uneven, S. as a lyric poet, a symbolist dramatist, and the author of *Melky bes*, on which his international reputation rests, remains one of the outstanding exemplars of Decadence in Russian literature of the 20th c.

FURTHER WORKS: *Zhalo smerti* (1904); *Sobranie stikhov* (1904); *Kniga skazok* (1905); *Politicheskie skazochki* (1906); *Rodine* (1906); *Zmy* (1907); *Istlevayushchie lichiny* (1907); *Liturgia mne* (1907); *Kniga razluk* (1908); *Vanka-klyuchnik i pazh Zhean* (1909); *V tolpe* (1909); *Kniga ocharovany* (1909); *Sobranie sochineny* (12 vols., 1909–12); *Malenky chelovek* (1911); *Otrok Lin* (1911); *Voyna i mir* (1912); *Opechalennaya nevesta* (1912); *Sobranie sochineny* (20 vols., 1913–14); *Lyubov nad bezdnami* (1914); *Voyna* (1915); *Kamen, broshenny v vodu* (1915); *Yary god* (1916); *Alaya lenta* (1917); *Aly mak* (1917); *Pomnish, ne zabudesh, i drugie rasskazy* (1918); *Slepaya babochka* (1918); *Zaklinatelnitsa zmey* (1921); *Odna lyubov* (1921); *Nebo goluboe* (1921); *Soborny blagovest* (1921); *Fimiamy* (1921); *Tsaritsa potseluev* (1921); *Kostyor dorozhny* (1922); *Sochtennye dni* (1922); *Svirel* (1922); *Charodeynaya chasha* (1922); *Baryshnya Liza* (1923); *Veliky blagovest* (1923); *Stikhotvorenia* (1939); *Izbrannoe* (1965); *Stikhotvorenia* (1975). **FURTHER WORKS IN ENGLISH:** *The Old House, and Other Tales* (1915); *The Sweet-Scented Name, and Other Fairy Tales, Fables and Stories* (1915); *Little Tales* (1917); *The Shield* (1917, with Gorky Maxim and Andreev Leonid); *The Kiss of the Unborn and Other Stories* (1977)

BIBLIOGRAPHY: Bristol, E., "F. S.'s Postrevolutionary Poetry," *ASEER*, 19 (1960): 414–22; Holthusen, J., *F. S.s Roman Trilogie* (1960); Field, A., "The Theatre of Two Wills: S.'s Plays," *SEER*, 41 (1962): 80–88; Connolly, J. W., "The Role of Duality in S.'s *Tvorimaya legenda*," *WSl*: 19–20 (1974–75): 25–36; Gerould, D., "S. and the Theatre," *TDR*, 21, 4 (1977): 79–84; Barker, M. G., "Erotic Themes in S.'s Prose," *MFS*, 26 (1980): 241–48; Rabinowitz, S. J., *S.'s Literary Children: Keys to a Symbolist's Prose* (1980)

—C. HAROLD BEDFORD

SOLÓRZANO, Carlos

Guatemalan dramatist, critic, and novelist, b. 1 May 1922, San Marcos

Although a native of Guatemala, S. has resided since 1939 in Mexico, where he has published all his work. After receiving a doctorate in literature from Mexico's National University, he studied dramatic art in France from 1948–1950. During this time he was strongly influenced by Albert CAMUS and Michel de GHELDERODE, both of whom he knew well. Since 1962 he has taught Latin American literature at his alma mater.

Although he has published two psychological novels and numerous studies on the theater, S. is best known as a playwright. He began his career with *Doña Beatriz* (1951; Doña Beatriz), a dramatization of an episode during the Spanish conquest of Guatemala. The proud, fanatically religious protagonist, wife of the conqueror Pedro de Alvarado, embodies long-standing European tradition, whereas her strong-willed husband symbolizes the dynamic vitality of the Renaissance transported to the New World. The future of Latin America, moreover, is represented by Pedro's mestizo daughter Leonor, who survives the climactic deluge that brings the play to its conclusion.

In S.'s most widely acclaimed drama, *Las manos de Dios* (1957; *The Hands of God*, 1968), a peasant girl named Beatriz accepts the aid of the devil to free her unjustly incarcerated brother. The devil emerges not as the traditional embodiment of evil, however, but rather as a symbol of rebellion against oppression. At the instigation of the priest, the townspeople, who serve as a kind of chorus reminiscent of Greek tragedy, sacrifice Beatriz for her "crimes" against the Church, but the devil remains committed to the cause of individual freedom.

S. ventures into the THEATER OF THE ABSURD with *Los fantoches* (1959; the puppets), a symbolic depiction of the human condition based on biblical myth and Mexican folklore. The characters include a blind, deaf-mute puppet maker; his daughter, who enters from time to time in order to select at random the next puppet to perish; and El Cabezón (Big Head), who never manages to comprehend why the puppets have been created, confined to their drab abode, and destined to destruction and nothingness.

Other representative S. plays are *El hechicero* (1955; the magician), which portrays man's quest for divine omniscience and immortality; *El crucificado* (1957; the crucified), a denunciation of the Christian doctrine of sacrifice and suffering; *Mea culpa* (1956; Latin: my fault), in which a sinner in search of absolution hears the confession of a mad bishop; and *Cruce de vías* (1959; railroad crossing), an absurdist representation of two would-be lovers buffeted by the forces of time and deceived by the illusory nature of reality.

One of Latin America's foremost dramatists, S. has been instrumental in the development of an avant-garde theater of ideas designed to replace realistic regionalism with a more poetically conceived, universal art form. An eclectic by nature, he has assimilated elements of classicism, EXPRESSIONISM, and psychoanalysis, but his primary preoccupations echo those of the French EXISTENTIALISTS of the post-World War II era. Thus, in S.'s mythology freedom emerges as the equivalent of good, oppression as synonymous with evil, and religion as an escape from responsibility. His works universalize the Latin American experience by dramatizing the intellectual and psychic currents undermining the established order of today's world.

FURTHER WORKS: *Del sentimiento de lo plástico en la obra de Unamuno* (1944); *Espejo de novelas* (1945); *Unamuno y el existencialismo* (1946); *Novelas de Unamuno* (1948); *La muerte hizo la luz* (1951); *Dos obras* (1957, with Carlos Prieto); *Tres actos* (1959); *El sueño del ángel* (1960); *Teatro latinoamericano del siglo XX* (1961); *El teatro latinoamericano en el siglo XX* (1964); *Los falsos demonios* (1966); *El visitante* (1966); *El zapato* (1966); *Teatro breve hispanoamericano contemporáneo* (1970); *Las celdas* (1971); *Testimonios teatrales de México* (1973); *Teatro breve* (1977)

BIBLIOGRAPHY: Dauster, F., "The Drama of C. S.," *MD*, 7 (1968–1969): 89–100; Rivas, E., *C. S. y el teatro hispanoamericano* (1970); Schoenbach, P. J., "La libertad en *Las manos de Dios*," *LATR*, 3, 2 (1970): 21–29; Radcliff-Umstead, D., "S.'s Tormented Puppets," *LATR*, 4, 2 (1971): 5–11; Rodríguez, O., "C. S.: Cronología bibliográfica mínima," *Chasqui*, 1, 1 (1972): 12–19; Uría-Santos, M. R., "El simbolismo de *Doña Beatriz*: Primera obra de C. S.," *REH*, 6 (1972): 63–70; Richards, K. C., "The Mexican Existentialism of S.'s *Los fantoches*," *LALR*, 9 (1976): 63–69

—GEORGE R. MCMURRAY

SOLOUKHIN, Vladimir Alexeevich

Russian poet, short-story writer, novelist, essayist, and journalist, b. 14 June 1924, Alepino; d. 4 Apr. 1997, Moscow

The son of a peasant, S. grew up on a collective farm in Vladimir province. He graduated from the Vladimir Technical College in 1942 and in 1951 from the Gorky Institute of Literature. From 1951 to 1957 he worked as a journalist for *Ogonyok* and for several years served on the editorial board of *Literaturnaya gazeta*. Since 1964 he has been coeditor of the literary journal *Molodaya gvardia*.

S. has written both conventional poems and experimental ones using highly original blank verse, eliminating strict rhythmic patterns and meter, and shunning metaphors. His poems often read like heightened prose in which emotive effects are achieved by repetition of words, or groups of words, or by syntactical devices. Avoiding intellectual abstractions, he focuses on particulars, searching for a fresh expression of felt experiences.

S.'s numerous prose works comprise travel sketches, short stories, a novel, and countless journalistic pieces dealing with literature, art, and such matters as mushrooms and ice fishing. In his most significant books, *Vladimirskie prosyolki* (1957; *A Walk in Rural Russia*, 1967) and its sequel, *Kaplya rosy* (1960; a drop of dew), he leads the reader through his native region. Here, as well as in many of his short stories, S., who is at heart a romantic, cannot hide his enchantment with the natural and human marvels he helps the reader to encounter on his travels and visits. S. combines the talents of an amateur ethnographer and closely observant naturalist with the eyes and ears of a passionate "collector" of memorable, often eccentric folk characters.

His short stories show his many-sided artistic personality—his subtle and laconic irony, his preference for concluding his tales with sudden revelations of unsuspected physical or moral strength in his characters, and his penchant for depicting the capricious and seemingly irrational in human behavior. By and large, he views the people he chooses to present in heroic terms, an attitude that is a source of some sentimentality. On the other hand, he avoids glossing over the ugliness, stupidity, and insensitivity he finds in the villages.

S. has searched out not only his own past but also the roots of Russian art produced in monasteries and village churches. Two works that were generated by this interest aroused much controversy in the Soviet Union. In *Pisma iz Russkogo Muzeya* (1966; letters from the Russian Museum) and in *Chornye doski* (1969; *Searching for Icons in Russia*, 1972) S. deplores the official indifference to old frescoes, icons, and other examples of religiously inspired folk art, and he pleads for the restoration of what could still be salvaged. Most significantly, he advocates a more sympathetic treatment of religious art and an appreciation of its aesthetic and spiritual fervor. In the latter book S. acts as the passionate icon collector and traveling sleuth who more often than not experiences disappointment rather than success. This technique allows for suspenseful narration and in addition brings the reader face to face with the shockingly neglectful as well as anachronistically pious attitudes toward religious objects. S.'s attempts to rekindle interest in this area must be viewed in conjunction with his generally nostalgic attachment to rural life and its inherent values. He has been associated with the so-called "village writers," whose typical quasi-Slavophile, antiurban, anti-Western, and nationalist views S. shares to some extent.

S.'s emphasis on the simple, rural individual and on often hidden, irrational, or unpredictable spiritual resources, on folk wisdom and traditional customs, on spontaneity and even naïveté, and on the ethical value of all things beautiful, reveals a humanism devoid of the usual orthodox, ideological overlay. In regard to form, S.'s stories and sketches are significant contributions to the genre in that they successfully combine the often lyrical, emotionally committed voice of the author narrator with the stance of a journalistic feature writer, fusing passion and information.

FURTHER WORKS: *Dozhd v stepi* (1953); *Rozhdenie Zernograda* (1955); *Zolotoe dno* (1956); *Za sin-moryami* (1956); *Razryv-trava* (1956); *Ruchi na asfalte* (1958); *Zhuravlikha* (1959); *Stepnaya byl* (1959); *Veter stranstvy* (1960); *Kak vypit solntse* (1961); *Otkrytki iz Vietnama* (1961); *Imeyushchy v rukakh tsvety* (1962); *Svidanie v Vyaznikakh* (1964); *Slavyanskaya tetrad* (1964); *Mat-machekha* (1964); *Tretya okhota* (1965); *S liricheskikh pozitsy* (1965); *Zimny den* (1969); *Olepinskie prudy* (1973); *Izbrannye proizvedenia* (1974); *Myod na khlebe* (1978). FURTHER WORKS IN ENGLISH: *White Grass* (1971)

BIBLIOGRAPHY: Holthusen, J., *Twentieth-Century Russian Literature* (1972): 243–46; Kasack, W., *Lexikon der russischen Literatur ab 1917* (1976): 373–75; Brown, D., *Soviet Russian Literature since Stalin* (1978): 237–43

—W. R. HIRSCHBERG

SOLSTAD, Dag

Norwegian novelist, short-story writer, and dramatist, b. 16 July 1941, Sandefjord

S. is known as a leader in the so-called *Profil* generation, a group of writers associated with a student magazine who came to the fore in the late 1960s. Like most of the other members of the group, S. considered himself a Marxist-Leninist, and throughout the 1970s he consciously placed his art in the service of a hoped-for proletarian revolution in Norway. Many of his erstwhile compatriots have since given up on their radical politics, but S. has not been deterred by the absence of a Marxist revolution.

S. had his debut in 1965, when he published *Spiraler* (spirals), a Kafka-inspired volume of short stories dealing with loneliness and isolation. A collection of short prose, *Svingstol* (1967; a turning chair), followed; its terse style is reminiscent of that of Tarjei VESAAS. S.'s first novel was *Irr! Grønt!* (1969; patina! green!). Its protagonist is a student from the country who is searching for liberation by consciously playing roles. The author got this idea from the Polish writer Witold GOMBROWICZ, whom he also introduced in an article in the literary periodical *Vinduet* in 1969. S. found that liberation cannot be achieved, however, for everybody is subject to the roles that are imposed on them by late capitalism. S.'s next novel, *Arild Asnes, 1970* (1971; Arild Asnes, 1970), portrays an attempt at a far more radical break with society. Asnes, a writer, is a socialist intellectual who, paradoxically, is given freedom to write in order that he may confirm the basis for existence under capitalism. An important aspect of the story is how Asnes overcomes his distasne for the simple and direct language of the Marxists and, in the end, becomes able to make it his own.

Arild Asnes, 1970 created a big stir, but even more so did S.'s next novel, *25. september-plassen* (1974; the 25th of september square). It is a chronicle of the postwar era in Norway, in which the author wants to show that the working class was betrayed by its Labor Party leaders, who abandoned true socialism and collaborated with American capitalist interests. This novel was followed by a trilogy that consists of the volumes *Svik. Førkrigsår* (1977; betrayal: prewar years), *Krig. 1940* (1978; war: 1940), and *Brød og våpen* (1980; bread and weapons). Here S. gives his Marxist-inspired version of events before and during World War II, attempting, among other things, to show that the Norwegian Nazis, the German occupants, and the Norwegian bourgeoisie had common interests. But the story is also a highly readable one that contains skillfully drawn portraits of members of the working class and their lives during trying times.

At the end of the 1970s it became apparent both that the Norwegian working class had no desire for a Marxist-Leninist revolution and that it was extremely unlikely that such a desire could be generated despite the best efforts of the committed revolutionary writers. A number of committed writers found it necessary to pause and review their earlier activities and the ideology behind them. S.'s attempt at such an examination of his past came under the unwieldy title *Gymnaslaerer Pedersens beretning om den store politiske vekkelsen som har hjemsøkt vårt land* (1982; highschool teacher Pedersen's account of the great political revival that has visited our country). S.'s next novel, *Forsøk på å beskrive det ugjennonntrengelige* (1984; an attempt to describe the impenetrable), on the other hand, represents a return to one of the author's earlier themes: The Labor Party has created a society in which it is impossible for decent human beings to exist.

S.'s most recent book, simply titled *Roman 1987* (1987; novel 1987), earned him the Nordic Literary Prize the following year. It is another review of the history of the Marxist-Leninist movement and is, like *Gymnaslaerer Pedersens beretning*, told in the first person. The protagonist abandons a promising career in teaching and research to become one with the working class by becoming a factory worker. His attempt fails, but he insists that the experience was nevertheless worth the effort. An apologia in the form of a novel, *Roman 1987* thus shows that S. has remained true to his convictions.

Most critics and literary historians would agree that S. is one of the most significant writers of contemporary Norway, second only to Kjartan FLØGSTAD. He is clearly the outstanding representative of the politically committed writers who flourished in the 1970s,

and his work in the 1980s has become even more interesting than his earlier books.

FURTHER WORKS: *Kamerat Stalin eller familien Nordby* (1975); *Artikler om litteratur* (1981); *Sleng på byen* (1983)

BIBLIOGRAPHY: Sehmsdorf, H. K., "From Individualism to Communism: The Political and Esthetic Transformation of D. S.'s Authorship," *PPNCFL*, 27, 1 (1976): 130–32; Sjåvik, J., "Language and Myth in D. S.'s *Arild Asnes, 1970,*" *PCP*, 18 (1983): 30–36; Rønning, H., "History, Identity, Communication: Trends in Recent Norwegian Fiction," *ScanR*, 76, 2 (1988): 95–102; Garton, J., "New Directions in Norwegian Literature," *RNL*, 12 (1989): 163–84; Kittange, A., *Allegory, Intertextuality and Irony in D. S.* (1989)

—JAN I. SJÅVIK

SOLZHENITSYN, Aleksandr Isaevich

Russian novelist, short-story writer, essayist, dramatist, and poet, b. 11 Dec. 1918, Kislovodsk

Born after his father had been killed in a hunting accident, S. was brought up by his mother in impoverished circumstances. During his youth in Rostov-on-Don, S. succumbed to the ideological fervor typical of the Soviet 1930s, abandoning the religious and patriotic values of his home for Marxism. An outstanding mathematics graduate of Rostov University (1941), S. seemed a young man of great promise in Soviet terms, especially after becoming a decorated commander of a front-line artillery unit during World War II. But his life and views were altered permanently by a sudden arrest in 1945 for critical comments about Stalin and by the eight-year prison term that followed.

At first his health deteriorated alarmingly in the camps; he was saved by an unexpected summons to work as a mathematician in a series of prison research institutes (1946–50) but was later flung back just as precipitously into the camp system. Release from camp in 1953 was followed by "perpetual exile" in a remote Central Asian hamlet. Clandestine writing now occupied all his available time, but these literary labors seemed doomed in the face of a diagnosis of terminal cancer. Against all expectations the disease was cured in 1954; in 1956 came release from exile and then full rehabilitation.

At the height of Khrushchev's de-Stalinization campaign (1961), S. risked submitting the work now known as *Odin den Ivana Denisovicha* (1962; *One Day in the Life of Ivan Denisovich*, 1963) to *Novy mir*, the leading Soviet literary monthly, then edited by Alexandr TVARDOVSKY. The very fact that a work depicting life in a Soviet forced-labor camp was allowed to appear in the U.S.S.R. caused a major sensation and assured S. of instant celebrity. But the official favor with which S. was at first viewed by the Soviet establishment proved to be short-lived, rapidly giving way to hostility and finally to vituperation and open harassment: the writer was able to publish only a few more short works in *Novy mir* before all legal means of appearing in print in his own country were denied him. Relying on the *samizdat* network (a system whereby texts are retyped and distributed chain-letter fashion by private individuals, with some copies usually finding their way abroad), S. nevertheless circulated a number of statements and open letters, becoming a prominent and eloquent opponent of the regime. At the same time, *samizdat* circulation and publication abroad of the novels *V kruge pervom* (1968; *The First Circle*, 1968) and *Rakovy korpus* (1968; *Cancer Ward*, 1968) conclusively established his literary reputation. S. was awarded the Nobel Prize for literature in 1970.

The appearance in Paris of S.'s indictment of the Soviet penal system, *Arkhipelag Gulag* (3 vols., 1973–75; *The Gulag Archipelago*, 3 vols., 1974–78), and the massive publicity generated by it moved the regime to direct action against S.: he was arrested, charged with treason, and forcibly deported to West Germany in 1974. He lived for a time in Zurich, then in 1976 moved to Vermont, where he has continued work on the cycle of historical narratives begun by *Avgust chetyrnadtsatogo* (1971; *August 1914*, 1972). In the Russian tradition that calls on writers to speak out on social issues, S. continues to make public statements, some of which have aroused intense controversy.

Because of the highly charged and politicized circumstances under which most of S.'s works have appeared, the critical response, perhaps inevitably, has often exhibited a similar degree of polarization. These abnormal pressures have even left their mark on the texts themselves. Many Western translations for example, are painfully deficient in quality because the publishers rushed them into print in an effort to capitalize on the latest sensation. More important, the original Russian texts (as published in the 1960s) were in some instances vitally affected. In *Bodalsya telyonok s dubom* (1975; *The Oak and the Calf*, 1980), S.'s autobiographical account of his struggle with the regime, he relates how he sometimes engaged in "self-censorship" in order to increase the chances of a work appearing in print in the U.S.S.R. This was true of *Odin den Ivana Denisovicha*, which S. abridged and softened, of *V kruge pervom*, which he rewrote entirely, and of one of his plays. The editions that appeared in print in the 1960s (and upon which the Western translations were based) therefore diverge in important ways from the texts as conceived and originally executed by the author. Clearly, a serious discussion of S.'s literary achievement must begin with reference to a firmly established canon. This is now being provided: in 1978 S. launched an authorized *Sobranie sochineny* (collected works); new translations made from this edition will eventually become available. It follows that English editions published before this date are in several instances textually obsolete; this is above and beyond the question of their reliability as translations. (In the latter regard, S.'s short fiction has fared especially poorly in English.)

A number of S.'s works are based directly on important episodes of his life and include major characters whose life histories and casts of mind are recognizably similar to the author's. This applies above all to Gleb Nerzhin, an inmate of the prison research institute depicted in *V kruge pervom*, and to Oleg Kostoglotov, a patient undergoing treatment for a stomach tumor in *Rakovy korpus*. In each case the novel presents a lightly fictionalized account of the author's own experience. The same is true also of several shorter works, for example, of "Matryonin dvor" (1963; "Matryona's Home," 1963), which reflects the writer's stint as a teacher in an isolated village. The autobiographical tendency seemingly exhibited here is in fact part of a more general literary gravitation toward the portrayal of real events and conditions. In this respect S. is heir to the legacy of the great 19th-c. Russian novelists who prided themselves on their truthful depiction of

Russian life and an accurate analysis of social currents. (The task is of course incomparably more difficult under Soviet conditions, where entire areas of the greatest social concern have been proscribed.) For S., as for his literary predecessors, the writer assumes the vital role of observer, chronicler, witness—and judge. Literature understood in this way is not mere "fiction"—an English word stressing the unreality of literary creation. On the contrary, in the Russian tradition to which S. belongs, art is seen as one of the ways to approach truth. Nor is the purely literary dimension downgraded in the process, for only high art, in this view, can achieve the breakthrough to a comprehensible and palpable vision of reality. The writer needs aesthetic insight and literary craftsmanship in order to select and structure his data, to discern connections and patterns inaccessible by any other means, and, of course, to communicate this knowledge to his readers.

A striking example of this method is *Arkhipelag Gulag*, a work significantly subtitled *Opyt khudozhestvennogo issledovania* (essay in artistic investigation). S. is convinced that a conventional history of Soviet prisons and camps can never be written: the facts have for too long been suppressed and distorted, documents have been destroyed and falsified, and the victims are mostly dead or too cowed to speak out. S. therefore turned to the techniques of art to organize and present the available data. Large overarching metaphors hold together facts and events and infuse them with a new meaning. Aesthetic intuition thus permits S. to generalize and extrapolate from individual case histories, while the narrative itself is a complex interweaving of historical exposition, autobiographical account, and numerous personal testimonies, everywhere interspersed with ironic or bitter comments, exhortations, questions to the reader, and so forth, all of which serve to dramatize the material.

The same methodological principles underlie S.'s vast and long-nurtured plan to chronicle the history of the Russian revolution. The cycle of historical narratives that begins with *Avgust chetyrnadtsatogo* is based on prodigious research (including a great deal of work with unpublished memoirs and archival materials, as well as interviews with surviving witnesses), but is presented in the framework of literature. The form is basically that of the historical novel, with inserted sections of purely historical exposition. The cycle is collectively called *Krasnoe koleso* (the red wheel) and subtitled *Povestvovanie v otmerennykh srokakh* (a narrative in segments of allotted time). It was originally conceived as consisting of four acts subdivided into twenty "knots" and covering the period between August 1914 and the spring of 1922. In addition, five epilogues were to bring the story up to 1945. (The term "knot" [*uzel*], used by S. in lieu of "volume," is derived from the mathematical concept of "nodal point," and suggests a moment in history where the central issues of the time reach their sharpest focus.) In 1982 S. announced that he had completed the first three "knots" that together constitute Act I of his narrative and focus on events leading up to the Bolshevik Revolution: *Avgust chetyrnadtsatogo, Oktyabr shestnadtsatogo* (October 1916), and *Mart semnadtsatogo* (March 1917). (It should be noted that since its first publication in 1971, Knot I has been rewritten and expanded to twice its original length by the incorporation of material bearing on the period before 1914.) The fifth epilogue, the end of S.'s planned cycle, was composed in 1952–53: this is a play written partially in verse and titled *Plenniki* (1981; *Prisoners*, 1983), in which Colonel Vorotyntsev, a central character in Knot I, learns that he is to be hanged in a Soviet prison in 1945.

The earliest work of S.'s that has so far appeared in print is *Prusskie nochi* (1974; *Prussian Nights*, 1977), a narrative poem composed in camp in 1950, and originally part of a much longer poetic text. It deals with the tumultuous advance of the Red Army into East Prussia late in World War II, and exhibits thematic patterns that are characteristic of S.'s work in general, including the figure of a searcher after truth, in this case the narrator, who is confronted by a kaleidoscopic sequence of events and impressions that he struggles to assimilate into some kind of moral framework. Within the confines of the poem he fails, but the sins of commission and omission into which he is drawn are recorded with a searing intensity that points ahead to a permanently awakened conscience. Many of S.'s works are variations on this theme of a defeat that represents a gain on a different level. The examples that could be adduced are so numerous, in fact, that a profound link seems to exist here to the author's world view. Nerzhin is shipped off to probable death in the camps at the end of *V kruge pervom*, but in his own terms the departure is a spiritual victory and an act of purification. Kostoglotov in *Rakovy korpus* despondently abandons all hope for earthly happiness but knows that this is the only morally honest decision. The camp uprising depicted in the screenplay *Znayut istinu tanki* (1981; tanks know the truth) is brutally crushed, but the liberating assertion of freedom, short as it was, lives on to inspire others. The heroine of "Matryonin dvor" dies in a needless accident after what seems to be a completely unsuccessful life, but her death reveals her true moral stature to the narrator. Many of the individual parts of *Arkhipelag Gulag* can also be shown to be structured around the same motif. A good illustration is the chapter entitled "Bely kotyonok" ("The White Kitten")— Vol. 3, Part V—a tale of two convicts who manage to break out of a camp but who ultimately fail in their escape attempt because at a critical moment they were moved by human compassion. S. never attempts to minimize the bitter cost of defeat, either in this instance or in the other examples cited. The magnitude of the loss is shown in vivid and often pitiless detail, and there is no appeal to any mystical epiphany. Yet the very fact that S. can offer something beyond despair in such contexts points unambiguously to the Christian roots of his vision of tragedy.

Although S. considers himself a traditionalist in matters of form ("modern" techniques are to him no more than tools to accommodate his material), his views on language and style are quite unconventional. More consistently than other contemporary Russian writers, S. eschews the barbarisms and clichés that have invaded and disfigured the Russian language of the Soviet epoch. He seeks to enrich his own vocabulary and syntax by drawing on "popular" or "substandard" speech, much of it culled from, or based on, the glossary of Vladimir Dal, a 19th-c. lexicographer whose massive compilation abounds in folk sayings and the popular idiom in general. One notes in this connection S.'s admiration for Russian proverbs, which are valued as much for their verbal compactness as for their wisdom. Thus Nerzhin, in *V kruge pervom*, in his quest for ethical standards, learns the most profound lesson of all from a proverb uttered by an uneducated peasant. In *Avgust chetyrnadtsatogo* and its sequels, a number of proverbs appear as independent entries between chapters, serving a structural function akin to that of the chorus in Greek tragedy: they pass a "folk" judgment on the events depicted. And S. relates in *Bodalsya telyonok s dubom* (the title itself comes from a folk saying) how he derived comfort in times of difficulty from reading collections of Russian proverbial expressions.

Another typical feature of S.'s writing style is the technique of shifting from a "neutral" third-person narrative to a direct transcription of the unuttered thoughts of his protagonists. This allows S. to illustrate the point of view of a character without necessarily having him speak, yet at the same time without sacrificing the potential for ironic distance that the third-person account possesses. *Odin den Ivana Denisovicha*, for example, while not presented as an oral first-person narrative, nonetheless reflects the verbal style and mental attitude of the main hero: the camp is seen through the eyes of a hardy peasant and veteran prisoner. The situation is more complex in *V kruge pervom*, with its large cast of articulate characters. Although technically retaining the third-person narrative throughout the novel, S. manipulates the point of view, shifting it to agree with that of the protagonist who happens to have center stage. The same technique is evident in *Rakovy korpus* and *Avgust chetyrnadtsatogo*. S. has referred to this method as "polyphony," but this term should not be taken to mean, as some critics have assumed, that the author's own viewpoint is impossible to extract from the text.

S. is a major figure in the history of Russian literature. Undoubtedly the most powerful talent in the field of Russian narrative prose since World War II, he also emerged as the most prominent adversary of the Soviet regime, an eloquent exposer of its past and present crimes. These two qualities—the prominence and the talent—are inseparable. "The ethical force with which he has pursued the indispensable traditions of Russian literature" (to quote the Nobel Prize citation) would have been ineffective if S. had not simultaneously demonstrated the highest standards of literary art.

FURTHER WORKS: *Nobelevskaya lektsia po literature 1970 goda* (1972; *The Nobel Lecture*, 1973); *Pismo vozhdyam Sovetskogo Soyuza* (1974); *Lenin v Tsyurikhe* (1975); *Skvoz chad* (1979). **FURTHER WORKS IN ENGLISH:** *Warning to the West* (1976); *East & West* (1980); *The Mortal Danger* (1980; enlarged ed., 1981); *Victory Celebrations* (1983)

BIBLIOGRAPHY: Nivat, G., and Aucouturier, M., eds., *S.* (1971); Brown, E. J., "S.'s Cast of Characters," in Brown, E. J., ed., *Major Soviet Writers: Essays in Criticism* (1973): 351–66; Fiene, D. M., *A. S.: An International Bibliography of Writings by and about Him* (1973); Labedz, L., ed., *S.: A Documentary Record*, 2nd ed. (1974); Dunlop, J. B., Haugh, R., and Klimoff, A., eds., *A. S.: Critical Essays and Documentary Materials*, 2nd ed. (1975); Moody, C., *S.*, 2nd ed. (1975); Feuer, K., ed., *S.: A Collection of Critical Essays* (1976); Carter, S., *The Politics of S.* (1977); Clément, O., *The Spirit of S.* (1977); Rzhevsky, L., *S.: Creator and Heroic Deed* (1978); Berman, R., ed., *S. at Harvard: The Address, Twelve Early Responses, and Six Later Reflections* (1980); Ericson, E. E., Jr., *S.: The Moral Vision* (1980); Krasnov, V., *S. and Dostoevsky: A Study in the Polyphonic Novel* (1980); Lakshin, V., *S., Tvardovsky, and "Novy Mir"* (1980); Nivat, G., *S.* (1980); Pomorska, K., "The Overcoded World of S.," in Burnbaum, H., and T. Eekman, eds., *Fiction and Drama in Eastern and Southeastern Europe* (1980): 327-35; *S. Studies: A Quarterly Survey* (1980 ff.)

—ALEXIS KLIMOFF

One Day in the Life of Ivan Denisovich is not a document in the sense of being a memoir, nor is it notes or reminiscences of the author's personal experiences, although only such personal experiences could lend this story its sense of genuine authenticity. This is a work of art and it is by virtue of the artistic interpretation of this material from life that it is a witness of special value, a document of an art that up to now had seemed to have few possibilities.

The reader will not find in A. S.'s story an allencompassing portrayal of that historic period that is particularly marked by the bitter memory of the year 1937. The content of *One Day* is naturally limited in time and place of action and the horizons of the main hero of the story. But in the writing of A. S., who here enters the literary scene for the first time, one day in the life of the camp prisoner, Ivan Denisovich Shukhov, develops into a picture which gives extraordinary vitality and fidelity to the truthfulness of its human characters. Herein above all lies the uncommon power of the work to impress. The reader can visualize for himself many of the people depicted here in the tragic role of camp inmates in other situations—at the front or at postwar construction sites. They are the same people who by the will of circumstance have been put to severe physical and moral tests under special and extreme conditions.

In this story there is no deliberate concentration of terrible facts of the cruelty and arbitrariness that were the result of the violation of Soviet legality. The author chose instead to portray only one of the most ordinary of days in the life at camp from reveille to retreat. Nevertheless this "ordinary" day cannot but arouse in the heart of the reader a bitter feeling of pain for the fate of the people who, from the pages of this story, rise up before us so alive and so near. Yet the unquestionable victory of the artist lies in the fact that the bitterness and the pain have nothing in common with a feeling of hopeless depression. On the contrary, the impression left by this work is so extraordinary in its unvarnished and difficult truth that it somehow frees the soul of the burden of things unsaid that needed to be said and at the same time it strengthens one's manly and lofty feelings.

This is a grim story—still another example of the fact that there are no areas or facts of reality that can be excluded from the sphere of the Soviet artist in our days or that are beyond truthful portrayal. Everything depends on the capabilities of the artist himself. [1962]

Alexandr Tvardovsky, Foreword to *One Day in the Life of Ivan Denisovich* (1963), pp. 13–15

[In *The First Circle*] Nerzhin is concerned throughout with thinking his way out of physical and spiritual imprisonment, with discovering the personal resources to resist humiliation, to make the right choice, no matter how painful. He learns and develops through the course of the novel, but in a single, a "positive," direction. When the choice presents itself, he survives morally by refusing to support the secret police research into new ways of entrapping the innocent, thus inviting transportation to a far harsher area of the vast Gulag Archipelago. His costly, perhaps suicidal, victory carries much of S.'s statement, and functions in the novel as the emblem of *human* resistance to Stalin's nearly perfect apparatus of dehumanization.

But he covers a narrower range than Rubin, is less "interesting" fictionally than the man who never wholly comprehends his double allegiance—to art and culture and human spontaneity on the one hand, and to the rigidities of the system on the other.

By making Rubin a victim of the system, S. excuses him from complicity in its day-to-day brutalities, grants him the leisure and freedom, paradoxically, to contemplate his circumstances, and allows himself to be a blood brother of the community of prisoners. His defense of conditions he considers inevitable exposes to debate and refutation the deeper rationales of the Soviet system. When he acts spontaneously, he loathes his wardens and lifts the morale of his fellow victims with marvelous flights of imagination mocking the grotesque injustices of their situation; when he falls into abstractions, he defends the entire cosmology that justifies their detention. "They were right," he is forced to say, "to put us in prison."

Rufus W. Mathewson, Jr., *The Positive Hero in Russian Literature*, 2nd ed. (1975), pp. 281–82

[In *Cancer Ward*, a conversation] takes place while Vega is giving Kostoglotov a transfusion of blood, and a small detail on this occasion is a telling contrast to the episode with Zoya. As he lies trustfully on the table—and for him, who for so long has had to be watchful and suspicious, "to be able to trust, to give himself to trust" is a great luxury—in the quiet room, so quiet that he can hear the faint ringing of the bubbles in the glass balloon from which the lifegiving blood is entering his arm, Kostoglotov watches a bright patch of light on the ceiling above him. As Vega's indignant words send him flying back to his childhood, he remembers some popular books on the physiology of love he had read as a boy, books of "consistent, logical, irrefutable materialism," and discovers that she too has read them and that on her as on him they have had the same effect of vacuity and desolation. Oleg, still gazing at the ceiling, sees how "The strange patch of pale sunlight . . . suddenly began to ripple. A flashing cluster of silver spots appeared from somewhere. They began to move about," and realizes that this rippling, airy circle is none other than the reflection of a puddle outside the window. Bright and lovely, it is like his feeling for Vega or, for that matter, like the experience of any genuine human love, whatever its physiological basis might be, and indeed of any truly human relationship, and also of a man's conception of what he is and what he lives by.

Helen Muchnic, "*Cancer Ward*: Of Fate and Guilt," in John B. Dunlop et al., eds., *A. S.: Critical Essays and Documentary Materials* (1975), p. 285

A conscientious, reasonable, modest, and honest general [Samsonov in *August 1914*] becomes by the will of Providence at once the perpetrator and victim of the catastrophe which will result in the fall of Russia. He is not directly responsible for the disaster since he did not conceive the absurd plan involving a premature offensive; nevertheless, as commander-in-chief, he carries responsibility for it. With extraordinary psychological insight S. shows how Samsonov, sensing defeat, divests himself of everything he has accumulated during a long military career. He descends deeply into himself, to his childhood memories, and then rises upward in prayer, preparing himself for sacrifice. On this deep level Samsonov approaches a kinship with Christ, experiences his own Gethsemane. Like Dostoevsky, S. was not afraid to superimpose the image of Christ onto a protagonist of his novel—and onto the fate of a Russian general at that. While kneeling in prayer, Samsonov wipes off a heavy sweat—compare this to the bloody sweat of Christ in the Gospel account. Like Christ in the Gospel, Samsonov experiences an hour of absolute isolation. When he rises from prayer, "no one had come for him either with a pressing question or with a cheering or bad report." And descending even deeper, Samsonov is granted a vision of his own impending death.

> Nikita Struve, "The Debate over *August 1914*," in
> John B. Dunlop et al., eds., *A. S.: Critical Essays
> and Documentary Materials* (1975), pp. 398–99

S.'s first three novels, like most of his stories, are rigorously restricted in time and space. Time is particularly important in *One Day in the Life of Ivan Denisovich*. Its limited time span, from reveille to lights out, enhances the structural unity, intensity, and compression of the novel. More important, this one day—a relatively *good* one for Shukhov among the 3,653 to which he has been sentenced—becomes the ironic quintessence of the stagnant, hopeless, and preposterous camp existence. The ultimate, purposeless idiocy of the camps is quietly emphasized in remarks about how time passes: "It was a funny thing how time flew when you were working! He was always struck by how fast the days went in camp—you didn't have time to turn around. But the end of your sentence never seemed to be any closer." Time has become a traditional theme in Soviet literature, most notably in the industrial novel, which stressed rapid work tempos: time must not be wasted, time means progress. In *One Day*, time is an evil joke; the authorities have robbed men of it, simply to squander it in colossal quantities of meaningless activity.

> Deming Brown, *Soviet Russian Literature since
> Stalin* (1978), p. 323

According to Aristotle, the following features distinguish forensic rhetoric from the deliberative and epideictic varieties: 1) its province is the past, "for it is always with regard to things already done that the one party accuses and the other defends"; 2) its elements are accusation and defense, since "the parties to a legal action will necessarily be engaged in either one or the other"; and 3) its aim "concerns justice or injustice," with "other considerations subsidiary to these."

The Gulag Archipelago conforms in every respect to these criteria. From the title alone it is clear that the work's province is the past—the evolution of the prison camp system and its operations from 1917 to 1956. But the events of the past are recounted, not in the dispassionate words of the historian, but the impassioned language of one who seeks to sway his audience in a particular direction. That direction is unmistakable. We are involved in an act of prosecution . . . [S.] resurrects the past, submits it to his audience for judgment, and, through the narrative means at his disposal, forces the agents of repression to "confess" their crimes. What is on trial, then, is the system that created, nurtured and administered the camps; the "history" of those institutions is evidence in the case. It is based on an appeal to unwritten law, what Aristotle terms the "principles which are supposed to be acknowledged by all mankind."

> Ronald Vroon, "Literature as Litigation: A. S.'s
> *The Gulag Archipelago*," *Russian History*, 7, 1–2
> (1980), pp. 216–17

[In *The Oak and the Calf*] there are two S.s, one the believer, the sublime prig, the only man in step; the other, the novelist who watches himself as acutely as he does other people, who looks into himself and them with the penetrating eye of a Tolstoy, but also with the same worldly understanding, the same charity. Certainly, without drawing any other comparisons, one can see repeated in S. the same Tolstoyan dualism between novelist and prophetic sage. And Tolstoy as a novelist saw himself as clearly as he saw other people. . . . The novelist [in *The Oak and the Calf*] is always alive, never taking himself quite seriously, and the detailed account of his final expulsion is a masterpiece of humor. This, too, is its only retrospective element: the rest was written at top speed more or less at the time it was taking place. . . . So the somewhat gimcrack air, as of things and persons and thoughts disturbed and *couchés provisoirement*, is itself a proper part of the effect this memoir creates.

> John Bayley, "The Two S.s," *NYRB*, 26 June
> 1980, pp. 4, 8

SOMALI LITERATURE

Although an official orthography for the Somali language was not introduced until 1972, various private systems of writing had been devised, and were in limited use, in the hundred years or so before this date; from 1940 they were applied to the recording of oral poetry and prose. The poetry, alliterative in form and rich in literary sophistication and reflective thought, is preserved verbatim in the memories of its auditors and passed on faithfully by reciters, with the name of the poet always quoted, as if by an oral copyright law.

Although firmly rooted in the past, Somali oral poetry adapted itself to modern life. Since World War II a new genre called *heello* has developed; it is used extensively in radio broadcasting, in the theater, and in recordings. Its main themes are either love or topical matters concerning politics and public life, and it is usually recited with musical accompaniment. Authors embarking on literature in its written form have taken upon themselves three main tasks: to continue carefully to record and annotate this oral heritage, to incorporate it into modern written genres, and finally to introduce entirely new elements not previously found in Somali culture.

Three important collections of oral prose are *Hikmad Soomaali* (1956; Somali wisdom) by Muuse Haaji Ismaaʿiil Galaal (also spelled Muuse Xaaji Ismaaʿiil Galaal; 1920–1980), *Murti iyo sheekooyin* (1973; traditional wisdom and stories) by Cabdulqaadir F. Bootaan (b. 1949), and *Sheekooyin Soomaaliyeed* (1973; Somali stories) by Muuse Cumar Islaam (b. 1937). Both oral prose and poetry are found in *Gabayo, maahmaah, iyo sheekooyin yaryar* (1965; poems, proverbs, and short stories) by Shire Jaamac Achmed (also spelled Axmed; b. 1934) and in articles in the journal *Iftiinka aqoonta* (1966–67), which also contain materials on Somali history.

Three of the greatest poets have volumes containing their collected poems together with their biographies. In *Diiwaanka gabayadii Sayid Maxamed Cabdulle Xasan* (1974; a collection of the poems of Sayid Maxamed Cabdulle Xasan [1856–1921]) Jaamac Cumar Ciise (b. 1932) has annotated a corpus of oral poems of the national hero and Muslim religious leader, who with his Dervish army waged war on the colonial occupiers until his death. The oral poems of Ismaaciil Mire (1862–1951), one of his generals and chief of intelligence in the Dervish army, are published in *Ismaaciil Mire* (1974; Ismaaciil Mire) by Axmed Faarax Cali "Idaajaa" (b. 1947). And in *Ma dhabba jacayl waa loo dhintaa?* (1975; is it true that people die of love?) Rashiid Maxamed Shabeele (b. 1950) writes of Cilmi Bowndheri (?–1941), an oral poet who is said to have died of unrequited love.

An example of oral poetry incorporated unchanged into original modern work is the play *Dabkuu shiday Darwiishkii* (1975; the fire that the Dervish lit) by Axmed Faarax Cali "Idaajaa" and Cabdulqaadir Xirsi "Yamyam" (b. 1946): the principal characters are Sayid Maxamed Cabdulle Xasan and Ismaaciil Mire, and the authors give to the two national heroes dialogue containing quotations from their poems. Faarax Maxamed Jaamac Cawl (b. 1937), in two historical novels, *Aqoondarro waa u nacab jacayl* (1974; *Ignorance Is the Enemy of Love*, 1982) and *Garbaduubkii gumeysiga* (1978; the shackles of colonialism), similarly weaves into his narratives poems that were composed at the time of the events he describes.

The scansion patterns and alliteration of oral poetry have been carried over intact into written poetry, even when it is concerned with current, mainly political, topics. Typical of such poetry is *Geeddiga wadaay* (1973; lead the trek) by Cabdi Muxumud Aamin (b. 1935), praising the ideals of the Somali revolution of 1969. A complete break with oral poetry and prose is found in those short stories and novels based on European models; the subjects and themes, however, are drawn from modern Somali life. The earliest example is the short story "Qawdhan iyo Qoran" (1967; Qawdhan and Qoran), by Axmed Cartan Xaange (b. 1936), which appeared in the literary journal *Horseed*. It is a love story ending in an elopement to save the heroine from being forced by her family to marry a man she does not want. Two short novels by Shire Jaamac Axmed, *Rooxaan* (1973; the spirits) and *Halgankii nolosha* (1973; life struggle), are, respectively, a bitter satire on the practice of

spirit divination, and the story of a young boy's unhappy life as an unwanted stepchild. Much new fiction is serialized in the literary pages of the national daily newspaper; typical of this work are *Waa inoo berrito* (1977; we shall see each other tomorrow) by Axmed Faarax Cali "Idaajaa," about a civil servant engaged in illegal currency deals, and *Wacdaraha jacaylka* (1977; the vicissitudes of love) by Yuusuf Axmed "Hero" (dates n.a.), a love story reflecting the modern feminist trend in Somali society.

A number of works have been produced in languages other than Somali. Somalis writing in Arabic are concerned mainly with religious themes, such as the lives of Muslim saints. In English, Nuruddin FARAH has published four novels of life in modern Somalia, which show great psychological depth and poetic vision: *From a Crooked Rib* (1970), which is particularly interesting as a male writer's insight into a Somali woman's experiences; *A Naked Needle* (1976); *Sweet and Sour Milk* (1979); and *Sardines* (1982). William J. F. Syad (b. 1930) writes lyrical and political poems in French and has published four volumes: *Khamsin* (1969; the khamsin wind), *Harmoniques* (1976; harmonics), *Cantiques* (1976; canticles), and *Naufragés du destin* (1978; destiny's shipwreck victims). Mohamed Said Samantar (b. 1928) writes poetry in both French and Italian, and in the bilingual *La pioggia è caduta/Il a plu* (1973; rain has fallen) he is concerned with the problems of Somalia and with pan-Africanism.

Unlike neighboring Ethiopia during the tumultuous years of the 1970s when the writing and publishing of fiction came to a standstill, the Somali civil war gave a new impetus to fiction writing. Somali writers, who had earlier felt constrained by stringent censorship laws, felt free to express themselves during the civil war. Much of their writing, however, is documentary and autobiographical. In *Maydinkiiba?* (1994; is that you?) Axmed Muuse Axmed Kayd (b. 1937) depicts the trials and tribulations of a young government employee, who, despite his initial shock at the malaise around him, slowly develops a wry sense of humor to protect himself from the hedonistic tendencies of his peers.

Ahmed I. Barkhadle (dates n.a.) ingeniously relates in *Miyi iye Qurbo* (1993; countryside and exile) the sad fate of his heroine—first as a maid in Italy, then as a refugee bride in Canada—to that of her mother, who, as a child, was abducted from her family by a band of roving camel rustlers.

The Somali civil war is exhaustively dealt with in three books written in English by renowned Somali journalist Mohamoud M. Afrah (b. 1933). The books are: *Target: Villa Somalia* (1991); *Mogadishu: Hell on Earth* (1993); and *The Somali Tragedy: The Gang Rape of a Nation* (1994). Based on factual experience but fictitiously narrated by Ali Dhuhul, a nom de plume, the books give a comprehensive view of the civil war from the fall of the late Somali dictator to the arrival and subsequent departure of the U.S. Marines, to the plight of Somali refugees in the diaspora. Even though a great deal of Somali experience is stored in the bardic memory, written poetry is few and far between. Maxamed Ibraahim Warsama "Hadraawi" (b. 1943) composed a great deal of poetry between 1970 and 1990, collected in a volume entitled *Hal-Karaan* (1993). Mohamoud S. Togane (dates n.a.) writes lyrical and political poetry in English and has published two volumes: *The Bottle and the Bushman: Poems of the Prodigal Son* (1986), and *This Devil's Concoction of Clans* (1998).

Although Somali written literature is of such recent origin, it has already reached a standard of excellence that gives hope for a bright future. Contemporary writers, creative, imaginative, and self-confident, share with the oral poets and narrators a high degree of awareness of the potentialities of language as a medium of artistic expression. In 20th-c. world literature Somalia presents an example of the coexistence of innovative trends with filial piety toward the cultural past.

BIBLIOGRAPHY: Andrzejewski, B. W., and I. M. Lewis, eds., Introduction to *Somali Poetry: An Introduction* (1964): 3–60; Johnson, J. W., *Heellooy Heelleellooy: The Development of the Genre Heello in Modern Somali Poetry* (1974); Andrzejewski, B. W., "The Veneration of Sufi Saints and Its Impact on the Oral Literature of the Somali People and Their Literature in Arabic," *AfrLS*, 15 (1974): 15–53; Andrzejewski, B. W., "The Rise of Written Somali Literature," *ARD*, Nos. 8–9 (1975): 7–14; Andrzejewski, B. W., "Modern and Traditional Aspects of Somali Drama," in Dorson, R. M., ed., *Folklore in the Modern World* (1978): 87–101; Beer, D. F., "Somali Literature in European Languages," *Horn of Africa*, 2, 4 (1979): 27–35; Gérard, A., *African Language Literatures* (1981): 155–70; Andrzejewski, B. W., "The Survival of the National Culture in Somalia during and after the Colonial Era: The Contribution of Poets, Playwrights and Collectors of Oral Literature," *N.E.A.: Journal of Research on North East Africa*, 1, 1 (1981): 3–15; Andrzejewski, B. W., "Alliteration and Scansion in Somali Oral Poetry and Their Cultural Correlates," *JASO*, 13, 1 (1982): 68–83

—B. W. ANDRZEJEWSKI;
UPDATED BY ALI JIMALI AHMED

Susan Sontag

SONTAG, Susan

American essayist, critic, novelist, short-story writer, and screenwriter, b. 16 Jan. 1933, New York, N.Y.

Raised in Tucson and Los Angeles, S. attended the universities of California and Chicago and later Harvard, Oxford, and Paris. Briefly married to social psychologist Philip Rieff, S. has taught, lectured, and worked as a journalist and editor. Her didacticism and seriousness of approach have reflected a high degree of intelligence on any subject about which she has written, whether literary, artistic, philosophical, political, or ethical, and in recent years she has increasingly turned to photography and to writing for and directing films.

Her first novel, *The Benefactor* (1963), was both praised and criticized for its subtle use of dream and reality; in it S. presents as protagonist a wealthy, introverted man who attempts to make his daily life conform to his bizarre dreams and to have them serve as solutions to his daytime dilemmas. So devoted to his dreams is he, in fact, that he rejects all well-meaning attempts to explain or divert them. A heavily symbolic work, the book itself takes on a nightmarish, Kafkaesque quality, with its introspective confusion of waking and sleeping hours, its limited action, and its extreme self-consciousness of character. *Death Kit* (1967), by contrast, is less self-consciously intellectual although still about a fragmented protagonist who cannot always distinguish between dream and reality, in this case with a crucial ambiguous act, a murder, leading to the protagonist's madness.

S.'s criticism has received more attention than her fiction and has been the subject of far more controversy. Much of this criticism, as in *Against Interpretation* (1966), reflects her contention that traditional content and meaning in the arts are no longer

important, that the "philistine" act of interpretation is itself an improper attempt to deny the integrity and uniqueness of the work of art. *Against Interpretation* evinces S.'s serious (if somewhat pretentious) approach to culture, one that helped illumine then-current avant-gardism for those who found confusing the proliferation of competing forms of culture, especially those emanating from Europe. *Styles of Radical Will* (1969) continues S.'s forays into contemporary culture, emphasizing such phenomena as drugs, pornography, cinema, and the work of such artists as the painter Andy Warhol, the composer John Cage, the film directors Jean-Luc Godard and Ingmar Bergman, and the dramatist Samuel BECKETT. *Trip to Hanoi* (1969) is important as a revelation of S.'s shift from a leftist but nondoctrinaire stance to one concerned with reassessing the meaning of the American Revolution and its consequences for the present.

S.'s sensitive, inquisitive explorations of contemporary culture, while as forcefully argued as they are passionately disputed or praised by her readers, have increasingly taken a personal turn in recent years, as suggested by *Illness as Metaphor* (1978), based on her own experiences with cancer surgery; the book was revised and expanded as *AIDS and Its Metaphors* (1988). Critics have accused her, on the one hand, of a grim, humorless, and abstract aestheticism derived from French "new wave" cinema and fiction, and on the other of a self-conscious celebration of whatever interests her at a particular moment. Her intelligence is admitted by both attackers and defenders, although her significance is endlessly debated and her attempts to deride literary and cultural movements while simultaneously drawing upon these currents for her own substance and style are at best self-contradictory. A complex, honest, but frustratingly ambiguous and inconsistent writer, S. is likely to endure more on the basis of a few landmark essays than on anything else.

FURTHER WORKS: *Freud: The Mind of the Moralist* (1959, with Rieff Philip); *Literature* (1966); *Duet for Cannibals* (1970); *Brother Carl* (1974); *On Photography* (1976); *I, Etcetera* (1978); *Under the Sign of Saturn* (1980); *A S. S. Reader* (1982); *I, Etcetera* (1978); *Story of the Eye* (1979); *Italy: One Hundred Years of Photography* (1988, with Cesare Colombo); *Cage-Cunningham-Johns: Dancers on a Plane, in Memory of Their Feelings* (1990, with Richard Francis); *The Way We Live Now* (1991, with Howard Hodgkin); *The Volcano Lover: A Romance* (1992); *Violent Legacies* (1992, with Richard Misrach); *Alice in Bed: A Play in Eight Scenes* (1993); *Conversations* (1995); *Homo Poeticus: Essays* (1995)

BIBLIOGRAPHY: Koch, S., "On S. S.," *TriQ*, 7 (1966): 153–60; Holbrook, D., "What New Sensibility?," *CQ*, 3 (1968): 153–63; Gilman, R., "S. S. and the Question of the New," *New Republic*, 3 May 1969: 23–28; Bellamy, J. D., *The New Fiction* (1974): 113–29; Rubin, L. D., Jr., "S. S. and the Camp Followers," *SR*, 82 (1974): 503–10; Kher, P. R., "S. S.'s Aesthetic: A Moral Point of View," *OJES*, 15 (1979): 55–64; Nelson, C., "Soliciting Self-Knowledge: The Rhetoric of S. S.'s Criticism," *CritI*, 6 (1980): 707–26; Sayres, S., *S. S.: The Elegiac Modernist* (1990)

—PAUL SCHLUETER

SORBIAN LITERATURE
See Lusatian Literature

SØRENSEN, Villy

Danish short-story writer, essayist, and philosopher, b. 13 Jan. 1929, Copenhagen

S. grew up in a lower-middle-class home in Copenhagen. Shortly after his university studies (1947–53), he established himself not only as a writer of unusual short stories but also as a major figure in Danish intellectual life, who has taken an active part in shaping its course during the post-World War II period through his literary and social criticism. From 1959 to 1963 he also played a significant role as coeditor of *Vindrosen*, a leading Danish cultural and literary journal of its time. His studies in philosophy and psychology at the universities of Copenhagen and Freiburg (Germany) are evident in S.'s work and have also resulted in a number of books on major philosophers such as Nietzsche, Schopenhauer, and Seneca, and in translations of selections from Erasmus's and Seneca's works. S.'s own pronounced philosophical views are an integral part of his fictional work, which is quantitatively small. Although he has published only three collections of short stories, there is no doubt about the stories' significance for postwar Danish literature.

At the time of its publication, his first collection, *Sære historier* (1953; strange stories), was viewed as a renewal of the fantastic

mode of narration, which until then had been represented mainly by the short fiction of Isak DINESEN. But unlike Dinesen, S. does not merely focus on fantastically strange events; his stories exemplify in a parabolic way his predominant theme of the divided personality and stress the individual's confrontation with the absurd. With its numerous variations, this theme unifies *Sære historier* with the later collections, *Ufarlige historier* (1955; harmless stories) and *Formynderfortællinger* (1964; a guardian's tales). S. derived the title of his second collection from a statement by Aristotle that the terrible is funny when it is harmless, and S. himself adds a humorous touch to his stories primarily by the use of irony and linguistic ambiguity; but the comic is always blended with the tragic.

The stories, some of which are quite long, are like case histories where critical close-up views are given of confrontations between opposing forces in a social environment that reflects and promotes cold and even cruel relationships among people; thus, S. opens uncanny perspectives into past and future societies alike. One recurring motif, murder, is indicative of the loss of a human dimension, as in "De forsvundne breve" (the missing letters). In a highly technological world that has made letters nearly obsolete, a mailman is murdered by a man desiring the human contact that the letters symbolize. Other stories explore a theme S. had discussed in connection with Kierkegaard's similar concern: an individual's deprivation of the experiences of childhood.

At times S. portrays suppressed thoughts and wishes, which reemerge when they finally must be dealt with, by using symbols such as a tiger appearing suddenly in a kitchen in "Tigrene" (1953; "The Tigers," 1957). Or he presents an individual caught psychologically between opposing forces like emotion and intellect or good and evil, by means of an actual physical split.

In S.'s fiction, if any human dimension is suppressed, it will resurge and have to be faced at some point in life, because of the underlying disruption of personal unity, exemplified by the Christian myth of the lost paradise. Both in stories set in a recognizably modern society and in those depicting fantastic events of folktale and legend, bold exaggeration tending to the grotesque is a major device in depicting psychological states. In his essays as well as his fiction, S. continues the process of interpreting human existence with all its suppressed and resurging traumas, as well as endeavors to overcome them in a socially responsible way, with an emphasis on the latter. In *Vejrdage* (1980; weather days), a collection of reflections in verse and prose in the form of diary entries from the summer of 1979, S. directly expresses his deep concern for the human and political situation worldwide.

FURTHER WORKS: *Digtere og dæmoner* (1959); *Hverken-eller* (1961); *Nietzsche* (1963); *Kafkas digtning* (1968); *Schopenhauer* (1969); *Mellem fortid og fremtid* (1969); *Midler uden mål* (1971); *Uden mål—og med* (1973); *Seneca* (1976); *Oprør fra midten* (1978, with Niels I. Meyer and K. Helweg-Pedersen; *Revolt from the Center*, 1981); *Den gyldne middelvej, og andre debatindlæg i 1970erne* (1979); *Aladdin* (1981); *Ragnarok* (1982); *Røret om oprøret* (1982, with Niels I. Meyer and K. Helweg-Pedersen). FURTHER WORKS IN ENGLISH: *Tiger in the Kitchen, and Other Strange Stories* (1957)

BIBLIOGRAPHY: Mitchell, P. M., *A History of Danish Literature*, 2nd ed. (1971): 305–6; Rossel, S. H., *A History of Scandinavian Literature, 1870–1980* (1981): 325–26

—LEONIE MARX

SORESCU, Marin

Romanian poet, dramatist, novelist, translator, and essayist, b. 29 Feb. 1936, Bulzeşti, Dolj County; d. 8 Dec. 1996, Bucharest

One of the most widely read and translated contemporary Romanian poets, S. was born in Bulzeşti, southern Romania, to a family of peasants with literary interests. After receiving his degree in philology from the University of Jassy (1960), S. worked as an editor for *Viaţa studenţească* and *Luceafărul*, where he also published his first poems. Between 1966 and 1972 he served as editor in chief of the Animafilm studio. Since 1978 he has been editing the literary magazine *Ramuri*. After his participations in the Edinburgh Festival (1971) and the International Writers' Program at the University of Iowa (1972), S.'s work has been published in several English translations. Among his many literary distinctions are the Poetry Prize of the Academia delle Muze, Florence (1978) and the International Fernando Riello Prize in Madrid (1983).

Singur printre poeţi (1964; alone amongst poets), a collection of spirited poetic parodies, and *Poeme* (1965; poems) announced S.'s exceptional gift for ironic observation. This gift was put to more earnest uses in *Moartea ceasului* (1966; the death of the clock) and *Tinereţea lui Don Quijote* (1968; *Don Quijote's Tender Years*, 1979), volumes that "defamiliarize" the familiar, constructing a new, self-ironic mythology from everyday realities. An instant favorite with readers, S.'s nonconformistic poetry contributed to the revival of poetic imagination in Romania after a decade of socialist pseudoart.

If the existential and metaphysical themes, such as life, death, creation, time—erotic love is conspicuously absent—predominate in the early poems, the following volumes balanced them with sociocultural concerns. *Tuşiţi* (1970; cough), *Suflete, bun la toate* (1972; soul, good for everything), *Astfel* (1973; thus), *Sărbători itinerante* (1978; movable feasts), probe psychological stereotypes, social fallacies, and skewed moral perspectives. The typical S. poem begins with a witty, pointed narrative that opens unexpected vistas of thought. This successful construction was imitated in the 1970s by lesser poets. Fortunately, at a time when S.'s poetry seemed inescapably caught in its own formula, the poet managed to surprise his readers with a collection of ironic love poems, *Descîntoteca* (1976; an archive of incantations), and with three volumes of prose-poetry entitled *La lilieci* (3 vols., 1973, 1977, 1981; among the lilacs), which recreated the mythic-autobiographical universe of S.'s native village from the perspective of a child, but with the refined self-consciousness of a postmodern poet who mixes archaic and contemporary idioms.

Though overshadowed by his success as a poet, S.'s playwriting has been remarkably innovative, bringing Romanian drama closer to the imaginative excellence of poetry. Under the influence of EXISTENTIALISM, S.'s plays are concerned with the struggle of the self in a hostile environment, with survival and spiritual questing. *Iona* (1965; Jonah) rewrites a well-known myth, focusing on various forms of modern entrapment. In a dramatized monologue, the fisherman Jonah debates his position in time and space, seeking to recover the freedom of the outside world, but each effort projects him into the belly of a larger fish. *Paraliserul* (1970; the sexton) is another one-man play that explores the tensions between faith and historical change. Locked up inside an abandoned cathedral, the sexton burns candles and eventually his own body in a metaphoric-absurd attempt to restore a blackened glory to his church. *Matca* (1973; the matrix) portrays a more hopeful postdiluvian world in which contraries (youth and age, creation and destruction, male and female) strike a fragile balance that perpetuates life. The play's humble villagers are caught in a cosmic drama that ends with the reassertion of the life-giving "matrix" of motherhood.

Republished as *Setea muntelui de sare* (1974; *The Thirst of the Salt Mountain*, 1985), these "ontological tragedies" established S.'s reputation as Romania's foremost metaphysical playwright. As if to challenge this description, S. wrote simultaneously comedies that explored the absurd face of contemporary urban culture: *Există nervi* (1968; folks have nerves) and *Pluta meduzei* (1970; Medusa's raft). More recently, S. has taken an interest in recreative historical drama: *Răceala* (1976; *A Cold*, 1978) and *A treia ţeapă* (1978; *Vlad Dracula, the Impaler*, 1987) are well-documented plays with a large cast of characters and an anticonventional treatment of history that suggest ingenious parallels between the bloody medieval times of Vlad the Impaler and Ceauşescu's Romania.

S. has also published a novel, *Trei dinţi din faţă* (1977; three front teeth), an anthology of translations, *Tratat de inspiraţie* (1985; treatise on inspiration), and several volumes of critical essays: *Teoria sferelor de influenţă* (1969; the theory of impacting spheres), *Starea de destin* (1976; state of destiny), and *Uşor cu pianul pe scări* (1985; easy with that piano down the stairs). S.'s reputation, however, remains primarily linked to the "poetic revival" of the 1960s and 1970s. Often compared to Henri MICHAUX, Jacques PRÉVERT, or Eugène IONESCO, S. is perhaps best seen as the skeptical-imaginative voice of an eastern Europe in pursuit of new cultural "transparencies" and connections.

FURTHER WORKS: *O aripă şi-un picior—Despre cum era să zbor* (1970); *Unghi* (1970); *Insomnii; Microeseuri* (1971); *Ocolul infinitului mic* (1973); *Norii* (1975); *Ceramică; Versuri* (1979); *Fîntîni în mare* (1982); *Poezii* (2 vols., 1990, 1992); *Traversarea: poezii* (1994); *Desfacerea gunoaielor; teatru* (1995). FURTHER WORKS IN ENGLISH: *Frames* (1972); *This Hour* (1982); *Symmetries* (1982); *Selected Poems* (1983); *Let's Talk about the Weather* (1985); *The Biggest Egg in the World* (1987); *Hands behind My Back: Selected Poems* (1991)

BIBLIOGRAPHY: MacGregor-Hastie, R., Introduction to *Frames* (1982): 9–14; Hamburger, M., Introduction to *Selected Poems* (1983): 5–8; Silkin, J., Introduction to *Let's Talk about the Weather* (1985): viii–xi; Catanoy, N., on *Symmetries, Miorita*, 9: 1–2 (1985): 93; Dorian, M., on *M. S.: Selected Poems, WLT*, 59, 1 (Winter 1985), 86; Munteanu, R., "La poésie de M. S.," *La civilisation des livres* (1986): 263–79

—MARCEL CORNIS-POPE

SORIANO, Osvaldo

Argentine novelist and journalist, b. 6 Jan. 1943, Mar del Plata; d. 29 Jan. 1997, Buenos Aires

A best-selling novelist and prolific journalist, S. was a self-proclaimed "autodidact" and perhaps the most popular Argentine writer of the late 20th c. He published seven novels that were widely read both in his own country and abroad, and yet he never gave up his journalistic endeavors. S. was born in Mar del Plata, a resort town near Buenos Aires, but his childhood found him traveling through the south of his country due to his father's work. S. began writing as a journalist in the early 1970s when he arrived in Buenos Aires, but his first novel was not published until he was thirty. S. spent the years of Argentine military dictatorship and harsh repression in exile, first in Brussels and then in Paris, from 1976 to 1984. This period had a profound effect on S., and his novelistic and journalistic production were, in many ways, thereafter concerned with the issues of exile, solitude, political violence and national identity.

S.'s first novel, *Triste, Solitario y final* (1973; Sad, Alone, and Final), shows its roots in popular genres such as the hardboiled detective novel in the style of Raymond CHANDLER and early Hollywood film, two genres that have been extremely popular with other Argentine writers as well. S.'s stylistic techniques are already evident: crisp, cinematographic narrative action, constant dialogue with extremely Argentine speech patterns, black humor and slapstick comedy, violence, and exaggerated parody. Besides appearing as a character in the novel, S. includes several figures from early Hollywood, such as Laurel and Hardy, Philip Marlowe, Charlie Chaplin, and numerous others.

No habrá más penas ni olvido (1982; *A Funny Dirty Little War*, 1986) and *Cuarteles de invierno* (1982; *Winter Quarters*, 1989) are short-allegorical novels that take place in the fictive town of Colonia Vega. Both of these novels were made into films (the latter twice). The small provincial town of Colonia Vega can be read both as a microcosmic allegory for Argentina and for the difficult transference of local action and responsibility to a distanced and remote domain. As in many of his other narratives, the novels begin with the backdrop of an everyday scene of normality and spiral into violence of parodic proportions The novels investigate individual and group responses to certain aspects of Argentine reality (the splintering of the Peronist movement in the former and the repressive atmosphere of military rule and its encroachment into the popular sector) through fast-paced plot development and the use of the anti-hero loner whose heroic actions give a glimmer of hope to a debased and hostile reality.

S.'s last four novels were written after his return from exile, and in many ways develop further the author's contemplation of Argentine national identity in the wake of the dictatorship years. The titles themselves seem to be a condensation of national identity, echoing Argentine tangos, lines from the national anthem, or popular sayings. In the novels, while parodic humor is still a constant, there is a definite air of nostalgia and even of apocalyptic futility, as if the narratives were roaming across the ruins of a shattered society in search of a trace of hope. *A sus plantas rendido un león* (1988; At Their Feet a Conquered Lion) is perhaps the lightest and most eccentric of his narratives, parodically reenacting the Falkland Islands dispute between two diplomats in a remote African country and conjuring up mock revolutionary figures. He returns to the question of exile and the Argentine identity abroad in his sixth novel, *El ojo de la patria* (1992; The Eye of the Homeland), which takes up the genre of the spy novel, although in this case the smuggled object is the cybernetic corpse of a 19th-c. Argentine hero. In these last three novels S. adopts conventions of the road novel in which the protagonists experience a transformation while simultaneously the narrative transforms the culture described. In a nostalgic effort to return to a simpler past, S. relocates the essence of Argentine culture from the urban center to the small town. *Una sombra ya pronto serás* (1990; Shadows, 1993) and his last novel, *La hora sin sombra* (1995; The Hour without Shade), take place on the back roads of the nation's landscape, at the crossroads of conflict in which Argentina encounters itself and its changing cultural reality. The land is desolate and uninviting, and the protagonists seem to experience a post-apocalyptic inner exile, an alienation which renders the characters lost and adrift in a hostile and unstable environment.

S. wrote for such important newspapers as *La Opinión* in the 1970s and *Página/12* from the 1980s to his death. Many of the articles were later collected into published collections of works. S. wrote short fictional pieces as well as commentary on pieces ranging from literature and politics to sports and family. While he never lost his popular roots in journalistic writing, his novelistic production became more subtle and multidimensional in his later works. His last novel is perhaps the most sophisticated and complex of his prolific production, and the first which has a clear metafictional style. S. leaves us with a novel that is rich and complex in its literary form, while still telling "a good story" and constructing a well-structured narrative.

FURTHER WORKS: *Artistas, Locos y crimiales* (1984); *Rebeldes, soñadores y fugitivos*(1988); *Cuentos de los años felices* (1993); *Piratas, fantasmas y dinosaurios* (1997)

BIBLIOGRAPHY: Catelli, N., "Desde el vértigo hacia el abismo," *Quimera*, 19 (1982): 43-46; Barr, L., " *Cuarteles de invierno:*The Reign of the Unrighteous," *REH*, 19 (1985): 49-59; Gandolfo, E. "O. S.: cómo contar la historia," in Petronio, G., et al., eds., *"Los héroes difíciles": La literatura policial en la Argentina y en Italia* (1991): 147-65; Lorente-Murphy, S., "Aproximación a una definición del proceso militar en Argentina: S., Viñas, Valenzuela," *Confluencia*, 10 (1995): 94-103; Guntsche, M., "El cronotopo de la cárcel laberíntica en *Una sombra ya pronto serás* de O. S.," *MRRM*, 11 (1995): 302-15

—LORI HOPKINS

SOROMENHO, Fernando Monteiro de Castro

Portuguese-Angolan novelist, short-story writer, and journalist, b. 31 Jan. 1910, Chinde, Mozambique; d. 18 June 1968, São Paulo, Brazil

Son of an upper-echelon official of the Portuguese African civil service, S. spent his first five years in Africa. He went to school in Lisbon for ten years and returned to Africa in 1925, remaining there until 1937, except for one stay in Portugal. During these years he was employed by a diamond company; he then worked in the civil service and was in constant contact with both the native population and the Portuguese civil servants, as well as with immigrant shopkeepers. He traveled through native villages in the district of Luanda, and although he did not speak the indigenous language, Kimbundu, he was able, with the aid of an interpreter, to gather folktales and other ethnographic materials, which he was later to use in his fiction. A sufferer from chronic asthma, in 1937 he left Angola because of its climate, returning to Portugal.

As a journalist, S. wrote for *O mundo português*, an official government publication, from 1939 to 1945. In 1942 he won first prize in the annual contest of the General Colonial Agency with his novel *Homens sem caminho* (1942; men without destiny). At the end of World War II, believing that the victorious allies would favor the establishment of democracy in Portugal, he joined an opposition party and lost his government connection together with his means of support. Unable to publish in Portugal, he went to Brazil, where *Terra morta* (1949; the dead land) appeared. A novel of social criticism, it was hailed as a masterpiece of NEOREALISM, which had become the dominant school in Portuguese fiction. It won international recognition after it had appeared in a French translation, as *Camaxilo* (1956). S. lived briefly in Paris in poverty, visited Russia at the invitation of the Soviet government, and in 1964 collaborated on a Russian anthology of Angolan literature. He then went back to Brazil and was given a full-time position at the University of São Paulo; he was finally at the point of earning a fair livelihood when he died of a cerebral hemorrhage.

S.'s fiction can be divided into two periods. The work of the first deals with black Africans living in their native milieu and following their old traditions. This is the subject of *Lendas negras* (1936; negro legends) and *Nhari: O drama da gente negra* (1938; Nhari: the drama of black folk), both collections of short fiction; of *Noite de angústia* (1939; night of anguish) and *Homens sem caminho*, both novels; and of two more collections of short stories, *Rajada, e outras histórias* (1943; the big wind, and other tales) and *Calenga* (1945; Calenga). In these beautifully written works there is a tendency to stress the exotic nature of the material.

Terra morta marks the beginning of S.'s second period, in which he turned his attention to the confrontation of two races and the consequent degradation of both. The exotic note disappears, and there is less stress on artistic technique and style. *Terra morta* was followed by *Viragem* (1957; the turning point) and the posthumously published *A chaga* (1970; the wound); this impressive trilogy makes clear the impossibility of continued colonial rule in Angola.

S.'s fiction presents a distinctive and intimate picture of a life that few Europeans knew and still fewer wrote about. He was a fine stylist who created characters with depth and who left a lasting record of a crucial stage of Angolan civilization.

FURTHER WORKS: *Imagens da cidade de São Paulo de Luanda* (1939); *A aventura e a morte no sertão* (1943); *Sertanejos de Angola* (1943); *Mistérios da terra* (1944); *A expedição ao país do oiro branco* (1944); *A maravilhosa viagem dos exploradores portugueses* (12 parts, 1946–1948); *Histórias da terra negra* (1960)

BIBLIOGRAPHY: Bastide, R., *L'Afrique dans l'œuvre de C. S.* (1960); Moser, G., "C. S.: An Angolan Realist," *Essays in Portuguese-African Literature* (1969): 42–60; Hamilton, R. G., *Voices from an Empire: A History of Afro-Portuguese Literature* (1975): 34–40; Moloney, R. L., "C. S.'s Africa," in T. Beardsley, T., Jr., et al., eds., *Studies in Honor of Lloyd A. Kasten* (1975): 175–84

—RAYMOND S. SAYERS

SOSA, Roberto

Honduran poet. b. June 1930, Yoro

S.'s early years coincided with the dictatorship of Tiburcio Carías Andino, a time of violence and repression when poor families like the Sosas suffered extreme privation. S.'s father

worked as a *venero* or fumigator on a Standard Fruit banana plantation and eventually contracted blue lung. S.'s mother taught him to read and write, but food was scarce, and at the age of five he had to go to work selling bread on the morning train that carried banana workers to a plantation. In time he was able to attend school, where in the fifth grade a small anthology of poetry, hand copied by the teacher for his pupils, changed his life forever: "I learned then that pages of poetry have the power to console." Denied a scholarship to attend high school by one of the dictator's henchmen, he continued to read voraciously on his own and in time found his way to Tegucigalpa, just as the Carías regime was ending. Working as a journalist, he made the acquaintance of many writers and began to publish poems in small magazines and literary supplements. In 1979 he received an M.A. in Hispanic literature at the University of Cincinnati. He has taught literature at the Autonomous University of Honduras and in 1987 was Fulbright professor at Montclair State University in New Jersey. He is a member of the Royal Academy of the Language.

S.'s early books, *Caligramas* (1959; Caligrams), *Muros* (1966; Walls), and *Mar interior* (1967; Inner Sea), attracted critical attention, but it was not until the publication of *Los pobres* (1969; The Poor) and *Un mundo para todos dividido* (1971; A World for All Divided) that S. received international acclaim. *Los pobres* won the Adonais Prize in Spain and *Un mundo para todos dividido* won the Casa de las Américas Prize in Cuba. Within a short time S. was recognized throughout Latin America as a major poetic talent, compared to both Pablo NERUDA and César VALLEJO. Like them S. portrays the physical and spiritual suffering of the poor and condemns the injustice and corruption that perpetuate it. A sign of the power of these poems is that publication of *Un mundo para todos dividido* was halted by the government. The military declared S.'s poetry "highly dangerous," and he received a number of death threats. However, even though the book was banned, the poems circulated in clandestine manuscripts and were frequently recited by students and artists in cafes and clubs throughout the country. Ironically, many of these poems are now required reading in public schools in Honduras.

As the 1970s progressed, the increasingly humiliating role played by Honduras in the Central American conflicts gave rise to a book entitled *Secreto militar* (1984; Military Secret), in which S. gave vent to long pent-up political ire. His caricatures of Latin America's military dictators are both grotesque and meticulously accurate. The caustic portraits of Carías, Duvalier, Somoza, Trujillo, Stroessner, and Pinochet provided a necessary exorcism. While never losing sight of his original socioethical commitment, in subsequent books S. embraced a wider range of poetic themes.

Two books of the 1980s, *El llanto de las cosas* (1984; The Weeping of Things) and *Máscara suelta* (1986; The Lifted Mask), were conceived together and complement one another in many ways. Fruit of the poet's literary and poetic maturity, they distilled all he had learned of life and art. Each represents a pole of his artistic creation. Although all the poems are about love, the *Llanto* poems center around selfless, unconditional love or agape, while the *Máscara* cycle celebrates eros, a realm seldom explored in S.'s previous poetry. *El llanto de las cosas*'s title is an allusion to *lacrimae rerum* (the tears of things), a phrase from the *Aeneid* that refers to the sadness that seems to emanate from all things in the wake of a major tragedy. For Honduras the context is both the irrevocable sense of loss that is the legacy of the Conquest and grief for the suffering that convulsed the isthmus during the decade of the 1980s. An elegiac tone pervades; alongside moving tributes to friends who have died, there are "elegies in life," such as the title poem dedicated to S.'s mother, "she, delicate balance / between / human hardness and the weeping of things." *El llanto de las cosas* pays homage to integrity and valor in the struggle for justice; "Los pesares juntos" (The Common Grief), for example, honors the mothers of the disappeared who demand to know the fate of their loved ones. Several poems express intense tenderness for of Honduras, a country so little "it hasn't even learned how to rain."

The poems in *Máscara suelta* are of a different inspiration. The sensual language and erotic imagery of these poems are a lyrical invocation of woman, perhaps as metaphor for all beauty. In her multiple refractions as lover, companion, defender of hearth and country, this woman is not the object of the poet's gaze but rather a living subject of history, vibrant, committed and fully realized. The elegant syntax and intricate codes of these poems point to a new direction in the S.'s poetic language.

For S., aesthetics and ethics form an inseparable whole. He has stated that he writes "to dignify human beings—why else would one write?" According to Honduran critic Andrés Morris, "S. represents absolute authenticity . . . an authenticity we have not known since Antonio Machado and César Vallejo." Carolyn Forché observes that his poems are like the sound of a shot that goes straight to the center of our hearts." Of his most recent work, Sam Hamill has said, "these elegiac and erotic lyrics present a voice as personal, as elegant and as timeless as the great poets of the T'ang dynasty and the Greek Anthology. S. joins passion and humility, ecstasy and grief, clarity and wisdom, to make poems as lucid an incandescent as anyone writing today."

FURTHER WORKS: *Prosa armada* (1981); *Hasta el sol de hoy* (1987); *Les larmes des choses* (1990); *Obra completa* (1990). FURTHER WORKS IN ENGLISH: *The Common Grief* (1994)

BIBLIOGRAPHY: Bardini, R., "R. S.: Poesia y politica en Honduras," *Plural*, 11 (May 1982): 13-15; Engelbert. J., Introduction to *The Common Grief* (1994): 7-10

—JO ANNE ENGELBERT

SOTHO LITERATURE

See Lesotho Literature and South African Literature: In South Sotho

SOTO, Gary

American poet and essayist, b. 12 Apr. 1952, Fresno, California

Born and reared in California, S. has his origins in the migratory Mexican working experience of the San Joaquin Valley, and his poems keenly reflect his life in these small rural communities. While a spokesman for the American working class, S.'s work more accurately explores the Chicano worldview, and by weaving together a cross-cultural diversity, S. provides a complex vision for a modern California. His writing has been widely anthologized, and has also appeared in such diverse journals as *The Nation*, the *New Republic*, and the *Bloomsbury Review*.

S. completed his M.F.A at the University of California—Irvine in 1976. Almost immediately, he returned to his roots to explore his own identity and that of his community. S.'s first important poem was "The Elements of San Joaquin" (1977), a long rumination on the multifaceted nature of life in Fresno. S.'s poem outlined the violence lurking behind the lives of the Chicano working class, shifting from the brutalities of urban living to the exhaustion of the rural community. Layering thinly disguised political outrage with more elemental symbolism, S. provided important insight into the nature of race and class in the American experience, suggesting that hatred and brutality was a central feature of the landscape. Using a hard, economical language, S.'s poem weaved through the narrator's consciousness, expanding outward to put down roots into a forbidding soil. This complex shifting between the regional and the personal offered a vital new perspective on the Chicano experience. S.'s poetic achievement was recognized in 1976, when he won the U.S. Award from the International Poetry Forum.

S.'s next poem series, *The Tale of Sunlight* (1978), offered a thematic continuity while it broadened its scope beyond the California context. This sweeping epic looked toward the dynamic influences of Latin American life. Dedicated to Gabriel GARCÍA MÁRQUEZ, S.'s poem relied upon a magical realist style which transformed the mundane everyday experiences of its characters, and turned them into beautiful, poignant moments of contemplation. The routines of peasant life become the truths of S.'s vision. The poem follows Molina, a Chicano everyman, through his thoughtful morning, exploring identity and working-class politics. This poem contributed to S.'s growing reputation, and in recognition of this, S. won the Bess Hokin Prize from *Poetry* in the same year.

S.'s prolific output continued with *Father Is a Pillow Tied to a Broom* (1980), *Where Sparrows Work Hard* (1981), and *Black Hair* (1985). In these works S.'s poetry is pared down to a language of hard facts, offering a direct line to his previous work. Following the same thematic concerns, these collections ruminate on the Chicano factory experience, using the working-class life as a basis for more metaphysical concerns. During this period, S.'s reputation as a major poet was enhanced when he won a Guggenheim Fellowship in 1980, a creative writing fellowship from the National Education Association, and the Levinson Award from *Poetry* in 1984. The following year S. became associate professor of English and Chicano studies at the University of California—Berkeley.

In the mid-1980s S.'s writing moved away from his traditional poetic concerns, and became more formally experimental. Choosing to focus on the prose form, S. wrote a series of autobiographical essays collected as continuous vignettes. Exploring the possibilities of an almost documentary language, *Living up the Street: Narrative Recollections* (1985) was the first of these departures. A set of narrative recollections, these prose stories show S.'s childhood in all of its poverty, but they never draw an explicit conclusion or political lesson from the material. While S.'s concern was to present his life the way it was lived, he assiduously avoided the role of propagandist. S.'s success was crowned when he won the American Book Award in the same year.

Small Faces (1986) and *Lesser Evils: Ten Quartets* (1988) intertwine S.'s Catholicism and a growing acceptance of domestic tranquillity. While these works represented a move onto new ground, there was a cooling of S.'s political ardor. Less concerned with the harsh realities of Chicano life, these later works offer a mellow perspective on his new middle-class life. S. is an important Chicano writer, whose work reflects the thoughts and politics of California's working-class minorities. While establishing a strong sense of ethnic identity, S. never relies on this as the sole focus of his work. Instead, he develops a broader creative base for the consideration of the American experience.

FURTHER WORKS: *The Cat's Meow* (1987); *Baseball in April* (1990); *Who Will Know Us* (1990)

BIBLIOGRAPHY: Buckley, C., "Keeping in Touch," *Abraxas* (1978): 16-17; Williamson, A., "In a Middle Style," *Poetry*, 135 (1980): 348-54; Bruce-Novoa, J., *Chicano Poetry: A Response to Chaos* (1982); Pérez-Torres, R., *Movements in Chicano Poetry* (1995)

—PAUL HANSOM

SOTO, Pedro Juan

Puerto Rican novelist and short-story writer, b. 11 July 1928, Cataño

S. earned degrees from Long Island University and Columbia University in New York, and from the University of Toulouse in France. At present he teaches at the University of Puerto Rico. In 1978 one of his sons, Carlos Enrique, was killed by the police in Puerto Rico. This incident has taken a toll on S.'s literary work, since he has been involved in litigations against the Puerto Rican and U.S. governments.

S.'s residence in New York between 1946 and 1955 is a key factor in understanding his literary oeuvre. In New York he learned about the plight of Puerto Rican immigrants as victims of poverty and racism. On the positive side, he was introduced to the works of William FAULKNER, Ernest HEMINGWAY, and John DOS PASSOS, as well as those of European writers like Albert CAMUS, Jean-Paul SARTRE, and Aldous HUXLEY.

S.'s best-known work of fiction is the collection of short stories *Spiks* (1956; spics). The ironic title is a pejorative epithet for Puerto Ricans in New York. The characters' marginal existences are vividly portrayed. S. realistically presents archetypal "newyoricans" (Puerto Ricans born and/or raised in New York) and, more importantly, shows the evolution of his antihero-characters torn between opposing forces—assimilation or acculturation. This same conflict is present in his novel *Ardiente suelo, fría estación* (1961; *Hot Land, Cold Season*, 1973), in which the main protagonist is torn between two societies—those of New York and Puerto Rico—and his conflicting perceptions of them. In the denouement he is forced to realize, like many of the characters in *Spiks*, that he is a man without a country.

The dualities of *Spiks* and *Ardiente suelo, fría estación* are also present in one of S.'s best novels, *Usmaíl* (1959; Usmaíl [i.e., U.S. Mail]). In this work, however, the story of the main character, Usmaíl, is told as a counterpoint to that of the destruction by the U.S. military of his native Vieques, an island off the coast of Puerto Rico. Vieques is a microcosm of all Puerto Rico, as Usmaíl is representative of all Puerto Ricans. The conflicts of Usmaíl—enclosed within a foreign political identity (signaled by his given name) and a hybrid, undefined racial identity (white father, black mother)—are solved at the end when he renames himself "Negro," denounces matriarchal upbringing, and declares himself a self-made man.

El francotirador (1969; the sniper) is, from the point of view of technique, S.'s finest novel. Tomás Saldívia, the protagonist, a Cuban exile living in Puerto Rico, is, like the characters in S.'s

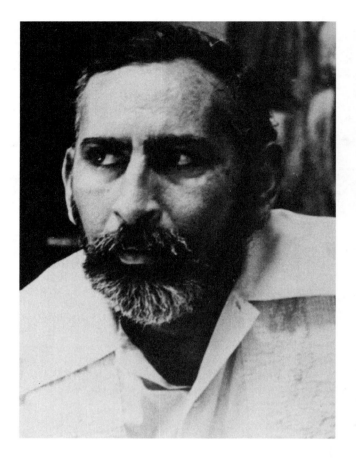

Pedro Juan Soto

other novels, a divided man. His internal conflict results from having left Cuba before Castro rather than staying to fight in the revolution. Within Saldívia's story, there is a second one—an imaginary novel relating Saldívia's own fantasy return to Cuba. The reader must choose between reading the two narratives as separate entities and perceiving the second one as a metafiction, a reflection of the first one.

Baldomero Freire in *Temporada de duendes* (1970; the season of elves) is also an escapist and a man-in-between. Caught up between fantasies (the movies and consumerism in Puerto Rico) and realities (U.S. power and colonial oppression), he commits suicide as a self-vindication for being a middle man and a traitor to his countrymen. In *Un decir . . .* (1976; a saying . . .), a collection of short stories, language is used as a biting, ironic tool for the destruction of myths adopted by the Puerto Ricans from the U.S. and for the exposure of the hybrid nature of the speakers' homeland and the dividedness of the Puerto Rican people. Dualities are no longer present; on the other hand, the possibility of coexistence and perpetual harmony between two distinct cultures is an illusion that S. continues to unmask.

S.'s fiction is written in a realistic language, but his style is deceptive, since it conceals complex structures and characterizations. His later works are more complex, reflecting perhaps STRUCTURALIST and poststructuralist theories of literature. Critics have, nevertheless, tended to study his work from a sociohistorical perspective or to point to EXISTENTIALIST themes. A reading of S.'s works in light of newer critical theories will undoubtedly establish him as one of the most advanced contemporary Puerto Rican writers of fiction.

FURTHER WORKS: *El huésped* (1955); *A solas con P. J. S.* (1971); *Un oscuro pueblo sonriente* (1982)

BIBLIOGRAPHY: Boring, P. Z., "Escape from Reality in the Fiction of P. J. S.," *PLL*, 8 (1972): 287–96; Boring, P. Z., "Usmaíl: The Puerto Rican Joe Christmas," *CLAJ*, 16 (1973): 324–33; Bonilla, E. S., "On the Vicissitudes of Being 'Puerto Rican': An Exploration of P. J. S.'s *Hot Land, Cold Season*," *RevI*, 8 (1978): 116–28; Miller, J. C., "The Emigrant and New York City: A Consideration of Four Puerto Rican Writers," *MELUS*, 5, 3 (1978): 82–99; Umpierre, L. M., "Entrevista con P. J. S.," *RC-R*, 7 (1979): 29–31; Umpierre, L. M., "Corrientes ideológicas en el *Usmaíl* de P. J. S.," *BR/RB*, 8 (1981): 62–74; Umpierre, L. M., *Ideología y novela en Puerto Rico (un estudio de la narrativa de Zeno, Laguerre y S.)* (1983): 81–119, 147–51

—LUZ MARÍA UMPIERRE

SOUPAULT, Philippe

French poet, novelist, and essayist, b. 2 Aug. 1897, Chaville

S. was profoundly affected by the loss of his father at the age of seven and gradually became estranged from his upper-middle-class family, who neither understood nor took seriously his writing and his hostility to his class. He was wounded in World War I. In 1917 he met Guillaume APOLLINAIRE, who was an important influence on him, and André BRETON. The following year he and Breton, in company with Louis ARAGON and Paul ÉLUARD formed the nucleus of the first SURREALIST group in Paris. In 1919 S. contributed to a DADAIST anthology and to the first issues of the surrealist review *Littérature*. Until 1927 he published regularly in *La révolution surréaliste*, but by then he had become dissatisfied with the political entanglements of the movement and Breton's efforts to codify surrealist theory. S.'s expulsion from the surrealist group was clearly stated in Breton's *Second Manifesto of Surrealism*. S. later became a journalist and radio broadcaster and traveled extensively in Europe, Asia, Africa, and America in this capacity and on behalf of UNESCO.

S.'s first collection of poems, *Aquarium* (aquarium), appeared in 1917. The novel *Les champs magnétiques* (1920; magnetic fields), which he coauthored with Breton, was the first major text of the surrealist movement and the first example of automatic writing to gain the approval of the other surrealists. Today, however, the vocabulary and images seem quite conventional.

Other novels of the 1920s, like *Le bon apôtre* (1923; the good apostle) and *Le voyage d'Horace Pirouelle* (1925; Horace Pirouelle's trip), treat the attempts by various youths to escape from the dull bourgeois life of postwar France. *Les frères Durandeau* (1924; the Durandeau brothers), probably S.'s best novel and a runner-up for the Goncourt Prize, and *Un grand homme* (1929; a great man) are harsh satires of the upper middle class, their materialism and disregard for human life. The "great man" of the latter book is based on Louis Renault, the automobile magnate, who was S.'s uncle.

S. has also written "presentations" of poets and painters who were particularly important to him, such as *Henri Rousseau, Le Douanier* (1927), *Guillaume Apollinaire; ou, Les reflets de l'incendie*

(1927; Guillaume Apollinaire; or, the reflections of the fire), *Lautréamont* (1927), and *Ucello* (1929). They tend, however, to be personal rather than objective in the treatment of their subjects.

S.'s best volumes of poetry were published in the early years of surrealism. *Rose des vents* (1920; rose of the winds) expresses the need for flight from the material universe with bold images of modern technology, and *Westwego* (1922; Westwego) continues to convey the desire to stretch the limits of reality, combining this with evocations of London and Paris. *Georgia* (1926; Georgia) reflects more clearly the excitement of the surrealists' quest for the unattainable goal.

S.'s poetry retains the spontaneous, mysterious, unexpected elements of surrealism. It also reflects the fluidity and transparency of Apollinaire's poetry. S. states that his poetry is "given" to him, and it seems sometimes to be derived from the secrets of his inner life and at others to express indirectly the poet's experience in the world.

FURTHER WORKS: *Premières chansons* (1920); *S'il vous plaît* (1920; *If You Please*, 1964); *L'invitation au suicide* (1922); *À la dérive* (1923); *Wang-wang* (1924); *Le bar de l'amour* (1925); *En joue!* (1925); *Corps perdu* (1926); *Carte postale* (1926); *Le nègre* (1927); *Histoire d'un blanc* (1927); *Le cœur d'or* (1927); *William Blake* (1928; *William Blake*, 1928); *Jean Lurçat* (1928); *Le roi de la vie* (1928); *Terpsichore* (1928); *Les dernières nuits de Paris* (1928; *The Last Nights of Paris*, 1929); *Bulles, billes, boules* (1930); *Baudelaire* (1931); *Charlot* (1931); *Les moribonds* (1934); *Il y a un océan* (1936); *Poésies complètes, 1917–1937* (1937); *Souvenirs de James Joyce* (1943); *Tous ensemble au bout du monde* (1943); *Le temps des assassins* (1944; *Age of Assassins*, 1946); *Ode à Londres bombardée* (1944; *Ode to a Bombed London*, 1944); *Eugène Labiche* (1945); *Odes* (1946); *L'âme secrète* (1946); *Journal d'un fantôme* (1946); *Message de l'île déserte* (1947); *Chansons* (1949); *Essai sur la poésie* (1950); *La fille qui a fait des miracles* (1950); *La parasite* (1951); *Sans phrases* (1953); *Alfred de Musset* (1957); *Helman* (1959); *Rendez-vous* (1960); *Profils perdus* (1963); *L'amitié* (1964); *Le vrai André Breton* (1966); *Le sixième coup de minuit* (1972); *Alibis* (1972); *Poèmes et poésies 1917–1973* (1973); *Collection fantôme* (1973); *Apprendre à vivre: 1897–1914* (1977); *Écrits de cinéma 1918–1931* (1979); *Vingt mille et un jours: Entretiens avec Serge Fauchereau* (1980)

BIBLIOGRAPHY: Clancier, G. E., *Panorama critique de Rimbaud au surréalisme* (1953): 450–55; Dupuy, H.-J., *P. S.* (1957); Matthews, J. H., *An Introduction to Surrealism* (1965): 33–50; Nadeau, M., *The History of Surrealism* (1965): 43–124; Sanouillet, M., *Dada à Paris* (1965), passim; Gershman, H. J., *The Surrealist Movement in France* (1969): 33–145

—CHARLES G. HILL

SOUTAR, William

Scottish poet and diarist, b. 28 April 1899, Perth; d. 15 Oct. 1943, Perth

Although he spent most of his adult life as a bedridden invalid, S. wrote poetry and prose until the day he died. After serving in the navy, when his crippling disease first manifested itself, he studied English literature at the University of Edinburgh. Despite poor health and paralysis, S. retained a concern for cultural and political issues, becoming a socialist, pacifist, and Scottish nationalist. He corresponded with and was visited by all the literary Scots of his day.

S. wrote poetry in both English and Scots. His early work in English is derivative and conventional, relying on abstraction and self-consciously poetic diction. Influenced by D. H. LAWRENCE and Wilfred OWEN, he later developed a more direct and contemporary style. His dominant themes are nature's beauty, the pathos of human betrayal of both nature and mankind, and an affirmation of faith in life. In *A Handful of Earth* (1936), *In the Time of Tyrants* (1939), and *The Expectant Silence* (1944), these combine with his mature style to produce many successful poems. On the whole, however, S.'s English verse remains undistinguished.

Influenced by Hugh MACDIARMID's vernacular poetry and the idea of a Scottish Renaissance, S. began in 1923 to write lyrics in Scots. Unlike his English verse, his poems in Scots use concrete, colloquial language and vivid imagery. Believing that hope for a renaissance lay in the future, he wrote many of his poems for children. *Seeds in the Wind* (1933; rev. and enlarged ed., 1943), a collection of these "bairnrhymes," has been called a minor classic. It contains humorous tales, wry characterizations, and beast fables as well as nursery songs. S.'s talent for comic verse is evident as well in poems he called "whigmaleeries" (whims or fantastical notions). In his Scots poems S. retained his focus on nature and human character, but here they are individualized and closely observed. He used Scots vocabulary to express distinctively Scottish moods and attitudes, including a union of realism and fancy, an ironic undercutting of pomposity, and an interest in the grotesque and supernatural. Like MacDiarmid, he wrote a "synthetic Scots," using words from all regions and times, and studied dictionaries to extend his range.

Although S. limited himself technically, relying heavily on the ballad stanza, his verse includes a broad range of tone and mood, becoming satiric, comic, lyrical, whimsical, and contemplative by turns. Preferring brief forms, he wrote riddles, epigrams, short lyrics, and a form he devised called "theme and variation" that reworks themes suggested by other poems. In addition to poetry he wrote journals, diaries, and a record of his dreams over twenty years. The posthumously published *Diaries of a Dying Man* (1954) is a remarkable documentation of inner experience in the face of death.

An important figure in the Scottish Renaissance, S. is probably second only to MacDiarmid as a writer of modern poems in Scots. His "whigmaleeries" are an original contribution to Scottish literature, and despite the limits of his traditional forms, he developed in Scots a fresh and distinctive voice.

FURTHER WORKS: *Gleanings by an Undergraduate* (1923); *Conflict* (1931); *The Solitary Way* (1934); *Brief Words* (1935); *Poems in Scots* (1935); *Riddles in Scots* (1937); *But the Earth Abideth* (1943); *Collected Poems* (1948); *Poems in Scots and English* (1961)

BIBLIOGRAPHY: MacDiarmid, H., Introduction to *Collected Poems* (1948): 9–21; Young, D., "W. S.'s Purpose in Poetry," *Poetry Scotland*, 2 (1945): 51–60; Scott, A., *Still Life: W. S. 1898–1943* (1958); Wittig, K., *The Scottish Tradition in Literature* (1958): 289–92; Buist, A., "*Still Life*: An Appreciation of W. S.," *PRev*, 52 (1961): 89–93; Bruce, G., *W. S.: The Man and the Poet* (1978); Scott, A., "Makar/Poet: W. S.," *ScotR*, No. 11 (1978): 31–37

—NANCY K. GISH

SOUTH AFRICAN LITERATURE

In Afrikaans

Afrikaans literature belongs almost totally to the 20th c., since the written language achieved recognition and acceptance only around the turn of the century. The language of the first European colonizers of the southern tip of Africa (beginning in 1652) was Dutch, from which Afrikaans developed, as a result of the intermingling of different cultures and eventually because of political forces.

After the discovery of diamonds and gold (1870–86), the impact of British imperialism on the Afrikaners had tragic consequences, culminating in the second Anglo-Boer War (1899–1902). Literature early in the century was dominated by this event, and the poetry of C. Louis Leipoldt (1880–1947) is considered the most impressive poetic document of that suffering and the most powerful protest against the physical and spiritual effects of war. Leipoldt and J. F. W. Grosskopf (1885–1948) are considered to be the founders of Afrikaans drama. But the most important writers at the beginning of the 20th c. were poets. The major ones, in addition to Leipoldt, were Jan F. E. Celliers (1865–1940), Totius (pseud. of Jacob Daniel du Toit, 1877–1953), and Eugène Marais (1871–1936). It was a time that demanded the immediacy of poetry; and when the poets sought respite from the atrocities of war, they worshiped nature, although the best work of A. G. Visser (1878–1929) was his lyrical love poetry.

The economic disruption after the war—poverty, land dispossession, urbanization, and the beginnings of the proletarianization of the Afrikaners—became a persistent theme in the fiction of the 1920s and 1930s. Novels glorifying the idyll of farm life and the work ethic and extolling the superiority of country over city were produced by D. F. Malherbe (1881–1969) and C. M. van den Heever (1902–1957), whose *Somer* (1935; *Harvest Home*, 1945) is typical of the treatment of this theme. The poetry of Toon van den Heever (1894–1956) also reflects the problems and conflicts facing the Afrikaner during this period. The most important realist—almost a naturalist—was Jochem van Bruggen (1881–1957), who portrayed the helplessness of a people being forced unwillingly into proletarianization, the destruction of the feudal system, and the poverty of tenant farmers. Mikro (pseud. of C. H. Kühn, 1903–1968), on the other hand, wrote comic novels and sketches of life in the Cape Province.

Projects by newly formed organizations working for the economic rehabilitation of the Afrikaners and the strengthening of nationalism during the 1930s did not have a direct influence on the literature of the time. But the attempts to liberate the Afrikaners economically and politically did bring with them a cultural uplifting, of which a sophisticated literature was part.

The most important figure of the group that came to prominence during the 1930s (known as the Dertigers) was N. P. van Wyk Louw (1906–1970), primarily a poet, but also a dramatist and literary essayist. Through popular means such as radio broadcasts, he educated his people about the nature of literature and criticism, about the aesthetics of poetry, and politically about the necessity of a "liberal" nationalism. His early poetry is individualistic and at times nihilistic; in his second phase, for example in the narrative poem *Raka* (1941; *Raka*, 1941), he turned to folk themes and styles; what is considered his third period is again personal, but with a sense of affirmation. His best play is the verse drama *Germanicus* (1956; Germanicus). A selection of his poetry is available in the bilingual collection *Oh, Wide and Sad Land* (1975). Other important poets of the same generation are Elisabeth Eybers (b. 1915), who is still producing work in Afrikaans although for a number of years she has lived outside the country, W. E. G. Louw (1913–80), and Uys Krige (1910–87), all writers of lyric verse.

During the 1930s poetry came to be regarded as an aristocratic ideal, a sublime trade—the word being man's sole instrument for the attainment of high truths of human existence. Ever since, Afrikaans poetry has retained this isolation of aestheticism, and those who in later decades have attempted to move toward social or political verse often met severe criticism.

The poets of the 1940s, particularly Ernst van Heerden (b. 1916), furthered the quest for the aesthetic word and image. Van Heerden employed complex metaphorical structures. But D. J. Opperman (1914–80), who, in addition to being the most important poetic voice after the death of van Wyk Louw, was also a playwright and critic, took images from everyday modern life. His metaphors and his choice of themes show a consciousness of Africa and of the South African social and political realities, of urbanization, and of the Afrikaners' growing nationalism. The degree of political commitment that did enter Afrikaans poetry, despite efforts to oppose it, can be traced to Opperman.

In 1948 the Afrikaner Nationalist Party came to power in South Africa. The Afrikaners' rise to political control culminated in the declaration of the Republic in 1960. There was a shift in fiction, away from what had been, since the 1920s, a literature idealistically supportive of the nationalist project, dealing with themes such as urbanization, poverty, the Boer War, and racial differences—often didactically, as in the work of G. H. Franz (1896–1956), M. E. R. (pseud. of Mimie E. Rothman, 1875–1975), and Johannes van Melle (1887–1953). Now there was protest writing, directed at the authoritarian power structure, apartheid, and the inherent discrimination at the core of this ideology. Much of this writing came from the Sestigers, those who began their careers in the 1960s.

These innovative young writers of fiction, poetry, and drama had precursors in van Wyk Louw in his later poetry, the cynical satiric poet Peter Blum (1925–92), the dramatist Bartho Smit (1924–86), the polemicist, novelist, and short-story writer Jan Rabie (b. 1920), and the novelist Étienne Leroux (pseud. of Stephanus Petrus Daniel le Roux, 1922–89). The first short stories of Rabie, published in the early 1950s, influenced by European SURREALISM and SYMBOLISM, showed the way.

The influence of Europe was strong on the Sestigers. Many of them went to Europe and lived there for considerable periods of time. Their experiments in technique and theme therefore to a great extent represented a transference to Afrikaans literature of the more recent literary movements in Europe. This self-proclaimed group has sometimes been criticized for being all-male, all-white, and for looking toward Europe for their literary models. The subsequent developments in Afrikaans literature, however, are to be seen in light of these initial challenges to the religious and moral values of the Calvinist fathers.

Leroux is the most distinguished novelist of the Sestiger group, best known for the Welgevonden trilogy—*Sewe dae by die*

Silbersteins (1962; *Seven Days at the Silbersteins*, 1964), *Een vir Azazel* (1964; *One for the Devil*, 1969), and *Die derde oog* (1966; *The Third Eye*, 1969)—in which, using experimental techniques and Carl JUNG's concept of archetypes, he explores the psychology of the Afrikaner. He comments on the loss of myths and satirizes some aspects of South African society.

André P. BRINK is one of the most popular contemporary Afrikaans novelists, and during the politically turbulent 1970s and 1980s, his novels were the most politically committed writing in Afrikaans, protesting against the injustices of apartheid, the falseness of the new Afrikaner capitalism, the power of the police, and the heritage of slavery. Some of his books were banned, unusual for an Afrikaans writer. Brink is bilingual and writes the English versions of his novels himself; these include *Kennis van die Aand* (1973; *Looking on Darkness*, 1975), *'n Oomblik in die wind* (1977; *An Instant in the Wind*, 1977), *Gerugte van reën* (1978; *Rumours of Rain*, 1978), *'n Droë wit seisoen* (1979; *A Dry White Season*, 1980), *Houd-den-bek* (1982; *A Chain of Voices*, 1982), and *Sandkastele* (1995, *Imaginings of Sand*, 1995).

In drama, Chris Barnard and André P. Brink attempted a transposition of the THEATER OF THE ABSURD into Afrikaans. But the plays of Bartho Smit, as well as the later works of Brink, epitomize the 1960s: an awareness of the techniques of playwriting, combined with the presentation of relevant political themes.

The short story became an important genre in the 1960s. Rabie's influence cannot be underestimated in the often poetic, highly concentrated and daring ventures into the darker side of the human psyche by Abraham H. de Vries (b. 1937), Chris Barnard (b. 1939), and John Miles (b. 1938), developing eventually into the portrayal of violence by later writers, as in the work of P. J. Haasbroek (b. 1943), as well as the first depictions of homoerotic desire in Afrikaans fiction, by Hennie Aucamp (b.1934).

Politically and aesthetically the most significant Sestiger writer is the poet and painter Breyten BREYTENBACH, who considered Paris as his home after his political self-exile because of his opposition to apartheid laws. The Zen Buddhist and Tantric aspects of his poetry stunned his traditional Calvinist readers; his opposition to the Afrikaners' ideology angered them. Returning to South Africa in 1975 in disguise, he was arrested and sentenced to nine years' imprisonment on a charge of "terrorism"; he was released in 1983 and returned to Paris. He now spends part of each year living and teaching in South Africa.

Even while in prison he managed to publish a number of volumes of his brilliant, innovative poetry. Two bilingual collections of his poetry, *And Death White as Words: An Anthology of the Poems of Breyten Breytenbach* (1978) and *In Africa Even the Flies Are Happy: Selected Poems 1964–1977* (1978), offer a representative selection. His *'n Seisoen in Paradys* (1976; *A Season in Paradise*, 1980) is a half-real, half-imaginary travelogue in poetic prose that is, ultimately, a meditation on South Africa. His imprisonment left Afrikaans literature—where there has always been the "guiding force" of a single strong creative personality—in a desert between commitment on the one hand and ivory-tower aestheticism and private obsessions on the other. Breytenbach's work represents a watershed in Afrikaans literature. He has, since the election of the first democratic government in South Africa, expressed feelings (representative of the sentiments of many) of disillusionment with the African National Congress Party-led government. He has also announced his intention not to publish anything written in Afrikaans again. His most recent work is a collection of autobiographical and critical pieces called *The Memory of Birds in Times of Revolution* (1996).

In addition to Breytenbach, leading poets of the 1970s were Wilma STOCKENSTRÖM and Sheila Cussons (b. 1922). Cusson's work is in the tradition of poetic refinement started by the Dertigers. Stockenström is also a novelist, whose most famous work is *The Expedition to the Baobab Tree* (1983), originally published as *Die Kremetartekspedisie* in 1981 and translated into English by South African writer J. M. Coetzee. Her work is in turn fiercely satirical of the monster, humankind, and nostalgic for a time when nature (and the African landscape in particular) revealed its own significance.

The most meaningful recent developments in Afrikaans literature have been in fiction, specifically the "political" novel initiated and continued by Brink. There has been an attempt at the documentary novel, by Elsa JOUBERT in *Die swerfjare van Poppie Nongena* (1978; *The Long Journey of Poppie Nongena*, 1980), the actual life story of a woman suppressed by apartheid. John Miles (b. 1935) and Karel Schoeman (b. 1939) have explored various possible South African political scenarios: their fictional visions are bleak.

More recently a number of works have appeared that attempt to come to terms with the ways in which apartheid was experienced by white South Africans. Marlene van Niekerk's *Triomf* (1994) is set in the Johannesburg suburb of Triomf, a development that replaced Sophiatown. The members of a dysfunctional Afrikaans family are depicted in the days before the first democratic elections; their naivete about the political situation evokes both horror and sympathy in the reader.

The future of Afrikaans remains uncertain. The status of the language has changed: from being the dominant language in parliament and in public discourse, it has had to take its place as one of eleven official languages. This changed status does not seem, however, to have had an adverse effect on the production of literary works. The last two decades have seen an increasing popularizing trend in Afrikaans fiction, perhaps in an attempt at gaining a wider readership.

BIBLIOGRAPHY: Coetzee, J. M., *Giving Offense: Essays on Censorship* (1966); Cope, J., *The Adversary Within: Dissident Writers in Afrikaans* (1982); Coetzee, J. M., "The Great South African Novel," *Leadership SA* (1982):74–79; Brink, A. P., *Mapmakers: Writing in a State of Siege* (1983); Daymond, M. J., J. U. Jacobs, and M. Lenta, eds., *Momentum: On Recent South African Writing* (1984); special South Africa issue, *ArielE*, 16, 2 (1985); Breytenbach, B., *End Papers: Essays, Letters, Articles of Faith, Workbook Notes* (1986); Brink, A. P., and J. M. Coetzee, introduction to *A Land Apart: A South African Reader* (1985): 7–15; Coetzee, J. M., *White Writing: On the Culture of Letters in South Africa* (1988)

—CARLI COETZEE

In English

Despite the increasingly severe political repression and the poor economic climate, South African literary production has grown substantially over the last decade, partly because of developing interest in local writing, both in South Africa and abroad, partly because of an expansion of local resources in the face of the cultural boycott, and partly because of an articulated relation between revolutionary struggle and cultural activism. Writing and drama workshops started reaching out to aspirant writers, sometimes combining with literacy projects (South Africa has a fifty-percent

illiteracy rate); performance poetry and popular theater have flourished; additional publishing companies have established themselves, as have a few more local journals and little magazines, some specifically devoted to black writing; and a large number of anthologies have been published, their focus often on current writing from marginalized groups or on hitherto neglected voices from the past.

During the last ten years, then, the contours of South African literature and literary history have begun to be radically revised. The recent unbanning of oppositional political organizations and the return of exiles promise to unite two strands of South African writing: writing produced, published, and marketed within the country, and writing produced and published beyond its boundaries or forced underground. Moreover, the category of "English writing" is continually becoming adjusted and expanded, both through the multilingual references of some contemporary black writing and through the turn made by certain Afrikaans writers, notably Breyten Breytenbach and Andre Brink, to writing in English.

Cultural activism is most in evidence in popular theater and in performance poetry. Popular theater is a continuation of African oral tradition, whose religious rituals, praise poems, and imaginative narratives included well-developed dramatic elements; using song and dance, and often remaining unscripted, popular theater attracts a wide, often not literate, audience, playing in local community halls as well as commercial theaters. After Zakes Mda and Gibson Kente (b. ca. 1945), whose plays tend to idealize black South African community life, younger playwrights often deal with class and ethnic differences within this community. Performance poetry, which also reaches back to oral tradition, is delivered rather than read, often with bodily gesture and movement, the spoken words sometimes combining with chants, ululations, and songs. It is performed at mass meetings, trade union and community gatherings, funerals, and other public and political occasions. While much performance poetry is in African languages, with some multilingual work (as in popular theater), some is in English, notably by Mzwakhe Mbuli (b. 1959?) and Nise Malange (b. 1960). Malange is one of the very few women cultural workers associated with COSATU (Congress of South African Trade Unions).

South African cultural debate typically revolves around the political responsibility of writers and critics, and the relation between writing and history. A semblance of historical veracity combined with political optimism is the preferred mode in fiction and drama; and in poetry, the exhortative and declamatory takes precedence over the lyric voice. Nadine GORDIMER and J. M. COETZEE, South Africa's two best-known novelists, are used to represent different literary and political directions in this debate. Coetzee's writing treats history as myth, both in his earlier work and his three most recent novels, *Life & Times of Michael K* (1983), *Foe* (1986), and *Age of Iron* (1990). Unlike Gordimer, he does not confine his vision to southern African themes. Gordimer—who was awarded the 1991 Nobel Prize in literature—is overtly concerned with "truth-telling" in relation to closely specified political moments in recent South African history; she follows what she sees as a more committed and more optimistic political line than Coetzee's. Her most recent novels are *July's People* (1981), *A Sport of Nature* (1987), and *My Son's Story* (1990); she has also published a novella, *Something Out There* (1984), and *Jump and Other Stories* (1991). Although many of the stories offer a positive political vision, some, unlike the novels, are dominated by despair.

Gordimer's and Coetzee's international successes, as well as the recognition of South Africa's leading playwright, Athol

FUGARD—whose most recent works include *A Lesson for Aloes* (1981), *"Master Harold" . . . and the Boys* (1982), and *The Road to Mecca* (1988)—have tended to eclipse other novelists and short-story writers of the same race and generational span, although some, like Dan JACOBSON, made careers after leaving South Africa. Among the best-established "minor" writers are Lionel Abrahams (b. 1928), Jillian Becker (b. 1932), Stephen Gray (b. 1941), Christopher Hope (b. 1944), Sheila Roberts (b. 1937), Peter Wilhelm (b. 1943), and Rose Zwi (b. 1928); many write satirically about white South African life. From a younger generation, two novels by Menán du Plessis (b. 1948)—*A State of Fear* (1983) and *Longlive* (1989)—continue in the tradition of Gordimer, where the personal and political become deeply interfused in the life of a white South African woman. Yet *Longlive* makes a particular turn Gordimer's work only points to: It portrays a community that represents itself by means of multiple, heterogeneous voices, and whose mode of existence breaks down the categories of apartheid. The text's use to political slogans, religious chants, graffiti, street-vendors' cries, along with dialogue, places it is part of a new South African writing that strives, to use the words of poet Jeremy Cronin, to "learn how to speak/With the voices of this land."

In poetry, too, generational difference makes itself felt in the course of the 1980s. After a strong set of poets, who are still writing, including Guy Butler, Patrick Cullinan (b. 1932), Jean Lipkin (b. 1926), Douglas Livingstone, and others, such as Ruth Miller (1919–1969), a younger generation looks back, self-critically and often satirically, at being brought up "white" in an apartheid culture. Particularly noteworthy among the younger generation are Jeni Couzyn (b. 1942). Ingrid de Kok (b. 1951), and Stephen Watson (b. 1953).

Whereas contemporary white writing tends to deal with white mythology, the social construction of whites in an apartheid culture, the possibilities of reconciliation between black and white, and (sometimes) the forging of a new, nonracial culture, black writing—counteracting the literary imbalances of the past—tends to focus on black communities and the possibilities of revolutionary change from within those communities. Black-consciousness writing, which began in the 1970s and continues into the present, takes its major philosophical position from an "African communalism" as opposed to "Western individualism." Mongane Serote's novel *To Every Birth its Blood* (1981) bases its fictional dynamic upon this distinction, turning, in the second half of the novel, to the revolutionary rebirth of a nation that has regained contact with its African heritage. Many black-consciousness novels, like Serote's, also give a close account of daily events in the life of those engaged in political struggle, including details of the intense physical and psychological torture inflicted on political detainees. Plot resolutions generally take the form of moments of deferral: Freedom is in the not-so-distant future. Sipho Sepamla's *A Ride on the Whirlwind* (1981) figures the return from exile as a "second coming."

Black consciousness has proven hospitable to black women writers, despite its explicit patriarchalism. After Noni Jabavu (b. 1919), whose work formed a (marginalized) part of what has been called a black literary renaissance in the 1960s and 1970s, the first wave of writing in English by black women in South Africa concerns itself with the supportive role of women in the struggle, both practically and as emblems of Mother Africa. Lauretta Ngcobo's (b. 1932) *Cross of Gold* (1981) and Miriam TLALI's *Amandla* (1981) address these themes from slightly different political perspectives. In later writing, including political autobiographies, and poems and short stories in anthologies, as well as a second novel

from Ngcobo, *And They Didn't Die* (1990), and recent short stories by Tlali, *Footprints in the Quag*, also published under the title *Soweto Stories* (1989), the female subjects take on more active and powerful roles, sometimes in response to the disempowerment of black men. The title of *Call Me Woman* (1985) by Ellen Kuzwayo (b. 1914) is an ironic allusion to Mtutuzeli Matshoba's (b. 1950) *Call Me Not a Man* (1979). Like much other black-consciousness writing, Kuzwayo's text refers, with mingled pride and anxiety, to the changed relations between parents and children after the school children's rebellion of 1976 and its aftermath.

Although the norm in black writing is to convey a close and unproblematic relation between writing and history, recent sets of short stories by Njabulo S. NDEBELE and Zoë Wicomb (b. 1948) complicate the picture. Wicomb's *You Can't Get Lost in Cape Town* (1987) focuses on acts of representation rather than on an "objective" reality. Ndebele's *Fools and Other Stories* (1983) shows an interest in releasing forms of cultural expression rather than in simply documenting oppression. Both writers represent an important moment in black South African writing: deeply committed to local political issues, yet at the same time part of an international intellectual debate.

Standard divisions between "black" and "white" writing are beginning to break down, most obviously in the broadly defined genre of political writing, which includes political autobiographies, collections of life-stories and interviews, and prison memoirs, and which incorporates, for instance. Mary Benson's (b. 1919) *A Far Cry: The Making of a South African* (1989), Hugh Lewin's (b. 1939) *Bandiet* (1981), and Emma Mashinini's (b. 1929) *Strikes Have Followed Me All My Life* (1989). Two major texts, both volumes of poems, to come out of prison experience are Jeremy Cronin's (b. 1949) *Inside* (1983) and Breyten Breytenbach's *Judas Eye* (1988).

During the course of the last decade, new reputations have been made. Most notable in this regard is Bessie HEAD, who left South Africa in 1963, and who lived in and wrote about Botswana as a part of an African past and future not available to her in the land of her birth. Head wrote three novels, *When Rain Clouds Gather* (1967), *Maru* (1971), and *A Question of Power* (1973), a set of short stories, *The Collector of Treasures* (1977), and two works of nonfiction, *Serowe: Village of the Rain Wind* (1981) and *A Bewitched Crossroad* (1984). She is one of Africa's most ambitious, energetic, and challenging writers, not least for her interest in race and gender oppression and her simultaneous refusal of orthodox political positions. Two collections of her writing have been posthumously published: *Tales of Tenderness and Power* (1989) and *A Woman Alone* (1990), along with a set of letters, *A Gesture of Belonging* (1991).

Finally, South African literary criticism has also come into its own, not least because of a set of critical texts written by South African writers themselves.

BIBLIOGRAPHY: Barnett, U. A., *A Vision of Order: A Study of Black South African Literature in English 1914–1980* (1983); Gray, S., ed., *The Penguin Book of Southern African Stories* (1985); Adey, D. and et al., *Companion to South African English Literature* (1986); Coetzee, J. M. and A. Brink, eds., *A Land Apart: A South African Reader* (1986); Bunn, D. and J. Taylor, *From South Africa: New Writing, Photographs and Art* (1987); Coetzee, J. M., *White Writing: On the Culture of Letters in South Africa* (1988); Gray, S., ed., *The Penguin Book of Southern African Verse* (1989); Driver,

D., "South Africa," *JCL*, Dec. issue each year; Smith, M. van W., *Grounds of Contest: A Survey of South African English Literature* (1990); Trump, M., ed., *Rendering Things Visible: Essays on South African Literary Culture* (1990); Lockett, C., ed., *Breaking the Silence: A Century of South African Women's Poetry* (1990); Van Niekerk, A., ed., *Raising the Blinds: A Century of South African Women's Stories* (1990)

—DOROTHY DRIVER

In Pedi

Although the Pedi (Northern Sotho) written alphabet goes back to 1861, the first literary works were not published until the 20th c. One of the early publications was Mampše Phala's (dates n.a.) *Kxomo 'a tshwa* (1935; the cow spits), a collection of traditional praise poems. This work served as an example for many later poets, who, even though they composed original poems, kept close to the practice of oral poetry.

While the praise poem is still held in high esteem, some changes have taken place. Poetry has become subjective and emotional, and the works of Phorohlo Mamogobo (b. 1926), Nonyane Tseke (b. 1947), Nkopodi Tseke (b. 1934), and Matome Fela (1918-1987) contain some of the most moving and dramatic passages in Pedi literature. Changes in tone have paralleled a new outlook on life: themes include man's destiny, social evils, and nationalistic or political topics. Some experiments with rhyme were undertaken but then abandoned. A more recent trend has been verse whose meter is rather loosely knit.

In the 1960s and early 1970s Pedi literature was dominated by Kgadime Matsepe (1932-1974), a master of irony who satirized man's complacency. His oeuvre includes six collections of poetry and nine novels. The complex structure of his novels, which are set against a background of traditional life, is a culmination of a development that can be traced to the early 1950s, with the short stories of Mogagabise Ramaila (1897-1962), which expose the evils of contemporary urban life.

In the 1980s and 1990s the new generation of authors dealt with modern urban life. Sonty Monakhisi's (b. 1954) *Tšeang malebiši* (1988; take heed) is a family saga; Mafori Mphalele (b. 1932) exploits the malpractices of the apartheid era in his *Letsogo la Molao* (1984; the arm of the law). The women writers of importance are Ramadimetja Phasha (b. 1963) and Matshidiso Kekana (b. 1958). Kekana's *Nonyana ya tokologo* (1985; bird of freedom) touches on feminism. Detective stories gained popularity. Books for juveniles were published, and Diphete Bopape's (b. 1957) *Ditsietsi* (1995; Ditsietsi) ranks with the best written in this genre. The short stories of Nyahlane Nkadimeng (b. 1947) and Malose Mpepele (1960-1991) are of major stylistic innovation, dealing with trifling events from daily life. The reflective essays of Lesiba Mahapa (b. 1933) and Sehlodi Mabitje (b. 1946) describe several places in Lebowa.

By comparison with poetry and fiction, Pedi drama still lags behind. Maje Serudu (b. 1935) and Samuel Puleng (b. 1958) gained some success. Several radio dramas of merit were published during the 1990s. The exception is Elias Matlala's (1913-1989) tragedy in verse, *Tšhukudu* (1941; rhinoceros); based on the Samson and Delilah story, it is a monumental drama.

BIBLIOGRAPHY: Mokgokong, P. C., "A Brief Survey of Modern Literature in the South African Bantu Languages—Northern Sotho,"

Limi, No. 6 (1968): 60-67; Gérard, A. S., *African Language Literatures* (1981): 220-23; Gérard, A. S., *Comparative Literature and African Literatures* (1983): 155-68; Ntuli, D. B., and Swanepoel, C. F., *Southern African Literature in African Languages* (1993); Smit, J. A., van Wyk, J., and Wade, J. P., *Rethinking South African Literary History* (1996)

—P. S. GROENEWALD

In South Sotho

Linguistically, stylistically, and even thematically, South African writing in South Sotho parallels literature published in that language in Lesotho. It is hard to separate South Sotho writers living in South Africa from those in Lesotho except by checking birthplace and residence. Moreover, major Lesotho writers like Attwell Sidwell Mopeli-Paulus (1913-1960) and Benjamin Leshoai (b. 1920) have lived in South Africa for extended periods.

The earliest published South Sotho writer in South Africa was Zakea Dolphin Mangoaela (1883-1963). He began by producing elementary-school readers and religious tracts, but he also published one work of fiction, a collection of folk tales *Har'a libatana le linyamat'sane* (1912; among the wild animals large and small). In later life he turned primarily to religious subjects and traditional literature, including the first publication of Sotho oral praise poetry on written form, *Lithoko tsa marena a Basotho* (1921; praises of the Sotho chief).

Like Mangoaela, most South Sotho writers took up teaching as the most available career. They first published translations and school texts. When they turned to creative writing, they showed themselves as amateurs by displaying no special affinity for a particular genre. Typical of such writers are James Jantjies Moiloa (b. 1916), who was a lecturer in Bantu languages before publishing volumes of poetry and short stories, a play, and a novel. A. C. J. Ramathe (1907-1958) was a supervisor of Bantu schools before publishing a novel *Tsepo* (1957; hope). Jacob Russell Saoli (b. 1914), while a school principal, published a collection of songs, *Meloli ea tumelo* (1951; songs of faith).

The most able of South African writers in South Sotho was Sophonia Machabe Mofokeng (1923-1957), a linguist who earned his doctorate with a dissertation on Sotho literature. His creative work includes *Senkatana* (1952; Senkatana), a play dealing with the legend of a many-headed monster Kgodumodumo, who is killed by the heroic young Senkatana; the collection *Leetong* (1954; on the road), which was the first real attempt in South Sotho to produce modern short stories; and a collection of essays, *Pelong ya ka* (1961; in my heart).

Samson Mbizo Guma (b. c. 1923) turned to history for his two novels: *Morena Mohlomi, mor'a Monyane* (1960; Chief Mohlomi, son of Monyane) about the conflict between traditional and modern custom regarding the killing of twins; and *Tshehlana tseo tsa Basia* (1962; the light-colored Basia girls), about a crisis in a tribe following a chief's death. Samson Rasebilu Machaka (b. 1932), after years of teaching, published *Meholdi ya polelo* (1962; the flavor of the language) and several more collections of verse.

In a more modern vein, Dyke Sentso (b. 1924) wrote several short stories and a volume of verse, *Matlakala* (1948; bits of grass), and contributed to the pioneering anthology *African Voices* (1959), edited by Peggy Rutherford. J. G. Mocoancoeng's (c. 1914-?) play *Tseleng ea bophelo* (1947; the path of life), set in an African township in the Orange Free State, deals with the contemporary problem of a husband who is led astray by city temptations and becomes a drunkard.

The most prolific recent writer is Ephraim Alfred Lesoro (b. 1929), with several radio plays, numerous books of poetry and, most notably, two novels. *Leshala le tswala molara* (c. 1960; charcoals make ashes) and *Pere ntsho Blackmore* (1968; Blackmore, the black horse), both edifying tales suitable for the moral education of the young.

The emphasis on education in the mother tongue, advocated, ironically, with equal intensity and diametrically opposed motivation in both South Africa and Lesotho, seems likely to maintain both market and audience for a continuing modern literature in the South Sotho language.

BIBLIOGRAPHY: Beuchat, P.-D., *Do the Bantus Have a Literature?* (1963); Guma, S. M., *The Form, Content and Technique of Traditional Literature in Southern Sotho* (1967); Gérard, A. S., "Southern Sotho Literature Today," *African Digest*, No. 15 (1968): 25-29; Lenake, J. M., "A Brief Survey of Modern Literature in the South African Bantu Languages: Southern Sotho," *Limi*, No. 6 (1968): 75-81; Moloi, A. J., "The Germination of Southern Sotho Poetry," *Limi* No. 8 (1969): 28-59; Gérard, A. S., *African Language Literatures* (1981): 190-223

—JOHN POVEY

In Tsonga

Swiss missionaries in South Africa started working among the Tsonga people in 1875 and soon thereafter translated the Bible into Tsonga, thereby creating a written language.

Daniel Cornel Marivate (b. 1897) wrote the first Tsonga novel, *Sasavona* (1938; Sasavona), whose central theme is the condemnation of irresponsibilty and wrecklessness, which Marivate seems to attribute to lack of education and refusal to adopt the Christian faith. Although Marivate dealt with social problems, the religious orientation prevailed in Tsonga fiction through the 1950s. For example, Samuel Jonas Baloyi's (1918-1980) novelette *Murhandziwani* (1949; Murhandziwani) depicts the evil effects of city life on young rural converts. H. W. E. Ntsanwisi's (b. 1922?) *Masungi* (1954; Masungi) was an attempt to depart from the moralistic and religious tendency: he describes the clash between traditional Tsonga culture and Western innovations.

In the early 1960s socioeconomic themes emerged. Love, as well as the clash of old and new, also began to receive more attention. B. K. M. Mtombeni's (1926-1976) novel *Mibya ya nyekanyeka* (1967; the straps of the baby sling are loose) shows that each individual must lead his own life, but it also demonstrates that nobody, including pastors, is immune to temptation. His novel *Ndzi tshikeni* (1973; leave me alone) depicts a man who dies as a result of avenging the murders of his wife and son.

Another noteworthy writer of fiction is F. A. Thuketana (b. 1933), whose novel *Xisomisana* (1968; Xisomisana) asserts that Christianity brings salvation. His other novel, *N'waninginini ma ka tindleve* (1978; N'waninginini does not listen), shows that disregarding parental advise leads to disaster.

Tsonga drama emerged only in 1960, but has developed considerably during the last decade. *Xaka* (1960; Chaka), by Samuel Jonas Baloyi, the first published Tsonga play, is a historical drama

portraying the great Zulu king. Most Tsonga plays have social themes. For example, *Ririmi i madlayisanti* (1964; the tongue gets you killed) by H. A. Mangwane (b. 1932) illustrates marital difficulties when one partner, especially the woman, is better educated than the other. *Gija wanuna wa matimba* (1965; Gija, the strong man), by H. S. V. Muzwayine (b. 1923) and Bill T. Mageza (b. 1926), depicts family problems caused my migratory labor. B. K. M. Mtombeni's *Malangavi ya mbilu* (1966; flames of the heart) artfully portrays the futility of deceit in love affairs. P. M. Makgoana's (b. 1948) *Vugima-musi* (1975; the horizon) criticizes parents who interfere in their children's choice of a marriage partner.

Eric Mashangu Nkondo's (b. 1930) play *Muhlupkeki Ngwanazi* (1974; Muhlupheki Ngwanazi) has a political subject: the attempts of Tsongas to free themselves from white oppression. E. G. W. Mbhombi's (b. 1940) *Madumelani* (1976; Madumelani) uses a plot reminiscent of *Macbeth*, adapted to a Tsonga rural community.

E. P. Ndhambi's (b. 1913) pioneering collection of poetry *Swiphato* (1949; praises) uses the traditional praise-poem style. P. E. Ntsanwisi (b. 1923), in *Vuluva bya switlho-kovetselo* (1957; flowers of praises), followed Ndhambi's style. The poetry of tis period was descriptive and objective.

Since 1965 poets have tended to write subjectively about socioeconomic problems in a changing world; B. J. Masebenza's (b. 1933) *Chochela-mandleni* (1965; fuchsia bush) was a trailblazing collection in this mode. The approach was developed by the Nkondo brothers, whose poetry reveals depth of insight and concentration on spiritual content. Eric Mashangu Nkondo's poetry treats a variety of themes, including a black man's frustrations and aspirations in South Africa. Even more profound is Winston Zinjiva Nkondo (b. 1941?), as revealed in his *Mbita ya vulombe* (1969; pot of honey). Another poet of great insight is M. M. Marhanele (b. 1950?).

BIBLIOGRAPHY: Marivate, C. T. D., "Publications to End of 1965 (Tsonga)," *Limi*, No. 2 (1966): 36-39; Marivate, C. T. D., "Publications to End of 1966 (Tsonga)," *Limi*, No. 4 (1967): 18-19; Marivate, C. T. D., "A Brief Survey of Modern Literature in South African Bantu Languages (Tsonga)," *Limi*, No. 6 (1968): 36-44; Marivate, C. T. D., "Tsonga Publications, 1970-1972," *Limi*, 3, 2 (1975): 71-73; Marivate, C. T. D., "Book Reviews (Tsonga)," *Limi*, 7, 1-2 (1980): 61-72; Gérard, A. S., *African Language Literatures* (1981): 203-4, 218-20

—C. T. D. MARIVATE

In Tswana

Until the end of the first quarter of the 20th c., publication in Tswana consisted mainly of translations of the Bible and other religious material by white missionaries endeavoring to convert the Tswana to Christianity.

A pioneer in creative writing was Sol T. Plaatje (1875-1932), although his novel *Mhudi* (1930) was published in English, presumably because he wanted to reach a wider readership. He did, however, translate some of Shakespeare's plays into Tswana, and his translations show considerable command of his native language.

The man considered the father of Tswana literature is D. P. Moloto (b. 1910). In his first novel, *Mokwena* (1940; Mokwena), he describes the customs of the Bakwena, a Tswana subgroup, and depicts in a matter-of-fact style the upbringing of a chief's son. This novel shows the influence of traditional Tswana storytelling. In his second novel, *Motimedi* (1953; the lost person), he focuses on the plight of the Tswana and other African groups living in urban areas; they have discarded their old ways of life and have thus lost some of their moral fiber.

Didactic Christian themes mark the work of several Tswana writers. Foremost among them is S. A. Moroke (b. 1912), and ordained Methodist minister whose main subject in his novels, short stories, plays, and poems is sin and redemption. His novel *Sephaphati* (1959; Sephaphati) is based on the Biblical story of the prodigal son. In his play *Lobisa Radipitse* (1962; Lobisa Radipitse) the chief character dies because of excessive drinking. Moroke moralizes to such an extent that his works are more like sermons than literature.

The most influential writer, in both his use of the Tswana language and his themes, has been D. P. Semakaleng Monyaise (b. 1921). A truly creative writer with a distinctive and interesting conversational style, he is primarily concerned with man's helplessness against the forces of evil, as in the novels *Marara* (1961; confusion) and *Go ša baori* (1970; those who sit by the fire get burned).

Monyaise sees life as inherently cruel, while J. M. Ntsime (b. 1930) is deeply concerned with man's relationship with God. He juxtaposes Christianity, which he sees as bringing saving grace, with witchcraft, which in his view leads to destruction. These opposing forces come into contact in his plays *Kobo e ntsho* (1968; the black robe) and *Pelo e ntsho* (1972; the black heart), with Christianity offering happiness and redemption.

Two important recent writers have focused on the problems of the young. Masego T. Mmileng (b. 1951), in his novels *Mangomo* (1971; despair) and *Lehudu* (1980; hollow place used for stamping corn), is concerned with the consequences of a harmful upbringing. R. M. Malope (b. 1944) shows how ignorance hampers young people. His style is so learned that his fiction, such as the novel *Matlhoko, matlhoko* (1980; sorrows, sorrows) and the short-story collection *Mmualebe* (1982; Mmualebe), is rather artificial.

Although Tswana literature has advanced steadily, most writers have focused on social and religious issues, disregarding politics and economics. There is good reason to hope, however, as evidenced by the work of Monyaise, that Tswana creative writing will develop further.

BIBLIOGRAPHY: Malepe, A. T., "A Brief Survey of Modern Literature in Tswana," *Limi*, No. 6 (1968): 68-75; Gérard, A. S., *African Language Literatures* (1981): 194-95, 202-3, 217-18

—A. T. MALEPE

In Venda

Since earliest times the Venda people, who live in northeastern Transvaal, have had an oral literature. Only with the coming of Lutheran missionaries, however, did written Venda literature come into being. The first printed work was a school reader published in 1899. In 1913 the missionary Theodor Schwellnus (?-1923) collected Venda folktales and fables in *Ndede ya luambo lwa Tshivenda* (a guide to the Venda language). A complete Venda Bible, translated by Paul Erdmann Schwellnus (?-1946) appeared in 1937; it set

the standard for written Venda. P. E. Schwellnus may be called the father of Venda literature, since he also tried various imaginative genres, with a fair amount of success.

A modern Venda literature began in the mid-1950s with the publications of several works of fiction. The first Venda "novel" was *Elelwani* (1954; remember), really a novella, by Titus N. Maumela (b. 1924), about tribal marriage customs. Maumela published several more short novels, dealing primarily with the clash between tradition and new ideas. E. S. Madima (b. 1922) depicted the evils of city life in his first short novel *A si ene* (1955; it is not he). Later, in *Maduvha ha fani* (1971; the days are not the same), he wrote about success in the city. M. E. R. Mathivha (b. 1921), in the long short story *Tsha ri vhone* (1956; let us see), focused on the conflict of generations. And in *Nungo nzi mulomoni* (1958; strength is in the mouth), by Paul Selaelo Mosehle Masekela (b. 1925), the hero is a young teacher born in the city who goes to live among his own people.

Maumela was also the founder of Venda drama. His *Tshililo* (1957; Tshililo), like his first novel, deals with tribal marriage customs. Other playwrights are M. E. R. Mathivha, whose *Mabalanganye* (1963; Mabalanganye) is about a prince who tries to gain power by foul methods, and Elias S. Netshilema (b. 1928), author of *Vha Musanda Vho-Dzegere* (c. 1957; Lord Dzegere).

The pioneer in modern Venda poetry was P. H. Nenzhelele (b. 1908), who published his first collection, *Zwirendo na zwimbo* (praises and songs), in 1958. The natural beauty of Vendaland inspired the poems of R. R. Matshili (b. 1933) in *Zwiala zwa Venda* (1967; medals of Vendaland). The publication of the collection *Tsiko-tshiphiri* (1971; secret creation) by W. M. R. Sigwavhulimu (b. 1937) heralded a new type of Venda poetry, which deals with nontraditional themes. Other poets of note are D. M. Ngwana (b. 1933), Michael N. Neumukovhani (b. 1945), and Paul Tshindane Mashuwa (b. 1945). The future of Venda poetry seems to be a blending of traditional themes and forms and modern techniques and subjects, such as urban life and war.

BIBLIOGRAPHY: Dau, R. S., "A Brief Survey of Modern Literature in the South African Bantu Languages: Venda," *Limi*, No. 6 (1968): 44-60; Mathivha, M. E. R., *History of Venda Literature* (1970); Mathivha, M. E. R., *An Outline History of the Development of Venda as a Written Language* (1973); Gérard, A. S., *African Language Literatures* (1981): 223-25

—M. E. R. MATHIVHA

In Xhosa

Spoken by some five and a half million people in the Republic of South Africa and the "homelands" of Transkei and Ciskei, Xhosa is one of the most important Bantu languages of southern Africa. It was also the first to be affected by the literary impact of the West. The earliest work on record is an early-19th-c. Christian hymn composed orally by a pre-literate convert named Ntsikana (c. 1783-c. 1820). Until the conquest of Xhosaland was completed in 1877, hymn writing and Bible translation were the main literary activities. During the last quarter of the 19th c., scattered poems in the vernacular journals issued by missionaries testified to increasingly articulated doubts about the benefits to be derived from the white man's presence.

The first major Xhosa author was Samuel Edward Krune Mqhayi (1875-1945), a highly esteemed oral poet as well as a prolific writer. After *Ityala lamawele* (1914; *The Case of the Twins*, 1966), a tale in defense of traditional law, his most ambitious published work was a utopian novel, *U-Don Jadu* (1929; Don Jadu), which projects his vision of a multiracial Africa.

Xhosa literature came into its own between the two world wars. Mqhayi's less gifted followers produced moralizing popular novelettes such as *U-Nomalizo* (1918; *Nomalizo*, 1928) by Enoch S. Guma (1896-1918), but Guybon B. Sinxo (1902-1962) wrote several realistic novels describing the misery and moral degradation of native slum life in the emergent industrial cities; his *Imfene kaDebeza* (1925; Debeza's baboon) was the first play in Xhosa. But serious drama did not appear until James J. R. Jolobe (1902-1976) published *Amathunzi obomi* (1958; the shadows of life), which focuses on the traumas of urban experience. Jolobe, a Protestant minister, is better know, however, as a lyric poet. His famed *Umyezo* (1936; *Poems of an African*, 1946), a collection of deeply Christian poems, introduced descriptive motifs unknown to the oral tradition of praise poetry; while some of the poems focus on important events in the past of the Xhosa, others contain oblique criticism of white racism.

The best Xhosa novel is *Ingqumbo yaminyanya* (1940; *The Wrath of the Ancestors*, 1980), the only imaginative work of Archibald C. Jordan (1906-1968). A breathtaking story of social and cultural upheaval in a Xhosa chiefdom, it is a perceptive and genuinely tragic treatment of two major themes in modern African literature: the conflict between tradition and the need for modernization; and the rejection of clan authority by the literate young in favor of individual choice in matters of love and marriage.

The Bantu Education Act of 1953 had highly ambiguous consequences for Xhosa as for the other vernacular literatures of South Africa. On the one hand, the enforced development of vernacular education suddenly created a vast potential audience of younger readers and thus an unexpected market for writers. On the other hand, because of the predominance of an immature readership and the hardening of censorship, there was no corresponding improvement in literary quality. The new market made it possible for older writers to reach print: R. M. Tshaka (b. 1904) had his first collection of poetry published in 1953. The only novel of Godfrey Malunga Mzamane (1909-1977) *Izinto zodidi* (1959; things of value) is just a sample of much edifying prose fiction that followed in the wake of Sinxo's prewar stories. This trite vein was also exploited by Witness K. Tamsanqa (b. 1928), one of the most prolific and popular Xhosa writers, who is more notable for his contribution to the growth of drama, especially plays. The most promising writer who emerged in the 1970s was Zitobile Sunshine Qangule (1934-1982): the intellectual content of his collection of poetry *Intshuntshe* (1970; a spear) and the sense of personal tragedy in his novel *Izagweba* (1972; fighting sticks) held out a promise of renewal that was unfortunately thwarted by his untimely death.

BIBLIOGRAPHY: Qangule, S. Z., "A Brief Survey of Modern Literature in the South African Bantu Languages: Xhosa," *Limi*, No. 6 (1968): 14-28; Gérard, A. S., *Four African Literatures* (1971): 21-100; Jordan, A. C., *Towards an African Literature: The Emergence of Literary Form in Xhosa* (1973); Mahlasela, B. E. N., *A General Survey of Xhosa Literature from its Early Beginnings in the 1800s to the Present* (1973); special Xhosa section, *South African Outlook*, No. 103 (1973): 93-137; Opland, J., "Imbongi Nezibongo: The Xhosa Tribal Poet and the Contemporary Poetic Tradition," *PMLA*, 90 (1975): 185-208; Gérard, A. S., *African Language Literatures* (1981): 186-201, 211-14

—ALBERT S. GÉRARD

In Zulu

Apart from their "homeland," Kwazulu, the Zulu people, about five and a half million in number, make up much of the population of the province of Natal, South Africa. They were not fully brought under colonial rule until the beginning of this century. Literacy, therefore, lagged; and, unlike the Xhosa and Sotho peoples, the Zulus did not start creating a written literature until the early 1920s, when some one-act plays, dramatizing folktales, were published in the Natal *Native Teachers' Journal*.

The first Zulu writer of note was John L. Dube (1871-1946). Although he belonged to the same generation as the Sotho novelist Thomas MOFOLO and the Xhosa writer S. E. K. Mqhayi (1875-1945), he did not embark on imaginative writing until 1933, when he published the first Zulu novel, *Insila kaTshaka* (*Jeqe, the Body-Servant of King Shaka*, 1951), a lively story dealing with Shaka, an early-19th-c. Zulu conqueror. Dube's earlier *U-Shembe* (1930; Shembe) was a biography of Shembe (c. 1865-1935), the founder of a dissident African church. A distinguishing feature of Zulu literature is that much of it consists of more or less fictionalized biographies of the nation's leaders.

Whereas Dube was the only author of his own generation, a number of gifted and ambitious younger writers came to the fore in the 1930s. R. R. R. Dhlomo (1901-1971) began his literary career with a novella in English, *An African Tragedy* (1928), which presented a somber picture of native life in city slums but also offered some cogent criticism of such customs as the bride-price. The true founder of Zulu literature in English, however, was his younger brother Herbert I. E. Dhlomo (1905-1956), author of *The Girl Who Killed to Save* (1936), *The Valley of a Thousand Hills* (1951), and many other works as yet unpublished.

Meanwhile, R. R. R. Dhlomo turned to writing in Zulu and over the years wrote a number of biographical accounts of 19th-c. chiefs. With *Indlele yababi* (1948; the path of the wicked ones), a novel of Zulu life in the native townships of Johannesburg, he reverted to his early inspiration. E. H. A. Made (1905-1978) initiated the edifying novel with *Indlafa yaseHarrisdale* (1940; the heir of Harrisdale).

Benedict W. Vilakazi (1906-1947), the best Zulu poet, was also a linguist and a student of traditional Zulu poetry. After some experiments with European verse forms, he returned to African forms in two collections: *Inkondlo kaZulu* (1935; Zulu poems) and *Amal'ezulu* (1945; *Zulu Horizons*, 1962). Of his two novels, the better is the posthumously published *Nje nempela* (1955; just how!), which deals with the 1906 Zulu uprising.

The 1950s saw the emergence of C. L. S. Nyembezi (b. 1919), who is usually regarded as the best Zulu novelist. His *Mntanami! Mntanami!* (1950; my child! my child!) is about the snares of city life; the humorous *Inkinsela yaseMgungundlovu* (1961; the tycoon from Pietermaritzburg) satirizes the black bourgeoisie.

In contemporary Zulu writing anecdotes about Zulu kings are popular, and nostalgia for past freedom and traditions is an abundant source of inspiration. Such themes appear in many tales by

Kenneth Bhengu (b. 1916), Joice J. Gwayi (b. 1928), and Moses Ngcobo (b. 1928). But following in the wake of Nyembezi's work, many recent novels focus on city life and the clash of cultures; this theme often takes the form of a conflict between generations on matters of love relations and marriage, as in the works by Jordan K. Ngubane (b. 1917), E. E. N. T. Mkhize (b. 1931), Z. Kuzwayo (b. 1935), and I. S. Kubheka (b. 1933).

Zulu drama, which was initiated in 1937 by Nimrod Ndebele (b. 1913), was slow to develop. Seldom designed for actual stage production, the plays often focused on episodes in some chieftain's life or anecdotes about the culture clash. The more significant dramatists are Elliot Zondi (b. 1930) and especially D. B. Z. Ntuli (b. 1940), whose radio plays have appeared in book form.

Although about forty anthologies of poetry have been issued since the death of Vilakazi, Zulu poetry lacks distinction. It is hampered by censorship, by the fact that its main outlet is the school audience, and by an unfortunate zeal for imitating European prosody. Among the few noteworthy recent poets are John C. Dlamini (b. 1916), O. E. H. Nxumalo (b. 1938), C. T. Msimang (b. 1938), and D. B. Z. Ntuli.

Several Zulu writers living in exile have turned to English. The most notable are Lewis Nkosi (b. 1936), a critic and playwright; Jordan K. Ngubane, who wrote *Ushaba: The Hurtle to Blood River* (1974), a novel that evisions how South African blacks will begin the process of overcoming their white oppressors; and Mazisi Kunene (b. 1936), author of two impressive Zulu epics: *Emperor Shaka the Great* (1979) and *Anthem of the Decades* (1981).

BIBLIOGRAPHY: Nyembezi, C. L. S., *A Review of Zulu Literature* (1961); Ntuli, D. B. Z., ''A Brief Survey of Modern Literature in the South African Bantu Languages: Zulu,'' *Limi*, No. 6 (1968): 28-36; Gérard, A. S., *Four African Literatures* (1971): 181-270; Gérard, A. S., *African Language Literatures* (1981): 192-201, 214-17

—ALBERT S. GÉRARD

SOW FALL, Aminata

Senegalese novelist (writing in French), b. 1941, Saint-Louis

Born of middle-class parents, S. F. spent her childhood in Saint-Louis, the old Senegalese capital city. She completed her secondary education in Dakar where her mother had sent her to help an older sister. After reading literature and translation in France, she completed a teaching diploma before returning to Senegal where she became a French teacher. Seconded to the French Language Teaching Reform Committee, she soon became the Head of Letters and Intellectual Property with the Ministry of Culture where she stayed for ten years. S. F. was a founder of both the African Center for Animation and Cultural Exchanges and the Khoudia Publishing House. She also runs a bookstore in the center of Dakar's suburb of Fann.

An avid reader, seduced by Baudelaire and the French classics from an early age, S. F. had the privilege to discover the French masters in her father's reading room. Her own writing spans some twenty-five years and started in earnest with the publication of her first novel *Le revenant* (1976; The Ghost). This novel deals with the issue of Senegalese society's greed, money, selfishness, and consumerism as observed by S. F. upon her return to Dakar after her years of study in France. Although *Le revenant* is not the first

book written in French by an African woman writer, its publication heralded the beginning of international recognition for Senegalese women novelists and poets. Interest in their work was further heightened with S. F.'s second novel, *La grève des bàttus* (1979; *The Beggars' Strike*, 1986), which was nominated for the prestigious French *Prix Goncourt*. This novel deals with the role beggars play in African, predominantly Muslim cities such as Dakar, and the ambivalent attitude of the local population towards them. *L'appel des arènes* (1982; The Call of the Arena) was also very successful in dealing with the dilemma facing people confronted simultaneously with European and African traditional values. *L'ex-père de la nation* (1987; The Former Father of the Nation) departs from purely social issues towards the realm of political intrigues and neocolonialism. It explores the rise and fall of a man who symbolizes a whole generation; one whose hopes of bettering their country are dashed by bloody dictatorships.

S. F.'s work is rooted in Senegalese culture but the author stresses that her writing has to be judged for its literary and aesthetic qualities rather than its socioeconomic concerns. This may explain in part her rejection of the "feminist label" and the fact that in line with the French canon that impressed her during her formative years, role models tend to be male rather then female. However, in *Le jujubier du Patriarche* (1993; The Tree of the Patriarch) S. F. attempts to reconcile tradition and modernity. According to the author, *Le jujubier du Patriarche* is like a dream, a song, a timeless tale, a myth in which a magician is asking the Patriarch to give him back his daughter. It is by far the most challenging of S. F.'s novels in terms of its narrative structure, and compared to her previous works more akin to the realist tradition. But it is her earlier novels for which she first gained recognition that remain the most significant contribution to a new contemporary African literary canon.

BIBLIOGRAPHY: Herzberger-Fofana, P., *Ecrivains africains et Identités culturelles* (1989): 103-7; Bobia, R., and C. Staunton, "A. S. F. and the Centre Africain d'Animation et d'Echanges Culturels in Senegal," *JMAS*, 29, 3 (1991): 531; Volet, J.-M., *La parole aux Africaines* (1993): 71-96; Busby, M., *Daughters of Africa* (1993): 525-32; d'Almeida, I. A., *Francophone African Women Writers: Destroying the Emptiness of Silence* (1994): 40-154

—JEAN-MARIE VOLET

SOYFER, Jura

Austrian dramatist, poet, storyteller, and essayist, b. 8 Dec. 1912, Kharkov, Russia; d. 6 Feb. 1939, Buchenwald, Germany

S. was born as the son of a wealthy businessman in the Russian steel industry. In late 1920 the family fled from the Bolshevik Revolution and reached Vienna in March of the following year. As a schoolboy S. experienced the political strife of Austria and became a leftist activist at an early age, writing poems, prose sketches, and reviews. After graduating from a *Gymnasium* in 1931 and taking courses at the University of Vienna, S. increasingly devoted himself to political journalism and contributed to *Arbeiter-Zeitung*, the organ of the Social Democratic Party. S.'s response to the events of February 1934 and clericofascist suppression was membership in a clandestine communist group. His best and most enduring work was done for the *Kleinkunst* stages of Vienna, the "little theaters" that presented political cabaret, such as ABC and Literatur am Naschmarkt, to which he contributed *Mittelstücke*, the centerpieces of their programs. These short dramas highlighted Austria's stature as a "proving ground for the destruction of the world," to use a phrase of Karl KRAUS, one of S.'s mentors. After three months of political imprisonment, S. was trapped by the Nazi invasion of Austria. He was taken to Dachau and from there to Buchenwald, where he died of typhoid fever at the age of twenty-six.

One reason why S. sometimes used such pseudonyms as Jura, Georg Anders, Fritz Feder, Norbert Noll, and Walter West may have been his sensitivity about the fact that his last name was a homonym of the German word *Säufer*, "drunkard." In his writings, moral indignation, cynical bitterness, and critical wit are coupled with lyrical lightness and poignant pathos. S.'s inspired use of language is reminiscent of his idols Krams and Johann Nestroy (1801–1862) as he wedded elements of the old Viennese popular theater to the hard-hitting topical revue. His four plays, unpublished in his lifetime, are modern morality plays, powerful parables, and dramatic tracts for the times that move on both a realistic and a surrealistic plane. For example, in *Der Lechner-Edi schaut ins Paradies* (1936; *Eddie Lechner's Trip to Paradise*, 1971), a play that presents a down-and-outer chopping away at the capitalistic system, an attempt is made, during a backward ride on a sort of time machine, to undo centuries of so-called progress. *Astoria* (1937; *Astoria*, 1977), a face with a factual basis about the promotion of a nonexistent state, a swindle turned into a Utopia, is still relevant in an age of wholesale delusion via manipulation and exploitation by the mass media and political packaging. *Weltuntergang* (1936; *The End of the World*, 1972) is a mordant cosmic farce in the spirit of Kraus and Nestroy, and *Vineta* (1937; *Vineta*, 1977) is based on a north German legend about a dead city. Among the most noteworthy of S.'s poems are "Das Lied von der Ordnung" (1932; "The Song of Order," 1977), "Lied des einfachen Menschen" (ca. 1936; "Song of the 20th Century Man," 1977), and "Dachau-Lied" (1938; "Song of the Austrians in Dachau," 1977).

S. devoted his tragically brief life to a futile fight against Austrian fascism and the deleterious slackness, apathy, and fatalistic resignation of his compatriots. Only in recent years has this fearless spokesman for a dispossessed generation emerged in his full stature as a major political and social satirist who illuminates a dark chapter in European history.

FURTHER WORKS: *Vom Paradies zum Weltuntergang: Dramen und Kleinkunst* (1947); *Von Paradies und Weltuntergang* (1962); *Das Gesamswerk* (1980); *Sturmzeit. Briefe 1931-1939* (1991); *Gesammelte Werke* (1993). FURTHER WORKS IN ENGLISH: *The Legacy of J.S., 1912–1939: Poems, Prose and Plays of an Austrian Antifascist* (1977); *It's Up to Us!* (1996)

BIBLIOGRAPHY: Lehmann, J., *The Whispering Gallery* (1955): 294–302; Steinmetz, S., "J. S.," *Weg und Ziel* (Feb. 1959): 149–56; Wellwarth, G. E., "J. S.: An Attempt at Rehabilitation," *American-German Review*, 35 (1969): 22–26; Jarka, H., "Politik und Zauberei: Die Stücke J. S.'s," *MAL*, 5 (1972): 96–143; Jarka, H., *J. S.: Leben, Werk, Zeit* (1987); Jarka, H., "J. S.: A Jewish Writer under Austro-Fascism," *Shofar*, 5 (1987): 18–27; Scheit, G., *Theater und revolutionärer Humanismus: Eine Studie zu J. S.* (1988); Arlt, H., et. al., eds., *Die Welt des J. S.* (1991); Daviau, D. G., ed., *J. S. and His Time* (1995)

—HARRY ZOHN

SOYINKA, Wole

Nigerian dramatist, poet, novelist, essayist, and translator (writing in English), b. 13 July 1934, Abeokuta

S. was educated at University College, Ibadan, and the University of Leeds, where he studied English literature. He has held teaching positions at the University of Ibadan, the University of Lagos, and the University of Ife, and has served as a visiting professor at Cambridge and the University of Sheffield in England and at Yale, Duke, and Harvard. During the Nigerian-Biafran war he spent twenty-two months in prison as a political detainee. Currently he is Woodruff Professor of the Arts at Emory University.

One of the most versatile and innovative of African writers, S. is known primarily for his plays, which range from high comedy and burlesque to fateful tragedy, biting social and political satire, and the THEATER OF THE ABSURD. His plays reflect the influence of both traditional African and modern European drama, and they invariably contain penetrating social criticism based on a profound understanding of human nature. S. has been a vital, moving force in the development of contemporary Nigerian theater, often serving as director, producer, and actor in professional stage companies that perform in the Yoruba language as well as in English.

In S.'s lightest comedy, *The Lion and the Jewel* (perf. 1959, pub. 1963), tradition triumphs over modernity: a wily old chief outmaneuvers a foppish young schoolteacher to win the hand of the village belle. Cunning and wit are also well rewarded in *The Trials of Brother Jero* (perf. 1960, pub. 1963) and its sequel, *Jero's Metamorphosis* (pub. 1973, perf. 1974), farces built around the antics of a fraudulent beach prophet. A more trenchant kind of satire can be found in *A Dance of the Forests* (perf. 1960, pub. 1963), an ironic celebration of Nigeria's independence, and in *Kongi's Harvest* (perf. 1965, pub. 1967), an attack on tyranny and megalomania in postcolonial Africa. S.'s sourest satire, *Madmen and Specialists* (perf. 1970, pub. 1971), published after the Nigerian civil war, deals with man's inhumanity and rapacity in times of severe stress. There has been a tendency toward increasingly dark humor in S.'s comic drama.

His serious philosophical plays explore less topical issues. *The Strong Breed* (pub. 1963, perf. 1966) and *The Swamp Dwellers* (perf. 1958, pub. 1963) examine the integrity of tradition and the nature of social responsibility in a confused world. *The Road* (1965), an intriguingly enigmatic work, deals with the meaning of death in the context of a seemingly meaningless, transitory existence. *Death and the King's Horseman* (pub. 1975, perf. 1976) investigates the notion of self-sacrifice and loyalty to a long-established ideal even in the face of cultural transformation. All these works are concerned in one way or another with man's efforts to come to terms with change and transition.

S. has adapted a few European plays for the African stage, infusing them with local relevance while retaining their basic structure and moral thrust. *The Bacchae of Euripides* (1973) includes scenes modeled upon contemporary Nigerian happenings, and *Opera Wonyosi* (perf. 1977, pub. 1981), based on John Gay's (1685–1732) *The Beggars' Opera* and Bertolt BRECHT's *The Threepenny Opera*, is set in a slick but tawdry African gangster world. Jean GENET's *The Balcony* provided the model for *A Play of Giants* (1984), which burlesques the sadistic antics of four African dictators—Nguema, Bokassa, Mobutu, and Amin. S. adroitly uses these foreign vehicles to drive home important social messages.

His recent plays have continued to treat social and political themes in a farcical and sharply satirical manner. *Requiem for a Futurologist* (1985), inspired in part by an anecdote by Jonathan Swift, deals with religious chicanery, and *From Zia, with Love* (1992), *A Scourge of Hyacinths* (1992) and *The Beatification of Area Boy* (1995) focus on the arbitrary injustices and cruelties of military rule. S. appears to have been stimulated to parody on stage some of the most topical absurdities of life in contemporary Nigeria, where soldiers, sycophants and charlatans thrive in an ambience of blatant corruption.

S.'s poetry is more serious but equally wide-ranging and morally committed. In *Idanre, and Other Poems* (1967) he proves himself the master of many different poetic moods, some of them inspired by the events that led to the Nigerian civil war. Gloom, depression, and grief are balanced by comic invective, mordant irony, and tender, lyrical reflections on death. *Poems from Prison* (1969), a pamphlet published while he was in detention, contains thoughts on his loss of freedom, and *A Shuttle in the Crypt* (1972) extends such encapsulated ruminations into the domain of metaphysics, religion, and ritual. One finds a yearning for liberty and light in these solemn songs of incarceration. *Ogun Abibiman* (1976), a single long poem, is a panegyric celebrating Mozambique's declaration of war on white-ruled Rhodesia, and many of the verses in *Mandela's Earth and Other Poems* (1988) either extol steadfast resistance to oppression or mourn the victims who gave their lives in the struggle for freedom.

S.'s novel *The Interpreters* (1965) is the most complex narrative work yet written by an African. Frequently compared with works by James JOYCE and William FAULKNER, it has an intricate, seemingly chaotic structure, a dense and evocative verbal texture, and a throng of tantalizingly emblematic characters. It focuses on a group of Nigerian intellectuals—an engineer, a journalist, an artist, a teacher, a lawyer, an aristocrat—who meet fortnightly at clubs in Ibadan and Lagos and get drunk together. Between binges they lead ordinary disorderly lives that bring them into contact with people from all parts of Nigerian urban society. Together or alone, in unison or at odds, these six intellectuals interpret and reinterpret their experiences and the world in which they live, leaving the reader to interpret the interpreters and their interpretations.

His second novel, *Season of Anomy* (1973), contains a more straightforward story line but is enriched by symbolic associations with the Orpheus and Eurydice myth and with narratives about Ogun, a revolutionary Yoruba deity. Like much of his writing in the early 1970s, this book reflects a number of the social attitudes and ideals S. formed while in prison.

S. has written four autobiographical works: *The Man Died: Prison Notes* (1972), a record of his imprisonment; *Aké: The Years of Childhood* (1981), a reconstruction of his early years; *Ìsarà* (1989), subtitled *A Voyage around "Essay,"* his father, whose world the book evokes; and *Ibadan: The Penkelemes Years* (1994), a memoir covering 1946-1965, the years of his own schooling, university education, and early theatrical work.

Some of S.'s ideas about literature and drama are recorded in *Myth, Literature and the African World* (1975), and a fuller, retrospective collection of his essays on literary and cultural matters can be found in *Art, Dialogue and Outrage* (1988). S.'s prose is often pungent and feisty, especially when he is answering critics or championing a cause. He is a formidable opponent in debate.

S.'s *The Open Sore of a Continent: A Personal Narrative of the Nigerian Crisis* (1996), an angry denunciation of military and

Wole Soyinka

civilian rule in his homeland, was prompted by the annulment of Nigeria's presidential election in 1993 and the execution of Ken Saro-Wiwa (1941-1995). S. questions whether such a callously abused polity, headed now by a murderous tyrant, can continue to hold together as a nation. This is an impassioned piece of vituperative writing.

S.'s multifarious works provide a kaleidoscopic view of human life in modern Africa; they also serve as graphic illustrations of his belief that the African artist should function "as the record of the mores and experiences of his society and as the voice of vision in his own time."

FURTHER WORKS: *Before the Blackout* (perf. 1965, pub. c. 1971); *Camwood on the Leaves* (perf. 1965, pub. 1973); *Collected Plays* (2 vols., 1973–1974); *The Critic and Society: Barthes, Leftocracy and Other Mythologies* (1980); *The Credo of Being and Nothingness* (1991); *Beyond the Berlin Wall* (1993)

BIBLIOGRAPHY: Moore, G., *W. S.* (1971); Jones, E., *The Writing of W. S.* (1973); Udoeyop, N. J., *Three Nigerian Poets: A Critical Study of the Poetry of S., Clark and Okigbo* (1973): 19–56; Graham-White, A., *The Drama of Black Africa* (1974): 117–45; Ogunba, O., *The Movement of Transition: A Study of the Plays of W. S.* (1975); Böttcher-Wöbcke, R., *Komik, Ironie und Satire im dramatischen Werk von W. S.* (1975); Bejlis, V. A., *W. S.* (1977); Page, M., *W. S.: Bibliography, Biography, Playography* (1979); Gibbs, J., ed., *Critical Perspectives on W. S.* (1980); Larsen, S., *A*

Writer and His Gods: A Study of the Importance of Yoruba Myths and Religious Ideas to the Writing of W. S. (1983); Gibbs, J., *W. S.* (1986); Gibbs, J., and B. Lindfors, eds., *Research on W. S.* (1993); Maja-Pearce, A., ed., *W. S.: An Appraisal* (1994); Wright, D., *W. S.: Life, Work, and Criticism* (1996)

—BERNTH LINDFORS

SPANISH LITERATURE

Seldom does the turn of a century coincide so closely with a new literary consciousness as in Spain in 1900. The disastrous defeat suffered by Spain in the Spanish-American War of 1898 triggered profound psychological reactions and far-reaching literary reverberations, particularly among the diverse personalities of the so-called Generation of '98. Common concern with the "decadence" of Spain and a search for its causes united a group whose artistic goals often varied significantly. Led by Miguel de UNAMUNO, they sought to analyze national problems, most frequently in the essay. Their introspective self-criticism led to some of the most significant literature ever written in Spain, with influences still felt in the final third of the century. Many critics consider this era a second Golden Age of Spanish letters.

Spanish writers of the 20th c. are usually divided into several chronological divisions: (1) the Generation of '98 includes writers born between 1864 and about 1880; (2) the Generation of 1925 (also called the Generation of José ORTEGA Y GASSET, the Generation of 1927, and the Generation of the Dictatorship) includes writers born between about 1880 and 1900; (3) the Generation of 1936 (writers born between 1900 and about 1920) is also called the Generation of the Republic, although the politics of its members varied widely, and there is little unity beyond the profound effects upon all of the Spanish Civil War (1936–39); the largest number of combatants, political exiles, political prisoners, and casualties come from this group; (4) constituting the postwar generations, until recently treated as a single group, are writers born from the end of World War I onward. Three rather clear divisions may be established, groups aesthetically and chronologically different: (a) writers appearing in the 1940s, cultivators of *tremendismo* (so called because of the "tremendous" horrified reactions it elicited); (b) writers emerging from the early 1950s to the mid-1960s, mostly children during the civil war, exponents of social literature and "objectivism"; (c) writers who came to the fore from the late 1960s through the early 1980s, including the first of those born after the civil war and so not directly affected by it. These are experimentalists of varying hues, of which the most important current is neobaroque.

Writers under all the governments of the 20th c., excepting the Republic, faced varying degrees of censorship. Repression was harshest under the dictatorship of Primo de Rivera (1923–30) and during the early post-civil-war years (the first quarter-century under Franco), and many writers grew up in near-total ignorance of the literary heritage of the 19th and early 20th cs. because for a time all moderate and progressive or liberal works were banned.

The Generation of 1925, under the intellectual leadership of Ortega y Gasset, was more subjective and self-consciously aesthetic than the Generation of '98. Less concerned with national problems, these writers were influenced by European experiments with EXPRESSIONISM, FUTURISM, SURREALISM, and the application of impressionism and psychoanalysis to literature. Ortega y

Gasset analyzed these trends in his controversial essay *La deshumanización del arte* (1925; *The Dehumanization of Art*, 1948), often misread as a mandate to follow the tendencies examined.

The civil strife interrupted significant literary activity for several years and marked postwar writing with political animosity and undertones, imposing certain themes and forms from which Spanish literature was to struggle for decades to free itself. Studies of the period after the Republic often omit writers and works for ideological reasons, and in addition there was a loss of contact between the intellectuals within Spain and those in exile. Consequently, the exiles' works of criticism and literary history initially gave the impression that Spanish literature ended in 1936, while those writing in Spain omitted reference not only to the exiles, but to others who were tainted in varying degrees by liberalism or republican associations (for many years, the Generation of '98 could be mentioned only in the context of hostile diatribe, and the vanguardist experiments of many members of the Generation of 1925 were anathema to the regime). This mutual hostility must be borne in mind when consulting much of the critical writing produced in the quarter-century after 1936, and the impressions conveyed discounted accordingly.

The Generation of 1936 (a controversial label) includes both young writers whose first works appeared under the Republic and contemporaries who published nothing until after the war. Many fought on opposing sides, some died, and those who went into exile were scattered widely, making any generalization concerning this group somewhat risky. Less inclined to experiments in aesthetics than their predecessors, moderate and eclectic, they began to turn away from art for art's sake toward more utilitarian art, social commitment, and neorealism (a trend resumed by many after the war).

The postwar literary scene, like that of other periods, consisted not only of one generation but of several age groups coexisting. While many of the Generation of '98 were dead or in exile by the war's end, others—Azorín, Pío BAROJA, Jacinto BENAVENTE, and lesser figures—continued to reside in Spain and to write. Some established members of the Generation of 1925 also formed part of the postwar scene. Works published during the war and immediate postwar years were often subliterary—propagandistic while the conflict continued and an outburst of self-glorification by the victors during several years following. Not until nearly 1970, when those born after the war's end began to publish, did the civil strife cease to be a major factor in the mentality and writing of Spanish intellectuals, even though it was not feasible to express dissidence openly until after abolition of the censorship (December 31, 1978) under the restored monarchy. Dissent or criticism of the regime had to be expressed obliquely or published outside Spain. Franco's supporters, conservative or traditionalist writers, mostly belonging to older generations, managed considerable productivity, but works produced by this faction have rarely been seen as significant; artistic innovation and the initiation of movements are the province of the more liberal writers, members in varying degrees of the opposition.

Philosophy, Criticism, and the Essay

After generations of relative obscurity in the field of philosophy, Spain produced two world-famous thinkers, José Ortega y Gasset and Miguel de Unamuno, as well as a host of significant lesser lights. Among prominent figures of the early 1900s were the teacher and literary theorist Francisco Giner de los Ríos (1839–1915); Santiago Ramón y Cajal (1852–1934), an important essayist on national problems and winner of a Nobel Prize for medicine; the conservative, Catholic critic, literary historian, and dogmatist Marcelino Menéndez y Pelayo (1856–1912); and Azorín, author of highly personal criticism and reinterpretations of Spanish classics, and of essays evocative of Spanish history and landscape. Ramón Menéndez Pidal (1869–1968) was a specialist in medieval literature and the father of systematic or scientific criticism in Spain. The journalist and conservative political theorist Ramiro de Maeztu (1875–1936) established much of the thought adopted by the Falange, which considered him a martyr for the reactionary cause.

Manuel García Morente (1886–1942), a collaborator in Ortega y Gasset's campaign to introduce significant European letters and thought to the Spanish public, was a notable thinker and educator in his own right. Américo Castro (1885–1972) is best known for his interpretations of the Spanish language, literature, and culture, an area also treated by the politician, essayist and polemicist Salvador de Madariaga (1886–1978) and the scientist, historian, sociologist and cultural theorist Gregorio Marañón (1887–1960). Slightly younger cultivators of interpretive prose include the thinker, essayist, author of aphorisms and literary doctrine, and long-term exile José Bergamín (1897-1983); the critic, essayist, and expert on bullfighting José María de Cossío (b. 1895), and the literary critic, historian, and biographer Melchor Fernández Almagro (1895–1966), one of the most moderate and rational voices among early interpreters of postwar literature. Important contributions to the essay were also made by the art historians and critics Juan António Gaya Nuño (dates n.a.) and Enrique Lafuente Ferrari (b. 1898), and the theorist of avant-garde movements Ernesto Giménez Caballero (b. 1899). Influence was exerted for a time by the political essayist José Antonio Primo de Rivera (1902–1936), son of the dictator, whose life and works formed a major basis of Falangist doctrine.

Unamuno and Ortega y Gasset anticipated several aspects of EXISTENTIALISM, as in their concern with the inadequacy of reason to explain the enigmas of life, but Unamuno chooses irrationality (faith) while Ortega y Gasset goes beyond existentialism, attempting to resolve the perennial opposition between reason and "life" (that is, irrationality), creating a dynamic fusion that he called "vital reason," as set forth in *El tema de nuestro tiempo* (1923; *The Modern Theme*, 1933). For both thinkers, the point of departure is individual human existence, which has no abstract meaning apart from that which man creates.

Unamuno was closer to the Danish philosopher Søren Kierkegaard (1818–1855) in that the problem for him is basically religious, a longing for immortality, and anguish at the prospect of death. Although a professor of metaphysics, Ortega y Gasset devoted little attention to the hereafter; his personal and emotional involvement was less than Unamuno's, but his concept of *naufragio* (shipwreck) resembles existential anguish.

Ortega y Gasset and Unamuno avoid the extreme nihilism and hopelessness of some later existentialists, concentrating on investing existence with significance. Unamuno finds meaning in the search itself, in the struggle against eternal mystery, as in *Mi religión, y otros ensayos* (1910; my religion, and other essays). Ortega y Gasset emphasizes ethical questions, postulating an imperative of excellence and the preservation of individuality in a mass society in *La rebelión de las masas* (1930; *The Revolt of the Masses*, 1932). Ortega y Gasset deals with radical solitude and the problematic relation of the individual to the other in the posthumous volume *El hombre y la gente* (1957; *Man and People*, 1957);

his concept of history in *Historia como sistema* (1941; *Toward a Philosophy of History,* 1941) anticipates that of Jean-Paul SARTRE, while his analysis of the lack of effective national leadership in *España invertebrada* (1921; *Invertebrate Spain*, 1937) continues a basic preoccupation of the Generation of '98. Ortega y Gasset is also important as a literary critic and interpreter of other philosophers.

For the first time since the Middle Ages, a philosophical school appeared in Spain. Many members of the so-called School of Madrid embody to some degree the ideas and teachings of Ortega y Gasset. Perhaps most important is Xavier Zubiri (b. 1898), erudite, esoteric and more obscure in his concepts and language than Ortega y Gasset, followed closely by José Luis Aranguren (b. 1909). A professional philosopher with special training in theology, Aranguren represents advanced European Catholic thought. The leading interpreter of the thought of Ortega y Gasset, Julián Marías (b. 1914), is also the author of a number of philosophical studies with some claim to fame as a thinker in his own right. Unamuno and Ortega y Gasset continue to influence new generations.

María ZAMBRANO, another disciple and interpreter of Ortega, has become something of an icon for younger writers (especially poets) in the last two decades of the 20th c. A liberal Republican activist during the Republic and Civil War, she spent most of her life thereafter in exile (1939-84), elaborating her own very personal metaphysics which owe more to Unamuno and Antonio MACHADO than to Ortega. Her mystic synthesis of thought, dream and revelation (termed "poetic reason") has drawn most attention.

Drama

The two principal tendencies of 19th-c. drama, the realistic (realism and naturalism) and the antirealist (neoclassicism, romanticism), continue to exist in varying degrees in the modern Spanish theater. The realistic tradition, represented by Benito PÉREZ GALDÓS, Jacinto Benavente, Carlos ARNICHES, the *costumbristas* (those concerned with describing the local color, folklore, and customs of a given region), the *género chico* (a short theatrical piece, often with music, in the *costumbrista* tradition), and Pedro Muñoz Seca (1881–1936) predominated during the first three decades. The pseudo-objectivist social theater of the 1950s (more successful with critics than with the general public) is a form of neorealism. In the antirealistic vein are José ECHEGARAY; the MODERNISTS; the cultivators of verse drama, Eduardo Marquina (1879–1946) and Francisco Villaespesa (1877–1936); the lyric theater of the brothers Manuel Machado (1874–1947) and Antonio Machado; Jacinto GRAU; and much of the theater of Federico GARCÍA LORCA.

Echegaray, winner of the Nobel Prize in 1904, dominated the Spanish stage during the last quarter of the 19th c. His melodramas, of the most exaggerated romanticism, continued to attract the public until after the beginning of the 20th c. Echegaray left no disciples, and his importance is now considered primarily historical.

The novelist Pérez Galdós is known as the Spanish Ibsen for his introduction of the drama of ideas, in which the individual is shown in conflict with society or conventions. Although few of his plays were box-office successes, Pérez Galdós is noted for his use of analytical dialogue and for the psychological content and realistic atmosphere of his plays. In his attempt to modify certain aspects of society, Pérez Galdós may be regarded as an antecedent of the social theater.

The plays of Benavente, winner of the 1922 Nobel Prize, represent the antithesis of the theater of Echegaray. Action in his dramas is subtle, ironic, and understated, with sly or witty dialogue replacing the cloak-and-sword intrigues. He satirizes the pretentious artificiality of the upper and middle classes, although never so severely as to prevent their constituting his most faithful audience. Elegant, malicious, caustic, and clever, Benavente is basically conservative, his criticism nonrevolutionary, and his theater intended primarily for entertainment.

Subordinating theatricality to ideas, and action and character to mastery of language, Benavente inspired a host of imitators, the most important being Gregorio MARTÍNEZ SIERRA. His unacknowledged collaborator, his wife María, appears to have been the more talented of the two. The theater of Martínez Sierra differs from that of Benavente primarily in the emphasis upon portraying feminine problems and personalities, and in a pronounced tendency to sentimentalism.

Carlos Arniches enjoyed great popularity with the humble people of Madrid, whom he made the protagonists of his plays. In the *costumbrista* tradition and independently of Benavente's reforms, Arniches portrayed the characters, customs, and environment of Madrid, much as the brothers Joaquín and Serafín ÁLVAREZ QUINTERO portrayed those of Andalusia. Pedro Muñoz Seca could be cruel and bitterly sincere in his extravagantly comic farces in which he exposed moral bankruptcy.

While not often successful commercially, the experiments of UNAMUNO, Ramón del VALLE-INCLÁN, and Azorín, none of them primarily a dramatist, kept Spanish theater in line with the more advanced movements of European theater. Each questioned the nature of reality, attempting to fuse realist and nonrealist currents. Unamuno dealt with the problems of personality, perspective, and the multifaceted nature of reality, showing the impossibility of apprehending the truth completely. For Unamuno, as for the Italian dramatist Luigi PIRANDELLO, the identity of character depended on constant creation.

Valle-Inclán attempted to give dramatic representation to the intrinsic values or essence of Spanish life, which he viewed as a grotesquely distorted reflection of European life, as seen especially in the exaggerated sense of honor, religious fanaticism, and false pride. Believing that this attitude could be conveyed only by systematic deformation, he created the *esperpento*, a usually brief dramatic form that he defined as the representation of traditional values and heroes as seen through a distorting mirror. His work, in its attempt to give a visual representation of the "soul" or emotions of a situation, showing the internal reality without showing the external appearance mimetically, coincides essentially with expressionism.

The techniques of another artistic movement, surrealism, were first applied to Spanish drama by Azorín, who attempted to incorporate tenets of psychoanalysis in his portrayals of dreams and the subconscious. Azorín thus anticipated aspects of García Lorca's theater, as he did to a certain extent also in his experiments with time and space.

Jacinto Grau, who wrote his most significant works in exile, ignored contemporary reality and produced exquisitely polished plays. His themes are universal and eternal, comprising the great myths and transcendental problems: Don Juan, good and evil, love and death, and human destiny. Grau's lofty, poetic, often archaic language, and his concept of his art as essentially tragic were barriers to popularity. Despite excellent literary qualities, his work is little known and infrequently performed.

García Lorca is regarded as one of the outstanding dramatists of the 20th c. His works, usually placed in rural settings, are characterized by formal perfection and dramatic intensity. Lyrical, dynamic

dialogue and a variety of symbols and myths are strikingly combined with music, dances, poetry, and song based upon Andalusian folklore. Characters in his mature works are primitive, larger than life, and often depersonalized, identified by role (for example, the Mother, or the Groom); they may be archetypes or incarnations of abstract elements such as maternal instinct or death. The passions, lyrically or symbolically transformed, are elemental and biological, instinctive, semi-or subconscious, obsessive and destructive. García Lorca conceived the theater in its totality, writing music, sketching sets, designing scenery, and giving expert attention to technical aspects, including costumes, lighting, casting, and direction. He has been called the only Spaniard of the century fully endowed for the theater. He was murdered at the outbreak of the civil war.

Alejandro CASONA, another gifted folklorist and innovator, lived in exile in Argentina from 1936 to 1962. Like García Lorca, he combined realism with poetic vision, offered original adaptations of eternal themes, and incorporated legend and a sense of timelessness into their works. A moralist who dealt repeatedly with the problem of personal happiness, Casona questioned whether contentment can be found in deceit, escape, or madness, or rather in the acceptance of reality and responsibility. Reality always triumphs in his plays, but post-civil-war critics who advocated critical neorealism and combative works classed his works with the "theater of evasion" (a pejorative label applied to almost all nonpolitical works). During the reign of social realism and its necessarily oblique political criticism, the label of evasiveness produced undeserved scorn for this master of theatrical technique and resources.

As is also the case with the novel and poetry, postwar Spanish drama may be divided into two groups: that of sociopolitical commitment, and that with other goals. The goals of "noncommitted" dramatists were not necessarily all the same or even compatible; it was simply that all dramas whose intent differed from the purposes of committed dramas were lumped together as a result of the lingering belligerence just beneath the surface of the literary scene. Social theater intended, by indictment of economic injustices, to expose ideological weakness or inconsistency of the political leadership, identified with preservation of the existing social order. "Evasiveness" was attributed to all works wherein the writer was motivated not by a wish to change society but by artistic considerations, moral or metaphysical concerns, or the simple desire to entertain. That the categorizing was not purely literary was evident in the fact that social dramas were the work of opponents of the Franco regime.

In the early years following the civil war, the propagandistic "theater of victory" glorified the winners. When the militaristic euphoria faded, there were revivals of classics and of Benavente, while contemporary plays were subjected to censorship stricter than that of any other genre. Works with no purpose except entertainment, those lacking social (political) intent, found easier approval and production. Among these "evasive" works are some dramas with admirable artistic qualities, including even some plays by Antonio BUERO VALLEJO. The most typical works of the theater of evasion, however, are of little substance, conventional, and innocuous; they are exemplified by the plays of the prolific Alfonso Paso (b. 1926). These years also saw works by more talented playwrights, particularly Enrique Jardiel Poncela (1901–1952) and Miguel Mihura (b. 1905), who anticipated aspects of the THEATER OF THE ABSURD, which was unable to develop in the reactionary atmosphere of Franco's Spain.

Among the most significant postwar dramatists are Buero Vallejo, Lauro Olmo (b. 1922), Alfonso SASTRE, Ricardo Rodríguez Buded (b. 1930), and Carlos Muñiz (b. 1930). While some have evolved subsequently, their best-known works are realistic, critical, and motivated by strong disagreement with prevailing political, social, and economic policy. Government censorship limited them to the "objective" or impassive presentation of seemingly nonpolitical situations. Typical themes of these plays are poverty, inadequate housing or employment, and exposure of the ways in which substandard conditions and opportunities rob the individual of his dignity, affect him psychologically, or bring family tragedy.

Buero Vallejo is considered to have initiated social theater with *Historia de una escalera* (1950; story of a staircase). He is, however, not one of the most extreme proponents of commitment. Aware of contemporary developments in theater elsewhere in Europe, he attempted to adapt these advances to Spanish circumstances, and to update the concept of tragedy, making it depend more upon the social context. Buero Vallejo used myths, occasional foreign settings, the historical past, and even a sort of "science fiction" future context for his plays, but despite such caution, his works were often censored.

Like Buero Vallejo, Sastre is a dramatic theorist, the author of numerous articles and lengthy critical essays. He is, with Buero Vallejo, one of the two foremost postwar dramatists in Spain. Sastre's moderately revolutionary theater, although characterized by a necessary restraint and seeming impassivity, embodied enough identifiable Marxist ideology that it brought not only prohibition of the plays but fines and imprisonment for the playwright. Nonetheless, Sastre believes firmly in maintaining the distinction between art and propaganda.

Fernando ARRABAL became a voluntary expatriate in the early 1950s when his first theatrical efforts were met with incomprehension and hostility in Spain. Moving to Paris, he managed to become known for his contributions to the Theater of the Absurd (although he himself preferred to call his works "Theater of Panic"). Until after the election of 1977 and the abolition of the censorship, Arrabal's work was unknown in Spain, and he wrote in French as a protest against conditions in Spain. His works have been compared with those of Eugène IONESCO and Samuel BECKETT, and like them, he frequently utilizes infantile or subnormal perspectives, portraying a disconcertingly amoral situation.

A substantial number of "new" playwrights during the 1960s and 1970s were unable to obtain authorization for performance of their works, or to find producers willing to risk presenting them even after restrictions began to be relaxed a year or two before Franco's death. These writers are referred to collectively as the "subterranean theater," an underground group that has remained essentially unknown despite the demise of the censorship. While they do not form a self-conscious school, the dozen or more silenced playwrights share certain common tendencies: their works are usually abstract, political allegories, concerned less with specifically Spanish settings than international or futuristic ambiences, and aimed at problems transcending national boundaries. The best known of these dramatists are José Ruibal (b. 1925) and Eduardo Quiles (b. 1940).

The 1970s saw increased experimentalism (never especially popular with Spanish producers or audiences), with some influences from models such as the "theater of cruelty," the "happening," and theater-in-the-round. Severely restricted by a puritanical censorship during the Franco regime, Spanish theater was flooded by a wave of eroticism verging on pornography when restrictions were relaxed, a wave abating only in the early 1980s.

Poetry

The major currents in Spanish poetry at the turn of the century were the aesthetic and experimental, on the one hand, and on the other, the sociophilosophical. The former is derived from French SYMBOLISM and the classic tradition emphasizing form, the search for ideal beauty, submission to aesthetic formulas, the concept of art as an end in itself, and a turning away from everyday reality. The latter is derived from romanticism, taking man as its theme and end, emphasizing the communication of content, sentiment, and relatively unembellished reality. The 20th c. may be seen as a pendular movement or alternation between these two tendencies: initial aestheticism, with some adherence to modernism, yielding to the existential and metaphysical emphasis of the Generation of '98, which is followed by the early Gongorist phase of the Generation of 1927. Postwar poetry evolves in a direction counter to the aestheticism and vanguardist experimentation of the prewar poets, moving from the political commitment of the war years through escapism to religious, philosophical, and social concerns during the 1950s and early 1960s. After the utilitarian extremes reached by social poets, since the mid-1960s, poets once again show a preoccupation with language as such, and the new avant-garde revives surrealism, the cult of the metaphor, the play with language as sound divorced from meaning.

The mature Antonio Machado, Unamuno, and poets representative of the dominant trends in the 1950s and 1960s depict recognizable, sometimes prosaic realities. Their poetry, directed to humanity as a whole, is conceived of as communication, a means to an end. Thus, they employ simple, sometimes colloquial language and strive for clear meanings.

Modernism affected formal elements and vocabulary to a certain extent, but its themes did not outlive it. By contrast, Unamuno and Antonio Machado have continued to make an impact upon poetic intent and substance through most of the century. While not known originally as a poet, Unamuno wrote an extensive lyric corpus much admired by other poets for its intensity. He is one of the major sonneteers of modern Spain, as well as one of the explorers of potential uses of free verse, internal rhyme, and secondary accents. His inspirations are his personal life, the family, national life and history, and religion, the last of which Unamuno rehabilitated as a poetic theme.

Antonio Machado believed firmly in the spoken language as poetic medium. He anticipated García Lorca in the attempt to write a new *romancero* (collection of legendary tales in verse), and in drawing upon folklore and popular culture. His outspoken, critical patriotism has inspired much postwar poetry, with echoes in fiction as well. Machado's metaphysical concern with time prefigures a preoccupation of many contemporary poets. Although one volume comprises all his poetry, he is generally regarded as one of the greatest Spanish poets of this or any century, with a magnificently sober and noble expression, a deceptively simple appearance, and a profound philosophical doubt underlying even his lightest verses.

Juan Ramón JIMÉNEZ was extremely sensitive, solitary, of exquisite and cultivated taste. He lived for his art, constantly purifying and refining it, collecting and destroying his early books in order to leave a more perfect legacy to posterity. The poet of

Andalusian landscape, gardens, and fountains, of delicate melancholy and vague pantheism, he exercised a veritable poetic hegemony in the period 1915–30.

A reaction against the sentiment of tardy romanticism, on the one hand, and the superficiality and stylization of modernism on the other is responsible for both the neo-Gongorism and subsequent surrealist experimentation by members of the Generation of 1927. The best known and most significant among this large group of poets were Pedro SALINAS, Jorge GUILLÉN, Dámaso ALONSO, Vicente ALEIXANDRE, Rafael ALBERTI, Luis CERNUDA, and poet-dramatist García Lorca. Attempting to free pure emotion from the control of logic, they made a cult of the metaphor. Their often hermetic expression, further complicated by the presence of elements of FREUD's psychoanalytic theory, bordered at times upon obscurity. Free association of words, images, and ideas formed an important part of this poetic process, and these poets, without reaching the extremes attained by poetic surrealism in other parts of Europe, did develop a modified Spanish version of the movement, exemplified primarily in the works of Aleixandre, Alberti, and García Lorca.

The group is best known as the Generation of 1927, the year in which they revived and rehabilitated the elaborate style exemplified in the works of the poet Luis de Góngora (1561–1627). The baroque "angel of darkness" dominated an early phase of development, after which the generation's members sought increasingly personal modes of expression. Their various phases are epitomized in the work of García Lorca, whose poetry evolved metrically from classic forms to free verse and from the influence of Góngora and of regional folklore to a surrealistic vanguardism, resulting eventually in his unique, personal tone, a blend of subjectivism, pantheism, myth, expressionism, and suppressed rebellion.

Alberti, like García Lorca a dramatist and painter, resembles him in the use of popular elements and Andalusian settings, but differs in temperament, in the greater spontaneity of his early works and in the irony and political charge of later works, especially the proletarian elements characterizing much of his verse after 1930. Cernuda and Alonso similarly progress toward the social and humanitarian attitudes of the postwar writers; indeed, Alonso's *Hijos de la ira* (1944; *Children of Wrath*, 1970) is considered a major landmark in the revitalization of the lyric after the war's end.

Aleixandre, probably Spain's greatest poet since the Generation of '98, received the Nobel Prize in 1977. Essentially romantic in his vital preoccupation with love and death, he made poetry of his most intimate personal experience, from amorous emotion to cosmic thought. Positive and constructive, he used the idea of life as his central motif. Of all the surviving major prewar poets, only Alonso and Aleixandre remained in Spain after the conflict. So great was Aleixandre's impact on successive generations of new poets that two of his best-known works, *Sombra del paraíso* (1944; shadow of paradise) and *Historia del corazón* (1954; history of the heart), have been called the "Bible" of postwar lyricists. Aleixandre continued to explore new channels of expression well into his seventies.

Miguel HERNÁNDEZ is considered the poet par excellence of the civil war, and few poems are more powerfully moving than those he penned for his wife while he was a soldier at the front. He is perhaps the most gifted member of the Generation of 1936, but death while a political prisoner cut short his career in 1942. Other significant poets of this generation include Gabriel CELAYA and Blas de OTERO, leaders of the so-called social poets, or authors of poetry of sociopolitical commitment, especially during the 1950s.

Dionisio Ridruejo (1912–1975), one of the most admirable spirits of this generation, likewise wrote war poetry. Less concerned with form and beauty than with human destiny and the economic and religious problems of men, poets of this group considered such problems from an individual and sometimes existential viewpoint. A more contemplative, philosophical, or meditative atmosphere is found in the works of Vicente Gaos (1919-1981) and Carlos Bousoño (b. 1923), one of the most original of contemporary critics of poetry.

Younger poets who joined members of the Generation of 1936 to produce social poetry conceived of human problems as essentially collective, and emphatically linked to the specific Spanish historical moment and context. The changing concept of poetry is reflected in the dedication of one of Otero's books to the "immense majority" and in a statement of Celaya's, echoed by many, to the effect that poetry is not an end in itself, but "an instrument to transform the world." Notes of social protest dominate in the poetry written in the 1950s and 1960s, much as is the case with the theater and with fiction; themes include social injustice, class problems, the work, sufferings, and aspirations of men—especially laborers—in our time. Another poet important in these years is José Hierro (b. 1922), whose major work was collected in *Cuánto sé de mí* (1975; how much I know about myself). "Social" poets characteristically seek the lyric potential of everyday life.

Much as with drama and fiction, the period of poetic commitment was followed by a more aesthetic countercurrent, a new preoccupation with the nature of poetry itself, with language and style for their own sakes (divorced from potential social impact), and with poetry as discovery, an instrument of epistemological investigation. Jaime Gil de Biedma (b. 1929) and Francisco Brines (b. 1934) are characteristic of this tendency, and among the better proponents of this concept of lyric creation or experience as exploration or quest for insight into life's ultimate mysteries. Social poetry, its altruistic and humanitarian motives notwithstanding, was essentially propagandistic and antipoetic, an inherent limitation of its own duration. The subsequent "poetry of discovery" and more recent Novísimos (the newest of the new) group do not renounce social commentary completely, but they return to more specifically lyric ends and techniques.

Not until the 1970s did poets appear who had been born after the end of the civil war, and who wished as a consequence to transcend the atmosphere of tendentiousness, protest, and lingering belligerence they perceived as characterizing much postwar literary production in Spain. Seeking new themes and sources of inspiration, they turned away from narrowly Spanish problems and political ills to more subjective and personal matters, sentiments, and memories. Their own childhood and adolescence, growing up in Franco's Spain, particularly in relationship to the personality development and sexual education of the individual writers, provided one focal point. Another was the invasion of an exhausted or economically weak Spanish culture by the new cultural and commercial powers, especially the U.S. Many poems by these writers reflect the transition to consumerism. Other foreign cultures, especially French and British, have also left their marks on Spanish cultural manifestations, and these, too, are mirrored in the poetry of the Novísimos, as is the progressive bastardization of the language under the impact of an influx of foreign words and expressions and imported technology, goods, and advertising. Vocabulary, syntax, and many rhetorical figures of these poets are neobaroque. Two representative members of the Novísimo group are Manuel Vázquez Montalbán (b. 1939) and José María Álvarez (b. 1942).

Although Spain has produced women poets throughout the ages, the 20th c. witnessed an extraordinary proliferation of women lyricists, largely ignored or forgotten by canonical literary historians. From early 20th-c. modernist beginnings, Sofía Casanova (pseud. of Sofía Pérez Casanova de Lutoslawski, 1861-1958) evolved toward feminist concerns, becoming a journalist and brilliant foreign correspondent during World War I. Women poets of the vanguard years include novelist-essayist Rosa CHACEL; Clementina Arderiu de Riba (1899-1976), who produced post-symbolist verse in Catalan; Ernestina de CHAMPOURCIN who evolved from early erotic poetry expressed in Surrealist metaphor to a quasi-mystic metaphysical emphasis in her mature years; Concha Méndez (1898-1986), much involved in publishing ventures of the Generation of 1925 and a brilliant poet in her own right, who developed from pre-war vitalism to anguished poetry of war and exile, articulating loss, pain, and despair. Pilar de Valderrama (1894-1979), the ''Guiomar'' of Antonio Machado's mature years and somewhat his disciple, expresses war's suffering and sorrow. The major woman poet of the 20th c. is Carmen CONDE, the first woman elected to the Royal Spanish Academy (1983). Conde authored nearly one hundred books, including more than forty volumes of poetry, ranging from early vanguard experimentation to intense autobiographical subjectivism, works of pacifist horror, expressed in free verse during the war years, and works of social commitment. Relegated to oblivion by Francoist censors, Conde emerged in her last years as a towering figure, especially for the daring feminist critique contained in her most significant collection, *Mujer sin Edén* (1947; trans. *Woman without Eden*, 1986). Other prominent women lyricists of the Franco era include Angela Figuera (1902-1984), known primarily as a poet of social protest; Gloria Fuertes (b. 1918), who moved from early post-Surrealist experimentation to social, feminist, and ludic themes; and Concha ZARDOYA, arguably the most eloquent of women poets of war and exile.

Fiction

While the panorama of the narrative at any given moment would inevitably include representatives of several generations and movements, evolution of the genre since 1900 is divisible into the following periods: (1) the concern with national decadence, backwardness and other problems, spiritual and intellectual, permeates the characteristic fictional creations of the Generation of '98, usually an introspective, discursive narrative of meditative or philosophical bent, containing as much of the essay as of the novel; (2) the exploration of psychology, the creation of unusual or interesting psyches, and the application of "dehumanized" aesthetics characterizes the novel of the Generation of 1925; (3) a combination of vanguardist experimentation and rejection of dehumanized fiction is found in early writings of the Generation of 1936, which initiates a timid return to mimetic and relatively traditional realism; (4) postwar *tremendismo* during the 1940s combines aspects of neonaturalism with expressionist distortion and existential sentiments of anguish and absurdity; (5) during the 1950s, objectivism is adapted as a means to circumvent the censorship and used by opponents of the regime; (6) after the publication of Luis MARTÍN-SANTOS's *Tiempo de silencio* (1962; *Time of Silence*, 1964), which put an end to the simplistic dualism of most critical neorealism, there begins a new experimentalism, whose most characteristic expression is neobaroque.

In 1912 Pérez Galdós completed his *Episodios nacionales* (national episodes), five series of novels based on national history, combining fact and fiction. His most significant works were published before 1900, but Pérez Galdós continued to influence writers in the 20th c., including several novelists in the postwar era. Also beginning in the previous century, Emilia de PARDO BAZÁN introduced into Spain a modified naturalism, inspired by the doctrines of the French novelist Émile Zola. A stronger personality and more conventional naturalism are evident in the novels of Vicente BLASCO-IBÁÑEZ, whose best-known works utilize a Valencian setting for tales of passion and violence. Despite the low esteem in which he is held by Spanish critics, he is one of the country's best-known novelists internationally.

The *nivolas* of Unamuno—he invented the word in reaction to critics who said his works of fiction were not novels (*novelas*)— were significant experiments excluding the standard realistic description and environmental detail to concentrate on dialogue, action, and characterization. In his much-discussed *Niebla* (1914; *Mist*, 1929) The questions the relationship of literary character to creator, and implicitly man's relationship to God, or in other words, the issue of mortality versus immortality. Unamuno, who frequently professed scorn for matters of aesthetics, might have been amused (if not horrified) to find the *nivola* taken as a serious aesthetic statement. The problems of envy, personality, and identity are analyzed in *Abel Sánchez* (1917; *Abel Sanchez*, 1956), and the problems of personality and identity are reexamined in several other narratives. Unamuno's questioning and introspective analysis culminate in *San Manuel Bueno, mártir* (1931; *Saint Manuel Bueno, Martyr*, 1954), considered his definitive religiophilosophical statement; the principal virtue of the protagonist is his self-sacrificing struggle to maintain in others the faith that he himself lacks.

In the four *Sonatas* (1902–05; *The Pleasant Memoirs of the Marquis de Bradomin: Four Sonatas*, 1924) of Valle-Inclán, a modernist perfection of style and a refined, decadent sensuality are combined with human, natural, and cultural elements of great beauty. The writer's initial aestheticism evolved through a trilogy, *La guerra carlista* (1908–9; the Carlist war), mingling historical interest with a somewhat sentimental defense of Carlism, to *Tirano Banderas* (1926; *The Tyrant*, 1929) and *El ruedo ibérico* (1927–28; the Iberian bull ring), an incomplete and little-known series employing the systematic degradation of reality characteristic of the *esperpento*.

From 1900 until his death in 1956, Pío Baroja published nearly seventy novels, in addition to memoirs and essays. Unquestionably one of the country's major novelists, he has been considered leftist, anarchist, and revolutionary, and his negative criticisms of traditional Spain were combined with moral skepticism. His views of human selfishness and cowardice are so cynical that the frequent label of revolutionary fails to convey the full character of his work. Baroja's style, criticized by some as careless, monotonous, and grammatically incorrect, is nevertheless clear, rapid, and intelligible. Baroja conceived of the novel as multiform and formless, a protean genre in which anything was legitimate. His narratives are loosely constructed, with few unified plots and often without perceptible continuity. The structuring constants in his novels include environment, the preference for action, and a rather uniform psychology in his protagonists. Baroja's "heroes," although surprisingly real, lack tenacity, will, and psychic profundity, and are often frustrated, maladjusted, or impotent.

The experimental novels of Azorín consist largely of description and evocation, lacking action but achieving an illusion of movement through variations in descriptive technique. His characters, settings, and temporal backgrounds nonetheless often appear motionless. The best fruits of his novelistic technique are found in *Doña Inés* (1925; Doña Inés), although theoretical critics prefer *La isla sin aurora* (1943; island without dawn), one of the few early examples of the application of surrealism to the narrative.

Stylistic preoccupations of modernism and Azorín's timelessness and static impressionism are combined with the aesthetic concerns of the Generation of 1925 in the work of Gabriel MIRÓ. This master of prose style displays a love of landscape in novels pervaded by melancholy, sensualism, and exquisite auditory, visual, and tactile impressions. His work generally lacks ideas, however, and offers little excitement.

Ramón PÉREZ DE AYALA created an intellectual scandal with *A. M. D. G.* (1910; A. M. D. G.), a cruel interpretation of Jesuit education, blending characteristic irony and early realism in the vein of Pérez Galdós. Intellectual, didactic, and moralistic, this disciple of Ortega y Gasset experimented with perspectivism in *Belarmino y Apolonio* (1921; Belarmino and Apolonio, 1971) and with simultaneous action and contrapuntal technique in *Tigre Juan* (1926; tiger Juan). Still more innovative was Ramón Gómez de la SERNA, who produced plays, criticism, biography, and autobiography—*Automoribundia* (1948; autodeathography)—as well as novels. His special creation is the *greguería*, a short semiaphoristic statement combining humor with metaphor. His work is fragmentary and chaotic, in his own words, "reflecting the disorder of the world," but shows exceptional linguistic vitality. The talent of another novelistic innovator, Benjamín JARNÉS, was obscured by his ambitious experiments in the "dehumanized" narrative, resulting in a voluptuous confusion of formal brilliance, sensual imagery, and metaphors that retard action and obscure character.

Significant novelists in the period immediately before the war include Ramón Sender and Francisco Ayala, both exiles, and the early narratives of Max AUB and Segundo Serrano Poncela (b. 1912). Most prolific of the exiles was Sender, whose early works were permeated by revolutionary combativeness. Many of his novels are autobiographical, chronicling his participation in strikes, revolutionary activities, and the civil war, as well as his own youth and adolescence. One of his most polished narratives is *Réquiem por un campesino español* (1960; Requiem for a Spanish Peasant, 1960), which symbolically personifies conflicting social elements. Aub's greatest accomplishment is an epic cycle of novels and tales collected as *El laberinto mágico* (1943–68; the magic labyrinth). Ayala turned from prewar surrealism to ironic and humorous critiques of the alien environment of exile in *Muertes de perro* (1958; Death as a Way of Life, 1964) and *El fondo del vaso* (1962; the bottom of the glass).

Exiles and novelists inside Spain alike are obsessed by the civil war; the need to understand the conflict and its causes has produced hundreds of novels (one bibliography in progress includes nearly eight thousand works on the subject, spanning many countries). The first supposedly objective explanation of the ideological bases of the conflict is a study of prewar Gerona by José María GIRONELLA, whose lengthy novel *Los cipreses creen en Dios* (1953; The Cypresses Believe in God, 1955) became the best seller of the postwar period. Notable interpretations of the civil war are also found in *Las luciérnagas* (the fireflies) of Ana María MATUTE, which was prohibited by the censors, then published in an expurgated version entitled *En esta tierra* (1955; in this land), a prelude

to her masterful poetic vision of the conflict's human causes in *Los hijos muertos* (1958; The Lost Children, 1965).

The first significant movement in the postwar period, *tremendismo*, derives from naturalism, and more remotely from the classic tradition of the picaresque, especially as interpreted by the satirist Francisco Gómez de Quevedo (1580–1645). A much-imitated novel, *La familia de Pascual Duarte* (1942; The Family of Pascual Duarte*, 1964), by Camilo José Cela, typifies the violence of the movement it spawned, as well as the sordidness of its environments. Cela, often considered more a caricaturist than a novelist, is a tireless experimenter with form and technique, whose innumerable characters are usually fragmentary. *La colmena* (1951; The Hive, 1953), considered his masterpiece, influenced many younger writers in choice of environment and types. *Nada* (1945; Nada, 1958), by Carmen LAFORET, represents the comparatively restrained, psychological variant of *tremendismo*. *La noria* (1952; the water-wheel), by Luis Romero (b. 1916), like much of Cela's work, lacks plot and protagonists, and further illustrates the movement.

The crimes of violence typical of *tremendismo*, the sordidness and amorality usually portrayed, reflected the despair and sense of absurdity experienced by Spanish intellectuals, unable to refer more explicitly to the atrocities of the civil strife and its aftermath. By the early 1950s, however, a new trend was perceptible: objectivism, adapted from the French NEW NOVEL, employed cinematic techniques and a pseudoscientific impassivity in its depiction of social problems. Objectivism had begun in France as a reaction against the literature of commitment and was an experimental movement. In Spain, however, it became a form for circumventing the censorship: apparently neutral, impassive, and without sermonizing or explicit value judgment, it presented on the face of things an absence of censorable content. Soon, however, the appearance of objectivity was negated by a deliberate and all but exclusive focus on injustice, poverty, and the most serious ills of Spanish society (of which the regime was considered the defender).

For the most part, then, objectivism in Spain is little more than a technique of the novel of sociopolitical criticism. The two most accomplished examples of the movement from the technical standpoint are *El Jarama* (1956; The One Day of the Week, 1962), by Rafael SÁNCHEZ FERLOSIO, and *Gran Sol* (1959; Grand Banks), by Ignacio Aldecoa (1925–1969). The period from the early 1950s to the early or mid-1960s, the heyday of critical neorealism, produced a literature known both as objectivism and the social novel, actually a literature of commitment whose cultivators were opposed to the regime and belligerently dedicated to political and economic reforms. After the resounding impact of Martín-Santos's *Tiempo de silencio*, which reacted against the simplistic portrayals and moral dualism of the social novel, many of the movement's former devotees began to seek other, more personal, and more artistic forms of expression.

Not all significant fiction writers subscribed to the tenets of objectivism; some continued to cultivate other forms of the novel. Gonzalo Torrente Ballester (b. 1910), also a critic and playwright, first excelled as a novelist in a neo-Galdósian, psychological vein, exemplified in his trilogy *Los gozos y las sombras* (1957–62; pleasures and shadows). Not until the 1970s did Torrente Ballester achieve popular or critical success; recognition came with publication of his mammoth work, *La saga/fuga de J. B.* (1973; the saga/fugue of J. B.), which is simultaneously an experimental New Novel and a parody of that genre. Torrente Ballester, the most honored novelist of the 1970s in Spain, triumphed again in

Fragmentos de apocalipsis (1977; fragments of apocalypse) and *La isla de los jacintos cortados* (1981; the isle of cut hyacinths), both combining vanguard trends and ironic parody of intellectual fads, critical styles, and literary practice and theory.

Another of Spain's more significant contemporary novelists, Miguel DELIBES, likewise remained independent of both *tremendismo* and objectivism, although expressing his own criticism of sociopolitical conditions in Spain. From traditional beginnings as a regional novelist of Castile, Delibes produced veritable masterpieces in *El camino* (1950; *The Path*, 1961), *La hoja roja* (1959; the red leaf), and *Las ratas* (1962; *Smoke on the Ground*, 1972). In all, Delibes calls attention to the backwardness, neglect, and subhuman living conditions in the forgotten villages of the bleak plateau. A more subjective approach is employed in *Cinco horas con Mario* (1966; five hours with Mario), a subtle exposé of the hypocrisy of the triumphant reactionary mentality, and his experimental *Parábola del náufrago* (1969; parable of the drowning man), a Kafkaesque existential fable of the perils of dehumanization.

Juan GOYTISOLO, long an expatriate residing in Paris, shifted from early neorealism to an increasingly subjective, analytical, and symbolic approach in his complex Mendiola trilogy, comprising *Señas de identidad* (1966; *Marks of Identity*, 1969), *Reivindicación del Conde Don Julián* (1970; *Count Julian*, 1974), and *Juan sin tierra* (1975; *Juan the Landless*, 1977). In these works Goytisolo seeks to destroy a series of national myths: machismo, the innocence of childhood, the sanctity of the home, and the "purity" of the language.

Juan BENET, a one-time associate of Martín-Santos and Sánchez Ferlosio, remained little known as a novelist until after the demise of neorealistic objectivism and the social novel. With the publication of his first full-length novel, *Volverás a Región* (1967; you'll return to Región), Benet became the leader of a new novelistic vanguard. Many of his novels treat the unreal, myth-filled area of Región, which is a microcosm of all that is most static and impenetrable in Spain. Topographical mythification is carried to the extreme in *Una meditación* (1969; *A Meditation*, 1982), *La otra casa de Mazón* (1972; Mazón's other house), and *Un viaje de invierno* (1971; a winter journey). Benet is indirect, self-contradictory, and deliberately obscure, traits found in many other neobaroque writers. His language is an outstanding example of neobaroque style.

The Spanish novel in the 1970s and early 1980s is characterized by multiplicity of formal and linguistic experiments, of which the neobaroque appears to be the most frequently attempted. However, there have been several interesting experiments in other directions. J. Leyva (b. 1938) blends Kafkaesque expressionism with surrealism and formalist principles in *Leitmotiv* (1972; leitmotif), while proceeding on several levels to a systematic demolition of the narrative discourse, as seen most clearly in *La calle de los árboles dormidos* (1974; the street of sleeping trees). Another experimental direction appears in the avant-garde writings of Manuel Antolín Rato (b. ca. 1945), exemplifying a fragmentation so extreme that rather than narratives, his texts are a collage of atoms in which theme is exploded, continuity abolished, and the literary language pulverized. *Cuando 900 mil mach aprox* (1973; when at approx. 900,000 mach) and *De vulgari Zyklon B manifestante* (1975; transmitting from vulgari Zyklon B) are chaotic, irrational, and esoteric, like their titles, with an abundance of allusions to contemporary culture and science characteristic of groups such as the Novísimos in poetry, and the practitioners of *nova-expresionismo* in prose, who coined their name from William BURROUGHS's *Nova*

Express and use avant-garde techniques. There is no single, dominant mode at present; the climate is one of experimentation and searching.

Women novelists are well represented in 20th c. Spain. Emilia Pardo Bazán, credited with introducing Naturalism to Spain, continued writing until her death, publishing half a dozen long novels, several novelettes, and some ten volumes of short stories in this c. Carmen de Burgos Colombine (1879-1932), an active suffragist and protofeminist, published some dozen long novels, numerous novelettes, and more than fifty stories, as well as hundreds of articles. Concha Espina (1869-1955), Spain's first female best-seller, twice nominated for the Nobel Prize, was highly regarded during the first three decades of this c. She authored some fifty books (novels, plays, and poetry), divided between postromantic sentimentalism and realism. Rosa Chacel, philosophically a disciple of Ortega y Gasset and literarily a disciple of James Joyce, was the major woman narrator of the vanguard generation, much influenced by European modernism. She produced a score of highly intellectualized, finely polished novels, story collections and lengthy essays emphasizing the feminine condition.

In the postwar period, a sizeable group of women novelists emerged, including Elena Soriano (1917-1997), a significant intellectual and feminist, whose work was prohibited until after Franco's death; Dolores Medio (1914-1997), a disciple of Ortega y Gasset, with interests in philosophy and pedagogy; Elena Quiroga (1921-1996), who developed from traditional realist beginnings through experimentation with perspectivism and became the second woman elected to the Royal Spanish Academy; Carmen Laforet, a novelist of the lives of women and adolescents, whose greatest recognition came with her first work; Ana María Matute, one of the postwar era's most honored women writers, a subjective, lyrical stylist with a powerful social conscience, presently the third woman in the Royal Spanish Academy; and Carmen MARTÍN GAITE, who has emerged as the country's leading woman writer in the final decade of the 20th c., her generation's best analyst of the post-Franco "new Spain," and a persuasive voice for feminist concerns.

Spanish Literature since 1970

Franco's death in November of 1975 ended the post-Civil War era of nearly four decades. Censorship in the totalitarian first quarter century was capricious and harsh—extremely so at first and moderately so later; by the mid-1960s, the regime began to become more pragmatic. In the 1960s and 1970s, expanding relations with the U.S., large-scale tourism, and economic development brought relaxed censorship and, in Franco's declining years, *aperturismo* (opening)—a move to accommodate internal diversity and resume relations with countries on the political left. Early 1970s educational reform legislation reestablished the legal status of Spain's vernaculars—Catalan, Galician, Basque—authorizing daily newspapers in these languages and their instruction in the schools. Together with women's recuperation of rights lost when the Republic fell, these events profoundly affect post-Franco culture and literature. One of the most significant developments of the past two decades in Spain has been the flowering of vernacular cultures and literatures, not only in Catalan and Galician, whose literary histories date from the late Middle Ages, but in Basque (heretofore primarily an oral culture), and dialectical areas threatened with total assimilation: Leonese, *Andalán* (Aragonese), *Bable* (Asturian), and even regional cultures not clearly differentiated on the linguistic level such as Extremaduran and Andalusian. The regional autonomy movements that go hand-in-hand with such geographically specific cultural phenomena are not merely a reaction to the four decades of Francoist repression of local autonomy but belong to a centrifugal tradition of centuries, going back to the 15th c. when linguistically and culturally distinct kingdoms were forcibly united under Ferdinand and Isabel.

Spanish literature under Franco exhibited several distinct aesthetic moments, all but the final one being representational. The Civil War years and those immediately following (1936–1942) are marked by *triunfalismo* (provictory propaganda) with its defiant Fascist rhetoric and glorification of violence and of Falangist values. An orgy of self-aggrandizement (with opposing voices silenced or in exile), *triunfalismo* produced no enduring masterworks, and quickly alienated most Spanish intellectuals. Although the dominant mode, it was not exclusive (several trends coexist throughout the Franco and post-Franco eras). *Tremendismo*, the most notorious mode of the 1940s and early 1950s, was named for the "tremendous" reader reaction elicited by accumulated violence, degradation, poverty, perversion, filth, and deformity. Derived from NATURALISM, without the scientific grounding, and the *esperpento*, an expressionistic aesthetic of deformation invented by Ramon María del VALLE-INCLÁN, *tremendismo* was exploited by some writers to reflect their anguish at war's atrocities; akin to EXISTENTIALISM, it was censored in Spain on religious grounds. "Social" literature or "critical realism," the first postwar movement affecting all genres, held sway from around 1950 until the late 1960s, featuring generic or collective protagonists, economic injustices, and social-class problems. "Social" meant political: Themes constituted a laundry list of things wrong with Spain, initiated or perpetuated by Franco. French objectivism and the techniques of Alain ROBBE-GRILLET were adapted as a methodology; skirting censorship was facilitated by an impassive stance, objective or pseudoscientific descriptions, and the absence of editorializing. Peninsular writers' ends differed, however, with techniques of studied indifference being employed only to spotlight cancers on Spain's body politic. Raised and educated under a repressive regime that had expunged liberal and progressive writers from the canon and excised their works from libraries and bookstores, some postwar writers "reinvented" naturalism, while others more closely followed György LUKÁCS, usually known indirectly via French writers or translations.

What these varied literary modes or moments shared, ideological differences notwithstanding, was the predominance of content over form. Variants of NEOREALISM have a testimonial thrust and a propagandistic ax to grind, though techniques and methods diverge. Covert belligerence is a major motivating force of post-Civil War writing, possibly explaining why aesthetic considerations were slow in returning. In the 1960s, however, with the works of Luis MARTÍN-SANTOS and Juan BENET, the obligatory pedestrian style, simplistic techniques, and repetitive themes of *engagée* literature, yield to new interest in literary artistry. Increasingly during the final post–Civil War decade and most emphatically in the post-Franco period, aestheticism, questions of form and language per se, experimentalism, and interest in literary theory replace emphasis on content. Whether neobaroque, postmodern, or neovanguardist, aesthetic experiments constitute the primary literary link between the post-Civil War and post-Franco periods.

Some critics term the "mid-century generation" (cultivators of "social" literature) the "new romantics"; their obsession with national ills also links them to Spain's "Generation of 1898." By contrast the immediately following neobaroques, postmoderns, or experimental postneorealists (critics have yet to agree on a name) have closer ties to Spain's "Generation of 1927" (neo-Gongorists, late modernists, vanguardists, and surrealists). The analogic fit is imperfect but suggestive. Experimentalism, the most highly visible mode in the post-Franco era, shares the stage with surviving members of the Generation of 1927: Rosa CHACEL, the late Nobel laureate Vicente ALEIXANDRE, Rafael ALBERTI, María Teresa León (b. 1904), Ernestina de CHAMPOURCÍN, and Clementina Arderiu (1899–1976); and returned exiles, notably Francisco AYALA; Mercè RODOREDA, the greatest of contemporary Catalan novelists; Manuel Andújar (b. 1913); Teresa Pàmies (b. 1919); and Gonzalo TORRENTE BALLESTER from the "Generation of 1936." Still active are many established writers of the post-Civil War era—Camilo José CELA, Miguel DELIBES, Juan GOYTISOLO, and Juan Benet—joined by an exceptional number of women writers from both the postwar and post-Franco eras: poets Carmen CONDE, Concha ZARDOYA, Gloria Fuertes (b. 1918), María Victoria ATENCIA, Ana María Fagundo (b. 1938), Clara Janés (b. 1940), and Elena Andrés (b. 1931), among others; novelists Ana María MATUTE, Carmen LAFORET, Mercedes Ballesteros (b. 1913), Dolores Medio, Mercedes Salisachs (b. 1916), Elena Quiroga, Elena Soriano, Concha Alós (b. 1922), Carmen MARTÍN GAITE, and Maria Aurèlia Capmany (1918–1992) from the Franco era plus Esther Tusquets (b. 1936), Ana María Moix (b. 1947), Marina Mayoral (b. 1942), Lourdes Ortiz (b. 1943), Rosa Montero (b. 1951), Carmen RIERA, Maria Antònia Oliver (b. 1946), Soledad Puértolas (b. 1947), Paloma Díaz-Mas (b. 1954), and Carmen Gómez-Ojea (b. 1945); dramatists Ana Diosdado (b. 1938), Pilar Enciso (b. 1926), Lidia Falcón (b. 1935), Maribel Lázaro (1949), Paloma Pedrero (b. 1957), Carmen Resino (b. 1941), and María Manuela Reina (b. 1958).

Spain's "new novel" of the 1970s is only indirectly indebted to prior experiments of the French NEW NOVEL. The term was used previously and more appropriately to refer to Objectivist texts of the 1950s and 1960s; subsequent aesthetic renovation owes more to recuperation of the works of modernist and vanguardist exiles, including Mercè Rodoreda, Rosa Chacel, Francisco Ayala, and many others, almost unknown because their works appeared outside Spain. A slightly prior impetus derives from the influence of the Latin American "boom"—writers from Jorge Luis BORGES through Gabriel GARCÍA MÁRQUEZ. Linguistic and structuralist theory also produced literary echoes, and a renewed emphasis on culture: Writers who accepted the depersonalized authorial unobtrusiveness imposed by ideologues during the *engagé* period revel in their distinct identities, cultural heritage, artistic expertise, and technical virtuosity. The phenomenon is best observed in fiction and poetry, although a somewhat distant parallel occurs in the "underground theater" of abstract political allegory. Survivors of MODERNISM and vanguardism of the 1920s offer precedents and parallels for much postneorealist experimentation of the 1970s and 1980s. In the 1970s *novísimos* poets (as in the "new novel"), themes expand beyond the narrow realm of social literature to the subjective, intellectual, imaginative, speculative, and metaphysical. Problems become more typical of 20th-c. Western civilization, no longer restricted to Spain's politicoeconomic circumstances. Themes grow more abstract; vocabulary turns complex and international—neologisms abound, and foreign or scientific terms proliferate. Typographical and visual experimentation, arbitrary punctuation, suppression of conventional syntax, new structures and subdivisions, and baroque contorsions of language become almost commonplace. Non-Spanish characters and settings—foreign, international, fantastic, or allegorical personae and geography—appear, and temporal exoticism replaces the "here and now" ambience of prior neorealist modes. Everyday life ceases to dominate; the author, with his culture, his rhetoric, and his personal weltanschauung comes increasingly to the fore. No longer brandished as an instrument for changing society, literature escapes from utilitarian preoccupations, and theoretical concerns replace thesis (message) to the detriment of clarity.

Philosophy, Criticism, and the Essay

The legacy of José Ortega y Gasset colors most subsequent thought, beginning with disciples from the Generation of 1927, Xavier Zuburi (b. 1898), José Gaos (b. 1902), María Zambrano (b. 1905), and from the Generation of 1936, Julián Marías (b. 1914), Manuel Granell (b. 1906), Paulino Garagorri (b. 1916), José Luis Aranguren (b. 1909), and others of the "School of Madrid." Dispersed by the Civil War, many have returned to newly democratic Spain and continue writing. Equally indebted to Ortega's "vital reason" are Zubiri's profound metaphysics, the medical anthropology of Pedro Laín Entralgo (b. 1908), and much contemporary Spanish historiography, sociology, and aesthetics. Laín—one-time psychiatrist, professor of medical history, and author of numerous scientific treatises—also draws on Martin HEIDEGGER, Wilhelm Dilthey (1833–1911), and Max Scheler (1874–1928) for his own anthropological, Christian humanism in such works as *Teoría y realidad del otro* (1983; theory and reality of the other), *Antropología médica para clínicos* (1984; medical anthropology for clinicians). *La espera y la esperanza* (1984; waiting and hoping), *Teatro del mundo* (1986; theater of the world), and *Sobre la amistad* (1986; on friendship). Zubiri's Catholic liberalism, likewise derived from PHENOMENOLOGY and Heidegger, finds maximum expression in his massive trilogy, *Inteligencia sentiente* (1981; feeling intelligence), *Inteligencia y logos* (1982; intelligence and Logos), *Inteligencia y Razón* (1983; intelligence and reason), and his masterpiece, *Naturaleza, Historia, Dios* (9th ed., 1987; nature, history, God). Julián Marías, Ortega's major interpreter, adapts and develops the master's concept of historical reason, describing human life in its general and theoretical structures in *Antropología metafísica* (1970; metaphysical anthropology), echoed on the personal level with his three-volume memoirs, *Una vida presente* (1988–89; present life), and on the national plane with *España inteligible: razón histórica de las Españas* (1985; intelligible Spain: historical reason of the Spains). With generation peers, namely, Rof Carballo (b. 1906), leading spokesman for Catholic psychoanalysis of Eros and culture, José Antonio Maravall (b. 1911), José Ferrater Mora (b. 1912), and others, Marías represents the effort to impose order upon the received and to follow the imperative of reason. Under the aegis of Ortega and modernism, novelist Rosa Chacel contributes important essays on eroticism in *Saturnal* (1972) while María Zambrano treats themes ranging from Seneca to liberalism, from the divine to democracy, from Spain as problem to love and knowledge of the soul. Indirectly influenced by German phenomenology, her primary study is of "poetic reason" or poetic intuition as a philosophical method, in works such as *Claros del bosque* (1978; clearings in the forest) and *Dos fragmentos sobre el amor* (1982; two fragments on love). Spain's most significant woman philosopher and essayist, Zambrano returned in 1984 from exile in Mexico, Cuba, Italy, and France to become the first female recipient of the Cervantes Prize (1988),

Spanish literature's most prestigious literary award. *De la aurora* (1986; concerning dawn) metaphorically alludes to new life and perpetual rebirth and is symbolic of a new ontology, mystic expression of new ways of knowing. Countess María de Campo Alange (b. 1902), Teresa Pàmies (b. 1919), Lidia Falcón (b. 1935), and Maria Aurèlia Capmany, exponents of Spanish feminism, are also concerned with political ideologies and social problems. Pàmies, a revolutionary activist who spent more than thirty years in exile, has published some two dozen novels and collections of memoirs in Catalan since her return to Catalonia at the end of the Franco era.

Young thinkers of the democratic era, Fernando Savater (b. 1938), Eugenio Trías (b. 1942), Xavier Rubert de Ventós (b. 1943), and Eduardo Subirats (dates n.a.) attempt to transcend limitations of earlier generations and incorporate existentialism, Marxism, psychoanalysis, structuralism, poststructuralism, and other important European currents. Partially synthesizing antagonistic intellectual postures from the Franco era, they move between Christian humanism and antihumanist Marxism as represented by Enrique Tierno Galvan (b. 1918), an agnostic socialist who evolved from neopositivism to become a marxist opponent of vitalism and existentialism. The anarchist thought of Augstín García Calvo (b. 1926) also attracts some younger Spaniards, but many follow Tierno (enthusiastic proponent of a secular, rational, scientifically controlled society), who offers an extreme solution to the conflict between personal autonomy and the state in favor of identifying the individual with the species. Younger Spanish thinkers' neoromantic defense of the empirical subject's passional nature and liberty attempts to rescue the subject from all politically and socially restrictive theory. Brandishing the metaphor of the ideal city, they react against system, authority, and ideology. Savater, influenced by Friedrich NIETZSCHE and Michel FOUCAULT is especially concerned with society's peril for the individual in *Panfleto contra el Todo* (1982; pamphlet against the whole) and *La tarea del héroe* (1983; the hero's task). Rubert, with a cultural critique in the line of Savater, warns of danger in abstractions such as power, progress, unity, and history—powerful collective symbols that absorb the individual—and combats bureaucracy, the collectivity, and utopianism of whatever hue. Subirats plumbs the relationship between Eros and culture, attempting to strengthen principles of critical reason against dogmatic abstraction in *La ilustration insuficiente* (1981; the insufficient Enlightenment), *El alma y la muerte* (1983; the soul and death), *La crisis de las vanguardias y la cultural moderna* (1985; the crisis of vanguards and modern culture), and *La floor y el cristal: Ensayos sobre arte y arquitectura* (1986; flower and crystal: essays on art and architecture). Trías, in dialogue with Heidegger and Nietzsche, offers anthropological and ontological analyses of human passions and creativity, incorporating neo-Freudian metapsychology, philosophical dualism, and binary systems in *El artista y la ciudad* (1976; the artist and the city), *Tratado de la pasión* (1979; treatise on passion), *Lo bello y lo siniestro* (1982; the beautiful and the sinister), *La filosofía y su sombra* (1983; philosophy and its shadow), and *Filosofía del futuro* (1983; philosophy of the future). Common to all is a neoromantic concern for individual freedom and a rejection of absolutist thought in any form.

While no predominant new voice has emerged to speak for Spanish philosophy, arguably the most noteworthy change in Spain's panarama of essay production during the final decades of the 20th c. has been the emergence of a substantial cadre of women essayists, writing on a wide variety of legal, sociological, cultural,

Fiction

Camilo José Cela, Spain's most controversial and visible post-Civil War novelist, was awarded the Nobel Prize for literature in 1989, largely thanks to his best-known early works, *La familia de Pascual Duarte* (1942; *The Family of Pascual Duarte*, 1964) and *La colmena* (1951; *The Hive* 1953). The comparably little-known novels after *San Camilo, 1936* (1969; Saint Camilo's Day, 1936) are much more experimental and less representational, especially *Officio de tinieblas, 5* (1973; service in darkness, 5) and *Mazurka para des muertos* (1983; dance for two cadavers). The latter, inspired like *San Camilo* by the Civil War, is set in Galicia and moves hostilities to the realm of myth. *Cristo versus Arizona* (1988; Christ against Arizona), Cela's most recent novel to date, continues the fragmentary, lyric techniques of *Oficio* and *Mazurka*, adding little new save the setting. *Madera de boj* (boxwood) has been announced for release several times without being completed. Also extremely productive in the post-Franco era is Gonzalo Torrente Ballester, who received the Cervantes Prize in 1985; a master of erudite humor and metaliterary satire, he came to prominence with *La saga/fuga de J. B.* (1973; J. B.'s saga and fugue), first part of a "fantastic trilogy" comprising *Fragmentos de apocalipsis* (1977; pieces of apocalypse) and *La isla de los jacintos cortados* (1980; the isle of cut hyacinths). Two-time winner of the Critics Prize, professional critic Torrente mocked Francoist power manipulation in *La princesa durmiente va a la escuela* (1983; Sleeping Beauty goes to school) and *La rosa de los vientos* (1985; the compass) and satirized international intrigue leve el viento al infinitvel el viento al infinito (1984; perhaps the wind will take us to infinity). Academic criticism is parodied in *Yo no soy yo, evidentemente* (1987; I'm not me, evidently), a literary mystery based on the multiple heteronyms of Fernando PESSOA. The numerous post-Franco works of Juan Benet include *En ciernes* (1976; in bloom), *El ángel del Señor abandona a Tobías* (1976; the angel of God abandons Tobias), *En el estado* (1977; in the state), *Del pozo y del numa* (1978; of the well and the guardian), *Saúl ante Samuel* (1980; Saul before Samuel), and a series of three novels entitled *Herrumbrosas Lanzas* (1983–1987; rusty spears), which revisit his mythical world of Región, to examine once again the microcosm of Spain and of the Civil War. Although seemingly simpler than novels of the Región series—maps, battle plans, and a more straightforward syntax deceptively suggest that the later books will clarify the ambiguities of Región—abundant contradictions, omissions, and ambiguities reflect Benet's conviction that knowledge and communication are impossible Miguel Delibes continues probing impoverished rural Castile's forgotten and half-abandoned villages with their xenophobia, backwardness, and varishing values in *Los santos inocentes* (1981; the holy innocents), *El tesoro* (1985; treasure), and *Castilla habla* (1986; Castile speaks). *Cartas de amor de un sexagenario voluptuoso* (1983; love-letters by a voluptuous sexagenarian) explores the anguish of aging, as Delibes did in *La hoja roja* (1959; the red leaf). Most significant is 377 A, *madera de héroe* (1987; 377A, of the stuff of heroes), Delibes's exploration of the meaning of heroism in the context of wartime Fascist rhetoric. Juan Goytisolo revels in Arabic culture and life-styles in *Makbara* (1979; *Makbara*, 1981),

while his *Paisajes des pués de la guerra* (1982; landscapes after war) presents an apocalyptic vision of an Arabic "invasion" of the Sentier section of Paris where Goytisolo has lived for many years. *Coto vedado* (1985; no hunting), the first volume of this member, demystifies his family and class, while *Las virtudes del pájaro solitario* (1987; virtues of the solitary bird) blends Spanish and Arabic mysticism with contemporary homosexuality and AIDS in a nightmarish experiment filled with bitter humor. Luis Goytisolo (Juan's brother, b. 1939), has lately emerged as a major novelist, thanks to completion of this tetralogy, collectively known as "Antagonía" (1973–1981): *Recuento* (recount). *Los verdes de mayo hasta el mar* (May green to the seal). *La cólera de Aguiles* (Achilles wrath), and *Teoría des conocimiento* (theory of knowledge), dense novels of complex psychological exploration in a Joycean vein that offer parody, satire, and radically innovative literary experimentation, functioning simultaneously on the levels of personal experience, political recapitulation, metaphysical inquiry, eroticism, and moral reflections. *Estela del fuego que se aleja* (1984; distant wake of fire) and *La paradoja del ave migratoria* (1987; paradox of the migratory bird) may be seem as implied responses to his brother's memoirs and latest novel. Francisco Ayala, Spain's most talented and significant exile, reestablished in Madrid in the post-Franco era and belatedly elected to the Royal Academy, has published dense volumes of essays and memoirs—*Las plumas del fénix* (1989; the feather of the phoenix) and *El escritor en su siglo* (1990; the writer in his century)—and more short fiction, but no new novels. Returned expatriate Rosa Chacel continues, as in the 1920s and 1930s, slowly perfecting her modernist novels in the style of James JOYCE. The autobiographical *Barrio de Maravillas* (1976; *The Maravillas District*, 1992) and *Desde el amanecer* (1972; since dawn) are supplemented by her diary, *Alcancía* (1982; potpourri), *Acrópolis* (1984; the acropolis), and a collection of articles, and *Rebañaduras* (1986; slices), with *Ciencias naturales* (1988; natural sciences) closing the autobiographical trilogy of her generation. Deserving more than passing mention is Carmen Martín Gaite, one of Spain's most respected, translated, and studied women novelists and essayists. Typical of feminist concerns in more than a dozen of her books are the novels *Entre visillos* (1958; *Behind the Curtains*, 1990) and *El cuarto de atrás* (1978; *The Black Room*, 1983). Other important writers who, like Martín Gaite, began writing "social" novels under the aegis of neorealism but have evolved, matured, and moved toward more aesthetically oriented narratives are Juan García Hortelano (b. 1928) and Juan Marsé (b. 1933), prolific and popular winners of numerous prizes for fiction. Marsé's *Ronda del Guinardó* (1984; Guinardo patrol) exploits the vogue of the thriller while constructing an artistic parable of wartime victory and defeat. Also from this period comes Catalan humorist, poet, and satirist Juan Perucho (b. 1920), whose novels and short stories have become known in Spain since the legalization of the vernaculars in the 1970s. Carlos Rojas (b. 1928) has carved a niche for himself by creating fantastic (de)mythologizations of well-known episodes of Spanish history. Lexicographer, art scholar, and poet José María Caballero Bonald (b. 1926) emerged as an original novelist of Andalucía with *Toda la noche oyeron pasar pájaros* (1981; they heard birds overhead all night) and *En la casa del padre* (1988; in the father's house). Francisco Umbral (b. 1935), a cultivator of the "new journalism" and an exceptional, highly personal stylist, has published more than sixty volumes: novels, essays, memoirs, literary portraits, and chronicles.

The current narrative scene is crowded not only with active survivors of the generation of Ortega (or of 1925) and generation of

1936 (ex-combatants and returned exiles), but also features ongoing activity by representatives of the several post-Civil War trends (*tremendismo*, social novel, neobaroque, or neovanguardist), together with newer writers who have appeared in the post-Franco era. Postneorealist emphasis on form over content demands more of the reader, offers more cosmopolitan and intellectual fare, and requires readers knowledgeable in narrative theory, intertextuality, and creative processes. In the post-Franco era, especially during the first five to seven years of transition to democracy, an explosion of interest in areas previously censored resulted in a porno-political fad and a renewed fascination with the Spanish Civil War viewed from the unaccustomed anti-Franco perspective, as well as works of exile. *Franquismo* per se likewise became a thematic nucleus, and memoirs (previously a genre little cultivated in Spain) gained in popularity, especially memoirs of war exile, and clandestine opposition during the dictatorship.

The post-Franco era witnesses the emergence of the metanovel as a genre, an enormous use of intertextuality, and the cultivation of a new historical novel. For the first time, detective fiction, the thriller, and science fiction begin to be cultivated by major Spanish writers. Significant, mature authors from diplomatic or professional circles have moved into the narrative, offering original perspectives and intellectual verve, including philosopher José Ferrater Mora (1912–1991), banker-diplomat José Luis Sampedro (b. 1917), naval officer, essayist, and novelist Antonio Menchaca (b. 1921), educator Josefina Aldecoa (b. 1926), and essayist José Jiménez Lozano (b. 1930), whose themes in both historical investigation and the novel are drawn from a variety of religions and their recondite or esoteric backgrounds. Recently recognized as a distinct group, the "Generation of 1968" includes Juan J. Armas Marcelo (b. 1946), José María Guelbenzu (b. 1944), Ana María Moux (b. 1947), Esther Tusquets (b. 1936), Juan José Millás (b. 1946), Luis Mateo Díez (b. 1945), José María Merino (b. 1944), Juan Pedro Aparicio (b. 1942), Lourdes Ortiz (b. 1943), Marina Mayoral (b. 1942), Cristina Fernández Cubas (b. 1945), and Soledad Puértolas (b. 1947). Writing in Catalan are Miquel Angel Riera (1930-1996), Baltasar Porcel (b. 1936), Manuel Vázquez Montalbán (b. 1939), Robert Saladrigas (b. 1940), Terenci Moix (b. 1943), and Pau Faner (b. 1949), who appeared in Franco's twilight years. In the forefront of Galician fiction in the post-Franco era are Carlos Casares (b. 1941), Xosé Neira Vilas (b. 1939), X. L. Méndez Ferrín (b. 1938), Camilo Gonsar (b. 1931), and María Xosé Queizán (b. 1939). Writing in Castilian are Ramón Hernández (b. 1943), Germán Sánchez Espeso (1940–1991), Raul Guerra Garrido (b. 1935), José María Vaz de Soto (b. 1943), José Leyva (b. 1938), Enrique Villa-Matas (b. 1948), Vicente Molina Foix (b. 1946), Pedro Zarraluki (b. 1940), and Javier Tomeo, each having authored at least a half-dozen works, garnering significant prizes or critical recognition; there is no common denominator among them; some began as vanguardists or experimentalists and others as neorealists. Important new writers achieving acclaim in the 1980s include Alvaro Pombo (b. 1939), Félix de Azúa (b. 1944), Javier Marías (b. 1951), Mariano Antolín Rato (b. 1943), Ignacio Martínez de Pisón (b. 1960), Enrique Murillo (b. 1944), and Paloma Díaz-Mas (b. 1954). Whether subverting the narrative conventions of realism via paradox and enigma, diffusion of meaning, or absence of a sense of closure, through metaphorical density, ellipsis, structural manipulation, fundamental incongruity, or multivalent and contradictory meaning, most post-Franco narratives challenge the reader and elude easy classification.

The 1990s have witnessed a renewed acceptability of more traditional styles side by side with experimentalism, radical innovations, and outrageous postures. Formerly clandestine erotic fiction has solidified a market share, with at least three publishers devoting series to tales of titillation. Eroticism has become increasingly pervasive in so-called serious fiction as well, along with the heightened visibility of gay and lesbian themes and sexuality. Of special interest is the increase in erotic works by women writers, notable Esther Tusquets, Carme Riera, Ana Rossetti, Paloma Díaz Mas, Almudena Grandes, and Mercedes Abad. The Work of Republican exiles (much of it prohibited until after the end of the Franco regime) continues to hold public interest, with publishers bringing out numerous new editions of fiction from the years of war and expatriation—previously published outside Spain—as well as initiating publication of the complete works of various prominent former exiles. Spanish women writers are publishing in quantity and variety, including feminist fiction of exceptional quality by Carmen Martín Gaite, Josephina R[odríguez] Aldecoa, Cristina Fernández-Cubas, Rosa Montero, Carme Riera, Maria Antonia Oliver, and Ester Tusquets. The New Historical novel has also enjoyed particular success, and writers in Galician and Catalan exploiting this vein have achieved mainstream acclaim. Examples include Alfredo Conde's National Literature Prize for *El Grifón* (1986; The Gryphon)—the first time this award was won by a novel in Galician—and Carme Riera's receipt of the same prize in 1995 for *En el último azul* (In the Farthest Blue), the first time the national award went to a novel whose original language was Catalan. Spain's institutionalized culture thereby officially embraces diversity, contrasting with the monolithic norms imposed five-hundred years ago by Ferdinand and Isabel. The Spanish novel is now plural, or multiple, not only formally and thematically but linguistically, as is the country—as attested by the growing strength of its autonomous regional governments and cultures—and can be expected for diverge even further from linguistic purity as Spain becomes more fully integrated into the European union, already rendering Peninsular discourse more cosmopolitan and pluralistic.

Poetry

A major event for Spanish poetry was the long-awaited return from exile of Rafael Alberti; and of comparable import was the death of Nobel Prize-winning poet Vicente Aleixandre in 1984. Carmen Conde began publishing poetry of note in the 1920s, but her association with the Republic brought hard times under Franco. Today the dean of living Spanish women poets, she has published more than forty books, including some novels and essays, and in 1978 became the first woman elected to the Spanish Royal Academy. The half-dozen poetry collections in Catalan by Clementina Arderiu (1889–1976) span some six decades from 1916 until her death; returned exile Ernestina de Champourcín likewise has a poetic career of over sixty years. *Primer exilio* (1978; first exile) brings together memories of some three decades in Mexico, while *La pared transparente* (1984; the transparent wall) seeks a "naked" poetry to communicate religious insights. The recent deaths of Angela Figuera, Blas de OTERO, and Gabriel CELAYA removed the leaders of the "social poets," a much-studied movement that had essentially run its course by 1970 with the highly touted launching of the *novísimos* ("newest") poets who rejected neorealist *engagement* in favor of experimental modes ranging from surrealist to camp. Others made of poetry an existential inquiry, an epistemological methodology, or a linguistic avenue to confront life's basic verities; imbricated in this trend are Francisco Brines (b. 1932), Eladio Cabañero (b. 1930), Angel Crespo (b. 1926), Gloria Fuertes (b. 1918), Jaime Gil de Biedma, Angel González (b. 1925), Manuel Montero (b. 1930), Claudio Rodríguez (b. 1934), Carlos Sahagún (b. 1938), and José Angel Valente (b. 1929), all of whom published their major works between 1956 and 1971. Numerous new poets were on the scene at the death of Franco, several coming from the *novísimos* group and all born between 1939 (the end of the Civil War) and 1951; Antonio Martínez Sarrión (b. 1939), Jesús Muñárriz (b. 1940), José María Alvarez (b. 1942), José Luis Giménez Frontín (b. 1943), Félix de Azúa (b. 1944), José Miguel Ullán (b. 1944), Pere Gimferrer (b. 1945), Marcos Ricardo Barnatán (b. 1946), Antonio Colinas (b. 1946), Vicente Molina Foix (b. 1946), Genaro Talens (b. 1946), José Luis Jover (b. 1946), Guillermo Carnero (b. 1947), Leopoldo María Panero (b. 1948), Jaime Siles (b. 1951), and Luis Antonio de Villena (b. 1951). In the decade just ended, María Victoria Atencia, Elena Andrés (b. 1931), Pureza Canelo (b. 1946), Juana Castro (b. 1945), Clara Janés (b. 1940), Paloma Palao (1944–1986), María del Carmen Pallarés (b. 1950), and Luzmaría Jiménez Faro (b. 1937) are among the better-published women poets writing in Castilian, with Ana Rosetti (b. 1950) being noteworthy for her erotic verse. Marta Pessarrodona (b. 1941) and María Mercè Marcal (b. 1952) are the major women poets writing in Catalan.

Theater

"Social" playwrights who have evolved beyond neorealist beginnings and continues to be important in the post-Franco era include Carlos Múñiz (b. 1927), José Martín Recuerda (b. 1925), and José María Rodríguez Méndez (b. 1925). Andalusian Antonio Gala (b. 1936) cultivates a more lyric, tragicomic vein in the tradition of CASONA, marked by wit and a plea for individual and sexual freedom. Jaime Salom (b. 1925), one of the few Catalans to achieve success on the Madrid stage under Franco, has evolved from conservative Catholicism to a libertarian stance. Cultivators of abstract political allegory and social satire, the "underground" dramatists such as José Ruibal (b. 1930), Antonio Martínez Ballesteros, and Eduardo Quiles continue to be ignored by the Spanish theatrical establishment, although other previously unknown dramatists have experienced varying degrees of acceptance: Miguel Romero Esteo (b. 1928), Francisco Nieva (b. 1927), Francisco Rojas Zorrilla, Angel García Pintado, Jesús Campos, Juan Antonio Castro, José Luis Alonso de Santos (b. 1942), Marcial Suárez, Jerónimo López Mozo (b. 1938), Domingo Miras, Alberto Miralles, Fermín Cabal (b. 1948), Luis Matilla, and Luis Riaza (dates n.a.). Post-Franco revivals of plays from the first third of the century, especially by pro-Republican writers—GARCÍA LORCA, VALLE-INCLAN. Manuel Azaña (1880–1940), and returned exile Rafael Alberti—share the boards with contemporary versions of classics done by writers well-known outside the theater, like Gonzalo Torrente Ballester, Carmen Martín Gaite, and others. Established post-Civil War luminaries Buero Vallejo and Alfonso SASTRE have enjoyed productions both of new works and plays previously censored. Only limited success was accorded Fernando ARRABAL when he returned from self-imposed exile. As a result of a more favorable cultural climate, a Centro Drámatico Nacional was created in the mid-1980s, and the theatrical review *Primer Acto* (suspended in 1975) was resucitated at the same time that other specialized journals were founded, including *Pipirijaina, El Público*, and *Segismundo*. Significant trends during the 1980s included decentralization (moving theater beyond traditional established centers in Madrid and Barcelona), official stimulation of children's theater, and the emergence of a number of younger dramatists such as Fermín Cabal (b. 1948), Alvaro del Amo, Ernesto Caballero, Julián Egea (dates n.a.), and an unusual number of women, headed by Lourdes Ortiz (b. 1943), Paloma Pedrero (b. 1957), and María Manucla Reina (b. 1958). A thriving theater in Catalan presented not only established contemporaries such as Manuel de PEDROLO, but also Ricard Bofill (b. 1940), Albert Boadella (b. 1943), Josep M. Benet i Jornet (dates n.a.), and many other newcomers.

Quite possibly the most significant trend in the post-Franco era is decentralization, the absence of any single literary or cultural dogma, the proliferation of cultures, norms and voices, together with the literary empowering of many previously suppressed and silenced constituencies: women, exiles, and representatives of the regional or vernacular languages.

BIBLIOGRAPHY: Cernuda, L., *Estudios sobre poesía española* (1957); Alborg, J. L., *Hora actual de la novela española* (2 vols., 1958–1962); de Nora, E. G., *La novela española contemporánea* (3 vols., 1958–1969); Eoff, S. H., *The Modern Spanish Novel* (1961); Marra López, J. R., *Narrativa española fuera de España, 1939–1961* (1963); Ley, C. D., *Spanish Poetry since 1939* (1962); Alonso, D., *Poetas españoles contemporáneos* (1965); Debicki, A. P., *Estudios sobre poesía española contemporánea* (1968); Gil Casado, P., *La novela social española (1942–1968)* (1968); Torrente Ballester, G., *Teatro español contemporáneo*, 2nd ed. (1968); Ilie, P., *The Surrealist Mode in Spanish Literature* (1968); Zardoya, C., *Poesía española del '98 y del '27* (1968); Benedikt, M., Introduction to Benedikt, M., and Wellwarth, G., eds., *Modern Spanish Theatre* (1969): ix–xx; Morris, C. B., *A Generation of Spanish Poets, 1920–1936* (1969); Torrente Ballester, G., *Panorama de la literatura española contemporánea*, 4th ed. (1969); Wellwarth, G., ed., Introduction to *The New Wave Spanish Drama* (1970): ix–xviii; Ruiz Ramón, F., *Historia del teatro español, 2: Siglo XX* (1971); Guillermo, E., and Hernández, J. A. *La novelística española de los 60* (1971); Brown, G. G., *A Literary History of Spain: The Twentieth Century* (1972); Wellwarth, G., *Spanish Underground Drama* (1972); Holt, M., *The Contemporary Spanish Theater (1949–1972)* (1975); Rosenthal, M., *Poetry of the Spanish Civil War* (1975); Sobejano, G., *Novela española de nuestro tiempo*, 2nd ed. (1975); Cobb, C. W., *Contemporary Spanish Poetry (1898–1963)* (1976); St. Martin, H., ed., Introduction to *Roots and Wings: Poetry from Spain, 1900–1975* (1976): 1–13; Spires, R., *La novela española de postguerra* (1978); Martínez Cachero, J. M., *La novela española entre 1936 y 1975: Historia de una aventura* (1979); Soldevila Durante, I., *La novela desde 1936* (1980); Amorós, A., *Introduction a la novela contemporánea* (1981); García Lorenzo, L., *Documentación sobre el teatro español* (1981); Ilie, P., *Literature and Inner Exile: Authoritarian Spain, 1939–1975* (1981); Ruiz de la Pena, A., *Introducción a la literatura asturiana* (1981); Concha, V., García de la, *El surrealismo* (1982); Debicki, A. P., *Poetry of Discovery: The Spanish Generation of 1956–1971* (1982); Sarasola, I., *Historia social de la literatura vasca* (1982); Triadu, J., *La novela catalana de posguerra* (1982); Alonso, S., *La novela en la transición* (1983); Daydí-Tolson, S., *The Post Civil War Spanish Social Poets* (1983); Pérez, J., *Novelistas femeninas de la postguerra española* (1983); Pérez Stansfield, M. P., *Direcciones de teatro español de posguerra* (1983); Fortes, J. A., *La novela joven en España* (1984); Besas, P., *Behind the Spanish Lens:*

Spanish Cinema under Fascism and Democracy (1985); Cabal, F., and J. L. Alonso de Santos, eds., *Teatro español de los 80* (1985); Edwards, G., *Dramatists in Perspective: Spanish Theater in the Twentieth Century* (1985); Galerstein, C. L., ed., *Women Writers of Spain: An Annotated Bio-Bibliographical Guide* (1986); Mantero, M., *Poetas española de posguerra* (1986); Villena, L. A. de., ed., *Postnovísimos* (1986); Fernández Heliodoro, A., *La novela española dentro de España* (1987); Fortes, J. A., *Novelas para la transición política* (1987); Landeira, R., and González-del-Valle, L. T., eds., *Nuevos y novísimos: Algunas perspectivas críticas sobre la narrativa española desde la década de les 60* (1987); Mangini González, S., *Rojos y rebeldes: La cultura de la disidencia durante el franquismo* (1987); Palomero, M. P., *Poetas de los 70* (1987); Rodríguez-Puértolas, J., *Literatura fascista española* (1987); Amell, S., and García Castañeda, S., eds., *La cultura española en el posfranquismo* (1988); Halsey, M. T., and P. Zatlin, eds., *The Contemporary Spanish Theater: A Collection of Critical Essays* (1988); Mainer, J.-C, *Historia, Literatura, Sociedad* (1988); Manteiga, R. C., et al., eds., *Feminine Concerns in Contemporary Spanish Fiction by Women* (1988); O'Connor, P. W., *Dramaturgas españolas de hoy* (1988); Pérez, J., *Contemporary Women Writers of Spain* (1988); Provencio, P., *Poeticas españoles contemporáneos. La generación del 50* (1988); Vázquez de Gey, E., *Queimar as Meigas (Galicia: 50 años de poesía de mujer)* (1988); Oliva, C., *El teatro desde 1936* (1989); Gil Casado, P., *La novela deshumanizada española (1958–1988)* (1990); Pérez, G. J., and Pérez, J., eds., *Monographic Review: Hispanic Women Poets* (1990); Valis, N., and C. Maier *In the Feminine Mode: Essays on Hispanic Women Writers* (1990); Brown, J. L., ed., *Women Writers of Contemporary Spain* (1991); Fortes, J. A., *La nueva narrativa andaluza* (1991); Perna, M. L., ed., *DLB: Twentieth Century Spanish Poets* (1991); Pérez, J., *Modern and Contemporary Spanish Women Poets* (1996); Glenn, K. and M. M. de R., *Public Forums—Private Views: Women Essayists of Spain* (1998)

—JANET PÉREZ

Basque Literature

The Spanish Civil War divides Basque literature in 20th-c. Spain into two distinct periods. In the first part of the century literary production was influenced by the loss of Basque autonomy as a result of the Carlist wars during the second half of the 19th c. Three genres predominated: lyric poetry, the novel, and the short story.

Xabier de Lizardi (pseud. of José María de Aguirre, 1896–1933) was the best lyric poet of the period preceding the civil war. In *Biotz-begietan* (1932; in the heart and in the eyes) Lizardi takes the role of hard of nature. His poetry is learned, conceptual, and stylistically dense. He creates new words and succeeds in expressing very subtle ideas in Basque, a language some consider ill-equipped for modern literature. Lauaxeta (pseud. of Esteban Urkiaga, 1905–1937) was another poet of note. His best works are *Bide barriak* (1931; new ways) and *Arrats-beran* (1935; in the late afternoon), which have traditional subjects, such as love, ideals, frustration, suffering, and death. His linguistic innovations often make his poetry difficult.

Domingo de Aguirre (1864–1920) is generally considered the best Basque novelist in the postromantic mode. *Kresala* (1906; the water of the sea), written in the Biscayan dialect, describes the life of fishermen. *Garoa* (1912; the fern), in the Guipúzcoan dialect, is a narrative of rural life full of detailed descriptions.

Kirikiño (pseud. of Ebaristo Buztinza, 1866–1929) excelled in the short story. Using the vernacular, he captured the subtle Basque sense of humor in the collections *Abarrak* (1918; branches) and *Bigarrengo abarrak* (1930; second branches).

The dramatist Toribio Alzaga (1861–1941) was a pioneer in Basque theater; his plays, such as *Axentxi ta Kontxesi* (1914; Assumption and Conception) and *Bernaiño'ren larriyak* (1915; Bernaiños afflictions), have a distinctly Basque flavor.

During the first ten years after the civil war no Basque books were published in Spain. Among the writers who worked in exile, Orixe (pseud. of Nicolás Ormaechea, 1888–1961) exerted a great influence on today's writers. His epic poem *Euskaldunak* (completed 1934, pub. 1950; the Basques), describes rural life.

The revival of Spanish-Basque literature began around 1960. The separatist movement "Basque Homeland and Liberty" was born in 1959, and modern writers are often political and cultural militants. Most reject traditional subjects, preferring to write about social and political issues; nationalism, the Basque language, socialism, and Marxism. Poetry, the essay, and the novel are the chief genres.

Gabriel de Aresti (1933–1975) was the first social-minded poet of this period. The influence of Blas de Otero (1916–1979) on him is apparent, and, like his mentor, Aresti espoused radical ideas. His book of poems *Harri eta herri* (1964; stone and country) was a significant departure from traditional subjects and forms. *Hiru gizon bakarka* (1974; three men by themselves) by Bitoriano Gandiaga (b. 1928) deals with social and political problems. His poetry reflects the will for survival of a minority.

The novel *Leturiaren egunkari ezkutua* (1957; the secret journal of Leturia) by Txillardegi (pseud. of José Luis Alvarez Enparantza, b. 1929) introduced the EXISTENTIALIST thinking of Sartre and Camus into Basque fiction. Ramón Saizarbitoria (b. 1944) used the techniques of the French NEW NOVEL in *Egunero hasten delako* (1969; because it starts every day).

Iñurritza (pseud. of Salbatore Mitxelena, 1919–1965) brought the essay to Basque literature with *Unamuno ta Abendats* (1958; Unamuno and the Spirit of the Race), a book in which he refuted Miguel de UNAMUNO's argument that the Basque language was not suited to modern life. Txillardegi presented his nonconformist and existentialist attitudes in *Huntaz eta hartaz* (1965; on this and that). José Azurmedi (b. 1941), with his vast literary, philosophical, and sociopolitical knowledge, has written important critical essays as well as distinguished poetry.

With the opening of Basque schools, the literature seems to have been given a new lease on life.

BIBLIOGRAPHY: Michelena, L., *Historia de la literatura vasca* (1960); Villasante, L., *Historia de la literatura vasca* (1961); Lecuona, M., de, *Literatura oral vasca* (1965); Cortázar, N., de, *Cien autores vascos* (1966); San Martín Ortiz de Zárate, J., *Escritores euskéricos* (1968); Torrealday, J. M., *Historia social de la lengua y literatura vascas* (1977)

—GORKA AULESTIA

Catalan Literature

The Castilian cultural and linguistic colonization of Catalonia began with the absorption of the Kingdom of Catalonia and Aragon by the Kingdom of Castile in the late Middle Ages. The despotic Bourbon dynasty that came to power in the 18th c. might have made the colonization total had not romanticism, with its emphasis on nationalism, triggered the Catalan Renaixença (rebirth). Despite continual interference from Madrid, Catalan literature continued to develop during the MODERNIST movement. Catalan modernism differed from the Spanish American and the Spanish peninsular varieties in its nationalistic overtones and in its deeper regard for artistic intuitiveness.

Before 1906 even the most original Catalan writers were related in one way or another to the Renaixença. With the poet Joan Maragall (1860–1911), however, a new sense of the relationship between politics and culture entered Catalan writing. Economic hardships following the Spanish-American War of 1898 and a growing sense of alienation from the central government resulted in a host of Catalan nationalistic writings—political, cultural, and linguistic—such as Enric Prat de la Riba's (1870–1917) *La nacionalitat catalana* (1906; the Catalan nationality) and the first important works of Eugeni d'Ors (pseud.: Xènius, 1882–1954) and Josep Carner (1884–1970), two of the leaders of the movement that came to be known as Noucentisme (the movement of the 20th c.).

The Noucentistes advocated a complete break with what Eugeni d'Ors called the "rusticity" of 19th–c. Catalan literature. Noucentistes rejected the Renaixença and advocated going back to the last great Catalan writers before Castilian interference—Joanot Martorell (ca. 1413–1468) and Joan Roiç de Corella (ca. 1438–1497)—while at the same time adapting literature to the modern age and using the newly standardized language.

The aims of the Noucentista poets are given in Ors's preface to *La muntanya d'ametistes* (1908; the amethyst mountain), the first book of poems by Guerau de Liost (pseud. of Jaume Bofill i Mates, 1878–1933). They wished a less impressionistic and more detailed view of the landscapes than the modernists. They advocated a cultivation of aesthetic values through intellectual rigor and precision of language. Since the Noucentistes believed that art should stress collective responsibility, some of the best works dealt with the concept of the ideal city, for example, Liost's *La ciutat d'ivori* (1918; the ivory city) and Carner's *Els fruits saborosos* (1906; the savory fruits). The Noucentista poets' desire to link themselves with the great Catalan literary tradition of the Middle Ages is seen most eloquently in Liost's Somnis (1913; dreams), in Carner's *Els fruits saborosos*, with its pastoral melancholy, and in Carles RIBA's *Primer libro d'estances* (1919; first book of stanzas), with its echoes of Ausiàs March (1397?–1459) and other medieval poets.

The civilized humor, balance, and assurance of Carner's early poems set the tone for the literary atmosphere of the period. His poems after 1921, written in exile in Belgium, display a deeper sense of compassion and a leaning toward metaphysical speculation. In *Nabí* (1914; Nabí) Carner masterfully uses the biblical story of Jonah to express his own deep conflict of doubt and faith.

No other poet responded more singlemindedly to the cultural challenges of Noucentisme than Carles Riba. Yet when he used medieval models, he seems to have done so more because they fitted his own interests than because of a calculated attempt to be in line with the Noucentista prescriptions. Riba's work has a closely knit structure and an openness to experience that place him among the major poets of SYMBOLISM.

Until very recently the best Catalan poetry reflected the influence of Carner and Riba. Among the dozen or so important poets of the period between World War I and the Spanish Civil War, Josep M. López Picó (1886–1959), Marià Maneni (b. 1898), and Tomàs Garcés (b. 1901) stand out for their purity of language, precision of imagery, and adoption of the best of the symbolist techniques. The eclectic Noucentistes included Josep Sebastià Pons (1886–1962), from Roussillon, France, who wrote the sublime *El aire i la fulla* (1930; the air and the leaf), Jaume Agelet (1888–1981), and Ventura Gassol (1893–1980). Less attuned to this trend were poets like Clementina Arderiu de Riba, whose feminine spontaneity cannot be traced to any clear literary model, and the more traditional and egocentric lyrics of Josep M. de Sagarra (1894–1961).

Such avant-garde movements as CUBISM, FUTURISM, and DADAISM also had an impact during the period roughly coinciding with the time of political unrest in Spain from the death of Prat de la Riba in 1917 to the establishment of Primo de Rivera's dictatorship in 1923. Among many good avantgarde poets, like Carles Salvador (1893–1955), the most important was Joan Salvat-Papasseit (1894–1924), whose early experimental satirical compositions were concerned with the liberty and dignity of man. The best of his later poetry shows an acceptance of his "proletarian" status. His love poems in *La rosa als llavis* (1923; the rose in the lips) are the most genuinely erotic lyrics in modern Catalan. J. V. FOIX, a major poet, skillfully bridged the seeming incompatibility of Noucentisme and avant-garde poetic sensibilities.

Noucentisme favored poetry over all other genres, in part because the movement strove to purify the language itself. There was relatively little drama written in Catalan during the two decades before the civil war. The most popular dramatists were the older Santiago Rusiñol (1861–1931) and Ignasi Iglésies (1871–1928). Angel Guimerà's (1845–1924) plays after 1900, more symbolic than his earlier ones, are not as brilliant as his rural plays such as *Terra baixa* (1897; *Marta of the Lowlands*, 1914), but in such later plays as *La reina jove* (1911; the young queen) he continued to display superb craftsmanship. Perhaps the most talented dramatist of the 1920s and 1930s was Josep M. de Sagarra, who wrote romantic and lyrical plays such as *La filla del Carmesí* (1929; Carmesí's daughter). A more realistic playwright was Joan Puig i Ferreter (1882–1956). In high comedy, not a Noucentista genre but seen by the movement as filling a need, Carles Soldevila (1891–1967) and Josep M. Millàs-Raurell (1896–1971) excelled. The scant Noucentista drama ended with the outstanding, down-to-earth play *Allò que tal vegada s'esdevingué* (1936; what perhaps happened) by Joan Oliver (b. 1899)—who used the pseudonym Pere Quart for his poetry.

In the early 20th c. there was only one full-fledged novel, Narcís Oller's (1846–1930) *Pilar Prim* (1906; Pilar Prim), a pessimistic work of environmental determinism. The relatively small number of narratives written up to 1910 were of the "fragmentary" or episodic type, in the modernist style. Examples are the morbid short works by Santiago Rusiñol, although his comic minor masterpiece, *L'auca del senyor Esteve* (1907; Mr. Esteve's broadsheet tale), is historically interesting for presenting both a criticism of values of modernism and a solution to its ills. Other novelists of the decade dwelled on the highly "decadent" aspects of romanticism. The erotic mysticism of the early novels of Prudenci Bertrana (1861–1942) represented an attempt to break through the limitations of realistic narrative into a more subjective and "poetic" world.

The dominant mode of fiction between 1900 and 1907, however, was the rural novel, which tended toward grimness and had elements of fantasy and symbolism. Its chief exponents were Ramon Casellas (1855–1910) and Víctor Català (pseud. of Caterina

Albert, 1869–1966), both of whom attempted to transform older realism through modernist techniques. Josep Pous i Pagès's (1873–1952) *La vida i mort d'En Jordi Fraginals* (1912; the life and death of Jordi Fraginals) marks the passing of modernism in Catalan fiction. The antiruralism of Noucentisme, with its shunning of romantic imprecision and with its notion that prose should be cultivated separately from the novel, had its negative effects. Although Eugeni d'Ors's celebrated *La ben plantada* (1912; the good-looking young lady) is sometimes cited as a Noucentista novel, it is in fact a symbolic meditation. Joaquim Ruyra (1858–1939), however, incorporated the linguistic aims of Noucentisme into true fiction in his collection of stories *Pinya de rosa* (1920; the pine-cone [or roselike] sailor's knot).

The portrayal of complex human relations, absent from Catalan fiction since Narcís Oller, took root again around 1925 in the work of Carles Soldevila and Joan Oliver, and especially in Miquel Llor's (1894–1966) *Laura a la ciutat dels sants* (1913; Laura at the city of the saints) and Llorenç Villalonga's (b. 1897) *Mort de dama* (1931; death of a lady). The widening of scope in Noucentista fiction during the 1930s can be seen in such works as the trilogy *Novelles de l'Ebre* (1932–47; novels of the Ebro River region), by Sebastià Juan Arbó (1902-1984), which made a strong case for the continuing relevance of the rural novel as a means of presenting unfamiliar areas of life. But the most striking portrayals of the geographical and social variety of Catalonia is found in the works of the prolific Josep Pla (1897–1981). He wrote fiction and biographies as well as essays, with a style that was forceful yet often lyrical; he was one of the most astute social observers of his time.

The end of civil war of 1936–39 marked the end of Catalan political institutions, and to a great extent of the cultural traditions that had been built up over the previous forty years. The war itself produced fine poetry, notably by two gifted writers who died young, Bartomeu Rosselló-Pòrcel (1913–1938) and Màrius Torres (1910–1942). After the Republican defeat, many writers went into exile. In the early 1940s there was practically no literary activity. The language had been banned in the schools, and all other Catalan cultural manifestations were prohibited. By the mid-1950s, however, the situation improved somewhat, and two types of literary expression emerged: the bland writing of those who accommodated themselves to the status quo; and the writing of those who, risking fines or imprisonment, subtly began to tackle serious social issues. To the second group belong the two most influential poets of the postwar period: Pere Quart (Joan Oliver) and Salvador ESPRIU. The untimely death in 1959 of Carles Riba, whose *Elegies de Bierville* (1943; enlarged ed., 1949; elegies of Bierville) were the finest symbolist poems to come out of the civil war, was a great loss to the literary community.

Pere Quart, a colloquial and unrhetorical playwright and poet, became the most accomplished satirist of his generation. The more refined and complex Salvador Espriu shares with many other writers a controlled anger at the false values of the urban middle class. His best poetic collection, *La Pell de brau* (1960; the bull's skin), where the situation of the peoples of Spain is focused through images taken from the history of the Jews in exile, made him the spokesman of the postwar generation. Most of the best of the new poets, however, such as Gabriel Ferrater (1922–1972) in *Les dones i els dies* (1968; the women and the days), stressed personal experiences, private convictions, and inner struggles. Joan Brossa (b. 1919) shows superb, near-surrealistic artistry in his "visual"

poetry. Joan Perucho (b. 1920) presents an oneiric world in his somewhat surrealistic poetry; his fiction is a blend of symbolism, fantasy, and science fiction. Vicent Andrés Estellés (b. 1924) exalts eroticism as the basic motivation of life. Pere Gimferrer (b. 1945) treats man's destiny and the passage of time with freshness and technical mastery.

Characteristic of postwar Catalan literature are the numerous multigenre writers, especially novelists who are also playwrights. Many older writers have published some of their best work since 1950, for example Llorenç Villalonga's novels about decadent Mallorcan society, and Mercè RODOREDA's novels about human solitude. Rodoreda's *La Plaça del Diamant* (1962; *The Time of the Doves*, 1980), a straightforward, moving account of a working-class woman in the Barcelona of the 1930s and 1940s, is one of the unquestionable masterpieces of post-civil-war Catalan fiction, the other being Manuel de PEDROLO's *Totes les bèsties de càrrega* (written 1965, pub. 1967; all the beasts of burden). Pedrolo is the greatest as well as the most prolific experimental novelist. Sebastià Juan Arbó continued to write important naturalistic novels, such as *L'espera* (1968; the wait). Vicenç Riera Llorca's (b. 1903) novels, such as *Amb permís de l'enterramorts* (1970; with the gravedigger's permission), depict people displaced by the civil war. Pere CALDERS's novels, mostly on Mexican subjects, like *L'ombra de l'atzavara* (1964; the shade of the agave), explore social problems. Avellí Artís Gener's (b. 1912) best novels are characterized by cosmopolitanism (he lived in exile in Mexico until 1965). In *Prohibida l'evasió* (1969; escape prohibited) he used cinematic and avant-garde techniques. Maria Aurèlia Capmany's (b. 1918) novels, such as *Un lloc entre els morts* (1967; a place among the dead), are distinguished by their dynamism, variety of topics, and fine psychological insight into the female characters. Teresa Pàmies's (b. 1919) novels, such as *Quan erem refugiats* (1975; when we were refugees), are remarkable personal testimonies of the events she experienced. Terenci Moix's (b. 1943) novels forcefully treat the conflict between the old and the young.

The achievement of post-civil-war Catalan theater is not so great as that of the novel. The most influential play has been Salvador Espriu's *Primera història d'Esther* (1948; first history of Esther). Conceived of as an epitaph for the Catalan language, it became a symbol of renewal. Despite all obstacles, a substantial number of interesting dramatists have appeared, some also novelists or short-story writers, such as Maria Aurèlia Capmany, Manuel de Pedrolo, and Baltasar Pòrcel (b. 1937). Pedrolo and Joan Brossa have made contributions to the THEATER OF THE ABSURD. Josep Maria Benet i Jornet (b. 1940) is more traditional; in plays such as *La nau* (1970; *The Ship*, 1976) he deals obliquely with collective problems in Catalonia. Other younger dramatists, many experimenting with highly original methods, are more politically oriented. Jordi Teixidor's (b. 1939) best play, *El retaule del flautista* (1970; *The Legend of the Piper*, 1976), is a clever adaptation of the legend of the Pied Piper of Hamelin, with social overtones and Brechtian techniques.

The Catalan essay flourished during the modernist period. Its great early exponents, Gabriel Alomar (1873–1941) and Eugeni d'Ors, were followed by Carles Riba and Joan Creixells (1896–1926). Outstanding essayists of more recent times are Josep Ferrater i Mora (b. 1912), a renowned philosopher; Jaume Vicens Vives (1910–1960), a fine historian; and Joan Fuster (1922-1991), an important literary critic whose *El descrèdit de la realitat* (1955; the discredit of reality) is in the tradition of Ors and José Ortega y

Gasset. Other exceptional critics are Joan Teixidor (b. 1913); Joan Triadú (b. 1921), author of *Una cultura sense llibertat* (1978; a culture without freedom); and Joan Ferraté (b. 1924), who has adapted American New Criticism to his theoretical writings.

The democracy of King Juan Carlos I has brought about the reestablishment of the teaching of Catalan in the schools and a degree of political autonomy. As a result, there is at present an explosion of literary activity.

BIBLIOGRAPHY: Terry, A., *A Literary History of Spain: Catalan Literature* (1972); Durán-Gili, M., "Catalan Literature," in Ivask, I., and G. von Wilpert, eds., *World Literature since 1945* (1973): 623–27; Wellwarth, G. E., Introduction to 3 *Catalan Dramatists* (1976): 1–7; Roca-Pons, J., *Introduction to Catalan Literature* (1977): 49–91; Rosenthal, D. H., Introduction to *Modern Catalan Poetry: An Anthology* (1979): 13–28; Solanas, J. V., *Historia de la literatura catalana* (1980); Cocozzella, P., "Konilòsia and Sepharad: The Dialectic of Self-Realization in Twentieth-Century Catalan Literature," *WLT*, 54 (1980): 208–13; Rosenthal, D. H., "Homage to Catalonia," *Village Voice* (5 Oct. 1982): 39, 41

—ALBERT M. FORCADAS

Catalan Literature since 1975

The death of Spanish Head of State General Francisco Franco Bahamonde (1898-1975) was followed by a reconfiguration of the Spanish system of government, including the dismantling of the Francoist political apparatus. After a period of transition, characterized by high expectations and tension, the legal foundations of the new government were overwhelmingly approved in a nation wide referendum. The Constitution of 1978 recognized the cultural plurality of the Spanish State, and made provisions for the creation of autonomous regions based, among other criteria, on ethnic and historical reasons. Catalonia's autochthonous cultural identity was thus officially recognized for the first time since the Second Republic (1931-39).

Although critics are in disagreement regarding the direct effect that the former dictator's death may have had on Catalan cultural production, it is evident that there was a considerable increase in the publication of books in the non-Castilian languages of Spain (Catalan, Basque, and Galician) following his demise. In any case, restrictions by the Franco regime on Catalan cultural expression had already eased in the 1960s and early 1970s setting in motion a resurgence of literary activity that would gain momentum after 1975.

An immediate consequence of the new political situation was the proliferation of testimonial narratives whose intent was to recover the voices of those silenced during the Franco years. In Vicenç Llorca's (dates n.a) *El meu pas pel temps 1903-1938* (1979; My Passage through the Years 1903-1938), for example, historical facts and personal recollections of the Spanish Civil War (1936-39) are intermingled to offer a version of events that challenge what had been the official position of the government.

In the first years of the transitional period, Catalan narrative follows a course of experimentalism that is in tune with the breaking with tradition that defines most of the decade. Some exponents of this fragmented, form driven, transgressive narrative are Ferran Cremades i Arlandis (b. 1950) in *Coll de serps* (1977; Gorge of Snakes), Biel Mesquida (b. 1947) in *Puta Marés* (ahí)

(1978; Sailor's Whore [there]), and Isa Tròloc (b. 1945) with *Ramona-Rosbif* (1976; Ramona-Roastbeef). Most importantly, these authors challenge traditional Catalan myths and go as far as incorporating plurilingual voices into their works. Following the restoration of the Generalitat 1980, with its corresponding Ministry of Culture, the struggle to preserve Catalonia's national identity, which had led intellectuals to the Social Realism of the 1960s and the counter culture experimentalism of the 1970s, becomes institutionalized. Released from militant political compromise, writers are allowed to express themselves through a variety of literary channels.

By the 1980s, the recovery of narrativity and plot becomes the primary focus for novelists. The fiction of Jaume Cabré (b. 1947) is representative of this new attitude, in novels like *Fra Junoy o Í agonía dels sons* (1984; Friar Junoy or the Agony of Dreams) and *Senyoria* (1991; Sire), an historical piece that explores the abuses of power in the 18th c. More extravagant is Jesus Moncada (b. 1941) who recreates a mythical reality in *Camídesirga* (1988; River Rope Course) and *La galería de les estatues* (1992; The Gallery of the Statues). In this last piece, an epic tone is ultimately deconstructed by the ironic subtext.

An interest in history is also present in the novels of Jordi Tiñena (b. 1955) where fictional characters interact with historical figures in a carefully researched setting. In *La dona del grill* (1996; The Cricket Woman), for example, he rescues the previously published account of a famous 15th-c. trial to create an intriguing love story. Although most of Tiñena's narrative centers on the Catalan historical experience—*El comediant de Perpinya* (1997; The Comedian from Perpignan), *Els vespres de don Magí Casterllanau* (1995; Don Magí Casterllanau's Evenings)—recently he has also used episodes of contemporary European history in *Un dia en la vida d'Ishak Butmic* (1995; A day in the Life of Ishak Butmic) about the siege of Sarajevo.

A writer of considerable sophistication is Sergi Pàmies (b.1960) whose collections of urban based short stories *T'hauria de caura la cara de vergonya* (1986; You Should be Ashamed) and *Infecció* (1987; Infection) demonstrate his ability to fuse fantasy with contemporary reality. His characters are trapped by the monotonous and incoherent absurdity of daily life. These elements, however, do not reduce the impact of the humor in his prose, nor do they limit the development of entertaining, well-designed plots. *L'instint* (1992; Instinct) and *Sentimental* (1995; Sentimental) are his latest pieces.

Quim Monzó (b.1952) shares a similar urban thematic content and humoristic propensity. In the pivotal *Uf, va dir ell* (1978; Gosh, He Said), and *Olivetti, Moulinex, Chaffoteaux et Maury* (1980; Olivetti, Moulinex, Chaffoteaux and Maury) he establishes a style influenced by American Postmodern Fiction. Monzó's short stories revolve around an initial key concept, which usually leads to a surprise ending of comical, absurd, or realistic character.

The fiction of Terenci Moix combines popular art forms like film and rock music with a decadently rich prose. Moix is credited with introducing previously barred topics like homosexuality and sado-masochism into the literary mainstream. His intention is to chronicle Catalan society in the Galdosian manner. A constant in his texts is the theme of hypocrisy and its implications. Moix's most significant works in the post-Franco era are *La caiguda de l'imperi sodomita i altres histories heretiques* (1976; The Fall of the Sodomite Empire and Other Heretical Stories), and *El sexe dels Àngels* (1992; The Sex of Angels), a parodic satire about Catalan culture in the sixties.

Still within the sphere of modernity is Robert Saladrigas whose literary discourse maintains an affinity with Marcel PROUST and Henry JAMES. There is, however, a testimonial dimension in some of his works like *Sóc Emma* (1983; I Am Emma) about the 1960s.

Congruent with the manifestations of postmodernity, the last two decades have also witnessed the erasure of traditional borders that separate high literature from popular subgenres. Thus the romance, mystery, science fiction, and erotic novels have found themselves side by side with more conventional forms. Many established writers indulge in these previously disdained genres incorporating them into their body of work.

Perhaps, no other popular genre has enjoyed more acceptance by Catalan readers and critics alike than hardboiled fiction. The inequities of the then newly formed Spanish democratic society, where economic opportunity and political freedoms coexisted with unemployment, drug addiction, and a vigorous market for sex, offered the perfect setting for crime centered narratives.

Jaume Fuster (b. 1945) is considered to be the initiator of the detective novel in Catalonia with the best seller *De mica en mica s'omple la pica* (1972; Little by Little the Sink Fills Up). Four years later he published what most critics believe to be his best novel *Tarda, sessió continua, 3.45* (1976; Afternoon, Double Feature, 3:45) in which ideological concerns of nationalistic dimensions are present. Fuster's favorite protagonist, Enric Vidal, the Catalan equivalent of Mickey Spillane's Mike Hammer returns in *La corona valenciana* (1982; The Valencian Crown) although he is now ten years older and has lost the ideological militancy of earlier works. Fuster's detective is in fact mirroring the changes in mainstream Catalan society. In *L'illa de les tres taronges* (1983; The Island of the Three Oranges), Fuster adopts a different style creating a universe of fantasy, mystery, and adventure similar to the one in TOLKIEN's trilogy.

Another major developer of hardboiled fiction is Ferran Torrent (b. 1951), whose contributions to the genre include variations in narrative point of view, a realistic development of characters, and an accurate representation of urban life in Valencia during the years of transition. Especially significant is Torrent's innovative use of rapid dialogue and of humor as a remedy to the slower moments of his narratives. In *No emprenyeu el comissari* (1984; Don't Upset the Police Commissioner), and *Penja els guants, Butxana!* (1985; Hang Up Your Gloves, Butxana!), Torrent concludes that the contradictions inherent in an unjust society make it impossible to behave ethically. Other noteworthy contributors to the genre are Andreu Martín (b. 1949), Antoni Serra (b. 1936), and Xavier Moret (b. 1952).

A major aspect of contemporary Catalan letters is the proliferation of works by women writers. Their inclusion into the literary canon has revolutionized such areas as narrative perspective, thematic variation, and the protagonist's gender and development. The success of Merce RODOREDA's *La Plaça del Diamant* (1962; *The Pigeon Girl*, 1967; *The Time of the Doves*, 1983) establishes the Barcelona-born writer at the forefront of the post-civil war Catalan novel. Her literary activity, however, transcended Franco's rule, and in 1978 she published a short story collection entitled *Semblava de seda i altres contes* (It Seemed Like Silk and Other Stories). This work engages in the same preoccupations that are a constant in Rodoreda's narrative, which revolve around the psychological complexities of characters that are confronted with a socially oppressive and sexist, historically based reality. A recurrent theme is the idea of prostitution as a desperate, yet ineffective,

means to fulfill dreams of economic and emotional stability. This can be seen in "El billet de mil" (The Thousand Franc Note) and in "Ada Liz." Man's inhumanity to man is the context for a series of war related tales including "Nit i boira" (Night and Fog), which takes place in a concentration camp, and "Orleans 3 quilometres" (3 Kilometers to Orleans), autobiographically inspired, about the Nazi occupation of France. Oniric and other surrealistic elements offer solace to a wounded soldier in "En una nit obscura" (On a Dark Night). Her last novel, *Quanta, quanta guerra* (1980; So Much War), is a picaresque like travel narrative that traces the life of a young boy who goes off to war. As in previous works, Rodoreda employs a bildungsroman sequence with strong lyrical and symbolist overtones that contrast with the brutality of military conflict.

A writer influenced by the intimism displayed in Rodoreda's works is Monserrat Roig (1946-1991) whose narrative falls within the Catalan realist tradition. In *Ramona Adeu* (1972; Goodbye, Ramona) she begins her trilogy about the lives of three generations of women named Ramona, through eighty years of Catalan history. It is a novel of significant complexity with alternating narrative devices, which include the use of dialogue, a first person diary, and an omniscient account. The second volume, *El temps de les cireres* (1977; The Time of Cherries) deals with a woman's attempt to recover her past by returning to the family she abandoned a decade before. The psychological alienation felt by the characters reinforces the authors attempt to provide a sociological chronicle of Catalan society. Roig's journalistic background is very evident in *L'hora violeta* (1980; The Violet Hour), the most feminist oriented novel of the trilogy. Multiple perspectives offer a denunciatory and pessimistic evaluation of the feminine condition.

Majorcan author Carme Riera revives the narrative techniques of noucentisme in her collection of brief fiction *Te deix amor, la mar com a penyora* (1975; I Leave you, Love, the Sea as Token), which became one of the early best sellers of post-Franco Catalan literature. Riera's debt to the style of the great Latin American short story writers of the Boom is demonstrated in *Jo pos per testimoni les gavines* (1977; I Call the Seagulls as My Witness). Her first novel *Una primavera per a Doménico Guarini* (1980; A "Primavera" for Domenico Guarini) is experimental in nature combining a propensity towards neobaroque language and the use of various forms of discourse with a detectivesque plot. Of a different thematic basis are the stories in *Epitelis Tendrissims* (1981; Exquisite Epithelia) where a Balearic hotel provides the background for a series of erotic adventures. Other works of Riera include *Joc de miralls* (1989; Game of Mirrors) and several non-fictional studies, Els cementiris de Barcelona (1980; Barcelona's Cemeteries), and *Quasi be un conte, la vida de Ramon Llull* (1980; Almost a Story: The Life of Ramon Llull) about the 13th-c. Majorcan intellectual.

The search for an uncompromised female identity occupies much of Maria Antónia Oliver's narrative. *Vegetal i Muller que cerca espill* (1982; Vegetable and Woman in Search of a Mirror) is a book that contains two television screen plays with fantasy oriented plots. In the Kafkaesque *Vegetal i Muller que cerca espill* the effects of her prolonged oppression by her late husband eventually transform a woman into a plant. In the second screenplay the social constraints imposed on an aspiring actress force her to choose marriage over her dreams of self-realization. A message of frustration and hopelessness combined with rapid socioeconomic change is present in *Crinères de foc* (1985; Manes of Fire) a novel in which postmodern elements, such as the use of pastiche and parody, as well as a multiplicity of discourses are prevalent. Following this trend she published *Estudi en lila* (1987; Study in Lilac) where the subject of rape is examined within the structure of a detective novel. This fusion of feminist issues with a popular novelistic genre is made even more interesting by the use of predominantly female characters, including the detective. Nuria Serrahima (b. 1937), Maria Barbal (b. 1949), Maria Angels Anglada (b. 1930), and Joana Escobedo (b. 1942) further enhance the list of contemporary women writers.

The evolution of Catalan poetry in the post–Franco era, reflects a decline in both production and consumption when compared to the prestige it had enjoyed as a form of resistance. By the late 1970s the Metapoetic, Surrealist, and Avant-garde inspired compositions of poets like Carles Mor (b. 1940), Miquel Bauçá (b. 1940), and Ramon Pinyol (b. 1950) are gradually replaced by a return to lyricism and human experience with an emphasis on metaphor. Although some diluted forms of experimentalism persist well into the 1980s, many previously committed, experimental poets rediscover reality as a source of expression.

In this vein, Joan Margarit (b. 1938) explores the passage of time, solitude, and the evocative power of memory in *El passat i la joia* (1982; The Past and Joy). Of similar content is *L'edat d'or* (1983; The Golden Age) by Francesc Parcerisas (b. 1944) where the delicate nature of the human condition is redeemed through beauty. In *Focs d'octubre* (1992; Fires of October) a melancholic tone compliments reflections on living in a postmodern world.

Another innovator of modern Catalan verse is Narcís Comadira (b. 1942) whose early formalist tendencies and interest in the recovery of the sonnet, evolve into an obsession with breaching the gap between signified and signifier. His attempt to arrive at the true essence of things is best demonstrated in *En quarentena* (1990; In Quarentine).

Pere Gimferrer (b. 1945) maintains the legacy he had initiated in the 1960s with his search for an autonomous artistic form. Never fully relinquishing the modernist influences of his early production, his amorous poetry persists in pursuing a baroque style, as exemplified in *L'espai desert* (1977; The Deserted Space) and *La llum* (1991; Light). In his prose he upholds the break with tradition through the incorporation of experimental techniques in the model established by the Noveau Roman, as detected in *Fortuny* (1983; Fortuny).

The same concern for poetic form along with a propensity towards a satiric and melancholic tone is present in *Mares del desig* (1979; Mothers of Desire), and *El somriure del tigre* (1989; The Tiger's Smile) by Salvador Oliva (b. 1942). The poetry of Olga Xirinacs (b. 1936), whose love poems are defined by their intimate images and lyric content, responds to an attempt to popularize the genre. Her narrative production includes *Al meu cap una llosa* (1985; A Gravestone at my Head), set in wartime England, and *Zona maritima* (1986; Maritime Area) which was awarded the Ramon Llull prize.

As an example of the confluence of paradigms, Maria Mercè Marçal (1952) offers an ideologically charged poetry of feminist concerns with shades of surrealism in *Bruixa de dol* (1979; Witch of Mourning), while life as an ascetic endeavor permeates the poetic production of Agustí Pons (b. 1947) in titles like *Signe i desig* (1987; Sign and Desire). During the 1980s a new generation of poets begins to include in their works contextualized references of the mythological, Greco-Roman, and Catalan classical traditions. They are drawn by the perennial qualities inherent in those

texts. An excellent example of this trend is Andreu Vidal's (b. 1959) *Els dies tranquils* (1988; The Peaceful Days) which offers a modern interpretation of mythological referents. On the other hand, Jaume Subirana (b. 1963) and Jordi Cornudella (b. 1962) extract lyrical inspiration from everyday life experiences, seeking to poetize colloquial forms of expression. A much more profound thematic content is present in the works of Carles Torner (b. 1963) whose *Als limits de la sal* (1984; The Limits of Salt) won the prestigious Carles Riba Award. Torner combines a careful metric construction based on Renaissance forms with an existentialist and religious focus. Other works by Torner include *L'angel del saqueig* (1990; The Angel of Pillage), and a novel, *L'estrangera* (1997; The Foreigner). Margalida Pons (b. 1966) breaks into the literary scene with *Sis bronzes grisos d'alba* (1985; Six Gray Bronzes of Dawn) an exercise in the creation of evocative images of considerable aesthetic value. The intimate and elegant use of language displayed by Pons shows the influence of Salvador Espriu and Joan Vinyoli (1914–1984), to both of whom she pays tribute by including quotes from their works. In Isidre Martinez i Marzo's (b. 1964) *Inici de les hores*(1986; Beginning of the Hours) traditional themes, such as love and time, are subjected to a wide range of lexical possibilities. In fact, this flexibility and depth of expression has increased in the poetic production of the last two decades as the Catalan language has become mandatory in schools, and as vernacular media becomes more diffused. Martinez i Marzo is also the author of two other books of poems *L'altre encara* (1994; Still the Other) and *Camí de tornada* (1996; Return Path). Other active contemporary poets are Encarna Sant-Celoni (b. 1959), Arnau Pons (b. 1965), Rafael Vallbona (b. 1960), Marta Pessarrodona (b. 1945), and Perejuame (b. 1957).

The victim of the most rigorous censorship inflicted upon Catalan letters during the Franco era, Catalan drama has had a less than spectacular evolution after 1975. Its trajectory finds its origins in the independent drama companies that flourished in the late 1960s. Groups like Fura dels Baus, La Cubana, Els Comediants, and Els Joglars resort to visually driven, spectacle centered, and for the most part, textless representations. Some groups like Putxinel•lis Claca in *Moriel Merma* (1978; Death to Merma) incorporate the use of puppets into their productions. Others, like Els Comediants base their plays on concepts borrowed from popular and religious festivals as is the case in *Plou i fa sol* (1976; It's Raining and the Sun Is Shining). In *Els virtuosos de Fontainebleau* (1985; The Virtuous Ones from Fontainebleau) and *Teledeum* (1984; Teledeum) by Els Joglars, humor and satire are the vehicle for an analysis of contemporary values. Both of these works signal the gradual transformation of Catalan theater towards a more content-based orientation.

Founded in 1976, the Teatre Lliure (Free Theatre) has been influential in bringing to the stage modified works of canonical foreign playwrights, as well as a few from native authors. Although criticized for its universal pretensions, it has proven that it can create an original style in the areas of performance and interpretation. The efforts of this independent organization, however, were not sufficient to create a solid popular base of interest in the autochthonous theater.

Directly related to the undermining of political power that had produced the theater cooperatives is the virtual disappearance of authored plays during the 1970s and most of the 1980s. Authored texts were associated with forms of authoritarian expression and were therefore disfavored. During these years few scripts by playwrights writing in Catalan actually made it to the stage.

A notable exception are those by the Sirera brothers, Rodolf (b. 1948) and Josep Lluis (b. 1945), who collaborated in pieces such as *El cólera dels deus* (1980; The Wrath of the Gods) and *El capvespre dels tròpics* (1980; The Dawn of the Tropics). Their works explore sociopolitical concerns related to their native Valencia or more frequently deal with issues relating to their artistic medium and its representation. Rodolf Sirera has also written *Bloody Mary Show*(1980; Bloody Mary Show) a play that combines several types of spectacles like the circus and the music hall.

Josep M. Benet i Jornet (b. 1940) is another playwright who is able to overcome the difficulties of the early post-Franco years. His *El somni de Bagdad* (1976; Baghdad's Dream) became a popular children's play. *Quan la ràdio parlava de Franco* (1979; When the Radio Used to Speak About Franco) is a sociological study typical of the years of transition and his biographical piece *El manuscript d'Alí Bei* (1985; Alí Beis's Manuscript) deals with the unlimited strength of human will.

The success of this last work coincides with the fact that toward the end of the 1980s the public demand for a return to a type of dramatic representation that addresses the problems of the individual. New playwrights begin to emerge and their plays reflect a tendency toward a new realism that respects formal elements. This resurgence not only reinstates the authored play, but it also modifies several technical aspects that had become obsolete. Dialogue, for example, is given a new dimension. Its function now becomes to transcend the isolation present in a hostile and dehumanized society. This new dialogue is reflective of the chaos inherent in postmodernity and thus it is ambiguous, fragmented, and repetitive.

Sergi Belbel (1963) is one of the principal representatives of the new trends. In his *Elsa Schneider* (1987; Elsa Schneider) a formalist structure reinforces the themes of loneliness and anguish. A more complex situation is present in *Dins la seva memòria* (1987; In His Memory) where the guilt felt by the protagonist over his brother's death leads him to desperation. Belbel's use of a tripartite interior monologue demonstrates his effective assimilation of the new dramatic techniques. Following a new trend in Catalan dramaturgy, Belbel has written several film screenplays based on his plays including *Caricies* (1996; Caresses). *Titànic 92* (1988; Titanic 92) by Guillem-Jordi Graells (1950), *Quan els paissatges de Cartier-Bresson* (1993; When the Landscapes of Cartier-Bresson), by Josep Pere Peyró, and *Accident* (1996; Accident) by Lluïsa Cunillé (b. 1961) are some of the outstanding pieces of recent years.

Despite its remarkable recovery, Catalan literature is not without its problems. Competition for readership from Castilian publications, especially from other sources of entertainment like film and television, have affected the Catalan book industry. The presence of large segments of non-Catalan speakers within the Catalan areas have also retarded, somewhat, the progress of Catalan letters. Nevertheless, the diversification of literary production, with more and more writers emerging from French Catalonia, Andorra, and the traditional areas, indicate a promising future.

BIBLIOGRAPHY: Porqueras-Mayo, A., *The New Catalan Short Story: An Anthology* (1983); Prado, J. M., and Vallverdú, F., *Historia de la Literatura Catalana* (1984); Pérez, J., *Contemporary Women Writers of Spain* (1988): 176-196; Zubatsky, D., *Spanish, Catalan and Galician Literary Authors of the Twentieth Century* (1992); Espadaler, A., *Historia de la Literatura Catalana* (1993); Rosenthal, D., *Four Postwar Catalan Poets* (1994); McNerney, K. and E. Salamanca, *Double Minorities of Spain: a Bio-Bibliographic Guide to Women Writers of the Catalan, Galician and Basque Countries* (1994); Solá-Solé, J. M., *Modern Catalan Literature* (1995)

—DIONISIO VISCARRI

Galician Literature

Although Galician-Portuguese was *the* medieval literary language of the Iberian peninsula, its reign was eclipsed with the independence of Portugal, the centralization of Spain, and the consequent development of both Portuguese and Spanish. Galician literature has always shared with Portuguese literature the predominance of poetry and an emphasis on rural themes.

It was not until the middle of the 19th c. that Galician once again became a productive literary vehicle; thus began the *Rexurdimento*, the Galician literary renascence. Galician literature in the 20th c. however, has faced major cultural difficulties. Owing to the language's regional use and its prohibition during the Franco dictatorship, Galician writers have been forced to adapt a Galician/Spanish bilingualism; some have even created two distinct literary/linguistic identities, while still others have abandoned their native Galician language to reach a wider audience in Spanish, for example, Camilo José CELA. Further, many writers who were politically outspoken were forced to emigrate to Argentina, Cuba, and Uruguay, where Galician cultural activities have flourished.

The consciousness of the Galician cultural heritage not only links writers of the 19th and 20th cs. but also has served to buffer contacts with foreign literary trends. In Manuel Leiras Pulpeiro's (1854–1911) *Cantares gallegos* (1911; Galician songs) the rural themes and customs popularized by Rosalía de Castro (1837–1885) reappeared. Antonio Noriega Varela (1869–1947) also used these humble, idyllic traditions in some of his verse but then turned to an almost pantheistic interpretation of life.

Ramón Cabanillas (1876–1959) attempted to break these lyrical limits. Although his first work, *No desterro* (1913; in exile), was written in Cuba and invoked the tradition of *morriña* (nostalgia) as a tribute to an earlier exiled poet, Manuel Curros Enríquez (1851–1908), his later volumes, for example *Do ermo* (1920; from the wilderness), evidenced his knowledge of Spanish American MODERNISTS. The poetry of Aquilino Iglesia Alvariño (1910–1961) had a similar thematic and technical development.

The French avant-garde movements of the early 20th c. influenced two recently "rediscovered" poets: Manuel António Pérez Sánchez (1900–1930) and Lois Amado Carballo (1901–1927). The Irmandades da Fala (Brotherhoods of the Language), local literary associations dedicated to the preservation, study, and development of Galician language and literature, as well as to the promotion of a Galician regional political and social identity within a Spanish national perspective, thrived during the 1920s. Still other poets adapted their lyric personalities to different themes and directions: Fermín Bouza Brey (1901–1973) wrote poetry reminiscent of medieval Galician-Portuguese verse; his followers included Álvaro CUNQUEIRO and Xosé Díaz Jácome (b. 1910).

Recent Galician poets have sought more flexible means of expression and have opened their works to nontraditional social themes. Celso Emilio Ferreiro (1914–1979), who has been called the "patriarch" of Galician poetry, subtly censured the harsh conditions of Galician life and the exploitation of the people. His collection of committed poetry *Longa noite de pedra* (1962; long night of stone) has been the all-time best-selling book of Galician poetry. Other significant social poets include Luis Seoane (1910–1979), Xosé Neira Vilas (b. 1928), and Xohana Torres (b. 1931).

Modern Galician fiction has its roots in the folktales and popular history of Galicia. The first literary endeavors of Alfonso Rodríguez Castelao (1886–1950) were captions for his pictorial sketches and caricatures of Galician life; he went on to cultivate all literary genres. With Vicente Risco (1884–1963) he cofounded the review *Nós* in 1920. Risco was an important novelist, essayist, and ethnologist. Ramón Otero Pedrayo (1888–1976) remains best known for his finely crafted stories of Galician life, *Contos do camiño e da rúa* (1932; tales of the road and the streets). Álvaro Cunqueiro has successfully broken down the language barrier by translating his own novels from Galician into Spanish. Eduardo Blanco-Amor (1897–1979) described his native village in his fiction, while Carlos Casares (b. 1941) and X. L. Méndez Ferrín (b. 1938) have presented life in Galicia during the Spanish Civil War in their post-Franco-era novels.

Drama during the early years of the century was also folkloric; Ramón Cabanillas, Alfonso Rodríguez Castelao, and Leandro Carré Alvarellos (1888–1976), however, introduced social concerns. The influence of the Spanish-language plays of the Galician Ramón María del Valle-Inclán has resulted in the strong SYMBOLIST orientation of modern Galician drama. Examples are *A fiestra valdeira* (1927; the empty window) by Rafael Dieste (1899–1981), Cunqueiro's *O incerto señor D. Hamlet* (1959; the uncertain Mr. Hamlet), and the works of Manuel Lourenzo (b. 1943) and Daniel Cortezón (dates n.a.).

Galician literature has faced an uphill battle for its self-affirmation. In the post-Franco era, however, Galicians have greater political autonomy. Because of renewed interest and opportunity, Galician language and culture have a bright future. Respected magazines, such as *Galaxia*, and newspapers in Galician have appeared, and there are fruitful new contacts with Portugal.

BIBLIOGRAPHY: Bell, A. F. G., *Portuguese Literature* (1922): 347–57; Díaz, J. W., "Spain's Vernacular Literatures in the Post-Franco Era," *WLT*, 53 (1979): 214–19, passim; *The Spanish Literary Year: 1974–1978* (1979); Cuesta, P. V., "Literatura gallega," in J. M. Díez Borque, ed., *Historia de las literaturas hispanicas no castellanas* (1980): 621–896

—IRWIN STERN

SPANISH-CARIBBEAN LITERATURE

Cuba, the Dominican Republic, and Puerto Rico share a colonial history that began in 1492 when Christopher Columbus landed in the Caribbean in search of a new route to the Far East. All three territories remained Spanish colonies until France began to colonize the western side of Hispaniola. At present the Dominican Republic and Haiti share, although not always comfortably, the island known as Hispaniola. The Spanish-American War of 1898 marked the beginning of a phase of profound social and political change in Cuba and Puerto Rico that included an increased North

American presence. While Puerto Rico remains a territory of the U.S., Cuba has developed its own brand of communism under the leadership of Fidel Castro. The literature of the Spanish-speaking Caribbean and that of its diaspora reflects and contributes to the region's ongoing struggle for self-definition.

Cuba

A discussion of 20th-c. Cuban literature and nationality cannot begin without mentioning José Martí known for his revolutionary leadership and his writings. His complete works, including the novel *Amistad Funesta* (Fatal Friendship), were published in 1911 by Gonzalo de Quesada. The Spanish-American War was followed in Cuba by a period of increased American presence and decadence culminated by the dictatorship of Fulgencio Batista. During this time poets escaped the realities of their country by writing lyrical, decorative poetry. Names associated to this period are Dulce María Borrero (1883-1945) and Mariano Brull (1908-1954). At that time, groups such as the *Minoristas* and *Orígenes* promoted women's poetry. Fina García Marruz was a contributor of *Orígenes* (1944-56), a magazine edited by José LEZAMA LIMA. Her works include *Transfiguración de Jesus en el monte* (1947; Jesus's Transfigurations on the Mountain), *Las miradas perdidas* (1951; The Lost Looks), and *Visitaciones* (1970; Visitations). Other contributors to *Orígenes* were José Rodrígez Feo (b. 1920) and Cintio Vitier (b. 1921). Lezama Lima's importance to Cuban poetry cannot be sufficiently underscored. His works include *Muerte de Narciso* (1937; Narcissus's Death), *Enemigo rumor* (1941; Enemy Rumor), *Aventuras Sigilosas* (1945; Secret Adventures), and *Fragmentos a su imán* (1977; Fragments to His Magnet) and the novel, *Paradiso* (1966; Paradise). While Lezama Lima displays elitist tendencies in his poetry, Nicolás GUILLÉN became best known for his rhythmically sonorous Afro-Cuban poetry in collections such as *Songoro cosongo* (1931), *El son entero* (1947; The Whole Rhythm), and *El gran zoo (¡Patria o muerte!)* (1967; The Great Zoo [Nation or Death!]).

The creation of a new republic in 1902 gave rise to novels that defined local social problems and searched for possible solutions. Among the novelists of this time are Emilio Bacardí Moreau (1844-1922), Jesús Castellanos (1879-1912), Carlos Loveira (1882-1928), and Miguel de Carrión (1875-1929). Carrión's *Las impuras* (1919; Impure Women) and *Las honradas* (1918; Honorable Women) with their questioning of women's role in society exemplify the novels of the time. The 1930s gave rise to a new generation of writers that included Alejo CARPENTIER and Lydia CABRERA. In his narratives Carpentier shows his interest in music and history so that works as *El reino de este mundo* (1949; *The Kingdom of this World*, 1957) and *El acoso* (1956; *Manhunt*, 1959) are actually designed with symphonic modes in mind while *El siglo de las luces* (1962; *The Kingdom of the World*, 1957 and *The Explosion in a Cathedral*, 1963) explore the makings of the first black republic in the Americas—the Haitian revolution. Cabrera's *Cuentos negros de Cuba* (1940; Cuban Black Stories), *¿Por qué?: Cuentos negros de Cuba* (1948; Why?: Cuban Black Stories), *El monte* (1948; The Mountain), and *La sociedad secreta Abakuá narrada por viejos adeptos* (1959; The Secret Abakuá Society Narrated by the Initiated) represent Afro-Cuban traditions.

The 1959 revolution has had a significant effect on Cuban literature. The new political system encouraged education and made it possible for a large number of Cubans to acquire a university degree thus increasing the pool of writers and readers interested in serious literature. The new regime also encouraged the production of literature through the *UNEAC—Unión de Escritores y Artistas de Cuba* (Union of Cuban Writers and Artists) and *Casa de las Américas* (America's House) which sponsor annual writing contests although prizes are not always given to the best productions but to those more ideologically in line with the Revolution. The communist regime also gave rise to a system of production in which authors were paid by the number of pages or verses written and were assured of publication. These factors sometimes make it difficult to judge literary production in Cuba, but undoubtedly, a large number of texts have been produced and published by Cuban writers inside and outside the island in the last half of the 20th c. An important author whose publications began before the Revolution but continued writing throughout the Castro regime was Dulce María Loynaz (1902-1997) who in 1992 won the top literary award in the Spanish-speaking world, the Miguel de Cervantes award. Loynaz's poetry collections include *Poemas sin nombre* (1953; Poems without Name), *Últimos días de una casa* (1958; Last Days of a House), and *Poemas náufragos* (1991; Poems Adrift). In prose she published *Jardín* (1951; Garden), *Un verano en Tenerife* (1958; A Summer in Tenerife), and *Yo fui (feliz) en Cuba . . . Los días cubanos de la Infanta Eulalia* (1993; I was (happy) in Cuba . . .The Cuban Days of the Infant Eulalia). Some notable contemporary writers are Nancy Morejón (b. 1944) and Georgina Herrera (b. 1936). Morejón is actually Cuba's most widely recognized black poet. Her works include *Mutismos* (1962; Silences), *Parajes de una época* (1979; Conditions of a Time), *Cuaderno de Granada* (1984; Notebook of Granada), *Piedra Pulida* (1986; Polished Stone), and *Baladas para un sueño* (1989; Ballads for a Dream). Herrera is also a black poet and radio scriptwriter whose works include *G. T.* (1963; G. T.), *Gentes y cosas* (1974; People and Things), *Granos de sol y luna* (1977; Grains of Sun and Moon), *Grande es el tiempo* (1989; Great is the Time), and *Gustadas sensaciones* (1996; Likened Sensations). Another important post-revolutionary writer is Roberto Fernández Retamar (b. 1930) whose poetry publications include *Elegía como un himno (A Rubén Martínez Villena)* (1950; Elegy like a Hymn), *Cuaderno paralelo* (1973; Parallel Notebook), and *Juana, y otros poemas personales* (1980; Juana, and Other Personal Poems). Dora Alonso (b. 1910), Mirta Yáñez (b. 1947), and Aida Bahr (b. 1958) are best known for their novels and short stories, which include *Tierra Inerme* (1961; Unarmed Earth), *La hora de los mameyes* (1983; The Time of the Mammee), and *Hay un gato en la ventana* (1984; There Is a Cat at the Window). Other noteworthy prose writers and their novels are Edmundo Desnoes's (b. 1930) *Memorias del subdesarrollo* (1965; Inconsolable Memories, 1967), Virgilio PIÑERA's *Presiones y diamantes* (1968; Pressures and Diamonds), Severo SARDUY's *Gestos* (1963; Gestures), and Heberto PADILLA's *Fuera del juego* (1968; Out of the Game), which won an *UNEAC* award. Ironically, while Sarduy became another writer in exile, Padilla was imprisoned in Cuba in 1971 as part of a series of repressive measures taken against artists.

Since 1959 a considerable number of Cubans have left the island because of political and economic reasons. Many writers and scholars are among those who have left Cuba and live in exile. While some of these still write in Spanish, others have chosen to write and publish in English. Guillermo CABRERA INFANTE directed the weekly review *Lunes de revolución* (Revolutionary Mondays) from 1959 to 1961 in Cuba but in 1965 left the island. He is best known for his essays on film and his innovative novels *Tres tristes tigres* (1964; *Three Trapped Tigers*, 1971) and *Vista del amanecer en el trópico* (1974; View of Daybreak in the Tropics). Among those writing outside the island in Spanish are Hilda Perera (b. 1926) who began her literary career at seventeen when she published *Cuentos de Apolo* (1943; Stories of Apollo). Her novels include *Mañana es 26* (1960; Tomorrow Is 26), *El sitio de nadie* (1973; Nobody's Place), *Felices Pascuas* (1977; Merry Christmas), and *Plantado* (1981; Political Prisoner), which narrates the experiences of a Cuban revolutionary who in turn becomes a victim of the revolution and a political prisoner from 1962 to 1974. Antonio BENÍTEZ ROJO, another Cuban writing in exile, has published articles of literary criticism as well as stories and novels. His collection of short stories *Tute de Reyes* (1967; Kings' Work) won the 1967 Casa de las Américas prize. His other publications include *El escudo de hojas secas* (1968; Shield of Dry Leaves), *Recopilación de textos de Juan Rulfo* (1969; Collection of Texts by Juan Rulfo), *Quince relatos de la América Latina* (1970; Fifteen Accounts of Latin America), *El mar de las lentejas* (1979; Sea of Lentils, 1990), and *La isla que se repite: El Caribe y la perspectiva posmoderna* (1989; *The Repeating Island: The Caribbean and the Postmodern Perspective*, 1992). Mayra Montero (b. 1952) is another writer born in Cuba but raised in Puerto Rico who has received international acclaim with her novels *La trenza de la hermosa luna* (1987; The Braid of the Beautiful Moon) and *La última noche que pasé contigo* (1991; The Last Night That I Spent with You). Cristina GARCÍA was born in Havana in 1958 but has lived most of her life in the U.S. In her novel, *Dreaming in Cuban* (1992), she portrays the effects of Cuba's politics on the inhabitants of the island and those forced into exile.

Dominican Republic

Dominican literature in the 20th c. has been best known through its poets who have led a series of poetry movements. The *Vedrinismo* movement received its name from Otilio Celestino Vigil Díaz (1880-1961). Domingo Moreno Jiménez (1894-1979) was the creator of the *Postumismo* movement and his *Psalmos* (1921; Psalms) revolutionized Dominican poetry. Tomás Hernández Franco (1904-1952), Manuel del Cabral (b. 1907), Héctor Incháustegui Cabral (1912-1979), and Pedro Mir (b. 1913) are known as the *Poetas Independientes del 40* (Independent Poets of the 40's). Mir has used his poetry to protest injustice, as in *Hay un país en el mundo* (1949; *There Is a Country in the World*, 1993) in which he discussed the problems of the landless peasants and in *Amén de mariposas* (1969; *Amen to Butterflies*, 1993) in which he eulogized the Mirabal sisters who were assassinated by Trujillo's orders. La *Poesía Sorprendida* (Surprised Poetry) group included Franklin Mieses Burgos (1907-1976), Freddy Gatón Arce (1920-1994), Manuel Rueda (b. 1921), Antonio Fernández Spencer (1922-1994), and Aída Cartagena Portalatín (1918-1994). They produced hermetic poetry that belies the general oppressive political atmosphere during the 1940s and 1950s when Trujillo was in power. This group was followed by the Generation of '48 that included Máximo Aviles Blonda (1931-1988), Lupo Hernández Rueda (b. 1930), and Victor Villegas (b. 1922). Straddling this generation and the next is Marcio VELOZ MAGGIOLO who is a poet, but moreover, who after Juan Bosch (b. 1909) is considered the most important Dominican contemporary narrator. His novel, *De abril en adelante* (1975,

From April On), was a finalist for Spain's Seix Barral Prize, and a collection of short stories, *La fértil agonía del amor* (1980, The Fertile Agony of Love) won the National Award for Short Stories in 1980. After Trujillo's death and the 1965 war various poetry groups emerged, such as *La Isla*, *El Puño*, and *La Antorcha*, which produced what is known as *Poesía de Postguerra* (Postwar Poetry). This was followed by *Joven Poesía* (Young Poetry) to which Jeannette Miller (b. 1944) and Soledad Álvarez (b. 1949) belonged.

Some early 20th-c. novels are Amelia Francisca de Marchena's (1850-1941) *Francisca Martinoff* (1901), Federico García Godoy's (1857-1924) *Rufinito* (1908), *Alma dominicana* (1911; Dominican Soul), and *Guanuma* (1908-14), and Tulio Cestero's (1877-1955) *La sangre* (1914; Blood). Among the prose writers, Juan Bosch and Pedro Mir (b. 1913) have been dominant figures and both have shown through their actions and writings an intense concern for their country and people's welfare. Bosch published a novel in 1936, *La mañosa* (The Wily One), and another in 1976, *El oro y la paz* (Gold and Peace). He has also published short story collections, *Cuentos escritos en el exilio* (1976; Stories Written in Exile) and *Cuentos* (1983; Stories), and many long essays such as *Judas Escariote, El Calumniado* (1955; Judas Iscariot, Slandered), *De Cristóbal Colón a Fidel Castro (El Caribe, frontera imperial)* (1969; From Christopher Columbus to Fidel Castro (The Caribbean, Imperial Frontier), and *Capitalismo tardío en la República Dominicana* (1986; Delayed Capitalism in the Dominican Republic). Throughout his writings Mir has shown an interest in history and historiography as in *El gran incendio* (1969; The Great Fire), *Las raíces dominicanas de la doctrina de Monroe* (1974; The Dominican Roots of the Monroe Doctrine), and *La noción de período en la historia dominicana* (1981-1983; The Concept of Period in Dominican History). In his novel, *Cuando amaban las tierras comuneras* (1978; When Communal Lands Were Loved), Mir portrays his country's history as a series of populist struggles. Other noteworthy contemporary prose writers are Pedro Vergés (b. 1945), whose novel, *Sólo cenizas hallarás (bolero)* (1980; You Will Only Find Ashes [Spanish Dance]), won several prizes in Spain, René Rodríguez Soriano (b. 1950), who was awarded the 1997 National Literature Prize for his collection of short stories, *La radio y otros boleros* (1996; The Radio and Other Spanish Songs), and Avelino Stanley (b. 1959) who also was awarded the 1997 National Literature Prize for his novel, *Tiempo muerto* (1997; Dead Time).

The two major female voices in 20th-c. Dominican letters are Aída Cartagena Portalatín and Hilma Contreras (b. 1902). Cartagena Portalatín was a prolific writer whose works include *Una mujer está sola* (1955; A Woman Is Alone), *La tierra escrita: Elegías* (1967; The Written Earth: Elegies), *la tarde en que murió estefanía* (sic) (1983; The Afternoon in which Stefani Died), and the novel, *Escalera para Electra* (1969; A Staircase for Electra), which received an honorable mention in the Seix Barral Prize competition. In 1953 Hilma Contreras published her first collection of short stories, *Cuatro Cuentos* (Four Stories), and this collection was followed by a novel in 1986, *La tierra está bramando* (The Earth Is Roaring), and another collection of short stories in 1993, *Facetas de la vida* (Facets of Life). Carmen Quidiello de Bosch (b. 1916), author of the theater piece *La eterna Eva y el insoportable Adán* (1995; The Eternal Eve and the Insufferable Adam), and Aída Bonnelly (b. 1926), author of the novel *Variaciones* (1984; Variations), are also important female figures in 20th century Dominican letters. Moreover, since the 1970s there has been a boom of women

writers in the Dominican Republic. Some of these are Aurora Arias (b. 1962), Angela Hernández (b. 1954), Carmen Imbert Brugal (b. 1954), Hortensia Paniagua (b. 1953), Emilia Pereyra (b. 1963), Ylonka Nacidit-Perdomo (b. 1965), Martha Rivera (b. 1960), Marisela Rizik (b. 1958), Sabrina Román (b. 1956), Carmen Sánchez (b. 1960), Sherezada (Chiqui) Vicioso (b. 1948), and Dulce Ureña (b. 1960).

Migration between the Dominican Republic and the U.S. increased after 1965 and as Dominicans have settled in the U.S. they have begun to publish in English. The most notable among these writers are Julia Álvarez (b. 1950), author of the poetry collection, *Homecoming* (1984), and the novels, *How the García Girls Lost Their Accents* (1991), *In the Time of the Butterflies* (1994), and *¡Yo!* (1997), and Junot Díaz (b. 1968) whose *Drown* (1996) was named a Notable Book of 1996 by the *New York Times Book Review*.

Puerto Rico

As with Cuba, Puerto Rico's 20th-c. history begins in 1898 with the Spanish-American War and the subsequent new political status. Puerto Rico became a colony of the U.S. as the new century dawned. The island suffered a military government, the English language was imposed, and the spelling of its name was even anglicized to Porto Rico. These and other factors obviously affected the literary production on the island and set up the situation for a future Puerto Rican diaspora that was to flourish on the mainland as the century progressed. This diaspora has developed its own brand of Spanish/English language, literature, and culture. Some Puerto Rican writers actually producing literature in the U.S. in English or a combination of English and Spanish are Nicholasa Mohr (b. 1935), Judith Ortiz Cofer (b. 1952), Piri Thomas (b. 1928), Pedro Pietri (b. 1944), Victor Hernández Cruz (b. 1949), and Tato Laviera (b. 1950).

Key Puerto Rican literary figures of the first half of the century are Eugenio María de Hostos (1839-1903), Salvador Brau (1842-1912), Lola Rodríguez de Tió (1843-1924), and Manuel Zeno Gandía (1855-1930). Zeno Gandía was a prolific poetry and prose writer best known for a series of novels entitled *Crónicas de un mundo enfermo* (Chronicles of a Sick World) and which include *La Charca* (1894; *La Charca*, 1982) and *El negocio* (1922; The Business). He is often compared to Emile Zola and became known as the best writer in Spanish America because he was able to fuse the three main tendencies of the romantic movement: naturalism, regionalism, and realism. Moreover, Zeno Gandía left a group of followers: Ramón Juliá Marín (1878-1917), Matías González García (1866-1938), and José Elías Levis (1871-1942). Contemporaneous to these Naturalists writers arose a group of modernists, José de Diego (1866-1918), Nemesio Canales (1878-1923), and Luis Lloréns Torres (1878-1944) who also made inroads into the avant-garde movement. While the Naturalists narrated the impact of the new North American presence on the island, the Modernists stressed the construction of the definition and symbols of Puerto Rican culture. In this construction the white *jíbaro* (rural peasant) becomes a key figure with connections to Spain but also to the Puerto Rican landscape. The Generation of 1930 continued to define Puerto Rican society as descended from Western culture excluding recognition of its African cultural roots. Perhaps this can be understood when one realizes that these writers tried to construct an image of Puerto Rican culture that could be used as a defensive weapon against the encroaching North American culture. Writers of the Generation of 1930 include Antonio S. Pedreira (1899-1939), Margot Arce (1904-1990), Concha Meléndez (1895-1984), Francisco Manrique Cabrera (1908-1978), Enrique LAGUERRE, Emilio S. Belaval (1903-1972), and Abelardo Díaz Alfaro (b. 1919). On the other hand, Luis Palés Matos (1898-1959) emphasized African elements in his poetry and held that Puerto Rican culture was richly infused by African culture. His best known work is *Tuntún de pasa y grifería* (1937), a book that portrays the beauty of an African heritage. As could be expected, Palés Matos's ideas caused a great polemic among Puerto Rican intellectuals and gave rise to well known essays such as Tomás Blanco's (1897-1975) *El prejuicio racial en Puerto Rico* (1942; Racial Prejudice in Puerto Rico).

There have been several poetry movements in Puerto Rico during the 20th c. Evaristo Ribera Chevremont (1896-1976) and Antonio Corretjer (1908-1985) are representative of the avantgarde movement. Corretjer was especially committed to finding a solution to Puerto Rico's political situation. Another poet who displayed an acute social commitment was Julia de Burgos (1914-1953). Her best known work is collected in *Poema en veinte surcos* (1938; Poem in Twenty Furrows), *Canción de la verdad sencilla* (1939; Song of the Simple Truth), and *El mar y tú* (1954; The Sea and You), and a selection of her poetry has been translated in the bilingual edition *Rosas en el espejo/Roses in the Mirror* (1992). Clara Lair (1895-1974) is also another important female poet of the first half of the century. Both of these women explored the metaphysical and surrealists worlds in their poetry.

The 1940s and 1950s brought to Puerto Rico many changes including the end of a government appointed by the U.S., the Popular Democratic Party (PPD), the first freely elected Puerto Rican governor, Luis Muñoz Marín, and Operation Bootstrap, a project of rapid cultural and industrial development. This project brought urban overcrowding and high rural unemployment, which in turn made many Puerto Ricans emigrate to the U.S. in search of work and better living conditions. These factors gave rise to a generation of writers, sometimes known as the Generation of 1945 or 1950, who developed an urban literature and portray the conditions of the Puerto Rican emigrants to the U.S. Among these are Abelardo Díaz Alfaro (b. 1919), José Luis González (b. 1926), René MARQUÉS, Pedro Juan SOTO, José Luis Vivas Maldonado (b. 1926), and Emilio Diaz Valcárcel (b. 1929).

The 1960s brought change to Puerto Rico as to the rest of the world. Operation Bootstrap, greater social mobility, an increase in the number of women working outside the home and gaining access to higher education, and the victory of the pro-statehood *PNP* (New Progressive Party) in 1968 are some of the factors affecting the island's society in that decade. Some important writers of the time are Ana Lydia VEGA, Magali García Ramis (b. 1946), Rosario FERRÉ, Edgardo Rodríguez Juliá (b. 1946), and Luis Rafael SÁNCHEZ. Sánchez's *La guaracha del Macho Camacho* (1976; *Macho Camacho's Beat*, 1981) reopened the discourse about Puerto Rican culture and the symbols used to construct it. Texts dealing with similar subject matter are Vega's *Encancaranublado y otros cuentos de naufragio* (1983; *Overcast Sky and Other Disaster Stories*. Some translations appear in *Her True-True Name: An Anthology of Women's Writing from the Caribbean*, 1989, and in *True and False Romances*, 1994), Ferré's *Maldito Amor* (1986; *Sweet Diamond Love and Other Stories*, 1988), García Ramis's *Felices días, tío Sergio* (1986; *Happy Days, Uncle Sergio*, 1995),

and Rodríguez Juliá's *La noche oscura del niño Avilés* (1984; The Child Avilé's Dark Night). These writers satirize a people whose values have been distorted and even lost in an Americanization process.

Women have been extremely active in the Puerto Rican literary scene in the last thirty years. The literary magazine *Asomante* (1945-72) was edited by Nilita Vientos Gastón (1908-1989) and Monelisa Lina Pérez Marchand (b. 1910), and the literary magazine *Zona de Carga y Descarga* (1971-75) was edited by Ferré and Olga Nolla. Women currently writing in Puerto Rico are Iris Zavala (b. 1936), Clara Cuevas (b. 1937), Olga Nolla (b. 1938), María Arrillaga (b. 1940), Ángela María Dávila (b. 1944), Marta Magaly Quiñones (b. 1945), Etna Iris Rivera (b. 1949), Luz Ivonne Ochart (b. 1949 or 51), Vanessa Droz (b. 1952), and Lilliana Ramos (b. 1954). Moreover, Loreina Santos Silva's (b. 1933) space poetry and innovative biography, *Este ojo que me mira* (1996; *This Eye That Looks at Me*, forthcoming) have attracted international attention, while Mayra Santos Febress's (b. 1966) collection of short stories, *Pez de Vidrio* (1995; *Urban Oracles*, 1997), won the *Letras de Oro* prize for 1993-94.

BIBLIOGRAPHY: Menton, S., *Prose Fiction of the Cuban Revolution* (1975); Collins, J. A., *Contemporary Theater in Puerto Rico* (1979); Acosta-Belen, E., "Notes on the Evolution of the Puerto Rican Novel," *L ALR*, 8, 16 (1980): 183-195; Gónzalez, J. L., *El país de cuatro pisos y otros ensayos* (1980); Morfi, A., *Historia crítica de un siglo de teatro puertorriqueño* (1980); Morales, J. L., ed. *Poesía afroantillana y negrista: Puerto Rico, República Dominicana, Cuba* (1981); Collins, J. A., *Contemporary Theater in Puerto Rico: The Decade of the Seventies* (1982); Rivera de Alvarez, J., *Literatura puertorriqueña: Su proceso en el tiempo* (1983); Sommer, D., *One Master for Another Populism as Patriarchal Rhetoric in Dominican Novels* (1983); Fowlie-Flores, F., ed., *Index to Puerto Rican Collective Biography* (1987); Flores, J., "Puerto Rican Literature in the United States: Stages and Perspectives," *ADE Bulletin*, 91 (1988): 39-44; special Dominican Literature issue, *RI*, 142 (1988); Kanellos, N., ed., *Biographical Dictionary of Hispanic Literature in the United States: The Literature of Puerto Ricans, Cuban Americans, and Other Hispanic Writers* (1989); Foster, D. W., *Cuban Literature: A Research Guide* (1985); Martínez, J. A., *Dictionary of Twentieth-Century Cuban Literature* (1990); Bejel, E., *Escribir en Cuba: Entrevistas con escritores cubanos: 1979-1989* (1991); De Filippis, D. C., ed., *The Women of Hispaniola: Moving Towards Tomorrow* (1993); Martínez Masdeu, E., ed., *22 Conferencias de Literatura Puertorriqueña* (1994); de la Hoz, L., *La poesía de las dos orillas: Cuba (1959-1993)* (1994); Torres-Saillant, S., "Dominican Literature and Its Criticism: Anatomy of a Troubled Identity," in Arnold, A. J., ed., *A History of Literature in the Caribbean*, (1994): 49-64; Yáñez, M., and M. Bobes, eds., *Estatuas de sal: Cuentistas cubanas contemporáneas* (1996)

—LINDA M. RODRÍGUEZ GUGLIELMONI

SPARK, Muriel

Scottish novelist, short-story writer, poet, dramatist, biographer, and critic, b. 1918, Edinburgh

S. spent the first eighteen years of her life in Edinburgh. She then lived in South Africa for eight years, returning to Britain in

Muriel Spark

1944. Working as a London-based writer and editor, she established herself as a literary figure of consequence with her first novel, *The Comforters* (1957). Three years earlier S. had converted to Roman Catholicism. She now lives in Rome and, while continuing to publish short stories and poetry, remains best known for her novels.

Since, as Francis Hart observes, the conversion "just preceded and in some ways occasioned her appearance as a novelist," and since the plots of her novels frequently involve supernatural phenomena with theological implications, S. has come to be regarded as a Catholic novelist. Because she also tends to handle her characters satirically, she seems to many readers and critics a disciple of Evelyn WAUGH. Of her more successful novels, the one giving clearest expression to her Roman Catholic belief is *Memento Mori* (1959), in which several octogenarians are disturbed by incessant telephone calls reminding them that they must die. They view the caller as someone to be tracked down by the police, but the "mystery" in this pseudodetective story turns out to be of the divine variety: the calls have a more than human source.

There are, however, many significant elements in S.'s novels that are not specifically Catholic, for example, her insightful treatment of the behavior of women in groups, especially in *The Prime of Miss Jean Brodie* (1961) and *The Girls of Slender Means* (1963). The former traces the long-term impact of Jean Brodie, a colorfully charismatic teacher at a girls' school in Edinburgh, on her six favorite pupils; the latter presents the intensely social life of the May of Teck Club, a London hostel for young women who have

family connections but lack funds. Both novels focus on the betrayal of the values of the group by a single member, a betrayal that results in a religious conversion.

S.'s use of Scottish lore and her affinities with earlier Scottish writers are also important aspects of her work. Jean Brodie claims descent from the same Deacon Brodie (an actual figure in Edinburgh history) on whom Robert Louis Stevenson based his celebrated Dr. Jekyll. The other product of Edinburgh to figure prominently in S.'s novels is Dougal Douglas in *The Ballad of Peckham Rye* (1960); he journeys to London to become the diabolical instigator of bizarre and ultimately violent goings-on, including a nervous breakdown, an attempt at blackmail, a brawl, and a gruesome murder. He thus joins the long line of characters in Scottish literature who resemble the Devil closely and may in fact be the Devil himself.

Memento Mori, The Ballad of Peckham Rye, The Prime of Miss Jean Brodie, and *The Girls of Slender Means* constitute S.'s best work to date; and, because the latest of them appeared in 1963, her reputation has somewhat declined. But at least one of the more recent novels gives good reason to expect that S. may fully regain her powers at any time. *The Takeover* (1976) treats a subject both so complex and so mundane (and therefore seemingly devoid of spiritual content) that her ambition is everywhere apparent: it is, as S. writes in the book, the "change in the meaning of property and money," "such a sea-change in the nature of reality as could not have been envisaged by Karl Marx or Sigmund Freud." Yet she masters this subject thoroughly. Such controlled virtuosity confirms the belief that S. remains a major figure in contemporary British fiction.

FURTHER WORKS: *Child of Light: A Reassessment of Mary Wollstonecraft Shelley* (1951); *The Fanfarlo, and Other Verse* (1952); *Emily Brontë: Her Life and Work* (1953, with Derek Stanford); *John Masefield* (1953); *Robinson* (1958); *The Go-Away Bird, and Other Stories* (1958); *The Bachelors* (1960); *Voices at Play* (1961); *Doctors of Philosophy* (1963); *The Mandelbaum Gate* (1965); *Collected Poems I* (1967); *Collected Stories I* (1967); *The Public Image* (1968); *The Very Fine Clock* (1968); *The Driver's Seat* (1970); *Not to Disturb* (1971); *The Hothouse by the East River* (1973); *The Abbess of Crewe* (1974); *Territorial Rights* (1979); *Loitering with Intent* (1981)

BIBLIOGRAPHY: Stanford, D., *M. S.* (1963); Malkoff, K., *M. S.* (1968); Kermode, F., *Continuities* (1968): 202–16; Auerbach, N., *Communities of Women: An Idea in Fiction* (1978): 167–81; Hart, F., *The Scottish Novel* (1978): 294–310; Ray, P., "Jean Brodie and Edinburgh," *SSL*, 13 (1978): 24–31; Whittaker, R., *The Faith and Fiction of M. S.* (1982)

—PHILIP E. RAY

SPENCER, Elizabeth

American novelist and short-story writer, b. 19 July 1921, Carrollton, Mississippi

Raised in a family whose Mississippi roots date back to the early 1800s, S. received her B.A. from Belhaven College and M.A.

from Vanderbilt University, where she studied under Donald Davidson (1893-1968). While teaching at the University of Mississippi, she published her first novel, *Fire in the Morning* (1948). Her second novel, *This Crooked Way* (1952), led to a writing grant from the National Institute of Arts and Letters. With two widely reviewed novels to her credit, S. received a Guggenheim Award in 1953 and traveled to Italy where she met John Arthur Blackwood Rusher, whom she married. They moved to Canada in 1958 where they resided for more than thirty years before moving to Chapel Hill, North Carolina. Continuing to write novels while moving more toward short fiction, S. received a *Kenyon Review* Fellowship in 1957 and citations from the American Academy of Arts and Letters in 1956 and again in 1983. She remains a writer well respected for her novels and short fiction, and her 1998 memoir, *Landscape of the Heart*, has been praised for its narrative of the 20th-c. South and insight into the lives of fellow Southern writers Eudora WELTY, Robert Penn WARREN, and Walker PERCY.

Set in the hill country of Mississippi and with the prevailing sense that violence might erupt at any moment, S.'s *Fire in the Morning* is clearly in FAULKNER's fictional realm; to her credit, the novel invites such comparisons without seeming to be thematically derivative. It addresses a two-generation feud over property in a small Mississippi town. Using modernist narrative techniques such as multiple points of view and flashbacks, S. holds a strong command over a large cast of characters while maintaining a sharp focus on her protagonist, Kinloch Armstrong. *This Crooked Way* is also set in the hills of Mississippi in the early part of this century. After *The Voice at the Back Door* (1956), which concerns racial equality and came out on the heels of the *Brown* decision, S. shifted away from historical novels of the Southern Renaissance tradition. While remaining highly descriptive, her writing style also moved more toward the tradition of HEMINGWAY than Faulkner.

Having written of the South while living in Italy, S. turned her thoughts to Italy while in Canada and found rich literary territory. As did Robert Penn Warren and Allen TATE in poetry and William STYRON and Pat Conroy (b. 1945) in popular novels, S. addresses the subject of Southerners in Italy in several short novels and stories. Her finest such work, *Light in the Piazza* (1960), confronts many of the same issues as Henry JAMES's short masterpiece, *Daisy Miller*. S.'s novel centers on a wealthy American mother and her decision whether or not to let her mentally-impaired daughter marry a young Italian man they meet while in Florence. The marriage would grant the daughter happiness and the mother freedom, but it would also be an act of deceit to the young suitor who knows nothing of his love's impairment. After a last-minute negotiation between the American mother and a knowing Italian father, the longevity of the marriage seems assured on the basis of the youths' mutual love, the American girl's dowry, and the useful language barrier.

Beginning her writing career with historical novels set in the hills of Mississippi, then moving to contemporary stories set in Italy and Canada, S. has also written with great insight and sensitivity about the ever-changing Gulf of Mexico coastal towns in *Ship Island and Other Stories* (1968) and *The Salt Line* (1984), among other works. As her writing returned again to the American South, so did S. herself after living for decades in Canada and abroad. In *Landscape of the Heart* she stresses the importance of kinship and family traditions and how deeply growing up in the Deep South shaped her life and writing. Recognized internationally for her distinguished body of literature written over five decades,

Light in the Piazza, *Landscapes of the Heart*, and *The Stories of E. S.* (1981) best represent her profuse talent.

FURTHER WORKS: *Knights and Dragons* (1965); *No Place for an Angel* (1967); *The Snare* (1972); *Marilee* (1981); *Jack of Diamonds* (1988); *Night Travelers* (1991); *On the Gulf* (1991)

BIBLIOGRAPHY: Burger, N. K., "E. S.'s Three Mississippi Novels," *SAQ*, 63 (Summer 1964): 351-62; Jones, J. G., *Mississippi Writers Talking* (1982): 95-129; Prenshaw, P. W., *E. S.* (1985); Inge, T. B., ed., *Southern Women Writers* (1990); Prenshaw, P. W., ed., *Conversations with E. S.* (1991); Roberts, T., *Self and Community in the Fiction of E. S.* (1993)

—JON PARRISH PEEDE

SPENDER, Stephen

English poet, essayist, critic, and translator, b. 28 Feb. 1909, London; d. 16 July 1995, London

Educated at University College, Oxford, S. came to be associated with other writers then at Oxford—W. H. AUDEN, C. Day LEWIS, and Louis MACNEICE. These were linked chiefly by the dominant influence of Auden on subject matter and imagery. Although S. shared their social consciousness, the reference of his early poetry is personal, even when the matter is political. During his years at Oxford, S., interested in his German-Jewish heritage, traveled much in Germany, in part to obtain relief from feeling "like a foreigner" in his own country. His acquaintance with German literature resulted in translations of works by Rainer Maria RILKE, Ernst TOLLER, Frank WEDEKIND, Büchner's *Danton's Death* (1939), and Schiller's *Mary Stuart* (1958).

S.'s third volume of verse, *Poems* (1933), established his reputation. In it he expresses his beliefs that the poet must realize in concrete images aspects of his inner life which are also significant to the public world, and that the imagination can move events—but not through "propaganda poetry."

In *The Destructive Element* (1935) S. analyzes the work of Henry JAMES, T. S. ELIOT, James JOYCE, and others for their concern with factors threatening civilization and their emphasis on the importance of individual solutions to moral and artistic problems. S.'s commitment to this idea shaped his response to communism and fascism. Although for a short time he became a communist after the publication of *Forward from Liberalism* (1937), his writings and talks stressing the individual's responsibility as opposed to doctrinaire policy kept him in disrepute with English communists. The long poem *Vienna* (1934) is characteristic of S.'s interlacing of public and private events, and the idea that public conflict and disease is reflected in personal life. *Trial of a Judge* (1938) is a play about the "tragedy" of a liberal judge defeated by both communism and fascism.

The poetry collection *The Still Centre* (1939) renewed his attempt to give private images universal significance. These poems reveal his continuing search for a faith to live by but also exhibit the technical shortcomings that characterize his work through *The Generous Days* (1971): labored images, inversion of word order to make a rhyme, and overextended development.

Coeditorship of *Horizon* with Cyril Connolly (1903–1974) in 1939 ended two years later in disagreement over editorial policy. From this time until the end of the war he was in the National Fire Service. After the war he traveled widely. *European Witness* (1946), a report on his trip to the British-occupied zone of Germany, analyzes the condition of German intellectuals under Hitler. *Learning Laughter* (1952) is an account of his visit to Israel. In 1953 he joined with Irving Kristol (b. 1920) to edit *Encounter*, from which S. resigned in 1968 because of the magazine's CIA connections.

In *Engaged in Writing* and *The Fool and the Princess* (1958)—two short novels—S. satirizes as a dissipation of creative energies such meetings as the International Writers' Conference, which he had attended in Spain in 1937. S.'s search for the relationship between private belief and public conduct took him in 1968 to Prague, Berlin, Paris, and New York to speak with student demonstrators. His report on that journey, *The Year of the Young Rebels* (1969), concludes with an analysis of the changing role of the university as it shapes and is shaped by youthful activists. In 1970 S. accepted a chair in English literature at University College in London.

In *Love-Hate Relations: A Study of Anglo-American Sensibilities* (1974) S. compares aspects of English and American literary activity—the American not as acutely as the English, although his observations on the institutionalizing of literature in the American university underscores the dangers, as S. sees it, of confusing values with expediency. This work restates a view set forth in his autobiography *World within World* (1951), that the only true hope for civilization is the individual's belief that his inner life can influence the course of outward events.

The Thirties and After: Poetry, Politics, People, 1933–1970 (1978) is an appendix to the autobiography, more episodic and less confessional, which again expresses S.'s belief in the mediating potential of art in public affairs. *Letters to Christopher* (1980), which includes, in addition to correspondence with Christopher ISHERWOOD, two of S.'s journals—of 1932 and 1939—documents portions of *World within World*, less effectively than if Isherwood's replies were included.

S.'s critical reception has always been divided. But the poetic production of over fifty years has remained stubbornly idiosyncratic, representing the central thesis of his work, both prose and poetry, that the inner life is of paramount value, and that the individual conscience can still exercise its function of criticism for self and for the common good.

FURTHER WORKS: *Nine Experiments* (1928); *Twenty Poems* (1930); *The Burning Cactus* (1936); *Poems for Spain* (1939); *The New Realism* (1939); *The Backward Son* (1940); *Selected Poems* (1940); *Ruins and Visions* (1942); *Life and the Poet* (1942); *Citizens in War and After* (1945); *Poems of Dedication* (1946); *Poetry since 1939* (1946); *Returning to Vienna 1947: Nine Sketches* (1947); *The Edge of Being* (1949); *Shelley* (1952; rev. ed., 1960); *The Creative Element* (1953); *Sirmione Peninsula* (1953); *Collected Poems, 1928–1953* (1955); *The Making of a Poem* (1955); *Inscriptions* (1958); *The Struggle of the Modern* (1963); *Selected Poems* (1964); *T. S. Eliot* (1975); *Henry Moore: Sculptures in Landscape* (1978, with Shakerley Geoffrey); *China Diary* (1983, with David Hockney)

BIBLIOGRAPHY: Seif, M., "The Influence of T. S. Eliot on Auden and S.," *SAQ*, 53 (1954): 61–69; Jacobs, W. D., "The Moderate Poetical Success of S. S.," *CE*, 17 (1956): 374–78; Maxwell, D. E. S., *Poets of the Thirties* (1969), passim; Weatherhead, A. K., *S. S. and the Thirties* (1975); Kulkarni, H. B., *S. S., Works and Criticism: An Annotated Bibliography* (1976); Hynes, S., "What Is a Decade? Notes on the Thirties," *SR*, 88 (1980): 506–11; Stitt, P., "S. S.: An Interview," *Paris Review*, No. 77 (1980): 118–54

—MANLY JOHNSON

SPERBER, Manès

Austrian novelist, memoirist, and essayist (writing in German, French, and English), b. 12 Dec. 1905, Zablotow, Austro-Hungarian Empire (now in Russia); d. 5 Feb. 1984, Paris, France

S. was born in a small Jewish town in Galicia. The family fled during World War I and eventually settled in Vienna. As a young man there S. was active in the Zionist youth movement, which proved significant for his later development. He became associated professionally with Alfred Adler, the noted Austrian psychiatrist whose approach to psychotherapy was based on the notion that the biological and psychological aspects of the individual form an integral unity. After publishing *Alfred Adler: Der Mensch und seine Lehre* (1926; Alfred Adler: the man and his teaching), S. moved to Berlin, where he taught psychology and edited a professional journal.

An outspoken communist, S. fled to Paris when Hitler came to power. He became disillusioned, however, and broke with the Communist Party in 1937. During the occupation he lived a lonely life in constant fear of the myrmidons of the Vichy regime. Thereafter he began his literary career, later becoming a director of the Paris publishing house Calmann-Lévy. This position paved the way for the publication of his novel trilogy in French translation (1949, 1950, 1953) before it appeared in the German original. In 1976 S. received the Georg Büchner Prize. In his later years he devoted himself primarily to compiling his memoirs and writing philosophical essays, although one additional novel, *Der schwarze Zaun* (1986; the black fence), was published posthumously.

Like other exiles, S. felt the inner need to grapple with the major social and political problems dominating Europe in the 1930s. *Der verbrannte Dornbusch* (1950; *Burned Bramble*, 1951), the first part of the trilogy, reflects the inner turmoil of S.'s own early commitment to Marxism. Experiences of three communist activists serve as a focus for the work. Through their eyes S. presents the communist underground as he himself experienced its activities. The disenchantment of the two younger characters projects the doubts and uncertainties that drove S. from the Party.

From a literary point of view, the work has certain weaknesses. The extensive panorama of characters, scenes, and situations is often disjointed and confusing. The attempt to offer a broad spectrum of relationships and events, interspersed with substantial dialectic, causes the novel to founder under the weight of sheer bulk. The structure is somewhat akin to that used more successfully by Anna SEGHERS in her novels, a technique involving multiple parallel strands of plot.

The failings of *Der verbrannte Dornbusch* are somewhat offset by its documentary value. S. is unquestionably successful in bringing the reader face to face with the realities of prewar European communism. If the novel only helps us understand the painful events of that period and the people who experienced them, it has in that accomplishment alone its raison d'être.

The second book of the trilogy, *Tiefer als der Abgrund* (1961; *The Abyss*, 1952), continues his examination of the communist experience during the 1930s and 1940s. A story of isolation and spiritual annihilation, the work focuses on the personal despair of one of the central figures of the earlier novel. Although the second book is less autobiographical, the internal conflicts, attitudes, and feelings of the main character clearly express S.'s own innermost concerns. Like its predecessor, *Tiefer als der Abgrund* is weakened by its overemphasis on political dialectic. Because it is not able to stand as an independent piece of fiction in its own right, it is the least satisfying part of the trilogy.

From a literary point of view, the third novel, *Die verlorene Bucht* (1955; *Journey without End*, 1954), is the most successful. It possesses a degree of dramatic power not found in the earlier novels, and therefore involves the reader emotionally in the anguish of the European situation. Set in Yugoslavia and Poland during the last part of World War II, the story moves through the violent spectacle of the collapse of Europe. One section, initially published independently in French as *Qu'une larme dans l'ocean* (1952; like a tear in the ocean), is particularly moving in its presentation of the extermination of Polish Jews in Volhynia. The vividness and accuracy of the portrayal is imbued by S.'s deep empathy for the Jewish situation. A definitive edition of the trilogy was published under the collective title *Wie eine Träne im Ozean* (*Like a Tear in the Ocean*, 1987 ff.) in 1961.

Organically connected to the novel trilogy are the three volumes of S.'s autobiography: *Die Wasserträger Gottes* (1974; *God's Water Carriers*, 1987), *Die vergebliche Warnung* (1975; *The Unheeded Warning*, 1991), and *Bis man mir Scherben auf die Augen legt* (1977; *Until My Eyes Are Closed with Shards*, 1994). In approaching once more the personal experiences that inform his novels, S. emphasizes the concept of the dignity of man as the key to human survival. His memoirs of his childhood, youth, and exile combine elements of lament at the passing of an earlier form of Jewish existence, defense of moral necessity, warning against the dilemmas of political activity, to form a powerful, if sometimes tedious, chronicle of an era.

S. has at times been compared to Arthur KOESTLER. Although he neither enjoys Koestler's reputation nor his strength of introspection, he succeeds, like Koestler, in evoking the reader's compassion with his portrayal of a world little understood. For that achievement he merits our gratitude.

FURTHER WORKS: *Zur Analyse der Tyrannis: Das Unglück, begabt zu sein* (1938); *Le talon d'Achille* (1957; *The Achilles Heel*, 1971); *Alfred Adler; oder, Das Elend der Psychologie* (1970; *Masks of Loneliness: Alfred Adler in Perspective*, 1974); *Leben in dieser Zeit* (1972); *Individuum und Gemeinschaft* (1978); *Churban; oder, Die unfaßbare Gewißheit* (1979); *Nur eine Brücke zwischen gestern und morgen* (1980); *Essays zur täglichen Weltgeschichte* (1981); *Gesammelte Werke in Einzelausgaben* (1981 ff.); *Die Wirklichkeit der Literatur des 20. Jahrhunderts; Der Freiheitsgedanke in der europänischen Literatur* (1983); *Ansprachen aus Anlaß der Verleihung des Friedenspreises des deutschen Buchhandels* (1983); *Ein politisches Leben: Gespräch mit L. Reinisch* (1984); *Wolyna* (1984); *Gefährdung der Demokratie* (1984); *Geteilte Einsamkeit: Der Autor und sein Leser* (1985); *Sein letztes Jahr* (1985); *Die Tyrannis und andere Essays aus den Jahren der Verachtung* (1987); *Sokrates* (1988); *Wie mächtig ist die Macht* (1991);

Anpassung und Widerstand (1994). FURTHER WORKS IN ENGLISH: *Man and His Deeds* (1970)

BIBLIOGRAPHY: Sinclair, U., on *Burned Bramble, NYTBR*, 18 March 1951: 1, 20; Barrett, W., on *The Abyss, NYTBR*, 1 June 1952: 4; Hicks, G., on *Journey without End, NYTBR*, 23 May 1954: 5; Koestler, A., *The Trial of the Dinosaur, and Other Essays* (1955): 60–65; Lehrmann, C. C., *The Jewish Element in French Literature* (1971): 263–66; Kraus, W., ed., *Schreiben in dieser Zeit: Für M. S.* (1976); Magris, C., "Ein Versuch aus dem Nirgends: Zu M. S. und seinem Werk," *MAL*, 12, 2 (1979): 44–66; Sternberg, C., *Ein treuer Ketzer* (1991); Corbin-Schuffels, A.-M., *M. S.* (1996)

—LOWELL A. BANGERTER

SPITTELER, Carl

Swiss poet, novelist, and essayist (writing in German), b. 24 April 1845, Liestal; d. 28 Dec. 1924, Lucerne

Although convinced of his poetic calling since the age of seventeen, S. obliged his father, a high state official, by taking a degree in theology. Not willing to be a Protestant minister, he served as a private tutor in Russia (1871–79), a high school teacher in Bern and Neuveville (1879–85), a journalist in Basel (1885–90), and literary editor of the renowned *Neue Zürcher Zeitung* (1890–91) in Zurich. Thereafter, an inheritance from his father-in-law gave him financial independence. In late 1914, at the beginning of World War I, S. became widely controversial when he advocated the position that politically neutral Switzerland should refrain from taking sides intellectually with Germany or France. He was awarded the Nobel Prize for literature in 1919.

Unconcerned with contemporary realism and naturalism, S. chose the mythological epic as his main form for exhibiting the mysteries of the human psyche in a world controlled by inimical fate. He gave psychological interpretations to Greek and Judeo-Christian myths. *Prometheus und Epimetheus* (1881; *Prometheus and Epimetheus*, 1931), S.'s first completed work, contrasts the profound Prometheus, devoted to his soul's ideals, with King Epimetheus, whose conscience knows only conventional dogmas asserted by sick and warring deities. The work's power derives from S.'s idiosyncratic symbolism and his use of iambic prose rhythms. Late in life, he recast the work in rhymed iambic hexameters as *Prometheus der Dulder* (1924; Prometheus the long-suffering), showing Prometheus as an artist painfully struggling to overcome unbound subjectivism.

Der olympische Frühling (4 vols., 1900–1904; rev. ed., 1909; Olympian spring) portrays a whole generation of new gods as they ascend to Olympus, fight for power, and lose it to inexorably destructive fate. Using pliable rhymed iambic hexameters, S. deploys colorful, idyllic, and dramatic scenes on a pessimistic background brightened only by Herakles, who embodies S.'s lifelong trust in the human soul's productive power.

The autobiographical novel *Imago* (1906; imago) probes satirically the friction between the uncompromising writer and Swiss bourgeois society. By splitting the protagonist Viktor's once beloved Theuda into her false married part (Pseuda) and her true self as an ideal inspiration (Imago), S. provides an incisive literary representation of the psychoanalytical concept of the imago. His memoirs, *Meine frühesten Erlebnisse* (1914; my earliest experiences), recall his childhood in striking archetypal images that shaped his mythological visions of psychic realities.

An exponent of important new currents in his time, S. in *Prometheus und Epimetheus* anticipated Nietzsche's *Thus Spake Zarathustra*, while his original conceptions of psychic processes connect him with FREUD and JUNG. Yet his insistence on the obsolete epic genre impairs the fusion of form and content; in this, he resembles the Swiss painter Arnold Böcklin (1827–1901), whose conventional portrayal of mythological figures also obscures his modern statements. Deliberately unorthodox, S. has been unfairly neglected; he deserves recognition not only for his prose but for a final bold attempt to adapt the old epic form to 20th-c. concepts.

FURTHER WORKS: *Extramundana* (1883); *Der Parlamentär* (1889); *Schmetterlinge* (1889); *Friedli der Kolderi* (1891); *Literarische Gleichnisse* (1892); *Gustav* (1892); *Der Ehrgeizige* (1892); *Balladen* (1896); *Der Gotthard* (1897); *Lachende Wahrheiten* (1898; *Laughing Truths*, 1927); *Conrad der Leutnant* (1898); *Glockenlieder* (1906); *Gerold und Hansli, die Mädchenfeinde* (1907; *Two Little Misogynists*, 1922); *Meine Beziehungen zu Nietzsche* (1908); *Rede über Gottfried Keller* (1919); *Das entscheidende Jahr* (1925); *Briefe von Adolf Frey und C. S.* (1933); *Gesammelte Werke* (11 vols., 1945–1958); *Kritische Schriften* (1965). FURTHER WORKS IN ENGLISH: *Selected Poems* (1928)

BIBLIOGRAPHY: Muirhead, J. F., "S. and the New Epic," *Transactions of the Royal Society of Literature of the United Kingdom*, 10 (1931): 35–57; LoCicero, V., "A Reappraisal of S.'s View of Schopenhauer," *GR*, 39 (1964): 37–49; Rommel, O., *S.'s "Olympischer Frühling" und seine epische Form* (1965); Paoli, R., "Die literarische Gestalt C. S.s," *LJGG*, 13 (1972): 307–29; Stauffacher, W., *C. S.* (1973); McHaffie, M., "Prometheus and Viktor: C. S.'s *Imago*," *GL&L*, 31 (1977): 67–77; Burkhard, M., "Blick in die Tiefe: S.s Epos *Prometheus und Epimetheus*," *ABnG*, 9 (1979): 111–30

—MARIANNE BURKHARD

SPOTA, Luis

Mexican novelist, b. 13 July 1925, Mexico City; d. 20 Jan. 1985, Mexico City

The son of an Italian merchant who immigrated to Mexico in the late 19th c. and a Mexican woman of Spanish descent, S. dropped out of school after finishing the sixth grade. In his struggle to support himself he worked as a bullfighter, a waiter, a sailor, a wetback in the fields of Texas, an encyclopedia salesman, an office boy, and a journalist. This broad experience, along with his voracious reading and keen observation of human behavior, enabled him to become Mexico's best-selling novelist as well as a major newspaper and televisions commentator. Although some critics consider him shallow and unworthy of serious literary investigation, his vivid portraits of contemporary Mexican society, including a total of twenty-eight novels, have elicited comparisons with Balzac's oeuvre.

S.'s second novel, *Murieron a mitad del río* (1948; they died in the middle of the river), epitomizes its author's writings in several respects: It dramatizes a well-known sociopolitical issue, in this case the maltreatment of wetbacks; it emphasizes dialogue and action rather than description and character development; and it holds the reader's attention from beginning to end. This novel portrays three young wetbacks, one of whom (José Paván) is probably a fictionalized portrait of the author himself. Although only one of them dies in a physical sense, they all experience a spiritual demise as a result of their encounter with injustice. Another of S.'s best early works is *Más cornadas da el hambre* (1951; *The Wounds of Hunger*, 1957), an exciting tale about bullfighting. Here too the protagonist exhibits characteristics of the author, who describes the triumphs and reverses of a young torero following the bullfighting circuit in provincial towns throughout Mexico. Perhaps S.'s best novel, *Casi el paraíso* (1956; *Almost Paradise*, 1964), is a clever satire of Mexico's greedy, shallow nouveaux riches. Although the characters emerge as sketchily drawn types, their actions and dialogues rivet the reader's attention throughout. Another important aspect of this novel is its structure, which alternates between the protagonist's present and past, enhancing suspense and irony. S.'s diverting exposé of the rampant corruption among Mexico's social climbers, politicians, and police has made this his most widely read work. Whereas *Casi el paraíso* flays Mexico's upper class, *La sangre enemiga* (1959; *The Enemy Blood*, 1961) stands out as a sordid, condemnatory portrayal of the urban poor. Like its predecessor, *La sangre enemiga* experiments with innovative structural techniques, shifting between different time frames and thus requiring greater reader participation. One of the major themes is jealousy and its disastrous ramifications, including deceit, murder, and police brutality. As in many of S.'s works, sex drives much of the action. Condemned is the strong element of *machismo* in Mexican society, that is, the harsh treatment of women by the insensitive, domineering male.

El tiempo de la ira (1960; the time of wrath) is one of many fine portraits of dictators in Latin American literature. Here S. presents a chronological account of César Darío's political career, including his eight-year dictatorial reign. Despite the length of this work (more than 500 pages), the reader's interest never flags, perhaps because of the vivid descriptions of setting and greater attention to character development. *El tiempo de la ira* marks the beginning of S.'s maturity as a writer.

Between 1975 and 1980 S. published a series of six political novels entitled *La costumbre del poder* (the custom of power). Although the setting of these traditionally structured, gripping tales is an unnamed Latin American country, they obviously depict conditions that have existed in Mexico. Critics have generally hailed *Palabras mayores* (1975; important words), the second of the series, as the best.

S. has been accused by critics of neglecting literary art to please the tastes of the unsophisticated reader, and it is true that, with a few notable exceptions, his novels are written in a direct, unadorned, almost journalistic style. He is nevertheless an exceptionally gifted storyteller whose suspenseful plots and forceful attacks on corruption have made him a highly visible and significant figure in contemporary Mexican fiction.

FURTHER WORKS: *José Mojica, hombre, artista, y fraile* (1944); *De la noche al día* (1945); *El coronel fue echado al mar* (1947); *Miguel Alemán en una semblanza* (1947); *Dos obras de teatro* (1949); *La estrella vacía* (1950); *Vagabunda* (1950); *Las grandes aguas* (1953); *Las horas violentas* (1958); *El aria de los sometidos* (1962); *La carcajada del gato* (1964); *La pequeña edad* (1964); *Los sueños del insomnio* (1966); *Lo de antes* (1968); *La plaza*

(1972); *¿Qué pasa con la novela en México?* (1972); *Las cajas* (1973); *El viaje* (1973); *Retrato hablado* (1975); *Sobre la marcha* (1976); *El primer día* (1977); *El rostro del sueño* (1979); *La víspera del trueno* (1980); *Mitad oscura* (1982); *Los días contados* (1983); *Paraíso 25* (1983); *Días de poder* (1985)

BIBLIOGRAPHY: González, M. P., "L. S., gran novelista en potencia," *RHM*, 26 (January-April 1960): 102–6; Selva, M. de la, "Tres novelistas de nuestra América," *CA*, 114, 1 (January-February 1961): 283–95; Ocampo de Gómez, A. M., and E. Prado Velázquez, eds., *Diccionario de escritores mexicanos* (1967): 374–75; Brown, D. F., "*Germinal's* Progeny," *Hispania*, 51, 3 (September 1968): 424–32; Langford, W. M., *The Mexican Novel Comes of Age* (1971): 103–26; Foster, D. W. and V. R. Foster, eds., *Modern Latin American Literature* (1975), Vol. 2: 356–63; Selva, M. de la, "Actualidad de L. S.," *CA*, 204, 1 (January-February 1976): 225–35; Trejo Fuentes, I., "¿Conoce usted a L. S.?: Un acercamiento a su obra," *La Semana de Bellas Artes*, 79 (6 June 1979): 12–14; Sefchovich, S., *Ideología y ficción en la obra de L. S.* (1985); Slick, S., on *Días de poder, WLT*, 60, 2 (Spring 1986): 291–92; García Nuñez, F., "Notas sobre la frontera norte en la novela mexicana," *CA*, 2, 4 (1988): 159–68; Cota-Cárdenas, M., "Visión de la frontera México-Texana, 1959: *Murieron a mitad del río por* L. S.," *ExTL*. 18. 1 (1989–1990): 72–87; Vélez, J. F., *Escritores mexicanos según ellos mismos* (1990): 11–18

—GEORGE R. MCMURRAY

SRANAN TONGO LITERATURE

See Dutch-Caribbean Literature

SRI LANKAN LITERATURE

In Sinhala

Modern Sinhalese literature emerged during the latter half of the 19th c., mainly because of the impact of the new system of education and other changes in the administrative system introduced under British rule to the island formerly known as Ceylon. This new educational system was designed to train local people for employment in the civil service; however, some of these local scholars who had cultivated a taste for English literature spearheaded a movement to create a new literature in Sinhalese. The translation of a large number of Christian books (including the Bible) and popular English works of fiction such as John Bunyan's *Pilgrim's Progress* and Jonathan Swift's *Gulliver's Travels* along with the publication of a series of journals and newspapers in Sinhalese helped to popularize the modern fiction. These factors also encouraged Sinhalese writers to create literary works based on European models.

The initial attempts at writing prose fiction were made by Isaac de Silva (1844-1907) with two stories, "The Fortunate Family" and "The Miserable Family," published in 1864, in which he shows how those who are genuinely faithful to Christianity prosper, while others who are dishonest and unfaithful, are reduced to poverty. In these two stories de Silva criticizes traditional Sinhalese customs and beliefs and promotes new values borrowed from the West.

Decades later Buddhist writers like Piyadasa Sirisena (1875-1946) made use of the same medium of fiction to challenge the activities of Christian missionaries and to attack those who blindly imitated Western culture. Poets and dramatists also joined writers of fiction in expressing religious and patriotic sentiments through their chosen media.

Some of the well-known novelists of the early period, such as Simon de Silva (1874-1920), W. A. Silva (1890-1957), and M. C. F. Perera (1879-1922), produced a large number of romances, thrillers, and detective stories in which religious and patriotic ideas predominate. W. A. Silva, an outstanding writer who dominated the Sinhalese literary scene throughout the first half of the 20th c., helped to create a readership for the novel and the short story despite strong opposition from the Buddhist clergy and others with a conventional outlook. Silva also produced ingenious adaptations of Richard Brinsley Sheridan's *Pizarro*, Rider Haggard's *She,* and Moliere's *Le bourgeois gentilhomme* in addition to his own original narratives.

Sinhalese writers did not begin to create interpretive literature until Martin Wickramasingha (1891-1971) paved the way with his collection of short stories, *Gahaniyak* (A Woman), in 1921. In his introduction to this work, Wickramasingha states clearly that the aim of the serious writer should not be to entertain, but to depict life realistically. He wished to break away from the popular, "run off the mill" type of fiction contemporary writers had been indulging in to please the readers most of whom did not have a proper understanding of good literature. Further, Wickramasingha published the novel, *Gamperaliya* (1942; The Change in Village), which was soon recognized as the first truly realistic Sinhalese novel. With this work he established himself as the leading writer in modern Sinhalese literature.

Ediriweera Sarachchandra (1914-1996), who followed closely behind Wickramasingha, especially in promoting literature and literary criticism as a university subject, pursued his experiments in the field of drama and later won recognition as the pioneer of modern Sinhalese drama. Sarachchandra was the teacher and mentor of most of the young poets, novelists, and critics who received their education at the University of Ceylon and who dominated the literary scene since 1956. He produced masterpieces of poetic drama with *Maname* (1956; Maname) and *Sinhabahu* (1961; Sinhabahu) and the novels, *Malagiya Atto* (1959; The Departed) and *Malavunge Avarudu Da* (1965; The Festival Day of the Departed). Sarachchandra's contributions inspired a new era in Sinhalese literature. The next generation of writers and poets—most of whom claimed Sarachchandra as their guide—were also influenced by the great masters of Russian and European literatures. They experimented with new forms, techniques, and styles. Siri Gunasingha (b. 1925), an academic with postgraduate training in Paris, introduced the STREAM-OF-CONSCIOUSNESS novel with his maiden novel, *Hevanalla* (1961; The Shadow), and spearheaded the free-verse movement in Sinhalese poetry with the anthology entitled *Mas Le Nati Ata* (1956; Bones without Flesh and Blood). This new form of poetry gained popularity, and soon replaced the traditional, stereotyped quatrains with end rhymes.

A new generation of writers, taking renowned Europe and American authors for their models, have drawn their themes and subject matter from a wide range of social, political, economic, and personal issues. Unlike the Sinhalese writers of the early period, these writers are free of religious and nationalistic obsessions and obligations. Their main concern is the improvement of the artistic quality of their work. In the contemporary Sinhalese novel, we often find situations in which educated young men and women are in perpetual conflict with their parents, as they try in vain to reconcile their Western education with a society that is still ruled by tradition.

More recently, Sinhalese writers have been depicting experiences drawn from current economic, political, and cultural developments in the country. A plethora of novels, poems, and plays have appeared during the past two decades on themes such as the new open economy, the two insurrections, and the on-going civil war. The trend for creating literary works on the concept of SOCIALIST REALISM, which was in vogue in the 1970s, has diminished with the disillusionment brought about by the collapse of the former Soviet Union. However, the interest for reading and translating novels from Africa and Latin America seems to be ever increasing.

Another important feature in modern Sinhalese literature is the emergence of women writers. In the early decades of the 20th c. there were no women writers or poets except for a few who expressed romantic sentiments in verse. Since the 1960s, however, a number of talented women have expressed themselves through the media of fiction, poetry, and drama. For example, Eva Ranaweera (dates n.a) in her novels, *Layisa* (1967; Layisa) and *Sedona* (1975; Sedona), depicts the plight of rural women from a feminist point of view. Sumithra Rahubaddha (dates n.a.) has established herself as the leading female novelist with award-winning novels such as *Bumuturunu* (1978; Rugs), *Udanaya* (1979; Joy of Victory), and *Dala Rala Pela* (1981; Strong High Waves). Among other contemporary women writers, Rupa Kodituvakku (dates n.a.), Anula Wijeratna Menike (dates n.a.), and Soma Jayakody (dates. n.a.) have treated similar issues and polemic subjects such as child abuse and the involvement of politicians in drug trafficking and crime.

Romantic, realistic, surrealistic, neorealistic, socialist, and psychoanalytic traditions have influenced modern Sinhalese literature in different ways. With access to high-tech printing methods, the increased availability of state and private funds for publishing, and the reintroduction of literature as a school subject, modern Sinhalese writers are encouraged to produce literary works at a scale unsurpassed at any time in the past.

BIBLIOGRAPHY: Sarachchandra, E. R., *The Sinhalese Novel* (1950); Wickramasuriya, S., *Sinhala Navakatavata Magapedima*, (1970); Rajakaruna, A., *Sinhala Navakatave Arambhaya* (1972); Ranjini Obeysekera and Chitra Fernando, eds., *Anthology of Modern Writing from Sri Lanka* (1981); *An Anthology of Sinhalese Literature of the Twentieth Century*, selected by the UNESCO National Commission of Sri Lanka (1987); Meddegama, U. P., "The Political Novel in Sinhalese," *SLJH*, 16, 1-2 (1990): 67-86

—U. P. MEDDEGAMA

In Tamil

Tamil literature in Sri Lanka, which has always been rooted in the Sri Lankan social, cultural, and political contexts, includes poetry, fiction, drama, criticism, and miscellaneous works.

The universities had a definite role in shaping Sri Lankan Tamil literature. Swami Vipulananda (1892-1957), K. Kanapathipillai, S. Chelvanayagam, S. Vithiananthan, A. Sathasivam, S. Thananjyarajaingham, A. Velupillai, K. Kailasapathi, K. Sivathamby, P. Poologasingham, and A. Shanmugadas (dates n.a.), among others, were influential in developing generations of Tamil writers. Major critical studies of Tamil literature include Sillayoor Selvarasan's *Eelathil Thamil Naaval Valarchi* (1967; Growth of the Tamil Novel in Sri Lanka); K. S. Sivakumaran's *Tamil Writing in Sri Lanka* (1974); N. Subramaniya Iyer's *Eelathu Thamil Naaval Ilakkiyam* (1978; Sri Lankan Tamil Novel), which discusses in brief nearly 450 Sri Lankan Tamil novels written between 1885 and 1977; and M. A. Nuhman, S. Mownaguru, and M. Chitraleka's *Irupatham Noottandu Eelaththu Thamil Ilkkiyam* (1979; Twentieth-Century Sri Lankan Tamil Literature).

Of the trends in Tamil literature K. Kailasapathy writes: "Both in Sri Lanka and South India postindependence problems created the conditions for the emergence of a brand of writers who came from the traditionally oppressed section of Tamil society, that is the lower castes. Many of them were attracted to Marxism and communist organizations that provided them with a worldview and also the confidence to struggle against exploitation and articulate their thoughts and feelings firmly. . . . As might be expected, their level of literary education was somewhat low. But they ushered in new experiences and visions into fiction, poetry, and drama using hitherto unheard of dialects, idioms, and expressions." Thus, Sri Lankan Tamil literature of the 1960s and 1970s mainly reflected the political and social conditions that were prevalent. The Progressive Writers Association functioned as a center for writers and artists, even if they did not subscribe to its Marxist or socialist ideologies.

The period between 1965 and 1970 saw the weakening of progressive forces, and the emergence of two important writers, S. Ponnuthurai and M. Thalayasingam (dates n.a.). The former is a talented craftsman and a stylist in language, known primarily for his short stories. Thalayasingam was an innovative thinker, a critic, and a remarkable creative writer, who attempted to transcend the narrow confines of Marxism with the assimilation of integrated yoga as professed in the Sarvodaya philosophy of Aurobindo. Among other notable writers are the poets Mahakavi (pseud. of T. Rudramoorthy), R. Murugaiyan, and Neelavanan (dates n.a.).

The generation of writers emerging in the 1980s and the early 1990s, in the wake of the internecine warfare among the Sri Lankans, include poets such as Cheran, V. I. S. Jeyapalan, Shanmugam Sivalingan, S. Sivasegeram, and Vilvaratnam; short-story writers such as Saddanatahn, A. Santhan, M. Kanagarajan, and Kohila Mahendran, as well as Uma Varatharajan, Ranja Kumar, and Thirukovil Kaviyugan; and novelists such as Selliah Ganeshalingan, K. Daniel, Chengai Aaaliyan, Deniyan, Arul Subramaniam, S. Yoganathan, and Bala Manoharan (dates n.a.).

BIBLIOGRAPHY: Selvarajan, S., "A Note on the Tamil Novel in Ceylon," *Community*, 5 (1963): 155-62; Vithiananthan, S., "Trends in Ceylon Tamil Writing," *Community*, 6 (1963): 155-62; Sivathamby, K., "Ceylonese Tamil Writing," *LAAW*, 24-25 (1975): 134-37; Halpé, A., and K. N. O. Dharmadasa, "Literature and the Arts," in de Silva, K. M., *Sri Lanka: A Survey* (1977): 434-65; Sivakumaran, K. S., *Major Trends in Contemporary Writing in Tamil in Sri Lanka* (1991)

—K. S. SIVAKUMARAN

In English

The English language was formally introduced to Sri Lanka after the Colebrooke-Cameron Constitutional Reforms of 1832 in order to create a local elite who would function as middle-level administrators. While the standard of English deteriorated with the increasing nationalism after independence in 1948 and the Sinhala Only Bill of 1958, recent governments, realizing the importance of English, have made strenuous efforts to reverse this trend.

Since the objective in introducing English was primarily functional, the literary work produced initially was meager and inferior so much so that *The Village in the Jungle* (1913) by Leonard Woolf (1880-1969), a British civil servant, was until recently considered the best Sri Lankan novel for its style, realism, and sympathetic portrayal of peasant life. Contemporary critics have established, however, that the novel is affected by colonialist thinking. During the first thirty years of the 20th c. a coterie of Ceylonese, notably Lucian de Zilwa and S. J. K. Crowther (dates n.a.), among others, who felt sufficiently confident about using English for creative work, produced romantic novels and lighthearted satires in a stilted (though very correct) form of English that were vitiated by an Orientalist attitude towards "the native."

The first major, modern novelists began their careers at a time when Sri Lankan creative writing in English was either ignored by the general public or condemned by academics for not meeting Western standards of excellence. Punyakante Wijenaike (b. 1933), who portrays the perils of village life in *The Waiting Earth* (1966) and the degeneration of feudal families in *Giraya* (1971), is prone to sentimentality and sensationalism. Even her award-winning novel, *Amulet* (1994), displays some angularities. Yet the versatility with which she explores themes such as child abuse, incest, marital rape, and madness neutralizes these shortcomings. James Goonewardena's (1921-1997) early novels, *A Quiet Place* (1968) and *The Call of the Kirala* (1971), are flawed by "pastoral longings," but later efforts including *One Mad Bid for Freedom* (1990) and *The Tribal Hangover* (1995) employ modernist techniques to explore issues of identity and the pressures faced by those Sri Lankans whose idealism is tested by chauvinism and cynicism. While Raja Proctor (1921-1991) explores social injustice in relation to the 1971 insurgency from the peasant's point of view in *Waiting for Surabiel* (1981), Ediriweera Sarachchandra (1914-1996) in *Curfew and a Full Moon* (1983) scrutinizes the insurgency from the perspective of a professor who is ambivalent towards a movement that he can neither identify with, nor ignore. Sarachchandra's other novels, *With the Begging Bowl* (1980) and *Foam upon the Stream* (1987), are romantic in conception. P. B. Rambukwelle's (dates n.a.) *The Desert Makers* (1985) is an experimental novel that describes the destruction of villages by an exploitative urban society. Combining fact and fiction, employing salacious humor, and celebrating the zest for living that he feels is consonant with Burghers, Carl Muller's (b. 1935) Von Bloss trilogy and *Colombo* (1995) have added a new dimension to Sri Lankan fiction. Rajiva Wijesinha's (b. 1954) novels largely focus on the social transition of recent years, but *An English Education* (1996) deals concurrently with political change, the evolution of the university system, the dissemination of English, and a complex of other issues.

The Sri Lankan migrant novel emerged with Michael ONDAATJE's *Running in the Family* (1982), a semiautobiographical work that captures the quirks and the living habits of Burghers in the 1950s and 1960s. Yasmine Gooneratne's (b. 1935) *A Change of Skies* (1992), while foregrounding the reasons for emigration and resultant tensions also demonstrates how immigrants can forge a meaningful identity for themselves through sensible compromise. *The Pleasures of Conquest* (1995) presents with satire the manner in which Amnesia—presumably meant to be Sri Lanka—has been

subjected to exploitation of various kinds from colonial times to the present. Romesh Gunesekera's (b. 1954) *Reef* (1994) contrasts the natural beauty of the island with the increasing tensions of the 1970s and 1980s, which only immigration can relieve. Shyam Selvadurai's (b. 1965) *Funny Boy* (1994) explores the problems that beset those who are doubly marginalized because of their race and sexual orientation. From a subaltern perspective, Sivanandan's (dates n.a.) *When Memory Dies* (1997) captures the serendipity and the peaceful coexistence among communities that prevailed despite colonial rule in the first half of the 20th c., while indicting successive Sri Lankan governments since independence for pursuing policies that have destroyed values, polarized communities, and brought about anarchy.

Sri Lankan literature in English was best known for its poetry until it was outstripped by fiction. The poetry ranged from the lyrical to the ironic, the romantic to the realist, and the formal to the experimental. George Keyt (1901-1993), better known for his paintings, is one of the country's first modern poets. Walter S. Senior (dates n.a.), a missionary attached to Trinity College, Kandy, wrote a few volumes of poetry that were Tennysonian in mood and style. The so-called "Kandy Lake Poets" produced work that was occasionally memorable but on the whole enervated by the worst tendencies of 19th-c. English verse. Poetry became more critical and self-reflexive in the 1940s and 1950s, perhaps influenced by E. F. C. Ludowyk's introduction of New Critical practices into the college's English Department. Patrick Fernando (1931-1982), a Roman Catholic steeped in the classics, wrote carefully crafted, ironic poetry in *The Return of Ulysses* (1955). Yasmine Gooneratne, a prolific poet until she turned to fiction, is Augustan in mood and in her attention to form. Although the satire in *Word Bird Motif* (1971) and *The Lizard's Cry* (1972) is devastating at times, she also shows considerable compassion and sensitivity in some of the poems that depict the 1971 insurgency. Her collection entitled *6000 Foot Death Dive* (1981) focuses on the experience of exile.

The cross-cultural impact on poetry has been aesthetically rewarding. Anne Ranasinghe (b. 1925), a German Jew who was educated in England and now resides in Sri Lanka, draws on her cosmopolitan background to generate poems on such themes as the holocaust, the insurgency, the exilic experience, and aging in collections such as *At What Dark Point* (1991) and *You Ask Me Why I Write Poems* (1994). Jean Arasanayagam (b. 1940), a Dutch Burgher who married a Hindu Tamil, uses "hybridity" to her advantage. The problems of finding acceptance in a different community, her Dutch heritage, and her reaction to Sri Lankan landscape and culture, however, have been partially supplanted by other themes after her experiences in a refugee camp during the riots of 1983, and her horror at the continuing violence in the country. Nonetheless, her collection, *Shooting the Floricans* (1994), suggests that the intensity that characterized her early work has been replaced by a sense of equanimity. Lakdasa Wikkramasinha's (1941-1978) five volumes of poetry include vitriolic pieces against colonizers, which though brilliant at times, are occasionally impaired by faulty construction. Those poems that deal with feudal society and the plight of the underprivileged are less potent but equally compelling. Ashley Halpé (b. 1933), Peter Scharen (dates n.a.), Basil Fernando (b. 1944), Kamala Wijeratne (b. 1939), and Gamini Seneviratne (b. 1938) are other important Sri Lankan poets.

Sri Lanka has not produced many playwrights, although it had a vibrant English theater in the 1950s and 1960s. Many original efforts were mildly critical of human foibles and provided light entertainment, but their humor often reveals elements of class snobbery. Gamini Gunawardena's (b. 1930) *Rama and Sita* (1964), a reworking of the *Ramayana* as poetic drama, was too ponderous to succeed in the theater. Ernest MacIntyre (b. 1935), who now resides in Australia, is Sri Lanka's best-known playwright in English. While *The Loneliness of the Short-Distance Traveller* (1971), influenced by the absurdist theatre, deals with issues like alienation and rootlessness, *Let's Give Them Curry* (1985) dramatizes the stresses and strains faced by Sri Lankan immigrants in Australia. *Rasanayagam's Last Riot* (1993) examines the tensions undergone by a Sinhala/Tamil couple against the background of a race riot. Regi Siriwardena's (dates n.a.) two collections of plays, *The Almsgiving and Other Plays* (1994) and *Octet* (1995), are primarily comedies with more dialogue than action where the influence of the realist dramatists is patent.

Literary journals such as *Navasilu* (1976), *Channels* (1989), and the *New Lankan Review* (1983), like their predecessors *Community* (1954-58, 1962-63), *Poetry Peradeniya* (1957-63), and *New Ceylon Writing* (1970-76), continue to provide a forum for creative and critical writing assisted by the *Sri Lanka Journal of the Humanities* (1970) and *Nethra* (1996), which accommodate literary criticism and reviews.

BIBLIOGRAPHY: Halpé, A., "Creative Writing in English," in de Silva, K. M., *Sri Lanka: A Survey* (1977): 446-54; Gooneratne, Y., "The English Poetry in Sri Lanka," *Diverse Inheritance: A Personal Perspective on Commonwealth Literature* (1980): 160-73; Goonetilleke, D. C. R. A., "Sri Lankan Poetry in English: Getting Beyond the Colonial Heritage," in Rutherford, A. ed., *From Commonwealth to Postcolonial* (1992): 333-43; Jayasuriya, W., *Sri Lanka's Modern English Literature: A Case Study in Literary Theory* (1994); Wijesinha, R., "Forms of Alienation: Sri Lankan Fiction in English," *Navasilu*, 11, 12 (1994): 102-13; Kandiah, T., "Inadequate Responses and the Attenuation of Creativity: Sri Lankan English Fiction of the Insurgency of 1971," in Thumboo, E., and T. Kandiah, eds., *The Writer as Historical Witness: Studies in Commonwealth Literature* (1995): 393-408; Gunawardena, S., *This Total Art: Perceptions of Sri Lankan Theatre* (1995)

—S. W. PERERA

STĂNESCU, Nichita

Romanian poet, b. 31 March 1933, Ploeşti; d. 13 Dec. 1983, Bucharest

Of mixed aristocratic Russian (through his mother) and middle-class Romanian descent, S. went to grammar school and then to the best secondary school in his native city. He was graduated from the University of Bucharest in 1957. A winner of the International Herder Prize (Vienna, 1975) and one of the finalists among the Nobel Prize nominees for 1979, S., whose poems have been translated into many languages, first became known to the English-speaking world through his impressive reading at the Poetry International Festival in London in 1971.

S.'s first volume, *Sensul iubirii* (1960; the meaning of love) was seen by liberal Romanian intellectuals as a timid but undeniable sign of spring in the midst of a period of ideological freeze and overall cultural re-Stalinization (1958–62). S. came into his own as

poet with his second book, *O viziune a sentimentelor* (1964; a vision of sentiments), and his poetic personality defined itself during the following years of partial liberalization (1964–71), when some of his most characteristic collections were published: *Unsprezece elegii* (1966; eleven elegies), *Oul şi sfera* (1967; the egg and the sphere), *Laus Ptolemaei* (1968; Latin: a eulogy of Ptolemy), *In dulcele stil clasic* (1970; in the sweet classic style). The more recent changes of the intellectual climate in his country (the regime's repeated attempts to launch a "cultural revolution"), have left him untouched, protected as he has been by his growing international reputation. *Epica magna* (1978; partial tr., *Unfinished Work*, 1979) is one of his finest and freest works.

S.'s poetry, which has been sometimes compared with Dylan THOMAS's, is both powerful and elusive, delicately concrete and cruelly abstract, protean and dogmatic, enigmatically joyous and passionately austere. In its complex and fascinatingly contradictory totality, it can be best described as an effort to rethink poetically the nature and sources of poetry in our postmodern age. Its recurrent themes and obsessions are typical of the postmodernist imagination: language and antilanguage—one of his volumes bears the significant title *Necuvintele* (1969; the unwords); diffusion and derealization of the self; an inescapable sense of indeterminacy; apocalyptic playfulness. But what makes S.'s poetry distinctive (essentially untranslatable yet powerfully attractive even in literal translation) is the extraordinary verbal gift of the poet, his precise use of ambiguity, his intuition of the secret metaphoric potential of common words and phrases, his ability to disrupt ordinary language in an inspired, seductively visionary, fashion.

FURTHER WORKS: *Dreptul la timp* (1965); *Alfa* (1967); *Roşu vertical* (1967); *Un pămînt numit România* (1969); *Cinci degete* (1969); *Poezii* (1970); *Cartea de recitire* (1972); *Măreţia frigului* (1972); *O literă în oglindă* (1972); *Belgradul în cinci prieteni* (1972); *Clar de inimă* (1973); *Starea poeziei* (1975); *Operele imperfecte* (1979). FURTHER WORKS IN ENGLISH: *The Still Unborn about the Dead* (1974)

BIBLIOGRAPHY: Popescu, P., Introduction to N. S., *The Still Unborn about the Dead* (1974): 7–12

—MATEI CALINESCU

STANGERUP, Henrik

Danish novelist, screenwriter, and critic, b. 1 Sept. 1937, Frederiksberg/Copenhagen

After four years' study of theology at the University of Copenhagen, S. began in 1960 a career as a journalist and a literature and film critic with various Copenhagen newspapers. As a reporter he has traveled extensively throughout Europe, in particular in France, where he studied film in 1964, and he feels strongly affiliated with pan-European sentiments and movements as well as the new French, anti-Marxist philosophers, such as Bernard-Henri Lévy (b. 1948). Journeys to Brazil in the 1970s have provided S. with new inspiration for a juxtaposition of exotic zest for life and European tepidity and sober-mindedness.

S.'s first and only short-story collection, *Grønt og sort* (1961; green and black), is written in the neorealistic style that dominated

Danish literature in the early 1960s. The focus is primarily on problems caused by the modern welfare state among young people from the upper class. Under their polished surface S. discovers glimpses of madness and ferocity that forcefully break through in the characters of his later writings.

The transition to the following self-centered novels took place with the humorous and selfironic stories and reportage in the travelogue *Veritabel pariser* (1966; a veritable Parisian) based on S.'s previous experiences in France. Autobiographical elements also dominate the novels Slangen i brystet (1969; the snake in the breast). S.'s breakthrough work, and *Løgn over Løgn* (1971; lie upon lie). The first novel is a penetrating psychological study of paranoia and existential insecurity. The protagonist is a middle-aged Danish correspondent stationed in Paris and fighting against the envy and criticism of his colleagues and against destructive forces in his environment and, in particular, in himself. The vague attempts at rebellion, which are also those of S. himself, erupt in his second novel. The previous satirical tone becomes more extrovert in a violent attack on the "politically correct" Danish cultural elite and their exploitation of other human beings.

With *Manden der ville være skyldig* (1973; *The Man Who Wanted To Be Guilty*, 1981), a major European success, S. combines the genre of the political novel in the tradition of Aldous HUXLEY and George ORWELL with science fiction. He departs from his former subjectivity and widens the scope of his polemic, focusing it on the social and political development, the final goal of which is the authoritarian state. His antidogmatic attitude, advocating the freedom and rights of the individual, is more directly voiced—also against reactionary conservatism—in several collections of essays and articles throughout the 1970s.

The final step into pure confession, related to S.'s first two novels, is taken with *Fjenden i forkøbet* (1978; anticipating the enemy). However, in contrast to these works, the depression and collapse lead to a state of clarification—the work is an exercise both in self-accusation and in self-defense. S. finds himself both as an artist and as a human being inspired by his experiences in Brazil. *Fjenden i forkøbet* concludes with a hymn to this newly discovered sensuous and colorful reality, which is juxtaposed to the one-dimensional Danish everyday grayishness.

This daily routine is brought up for discussion from a theological point of view in S.'s first feature film, *Giv Gud en chance om søndagen* (1970; give God a chance on Sunday), and from an erotic perspective in his next film, *Farlige kys* (1972; dangerous kisses), in which S. analyzes the attitude of his own generation toward love and sexuality. Later in his career as a film director S., together with the Brazilian writer Fausto Wolff (dates n.a.), reworked an 18th-c. comedy by the Danish dramatist Ludvig Holberg (1684–1754), *Erasmus Montanus*, into an imaginative movie influenced by the commedia dell'arte about a Brazilian student who returns from Portugal in the mid-17th c. The script was published in 1976, entitled *Jorden er flad* (the earth is flat); the film itself was a fiasco in Denmark and a success in France.

Brazil is also the setting for *Vejen til Lagoa Santa* (1981; *The Road to Lagoa Santa*, 1984), which marks a new development in S.'s writing, taking it to an absolute zenith and opening it up to an international audience. The volume is the first in a series of three documentary novels, in fact a trilogy, based on painstaking research of source material and structured on the three stages in Søren Kierkegaard's philosophy. They have in common three Danes whose destiny is defined through their wrestling with foreign environments, three historical figures who in S.'s universe become

three spiritual types given mythic dimensions. For *Det er svært at dø i Dieppe* (1985: The Seducer: *It Is Hard To Die in Dieppe*, 1990) S. has chosen an opposite character, the prolific 19th c. man of letters P. L. Møller, an aesthetic character in a Kierkegaardian sense, attempting to live in the moment but perpetually dissatisfied and, like the protagonists of S.'s earlier novels, in a permanent state of catastrophe. With *Broder Jacob* (1991; *Brother Jacob*, 1993) S. has reached the highest Kierkegaardian category, the religious stage. Jacob, the brother of the Danish Renaissance king Christian II, becomes a representative of the Catholic Church, not only its faith but also its spiritualism and cosmopolitan outlook that he could not find in Denmark. With a superbly developed stylistic beauty and narrative skill S. has returned to his initial cultural criticism of Danish mentality, against its rationalism, pettiness, and puritan sense of guilt.

Here, as well as in his entire oeuvre, S. centers on the relationship between the individual and his confining, hypocritical, and, in the final account, destructive environment. Whereas S. originally was unable to point to a way to escape from chaos and catastrophe, his last novel suggests a metaphysical solution represented by Catholicism, which has succeeded in incorporating the physical world, art, and longing in a universal utopia.

FURTHER WORKS: *Lille Håbs rejse* (1958); *Kunsten at være ulykkelig* (1974); *Mens tid var* (1978); *Retten til ikke at høre til* (1979); *Fangelejrens frie halvdel* (1980); *Samba* (1982)

BIBLIOGRAPHY: Monty, I., "An Unsentimental Dane," *Danish Journal*, 72 (1972): 14–19; Lasky, M. J., "In the Shadow of Northern Lights. A Conversation with the Danish Novelist, H. S.," *Encounter*, 63, 2 (1984): 97–123

—SVEN HAKON ROSSEL

STEAD, Christina

Australian novelist, b. 17 July 1902, Sydney; d. 31 March 1983, Sydney

After training at Sydney Teachers' College and working as both a teacher and a psychological tester, S. went to business school and then worked as a secretary to save the money she needed to leave Australia for Europe. In 1928 she sailed to England. She found work as a secretary with a firm of grain merchants, where she met the manager, William Blake, an American Marxist economist, with whom she remained until his death in 1968. During the 1930s and 1940s she lived in Paris, New York, and all around Europe; she settled in England in 1953. In 1974 she returned to Australia.

S. was a writer of startling and paradoxical originality. Her brilliant extravagance of language and form has at its core a ruthlessly unsentimental vision that penetrates the surface of human relationships to unmask the often violent interplay beneath. In their central interest in character, their social scope, and their texture of imagery, her novels belong to the 19th c.; but in their integration of the insights of Marx and FREUD and their stylistic innovation, they are clearly of the 20th.

S.'s fiction is made out of her understanding of the interconnections of private personality and the political-social structure. In her autobiographical novel *The Man Who Loved Children* (1940), considered her masterpiece, she shows us the family as the crucible and microcosm of the social world, and similarly ruled by power politics. The novel takes as its hero no one individual but the entire family, realized as a dynamic organism with a collective self-image and way of functioning. This family feeds on its children more than it nurtures them; the father particularly makes the children he "loves" figures in his own self-aggrandizing drama.

The members of this family are typical S. characters. Jules Bertillon in *House of All Nations* (1938), a satiric tour de force exposing the corrupt world of international banking, like Sam Pollit in *The Man Who Loved Children*, is a "charmer who deceives." S. is fascinated by obsessive characters who bewitch others with their talk. Nellie Cotter Cook, the working-class English journalist in *Dark Places of the Heart* (1966; Br., *Cotter's England*), preaches socialism and feminine sympathy while she preys on her listening victims to satisfy her own needs.

Emerging from the violent intimacies of the family, which S. portrays in its enormous and complex vitality, is another of her recurring characters, the independent woman. Each early heroine struggles with her image as a passive Sleeping Beauty, drowned in melancholy self-absorption, sensual primarily in her fantasy life. In her heroic odyssey from Australia to England, and toward adulthood, Teresa Hawkins in the autobiographical *For Love Alone* (1944) has the heroic strength of will to accept the isolation of breaking free from the conventional demands of family and society to follow her own determined vision of love and work. In S.'s late work, however, the stoicism she prized in her heroic women becomes just one more strategem in the general human endeavor to take as much while giving as little as possible. In her late tales, old women manipulatively wring from others the love they fail to find in families they fail to form. S.'s narratives became increasingly ironic. In *The Man Who Loved Children* and *For Love Alone* she achieves a balance of involvement and ironic detachment. In her later work her narrator assumes a more dispassionate distance, from which she observes the idiosyncratic details of the human comedy.

While the emphasis shifts, fantasy always mingles with realism. S.'s earliest stories, *The Salzburg Tales* (1934), are frequently overtly gothic, as are some of her last. But an acute sense of natural and social milieu balances her relentless introspection and fertile imaginative fantasy. S.'s writing is persistently particular, full of specific, detailed observations, and also of abundant digressions and repetitions. Hers is a style of excess: exuberant, rich, sometimes uncontrolled.

Although she sympathized with the oppressed, S. always directed her final caveat against the tyrannies of egotism. Her vision is dark, but not despairing. She had a zest for observation; her range of interests was as wide as her travels. Her novels treat poor working-class characters in Australia and England, rich businessmen in Paris and New York, American journalists, European expatriates, and bourgeois families. With the respect for individual integrity her characters rarely show to each other, S. accepted a great variety of human idiosyncracy.

After the peak achievement of her two autobiographical novels of the 1940s her writing diminished in power; for nearly fourteen years she ceased publishing. With the reissue of *The Man Who Loved Children* in 1965, S., in her sixties, resumed what seemed almost a second career. Few novels, as Susan SONTAG has observed, match the enduring eminence of *The Man Who Loved Children*.

FURTHER WORKS: *Seven Poor Men of Sydney* (1934); *The Beauties and Furies* (1936); *Letty Fox: Her Luck* (1946); *A Little Tea, a Little Chat* (1948); *The People with the Dogs* (1952); *The Puzzleheaded Girl: Four Novellas* (1967); *The Little Hotel* (1975); *Miss Herbert (The Suburban Wife)* (1976); *A C. S. Reader* (1978)

BIBLIOGRAPHY: Geering, R., *C. S.* (1969); Burns, G., "The Moral Design of *The Man Who Loved Children*," *CR*, 14 (1971): 36–61; Boyers, R., "The Family Novel," *Salmagundi*, 26 (1974): 3–25; Sturm, T., "C. S.'s New Realism," in Anderson, D., and Knight, S., eds., *Cunning Exiles* (1974): 9–35; Ricks, C., "Fathers and Children," *NYRB*, (26 June 1975): 13–15; special S. issue, *Southerly*, 38, 4 (1978); Lidoff, J., *C. S.* (1982)

—JOAN LIDOFF

STEFANYK, Vasyl

Ukrainian short-story writer and essayist, b. 14 May 1871, Rusiv (then in Austro-Hungarian Empire); d. 7 Dec. 1936, Rusiv (then in Poland; now in Ukraine)

Born into a family of wealthy landowners living in the part of the Ukraine known as Pokuttya (then under Austro-Hungarian control), S. had a hard childhood and a difficult life. Conflict with his tyrannical father, the scorn and derision he suffered from Polish students and teachers that eventually forced him to leave the high school at Kolomyya (in 1889), the sudden deaths of family members and friends, a frustrating love affair, his arrest in 1895 by Austrian authorities for his political activities, and frail health contributed to the minor key in which most of his stories are written. Very few of his works, however, are autobiographical.

During the years 1892–1900, while studying medicine in Cracow at the insistence of his father, S. met a number of leading Polish writers and intellectuals in whose company he acquired a degree of artistic sophistication and an appreciation for Western literature. His earliest Ukrainian mentor was the satirist Les Martovych (1871–1916), and later he developed a friendship with Ivan FRANKO. S. lived in the village of Stetsiv from 1904 to 1909, and from 1909 until his death in Rusiv. After the Communist victory in the Civil War following the Russian revolution, S. established friendly contacts with several Soviet writers and intellectuals, and in 1927 the Soviet government allotted him a pension, which he continued to receive until 1932, when he broke off all relations with the Soviet Ukraine.

S.'s unusual literary career can be divided into two major periods. The first extends from 1890, when he began to write short articles and reports while still in high school, to 1905, the date of the appearance of his fourth collection of stories. The years 1905–16 were a period chiefly of political activism. He resumed writing in 1916, and in this second period, lasting until his death, he published some twenty works, including his fifth story collection, *Zemlya* (1926; the earth).

S.'s stories, written for the most part in local dialect, sometimes only a page in length, are stylistic masterpieces and gems of literary economy—succinct in expression and highly dramatic in structure. These miniatures offer profound insight into the soul of the Ukrainian peasant of the Pokuttya region and a vividly realistic depiction of peasant life in all its misery and tragedy. Good examples of S.'s early work are the stories "Pobozhna" (1899; "The Pious Woman," 1973), a concise analysis of a senseless marital conflict; and "Novyna" (1899; "The News," 1973), a sketch of a peasant bent on drowning his children because he is unable to feed them.

S.'s stories of the second period are generally more mature and moving in their laconic expression than those of the first, although the subjects and themes remain the same. Perhaps the best example is "Syny" (1922; "The Sons," 1971), the story of an old man who, having lost his two sons in the war, tries to share the burden of his grief with the Mother of God.

Although regarded by some critics as merely a "bard of the Ukrainian village," S. is a consummate artist whose highly polished prose has no equal. He was able to focus on man's most basic anguish and to express it, bare and unembellished, with a few bold strokes.

FURTHER WORKS: *Synya knyzhechka* (1899); *Kaminny khrest: Studiyi i obrazky* (1900); *Moye slovo* (1905); *Opovidannya* (1919); *Klenovi lystky* (1924); *Leseva familya ta inshi opovidannya* (1926); *Vybrani tvory* (1927); *Tvory* (1927); *Vybrani tvory* (1928); *Vistuny; Osin; Novyna* (1928); *Paly; May* (1928); *Pobozhna* (1931); *Publitsystyka* (1953); *Povne zibrannya tvoriv* (3 vols., 1954); *Katrusya: Vybrani tvory* (1965); *Tvory* (1972). FURTHER WORKS IN ENGLISH: *Articles and Selections* (1971); *The Stone Cross* (1971); *Maple Leaves and Other Stories* (1988)

BIBLIOGRAPHY: Manning, C. A., *Ukrainian Literature: Studies of the Leading Authors* (1944): 103–11; Andrusyshen, C. H., Introduction to V. S., *The Stone Cross* (1971): 4–19; Struk, D. S., *A Study of V. S.* (1973); Mihailovich, V. D., et al., eds., *Modern Slavic Literatures* (1976), Vol. 2: 509-13

—LEONID RUDNYTZKY

STEGNER, Wallace

American novelist, short-story writer, and essayist, b. 18 Feb. 1909, Lake Mills, Iowa; d. 13 Apr. 1993, Santa Fe, New Mexico

S. was born in Lake Mills, Iowa, the second and youngest son of George and Hilda Paulson Stegner. Following his father's search for wealth and success, the family moved repeatedly. During his first five years, they lived in Iowa, North Dakota, and Washington State. For six years they lived in East End, a small remote village on the plains of southern Saskatchewan. They moved to Great Falls, Montana and later to Salt Lake City, Utah. Even in this final location, the family was rootless, moving ten times in ten years. S. endured a tense, tempestuous, and complicated relationship with his restless father, who was driven by a code of behavior drawn from the Western idealism of the 19th c. S.'s father sought constantly to achieve the "American Dream" for himself and his family in a variety of risky ventures, some legal some illegal. His mother provided a sense of stability and humanity, recognizing early a sensitivity, an artistic and intellectual capacity in S. that was perhaps unsuited to frontier living.

After entering the University of Utah, S. was "discovered" by the professor of his freshman writing class, the novelist Vardis

Fisher (1895-1968), who encouraged him to develop his writing talents. While an undergraduate, S. wrote stories and essays for writing courses and did some reporting for the *Salt Lake Tribune*. He began writing seriously while a graduate student at the University of Iowa, under the guidance and encouragement of Norman Foerster. He completed his master's thesis (consisting of several short stories) in 1932. After studying at the University of California, Berkeley, he returned to Iowa to receive his Ph.D. in literary studies in 1935. As a graduate student, S. began his long and distinguished teaching career. He taught at Augustana College in Rock Island, Illinois, the University of Utah, and the University of Wisconsin. He achieved national attention as a writer with *Remembering Laughter* (1937) and in 1939 he joined the staff of the Bread Loaf Writers' Conference, where he became friends with Bernard DeVoto (1897-1955) and Robert FROST. He taught at Harvard until 1944, and he directed the writing program at Stanford University from 1945 until 1971. He continued writing until his death in 1993.

Remembering Laughter concerns the troubled relationship of two adult sisters. The novel introduces the related themes of family and community in S.'s characteristically lean, spare, and dramatic prose. *On a Darkling Plain* (1940) explores the life of a wounded World War I veteran, Edwin Vickers, who retreats to the plains of Saskatchewan to live a secluded life only to find that the flu epidemic of 1918 forces him into contact with others, redeeming and humanizing him at the cost of his own life. *The Big Rock Candy Mountain* (1943) established S. as an important American writer. This sweeping modern epic is self-consciously autobiographical, drawing heavily from the author's own family and their experiences as transient Westerners in the early 20th c. The novel recounts the experiences of the Mason family: Bo, Elsa, and their sons Chester and Bruce, as they follow Bo's desperate dream of riches and success. The story is told from the point of view of each character, a remarkable strategy that allows S. to plumb the depths of his own experience while at the same time making it representative of 20th-c. American life. Like many novels of its time, *The Big Rock Candy Mountain* portrays the failure of the American Dream but culminates as the lone survivor, Bruce (S.'s fictional self), finds meaning by recognizing the dark, shaping influences of family and community. These themes continue in many novels, including the Pulitzer Prize-winning *Angle of Repose* (1971). Here S. displays an almost Hawthornian sense of the influence of history and heritage. A retired history professor, Lyman Ward, struggles to sort out the complexities of his own family relationships by editing the papers of his grandmother, Susan Burling Ward, who was a successful illustrator and writer. S. attempts to explore what he sees as the hidden often mysterious continuities between a family's past and present and the manner in which history shapes individual lives.

In all of his fictional works S. places an emphasis on the development of character within the context of time and place. His works are notable and distinctive because they retain the possibility of redemption, finding meaning and order in the seeming chaos of 20th-c. American life. Although S. was a prolific writer of criticism, biography, and nonfiction, he is best known as a novelist. Over the span of fifty years he managed to create a series of remarkable novels that explore from various perspectives the essential rootlessness of American life in the 20th c. Perhaps because his works are firmly grounded in place—South Dakota, Saskatchewan, Utah, Grass Valley, California—he is often characterized as a "Western" writer. But S.'s characters, most of which are remarkably well developed and distinctive, portray a complex geography of mind that lift them far beyond region. Writing within a period dominated by modernism, his fictions were in a sense unfashionable, insofar as they display an enduring concern for the family and community, for the complex emotional relationships between husbands and wives, parents and children. Although his characters suffer the traumas of existential isolation, they often find meaning in a world that is ultimately ordered and purposeful.

FURTHER WORKS: *Clarence Edward Dutton: An Appraisal* (1935); *The Potter's House* (1938); *Fire and Ice* (1941); *Mormon Country* (1942); *One Nation* (1945, with the editors of *Look*); *Second Growth* (1947); *The Preacher and the Slave* (1950); *The Women on the Wall* (1950); *Joe Hill* (1950); *The Writer in America* (1951); *Beyond the Hundreth Meridian: John Wesley Powell and the Second Opening of the West* (1954); *The City of the Living, and Other Stories* (1960); *The Papers of Bernard DeVoto: A Description and Checklist of his Work* (1960); *A Shooting Star* (1961); *Wolf Willow: A History, a Story, and a Memory of the Last Plains Frontier* (1962); *The Gathering of Zion: The Story of the Mormon Trail* (1964); *Teaching the Short Story* (1965); *All the Little Live Things* (1967); *The Sound of Mountain Water* (1969); *Discovery! The Search for Arabian Oil* (1971); *Variations on the Theme of Discontent* (1972); *Robert Frost and Bernard DeVoto* (1974); *The Uneasy Chair: A Biography of Bernard DeVoto* (1974); *The Spectator Bird* (1978); *Recapitulation* (1979); *Crossing to Safety* (1987); *Where the Bluebird Sings to the Lemonade Springs: Living and Writing in the West* (1992)

BIBLIOGRAPHY: Flora, J. M., *A Literary History of the American West* (1987); Lewis, M., and L. Lewis, *W. S.* (1972); Robinson F. G., and M. G. Robinson, *W. S.* (1977); Benson, J. J., *W. S.: His Life and Work* (1996)

—STEVEN FRYE

STEIN, Gertrude

American novelist, poet, dramatist, and critic, b. 3 Feb. 1874, Allegheny, Pa.; d. 27 July 1946, Paris

Born into a moderately wealthy family, S. was raised in Oakland, California. In 1893 she entered the Harvard Annex (Radcliffe College), where she studied psychology with William James and Hugo Munsterberg. Her first publications appeared in the *Psychological Review* (1896 and 1898). In 1897 she began medical school at Johns Hopkins but left in 1902 without a degree. In 1902 she went abroad and the following year settled in Paris, where she lived the rest of her life.

S. was long known principally as a Paris aesthete, a friend of the famous, a patron of the arts, and an "experimental" writer whose importance lay more in her influence on others than in her own work. Recent criticism has taken S.'s work more seriously, a judgment corroborated by the many books by her still in print.

In the early years Gertrude and her brother Leo, along with another brother, Michael, and his wife Sarah, began to amass an important collection of 20th-c. painting, and S. established a lifelong friendship with Pablo Picasso. She began to write, producing in 1902–3 a novella, *Quod Erat Demonstrandum* (pub. 1950 as

Things as They Are). This autobiographical work about a lesbian love triangle is a more or less conventional narrative, somewhat in the manner of the later Henry JAMES.

After this apprentice work, S. began the extensive character studies she used in *The Making of Americans* (pub. 1925). The writing of that massive novel, however, had to wait until the completion of *Three Lives: Stories of the Good Anna, Melanctha, and Gentle Lena* (1909), composed during 1905–6, when she was sitting for the famous portrait by Picasso. *Three Lives* remains one of S.'s most popular books. Its lengthy middle tale, "Melanctha," is the first work to exhibit the characteristic signs of her abstractionism: her use of repetition and the present participle, the diminution of background and setting, the slowing down of narrative movement, and circumlocution.

Before 1914 S. wrote a series of long works in which she developed her abstract style by using the CUBIST qualities of distortion and fragmentation. These works include *The Making of Americans, A Long Gay Book* (pub. 1933), *Matisse Picasso and Gertrude Stein with Two Shorter Stories* (pub. 1933), and *Tender Buttons: Objects, Food, Rooms* (1914), the last a prose poem that attempts to parallel cubist collage. Also at this time S. began to write "portraits," verbal impressions of individuals often containing little reference to their ostensible subjects. It was during these years preceding World War I that Alice B. Toklas joined the S. household and Leo eventually moved out. The relationship of S. and Toklas remained intact until S.'s death.

After the war S. became a public figure. She was sought out by many expatriate American writers of what she dubbed the "lost generation." Among them were Sherwood ANDERSON, F. Scott FITZGERALD, Ezra POUND, and Ernest HEMINGWAY. Hemingway came strongly under her influence, as one can see in the stylized repetitions and calculated simplicity of much of his work. He was also instrumental in getting sections of *The Making of Americans* published in *Transatlantic Review*. The publication of the full huge novel in 1925 augmented her reputation. In the same year she lectured at Oxford and Cambridge, and the book that grew out of these lectures, *Composition as Explanation* (1926), was the first of a series of critical essays that appeared during the next two decades.

Before 1925 S. had written many plays and opera librettos, all of which defied the conventions of those genres. Her dramatic structures and use of "absurdist" dialogue anticipated many elements of modern experimental drama, but these plays remained unproduced for years. In the late 1920s the American composer Virgil Thomson wrote, in collaboration with S., the opera *Four Saints in Three Acts*. Her libretto, which is essentially plotless, is a celebration of the life of Saint Theresa of Ávila. Published in 1934, it was produced in the same year under the direction of John Houseman with an all-black cast, and achieved an extended New York run. That opera and her final one, *The Mother of Us All* (1946), are now produced with some regularity. *The Mother of Us All* is a valedictory statement in which S. projects her own life and personality onto that of Susan B. Anthony.

The Autobiography of Alice B. Toklas (1933) is, of all S.'s books, the most well known, widely read, and readily accessible. It is ostensibly written by Alice Toklas rather than S. This pretense allows S. to let the reader view her from the perspective of someone else, and also gives full expression to her considerable ego. The work is a much-embellished, personalized memoir of life among the modernists, at the hub of which is always S. herself.

After *The Autobiography of Alice B. Toklas* was serialized in *The Atlantic* and then published in book form, S.'s fame was assured. In 1934–35 she made a triumphant lecture tour of the U.S. during which she became a media celebrity. *Lectures in America* (1935) and *Narration* (1935), both based on the talks she gave, contain S.'s critical statements on such topics as painting, poetry and grammar, and the history of English literature.

In her final decade S. continued to work in the genres she had previously explored. Her major work of reminiscence is *Everybody's Autobiography* (1937), a straightforward continuation of *The Autobiography of Alice B. Toklas*, narrated by S. in her own voice. The posthumously published novel *Mrs. Reynolds* (1952) is an extended work in her abstract, repetitive style. Written during World War II, it has the menace of Hitler in the background. *The Geographical History of America* (1936) is an abstract meditation on a distinction important to S.—that between "human nature" and the "human mind." Her final dramas are collected in *Last Operas and Plays* (1949). They include experimental works as well as more conventional plays such as *Dr. Faustus Lights the Lights* (1938). Following her death, her unpublished works were released in eight volumes under the general title *The Yale Edition of the Unpublished Writings of G. S.* (1951–58).

There is still no consensus about S., but she is increasingly ranked as a major 20th-c. writer, and her work is receiving much critical attention. Her verse, while not known in her lifetime, is now seen as a major lesbian document, particularly the long poem "Lifting Belly" (1917). Overall, she is, with James JOYCE, the 20th-c. writer who most completely explored the implications of literary modernism.

FURTHER WORKS: *Geography and Plays* (1922); *Useful Knowledge* (1928); *Lucy Church Amiably* (1930); *Before the Flowers of Friendship Faded Friendship Faded* (1931); *How to Write* (1931); *Operas and Plays* (1932); *Portraits and Prayers* (1934); *Picasso* (1938); *The World Is Round* (1939); *What Are Masterpieces* (1940); *Paris France* (1940); *Ida, a Novel* (1941); *Wars I Have Seen* (1945); *Brewsie and Willie* (1946); *Selected Writings* (1946); *Four in America* (1947); *Blood on the Dining Room Floor* (1948); *Two: G. S. and Her Brother, and Other Early Portraits* (1951); *Bee Time Vine, and Other Pieces* (1953); *As Fine as Melanctha* (1954); *Painted Lace, and Other Pieces* (1955); *Stanzas in Meditation, and Other Poems* (1956); *Alphabets and Birthdays* (1957); *A Novel of Thank You* (1958); *Fernhurst, Q.E.D., and Other Early Writings* (1971); *A Primer for the Gradual Understanding of G. S.* (1971); *Sherwood Anderson-G. S.: Correspondence and Personal Essays* (1972); *Reflections on the Atomic Bomb* (1973); *How Writing Is Written* (1974); *The Yale G. S.: Selections* (1980)

BIBLIOGRAPHY: Wilson, E., *Axel's Castle* (1931): 237–56; Sutherland, D., *G. S.: A Biography of Her Work* (1957); Brinnin, J. M., *The Third Rose: G. S. and Her World* (1959); Hoffman, F. J., *G. S.* (1961); Hoffman, M. J., *The Development of Abstractionism in the Writings of G. S.* (1965); Stewart, A., *G. S. and the Present* (1967); Weinstein, N., *G. S. and the Language of the Modern Consciousness* (1970); Bridgman, R., *G. S. in Pieces* (1970); Mellow, J. R., *Charmed Circle: G. S. & Company* (1974); Hoffman, M. J., *G. S.* (1976); Steiner, W., *Exact Resemblance to Exact Resemblance: The Literary Portraiture of G. S.* (1978)

—MICHAEL J. HOFFMAN

Gertrude Stein

STEINARR, Steinn

(pseud. of Aðalsteinn Kristmundsson) Icelandic poet, b. 13 Oct. 1908, Laugaland; d. 25 May 1958, Reykjavík

Born in northwest Iceland and raised in poverty, S. received little formal education, attending a folk high school for only one year. He was physically handicapped and thus poorly suited for manual labor. By 1930 he had moved to Reykjavík, which was then in the throes of an economic depression, with heavy unemployment and great suffering for working-class people.

Both his own personal circumstances and the disorder of the social scene that he witnessed are strongly reflected in S.'s first volume of verse, *Rauður loginn brann* (1934; red burned the flame), which contains many poems asserting the cause of the proletariat and bitterly attacking those in power. In form, the poems are mostly traditional, although there are a few examples of free verse with dense images. The influence of Jóhannes úr KÖTLUM and Tómas GUÐMUNDSSON can be seen, for example, in the frequent use of paradoxes. The satirical and cynical tone that characterizes so many of the poems was to remain the hallmark of S.'s poetry throughout his life.

His second book, *Ljóð* (1937; poems), indicated a shift in S.'s concerns: the intense social criticism gave way to a concern with philosophical issues and private psychological problems. With this collection S. set forth a strong view of the human condition—that life has no purpose. The red flame of revolution of his first book had yielded to the white fire of skepticism and a sense of futility—a stance that was symbolically reiterated in the titles of his next two collections: *Spor í sandi* (1940; footprints in the sand) and *Ferð; án fyrirheits* (1942; journey without promise). Although many of the poems in *Spor í sandi* and *Ferð; án fyrirheits* are traditional in form, S. was the most important pioneer of modernism in Icelandic verse; his innovativeness is evident in his density of images, his crafting of a new poetic diction, and his use of fresh symbols and nonlogical associations.

S.'s stylistic development culminated in *Tíminn og vatnið;* (1948; enlarged ed., 1956; *Time and Water*, 1972), a lengthy cycle of poems written just when S. had become acquainted with modern Swedish verse and had grown especially fond of *The Waste Land* by T. S. ELIOT. The imagery of this last work of his also resembles the techniques of abstract painting. While its outward form is simplicity itself, *Tíminn og vatnið* is a complex and difficult work. There are three central thematic elements—the poet's ego, time, and water—whose symbolic values defy precise interpretation. Intertwined with these themes are mythological motifs. Taken as a whole, this cycle may be regarded as a final settlement of accounts: the poet, through his art, has made his peace with the world of futility and has thus united himself with eternity.

FURTHER WORKS: *100 kvæði* (1949); *Kæðasafn og greinar* (1964)

BIBLIOGRAPHY: Einarsson, S., *A History of Icelandic Literature* (1957): 324–25; Rossel, S. H., *A History of Scandinavian Literature 1870–1980* (1982): 372

—SVEINN SKORRI HÖSKULDSSON

STEINBECK, John

American novelist, dramatist, short-story writer, screenwriter, and essayist, b. 27 Feb. 1902, Salinas, Cal.; d. 20 Dec. 1968, New York, N.Y.

Athlete, senior-class president, and writer in high school, S. attended Stanford University erratically (1920–25), mostly taking courses in the biological sciences. After working for a short time as a laborer and reporter in New York City while writing but failing to publish, he returned to California, the setting for most of his fiction, where he lived until 1943. His travels during this time related to film-making in Mexico, to a specimen-collecting expedition with marine biologist Ed Ricketts (1897–1948)—the friend and some-time collaborator who helped shape the biological, nonjudgmental vision of humanity that guided S.'s middle-period fiction—and to various journalistic projects, including coverage of the drought-driven Oklahoma farmers who poured into California in the 1930s, and a book-length report on a bomber team for the Army Air Corps. During World War II he wrote newspaper stories from England and Europe. In 1943 he moved to New York City, his home for the rest of his life. Summers at Sag Harbor, expeditions to England, and extensive travels in Europe took him still farther from his native California. He wrote speeches for Adlai Stevenson during the 1956 presidential campaign. In 1962 he received the Nobel Prize for literature and in 1964, the Presidential Medal of Freedom. His travels around the U.S. with his poodle, Charley, led directly to the last two of his books published during his lifetime: *Travels with Charley in Search of America* (1962) and *America and Americans* (1966).

Cup of Gold (1929), *The Pastures of Heaven* (1932), and *To a God Unknown* (1933), his first three published novels, established the pattern of formal and thematic variety that characterizes S.'s work. The first has the form of a swashbuckling adventure story, seeming to tell of Sir Henry Morgan's life and piratical adventures. Its major concern, however, is with the coming of melancholy wisdom as the old pirate-turned-respectable-administrator realizes that his early dreams have turned to cheap illusions. In *The Pastures of Heaven*, probably the most appealing of the three, S. put together a number of short stories centering around one man and his inadvertent blighting of a small community. The novel—for so the book indeed is—specifies interconnections of influence and a strong sense of place, of the California valley that gives the book its title. Evocation of the land itself, and of what it signifies to those who work it and live upon it, was to become a strong mark of many of S.'s later works, and of none more forcibly than *To a God Unknown*, in fact written before *The Pastures of Heaven*. Here, the family and its ambivalent pressures (another concern in later S. books) come alive for the first time in S.'s fiction. Through Joseph Wayne's mystical oneness with the land, S. began to probe into atavistic patterns and conflicts that make myth possible.

These early novels received almost no positive critical recognition and had abysmal sales. S.'s only recognized success was in the writing of the short story, a form in which he enjoyed working all his life and of which he became one of America's masters. Then, in 1935, the firm of Covici-Friede published *Tortilla Flat*, and S. found in Pascal ("Pat") Covici (1885–1964) the editor with whom his name is now associated. Once more writing a book different from its predecessors, S. in *Tortilla Flat* presented the *paisanos* of Monterey in a comic exaggeration of Arthurian motifs that achieved some critical and considerable popular acclaim. Although the characters in this humorous extravaganza exemplify what one might label an underprivileged existence, their gusto and their author's sense of fun mark a total break in tone from the books S. wrote before and show a sharp contrast to those he wrote immediately after.

In Dubious Battle (1936), *Of Mice and Men* (1937), and *The Grapes of Wrath* (1939)—the last of which won a Pulitzer Prize in 1940—established S.'s reputation as a writer with sympathy for underdogs like the exploited farm workers of California. This reputation, while certainly deserved, allowed some readers to undervalue S.'s work as having a merely social significance. Today, *In Dubious Battle* is regarded not only as the prime example of a 1930s strike novel but also as a structurally fascinating and emotionally rewarding presentation of deeply ambivalent and indecisively held positions that at first appear to be firm convictions. For what sort of cause will a man reasonably die? How do groups function? What are the limitations of herd mentality? In the character of Doc Burton, Steinbeck created his first detached observer, a figure to a degree derived from his speculative friend, Ed Ricketts, to reappear, with changes, in almost every subsequent novel S. was to write, most prominently simply as "Doc" in *Cannery Row* (1945) and *Sweet Thursday* (1954).

Of Mice and Men was the first and most successful of S.'s three efforts to write a novel that could serve as script for a play. (The other two are *The Moon Is Down* [1942] and *Burning Bright* [1950].) It presents Lenny and George as larger-than-life representatives of ordinary "working stiffs" who want, some day, a place of their own. Lenny, the gigantic idiot, draws comfort from images of that small house, with garden and rabbits, that George knows they can never achieve. When Lenny dies, shot by George to save him from a lynch mob, reader and audience know that George is doomed to a future with no hope.

The Grapes of Wrath, along with *East of Eden* (1952) and *The Winter of Our Discontent* (1961), confirmed S.'s mastery of complex storytelling. Alternating discursive interchapters with the travails of its west-ward-bound Okies, the Joads and their fellows, *The Grapes of Wrath* brings to light the predicament of hard-working, independent, ill-educated people caught in the trap of circumstances that they struggle to understand. It is also a major exploration of man's rootedness to the land and of the effects of natural, social, biological, and economic forces upon people. In subsequent works the biological metaphor controlling most of S.'s writing through *The Grapes of Wrath* gives way to a fascination with the human ability to overcome conditioning, to make choices that transcend innate ignorance or weakness or wickedness. *East of Eden*, although a moving family saga in which young John Ernst Steinbeck is himself a minor character, is in essence a book about moral choice and responsibility. Only recently have critics begun to appreciate the satisfyingly rich texture of the interwoven stories of the Trask family, the Hamilton family, and a changing America from the Civil War to World War I.

S.'s last major novel, *The Winter of Our Discontent*, continues his exploration of the moral dilemmas involved in being fully human, this time in contemporary America, where choices between genteel poverty and corrupt comfort press in upon the protagonist with a force and reality that suggest no easy resolution. The posthumously published *The Acts of King Arthur and His Noble Knights* (1976), written from a similar moral perspective, tries to bring to life the Arthurian world that S. discovered early and loved long. The substance and spirit of Malory's *Le Morte Darthur* have infused much of S.'s fiction, but one cannot say that S.'s affectionate effort to put Malory into modern fictional form succeeded.

Although many critics wondered at S.'s receiving the Nobel Prize in 1962, S.'s contributions to the craft and canon of American writing have become increasingly apparent. The high regard in which his fiction is held worldwide and the frequent revival in America of cinematic and theatrical versions of his works suggest that his reputation may have stabilized. If not in the very first rank of American writers, he certainly belongs among the enduringly readable and significant.

FURTHER WORKS: *The Red Pony* (1937, 3 parts); *Their Blood Is Strong* (1938); *The Long Valley* (1938; includes all 4 parts of *The Red Pony*); *Sea of Cortez: A Leisurely Journey of Travel and Research* (1941, with Edward F. Ricketts); *The Forgotten Village* (1941); *Bombs Away: The Story of a Bomber Team* (1942); *The Portable S.* (1943; new eds., 1946, 1971); *The Pearl* (1947); *The Wayward Bus* (1947); *A Russian Journal* (1948, with photographs by Robert Capa); *Viva, Zapata!* (1950, screenplay); *The Log from the Sea of Cortez* (1951); *The Short Novels of J. S.* (1953); *The Short Reign of Pippin IV: A Fabrication* (1957); *Once There Was a War* (1958); *Journal of a Novel: The "East of Eden" Letters* (1969); *S.: A Life in Letters* (1975)

BIBLIOGRAPHY: Moore, H. T., *The Novels of J. S.: A First Critical Study* (1939); Tedlock, E. W., Jr. and C. V. Wicker, eds., *S. and His Critics* (1957); Lisca, P., *The Wide World of J. S.* (1958); French,

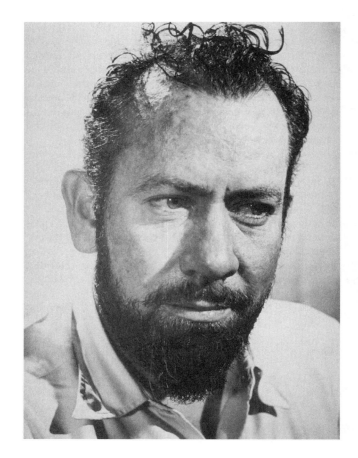

John Steinbeck

W., *J. S.* (1961; rev. ed., 1975); Watt, F. W., *J. S.* (1962); Fontenrose, J., *J. S.: An Introduction and Interpretation* (1963); Covici, P., Jr., Introduction to *The Portable S.* (1971): xi–xlii; Astro, R., *J. S. and Edward F. Ricketts: The Shaping of a Novelist* (1973); Fensch, T., *S. and Covici: The Story of a Friendship* (1979); McCarthy, P., *J. S.* (1980); Benson, J. J., *The True Adventures of J. S., Writer* (1983)

—PASCAL COVICI, JR.

STEINER, George

American literary and social critic, journalist, and writer of fiction, b. 23 April 1929, Paris, France

Born of Austrian parents and raised in France, S. became a naturalized American in 1944. He pursued his education both in the U.S.—at the University of Chicago (B.A.) and at Harvard (M.A.)—and abroad, earning advanced degrees at the Sorbonne and at Balliol College, Oxford, where he was a Rhodes Scholar. His academic career has included positions at a number of prominent American universities. Since 1961 S. has also been associated with Churchill College, Cambridge. He currently holds the Chair of English and Comparative Literature at the University of Geneva in Switzerland.

S.'s principal production has been several volumes of literary and social criticism. His own international background has determined his perspective as a writer. At home in many languages, a cosmopolitan and champion of culture in the face of more provincial modes of interpretation, S. takes a strong traditionalist stance, invigorated by his central-European heritage, which lends his pronouncements on the necessity of safeguarding and confirming Western civilization a tone of warmth and urgency, at times of messianic ardor.

His position became apparent in his first major work, *Tolstoy or Dostoevsky: An Essay in the Old Criticism* (1959), which claims for the twin giants of Russian fiction older, more traditional categories of form and value, and translates their fictions into two opposing visions of existence: as a son of Homer, Tolstoy's vision is inherited, communal, committed to this earth; as a son of tragedy, Dostoevsky is apocalyptic, alienated, diabolically striving for a world beyond. But both, as S. sees them, are equally dedicated to the potentials of the human spirit.

S.'s second major work, *The Death of Tragedy* (1961), is part elegy and part a story of renewal. First he laments the passing of the tragedies of classical antiquity and Shakespeare—the high mimetic drama that mirrored a culture's anxieties and aspirations and disappeared with the collapse of humanistic intelligence, the incursions of progress, and the splintering of society into private sensibilities. But S. praises later shifts of the tragic impulse into the more experimental forms of Goethe and the romantic drama of Büchner and Byron, of Ibsen and of CHEKHOV later in the 19th c., and more recently in BRECHT, although the eccentricities of their work reveal that the *polis*, the just city of Aeschylus and Shakespeare, has lost its health and wholeness too.

That is the fact S. addresses in the first large assembly of his articles, *Language and Silence: Essays on Language, Literature and the Inhuman* (1967). From this manifesto on the crucial bond between humane literacy and civilization, S. emerges as a challenging critic of literature and its social context, who threads his way from silence to articulation. Few have defended the aesthetics of silence as outspokenly as S.—the silence that should reflect the failure of our literacy to stem contemporary barbarisms, and the lethal silence that, at the close of the last war, provoked Günter GRASS and others to re-create the German language from its ashes, and the survivors of the deathcamps to reassert their voices in defiance. The three compelling stories in *Anno Domini* (1964) dramatize the death of the heart that completes the ravages of combat. His powerful novella *The Portage to San Cristóbal of A. H.* (1979) is S.'s resuscitation of the ghost of Adolf Hitler as a spirit that refuses to be silent, however deftly history refuses to register his impact and comprehend his brutal mission. It has been adapted for the stage as well as translated into many languages, and its effects have been extraordinarily strong. For S., the other victors over silence remain the "para-Marxists," György LUKÁCS, Walter BENJAMIN, and Theodor W. ADORNO, who would release literature from crabbed, partisan ideologies while rooting it, once again, in the matrix of human sentiment and the meaning of the Logos.

That meaning must now come, as S. sees it, from new semantic centers, free from earlier jurisdictions. In *Extraterritorial: Papers on Literature and the Language Revolution* (1971) he supports the writers of exile, Jorge Luis BORGES, Vladimir NABOKOV, and Samuel BECKETT, and the linguistic schools of Moscow and Prague, which brought their methods to the task of defining human identity. What S. appeals for, in one of his strongest essays, "The Language Animal," is a union between linguistics and literature.

S. faces the possibility that our lives can no longer be defined linguistically in *In Bluebeard's Castle: Some Notes toward the Redefinition of Culture* (1971). For S., World War II, in particular the destruction of European Jewry, constitutes a Second Fall so catastrophic that all accounts of our history may have to be rewritten in utterly new codes, musical or scientific, exhilarating or grimly disenchanting—promising a new literacy if not a new culture. These are the unopened doors in Bluebeard's Castle, and whatever dangers they may enclose, S. would fling them open with a kind of Nietzschean enthusiasm for inquiry and adventure.

For what concerns him most is the "classic contract between word and world"—ultimately broken in the last war, but nevertheless recoverable in countless acts of translation from one language to another. The poetics of translation is his constant and recurring theme, especially in his most recent works: *After Babel: Aspects of Language and Translation* (1975), *On Difficulty, and Other Essays* (1978), and *Martin Heidegger* (1978), his cogent introduction to the German philosopher. *After Babel* is a book of large, generous dimension and cultural reach, perhaps the fullest attempt in our time to make a summary statement about the act of translation, as well as one of the most impassioned pleas for responsible literacy, a plea that has led many to place S. in the company of R. P. BLACKMUR, Malcolm COWLEY, and Edmund WILSON; S., like Wilson before him, writes reviews for *The New Yorker*. Others, compelled by the voice of conscience S. sounds in the wake of the Holocaust, and by his equipoise between the specialist's techniques and the crisis of the beleaguered *polis*, will ally him with the para-Marxists who insist upon the symbiosis of poetry and politics—the heirs of the great European tradition, whom S. has celebrated for possessing "a central humanism, classical in background, radical of bias," a description that will serve for S.'s lineage and affiliation too.

FURTHER WORKS: *Fields of Force: Fischer and Spassky at Reykjavik* (1974)

BIBLIOGRAPHY: Burgess, A., *Urgent Copy* (1968): 184–92; Rosenfeld, A. H., "On Reading G. S.," *Midstream*, (February 1972): 70–80; Carruth, H., "Fallacies of Silence," *HudR*, 26 (1973): 426–70; Strawson, P. F., on *Martin Heidegger* and *On Difficulty*, *NYRB*, (17 April 1979): 35; Rosenfeld, A. H., "S.'s Hitler," *Salmagundi*, Nos. 52–53 (1981): 160–74

—ROBERT FAGLES

STEPHENS, James

Irish novelist, short-story writer, and poet, b. 9 Feb. 1880?, Dublin; d. 26 Dec. 1950, London, England

S. chose to obscure his parentage and birthdate, claiming (fancifully) to have been born on the same date (February 2, 1882) and even at the same hour as James JOYCE. The first fact about him known for certain is that at age six he was committed to a home for orphaned or abandoned boys. Here he received rudiments of formal education and vocational training. In 1896 he took employment as clerk-typist in a law office. By 1907 his writing had attracted George RUSSELL, who encouraged him in the study of Eastern philosophies and introduced him to the major figures of the Irish Literary Revival. An ardent nationalist, S. became active in the

Sinn Fein, learned Gaelic, and immersed himself in the native folklore and sagas. After a long succession of clerical jobs, in 1915 he was appointed Registrar of the National Gallery of Ireland. In 1924 he resigned from the National Gallery, thereafter making his home in Paris and London, with frequent tours of America for lectures and poetry recitals. Although suffering recurrent physical and psychological afflictions in his last years, he delivered a captivating series of talks over the British radio network.

S.'s strength as a writer is in his prose, a personalized expression of his belief in the themes of William Blake and the teachings of theosophy. His first three novels—*The Charwoman's Daughter* (1912; Am., *Mary, Mary*), *The Crock of Gold* (1912), and *The Demi Gods* (1914)—present life in Ireland's slums and adjoining countryside as he had encountered it. Scenes of hunger, illness, and hostility interact with moments of love, wish-fulfillment, and joy among flowers. Mundane and supernatural beings mingle unself-consciously; dichotomies of man-woman, city-country, ancient-modern, substance-illusion are buoyantly explored. S. decried the constriction of the individual by a despotic society, and strove by persuasive use of whimsy and fantasy to circumvent the actuality. In each of these three novels a young Irish girl (representing Ireland) undergoes an arduous progress from innocence through experience to self-realization and transcendence. Exercising the oral traditions of song and storytelling, sudden caprices of plot, anthropomorphic byplay, and a beguiling array of godlings, toilers, children, warriors, and philosophers, S. educed a world in which goodness may be rewarded and dreams might come true.

Deirdre (1923) and *In the Land of Youth* (1924) represent S.'s attempt to construct a modern mythology on the base of two well-known Irish sagas. By freely interpolating fragments from other tales, new situations, contemporary characters, and a strain of humor, he pared down these versions to human dimensions.

S.'s short stories are crowded with ill-favored, frustrated people locked in mutually destructive domestic strife. In the collection *Here Are Ladies* (1913) the tone is comic, the form casual. The stories in *Etched in Moonlight* (1928) are grim and stringent, indictments of society's indifference to privation.

As a poet, S. drew from Blake, Wordsworth, Burns, Browning, and Emerson, never developing a distinct voice or technique. His verses exude charm and are marked by simple, melodic diction, fluent rhythms, and a sense of the wonder of creation—a poetry not of intellect but of observation and feeling. The range of topics includes social and religious protest and caustic, colloquial portraits in *Insurrections* (1909) and *The Hill of Vision* (1912); bliss in nature and the primacy of imagination over reason in *Songs from the Clay* (1915); and politics, patriotism, and literary antecedents in *Green Branches* (1916) and *Reincarnations* (1918).

Three decades after his death S.'s reputation lies in *The Crock of Gold*, a truly original work, plus a slender selection from his lyrics and short stories in anthologies. Critical emphasis on his lightness of manner and eccentric perspectives has deflected attention from his artful mixture of mysticism, naturalism, and pastoral; his enduring innovations in prose forms; and his unflagging advocacy of the individual against society. S. asserted the spirituality of human nature and broached some engaging ways of repossessing it.

FURTHER WORKS: *The Lonely God, and Other Poems* (1909); *Five New Poems* (1913); *The Adventures of Seumas Beg; The Rocky Road to Dublin* (1915); *The Insurrection in Dublin* (1916); *Hunger: A Dublin Story* (1918, under pseud. James Esse); *Irish Fairy Tales* (1920); *Arthur Griffith, Journalist and Statesman* (1922);

Little Things, and Other Poems (1924); *A Poetry Recital* (1925); *Collected Poems* (1926; 2nd enlarged ed., 1954); *On Prose and Verse* (1928); *Dublin Letters* (1928); *Julia Elizabeth: A Comedy in One Act* (1929); *Theme and Variations* (1930); *Strict Joy* (1931); *Kings and the Moon* (1938); *J. S.: A Selection* (1962; Am., *A. J. S. Reader*); *James, Seumas & Jacques: Unpublished Writings of J. S.* (1964); *Letters of J. S.* (1974); *Uncollected Prose of J. S.* (2 vols., 1983)

BIBLIOGRAPHY: [George Russell], A. E., *Imaginations and Reveries* (1915): 34–44; Bramsbäck, B., *J. S.: A Literary and Bibliographical Study* (1959); special S. issue, *CLQ*, Series 5, No. 9 (1961); Pyle, H., *J. S.: His Work and an Account of His Life* (1965); Martin, A., *J. S.: A Critical Study* (1977); Finneran, R. J., *The Olympian and the Leprechaun: W. B. Yeats and J. S.* (1978); McFate, P., *The Writings of J. S.* (1979)

—RICHARD CARY

STERNHEIM, Carl

German dramatist, novelist, and essayist, b. 1 April 1878, Leipzig; d. 3 Nov. 1942, Brussels, Belgium

The son of a financier with literary aspirations, S. studied law, literature, philosophy, and art history at Munich, Leipzig, and Göttingen. His second marriage, to Thea Bauer, brought him considerable wealth. Together with Franz Blei (1871–1942), he founded the journal *Hyperion* in 1908. S. was never affiliated with any of the artistic circles of his time. In 1930 he was married a third time, to Pamela Wedekind, the daughter of Frank WEDEKIND. During the same year he moved to Belgium, where he spent the rest of his life in near-obscurity, suffering from nervous disorders.

S.'s unsuccessful early tragedies up to *Don Juan* (1909; Don Juan) are études in the romantic vein and of little significance. When he turned to comedies, he was, after the tumultuous premiere of *Die Hose* (1911; *A Pair of Drawers*, 1927; later trs., *The Underpants*, 1960; *The Bloomers*, 1970) catapulted to literary fame overnight and subsequently hailed as the "modern Molière" and leading satirist of his day. In his drive for a new enlightenment, S. was influenced by Nietzsche's contempt for the bourgeois. His literary models include Wedekind, Heinrich MANN, Molière, and, more indirectly, Heine, Lessing, Voltaire, and Wilde. As a vehicle for his incisive diagnosis of Wilhelminian society, he created a new form of comedy (*bürgerliches Lustspiel*), which delivers its merciless attack on bourgeois hypocrisy through suprarealistic and grotesque effects. The self-proclaimed "physician for the maladies of his time" denounced egoism on all levels, at the same time stressing the necessity of a powerful "new vision" beyond the present debacle.

S.'s most acclaimed comedies, later to be collected under the title *Aus dem bürgerlichen Heldenleben* (1922; *Scenes from the Heroic Life of the Middle-Classes*, 1970), form a thematically coherent circle. In *Die Hose*, the Maske family is introduced as a mainstay of petit-bourgeois cunning and greed. *Der Snob* (1914; *A Place in the World*, 1927; later trs., *The Snob*, 1949, 1970) and *1913* (1915; *1913*, 1939) trace the ruthless ascent of Maske's son and grandchildren to power and wealth. The later *Das Fossil* (1923; *The Fossil*, 1970) brings the Maske tetralogy, a brilliant sociohistorical documentation of an epoch, to a conclusion. As a whole, it is an impressive pathography of Wilhelminian society, its commercialism and its caste system.

The other plays of the series, all of which were among the most frequently performed on the German stage up to the early 1920s, also center around selfishness and brutal opportunism: *Die Kassette* (1912; *The Strongbox*, 1963), *Bürger Schippel* (1913; *Paul Schippel, Esq.*, 1970), *Der Kandidat* (1914; the candidate), *Tabula rasa* (1916; tabula rasa) and *Der Geizige* (1916; the miser). The overall effect of the plays is at times chilling and often ambivalent. They unmask the contradictions between hypocritical bourgeois morality and the actual deeds spawned by greed and ambition. S.'s character types proudly exhibit what he termed the "courage to stand by their own reality": the quality of the Nietzschean *Übermensch*, ready to establish a new order beyond good and evil. In this light, the plays tend to glorify the protagonists to some extent. Their grotesquely outrageous social Darwinism, on the other hand, while not explicitly condemned, nevertheless speaks for itself.

S.'s satirical wit and his lack of pathos set him apart from EXPRESSIONISM. He shared with most of the expressionists, however, strong antinaturalist tendencies, a concern for the "essential," and the vision of a "new man." This vision is strikingly expressed in *1913* and in the short story "Busekow" (1913; Busekow). An equally cogent link is formed by his two-pronged drive for social and artistic renewal: while castigating society for deforming the individual, he simultaneously purged from his language all crippling elements (cliché, metaphor) and arrived, like Georg KAISER and August STRAMM, at an artificially compressed, intense, and superbly precise style reminiscent of FUTURISM. His innovative prose, later collected as *Chronik von des zwanzigsten Jahrhunderts Beginn* (1918; chronicle of the beginning of the twentieth century), and his novel *Europa* (1920; Europe) bridge the gap between expressionism and the sober postwar literary trends.

During the Weimar years, S.'s plays lost touch with a rapidly changing society. His writings after 1920 met with little acclaim, and around 1931 his productivity waned. In his late autobiography *Vorkriegseuropa im Gleichnis meines Lebens* (1936; prewar Europe as an allegory of my life), S. vacillates between self-glorification and obvious resignation to the fact that the much-hoped-for new enlightenment had not taken place. The 1960s witnessed an international revival of his comedies. S. remains a controversial, equivocal figure. Although berated by some critics as a snob, a parvenu or a bourgeois in the wolf's clothing, he is recognized by most not only as the master of an inimitable style, but as the creator of a highly original concept of comedy fit to plausibly assail a sick society.

FURTHER WORKS: *Der Heiland* (1898); *Fanale!* (1901); *Judas Ischarioth* (1901); *Auf Krugdorf* (1902); *Ulrich und Brigitte* (1907); *Napoleon* (1915); *Das leidende Weib* (1915); *Der Scharmante* (original title: *Zwischen den Schlachten*, 1915); *Schuhlin* (1916); *Meta* (1916); *Mädchen* (1917); *Der Stänker* (original title: *Perleberg*, 1917); *Die Marquise von Arcis* (1918; *The Mask of Virtue*, 1935); *Ulrike* (1918); *Prosa* (1918); *Die deutsche Revolution* (1919); *Der entfesselte Zeitgenosse* (1920); *Berlin; oder, Juste Milieu* (1920); *Tasso; oder, Kunst des Juste Milieu* (1921); *Fairfax* (1921; *Fairfax*, 1923); *Manon Lescaut* (1921); *Libussa, des Kaisers Leibroß* (1922); *Der Nebbich* (1922); *Der Abenteurer* (1922); *Gauguin und van Gogh* (1924); *Oscar Wilde* (1925); *Die Schule von Uznach; oder, Neue Sachlichkeit* (1926); *Lutetia: Berichte über europäische*

Politik, Kunst und Volksleben 1926 (1926); *Die Väter; oder, Knock Out* (1928); *John Pierpont Morgan* (1930); *Aut Caesar aut nihil* (1930); *Kleiner Katechismus für das Jahr 1930/31* (1930); *Gesamtwerk* (10 vols., 1963–1976)

BIBLIOGRAPHY: Karasek, H., *C. S.* (1965); Wendler, W., *C. S.: Weltvorstellung und Kunstprinzipien* (1966); Emrich, W., "Die Komödie C. S.s," in Steffen, H., ed., *Der deutsche Expressionismus*, 2nd ed. (1970): 115–37; Myers, D., "C. S.: Satirist or Creator of Modern Heroes?," *Monatshefte*, 65 (1973): 39–47; Schwerte, H., "C. S.," in Wiese, B. von, ed., *Deutsche Dichter der Moderne*, 3rd ed. (1975): 476–91; Gittleman, S., "S., Wedekind, and *Homo Economicus*," *GQ*, 49 (1976): 25–30; Durzak, M., *Das expressionistische Drama: C. S.—Georg Kaiser* (1978): 43–101

—GERHARD P. KNAPP

STEVENS, Wallace

American poet, b. 2 Oct. 1879, Reading, Pa.; d. 2 Aug. 1955, Hartford, Conn.

S. was always highly reticent about the details of his personal life, and they impinge only obliquely on his poetry, where autobiography is subsumed within the imaginative life lived in the poems themselves. S. grew up amid comfortable and conventional surroundings in an educated middle-class family of Dutch and German descent. He studied at Harvard from 1897 to 1900 as a special (non-matriculated) student. Here he encountered an intellectual environment stamped by George SANTAYANA and William James (1842–1910), to both of whom S.'s later thinking shows an indebtedness, and began his literary apprenticeship writing verse for the *Harvard Advocate*. After a brief fling as a journalist did not pan out, he attended law school, was admitted to the New York bar in 1904, and practiced law in New York City until he entered a bonding firm in 1908. In 1916 he joined the Hartford Accident and Indemnity Company as a specialist in investment banking, becoming a vice-president of the company in 1934. For most of his adult life, S. successfully pursued parallel careers as a business executive and a poet, finding them suited to the practical and imaginative sides of his personality.

After the initial flurry at Harvard, S. wrote little poetry until a renewed creative outburst, beginning around 1913–14 and lasting about ten years. During this time he came in touch with the artistic activity centered in Greenwich Village, although he remained somewhat aloof from it; he became acquainted with other emerging poets like William Carlos WILLIAMS and received particular encouragement from Harriet Monroe (1861–1936), editor of *Poetry: A Magazine of Verse*. S.'s poems began to appear in *Poetry* and other little magazines that fostered modern verse. In 1923, at the age of forty-four, he brought out his first book, *Harmonium*, which was reissued in an enlarged version in 1931. After another hiatus during the remainder of the 1920s, S.'s poetic career resumed in the next decade, and a steady output of poems in the quarter of a century until his death resulted in five more more collections— *Ideas of Order* (1935; rev. ed., 1936), *The Man with the Blue Guitar* (1937), *Parts of a World* (1942), *Transport to Summer* (1947), and *The Auroras of Autumn* (1950)—and climaxed with the *Collected Poems* (1954). These works have been supplemented since his death by *Opus Posthumous* (1957) and by a chronologically arranged selection of poems from his entire career, *The Palm at the End of the Mind* (1971). Growing recognition came to S. in his late years, when he received such honors as the Bollingen Prize for Poetry (1950), the National Book Award (1951), and the Pulitzer Prize (1955).

S.'s early poetry displays various themes, moods, and tones, but its chief defining quality is the distinctive poetic sensibility it projects through its style. With its unusual images and conceits, its penchant for vivid colors, its fondness for quirky words and phrases, its cosmopolitan mingling of things foreign and things American, and its elegant wit that revels in erudite word-play, comic juxtapositions, and eccentric titles, the verbal virtuosity of *Harmonium* earned the epithet "gaudy" and gave S. his initial reputation as a poetic "dandy." These appellations, however, belie the underlying seriousness of most of the poems. Some of the finest express S.'s conviction that the mutable natural world is the only one available to humankind. "Sunday Morning" (1915), perhaps S.'s most familiar work, is a meditation that counters the traditional Christian ideas of heaven and immortality with a celebration of an earthly and human paradise, where life and death are both parts of the continuum of being, and where the perishable bliss that living affords is the true basis of human fulfillment. The more difficult "Le Monocle de Mon Oncle" (1918), recasts similar themes in a seriocomic disquisition on the waning of passion and beauty felt by two middle-aged lovers, and finds in the power of poetry what recompense it can for the recognition that fulfillment and loss are inextricably intertwined in human experience. Several other poems, including "Peter Quince at the Clavier" (1915), "Thirteen Ways of Looking at a Blackbird" (1917), "Anecdote of the Jar" (1919), "The Snow Man" (1921), "A High-Toned Old Christian Woman" (1922), and "The Emperor of Ice-Cream" (1922), are among the frequently anthologized pieces by which many readers know S. best. The dialectic between reality and the imagination that becomes the explicit subject of the later poetry is an implicit but nonetheless central thread in the early verse, which vibrates between a zest for the tangible in all its sensuous particularity and an equally keen susceptibility to the "fictive music" that hovers about the human engagement with the phenomenal world. Much of the poetry is characterized by an acute sensitivity to the elusive and ever-changing qualities of human perception, and by a playful manipulation of objective reality that reflects an imaginative freedom and ebullience in the aesthetic confrontation with that world, although the bright surface also has its darker shadings.

Harmonium also included the first of the major long poems that punctuate S.'s career. "The Comedian as the Letter C" (1922) surveys S.'s poetic development and the general predicament of the modern poet from a comic perspective, as its traces the meandering journey of the unheroic Crispin through the several stages of his confrontation with the world and his final accommodation to this "insoluble lump." The ironic deflation of the romantic visionary quest and S.'s distanced, often self-mocking stance toward his persona exhibit the ironic and impersonal mode of early modernism.

S.'s poetry underwent a marked change in the 1930s. He found himself reexamining against a backdrop of worldwide crisis his personal conception of the place and function of poetry. The chaos and violence of contemporary life called forth a fuller awareness of the social-historical component of reality. S. addressed the current turmoil most directly in the long poem *Owl's Clover* (1936), a counteroffensive against the widespread assault on poetry that was not politically purposive and the more specific criticism by literary

Wallace Stevens

Marxists that his own art, having once been insulated from the class struggle, was now confused by it. The poem voices S.'s innermost convictions about poetry, but in polemical and overwrought verse that is uncongenial to the poet. His other works of this period express his coming to terms with the conflicting demands of poetry and history more felicitously.

The paramount issues for S. were to keep poetry alive and affirm the imaginative act in the face of their being overwhelmed by the antipoetic pressures of the present moment. The disintegration of all forms of order in the world around him made more imperative the "blessed rage for order" that manifests itself in poetry. "The Idea of Order at Key West" (1934), probably S.'s best-known poem aside from "Sunday Morning," poignantly celebrates his fundamental recognition that the individual human imagination is the "single artificer" of order through the personal vision it imposes on the tumultuous forces that lie outside the self. Repeatedly, in the poems of these years, S. considers the demise and rejuvenation of imaginative endeavour, strikingly figured in the metaphor of "the man on the dump." Imaginative appropriations of the world grow stale, and one returns to the disordered miscellany of reality, yet simultaneously the imagination renews itself by hewing closely to this detritus.

All of these concerns pervade "The Man with the Blue Guitar" (1937), S.'s best long work of the 1930s. The poem formulates the relationship between the imagined and the real in a series of thirty-three short songs, composed in a plain style and bare two-line stanzas that are consonant with the focus on a struggle reduced to its rudiments; the songs pose the poet-singer against "things as they are" and elaborate the contest between them in its alternations of intercourse and opposition. The demand that the music-maker fashion "a tune beyond us, yet ourselves" proclaimed the quintessential responsibility of poetry in our time, as S. saw it. In 1940, as war engulfed the world, S. (in "Of Modern Poetry") called for "the poem of the act of the mind" in its effort to find "what will suffice" to sustain the act of ordinary living, and declared (in "Asides on the Oboe") that nothing less would serve than an adequate conception of ourselves, a "central man."

These aspirations define the direction of his later poetry, to which "Notes toward a Supreme Fiction" (1942) is the great prolegomenon. As the tentativeness of the title implies, the poem does not propound a supreme fiction, but rather grounds its possibility in the poetic act itself. The three main sections postulate and explore the necessary properties of any such fiction or ideal— "It Must Be Abstract," "It Must Change," "It Must Give Pleasure"—and establish the poem's argumentative framework. Yet this structure, although it reflects the later S.'s more theoretical cast of mind, becomes in his hands not a vehicle for reasoned, logical exposition, but for the metaphorical enactment of the argument, allowing ample room for the rich interplay of language and tropes at which S. excels. This philosophical and discursive mode reflecting the movements of the mind is that of the later long poems as well. "Esthétique du Mal" (1944) projects the modern secular imagination grappling with the problem of evil, and validates S.'s view of the essentially moral nature of his aesthetic approach to life. "Credences of Summer" (1946), "The Auroras of Autumn" (1948), and "An Ordinary Evening in New Haven" (1949) extend S.'s self-reflexive meditation on poetry and its relation to life, elaborating his complex vision in verse that has great intellectual and emotive force in spite of the sometimes obscure and private quality of its musings. Critics differ on the merits of the individual long works after "Notes toward a Supreme Fiction," but taken as a whole they constitute a substantial achievement.

S.'s last years produced a distinguished group of shorter poems, including "The Rock" (1950) and several splendid contemplative lyrics. These pensive celebrations of the life-death continuum, with their simultaneous acceptance of nothingness and affirmation of the triumphs of the "august imagination," stand as S.'s final testament of poetic faith. Reflecting the mood and tenor of these poems, S.'s late style moves toward "a plain sense of things" that largely eschews the showier verbal effects of the earlier verse, but shimmers instead with a quiet elegance and luminosity.

No brief summary can do justice to the profound contemplation of the life of the imagination that finds expression in S.'s later poetry, as well as in his occasional essays collected in *The Necessary Angel* (1951). A skeletal outline of certain key informing ideas, such as is offered here, serves only to direct readers back to the poems themselves. S. proceeds from the premise that, in a world in which the old myths and the old gods are dead, the locus of the human search for order and meaning must be the interchange between reality and the individual imagination. He views the two as equals, each dependent upon the other in shaping the nature of human experience. If they are interdependent, so too are they mutually resistant, with the consequent result that all imaginative activity oscillates perpetually between the stark idea of the real as it exists in itself apart from any human presence (paradoxically an idea that, from the human standpoint, has to be imagined) and the augmented world as it is conceptualized by the mind. S.'s dominant metaphor for this fluctuation is the seasonal cycle in nature, which

adumbrates the constant alternation of renewal-communion-with-drawal-absence that characterizes the contact between the imagination and reality. As S. anatomizes this pattern in all its shifting phases, the view that either side of the traditional subject-object dichotomy is primary dissolves, and their interaction itself becomes the crucial entity, or as S. himself once put it, "the real world seen by an imaginative man may very well seem like an imaginative construction."

For S., human endeavor rests on a belief in fictions, acknowledged as fictions, by which we know our world. The putative end of this endeavor, a supreme fiction, must both contain reality and image a complete and normative humanity, a potential common to every person and realizable by the imagination of each individual. S. comes to see this ideal as the basis for human possibility and individual freedom within the actual world. It does not result in final forms or a finished body of beliefs beyond the self. It resides, instead, in the act of living through the imagination in a world governed by change. The act of poetry, traced so ardently and arduously in S.'s later poems, mirrors this process and is thus synonymous with self-realization.

Once admired largely by certain critics and fellow poets and thought to be something of an anomaly among his literary peers, S. is now regarded as one of the foremost modern poets. During the course of his career, it was difficult to discern clearly the inner coherence with which his poetry gradually unfolded his sensibility, and critics responded primarily to his immediate phases and shifts in direction or to individual poems. Since his death, however, growing critical attention has amply revealed the centrality of purpose and the contours of its evolving realization in his entire canon, and has taken fuller measure of his place as a poet. Although S. has strong affinities with romantic and Transcendentalist predecessors like Keats and Emerson, his way of seeing and thinking belongs distinctly to the 20th c. He ranks alongside T. S. ELIOT, Ezra POUND, and William Carlos Williams as a seminal force in modern American verse. Whereas Eliot and Pound, however, sought to wrest a viable poetic answer to the modern cultural predicament from the heritage of the past, S. looked instead to the exertions of the individual imagination within the present. Like Williams, he sought to discover through poetry the reality of his own time and place independent of literary tradition, but, unlike Williams, he located that reality not in the world of things, but in the mind and the fictions by which it endows that other world with human shape. Few other poets have provided as extensive, searching, and eloquent a defense of poetry in our age.

FURTHER WORKS: *Letters of W. S.* (1966)

BIBLIOGRAPHY: Kermode, F., *W. S.* (1960); Pearce, R. H., *The Continuity of American Poetry* (1961): 376–419; Miller, J. H., *Poets of Reality* (1965): 217–84; Pearce, R. H., and J. H. Miller, eds., *The Act of Mind: Essays on the Poetry of W. S.* (1965); Riddle, J. N., *The Clairvoyant Eye: The Poetry and Poetics of W. S.* (1965); Doggett, F., *S.'s Poetry of Thought* (1966); Buttel, R. W., *W. S.: The Making of "Harmonium"* (1967); Baird, J., *The Dome and the Rock: Structure in the Poetry of W. S.* (1968); Vendler, H., *On Extended Wings: W. S.'s Longer Poems* (1969); Morse, S. F., *W. S.: Poetry as Life* (1970); Benamou, M., *W. S. and the Symbolist Imagination* (1972); Litz, A. W., *Introspective Voyager: The Poetic Development of W. S.* (1972); Edelstein, J. M., *W. S.: A Descriptive Bibliography* (1973); Beckett, L., *W. S.* (1974); Middlebrook, D. W., *Walt Whitman and W. S.* (1974); Morris,

A. K., *W. S.: Imagination and Faith* (1974); Bloom, H., *W. S.: The Poems of Our Climate* (1977); Stevens, H., *Souvenirs and Prophecies: The Young W. S.* (1977); Weston, S. B., *W. S.: An Introduction to the Poetry* (1977); Willard, A. F., *W. S.: The Poet and His Critics* (1978); Borroff, M., *Language and the Poet: Verbal Artistry in Frost, S., and Moore* (1979): 41–79; Doggett, F., *W. S.: The Making of the Poem* (1980); Doggett, F., and Buttel, R. W., eds., *W. S.: A Celebration* (1980)

—PETER W. DOWELL

Those phrases [from T. S. Eliot's essay on "The Metaphysical Poets"], so full of insight, "a direct sensuous apprehension of thought, or a re-creation of thought into feeling," precisely define the quality of S.'s poetry that has confused [some] readers. . . .According to Eliot's definition, S. is an intellectual poet. For that reason, though "the value of his poetry cannot be measured in intellectual terms" *alone*, neither can it be appreciated without an equal understanding of both its intellectual component and its element of sheer sensibility. Most of those who have written about his work have assumed that he was a lyricist in the nineteenth-century tradition. To the contrary, not the least of his distinctions is that he created for himself a genre that was new in its time, except insofar as Ezra Pound and Eliot did likewise: a type of poem that may be called a lyric of ideas, an intellectual lyric. S. is one of the originators of the Metaphysical trend in the poetry of our time.

Hi Simons, "The Genre of W. S.," *SR*, 53
(1945), p. 569

When the reader comes to aberrant poems like "Page of a Tale" and "A Rabbit as King of the Ghosts," he realizes how little there is in S., ordinarily, of the narrative, dramatic, immediately active side of life, of harried actors compelled, impelled, in ignorant hope. But how much there is of the man who looks, feels, meditates, in the freedom of removedness, of disinterested imagining, of thoughtful love! As we read the poems we are so continually aware of S. observing, meditating, creating, that we feel like saying that the process of creating the poem is the poem. Surprisingly often the motion of qualification, of concession, of logical conclusion—a dialectical motion in the older sense of *dialectical*—is the movement that organizes the poem; and in S. the unlikely tenderness of this movement—the one, the not-quite-that, the other, the not-exactly-the-other, the real one, the real other—is like the tenderness of the sculptor or draftsman, whose hand makes but looks as if it caressed.

Randall Jarrell, on *The Collected Poems of W. S.*,
YR, 44 (1955), pp. 345–46

S.'s vision, for it is almost that, is of living and unliving—a term which seems closer to his ideas than dead—men joined together in admiration, whether vocal or mute, of being. Being is the great poem, and all our lesser poems only approximate its intensity and power.

The sun is this primal force of being, reflected alike by living and unliving, by people and by things. Our dualisms disguise their single origin. It can be called God or the Imagination . . . though these terms are also only metaphors for what is ultimately a mystery to be worshipped rather than fathomed. The beauty that the sun creates antedates human life; long before we came on the earth the sun was covering the rock of reality with leaves, but once arrived here, we too participate in it. The sun is the Ulysses to which we and the world are the faithful Penelope. Its force is constant, and anchors in repetition all the changes which occur in the world, as the ever-changing gleams of sunshine stem always from the same burning source.

Richard Ellmann, "W. S.'s Ice-Cream," *KR*, 19
(1957), pp. 101–2

You sit in a chair, say, admiring the beauty of your four-year-old daughter: you call to mind certain resemblances between her and her absent mother, between her and your imagined image of yourself, between her and your memories and pictures of grandparents. You think, too, of certain painted images of children by Renoir or Romney; you think of Andrew Marvell's "Picture of Little T. C. in a Prospect of Flowers"; you think of the dogwood that bloomed last spring and of the zinnias now blooming outside. And for a moment the object toward which all these resemblances converge, or from which they infinitely extend—for a moment the object becomes a luminous center by which the sense of life is composed, "completed in a completed scene," as S. says. Such is W. S.'s "World as Meditation," a world where the poet may adopt the words of Valéry's Architect and say, "By dint of constructing . . . I truly believe that I have constructed myself."

Louis L. Martz, "W. S.: The World as
Meditation," *YR*, 47 (1958), p. 536

S. has most often been described as at worst a dandy and a connoisseur of chaos . . . and at best a poet so "pure" as to be bereft of any significant affiliation with the tradition of American poetry. The tendency, on the whole, has been to interpret him as a kind of post-post-*symboliste*, dwelling by choice in the universal intense inane. Whereas it has been not too difficult to accommodate a Williams on the one hand and an Eliot on the other to our conception of the evolution of poetry and poetics in the United States, only now we are beginning to realize that S. has an important place in that conception too—along with Eliot's, perhaps the most important of all. For in his work—if only we will at last give it the devoted study we have given to Eliot's—the continuity of the most deeply rooted tradition of American poetry, what I have called its Adamic phase, reaches the point of no return. "I'm ploughing on Sunday,/Ploughing North America," he wrote in an early poem "Ploughing on

Sunday" and so defined his major concern—to deal with Sunday, not workaday, matters: aspiration, understanding, belief, commitment in the North American portion of the modern world.

Roy Harvey Pearce, *The Continuity of American Poetry* (1961), p. 376

The critic of S. is confronted with a number of basic contradictions. He is and is not an intellectual poet, is and is not a "pure" poet. He is a romantic, but disconcertingly impersonal; a traditional poet, yet experimental; an imagist, but also a symbolist of sorts; a lyrical and meditative poet who wears equally well the masks of clown and pedagogue. The fact is, he can be at any one time any and all of these, which should, I think, give pause to those who would either praise his poetics or censure his obsession with one limited and vague idea. S. resolves the contradictions in a poetry which is neither pure lyric nor intellectual argument, but which at any one time may pose as either. Accused, especially in his early poetry, of being a hedonist pure and simple, S. was no less a reflective poet from first to last. The experience of his poetry, even at its most militantly antirational, is within the mind rather than at the tip of the senses.

Joseph N. Riddel, *The Clairvoyant Eye: The Poetry and Poetics of W. S.* (1965), p. 11

Though W. S.'s idiosyncratic vocabulary and imagery have been blamed and praised ever since his first poems appeared in print, his equally odd syntax has been less noticed. It shares nevertheless in his act of the mind, and differentiates him noticeably from other poets, whether the Romantic poets whose dependent heir he is, or his contemporaries in England and America. Abstractly considered, S.'s "themes" are familiar, not to say banal, ones, but his poetry reproduces them in a new form, chiefly in an elaborately mannered movement of thought, which changes very little in the course of the *Collected Poems*. It is, needless to say, expressive of several moods, but three large manners can be distinguished, all of them present in S.'s long poems. The first, in an ecstatic idiom, proclaims, sometimes defiantly, the pure good of being, the worth of vigorous life, the earthy marriages, the secular joys of ploughing on Sunday. The second, despairingly and in tones of apathy, anatomizes a stale and withered life. The third and most characteristic form is a tentative, diffident, and reluctant search for a middle route between ecstasy and apathy, a sensible ecstasy of pauvred color, to use S.'s own phrase.

Helen Vendler, *On Extended Wings: W. S.'s Longer Poems* (1969), p. 13

Like Emerson and Whitman before him, S. persuades himself by his own rhetoric that momentarily, in his poem, his ontological self and his empirical self have come together. Nietzsche, until he went mad, did not confuse himself with his own Zarathustra.

The Transcendental strain in S. is the native strain in our poetry, and it exacted of S. a rich philosophical confusion upon which everything that is strongest in American poetic tradition is founded. Nothing is got for nothing, and it need not surprise us that S.'s last poem sublimely celebrates a "Mere Being" that is beyond not only reason but also beyond all "human meaning" and even "human feeling." The American Sublime ends as the abyss, as the void beckoning just beyond the palm at the end of the mind. There is a great chill in Emerson, and in his children voluntary and involuntary—in Whitman, Thoreau, Dickinson, as in Hawthorne, Melville, James. But there is no chill in all of these so absolute and so Sublime as in the final vision of the Transcendental strain in W. S.

Harold Bloom, *Poetry as Repression* (1976), pp. 292–93

STOCKENSTRÖM, Wilma

South African poet, novelist, and playwright, b. 1933, Napier, Cape Province

S. is arguably South Africa's foremost Arikaans language poet. To English-speaking readers she is most famous for her novel *Die Kremetartekspedisie* (1981), published in English in 1983 as *The Expedition to the Baobab Tree*. S. has been awarded numerous prizes, both in South Africa and internationally.

In her work S. returns to the themes of landscape and nature. Her interpretations of these themes includes a rewriting of the Afrikaans farm novel, with its obsession with the natural bond between the white farmer and the land. S.'s protagonists in her farm novel *Uitdraai* (1976; Turn-Off) are the white daughter of the farmer and her unacknowledged half-brother, son of one of the black women who works on the farm. In *Die Kremetartekspedisie* S. seeks to confront her own complicity with what she regards as the destructive and reductive human desire to map and interpret landscapes through language and especially through print. In her prose and poetry the poet figure is often metaphorically represented as an intruder and destroyer, someone whose desire to acquire knowledge and express a relation with nature destroys that which it probes. Thus in *Die Kremetartekspedisie* S. is less concerned with writing about the political significance of land—although this theme is touched on elsewhere in her work—than to find a radically new way in which her narrator can relate to nature. The narrative is set on the east coast of Africa, during the 14th century, although both space and time remain indeterminate. The narrator, a woman who had been captured by slave-dealers as a child and worked as a slave in a city on the east coast of Africa, is abandoned by one of her owners to die in the desert. As she dies, she imagines herself diving into a new consciousness, which will be shaped like a baobab tree—the roots mirroring the branches above ground.

S.'s work is not overtly political, but it is concerned with the signification of land and nature, and returns obsessively to a consideration of forms of power, of which language—European and African languages alike—is the prime example.

FURTHER WORKS: *Vir die bysiende leser* (1970); *Dawid die dik dom kat* (1971); *Trippens se patatta* (1971); *Spiel van Water*

(1973); *Van vergetelheid en van glans* (1976); *Laaste middagmaal* (1978); *Eers Linkie dan Johanna* (1979); *Monsterverse* (1984); *Kaapse Rekwisiete* (1987); *Die heengaanrefrein* (1988); *Aan die Kaap geskryf* (1994)

BIBLIOGRAPHY: Du Plessis, M., "Bodies and Signs: Inscriptions of Femininity in John Coetzee and W. S.," *JLSTL*, 4, 1 (1988); Gray, S., "Some Notes on Further Readings of W. S.'s Slave Narrative, *The Expedition to the Baobab Tree*," *Literator*, 12, 1 (1991); Brink, A., "Woman and Language in Darkest Africa: The Quest for Articulation in Two Postcolonial Novels," *Literator*, 13, 1 (1992)

—CARLI COETZEE

STOESSL, Otto

Austrian novella writer, novelist, poet, essayist, and dramatist, b. 2 May 1875, Vienna; d. 15 Sept. 1936, Vienna

The early death of S.'s father, a physician, clouded his youth. And the unburdening of oppressive childhood remembrances—the memory of a beloved father so early lost and of an unmotherly mother—is a recurring motif in his writings.

S.'s early literary endeavors and successes—he published his first long novella *Leile* (Leile) in 1898—brought him into contact with Peter Altenberg (1859–1919), Karl KRAUS, and the architect Adolf Loos (1870–1933). He contributed to Kraus's periodical *Die Fackel* until 1911, when Kraus began to do all the writing for the journal himself. In spite of his aspirations to establish himself as a writer, S. continued his studies at the University of Vienna and earned a degree as a doctor of law in 1900. The insecurity of a writer's existence prompted him to work for a rail company. The problem of such division of an artist's life appears in various guises in S.'s writings. After 1919 he was the Burgtheater critic for the *Wiener Zeitung*. He left his railroad position in 1923. In the same year he was the first recipient of the Prize of the City of Vienna.

The decade before World War I was the happiest and most productive of S.'s life. At first he was drawn to the drama and toward naturalistic social criticism, but he soon turned his attention to fiction. His models were the past masters of poetic realism, Gottfried Keller (1819–1890), Conrad Ferdinand Meyer (1825–1898), and Adalbert Stifter (1805–1868), about whom he wrote superb critical essays. S. carried on this tradition of the Austrian novella. What gives his novellas their vigor and conviction is, beyond all aesthetic merits, their profound humanity.

S. did not want to be anything but a quiet observer, who, from his window, watched people's lives with a keen but kindly eye. What compelled his greatest compassion were the strangely blurred border areas of a seemingly solidly built society and the people who lived in an oddly hazy, indescribable twilight. These outsiders, who despised bourgeois life yet were caricatures of its members, are his favorites. Such characters are Heinrich Frantzel in *Das Haus Erath* (1920; the house of Erath)—the Frantzels are to Austria what the Buddenbrooks and Forsytes are to Germany and England; Lieutenant Roszkowski, master of the art of living, in *Sonjas letzter Name* (1908; Sonja's last name); and that funniest specimen of an ingenious heel, Egon de Alamor, in *Egon und Danitza* (1911; Egon and Danitza). In addition to buffoons, hypocrites, and adventurers, there are such wondrously fine women as the patiently suffering Antonia and the angelic Agnes in *Das Haus Erath*.

The end of World War I and the collapse of the Austro-Hungarian empire seemed to deprive S. of the main elements of his life and art. But his unbroken creative energy turned this painful experience into a subject of artistic creation. The novel *Das Haus Erath* shows this collapse by means of presenting the fate of three generations of a widely branched-out, originally solid and wealthy family; its moral and financial decline represents the degeneration of the middle class generally and so attests to the empire's ruin. Rich in psychological insight, breadth of ideas, and beauty of language, *Das Haus Erath* is justly considered S.'s main achievement.

When, in 1933, the first volume of his *Gesammelte Werke* (4 vols., 1933–37; collected works) appeared, S. titled it *Arcadia*, gathering in it a series of poetic creations almost all of which deal with classical antiquity or are rooted in antiquity. The typical Austrian—a synthesis of German and Mediterranean elements, of antiquity and Christianity—pervades S.'s work. This is particularly apparent in his *Griechisches Tagebuch* (1930; Greek diary), which combines Goethe's wide vision with the realism of Franz Grillparzer's (1791–1873) notes on a similar journey through Greece.

For the volumes comprising his novellas S. planned a division into *Schöpfer* (creators) and *Geschöpfe* (creatures). He did not live to see their publication. Only the volume *Schöpfer* appeared, in 1937, after S.'s death. With the emigration of his publisher in 1938 this edition of his collected works came to an end.

Behind every poetic creation of S., a spiritual, moral force is operative. He believed that "the homeland of all morality is art. It gives direction and uniqueness, it enlivens man's wretched life through its manifold interpretations, it provides variety for the moments of perpetual tension and so lightens the burden on his shoulders."

FURTHER WORKS: *Ware* (1897); *Tote Götter* (1898); *Kinderfrühling* (1904); *Gottfried Keller* (1904); *Conrad Ferdinand Meyer* (1906); *In den Mauern* (1907; repub. as *Das Schicksal pocht an die Pforte*, 1956); *Negerkönigs Tochter* (1910); *Allerleirauh* (1911); *Morgenrot* (1912); *Was nützen mir die schönen Schuhe* (1913); *Unterwelt* (1914); *Lebensform und Dichtungsform* (1914); *Basem, der Grobschmied* (1916); *Der Hirt als Gott* (1920); *Irrwege* (1922); *Sonnenmelodie* (1923); *Opfer* (1923); *Adalbert Stifter* (1925); *Johannes Freudensprung* (1926); *Nachtgeschichten* (1926; repub. as *Menschendämmerung*, 1929); *Die Schmiere* (1927); *Antike Motive* (1928); *Die wahre Helena* (1931); *Nora, die Füchsin* (1934)

BIBLIOGRAPHY: Magris, C., *Der habsburgische Mythos in der österreichischen Literatur* (1966): 246; Domandi, A. K., ed., *Modern German Literature* (1972), Vol. II: 285–89; Stoessl, F., "O. S.: Ein Porträt," *ÖGL*, 17 (1973): 231–50

—FREDERICK UNGAR

STONE, Robert

American novelist and screenwriter, b. 21 Aug. 1937, New York, New York

S. was born and reared in New York, but his travels, journalistic and otherwise, have taken him to the far reaches of the American empire and beyond—New Orleans, Saigon, London, Israel, even Hollywood. After dropping out of high school and serving in the navy in the late 1950s, S. observed firsthand, and lived, much of the cataclysmic change of the 1960s, in the Vietnam War and the West Coast of the Merry Pranksters. Reporting back to us first as a freelance journalist and later as a novelist, he continues to report from near and far on the state of the world and the search for transcendence beyond the tangled labyrinths of its murderous but mundane intrigues.

In six novels published over a span of thirty years, S. has become one of America's foremost political writers, a novelist whose explorations have taken him deep into the heart of America's darkness, wherever it is to be found. In the midst of his examinations of America and American influence, S. reveals, beneath the cynicism so proudly worn by many of his characters and so well earned by the events and ideas they encounter, a negative vision that reaches toward allegory. This combination of ironic negation and apocalyptic quest for transcendent meaning has drawn comparisons to Flannery O'CONNOR and Nathanael WEST, while S.'s eye for imperialism, as well as his Neitzschean fascination with the dark side of human nature, has earned comparisons to Joseph CONRAD.

S.'s main characters are, while varied, are all in extreme states, at the end of their financial, legal, mental, ideological, spiritual, or pharmaceutical ropes. Their stories are driven by attempts to extricate themselves from complications, often labyrinthine, that they and others have made as they try to maneuver in a world they have the sense to know they can't understand. The second motor driving their stories is the search not to extricate themselves from their plots but from the cynicism that has contributed to their current states: true success, a success for the most part barely imaginable, would be to free themselves and to believe. In this second drive S. manifests what seems to lay behind his own drive toward the apocalyptic, in its true derivation—an uncovering. Without cynicism, there would be no uncovering; without faith that there must be something else to be uncovered, there is nothing.

S.'s main characters have from the beginning fought in this struggle, choosing to ignore it, drink and drug it away, disbelieve in it, or lose their minds and sometimes their lives in attempts to win it. All of his novels contain some kind of battle-to-the-death, in which more is at stake. *Hall of Mirrors* (1967) has a New Orleans race war. *Dog Soldiers* (1974) quite literally brings the Vietnam War home to America, with the disillusioned cynicism, violence, and heroin that accompanied it while it was still in the jungle. *A Flag for Sunrise* (1981) follows the wars of American involvement in Central America. *Children of Light* (1986) moves Kate Chopin's (1851-1904) *The Awakening* (1899) to Hollywood, again quite literally, and over the course of that novel's being turned into a film tracks the violence wrought by this new world on a new version of its fierce but fragile heroine. *Outerbridge Reach* (1992) features the struggle between a man and his better and worst selves in a world whose moral channels are not clearly charted, writ largely in his struggles for his wife and against the sea. In *Damascus Gate* (1998) the connection between violence and belief is drawn most plainly, in the violence that occurs in Jerusalem's Old City and environs and results from the belief of individuals that they are working from divine instruction, whether that instruction be Jewish, Muslim, or Christian.

S. has been criticized for the prominence of politics and history in his novels; many have seen them as hampered by overly mechanical manipulation of character and event and excessive incorporation of authenticating detail—efforts motivated by attempts to master a new, foreign setting. This suggestion that S. engages in a form of artistic imperialism has been echoed in suggestions, particularly about *Damascus Gate*, that many of his realistic fictional situations are turned into struggles of the ultimate kind, that even a simple drug deal or boat race, in his hands, becomes romance. Turned around, these criticisms could be seen as simple description: working the vein of Herman Melville and Nathaniel Hawthorne, S. manages to examine real-world conflicts and to portray the explosive physical and psychic violence they wreak on people's lives, and in so doing manages to tackle the big questions without resorting to distant pasts or isolated whaling boats. Viewed from this angle, S. the American artistic imperialist can be seen instead as a novelist of the highest literary ambition.

FURTHER WORKS: *WUSA* (1970); *Who'll Stop the Rain* (1978)

BIBLIOGRAPHY: Shelton, F. W., "R. S.'s *Dog Soldiers*: Vietnam Coming Home to America," *Crit*, 24, 2 (1983): 74-81; Parkes, J. G., "Unfit Survivors: The Failed and Lost Pilgrims in the Fiction of R. S.," *CEA*, 53 (1990): 52-57; Solotaroff, R., *R. S.* (1994)

—SAM COHEN

STOPPARD, Tom

English dramatist, b. 3 July 1937, Zlín, Czechoslovakia

S.'s family left their native country for Singapore in 1939, the year in which the Nazis began their occupation. In 1942 his father, forced to remain behind in Singapore, sent the family to India. During the fighting he was killed by the Japanese. In 1946 S.'s mother married a British officer who later took the family to England. In 1954, at the age of seventeen, S. took a job with a Bristol newspaper; by 1958 he was a second-string drama critic. He began writing plays in 1960, at first for radio and television. In 1967 *Rosencrantz and Guildenstern Are Dead* was performed at the Old Vic in London, instantly establishing S. as an important dramatist. His most ambitious full-length plays since then are *Jumpers* (1972) and *Travesties* (perf. 1974, pub. 1975), and of his many short farces the most notable is *The Real Inspector Hound* (1968). In addition to his original works, S. has adapted several plays by other dramatists and, like his friend Harold PINTER, has written screenplays that display his mastery of spoken English.

Rosencrantz and Guildenstern Are Dead brings two of the least important characters in Shakespeare's *Hamlet* to the center of the stage, where they are baffled by the glimpses they catch of the tragedy that is unfolding at Elsinore. Like the two tramps in *Waiting for Godot* by Samuel BECKETT, Rosencrantz and Guildenstern pass the time as best they can, playing games and trying to be rational about their situation. While Beckett's characters are in a static situation, however, S.'s two characters move inexorably toward their fate, which is spelled out in the title of the play.

Rosencrantz and Guildenstern Are Dead has been given innumerable interpretations, many of them centering around EXISTENTIALISM. Perhaps the best formulation of the play's theme was made by C. J. Gianakaris: "Man is an actor in a play not wholly of his own making." While that idea may be a familiar one, S. makes it seem new by illustrating it literally: the only identity that his central characters have is that they are dispensable characters in someone else's play. A contrast is repeatedly drawn between Rosencrantz and Guildenstern, each of whom must play out *his* part whether he wishes to do so or not, and a troupe of strolling players, the members of which will perform any parts if the fee is sufficient. The most memorable moment in the play comes when an enraged Guildenstern stabs the leading Player, who dies an agonizing death—but rises up again. He was stabbed with his own knife, which of course is only a "play" knife. The deaths lying in wait for Rosencrantz and Guildenstern, in contrast, are only too "real."

The theme of man-as-actor runs through *Lord Malquist and Mr. Moon* (1966), an uneven novel that nevertheless is a marvelous storehouse of S.'s wit and imagination. Mr. Moon is described in the novel as standing "like a stranded actor denied the release of an exit." In the one-act comedy *The Real Inspector Hound*, a second-string critic leaves his comfortable seat in the theater, where he is reviewing a play, and takes a very uncomfortable role in the play on stage.

In *Jumpers*, the moon, barren and desolate, is a symbol of what the world is coming to resemble, now that there are no moral values acknowledged to be objectively valid. The central character is a Professor of Moral Philosophy who is outside the mainstream of modern philosophy; he tries desperately to prove the existence of moral absolutes by using logical reasoning. A constant theme in S. is that while the most wildly surrealistic situations turn out to have perfectly logical explanations, the situations encountered in the real world are impervious to any logical analysis.

S.'s announced intention in *Jumpers* and *Travesties* was to "end up by contriving the perfect marriage between the play of ideas and farce, or perhaps even high comedy." His characters have serious discussions about modern philosophy (*Jumpers*) or the nature and function of art (*Travesties*), and the discussions give rise to as much laughter as the crassest commercial comedy. S.'s most recent works, which take a direct political stand in favor of freedom of expression in totalitarian societies, have seemed to many critics a retreat from the dazzling brilliance of those earlier plays. In *Night and Day* (1979) a rebellion in a fictitious African country serves as background for an ironic debate about the crucial informative role played by journalism, despite its invasions of privacy and its scoop-hungry reporters. Two highly original works set in Communist-bloc countries, *Every Good Boy Deserves Favor* (perf. 1977, pub. 1978) and the television play *Professional Foul* (perf. 1977, pub. 1978), stem in part from S.'s meditation upon the fate that might have been his had he remained in his native country. In the first play, a political dissident who is placed in a mental institution shares a room with a genuine mental patient who plays the triangle in an imaginary orchestra—and in S.'s play, which places an entire symphony orchestra on the stage, the pastiche of Russian music composed by André Previn is as important as S.'s dialogue. In *Professional Foul* a British philosopher, visiting Prague for a colloquium (and—of greater importance to him—a soccer match), is reunited with one of his former students, whose difficulties with the Czech police make the philosopher reexamine the conflicting claims of disinterested thought and social intervention.

There is no doubt that S.'s career to date can be divided into two parts—the break seems to come when Lenin steps on stage at the beginning of the second act of *Travesties*—and that his more recent work has distinct political overtones. What all of S.'s plays share, however, is their overwhelming tendency to be hilariously funny. His sternest critics, who claim that S.'s dramatic devices are secondhand and his philosophy second-rate, have never denied that S. is one of the wittiest dramatists now writing in English.

FURTHER WORKS: *Enter a Free Man* (1968); *Albert's Bridge, and If You're Glad I'll Be Frank* (1969); *After Magritte* (1971); *Artist Descending a Staircase, and Where Are They Now?* (1973); *Dirty Linen, and New-Found-Land* (1976); *Dogg's Hamlet, Cahoot's Macbeth* (1979); *Undiscovered Country* (1980; adaptation of Arthur Schnitzler's *Das weite Land*); *On the Razzle* (1981; adaptation of Johann Nestroy's *Einen Jux will er sich machen*); *The Real Thing* (1982)

BIBLIOGRAPHY: Brustein, R., *The Third Theatre* (1969): 149–53; Gianakaris, C. J., "Absurdism Altered: *Rosencrantz and Guildenstern Are Dead*," *Drama Survey*, 7: 1–2 (1968–1969): 52–58; Taylor, J. R., *The Second Wave* (1971): 94–107; Bigsby, C. W. E., *T. S.* (1976); Hayman, R., *T. S.* (1977); Cahn, V. L., *Beyond Absurdity: The Plays of T. S.* (1979); Tynan, K., *Show People* (1979): 44–123; Dean, J. F., *T. S.: Comedy as a Moral Matrix* (1981); Londré, F. H., *T. S.* (1981); Hunter, J., *T. S.'s Plays* (1983)

—MICHAEL POPKIN

STOREY, David

English novelist and dramatist, b. 13 July 1933, Wakefield

The son of a Yorkshire mine worker, S. played rugby professionally with the Leeds Rugby League Club to finance his study at the Slade School of Art in London. He also worked for a tent-erecting firm and as a teacher. Much of S.'s own experience appears in his works.

S.'s novels and plays reflect his sense of conflict between body and soul in contemporary life. Related to this theme are his concern with mental breakdown, a search for wholeness, and the excessive and bewildering demands of parents on their children, particularly those of the working class. His fiction and drama provide vivid, realistic depictions of the places and activities with which he was familiar. Yet, while his works are grounded in meticulous detail, they often suggest various symbolic meanings.

S. first gained recognition for his novel *This Sporting Life* (1960), which combines realistic accounts of the day-to-day life of a rugby player with the strange love affair between the footballer Arthur Machin (body) and his middle-aged, widowed landlady (soul). She is determined to meet his advances with indifference. But after she is separated from Machin, she shows symptoms of strain and withdrawal, and ultimately dies. *Flight into Camden* (1961) is a first-person account of an unmarried secretary (soul) who goes to live in London with a married art teacher (apparently body, but really soul) who is undergoing a mental breakdown. But she realizes that he will drift back to his wife and that she will return to her disapproving parents. *Pasmore* (1972) presents a similar story from the male point of view; the character Pasmore is suffering a collapse, tries to escape his marriage, is blocked by stern parental opposition, and fails to escape. *Saville* (1976) deals with a talented young man who, wrenched from his background in a coal-mining community, finds himself classless and without a sense of identity.

S.'s novels generally are free of traditional middle-class restraints; the lustiest, *Radcliffe* (1963), is a violent homosexual love story. Radcliffe (soul), a descendant of the aristocracy, needs the working-class vitality of Tolson (body) to achieve wholeness, but in the end kills him. In *Radcliffe* the incompatibility of the soul and body has social and religious as well as psychological dimensions.

S. is probably best known for his plays, particularly *Home* (1970) and *The Changing Room* (1972). His first play, *The Restoration of Arnold Middleton* (1964), like several of S.'s novels, deals with the break-up of a marriage and with mental breakdown; but here the central character overcomes his mental illness and is restored. *In Celebration* (1965) provides S.'s fullest picture of the generation gap and of the disturbing demands of parents upon children. Three sons, including one long dead, had been expected to justify the hasty marriage of the pregnant mother to a miner beneath her class.

S.'s next three plays have been compared by some critics with those of Chekhov. Individuals come together to form a group with its own rhythms and life; a spell is cast, a mood is evoked, symbolic meanings are suggested. Productions of these plays have profited from the sensitive direction of Lindsay Anderson. In *The Contractor* (1970) five men erect a tent for a wedding breakfast for their boss's daughter, then take it down the next day. In *Home* two men and two women come together and talk, almost aimlessly; this conversation is interrupted by some long silences and by some tears. Gradually the audience perceives that the "home" is an asylum and that perhaps the asylum is modern Britain. The play is a distillation of S.'s early concern with mental illness. *The Changing Room*, a more complex play, about the members of a rugby team, has more realistic detail and twenty-two characters, including an aging coach, a badly injured player, and the handy-man who never leaves to watch the game, since his place is in the changing room. These characters are separate entities, yet they become one organism as we see them before a game, during the interval, and at the end. A sense of wholeness has been achieved.

S. holds a distinctive position in contemporary English literature. From the working-class perspective of miner, rugby player, or tent erector, he has provided a realistic view of a certain part of English society. He has brought personal intensity to the exploration of the body-soul relationship, of mental illness, and of the generation gap. In his later plays realism and feeling have been suffused with a poetic vision.

FURTHER WORKS: *Cromwell* (1973); *The Farm* (1973); *A Temporary Life* (1973); *Edward* (1973); *Life Class* (1974); *Mother's Day* (1976); *Sisters* (1978); *Early Days* (1980); *A Prodigal Child* (1982)

BIBLIOGRAPHY: McGuinness, F., "The Novels of D. S.," *London*, 3, 12 (1964): 79–83; Shrapnel, S., "No Goodness and No Kings," *CQ*, 5, 2 (1970): 181–87; Free, W. J., "The Ironic Anger of D. S.," *MD*, 16 (1973): 307–16; Taylor, J. R., *D. S.* (1974); Quigley, A. E., "The Emblematic Structure and Setting of D. S.'s Plays," *MD*, 22 (1979): 259–76; Rosen, C., "Symbolic Naturalism in D. S.'s

Home," *MD*, 22 (1979): 277–89; Shelton, L. E., "D. S. and the Invisible Event," *MQ*, 22 (1981): 392–406

—JOSEPH E. DUNCAN

STRACHEY, Lytton

English biographer, essayist, and critic, b. 1 March 1880, London; d. 21 Jan. 1932, Inkpen

S. was born into an upper-middle-class family; his father was a general in the British Army with extensive service in India as a soldier and civil administrator. In 1899 S. matriculated at Trinity College, Cambridge University, where he met many of the writers and intellectuals who, with S., were later to form the nucleus of the Bloomsbury Group: Clive Bell (1881–1964), Leonard Woolf (1880–1969), John Maynard Keynes (1883–1946), and E. M. FORSTER. In 1907 S. became a reviewer for *The Spectator* and the *New Quarterly*. His first book, *Landmarks in French Literature* (1912), is written in an urbane, graceful style that anticipates the greater works to come.

With *Eminent Victorians* (1918), consisting of biographical essays on Florence Nightingale, Cardinal Manning, General Charles George Gordon, and Dr. Thomas Arnold, S. achieved immediate fame, but the book also incurred the wrath of some reviewers and professional historians, for S. had rejected traditional conventions of biography and had injected irony and psychological analysis into a consciously designed dramatic framework. For S., biography was not simply the organization of historical fact designed to reveal the noble qualities of revered figures but an artistic design expressing the biographer's personal vision. Thus, through S.'s exposure of the less admirable qualities of his subjects, even the title *Eminent Victorians* was clearly ironic.

S.'s next major work, *Queen Victoria* (1921), is decidedly less ironic, less a deliberate attempt to reduce myth to human proportions. Stylistically, the narration has greater maturity; and since S. was dealing with only one major figure, the narration results in an aesthetically satisfying unity. Although *Queen Victoria* has come to be regarded as S.'s masterpiece, it has had less of an influence on historical writing than has *Eminent Victorians*.

In *Elizabeth and Essex: A Tragic History* (1928), a work more of historical drama than of historical research, S. presents imaginatively conceived truth rather than scholarly fact. In addition, there are obvious Freudian (and personal) implications in, for example, the treatment of the mother-son relationship between the Queen and Essex, an idea no doubt derived from S.'s brother, James, who had studied with FREUD and, in fact, translated his works. A popular success, *Elizabeth and Essex* was regarded by many historians as a mere trifling with history. Indeed, it has been facetiously called S.'s only work of fiction.

Although S.'s reputation declined after his death, his influence as a biographer continued to be widely felt. S.'s main contribution was his insistence that truth must be imaginatively and intuitively grasped. The recent revival of interest in S. indicates that, as historian and critic, he remains an enduringly interesting creative artist.

FURTHER WORKS: *Books and Characters: French and English* (1922); *Pope* (1925); *Portraits in Miniature, and Other Essays*

(1931); *Characters and Commentaries* (1933); *The Collected Works* (6 vols., 1948); *Virginia Woolf and L. S.: Letters* (1956); *Spectatorial Essays* (1964); *Ermyntrude and Esmeralda* (1969); *L. S. by Himself: A Self-Portrait* (1971); *The Really Interesting Question, and Other Papers* (1972); *The Shorter S.* (1980)

BIBLIOGRAPHY: Dobree, B., "L. S.," in W. R. Inge, ed., *Post Victorians* (1933): 572–89; Iyengar, K. R. S., *L. S.: A Critical Study* (1939); Sanders, C. R., *L. S.: His Mind and Art* (1957); Kallich, M., *The Psychological Milieu of L. S.* (1961); Holroyd, M., *L. S.: A Critical Biography* (2 vols., 1967–1968); Edel, L., *Bloomsbury: A House of Lions* (1979), passim

—KARL BECKSON

STRAMM, August

German poet and dramatist, b. 29 July 1874, Münster; d. 1 Sept. 1915, Gorodenka, Russia

The son of a postal official, S. had a career as civil servant in the postal service. After studying philosophy and economics, he received his doctorate in 1909 for his dissertation on the unification of international postal rates. Having served as captain in the army reserve, he was killed in action on the Russian front during World War I.

For several years S.'s literary endeavors had been rejected by German publishers until in 1913 he met Herwarth Walden (1878–1941), the editor of the EXPRESSIONIST magazine *Der Sturm* and leader of the Storm Circle. S. immediately became the leading poet of this group, whose members included writers like Alfred DÖBLIN and Else Lasker-Schüler (1876–1945) and painters like Oskar Kokoschka (1886–1980) and Franz Marc (1880–1916). The linguistic theories and practices of Filippo Tommaso MARINETTI and the aesthetic principles of Wassily Kandinsky (1866–1944) underwent a radical transformation in S.'s writings. His brief poems of a few lines reduce language to a small number of symbolic key words, which are arranged in repetitive or parallel patterns to form rhythmic structures. Thus, meaning is expressed by the positioning of a word. In his first collection of poems, *Du: Liebesgedichte* (1915: thou: love poems), love as a cosmic experience is treated in all its erotic manifestations, from the sacred to the profane. His last poems, impressionistic sketches of war and death or abstract word groupings, were published posthumously by Walden in *Tropfblut* (1919; drip-blood), together with his earliest poems.

As a dramatist S. began with naturalistic one-act plays in the style of Arno Holz (1863–1929) and Johannes Schlaf (1862–1941). After these simple milieu studies he turned to the poetic atmosphere and erotic mysticism of Maurice MAETERLINCK in *Die Haidebraut* (1914; *The Bride of the Moor*, 1914) and *Sancta Susanna* (1914; *Sancta Susanna: The Song of a May Night*, 1914). The latter play provided Paul Hindemith with the libretto for his opera of 1921. S.'s last plays, *Erwachen* (1915; awakening), *Kräfte* (1915; forces), and *Geschehen* (1916; happening), are brief condensations of his cosmic philosophy. They re-create the dualistic struggle of light and darkness and of hate and love, and they offer hope of ultimate salvation through a messianic figure of light.

Lytton Strachey

These sketchy allegories are reminiscent of Kokoschka's and Kandinsky's experimental plays. S. aims at a synthesis of light and sound, of gesture and motion. Language no longer serves as verbal communication; it becomes a series of sound symbols that are integrated within an abstract stage composition. Likewise, the actor is reduced to a structural element, a mere body in motion.

Like the Italian FUTURISTS, S. developed his own radical technique of liberating the single word and thus energized language. The explosive quality of his poems is the result of a long and painstaking process of deforming and reshaping conventional speech and of arranging rhythmic lines in repetitive patterns in order to achieve the greatest effects with a minimum of words. His linguistic alchemy places him into the esoteric tradition of Stéphane Mallarmé or close to the CUBIST constructivism of Guillaume APOLLINAIRE; he resembles the laboratory poet in Gottfried BENN's theory of modern poetry. With his dissolution of language he influenced DADAISM, while his constructivism foreshadowed the techniques of modern concrete poetry.

FURTHER WORKS: *Rudimentär* (1914); *Die Unfruchtbaren* (1916); *Die Menschheit* (1916); *Dichtungen in drei Bänden* (1918–1919; only first 2 vols. pub.); *Dein Lächeln weint* (1956); *Das Werk* (1963). FURTHER WORKS IN ENGLISH: *22 Poems* (1969)

BIBLIOGRAPHY: Radrizzani, R., Postscript to *A. S.: Das Werk* (1963): 399–489; Adler, J. D., "On the Centenary of A. S.," *PEGS*,

44 (1973–1974): 1–40; Marx, H., "A. S.," *TDR*, 19, 3 (1975): 13–33; Perkins, C. R. B., "A. S.: His Attempts to Revitalize the Language of Poetry," *NGS*, 4 (1976): 141–55; Adler, J. D. and J. J. White, eds., *A. S.: Kritische Essays und unveröffentlichtes Quellenmaterial aus dem Nachlaß des Dichters* (1979)

—CHRISTOPH HERIN

STRAND, Mark

American poet, b. 11 Apr. 1934, Summerside, Prince Edward Island, Canada

Like many American poets who are also professors of literature, S. has led a peripatetic life. He received his B.A. from Antioch College (1957); a B.F.A. from Yale University (1959) and his M.A. from the University of Iowa (1962). In the course of a distinguished career he has taught at such colleges and universities as Mount Holyoke, Columbia, Brooklyn College, Yale, Brandeis, Princeton, Harvard, and the universities of Iowa, Washington, Virginia, California, and Utah. In 1960–1961 he was a Fulbright scholar in Italy; in 1965–1966, a Fulbright lecturer in Brazil. In 1990 he was named America's fourth poet laureate—the first laureate to be appointed at the height of his career.

S.'s poetry is distinguished from that of his contemporaries primarily by its persona, who is so alert to ontological mysteries that he experiences himself as double. In the collection *Sleeping*

Mark Strand

with *One Eye Open* (1964), S. makes clear that one of the two selves of his persona lives in the objective, physical world; the other self (the vehicle of consciousness in the poems) seems real only in the narrator's subjective awareness. The poem "Keeping Things Whole" defines the persona famously as a not-field moving through a field of reality and keeping the field whole by moving on, careful not to displace any aspect of the field with his comparatively insufficient being. The extraordinary impact of such poems derives from the coolness with which the persona recounts his sense of double existence. While he is clearly harrowed by his relationship to nothingness, his tone is far from being confessional. He affects to stand outside his trauma even while he strives conversationally to give it definition and even while he experiences it as personal dissolution.

Such ontological awarenesses are rendered surrealistically in the poems of *Reasons for Moving* (1968). The persona is awakened at midnight by a weeping mailman who seems his alter ego; he is run over by a train whose engineer whispers intimately in his ear; he leaves Rio de Janeuro in a death bus, comforted by a woman with tombstones in her eyes. In "The Man in the Mirror" he confronts an alter ego in the glass, frightened both that the image will desert him and that it will endure. Such poems extend the imaginative reach of *Sleeping with One Eye Open* and advance considerably its level of technique. Indeed, the increasing "disease" of the poet's vision and the gathering ease of his craft become in *Reasons for Moving* an important counterpoint.

Several of the poems in *Darker* (1970) more than justify their collective title, notably such poems as "My Life By Somebody Else" and "The Way It Is," in both of which the persona continues to probe a nothingness that seems to contain the secret of his being. But other poems, like "Breath," "From a Litany," and especially. "The New Poetry Handbook," look to poetry as an alternative to nothingness. Poetry is not in these texts a vehicle of expressing the self but a process of being that authenticates being. The S. persona subsequently approaches reality not so much through his shadow of nothingness as through his creative imagination. Indeed, the seven relatively long poems of *The Story of Our Lives* (1973) drift from the propositional mode to the interrogative as the persona strives to create a substantial world out of his emptiness. A new and daunting balance of ontologies is the result in poems like "Elegy for My Father" and "The Untelling."

The Monument (1978) is in many ways the persona's ultimate statement of selfhood as a non-experience. A sequence of fifty-two prose statements, it intermingles almost seamlessly the voice of the S. persona and quotations from Shakespeare, Sir Thomas Browne, William Wordsworth, Friedrich Nietzsche, Wallace STEVENS, and others. Ostensibly engaged in creating a monument to selfhood—addressing, even, his future translator (the texts affect to be already translated)—the persona moves from an initial show of egotism to a self-effacement so entire that it is impossible to discern where he exits the sequence and fades into the voices of literary tradition. Ultimately, the volume is both monument and antimonument: a developing tabula rasa that configures the presence-through-absence of the persona's essential being.

In the wake of *The Monument*, the poems of *The Late Hour* (1978), of a "New Poems (1980)" section in the *Selected Poems* (1980), and of *The Continuous Life* (1990) seem the gentle aftermath of a storm. The concerns of the poems are more varied than before and less ontologically harrowed; the author's trademark commitment to self-effacement is only a sporadic concern; the persona is notably older, hopeful, almost at peace; his eruptions of anxiety are governable. There is no apparent rejection of the persona's earlier stance, for a poem like. "An Old Man Awake in His Own Death" worries questions of ego and anonymity as much as the earlier poems. In the majority of these poems, however, the persona has abandoned his lonely vigil at the abyss of nothingness for more comfortable, even domestic terrain. One of the effects of this domestication is a more affective level of statement. Poems like "For Jessica, My Daughter," "My Mother on an Evening in Late Summer," and the almost blithesome "Night Piece" have enormous authority as testaments of felt experience, their authority all the greater for the poet having deferred affective statements for so long.

S. is generally recognized as an austerely eloquent and spiritually intrepid poet in the tradition of his acknowledged mentors, Elizabeth BISHOP and William Carlos WILLIAMS, but his voice is entirely his own: subdued and quietly intense in the best manner of recent poetry; but plainer, sterner, and more spiritually harrowed than that of his mentors and of his contemporaries alike. Few voices in American poetry seem more authentic today, and few command a more respectful audience.

FURTHER WORKS: *The Sargeantville Notebook* (1973); *Elegy for My Father* (1978); *The Planet of Lost Things* (1982); *Art of the Real: Nine American Figurative Painters* (1983); *Mr. and Mrs. Baby and Other Stories* (1985); *The Night Book* (1985); *Rembrandt Takes a Walk* (1986); *William Bailey* (1987)

BIBLIOGRAPHY: Howard, R., *Alone with America: Essays on the Art of Poetry in the United States since 1950* (1969): 507–16; Crenner, J., "M. S.: Darker," *Seneca Review*, 2 (April 1971): 87–97; Bloom, H., "Dark and Radiant Peripheries: M. S. and A. R. Ammons," *SoR*, 8 (Winter 1972): 133–41; Gregerson, L., "Negative Capability," *Parnassus: Poetry in Review*, 9 (1978): 90–114; Kirby, D., "The Nature of No One," *TLS*, (15 September 1978): 1009; McClanahan, T., "M. S.," in D. J. Greiner, ed., *DLB: American Poets since World War II*, Part 2 (1980): 303–9; Shaw, R., "Quartet," *Poetry*, 139 (1981): 171–77; Stitt, P., "Stages of Reality: The Mind/Body Problem in Contemporary Poetry," *GaR*, 37 (1983): 201–10; Olsen, L., "Entry to the Unaccounted for: M. S.'s Fantastic Autism," in P. D. Murphy and V. Hyles, eds., *The Poetic Fantastic: Studies in an Evolvine Genre* (1989): 89–96; Kirby, D. K., *M. S. and the Poet's Place in Contemporary Culture* (1990)

—ROBERT F. KIERNAN

STREAM OF CONSCIOUSNESS

Critics use a variety of terms—often interchangeably—to describe attempts by authors to convey to the reader the contents of the mind of a character: stream of consciousness; silent, internal, or interior soliloquy or monologue (*monologue intérieur*); narrated monologue (*erlebte Rede, style indirect libre*). Such sections in a novel can range from an occasional question, fully verbalized, that a character silently puts to himself or herself to whole chapters in which a writer attempts to present the full workings of a character's mind.

Although writers developed the stream-of-consciousness technique and the other similar techniques in the early decades of the 20th c., bringing them to a full flowering in the 1920s, antecedents have been traced back into the 18th c. and even earlier. Some see Shakespearean soliloquy as the earliest precursor. Others offer the following as important forerunners: in the English novel, Laurence Sterne's *Tristram Shandy* (1760–1967), Charles Dickens's *The Pickwick Papers* (1837), George Meredith's (1828–1909) *The Egoist* (1879), much of the later work of Henry JAMES, and Joseph CONRAD's *Lord Jim* (1900) and *Chance* (1913); in the European novel, Gustave Flaubert's *Madame Bovary* (1857), Édouard Dujardin's (1861–1949) *Les lauriers sont coupés* (1887; *We'll to the Woods No More*, 1938), Fyodor Dostoevsky's *Notes from Underground* (1864) and *Crime and Punishment* (1866), and various works by Leo Tolstoy.

The ideas of certain philosophers, psychologists, and psychoanalysts also contributed to the development of the stream-of-consciousness and similar techniques: William James (1842–1910) and Henri BERGSON; Sigmund FREUD and Carl Gustav JUNG.

The stream-of-consciousness technique can be seen as the culmination of the tendency to "interiorize" the novel, first described by Percy Lubbock (1879–1965) in *The Craft of Fiction* (1921). One can see now how the growing interest of the 19th-c. novelists in "point of view" led to the novels of James and Conrad, in which the story is told by one of the characters in the novel rather than by an omniscient author, or at least is seen from the point of view of a single character. The logical next step was for the author to attempt to deposit the reader in the mind of a character, to offer the reader some version of the character's stream of consciousness.

Clear steps in that direction appeared about the time of World War I in Marcel PROUST's *Du côté de chez Swann* (1913; *Swann's Way*, 1922), the first of the seven volume *À la recherche du temps perdu* (1913–27; *Remembrance of Things Past*, 1922–32); Dorothy Richardson's (1873–1957) *Pointed Roofs* (1915), the first of the twelve-volume *Pilgrimage* (1915–38); and James JOYCE's *A Portrait of the Artist as a Young Man* (1916).

The flowering of the stream-of-consciousness and similar techniques, and probably their fullest exploitation, occurred during the 1920s with James Joyce's *Ulysses* (1922), Virginia WOOLF's *Mrs. Dalloway* (1925) and *To the Lighthouse* (1927), William FAULKNER's *The Sound and the Fury* (1929), and Alfred DÖBLIN's *Berlin Alexanderplatz*, (1929; *Alexanderplatz, Berlin*, 1931). Novelists since then have continued to use the stream-of-consciousness technique and its variations. Indeed, they have become standard devices in the novelist's bag.

In analyzing the stream-of-consciousness technique, one must recognize that the novelist can use only language in presenting a character's stream of consciousness; and language is linear and additive: word + word + word . . . , sentence + sentence + sentence . . . . The psychological stream of consciousness, the actual stream of consciousness in the human mind, is multidimensional; it involves three dimensions of space in addition to time. The human stream of consciousness is a flow of concurrencies through time: the sensations that arrive at the mind from the various sense organs and the perceptions into which the mind organizes them; fragments of thought; carefully articulated ideas; flashes of memory; fully remembered scenes or episodes; orientations of space, time, or purpose—some or even much of it preverbal (or perhaps, some critics suggest, even preconscious). A novelist cannot present a stream of consciousness, therefore, but can at best only simulate it.

Some of the early stream-of-consciousness novelists, however, seem to have had little doubt that they were reproducing the psychological stream of consciousness. In *A Portrait of the Artist as a Young Man* Joyce has Stephen Dedalus say, "The artist, like the God of the creation, remains within or behind or beyond or above his handiwork, invisible, refined out of existence, indifferent, paring his fingernails." A writer who wants to be invisible to the reader must not leave authorial traces that intrude on the reader's consciousness. The best way for the author to "disappear" is to persuade the reader that he (the reader) is in the mind of one of the characters, and that is what Joyce tried to do. As he told Djuna BARNES, "In *Ulysses* I have recorded simultaneously, what a man says, sees, thinks, and what such seeing, thinking, saying does, to what you Freudians call the subconscious."

Virginia Woolf, attempting to explain how she and some of her contemporaries, including Joyce, differed from their immediate predecessors like Arnold BENNETT, John GALSWORTHY, and H. G. WELLS, wrote in the *Times Literary Supplement* in 1919:

"Examine for a moment an ordinary mind on an ordinary day. The mind receives a myriad of impressions—trivial, fantastic, evanescent, or engraved with the sharpness of steel. From all sides they come, an incessant shower of innumerable atoms; and as they fall, as they shape themselves into the life of Monday or Tuesday, the accent falls differently from of old; the moment of importance came not here but there; so that, if a writer were a free man and not a slave, if he could write what he chose, not what he must, if he could base his work upon his own feeling and not upon convention, there would be no plot, no comedy, no tragedy, no love interest or catastrophe in the accepted style, and perhaps not a single button sewn on as the Bond Street tailors would have it. Life is not a series of gig-lamps symmetrically arranged; life is a luminous halo, a semi-transparent envelope surrounding us from the beginning of consciousness to the end. Is it not the task of the novelist to convey this varying, this unknown and uncircumscribed spirit, whatever aberration or complexity it may display, with as little mixture of the alien and external as possible? . . . Let us record the atoms as they fall upon the mind in the order in which they fall, let us trace the pattern, however disconnected and incoherent in appearance, which each sight or incident scores upon the consciousness."

The emphasis here is clearly on the attempt to present as directly as possible the individual sensation and perception, not a character's verbal report of what he or she thinks or feels.

The following continuum describes from smallest to greatest the degree to which the author appears—or disappears—in a novel, the degree, that is, to which the author attempts to simulate what happens in his or her character's mind: (1) statement by an obviously intrusive author; (2) summary statement by an omniscient author; (3) narrated monologue (*erlebte Rede*, or *style indirect libre*); (4) spoken soliloquy or monologue; (5) silent, internal, or interior soliloquy or monologue (*monologue intérieur*); (6) (simulated) stream of consciousness. Critics have variously called "stream of consciousness" any or all of the last four techniques distinguished in the continuum. Lumping them all together, however, destroys some useful distinctions and does not encourage the critical reader to try to understand what an author is attempting.

Dorrit Cohn, in *Transparent Minds: Narrative Modes for Presenting Consciousness in Fiction* (1978), rejects this model and the work of many of the students of the stream-of-consciousness technique on the grounds that they confuse "manner with matter" and that they assume "that only disorganized language can render disorganized minds." She proposes instead the following model: (I) Consciousness in third-person context: (A) psycho-narration—the narrator's discourse about a character's consciousness; (B)

quoted monologue—a character's mental discourse; (C) narrated monologue—a character's mental discourse in the guise of the narrator's discourse; (II) consciousness in first-person texts: from self-narration to various kinds of monologue, including forms in between.

There is space here only for a few quick examples of the various "levels" in the first model. The following passage from "Lestrygonians," the eighth chapter in Joyce's *Ulysses*, shows three:

"Some chap with a dose burning him.
"If he . . .
"O!
"Eh?
"No . . . No.
"No, no, I don't believe it. He wouldn't surely?
"No. No.
"Mr Bloom moved forward raising his troubled eyes."

The first and sixth lines are silent or internal monologue. Lines two through five are stream of consciousness, in this instance attempts to simulate Leopold Bloom's feelings, psychological and visceral, as they flood in and overwhelm him. The last line is a summary statement by the author. Chapters in *Ulysses* like "Proteus" and "Lestrygonians" that make the most use of the stream-of-consciousness technique all contain, also, internal monologue and omniscient author's statements. The last chapter, "Penelope," is entirely internal monologue or soliloquy.

Joyce's *A Portrait of the Artist as a Young Man* contains many instances of narrated monologue: the omniscient author's presentation of a character's thoughts in the language and style of the character himself. In the following passage, for example, the first two sentences are narrated monologue, the last omniscient author's statement:

"It made him very tired to think that way. It made him feel his head very big. He turned over the flyleaf and looked wearily at the green round earth in the middle of the maroon clouds."

Joyce does not intrude the way 19th-c. novelists frequently did: "But let the gentle-hearted reader be under no apprehension whatever . . . ." In *Ulysses*, however, he obviously intrudes in other ways—in sentences that clearly come from a playful author rather than from the mind of one of the characters:

"He came a step a sinkapace forward on neatsleather creaking and a step backward a sinkapace on the solemn floor."

"As said before, he [Bloom] ate with relish the inner organs. . . ."

"Some man that wayfaring was stood by housedoor at night's oncoming."

Despite Joyce's example, however, novelists who use the stream-of-consciousness technique and other similar techniques tend not to intrude, tend to remain "invisible, refined out of existence."

In an age of continued interest in matters psychological, it is not surprising that stream of consciousness and its variants have become standard techniques for the writer of fiction. What in the 1920s were seen as daring experiments that often outraged conservative critics have, in the ensuing years, become almost routine. Even in popular fiction today—detective stories, spy thrillers, romances—the reader frequently finds himself in the consciousness of one of the characters, recording the "atoms as they fall upon the mind."

BIBLIOGRAPHY: Humphrey, R., *Stream of Consciousness in the Modern Novel* (1954); Edel, L., *The Psychological Novel* (1955), passim; Friedman, M., *Stream of Consciousness: A Study in*

Literary Method (1955); Booth, W., *The Rhetoric of Fiction* (1961), passim; Souvage, J., *An Introduction to the Study of the Novel* (1965), passim; Dahl, L., *Linguistic Features of the Stream-of-Consciousness Technique of James Joyce, Virginia Woolf, and Eugene O'Neill* (1970); Steinberg, E., *The Stream of Consciousness and Beyond in "Ulysses"* (1973); Cohn, D., *Transparent Minds: Narrative Modes for Presenting Consciousness in Fiction* (1978); Steinberg, E., ed., *The Stream-of-Consciousness Technique in the Modern Novel* (1979)

—ERWIN R. STEINBERG

STREUVELS, Stijn

(pseud. of Frank Lateur) Belgian novelist and short-story writer (writing in Flemish), b. 3 March 1871, Heule, d. 15 Aug. 1969, Ingooigem

S.'s father was a tailor. His mother, a sister of the great poet Guido Gezelle (1830–1899), raised her children strictly and rigidly in the Catholic faith. S. left school early and was apprenticed to a baker. Until his marriage in 1905 he worked with his father, who had in the meantime taken over a bakery in Avelgem.

Self-taught, S. read widely and studied German, English, French, and Norwegian; he also became acquainted with Scandinavian and Russian literature. He was interested in cultural life in his village (theater and music), wrote for many literary periodicals, and was invited by *Van nu en straks*, the leading literary magazine at the turn of the century, to contribute on a regular basis. His extraordinary narrative talent met with critical and popular acclaim very early. From 1905 on he lived in Igooigem, devoting himself full time to writing.

The whole of S.'s oeuvre is closely related to his native territory, the southern part of West Flanders. Yet he cannot be classified as a mere regionalist. He gave an authentic picture of the everyday life of people in close contact with nature, sometimes through detailed, often pitiless descriptions, sometimes through subjective and lyrical visions, always in a very personal and astonishingly rich dialectal language. With Felix TIMMERMANS and Ernest CLAES, S. is one of the most frequently translated Flemish writers.

Apart from fiction, S. also wrote essayistic prose, travel books, and two short plays, and did many translations (from French, German, and Norwegian) and adaptations from chapbooks and sagas. His autobiographical writings, such as *Heule* (1942; Heule), *Avelghem* (1946; Avelgem), *Ingoyghem* (2 vols., 1951, 1957; Ingooigem)—the last two titles use old-style spelling—*Kroniek van de familie Gezelle* (1960; chronicle of the Gezelle family), are interesting not only for their background information but also because of the valuable light they shed on important events of the time. This is especially true of his war diaries, *In oorlogstijd* (5 vols., 1915–16; in wartime), which have only very recently been published in complete form (1979).

The early short-story collections *Lenteleven* (1899; *The Path of Life*, 1915), *Zomerland* (1900; summer country), and *Zonnetij* (1900; sun tide) have visionary dimensions. The story "De oogst" (the harvest) in *Zonnetij*, relating how a poor Flemish seasonal worker is fatally stricken by the sun while harvesting, established

S.'s fame. *Langs de wegen* (1902; *Old Jan.* 1936), his first novel, relates harsh circumstances in a fatalistic tone, qualities also characteristic of his early shorter fiction, which was written in solitude and under the influence of naturalism. *Langs de wegen* is the life story of a horse groom, presented as having a cyclical pattern dominated by fate and death: after marrying and struggling to support his wife and children, the main character, at the mercy of nature, is finally defeated by the small patch of land he worked on. A gloomy and pessimistic tone is also evident in his next novel, *Minnehandel* (1903; love trade), in which man and nature are seen as part of one cosmic unity. Love and destiny are controlled only by the claims of the land.

In S.'s more mature novels he perceived a harmony between man and nature, although not between man and man. In *De vlaschaard* (1907; the flax field), his best-known novel, human passions are still regulated by the succession of the seasons, but there is room for the drama of individual characters: here the central conflict between a farmer and his son is knitted with the course of nature.

S. subsequently focused on a wider range of problems, including social and moral conflicts. He analyzed the child's mind in the novella *Kerstekind* (1911; Christmas child) and in the short novel *Prutske* (1922; Prutske). The hallucinatory story "Het leven en de dood in den ast" (life and death in the kiln house), in the collection *Werkmensen* (1926; laborers), is a masterpiece of psychological insight. This story conjures up a night in a kiln house, interweaving the thoughts and dreams of the workers, who are half-consciously threatened by the presence of death. S.'s full creative powers are also evident in *De teleurgang van de waterhoek* (1927; the loss of the river edge), a full-fledged novel in which he portrays a primitive and rough agrarian community rebelling against the construction of a bridge. The gradual weakening of the older generation and the triumph of the younger one and of progress is counterbalanced by a passionate love affair.

FURTHER WORKS: *Dodendans* (1901); *Dagen* (1902); *Soldatenbloed* (1904); *Dorpsgeheimen* (2 vols., 1904); *Openlucht* (1905); *Stille avonden* (1905); *Het uitzicht der dingen* (1905); *Reinaert de vos* (1907); *Najaar* (1909); *De blijde dag* (2 vols., 1909); *Het glorierijke licht* (1912); *Morgenstond* (1912); *De workman* (1913); *De landse woningen in Vlaanderen* (1913); *Dorpslucht* (2 vols., 1914–1915; rewritten as *Beroering over het dorp*, 1948); *Genoveva van Brabant* (2 vols., 1919–1920); *Grootmoedertje* (1922); *Vertelsels van 't jaar nul* (1922); *Land en leven in Vlaanderen* (1923); *Herinneringen uit het verleden* (1924); *Tristan en Isolde* (1924); *Op de Vlaamse binnenwateren* (1925); *Drie koningen aan de kust* (1927); *Kerstwake* (1928); *Kerstvertelsel* (1929); *Alma met de vlassen haren* (1931); *De rampzalige kaproen* (1933); *IJslandse godensagen* (1933); *Sagen uit het hoge noorden* (1934); *Zeelieden en zeevisserij* (1934); *Prutskes vertelselboek* (1935); *Levensbloesem* (1937); *De terechtstelling van een onschuldige* (1940); *De maanden* (1941); *Volledige werken* (12 vols., 1950–1955); *In levenden lijve* (1966); *Volledig werk* (4 vols., 1971–1973)

BIBLIOGRAPHY: Mallinson, V., *Modern Belgian Literature 1830–1960* (1966): 43–46; Lissens, R. F., *Flämische Literaturgeschichte des 19. und 20. Jahrhunderts* (1970): 104–11; Meijer, R. P., *Literature of the Low Countries* (1971): 276–79

—ANNE MARIE MUSSCHOOT

August Strindberg

STRINDBERG, August

Swedish dramatist, novelist, short-story writer, essayist, and poet, b. 22 Jan. 1849, Stockholm; d. 14 May 1912, Stockholm

Perhaps one of the most charismatic figures in world literature, S. and his oeuvre portray a consummate blending of life and art, representing the 19th-c. dictate that the goal of life is to become art. Born as the fourth of eleven children of a lower-middle class shipping agent and a servant woman, S. was a hypersensitive child who after his mother's death and father's remarriage came to hate his stepmother—see the autobiographical novel *Tjänstekvinnans son* (1886; *Son of a Servant*, 1913). The desperate need for maternal affection and the concomitant resentment aroused by this dependency led in S. to an ambivalent attitude toward women, which was to suffuse and inform both his life and his art. It is perhaps not surprising that S. should marry three times and each time a woman eminently unsuited to him (Siri von Essen, 1877; Frida Uhl, 1893; Harriet Bosse, 1901). Career women who were attractive, intelligent, and ambitious, his wives refused to relegate themselves to the role of the simple domestic housewife that S. so keenly wanted. This ambivalence toward women and the tension that S. always felt between his father's middle-class and his mother's lower-class origins pervade both the plays and the prose of the 1880s.

Fadren (1887; *The Father*, 1907), influenced by both Nietzsche and the French psychologists, depicts a battle between the Captain and his wife Laura over the future of their child. By virtue of his integrity and moral principles, the father is incapable of stooping to the insidious and demeaning tactics his wife employs in her struggle for control of the daughter; finally he is reduced to a whimpering child, begging comfort from his nanny, as he is taken off to an insane asylum. What is especially interesting in this, as in any S. drama, is the tremendous strength and passion that the combatants bring to their struggle, their mutual love for the child, and the sense in which they are involved less in a particular marital disagreement than in a pitched battle between the sexes. In all the plays and prose of this period, S.'s style is spare and ascetic, representing his rebellion against the artificial French-influenced theater that had dominated the Swedish stage for most of the 19th c. But none of the works of the 1880s, despite his dubbing them "realistic" and/or "naturalistic," is without a certain visionary tendency. Act I of *Fadren* begins with a scientific and psychological frame of reference for his characters, but the play gradually glides into the "EXPRESSIONIST" characterization, whereby the figures become wounded souls who cry their despair or triumph aloud to the void.

S.'s next major drama, *Fröken Julie* (1888; *Miss Julie*, 1913), which S. subtitled "a naturalistic tragedy," expands the motif of the battle between the sexes and couples it with a social struggle as well. Alternately aristocratic and socialist in his sympathies, S. is deeply concerned with the dissolution of the nobility and the emergence of the lower classes. Enfeebled and enervated by her parents (her mother is a man-hating feminist and her father a weak aristocrat), Julie encounters her father's servant Jean, a lackey who has received some education and is socially on the rise. Intoxicated by the midsummer atmosphere, Julie allows herself to be seduced by Jean and must then confront her mistake, but since she is unable to arrive at any reasonable plan of flight, she orders Jean to hypnotize her into committing suicide. S. was particularly proud of the naturalistic innovations he incorporated into this drama, enumerating in his preface the multiplicity of motive, the concept of the "characterless" character, the realistic production values, and the Darwinian survival-of-the-fittest motif in the play. But its continued success on the stage lies less in its capacity as a doctrinaire piece of naturalism than in its blending of naturalism and expressionism. The dreams Jean and Julie recount to each other and the almost comalike state to which fatigue, inner tension, dishonor, and the aphrodisiacal atmosphere of the evening reduced Julie have the effect of hypnotizing the audience into a dreamlike awareness of the dramatic proceedings. The spectators become as blurred and vague in their perception as Julie and are compelled toward the final resolution as inexorably as she is.

But the early S. (pre-1892) is by no means limited to realistic-naturalistic drama. Extraordinarily prolific, he also wrote one excellent historical drama, *Mäster Olof* (1872; *Master Olof*, 1959); many essays on Swedish life and letters; several folk dramas; five autobiographical novels; two collections of short stories on married life; pseudoscientific essays; some fine novels on Swedish folk life—*Hemsöborna* (1887; *The Natives of Hemsö*, 1965) and *Skärkarlsliv* (1888; life in the skerries); the Nietzschean novel *I havsbandet* (1890; *By the Open Sea*, 1913); a large collection of one-act plays in the manner of André Antoine's Théâtre Libre; and some less than remarkable poetry.

After 1892 the seemingly compulsively productive S. became strangely silent. The reason for this silence is that during this period S.'s separation from Siri von Essen became final, and he began to conduct chemical and alchemical experiments that occupied all his free time. He was also spending time in both Berlin and Paris, where, removed from the support system of his Swedish family and friends, he underwent his Inferno crisis, documented in *Inferno* (1897; *Inferno*, 1913) and *Legender* (1898; *Legends*, 1912). Haunted by guilt about deserting his children and persecuted by his critics (even to the extent that he was brought up on charges of blasphemy), he became possessed of a persecution mania, convinced that his enemies were trying to kill him with electromagnetic fields and that he was being pursued by a group of avenging furies whom he called "the powers," whose purpose was to humiliate and chastise him. With the help of his Swedenborg studies, however, he emerged from his crisis in 1897–98 to commence a vital and revolutionary period in his artistic production.

Having gained a new religious philosophy that stressed resignation, compassion, and the inevitable suffering of mankind, S. inaugurated what critics have subsequently called his "expressionistic" period. The first of his dramas after the Inferno experience, *Till Damascus, I-II* (1898; *To Damascus*, I-II, 1933), presents a protagonist called the Stranger, who is everyman and everything, possessing within his character the entire range of human experience and representing S.'s conception of man in combat with his fate and man in search of himself. He is possessed of a subconscious that drives him forth to self-confrontation as he passes from station to station on his penitential journey toward salvation, encountering people from the past whom he has injured and who demand restitution from him. The Stranger is in the drama both dreamer and dreamed, perceiver and perceived. He pits various of his "selves" against one another in an attempt to bridge the gap between subject and object, to achieve a balance between them as he tries to uncover a more whole Self; all this takes place in an atmosphere of free association that functions to give the work the fluidity appropriate to dream. Rife with biographical detail, the play depicts a movement inward, which is then duplicated precisely in the second half of the drama in such a way that the final scene takes place where the first one did, the play thereby forming a circular pilgrimage that imparts a necessary insecurity in both the Stranger and the audience as to whether or not the entire proceedings have been a dream journey into the depths of the subconscious and back again. All the characters are dreamlike and shadowy, and because they represent certain aspects of S.'s personality rather than real human beings, they are impersonal and nameless. Even the unities of time and space are summarily dismissed as being irrelevant in a world in which dream consciousness reigns supreme. The entire drama is an effort to bring about a reconciliation of the different levels of consciousness into one cohesive awareness of self, on a plane where the laws of external logic are set aside in favor of the more elemental and spontaneous dream logic. The emphasis on subjectivity that pervades the post-Inferno dramaturgy was to become a vital part of all subsequent Western drama.

Taking the dramatic tenets he established in 1898 as a starting point, S. embellished on this journey format with what is probably his most influential drama, *Ett drömspel* (1901; *A Dream Play*, 1912). In his preface S. says that he has tried "to imitate the disconnected but apparently logical form of a dream . . . a blending of memories, free inventions, absurdities, and improvisations. . . . The characters split, double, redouble, evaporate, condense, scatter, and converge. But one consciousness remains above all of them: the dreamer's." Time and space do not exist in S.'s dream dramaturgy. They are replaced by consciousness following its own wayward paths. All thoughts, attitudes, and perceptions emanate from a single individual's unconscious, as do the "characters" and events, through the dreamer's distortion of their objective reality. These have been sifted through his psyche and become appropriated by him. In an attempt to bridge the gap between the conscious and unconscious, S. portrays a dream state in which the elements of consciousness (the past and familiar people) are placed in an atmosphere of unconsciousness (wish fulfillment, extrasensory perception, and *déjà vu*) in order to form a synthesis whereby the two are reconciled with each other. Prefiguring FREUD in this regard, S. postulates that through the unconscious we can come to confront most effectively ourselves and our God. The protagonist, Indra's Daughter (S. had actively studied Eastern mysticism during the Inferno), descends to earth in order to ascertain for her father whether or not the complaints of mankind are justified. Like *Till Damaskus, Ett drömspel* is a pilgrimage drama, but here the heroine is involved with three different men, all of whom represent various stages in mankind's development: the Officer is the optimistic, idealistic young lover; the Lawyer is the mature man who struggles against a world of injustice in his business and against the inherent battle between the sexes in his marital life; and the Poet is the seer, the visionary who tries to impart order and beauty to the chaos about him.

The dream, as an individual psychological and as a dramatic form, functions for S. as a way to encounter and resolve our personal and historical cultural pasts. Only by integrating and defusing the past can we attain the freedom of futurity. The individual characters in the drama become archetypes without names—allegorical, psychological, and historical functions through which we can define ourselves. They are extensions of various facets of a single theme or motif in the personality of the dreamer, not viable individual characters. Scenically, S. opts for the use of setting as an image symbolic of the dreamer's state of mind. S. prescribes for *Ett drömspel* flexible wings, which serve as space, architecture, and landscape. Objects markedly change their nature and appearance from scene to scene: the door and coatrack remain in the retina of the observer's eye, as everything else about him shifts shape and function, scenes fading indeterminately into each other. At the conclusion of the play, all the major characters reappear, casting the symbols of their trials and tribulations onto a purifying fire. As Indra's daughter counsels tolerance and compassion, the heat from the fire fed on wickedness compels a giant chrysanthemum to burst into bloom in a heavenward ascent. Although S. recognizes the suffering inherent in the human condition, he also postulates a transcendence into the divine.

The strong reverberations of Lutheran dogma that pervade the post-Inferno production are, then, accompanied by an increasing interest in history and the role it plays in the development of individuals and cultures, an interest that is evident in the nine historical plays he wrote during this period. Although they have not received the attention abroad they deserve (presumably because of their ostensibly obscure subject matter—Swedish history), they all incorporate the fundamental Strindbergian tension between an individual's public and private callings, between his epic and psychological destinies. They, like the rest of the post-Inferno works, portray in dreamlike fashion the immutable conflicts of consciousness.

S.'s last major contribution to the body of world literature lies in the revolutionary experiments he undertook during 1907–8, in order to establish an intimate theater and create a body of drama suitable for it. Basing his innovations on the form of chamber music, S. sought to create a drama that would, in a reduced and concentrated form, consist of a motif and variations, eliciting in the spectator less an intellectual recognition than an atmosphere, a mood. To this end, he wrote four chamber plays in 1907; *Oväder* (*The Thunderstorm*, 1913), *Brända tomten* (*After the Fire*, 1913; later trs. titled *The Burned House, The House That Burned*), *Spöksonaten* (*The Spook Sonata*, 1916; later trs. titled *The Ghost Sonata*), and *Pelikanen* (*The Pelican*, 1962). In his use of a musical model, S. was trying to expand the generic boundaries of his medium and to impart an extra dimension of subliminal involvement to his art. One of the ways in which S. achieved this involvement is by discarding the single protagonist in favor of a small group of equally important characters, all of whom together form a kind of dramatic distillate. Indicative of this new dramatic style is that people are less the protagonists of these dramas than are houses, houses that over many years have absorbed into themselves all the evil and sins of their inhabitants and have become metaphors for the total individual.

The houses are falling apart or burned down or are dirty or drafty, reflecting the moral depravity of those who dwell there. The individuals who people these dramas are automatons, paralyzed by their guilt into absurd and stiff roles and postures. Their language is one of fear and hostility: words cover up terror and hide reality. Language becomes a smokescreen the individual throws up around himself to prevent the world from knowing him. Actions, too, are simply the manifestations of the self-imposed roles these characters have assumed to shield themselves from reality. But this role-playing is ultimately a falsification, and each individual must come to a traumatic reckoning with his soul and his past in order to dispel the aura of introspective pity in which he wallows. Sickness and death abound; the characters are as ill as they are corrupt, tormented both; spiritually and physically by the sins of their pasts.

But in contrast to most of the characters, S. places the figure of the "Sunday child," the individual who is capable of perceiving supernatural phenomena, of divining the truth, and of stripping away the facades of lies and deceits that other characters project. It is these "Sunday children" who precipitate the crisis in these dramas, by psychologically excoriating the other characters, unmasking their evil, and compelling them to confront the moral paucity of their lives. There is a basic transformation in this dramaturgy from the earlier emphasis on emotion and cognition to sense perceptions and sensations. Thunder, lightning, heat, and cold oppress our senses and those of the characters. A more direct and immediate mode of drama has been born.

S.'s impact on 20th-c. drama is perhaps equaled only by that of his fellow Scandinavian Ibsen. But whereas Ibsen influenced the realistic school of Bernard SHAW, S. is the model for much of the drama of Eugene O'NEILL, Luigi PIRANDELLO, Eugène IONESCO, Friedrich DÜRRENMATT, Edward ALBEE, Tennessee WILLIAMS, and Samuel BECKETT, to say nothing of the German expressionists, for whom he was a constant source of imitation and inspiration. Indeed, one can discern S.'s rich and compelling production behind virtually all that is most modern in modern theater.

FURTHER WORKS: *Fritänkaren* (1869); *En namnsdagsgåva* (1869); *I Rom* (1870); *Hermione* (1870); *Den fredslöse* (1871; *The Outlaw*, 1969); *Anno fyrtioåtta* (1876); *Från Fjärdingen och Svartbäcken* (1877); *Röda rummet* (1879; *The Red Room*, 1913); *Gillets hemlighet* (1880); *Gamla Stockholm* (1880); *Lycko-Pers resa* (1882; *Lucky Pehr*, 1912; later tr., *Lucky Per's Journey*, 1965); *Svenska folket* (1882); *Nya riket* (1882); *Svenska öden och äventyr* (1882–1892); *Dikter på vers och prosa* (1883); *Sömngångarnätter på vakna dagar* (1884); *Giftas I* (1884; *Getting Married*, 1972); *Utopier i verkligheten* (1885); *Giftas II* (1886); *Jäsningstiden* (1886; *The Growth of a Soul*, 1914); *I röda rummet* (1886); *Författaren* (1886); *Marodörer* (1887); *Kamraterna* (1887; *Comrades*, 1919); *Vivisektioner* (1887–1890); *Tschandala* (1888); *Le plaidoyer d'un fou* (1888; Swed., *En dåres försvarstal*, 1895; *The Confessions of a Fool*, 1912; later tr., *A Madman's Defense*, 1967); *Fordringsägare* (1888; *Creditors*, 1910); *Paria* (1889; *Pariah*, 1913); *Samum* (1889; *Simoom*, 1969); *Bland franska bönder* (1889); *Den starkare* (1889; *The Stronger*, 1964); *Första varningen* (1892; *The First Warning*, 1969); *Debet och kredit* (1892; *Debit and Credit*, 1969); *Inför döden* (1892; *In the Face of Death*, 1969) *Moderkärlek* (1892; *Mother Love*, 1969); *Leka med elden* (1892; *Playing with Fire*, 1969); *Himmelrikets nycklar* (1892; *The Keys of Heaven*, 1965); *Bandet* (1892; *The Bond*, 1960); *Ockulta dagboken* (written 1896–1908, pub. 1963; *From an Occult Diary*, 1965); *Advent* (1898; *Advent*, 1912); *Brott och brott* (1899; *Crimes and Crimes*, 1960); *Folkungasagan* (1899; *The Saga of the Folkungs*, 1959); *Gustav Vasa* (1899; *Gustav Vasa*, 1916); *Erik XIV* (1899; *Erik XIV*, 1931); *Gustav Adolf* (1900; *Gustav Adolf*, 1957); *Midsommar* (1900; *Midsummertide*, 1912); *Kaspers fet-tisdag* (1900); *Påsk* (1900; *Easter*, 1912); *Dödsdansen I, II* (1900; *The Dance of Death*, 1912); *Till Damaskus III* (1901; *To Damascus III*, 1935); *Kristina* (1901; *Queen Christina*, 1955); *Carl XII* (1901; *Carl XII*, 1964); *Engelbrekt* (1901; *Engelbrekt*, 1949); *Kronbruden* (1901; *The Bridal Crown*, 1916; later tr., *The Crownbride*, 1981); *Svanevit* (1901; *Swanwhite*, 1914); *Fagervik och Skamsund* (1902); *Gustav III* (1902; *Gustav III*, 1955); *Ensam* (1903; *Alone*, 1968); *Näktergalen i Wittenberg* (1903; *The Nightingale of Wittenberg*, 1970); *Världshistoriens mystik: Genom öknar till arvland; Hellas; Lammet och vilddjuret* (1903; *World Historical Plays: Through Deserts to Ancient Lands; Hellas; The Lamb and the Beast*, 1970); *Götiska rummen* (1904); *Svarta fanor* (1904); *Historiska miniatyrer* (1905); *Taklagsöl* (1905); *Ordalek och småkonst* (1905); *Hövdingaminnen* (1906); *Syndabocken* (1906; *The Scapegoat*, 1967); *Nya svenska öden* (1906); *Toten-Insel* (1907); *Blå boken* (4 vols., 1907–1912; *Zones of the Spirit*, 1913); *Siste riddaren* (1908; *The Last of the Knights*, 1956); *Riksföreståndaren* (1908; *The Regent*, 1956); *Öppna brev till Intima teatern* (1908; *Open Letters to the Intimate Theater*, 1966); *Bjälbojarlen* (1908; *Earl Birger of Bjälbo*, 1956); *Abu Cassems tofflor* (1908); *Svarta handsken* (1909); *Stora landsvägen* (1909; *The Great Highway*, 1965); *Fabler* (1909); *Religiös renässans* (1910); *Samlade skrifter* (55 vols., 1912–1920); *Samlade otryckta skrifter* (5 vols., 1918–1921); *Skrifter* (14 vols., 1946); *S.s ungdomsjournalistik* (1946); *Från Fjärden till blå tornet* (1947); *Brev* (15 vols., 1948 ff.); *Brev till min dotter Kerstin* (1961). FURTHER WORKS IN ENGLISH: *The University of Washington Press S.* (1955 ff.); *Five Plays* (1960); *Seven Plays* (1960); *The Chamber Plays* (1962); *Selected Plays and Prose* (1964); *Eight Expressionistic Plays* (1965); *Inferno, Alone, and Other Writings* (1968); *The S. Reader* (1968); *S.'s One-Act Plays* (1969); *S.: Three Experimental Plays* (1975); *The Plays of S.* (2 vols., 1976); *Five Plays* (1983)

BIBLIOGRAPHY: Dahlström, C. E. W. L., *S.'s Dramatic Expressionism* (1930); McGill, V. L., *A. S.: The Bedeviled Viking* (1930); Campbell, G. A., *S.* (1933); Mortenson, B. M. and B. W. Downs,

S.: An Introduction to His Life and Work (1949); Sprigge, E., *The Strange Life of A. S.* (1949); Borland, H., *Nietzsche's Influence on Swedish Literature* (1956): 17–46; Madsen, B. G., *S.'s Naturalistic Theatre* (1962); Johnson, W., *S. and the Historical Drama* (1963); Klaf, F. S., *S.: The Origin of Psychology in Modern Drama* (1963); Valency, M., *The Flower and the Castle* (1963); Brustein, R., *The Theatre of Revolt* (1964): 87–134; Johanneson, E., *The Novels of A. S.* (1968); Lamm, M., *A. S.* (1971); Ollén, G., *A. S.* (1972); Steene, B., *The Greatest Fire: A Study of A. S.* (1973); Brandell, G., *S. in Inferno* (1974); Gilman, R., *The Making of Modern Drama* (1974): 83–115; Ward, J., *The Social and Religious Plays of A. S.* (1980); Blackwell, M. J., ed., *Structures of Influence: A Comparative Approach to A. S.* (1981); Carlson, H., *S. and the Poetry of Myth* (1982); Sprinchorn, E., *S. as Dramatist* (1982); Tornqvist, E., *Strindbergian Drama: Themes and Structure* (1982)

—MARILYN JOHNS BLACKWELL

Naturalism's great genius—S.—who after all was not a naturalist, never became ensnared by this form [the beautiful mist of symbolism] even though the new need for which symbolism was an expression was also evident in him, and despite the fact that the appearance of symbolism coincided with a crisis in his life similar to the religious emergence which influenced other writers to follow the new movement. He had too many associations with strong contemporary currents, even if he often went against them, to be content with this casually arranged form. And so he becomes instead, as a dramatist, the creator of a new, deeply personal form, entirely the outgrowth of inner compulsion, wholly a ruthless, personal expression, but none the less conditioned by the time itself. . . .

And it is a fact that he has meant the renewal of the modern drama, and thereby also the gradual renewal of the theatre. It is from him and through him that naturalism received the critical blow, even though it is also S. who gave naturalism its most intense dramatic works. If one wishes to understand the direction in which the modern theatre is actually striving and the line of development it will probably follow, it is certainly wise to turn to him first of all. . . .

S.'s drama such as it gradually became signifies in all respects revolt and renewal. And one cannot imagine that it will have anything else but a revolutionary effect on modern drama because it so completely destroys the old foundations, creates new ones instead, and so clearly shows a way which leads forward. [1918]

Pär Lagerkvist, *Modern Theatre* (1966), pp. 24, 27

S. still remains among the most modern of moderns, the greatest interpreter of the theater of the characteristic spiritual conflicts which constitute the drama— the blood—of our lives today. He carried Naturalism to a logical attainment of such poignant intensity that, if the work of any other playwright is to be called "naturalism," we must classify a play like *The Dance of Death* as "super-naturalism," and place it in a class

by itself, exclusively S.'s since no one before or after him has had the genius to qualify.

Yet it is only by means of some form of "supernaturalism" that we may express in the theater what we comprehend intuitively of that self-defeating self-obsession which is the discount we moderns have to pay for the loan of life. . . .

S. knew and suffered with our struggle years before many of us were born. He expressed it by intensifying the method of his time and by foreshadowing both in content and form the methods to come. All that is enduring in what we loosely call "Expressionism"—all that is artistically valid and sound theater—can be clearly traced back through Wedekind to S.'s *The Dream Play, There Are Crimes and Crimes, The Spook* [*Ghost*] *Sonata*. [1924]

Eugene O'Neill, "S. and Our Theater," in Helen Deutsch and Stella Hanau, *The Provincetown: A Story of the Theatre* (1931), pp. 191–92

When one has portrayed S.'s personality one has already given a descriptive account of his authorship. In world literature there are assuredly very few writers in whom life and literature so wholly intertwine. If his personality is nothing else than the disemboguement of his violently vital and intense temperament, then his literary product is essentially nothing more than the image of his temperament on paper. The explanation of the powerful influence he has exercised both among us and in foreign countries rests in no small degree in his astonishing immediateness. To read him is the same as to live with him.

Martin Lamm, *S.s dramer*, Vol. I (1926), p. 19

S.'s life and works are so intertwined that it is extremely difficult to determine whether his life is a gesture from his works or his works purely radiation from his life. S. so lives in his literature and his life that his concept of reality in the one is conditioned by his concept of reality in the other.

It is here that we encounter distortion of observed reality because of inner experience. But even more than that S. baffles us at times by presenting observed reality and inner experience in a combination that permits the spectator or the reader to see both at once. His works are by no means the result of "thoroughgoing introversion" in which the bridges between subject and object are completely broken. It is this "half-reality" that S. presents, a standing *on the bridge* with complete uncertainty regarding the direction he will take, even as the Unknown stands on the street corner at the opening of *To Damascus*.

For the Unknown, reality has changed from the mere report of observations to a contemplation of meanings. He no longer sees objects and incidents, but thoughts and meanings. Moreover, the whole universe ceases to be a chaos of chance objects and chance occurrences; it is now the manifestation of a purpose. . . . In *To Damascus* . . . we must credit the

Unknown with his own expressionistic nature; he seeks for the heart of reality behind the superficial objective manifestations.

Carl Enoch William Leonard Dahlström, *S.'s Dramatic Expressionism* (1930), pp. 143–44

S. . . . is less interested in revelation than in the free composition of a universe of pure expressiveness. He wishes to re-produce a universe in which the empirical laws of causality and relationship are suspended and only a single purpose rules: the will to express an invisible situation. The Expressionist dramatist, like the dreamer, concentrates entirely on the purpose of expressing an inner world and refuses to let conformity to external reality divert him from this purpose. The physical stage, the protagonist's environment, ceases to be a fixed frame of a scene or act and becomes a projection of his inner self. For the idea of the set stage implies the concept of a fixed external nature in which the actions that art imitates take place. S. and the Expressionists conceive of the world to be expressed in art not as a given space of nature but as a field of magnetic and gravitational forces radiating from the soul.

Walter Sokel, *The Writer in Extremis* (1959), p.38

Outside Scandinavia A. S. has been known almost exclusively as the half-mad Swedish genius who wrote a number of highly arresting dramas and auto-biographical works and who otherwise distinguished himself by recording some views on women which are anything but gallant. This one-sided capsule view of one of Sweden's greatest authors, and the only Swedish author who occupies an important place in world literature, has in recent years been somewhat rectified by those critics outside Sweden who have taken the trouble to examine more closely than had previously been the case S.'s general significance for modern drama. . . .

Few authors are as difficult as S. to fit into a summary literary formula. His genius is too volatile and his interests too many-sided to be accommodated for any length of time to a particular literary group or a fixed literary program. In the course of his career he is continuously involved in extricating himself from tentative earlier positions, restlessly searching for a way of life and a literary form which is inherently his own. In every genre which he employs he is the born experimenter, never satisfied with the form as he finds it, always giving to it the stamp of his own restive genius. This is particularly true in the drama, where his mastery is most impressive and his experimental proclivities most daring and fruitful. Though not all Swedish critics are equally impressed by some of the more extremely experimental aspects of S.'s later work, they are without exception in agreement that his handling of language is one of the chief miracles of Swedish literature. No Swedish author has the stylistic variety and range, the spontaneity,

directness, and economy of phrasing that S. commands. He shook Swedish prose completely loose from its earlier ceremonious, rhetorical propensities, bringing to it a pulsive aliveness and driving intensity which have provided the point of departure for all modern developments in Swedish prose style.

Alrik Gustafson, *A History of Swedish Literature* (1961), pp. 254–55

[S.'s] techniques in the twelve major [historical] plays are, of course, primarily realistic-naturalistic, shifting to the expressionistic when necessary, of course, to convey aspects of the human experience that a purely realistic technique of characterization could not suggest. On the whole, however, his technique of characterization is to present his central characters from as many points of view and in as many sorts of situations as his intentions and his plot permit; to a remarkable degree, the same procedure applies to his secondary and minor characters. We "see" the central characters as men and women limited by the human condition, involved in numerous roles besides that of king, queen, regent, or leader struggling for power to carry through a program. . . . But what does emerge from Strindbergian characterizations of central characters, whom he considered exceptionally gifted human beings, is that they are not flawless paragons but flesh and blood human beings in both their greatness and their littleness, in other words, perfectly believable people, who shared with the rest of humanity the limitations of the human condition. . . .

It is the cycle about Swedish rulers that stamps S. as the major modern contributor to the genre [of the historical drama], and no objective reader who examines these plays with care is likely to fail to recognize them as a unique contribution, not only to Swedish literature and the Swedish stage but also to world literature and . . . to world theater.

Walter Johnson, *S. and the Historical Drama* (1963), pp. 283–84, 292

It is a fact worth noting that S. composed *The Ghost Sonata* and liberated drama from its long enslavement to character and motivation in the same year that Picasso painted *Les Demoiselles d'Avignon* and shattered the old concepts of the relationship of art to nature. The unresolved contradictions and un-nerving dislocations in these works signalized a new epoch in the arts and possibly in Western culture. A revolutionary year in many ways, 1907 was also a year of strange coincidences. While Picasso painted *Les Demoiselles*, Schönberg set to work on his Second String Quartet, which was to lead him to upset the traditional concepts of musical harmony and rhythm. And at about the same time Einstein had what he later called "the happiest thought of my life": the flash of insight that led him to develop the general theory of relativity and to overturn the accepted notions of gravity, space, and time. What Picasso did for painting, Schönberg, for music, and Einstein, for science, S. did for the drama.

Evert Sprinchorn, *S. as Dramatist* (1982), p. 276

STRITTMATTER, Erwin

German novelist, dramatist, and short-story writer, b. 14 Aug. 1912, Spremberg; d. 31 Jan. 1994, Dollgow

Unlike most modern East German writers, S. is a "true son" of the working class. After attending a technical school he became a baker's apprentice. While working at various occupations, S. pursued self-education vigorously and engaged in early literary efforts. As a member of the Young Socialist Workers he was imprisoned briefly in 1934 but was not deterred from political activism. After World War II he returned to his work as a baker, joined the Socialist Unity Party in 1947, and was appointed an administrator over seven villages. He also worked as a correspondent during the late 1940s and eventually became a newspaper editor in Senftenberg. After achieving success as a writer in the 1950s, S. became first secretary of the German Writers' Union in 1959, and deputy chairman in 1961. Beginning in 1958, he lived and worked in the village of Dollgow, where he belonged to a farm commune and raised ponies. Among the awards that he received for his literary efforts were the National Prize of the German Democratic Republic (1953, 1955, 1964, 1976), the Lessing Prize (1961), and the Fontane Prize (1966).

Taken as a whole, S.'s works strongly reflect both his closeness to the people and his adherence to the Socialist Unity Party line. Yet despite the programmatic nature of many of his writings, an earthy honesty, a quiet homespun humor, and a degree of complex reality lend unusual charm, interest, and readability to his works.

S.'s first novel, *Der Ochsenkutscher* (1951; the oxcart driver), is intensely autobiographical. The portrayal of Lope's childhood and youth reflects S.'s personal development of social consciousness and presents his view of the decadent social order that made necessary the system to which he credits his own literary success.

Two of S.'s novels, *Tinko* (1954; Tinko) and *Ole Bienkopp* (1963; *Ole Bienkopp*, 1966), won East German national prizes. In a sense they are ideological sequels to *Der Ochsenkutscher*. *Tinko* places strong emphasis on the historical circumstances marking the death of the old capitalist era and the birth of the new order, while *Ole Bienkopp*, S.'s most important early novel, is concerned with the evolution of the new society. In portraying the life of Ole Hansen (nicknamed Bienkopp), S. endeavored to illustrate that the new society cannot be built by the individualist. Ole, who frequently finds himself in conflict with party representatives and policies, eventually allows his individualism to kill him, by relying only upon himself to do a job that could better have been done by the group.

S.'s most ambitious creation is the novel *Der Laden* (3 vols., 1982-1992, the store), which, like most of his successful works, derives its intensely human power from the thinly veiled but sensitive presentation of deeply personal experience. Around the central symbol of the general store that is run by the protagonist's mother, S. constructed a literary mosaic that fluidly integrates elements of commentary and reflection about literature, writers, political progress, environmental problems, party politics, and the practical dimensions of ethnic minority experience in a communist society into the portrayal of greed, opportunism, and other characteristics of petit-bourgeois and rural life in eastern Germany beginning in the 1920s.

Among S.'s warmest and most human works are the autobiographical stories in the collections *Die blaue Nachtigall; oder, Der Anfang von etwas* (1973; the blue nightingale; or, the beginning of something) and *Meine Freundin Tina Babe* (1977; my lady friend, Tina Babe). The title story of the latter book is representative of these narratives. It reveals in lighthearted fashion the love of people that informed his work and shaped his basic attitudes toward his literary craft.

S. also won some acclaim in East Germany as a dramatist. In 1953 he received a national prize for *Katzgraben* (1954; Katzgraben), which was staged through the encouragement of Bertolt BRECHT by the Berliner Ensemble. Neither *Katzgraben* nor another prize-winning play, *Die Holländerbraut* (1961; the Dutch bride) were particularly successful on the stage. Yet they contain the realistic portrayal of the life of the common man that made S. one of East Germany's most prominent writers. In his ability to portray the proletarian milieu S. was second only to his East German contemporary Johannes BOBROWSKI.

FURTHER WORKS: *Der Wald der glücklichen Kinder* (1951); *Eine Mauer fällt* (1953); *Paul und die Dame Daniel* (1956); *Der Wundertäter* (3 vols., 1957–1980); *Pony Pedro* (1959); *Schulzenhofer Kramkalender* (1966); *Ein Dienstag im September* (1969); *¾ hundert Kleingeschichten* (1971); *Damals auf der Farm, und andere Geschichten* (1974); *Sulamith Mingedö, der Doktor und die Laus* (1977); *Briefe aus Schulzendorf* (1977); *Analysen, Erörterungen, Gespräche* (1980); *Selbstermunterungen* (1981); *Als ich noch ein Pferderäuber war* (1982); *Der Laden* (1982); *Wahre Geschichten aller Ard(t)* (1982); *Zirkus Wind* (1982); *Grüner Juni* (1985); *Die Nachtigall-Geschichten* (1987); *Lebenszeit* (1987); *Die Lage in den Lüften* (1990); *Nur was ich weiß und fühle* (1994); *Wege zu Lautse* (1994); *Vor der Verwandlung* (1995); *Ponyweihnacht* (1996); *Wie ich meinen Großvater kennenlernte* (1996)

BIBLIOGRAPHY: Andrews, R. C., "Re-education through Literature: E. S.'s *Tinko*," GL&L, 14 (1960–61): 204–9; Reich-Ranicki, M., *Deutsche Literatur in West und Ost* (1963): 411–21; Haase, H., "Komisches und Tragisches in E. S.s 'Ole Bienkopp,'" NDL, 12, 3 (1964): 130–41; Huebener, T., *The Literature of East Germany* (1970): 89–95; Brettschneider, W., "E. S.," in Wiese, B. von, ed., *Deutsche Dichter der Gegenwart* (1973): 250–60; Einhorn, B., *Der Roman in der DDR 1949–1969* (1978): 178–211: 273–316; Löffler, A., "Zu E. S.," in Löffler, A., ed., *. . . an seinem Platz geprüft* (1979): 216–32; Reso, M., et al., *E. S.: Leben und Werk* (1984); Hillich, R., "E. S.: A Political Philosopher from the Land of *naivitas*," in Kane, M., ed., *Socialism and the Literary Imagination* (1991): 41-59

—LOWELL A. BANGERTER

STRUCTURALISM

In its broadest sense structuralism is a 20th-c. movement in the humanities and social sciences that attaches relatively little importance to causal explanation and maintains that to understand a phenomenon one must describe both its internal structure—the relations among its parts—and its relations with other phenomena, with which it forms larger structures. In its more precise sense, however, the term structuralism is generally restricted to schools of thought in modern linguistics, anthropology, and literary criticism. Structuralism in these three fields involves the attempt to reconstruct the systems that underlie actual phenomena and that stipulate their possible forms and meanings.

Ferdinand de Saussure (1857–1913), the father of modern linguistics, is generally regarded as the founder of structuralism. Distinguishing between concrete speech acts (*parole*) and the underlying system that one acquires when one learns a language (*langue*), Saussure argued that linguistics must concentrate on the latter and must define the elements of this system in terms of their relations with one another. A language is a system not of positive elements but of structures, purely relational units. Structuralism has been the main current of modern linguistics, and even the transformational-generative grammar developed by Noam Chomsky (b. 1928) is only a more sophisticated version of the basic structuralist approach.

Claude LÉVI-STRAUSS, one of the central figures of structuralism, argued in his pioneering article "L'analyse structurale en linguistique et en anthropologie" (1945; "Structural Analysis in Linguistics and Anthropology," 1963) that anthropologists should follow the lead of linguists and treat social and cultural phenomena as manifestations of underlying systems that govern their form and meaning. His studies of primitive logic, totemism, and myth are attempts to reconstruct a "logic of the concrete": instead of trying to explain individual practices or stories in terms of their social function, he considers them as elements of a "language," a conceptual system in and through which people organize the world.

In the 1950s and 1960s structuralism became an important movement in literary criticism, first of all in France and then, through the dissemination of the writings of Roland BARTHES in particular, in many other countries. The flourishing of structuralist literary criticism in the 1960s coincides with a popular success that made structuralism the successor to EXISTENTIALISM: it was no longer simply a method in particular disciplines but a general way of thinking about man and his culture. Structuralism thus relates to literary practice in three ways: first, as part of the general intellectual ethos of the 20th c., it occasionally provides a precise statement of themes and attitudes more diffusely present in literary works of the period; second, as a theory of literature and method of criticism particularly attuned to modern developments in literature, it offers an account of the modes of literary discourse; and finally, as part of the intellectual climate of the 1960s, it began to have discernible effects on literary practice.

The two fundamental insights on which structuralism is based are (1) that social and cultural phenomena do not have essences but are defined both by their internal structure (the relations among their parts) and by their place in the structures of the relevant social and cultural systems, and (2) that social and cultural phenomena are not just objects and events but objects and events with meaning, and therefore can be studied as signs. Consequently, structuralism is not inclined to think of individuals as the authors or creators of meaning but focuses instead on the interpersonal and hence impersonal systems that individuals assimilate and that themselves contain the possibilities of meaning. Its opponents criticize structuralism for being antihumanistic, and there is a measure of truth in this. One might say, in fact, that structuralism expresses an important trend in modern literature, which has come to deal less and less with full, rich characters actively engaged in making their destiny and ordering the world to their projects, and has set in their place the faceless antihero who is produced and controlled by a variety of social and cultural systems over which he exercises little control and which may even remain opaque to him. Robert MUSIL's *Der Mann ohne Eigenschaften* (1930–43; partial tr., *The Man without Qualities*, 1953) and the works of Franz KAFKA are only major examples of a trend that one might bring under the heading of what José ORTEGA Y GASSET called the "dehumanization of art."

The rise of abstract, nonrepresentational art has been another important aspect of this trend, and here too structuralism offers an explicit statement and justification of themes that have governed literary and artistic practice. The basic activity of the human mind is that of imposing form upon the objects of experience, and consequently, the formal imagination becomes the focus of interest. It is not that structuralism concentrates on form at the expense of content but rather that it tends to treat all content as form, or at least to think of content as a technical device that enables the completed form (the work itself) to come into existence. Stéphane MALLARMÉ's statement that "the world exists to give rise to a book" is the extreme version of this position: in general, the goal of art is not the representation of objects, and those objects represented are used in order to create a formal pattern. In literature, imitation of the world becomes less important than the exploration of the process of organizing the world both in life and in literature. And hence the idea of the world as language, of the world as a linguistic construct, has played an important role in the most radical modernist texts: those of Lautréamont (1847–1870), Mallarmé, and later James JOYCE and Raymond ROUSSEL. If we think of language as a system that organizes the world, then literature becomes an experiment in transforming the world through dislocation or modification of language and its forms of coherence.

Finally, structuralism, in its attempt to make explicit the conventions which enable things to have meaning, reflects the increasing self-consciousness of 20th-c. art and literature, the desire to recognize conventions as conventions so as to question them or deliberately employ them to unusual ends. Schönberg's and Stravinsky's experiments with new musical conventions have their literary analogues in the self-conscious play of André GIDE's *Les faux-monnayeurs* (1926; *The Counterfeitors*, 1927), Joyce's *Ulysses* (1922), and the fictions of Jorge Luis BORGES. Literature is no longer thought of as expression by an author in a medium taken as natural; it is an ironic process of construction in which one outplays the conventions.

Although structuralism may be a reflection of the *Zeitgeist*, it is also, and more specifically, a theory of literature and a method of criticism. In France, structuralist criticism represented a revolt against the particular types of erudition—literary history and biographical criticism—that were dominant in French universities. Like Anglo-American New Criticism, structuralism sought to return "to the text itself," but unlike the former, it assumed that one could not discover structures without a methodological model—a theory that enabled one to identify structures. Hence, instead of persuading themselves that one could read and interpret each text on its own terms and without preconceptions, structuralists sought to understand how literary discourse operates. And instead of making the interpretation of individual texts their goal, structuralists saw the encounters with particular texts as a way of studying the operations of literary discourse and the process of reading itself. In *Critique et vérité* (1966; criticism and truth) Roland Barthes distinguished between a criticism that places the text in a context and assigns meaning to it and a science of literature or poetics that studies the conditions of content: the formal structures that organize the text and make possible a range of meanings. A poetics of this kind would stand to literature as linguistics stands to language. That is to say, although literature uses language, it is also itself a language in that its meanings are made possible by systems of convention that the analyst must attempt to describe. Pursuing this enterprise, structuralist poetics has developed a series of concepts designed to account for the operation of literature as a system.

The first principle is that literature may be studied as a system of signs. Sentences, themselves linguistic signs, will have different meanings according to the conventions of the literary context within which they appear, and thus, within the literary system they become signifiers or forms whose signifieds are their special meanings within literary discourse. A culture prefers to think of its signs as natural, to motivate the relationship between signifier and signified so that meanings will seem to be intrinsic rather than the result of convention, but structuralism emphasizes that in order to understand the workings of cultural systems, we must remain aware of the artificiality, even arbitrariness, of signs. It is only then that we can grasp the nature of the operative conventions. The conventions that give sentences additional meanings are those of an *écriture*: a particular mode of writing founded on an implicit contract between author and reader. These modes of writing involve various codes, according to which we read the text. Some of these codes are models of human behavior as treated in literature: notions of personality, of relations between action and motive, of causality. Others are models of literary intelligibility: notions of coherence and incoherence, of plausible and implausible symbolic extrapolation, of significance and insignificance. These codes, which indicate possible meanings provided by the institution of literature, enable us to move from the text itself to plausible, or *vraisemblable*, readings of the text.

The process of interpretation is an attempt to bring the text within a logical discursive order by making it the expression of a meaning, and although structuralism seeks to describe this process by analyzing the conventions and codes on which it depends, it also would emphasize that the most interesting aspects of literary works are not the meanings that can be drawn from them by interpretation but the ways in which they resist or comply with the activity of interpretation. A structuralist analysis of a particular work thus aims less at interpreting it and making it the expression of a meaning than at examining the ways in which it responds to the reader's attempt to make it coherent and unified. The critic does not discover structure so much as observe the process of structuration, and he values not a positive meaning but the difficulties, the detours, and the indeterminacies that the text offers, as one attempts to organize it. He is less attracted by complete signs, where a form is correlated with a determinable meaning, than by empty signs, where the signifier holds out a promise of meaning but where the meaning remains a formal promise only, where the forms of a text are marked as signs but where there is always too much or too little meaning. Structuralism thus distinguishes between the readable (*lisible*) text—which we know how to read because it is written in compliance with conventions with which we are familiar—and the unreadable or writable (*scriptible*) text—that which can be written but which eludes us when we try to read it—and it values the latter for the challenge it poses to our accepted ways of ordering and interpreting experience. But despite its stated preference for difficult modern texts, whose difficulties it can characterize in terms of

the expectations that are frustrated, structuralism is more successful in discussing older, readable texts, because there the codes and conventions that it analyzes have fuller play.

A structuralist approach to literature thus involves a critique of both a representational aesthetic, which locates value in what is represented, and an aesthetic of expression, in which the text is designed to provide access to a meaning. The important relationship between the literary work and the world, it would say, lies not in similarity of content (the novel represents a world, the poem expresses an experience) but in homology of form: the activity of reading and structuring a work is analogous to the activity of structuring and making sense of our experience. And consequently literature is valued for the ways in which it challenges the interpretive procedures by which we make the world intelligible for ourselves. The obstacles literature poses to interpretation, the self-conscious playing with and against conventions, make us aware of the contingent and conventional nature of the models by which we are accustomed to read our own experience. The value of literature is thus related to its implicit recognition of the arbitrary nature of the sign: undermining culture's incessant attempt to make us think of meanings as natural, literature asserts its own condition as artifice and produces in the reader a self-conscious exploration of his ways of ordering experience.

There was always within structuralism a productive tension between the attempt to describe, systematically and scientifically, the codes on which cultural practices depend and the interest in how complicated texts escape or undermine those codes. Increasingly in the 1970s, however, these two concerns received different names: the systematic investigation of codes was called "semiotics" (the science of signs), and the exploration of works' resistance to codes was called "poststructuralism." Poststructuralism is something of a catchall term under which are grouped various critical and theoretical investigations that owe much to structuralism but are skeptical about the possibility of a comprehensive science of signification. The writings of some structuralists, such as Roland Barthes's *S/Z* (1970; *S/Z*, 1974), mix semiotic and poststructuralist concerns, analyzing literary codes while insisting that such analyses can never lead to a scientific mastery of meaning. The most prominent poststructuralist is Jacques DERRIDA, whose analyses of a range of literary and nonliterary works show how these works subvert the assumptions on which they rely. What Derrida calls "deconstruction" is a form of poststructuralism that encourages, in literary criticism, the teasing out of contradictory logics of signification within literary works.

The spread of structuralist and poststructuralist reflections on literature has encouraged the creation of literary works that set out to challenge or subvert the reader's expectations and the logic of signification on which those expectations are based. Indeed, structuralist theory developed partly as a response to the most challenging works of French literature, some of which (by Mallarmé, Lautréamont, Roussel) were already old, but others of which, particularly the novels of Alain ROBBE-GRILLET, were being written concurrently with the rise of structuralism. Robbe-Grillet himself saw his novels as attacks on old conceptions of plot, character, and theme, and the directions taken by his work and that of his fellow practitioners of the NEW NOVEL, Claude SIMON and Michel BUTOR, were conditioned by structuralist accounts of the New Novel. Writers such as Philippe SOLLERS and Jean RICARDOU, who write both novels and criticism, have produced texts designed to illustrate or apply structuralist theory: in these works the difficulty of identifying characters and themes or grasping a dominant register of discourse heightens the reader's awareness of the conventions on which intelligibility depends. The interdependence of structuralism and recent French fiction is shown by the fact that one of the best accounts of structuralism is Stephen Heath's *The Nouveau Roman: A Study in the Practice of Writing* (1972).

Outside France the influence of structuralism on literature is more difficult to assess. The clearest instance of direct influence is Anthony BURGESS's *MF* (1971), an elaborate play on themes from Lévi-Strauss that not only presupposes structuralist modes of analysis but also assumes the importance of literary reflection on systems of meaning. American novelists such as John BARTH, John CHEEVER, and Kurt VONNEGUT, Jr. have also been called structuralist by some critics, but this seems the result of general thematic similarities, particularly in the treatment of character, rather than direct influence. Structuralism no doubt bears some responsibility for "open-ended fictions," such as John FOWLES's *The French Lieutenant's Woman* (1969), but once again it is difficult to distinguish the influence of structuralist writings from the effects of the cultural climate out of which structuralism emerged. One might conclude that while structuralism has been responsible for the most radical strains in contemporary French writing, in other countries it has been primarily a mode of analysis and a reflection of modern sensibility.

BIBLIOGRAPHY: Robbe-Grillet, A., *For a New Novel* (1965); Lévi-Strauss, C., *The Savage Mind* (1966); Lévi-Strauss, C., *The Raw and the Cooked* (1969); Ehrmann, J., ed. *Structuralism* (1971); Barthes, R., *Critical Essays* (1972); Heath, S., *The Nouveau Roman: A Study in the Practice of Writing* (1972); Robey, D., ed. *Structuralism: An Introduction* (1973); Barthes, R., *S/Z* (1974); Culler, J., *Structuralist Poetics* (1975); Hawkes, T., *Structuralism and Semiotics* (1977); Derrida, J., *Writing and Difference* (1978); Genette, G., *Narrative Discourse* (1979); Sturrock, J., ed., *Structuralism and Since* (1979); Lentricchia, F., *After the New Criticism* (1980); Todorov, T., *Introduction to Poetics* (1981)

—JONATHAN CULLER

STRUNGE, Michael

Danish poet, b. 19 June 1958, Copenhagen; d. 9 Mar. 1986, Copenhagen

S. is considered one of the most important Danish poets of the 1980s, and his sudden death in 1986 made a strong impression on his readers and fellow poets. S. grew up in a working-class family in Hvidovre, a suburb to Copenhagen, and the rhythms of the suburb and of the city became important elements of his poetry.

S. made his debut with the collection *Livets hastighed* (1978; Speed of Life), but it was especially his poems from the 1980s that gave him his reputation as the poet of a young generation. *Skrigerne* (1980; The Screamers) is inspired by English and Danish punk music. The ugly rhymes and rhythms of the poems sneer at society, pop- and disco-culture as well as at the old rebels of the 1960s. The following collection, *Vi folder drømmens faner ud* (1981; Let's Unfold The Banners of Our Dreams), is inspired by SURREALISM and focuses on the nightlife of the city where youngsters dance, make love, and exchange hearts and dreams. The poet predicts a new intensive life that will pull down the walls of society and the

repressive norms and morals of the older generation. The musician and poet David Bowie's vision of the heros by the Berlin Wall and his "space-rebels" inspired *Fremtidsminder* (1980; Future Memories).

In 1981 S. began *Sidegaden* (The Side Street), a punklike and postmodern periodical, that in a posh layout presented new music, art, and poetry to a young audience. The European and American avant-gardes and neo-avant-gardes from Arthur Rimbaud to Lou Reed were also important topics of *Sidegaden*. In the mid-1980s S. also became a literary critic at leading papers and mingled in the cultural debate attacking the conversative debaters as well as the dated 1960s rebels. In S.'s opinion they had betrayed their cause and sold out the revolutionary ideals and dreams. S.'s poetry protested against the left-wing culture of the 1970s and its idealization of a socialrealistic art and literature. According to S., art and literature should be visionary, experimental, and suggestive. He wanted to create poems of an intense beauty and energy, and he had an ear for the sonority of words, syllables, and alliterations. In his opinion the poem should be the instantaneous utopia of body and soul. S. was both a romanticist and a dreamer and a postmodernist, very interested in staging his art and his public life. He was good-looking, introduced new fashions, wore makeup, and made a very intense impression when he recited his poems to an audience. His later poems concentrated on the basic experiences of life: love, joy, sorrow, depression, and the consciousness of death. In *Ud af natten* (1982; Out of the Night) the visions are described as "nightorgasms of the sight" that eliminate the emptiness, depression, and silence of modern life.

He saw his ninth collection, *Væbnet med vinger* (1984; Armed with Wings), as his last. He stated that from then on he just wanted to live an anonymous life. He had fallen in love and was very happy with his girlfriend. He felt that he no longer needed poetry, and explained that he had used poetry to defeat his own depressions and get access to reality. He felt that he had already made his best artistic contributions and wanted to stop his career. S. thought that if he continued he could end up repeating himself. He went to South America with his girlfriend, but the heat and the light of the tropical climate depressed him and they soon returned to Denmark. He started to write poems again, and—under the pseudonym Simon Lack—S. published a new collection of poems, *Verdenssøn* (1985; The Son of the World). S. had a sense of humor and he succeeded in reviewing his own book in a leading paper before it was brought to public knowledge that he was the author. But though the appearance of *Verdenssøn* became a humorous disclosure of literary criticism, the subject of the poems was serious. In *Verdenssøn* S. sought an ultimate truth of life. He sneered at his own former poetic attitudes and manners and tried to reach out for a new artistic beginning and for new sparks of life. *Verdenssøn* is one of the most important collections of contemporary Danish poetry, full of despair and love and longing. On 9 March, 1986 S. committed suicide and the memorial poems of his fellow poets and fans showed that his poems lived in many young hearts.

S.'s collection of poems was published in 1994, and the beautiful black book became a tremendous success. It was obvious that S. had become a classic of young Danish poetry in the 20th c.

FURTHER WORKS: *Nigger 1* (1982); *Nigger 2* (1983); *Popsange* (1983); *Billedpistolen* (1986); *Mai Strunge. Samtaler m.m.* (1986, with Anne-Marie Mai); *Sidegader. Prosa 1978-1986* (1996)

BIBLIOGRAPHY: Skyum-Nielsen, E., "Subkulturelle stemmer," in Brostrøm, T., and A. Winge, eds., *Danske digtere i det 20.*

århundrede (1982), Vol. 5: 351-89; Schnack, A., and J. G. Brandt, *80 moderne danske digtere* (1988): 252-57; Davidsen, M., "Væbnet med romantik," in Mai, A. M. ed., *Digtning fra 80'er til 90'er* (1993): 33-47; Stidsen, M., "Mit hjerte er en termokande," *Kritik*, 91-92 (1990): 54-74; Stein Laren, P., *Digtets krystal* (1997): 13-52

—ANNE-MARIE MAI

STUS, Vasyl

Ukrainian poet, literary critic, and translator, b. 8 Jan. 1938, Rakhmanivtsi, Vinnytsya region; d. 4 Sept. 1985, Concentration Camp Nr.36-I Perm, Ural Region, Russia

Born into a rural Ukrainian family, S. was destined to become his country's leading intellectual poet and the unrelenting champion of its national resistance movement. After studying at the Donetsk Pedagogical Institute, S. served in the Soviet army and, upon his discharge, taught school and worked as a journalist. In 1964 he joined the Institute of Literature of the Ukrainian S.S.R. in Kiev, but lost his position in 1965 because of his repeated intercessions on behalf of persecuted Ukrainian intellectuals. In 1966 he obtained a position with the State Archives of History, but was dismissed from it later that year. S. was first arrested in 1972, and after nine months of interrogation in Kiev was sentenced to five years of forced labor and three years of exile. Having served the imprisonment in Mordovia and two years of exile in Kolyma, S. returned to Kiev in August of 1979 unbroken in spirit but with severely impaired health. In October 1979 he joined the Ukrainian Helsinki Group, was rearrested in May for "anti-Soviet agitation and propaganda," and was sentenced on August 1980 to fifteen years of forced labor. His plight attracted considerable attention, both in Ukraine and in the West, and his death in the concentration camp, where he was deprived of medical treatment and tortured, rendered him a martyr of the Ukrainian cause.

S. began publishing poetry and articles on literature as early as 1959 in the Kiev-based literary journal *Dnipro*. Because of his activities on behalf of human rights, he soon became a dissident poet whose works could not be published in the Soviet Union. As a result, his major collections have appeared in the West, having been smuggled out of the Soviet Union, while hundreds of his poetic works have been destroyed by his jailers, and are thus irretrievably lost.

A highly original and powerful poet, S. combines autobiographical and patriotic motifs with intellectual introspection. Already his first collection, *Zymovi dereva* (1970; trees of winter), published in Brussels, manifests his extraordinary, Rilkean talent to transform life into poetry. Motifs of love for his native land and its beautiful natural settings, of joy and suffering, of love and hatred, and eternal questions concerning the human condition are almost always presented *sub specie aeternitatis*. S.'s poetry, even while intensely autobiographical or national, never fails to transcend personal and geographical confines and soars into the universal realm of thought and human spirit. In this sense, S. is an intensely religious poet, whose work is often a hymn to the Creator.

While S.'s early poetry is characterized by an ever-present *amor fati*, his later work, especially that written in prison, is informed by an intensely tragic sense of life. In the collection *Svicha v svichadi* (1977; a candle in a mirror), published in New York, motifs of manliness and courage vie for supremacy with feelings of sorrow and despair. His poetic farewell to Ukraine, for example, entitled significantly "Ostannya pisnya" (the last song), and his nine-line poem "Synovi" (to my son) from the collection with the revealing title *Vesely tsvyntar* (1971; the joyful cemetery), reflect what he ascribed to Beethoven: the "harmonized suffering" of his own "many-troubled soul" and his quest to preserve within himself the pristine purity of the human spirit.

Like Rilke and Goethe, whose work S. admired and translated (the bulk of these translations, too, was lost in the concentration camps), S. perceived in poetry a redemptive quality endowed with the power to change the world and the self. To S. poetry was both "beauty and delight" without which life was hardly imaginable; he sought it within himself, in his own Ukrainian tradition, and in the Western world from which he was separated. Within prison walls, poetry became a way of life, a world unto itself without vanity and terror. At times it was perhaps more real than the cruel reality surrounding him because it reflected more accurately his true state of being. S. the poet often dwelled on sorrow and even despair; S. the man was always uncompromisingly heroic. For a while, his heroic biography tended to overshadow his poetic achievement. However, the continued interest in his poetry and its translation into many foreign languages, including English and German, provide assurance that his poetic oeuvre will endure and prevail.

FURTHER WORKS: *Palimpsesty* (1986); *Doroha bolya* (1990). FURTHER WORKS IN ENGLISH: *Selected Poems* (1987)

BIBLIOGRAPHY: Wolffheim, E., "Unter der Eisscholle schlägt das Herz der Erde," Introduction to *Du hast dein Leben nur geträumt* (1982): 5–11; Horbatsch, A., "Sein Verbrechen ist der Widerstand," Introduction to *Ein Dichter im Widerstand. Aus dem Tagebuch des Wassyl Stus* (1984): 5–7; Levytsky, M., "V. S.: Doomed to Death and Immortality," *Religious Rights*, 1 (1985): 6–7; Shevelov, G. Y., "Potion and Poison," Introduction to *Selected Poems* (1987): xv–xxx; Rudnytzky, L., "V. S. und die deutsche Dichtung," *Jahrbuch der Ukrainekunde* (1988): 162–76

—LEONID RUDNYTZKY

STYRON, William

American novelist, b. 11 June 1925, Newport News, Va.

S. has lived outside the South ever since graduation from Duke University in 1947; yet his hometown of Newport News figures importantly (as "Port Warwick") in his novels, and the Southern white's treatment of blacks, among other topics associated with "Southern literature," is a recurrent issue in his work. After a brief stint as a publishing-house editor, S. turned his hand to writing for a living. On the basis of his first novel, *Lie Down in Darkness* (1951), he was awarded a year's fellowship in Rome: Italy later provided the backdrop for *Set This House on Fire* (1960). S.'s interest in the military, expressed to varying degrees in all his novels, but especially in *The Long March* (1953), derives from his experiences in the marines. A lifelong fascination with Nat Turner, the 19th-c. black slave whose insurrection took place near S.'s Tidewater Virginia home, reached fruition in the 1960s, when S.'s friendship with the black writer James BALDWIN provided the final stimulus for the creation of *The Confessions of Nat Turner* (1967), a Pulitzer Prize-winning, highly controversial novel. The retrospective *Sophie's Choice* (1979) centers on an immature author very like the young S. himself, writing his first novel and gaining the dark vision of life that will henceforth impel and color his art.

Lie Down in Darkness, highly indebted to William FAULKNER and James JOYCE, reconstructs the past through a complex series of interior monologues that locate the causes of a young woman's suicide in the failings of her parents; yet the parents, too, have been misguided, by the inadequate codes of Southern gentlemanliness and blood-and-guts militarism. Although the novel despairs of human happiness, its gloom is tempered by the author's affirmation of the ability to make choices and fulfill responsibilities, and thus to ease the way in a forlorn, incomprehensible universe.

S.'s simplest and most straightforward work, *The Long March*, concerns a thirteen-hour forced march in a marine reserve camp in North Carolina. The senseless orders challenge one reservist to preserve his manhood by outdoing all others in the tenacity with which he marches; thus, within the parameters of the military establishment he defiantly rebels against attempts to break his sense of uniqueness and worth. Through him, for at least a moment, the company is empowered and hopeful, in control of outside forces.

Set This House on Fire presents a nightmare vision of the enslavement and disintegration of a masochistic, would-be artist. Alienated from God and family, lacking any sense of identity, he readily falls prey to a malevolent personality representative in part of American materialism. His moral sensibilities regenerate and he rejoins humanity only after accepting personal responsibility for the needs of others and his own criminal activities.

The Confessions of Nat Turner is an ambitious meditation on the institution of slavery through an imaginative, first-person rendition of Nat Turner's motivations for insurrection. Confronted on all sides with the hypocrisies of orthodox Christianity, Turner is driven to seek salvation by asserting his identity—his personhood—through rebellion and murder. His failure as a revolutionary brings success as a human being: he achieves a kind of redemption by recognizing that a white woman he has slaughtered had a right to live.

The heroine of *Sophie's Choice* has also been deprived of her identity, first by her tyrannical father, then by the Nazis, and finally by her crazed lover. Her choices have been numerous, bitter, and, ultimately, defeating; for at no stage has she mustered the courage to do the heroic tasks demanded of her, nor are her moral imperatives really clear. S. relates these personal failures to the larger failures of modern society and to the guilt that all must share for their treatment of others. Yet through the autobiographical narrator he also bears witness to the possibilities for grace and love.

All of S.'s works are concerned with victimization and rebellion, and all portray human beings *in extremis*. There is a heightened quality to the novels, for the central characters, engaged in violent acts, appear more heroic or degraded—certainly larger—than life, and the style, with its intricate syntax and polysyllabic vocabulary, can only be described as grand. This combination of theme, characterization, and rhetoric is in many respects "Faulknerian"; but S. has a distinctly un-Faulknerian sense of religion, community, and history as well as a set of different concerns, including sexual perversion masquerading as religious fanaticism or Freudian chic.

S. has taken great risks in his tackling of large philosophical issues like the meaning of evil, and historical phenomena of such magnitude as atomic warfare, black slavery, and the Holocaust. Many have criticized as unhistorical and even outrageous his

attempt as a white man in the racially turbulent 1960s to characterize Nat Turner and the black experience. On purely literary grounds, S. can be faulted for a certain heavy-handedness in his melodramatic turns of plot and turgidity of prose. But S. is unequaled for the passion with which he inveighs against bureaucracy and slavery of any sort. And he always tells a good story, combining the high seriousness of a morality play, the biting observations of social satire, the suspense of a mystery thriller, and the comic absurdities of an existentialist fable.

FURTHER WORKS: *In the Clap Shack* (1973); *This Quiet Dust, and Other Writings* (1982)

BIBLIOGRAPHY: Clarke, J., ed., *W. S.'s "Nat Turner": Ten Black Writers Respond* (1968); Hoffman, F. J., "The Cure of 'Nothing!': The Fiction of W. S.," in Browne, R. B., et al., eds., *Frontiers of American Culture* (1968): 69–87; Mackin, C., *W. S.* (1969); Friedman, M., and Malin, I., eds., *W. S.'s "The Confessions of Nat Turner"* (1970); Galloway, D., *The Absurd Hero in American Fiction*, rev. ed. (1970): 51–81; Pearce, R., *W. S.* (1972); Friedman, M., *W. S.* (1974); Morris, R., and Malin, I., eds., *The Achievement of W. S.* (1975; rev. ed., 1981); special S. section, *MissQ*, 34, 1 (1980–81): 3–59; Casciato, A. D., and West, J. L. W., eds., *Critical Essays on W. S.* (1982)

—JUDITH RUDERMAN

SU Man-shu

(born Su Chien; also known as Su Yüan-ying and Su Hsüan-ying) Chinese poet and novelist, b. 1884, Yokohama, Japan; d. 2 May 1918, Shanghai

Son of a Cantonese merchant in Yokohama and a Japanese mother, S. was five years old when he was taken to Chung-shan in southern Kwangtung province to live with his father's clan. There he received a traditional Chinese education. At fourteen he went back to Japan to study in Yokohama and Tokyo. He participated in a movement of Chinese students to overthrow the Manchu government in China. In 1903 he went to Shanghai for teaching and newspaper work. In 1904, while on a trip to Kwangtung, he became a Buddhist monk, taking the name Man-shu. He spent the remaining fourteen years of his life writing, teaching, and traveling. He shuttled between Shanghai and Tokyo, visited Thailand, Ceylon, and Java, but never stayed long in any one place. In China he made friends with prominent men of letters, particularly members of a revolutionary literary society known as Nan-shê, and with leaders of the Nationalist Party. Disillusionment with political events in the country after the 1911 revolution and failing health made him pessimistic and melancholic during the last years of his life.

S. wrote extensively on a variety of topics, ranging from Sanskrit grammar to the flora of the Western hemisphere. He prepared a Chinese-English dictionary as well as the geographical terms and itinerary charts for the travelogues of two Buddhist pilgrims. He also compiled three anthologies of English translations of Chinese poems and essays. A fine painter, his landscapes were treasured by friends and other contemporaries.

As a poet, S. specialized in the *chüeh-chu*—a four-line lyric with five or seven words to the line. His poems, although written in traditional Chinese forms, are delicate, refreshing, and spontane-ous. They show the sensitivity of a young poet in love with women and nature, all presented with consummate skill. Especially origi-nal and exquisite are his descriptions of rural scenery in Japan: the ice flag atop a thatched store signaling a nearby market; himself with straw sandals and a broken alms bowl, walking across bridges where cherry blossoms bloom. Buddhist attitudes also influence the mood and tone of his poetry.

The best-known of S.'s works, *Tuan-hung ling-yen chi* (1912; *The Lone Swan*, 1924), is a seemingly autobiographical narrative. It describes the tender love affair between Su San-lang—a Chinese youth of Japanese origin, who has become a Buddhist monk—and his Japanese cousin. Torn by the conflict between his affection for her and his vow of celibacy, San-lang assumes a heroic stature at the end when, casting aside his doubts and timorous desires, he resolutely renounces his mundane attachments and decides to roam like a "lone swan" in this floating world. The delineation of delicate and yet poignant emotions, the novelty of a Sino-Japanese love affair, and the theme of the conflict between love and religion made the novel an instant success.

S.'s other literary works include the collection of miscellaneous writings *Yen-tzu-han sui-pi* (1913; random notes from a swallow's mausoleum). Although written in traditional style, these notes differ from their prototypes in content and substance. Their interest lies in the author's knowledge of Western languages and litera-tures, his familiarity with Sanskrit and with India, and his experi-ences in Japan and southeast Asia.

A "Sino-Japanese genius," S. bridged the cultural gap between China and Japan and contributed to the development of East-West literary relations, as well as to Chinese knowledge of Western literature through his translations of Hugo's *Les misérables* and poetry by Byron, Shelley, and others. His works were immensely popular and influential from the 1920s to the 1940s; his melan-choly, romantic mood fascinated the young people of that period. S.'s writing occupies a prominent place in the literature of 20th-c. China.

FURTHER WORKS: *Wen-hsüeh yin-yüan* (1908); *Ch'ao-yin* (1911); *Han-Ying san-mei chi* (1914); *S. M. ch'üan-chi* (5 vols., 1928–1931); *S. M. ta-shih chi-nien chi* (1943)

BIBLIOGRAPHY: McAleavy, H., *S. M.: A Sino-Japanese Genius* (1960); Wu-chi, Liu, *S. M.* (1970); Lee, L., *The Romantic Genera-tion of Modern Chinese Writers* (1973): 58–78

—LIU WU-CHI

SUAREZ, Clementina

Honduran poet, b. 12 May 1902, Juticalpa; d. 9 Dec. 1991, Tegucigalpa

Born in Juticalpa, the isolated capital of the Department of Olancho, Honduras, S. left her hometown at age twenty-one. Once on her own, she began to publish her poetry and to develop a lifestyle unique for a Central American woman in the early decades of the 20th c. She traveled, lived and worked throughout Central America, Mexico and Cuba, gaining notoriety for her rebellious, woman-centered poetry, her bohemian lifestyle, and her activities

as a dedicated promoter and collector of Central American art. She spent the final decades of her long life in Tegucigalpa, where she owned and operated an art gallery. She was killed at her home by unknown intruders in 1991.

S.'s poetry is characterized by growth and change, as she was influenced by a number of the literary currents prevalent in Latin America, including romanticism, MODERNISM, the avant-garde, and the poetry of social commitment. Her first volume of poetry, *Corazón sangrante* (1930; Bleeding Heart), is a carefully crafted collection that has the distinction of being the first book of poetry by a woman to be published in Honduras. Its themes are nature, melancholy, and impossible love. The following year she pub-lished three more books of poetry, one of which, *Los templos de fuego* (1931; Temples of Fire), contains some of her most frequent-ly quoted and anthologized poems. They are formally much freer than her first poems and some of them were clearly written with performance in mind, as S. often recited her poetry for audiences. The lyric voice of these volumes is that of a woman rebelling against the strictures of a provincial, patriarchal society and cele-brating her sexuality.

While living for a time in Cuba in the mid-1930s, S. was deeply impressed by the political and social commitment of the Cuban writers and began to write poetry of a more political nature. *Veleros* (1937; Sailing Ships) represents her initial experimentation in the development of a socially conscious poetry. Subsequent volumes show that while S. never abandoned the intensely personal first-person, her poetry became the voice of a woman struggling to identify herself with the ideals of a revolutionary consciousness, yet persistently aware of the numerous forces militating against the realization of this in practice.

As Central America suffered through decades of dictatorships, S.'s poetry reflected the militancy, anger, and hope of many of the region's writers. The centerpiece of her oeuvre, *Creciendo con la hierba* (1957; Growing with the Grass), is a single long poem in eight parts that explores the nature of passionate love and revolu-tionary idealism. The lyric female voice addresses her lover, telling him that she has grown and changed, that her voice is no longer that of the simple lover, but has taken upon itself the reality of all women who suffer injustice. She asks him to accompany her in a new adventure of awakened consciousness, wanting a comrade as well as a lover, but he insists that he prefers her as she was. Unwilling to return to the past, she mourns her loss yet celebrates her transformation.

Her next book, *Canto a la encontrada patria* y *su héroe* (1958; Song of the Found Fatherland and Its Hero), is a highly original lyric-epic poem that celebrates Honduras and its foremost patriot, Francisco Morazán, while at the same time cleverly inverting expectations and identifying the female lyric voice with the fatherland.

In the last decades of her life S.'s poetry continued to confront the social and political realities of Central America, but she also began to write poems of a more contemplative nature, reflections on love, age, memory, and solitude. The felicitous conjunction of the autobiographical impulse and the outward-looking concern for her country and for humanity in general has given S.'s poetry a wide readership and an enviable visibility in Central America.

When S. first began publishing and performing her poetry, she was considered scandalous to Honduran society, unused to women openly expressing their sexuality, their politics or their independ-ence. During her lifetime she gradually gained acceptance and recognition and received numerous literary awards, including the

Honduran National Literary Award, her country's highest praise. Even after her death she continues to be an inspiration to new generations of women writers who admire her lifelong dedication to her art as well as her strength and independent spirit.

FURTHER WORKS: *Iniciales* (1931); *De mis sábados el último* (1931); *Recital en el Teatro Nacional* (1931); *Recital para Marco A. Ponce* (1932); *Engranajes* (1935); *De la desilusión a la esperanza* (1944); *El poeta y sus señales* (1969); *Antología poética* (1984); *Con mis versos saludo a las generaciones futuras* (1988)

BIBLIOGRAPHY: Price, J., *Faces of Rebellion: Critical Commentary and Translation of the Poetry of Julia de Burgos, Rosario Castellanos and C. S.* (1981); Salinas, M., "El mundo poético de C. S.," in Salinas, M., *Literatura hondureña contemporánea* (1991); Gold, J., *C. S.: Her Life and Poetry* (1995)

—JANET N. GOLD

SUDANESE LITERATURE

The rise of the Mahdist state in the Sudan in the late 19th c. provided Sudanese writers, particularly poets, with new themes. The poetry of this period, mainly epic in form, primarily sought to glorify the Mahdī and his followers. Despite this new subject, the cliché-ridden traditional style of Arabic poetry prevailed, except for a few poems. The most prominent poets were 'Abd al-Ghanī al-Salawī (1822–?), al-Shaykh Husayn al-Zahrā' (1833–1894), and Muhammad 'Umar al-Banna (1848–1919).

Most prose writing of the period consisted of religious or linguistic treatises. The only exceptions were the manifestos and letters of the Mahdī himself.

Poetry

The most characteristic genre in Sudanese literature remains poetry. The major currents since the beginning of this century have been neoclassicism, romanticism, and realism. One should be cautioned, however, that these three terms do not have the same meanings as in European literature.

Important representatives of the neoclassical current were 'Abdallāh al-Banna (b. 1890) and 'Abdallāh 'Abd al-Rahmān (1891–1964), and especially Muhammad Sa'īd al-'Abbāssī (1880–1963). Their poetry is characterized by carefully chosen diction, clarity of style, and enchanting musicality. The poets of this period, following World War I, were influenced by the Egyptian poets who had forged a renascence in Arabic literature. Although many were later affected by the romanticism of the 1930s, others remained faithful to classical style. Among later writers, 'Abdallah al-Tayyib (b. 1921) is a good representative of the neoclassicists, who looked for models in Arabic poetry of the golden age. They rejected Western civilization and conceived of nationalism not as confined to the modern Sudan but as embracing the whole Arab and Muslim world. Their clinging to the classical style was in itself a rejection of Westernization.

Al-Amīn 'Alī Madanī (b. 1910) was the first to attack neoclassical poetry. Hamza Tambal (1893–1960) rejected all traditional verse and called for a new, "genuine" poetry. Along with Tambal, the most prominent romantic poets were Tījānī Yūsuf Bashīr (1910–1936), Idrīs Jammā' (1922–1980), and Muhammad Ahmad Mahjūb (1910–1976). Both Tambal and Mahjūb insisted on the value of local color, then a new element. Some romantic poets were influenced by Arab poets living in America, such as Kahlil GIBRAN (Khalīl Jubrān); others, by the English romantic poets Shelley, Keats, and Wordsworth. Unlike the neoclassicists, the romantics were receptive to Western influences in both form and content. Many of their works had a somewhat morbid tone.

With the shattering disillusionment of World War II, the romantic tide started to ebb, giving way to realistic expression. The forerunner of this trend was Husayn Mansūr (b. 1915), author of *Al-Shāti' al-sakhrī* (n.d.; the stony beach), a collection of poems. Muhammad al-Mahdī al-Majdhūb (b. 1919), author of the poetry collection *Nār al-Majādhīb* (1973; the fire of Majādhīb), and Ismā'īl Hasan (?–1982) are considered the best representatives of realism. These poets sometimes used free forms. Al-Majdhūb, however, wonderfully blended all three currents: neoclassicism, romanticism, and realism.

Poetry with a socialist purpose is an offshoot of the realistic trend. The major leftist poets are Salāh Ahmad Ibrāhīm (b. 1933), Tāj al-Hasan (b. 1929), Jaylī 'Abd al-Rahmān (b. 1930), and Muhyī al-dīn Fāris (b. 1936). Most outstanding is Salāh Ahmad Ibrāhīm, with his volumes *Ghābat al-Abanus* (1963; the wood of Abanus) and *Ghabdat al-Hababai* (1965; anger of Hababai). His style is subtle and sophisticated yet spontaneous, and his poetry is solidly intellectual and humane. These socialist poets tend to generalize from their personal experiences, to embrace people in similar situations. They also favor specifically African imagery and have introduced new vocabulary and narrative forms.

The Essay

At the turn of the century prose writing in the Sudan was a weak imitation of classical Arabic works. It was characterized by a flowery style that treated language as an object in itself. The first real newspaper, *Al-Hadara*, founded in 1919, became the training ground for Sudanese essayists and journalists. The influence of Egyptian and Syrian writers was particularly strong on journalists. The two major literary periodicals of the 1930s were *Al-Nahda* and *Al-Fajr*.

The most distinguished essayists of the 1930s were Muhammad Ahmad Mahjūb, Muhammad 'Ashrī al-Siddīq (1908–1972), and Mu'awiya Nūr (1919–1942). Mahjūb's style combines the clarity of classical Arabic with the fluency of the English language. He was influenced by British essayists in both approach and style, as was al-Siddīq. Nūr, however, emulated Egyptian writers (he lived most of his life in Egypt). The romanticism that dominated Sudanese literature during the 1930s appeared first in criticism and only later in poetry. Most essayistic writing of this period discussed social problems or literature, since political writings were forbidden under colonial rule.

Since independence in 1956, politics and the autonomy of Sudanese culture have become popular topics. A leading critic of pan-Arabist orientation is 'Abdallah al-Tayyib.

Fiction

Sudanese fiction first appeared in the journals *Al-Nahda* and *Al-Fajr*. The short story, born during the height of romanticism, had as its principal early theme the obstacles that stand between lovers in a closed society.

The foremost short-story writers are 'Uthmān 'Alī Nūr (b. 1923) and Mu'awiya Nūr. The stories of 'Uthmān 'Alī Nūr—collected in *Ghādat al-qarya* (1953; the village beauty), *Al-Bayt al-maskūn* (1955; the haunted house), and *Al-Hubb al-kabīr* (1958; the great love)—deal with social problems in the style of folktales. The simplicity of his technique made his stories widely popular.

Although Abū Bakr Khālid (1934–1976) evokes Sudanese customs and landscapes, he seems to direct his stories to readers in the Arab world in general rather than to a specifically Sudanese audience. Country life is a prominent subject in his stories, and his style is a mixture of classical Arabic and colloquial Sudanese, particularly so in dialogue. Often his stories end with a moral drawn from the events narrated.

Romanticism gradually gave way to the realism that dominated the literary scene in the 1950s and 1960s. The three leading writers of fiction in this mode are al-Tayyib Zarūq (b. 1935), Salāh Ahmad Ibrāhīm, and 'Alī al-Mak (b. 1937). Zarūq's two collections, *Hayāt saghīra* (1957; a small life) and *Al-Ard al-safrā'* (1961; the yellow land), are marked by simple, straightforward realism. Both Ibrāhīm and al-Mak, the coauthors of the short-story collection *Al-Būrjwaziyya al-saghīra* (1958; the petite bourgeosie), are representative of SOCIALIST REALISM. They criticized the new bourgeois class that ruled after the British left.

The major literary figure, not belonging to any trend or school is al-Tayyib Sālih (b. 1929). The masterpiece of Sudanese fiction is his novel *Mawsim al-hijra ilā al-shimāl* (1966; *Season of Migration to the North*, 1969), whose main theme is the encounter of Afro-Arab and European cultures, an encounter represented by the behavior of the principal character, Mustafā Sa'īd, who as a Sudanese is a mixture of Africa and Arabia. The African side appears in the color of his skin, his Arabism in his Islamic background. He both hates and respects European culture. This conflict results in a kind of split personality. Since neither complete integration in nor total rejection of European culture is possible or desirable, the question confronting him is what to take of it and what to leave—the dilemma, indeed, of all African Arab intellectuals who have to deal with European civilization. Although in Sālih's other novels and in his short stories he is at times rather provincial, his works are always rich in symbol and metaphor, and he has achieved an international reputation.

At present there is a host of young short-story writers and novelists; the short story in particular is experiencing a great vogue.

Sudanese literature in the 20th c. has had a development similar to that of other Arab countries, but it has its own distinctive features. The influence of both Egyptian and English writers has been especially strong. Although it was very imitative of both at the beginning of this century, it has now established itself as an independent literature. In all genres except the drama, which has not yet taken hold, much writing of high quality is being produced.

BIBLIOGRAPHY: Jayyusi, S. K., *Trends and Movements in Modern Arabic Poetry* (1977), Vol. II: 452–64; Marchand, B., "Écrivains soudanais," *Maghreb-Machrek*, No. 76 (1977): 67–69; Ahmed, O. H., ed., Introduction to *Sixteen Sudanese Short Stories* (1981): 1–5; Abdul-Hai, M., *Tradition and English and American Influences in Arabic Romantic Poetry* (1982), passim

—IBRAHIM AL-HARDALLO

SUNDANESE LITERATURE

See under Indonesian Literature

SUNDMAN, Per Olof

Swedish novelist and short-story writer, b. 4 Sept. 1922, Vaxholm; d. 9 Nov. 1992, Stockholm

After completing his secondary education and military service in Stockholm, S. spent fourteen years (1949–63) as the owner of a tourist hotel in the northern province of Jämtland. Concurrently with his writing, S. involved himself actively in local politics as a member of the Center Party. From 1968 to 1979 he held a seat in the Swedish Parliament and served on a number of boards dealing with cultural affairs. In 1975 S. was elected a member of the Swedish Academy. He has been the recipient of a number of literary prizes.

The vast and sparsely populated areas of northern Sweden provide the setting for a number of S.'s works, most of which take the form of explorations through which individuals and their interrelationships reveal themselves in sharp outlines. In his first collection of short stories, *Jägarna* (1957; the hunters), the absence of traditional plots and the often inconclusive endings force the reader's attention to the process of observation itself. The novel *Undersökningen* (1958; the investigation) describes the futile attempts of a member of a rural temperance board to arrive at any definite "truth" about a case he has been commissioned to investigate. The investigator's efforts to avoid personal value judgments and preconceived notions express the author's own concerns with objectivity; the difficulties of the investigation illustrate his theory about the basic inaccessibility of fellow humans.

In the novel *Skytten* (1960; the marksman) the mystery surrounding the death of a member of a hunting party is never solved, but through the protagonist's wanderings on the day following the event there emerges a detailed description of a northern community, the forces behind its transformation from a rural village into a technological society, and the social, economic, and political implications of the change. The same shift from what is ostensibly the main plot can be observed in the novel *Två dagar, två nätter* (1965; *Two Days, Two Nights*, 1969), in which a country sheriff and the local school-teacher track down a young murderer in the wilderness. The story, as told by the school-teacher, turns into a penetrating study of the two protagonists and their relationship; inadvertently the narrator gives a damning protrait of himself and reveals in his person some fundamental mechanisms behind violence.

S. scored his first international success with the novel *Expeditionen* (1962; *The Expedition*, 1967). Although the novel is based on H. M. Stanley's relief expedition to rescue Emin Pasha, S. cautions his readers that the story is not about this expedition. Through the observations of the two narrators, the European Laronne and the Eastern Jaffar Topan, the extravagant undertaking is viewed in a double perspective, with the interest focused on the enigmatic leader of the expedition. By the time the story abruptly ends in mid-jungle, the expedition has become an end in itself. Although the book could be read as a clever pastiche of 19th-c. conceits, it is closer to the author's intentions to view it as a scathing indictment of Europe's relations to other continents.

S.'s most ambitious and most widely translated work, *Ingenjör Andrée's luftfärd* (1967; *The Flight of the Eagle*, 1970), also presents an ideological critique of 19th-c. attitudes with ominous extensions into our century. Based on the ill-starred attempt by S. A. Andrée to reach the North Pole by balloon in 1897, the novel is the tragic story of an absurd adventure, a modern variation on the Icarus myth, and an allegory about Western man and his technological hubris.

S.'s literary method is characterized by an extreme verbal economy and a deliberate and painstaking cultivation of the art of reduction. Basically a behaviorist, S. limits himself to surface observations and consistently avoids psychological interpretations or speculations about inner processes of his narrators and fictional characters. His admiration for the stark and laconic narrative style of the Icelandic sagas is reflected in his own prose. In S.'s explorations of reality, his accuracy of observation and attention to facts and details of indisputable authenticity lend weight and immediacy to characters and objects.

FURTHER WORKS: *Sökarna* (1963); *Resa* (1965); *Människor vid hav* (1966); *Ett år* (1967); *Ingen fruktan, intet hopp* (1968); *Kontrollanten* (1973); *Lofoten, sommar* (1973); *Berättelsen om Såm* (1977); *Ishav* (1982)

BIBLIOGRAPHY: Dembo, L., "An Interview with P. O. S.," *ConL*, 12 (1971): 267–75; Sjöberg, L., "P. O. S. and the Uses of Reality," *ASR*, 59 (1971): 145–54; Sjöberg, L., "P. O. S.: The Writer as a Reasonably Unbiased Observer," *BA*, 47 (1973): 253–60; Warme, L., "The Quests in the Works of P. O. S.," *PPNCFL*, 28 (1977): 108–11; Warme, L., "P. O. S. and the French New Novel— Influence or Coincidence?" *SS*, 50 (1978): 403–13; Stendahl, B., "P. O. S. on the Expedition of Truthtelling," *WLT*, 55 (1981): 250–56

—LARS G. WARME

SUPERVIELLE, Jules

French poet, novelist, short-story writer, and dramatist, b. 16 Jan. 1884, Montevideo, Uruguay; d. 17 May 1960, Paris

Born into a French-Basque family living in Uruguay, S. was orphaned at an early age and was raised by an uncle. He spent a relatively happy childhood on the pampas, often evoked in his poems and fiction. When he was ten, he was sent to Paris for his education and later attended the Sorbonne. Except for the years during World War II, which were spent in Uruguay, he resided as an adult in Paris, although he did make frequent visits to Uruguay.

S.'s fame rests primarily on his poems. Viewed within the framework of contemporary French poetry, his verse is characterized by an unusual intimacy and lightness of touch. As it reaches beyond the self, his quest appears devoid of sentimentality, introspection, and dramatization. S. sought to create both an inner and an outer landscape. The poet remains at the center, fashioning a network of mysterious correspondences and exchanges, abolishing walls and barriers. He moves "beyond silence" or shows the way from the surface to the secret recesses of the heart.

S.'s themes are the eternal ones of lyric poetry: love, solitude, remembrance, nature, and death. Man's anguish, according to S., stems from a deceptive, insufficient knowledge of himself and the universe. The worlds of reality and dream, of the dead and the living, belong to one vast organism where everything yearns for communion. He represents man in images of eyes that seek to open,

hands stretched out, hearts whose beats are barely perceptible—all exemplifying the need for love and understanding. This resemblance of all living creatures to one another does not, however, make for familiarity; man feels uneasy with other creatures. S. seeks to enter into a dialogue with the creatures he encounters, whom he addresses in colloquial language. He endows even God with a human voice and reveals His dependence on man as much as man's dependence on God.

Oblivion, above all, haunts the poet. He forgets, but at least he "knows" that he forgets. Those who are "under the waters" or in the grave appeal to the poet to speak to them, so that they are not forgotten. Thus, for example, *Oublieuse mémoire* (1943; forgetful memory) is the significant title of one of S.'s poetry collections. In *Les amis inconus* (1934; unknown friends) S. reveals his fear of not recognizing the more intimate features of man and the world. This fear explains his desire to bring remoteness within reach, to change the cosmic into the intimate: God into a benign or sad man, the sun into a daisy. Metamorphosis constitutes a continuous process where the unexpected is coupled with the recognizable.

Repeatedly S. seeks to grasp the origins of creation. In *La fable du monde* (1938; the fable of the world) he strives to retrieve true innocence as well as the initial poetic gesture. The poet is not entirely devoid of irony and humility as he equates divine and poetic creation.

S.'s tales and plays have a delicacy of language and imaginative plots that sometimes unfold with deliberate unreality. The heroes and heroines find themselves in bewildering dilemmas because they usually belong to two worlds: that of the present and that of the legendary past in his play *La belle au bois* (1932; the beauty in the woods); that of the high seas and of everyday reality in the short stories of *L'enfant de la haute mer* (1931; the child of the high seas); that of biblical tradition and of modern speed in the stories included in *L'arche de Noé* (1938; Noah's ark). When he borrowed from European and Oriental traditions, S. modified the tales so as to enhance the imaginary realm and to discount social, metaphysical, and moral implications. As a storyteller, S. rejected mimesis, chronology, and causality, substituting for them a purely poetic coherence stated by means of paradox. As his hero in *Le forçat innocent* (1930; the innocent convict) illustrates, S. bypasses established systems, codes, and values. With subtle irony he animates the characters of old legends, endowing them with their own peculiar poetic sensitivity, innocence, and awe.

S.'s novels are narrated in an intimate, witty tone. In his fictional masterpiece *Le voleur d'enfants* (1926; *The Man Who Stole Children*, 1967) he evokes the ambiguity of family relationships. The whole range of love—filial, paternal, maternal, brotherly, sisterly—goes through subtle transformations and revelations. Most of the central figures are children in the process of growing up and changing milieus. Shifts and reversals between dream, desire, and reality encompass the world of the pampas as well as the streets of Paris.

In S.'s works we rediscover not only our fear of grasping nothing in a world of erosion and constant metamorphosis but also our need to marvel at and in a sense relive the day of creation.

FURTHER WORKS: *Brumes du passé* (1900); *Comme des voiliers* (1910); *Les poèmes de l'humour triste* (1919); *Poèmes* (1919); *Debarcadères, La Pampa, Une paillotte au Paraguay, Distances, Flotteurs d'alarme* (1922); *L'homme de la pampa* (1923); *Gravitations* (1925); *Oloran-Sainte-Marie* (1927); *Saisir* (1928); *Le survivant* (1928; *The Survivor*, 1951); *Uruguay* (1928); *Boire à la source*

(1933); *Première famille* (1936); *Phosphorescences* (1936); *Bolivar* (1936); *Poèmes de la France malheureuse* (1942); *Le petit bois, et autres contes* (1942); *Orphée, et autres contes* (1946); *Dix-huit poèmes* (1946); *À la nuit* (1947); *Choix de poèmes* (1947); *Robinson* (1949); *Shéhérazade* (1949); *Premiers pas de l'univers* (1950); *Naissances* (1951); *Le jeune homme du dimanche et des autres jours* (1955); *L'escalier* (1956); *Le corps tragique* (1959); *Les suites d'une course* (1959); *Correspondance J. S.-René Étiemble* (1969). FURTHER WORKS IN ENGLISH: *Along the Road to Bethlehem* (1933); *The Ox and the Ass at the Manger* (1945); *The Shell and the Ear* (1951); *The Night Lover* (1961); *S.* [poems] (1967, bilingual); *Selected Writings* (1967, bilingual)

BIBLIOGRAPHY: Greene, T., *J. S.* (1958); Blair, D., *J. S.* (1960); Étiemble, R., *S.* (1960); Hiddleston, J., *L'univers de J. S.* (1965); Jones, L., *Poetic Fantasy and Fiction: The Short Stories of J. S.* (1973); special S. issue, *FR*, 46, 5 (1973); Martin, G., "J. S.: A Poetry of Diffidence," in R. Cardinal, ed., *Sensibility and Creation: Studies in Twentieth-Century French Poetry* (1977): 103–21

—RENÉE RIESE HUBERT

SURINAM LITERATURE
See under Dutch-Caribbean Literature

SURREALISM

As defined by its founder and chief exponent, André BRETON, in his first *Manifeste du surréalisme* (1924; *Manifesto of Surrealism*, 1969), surrealism has two meanings. In one sense, it is a form of psychic automatism intended to liberate the modes of literary and artistic expression from the traditional limits set by reason: in a more general sense, it is a philosophical belief that a superior reality can be achieved by human imagination through the free use of those forms of verbal and pictorial associations that tend to break the barrier of the dream.

In the aftermath of World War I surrealism crystallized into doctrine a series of avant-garde movements that had attracted to Paris writers and artists from all parts of Europe to participate in the artistic renewal previously heralded by both ROMANTICISM and SYMBOLISM. In painting, CUBISM had cleared away many of the conventions of form earlier in the 20th c., and FUTURISM and DADAISM had challenged bourgeois morality and taste in literature and art. Proceeding beyond the revolutionary nihilism of Dada, surrealists were joined by erstwhile cubists and Dadaists in a concerted effort to evolve a positive credo and an affirmative technique to add depth and breadth to the aesthetic domain.

Breton borrowed the word "surrealist" from the preface of a fragmentary, experimental play, *Les mamelles de Tirésias* (1917; *The Breasts of Tiresias*, 1961), by Guillaume APOLLINAIRE. The surrealists hailed Apollinaire as the foremost poet of the new century because as the spokesman of cubism he had tightened the link between art and poetry and had foreseen a superior destiny for the poet who, in the new spirit, would become "more pure, more live, and more learned."

According to the surrealists, the "great modern tradition" had been launched by Charles Baudelaire (1821–1867) in the last two lines of his poem "Le voyage" ("The Voyage") in the 1861 edition of *Les fleurs du mal* (*Flowers of Evil*, 1931 and numerous later translations), in which he called upon man to turn the ordinary voyage into an adventure into the abysses of the unknown, whether the journey led to heaven or to perdition. Because science in the latter part of the 19th c. had made the metaphysical infinite a less than satisfactory objective for seekers of the absolute, the poet aimed to free the notion of reality from the restrictions of what the logical mind called "reason" and "nature."

Early evidences of the cult of the irrational were apparent in French poets who around 1870 had best expressed the spiritual crisis of the epoch: the hallucinatory writings of Lautréamont (1846–1870), *Les illuminations* (1887; *Illuminations*, 1946) of Arthur Rimbaud (1854–1891), and Stéphane Mallarmé's (1842–1898) *Un coup de dés jamais n'abolira le hasard* (1897; *Dice Thrown Never Will Annul Chance*, 1965), the most esoteric poem of the 19th c.

The surrealists also found support in the occultists and oneirocritics among the German romantics, such as Achim von Arnim (1781–1831), Novalis (1772–1801), Friedrich Hölderlin (1770–1843), Jean Paul (1763–1825), and E. T. A. Hoffmann (1776–1822). They defined the poet as any man who was endowed with imagination and had a passion for liberty, who was ready to substitute for the theological beyond the infinite possibilities of the concrete world, in a daring transgression of form and of the rational processes of cause and effect. This was the materiomystical climate of surrealism.

Among the French writers, in addition to Breton, who at some time during the period 1924–39 assumed the surrealist trademark were Louis ARAGON, Tristan TZARA, Antonin ARTAUD, Robert DESNOS, Paul ÉLUARD, Henri MICHAUX, Philippe SOUPAULT, Jacques PRÉVERT, and Benjamin Péret (1899–1959). Artists of various nationalities became their associates: Salvador Dalí, Marcel Duchamp, Max Ernst, Alberto Giacometti, Valentine Hugo, René Magritte, Joan Miró, Francis Picabia, Yves Tanguy. Pablo Picasso, if never literally a surrealist, was closely affiliated with both Breton and Éluard.

Beginning with *Les champs magnétiques* (1920; magnetic fields), co-authored by Breton and Soupault, surrealism maintained itself as a distinct literary movement all through the period between the two world wars. The principal journals were *Révolution surréaliste* (1924–30), transformed into *Le surréalisme au service de la révolution* (1930–33); *Minotaure* (1933–38); *Cahiers GLM* (1936–39); *VVV* in New York during World War II, when Breton temporarily exiled himself in America; and the short-lived *Médium* in France (1953–54).

Surrealism had its polemics, metaphysics, and poetics. Its polemics, given free expression in the periodicals and in Breton's *Second Manifeste du surréalisme* (1930; *Second Manifesto of Surrealism*, 1969), centered around the disloyalty of certain of the early surrealists and the short-lived political affiliations with that other dream of transforming the world, a dream that had been implied in early forms of communism. The metaphysics is most directly stated in Breton's first manifesto of 1924—which had taken him five years to formulate and which marked the official birth of the movement—and his *Nadja* (1928; *Nadja*, 1960) and *Les vases communicants* (1932; communicating vessels); in Aragon's *Le paysan de Paris* (1926; the peasant of Paris); in René Crevel's (1900–1935) *L'esprit contre la raison* (1927; spirit against reason); and in Éluard's *Le dessous d'une vie; ou, La pyramide humaine* (1926; the underpart of a life; or, the human pyramid).

These works crystallized in a fusion of poetry and prose the new philosophy of reality. Inspired by Hegel's monistic notion of the universe, they aimed at a synthesis of the spiritual and the material, believing in the continuity of the state of consciousness and the dream, of life and death. They conceived of existence as the composite of two connected urns, a conciliation between apparent contradictions in form and phenomena. Refuting all notions of a spiritual order in nature, they accepted hazard or chance as the manifestation of a "divine disorder." According to Aragon in *Le paysan de Paris*, "the concrete form of disorder is the outer limit of the mind." If the mind can sufficiently free itself from logic to be receptive to this disorder, then it will have pierced the outer shell of reality and arrived at a more comprehensive notion of the material world.

The poetics is also clearly set forth in Breton's first and second manifestos as well as in Aragon's *Traité du style* (1928; treatise on style) and Tzara's "Essai sur la situation de la poésie" (1931; essay on the situation of poetry). A radical blow was dealt to descriptive writing and at the same time to the abstract imagery and analogy of correspondences of symbolist writing.

Abandoning the imitation of nature to photography, the surrealists attempted to make of art an act of creation rather than of representation. The creative role of language was stressed. The poem became the composite of a series of images that were not dependent on any central subject: "Images think for me," said Éluard.

It was Breton's belief, also explained in *Qu'est-ce que le surréalisme* (1934; *What Is Surrealism?*, 1936), that words brought together by creative intuition could form a dynamic image whose effect would be much more provocative than that of abstract thoughts groping for words to give them a countenance.

In restoring language to a state of effervescence, the surrealist poet investigated the potential meaning captive within words that had become tired and shopworn through abuse. Even more important than the choice of words was the combination of words. Poetic analogy was replaced by the juxtaposition of the farfetched chance encounters of two images.

This concept of the new metaphor had been suggested in the presurrealist era by Pierre REVERDY in a statement that was to be quoted often: "The image is purely a creation of the mind. It cannot be produced by comparison but by bringing together two more or less distant realities." Images thus constructed contain a dose of absurdity and an element of surprise that in the opinion of Apollinaire was one of the fundamental resources of the modern mind. The surrealist poets and artists found themselves in a magnetic field where, by the attraction of one image to another, the objects of reality deviated from their traditional roles. The result is an incongruous unit—fashioned out of sensory data but in combinations undecipherable to the outsider—that establishes an intimate link between the subject and the object.

As a young medical student in mental hospitals during World War I, Breton had become acquainted with the work of the French neurologist Jean-Martin Charcot (1825–1893) and of Sigmund FREUD. Later, with his surrealist colleagues, he explored Freudian methods as means of preparing the subconscious mind for creative writing and painting. Among these activities was automatic writing. These "surrealist texts" were not poems. They served to enrich poetic consciousness and break down traditional word associations too deep-set to be avoided by the rational mind.

The surrealists also participated in group sessions designed to promote collective dreaming and the uninhibited interpretation of dreams. Breton noted that the effect of the dream on imagery—the disorientation of objects, the distortion of events, the verbal condensation of the dream—provided a transfiguration of reality worthy of poetic transcription.

Freudian influence also accounted for the surrealists' interest in the mentally deranged. *L'Immaculée Conception* (1930; the Immaculate Conception), a collaboration between Breton and Éluard, set out to imitate delirium and to simulate the various stages of insanity. Breton's novel *Nadja* presents a mentally disturbed heroine who makes no distinction between reality and hallucination as she gracefully hides her fern-colored eyes behind the imaginary feather of her hat and sees a blue wind passing through the trees. The surrealists considered that the study of these aberrations served as a gateway to a better comprehension of the total working of the human intellect. Breton put his faith in the unexpected, in psychic spontaneity; logic having so obviously failed, the world might well be transformed, he thought, through the liberation of the irrational forces in man.

Surrealism essentially attempted to capture the state of the "marvelous," to express the disordinate in nature as perceived by the irrational qualities of the mind. This is the driving vision of Breton's poetry in collections such as *Clair de terre* (1923; earthlight) and *Le revolver à cheveux blancs* (1932; the revolver with white hair), in Éluard's *Capitale de la douleur* (1926; *Capital of Pain*, 1973) and *Défense de savoir* (1928; learning forbidden), in Péret's *Le grand jeu* (1928; the great game), and in Tzara's *L'homme approximatif* (1931; *Approximate Man*, 1973).

World War II had the double effect of dissolving the surrealist coterie, already depleted in the 1930s, and of disseminating the surrealist style abroad. Aragon and Éluard, who had committed themselves to the Resistance and to communist affiliations, reverted to a more directly communicative lyricism that retained much of the surrealist type of imagery while abandoning its ideology.

The transformations in French poetic language gradually encouraged similar mutations in the literature of other countries. Surrealist magazines outside France included *Surrealismus* in Czechoslovakia, *Nadrealizam danas i ovde* in Yugoslavia, *Gaceta de arte* in Spain, *Konkretion* in Denmark, and *Negro sobre blanco* in Argentina.

A direct link between French surrealism and the New World is the early surrealist poetry of the Martinican Aimé CÉSAIRE, who studied in Paris in the 1930s and became associated with Breton's circle. In Europe, the country most profoundly influenced by surrealism was Spain. In the 1920s and early 1930s, before the civil war, a great deal of French surrealist writing was translated into Spanish. AZORÍN, Rafael ALBERTI, Federico GARCÍA LORCA, Luis CERNUDA, Vicente ALEIXANDRE, Benjamín JARNÉS, Ramón GÓMEZ DE LA SERNA, and the Catalan J. V. FOIX all wrote in a surrealist vein. Two Spaniards, Dalí and Luis Buñuel, collaborated on the famous surrealist films *Un chien andalou* (1929) and *L'âge d'or* (1930). Surrealism also made itself felt in Spanish America, particularly in the work of Octavio PAZ, César VALLEJO, and Pablo NERUDA. The dreamlike quality of some of the Argentine Julio CORTÁZAR's writing links him to surrealism as well.

Surrealism as an organized movement never gained much of a foothold in the English-speaking world, but its influence was felt. In Britain David Gascoyne (b. 1916) translated French surrealist poetry and wrote *A Short Survey of Surrealism* (1935) as well as his own surrealist verse. Other members of the British surrealist group were Hugh Sykes Davies (b. 1909) and Ruthven Todd (b. 1914). Sir Herbert READ promoted surrealism in painting and literature, and he edited a collection, *Surrealism* (1936), with essays by Breton, Éluard, and others; Read's introduction to the volume is his own important statement on the subject. Dylan THOMAS was probably the British poet most strongly influenced by surrealism.

There was no surrealist movement per se in America, although in the 1930s Charles Henri Ford (b. 1913) attempted to found one. But elements of surrealism can be found in the poetry of Hart CRANE, e. e. CUMMINGS, and William Carlos WILLIAMS, and it has had a strong impact on the post-World War II generation of American poets, including Robert BLY and Frank O'HARA.

The repercussions were more far-reaching in the realm of the plastic arts and cinema (see Film and Literature) than in literature, and surrealist exhibits were organized in most countries. Twenty-four nations were represented in the International Surrealist Exposition in Paris in 1949. The vertiginous freedom of expression unleashed by surrealism eventually affected the form and technique of the novel, and Artaud's *Le théâtre et son double* (1938; *The Theater and Its Double*, 1958) provided the THEATER OF THE ABSURD with many of its techniques.

The philosophy of surrealism, however, became more specifically involved with the destiny and presence of Breton, whose later writings, such as *Fata Morgana* (1940; Morgan le Fay) and *Ode à Charles Fourier* (1947; *Ode to Charles Fourier*, 1970), identified him more and more with the hermetic tradition, that is, with the desire to comprehend the great circuit of creation, to establish a firmer bond between sense perceptions and the power of intellectual metamorphosis. The "convulsive beauty" he discerned in the unpredictability of universal phenomena found confirmation in the scientific doctrines of probability and non-Euclidean geometry. Exceeding its historical moment, surrealism became a style and philosophy attuned to the inventive spirit of 20th-c. science. As the antithesis of both the literature of escape and the literature of despair, surrealism expressed a consuming desire to master the human condition.

BIBLIOGRAPHY: Lemaître, G., *From Cubism to Surrealism in French Literature* (1941); Balakian, A., *The Literary Origins of Surrealism: A New Mysticism in French Poetry* (1947); Raymond, M., *From Baudelaire to Surrealism* (1949); Fowlie, W., *The Age of Surrealism* (1950); Balakian, A., *Surrealism: The Road to the Absolute* (1959; rev. ed., 1970); Duplessis, Y., *Surrealism* (1962); Alquié, F., *The Philosophy of Surrealism* (1965); Matthews, J. H., *An Introduction to Surrealism* (1965); Nadeau, M., *The History of Surrealism* (1965); Matthews, J. H., *Surrealism and the Novel* (1966); Gershman, H., *The Surrealist Revolution in France* (1968); Ilie, P., *The Surrealist Mode in Spanish Literature* (1968); Matthews, J. H., *Surrealist Poetry in France* (1969); Caws, M. A., *The Poetry of Dada and Surrealism* (1970); Ray, P. C., *The Surrealist Movement in England* (1971); Bigsby, C. W. E., *Dada and Surrealism* (1972); Morris, C. B., *Surrealism and Spain 1920–1936*, (1972); Sandrow, N., *Surrealism: Theater, Arts, Ideas* (1972); Matthews, J. H., *Theatre in Dada and Surrealism* (1974); Orenstein, G., *The Theater of the Marvelous: Surrealism and the Contemporary Stage* (1975); Matthews, J. H., *Toward the Poetics of Surrealism* (1976); Germain, E. P., ed., Introduction to *English and American Surrealist Poetry* (1978): 25–55; Jean, M., ed., *The Autobiography of Surrealism* (1980); Caws, M. A., *A Metapoetics of the Passage: Architextures in Surrealism and After* (1982)

—ANNA BALAKIAN

SUTHERLAND, Efua Theodora Morgue

Ghanaian dramatist (writing in English), b. 27 June 1924, Cape Coast

Born and educated in what was then the Gold Coast, S. earned a B.A. in education at Cambridge and studied at the School of Oriental and African Studies at the University of London. This mixture of indigenous and Western knowledge marks her work as a dramatist. Upon her return to Ghana, S. became a teacher; the three children she had with her American husband, William Sutherland, combined to develop her interest in working dramatically with children. That interest also involved developing an awareness of African traditional performative structures, which S. not only researched but actively promoted herself. In 1958 S. began the Experimental Theater Players group, and later, with funding from Ghana's art council and the Rockefeller Foundation in the U.S., developed the Ghana Drama Studio. Supported by Ghana's independence, the Studio was a success and became part of the University of Ghana's Institute of African Studies. The Studio's purpose was to perform plays that could rouse the people; it, like the Experimental Theater group, wanted to take drama out of a classical theatrical setting and to the people: these goals led S. to dramatic innovations in her dramaturgy.

S.'s concern for children who are caught in the conflicts of contemporary Ghana is evident in the society for children's writing that she established. Although only a few of her works for children are published, they provide a reading audience with some sense of the techniques used to educate and entertain juvenile audiences. *Vulture! Vulture!* and *Tahinta*, published in 1968, are rhythm plays, and as such they are brief and rely heavily on musical rhythm to maintain their dynamism. Children are kept involved through participation and through the use of a chorus that comments on the action.

A chorus also plays a role in S.'s two most popular plays, *The Marriage of Anansewa* (1975) and *Edufa* (1967). Based on Ananse, the African spider or trickster figure, *The Marriage of Anansewa* uses the folk element to explore the tensions facing a young woman growing up between traditions. Anansewa, Ananse's daughter, is a Western-educated urban young woman. She is taking a secretarial course when her father, desperate for money, sets out to gain wealth from her potential as a bride. During the complex and humorous negotiations with four suitors that form the heart of the play's plot, Anansewa experiences traditional women's ceremonies that her father had previously considered superfluous. Anansewa, however, finds them surprisingly fulfilling. As befits a comedy, all ends happy, and the audience takes away a sense that traditions need not be lost in pursuit of modern accouterments. In another twist the play has also been read as an allegory of Ghana's receipt of foreign aid from competing Western suitors. The play's style dramatizes the play's responsiveness to its locale. S. incorporates elements of the *Anansesem*, or storytelling, techniques from which the characters are derived, into her sense of traditional theater, or *Anansegoro*. Interruptions pepper the play, as performers and the audience sing or recount *mboguo*, brief tales that comment on the play's action. The chorus reacts to the events that are unfolding, and the split between performers and audience is blurred with the audience invited to participate in songs.

Edufa offers a seemingly pointed contrast. Rather than being based on a folktale, as is S.'s other best-known play, *Foriwa* (1968), *Edufa* echoes *Alcestis*, by the classical Greek dramatist

Euripides. S.'s version changes the names as well as the focus; rather than exploring the demands of proper mourning versus hospitality, S.'s play continues her concern with imported attitudes and values as opposed to those rooted in the tradition of the region. *Edufa*'s tribute to Euripides can also be seen as a tribute to Ghana. This play, as S.'s others, unapologetically incorporates words from the Akan language; indeed, *Foriwa* was first produced in the language Twi. Throughout her oeuvre, S.'s awareness of Western traditions is subordinated to her interest in her audience's local context.

S.'s importance to African drama, and to Ghanaian drama in particular, can hardly be overstated. Not only through her published work, but through the many plays produced only in performance as well as in her work developing workshops and schools to train young dramatists, S.'s effect has been inestimable. Furthermore, S.'s work provides pioneering investigations into the complexity of human action caught in changing cultures; her characters live through these pressures, and S. masterfully incorporates those tensions into her dramatic style that weaves together Ghanaian oral and performative influences.

FURTHER WORKS: *Playtime in Africa* (1960, with Willis Bell); *The Roadmakers* (1961, with Willis Bell); *You Swore an Oath, Anansegoro* (1964); *Odasani* (1967); *The Original Bob: The Story of Bob Johnson, Ghana's Ace Comedian* (1970, with Willis Bell); *Anansegoro: Story-telling Drama in Ghana* (1975); *The Voice in the Forest: A Tale from Ghana* (1983)

BIBLIOGRAPHY: Okafor, C., "Parallelism Versus Influence in African Literature: The Case of S.'s *Edufa*," *Kiabàrà*, 3 (1980): 165–7; Etherton, M., *The Development of African Drama* (1982): 215–27; Talbert, L. L., "*Alcestis* and *Edufa*: The Transitional Individual," *WLWE*, 22, 2 (1983): 183–90; Pearce, A., "The Didactic Essence of S.'s Plays," *ALT*, 15 (1987): 71–81; Wilentz, G., "Writing for the Children: Orature, Tradition and Community in S.'s *Foriwa*," *RAL*, 19, 2 (1988): 182–96

—VICTORIA CARCHIDI

SUTSKEVER, Avrom

Yiddish poet and short-story writer, b. 15 July 1913, Smorgon, Russian Empire (now in Byelorussia)

S. has had a life of flight. His upbringing and education were disjointed because of military invasions and occupations. Beginning his studies in a Jewish elementary school, S. continued in a Polish-Jewish secondary school, later taking courses in literature and criticism at Vilna University. He began to write poems in 1927. Invited to join the literary group Young Vilna, he published his first poems in 1933; these attracted the attention of Aron Glants-Leyeles (1889–1966), who invited S. to contribute to his monthly *In zikh*. S.'s first book, *Lider* (1937; poems), was hailed as the work of a virtuoso of language and style. His second collection, *Valdiks* (1940; forests), was seen as a major achievement.

Toward the end of World War II S. joined the guerrillas of the Vilna ghetto and in March 1944 was honored by the Moscow government as a poet and a partisan. In 1946 he left Russia and settled in Palestine in 1947. His *Gaystike erd* (1961; spiritual soil) chronicles his first encounters with the land of his forebears, while his stylized ten-poem sequence *In midber Sinay* (1957; in the Sinai

desert) conveys his sense of wonder with a vocabulary influenced by ancient prayerbooks. Since 1949 S. has edited the premier Yiddish literary journal, *Di goldene keyt*. He represented the State of Israel at the International Poetry Congress in the Netherlands in 1976.

One of the earliest and most articulate poets of the Holocaust, S. is the voice of a collective lament, writing with great tenderness of the ineffable loss. Everything he saw, heard, and experienced as a child in Siberia and as an adult in interwar Poland, in the Vilna ghetto, and in war-threatened Israel is re-created in his writings: *Sibir* (1953; *Siberia*, 1961), with illustrations by Mare Chagall; *Fun vilner geto* (1946; from the Vilna ghetto); and *Tsaytike penimer* (1970; ripened faces).

Further mastery of language and imagery emerged in S.'s *Firkantike oysyes un moyfsim* (1968; square letters and miracles). His rich use of color and shading produces images that call up memories and visions he has observed and lived through. He searches for answers to the mystery of suffering and presents life's struggles in a pantheistic spirit.

S.'s oeuvre is of epic breadth. Nature, the desert, the nightmares of the ghetto, the woods of Vilna, physical agony, and a ceaseless quest for beauty—all these are interpreted in his work, in a way that sparks the intellect and elevates the spirit. His poetic achievement and his creative editorship of *Di goldene keyt* assure him a prominent place in the history of Yiddish literature. Major accolades, including the Israeli Government Award, testify to the wide recognition of his accomplishment.

FURTHER WORKS: *Di festung* (1945); *Vilner geto 1941–1944* (1945); *Lider fun geto* (1946); *Geheymshtot: Poeme* (1948); *Yidishe gas* (1948); *In fayer-vogn* (1952); *Ode tsu der toyb* (1955); *Oazis* (1960); *A. S.: Poetishe verk* (2 vols., 1963); *Lider fun yam hamoves* (1968); *Di fidlroyz* (1974); *Griner akvarium, un andere dertseylungen* (1975; partial tr., *Green Aquarium*, 1982); *Lider fun togbukh* (1977); *Di ershte nakht in geto* (1979); *Dortn vu es nekhtikn di shtern* (1979)

BIBLIOGRAPHY: Madison, C., *Yiddish Literature: Its Scope and Major Writers* (1968): 510–14; Biletsky, I. C., *Essays on Yiddish Poetry and Prose Writers* (1969): 207–32; Leftwich, J., *A. S.: Partisan Poet* (1971); Liptzin, S., *The Maturing of Yiddish Literature* (1970): 267–71; Nowersztern, A., *A. S. Bibliography* (1976); Wisse, R. R., "*A. S.: Green Aquarium,*" *Prooftexts*, 2, 1 (1982): 95–97

—THOMAS E. BIRD

SVEVO, Italo

(pseud. of Ettore Schmitz) Italian novelist, short-story writer, and dramatist, b. 19 Dec. 1861, Trieste; d. 13 Sept. 1928, Motta di Livenza

S. was born to a German-Italian-Jewish family in Trieste, then an important international port of the Austro-Hungarian Empire. His pen-name—Svevo means Swabian—testifies to his double social identity and his mixed cultural affiliations. Young Schmitz was educated in a German school near Würzburg and later attended a business school in Trieste, but his family's precarious financial affairs forced him to take a job in the local branch of the Viennese Union Bank at the age of nineteen. From then on his life was spent in business, for which he felt he had neither the talent nor the ambition. The circumstances of S.'s career as a nonprofessional writer have had much to do with what has come to be known as the "Svevo case"—an expression that has become emblematic of the belated recognition of an unjustly neglected writer.

S.'s first novel, *Una vita* (1892; *A Life*, 1963), attracted little interest, and his second, *Senilità* (1898; *As a Man Grows Older*, 1932), met with the same indifference. Bitterly disappointed, S. gave up his literary vocation, or so it seemed, for a long time. Between *Senilità* and *La coscienza di Zeno* (1923; *The Confessions of Zeno*, 1930), the third and best of his novels, there is an interval of twenty-five years. But he never quite put down his pen. His diary, letters, short stories, fables, and plays, dating from the years of self-imposed silence, reflect his artistic development. The friendship of James JOYCE, which began in 1907, no doubt gave him renewed confidence in his ability as a writer. Joyce's unfailing support was also largely responsible for the warm reception accorded to *La coscienza di Zeno* in avant-garde French literary circles.

In the last years of his life S. wrote some of his most famous shorter narratives, such as *Una burla riuscita* (1929; *The Hoax*, 1929), *Vino generoso* (1929; *Generous Wine*, 1930), and various sections of a projected sequel to *La coscienza di Zeno*. None of these novel-fragments was published in S.'s lifetime. The opening of the novel "Il vecchione" (the old, old man) first appeared in the collection *La novella del buon vecchio e della bella fanciulla, ed altri scritti* (1929; *The Nice Old Man and the Pretty Girl, and Other Stories*, 1930), the other pieces in the volume *Corto viaggio sentimentale, e altri racconti inediti* (1949; short sentimental journey, and other unpublished stories). English renderings of the five surviving fragments and drafts of the never-completed fourth novel have been collected in the volume *Further Confessions of Zeno* (1969). S. died of injuries sustained in an automobile accident.

The first of S.'s major works, *Una vita*, the most directly autobiographical of S.'s novels, relates the story of a young man from the provinces, Alfonso Nitti, who comes to Trieste to work as a clerk in a bank. Nitti, who has a degree in philosophy and entertains literary ambitions, proves unable to cope with the pressures of his tedious job and seeks refuge in daydreams about self-mastery, wealth, and happiness. His main effort is a prolonged and stormy love affair with his employer's daughter, which he is powerless to continue. This narrative about a twenty-year-old suicide is still, both in theme and technique, anchored in naturalism. The protagonist is primarily concerned with succeeding in business and life, and is ready to blame society for failures that could only be attributed to his own ineptness.

That S. possessed an unusual gift for self-analysis and introspection can be seen even more clearly in *Senilità*, in which the protagonist, Emilio Brentani, who lives with his spinsterish and hysterical sister Amalia, becomes involved with Angiolina, a young and sensuous working-class girl, in a futile attempt to find his identity. Brentani is a further refinement of the introspective, unheroic S. hero, sufferer, at age thirty-five, of a premature sense of senility, who tries to impose his dreams and illusions on reality. Structurally, the well-made novel is built around the contrasts between two sets of characters: Emilio and Amalia, representing disease, contemplation, the negation of life, are opposed to Stefano Balli, the hero's only friend and mentor, and Angiolina, representing health, youth, and action.

The central figure of *La coscienza de Zeno* is similarly doubting, guilt-ridden, and tenaciously self-analytical, but he is also the man who manages to construct through his ability to rationalize an operable reality, the supports of which are compromise and deceit. The basic action of *La coscienza di Zeno* revolves around a resistance to Freudian psychoanalysis. Zeno's doctor suggests that he write his memoirs, and so Zeno relates, or rather reinvents, the major events of his life. The most prevalent thematic element in the novel is announced by the ambiguous Italian word in the title, *coscienza*, which may signify either conscience or consciousness. Admittedly, the novel is considerably more than a confession and a treatment of Zeno's conscience. The *coscienza* investigated is Zeno's range of awareness, from that of himself and his life to a growing consciousness of the dimensions that frame human life in general. Time as linear succession is questioned here as an effective ordering process for human behavior. By continually slipping in and out of different verb tenses Zeno creatively reconstructs "time" to his own advantage.

The importance of S.'s shorter works of fiction can hardly be exaggerated. The author's favorite fictional themes, his typical characters are present even in the minor narrative works. S.'s best short stories are those written in his last years and akin, in subject and method, to his masterwork. With their open form and their all-accepting spirit, they represent S.'s most rounded statement, ideologically and technically, about a lifetime of groping with the potentials of language and the absurdities of the human condition.

If S.'s reputation as a major figure in the mainstream of the modern European narrative tradition is securely established, his theater has been, and still is, a problem for critics. To be sure, his plays never went beyond the stage of literary experimentation; only one of them, the one-act comedy *Terzetto spezzato* (1925; the broken triangle) was produced during his lifetime, in Rome in 1927. The reaction to the dramatic effectiveness of his plays has been for the most part negative, and critics have been content with examining them for the light they shed on S. the fiction writer.

FURTHER WORKS: *Inferiorità* (1931; *Inferiority*, 1969); *Corrispondenza con gli amici di Francia* (1953); *Saggie e pagine sparse* (1954); *Commedie* (1960; expanded ed., 1979); *Diario per la fidanzata* (1962); *Lettere alla moglie* (1963); *Epistolario* (1966); *Racconti; Saggi; Pagine sparse* (1968); *Romanzi* (1969); *Carteggio con James Joyce, Valery Larbaud, Benjamin Crémieux, Marie Anne Comnène, Eugenio Montale, Valerio Jahier* (1978). FURTHER WORKS IN ENGLISH: *Short Sentimental Journey, and Other Stories* (1967)

BIBLIOGRAPHY: Furbank, P. N., *I. S.: The Man and the Writer* (1966); Staley, T. F., ed., *Essays on I. S.* (1969); special S. issues, *MFS*, 18, 1 (1972); Fusco, M., *I. S.: Conscience et réalité* (1973); Moloney, B., *I. S.: A Critical Introduction* (1974); Biasin, G.-P., *Literary Diseases: Theme and Metaphor in the Italian Novel* (1975): 63–99; Lebowitz, N., *I. S.* (1978)

—ALBERT N. MANCINI

SWAHILI LITERATURE

See under Kenyan Literature and Tanzanian Literature

SWEDISH LITERATURE

Swedish literature in the 20th c. reflects the political and scientific developments of the 19th c. The biological, social, and economic significance of Marx's and Darwin's determinist theories were expressed in the works of writers such as August STRINDBERG. His naturalist dramas *Fadren* (1887; *The Father*, 1907) and *Fröken Julie* (1888; *Countess Julie*, 1912; numerous later trs. as *Miss Julie, Lady Julie*) are an offshoot of Émile Zola's application of Darwin's ideas to literature. But Strindberg changed rapidly, and his later EXPRESSIONIST plays had an immense influence on 20th-c. world drama. Additionally, Strindberg's political activism and his intense involvement in contemporary public life established a pattern followed by many 20th-c. Swedish literary figures. Like him, other Swedish writers of the 1880s were involved in public debates about industrialism, science, and education.

Resisting this tide, writers of the 1890s, such as Selma Lagerlöf (1858–1940), who achieved worldwide fame, focused on fantasy, antiquity, and nationalism. Verner von Heidenstam (1859–1940) typifies the aesthetic, subjective, and nationalistic quality of the writers of the 1890s, called Nittiotalister (literally, writers of the 1890s). Lagerlöf, Heidenstam, and Erik Axel Karlfeldt (1864–1931) all won Nobel Prizes. Along with Gustaf Fröding (1860–1911), these writers portrayed regional aspects of rural Sweden and opposed the pessimism of the 1880s. Heidenstam turned to the past, while Lagerlöf and Fröding, the latter a moody lyrical poet, were most effective in focusing on Swedish nature and the rural population. Karlfeldt described with feeling and profundity the Dalarna region of Sweden.

The fantasy and nationalism of the 1890s turned in two directions in the 20th c.: toward economic and social progress, consistent with the interests of the 1880s, on the political left; and toward old-fashioned individualism on the right. Writers around the end of the century proffered a jaded individualism, almost a sense of indifference and helplessness. Hjalmar SÖDERBERG is the best representative of this group. His gemlike stories and novels reveal both the first stages of the new century and the remnants of the Decadent aesthetic style of the 1890s. Similar to the "flaneurs" (named after the French dandies who promenaded the streets), Söderberg represents the passive observer, the pessimist who sees man's inability to have any real control over his own life. Söderberg's most famous novel, *Doktor Glas* (1905; *Doctor Glas*, 1963), aroused controversy because it deals with a doctor who secretly poisons the abusive husband of the woman he loves, even though he knows the woman loves another man and the murder will accomplish nothing for him personally and perhaps little for the woman. The poet and prose writer Bo Bergman (1869–1967) held a similarly pessimistic view of life, also seeing man as a helpless puppet. Oscar Levertin (1862–1906) was both a typical author of the time and an important critic. Like Söderberg and Levertin, Per Hallström (1866–1960) wrote of urban life, specializing in brooding, intense short stories.

Vilhelm EKELUND, the most important poet at the turn of the century, came from the tradition of the SYMBOLISTS and followed in the path of his fellow southern Swedish Decadent author, Ola Hansson (1860–1925). Combining the presentation of Swedish landscapes with idealistic philosophies, Ekelund in free verse captured the delicate secrets of the countryside of Sweden. Devoted to beauty, Ekelund gradually withdrew into a world of classicism, but his innovations in verse influenced later generations.

Anders Österling (1884–1981) started as a symbolist but turned to a more popular regional poetry. He combined romantic and realistic images from everyday life. Albert Engström (1869–1940), successful both as a caricaturist and author, anticipates later Swedish realism in his Småland descriptions.

By 1910 a new group of writers who were describing changing Swedish society had appeared on the scene. These middle-class, realist Tiotalister (writers of the 1910s) wrote casual, flowing prose portraying life in the countryside and towns. Gustaf Hellström (1882–1953), Sigfrid Siwertz (1882–1970), Ludvig Nordström (1882–1942), and Hjalmar BERGMAN captured the love and enmity between generations of families, the hopes for education that generations past had been denied, and the rise of the middle class in growing Swedish towns.

Bergman's work stands above the others in its depth and diversity. A playwright and novelist, he examined both the humorous and terrifying aspects of the human condition. Creating a city, Wadköping, modeled after his home town, Bergman wrote a series of pessimistic works about the love affairs and economic disasters of small-town families. Hellström made good use of his experiences as a journalist in his novels, while Siwertz wrote of the transition from the "flaneur's" passive mentality to that of the social activist. Nordström used northern Sweden to concentrate on social and economic problems.

All these writers represented and wrote about the developing Swedish middle class. The "proletarian" writers, such as the novelist Martin Koch (1882–1940) and the poet Dan Anderson (1888–1920), were among the first literary figures from the working class. Although their works are not major, they marked a turning point in Swedish literature.

But before proletarian writers came to dominate the literary scene, MODERNISM entered Swedish literature. Three writers, the Finland-Swedish poet Edith SÖDERGRAN, Pär LAGERKVIST, and Birger Sjöberg (1885–1929), made the Swedish language more expressive and personal; at times they cast aside grammar, meter, traditional imagery, and even logic.

Sjöberg wrote about the problems of the developing upper middle class, but his work is known both for his affectionate portrayal of small-town life and for his major innovations in writing. His literary career flashed briefly but brilliantly from 1922 to 1929, and his first volume, *Fridas bok* (1922; Frida's book), a collection of humorous and ironic song-poems, made him a beloved figure in Sweden's tradition of author-composers. Later, in *Kriser och Kransar* (1926; crises and garlands), his idyllic verse broke into the violent dissonance of modern times, and his complex expressionism reveals the tortures of his life. Södergran, with her startling and original verse, is perhaps the most important Swedish-language poet of the first quarter of the 20th c.

Lagerkvist stands as one of the major figures of 20-c. Scandinavian literature. His work ranges from expressionist poems and plays to metaphysically and religiously oriented novels and plays. The power of evil is characterized in *Dvärgen* (1944; *The Dwarf*, 1945), while *Barabbas* (1950; *Barabbas*, 1951) and *Sibyllan* (1956; The Sibyl, 1958) probe with simplicity and strength the mystery of faith and the potential of the human spirit. Lagerkvist received the Nobel Prize in 1951.

In contrast to Lagerkvist, many Swedish writers continued in the socially committed tradition of Strindberg. Influenced by the early Swedish feminist Ellen Key (1849–1926), Elin Wägner (1882–1949) fought for women's rights and wrote novels sympathetically describing the lives and problems of women. Although there were traditional poets, such as Erik Blomberg (1894–1965) and Bertil Malmberg (1889–1958), during the years between the world wars, experimental or proletarian authors dominated the literary scene. During the late 1920s and early 1930s working-class literature continued to develop, but the separation between popular and serious literature widened. Simultaneously, literary movements from the European mainstream, such as SURREALISM, gained adherents in Sweden.

Ivar LO-JOHANSSON and Jan Fridegård (1897–1968) typify lower-class, *statarskolan* (sharecropper) writers. Lo-Johansson made his debut with *Godnatt, jord* (1933; *Breaking Free*, 1990), a description of the almost slavelike conditions of farmers working land they do not own, who are paid with a percentage of what they grow. Lo-Johansson has continued to write naturalist, documentary-style novels on various aspects of his native Sörmland, as well as about Stockholm. Fridegård's work differs from Lo-Johansson's in its focus on the individual. His trilogy *Lars Hård* (1935–36; *I, Lars Hård*, 1983; *Jacob's Ladder*, 1987; *Mercy*, 1987) is about the development of a boy who grows up in rural poverty. Somewhat autobiographical and filled with descriptions of brutality, the novels attack social injustices. A woman's view of this sharecropper's world appears in the writing of Moa Martinson (1890–1964).

Vilhelm MOBERG attained world recognition for his novels about Swedish emigrants to America. He, too, grew up in the poorest of farm country in Småland, and he started at an early age writing popular literature and journalism. His lifelong concern with individualism and freedom appears in his novels of the 1940s. The emigrant novels—*Utvandrarna* (1949; *The Emigrants* 1951), *Invandrarna* (1951; *Unto a Good Land*, 1954), *Nybyggarna* (1956; *The Settlers*, 1978), and *Sista brevet till Sverige* (1959; *The Last Letter Home*, 1961)—demonstrate his interest in history and his love of individual freedom. Frans G. BENGTSSON, a poet, essayist, and novelist from Lund, became widely known through his two-volume novel about the Vikings, *Röde Orm* (1941, 1945; *The Long Ships: A Saga of the Viking Age*, 1954). Fritiof Nilson Piraten (1895–1972) wrote novels about Bombi Bitt, a character reminiscent of Mark Twain's Huckleberry Finn.

Eyvind JOHNSON, like many others who started publishing in the 1930s, began his career as a proletarian writer, but he soon turned to the most sophisticated literary techniques. One of the leading intellectual and experimental writers of this generation, Johnson ranges in his work from the autobiographical tetralogy known as *Romanen om Olof* (1934–37; the novel about Olof), which is a series of proletarian *Norrländsk* (northern Swedish) novels, to a retelling of the *Odyssey, Strändernas svall* (1946; *Return to Ithaca*, 1952).

Johnson exemplifies the transition that occurred in Sweden between 1920 and 1940. With the institution of universal suffrage in 1918, Sweden had become a fully democratic society; recession and unemployment led to a Social Democratic government in 1932. Thus, not only did working-class writers come into prominence, but middle- and upper-class writers criticized bourgeois society. Agnes von Krusenstjerna (1894–1940) came from an upper-class family and intimately described in her novels what it was like to grow up in that milieu. The explicit erotic descriptions in her novels caused intense public discussion. Olle Hedberg (1899–1974) bitterly criticized the bourgeois life style in his novels and offered his own form of mysticism.

The 1930s, then, presented a wide variety of writing, including surrealist works and those tinged with Marxism and the theories of FREUD and JUNG. The new modernist techniques appeared in the journal *Spektrum*, published by the Marxist group named Clarté, as well as in an anthology titled *Fem unga* (1929; five young men). Of the Clarté group, Karin BOYE made the greatest impact. Blending love of nature and the experience of psychoanalysis, Boye, torn by sexual conflicts, is one of the most personal of Swedish poets. Fresh attitudes toward sex, influenced by FREUD and D. H. LAWRENCE, marked the Fem Unga writers. Several of them brought a new primitivism, or *livsdyrkan* (life-worship), to Swedish literature.

Artur LUNDKVIST and Harry MARTINSON, the major Fem Unga authors, came from lower-class backgrounds, traveled extensively, and brought a rich sense of the exotic into their writings. Lundkvist's plea for spontaneity and freedom mirrored similar sentiments in other literatures, but he added a Gauguin-like sensuality as well as a feeling for the rhythms of the city. Over the years Lundkvist, as much a public figure as a major writer, has written travel books and, through his essays, has introduced many foreign writers to the Swedish reading public. Martinson established himself as the most important member of the group, ranking with Lagerkvist and Johnson as one of the three most powerful Swedish writers of the first half of the century. Martinson's novel *Nässlorna blomma* (1935; *Flowering Nettle*, 1936) describes his own childhood as an orphan. Profound humanism and detailed, almost scientific observation characterize his writing. The culmination of his work is an epic poem about a lost space ship, *Aniara* (1956; *Aniara*, 1963; new tr., 1991). Martinson and Eyvind Johnson shared the Nobel Prize in 1974.

Other significant writers of the 1930s and 1940s include Tage AURELL, whose tightly crafted prose objectively probes the often tragic lives of people from Värmland, and Thorsten Jonsson (1910–1950). Through his translations and essays Jonsson introduced American writers such as HEMINGWAY, FAULKNER, and STEINBECK to Sweden. Jonsson's own works reflect their influence, but, continuing the naturalist tradition, he also used actual criminal records as sources for some of his stories. Walter Ljungquist (1900–1974) experimented with a Hemingwayesque style, then turned to a more psychological and symbolic technique.

There were also many developments in Swedish poetry during this period. Johannes Edfelt (b. 1904) and Hjalmar GULLBERG wrote major volumes of verse during the 1930s. Both men combined aspects of modernist poetry with traditional verse forms. Gullberg, an elegant, if pessimistic poet, often used classical themes. Nils FERLIN enjoyed wide popularity with his melodious folk poetry and bohemian image.

The major poetic force to appear in the 1930s, however, was the poetry of Gunnar EKELÖF, whose *Sent på jorden* (1932; late on the earth) started one of the most creative and experimental oeuvres in modern Swedish literature. Associated for a time with the writers publishing in *Spektrum*, Ekelöf was dubbed a surrealist by them, but he rejected the label. Ekelöf's lifelong concerns were those of the mystic, the man seeking the unconscious, the outsider who feels alien even to his own country. With associative imagery, musical forms, nonsense poetry, and dream poems, Ekelöf explored for over thirty years man's paradoxical nature.

While many of the writers thus far discussed continued to publish into the 1950s, an important younger group appeared during the 1940s. Two of the major poets of these war-torn years, Erik LINDEGREN and Karl Vennberg (1910–1995), are often linked. The Fyrtiotalister (writers of the 1940s) were quickly heralded as important innovators who reflected the pessimism and despair of World War II. Lindegren's *Mannen utan väg* (1942; the man without a way), with its forty dense fourteen-line poems, exemplifies the poetry of this decade. Consciously modern, so complex as to be obscure, Lindegren succeeds in creating a strong sense of structure within a seemingly disharmonious and illogical language. In *Halmfackla* (1944; straw torch) Vennberg, a poet and critic, opposed idealism and showed man's isolation broken only by brief idyllic moments. His later works portray in rich and sometimes playful tones both man's irony and his stoicism.

Another fine poet of this period, Werner ASPENSTRÖM, cultivates a philosophical art of the miniature, a clarity perhaps related to IMAGISM. Ragnar Thoursie (b. 1919) followed in the 1940s tradition, but led the way back to a slightly more optimistic but less dramatic world of suburbia. Rather than look at the pessimism of his contemporaries, Sven Alfons (b. 1918), a painter as well as a poet, tried to look, if hesitantly, back to happier days.

The fiction writers of the 1940s share the pessimism of the poets. A sense of futility and impotence characterizes much of their work. One of the most influential writers of this group was Stig DAGERMAN. Born into a working-class family and active as a journalist for a socialist newspaper, Dagerman wrote finely chiseled prose describing in depressing imagery man's terrors and his inability to sustain a stable society.

Almost as an answer to the dark anguish of his fellow writers, Lars AHLIN confronts man at a zero point, an absolute emptiness from which he may be able to develop. An overtly religious writer, Ahlin struggles with man's fate, trying to wrest from language itself and from man's ability to love whatever chance of salvation mankind may have. The novelists Ulla Isaksson (b. 1916) and Sivar ARNÉR question the moral and psychological identity of man.

If the 1940s have a relatively clear profile, the 1950s do not. The trends of the 1940s continued; earlier major writers produced new works. In essence, the 1950s may be considered the aesthetic calm before the political storm and literary renascence of the 1960s. Lars GYLLENSTEN's works reflect one aspect of this period, the postwar moral and existential crisis. Philosophical and antidogmatic, Gyllensten satirizes the equivocal or multiple nature of truth. Often classical, biblical, or mythological in subject matter, Gyllensten's novels offer new and unusual views of mythological personages. Sven Fagerberg (b. 1918), in his novels, is influenced by James JOYCE, Zen Buddhism, and his own experience as a businessman. Willy Kyrklund (b. 1921) and Arne Sand (1927–1963) tried to turn away from the sophisticated tone of the 1940s to a new naïvism.

Several major writers of the 1950s shared an initial interest in voyages, expeditions to unfamiliar countries. Per WÄSTBERG, who wrote a number of brilliant novels, typifies the transition from the 1950s to the 1960s: he explored the contrast between Sweden's secure little world and the oppression in other lands. Sara LIDMAN shows even more strongly the same transition as her works progressed from traditional novels to intense sociopolitical critiques. Like Wästberg, she was stunned at the oppression in Africa and later became a major spokesperson against the war in Vietnam. The Third World also functions as a thematic aspect of some of Per Olof SUNDMAN's writing. Sundman, however, tends to focus on the balances of power within society. As a novelist, but, far more importantly, as a nonfiction writer who traveled in and wrote about Asia, Jan Myrdal (b. 1927) became a leading proponent of the political consciousness that began to dominate Swedish literature in the 1960s.

In poetry, Lars FORSSELL and Tomas TRANSTRÖMER are the leading figures. Forssell's translations of Ezra POUND parallel Forssell's own use of "personae," characters through whom he speaks. Using different narrators, he strives for a simplicity and directness new to Swedish poetry. Tranströmer's first volume of poetry, *17 dikter* (1954; 17 poems), was acclaimed as a major work. Few poets have influenced their own generation as strongly and rapidly or have been translated as extensively. Tranströmer's clear imagery partially explains his success abroad; within Sweden his use of everyday images to create surprisingly new metaphors is distinctive. Östen Sjöstrand (b. 1925) and the popular Bo Setterlind (1923–1991) wrote religious poetry, while Folke Isaksson (b. 1927), although at times writing an ironic and playful poetry, made the same transition to political involvement in the 1960s that is typical of Swedish writers of the period. One of the strongest socially committed poets was Sonja ÅKESSON, one of Sweden's leading feminist writers.

The 1960s may one day be seen as a golden age in Swedish literature. This renascence partially took its shape from the growing awareness of the social and economic problems of the Third World and from the bitterness felt about America's role in the Vietnam War. Given Sweden's history, and the literary tradition of socially involved writers, this new and intense tie between politics and art was not surprising. What distinguishes the period is the relatively large number of politically liberal, often leftist, writers and also the high quality of their work. Writers debuting in the early 1960s used traditional techniques and subjects, but they gradually shifted to documentary and political works, such as Sara Lidman's novel on South Africa, *Jag och min son* (1961; rev, ed., 1963; I and my son) and Jan Myrdal's collection of interviews, *Rapport från en kinesisk by* (1963; *Report from a Chinese Village*, 1965).

Some writers from this group have continued to create important new works in various genres. Lars GUSTAFSSON, P. C. JERSILD, Per Olov ENQUIST, Sven DELBLANC, and Stig Claesson (b. 1928) are among the major figures of this modern renascence, and each of them has added a different dimension to Swedish literature. For a time, however, all of them wrote works that were directly related to contemporary social, economic, or political problems.

Gustafsson's writings are more philosophically than politically oriented. In his poetry, plays, and novels he probes the nature of man's being and his ability to learn the truth about himself. Jersild warmly, satirically, and brilliantly focuses on modern man caught in the web of bureaucracy. Endowed with a vivid imagination and sharp wit, Jersild may also be the finest magician of words among the new writers. Enquist, a journalist, novelist, and playwright, stands in the forefront of the socially committed writers. His *Legionärerna* (1968; *The Legionnaires*, 1973) is one of the best of the many fine documentary novels written in Sweden over the last two decades. His play *Tribadernas natt* (1975; *The Night of the Tribades*, 1977) was performed throughout the world. Delblanc, probing the relation between the writer, his language, and his world, has focused on the ambivalent position of the socialist artist. Like Jersild and Enquist, Delblanc is acutely concerned with man's responsibility to his fellow man. Claesson, one of the most prolific and wide-ranging writers of this group, often uses Stockholm as the background of his novels; one of his principal subjects is the gradual depopulation of rural Sweden. Another writer who turned to political themes is Kerstin EKMAN, an important figure in Sweden's tradition of feminist writers; she shifted from detective fiction to documentary novels. Most Swedish writing between 1963 and the early 1970s was intensely political.

Since the mid-1970s many of the major Swedish writers have returned to more traditional fiction and poetry. Several have written long autobiographical works. Still, concern with social issues, ranging from bureaucratic expansion to economic exploitation and development of nuclear energy and arms, continues as a basic characteristic of modern Swedish writing.

Poets, too, have followed the political trend. Göran Sonnevi (b. 1939), Lars Norén (b. 1944), and Göran Palm (b. 1931) have received substantial recognition. Other well-known poets are Björn Håkanson (b. 1938), Reidar Ekner (b. 1929), Kjell Espmark (b. 1930), Gunnar Harding (b. 1940), and Tobias Berggren (b. 1940).

One of the most influential figures of modern Swedish literature is the famous filmmaker and stage director Ingmar Bergman (b. 1918). Bergman's career seems even more remarkable in light of the limited number of important Swedish playwrights in this century. After Strindberg, only a few Swedish writers produced genuinely significant plays. Hjalmar Bergman wrote some exceptional plays in the early part of the century, while Pär Lagerkvist's expressionist plays established him as one of the most important Swedish dramatists after Strindberg. Sigfrid Siwertz and Vilhelm Moberg wrote successful plays; they were followed by the EXISTENTIALIST works of Stig Dagerman in the 1940s. In the 1950s and 1960s, among others, Werner Aspenström experimented with absurdist drama and Lars Forssell wrote historical, yet antiheroic plays. Most recently, Per Olov Enquist and Lars Norén have gained wide recognition as important playwrights. But drama remains a lesser genre in Sweden, and hence Bergman's accomplishments stand out still more clearly. Almost every Swedish writer of the past twenty to thirty years has been influenced by Bergman's intense cinematic exploration of characters in search of a psychological and metaphysical identity.

Swedish Literature since 1980

Toward the end of the 1970s, Swedish literature is marked by tenuous orientations in new directions after the unprecedented rallying around the radical leftist banners that took place in the period from the mid-1960s to the mid-1970s. As many of the ideologues and "culture workers" of the so-called Generation of '68 doffed their Mao jackets for equally becoming garments boasting Pierre Cardin labels and replaced the Fidel Castro and Che Guevara posters on their walls with art works of greater financial investment value, the benefits or casualties of the recent cultural revolution still remained to be evaluated—computed may be a better term in the age of electronics, which Sweden embraced more readily and thoroughly than most nations. It is still debatable whether the politicizing of literature and art in general provided a new and salutary definition of the whole concept of "culture" as intended or whether it constituted an act of vandalism through a radical break in the continuity of the cultural heritage. This heritage, kept alive under siege through the undaunted efforts of already established writers, had come to be viewed as a luxury or even as one more instrument of oppression and exploitation; the "difficulty," inaccessibility, or political irrelevance of traditional art for an imagined "average consumer" was seen as a further sign of the inequality inherent in the class society, even in the Swedish welfare state. The term finkultur (exclusive culture) was used as opposed to the new gospel that "everything is culture." The attempts to lower the standards to the imagined needs of the culturally "underprivileged" were often unwittingly condescending albeit well-meaning. The Swedish Academy, more than ever viewed as the stronghold of conservatism, weathered the storm and was able to celebrate its two hundredth anniversary in 1986. The literary legacy of the rebellious decade—"new simplicity" in

poetry and in general contempt for traditional poetic expression, denial of existential-metaphysical dimensions of the novel in favor of political demonstration, and agitprop and "happenings" as substitutes for drama (in 1991 Ingmar Bergman laments the loss of a whole generation of professionally trained and disciplined actors and directors)—presented a shaky foundation for growth and development of the literary genres in the POSTMODERNIST era.

A further threat to the future of Swedish literature was economic: The modest size of the population with a proportionately small readership in combination with very high production costs makes book publishing unprofitable. Few authors in Sweden are able to support themselves solely from the results of their creative writing. Contributing factors are also competition from literature in translation and readily available sources of entertainment in the electronic media age. In this situation, a national "cultural policy" was adopted in 1975 involving among other things government support of literature aimed at safeguarding the variety and the quality of Swedish literature; the fact that the government has only a minority voice in determining the ultimate worthiness of recipients is of course crucially important.

In the last decade, there have been three highly publicized collective undertakings in Sweden that could be viewed as signs of a different climate or a major effort to restore and to summarize a battered cultural heritage: the initiation of a new national encyclopedia; the completion in 1990 of the seven-volume richly illustrated history of Swedish literature, Den svenska litteraturen; and the mammoth so-called National Edition of August Strindberg's works, which will comprise seventy-four annotated volumes when completed.

In a speech given in England in 1983, Swedish critic Ruth Halldén (b. 1927) compared the novel in Sweden and in Britain: "Swedish novelists have a different temperament and rarely seek recognition as entertainers and wits. They have less respect for common sense, and tend to be of a more mystical or revolutionary turn of mind, aspiring to the immodest heights of a genius, a saint, or a savior. Whereas an English writer is content to produce novels with an exciting plot elegantly and competently narrated, and selects another literary form if he wishes to argue a case, defend a cause, or put forward a new theory, a Swedish writer is likely to use the novel for such purposes." The observation is astute, and it may explain the readiness with which the Swedish novel became an instrument of radical political propaganda in the 1960s and 1970s, when documentary novels and a large number of "report books" threatened to obliterate the distinctive features of the various genres. Voices continued to proclaim the imminent death of the novel, or the "sclerosis of the Swedish novel" in the words of Lars GUSTAFSSON, himself a major novelist whose position as an observer in Austin, Texas, provides him with a critical distance to his native land and its literature. Notwithstanding such dire predictions, the novel has continued to defend its position and to develop in new directions.

One such direction, uniquely Swedish at this time, is a significant trend to explore a fairly recent past. Some of the best novelists set their clocks back from a critical today and its utopian concerns for tomorrow to a historical yesterday. A number of impressive multivolume works were produced in which social and family history and myth were built into stories around fictive characters in meticulously authentic historical settings. Per Anders Fogelström (b. 1915) had already presented an immensely popular traditionally realistic five-volume series about Stockholm during the last hundred years from a proletarian perspective (1960–1968); in the 1980s he extends the chronicle in four additional novels to include well-researched accounts of life in 18th- and 19th-c. Stockholm. Sven DELBLANC, more experimental in his narrative style, who wrote a tetralogy centered on a rural Hedeby (1970–1976), now continues in another tetralogy (1981–1985) to trace a dark saga about the ancestor Samuel and his descendants, partly based on the author's own family. Kerstin EKMAN follows three successive generations of women from the 1870s to the present in a tetralogy (1974–1983) against the background of the growth and development of the town of Katrineholm. Perhaps most remarkable of all these historical chronicles is Sara LIDMAN's five-volume series (1977–85) about the building of the railroad and colonization of her native province Västerbotten close to the arctic circle. Other writers also found their material in the recent past of their native regions: Göran Tunström (b. 1937), whose Värmland figures prominently in his novels, and Torgny LINDGREN, another native of Västerbotten. More personal explorations of the past are undertaken in Jan Myrdal's recreation of his childhood in three volumes (1982–1989) or in Heidi von Born's (b. 1936) basically autobiographical tetralogy (1981–1989) set in Stockholm, while Sigrid Combüchen (b. 1942) presents a remarkable "metafictional" biography of Lord Byron (1988). In most of these novels, as well as the novels of Per Olov ENQVIST, traditional realism is undermined by a high degree of narrative artistry or flights of imagination, at times reminiscent of Latin American MAGIC REALISM.

Critic Halldén's comment on the traditional neglect of entertainment aspects in the Swedish novel is countered by a number of works in the 1980s, which justify the term *berättandets återkomst* (the return of storytelling). P. C. JERSILD remains one of the most popular writers; his social criticism is tempered with ironic humor in novels of high literary merit. Göran Hägg (b. 1947) writes eminently readable satires of intellectual life in Sweden. Lars Gustafsson experiments with such popular genres as the spy thriller and science fiction, Delblanc even writes a novel in the style of a Jackie Collins best-seller, and Klas Östergren (b. 1955) presents an adventure story about smugglers; in all of these novels, the popular form is a deceptive front for a continued discussion of more serious moral, social, and literary issues.

A number of novels in the 1980s have religious or metaphysical undertones. Lars AHLIN, one of the great novelists of the century, made his literary comeback in the early part of the decade after a silence of over twenty years. Birgitta TROTZIG continues offering a specifically Catholic perspective in her novels. A note of Job-like lamentation coupled with implied social protest in the face of inhuman sufferings is noticeable in her works, and also in those of Delblanc, Tunström, and Lindgren. Of interest is the specifically religious vision, the "Christian socialism," in the novels of Hans Granlid (b. 1926). From an agnostic-existentialist position Lars GYLLENSTEN continues his Kierkegaardian explorations of the human condition with an increased employment in the 1980s of religious "models" in intertextual dialogues with, among many others, Pär LAGERKVIST's works.

The large number of immigrants in Sweden will undoubtedly add significantly to the texture and variety of Swedish literature in years to come. A leading position among the immigrant writers is held by Theodor Kallifatides (b. 1938), whose work alternates between contemporary descriptions of life in his adopted country and reminiscences from his native Greece.

Several authors who made promising debuts in the previous decade consolidated their positions in the 1980s, among them Inger Alfvén (b. 1940), Jacques Werup (b. 1945), Ernst Brunner (b. 1950), and Lars Andersson (b. 1954). Stig Larsson (b. 1955), active

in all the major literary genres, is the foremost interpreter of a postmodernist sensibility and the writer who has most radically broken with established narrative conventions.

The shift in attitude toward poetry from the 1960s to the 1980s is illustrated in the fate of one of the great poetic geniuses of the century: Harry MARTINSON, who fell silent, or was silenced, in the harsh public-media climate of the 1960s, a rich harvest of his unpublished poetry has appeared posthumously in the more appreciative 1980s. In this decade, poetry shows greater individual variations than prose fiction. In general, the poets are more concerned with existential probings than social issues. The earlier political involvement has all but disappeared; if "issues" are discussed, they tend to concern ecology. One of the most visible poets of the 1960s, Göran Palm, writes a broad and satirical epic in blank verse: *Sverige—en vintersaga* (1984; Sweden—a winter's tale). When he returns in 1989 with a second part, he expresses concern for the threatened environment. Similar ecological concerns are found in the poetry of Elisabet Hermodsson (b. 1927), Bengt Emil Johnson (b. 1936), and Ulf Eriksson (b. 1958). The poetic scene is still dominated by such masters as Tomas TRANSTRÖMER and Lars Gustafsson, both widely translated. Tranströmer's poetry is the subject of a study by Kjell Espmark (b. 1930), himself an outstanding poet and, as a professor of literature, the author of brilliant works about poetry. Lars FORSSELL again proves his versatility with a noted epic-dramatic poem, which was set to music; it is based on the Book of Ruth in the Old Testament. Nikias Rådström (b. 1953) displays stylistic brilliance in poems full of paradoxes, while Kristina Lugn's (b. 1948) poetry offers a specifically feminine perspective of self-mocking irony. As in his prose fiction, Stig Larsson performs acts of linguistic sabotage in his poetry. A problematic relationship to language is also evident in the tentative explorations of reality in the poetry of Katarina Frostenson (b. 1953).

Sweden is a theatergoing nation. Stockholm has a higher density of theaters than any capital in the world. One reason may be that interest is early fostered through Sweden's tradition of excellent children's theater. Ingmar Bergman retired from filmmaking with *Fanny and Alexander* and returned to his first love, theater. He remains a towering presence. As director at Dramaten, Sweden's national stage, he produced in the 1980s a line of brilliant interpretations of classics—Shakespeare, Ibsen, Strindberg, and O'Neill. Per Olov Enquist and Lars NORÉN consolidated their reputations as Sweden's leading and most exportable contemporary dramatists. Agneta Pleijel (b. 1940), Stig Larsson, and Staffan Göthe (b. 1944) have added to the native repertoire, while a number of works by novelists, such as Anders Fogelström and Inger Alfvén, have been dramatized for the stage or the screen.

For the Swedish literature of Finland, see Finnish Literature.

BIBLIOGRAPHY: Mortensen, B., "Swedish Literature 1870–1950," in Bredsdorff, E., et al., *An Introduction to Scandinavian Literature* (1951): 181–209; Wizelius, I., *Swedish Literature 1956–1960* (1960); Gustafson, A., *A History of Swedish Literature* (1961); Sundberg, K., *New Swedish Books 1973–1974* (1974); Scobbie, I., ed., *Essays on Swedish Literature* (1978); Frick, L., *New Swedish Books 1975–1978* (1979); *Swedish Books* (1979 ff.); Wrede, J., et al., eds., *20th Century Drama in Scandinavia: Proceedings of the 12th Study Conference of the International Association for Scandinavian Studies, Helsinki, August 6–12, 1978* (1979); Printz-Påhlson, G., "The Tradition of Contemporary Swedish Poetry," introduction to *Contemporary Swedish Poetry* (1980): 9–16, special Sweden issue, *WLT*, 55, 2 (1981); Rossel, S., *A History of Scandinavian Literature, 1870–1980* (1982); Andersen, F. Egholm, and Weinstock, J., eds., *The Nordic Mind: Current Trends in Scandinavian Literary Criticism* (1987); Scobbie, I., ed., *Aspects of Modern Swedish Literature* (1988); Algulin, I., *A History of Swedish Literature* (1989); Zuck, V., ed., *Dictionary of Scandinavian Literature* (1990); Warme, L. G., ed., *A History of Swedish Literature* (1996)

—ROSS P. SHIDELER

SWISS LITERATURE

In German

About seventy percent of the population of Switzerland speaks one of several German dialects, and the literature produced by its German-speaking authors in the twentieth century has been copious and diverse. Nevertheless, this literature has rarely been able to gain a foothold in other German-speaking parts of Europe. Even today it is unfortunately viewed by many as an unimportant provincial appendage. The reasons for this attitude are many. German-Swiss writers tend to address local audiences and to concentrate on personal problems set in a specific Swiss locality, thus evoking the criticism that they have "narrow horizons." For all authors, the standard written German language (the *Hochsprache*) is a foreign medium—vastly different from their dialect—which must be painstakingly acquired: this situation leads some critics and even some writers to view the literature as substandard. A whole generation of Swiss writers was shut off from German readers during the Nazi era. And Swiss authors tend to be more heavily bound to tradition and slower to accept innovations. There are those, of course, who have been able to break out of this mold, and since 1945 more and more German-Swiss writers have found a readership outside their native country. Today, acceptance by a publishing house in West Germany is almost a financial necessity, given the limited market in Switzerland.

Fiction

The novel and the short story are by far the most important genres in German-Swiss literature. This direction was determined in the 19th c. by the great prose writers Jeremias Gotthelf (1797–1854), Gottfried Keller (1819–1890), and Conrad Ferdinand Meyer (1825–1898). In the early part of the 20th c. most writers, such as Ernest Zahn (1867–1952) and Jakob Christoph Heer (1859–1925), restricted themselves to narratives with a strong local color, or they wrote stories with heavy religious overtones, like Heinrich Federer (1866–1938), Meinrad Lienert (1865–1933), and, a bit later, Josef Maria Camenzind (1904-1984). A notable exception is the work of Robert WALSER, which, after decades of neglect, has received enormous scholarly attention in recent years. In *Jakob von Gunten* (1909; *Jakob von Gunten*, 1969) and other novels Walser displays the typical Swiss penchant for using a narrow focus and eschewing great themes and general ideologies. Yet, through masterfully crafted and ironic prose, he is able to turn his microcosm into a mirror for the world at large.

The various trends of European modernism left their traces in Switzerland. For example, Jakob Bosshart (1862–1924), Otto Wirz (1877–1946), Max Pulver (1889–1952) and Adrien Turel (1890–1957) wrote in a style very reminiscent of German EXPRESSION-ISM. Rudolf Jakob Humam's (1895–1977) novel *Die Inseln* (1936; the islands) questions the very art of writing; it enjoyed a rediscovery in the 1950s because of its modernist approach. There were also a number of novels critical of society, the best being *Wenn Puritaner jung sind* (1941; when puritans are young) by Albert J. Welti (1894–1965). Ludwig Hohl's (1904–1980) small oeuvre of experimental works in the 1930s and 1940s, although it found no echo at the time, was admired by the members of the "concrete" school after 1950.

Most writers, however, continued in the traditional, classical vein. Arnold Kübler (1890–1983) wrote *Entwicklungsromane* (novels of development); Kurt Guggenheim (1896–1983) wrote about city life in Zurich; Friedrich Glauser (1896–1938) wrote sophisticated detective novels; Meinrad Inglin (1893–1971) created in his *Schweizerspiegel* (1938; Swiss mirror) a detailed panorama of Swiss society during World War I; and Albin Zollinger (1895–1941) examined the role of the artist in society and the difficulties an individual encounters when confronting societal constrains. A few writers, like Jakob Schaffner (1875–1941), even had strong leanings toward the German Nazi party.

The early postwar period was dominated by the EXISTENTIAL-IST novels of Max FRISCH. In such works as *Stiller* (1954; *I'm Not Stiller*, 1958) and *Homo Faber* (1957; *Homo Faber*, 1959) Frisch faces his own and western Europe's identity crisis resulting from World War II. His characters deny their existence and try to find avenues of escape, only to be confronted in the end by harsh reality.

Around 1959 a new generation of novelists emerged who completely reshaped the German-Swiss literary scene. They developed new narrative structures based partly on a skepticism toward the capacity of the standard language to carry meaning, and they set their novels in contemporary society. Many of the works of this new generation are indebted to the NEW NOVEL, such as Otto F. WALTER's *Der Stumme* (1959; *The Mute*, 1962) or Peter BICHSEL's *Jahreszeiten* (1967; seasons). Bichsel is perhaps the most popular of these new writers. His prose text *Eigentlich möchte Frau Blum den Milchmann kennenlernen* (1964; *And Really Frau Blum Would Very Much Like to Meet the Milkman*, 1969) won the prize of the West German Group 47; his collection of short prose pieces *Kindergeschichten* (1969; *There Is No Such Place as America*, 1970) explores the connections between language and action.

Some writers follow the style of the documentary novel, such as Walter's *Die Verwilderung* (1977; gone wild) or Jürg Federspiel's (b. 1931) *Museum des Hasses* (1969; museum of hate). Many, like Adolf MUSCHG, Walter Matthias Diggelmann (1927–1979), and Gerold Späth (b. 1939), write novels critical of the social-political nexus. For example, Muschg examines such subjects as alienation in his novel *Fremdkörper* (1968; foreign bodies) and an intellectual's reaction to the student uprisings in the late 1960s in *Albisser's Grand* (1974; Albisser's reason). Diggelmann concentrates on the negative influences that society can exert on youth, as in *Die Vergnü gungsfahrt* (1969; the pleasure trip), and on the demoralizing effects of the mass media, as in *Das Verhör des Harry Wind* (1962; the interrogation of Harry Wind).

Other writers, such as Paul Nizon (b. 1929), Hugo Loetscher (b. 1929), or E. Y. MEYER, are concerned primarily with the individual and his response to his environment. Regardless of the degree of linguistic or literary experimentation in the works of these writers, at their core generally lies a realistic story that tries to define or confront those diverse elements comprising the Swiss national identity. Writers feel that this search for "Swissness" is essential to offset the strong historical and cultural links with Germany.

Since around 1970 a group of women fiction writers has had an impact. It includes Gertrud Wilker (1924–1984), Erica Pedretti (b. 1930), Maja Beutler (b. 1936), Ingeborg Kaiser (b. 1935), Elisabeth Meylan (b. 1937), Margrit Schriber (b. 1939), and Gertrud LEUTENEGGER. Most started writing later in life because of family obligations and tend to concentrate on interactions within the confines of the home.

Drama

The most notable pre-1945 dramatist was Cäsar von Arx (1895–1949). His works, frequently in the form of "festival plays," celebrated events from Swiss history. They were meant to have a popular appeal but contained such ponderous and artificial dialogue that they were soon forgotten. Other dramatists of the time created conventional historical dramas or period pieces. The one exception was Jakob Bührer (1882–1975), who wrote from a committed socialist perspective.

The real breakthrough in German-Swiss drama came after World War II, through the achievements of Max FRISCH and Friedrich DÜRRENMATT, both of whom not only dominated the German-language stage for many years but were also successful internationally. Frisch is concerned with contemporary problems on a global scale. His early plays deal with World War II and its victims, as in *Nun singen sie wieder* (1946; now they sing again). He was later greatly influenced by Bertolt BRECHT's theories on the theater and wrote several "parables" in the Brechtian style: *Biedermann and die Brandstifter* (1958; *The Firebugs*, 1959) depicts the confrontation between modern man and the uncontrollable terror that society can unleash, and *Andorra* (1961; *Andorra*, 1962) is an exploration of anti-Semitism. Dürrenmatt has been even more prolific than Frisch and also prefers to write parables, often with comic overtones, on the topics of guilt, justice, and punishment. In *Romulus der Große* (1949; *Romulus the Great*, 1965) and *Die Ehe des Herrn Mississippi* (1952; *The Marriage of Mr. Mississippi*, 1965) Dürrenmatt explores the difficulties man has in controlling his destiny. *Der Besuch der alten Dame* (1956; *The Visit*, 1962) is a powerful examination of crime and punishment in a corrupt capitalist society, and *Die Physiker* (1962; *The Physicists*, 1965) investigates the responsibility of scientists toward society. Both Frisch and Dürrenmatt usually do not specify time and place, and thus their plays assume universal dimensions with widespread appeal. They also had great influence on the development of the theater in West Germany.

Since the early 1970s, when Frisch and Dürrenmatt turned away from the theater, other dramatists have tried to fill the vacuum. Herbert Meier's (b. 1928) plays blend contemporary problems and inner conflicts. Hansjörg Schneider's (b. 1938) dramas in standard German and in dialect examine the linguistic parameters of contemporary culture. And Walter Vogt (1927–1988), a psychiatrist, excels in intimate scenes depicting mental crises and anxieties. These dramatists, unfortunately, have not succeeded in gaining the recognition of their illustrious predecessors.

Poetry

Carl SPITTELER was the most successful poet at the turn of the century. His unique blend of mythology, allegory, and philosophy earned him the Nobel Prize for literature in 1919 and the acclaim of an international public. During the next few decades, however,

poetic creation declined drastically and was limited mainly to verses in the local dialects. Some poets did write in the expressionist style, such as Albin Zollinger (1895–1941), Max Pulver (1889–1952), Adrien Turel (1890–1957), and Karl Stamm (1890–1919). Stamm's verses are full of pathos, running the gamut from religious ecstasy to depictions of the horrors of war, which he experienced firsthand.

The 1930s and 1940s saw the resurgence of traditional lyricism: Hermann Hiltbrunner (1893–1961) stressed the personal, private, religious side of life, Werner Zemp (1906–1959) preferred ornamental and romantic images, and Paul A. Brenner (1910–1967) tried to emulate 19th-c. forms. Of all the genres in the first half of the 20th c., poetry was the least productive, and the relative tranquility of Switzerland during this time of political turmoil in the rest of Europe contributed to the maintenance of the status quo.

It is thus all the more surprising that for a time after the war Switzerland was to be a leader in world poetry in the person of Eugen GOMRINGER. Gomringer is the acknowledged father of the "concrete" school. He helped give the movement direction through a new kind of poem, the "constellation," and through his theoretical writings; he is responsible for the spread of this type of poetry to West Germany and Austria. His most important writings can be found in *Worte sind schatten* (1969; words are shadows). Gomringer's influence can be seen in the works of Kurt Hutterli (b. 1943), who writes prose poems, and Beat Brechbühl (b. 1939), who combines elements of pop art and SURREALISM.

Traditional poetic styles were still popular after World War II. Silja Walter (b. 1919) continues the romantic tradition, Urs Oberlin (b. 1919) uses motifs from antiquity, Erika Burkart (b. 1922) explores a highly subjective thematic range, and Gerhard Meier (b. 1917) and Walter Gross (b. 1924) primarily write nature lyrics. Since most contemporary German-Swiss writers produce poetry only as a sideline, they do not have time to develop new approaches, and therefore these anachronistic forms have enjoyed a longer life span than might be expected.

In the course of the 20th c. German-Swiss literature has emerged from the narrow confines of pastoral idylls and dialects to become a nearly equal partner of German and Austrian literature. In recent years it has at times even succeeded in being in the forefront of the avant-garde. Traditional forms, of course, still abound, and many works do not have global ramifications. Yet in describing their own milieu German-Swiss writers have gradually been able to produce works that not only appeal to the native population but are admired and appreciated by non-Swiss readers.

BIBLIOGRAPHY: Faesi, R., *Gestalten und Wandlungen schweizerischer Dichtung* (1922); Korrodi, E., *Schweizerdichtung der Gegenwart* (1924); Ermatinger, E., *Dichtung und Geistesleben der deutschen Schweiz* (1933); Friedrich, W. P., "Chief Traits in Swiss Literature," *SAQ*, 48 (1948): 173–85; special Switzerland issue, *GL&L*, 12, 1 (1958); Schmid, K., *Unbehagen im Kleinstaat* (1963); Zbinden, H., *Schweizer Literatur in europäischer Sicht* (1964); Pulver, E., "Die deutschsprachige Literatur der Schweizseit 1945," in Gsteiger, M., ed., *Die zeitgenössischen Literaturen der Schweiz* (1974): 143–406; Waidson, H. M., "Some Contemporary German-Swiss Short Stories," *BA*, 48 (1974): 491–502; Fringeli, D., *Von Spitteler zu Muschg* (1975); Burkhard, M., "Gauging Existential Space: The Emergence of Women Writers in Switzerland," *WLT*, 55 (1981): 607–12; Obermüller, K., "Die Literatur der Gegenwart in der Schweiz," in Durzak, M., ed., *Deutsche Gegenwartsliteratur* (1981): 620–31; Stern, M., "Literarischer Expressionismus in der

Schweiz, 1910 bis 1925," in Stern, M., ed., *Expressionismus in der Schweiz* (1981), Vol. 2: 223-91

—ROBERT ACKER

In Swiss-German

The colloquial language of the Germanic population of Switzerland is Swiss-German (Schwyzertütsch), actually several different Alemannic dialects. It constitutes one of the national links because it is the language of a folk literature strongly rooted in the growth of Swiss federalism. During the romantic period the folksong was rediscovered, and even such a cosmopolitan scholar as Jakob Burckhardt (1818–1897) wrote dialect poetry. Early in the 20th c. the dialect of Bern was elevated to literary prominence by three writers. Otto von Greyerz (1863–1940) published the influential anthology *Im Röseligarte* (6 vols., 1908–12; in the rose garden) and in 1914 founded a theater group in Bern for which he wrote dialect comedies. Simon Gfeller (1863–1943) captured the language and spirit of cheese-makers and farmers in his rustic stories of the Emme valley. The greatest Swiss dialect writer, Rudolf von Tavel (1866–1934), regarded the speech of the city of Bern as eminently suitable for artistic expression. A strong awareness of regional history and Protestant traditions, as well as a vein of humor, permeate his novels, such as *Der Houpme Lombach* (1903; Captain Lombach), *Ring i der Chetti* (1931; links in the chain), and *Meischter und Ritter* (1933; masters and knights).

In the canton of Schwyz, the cradle of Swiss democracy, Meinrad Lienert (1865–1933) found fertile ground for his simple, very lyrical poems, collected in *'s Schwäbelpfyffli* (3 vols., 1913–20; the little pipe of Schwäbel). In the canton of Solothurn, Josef Reinhart (1875–1957) was a successful short-story writer. In the canton of Thurgau, Alfred Huggenberger (1867–1960) injected subtle irony into his comedies of farm life. A perfect language for satire is the rapid, witty Basel dialect in which Dominik Müller (pseud. of Paul Schmitz, 1871–1953) wrote and staged humorously biting plays about the mores of his city's burghers, which were collected as *Basler Theater* (1922; Basel theater).

During World War II, dialect literature became synonymous with the moral defense of the country. The spirit of the 1939 National Exposition in Zurich inspired an extensive use of the vernacular in journalism, juvenile literature, radio, cabaret, and later in television.

Today the use of Swiss-German is an indication of an authentic Swiss quality. Thus, dialect writing enjoys substantial popularity, especially in the theater and on television. An outstanding contemporary dialect poet is Kurt Marti (b. 1921), a Protestant minister from Bern who modernized the Alemannic poem, removing it from the sentimental pastoral tradition; he gained fame with *rosa loui* (1967; rosa loui). Julian Dillier (b. 1922) from Schwyz and Stefan Keller (b. 1958) from the canton of Thurgau have also written modern poetry in dialect. Ernst Eggiman (b. 1936) uses the dialect as the basis of his "concrete" poetry.

Since dialect writing is strictly for home consumption, many, especially essayists and novelists, also use standard German to reach a larger audience.

BIBLIOGRAPHY: Greyerz, O. von, *Die Mundartdichtung der deutschen Schweiz* (1924); Greyerz, O. von, "Alemannische Mundartliteratur," in P. Merker W. Stammler, ed., *Reallexikon der deutschen Literaturgeschichte*, Vol. 1 (1925): 9–16; Nadler, J., *Literaturgeschichte der deutschen Schweiz* (1932); Senn, A., "Verhältnis von Mundart and Schriftsprache in der deutschen Schweiz," *JEGP*, 34 (1935): 42–58; Senn, A., "Swiss Literature in Alamannic" (sic), in H. Smith, ed., *Columbia Dictionary of Modern European Literature* (1947): 801–2; Pulver, E., "Von der Mundartliteratur zu Gedichten in Schweizer Umgangssprache," in M. Gsteiger, ed., *Die zeitgenössischen Literaturen der Schweiz* (1974): 328–42

—UPDATED BY RITA STEIN

In French

French, the first language of about twenty percent of the population, is spoken in the western part of Switzerland, called Romandie, which includes the cantons of Vaud, Geneva, and Neuchâtel and parts of the Valais, Fribourg, and Bern.

French-Swiss literature began to take a distinctive form in the 19th c. with the writings of Henri-Frédéric Amiel (1821–1881), a philosopher and poet whose great work is his posthumously published *Journal intime* (definitive ed., 3 vols., 1923; *The Private Journal*, 1935); of the poet Juste Olivier (1807–1876); and of the novelist and critic Édouard Rod (1857–1910). With the founding of three important literary journals, *La voile latine* (1904–10), *Cahiers vaudois* (1914–18), and *La revue de Genève* (1920–30), French-Swiss writers asserted their independence, although there have always been strong ties to French culture, and many French-Swiss writers spend much time in Paris or move permanently to France.

Fiction

The major writer of 20th-c. Romandie is Charles-Ferdinand RAMUZ. After disappointing contacts with academic life, he retreated to the Vaud on Lake Geneva, finding inspiration there for his novels about wine-growers, fishermen, and mountain people. The struggle of these people with nature, and the sense of one's inescapable destiny, form the central themes of Ramuz's novels. His style is that of a visionary poet writing in prose.

Guy de Pourtalès's (1881–1941) masterpiece, *La pêche miraculeuse* (1937; *Shadows around the Lake*, 1938), reflects the novelist's aristocratic background and the conflict between his Swiss nationalism and his broader European outlook. Paul Budry (1883–1949) wrote lively anecdotal short stories with Swiss settings; he was a perceptive art critic as well. Robert de Traz's (1884–1951) novels deal with moral conflicts and social problems, as in *Les heures de silence* (1934; *Silent Hours*, 1934). Jacques Chenevière (1886–1976) is known for novels depicting feminine psychology, notably *Connais ton cœur* (1935; know your heart).

Maurice Zermatten (b. 1910) was one of the first novelists to write of the Valais; his works, such as *Le colère de Dieu* (1940; the wrath of God) and *La fontaine d'Aréthuse* (1958; the fountain of Arethusa), show the influence of Ramuz. Jacques Mercanton (b. 1910), a convert to Catholicism, is preoccupied with psychological and religious conflicts, notably in *Thomas l'incrédule* (1942; doubting Thomas) and *Christ au désert* (1948; Christ in the wilderness). Georges Borgeaud (b. 1914) recalled details of his youth spent in Romandie in his novel *Le préau* (1952; the playground). Two outstanding novels of the 1950s were *La clarté de la nuit* (1956; the brightness of the night) by Jean-Pierre Monnier (b. 1921) and *Je* (1959; I) by Yves Velan (b. 1925).

The best-known woman novelist of Romandie is Monique Saint-Hélier (1895–1955), whose work was influenced by her acquaintance with Rainer Maria RILKE. Alice Rivaz (b. 1901) describes the solitude of women in her novels, and S. Corinna Bille (1912–1979) wrote fiction about the Valais.

Among younger novelists, the major writer is Jacques Chessex (b. 1934), who began as a contemplative poet. His *La confession du Pasteur Burn* (1967; the confession of Pastor Burn) is in essence a self-analysis; his novel *L'ogre* (1973; *A Father's Love*, 1975) won the Goncourt Prize in France; the nonfiction *Portrait des Vaudois* (1969; portrait of the people of the Vaud) goes beyond regional description to meditate on universal questions. Anne-Lise Grobéty (b. 1949), author of *Pour mourir en février* (1970; to die in February), is a talented younger novelist.

Blaise CENDRARS can be numbered among French-Swiss writers only insofar as he was born in Switzerland; his true literary milieu was the Paris avant–garde.

The Essay and Literary Criticism

Most of the literary and publishing activities in Romandie take place in the old university cities: Geneva, Lausanne, Sion, Neuchâtel, Fribourg, and Porrentruy. Scholarship is closely associated with publication in literary magazines and editorial work on books and periodicals. The literary men and women of Romandie, although closely identified with the cultural heritage of the region, are not parochial.

A notable example of a European-oriented Romandie writer is Gonzague de Reynold (1880–1970). Because of his strong ties to his ancestral home in the hills of Fribourg, he was bound to both the French and German traditions of Swiss culture. His masterpiece, *Cités et pays suisses* (3 vols., 1914–20; Swiss cities and countries), is a lyrical evocation of the history of the four Swiss cultures. In many other writings Reynold glorifies Swiss federalism.

Edmond Gilliard (1875–1969) wrote important essays on Rousseau, Ramuz, and other French-Swiss writers. Charles-Albert Cingria (1883–1954), who divided his time between his native city of Geneva and Paris, is known especially for his imaginative books about his travels.

Denis de Rougemont (1906–1985) participated in intellectual movements concerned with promoting the unity of Europe. His books deal with topics ranging from Swiss and European themes in *L'attitude fédéraliste* (1946; the federalist attitude) and *Vingt-huit siècles d'Europe* (1961; twenty-eight centuries of Europe) to American impressions in *Vivre en Amérique* (1947; living in America). In America he is especially known through translations of two thought-provoking books: *L'amour et l'occident* (1939; *Love in the Western World*, 1940) and *Comme toi-même: Essais sur les mythes de l'amour* (1963; *Love Declared: Essays on the Myths of Love*, 1963).

Other notable critics are Léon Bopp (1896–1977), known for his *Philosophie de l'art* (1954; philosophy of art); Charly Guyot (b. 1898), who wrote *Écrivains de Suisse française* (1961; writers of French Switzerland); and Albert Béguin (1901–1957), author of *L'âme romantique et le rêve* (1937; the romantic soul and the dream). *Les Saintes Écritures: Critique* (1972; the Holy Scriptures: criticism) by Jacques Chessex, is, despite its title, a collection of essays on contemporary French-Swiss writers.

What has come to be known as the Geneva School of Criticism has produced some internationally recognized literary critics, such

as Marcel Raymond (1897–1957), Jean Rousse (b. 1910), and Jean Starobinski (b. 1920).

Poetry

Poetry in French Switzerland has developed slowly; only since 1920 has it been of any significance, and it has not enjoyed an outstanding position in Romandie literature. Nevertheless, in the Vaud three poets produced some fine verse. Pierre-Louis Matthey (1893–1970) translated Shakespeare, Blake, and Keats; his own poetry is influenced by the English romantics. Gustave Roud (1897–1976), a mystic influenced by romanticism, wrote poetic prose from his seclusion in a village high above Lake Geneva. The tragedy of Edmond-Henri Crisinel's (1897–1948) own mental illness is recorded in his haunting, mystical, yet controlled poetry.

Important poets of later generations include Maurice Chappaz (b. 1916), author of *Testament du Haut-Rhône* (1953; testament of the Haut-Rhône), Jacques Cuttat (1916–1993), Marc Eigeldinger (1917–1991), Georges Haldas (b. 1918), Philippe Jacottet (b. 1925), and Alexandre Voisard (b. 1930).

Drama

In 1908 René Morax (1873–1963), founder of the Romand theater, began to stage outdoor drama in Mézières, a village in the Vaud. For his popular theater Morax restricted himself to legendary and historical themes of local or national history, such as a play about William Tell. The Fribourg festivals had similar patriotic appeal, with writers such as Gonzague de Reynold contributing texts for musical spectacles. On the modern stage Alfred Gehri (1895–1972) attained international success with *Sixième étage* (1937; sixth floor). Other playwrights are Robert PINGET, also an important avant-garde novelist, who lives in France, Walter Weideli (b. 1927), Henri Debluë (1924–1988), and Louis Gaulis (1932–1978).

BIBLIOGRAPHY: Martinet, E., *Portraits d'écrivains romands contemporains* (2 vols., 1944, 1954); Weber-Perret, M., *Écrivains romands 1900–1950* (1951); Guyot, C., *Écrivains de Suisse française* (1961); Berchtold, A., *La Suisse romande au cap du XXe siècle* (1963); Tougas, G., *Littérature romande et culture française* (1963); Jost, F., "Y a-t-il une littérature suisse?," *Essais de littérature comparée*, Vol. I (1964): 315–38; Perrochon, H., *De Rousseau à Ramuz* (1966); Guyot, C., "The Literature of French-Speaking Switzerland in the Twentieth Century," in Natan, A., ed., *Swiss Men of Letters* (1970): 59–75; Chessex, J., *Les Saintes Écritures: Critique* (1972); Sorell, W., *The Swiss: A Cultural Panorama of Switzerland* (1972): 79–93; Secretan, O., *La Suisse alémanique vue à travers les lettres romandes de 1848 à nos jours* (1974); Gsteiger, M., *La nouvelle littérature romande* (1978); *Swiss-French Studies* (1980 ff.)

—UPDATED BY RITA STEIN

In Italian

The Italian-speaking population of Switzerland (about nine percent) lives mostly in the southern part of the country, in the canton of Ticino and in sections of Graubünden (Grisons). A passion for rhetoric and a preoccupation with a workable synthesis of Swiss nationality and Italian linguistic and cultural heritage have produced statesmen, orators, and essayists of national stature. Stefano Franscini (1796–1857), a historian, economist, and educator, set the liberal foundations for this development. The major followers of his sociopolitical and humanitarian ideas were Romeo Manzoni (1847–1919) and Brenno Bertoni (1860–1945). Conservative attitudes were represented by Giuseppe Motta (1871–1941), the multilingual Swiss president with a truly European outlook.

With Francesco Chiesa (1871–1973) Ticinese literature attained national importance in Switzerland and recognition in Italy. Chiesa was a teacher, poet, novelist, and short-story writer. His *Calliope* (3 vols., 1903–7; Calliope) is an epic lyrical work on the evolution of civilization, comprising *La cattedrale* (the cathedral), evoking the Middle Ages; *La reggia* (the royal palace), about the Renaissance; and *La città* (the city), dealing with the modern period. In his fiction Chiesa was deeply involved with nature and man's relationship to it. Some of his best narratives are *Racconti puerili* (1920; youthful stories), the novel *Tempo di marzo* (1925; March weather), and *Racconti del mio orto* (1929; stories of my east), all rich in local color and autobiographical material. Religion figures prominently in the novel *Sant'Amarillide* (1938; Saint Amaryllis).

Angelo Nessi (1873–1932) wrote satirically and humorously; his masterpiece is the autobiographical novel *Cip* (1934; Cip). The poet, essayist, critic, and novelist Giuseppe Zoppi (1896–1952) wrote lyrically about mountain life in *Il libro dell'Alpe* (1922; the book of the Alps). The many-faceted Reto Roedel (b. 1898) has written important criticism as well as fiction and plays. Piero Bianconi (1899–1984) favored the fragmentary sketch, written with a strong sense for artistic observation, as in *Ritagli* (1935; cuttings) and *Cartoline locarnesi* (1959; Locarno postcards). Bianconi is also the author of many works on art and folklore. His pupil, Mario Agliati (b. 1922), writes especially of Lugano.

Elena Bonzanigo (b. 1897) is best known for the historical novel *Serena Seròdine* (1944; Serena Seròdine). Piero Scanziani (b. 1908), who moved to Rome and is also a journalist, is a writer of sophisticated technique whose novels are set on a grand historical and philosophical scale. Carlo Castelli (b. 1909) wrote several volumes of short stories but is better known for his television and radio plays. Felice Filippini (1917–1988), also a painter, depicts rural life in his stories, novels, and essays. Martino della Valle (b. 1922) writes tales of the Ticino valleys. Adolfo Jenni (b. 1911), also a critic and poet, creates what he calls *prose di romanzo*, somewhere between fiction and criticism. Giovanni Bonalumi (b. 1922), a literary scholar and critic, is the author of *Gli ostaggi* (1954; the hostages), a novel about religious doubt set in a seminary. Enrico Filippini (b. 1934), considered Swiss although he settled in Milan, has written several unconventional essays and novels. He has also translated a number of important German-language writers into Italian.

In poetry, Valerio Abbòndio (1891–1958) ranged from sensitive descriptions of nature to human and transcendental themes. The religious poet Felice Menghini (1909–1947) is known for *Parabola* (1943; parabola). Giorgio Orelli's (b. 1921) poetry is reminiscent of that of Giuseppe UNGARETTI; Plinio Martini (1923–1979) is another talented lyric poet.

A prominent place among scholars and essayists is held by Guido Calgari (1905–1970), whose works express the need for strong cultural links between the Italian-Swiss and the Italians. His *Storia delle quattro letterature della Svizzera* (1958; new ed., *Le 4 letterature della Svizzera*, 1968; [history of] the four literatures of Switzerland) is a standard work.

BIBLIOGRAPHY: Calgari, G., "Italian Switzerland and National Literature," in Natan, A., ed., *Swiss Men of Letters* (1970): 79–100; Sorell, W., *The Swiss: A Cultural Panorama of Switzerland* (1972): 93–99; Vollenweider, A., "Die italienischsprachige Literatur der Schweiz seit 1945," in Gsteiger, M., ed., *Die seitgenössischen Literaturen der Schweiz* (1974): 549–607

—UPDATED BY RITA STEIN

In Romansh

On 20 February 1938, a referendum of the Swiss people recognized Raeto-Romance (commonly known as Romansh), spoken in the canton of Graubünden (Grisons), as Switzerland's fourth national language. About fifty thousand Swiss, one percent of the population, speak the language, which has four main dialects (each with subdialects): Ladin (or Engadine Romansh), Sursilvan, Sutsilvan, and Surmiran.

The first modern Ladin writer of note was Peider Lansel (1863–1943). Born in Italy of an emigrant family, he was educated in Switzerland, where he later lived. He was dedicated to preserving and rejuvenating the language, and his lyric poetry has had an enduring influence. Schimun Vonmoos (1868–1940) abandoned the traditional folkloric basis of Romansh fiction to concentrate on more universal matters; he is known especially for his short stories, such as "La vacha cranzla" (1934; "The Curly-Horned Cow," 1971). Men Rauch's (1888–1958) enthusiasm for hunting is reflected in the stories of *In bocca d'luf* (1941; in the jaws of the wolf), and his musical verse is evident in *Chanzuns per guitarra* (1925; songs for guitar). Gian Gianet Cloetta (1874–1965) wrote tales about emigrants from Graubünden and about mountain peasants. Eduard Bezzola (1875–1948), author of songs and plays, devoted himself to preserving Romansh language and literature.

Artur Caflisch (1893–1972) was an important Ladin lyric and satirical poet. The short stories and novels of Gian Girun (pseud. of Ursina Clavuot-Geer, b. 1898) portray childhood and nature with lyrical realism. Reto Caratsch (1901–1978) had a highly original prose style; his satires are Rabelaisian in tone.

Among more recent Ladin writers, Jon Semadeni (1910–1981) is considered the founder of modern Romansh drama; he eschewed the romantic tradition of historical drama in favor of realism. Cla Biert (1920–1981), one of the founders, in 1953, of the first Romansh cabaret, La Panaglia (the butter churn), has written fiction marked by sensuality and at times vulgar humor. *Only a Game* (1969) is a collection of his stories in English translation. Andri Peer (1921–1985) is the most important writer in Ladin today. Although chiefly a lyric poet, he has also written numerous short stories and several volumes of essays and criticism.

A key figure in the development of Sursilvan literature was Giachen Caspar Muoth (1844–1906), whose epics and ballads celebrate the struggles of the peasantry. Flurin Camathias (1871–1946), primarily a poet, represents romanticism in defense of religion, an important theme in Romansh literature. Sursilvan fiction was developed by Giachen Michel Nay (1860–1920), who vividly portrayed mountain life, and by Maurus Carnot (1865–1935), who wrote poetry and philosophical works in addition to regionalist novels. Gian Cadieli (1876–1952) wrote ballads and was one of Surselva's few satirists. Gian Fontana (1897–1935) joined a personal lyricism to portraits of village and peasant life in his poetry and short stories, while Michel Maissen (1901–1979) also used the popular theme of Alpine life in his fiction.

Later Sursilvan writers include Toni Halter (1914–1986), who depicts Surselva in different periods in his fiction; Flurin Darms (b. 1918), whose poetry deals with the unfathomable small actions of men and animals and the lonely life in the mountains; Theo Candinas (b. 1929), who has written poetry, novels, and plays about loneliness, desolation, and despair; and Hendri Spescha (1929–1982), whose introspective poetry reveals an ironic preoccupation with death.

In Sutsilvan, Steafan Loringett (1891–1970) was a poet who increasingly identified himself with the Romansh cause, and Gion Tscharner (b. 1933) has written poetry with fresh and innovative imagery. In the Surmiran dialect, Father Alexander Lozza's (1880–1953) lyric poetry and short stories deal with the question of good and evil, and Peder Cadotsch (b. 1922), a short-story writer and poet, has moved from historical subjects to modern ones.

A project begun in 1982 to create a common written language, "Rumantsch Grischun," may eventually eliminate the distinctions among these dialects. The paradox of Romansh culture is the desire to be separate but the need to be one.

BIBLIOGRAPHY: Bezzola, R., *La littérature en Suisse rétoromanche* (1964); Peer, A., "Rhaeto-Romanic Literature," in Natan, A., ed., *Swiss Men of Letters* (1970): 103–17; Mützenberg, G., *Destin de la langue et de la littérature rhéto-romanes* (1974); Uffer, L., "Die rätoromanische Literatur der Schweiz: Ein Überblick bis heute," in Gsteiger, M., ed., *Die zeitgenössischen Literaturen der Schweiz* (1974): 611–78; Camartin, I., *Rätoromanische Gegenwartsliteratur in Graubünden* (1976); Van Eerde, J., "The Predicament of Romansh Literature," *BA*, 50 (1976): 341–45; Gregory, D., *Romontsch Language and Literature* (1982)

—JOHN VAN EERDE

SYMBOLISM

Symbolism, in the narrow sense, designates a school of French poets who in the mid-1880s repudiated Parnassian descriptive techniques and turned to a nonrepresentational mode. Coined by Jean Moréas (1856–1910) in 1885, the term served to defend a group of poets deemed excessively pessimistic, hence decadent, by some critics; it called attention to the Decadents' positive goal, the pursuit of ideal beauty by means of the "eternal symbol." Moréas's claims, restated in 1886 in a formal manifesto in *Le Figaro*, signaled a decade of intense debates, which popularized the name *symboliste* but did not establish a coherent doctrine or produce a poet of major significance.

In a broader sense, symbolism designates a change in poetic sensibility brought to the status of a literary movement by Charles Baudelaire (1821–1867), Arthur Rimbaud (1854–1891), Paul Verlaine (1844–1896), and Stéphane Mallarmé (1842–1898). It encompasses French postromantic poetry of the second half of the 19th c. and represents a shift in the way poets apprehended reality. The romantics viewed experience in terms of feelings; symbolists extended poetry's domain to psychological states, to the mind and the senses, giving poetry the status of a philosophical or mystical venture that can take man beyond sense experience to the essence of things. The predominant outlook was a negative one, anchored

in the poets' profound disaffection with the spirit of positivistic science and bourgeois values. Rejecting the world, the symbolists rejected literary traditions and advocated complete freedom of expression. They evolved not a single doctrine but a way of writing that enhanced the poem's power to communicate meaning indirectly and elevated it to the level of an art object. Instead of description, allegory, rhetoric, and didacticism, symbolists relied on techniques of suggestion: word association, effects of blurring and synesthesia, verbal harmonies, structures imitating music, the projection of inner states upon external objects.

Baudelaire's *Les fleurs du mal* (1857; *Les Fleurs du Mal*, 1926) set the direction taken by the symbolists. In this revolutionary collection, Baudelaire undertook to explore the inner chaos of man, his spiritual apathy, his despair, his fascination with both evil and the ideal, and by emphasizing the negative experience of the abyss, the *gouffre*, crystallized the attitude that under the name of decadence became identified with symbolism. The poem "Correspondances" ("Correspondences"), later hailed as a symbolist manifesto, grounded poetry in the notion of relationships that bridge the gap not only between the natural and spiritual worlds but also between external reality and the poet's inner realm, thereby transforming nature into a storehouse of images that mirror the human.

Although Rimbaud did not significantly influence the early phases of symbolism, his spiritual orientation assumes symbolist characteristics, evident most clearly in his scorn for society and the parallel quest for the unknown. As did Baudelaire, Rimbaud made poetry the instrument of knowledge. Combining sound, taste, color, violent rhythms, images uncomplicated by reflection, and dream sequences, he delved into the self and claimed to have discovered a poetry that touches all the senses. Going beyond Baudelaire, Rimbaud sought to heighten his powers of vision by means of the conscious disturbance of the senses and hallucination, thus injecting into his work a high degree of irrationality.

At first a Parnassian, Verlaine discovered quickly the art of suggestive writing, bringing it to maturity in *Romances sans paroles* (1874; *Romances without Words*, 1921), his most symbolist collection. As Verlaine saw it, poetry mirrors the author's subjectivity; it is a harmony of sound and color, imprecise, muted, as fugitive as the scent of mint, drawing its melody from assonance and aesthetic asymmetry. He projected upon finely drawn landscapes moods of bittersweet melancholy and created a widely imitated impressionistic style, based on carefully contrived effects of vagueness, nuance, blurred lines, delicate melodies, and colors in half-tones. Prolific and spontaneous, he supplied a universally accessible poetic model of incomparable musicality, and through his study *Les poètes maudits* (1884; the damned poets) introduced the younger generation to the symbolists Tristan Corbière (1845–1875) and Villiers de l'Isle-Adam (1838–1889), among others.

Mallarmé gave symbolism a sense of direction both through his writing and the Tuesday gatherings he held for writers and artists beginning around 1884. His own theories, however, went far beyond those of his contemporaries and reflected his search for a pure symbolic language severed from external circumstance. If Verlaine identified the symbol with the subjective landscape, Mallarmé made it the very condition of creativity, the essence of the art of evocation. Proceeding systematically, Mallarmé abstracted words from their habitual contexts, violated the natural rhythms and grammatical sequences, used extreme forms of condensation, and looked to music for structural models. He hoped to achieve in poetry a juncture of sight and hearing that bypasses logic and yields intuitive understanding. Distance from reality, the core of Mallarmé's poetic concepts, informs his poems. Inactivity, fear of life, confrontation with the void are the dominant themes in Mallarmé; they confirm his sense of the artist as a solitary having no real function in society.

A new generation of poets came to prominence in 1885. It drew inspiration from its predecessors but, unable to respond to the deeper elements of symbolism, concentrated on formal innovations. René Ghil (1862–1925) attempted to reduce poetry to pure sound, Gustave Kahn (1859–1936) replaced the traditional syllabic numeration by accentuated verse patterns or free verse, and American-born Stuart Merrill (1863–1915) and Francis Viélé–Griffin (1864–1937) sought to reproduce in French the euphonies of English poetry. Jean Moréas, tiring of symbolism, returned to classical forms, while Émile VERHAEREN, a Belgian, exploited the theme of the modern city to give his work a sense of energy. Jules Laforgue (1860–1887), the most talented among the younger symbolists, expressed the essential themes of decadence and, believing that words do not respond to any transcendent reality, hoped to purify language by ridding it of both its earthly tonalities and its mysticism.

Applying Mallarmé's principles, symbolists created a theater closely related to poetry, dependent on atmosphere, loosely woven occurrences, the interplay of light and sound, silences, symbolic use of objects and settings, action suggested through its effects, and characters subservient to theme and author. Villiers de l'Isle-Adam was the first to try new forms, and even though his techniques remained conventional, his protagonist Axel in the play *Axel* (1890; *Axel*, 1925) became identified with the image of the decadent. Maurice MAETERLINCK, a Belgian, author of *Pelléas et Mélisande* (1892; *Pelléas and Mélisande*, 1894), made the most effective use of symbolist devices. His plays, with their dreamlike atmosphere and preoccupation with death, influenced Gerhart HAUPTMANN, a German, and the Austrian Hugo von HOFMANNSTHAL, both of whom subordinated plot and character to tone. By contrast, the symbolist contribution to fiction was less significant, with Joris-Karl Huysmans's (1848–1907) *À rebours* (1884; *Against the Grain*, 1922) being the most notable exception.

After 1900 symbolism survived not as a movement but a legacy of attitudes and principles deriving essentially from the four major figures and often modified by new poetic currents. It is discernible in the early works of André GIDE and in Paul CLAUDEL's dramatic pieces. Paul VALÉRY's *Le cimetière marin* (1920; *The Graveyard by the Sea*, 1932), with its systematic coupling of inner perception and outer landscape, and structures organized in the manner of musical variations, represents the high point of symbolist influence in the 20th c. Poets as diverse as the SURREALISTS and Saint-John PERSE, a master of disciplined cadences, were responsive to the symbolist heritage and extended it into the 1920s.

Symbolist conventions, enriched and altered by foreign writers as early as the 1890s, gave rise to an international movement that touched the literatures of western and eastern Europe and persisted well into the 1920s and 1930s. Stefan GEORGE transplanted the new aesthetic to Germany and influenced Rainer Maria RILKE, whose poetry suggests best among the German poets an affinity with symbolism. The work of the Italians Gabriele D'ANNUNZIO, Giuseppe UNGARETTI, and Ugo BETTI is sometimes tinged with symbolism. To a degree, symbolist influences can also be traced in the American poets Hart CRANE and Wallace STEVENS. In England, symbolist influences brought into focus the artist's separation from society and his desire for artistic freedom, associated in

particular with Oscar Wilde (1854–1900) and Arthur Symons (1865–1945). Symons, author of *The Symbolist Movement in Literature* (1899), directed many English writers toward symbolism, among them William Butler YEATS, who expanded symbolist resources by tapping into Celtic legends, and T. S. ELIOT, in whose early work one detects a symbolist affiliation with music and the intermingling of inner states and concrete images.

The stimulating effect of symbolism in Russia initiated a cultural renascence. It brought to the forefront questions of literary form, recast significantly the thematic matter, and renovated literary criticism. In the 1890s writers elaborated techniques based on French sources. Fyodor SOLOGUB exalted beauty over life and cultivated an extreme form of egotism; Konstantin BALMONT was best known for his rhythmic inventions; Valery BRYUSOV, an excellent polemicist, emerged as the movement's foremost apologist. Later poets, associated with *Vesy* (1904–9), the principal organ of Russian symbolism, rediscovered Russian sources. They combined the aestheticism of the 1890s with a mysticism of native vintage, thus elaborating a unique synthesis of poetry and religion, represented by Andrey BELY's attempts to equate symbolization with the creation of values, and by Vyacheslav IVANOV's concept of a collective religious intuition. Alexandr BLOK, a master of imagery and verbal melodies, drew inspiration from everyday realities and, in his mature years, from the religious searchings of the Russian people. Blok did much to reshape the language and prosody of Russian poetry. Russian symbolism did not survive past the Bolshevik revolution.

By contrast, in the Spanish-speaking countries symbolism was at once more diffuse and longer–lasting, not so much a movement as a clustering of techniques and tendencies, intertwined with the larger current of MODERNISM. Symbolism accounts for some of modernism's most durable features: musicality, ambiguity, suggestiveness, and mysticism, seen in the aspiration to universal harmony of the Nicaraguan Rubén DARÍO, the Mexican modernist Amado NERVO, and the Argentine Leopoldo LUGONES. Julián del Casal (1863–1893), a Cuban poet, professed disenchantment with reality, as did the lyric Colombian poet José Asunción Silva (1865–1896) and Julio HERRERA Y REISSIG, a native of Uruguay. Among the Spanish poets, Federico GARCÍA LORCA had the Baudelairean gift of transmuting sensuality into mysticism, Juan Ramón JIMÉNEZ thought of poetry as a symbolic mirroring of the universe, and Antonio MACHADO, an admirer of Mallarmé, perfected the art of expanding natural images into complex symbolic systems. Symbolist techniques also surface in the Spanish American narrative, less often in the prose works of Spanish writers, even though such figures as Miguel de UNAMUNO and Ramón VALLE-INCLÁN shared the symbolists' synthesizing vision of art and language.

Within Luso-Brazilian literature symbolism remained a distinct category. It marks a stage in the development of Eugénio de Castro (1869–1944), the first to espouse symbolism in Portugal, Antonio Patricio (1878–1930), Mário de SÁ-CARNEIRO, and Camilo Pessanha (1867–1926), the best known of the Portuguese symbolists. In Brazil, symbolism found its most original exponent in the hypnotic and deeply felt verse of the black poet João da Cruz e Sousa (1861–1898).

On the international scale, mingling freely with native currents, symbolism was a vigorous force for renovation, a fountainhead of much of modern poetry. Its longevity and influence derived from the poets' ability to transcend direct, limited meanings through the use of the symbol-image and both to open up new possibilities and to give voice to a mood of metaphysical restlessness.

BIBLIOGRAPHY: Symons, A., *The Symbolist Movement in Literature* (1899); Wilson, E., *Axel's Castle: A Study in the Imaginative Literature of 1870–1930* (1931); Bowra, C. M., *The Heritage of Symbolism* (1943); Cornell, K., *The Symbolist Movement* (1951); Chiari, J., *Symbolism from Poe to Mallarmé: The Growth of a Myth* (1956); Cornell, K., *The Post-Symbolist Period* (1958); Donchin, G., *The Influence of French Symbolism on Russian Poetry* (1958); Lawler, J., *The Language of Symbolism* (1969); Kugel, J. L., *The Techniques of Strangeness in Symbolist Poetry* (1971); Anderson, D. L., *Symbolism: A Bibliography of Symbolism as an International Multi-Disciplinary Movement* (1975); Balakian, A., *The Symbolist Movement*, 2nd ed. (1977); Grass, R. and W. R. Risley, eds., *Waiting for Pegasus: Studies of the Presence of Symbolism and Decadence in Hispanic Letters* (1979); Valency, M., *The End of the World: An Introduction to Contemporary Drama* (1980); Balakian, A., ed., *The Symbolist Movement in the Literature of European Languages* (1982)

—VIKTORIA SKRUPSKELIS

SYNGE, John Millington

Irish dramatist, essayist, and poet, b. 16 April 1871, Rathfarnham; d. 24 March 1909, Dublin

S.'s barrister father died a year after the boy's birth, and S. grew up under the stern dominion of his mother. The maternal tutelage was that of strict Protestant discipline and devotion to God. S. was taught that the wages of sin was certain damnation. Early in his teens, however, he discovered Darwin and suffered a crisis of faith from which he was never fully to recover. His resulting agnosticism isolated the youth from family and friends, contributing to the withdrawn and solitary nature for which he was known.

S. entered Trinity College, Dublin in 1888 in order to study law, but he quickly discovered the joys of literature and music. An indifferent scholar at best, he earned in 1892 a pass, or "gentleman's," degree, having met the minimum requirements of the college without special distinction. Music was S.'s chief passion during and immediately after his college years. He studied theory and composition at the Royal Irish Academy of Music, learned to play the violin, and performed occasionally in the Academy's orchestra.

S. first left Ireland in 1893 for trips to Germany, Italy, and France, cultivating an interest in Continental literature. It was in France in 1896 that he first met his countryman W. B. YEATS, a writer who was to have a profound influence on S. and remain a lifelong friend. Yeats advised him to abandon his pursuit of the study of French literature and return to Ireland to study Celtic culture and the Gaelic language.

Heeding Yeats's counsel, S. went back to his native country and undertook a series of visits to the Aran Islands off the west coast of County Clare. He first set foot on Aranmor on May 10, 1898, and found there a culture largely untouched by modern civilization and a people steeped in the Celtic superstitions and folklore of previous centuries. He visited the islands four times between 1898 and 1901, living with the people of Aran and learning Gaelic. In 1907 he published *The Aran Islands*, a lengthy narrative account of his adventures, and his major prose work.

His experiences among the peasants of Aran and of the west of Ireland revealed to S. a life and a language that were to serve as the inspiration for almost all his dramatic works. All of S.'s plays save one embody Irish peasant life, and all employ a richly poetic Anglo-Irish dialect that is uniquely his.

In 1898 Yeats introduced S. to Lady Gregory (1859–1932) and Edward Martyn (1859–1923), cofounders with Yeats of the Irish Literary Theatre (later the Irish National Theatre Society). Thus began S.'s interest in the theater. In 1903 his first acted play, *In the Shadow of the Glen* (pub. 1904), was produced in Dublin by Yeats and Lady Gregory. (An earlier S. play, "When the Moon Has Set," written in 1901, was never produced or published.)

In the Shadow of the Glen is a short one-acter—little more than a dramatic sketch—but it clearly reveals S.'s technique as a dramatist and prefigures the style of his later plays. In this ironic comedy, S. exhibited a keen sense of the comic and demonstrated the distinctive blend of farce, satire, and plaintiveness that is so characteristic of his comic mode. The comedy's protagonist is Nora Burke, the first of S.'s headstrong young heroines who dramatize the unhappy plight of the Irish peasant girl at the turn of the century. Nora, trapped in a loveless marriage to an aging farmer, abandons her husband to run off with a young tramp who promises romance and adventure.

This play offended the Dublin audiences, who saw it as an attack upon Irish womanhood. But the critical furor it occasioned was only the first in a series of controversies that were to rage over S.'s plays.

Riders to the Sea (pub. 1903, perf. 1904), S.'s next play, is perhaps the finest one-act tragedy in English. Set on the rugged coast of one of the Aran Islands, it is a deeply moving essay in grief. Its protagonist, old Maurya, has lost five sons to the cruel sea, and we see her at the moment when she learns of the drowning of her sixth and last. The play evokes the poetic and mythic reverberations of Greek tragedy as it blends both Christian and pre-Christian elements, strongly suggesting the supernatural. *Riders to the Sea* established S. as an important modern dramatist, and in 1905 he became a director, together with Yeats and Lady Gregory, of the Irish National Theatre Society.

The Well of the Saints (1905), S.'s first full-length play, is a parable in which a middle-aged blind couple have their sight miraculously restored by a healer, only to discover that they cannot bear the sight of one another. Their marriage destroyed, each suffers loneliness and despair until their blindness returns and they are reunited, happy once again and considerably wiser. S.'s point is that the Saint's "miracle" is not nearly so profound as is the self-knowledge gained by Martin and Mary, who learn to "see" the true meaning of their life together. Although flawed by a lack of physical action and an emphasis on psychological states, the play deftly blends the comic, the tragic, and the lyrical. It is perhaps S.'s strongest statement of the need—indeed, the right—of the individual to shape and define his own life view, free from conventional ideas of morality and religion. It is a theme that runs throughout the S. canon.

The Tinker's Wedding (pub. 1908, perf. 1909), a rollicking two-act farce, is the brightest of S.'s creations. Like *In the Shadow of the Glen*, it concerns a young girl for whom the limitations of good Catholic morality are in conflict with the impulses of nature. Sarah Casey wants to wed her young tinker beau, but she cannot convince the local priest, a pious, pompous fool, to perform the ceremony. In the end she and her intended overpower the priest and bind him in a sack, rendering him utterly ridiculous. This play is perhaps S.'s most outspoken criticism of the Irish-Catholic clergy. Yeats felt that it was "too dangerous for the theatre," and S. himself admitted in 1906 that it was "never played here [Dublin] because it is thought too immoral and anticlerical." Nevertheless, *The Tinker's Wedding* is a delightful romp, somewhat reminiscent of Boccaccio in its good-natured lambasting of conventional religion and "establishment" clergy.

S.'s finest and most famous play is *The Playboy of the Western World* (1907), a comedy that provoked riots during its initial Dublin performances and prompted most of the Irish urban populations of Ireland, England, and America to condemn S. as—at best—a scoundrel and—at worst—a traitor. Once again set among the peasantry of the West (County Mayo), *The Playboy of the Western World* recounts the fanciful tale of a young ne'er-do-well, Christy Mahon, who, believing that he has killed his father, seeks refuge among the group of Mayo peasants. Starved for romance and adventure, the Mayo people take him in as a hero and exalt his gallant deed. Chief among the group is Pegeen Mike, S.'s finest characterization of the headstrong Irish peasant girl. When Christy's father appears, wounded but very much alive, Pegeen and the others turn against the boy, and in desperation he tries once again to kill his father to regain Pegeen's affection. This only further infuriates her, and it is only the survival and hilarious second resurrection of the father that saves Christy from the gallows. From this experience, the boy evolves from a sniveling coward to a self-determined man who takes charge of his own life, having learned something of the fickleness of human nature.

The Playboy of the Western World is skillfully plotted, rich in effective characterization, and couched in dialogue that, although written as prose, frequently soars into the realm of lyrical verse. In no other play was S. able so effectively to combine naturalism with fancy. It is, justifiably, one of the most frequently produced of Irish plays.

S. wrote only one play after *The Playboy of the Western World*; his illness, Hodgkin's disease, had advanced, and he undoubtedly knew that he was dying. In 1906 he had fallen in love with the actress Molly Allgood (stage name, Maire O'Neill) and wanted to write "something quiet and stately and restrained" for her to act. The result was *Deirdre of the Sorrows*, published posthumously in 1910. It is a somber and brooding tragedy, based upon an Irish myth dating from the 8th or 9th c.

Deirdre of the Sorrows, the most poetic of S.'s plays, tells of a young girl who is fated by a prophecy to grow to great beauty and bring about the destruction of the House of Usna and the deaths of many men. Although betrothed to a king, she goes off with a lover and, in the end, returns to the king, who treacherously orders the murders of her lover and his brothers. The prophecy having been fulfilled, Deirdre kills herself. The play has moments of considerable beauty, chiefly in its lyrical dialogue, but it offers little in the way of dramatic tension. Its protagonist, unlike most tragic figures, seems resigned throughout to her fate and offers little resistance or defiance of the prophecy. S.'s final tragedy lacks the vitality and urgency of his comedies.

S.'s nondramatic works consist of the aforementioned *The Aran Islands*, a number of essays on Irish life, and a small body of lyrical verse, the last published in *Poems and Translations* (1909). His poems, a mere two dozen in number, are short, rhymed lyrics in fairly regular meter. Quite personal in content, they display a masculine vitality and earthiness, as well as a sardonic humor. Also noteworthy are the dozen sonnets by Petrarch that S. translated into English prose.

Throughout his unhappily brief career as a dramatist, S. repeatedly provoked the ire of his audiences because he depicted the Irish peasants as he knew them, without idealization, thereby challenging the romantic illusions about "Irish life" so dear to the Dubliners. He refused always to compromise with those who placed Irish nationalism above artistic integrity. Today he is recognized as a major force in the birth of the modern drama and as a true spokesman for the Irish spirit of his time. *The Playboy of the Western World* and *Riders to the Sea* at least are modern masterpieces that will surely endure.

FURTHER WORKS: *Works of J. M. S.* (4 vols., 1910); *Plays by J. M. S.* (1932); *J. M. S.: Collected Works* (4 vols., 1962–1968); *Letters to Molly: J. M. S. to Maire O'Neill* (1971); *The S. Manuscripts in the Library of Trinity College, Dublin* (1971); *J. M. S. to Lady Gregory and W. B. Yeats* (1971); *The Collected Letters of J. M. S., Vol. I: 1871–1907* (1983)

BIBLIOGRAPHY: Bourgeois, M., *J. M. S. and the Irish Theatre* (1913); Corkery, D., *S. and Anglo-Irish Literature* (1931); Ellis-Fermor, U., *The Irish Dramatic Movement* (1939; 2nd ed., 1954): 163–86; Greene, D. H., and E. M. Stephens, *J. M. S.* (1959); Price, A., *S. and the Anglo-Irish Drama* (1961); Gerstenberger, D., *J. M. S.* (1964); Saddlemyer, A., *J. M. S. and Modern Comedy* (1968); Skelton, R., *The Writings of J. M. S.* (1971); Bushrui, S. B., ed., *A Centenary Tribute to J. M. S., 1871–1909: Sunshine and the Moon's Delight* (1972); Harmon, M., ed., *J. M. S.: Centenary Papers 1971* (1972); Grene, N., *S.: A Critical Study of the Plays* (1975); Fallis, R., *The Irish Renaissance* (1977): passim; Worth, K., *The Irish Drama of Europe from Yeats to Beckett* (1978): 120–39; Kiberd, D., *S. and the Irish Language* (1979); Kopper, E. A., Jr., *J. M. S.: A Reference Guide* (1979); Thornton, W., *J. M. S. and the Western Mind* (1979)

—JACK A. VAUGHN

Mr. S. has in common with the great theatre of the world, with that of Greece and that of India, with the creator of Falstaff, with Racine, a delight in language, a preoccupation with individual life. He resembles them also by a preoccupation with what is lasting and noble, that came to him, not as I think from books, but while he listened to old stories in the cottages, and contrasted what they remembered with reality. The only literature of the Irish country-people is their songs, full often of extravagant love, and their stories of kings and of kings' children. "I will cry my fill, but not for God, but because Finn and the Fianna are not living," says Oisin in the story. Every writer, even every small writer, who has belonged to the great tradition, has had his dream of an impossibly noble life, and the greater he is, the more does it seem to plunge him into some beautiful or bitter reverie. Some, and of these are all the earliest poets of the world, gave it direct expression; others mingle it so subtly with reality, that it is a day's work to disentangle it; others bring it near by showing us whatever is most its contrary. Mr. S., indeed, sets before us ugly, deformed or sinful people, but his people, moved by no practical ambition, are driven by a dream of that impossible life. That we may feel how intensely his woman of the glen dreams of days that shall be entirely alive, she that is "a hard woman to please" must spend her days between a sour–faced old husband, a man who goes mad upon the hills, a craven lad and a drunken tramp; and those two blind people of *The Well of the Saints* are so transformed by the dream, that they choose blindness rather than reality. He tells us of realities, but he knows that art has never taken more than its symbols from anything that the eye can see or the hand measure.

It is the preoccupation of his characters with their dream that gives his plays their drifting movement, their emotional subtlety. In most of the dramatic writing of our time, and this is one of the reasons why our dramatists do not find the need for a better speech, one finds a simple motive lifted, as it were, into the full light of the stage. The ordinary student of drama will not find anywhere in *The Well of the Saints* that excitement of the will in the presence of attainable advantages, which he is accustomed to think the natural stuff of drama, and if he see it played he will wonder why Act is knitted to Act so loosely, why it is all like a decoration on a flat surface, why there is so much leisure in the dialogue, even in the midst of passion. [1905]

> W. B. Yeats, Preface to the First Edition of *The Well of the Saints*, in *Essays* (1924), pp. 375–77

No one who knows Ireland at all would hold that S.'s plays are typical of the Irish peasant generally, but any one who knows Irish literature at all, and the life of the roads in Ireland, will admit that wildness and extravagance are to be found in that literature from the beginning and in that life even at this day of supposed civilization. . . .

Always the joy of making something beautiful out of his experience and dream of life is what inspires S. to write, and though the intention to read life truly is a passion with him, there is never a suggestion of didacticism, or even of moralizing, though *The Well of the Saints* is unquestionably, whether he wills it so or not, a symbol of man's discontent with things as they are, his preference in some things of the lie to the truth. I think that S. did not will to make *The Well of the Saints* a symbol, and that the play was to him but a reading of life, as life is, in his characteristic, exalted, ironic, extravagant way of writing, and that if he was aware of the symbolism, he was not keenly aware of it or much interested in it. He gives us life untroubled by the passing agitation of the day, and for that we should be thankful, and thankful, too, that he has given in his plays "the nourishment, not very easy to define, on which our imaginations live." His irony, as desolating to some as the irony of Swift, gives pause to all, as insight always will, but to me his extravagance is a joy unalloyed, and his exaltation, so rare a thing in modern literature, should bring to all men delight and refreshment of spirit. No reading, or seeing and hearing, of his plays leaves me without a feeling of richness or without wonder and large content. He gives back my youth to me, both in the theatre and in my library, and, in the glow that is mine

in such recapture, I call him the greatest dramatist in English that our stage has known in a century.

> C. Weygandt, *Irish Plays and Playwrights* (1913), pp. 171, 196–97

The exotic appeal of S.'s work can scarcely be exaggerated; and it is another aspect of his romantic and lyrical character. I think there can be no doubt that S. himself experienced the language and life he found in the Aran Islands as something rare and strange, beautiful because it was unsophisticated, remote, elemental. It awoke the artist in him, as Paris had not been able to do, because he was a romantic. And in this S. is the pure artist, without any admixture of the political intentions that have always to be reckoned with in Yeats and other adherents of the Celtic renaissance. Yeats it was who sent S. out to the West, helping a genius to find his line, but also making a démarche in the political cause of Irish nationalism. It is clear that S. was independent of causes; an unpolitical artist, whatever use others made of his work once it was done. His pleasure in observing his primitives and in savouring their musical and picturesque language was from any point of view but the artistic irresponsible and non-commital. The storm about *The Playboy of the Western World* arose because there were many Irishmen who could not emulate such detachment.

As far as the Anglo-Saxons are concerned, I think Max Beerbohm came nearest to the truth when he stressed the exotic as the source of our greatest pleasure in S. It is, however, a judgement that has been obscured by more frequent tributes to his pure dramatic genius. No one would deny his natural sense of drama and theatre, his powers in comedy and tragedy. If he were without them his more personal charms would be thin and vapid perhaps. But he did not possess those powers in an astonishing degree, and they alone certainly do not make the S. to whom we are endeared. They are the excellent soil above which the rare bloom raises its head. S.'s greatest distinction, the thing that gives our acquaintance with him its particular flavour, is his wonderful language, which pleases us not as a heightened form of the language we ourselves use, but as a picturesque deviation from it. Two things support each other; the setting of Irish character, atmosphere and speech is itself exotically attractive, and it is made more so, pointedly so, by S.'s exquisite and subtle handling of the imaginative language he discovered in the West.

> Ronald Peacock, *The Poet in the Theatre* (1946), pp. 110–11

S. is the only great poetic dramatist of the [Irish dramatic] movement; the only one, that is, for whom poetry and drama were inseparable, in whose work dramatic intensity invariably finds poetic expression and the poetic mood its only full expression in dramatic form. All the other playwrights of the movement seem, in the last analysis, to have been either dramatists in whom the instinct for dramatic expression sometimes brought with it the poetry of diction, imagery or cadence, or poets who turned for a time to the dramatic form, returning, sooner or later, again to other forms. But it is hard to imagine this separation in S.: poetic and dramatic expression in him are one and simultaneous, as they appear to have been with Shakespeare and with Webster, in whom the presence of a high degree of one mood meant the presence of a high degree of the other, whether the form were prose or verse, the matter comedy or tragedy.

Yet there is a paradox in S.'s genius, a dualism of a different and a rarer kind. For while he is essentially a dramatic poet, one of the roots of his poetry is mysticism, such as he recognized in the mountain and sea-faring Irish peasants living far enough out of reach of civilization to respond to and reflect the nature about them. And mystical experience, particularly the extreme form of nature-mysticism that we find in S., is in itself as nearly as possible incompatible with dramatic expression. Yet the presence of nature is as strongly felt in the plays as in *The Aran Islands* and *In Wicklow and West Kerry* and it is not there as a digression, irrelevant or undramatic. Nature is a protagonist in *In the Shadow of the Glen* and *Riders to the Sea*, so filling the minds of the characters as to shape their actions, moods and fates; it is the ever-present setting, genially familiar, of *The Well of the Saints* and *The Tinker's Wedding*; it remains as a continual and surprising source of imagery and incidental reference throughout *The Playboy of the Western World* and becomes again a poetic protagonist in *Deirdre of the Sorrows*. When S. began to draw his material from the Aran Islands he had found, by one of those accidents of fortune which sometimes save genius from extinction, the people who alone could stimulate his imagination and offer him something on which this strange combination of dramatist and nature-mystic could work. They were the human theme which drama must have and yet they were in part at least nature itself.

Una Ellis-Fermor, *The Irish Dramatic Movement*,
2nd ed. (1954), pp. 163–64

It is worth noting how closely bound into one main theme are the three elements of tension between dream and actuality, interaction between Man and the natural world, and awareness of mutability. All the sympathetic figures in S.'s plays are driven by an impossible dream; each, with a single-minded, intense, almost child-like longing to become "a wonder" is continually reaching out for a finer and fuller life. Imagination is creative in each of them, and it gives them a vision of some good beyond the poverty or drabness or terror which surrounds them; towards that vision, that dream, they strive. Yet they are nearly always frustrated. Only in *The Playboy of the Western World* does the power of the imagination make dream and actuality one, and accordingly this play is the richest and most joyous that Synge wrote. *The Tinker's Wedding* too is largely happy, because

Sarah's dream is of something worse than her normal life and she gets rid of it in the end and returns thankfully to her proper station. But in *In the Shadow of the Glen*, although it is clearly implied that Nora's choice was the right one, it is not asserted that she and the Tramp attain what they seek, and in the other plays and in the prose works and the poetry the dream is invariably overcome by actuality. Hence the tragic undertones, the sombreness and the awareness of mutability pervading S.'s work.

Alan Price, *S. and the Anglo-Irish Drama* (1961),
p. 216

Freed of the Yeatsian vision, let us look at reality through S.'s eyes. It must be sought in a "comprehensive and natural form," he tells us in his preface to *The Playboy of the Western World*. In Ireland there are still places where this reality is superb and wild, and therefore joyous—even to the point of the Rabelaisian. But always, for it to remain valid, this joy must be rooted in its natural form, must, in fact, flow from the imagination of the people. When one is true to the folk imagination, it follows that one will be true to their mode of expression. The richer the imagination, the richer and more copious the language. And always, for the artist to remain true to his subject, the delicate balance must be perceived and tested, the tension between form and spirit preserved. The artist must never become so carried away with a wild joyousness that he loses sight of the form which contains it. "The strong things of life are needed in poetry also," he warns us, "to show that what is exalted or tender is not made by feeble blood." The Rabelaisian may even incorporate the brutal. Nor can there be true affirmation without testing all verities. In wit, as Oscar Wilde has taught us, forcing the verities to walk a tightrope leads to paradox. In drama, S. shows us it leads to irony, both in choice of subject and technique.

Ann Saddlemyer, *J. M. S. and Modern Comedy*
(1968), pp. 12–13

It is my view that J. M. S. was far from being the objective and sardonic observer of the Irish scene that some have thought him, and equally far from being the passionate devotee of all things simple and rural that others have supposed. He was a man who transformed every significant personal experience and encounter into literature, transfiguring all into fable with the energy of his imagination. He could not comfortably see the smallest evidence of human dignity, depravity, or passion without setting it in the context of the predicament of a human race granted both the potential of passionate life and the knowledge of ultimate death. He could not allow the existence of the commonplace, and though his natural bent was for bitter comedy, he saw the heroic in everything he met. Early troubled by the narrow savagery of the evangelical Protestant ethic and the blinkered complacency of Ascendancy bourgeois attitudes, he took up the cause of individual freedom and celebrated the anarchy of the passionate heart wherever he could find it. Disturbed by thoughts of his own mortality from an early age, he brought to his writings a vivid awareness of life's insecurity together with an intense relish for the gaiety and absurdity of its enjoyments, and created works whose richness and tension few have equalled.

Robin Skelton, *The Writings of J. M. S.* (1971),
p. 171

For many readers S. scarcely seems a very modern playwright. He stands so much apart from the mainstream of the drama that our sense of his historical position is very vague, but there is a general feeling that he is well back towards the beginning of the century, certainly a long way from the modernity of the absurdists. Ironically, it may be S.'s success which makes him so unobtrusive, where dramatists who have produced experimental failures look more significant. The techniques used in the comedies are simple and unostentatious so that the plays seem to be no more than they appear on the surface, realistic sketches of peasant life. Yet when we have considered their structure in detail, it is clear that they involve a complicated interplay between dramatic modes which links them with more obviously experimental plays of a later period. If the fragmented and disparate movements of modern drama can be said to have a central direction it is in the quest for an image of man—a man who can no longer fill the centre of a tragic universe, nor participate in an assured social order. It is in this context that the four "unhappy comedies" of S. may be seen as significantly the work of a modern dramatist.

Nicholas Grene, *S.: A Critical Study of the Plays*
(1975), p. 159

SYRIAN LITERATURE

For understanding the nature of modern literature in Syria, it is probably necessary to note that the term "Syrian Literature" is not quite familiar among Syrian writers who generally tend to maintain that the outcome of their literary production could better be defined as "arabic literature in /of Syria." For many of them this terminology is apparently meant to stress the Arab national character of the mainstream of culture in Syria, but it also serves to underline a paradox latent in the very being of this literature in the sense that it is, at one and the same time, old (since it is the legal descendant of classical Arabic literature) and young (since it is virtually the literature of a young state that emerged in the aftermath of World War II and the evacuation of French mandate forces in 1946). To draw on Edward Said's *Beginnings* (1975), this fact may well explain the ambivalent line of development that has so far governed the march of literature in Syria, i.e. to keep balance between the vehement quest for maintaining the historical national identity and to respond at the same time to the successive waves of Westernization first and modernization later. The same ambivalence applies to the

language of this literature, which has always fluctuated between the deep rooted conservatism and rhetoric of classical Arabic on one hand and the need for new literary diction, flexible grammar, and fresh structures necessary to meet the challenges of modern writing on the other.

The Syrian literary production developed rather slowly during the first half of the 20th c. with limited span of subjects mainly traditional with very little special local color and with limited signs of adventure. In fact the few adventurous experiments came from those writers who had chance to study in Europe, mainly France the colonizing power. With them came into Syria the first wave of Western influences through direct contact and adaptation or—to a lesser degree—through translation, first from French literature and gradually later from English, German and Russian, but mostly through French. Throughout this period there was hardly a difference between Westernization and modernization. The West being the only available model, the elite did not consider any other choice but to follow the path of European civilization, though traditional writing went on as strongly as ever. In the few years that followed the end of World War II many signs of change started to appear, especially on the pages of the newly established newspapers and magazines that were the mouthpiece of the new avant-garde who became later the champions of change.

From the early 1950s winds of change became gradually stronger with the new open-door cultural policy of the young state. Monopoly of the French language was broken, Anglo-American influences were welcome and soon followed by Soviet and East European influences. Literary translation flourished slowly but steadily, and with the rapid expansion of education more and more talents had chance to contribute to the literary scene. Gradually the traditional dominance of poetry started to give way to the challenge of narrative forms borrowed from the West, either directly or indirectly, through contact with the Egyptian and Lebanese pioneers who were ahead of Syrians in assimilating Western literary influences. The rise of the middle class hastened transformation. To borrow the words of H. Gibb, it was "not just a matter of a few influences, limited in greater or lesser degree, but of a complete social revolution." Literature was an active agent of this revolution and also a major beneficiary since the soil was now prepared for adventure and experiment.

The 1950s and 1960s witnessed the gradual growth of narrative genres, the short story first and then the novel, with dramatic writing slowly developing as was the case in the most adjacent Arab countries. Literary schools came to be known and modeled after the Western experience: romanticism coming very early, then symbolism as a school limited to few sophisticated poets, then realism and socialist realism strongly dominating as a result of political changes. Then in the late 1960s came the wave of modernism with varied individual situations and new forms; all this led the way to harmony with the Western or rather international atmosphere of open unlimited experimentalism.

However, all these changes have taken place within a framework of relative conservatism regarding both identity and language. Modernism and innovation in the West has in general taken place within a context of individualism and in many cases discomposure and alienation. Due to heated nationalism and social ideologies that have dominated the contemporary Arab history (and par excellence Syria), almost all existentialist and modernistic ideas have been transformed—sometimes drastically—to suit national and sociopolitical commitments widely spread among Arab (particulary Syrian intellectuals), to the extent that the content and the ideological message of the literary work have always taken the fore and pivoted its shaping. It was only in the late 1980s that part of the literary production started to reflect rather personalized and daring experimental ventures in expression and form. It will be for the 21st c. to decide whether this tendency is bound to form a real challenge to the whole bulk of literature in Syria, which has generally remained closer to the tenets of Neo-Classicism.

Poetry

The first wave of Syrian poetry after World War I was characterized with strict classicism emphasized by strong yearning to have the glory of both the nation and poetry revived exactly along the lines of the past, content, and form. Even poetic diction had its archetype in the pre-Islamic and Abbasid periods. The only new thing, perhaps, was the national content and the stress for independence and liberty through the poem of occasion. Major representatives of this school were: M. Al-Bizm (1887–1955), Khalīl Mardam (1895–1959), Khayr al-dīn al Zirklī (1893–1967) and Shafīq Jabrī (1898–1980). Jabrī gradually sought moderate innovation through his smooth language and delicate, though conventional imagery. Muhammad Sulaymān al-Ahmad (known as Badawi al-Jabal, 1904–1980) later came to be the peak of this current.

It was not easy for the next generation to take the necessary step forward. Thanks to 'umar Abū Rīsha (1910–1990) the gap was bridged through his poetic talent, modern education (American University of Beirut), contact with English Romantic poetry and later Indian poetry and over all, his mastery of poetic diction. Moreover he succeeded in giving direction to his short poems and subsequently providing a sort of organic unity. He also gave a relative frankness in the hitherto reserved love poetry. Furthermore, his neo-classicism was mixed with romantic elements that came to be clearer in the poetry of his fellow neo-classicist Anwar al-'attar (1908–1972). Neo-Classicism persisted, however, enjoying the atmosphere of change already initiated by the Syro-American current (Mahjar), which from the late 1930s gained popularity in Syria by introducing fresh experiences to Arabic poetry coupled with limited flexibility in form and prosody elicited by American influences and conditions of migration to the Americas.

Another important example of the combination of new-classicism and romanticism is the rather peculiar widespread current that started in the 1940s and went on strongly until the end of the century and can be termed as "Platform poetry." This is a national poetry usually recited on political occasions. It is probably best represented by Sulaymān al-'īssā (b. 1923). He has devoted his long poetry life to Arab national causes and particularly to Palestine and Arab unity. Characterized by verbal overtones and enthusiasm, this current appealed to the sympathies of the widest readership. He has later turned to children literature rarely cultivated in Syria before.

The 1950s began with a wave of realism that has changed the classical ideal commitment to a concrete probe of social and political conditions with an avowment to change them for the better, explicitly by socialist realists and implicitly by critical realists. Due to the spread of education and rise of middle and lower-middle classes the appeal to realistic writing was overwhelming. Young writers of all political parties were involved in the sociopolitical and ideological struggle. The success of their poetry was ephemeral and their output was more to quantity than to quality. Among them Shauqī Baghdādī (b. 1928) deserves mention due to his honesty, spontaneity, and continuous quest for making

up a balance between his subjective conscience and his objective country and everywhere else, with a tone of sensitivity and tenderness steadily increasing in his late poems *Shay'un yakhussu 'l-rūh* (1996; Something That Belongs to the Soul).

In the 1960s the appeal of realism was challenged by the perplexing temptation of modernism. The Shi'r Group in Beirut, led by the Syro-Lebanese poet ADUNĪS, called for a new poetry to be a rebellion against the forms and methods of the old poetry, a rejection of its attitudes and styles which have outlived its usefulness. He went on with his rebellion inexorably dreaming of revolutionizing Arab life through poetry. His prose is as important as his poetry. In his poetry, however, he succeeded in creating a new style of experimental writing that has never been known in Arabic before. He also introduced the prose poem, which has been the subject of great controversy since the early 1960s.

Adunīs has influenced, directly or indirectly, waves of young poets all over the Arab World. He is controversial and his followers have different interpretations of his views. Unfortunately, most of his imitators lacked his mastery of language, his broad cultural background, his deep familiarity with European poetry (Saint–John Perse in particular), his astonishing wild imagery, his involvement in Sufism and other occult philosophies, and at last his own unique talent of molding all these and similar cultural and literary qualifications through deep perception and piercing vision. His imitators have mostly resorted to obliquity in their quest to follow the prototype.

The scene in the 1970s onward is one of the intermingled ideas and experiences. Almost all tendencies mentioned above have survived but not without drastic changes as a result of both struggle and interaction with each other: The domination of the wave of modernism cannot be denied but its applications give the impression that the new generation of modernists tend to be eclectic and iconoclast. An age of experimentation is coming through with all the pros and cons of knowing just what you do not want and hoping that what lies ahead could be reached through trial and error and without any sort of vision. The result, after all, is mostly obliquity and introvertionism, leading of course to the confinement of public interest in poetry to the least standards. The Syrian scene at the turn of the century is producing many an earnest poet ranging from Realists to Sufists to legend fans, to modernists and more often to a mixture of all tendencies, with always a touch of SYMBOLISM. Zealous traditionalists are there also. Many earnest endeavors deserve mention here, but the most representative of the recent scene may be: Muhammad 'Umrān (1943–1996), Mamdouh 'Adwān (b. 1941), Fāyez Khaddour (b. 1942), Shākir Mutlaq (b. 1938), Mamdouh Skāf (b. 1938), Nazīh Abū 'afash (b. 1946), Khālid M. al-Barād'i (b. 1934), Abd al-Qādir al-Hisnī (b. 1953), among others.

The passing away of Nizār QABBĀNĪ has marked the end of the era of Syrian poetry in the 20th c. Qabbānī has been throughout the century the best seller and the most famous Arab poet. He started in the 1940s as a poet of frivolous and hedonic love thus arousing the wrath of conservatives, but soon developed his subjects and tools to be the poet of the avant-garde. After the 1967 Arab defeat he changed the whole tune and confronted both rulers and ruled with harsh criticism. Discarding Syria to Lebanon, then to Europe and lastly to London, he has been prepared to develop his language always towards vividness and spontaneity, borrowing from the Damascene dialect and folkloric expressions the most poignant vocabulary. In his late poems written in London he fascinated his audience through having both picture and language of the Arab East, probably suggesting that East is still East and West is still

West albeit they are mixing together in the contemporary pot of technology and information in such a way that has never been dreamt of before.

Finally, it is obvious that not a single female name has been mentioned in spite of the real advancement in the field of woman emancipation in Syria. Apart from the late Hind Haroun (1928–1996), known as the poetess of motherhood, it is difficult to mention any other woman in her own right. A few female names will be mentioned, however, in the following section on prose fiction.

The Novel and Short Story

The novel and the short story had no such glorious past as poetry. Instead of revival they had to be born, and with them the drama. Early translations were the midwives. Clash with the West and Social change that followed hospitalized the birth. At the beginning of the 20th c. writers began to imitate the widely spread translations or to borrow directly from Europe. In 1913 *Zainab* appeared in Egypt to be the first Arabic novel. Syria had to wait until 1937 to welcome the birth of *Naham* (Gluttony) by Shakīb al-Jābirī (1912–1996) who was educated in Germany. Before *Naham*, there were few historical and love novels with only historic value. In 1939 Jābirī published his second novel, *Qadarn yalhū (Fate at Play)*, to be followed by a sequel, *Qaws quzah* (1946; Rainbow), both relating a romantic love between a young Arab and a German girl and professing the necessity of East and West to meet and build up a new civilization. But the end was tragic.

During the same period the short story also had its beginnings. In 1931 'Alī Khuluqī (1911–1984) published the first collection of stories: *Rabī' wa kharīf* (Spring and Autumn). In 1937 the second collection *Fī Qusūr Dimashq* (In Damascus Palaces) came out. Both had a common theme of naive social criticism.

More solid short stories were also published mainly by Fu'ād al-Shāyib (French educated) treating the confrontation between East and West and other intellectual questions, later collected under the title *Tārīkh Jurh* (1944; History of Wound). In 1948 'Abd al-Salām al-'Ujaylī (b. 1925) published *Bint al-Sāhira* (The Daughter of the Sorceress). Both collections were promising.

Owing to social change, heated political struggle, and new Russian and socialist influences, a sudden flourishment of short-story writing took place with an average publication of four collections yearly, and improvement in both form and content. Al-'Ujaylī published *Qanādīl Ishbīliah* (1956; Lanterns of Seville) to be followed almost every two years by a new collection, thus asserting his mastery and devotion up to the end of the century. Most of these works have centered around change of social beliefs and behavior through the game of rivalry between science and superstition, village and town, educated and illiterate. A born story-teller, he never fails to enchant his reader and weave his plot after the Guy de Maupassant model dexterously and always with a touch of sense of humor.

Zakariyyā TĀMIR, who later became one of the very few writers totally devoted to the short story, soon established himself as the main rival to al-'Ujaylī. Coming up from the lower-middle class, and with very little schooling, with no knowledge of a foreign language he, alas, proved to be the one destined to change the whole course of short story in Syria from concentration on external sociopolitical conditions to the inner suffering of human soul and the tragedy of existence. He has also changed the medium of narration from concrete stiff language to dreamy and floppy diction. The influence of SURREALISM, EXISTENTIALISM, and literature of alienation is evident in his works. His first collection, *Sahīl al-jawā al-abyad* (1960; Neigh of the White Horse), and other stories reveal a deep familiarity with modern psychology. In his masterpiece *'Wajh al-qamar* (1973; The Face of the Moon) he efficiently applies Freudian psychoanalysis to help the protagonist, a divorced young woman, restore her oppressed feminism through external influences that bring back the reminiscences of a rape incident in her childhood. Tāmir left Syria for Beirut and then Europe (London) where he published his collection *Nidā' Nūh* (1994; The Appeal of Noah).

In the 1950s the novel lagged behind with a poor average of one title yearly, overloaded mostly with political and ideological preaching or with sentimentalism and highly refined language. Due to natural literary growth, a relative flourishment in the production of novels was evident. Influences from Anglo-American literature entered rivalry with previous existentialist and socialist influences, laying the basis for future stages of openness to different international experiences. At the same time most writers did not neglect the short story. They charged both genres with social or intellectual messages. The construction of prose fiction in general heavily centered around events with constant claim that they were true stories. Sometimes the ideological preaching was the center, as in Mutā' Safadī (b. 1929) who tried to work out a nationalist Arab theory through rather strange intermarriage between national zeal and existentialist commitment, quite outspoken in his collection *Ashbāh abtāl* (1959; Ghosts of Heroes) and his two novels *Jīl al qadar* (1960; The Generation of Destiny) and *Thā'ir muhtarif* (1961; A Professional Rebel).

At the beginning of this stage al-Jābirī published his fourth and final romantic novel, *Wadā'an y Afāmyā* (1960; Farewell to Afamya), continuing his theses on the necessary embrace between East and West with clear maturity both in intellectual treatment and in success of employing modern techniques of narration such as flashbacks, foreflashes, scenic juxtaposition, montage, and others.

Hannā MĪNA, who later proved to be Syria's foremost novelist, published his second novel *Al-shirā' wa 'l-'āsifa* (1966; The Sail and the Tempest) after his first novel of the 1950s, *Al-masābīh al-zurg* (1954; Blue Lamps), introducing in both novels a successful simple approach to socialist realism ideas that became familiar and mechanically applied by many of his fellow realists. He laid down also the basis of his major theme to be consistent in most of his future novels; the portrayal of the suffering of the downtrodden and poor as individuals, families and class, with very special attention to life and struggle in the seaports (literature of the seas-adab al bahr). Mīna excelled in both content and form based on honesty, sincerity and spontaneity, all expressed without ostentation or trick but through a very simple, easy style colored by local terms and expressions especially from the peasantry and seamen vernacular. Mīna continued to write from time to time the short story, the article, and the autobiographical narrative, but always remained loyal to the novel proper. He is a best seller and widely read all over the Arab world. Most of his works are translated into European and other languages.

Another suprising voice was the young student of English, Hānī al-Rāhib (b. 1939), whose first novel, *Al-mahzūmūn* (1961; The Defeated), gave a report on the life and views of university students. It was followed by *Sharkh fī tarīkh tawīl* (1970; Crack in a Long History). In his third novel, *Alf layla wa laylatān* (1977; One Thousand and Two Nights), he treated another political issue (unity between Syria and Egypt) and took an important step to modernize novel writing through relatively discarding the event and relying on cycles reminiscent of the Arabian nights free narration. Later, he followed the same line of open narration but with inclination to write lengthy novels, which complicated his control over this approach, as is clear in his next novel, *alwabā'* (1982; The Plague), and later novels. He is also well known for his daring short stories.

The voices of female writers added importance to the 1960s. Colette Suhail Kurī published her controversial short novel *Ayyām ma'ahu* (1959; Days with Him) to be followed by *Layla wāhida* (1961; One Night) and other novels treating the theme of love and adding a new female flavor to the literary scene.

Ghāda al-Sammān (b. 1942) figures as an important writer of fiction and essay. Another graduate of English, emancipated and outspoken, she has had great influence in Syria and the Arab world. She left Syria in an early state after she made her reputation through her daring short stories. Her first collection, *Aynāka qadarī* (1962; Your Eyes Are My Fate), aroused varied discussions and revealed her existentialist modernistic bent with very rich psychological and philosophical dictionary. Later, she added the theme of Lebanon's civil war, especially in her two novels *Beirut 75* (1975) and *Kawābīs Beirūt* (1976; Beirut Nightmares). In her later novels and essays, she has returned to themes of love, existence, and high-class life.

Both the short story and the novel are advancing steadily. Writers leap from one genre to another, with rare exceptions (Tāmir's utter devotion to the short story). Furthermore, many writers try their hands at writing plays, such as W. Ikhlāsī who always shifts between the three genres. Every individual writer spreads his or her theme and technique priorities to the two or three genres. The borders between currents and tendencies are no more clear-cut.

Individualism is gradually growing together with more interest in the inner world of man. It is a movement from the outside reality to the inside without forgetting that the conditions around have the upperhand in deciding the behavior of the individual and the masses. The line of departure from the early stages is very delicate. As if before it was thought that through ideology and open struggle change could be achieved, hence the overwhelming wave of realism in its different forms. After all those frustrations, national, societal and individual, writers came to believe that the only chance left was to manipulate the dimensions of reality and build up the substitute: a dreamy world, not quite cut off from the realities on earth and at the same time kept open for the desired change. Thus, a great part of contemporary Syrian prose fiction belongs to magic realism with clear bents toward symbol and myth.

The diction of all groups is now simple Arabic, smooth and enriched by special words and expressions from the vernacular and folklore. Furthermore, the autobiographical is now diluted and employed as an organic part of narration. The stiff traditional ego is less noticed, and the first pronoun has mostly a collective sense. Naturally this reading applies more to the younger generation of writers. As for the elder generation, they have kept their previous predilections but variedly modified in content and form to suit the new spirit of writing.

In the short story, major representatives of the generations of the 1970s onward may be: Walīd Mi'marī (b. 1941), Mohammed Kāmil al-Khateeb (b. 1949), Zuhair Jabbour (b. 1942), Nayrouze Mālik (b. 1943). From the younger generation it is still difficult to single out names, but it is necessary to mention that they are very earnest in the cultivation of the short story, and this meager genre is still overloaded with serious problems of existence and human condition as it was with their predecessors. One example is "Zahrat

al-Sukhū al-Barriyya; The Flower of Wild Rocks," a short story by Mi'marī, published in 1980. Using the first person plural, the narrator tells his fellow villagers how a group of young men went to hunt but found nothing but a strange blue wild flower. Was it a good omen or an uncanny sign? The story is an open text with no suggestions. All characteristics mentioned above apply to it, besides economy in expression and the consistent presence of human tenderness.

Some other elder writers show little change in their approach and style, such as the two realist pioneers: Ulfat al-Idilbī (b. 1913) and Fāris Zarzūr (b. 1930) and the romantic stylist master Badī' Haqqī (b. 1922).

Novel writing is, naturally, still in the hands of the elder generation with few exceptions. Representative of the 1970s onward may be, in addition to major pioneers mentioned before: Khayrī al-Dhahabī (b. 1946). Devoted to establishing a special flavor for the Arabic novel, he started early with *Malakūt al-Busatā* (1976; The World of the Simple People). Other novels followed suit. His most recent production is a trilogy (very familiar practice nowadays). The major title is *Tahawwulāt* (Metamorphoses). Part I is entitled *Hasība* (1987; Mother), Part II *Fayyād* (Father), and Part III *Hishām* (1998; Son). It is an epic of a family's struggle with the time and place. Old life in Damascus is the setting. Narration is quasi-historical, loaded with symbols and not without a touch of myth and magic.

Other representatives of the modified realism of earlier stages are 'Abd al-Nabī Hijazī (b. 1938), Ahmad Yusuf Dawoud (b. 1945), Nabīl Sulaymān (b. 1945). Finally, it is important to note that direct realism persists. Its representatives also prefer the lengthy novel or the trilogy. In the mid 1990s it is represented by Abd al-Karīm Nasīf (b. 1939). Nādia Khost (b. 1935), a pioneer of women's writing, started with essays, then short stories, and turned to novels quite lately. Her *Hubb fī bilād al-Shām* (1995; Love in the Sham Land) is a lengthy novel tracing the history of life in the 20th c.

Drama

The position of drama in the Arab world, including Syria, is far less encouraging than that of the narrative genres. In spite of successive efforts made by governments and individuals to change the situation, the results until the late 1990s are not sufficiently encouraging. A multiplicity of factors, historical, social, cultural, and political are usually given to explain the situation.

In Syria, Mārūn al-Naqqāsh (1817–1898) presented his plays, partly adapted from French, as early as mid 19th c., to be followed later by Abū Khalīl al-Qabbānī (1833–1903) who tried to establish a local theater based on music and singing as substitute for European adaptations. But he had to leave Syria for Egypt where his theater flourished and was considered the basis for the original desired pattern.

The social reasons for al-Qabbāni's expulsion from Syria remained active years after his departure. In the 1960s government attention was given to development of the theater supported by the intellectual public opinion. Government plans went on vigorously. The national theater was founded by the Ministry of Culture, and play writing was encouraged. Gradually writers and poets tried their hands at writing dramas with clear inclination to poetic drama or to flowery language in prose. Later, they came to adopt simple language. Poets and writers wrote plays from time to time. The more enthusiastic were Mamdūh 'Adwān and Walīd Ikhlāsī. Some dramatists had some chance to have their works performed, though partially. Among them are Riyād 'Ismat (b.1947), 'Ali 'Uqla 'Ursān (b.1940), and Farhān Bulbul (b.1937).

The tragic death of Sa'dallāh WANNŪS has been a great loss for the cause of drama and literature in general. He was a born dramatist and a committed intellectual who devoted himself to theater. Critics divide his works into two phases, the first what Wannūs had termed as the "theater of politicization," the second his works of the 1990s. *Haflat samar min ajl khamsa huzaīrān* (1968; An Evening's Entertainment for June the Fifth) came as direct response to the 1967 defeat. Owing to the scenic structure, the reproduction of one of the war fronts, the questions leaping from every movement, and the depth and audacity of discourse, its performance enticed and captured a consciousness of the tragedy.

Then came—after two plays in 1969—*Mughāmarat ra's almamlūk Jābir* (1970; The Adventure of the Head of Slave Jābir) as an artifice abounding in symbols and moving within a multiplicity of times and references. The tragedy was there in the initiative of Jābir who through his action has lost the power of action because his head became a written tool in the hands of the plotting *vazier*.

In *Al-malik huwa al-malik* (1977; The King Is the King) he drew on a famous folkloric tale, and rebuilt the original characters to carry out his treatment of the question of power. In this play and in *sahra ma' Abū Khalīl Al-Qabbānī* (1973; A Soiré with Abū Khalīl Al-Qabbānī), he plays the game of a theater inside a theater, thus taking advantage of two levels of signification and creating double effect. With *Tuqūs al-ishārāt wa 'l-tahawwulāt* (1994; The Rituals of Signs and Metamorphoses) and *Ahlām sharqiyya* (1995; Unhappy Dreams) we come to the second phase where he exposes the psyche, dramatizes its caprices and goes down deep into the core of inner struggle. Female characters are brought to the fore and their hidden secrets revealed to say what is usually not said. The end is being approached.

BIBLIOGRAPHY: Landau, J., *Studies in the Arab Theater and Cinema* (1958); Gibb, H., *Studies in the Civilization of Islam* (1962); Khateeb, H. A., *Prosefiction in Syria with Special Reference to Foreign Influences* (1969); Said, E., *Beginnings: Intention and Method* (1975); Boullata, I., J., *Modern Arab Poets (1850–1975)* (1976); Khadra Jayyusi, S., *Trends and Movements in Modern Arabic Poetry I, II* (1977); Khateeb, H. A., "The European Relations of Modern Arabic Literature," VIIIth ICLA Congress, Stuttgart (1980): 31–46; Allen, R., *The Arabic Novel: An Historical and Critical Introduction* (1982); Khateeb, H. A., "Political Factors Influencing the Rise of the Short Story in the Syrian Fifties," *Neohelikon*, 14, 2 (1987): 287–297

—HUSSAM AL KHATEEB

SZABÓ, Lörinc

Hungarian poet, journalist, and translator, b. 31 March 1900, Miskolc; d. 3 Oct. 1957, Budapest

Son of a locomotive engineer, S. started writing poetry while still attending school and began contributing to the literary journal *Nyugat* in 1919. He studied engineering and philosophy but did not take a degree; he eked out a living as a journalist, editor, and translator. S. received the Baumgarten Prize for poetry in 1932, 1937, and 1944. After years of official neglect by the Communists, he was awarded the Kossuth Prize in the last year of his life.

The two years S. spent as a member of Mihály BABITS's household left its mark on his first volume, *Föld, erdő, isten* (1922; earth, forest, god), which is characterized by idyllic portrayals of nature and an austere mastery of form. In *Kalibán* (1923; Caliban) the Satanism of Baudelaire and a defiant Decadence echoing Endre ADY replace the balanced discipline of the earlier volume. Man and his world are increasingly at opposite poles of a dualistic universe. Exceptions to the prevailing tone are the love lyrics and two great religious works, the poem "Az eretnek tragédiája" (the heretic's tragedy) and the cycle "Testvérsiratók" (brother mourners).

Fény, fény, fény (1925; light, light, light) continues to explore the relationships of man and technology, but from a more positive viewpoint: instead of opposing the New Age of Iron, the poet now accepts it. This volume evinces S.'s interest in the German EXPRESSIONISTS, whom he was translating at the time. In *A Sátán műremekei* (1926; Satan's masterpieces) there is an explosion of form: S. now uses a proselike, monotonous free verse almost indistinguishable from everyday speech. The whole volume resembles a *Bildungsroman*, with the poet's persona assuming the role of the hero of a novel in search of his own identity. The love poetry is sensuous and passionate.

Te meg a világ (1932; you and the world) continues the process begun six years earlier. The poet now claims that fulfillment may be found in nothing but the self, but his deepseated puritanism breaks through the veneer of hedonism. With *Különbéke* (1936; a separate peace) a new humanism emerges. The poet can look at the poor with compassion and his own near-poverty with gentle irony. The naturalism of the earlier period yields to Oriental philosophy. The "separate peace" of the volume's title reflects this change. Life is just as bad as he had always thought it, probably worse, but now he can accept it.

The short volume *Reggeltől estig* (1937; from morning to night) is the poetic record of a day's journey from Hungary to Switzerland and back in 1936, in the early days of commercial aviation; it was later included in *Harc az ünnepért* (1938; struggle for a day of celebration), a collection that later became controversial because it contained S.'s 1928 poem "Vezér" (leader). Although written five years before Hitler's rise to power, the poem was thought by some to glorify the Nazi leader and was the chief cause of S.'s subsequent blacklisting and harassment under the postwar Communist regime. For the collection *Régen és most* (1943; then and now), first published as a section of *Összes versek* (1943; complete poems), S. revised his pre-1926 poems to provide an "authorized version."

A huszonhatodik év: Lirai requiem százhúsz szonettben (1957; the twenty-sixth year: lyric requiem in 120 sonnets) is the record of the poet's grief when his mistress of twenty-five years committed suicide. Regret, nostalgia, self-accusation, tenderness, passion, and eventual acceptance of the inevitable are gathered here in a great lyric diary.

No discussion of S. should overlook his distinguished career as a translator. His translations of Shakespeare, Burns, Wordsworth, Coleridge, Blake, Villon, Baudelaire, Verlaine, Goethe, Stefan GEORGE, Omar Khayyam, Pushkin, and many others have become parts of the Hungarian poetic canon and validate the title of his gigantic two-volume anthology of translations: *Örök barátaink* (1941–48; our friends forever).

FURTHER WORKS: *Tücsökzene* (1947); *Válogatott versei* (1956); *Összegyűjtött versei* (1960); *Válogatott műfordításai* (1960); *Kicsi vagyok én. . .* (1961); *Válogatott versei* (1963)

BIBLIOGRAPHY: Klaniczay, T., et al., *History of Hungarian Literature* (1964): 236–37; Reményi, J., *Hungarian Writers and Literature* (1964): 378–82

—DALMA H. BRUNAUER

SZICHMAN, Mario

Argentine novelist and essayist, b. 2 Jan. 1945, Buenos Aires

S., born into an Argentine Jewish family, now lives in New York, where he is an editor in the Latin American department of Associated Press. In addition to his work in fiction, he has been a correspondent and editor for several newspapers and journals in Latin America, the U.S., and Israel. S. lived in Venezuela from 1967 to 1971, where he worked as a news editor, then returned to Buenos Aires. He left Argentina in 1975, living again in Venezuela until 1980, where he was an editor and a professor of Hispanic American literature at the Universidad Andrés Bello in Caracas. While in Venezuela, he published two socially conscious studies on Venezuelan writers Arturo USLAR PIETRI and Miguel Otero Silva (1908–1985): *Uslar: cultura y dependencia* (1975; Uslar: culture and dependence) and *Miguel Otero Silva: mitología de una generación frustrada* (1975; Miguel Otero Silva: mythology of a frustrated generation). In 1980 he directed the cultural supplement of the newspaper *Últimas Noticias* in Caracas; the supplement won the National Prize for journalism that year. He left Caracas in 1980 for the U.S., where he has worked as a journalist, including, from 1981 to 1987, as editor in the Latin American department of United Press International in New York and then in Washington. Besides his journalistic work, he has published numerous stories, especially in the journal *Hispamérica*.

S. continues the prolific 20th-c. tradition of Argentine Jewish writing but, as commentators such as Naomi Lindstrom have noted, with a more radical and cynical stance than many of his predecessors such as Alberto Gerchunoff (1884–1950). His first effort as a novelist, *Crónica falsa* (1969; false chronicle), is now seen by him as an apprentice work; he revised it as *La verdadera crónica falsa* (the true false chronicle) in 1972. The revision represents the first in a series of novels that employ cinematic devices (such as traveling shots), techniques from vaudeville, Yiddish humor, and other radical narrative techniques to detail the efforts of the Pechof family, Polish-born Jewish immigrants to Argentina, to maintain their identity within a nationalistic Argentine culture. At the same time, the nature of their Jewish cultural identity is questioned, examined, falsified, or shown to be historically elusive though perhaps "true" in the memory of the protagonists (thus the "true false chronicle").

A striking aspect of the work of S. is his rather bizarre, Marx-Brothers-like humor in presenting the saga of the Pechofs through several generations of Argentine life in the 20th c. The Pechof "saga" is presented in three novels: *La verdadera crónica falsa; Los judíos del Mar Dulce* (1971; the Jews of the freshwater sea); and *A las 20:25, la señora entró en la inmortalidad* (1981; *At 8:25 Evita Became Immortal*, 1983). A fourth novel in the series, *La tercera fundación de Buenos Aires* (the third founding of Buenos

Aires), will soon be published. The novels are set against the backdrop of Argentine cultural and political history and especially of the rise and decline of Peronism and its cultural mythology, which is severely questioned. The use of Yiddish phrases, epithets, and scatological humor realizes the ethnic ambience of the characters and lends them individuality; one protagonist, for instance, normally reveals his foreignness by substituting "g" for "r" in his speech. But S. eschews any cheap sentimentalization or endearment of his characters; while memorable and attractive as human creations, they are subject to sharp criticism and revelation of their faults.

S. is now at work on a new novel, *Botín de guerra* (war booty), concerning one of the characters from *A las 20:25*. His work is an important part of the ongoing critical reevaluation by Argentine Jews concerning their history and their place within Argentine culture. As the criticism on S. has pointed out, his novels also contribute in a substantial way to the evaluation of the Peronist period, critiquing the effects of the cult of Juan Perón and his wife Eva on the politics and social relationships of Argentines.

BIBLIOGRAPHY: Sarlo, B., "Judíos y argentinos: el linaje de la literatura," *Quimera*: 21–22 (July-August 1982): 70–73; Lindstrom, N., "Problems and Possibilities in the Analysis of Jewish Argentine Literary Works," *Latin American Research Review*, 18, 1 (1983): 118–26; Senkman, L., *La identidad judía en la literatura argentina* (1983): 269–83; Sosnowski, S., "Latin American Jewish Writers: A Bridge toward History," *Prooftexts*, 4, 1 (1984): 71–92; Lipp, S., "Jewish Themes and Authors in Contemporary Argentine Fiction," in R. S. Minc, ed., *El Cono Sur* (1985): 49–55; Morello-Frosch, M., "Textos inscriptos al margen de la literatura argentina: *A las 20:25, la señora entró en la inmortalidad*, de M. S.," in R. S. Minc, ed., *El Cono Sur* (1985): 137–45; Senkman, L., "De la legitimación del israelita argentino a la asunción de la identidad de algunos escritores judeoargentinos," in R. S. Minc, ed., *El Cono Sur* (1985): 56–71; special issue on Jewish writers, *Folio*, 17 (1987): 24–56; Gardiol, R. M., "Jewish Writers: An Emerging Force in Contemporary Argentine Literature," *Hispano*, 31, 1 (1987): 65–76; Lindstrom, N., *Jewish Issues in Argentine Literature: From Gerchunoff to S.* (1989): 146–57, 181

—KENNETH E. HALL

SZYMBORSKA, Wisława

Polish poet, b. 2 July 1923, Prowent-Bnin

Born near Poznań, S. moved with her family to Cracow at the age of eight and has lived there since. She studied sociology and Polish philology at Jagellonian University and made her debut as a poet in 1945. In 1952 she joined the editorial staff of the literary weekly *Życie literackie*, where she published many book reviews between 1967 and 1972. Although not a prolific poet—she has produced some 180 poems altogether, only 145 of which she acknowledges as her mature work—S. has published poems regularly and is also a distinguished translator of French poetry. In 1996 S. was awarded the Nobel Prize for literature.

S. was caught up in the SOCIALIST REALISM controversy shortly after her debut. *Dlatego żyjemy* (1952; that is what we live for) and *Pytania zadawane sobie* (1954; questions put to myself) are the most Socialist Realist of her works, although this style came to her

Wisława Szymborska

shared by Polish writers during the latter half of the 1970s. But S. is not merely a political writer, and her later poems join with earlier works to weave a subtle and erudite fabric of "sounds, feelings, thoughts" (the title of a volume of her poems in English translation).

FURTHER WORKS: *Sól* (1962); *Wiersze wybrane* (1964); *Poezje wybrane* (1967); *Poezje* (1970; 2nd ed., 1977); *Wszelki wypadek* (1972); *Lektury nadobowiązkowe* (1973); *Wielka liczba* (1976). FURTHER WORKS IN ENGLISH: *Sounds, Feelings, Thoughts: Seventy Poems by W. S.* (1981)

BIBLIOGRAPHY: Krynski, M. J., and R. Maguire, Introduction to *Sounds, Feelings, Thoughts: Seventy Poems by W. S.* (1981): 3–18; Levine, M. G., *Contemporary Polish Poetry 1925–1975* (1981): 92–104

—ALICE-CATHERINE CARLS

SZYSZKOWITZ, Gerald

Austrian novelist and dramatist, b. 22 July 1938, Graz

Born in Graz, S. began his literary career while still a student in his hometown. After receiving a Ph.D. in theater history and German from the University of Vienna in 1960, he traveled extensively to such exotic places as Martinique, Tokyo, Rangoon, and Calcutta. Subsequently he held positions at a number of theaters in West Germany—Bonn, Dortmund, Wilhelmshaven—initially as a director's assistant, later as a director. In 1968 he returned to Graz to become senior producer and director at the local state theater. Four years later, he joined the drama department of the Austrian Television Company. Having been responsible for numerous highly regarded, internationally acclaimed productions, S. is still better known as a television producer than as an author in his own right.

S. has taken a rather independent literary course, ignoring trends, distancing himself from experiments and extremes, avoiding firm programs and rigid theories but following, instead, a tradition of 19th- and early 20th-c. novelists such as Theodor Fontane (1819–1898) and Joseph ROTH, two of his favorite writers. S. is, above all, a storyteller, a literary chronicler of Austria's recent past. In all of his novels he has skillfully combined historically accurate events with fictitious portrayals of convincingly pictured individuals.

S.'s first novel, *Der Thaya* (1981; Mr. Thaya), and the fifth one, *Puntigam oder Die Kunst des Vergessens* (1988; *Puntigam or The Art of Forgetting*, 1990), are his masterpieces. *Der Thaya* is the first part of a trilogy in which the author describes the life and the gradual decline of a manorial family from northern Austria. The trilogy captivates its readers not only through a well-defined, action-filled plot—family idylls are skillfully interwoven with odysseys of refugees and melodramatic love affairs—but also through its atmosphere. The basic tone is melancholy, overlaid with humor and subtle irony. While *Der Thaya* portrays the family patriarch, its sequel, *Seitenwechsel* (1982; changing sides), describes the attempts of his daughter-in-law to break out of the confinements of her marriage. The final volume, *Osterschnee* (1983; Easter snow), focuses on the younger Thaya's increasing

with some difficulty. S. freed herself from the officially encouraged political overtones in *Wołanie do Yeti* (1957; calling out to Yeti), but it was only with *Sto pociech* (1967; a hundred consolations) that her mature period began. This versatile, "nonspecialized" poet, as S. has called herself, has been able to examine the human condition. Philosophical concerns, however, are presented in a seemingly casual manner through the vehicle of images related to everyday life.

S.'s poetry is immediately accessible, but misleadingly easy. Hers is a refreshingly female, but not feminist, verse that lets the reader see the world through the eyes of a woman poet. While one of her major themes is pessimism about the future of mankind, a pessimism based on historical evidence, and while some of her best tools are acute irony and a tone of detachment, her poems convey the buoyancy of life and the joy of creativity. Her main distinction may well lie in the way she demonstrates the delicate balance between love of life and a rational skepticism, while making the reader keenly aware of the power of words, fragile but ultimately victorious.

One of the reasons why S.'s poems are so few in number is her insistence on carefully crafting each one, as well as her awareness of the limitations of language. In her case, this dilemma has political implications, for she belongs to a generation in Poland that was confronted at the outset by the political consequences of writing. At first a Socialist Realist S. matured two decades later into an opponent of Communism. Her more recent works focus again on political issues, now seen with a cynicism and desperation alienation. Following the breakup of his marriage and disillusioned by the lethargy and the corruption in his country, he commits suicide. In *Osterschnee* S. shows the dilemma of what he calls the "sandwich generation," those men standing between their powerful fathers, who rebuilt Austria after World War II, and the younger, more dynamic generation. In *Furlani oder Die Zährtlichkeit des Verrats* (1985; Furlani or the tenderness of betrayal) S., remaining faithful to his montage technique, combines political events of the 1980s with a spy thriller and a romance.

A best-seller in Austria, *Puntigam oder Die Kunst des Vergessens* exposes what many consider the Austrians' collective amnesia about their Nazi past. Moving between the present and the war years and including many allusions to the controversy surrounding Austrian President Kurt Waldheim, the novel portrays events following Hitler's annexation of Austria in 1938 from three points of view: old Puntigam, who operates a mill in Graz and welcomes the economic upsurge; his daughter, Marianne, who struggles to keep her Austrian identity; and her opportunistic, mindless cousin, Friedemann, the ultimate "artist of forgetfulness." Rightly, *Puntigam* has been called a "courageous and much-needed book." A stage play version of the novel was released in 1991.

It is against the background of international politics that S. presents two compelling love stories in two novels written in the early 1990s. *Auf der anderen Seite* (1990; *On the Other Side*, 1991) deals with the opening of the Austro-Czechoslovakian border. *Moritz und Nathalie oder Die Angst vor der Sehnsucht* (1991; Moritz and Nathalie or fear of longing) is set during the war in Yugoslavia that followed Slovenia's declaration of independence in the summer of 1991.

All the fiction S. has written since then shows characteristics of previous novels. *Der Liebe lange Weile* (1992; love's leisure) and *Lieben wie gedruckt oder Die Herren der Herrengasse* (1993; Loving and lying or the gentlemen from Herrengasse) revolve around love and politics in Austria. *Die Badenweiler oder Nichts wird bleiben von Österreich* (1995; Die Badenweiler or nothing will remain of Austria) is a love story covering three generations and set in Austria between 1905 and 1995 with a brief appearance by Adolf Hitler. *Anna oder Der Flügelschlag der Freiheit* (1996; Anna or the wings of freedom) has been interpreted as a roman à clef presenting thinly veiled portraits of prominent families in S.'s home town of Graz. In the 1990s S. published two volumes of short prose, *Der Vulkan* (1994; the volcano) and *Lesereisen* (1998; reading tours).

The majority of S.'s plays, with their very Austrian tone, are a sequence of variations on one theme: Interpersonal relationships are generally unhappy. *Grillparzer oder Die drei Schwestern* (1991; Grillparzer or the three sisters) is about unrequited love; *Am Irrsee* (1991; on Lake Irrsee) shows the disappointments and the despair of five women, while *Der Liebe lange Weile* (1989; love's leisure) centers on the erotic adventures of students amidst political turmoil.

S. is a genuinely gifted author, whose books provide enjoyable reading and reflect his basic philosophy: A good novel must present an essential theme as "entertainingly as possible."

FURTHER WORKS: *Theater-Stücke* (1991)

BIBLIOGRAPHY: *G. S.: Beiträge und Materialien* (1988); Binder, C. H., "Anmerkungen zum Roman *Puntigam oder Die Kunst des Vergessens* von G. S.," *MAL*, 23, 3–4 (1990): 155–66; Koppensteiner, J., "Gespräch mit G. S.," *Deutsche Bücher*, 2 (1990): 85–97; Koppensteiner, J., Afterword to *Puntigam or The Art of Forgetting* (1990): 261–66; Koppensteiner, J., Afterword to *On the Other Side* (1991): 135–39; Zeyringer, K., ed., *G. S. oder Die Kunst des Erinnerns* (1993)

—JÜRGEN KOPPENSTEINER

T

TABASARAN LITERATURE

See North Caucasian Literatures

TABIDZE, Galaktion

Georgian poet, b. 18 Nov. 1892, Chkviisi; d. 17 March 1959, Tbilisi

T.'s family was connected with the Georgian Orthodox Church; his father was a priest and teacher. In 1908 T. entered the Tbilisi Religious Seminary, at that time a center of revolutionary ferment. That same year his poetry began to appear in the journal *Chveni kvali* and the newspaper *Amirani*. His first book of poems, *Leksebi* (1914; poems), received wide acclaim. Its tone is introspective and pessimistic; the poems demonstrate an unusual fluency in form and expression, thus immediately establishing T. as the foremost Georgian poet of his generation.

In 1915 T. traveled to Moscow, where he met a number of prominent Russian SYMBOLIST poets. When he returned to Georgia the following year, he began to contribute to the journal of the symbolist Blue Horn movement. During the period of Georgian independence (1918–21) T. tried out new forms and devised an aesthetic philosophy heavily influenced by French and Russian symbolism. He set down his ideas in a book written in Georgian, but with a French title, *Crâne aux fleurs artistiques* (1919; skull with the flowers of art). His collection of poems published in the same year, *Artistuli leksebi* (artistic poems), is the creative embodiment of his theoretical work.

The Soviet invasion of Georgia in 1921 put an end to T.'s involvement with symbolist forms. Not wishing to go into exile, the poet came to terms with the new regime, and in recognition of his leading position in Georgian letters, he was given editorial charge of several journals, one of which was called *Galaktion Tabidze*. In 1924 he cofounded *Mnatobi*, which has remained the major literary journal in Georgia ever since.

Despite the limitations on his art imposed by the Soviet regime, T. wrote prolifically. During the late 1920s and early 1930s several long cycles of poems appeared, such as "Epokha" (1930; the epoch), "Patsipizmi" (1930; pacifism), "Presa" (1930; the press), and "Revoltsionuri Sakartvelo" (1931–32; revolutionary Georgia).

During World War II, T. wrote a great many obligatory antifascist and patriotic poems. In the late 1940s several lyric poems on historical themes permitted T. to avoid politics as such, although even these are marked by typical communist themes of "anticolonialism" and "people's struggle." His death under mysterious circumstances (he fell from a window) was officially declared to have been an accident, but he was known to have been deeply depressed, and his close friends were convinced that he had committed suicide.

T.'s genius was such that his sense of pure poetics may be said to have transcended the burden of official literary policy under which he was forced to labor most of his life. In his poems the subject matter is frequently secondary to the beauty of the language and rhythm. T.'s influence on three generations of Georgian poets was enormous, and his stylistic innovations will undoubtedly continue to affect the work of writers in Georgian.

FURTHER WORKS: *Tkhzulebani* (12 vols., 1966–1973).

—LEONARD FOX

TABUCCHI, Antonio

Italian novelist and short-story writer, b. 24 Sept. 1943, Pisa

T. is one of the most critically acclaimed and popularly successful writers of his generation. After graduating from the University of Pisa, he conducted research at the prestigious Scuola Normale in that city, taught at the University of Genoa, and became a professor of Portuguese Language and Literature at the University of Siena. As a scholar and translator, he is best known for his work on the poet Fernando PESSOA, whose poems, entitled *Una sola moltitudine* (2 vols., 1979–84; A Single Multitude), he edited in Italian. In addition to being the subject of numerous critical studies, some collected in *Un baule pieno di gente* (1990; A Trunk Full of People), and of a short work of fiction, *Gli ultimi tre giorni di Fernando Pessoa. Un delirio* (1994; The Last Three Days of Fernando Pessoa. A Delirium), Pessoa is a constant presence in all of T.'s fiction. The elusiveness and the fragmentation of identity that mark the writings of the Portuguese poet are also recurrent elements of T.'s own oeuvre and, in particular, characterize his highly self-conscious narrators. A voracious reader, in his writings T. openly acknowledges the influence of his poetic fathers, who include Luigi PIRANDELLO, Jorge Luis BORGES, Robert Louis Stevenson, Herman Melville, Joseph CONRAD, and Henry JAMES, while at the same time maintaining a voice which is unique in the landscape of contemporary Italian literature. Particularly important is the inspiration derived from the figurative arts; specific works, from Diego Rodriguez de Silva y Velázquez's *Las Meninas* to the frescos of Fra Angelico, have often provided a hermeneutical key to his stories.

T. made his debut as a narrator in 1975 with *Piazza d'Italia* (Square of Italy), a novel which, as the author put it, sought to chart "a short history of the last hundred years of Italy, in tragicomic style" by following three generations of a Tuscan family from Unification to the reconstruction following World War II. Like his second novel, *Il piccolo naviglio* (1978, The Little Ship), *Piazza d'Italia* is concerned with the intermeshing of private stories and the warp of history. The mythical dimension of the passing of the generations against which the historical events are set is emphasized by the cyclical structure of the narrative—critic Cesare Segre called *Piazza d'Italia* "a popular fable."

T.'s third work of fiction, the collection of short stories *Il gioco del rovescio* (1981, rev. ed., 1988; *Letter from Casablanca*, 1986) marks the beginning of a new phase. In spite of his recent return to the novel T. is a master of the short story and of the novella, and this volume already displays several of the major themes and concerns of his mature fiction. In the short story that opens the collection, "The Game of Backwards," the narrator returns to Lisbon after being informed that his lover, a collaborator in the underground opposition to Salazar's regime, has died. The temporal plane of the narrative shifts back and forth between the present of the narrator's journey and the past of his relationship with the woman, and as the two converge the possibility of reconstructing a coherent, seamless account of the events lived by the two characters is called more and more into question. The narrator's reference to the character in the background of Velázquez's *Las Meninas*, who, being placed at the vanishing point of the painting, perceives a scene that is the reverse of that beholden by the viewer, effectively describes T.'s poetics. Writing is a "game of backwards," a way to undermine the superficial clarity and coherence of reality by bringing into relief its reverse, those liminal experiences that constitute its "other": memories, dreams, mirages, and hallucinations. The same imperative drives T.'s stylistic research. His writing is characterized by great clearness and precision, and yet it is at the same time highly evocative and allusive. What matters is often not what the discourse says but what it leaves unsaid, what reverberates at the interstices between words, and in the gaps and discontinuities of the narrative. In the title story of *Donna di Porto Pim* (1983; *The Woman of Porto Pim*, 1991), a collection of prose fragments and stories that the author himself describes as an idiosyncratic and *sui generis* travel book, a tale of betrayal and murder is told by focusing on the minimal, everyday acts which surrounded the putatively major events that lead up to the homicide of the narrator's lover, and that are instead consigned to silence. Told by the protagonist to an unnamed listener, this story is an especially fine example of monologue, a genre that T. uses to great effect in both his fiction and in his two theatrical works, *Il signor Pirandello è desiderato al telefono* (Mr. Pirandello Is Kindly Requested to Come to the Phone) and *Il tempo stringe* (Time Is Running Out), both collected in *I dialoghi mancati* (1988; Failed Dialogues).

T.'s second major collection of short stories, *Piccoli equivoci senza importanza* (1985; *Little Misunderstandings of No Importance*, 1987), continues to elaborate the themes of memory, in particular memory tinged by the melancholy that the Portuguese know as *saudade*, and of the deceptiveness of surface reality. In the eponymous story, the love and friendship that link the characters is projected into an irretrievable past as one of them is put on trial for his involvement in terrorist activities. "Spells" exemplifies T.'s ability to shift perspectives and points of view: seen by a child, the difficulties of his cousin's family, with whom he is spending the summer holidays, turn into the workings of a mysterious and all-pervasive evil force, all but invisible to the adults.

Donna di Porto Pim introduces another central theme in T.'s narrative, that of the journey. Whether they travel physically through space or mentally through the landscape of memory, T.'s protagonists are often in search of something or someone which in the end is revealed to be their own self. Thus, the journey is always an existential one. This is the case of the two novellas published in the 1980s, *Notturno indiano* (1984; *Indian Nocturne*, 1988) and *Il filo dell'orizzonte* (1986; *The Edge of the Horizon*, 1990). *Notturno indiano*, described by T. as "a novel built on absence," is one his most accomplished works, in which the "game of backwards" is elevated to a structural and thematic principle: though he remains always the outsider, the narrator travels through an India which is the "backwards" of that of tourists' brochures and travel books, in a

series of nocturnal scenes that lead him to such locations as a cockroach infested hospital in Bombay, the Madras headquarters of the Theosophical Society, or a bus stop "about 50 kilometers from Mangalore, place name unknown." The object of his quest is Xavier, "a Portuguese who lost his way in India," but in the course of the narrative it is the identity of the narrator himself that undergoes a process of questioning and redefinition, and the quest is suspended—"the book is finished," the narrator says—once the process of identification between the protagonist and Xavier is accomplished and the person lost in India becomes the narrator himself. *Il filo dell'orizzonte* adopts the form of the detective novel but turns the epistemological thrust of the genre into an existential one. Spino, the protagonist, investigates the death of Carlo Noboldi, but his investigation hinges more on who Noboldi was than on who killed him. As he reconstructs the victim's identity by putting together apparently inconsequential details, Spino also attempts to reconstruct larger patterns of meaning in the universe. In a typical gesture, the novel concludes with the protagonist stepping into the darkness of a warehouse to find the solution to a mystery which remains, to the reader, open.

In recent years T.'s narrative has focused more sharply and earnestly on social and political concerns, and history has often returned to occupy the foreground of his fiction. In 1991, in addition to *Requiem. Uma alucinação* (Requiem. A Hallucination), the story of an oneiric and hallucinatory wandering through Lisbon written in Portuguese, he published *L'angelo nero* (The Black Angel), a collection marked by a stronger sense of evil and by a somber, foreboding tone. But it was with the novel *Sostiene Pereira. Una testimonianza* (1994; *Pereira Declares. A Testimony*, 1995), which quickly became a bestseller, that T. offered his most sustained engagement with politics and history. Set in Salazar's Lisbon in 1938, the novel is the report of yet another unnamed narrator who relates the testimony of the protagonist, Pereira, the cultural editor of a minor Lisbon newspaper. With the unfolding of his relationship with his newly-hired assistant, Francesco Monteiro Rossi, and his girlfriend Marta—both of whom are involved in underground activities in support of the Republican side in the Spanish civil war—the journalist slowly begins to develop a political consciousness that frees him from the aestheticism in which he had found refuge from everyday events and offers him a way out of the sterility of his life. In spite of its phenomenal success the novel is flawed; T.'s review of the cultural landscape of the 1930s, for instance, strikes as manichean, and the search for a more rhythmic and lyrical prose verges at times on self-parody, as is the case with the much repeated refrain "Pereira declares." Some of the structural and stylistic subtlety of the short stories and novellas seems lost to the necessities of the architecture of a more sustained narrative. While *La testa perduta di Damasceno Monteiro* (1997; The Missing Head of Damasceno Monteiro), is not free of the problems of *Sostiene Pereira*, T.'s continued engagement with a more extended narrative form attests to an ongoing research whose best fruits are perhaps still to come.

T.'s fiction has been very well received outside of Italy, and his works have been translated into English, French, Spanish, and Portuguese. There have been film adaptations of two of his novels: *Notturno indiano* (1989), directed by Alain Corneau, and *Sostiene Pereira* (1995), directed by Roberto Faenza, and starring Marcello Mastroianni. He has been awarded numerous Italian and international prizes, including the French "Médicis Etranger" (1987) and the Viareggio and Campiello Prizes (1994). In 1989 he was conferred the title of "Comendador da Ordem do Infante Dom Enrique" by the President of the Portuguese Republic, Mario Soares, and in 1996 that of "Officier des Arts et Lettres" in France.

FURTHER WORKS: *I volatili del Beato Angelico* (1987; *The Flying Creatures of Fra Angelico*, 1991); *Sogni di sogni* (1992). FURTHER WORKS IN ENGLISH: *Vanishing Point* (1991)

BIBLIOGRAPHY: Francese, J., "The Postmodern Discourse of Doctorow's *Billy Bathgate* and T.'s *I dialoghi mancati*," *Annali d'italianistica*, 9 (1991): 182–97; Lepschy, A. L., "Filling the Gaps: Dreams in the Narrative Fiction of A. T.," *Romance Studies*, 18 (1991): 55–64; Lepschy, A. L., "A. T.: Splinters of Existence," in Baránski, Z., and Pertile, L., eds., *The New Italian Novel* (1993): 184–99; Biasin, G. P., "Other Foods, Other Voices," *MLN*, 109.5 (1994): 831–46; Botta, A., "An Interview with A. T.," *ConL*, 35, 3 (1994): 421–40; Wilson, R., "A Reading of A. T.'s *Il filo dell'orizzonte*," *Studi d'italianistica nell'Africa Australe/Italian Studies in Southern Africa*, 9, 1 (1996): 72–87; Klopp, C. D., "A. T.: Postmodern Catholic Writer," *WLT*, 71, 2 (1997): 331–34; Ferraro, B., and Prunster, N., eds., *A. T. A Collection of Essays* (1997)

—LUCA SOMIGLI

TADJO, Véronique

Ivoirian novelist, poet, and short-story writer, b. 1955, Paris, France

Educated in France and in Côte d'Ivoire, T. has ties to three or more continents. Her mother, a sculptor and painter, is French, while her father is a highly placed official in the Ivoirian government. She has a doctorate in African-American culture and literature from the Sorbonne, and has traveled widely in Africa, Europe, Latin America, and the U.S. She teaches at the National University of Côte d'Ivoire in Abidjan.

Although T. has received literary prizes from the French Agency for Cultural and Technical Cooperation (ACCT) and from UNESCO, her work remains almost unknown to readers and critics outside of the circle of specialists in African literature. In the context of sub-Saharan African literature, her work stands out because of its dense, poetic texture and its genre-bending qualities.

This inventive attitude toward issues of language and style puts T. into the company of other West African writers who choose to experiment with form without necessarily opting for a creolized language. Similar to her Ivoirian compatriot, Jean-Marie Adiaffi (b. 1941), T. has shown that it is indeed possible to remain politically and socially engaged while transforming the artistic discourse of engagement.

In her intensely emotional poetry and short stories, she contrasts inner life with external problems such as poverty. T.'s work makes the link between the personal and the political very strongly. In the context of Francophone African writing, her emphasis on personal relationships and love in the poems collected in *Latérite* (1984; Laterite) and the short stories of *A vol d'oiseau* (1992; As the Crow

Flies) is striking and unusual. Moreover, she does not approach the issues in standard fashion, by focusing on social institutions such as marriage and polygyny, as other Francophone writers have done.

Her turn toward a West African form of MAGIC REALISM represents a more successful resolution of the dilemma. In *Le royaume aveugle* (1990; The Blind Kingdom) the apocalypse simply opens upon a new chapter of suffering, as dictators who are literally blind conquer and dominate an unnamed kingdom that clearly represents Côte d'Ivoire. T. attacks the blindness, corruption, and filth in the kingdom, but also indicates that even the blind may see the truth if they so choose.

The critic Irène d'Alméïda writes that T. presents a message of hope that positive values will repair the damaged social fabric, yet also shows the difficulties and ambiguities of this situation. Perhaps this delicate balance between ambiguity and engagement best describes T.'s work and its importance in the context of Francophone African writing.

FURTHER WORKS: *Lord of the Dance* (1988); *La chanson de la vie* (1989); *Mamy Wata et le monstre* (1993)

BIBLIOGRAPHY: Cazenave, O., *Femmes rebelles: Naissance d'un nouveau roman africain au féminin* (1996): 310–17; d'Alméïda, I., *Francophone African Women Writers: Destroying the Emptiness of Silence* (1994): 154–68; Ormerod, B., and J.-M. Volet, eds., *Romancières africaines d'expression française: Le sud du Sahara* (1994): 139–40; Kom, A., ed., *Dictionnaire des oeuvres littéraires de langue française en Afrique au Sud du Sahara* (1996): 298–99

—LISA MCNEE

TAFDRUP, Pia

Danish poet, b. 29 May 1952, Copenhagen

During the 1980s, T. clearly emerged as one of Denmark's most outstanding poets, and in 1988, at a remarkably young age, she became a member of the prestigious Danish Academy. She graduated in 1977 from the University of Copenhagen; she has traveled widely, including the U.S., and her experiences as a traveler have echoed in her poetry.

T.'s debut, *Når det går hul på en engel* (1981; when an angel has been grazed), reflects a young person's double experience of knowing that the world is fragmenting—wars, relationships, sudden death—and of being able to probe that world with and through words: to write poetry. This dual attitude, simultaneous desperation and joy, marks T.'s body of poetry and gives it an undeniable tension. T. is, however, not an ideological or philosophical writer, for her emphasis is always on experience—often in its minutest nuances. In particular, she devotes much detail and attention to sexual desire and that awareness of the body, or bodies, to which such sensuality leads. Perceptively, she has characterized her own poetry in that vein as not merely trying to write about desire but to demonstrate it through language—what she calls "the syntax of desire."

T.'s collections of poetry—*Intetfang* (1982; nohold), *Den inderste zone* (1983; the innermost zone), *Springflod* (1985; *Springtide*,

281

1989), *Hvid feber* (1986; white fever), and *Sekundernes bro* (1988; the bridge of the seconds)—may not startle the reader with any abrupt changes in form or outlook, but the language gradually seems more vibrant and rhythmical. T. is a skilled performer of her own texts, and the oral quality of them suggests very strongly that they be read aloud and not merely read. As is the case in all oral poetry of quality, the full impact of the nuance of detail, the suggested pauses, the implied intonation are realized only when the text is given voice.

T., whose background in literature is impressive, once in an article—which might be seen as the draft for a poetics—noted that aesthetics should not be perceived as a straitjacket from which the poem dreams of being liberated; aesthetics is, rather, the reason why the poem is not destroyed by chaos. T.'s texts may be seen as acts of resistance against chaos, and in her exploration of desire and the language of desire, the moments of lust, ecstasy, intimacy, and joy grant her a sense of a fullness and fulfillment that, at least momentarily, keeps the existential darkness at bay. In some ambitious poems she attempts, as did the poets of yore, to reach for the unfathomable. Such sensual moments offer, in addition, a sense of self and self-assurance, which permit an openness and sensitivity to a partner; thus, T.'s poetry, even if it records much loneliness, cherishes a sense of togetherness.

Such moments, however, never make T.'s experience of the world simplistic or idyllic, for she is astutely aware that her world, as well as the world in general, is fragile and that death may be imminent. In fact, her rhythmic, sensuous language—laden with rich, innovative images—refutes any clear-cut, mundane perception of existence but conjures up, rather, the complexity and richness of the experience of the one whose senses are open to the world.

Lately, T. has tried her hand at drama. *Døden i bjergene* (1988; death in the mountains), and with *Jorden er blå* (1991; Earth is blue), she continued her exploration into that genre dealing with the issue of individual responsibility.

T. made her astute awareness of her vocation an issue in *Over vandet gårr jeg* (1991; I walk on water), a poetics. Her ensuing collections of poetry suggest that she continues to expand her horizons. *Krystalskoven* (1992; The crystal forest) depicts forests and trees as being very real but as referring simultaneously to a mental reality.

T. is undeniably one of Denmark's leading poets. Her quest for fulfillment is rendered with a burning, pleading, proud, painful, and joyful intensity; thus, she has found for desire a language that is her own.

FURTHER WORKS: *Territorialsang* (1994). FURTHER WORKS IN ENGLISH: *Spring Tide* (1989)

BIBLIOGRAPHY: Wamberg, B., ed., *Out of Denmark* (1985): 149–50; Heitmann, A., ed., *No Man's Land: An Anthology of Modern Danish Women's Literature* (1987): 11–12; Houe, P., in Rossel, S., *A History of Danish Literature* (1992): 540-41

—NIELS INGWERSEN

TAGALOG LITERATURE

See Philippine Literature

Rabindranath Tagore

TAGORE, Rabindranath

(Anglicized form of Thakur) Indian poet, dramatist, novelist, short-story writer, essayist, and philosopher (writing in Bengali and English), b. 7 May 1861, Calcutta; d. 7 Aug. 1941, Calcutta

T. came from a prosperous and cultivated Hindu family. His father, Devendranath, was an ardent supporter of the Brahmo Samaj movement for the reformation of Hinduism. At the age of seventeen T. was sent to England to study; he attended school at Brighton and in 1879 was admitted to University College, London, but returned to India in 1880 without completing his studies. In 1883 he married and was later put in charge of the family estates by his father.

In 1901, having already published numerous volumes of poems, stories, and dramas and having served as editor of several Bengali journals, T. founded Santiniketan ("abode of peace"), a school that later developed into the international university called Visva-Bharati ("universal voice"). The school was to serve as a bridge between the cultures of the East and the West; its motto was "Where the whole world forms its single nest." Being a humanist in the cosmic sense of the term, T. was highly critical of what was called "education" in British India and described it as "the stuff that was crammed into our intellectual vacancy," as if "we had bought our spectacles at the expense of our eyesight." He wanted Indians to go back to what they once possessed, namely, "such a thing as our own mind."

In 1913 T. received the Nobel Prize for literature. In 1915 Gandhi visited him at Santiniketan, and in the same year T. was knighted by the King of England, although in 1919 he renounced the knighthood as a protest against the Amritsar massacre by the British police, in which about four hundred people were killed. In 1930 he gave the Hibbert Lectures at Oxford.

T. hailed Gandhi as the "wielder of that rod" that could "awaken India in Truth and Love" but criticized Gandhi's policy of non-cooperation. Although a patriot—he said, "I shall be born in India again and again, with all the poverty, misery, and wretchedness"—T. sided with England on the eve of the war in 1939, declaring that "no Indian can wish England to lose the war she is fighting for the sake of liberty." Nevertheless, he ultimately accepted Gandhi's views about the exploitation of the Indian people.

A painter and musician as well as a prolific and versatile writer, T. made notable contributions to all the genres in which he wrote. But it was essentially as a lyric poet that he was hailed by W. B. YEATS and Ezra POUND on the publication of *Gitanjali (Song Offerings)* (1912), a collection of English prose translations by the author of a selection of poems from several of his Bengali collections, including *Gitanjali* (1910; song offerings). In his introduction to the volume Yeats said that it was a work of supreme culture and had stirred his blood as nothing had for years; Pound wrote an article in the *Fortnightly Review* praising T.'s work. In this volume the poet's spiritual and cosmic philosophy of life, far from obstructing the lyric flow and movement of his verse, confers upon it a rare beauty of rhythm, accents, and imagery. T. looks upon the whole cosmic and temporal process as a ceaseless fulfillment of some "eternal dream." He was a poet more religious than philosophical, and more mystical than religious—his translation into English of works by a mystical poet of the 15th c., *One Hundred Poems of Kabir* (1914), is a case in point. The poems in the English *Gitanjali*—the poet's colloquies with God—seek to define and at the same time to transcend the dichotomy between "I" and "Thou," between the contemplator and the contemplated. In exploring this theme, T. belongs to the lyric tradition of Vaishnava Hinduism, which focuses on the personal relationship between man and his Creator. Like Kabir, T. brought to an extremely intimate personal realization of God a musical as well as a lyrical skill, an imagery at once realistic and evocative, and a wealth of symbols and concepts from the most disparate faiths and philosophies.

Gitanjali is T's masterpiece and his most characteristic book. None of his subsequent volumes of poetry, which deal, variously, with divine and human love, inner exploration, and cosmic philosophy, achieves the same freshness and subtlety of creative inspiration, together with technical mastery, as this book; nor do they add anything to the poetic and mystical philosophy so superbly expressed in *Gitanjali*.

While T.'s philosophy is his own, it is largely the result of his intermingling of the essence of Hinduism, absorbed from study of classic religious texts and the works of early Indian philosophers and poets, with what he acquired from his admiring familiarity with Western thought and modern European—especially English—literature, and his combining of both with his own intuitional faith, a belief in divine immanence in all things. This rich synthesis, which also incorporates traditional Bengali literature, underlies all his work and translates itself into the kind of symbolism and allegory found in his more successful plays, novels, and short stories; his philosophy also goes a long way toward accounting for,

and to some extent justifying, the lack of real action and well-conceived plots in his fiction and drama.

Among T.'s important plays are *Chitrangada* (1892; *Chitra*, 1913), *Dakghar* (1912; *The Post Office*, 1914), *Raja* (1910; *The King of the Dark Chamber*, 1914), *Phalguni* (1916; *The Cycle of Spring*, 1917), and *Rakta-karabi* (1924; *Red Oleanders*, 1925), all of which center around the conflict between the vital urge represented by the human personality and the impersonal and mechanical force represented by industrialization, with the ultimate triumph of personality. From the point of view of lyric effusiveness, *Chitrangada*, which T. translated into English himself, is generally regarded as his loveliest play. *Dakghar* depicts the yearnings and thoughts of a child, Amal; T. regarded it as a truthful evocation of his own childhood. *Raja* is inspired by his belief in the realization of the divine by the human being in the form of a kind and benevolent king as the head of a government. *Phalguni* has for its theme the celebration of youth and its bliss, whereas in *Rakta-karabi* T. depicts life in a modern industrial society and its warping effects on man's inner nature. In his old age he invented a form of dance drama with music.

Among T.'s novels, *Gora* (1910; *Gora*, 1924) and *Ghare-baire* (1916; *The Home and the World*, 1919) are the best known. *Gora* deals with the desire for political independence, with the mentality of the subject nation, and with the wish for social justice struggling against the power and privilege of a class- and caste-ridden society. In *Ghare-baire* T. focuses on the cult of violence against the British as a political weapon and as a means of achieving independence, and the growing appeal of such a course in the minds of Indians; hence, to some extent, the novel allegorizes the emergence of India into a new and restless world of social upheaval and political turmoil.

As a short-story writer, too, T. was a pioneer in Bengali literature. His stories are studies in psychology or impressionistic sketches depicting village life in East Bengal.

Of his literary, political and philosophical essays, the most noteworthy are *Sadhana: The Realisation of Life* (1913), *Nationalism* (1917), and *Personality* (1917), lectures in English; *Creative Unity* (1922), essays and lectures in English; *The Religion of Man* (1931), the Hibbert Lectures delivered at Oxford; and *Shabhyatar shangkat* (1941; *Crisis in Civilization*, 1941), an address delivered on the occasion of his eightieth birthday. All of these works show his optimistic faith and idealism.

T. traveled all over the world and met most of the eminent writers, thinkers, and artists of his day. A few months before his death the University of Oxford conferred upon him the honorary degree of Doctor of Letters; since T. was too ill to go to Oxford, the university sent its two distinguished representatives to India to present it to him—a rare honor. T. was a humanist and a humanitarian who sought above all to reconcile material and spiritual values.

FURTHER WORKS: *Bau-thakuranir hat* (1883); *Prabhat sangit* (1883); *Rajarshi* (1887); *Raja o rani* (1889; *The King and the Queen*, 1918; later tr., *Devouring Love*, 1961); *Visargan* (1890; *Sacrifice*, 1917); *Manasi* (1890); *Iurope-jatrir diari* (2 vols., 1891, 1893); *Valmiki pratibha* (1893); *Sonar tari* (1894); *Katha* (1900); *Kahini* (1900); *Kalpana* (1900); *Kshanika* (1900); *Naivedya* (1901); *Nashtanir* (1901; *The Broken Nest*, 1971); *Chokher bali* (1903; *Eyesore*, 1914; later tr., *Binodini*, 1959); *Kheya* (1906); *Naukadubi* (1906; *The Wreck*, 1921); *Saradotsava* (1908; *Autumn Festival*, 1920); *Chinnapatra* (1912; expanded ed., *Chinnapatrabali*,

1960; *Glimpses of Bengal*, 1921); *Viday-abhisap* (1912; *The Curse at Farewell*, 1924); *Jivansmriti* (1912; *My Reminiscences*, 1917); *Ghitimalya* (1914); *Gitali* (1914); *Balak* (1916; *A Flight of Swans*, 1955); *Chaturanga* (1916; *Chaturanga*, 1963); *Palataka* (1918); *Japan-jatri* (1919; *A Visit to Japan*, 1961); *Lipika* (1922); *Mukta-dhara* (1922; *Mukta-dhara*, 1922; later tr., 1950); *Grihaprabesh* (1925); *Natir puja* (1926; *Natir Puja*, 1926; later tr., 1950); *Sesher kavita* (1929; *Farewell, My Friend*, 1946); *Mahua* (1929; *The Herald of Spring*, 1957); *Jatri* (1929); *Yogayog* (1929); *Rashiar chithi* (1931; *Letters from Russia*, 1960); *Punascha* (1932); *Dui bon* (1933; *Two Sisters*, 1945); *Chandalika* (1933; *Chandalika*, 1938; later tr., 1950); *Malancha* (1934; *The Garden*, 1956); *Char adhyaya* (1934; *Four Chapters*, 1950); *Bithika* (1935); *Shesh saptak* (1935); *Patraput* (1936); *Syamali* (1936; *Syamali*, 1955); *Khapchara* (1937); *Prantik* (1938); *Senjuti* (1938); *Prahasini* (1939); *Pather sancay* (1939); *Akaspradip* (1939); *Syama* (1939); *Nabajataka* (1940); *Shanai* (1940); *Chelebela* (1940; *My Boyhood Days*, 1940); *Rogshajyay* (1940); *Arogya* (1941); *Janmadine* (1941); *Galpasalpa* (1941); *Gitabitan* (1960); *Galpaguccha* (4 vols., 1960–1962); *Bicitra* (1961); *Rabindra-racanabali* (27 vols., 1964–1966). FURTHER WORKS IN ENGLISH: *Glimpses of Bengal Life* (1913); *The Gardener* (1913); *The Crescent Moon* (1913); *Fruit Gathering* (1916); *The Hungry Stones and Other Stories* (1916); *Stray Birds* (1916); *Sacrifice, and Other Plays* (1917); *Mashi and Other Stories* (1918); *Lover's Gift and Crossing* (1918); *Stories from T.* (1918); *The Fugitive* (1921); *Thought Relics* (1921; enlarged ed., *Thoughts from T.*, 1929); *Poems from T.* (1922); *Letters from Abroad* (1924); *Broken Ties and Other Stories* (1925); *Talks in China* (1925); *The Augustan Books of Modern Poetry: R. T.* (1925); *Fireflies* (1928); *Lectures and Addresses* (1928); *Letters to a Friend* (1928); *The T. Birthday Book* (1928); *The Child* (1931); *Mahatmaji and the Depressed Humanity* (1932); *The Golden Boat* (1932); *Collected Poems and Plays of R. T.* (1936); *Man* (1937); *Poems* (1942); *The Parrot's Training and Other Stories* (1944); *Rolland and T.* [letters and conversations] (1945); *Three Plays* (1950); *Sheaves* (1951); *More Stories from T.* (1951); *Tales from T.* (1953); *A. T. Testament* (1953); *More Tales from T.* (1956); *Our Universe* (1958); *The Runaway and Other Stories* (1959); *Wings of Death* (1960); *R. T. Pioneer in Education* (1961, with Leonard Elmhirst); *A. T. Reader* (1961); *Towards Universal Man* (1961); *The Housewarming and Other Selected Writings* (1965); *Imperfect Encounter: Letters of William Rothenstein and R. T., 1911–1941* (1972); *Later Poems of R. T.* (1974)

BIBLIOGRAPHY: Pound, E., "R. T.," *Fortnightly Review*, 1 March 1913: 571–79; Thompson, E., *R. T.: Poet and Dramatist* (1926; rev. ed., 1948); Guha-Thakurta, P., *The Bengali Drama: Its Origin and Development* (1930): 177–223; Ghose, S., *The Later Poems of T.* (1961); Mukerjee, H., *Himself a True Poem: A Study of R. T.* (1961); Sahitya Akademi, *R. T., 1861–1961: A Centenary Volume* (1961); Bose, B., *T.: Portrait of a Poet* (1962); Kripalani, K., *R. T.: A Biography* (1962; rev. ed., 1980); Khanolkar, G. D., *The Lute and the Plough: A Life of R. T.* (1963); Ray, N., *An Artist in Life: A Commentary on the Works of R. T.* (1967); Banerjee, H., *R. T.* (1971); Chakravorty, B. C., *R. T., His Mind and Art: T.'s Contribution to English Literature* (1971); Lago, M. M., *R. T.* (1976)

—G. SINGH

These lyrics—which are in the original, my Indians tell me, full of subtlety of rhythm, of untranslatable delicacies of colour, of metrical invention—display in their thought a world I have dreamed of all my life long. The work of a supreme culture, they yet appear as much the growth of common soil as the grass and the rushes. A tradition, where poetry and religion are the same thing, has passed through the centuries, gathering from learned and unlearned metaphor and emotion, and carried back again to the multitude the thought of the scholar and of the noble. . . .

A whole people, a whole civilisation, immeasurably strange to us, seems to have been taken up into this imagination; and yet we are not moved because of its strangeness, but because we have met our own image, as though we had walked in Rossetti's willow wood, or heard, perhaps for the first time in literature, our voice as in a dream.

W. B. Yeats, Introduction to R. T., *Gitanjali (Song Offerings)* (1912), pp. xii–xiv, xvi–xvii

The movement of his prose [in *Gitanjali (Song Offerings)*] may escape you if you read it only from print, but read it aloud, a little tentatively, and the delicacy of its rhythm is at once apparent.

I think this good fortune is unconscious. I do not think it is an accident. It is the sort of prose rhythm a man would use after years of word arranging. He would shun kakophony almost unwittingly.

The next easiest things to note are the occasional brilliant phrases, now like some pure Hellenic, in "Morning with the golden basket in her right hand," now like the last sophistication of De Gourmont or Baudelaire.

But beneath and about it all is this spirit of curious quiet. We have found our new Greece, suddenly. As the sense of balance came back upon Europe in the days before the Renaissance, so it seems to me does this sense of a saner stillness come now to us in the midst of our clangour of mechanisms. . . .

There is in him the stillness of nature. The poems do not seem to have been produced by storm or by ignition, but seem to show the normal habit of his mind. He is at one with nature, and finds no contradictions. And this is in sharp contrast with the Western mode, where man must be shown attempting to master nature if we are to have "great drama." It is in contrast to the Hellenic representation of man the sport of the gods, and both in the grip of destiny.

Ezra Pound, "R. T.," *Fortnightly Review*, 1 March 1913, pp. 573–74

Gitanjali brings the poet into closer and more familiar contact with the natural world than any previous book. This is not to say that its natural effects are truer or brighter or lovelier than many that have been attained by him before. It is a matter of atmosphere, of being steeped in sound and sight and colour. The book's mood is grey, its key is almost always minor, its pictures mournful, or, at best, untouched by exhilaration. Probably the impression of monotony comes from this oneness of mood, an impression as of a wind wailing through rainy woods, and from the fact that the book gets its effects out of the merest handful of illustrations. Rarely was fine poetry, one thinks, made out of less variety; rain and cloud, wind and rising river, boatmen, lamps, temples and gongs, flutes and *vinas*, birds flying home at dusk, travellers tired or with provisions exhausted, flowers opening and falling. It is astonishing what range the poet gets out of these few things—they are far too naturally and purely used here to be called properties, as they justifiably might be in much of his work. . . .

It was through the English *Gitanjali* that I got my first introduction to his poetry, and I confess myself to this day so under its spell that I cannot appraise it with any degree of accuracy. The book has spoken to countless hearts, has been a revelation of what they felt and experienced, and cannot ever be forgotten.

Edward Thompson, *R. T.: Poet and Dramatist*, rev. ed. (1948), pp. 217–18

We have in English literature romantic poets like Shelley and Keats, religious poets like Francis Thompson and realists like Eliot, Auden and Spender. But T. holds a unique position in the realm of poetry on account of the fact that he has combined in himself the romanticism of Shelley, the mysticism of Francis Thompson and the realism of Eliot, Auden and Spender. He has given us the songs of childhood in *The Crescent Moon*, the songs of human love in *The Gardener*, the songs of divine love in *Gitanjali* and the songs of common humanity in *Poems*. These works have enriched the English language and are his lasting contributions to English literature.

Throughout his poetic career, he has never lost his sense of balance and proportion. His romanticism has always been tinged with realism, his realism has never sunk down to the level of sordid materialism and his mysticism has never denied the claims of humanism. During the twenties and thirties of this century, when the English poets like Eliot, Auden, Spender and Day Lewis were baffled by the greatest spiritual crisis in human history, he alone retained his faith in the divinity of man. He has shown in his *Poems* how to reconcile the claims of the material and spiritual values of life. He has explained in *Creative Unity* how mankind can be united only by the spiritual bond of love and friendship. He has asserted in *The Religion of Man* that the only religion of man is service to humanity.

Gitanjali gave R. [T.] the place of a mystic in the world of letters. I have no doubt in my mind that the day has come when he will be regarded by the English-speaking world as a great realist who has also been the greatest exponent of the divinity in man.

B. C. Chakravorty, *R. T., His Mind and Art: T.'s Contribution to English Literature* (1971), pp. 298–99

[T.] was a very lonely man. Buddhadeva Bose says: "He had no rivals, and no examples of styles different from his; there was no criticism by which he could profit, and scarcely a literary friend whom he could treat as an equal. . . . And this, I think, was a misfortune." He was a captive of his own genius. As Buddhadeva says: "Little things which he did playfully, or because there was nobody else to do them, turned out to be stages in the development of Bengali poetry." Continual awareness of such a responsibility becomes like a physical burden. His lecture tours abroad were an economic necessity for his school; they were also a psychological necessity for T., who was always hungry for occasions like the memorable one at Cambridge. Behavior that appeared to be—and was—quixotic, such as his impulsive cancellations of lecture engagements, was the result of a cumulative exhaustion brought on by intellectual over-excitement and sheer overwork. Critics who have kept him on a pedestal designed for a god have done him a disservice. When he is reduced to human scale his achievements are enhanced: it does not seem possible that one man, even by living for eighty years, could have done so much.

It is important now that he be considered, and reconsidered, in the roles in which he saw himself. He is a literary figure, not a sociological model, although his experience and his works illuminate Indian social history. The West knew him only briefly and imperfectly. A renewed if belated effort to know him more fully would provide its own rewards.

Mary M. Lago, *R. T.* (1976), pp. 146–47

The basic and most robust characteristic of T.'s philosophy of life was his emphasis on the development of the human personality and his deep-set conviction that there is no inherent contradiction between the claims of the so-called opposites—the flesh and the spirit, the human and the divine, love of life and love of God, joy in beauty and pursuit of truth, social obligation and individual rights, respect for tradition and the freedom to experiment, love of one's people and faith in the unity of mankind. These seeming opposites can and must be reconciled, not by tentative compromises and timid vacillation but by building a true harmony out of the apparent discordance. This faith runs through all his poetry in a thousand echoes. . . .

The religious, moral, aesthetic and intellectual aspects of T.'s own personality were so well developed and matched that of no one was it more true than of him that he saw life steadily and saw it whole. . . .

If T. had been nothing more than a poet and writer, the quality and output of his contribution to his people's language and literature would still entitle him to be remembered as one of the world's truly great immortals. But he was something much more. He was an artist in life. His personal life was as harmonious and noble as his verse is simple and beautiful. He lived as he wrote, not for pleasure or profit but out of joy, not as a brilliant egoist but as a dedicated spirit, conscious that his genius was a gift from the divine, to be used in the service of man.

Krishna Kripalani, *R. T.: A Biography*, rev. ed. (1980), pp. 5–6

TAIWANESE LITERATURE

See Chinese Literature

TAJIK LITERATURE

At the beginning of the 20th c. Tajik literature still bore the stamp of its Persian and Central Asian heritage. Traditional forms and subjects predominated, and the literary language favored abstractions and Arabisms rather than vernacular speech. Poetry was the preferred medium of expression, while prose was limited to the short tale.

The Russian Revolution and subsequent policies of the Soviet state set Tajik literature on a new course. After a period of experiment with content and form in the 1920s, the Communist Party imposed on writers a set of ideological and aesthetic guidelines (they were never separate) usually known as SOCIALIST REALISM. Henceforth, literary dogma, rather than personal artistic inclinations, determined the writer's choice of subject and handling of character. He was expected to depict mass social movements and the individual personality from the standpoint of the prevailing interpretation of Marxism-Leninism. He had to show how social change took place and why it must inevitably lead to a communistic "better world." In delineating character, he was obliged to idealize the "progressives" and to excoriate their opponents. Finally, he had to remember that good art was not merely a reflection of reality but also a powerful instrument for changing that reality.

Poetry

Poetry in the 1920s and 1930s reflected the growing pains of Soviet Tajik literature. Many poets, primarily those who had come to maturity before the revolution, preserved traditional forms and meters and ignored the new utilitarian role assigned to poetry. Foremost among them was Muhammad Zufarkhon Javhari (1860–1945), whose poems were filled with abstract images and metaphors. On the other hand, there were poets who fused classical prosody with revolutionary subject matter, such as Abulqasim LAHUTI, the first major Soviet Tajik poet. In sometimes strident verse he extolled socialist construction, but at the same time he wrote *ghazals* (love poems) of exquisite delicacy. A master of the classical *aruz* (a meter based upon the regular alternation of long and short syllables), he also fostered such innovations as blank verse. A good example of his method is "Taj va bayraq" (1935; crown and banner), a *doston* (a longer epic-lyrical poem) that described socialist competition on a collective farm in meters borrowed from the classical Persian masterpiece *Shahnama*.

The postrevolutionary generation of poets adhered faithfully to the canons of social poetry. They drew upon economic plans for their themes, and they wrote in a language close to the vernacular. Their leader was Mirzo TURSUNZODA, whose first major poem, *Khazon va bahor* (1937; autumn and spring), contrasted the unhappy past life of the peasantry with the bright future promised by the collective farm. During World War II he and his colleagues placed their art fully in the service of the fatherland. Tursunzoda himself composed tirelessly on the theme of the brotherhood of Soviet peoples, and Mirsaid Mirshakar (b. 1912) glorified the patriotism of Soviet miners in *Odami az bomi jahon* (1943; men from the roof of the world), one of the most original poems to come out of the war. Mirshakar also skillfully combined folk legend with socialist construction in *Qishloqi tilloi* (1944; the golden village), a reworking of the Pamir tale about the land of eternal happiness.

Utilitarian themes also dominated postwar poetry. In *Hasani arobakash* (1954; Hasan the cart driver), a *doston*, Tursunzoda described the impact of revolutionary struggle on community attitudes and individual psyches, and in *Dashti laband* (1961; the lazy steppe) Mirshakar proclaimed the superiority of collective labor. But change was in the air. Ghaffor Mirzo (b. 1929), perhaps the most important of the new poets, abandoned the *aruz* and treated the problems of contemporary Soviet society with unaccustomed candor in *Sesadu shastu shash pahlu* (1962; 366 degrees).

Fiction

The dominant figure in postrevolutionary Tajik fiction has been Sadriddin AINI, the founder of the Tajik novel. His first novel, *Odina* (1924; Odina), revealed his debt to tradition. While the action is focused on the immense changes taking place in Soviet society, the central characters are a pair of lovers who meet a tragic fate, a theme found in several classical Eastern romances. In *Dokhunda* (1930; Dokhunda) simplicity and directness characterize Aini's style, and in his description of men and events realism is the dominant mode. His later novels, *Ghulomon* (1934; the slaves), perhaps his best, and *Margi sudkhör* (1937; usurer's death), a psychological study, were broad panoramas of Central Asian society, which firmly established long fiction as a major genre of Tajik literature.

Despite Aini's example, short stories dominated fiction until the end of World War II. They concentrated on the new problems of Tajik society in loosely constructed plots and often stereotyped characters. Depicting workers and peasants in production or in conflict with class enemies, these stories generally ignored inner feelings and motivations. The war exacerbated these shortcomings, since the declared purpose of fiction was to arouse Soviet patriotism and exhort the populace to all manner of sacrifices.

After the war the novel grew in importance, but theme and character remained within the bounds imposed by Socialist Realism. Novelists were preoccupied especially with the creation of the positive hero. He was invariably drawn from among the laboring classes and was a product of revolutionary struggle or Soviet institutions. Idealized as the builder of the communist future, he resembled the figures of a medieval hagiography. Like the central figure in Jalol Ikromi's (b. 1909) *Shodi* (1957; Shodi), an otherwise revealing examination of Tajik society, he was often the personification of ideology rather than a creature of flesh and blood.

Whether it be an autobiographical work like *Subhi javonii mo* (1954; the dawn of our youth) by Sotim Ulughzoda (b. 1911) or a historical panorama of prerevolutionary Bukhara like Ikromi's *Duktari otash* (1961; the daughter of fire), the spiritual core of the novel was the transformation of communities and individual personalities wrought by revolutionary struggle. "Progressive forces" unfailingly triumphed because, as Rahim Jalil (b. 1909) showed in *Odamoni jovid* (1949; immortal people), they alone were in step with history.

The thaw in intellectual life following Stalin's death allowed novelists to diversify their subject matter and to experiment with form. Indicative of the new trend was Ikromi's examination of family life and love, *Man gunahgoram* (1957; I am guilty), and Fazliddin Muhammadiev's (1928–1986) unconventional treatment of the generation gap, *Odamoni kuhna* (1962; old people). Before the publication of *Odamoni kuhna* the elderly had usually been depicted as merely the remnants of a society whose day has passed, while the young were hailed as the true bearers of communism. Muhammadiev was at pains to show that both generations were united by an unshakable devotion to socialist construction.

Drama

A Tajik drama in the modern sense of the term did not exist until 1929, when a national theater was founded. As with poetry and fiction, drama, too, was expected to serve economic and political goals: the struggle against nationalist opponents of the Soviet system, as in Tursunzoda's *Hukm* (1934; the verdict), and the triumph of the new over the old, as in Ulughzoda's collective-farm play, *Shodmon* (1939; Shodmon). During World War II dramatists turned out dozens of plays to support the war effort, most of them hastily written one-acters. In the immediate postwar period playwrights usually stuck to the five-year-plan formula, but occasionally a work of uncommon interest emerged, such as Mirshakar's *Shahri man* (1951; my city), which explored the rivalry between two urban planners over the architectural style of their new city.

Since 1960 Tajik dramatists have broadened their themes and have made their heroes, and even villains, more human as they probed the complexities of individual behavior. Ulughzoda's comedy *Gavhari shabcharough* (1962; the precious jewel) depicts the foibles of human character in a lighthearted manner far different from the heavy-handed censure of the Stalin era, and Ikromi explored the psyches of Tajik intellectuals in *Khor dar guliston* (1964; a thorn among the roses).

Although Tajik literature since the 1930s has been subject to the homogenizing effects of ideological and aesthetic control exercised from Moscow, it has, nonetheless, preserved a specific character that distinguishes it from other Soviet literatures. Its creators have continued to be inspired by classical Tajik and Persian literature and by a rich local folklore, and the best among them have interpreted the Soviet experience in accordance with national traditions and sensibilities. In the later 1960s and 1970s significant innovation occurred, especially in prose. Fazliddin Muhammadiev's *Dar on dunyo* (1966; in that world) suggests how far the novel has come since the 1930s. In describing the pilgrimage of Muslims to Mecca, he dwells upon the eternal themes of the meaning of human existence and the nature of happiness, and Muhiddin Khojaev (b. 1938) in *Ob-rushnoi* (2 vols., 1973–75; water-light) abandons timeworn formulas of plot and character to probe the emotional and spiritual life of heroes and villains. In the 1980s and 1990s, especially after the collapse of the Soviet Union,

Tajik writers turned increasingly to classical Tajik-Persian literary traditions and sought themes based on national history and contemporary political and cultural struggles, as in the poetry of Bozor Sobir and Askar Hakim.

BIBLIOGRAPHY: Bečka, J., "Tajik Literature from the 16th Century to the Present," in J. Rypka, et al., *History of Iranian Literature* (1968): 525–605; Bečka, J., "The Tajik Soviet Doston and Mirzo Tursunzoda," *ArO*, 44 (1976): 213–39; Hitchins, K., "Modern Tajik Literature," in Yarshater, E., ed., *Persian Literature* (1988): 454–75

—KEITH HITCHINS

TAKDIR Alisjahbana, Sutan

Indonesian novelist, poet, critic, and essayist (also writing in English and Dutch), b. 11 Feb. 1908, Natal, North Sumatra

T.'s name is generally prefaced with Sutan, an aristocratic title of the West Sumatran Minangkabau people. After being an undistinguished student in Dutch-language high schools and a failure as a schoolteacher, in 1930 T. joined the editorial staff of the Netherlands Indies Government publishing house Balai Pustaka, a position which he held until the beginning of the Japanese occupation in 1942. Between 1942 and 1950 he was a key figure in the modernization of the Indonesian language, publishing in 1949 what became a standard grammar. Between 1945 and 1949 he was also a member of the interim parliament of the Republic of Indonesia, and from 1957 until 1960 a member of the Indonesian Constituent Assembly. During the 1950s he established and managed a successful publishing firm and lectured in philosophy and literature at a private institution he founded, the National University in Djakarta. Between 1958 and 1962 he studied cultural theory in Europe and the U.S. Finding the political climate of President Sukarno's Indonesia in the early 1960s uncongenial, he remained abroad. In 1963 he became professor and head of the Department of Malay Studies at the University of Malaya in Kuala Lumpur, Malaysia, angering the Indonesian government. He returned to Indonesia in 1968 and reassumed leadership of the National University. With characteristic energy he established the Toyabungkah Art Center on the island of Bali in 1973.

It is doubtful whether any figure in contemporary Indonesian letters is as important as T. In 1933 he became a founding editor of the independent cultural monthly *Pujangga baru*, which, despite its small circulation, exerted a profound influence on the development of modern Indonesian literature. Through the pages of this journal T. initiated a debate on the direction of Indonesia's cultural development. T. held that prior to the appearance in Indonesia of European technology and liberal values, the country had lived in a dark age of ignorance and feudalism that was best forgotten. T. rejected this past as a basis for Indonesia's national identity and cultural development, and argued that in all fields Indonesia needed to model itself on Europe if it were to have any hope of creating a dynamic and modern future.

In his novel *Layar terkembang* (1936; under full sail) T. attempted a literary formulation of his views. The novel was the first in Indonesian to attempt a thoroughgoing adaptation of the conventions of European realism. Thematically it deals with the contrast between two sisters: one independent, dynamic, and progressive; the other domestic and traditionally feminine. The comparison, while not denigrating the latter, emphatically favors the former. In the novel *Kalah dan menang* (1978; defeat and victory) T. paints a panoramic portrait of Indonesia during the Japanese occupation. He contrasts the ideologies of European bourgeois liberalism, Javanese feudal mysticism, and Japanese fascist militarism. His sympathies lie firmly with the first, and it is not hard to see in the novel an oblique attack on Indonesia's current social and political order, dominated as it is by a military government top-heavy with conservative Javanese officers.

T.'s interest in cultural polemics and the development of a standard Indonesian language is all too evident in his major works of fiction. They are marred by intrusive, tedious, and in many cases decidedly dated debates. Stylistically they are ponderous, pointedly using only the formal register of Indonesian, which T. has consistently promoted as the national standard.

Although it might cause him some consternation, it seems likely that T.'s literary reputation may come to rest primarily on his poetry, represented in two small collections, *Tebaran mega* (1935; scattered clouds) and *Lagu pemacu ombak* (1978; song of a surfboard rider), and on three early prose romances, *Tak putus dirundung malang* (1929; dogged by endless misfortune), *Dian yang tak kunjung padam* (1932; the undimmed flame), and *Anak perawan di sarang penyamun* (written 1920s, pub. 1941; the virgin and the bandits). The romances, all set in Sumatra, have in common the theme of youthful spirit confronting adversity; they are tinged with a pleasantly sentimental sadness. His poetry is notable for an emotively personal touch expressed with a directness and conciseness conspicuously absent in his more ambitious prose works.

FURTHER WORKS: *Kamus istilah* (1945); *Pembimbing ke filsafat* (1945); *Puisi lama* (1946); *Puisi baru* (1946); *Tatabahasa baru Bahasa Indonesia* (1949); *Soal kebudayaan Indonesia di tengah-tengah dunia* (1950); *Museum sebagai alat pendidikan zaman moderen* (1954); *Sejarah Bahasa Indonesia* (1956); *Krisis akhlak pemuda Indonesia* (1956); *Dari perjuangan dan pertumbuhan Bahasa Indonesia* (1957); *Perjuangan untuk autonomi dan kedudukan adat di dalamnya* (1957); *Indonesia in the Modern World* (1961; rev. expanded ed., *Indonesia: Social and Cultural Revolution*, 1966); *The Failure of Modern Linguistics in the Face of Linguistic Problems of the Twentieth Century* (1965); *Values as Integrating Forces in Personality, Society and Culture* (1966); *Kebangkitan puisi baru Indonesia* (1969); *Grotta Azzura: Kisah cita dan cinta* (3 vols., 1970–1971); *Perkembangan sejarah kebudayaan dilihat dari jurusan nilai-nilai* (1975); *Language Planning for Modernization: The Case of Indonesian and Malaysian* (1976); *Dari perjuangan dan pertumbuhan Bahasa Indonesia sebagai bahasa moderen* (1977); *Perjuangan tanggung jawab dalam kesusasteraan* (1977); *Amir Hamzah sebagai penyair dan uraian sajak Nyanyian sunyi* (1978)

BIBLIOGRAPHY: Raffel, B., *The Development of Modern Indonesian Poetry* (1967): 56–61; Sutherland, H., "Pujangga Baru: Aspects of Indonesian Intellectual Life in the 1930s," *Indonesia*, No. 6 (1968): 106–27; Aveling, H., *A Thematic History of Indonesian Poetry: 1920 to 1974* (1974), passim; Friedus, A. J., *Sumatran*

Contributions to the Development of Indonesian Literature, 1920–1942 (1977): 37–41; Udin, S., ed., *Spectrum: Essays Presented to S. T. A. on His Seventieth Birthday* (1978); Teeuw, A., *Modern Indonesian Literature*, rev. ed. (1979), Vol. I: 31–41, 65–66, and passim, Vol. II: 165–67 and passim

—GEORGE QUINN

TAKTSIS, Costas

Greek novelist, poet, and translator, b. 8 Oct. 1927, Thessalonike; d. 28 Aug. 1988, Athens

Born in Thessalonike, T. moved with his family to Athens when he was a boy, and he spent there most of his life in Greece. In the late 1940s he studied law for three years without earning a degree. He traveled extensively during 1954–1964 and again in 1968–1969. He visited, or lived in, France, England, the U.S., Australia, and Africa. While overseas, he supported himself by doing all sorts of odd jobs, just as he had done in Athens, although at the same period he published several books. During 1964–1967 he worked for the literary magazine *Pali*. In 1969 he openly opposed the military régime in Athens as he had done while abroad. Apart from writing and temporary positions he also did excellent translations of Aristophanes and some modern authors until his sudden death: He was found murdered in his apartment. Although the exact circumstances of his loss have not been unraveled, the consensus attributes it to homosexual foul play.

T.'s first literary publication was the verse collection *Deka poiemata* (1951; ten poems), followed by two other collections in 1952 and 1953. Later he quietly disavowed them. Another two books of poetry appeared in 1954 and 1958, but he never made a reputation as a poet although some of his pieces reflected personal experiences from the literary Café Byzantion and the homosexual circle of Café Brazilian in postwar Athens. Giving up poetry, he worked on his only novel, *To trito stephani* (1962; *The Third Wedding*, 1967; repub. as *The Third Wedding Wreath*, 1985), a tour de force of psychological fiction, which became a best-seller and was soon translated into English, French, German, Polish, and Hungarian. The great success of *To trito stephani* was due to T.'s unsurpassed skill in recording the sensibility and behavior of his spirited women protagonists through a sequence of interior monologues offering varying or conflicting viewpoints on personal, family, and national happenings over a time span covering the first half of this century in Greece. His heroines bring to mind Euripides's Hecuba and other tragic characters from the Trojan War cycle, as do some of the motifs and analogues in the complex plot. However, T.'s purpose was not to modernize the classical myth or to recreate a tragic saga, but to achieve a relentless and compassionate exposure of the female psyche in reaction to an intensely felt sequence of national agonies. "Read this book and you will know more about Greece than you could learn from a dozen histories," commented Dilys Powell. "It makes you think of Charles du Bos's remark on *Anna Karenina*: 'This is how life would speak, if it could speak!'" observed Robert André, and Seymour Smith wrote that this novel "shows a creative wisdom that places T. in the forefront of contemporary European writers."

T.'s only book of short stories, *Ta resta* (1972; the rest), was inspired by experiences of his adventurous youth. His last two books were nonfiction: sketches and anecdotes from Athenian life entitled *He yiayia mou he Athena* (1979; my grandmother Athens), plus his controversial memoirs, *To phovero vema* (the terrible tribune), posthumously published in 1989.

FURTHER WORKS: *Mikra poiemata* (1952); *Perihoran dodekaten* (1953); *Symphonia tou Brazilian* (1954); *Kafeneio to Vyzantio* (1958)

BIBLIOGRAPHY: Mackridge, P., on *He yiayia mou he Athena*, WLT, 55, 2 (Spring 1981): 359–60; Chioles, J., Introduction to *The Third Wedding Wreath* (1985): i–xiii

—M. BYRON RAIZIS

TALEV, Dimitur

(born Dimitur Talev Petrov) Bulgarian novelist, short-story writer, and dramatist, b. 14 Sept. 1898, Prilep, Ottoman Empire (now in Yugoslavia); d. 20 Oct. 1966, Sofia

T. was born and grew up in Macedonia, then still part of the Ottoman Empire. As a child he experienced the feverish preparation of the Macedonians for the uprising of 1903. This struggle against the Turks became a central theme of his writings. The troubles in the Balkans disrupted his education: T. studied in Prilep, Bitola, Skopje, Zagreb, Vienna; in 1924 he graduated from the University of Sofia with a degree in Slavic philology. He made his home in Sofia, but his travels in Italy and France are reflected in his short fiction.

T. was an inspired patriot whose works are an intense expression of his love for Macedonia, the history of the Bulgarian state, and the moral values of the Bulgarian tradition. Because of his strong nationalist feelings and independent stance, he was for some time out of favor with the Communist government; but in 1966 he was named People's Cultural Worker of Bulgaria. This pattern is also exemplified by his expulsion from the official Writers' Union for a time, and later his appointment as its president. T.'s writings achieved great popularity and international recognition, the best of his works having been widely translated. Years of poorly paid jobs and subsistence existence ruined his health: T. experienced the agony of a slow death.

The short-story collections *Zlatniyat klyuch* (1935; the golden key), *Starata kushta* (1928; the old house), and *Zavrushtane* (1944; the return journey) draw a vivid panorama of the Macedonian ethos, with its patriarchal structures, and celebrate the enduring spirit of the people of greater Bulgaria. There is a distinct emphasis on character development limning the quintessential national personality in the natural order of man's lot. And, as in his novels, a striking characteristic is the presence of female Christ-like figures who transform the lives of embittered, hurt, or lost men.

T.'s masterpiece is the trilogy consisting of *Zhelezniyat svetilnik* (1952; *The Iron Candlestick*, 1964), *Ilinden* (1953; *Ilinden*, 1966), and *Prespanskite kambani* (1954; *The Bells of Prespa*, 1966). These novels trace a Macedonian family and its community from the 1870s to independence from Ottoman rule. In the manner of the roman-fleuve, the characters' lives are interwoven against the background of the historical forces that shaped the Balkan peninsula.

Important literary influences on T. were two major Bulgarian writers, Ivan VAZOV and Yordan YOVKOV, Tolstoy, and some 19th-c. French realists. Although T.'s themes are regional with a very specific local color, they go beyond provincialism. The world of his fiction is populated by timeless personages, and the sum of his work presents the human predicament in its complexities, the forces that mold destinies, and the processes that enlighten people.

FURTHER WORKS: *Sulzite na mama* (1925); *Usilni godini* (3 vols., 1928–1930); *Pod mrachnoto nebe* (1932); *Velikiyat tsar* (1937); *Na zavoy* (1940); *Gotse Delchev* (1942); *Grad Prilep: Borbi za rod i svoboda* (1943); *Kiprovets vustana* (1954); *Ilindentsi* (1955); *Samuil* (3 vols., 1958–1960; rev. ed., 1965); *Bratyata ot Struga* (1962); *Povesti i raskazi* (1962); *Khilendarskiyat monakh* (1962); *Glasovete vi chuvam* (1966); *Suchineniya* (II vols., 1972–1978)

BIBLIOGRAPHY: Mihailovich, V. D., et al., eds., *Modern Slavic Literatures*, Vol. II (1976): 23–26

—Y. V. KARAGEORGE

TALVIK, Heiti

(pseud. of Heiti Talviken) Estonian poet, b. 9 Sept. 1904, Pärnu; d. 18 July 1947? in a Soviet labor camp on the Ob River, Siberia

T.'s father was a professor of forensic medicine, his mother a pianist. His father's discussion of crime, disease, and suicide, combined with his mother's interest in classical music and literature, helped produce the conflicting background of T.'s poetry. While he was a student at Tartu University from 1926 to 1934, his main interests were SYMBOLIST poetry, the philosophy of pessimism, and, later, comparative religion, particularly the antidogmatic Judaism of Lev Shestov (1866–1938). The poets who inspired T.'s restless thought were Alexander Blok, Léon-Paul FARGUE, Paul CLAUDEL, and Georgy Ivanov (1894–1958). In 1937 T. married the poet Betti ALVER.

T.'s known works—all written between 1924 and 1942—consist of 99 predominantly short, severely crafted, yet powerful poems, contained in two books, *Palavik* (1934; fever) and *Kohtupäev* (1937; doomsday), and five uncollected poems. An unspecified number of poems were destroyed by T. himself, who was very critical of his own work, and in the end his papers were seized by the Soviet secret police and have never been recovered. This poetry forms both an extended allegory of T.'s youth and an autobiography of a soul in its journey through the chaos of our century. There is a contrast in the poems between the disasters of war, Nazism, and the "bloody sun" of Lenin's October on the one hand, and on the other T.'s own private spiritual torments, the corrosive effects of dreariness sapping the will.

From these self-centered limits, which too easily justify psychic as well as physical drunkenness, T. moved in his philosophical poetry toward more universal experience and more objective perception. He devoted his talent and energy to exposing the spread of fascism, and in the cycle of poems "Dies irae," written as early as 1934 and published in *Kohtupäev*, he recognized Nazism for the death sentence it was.

Once he had perceived the doom of modern Europe, T. engaged in a struggle to preserve artistic unity. He thought that purism in prosody—mathematical principles of control in metrics and language—could save man from becoming utterly inhumane. In his late poetry, form becomes content, just as spiritual obedience and asceticism-in-faith becomes liberty. But T. paid dearly for his love of EXISTENTIALIST freedom. He was not allowed to publish under Soviet rule, although strangely enough three of his poems were printed in the anthology *Ammukaar* (curve of the bow) in 1942 during the German occupation. After the Soviet reoccupation of Estonia in 1944, he was arrested by the Soviet police and ultimately was sent to a camp on the Ob River. The actual date of his death is uncertain; in the official publications of Estonia, the year is variously given as 1945, 1946, or 1947.

BIBLIOGRAPHY: Matthews, W. K., "Phases of Estonian Poetry," in Matthews, W. K., ed., *Anthology of Modern Estonian Poetry* (1953): xv–xxix; Ivask, I., "H. T.: Day of Judgement," in Kõressaar, V., and Rannit, A., eds., *Estonian Poetry and Language: Studies in Honor of Ants Oras* (1965): 283–87; Rannit, A., "H. T., an Estonian Poet (1904–1947): From Decadent Dream to Martyrdom," in *Proceedings of the 39th International Congress of P.E.N. Clubs, Jerusalem* (1976): 55–64; Aspel, A., "Baudelaire and the Poetry of H. T.," in Leitch, V., ed., *The Poetry of Estonia: Essays in Comparative Analysis* (1983): 171–88

—ALEKSIS RANNIT

TALVIO, Maila

(pseud. of Maria Mikkola) Finnish novelist, b. 17 Oct. 1871, Hartola; d. 6 Jan. 1951, Helsinki

T. was born the seventh child of a village parson and spent her early childhood in a rural setting. After four years of high school in Helsinki, she graduated at sixteen and returned home to teach her siblings. A great need to express herself first inspired her to pursue a career in music, but lacking a good teacher, she turned to writing instead. Her first stories were published in the late 1890s, serialized in the newspaper *Päiväiehti,* among them her first novel, *Haapaniemen keinu* (1895; The Swing at Haapaniemi).

The latter part of the 19th c. and the early 1900s witnessed a rising nationalism in Finland, which was still a Grand Duchy under Russian rule. T. joined other Finnish artists and politicians in protest against increasing Russian suppression, making passionate speeches, joining demonstrations, and writing articles full of patriotic fervor. Starting out as a neoromantic, T. believed in the inherent goodness of common folk. She had personally witnessed their abuse at the hands of big landowners and even clergy. In her breakthrough novel, *Pimeänpirtin hävitys* (1901; The Destruction of Pimeäpirtti), the tensions between the Finnish-speaking tenant farmers and their Swedish-speaking landlords provide the background for an incest drama. Having first played up the plight of basically good people, T. soon became impatient with the laziness and drunkenness prevalent among the agrarian proletariat. Her next books portray characters whose vices bring them to a sorry end. *Niniven lapset* (1915; The Children of Niniveh) shows what happens when naive boys and girls leave the farm and seek easier employment and a good time in the "sinful" big city of Helsinki.

The turn of the century saw the rise of the labor movement in Finland. T. portrayed factory workers with sympathy but remained distrustful of socialism and communism. The Finnish Civil War of 1918 with its strikes, riots, and brutal killings provided the background for books T. published from 1918 to 1928, which are uncharacteristically pessimistic. T. suffered a bout of depression, but by 1929 her fundamental optimism had returned, and she entered a new phase in her writing. The preacher and moralist was replaced by an objective student of character, who described the foibles and triumphs of her fictional characters, often with a touch of humor.

T. had discovered that her true talent lay in writing historical novels, the material for which she found in the past generations of her own family. T.'s maternal ancestors came from Helsinki, and among them she found a 17th-c. burgher who became the main character of the first part of a trilogy depicting the life and times of the people of Helsinki. *Iltämeren tytär* (1929; Daughter of the Baltic) was followed by *Hed-Ulla ja hänen kosijansa* (1931; Hed-Ulla and Her Suitors) and *Hopealaiva* (1936; The Silver Ship). In 1940 they were republished as a three-volume work under the title of the first volume. *Linnoituksen iloiset rouvat* (1941; The Merry Wives of the Fortress) brought the story and some of the characters up to the war of 1808–09 and the surrender, by treason, of the mighty fortress of "Sveaborg" in Helsinki harbor.

In addition to novels, T. wrote nearly a dozen plays, generally failures on stage. Her passionate espousal of causes such as temperance, the fight against tuberculosis (a major killer at the time), the Finnish language, and patriotism in general moved her to write numerous articles on these topics, and she was a sought-after speaker. She founded a tuberculosis sanitarium and wrote a novel, *Ne 45000* (1932; Those 45,000), which dealt with the problem of tuberculosis. The home she shared with her husband, the linguist J. J. Mikkola, in the Meilahti suburb of Helsinki became the "Finnish cultural home" most likely visited by foreign cultural dignitaries. For years she conducted a literary "salon" in her home and held "open house" for students from her husband's home province studying in Helsinki.

When the city of Helsinki celebrated its 400th anniversary in 1950, T. was awarded an honorary doctorate by Helsinki University. Prior to that, she had received the State Literature Prize in 1936 and the Aleksis Kivi Literary Prize in 1940. T. was also a translator of foreign language literature into Finnish, and some of her own books have been translated, mostly into Swedish and German, earning her the Golden Wreath of the Polish Academy and the Heinrich Steffens Prize of Hamburg University

T.'s descriptions of the beautiful nature of Finland are almost unequaled, and she often used nature to express human emotions. Her place in Finnish literature has been earned primarily by her historical novels. The colorful spectacle of life, tragedy alternating with soaring happiness, give T.'s historical novels their spectacular appeal. Earlier Finnish historical novelists had been of the "great man of history" school, but T. saw crowds, large numbers of individuals, as the real movers of history. T.'s descriptions of the past are so realistic and so rich with detail that the reader is swept along by the torrent of events that make up the story. T. was nearly eighty when she died, and her literary production fills thirteen volumes. A speaker at her graveside called T. a "unique Phenomenon" in Finnish cultural history.

FURTHER WORKS: *Nähtyä ja tunnettua. Kertomuksia ja kuvauksia* (1896); *Aili. Kertomus* (1897); *Kaksi rakkautta* (1898); *Suomesta*

pois. *Kuvaus keväätä 1899* (1899); *Johan Ludvig Runeberg* (1900); *Kansan seassa* (1901); *Juha Joutsia* (1903); *Muuan diti. Kertomus* (1904); *Kauppaneuvoksen kuoltua* (1905); *Louhilinna. Tarina vanhasta talosta* (1906); *Eri teitä* (1908); *Puheita* (1908); *Anna Sarkoila* (1910); *Tähtien ala* (1910); *Kirjava keto* (1911); *Elinan häät* (1912); *Hämähäkki ja muita kertomuksia* (1912); *Kun meidän kaivosta vesi loppuu* (1913); *Talonhuijari* (1913); *Yölintu. Kuvauksia menneiltä ajoilta* (1913); *Huhtikuun-Manta* (1914); *Elämänleikki ynnä muita puheita maalaisille* (1915); *Lempiäniemen tyttäret* (1915); *Elämän kasvot* (1916); *Kultainen lyyra. Katkelmia naisyioppilaan elämästä* (1916); *Kootut teokset* (8 vols., 1917–26); *Silmä yössä* (1917); *Näkymätön kirjanpitäjä. Kertomuksia* (1918); *Kurjet* (1919); *Yötä jä aamua. Puheita vapautemme huomenhetkinä* (1919); *Valkea huvila* (1920); *Kihlasormus. Kertomus* (1921); *Kirkonkello* (1922); *Viimeinen laiva* (1922); *Opin sauna* (1923); *Sydämet. Kertomuksia* (1924); *Hiljentykäämme. Puheitaa kertoelmia* (Speeches, 1929); *Terveisiä* (1936); *Rukkaset ja kukkaset. Muistinäkyä* (1947); *Juhlavalkeat* (1948); *Lokakuun morsian. Kertomuksia* (1948); *Rakkauden riemut ja tuskat* (1949); *Kootut teokset* (13 vols., 1951); *Valitut teokset* (1953); *Linnoituksen iloiset rouvat & Yölintu* (1982)

BIBLIOGRAPHY: Ahokas, J., *A History of Finnish Literature* (1973): 171–74; Koskenniemi, V. A., Introduction to *Valitut Teokset* (1953): 5–15; Jäntti, Y., ed., *Suomen Sana. Kansalliskirjallisuutemme valioukemisto* (1966), Vol. 20: 546–61; *M. T. ja hänen teoksensa* (1933); Tuulio, T., "M. T.," in Pohjanpalo, S., et al., eds., *Suomalaisia vaikuttajanaisia* (1978): 87–97; Rintala, R., ed., *Suomalaisia kirjalijoita 1500-luvulta nykypäiviin* (1994)

—MARGARETA MARTIN

TAMIL LITERATURE

See Indian Literature, Malaysian Literature, Singapore Literature and Sri Lankan Literature

TĀMIR, Zakariyyā

Syrian short-story writer and journalist, b. 1931, Damascus

One of the most accomplished writers of short stories in the Arab world in recent decades, T. has devoted his career as a litterateur to this single genre. Apparently self-taught to a large extent, he has worked in television and journalism; among other posts within the government's cultural apparatus, he has served as editor of the prominent Syrian literary journal *Al-Ma'rifa*. The offer of a position in journalism at an Arab newspaper in London took him away from his homeland, and he now resides in Oxford.

A prolific writer of instinctual genius, T. produced a number of short stories of the highest quality beginning in the late 1950s. They are characterized by an extremely economical and clear style, one that often makes use of the techniques of the visual media in which he had worked, as, for example, in "Sayf" (1960; "Summer," in *Modern Arabic Short Stories*, 1974), in which he brings together a cluster of minor incidents that take place as a young man is endeavoring to seduce a young woman during the heat of summer. While T.'s allegorical and allusive style has enabled him to produce some of the most notable additions to the corpus of modern Arabic short stories, this very same quality has also made him a successful writer of stories for children, as in the collection *Li-mādhā saqat al-nahr* (1973; why did the river fall), which contains many examples of allegorical fables.

It is clearly a reflection of T.'s impoverished upbringing and the kind of society in which he and many of his fellow authors have had to write for many years that allegory and symbol are used in his fictions to create nightmarish worlds full of alienated, oppressed people and oppressors of singular callousness. In stories of disconcerting terseness T. manages to capture the tragedy of human failure, demolishing the world of reality as he fashions scenarios where spite and injustice are the governing principles and the logic of normal life is absent. Any number of stories could be cited as reflections of these facets of his style. The effects of political oppression on the individual are seen in a story such as "Mulakhkhas ma jarā li-Muhammad al-Mahmūdī" (1978; pub. in English as "A Summary of What Happened to Mohammed al-Mahmoudi," in *Tigers on the Tenth Day and Other Stories*, 1985, and as "What Happened to Muhammad al-Mahmūdī," in *JArabL*, 13, 1982). "Al-A'dā" (1978; "The Enemies," 1981) shows some of the consequences of such societal priorities, constituting a wholesale condemnation of the Arab nation in the wake of the June 1967 defeat couched within a sequence of numbered sections that make use of the most withering sarcasm.

Another subject to which T. has often turned his attention is the sexual morality that is forced upon both men and women in Middle Eastern society and the resulting psychological tensions. This is seen at its most powerful in "Wajh alqamar" (1973; pub. in English as "The Face of the Moon," in *JArabL*, 3, 1972, as "The Moon Unmasked," in *JArabL*, 16, 1985, and as "The Face of the Moon," in *Tigers on the Tenth Day and Other Stories*, 1986), a story that is remarkable both for its creative use of symbols and for examples of that imagery for which T.'s writing is justifiably famous, as, for example, when the eyes of a madman in the street seem to Samīha, a young woman whose emerging sexuality is the subject of the story, like "two sick tigers drowsing on the grass of some thick jungle."

Since leaving Syria T. has devoted himself to journalism, something that has deprived readers of Arabic short fiction of one of its most excellent practitioners. Fortunately, he has left a large collection of short stories of considerable variety and quality to serve as a basis on which future generations may build. For, while the short story may be the most popular literary genre in the Arab world today, the number of those who may be counted as its masters, as T. undoubtedly is, are relatively few.

FURTHER WORKS: *Sahī al-Jawaād al-Abyad* (1960); *Rabi' fī al-ramād* (1963); *Al-Ra'd* (1970); *Li-mādhā saqat al-nahr* (1973); *Dimashq al-harā'iq* (1975?); *Nidā' Nūh* (1994)

BIBLIOGRAPHY: Allen, R., ed., *Modern Arabic Literature* (1987): 313–17; al-Khateeb, H., "A Modern Syrian Short Story: 'Wajh alqamar,'" *JArabL*, 3 (1972): 96–105; Baldissera, E., "La formation du récit moderne en Syrie," *Quaderni di studi arabi*: 5–6 (1987–88): 83–90

—ROGER ALLEN

TAMMSAARE, A. H.

(pseud. of Anton Hansen) Estonian novelist, short-story writer, dramatist, translator, essayist, and critic; b. 30 Jan. 1878, Albu; d. 1 March 1940, Tallinn

T. was one of many children of a farmer. After graduating from high school in 1903, he first worked as a journalist, then from 1907 to 1911 studied law at the University of Tartu, but he did not complete his final examinations because he fell ill with tuberculosis. He recovered and became a full-time writer in Tallinn from 1919 until a fatal heart attack in 1940.

T. began publishing in 1900, and his early works are characterized by rural "poetic" realism; his best short story of this period is the partly naturalistic "Vanad ja noored" (1903; the old and the young). During his second, impressionistic period, lasting from 1908 to 1919, he wrote several short urban novels and a collection of miniatures, *Poiss ja liblik* (1915; *The Boy and the Butterfly*, 1977), influenced by Oscar Wilde, in which T. stressed the values of art over life.

In his search for truth and righteousness T. was a passionate observer, vehemently anticlerical, insisting on and practicing incorruptible morals. His works of the 1920s, during which he achieved wide recognition, explore his moral concerns. The powerful tragic drama *Juudit* (1921; Judith), in which the heroine kills Holofernes for egoistic motives, was followed by the short novel *Kõrboja peremees* (1922; master of Kõrboja), an example of psychological realism and neoromanticism, a story of unsuccessful love and suicide that nevertheless ends with life going on. T.'s magnum opus and the most epic of Estonian novels, *Tõde ja õigus* (5 vols., 1926–33; truth and righteousness), which is partly autobiographical, deals with crucial phases of urbanization in Estonia. According to T. himself, the first volume depicts man's struggle with the earth, the second with God, the third with society, and the fourth with himself; the fifth volume is marked by resignation. In the first three volumes, romanticism and realism convincingly blend into a unified style, but in the fourth and fifth the epic, which consistently prefers the individual to the typical, suffers from long, garrulous philosophizing, unfunctional detail, and verbosity that weaken the style and structure. *Tõde ja õigus* typifies T.'s thought throughout his life: a humanist idealism and a plenitude of lively aphorism notwithstanding, T. was skeptical and pessimistic, and in general saw things as a natural scientist would, his approach being biological rather than psychological.

T.'s works of the 1930s include two shorter neorealistic novels analyzing love and marriage, *Elu ja armastus* (1934; life and love) and *Ma armastasin sakslast* (1935; I loved a German), and a satiric play, *Kuningal on külm* (1936; the king is cold), dealing with democracy and dictatorship. His last and most artistic work was the surreal, psychosocial novel *Põrgupõhja uus vanapagan* (1939; *The Misadventures of the New Satan*, 1978), a brilliant indictment of selfishness and demagogy in society.

A prolific translator, T. ably rendered into Estonian the works of Joseph CONRAD, John GALSWORTHY, George Bernard SHAW, Dostoevsky, Ivan Goncharov (1812–1891), Oscar Wilde, and T. E. Lawrence (1888–1935). Of these, Dostoevsky, Wilde, and Shaw, as well as Gogol and Knut HAMSUN influenced his own work.

FURTHER WORKS: *Kaks paari ja üksainus* (1902); *Uurimisel* (1907); *Raha-auk* (1907); *Pikad sammud* (1908); *Noored hinged* (1909); *Üle piiri* (1910); *Kärbes* (1917); *Varjundid* (1917); *Põialpoiss* (1923); *Meie rebane* (1932)

BIBLIOGRAPHY: Judas, E., *Russian Influences on Estonian Literature* (1941): 89–138; Jänes, H., *Geschichte der estnischen Literatur* (1965): 136–45; Nirk, E., *Estonian Literature* (1970): 208–18; Siirak, E., *A. H. T. in Estonian Literature* (1978)

—ALO RAUN

TAMMUZ, Benjamin

Israeli novelist, short-story writer, and art critic, b. 10 July 1919, Karkov, Ukraine; d. 20 July 1989, Tel Aviv

T. reached Palestine in 1924, growing up in Tel Aviv. He was active in the "Canaanite" movement as a young man, and then studied art at the Sorbonne in Paris. He was always active in journalism, at an early stage editing the youth journal *Haaretz shelanu* and, from 1965, serving as literary editor of *Haaretz*.

His first literary genre was the short story, and his first collection, *Holot hazahav* (1950; golden sands), attracted considerable attention and critical acclaim. In these stories, the central figure is usually a boy, growing up with his immigrant parents in the emergent yishuv (Jewish entity in Palestine), seeing himself as doubly alienated, from his family on the one hand, and from the crass environment of his peers on the other. Such themes preoccupied the author in other guises in later works. His trilogy, *Hayey elyakum* (1963; life of Elyakum), *Bsof maarav* (1966; *Castle in Spain*, 1973), and *Sefer hahazayot* (1969; the book of hallucinations), pursues an individual trying to establish his own identity, often by removing himself from his own natural environment. In the third volume of the trilogy, the narrator returns narcissistically to his primary subject, himself. T. is the archetypal creator of a characteristic figure of the Israeli fiction of the 1960s, the antihero.

In the 1970s, T. sought new subjects and new ways of treating them. First, he wrote a long autobiography in fictional form, *Yaakov* (1971; Jacob). The author adopts as his hero one Jacob, but this name and the circumstances of his life act as a thinly veiled disguise for the author's own, from his birth, through his childhood emigration, his youth, and his maturity. One of T.'s fictional preoccupations is the question of national identity, of his own people and the status of Israel. Just as Jacob serves as the hero of the novel by that name so *Hapardes* (1972; *The Orchard*, 1984) is written in the manner of a parable concerning the ownership of an orchard. T. was much occupied in his writing with relations between Jew and Arab, which can be seen as rivalry between siblings over the birthright. *Hapardes* is open-ended, concluding with a tentatively expressed Messianic hope for a "solution."

The final phase of T.'s writing, in the 1980s, is more abstract. *Minotaur* (1980; *Minotaur*, 1981), perhaps his most achieved novel, is about a secret agent, and has the shape of a detective story. Typically, the female figure in the novel, his beloved Thea, is the idealized woman, adored but distanced by the Minotaur, the secretive hero. He loves her, but they must never meet. T.'s final work, *Haziqit vehazamir* (1989; the chameleon and the nightingale), is not only a puzzling amalgam of tales, but also presents a view of Jewish history through two types or approaches. One is the chameleon, who slots into his environment inconspicuously, and the other is the nightingale, who adds color to life. For all the suggestive allegorization of this story, it is the strong narrative line that gives the text its thrust and forces the reader to read on. As with so many of T.'s works, the practice can override a rather unsatisfactory theory.

FURTHER WORKS: *Mishley baqbuqim* (1975; *A Rare Cure*, 1981); *Reqviem Inaaman* (1978; *Requiem for Naaman*, 1982); *Pundaqo shel yirmiyahu* (1984)

BIBLIOGRAPHY: Yudkin, L. I., *Escape into Siege: A Survey of Israeli Literature Today* (1974): 91–92: 174–6; Yudkin, L. I., *1948 and After: Aspects of Israeli Fiction* (1984): 153–54: 159–60; Chertok, H., "The Number Two Canaanite in the World; a Conversation with B. T.," *Jewish Frontier*, 53, 3 (April-May 1986): 9–12

—LEON I. YUDKIN

TANEDA Santōka

(pseud. of Taneda Shōichi) Japanese poet, b. 3 Dec. 1882, Hōfu; d. 11 Oct. 1940, Matsuyama

Son of a well-to-do landowner in western Japan, T. became interested early in traditional haiku poetry, with its five-seven-five-syllable pattern. In 1902 he was admitted to Waseda University in Tokyo to study literature, but he dropped out of school after a year because of a serious drinking problem, which was to plague him throughout his life.

In 1911 T. came under the influence of Seisensui Ogiwara (1884–1976), the leader of the New Tendency School of haiku, which discarded the traditional seasonal imagery and the fixed syllabic pattern for a freer verse form. While T. contributed sporadically to Seisensui's poetry journal *Sōun*, he drifted from job to job and in 1924 tried to commit suicide, an action that led to his taking vows as a Zen priest the following year. Thereafter known in Japan by his Buddhist priest's name Santōka, he spent the remaining fifteen years of his life wandering through Japan, writing free-verse haiku about his experiences.

T.'s literary reputation derives from this final quarter of his life, when he walked thousands of miles as a mendicant priest and wrote thousands of poems, sometimes only two or three words long and few longer than ten words, describing the natural scenes he encountered and how he related to them. In 1930 he began publishing a poetry journal, *Sambaku*, named after a boarding house in Kumamoto City, and in 1932, with the financial backing of other poets, he published his first book of poems, *Hachi no ko* (the begging bowl).

T. evinces in his poetry the deeply ingrained Japanese tradition of seeking in nature a release from anxieties caused by society and an entry into spiritual enlightenment. Like the great 12th-c. priest-poet Saigyō and the early 19th-c. Zen master Ryōkan, T. sees nature both as a place of serenity and as an arena in which to do battle with his inner conflicts. In some of his poems T. exorcises the demons within himself by surrendering to the inevitable cycles of the natural world.

While they follow a much–trodden literary path, T.'s poems are free from the literary allusions and multilayered images that can make traditional Japanese poetry so abstruse. Although T. in 1936 did retrace the route taken by the famous haiku poet Bashō (1644–1694) in *Narrow Road to the Deep North*, his poetry remains firmly fixed in the 20th c. Like walking and drinking sake, T. said, writing haiku was a cathartic experience through which he transcended his personal flaws in search of more permanent truths. He dreamed of taking the artifice out of art, of making his poems sing "like the floating clouds, like the flow of water, like a small bird, like the dancing leaves."

Unknown outside of a small circle during his lifetime, T. has gained a wide following in the past twenty years. Readers admire both his use of nature as the principal image and his probings of the tensions of modern man. T. was both possibly the last in a thousand-year-old tradition of roving priest-poets and a pioneer in the use of unadorned, profoundly simple free-verse haiku.

FURTHER WORKS: *Sōmokutō* (1933); *Sangyō suigyō* (1935); *Zassō fūkei* (1936); *Kaki no ha* (1938); *Kōkan* (1940); *Karasu* (1940). FURTHER WORKS IN ENGLISH: *Mountain Tasting: Zen Haiku by S. T.* (1980)

BIBLIOGRAPHY: Blyth, R. H., *A History of Haiku* (1964), Vol. 2: 173-88; Abrams, J., "Hail in the Begging Bowl: The Odyssey and Poetry of Santōka," *MN*, 3 (1977): 269–302; Stevens, J., Introduction to *Mountain Tasting: Zen Haiku by S. T.* (1980): 9–29

—JAMES ABRAMS

TANIZAKI Jun'ichirō

Japanese novelist, short-story writer, essayist, and dramatist, b. 24 July 1886, Tokyo; d. 30 July 1965, Yūgawara

Eldest surviving son of a declining merchant family in Tokyo, T. was in his formative years while Japan was emerging as a world power. Owing to his father's business failure and the family's precarious economic situation, he received schooling only through the charity of friends and relatives and the encouragement of teachers who recognized his talent. Having previously studied law and English, he entered Tokyo University's Department of National Literature in 1908 with the intention of becoming a writer. This was "the most convenient way of slacking off my school work," he later wrote. In 1910 he was expelled from the university for failure to pay tuition. Following the great earthquake of 1923, in a move symbolic of a return in spirit to traditional Japan, T. rejected his native city of Tokyo and retreated to the quieter, old-fashioned world of the Kansai area, around Kyoto and Osaka, where some of his most characteristic works were written. After World War II, once again living near Tokyo, T. had a final outburst of creativity.

Although most important for his fiction, T. early in his career also wrote many plays—particularly between 1911 and 1924—and in 1920 he became a consultant for a budding motion picture company, for which he wrote scenarios.

In 1910 T. published the best known of his early stories, "Shisei" ("The Tattoo," 1914), a tale that reveals in embryonic form his central theme, which he was to develop for more than half a century: beauty is feminine, beauty is strength. During the years that immediately followed, he devoted himself to writing and found his literary identity. "Who was it," he wrote in "Itansha no kanashimi" (1917; the sorrows of a heretic), an autobiographical story, "that created in me the strange propensity to be more deeply concerned not about what is good but rather what is beautiful?"

The tale "Manji" (1928; whirlpool) portrays a femme fatale, a beautiful young art student who is the model for a drawing of a Buddhist saint. Her actual character, however, is perverse, deceptive, and destructive, as she seduces both a mild-mannered lawyer and his aggressive wife. The Osaka setting, rich with the flavor of old Japan, and the feminine Osaka dialect help to evoke the languorous charm of traditional culture, which is juxtaposed to a bizarre confession. In several ways "Manji" foreshadowed the novel *Tade kuu mushi* (serial pub. 1928–29; *Some Prefer Nettles*, 1955), which is about a hopeless marriage and a conflict between the old and new ways of life, also set in the Kansai area. Both works deal with contrasting concepts of the idealized woman, on the one hand, and the everyday woman of reality, on the other.

Representative of the most polished and skillful of the tales that T. wrote is the novella *Shunkinshō* (1933; *The Story of Shunkin*, 1936; later tr., *A Portrait of Shunkin*, 1963), which tells of how a devoted servant blinds himself in order to perfect his art and remain always with his believed mistress, who is a blind musician. The tale is a psychological study of how devotion may curdle into a neurotic fixation. T.'s long essay *In'ei raisan* (serial pub. 1933–34; *In Praise of Shadows*, 1977), which celebrates his rejection of Tokyo and his retreat to the more traditional world of Kyoto and Osaka, expresses his view that classical Japanese art flourished in the shade and that the dazzle of the modern world destroys it. Therefore one must dim the lights.

At the peak of his creative powers, T. published serially (1939–41) a modern version of the 11th-c. classic *The Tale of Genji*, the greatest work in Japanese literature.

Sasame Yuki (3 vols., 1946–48; *The Makioka Sisters*, 1958), an elegy to a vanished era and his longest novel, stands out not only among T.'s works but also from the whole corpus of 20th c. Japanese literature. He had actually begun to publish it serially in 1943, but it was suppressed at the time by the military authorities. Within an old but declining merchant family, which clings to the belief that suitably arranged matches preserve one's heritage and social position, two unmarried sisters, the younger of four, display conflicting styles of life. The older of the pair, Yukiko (literally, "Snow-Child," the heroine denoted in the Japanese title), emerges as a quiet, traditional woman. The younger, Taeko, scandalously impulsive and modern, indulges in various escapades and adventures. It is as if T.'s prototypical woman has split into two; she who is outwardly strong and she who is outwardly feminine. Yet, ironically, the willful Taeko dies and the apparently placid Yukiko survives.

Kagi (1956; *The Key*, 1961) is a study of adultery and middle-aged depravity set in Kyoto. In this novel, a complex web of reality and fantasy, the parallel diaries of a husband and wife, largely about their sexual experiences, convey surprising narrative rhythms and a distinctive tone. One of T.'s last novels, *Fūten rōjin nikki* (1962; *The Diary of a Mad Old Man*, 1965), presents the satirical portrait of an ill but unruly patriarch, revealing a childish and obdurate sensibility long attuned to art, to the nuances of sexuality, and to the imminence of death.

Nothing that occurred in the world around T. deterred him from his quest for the "eternal woman" of traditional Japan, whom he deified. Concurrently, he wrote with fondness of the past and of the losses suffered in the course of modernization. Translating the conflict between old and new from the world of thought into the realm of feeling, he reduced it to sexual terms. A prolific writer and painstaking craftsman, he desired to entertain, enlighten, and shock his audience. The alarming implications of his art and his skill in revealing disturbing truths to the reading public evoked wide attention. T. explored human life with daring, sensitivity, and psychological acumen. His writing appeals readily to Western readers, and he deserves to be remembered as one of the preeminent writers of the 20th c.

FURTHER WORKS: *Shisei* (1911); *Akuma* (1913); *O'Tsuya-goroshi* (1915; *A Springtime Case*, 1927); *Itansha no kanashimi* (1917); *Haha o kōru ki* (1919); *Kyōfu jidai* (1920); *Mumyō to Aizen* (1924); *Chijin no ai* (1924–1925); *Jōzetsuroku* (1930); *Yoshino kuzu* (1931; *Arrowroot*, 1982); *Mōmoku monogatari* (1932; *A Blind Man's Tale*, 1963); *Ashikari* (1932; *Ashikari*, 1936); *Seishun monogatari* (1933); *Bushū-kō hiwa* (1935; *The Secret History of the Lord Musashi*, 1982); *Neko to Shōzō to futari no onna* (1937); *Yōshō-jidai* (1957); *Yume no ukihashi* (1960; *The Floating Bridge of Dreams*, 1963); *Mitsu no baai* (1961); *Daidokoro taiheiki* (1963); *Nihon no bungaku: T. J.* (1964); *T. J. zenshū* (28 vols., 1966–70). FURTHER WORKS IN ENGLISH: *Seven Japanese Tales by J. T.* (1963)

BIBLIOGRAPHY: Olson, L., "*The Makioka Sisters*," *American Universities Field Staff: East Asia*, 9, 5 (1964): 533–41; Chambers, A., "T. J.'s Historical Fiction," *JATJ*: 8 (1972): 34–44; Fernandez, J., "A Study of T.'s *The Key*," and Tsukimura, R., "The Sense of Loss in *The Makioka Sisters*," in K. Tsuruta and T. E. Swann, eds., *Approaches to the Modern Japanese Novel* (1976): 215–40; Gangloff, E. J., "T.'s Use of Traditional Literature," *JATJ*, 11 (1976): 217–34; Ueda, M., *Modern Japanese Writers and the Nature of Literature* (1976): 54–84; Rimer, J. T., *Modern Japanese Fiction and Its Traditions* (1978): 22–37; Petersen, G. B., *The Moon in the Water: Understanding T., Kawabata, and Mishima* (1979): 44–120; Lippit, N. M., *Reality and Fiction in Modern Japanese Literature* (1980): 55–69, 82–103; Chambers, A. H., "A Study of T.'s *Yoshino kuzu*," *HJAS*, 41 (1981): 483–505; Merken, K., "T. J.:'Tattoo,' 'The Tale of Shunkin,' 'The Bridge of Dreams,'" in T. E. Swann and K. Tsuruta, eds., *Approaches to the Modern Japanese Short Story* (1982): 319–38

—LEON M. ZOLBROD

TANSI, Sony Labou

(pseud. of Marcel Ntsoni) Congolese novelist, poet, and dramatist (writing in French), b. 5 July 1947, Kimwanza, Belgian Congo (now Democratic Republic of Congo); d. 14 June 1995, Foufoudou

Born in Kimwanza, T. was the oldest of seven children. At twelve he came to Brazzaville, living in Congo all the rest of his life except for 1993 when, during Congo's civil war, he lived in France. He attended college at Boko, and in 1971 was appointed to teach French and English at Kindauba. In 1971 he began seriously to write and produce plays but quickly fell under criticism of Congo's *Parti Congolais du Travail* for producing work that wasn't sufficiently communist. He continued to write and direct, however, and in 1980 cofounded the *Rocado Zulu Théâtre* in Brazzaville. T. was one of the founders of M.C.D.D.I., a group opposed to Congo's single political party system. In 1995 T. died of AIDs-related illness.

T. is perhaps best known as a novelist. He had a stylistic exuberance and originality that caught the attention of critics, who saw connections of his work to François Rabelais, Gabriel GARCÍA

MÁRQUEZ, and Alfred JARRY. His best novels, such as *La vie et demie* (1979; Life and a Half), *Les septs solitudes de Lorsa Lopez* (1985; *The Seven Solitudes of Lorsa Lopez,* 1995), and *Les yeux du volcan* (1988; The Eyes of the Volcano), employ a carnivalesque and maximalist style, using a rollicking syntax and cramming sentences full of details, rapidly switching perspective and point of view.

Throughout his work, T. exhibits a fascination with the corruptions of power and with the possibilities of resistance. T.'s first novel, *La vie et demie*, takes place in an imagined African dictatorship governed by a self-acclaimed "providential guide." The guide has no qualms about having his chief opposition killed, but though killed and even reduced to a paste the opposition leader continues to speak and to torment the guide. Part science fiction, part vicious burlesque, the novel is nonetheless a powerful book about the persistence of resistance in the face of extreme politics. Similarly, *L'etat honteux* (1981; The Shameful State) charts the reign of a megalomaniac president, providing a critique of politics after African independence.

Two other books broaden these concerns, moving away from a focus on governmental heads and into a wider consideration of the individual's relation to power. *Les septs solitudes de Lorsa Lopez* concerns the murder of a woman by her husband and all its contingent repercussions, worked out through elaborate political machinations, prophecies, and the struggle between two different local peoples. In *Les yeux du volcan* a mysterious colossus arrives to throw the town of Hozanna into chaos, eventually unveiling himself as the forerunner of a revolution.

L'antepeuple (1983; *The Antipeople*, 1988) and *Commencement des douleurs* (1995; The Beginning of Sorrow) examine lives ruined by passion. In the first a director of a girl's school is accused in a suicide note of having made a girl pregnant. As a result he is jailed and loses his family. The second concerns an old sage thrown into jail for years for having given a young girl too long of a kiss. Despite T.'s political approach masking a sometimes derogatory treatment of female characters, these are powerful novels, *L'antepeuple* receiving the prestigious Grand Prize of Afrique Noire.

T.'s drama has found similar acclaim, and he has received the Ibsen Prize and the Francophonie Prize. Valérie Layraud sees his theater as falling into two chronological groupings: his earlier plays create a revolutionary theater that denounces neocolonialism; his later plays, however, tend to be SYMBOLIST, dealing with larger themes such as life and death, love and revolt, sometimes at the expense of national critique. In the first group is *La paranthèse de sang* (1978; *Parenthesis of Blood*, 1986), about a troop of comic but brutal soldiers sent to kill a famed rebel leader who is already dead. From the second is *Qui a mangé Madame d'Avoine Bergotha* (1989; Who Ate Madame d'Avoine Bergotha?), about a self-acclaimed dictator who kicks all males except for himself and his officially designated inseminators out of the country. T.'s poetry is less well known, though it has been praised by such poets as Édouard Maunick (b. 1931).

His reputation as the strongest and most incendiary Congolese novelist has grown even stronger since his death. Always political, T.'s literary work is stylistically as well as politically nonconformist, blending satire of African politics with a warped vision of the world.

FURTHER WORKS: *Conscience de tracteur* (1979); *S. L. T.: un citoyen de ce siecle* (1986); *Poèmes et vents lisses* (1995); *Théâtre* (1995); *L'autre monde: écrits inédits* (1997)

BIBLIOGRAPHY: Osazuwa, S., *La fonction critique de l'œuvre romanesque de S. L. T.* (1991); Cakabakulu, M., *Introduction á l'œuvre de S. L. T.* (1995); Devésa, J.-M., *S. L. T.: Ecrivain de la honte et des rives magiques du Kongo* (1996); Mbanga, A., *Les procédés de création dans l'œuvre de S. L. T.* (1996); Updike, J., "The Works of S. L. T.," *New Yorker*, 5 February 1996: 70

—BRIAN EVENSON

TANZANIAN LITERATURE

Until recently scholars erroneously regarded Tanzania—a nation born in 1964 of the union of Zanzibar and other islands with mainland Tanganyika, which had won independence from Great Britain in 1961—as the driest patch in a supposed East African literary desert.

Tanzania's "socialist" path, outlined by President Julius Nyerere in the Arusha Declaration of 1967, has drawn the world's attention to all spheres of Tanzania's life as a social laboratory. Its literature, and a body of scholarship that nurtures it, are conscious parts of the Tanzanian experiment. Since the Arusha Declaration the country has been developing a distinct national literature out of three preindependence currents: (1) traditional Swahili literature; (2) writing in the English language; (3) the oral literatures of over 120 linguistically distinct ethnic groups.

In Swahili

Swahili did not obtain the designation of the Tanzanian national language until 1966, yet the oldest continuous tradition of written literature in Africa is the Swahili epic poetry of the East African coast, dating back several hundred years. Extant pre-19th-c. examples deal mainly with Islamic religious themes in an esoteric language. Recent scholarship, much of it coming from the Institute of Kiswahili Research at the University of Dar es Salaam, has begun to demolish earlier assertions generated by European scholars, and is now showing that most likely Swahili literature has not all derived from and imitated Arabic culture. Its African basis is now being established and explored.

Among the writing that prepared the way for the emerging Tanzanian national literature in the Swahili language are a number of *tenzis* (roughly, "epics") chronicling resistance struggles against foreign occupiers. Around 1905 Hemed Abdallah (dates n.a.) wrote *Vita vya Wadachi kutamalaki mrima* (war between the Germans and the coastal people), describing the Abushiri war from a united African-Arab point of view. The Maji Maji war of resistance against German colonialism, led by Kinjeketile Ngwale from 1905 to 1907, was told from the vantage point of the valiant oppressed and from a national, nonethnic perspective in *Vita vya Maji Maji* (written c. 1912; the Maji Maji war) by Abdul Karim (dates n.a.).

Following suppression of the Maji Maji uprising, nationalist sentiment disappeared from poetry, and a vacuum of apathy was filled with religious and escapist verse until the rise of the nationalist movement in the late 1940s. This new flowering saw the emergence of East Africa's "Shakespeare," Shaaban ROBERT. In 1934 he began writing Swahili verse in a conservative vein, but he soon adopted progressive nationalist themes.

In the epic tradition, other harbingers of a national poetry were Amri Abedi (dates n.a.), Saadan Kandoro (dates n.a.), and Akilimali (dates n.a.). A great boost was given to this cultural awakening in 1954 with the publication of Amri Abedi's *Sheria za kutunga mashairi na diwani ya Amri* (Amri's rules and advice for composing poetry), which for the first time put the rules of Swahili versification into print.

In the postindependence period the *tenzi* survives in Tanzania as a living, now national, tradition of commemoration. Recent examples are *Karume* (1966; Karume), a chronicle of the life and achievements of Karume, the leader of the Zanzibar revolution in 1964, by Z. H. Mohammed (dates n.a.); *Jamhuri ya Tanzania* (1968; the Republic of Tanzania) by R. Mwaruka (dates n.a.); and *Zinduko la ujamaa* (1972; the awakening of socialism) by Z. H. Lesso (dates n.a.).

Second in stature as a poet only to Shaaban Robert was Mathias E. Mnyampala (?–1969), who wrote an epic on the life of Christ, *Utenzi wa Injili* (c. 1960; epic of the Holy Gospel) and who revived another traditional form, the *ngonjera*, a kind of poetic debate. Answering President Nyerere's 1968 call for poets and writers to become propaganda mouthpieces for the Arusha Declaration's principles of "socialism," Mnyampala produced two volumes of *ngonjera* in the last year of his life.

While Mnyampala's example was lauded and his verse was of very high quality, it was composed in a style too arcane to catch on with a mass audience. Nevertheless, the Arusha Declaration has spawned many volumes of popular poetry.

The founder of a major new trend in Swahili poetry, Euphrase Kezilahabi (b. 1945?), has broken not only with traditional themes but, more importantly, with traditional forms. His collection *Kichomi* (1974; heartburn) has inspired many other poets to abandon the ancient rigid conventions for composing Swahili verse and to explore the expressive capacities of free verse. The grip of the coastal tradition and its conventions broken, Swahili poetry in Tanzania is now a national poetry. Politics, and not religious moralizing, is the main theme. Unlike Swahili verse in other countries, in Tanzania it has become a force of social mobilization instead of maintaining the status quo. Poetry remains the most important literary genre. The "novels" of Shaaban Robert reflect this fact, for they are in conventional Swahili verse.

The first "modern" Swahili novel is James Mbotela's (dates n.a.) *Uhuru wa watumwa* (1934; freedom of the slaves). It praises the British for having "freed" African slaves from Arab chains. Having a very small audience until only very recently, Swahili prose literature in Tanzania before 1970 was primarily confined to simple stories of crime and passion.

The main focus of the more sophisticated contemporary Tanzanian Swahili prose writers is also social. Primary themes are wars of liberation, village versus city life, and the building of socialism. Among the better known novels are F. Nkwera's (dates n.a.) *Mzishi wa Baba Ana Radhi* (1967; Baba Ana Radhi's undertaker), a utopian view of village life that resembles the Guinean novelist Camara LAYE's seminal *The Dark Child*; J. M. Simbamwene's (dates n.a.) love-and-intrigue works *Mwisho wa mapenzi* (1971; the end of love) and *Kwa sababu ya pesa* (1972; because of money), the latter a condemnation of city life as the root of all evils; M. S. Abdulla's (dates n.a.) detective novels *Kisimi cha Giningi* (1968; Giningi's fountain [or, well]), *Siri ya sifuri* (1974; secret of zero), and *Duniani kuna watu* (1974; it takes all kinds), nonsocialist works in which the worthy propertied people are protected from the rabble by shrewd sleuths; E. A. Musiba's (dates n.a.) *Kufa na kupona* (1974; life and death), in which detective work supports the liberation of struggle; C. K. Omari's (dates n.a.) *Mwenda kwao* (1976; return of the prodigal), the chronicle of the breakdown of a marriage between a Tanzanian and his American wife; J. K. Kiimbila's (dates n.a.) *Ubeberu utashindwa* (1971; imperialism will be vanquished), set in Mozambique; N. Balisidya's (dates n.a.) *Shida* (1975; hardship), a female *Bildungsroman* on the town-versus-country theme; and F. E. M. K. Senkoro's (dates n.a.) *Mzalendo* (1977; the patriot), a novelistic demonstration that the victory of the masses is inevitable. Two recent works frequently pointed to as establishing a new trend in which oppression of Africans by Africans is defeated by class struggle are *Nyota ya Rehema* (1976; Rehema's star) by M. S. Mohamed (dates n.a.) and *Asali chungu* (1977; bitter honey) by S. A. Mohamed (dates n.a.).

Tanzania's major novelist is Euphrase Kezilahabi. His best-known work is *Rosa mistika* (1971; mystic rose), about a girl's odyssey from purity to whoredom to death and a dialogue with God. Stigmatized by some compatriot critics as an existentialist because of his pessimistic tendencies and his emphasis on anxiety, loneliness, and absurdity, Kezilahabi has responded by gradually increased militancy. Critics are now discovering the subtlety of even his early works, seeing that his present preoccupations with the theme of corruption in the ruling class and of its gulling of the people with pseudorevolutionary posturing were latent from the outset of his career in fiction.

Activity in drama has not been significant in Tanzania. Only one playwright, Ebrahim Hussein (dates n.a.), has had international exposure, largely due to a translation into English of his *Kinjeketile* (1969; *Kinjeketile*, 1970), a powerful dramatization of interethnic unity in the Maji Maji war. Tanzania's only other important dramatist is Penina Muhando (dates n.a.). Although unknown abroad, she has had greater domestic impact than Hussein because her concerns are closer to those of the masses. In her often controversial plays she has dealt with political themes and with the oppression of women.

As a way of disarming detractors of Swahili who said it could not be the vehicle of science and high culture, and who were opposed to its adoption as a national language, President Nyerere translated Shakespeare's *Merchant of Venice* and *Julius Caesar* into Swahili in the 1960s, thus assisting the meteoric rise of literature in Swahili to its stature as a national literature today, and cautiously asserting that some things in the former colonialist's culture might be of value in the formation of Tanzanian national culture.

In English

Tanzanian literature in English gives a distorted image of the country, but it too has taken on a distinct national flavor. It began with Martin Kayamba's (1891–1940) posthumously published *An African in Europe* (1948) and *African Problems* (1948), accounts of his travels to England beginning in 1931, and of his British-tutored notions of how to "civilize" Africa.

The brief period from independence in 1961 to the Arusha Declaration in 1967 saw English-language literary activity centered at the University of Dar es Salaam, with many works from this time being published in the literary magazine *Darlite* (1966–70). Most of this apprentice work stiffly aped British romantics. By 1970, soon after the Arusha Declaration, when *Umma* (masses) replaced *Darlite*, the rootless cosmopolitanism of "commonwealth" writing gave way to distinctly national, socially committed writing.

No major figures have yet emerged in English, and several who began in that language in *Darlite* and *Umma* have gone on to establish themselves in Swahili. It is only from novels in English, however, that a Western audience can gain any accurate insight into Tanzanian literature. Peter Palangyo's (dates n.a.) *Dying in the Sun* (1968) was first to appear; its main themes are generation conflict, alienation, and love. Gabriel Ruhumbika's (dates n.a.) *Village in Uhuru* (1969) focuses on difficulties in breaking tribal and regional identities in order to build a nation. Barnabas Katigula's (dates n.a.) *Groping in the Dark* (1974), an excellent novelette, grapples with individual problems understood as social problems from the nonrevolutionary, reformist point of view of *ujamaa* (socialism). Ismail Mbise's (dates n.a.) *Blood on Our Land* (1974) blends fiction with documentary more skillfully than Ruhumbika's novel. Although a gripping account of the events leading up to the expulsion of the Wameru people from their ancestral lands by the British in 1951, it fails in its attempt at allegorical evocation of the neocolonial situation of most of contemporary Africa, including Tanzania. W. E. Mkufya's (dates n.a.) *The Wicked Walk* (1977) is about the corruption of city-based bureaucrats in Dar es Salaam. It is the first fully urban Tanzanian novel in English, and in it an ideological convergence of the Tanzanian literatures in English and Swahili can definitely be seen.

Oral Traditions

Government policies have clearly given shape to trends that distinguish Tanzanian literature from those of its East African neighbors. Currently a tremendous amount of oral material from more than one hundred ethnic groups is being gathered under government sponsorship, and the results of this campaign will definitely further enrich the hybrid culture being forged.

Since about 1975 a serious group of critics based in Tanzania has been establishing a necessary, salutary, symbiotic relationship with the country's writers. The locally topical nature of the national literature is now being brought to maturity by aesthetic as well as ideological scrutiny, and soon translations will reveal to the world what a ripening, dynamic literature has developed in a very short time.

BIBLIOGRAPHY: Mulokozi, M., "Revolution and Reaction in Swahili Poetry," *Umma*, 4 (1974): 118–38; Knappert, J., *Four Centuries of Swahili Verse: A Literary History and Anthology* (1979): 264–310 and passim; Parker, C., "What Is Swahili Literature?: More Questions than Answers," *The Gar* 33 (1979): 28; Arnold, S. H., "Popular Literature in Tanzania: Its Background and Relation to 'East African' Literature," in C. Parker, et al., eds., *When the Drumbeat Changes* (1981): 88–118; Gérard, A. S., *African Language Literatures* (1981): 93–153; Senkoro, F. E. M. K., "Ngombe Akivundika Guu. . . : Preliminary Remarks on the Proverb-Story in Written Swahili Literature," in D. Dorsey, et al., eds., *Design and Intent in African Literature* (1982): 59–69; Arnold, S. H., "A History of Tanzanian Literature in English," in A. S. Gérard, ed., *History of African Literatures in European Languages* (1983): 1877–1902

—STEPHEN H. ARNOLD

TARDIEU, Jean

French dramatist and poet, b. 1 Nov. 1903, Saint-Germain-de-Joux; d. 27 Jan. 1995, Créteil

T., whose father was a painter and mother a musician, studied at the Lycée Condorcet and the Sorbonne in Paris. Although he began writing plays early, he abandoned the theater for a long time to turn his attention to poetry. During World War II he was active in the Resistance. After the liberation he joined the drama section of the French broadcasting organization, later heading its experimental dramatic workshop. He is a Chevalier of the Legion of Honor and received the Grand Prize in Poetry of the French Academy in 1972.

T. made his debut as a poet with *Le fleuve caché* (1933; the hidden river), but he first attracted wide notice with *Accents* (1939; accents), a collection of evanescent, suprarational poetry that also contained translations from the German poet Hölderlin (T. translated some works by Goethe as well). The lyrical verse of *Le témoin invisible* (1943; the invisible witness), *Figures* (1944; figures), *Poèmes* (1944; poems), *Le démon de l'irréalité* (1946; the demon of the unreal), *Les dieux étouffés* (1946; smothered gods), and *Jours pétrifiés 1942–1944* (2 vols., 1947–48; petrified days 1942–1944)—inspired by his activities in the Resistance—were marked by pulsing rhythms.

After the war T. began experimenting with language in both his poetry and plays. The influence of Raymond QUENEAU and Jacques PRÉVERT can be seen in his work, which frequently has a SURREALIST flavor. Some of his best plays are collected in the significantly titled *Théâtre de chambre, I* (1955; enlarged ed., 1966; chamber theater, I) and *Théâtre II: Poèmes à jouer* (1960; theater II: poems for acting): his plays for the most part are very short, almost sketches, meant for intimate theaters, and are as much poems as plays. They also resemble chamber music, with the human voice acting as a musical instrument. In his plays people find themselves at the mercy of forces beyond their control. The injection of the bizarre into ordinary occurrences, the satirical treatment of the theme of man trapped in situations stemming from his own social structures, the combination of pathetic or tragic implications with at times very funny action, and the experimental use of language have caused many critics to dub T. one of the founders of the THEATER OF THE ABSURD.

An outstanding play in *Théâtre de chambre, I, La serrure* (the keyhole) is a bold two-character vignette about a voyeur and a prostitute; as she strips, she sheds her flesh as well, revealing a skeleton, symbol of death. In *Le guichet* (1955; *The Enquiry Office*, 1968) death also plays a role: a man trying to get information about a train is instead given a horoscope, informing him he is scheduled to die.

T.'s best play is probably *Les amants du métro* (1952; *The Underground Lovers*, 1968), a bittersweet Romeo and Juliet dream play that takes place in the Paris subway. In it the word patterns are highly musical, as they are in *La sonate et les trois messieurs* (1955; *The Sonata and the Three Gentlemen*, 1968), whose structure is based on the sonata form and in which characters function as instruments, reciting the text in various prescribed tempos. Ultimately, T.'s concern is the enigma of language on stage and its relationship to pure feeling.

T. is also an experienced art and music critic. He has written studies on art theory and European painting: *De la peinture que l'on dit abstraite* (1960; about painting that is called abstract), *Hans Hartung* (1962; Hans Hartung), and *Hollande* (1963; Holland).

FURTHER WORKS: *La politesse inutile* (1946; *Courtesy Doesn't Pay*, 1968); *Qui est là?* (1947; *Who Goes There?*, 1968); *Il était une fois, deux fois, trois fois* (1947); *Un geste pour un autre* (1951; *One Way for Another*, 1964); *Un mot pour un autre* (1951); *Conversation-Sinfonietta* (1951; *Conversation-Sinfonietta*, 1968); *Monsieur, Monsieur* (1951); *Monsieur Oswald et Zénaïde; ou, Les apartés* (1951); *Ce que parler veut dire* (1951); *Faust et Yorick* (1951; *Faust and Yorick*, 1968); *La première personne du singulier* (1952); *Il y avait foule au manoir* (1952; *The Crowd Up at the Manor*, 1968); *Eux seuls le savent* (1952; *They Alone Know*, 1968); *Le meuble* (1954); *La Société Apollon; ou, Comment parler des arts* (1955; *The Apollo Society; or, How to Talk about the Arts*, 1968); *L'ombre du cavalier et Hiver* (1956, with A. Husson); *Les temps du verbe; ou, Le pouvoir de la parole* (1956); *L'espace et la flûte* (1958); *L'ABC de notre vie* (1959); *Rythme à trois temps* (1959); *Choix de poèmes* (1961); *Le fleuve caché: Poésies 1938–1961* (1968); *Les portes de toile* (1969); *Grandeurs et faiblesses de la radio* (1969); *La part de l'ombre, suivi de La première personne du singulier et Retour sans fin* (1972); *L'obscurité du jour* (1974); *Théâtre III* (1975); *Bazaine* (1975); *Formeries: Poèmes pour la main droite* (1976); *Infra-critique de l'œuvre du Prof. Froeppel* (1976). **FURTHER WORKS IN ENGLISH:** *The Underground Lovers, and Other Experimental Plays* (1968)

BIBLIOGRAPHY: Esslin, M., *The Theatre of the Absurd* (1961): 168–76; Pronko, L. C., *Avant-Garde: The Experimental Theater in France* (1962): 155–58; Noulet, E., *J. T.* (1964); Wellwarth, G. E., *The Theater of Protest and Paradox*, rev. ed. (1971): 97–110; Kinds, E., *J. T.; ou, L'énigme d'exister* (1973); Henning, S. D., "J. T. and the Structure of the Grotesque," *RomN*, 19 (1978): 146–51; Vernois, P., *Le dramaturgie poétique de J. T.* (1981)

—KENNETH S. WHITE

TATAR LITERATURE

Tatars of both the Volga basin and Crimea began to create a modern literature in the late 19th c., supplementing the omnipresent poetry with novels, plays, and other Western genres before 1900. By the end of World War I nationalist and pan-Turkic influences had become strong. Early in the century Tatar reformists argued with conservatives over cultural, social, and aesthetic values. According to local critics, the most effective of the reformist authors in the Volga region were Muhammad Ghayaz Is'haqi (1878–1954) and Ghalimjan Girfan-uli Ibrahimov (1887–1938); Ibrahimov later joined the Communist Party. Preeminent among young Tatar poets in the early part of the 20th c., Ghabdullah Tuqay (1886–1913), like Is'haqi and Ibrahimov, wrote for magazines and newspapers at the same time he was creating imaginative works. Tuqay's poetry—for example, "Shürälä" (1907; a wood goblin)—was in a new style but with occasional older verse forms, such as the *ghazal*. Tuqay became enormously popular outside Tatarstan, in part because of his many children's poems. Most of his poetry was gathered in *Shighirlär mäjmughasï* (1915; a collection of verse).

Among the prose works Is'haqi published before he emigrated in 1918 are a short novella about the fate of defenseless girls, *Käläpushche qïz* (1900; the skullcap girl), and a long novel, *Telänche qïzï* (3 vols., 1906–14; the beggar's daughter). He also wrote many plays, the earliest being *Ike ghishïq* (1903; two loves) and *Öch khatïn berlän tormïsh* (1908; life with three wives). Ibrahimov wrote a number of novels, including *Qazaq qïzï* (1909; a Kazakh girl), and *Bezneng könnär* (1913–14; our days). After the 1917 revolution he published much more fiction and nonfiction and also wrote some drama, but he was often subjected to sharp political criticism for "nationalist" views. Russian secret police arrested him in 1937, and he died the next year in a Kazan prison.

Ibrahimov's pointless death was one of the many cruelties that pervaded Soviet literary life until Stalin died in 1953. The stifling SOCIALIST REALISM of these decades was gradually superseded by attention to real Tatar history and life. Three writers were particularly important in nursing Tatar literature back to health. Fatikh Khösni (b. 1908) wrote short stories, plays, and a few major novels, such as *Utïzïnchï yïl* (1958; the year 1930). Ämirkhan Yeniki (b. 1909) has looked closely at family life and romantic love in novellas like *Yöräk sere* (1958; the heart's secret). His more controversial *Räshä* (1965; mirage) is a novel that expresses opposition to Stalinism. Ghömär Bäshir (b. 1901) is fairly widely read. His *Namus* (1948; *Honor*, 1951) is a Socialist Realist novel. A later work, *Tughan yaghïm—yäshel bishek* (1967; my native land is a green cradle), is an autobiographical novel well received by Tatars for treating in detail both their life before the revolution and the rigorous Sovietization and for scrutinizing the ideals of young people.

Poetry has kept its place in the hearts of the public. Äkhsän Bayanov (b. 1927), the satirist Salikh Battal (b. 1905), and the village writer Ghamil Afzal (b. 1921) typify those who have offered purposeful verse acceptable to official critics and ideologists; many others have written personal poetry. Räshit Gäräy (b. 1931) has written some elegant poems, as in the collection *Tughan yaq shigherläre* (1978; verses of the native land). In the most recent Tatar poetry styles and themes are mixed, with ideological poets occasionally offering personal verse and lyric poets expressing Tatar patriotism in the pages of the main literary magazine, *Qazan utlarï*.

Crimean Tatar writers, appreciably fewer than Volga Tatars in this century, were prominently represented by Omer Ipchi (?–c. 1937). He began writing before the revolution but gained attention later for his plays about ethnic problems, such as *Fahishä* (1925; the prostitute), about a Russian girl and a Karaim merchant, and *Azad khalq* (1927; a free people). Bekir Sidqi Chobanzade (1893–c. 1935) was a recognized scholar and poet whose small volume *Boran* (1928; the tempest) contains poems written abroad and at home between 1916 and 1926. Both writers perished during the purges of the 1930s. On May 18, 1944, Stalin exiled the entire Crimean Tatar people from its homeland to Central Asia for alleged treason. Literature began to revive several years before September 9, 1967, when Communist authorities officially exonerated the group. A few Crimean Tatar poets had by then issued, in Tashkent, small books of verse, such as *Sevem seni, omyur!* (1964; life, I love you!), by Riza Khalid (dates n.a.).

By 1979 the combined Tatar population of the former U.S.S.R. exceeded 6.3 million, promising a large and literate pool of readers and potential writers for the years ahead.

BIBLIOGRAPHY: Davletshin, T., *Cultural Life in the Tatar Autonomous Republic* (1953); Musabai, B., "Contemporary Tatar Literature," *ETR*, 1 (1958): 59–69; Battal-Tay-mas, A., "La littérature des Tatars de Kazan" and "La littérature des Tatars de Crimée," *Philogiae Turcicae Fundamenta*, 2 (1964): 762–78: 785–92; Burbiel,

G., "Tatar Literature," in G. Luckyj, ed., *Discordant Voices: The Non-Russian Soviet Literatures* (1975): 89–125

—EDWARD ALLWORTH

TATARKA, Dominik

Slovak novelist and essayist, b. 14 Mar. 1913, Drienové; d. 10 May 1989, Bratislava

T. was born into a middle-class family in west central Slovakia, and studied languages in Prague and at the Sorbonne. He briefly taught on the high school level, then became an editor of various papers and journals, and for a short time worked as a screenwriter. His first novels, though controversial, brought him the title "Worthy Artist" in the liberal days of 1969, but ten years later he was one of the few Slovak dissidents who signed Charter 77, and his last works brought charges of pornography as well as political condemnation and isolation. T.'s novels to a certain extent illustrate the range of Slovak fiction during and after World War II. His first book, *V úzkosti hľadania* (1942; In the Anxiety of Searching), collects youthful reminiscences and personal experiences with vestigial prewar naturism. His *Panna zázračnica* (1944–45; The Miraculous Virgin), a portrait of a free-spirit valorized by a group of students, hints at the SURREALISM then at its height in Slovak poetry. Along with the immediate postwar Communist influence and eventual takeover of Czechoslovakia in 1948, T. accepted the theory and techniques of SOCIALIST REALISM. His controversial novel *Farská Republika* (1948; The Parish Republic) not only satirized the wartime government of Slovakia dominated by Nazi Germany, but created a positive hero who turns to socialism. Even more schematic were T.'s "construction novels" *Prvú a druhú úder* (1950; First and Second Blow) and especially his *Radostník* (1954; Celebration Cake) and *Družné letá* (1954; Times of Comradeship). T.'s work turned dramatically after the death of Joseph Stalin and the Soviet admission of his crimes during the "cult of personality." In 1956 T. published *Démon súhlasu* (1987; The Demon of Conformism), a strikingly sharp satire of Stalinist society through the monologue and manifesto of a late collaborator in that society, who comes back to life after an airplane crash to warn his former colleagues and friends of their demonic possession by the devils of conformism with its hypocrisy, cynicism, lies, and cruelty.

Grotesque in its description of colleagues who burn with desire to mingle their brains into borrowed brains, the satire was highly praised morally as well as aesthetically. T.'s new recognition of Stalinism altered also the form of his next fiction, two novellas in *Rozhovory bez konca* (1959; Endless Conversations), which became reflective analyses of individual and family relations. This personalist emphasis returned T. to his youth as a student in Paris with a young woman in 1938, through lyrical evocation of the last year before the war, in *Prútené kreslá* (1963; Wicker Chairs). In this same spirit T. wrote the screenplay for the film of his earlier *Panna zázračnica*. The Soviet invasion of Czechoslovakia to stop the reform movement led by Alexander Dubček in 1968 found T. unready to "normalize" and reject the former liberalization, and he became one of the few Slovaks to sign the Charter 77 manifesto of civic and artistic freedoms. During his two decades of official silence, persecution, and isolation, T. was active unofficially as he published essays and miscellaneous pieces in the Czech dissident press and in the West. This time T.'s new content emerged in his most radical generic innovations. Not allowed to publish in the official press, T.—and sometimes his friends abroad—published his diary jottings and tape-recorded interviews and conversations under the general titles of *Pisačky* and *Nahrávačky* respectively before their collected publication in three volumes: *Pisačky* (1984; Jottings), *Sám proti noci* (1984; Alone against the Night), and *Listy do večnosti* (1984; Letters to Eternity). Autobiographical, utterly unrestrained in language and content, polythematic, symbolic, playfully inventive, rhapsodic, sensual, naturalistically erotic, repetitive and loquacious, these works have been called lyrically transcendent by some critics and pornographic by others. The prominence given to a series of mistresses, remembered and new, and also given to T.'s beloved mother and his sisters, has suggested that woman is his closest personification of nature. Alternatively, T. is said to have called his work a revelation of the ultimate human betrayal through lovers sent to him by the secret police, and of the power of eros to overcome the degradation of such betrayal.

FURTHER WORKS: *Človek na cestách* (1957); *Naša brigáda* (1962); *Proti démonom* (1968); *Vybrané spisy*, Vol. 1 (1971)

BIBLIOGRAPHY: Šutovec, M., "Démon sa vracia," *SlovP*, 80 (1964): 5, 122-28; Mlynárik, J., Afterword to *Listy do večnosti* (1984): 155-59; Petro, P., "*Pisačky*ako literatúra vypovedania," *Proměny*, 3 (1985): 84-88; special T. section, *Proměny*, 5 (1989): 3-30; Petro, P., "The Audacity of T.," in Pynsent, R. B., ed., *Modern Slovak Prose* (1990): 50-58; Petro, P., *History of Slovak Literature* (1995): 145-46

—NORMA LEIGH RUDINSKY

TATE, Allen

American poet, essayist, critic, novelist, and biographer, b. 19 Nov. 1899, Winchester, Ky.; d. 9 Feb. 1979, Nashville, Tenn.

Born into a family that took pride in its Virginia and Maryland background, T. was from his youth aware of the problems that faced the American South. In 1921, during his undergraduate days at Vanderbilt University in Nashville, Tennessee, he became associated with a brilliant group of young writers who contributed to *The Fugitive*, a "little magazine" whose name has come to stand for an important literary movement. Active in the circle was John Crowe RANSOM, T.'s professor of English, who, along with Donald Davidson (1893–1968), Robert Penn WARREN, and other "Fugitives," became his lifelong friend. In 1930, with other members of this group, T. contributed "Remarks on the Southern Religion," later republished as "Religion and the Old South," to a collection of essays entitled *I'll Take My Stand: The South and the Agrarian Tradition*, which brought the Southern Agrarian movement to the attention of the American literary public. The writers urged the South to resist the expansion of northern industrialism and its resultant way of life, which in their view threatened to cheapen manners and family life, narrow human sympathies, and impoverish religion and the arts.

In 1924 T. had moved to New York, supporting himself as a free-lance reviewer, while he and his first wife, the novelist Caroline GORDON, began to move in the city's literary circles. T.'s first volume of commercially published verse, *Mr. Pope, and Other Poems*, appeared in 1928. The formal discipline and eloquent intensity of these poems soon received critical recognition.

During his long career T. held a number of temporary academic appointments, including posts at Princeton, Chicago, Oxford, Vanderbilt, and Indiana universities, the University of the South, and the Library of Congress. From 1951 until his retirement in 1969 he held a professorship in English at the University of Minnesota. He served in editorial capacities on *Hound and Horn*, *The Sewanee Review*, and *The Kenyon Review*. Among his many awards and honors were the Bollingen Prize in Poetry (1956) and the National Medal for Literature (1976).

T.'s critical theory developed along with his poetic practice. His point of departure seems to have been Baudelaire's theory of correspondences, which T. recognized as especially applicable to the practice of the Elizabethan dramatists. As a result of this view, he stood firmly in opposition to romantic theory and practice. He was convinced that the poet should not, in the spirit of a Wordsworth or a Shelley, indulge in a spontaneous expression of his own feelings. He would do better to aim at influencing, even at controlling, the consciousness of the attentive reader. Nevertheless, T. was not given to concealing the intensity of his own commitments. Much of his own verse was motivated—perhaps one might say "inspired"—by his ardent repudiation of what he took to be the gilded and grandiose decadence of American civilization held in ignominious thralldom by a monster more insidious than the bitch goddess of Matthew Arnold.

This attitude was intensified by his sympathy for both the indignant and the contrite survivors of the Old South. This sympathy seems to have been strengthened by condescending reactions in the North to the Tennessee "monkey trial" of 1925. As his thought took shape, however, T. made his way toward a more universal philosophy, which drew support from his study of Dante, of Vergil, and of the Greek classics. This reading led him toward acceptance of the traditional wisdom of Roman Catholicism, to which he converted in 1950. His novel *The Fathers* (1938) anticipated this development, which parallels in its own way the cultural criticism of William Butler YEATS and T.'s friend T. S. ELIOT. In this philosophy the poet, as teacher and as artist, must find his place in a cultural tradition that he may strive in all humility to clarify and enrich, seeking a "unity of view and a confidence of judgment" that will reconcile art and life.

Recognition of our failure to reach such heights of vision is in itself an important moment of self-realization. This insight constitutes the message of "Ode to the Confederate Dead" (final version, 1930), perhaps the best known and most discussed of T.'s poems. Here, in a restless interplay of image and metaphor, often obscure at a first reading, the poet begs our sympathy for those who find themselves painfully at odds with a world they cannot escape or ignore; at the same time, he quietly reminds us that in our own way we share their predicament.

In later years T.'s poetry came increasingly to reflect his Roman Catholic sympathies and his profound admiration for Dante, whose philosophy and poetic practice increasingly held his attention. This is evident in some of his finest poetry, including "Seasons of the Soul" (1944), "The Maimed Man" (1952), and "The Buried Lake" (1953), which carry one beyond the painful bewilderment of "Ode to the Confederate Dead." T.'s masterpiece is perhaps "The Swimmers" (1953), a canto in narrative form about the poet's witnessing, as a boy of eleven, the grisly aftermath of a Kentucky lynching.

Allen Tate

This experience is recorded with Dantesque lucidity, as the sequence of past events is calmly and wisely revisited.

FURTHER WORKS: *The Golden Mean, and Other Poems* (1923, with Wills Ridley); *Stonewall Jackson, the Good Soldier: A Narrative* (1928); *Jefferson Davis, His Rise and Fall: A Biographical Narrative* (1929); *Three Poems: "Ode to the Confederate Dead," Being the Revised and Final Version of a Poem Previously Published on Several Occasions; To Which Are Added "Message from Abroad" and "The Cross"* (1930); *Poems, 1928–1931* (1932); *Reactionary Essays on Poetry and Ideas* (1936); *The Mediterranean, and Other Poems* (1936); *Selected Poems* (1937); *Reason in Madness: Critical Essays* (1941); *Sonnets at Christmas* (1941); *Invitation to Learning* (1941, with Cairns Huntington and Mark Van Doren); *Vigil of Venus: Pervigilium Veneris* (1943); *The Winter Sea: A Book of Poems* (1944); *Poems, 1920–1945: A Selection* (1947); *Poems, 1922–1947* (1948); *On the Limits of Poetry: Selected Essays, 1928–1948* (1948); *The Hovering Fly, and Other Essays* (1949); *Two Conceits for the Eye to Sing, If Possible* (1950); *The Forlorn Demon: Didactic and Critical Essays* (1953); *The Man of Letters in the Modern World: Selected Essays, 1928–1955* (1955); *Collected Essays* (1959); *Poems* (1960); *Essays of Four Decades* (1968); *The Swimmers, and Other Selected Poems* (1971); *The Translation of Poetry* (1972); *The Literary Correspondence of Donald Davidson and A. T.* (1974); *Memoirs and Opinions, 1926–1974* (1975); *The Fathers and Other Fiction* (1977); *Collected Poems, 1919–1976* (1977); *The Republic of*

Letters in America: The Correspondence of John Peale Bishop and A. T. (1981); *The Poetry Reviews of A. T., 1924–1944* (1983)

BIBLIOGRAPHY: "Homage to A. T.," special section, *SR*, 67, 4 (1959): 528–631; Meiners, R. K., *The Last Alternatives: A Study of the Works of A. T.* (1963); Hemphill, G., *A. T.* (1964); Stewart, J. L., *The Burden of Time: The Fugitives and Agrarians* (1965): 307–426 and passim; Bishop, F., *A. T.* (1967); Squires, R., *A. T.: A Literary Biography* (1971); Squires, R., ed., *A. T. and His Work: Critical Evaluations* (1972); special T. section, *SoR*, 12, 4 (1976): 685–797

—NEWTON P. STALLKNECHT

TATE, James

American poet and scholar, b. 8 December 1943, Kansas City, Missouri

Poet T. is equally at home with topics of war, loss, appreciation, or gardening, which he treats through challenging techniques including stream of consciousness and nonsense. T.'s style has been likened to Dadaism and the comparison is apt, but beyond the difficulty of his language lies a sense of humor and a sheer sense of enjoyment in his craft. His subjects reflect the concerns of T.'s generation and the concerns of his readers of all generations; contemporary topics are the norm in each decade he has published. His very first book, *The Lost Pilot*, was the Yale Younger Poets selection in 1967 and established him as a serious poet. T. won the 1992 Pulitzer Prize for his *Selected Poems*, the 1994 National Book Award for *Worshipful Company*, and the 1995 Tanning Prize from the Academy of American Poets.

T. once alluded to Walt Whitman and William Carlos WIL-LIAMS as poets with whom he has an affinity. His selection of two very unique voices from the American literary canon is not surprising. While his use of SURREALISM in the 1970s was not unlike the work being produced by other poets in literary magazines, he managed to set himself apart through such poems as "Stray Animals" (1968). In this poem T. celebrates being alone: the narrator notices things he might not notice had he company. His thoughts drift from stray animals on the porch to smells of burning leaves, shadows on his forehead, and bees in a mimosa tree. These perceptions end with "This is a house of unwritten poems, / this is where I am unborn." The final line disrupts the drowsy calm of the rest of the poem and is typical of T.'s desire to create what he has called "the agony of communication" by drawing the reader into the poem and then throwing in a line that causes confusion. T. has said that language must sometimes be manipulated in whatever direction the poem goes in order to squeeze out the meaning. He has adhered to this modernist belief even into the last decade of the 20th c.

The last decade of the 20th c. is especially significant for T. and his readers. He won three major awards and published his twelfth book of poetry, *The Shroud of the Gnome*. Although there have not been great shifts in style or subject matter from each book of poems to the next, this most recent collection seems more self-conscious; in poems such as "Faulty Diction" the title is almost painfully conscious of what's to come in lines such as "My, but don't you look positively zodiacal today!" Again, T. has fun playing with words and delights in making the reader work to earn the reward of

understanding. The point of doing this is to make the reader stop and look at common words in a new way; rather than creating new words, T. uses everyday words in uncommon situations that force the reader to stop and see them with fresh eyes.

T.'s poems are not only about language, but it is his use of language and his keen ability to see into the heart of things that keeps his readers coming back for more. He admits that he wants to get at the truth of things by creating juxtapositions and nonsense, but even neophytes to his work know that his genius lies in the way he mesmerizes us with his images and his brutal honesty. Not all his poems are silly or even funny, but all are heartfelt and enduring.

FURTHER WORKS: *The Torches* (1968); *Shepherds of the Mist* (1969); *Wrong Songs* (1970); *Absences: New Poems* (1972); *Viper Jazz* (1976); *Riven Doggeries* (1979); *Land of Little Sticks* (1981); *Hints to Pilgrims* (1982); *The Oblivion Ha-Ha: Sixty Poems* (1984); *Reckoner* (1986); *Distance from Loved Ones* (1990)

BIBLIOGRAPHY: Bellamy, J., ed., *American Poetry Observed: Poets on their Work* (1984): 248-65; Revell, D., "The Desperate Buck and Wing: J. T. and the Failure of Ritual," *WHR*, 38 (1984) 372-379; Upton, L. "The Masters Can Only Make Us Laugh: Authority in the Poetry of J. T.," *South Atlantic Review*, 55 (1990): 78-86

—MARCY TANTER

TAYLOR, Peter

American novelist, short-story writer, and dramatist, b. 18 Jan. 1917, Trenton, Tennessee; d. 2 Nov. 1994, Charlottesville, Virginia

T. was a son of the Southern gentry, the grandson of a governor, the product of an early education at Vanderbilt University. There he studied with Allen TATE and John Crowe RANSOM and befriended Robert Penn WARREN, Randall JARRELL, and Robert LOWELL. After completing his education, and serving in the army during World War II, in England, T. commenced a career of writing and teaching that spanned nearly fifty years.

In spite of his three well-received novels—*A Woman of Means* (1950), *A Summons to Memphis* (1987), which earned T. the Pulitzer at seventy years old, and *In the Tennessee Country* (1994), published months before his death—T. is most celebrated as a writer of short stories. Those stories, published in collections in five decades, starting with *A Long Fourth and Other Stories* (1948) and winning a PEN/Faulkner Award for *The Old Forest and Other Stories* (1985), are cited by other writers of fiction and by critics as masterpieces of the form. Characterized by an ear for the rhythms of speech and emotion, an eye for the telling detail, and a feel for narrative pace and movement, T.'s stories endure as writerly accomplishments. As empathetic art, they also have earned appreciation; his finely observed characters are rarely judged, but instead understood. At times they even come to some kind of understanding of themselves, though the epiphany, however explosive the situation that occasions it, is usually a quiet one.

T. was the poet of the vanishing upper crust of a vanishing Upper South. Over the course of his long career, in his stories and novels and plays, T. chronicled the latter and the last days of this Southern genteel class, at a time when many of its members hadn't realized yet that they were the last of a species headed toward extinction. T.'s natural history of this species, of its hunting and mating patterns, and of its adaptations to the loss of its natural environment, is however anything but clinical. While far from wholeheartedly affectionate, T.'s history isn't naturalistically heartless, either; his fading Southern gentry, flawed and sometimes deserving of their fates, are still appreciated for their gentlemanly dreams and for their fateful attempts to keep them alive, or for their often futile attempts to escape them.

The deservedly famous T. voice remains his strongest legacy. It is a voice that runs through his work, addressing his readers in an intimately reserved, conversationally formal way, in a way through which the presence of the storyteller is felt. T. thus refutes, without perhaps thinking of it in these terms, Walter BENJAMIN's famous obituary for the storyteller in modern literature; in T.'s voice we do feel part of the storytelling circle, even if the community from which he speaks is not ours, and even if the community itself is gently disintegrating.

The "Tennessee country" of T.'s last title was the country of this community, the country of the Southern ruling class of money and power, whose membership is determined by birth and breeding. Born into this class himself, T. knew these bankers and senators and governors, the women who were restricted to ruling the social world, and their privileged yet constrained children. This knowledge allowed him to capture the ambition, the thwarted imagination, and the desperate attempts to suppress or release the urge to escape this world. Living into the 1990s and seeing the Old South turn into the new South of chain hotels and new money allowed T. to capture the changes wrought on the elevated yet confining positions of his characters. Writing as sensitively and warmheartedly as he did allowed him to chronicle this passage with neither rancor nor celebration, but instead elegiacally.

FURTHER WORKS: *The Widows of Thornton* (1954); *Happy Families Are All Alike: A Collection of Stories* (1959); *A Tennessee Day in St. Louis* (1959); *Miss Leonora When Last Seen and Fifteen Other Stories* (1963); *A Stand in the Mountains* (1965); *The Collected Stories of P. T.* (1969); *Presences: Seven Dramatic Pieces* (1973); *In the Miro District and Other Stories* (1977)

BIBLIOGRAPHY: Robison, J. C., *P. T.: A Study of the Short Fiction* (1988); McAlexander, H. H., ed., *Critical Essays on P. T.* (1993); Stevens, R. C., and L. B. Salamon, eds., *The Craft of P. T.* (1995); Peters, J., "A Man of Good Character: Remembering P. T.," *NER*, 18 (1997): 64-68

—SAM COHEN

TAYMŪR, Mahmūd

Egyptian novelist, short-story writer, dramatist, literary historian, and critic, b. 16 June 1894, Cairo; d. 25 Aug. 1973, Lausanne, Switzerland

T. is one of the most prolific Egyptian writers, with more than 300 short stories, seven novels, and numerous plays to his credit, as well as studies on literary history, literary criticism, language, aesthetics, and travels. On 5 April 1947 he was elected to the Egyptian Academy.

He is a scion of an aristocratic family, whose members held senior positions at the court of Egypt's rulers throughout the 19th c. and were noted for their interest in literature. Three other members of the family preceded T. as creative writers: the poet 'Ā'isha al-Taymūriyya (1840–1902), T.'s aunt, Ahmad Taymūr (1871–1930), his father, and Muhammad Taymūr (1892–1921), his older brother.

The last, who had considerable influence on the writers of his generation, strove to create authentic Egyptian literature, which he tried to do both in his short stories and plays. To make his writing truly Egyptian he made liberal use of 'āmmiyyah (the spoken dialect), thus challenging the convention that literature should be written in the *fushā*, literary language, only. His influence on his younger brother, T., was immense. As described by T., his brother aroused in him the passion for creating an "Egyptian literature to the core" that would reflect "national features, national events, national spirit, where the national character would be emphasized in expression and description." It was not a call to shun European literature, which they both read and admired, but a reaction against the then current tendency to imitate it. His brother's early death left T. helpless and fearful that his brother's dream might remain unrealized. Eventually he recovered and determined to continue his brother's work by putting his ideas into practice. Thus he started his long literary career, never relenting in his efforts to bring Egyptian literature up to a level equal to the best in the world's literature. His works were translated extensively into a large number of languages.

The notion that a realistic Egyptian literature should depict Egyptian characters speaking 'āmmiyyah was initially self-evident to T. He felt that making his characters speak *fushā* would give the story a false ring. Yet, writing in 'āmmiyyah violated an age-old canon; so gradually he gave up the use of 'āmmiyyah and systematically rewrote his stories and plays in *fushā*. Explaining his belated preference for the *fushā*, T. pointed out that in the earlier period of his creative writing *fushā* was too lofty for the ordinary reader and sounded too artificial in modern stories. But in time *fushā* had become simplified, while the rising level of education in Egypt made it easier for the readers. But even then he maintained that plays should be written in 'āmmiyyah when depicting the present (thus excepting historical plays)—meant to be performed on the stage—because the 'āmmiyyah is the language that people are used to hearing, whereas *fushā* is the language they are used to reading. A result of this vacillation is that many of T.'s plays and stories are available in two versions. In many cases the titles, too, were altered to *fushā* or 'āmmiyyah. No systematic analysis of all of T.'s double versions has been made yet.

Critical comments on this dual procedure were voiced when the story "Abū 'Alī 'āmil artiste," first published in 1934, was turned in 1954 into "Abū: 'Alī al-fannān" (Abu Ali the artist), questioning the author's right to alter a work that has become part of a people's literary stock. T. replied that he felt he had every right to reshape his works in a manner conforming to his more mature understanding of the requirements of good literature.

In his many years of creative writing, T. felt free to adopt any literary trend that seemed to him appropriate for the piece at hand. So we can find pieces written in the romantic, the realist, and even the SURREALIST vein. For his mode of narrative he has adopted, as the case may be, straight third-person narrative, first-person narrative, interior monologue, or any combination of them. With the advent of the psychological novel he had shown great interest in Freudian psychoanalysis and delved into his protagonists' subconscious. His way of writing has been, therefore, labeled *al-lā madhhabiyya*, or nondoctrinal.

FURTHER WORKS: *Al-shaykh jum'a* (1925); *'Amm Mitwallī* (1927); *Al-shaykh sayyid al-'abīt* (1928); *Tāriq al-andalusī* (1930); *Al-mawkib* (1932); *Al-atlāl* (1934); *Nidā' al-majhūl* (1939); *Fir'awn al-saghīr* (1939); *'Arūs al-nīl* (1941); *Al-makhbā' raqam 13* (1942); *Qanābil* (1943); *Salwā fi mahabb al-rīh* (1944); *Kull 'ām wa-antum bi-khayr* (1950); *Abū al-shawārib* (1953); *Abū 'ali al-fannān* (1955); *Shamrūkh* (1958); *Anā al-qātil* (1961); *Ma'būd min tīn* (1969); *Zawjatī al-mazād* (1970)

BIBLIOGRAPHY: Widmer, G., *M. T.* (1932); Johnson-Davies, D., comp., *Modern Arabic Short Stories* (1967): 169–75; Haywood, J., *Modern Arabic Literature, 1800–1970* (1971): 204–5: 235–40; Stetkevych, J., "Classical Arabic on Stage," in Ostle, R. C., ed., *Studies in Modern Arabic Literature* (1975): 152–78; Peled, M., "Reading Two Versions of a Story by M. T.: A Study in the Rhetoric of Fiction," *Israel Oriental Studies*, 7 (1977): 309–30; Badawi, M. M., *Modern Arabic Drama in Egypt* (1987): 88–111; Allen, R., ed., *Modern Arabic Literature* (1987): 317–23

—MATTITYAHU PELED

TCHERNICHOWSKY, Saul

Hebrew poet, b. 20 Aug. 1875, Mikhailovka, Russia; d. 14 Oct. 1943, Jerusalem, Palestine

T. was born and raised in a Russian village in the Crimea, and this background influenced his work in three ways. In his hometown he absorbed Orthodox Jewish traditions, was exposed to western European and Russian culture, and developed a lasting sensitivity to nature and landscape. T.'s adult biography, however, is a record of restless wanderings. These, together with the events that prompted them, further determined the character of his poetry and necessitate treating it chronologically.

Between 1890 and 1899 T. studied in Odessa, where he voraciously read works in European languages (German, French, English, Greek, and Latin), especially poetry, and came into contact with the emergent Zionist movement. These two influences had a decisive and immediately apparent effect. His first book of verse, *Chezyonot umanginot* (1898; visions and melodies), reflects his deep involvement with the poetry of different nations, as well as his emphasis on the formal elements of language and versification. Unlike most of his contemporaries writing in Hebrew, T. did not struggle with the stock phrases of classical sources but rather attempted to weld biblical language to images drawn from direct observation. His reflective poems of the same period, such as "Beleil Chanukah" (1896; "A Night in Chanukah," 1923), criticize Diaspora life and thus exemplify his Jewish nationalism. These two motifs are expanded in the second volume of *Chezyonot umanginot* (1901) and in *Shirim* (1920; poems), the latter written between 1899 and 1906 in Heidelberg and Lausanne, where T. studied medicine (the source of his livelihood for the rest of his life).

During T.'s "Russian period" (1906–22) he held various medical posts, serving in the Russian army during World War I. His war experiences, and his earlier arrest for political agitation in 1907, considerably affected his writings. His sonnet sequences express his awareness of the contrast between his love of life—an example is "Lashemesh" (1919; "To the Sun," 1978)—and his despair over the sufferings of humanity, as in "Al hadam" (1922; concerning

blood). His attempted detachment from reality is apparent in his adherence to the rigorous forms of the sonnet and, in his long narrative poems, in his recollections of childhood tranquillity, as in, for example, "Chatunatah shel Elka" (1920; partial tr., "Elka's Wedding," 1966).

From 1922 to 1931 T. lived in Berlin. There he wrote some prose and translated into Hebrew numerous plays (by Molière, Shakespeare, Sophocles) and poems (by, among others, Homer and Longfellow). His personal and national poetry of the period became more tragic and reflects his awareness of his fate as an eternal wanderer.

In 1931 T. moved to mandated Palestine. His poetry of this period indicates his attempts to integrate local life and scenery into his work. Simultaneously, however, he sought refuge in the scenes of his youth. Also striking is his attempt at a synoptic view of his personal and national fate: of the world of the child and the old man and of Palestinian and European landscapes.

T. was an outstanding representative of the transformation in Hebrew poetry between the 19th-c. "national awakening" and the modern era. What is distinctive in the form of his verse is his consistent tendency to break the constricting bounds of previous Hebrew literature and his concern with its adoption of European aesthetics. The content of his poetry is characterized by perceived tension between opposing poles: an idyllic attitude toward Jewish tradition versus a contempt for the stagnation of Jewish Diaspora culture; an affirmation of life versus despair over the human race; and a feeling of oneness with nature versus alienation from natural surroundings.

Besides contributing to the development of Hebrew literature, T. also strengthened the bonds between Hebrew and European literature. As both a prolific translator and a poet, he refined the Hebrew language, and also its poetics and genres, in accordance with European models. Although aware of the tensions resulting from the colliding of two cultures, T. eventually came to accept his people's heritage within the framework of European civilization.

FURTHER WORKS: *Shirim chadashim* (1923); *Bar Kochba* (1923); *Machberet hasonetot* (1925); *Kitve S. T.* (10 vols., 1929–1934); *Shloshim ushloshah sipurim* (1941); *Asher haya velo haya* (1941); *Shirim* (1943); *Kochve shamayim rechokim* (1944). FURTHER WORKS IN ENGLISH: *S. T.* (1978)

BIBLIOGRAPHY: Snowman, L. V., *T. and His Poetry* (1929); Waxman, M., *A History of Jewish Literature* (1941), Vol. 4: 259–81; Ribalow, M., *The Flowering of Modern Hebrew Literature* (1959): 88–122; Silberschlag, E., *S. T.: Poet of Revolt* (1968)

—TOVA COHEN

TCHICAYA U TAM'SI

(born Gérald Félix Tchicaya) Congolese poet and novelist (writing in French), b. 25 Aug. 1931, M'Pili; d. 22 Apr. 1988, Paris, France

T. came from a prominent Congolese family. His father, Félix Tchicaya, became a deputy to the French national assembly in 1946, with the result that T. spent his formative years in Paris. He attended the Lycée Janson-de-Sailly and, after holding various jobs, joined UNESCO, where he worked until 1985. T., who had been in ill health, died of cardiac arrest during the night of 21–22 April 1988.

T.'s poetry is characterized by oneiric imagery, elliptical discourse, and semantic discontinuities, due in part, no doubt, to the blend of, on the one hand, African objective referents, linguistic cadences, and narrative predilections, and, on the other hand, European literary influences, such as the work of Arthur Rimbaud (1854–1891).

T. gained recognition in his mid-twenties with the publication of his first collections of poems. *Le mauvais sang* (1955; bad blood) and *Feu de brousse* (1957; *Brush Fire*, 1964). With the English translation of *Brush Fire*, published by the small but prestigious Mbari Publications press in Ibadan, Nigeria, as well as a *Selected Poems* (1970) in Heineman's widely-distributed African Writers Series, T. became known throughout the world as one of Africa's leading poets. Other collections, in the same mode as that of the first two, include *Á triche-coeur* (1958; a game of cheat-heart), *Epitomépitomé* (1961; epitome), *Le ventre* (1964; the belly), and *La veste intérieure suivi de notes de veille* (1977; the indoor coat followed by waking notes).

T.'s career took a significant turn in 1980 with the publication of his first novel, *Les cancrelats* (the roaches). This brilliant work had, according to T., been composed in the 1950s but had been repeatedly rejected by publishers. *Les cancrelats* is the first volume of a loosely knit tetralogy spanning Congolese history in the 20th c. This novel interweaves the stories of two families over two generations during the first half of the century: a French colonial family and the family of one of its servants. It was followed by *Les méduses ou les orties de la mer* (1982; *The Madman and the Medusa*, 1989), which takes place against the somewhat remote backdrop of World War II. *Les phalènes* (1984; the moths), among whose main characters we find the children of the servant in *Les cancrelats*, covers the years from the rescission in 1946 of the double-standard legal system, known as the *Indigénat* to Congolese independence in 1960; and *Ces fruits si doux de l'arbre à pain* (1987; those sweet, sweet fruits of the breadwood tree) deals with the tumultuous postindependence years during and immediately following the presidency of Abbé Fulbert Youhou (who appears in the novel as Abbé Lokou) and is an indictment of the period's loss of traditional values and of the corruption that overwhelms and destroys the book's honorable characters.

Though more accessible to the general reader than his poetry, T.'s novels do contain labyrinthine subplots and mysterious happenings reminiscent of supernatural events found in African folktales. Couched in a highly charged poetic prose and recounting hauntingly enigmatic tales, the novels warrant placement of T. among the major novelists of the world.

T. also wrote short stories, collected in *La maun sèche* (1980; the dry hand), and plays: *Le Zulu, suivi de Vwène le fondateur* (1978; the Zulu, followed by Vwène the founding father) and *Le destin glorieux du maréchal Nnikon Nniku* (1979; *The Glorious Destiny of Marshal Nnikon Nniku*, 1986).

T.'s work as a whole is bold in style and often surreal in content. He compellingly intertwines narration of the experiences of individuals with the cultural givens of their society and the larger political events that impact on their lives. Despite T.'s extensive European experience and consummate manipulation of the French language, the main thrust of his work remains Afrocentric.

FURTHER WORKS: *Arc musical précédé de Épitomé* (1970); *Le pain et la cendre, Le ventre* (1978); *Légendes africaines* (1979)

BIBLIOGRAPHY: Herdeck, D. E., *African Authors* (1973): 450–52; Blair, D. S., *African Literature in French* (1976): 171–78; Kom, A., ed., *Dictionnaire des œuvres littéraires négro-africaines de langue française* (1983), passim; Zell et al., H. M., eds., *A New Reader's Guide to African Literature*, rev. 2nd ed. (1983): 284–85, 503–6; Sellin, E., Introduction to *The Madman and the Medusa* (1989): xi–xvi; O'Grady, B., "Tchicayu U Tam'si: Some Thoughts on the Poet's Symbolic Mode of Expression," *WLT*, 65, 1 (Winter 1991): 29–34

—ERIC SELLIN

TEILLIER, Jorge

Chilean poet and editor, b. 24 June 1935, Lautaro; d. 22 April 1996

The grandson of French immigrants to southern Chile, T. has chosen his homeland in the agricultural south as a setting for most of his poetry, even though Santiago has become a second home. He had been preparing to be a history professor when an older writer, Teófilo Cid (1914–1964), poet of the Generation of 1938, introduced T. to SURREALISM and inspired him to abandon history for poetry. One writer hinted that Cid may also have infected T.'s soul at the same time with his own devastating disease: alcoholism. His father's being a militant communist has caused T. anguish because he prefers to omit propaganda from his writings, feeling that ideology and poetry do not mix. (One critic jokingly said that the only Marx influence in his writings is high-brow slapstick from the Marx brothers.) Although he has not been a militant leftist in verse, T. sympathized with the Popular Front and suffered the loss of a daughter to exile.

T. says that much of the poetry of his first book, *Para ángeles y gorriones* (1956; for angels and sparrows), was composed at his student desk during high school. The book was widely reviewed in Chile. In the press it received much praise, as a masterpiece for such a young poet. There are images in T.'s early writing that several critics attribute to Pablo NERUDA. Such motifs appear in his poetry as a combination of negative images—a world that falls apart—which can be seen, for example, in the title of his second book, *El cielo cae con las hojas* (1958; the heavens fall with the leaves). Yet for the most part T. has devised his own special poetic vision of the world. In 1962 he won the Municipal Prize of Santiago for Poetry and the Gabriela Mistral Prize for his third book, *El árbol de la memoria* (1961; the memory tree). In *Poemas del país de nunca jamás* (1963; poems from never-never land), T. continues the creation of fanciful metaphors of the Chilean southland which he had learned to evoke in his early writings. The predominant setting in these works is a landscape that is magical. It comes from the poet's own "metarealism" or secret realism in that it invokes memories, images, mystery, and daydreams that are innovative and very subjective. These elements can also be interpreted as tricks or secrets in his composition whereby he uses signifiers that have hidden meanings for other realities. For example, death is often disguised. *Los trenes de la noche* (1964; trains of the night) was written during an all-night train ride from Santiago south to Lautaro. The poet views his magic land at night, but also recalls other train rides. Trains have become motifs in many poems in his books.

Muertes y maravillas (1971; death and marvels) is an important anthology of his first twelve years of writing. It also includes a short autobiography, a complete bibliography to 1970, and a short criticism by Alfonso Calderón (b. 1929).

In some of his later writing T. continues his frustration with lost dreams. For example, in *Cartas para reinas de otras primaveras* (1985; letters for queens of other springs) his disillusionment continues to surface. But now he is less apt to stay in his southern microcosm, first writing of a burlesque hall in Panama and later about problems of censorship with the Pinochet military dictatorship. Some poems have beautiful, striking images, but, on the whole, this book is not as strong as his earlier efforts.

Fernando ALEGRÍA and others have included T. in the Generation of 1950, but even though he is a close friend of many of the writers, he does not identify with that group, which he considers too bourgeois. T. did belong to the Trilce Group (at the Austral University in Valdivia) and the Poets of the Lar. If one were to classify T.'s poetry, it would basically be romantic in theme with an occasional vanguardist metaphor. T. is a brilliant, erudite poet, who has read and traveled extensively. For some readers his setting may be limited, because he prefers to write about the land of his inheritance, but he is an artful poet who can capture the reader's imagination with his innovative images.

FURTHER WORKS: *Romeo Murga, poeta adolescente* (1962); *Otoño secreto* (1964); *Actualidad de Vicente Huidobro* (1964); *Poemas secretos* (1965); *Crónica del forastero* (1968); *Cuando todos se vayan: homenaje a Ray Bradbury* (1968); *El pasajero del Hotel Usher* (1975); *Los trenes que no has de beber* (1977); *Para un pueblo fantasma* (1978); *El molino y la higuera* (1993); *Conversaciones con J. T.* (1993); *En el mudo corazón del bosque* (1997). FURTHER WORKS IN ENGLISH: *From the Country of Nevermore: Selected Poems of J. T.* (1990); *In Order to Talk with the Dead: Selected Poems of J. T.* (1990).

BIBLIOGRAPHY: Sánchez Latorre, L., *Los expedientes de Filebo* (1965): 161–65; Alegría, F., *Literatura chilena del siglo XX* (1967): 53–54; Mengod, V., *Historia de la literatura chilena* (1967): 121–22; Villegas, J., "La mitificación de la pobreza en un poema [Aparición de Teófilo Cid] de J. T.," *Inti*, 9 (Spring 1979): 13–25; Guerra-Cunningham, L., "The Concept of Marginality in 'To a Ghost Town' by J. T.," *PCP*, 16 (1981): 45–55; Valdés, E., "Cincuenta años en la poesía de J. T.," *RCLL*, 13, 25 (1987): 185–88; Stojkov, T. R., "J. T.: The Vocation of a Poet," *WLT*, 70, 2 (Spring 1996): 311–15; Sarmiento, O., "J. T.," *Hispamérica*, 25, 3 (Apr. 1996): 59–68

—LON PEARSON

TEIRLINCK, Herman

Belgian novelist, dramatist, and essayist (writing in Flemish), b. 24 Feb. 1879, Sint Jans Molenbeek; d. 4 Feb. 1967, Beersel-Lot

T. had a long career as a public official. He taught literature and the dramatic arts in the public schools of Brussels and advised three Belgian kings on matters concerning Flemish culture. He was the cofounder and director of what is still one of the most important literary periodicals in Belgium, *Nieuw vlaams tijdschrift* (founded in 1946). Among many other awards and prizes, T. received in 1956 the Prize for Dutch Letters established by the combined governments of the Netherlands and Belgium.

T. was the most prolific and protean of 20th-c. Flemish writers. In novels, plays, tales, countless essays, speeches, and introductions, he rallied to the standard of his friend August VERMEYLEN, who said, "We want to be Flemings in order to be Europeans." Unlike his compatriots Maurice MAETERLINCK and Émile VERHAEREN, who wrote in French, T. opted for writing in his mother tongue, in spite of the inevitable limitation in readership inherent in writing in a lesser-known language.

After an initial volume of poems, *Verzen* (1900; poems), T. published three regional novels: *De wonderbare wereld* (1902; the miraculous world), *Het stille gesternte* (1903; the silent constellation), and *De doolage* (1905; the swamp). The stylistic virtuosity that is a hallmark of T.'s work is most evident in his elegant novel *Mijnheer J. B. Serjanszoon, orator didacticus* (1908). In this ironic portrait of an 18th-c. epicure, written in an extravagantly ornamental style, T. presents a dilettante whose dazzling verbal mask cannot protect him from loneliness and fear of death. *Het ivoren aapje* (1909; the ivory monkey) was the first Flemish novel to deal exclusively with the metropolis. Reminiscent of Alfred DÖBLIN'S *Berlin Alexanderplatz*, it portrays the teeming life of Brussels around 1900.

Other novels followed, but in 1922 T. temporarily stopped writing fiction and turned to the theater. For over a quarter of a century his EXPRESSIONIST plays and his influence as a theoretician and director dominated the development of the Flemish stage.

T. saw plays not as mirrors of everyday reality but as independent structures of ideas. He boldly discarded threadbare techniques and topics and introduced a concept of total theater in which dance, mime, recorded music, and cinematic effects were utilized to break down the barrier between the spectators and the stage. Examples of plays employing these techniques are *De vertraagde film* (1922; the slow-motion film), *Ik dien* (1923; I serve), *De man zonder lijf* (1925; the bodiless man), *Ave* (1928, Latin: hail), and *De ekster op de galg* (1937; the crow on the gallows). T.'s desire to duplicate the union and intimacy of the medieval miracle plays is evident in his scenarios for outdoor theater and an adaptation of the classic *Everyman* (1934). In later years, T. wrote an impressive adaptation of Aeschylus's *Oresteia* (1946).

T. returned to fiction during World War II. *Maria Speermalie* (1940; Maria Speermalie) and *Het gevecht met de engel* (1952; the fight with the angel) are masterpieces that celebrate the primitive forces of nature. The latter novel is a particularly fine presentation of the major themes that occupied T. throughout his life: sexual passion and perversion; the fierce majesty of the female; and the exuberant eternality of nature. In both novels the celebration of the blood and the atavistic mystery of nature reminds one of D. H. LAWRENCE, Jean GIONO, and Knut HAMSUN. T. shared Lawrence's interest in pitting decadent civilization against the forces basic to mankind and to nature, although the Lawrentian figures pale beside the ebullient primitives of T.

In his final novel, *Zelfportret of het galgemaal* (1955; *The Man in the Mirror*, 1963), T. investigated the anatomy of the modern psyche. Its hero, Henri M., is a far more complex Serjanszoon. Aware of his masks, he scrutinizes the various roles he plays. A psychoanalytical novel, *Zelfportret* makes use of all T.'s stylistic powers, profound psychological insights, and ironic subtlety to describe the discontented winter of a life in which there is no hope of spring.

Although he hedonistically put imagination ahead of reality, T. succeeded in speaking directly to a large audience in novels and plays that deal with every level of society. His lyric imagination, the tragic dimension of his characters, and the dramatic conflict between the sexes and between nature and modern civilization culminate in a positive vision that gives T.'s work a quality that is both of our time and beyond it.

FURTHER WORKS: *Landelijke historiën* (1901); *Het bedrijf van den kwade* (1904); *Zon* (1906); *De kroonluchter* (1907); *Het avontuurlijk Leven van Lieven Cordaat* (1907); *Johan Doxa* (1917); *De nieuwe Uilenspiegel* (1920); *De wonderlijke mei* (1926); *De lemen torens* (1928); *Elckerlyc* (1937); *Griseldis* (1942); *Rolande met de Bles* (1944); *Verzameld Werk* (9 vols., 1955–1973); *Taco* (1958)

BIBLIOGRAPHY: Brachin, P., *L'expressionisme dans le théâtre de H. T.* (1958); Meijer, R. P., *Literature of the Low Countries*, new ed. (1978): 280–82

—E. M. BEEKMAN

TEIXEIRA DE PASCOAES

(pseud. of Joaquim Pereira Teixeira de Vasconcelos) Portuguese poet and essayist, b. 2 Nov. 1877, São João do Gatão Portuguese; d. 14 Dec. 1952, São João do Gatão Portuguese

T. de P., from a prominent family, studied law at the University of Coimbra. From 1906 to 1908 he was an attorney in Oporto, while he also devoted himself to literature, the republican cause, and the management of his family's properties. In 1911, a year after Portugal was proclaimed a republic, T. de P. helped establish the Portuguese Renascence, an organization devoted to enriching the cultural life of the nation. He was director of its journal, *A águia*, until 1917, when he returned to his family estate, where he resided the rest of his life.

T. de P.'s literary production was vast; some seventy-five works of poetry, fiction, drama, memoirs, biography, and essays appeared from 1896 to 1953. The main concern of practically all of his writings is to define man's place in the universe, on a cosmic, transcendent scale. He envisions man on a journey beginning at the moment of creation and ending in a future time when, strengthened by the tests he has suffered, he will be one with the universe. T. de P.'s idea of the universe is partly in the biblical tradition, but it also takes in nonhuman beings from the pagan tradition, such as Pan, and perceives life in even apparently insentient forms.

The catalyst that helps man toward this goal of harmony is the Portuguese concept of *saudade*: T. de P. believed that memories of the past and remembrances of origins would provide the foundation for a better future. The process was also relevant on a national level. T. de P. wanted Portugal to realize its potential by being its authentic self, and he believed that the fresh start brought about by the proclamation of the republic was a good opportunity. A remembrance of the past and a rediscovery of genuinely Portuguese institutions would lead to an appropriate future for the nation.

The guide on this quest for personal and national harmony was T. de P. himself, who used his own experiences to map the course.

The landscapes of his works are based on his native Marão region, and many of the figures that appear are people from his childhood. In addition, the persona he adopts derives from his notion of the ascetic seer who reveals truths to humanity.

T. de P.'s best and most representative writings were largely in verse and completed by 1915. *Sempre* (1898; always) and *Terra proibida* (1899; forbidden land) both recall the region of this birth and establish the poet as the revealer of truths. *Jesus e Pã* (1903; Jesus and Pan) develops his view of nature as a cover for hidden, vital forces and the shadows of beings from the past, as does *As sombras* (1907; the shadows). Two long narrative poems, *Marânus* (1911; Marânus) and *Regresso ao Paraíso* (1912; return to Paradise) complete T. de P.'s poetic statement. *Marânus* chronicles the title figure's life, death, and transfiguration into one of the shadows of the landscape. *Regresso ao Paraíso* tells of the return of Adam and Eve to Paradise after the Last Judgment, to begin a new cosmic cycle. The essay *A arte de ser português* (1915; the art of being Portuguese) encapsulates his thinking on the specifically Portuguese aspects of the quest for harmony.

T. de P. is not so highly regarded as he once was. His poetry is most advantageously read in anthologies, while most of his prose offers little to readers of the late 20th c. Because of his language and lofty philosophical tone, T. de P. may be viewed as one of the last 19th-c. Portuguese poets; but his desire to give a philosophical transcendence to regional experience may be seen as a way of dealing with the disquieting uncertainties of the 20th c.

FURTHER WORKS: *Belo* (1896); *À minha alma* (1901); *À Ventura* (1901); *Para a luz* (1904); *Vida etérea* (1906); *Senhora da noite* (1909); *Elegias* (1912); *O espírito lusitano e o saudosismo* (1912); *O doido e a morte* (1913); *O génio português na sua expressão filosófica, poética e religiosa* (1913); *Verbo escuro* (1914); *A era lusíada* (1914); *A Beira num relâmpago* (1916); *Os poetas lusíadas* (1919); *Elegia da solidão* (1921); *Cantos indecisos* (1921); *O bailado* (1921); *A caridade* (1922); *A nossa fome* (1923); *O pobre tolo* (1924); *Elegia do amor* (1924); *Londres* (1925); *Cânticos* (1925); *D. Carlos* (1925); *Sonetos* (1925); *Livro de memórias* (1928); *São Paulo* (1934); *Painel* (1935); *São Jerónimo e a trovoada* (1936); *O homem universal* (1937); *Napoleão* (1940); *O duplo passeio* (1942); *O penitente* (1942); *Santo Agostinho* (1945); *Pró-paz* (1950); *Versos da noite* (1950); *Dois jornalistas* (1950); *O empecido* (1950); *Últimos versos* (1953); *Obras completas* (11 vols., 1965 ff.)

BIBLIOGRAPHY: Figueiredo, F. de, *Historia literaria de Portugal*, Vol. 3 (1949): 134–35; Régio, J., "Introduction à T. de P.," *BEPIF*, 17 (1952): 187–98; Frèches, C.-H., *La littérature portugaise* (1970): 114; Saraiva, A. J., *Breve historia de la literatura portuguesa* (1971): 251–53; Roberts, W. H., "Notes on the Poetry of T. de P.," *JAPS*, 9 (1975): 9–17

—GREGORY MCNAB

TELLES, Lygia Fagundes

Brazilian novelist and short-story writer, b. 19 Apr. 1924, São Paulo

T. holds a position of prominence in contemporary Brazilian letters. She has been compared in stature to the late Clarice

LISPECTOR and is one of three women in the Brazilian Academy of Letters. She has over twenty published books, many of which are translated into several languages. Although her concern is with modern Brazilian women in an urban setting, T. grew up in the interior of the state of São Paulo in small cities, where her father served as judge. She completed her studies in the capital, where she graduated in law from the University of São Paulo. She began to write at an early age, but she dismisses these first efforts as products of a too-innocent girlhood. Her writing has been a process of empowerment, overcoming what she terms the ignorance and fear of her girlhood.

T.'s first published novel, *Ciranda da pedra* (1954; *The Marble Dance*, 1986), introduced the dialectic of imprisonment and liberation that moves through her entire oeuvre. Like in Clarice Lispector's fiction, family ties are prison chains that impede the protagonists from achieving growth. This theme is encapsulated in the metaphor of the aquarium in *Verão no aquário* (1963; summer in the aquarium), which in the novel signifies the childhood that dooms the protagonist to dependency. The claustrophobic social ambience of most of T.'s narratives is that of an upper middle class bankrupt of both money and morals. T. documents the inner turmoil of women who need to escape but are ill equipped to function in a rapidly changing world.

T. is best known for her novel *As meninas* (1973; *The Girl in the Photograph*, 1982), which opens new directions in her prose style and introduces the element of specific political protest against the military dictatorship, then in one of its most repressive phases. The three women in this story are inmates not of the family home but of a pension in São Paulo. The fluid, alternating narrative perspectives of the novel offer intimate portraits of lives complicated by the contradictory dynamics of megacity life in a regressive moment of Brazilian history.

T.'s most recent work is *As horas nuas* (1989; the naked hour), which continues the revolutionary path of *As meninas* and has been compared to Clarice Lispector's *A hora da estrela* (1977; *The Hour of the Star*, 1986). This book, which won the Pedro Nava Prize for best novel of 1989, is the story of an aging alcoholic actress, a character as "polluted" and devastated as the country Brazil, for which she is clearly a symbol. The vision of São Paulo is one of prevailing misery; the city is "occupied" by street people, economic refugees of ecological and economic decline. One of the several narrators is Rahul, the cat, who gazes on the chaos with a calm, experienced eye.

T. distinguishes herself from peers such as Lispector and Nélida PIÑON with a direct testimonial prose that contrasts with the famous abstract approaches of Lispector and Piñon to the themes shared by these three writers. T. offers keen observations on contemporary Brazilian society and politics, addressing the precarious situation of women in this aggressive environment. While they are very different stylists, T. and her colleagues find common ground in their commitment to social change.

FURTHER WORKS: *Histórias do desencontro* (1958); *Antes do baile verde* (1971); *Seminário dos ratos* (1977; *Tigrela and Other Stories*, 1986); *A disciplina do amor* (1980); *Mistérios* (1981)

BIBLIOGRAPHY: Oliveira, K., *A técnica narrativa em L. F. T.* (1972); Silverman, M., *Moderna ficção brasileira 2: ensaios* (1981): 162–84; Tolman, J., "New Fiction: L. F. T.," *Review*, 30 (1981): 65–70; Burgin, R., on *Seminário dos ratos*, "Tigrela and Other Stories," *NYTBR*, (4 May 1986): 40; Stern, I., ed., *Dictionary of Brazilian Literature* (1988): 337–38; Abreu, C. F., on *As horas nuas*, "As horas de Lygia," *Isto É/Senhor* (6 June 1989): 88

—ELIZABETH LOWE

TELUGU LITERATURE
See Indian Literature

TENDRYAKOV, Vladimir Fyodorovich

Russian short-story writer and novelist, b. 5 Dec. 1923, Makarovskaya; d. 3 Aug. 1984, Moscow

Son of a district official, T. grew up in the Vologda region. He served in World War II, became a member of the Communist Party in 1948, and graduated from the Gorky Institute of Literature in 1951. He began to publish in 1947 but did not achieve prominence until the liberal post-Stalin "thaw" period, when, along with other "village prose" writers, he portrayed the weaknesses and abuses in Soviet agriculture that Khrushchev wanted exposed.

Although T. has written two full-length novels, some science fiction, and plays and screenplays, his forte is the short novel or novella (*povest*), which he organizes around a moral crisis or test, usually in connection with an accident or crime. The best of them are well-constructed, suspenseful narratives, marked by an authentic, usually rural or small-town setting, and by vivid, individualized language. Many of his works suggest a basically tragic vision of the life of ordinary people, who find themselves helplessly wedged in between social or environmental forces and an awakened moral or spiritual awareness that leaves them with a sense of frustration, futility, and failure. They distrust modern technological civilization and its social institutions, which fail to relieve man's spiritual and existential anguish.

With the long story *Ukhaby* (1956; "Potholes," 1957) T. began to focus on psychological problems tied to man's moral nature, addressing himself to questions of duty, conscience, and guilt. In general, he presented people who felt inadequate and bewildered. In *Ukhaby*, a man dies as a result of an accident; T. dwells not on the bureaucrat who could have saved the man but on the guilt feelings and self-recrimination of the truck driver who was responsible for the accident. In *Troyka, semyorka, tuz* (1960; "Three, Seven, Ace," 1973), an innocent man will end up in prison because of the failure of a young logger to muster the courage to give self-incriminating evidence. In *Sud* (1961; "Justice," 1973), a fatal hunting accident leads to a farcical investigation and pointless trial, as a result of which the leader of the hunting party, feeling humiliated and defeated in front of his village, remains alone with his guilt and sense of bewilderment vis-à-vis the ironic twists of events. The luckless collective-farm worker in *Podyonka-vek korotky* (1965; "Creature of a Day," 1973) cannot evade the ruinous consequences of a small crime—misstating the number of pigs in her piggery—which escalates into arson and thus destroys her short-lived fame and happiness that the original lie established and helped maintain.

In recent years T.'s outlook has become increasingly gloomy. *Konchina* (1968; the death) deals with desolate rural life under

Stalin and ends on a deeply pessimistic note, while *Apostolskaya komandirovka* (1969; on apostolic business) and *Zatmenie* (1977; eclipse) present the outwardly successful contemporary Soviet intelligentsia as beset by an existential malaise, which they try to cure by exploring the metaphysical dimensions of life, including religion.

FURTHER WORKS: *Delo moego vzvoda* (1947); *Padenie Chuprova* (1953); *Pod lezhach kamen* (1954); *V severnom krae* (1954); *Ne ko dvoru* (1954; *Son-in-Law*, 1956); *Nenastie* (1954); *Rytsar tyutelki* (1956); *Tugoy uzel* (1956); *Chudotvornaya* (1958); *Za begushchim dnyom* (1959); *Chrezvychaynoe* (1961); *Bely flag* (1962); *Korotkoe zamykanie* (1962; "Short Circuit," 1964); *Rasskazy radista* (1963); *Puteshestvie dlinoy v vek* (1963); *Putevye zapiski* (1964); *Svidanie s Nefertiti* (1964); *Nakhodka* (1965); *Onega* (1969); *Molilas li ty na noch, Dezdemona?* (1971); *Vesennie perevyortyshi* (1973); *Tri meshka pshenitsy* (1973); *Noch posle vypuska* (1974); *Rasplata* (1979); *Sobranie sochineny* (4 vols., 1978–1980). FURTHER WORKS IN ENGLISH: *Three, Seven, Ace, and Other Stories* (1973); *A Topsy-Turvy Spring* (1978)

BIBLIOGRAPHY: Garrard, J. G., "V. T.," *SEEJ*, 9 (1965): 1–18; Ninov, A., "V. T.," *SovL*, No. 6 (1968): 162–65; Holthusen, J., *Twentieth-Century Russian Literature* (1972): 239–43; Brown, D., *Soviet Russian Literature since Stalin* (1978): 169–82; Shneidman, N. N., *Soviet Literature in the 1970's* (1979): 21–23; Hosking, G., *Beyond Socialist Realism* (1980): 84–100

—W. R. HIRSCHBERG

TENNANT, Emma

(pseud.: Catherine Aydy) British novelist, b. 20 Oct. 1937, London

T. is a leading exponent of British "New Fiction," a loose aggregate of science-fiction writers and postmodernists, and employs a highly self-conscious sense of parody in her works. Interested in the fictive nature of fiction, T. blurs traditional genres and exploits the conventions used in mainstream forms to produce a highly original vision. Feminism, gender, class relations, and social politics are all mediated through her peculiar style, leaving a view of contemporary Britain distinctively askew.

After an abortive first novel, T.'s career took off with *The Time of the Crack* (1973) and *The Last of the Country House Murders* (1974), two novels that meld the sensationally apocalyptic to a more sobering social analysis. The first uses the metaphor of a crack in the river Thames to explore the changing nature of British class relations. As the river slowly drains away, new questions and horrors are left in clear view for all those who wish to take notice. In the same way these observations on national disintegration and political decline and fall are carried over into the second novel. Essentially a parody of the country-house form of detective fiction, the novel begins as a murder mystery planned by the government to attract tourists. Yet this initial guise slowly dissolves to reveal a more sophisticated rumination on the future of the British ruling class at a time of possible revolution.

Yet T.'s concerns also reveal a profound interest in the nature of fiction itself and the possibilities of influencing the way we see the world by calling into question familiar structures of meaning. *Hotel de Dream* (1976) hilariously explores the irritation experienced by fictional characters themselves who hate what the writer is doing to

them. In an act of rebellion the fictional characters erupt into real life and try to take control of their own story. *Wild Nights* (1979), *Alice Fell* (1980), and *Queen of Stones* (1982) continue T.'s interest in blurring reality by relying on the eruptions of magical incident into the everyday. T. literally borrows story structures from classic novels and myths. *The Arabian Nights*, *Alice's Adventures in Wonderland*, and *Lord of the Flies* become new sites for her creative ability, turning familiar aspects of these stories on their heads, thus providing a new perspective. These borrowings add a new dimension to the originals and tend to channel the drama along gendered lines.

T. is also interested in questions of feminist identity and the ways in which the idea of the female is shaped by culture. By altering the familiar assumptions surrounding women's identities, T. not only offers alternatives but questions the ways in which these identities are policed. *The Bad Sister* (1978), a close copy of James Hogg's (1770–1835) *Confessions of a Justified Sinner* (1824), flips the sex of the main characters as the novel explores the limits of being a woman in an urban, political context. Because the central character has a split personality, her identity undergoes a radical transformation in this tale of duality, fanaticism, and the schizoid nature of modern women. T.'s interest in the dual nature of identity and reality is continued in *Woman Beware Woman* (1983), a feminist revenge tragedy, where myths and reality change places, subconscious drives erupt into the waking world, and thwarted love allied to resentment result in suppressed passion.

This duality is continued in *Two Women of London: The Strange Case of Ms. Jekyll and Mrs. Hyde* (1989). A reworking of Robert Louis Stevenson's story, the two female protagonists live split lives, reconciled with the use of antidepressant drugs. The novel explores the divided self and the pressures on women in a competitive society where poverty and conspicuous consumption coexist. It also calls into question the popularization of Victorian values and self-help ideologies to alleviate chronic social problems. Similarly, *Sisters and Strangers* (1990) offers a comprehensive survey of the lives, lies, and contradictions central to women's lives, in what is essentially a history of woman. An Eve story blended with 20th-c. realities, it outlines the recurring roles offered to women socially, in this disturbing postfeminist analysis especially concerned with love and romance through which women are expected to live.

T.'s cannon of work is both difficult and disturbing, mainly because she takes on trying questions. This, allied to her constant commitment to breaking down the traditional novel form, make T. a formidable modern writer. Yet T. is no mere aesthetician, and her work carefully reflects the painful unease at a time of major social transformation in which familiar stories collapse into something else entirely. A feminist and a political thinker, T. has pushed the British novel into exciting new directions.

FURTHER WORKS: *The Color of Rain* (1964); *Black Marina* (1985); *The Adventures of Robina, by Herself* (1986); *The House of Hospitalities* (1987); *A Wedding of Cousins* (1988); *The Magic Drum* (1989); *Faustine* (1991)

BIBLIOGRAPHY: Davis, R., *Possibility Fictions* (1988): 172–78; Marks, J., *The New Wave* (1989): 64–70; Cocker, N., *Grand Illusions* (1990): 3–7; Indiana, G., "E. T.'s Higher Powers," *Let It Bleed* (1996): 202-14

—PAUL HANSOM

TERZAKIS, Anghelos

Greek novelist, short-story writer, dramatist, essayist, and critic, b. 16 Feb. 1907, Nauplia; d. 3 Aug. 1979, Athens

Born into a wealthy family, T. studied law at the University of Athens; but, although admitted to the bar in 1929, he gave up practicing law for writing. From 1928 to 1930 he edited the literary magazines *Pnoi* and *Loghos*. Beginning in 1937 he served as secretary, then director of repertory, of the Greek National Theater; he eventually became general director of the dramatic school of that theater. From 1963 to 1967 he also edited the outstanding Athenian cultural monthly *Epohes*. He was awarded several important prizes and was elected to the Academy of Athens.

Two early collections of short stories showed the influence of the SYMBOLIST writer Konstandinos Hadzopoulos (1868–1920), but T. then turned to realism, focusing in most of his fiction on the economic and social problems of the lower middle class. Of his early novels in this vein, the most accomplished is *I menexedhenia politia* (1937; violet city). In his masterpiece, *I pringipessa Izabo* (1945; Princess Isabeau), however, T. deviated from this theme, turning to the historical novel. Through the romance between a Frankish princess and a young Greek, he vividly re-creates their world, portraying ethnic contrasts and the conflict between the declining Frankish rulers and the rising dynamism of their Greek subjects in the 13th-c. Peloponnese.

In subsequent novels and short stories T. returned with even greater skill—and pessimism—to the depiction of the deprivations, doubts, frustrations, and hopelessness of lower-middle-class life. In his last two masterful novels, *Dhihos Theo* (1951; without God) and the obviously confessional *Mystiki zoi* (1957; secret life), extraordinary narrative skill is combined with astute psychological observation in T.'s portrayal of families—studies of weak souls victimized by circumstance and self-imposed fate. In these works naked realism is enriched with symbolic and lyrical elements. *Dhihos Theo*, dealing with the troubled years between the two world wars, encompasses a wide variety of human types while dealing with modern political and social ideology, big-city alienation, and the sufferings of a lost generation. The more introspective *Mystiki zoi* uses modernist techniques such as the STREAM OF CONSCIOUSNESS and flashbacks to represent the search for an elusive truth of a man and a woman, who at the end fail to communicate.

Some consider T.'s dramatic work more important than his novels. His eleven plays were a major contribution to modern Greek drama in its developmental period. In *Aftokrator Mihail* (1936; Emperor Michael), *O stavros ke to spathi* (1939; the cross and the sword), and *Theofano* (1956; Theofano) he uses subjects from Byzantine history to depict the failure of mediocre leaders to connect their lives effectively with the great events of their times. Similar dialectics are dramatized in the biblical play *Thomas o dhipsyhos* (1962; Thomas of the divided soul) and in other dramas.

T. was also an essayist and literary critic of considerable reputation. In the numerous articles he contributed to newspapers and magazines he deals with a wide range of contemporary issues, and he also wrote insightfully about the drama. His creativity, combined with his intellectual and social awareness and his incessant activism, made him a leading figure in Greek literature.

FURTHER WORKS: *O xehasmenos* (1925); *Fthinoporini symfonia* (1929); *Dhesmotes* (1932); *I parakmi ton Skliron* (1933); *Ghamilio emvatirio* (1937); *Ilotes* (1939); *O exousiastis* (1942); *Tou erota ke tou thanatou* (1943); *I storyi* (1944); *To meghalo pehnidhi* (1944); *Taxidhi me ton Espero* (1946); *Aprilis* (1946); *Aghni* (1949); *Nyhta sti Mesoyio* (1958); *Prosanatolismos ston eona* (1963); *To mystirio tou Iaghou* (1964); *Helliniki epopiia* (1964); *O proghonos* (1970); *Afieroma stin trayiki mousa* (1970; *Homage to the Tragic Muse*, 1978)

BIBLIOGRAPHY: Demaras, C., et al., "A. T.: A Critical Mosaic," *The Charioteer*, No. 4 (1962): 50–54; Proussis, C. M., "The Novels of A. T.," *Daedalus*, 95 (1966): 1021–45; Vitti, M., "Family and Alienation in Contemporary Greek Fiction," in P. Bien and E. Keeley, eds., *Modern Greek Writers* (1972): 219–31 and passim; Politis, L., *A History of Modern Greek Literature* (1975): 257–58, 265–66

—ANDONIS DECAVALLES

THAHKIN KO-DAW HMAING

(pseud. of U Lun; other pseuds.: Maung Lun, Mit-sata Maung Hmaing) Burmese poet, dramatist, and novelist, b. 23 March 1876, Wale; d. 27 July 1964, Rangoon

T. K. H. was sent at an early age to Mandalay for a monastic education but returned in 1895 to his native Lower Burma to work on newspapers. Writing under the pseudonym of Maung Lun, he had by 1910 reached a wide audience through numerous traditional stage plays in verse on themes drawn from Burmese history and legend. Few survive, as he did not want to become known by such unserious works.

In 1911 T. K. H. became interested in politics through working on the newly established newspaper *Thu-ri-ya*; from then on he regularly wrote articles and poems commenting on contemporary events for this paper and other publications, such as the magazine *Dagon*, of which he later became editor. A master of Burmese classical literature, he wrote a great many works in verse (or in mixed verse-prose style), brilliantly presenting satires in the form of learned religious commentaries (*tika* in the Pali language) on worldly subjects, such as the series called *Hkwei ti-ka* (1925–27; commentary on dogs), in which he reproves Burmese politicians for wasting their efforts against the British in futile squabbling.

For his single novel, *Mit-sata Maung Hmaing hma-daw-bon wut-htu* (1921; the epistles of Mr. Maung Hmaing), he used a pen name which made fun of those Burmese who aped their British masters by using "Mr." in front of their names. Maung Hmaing was the name of a notorious rascal in an early Burmese novel, *Maung Hmaing wut-htu* (1904; the story of Maung Hmaing) by U Kyi (1848–1908). T. K. H. became known by his regular pseudonym in 1934, when he joined the Do-bama party (a group of young Burmese nationalists who called themselves "Thahkin," or "master").

T. K. H. is considered to be unequaled in the *lei-gyo-gyi*, a traditional poetic form to which he gave striking new content with great popular appeal, and through which he was an inspiration to the younger generation of Burmese nationalists. He fostered their interest in history, aroused their pride in their language and culture, urged them to take positive action such as student strikes—as in *Bwaing-kauk ti-ka* (1927; boycott commentary)—but also mocked those who were mere political opportunists. After World War II he wrote less, devoting his energies to persuading his fellow citizens to live in peace and unity in independent but politically divided Burma.

The allusive and highly memorable style of his poems made them very popular with his fellow countrymen while at the same time preserving them from British government censorship. A man of many skills—a true Buddhist and a staunch patriot; poet and playwright; historian and teacher; pioneer writer and satirist— T. K. H. is the single most revered literary figure in modern Burma.

FURTHER WORKS: *Bo ti-ka* (1920); *Myauk ti-ka* (1923); *Galon-byan di-pani tika* (1930); *Thankin ti-ka* (1934)

BIBLIOGRAPHY: Tin Htway, U., "The Role of Literature in Nation Building," *JBRS*, 55, Parts 1–2 (1972): 19–46

—ANNA J. ALLOTT

THAI LITERATURE

Literature in the Thai language goes back to the 13th c. Before the second half of the 19th c., when Thailand (formerly Siam) came into close contact with Western civilization, imaginative writing had appeared in three main genres: songs and lyric poems, narrative poetry, and dance drama. Prose was used chiefly for practical purposes, such as recording history and promulgating laws.

Literature in 20th-c. Thailand is usually written in the national language, but regional oral literatures can still be found in other languages: Mon, Khmer, Karen, and Chinese. During the modernization of Thailand in the Chulalongkorn period (1868–1910) new forms, techniques, subjects, ideas, and goals were introduced into literature, and several new genres emerged.

The Novel

The Thai novel has generally been aimed more at the senses than at the intellect. Nevertheless, some novelists have dealt with serious issues and have presented more diversified subjects, including a broader spectrum of Thai society.

In *Lakhon haeng chiwit* (1929; the circus of life), the first Thai autobiographical novel, Prince Akatdamkoeng Raphiphat (1905–1932) deals with alienation. The protagonist sees his homeland as in serious need of development, a country whose cultural system has deprived him of personal fulfillment. After working abroad as a journalist, he returns home, becomes a novelist, and hopes through his work to bring about a better-educated society.

The most famous humorist, P. Intharapalit (Pricha Intharapalit, 1910–1968), had a large readership, encompassing adults and school-children, intellectuals and the common people. His most popular work is his series of unconnected, self-contained episodes about the "Trio"—Phon, Nikon, and Kim-ngaun—whose behavior and attitudes reflect the development of Thai society since the end of World War II.

Suwanni Sukhontha (Suwanni Sukhonthiang, b. 1932), a painter turned novelist, became well known for her novel *Khao chu Kan* (1970; his name is Kan), whose protagonist is an idealistic physician who has left Bangkok for a job in the provinces. Confronted by many problems, social as well as personal, his efforts fail, and he dies in the end.

The life of the old upper class is portrayed by such writers as M. R. Kukrit PRAMOJ, also a prominent journalist and politician. His greatest novel, *Si phaendin* (1953; *Four Reigns*, 1981), is a saga centered on an upper-class woman. Botan (pseud. of Supha Lusiri Sirising, b. (1945), of Chinese descent, was the first writer to express the pride of her ethnic group in novel form. Her *Chotmai chak muang Thai* (1969; *Letters from Thailand*, 1977), which depicts the lives of Chinese immigrants making their fortune in Thailand, won a SEATO award for the best novel of 1969, although it aroused great conroversy.

Among novelists focusing on the country-side, Nimit Phumithawon (1935–1981), a schoolteacher in the northern part of the central plain, often depicted the local people. *Dae khun khru duai khom faek* (1969; to sir with a club), tells how a young schoolteacher in rural Thailand faces and overcomes severe educational and social problems. Villagers in the northeast are portrayed by Khamphun Bunthawi (b. 1928). His *Luk i-san* (1971; a son of the northeast) shows how the peasants suffer from poverty yet still manage to enjoy life.

The spiritual confusion arising from rapid social change and disintegrating morality finds expression in the works of Buddhist scholars, such as Wasin Inthasara's (b. 1934) *Phra A-non Phuttha anucha* (1965; Phra Anon, the brother of the Lord Buddha), in which he discusses aspects of Buddhism applicable to modern life, in a language that can be grasped by laymen.

Some writers use the novel as an instrument for social change, for example, SIBURAPHA (pseud. of Kulap Saipradit) and Seni Saowaphong (pseud. of Sakchai Bamrungphong, b. 1918). These writers want the voice of the people to be heard and their needs to be felt. In the unfinished novel *Lae pai khang na* (2 parts, 1955, 1957; look forward) Siburapha shows his admiration for the People's Party, which was successful in bringing about a constitutional monarchy in 1932, and his antipathy toward dictatorial government. Seni Saowaphong's novel *Pisat* (1944; the ghost) tells of a country youth who comes to Bangkok to study, earns a law degree, and returns to the countryside, where he feels he is more needed. Seni shows the hardships of Thai farmers, struggling against poverty and debt. Both Seni and Siburapha point out the error of the old upper class in trying to preserve the status quo.

Concern for better social conditions also features prominently in *Raya* (1955; Raya) by Sot Kuramarohit (1908–1978), which takes place during and after World War II. Raya is a country youth determined to fight against evil. During the war he joins the Free Thai Movement and afterward battles corruption and wickedness in politics. Sot suggests that a cooperative system could solve economic problems.

The leading woman novelist has been Dokmai SOT, whose works, mainly dealing with upper-class women, are conservative in outlook. Unlike most women novelists, who emulate Dokmai Sot in her choice of domestic subjects, Boonlua (M. L. Boonlua Debyasuvarn, 1911–1982), Dokmai Sot's sister, created in *Surat nari* (1971; women of Surat) an imaginary country in which women are in control and progressive-minded men campaign for equal rights. This satirical novel reflects many aspects of contemporary Thailand.

The Short Story

In the early part of the century most short stories were didactic, often sentimental, with love as the principal subject. Later, as with the novel, subjects and themes became more varied. Nearly all Thai novelists have tried their hands at the genre, but a few writers are noted primarily for their stories. Manat Chanyong (1907–1965) published over a thousand short stories. Although he wrote about a variety of middle- and lower-class types, his most famous works are those about country folk. The way of life Manat portrays preserves the old values, when rural people lived simply and in harmony with their surroundings. Friendship, gratitude, and integrity govern the community.

Lao KHAMHOM (pseud. of Khamsing Sinok), who also writes about country people, presents a different view. In his two small volumes—*Fa bo kan* (1958; the sky bars none), a collection of short stories, and *Kamphaeng* (1974; the wall), containing short stories and other writings—he depicts the poor and superstitious peasants of the northeast, who are virtually isolated from the modern world. Twelve of his stories were published in English translation as *The Politician, and Other Stories* (1973).

A-chin Panchaphan (b. 1927) draws his subjects from his own experiences in the tin mines in southern Thailand. His mine stories focus on an engineering student who has dropped out of the university to work in the mines.

The most unusual short-story writer has been Rong Wong-savun (Narong Wong-sa-vun, b. 1932), who began as a journalist and photographer. His distinctive style is characterized by word coinages, new expressions, and unusual images. His subject matter is wide-ranging, and his stories are set in a variety of places: a café in Bang Lamphu Square in the heart of old Bangkok, the Thai countryside, a clean street in Peking, an expensive nightclub in the "concrete jungle" of San Francisco.

Poetry

Although the Thais still think of themselves as a poetry-minded people, there are not many who have composed substantial works in the 20th c. Historical narratives have sometimes been used in Thai verse. A remarkable work of this kind is the posthumously published *Sam krung* (1952; the three capital cities), in which Prince Bidya-lankarana (1876–1945), also a short-story writer of note, not only employed all the Thai verse forms but also invented a new one, as well as using the punctuation marks of Western grammar. The poem begins in 1767, the year the capital city of Ayutthaya was destroyed by the Burmese, and ends shortly before the close of World War II, *Sam krung* is remarkable not only for its style but for its humor and sharp wit.

Buddhist ethics pervade much of Thai poetry. Using a variety of conventional *chan* forms, Nai Chit Burathat (1896–1942), in *Samakkhi phet kham chan* (1915; unity destroyed), asserts that once unity is lost, no matter how strong a state had been, its destruction is inevitable.

A new note in poetry was sounded with the publication in 1964 of the collected poems of the revolutionary Ang-khan Kalayanaphong (b. 1926), who broke with the old conventions. His love of nature, art, and poetry itself is set against his disgust with modern society, which caused him anguish and bitterness. Ang-khan has been accused of corrupting the beauty of Thai poetic diction by using "unpoetic" and vulgar language. But this very technique enables him to express emotions and ideas strikingly. A number of his poems have been published in English translation in journals. Also a visual artist, Ang-khan sometimes uses elaborate calligraphy.

After the student-led popular uprising in October 1973, lyric poetry with overtones of Maoist theories of art and literature filled book stands in Bangkok. Some poets drew their material from the uprising, including eulogizing those who died in it. Works of this sort vanished after October 6, 1976, the chaotic day when the elected government was ousted; a number of prominent figures fled the country, and a few days later a military-supported government took power. This regime imposed strict censorship and banned leftist books.

In the past two decades graffiti has become an important form of poetry. The scribblers use the conventional forms of proverb, saying, and aphorism, but with fresh content. These often humorous writings—on walls and vehicles—reflect problems of contemporary society and also affirm the traditional Thai penchant for poetry amid the influx of foreign influences and rapid social change.

Recently another new form of expression has appeared—concrete or visual poetry. This kind of work is still in an experimental stage in Thailand and appeals more to students than to the general public.

Drama

After Crown Prince Vajiravudh (1881–1925) returned from England, where he had been educated, he introduced Western-style prose drama to Thailand. He encouraged translations and adaptations of European plays and wrote a number of original plays himself (as well as an epistolary narrative).

There were also innovations in the classical dance drama, moving it in the direction of musical drama and opera. Prince Vajiravudh, who later became king, and other princes and noblemen established their own repertory theaters. In more recent times films and television have become more popular than theater. Many novels are dramatized for these media. It is thus left to the universities to promote stage plays.

Modern Thai literature also encompasses children's literature and many forms of non-fictional prose: autobiographies, biographies, essays, diaries, letters, memoirs, travel books, and literary criticism.

Literature in this century has become increasingly public. Poetry readings, lectures, discussions about literature, and contests of impromptu poetry have become frequent. Book fairs are held from time to time, with prizes awarded to the best works. This lively activity bodes well for the future of Thai literature.

BIBLIOGRAPHY: Jumsai, M. L. M., *History of Thai Literature* (1973); Rutnin, M., ed., *The Siamese Theatre: A Collection of Reprints from the Journal of the Siam Society* (1975); Senanan, W., *The Genesis of the Novel in Thailand* (1975); Umavijani, M., *The Domain of Thai Literature* (1978); Chitakasem, M., "The Development of Political and Social Consciousness in Thai Short Stories," in Davidson, J. H. C. S., and H. Cordell, eds., *The Short Story in South East Asia: Aspects of a Genre* (1982): 63–99

—WIBHA SENANAN KONGKANANDA

THAW-DA HSWEI

(pseud. of U Kyin Hswei) Burmese short-story writer, humorist, and satirist, b. 26 May 1919, Kyo-bin village, Paung-de township

The eldest son of a well-to-do paddy farmer in Lower Burma, T. H. finished secondary school and was studying English when war broke out. He worked as a pony-cart driver, then tried trading, lost money, lived an irregular life, and finally turned to writing, with a very funny story, "Baran-di tapalin" (1947; a bottle of brandy) in the newly established magazine *Shumawa*. Encouraged by the success of his story, T. H. began writing regularly, first humorous stories, then, in the 1950s, realistic accounts of urban and country life.

In his earliest stories T. H. was rarely able to resist a laugh, a pun, or a vulgar joke; but he soon turned to satire, presenting sometimes quite unflattering portraits of his fellow writers, more often powerful condemnations of human stupidity, greed, and cruelty. Thus, in the collection *Bawa hto hto* (1961; many lives), based on his wartime experience of running a tea shop, he shocks the reader with the life story of a young prostitute whom he had befriended. This story, "Lu lu-gyin kaik-sa-nei-gya-ba-thi" (man preys on man), describes without a trace of sentimentality, how heartlessly local menfolk look forward to the death of the exhausted young prostitute, as her funeral will be the excuse for seven days of gambling and feasting.

T. H.'s full and varied life style provides rich material for his many-sided talent as a storyteller. He can vividly evoke a typical Burmese scene by the brief description of sights, sounds, and smells; he can conjure up the inhabitants of both town and countryside by means of a few lines of dialogue or a brief account of an incident. Two prize-winning collections, *Thadawa-do-i than-thaya* (1964; all creatures that on earth do dwell) and *I law-ka myei mahi-we* (1970; life on this earth), depict many of the less pleasant realities of country life such as theft of animals and brigandage.

In a country in which the writer's role is, by tradition and by present government policy, a didactic one, T. H. is unusual in refusing to offer himself as a model. On the contrary, many of his most popular stories are honest accounts of his own sins, written with such self-mockery and humor that all criticism is disarmed. In the collection *Pyei myan-ma pya-yok-mya* (1962; what life is like in Burma) he turned his satire against the cruelty of antigovernment insurgents who have been active since Burma's independence was declared in 1948.

In Burma T. H. is particularly liked for his sincerity and forthrightness. Recent stories either deal with basic moral dilemmas or are episodes from his own life, since present political conditions have made it difficult even for such well-established authors as T. H. to write of life exactly as it is.

FURTHER WORKS: *Lu-bon hkan-wa* (1966); *Lawka lu-pyei* (1968); *Kyun-daw bawa-zat-kyaung* (1972 ff.)

BIBLIOGRAPHY: Chit, Khin Myo, "Thaw-dar-swe," *The Guardian Magazine*, Oct. 1957: 19–20; Allott, A. J., "The Short Story in Burma, with Special Reference to Its Social and Political Significance," in J. H. C. S. Davidson and H. Cordell, eds., *The Short Story in South East Asia* (1982): 101–39

—ANNA J. ALLOTT

THEATER OF THE ABSURD

The term "Theater of the Absurd" became current after the appearance in 1961 of a book with this title by the present author. It has been applied to the work of a group of playwrights who created something like a new convention in drama in France during the 1950s—Arthur ADAMOV, Eugène IONESCO, Samuel BECKETT, Jean GENET—and to a number of younger dramatists who subsequently began to write in this style: the Spanish dramatist Fernando ARRABAL; Harold PINTER, N. F. Simpson (b. 1919), David Campton (b. 1924), and Tom STOPPARD in England; Günter GRASS and Wolfgang HILDESHEIMER in West Germany; Sławomir MROŻEK and Tadeusz RÓŻEWICZ in Poland; Václav HAVEL in Czechoslovakia; and Edward ALBEE, Arthur Kopit (b. 1937), and Jean-Claude Van Itallie (b. 1936) in the U.S., to name only the most prominent.

The writers who are often referred to by the term have never formed a conscious grouping or literary movement. They are all highly individualized personalities, and in no way have they themselves acknowledged that they constitute a school of dramatists. Yet they have some basic features and techniques in common.

In plays like Beckett's *En attendant Godot* (1952; *Waiting for Godot*, 1954) or Ionesco's *Le rhinocéros* (1959; *Rhinoceros*, 1960), there is no pretense that the action on stage is aiming at realism: two men waiting endlessly by a lonely tree for the coming of someone with whom they may or may not have an appointment—two men whose previous life or way of earning a livelihood is never disclosed; or a strange disease that turns a whole population into raging pachyderms, could not possibly convincingly exist in the real world. Yet the audience is never told whether what they are witnessing is meant to be a dream, allegory, or symbolism. Nor is such interpretation at all essential: the images presented by these plays are *metaphors* for aspects of human existence; like metaphors in poetry their function is to evoke states of mind, feelings in all their complexity, with all the clusters of associations, hopes, and anxieties that are experienced when we are suffering the agony of *waiting*, or the equal agony of seeing our best friends being brainwashed into becoming the tools of some totalitarian political party or religious ideology.

The writers of the Theater of the Absurd are, essentially, trying to transfer some of the methods of poetry to the stage. A lyric is a structure of metaphors; it does not aim at telling a story but merely at evoking feelings. Drama, on the other hand, has traditionally relied on the elements of fiction—plot and character—in order to hold an audience's attention and to create the desire to find out what is going to happen next—in short, suspense. How can an accumulation of mere metaphorical images create the suspense needed to keep an audience in their seats? In these absurdist plays the characters are vague or unstable (men change into rhinos), and the action often is without rational or psychological motivation. Yet, in defiance of all traditional expectations, the plays of Beckett, Ionesco, Adamov, and Pinter have achieved considerable and lasting success in the Theater. They have done so by creating a new type of suspense. In the conventional theater the audience has to ask itself from scene to scene: "What is going to happen next?" In the Theater of the Absurd they must ask themselves: "What *is* happening?" In other words, these playwrights have achieved the extremely difficult feat of creating situations so mysterious and yet fascinating that the audience is made to want to unravel the mystery, or at least to watch the unfolding of the completed structure of metaphorical images of which the play is composed. What is more, through the brilliance of their dialogue these writers are able to rivet the audience's attention and evoke their amusement from sentence to sentence. The characters may be undefined in *Waiting for Godot* and literally nothing happens in the play, which ends exactly as it began, but from moment to moment the dialogue is amusing and witty and there is always something happening—however mysterious or nonsensical.

The emergence of a considerable number of major dramatists who, in pursuing their individual visions and inclinations, have all hit upon what is basically a new convention of dramatic structure and technique, points to the fact that the Theater of the Absurd met a need of its period, responded to the *Zeitgeist*. And indeed, the disillusionment with any fixed ideological interpretation of the world, religious or political, after World War II—a disillusionment that led to Jean-Paul SARTRE's and Albert CAMUS's EXISTENTIAL-ISM, a view of the world as essentially without a meaning accessible to mankind and hence "absurd" (in the philosophical sense of the term)—is reflected in the bleak world view of the absurdist playwrights. Moreover, modern psychology and philosophy have thrown the classical concept of human character and identity into question, while other dominant tenets of modern philosophy, such as logical positivism, have equally powerfully questioned the ability of human language to arrive at an adequate representation of reality. All these trends are, subconsciously rather than consciously, reflected in the work of the dramatists of the Theater of the Absurd.

The subject matter of the plays of the Theater of the Absurd is consequently derived from basic human anxieties and concerns: the nature of the self and the problematic definition of an individual's identity; the inexorable presence of death facing human beings at any moment of their lives; the difficulties of genuine communication among people imprisoned in their own perceptions of "the other"; the nature of time in its irreversible flow; the absence, in our over organized and computerized world, of what Ionesco calls a "metaphysical dimension"; the alienation of mankind through greed and materialism and the continued subconscious yearning for a religious experience; the illusory nature of the power structures of our world (which Genet sees as the expression of the sexual fantasies of those in charge of institutions); and, pervading it all, the imperfections and pitfalls of language, the medium that often distorts and dictates our thinking and feeling.

Yet these serious matters tend to find expression in forms that are grotesquely comic and farcical; the plays are often labeled as "tragic farce," "antitheater," "grotesque." They thus represent an extreme form of the tendency of modern drama toward the mixed genre of "tragicomedy." In a world without ultimate discernible purpose, even the most serious matters become in some way ridiculous: BLACK HUMOR is the only possible response to such a world, the only way to assert human dignity in the face of despair and hopelessness. The courage to face the world in all its incomprehensibility thus becomes, for writers like Beckett, Adamov, Ionesco, and Genet, the highest of ethical values.

The Theater of the Absurd had its heyday after the success of Beckett's *Waiting for Godot* in Paris in 1953, Ionesco's *Rhinoceros* in London in 1960, Pinter's *The Caretaker* in London (1960), and the 1960 Paris production of Genet's *Le balcon* (1956; rev. ed., 1960; *The Balcony*, 1957). In the 1970s the apathy engendered in France and elsewhere by the collapse of the revolutionary movements of the late 1960s led to a decline in interest in the problems raised by the playwrights of the absurd and a return to a more realistic (and materialistic) style of drama, while the avant-garde turned to more formal experiments with the theatrical space.

The Theater of the Absurd has, however, contributed a great deal to the enrichment of the permanent vocabulary of theater. Techniques that would previously have been regarded as impracticable or highly unconventional have become familiar and acceptable to audiences: the introduction of dream and fantasy scenes into realistic drama; the use of sudden transitions from one plane of reality to another; dialogue arising from incomprehension, misunderstanding of vocabulary, or grotesque heightening of language. All these have now become almost commonplaces of mainstream drama and even have affected the mass media.

The Theater of the Absurd, which had its origins in certain aspects of the literary-dramatic tradition—the use of powerful stage metaphors (like the image of naked King Lear confronting the storm); clowning and mad scenes; SURREALISTIC imagery and nonsense poetry; medieval and Renaissance allegory; the EXPRES-SIONISM and dream plays of STRINDBERG—has thus now reunited with that tradition, enriching and enlarging it. Hardly any play written since the phenomenon arose is entirely free from its influence.

BIBLIOGRAPHY: Camus, A., *The Myth of Sisyphus* (1955); Grossvogel, D., *The Self-Conscious Stage in Modern French Drama* (1958); Esslin, M., *The Theatre of the Absurd* (1961; 3rd updated ed., 1980); Guicharnaud, J., *Modern French Theatre from Giraudoux to Beckett* (1961); Grossvogel, D., *Four Playwrights and a Post-script* (1962); Pronko, L. C., *Avant-Garde: The Experimental Theater in France* (1962); Wellwarth, G., *The Theatre of Protest and Paradox* (1964; rev. ed., 1971); Fletcher, J., ed., *Forces in Modern French Drama* (1972); Jacquart, E. C., *Le théâtre de la dérision* (1974)

—MARTIN ESSLIN

THEIN HPEI MYINT

Burmese novelist, short-story writer, essayist, and journalist, b. 10 July 1914, Bu-dalin; d. 15 Jan. 1978, Rangoon

Son of a minor government official, T. H. M. began writing fiction while a student at the University of Rangoon. He took up journalism while studying law in Calcutta, where he came in touch with Bengali Communists and made a lifelong commitment both to writing with a social purpose and to left-wing politics.

His first novel, *Tet hpon-gyi* (1937; the modern monk), created a sensation because of its portrayal of certain Buddhist monks as corrupt and sexually immoral. Angry monks demanded that the work be banned. In 1938 he helped found the Nagani (Red Dragon) Book Club, whose first title was T. H. M.'s biography of the revered nationalist writer, Thakhin Ko-daw HMAING, entitled *Hsaya Lun ahtok-pat-ti* (1938; biography of U Lun).

His prewar experiences with the nationalist movement as a student, his extensive travels inside and outside Burma, especially after the war, his expulsion from the Burmese Communist Party, and his involvement in political and social matters have been used by him as material for several major novels and thirty or so important short stories; he has also chronicled his experiences in numerous memoirs and travelogues and in an autobiography, *Kyun-daw-i ahcit-u* (1974; literature, my first love).

Thabeik-hmauk kyaung-tha (1937; the student boycotter) gives a picture of the 1936 students' strike at Rangoon University; *Lanza paw-bi* (1949; the way out) covers the confused period of 1945–47; *Ashei-ga nei-wun htwet-thi-pama* (1958; as sure as the sun rising in the east) captures the excitement of the growing anti-British nationalist movement between 1936 and 1942. All three of these are novels, but they are based on events in T. H. M.'s own life. *Wuthtu-do baung-gyok* (1966; collected short stories) contains stories written between 1934 and 1966 on such themes as the poverty that leads to dishonesty and prostitution, the plight of refugees fleeing from insurgent attacks, and the corruption of politicians.

T. H. M. is one of the most widely read writers in Burma today and probably one of the most influential. He applied his versatile talents to a wide range of subjects and never hesitated to deal with controversial matters—venereal disease in *Tet-hkit Nat-hso* (1938; evil spirits of modern times), alcoholism in *Thu-do lin-maya 34 hnit* (1978; married for thirty-four years)—or to criticize segments of the community that might have preferred to remain unchallenged, such as the *sangha* (Buddhist monkhood) and the government. He was never content to approach literature merely as a diversion; he rarely wrote humorously but nearly always sought to provoke and to convince, to inform and to influence his readers.

FURTHER WORKS: *Ngaing-nganyei atwei-akyon-mya* (1956); *Sit-atwin hkayi-the* (1966). FURTHER WORKS IN ENGLISH: *Selected Short Stories* (1973)

BIBLIOGRAPHY: Milne, P. M., Introduction to T. H. M., *Selected Short Stories* (1973): 1–19; Allott, A. J., "The Short Story in Burma, with Special Reference to Its Social and Political Significance," in Davidson, J. H. C. S., and Cordell, H., *The Short Story in South East Asia* (1982): 101–39

—ANNA J. ALLOTT

THEOTOKAS, Yorghos (George)

Greek novelist, dramatist, and essayist, b. 27 Aug. 1905, Constantinople, Ottoman Empire (now Istanbul, Turkey); d. 30 Oct. 1966, Athens

T.'s family came from the island of Chios. After the Asia Minor disaster in 1922, whereby Greece lost territories to Turkey that had been recognized as Greek in 1920, T. settled with his parents in Athens and earned a law degree there in 1926. He practiced law in Athens and in 1956 ran for parliament, but did not win. T., who in *Dhokimio yia tin Ameriki* (1954; essay about America) expressed admiration for Franklin Roosevelt and the New Deal, was in his political orientation a social democrat. In 1961 he supported Prime Minister Yorghos Papandreou, and when, in 1963, King Constantine dismissed Papandreou, T., in articles in the newspaper *To vima*, later collected in *I ethniki krisi* (1966; the national crisis), warned against the threat of a military dictatorship, which came to pass a year after his death.

In most of his fiction T. favored a formal, epiclike style and always wrote in the demotic. He liked to gather in one narrative, as if on a mural, many characters of contrasting backgrounds and personalities. In his first epic-length and, to many, most interesting novel, *Argho* (1936; *Argo*, 1951), he juxtaposes a wheeling-and-dealing politician, Pavlos Skinas, and an idealistic seminarian-turned-communist, Dhamianos Frantzis. These opposite characters, like others in T.'s works, illustrate his concern with the recurrent disparity between ideology and reality. He had already called on Greek writers to reject easy dogmatisms in his long essay *Elefthero pnevma* (1929; free spirit), and this document became the manifesto of T. and other writers who came to be known as the Generation of the Thirties.

In *Argho*, a novel about intellectual ferment in Athens, T. depicts the ideological and psychological turmoil that resulted from the frustration of long-held political aspirations because of the 1922 disaster, as well as from the social tensions generated in neighboring European nations polarized by fascism and communism.

World War II, the civil war, and other upheavals further shook the Greek nation. In 1964 T. published another epic-length novel, *Asthenis ke odhipori* (1964; invalids and travelers). As in *Argho*, T. portrays characters caught in a maelstrom of conflicting creeds while they attempt to remain true to both their national tradition and their inner selves.

T. was active in the advancement of the modern Greek theater. He wanted to create a theater of ideas and drew his material from the whole of Greek tradition: from antiquity, as in *Alkiviadhis* (1957; *Alcibiades*, 1966); from Byzantine history, as in *I Lakena* (1944; the Lakonian woman); from modern history, as in *Andara st' Anapli* (1942; revolt at Anapli); from Karaghiozis shadow-theater, as in *To kastro tis orias* (1944; the castle of beauty). During two short intervals (1945–46 and 1950–52) T. complemented his success as a playwright with the directorship of the Greek National Theater.

Ideas and their power to orient or disorient nations and individuals remained T.'s chief concern. Undoubtedly it was because of this intellectual focus that some critics characterize his narratives and dramas as "cold" and "cerebral." But the issues that T. pondered grew naturally out of his time and place. Moreover, T. could adopt, when appropriate, a more subjective, even lyrical style—most notably in the novella *Leonis* (1940; Leonis), in which he portrays the life of the Greek bourgeoisie of Constantinople in their last happy years, simultaneously describing the pangs of Leonis's first love, a private event no less disorienting to him than his politically caused displacement to Athens. For T., the forces that affected humankind were numerous, complex, and ultimately not analyzable.

FURTHER WORKS: *Ores arghias* (1931); *Embros sto kinoniko provlima* (1932); *Fylla imeroloyiou* (2 vols., 1934); *Evripidhis Pendozalis ke alles istories* (1937); *To dhemonio* (1939); *Imeroloyio tis "Arghos" ke tou "Dhemoniou"* (1939); *Pefti to vradhi* (1941); *To yefiri tis Artas* (1942); *Oniro tou Dhodhekamerou* (1943); *To pehnidhi tis trelas ke tis fronimadhas* (1944; "The Game of Folly versus Wisdom," 1969); *Sto katofli ton neon keron* (1945); *Synapandima stin Pendeli* (1947); *To timima tis lefterias* (1948); *Provlimata tou kerou mas* (1956); *Sklires rizes* (1956); *I akri tou dhromou* (1960); *Pnevmatiki poria* (1961); *Taxidhi sti Mesi Anatoli ke sto Ayion Oros* (1961); *O telefteos polemos* (1964); *Theatrika ergha* (2 vols., 1965–1966); *I kambanes* (1970); *Taxidhia* (1971); *Allilografia: 1930–1966* (1975, with George Seferis); *I orthodhoxia ston kero mas* (1975); *Politika kimena* (1976); *Simees ston ilio* (1985). FURTHER WORKS IN ENGLISH: *Leonis: A Novel* (1985)

BIBLIOGRAPHY: Panayotopoulos, I. M., Karandonis, A., and Sahinis, A., "G. T.: A Critical Mosaic," *Charioteer*, 5 (1963): 60–64; Seferis, G., "Conversation with Fabrice," *Agenda*, 7, 1 (1969): 50–57; Mackridge, P., "Bibliography of G. T.," *Mantatophoros*, No. 3 (1973): 18–20; Doulis, T., *G. T.* (1975); Doulis, T., *Disaster and Fiction: The Impact of the Asia Minor Disaster of 1922 on Modern Greek Fiction* (1977): 90–96: 106–9: 166–68; Richer, R., *L'itinéraire de G. T.* (1979)

—EDWARD PHINNEY

THERIAULT, Yves

Canadian novelist, short-story writer, radio and television scriptwriter, dramatist, and essayist (writing in French), b. 28 Nov. 1915, Quebec; d. 20 Oct. 1983, Rawdon, Province of Quebec

T. received his education in Montreal at the Notre-Dame-de-Grâce Parochial School and the MontSaint-Louis School before embarking on a number of professions, as trapper, truck driver, boxer, salesman, radio announcer, and scriptwriter, carrying out these activities in various cities, among them Montreal, Trois-Rivières, and Hull. A grant from the French government enabled him to go to France in 1950; from there he left on a trip around the world. Following this period of exploration and self-discovery, he devoted himself to literature, except for interruptions brought about by his work for the government—from 1965 to 1967 he was director of cultural affairs in the ministry of cultural affairs—and by illness—in 1970, a heart problem forced him to cease all activities temporarily.

T. is Quebec's most prolific and one of its most successful writers, among the few to live exclusively from writing. His first book, *Contes pour un homme seul* (1944; tales for a man alone), a collection of short stories, was a popular success and set him on the road to his literary career. In it, we find rebellious individuals with larger-than-life temperaments, the very type of psychological and physical traits that can be seen in characters in his later novels, works such as *Le dompteur d'ours* (1951; the bear tamer), *Aaron* (1954; Aaron), *Agakuk* (1958; *Agakuk*, 1963), *Ashini* (1961; *Ashini*, 1972), *Cul-de-sac* (1961; *Cul-de-sac*, 1973), and *Kesten* (1968; *Kesten*, 1973).

Many of his works can be read in the context of the recent history of Quebec, with the isolation of the Francophones in a sea of Anglophones, the opposition of two cultures in one nation, the group's oppression of the individual, and the gradual fulfillment of individuals confronted by forces tugging at them. In addition to societal polarizations, sexual opposition and harmony are repeatedly explored in T.'s works.

T. presents the reader with "outsiders" who must constantly struggle to assert their identity. In *Aaron*, Jews are the protagonists. Moishe, with orthodox values, confronts not only the "other" world around him, but, within his own, Aaron, his grandson, who rejects his heritage. Aaron in turn seeks to liberate himself from his surroundings in a poor section of Montreal and to become part of the English world. Transposed into the traditional Catholic world of Quebec, we have the confrontation of the upholders of tradition against the newer generation eager for change and for the world of the future.

In T.'s most successful work, *Agakuk*, which has been translated into approximately twenty languages, the hero, an Inuit, leaves the traditional life of the village to go live alone with his wife Iriook, herself an outsider, a bearer of different customs and outlooks, in a remote arctic area several days' journey away. There he carries on the struggle for survival against nature, the wilderness, aided by Iriook, who is more instructed than ordinary Inuit women, more resourceful, and more independent-minded. The oppositions are between the individual and the group, the native culture and the white world with its different values, laws, and degrees of civilization, and, not least, between a husband and his wife. Rich in detail about the daily life of the residents of inhospitable climates, with vivid descriptions of the hunt, the building of living quarters, the sexual life of the couple, and the birth of their

children, the work portrays the successful self-fulfillment of Agakuk, who is nevertheless forced to accept the nontraditional values of his wife, who is every bit as successful and even more evolved than he.

In recognition of the quality and quantity of his work—forty novels and stories, twenty books for children, numerous plays, over one thousand scripts for radio and television—T. has been the recipient of many awards, for example, from the Province of Quebec in 1954 and 1958, and from the governor general in 1960. In 1959 he was elected to the Royal Society of Canada. Although not known for modern approaches to creative writing, T. has nonetheless succeeded in developing a lively, energetic style appropriate to his narratives, and he has treated topics that have had a wide appeal. He has been called the father of Quebec letters.

FURTHER WORKS: *Roi de la côte nord* (1960); *Le vendeur d'étoiles* (1961); *Séjour à Moscou* (1961); *Si la bombe m'était contée* (1962); *La rose de Pierre* (1964); *N'Tsuk* (1968; *N'Tsuk*, 1972); *Tayaout, fils d'Agakuk* (1969); *Le haut pays* (1973); *Agoak, l'héritage d'Agakuk* (1975; *Agoak, The Legacy of Agakuk*, 1979); *Œuvre de chair* (1975; *Ways of the Flesh*, 1977); *Le partage de minuit* (1980); *L'étreinte de Vénus. Contes policiers* (1981); *La femme Anna et autres contes* (1981); *Valéric et le grand canot. Récits* (1981); *L'herbe de tendresse. Récits* (1983)

BIBLIOGRAPHY: Bessette, G., "French Canadian Society As Seen by Contemporary Novelists," *QQ*, 69 (1962): 177–97; Robidoux, R., and A. Renaud, *Le roman canadien-français du vingtième siècle* (1966): 92–103; Edmond, M., *Y. T. et le combat de l'homme* (1973); Carrier, D., *Bibliographie analytique d'Y. T. 1940–1984* (1985); Cagnon, M., *The French Novel of Quebec* (1986): 55–59; Talbot, E. J., "T.'s *Agakuk:* The Matter of Closure," *Québec Studies*, 4 (1986): 127–34; Lemire, M., et al., *Dictionnaire des œuvres littéraires du Québec* (1982), Vol. 3, passim; (1984), Vol. 4, passim; (1987), Vol. 5, passim; Hamel et al., R., *Dictionnaire des auteurs de langue française en Amérique du Nord* (1989): 1283–86

—PAUL BARRETTE

THEROUX, Paul

American novelist and travel writer, b. 10 Apr. 1941, Medford, Mass.

T. began his career as a novelist with the publication of *Waldo* (1967), a work that satirizes father-son relationships, academic life, the popular press, psychiatry, and contemporary sexual mores via the adventures of Waldo, the title character. *Waldo* was quickly followed by three novels that grew out of T.'s experiences in Africa: *Fong and the Indians* (1968), *Girls at Play* (1969), and *Jungle Lovers* (1971). These African novels, which have been collected in a single volume entitled *On the Edge of the Great Rift* (1996), established T. as an author interested in postcolonial life in Third World nations, the clash between cultures, and the dilemmas faced by individuals who live in alien lands. Each of T.'s African novels examines the roles of "Others" in Africa. *Fong and the Indians* deals with the experiences of Asians in East Africa and, in addition to attacking the racist treatment of Asians living in postcolonial African nations, also criticizes America's inane Cold

War foreign policy. *Girls at Play* describes the situations encountered by white women in postcolonial Kenya and debunks popular Western conceptions about Africa. *Jungle Lovers* dramatizes the exploits of an American insurance agent and a French-Canadian insurgent in Malawi and shows that neither capitalism nor communism—the ideological alternatives offered by the West to Africa—offers viable solutions to Africa's problems.

While T.'s early novels and the others that quickly followed were well received critically, it was not until the publication of his first travel book, *The Great Railway Bazaar: By Train through Asia* (1975), that T. gained literary fame and financial success. T. has always recognized the connection between travel and writing; indeed, for T. travel fuels writing and writing, which requires long months of work that sometimes result in "cabin fever," sparks the need to travel. The charm of T.'s travel writing resides in his willingness to interject his own character into the scenes he describes and in his ability to make observations about the political situations and cultural clashes he encounters on his travels. T.'s travel writings also reflect his interest in railroads and rail travel. *The Great Railway Bazaar*, which chronicles T.'s journey from Victoria Station in London through India and Asia to Tokyo Central, was followed by two other books that describe transcontinental rail travel: *The Old Patagonian Express: By Train through the Americas* (1979) and *Riding the Iron Rooster: By Train through China* (1989), which won the Thomas Cook Travel Book Award.

T. is a prolific writer who continued to produce a novel every year or two even while publishing his travel books. Among the most notable of his novels published in the 1980s is *The Mosquito Coast* (1982), the story of Allie Fox, an inventor who moves his family from Massachusetts to Honduras to start a new life free of the constraints of American politics and consumerism. The novel features a number of characteristics that frequently grace T.'s fiction: attention to the details of setting, a concern with characters who find themselves in alien lands and challenging situations, the relationship of fathers and sons, and an interest in the clash between personal illusion and reality. T. has also published *My Other Life* (1996), a novel that traces the adventures of a writer named Paul Theroux as he moves, during a thirty-year period, from Massachusetts to Africa to Singapore to London, writing novels, marrying and losing a wife, and finding himself alone at fifty. *My Other Life* is one of T.'s most postmodern works; it merges fiction and autobiography, implies that memory shapes reality, includes an element of metafiction, and showcases writing that borders on self parody.

In a career spanning three decades T. has won critical acclaim and popular recognition for his novels, short stories, travelogues, and literary criticism. T.'s many books are largely an attempt to deal with the emptiness that threatens to overwhelm individuals as they deal with the vastness of geographical space—the steppes of Asia or the wilds of Patagonia—or struggle with alien environments and the harshness of reality in the Third World. He takes his readers, both in his fiction and in his travelogues, to the rough places of the planet and the soul without romanticizing either.

FURTHER WORKS: *Murder at Mount Holly* (1969); *Sinning with Annie and Other Stories* (1972); *Saint Jack* (1973); *The Black House* (1974); *The Family Arsenal* (1976); *The Consul's File* (1977); *Picture Palace* (1978); *A Christmas Card* (1978); *World's End and Other Stories* (1980); *The London Embassy* (1983); *The Kingdom by the Sea: A Journey around Great Britain* (1983); *Sailing through China* (1983); *Half Moon Street* (1984); *Sunrise*

with Seamonsters: Travels and Discoveries (1985); *O-Zone* (1986); *My Secret History* (1989); *Chicago Loop* (1990); *The Happy Isles of Oceania: Paddling the Pacific* (1992); *Traveling the World* (1992); *Milroy the Magician* (1994); *The Pillars of Hercules: A Grand Tour of the Mediterranean* (1995); *Kowloon Tong* (1997); *The Collected Stories* (1997)

BIBLIOGRAPHY: Towers, R. "A Certified American in a Highly English Mode," *NYTBR*, 24 Aug. 1975: 1-2; Ruas, C., *Conversations with American Writers* (1985): 244-64; Coale, S., *P. T.* (1987); Glaser, E., "The Self-Reflexive Traveler: P. T. on the Art of Travel and Travel Writing," *CenR*, 33 (1989): 193-206; Upchurch, M., "P. T.: Novelist as Shapeshifter," *Glimmer Train*, 12 (1994): 13-31

—DAVE KUHNE

THOBY-MARCELIN, Philippe

Haitian novelist and poet (writing in French), b. 11 Dec. 1904, Port-au-Prince; d. 13 Aug. 1975, New York, N. Y., U.S.A.

MARCELIN, Pierre

Haitian novelist (writing in French), b. 6 Aug. 1908, Port-au-Prince

Brothers T.-M. and M. were born into a family of long-standing literary and political traditions. Their grandfather, Armand Thoby, was a writer and statesman. Following Haitian custom, Philippe prefixed his mother's maiden name to his own. Both brothers were educated in Catholic schools, studied law, and became public officials in Haiti. Of the the two brothers, T.-M. is generally better known for his cultural activities and literary accomplishments. During the renascence of Haitian letters and arts in the 1920s he was an active member of the group of intellectuals rallying around the magazine *La revue indigène,* which took a strong stand against imitating French literary models and advocated assertion of the Haitian cultural heritage. In 1949 T.-M. came to Washington, D.C., where he served as a translator at the Pan American Union.

T.-M.'s first literary medium was poetry. Later he turned to prose and, in collaboration with M., started to write novels dealing with Haitian peasant and middle-class life. Their first novel, *Canapé-Vert* (1944; *Canapé-Vert,* 1944), the first piece of Haitian fiction translated into English, won the second Latin American Literary Prize Competition. The brothers collaborated on three additional novels, all translated into English and well received by both the public and critics, including Edmund WILSON, who wrote an appreciative introduction to the English translation of *Le crayon de Dieu* (1952; *The Pencil of God,* 1951). For the background of their novels, both brothers pursued extensive studies in Haitian folklore and anthropology. Written in simple, occasionally colloquial style, with a penchant for realistic detail, the novels evoke an ambience of myth and misery where voodoo mysticism vies with bourgeois urbaneness. The primitive economic conditions of the people contrast sharply with the riches of popular imagination, which conjures up a supernatural world whose workings accord meaning to human existence.

Next to their interest in the Haitian ethos is their concern with the bitter strife between the Catholic Church and the practitioners of voodoo. There are also allusions to the corrupt state of Haitian politics and bureaucracy. But generally, the authors do not indulge in overt didacticism, and most of their characters remain detached from class consciousness or revolutionary spirit.

This want of ideological import has occasioned criticism on the part of more militant minds who see little merit in the authors' stance as observers of skeptical aloofness. But obviously, as evidenced by the appended glossaries, the intended reader is the non-Haitian who, although confronted with something quaintly exotic, recognizes a dimension of universality in the authors' compassionate irony that pleads for tolerance and understanding among all men.

FURTHER WORKS: *La bête de Musseau* (1946; *The Beast of the Haitian Hills*, 1946); *Contes et légendes d'Haïti* (1967; *The Singing Turtle and Other Tales from Haiti*, 1971); *Tous les hommes sont fous* (1970; *All Men Are Mad*, 1970). T.-M.: *Lago-Lago* (1930); *La négresse adolescente* (1932); *Dialogue avec la femme endormie* (1941); *À fonds perdu* (1953)

BIBLIOGRAPHY: Bontemps, A., on *The Beast of the Haitian Hills, NYTBR*, 24 Nov. 1946: 5; Wilson, E., Introduction to *The Pencil of God* (1951): v–xvii; Hughes, L., on *The Pencil of God, NYTBR*, 4 Feb. 1951: 32; Wilson, E., Introduction to *All Men Are Mad* (1970): vii–xii; Clark, J., on *All Men Are Mad, America*, 26 July 1970: 46–47; Larsen, C., on *All Men Are Mad, BA*, 45 (1971): 363–64; Knight, V.K., "M. and T.-M.: Sensationalism or Realism?" *BlackI*, 2, 1973: 30–42; Dash, M., *Literature and Ideology in Haiti* (1981)

—JURIUS SELENIEKS

THOMAS, Dylan

Welsh poet, short-story writer, and novelist (writing in English), b. 27 Oct. 1914, Swansea; d. 9 Nov. 1953, New York, N.Y., U.S.A.

After grammar school in Swansea, where his father was senior English master, T. worked as a journalist for the *Herald of Wales* and the *South Wales Evening Post*. By the age of twenty-two he had published two volumes of verse. During World War II he lived in London and worked sporadically for the BBC as a scriptwriter. In 1948 he returned to Wales. Financial problems induced him to go on a reading tour of the United States. A powerful reader, especially of his own verse, T. was lionized for his public appearances on American college campuses in 1950, 1952, and 1953. He gained considerable notoriety in literary circles for his charismatic, sometimes outrageous personality, often hostile to academe while at the same time receptive to praise. He drank excessively, and his death resulted from his alcoholism.

While poets like W. H. AUDEN and Stephen SPENDER dominated the literary scene in England after T. S. ELIOT'S primacy in the 1920s and wrote poetry committed to their version of leftist politics, T. announced himself as a wholly different sort of poetic voice with his first volume, *18 Poems* (1934). Intensely subjective, associatively organized, richly sensuous, aural and private, these poems concern elemental, archetypal experiences: birth, sex, and death. Seemingly impenetrable on the level of plain sense, they communicate, before they are understood, a kind of audacious vitality and music. They offer obscure juxtapositions of warring

images that connote a Freudian dream world. Nevertheless, T.'s admittedly self-conscious control of a dialectical poetic process and his careful revisions confirm that he should not be labeled a SURREALIST. To the poet-persona, natural man is an extension of the external world, which, like himself, reflects the life cycle, itself a creative-destructive continuum of Eros and Thanatos. Form is content; imagery and sound cannot be divorced from meaning, itself elemental as the air, earth, water, and fire imagery that abounds. Birth, the life force, onanism are among T.'s subjects, as are references or oblique allusions to the Bible of Nonconformist Christianity and biblical archetypes such as Adam and Christ that ambiguously couple the sacred and the profane. The persona dreams his "genesis" and recognizes that "the force that through the green fuse drives the flower" also drives him.

Twenty-five Poems (1936) reveals little change of style or theme, but *The Map of Love* (1939), whose subject is announced in the title, suggests a shifting emphasis, which becomes more pronounced in *Deaths and Entrances* (1946), whose title implies a new covenant with a sacred world beyond self. Early poems embody the correspondence of nature and body with the dramatic center in the self, whereas later poems increasingly use the same correspondence to emphasize the response of the poet to nature. Early and late, time and transience track the poet down. The modern romantic solemnizes, however, the deaths of others in "After the Funeral" (1939) and "A Refusal to Mourn the Death by Fire of a Child in London" (1946). Tormented by the paradox that living is dying, T. in later poems blesses and clings to life, despite the shadow of death that falls in poems such as the finely wrought villanelle for his dying father, "Do Not Go Gentle into That Good Night" (1946).

The poems of T.'s last decade, often grounded in specific occasions or places, are more direct and resonant than early poems. The pastoral odes "Poem in October" (1946) and "Fern Hill" (1946) express a Wordsworthian nostalgia for lost youth, as well as T.'s awful joy at being caught up in the terrifying but beautiful process of what must be God's universe. In "Poem in October" he celebrates his thirtieth birthday, admiring water and birds on a rainy autumn day until the weather reminds him of childhood pleasures that can never be reclaimed. "Fern Hill," a nostalgic paean of praise for rural childhood, lush in its images of animals, fertile crops, and streams, is carefully controlled (although deceptively loose and flowing) by associations both overt and oblique between the farm Fern Hill and Eden; the "green" boy, an Adam in Paradise, is inevitably led by time to the loss of innocence and carefree childhood. The blessings of the "prince of the apple towns" are shadowed by the loss of grace that comes with growing up and awaking to "the farm forever fled from the childless land." In similarly rich, synaesthetic nature imagery and musical lines lush in alliteration, internal rhyme, and off-rhyme, "Poem on His Birthday" (1952) celebrates the bounty and beauty of an elemental world affirmed by holiness, as the persona sails "out to die." This ode on T.'s thirty-fifth birthday expresses his medium and message: "Four elements and five/Senses, and man a spirit in love/Tangling through this spun slime/To his nimbus bell cool kingdom come. . . ."

Influenced by John Donne and Gerard Manley Hopkins (although not derivative), T. did not at first share their religious enthusiasms. In 1951, still uncertain, he said that the late poems were written "in praise of God's world by a man who doesn't believe in God." In a note prefacing *Collected Poems* (1952) T.

indicated that his poems "with all their crudities, doubts and confusions" were written "for the love of man and in praise of God, and I'd be a damn' fool if they weren't." Critics, finding evidence of religious feeling in the poems, describe them as mystical, visionary, sacramental, or pantheistic. Such difficult poems as the "Altarwise by Owl-Light" sequence (1936), "The Conversation of Prayer" (1946), "Vision and Prayer" (1946), and "There Was a Saviour" (1946) manifest T.'s religious concerns. For T., "Dark is a way and light is a place,/Heaven that never was/Nor will be ever is always true" ("Poem on His Birthday"). Although he at first rejected the Nonconformist Christianity of his mother, the poetry communicates religious awe of the created universe and the artist's task as suffering, redeeming creator in that world—the conscious craftsman who, as he writes in "In My Craft and Sullen Art" (1946), makes poems for the heedless "lovers, their arms/Round the griefs of the ages. . . ." In poems T. ritualizes man's passage through a world of lacerating beauty. The canon of his work reveals his gradual emergence from the womb of self to winged flight in pastoral nature that cries out for praise and prayer.

Although primarily a poet, T. wrote autobiographical fiction (emulating James JOYCE) in the short stories in *Portrait of the Artist as a Young Dog* (1940), experimental stories included in *The Map of Love*, the charming winter's tale *A Child's Christmas in Wales* (1955), and a roman à clef in his unfinished novel *Adventures in the Skin Trade* (1955). Whereas his fiction written before 1939 was experimental fantasy only slightly more in contact with external reality than his early poems, the later narratives are vigorously realistic and often comic. The nostalgic *A Child's Christmas in Wales* captures the climate of Welsh family life from the point of view of a mischievous boy. His film scripts concern less personal subjects: *The Doctor and the Devils* (1953), for example, is about the dilemmas of a doctor who, in the interests of science, uses murder victims as cadavers for dissection. T.'s well-known BBC radio script *Under Milk Wood* (1954) is a playfully exuberant return to the Welsh landscape; it celebrates the domestic life and dreams of ordinary people.

FURTHER WORKS: *The World I Breathe* (1939); *New Poems* (1943); *Selected Writings* (1946); *Twenty-Six Poems* (1950); *In Country Sleep* (1952); *Quite Early One Morning* (1954); *A Prospect of the Sea* (1955); *Letters to Vernon Watkins* (1957); *The Colour of Saying* (1963); *Miscellany: Poems, Stories, Broadcasts* (1963); *The Beach of Falesá* (film script, 1963); *Twenty Years A–Growing: A Film Script from the Story by Maurice O'Sullivan* (1964); *Rebecca's Daughters* (1965); *Me and My Bike* (film script, 1965); *Selected Letters* (1966); *Miscellany Two: A Visit to Grandpa's and Other Stories* (1966); *The Notebooks of D. T.* (1967); *Twelve More Letters of D. T.* (1970); *D. T.: Early Prose Writings* (1971); *D. T.: The Poems* (1971); *The Death of the King's Canary* (1976, with John Davenport); *Miscellany Three: Poems and Stories* (1978)

BIBLIOGRAPHY: Treece, H., *D. T.: "Dog among the Fairies"* (1949); Olson, E., *The Poetry of D. T.* (1954); Stanford, D., *D. T.* (1954); Brinnin, J. M., *D. T. in America* (1955); Brinnin, J. M., ed., *A Casebook on D. T.* (1960); Tindall, W. Y., *A Reader's Guide to D. T.* (1962); Maud, R., *Entrances to D. T.'s Poetry* (1963); FitzGibbon, C., *The Life of D. T.* (1965); Korg, J., *D. T.* (1965); Cox, C. B., ed., *D. T.: A Collection of Critical Essays* (1966); Davies, A. T., *Dylan: Druid of the Broken Body* (1966); Burdette, R. K., *The Saga of Prayer: The Poetry of D. T.* (1972); Kidder,

Dylan Thomas

R. M., *D. T.: The Country of the Spirit* (1973); Ferris, P., *D. T.: A Biography* (1977); Ackerman, J., *D. T.: His Life and Work* (1996)

—MARTHA FODASKI-BLACK

THOMAS, Edward

English poet, essayist, and critic, b. 3 March 1878, London; d. 9 April 1917, Arras, France

The son of "mainly Welsh" parents, T. grew up in London, yet cultivated a love of the countryside and of rural literature. Influenced by Richard Jefferies (1848–1887), he published *The Woodland Life* (1897) while still less than twenty. After earning a history degree at Oxford in 1900, T. became a full-time writer, living in the country, chiefly near Steep, Hampshire. Always in financial straits, and trying to support a wife and three children, T. was forced to undertake much commissioned writing, besides producing over a million words of reviews between 1900 and 1914. This treadmill caused depression and breakdown, reflected in T.'s *Letters to Gordon Bottomley* (1968).

His life was changed, however, both by friendship with the American poet Robert FROST and, paradoxically, by World War I. These events, together with other factors, turned T. into a poet at the age of thirty-six. Having championed Frost's poetry, he learned from Frost how to give poetic shape to his own prose nature sketches. The war awoke in T. a still more urgent imaginative response to England, one that eventually led him to join the Artists' Rifles in July 1915. He wrote over 140 poems between December 1914 and his death in the Battle of Arras.

T. characteristically mocked himself as "a doomed hack," but his prose works should not be dismissed as potboilers. All his rural books, especially such compilations as *The South Country* (1909) and *In Pursuit of Spring* (1914), contain impression and perceptions that T. later transmuted into poetry. His prose style gradually threw off its influences, including that of Walter Pater (1839–1894), whose preciosities infect the meditative and fanciful essays collected under the title of *Horae Solitariae* (1902). The autobiographical *The Childhood of E. T.* (written 1914, pub. 1938) achieves a lucid, supple, modern style. So does T.'s critical work, whose value is now being increasingly recognized. A leading reviewer of new poetry, and a believer in the poetry of the new age, he was ahead of his time in appreciating the qualities not only of Frost but also of W. B. YEATS, D. H. LAWRENCE, and others. In full-length critical studies, like *Algernon Charles Swinburne* (1912) and *Walter Pater* (1913), he explored the relation of language to life, an issue that was centrally relevant to the exorcism of 19th–c. literary modes. And his many considerations of "country books," for instance, *Richard Jefferies* (1909) and *George Borrow* (1912), reveal an unparalleled absorption of the tradition of rural prose. T.'s poetry reaps the harvest of this previous critical as well as creative activity.

Apart from a selection in *An Annual of New Poetry* (1917), all T.'s poetry was published posthumously, at first in *Poems* (1917) and *Last Poems* (1918). He shared Frost's insistence on "absolute fidelity to the postures which the voice assumes in the most expressive intimate speech." Compared to Frost, however, he concentrated more exclusively on lyric forms, and created a more complex psychological landscape, where, as F. R. LEAVIS says, "the outward scene is accessory to an inner theatre." T.'s poetry explores a tension between positive and negative perspectives that has cultural as well as personal dimensions. On the positive side, such poems as "The Manor Farm," "Lob," and "Words" celebrate the English tradition as a continuing fusion of environment, people, folklore, and language. On the other hand, images of derelict buildings and dark forests evoke death or an "unknown" future. Frost said that T.'s poems should be called "Roads to France." And although he was killed before he could write any trench poetry, he symbolically expresses the transition between the prewar and postwar worlds.

T. has recently taken his rightful place as the progenitor of a distinctively English line in 20th–c. poetry. His importance had earlier been obscured by his oblique techniques, late development, early death, and the advent of modernism. Since the generation of Philip LARKIN and Ted HUGHES, contemporary poets in England have been influenced by his subject matter, approach, and revitalization of traditional forms.

FURTHER WORKS: *Oxford* (1903); *Rose Acre Papers* (1904); *Beautiful Wales* (1905); *The Heart of England* (1906); *Rest and Unrest* (1910); *Feminine Influence on the Poets* (1910); *Windsor Castle* (1910); *The Isle of Wight* (1911); *Light and Twilight* (1911); *Maurice Maeterlinck* (1911); *Celtic Stories* (1911); *The Tenth Muse* (1911); *Lafcadio Hearn* (1912); *Norse Tales* (1912); *The Icknield Way* (1913); *The Country* (1913); *The Happy-Go-Lucky Morgans* (1913); *Four-and-Twenty Blackbirds* (1915); *The Life of*

the Duke of Marlborough (1915); *Keats* (1916); *A Literary Pilgrim in England* (1917); *Cloud Castle* (1922); *The Last Sheaf* (1928); *The Prose of E. T.* (1948); *Collected Poems* (1949); *Poems and Last Poems* (1973); *Collected Poems* (1978); *A Language Not to Be Betrayed: Selected Prose of E. T.* (1981)

BIBLIOGRAPHY: Thomas, H., *As It Was* (1926); Thomas, H., *World without End* (1931); Moore, J., *The Life and Letters of E. T.* (1939); Coombes, H., *E. T.* (1956); Farjeon, E., *E. T.: The Last Four Years* (1958); Cooke, W., *E. T.: A Critical Biography* (1970); Thomas, R. G., *E. T.* (1972); Motion, A., *The Poetry of E. T.* (1980)

—EDNA LONGLEY

THOMAS, R(onald) S(tuart)

Welsh poet (writing in English), b. 1913, Cardiff

After receiving a degree in Latin from the University College of North Wales at Bangor, T. became a priest of the Church of Wales, taught himself to speak Welsh, and chose to serve in the Welsh countryside, which has provided much of the substance for his verse.

Although he had published three earlier volumes of poetry, T. first gained wide recognition with *Song at the Year's Turning* (1955), which included many of the poems from his earlier books. The volume appeared at a time when British poetry was undergoing a strong reaction against the modernist poetics of T. S. ELIOT and Ezra POUND. Although T.'s was a thoroughly individual voice, he did share with such contemporaries as Donald Davie (1922-1995) and Philip LARKIN a commitment to poetry of direct statement, firmly rooted in the common language. Rejecting the discontinuous style and the verbal complexities of modernist verse, T. employed traditional lyric and narrative verse forms in his lucid, and often bitterly ironic, depletion of life on the harsh, lonely farms of the Welsh hill country.

Song at the Year's Turning established the fundamental terms of T.'s poetic vision: harsh nature only occasionally touched with a softer beauty, industrial progress eroding the older culture of the land, men and women falling into deeper and deeper spiritual poverty in their struggle to survive. The figure of a peasant, Iago Prytherch, recurs through these poems, and T. uses him to focus the qualities of a people who seem to have little more humor, sympathy, or imagination than the stony fields they work. T. is deeply ambivalent in his presentation of this stark figure of a man whose vacancy of mind can be frightening, yet who seems almost mythic in his oneness with nature. For T., nature is the ground against which his characters are defined, manifesting itself primarily in the sunless skies, the poor soil, and the chilling wind of the Welsh hills. This harsh world often seems to condition the emotional lives of T.'s characters, who work alone in the fields and spend their days without passion, or consciously felt loneliness, and without sign of curiosity about the world beyond their narrow sphere. Against this bleak picture, however, T. occasionally suggests the enduring vitality and beauty of nature—even in so stark a setting—and he sees in that apparent contradiction a condition of salvation: the men and women who have been made less than human by their closeness to a cold and barren nature are already equally close to the contrary fruitfulness that this harsh nature so strangely contains.

In subsequent books—*Poetry for Supper* (1958), *Tares* (1961), and *The Bread of Truth* (1963)—T. developed his vision. If harsh nature was a timeless condition of life in Wales, there was another threat of more recent origin in the modern, technological society that was steadily encroaching on the simpler life of isolated farm and village. Almost uniformly through his work, T. uses images of mechanism in ways that emphasize cold, inhuman qualities. In countless ways industrial society makes its way into the lives of the people: cheap, useless goods attract them, the excitement of the city calls them down from the hills, the need for money entangles them in new constraints. And beyond the generalized opposition of town and country, old and new, there is an awareness that this new urban, industrial culture is essentially English, and that it represents still another step in England's domination of Wales.

During the 1970s T.'s tone became even darker. In *H'm* (1972) and *Laboratories of the Spirit* (1975) T. pursued the same questions of spiritual poverty and doubt of earlier volumes, but rather than describing the barren lives of isolated individuals, his inquiry became more general, and more negative. These later poems present a God who is often cruel and capricious—when he is not absent altogether. T. creates a narrator painfully aware of his own contingency, seeking in loneliness and ignorance for any sign—even a negative one—of a presence beyond himself.

In the 1980s, T.'s gradual movement away from the stark realism of his earlier verse became noticeable, as he constructed his poems around a widening range of references to modern art, to science, and to the work of other writers, such as Wallace STEVENS. *Between Here and Now* (1981) and *Later Poems* (1983), in particular, contain numerous poems about paintings (from Monet through Gauguin, Van Gogh and Picasso, to Magritte and Ernst), which, taken together, constitute a kind of meditation on the emergence of modernism in art. While questions of Welsh identity are still present in the later poems, the intrusions into traditional Welsh culture, which T. had always represented as vanishing, are likely to come not so much from English consumer goods, as from a globalized technology of space travel and looming nuclear winter. If the scope of T.'s later volumes is wider than that of the early Prytherch poems, with their stony and claustrophobic fields, the effect still provides an image of negativity which is the occasion for poems of religious questioning.

The poetry of T. was once seen primarily as redeeming a verse tradition temporarily obscured by the modernists. More recently, however, T. has come to be seen as one of the major voices of the Welsh nation in this century, and a writer whose relentless scrutiny of the human costs of modernity make him far more than a regional poet.

FURTHER WORKS: *The Stones of the Field* (1946); *An Acre of Land* (1952); *The Minister* (1953); *Judgement Day* (1960); *The Mountains* (1963); *Words and the Poet* (1964); *Pietà* (1966); *Not That He Brought Flowers* (1968); *Young and Old* (1972); *Selected Poems 1946–1968* (1973); *What Is a Welshman?* (1974); *The Way of It* (1977); *Frequencies* (1978); *Between Here and Now* (1981); *Later Poems 1972–1982* (1983); *Ingrowing Thoughts* (1985); *Destinations* (1985); *Experimenting with an Amern* (1986); *Welsh Airs* (1987); *A Blackbird Singing* (1989); *Counterpoint* (1990); *Mass for Hard Times* (1992); *Collected Poems, 1945-1990* (1993); *No Truce with the Furies* (1995); *Selected Prose* (1995); *Autobiographies* (1997)

BIBLIOGRAPHY: Knapp, J. F., "The Poetry of R. S. T.," *TCL,* 1 (1971): 1–9; Bedient, C., "On R. S. T.," *CritQ,* 14 (1972): 253–68; Humfrey, B., "The Gap in the Hedge: R. S. T.'s Emblem Poetry," *AWR,* 26 (1977): 49–57; Herman, V., "Negativity and Language in the Religious Poetry of R. S. T.," *ELH,* 45 (1978): 710–31; Dyson, A. E., "The Poetry of R. S. T.," *CritQ,* 20 (1978): 5–31; Merchant, W. M., *R. S. T.* (1979); Meir, C., "The Poetry of R. S. T.," in Jones, P., and Schmidt, M., eds., *British Poetry since 1970: A Critical Survey* (1980): 1–13; Phillips, D. Z., *R. S. T.: Poet of the Hidden God* (1986); Davis, W. V., ed., *Miraculous Simplicity: Essays on R. S. T.* (1993); Thomas, M. W., ed., *The Page's Drift: R. S. T. at Eighty* (1993); Shepherd, E., *R. S. T.: Conceding an Absence; Images of God Explored* (1996)

—JAMES F. KNAPP

THÓRÐARSON, Thórbergur

Icelandic poet, essayist, and biographer, b. 12 March 1889, Suðursveit; d. 12 Nov. 1974, Reykjavík

T. was the son of a poor farmer and grew up in an isolated area in southeastern Iceland. At seventeen he began to work as a fisherman and laborer; three years later he entered the Teachers' Training College in Reykjavík. Motivated by a desire for wisdom and spiritual values, he was disappointed with the dry facts presented to him at school and soon left. Although at times near starvation, he dedicated himself to self-education, taking on odd jobs to earn his living. Later he was exempted from the formal requirements for enrollment at the University of Iceland, where he studied Icelandic language and literature for five years. After some years of teaching, he devoted himself entirely to literary work.

T.'s first publications were three volumes of humorous verse, in which he caricatures the sentimental rhetoric of the poetry then popular in Iceland. In these poems his favorite device is the sudden anticlimax.

T.'s literary breakthrough came with *Bréf til Láru* (1924; a letter to Lára), a book totally different from anything published in Iceland up to that time. In part the book functions as a pamphlet wherein T. boldly attacks the injustices of capitalist society and the conservatism of the church—the Roman Catholic Church especially—as well as the conservatism and chauvinism of the peasant culture then dominating Iceland. But the book's originality lies in the author's descriptions of himself. He exposes his eccentricity, superstition, and weird imagination while at the same time remaining arrogantly assured of his own intellectual vigor and honesty. Humor and irony are the keynotes of this work; the style is lucid and unconventional, mixing high rhetoric and colloquial language.

Attacks came quickly from politicians and churchmen. T. was accused of blasphemy and lost his teaching post. Nevertheless, his stylistic brilliance was recognized by everyone.

This mode of humorous and ironic self-description was continued in T.'s masterpiece, the autobiographical works comprising *Íslenzkur aôall* (1938; *In Search of My Beloved*, 1967) and *Ofvitinn* (2 vols., 1940–41; the eccentric [lit., the all–too–wise]). Here T. gives a vivid picture of his youth in Reykjavík, with his hopes and his disappointments. He describes the political atmosphere of the years before World War I, when national independence was the crucial political issue in Iceland; his awkward initiation to sexual life; and his ethereal love for a country girl. These books are built around innumerable witty and picturesque sketches and anecdotes, frequently passing the boundaries of the absurd, unified by the quixotic figure of the protagonist, utterly naïve in many ways, but uncompromising in his search for wisdom and his struggle for justice.

In the Icelandic popular tradition of oral narrative one of the favorite genres is the anecdote about "strange persons." T.'s skill in committing this narrative form to paper is unequaled. Particularly fine examples of this are found in *Ævisaga Árna prófasts Þórarinssonar* (4 vols., 1945–50; the life of Reverend Árni Þórarinsson), the biography of a retired clergyman as told by himself to T. This old man was an orthodox Lutheran, while at the same time a firm believer in all sorts of supernatural phenomena and in the essential wisdom of the common people (beliefs shared by T.). Reverend Árni had a great memory and was a master of oral narration. His collaboration with T. vividly recalls the daily life of a past era, a life that, although beset by harsh conditions, still overflows with humor and variety.

In his later years T. drew the material for his writing mainly from his own life, but gradually became more objective. Through half a century he was one of Iceland's finest essayists, writing on political and cultural matters and on literature. He was an arch foe of oppression and hypocrisy, and he championed sincerity and simplicity. Yet although his own sincerity cannot be doubted, the seeming simplicity of his essays is deceptive. Their style is always profoundly ironic.

T.'s style strongly influenced his Icelandic contemporaries. Although the bulk of his writing is biographical or autobiographical in character, his way of re-creating the past is an imaginative triumph. His skill at humor and irony is unsurpassed in Icelandic literature.

FURTHER WORKS: *Hálfir skósólar* (1914); *Spaks manns spjarir* (1915); *Ljós úr austri* (1920); *Hvítir hrafnar* (1922); *Alþjóðamál og mátleysur* (1933); *Pistilinn skrifaði* (1933); *Rauða hættan* (1935); *Refskák auðvaldsins* (1939); *Edda Þórbergs Þórðarsonar* (1941); *Indriði miðill* (1942); *Viðfjarðarundrin* (1943); *Sálmurinn um blómið* (2 vols., 1954–55); *Steinarnir tala* (1956); *Urn lönd og lýði* (1957); *Rökkuróperan* (1958); *Marsinn til Kreml* (1962); *Í Unuhúsi* (1962); *Einar ríki* (2 vols., 1967–68); *Í Suðursveit* (1975); *Ólíkar persónur* (1976)

BIBLIOGRAPHY: Einarsson, S., *History of Icelandic Prose Writers* (1948): 212–19; Einarsson, S., *A. History of Icelandic Literature* (1957): 302–4; Einarsson, S., "T. T., Humorist: A Note," *SS*, 35 (1963): 59–63; Hallmundsson, H., ed., *Anthology of Scandinavian Literature* (1966): 248; Karlsson, K., Introduction to *In Search of My Beloved* (1967): 7–17; Bandle, O., "*Íslenzkur aðall* als Boheme–Roman," in *Minjar og menntir: Afmælisrit helgað Kristjáni Eldjárn* (1976): 32–46

—VÉSTEINN ÓLASON

THURBER, James

American short-story writer and essayist, b. 8 Dec. 1894, Columbus, Ohio; d. 4 Nov. 1961, New York, N.Y.

T. was born in Columbus, Ohio, where he spent most of an unhappy childhood. Accidentally blinded in his left eye by his brother William, T. was unable to participate in games and sports with other children. This isolation caused him to develop a rich fantasy life through books and daydreams, which would serve to inspire his later fiction. As a young man T. worked in France for some time as a reporter for the Paris edition of the *Chicago Tribune* before returning to the U.S. in 1926. In 1927 T. was hired as an editor-writer for the then fledgling *New Yorker* magazine. Although he disdained the editorial tasks, T. would find this experience valuable for his later literary career. It was during his time at the *New Yorker* that T. developed the clear, concise prose style for which he (and the magazine as well) would become famous.

In 1929 T. published his first book in collaboration with his friend and fellow *New Yorker* staffer E. B. WHITE. *Is Sex Necessary? or Why You Feel the Way You Do* is a spoof of contemporary theorists who had been attempting to reduce sex to a scientifically and psychologically understandable level. White and T., assuming the personae of Drs. Walter Tithridge and Karl Zaner, wrote alternating chapters of the book, explaining such topics as White's "How To Tell Love from Passion" and T.'s "The Nature of the American Male" (a title that anticipates a theme prevalent throughout a great deal of T.'s later fiction). The book met with great popular success and instantly established T. as a true comedic talent.

The publication of *My Life and Hard Times* (1933) brought critical acclaim and public recognition of T. as a major American literary figure, and prompted Ernest HEMINGWAY to call T.'s writing "the best . . . coming out of America." *My Life and Hard Times* is a collection of semiautobiographical essays that ostensibly tell of T.'s life growing up in Ohio. The pieces establish T.'s "family" as perhaps the oddest in American history, including "Grandfather," a sporadically senile old man who lives half his life in early-20th-c. Columbus and half in the Civil War era. The humor of these essays springs from T.'s craftsmanlike use of irony in narrative and tone. The characters are comical due to their ironic preoccupations with events that are feared but never happen. The subdued narrative ironically undercuts the frantic action of the narrative to create a humorous effect.

T.'s fiction generally deals with the themes of man versus woman and imagination versus reality. These two themes often merge in his short stories, and the best-known example is "The Secret Life of Walter Mitty" (1939)—far and away T.'s most famous short story. "The Secret Life of Walter Mitty" tells the story of the title character, a meek, mild-mannered, henpecked husband who escapes from the tedium and hopelessness of his everyday existence through a series of swashbuckling, escapist fantasies. Although the story is just over 2,000 words long, T. spent more than eight weeks writing it. The care he put into its construction is evident in the flawless way Mitty's dream sequences are blended with real-world events: A newsboy shouting about a spectacular murder trial causes Mitty to imagine himself as the defendant; a subsequently imagined courtroom outburst—"You miserable cur!"—causes the "real" Walter Mitty to remember a shopping errand for "puppy biscuit." The terms "Walter Mitty" and "Walter Mittyish" have gained generic status and today can be found as entries in English dictionaries—denoting an unassuming person who escapes from reality by dreaming of being heroic or successful. "Mittyish," or "Mittyesque," characters appear throughout T.'s fiction, for example, in "The Curb in the Sky" (1931), "The Unicorn in the Garden" (1939), "The Catbird Seat" (1942), and "The Lady on 142" (1943).

In addition to his fame as a writer, T. was a highly respected artist and cartoonist as well. Compared to such legendary figures as Pablo Picasso and Henri Matisse, T.'s surreal sketches first appeared in *Is Sex Necessary?* and were thereafter a regular feature of the *New Yorker*, where they became the prototypes for the offbeat sophisticated cartoons that appear in that magazine today. T.'s cartoons are best described as minimalist nonsequitur snapshots, which defy attempts at conventional explanation. The "title piece" in the collection *The Seal in the Bedroom and Other Predicaments* (1932) is a good example. A man and woman are in bed, the woman lecturing the man who stares despondently in the opposite direction. Above the headboard is a bemused looking seal who gazes off in the opposite direction from the man and woman. The caption has the woman saying "All right, have it your way—you heard a seal bark." The humor lies in the utter inexplicability of the situation, and T. himself was often hard-pressed to explain the origin of his cartoon ideas.

In 1941 T. became totally blind and this obviously affected his later work. From that point on, he mainly confined his writing to more "simplistic" or childlike forms: fables and children's books, including *Fables for Our Time and Famous Poems Illustrated* (1940–1941), *Many Moons* (1942), *The Great Quillow* (1944), *The White Deer* (1945), *The 13 Clocks* (1950), *Further Fables for Our Time* (1956), and *The Wonderful O* (1957). It seems that he was unable or unwilling to deal with his personal crises, and thus he withdrew, Walter Mitty-like, into a childlike realm of fantasy. However, despite the innocent nature of these later genres, T.'s work at this time does show a great deal of bitterness. His fables frequently end with bleak morals of death and/or apocalyptic destruction. His children's tales, although more overtly optimistic, also display a cynical undercurrent, particularly *The White Deer*, whose heroes' "valiant deeds" are undermined by the ironic ease with which they are accomplished and the ultimate absence of any real danger in accomplishing them.

T. died in 1961, but his works have stood the test of time. His stories, with their elements of SURREALISM and fantasy, influenced later writers such as Kurt VONNEGUT, JR., and Joseph HELLER. T. is generally acknowledged as the greatest American humorist since Mark Twain (1835–1910) and one of the most important figures in 20th-c. American literature.

FURTHER WORKS: *The Owl in the Attic and Other Perplexities* (1931); *The Middle-Aged Man on the Flying Trapeze* (1935); *Let Your Mind Alone!* (1937); *The Last Flower* (1939); *The Male Animal* (1939, with Elliott Nugent); *My World—And Welcome to It* (1942); *T.'s Men, Women and Dogs* (1942); *The T. Carnival* (1945); *The Beast in Me and Other Animals* (1948); *The T. Album* (1952); *T. Country* (1953); *T.'s Dogs* (1955); *Alarms and Diversions* (1957); *The Years with Ross* (1959); *Lanterns and Lances* (1961); *Credos and Curios* (1962); *Vintage T.* (1963); *T. and Company* (1966); *Selected Letters of J. T.* (1981)

BIBLIOGRAPHY: Morsberger, R. E., *J. T.* (1964); Tobias, R. C., *The Art of J. T.* (1969); Black, S. A., *J. T., His Masquerades: A Critical Study* (1970); Holmes, C. S., *The Clocks of Columbus: The Literary Career of J. T.* (1972); Holmes, C. S., ed., *T.: A Collection of Critical Essays* (1974); Bernstein, B., *T.: A Biography* (1975); Kenney, C. M., *T.'s Anatomy of Confusion* (1984); Maharg, R. A., "The Modern Fable: J. T.'s Social Criticisms," *CLAQ*, 9 (1984): 72–73; Long. R. E., *J. T.* (1988); Sheed, W., *Essays in Disguise* (1990): 90–95; Grauer, N. A., *Remember Laughter: A Life of J. T.* (1994); Kinney, H., *J. T.: His Life and Times* (1995)

—JASON BERNER

James Thurber

TIBETAN LITERATURE

Tibetan literature in the 20th c. reflects adaptation—for the most part deliberate and restrained—to life without the ancient Tibetan cultural traditions. This is particularly true of the period from 1959 to the present, following the Chinese invasion. A discussion of contemporary works must be limited to those of the refugees who have lived in India since the Chinese takeover; literary production inside Tibet since 1959 is little known and inaccessible to most outsiders.

Tibetan literature—a body rivaling that of the Arabs or Chinese in size—is overwhelmingly religious and thus neither "fiction" nor "nonfiction" as commonly defined. On a more popular level are the oral tales about A-khu Ston-pa, an often obscene Falstaffian figure, and about Gesar, Tibet's favorite heroic personage. These tales are secular in origin, with much narrative description of peasant or nomad life. An interesting example of a recent creation is Don-brgyud-ñima's (dates n.a.) *Dzam-glin Ge-sar* (1961; Gesar conquers Germany), inspired by recent military history. Transcribed oral versions of the Gesar epic are important literary documents; as opposed to written literature, some of these works have escaped tampering by monastic censors, who controlled the printeries and thus, to a great degree, what emerged from them.

Perhaps the most important literary figure in the first half of this century was Dge-'dun-chos-'phel (1895–1951), an artist, poet, and literary critic. Unfortunately, his revolutionary views on the art of creative writing seem not to be available, if they have survived. Today many Tibetans see him as a prophet in the realm of literary innovation. He wrote of sex and physical love in a personal manner that shocked Lhasa authorities, who referred to him as a madman. His views on the limits and forms of Tibetan literature are no doubt a key to understanding the foment among Tibetan intellectuals caused by British and other foreign influences in this century.

Contemporary refugee literature remains predominantly religious—for example, exegeses on Buddhist texts. Little fiction has been produced, but Tshe-dban-don-ldan (dates n.a.) wrote a novel, *Mig gi gra mag* (c. 1978; drama of the eyes), set in Ladakh, in the Himalayas. It is consciously based on Hindi texts and Western fiction. Emotional situations are played out through a series of dialogues, with character development and psychological analysis less important than the events themselves. The fact that the author, as a Ladakhi, is probably not a refugee may be significant in his acceptance of outside influences.

External forces are destined to become more important in Tibetan refugee literature as well, while older authors publish collections or separate works written before their exile. Mkhas-btsun-bzari-po's (dates n.a.) *Gtam dpe sna tshogs dan gźas tshigs kha śas* (1974; some songs and stories) is a collection of great beauty and interest, containing everything from drinking songs and acrostics to reverential works. Several are similar in form to the famous love poems of the sixth Dalai Lama, Tshans-dbyans-rgya-mtsho (1683–1706), *Mgul glu (Love Songs of the Sixth Dalai Lama*, 1930), often cited as early examples of purely romantic poetry.

BIBLIOGRAPHY: Richardson, H., *Tibet: Past and Present* (1967); Snellgrove, D. L. and H. Richardson, *A Cultural History of Tibet* (1968; rev. ed., 1980); Stein, R. A., *Tibetan Civilization* (1972)

—MICHAEL L. WALTER

TIKKANEN, Märta

Finnish novelist (writing in Swedish), b. 3 Apr. 1935, Helsinki

The daughter of a distinguished educator, T. was employed as a young woman at Finland's leading Swedish-language newspaper, *Hufvudstadsbladet*, and then followed the pedagogical career of both her parents, teaching at an upper school and becoming director of an institute for adult education. A first marriage ended in divorce; a second union, in 1963, with the writer and artist Henrik Tikkanen (1924–1984), wrought a profound change in her life. Deeply devoted to her gifted and difficult husband, she was nonetheless drawn to the feminist movement and emerged, in time, as a leading northern European advocate of women's liberation; however, her militancy has been tempered all along by a sense of her individualism and a distinct pride in her role as the mother of five children.

Her first two novels, *Nu imorron* (1970; now tomorrow) and *Ingenmansland* (1972; no-man's land), deal with a couple, easily recognized—with the aid of her own later works and her husband's autobiographical books—as a somewhat fictionalized portrayal of their marriage. The wife's situation is made ever more difficult by the husband's alcoholism, erotic adventures, and jealousy, and by

her constant exhaustion (as a working woman, a mostly loving wife, and a conscientious mother), her growing awareness of male domination, and her sense that she is wasting her own gifts. T.'s next two books, sometimes characterized as "pamphlet novels," turn away from immediate personal concerns to other problems of oppressed or neglected women. In *Vem bryr sej om Dori Mihailov?* (1974; who cares about Doris Mihailov?) the central if invisible figure is a lonely and emotionally damaged single parent; the story of her life is pieced together by a female television reporter and a self-centered male psychiatrist. T.'s *Män kan inte väldtas* (1975; *Manrape*, 1977) marked her entrance into international fame, not least because of its sensational nature: Raped by a man whom she has accompanied to his apartment, a divorcee plots and triumphantly (if somewhat unbelievably) inflicts a counterrape on her assailant. Widely translated, the book was made into a film (1978) by Jörn DONNER. From this *succès de scandale* T. went on to *Århundradets Kärlekssaga* (1978; *Love Story of the Century*, 1984), in which, using what might be called a narrative series of prose poems, she took revenge on her husband for his complaints about her emotional coldness and aggressiveness. Concentrating not only on the husband's drunkenness but his egocentricity, the book (and a subsequent dramatization) reached a huge audience of women who found it a reflection, in some measure, of their own marital lot; T.'s remarkable reputation in Germany in particular was built upon her bitter story of an unbearable but evidently inescapable relationship.

As the health of her husband declined, T.'s attention went to other domestic miseries. In *Mörkret som ger glädjen djup* (1981; the darkness that gives happiness depth) she interlarded—in still more narrative-lyrical poems—the account of a contemporary adolescent's emotional illness with the tale of the devotion, and self-accusation, of the mother of Josef Julius Wecksell (1838–1907), a Finland-Swedish poet who had gone incurably insane while still in his early twenties. A companion work, in topic if not in tone, *Sofias egen bok* (1982; Sofia's own book), was the factual chronicle of the illness and treatment of her youngest child, afflicted with minimal brain dysfunction. With *Rödluvan* (1986; Little Red Ridinghood) T. took up her own case for analysis: the little girl with a gently domineering father and a compliant mother who moved into the lair of a demanding husband, a shaggy wolf more vulnerable in life than in the fairy tale. Nonetheless, aware though she was of the childhood situation that, she believed, created her acquiescence to male tyranny, and proud of her revolt, she told, in *Storfångaren* (1989; the great huntsmen), of her longing for her new love, a distinguished Danish author, during a visit to women's centers in Greenland.

T. is one of Finland's best-known authors, because of her ability to combine feminist messages with personal revelations in a variously passionate, wry, or sentimental way. Her ejaculatory style is a particularly apt instrument for attracting and holding her readership: Extremely conversational at the start of her career, her verbal mode has grown more and more exalted with the years, so that it is almost impossible (save in the case history of her daughter) to draw a line between prose and poetry. Similarly, the genre description "novel" on the dust jacket of what is probably her best book, *Rödluvan*, seems to be a misnomer for what is part of her own ongoing autobiography.

FURTHER WORKS: *Henrik* (1985)

BIBLIOGRAPHY: Koch-Klenske, E., "Über M. T.s Roman, 'Wie vergewaltige ich einen Mann'" *Das häßliche Gesicht der schönen Frau: Literarische Porträts* (1982): 191–251

—GEORGE C. SCHOOLFIELD

TIMMERMANS, Felix

Belgian novelist and short-story writer (writing in Flemish), b. 5 July 1886, Lier; d. 24 Jan. 1947, Lier

To ward off bad luck that might come to the thirteenth child of the family, T.'s parents christened him Felix (the happy one). His native town is known for its Béguinage, the section reserved for lay Catholic sisters who devote themselves to helping the sick, praying, and doing lacework; T.'s father was a traveling lace salesman. T. quit school at fourteen, although he later occasionally attended classes at the art school of Lier. His spontaneous, informal style is partly attributable to his being an autodidact without a solid training in grammar. All the same, he was elected in 1931 to the Royal Academy of Flemish Letters. He spent nearly his entire life in Lier, writing as well as drawing and painting in his small studio in a corner of the Béguinage. T. illustrated many of his own works. His drawings are rarely larger than a few square inches and possess an engaging clarity characterized by a clean line.

Some of T.'s works have been translated into twenty-five languages, an extraordinary achievement for a Flemish writer. Always a *flamingant*, one of the militant northern Belgians who demand Flemish supremacy, T. was persona grata during the Nazi occupation of Belgium; after the liberation, there were suggestions that he was a collaborationist. The distress these accusations caused him probably triggered the heart ailment that made him an invalid for the final thirty months of his life.

Pallieter (1916; *Pallieter*, 1924) was published during World War I, when the first German occupation was causing starvation in Belgium. A series of lyrical nature sketches, the book lifted the nation's morale, and *pallieter*, the name of the book's hero, has been added to the Flemish vocabulary to describe the joy of living. Pallieter is a young miller, an exuberant brute of a man, devoid of intellectual pretensions, who has the insouciant laughter of an honest person who notices that birds sing for rich and poor alike. T. calls him a *dagenmelker*, one who milks all the enjoyment he can out of each day, whether working, chatting, drinking, or making love. The book's language, with frequent use of dialect, is rich and innovative.

In *Het kindeke Jesus in Vlaanderen* (1917; *The Christ Child in Flanders*, 1960) T. portrayed the adventures of the child Jesus and of Mary and Joseph against a backdrop of medieval Flanders. He captures through prose the simple beauty of the Nativity scenes of the great Flemish painters. *Pieter Bruegel* (1928; *Droll Peter*, 1930) is a romanticized biography of the Rabelaisian 16th-c. artist. *De harp van Sint Franciscus* (1932; *The Perfect Joy of St. Francis*, 1952) is a novel that presents with poetic feeling the temporal and spiritual events of the saint's life. In both of these books, T. projects some of his own naïve piety and sensuous delight, as well as his genuine love of nature and mankind.

Boerenpsalm (1935; psalm of the farmer) is T.'s most accomplished work. The psychology is more penetrating than in earlier works, and the style, although it remains regional, is more controlled in telling the life of the primitive, sporadically brutal

peasant Wortel, who, with a simple faith in God and invincible determination, contends with the elements, harvests the fruit of the land, and experiences the joys and sorrows of marriage and paternity. This work represents the height of T.'s ability to pinpoint the revealing character trait, the distinctive superstition, and the universal emotion.

Although a melancholy man in private life, T. produced a bright, delightful opus. Most of his work makes one smile because it is spiced with humor and mischief. In folksy, luminous language he presents a story simply. Yet his fiction is, surprisingly, larded with meaningful commentary on history, faith, and human foibles; and it yields ethical guides. He has a knack for integrating grossness and delicacy.

T.'s sympathetic portrayal of rural and small-town life in Flanders enriched its literature with a number of likable, credible characters. His narrative skill, his unbridled imagination, his evocative and personal style made him the best Flemish prose writer between the two world wars. Critics have tended to slight him for being simplistic and provincial. But T. never pretended to be anyone other than pipe-smoking Felix from the Béguinage of Lier, raconteur par excellence.

FURTHER WORKS: *Schemeringen van den dood* (1910); *Begijnhofsproken* (1911); *Boudewijn* (1919); *Anne-Marie* (1921); *De vier Heemskinderen* (1922); *De zeer schoone uren van juffrouw Symforosa, begijntje* (1922); *Uit mijn rommelkas* (1922); *Driekoningentryptiek* (1923; *The Triptych of the Three Kings*, 1936); *Mijnheer Pirroen* (1923); *De pastoor uit den bloeyenden wijngaerdt* (1923); *Het keerseken in de lanteern* (1924; *Leontientje* (1926); *Naar waar de appelsienen groeien* (1926); *Het hovenierken Gods* (1927); *De hemelsche Salome* (1930); *Bij de krabbekoker* (1934); *Pijp en toebak* (1937); *Ik zag Cecilia komen* (1938); *De familie Hernat* (1941); *Minneke poes* (1942); *Vertelsels* (3 vols., 1942–1945); *Adagio* (1947); *Adriaan Brouwer* (1948)

BIBLIOGRAPHY: de Backer, F., *Contemporary Flemish Literature* (1934): 45–46; Greshoff, J., *Belgian Literature in the Dutch Language* (1945): 296–97; Streicher, S., *T. der ewige Poet* (1948); Jacobs, K., *T.: Lebenstage und Wesenszüge eines Dichters* (1949); Timmermans, L., *Mein Vater* (1952); Mallinson, V., *Modern Belgian Literature* (1966): 93–94; Meijer, R. P., *Literature of the Low Countries*, new ed. (1978): 329

—HENRI KOPS

TIMRAVA

(pseud. of Božena Slančíková) Slovak short-story and novella writer, b. 2 Oct. 1867, Polichno; d. 27 Nov. 1951, Lučenec

T. was born, matured, and died in the southwest region of Slovakia where she set all her works. The daughter of an impoverished Lutheran pastor with a large family, she lived in a rural parsonage that centered in the village intelligentsia. This class and the contrasting village peasantry created the primary tension of her work. Unmarried in an old Protestant society that viewed women as only helpmates and mothers, T. also expressed the new view of women as activists in the national ferments preceding the demise of the Austro-Hungarian Empire in World War I and its aftermath in the establishment of Czechoslovakia in 1919. She was awarded the title of National Artist in 1947.

T.'s first literary effort brought girlish sentimental verse circulated among family and friends in nearby parishes, but she soon found her distinctive ironic voice in two kinds of short fiction. Realistic and traditionally plotted narratives of the local peasants portray their births, marriages, and deaths motivated and often corrupted by tragic obsession with land and property in "Žiadna radosť" (1911; "No Joy at All," 1992), by paternalist dogmatic conservatism in the almost naturalistic "ťapákovci" (1914; "The ťapák Clan," 1992), or by decimating emigration to America in "Tá zem vábna" (1907; "That Alluring Land," 1992). T.'s fifty-odd stories and novellas are almost evenly divided between the peasant class and the parsonage intelligentsia, but her bitterly caricaturic novella about World War I, *Hrdinovia* (1918; "Great War Heroes," 1992), effectively interlaces and balances the callous chauvinism, helpless sorrows, and sham heroics of both classes. The chief contrast appears between the bombastic cowardly notary and the idealistic but passive vice notary. The egotism of numerous female villagers equals that of the young ladies of the area. This compact tragicomedy with pacifist subtext received a substantial prize from the Slovak women's organization Živena.

Still realistic and conventionally plotted is T.'s autobiographical *Všetko za národ* (1930; Everything for the Nation), her longest work and the only one primarily about the Slovak national movement. A similar though much shorter piece, "Skúsenos" (1902; Experience), was radically edited and the original manuscript is now lost, but its ironic self-parody is clear.

These two works somewhat share in the formal experimentation of T.'s second type of fiction. Her most original texts show middle-class young women whose rebellious though unspoken consciousness provokes the movement of each story. In part T.'s "Nemilí" (1897; The Unpleasant [People]), "Boj" (1900; "Battle," 1992), "Bez hrdosti" (1905; Without Self-respect), "Veľke šťastie" (1906; Good Fortune), and "Strašny koniec" (1912; The Awful Ending) approach stream-of-consciousness narrative, though without such radical linguistic experiments as demonstrated by Virginia WOOLF. In the epiphany of "Bez hrdosti" Milina sees through the pretensions of her intended and rejects him, and in "Veľke šťastie" four young women accept their marriages with varying degrees of resignation but the same clear-eyed perception of how little they are receiving. Romantically these women want to refuse the pragmatic financial side of a "good match," and feel their forced choice is unjust, unjustifiable, and often even unexplainable. T.'s impressionistic stories are partly autobiographical, but they capture a widely recognizable and significant moment in women's social trend toward feminism.

Much praised by Czechoslovak Marxist critics for her early and very perceptive identification of many of the contradictions of capitalism, T. is equally striking for her originality in representing the rebellious interior monologues of incipient feminists in her time and place.

FURTHER WORKS: *Dve doby* (1937); *Zobrané spisy* (12 vols., 1921-45); *Korešpondencia Timravy a Šoltésovej* (1952); *Zobrané spisy* (7 vols., 1955-59); *Dielo* (1971). FURTHER WORKS IN ENGLISH: *That Alluring Land, or Slovak Stories by T.* (1992)

BIBLIOGRAPHY: Kusý, I., ed., *T. v kritike a spomienkach* (1958); Gáfrik, M., "T. a slovenská moderna," *SlovLit*, 15 (1968): 174-79; Strmeň, K., "Slovak Literature: A Brief History," in Cincura, A., ed., *An Anthology of Slovak Literature* (1976): xl-xli; Števček, J., *Esej o slovenskom romane* (1979): 224-44; Rudinsky, N. L., *Incipient Feminists* (1990): 167-80; Rudinsky, N. L., "Božena Slančíková," in Wilson, K. M., ed., *Encyclopedia of Continental Women Writers* (1991), Vol. 2: 1161-62; Petro, P., *History of Slovak Literature* (1995): 114-17

—NORMA LEIGH RUDINSKY

TING LING

(pseud. of Chiang Ping-chih) Chinese novelist and short-story writer, b. 1904?, Li-ling, Hunan Province; d. 4 March 1986, Beijing

Born into a small-town landowning family, T. L. lived with her widowed mother until adolescence, when she left home for Shanghai, where she was exposed to new, revolutionary ideas. In 1930 she became a member of the League of Leftist Writers, headed by Lu HSÜN. Two years later she joined the Chinese Communist Party. She was arrested and imprisoned from 1933 to 1936. During the Sino-Japanese War (1937–45) she went to Yenan and was active in the Communist literary circle. When the Communists came to power in 1949, she was the leading writer of the new regime. Her international fame and her high position in the Communist literary hierarchy, however, did not prevent her from being purged as a revisionist in 1957. She disappeared from the Chinese literary scene until her reemergence in 1979.

T. L.'s early stories and novels (1927–30) are noted for their bold depictions of youthful love and the conflict between body and mind. The short story "So-fei nü-shih ti jihchi" (1928; "The Diary of Miss Sophia," 1974) is an outcry of the agonizing soul of a "new woman" fighting for emancipation from the rigid traditional conventions governing relationships between the sexes in China. Its frank revelation of the protagonist's passionate sexuality startled the Chinese literary world of that time. The conflict between love and revolution is the theme of the novels *Wei Hu* (1930; Wei Hu) and *Ichiu san-ling nien ch'un Shang-hai* (1930; Shanghai, spring 1930), in both of which the young protagonist sacrifices love for the revolutionary cause.

The novella *Shui* (1931; *The Flood*, 1936), first published in *Pei-tou*, a literary organ of the League of Leftist Writers edited by T. L. herself, marks the beginning of her second phase (1931–36), the main goal of which was to present the life of the peasant masses. *Shui* is a powerful story of the struggle during a devastating flood of a group of destitute villagers, who later turn into a revolutionary force "fiercer than the flood." The work has no outstanding individual characters but portrays the masses as a composite protagonist. Since T. L. had no actual experience and contact with the peasants, however, her descriptions and characterizations are superficial, and she was criticized for her brand of romantic revolutionism.

This failure in her early attempt at SOCIALIST REALISM T. L. remedied in *T'ai-yang chao tsai Sang-kan-ho shang* (1948; *The Sun Shines over the Sangkan River*, 1954), the major novel of her third period (1937–57). Living among the peasants in Communist-controlled areas in north China, T. L. personally witnessed and actively participated in land-reform work in 1946 and 1947. The novel, which won the Stalin Prize, is a realistic presentation of the class struggle between peasants and landlords in a farming village, the breaking up of the feudal landowning system in Chinese society on the eve of the Communist victory, and the vital role of the Party cadres in land reform. Here again the protagonists are groups of peasants and Party workers. For its successful creation of new heroic images, for its fidelity to life, and for its artistry, the novel has been hailed by Communist critics as an "epic of our great land reform." It has been translated into thirteen languages.

In addition to fiction, T. L. wrote numerous essays, war reports, biographical sketches, and plays. In the critical essay "Life and Creative Writing" (1957), published in the Peking English-language periodical *Chinese Literature*, she urges writers to "go out to experience life" and, in keeping with the Party directive, to live among the masses and establish friendly relations with them.

The "correctness" of her ideology notwithstanding, T. L., once dubbed the "woman warrior of New China," eventually incurred the displeasure of Party authorities by her independent spirit and, perhaps, by her arrogance. For more than twenty years she was thrown into the limbo of ignominy until she was rehabilitated in early 1979. The announcement that she was working on a selected-works volume and a sequel to *T'ai-yang chao tsai Sang-kan-ho shang* perhaps signals a relaxation of government control over literature, although to date she has published nothing more of significance.

FURTHER WORKS: *Tsai heh-an chung* (1928); *Tzu-sha jih-chi* (1929); *I-ko nü-hsing* (1930); *Yeh-hui* (1933); *Mu-ch'in* (1933); *I-wai chi* (1936); *I-k'o wei-ch'u-t'ang ti chiang-tang* (1939); *T'uan-chü* (1940); *Wo tsai Hsia-ts'un ti shih-hou* (1946; *When I Was in Sha Chuan and Other Stories*, 1946); *Yao-kung* (1949); *T. L. wen-chi* (1949); *K'ua-tao hsin ti shih-tai lai* (1951); *T. L. hsüan-chi* (1952); *Yen-an chi* (1954); *T. L. tuan-p'ien hsiaoshuo* (1954); *T. L. ming-chu hsüan* (1965). FURTHER WORKS IN ENGLISH: *I Myself Am a Woman: Selected Writings of T. L.* (1989)

BIBLIOGRAPHY: Feng Hsüeh-feng, Introduction to *The Sun Shines over the Sangkan River* (1954): 335–46; Hsia, C. T., *A History of Modern Chinese Fiction* (1971): 262–72, 484–92; Nieh, H., *Shen Ts'ung-wen* (1972): 46–64; Feuerwerker, Y. M., "The Changing Relationship between Literature and Life: Aspects of the Writer's Role in Ding Ling," in Goldman, M., ed., *Modern Chinese Literature in the May Fourth Era* (1977): 281–307; Feuerwerker, Y. M., *Ding Ling's Fiction: Ideology and Narrative in Modern Chinese Literature* (1982)

—LIU WU-CHI

TLALI, Miriam Mesoli

South African novelist and short-story writer (writing in English), b. 1933, Doornfontein, Johannesburg

The context in which T. grew up has importantly shaped her writing. Born into a nonwhite area outside of Johannesburg, T.'s education was interrupted by removals that destroyed communities such as Sophiatown, which marked South Africa's racially stratified society. T.'s early years were spent in Soweto, later known for the riots against inadequate education that form the subject of T.'s second novel, *Amandla* (1980). T. has commented that she had very limited access to books as she was growing up, despite her parents' encouragement: her father left her his books at his death and her mother supported her efforts to write about her life. T.

attended St. Cyprian's Anglican School and Madibane High School, and as a young adult entered the University of Witwatersrand to study medicine. There T. was able to read more widely than before, in part from work smuggled in by students studying outside South Africa's borders. It was not until T. began traveling outside her country that she had easy access to literature by her contemporaries. As a result, T. insisted that her two children pursue their studies outside South Africa to avoid limitations created by the apartheid regime. Nonetheless, T. maintains her commitment to her country, remaining a Soweto writer, and resisting any temptation to write of South Africa from afar.

After two years, T. had to leave Witwatersrand. She briefly studied at Roma University in Lesotho, but when her funds ran out, used skills in bookkeeping and typing to find a position in an electrical appliance shop. These experiences shaped her first novel, *Muriel at Metropolitan* (1975). The opportunity to write the novel came after T.'s mother-in-law fell ill; while nursing her, and on an old typewriter found for her by her husband Stephen Lehutso, T. wrote the book. The support of T.'s husband was essential for a publisher to accept the manuscript, as the laws at the time held T. to be legal minor. Written by 1968, *Muriel* did not get published until 1975, and when it did appear, from Ravan Press, it was with some excisions of portions that were deemed to be potentially too objectionable. Despite that caution, the novel was censored. *Amandla*, T.'s second novel, a fictionalized account of the Soweto uprising, was also banned within six weeks of its publication.

Although loosely autobiographical, *Muriel* is marked by a dispassion that has intrigued critics: some argue it understates the anger and rage created in an apartheid setting, others claim its disengaged quality renders its depictions of the multilayered levels of hatred and contempt between men and women in a strict hierarchy of status and power all the more inescapably potent. The novel's first title, and the one under which its latest edition is sold, is *Between Two Worlds*. As this title suggests, the novel explores the divisiveness of apartheid. From her position as a black woman working in a shop that sells to both black and white customers, Muriel is able to see the discriminatory hire-purchase practices her Jewish employer uses against the less-educated black patrons. Through her eyes the novel documents hierarchies among the white staff, and the workers' quests for a sense of themselves through local notoriety, petty thievery, or ethnic affiliations. Although the novel's structure follows a chronological progression, each chapter conveys new episodes almost as isolated vignettes. This structure creates a cumulative effect: each scene first resonates in itself, then ripples outward to indict the wholesale degrading effects of racism and sexism and bigotry on victims and perpetrators alike. In this way the novel powerfully demonstrates the interconnection of personal and public behavior and decisions.

A similar crystalline structure marks T.'s collection, *Mihloti* (1984), though here less a stylistic decision than one created by the fact of an anthology. *Mihloti*, the Shangane word for tears, brings together a number of different short pieces, many of them written for *Staffrider* magazine. Nonfiction and fiction, interviews and short stories, are juxtaposed against each other, and these seemingly independent drops flow together to form a flood of tears, recording the double affliction for black women of racial and sexual oppression. T.'s collection of short stories, *Footprints in the Quag: Stories and Dialogues from Soweto* (1989), expands her use of the isolated yet connected form of her earlier work.

Some critics find dissatisfaction in the lack of formal rigor in T.'s work, an element explained by some difficulties shaping

English to her experiences. However, T.'s rough documentary style follows her concerns, and permits expression of nuances that would lose their emphasis through a more polished style. T. has pointed out the difficulty of becoming a writer in conditions that stripped writers of their sense of a literary tradition. Along with other writers from the last two decades, T. is part of the new and rich literary oeuvre coming out of the country, forming a living tradition to which younger writers can aspire.

FURTHER WORKS: *Crimen Injuria* (1986)

BIBLIOGRAPHY: Rive, R., "T.," *IonC*, 13, 6 (1984): 23; Sole, K., "The Days of Power: Depictions of Politics and Community in Four Recent South African Novels," *RAL*, 19, 1 (1988): 65-88; Lockett, C., "The Fabric of Experience: a Critical Perspective on the Writing of T.," in Clayton, C., ed., *Women and Writing in South Africa* (1989): 275-85; Lenta, M., "Two Women and Their Territories: Sheila Roberts and T.," *TSWL*, 11 (1992): 103-11; Dean, J., "Interview with T.," *NLitsR*, 27 (1994): 45-56; Omokore, O., "Images of Women in T.'s *Amandla*," *Bridges*, 6 (1995): 1-9; Nfah-Abbenyi, J., *Gender in African Women's Writing: Identity, Sexuality, and Difference* (1997): 123-35

—VICTORIA CARCHIDI

TOBINO, Mario

Italian novelist, poet, and short-story writer, b. 16 Jan. 1910, Viareggio

T. spent his early youth in a carefree, middle-class environment. He studied medicine at the University of Pisa for two years, then transferred to the University of Bologna, where, in 1936, he received his medical degree. In 1938–39, after his discharge from military service, he continued his studies at the psychiatric hospital of Bologna, specializing in neurology and psychiatry. In 1940, following short assignments in the hospitals of Ancona and Gorizia, he was drafted and sent to the war zone in North Africa. Upon his discharge, he joined the Resistance movement. From 1942 until 1980 he served as resident psychiatrist in the mental hospital at Maggiano, near Lucca.

In much of T.'s work, autobiography and imagination interact as essential ingredients of a literary process that seeks to integrate personal experiences with the fabric of the narrative. What results is a composite structure in which the author's persona acts as participant or witness to objective events transformed into fictional material. Thus, *Bandiera nera* (1950; black flag) deals obliquely with T.'s youthful exposure to university life under fascism, with its intellectual sterility and unmasked subservience to the regime. In *Il deserto della Libia* (1952; *The Deserts of Libya*, 1967) the book's discontinuous narrative and iconoclastic display of formal structures stand out as graphic coordinates of ideological disposition, namely aversion to Mussolini's military adventures in Africa and a despairing consciousness of the futility of war. The ordeal of World War II reappears in T.'s volume of poetry *L'asso di picche* (1955; the ace of spades), and in *Il clandestino* (1962; *The Underground*, 1966), which is not the novel of epic dimensions the author intended it to be, but a large collection of loosely structured episodes held together by the underlying vision of the Resistance as a popular struggle against oppression.

T.'s activity as a psychiatrist in the women's ward of a mental institution is reflected in *Le donne libere di Magliano* (1953; *The Women of Magliano*, 1954), a dense, thought-provoking work devoid of the exuberance and impulsiveness that surface in many of T.'s narratives. The book owes its strength to the fact that the author downplays the clinical aspect of insanity in favor of a sensitive, multifaceted portrait of mental patients that is designed to elicit understanding and compassion. Motivated perhaps by the favorable reception of this work, T. returned to the same subject, although with less success, in *Per le antiche scale* (1972; up the ancient staircase) and in the collection of short stories *La bella degli specchi* (1976; the beauty of the mirrors).

Closely tied to T.'s experiences are *Il figlio del farmacista* (1942; the pharmacist's son), *La brace dei Biassoli* (1956; the embers of the Biassoli family), and, most importantly, *Una giornata con Dufenne* (1968; a day with Dufenne). In these three works memory is present as a cognitive, analytical vehicle governing the writer's retrospective account of his adolescent experiences and the social environment in which they unfolded.

T.'s work is distinguished by a systematic effort to transform individual experience into an art form that never compromises with life. His factually based yet highly personal narrative constitutes, above all, a commitment—the commitment of a writer-psychiatrist who seeks to understand society and contribute to its betterment.

FURTHER WORKS: *Poesie* (1934); *Amicizia* (1939); *Veleno e amore* (1942); *La gelosia del marinaio* (1942); *'44–'48* (1949); *L'angelo del Liponard* (1951); *Due italiani a Parigi* (1954); *Passione per l'Italia* (1958); *L'Alberta di Montenero* (1965); *Sulla spiaggia e di là dal nolo* (1966); *Biondo era e bello* (1974); *Veleno e amore secondo* (1974); *Il perduto amore* (1979); *Gli ultimi giorni di Magliano* (1982)

BIBLIOGRAPHY: Internoscia, D., on *Due italiani a Parigi*, *BA*, 29 (1955): 468; Pacifici, S., on *Il clandestino*, *BA*, 37 (1963): 328; Caputo-Mayr, L., on *Per le antiche scale*, *BA*, 47 (1973): 544; Musumeci, A., on *L'asso di picche; Veleno e amore secondo*, *BA*, 49 (1975): 103; Capozzi, R., on *La bella degli specchi*, *WLT*, 51 (1977): 263

—AUGUSTUS PALLOTTA

TOGOLESE LITERATURE

The German colony of Togoland was occupied by Britain and France at the beginning of World War I, and was divided between the two countries by the League of Nations after the war. What became British Togoland—the western part—was administered by the Gold Coast (now Ghana) and merged with it in 1956. French Togo, the larger and poorer eastern area, became the independent republic of Togo in 1960.

During their thirty-year stay, the Germans had done intensive linguistic research and encouraged the Togolese to write and study their own languages. It was therefore not surprising that a western Togolese, Kwasi Fiawoo (1891–1969), became the first West African to write and publish a play in an African language, Ewe: *Toko atolia* (1937; *The Fifth Landing Stage*, 1943). This was the first of a long series of dramatic and novelistic works in Ewe, a noteworthy example being Sam Obianim's (b. 1920) novel *Amegbetoa; alo, Agbezuge fe nutinya* (1949; humanity; or, the struggles of Agbezuge).

Writing and publishing in Ewe was rather widespread in British Togoland and continues today in Ghana. In French Togo, where the colonial language was encouraged, it took several decades for a French-speaking intelligentsia to emerge. The rise of Togolese nationalism after World War II led to the development of an active press, which, thanks to the United Nations trusteeship, was kept alive and fighting against French colonialism. The first Togolese novel written in French was not, however, an anticolonial tract but a Church-inspired ethnographic novel, *Le fils du fétiche* (1955; the son of the fetish) by a schoolteacher, David Ananou (b. 1917).

After independence, Editogo, the national publishing house, issued its first novel, *Les secrets d'Éléonore* (1963; Éléonore's secrets), by Benin-born Félix Couchoro (1900–1968). The only daily newspaper, *Togo-Presse*, published serially nineteen novels by Couchoro. A tradition of journalistic novelettes was born; Victor Aladji's (b. 1941) *L'équilibriste* (1972; the tightrope walker) is typical of the genre.

Poetry in French is mainly written by students and schoolteachers and very seldom finds its way into print; an interesting and fairly representative selection has been made by Yves-Emmanuel Dogbe (b. 1939), himself a poet, in *Anthologie de la poésie togolaise* (1980; anthology of Togolese poetry).

Dramatic writing in Ewe, especially religious plays and musical comedies (called *kantatas*) influenced playwriting in French. Senouvo Nestor Zinsou's (b. 1946) *On joue la comédie* (1972; let's act) is certainly one of the most brilliantly written plays to have come out of French-speaking Africa. It has also been very successful on the stage.

BIBLIOGRAPHY: Amegbleame, S. A., *Le livre ewe: Essai de bibliographie* (1975); Baratte-Eno Belinga, T., et al., *Bibliographie des auteurs africains de langue française,* 4th ed. (1979): 164–68; Amegbleame, S. A., "La fiction narrative dans la production littérature ewe: La nouvelle et le roman," *AfricaL*, 50 (1980): 24–36

—ALAIN RICARD

TOLKIEN, J(ohn) R(onald) R(euel)

English novelist and scholar, b. 3 Jan. 1892, Bloemfontein, South Africa; d. 2 Sept. 1973, Bournemouth

T. was educated at Exeter College, Oxford, and served in World War I. He taught at the University of Leeds and then from 1925 until his retirement in 1959 at Oxford. In 1972 he was made a Commander of the British Empire.

Of his many scholarly publications and editions, the best known are *A Middle English Vocabulary* (1922), *Chaucer as a Philologist* (1924), *Sir Gawain and the Green Knight* (edited in collaboration with E. V. Gordon, 1925), and *Beowulf: The Monsters and the Critics* (1937).

To most readers T. is known as the creator of an extensive and elaborate romance epic concerning a struggle for power during the third age of "Middle Earth." The central participants in this final conflict are certain hobbits, an "unobtrusive, but very ancient

J. R. R. Tolkien

people," small, somewhat human in form, comfort-loving, modest, and peaceable, but in time of need capable of heroic feats.

The story had its inception in *The Hobbit* (1937), in which Bilbo Baggins gains possession of a ring that bestows unimaginable power. This master ring is coveted by the malign forces of Sauron, the dark lord of Mordor, for possession of it will give him control of Middle Earth. It becomes the duty of Bilbo's heir, Frodo, to retain the ring, fighting off the efforts of organized evil to obtain it, until he can destroy it by throwing it into the cracks of doom in the fire mountain Orodruin.

The trilogy *The Lord of the Rings*—comprising *The Fellowship of the Ring* (1954), *The Two Towers* (1954), and *The Return of the King* (1955)—details the completion of the quest and the rescue of Middle Earth from Sauron's threatened tyranny. In their effort the hobbits are assisted by wizards, magicians, elves, dwarves, rangers, Ents—very rarely by human beings. They are opposed by trolls, orcs, ringwraiths, black riders, and other embodiments of ultimate force and fraud. The tenets of the literary theory on which T. based his trilogy are described in a long discourse, "On Fairy Stories," written in 1938 and published in a volume called *Essays Presented to Charles Williams* (1947).

T.'s extraliterary purposes, however, are less clearly indicated. He himself denied that the work is an allegory or that he intended "any inner meaning or 'message.'" He conceded that readers may apply the story to their own knowledge, thought, and experience. Accordingly, many readers see in T.'s fiction a projection of a cosmic conflict of good and evil within the framework of a created mythology that has affiliations with traditional mythologies. This interpretation seems all the more plausible because of T.'s personal friendship with Charles Williams (1886–1945) and C. S. Lewis, both avowed propagators of the Christian faith through fiction, and because of the consistency, if no more, of T.'s formulations, with their Christian orthodoxy in dogma, ethics, psychology, and view of history. All three were writers of what may be called "theological romance."

With the posthumously published *The Silmarillion* (1977) T. brought nearer to completion a "mythology for England." The lack of such a work he had long regretted and had through the years labored to create. Indeed, this effort was probably T.'s main contribution in imaginative writing. His fantasies, which show apparently endless inventiveness, and his scholarship are ultimately of a piece.

FURTHER WORKS: *Fairy Stories: A Critical Study* (1946); *Farmer Giles of Ham* (1949); *The Adventures of Tom Bombadil* (1962); *Tree and Leaf* (1964); *The T. Reader* (1966); *Smith of Wootton Major* (1967); *Unfinished Tales of Númenor and Middle Earth* (1980); *Letters of J. R. R. T.* (1981); *"Finn and Hengest": The Fragment and the Episode* (1983); *Poems and Stories* (1994)

BIBLIOGRAPHY: Isaacs, N. D., and R. A. Zimbardo, eds., *T.: New Critical Perspectives* (1968); Kocher, P. H., *Master of Middle Earth: The Fiction of J. R. R. T.* (1972); Helms, R., *T.'s World* (1974); Carpenter, H., *T.: A Biography* (1977); Nitzsche, J. C., *T.'s Art: A "Mythology for England"* (1979); Salu, M., and Farrell, R. T., ed., *J. R. R. T., Scholar and Storyteller: Essays in Memoriam* (1979); Crabbe, K. F., *J. R. R. T.* (1981); Helms, R., *T. and the Silmarils* (1981)

—W. R. IRWIN

TOLLER, Ernst

German dramatist, essayist, and poet, b. 1 Dec. 1893, Samotschin (now Szamocin, Poland); d. 22 May 1939, New York, N.Y., U.S.A.

T., as the son of a Jewish merchant in the province of Posen in East Prussia, experienced early the isolation of an outsider. After military service in World War I, T. finished his studies in Munich and Heidelberg, during which time (1917–18) he met prominent socialist activists, among them Kurt Eisner, whom he followed to Munich; there he joined the USPD (Independent Social Democratic Party), organizing students and workers. T. played an important role in Eisner's revolutionary socialist republic in Munich (November 1918). When Eisner was murdered (February 1919) and the revolution brutally suppressed, T. was sentenced to five years' imprisonment. Upon his release in 1924 T. pursued his leftist-pacifist political activity. His anti-Nazi stance forced him to flee Germany in 1933. Through his tireless lecturing he became one of the most articulate spokesmen of the German exiles. By 1937 the obvious futility of the antifascist cause contributed to T.'s growing depression. In 1938 he separated from his wife, left Hollywood (where he had worked as a scriptwriter), and devoted himself to the cause of the Spanish Republic. T.'s failed marriage, peripatetic existence, and depressed state contributed to his suicide in New York City.

T.'s political activity is the context for his literary production. His first play, *Die Wandlung* (1919; *Transfiguration*, 1935), uses the scenic tableaux of EXPRESSIONIST drama rather than a chronologically unfolding plot. It explores problems of the outsider identity of the German Jew (the hero, Friedrich, wishes to obliterate his Jewishness), and contains a pacifist rejection of war and of nationalism. It ends with the hero's transformation from social alienation to an awareness of the working people, and an exhortation to a bloodless revolution to free mankind. The characters function allegorically, representing types rather than individuals, a device T. used in subsequent plays as well.

Masse Mensch (1921; *Man and the Masses*, 1924) is T.'s immediate response to the uprising in Munich. The play depicts how the ideals of revolution are perverted into bloodthirsty tactics. The contradiction between individualism and social integration is a central issue in the drama—one that T. had experienced personally. *Die Maschinenstürmer* (1922; *The Machine Wreckers*, 1923) has as its historical material the Luddite riots of 1815 in Nottingham, events through which T. explores the problems of politicizing and organizing workers in the wake of growing industrialization. *Der deutsche Hinkemann* (1923; retitled *Hinkemann; Brokenbow*, 1926; later tr., *Hinkemann*, 1935) is the story of a veteran emasculated in the war who sacrifices himself (by taking a degrading job) for love of his wife, whom he cannot fulfill sexually. Here T. departed from his earlier expressionist pathos: the play is traditionally Aristotelian in structure and explores not sociopolitical themes but individual emotional problems.

T. continued to write plays (his comedies remain too little known), poetry, and prose (journalism and travel sketches) up until his emigration. His autobiography, *Eine Jugend in Deutschland* (1933; *I Was a German*, 1934), covers his life from youth to his release from prison and interprets the Nazi regime as the inevitable fulfillment of historical processes. It is T.'s most mature work as well as one of the outstanding documents of German exile literature.

FURTHER WORKS: *Der Tag des Proletariats: Ein Chorwerk; Requiem den erschossenen Brüdern: Ein Chorwerk* (1921); *Gedichte der Gefangenen* (1921); *Der entfesselte Wotan* (1923); *Das Schwalbenbuch* (1924; *The Swallow-Book*, 1924); *Vormorgen* (1924); *Die Rache des verhöhnten Liebhabers; oder, Faulheit und Männerlist* (1925; *The Scorned Lover's Revenge; or, The Wiles of Women and Men*, 1935); *Hoppla, wir leben* (1927); *Hoppla*, (1928; later tr., *Hoppla! Such Is Life*, 1935); *Deutsche Revolution* (1927); *Justiz: Erlebnisse* (1927); *Feuer aus den Kesseln* (1930; *Draw the Fires*, 1935); *National-Sozialismus* (1930, with Alfred Muhr); *Quer durch: Reisebilder und Reden* (1930; *Which World—Which Way?: Travel Pictures from America and Russia*, 1931); *Die blinde Göttin* (1933; *The Blind Goddess*, 1934); *Wunder in Amerika* (1931, with Hermann Kesten; *Mary Baker Eddy*, 1935); *Briefe aus dem Gefängnis* (1935; *Look through the Bars*, 1937); *Nie wieder Friede!* (1936; *No More Peace!*, 1937); *Pastor Hall* (written 1937, pub. 1946; *Pastor Hall*, 1938); *Blind Man's Buff* (1938, with Denis Johnston); *Ausgewählte Schriften* (1959); *Prosa, Briefe, Dramen, Gedichte* (1961); *Gesammelte Werke* (5 vols., 1978). **FURTHER WORKS IN ENGLISH:** *Seven Plays* (1935)

BIBLIOGRAPHY: Sokel, W., *The Writer in Extremis* (1959), passim; Beckley, R., "E. T.," in A. Natan, ed., *German Men of Letters*, vol. III (1964): 85–106; Spalek, J., *E. T. and His Critics: A Bibliography* (1968); Petersen, C., "E. T.," in W. Rothe, ed., *Expressionismus als Literatur* (1969): 582–84; ter Haar, C., *E. T.: Apell oder*

Resignation (1977); Lamb, S., "E. T. and the Weimar Republic," in K. Bullivant, ed., *Culture and Society in the Weimar Republic* (1978): 71–93; Pittock, M., *E. T.* (1979)

—THOMAS SVEND HANSEN

TOLSTAYA, Tatyana

Russian short-story writer, b. 3 May 1951, Leningrad (now St. Petersburg)

If heredity influences choice of vocation, T.'s literary genealogy preordained her role of writer. On her father's side, she is the great-grandniece of Lev Tolstoy (1828–1910) and the granddaughter of the novelist Aleksey N. TOLSTOY and the poet Natalia Krandievskaya (1888–1963). Her maternal grandfather, Mikhail Lozinsky (1886–1955), translated the plays of Shakespeare and Molière, among others, and produced the acclaimed standard Russian version of Dante's *Divine Comedy*. Half a dozen lesser-known literati are also among the ancestors of T.'s highly cultured family. At Leningrad State University, T. specialized in classics in the School of Languages and Literatures. Upon graduation in 1974, she moved to Moscow and worked for eight years at the publishing house Naka before making her debut with "Na zolotom kryltse sideli . . ." (1983; "On the Golden Porch," 1989). Readers' enthusiastic reception of her story "Peters" (1986; "Peters," 1989) three years later established T.'s reputation as a unique voice in contemporary Russian fiction and launched her career. Her collection of stories, *Na zolotom kryltse sideli . . .* (1987; *On the Golden Porch*, 1989), translated into ten languages, brought her international fame. Since 1988 she has divided her time between Moscow and the U.S., where she teaches, lectures on Russian culture, and writes review essays for mainstream publications.

Time, language, and imagination are the reigning divinities of T.'s fictional universe. With the aid of myth, folklore, and numerous intertexts, her inordinately condensed narratives offer meditations on eternal universal concerns: the elusive significance of a given life in "Sonia" (1984; "Sonia," 1989), "Peters," "Samaia hubumaia" (1986; "Most Beloved," 1991), "Somnambula v tumane" (1988; "Sleepwalker in a Fog," 1991); the isolation of the individual personality in "Peters," "Spi spokoino, synok" (1986; "Sweet Dreams, Son," 1989), "Krug" (1987; "The Circle," 1989); the conflicting claims of spirit and matter in "Okhota na mamonta" (1985; "Hunting the Wooly Mammoth," 1989), "Ogon' i pyl' " (1986; "Fire and Dust," 1989), "Poet i muza" (1986; "The Poet and the Muse," 1990); the complex nature of, and interplay between, perception and language in "Na zolotom kryltse sideli . . ." "Fakir" (1986; "The Fakir," 1989). "Noch" (1987; "Night," 1990), and "Liubish—ne liubish" (1987; "Loves Me, Loves Me Not," 1989); and the transforming power of imagination and memory in "Na zolotom kryltse sideli. . . ," "Svidanie s ptitsei" (1983; "Date with a Bird," 1989), "Reka Okkervil" (1985; "Okkervil River," 1989), and "Milaia Shura" (1985; "Sweet Shura," 1989). Yet throughout her oeuvre, as T. herself has acknowledged, style has primacy over thematic novelty and psychological insight.

T.'s narratives move at an irregular pace, combining minimal plots and sparse dialogue with extravagant poetic description as they slip unobtrusively in and out of temporal frames and characters' thoughts through quasi-direct discourse. Those characters, often situated at the two extremes of the age spectrum, are rendered memorable through T.'s vividly grotesque depiction of their simultaneously risible and pitiable features. A comparably synthetic technique for portraying "losers" in amorous endeavors allows T. to demythologize romance, as in "Peters" and "Vyshel mesiats iz tumana" (1987; "The Moon Came Out," 1992), just as multiple perspectives on a given individual destabilize a single, unilinear interpretation of character. T.'s fiction teems with dreamers, self-abnegators, failures, pragmatists, egotists, and misanthropes shuttled between largely unrealizable desires and brute reality. That gap may be bridged by the transfiguring capacities of the imagination, which flourishes virtually unchecked in childhood, but diminishes with time's passage. Hence the melancholy sense of loss and helplessness that permeates T.'s texts.

T. compensates for her protagonists' deprivations by conjuring up for the reader an Aladdin's cave of stylistic riches. To enter Tolstayaland is to step simultaneously into the magical realm of the fairy tale and the oppressive dinginess of a grimy kitchen. The endless array of startling contrasts yields not only sensual pleasure, but also fresh perspectives on phenomena that acquire multiple dazzling hues. Scrambling temporal and spatial categories, alternating poetic lyricism with satirical irony, shifting from one narrative perspective to another, leaping from colloquialisms and popular slogans to elevated diction and citations from "sacrosanct" sources, T. packs her kaleidoscopic narratives to the brim. Critics have responded above all to the bold originality of her metaphors, which sometimes swell to Homeric proportions; to her breathtakingly unconventional, subversive juxtapositions; to her idiosyncratic, garrulous Sternian narrator; and to her skill at creating a densely palpable atmosphere through eloquent detail and accumulation of rhetorical devices. Her iridescent, luxurious prose—laden with vivid tropes, apostrophes, exclamations, rhetorical questions, and allusions—isolates her stylistically from the majority of contemporary Soviet authors. It allies her with such creative innovators of the 1920s as Yury OLESHA and Isaak BABEL, as well as Nikolay Gogol (1809–1852), Ivan BUNIN, Andrey BELY, and Vladimir NABOKOV. Moreover, it corroborates T.'s claim that the desire to display the spectacular range of the Russian language, to explore its boundless expressive powers, was the chief stimulus for her metamorphosis into a writer.

Early in her career T. focused on the lost paradise of childhood, relying on the Edenic myth as algorithm. Whatever the diversity of her subsequent narratives, including experiments in moral allegory, notably "Serafim" (1986; "Serafim," 1992) and "Chistyi list" (1984; "A Clean Sheet," 1989), they never addressed nakedly political issues or engaged in topical debates. In that regard, her latest publication, "Limpopo" (1991; "Limpopo," 1992), signals a dramatic reorientation. Longer, more digressive, and less tightly constructed than any of her previous stories, it verges on a novella and offers transparently ironic commentary on Russia's current situation of impotent chaos and spiritual indigence: Crushed by a compromised past, Russians foresee no tenable future and dwell in anomie. Its verbal pyrotechnics and hilariously comic passages notwithstanding, "Limpopo" has affinities with the apocalyptic strain of literature that has proliferated during Gorbachev's policy of glasnost.

Since her debut in 1983, T.'s texts have grown progressively longer. One could reasonably classify her last two publications, "Somnambula v tumane" and "Limpopo," as *povesti* (novellas) rather than short stories. If her recently professed intention of authoring a novel in the near future signals a search for new directions, then the first phase of her creative development unequivocally guarantees her status as the stylistically most venturesome and complex modernist practitioner of the short story in Russia during the 1980s. Although modest in quantity, her oeuvre amply justifies Joseph BRODSKY's assertion that T. is "[t]he most original, tactile, luminous voice in Russian prose today."

FURTHER WORKS: *Somnambula v tumane* (1992). FURTHER WORKS IN ENGLISH: *Sleepwalker in a Fog* (1992)

BIBLIOGRAPHY: Goscilo, H., "T. T.'s 'Dome of Many-Coloured Glass': The World Refracted through Multiple Perspectives," *SlavR*, 47, 2 (1988): 280–90; Barker, A., "Are Women Writing Women's Writing in the Soviet Union Today? T. and Grekova," *Studies in Comparative Communism*, 21: 3–4 (1988): 357–64; Goscilo, H., "Tolstajan Love as Surface Text," *SEEJ*, 34, 1 (1990): 40–52; Goscilo, H., "Paradise, Purgatory, and Post-Mortems in the World of T. T.," *Indiana Slavic Studies*, 5 (1990): 97–113; Goscilo, H., "Tolstaian Times: Traversals and Transfers," in Sharma, S., ed., *New Directions in Soviet Literature* (1992): 36–62

—HELENA GOSCILO

TOLSTOY, Alexey Nikolaevich

Russian novelist, short-story writer, dramatist, and poet, b. 10 Jan. 1883, Nikolaevsk (now Pugachyov); d. 23 Feb. 1945, Moscow

Born into an aristocratic family distantly related to Lev Tolstoy and Ivan Turgenev, T. grew up on a Volga estate near Samara. He moved to St. Petersburg in 1901, attending the Technological Institute and frequenting bohemian and SYMBOLIST literary groups. He served as a war correspondent (1914–16), sided with the Whites during the civil war, and emigrated to Paris in 1919. Later he became literary editor of the Berlin Bolshevik newspaper *Nakanune* and was influenced by the Change-of-Landmarks movement, a group of young exiles seeking rapprochement with Soviet Russia, where he returned in 1923.

T. entered Russian literature as a promising poet influenced by the Decadents. His only verse collections, *Liriki* (1907; lyric poetry) and *Za sinimi rekami* (1911; beyond blue rivers), focus on nature and popular Russian legends, told with an irrepressible vitality. Following the MODERNISTS Fyodor SOLOGUB and Alexey REMIZOV, he published a collection of prose folktales, *Sorochyi skazki* (1910; magpie tales). The fullest expression of his lifelong interest in Russian folklore was a posthumously published collection of sixty reworked folktales, *Russkie narodnye skazki* (1946; *Russian Tales for Children*, 1947).

T.'s talent for witty narration, his predilection for the fantastic and grotesque, and his mastery of a racy, colloquial Russian style found best expression in his colorful stories about cantankerous, eccentric landowners who lived in the forests beyond the Volga; these stories linked him to the neorealist tradition of Mikhail PRISHVIN, Yevgeny ZAMYATIN, and REMIZOV. Unlike the others, however, T. early displayed divergent tendencies for the boisterous adventure tale, such as his *Priklyuchenia Rastyogina* (1913–14; the adventures of Rastyogin), and for stories of life and love amid the general decline of the landed gentry, such as *Khromoy barin* (1912; *The Lame Prince*, 1958). The fictionalized autobiography written abroad, *Detstvo Nikity* (1922; *Nikita's Childhood*, 1945), may well be T.'s best work. The plotless narration of various childhood episodes sustained throughout with charm and naïve joy remains unmarred by philosophic pretension.

Concurrently, T. wrote *Syostry* (1922; *The Road to Calvary*, 1923), the first part of an ambitious trilogy, *Khozhdenie po mukam* (1922–41; Parts 1–2, *Darkness and Dawn*, 1935; Parts 1–3, *Road to Calvary*, 1946; later tr., *Ordeal*, 1953). The first attempt in Russian literature to create a broad canvas of Russian society on the eve of the revolution, *Syostry* (sisters) contains vivid descriptions of events and fine character depictions but lacks objectivity, depth, and historicity. By contrast, the second part, *1918* (1927–28), is a historical novel presenting a vast panorama of the civil war characterized by colorful dialogue, uncommon variety of situation, bright albeit superficial characterization, and relatively detached objectivity. In the third part, *Khmuroe utro* (1941; bleak morning), the characters have become stereotyped, and the style has regressed from adult realism to adolescent make-believe stagecraft.

Upon returning to Russia, T. abstained from portraying the new milieu and wrote entertaining novels: *Aelita* (1923; *Aelita*, 195?), a romance in the manner of H. G. WELLS whose flat, absurd scientific portions add nothing to the themes of eternal love and irrational, elemental revolt; *Giperboloid inzhenera Garina* (1927; *The Death Box*, 1936; later tr., *The Garin Death Ray*, 1961), a thriller involving an unscrupulous inventor who seeks to enslave Europe with his death ray; and *Pokhozhdenie Nevzorova; ili, Ibikus* (1925; the adventures of Nevzorov; or, Ibycus), a satiric tale of unbelievable adventures among the lower depths of Russian émigrés.

The unfinished monumental biography *Pyotr Pervy* (1929–45; Part 1, *Peter the Great*, 1932; Parts 1–2, 1936; Parts 1–3, *Peter the First*, 1959) displayed solid historical authenticity, rendering a fine psychological and physical portrait of the genius Peter against a backdrop of a turbulent, critical period in Russia's past. T. also wrote sycophantic political novels such as *Chornoe zoloto* (1932; black gold), full of uncharitable caricatures of Russian émigrés, and *Khleb* (1937; *Bread*, 1937), in which history was shamelessly falsified to laud Stalin and denigrate Trotsky.

T.'s favorite themes and techniques were also reflected in numerous plays: beginning by describing the declining gentry in *Nasilniki* (1911; ravishers), he shifted to adventure and melodrama, depicting the last days of the monarchy in *Zagovor imperatritsy* (1925; the empress's conspiracy) and the infamous double agent in *Azef* (1926; Azef). In his last plays, *Oryol i orlitsa* (1942; the male and female eagles) and *Trudnye gody* (1943; difficult years), he idealized Ivan the Terrible and then drew transparent parallels between him and Stalin.

Officially revered in the Soviet Union as a classic on a par with Mikhail SHOLOKHOV, T. is usually viewed by Western critics as a talented but shallow writer. His remarkable narrative flair and stylistic mastery are best exemplified in his early stories and childhood autobiography, and these and his major novels have earned him a place in world literature.

FURTHER WORKS: *Sochinenia* (2 vols., 1910–1912); *Rodnye mesta* (1912); *Vystrel* (1914); *Molodoy pisatel* (1914); *Arkhip; V lesu; Stranitsa iz zhizni* (1915); *Den bitvy* (1915); *Dni voyny* (1915); *Obyknovenny chelovek* (1915); *Kasatka* (1916); *Nechistaya sila* (1916); *Orion* (1916); *Gorky tsvet* (1917); *Ovrazhki* (1917); *Mest* (1918); *Na podvodnoy lodke* (1918); *Prekrasnaya dama* (1918); *Soldat i chort* (1918); *Lyubov kniga zolotaya* (1919); *Navazhdenie* (1919); *Rozh* (1919); *Smert Dantona* (1919); *Neobyknovennoe priklyuchenie* (1921); *Den Petra; Dlya chego idet sneg?* (1922);

Kitayskie teni (1922); *Lunnaya syrost* (1922); *Niskhozhdenie i preobrazhenie* (1922); *Prekrasnaya dama; Pod vodoy* (1922); *Utoli moi pechali* (1922); *Dikoe pole* (1923); *Pod starymi lipami* (1923); *Privorot* (1923); *Rukopis, naydennaya sredi musora pod krovatyu* (1923); *Bunt mashin* (1924); *Chernaya pyatnitsa* (1924); *Ubystvo Antuana Rivo* (1924); *Chudaki* (1925); *Golubye goroda* (1925); *Kak ni v chyom ne byvalo* (1925); *Soyuz pyati* (1925); *Moskovskie nochi* (1926); *Sem dney, v. kotorye byl ograblen mir, i drugie rasskazy* (1926); *Anglichane, kogda oni lyubezny* (1927); *Drevny put* (1927); *Velikosvetskie bandity* (1927); *Zavolzhie* (1927); *Radiovreditel* (1928); *Sto tysyach* (1928); *Vasily Suchkov* (1928); *Zhivye teni* (1928); *Gadyuka* (1929); *Eto budet* (1931); *Neobychaynye priklyuchenia na volzhskom paroxode* (1931); *Puteshestvie v drugoy mir* (1932); *Patent 119* (1933); *Povest smutnogo vremeni* (1936); *Zolotoy klyuchik; ili, Priklyuchenia Buratino* (1936); *Zolotoy klyuchik: Piesa* (1939); *Put k pobede* (1940); *Russkie skazki* (1940); *Blitskrig ili blitskrakh* (1941); *Ya prizyvayu k nenavisti* (1941); *Chto my zashchishchaem* (1941); *Rasskazy Ivana Sudareva* (1942); *Rodina* (1942); *Mat i doch* (1943); *Stati* (1944); *Kozadereza* (1946); *Polnoe sobranie sochineny* (15 vols., 1946–1953); *Po shchuchiemu velenyu* (1950); *A. T., o literature* (1956); *Sobranie sochineny* (10 vols., 1958–1961). FURTHER WORKS IN ENGLISH: *Daredevils, and Other Stories* (1942); *My Country: Articles and Stories of the Great Patriotic War of the Soviet Union* (1943); *The Making of Russia* (1945); *Selected Stories* (1949); *A Week in Turenevo, and Other Stories* (1958); *Tales of Courage and Conflict* (1958)

BIBLIOGRAPHY: Mirsky, D., *Contemporary Russian Literature, 1881–1925* (1926): 291–95; Koutaissoff, E., "Style as a Reflection of Social Change: A. N. T.," in P. Böckmann, ed., *Stil- und Formenprobleme in der Literatur* (1959): 468–73; Jünger, H., *A. T.: Erkenntnis und Gestaltung* (1969); Rühle, J., *Literature and Revolution* (1969): 102–8; Struve, G., *Russian Literature under Lenin and Stalin, 1917–1953* (1971): 141–43, 175–77, 335–39; Reavey, G., Introduction to A. T., *A Week in Turenevo, and Other Stories* (1975): 1–12; Slonim, M., *Soviet Russian Literature: Writers and Problems, 1917–1977* (1977): 144–54

—ALEX M. SHANE

TOMASI DI LAMPEDUSA, Giuseppe

Italian novelist and essayist, b. 23 Dec. 1896, Palermo; d. 23 July 1957, Rome

T. di L., Duke of Palma and Prince of Lampedusa, belonged to one of the oldest families of Sicily, Little is known about his private life, except that he served in both world wars, traveled widely throughout Europe, married the Baroness Alessandra Wolff-Stomersee, a Latvian exile whom he met in London where his uncle was Italian ambassador, and attended a literary meeting in northern Italy in 1954, at which his cousin, Lucio PICCOLO, was awarded a prize for his poetry, which had just recently come to the attention of Eugenio MONTALE. Upon T. di L.'s return from that meeting, he began writing the novel which he had had in mind for many years and which posthumously catapulted him to worldwide fame. More than a million copies of *Il gattopardo* (1958; *The Leopard*, 1960) have been sold in Italy, and the book has been translated into fifteen languages. Even T. di L.'s collection of short prose pieces, *Racconti*

(1961; partial tr., *Two Stories and a Memory*, 1962), a difficult kind of book to find a market for, has been widely translated, proof of the spectacular appeal of *Il gattopardo*.

T. di L.'s other published writings consist of three articles that appeared in a Genoese periodical in 1926–27; a series of brief introductions to French writers of the 16th c., *Invito alle lettere francesi del Cinquecento* (1970; an invitation to 16th-c. French literature), and *Lezioni su Stendhal* (lessons on Stendhal), which appeared in the literary review *Paragone* in 1959 and in book form in 1977. The three articles indicate an early literary vocation, which was cut short and taken up again only in the last years of his life; the other two works are connected with his teaching activity—private discussions of French literature that he held for a group of young friends in 1954–55, among whom was the young man he and his wife later adopted.

Lezioni su Stendhal is an important text for understanding many aspects of *Il gattopardo* that puzzled its first reviewers, who were often motivated by ideological rather than literary considerations. It is also proof of T. di L.'s thorough acquaintance with the cosmopolitan, European tradition of 20th-c. discussions of the novel, a tradition that goes back to Henry JAMES, passes through E. M. FORSTER's *Aspects of the Novel* (1927), and finds its major authors in Thomas Mann, Marcel PROUST, and James JOYCE. T. di L. admired all of Stendhal's works, but his special enthusiasm went to *The Red and the Black* and *The Charterhouse of Parma*, which together represent the apparently contradictory qualities of *Il gattopardo*: that of historical novel and of "lyrical" outpouring of its author's sentiments. T. di L.'s style is more florid than Stendhal's, but he is capable of the same concentration, the same paring away of the superfluous in selected understated moments in the narrative, to which his analysis of Stendhal calls attention.

Il gattopardo consists of eight chapters, not all of which were part of the original conception. This composition by blocks no doubt left its trace on the work as we have it, accounting for those disproportions and seeming digressions that some critics have attributed to T. di L.'s presumed inexperience as a novelist and to the possibility that his completion and revision of the manuscript were interrupted by illness and death. A more careful reading, however—one for which the observations on narrative technique in *Lezioni su Stendhal* can serve as guide—reveals a tightly structured network of balanced episodes, moods, and meditations, which forms a unified pattern.

Each of the chapters is marked by a date, the first and last being May 1860 and May 1910, thus rounding out a fifty-year span for the action. In all the chapters except the fifth and the last, center stage is occupied by the protagonist, Don Fabrizio Corbera, Prince of Salina. (The rampant leopard of the title is the emblem of the family coat of arms, and also refers to the prince himself.) The first four chapters are all dated 1860, the year of Garibaldi's "liberation" of Sicily from Bourbon rule, of the plebiscite that sanctioned the annexation of the Kingdom of the Two Sicilies to the Kingdom of Sardinia, and of the first efforts by the Piedmontese—the artificers of unification—to enlist the cooperation of Sicily's old nobility in the formation of the government of the new nation. The setting shifts from the prince's palace in Palermo to his country residence at Donnafugata, where the social and political novelties of the new regime stand out more dramatically against the timeless, quasi-feudal environment in which he feels most at home. It is at Donnafugata that the prince watches his nephew Tancredi, more beloved by him than his own son, fall in love with Angelica, the beautiful daughter of Don Calogero Sedàra, the vulgar, grasping entrepreneur who is on his way to wealth and political power. In his deep, tolerant disenchantment, born of aristocratic detachment, declining vitality, and cultivated, refined taste, the prince favors the union of Tancredi and Angelica, even at the cost of disappointing his gentle daughter Concetta. Angelica, not Concetta, is the suitable mate for the young man who has joined Garibaldi against his own class because he has understood that the Bourbons must go.

Chapter 6 is dated November 1862; it is the ball scene, a virtuoso piece built on the interplay of funereal and festive motives, of intimations of death and disintegration in the midst of the brilliant lights, the euphoric dance music, the crinolines and starched shirt fronts that signify youthful energy and the pursuit of pleasure. Its somber notes carry over into Chapter 7, the prince's deathbed scene (July 1883), in which in a last weighing of the meaning of life he sums up the infinitesimally small number of joyful hours as against his seventy years of boredom and pain. Chapter 8 is a coda, the "end of everything," the great family chapter of the book, the point at which the historical novel most clearly makes way for the deep psychological insights of the bourgeois novel.

Il gattopardo represents a variation on the classical form of the historical novel in that the narrative voice does not aim at objectivity but, on the contrary, permits the present to intrude into the past. Thus, the omniscient narrator is not content with knowing everything there is to know about his characters but also hints at what will happen after the story is finished. The fictional world chronicled is thus imbued with a strong sense of immediacy and is given continued life in the present. For its narrative sweep and emotional impact *Il gattopardo* has sometimes been compared to *Gone with the Wind*. Unlike *Gone with the Wind*, however, it has already become the object of serious critical analysis.

BIBLIOGRAPHY: Kermode, F., "Old Orders Changing," *Puzzles and Epiphanies* (1962): 131–39; Colquhoun, A., "[T. di] L. in Sicily: The Lair of the Leopard," *Atlantic*, (February 1963): 91–110; Gilbert, J., "The Metamorphosis of the Gods in *Il gattopardo*," *MLN*, 81 (1966): 22–32; Pallotta, A., "*Il gattopardo*: A Theme-Structure Analysis," *Italica*, 43 (1966): 57–65; Ragusa, O., "Stendhal, T. di L., and the Novel," *CLS*, 10 (1973): 195–228; Lansing, R., "The Structure of Meaning in [T. di] L.'s *Il gattopardo*," *PMLA*, 93 (1978): 409–22; Lucente, G. L., "[T. di] L.'s *Il gattopardo*: Figure and Temporality in an Historical Novel," *MLN*, 93 (1978): 82–108

—OLGA RAGUSA

TONGA LITERATURE

See Zambian Literature

TOOMER, Jean

American fiction writer and poet, b. 26 Dec. 1894, Washington, D. C.; d. 30 March 1967, Doylestown, Pa.

The grandson of P. B. S. Pinchback, a prominent political figure during the Reconstruction era, T. studied briefly at several universities—including the University of Wisconsin, the University of

Chicago, and New York University—as he considered various careers before turning to literature in 1920. In 1923, before *Cane* (1923) was published, T., whose early studies examined diverse philosophies, became interested in the philosophy of Georges Gurdjieff (1877–1949), who urged a spiritual reform that would bring people into harmony with themselves. Subsequently, both while he was a leader of the Gurdjieff movement in America and afterward, T. attempted to write fiction, poetry, drama, and nonfiction that would promote a spiritual regeneration of America; but publishers rejected his didactic novels and his autobiographical works. Insisting that the rejections were based on the identification of him as a Negro and the consequent belief that he should write another *Cane*, T., in essays such as "A Fiction and Some Facts" (privately printed, 1931) and in his autobiographical writings, argued that Americans represented a new race for which the earlier racial identifications of European or African were irrelevant. Before his death, T. completed several autobiographies, collections of stories and poems, novels, dramas, and book-length works of nonfiction, none published in his lifetime. Some of these materials have been published in *The Wayward and the Seeking: Selected Writings of J. T.* (1980).

During the early 1920s, T. was heralded as one of the most promising writers of America. The promise seemed to have been realized with the publication of *Cane*, a collection of lyric, impressionistic stories, sketches, and poems primarily about black Americans living in rural Georgia or Washington, D.C. After 1923, however, T.'s only book-length publication was the privately printed *Essentials* (1931), a collection of aphorisms and maxims about the spiritual, intellectual, and emotional needs of Americans. Despite occasional publication in periodicals during the following three decades, T. faded into obscurity until a resurgence of interest in Afro-American literature during the 1960s promoted the rediscovery of *Cane* and a restoration of T.'s early reputation.

In *Cane*, T.'s masterpiece, sensuous metaphors, impressionistically realistic characterization, and lyric style merge into sometimes enigmatic sketches evoking a world of people in conflict with the mores prescribed by society. T. wrote that it was an attempt to present the swan song of a dying way of life.

The first section, set in Georgia, focuses on women caught between the compulsions of nature and the taboos of society. For example, before she has entered her teenage years, men approve the mischievous behavior of Karintha, who learns and practices sex at an early age. As a woman, unmarried Karintha secretly gives birth to a child whom she kills or permits to die. Nine-year-old Esther, fairskinned daughter of the richest Negro in the town, responds emotionally to a powerful, dark-skinned adult, King Barlo. Having been taught that well-behaved women do not have physical needs for sex, Esther at sixteen conceals her desires, withers at twenty-two because of the lack of passion and reality in her life, and at twenty-seven withdraws from reality after Barlo's rejection. Becky, a white woman, transgresses so drastically against Southern taboos by giving birth to two black children that even the blacks and whites who help her must pretend to themselves that she does not exist.

The second section, set in Washington, D.C., except for one story located in Chicago, reveals individuals removed from the soil, who are less willing to defy society's mores. John, brother of a theater manager in the black section of Washington, is attracted to Dorris, a chorus girl; but he does not even try to talk with her because he cannot transcend the conflict between his awareness that society will consider his interest sexual and his desire to assure himself that it is merely spiritual and intellectual. Bona, a young white woman from the South, and Paul, who is "passing" for white, are attracted to each other. Although she suspects his Afro-American ancestry, Bona, surrendering to her emotions, accepts a date with him. Paul loses her, however, when he stops to assure a black doorman that their relationship is not sexual.

The final section of *Cane* is the novelette "Kabnis." Ralph Kabnis, a Northern-reared Afro-American, has come South to discover his heritage but experiences only fear and disillusionment. Reared to believe in the power of education, he learns to distrust the form personified by the hypocritical principal Hanby, who is more interested in acquiring power in a segregated society than in educating blacks. From listening to Layman, a journeyman preacher, Kabnis learns that religion merely teaches blacks to try to ignore oppression. Fired from his teaching position because he drinks whiskey and smokes cigarettes, Kabnis accepts a job as apprentice to Halsey, a wagon maker—just at the time that America was moving into the automobilé age.

FURTHER WORKS: *The Collected Poems of J. T.* (1988)

BIBLIOGRAPHY: Fullinwinder, S., "J. T., Lost Generation or Negro Renaissance?" *Phylon*, 27 (1966): 396–403; Turner, D. T., *In a Minor Chord: Three Afro-American Writers and Their Search for Identity* (1971): 1–60; Farrison, W. E., "J. T.'s *Cane* Again," *CLAJ*, 15 (1972): 295–302; Baker, H. A., Jr., *Singers of Daybreak: Studies in Black American Literature* (1974): 53–80; Reilly, J., "J. T.: An Annotated List of Criticism," *RALS*, 4, 1 (1974), 27–55; Turner, D. T., Introduction to *Cane* (1975): ix–xxv; O'Daniel, T. B., ed., *J. T.: A Critical Evaluation* (1983)

—DARWIN T. TURNER

TORBERG, Friedrich

Austrian novelist, essayist, and poet, b. 16 Sept. 1908, Vienna; d. 10 Nov. 1979, Vienna

T. was educated in Vienna and in Prague, in the latter of which his family lived from 1922 on. He published poems, stories, and a novel at an early age. The name he legally adopted in 1930 is derived from the names of his father, Alfred Kantor, and his maternal grandfather, Simon Berg. His early mentor Max BROD encouraged him in his lifelong positive attitude toward his Jewishness and in his Zionist orientation. Following some years of freelance work for a number of newspapers and periodicals in Prague, Leipzig, and Vienna, T. emigrated to Zurich in 1938, and later to Paris. After serving in the Free Czech Army for a year, T. fled to Spain and Portugal, and in late October of 1940 he arrived in the U.S. For several years he lived in California working as a screenwriter, but only one of his screenplays, *Voice in the Wind* (1944), was filmed. In 1944 T. moved to New York, where he contributed to a number of journals and worked on a German edition of *Time*. Having become a U.S. citizen in 1945, T. returned to Vienna in 1951, and from 1954 to 1965 he edited *Forum*, a cultural-political monthly sponsored by the Congress for Cultural Freedom, in addition to being active as a drama critic. A staunch anti-Communist, he carried on protracted polemics against performances of Bertolt BRECHT's plays. His death, following an operation, occurred a month after he had received the Great Austrian State Prize for Literature.

Franz WERFEL, a devoted friend, once characterized T. as one of the few contemporary writers "who have something to say and know how to say it." T.'s greatest international success, both critical and popular, was his first novel, *Der Schüler Gerber hat absolviert* (1930; *The Examination*, 1932), a sensitive portrayal of a secondary-school senior in whom the ordinary tensions and conflicts of adolescence are exacerbated to the point of despair by an unfeeling environment. Kurt Gerber's suicide, one of many such "school graduations" in real life, is caused by a repressive society and an autocratic school system, in particular a sadistic teacher, "Gott" ("God") Kupfer. T.'s novel *Die Mannschaft* (1935; the team) has a sports setting and reflects some of the author's experiences as a swimmer and water-polo player.

One of the youngest members of the circle around Karl KRAUS, T. was inspired by the satirist to develop his moral and political conscience as well as his critical intelligence and his stylistic virtuosity. The great themes of his later novels are totalitarianism versus freedom and opportunistic compromise versus the exigencies of emigration and exile. T.'s novella *Mein ist die Rache* (1943; vengeance is mine) explores the moral conflict of a rabbinical student who, having preached divine retribution, shoots the brutal commandant of his concentration camp and is henceforth haunted by guilt feelings. *Hier bin ich, mein Vater* (1948; here I am, father) is the confession of a Viennese Jew who becomes a spy for the Gestapo in a misguided attempt to get his father released from Dachau and who then experiences progressive degradation and dissolution. *Die zweite Begegnung* (1950; the second encounter) tells the story of an ex-officer and student who manages to escape to freedom from communist Czechoslovakia. *Süsskind von Trimberg* (1972; Süsskind von Trimberg), a very personal book, is yet another parable of the Jew in a hostile world and a kind of epitaph of the German-Jewish symbiosis. In writing a poetic biography of a minor Minnesinger of the 13th c., the first Jew to make a contribution to German literature, T. makes it poignantly plain that he regards himself as one of the last to make such a contribution.

PPP: Pamphlete, Parodien, Post Scripta (1964; polemics, parodies, glosses) is a lively compendium of short prose works, and *Das fünfte Rad am Thespiskarren* (2 vols., 1966–67; the fifth wheel on the Thespian carriage) brings together the author's drama criticism. T. was also active as an editor and translator, producing a four-volume edition (1957–63) of the novels, stories, and plays of the Austrian writer Fritz von Herzmanovsky-Orlando (1877–1954) and translating from the English several books by the Israeli satirist Ephraim Kishon (b. 1924). T.'s last great success was *Die Tante Jolesch; oder, Der Untergang des Abendlandes in Anekdoten* (1975; Aunt Jolesch; or, the decline of the West in anecdotes), a witty book of memoirs and other short pieces. This book and its sequel, *Die Erben der Tante Jolesch* (1978; the heirs of Aunt Jolesch), are brilliant and diverting evocations of a bygone world.

FURTHER WORKS: *Der ewige Refrain* (1929); —*und glauben, es wäre die Liebe* (1932); *Abschied* (1937); *Lebenslied* (1958); *Mit der Zeit—gegen die Zeit* (1965); *Golems Wiederkehr* (1968); *Apropos: Nachgelassenes—Kritisches—Bleibendes* (1981); *In diesem Sinne: Briefe an Freunde und Zeitgenossen* (1981); *Kaffeehaus war überall: Briefwechsel mit Käauzen und Originalen* (1982); *Pagasus im Joch* (1983); *Auch das war Wien* (1984); *Auch Nichtraucher müssen sterben* (1985); *Liebste Freundin und Alma* (1987); *eine tolle, tolle Zeit* (1989); *Voreingenommen wie ich bin* (1991)

BIBLIOGRAPHY: Siedler, W. J., "Die Freiheit der Entscheidung: Zum Werke F. T.s," *Der Monat*, April 1953: 77–81; Ahl, H., *Literarische Porträts* (1962): 93–100; Eisenreich, H., Introduction to F. T., *Mit der Zeit—gegen die Zeit* (1965): 5–13; Reich-Ranicki, M., *Literarisches Leben in Deutschland* (1965): 142–45; Strelka, J. P., "F. T." in Strelka, J. P., and Spalek, J., eds., *Deutsche Exilliteratur seit 1933: Kalifornien* (1976): 616–32; Strelka, J. P., ed., *Der Weg war schon das Ziel: Festschrift füur F. T. zum 70. Geburtstag* (1978); Schönwiese, E., *Literatur in Wien zwischen 1930 und 1980* (1980): 159–65; Hackel, F.-H., *Zur Sprachkunst F. T.'s* (1984); Rickels, L., "F. T.," in Daviau, D. G., ed., *Major Figures of Modern Austrian Literature* (1988): 397–422; Axmann, D., ed., *Und lächeln ist das Erbteil meines Stammes* (1988); Tichy, F., *T. Ein Leben in Widersprüchen* (1995)

—HARRY ZOHN

TORGA, Miguel

(pseud. of Adolfo Correia da Rocha) Portuguese short-story writer, novelist, diarist, poet, and dramatist, b. 12 Aug. 1907, São Martinho de Anta; d. 17 Jan. 1995, Coimbra

A full account of T.'s early life is given in his multivolume autobiographical work *A criação do mundo* (the creation of the world). The first volume, *Os dois primeiros dias* (1937; the first two days), is divided into two major parts: "O primeiro dia" (the first day) describes T.'s childhood, which was spent in the mountains of the Trás-os-Montes province where he was born, and in a nearby city. "O segundo dia" (the second day) retells his adolescence, during which he worked on the plantation of wealthy relatives in Brazil in order to be able to continue his education. The second volume, *O tercero dia da criação do mundo* (1938; the third day of the creation of the world), treats, for the most part, the years at the university in Coimbra and his work as a country doctor. *O quarto dia da criação do mundo* (1939; the fourth day of the creation of the world), the third volume of the series, deals with his brief journey through Spain, Italy, and France at the time of the Spanish Civil War, his visit in France with Portuguese émigrés, and his return to Portugal. T.'s autobiographical writings reveal his struggle to be himself. With his outspoken independence of mind, this means not only challenging the world as it is but life itself, its dependence on chance, its brevity and futility.

Since 1941 T. has been publishing in installments his *Diário* (12 vols., 1941–77). These diaries, which he started to keep in 1932, appear every few years. His thoughts on national and world problems are sometimes narrowly Iberian in spirit, but his work as a whole has universal appeal. These volumes contain insightful prose and the best of his lyric poetry.

T.'s finest achievements are his short stories, particularly those in his two collections *Contos da montanha* (1941; mountain tales)

and *Novos contos da montanha* (1944; new mountain tales). All these stories, set in the remote and backward province of Trás-os-Montes, depict the harshness of its people. Their lives are untouched by brotherly love and the humanizing influence of civilization. The basic impulse that motivates these rural people is self-preservation, although the actions prompted by this need are put forth as actions prompted by morality. T.'s astute analysis of these people, combined with his sense of irony and the terseness and precision of his style, make these short stories masterpieces.

Highly admired among T.'s works are the animal stories collected in *Bichos* (1940; *Farrusco the Blackbird, and Other Stories from the Portuguese*, 1950). Most are told from the animals' point of view, although the animals are allowed to experience human emotions.

T.'s many volumes of poetry are filled with the despair of a humanist who loves mankind. In *O outro livro de Job* (1936; the other book of Job) T. movingly laments man's insurmountable isolation in mass society. Although he sees this isolation as an evil to be struggled against, he defiantly proclaims it for himself. *Câmara ardente* (1962; burning chamber) is the expression of a Christian tormented by religious disbelief.

In recent years T. has revised some earlier published works and occasional, mostly political, articles written since 1945 but prohibited from publication during the Salazar regime, which was in power until 1974. Now gathered and published as *Fogo preso* (1977; shackled fire [or, fireworks that cannot rise]), these writings express his struggle against the oppressive political situation in his homeland and reveal T. as the "prophet of the Portuguese revolution."

The genius of T. is revealed in his style, unique in Portuguese, of short sentences and perfectly chosen words that concisely express vivid and dramatic scenes. It is sturdy and strong yet lyrical, almost simple, just like the *torga* (a regional term), the lovely heath that grows wild on uncultivated land.

The popularity of his books, his nomination twice for the Nobel Prize (1960 and 1978), and his winning of the 1976 Belgian Knokke-Heist International Grande Prize of Poetry attest to the high regard in which T. is held. He is not only the best recorder and interpreter of his native region but also the most important living poet of his country. A writer of universal appeal, his works have been translated into English, Spanish, French, Italian, and German.

FURTHER WORKS: *Ansiedade* (1928); *Rampa* (1930); *Tributo* (1931); *Pão Ázimo* (1931); *Abismo* (1932); *A terceira voz* (1934); *Um reino maravilhoso* (1941); *Mar* (1941); *Terra firme* (1941); *Rua* (1942); *Lamentação* (1943; *Lamentation*, 1961); *O Senhor Ventura* (1943); *Libertação* (1944); *O Porto* (1944); *Vindima* (1945); *Odes* (1946); *Sinfonia* (1947); *Nihil sibi* (1948); *O Paraíso* (1949); *Cântico do homem* (1950); *Portugal* (1950); *Pedras lavradas* (1951); *Alguns poemas ibéricos* (1952); *Penas do purgatório* (1954); *Traço de união* (1955); *Orfeu rebelde* (1958); *Poemas ibéricos* (1965); *O quinto dia da criação mundo* (1974); *O sexto dia da criação mundo* (1981). FURTHER WORKS IN ENGLISH: *Open Sesame, and Other Stories from the Portuguese* (1960)

BIBLIOGRAPHY: Brass, D., Introduction to *Farrusco the Blackbird* (1950): 7–14; Vidigal, B. D. S., "Contemporary Portuguese Writing," in Livermore, H. V., ed., *Brazil and Portugal: An Introduction* (1953): 143; Brass, D., "M. T.: A New Portuguese Poet," *Dublin Review*, 229 (1955): 402–16; Ricard, R., "*Despenador et abafador*; ou, La fortune d'un thème macabre de Ventura García

Calderón a M. T.," *BEPIF* 20 (1958): 211–19; Brass, D., "The Wisdom of the Soil," *TLS*, 7 Oct. 1977: 1168; Clemente, A., "The Portuguese Revolution Seen through the Eyes of Three Contemporary Writers," *Proceedings of the Fourth National Portuguese Conference* (1979): 24–51

—ELIZABETH R. SUTER

TORRENTE BALLESTER, Gonzalo

Spanish novelist and essayist, b. 13 June 1910, Ferrol

T. B. has spent most of his professional life as a teacher in high schools in Spain, with a short stay at the State University of New York at Albany (1966–1970) as a professor of literature. Although he has won recognition as a critic and literary historian, and is a member of the prestigious Royal Academy of the Spanish Language, his prominence stems primarily from his novels.

T. B. cannot be placed easily into a generation of writers or be viewed as a member of a specific literary movement in post–Civil War Spain. Rather, he stands radically apart from most authors of his time during nearly fifty years of writing literature. Even when he has drawn upon dominant trends of literary fashion in Spain—the social realism of the 1950s or the experimental techniques of the 1970s—he has reshaped them in unique ways and enriched their potential for complexity. Although his early works have at times a clear political and social component, as did the novels of many Spanish novelists during the Franco regime, T. B.'s fiction is most consistently shaped by the recurrent concern for myth, parody, the writing of history, and the nature of literary characterization.

Many of T. B.'s early novels have been praised in recent critical writing but received scant attention when first published. His first significant body of work is the trilogy *Los gozos y las sombras* (joys and shadows): *El señor llega* (1957; the master arrives), *Donde da la vuelta el aire* (1960; where the air turns around), and *La Pascua triste* (1962; the sad Easter). These novels are set in T. B.'s native Galicia in northwest Spain and focus on the material-spiritual conflict between a physician who has returned to his hometown after studying abroad, and an engineer who has lived in the town all of his life. Two other novels of the 1960s, although relatively unknown during the time of their publication, are important in the author's development. *Don Juan* (1963; Don Juan) hints at the imaginative play that will eventually dominate T. B.'s novels after 1970, while *Off-Side* (1969; title in English) reveals the realistic undercurrent of pessimism that several critics attribute to the early years of his writing.

With the publication of *La saga/fuga de J. B.* (the saga/fugue of J. B.) in 1972, winner of the National Novel Prize (1972), T. B. moved to the forefront of Spanish novelists. The work represents less a break with his previous novels than a complex elaboration of the principal narrative determinants that shape his earlier fiction: concern for the theory of narration; multiple perspectives on the real and the invented in the telling of a story; the fragmentation of time; parody of literary modes; and the play of history amid reality and imagination. The thin story line of the novel resists synthesis but turns upon the life of Jos Bastida and his growing awareness of his mythical status in the city of Castroforte. The novel ultimately destroys many of the myths upon which Spain has constructed its

own image (T. B. attacks social institutions, sexual mores, religion) and parodies recent critical theories that seek to reduce fiction to mere structure or psychological case studies. Above all, however, *La saga/fuga* stands at the forefront of post-Civil War narrative that promotes the postmodern expression of ambiguity and chaos as essential values of the novelistic process.

The late 1970s to the present represent the most productive and inventive period of T. B.'s career. In a series of novels that intensify the metafictional pattern and technical complexity established in *La saga/fuga* T. B. explores the nature of the literary process and the contingencies of narration. *Fragmentos de apocalipsis* (1977; fragments of apocalypse), awarded the Critics' Prize (1977), and *La isla de los jacintos cortados* (1981; the isle of cut hyacinths) both examine how characters are at once fictional and real, and both explore T. B.'s interest in historiography and the way that events in past time are framed by narration and given meaning in the present as components of a story. *La rosa de los vientos* (1985; the rose of the winds) focuses more specifically on the nature of history and reveals how the real and the imaginary are enmeshed in similar narrative structures. T. B.'s most recent novel, *Yo no soy yo, evidentemente* (1987; it's not me, obviously), represents a summing up of his intensely theoretical concerns. The novel undercuts the creation of characters in fiction by placing their very existence in doubt, and also parodies textual exegesis and the industry of literary criticism that produces meaning in fiction.

T. B. has played a significant role in bringing contemporary fiction in Spain into the mainstream of postmodern writing. His forceful imagination stands behind a theory of the novel that seeks to commingle literature and life, meaning and being. He frequently parodies the fictional process, not to destroy it, but to reveal the richness of its workings and the contingency of its meanings. Indeed, his parodies do not disparage the novel, but rather celebrate its pleasures and bring to the fore its existential importance.

FURTHER WORKS: *El viaje del joven Tobías* (1938); *El casamiento enganoso* (1939); *Lope de Aguirre* (1941); *Siete ensayos y una farsa* (1942); *Javier Mariño* (1943); *República Barataria* (1944); *El retorno de Ulises* (1946); *El golpe de estado de Guadalupe Limón* (1946); *Compostela* (1948); *lfigenia* (1949); *Literatura españõla contemporánea (1898–1936)* (1949); *Farraquino* (1954); *Panorama de la literatura española contemporánea* (1956); *Teatro español contemporáneo* (1957); *El "Quijote" como juego* (1975); *Cuadernos de La Romana* (1976); *Nuevos cuadernos de La Romana* (1976); *Obra completa, 1* (1977); *Acerca del novelista y de su arte: Discurso* (1977); *Las sombras recobradas* (1979); *Teatro, I, II* (1982); *Ensayos críticos* (1982); *Cuadernos de un vate vago* (1983); *Daphne y ensueños* (1983); *La princesa durmiente va a la escuela* (1983); *Quizá nos lleve el viento al infinite* (1984); *El "Quijote" como juego y otros trabajos críticos* (1984); *Cotufas en el golfo* (1986); *Hombre al agua* (1987); *lfigenia y otros cuentos* (1987)

BIBLIOGRAPHY: *Homenaje a G. T. B.* (1981); Becerra, C., *G. T. B.* (1982); Giménez González, A., *T. B. en su mundo literario* (1984); Perez, J., *G. T. B.* (1984); Blackwell, F. H., *The Game of Literature: Demythification and Parody in Novels of G. T. B.* (1985); special T. B. issue, *Anthropos*: 66–67 (1986); Pérez, J., and Miller, S., eds., *Critical Studies on G. T. B.* (1989); Loureiro, A. G., *Mentira y seducción: La trilogía fantástica de T. B.* (1990)

—DAVID K. HERZBERGER

TÓTH, Árpád

Hungarian poet, translator, journalist, critic, and short-story writer, b. 14 April 1886, Arad (then in Austro-Hungarian Empire, now in Romania); d. 7 Nov. 1928, Budapest

Son of a sculptor who later fell upon hard times, T. lived his whole life under the double shadow of poverty and tuberculosis. Although a good student, he was unable to finish his university studies; he supported himself as a journalist and later as a literary critic. He was a founding member of the important magazine *Nyugat*.

T.'s first volume of poetry, *Hajnali szerenád* (1913; serenade at dawn), is a profound study in melancholy and resignation. The title poem is one of the greatest love lyrics in Hungarian. Throughout the volume, lassitude is expressed through such techniques as slow iambs mixed with spondees, assonance, feminine and approximate rhymes, and frequent enjambments. His imagery is arresting, full of vitality, providing a variety of subject matter to contrast with the prevailing sadness of tone. At other times, his poetry dazzles with virtuoso rhymes and word-music.

With his second volume of poems, *Lomha gályán* (1917; on a sluggish galley), T. steps from the ivory tower of his self-imposed isolation and freely embraces mankind. The horrors of war are balanced against beauties of nature and of a simple, full life. In this volume T. the courageous journalist and the gentle poet fuse to achieve a vision of a better world to come. During this period T. translated Shelley's "Ode to the West Wind." The translation was so masterful that Mihály BABITS once said that he considered it the best Hungarian poem. In the early 1920s T. also did superb translations of the medieval French poem *Aucassin and Nicolette* and of poems by Milton, Oscar Wilde, and Baudelaire, among others. These were collected in *Örökvirágok* (1923; eternal flowers).

Az öröm illan (1922; joy evaporates) indicates by its very title that the poet's mood had darkened. Like Dezső KOSZTOLÁNYI, T. learned the difference between the sweet melancholy of immature youth and the true sorrow of the adult. But he never lost hope. The title poem of *Lélektől lélekig* (1928; from soul to soul), however, shows an increasing sense of isolation, as he compares the distance between individual human souls to the distance between stars, with the "immense, icy void between."

Throughout his career, T.'s technical mastery increased. His verse forms became more and more varied, and he was able to achieve striking effects with the simplest of means. His later poems sometimes speak with the simplicity of folk songs, the deceptive simplicity characteristic of great art. Strong, songlike rhythms, memorable diction, arresting imagery impress themselves on the reader's mind. Up until the end he never relinquished the sense that life was magical, that it was beautiful, and that there was a mystical design in the cycle of life and death.

T. also left behind a small body of prose writings, which have been collected in *Novellái és válogatott cikkei* (1960; short stories and selected articles). In the stories a fastidious artist, an imaginative and truly poetic soul, spins enchanting tales. Often they verge on the fantastic, but they are always what the poems are—profound human documents.

FURTHER WORKS: *Bírálatok és tanulmányok* (1939); *Összes versei és versfordításai* (1958); *Novellái és válogatott cikkei* (1960); *Összes versei, versfordításai és novellái* (1962); *Összes mű vei* (2 vols., 1964); *T. Á. válogatott mű vei* (1964)

BIBLIOGRAPHY: Klaniczay, T., et al., *History of Hungarian Literature* (1964): 206–8; Reményi, J., *Hungarian Writers and Literature* (1964): 292–97

—DALMA H. BRUNAUER

TOURNIER, Michel

French novelist, b. 19 Dec. 1924, Paris

T. did graduate work in philosophy in Germany immediately after World War II. After his return to France he failed the final examination that would have enabled him to become a professor of philosophy, and he was forced to take up a series of positions in communications and publishing. Among the many volumes he translated from German to French were the novels of Erich Maria REMARQUE, which, characteristically, he took it upon himself to revise when he felt he could make an improvement.

After three novels of his own had gone unpublished—he did not consider them worthy of being offered for publication—T. wrote *Vendredi; ou, Les limbes du Pacifique* (1967; *Friday*, 1969), which was awarded a prestigious prize. In this idiosyncratic recasting of Defoe's 18th-c. novel, Robinson Crusoe forms his own utopian community and forces his man Friday to obey its arbitrary laws. But when an accidental explosion destroys "civilization" on Crusoe's island, the master decides to put himself in the hands of his slave: the two switch roles and the European begins to learn from the native.

Even more ambitious was *Le roi des aulnes* (1970; *The Ogre*, 1972), set in Germany during World War II and partly inspired by Goethe's famous ballad "The Erl King." Abel Tiffauges, the protagonist, plays in turn each of the three roles in that ballad: as a French schoolboy, he is the young child hidden in his father's cloak; as a French soldier in charge of carrier pigeons, he is the father on horseback attempting vainly to protect his son from the Erl King; and as a German prisoner after 1940, he becomes the Erl King himself, snatching the child from the arms of his father. (Although still a prisoner, he is put in charge of selecting young students for one of Hitler's elite military academies.) As Tiffauges rides about the countryside choosing his victims and sometimes forcibly carrying them off, he is not only an embodiment of the Erl King but also an embodiment of Hitler as well. *Le roi des aulnes* is the only novel ever to be awarded the Goncourt Prize by a unanimous vote; shortly thereafter T. himself was chosen as a member of the Goncourt jury.

Les météores (1975; *Gemini*, 1981) stirred up more controversy than his earlier novels, primarily because of the flamboyant character Alexandre. As a homosexual he bitterly attacks the heterosexual world, and as manager of a disposal company his domain includes the largest refuse dumps in France. The novel loses a great deal of its vitality about two-thirds of the way through, when Alexandre departs from it, but T. seems to be making an important point about the way characters with a unique human identity are disappearing from modern literature. T. moves from Alexandre to his twin nephews because T. sees identical twins as "a single being with the monstrous faculty of occupying two different positions in space." Jean and Paul form one being and share one identity; others see them indistinguishably as "Jean-Paul." When one twin abandons

337

the other, the survivor cannot exist without the reflected confirmation of his identity, and must seek through the world for his other half. In an astonishing conclusion, the surviving twin is almost literally cut in two, later to be "extended" into the larger world of meteorological phenomena.

In between his third novel and his fourth, T. published major works in three completely different genres. *Le vent paraclet* (1977; the holy spirit) is an intellectual autobiography that begins with childhood experiences but moves on to general philosophical issues and finally to a dispassionate analysis of T.'s own earlier novels. *Le coq de bruyère* (1978; the grouse) is a collection of short stories ranging from yet another Robinson Crusoe variation to the surprisingly old-fashioned title story, dealing with the last fling of a retired army officer. *Des clefs et des serrures* (1979; on keys and locks) contains forty brief essays, each one stimulated (or sometimes simply illustrated) by the work of a famous photographer. T. himself is an amateur photographer, and his interest in the art form is illustrated by the character in his fourth novel who is searching for a new dispensation that would end the Old Testament prohibition on graven images.

Gaspard, Melchior & Balthazar (1980; *The Four Wise Men*, 1982) retells the story of the three magi of the New Testament. On another level, the novel is a meditation about the nature of signs and narrative. Each king draws a different moral from the story told them by King Herod and later from the encounter with the infant Jesus. The fourth king, Taor, who goes unmentioned in the Gospel account because he arrived in Bethlehem too late, seeks his own meaning in the incarnation and stands for T.'s readers, each of whom must also seek a personal meaning in the modernized myth.

At the heart of this novel is a short story, "Barbedor" ("King Goldbeard") presented as such—and, significantly, it takes the form of a fairy tale for children. For T. the primary childlike aspect of a myth is as essential to it as its metaphysical summit, and at his best T. combines both of those levels with innumerable intermediate ones. He has not only written for adults but has also produced a parallel series of books for young readers. T. deals with myths because their very simplicity allows them to serve as the framework for a complex web of symbols and ideas. His novels have therefore been praised for their depth but also severely criticized for their pretentiousness. Whether they are seen as fascinating revitalizations of myth or as arid games will depend upon the reader's temperament, but there is no question about T.'s goal. "A dead myth is called an allegory," he writes. "The writer's function is to prevent myths from turning into allegories."

FURTHER WORKS: *Vendredi; ou, La vie sauvage* (1971; *Friday and Robinson: Life on Speranza Island,* 1972); *Canada: Journal de voyage* (1977); *Pierrot; ou, Les secrets de la nuit* (1979); *Le vol du vampire* (1981); *Gilles et Jeanne* (1983)

BIBLIOGRAPHY: Sissman, L. E. on *The Ogre, New Yorker,* (30 December 1972): 68–70; White, J. J., "Signs of Disturbance: The Semiological Import of Some Recent Fiction by M. T. and Peter Handke," *JES,* 4 (1974): 233–54; Bray, B. on *Gemini, TLS,* (22 August 1975): 950; special T. section, *Magazine littéraire,* No. 138 (1978): 10–25; Hueston, P., Interview with T., *Meanjin,* 38 (1979): 400–405; special T. issue, *Sud,* numéro hors-série (1980); McDowell, D. on *Gaspard, Melchior & Balthazar, WLT,* 55 (1981): 428–29; Shattuck, R., "Why Not the Best?" *NYRB,* (28 April 1983): 8–15

—MICHAEL POPKIN

TOZZI, Federigo

Italian novelist and short-story writer, b. 1 Jan. 1883, Siena; d. 21 March 1920, Rome

T.'s personality and his fiction were strongly influenced by the circumstances surrounding his childhood. He was the only surviving child after eight siblings had died shortly after birth. His mother, melancholy but loving and protective, died when T. was twelve, leaving him to the care of his father, a dynamic but crude and insensitive person who regularly beat and chastised his son. The young T. was often ill, completely inept at working in his father's very successful restaurant, and unsuccessful in a series of technical schools. During his teenage years his first love experience ended in bitter disillusionment when the peasant girl that he loved became pregnant by another man. After his father's death T. left his job as a railroad clerk to undertake the frustrating and unsuccessful management of the family property. During World War I he lived in Rome, where he worked with the Italian Red Cross. His untimely death, from pneumonia, came just before the publication of his major novels.

The ineptitude for practical living that characterized T.'s life dominates his short stories and novels, which are relentlessly somber and depressing. He seems to express a sense of life's utter futility. His protagonists are condemned by fate to mediocrity and defeat from which there is no escape. They are isolated within themselves and are incapable of meaningful communication. Yet they struggle against their destiny, thus becoming tragic figures who poignantly express T.'s sense of lost opportunities.

Con gli occhi chiusi (1919; with closed eyes) is an autobiographical novel about a disillusioning love affair. Pietro Rosi, an idealistic and naïve young man, proposes marriage to Ghisola, a peasant girl whom he believes to be pure and innocent but who in reality has a number of lovers. He rejects every indication of the truth until his eyes are opened by his discovery that Ghisola is pregnant by another man. Although this is a terrible blow to Pietro, *Con gli occhi chiusi* is T.'s least pessimistic novel, because its ending suggests that the protagonist, toughened by experience, will be better equipped to cope with the realities of life.

The defeat of the protagonist is more unequivocal in *Il podere* (1921; the farm). On his father's death, Remigio, a well-intentioned and sensitive but inept young man, comes home to manage the family farm. His father's apparent indebtedness, the ill will, greediness, and cunning of virtually everyone around him, and even nature combine to cause his financial and spiritual failure. His violent death at the hands of a resentful farmhand is the last of a series of seemingly predestined disasters.

Tre croci (1920; *Three Crosses,* 1921) is the least directly autobiographical of T.'s novels. Based on real events, it is the story of three brothers who, unsuccessful in their meager efforts to earn a living from their failing bookstore, are nevertheless unwilling to give up their standard of living. Faced with bankruptcy, they postpone the inevitable collapse by forging a friend's signature on a promissory note. When the truth is revealed, Giulio hangs himself. Shortly thereafter, Niccolò dies from a stroke and Enrico languishes and dies in a poorhouse.

Having neither the bombastic sensuality of Gabriele D'ANNUNZIO nor the cerebral probing of Luigi PIRANDELLO, both in vogue in the 1920s, T.'s fiction was not warmly embraced by his contemporaries. Since his works were also completely lacking in social context, it was not until after the postwar period of NEOREALISM that T. was "rediscovered" and placed on a level with Giovanni VERGA and Italo SVEVO. His importance lies in his ability to give artistic expression to his feelings of essential human tragedy.

FURTHER WORKS: *La zampogna verde* (1911); *Antologia d'antichi scrittori senesi dalle origini fino a Santa Caterina* (1913); *La città della vergine* (1913); *Mascherate e strambotti della Congrega dei Rozzi di Siena* (1915); *Bestie* (1917); *Le cose più belle di Santa Caterina da Siena* (1918); *Giovani* (1920); *L'amore* (1920); *Gli egoisti; L'incalco* (1923); *Novale* (1925); *Ricordi di un impiegato* (1927); *Realtà di ieri e di oggi* (1928); *L'immagine, e altri racconti* (1946); *Nuovi racconti* (1960); *I romanzi* (1969; new ed., 1973); *Adele* (1979)

BIBLIOGRAPHY: Vittorini, D., *The Modern Italian Novel* (1930): 210–16; Debenedetti, G., "F. T.: A Psychological Interpretation," in S. Pacifici, ed., *From Verismo to Experimentalism: Essays on the Modern Italian Novel* (1969): 102–19; Cassola, C., "The Overdue Discovery of F. T.," *Newsletter of the Istituto Italiano di Cultura*, 28 (1970): 1–4; Rimanelli, G., "F. T.: Misfit and Master," *IQ*, 14, 56 (1971): 29–76; Pacifici, S., *The Modern Italian Novel from Capuana to Tozzi* (1973): 136–64; Klopp, C., "Federigo's Ark: Beasts and Bestiality in T.," *IQ*, 21, 81 (1980): 55–62; Pedroni, P. N., "F. T.: Autobiography and Antinaturalism," *Italica*, 60 (1983): 10–23

—PETER N. PEDRONI

TRAKL, Georg

Austrian poet, b. 3 Feb. 1887, Salzburg; d. 3 Nov. 1914, Cracow, Austro-Hungarian Empire

T. was the fifth child of a prosperous hardware dealer. He was raised as a Protestant in the predominantly Catholic city of Salzburg. Aside from two putative suicide attempts, he had a relatively normal childhood. T.'s younger sister Margarethe, or Gretl, was the member of the family closest to him.

T. entered secondary school in 1897. In 1905 he left school prematurely, with the consequence that the only dignified profession open to him was pharmacy. T. had already begun to drink heavily as well as to experiment with chloroform and other intoxicants. His addiction worsened through the rest of his life. It seems likely that T. and Gretl began their incestuous relationship about this time. T. later introduced her to the use of drugs, an act that seems to have intensified his feelings of guilt.

During his pharmaceutical training (1906–10) he began to publish verse. In 1906 his two one-act plays, *Totentag* (All Souls' Day) and *Fata Morgana* (fata morgana) were performed in Salzburg. Toward the end of 1910 T. discovered and began to cultivate his own lyric voice. But at the same time he found it impossible to settle down and hold a job. He spent the last years of his short life moving between Vienna, Salzburg, and Innsbruck. In Innsbruck he found a patron and friend in Ludwig von Ficker (1880–1967), editor of the distinguished literary periodical *Der Brenner*. Nearly all of T.'s enduring work was written after he became acquainted with Ficker, who recognized T.'s genius. Ficker published T.'s work and in July 1914—acting as agent for the philosopher Ludwig Wittgenstein (1889–1951), who had given Ficker a large sum from

his inheritance to distribute to worthy writers—awarded T. a grant of twenty thousand kronen, a small fortune at the time.

T. was never to draw on that sum. In August he was called to serve as a medical corpsman at the front in Galicia. The bloody battle of Grodek in September, the summary hanging of civilians, and the suffering of severely wounded soldiers in the absence of doctors and all medication—these experiences aggravated T.'s psychosis and led to his suicide by an overdose of cocaine. He died in the psychiatric section of a military hospital. Kurt Wolff (1887–1963), publisher of *Gedichte* (1913; poems), T.'s first volume of verse, issued a second, *Sebastian im Traum* (1915; Sebastian in a dream), which T. had completed eight months before his death.

What little is known about T.'s life seems important for the understanding of his work. The suicide, for example, is the expression of his enduring obsession with narcosis and death. On the other hand, his verse is altogether autonomous. Patterns of rhythm and sound, the arrangement of images, and aesthetic effect in general were T.'s prime concern, not the conveying of ideas or personal experience. His poems suggest a wide range of meanings despite, or perhaps because of, their taut, hermetic structure. He aimed to write poetry full to bursting with movement and visions, and his best work carries a shock effect.

T.'s early verse uses familiar images and motifs strung together and organized into conventional rhymed strophes. Then, under the influence of Rimbaud, he developed a free-verse style with long lines. His most mature poems are written with short lines and free rhythms. As he developed he showed a tendency toward greater simplicity, visualization, and immediacy.

At his best, T. worked with great economy of means, constructing patterns with a relatively small stock of motifs: sister, pain, narcosis, the Sacraments, shepherds, the moon, wild game, the basic colors, among others. The tension in his poetry arises from the fusing of conflicting elements, which might be categorized as malign and benign.

T.'s early work speaks of the decay of a world where there are still vestiges of Christian wholeness. In the later poems the discrepancy between salvation and destruction grows sharper and takes on cosmic proportions. The poem "Klage" (pub. 1915; "Lament," 1957), written shortly before his death, shows him at the height of his powers. In twelve short, unrhymed, metrically irregular lines he compresses a vision of immense breadth and import. Within this compact unit there are three abrupt shifts from the personal realm to infinities of time and space; syntactically rough lines sing with the music of assonance and alliteration; and the extremes of violent collision and frozen stasis stand side by side. Death by water occurs three times, and we are left in the end beneath the vacant indifference of night and stars. The whole complex is held together by "the dark voice above the sea" singing its lament with melancholy, disembodied beauty.

T. shared with contemporary German EXPRESSIONISTS their striving for explosive effect and their preoccupation with imminent apocalyptic disaster. His talent was just beginning to be recognized at the time of his death. Since then he has come to be considered among the greatest of German lyric poets. His work belongs in the vatic tradition and has served as a model for two succeeding generations of writers.

FURTHER WORKS: *Die Dichtungen* (1917); *Der Herbst des Einsamen* (1920); *Gesang des Abgeschiedenen* (1933); *Aus goldenem Kelch: Die Jugenddichtungen* (1939); *Offenbarung und Untergang:*

Prosadichtungen (1947); *Nachlaß und Biographie* (1949); *Dichtungen und Briefe* (2 vols., 1969); *Song of the West: Selected Poems of G. T.* (1988); *Autumn Sonata: Selected Poems of G. T.* (1989). **FURTHER WORKS IN ENGLISH:** *Twenty Poems of T.* (1961); *Selected Poems* (1968); *Poems* (1973); Appendix in Sharp, M. J., *The Poet's Madness: A Reading of G. T.* (1981)

BIBLIOGRAPHY: Hamburger, M., *Reason and Energy: Studies in German Literature* (1957): 239–71; Sokel, W., *The Writer in Extremis* (1959): 72–78; Casey, T. J., *Manshape That Shone: An Interpretation of T.* (1964); Lindenberger, H., *G. T.* (1971); Saas, C., *G. T.* (1974); Sharp, M. J., *The Poet's Madness: A Reading of G. T.* (1981)

—EDSON M. CHICK

TRANSTRÖMER, Tomas

Swedish poet, b. 15 April 1931, Stockholm

T. was born and educated in Stockholm, receiving a degree in psychology from the University of Stockholm in 1956. He first worked for the Psychotechnological Institute at this university, then took a position as a psychologist at Roxtuna, an institution for juvenile offenders, in 1960. Since 1966 he and his family have lived in Västerås, a city about sixty miles west of Stockholm. For the last few years, T. has worked only part time as a psychologist in order to give more time to his writing. He was the 1981 recipient of the West German Petrarca Prize for poetry.

Since the publication of his first book, *17 dikter* (1954; 17 poems), T. has occupied an important and influential position in Swedish literature. This first collection includes metrical experiments in blank verse and sapphic stanzas. The free verse that is T.'s usual form has exceptionally strong rhythmic qualities, perhaps connected with T.'s love of music: he is an accomplished amateur musician, and many poems have titles that refer to music.

What has made T. perhaps the most imitated of living Swedish poets is, however, not his prosody but his imagery. T.'s poems are often built around a single, concrete image that serves to reveal some truth, often psychological. A typical T. poem is either a "snapshot of something in violent motion"—as he himself puts it in "I det fria" ("In the Clear," 1972; also tr. as "Out in the Open," 1975) from *Klanger och spår* (1966; sounds and tracks)—or a description of something immobile that then suddenly starts moving, bringing a sense of release and of life. Inanimate objects are often described in metaphors of animate, even human, life, and stationary objects, like a forest or a group of islands, are often subject to "violent motion." "Sweden is a hauled-up, unrigged ship," probably T.'s most celebrated metaphor (in "Epilog" ["Epilogue," 1972], from *17 dikter*), contrasts the stagnant state of Swedish society with the life and movement of the Swedish landscape. In this poem, the landscape—one that frequently occurs in T.'s poetry—is the Baltic coast east of Stockholm.

Östersjöar (1974; *Baltics*, 1975), T.'s longest poem and the only one published as a separate volume, celebrates the Baltic archipelago, which has strong personal associations for T. His maternal grandfather, we are told in the poem, was a pilot in these waters, and T. spent his childhood summers on an island in this

Georg Trakl

archipelago. *Östersjöar*, probably the finest example of T.'s musical virtuosity in poetry, uses the sea as a symbol of movement and recurrence. The battle between sea and land suggests other contrasting concepts, such as war and peace, political freedom and totalitarianism, humans in harmony with nature and at odds with nature. In *Östersjöar*, the abrupt stops and starts frequent in the earlier poems have largely been replaced by the continuous movements of sea and wind. Memories of World War II are used as images reflecting present political conditions in the Baltic states, where T. has traveled extensively.

In some of the collections between *17 dikter* and *Östersjöar*, particularly *Hemligheter på vägen* (1958; secrets on the way) and *Den halvfärdiga himlen* (1962; the half-finished heaven), many poems have settings outside of Sweden, for example in Greece and Italy.

T.'s profession as a psychologist, as well as his travels, have influenced poems such as "Efter anfall" ("After an Attack," 1972) in *Hemligheter på vägen*. *P.S.* (1980; P.S.) continues the interest in words and language evidenced in *Östersjöar*. In *Östersjöar* people are able to communicate in spite of having only rudimentary knowledge of a common language, or in spite of their fear of being overheard by political spies; in P.S. speakers offer words but no language, signifying lack of communication and perhaps also lack of individual expression.

In spite of his frequent use of specifically Swedish settings and situations, the directness of T.'s language and the power of his images have attracted more translators to T.'s works than to those of any of his Scandinavian contemporaries. In the English-speaking world in particular, he has a reputation as one of the most outstanding of living poets.

FURTHER WORKS: *Kvartett* (1967); *Mörkerseende* (1970; *Night Vision*, 1971); *Stigar* (1973); *Sanningsbarriären* (1978; *Truth Barriers*, 1980); *T. T.: Selected Poems* (1987); *For the Living and the Dead* (1995). **FURTHER WORKS IN ENGLISH:** *Fifteen Poems* (1966); *Twenty Poems of T. T.* (1970); *Night Vision* (1971); *Windows & Stones: Selected Poems* (1972); *Selected Poems* (1974; enlarged ed., 1981); *Friends, You Drank Some Darkness: Three Swedish Poets—Harry Martinson, Gunnar Ekelöf, T. T.* (1975)

BIBLIOGRAPHY: Steene, B., "Vision and Reality in the Poetry of T. T.," *SS*, 37 (1965): 236–44; Sellin, E., "T. T. and the Cosmic Image," *SS*, 43 (1971): 241–50; Sellin, E., "T. T., Trafficker in Miracles," *BA*, 46 (1972): 44–48; Sjöberg, L., "The Poetry of T. T.," *ASR*, 60 (1972): 37–42; Bly, R., and Transtroömer, T., "Two Poets Translating," *Translation*, 4 (1977): 47–58; Gustafsson, L., *Forays into Swedish Poetry* (1978): 33–37; special T. issue, *Ironwood*, 13, 1 (1979)

—YVONNE L. SANDSTROEM

TRAVEN, B.

(pseud.; exact identity unknown; other pseuds.: Ret Marut, Richard Maurhut, F. Torsvan, T. Torsvan, Hal Croves, etc.) novelist, short-story writer, essayist, and journalist of as yet undetermined nationality, b. 1882?; d. 26 March 1969, Mexico City, Mexico

Although T. claimed to be American, his most important works were published in Germany during the 1920s and 1930s, before some of them appeared in translation in England and three manuscripts, presumably written in English but curiously Germanic, arrived in New York for publication in the U.S.; these were heavily edited to make them sound more colloquially American. Nothing definitive is known about T.'s origin. He may have been the son of a German pottery worker from Schwiebus (now Świebodzin, Poland), and his real name may have been Otto Feige. An earlier supposition, however, that he was related to Kaiser Wilhelm II, cannot yet be altogether dismissed. That he lived in Germany between 1907 and 1922 under the name Ret Marut is the only thing we know for certain. If circumstantial evidence (Marut's disappearance from Europe in 1924 and the first publication of T.'s stories in 1925, the manuscripts having arrived from Mexico) does not prove beyond a shadow of a doubt that Marut became T., similarity of styles and themes in the writings of Marut and T. does.

Marut had been an itinerant actor on German stages between 1907 and 1915 and even then claimed to be American. He published stories and anecdotes in German newspapers and magazines between 1912 and 1919. Between 1917 and 1922 he brought out his own anarchist journal, *Der Ziegelbrenner*. He was involved in the uprising in Munich in 1919 which led to that city's short-lived Räterepublik. On May 1 of that year White Guard soldiers, according to his own later account in *Der Ziegelbrenner*, arrested him, but before being summarily tried and condemned to death and shot as a traitor, Marut was able to escape. Between 1915 and 1924,

he attempted repeatedly but in vain to obtain American papers; once he also applied unsuccessfully for German citizenship; in 1923 he was picked up in London as an unregistered alien. In the spring or early summer of 1924 he went to Mexico. From there he began sending manuscripts to German periodicals. In 1925 his first stories under the name T. were published and, in 1926, his first novel, *Das Totenschiff (The Death Ship*, Am. 1934, Br. 1934), the story of an American sailor who, because he has no identity papers and is unable to find work in Europe, ends up shoveling coal on a ship destined to go to the bottom of the sea for insurance money. The book became an instant best seller. In Mexico T. presumably used the names Torsvan and Croves.

Although his work is well known in Europe and Latin America, T. has never become popular in the U.S. and is still primarily known as the author of the novel *Der Schatz der Sierra Madre* (1927; *The Treasure of the Sierra Madre*, Br. 1934, Am. 1935), on which the famous movie was based. His early novels and stories deal with tramps either looking for work or having found it temporarily, and with their plight as "innocents" caught in a worldwide exploitative system, although oil company executives and *montería* (mahogany land) owners are likewise involuntary puppets of the same system and not necessarily innately evil. Evil for T. is the state. T. criticizes capitalist and imperialist exploitation of the poor the world over from an anarchist point of view. Nationalism, the Catholic Church (and occasionally American Protestant churches and sects), and the military are often incidentally attacked and condemned. T.'s anarchism is strongly influenced by Max Stirner (1806–1856) in its denial of the hegemony of institutions, material and spiritual, over individual humans, and in its insistence on personal indignation, rigorous self-knowledge, and self-expression; it is influenced also by Gustav Landauer (1870–1919) in its vision of communes as a form of social organization preferable to the state.

T.'s series of six novels dealing with the social structure of Indians and whites in the south-Mexican state of Chiapas during the regime (1876–1911) of Porfirio Díaz and with the exploitation of Indians by mestizos and whites and their enslavement on *monterías* constitutes an almost systematic and complete sociology whose value is just beginning to be recognized by historians, anthropologists—and literary critics.

T.'s use of English words in the German texts and his unsuccessful attempts to render American idioms in German, his frequent use of English syntax in German sentences, and his evident familiarity with American mainstream writers to whom he alludes consciously and, what is more important, unconsciously, has led some critics to the conviction that Marut, who demonstrably did not know idiomatic English well, translated into German manuscripts originally written by an American in English. Marut then interpolated his own philosophy and perhaps determined the structure of the works. For these critics, T.'s works are thus the product of a collaboration. The question is still open; seen in this light, however, T. may be considered an American *and* German writer.

A realist concerned with the American working-class pariah and with the almost equally despised Mexican Indian, T. created a lumpen-proletarian fiction of the highest order: infused with humane values, yet easy to read; full of humor but also of detailed descriptions of work processes; rich in archetypal experiences (for instance, dying and rebirth), yet never poor in understandable human motivation; replete with reflective irony, but bursting also with down-to-earth adventure.

FURTHER WORKS: As Ret Marut: *Der Ziegelbrenner* (facsimile ed., 1967; 2nd ed., 1976); *Die Geschichte vom unbegrabenen Leichnam* (1980). As Richard Maurhut: *An das Fräulein von S . . .* (1916; *To the Honorable Miss S . . . ,* 1981). As B. Traven: *Der Wobbly* (1926; retitled *Die Baumwollpflücker,* 1929; *The Cotton-Pickers,* Br. 1956, Am. 1969); *Land des Frühlings* (1928; rev. eds., 1950, 1982); *Der Busch* (1928; expanded ed., 1930); *Die Brücke im Dschungel* (1929; *The Bridge in the Jungle,* 1938); *Die weiße Rose* (1929; *The White Rose,* Br. 1965, Am. 1979); *Der Karren* (1931; *The Carreta,* Br. 1936, Am. 1970); *Regierung* (1931; *Government,* Br. 1935, Am. 1971); *Der Marsch ins Reich der Caoba* (1933; Br., *March to Caobaland,* 1961; Am., *March to the Monteria,* 1964); *Die Troza* (1936); *Die Rebellion der Gehenkten* (1936; *The Rebellion of the Hanged,* Am. 1952, Br. 1972); *Sonnenschöpfung* (1936; *Creation of the Sun and Moon,* Am. 1968, Br. 1971); *Ein General kommt aus dem Dschungel* (1940; *General from the Jungle,* Br. 1954, Am. 1972); *Macario* (1950; retitled "Der dritte Gast" as pub. in collections; "The Third Guest," 1954); *Aslan Norval* (1960). **FURTHER WORKS IN ENGLISH:** *Stories by the Man Nobody Knows* (1961); *The Night Visitor, and Other Stories* (1966); *The Kidnapped Saint, and Other Stories* (1975); *To the Honorable Miss S . . . and Other Stories* (1981)

BIBLIOGRAPHY: Chankin, D. O., *Anonymity and Death: The Fiction of B. T.* (1975); Baumann, M. L., *B. T.: An Introduction* (1976); Recknagel, R., *Beiträge zur Biographie des B. T.,* 3rd ed. (1977); Stone, J., *The Mystery of B. T.* (1977); Baumann, M. L., "B. T.: Realist and Prophet," *VQR,* 53 (1977): 73–85; Raskin, J., *My Search for B. T.* (1980); Wyatt, W., *The Secret of the Sierra Madre: The Man Who Was B. T.* (1980)

—MICHAEL L. BAUMANN

Michel Tremblay

TREMBLAY, Michel

Canadian dramatist, novelist, short-story writer, screenwriter, and translator (writing in French), b. 25 June 1942, Montreal

T. studied until the eleventh grade at the Saint-Stanislas School, at which point he became a linotypist and then a worker in the costume department of Radio Canada, 1966–1967. After writing a play and a collection of short stories, *Contes pour buveurs attardés* (1966; *Stories for Late Night Drinkers,* 1977), T. exploded onto the literary scene with his play *Les belles sœurs* (1968; *The sisters-in-law,* 1974), written in 1965 and first performed in 1968. Subsequent plays in the same vein, referred to as the cycle of the *Belles-Sœurs,* made him the most important theatrical figure in Canada; the many performances of his works outside of the country have added an international dimension to his fame.

Les belles-sœurs originally met with resistance on the part of theater directors who all refused to perform it when it was first proposed to them; even after its overwhelmingly positive popular reception, it was denied support by the provincial and federal governments for performance in France. In both instances, the decisions were made because of the "vulgarity" of the language spoken by the women from the working-class neighborhood of Montreal. Nevertheless, when it finally appeared before the public in March 1968, it was immediately recognized as a turning point in

Quebec theater. Ostensibly the representation of a party given by Germaine Lauzon to have fifteen of her friends help her glue the one million green stamps she won in a contest into stamp books, the dialogues—duets, trios, choruses—soon reveal the lives of the many *belles-sœurs,* solidly anchored in their trivialities, pushed around by men and the religious establishment, stealing small pleasures by watching television, becoming involved with a brush salesman, having a drink at a club once a week, being addicted to bingo, or being torn by personal conflicts. Many of them, in the course of the evening, steal filled stamp books for themselves. In addition to the novelty of representing this slice of society, the play's striking feature is the use of the language of the common people, *joual,* with its colorful imagery, its Anglicisms, its unusual grammatical turns, and its provincial-dialectal pronunciation. The public immediately recognized itself in these women, found the work unique, and observed, between laughs, some unsettling elements of their lives and society.

Among T.'s other plays are *À toi, pour toujours, ta Marie-Lou* (1971; *Forever Yours, Marie-Lou,* 1975), a much more somber work, pitting Carmen against her sister Manon and in confrontation with their dead parents—Carmen, intending to free herself from her oppressive surroundings, Manon clinging to her millieu. Despite the overwhelming tragic atmosphere, the play was a great success, the most successful of the cycle after *Les belles-sœurs.* Carmen reappears in *Sainte Carmen de la Main* (1976; *Sainte Carmen of the Main,* 1981), in which she tries to launch a career as a countrywestern singer. *Damnée Manon, sacrée Sandra* (1977;

Damnée Manon, Sacrée Sandra, 1981) brings the series to an end, although the same cycle spirit is taken up again in *Albertine, en cinq temps* (1984; *Albertine in Five Times*, 1986).

Following his many theatrical successes, T. turned to the novel, creating a series, *Chroniques du Plateau Mont-Royal*, in which many of his best known characters reappear: *C't'à ton tour, Laura Cadieux* (1973; it's your turn, Laura Cadieux), *La grosse femme d'à côté est enceinte* (1978; *The Fat Woman Next Door Is Pregnant*, 1981), *Des nouvelles d'Édouard* (1984; news from Edward), *Le Cœur découvert: Roman d'amours* (1986; open heart: novel of love). As is the case with his plays, we find the characters speaking the language of the people, with the structure sometimes betraying a certain theatricality, and these novels sometimes contain sections that seem to have been written for the stage; indeed, some have been presented as dramatic readings.

The society represented by T. reveals not only the problems found in everyday life, but represents the greater problems of Quebec society, where individuals living lives as Canadians are alienated, never quite fitting in because of their otherness.

Recognized as one of Quebec's most important writers, T. has been the recipient of numerous awards, among them that of being named the most important theatrical figure in Montreal in the preceding twenty years in 1978, receiving the France-Québec Prize in 1981, and being named Chevalier de l'Ordre des arts et des lettres de France in 1984.

FURTHER WORKS: *Demain matin, Montréal m'attend* (1972); *Hosanna (suivi de) La Duchesse de Langeais* (1973; *Hosanna*, 1974); *La Duchesse de Langeais and Other Plays* (1976); *Bonjour, là, bonjour* (1974; *Bonjour, là, bonjour*, 1975); *Mademoiselle Marguerite* (1975); *L'impromptu d'Outremont* (1980; *The Impromptu of Outremont*, 1981); *Thérèse et Pierrette à l'école des Saints-Anges* (1980; *Thérèse and Pierrette and the Little Hanging Angel*, 1984); *Les anciennes odeurs* (1981; *Remember Me*, 1984); *La duchesse et le roturier* (1982); *Le Premier quartier de la lune* (1989); *Marcel poursuivi par les chiens* (1992); *En circuit fermé* (1994); *Messe solennelle pour une pleine lune d'été* (1996)

BIBLIOGRAPHY: Dorsinville, M., in New, W. H., ed., *Dramatists in Canada: Selected Essays* (1972): 179–95; Usmiani, R., "The T. Opus: Unity in Diversity," *CTR*, 24 (Fall 1979): 12–25; Ripley, J., "From Alienation to Transcendence, the Quest for Selfhood in M. T.'s Plays," *CanL*, 85 (1980): 44–59; Usmiani, R., *M. T.* (1982); Lemire, M., et al., *Dictionnaire des œuvres littéraires du Québec* (1984), Vol. 4: passim; (1987), Vol. 5: passim; Weiss, J. M., *French-Canadian Theater* (1986): 27–48; Hamel, R., et al., *Dictionnaire des auteurs de langue française en Amérique du Nord* (1989): 1301–4; New, W. H., *A History of Canadian Literature* (1989): 248–50

—PAUL BARRETTE

TREVOR, William

(pseud. of William Trevor Cox) Irish novelist and short-story writer, b. 24 May 1928, Mitchelstown

An Irishman who has lived most of his adult life in England, T. first established himself as an acute, ironic observer of contemporary English society, but in recent years has increasingly written

William Trevor

about his native country. He was born into a middle-class Protestant family in County Cork, and earned a degree in history from Trinity College, Dublin, in 1950. After teaching school for several years in Dublin and in Northern Ireland, he moved to London and devoted himself to sculpting and, later, writing while working as an advertising copywriter. After his reputation as a writer was secured, he settled in the Devon countryside, where he still lives.

T.'s novels published in the 1960s are characterized by a precise, wry, understated brand of irony that caused him to be associated with Evelyn WAUGH and Kingsley AMIS. Typical of these is the novel that first put T. on the literary map, *The Old Boys* (1964), a satirical, often extremely comic portrayal of various intrigues among a group of elderly Englishmen who attended the same public school. A number of T.'s English novels are, however, considerably broader and more ambitious than this. *The Boarding-House* (1965), *Miss Gomez and the Brethren* (1971), and *Elizabeth Alone* (1973) rely on large, somewhat Dickensian, casts of characters and cut across many segments of English society: from upper-middle-class suburban life to the seedy underside of contemporary London, a world of petty criminals, con artists, and lonely men and women living in bed-sitters that T. has made his own. Through them all runs T.'s view of contemporary life as fundamentally alienated, a view that is countered to some extent by an essentially humanistic fair in the principles of compassion and connection. In his last two English novels, *The Children of Dynmouth* (1976) and *Other People's World* (1980), this view is worked out in part through a critique of the divisiveness of the class system.

Although these novels never shrink from exposing bleak corners of contemporary life, their pessimism is tempered by a fine sense of comedy, as well as by T.'s humanism. T.'s short stories, however, tend to be darker; in them, characters rarely discover the means of breaking out of their moral and social alienation, or of overcoming the crippling illusions with which they mask their various inadequacies. One of T.'s most impressive achievements in this genre is a sequence of three stories entitled "Matilda's England," from *Lovers of Their Time, and Other Stories* (1978), in which the madness that steadily descends on the protagonist is seen to be the madness of a civilization irreparably maimed by two world wars.

T.'s Irish fiction, which accounts for most of his work in the 1980s and 1990s, falls into two categories. There are a number of short stories, including the well-known "The Ballroom of Romance," one novella, *Nights at the Alexandra* (1987), and the highly regarded novel *Reading Turgenev* (1991) that examine the middle-class provincial Ireland that T. knew growing up—the territory of much of the fiction of Frank O'Connor—depicting it as morally, socially, and emotionally paralyzed. In his more politically conscious fiction about Ireland—*Fools of Fortune* (1983), *The Silence in the Garden* (1988), and several short stories—T. indirectly but powerfully exposes the cultural, historical, and emotional forces that lie behind the violence in contemporary Northern Ireland.

Although T. has often been described as an ironist preoccupied with society's losers and eccentrics, there is an impressive range to his writing. He has written, for example, as much about life in middle-class suburbs as he has about people wasting away in London's down-and-out quarters or Ireland's remote provinces. He has also written convincingly about love and marriage, a central concern of his fiction, at all levels of society. Finally, and perhaps most important, he has written with genuine depth about some of the most pressing social issues of his day, including those in Northern Ireland. There is a remarkable consistency of quality in all of T.'s work, but it seems likely that in the long run his writing about Ireland will be that for which he is most justly acclaimed.

FURTHER WORKS: *A Standard of Behaviour* (1958); *The Love Department* (1966); *The Day We Got Drunk on Cake, and Other Stories* (1967); *Mrs. Eckdorf in O'Neill's Hotel* (1969); *The Ballroom of Romance, and Other Stories* (1972); *Angels at the Ritz, and Other Stories* (1975); *The Stories of W. T.* (1983); *Family Sins, and Other Stories* (1990); *W. T.: The Collected Stories* (1992); *Excursions in the Real World* (1993); *Felicia's Journey* (1994); *After Rain* (1996)

BIBLIOGRAPHY: Mortimer, M., "W. T. in Dublin," *EI*, 4 (1975): 77–85; Gitzen, J., "The Truth-Tellers of W. T.," *Crit*, 21, 1 (1979): 59–72; Rhodes, R., "W. T.'s Stories of the Troubles," in Brophy, J. D., and R. J. Porter, eds., *Contemporary Irish Writing* (1983): 95–114; Mortimer, M., "The Short Stories of W. T.," *EI*, 9 (1984): 161–73; Stinson, J., "Replicas, Foils, and Revaluation in Some 'Irish' Short Stories of W. T.," *CJIS*, 11, 2 (1985): 17–26; Morrison, K., "W. T.'s 'System of Correspondence,'" *MR*, 28 (1987): 489–96; Schirmer, G. A., *W. T.: A Study of His Fiction* (1990); Paulson, S. M., *W. T.: A Study of the Short Fiction* (1993); Morrison, K., *W. T.* (1993)

—GREGORY A. SCHIRMER

TRIANA, José

Cuban dramatist, b. 4 Jan. 1931, Hatuey, Camaguey

T. spent the early part of his life in a number of small towns around the Cuban countryside before moving to Madrid in the mid-1950s. Like many other young Cuban writers. T. sought to leave behind the repression of the Batista regime, which held power until the Marxist revolution of 1959. Afterward T. returned to his native country, where his career flourished during the 1960s due to the Castro government's support of a national Cuban artistic program. In 1966 T.'s most significant work, *La noche de los asesinos* (1965; *The Criminals*, 1971), was produced in Havana, firmly establishing T. as an influential voice in 20th-c Latin American literature.

As a young man in Cuba, T. worked as a teacher and studied liberal arts at the University of Oriente. It was not until moving to Europe in 1955 that he committed himself to a literary career. In 1957 he wrote *El mayor general hablará de teogonia* (1962; the major general will speak of theogony), which was first produced in 1960. This play features several characteristics of the THEATER OF THE ABSURD, which places characters in surreal and occasionally horrifying situations in an attempt to represent the futile nature of human existence. The play tells the story of a lower-class Cuban family that has been supported by the charity of its landlord (the major general). The family anxiously anticipates a visit from the general, who is perceived variously by the wife as a figure of divine generosity, and by the husband and his sister-in-law as a figure of divine retribution. Upon the general's arrival, it becomes apparent that the deified figure has nothing more than a sort of disinterested contempt for his idolators, and thus the play succeeds mainly as a satirical attack upon weak-willed worshipers of a supreme being.

After the success of this first play, T. went on to produce three more dramas set among the lower classes of Cuban society. *Medea en el espejo* (perf. 1960, pub. 1962; Medea in the mirror) is a modern retelling of Euripides's *Medea* set in the slums of Cuba. *El Parque de la Fraternidad* (1962; brotherhood park) deals with the failure of three stock characters of Cuban drama to establish meaningful communication. *La muerte del ñeque* (perf. 1963, pub. 1964; the death of the bogeyman) is another play reminiscent of Greek tragedy, wherein a gangster is killed by three other criminals who symbolize the three fates of Greek drama. All three plays lend a mythic status to the everyday occurrences of postrevolutionary Cuba.

In 1966 T. produced his most critically acclaimed work, *La noche de los asesinos*. The drama takes place in a run-down basement, where three Cuban youths engage in a bizarre role-playing game: They pretend to murder their parents, and then go on to enact their own arrest and trial. The youngsters play all the parts in the surreal drama, including parents, police, and courtroom figures. When their "story" is over, the teenagers switch parts and begin the role-playing again. Like *El mayor general hablará de teogonia*, *La noche de los asesinos* is an absurdist work that deals with the issues of guilt and innocence. The play won the prestigious Casa de las Américas Prize for drama (1965) and the Gallo de La Habana Award for best play (1966).

T.'s career as a dramatist flourished in the late 1960s. He served as literary adviser to the Consejo Nacional de Cultura, the Instituto Cubana del Libro, and the publishing house of Letras Cubanas, and in 1967 he traveled to Europe for the international premiere of *La noche de los asesinos*. This prestige, however, was short-lived, as hard-liners in the Cuban government questioned the value of absurdist works to revolutionary ideals. Since absurdism, by definition, does not deal overtly with recognizable elements of everyday life, it was deemed worthless by those in power, who encouraged artistic works that featured Marxist propaganda. Furthermore, *La noche de los asesinos* was perceived as a thinly veiled attack on authoritarianism, and thus it and T.'s other plays were officially banned. T. himself was sentenced to a life of manual labor until 1980, when Castro allowed Cuban dissidents to leave the country, and T. voluntarily exiled himself to France, where he has lived ever since. T. came to the U.S. in 1981 as a visiting professor at Dartmouth College, and received a Cintas Fellowship for 1985–1986. In 1986 T.'s *Worlds Apart*, translated from the Spanish, premiered in London.

Despite his eventual discontent with the outcomes of the 1959 revolution and the subsequent exile from his homeland, T. remained committed to socialist ideals both personally and artistically. He is recognized as one of the most powerful literary voices of postrevolutionary Cuba.

FURTHER WORKS: *De la madera de los sueños* (1958); *La casa ardiendo* (perf. 1962); *La visita del angel* (perf. 1963); *Ceremonial de guerra* (1989)

BIBLIOGRAPHY: Dauster, F. N., "The Game of Chance: The Theatre of J. T.," *LATR*, 3, 1 (1969): 3–8; Miranda, J., "J. T. o el conflicto," *CHA*, 230 (1969): 439–44; Murch, A. C., "Genet-T Kopit: Ritual as 'Danse Macabre,'" *MD*, 15, 4 (1973): 369–81; Dauster, F. N., "J. T.: El Juego violento," *Ensayos sobre teatro hispanoamericano* (1975): 9–36; Palls, T. L., "The Theatre of the Absurd in Cuba After 1959," *LATR*, 4, 7 (1975): 67–72; Nigro, K., "*La noche de los asesinos*: Playscript and Stage Enactment," *LATR*, 11, 1 (1977): 45–57; Campa, R. V. de la, *J. T.: Ritualización de la sociedad cubana* (1979); Neglia, E., "El asedio a la casa: Un estudio del decorado en *La noche de los asesinos*," *RI*, 46, 110 (1980): 139–49; Dauster, F. N., "J. T.," in C. A. Sole, ed., *Latin American Writers* (1989), Vol. 3: 1415–18; Escarpenter, J. A. and L. S. Glaze, "J. T.," in J. A. Martinez, ed., *Dictionary of Twentieth Century Cuban Literature* (1990): 466–70

—JASON BERNER

TRIFONOV, Yury Valentinovich

Russian novelist and short-story writer, b. 28 Aug. 1925, Moscow; d. 28 March 1981, Moscow

The central event of T.'s childhood was the arrest and execution of his father, a Party functionary, in 1937, at the height of the Stalinist terror. After finishing secondary school in Tashkent in 1942, T. returned to Moscow, where he worked at a number of wartime jobs. In 1944 he entered the Gorky Literary Institute, graduating in 1949. Soon thereafter T. published his first novel, *Studenty* (1950; *Students*, 1953), which earned him the dubious distinction of a Stalin Prize.

T.'s novels and short stories of the 1950s and 1960s gave little cause for critical attention. The collections *V kontse sezona* (1961; at the end of the season) and *Fakely na Flaminio* (1965; torches on Flaminio), for instance, contain quite conventional stories about sports. The documentary novel *Otblesk kostra* (1965; reworked

1966; the fire's reflection) traces the fate of T.'s father. The long novel *Utolenie zhazhdy* (1963; the quenching of a thirst) is a fairly typical late "thaw" work set at a construction site in Central Asia.

T. came into his own in the 1970s with two kinds of works: accounts of contemporary life among the Moscow intelligentsia and mosaic novellas about the past. The so-called Moscow novellas— *Obmen* (1969; *The Exchange*, 1977), *Predvaritelnye itogi* (1970; *Taking Stock*, 1977), *Dolgoe proshchanie* (1971; *The Long Goodbye*, 1977), and *Drugaya zhizn* (1975; *Another Life*, 1983)— chronicle the way the upper stratum of the Soviet intelligentsia has become bourgeois and the accompanying disintegration of family life and traditional morality. T. deals with his subject matter in a masterly way, achieving great profundity of characterization.

T.'s other important works of the last decade of his life, *Dom na naberezhnoy* (1976; *The House on the Embankment*, 1983), *Starik* (1978; the old man), and *Vremya i mesto* (1981; time and place), center on older protagonists who meditate on the past. In so doing, the characters attempt to understand both the past and the present, and in all cases they uncover a morass of ugly, compromising facts and incidents. Whatever truths they discover are negative ones, and this aspect of T.'s mature works sets him apart from the mainstream of Russian literature published in the U.S.S.R. in the 1970s.

T.'s best works represent a major contribution to 20th-c. Russian literature. In his command of narrative structure and psychological portraiture as well as in his efforts to get at the truth of the Russian experience he belongs to the most distinguished traditions of Russian writing. His relatively early death, the unexpected consequence of routine kidney surgery, robbed contemporary Russian literature of one of its major talents.

FURTHER WORKS: *Pod solntsem* (1959); *Kepka s bolshim kozyrkom* (1969); *Igry v sumerkakh* (1970); *Neterpenie* (1973; *The Impatient Ones*, 1978)

BIBLIOGRAPHY: Schneidmann, N., "Jurij T. and the Ethics of Contemporary Soviet City Life," *CSP*, 19 (1977): 3–21; Kasack, W., *Die russische Literatur 1945–1976* (1980): 41–42; Hosking, G., *Beyond Socialist Realism* (1980): 183–87; Brown, E. J., *Russian Literature since the Revolution*, rev. ed. (1982): 313–19

—DAVID A. LOWE

TRILLING, Lionel

American critic, essayist, editor, novelist, and short-story writer, b. 4 July 1905, New York, New York, d. 5 Nov. 1975, New York, New York

T. was born and reared in New York City, the son of immigrant parents. His father emigrated from Bialystok, Poland when he was about thirteen years old. T.'s mother was born and reared in London's East End, the daughter of Eastern European immigrant parents; she emigrated to New York at age sixteen or seventeen. T.'s mother was a highly intelligent woman, a voracious reader, and an Anglophile. During his youth, the Trillings were a middle-class, Jewish family, although the failure of his father's manufacturing business forced T. to take on the burden of supporting them while still a graduate student. T. took his undergraduate and graduate degrees in English at Columbia University, his B.A. in 1925, his M.A. in 1925, and his Ph.D. in 1938. T. served as an instructor at Columbia while still a graduate student, but after publication of his first book, *Matthew Arnold* (1939), he was promoted to assistant professor. In total, T. was engaged in education at that institution for forty years. His book on Arnold, widely well received, served to first establish T. as a critic and scholar of some repute. T. continued to publish prodigiously, producing influential book-length studies of E. M. FORSTER and Sigmund FREUD, and as an editor and essayist, contributing regularly to the *Kenyon Review* and *Partisan Review*. Long before the end of his distinguished academic career, T. was recognized as one of the foremost thinkers in American academic literary history.

T.'s most influential work, *The Liberal Imagination: Essays on Literature and Society*, was published in 1950. The essays collected in that work were all written by T. in the 1940s, and served to delineate as clearly as has ever been possible T.'s critical approach. T.'s critical model was Matthew Arnold and *The Liberal Imagination*—a sort of contemporary *Culture and Anarchy* in which T., a liberal humanist himself, essentially takes to task the political oversimplifications of the liberal intellectualism of his era. In addition, T. suggested that modernist literature could provide a remedy to the tedium of contemporary liberalism. Yet his overarching concern in *The Liberal Imagination* and in his long career overall, is with the explication of American culture and the relation of culture to the individual.

Like Arnold, literary study was for T. fundamentally a study of life, and its relation to the self and society is revealed for him in what he called the "animus" (animating force) of the author; as he explains in his essay "On the Teaching of Modern Literature," when he approaches a literary text, he begins with "the animus of the author, the objects of his will, [and] the things he wants or wants to have happen." The motivations and intents of the author spoke to T. about "moral issues," which he saw as the foundation of culture. Thus the study of literature was not, for T. a study of the text as an isolated aesthetic object, but rather necessarily widened to a contemplation on the psychological, social, and cultural implications of the literary text.

T.'s preference for seeking to explain the most complex cultural levels of a literary text often pushed him into ambiguity, for again like Arnold, T. tended to seek, even idealize, a centrist position. T. always sought to fully explore both sides of any issue, and this was often accomplished, as his critics at times observed, at the price of never seeming to have an identifiable position on anything. His seeming ambivalence was a product of his hesitance to polemicize, a hesitancy born of his recognition of the overwhelming intricacy and depth of most human problems, as well as his consistent rejection of the political oversimplifications of the literary Left; one of T.'s favorite phrases, in fact, is reported to have been, "it's complicated, it's very complicated."

The Opposing Self: Nine Essays in Criticism (1955) illustrates another one of T.'s enduring interests, the 19th-c. novel, and in particular, its moral perspective and concerns with social manners. Perhaps one of the things that T. admired most about Arnold was his consistent dedication to moral purpose in literature. Indeed, T. believed that literature, and therefore the literary artist, could and did shape cultural attitudes, as well as individual values and behaviors. For T., authors like William Dean Howells and George ORWELL exemplified the moral perspective he found most valuable to the culture at large, authors who in his words, "live their visions as well as write them, who *are* what they write, whom we think of as standing for something."

FURTHER WORKS: *E. M. Forster* (1943); *The Middle of the Journey* (1947); *Freud and the Crisis of Our Culture* (1955); *A Gathering of Fugitives* (1956); *The Experience of Literature* (1967); *Sincerity and Authenticity* (1972); *Mind in the Modern World* (1972); *The Last Decade: Essays and Reviews, 1965–1975* (1979); *Of This Time, of That Place and Other Stories* (1979); *Prefaces to The Experience of Literature* (1979); *Speaking of Literature and Society* (1980)

BIBLIOGRAPHY: Lewis, R., "L. T. and the New Stoicism," *HudR*, 3, 2 (1950): 313-17; Scott, N., *Three American Moralists: Mailer, Bellow, T.* (1973); Wellek, R., "The Literary Criticism of L. T." *NER*, 2 (1979): 26-49; Chace, W., *L. T.: Criticism and Politics* (1980); Krupnick, M., *L. T. and the Fate of Cultural Criticism* (1986); Tanner, S., *L. T.* (1988); Klingenstein, S., "A Professor of Literature," *Jews in the American Academy, 1900-1940: The Dynamics of Intellectual Assimilation* (1991): 137–98; Trilling, D., *The Beginning of the Journey: The Marriage of Diana and L. T.* (1993)

—MARSHA WATSON

TRINIDADIAN LITERATURE
See English-Caribbean Literature

TROTZIG, Birgitta

Swedish novelist, short-story writer, and essayist, b. 29 Sept. 1929, Gothenburg

T. was raised in Sweden's southernmost province, Skåne, which provides the setting for a number of her works, a landscape of bleak plains, an undramatic Baltic coastline, and often oppressive skies. With her artist husband, T. lived in France from 1954 to 1969; in the words of Adma d'Heurle (b. 1924), "Her intimate knowledge of the art world, her continuing interest in world affairs, and her identification with the poor and oppressed of the world were intensified throughout this period of expatriation. It was also at this time that T. came in contact with the vigorous progressive Catholic movements of the 1950s and joined the Catholic church." From her debut in 1951, T.—unaffected by the vagaries of literary fashion—has remained faithful to an original vision of existence and presented a profile uniquely her own. She is the recipient of a number of prestigious literary prizes, among them the Selma Lagerlöf Prize (1984) and the Pilot Prize (1985), and has enjoyed critical acclaim, not least in France.

T.'s vision of existence is basically religious, but her novels and short stories (she often refers to the latter as fairy tales or legends) are not vehicles for abstract theological discourse; they are palpably and painfully concrete; the concept of God-made-flesh is fundamental in her works. Her early novel *De utsatta* (1957; the exposed) is set in Skåne against a background of war in the 17th c. The novel *En berättelse från kasten* (1961; a tale from the coast) is set in Skåne in the Middle Ages. Her later novels, *Sveket* (1966; the betrayal), *Sjukdomen* (1972; the illness), and *Dykungens dotter* (1984; the marsh king's daughter), are set in more recent times. In most of T.'s stories the protagonists are from the lowest strata of society, people who are poor, downtrodden, and betrayed by life and fellow beings. They are suffering pain, hardships, and indignities, sometimes to the limits of the endurable; the pessimistic vision of existence that emerges through T.'s descriptions is relentless and seemingly unrelieved by grace and only redeemed by the dark intensity of her language. Critics have suggested that T. has made her uncompromising vision an end in itself, effective and compelling, but ultimately aesthetic. It may also be tempting to suggest a deliberate "pious manipulation" behind the creation of such a bleak, implacable, and hopeless universe in order to offer redemption through Christ as the only possible salvation. T. had an early traumatic experience of unmitigated evil when confronted with the exposed horrors of Nazi concentration camps; she also repeatedly points to the predominance of hunger, poverty, oppression, and torture in the world at large as ample justification for her vision. The suffering of children in particular makes T. approach the timeless theodicy problem: how to reconcile the concept of a loving God with the existence of so much evil. Although T.'s political orientation toward a socialist-Marxist worldview may at times conflict with her religious convictions, the search for justice, divine or social, remains a constant. The descriptions in T.'s stories are often unstated indictments of intolerable social conditions; *Dykungens dotter*, for example, is on the mythical and allegorical level patterned on the Hans Christian Andersen fairy tale of the same title; on the realistic level it offers a highly critical account of the social development in Sweden, seen from the perspective of three generations of disenfranchised people. *De utsatta* is more than a historical novel; the descriptions of war in 17th-c. Skåne reverberate with the author's strong emotional involvement with contemporary events in Algeria. The malady implied in the title of the novel *Sjukdomen* is not only that of the mentally retarded protagonist: his birth in 1914 and his first internment in 1939 are significant dates in his life, but also in world history. T. admits that she intended the novel to be both an individual story and a myth of our century.

T.'s primary concern, however, is to depict the individual at the intersection of life and death, order and disorder, hope and despair. The ritual movement is downward, to the lowest and the most degraded state, in an imitation of or rather identification with the passion of Christ toward metamorphosis and resurrection.

In her essays T. offers comments on her own activity as an author. Repeatedly she asserts her belief in the potentials of art and in the power of the artist as outsider and rebel: Unfettered art is one of the most effective weapons against what she terms "the insufferable order."

FURTHER WORKS: *Ur de älskandes liv* (1951); *Bilder* (1954); *Ett landskap, dagbok—fragment 54—58* (1959); *Utkast och förslag* (1962); *Levande och döda* (1964); *Ordgränser* (1968); *I kejsarens tid* (1975); *Berättelser* (1977); *Jaget och världen* (1977); *Anima* (1982)

BIBLIOGRAPHY: d'Heurle, A., "Introducing B. T." *SBR*, 1 (October 1983): 24–26; d'Heurle, A., "The Image of Woman in the Fiction of B. T.," *SS*, 55, 4 (1983): 371–82; Algulin, I., *A History of Swedish Literature* (1989): 266–67; Zuck, V., ed., *Dictionary of Scandinavian Literature* (1990): 626–28

—LARS G. WARME

TS'AO YÜ

(pseud. of Wan Chia-pao) Chinese dramatist, b. 26 Oct. 1910, Tientsin

Son of a well-to-do military official, T. obtained an early initiation in Western-style spoken drama while in high school, cultivating a special interest in Ibsen, GALSWORTHY, and Molière. After entering Tsinghua University in Peking in 1930, he expanded his technical and literary knowledge by studying the works of GORKY, CHEKHOV, SHAW, O'NEILL, Euripides, Aeschylus, and others. Upon graduation, T. taught English at various colleges throughout China, and after the Sino-Japanese War (1937–45) worked as a scriptwriter for films. Since the beginning of the Communist regime in 1949, T. has given active support to the Party's literary policies, holding several key posts in the state bureaucracy. He is at present head of the Peking People's Art Theater.

T.'s plays reflect a continuing struggle to find the means for regenerating the Chinese spirit in the midst of war and national modernization. His first three plays—*Lei-yü* (1934; *Thunder and Rain*, 1936; later tr., *Thunderstorm*, 1958); *Jih-ch'u* (1936; *The Sunrise*, 1940), and *Yüan-yeh* (1937; *The Wilderness*, 1979)— which are often considered a trilogy, demonstrate the beginning of a philosophical ripening for T., combining Western and Chinese thought. In *Lei-yü* he uses Hellenic fate—what T. has called "cosmic cruelty"—and the Aristotelian form of tragedy to examine frustrated love, adultery, and revenge in an oppressively traditional middle-class Chinese family. In *Jih-ch'u*, a story of men and women prostituting themselves to a corrupt system for the sake of false freedom and short-term gain, T. hints at a Taoistic truth: man is subject to the disinterested dynamics of a Godless universe, with which he must harmonize or else perish. Finally, in *Yüan-yeh*, which tells of an escaped convict taking revenge on the landlord clan that ruined his family, T. recapitulates and blends the themes of *Lei-yü* and *Jih-ch'u* into a Promethean protagonist *manqué*. By adding an expressionism that T. borrowed from O'Neill's *The Emperor Jones*, T. created a notable cross-cultural fusion of ideas and forms.

If the trilogy represented a period of philosophical growth for T. and highlighted the inequities of Chinese society in the Republican era, the remainder of T.'s plays before 1949 turned more to the objective changes that must occur for China to regain its strength. For example, *Pei-ching jen* (1941; Peking man), which is perhaps literarily the most sophisticated of T.'s works, presents a moving profile of a declining gentry family in Peking, the members of which are forced to decide how they should each reconcile the demands of tradition with those of modernity. And in T.'s last pre-Communist play, *Ch'iao* (1946; bridge), idealistic industrial engineers, in their conflict with self-seeking government officials after the war, show in concrete terms the need not only for a new spirit of sacrifice and national pride but also for innovative management techniques and a commitment to change. Although flawed artistically, *Ch'iao*, in its social-political message, is possibly the most mature of T.'s dramas.

T.'s plays after 1949, like those of other hopeful Republican playwrights who sided with the Communists, suffer artistically from Maoist literary strictures. One exception, perhaps, is *Tan chien p'ien* (1961; gall and sword), a historical play based on the traditional tale of Kou-chien, king of Yüeh (5th c. B.C.), avenging his defeat by Fu-ch'a, king of Wu, after many years of patient preparation. Although a play intended to illustrate the politically correct theme that a weak, oppressed nation such as China can eventually prevail over its imperialist overlords, T.'s skill in characterization and plot design makes this work extraordinary among usually mediocre Communist dramas.

There is little question that T.'s early plays place him among the best playwrights that China has produced in the 20th c. His talent for combining complex philosophical visions from both China and the West has made him a remarkable contributor to world literature. At the same time, by dramatizing the ideal of spiritual renascence in China, he was able to objectify his own people's dreams for fulfillment during a time of momentous national change.

FURTHER WORKS: *Hei tzu erh-shih-pa* (written 1938, with Sung Chih-tie, pub. 1945); *Cheng tsai hsiang* (1940); *Shui-pien* (1940); *Chia* (1942); *Yen-yang t'ien* (1948); *Minglang ti t'ien* (1954; *Bright Skies*, 1960); *Ying ch'un chi* (1958); *Wang Chao-chün* (1978)

BIBLIOGRAPHY: Ch'en, D. Y., "The Trilogy of T. Y. and Western Drama," in Frenz, H., ed., *Asia and the Humanities* (1959): 26–37; Ch'en, D. Y., "*The Hairy Ape* and *The Peking Man*: Two Types of Primitivism in Modern Society," *YCGL*, 15 (1966): 214–20; Ch'en, D. Y., "The Chinese Adaptation of Eugene O'Neill's *The Emperor Jones*," *MD*, 9 (1967): 431–39; Lau, J. S. M., *T. Y., the Reluctant Disciple of Chekhov and O'Neill: A Study in Literary Influence* (1970); Hu, J. Y. H., *T. Y.* (1972); Rand, C. C., Introduction to T. Y., *The Wilderness* (1979): vi-1

—CHRISTOPHER C. RAND

TSIRKAS, Stratis

(pseud. of Yannis Hadjiandreas) Greek prose writer, critic, and poet, b. 10 July 1911, Cairo, Egypt; d. 27 Jan. 1980, Athens

T. was a prolific writer of fiction and a pioneer commentator on the Alexandrian poet C. P. CAVAFY. After his graduation from the Ambeteios School of Commerce in Cairo (1928), he worked for a year in the National Bank of Egypt, then was an accountant in small cotton concerns of the Nile area until the late 1930s when he settled in Alexandria as manager of a tannery. His contact with communist circles started in 1930 and continued through the end of his life, although his books caused friction with party leaders of doctrinaire persuasions. He was very active in prewar antifascist and peace movements, helped Greek resistance fighters during World War II, and continued his political activism in the 1950s when he also traveled to France, Switzerland, Germany, and Greece. In 1963 he settled permanently in Athens, where he contributed the short story "Alaxokairia" ("Weather-Change") to the resistance volume *Dekaokhto Keimena* (1970; *Eighteen Texts*, 1972). His studies of the Cavafy era and his Middle East trilogy made him famous in Greece and abroad in the 1970s.

T.'s literary career began with the publication of a fairy tale, "To phengari" (1927; the moon), in the Alexandrian magazine *Panegyptia* when he was only sixteen. The first collection of short stories, *Hoi Fellahoi* (1937; the Fellahs), presented his leftist ideology both in subject matter and themes. His sympathy for the

poor, downtrodden, exploited, and those vanquished in personal or communal life continued to be the hallmark in his two books of verse, three volumes of short stories, and the novella *Noudendin Bompa* (1957; Nurendin Boba) that he published before settling in Athens.

T.'s narrative technique and style in realistic fiction were conventional although quite effective for his humanitarian concerns. In contrast, the pronounced Marxist coloration of his verse left it outside the aesthetic climate that was being developed by modernist poets like Angelos SIKELIANOS, George SEFERIS, and Odysseus ELYTIS, or the more sophisticated Marxists Kostas VARNALIS, Yannis RITSOS, and Nikiforos Vrettakos. T. won his reputation as a novelist of great breadth and cosmopolitan vision with the publication of the epic trilogy *Akyvernetes politeies* (*Drifting Cities*, 1974), which consists of the novels *He leskhe* (1961), *Ariagne* (1962), and *He nykhterida* (1965) (respectively *The Club, Ariagne,* and *The Bat* in the English translation of 1974). Comparable in spirit, narrative structure, and characterization technique to Lawrence DURRELL'S contemporaneous tetralogy *The Alexandria Quartet* (1957–1962) this *roman-fleuve*, in its 1971 French translation, won the prize for best foreign book of the French critics and publishers in 1972. Its English version offered the scenario for the international television serial released in the 1980s. By then, it had appeared in Spanish, Italian, and Romanian as well. Its arresting but not complex plot features a fascinating gallery of Greek and international characters from many walks of life as they go through dramatic crises set in wartime Jerusalem, Alexandria, and Cairo. T.'s well-rounded and colorful heroes and heroines are drawn into a vortex of intrigue, spying, fighting, and love affairs that are typical of the exotic locale and its nebulous atmosphere.

Encouraged by the popularity of his trilogy, he started working on a new one, set in Greece. He completed only the first novel, *He khamene anoixe* (1976; the lost spring), whose main hero, now a middle-aged, tired, and disappointed leftist activist, not unlike the author, becomes involved in the dramatic political developments of 1965 in Greece that led to the 1967 military takeover. In most artistic and thematic respects this last novel is a continuation of the commendable achievement of The Middle East trilogy. A French translation appeared in 1982.

T.'s reputation as a literary critic was secured with the publication of the treatise *Ho Kavaphes kai he epokhe tou* (1958; Cavafy and his times), which won a State Prize for essay. It explores, from a Marxist angle, the cultural milieu and sociopolitical events in the international society of early 20th-c. Egypt where Cavafy lived and wrote. This study was complemented by the volume of essays *Ho politikos Kavaphes* (1971; the political Cavafy), which offered additional information and, like the monograph that preceded it, provoked a spirited but enlightening dialogue with disagreeing scholars, Greek and foreign.

Apart from the translation of *Akyvernetes politeies* into five languages and of his Nile novella into French and Arabic, several of T.'s short stories appeared in these two languages plus English, German, Hungarian, Polish, and Russian. His poems were collected in a volume posthumously.

FURTHER WORKS: *To lyriko taxidi* (1938); *Allokoton anthropoi kai alla diegemata* (1944); *Proteleftaios apokhairetismos kai to ispaniko oratorio* (1946); *Ho Apriles einai pio skleros* (1947); *Ho hypnon tou theriste kai alla diegemata* (1954); *Ston kavon kai alla diegemata* (1966); *Ta hemerologia* (1973); *Ta poiemata* (1981)

BIBLIOGRAPHY: Raizis, M. B., on *He khamene anoixe, WLT*, 51, 4 (Autumn 1977): 658–59

—M. BYRON RAIZES

TSONGA LITERATURE
See under South African Literature

TSUSHIMA Yūko

(pseud. of Tsushima Satoko) Japanese novelist, short-story writer, and essayist, b. 30 Mar. 1947, Tokyo

T. is the daughter of Tsushima Shūji, who wrote under the pen name Dazai OSAMU, and his wife, Tsushima Michiko. After her father's death in 1948, when she was one year old, T. and her brother and sister were brought up by their mother. T. was close to her older brother, who had Down's syndrome, and who died when he was fifteen and she was twelve. The loss of the language-free world they had shared, and a desire to find value in human existence by some measure other than the intellect, led T. to begin writing fiction in her late teens while she was an English literature manor at Shirayuri Women's College. An important inspiration, for its innovations in style and form, was the work of William FAULKNER, particularly *The Sound and the Fury* (1929).

T.'s first published short story, "Rekuiemu—inu to otona no tame ni" (1969; requiem for a dog and an adult), was written in her senior year of college. Her early stories present a closed world of family relationships, often from a child's viewpoint; many contain macabre and surreal elements. Inevitably first identified as Dazai's daughter, T. soon began to establish an independent reputation. "Kitsune o haramu" (1972; conceiving a fox) was nominated for the Akutagawa Prize; the collections *Mugura no haha* (1975: the mother in the house of grass) and *Kusa no fushido* (1977; a bed of grass) were awarded the Tamura Toshiko Prize (1976) and the Izumi Kyūka Prize (1977), respectively; and the novel *Chūji* (1978; *Child of Fortune*, 1983) received the Women's Literary Award (1978).

The protagonist of *Chūji* is a thirty-six-year-old divorced mother who believes herself to be pregnant again. Through her experience of the pregnancy and the conventional attitudes of the people around her, the novel explores two of T.'s major themes: the tensions between motherhood and other dimensions of identity and sexuality, and the social marginality of a woman raising a family alone. (T. married in 1970 and divorced in 1976, when her daughter was four; her son was born the same year.) T.'s characteristic use of light and water images as symbols of vitality and sexuality is at its most effective in this work. T. has carried on the efforts of earlier women writers such as Okamoto Kanoko (1889–1939) and Enchi FUMIKO to portray sexual love as experienced by a woman. Often employing narrative techniques close to those of the confessional *shishūsetsu*, or "I-novel," she has reexamined the language available to express a woman's sexuality—a concern she shares with many contemporaries writing in other languages.

The newspaper serialization of her novel *Yama o hashiru onna* (1980; *Woman Running in the Mountains*, 1991) brought T. a wider audience, while the story "Danmari ichi" (1982; "The Silent Traders," 1984) earned her the Kawabata Yasunari Prize (1983). Both works employ vivid images of nature in the interstices of the city, and draw on folkloric sources. The novel's heroine, a young single mother, dreams of living like the indigenous hunter-gatherers of the far north. The deadening urban routine and the control of bureaucracy over her life (through records of her child's illegitimacy) can barely contain her intuitive, wild energy. Associations with the *yamanba*, or mountain witch, and Japan's preagricultural peoples give mythic force to a novel of minutely detailed realism.

After the sudden loss of her son in 1985, T. turned to an intensely personal contemplation of grief in which she strips away modern technological society's insulation from the inevitability of death. The novel *Yoru no hikari ni owarete* (1986: driven by the light of night) retells the 11th-c. romance *Yowa no nezame* (*The Tale of Nezame*, 1979). In three chapters in letter form, the contemporary narrator addresses the woman author of the tale, Sugawara no Takasue no Musume (1008–?). In her lifetime, death must have been an ever-present reality, yet her words have survived for nearly a thousand years—facts that sustain the narrator, herself a writer, as she resolves to continue her own work.

T.'s prolific output and the autobiographical basis of her writing have resulted in some repetitive reworking of materials in her short stories. Over her twenty-year career, however, her fiction has evolved a distinctive fusion of realistic social content, critically observed from the margins, and transcending elements of myth, dream, and natural imagery employed with considerable imaginative power.

FURTHER WORKS: *Shanikusai* (1971); *Dōji no kage* (1973); *Ikimono no atsumaru ie* (1973); *Waga chichitachi* (1975); *Toōmei kūkan ga mieru toki* (1977); *Yorokobi no shima* (1978); *Yoru no tī pātī* (1979); *Hyūgen* (1979); *Hikari no ryūbun* (1979); *Saigo no shuryū* (1979); *Moeru kaze* (1980); *Yoru to asa no tegami* (1980); *Shōsetsu no naka no fūkei* (1982); *Suifu* (1982); *Watakushi no jikan* (1982); *Hi no kawa no hotori de* (1983); *Danmari ichi* (1984); *Ōma monogatari* (1984); *Osanaki hibi e* (1986); *Mahiru e* (1988); *Yume no kiroku* (1988); *Hon no naka no shōjotachi* (1989); *Kusamura* (1989); *Afureru haru* (1990); *Ōinaru yume yo, hikari yo* (1991). **FURTHER WORKS IN ENGLISH:** *The Shooting Gallery, and Other Stories* (1988)

BIBLIOGRAPHY: Monnet, L., "Mord, Inzest und Schwachsinn: Die weibliche Mythologie Tsushima Yukos," in K. P. Portner and R. Schneider, eds., *Referate des VII. Deutschen Japanologentages in Hamburg* (1988), Vol. 3: 218–27; Dunlop, L. on *The Shooting Gallery, LitR*, 32 (1989): 288–93; Schierbeck, S. S., "T. Y.," *East Asian Institute Occasional Papers 5: Postwar Japanese Women Writers* (1989): 149–52; Drabble, M. and Tsushima Yūko, "Career and Family for the Woman Writer and in Women's Writing," in F. Takano, ed., *Margaret Drabble in Tokyo* (1991): 59–112; Cheever, S. on *Woman Running in the Mountains, Los Angeles Times Book Review* (26 May 1991): 2; Miyoshi, M., "T. Y.," *Off Center Power and Culture Relations between Japan and the United States* (1991): 212–16

—GERALDINE HARCOURT

TSVETAEVA, Marina Ivanova

(also transliterated Cvetaeva) Russian poet and essayist, b. 26 Sept. 1892, Moscow; d. 31 Aug. 1941, Yelabuga

Born into a highly cultivated family—her father was the founder of the Museum of Fine Arts, her mother a concert pianist—T. started writing poetry as a child. Her first volume of verse, *Vecherny albom* (1910; evening album), attracted the attention of such prominent poets as Nikolay Gumilyov, Valery Bryusov, and Maximilian Voloshin (1877–1932). It was followed by *Volshebny fonar* (1912; the magic lantern) and *Iz dvukh knig* (1913; from two books). All three books were a tribute to her childhood, the ideals of her youth, and the heroes of history and fiction whom she revered with a feeling akin to awe. With the collection *Vyorsty* (1922; miles) her verse achieved artistic and stylistic maturity.

The poems composed between 1917 and 1921 were published posthumously under the title *Lebediny stan* (1957; *The Demesne of the Swans*, 1980). Written during years of hardship and famine—one of her own daughters had died of starvation in 1920—they are among the most "political" of her poems in that they deal with the brutal realities of the revolution. In 1922 T. followed her husband, Sergey Efron, a former White Army officer, into exile, first to Prague and then to Paris. T.'s versatility and consummate mastery of her art can be perceived in much she wrote during those years. One of her collections, *Razluka* (1922; separation), so impressed the poet Andrey BELY that he began experimenting with T.'s style and entitled his next book of poems, *Posle razluki* (1922; after separation), after it. T.'s last important collection of poems, *Posle Rossii: 1922–1925* (1928; after Russia: 1922–1925), is considered by many serious critics her finest work. In 1933 her husband's activities as a Soviet agent turned the fanatically anti-Bolshevik Russian community of Paris against her, effectively blocking her already limited avenues of publication. Scorned and boycotted as a poet, she turned to prose. *Moy Pushkin* (1937; my Pushkin) is one of her better-known prose works, and one of her best.

In the summer of 1939, friendless and almost destitute, she decided to return to her homeland with her son and join her husband and daughter, who had preceded her there. Tragedy awaited her: her husband was soon arrested and later executed, and her daughter was sent to a labor camp. In 1941, after the German invasion, she was evacuated with her son to the small provincial town of Yelabuga. After ten days there, she hanged herself.

Like the art of her favorite poet, the SYMBOLIST Alexandr BLOK, T.'s lyrical output can be regarded as a diary of her spiritual life. More sensitively and truthfully than the numerous recollections of her by her contemporaries, her poems reflect the contradictions of her personality that caused many to misunderstand and mistrust her: her inability to separate her personal life from the vagaries of her fertile imagination; her passionate and erratic nature seemingly at odds with her highly disciplined, logical mind; the coexistence in her of the conservative political thinker with the rebellious, revolutionary innovator in poetics.

T. came to Russian poetry at the beginning of the 20th c. Although she could not escape the influence of contemporary trends during this fertile literary period, she stood apart and remained unmistakably original. Her tastes were eclectic, her choice of themes encompassed the wide range of her emotional and intellectual experiences. She explored classical myths and folklore, biblical and historical characters; she experimented with many styles, ranging from the "grand" 18th c. diction of Gavriil Romanovich Derzhavin (1743–1816) to imitations of peasant speech. Among her innumerable themes in prose and poetry, those of love and death prevail.

Her literary versatility is remarkable: she wrote dramas, memoirs, and critical and philosophical essays, and throughout her life engaged in a vast correspondence with some of the greatest figures of her times, such as Rainer Maria RILKE and Boris PASTERNAK. In her art one can recognize romantic, classical, symbolist, and FUTURIST influences, but no one single strain predominates. A willful independence of spirit prevented her from adhering to any established poetic school, and she never deviated from the principle to which she had committed herself in her youth: to be true to herself, her convictions, and her art regardless of the pressures of the times and milieu.

T.'s voice resounds distinctly in her lyrics, and in this respect and certain others she reminds one of Emily Dickinson: in T., too, we encounter the terse, aphoristic saying, the unexpected fresh metaphor, the incisive observation, as well as the contrasts and contradictions that cut through the deepest layers of consciousness. T.'s poetry, however, is more direct than Dickinson's, her diction harsher.

T.'s language is as complex and individualistic as her personality. Contracted syntax; paradoxes; the interplay of verbless, monosyllabic lines; ellipses; imitations of magic spells and incantations; coinages of new words and word combinations; onomatopoeic effect—all these devices enter at one time or another into T.'s lyrical experimentations.

Totally devoted to her art, fanatically disciplined, she weighed each word with the painstaking care of a painter choosing his hues. The sound, shape, and expressive possibilities of the word fascinated and challenged her. The search for the right word was a search for the authentic self, and creation was a kind of catharsis of the soul.

T.'s poetry both courts criticism and defies it. One of the most controversial personalities of 20th-c. Russia, she evoked profound indignation in certain people. They found her too intense, too eccentric; she overwhelmed people with the power of her emotions and antagonized them with her inflexibility. In fact, dispassionate comments about her art or personality can seldom be found. The poet Zinaida HIPPIUS refused to permit her own poems to appear on the same page with T.'s. All that Ivan BUNIN could perceive in her verse was "a flood of wild words and sounds." Pasternak, however, called her the "highest" and considered her a greater poet than Anna AKHMATOVA. Vladimir NABOKOV called her a "poetic genius."

T.'s fame is greater abroad than in her own country, which has still not forgiven her either her rejection of the revolution or her independent spirit. Pasternak wrote: "The greatest recognition and reevaluation of all awaits T., the outstanding Russian poet of the twentieth century." Among the younger generation and the more discriminating critics in the Soviet Union, T. enjoys popularity and prestige, but the limited publication of her works there suggests that the fulfillment of Pasternak's prophecy is still far off.

FURTHER WORKS: *Metel* (1918); *Preklyuchenie* (1919); *Konets Kazanovy* (1922); *Star devitsa* (1922); *Stikhi k Bloku* (1922); *Remeslo* (1923); *Psikheya* (1923); *Molodets* (1924); *Ariadna* (1924); *Proza* (1953); *Proza* (1969); *Pisma k Anne Teskovoy* (1969); *Neizdannye pisma* (1971); *Mat i muzyka* (1977); *Izbrannaya proza, 1917–1937* (2 vols., 1979); *Sochinenia* (2 vols., 1980); *Stikhotvorenia i poemy* (1980 ff.); *Krysolov* (1982). FURTHER WORKS IN ENGLISH: *M. T.: Selected Poems* (1971; rev. and enlarged ed., 1981); *A Captive Spirit: Selected Prose* (1980)

BIBLIOGRAPHY: Karlinsky, S., *M. Cvetaeva: Her Life and Art* (1966); Livingstone, A., "M. T. and Russian Poetry," *MelbSS*, 5–6 (1971): 178–93; Slonim, M., "Notes on T.," *RusR*, 31 (1972): 117–25; Taubman, J. A., "M. T. and Boris Pasternak: Toward the History of a Friendship," *RLT*, No. 2 (1972): 303–22; Mirsky, D. S., "M. S.," *TriQ*, 28 (1973): 88–93; Taubman, J. A., "T. and Akhmatova: Two Female Voices in a Poetic Quart," *RLT*, No. 9 (1974): 355–69; Livingstone, A., "T.s' 'Art in the Light of Conscience,'" *RLT*, No. 11 (1975): 363–78; Gove, A. F., "The Feminine Stereotype and Beyond: Role Conflict and Resolution in the Poetics of M. T.," *SlavR*, 36 (1977): 231–55; Vitins, I., "Escape from Earth: A Study of T.'s Elsewheres," *SlavR*, 36 (1977): 644–57; Proffer, E., ed., *T.: A Pictorial Biography* (1980)

—LUCY VOGEL

TSWANA LITERATURE

See Botswana Literature and under South African Literature

TUCHOLSKY, Kurt

German essayist, critic, and poet, b. 9 Jan. 1890, Berlin; d. 21 Dec. 1935, Hindås, Sweden

T., the son of a businessman, received his early schooling in Berlin and Stettin (now Szczecin, Poland). His father's untimely death and a strained relationship with his mother overshadowed his youth. After studying at the universities of Berlin, Geneva, and Jena, T. received a doctorate of laws from Jena in 1915. Shortly thereafter he was conscripted into the army, and his three and a half years of service during World War I (on the eastern front, in the Baltic area, and in Romania) turned him into an ardent pacifist.

In 1913 he began to contribute to *Die Schaubühne*, after 1918 called *Die Weltbühne*, one of the most distinguished cultural and political periodicals of the time. He was a close associate of its founder, Siegfried Jacobsohn (1881–1926), and its sometime editor, Carl von Ossietzky (1889–1938). Among the numerous other journals to which T. contributed were *Vossische Zeitung, Ulk*, and *Die Welt am Montag*. In addition to writing under his own name, the versatile T. used the pseudonyms Peter Panter, Theobald Tiger, Ignaz Wrobel, and Kaspar Hauser, calling this situation "gay schizophrenia." After 1924, when he went to Paris as a correspondent for *Die Weltbühne*, T. lived in Germany only sporadically, residing mostly in France, Sweden, and Switzerland, and considering Sweden his permanent home after 1929. In 1932 he stopped writing for publication ("I have success. But I have no effectiveness whatever"). In his last years T. was afflicted with severe sinus trouble that necessitated several operations. Two volumes of letters and diary entries published in recent years give a poignant picture of this cheerless and increasingly desperate exile period. Deeply depressed by the course of events in Germany and the madness of his time, T. committed suicide a few weeks before his forty-sixth birthday.

T. is widely regarded as one of the most powerful satirists of this century. His work consists mainly of lively, stylistically notable, and frequently witty essays, feuilletons, glosses, political and cultural commentaries, monologues, poems, book reviews, drama criticism, aphorisms, and chansons. His satirical sallies were directed at nationalism and militarism, deep-rooted flaws in the German national character, the encroachments and injustices of the great Moloch state, entrenched privilege, the dehumanizing forces of our age, and human stupidity, cupidity, and indifference in their myriad guises.

T.'s satiric oeuvre is flanked by two charming romantic idylls with autobiographical elements, *Rheinsberg: Ein Bilderbuch für Verliebte* (1912; Rheinsberg: a picture book for lovers) and *Schloß Gripsholm* (1931; *Castle Gripsholm*, 1985). An early volume of poems, *Fromme Gesänge* (1919; pious chants), was followed by much light verse, some of it in the Berlin vernacular. The typically clever title of T.'s first collection of satirical pieces, *Mit 5 PS* (1928), has a dual meaning: "under five pseudonyms" and "with five horsepower." Succeeding collections were characteristically titled *Das Lächeln der Mona Lisa* (1929; Mona Lisa's smile) and *Lerne lachen ohne zu weinen* (1932; learn to laugh without crying).

T.'s cabaret-type poetry was set to music by such composers as Hanns Eisler, Rudolf Nelson, Werner Richard Heymann, Friedrich Holländer, and Olaf Bienert, and in his lifetime it was presented in revues or cabarets by performers like Trude Hesterberg, Kate Kühl, Ernst Busch, Paul Graetz, Gussy Holl, and Rosa Valetti. *Ein Pyrenäenbuch* (1927; a book about the Pyrenees) shows to good advantage T. the sensitive traveler and outstanding reporter, but his only play, *Christoph Kolumbus; oder, Die Entdeckung Amerikas* (1932; *Christopher Columbus*, 1972), written in collaboration with Walter Hasenclever (1890–1940), was less successful.

One of T.'s most controversial works is *Deutschland, Deutschland über alles* (1929; *Deutschland, Deutschland über Alles*, 1972), a book containing prose and poetry by T. as well as numerous photos and John Heartfield's photomontages; it is a mordant assessment and hard-hitting exposure of many aspects of the Weimar Republic. Having left the Jewish fold in 1911, T. devoted thirteen prose sketches to the thoughts and doings of "Herr Wendriner," a depiction of an assimilationist, opportunistic, spiritually empty German Jew.

Since the end of World War II T.'s work has been deemed to be of undiminished timeliness and relevance, and the satirist was widely republished in both West and East Germany. This "T. renaissance" is due in large measure to the efforts of T.'s second wife, Mary Gerold-Tucholsky, who coedited his collected works and his letters as well as establishing exemplary archives. Three revues based on T.'s writings as adapted by Louis Golden and Harold Poor have been presented in this country: *Tucholsky!* (Waltham, Mass., 1971), *Tickles by Tucholsky* (New York, 1976), and *Berlin Kabarett* (Boston, 1983).

FURTHER WORKS: *Der Zeitsparer* (1914); *Träumereien an preußischen Kaminen* (1920); *Gruß nach vorn* (1946); *Zwischen gestern und morgen* (1952); *Na und—?* (1953); *Und überhaupt. . .* (1953); *Panter, Tiger & Co.* (1954); *K. T. haßt—liebt* (1957); *Man sollte mal. . .* (1957); *Gesammelte Werke* (3 vols., 1960–61); *So siehst du aus!* (1962); *Ausgewählte Briefe 1913–1935* (1962); *Warum lacht die Mona Lisa?* (1968); *Wenn die Igel in der Abendstunde* (1968); *Briefe an eine Katholikin, 1929–1931* (1970); *Briefe aus dem Schweigen, 1932–1935* (1977); *Die Q-Tagebücher, 1934–1935* (1978); *Unser ungelebtes Leben: Briefe an Mary*

(1982). FURTHER WORKS IN ENGLISH: *The World Is a Comedy: A T. Anthology* (1957); *What If—? Satirical Writings of K. T.* (1968); *Kleines Lesebuch/Little Reader* (1977, bilingual); *Germany! Germany! A K. T. Reader* (1990)

BIBLIOGRAPHY: Zohn, H., "K. T., the German-Jewish Satirist," *Jewish Forum*, Aug. 1956: 110–13; Schulz, K.-P., *K. T. in Selbstzeugnissen und Bilddokumenten* (1959); Poor, H. L., *K. T. and the Ordeal of Germany, 1914–1935* (1968); Laqueur, W. Z., "The T. Complaint," *Encounter*, Oct. 1969: 76–80; Brady, P. V., "The Writer and the Camera: K. T.'s Experiments in Partnership," *MLR*, 74 (1979): 856–70; Zwerenz, G., *K. T.: Biographie eines guten Deutschen* (1979); Grenville, B. P., *K. T.: The Ironic Sentimentalist* (1981); Ackermann, I., ed., *K. T. Sieben Beiträge zu Werk und Wirkung* (1981); King, J., *K. T. als politischer Publizist* (1983); Soldenhoff, R., *K. T. Ein Lebensbild* (1985); Austermann, A., *K. T. Der Journalist und sein Publikum* (1985); Wessling, B. W., *T. Ein deutsches Ärgernis* (1985); Raddatz, F. J., *T. Ein Pseudonym* (1989); Bemmann, H., *K. T.* (1990); Ackermann, I., et al., eds., *T. heute* (1991); Hepp, M., *K. T. Biographische Annäherungen* (1993); Schulz, K.-P., *Wer war T.?* (1996)

—HARRY ZOHN

TUMBUKA LITERATURE

See Zambian Literature

TUNISIAN LITERATURE

In Arabic

In the first half of the 20th c. the combined influence of *nahda* (cultural renaissance) and *salafiyya* (religious reformism), both of which originated in the Arab Mashriq (Middle East), gave a new life to Tunisian literature, which for centuries had been reduced to the puerile imitation of poets of the past.

The prime exponent of this new awakening was Tāhir Haddād (1901-1935). His original thinking, expounded in his two books, *Al-'Ummāl al-tunisiyyūn wa zuhūr al-haraka al-niqābiyya* (1927; Tunisian Workers and the Emergence of Trade Unionism) and *Imra'a-tunā fī al-sharī'a wa al-mujtama'* (1930; Our Women Before Sharia [body of Islamic law] and Society), influenced the platform of the nationalist Neo-Dustūr Party and have shaped important legislation in postindependence Tunisia.

Another leading figure of this rebirth was Abū al-Qāsim AL-SHĀBBĪ, Tunisia's best-known poet. He rebelled against traditional forms, with their trivial details, stock imagery, and clichés, and advocated inventiveness and originality, ideas he set forth in his famous lecture *Al-Khayāl al-shi'rī 'inda al-'Arab* (1929; The Poetic Imagination of the Arabs). He also directed his lyrical energies to awakening his people to their situation and debunking the colonial order. His collection of poems *Aghānī al-hayāt* (Hymns to Life), not published until 1954, reveals his stylistic and thematic preferences, as well as the affinities he shared with the European romantics and the poets of Al-Mahjar, that is, Arab poets living in the Americas in the late 19th and early 20th cs.

A truly national literature can be said to have emerged with the group Taht al-Sūr (Under the Ramparts), named after the café where its members met. The short story became the preferred literary genre. The group's most outstanding member was 'Ali Du'ājī (1909-1949), whose wit and love of life found full expression in his many exquisite tales about his native Tunis and its inhabitants. His short stories are collected in *Layālī al-samar* (1969; Nights of Insomnia). Du'ājī's imagination goes beyond the everyday, as in his fictionalized travel book *Jawla hawl hānāt al-bahr al-abyad al-mutawassit* (1935; A Tour of Mediterranean Bars).

Mahmūd MAS'ADĪ, who enjoyed the benefits of a Franco-Arabic education, departed radically from the preoccupations of his contemporaries, perceiving the Tunisian reality more speculatively and philosophically. His most acclaimed play, *Al-Sudd* (wr. 1942; pub. 1955; The Dam), is an existentialist drama in the vein of Jean-Paul SARTRE's theater of ideas. In this play, as well as in the novel *Haddatha Abū Hurayra . . . qāla* (1973; Thus Spake Abu Hurayra . . .He Said) and in the essay collection *Mawlid al-nisyān, wa ta'ammulāt ukhrā* (1974; The Birth of Oblivion, and Other Essays), Mas'adī employs the highly metaphorical language of the Koran.

Independence in 1956, followed by an expanded educational system, gave rise to a large intelligentsia whose literary concerns shifted from the binary perspective of colonizer-colonized to a multiple perception of an increasingly complex Tunisia; the quest for identity became the most prominent theme. Munawwar Smaddah (b. 1931), the most prolific of postindependence poets—he wrote ten volumes of poetry—was famous for his simple but classical lyricism that poignantly expressed his nationalistic feelings.

The novel made a tentative start with Bashīr Khurayif's (b. 1917) first full-length fictional work, *Iflās; aw, Hubbuki darabanī* (1959; Bankruptcy; or, Madly in Love with You), a didactic and moralistic work, written in the mode of social realism, as are his other novels, *Barg El-lil* (1960; Barg El-lil) and *Al-Daqala fī arājinihā* (1969; A Bunch of Dates). In a more populist vein is a novel by 'Abd al-Qādir ibn al-Shaykhn (Bencheik, b. 1929), *Wa nasībī min al-ufuq* (1970; My Share of the Horizon), which depicts the hardships of rural life in Tunisia. Other populist works are Rashād al-Hamzāwī's (b. 1934) *Boudouda māta* (1962; Boudouda Is Dead), Mustafā al-Fārisi's (b. 1931) *Al-Mun 'araj* (1966; The Bend), and al-'Arūsī al-Matwī's (b. 1920) *Al-Tūt al-murr* (1967; Bitter Mulberries).

The most innovative of postindependence writers is 'Izz al-dīn Madanī (b. 1938), a novelist, short-story writer, dramatist, critic, and essayist. His experimental plays—*Thawrat al-Zanj* (1970; The Rebellion of the Zanj) and *Al-Hallāj* (1973; Al-Hallāj)—are full of political undertones pertinent to Tunisia in particular and the Arab world in general. He combines distinctively Tunisian material with avant-garde methods. His many provocative essays, including *Asātir* (1968; Myths), add to his reputation as Tunisia's foremost writer.

Samīr 'Ayyādī's (b. 1947) short stories—for example, those in the collection *Sakhab al-samt* (1970; The Roar of Silence)—and his play *'Atshān yā sabāya* (1970; Maidens, Quench My Thirst) express the disenchantment with the status quo, a widespread sentiment among the educated.

Such feelings are explored through oneiric and fantastic imagery by a host of talented younger poets. Tāhir al-Hammāmī (b. 1947), in his experimental works *Al-Hisār* (1972; The Siege) and *Al-Shams tala'at ka-al-khubza* (1973; The Sun Rose like a Loaf of Bread), and Habīb Zannād (b. 1946), in *Al-Majzūm bi al-lām* (1970; The Negative Mode), resemble the European avant-garde.

In this context one should also note the bacchic and iconoclastic poetry of Sghayyer Ouled Ahmed (b. 1956), especially in *Nachîd al-ayyâm al-sitta* (1988; Song of the Six Days) and *Laysa lî muchkila* (1988; I Have No Problem).

Currently the most promising writer in Tunisia, Ridha Kéfi (b. 1950), a journalist and polemicist, embodies the perfect example of a new breed of writers in Tunisia who are well traveled and fully conversant in many languages and cultures. If Kéfi's creative writing is predominantly in Arabic—*Kharif* (1984; Autumn); *Khayt Aryân* (1987; Ariadne's Clew), *Nisâ'* (1987; Woman)—his journalistic and polemic essays are in French. His essay *La maison Tunisie* (1995; The House of Tunisia) is a lucid examination of the Tunisian predicament.

The review *Al-Fikr*, founded in 1955 by Muhammad Mazālī (b. 1926), Tunisia's former prime minister, for long the best forum for Tunisians writing in Arabic, ceased in 1986. It was replaced by *Al-Hayat Al-Thakafiyya*.

In French

Tunisia seems to have resigned itself to being the stepchild of North African literature in French. Albert MEMMI, a Tunisian Jew, is still unchallenged as the leading essayist and writer of fiction. In his largely autobiographical novels, *La statue de sel* (1953; The Pillar of Salt*, 1955) and *Agar* (1955; Agar), and his theoretical exegesis, *Portrait du colonisé, précédé du Portrait du colonisateur* (1957; The Colonizer and the Colonized*, 1965), Memmi expounds a sociology of oppression, which becomes more universalized in his later works. The theme of dominance and oppression marks *Portrai d'un Juif* (1962; Portrait of a Jew*, 1962), *La libération du Juif* (1966; The Liberation of the Jew*, 1966), and *L'homme dominé* (1968; Dominated Man*, 1968). His later novels, *Le scorpion; ou, La confession imaginaire* (1969; The Scorpion; or, The Imaginary Confession*, 1971), which makes use of stream-of-consciousness techniques, and *Le désert* (1977; The Desert) and *Le Pharaon* (1988; The Pharoah), which dwell on myths, symbols, and metaphors, address themselves to more universal questions. Memmi's only volume of poems, *Le mirliton du ciel* (1990; The Reed Pipe of the Sky), blends nostalgia and introspection.

Mustapha Tlili (b. 1937) depicts the brutalizations of the colonized in his novels: *La rage aux tripes* (1975; Fury in the Guts), *Le bruit dort* (1978; The Noise Sleeps), and *Gloire des sables* (1982; Glory of the Sands). Tlili, who lived for thirteen years in New York, offers in his novels a multidimensional investigation of his own past. In his most recent novel, *La montagne du lion* (1988; The Lion's Mountain), a poetic-political fable, Tlili indicts, with wit and humor, postindependence Maghrebian development policies that have ravaged the indigenous traditional culture in the name of progress.

The most promising novelists are Abdelwahab Meddeb (b. 1946) and Fawzi Mellah (b. 1946). Meddeb's *Talismano* (1979; The Talisman) is a major novel whose importance can be equated to that of the Algerian writer Kateb YACINE's *Nedjma* (1956; *Nedjma*, 1961). Meddeb attempts a deconstruction of Tunisian reality and, beyond that, contemporary Arab reality. The narrator revisits his native city, Tunis, and submits his observations and reminiscences to a thorough and meticulous examination, a sort of self-exorcism. In his second novel, *Phantasia* (1986), as well as in his poetry, notably *Tombeau d'Ibn Arabi* (1987; Ibn Arabi's Tomb) and *Les 99 stations de Yale* (1955; The 99 Stations of Yale), and in the play *La gazelle et l'enfant* (1922; The Gazelle and the

Child), Meddeb continues his exploration of such themes as the confrontation between East and West and the dynamics of the archaic and the postmodern, focusing especially on the poetic and philosophical legacy of the early Masters of Medieval Muslim Sufism (most notably Ibn Arabi) whose heretic and iconoclastic teachings are resurrected, revamped, reinvented, and couched in today's postdeconstructionist jargon.

Like Meddeb's, Mellah's fiction addresses the present by questioning the past. In *Le conclave des pleureuses* (1987; The Conclave of Weeping Women), Mellah examines tradition to explain the vicissitudes of the modern, whereas in *Elissa, la reine vagabonde* (1988; Elissa, the Vagabond Queen) history, myth, and legend are enlisted to shed a new and original light on the current Tunisian predicament. Mellah is also the author of several essays, collected in *De l'unité arabe* (1985; On Arab Unity) and plays, notably *Néron et les oiseaux de passage* (1974; Nero and the Passing Birds) and *Le palais du non-retuor* (1985; The Palace of No Return).

While drama in French is almost nonexistent, poetry is the most favored medium of expression. Hédi Bouraoui (b. 1932), Mohamed Aziza (pseud.: Chems Nadir, b. 1940), Salah Garmadi (1930-1982), Moncef Ghachem (b. 1946), Majid El-Houssi (b. 1942), and Tahar Békri (b. 1951) display undeniable talent. Bouraoui, however, is the only one whose work displays a unity, as can be seen in *Vésuviades* (1974; Vesuviads), *Sans frontières* (1979; Without Boundaries*, 1979), *Haïtuvois, suivi d'Antillades* (1980; [pun] Hey, You See, Followed by Antillades). Yet his poetry—and this is true for all Francophone Tunisian poets—has attracted little attention at home. The major obstacle is that it is rooted in a time and space beyond immediate Tunisian concerns.

Aziza's poetry is dominated by an obsession—his Arabness. His quest for an earlier and truer self is somewhat contrived. Aziza is more eloquent and persuasive in his essayistic works. Garmadi's poetry stems from his interest in linguistics. For him, the poetic exploration of language is the same as the quest for identity. Moncef Ghachem extols a poetics of violence: his verse is full of anger at the unfulfilled promises of independence and denunciation of those who use power for their own self-interest.

Majid El-Houssi, the most promising of the younger poets, draws on both the present—the traumas of the decolonized—and the past—the reactualization of the precolonial Arab, Berber, and Muslim heritage. In *Imagivresse* (1973; Drunkimages) and later with less success in *Ahméta-O* (1981; Ahméta-O) and *Iris ifriqiya* (1981) African Iris) the poet uses surrealist techniques to express the multiple layers of his own reality.

Tahar Bérki (b. 1951) is the most original poetic voice in the last decade. His poetry, both in French and Arabic, is marked in the first volumes, *Le laboureur du soleil* (1983; The Sun's Ploughman); *Le chant du roi errant* (1985; The Song of the Errant King); *Le coeur rompu aux océans* (1988; The Oceanworthy Heart), by the poet's painful experience of exile from the homeland for political reasons. His exilic trials are transcended later, especially in *La sève des jours* (1991; The Sap of Days) and *Les chapelets d'attache* (1993; The Rosary of Anchorage), to become a metaphor for the condition of the writer condemned to live, not without advantage, between cultures, languages, and countries.

Women writers in Tunisia have begun to gain recognition both as poets and novelists. A recent auspicious debut was made by Amina Saïd (b. 1953) with her collection of poetry *Nuit friable* (1980; Crumbling Night), in which a simple lyricism is used to explore the psyche, in particular that of the North African woman.

In both her essay *Désenchantement national* (1982; National Disenchantment) and her novel, *L'oeil du jour* (1985; The Day's Eye), Hélé Béji (dates n.a.) offers an insightful perspective on the problems facing women who are caught in the bind between tradition and modernity. This theme is treated with equal brio by Emna Bel Haj Yahia (dates n.a.) in *Chronique frontalière* (1990; Border chronicle).

BIBLIOGRAPHY: Khatibi, A., *Le roman maghrébin* (1968); Ghazi, F., *Le roman et la nouvelle en Tunisie* (1970); Zmerli, S., *Figures tunisiennes: Les contemporains et les autres* (1972); Yetiv, I., *Le thème de l'aliénation dans le roman maghrébin* (1972); Déjeux, J., *Littérature maghrébine de langue française* (1973); Fontaine, J., *Vingt ans de littérature tunisienne 1956–1975* (1977); Ostle, R. C., "Mahmūd al-Mas'adi and Tunisia's Lost Generation," *JArabL*, 8 (1977): 153–66; special issue, *O&C*, 4, 2 (1979); *La littérature maghrébine de langue française devant la critique*; Baccar, T., Introduction to T. Baccar and S. Garmadi, eds., *Écrivains de Tunisie* (1980): 11–54

—HÉDI ABDEL JAOUAD

TURÈLL, Dan

Danish poet, novelist, and essayist, b. 19 Mar. 1946, Copenhagen; d. 15 Oct. 1993, Copenhagen

Born in Copenhagen to working-class parents, T. moved with his family to the suburb of Vangede when he was seven years old. He finished school in 1964, took casual jobs, and wrote poems and columns for the local papers. T. was interested in jazz, in Ezra POUND's *Cantos*, and in the poems of the American beat generation, which he was introduced to by his close friend, the poet Peter LAUGESEN.

In 1966 T. published his first collection of poems, *Vibrationer* (Vibrations), at his own expense. He later deleted these poems from the list of his works because he thought them to be too influenced by Danish modernist poetry, and he considered the following collection *40 ark* (1969; 40 Sheets) as his debut. *40 ark* as well as *40 linier* (1969; 40 Lines) were duplicated, taped stencils. T.'s early "subpub-books" had self-invented publishers with spectacular and subtle names such as "Dracula Poetry Inc.," "Peace Eye Spirit," "Intergalactic Expansion of Visible Communications, Inc.," or the Andy Warhol-like "Soft Machine Productions." Today, these subpub-books—some of which are handwritten in different colors of Indian ink—are expensive collector's items like *Changes of Light* (1970; title in English). Many of T.'s collections have English titles and are partly written in English.

Though it was difficult for T. to get his first books accepted by the commercial publishing houses, he continued his way of writing poems, emphasizing the process itself. He tried to make new meanings of words and linguistic patterns emerge from the creative association. In *Manuskrifter* (2 vols., 1970; Manu-Scriptures) and *Bevægelser formålsløst cirklende* (1971; Pointless Circulating Movements) T. tried to elaborate a writing that could dissolve the hierarchy of meaning and give the reader and the poet himself a new linguistic experience.

T. was extremely productive, and from 1969 to 1975 he published thirty-five books, many at his own expense. *Sekvens af Manjana, den endeløse sang flimrende gennem hudens pupiller* (1973; A Sequence of Manjana, the Endless Song Shimmering through the Pupils of the Skin) was the turning point of his career and was soon recognized as a major work of contemporary Danish poetry. *Sekvens af Manjana, den endeløse sang flimrende gennem hudens pupiller* consists of several forms of text and genres— "poems, montages, transmissions, notes, exorcisms, hymns, projections, songs, fotos, performances, transcriptions, journals, films," as T. explained. The writing is supposed to shape itself freely, and the poet tries to create a poetic criticism that will end modern suppression of body and soul and make an exploration of the mind possible. The notion of writing seems inspired by both French structuralist and poststructuralist ideas of "l'écriture" and of Zen Buddhist philosophy. T. was very conscious of using various kinds of linguistic material and in opposition to modernist poets. He was fascinated by pop music, cartoons, and Westerns and often referred to cartoon figures and Western heroes in his texts. In 1974 T. published *Karma Cowboy* (title in English), and as the title indicates T. combined Western film-clichés and Eastern philosophy in a large and tangled text-album, partly written in English. The genres of *Karma Cowboy* are "the blues," "the common prayer," "the telegram," and the Japanese "Li-poem." The poet chants, sings, and recites his text and re-creates poems of Allen GINSBERG in Danish.

Karma Cowboy included T.'s first "Vangede" poems. The collection *Vangede billeder* (1975; Vangede Pictures) included humorous and warmhearted narrative prose poems on the neighborhood of his childhood, the suburb Vangede, and its inhabitants and shopkeepers. *Vangede billeder* made T. a very popular poet and with his black-polished nails, star-shaped earrings, and his cowboy hat he became a well-known and controversial figure in Danish cultural life. T. actually decided to wear black nail polish in order to get a public image and in a humorous way debate the mechanisms of postmodern image-making.

Vangede billeder showed T.'s linguistic mastery in the both touching and accurate portrait of his childhood days and neighborhood, and the book became a modern classic. T. mastered a refined linguistic game with phrases, platitudes, and original poetic imagery, and the kindness of his own personality characterized the whole book.

In the following years T. published poems, essays, and novels. He became a columnist at one of the leading papers and his weekly essays on the city of Copenhagen had their own elegant style, inspired by the Danish author Herman Bang (1857–1912), who introduced this impressionistic genre in Denmark in the beginning of the 20th c. T. also experimented with the crime novel; from 1981 to 1994 he published a series of twelve crime novels. Several of these novels have been translated into German, Dutch, and French. T. was extremely productive, always working on new projects and series of poems or essays and also performing and touring with his jazz band, Sølvstjernerne (The Silverstars). In the early 1990s— prior to his premature death from throat cancer at age forty-seven— T. and his wife, the actress Chili Turèll, performed with recitations of poems and pop songs. The most important of his many collections are his "city" trilogy, *Drive-in-digte* (1976, Drive-in-Poems), *3-D poems* (1977; Poems in Three Dimensions), and *Storby-Blues* (1977; The Blues of the City), the six volumes of *Medie-Montager* (1975–78; Media Montages), and the trilogy *Himalaya Hilton* (1991; title in English), *Gud & Gokke* (1992; God & Ollie), and *Tja-a Cha Cha* (1993; A Cha-Cha-Chat). T.'s writing is a moving and living rhythm, which forms a streaming and flowing text with wonderful improvisations, solos, and highlights.

FURTHER WORKS: *Occult Confessions* (1970); *Speed of Life* (1970); *Områder af skiftende tæthed og tomhed* (1970); *Manuskrifter om hvad som helst* (1971); *The Total-Copy System* (1971); *Sidste forestilling af bevidstløse trancebilleder* (1972); *A Draft of XXX Space Cantos* (1972); *Opsvulmede byer i sigtekornet flagrende skud i bevidstheden* (1972); *Feulliton* (8 vols., 1972-78); *Dobbeltskrift* (1973, with Peter Laugesen); *Film* (1973, with Henrik Have); *Lissom* (1973); *Onkel Danny's dadaistiske disc-jockey djellaba jazzjungle joysticks* (1973); *Onkel Danny's Deliristiske Jukebox Jitterbug* (1974); *Here Comes Your 19th Nervous Breakdown* (1974); *Another Draft of Space Cantos* (1974); *Third Draft of Space Cantos* (1975); *Nytår i Rom* (1976); *Onkel Danny fortæller* (1976); *Live-Show Feed-Back* (1976); *Livets Karrusel* (1977); *Onkel Danny fortæller videre* (1978); *Onkel Danny's små sorte sitrende skinnende swingende saxsoli sæbeboble-sange* (1978); *Alverdens vampyrer* (1978); *Onkel Danny fortæller i timevis* (1979); *Onkel Danny's Rullende Rallende Regnsvejs Ragtime Rhapsody* (1979); *D. T. i byen* (1979); *Møde i Garda* (1979, with Barry Wilmont); *Ulysses' Spejl* (1981, with Barry Wilmont and Henrik Nordbrandt); *Onkel Danny fortæller på talløse opfordringer* (1982); *D. T. i byen igen* (1982); *Alhambra Blues* (1983); *And All That Jazz* (1983, with Gorm Valentin); *Sort Film* (1984); *Kom forbi* (1984); *Don Dobbeltliv og andre historier fra Stjernecaféen* (1985); *D. T. i byen så det basker* (1985); *Jazz-digte, Nekrolog, Blues for Buddha* (1986–88, with Peter Hentze), *D. T. i byen i dén grad* (1988); *As Time Goes By . . .* (1989); *Forklædt til genkendelighed* (1989); *Undervejs med Copenhagen All Stars* (1991); *D. T. i byen—og i baggårdene* (1991); *Det døgn, da . . .* (1992); *D. T. i byen—for sidste gang* (1994); *Just a Gigolo* (1995)

BIBLIOGRAPHY: Højris, R., *D. T.—samtale og introduktion* (1977); Poulsen, P., "D. T.," in Brostrøm, T., and A. Winge, eds., *Danske digtere i det 20. århundrede* (1982), Vol. 5: 413–20; Schnack, A., and J. G. Brandt, *80 moderne danske digtere* (1988): 273–78; Bundgaard, P., *Superdan. Et portræt af D. T.* (1995)

—ANNE-MARIE MAI

TURKISH LITERATURE

Modern Turkish literature evolved under European influence during the second half of the 19th c., and its rise is connected with the cultural transformation that began in the wake of Westernizing reforms. The process of literary modernization was begun by a cadre of intellectuals who learned French in newly established schools in Turkey and developed an appreciation of European culture as a result of their travel and residence in Europe. The first literary innovators were socially committed reformists who sought to disseminate through their writings such ideas as freedom, equality, justice, progress, and patriotism. As such, they turned to journalism, introduced the essay, and employed literature as a means of educating the public, thus establishing a strong didactic trend. They were also Westernists who rejected traditional Turkish literary forms and introduced such genres as the novel and, in drama, tragedy and comedy. The highly abstract imagery and rigid verse forms of classical Turkish poetry, based on the AraboPersian models, were gradually abandoned in favor of a poetic idiom appropriate to convey ideas.

Two early leaders of Turkish literary Westernization were Ibrahim Şinasi (1826–1871) and Namik Kemal (1840–1888). Şinasi wrote the first Turkish play, *Şair evlenmesi* (1859; *The Wedding of a Poet*, 1981), a comedy about lower-middle-class urban life; Kemal published the first Turkish novel, *Intibah* (1876; awakening), and wrote Hugoesque tragedies with patriotic themes. Both Şinasi and Kemal took the position that the primary function of literature was to be of service to society, and what they preached in their essays, they practiced as poets as well.

Reaction against utilitarianism in literature gained momentum in the 1880s when an art-for-art's-sake movement arose. Sentimental lyricism replaced social concerns in the poetry of Recaizade Ekrem (1847–1914) and of Abdühak Hamit Tarhan (1852–1937). Both were committed Westernists, and Tarhan also wrote plays in imitation of Shakespearean and French neoclassical tragedies. The same period also witnessed a resurgence of traditionalism, while devastating polemics between innovators and defenders of classical verse dominated the literary scene.

Such polemics continued throughout the 1890s; Westernists who gathered around the influential periodical *Servet-i fünun* initiated a literary movement that took over postromantic trends in French literature. Influenced by the Parnassians and SYMBOLISTS, the poets of this group experimented with new verse forms, including the prose poem. Fiction of the period, on the other hand, was dominated by a search for realism.

The Turkish novel in the last quarter of the 19th c. reflected and documented the circumstances of rapid cultural and social change. Ahmet Mithat (1844–1912), who popularized the novel, employed the genre as a means of instructing the public. He defended the moral virtues of Turkish society but aimed to show the means of achieving material progress through imitating the European work ethic. Other novelists of the period shared similar concerns; they ridiculed the effete foppery of certain elite groups for whom Westernization simply meant fashionableness, and they reflected on the breakdown of the traditional family structure as a result of Europeanization. The novel gained more depth and subtlety in the 1890s. The principles of naturalism and Zola's theories were first introduced in 1885, and novelists began to pay greater attention to the psychological dimension of characters and to the influence of environment on the personality. The search for realism culminated in Halit Ziya Uşakligil's (1866–1945) *Aşk-i memnu* (1900; forbidden love), a novel that vividly depicts life in an upper-class Istanbul mansion and tensions among the members of the family. By the turn of the century, Western genres had been adopted in Turkish literature, and the principal currents of literary modernism had begun taking shape. The development of Turkish poetry, fiction, and drama in the 20th c. has been closely connected with ideological movements.

Poetry

Nationalism as an ideology predated the establishment of the Turkish Republic as a nation-state in 1923. In the face of the rapid disintegration of the Ottoman Empire and especially during the incessant wars between 1910 and 1922, poetry was called upon to inculcate a sense of patriotism and national solidarity. National consciousness replaced Ottomanism, which had been a patriotic movement that called for the protection of the Ottoman Empire as a multiethnic, multireligious, cosmopolitan entity. As a result, poets began turning to Turkish folklore as a source of inspiration. The quantitative meter borrowed from the Arabic was forsaken in favor of the simple syllabic meter of the minstrels. Nationalism also meant populism, and poets began using pure conversational Turkish rather than the formal literary language called Ottoman, cultivated by the elite over several centuries, which relied heavily on Arabic and Persian vocabulary.

Two leaders of the nationalist vein were Mehmet Emin Yurdakul (1869–1944) and Ziya Gökalp (1876–1924). Yurdakul wrote verse in imitation of folk poetry laden with references to the accomplishments of the Turkish nation. Gökalp, who was also the father of Turkish sociology, aimed to convey the principles of nationalism through simple, didactic poems. Riza Tevfik Bölükbaşi (1869–1949), who defined literature as a manifestation of national conscience, was far more successful in capturing the essence of folkloric poetry, its themes as well as melodies; he was the first urban poet to use the syllabic meter of the minstrels with ease, and his poems contained vivid pictures of rural Anatolia.

The rising interest in folklore as the basis of the new poetry culminated in the work of Orhan Seyfi Orhon (1890–1972), Enis Behiç Koryürek (1891–1949), Halit Fahri Ozansoy (1891–1971), Yusuf Ziya Ortaç (1895–1967), and Faruk Nafiz Çamhbel (1898–1973). All five began their careers under the influence of nationalism and were encouraged by nationalist leaders. Although their success as poets varied, they collectively confirmed that poetry could be written in a simple language and address itself to the popular taste. The combined influence of folklore and nationalism thus set a major trend that continued through the 1940s. The poems of Kemalettin Kamu (1901–1948), Ahmet Kutsi Tecer (1901–1967), Ömer Bedrettin Uşakh (1904–1946), and Behçet Kemal Çaglar (1908–1969) are inspired by a romantic sense of attachment to the land and to the people.

The trend of employing folkloric themes in literature was encouraged by the government. The state aimed at fostering a strong sense of national identity, and as a part of its nation-building program People's Houses were established in 1931, as the cultural arm of the ruling Republican People's Party. The People's Houses replaced the Turkish Hearths, founded earlier to disseminate panTurkish ideals, and in contradistinction to the Hearths, they promoted artistic and literary activity in keeping with the secular, populist, patriotic, and Westernist ideals of the Turkish Republic. The People's Houses served as social and cultural centers, and provided financial assistance to the artistic community. In 1932 the semiofficial Turkish Language Society was established; it helped accelerate the language-reform movement and encouraged poets in their search for a national idiom through the use of nonliterary, spoken Turkish.

The result, however, was not a domination of poetry by ideological trends. For many of the young poets who began publishing in the first two decades of the Republic, the language reform and the rejection of classical verse forms provided a means for experimentation and new departures. The questions of love, death, and time, and of deep psychological urges versus material aspects of human existence were explored in the poems of Ahmet Hamdi Tanpinar (1901–1962), Necip Fazil Kisakrürek (b. 1905), Cahit Sitki Taranci (1910–1956), and Ziya Osman Saba (1910–1957).

Meanwhile, the burden of the past was not to be ignored. Three poets kept alive the sense of aesthetics based on classical meter, although their art pointed in different directions. Mehmet Akif Ersoy (1873–1936), whose nationalism stemmed from his opposition to European imperialism, championed the cause of Islam as a regulative, moral force in society. Two stanzas of a poem he wrote during the War of Independence (1920–22) were adopted as the

Turkish national anthem in 1921. But ironically, because of his disagreement with the secular principles of the Republic, he left Turkey in 1924 and lived in Egypt until a few months before he died. His most interesting poems are those that depict lower-middle-class urban life, and he was the last craftsman who could make common people speak through the intricate metrics and rhyme scheme of classical verse. Ahmet Haşim (1884–1933) continued the trend of symbolism begun in the 1890s; the melancholy effect of his poems was achieved through an effective use of color imagery. Yahya Kemal Beyath (1884–1958), a neoclassicist, imitated the masters of the Ottoman and Persian classical tradition in a significant portion of his work, but his best-known poems are those that capture various scenes of Istanbul. His neoclassicism manifested itself not only in his preference for classical diction but also in his nostalgic references to the glories of the Ottoman past. The works of these poets constituted the only strong link between tradition and modernity in Turkish literature.

Nazim HIKMET was a true revolutionary in several senses of the word. He embraced communism as a student in Moscow in the early 1920s and began writing poems celebrating the struggle of the workers, peasants, and colonial peoples against imperialism. After spending several years in prisons in Turkey, he defected to the Soviet Union, where he died in exile. Hikmet, under the influence of Vladimir MAYAKOVSKY, revolutionized Turkish poetry by introducing free verse, thereby paving the way for a poetic idiom free from formal constraints. He was, however, a master craftsman who employed to advantage all the possibilities that the language could accommodate. Hikmet was above all a lyricist and a humanist; he wrote a number of intimate love poems, and his revolutionary poems reflect his love for the people.

The appearance of *Garip* (1941; strange), a small anthology consisting of poems by Orhan Veli Kamk (1914–1950), Oktay Rifat (b. 1914), and Melih Cevdet ANDAY, was a prelude to a new era of modernism. In the introduction to the volume, the contributors declared that poetry ought to be attuned to the taste of the masses and reflect their feelings and aspirations. The de-elitization of poetry constituted a final break with the tradition amid bitter objections and much controversy; but the wryly humorous tone and epigrammatic style of the *Garip* group nevertheless became widely popular. Kamk vividly conveyed the moods and dreams of individuals as well as depicting scenery by the use of concrete images. Rifat developed a satirical style and continued to experiment with free association of ideas, while his later poetry became more intellectual. Anday also turned to intellectual explorations in his poetry; his work has become more abstract as he probes the complexities of human life and man's relationships with nature while searching for a universal mythology.

The *Garip* movement was influential in setting a trend of poetic realism that lasted through the early 1950s. Poets developed a colloquial idiom shorn of all artifice. In general, poetry became descriptive and colorful; even social commitment was conveyed through ironic or satirical statements. After the mid-1950s, however, a reaction developed against the simple formulations and levity of the poetic realists. A group of younger poets rejected social realism as a viable base for poetry. On the one hand they derived their inspirations from Asaf Halet Çelebi (1907–1958), a pioneering SURREALIST who had defined the goals and methods of abstract poetry in the 1940s. On the other hand, they sought to go beyond surrealism by achieving total meaninglessness in poetry. Ilhan Berk (b. 1916), Cemal Süreyya (b. 1931), and Edip CANSEVER were the champions of obscurantist verse.

No single current or trend has dominated Turkish poetry since the 1960s, while experiments and departures in different directions have resulted in its enrichment. Regardless of fashionable currents and countercurrents, social engagement continued to be a strong trend. One of the leading contemporary poets, Fazil Hüsnü DAĞLARCA, has often returned to social and political topics. Although his vast output includes lyrical and metaphysical works, he has forcefully conveyed his condemnation of the existence of poverty and injustice, of the maltreatment of the disenfranchised, and even of the American involvement in Vietnam.

The individual was not neglected in the work of several poets who rejected social realism in favor of probing the individual's response to life. In Behçet NECATIGIL's work the feelings of hope and despair in the face of life's vicissitudes are explored. At different stages of their careers, Cemal Süreyya and Turgut Uyar (b. 1927) have explored psychological states, sexual urges, and attitudes toward the social and natural environment; Uyar has also experimented with traditional forms while eschewing antiquated vocabulary and classical meters. The influence of neosurrealism also remained and can be discerned in the technique and imagery employed by Ece Ayhan (b. 1931) and Ülkü Tamer (b. 1937). The multifaceted development of Turkish poetry thus continues, while younger poets explore different approaches and achieve new syntheses.

Fiction

With the rise of nationalism in the first decades of the 20th c., just as poets turned to folkloric themes and forms, novelists and short-story writers also began shifting the focus of fiction away from the upper-class life of the capital to the rural hinterland. A populist-nationalist movement began in 1911 with the initial publication in Salonika of a literary magazine, *Genç kalemler;* its contributors defended the use of the vernacular in literature and rejected a literary language separate from the spoken Turkish of the people. The leading writer of this group, Ömer Seyfettin (1884–1920), wrote anecdotal stories in which he captured the lifestyle and mentality of people in urban neighborhoods and rural towns. In this respect, his work complemented the trend of concrete realism set earlier by Hüseyin Rahmi Gürpinar (1864–1944) and Ahmet Rasim (1864–1932), who portrayed humorous aspects of Istanbul life by caricaturizing representative types. Both in his humorous vignettes and stories with nationalistic themes, however, Seyfettin aimed to present and defend the true values and virtues of Turkish society.

The transformation from empire to nation state and the attendant changes in society captured the imagination of novelists in the early decades of the Republic. Halide Edib ADIVAR wrote about traditionalist communities as well as the emerging modern society; she also wrote sagas of the War of Independence. Yakup Kadri KARAOSMANOĞLU's novels as a whole portray and document the transformation of Turkish society in the first half of the 20th c. His broad, panoramic view encompasses such themes as the breakdown of the traditional family, the changing political life, and the distance between urban and rural culture. The pathological aspects of the clash between conservative, traditionalist groups and ultra modernist elements were examined by Peyami Safa (1899–1961). The title of his novel *Fatih-Harbiye* (1931; Fatih-Harbiye) came to connote the syndrome of incompatibility between socially and culturally opposed segments of society: Fatih is the old part of Istanbul—lower-middle-class and traditional; Harbiye is a newer section—upper-middle-class, posh, Westernized.

In the same period, interest in Anatolia increased, and many urban novelists attempted to discover the rural heartland of the nation. Prior to World War I, only two authors had written about the village. In 1919 Refik Halit Karay (1888–1965), who had spent time in Anatolia as a political exile, published his first collection of realistic stories depicting life in villages and small towns: *Memleket hikâyeleri* (stories from the country). Others approached Anatolia with a romantic attitude, extolling the virtues of the peasant uncorrupted by the cynicism and egotism of urban life. In his popular *Çlikuşu* (1922; *The Autobiography of a Turkish Girl,* 1949), Reşat Nuri Güntekin (1889–1956) sent his idealistic heroine to Anatolia as a schoolteacher. In another novel, *Yeşil gece* (1928; green night), however, he focused on fanaticism and reaction as forces detrimental to social progress.

In the 1940s voices of protest began to emerge in fiction. Sabahattin Ali (1906–1948) presented a fundamentally different picture of rural Turkey, one in which the tragedy of the poor peasants and their struggle for existence was depicted. Social realism was taken up by a new generation of writers, among whom were younger people with rural backgrounds who had been educated in the Village Institutes—teacher-training schools established as a part of the educational mobilization program. They knew only too well the unpleasant realities of village life—the underdevelopment, the poverty, the plight of the landless sharecropper—and used the novel as a means to expose these realities. Thus was born an indigenous genre of social realism, called the "village novel."

Yaşar KEMAL's novels written between 1955 and 1975 forcefully convey the predicament of the peasant in the face of the changing economic order: they chronicle the incursion of capitalism into rural areas and depict the worsening plight of the nomad and the sharecropper as the old feudal landlords are gradually replaced by a greedier breed of investors. Kemal's novelistic art encompasses more than social realism; it is informed by a deep knowledge and appreciation of Anatolian culture and the legends of the oral tradition. Other village novelists have chiefly focused on the discrimination against the peasant and the collusion of the rich with the local officials to rob the peasant of his livelihood. In his prize-winning *Yilanlarin öcü* (1959; the revenge of the snakes) Fakir Baykurt (b. 1929), for instance, recounts the mortal struggle between a poor family and the village headman who allows a piece of their property to be taken over by an influential person.

Under the category of the village novel was also subsumed fiction dealing with the circumstances of the lumpen proletariat. Orhan Kemal (1914–1970) was the most influential among the writers who dwelt on the exploitation of the worker. He not only was critical of the capitalist developments in Turkey but also examined the impact of industrialization on the laborer, whose plight included dislocation from the village to urban centers, where he remained alienated and destitute. Literature of protest dominated Turkish fiction until recently, but few of the social realists achieved psychological depth in their novels.

Meanwhile, the cosmopolitan and urban tradition continued. A major figure of the 1940s was Sait Faik Abasiyanik (1906–1954), who explored the torments of the human soul and the agony of love and betrayal in romantic, almost lyrical stories that fully reflected the pathos of urban life and vividly depicted the denizens of the back streets, taverns, and waterfront of Istanbul. Abdülhak Şinasi Hisar's (1883–1963) work recalled with nostalgia life at the turn of the century. Orhan Hançerlioğlu (b. 1916) and Oktay Akbal (b. 1923), on the other hand, dwelt on the crises of contemporary urban life. Haldun Taner's (b. 1915) stories depict with great sympathy and humor absurd situations and eccentric types encountered in the cosmopolitan milieu. Turkish humor found its spokesman in Aziz NESIN, the prolific satirist of international fame who continues to poke fun at ludicrous aspects of everyday life and to assault the absurdities of officialdom.

Realists began to explore new possibilities and techniques in the 1960s and 1970s. Kemal Tahir (1910–1973), who started out as a village novelist, gradually turned to the historical novel as a means to explain the background of present social conditions. Several of his works dwell on the formation of social classes and groups in the recent past, but in his controversial *Devlet ana* (1967; mother state) he attempted to present a panoramic view of the emergence of the Ottoman state in the 13th c. Attila ILHAN began his career as a poet who successfully combined social realism with an optimistic outlook; since the 1960s, however, he has written fiction in which the social life and political climate of early-20th-c. Turkey are convincingly and vividly portrayed.

Two women novelists have made significant contributions to the realist novel. Sevgi Soysal (1936–1976) treated the differences between social classes through representative types; Adalet AĞAOĞLU has depicted social and political currents as reflected in the experience of the individual. Another woman writer, Füruzan [Selçuk] (b. 1935), has achieved fully developed character analysis within the framework of the short story. The regionalism of the village novel has been continued in the work of Bekir Yildiz (b. 1933), who depicted the harsh and ruthless conditions of the rural southeast. However, he has also dealt with the cultural alienation, loneliness, and discrimination experienced by Turkish guest workers in West Germany, a topic that is increasingly coming into vogue among young Turkish writers, some of whom live in West Germany.

Realism has been the mainstream of modern Turkish fiction, although there have been some notable attempts at abstract explorations of the states of mind through the use of the STREAM-OF-CONSCIOUSNESS technique.

Drama

Modern Turkish drama owes much to municipal and state support of theatrical activity. Most of the repertory of European-style playhouses established in the 19th c. consisted of translations, while Turkish authors attempted to grasp the techniques of playwriting and imitated a broad variety of Western dramatic genres. In 1914 the Istanbul Municipal Theater was established. Since the 1930s there has been governmental encouragement and support of playwriting and production through the People's Houses and State Theaters. The 1960s saw an upsurge of theatrical activity, as numerous private companies were formed. Since then, however, economic conditions and competition from the television and film industries have increased the dependence of repertory theaters on public support.

Playwriting in Turkey has yet to catch up with poetry and fiction on the one hand, and with the number and quality of theater companies that remain dependent on translations on the other. The majority of plays written before the 1960s consisted of satires and melodramas, although a few distinguished authors experimented with psychological drama, avant-garde plays, and folkloric themes.

The scope of dramatic writing has broadened over the last two decades as playwrights have begun treating a variety of themes explored by novelists. Paralleling the village novel, plays by Necati CUMALI and Cahit Atay (b. 1925) constitute dramatic versions of protest literature. Social criticism has also been presented in

comedies and satires, notably in the works of Cevat Fehmi Başkut (1908–1971) and Aziz Nesin. Orhan Asena (b. 1922), Turan Oflazoğlu (b. 1932), and Güngör DİLMEN have successfully written plays based on Ottoman history, folklore, and mythology. Haldun Taner's *Keşanh Ali destanı* (1964; *The Ballad of Ali of Keshan*,1976), a musical in the vein of BRECHT's *Threepenny Opera*, was an outstanding achievement of the early 1960s. Contemporary playwrights continue their explorations in several directions while they supply the stage with plays ranging from slick musical comedies to bitter exposés of the human condition.

See also under Cypriot Literature and Yugoslav Literature. For non-Turkish writing in Turkey, see Armenian Literature and Kurdish Literature.

BIBLIOGRAPHY: Karpat, K., "Social Themes in Contemporary Turkish Literature," *MEJ*, 14 (1960): 29–44, 153–68; Karpat, K., "Contemporary Turkish Literature," *LitR*, 4 (1961): 287–302; And, M., *A History of Theatre and Popular Entertainment in Turkey* (1963–1964); Rathbun, C., *The Village in the Turkish Novel and Short Story* (1972); Halman, T. S., "Turkish Literature in the 1960s," *LitR*, 15 (1972): 387–402; Halman, T. S., ed., special Turkey issue, *RNL*, 4, 1 (1973); Stone, F., *The Rub of Cultures in Modern Turkey* (1973); Halman, T. S., ed., Introduction to *Modern Turkish Drama* (1976): 13–51; Robson, B., *The Drums Beat Nightly: The Development of the Turkish Drama as a Vehicle for Social and Political Comment in the Post-Revolutionary Period: 1924 to the Present* (1976); Iz, F., ed., Introduction to *Modern Turkish Short Stories* (1978): 9–25; Menemencioğlu, N., ed., Introduction to *The Penguin Book of Turkish Verse* (1978): 47–57; Halman, T. S., "Literature of the Turkish Republic," in Halman, T. S., *Contemporary Turkish Literature* (1982): 21–36

—AHMET Ö. EVIN

Turkish Literature since 1980

The 1980s were an eventful decade in Turkey: ideological and economic turmoil, repressive military regime, multiparty parliamentary system dominated by a single party, transition to free market economy, restoration of democratic freedoms. Literature experienced, within ten years, the worst repression and the widest freedom. While academic freedom remained curtailed to some extent in the 1990s, literature enjoyed a virtually unprecedented ability to deal with any themes and ideas, including those that had sometimes brought retribution to literary figures in the past. Consequently, as the 20th c. draws to a close, Turkish literature enjoys ideological and erotic openness and brave innovations in substance, structure, and style. Its diversity seems wider and bolder than ever.

Poetry

Many of the prominent modern poets, including Fazil Hüsnü DAĞLARCA, Melih Cevdet ANDAY, Necati CUMALI, Ilhan Berk, and others, continue to be prolific and to explore new creative dimensions. Dağlarca, often referred to as "Turkey's leading living poet," published in the 1980s hundreds of lyric and philosophical poems remarkable for their luminosity. Anday pursued his interest in Near Eastern mythology as well as modern mythopoesis, while Cumali achieved an ever stronger synthesis of social concerns and private sensibilities. Berk, a foremost experimenter since the 1950s, produced several volumes, each one of which represents a striking innovation of poetic technique.

Several poets, highly promising in the previous two decades, fulfilled their potential. Of these, perhaps the most productive was Özdemir İnce (b. 1936), who published several volumes of his new powerful poems and translations of Ritsos, Lautréamont, Char, and others and first-rate criticism, became a member of the Mallarmé Academy, and organized the First Istanbul International Poetry Forum (1991). İnce's poems, full of fresh evocations, metaphors, and compelling human drama, exhibit an admirable virtuosity. One of his major accomplishments is a four-volume anthology of modern world poetry, which he edited together with Ataol Behramoğlu (b. 1942), who also achieved premier status in the 1980s with exquisitely crafted poems of love, exile, and protest.

Ahmet Oktay (b. 1933) stands as one of contemporary Turkey's eminent intellectual poets and masters of literary theory. His poetry shares some of the features of the best work of Wallace Stevens and Rilke. Hilmi Yavuz (b. 1936) enjoys considerable esteem for his stimulating blend of traditional Turkish aesthetic values and many of the values of European poetry. Perhaps the most original of the living Turkish poets is Ece Ayhand, who is renowned for his imaginative distortions of syntax, for calculated obscurantism, and strange syncopations. Sabahattin Kudret Aksal (b. 1920–1993), by contrast, is a poet of lucidity even when he deals with elusive themes.

Between 1985 and 1996, several prominent poets died: Edip CANSEVER, Oktay Rifat (1914–1988), Turgut Uyar (1927–1985), Metin Eloglu (1927–1985), Tahsin Sarag (1930–1989), Cemal Süreyya (1931–1990), and Sabahattin Kudret Aksal, all of whom had introduced to Turkey new dimensions of poetic experience.

In the early 1990s, ideologies and social protest became less of a force among Turkish poets compared with their dominance from 1960 to 1980. Nonetheless, political commitment continues to motivate many socialists, including Gülten Akin (b. 1933), Turkey's leading woman poet.

Neosurrealism, which was in vogue as an antipode to the social realists in the pre-1980 period, seems to have lost much of its appeal. Essentially, Turkish poetry has entered an era when no specific school or movement prevails. Also, there is a growing group of poets, including many young ones, who are creating ultramodern poems inspired by some of the basic values and aesthetic norms of classical Ottoman verse. Neoclassicism, which attempts to keep alive the stanzaic forms and the prosody of that tradition, is still going strong.

Fiction

A restless quest for fresh techniques and textures has characterized Turkish novels and short stories since the early 1980s. As the so-called "village fiction" of the earlier decades steadily lost ground, writers became more responsive to the modern fiction of Europe, the U.S., and Latin America. Translation activity, mainly from English and French, has gained momentum—as well as greater impact thanks to strides in the art of translation.

Yashar KEMAL, still Turkey's strongest Nobel candidate, has continued to write the saga of his southwestern Anatolian region in further volumes of *İnce Memed* (slim Memed), the first volume of which was translated into English as *Memed, My Hawk* (1961), and *Demirciler çarşısı cinayeti* (1974; *The Lords of Akchasaz: Murder in the Ironsmiths Market*, 1979). Much of Kemal's fiction since the

late 1970s has dealt with fishing communities and urban life. His books are being translated into numerous languages at an impressive rate. Most recent English translations, all by Thilda Kemal, include *Al Gözüm Seyreyle Salih* as *Seagull* (1981), *Deniz Küstü* (1978) as *The Sea-Crossed Fisherman* (1985), *Kuşlar da gitti* (1978) as *The Birds Have Also Gone* (1987), and *Yılanı Öldürseler* (1976) as *To Crush the Serpent* (1991).

The legendary satirist Aziz NESIN died in 1995, leaving behind over ninety books of short stories, essays, poems, and novels. Satire continues to fire the imagination of the Turkish public: Sales of humorous books (many of them with illustrations and cartoons) enjoy more substantial sales than virtually all other genres—and a whole new generation of humorists and satirists has emerged in recent years.

A remarkable development in fiction is the ascendancy of a large group of woman writers. This group, which includes Adalet AĞAOĞLU, Tomris Uyar (b. 1941), Pınar Kür (b. 1943), Nazlı Eray (b. 1945), Leylâ Erbil (b. 1931), Sevim Burak (1931–1983), Füruzan, Gülten Dayıoğlu (b. 1935), Ayla Kutlu (b. 1938), and others, has brought vitality to novelistic techniques. Aysel Özakın (b. 1942) has produced stories drawn on the experiences of the Turkish guest workers in Germany; one of her books is available in English translation: *The Prizegiving* (1988, trans. by Celia Kerslake). A first novel, *Sevgili arsız ölüm* (1983; dear shameless death) by Latife Tekin (b. 1957), burst on the literary scene with a gripping narrative and a brave new language steeped in quaint provincial expressions and an unaccustomed urban lumpen lingo. Hailed by many critics as nothing short of a small masterpiece, the Tekin novel documents the trials and tribulations of a rural family struggling to survive in the big city.

The 1980s also witnessed the meteoric rise of Orhan Pamuk (b. 1952). His first novel, *Cevdet Bey ve oğulları* (1982; Cevdet Bey and his sons), a family saga reminiscent of Thomas MANN's *Buddenbrooks*, is a sprawling conventional narrative. *Sessiz ev* (1983; the silent house) is a powerful Faulknerian novella and winner of the 1984 Madarali Award. Pamuk's *Beyaz kale* of 1985 has been a major success not only in Turkey but also in the English-speaking world when it came out in 1991 as *The White Castle*, translated by Victoria Holbrook, winning extensive praise from American critics (the *New York Times*, John Updike in the *New Yorker*, and many others). It is perhaps the most successful postmodernist Turkish novel. Set in Istanbul in the 17th c., it depicts the confrontation and merger of East and West in the persons of a young Italian and a Turkish intellectual who cooperate and sometimes conspire to find solutions for the Ottoman state. Pamuk's huge novel of 1990, entitled *Kara Kitap* (black book), which went through a dozen printings in one year, has established him as one of Turkey's great novelists. It is a masterful intellectual exercise in postmodernist fiction with vivid and elusive characters and an obscurantist plot.

Mobil Corporation's prestigious Pegasus Prize, however, for the best novel published in Turkey between 1980 and 1990, went to Bilge Karasu (1930–1995) for his intriguing novel *Gece* (1985; night). Karasu, a master of the STREAM-OF-CONSCIOUSNESS technique and a conjurer of modern myths, shares with Ferit Edgü (b. 1916), Selim Ileri (b. 1949), Murathan Mungan (b. 1955), and others a subtle aesthetics of narration and character portrayal.

The Turkish novel is currently enjoying a period of quest for regeneration based on an awareness of the best of world literature and the private and social crises of Turks at home and abroad.

Drama

Theater is vibrant in Turkish cities—with hundreds of plays, native and foreign, produced by the state, city, and independent theaters. Regional theatrical activity has also gained momentum.

Turkish playwrights have feverishly written about historical, mythological, and contemporary subjects in a wide variety of dramatic forms. A. Turan Oflazoğlu and Orhan Asena are among the leading figures of historical drama. Oflazoğlu has concentrated on Ottoman sultans in plays that have a Shakespearean structure and tone. Güngör DILMEN is a foremost playwright who has dealt with ancient myths and many phases of Turkish and non-Turkish history.

A major figure to emerge in the 1980s is Mehmet Baydur (b. 1952), whose ingenious plots, whimsical characters, and rich and sometimes lyrical dialogue have made his plays popular in Turkey and, some, in translation, in France. *Güneyli bayan* (1984; southern lady) by the woman playwright Bilgesu Erenus (b. 1943) attracted considerable attention. It is a poignant play based on the life of Lillian HELLMAN. Murathan Mungam (b. 1955) is the author of some striking modern plays as well as the one-actor dramatization of the life and poetry of Orhan Veli Kanık, which has been presented with great success by the prominent actor Müşfik Kenter.

As the 20th c. draws to a close, Turkish literature shows both maturity and a restless energy to introduce new creative dimensions. It seems secure and confident about its authentic cultural identity, and eager to embrace influences from abroad and to generate new aesthetic values from within its own resources.

BIBLIOGRAPHY: Halman, T. S., "Life of Literature and Death of Ideologies in Turkey," *Translation: The Journal of Literary Translation*, 19 (Fall 1987): 3–7; Güneli Gün, "Comets on the Turkish Literary Horizon: Woman Writers," *Translation: The Journal of Literary Translation,* 19 (Fall 1987): 76–82; Reddy, N. M., *Twenty Stories by Turkish Women Writers* (1989); Halman, T. S., *Living Poets of Turkey* (1989); Fergar, F. K., *Modern Turkish Poetry* (1992); Halman, T. S., "Turkish Poetry," in A. Premington and T. V. F. Brogan, eds., *The New Princeton Encyclopedia of Poetry and Poetics* (1993): 1311–14

—TALAT SAIT HALMAN

TURKMEN LITERATURE

During the first two decades of the 20th c. oral poetry continued to dominate Turkmen literature, although written verse, by those educated mainly in Bukhara and Khiva, dates from at least the 18th c. A transitional figure, Muhammed Qlïch (1885–1922), combined traditional themes with laments over the hard life and social injustice. His long poem *Bichare* (before 1917; the pauper) describes the unhappiness of a young woman given in marriage for a large bride price. That plight of women in Central Asian society recurred often in literature of the early part of the century, as can be seen in Agakhan Durdï's (1904–1947) stories "Bürgüt penjesinde bir gözel" (1927; a beauty in the eagle's talons) and "Bagtlï gïz Bagdatda" (1928; lucky girl in Baghdad).

The new medium of prose was quickly adopted by the poets Berdï Kerbaba-oghli (Russian: Kerbabaev; 1894–1974) and Ata Govshut (1903–1953), the former mainly for short stories and novels, the latter for dramas like *Ganlï jengngel* (1929; bloody thicket). Kerbaba, in the long story "Garshïlïklï guda" (1928; double wedding) and other writings, also turned to the troubling topic of the status of women.

Many Turkmens, including Kerbaba, the poet and dramatist Garaja Burun (b. 1898), and Abdulhäkim Qulmohammed-oghli (c. 1900–c. 1931), came under heavy political attack during the Soviet state's organization of all writers just prior to 1932. Qulmohammed-oghli, earlier recognized for his poetry, such as *Ümit yalqïmlarï* (1926; flames of hope), soon perished in Stalin's purges, but numerous Turkmen writers did survive the terror of the 1930s. Kerbaba, who had been imprisoned, went on to win the Stalin Prize for literature in 1948 for the novel *Aygïtlï ädim* (1940–47; *The Decisive Step*, 1948), which deals with the convulsions in Turkmen society between 1917 and 1921.

In Turkmen literary history since 1920, the Kekilov family provides a revealing chapter. At least two of its members have played strikingly different roles in literature. Shalï Kekilov (1906–1943) earned praise as a proletarian poet from Communist Party ideologists for satirizing Turkmen nationalists whose poetry employed Aesopean or allegorical techniques that had marked earlier mystic poetry. Known more for his political activity than his writing, Shalï Kekilov's small number of works are mostly topical Marxist propaganda, like the poems "Gïzïlarbat remont zavodïnda" (1932; at the Gïzïlarbat repair barns) and "Dada Ivan" (1943; uncle Ivan), about a Russian commander. He wrote some plays in a similar vein, including *Garrï bashda yäsh pikir* (1935; a new thought in an old head). Aman Kekilov (1912–1974), Shalï's brother, educated in Moscow, became a literary historian and folklorist as well as poet. Some of his early poetry appeared in *Goshgular yïgïndïsï* (1932; collection of poems). His major work, *Söygi* (3 vols., 1945, 1957, 1960; love), a long narrative poem with a Turkmen girl as protagonist, has been translated into Russian.

Annasoltan Kekilov (dates n.a.), perhaps related to Shalï and Aman, who published several books, including *Zenanlar: Goshgular* (1971; the women: poems), attracted wide attention when she openly complained about conditions in Turkmenistan, first to the Communist Party Central Committee in Moscow and then to the Twenty-fourth Congress of the Communist Party of the Soviet Union in April 1971. Turkmen authorities are reported to have blocked the printing of her fourth book of verse. Forced out of her job and committed to a psychiatric hospital until she would agree to renounce her complaints, she instead petitioned for emigration, which was not granted.

The Kekilov brothers each wrote plays, although drama reached Turkmenistan as a modern genre no earlier than the 1920s. After historical, nationalistic plays like B. Abdullin's (dates n.a.) *Soltan Sanjar* (early 1920s; Sultan Sanjar) played on Turkmen stages, some time elapsed before full-fledged local dramatists emerged. Best known are Guseyn Mukhtarov (1914–1980) and Gara Seyitliev (1915–1972), who coauthored a melodrama, *Chopan oglï* (1953; shepherd's son). *Allan Aganïng mashgalasï* (1949; Allan Aga's family), by Mukhtarov, was lauded by Soviet critics. Seyitliev, in addition to several other plays, including *Jakhan* (1946; Jakhan), wrote many poems.

BIBLIOGRAPHY: Köprülüzade, F., "Turkoman Literature," *Encyclopedia of Islam* (1934), Vol. IV: 898–99; Nikitine, B., "La littérature des Musulmans en U.R.S.S.: Turkemistan," *Revue des études islamiques*, No. 8 (1934): 342–48; Benzing, J., "Die türkmenische Literatur," *Philologiae Turcicae Fundamenta*, 2 (1964): 721–41; Allworth, E., "The Focus of Literature," in Allworth,

E., ed., *Central Asia: A Century of Russian Rule* (1967): 397–433; Murat, A. B., "Turkmenistan and the Turkmens," *Handbook of Major Soviet Nationalities* (1975): 262–82

—EDWARD ALLWORTH

TURSUNZODA, Mirzo

(Russian: Tursunzade) Tajik poet and journalist, b. 2 May 1911, Qarotogh; d. 24 Sept. 1977, Dushanbe

Belonging to the first generation of Tajiks brought up under the Soviet regime, T. headed the Writers' Union of Tajikistan from 1946 to his death. From 1959 on, he was also one of the secretaries of the All-Soviet Writers' Union and in the last two decades of his life one of the main figures of the Soviet-led Afro-Asian Solidarity Movement.

T. made his debut as a poet in 1929. His first collection, *Bayroqi zafar* (1932; victory banner), consists of poems, short stories, and documentary sketches imbued with the fervor of "socialist building" but lacking in artistry. With A. Dehoti he wrote the libretto for the first Tajik opera, *Shörishi Vose'* (1939; the Vose rebellion).

T. achieved renown with the cycle of poems *Qissayi Hinduston* (1947–48; Indian story). Classical in form and beautifully written, the cycle shows India as a land of staggering natural splendor, great cultural traditions, and sharp social contrasts—ensnared by international imperialism. India remained one of T.'s favorite subjects. In the epic poem *Sadoyi Osiyo* (1956; the voice of Asia) India is portrayed as a member of the great anti-imperialist alliance of Asian nations, joining forces with China and, naturally, the U.S.S.R. Although faithfully in line with the Soviet policy of its time, the poem has a very strong pan-Asiatic flavor.

T. also wrote poems about Soviet life, especially Tajik life. On the occasion of Stalin's seventieth birthday, he published a long panegyric, *Mavji tabrikho* (1951; stream of greetings); a great success initially, it has sunk into oblivion in the post-Stalin era. His longest poem, *Hasani arobakash* (1954; Hasan the cart driver), the first Tajik novel in verse, tells the story of an ordinary Tajik worker's adaptation to the Soviet way of life in the 1920s and early 1930s. The epic poem *Charoghi abadi* (1957; eternal light) is a tribute to Sadriddin AYNI in which that writer becomes a symbol of the first sovietized Tajiks. In *Joni shirin* (1960; sweet darling) lyrical passages on the poet's lifelong love and esteem for his wife are followed by sections on his love for the communist ideal, for his land, and for the awakening peoples of Asia and Africa.

T. was the first significant Tajik poet to belong completely to the Soviet period, and from the late 1940s until his death he dominated Tajik poetry. Through Russian translations of his works he has become one of the best-known non-Russian poets of the U.S.S.R. He is also fairly well known in the Third World, although largely because of his role in the Afro-Asian Solidarity Movement.

FURTHER WORKS: *Hukm* (1934); *Oftobi mamlakat* (1936); *Khisrav va Shirin* (1936, with A. Dehoti); *Khazon va bahor* (1937); *Vodiyi Hisor* (1940); *Pisari Vatan* (1942); *Tohir va Zöhro* (1943); *Aröz az Moskva* (1945); *Arös* (1946); *Man az Sharqi ozod* (1950); *Sulh bar jang ghalaba khohad kard* (1950); *Dar kishvari tojik* (1952); *Dukhtari muqaddas* (1957); *Az Gang to Kreml* (1970); *Dastovez* (1976). FURTHER WORKS IN ENGLISH: *My Day and Age: Selected Poems* (1977)

BIBLIOGRAPHY: Pankina, V., "Champion of Peace and Poet," *Culture and Life*, No. 10 (1966): 41–42; Ma'sumi, N., "Poem on the Transformation of Life," in *Yádnáme-ye Jan Rypka* (1967): 209–17; Bečka, J., in J. Rypka, et al., *History of Iranian Literature* (1968): 577–79; Osmanova, Z., "M. T.," *Culture and Life*, No. 6 (1971): 46; Bečka, J., "The Tajik Soviet Doston and M. T.," *ArO*, 44 (1976): 213–39

—MICHAEL ZAND

TUTUOLA, Amos

Nigerian storyteller (writing in English), b. 20 June 1922, Abeokuta; d. 7 June 1997, Ibadan

T. had six years of formal education in mission schools and worked briefly as a coppersmith and messenger before finding lifetime employment as a stock clerk in Nigeria's national broadcasting company.

In all his books T. uses the same basic narrative pattern. A hero (or heroine) with supernatural powers or access to supernatural assistance sets out on a journey in quest of something important but suffers incredible hardships before successfully accomplishing his mission. He ventures into unearthly realms, performs arduous tasks, fights with fearsome monsters, endures cruel tortures, and narrowly escapes death. Sometimes he is accompanied by a relative or by loyal companions; sometimes he wanders alone. But he always survives his ordeals, attains his objective, and usually emerges from his nightmarish experiences a wiser, wealthier man. The cycle of his adventures—involving a departure, an initiation, and a return—resembles that found in myths and folktales the world over.

T.'s first long narrative, *The Wild Hunter in the Bush of the Ghosts* (written c. 1948, pub. 1982), was originally submitted to a London publisher of photography books, from whose files it recently was recovered and put into print for the first time. Basically a Yoruba hunter's tale, it tells of marvelous adventures in bizarre bush towns and includes excursions to Heaven and Hell, the latter resembling a vast bureaucracy with an Engineering Department, Correspondence Section, and Employment Exchange Office. The story shows signs of having been influenced by the Yoruba narratives of D. O. Fagunwa (1903–1963) as well as by John Bunyan's *The Pilgrim's Progress*, but it is a bit cruder in conception and execution than T.'s later works.

T.'s first published book, *The Palm-Wine Drinkard and His Dead Palm-Wine Tapster in the Dead's Town* (1952), describing a hero's descent into an African underworld in search of a dead companion whom he wants to persuade to return to the land of the living, had a mixed critical reception. Written in a curiously expressive idiom that Dylan THOMAS termed "young English," this unusual story delighted European and American critics who tended to look upon its author as an extraordinarily imaginative native genius. However, it offended many educated Nigerian readers who recognized T.'s borrowings from oral tradition and from Fagunwa, disapproved of his bad grammar, and felt he was being lionized abroad by condescending racists. In much of the criticism written on T. since, there has been controversy over the merits and faults of this book, but it is still regarded as his most significant work and has been translated into many languages.

T.'s later books confirmed his reputation as an interesting but limited author who specialized in transmuting oral narratives into episodic adventure fiction about the wanderings of a resourceful human being in extraterrestrial domains. In *My Life in the Bush of Ghosts* (1954) the narrator-hero spends twenty-four years in an interesting African spirit world replete with towns, law courts, royal palaces, barber shops, and even a Methodist church, until a "Television-handed ghostess" helps him to escape to the human world he came from. *Simbi and the Satyr of the Dark Jungle* (1955) is the same kind of story, the major difference being that the chief character is a young lady who sets out on a quest for worldly experience because she wants to know the difficulties of poverty and punishment. This book was the first by T. to be organized into chapters and to be written in the third person; it was also his first to be populated with a number of non-African creatures—satyr, nymph, phoenix, imp, and so forth—a clear indication that he was supplementing his stock of Yoruba oral lore with readings in world mythology.

T.'s mode of storytelling gradually became more literary as he continued writing. In *Feather Woman of the Jungle* (1962), his most stylized work, he created an Arabian Nights structure by having a seventy-six-year-old chief entertain villagers every night for ten nights with accounts of his past adventures. In *The Brave African Huntress* (1958) and *Ajaiyi and His Inherited Poverty* (1967), he adopted the practice of citing one or more proverbs at the head of a chapter and then using the action in that chapter to illustrate the proverbs. Both of these narrative techniques may have entered written literature from oral tradition, but T. appears to have picked them up from his reading. In any case, they suited his material perfectly, providing him with ready-made vehicles for weaving together a group of disparate tales. His adoption of such conventions made him no less an oral raconteur in print. *The Witch-Herbalist of the Remote Town* (1981) and *Pauper, Brawler and Slanderer* (1987) manifest the same blend of African and Western stylistic and structural elements. In *Yoruba Folktales* (1986) T. tried telling traditional tales in a straightforward manner, without combining them into a single adventure-packed narrative.

T.'s reputation is now secure both at home and abroad, for he has come to be accepted as a distinctive phenomenon in world literature, a writer who bridges two narrative traditions and two cultures by translating oral art into literary art.

BIBLIOGRAPHY: Moore, G., *Seven African Writers* (1962): 39–57; Obiechina, E. N., "A. T. and the Oral Tradition," *PA*, No. 65 (1968): 85–106; Collins, H. R., *A. T.* (1969); Lindfors, B., "A. T.: Debts and Assets," *CEAfr*, No. 38 (1970): 306–34; Anozie, S. O., "A. T.: Littérature et folklore; ou, Le problème de la synthèse," *CEAfr*, No. 38 (1970): 335–51; Armstrong, R. P., "The Narrative and Intensive Continuity: *The Palm-Wine Drinkard*," *RAL*, 1 (1970): 9–34; Böttcher, K.-H., *Tradition und Modernität bei A. T. und Chinua Achebe: Grundzüge der westafrikanischen Erzählliteratur englischer Sprache* (1974); Lindfors, B., ed., *Critical Perspectives on A. T.* (1975); Dussutour-Hammer, M., *A. T.: Tradition orale et écriture de conte* (1976); Achebe, C., "Work and Play in T.'s *The Palm-Wine Drinkard*," *Okike*, 14 (1978): 25–33; Coates, J., "The Inward Journey of the Palm-Wine Drinkard," *ALT*, 11 (1980): 122–29; Balvaude, C. E., *A. T. et l'univers du conte africain* (1989); Quayson, A., *Strategic Transformations in Nigerian Writing* (1997)

—BERNTH LINDFORS

TUURI, Antti

Finnish novelist and short-story writer, b. 1 Oct. 1944, Kauhava

T. is one of Finland's most highly regarded postwar writers. Born in the western Finland province of Ostrobothnia and trained as an engineer, he brings these two elements into his literary output. He has worked in a number of jobs requiring a high level of technical skill, and even his rather flat and matter-of-fact style serves to juxtapose the impersonal industrial milieu he often chooses as the background for his stories and his all too human characters who try to survive in this world.

After T.'s early novels and short-story collections in the 1970s, his *Joki virtaa läpi kaupungin* (1977; a river flows through the town) presents a richer narrative technique. The lives of three people accidentally touch—a foreman who breaks loose from the shackles of technocracy, a fragile artist, and an old university professor who wishes to die naturally rather than have his life prolonged by the life-support systems of the modern hospital. In his short-story collection *Maailman kivisin paikka* (1980; the stoniest place in the world) T. uses the classical short-story technique of the narrator and the frame.

T. is convinced that people are shaped by their heredity, economic factors, and even the landscape they live in. Most of his characters come from Ostrobothnia, the flat "breadbasket" province of Finland. His novel *Pohjanmaa* (1982; Ostrobothnia) was awarded the Nordic Prize for literature in 1985. It describes the events of one summer day; a farm family has gathered for the reading of the will of a grandfather who emigrated to the U.S. in the 1920s. The tone is matter-of-fact and often ironic, the narrator viewing the activities of his relatives as a black comedy. The book has been translated into several languages (not including English) and was made into a film by the same title in Finland in 1988.

The Ostrobothnian province of Finland has probably contributed most to the Finnish emigration to the U.S. and Canada. T. has continued to explore the lives of his neighbors in several books that take them to the "new world" of which they had an idealized picture. *Ameriikan raitti* (1986; the American road), set in the present, describes the life of more recent Finnish emigrants in Florida, many of whom have fled there to avoid taxation in Finland. When the hero decides to visit the town where his grandfather had emigrated in the 1920s, he finds an entire parallel family they knew nothing about in Finland. The style is laconic and made more interesting still by the use of unusual verb forms, such as present and past perfect indicative. A Finnish movie was made of the book in 1990. The harsh reality of life in the Canadian mines where Finns were brought as strikebreakers in the 1930s is described in *Uusi Jerusalem* (1988; the new Jerusalem) and *Maam avaruus* (1989; the wide earth), where the Utopian community praised to the hero as harboring "no dogs, no witches, no whores, no murderers, and no idol worshipers" turns out to be the very opposite. Another topic that has occupied T. is World War II as it was fought in Finland. Again, Ostrobothnians play the main parts. When T. was doing his research, he discovered that almost all of the many books about the war were written by people above the rank of colonel, to whom the war seemed like a game of chess. The regimental diaries kept by sergeant majors or clerks provided a much more personal view of the war. In *Talvisota* (1984; the winter war), the soldier is an unassuming hero who carries out his killing as a job that must be done. Because of the narrative style chosen, the book has few named characters. When the Finnish movie of this book was made in 1989, T. collaborated in the writing of the script. In 1990 T. published *Rukajärven tiellä* (on the road to Rukajärvi) and its sequel, *Rukajärven linja* (1991; the Rukaärvi line), which describe the Continuation War (1941–1944).

T. is undoubtedly one of the major contemporary Finnish writers. Besides novels and short stories, he has published plays and written articles and documentary texts. Between 1971 and 1987 he was awarded thirteen literary prizes, and his novels and short stories have been translated into many languages, although the English-reading public still has to depend on a few short stories published in *Books in Finland* and some anthologies. The reason may be found in the specifically Finnish associative contexts of T.'s characters that may not be immediately clear to non-Finnish readers, who nevertheless would enjoy the laconic wry humor that these heroes exhibit in the absurd situations where life—and T.— places them.

FURTHER WORKS: *Asioiden suhteet* (1971); *Lauantaina illalla* (1971); *Seitsemän kertomusta* (1972); *Marraskltun loppu* (1973); *Vuosi elämästä* (1975); *Perhokalastuksen alkeet* (1978); *Asiantuntija* (1979); *Kertomus järvestä* (1981); *"Juhani Aho kalastuskirjailijana," Suomalaisia kirjailijoita* (1982); *Samuttajat* (1983); *Novellit* (1983); *Viisitoista metriä vasempaan* (1985); *Maakunnan mies* (1986); *Voiman miehet* (1986); *Vääpeli Matala lentää* (1987); *Maan avaruus* (1989)

BIBLIOGRAPHY: Salokannel, J., "Unusual Men," *WLT*, 54, 1 (Winter 1980): 24–27; Tarkka, P., "A. T.: The Engineer's Story," *BF*, 2 (1981): 46–48

—MARGARETA MARTIN

TUVAN LITERATURE

The Tuvans are a Turkic people living in eastern Siberia, to the west of the Mongolian People's Republic. The approximately 150,000 speakers of Tuvan employ a blend of Turkic structure and Mongolian vocabulary and thus are linguistically distant from the mainstream of the Central Asian Turkic peoples of the steppes. Until 1911 Tannu Tuva was part of Outer Mongolia; nominally independent from 1911 to 1914, it then came under Russian protection until the 1917 revolution; for a short time it was under Chinese rule, then became nominally independent again in 1921 as the Tuvan People's Republic, although under the influence of the Soviet Union, which annexed it in 1944. It became the Tuvan Autonomous Soviet Socialist Republic in 1961.

The Tuvans have a well-developed oral literature, consisting of tales, epics, lays, proverbs, riddles, and hymns—typical of the Mongolian and Turkic peoples surrounding them. In the centuries before literacy, the small numbers of educated people (from the Lama-Buddhist clergy and the nobility) among this pastoral and nomadic people learned to read and write in Mongolian.

Beginning in the mid-19th c. a number of ethnologists recorded a great deal of Tuvan folklore. After the founding of the People's Republic in 1921, organized scholarly efforts were made to collect and publish the folklore. From the 1920s on, the adoption of nationality policies favorable to preliterate minorities within the Soviet orbit meant that even small linguistic groups like the Tuvans were entitled to their own language, script, and literature, so long as

it was "national in form, socialist in content." In 1930 a Latin alphabet was introduced, and reading materials for schools and the public were printed. To make the transition to education under Russian administrative guidance, a modified Cyrillic alphabet was adopted in 1940. After the 1944 annexation a research institute for language, literature, and history was established, which among other activities sent people out to record the repertoires of bards and storytellers. Today a wide variety of writing is published in the tiny Tuvan A.S.S.R.

A modern socialist literature—including poems, short stories, novels, plays, and sketches—began in the late 1930s and has grown to maturity under the League of Tuvan Writers, which publishes the literary journal *Ulug-Khem*. The most prominent Tuvan writer has been Salchak Toka (1901–1973), son of a poor herdsman who rose to be a Party secretary and minister of education. His trilogy about nomadic life and the changes brought about by the communist system, *Arattyng sözü* (1950, 1956, 1964; a herdsman's story; Part I tr. as *A Shepherd's Tale*, n.d.), received the Stalin Prize for literature in 1951, was translated into Russian, and enjoyed popularity throughout the Soviet Union.

Other important writers are Stepan Sarygool (b. 1908), author of poems and epics; Oleg Sagan-ool (1913–1971), primarily a novelist; Yury Künzegesh (b. 1927), a poet; and Sergey Bakizovich Pürbü (b. 1913), who writes tales, plays, and verse stressing modern Tuvan life.

BIBLIOGRAPHY: Krueger, J. R., *Tuvan Manual* (1977); Taube, E., *Tuwinische Volksmärchen* (1978)

—JOHN R. KRUEGER

TUWHARE, Hone

New Zealand poet, short-story writer, and dramatist, b. 21 Oct. 1922, Kaikohe, Northland

T.'s childhood and adolescence spanned the worst of the Great Depression. His mother died when he was five and he and his father led an impoverished existence, moving from one place to another in the region of Auckland City, seeking work and shelter. His working-class identification and passion for social justice dates from these years and had an inevitable outcome in his move to communism in the early 1940s. Of equal importance is his dual cultural heritage: he learned Maori language, lore, and custom orally, through the songs, chants, yarns, and oratory of his people on the marae, in the streets, and in the home. At the same time, and equally, he acquired not only the oral but also the written and literary traditions of the English language. He was a voracious reader, first of the Bible and later of the contents of lending bookstores and libraries. His education was sporadic and did not extend past primary level. He was indentured as a boilermaker through the war years and it was that trade which sustained him in his early working life. Post-war, he served in Japan and saw firsthand the devastation of Hiroshima. He began to write and publish seriously in the late 1950s. As a writer, T. has traveled to Hawaii, China, Papua New Guinea, Australia, and Germany.

T.'s first collection of poems, *No Ordinary Sun* (1964), was a landmark publication, marking both the early stirrings of the renaissance in Maori writing and consciousness and also T.'s own determination of his future as poet and writer. Fellow-poet R.A.K.

Mason introduced him: "Here—and I think this is for the first time—is a member of the Maori race qualifying as a poet in English and in the idiom of his own generation, but still drawing his main strength from his own people." *No Ordinary Sun* had unprecedented success: the 700-copy print-run sold in ten days and ultimately ran to twelve printings over more than thirty years. It established T.'s themes: its *wairua* (spirit) resides in *aroha* (love) for the land and its people and is voiced in a range of poems from the very personal to the political, the latter best exemplified by the title poem "No Ordinary Sun," perhaps New Zealand's best-known antinuclear statement and a reflection of his experience in Japan. T.'s personal poems have echoes in traditional Maori forms such as *waiata whaiapo* (sweetheart poems, about physical and erotic love) or *waiata tangi* (laments or elegies, tributes to those who have died). His voice in this first volume is romantic, often rhetorical and lyrical.

Subsequent collections consolidated his position as a popular poet and continued to express both the personal and the political. T. was a member of the historic 1975 Maori land march, for instance, and marked the event in a number of poems in *Making a Fist of It* (1978). The small vernacular component in his early writing strengthened to become a major element; he wrote a number of short stories, and also moved in the direction of prose-poems. T.'s play, *On Ilkla Moor B'aht 'At* (1991), subtitled *In the Wilderness without a Hat*, examines issues of identity for Maori in a non-Maori world: it was produced to widespread acclaim in the late 1980s. Of particular importance in all T.'s writing is his link to the oral traditions of both of his cultures, Maori and non-Maori. He writes to the sound of the speaking and dramatized voice and early realized his own performance prowess; for many years he has augmented his income by readings of his work in schools, tertiary institutions, and in public.

The title of T.'s *Shape-shifter* (1997) alludes to Celtic myth but also neatly includes the mythic Maori shape-shifter, Maui, with whom T. himself shares much. Like Maui, T. is chameleonlike, drawing from wherever and whomever he is with; he is a prankster and comic on occasion, a lover, an artist, a man above all, who has lived vividly in his time and with his people and expressed that in his poetry. T.'s contribution to literature has been recognized and supported by a number of grants and awards, most notably Robert Burns Fellowships from the University of Otago (1969; 1974), a Hocken Fellowship (1983), a DAAD Fellowship (1985), a Writing Fellowship from the University of Auckland (1991), the Te Waka Toi Award (1991), a Leading Writers Grant (1992), and an honorary D. Litt. from the University of Otago (1998).

FURTHER WORKS: *Come Rain Hail* (1970); *Sap-Wood & Milk* (1972); *Something Nothing* (1974); *Selected Poems* (1980); *Year of the Dog: Poems New and Selected* (1982); *Mihi: Collected Poems* (1987); *Eel* (1988); *Short Back & Sideways: Poems and Prose* (1992); *Deep River Talk: Collected Poems* (1993)

BIBLIOGRAPHY: Fairbrother, P., "H. T.," *Te Ao Hou*, 48 (Sept. 1964): 4-5; Coad, J., "H. T.," *Affairs Magazine* (Aug. 1970): 322-25; Eruera, T., "Being Purely and Solely Alone," *New Argot*, 3 (1975): 2; Oppenheim, R., "Internal Exile: Continuity and Community in Maori Poetry," *JPS*, 92 (1983): 245-57; Manhire, B., "Ready to Move," *Landfall*, 42 (1988): 262-68; O'Brien, G., "H. T.," *Moments of Invention* (1988): 53-59; Manhire, B., "Dirty Silence: Impure Sounds in New Zealand Poetry," in McGregor, G., and M. Williams, eds., *Dirty Silence: Aspects of Language and Literature in New Zealand* (1991): 143-59; Stewart, F., Introduction to *Deep River Talk* (1994): 3-9; Hunt, J., *H. T.* (1998)

—JANET HUNT

TUWIM, Julian

Polish poet, b. 13 Sept. 1894, Łódź; d. 27 Dec. 1953, Zakopane

T. grew up in the pleasant atmosphere of a progressive middle-class family; his father was employed in a bank. T. received his secondary education in a Russian high school in Łódź, and his familiarity with Russian literature, later to develop into a lifelong love and admiration, seems to date from that time. In 1916 he began to study law at the University of Warsaw but after a couple of years found this not to be his real calling, and he embarked on a literary career. He was a cofounder and one of the most distinguished and popular members of Skamander, a group of young poets who gave a new direction to literature in interwar Poland.

T., in his own words, was "drunk with God's world." His poetry is characterized by a powerful emotional vitality, a zest for life, and a desire to participate in all its aspects with his five senses as well as with his eager mind. T.'s lyrics are tender, sincere, and free of sentimentality, and much of his verse is erotic; his satire, directed at obscurantism and social injustice, is aggressive, biting, and, on occasion, brutal. The appearance in 1918 in an avant-garde magazine of his poem "Wiosna" (spring) shocked readers of more refined taste, because of its naturalistic and brutal imagery; his long poem *Bal w operze* (1936; a ball at the opera), a savage satire on the rich and privileged that contrasts them with those living in abject poverty, was confiscated by outraged authorities and, while widely circulated in manuscript, appeared in full only in 1949.

T. delighted in things grotesque, bizarre, and unusual; he engaged in studies of the Polish lore of superstitions, witches, and devils. A "hunter of words," he had a craftsman's delight in words as both material and tools of his art. T.'s mastery of the Polish language was enriched through his interest in and use of folk dialects, the language of the old masters of Polish literature, and that of the city streets. He loved using words in new combinations, creating new words whose meaning (if any) was to be conveyed only through their sound. This last technique, attributed by some critics to the influence of Russian FUTURISM, was rather in the nature of an exercise in verbal virtuosity: otherwise, T., like other Skamandrites, preferred more traditional forms of verse, which, however, did not detract from their originality. He also excelled in translating poetry from foreign languages, not only rendering but actually adapting them into Polish.

In his youth T. enjoyed playing with words and rhymes, whether writing parodies and songs for Warsaw cabarets or charming verse for children, acting as a prankster or an "alchemist." At the same time he gave expression to his somber moods and his indignation in starkly realistic pictures of human suffering. His urbanism was of the down-to-earth kind, concerned with city slums rather than with palaces, dark alleys rather than elegant boulevards. He was the bard of human failures, of dull existence in small provincial towns; he wrote of the stolid, greedy bourgeoisie—"horrible inhabitants of horrible homes"—and of the life of the hungry poor in their miserable hovels.

T.'s volumes of verse between *Czyhanie na Boga* (1918; lying in wait for God) and *Słowa we krwi* (1926; words in blood) represent the lighter, happier period of his creative work. Those from *Rzecz czarnoleska* (1929; Charnolas speech) to *Treść gorejąca* (1936; burning essence) reflect the mature poet's disillusioned attitude toward life and an almost apocalyptic sense of the approaching world catastrophe. T. left Poland in 1939; he spent the war years in Brazil and New York, where he wrote his long poem *Kwiaty polskie* (1949; flowers of Poland), an epic reminiscent in form of Byron's *Don Juan*, Juliusz Słowacki's (1809–1849) *Beniowski*, and Pushkin's *Eugene Onegin*. The poem's plot is less important than its lyric digressions—nostalgic memories of a vanished youth, everyday life in Poland, and occasional political criticisms. Although showered with honors after his return to Poland in 1949, T. in his last years did not write any important poetry except for some excellent further translations from Pushkin, Vladimir MAYAKOVSKY, and the Russian SYMBOLISTS. T.'s original talent and his innovative virtuosity of form assure him a distinguished niche in the poets' gallery of interwar Poland.

FURTHER WORKS: *Sokrates tańczący* (1920); *Siódma jesień* (1922); *Wierszy tom czwarty* (1923); *Czary i czarty polskie* (1924); *Biblia cygańska* (1933); *Jarmark rvmów* (1934); *Cztery wieki fraszki polskiej* (1936); *Lokomotywa; Rzepka; Ptasie radio* (1938; *Locomotive; The Turnip; The Bird's Broadcast*, 1940); *Dzieła* (5 vols., 1955–64); *Cicer cum caule; czyli, Groch z kapustą* (3 vols., 1958–63)

BIBLIOGRAPHY: Szyjkowski, M., on *Cztery wieki fraszki polskiej, Slavische Rundschau*, 9, 6 (1937): 100–112; Dembowski, P., "J. T.," *CSP*, 1 (1956): 59–65; Miłosz, C., *The History of Polish Literature* (1969): 387–89; Krzyzanowski, J., *A History of Polish Literature* (1978): 86–88, 568–70

—XENIA GASIOROWSKA

TVARDOVSKY, Alexandr Trifonovich

Russian poet, essayist, and editor, b. 21 June 1910, Zagore; d. 18 Dec. 1971, Moscow

T.'s childhood in rural Smolensk province instilled in him a lifelong affection and reverence for village life and people. At the same time, he grew up championing the revolutionary regime. As reward for teenage newspaper work and poetry glorifying agricultural collectivization, T. was sent to the Smolensk Pedagogical Institute in 1934, and later to the Moscow Institute of Philosophy, Literature, and History, from which he graduated in 1939, after joining the Communist Party. His status as a special war correspondent from 1941 to 1945 enabled him to compose his main poetic work during the war years. While T. remained loyal to the state and to the cause of communism, he expressed misgivings about Stalinist excesses after the war and worked toward combining communism with open discussion and criticism. He used his subsequent prominent political positions to publicize the need for less propagandistic writing, thus becoming known as "Russia's civic conscience" at home and as a liberal communist abroad.

T.'s first widely successful work was the long poem *Strana Muravia* (1936; the land of Muravia), a parable about the changing peasant mentality during collectivization. While the content reflects Stalinist ideology, the style, rhythm, and structure echo folk epics and legends. T.'s reputation as a poet rests primarily on his war epic *Vasily Tyorkin* (1945; *Vasily Tyorkin*, 1975), a cycle loosely connected by the frontline experiences of an unpretentious peasant soldier who symbolizes the beleaguered but undaunted spirit of the Russian people. T. continued his chronicling of the Russian peasant with *Dom u dorogi* (1946; the house by the road), a lyrical tribute to the suffering of rural women, especially mothers, under enemy occupation.

Critical opinion about the quality of T.'s poetry remains divided: acclaim in the Soviet Union, echoed by C. P. SNOW, who compared T. to Alexander Pope in verbal inventiveness; moderate praise by most Western scholars, who see little that is new or original in his verse and consider his optimistic tone amid the horrors of war and Stalinism too attuned to SOCIALIST REALISM.

T.'s second and, in Western estimation, much more significant literary activity is his editorship of the journal *Novy mir*, which had published the philosophical and political views of prominent independent-minded literary figures after its founding in 1925. During the strict censorship of the Stalin period the journal largely reflected the ideology of the regime. With T.'s appointment in 1950, however, it regained its semiautonomy. The reimposition of severe discipline after the relaxed war years produced a subtle political reorientation in T., which found expression in *Novy mir*. Within months after Stalin's death in 1953 T. published a call to restore credibility to literature. This essay is generally accepted as marking the start of the "thaw" period. T.'s liberalizing efforts, coupled with a much more skeptical and sarcastic tone in his narrative poem *Tyorkin na tom svete* (written early 1950s, unofficially circulated 1953–54, published in a politically less tendentious version 1963; Tyorkin in the other world) resulted in his dismissal in 1954, officially for alcoholism. T. continued his poetic activity with *Za dalyu dal* (1953–58; distance beyond distance), a diary in verse published serially in which he describes his reactions to the sweeping changes Russia has undergone during Soviet rule.

Reinstated as chief editor of *Novy mir* in 1958, following Khrushchev's de-Stalinization policy, T. presided over the reform and liberalization of Soviet literature by publishing hitherto suppressed talented writers and critical essays supporting the new writing, while downgrading previous distortions of reality. His ability to combine political influence with progressive thought for almost two decades raised literature to a level still evident among writers of the 1980s. The high point of T.'s editorial activity is associated with Alexandr SOLZHENITSYN. T. marshaled all his influence and guile to get into print a series of controversial Solzhenitsyn works. Several factors contributed to T.'s forced resignation in 1970 and to *Novy mir*'s reorganization into a politically neutral publication: Khrushchev's ouster, government-sponsored conservative reaction to T.'s reforms, and Solzhenitsyn's public challenges to the entire Soviet system, which T. did not agree with.

T. the editor maintained a balance between what was politically possible and the demands of increasingly vocal dissident writers; he courageously and honestly refuted attacks on the new writing and sacrificed his political standing on its behalf; he grew in outlook from a popular, noncontroversial poet and government supporter to an active champion of diverse opinion.

FURTHER WORKS: *Put k sotsializmu* (1931); *Dnevnik predsedatelya kolkhoza* (1932); *Sbornik stikhov 1930–35* (1935); *Doroga* (1938);

Selskaya khronika (1939); *Zagore* (1941); *Frontovye stikhi* (1941); *Stikhi o voyne* (1942); *Iz liriki 1936–45* (1946); *Izbrannoe* (1946); *Rodina i chuzhbina* (1947); *Izbranno stikhotvorenia i poemy* (1947); *Stikhotvorenia* (2 vols., 1951); *Izbrannoe* (1957); *Stikhotvorenia i poemy* (1957); *Izbrannoe stikhotvorenia* (1958); *Stikhi o Sibiri* (1958); *Sobranie sochineny* (1959); *Stikhi iz zapisnoy knizhki* (1959); *Pechniki* (1959); *Stati i zametki o literature* (1961); *Kniga liriki* (1962); *Izbrannaya lirika* (1964); *Kak byl napisan Vasily Tyorkin* (1965); *Lenin i pechniki: Po predaniyu* (1966); *Sobranie sochineny* (5 vols., 1966–71); *Iz liriki etikh let 1959–67* (1967); *Poezia Mikhaila Isakovskogo* (1969). **FURTHER WORKS IN ENGLISH:** *Tyorkin and the Stove Makers* (1974)

BIBLIOGRAPHY: Roshchin, P., *A. T.* (1966); Glenny, M., *Novy Mir 1925–1967* (1972); Hotz, R., *Allein der Wahrheit verpflichtet: A. T.* (1972); Medvedev, Z., *Ten Years after Ivan Denisovich* (1973); Frankel, E., "The Return of T. to *Novy Mir*, July 1958," *RusR* 35 (1976): 155–72; Solzhenitsyn, A., *The Oak and the Calf* (1980); Lakshin, V., *Solzhenitsyn, T. and "Novy Mir"* (1980)

—MARGOT K. FRANK

TY-CASPER, Linda

Philippine novelist and short-story writer (writing in English), b. 17 Sept. 1931, Manila

As the daughter of a textbook writer for public schools and the operations manager of the Philippine National Railways, T.-C. was expected to prepare for a career of service in the postwar Philippines. She became valedictorian of the 1955 class at the University of the Philippines College of Law, and began to write short fiction while waiting for results of the bar examination. In 1956 she proceeded, on scholarship, to Harvard Law School where she received her LL.M. in 1957. At Widener Library meanwhile she discovered prejudicial statements about her country in supposedly authoritative sources. Consequently she decided neither to practice law nor to teach it, but to become an advocate for her people through researching and writing historical fiction. T.-C. became the first Filipina to receive a grant from the Radcliffe Institute (1974–1975); in 1984 she held a Djerassi Foundation in-residence grant in California; and in 1988 she received a Massachusetts Artists Foundation Award. With each opportunity she persisted in dramatizing the difficulty of Filipinos, during centuries of Spanish and American colonialism, to find satisfactory terms for self-definition and -determination.

The Peninsulars (1964) set a precedent for reconstructing confrontations in Manila, during the 19th c., between Spanish liberals and conservatives, which so weakened the colonial administration that incursions by the Dutch and later by the British were possible. In 1979, T.-C. published *The Three-Cornered Sun*, a novel of the ill-fated revolution of 1896–1898. Not only were the Spaniards far better equipped militarily than the Filipino insurgents, but the latter were divided into factions. The novel shows how aristocratic dilettantes, at first in combat as if at play, learned in their defeat the rightness of the national cause and the need for solidarity. The same pattern of naïveté gradually and painfully enlightened appears in *Ten Thousand Seeds* (1987). This time,

however, it is the Americans who, coming as liberators, found themselves substitute rulers instead, and understood such realities better only at the outbreak of the Philippine-American War in 1899.

T.-C.'s later novels have concentrated on oppression of Filipinos by their own countrymen who have put greed, nepotism, and factionalism before the national interest, especially during the martial-law years of President Ferdinand Marcos (1972–1981). *Dread Empire* (1980) reveals how a provincial strongman managed to imitate Marcos's tactics locally; *Hazards of Distance* (1981) pictures how ordinary citizens became caught between government violence and the Communist New People's Army; and *Fortress in the Plaza* (1985) dramatizes the impact on decent families of the political opposition's actual massacre, in a Manila public square, in 1972. As censorship tightened, T.-C. found her audience in London with *Awaiting Trespass* (1985), a novel of the martyrdom of a presumed wastrel secretly helping imprisoned detainees; and *Wings of Stone* (1986), a tale of an expatriate's return from America during the election of 1984, which, along with the 1983 assassination of a more illustrious returnee, Ninoy Aquino, ignited the final stages of revolt against Marcos. *A Small Party in a Garden* (1988) personalizes the régime's brutality through the gang rape of a politically neutral woman, one of Imelda Marcos's lesser staff, by men in uniform.

Despite marriage to an American, T.-C. has retained her Philippine citizenship. Yet she has tried not to be chauvinistic in her judgments, but to distinguish persons of good will among the Spaniards and Americans, as well as—when necessary—to indict Filipinos who have betrayed the ideals of self-sacrifice and service.

FURTHER WORKS: *The Transparent Sun, and Other Stories* (1963); *The Secret Runner, and Other Stories* (1974); *Common Continent, 19 Stories* (1991)

BIBLIOGRAPHY: Casper, L., *New Writing from the Philippines* (1966): 134–37; Galdon, J., ed., *Philippine Fiction* (1972): 193–202; Casper, L., *Firewalkers* (1987): 158–61; Valeros, F. B., and E. Valeros-Gruenberg, eds., *Filipino Writers in English* (1987): 52

—LEONARD CASPER

TYLER, Anne

American novelist, b. 25 Oct. 1941, Minneapolis, Minn.

T. was raised and educated in North Carolina and has lived in Baltimore for much of her adult life. She considers herself a Southern writer and has stated that the influence of Eudora WELTY was crucial in her decision to write fiction. The South is often the setting for her fiction and, in her hands, small-town Maryland is definitively part of that region. T. studied writing with Reynolds Price (b. 1933) at Duke University, but her major in Russian preserved her from what she calls the hardest time for many writers, "that dead spot after college . . . and before their first published work." After graduation from Duke, T. did graduate work in Russian studies at Columbia and worked, among other miscellaneous jobs, as a bibliographer, ordering books from the Soviet Union, before publishing her first novel, *If Morning Ever Comes* (1964). The professional "dead spot" was not only filled

Anne Tyler

with various lively activities, but was also notably brief. From that first book through *Saint Maybe* (1991), T. has published a total of twelve novels to increasing critical praise and public attention.

Despite her acknowledged debt to Welty, T. is not a Southern writer in the gothic sense of the term, nor does she write regional chronicles of loss. Rather, the South is the essential, realistically conceived background for snapshots of persons and places, images designed and executed with meticulous craft. All the commentators on her earlier work remarked on their sense of T.'s careful attention to the means of expression. Some of them saw it as excessive caution, the failure or deliberate refusal to take risks, whereas others admired the concern for technique. Only in the second part of her oeuvre did critics regularly begin to note T.'s subtle wit and the way it informs not only the writing itself but the rendering of character.

Since *Searching for Caleb* (1976), T.'s novels have been recognized for their power in combining comic and serious elements, and their frequent creation of a particular comic figure. Thus, Morgan Gower of *Morgan's Passing* (1980) is described by Stella Nesanovich in the *Southern Review* (1981) as "a genuine eccentric in an urban setting, a comic anti-hero." And Benjamin DeMott, writing in the *New York Times* (1982), calls *Dinner at the Homesick Restaurant* (1982) "an extremely beautiful book," and also characterizes it as "funny, heart-hammering, [and] wise." *The Accidental Tourist* (1985), which shares these qualities, had an even better reception, especially since it was adapted into a popular film without their being lost. In this and her work since, the

hallmark of sensitivity to the eccentric in the ordinary continues to develop, such that the pains T. takes are no longer perceived as a false or unfortunate emphasis, but rather an organic support for content that manages to embrace the tragic and the comic at once.

T. is one of the very few contemporary American writers whose work effortlessly crosses the boundary between "high" and "popular" fiction. As the themes of her novels frequently involve the quirks and eccentricities of characters or events in ordinary life, the experience of reading one of her novels also involves the sense of crossing over, this time from the mundane to the nearly surreal and back again.

FURTHER WORKS: *The Tin Can Tree* (1965); *A Slipping-Down Life* (1970); *The Clock Winder* (1972); *Celestial Navigation* (1974); *Earthly Possessions* (1977); *Breathing Lessons* (1988)

BIBLIOGRAPHY: Linton, K., *The Temporal Horizon: A Study of the Theme of Time in A. T.'s Major Novels* (1989); Voelker, J. C., *Art and the Accidental in A. T.* (1989); Stephens, C. R., ed., *The Fiction of A. T.* (1990); Petry, A. H., *Understanding A. T.* (1990); Willrich, P. O., "Watching through Windows: A Perspective on A. T.," *VQR*, 68, 3 (1992): 497-516; Petry, A. H., ed., *Critical Essays on A. T.* (1992); Evans, E., *A. T.* (1993); Salwak, D., ed., *A. T. as Novelist* (1994); Bennet, B. A., "Attempting to Connect: Verbal Humor in the Novels of A. T.," *SoAR*, 6, 1 (1995): 57-75

—LILLIAN S. ROBINSON

TZARA, Tristan

(pseud. of Samuel Rosenstock) French poet and critic (also writing in Romanian), b. 16 Apr. 1896, Moinesti, Romania; d. 24 Dec. 1963, Paris

The eldest son of a well-to-do family, T. had one sister, Lucie, referred to in some early poems. He completed his secondary education in Bucharest, where he met the poet Ion Vinea (1895–1964), who became a lifelong friend, and with whom he founded the magazine *Simbolul*, having been influenced by SYMBOLISM. When still in Romania T. had signed poems with the name "Tristan," inspired perhaps by Wagner's *Tristan und Isolde* as well as by the French poet Tristan Corbière (1845–1875). The name "Tzara," added later, recalls the Romanian word for land. (He adopted the name officially in 1925.)

T. changed his writing style when he emigrated to Zurich in 1915 and became one of the founders of DADAISM. He arrived in Paris in 1920, where his Dada soon clashed with the SURREALISM of André BRETON. As a member of the Communist Party, he went to Madrid during the Spanish Civil War. During World War II he directed Resistance literary activity in the south of France. Many writers associated with surrealism joined the Communist Party during this period, but only T. and Louis ARAGON remained loyal members for life.

T. was mainly a poet, although he wrote some dramatic texts, an unfinished novel, and several pieces of criticism, including an unpublished work on anagrams in the poetry of François Villon. A key critical text is "Essai sur la situation de la poésie" (1931; essay on the situation of poetry). Many of his texts, however, for example, *Grains et issues* (1935; seeds and outcomes), show a mixture of different levels of writing, such as the purely discursive and the poetic, and thus T. is among those 20th-c. writers who defy genre, using poetry as criticism and vice versa.

T.'s works from his Zurich days emphasize a revolt against traditional language and literature. In the brilliant Dada manifestos of 1916–20, published together in *Manifestes Dada* (1924; *Seven Dada Manifestos*, 1977), as well as in *Vingt-cinq poèmes* (1918; twenty-five poems), he experiments with sound, simultaneism, and juxtaposition. The ellipses, meaningless syllables, irony, and lines like broken outbursts in many of T.'s early texts might confound the reader—or spectator, in the case of cabaret performances. This is the desired effect, since he was denying signification and attacking the limitations of language. In subsequent volumes, published during the height of the surrealist movement, the more shocking techniques disappear, the poetic lines are often more controlled, and recurring images help to organize the poem. Always fond of parody, T. superimposed nonrational structures on rational ones, to give his own poetic brand of "automatic writing." But in this latter period, any incoherence has the character of practice, rather than the denial, of poetry.

L'homme approximatif (1931; *Approximate Man*, 1973) is not only the most representative work of this period, it is T.'s key poetical work and a recognized masterpiece of 20th-c. French literature. Here can be found the highest degree of integration of techniques and theme in all of T.'s poetry. This long poem, often referred to as an epic, has as its theme a struggle and search for a cosmic knowledge and language. Travel imagery contributes to the motif of searching, while religious references reinforce the metaphysical implications of the quest. Imagery that mixes organic and inorganic, human and nonhuman elements implies a unified cosmos, while more consistently than any other images or allusions, references to language appear everywhere in this poem.

In volumes published after 1935, a political significance is attached to the theme of struggle for a language. The long poems *Sans coup férir* (1949; without firing a shot) and *À haute flamme* (1955; on high flame) are completely organized around political implications, with specific allusions to World War II. While there is a general tendency toward realism and a simpler style, some of the later works, such as *De mémoire d'homme* (1950; within living memory) and *La bonne heure* (1955; the good time), recall the fulgurating lines of earlier volumes, precisely because T. is constructing a sort of poetical autobiography. Another innovation in this last period is the "perpetual poem" *La rose et le chien* (1958; the rose and the dog)—designed by Picasso, with his engravings—whose physical structure (three movable disks) becomes inseparable from the text.

T. never settled for one poetic voice, although he insisted on the continuity of his poetic work. This paradox can be understood through a major theme of his work: language—the critique of it and the quest for it. This theme ties his work to a general trend in modern French poetry. Indeed, through T.'s works one relives some of the greatest artistic, philosophical, and political events of the 20th c.

FURTHER WORKS: *La première aventure céleste de Monsieur Antipyrine* (1916); *Cinéma calendrier du cœur abstrait maisons* (1920); *Dada au grand air* (1921, with Hans Arp and Max Ernst); *Faites vos jeux* (1923); *Mouchoir de nuages* (1925); *Indicateur des chemins de cœur* (1928); *De nos oiseaux* (1929); *L'arbre des voyageurs* (1930); *Où boivent les loups* (1932); *L'antitête* (1933); *Primele poeme* (1934); *La main passe* (1935); *Sur le champ* (1937); *Vigies* (1937); *La deuxième aventure céleste de Monsieur Antipyrine* (1938); *Midis gagnés* (1939); *Ça va* (1944); *Une route seul soleil* (1944); *Entre-temps* (1946); *Le signe de vie* (1946); *Terre sur terre* (1946); *Le cœur à gaz* (1946); *La fuite* (1947); *Morceaux choisis* (1947); *Le surréalisme et l'après-guerre* (1947); *Phases* (1949); *Parler seul* (1950); *L'art océanien* (1951); *La première main* (1952); *La face intérieure* (1953); *Picasso et la poésie* (1953); *Miennes* (1955); *L'Égypte face à face* (1954); *Le temps naissant* (1955); *Le fruit permis* (1956); *Frère bois* (1957); *Juste présent* (1961); *De la coupe aux lèvres* (1961); *Lampisteries, précédées de Sept manifestes Dada* (1963; *Seven Dada Manifestos and Lampisteries*, 1977); *Premiers poèmes* (1965; *Primele poeme/First Poems*, 1976); *Œuvres complètes* (1975 ff.); *Jongleur de temps* (1976). FURTHER WORKS IN ENGLISH: *Thirteen Poems* (1969); *Destroyed Days* (1971); *Approximate Man, and Other Writings* (1973); *Cosmic Realities Vanilla Tobacco Drawings* (1975); *Selected Poems* (1975)

BIBLIOGRAPHY: Caws, M. A., *The Poetry of Dada and Surrealism* (1970): 95–135; Peterson, E., *T. T.* (1971); Caws, M. A., *The Inner Theatre of Recent French Poetry* (1972): 51–75; special T. issue *Europe*, Nos. 555–56 (1975); Tison-Braun, M., *T. T.; inventeur de l'homme nouveau* (1977); Browning, G., *T. T.: The Genesis of the Dada Poem* (1979); Caldwell, R. L., "From Chemical Explosion to Simple Fruits: Nature in the Poetry of T. T.," *PCL*, 5 (1979): 18–23

—RUTH L. CALDWELL

U

UDMURT LITERATURE

See Finno-Ugric Literatures

UGANDAN LITERATURE

The republic of Uganda resulted from the unification by the British of several nations speaking different languages. The most powerful of these was the kingdom of Buganda, whose language was given written form in the 1880s; the Ganda Bible (1896) was soon followed by the first books of native authorship; these were the work of the kingdom's *katikiro* (prime minister), Apolo (later Sir Apolo) Kagwa (1865–1927), and of his secretary, Ham Mukasa (1871–1956); they dealt with the history of the Ganda kings and the customs of the Ganda people, as did the memoirs that the *kabaka* (king) himself, Sir Daudi Chwa (1897–1939), published between the two world wars.

Although vernacular imaginative writing received some encouragement through the International African Institute competitions, it did not get a real start until the foundation of the East African Literature Bureau soon after World War II. Much of the Bureau's publications consisted of prose fiction designed for juvenile readers, such as *Muddu awulira* (1953; the obedient servant) by Michael Bazze Nsimbi (b. 1910). During the ensuing years creative writing in Ganda gradually diversified with such novels as *Zinunula omunaku* (1954; they buy a poor man) by Edward E. N. Kawere (dates n.a.) and the poetry of *Ennyimba ezimu* (1958; some songs) by Y. B. Lubambula (dates n.a.). By the time independence came in 1962, the foundations had thus been laid for a written art in Ganda.

The East African Literature Bureau was also concerned with literacy in other languages, especially Luo (which is also spoken in Kenya). The first literary publication in Luo was a novel in the Acholi dialect, *Lak tar miyo kinycro wi lobo* (1953; are your teeth white? then laugh) by Okot P'BITEK, whose next work, a long satirical poem, was to become famous in English as *Song of Lawino: A Lament* (1966) before the vernacular original, *War pa Lawino* (1968), could reach print. Several other Luo writers were prompted to use English, although J. P. Ocitti (dates n.a.) continued to write fiction in Luo, publishing *Lacan ma kwo pe kinyero* (1960; every dog has its day), a collection of tales, and other works.

One admittedly minor aspect of Uganda's first prime minister Milton Obote's determination to abolish Ganda supremacy was the spreading of literacy in yet other Ugandan languages. Even as early as 1955, the East African Literature Bureau had published an account of traditional history in Runyankore, *Abagabe b'Ankole* (the kings of Ankole), by A. G. Katate (dates n.a.) and L. Kamugungunu (dates n.a.). After independence Timothy B. Bazarrabusa (1912–1966) inaugurated modern fiction in Nyoro-Toro with *Ha munwa gw'ekituuro* (1963; the point of death), and E. J. Lyavala-Lwanga (dates n.a.) produced the first collection of folk stories in Soga, *Endheso dh'Abasoga* (1967; tales of the Basoga).

While such developments took place throughout British Africa, it is Uganda's peculiar distinction that it was where East African creative writing in English originated in the late 1950s. This development was due in part to the role played by David Cook of the English department of Makerere College, an interterritorial institution set up near Kampala in 1939 to serve the whole of British East Africa. The magazine *Penpoint* (founded 1958) was the launching pad for a number of budding writers, the majority of whom, admittedly, were Kenyans. At the Kampala conference of 1962 Anglophone writers from West and South Africa gave further encouragement to their young East African colleagues, and an anthology of *Penpoint* contributions, *Origin East Africa*, edited by David Cook, was published in 1965.

Ugandan creative writing in English began in earnest in the mid-1960s with *Kalasanda* (1965) and *Kalasanda Revisited* (1966), rather conventional tales of peaceful Ganda village life by Barbara Kimenye (b. 1939), and with Okot p'Bitek's *Song of Lawino*. The latter's immediate success encouraged several younger writers to experiment with loose forms mixing narrative and soliloquy, prose and verse. Okello Oculi (b. 1942) described his blank-verse story "Orphan" (1968) as a "village opera." In his novel *Prostitute* (1968) the narrative is interspersed with verse passages. *The Abandoned Hut* (1969) by Joseph Buruga (b. 1942) is a long poem denouncing the erosion of African values under Western influence. As for p'Bitek himself, after his initial plea for tradition, he somewhat hastily and feebly tried to show the other side of the coin in *Song of Ocol* (1970); but the *Two Songs* (1971) demonstrated the flexibility of a genre whose plain diction had proved capable of the most subtle irony: the desultory ribaldry of "Song of Malaya" is balanced by the committed concern of "Song of Prisoner," a poem inspired by the assassination of Tom Mboya.

Other writers, however, found the Western-type novel a more appropriate medium for the literature of a modern country. In *Return to the Shadows* (1969) Robert Serumaga (b. 1939) prophetically sets the story in a nation ridden by military coups; his play *The Elephants* (1971) deals with the predicament of an intellectual in a world of political violence. *The Experience* (1970) by Eneriko Seruma (pseud. of Henry Kimbugwe, b. 1944) provides a bitter image of the confusion and alienation of the Westernized African.

As a result of Idi Amin Dada's coup in 1971, the 1970s were particularly marked by the growth of a Ugandan literature in exile. A majority of writers found it advisable to leave their country for less lethal parts of the world, especially Kenya, where most Ugandan works were henceforth published. Although this situation contributed to restoring a sort of interterritorial mood among East African authors in Nairobi, Ugandan writing maintained its specific individuality.

While the poet Richard Ntiru (b. 1946) in *Tensions* (1971) rejected p'Bitek's example in favor of a more personal and more intellectual type of lyricism, nearer the examples of T. S. ELIOT and W. B. YEATS, the novel remained the most popular genre, exploring a wide range of themes.

Arcadian vignettes of village life figure prominently in novels by Ganda authors writing in English, like *The Outcasts* (1971) by Bonnie Lubega (b. 1930) and *A Son of Kabira* (1972) by Davis Sebukima (b. 1943), as well as in the fiction of non-Ganda novelists, such as Tumusiime-Rushedge's (dates n.a.) *The Bull's Horn* (1972), and *Pulse of the Woods* (1974) and other early works by Uganda's most prolific popular writer, Godfrey Kalimugogo (dates n.a.).

There is a stark contrast between these and the many novels that, in Uganda as in most successor states of British Africa, focus on the theme of political violence. This obsessive trend, initiated by Robert Serumaga and emphasized in his play *Majangwa* (1972), was taken up by John Ruganda (b. 1941) in the play *The Burdens* (1972) and by Davis Sebukima in the darkly satirical novel *The Half-Brothers* (1970).

Race relations—a major subject in a polyethnic country with a tradition of tribal rivalries and an economically important Asian (Indian) minority, and especially in the literary circles, where European expatriates used to be very visible—had been first explored in Eneriko Seruma's *The Experience*. His stories, collected in *The Heart Seller* (1971), concentrate on their sexual implications, as does *The People's Bachelor* (1971) by Austin S. Bukenya (b. 1944). Interracial sex is also central to a number of novels and plays by such Ugandans of Asian origin as Bahadur Tejani (dates n.a.) in *Days after Tomorrow* (1971) and Laban Erapu (b. 1955) and Jagjit Singh (b. 1949) in their popular radio plays. More prominence is given to the political problems that national independence raises for Asians in an important novel, *In a Brown Mantle* (1972), by Peter NAZARETH, a well-known creative writer and critic of Goan origin. By the mid-1970s greater explicitness in sexual matters and the example of Kenyan writers had given rise to a popular literature with an undisguised pornographic bent, as represented by *The Sobbing Sounds* (1975) by an as yet unidentified English-language Ganda writer who signs himself Omunjakko Nakibimbiri.

Along with Okot p'Bitek, who died in 1982, the most impressive writer Uganda has produced so far is Taban lo Liyong (b. 1938), whose family had migrated from the Sudan. By the late 1970s, when he left Uganda to acquire Sudanese citizenship and teach in Juba, he had published about a dozen books—essays and short-story collections, poetry, and recordings of oral art—including *The Last Word* (1969), a collection of essays; *Ballads of Underdevelopment* (1976); and *The Popular Culture of East Africa* (1979). Contrary to his fellow Acholi p'Bitek, and despite the eccentricity built into his outlook and literary style, Taban lo Liyong is all in favor of modernization. In his anger and bitterness at the ruptured condition of black Africa after two decades of independence, he proclaimed his conviction that "what we can write legitimately are fragments. . . . Never a story. Nor a tragedy."

As the 1970s came to a close with the collapse of the Idi Amin regime, there was some hope that Uganda might heal its wounds and once more offer its writers the shelter and the congenial atmosphere of a peaceful home. Continued disorder, however, has prevented such expectations from materializing during the ensuing years.

BIBLIOGRAPHY: Roscoe, A., *Uhuru's Fire: African Literature East and South* (1977): 32–87, 107–34, 260–65; Horn, A., "Uhuru to Amin: The Golden Decade of Theatre in Uganda," *LHY*, 19, 1 (1978): 22–49; Gérard, A. S., *African Language Literatures* (1981): 299–307

—ALBERT S. GÉRARD

Ugandan Literature since 1980

The passage of time does not only necessitate the continued recording of the ever-unfolding literary process in a given country,

but also requires the review of the already documented literary history, since previously isolated or seemingly negligible facts begin to acquire added meanings as they fall into settling patterns or constitute evolving trends. This is particularly true of emergent literatures, as illustrated by the national literature of Uganda.

Thus, the beginning of Ugandan literature in English should be fixed in 1904, when the translation of Ham Mukasa's *Uganda's Katikiro in England* was published. This travel account is a variant of the biographical genre, which was widely spread in African literatures during the nascent stage of their development, and which can now justifiably be defined as one of the earliest literary forms. In 1975 it appeared under a new title, *Sir Apolo Kagwa Discovers Britain*, edited by Taban lo Liyong. Following it was *The Story of an African Chief* (1935), also published in 1936 as *Africa Answers Back*, by Akiki Nyabongo (dates n.a.). *Desecration of My Kingdom* (1967) by Mutesa II, Kabaka of Buganda, is, on the other hand, similar in context to the writings by such nationalist leaders as Jomo Kenyatta and Julius Nyerere, which belong equally to historiography and literature, and whose subject matter is the anticolonial struggle.

In further retrospect the 1960s can be considered a golden decade in the history of Ugandan literature. They stand out not so much in terms of a voluminous literary output, but as a time dominated by intense intellectualism and a spirit of creativity, in which fictional writing became a felt need and a natural form of artistic expression. One of the factors that contributed to this was the presence of *Transition* magazine, founded in 1961 by Rajat Neogy (1938-1995). With its diverse orientation towards literature, culture, politics, and sociology, and under the brilliant editorship of Neogy, it became the most serious forum of its kind in Africa. In 1968 Neogy was detained and subsequently put on trial by President Milton Obote. Although acquitted, he could no longer function in the country, and *Transition* ceased publication. In an ironic shift of historic significance, *Transition* turned into an early example of the suppression of freedom, which was to play such a devastating role in Ugandan literary life. The journal *Dhana*, the successor to *Penpoint*, was also instrumental in stimulating literary productivity. It became defunct in the late 1970s, partly as a result of the gross encroachment on free speech under President Amin. Its resurrection in the late 1980s was a recognition of the gap it had left.

On the level of symbolism, the publication of several important works in the grim year of 1971 can now be seen as an anticelebration of Amin's rule and a pledge of resilience, notably Taban lo Liyong's *Frantz Fanon's Uneven Ribs: Poems More and More* (1971) and *The Uniformed Man* (1971), a book of fragmented prose. In 1969 Taban had published *Fixions and Other Stories*, followed in 1970 by *Meditations in Limbo* and *Eating Chiefs*, translations of folk tales, and a year later he produced *Another Nigger Dead*, an anthology of poetry and a piece of critical writing. He was becoming the most prolific and, perhaps, the most extraordinary Ugandan writer. *Thirteen Offensives against Our Enemies*, containing the author's ideological agenda for development, and some poems, came out in 1973. *Words That Melt a Mountain* (1996) is a collection of poems inspired by his sojourn in Japan during 1992-94. Taban also continued working as an essayist. In *Another Last Word* (1990) he comments, in part, on the role of the writer in African society. In *Culture Is Rutan* (1991) he insists on the conscious use of "African literary forms (and traditions) in modern African literary compositions."

Political writing, which is one of the most recognizable trends in Ugandan literature today, also has its origins in the 1970s. After Nazareth's *In a Brown Mantle* and Sebukima's *The Half-Brothers* set the critical tone in the treatment of political reality, exhibiting a predominantly negative disposition even to the political aspect of the commonly glorified national liberation movement, later writers proceeded to expose various post-colonial political malaises. *The Final Blasphemy* (1978) by Felix Okoboi (dates n.a.) refers, in part, to one of the numerous means that enable a corrupt regime to maintain its grip on power—the manipulation of the media.

Political repression, as an alternative means employed by antipopular regimes to sustain power, features in Grace Ibangira's (dates n.a.) novel *Bitter Harvest* (1980) and Godfrey Kalimugogo's (dates n.a.) *Sandu the Prince* (1982). The head of state in Cyprian Karamagi's (dates n.a.) *Bulemu the Bastard* (1980) condemns all forms of political punishment and declares that "keeping your influential enemy in an uninfluential corner is enough torture." In contrast to this "benevolent" dictatorship, some novels emphasize the extension of political repression to wanton brutality unleashed on the entire population. *The Rape of the Pearl* (1985) by Magala-Nyago (dates n.a.) and *The Seasons of Thomas Tebo* (1986) by John Nagenda (b. 1938) are the most striking examples in this category.

The deadly violence perpetrated by degenerated political regimes is at the center of action in the play *The Floods* (1980) by John Ruganda and the Lugand-language play *Olusozi lwa Batulege* (1986; The Hill of the Chequered Zebra) by Andrew Kibuuka (dates n.a.). Self-seeking politicians have been satirized by Byron Kawaddwa (?-1977) in the musical drama *Oluyimba lwa Wankoko*, written in Luganda in 1971 and published in English as *The Song of Wankoko* in 1976. In a similar vein, Elvania Namukwaya Zirimu (dates n.a.), in *When the Hunchback Made Rain* (1974), and Nuwa Sentongo (dates n.a.), in *The Invisible Bond* (1975), illustrate how politically bankrupt systems can be used by individuals within them for settling personal scores.

Alex Mukulu's (b. 1955) *30 Years of Bananas* (1993), which gives an account of Uganda's political history since independence, is one example of the new drama that emerged in the atmosphere of political emancipation which dawned after the victory of Yoweri Museveni's National Resistance Movement in 1986. It is characterized by a more realistic, direct form of expression. Olumidi Osinya's (pseud. of Horace Awori, dates n.a.) fable *The Amazing Saga of Field Marshal Abdulla Salim Fisi (Or How the Hyena Got His!)* (1977) and the novels *Target Amin* by Joseph Konrad (a pseudonym, dates n.a.), *Truckful of Gold* (n.d.) by the late S. Joshua L. Zake (dates n.a.), and *The General Is Up* (1991) by Peter Nazareth deal specifically with the Amin regime. In poetry Grace Akello's (dates n.a.) *My Barren Song* (1979) is the most powerful response to the abnormality of its occurrence.

Politics did not, however, obliterate all other concerns, and even some of the most politically conscious authors have written works with entirely different thematic preoccupations. Thus, Ruganda published *Black Mamba* (1973), a volume which, besides the title play, contains *Covenant with Death*, both of which center on problems of private life. Davis Sebukima put together his short stories in the collection *Growing Up* (1974). In it, "growing up" is presented as a lifelong process of an individual's spiritual, emotional, and mental development. This theme was taken up by Timothy Wangusa (b. 1942) in his tender coming-of-age novel, *Upon This Mountain* (1989). Wangusa is also the author of the volume of poetry entitled *Salutations* (1977).

Godfrey Kalimugogo, in *The Department* (1976) and *The Prodigal Chairman* (1979), exposes the corruption that erodes top-level bureaucratic power, and uses satire to etch the portraits of high-ranking executives. He also wrote *Pilgrimage to Nowhere* (1974), a story about a son "lost" in the big city. Similar to this novel are *A Man of Two Faces* (1978) by Henry Owino (b. 1942) and *The Eternal Problem* (1982) by Felix Okoboi. Okello Oculi published the book-length poem *Malak* (1976) and the novel *Kookolem* (1978). They treat, the former on a global, the latter on a private level, the themes of injustice, poverty, ignorance, disease, and brutality.

Cliff Lubwa p'Chong (1946-1997), an actor, poet, playwright, and literary editor, looked for themes and modes of writing in Acholi culture and poetic traditions. He is the author of a volume of two plays, *Generosity Kills and The Last Safari* (1975), and a collection of poems, *Words of My Groaning* (1976). He edited Okot p'Bitek's posthumously published books, *Acholi Proverbs* (1985), *Artist, the Ruler* (1986), and *White Teeth* (1989).

Bahadur Tejani, now a Ugandan writer in the diaspora, brings his new experiences to bear on his fiction. His recent short stories, for example, "Black Cosmos," published in *Wasafiri* (1990) in England, are oriented towards the American world. This is as much a new departure as a continued preoccupation with multiculturalism, and an expression of the author's humanist vision. He is also an author of children's stories, notably "Alice in Yankeeland" (1988) and "Freedom Star" (1990). Joseph M. Luguya's (dates n.a.) novel, *Payment in Kind* (1985), deserves mention for its unusual probing into matters of the human psyche.

As to be expected, young authors respond to topical issues of their time. Namige Kayondo (b. 1963) in his first novel, *Vanishing Shadows* (1995), depicts a world over which so many uncertainties cast their shadows, the most deadly being that of AIDS. But another young author has come to assert the contiguity of the literary process. Jane Okot p'Bitek (b. 1966), in her *Song of Farewell* (1994), has revitalized the tradition of the "song school" in East Africa started by her father. Yet, even she has demonstrated that the new generation has new songs to sing. What remains is the indestructibility of genuine talent, however much this talent remains unrevealed. "I happen to know that there are waiting in various publishing houses in Kampala literally hundreds of manuscripts," says Timothy Wangusa in a 1991 interview. When this material is sieved, and the writings that are of good literary quality eventually get published, yet another review of Ugandan literature would become necessary. It might considerably alter the present one, and come closer to the authentic portrayal of the literature of this East African country.

BIBLIOGRAPHY: Heron, G. A., *The Poetry of Okot p'Bitek* (1976); Wanjala, C., *For Home and Freedom* (1980); Nazareth, P., "Waiting for Amin: Two Decades of Ugandan Literature" and "Bibliyongraphy, or Six Tabans in Search of an Author," in Killam, G. D., ed., *The Writing of East and Central Africa* (1984): 7-35, 159-76; Sicherman, C., "Timothy Wangusa and Contemporary Ugandan Literature: An Interview," *WLWE*, 32, 1-2 (1992-93): 22-32; Breitinger, E., "Theater and Political Mobilization: Case Studies from Uganda," in Davis, G. V., ed., *Southern African Writing: Voyages and Explorations* (1994): 155-70; Mbowa, R., "Theater and Political Repression in Uganda," *RAL*, 27, 3 (1996): 87-97

—EMILIA V. ILIEVA

al-'UJAYLĪ, 'Abd al-Salām

Syrian novelist, short-story writer, travel writer, and essayist, b. July 1918 or 1919, Raqqah

U. was born at Raqqah on the Euphrates, and comes of a family that claims descent from the Prophet Muhammad. The absence of birth registration in Syria at the time of his birth has made it uncertain whether U. was born in 1918 or 1919. After schooling at Raqqah and Aleppo, he entered the University of Dasmascus to study medicine, and was admitted to the degree of Doctor of Medicine in 1945. Soon afterward, he entered politics, and was elected a representative for Raqqah in the Syrian National Assembly in 1947. For a brief period (April-September 1962) he was a minister in the Syrian government, but he does not seem to have relished political power and instead devoted himself to the practice of his profession of medicine.

U. has traveled widely, and he has written a number of travel books. Nevertheless he has continued to make his home in Raqqah, and has thereby retained close ties with the Syrian countryside and traditional Arab life only indirectly touched by Western influences.

U. made his first attempts at literary composition when he was only twelve, and his first published work, the bedouin story "Nūmān" (1936; Numan), appeared before he was twenty. Since then he has contributed to many literary genres, but most significantly to the essay, the novella, and the short story. His first collection of short stories. *Bint al-Sāhirah* (daughter of the sorceress), appeared in 1948. Examples of his work have been translated into a number of languages, including English, French, German, and Spanish. U.'s work has been the subject of a great deal of attention from Arab critics: the two published bibliographies devoted to him list nearly 400 critical articles and books by Arab authors dealing with his literary production.

U. sees human existence as a continual struggle between inadequate human strength and ineluctable fate. He is thus much influenced by the ancient Arab concept of *qadar* (predestination), but he believes at the same time in the stubborn resilience of humans in the face of a threatening universe.

U. sets a distance between himself and the play of human interests and human actions, while finding in them rich and fertile material for portrayal and comment. He is a keen-eyed observer of the social scene but has not tried to analyze the structure of social struggles or the clash of class interests in his fiction. One cause, however, about which U. feels deeply is that of the dispossessed Palestinians. He has dealt with this subject in political articles and in some of his short stories, notably "Nubū'āt al-shaykh Salmān" (1965; the prophecies of shaykh Salman), which portrays the almost mystical yearning of the Palestinians for their lost land.

U.'s attitude of detachment is closely connected with his engrained scepticism. This is well illustrated in his short story "al-Ru'yā" (1953; "The Dream," 1967), in which an ignorant village religious dignitary interprets the dream of one of the superstitious villagers as meaning that the man will shortly die. The local schoolmaster, appalled by this, fights fire with fire by persuading the man that with supernatural aid his imminent demise can be avoided. The ironic twist at the end of the story in no way detracts from the sceptical note struck throughout the narrative.

"Al-Ru'yā" deals with scepticism towards superstitious and religious obscurantism; the novella *Hikāyat majānīn* (1971; *Madness*, 1988) is informed with a more comprehensive scepticism. It takes the form of an account of a car ride in which the lives and careers of the passengers are contrasted with the life of a madwoman, and presents a comparison between two sorts of madness; madness in the sense of insanity and madness in the sense of the pursuit of futility and illusion. In this novella U. seems to have moved some way from his accustomed realism toward SYMBOLISM.

U.'s scepticism is, however, not totally unshakable. In one of the most interesting and suggestive of his essays, entitled "Ishhad yā tabīb" (1978; bear witness, o physician!), U. describes an extraordinary Sufi ceremony performed at his family residence in Raqqah. This ceremony involves the self-infliction of wounds on themselves by religious devotees, which leave no mark and leave the victims apparently none the worse physically. U. uses the inexplicable events of this so-called *darb* (blow) ceremony to point up the perplexity experienced by those like himself educated in Western science, who are brought face to face with phenomena and aspects of traditional Eastern life that cannot be reconciled with their scientific knowledge—and yet which cannot be refuted by it.

Much of U.'s work displays an attractive sardonic humor. This is seen to best advantage in his *Maqāmāt* (1962; assemblies), a collection of comic dramatic anecdotes in rhymed prose, in the Arabic tradition of Badī' al-Zamān al-Hamadhānī (968–1008) and al-Qāsim b. 'Alī-al-Harīrī (1054–1122).

U.'s style has changed little during his long career as an author, although his work as a whole shows great diversity of theme and treatment. He disposes of a very wide vocabulary, and writes exclusively in literary Arabic, eschewing the use of colloquial dialects favored by some modern writers of Arabic fiction. His literary output is large, and some of it will probably prove to be ephemeral, but there can be no doubt that among his contributions to the art of the short story and the essay there are works that will have a permanent place in Arabic literature.

FURTHER WORKS: *Sā'at al-mulāzim* (1954); *Ashyā' shakhsiyyah* (1968); *Ahādīth al-'ashiyyāt* (1971); *Fāris madīnat al-qantarah* (1971); *Qulūb 'alā al-aslāk* (1974); *al-Sayf wa-al-tābūt* (1974); *Azāhīr tishrīn al-mudammah* (1976); *al-Hubb al-hazīn* (1977); *'Iyādah fī al-rīf* (1978); *al-Maghmūrūn* (1979); *Fi kull wādin 'asa* (1984); *Fusūl Abī al-Bahā'* (1986); *Mawt al-habībah* (1987); *Hafnah min al-dhikriyyāt* (1987); *Jīl al-darabūkkah* (1990); *Filastīniyyāt* (1994)

BIBLIOGRAPHY: Young, M. J. L., "A. S. U. and his Maqāmāt," *Middle East Studies*, 14, 2 (1978): 205–10; Allen, R., ed., *Modern Arabic Literature* (1987): 329–32; Ramos Calvo, A. M., "Visión de España en la literatura árabe contemporanea: dos ejemplos sirios," in Agreda, F. de, ed., *La traducción y la crítica literaria: actas de las jornadas de Hispanismo árabe* (1990): 255–62

—M. J. L. YOUNG

UJEVIĆ, Tin (Augustin)

Yugoslav poet and essayist (writing in Croatian), b. 5 July 1891, Vrgorac, Austro-Hungarian Empire (now Croatia); d. 12 Nov. 1955, Zagreb

Having spent his childhood and adolescence in his native Dalmatia, U. went to Zagreb, then to Belgrade, and finally to Paris to study philosophy. During World War I he was an active member of pro-Yugoslav Serbian and Croatian émigré circles in Paris. Because of his antimonarchist views and political naïveté, he soon came into conflict with the royalist leaders of the emigration, was rejected by them and politically discredited. Deeply hurt, on returning to Yugoslavia in 1919 U. led a lonely life of a maverick poet in Belgrade in the 1920s, in Sarajevo and Split in the 1930s, and in Zagreb from the 1940s until his death. Once regarded as a controversial poet and an eccentric—often ridiculed and humiliated, and even proclaimed mentally unbalanced—U. is today considered one of the greatest, most original, and most influential Croatian poets of the 20th c.

U. achieved prominence during the early years of his writing career (1909–14), and a cycle of his poems was included in the prestigious anthology *Hrvatska mlada lirika* (1914; the new Croatian lyric poetry). During World War I, after having experienced great disappointments in his political and personal life in Paris, the proud poet suffered a deep emotional crisis that from then on would profoundly affect the tone and content of his poetry. His first two collections, *Lelek sebra* (1920; lament of a serf) and *Kolajna* (1926; a neck-piece), are in sharp contrast to his youthful, optimistic poetry. These collections are characterized by gloomy moods, a pessimistic outlook on life and man's fate, and a deep resentment toward our dehumanized and cruel world in which sensitive and honest men such as U. "grow old while still young" and feel "weak and powerless/and so alone, without a friend/so perturbed and desperate...."

Unable to cope with the absurdities of life, U. eventually turned inward. His rich and turbulent thoughts became the center of his poetic universe and his only reality. Through this prism the poet also contemplated the world outside. Over the years, U.'s poetry grew increasingly introspective and became confessional and egocentric in tone, although without losing anything of its originality, emotional richness, and intellectual depth.

Only during the 1930s did U.'s poetry brighten up. The calm and serene small-town atmosphere of picturesque Sarajevo and the Adriatic resort of Split affected him in a positive way. His appreciation for the beauties of nature grew deeper, as did his interest in and concern for deprived people and social outcasts like himself. Although critical of social injustices, U. remained a Utopian socialist, and contrary to his fellow Belgrade SURREALISTS of the 1920s, he never aligned himself with any organized and politically active socialist or communist group.

U.'s essays on Croatian, Serbian, and French literature and on Indian and Oriental philosophy are an important part of his literary work. They are indispensable for understanding the complexity of U. the man and the poet and the unusual, surreal world that he created for himself.

An intelligent, sensitive, and ethical man, U. was a strong individualist, and his almost superhuman inner strength and sense of dignity kept him going despite all the adversities that plagued his lonely life. It also made it possible for him to create a powerful poetic oeuvre that bridges the gap between the old and the new, the traditional and the conventional, the past and the future. Many Yugoslav poets after World War II were influenced by U.'s poetry, and many still look to it for inspiration.

FURTHER WORKS: *Nedjelja maloljetnih: Jedna podvrsta Moderne* (1931); *Dva glavna bogumila: Lev Tolstoj i Mahatma Gandhi* (1931); *Auto na korzu* (1932); *Ojadjeno zvono* (1933); *Pesme* (1937); *Ljudi za vratima gostionice* (1938); *Skalpel kaosa: Iskopine iz sedre sadašjice* (1938); *Rukovet* (1950); *Žedan kamen na studencu* (1954); *Izabrane pjesme* (1956); *Mamurluci i pobješnjela krava* (1956); *Mudre i lude djevice: Pjesničke proze* (1957); *Sabrane djela* (17 vols., 1963–67); *Izabrana djela* (3 vols., 1964); *Svakisdašnja jadikovka, i druge pjesme* (1981)

BIBLIOGRAPHY: Vanpotić, M., *Contemporary Croatian Literature* (1966): 34–37, 186–89; Nizeteo, A., "Whitman in Croatian: T. U. and Walt Whitman," *JCS*, 11–12 (1971): 105–51; Eekman, T., *Thirty Years of Yugoslav Literature (1945–1975)* (1978): 39–42

—BILJANA ŠLJIVIĆ-ŠIMŠIĆ

UKRAINIAN LITERATURE

Ukrainian literature in the 19th c. was dominated by romanticism, which reached its zenith in the poetry of Taras Shevchenko (1814–1861). His collection *Kobzar* (1840; *The Kobzar of the Ukraine*, 1922) not only reaffirmed that Ukrainian was a suitable literary language but also awakened the national consciousness. Following Shevchenko's death, the tsarist government attempted to eradicate Ukrainian language and culture completely. In 1876 Tsar Alexandr II issued the Ems Ukase, declaring that publishing books (with some minor exceptions), producing plays, or giving language instruction in Ukrainian was a crime against the state. Only in 1906 did the Russian Imperial Academy acknowledge Ukrainian as a separate language. Because of Russian oppression, Ukrainian intellectual life had shifted to the western Ukraine (Galicia), which, as part of the Austro-Hungarian Empire, enjoyed more freedom and provided greater opportunities for literary and cultural activities. Ukrainian writers living in tsarist Russia often sent their manuscripts to western Ukraine, and the published works were smuggled back to eastern Ukraine.

The Turn of the Century: Realism

Fiction

While poetry always has been the dominant genre of Ukrainian literature, 19th-c. realism encouraged the development of fiction. Among the leading writers were the late-romanticist Marko Vovchok (pseud. of Maria Vilinska-Markovych, 1834–1907), who combined ethnographic elements with a realistic depiction of peasant life; and Olena Pchilka (pseud. of Olha Drahomanov Kosach, 1849–1930), whose early-20th-c. works focus on the Ukrainian middle class. Also notable were Ivan Nechuy-Levytsky (1838–1918), whose novels accurately reflect peasant life during and after serfdom as well as the relationship between the common people and the intelligentsia; Borys Hrinchenko (1863–1910), whose tales and novels deal with the loss of Ukrainian identity among peasants and the clashes of various ideologies; and Panas Myrny (pseud. of Panas Rudchenko, 1849–1920), whose social novels, such as *Povia* (1919; the fallen woman), realistically depicted village life. Of paramount importance for the development of the Ukrainian novel were the fiction and criticism of Pantaleymon Kulish (1819–1897), the socialist ideology of Mykhaylo Drahomanov (1841–1895), and the writings of Ivan FRANKO.

Drama

The first permanent Ukrainian theatrical troupe was established by the actor-playwright Marko Kropyvnytsky (1840–1910) in the late 19th c. More so than fiction, the plays written then combined romantic motifs with realistic presentation. The repertoire was invigorated by the works of Mykhaylo Starytsky (1840–1904), whose popular historical dramas were rather melodramatic and tended to idealize the Ukrainian past, and by the plays of Karpenko-Kary (pseud. of Ivan Tobilevych, 1845–1907), the founder of Ukrainian social drama. Realistic drama culminated in the social plays of Ivan Franko and the poetic dramas and dramatic poems of Lesya UKRAYINKA.

Poetry

The realistic poets were for the most part also prose writers and dramatists. Such exclusively poetic talents as Pavlo Hrabovsky (1864–1902), Volodymyr Samylenko (1864–1925), and Sydir Vorobkevych (1836–1903) wrote lyrics, satirical songs, and revolutionary verse. Despite their high regard for Shevchenko, they generally ignored his formal innovations and were influenced instead by the poetic fables of Leonid Hlibov (1827–1893) and the satirical verse of Stepan Rudansky (1834–1873).

The Age of Modernism

With the legalization of the Ukrainian press within the Russian empire after 1905 and the infusion of western aesthetic ideas (such as art for art's sake and SYMBOLISM), Ukrainian literature began to take on a more cosmopolitan character. The traditional subjects of Ukrainian literature—village life, the role of the intelligentsia, and the concomitant themes of national liberation and social justice—were augmented by more universal motifs and by the search for new literary forms. Most writers synthesized the old and the new. Various literary groups came into being, such as Young Muse in Lviv (Lvov), and Ukrainian Home in Kiev. The most important factor in the growth of Ukrainian letters was the journal *Literaturno-naukovy visnyk*. In 1901 the Ukrainian MODERNISTS published their manifesto in this journal. They championed the poet's inalienable right to dwell subjectively on his personal experiences and to foster a cult of beauty above all else. The ensuing differences between the generations were most poignantly expressed in polemical discussions between Ivan Franko and Mykola Voronny (1871–1942).

Fiction

The leading writer of fiction was Mykhaylo KOTSYUBYNSKY. His novels—such as *Fata Morgana* (1910; *Fata Morgana*, 1976), an impressionistic study of human psychology set against social conflict in a village, and *Tini zabutykh predkiv* (1913; *Shadows of Forgotten Ancestors*, 1981), a moving portrayal of the Hutsuls (Carpathian mountain folk)—are deeply rooted in the soil, but written in a refined manner closely attuned to the fin-de-siècle mood. Vasyl STEFANYK, in his miniatures on peasant life, was Kotsyubynsky's equal in the analysis of the human condition and the poignant expression of the tragic sense of life, but quite different in manner.

Other modernist writers were Les (Olexandr) Martovych (1871–1916), known primarily for the short novel *Zabobon* (written 1911, pub. 1917; superstition), a somewhat caricatured view of life in a colorless Galician district; Marko Cheremshyna (pseud. of Ivan Semanyuk, 1874–1927), author of highly stylized stories of Ukrainian village life; and Stepan Vasylchenko (pseud. of Stepan Panasenko, 1878–1932), whose search for a new style for his tales led him to Gogol, E. T. A. Hoffmann, and Ukrainian folk poetry, thus paving the way for a romantic revival, which culminated in the works of Yury Yanovsky (1902–1954) and Todos Osmachka (1895–1962). Also of importance are the sketches in *Poezia v. prozi* (1902; poetry in prose) by Hnat Khotkevych (1877–1942); the historical novels of Katrya Hrynevych (1875–1947), set in the Middle Ages and written in an archaic, aristocratically refined style; the haunting romantic novels of Olha Kobylanska (1865–1942); and the social and historical novels, especially the tetralogy *Mazepa* (1926–29; Mazepa), by the melancholy poet-novelist Bohdan Lepky (1872–1941). New moral, psychological, and pathological motifs were added to Ukrainian fiction by Volodymyr VYNNYCHENKO.

Drama

The most important plays of the period were those of Ivan Franko, Lesya Ukrayinka, and Volodymyr Vynnychenko. Among poet-playwrights, Vasyl Pachovsky's (1878–1942) lyrical achievement completely overshadows his dramatic work, and Olexandr Oles's (pseud. of Olexandr Kandyba, 1878–1944) plays pale next to his turbulent verse. The dramas of the critic-essayist Lyudmyla Starytska-Chernyakhivska (1869–1941) range thematically from classical antiquity to the cossack-hetman period of Ukrainian history; Spyrydon Cherkasenko (1876–1940), who published stories and poems under the name Petro Stakh, also wrote fine verse dramas.

Poetry

Poetry of the early 20th c. reflects a more programmatic modernism in its (not always successful) attempts to reject traditional literary canons. A distinct contribution was made by such Young Muse members as Vasyl Pachovsky, whose poetry shows refined versification and striking tonal effects; Petro Karmansky (1878–1956), whose verse alternated between gloomy despair and vitriolic attacks on philistinism; Stepan Charnetsky (1881–1945), who wrote melancholy nature poetry and humorous feuilletons; and Vasyl Shchurat (1872–1948), whose poetry contains both religious overtones and social criticism.

A transitory Shevchenko-like prophet stature was achieved by Olexandr Oles with his collections *Z zhurboyu radist obnyalas* (1907; sorrow and joy embraced each other) and *Poeziyi* (2 vols., 1909–11; poems), while Mykola Voronny's writings substantially enriched the poetic vocabulary. Hryhory Chuprynka's (1879–1921) numerous collections mark the poetic apogee of that period.

Other poets include the linguist and Oriental scholar Ahatanhel Krymsky (1871–1941), whose reflective lyrics express disillusionment, existential loneliness, and a search for the exotic; and the self-declared modernist Mykola Chernyavsky (1867–1937), whose social verse and love poetry were nonetheless grounded in tradition. An early symbolist was Mykola Filyansky (1873–1937).

The Interwar Period

The demise of the Russian and Austro-Hungarian empires, the proclamation of an independent Ukraine (January 22, 1918), and the existence of that independent state (until 1922) induced a surge of Ukrainian culture, which continued even after the Soviet Russian takeover. Initially, literary life revolved around various journals, such as *Literaturnonaukovy visnyk*, which served mostly as a forum for established writers; *Shlyakh*, where many young poets such as Maxym RYLSKY and Yakiv Savchenko (1890–1937) published their works; *Knyhar*, edited by the classical scholar and neoclassicist poet Mykola Zerov (1891–1941); and *Mystetsvo*, whose chief editor was the FUTURIST poet Mykhaylo Semenko (1892–1939).

In addition to the groupings by aesthetic orientation, there were several communist literary groups of various ideological colorations, all of which were disbanded prior to the establishment of the Soviet Writers' Union in 1934. This period ended in massive purges of Ukrainian intellectuals.

In the western Ukraine, part of Poland after World War I, dynamic literary activity centered on *Literaturno-naukovy visnyk* (1922–32) and later *Visnyk* (1933–39), edited by the fiery journalist and essayist Dmytro Dontsov (1883–1973), the ideologue of Ukrainian nationalism. Among other groups was the Catholic Logos, whose chief representatives were the scholar, poet, and novelist Hryhory Luznytsky (b. 1903) and the mystical historical novelist Natalena Koroleva (1889–1966). The group centered around the journal *Nazustrich* (1934–39) and included the painter-poet Svyatoslav Hordynsky (b. 1909), the erudite literary critic Mykhaylo Rudnytsky (1889–1975), and the poet, prose writer, and dramatist Yury Kosach (b. 1909).

After the Soviet takeover in 1922, Prague and Warsaw became Ukrainian émigré centers. The Prague school, consisting mainly of poets, flourished in the 1920s. In the 1930s in Warsaw, a new group known as Tank was founded around the poet Yury Lypa (1900–1944) and the poet and novelist Natalia Livytska-Kholodna (b. 1902). The most important journal here was *My* (1934–39), which espoused the ideology of the nationalist leader Symon Petlyura (1877–1926).

Fiction

Novelists and short-story writers of the 1920s continued the experimentation of the previous decade and expanded the range of themes and styles. New subjects included the revolution, the city, Ukrainization (or rather, de-Russification of the Ukraine), and industrialization. Literary currents ranged from traditional realism, espoused by Petro Punch (b. 1891), to the avant-garde prose of the poet-linguist Mayk Yohansen (1895–1937). A new brand of romanticism appeared in Yury Yanovsky's fiction, especially the novel *Mayster korablya* (1929; the ship builder), which achieves a synthesis between the lofty poetic beauty of the sea and the Marxist notion of labor as an absolute. A romantic vision of the revolution alternated with an exposé of the drabness and filth of postrevolutionary life in the short stories of Mykola Khvylovy (pseud. of Mykola Fitilov, 1893–1933), who initially supported the revolution but later decried its degeneration and called for the Ukraine's spiritual independence from Moscow and a cultural union with Europe. A *sui generis* elegant romantic style, developed under the influence of French fiction, characterizes the short stories of Arkady Lyubchenko (1899–1945), who, in addition to writing on the revolution, satirized the intelligentsia of the NEP period in his novel *Obraza* (1927; the insult).

Representatives of impressionist prose were Hryhory Kosynka (1899–1934), whose lyrical stories glorify the Ukrainian peasant-insurgents; Valerian Pidmohylny (1901–1941), whose novel about

Kiev, *Misto* (1928; the city), became a favorite among the youth; Andry Holovko (1897–1972), whose novel *Buryan* (1927; *The Weeds*, 1976) deals with postrevolutionary life in the Soviet Ukraine; and Mykhaylo Ivchenko (1890–1939), whose stories show a profound tragic sense.

Naturalism was ably represented by the scholar-linguist Borys Antonenko-Davydovych (b. 1899) in his courageous novel *Smert* (1928; death), whose hero cannot reconcile his being Ukrainian with an acceptance of the Bolshevik revolution. EXPRESSIONISM received its due in Ivan Dniprovsky's (1895–1934) collection of stories *Za rady neyi* (1928; for her sake), dealing with the horrors and tragedies of war and revolution.

In contrast to the ornate impressionism and the explosive expressionism of his contemporaries, Olexa Slisarenko (1891–1937) presented sharply drawn characters, situations, and plots intensified by vivid imagery, as in the novel *Zlamany gvynt* (1929; the broken screw). Other significant writers were Yury Smolych (1900–1976), whose forte was adventure stories; Volodymyr Gzhytsky (1895–1973), known chiefly for the novel *Chorne ozero* (1929; the black lake), which deals with the Russian subjugation of the peoples of Asia; Oles Dosvitny (1891–1934), author of several novels with exotic settings; and the satirist Ostap Vyshnya (1889–1956), writer of popular tales and stories, a selection of which was translated into English under the title *Hard Times* (1981).

Drama

While the plays of Volodymyr Vynnychenko were being staged in the theaters of western Europe, Les Kurbas (1887–1942) founded the Berezil Theater (1922–34) in Kiev (moved to Kharkiv [Kharkov] in 1926). Kurbas's work with young dramatists, especially Mykola Kulish (1892–1942), stimulated and guided the development of the Ukrainian drama. Kurbas's liquidation during a subsequent purge and Kulish's arrest and deportation irreparably harmed the drama. Overcoming early ethnographic impulses, Kulish had created an impressive variety of expressionistic plays, most of which were banned from the Ukrainian stage. Another important, original playwright was the prolific Ivan Kocherha (1881–1952). A representative of SOCIALIST REALISM was Olexandr Kornychuk (b. 1902).

Poetry

The first group of poets of the interwar period were the symbolists, the most important of whom was Pavlo Tychyna (1891–1967). Tychyna displayed occasional flashes of genius even later, while writing within the framework of Socialist Realism. Other symbolists were Dmytro Zahul (1890–1938), whose career was cut short by exile to Russia's polar region; Yakiv Savchenko, whose verse is characterized by a morbid pessimism and mysticism, and who suffered the same fate as Zahul; Volodymyr Kobylyansky (1895–1919), whose only collection of verse, *My dar* (1920; my gift), was written under the influence of the German romantics; and Volodymyr Svidzinsky (1885–1941), whose poetry is characterized by vivid imagery and the selective use of rare words.

The most significant contribution to Ukrainian poetry of the period was made by the neoclassicists of Kiev, whose outstanding representative was Maxym Rylsky. They drew poetic sustenance from classical antiquity and modeled themselves on the French Parnassians; refusing to accede to the "revolutionary" demands of the time, they championed clarity, balance, and harmony. Their theoretician was Mykola Zerov. Other neoclassicists were the literary scholar Pavlo Fylypovych (1891–1937), the erudite critic and translator Mykhaylo Dray-Khmara (1889–1938), and Oswald Burghardt (1891–1947), who later used the pseudonym Yury Klen.

Impressionism in the 1920s was represented chiefly by the eclectic philosophical poetry of Yevhen Pluzhnyk (1898–1936). Futurism found expression in the often cacophonous and perplexing whimsical verse of Mykhaylo Semenko and the stylistically complex poetic compositions of Geo Shkurupy (1903–1934). Expressionism was typified by the fiery verse of the poet-novelist Todos Osmachka. Neoromanticism was championed by the popular Olexa Vlysko (1908–1934), whose recklessly enthusiastic and often poignantly critical verse brought about his execution by the regime. The poet-translator Mykola Bazhan (b. 1904) was to some extent a neoromanticist, but the most popular representative of this trend was Volodymyr Sosyura (1894–1965).

Between the two world wars the western Ukraine produced many powerful, original poets. Foremost was Bohdan Ihor Antonych (1909–1937), whose verse, characterized by whimsical metaphors and striking nature imagery, proclaims the unity of all things.

The émigré centers of Prague and Warsaw included such poets as the mystic Olexa Stefanovych (1899–1970), known for his historical verse, as was Yury Darahan (1894–1926), whose collection Sahaydak (1926; the quiver) glorified the ancient Ukrainian princes and cossacks; Leonid Mosendz (1897–1948), a short-story writer as well as author of philosophical poems that strive to synthesize the Ukraine with western Europe; and Oxana Lyaturynska (1902–1981), whose exquisite poetic miniatures deal with Ukrainian mythology and the heroic past. Of greater importance were Oleh Olzhych (pseud. of Oleh Kandyba, 1908–1944), whose idealistic, martial call for the liberation of the Ukraine was cut short by his death in the Sachsenhausen concentration camp; and another Nazi victim, Olena Teliha (1907–1942), whose lyric poetry, written under the influence of Lesya Ukrayinka, combines tenderness with revolutionary fervor. Significant poetic stature was achieved by Bohdan Kravtsiv (1904–1975) and Yury Lypa. Perhaps the most strikingly visionary poet of this generation was Yevhen Malanyuk (1897–1968).

After World War II

The ravages of the war brought about a relaxation of literary controls in the Soviet Ukraine. In 1946, however, charges of nationalism were once more leveled against many writers and critics, and in 1949 there began a campaign against "cosmopolitanism," that is, Jewish writers. These purges continued until the "thaw" period following Stalin's death in 1953.

Since the reimposition of strict literary controls around 1964 the phenomenon of samvydav ("self-publishing") has appeared. Literary, political, and even scholarly works are circulated clandestinely, and later often published in the West. The first major samvydav collection of both scholarly and literary merit was Vyacheslav Chornovil's (b. 1938) Lykho z rozumu (1967; The Chornovil Papers, 1968).

In September 1945 the Ukrainian Artists' Movement was established by émigrés in Fürth, in Allied-occupied Germany. By the mid-1950s the center of emigration had shifted to America, where the Ukrainian Writers' Association in Exile, known as Slovo, was formed.

The number of émigré writers and readers is steadily declining as a result of the natural course of assimilation. There is, however, ample evidence of growing scholarly interest in Ukrainian literature. Thus, some form of survival of Ukrainian literature in exile appears to be assured.

Fiction

During the war and immediately afterward, many Soviet Ukrainian writers of the older generation returned to literature, among them Yury Yanovsky, Petro Punch, and the filmmaker Olexandr Dovzhenko (1894–1956), whose autobiographical novel Zacharovana Desna (1954; abridged tr., The Enchanted Desna, 1970) is a masterpiece.

Quite naturally, the "Great Patriotic War" (World War II) and the advantages of the communist system became the topics of the day, as evidenced by Oles HONCHAR's messianic Praporonostsi (2 vols., 1947–48; The Standard Bearers, 2 vols., 1948–50) and Mykhaylo Stelmakh's (1912–1983) stylistically accomplished novel Krov lyudska—ne vodytsya (1957; Let the Blood of Man Not Flow, 1962). The historical novel once more became popular, with such works as Olexandr Ilchenko's (b. 1909) Kozatskomu rodu nema perevodu (1958; there is no end to the cossack breed) and the novels of Semen Sklyarenko (1901–1962), especially Svyatoslav (1959; Svyatoslav) and Volodymyr (1962; Volodymyr), set in the Kievan-Rus period.

Of considerable merit is the novel Dyky med (1963; wild honey) by Leonid Pervomaysky (pseud. of Illya Hurevych, 1908–1973), despite the author's annoying restraint in probing the metaphysical and spiritual dimensions of life. Also quite talented is Roman Ivanychuk (b. 1929), as evidenced by his historical novel Malvy (1968; the hollyhocks), but his more recent work displays conspicuous conformism. A leading contemporary Soviet Ukrainian novelist is Pavlo Zahrebelny (b. 1924); among his several monumental novels, Dyvo (1968; the marvel) is a Küunstlerroman set in the 10th and 20th cs. A subtle mixture of religious mysticism and science fiction marks the work of Oles Berdnyk (b. 1927), who has been jailed and whose work has been banned. The clandestinely published autobiographical novel Bilmo (1971; Cataract, 1976) by Mykhaylo Osadchy (b. 1936) is a moving account of human suffering. The work of Iryna Vilde (1907–1982) is significant as an example of Socialist Realism. Outstanding younger Soviet Ukrainian fiction writers are Petro Uhlyarenko (b. 1922), Hryhir Tyutyunnyk (b. 1931), and Yury Shcherbak (b. 1934).

Émigré prose is represented by such masters as Ulas Samchuk (b. 1905), who established his reputation as a novelist with the monumental trilogy Volyn (1932–37; Vol-hynia); and the poet-essayist Vasyl Barka (b. 1908), whose powerful novel Zhovty knyaz (1962; yellow prince) deals with the artificially created famine in the Ukraine (1932–33). His novel in verse, Svidok dlya sontsya shestykrylykh (1981; the witness for the sun of seraphim), is an attempt to re-Christianize Ukrainian literature. Other significant émigré novelists are Ivan Bahryany (1906–1963), whose Tyhrolovy (1947; The Hunters and the Hunted, 1955) enjoyed considerable popularity; Viktor Domontovych (pseud. of Viktor Petrov, 1894–1969) with Doktor Seraphicus (1947; Doctor Seraphicus); and especially Todos Osmachka, whose novels, such as Rotonda dushohubtsiv (1956; Red Assassins, 1959), re-create the inferno of the Ukraine's recent past.

Drama

The de facto colonial status of the Soviet Ukraine on the one hand, and the émigré existence of the Ukrainians in the free world on the other, precludes any real development of Ukrainian theater. Following the war, Olexandr Kornychuk continued to write Socialist Realist plays. Ivan Kocherha's historical drama *Yaroslav Mudry* (1944; Yaroslav the Wise) and his philosophical drama *Istyna* (1948; the truth) are substantial contributions. Also of interest are the plays of Olexandr Levada (b. 1909), especially *Faust i smert* (1960; Faust and death), which transposes the Faust theme to the space age.

Poetry

Among the major poets who resumed writing after the war were Maxym Rylsky, Pavlo Tychyna, and the prolific poet-critic Andry Malyshko (1912–1970). At that time, too, the Soviet war hero and now dissident Mykola RUDENKO began his career with such collections as *Z pokhodu* (1947; from the campaign) and *Leningradtsi* (1948; the people of Leningrad), which contrast strongly with his contemporary clandestine output, published in the West.

The greatest contribution to postwar Ukrainian poetry was made by the Generation of the 1960s, who, free from the fear of terror as a result of Khrushchev's de-Stalinization policies, began to assert their individualism. The leading poets of this generation are Ivan DRACH; Lina KOSTENKO, whose personal verse such as the collection *Mandrivky sertsya* (1961; the wanderings of the heart) as well as the historical novel in verse *Marusya Churay* (1979; Marusya Churay) display great power; and Vasyl Symonenko (1935–1963), whose passionately patriotic poetry found favor at home and abroad. Other outstanding poets are Vitaly Korotych (b. 1936) and Mykola Vinhranovsky (b. 1936).

Some of the best Soviet Ukrainian poetry is published only abroad, including the collections *Pidsumovuyuch movchannya* (1971; reassessing silence) by Ihor Kalynets (b. 1939) and *Svicha v. svichadi* (1977; a candle in the holder) by Vasyl STUS.

Ukrainian poetic output in the West continues. Still active are members of the older generation, such as Volodymyr Yaniv (b. 1908); the journalist and lyric poet Olexa Hay-Holovko (b. 1914); Ostap Tarnavsky (b. 1917), primarily a poet but also an essayist and short-story writer; and the poet-scholars Yar Slavutych (b. 1918) and Ihor Kachurovsky (b. 1918). Vadym Lesych (1909–1982) was a forerunner of the younger generation of poets, most of whom belong to the New York Group; outstanding among them are Yuriy Tarnavsky (b. 1934), Emma Andiyevska (b. 1931), Bohdan Boychuk (b. 1927), and Bohdan Rubchak (b. 1935). Bohdan Nyzhankivsky (b. 1909), who sometimes uses the pseudonym Babay, is the most talented contemporary Ukrainian humorist and satirist.

Ukrainian Literature since 1980

The historical events of the late 1980s and early 1990s have had a profound impact on the development of Ukrainian literature. Gorbachev's policy of glasnost and perestroika eventually led to the birth of the "Rukh" (movement), an umbrella organization for reformers that initially defined itself as "the Popular Movement in Support of Perestroika." Rukh was the child of poets. Its nine-man coordinating committee, which came into being in Kiev early in 1989, included personalities of Ukrainian literature such as the renowned poets Ivan DRACH and Dmytro Pavlychko (b. 1929), the literary scholar Vyacheslav Bryukhovetsky (b. 1947), the literary critic and editor Vitaly Donchyk (b. 1932), the writer Anatoly

Shevchenko (b. 1932), and the theater specialist Les Tanyuk (b. 1938). Rukh held its founding congress in Kiev in September 1989, with 1,109 delegates attending, representing some 280,000 members. Ivan Drach was elected as its first chairman, and the noted novelist Volodymyr Yavorivsky (b. 1942) chairman of its "Grand Council." The emergence of Rukh was a most important factor in Ukrainian literary and cultural life. The movement provided vigor and vitality to Ukrainian literature and set new directions for its future development. Additional important events that influenced literary life in Ukraine are the proclamation of Ukraine's independence on 24 August 1991 by the Ukrainian Rada (Parliament), and the subsequent overwhelming affirmation of that proclamation by a popular referendum. Perhaps the most important factor in the recent development of Ukrainian literature, however, was the tragedy of Chernobyl on 26 April 1986, which not only found wide reverberation in Ukrainian literature, both in Ukraine and in the diaspora, but also gave rise to a rage that engendered determined resistance.

As a result of these events, several important and very positive developments have occurred. Freedom of expression prevails, and the phenomenon of "dissidentism" has been relegated to history; the restoration of hundreds of writers whose names were taboo during the so-called era of stagnation is taking place—the Kiev-based literary scholar Mykola Zhulynsky (b. 1940) speaks of a total of 300 such individuals; and the task of the inclusion of Ukrainian émigré writers, both dead and alive, into the mainstream of literary life in Ukraine has been initiated. In light of these developments one can speak of a unification process of Ukrainian literature. If allowed to continue, this process will lead to an unprecedented unity of Ukrainian literature. For the first time in history, Ukrainian literature will be without any artificial barriers or divisions and without "forgotten" names or forbidden books.

Among the former dissidents who are now active are the poet Ihor Kalynets, the poet and essayist Yevhen Sverstyuk (b. 1928), the poet and critic Ivan Svitlychny (1929–1992), and the poet and novelist Mykola RUDENKO, who recently returned to Ukraine from the U.S. Among the deceased victims of Stalinism who have been rehabilitated are the writer and political activist Mykola Khvylovy, the dramatist Mykola Kulish, and the neoclassical poets Mykola Zerov and Mykhaylo Dray-Khmara, as well as the most recent victim, Vasyl STUS, whose posthumously published collection *Doroha bolyu* (1990; the way of pain) has been received with great acclaim. Heading the list of rehabilitated dead émigré literati is the novelist and dramatist Volodymyr Vynnychenko. He is followed by Yevhen Malanyuk, Olena Teliha, and Oleh Olzhych (pseud. of Oleh Kandyba)—all known previously as "bourgeois nationalist" poets—the neoclassicist poet Yury Klen (pseud. of Oswald Burkhardt), and the novelist Ivan Bahryany. The living émigré writers now appearing in print in Ukraine include Bohdan Boychuk and Bohdan Rubchak (b. 1935), both of the New York Group of Ukrainian poets, the Rio de Janeiro-based poet and dramatist Vira Vovk (pseud. of Vira Selyanska, b. 1926), whose plays have helped invigorate contemporary theater in Ukraine, and the poet and essayist Ostap Tarnavsky (1917–1992), the president of SLOVO, The Association of Ukrainian Writers in Exile.

Poetry

Traditionally the strongest genre in Ukrainian literature, poetry has experienced a tremendous revival in the late 1980s. A whole new coterie of poets known as *visimdesyatnyky* (the generation of the eighties) has come into being, united in love for the Ukrainian language and in their zest for innovation and experimentation, but at the same time highly individualistic and distinct, each with his or her own poetic profile. The leading voices of this generation are Yury Andrukhovych (b. 1960), Natalka Bilotserkivets (b. 1954), Pavlo Hirnyk (b. 1956), Oleksandr Hrytsenko (b. 1957), Viktor Kordun (b. 1946), Oleh Lysheba (b. 1949), Sofiya Maydanska (b. 1948), Viktor Neborak (b. 1961), Oksana Pakhlovska (b. 1956), Mykola Ryabchuk (b. 1953), Volodymyr Tsybulko (b. 1964), Oksana Zabuzhko (b. 1960), and Ihor Rymaruk (b. 1958), whose collection *Nichni holosy* (1991; voices of the night) reflects most succinctly the new directions of contemporary Ukrainian poetry.

Especially noteworthy are five women poets whose most important works were published between 1988 and 1990. Sofiya Maydanska's *Povnolittya nadiyi* (1988; hope coming of age), a collection of subjective lyrical poetry written in an optimistic mood celebrating life and beauty of nature, and her *Osvidchennya* (1990; declaration), which consists of seventy letters written to the reader, are fine examples of her art. The pithy and often compressed form of these poems enables the author to communicate to the reader in a highly poetic manner her intellectual and social concerns and her love for her country and her people. A vivid imagination coupled with a pleasant sense of humor characterizes the collection *Chayna tser-emoniya* (1990; tea ceremony) by Iryna Zhylenko, while Oksana Zabuzhko's *Dyryhent ostannoyi svichky* (1990; the bearer of the last candle) is informed by feelings of strong anger, a sense of profound sorrow, and an all-pervasive touch of bitter-sweet irony. Noteworthy is also Mariya Vlad's (b. 1940) poetry, such as her collection *Virshi ta poemy* (1990; poems and narrative poems), which is steeped in the natural beauty of the Hutsul region and its rich folklore tradition, but transcends aesthetically its regional confines. Lina KOSTENKO's *Vybrane* (1989; selected works) occupies a special place in this poetry written by women. Characterized by a universal, human concern, these works display no marked feminist tendencies; they are, for the most part, nonideological, apolitical, and intensely personal.

An important event in the annals of contemporary Ukrainian poetry is the publication of *Ikar na metelykovykh krylakh* (Icarus on the Wings of a Butterfly, 1991) by Vasyl Holoborodko (b. 1942), who made his literary debut in the 1960s, but whose work had been suppressed. The tragic history of Ukraine and the sufferings of its people form the subject matter of this collection, in which the author's personal reminiscences and observations are interspersed with historical motifs. Equally moving is Hryhory Chubay's (1949–1982) poetry with the revealing title *Hovoryty, movchary i hovoryty znovu* (1989; to speak, to be silent, and to speak again), which expresses the tragic ethos of the 1970s, while the collections *Pohulyanka odyntsem* (1990; walking alone) by Mykola Vorobyov (b. 1941) and *Khymera* (1989; chimera) by Vasyl Ruban (b. 1942) display an interesting bent for experimentation with language. Two books by Hennady Moroz (b. 1948), *Veresnevi dni* (1985; days of September) and especially his latest, *Zemlya* (1989; the earth), show great promise.

The thematic diversity of contemporary Ukrainian poetry is astounding. Religious themes and motifs abound. While some poets champion Christianity, others bemoan the passing of the pagan age and accuse Christianity of eliminating it. There are frequent allusions to ecological problems that beset contemporary Ukraine, and the vicissitudes of life in the 20th c. are confronted

there. The Ukrainian language and its sorrowful state are the subject of many poems and Ukraine's tragic plight throughout its history is acknowledged. Poetry in the 1980s and 1990s appears to serve as a form of catharsis, which enables both the poet and the reader to come to terms with personal and national dilemmas.

Fiction

Just like poetry, Ukrainian prose experienced a revival in the latter part of the 1980s. Roman Ivanychuk, author of significant historical prose, wrote a number of short stories, and was awarded the Shevchenko Prize (1985) for his latest novels, *Voda z kamenyu* (1982; water from the stone) and *Chetverty vymir* (1984; the fourth dimension). The prolific prize-winning novelist Yury Mushketyk (b. 1929) attracted considerable attention with his work *Yasa* (1987; Yasa), which celebrates in a heightened poetic manner the Ukrainian Cossack past. The novel portrays the Cossacks as fierce and brave warriors and their leaders as cultured, intelligent people whose heroic struggle against czarist Russian imperialism flows from the natural desire for freedom and sovereignty. The Chernobyl catastrophe, which received its due in poetry, notably by Drach, Kostenko, and Maydanska, among others, was best captured in prose by Volodymyr Yavorivsky's (b. 1942) novel *Mariya z polynom u kintsi stolittya* (1988; Maria with wormwood at the end of the century). Divided into 109 brief chapters (some of them less than half of a page), the work succeeds in conveying the suffering and sorrow of the simple people affected by the disaster. A kind of neo-Rousseauism informs the work of Oleksandr Hyzha (b. 1936) as evident from his two novels *Hlyboka mezha* (1987; the deep furrow) and its sequel, *Zhytni plachi* (1990; the laments of rye), which portray the Ukrainian peasants as simple yet noble human beings whose contact with the soil keeps them pure and unspoiled. In sharp contrast to the people are the dehumanizing forces of the collective system that cripple the human soul and destroy humanity.

Mykola Olynyk's (b. 1923) novel *Dochka Prometeya* (1990; daughter of Prometheus) and Valentyn Tarnavsky's (b. 1951) *Porozhny pedestal* (1990; the empty pedestal) are also works that will stand the test of time.

The thematic range of Ukrainian prose is just as wide as that of poetry. Traditional style alternates with "neo-avant-garde" mannerisms. Young authors attempt to establish themselves, and the older ones strive to reinvigorate or to restructure the creative process.

The Essay

The other avenues of literary expression—the essay and literary criticism—also flourish. Of special importance is Oles HONCHAR's *Chym zhyvemo: Na shlyakhakh do ukrayinskoho vidrodzhennya* (1991; how we live: on the path to a Ukrainian rebirth), a collection of essays, speeches, interviews, and notes written on various occasions from 1966 to 1991, which reflect the Zeitgeist of the three decades and chronicle the struggle of Ukrainian intellectuals for cultural and national independence; and Valery SHEVCHUK's *Doroha v tysyachu rokiv* (1990; the way into the millennium), which seeks to portray a deeper understanding of Ukrainian history and culture. A new rigorous scholarly approach is seen in Ivan Dzyuba's (b. 1931) examination of Taras Shevchenko's relations with the Slavophiles, *U vsyakoho svoya dolya* (1989; each has his own fate), and in Anatoly Pohribny's (b. 1942) trenchant studies of the writer and lexicographer Borys Hrinchenko (1863–1910), published in 1988 and 1990.

The new freedom has given rise to lively literary discussions on the pages of the *Literaturna Ukrayina* and in other journals. To reflect more accurately the new reality, some journals have changed their names. *Radyanske Literaturoznavstvo* (Soviet literary studies) has become *Slovo i Chas* (word and time), and many new literary journals and magazines have been founded. Among them is *Svito-Vyd* (the organ of the Kiev branch of the Writers Union and the New York Group, the first issue of which appeared in 1990), *Ternopil* (founded in January 1991), and a number of children's magazines.

Drama

The drama is traditionally the weakest genre of Ukrainian literature. Centuries of statelessness and the colonial status of Ukraine within the Soviet Union have precluded the development of a bona fide national theater. Such talented dramatists as Volodymyr Vynnychenko, Mykola Kulish, and to a lesser degree Ivan Kocherha were frequently not afforded the opportunity to see their plays on Ukrainian stages. On the other hand, the works of Oleksandr Kornychuk, written and produced in accordance with the doctrine of SOCIALIST REALISM, enjoyed considerable success, as did the plays of Mykola Zarudny (b. 1921), who is still active in the contemporary Ukrainian theater.

Among the leading dramatists in the 1980s are Larysa Khorolets (b. 1948), whose plays, such as *Trety* (1982; the third) and *V okeani bezvisti* (1985; in the ocean of obscurity), enjoy great popularity and have been translated into several languages; Oleksy Kolomiyets (b. 1919), whose plays *Uby leva* (1984; kill the lion) and *Zlyva* (1985; deluge) have received wide acclaim; and Vasyl Melnyk (b. 1937), author of numerous one-act plays, among them the vaudeville comedy *Molodyata* (the young couple) and the historical drama *Dolya i pisnya* (fate and song), about the life of the bard of Bukovyna, Yury Fedkovych (1834–1888).

Some contemporary dramatists write both for the theater and the film industry. Among these are Bohdan Chaly (b. 1924), Ihor Malyshevsky (b. 1936), Vsevolod Nestayko (b. 1930), and Yury Shcherbak. Nelya Sheyko-Medvedyeva (b. 1947) is successful as a children's dramatist as attested by her collection of plays, *Kvitka shchyastya* (1986; flower of happiness), and as a scholar of the theater and drama.

In an article aptly entitled "Istorychna patoheneza ukrayinskoyi dramy" (the historical pathogenesis of Ukrainian drama), published in the November 1991 issue of the journal *Sučasnist'* (Newark, New Jersey), Lina Kostenko analyzes the "catastrophic" state of Ukrainian theater and drama. Although focusing on the negatives of past and present, she nonetheless predicts an imminent revival of both theater and drama in Ukraine.

Even since the era of Gorbachev's glasnost (1987-90) and especially after the December 1991 referendum in which over 90% of the population of Ukraine voted for independence, there has been a constant and steady process of the unification of Ukrainian literature. Many writers, whose works were proscribed for various reasons, have been returned to the canon of Ukrainian literature. Similarly, the works of Ukrainian émigré authors, previously banned, have now become generally accessible to both scholar and layman in Ukraine. Ukrainian literature of the so-called "Near Abroad" (i.e., in such countries as Poland, the Czech and Slovak republics, Romania, and the former republics of Yugoslavia) has become more closely linked with the literature of Ukraine.

Freedom and democracy have had a great impact on Ukrainian literature of the 1990s. There is a new spirit of creativity embraced by a young generation of poets and critics known as the *visimdesyatnyky* (the generation of the eighties). Ranging from the irreverently vulgar to the child-like naive, from tradition to post-modernism and post avant-gardism with a penchant for outrageous experimentalism, these artists reflect a rich variety of styles, techniques, and thematic arrangements of great intensity. The best-known example is a group of avant-garde poets known as *Bu-Ba-Bu* (Burlesque, Farce, Buffoonery), which was formed in the 1980s by Yuri Andrukhovych (b. 1960), Oleksandr Irvanets (b. 1961), and Viktor Neborak (b. 1961). Other groups of intellectual rebels are *Propala hramota* (The Lost Charter), *Luhosad* (The Meadow Orchard) and *Nova degeneratisiya* (The New Degeneration), which has its roots in the Ukrainian futurism of the 1920s. A more traditionally oriented group of young writers is the Kyiv-based *Tvorcha Asotsiyatsiya "500"* (The Creative Association "500"), which published an anthology of Ukrainian literature after 1991 called *Imennyk* (the noun).

Along with the creative ferment there is also a spirit of cultural crisis and fin-de-siècle brought about by generational conflicts, social instabilities and economic woes of present-day Ukraine. Nonetheless, amidst these inimical and divisive forces thrives an energy and passion which seeks to come to terms with Ukraine's immediate past as well as embrace the Zeitgeist of the imminent millennium.

BIBLIOGRAPHY: Manning, C. A., *Ukrainian Literature: Studies of the Leading Authors* (1944); Luckyj, G. S. N., *Literary Politics in the Soviet Ukraine: 1917–1934* (1956); Andrusyshen, C. H., and Kirkconnell, W., eds. *The Ukrainian Poets: 1189–1962* (1962); Dzyuba, I., *Internationalism or Russification?: A Study in the Soviet Nationalities Problem*, 2nd ed. (1970); Shabliovsky, Y., *Ukrainian Literature through the Ages* (1970); Čyzevs'kyj, D., *A History of Ukrainian Literature* (1975); Luckyj, G. S. N., "Ukrainian Literature," in Luckyj, G. S. N., ed., *Discordant Voices: The Non-Russian Soviet Literatures* (1975): 127–38; Mihailovich, V. D., et al., eds., *Modern Slavic Literature* (1976), Vol. II: 448–532; Kuchar, R. V., "Ukrainian Émigré Literature after 1945," *UQ*, 33 (1977): 265–70; Pytlowany, M., "Continuity and Innovation in the Poetry of the New York Group," *JUKGS*, 2, 1 (1977): 3–21; Shtohryn, D. M., "Ukrainian Literature in the United States," in *Ethnic Literatures since 1776* (1978): 569–90; Kuchar, R. V., "Ukrainian Clandestine Literature in the USSR," *UQ*, 34 (1978): 276–82; Tarnawsky, M., "Ukrainian Literature for the American Reader," *WLT*, 52 (1978): 235–39; Grabowicz, G., "New Directions in Ukrainian Poetry in the United States," and Rudnytzky, L., "Commentary," in Magocsi, P. R., ed., *The Ukrainian Experience in the United States: A Symposium* (1979): 156–78; Tarnawsky, O., "Dissident Poets in Ukraine," *JUKS*, 6, 2 (1981): 17–27; Rubchak, B., "Homes As Shells: Ukrainian Émigré Poetry," in Rozumnyj, J., ed., *New Soil, Old Roots* (1983): 87–123; Zyla, W. T., "Recent Developments of Ukrainian Letters in the United States," *Ethnic Forum*, 3, 1–2 (1983): 48–65; Bahry, R. M., ed., *Echoes of Glasnost in Soviet Ukraine* (1989): 123–29, 151–70; Sajewych, G., and A. Sorokowski, eds., *The Popular Movement of Ukraine for Restructuring* (1989); Rudnytzky, L., "A Miracle in Continuity: Christian Themes and Motifs in Soviet Ukrainian Literature," *UQ*, 46 (1990): 34–44; Rubchak, B., "Because We Have No Time: Recent Ukrainian Poetry," *Agni*, 33 (1991): 278–304; Onyshkevych,

L. M. L., "On the Stages of Ukraine 1990: From Sholom Aleichem to Mykola Kulish," *Soviet and East European Performance: Drama, Theater, Film*, 11 (1991): 49–57; Luckyj, G. S. N., *Ukrainian Literature in the Twentieth Century: A Reader's Guide* (1992); Hogan, E., et al., eds., *From Three Worlds: New Ukrainian Writing* (1996); Čyževs'kyj, D., *A History of Ukrainian Literature*, 2nd ed. (1997); Lindheim, R. and G. S. N. Luckyj, eds., *Towards an Intellectual History of Ukraine: An Anthology of Ukrainian Thought from 1710 to 1995* (1996); Horbatsch, A.-H., *Die Ukraine im Spiegel ihrer Literatur: Dichtung als Überlebensweg eines Volkes. Beiträge* (1997)

—LEONID RUDNYTZKY

UKRAYINKA, Lesya

(pseud. of Laryssa Kosach Kvitka) Ukrainian poet, dramatist, short-story writer, translator, and critic, b. 13 Feb. 1871, Novohrad-Volynsky; d. 19 July 1913, Surami, Georgia

U.'s mother, Olena Pchilka (pseud, of Olha Drahomanov Kosach, 1849–1930), was a prominent writer. Her father, Petro Kosach (1841–1909), was an intellectual and patron of the arts. U. spent her early childhood in Volhynia, and the great natural beauty of that part of the Ukraine made a lasting impression on her. In 1881 she was stricken with tuberculosis; in a vain search for a cure, she later traveled all over Europe and even to Egypt. These travels, however, did enable her to acquire firsthand knowledge of various foreign cultures and literatures and to become proficient in several languages. In 1907 she married Klyment Kvitka (1880–1953), a court official, musicologist, and cultural ethnographer.

U. began to write at the age of nine. Her first three collections of poetry—*Na krylakh pisen* (1893; on the wings of songs), *Dumy i mriyi* (1899; thoughts and dreams), and *Vidhuky* (1902; echoes)—established her as the leading young Ukrainian poet of her time.

After being under the strong influence of Heinrich Heine, whose *Book of Songs* (1827) she translated in 1892, U. wrote poetry characterized by a wide range of emotions, from quiet sorrow and gentle yearning to defiant despair and proud scorn. Fighting a losing battle against an implacable disease, she challenged death and refused to submit to pain. Typical examples of her poetry of the 1890s are "Contra spem spero" (1893; "Contra Spem Spero," 1950) and "Horyt moye sertse" (1899; "My Heart Is Ablaze," 1963), which are imbued with her strong will to live and her determination to fight against oppression and enslavement.

U. was the first Ukrainian dramatist to go beyond strictly national subject matter. Her achievements in the drama were anticipated by her long dramatic poems. For example, *Robert Bryus, shotlyandsky korol* (1894; *Robert Bruce, King of Scotland*, 1968) glorifies the struggle for Scottish independence, showing U.'s increasing concern for social and civic problems. *Oderzhyma* (1901; a woman possessed) reveals her intense religious feelings and profound capacity to experience and express love and suffering.

Thematically connected with *Oderzhyma* is a cycle of works set in Old Testament times and during the early Christian era. It includes a short dialogue entitled "V domu roboty, v krayini nevoli" (1906; in a house of labor, in a country of servitude), the drama *Vavylonsky polon* (1908; *The Babylonian Captivity*, 1916),

and its sequel, *Na ruyinakh* (1908; *On the Ruins*, 1950), which poignantly express the idea that a nation remains spiritually strong as long as it struggles to survive. To this category also belong the play *U katakombakh* (1906; *In the Catacombs*, 1971), about the quest of a Christian neophyte for self-realization; *Rufin i Pristsilla* (1911; Rufin and Priscilla) and *Advokat Martian* (1913; *Martianus the Advocate*, 1950), both of which deal with the conflict between religious convictions and love; and *Na poli krovy* (1911; on the field of blood), a sensitive probing of the psychology of Judas.

Other critical periods in history that play a prominent part in U.'s dramas are classical antiquity, the time of Mohammed, the Middle Ages, and the era of the Pilgrim settlers. All these works are historically objective and at the same time allude to Ukrainian problems at the turn of the century.

Quite different in content and style are U.'s naturalistic play *Blakytna troyanda* (1908; the blue rose), which deals in the manner of Ibsen and HAUPTMANN with inherited mental illness; the neoromantic dramatic fairy tale *Lisova pisnya* (1912; *Forest Song*, 1950), a paean to the beauty of the landscape and folklore of her regional homeland; and the psychological historical drama *Boyarynya* (1914; *The Noblewoman*, 1950), her most cogent and compelling statement on patriotism and the right of national self-determination. Of importance also is her rather original treatment of the Don Juan theme in the play *Kaminny hospodar* (1912; *The Stone Host*, 1968).

U.'s fiction consists of a large number of short stories, tales, and an unfinished novel, *Ekbal-hanem* (1913; Ekbal-hanem), which juxtaposes magnificent descriptions of its Egyptian setting with the waning beauty of an Arab woman and provides a keen psychological insight into the soul of the woman.

In addition to her work on Heine and her critical essays on various poets, U. also did highly accomplished translations from the works of Byron, Homer, Hugo, Turgenev, and Shakespeare; she also rendered into Ukrainian a number of Egyptian and Italian folksongs, as well as Indian epic tales.

Through the strength and the beauty of her verse, the psychological depth and thematic range of her dramatic works, the soundness of her critical writings, and most of all, her personal courage, U. established herself as an artist for all times.

FURTHER WORKS: *Nad morem: Opovidannya* (1908); *Kassandra* (1908); *Yohanna, zhinka Khusova* (1910); *Tvory* (1911); *Poeziyi* (1914); *Narodni melodiyi* (1917); *Starodavnya istoria skhidnykh narodiv* (1918); *Tvory* (10 vols., 1923–25); *Tvory* (12 vols., 1927–30); *Povne vydannya tvoriv* (6 vols., 1939); *Neopublikovani tvory* (1947); *Tvory* (5 vols., 1951–56); *Tvory* (10 vols., 1963–65); *Zibrannya tvoriv* (12 vols., 1975–78); *Poemy i dramy* (1980); *Dramatychni poemy* (1983); *Tvory v dvokh tomakh* (2 vols., 1986-87). FURTHER WORKS IN ENGLISH: *Spirit of Flame: A Collection of the Works of L. U.* (1950); *L. U.: Life and Work; Selected Works* (1968); *Hope: Selected Poetry* (1975, bilingual)

BIBLIOGRAPHY: Bida, C., ed., *L. U.: Life and Work; Selected Works* (1968): 4–84; Pazuniak, N., "L. U.: Ukraine's Greatest Poetess," *UQ*, 3 (1971): 237–52; Zyla, W., "A Ukrainian Version of Scotland's Liberator, Bruce," *SSL*, 11 (1973): 3–12; Čyževs'kyj, D., *A History of Ukrainian Literature* (1975): 614–18; Rudnyćkyj, J. B., "Africa in the Life and Work of L. U.," in Cadot, M., et al., *Proceedings of the 6th Congress of the International Comparative Literature Association* (1975): 643–47; Mihailovich, V. D., et al., eds., *Modern Slavic Literatures* (1976), Vol. II: 518–23; Zyla, W., "A Prophetess Fated to Be Disbelieved: *Cassandra* by L. U.," *Mitteilungen*, 14 (1977): 134–43

—LEONID RUDNYTZKY

ULTRAISM

Ultraism, a term derived from Latin *ultra* (beyond), was a short-lived but important literary movement which shaped Spanish and, to a certain extent, Spanish-American poetry between roughly 1918 and 1924, that is, between the disintegration of MODERNISM and the emergence of Federico GARCÍA LORCA's Generation of 1927. There were numerous ultraist manifestos, almost as many as poets belonging to the core group—and ultraism was not really a formal school with coherent principles of its own. Rather, it was an artistic movement that, nurtured by all the major isms of the time—FUTURISM, DADAISM, CUBISM, EXPRESSIONISM, Vicente HUIDOBRO's creationism—sought the incorporation of Hispanic literature into the mainstream of European art, an ambitious task, later completed by the 1927 Spanish group of poets.

Like other isms, ultraism vigorously attacked and rejected the norms and forms of the past while advocating new, more effective means of expression and more abrasive stylistic principles that would capture the free and often irrational flow of the poet's imagination. Guided by the prevailing idea of poetry as a game played by language and imagination, and strongly inspired by an iconoclastic spirit, the ultraist poet, with humor and frivolity, produced poems in which form always became an end in itself. This formalistic imbalance, of course, was deliberately caused by the poet's excessive manipulation of metaphor and by his capricious and often trivial elaboration of the poem not only as a verbal object but also as a visual representation of its content. Thus, ultraist poems would, for instance, assume the typographic form of a horse, a tree, a hat, and so forth. Ultraism also found poetic inspiration in trains, airplanes, automobiles, and many other creations of modern technology.

Fervor alone was not enough to produce notable and lasting works of art. On the whole, ultraism, with very few notable exceptions, such as the early poetry of Jorge Luis BORGES, Gerardo Diego (1896-1987), and Juan Larrea (1895–1982), was a sterile movement—in part because it was limited to poetry. Curiously, the ultraists, both in Spain and Latin America, never tried to work with either the novel or the drama. And most of the poems were not conceived as parts of a larger, major work, to be embodied in a book. As a result, a considerable amount of that poetic output has remained scattered and forgotten in the pages of the movement's journals, of which the most important were *Ultra, Grecia, Cervantes*, and *Alfar*. Two other reasons for the group's limited achievement were its short duration (it lasted no more than six years) and the lack of major talent in the group as a whole.

These factors, however, do not negate the importance of ultraism in the development of 20th-c. Hispanic literature. The movement created an innovative and enthusiastic climate for subsequent poets (the Generation of 1927 and later avant-garde groups in Latin America), whose poetry would never have been what it is without the influences of ultraism. From it they inherited the wish to search for new forms and to create a pure, metaphorical poetry, stripped of anecdotal descriptions and facile sentimental undertones.

BIBLIOGRAPHY: De Torre, G., *Literaturas europeas de vanguardia* (1965): 501–600; Videla, G., *El Ultraismo* (1971)

—VICENTE CABRERA

ULUGHZODA, Sotim

Tajik novelist, playwright, and literary historian, b. 11 Sept. 1911, Namangan, Uzbekistan; d. 1997, Moscow, Russia

U. was reared in a poor, rural family and received his early education in traditional schools. In 1929 he graduated from the Tashkent Teacher Training Institute, where he taught the following year. In 1930 he moved to Dushanbe and supervised the publication of the journals *Komsomol-i Tojikiston, Tojikiston-i Surkh*, and *Baro-i Adabiyyot-i Sosiolisti*. His graduate studies were interrupted by World War II when, between 1941 and 1944, he served as a war correspondent. From 1944 to 1946 he served as the head of the Writers Union of Tajikistan.

Beginning in 1930, U. wrote brief pieces for *Tojikiston-i Surkh* and *Baro-i Adabiyyot-i Sosiolisti*. These pieces dealt with the major literary figures of Tajikistan, including Abu Abdallah Rudaki (d. 940), Abu al-Qasim Firdowsi (935-1020 or 26), Abu Ali Sina (980-1037), Ahmad Donish (1827-1897), Sadriddin aini, and Abdusalam Dihoti (1911-1962). By the end of the 1930s, however, U.'s attention was increasingly being attracted to the stage. His two plays, *Shodmon* (1939; Rejoicing), depicting the conflict between the new order and the old, and *Kaltadoron-i Surkh* (1940; Red Club Wielders), about the battles of the Red Army against the Basmachis, were received with great enthusiasm. In fact, the latter was staged in Moscow in 1941. Using his experience as a war correspondent, U. followed with his third play, *Dar Otash* (1944; In the Fire). The antifascist play, which was staged in Dushanbe in the Lahuti Theater, inaugurated a new phase in Tajik dramatic presentation. The second phase of U.'s career came to an end with a comedy entitled *Juyandagon* (1951; The Searchers). The play, dealing with the activities of geologists commissioned to look for precious stones, was not received well; it degraded the image of Soviet women in the media.

U.'s first major novel, *Navobod* (1948-53; The New Settlement), established the *kolkhoz* system as a way of life. More importantly, it analyzed the complex relations obtaining between the *kolkhoz* director and his workers. With *Subh-i Javoni-i Mo* (1954; The Prime of Our Youth), reminiscent of Sadriddin Aini's *Yoddoshtho*, U. continued his career as a novelist and literary historian by documenting the events of his early youth (1916-29) and by dwelling on family ties and networking with friends. His portrayal of the mutual support system that sustains Tajik families in dire circumstances is noteworthy. Also noteworthy is the interaction between the rich and the poor in pre-Soviet times contrasted with the rule of the peasants and workers after 1917. U. paints a thorough picture of the gradual but steady growth of communist thought and anti-Islamic ideas in youthful minds.

While Aini dwells on Bukhara, Samarqand, and the Hissar region before the revolution, U. deals with Tashkent and the Ferghana valley to the east. The contrast is striking. Tashkent was equipped with new-method schools while the south debated the modernization issue amid political and ideological intrigue. Similarly, the north was protected by the Red Army while the south, allegedly helping the Basmachi movement, was being devastated by both the Basmachi rebels and the Red Army.

The Soviets praised U. for his play entitled *Rudaki* (1958; Rudaki), a portrayal of the famous 10th-c. poet. U. was awarded special praise for the versatility that he had afforded the character in proving his love for the oppressed Nigina. While *Rudaki* is a most praiseworthy endeavor—the production based on it captured the Golden Eagle Prize—it is U.'s *Vosse* (1980; Vosse) that must be regarded as his major achievement. Written between 1961 and 1967, *Vosse* portrays not only the life of a revolutionary peasant but the circumstances that led the illiterate farmer to rise against Amir Abdul Ahad, who ruled from 1885 to 1910. To gather materials for the novel, in addition to consulting the histories and the *soruds* about the insurrection, U. visited the region of Khavaling, village by village, talking to the old people who still remembered the event.

U. is the third most important contemporary Tajik novelist, the other two being Aini and Jalol Ikromi (1909-1993), respectively. He is the least conformist of the contemporary Tajik authors. As an investigative reporter and fiction writer, he had every opportunity to promote socialism. But, instead, he chose to use his talent for the promotion of indigenous Tajik culture by illuminating some of its more obscure facets. Working in a vacuum, however, made him vulnerable to a great deal of degradation and mental anguish doled out by the government and his peers. The most misunderstood author of present-day Tajikistan, U. disclosed not only the nature of the socialists' recruiting policies in Islamic lands, but the manner in which those policies were implemented. In addition, by portraying the courage of the Tajiks who had taken a stand against oppression, he underscored the futility of contemporary exploitative socialist schemes at work in his homeland.

FURTHER WORKS: *Asarho-i Muntakhab* (4 vols., 1967-76); *Muntakhibot* (2 vols., 1982)

BIBLIOGRAPHY: ''S. U.,'' in *Ocherk-i Ta'rikhi-i Adabiyyot-i Soveti-i Tojik* (1959), Vol. 2: 365-403; Demidchik, L. N., *Tadzhikskaya Dramaturgiya, 40-50 godov* (1965); Qodiri, A., *Adibon-i Tojikiston* (1966): 232-37; Kenjaboi, Y., *S. U. ve Povest-i Tarjimaholi-i U "Subh-i Javoni-i Mo"* (1968); Harri, J., ed., *The Literatures of the Soviet Peoples: A Historical and Biographical Survey* (1970): 455; Shukurov, M. "U.," *Ensaiklopidio-i Soveti-i Tojik* (1987), Vol. 7: 481-83

—IRAJ BASHIRI

UNAMUNO, Miguel de

Spanish philosopher, novelist, essayist, poet, and dramatist, b. 29 Sept. 1864, Bilbao; d. 31 Dec. 1936, Salamanca

At the age of ten U. personally experienced, during the cruel siege of Bilbao by the reactionary Carlist army, the ongoing rift and violence between traditionalist and progressive forces, a struggle that had eternally plagued Spain. As a young man U. showed a fervid intolerance and impatience toward dogmatism and political cant and as a student exercise translated *The French Revolution* of Thomas Carlyle, a writer he greatly admired. In 1880 he enrolled at the University of Madrid, where four years later he received a

Miguel de Unamuno

doctorate; his dissertation dealt with the origins and prehistory of his Basque ancestors.

U. had great difficulty in obtaining a university position. Finally, in 1891, he was appointed professor of Greek at the University of Salamanca, and in 1901 he was named rector, a post that he intermittently held until his death, depending upon his compatibility with the government and his ability to refrain from haranguing the authorities. In fact, so vociferous were U.'s complaints against the Spanish monarchy and the military dictatorship of General Primo de Rivera that he was exiled in 1924 to Fuerteventura, in the Canary Islands, from where he soon escaped to France. He lived in Paris and then settled in Hendaye, a border town, so that he could contemplate his beloved Spain. U. finally returned in 1930 to a jubilantly cheering public.

At the outbreak of the civil war, U. declared himself in favor of Franco; however, soon after, at the University of Salamanca in October 1936, he took a strong public stand against the Franco forces, accusing them of peddling death and destruction. He warned: "You will conquer but not convince." He was removed from the rectorship for the last time and was confined to his home, where he died a few months later, a victim of his country's internecine strife.

Although his works are riddled with paradoxes, perplexities, and contradictions, U.'s suffering and agonizing are consistent and deeply serious. Whether writing about Spain as a whole or the individual consciousness, he demanded authenticity and sobriety. He sought the eternal in the temporal; it was not precisely Spain's history that interested U. but its "intrahistory"—the ongoing events that remained after pruning away the accidents of fleeting history. Nor was it man's psychology per se—the accidents of personality and situations—that interested U., but rather his naked soul, unadorned and vulnerable. He dealt with everything on its deepest level, where consciousness itself was rightfully the only proper subject matter. His works are the ultimate representations of conscience and consciousness.

It is ironic that although U. was so multitalented, writing in almost every genre, his work is so utterly monomaniacal. It is an anguished, eloquent articulation of the central themes of the tragedy of death in man's life and of his desire for immortality against all reason and reasonableness. An EXISTENTIALIST, who learned Danish expressly to read Kierkegaard in the original, U. realized that, in the face of death, man must struggle to create his own soul, even if first he has to create a God.

U. readily appropriated Don Quixote as a symbol of his struggle and an emblem of his own concerns. In *Vida de Don Quijote y Sancho* (1905; *Life of Don Quixote and Sancho*, 1927; new tr., 1967), he concludes that Don Quixote's sheer will, extraordinary faith, and contempt for a mechanistic world view are a corroboration of U.'s own skepticism and ultimate rejection of reason, science, and the antediluvian idea of progress that had once intrigued him. Don Quixote, through his own heroism, succeeds in reaching the point at which he can proclaim, "I know who I am." U., the existentialist, altered the quixotic pronouncement: "I know who I want to be," thus going from the realm of necessity to one of complete freedom. His interest in Don Quixote, however, did not stop at antirationalistic posturing. According to U., Don Quixote understands implicitly how to use his creator, Cervantes, to his own advantage and become the perfect autonomous character, even more real than the author.

U.'s greatest meditation on death and immortality is *Del sentimiento trágico de la vida en los hombres y en los pueblos* (1913; *The Tragic Sense of Life in Men and in Peoples*, 1921; new tr., *The Tragic Sense of Life in Men and Nations*, 1972). It is a quest for the faith that will reward U. with the consolation of immortality that reason so tragically has denied him. Here lies the essential paradox or dialectic—the dramatic irreconcilability between faith and reason. Through vitalistic irrationality, he hopes to save his soul and waits for his much desired theophany.

As a novelist, U. remained very much a philosopher and brought to the genre the same naked passions and ontological preoccupations that he had detailed in his other writings. After a rather conventional novel of observation and description, *Paz en la guerra* (1897; *Peace in War: A Novel*, 1983), an account of the bombardment and siege of Bilbao in 1874, he created a more philosophical, less realistic narrative, in which the idea of existence was placed in high relief.

A transitional novel is the rather forced but not altogether unsuccessful satire *Amor y pedagogía* (1902; love and pedagogy), a tragicomic portrait of the downfall of a neo-Comtian positivist, Avito, whose only religion is science. He tries to quantify man's deepest impulses—sexuality, love, death. Although Avito fails in the experimental upbringing of his son, who withers away into a passive death, he intends to try again with his grandson. In *Niebla* (1914; *Mist*, 1929), one of U.'s most successful novels, Avito appears as a minor character, and it is revealed that he has not gone through with his experiment on his grandson.

Niebla, a highly unconventional and multiperspective novel, underscores the belief of U.—who assumes the role of a god, since he has created his characters just as God has created mankind—that human beings must struggle for their dignity and authenticity. In Augusto's rebellion against U., the author, and in his fight for life as a character in the novel, U. reiterates the playful notion (cf. *Vida de Don Quijote y Sancho*) that an author (God) depends upon his characters (mankind) for existence and fame. However, Augusto dies—is "killed off" by U.—perhaps by suicide, a thought U. denies in the preface, or of a broken heart because of the cruel deception of Eugenia, whom he had deeply loved.

In *Abel Sánchez: Una historia de pasión* (1917; *Abel Sánchez*, 1956), U. recasts and modernizes the Cain and Abel story to expose the ontological insecurity of Joaquín (Cain) Monegro, whose entire existence is defined by his uncontrollable, extrahuman envy of Abel. It is an object lesson in the failure of self-actualization, of having essence—here deep envy—monopolize and ultimately destroy the ability of a human being to "become" or arrive at a comfortable sense of identity.

U.'s critically best-received work of fiction, *San Manuel Bueno, Mártir* (1931; *Saint Manuel Bueno, Martyr*, 1954), is an account with little external action of a country priest, Don Manuel Bueno, who ceases to believe in the basic tenets of the Catholic Church. This novella can be regarded, as U. himself suggested, as the final part of a trilogy, which began with *Del sentimiento trágico de la vida en los hombres y en los pueblos* and *La agonía del Cristianismo* (1925; *The Agony of Christianity*, 1928; new trs., 1960, 1974). Don Manuel's doubt about his own immortality is transformed into a creative and poetic uncertainty, and is never a destructive force. In spite of his burdensome tragic secret, he never eschews his ethical responsibility and continues to care for his parishioners and to act as if he were a believer. In his tragic sense of life the priest touches a young parishioner, Angela, and her brother Lazarus, whom he resurrects from a death of nonbelief to a compassionate life of tacit disbelief, the same disbelief shared by his mentor. Here creative doubt gives one authentic being.

This same theme of authenticity characterizes U.'s plays. He created a theater of existence, eschewing extraneous action, plot complications, superfluous characters, and elaborate stage designs. Particularly interesting is his mystery play *El otro* (1932; *The Other*, 1947), a taut and hard-edged parable about identity. It is yet another variant of the Cain and Abel theme. *El otro* deals with a set of twins, Cosme and Damián, one of whom lies dead, killed by his brother, who is now half-mad. The audience never learns who killed whom, as U. underscores the total confusion about the nature of reality and appearance, victim and victimizer.

The drama *El hermano Juan; o, El mundo es teatro* (1934; brother Juan; or, the world is a stage) is another manifestation of U.'s concern with immortality. Don Juan is not the self-assured suitor and ravager of women; he has contempt for himself and the women who throw themselves at him. He dies a friar, ironically aware of his doom to eternal life and fame, for he is part of the mythos and collective imagination of man. Yet he is hardly the legendary Don Juan, but rather a character of self-doubt and poetic consciousness.

U., who always held that poetry was the highest form of expression, brought to his verse, which he wrote throughout his life, concerns similar to those he explored in other genres. It has been suggested that U. was Spain's compensation for not having a great 19th-c. poet. In *Poesías* (1907; poems), he dispenses with the musicality of SYMBOLISM and MODERNISM, lest he be lulled into peacefulness. He wants to agonize. Thus, he uses harsh and crude sounds and unpoetic diction. His desire for immortality he felt might be fulfilled through his poems, which he called "children of his soul."

His long religious poem *El Cristo de Velázquez* (1920; *The Christ of Velázquez*, 1951) was written at a time when neither long nor religious poems were in vogue. The sobering beauty and intense profundity of the poem are overwhelming. It is a song to Christ, inspired by Velázquez's painting in the Prado, to the Christ who died so man could live on. U. questions the notion of the Trinity; he is sure that man had to create God so he could be assured of eternal life. The poem is like a shimmering cross upon which both Christ and man die and aspire to be reborn into eternity.

It is entirely fitting to call U. Spain's first contemporary writer, for he confronted ontological crises with unbridled courage. His undertaking, although enormous and unduly painful, was realized with great heroic fortitude and total commitment to both his country and his fellow man. His work, the result of an unselfish but not selfless obligation, exposes but does not solve the deep mysteries of human existence. No writer has more fearlessly confronted the tragedy of life or the menacing nothingness that death may offer. U.'s works are the summa of his suffering as a man of flesh and blood among other men of flesh and blood.

FURTHER WORKS: *En torno al casticismo* (1895); *Paisajes* (1902); *De mi país: Descripciones, relatos y artículos de costumbres* (1903); *Recuerdos de niñez y la mocedad* (1908); *La Esfinge* (1909); *Mi religión, y otros ensayos* (1910); *Por tierras de Portugal y de España* (1911); *Rosario de sonetos líricos* (1911); *Soliloquios y conversaciones* (1911; *Essays and Soliloquies*, 1925); *Contra esto y aquello* (1912); *El espejo de la muerte (Novelas cortas)* (1913); *Ensayos* (7 vols., 1916–18); *Tres novelas ejemplares y un prólogo* (1920; *Three Exemplary Novels and a Prologue*, 1930); *Fedra* (1921; *Phaedra*, 1959); *La tía Tula* (1921); *La venda* (1921); *Andanzas y visiones españolas* (1922); *Rimas de dentro* (1923); *Teresa: Rimas de un poeta desconocido* (1923); *De Fuerteventura a París: Diario íntimo de confinamiento y destierro* (1925); *Raquel encadenada* (1926); *Cómo se hace una novela* (1927); *Dos artículos y dos discursos* (1928); *Romancero de destierro* (1928); *Sombras de sueño* (1930); *Discurso leído en la solemne apertura del curso académico 1934–35 en la Universidad de Salamanca* (1934); *La ciudad de Henoc: Comentario 1933* (1941); *Antología poética* (1942); *El porvenir de España* (1942); *Ensayos* (2 vols., 1942); *Cuenca ibérica (Lenguaje y paisaje)* (1943); *Temas argentinos* (1943); *La enormidad de España* (1944); *Paisajes del alma* (1944); *Visiones y comentarios* (1949); *Mi Salamanca* (1950); *De esto y aquello* (4 vols., 1950–54); *Cancionero* (1953); *En el destierro (Recuerdos y esperanzas)* (1957); *Inquietudes y meditaciones* (1957); *Cincuenta poesías inéditas (1899–1927)* (1958); *Autodiálogos* (1959); *Mi vida y otros recuerdos personales* (2 vols., 1950); *Teatro completo* (1959); *Desde el mirador de la guerra* (1970); *Diario íntimo* (1970); *Obras completas* (16 vols., 1952–58). **FURTHER WORKS IN ENGLISH:** *Perplexities and Paradoxes* (1945); *Poems* (1952); *Abel Sanchez, and Other Stories* (1956); *Our Lord Don Quixote: The Life of Don Quixote and Sancho, with Related Essays* (1967); *The Last Poems of M. de U.* (1974); *The Agony of Christianity, and Essays on Faith* (1974); *Ficciones: Four Stories and a Play* (1975); *The Private World* (1985)

BIBLIOGRAPHY: Barea, A., *U.* (1952); Blanco Aguinaga, C., *El U. contemplativo* (1959); Ferrater Mora, J., *U.: A Philosophy of Tragedy* (1962); Rudd, M. T., *The Lone Heretic: A Biography of M. de U. y Jugo* (1964); García Blanco, M., *En torno a U.* (1965); Marías, J., *M. de U.* (1966); Martínez-López, R., ed., *U. Centennial Studies* (1966); Valdés, M., *Death in the Literature of U.* (1966); Young, H. T., *The Victorious Expression: A Study of Four Contemporary Spanish Poets* (1966): 3–31; Barcia, J. R., and Zeitlin, M. A., eds., *U.: Creator and Creation* (1967); Ilie, P., *U.: An Existential View of Self and Society* (1967); Basdekis, D., *M. de U.* (1969); Nozick, M., *de U.* (1971); Batchelor, R. E., *U. Novelist* (1972); Ouimette, V., *Reason Aflame: U. and the Heroic Will* (1974); Jurkevich, G., *The Elusive Self: Archetypal Approaches to the Novels of U.* (1991); Round, N. G., "Some Preliminary Thoughts on the Unamunian Speech Act," *Revista Canadiense de Estudios Hispanos*, 21 (1996): 217-36

—MARSHALL J. SCHNEIDER

When M. de U.'s volume of poetry [*Poesías*] appeared there were some expressions of admiration and infinite protests. How is it that this man who writes such strange paradoxes, this man who is called wise, this man who knows Greek, who knows a half-dozen languages . . . wants to be a poet also? The hangmen who love to pigeonhole, those who see a man as being good for only one thing, are furious.

And when I went on record in front of some of them that in my opinion M. de U. is, above all, a poet, and perhaps only that, they looked at me strangely and thought they had found an irony in this opinion.

Certainly U. is fond of paradoxes—I myself have become victim of some—but he is one of the most notable movers of ideas that there is today, and as I have said, in my opinion, a poet. Yes, to be a poet is to appear at the doors of the mysterious and to return from there with a glimmer of the unknown in one's eyes. And few men like that Basque put their soul in the deepest core of life and death. [May 2, 1909]

Rubén Darío, *Obras completas*, Vol. II (1950), pp. 787–88

U. transfigures the despised and comic person of Don Quixote. This symbol of his land's wrong-headed action becomes for U. the god of a new Order, the prophet of a new national revelation. Don M. de U. of the Basques identifies his cause of pure and personal effort with the crusade of the old hidalgo of La Mancha. Like that knight, he will construct his world platonically from the ideals of his inheritance and go forth *really* that it may prevail. As Quixote fought common sense, U. fights "business." The old windmills are now factories, the old inns are industrial cities, the old King's police are the votaries of Demos. Where all that is glorious has become so sterile, all that is serious so low, let Don Quixote be savior. The final jest of the bitter, broken Cervantes becomes our Man of Sorrows. . . .

So with inimitable verve and wit, U. identifies his will with the old body of Spain: and hobbles forth, like Quixote, to enact justice. He wants it for himself. But since Spain is in him, since Spain is his Rocinante, Spain must go along. Spain must wake, if only for his sake.

Waldo Frank, *Virgin Spain* (1926), pp. 284–85

U.'s novel puts us in contact with that true reality which is man. This is its principal role. Other modes of thought—for we are dealing with thought—have their point of departure in previous and abstract diagrams. For example, they consider human life from a biological point of view, based on the perhaps unconscious supposition of the fundamental unity of everything we call life, and therefore they cast human reality into modes of apprehension which are alien to it and which cannot contain it without deforming it. Or again, they move from the outset within the compass of what we could call "culture," leading us to an extremely deficient and nonessential view of man. U., on the other hand, tries to obtain the highest possible degree of nakedness and authenticity in the object to which he is trying to find access. He attempts to reach the very core of the human drama, and simply to recount it, letting it be just what it is. The purpose of the existential or personal novel is to make plain to us a person's history, letting his intimate movements develop before our eyes, in broad daylight, and thus uncovering his ultimate nucleus. The purpose is, simply, to show human existence in all its truth. [1942]

Julián Marías, *M. de U.* (1966), pp. 60–61

U. had an ardent wish to be recognised as a great poet in verse and prose. He insisted on an assessment of his writings which his greatest admirers were unable to endorse; for instance, he gave pride of place to his first novel, *Peace in War*, and he maintained that he would be best remembered by his poetry. His rough-tongued poems with their blend of fervour and contemplation brought indeed a new note into Spanish lyrical poetry at the turn of the century, but their poetic form was never strong enough to absorb the sentiments and thoughts that inspired them. It was not U. himself who found the right lyrical shape for his visions, but his much younger friend Antonio Machado. And yet U. was not wrong when he called himself a poet: he was a poet who had to create a world in his image so as to assure himself of his self. Taken in this sense, U.'s true poetic creation was the personality he projected into all his work; his "agony," his ceaseless struggle with himself and the universe, was the core of every one of his novels and stories, poems and essays.

If he sometimes failed as an artist, it was because he handled his tools clumsily; he often insisted on the rights of his thesis against the intrinsic demands of the tale which was to clothe it. What he wanted to write was not something that made "good reading," but something that penetrated below the surface of the truth.

Arturo Barea, *U.* (1952), p. 37

For sheer power and for bareness of literary devices, *Three Exemplary Novels* can hardly be compared with anything currently in vogue. In structure and tone they are closer to drama than to any form of narrative literature. Their harshness and their stifling atmosphere of passion are reminiscent of some of the plays of Strindberg (a writer very much influenced by Ibsen, as U. was in his youth) or of O'Neill. The significant difference is that Strindberg and O'Neill are naturalistic authors whose works are studies in hatred and lust, while U.'s aims are predominantly philosophical and metaphysical: he does not attempt to foster psychological understanding of human behavior but to give, as he would say, "glimpses of the deep mystery of man's soul and conscience." It is in this sense that his works are related to existentialist literature.

Angel del Río, Introduction to M. de U., *Three Exemplary Novels* (1956), pp. 26–27

To leave everything unfinished, whether a literary work or life itself, was one of U.'s constant aims. Small wonder that his works impress us as being a kind of continuous creation, a sort of "interminable poem." . . .

In the essentially unfinished character of U.'s works we encounter . . . that impulse to overturn, to pour out, to overflow . . . and which so faithfully represents U.'s temperament, his aims. Such an impulse is present even when, as in poetic forms fixed by tradition—like the sonnet—all would seem to end with the final verse. But if the last line of any of U.'s sonnets is a formal conclusion, it is also a new beginning; the poet has ceased to move his pen, but he keeps his spirit—and the spirit of his readers—mobile. Thus in the majority of cases—as in *Teresa*, in *The Christ of Velázquez*, in considerable portions of the *Book of Songs*—U. unequivocally adopts those poetic forms that are least encumbered by formal exigencies and abound with "loose ends" that can be resumed at any time—and developed indefinitely. Not that U. avoids rhythm; on the contrary, he finds it everywhere, even in Kant's *Critiques*! But this rhythm is the rhythm of life. It is not difficult to find hendecasyllables in *The Tragic Sense of Life*. But they are not intended as poetic ornament; they are meant to be songs. Perhaps, after all, U.'s writings are songs of a sort, sung by a soul made of living words. [1957]

José Ferrater Mora, *U.: A Philosophy of Tragedy* (1962), pp. 95–96

The central themes which implicitly pervade U.'s complete works are reducible to the human biped, God, and Spain and the world, perhaps in that order of importance. His essays, as well as his complete works on the whole, inevitably thread their way along a baroque course destined to crystallize in the form of these few considerations; lesser themes all owe their genesis and sustenance to omnipresent essentials. If the path toward these basics is often oblique, tortuous, and intentionally blurred, and if during our itinerary, we are sometimes treated to histrionics, harangues, effrontery, and other indelicacies, we eventually come to realize that these apparent defects are simply part of the ingredients of U.'s method whereby the obdurate provocateur seeks in every way conceivable to strain the attention of his readers to a point where each and every one of them is forced into a dialogic give and take; an exchange, sometimes a confrontation, between reader, author, and/or work. U.'s attempts, as one of its goals, to involve the reader-participant in an elaborate dialectic which would facilitate his role as a "co-laborator." Beneath the fractured, incoherent surface of his art, there lurks an exemplary lucidity; a coherent challenge which is the product of an apparently asystematic method. Ephemeral man versus immortal man, an abstract God versus an anthropomorphic God, Spain versus the universe, all embroiled in a vital tug of war, are thrust against a massive, dislocated canvas created to startle, seduce, and then transfix the reader to a few universal essentials.

Demetrios Basdekis, *M. de U.* (1969), p. 5

U. escapes intellectual appreciation but exercises a powerful fascination, for it is in the affective response to existence and in his emotional involvement with kindred spirits that he lived out the plenitude of his metaphysical struggle. He combines the imperious, warrior-like vitality of a Nietzsche with the intellectual paralysis of a Pirandello, the stirring pride of an Ibsen with the frustration of a Kafka, oscillating between his frenzied exaltation of the "man of flesh and blood" and the diaphanous concepts of dreams and shadows. The heroic adventurer plunged into the tragedy of impotence. U. relived the irreducible opposition of the real and the ideal, the all and the nothing that Don Quixote lived before him. He sought the quixotic in all things, whether in creative writing or in contemplation of other writers, and assumed with his patron saint Don Quixote the tragic contradiction of all the great "feelers" of Europe. He tussled incessantly with the attitudes and feelings of many literary giants, transforming them, by a strange osmosis, into an intimate experience. Like Nietzsche, he was romantically inclined but infinitely surpassed the Romanticism of the nineteenth century, wrestling with the spirit of yearning in order to forge for himself the ideal of the heroic existence. Again, like Nietzsche, he wrote with his blood for he saw language as the blood of the spirit, resolving the struggle for life in recreation through identification with others and personal confession.

R. E. Batchelor, *U. Novelist* (1972), pp. 11–12

UNDER, Marie

Estonian poet, translator, and essayist, b. 27 Mar. 1883, Tallinn; d. 25 Sept. 1980, Stockholm, Sweden

Daughter of a schoolteacher, U. studied German, French, and Russian extensively in her youth. In 1917 she became the leader of the rebellious poets of the Siuru group, and in 1924 she married one of them, Artur Adson (1889–1977), without whose encouragement her artistic and cognitive maturation would have been unthinkable.

U. started as a poet of flaming youth in the decorative fin-de-siècle style and a writer of experimental sonnets. Within that style she expressed the rebelliousness, erratic temperament, and emancipation of the 1910s: the fervent heart she gave voice to was even more dramatic than Anna AKHMATOVA's or Edna St. Vincent MILLAY's, with a much more demonstrative eroticism. Her first published book (the second she wrote), *Sonetid* (1917; sonnets), contained lines like "Oh, those [my] stockings that do not want to end," which shocked and delighted Estonian readers and critics. Her subjective approach to love themes continued in *Eelõitseng* (1918; first flowering) and in her most sensual book, *Sinine puri* (1920; blue sail); her use of broken yet musically convincing metrical schemes made her the fountainhead of 20th-c. Estonian neoromantic poetry. The initial swiftness of her thought and feeling was matched by a sometimes unfortunate haste of execution, but in general, even in her early, less significant poetry, the freedom and certainty of her pen made for vitality and freshness. As a young lyric poet she seldom had composure or repose, but her poetry is not purely emotional; it is abundant, even over-abundant, with thought.

Although critics have characterized her early work as impressionistic, U. lacked the impressionist trait of antimonumentality. She seldom used the technique of blurring the outlines of tonal progression of wording, and even as an impressionist she did not avoid hard, melodic edges and sudden, sharp contrasts of images. Thus, because she was a born poet of energy, it was easy for her to modulate her style and become an EXPRESSIONIST of strong rhythm (specifically, of innovative techniques in accentual verse) and of driving power of thought. U.'s collections *Verivalla* (1920; gaping wounds), *Pärisosa* (1923; heritage), and *Hääl varjust* (1927; voice from the shadow) express the full profundity of her anxiety and show her as a person feeling all emotions with authentic intensity. Prepared by her reading of Rimbaud, Whitman, and Émile VERHAEREN, U. accepted the aesthetic and spirit of the expressionists, especially of Georg Heym (1887–1912) and Georg TRAKL, and, applying their ideals to verse translation, she published the anthology *Valik saksa uuemast lüürikast* (1920; selection of new German poetry). Her dynamic lyricism found a new affirmation in *Õnnevarjutus* (1929; eclipse of happiness), a collection of ballads in a style to some extent reminiscent of those of the German poet Agnes Miegel (1879–1964).

It is with *Rõõm ühest ilusast päevast* (1928; joy at the beautiful day), and especially with *Kivi südamelt* (1935; the stone off the heart), that U.'s mental vigor found a more classical structure, although to the very end of her life she remained an emotionally and intellectually restless master of open form. In the choice and treatment of subject, *Kivi südamelt* also reflects the Christian fervor and philosophical, symbol-laden character of her late work. U. started producing political poetry under the Soviet and Nazi occupations (1940–41 and 1941–44) and, escaping from the second Soviet occupation to Sweden in the autumn of 1944, she continued to write it there. She showed remarkable mastery as a committed writer, working with precision and tension, but without calling the Nazis or Soviets by name; and although strongly tied in her dramatic nature lyrics to her native soil, she never even mentioned the name of her beloved Estonia in any of her poems. U.'s Christian attitudes kept her from becoming overly nationalistic, but her late verse has especially captured Estonian hearts and minds because it is the essence of her own humane patriotism, sense of right, and inward serenity.

One of U.'s finest collections is her last book, *Ääremail* (1963; in the borderlands), in which her metaphysical insight and symbolism found its final, somber, philosophical tonality. She fulfilled her task in her hours of gloom, showing again the true power of introspection and passion. She was a master of both inductive and deductive thinking, but throughout her life her verse was persuasive essentially because all of it is permeated with lyrical flow.

U. was active as a critic primarily in the 1920s; her special interest at the time was modernist theater. Later, and until her death, her sympathies in the arts lay more with Beethoven's music and El Greco's paintings. She was exceedingly active as a verse and prose translator, rendering 26 major works into Estonian, starting with Goethe and Schiller and ending with Pär LAGERKVIST and Boris PASTERNAK. She never imposed her own diction on any of her renderings, but tried to follow precisely the outer structure and integral style of the original.

U.'s popularity and reputation are constantly growing, and she is regarded as the foremost Estonian lyric and lyrophilosophical poet of the 20th c. As such, her achievements complement those of her follower Betti ALVER, Estonia's leading intellectual poet.

FURTHER WORKS: *Lageda taeva all* (1930); *Mureliku suuga* (1942); *Sädamed tuhas* (1954); *Südamik* (1957); *Kogutud luuletused* (1958); *Mu süda laulab* (1981). FURTHER WORKS IN ENGLISH: *Child of Man* (1955)

BIBLIOGRAPHY: Rannit, A., "Tribute to M. U. at Eighty," *BA*, 37 (1963): 125–31; Oras, A., *M. U.* (1963); Ivask, I., "M. U.: And the Flesh Became Word," in V. Kõressaar and A. Rannit, eds., *Estonian Poetry and Language: Studies in Honor of Ants Oras* (1965): 272–80; Aspel, A., "M. U.'s Quest of Transcendence," *BA*, 51 (1969): 363–65; Oras, A., "M. U. and Estonian Poetry," *SR*, 78 (1970): 247–68; Rannit, A., "M. U. and El Greco: An Attempt at Comparative Aesthetics," *Proceedings of the 7th International Congress of Aesthetics*, II (1977): 597–623; George, E. E., "M. U. and Goethe: Metaphysical Perspective and the Vanishing Point of Lyric Style," in V. B. Leitch, ed., *The Poetry of Estonia: Essays in Comparative Analysis* (1983): 107–42

—ALEKSIS RANNIT

UNDSET, Sigrid

Norwegian novelist, short-story writer, and essayist, b. 20 May 1882, Kalundborg, Denmark; d. 10 June 1949, Lillehammer

U.'s childhood and youth were spent chiefly in Norway's capital, Christiania (now Oslo). Her earliest artistic ambitions were directed at painting. From her archaeologist father, who died when she was eleven, she acquired an intense interest in medieval history and literature. Dissatisfied with her school environment and constrained by limited finances, U. turned to secretarial training and in 1899 took employment in an Oslo office. It was as a young career woman that U. began to nurture her literary talent. In 1909 she left her job to devote full attention to writing. Following several trips abroad, U. made her home at Lillehammer. There she reared her three children. She converted to Catholicism in 1924, at which time her marriage to the painter A. C. Svarstad was annulled. In 1928 she won the Nobel Prize for literature. In 1940 U. fled from the Nazis; during the war she lived in the U.S., where she continued her active opposition to Nazism and agitated on behalf of occupied Norway. She was awarded the Grand Cross of the Order of St. Olav in 1947.

U.'s writing encompasses both medieval and modern settings. The urban milieu of her youth provided fertile ground for her literary imagination; but because of her fascination with the cultural heritage of medieval Scandinavia, the historical novel held a special appeal. As a budding author, however, U. was advised by a publisher to invest her energies in contemporary rather than historical subjects. At first she dutifully and adeptly followed this advice. But in the 1920s she produced the towering novels of the Middle Ages that won her international fame; here human drama unfolded across broad, multivolume canvases with meticulous background detail. In the third phase of her career the modern world reemerged as the major focus.

U.'s first novel, *Fru Marta Oulie* (1907; Mrs. Marta Oulie), boldly tackles the subject of marital infidelity. A series of works dealing with the problems of modern women ensued. The most important of these, *Jenny* (1911; *Jenny*, 1921), is the story of a young painter whose dream of all-consuming love overshadows her artistic goals. But compromise and disappointment cloud Jenny's search. Her self-esteem withers in the face of flawed romances, and her sense of hope vanishes with the death of her child. Jenny's suicide illustrates the tragedy of intense idealism. It also underscores a major theme in U.'s fiction—the demands of love.

Typically, her modern heroines experience a painful conflict between the public and private spheres. In *Den lykkelige alder* (1908; the happy age) Uni chooses the role of wife and mother over a theatrical career; her family life and the consequences of her decision are explored in the story "Fru Hjelde" in *Splinten av troldspeilet* (1917; only "Fru Hjelde" tr. in *Images in a Mirror*, 1938). In *Vaaren* (1914; springtime) Rose comes to terms with a shaky marriage and acknowledges the primacy of domestic responsibilities. The short stories from this period, collected in *Fattige skjæbner* (1912; pitiful destinies) and *De kloge jomfruer* (1918; the wise virgins), offer sympathetic portrayals of working-class women from all stages of life. The emphasis rests on lonely, unmarried, or childless individuals who long for happiness and self-fulfillment. In all of U.'s depictions of female love and maturation, sexuality and motherhood receive frank and positive treatment. These bold endorsements of woman's biological nature were criticized by some contemporary feminists as reactionary.

The sweeping historical trilogy *Kristin Lavransdatter* (1920–22; *Kristin Lavransdatter*, 1923–27), set in 14th-c. Norway, stands as U.'s masterpiece. In the first volume, *Kransen* (1920; *The Bridal Wreath*, 1923), Kristin's passage to adulthood is marked by carefully crafted sequences of rising and falling suspense, which flow as naturally and inevitably as her passion for Erlend. The powerful evocation of external reality, through striking images and tangible everyday details, is complemented by glittering psychological insights, which bring the characters into sharp and memorable focus. Undergirding this technical triumph is the brilliant juxtaposition of the secular and the spiritual, the poles between which Kristin is pulled as she charts her path in life. In *Husfrue* (1921; *The Mistress of Husaby*, 1925) and *Korset* (1922; *The Cross*, 1927) the tale is carried forward through Kristin and Erlend's marriage to Kristin's final reckoning with God. The narrative retains its fundamental grandeur, although the sparkle of *Kransen* is not duplicated in the other two volumes.

A male figure dominates U.'s other ambitious medieval cycle, *Olav Audunssøn i Hestviken* (1925) and *Olav Audunssøn og hans børn* (1927; Eng. tr. of both: *The Master of Hestviken*, 4 vols., 1928–30). Like Kristin, Olav must come to terms with God's supremacy. His anguished relationship with the Creator derives from a secret murder he chooses not to confess. Olav struggles with his conscience; his only comfort can be God's bountiful mercy.

The interrelationship of social and religious responsibility is examined further in the novels from the 1930s, all but one of which have a present-day setting. Marriage as both sacrament and ethical commitment, a theme central to *Kristin Lavransdatter*, supplies the subject for *Den trofaste hustru* (1936; *The Faithful Wife*, 1937). Marriage and motherhood are also highlighted in *Ida Elisabeth* (1932: *Ida Elisabeth*, 1933) and in *Madame Dorthea* (1938; *Madame Dorthea*, 1940), an unfinished novel about the 18th c.

A devout Christian, U. wove religious themes into most of her later writings. The religious life is addressed most explicitly in two novels about Paul Selmer and his conversion to Catholicism—*Gymnadenia* (1929; *The Wild Orchid*, 1931) and *Den brændende busk* (1930; *The Burning Bush*, 1932)—as well as in biographies of saints like *Norske helgener* (1937; *Saga of Saints*, 1934) and the posthumously published *Caterina av Siena* (1951; *Catherine of Siena*, 1954). The essay collections *Et kvindesynspunkt* (1919; a woman's point of view), *Etapper* (1929; stages), and *Etapper: Ny række* (1933; *Stages on the Road*, 1934) provide additional insight into U.'s strong views on religion, modern morality, and the female role.

Glimpses into U.'s own life are offered by the childhood description *Elleve år* (1934; *The Longest Years*, 1935) and by two books written when she was in the U.S. and first published in English: *Tilbake til fremtiden* (1945; *Return to the Future*, 1942) describes her flight from Scandinavia through Russia and Japan; *Lykkelige dager* (1947; *Happy Times in Norway*, 1942) offers a heart-warming picture of family life in Lillehammer.

Early on U. tried her hand at both drama—*I grålysningen* (1908; in the gray light of dawn)—and verse—*Ungdom* (1910; youth)—but quickly recognized that fiction was her forte. Although she is sometimes labeled dogmatic, her literary achievement springs from her penetrating analyses of central human concerns. Stirring portraits of individual women and men illuminate universal questions of responsibility, faith, love, and commitment. Bridging the centuries with a powerful ability to capture everyday life, U. shows us the timeless nature of the human heart.

FURTHER WORKS: *Fortællingen om Viga-Ljot og Vigdis* (1909; *Gunnar's Daughter*, 1936); *Fortællinger om kong Arthur og ridderne av det runde bord* (1915); *Tre søstre* (1917); *Sankt Halvards liv, død og jertegn* (1925); *Katholsk propaganda* (1927); *Hellig Olav, Norges konge* (1930); *Sigurd og hans tapre venner* (1931 [in German]; 1955 [in Norwegian]; *Sigurd and His Brave Companions*, 1943); *Selvportretter og landskapsbilleder* (1938; *Men, Women and Places*, 1939); *Romaner og fortællinger fra*

Sigrid Undset

nutiden (10 vols., 1949); *Middelalderromaner* (10 vols., 1949); *Artikler og taler fra krigstiden* (1952); *S. U.s ungdomstegninger* (1960); *Kirke og klosterliv: Tre essays fra norsk middelalder* (1963); *Kjære Dea* (1979). FURTHER WORKS IN ENGLISH: *Christmas and Twelfth Night* (1932); *Four Stories* (1959)

BIBLIOGRAPHY: Gustafson, A., *Six Scandinavian Novelists* (1940): 286–361; Monroe, N., *The Novel and Society* (1941): 39–87; Winsnes, A., *S. U.: A Study in Christian Realism* (1953); McFarlane, J., *Ibsen and the Temper of Norwegian Literature* (1960): 158–68; Deschamps, N., *S. U.: ou, La morale de la passion* (1966); Dunn, M., "*The Master of Hestviken*: A New Reading," *SS*, 38 (1966): 281–94, and *SS*, 40 (1968): 210–24; Bayerschmidt, C., *S. U.* (1970); McCarthy, C., "S. U.," *Critic*, 32, 3 (1974): 58–64; Boland, M., "Rediscovering S. U.," *Commonweal* (7 November 1980): 620–23

—JANET E. RASMUSSEN

UNGARETTI, Giuseppe

Italian poet, essayist, and translator, b. 10 Feb. 1888, Alexandria, Egypt; d. 1 June 1970, Milan

The son of Tuscan emigrants, U. spent his early youth in Alexandria, where he attended a French school. In 1912 he went to

Paris to study at the Sorbonne. One of his teachers was Henri BERGSON, whose ideas left a mark on U.'s poetic development. No less influential was his exposure to Parisian intellectual and artistic life, represented by such figures as Guillaume APOLLINAIRE, Picasso, Braque, Modigliani, De Chirico, and Léger. In 1915 U. enlisted in the Italian infantry and was sent to the front. Following World War I, he returned to Paris as a correspondent for the daily *Il popolo d'Italia*. From 1921 to 1936 he lived in Rome, working in the Foreign Ministry and, beginning in 1931, as a journalist for *La gazzetta del popolo*. In 1936 U. was offered the chair of Italian literature at the University of São Paulo (Brazil), a post he held for six years. Upon his return to Italy in 1942, he was appointed professor of modern Italian literature at the University of Rome and held that position until 1962. The last years of his life were marked by extensive travels, including a trip to the U.S. shortly before his death.

U.'s cultural background, especially his familiarity with Baudelaire and Mallarmé, proved instrumental in his being able to break with tradition and provincialism, a break advocated by the FUTURIST poets, the periodicals *La voce* and *Lacerba*, and other innovative forces in early 20th-c. Italian literature. His first work, the slender book of verse *Il porto sepolto* (1916; *The Buried Port*, 1958), exemplified, in structure and aesthetic impulse, a novel approach to poetry. Eschewing traditional forms in favor of a cryptic, subdued, and musically conscious poetic diction, U. sought to wrest optimal suggestive value from a verse structure stripped of all unessential elements. Some aspects of this poetry, especially its elliptical and occasionally abstruse language, are identified with Italian HERMETICISM. *Il porto sepolto* and the work that followed, *Allegria di naufragi* (1919; *Joy of Shipwrecks*, 1958), reflect a distillation of the poet's war experiences marked by stark images of trench life and a mythical vision of his native city rooted in childhood memories. Correspondingly, the poet's existential disposition oscillates between experienced suffering borne with stoic resignation and the liberating quest for a higher state of consciousness in which the self acquires spiritual plenitude as "a pliant fiber/of the universe."

Sentimento del tempo (1933; *Sentiment of Time*, 1958) underlines the progression from experimentation to the recovery of traditional metric forms consistent, as U. put it, with "the expressive needs of today." The restructured verse betrays a retrospective process characterized by the assimilation of classical myths, the psychological dimension of time, and, more importantly, a marked affinity with Petrarch and Giacomo Leopardi (1798–1837). Conceptually, the work delineates the crisis of a restless spirit engaged in the elusive search for absolute truths. In the second part of the volume, this crisis takes the form of a confessional admission to the spiritual void of the self, an admission that attests as well to the insufficiency of individual commitment to art to achieve spiritual fulfillment; hence the attraction to a higher order of consciousness identified with religious faith. In *Il dolore* (1947; *Grief*, 1958) metaphysical preoccupations give way to intense grief and despair motivated by personal tragedies: the loss of his nine-year-old son, rendered with extraordinary lyrical force in the poem "Tu ti spezzasti" ("You Shattered"); the death of his brother; and the sight of Italy subjected to the devastation of World War II.

The last of U.'s major works, *La terra promessa* (1950; *The Promised Land*, 1958), reaffirms the coherence of a poetic vision nurtured by the quest for an Edenic "innocent country" that ultimately proves unattainable. But this is not a conclusive statement. In "Monologhetto" ("Short Monologue"), contained in *Un grido e paesaggi* (1952; *A Cry and Landscapes*, 1958), U. returns, with renewed vitality, to the theme of individual fulfillment. On the other hand, *Il taccuino del vecchio* (1960; *The Old Man's Notebook*, 1969) and *Dialogo* (1968; *Dialogue*, 1969) convey a desolate, disquieting view of existence, not devoid, however, of a glimmer of hope. These final lyrics underline U.'s irrepressible search for truth and his enduring faith in poetry as a vital, redeeming expression of human experience.

U. devoted considerable time to literary translations. Well known are his Italian versions of Shakespeare's sonnets, selected poems of Góngora, Mallarmé, and Blake, and Racine's drama *Phèdre*.

U.'s verse represents a milestone in 20th-c. Italian poetry. The title of his complete works, *Vita d'un uomo* (1969; life of a man), bears witness to a lifelong process of creative labor in which lyricism reaches new levels of intensity as it documents, through a relentless mythical quest for harmony and innocence, the inquietudes and aspirations voiced by a man of our time.

FURTHER WORKS: *L'allegria* (1931); *Poesie disperse* (1945); *Derniers jours—1919* (1947); *Il povero nella città* (1949); *Il deserto e depo* (1961); *Morte delle stagioni* (1967); *Lettere a un fenomenologo* (1972); *Saggi e interventi* (1974). FURTHER WORKS IN ENGLISH: *Life of a Man* (1958); *G. U.: Selected Poems* (1969); *Selected Poems of G. U.* (1975)

BIBLIOGRAPHY: Cambon, G., *G. U.* (1967); Cary, J., *Three Modern Italian Poets: Saba, U., Montale* (1969): 135–233; Sanavió, P., ed., special U. issue, *L'Herne*, No. 11 (1969); special U. issue, *Agenda*, 8, 2 (1970); special U. issue, *BA*, 44, 4 (1970); Genot, G., *Sémantique du discontinu dans "L'allegria" d'U.* (1972); special U. issue, *FI*, 6, 2 (1972); Jones, F. J., *G. U., Poet and Critic* (1977); Caroutch, Y., *U.* (1979)

—AUGUSTUS PALLOTTA

UPDIKE, John

American novelist, short-story writer, critic, and poet, b. 18 Mar. 1932, Shillington, Pa.

U. was the only child of Wesley Updike, a teacher in a small Pennsylvania-Dutch community, and Linda Hoyer Updike, a writer. While attending Harvard he edited the *Harvard Lampoon*, serving as both a writer and graphic artist. Upon graduation in 1954 U. attended the Ruskin School of Drawing and Fine Art in Oxford, England, for a year. His return to the U.S. in 1955 was occasioned by an offer to join the staff of *The New Yorker*, with which he has been affiliated ever since, first as a writer for the "Talk of the Town" column, subsequently as contributor of poetry, essays, fiction, and literary criticism. His many honors and awards have included the National Book Award for *The Centaur* (1963), membership in the American Academy of Arts and Letters, a Guggenheim Fellowship in poetry (1959), the Prix Médicis Étranger (1966), the O. Henry Award for fiction (1966), a Fulbright Fellowship to Africa (1972), and both a Pulitzer Prize and an American Book Award in 1982 for *Rabbit Is Rich* (1981).

From its very beginning U.'s literary career has been distinguished by an unassailable stylistic brilliance. Critics unanimously praise the careful polish of his prose, his sharp instinct for metaphor, his painterly ability to set a vivid scene, and his ear for both the music and the dissonance of American speech. Yet his customary subject matter—the daily life of the suburban middle class—has seemed too commonplace for the taste of many readers. He has often been accused, in effect, of lavishing million-dollar talents on two-bit themes.

Such criticism is perhaps valid for the bulk of his poetry. *Tossing and Turning* (1977) gathers together a congeries of rhyming puns, superficial conceits, overly clever aphorisms, and obscure anagrams; this collection (including, for example, several turgid paeans to swollen genitalia) displays little more than the glitter of empty preciosity.

In his novels and short stories, however, U. demonstrates a more appropriate mastery of skill and substance. His fiction transcends the sometimes trivial limitations of middle class characters and setting, turning domestic dramas into comprehensive and illuminating revelations of the human spirit.

U.'s three novels featuring the character of Harry "Rabbit" Angstrom—*Rabbit, Run* (1960), *Rabbit Redux* (1971), and *Rabbit Is Rich*—offer his most eloquent and sustained treatment of an Everyman-hero in middle America. In the first book of the series, Rabbit, an ex-high school athlete whose best moments in life were experienced on a basketball court, tries to come to terms with the tedium of his adult life, where there are no cheering crowds or scoreboards to tell him how he is doing. Much of *Rabbit, Run* finds Rabbit trying to escape from his recently acquired wife: by driving south as far as a full tank of gasoline will take him; by carousing with his former coach; by running—literally and figuratively—whenever crisis or ennui confronts him. Not until the climatic scene of the novel, in which his wife, Janice, accidentally drowns their newborn daughter, is the protagonist forced to confront and consider his life.

Rabbit's story is fleshed out by evocative descriptions of the details of daily life in the 1950s. The styles of that decade—in automobiles, music, television, clothing, and opinion—come to life around Rabbit, although he is often oblivious to them.

Rabbit Redux is set in the tumultuous 1960s. Vietnam protest, the moon landing, the drug culture, and radical black activism—all force themselves upon Rabbit's consciousness. Although the events in *Rabbit Redux* sound like those of many other dreary political novels of its era, U.'s vibrant language and sympathetic portrayal of character make this book not so much political as individual, not so much time-bound as universal. Events of the larger world intrude at every turn, but Rabbit's attention persistently focuses on the small-scale joys and crises of his wandering life. As a wanderer who eventually returns home, Rabbit is an American Odysseus. The plot of *Rabbit Redux* mirrors Homer's epic in many particulars: the lotus-eaters are recast as drugged flower children; the Cyclops holds forth in a neighborhood bar as a single large television eye: Penelope—Rabbit's wife, Janice—does not remain faithful, but she does confine herself to an affair with a Greek used-car salesman, thereby retaining at least a shadow of her legendary precursor.

Rabbit Is Rich shows the protagonist in his middle years as the successful owner of a Toyota automobile dealership. Rabbit continues, as in the earlier novels, to fail in his domestic relationships, to lament the shabbiness of the civilization around him, and to feel generally ill at ease. But there is a difference. Whereas the younger Rabbit behaved instinctively, as he reaches his middle years he becomes reflective. Rabbit could never be mistaken for an intellectual, but he possessed a keen, active mind. His problem is that he

John Updike

has little in the way of cultural experience to challenge himself with. In this novel Rabbit becomes an aesthetician of the shoddy and the false in his world. He constructs elaborate mental lists. Musically and visually poetic, these listings would not be unworthy of Walt Whitman, except that their subject matter is hopelessly drab: plastic, neon, concrete, and smoke dominate his landscape and therefore his mind. In Rabbit Angstrom U. has created an unlikely hero—honest, bewildered, bright, misplaced—and he has in the process chronicled three decades of American daily life with consummate fidelity to each era.

The Rabbit novels share twin obsessions with much of U.'s other fiction: theology and sex. U. describes Rabbit's sexual exploits explicity and often. He also pays a great deal of attention to Protestant Christianity as believed (although seldom practiced) by his protagonist. Elsewhere, especially in *A Month of Sundays* (1975), he suggests that the experience of an infinite God and the equally mysterious experience of physical passion are intimately connected. For his character Rabbit there is merely the uneasiness of juggling two large forces in his life, one sacred and one profane.

A strong autobiographical strain runs through many of U.'s short stories. The earlier stories are usually set in the Pennsylvania countryside where he grew up, and the families described are similar in sensibilities to the families he has described in autobiographical writings and interviews. In his novels this strain is artfully diffused, but it can often be seen there as well. Rabbit Angstrom, for example, can be taken as an alternative personality, the kind of person U. could have become if certain particulars of his life had been different. Rabbit is gifted, both in body and mind, but, sadly, he lives by his guts rather than his wits.

A more nearly autobiographical exercise appears in *Too Far to Go: The Maples Stories* (1979). These interconnected short stories (written over the course of several years while U. was divorcing his first wife) document the trauma of divorce in the family of Richard and Joan Maple. Richard Maple, unlike Rabbit Angstrom, is an intellectual, living much of his life in his mind. He confronts trouble with all the mental force he can muster. His life is probably no happier than Rabbit's, but he does emerge from his traumatic divorce with a tough, admirable self-knowledge utterly lacking in Rabbit.

The Maples stories are unrelenting in their depiction of the anguish, guilt, and cruelty attending Richard and Joan's bitter ceremony. Agonizing children ask questions their parents will not or cannot answer; civilized, bourgeois adults find their lives, like careening automobiles, dangerously out of control. The disasters of this drama are not, however, all-encompassing. They consist of vows unkept, of trust broken, of children wounded, of small domestic furnishings permanently scorched. But everyone survives the ordeal: the overriding perspective of these stories suggests that for Richard and Joan Maple bits and pieces of a saving grace can be found despite their tribulations. The final scene in the story "Here Come the Maples" demonstrates U.'s skill in balancing conflict and in restoring ravaged souls. As the Maples prepare to leave the courthouse where they have signed papers making their divorce final, Richard, on impulse, leans over and kisses Joan. The act seals their rupture, but it also affirms a ritual bond holding them within certain shared assumptions. In these short stories, as in all of his fiction, U. displays a rare talent for precision and a surehanded wisdom in creating and understanding his subjects.

FURTHER WORKS: *The Carpentered Hen and Other Tame Creatures* (1958); *The Poorhouse Fair* (1959); *The Same Door* (1959); *Pigeon Feathers, and Other Stories* (1962); *Telephone Poles, and Other Poems* (1963); *Olinger Stories: A Selection* (1964); *Of the Farm* (1965); *Assorted Prose* (1965); *The Music School* (1966); *Couples* (1968); *Midpoint, and Other Poems* (1969); *Bech: A Book* (1970); *Museums and Women, and Other Stories* (1972); *Six Poems* (1973); *Buchanan Dying* (1974); *Picked-Up Pieces* (1975); *Marry Me: A Romance* (1976); *The Coup* (1978); *Sixteen Sonnets* (1979); *Problems, and Other Stories* (1979); *Five Poems* (1980); *Hawthorne's Creed* (1981); *Rabbit Is Rich* (1981); *Rabbit, Run* (1981); *Bech Is Back* (1982); *The Beloved* (1982); *Hugging the Shore* (1983); *The Witches of Eastwick* (1984); *Facing Nature* (1985); *Roger's Version* (1986); *Just Looking: Essays on Art* (1989); *Rabbit at Rest* (1990); *Odd Jobs: Essays and Criticism* (1991); *Memories of the Ford Administration* (1992); *Collected Poems 1953-1993* (1993); *The Afterlife, and Other Stories* (1994); *Brazil* (1994); *Golf Dreams: Writing on Golf* (1996); *In the Beauty of the Lilies* (1996)

BIBLIOGRAPHY: Samuels, C. T., *J. U.* (1969); Hamilton, K., and Hamilton, A., *The Elements of J. U.* (1970); Burchard, R. C., *J. U.: Yea Sayings* (1971); Taylor, L. E., *Pastoral and Antipastoral Patterns in J. U.'s Fiction* (1971); Detweiler, R., *J. U.* (1972); Markle, J. B., *Fighters and Lovers: Theme in the Novels of J. U.* (1973); Vargo, E. P., *Rainstorms and Fire: Ritual in the Novels of J. U.* (1973); Thorburn, D., and Eiland, H., eds., *J. U.: A Collection of Critical Essays* (1979); Hunt, G. W., *J. U. and the Three Great Secret Things: Sex, Religion, and Art* (1980); Uphaus, S. H., *J. U.* (1980); Greiner, D. J., *The Other J. U.: Poems, Short Stories, Prose, Play* (1981); Macnaughton, W. R., ed., *Critical Essays on J. U.* (1982); Luscher, R. M., *J. U.: A Study of the Short Fiction* (1993)

—LARRY TEN HARMSEL

Though he is barely thirty, U. has already awakened themes dormant in American letters since Hawthorne and Melville. Surely many religious people feel their own childhood, their hopes and terrors, to the tips of their toes when they read him. Yet the established critics seem to miss what he is saying.

"The point to be made about U.," George Steiner wrote about *The Centaur*, "is tiresomely obvious. . . . It is, of course, the gap between formal, technical virtuosity and the interest or originality of what is being said." Yet U. is often writing about man's search for personal immortality. He sometimes takes Protestant Christianity with ruthless seriousness. He is willing to try to understand life in American small towns and suburbs as it is now lived; he is not a prophet of dangerous living, not a preacher of meaninglessness. He regularly refuses the values, the starting points, of the secular reformer. He does not take the lead in causes the critics like to support; he sometimes takes a direction they fail to see.

Michael Novak, "U.'s Quest for Liturgy," *Commonweal*, 10 May 1963, p. 192

There were many of us who felt that *Rabbit, Run* was U.'s most solid book—or at least until *Bech*—and now it looked as if he was going to fall back on it and try to milk it for whatever was left. A tour de force about a creep—that's about what I expected. And I was never so wrong. *Rabbit Redux* is the complete U. at last, an awesomely accomplished writer who is better, tougher, wiser and more radically human than anyone could have expected him to be.

In *Rabbit Redux*, U.'s ear is perfect and he has finally put together in his prose all the things that were there only separately. He has sacrificed none of his sensibility—simply translated it into gutsier, more natural but no less eloquent rhythms. He moves now with the sureness, grace and precision of the born athlete. Let me give you just one random example: Jill's mother—rich, ripe, spoiled—feels, when she finds out what happened to her daughter, "a grieved anger seeking its ceiling, a flamingo in her voice seeking the space to flaunt its vivid wings. . . ." But enough—for God's sake, read the book. It may even—will probably—change your life.

Anatole Broyard, "U. Goes All Out at Last," *NYT*, 5 Nov. 1971, p. 40

J. U. has been an enviable problem. Gifted at once with a supremely alert ear and eye for the pulse and sinew of contemporary American speech and with a passion for the rare word, for the jewelled and baroque precisions still vital beneath and around the current of common idiom, he has been able to write about literally *anything*. Whether it be the stubble in a Pennsylvania field, the swerve of a basketball under gymnasium lights, the rasp of a tire on gravel, the tightening at a man's temples under pressure of sexual fantasy, Mr. U. has made these planes of experience brilliantly his own yet true to the evidence, penetrative into the fabric of American discourse and gesture to a degree that future historians and sociologists will exult in. He has written of rich and poor, of urban and rural, of science and political intrigue, of gregariousness and cold solitude with an unforgiving yet strangely solicitous, almost tender intelligence. The critic and the poet in him (a minor but sparkling poet of occasion and humor of a kind infrequent now) are at no odds with the novelist; the same sharpness of apprehension bears on the object in each of U.'s modes. But it is precisely this ubiquity, the sheer range of whatever elicits his luminous dispassions, that has made it difficult for him to find a mastering theme.

> George Steiner, "Scarlet Letters," *New Yorker*, 10
> Mar. 1975, p. 116

His genius is best excited by the lyric possibilities of tragic events that, failing to justify themselves as tragedy, turn unaccountably into comedies. Perhaps it is out of a general sense of doom, of American expansion and decay, that U. works, or perhaps it is something more personal, which his extraordinary professional art can disguise: the constant transformation of what would be "suffering" into works of art that are direct appeals to [Nature's muse], not for salvation as such, but for the possibly higher experience of being "transparent"—that is, an artist. There has been from the first, in his fiction, an omniscience that works against the serious development of tragic experiences; what might be tragedy can be re-examined, re-assessed, and dramatized as finally comic, with overtones of despair. Contending for one's soul with Nature is, of course, the Calvinist God Whose judgments may be harsh but do not justify the term *tragic*.

Like Flannery O'Connor, who also studied art before she concentrated upon prose fiction, U. pays homage to the visual artist's "submission" to the physical stimuli of his world far more than most writers.

> Joyce Carol Oates, "U.'s American Comedies,"
> *MFS*, 21 (1975), p. 459

I would argue that *A Month of Sundays* attempts to redefine our religious heritage by creating a paradigm of the contemporary religious scene in America. By a paradigm I mean that the symbolic action of the novel traces the movements that U. feels have taken place in America's religious history. If we look at the novel in this way, Marshfield's progression among various women epitomizes the large movements of American religious history. Beginning with a long devotion, or marriage, to ethical action alone (Jane), it moves to a

brief hedonism (Alicia), to a commitment to otherworldly faith devoid of physical action (Mrs. Harlow), and finally to a unification of them all (Ms. Prynne).

The symbolic treatment of the desert and the omega both serve to reinforce my theory that U. intends for us to see this as paradigm of American religious history. The desert is the vast, at first glance meaningless and empty, post-Wasteland world to which we have come from the lush greenery of New England. The desert is, Marshfield realizes, our real environment, and it is growing rapidly, so that even the White House is inhabited by a scorpion. Marshfield writes, "the special world of God within the Bible is an oasis world; the world beyond, the world of the Lord's wider creation, is a desert." It is this world, this desert world, in which he learns to live.

> Suzanne H. Uphaus, *J. U.* (1980), p. 100

One should not draw final conclusions about an author as adept at so many different genres as J. U. To provide a summary statement at this stage of his career is presumptuous; to offer a prediction about his future is risky. U. delights because he surprises. One never knows what the next book will be. Alastair Reid's description of the multiple qualities of *The Coup*, U.'s latest novel at this writing, is to the point: "Call *The Coup* a caper, an indulgence, a tract, a chronicle, a fable—and it is all these things at different times—the fact is that U.'s sentences can be read with the pleasure that poetry can, and the fingers are more than enough to count the novelists of whom such a thing can be said. Whether imagining the presidency of a historical personage like James Buchanan, or creating the history of an imaginary country like Kush, U.'s sentences shine."

Yet many readers believe that the style outshines the substance. The catch phrases of the negative evaluations. . . continue to echo around this impressive canon: "All wind-up and no delivery"; "writes like an angel but has nothing to say"; "great issues aren't at issue in his work." What can one do except to shake his head and ask the reviewers to reread. U.'s reaction to this kind of carping is generally true: that many critics treat his books as disappointing versions of the ones they might have written if they had had the same material. But they do not have his material, and they do not have his style. Still, as he himself notes, there is no way a writer can please every reader. Author of more than twenty volumes, U. has pleased millions.

> Donald J. Greiner, *The Other J. U.* (1981), p. 261

UPPDAL, Kristofer

Norwegian novelist, poet, and essayist, b. 19 Feb. 1878, Beitstad, Nord-Trøndelag; d. 26 Dec. 1961, Oppdal, Sør-Trøndelag

U. is notable for his proletarian novels and lyric poetry, particularly his free verse, all of which he wrote in a version of New

Norwegian strongly influenced by the dialect of his native Trøndheim. Born in the northern Trøndelag region, U. spent his youth as a farm laborer, shepherd, and hired hand in his father's livery stable. After some brief studies in folk high schools in Norway and Denmark, he worked for the next twelve years as a miner and itinerant laborer, occasionally as a newspaper reporter, traveling the length and breadth of Norway. In 1899 U. joined Norway's burgeoning labor union, at the time perhaps the most radical in Europe, in which he later served in several elected positions. In his fiction U. set himself the task of recounting the unfolding saga of Norway's new industrial worker—the miner, the railroad worker, the union organizer. The period after World War I was one of rapid industrialization in Norway when men by the thousands were leaving their villages and joining railroad crews or flocking to the cities in search of factory jobs. For U. these men represented, at the least, a new phase in the history of class relations, if not a new type of humanity altogether. In U.'s view, these workers, thanks to their newly acquired skills and political power, could look forward to a degree of freedom and self-confidence that was greater than at any previous point in history.

U. embodied this vision in a series of ten novels with the collective title of *Dansen gjennom skuggeheimen* (1911–24; dance through the world of shadows). U.'s first novel, *Ved Akerselva* (1910; by Aker River), a realistic account of the life of an itinerant railroad worker, was originally conceived as an independent work, but after completing it U. conceived the idea for his larger work, and in 1923 he integrated the novel into the series in a revised version under the title of *Vandringa* (travels). While not autobiographical in a narrow sense, these ten novels retrace the course of U.'s life and career. In the first half of the series he tells the stories of young men as they grow up, leave home, and launch into life as itinerant laborers. In the latter half, particularly volumes seven and ten, U. focuses his attention on the complex relationships that arise between the worker and the labor union, the organization that both empowers and restricts him. The novels in their order of composition (not narrative sequence) are *Dansen gjennom skuggeheimen* (1911; dance through the world of shadows), *Trolldom i lufta* (1912; magic in the air), *Bas-Ola storbas og laget hans* (1913; big boss Ola and his crew), *Røysingfolke* (1914; people on the move), *Stigeren* (1919; the climber), *Kongen* (1920; the king), *Domkyrkjebyggaren* (1921; the cathedral builder), *I skiftet* (1922; the change), *Vandringa* (1923; travels), and *Herdsla* (1924; Herdsla). From an aesthetic standpoint, it is perhaps the first novel, from which the series derives its name, that is the most accomplished. The later novels, however, are interesting from the way in which they reveal the almost religious significance U. attributed to the labor movement in Norway, and his growing pessimism when it failed to meet his expectations.

U.'s first volumes of poetry, *Kvæde* (1905; lament) and *Ung sorg* (1905; young sorrow), are chiefly of historical value today, marked as they are by conventional language and naive, nationalistic sentiment. However, his subsequent volumes, *Sol-laug* (1905; sun league), *Villfuglar* (1909; wild birds), *Snø-rim* (1915; snow rhyme), *Solblødling* (1918; sun bleeding), *Elskhug* (1919; love), and *Altarelden* (1920; altar fire), show a steady progression in artistry and creative freedom. As in his fiction, U. directs his attention to the working man, portraying his passions and disappointments with immediacy and power, employing the technique of free verse long before it became popular in Scandinavia. In the earlier volumes, U.'s vision is informed by a kind of pantheistic eroticism; in the later volumes, certainly as a result of World War I,

his vision becomes darker, verging on the apocalyptic. U. devoted the final years of his life to an immense poetic work in three books, *Galgberget* (1930; gallows mountain), *Hagamannen* (1939; Haga man), and *Løysinga* (1947; the solution), published under the collective title *Kulten* (1947; Kulten). Kulten is the name of the protagonist of this epic work of dark Nietzschean prophecy. He is a farmer-prophet who preaches a dark religion of suffering and eternal return, and as such embodies the pessimistic conclusion of U.'s philosophical and religious speculation in his final years.

FURTHER WORKS: *Ved Akerselva, og andre forteljingar* (1910); *Jotunbrunnen* (1925); *Dikt i utval, 1878–1961* (1960); *Hestane mine; etterlatne dikt* (1963); *Om dikting og diktarar; litterære artiklar i utval* (1965)

BIBLIOGRAPHY: Solumsmoen, O., *K. U., Cathedral-Builder* (1967)

—WILLIAM E. MISHLER

URDU LITERATURE
See Indian Literature and under Pakistani Literature

URMUZ
(pseud. of Demetru Dem. Demetrescu-Buzău) Romanian writer, b. 18 Mar. 1883, Curtea de Arges; d. 23 Nov. 1923, Bucharest

The son of a doctor, U. was educated in Bucharest, where he went to one of the best secondary schools and then studied law. He subsequently served as a judge in several provincial cities. He fought in World War I and after the war was a registrar at the highest court of law in Bucharest. He was given the literary pseudonym "Urmuz" by Tudor ARGHEZI, who in 1922 published two of U.'s short prose pieces in the literary journal *Cugetul românesc*, which Arghezi edited. Shortly thereafter, for unknown reasons, U. committed suicide.

Although U.'s work is extremely scant—the complete works, brought out in 1930 by Sasa Pană, a prominent Romanian avant-garde editor and publisher, consist of a forty-seven-page volume entitled *Algazy & Grummer* (*Algazy & Grummer*, tr. in *Adam*, 33, 322–24, 1967)—his influence, reinforced by his apparently gratuitous suicide, was enormous. Practically all the representatives of the lively Romanian avant-garde were, at key moments in their careers, under the spell of U.'s nonsensical humor, with its unexpected metaphysical implications, its SURREALIST dream world, its strangely named pseudocharacters (Algazy, Grummer, Ismail, Turnavitu, Gayk, Cotadi), and its imaginatively grotesque use of the stalest and tritest linguistic clichés.

Even the fact that he wrote so little and that everything he cared to put down on paper was not only a mad parody but actually a systematic and curiously effective subversion of "normal" literature contributed to U.'s reputation as a bizarre genius, a prophet of universal decay, a metaphysician of absurdity and silence. He was a genuine precursor and an independent early practitioner of antiliterature and the literature of the absurd, in the same line as the Romanian-born Tristan TZARA, founder of DADAISM, and the French surrealists. He was not, however, a writer without predecessors, and some of his literary sources can be traced to the works of such a Romanian master of the comic as I. L. Caragiale (1852–1912) and to the experiments of certain French writers such as Alfred JARRY. But U.'s obsessive world, although less rich, is certainly different from the essentially farcical world of Jarry's *Ubu* plays.

Eugène IONESCO, who has translated U.'s pieces into French, is right when he remarks in his introduction to these translations that U., whatever his reasons, was one of the first Europeans to try consciously to "dislocate" language and to express, through adequately absurdist means, the consciousness of one who sees the world coming apart, as his "heroes" absurdly disintegrate before the eyes of the reader. U.'s anxious tragicomedy of language left its definite mark on the writing not only of the Romanian avant-gardists or quasi-avant-gardists who continued to express themselves in their native tongue but also on those who chose to emigrate to France, from Ilarie Voronca (1903–1946) to Ghérasim Luca (b. c. 1920), perhaps the last significant postwar French surrealist poet, to Ionesco himself.

BIBLIOGRAPHY: Ionesco, E., "Précurseurs roumains du surréalisme," *Les lettres nouvelles* (Jan.-Feb. 1965): 73–78; special U. issue, *Adam*, 33 (1967): 322–24; Ionesco, E., "Présentation de U.," *SFR*, 3, 3 (1979): 297–314

—MATEI CALINESCU

URUGUAYAN LITERATURE

The last years of the 19th c. were marked by intense literary activity in Uruguay. Intellectual and aesthetic currents that were to shape 20th-c. Uruguayan literature could be clearly seen in the journal *Revista nacional de literatura y ciencias sociales* (1895–97). Two of its editors, José Enrique Rodó and Víctor Pérez Petit (1871–1947), demonstrated the eclectic nature of the times; the former is considered the leading philosopher of Spanish American MODERNISM, and the latter wrote fiction, drama, and poetry that revealed realistic and at times naturalistic tendencies.

Rodó's essay *Ariel* (1900; *Ariel*, 1922) attempted to delineate the cultural contributions of Latin America's Greco-Roman heritage and to contrast these contributions with the emphasis on utilitarian materialism seen in the United States and its Anglo-Saxon traditions. This essay was viewed as a kind of spiritual manifesto for the modernist movement, and its opinions regarding the United States were still generally accepted by a majority of Spanish Americans decades after its publication.

Julio HERRERA Y REISSIG was one of modernism's leading poets. Founder of the literary cenacle Panoramic Tower, Herrera y Reissig produced romantic verse early in his career, but by 1900 he had espoused French SYMBOLISM, the use of synesthesia, and an abstruse, animistic view of the universe. With the passing of modernism's vogue, a more intensely personal poetry was seen in the works of Delmira Agustini (1886–1914) and Juana de Ibarbourou (1892-1979). Unrestrained sensual love was a trademark of their verse, and, as in the case of nearly all of the postmodernist poets of Uruguay, there was a spirit of experimentation with new metrical forms.

Florencio Sánchez was without a doubt the outstanding Uruguayan dramatist of the first half of the 20th c. An astute observer of both rural and urban tensions, Sánchez's early success began with *M'hijo el dotor* (1903; *My Son the Lawyer*, 1961) and

La gringa (1904; *The Foreign Girl*, 1942; later tr., *The Immigrant Girl*, 1961). The latter is a realistic picture of the struggle between Italian immigrants and the gaucho landowners. Although Montevideo was (and is) a city where theater was widely appreciated, Sánchez found a larger audience in Buenos Aires, where many of his greatest successes were staged.

It is in the field of the novel and the short story that Uruguay has made its most significant contribution to 20th-c. literature. The Generation of 1900 included writers who clearly rejected the idealism of the romantics both in prose and poetry; realism and positivism were widely accepted, as was the modernist aesthetic. Eduardo Acevedo Díaz (1851–1921), Uruguay's first important novelist, was still active during the early years of the century. His 19th-c. historical novels had turned the attention of other writers to native, rural themes. His work served to inspire the major novelists of the Generation of 1900, Carlos REYLES, Javier de Viana (1865–1926), and Justino Zavala Muniz (1898-1969).

The generation's best novelist, Reyles, wrote *El terruño* (1916; native soil), a masterpiece depicting the confrontation of two brothers that ends in the destruction of both. His best-known work is *El embrujo de Sevilla* (1922; *Castanets*, 1929). Set in Andalusia, this novel is an excellent example of the tempering influence of modernism on the sometimes heavy hand of realism and determinism so prevalent at the time. Javier de Viana's one novel, *Gaucha* (1899; *Gauchos*, 1925), followed the line of Zola's naturalism in its vivid picture of decadent rural life. Viana's forte, however, was the short story; his themes and style remained constant throughout his literary career. Justino Zavala Muniz wrote only three novels, all of high literary value. His *Crónica de un crimen* (1926; chronicle of a crime) shows the continuing presence of Acevedo Díaz and the predilection for rural and gaucho themes.

Horacio QUIROGA, Uruguay's best short-story writer, was another luminary of the Generation of 1900. As the leader of the literary group Council of Brilliant Knowledge, he early experimented with modernist verse, but his best writing was done after he went, in 1910, to the Argentine jungle province of Misiones. His tales of horror, tragedy, and death appear in various collections; the English collection *The Decapitated Chicken, and Other Stories* (1976) contains some of his finest stories in translation. Although Quiroga spent many years in Argentina, his literary production was not unlike that of his compatriots who by 1920 were dedicated primarily to the regional rural novel and short story. Javier de Viana's collection *Leña seca* (1911; dry wood) and a series of other collected short stories published between 1921 and 1925 place him beside the master Quiroga in the exploration of the rural scene, its tragedy and its tensions.

Adolfo Montiel Ballesteros (1888-1971), Vicente A. Salaverri (1887–1971), and Enrique AMORIM continued this interest in rural themes during the period between the two world wars. They all produced both short stories and novels, but in his later years Amorim, the most popular writer of this group, began to explore urban problems. *El caballo y su sombra* (1941; *The Horse and His Shadow*, 1943) is Amorim's best work concerning the social, economic, and spiritual plight of the gaucho. In his later years Amorim wrote novels with an urban setting that probed the problems of a bureaucratic, industrialized society.

By the end of World War II nearly a third of Uruguay's population was concentrated in Montevideo. Interest in literature and the arts flourished, and there was a thriving press both in the capital and in the provinces. Literary works began to abandon the rural scene and to explore the vicissitudes of urban life. Many have referred to these writers as the Generation of 1945. The short story and the novel continued as the genres preferred by this generation, and the experimental prose style popular throughout Spanish America after 1945 was evident in Uruguay as well.

Felisberto HERNÁNDEZ and Juan Carlos ONETTI both explored the world of solitary souls in the midst of the urban masses. Onetti, in his first work, *El pozo* (1939; the pit), attempts to reach the inner being of his characters. In *La vida breve* (1950; *A Brief Life*, 1976) he reaches into the fantastic in his analysis of the urban world. Carlos Martínez Moreno (b. 1917) and Angel Rama (b. 1926) also write novels and short stories that are studies of city life. Mario BENEDETTI is without doubt the most prominent member of the Generation of 1945. A novelist, short-story writer, dramatist, and critic, Benedetti is best known for his fiction dealing with middle-class office workers caught up in the routine pattern of daily bureaucratic life. *Montevideanos* (1959; people of Montevideo) contains his most important short stories. The novel *La tregua* (1960; *The Truce*, 1969) considers the plight of the office worker when retirement approaches. Benedetti's work as a critic has received international attention, and his penetrating analysis of Spanish American political and literary trends has made him one of Uruguay's leading writers.

In the late 1960s Uruguay entered a period of social and political disintegration, culminating in a twelve-year dictatorship from 1973 to 1985. This led to the imprisonment and oftentimes torture of many writers and intellectuals while others were forced into exile. As a result of the diaspora cultural life was nearly annihilated within Uruguay. Many writers, however, continued to publish in exile, and in 1985 with the restoration of democracy a new freedom has allowed Uruguay once again to produce literature of value, far in excess of many larger countries.

BIBLIOGRAPHY: Rela, W., *Contribución a la bibliografía de la literatura uruguaya, 1835–1962* (1963); Musso Ambrosi, L. A., *Bibliografía de bibliografías uruguayas* (1964); Englekirk, J., and Ramos, M. *La narrativa uruguaya* (1967); Benedetti, M., *Literatura uruguaya siglo XX*, rev. ed. (1969); Rela, W., *Fuentes para el estudio de la literatura uruguaya, 1835–1962* (1969); Torres Fierro, D., "Recent Uruguayan Literature: An Assessment," *NewS*, 5 (1975): 113–16; Bollo, S., *Literatura uruguaya 1807–1975* (1976); Young, C. M., *Afro-Uruguayan Expression: A Cultural Perspective* (1990); Zlotchew, C. M., *Voices of the River Plate: Interviews with Writers of Argentina and Uruguay* (1995)

—HARLEY D. OBERHELMAN

USIGLI, Rodolfo

Mexican dramatist, essayist, critic, poet, and novelist, b. 17 Nov. 1905, Mexico City; d. 18 June 1979, Mexico City

Born into a family of Italian and Polish origin, U. made his first stage appearance at the age of twelve and dedicated most of his life to the theater. In 1935 he received a grant from the Rockefeller Foundation to study dramatic composition at Yale University, after which he returned to Mexico City and began the most productive period of his career. He taught theatrical history and technique at the University of Mexico and held diplomatic posts in France, Lebanon, and Norway.

The bulk of U.'s theater can be divided into three broad categories. The plays in the first consist of social or political satire; those in the second deal with abnormal psychology; and those in the third depict dramatic episodes of Mexican history. *El gesticulador* (1943; the imposter) and *Corona de sombra* (1943; *Crown of Shadows*, 1947) are generally considered his best works. *El gesticulador*, a deft portrayal of an impecunious history professor named César Rubio who assumes the identity of a deceased revolutionary hero to gain fortune and political power, rails against the betrayal of revolutionary ideals and the fraud prevalent at all levels of Mexican life. The cyclical recurrence of events underscores the archetypal struggle between good and evil as well as the author's belief in the unalterable essence of the human condition. César Rubio, moreover, represents U.'s concept of the mythical hero—a charismatic leader who, at a crucial point in history, synthesizes conflicting currents and sets a new course for his nation.

Corona de sombra treats the attempt by Maximilian and Carlota to establish an empire in Mexico in the 1860s. An imaginative interpretation rather than a historical account, this play represents the royal couple as necessary victims in the course of Mexico's struggle against foreign intervention. The initial action takes place in 1927 in the demented Carlota's bedroom on the day of her death, but dimensions are expanded by skillfully manipulated flashbacks illuminating critical moments from the past. U. simplifies and poeticizes history in order to reveal fundamental aspects of human behavior and thus gain greater insight into the present.

Two of U.'s greatest popular successes were *El niño y la niebla* (1950; the child and the fog), an emotion-packed naturalistic tragedy of congenital insanity, and *Jano es una muchacha* (1952; Jano is a girl), which caused a scandal because of its candid treatment of prostitution and sexual hypocrisy. His later plays include *Los viejos* (1971; the old people) and *Buenos días, señor Presidente!* (1972; good morning, Mr. President), both of which dramatize the generation gap in contemporary Mexican society, the former contrasting the aesthetic tastes of the old and young, and the latter, their political ideals.

U. wrote extensively on the Mexican theater and dramatic theory, his most basic tenets being that Mexican playwrights should treat themes related to national realities and that the theater should not mirror reality but instead should strive for an artistic, fictionalized representation of its essential features. Although his plots are usually tightly structured, they are occasionally marred by contrived situations. In *El gesticulador*, for example, a young North American professor of Mexican history fortuitously arrives at the door of César Rubio and announces his intention to research the life of a revolutionary figure with the same name as that of his host. U. is obviously more interested in the presentation of ideas than in the development of characters in real-life situations.

Despite his stress on national themes, U. has enjoyed greater success abroad than any other Mexican playwright. He has also been influenced by numerous foreign authors, including the ancient Greeks, John Galsworthy, and Bernard Shaw. Above all, however, he is a Francophile, having read widely in French and having based several of his dramas on works by well-known French writers. For example, Molière's *The Misanthrope* inspired U.'s *Alcestes* (1963; Alcestes); the plot of U.'s *Un navío cargado. . .* (1961; a ship loaded with. . .) reflects that of Joris-Karl Huysmans's (1848–1907) novel *Against the Grain*; and *4 chemins 4* (1963; 4 roads 4), written in French, is a Mexican version of *Une vie secréte* (a secret life) by Henri-René Lenormand (1882–1951).

U. has also published lyrical poetry and an ingeniously constructed murder mystery, *Ensayo de un crimen* (1944; trial of a crime). In 1972 he received the prestigious National Prize of Letters. On this occasion he was recognized not only as the creator of the modern Mexican theater but also as one of Latin America's most distinguished dramatists.

FURTHER WORKS: *El apostol* (1931); *México en el teatro* (1932); *Caminos del teatro en México* (1933); *Conversacíon desesperada* (1938); *Medio tono* (1938); *La familia cena en casa* (1942); *Itinerario del autor dramático* (1942); *Otra primavera* (1947; *Another Springtime*, 1961); *La última puerta* (1948); *Vacaciones I* (1948); *La mujer no hace milagros* (1949); *Sueño de día* (1949); *Aguas estancadas* (1952); *Vacaciones II* (1954); *Mientras amemos* (1956); *Un día de éstos* (1957); *Antonio Ruiz et l'art dangereux de la peinture* (1960); *La exposición* (1960); *Estado de secreto* (1963); *Falso drama* (1963); *Noche de estío* (1963); *El presidente y el ideal* (1963); *Teatro completo* (2 vols., 1963–66); *Corona de luz* (1965); *Anatomía del teatro* (1966); *Corona de fuego* (1966); *La diadema* (1966); *Dios, Batidillo y la mujer* (1966); *Los fugitivos* (1966); *Las madres* (1966); *El testamento y el viudo* (1966); *El encuentro* (1967); *Juan Ruiz de Alarcón en el tiempo* (1967); *Voces: Diario de trabajo* (1967); *Carta de amor* (1968); *El gran circo del mundo* (1969); *Obliteración* (1973); *Conversaciones y encuentros* (1974); *Imagen y prisma de México* (1976)

BIBLIOGRAPHY: Howatt, C., "R. U.," *BA*, 24 (1950): 127–30; Beck, V. F., "La fuerza motriz en la obra dramática de R. U.," *RI*, 18 (1953): 369–83; Gates, E. J., "U. as Seen in His Prefaces and Epilogues," *Hispania*, 37 (1954): 432–37; Ragle, G., "R. U. and His Mexican Scene," *Hispania*, 46 (1963): 307–11; Tilles, S. T., "R. U.'s Concept of Dramatic Art," *LATR*, 3, 2 (1970): 31–38; Savage, R. V., "R. U.'s Ideas of Mexican Theatre," *LATR*, 4, 2 (1971): 13–20; Scott, W. P., "Toward an U. Bibliography (1931–1971)," *LATR*, 6, 1 (1972): 53–63

—GEORGE R. MCMURRAY

USLAR PIETRI, Arturo

Venezuelan novelist, short-story writer, dramatist, essayist, and biographer, b. 16 May 1906, Caracas

U. P.'s forebears were of German and Italian descent. His grandfather and father were generals. He began publishing in magazines and newspapers while still in high school. After receiving his doctorate from the Central University in Caracas, he was appointed to the staff of the Venezuelan embassy in Paris. When he returned to Venezuela he abandoned his earlier avant-garde style and focused on the political, economic, and social problems of Venezuela. He both taught and held government positions. A military coup forced U. P. into a four-year exile in New York in the late 1940s. After his return in 1950, his literary interest shifted from the novel and short story to the essay. Eventually he again participated actively in political life.

In his first and most famous novel, *Las lanzas coloradas* (1931; *The Red Lances*, 1963), U. P. vividly depicts the War of Independence in Venezuela during 1812–14, the height of the conflict. Historical figures function merely as leitmotifs and background. The plot revolves around a mestizo who revolts against his master.

Arturo Uslar Pietri

Ironically, the patriotic creoles (Spaniards born in the colonies) find themselves battling not only the royalist troops but also their own ex-slaves.

U. P.'s mythified biographical novel, *El camino de El Dorado* (1947; the road to El Dorado), narrates in a colorful and vigorous style the bizarre adventures of the 16th-c. tyrant conquistador Lope de Aguirre, who inspired a paralyzing fascination among his soldiers.

U. P. ranks among the foremost Spanish-American short-story writers. According to Luis Leal, the term MAGIC REALISM was first used in Latin American letters by U. P. (1948) as *realismo mágico*, denoting the "discovery of mystery immanent in reality." Among his best-known stories marked by magic realism are "La lluvia" (1936; "Rain," 1942), a masterpiece of the genre, and "El fuego fatuo" (1936; "Ignis Fatuus," 1948). *Treinta cuentos* (1978; thirty short stories) contains works of magic realism written in an impressionistic and avant-garde style rich in images.

Among the subjects of U. P.'s visionary or pragmatic books of essays are the existence of an independent Latin American culture; Venezuelan problems (oil, population, education, and ecology); literature and art; science and politics. Various essays deal with *mestizaje* or hybridization—the new fusion of Europeans, Africans, and American Indians—which he regards as the basis of Latin American originality, and a key to understanding it in the framework of world history; he also sees in *mestizaje* the answer to the search for identity, resulting in an exaltation of the Latin American spirit. U. P.'s main focus is on history as a pragmatic instrument for perceiving the present in order to chart the future of the country. He believes that history and literature can serve the moral and didactic function of educating his fellow countrymen to reform Venezuela and to build its future.

FURTHER WORKS: *Barrabás, y otros relatos* (1928); *Red* (1936); *Sumario de economía venezolana para alivio de estudiantes* (1945); *Letras y hombres de Venezuela* (1948); *Treinta hombres y sus sombras* (1948); *La ciudad de nadie* (1950); *De una a otra Venezuela* (1950); *Las nubes* (1951); *Otoño en Europa* (1952); *Apuntes para retratos* (1952); *Tierra venezolana* (1953); *Obras selectas* (1953); *Breve historia de la novela hispano-americana* (1954); *Historia de la rebelión popular de 1814* (1954); *Tiempo de contar* (1954); *Pizarrón* (1955); *Teatro* (1958); *Materiales para la construcción de Venezuela* (1959); *Chuo Gil y las tejedoras* (1960); *Del hacer y deshacer de Venezuela* (1962); *Sumario de la civilización occidental* (1962); *Un retrato en la geografía* (1962); *Valores humanos* (4 vols., 1964); *Estación de máscaras* (1964); *Hacia el humanismo democrático* (1965); *La palabra compartida* (1964); *Petróleo de vida ye muerte* (1966); *Pasos y pasajeros* (1966); *Oraciones para despertar* (1967); *Las vacas gordas y las vacas flacas* (1968); *La lluvia y otros cuentos* (1968); *Catorce cuentos venezolanos* (1969); *En busca del nuevo mundo* (1969); *Manoa* (1972); *Moscas, árboles y hombres* (1973); *Oficio de difuntos* (1973); *Fantasmas de dos mundos* (1979); *Los ganadores* (1980)

BIBLIOGRAPHY: Holmes, H. A., *Contemporary Spanish Americans* (1949): 184–98; Flores, A., *Historia y antología del cuento y la novela en Hispanoamerica* (1959): 634–41; Leal, L., "El realismo mágico en la literatura hispanoamericana," *CA*, 26 (1967): 230–35; Miliani, D., *U. P.: Renovador del cuento venezolano* (1969); Salgado, M. A., "Trends of Spanish American Fiction since 1950," *SAB*, 43, 1 (1978): 19–29; Peña, A., *Conversaciones con U. P.* (1978)

—JOHN FLASHER

USMAN Awang

(pseud.: Tongkat Waran [policeman's truncheon]) Malaysian poet, dramatist, short-story writer, and novelist (writing in Malay), b. 12 July 1929, Kota Tinggi

U. received an elementary education and some secondary schooling in his native state of Johore. He began working while very young, during the Japanese occupation (1942–45). In 1946, after the return of the British to Malaya, he became a policeman. He went to Singapore in 1951 to work as a newspaper and magazine proofreader; he later became an editor of several of these Malay publications. In 1963 he became an editor for the Language and Literary Agency in Malaysia, a position he holds to the present day.

U. is one of the writers credited with the development of modern Malay *sajak* (free verse) poetry in the early postwar years. Nevertheless, his early poetry, collected in *Gelombang* (1961; waves), showed the unmistakable characteristics of the older, traditional *pantun* and *syair* forms. Only in ideas and tone can U.'s early poetry be said to represent new directions. The collection *Duri dan api* (1967; thorn and fire) shows a development. The clarion call for independence, the cry of the struggling poor, the peasants, fishermen, and laborers; the difficult life in the cities,

especially for the workers; and the general social and political problems of the day are his favorite early subjects. Alongside these themes, which showed U. to be an angry young man, there were others that were simply human, personal, and romantic: love, peace, godliness, and family life.

In his early poetic experiments U. was groping in both form and theme. After his horizons were broadened by reading and travel, in addition to poems on local subjects he wrote on international themes, such as "Salam benua" (1970; greetings to the continents), which criticizes leaders of powerful nations for perpetuating a divided world, and "Darah dan doa" (1972; blood and prayer), a message of peace to all mankind.

U. is also a playwright. His best-known dramatic work is *Muzika Uda dan Dara* (1976; the musical play of Uda and Dara), with music by Basil Jayatilaka. It is a powerful drama of two young lovers thwarted by the evil designs of the girl's rich suitor.

The versatile U. has written fiction as well. Twenty-one short stories are collected in *Degup jantung* (1963; the heart beats). In these the reader can trace the author's development from a romantic and idealistic youth to a more mature writer concerned with social justice. His only novel, *Tulang-tulang berserakan* (1966; the scattered skeleton), is a less successful work. More an autobiography than a novel, it is based on U.'s experiences in Malacca and tells of a policeman who must fight communist insurgents without fully understanding the situation. This straightforward narrative is redeemed by its language and style.

U.'s primary importance is as a poet. Many younger writers have been influenced both by his style and by his passionate and committed treatment of social and political themes.

FURTHER WORKS: *Dari bintang ke bintang* (1965); *Serunai malam* (1966); *Tamu di Bukit Kenny* (1968); *Di bawah matahari* (1969); *Tirai zaman* (1969); *Kaki langit* (1971)

BIBLIOGRAPHY: Kirkup, J., Introduction to A. Majid and O. Rice, eds., *Modern Malay Verse*, 6th ed. (1971): x–xii; Osman, Mohd. Taib bin, "Modern Malay Literature: A Reflection of a Changing Society and Culture," *ASPAC Quarterly*, 5, 3 (1973): 23–37

—MOHD. TAIB BIN OSMAN

UYGHUR LITERATURE

The term "Uyghur" (more correctly, New Uyghur) was adopted in 1921, in Tashkent, at a meeting of emigrants of this Turkic group from the Chinese province of Sinkiang living in what was then the U.S.S.R. (There are today approximately two hundred thousand Uyghurs living in the former Soviet Union.) From the early 1930s the term was also used in Sinkiang, where the majority of Uyghurs (almost six million) live. The Uyghur literature of Sinkiang is now written in a modified roman alphabet based on the Chinese *pinyin*, although Arabic script continues to be used; the Uyghur minority of the U.S.S.R. uses a modified Cyrillic alphabet. In the People's Republic of China, Urumchi, the capital of Sinkiang province, and Kashghar, in the south, are the centers of Uyghur literary activity; in the U.S.S.R., the center is Alma-Ata in the Kazakh S.S.R.

Prior to 1921 Uyghur literature consisted partly of Islamic religious and moralistic works, available in manuscripts and lithographed editions, and partly of tradition-bound folklore, mainly tales, legends, and popular poetry. In the U.S.S.R. modern Uyghur literature developed along the lines of Soviet SOCIALIST REALISM. This meant a complete break with earlier literary patterns. Beginning with World War II a trend to explore the origins and history of the Uyghur people became noticeable—although it did not exclude the guiding principles of socialist ideology. An increased interest in subjects dealing with adjacent Sinkiang can also be noted. Leading writers of this period are Ilya Bakhtiya (dates n.a.), Khizmet Abdullin (dates n.a.), and Rozi Kadiri (dates n.a.). These and others have been discussed and analyzed by the literary historian M. K. Khamrayev (dates n.a.), who has been published in Russian as well as Uyghur.

Uyghur literature in Sinkiang can be said to begin after the uprising in 1932, when the works of Soviet-Uyghur authors, especially those of Umar Muhammadi (dates n.a.), were brought in and widely read. Only after the establishment of the Chinese Communist regime, however, did a genuine Sinkiang-Uyghur literature come into being, beginning with the literary journal *Tarim*. Short stories and novels were written in a realistic style, with themes deriving from the new ideology.

Since the end of the Cultural Revolution of the 1960s, which affected the Uyghurs as well as the other ethnic groups of China, Sinkiang-Uyghur literary production has increased considerably. An example of modern Sinkiang-Uyghur literature is Kayyum Turdi's (dates n.a.) novel *Kizil tagh itigida* (1976; at the outskirts of the red mountain), about the daily life of agricultural and irrigation workers living near the mountains of southern Sinkiang. Several anthologies of modern Uyghur literature have appeared, for example, *Hikayilir* (1980; short stories).

BIBLIOGRAPHY: Benzing, J., "Die usbekische und neu-uigurische Literatur," *Philologiae Turcicae Fundamenta*, 2 (1964): 700–720; Gabain, A. von, "Neu-uigurische Literatur," *Turcica*, 12 (1980): 156–60; Jarring, G., *Some Notes on Eastern Turki (New Uighur) Munazara Literature*, Scripta Minora, Royal Society of Letters at Lund (1981); Jarring, G., "The New Romanized Alphabet for Uighur and Kazakh and Some Observations on the Uighur Dialect of Kashgar," *CAsJ*, 25 (1981): 230–45

—GUNNAR JARRING

UZBEK LITERATURE

The language of the Uzbeks was called Turki or Turkistani until 1925, when the official designation was changed to Uzbek by Soviet authorities. The old oral art and the Chaghatay tradition (the Turkic tradition of written poetry and prose of Central Asia that flourished from the 14th to the 19th cs.) continued into the 20th c. in Uzbek literature, but modern, mainly didactic works began to be written. Marked by innovations in style, form, and genre, the new writing was at first devoted largely to various reforms and was later exploited for political indoctrination. Transitional verse, using standard prosody and both traditional and contemporary themes, was written by numerous poets, notably Muhammad Khoja-oghli Muqimiy (1850–1903).

Modern Uzbek drama originated with Mahmud Khoja BEHBUDIY's *Padarkush* (1911; *The Patricide*, 1979). Drama immediately became the chief new genre; representative plays were Hajji Mu'in

Shukrullahoghli's (dates n.a.) *Mäzlumää khatin* (1916; an aggrieved woman) and Hamza Hakimzada Niyaziy's (1889–1929) *Narmuhämmäd damläning kufr khätasi* (1916; the sacrilegious error of teacher Narmuhämmäd).

Some early dramatists also wrote fiction. The bilingual Abdalrauf FITRAT, who created the first Turki-language historical dramas—*Beggijan* (1917; Beggijan) and *Abul Fayz Khan* (1924; Abul Fayz Khan), among others—wrote in Tajik-Farsi (Persian) the controversial *Bayyanat-e sayyah-e hindi* (1912–13; tales of a Hindu traveler) and in Turki *Qiyamät* (1923; judgment day), both later translated into Russian and other languages. The first full-length Uzbek novel was *Otgän kunlär* (1925–26; days gone by) by Abdullah QADIRIY. He published another historical novel, *Mehrabdän chäyan* (1928; scorpion from the pulpit), about the Qoqan Khanate.

More recently, the foremost novelists have been AYBEK, winner of the Stalin Prize for the historical novel *Nävaiy* (1944; Nävaiy), and also author of, among many other works, an engrossing autobiographical novella, *Balälik* (1963; childhood); Asqad Mukhtar (b. 1920), whose *Apä-singillär* (1955; *The Sisters*, n.d.) is about women's emancipation; and the SOCIALIST REALIST writers Äbdullah Qähhar (1907–1968), whose *Särab* (1937; mirage) attacks nonconformist intellectuals, and Sharaf R. Rashidov (b. 1917), a Communist politician whose several novels include *Ghaliblär* (1951; *The Victors*, c. 1958), about collective farms, and *Qudrätli tolqin* (1964; mighty wave), about a Party functionary's private life.

New prose, both narrative and dramatic, is in greater demand than poetry, reversing older trends. Novels like Shatursun Ghulam's (dates n.a.) *Tazä häwa* (1978; the pure air) and stories by such writers as Rustäm Rahman (b. 1926), printed in the literary magazine *Shärq yulduzi*, reach a wide readership. Young writers of fiction, such as Nuräli Qäbul (dates n.a.) and Yaqut Rähim (dates n.a.), who writes about contemporary life, are often introduced in this magazine. Dramas are published less frequently and seldom treat current topics, probably because of severe censorship. During 1978, for example, only one new play was printed in *Shärq yulduzi*, Izzat Atakhan Sultan's (b. 1910) *Istehkam* (fortification), about a standard political-historical subject. Historical fiction by Mamadali Mahmud (b. 1945) and others has roiled the Marxist sensibilities of establishment critics by unabashedly admiring the physical, cultural, and spiritual inheritance of Central Asians. Mahmud's *Olmäs qayälär* (1981; perpetual cliffs), which ran in two successive installments in *Shärq yulduzi*, elicited harsh criticism in official circles and in the Uzbek S.S.R. press.

In the 20th c. poetry has been composed by many dramatists and writers of fiction as well as by those who are exclusively poets. Aybek began as a lyric poet, publishing the collection *Tuyghulär* (1926; sentiments). Toward the very end of his life he returned to verse, working on a grand, historical *dastan* (epic), *Temur* (1968; Tamerlane). Aybek was initially a protégé of illustrious poets like Batu (pseud. of Mähmud Hadi, 1904–1930), Cholpan (pseud. of Abdulhamid Suleyman, 1896–1938), Fitrat, and Elbek (pseud. of Mir Mashrik Yunus-oghli, 1898–1939), a quartet whose earliest avowedly Uzbek-language verse made up *Ozbek yash shairläri* (1922; young Uzbek poets) and who dominated Uzbek literature of the 1920s.

These poets and others were attacked by approved "proletarian" versifiers such as Ghayratiy (pseud. of Abdurahim Abdullah-oghli, b. 1902), who savagely criticized Cholpan, Qadiriy, and others in political rhymes. This led in the 1930s to the imprisonment and execution of Qadiriy, the four "young Uzbek poets," and many other talented writers, leaving mostly the conformist Socialist

Realists to hold sway for some twenty years. The revival in Uzbek verse that occurred in the 1960s and 1970s, therefore, has largely been the work of younger poets, among them women, earlier conspicuously absent from literature except for Manzura Sabir Aydin (1906–1953), Zulfiya Israil (b. 1915), and Saida Zunnun (b. 1926).

Interesting newcomers who have received prizes for poetry from the Communist Youth League of Uzbekistan include Hälimä Khudayberdi (b. 1948), whose slim volumes of verse, *Aq almälär* (1974; white apple trees), *Chämän* (1974; flower garden), and *Baba quyash* (1977; forefather sun), offer many short lyrical and personal poems, often dedicated to teachers or parents, along with occasional patriotic or topical verse. Gulchehra Nurullah (b. 1938), another young woman poet, devotes much of the delicate language in the short collections *Arzulärim qäqädi qänat* (1971; my desires take wing) and *Bäghishlaw* (1978; dedication) to beauty, love, and happiness, and to her children, sister, and mother. Outstanding newer male voices of the 1960s and 1970s include Rauf Parfi (dates n.a.) and Äziz Äbduräzzaq (b. 1928). Their poetry, too, appears often in *Shärq yulduzi*. "Official" poetry is well represented by Räz Babajan (b. 1921), who won a U.S.S.R. State Prize for *Ab-i häyat* (1969; water of life); he also writes comic plays. Notable, too, is the poetry of Räzzaq Äbduräshid (b. 1936), which appears in the collections *Käftimdäm aläm* (1969; the world on my palm), *Qälbim qolingdä* (1970; my heart in your hand), and others.

An exceptional case in current Uzbek literature is the work of Raim Farhadiy (b. 1942), which is of a type promoted by the Soviet regime: works by Central Asian writers composed not in their own language but in Russian. Many of Farhadiy's poems are collected in the Russian volumes *Freski Afrasiaba* (1970; frescoes of Afrasiab) and *Granitsa serdtsa* (1976; the heart's frontier).

Karakalpak Literature. The Karakalpaks, an ethnic group that since 1936 has been governed within the Uzbek S.S.R., have taken up written prose and verse after an exclusive preoccupation with oral art at the start of the century. Early playwrights were Qasïm Auezulu (1897–1937), author of *Tilek jolïnda* (1925; on the path of resolve); Äbdiraman Ötep (1904–1934), whose sixteen full-length plays long dominated Karakalpak drama; and Jolmurza Aymurza (b. 1910), whose plays, poetry, and fiction span the period from the 1920s to after World War II. Tölek (Tölepbergen) Qayïpbergen (b. 1929) published, among other works, the novelette *Mughallimge rakhmet* (1958; to the teacher, thanks) and the verse epic *Qaraqalpaq dastani* (1977 ff.; Karakalpak epic), translated into Uzbek and Russian. New verse includes small volumes of lyrics and narrative poems by Tölepbergen Mätmurad (dates n.a.) and Mäten Seytniyaz (dates n.a.).

BIBLIOGRAPHY: Allworth, E., *Uzbek Literary Politics* (1964); Benzing, J., "Die usbekische und neu-uigurische Literatur," *Philologiae Turcicae Fundamenta*, 2 (1964): 700–720; "La littérature karakalpak," *Philologiae Turcicae Fundamenta*, 2 (1964): 761; Allworth, E., "An Old Mood Returns to Central Asian Literature," *LE&W*, 11, 2 (1967): 149–54; Fierman, W., "Uzbek Feelings of Ethnicity: A Study of Attitudes Expressed in Recent Uzbek Literature," *CMRS*, 22, 2–3 (1981): 187–229

—EDWARD ALLWORTH

V

VĀCIETIS, Ojārs

Latvian poet, b. 13 Nov. 1933, County of Trapene; d. 28 Nov. 1983, Riga

V. was reared in the northeastern part of Latvia, near the Gauja River, which would exert a powerful attraction on the future poet and become a recurrent motif in his poetry. The war, which robbed his generation of its childhood, left an indelible mark on his psyche; it is a theme to which he returned more than once in his writing. His first publications attracted the attention of critics and other poets, and V. was invited to attend the Young Authors' seminar in Riga. His successful participation motivated him to begin studies at the University of Latvia. Although V. did not complete his studies, his years at the university allowed him to become familiar with the theory and history of literature. Beginning in 1958, V. held a number of jobs in the world of publishing and journalism and began to write critical reviews.

In early 1960 V. and his wife, the poet and translator Ludmila Azarova, moved to Riga, and in that same year V. published *Krāces apiet nav laika* (1960; No Time to Go around the Rapids). The principal subject of V.'s first important collection of poems is the question of the poet's and his generation's responsibility. It is a responsibility generated by the aftermath of World War II, a special consciousness that manifests itself as an intolerance of outward appearances and as a demand for honest work and truthfulness. The poems voice a sharp condemnation of hypocritical, demagogic, and totalitarian forms of thought. The poem "Einšteiniāna" (1962; Einsteinade) marks the beginning of a significant new phase in V.'s creativity. It is a work of great daring that left a profound mark on the subsequent development of Latvian literature. The innovation consists in calling for a widening and deepening of the artistic experience of time and space in poetry. The poem is notable, as well, for a stylistic expressiveness and intellectual power not found in earlier work. Contributing to the poem's tragic expressiveness is the sweeping survey of the contradictions, indifference, apathy, and cowardice that have become the defining characteristics of a totalitarian society. The poet appeals to the memory of past persecutions and, addressing himself to humanity's conscience, enjoins it to respect the genius of those who can see and reach beyond the limits of the commonplace.

In 1963 V. became a frequent target of criticism by the communist leadership and finally incurred an explicit prohibition to publish for five years. However, in 1968 critics greeted the collection *Dzegūžlaiks* (The Time of Cuckoos) as a work marking a new phase in the poet's creativity. They noted that the previous, largely critical outlook had given way to a more harmonious and optimistic perspective sustained by a growing faith in humanity's basic goodness. The poet's creativity also gave evidence of a thematic and stylistic evolution. The former emphasis on the global and universal was replaced by a concern for the ordinary, and daily, inner conflicts replaced struggles waged with the world outside. *Visāda garuma stundas* (1974; Hours of Every Length) is largely philosophical in its orientation. V. returns here to some of his favorite themes, among which, as the title suggests, is the notion of an inner, psychological time. In general, V.'s poetry of the mid-1970s is so rich and varied that it encompasses all the topics and problems to be found in the work of the Latvian poets of the time. His stylistic virtuosity is also evident in the vast range of tonalities he covers, going from the lyrical and heroic to satirical and journalistic modes,

The poetry of *Zibens pareizrakstība* (1980; The Orthography of Lightning) is described by critics as the awakening call that speaks to the consciousness of a people and of an era. The collection is marked by a harsh and bitter tone that often contrasts with expressions of a profound love the poet manifests for his people and his time. V.'s last collection, *Si minors* (1982; Si Minor), is written in the form of a diary that contains observations about daily existence as well as a meditation on the creative process. While the title suggests a melancholy mood, the poems mainly express the struggle for meaning in a life in which despair intermingles with renewed bursts of energy, even the joy of victory.

V. also published a number of collections of poetry for children. The purpose, as in his other works, is to energize the reader with the desire to find out more about the world and about oneself. V. is generally considered one of Latvia's most talented poets of the second half of the 20th c. His notable achievements are to have revived almost single-handedly interest in poetry following World War II and, later, to have played a key role in helping to maintain the vitality of the genre during the decades of Soviet occupation.

FURTHER WORKS: *Tālu ceļu vējš* (1956); *Ugunīs* (1958); *Tās dienas acīm* (1959); *Dziesmas par. . .* (1965); *Viņu adrese—taiga* (1966); *Elpa* (1966); *Sasiesim astes* (1967); *Aiz simtās slāpes* (1969); *Melnās ogas* (1971); *Punktiņš, punktiņš, komatiņš* (1971); *Gamma* (1976); *Kabata* (1976); *Antracīts* (1978); *Ar pūces spalvu* (1983); *Astoņi kustoņi* (1984); *Nolemtība* (1985); *Ex libris* (1988); *Kopoti raksti* (7 vols., 1989–95); *Es protu noņemt sāpes* (1993)

BIBLIOGRAPHY: Ķikāns, V., *Kur cilvēks sācies* (1974); Čaklais, M., *Saule rakstāmgaldā* (1975): 65–82; Admīdiņš, R., *Dzejas darbdiena* (1977): 37–84; Valeinis, V., *Latviešu lirikas vēsture* (1979): 305–22; Peters, J., *Kalējs kala debesīs . . .* (1981): 132–39; Kubuliņa, A., *Kontūras* (1981): 85–101; Garda, M., ed., *O. V.–50: Pers. Bibl. Rād.* (1983); Kronta, I., *Gadi. Darbi. Personības* (1986): 305–40; Ķikāns, V., *Tevī kāpj mīļums . . .* (1989); Kronta, I., ed., *Visums, sirds un tāpat . . .* (1993)

—KARLIS RACEVSKIS

VACULÍK, Ludvík

Czechoslovak novelist and essayist (writing in Czech), b. 23 July 1926, Brumov, near Valašské Klobouky

At the age of fifteen V. went to work in a shoe factory but at the same time continued his education, eventually studying journalism in Prague. For three years he was supervisor in a trade school. In 1953 he became a book editor, later took up radio journalism, and then became an editor of the Writers' Union's weekly journal, a position he held from 1965 until it was forced to suspend publication in 1969. Between 1969 and 1989 V. was under a publication ban in Czechoslovakia, and his work appeared only in the West. In the 1970s V. helped to organize the dissemination in manuscript copies of the work of banned writers and was frequently harassed and interrogated by the secret police.

In his first work, the novel *Rušný dům* (1963; a busy house), V. used his not too happy experience as an educator to present an unembellished picture of some of the practices he had witnessed. But the book, a kind of public complaint, attracted less attention than did V.'s radio programs and later his unconventional essays and articles.

It was only when *Sekyra* (1966; *The Axe*, 1973) was published that V. was also recognized as a novelist. This book appeared at a time of growing doubts about the performance of the Communist Party as a self-proclaimed leader of the nation. The main character in *Sekyra* (modeled evidently on V.'s father) is an idealist of strong moral sense who in the difficult years before and during World War II cherished his vision of justice and happy life for all under socialism. He enthusiastically sets about building the perfect society, dragging the hesitant into it by force if necessary. The means employed gradually corrupt the ideal, and he dies, having alienated those he wanted to help, a dreamer degraded to a Party official. *Sekyra* has a complex structure, with several time frames often blending in midsentence; its idiosyncratic style bespeaks the influence of the Moravian dialect both in syntax and in vocabulary.

In his skeptical view of recent history, V. by implication blamed the Party leadership for ills not specific to socialism, but shared by most industrial societies. He believed, however, that the socialist program had promised to do away with these ills and that the Party was in a position to carry out that pledge. This conviction was forcefully expressed in his address at the Fourth Czechoslovak Writers' Congress in 1967. Although the speech was immediately banned and V. expelled from the Communist Party, news of it quickly spread. In the best tradition of Czech writers, V. had spoken up on behalf of the nation. The speech also signaled the approaching conflict between the reformers and the dogmatists within the Party, which was to result in the short-lived liberalization of 1968. During that period, V. produced "Dva tisíce slov" ("Two Thousand Words"), an article published in several Prague newspapers and in translation in the Western press, calling for the speeding up of reforms and outlining the duties and the rights of the citizen. It attracted worldwide attention, became one of the classic documents of the human-rights movement, and a few months later was used by the Soviet Union as one of the pretexts for armed intervention. For some time to come it overshadowed V.'s importance as a writer.

V.'s next book, *Morčata* (1977; *The Guinea Pigs*, 1973), published in Czech in Canada, was long available only in a German translation, although it was written shortly after the 1968 invasion, the aftermath of which it obviously reflects in an indirect way. It presents a time out of joint, a world in which values are perverted and false perceptions are the order of the day. A Kafkaesque abstraction combined with V.'s customary earthiness and with BLACK HUMOR turn a cheerful little tale about a Prague family who keep guinea pigs for their sons' pleasure into a haunting allegory of helplessness and inescapable doom.

During the 1970s V., who was awarded the George Orwell Prize in 1976, wrote mainly sketches and essays inspired by the everyday experience of a dissident, some of which received wide publicity in the West. Some of these were published as *A Cup of Coffee with My Interrogator* (1986).

Český snář (1983; Czech book of dreams), also published in Canada, is, like *Sekyra* and *Morčata*, anything but a conventional novel. The characters are real people and bear their real names, and the events that are recounted actually took place; yet the order imposed on them by the author is that of a work of fiction. Written in the form of a diary, it describes the life of the isolated and closely knit community of political and literary dissidents in Prague. The merciless sincerity with which V. exposes all its aspects implicitly contrasts with the corruption and hypocrisy of the system that has forced them into a ghetto, although hardly any reference is made to the world at large and no criticism is offered.

V. acquired a considerable prestige in the 1960s for his uncompromising attitude to all kinds of official malpractices, which he castigated with the zeal of a grass-roots reformer. His popularity reached a peak in 1967, when he became almost a national hero. At the same time he helped to raise the level of Czech journalism. In his novels and other writings, marked by a characteristic style and humor, he evoked a personal, intriguing and provocative chronicle of life in Czechoslovakia over the past thirty turbulent years.

BIBLIOGRAPHY: Hamšík, D., *Writers against Rulers* (1971): 181–98; Liehm, A. J., *The Politics of Culture* (1972): 183–201; Mihailovich, V. D., et al., eds., *Modern Slavic Literatures* (1976), Vol. II: 209–13; French, A., *Czech Writers and Politics, 1945–1969* (1982): 233–36, 256–61, and passim

—IGOR HÁJEK

VAIČIULAITIS, Antanas

Lithuanian short-story writer, novelist, and critic, b. 23 June 1906, Vilkaviškis; d. 22 July 1992

V. studied Lithuanian and French literatures at the Lithuanian State University, Kaunas, before going to France to study at the University of Grenoble and the Sorbonne. After a number of years spent as a high-school teacher and university lecturer, in 1940 V. joined the staff of the Lithuanian embassy in Rome. Shortly afterward, he emigrated to the U.S. and later became associated with the Voice of America and the U.S. Information Agency.

A careful, unhurried artist, V. creates his artistic designs from the texture of day-to-day reality, but he is interested in nuances of human experience that often seem peripheral to the central concerns of most men. For example, in his stories people so identify with the human significance of things rendered obsolete by time that they prefer to follow them into oblivion; the sight of a yellow leaf falling in the autumn sunshine can be an emotionally overwhelming experience; and an illegitimate child personally accepts her mother's guilt and allows her own life to plunge toward tragedy.

V.'s one novel, *Valentina* (1936; Valentina), depicts a woman's retreat from love into the arms of death. The story is told from the viewpoint of her lover, Antanas, who becomes a vehicle for the author's personal sad and gentle visions. Valentina's fragile inner world collapses under the pressure of exterior reality when she is forced to choose between a man she loves and a strong, vulgar man to whom she is morally indebted. Unable to decide, she drowns herself in a lake during a summer storm. Since Antanas's love for her is essentially based on the ideal vision he has created, Valentina's death is the death of love itself to him, and the novel comes to an abrupt halt.

V. strives for symmetrical correspondence between emotional states and his characters' concrete environment; material reality therefore acquires a symbolic and prophetic significance. This is especially true of the world of nature—the principal medium through which V.'s protagonists become aware of the intensity and meaning of their personal emotions and relationships. In one of his best stories, "Moteris iš šiaurės" (1947; "The Woman from the North," 1965), the autumn floods create a tragic atmosphere in which a desperate love affair, in conflict with the established societal norms, ineluctably speeds to an unhappy end.

In V.'s writing, inanimate objects seem to acquire a life independent of natural laws. V. has experimented with genres that verge on fairy tales, even though nothing at all miraculous happens in these stories. He has also written true fairy tales, some of which are "prose fables," in which human passions are conveyed through animal protagonists, and legends of other times and places. He often expresses his moral and aesthetic concerns by using artists, saints, and philosophers as protagonists.

V. is one of the best Lithuanian prose stylists. Although in his work features of objective reality are made indeterminate by emotion, everything remains precise, and his tales retain a classical sense of proportion, order, and clarity.

FURTHER WORKS: *Vakaras sargo namely* (1932); *Vidudienis kaimo smuklėj* (1933; *Noon at a Country Inn*, 1965); *Mūsų mažoji sesuo* (1936); *Pelkių takas* (1939); *Kur bakūžė samanota* (1947); *Pasakojimai* (1955); *Auksinė kurpelė* (1957); *Gluosnių daina* (1968); *Ir atlėkė volungė* (1980)

BIBLIOGRAPHY: Šilbajoris, R., *Perfection of Exile: 14 Contemporary Lithuanian Writers* (1970): 56–76

—RIMVYDAS ŠILBAJORIS

VAILLAND, Roger

French novelist, essayist, and journalist, b. 16 Oct. 1907, Acy-en-Multien; d. 12 May 1965, Meillonnas

The elder of two children in a middle-class Catholic family, V. spent most of his youth in Reims and in Paris, where he attended the Sorbonne. An early passion for literature in general, and poetry in particular, led him and a group of friends—notably René DAUMAL and Roger Gilbert-Lecomte (1907–1943)—to create a literary review, *Le grand jeu* (1928–29), which was recognized and appreciated by the SURREALISTS. At about the same time, V. began writing for *Paris-Midi* and *Paris-Soir*. André BRETON used this journalistic career as a reason to banish V. and *Le grand jeu* from the inner circle of surrealism. The 1930s were a period of travel and prolific journalistic activity for him.

V.'s experiences with the Resistance furnished him with the setting and the material for the novel *Drôle de jeu* (1945; *Playing for Keeps*, 1948). During the next twenty years V. published eight novels and wrote three plays, one of which, *Héloïse et Abélard* (1949; Heloise and Abelard), won the Ibsen Prize. With another play, *Le colonel Foster plaidera coupable* (1951; Colonel Foster will plead guilty), he publicly sided with the Soviet Union in the Cold War; he joined the Communist Party in 1952. Most of his work between 1951 and 1956 bears witness to this ideological affiliation. Returning disillusioned from the Twentieth Party Congress in Moscow in 1956, he wrote *La loi* (1957; *The Law*, 1958),

which earned him the Goncourt Prize. V. also published accounts of his travels and wrote several filmscripts.

V.'s novels present his life and personality as part of French life during a critical historical period. *Drôle de jeu*, his Resistance novel, has a protagonist whose character develops in a changing environment; this kind of development is the subject of all his later novels. *Les mauvais coups* (1948; *Turn of the Wheel*, 1962) is the story of a man trapped in a marriage who succeeds in forcing his wife to commit suicide, an act that frees him from his past. *Bon pied, bon œil* (1950; hale and hearty), a sequel to *Drôle de jeu*, expresses disillusionment with postwar society, seen as merely a continuation of prewar class systems with the ever-increasing influence of professional journalism on the lives of private citizens. *Un jeune homme seul* (1951; a young man alone) portrays a middle-class man who is able to cure his solitude by joining with others in a common cause. V.'s next two novels, *Beau masque* (1954; handsome mask) and *325 000 francs* (1956; 325,000 francs), are "committed" novels with protagonists from the working class, while *La loi* is a description of contemporary Italy seen as a feudal society. His last two novels, *La fête* (1960; *Fête*, 1961) and *La truite* (1964; *The Trout*, 1965), deal directly with novelists and their relation to society.

The rich texture of V.'s novels and their increasing popularity are attributable to his ability to grasp ideological complexities and depict them in concrete situations, while at the same time he points to his literary heritage and his individuality.

FURTHER WORKS: *Un homme du peuple sous la Révolution* (1937, with Raymond Manevy); *Suède 1940* (1940); *La dernière bataille de l'armée de Lattre* (1945); *La bataille d'Alsace—novembre-décembre 1944* (1945); *Léopold III devant la conscience belge* (1945); *Quelques réflexions sur la singularité d'être français* (1946); *Esquisse pour le portrait du vrai libertin* (1946); *Le surréalisme contre la Révolution* (1947); *Boroboudour* (1951); *Choses vues en Egypte* (1952); *Expérience du drame* (1953); *Laclos par luimême* (1953); *L'éloge du Cardinal de Bernis* (1956); *Monsieur Jean* (1959); *Les liaisons dangereuses 1960* (1960); *Les pages immortelles de Suétone: Les douze Césars* (1962); *Le regard froid* (1963); *La Réunion* (1964); *Écrits intimes* (1968); *Œuvres complètes* (10 vols., 1968); *Lettres à sa famille* (1972); *Le Saint-Empire* (1978)

BIBLIOGRAPHY: Bott, F., *Les saisons de R. V.* (1969); Brochier, J.-J., *R. V.: Tentative de description* (1969); Chaleil, M., *Entretiens: R. V.* (1970); Recanati, J., *Esquisse pour la psychanalyse d'un libertin: R. V.* (1971); Picard, M., *Libertinage et tragique dans l'oeuvre de R. V.* (1972); Ballet, R. and E. Vailland, *R. V: Deux études* (1973); Flower, J. E., *R. V.: The Man and His Masks* (1975)

—JO ANN MCNATT

VALDEZ, Luis

American playwright (writing in English and Spanish), b. 26 June 1940, Delano, California

The son of a farm worker, V. was born in California into the bilingual, bicultural world of migrant workers that became the context and theme of his theater work. He studied theater at San

Jose State University, where he wrote *The Theft* (perf. 1961), a one-act play, and *The Shrunken Head of Pancho Villa* (perf. 1964, pub. 1967), a full-length play staged by the college. In 1964 he joined the San Francisco Mime Troupe, a political theater collective. In 1965 V. left the troupe to join the United Farm Workers and help César Chávez organize migrant farm laborers. V. and other union members used theatrical improvisations as a tool for understanding, communication, and resolution of issues. Out of this work, El Teatro Campesino (The Farmworkers' Theater) was born.

V. created many *actos*—one-act political pieces created through improvisation—for El Teatro Campesino. In 1967 he separated the theater group from the union, in order to focus more on the theatrical intent and broaden its focus to a wide range of Chicano issues. The company was earning artistic recognition: in 1968 they won an Obie Award, and in 1969 they performed in Europe.

El Teatro Campesino continued to create *actos*, but moved on to other work as well. In 1967 V. wrote *Dark Root of a Scream,* published in *From the Barrio: A Chicano Anthology* (1973), a passionate Vietnam War protest play, and 1970 saw production of *Bernabé,* published in *Contemporary Chicano Theater* (1975), an allegorical play about a village idiot who is in love with the Earth. V. called these plays *mitos* or myths: they use allegorical figures, historical and religious allusions, and a kind of epic distance to create a tone that is larger than life.

In 1974 V.'s *La carpa de los Rasquachis* (The Tent of the Underdogs) was performed to great acclaim. Using a combination of styles—comedy, musical, political allegory, realism—the play followed the experiences of a farm worker surviving a tough life in America. Performed with few actors playing many roles, the play drew on European street theater traditions like commedia dell'arte, as well as the Mexican tent theater tradition from which it takes its title.

V.'s next play, *Zoot Suit* (perf. 1978, pub. 1992), would be his best known and most instrumental toward mainstreaming Chicano theater. Based on an actual murder trial during World War II, when several young Chicano boys were sentenced—probably unfairly—to life in prison, *Zoot Suit* freely mixed Spanish and English, as well as combining realistic political theater with catchy musical numbers. It was a tremendous success in Los Angeles, and became the first Chicano play to open on Broadway. In 1982 V. adapted the play for film. V. also adapted and produced a melodrama by 19th-c. theater artist David Belasco, following it with an original melodrama entitled *Bandido!* (perf. 1980). *Corridos* (perf. 1983) was an exploration of the Mexican storytelling tradition, and *I Don't Have to Show You No Stinking Badges!* (perf. 1986) a realistic play about a middle-class Chicano family's assimilation into American culture.

V. directed several films and television specials during the 1980s and 1990s, most notably *La Bamba* (1987), the story of the Chicano pop singer Ritchie Valens. While enjoying his ability to engage in a wide variety of projects, V. continues to work with El Teatro Campesino and to create plays that address the political and social issues so fundamental to his early work. Admired for his originality and passionate themes, he is credited with having begun a revolution in Chicano theater that served as a forerunner for contemporary multicultural literature and performance.

FURTHER WORKS: *Actos* (1971); *Zoot Suit and Other Plays* (1992)

BIBLIOGRAPHY: Brown, E., "The Teatro Campesino's Vietnam Trilogy," *MV,* 4, 1 (1980): 29–38; Herms, D., "L. V., Chicano Dramatist: An Introduction and an Interview," in Bock, H. and A. Wertheim, eds., *Essays on Contemporary American Drama* (1981): 257–78; Huerta, J., Introduction to *Zoot Suit and Other Plays* (1992): 7–20; Babcock, G., "Looking for a Third Space: El Pachuco and Chicano Nationalism in L. V.'s Zoot Suit," in M. Maufort, ed., *Staging Difference: Cultural Pluralism in American Theatre and Drama* (1995): 215–25

—GINGER STRAND

VALENZUELA, Luisa

Argentine novelist, short-story writer, and journalist, b. 26 Nov. 1938, Buenos Aires

V. is one of the best-known, most critically acclaimed, and most translated contemporary Latin American authors. As the daughter of a successful Argentine novelist, Luisa Mercedes Levinson (1912–1988), V. grew up in an atmosphere of literary excitement and expectation. She worked as a journalist and editor, and published her first short story when she was eighteen. Her first novel, *Hay que sonreír* (1966; *Clara*, 1976), was written when she was homesick for Buenos Aires while living in Paris from 1959 to 1961. She participated in the University of Iowa's International Writers Program in 1969 while she wrote her second novel, *El gato eficaz* (1972; the effective cat). In 1978 V. settled in New York, where she has conducted creative writing workshops at New York University and Columbia University and has been the recipient of many grants and honors. In recent years, she has divided her time between New York City, Buenos Aires, and Tepoztlán, Mexico, all of which enter into her fiction. As well as being a prolific writer who has published six novels and five collections of short stories and novellas, V. is also vigorously involved in combating repression and censorship, both in her writing and as an active member of various international human rights organizations.

In all of her fiction, V. has focused on the interrelated themes of politics, language, and women. She often demonstrates how language can deform the reality it purports to describe and how it can be used to oppress and manipulate, on both personal and political levels. Concern for human rights and individual freedoms permeates V.'s writing, as does her interest in the social role of gender, the factors that determine the identity of women, and sexuality. She is fascinated by myths and by dreams, frequently weaving them into her multilayered fictions, which are often complex metaphors or parables of political and social realities.

Much of V.'s fiction is recognizably descriptive of Argentina. *Aquí pasan cosas raras* (1975; *Strange Things Happen Here,* 1979), written in Argentina during a period of political terrorism, focuses on the oppression of human beings by other human beings. In the title story, two poor men are torn between their desire to improve their lives and their terror of being noticed by the police. "Los mejor calzados" ("The Best Shod") is an ironic description of how the beggars of Buenos Aires wear elegant shoes because they can appropriate the footware of the bodies dumped in heaps by the torture squads.

Como en la guerra (1977; *He Who Searches,* 1977) is a novel of multiple simultaneous levels: a mythic journey, a search for truth, and an exploratory investigation of the essence of terrorism and the relationship of torturers and victims. Although the majority of stories in *Donde viven las águilas* (1983; *Up among the Eagles*, 1988) are abstract, magical, and metaphorical, many of them also have a powerful political component. In "Los censores" ("The Censors"), a dissident becomes a supporter of repression, even though it means his own execution, and "La historia de Papito" ("Papito's Story") is a moving tale of fear and empathy in the face of military violence. *Novela negra con argentinos* (1990; *Black Novel [with Argentines]*, 1992) is a surrealistic murder mystery, a metaphor of violence in contemporary Argentina, and *Realidad national desde la cama* (1990; *Bedside Manners*, 1995) recounts the startling experiences of a woman who returns to Argentina after an absence of ten years. In a series of hilarious, bizarre encounters, the horrors of inflation, poverty, and militarism are described, mocked, and made vivid.

V. has shown herself to be immensely skillful at both realistic and imaginative description, and nearly all of her fiction combines the two levels. She celebrates the capacity of human culture for myth and invention, while denouncing the repressive political misuses of these same powers. Each of her novels and short-story collections has enhanced her reputation as one of the most important voices in contemporary Latin American literature.

FURTHER WORKS: *Los heréticos* (1967); *Libro que no muerde* (1980); *Cambio de armas* (1982; *Other Weapons*, 1985); *Cola de lagartija* (1983; *The Lizard's Tail*, 1983); *Libro que no muerde* (1980); *Simetrías* (1993). FURTHER WORKS IN ENGLISH: *Clara: Thirteen Short Stories and a Novel* (1976); *Strange Things Happen Here: Twenty-Six Short Stories and a Novel* (1979); *Open Door: Stories by L. V.* (1988); *Stories by L.V.* (1988); *Blame* (1992)

BIBLIOGRAPHY: Martínez, Z. N., *El gato eficaz* de L. V.: La productividad del texto," *RCEH*, 4 (1979): 73–80; Picón Garfield, E., "Muerte-metamorfosis—modernidad: *El gato eficaz* de L. V.," *Insula*, 400–01 (1980): 17; Ordoñez, M., "Máscaras de espejos, un juego especular: Entrevista-associaciones con la escritora argentina L. V.," *RI*, 51, 132–33 (1985): 511–19; Paley Francescato, M., "*Cola de lagartija*: látigo de la palabra y la triple P.," *RI*, 51, 132–33 (1985): 875–82; special L. V. issue, *RCF*, 6, 3 (1986); Magnarelli, S., *Reflections/Refractions: Reading L. V.* (1988); Gazarian-Gautier, M.-L., "L. V.," *Interviews with Latin American Writers* (1989): 293–322; Magnarelli, S., "L. V.," in Marting, D. E., ed., *Spanish American Women Writers* (1990): 532–45; Guest, V., *Reweaving the Violated Marriage: Strategies for Confronting the Discourse of Political Terror in L. V.'s "The Lizard's Tail"* (1990); Cordones-Cook, J., *Poética de transgresión en la novelística de L. V.* (1991); Martínez, N. Z., *El silencio que habla: aproximación a la obra de L. V.* (1994)

—MARY G. BERG

VALÉRY, Paul

French poet and essayist, b. 30 Oct. 1871, Sète; d. 20 July 1945, Paris

Born of French-Italian parents, V. spent his childhood in the Mediterranean port town of his birth. He terminated his secondary schooling at Montpellier, where in 1888 he entered the university that today bears his name. While studying law, V. wrote poetry and became intensely interested in architecture, mathematics, and physics, the music of Richard Wagner, and the "scientific" poetics of Edgar Allan Poe. In 1889 V. discovered the Decadents and the poets Paul Verlaine and Stéphane Mallarmé. The following year he met the Parisian poet Pierre Louÿs (1870–1925), who introduced him to André GIDE; both were disciples of Mallarmé, whose poetry had the deepest effect on V. The example of Mallarmé was in fact soon to contribute to a blockage in V.'s own poetic creativity. During a Paris visit in 1891, V. was introduced to Mallarmé by Louÿs, who also began publishing in his review *La conque* some of V.'s poems, among them "Narcisse parle" (1891; "Narcissus Speaks," 1971), his first poem on the Narcissus theme, which permeates his work. The following year, V. underwent a severe emotional crisis from which he emerged with the determination to forsake all idols, including poetry, for scientific endeavors.

After terminating his law studies in 1893, V. moved to Paris where he regularly attended Mallarmé's Tuesday evening gatherings and soon became the older poet's favorite disciple. Living in an austere room whose sole decoration consisted of a blackboard, usually covered with calculations and equations, V. now wrote some of his most famous essays, like *La soirée avec Monsieur Teste* (1896; "An Evening with M. Teste," 1922), the first of the numerous pieces of the *Teste* cycle that was to preoccupy him throughout his life. Here he also wrote the first of his Leonardo da Vinci essays, *L'introduction à la méthode de Léonard de Vinci* (1895; "Introduction to the Method of Leonardo da Vinci," 1926), commissioned by *La nouvelle revue*. But most significantly, in 1894 V. began the first of the 257 *Cahiers* (notebooks) that he continued to write, at his privileged early hours of each day, for fifty years. These *Cahiers*, published posthumously in a 29-volume facsimile edition (1957–61), constitute a rich storehouse of ideas and inspirations from which V. drew throughout his life.

In 1897 V. was named to a position in the War Department, which he held until his marriage in 1900 to Jeannie Gobillard, niece of the Impressionist painter Berthe Morisot. He wrote an essay, "L'art militaire" (1897; military art), and his correspondence of those years reveals speculations about a *mathématique de la parole* (a mathematics of language), as well as plans for an *Arithmetica universalis* as a tool for the exploration of the mind. The year of his marriage V. left the War Department to become the private secretary of Edouard Lebey, a key executive of the news agency Havas. This position, which V. held until 1922, gave him exceptional insights into world affairs while leaving him much free time to pursue his own work.

In 1912 Gide approached V. on behalf of the publisher Gaston Gallimard with the request to submit his poems (scattered in diverse reviews) as well as some of his prose for publication. V. finally consented with the reservation that he "touch up" some of his old poems and submit some new ones for the volume. Thus he began to work on what was originally planned as a poem of some forty lines, a composition that eventually grew into the five hundred lines of *La jeune Parque* (1917; "The Young Fate," 1971). *La jeune Parque*, in the most rigorous classical prosody, orchestrates "a succession of psychological substitutions, the changes of a consciousness through the duration of a night," according to its author. In a letter also of 1917, V. relates its theme to one of Poe's key terms, "consciousness," in discussing this intellectual subject's lyric composition. Later V. recalled how, after the years of patient work on this poem, other poems burst forth almost spontaneously. What had originally been intended as a farewell came to mark his return to poetry.

Critical acclaim of *La jeune Parque*, his most hermetic poem, established V. as the most significant contemporary French poet. He soon became one of the most eminent public figures, receiving the highest official recognition and tributes from his own as well as other European countries. In 1923 he was named Chevalier, in 1931 Grand Officier, of the Legion of Honor; and in 1927 he became a member of the French Academy. From 1924 to 1934 he was president of the P.E.N. Club, and in 1935 he presided over the Arts and Letters group of the League of Nations' Committee for International Cooperation. In 1933 he was appointed one of the directors of the Mediterranean University Center, and in 1936 he assumed his professorship at the Collège de France, a chair in poetics specially created for him. As one of the most sought-after lecturers throughout Europe, V. had become the representative of his country's culture abroad.

The poems that followed *La jeune Parque* became V.'s major cycle of poems, *Charmes* (1922; 2nd ed., 1927; *Charms*, 1971), the second edition including "Fragments du Narcisse" ("Fragments of the Narcissus," 1971). With *Charmes* V.'s career as lyric poet reached its zenith. The best-known of the *Charmes* is the great elegiac meditation, "Le cimetière marin" (1920; "The Graveyard by the Sea," 1928), which first imposed itself on the poetic consciousness as a rhythm, then as a metric and strophic figure that needed to be "filled." V. called this poem his intellectual biography. Its protagonist is the Self divided, surrounded by a world of sun and sea, key symbols in V.'s poetry for intellect and affect. The setting is structured out of the poet's personal memories; it celebrates the universal archetypal elements of fire and water, symbols of mind and body. The lucid Self is alone, high up in the sun-drenched graveyard overlooking the sea, his mind aspiring to transcend the body that partakes of the universal mutability. In this soliloquy of the mind, the antithetical motifs of light and darkness, transcendent thought and material decomposition, timelessness and cyclical return, life and death, the universal and the personal, are contrapuntally invoked and interwoven in a poetic text V. called a fugue. Its themes are the contrasting moments of a dualistic Self, its ideal, angelic aspirations and its human limitations.

The publication of "Eupalinos; ou, L'architecte" (1921; "Eupalinos; or, The Architect," 1932) and "L'âme et la danse" (1921; "Dance and the Soul," 1951), both written on commission, distinguished V. as the master of yet another form of poetic expression, the Socratic dialogue. "Eupalinos; ou, L'architecte" is a "Dialogue of the Dead," in which the shades of Phaedrus and Socrates, now free of the bonds of space and time, nostalgically recall their mortal existence, freely evoking figures of the past, like Phaedrus's friend Eupalinos, the great architect and builder who had created temples inspired by love, metamorphosing life—and love—into art. "L'âme et la danse," as its title suggests, celebrates both body and soul, as Socrates, his physician Eryximachus, and Phaedrus, at a banquet, discourse on the most bodily of the arts, dance. V. returned to the dialogue form with "L'idée fixe; ou, Deux hommes à la mer" (1932; "L'Idée Fixe: A Dialogue at the Seaside," 1946) and "Dialogue de l'arbre" (1943; "Dialogue of the Tree," 1956). The former is about the mind obsessed by its "idée fixe," while the latter celebrates one of V.'s key symbols, the tree, which, with its roots deep in the earth and its crown reaching toward the sun, harmonizes the Dionysian Eros and its Apollonian sublimation.

Another genre that V. developed is the *mélodrame*, such as *Amphion* (*Amphion*, 1960), written to the music of Arthur Honegger and presented at the Paris Opera and Covent Garden in 1931, and *Sémiramis* (*Semiramis*, 1960), also written to Honegger's music,

Paul Valéry

presented at the Paris Opera in 1934. V.'s Narcissus last appeared in *Cantate du Narcisse* (1938; *The Narcissus Cantata*, 1960), written as a libretto to the music of Germaine Tailleferre.

V.'s many essays on subjects ranging from art, aesthetics, and literary criticism to pedagogy, philosophy, and politics, almost all of them commissioned work, were published in *Variété* (5 vols., 1924–44; *Variety*, 1968). *Tel quel* (2 vols., 1930–35; *Literature, Life and Letters*, 1936) consists of prose fragments, prose poems, and reflections on various subjects.

V., who did not consider himself primarily a poet, who disdained being "a man of letters," became, ironically, both *par excellence*, and countless passages in the *Cahiers* reflect this fundamental contradiction, an agon with his destiny. V.'s early poetry was influenced by the SYMBOLISTS, and some of the early pieces published in *Album de vers anciens 1890–1900* (1920; *Album of Early Verse*, 1971) reveal him as the most gifted of Mallarmé's disciples. However, the encounter with the work of Poe, whom V. admired principally as a theoretician and speculative thinker, led him early to reflect on literary technique—on the production rather than the product of the creative process. Throughout his life V. insisted that for him the mental process of creation was alone important, while he considered the poem a mere by-product or residue, a remnant or leftover for the others, the readers. Narcissus became a major symbolic figure for the divided self in which the mind beholds itself at work.

The functioning of the mind became V.'s principal interest after the 1892 crisis; and, although he eventually abandoned his projects of the "universal arithmetic" for the systematic exploration of the mind, the mind's functioning remained the dominant theme of his work.

Thus Teste, the "witness," is one of V.'s heroes of the intellect, a figure, V. tells us, formed of the "most intellectual moments" of a real being, an abstraction that could not exist in the concrete. The fragmentary nature of the persona is reflected in the form of this *roman moderne*, the fragments—letters, excerpts from notebooks, dialogues, sketches, and thoughts—that make up the *Teste* cycle. Teste, a "monster of the intellect," is the man of "the possible," of potency rather than act, who sees all without being seen, who reduces the world to an object without being object for another. And Teste's glance, which reduces the others to mere objects, includes the Self in the objectification. This ultimate degree of inner vision, of introspection and of "self-consciousness" (one of V.'s favorite words, inherited from Poe) underlies his lyric poetry as well, from the "Narcisse" compositions and *La jeune Parque* to "Le cimetière marin."

Another of V.'s heroes of the mind is his Leonardo da Vinci, "principal figure of this comedy of the intellect which has not yet found its poet." While Teste lives almost entirely in and by his mind, Leonardo is an artist, a creator who passionately explores and masters the phenomenal world. Unlike the *Teste* cycle, the *Leonardo* cycle originated from a commission; *L'introduction à la méthode de Léonard de Vinci* was republished in 1919, preceded now by a "Note et digression" ("Note and Digression") both of which were republished in 1933, along with a third essay, "Léonard et les philosophes" ("Leonardo and the Philosophers," 1972), all three texts now accompanied by marginal notes written between 1929 and 1933. This annotated trilogy of texts, dating from 1895, 1919, and 1929, constitutes an integral part of V.'s phenomenology of artistic perception and aesthetics. It celebrates not the historical Italian artist and inventor, but rather a universal self which reflects the poet's ideal.

The principal work of V.'s later years are the *Faust* fragments on which he began to work in 1940, but whose origins in the *Cahiers* reach back to the 1920s. *Études pour mon Faust* (1941; studies for my Faust), subsequently entitled "*Mon Faust*" (*Ébauches*) (*My Faust*, 1960), contains the three acts of "Lust la demoiselle de cristal: Comédie" ("Luste; or, The Crystal Girl: A Comedy") and the fragment of "Le solitaire; ou, Les malédictions d'univers: Féerie dramatique" ("The Only One; or, The Curses of the Cosmos: A Dramatic Fairy Tale"). In the *Faust* fragments, V.'s fundamental dialectic, the angelic aspirations and human limitations of a dualistic Self, is dramatized in the struggle of Eros and Nous (reason). The grand attempt to transform the one into the other and to harmonize human love and intellectual purity fails, and the text remained in fragmentary form. Faust represents V.'s last intellectual hero, one who succumbs to the temptations of a mind that destroys him.

V.'s work, the formal beauty of a poetry that embraces so many forms, the elegant essays that reflect the spectrum of contemporary knowledge, and the notebooks that recorded the life of a mind and of the world for fifty years, constitutes one of the most imposing literary monuments of the twentieth century.

FURTHER WORKS: *Degas danse dessin* (1934; *Degas, Dance, Drawing*, 1948); *Regards sur le monde actuel* (1938; *Reflections on the World Today*, 1948); *Mélange* (1939; *Mixture*, 1969); *Mauvaises pensées et autres* (1941; *Bad Thoughts and Not So Bad*, 1970); *Histoires brisées* (1950; *Broken Stories*, 1969); *Lettres à*

quelques-uns (1952); *André Gide-P. V.: Correspondance, 1890–1942* (1955; *Self-Portraits: The Gide-V. Letters, 1890–1942*, 1966); *P. V.-Gustave Fourmont: Correspondance, 1887–1933* (1957); *œuvres* (2 vols., 1957–60); *Cahiers* (2 vols., 1973–74). FURTHER WORKS IN ENGLISH: *Selected Writings* (1950); *The Collected Works of P. V.* (15 vols., 1956–75); *P. V.: An Anthology* (1977)

BIBLIOGRAPHY: Suckling, N., *P. V. and the Civilized Mind* (1954); Ince, W. N., *The Poetic Theory of P. V.: Inspiration and Technique* (1961); Mackay, A., *The Universal Self: A Study of P. V.* (1961); Lawler, J. R., *Lecture de V.: Une étude de "Charmes"* (1963); Robinson, J., *Analyse de l'esprit dans les Cahiers de V.* (1963); Hytier, J., *The Poetics of P. V.* (1966); Crow, C., *P. V.: Consciousness of Nature* (1972); Laurenti, H., *P. V. et le théâtre* (1973); Virtanen, R., *The Scientific Analogies of P. V.* (1974); Lawler, J. R., *The Poet as Analyst: Essays on P. V.* (1974); de Lussy, F., *La genèse de "La jeune Parque"* (1975); Yeschua, S., *V.: Le roman et l'œuvre à faire* (1976); Weinberg, K., *The Figure of Faust in V. and Goethe* (1976); Lazaridès, A., *V. pour une poétique du Dialogue* (1978); Livni, A., *La recherche de Dieu chez P. V.* (1978); Celeyrette-Pietri, N., *V. et le Moi des Cahiers à l'œuvre* (1979); Franklin, U., *The Rhetoric of V.'s Prose "Aubades"* (1979); Pietra, R., *V. directions spatiales et parcours verbal* (1981); Crow, C., *P. V. and the Poetry of Voice* (1982); Nash, S., *P. V.'s "Album de vers anciens": A Past Transfigured* (1982)

—URSULA FRANKLIN

The poem ["Palm Tree"] is controlled by a perception, not by a simple reverie. Think of "To the Plane Tree," which follows a different politics, a more rigid one. . . . It must be said that "Palm Tree" traverses an easier road: the palm tree stands for something other than itself; the plane tree stands only for itself. "Palm Tree" is a cosmic poem, while "To the Plane Tree" is an intimate one. . . .

Perhaps one or two readers . . . have been misled into expecting only cleverly rhymed philosophy from V. and have therefore missed his music. Indeed, there is not a single poem in *Charms* that does not make one understand that a song is primarily a song, and always a song. "Palm Tree" is but one more example. The rhythm summons the rhyme, by a harmony and balance of sonorities that extend from one line to the next. Who can guess how one line will rhyme with the preceding one or the following one? The feeling V. gives is always one of continuous harmony.

Alain, in P. V., *Charmes* (1929), pp. 240–44

Yeats, Rilke, and Eliot have written verses more memorable than V.'s; Joyce and Stefan George have made deeper modifications in their instrument (perhaps French is less modifiable than English and German); but behind the work of those eminent artisans is no personality comparable to V.'s. That his personality may be a kind of projection of his work does not diminish the fact. The meritorious mission that V. performed (and continues to perform) is that he proposed lucidity to men in a basely romantic age, in the melancholy age of Nazism and dialectical materialism, the age of the augurs of Freud's doctrine and the traffickers in surrealism.

At his death P. V. leaves us the symbol of a man who is infinitely sensitive to every fact and for whom every act is a stimulus that can arouse an infinite series of thoughts. A man who transcends the differential traits of the ego and of whom we can say, like William Hazlitt of Shakespeare, "He is nothing in himself." A man whose admirable texts do not exhaust, or even define, his all-embracing possibilities. A man who, in a century that adores the chaotic idols of blood, earth, and passion, always preferred the lucid pleasures of thought and the secret adventures of order. [1945]

Jorge Luis Borges, Other Inquisitions (1964),
p. 74

In the end, V., like everyone else, assigns the leading role to inspiration, and, when he seems to be attacking it, is in reality only attacking an extreme theory according to which all poetic activity is a dictation by some mysterious power, either internal or external, a thesis that has never been upheld to this point by anyone, and that never could be. V. is opposing the caricature of a theory without followers, or, at most, a naïve idea he encountered in people who had never given any thought to the composition of a poem. We may doubt, whatever he tells us, that he found it in real poets; even if many of them exaggerated the mysticism of inspiration, they always left a place for technical necessities.

Read V. and you will see that the argument is concerned not with the reality of inspiration but with its ability to create a work entirely on its own. [1953]

Jean Hytier, The Poetics of P. V. (1966), p. 134

It will very soon strike the attention of the perceptive reader, that much of what [V.] predicates of "poetry" is applicable only to his own poetry. The best approach [to V.'s poetic theory], I believe, is through a little essay, of very early date . . . entitled "On Literary Technique." The date [of composition] is 1889, but this early credo gives a clue to his later development. What it announces is no less than a new style for poets, as well as a new style for poetry. The satanist, the dandy, the poète maudit [cursed poet] have had their day: eleven years before the end of the nineteenth century V. invents the role which is to make him representative of the twentieth: "a totally new and modern conception of the poet. He is no longer the disheveled madman who writes a whole poem in the course of one feverish night; he is a cool scientist, almost an algebraist, in the service of a subtle dreamer. A hundred lines at most will make up his longest poems." . . .

V. in fact invented, and was to impose upon his age, not so much a new conception of poetry as a new conception of the poet. The tower of ivory has been fitted up as a laboratory—a solitary laboratory, for V. never went so far as to advocate "teamwork" in the writing of poetry. The poet is comparable to the mathematical physicist, or else to the biologist or chemist. He is to carry out the role of scientist as studiously as Sherlock Holmes did: this is the aspect of himself to which he calls the public's attention. Our picture of the poet is to be very like that of the austere, bespectacled man in a white coat, whose portrait appears in advertisements, weighing out or testing the drugs of which is compounded some medicine with an impressive name.

T. S. Eliot, Introduction to P. V., The Art of
Poetry, Collected Works, Vol. VII (1958), pp.
xviii–xx

It is clear to the reader of V.'s verse how much of himself he puts into it, despite its admirable control and impersonality. His poems are about his own life and thought, the splendeurs et misères of a certain kind of intellectual, ranging from the "comédie de l'intellect," that anguish and ecstasy of "awareness" which find expression in poems such as La jeune Parque or "Le cimetière marin," to the theme of poetic composition in many of the poems of Charmes. The controlled concentration of sound and sense, the tones of his poetry—exalted, sardonic, sombre, wistful, flippant, ironic, to mention a few—are, like the themes, an integral part of this self-expression. He was not usually eager to admit to what extent his most intimate preoccupations passed into his verse. He was not given to discussing very often what his poems were "about"; this is understandable if we recall his views on the relationship between sense and form in poetry and his dismissal of the sense of a poem such as La jeune Parque as "commonplaces." But he nevertheless explained with care on several occasions what was "in his mind" when he wrote certain poems; and an excellent idea can thereby be formed of the original and personal contribution he wanted to make and did make to French poetry.

W. N. Ince, The Poetic Theory of P. V.:
Inspiration and Technique (1961), p. 164

Spiritual and amusing, ["Silhouette of a Serpent"] is also one of the most profound of [the] Charms. It is a complex and condensed composition, at once theological, dramatic and burlesque. Like "The Pythoness" it is a monologue in octosyllabic verse. The character of the Serpent, half tragic and sinister, half farcical, was suggested by Wagner's Beckmesser in Die Meistersinger, and the means used by the musician may have inspired the poet's methods.

V. noted that the whole difficulty of the work lay in the changes of tone, and said that he had purposely exaggerated the assonances and the alliterations. Certainly in no poem has he more magically used the possibilities of language, or shown greater virtuosity in the choice of dominant harmonic values. The whole construction is a triumph of formal art.

The poem, for English readers, is in many ways a modern synthesis of Milton's Paradise Lost, seen entirely from the point of view of the Serpent, who here (as he might seem in Milton's poem) is the real hero of the drama. The central theme is the temptation of Eve, and the cosmogony is dealt with through Satan's reactions, that is to say the poet's. . . .

In his ironic acceptance of the myth, V. perceives that intuition becomes knowledge and that beyond knowledge there reigns an absence which is absolute.

Agnes Mackay, *The Universal Self: A Study of P. V.* (1961), pp. 190, 193

At the end of ["The Young Fate" the central character] is at a stage past the sluggish, unreflective happiness symbolised by Eve in "Silhouette of a Serpent"; past the discovery of a potentially tragic separation symbolised by Narcissus [in "Narcissus Speaks"]; and past the violent struggle against involuntary experience symbolised by the Pythoness [in "The Pythoness"]. In fact the Fate seems to exist as a companion figure to M. Teste, with the difference that the power made available to her by the survival of a crisis allows her at least to contemplate willingly acceptance of the kind of involvement he scorns or even fears.

The ending of "The Young Fate" naturally invites comparison with that of "The Graveyard by the Sea," the protagonist of which forms another major figure in V.'s expression of the drama of consciousness and nature. Where in the first poem, published in 1917, the sun is seen rising, in the later poem, a work of V.'s maturity published in 1920, the sun is already at its zenith and the mind of the speaker at a later stage of development. Where the Fate's experience is knife-edged in places, the "lover of abstractions" of "The Graveyard by the Sea" represents the achievement of a finer balance of his different mental exigencies. . . . The experience crystallised round the speaker here in a network of light and shade, calm and movement, is as deep as that attributed by the Fate to a preconscious existence, yet transferred to the fully conscious mind and expressed accordingly in the present tense.

The images through which this experience is created [are] the melting fruit, the tiny flecks of foam about to break out into movement, the relatively unchanging sky compared with the changing human consciousness, and so on. By the end of the poem they have each played a part in the triumphant upsurge of living energy with which, in the form of the vigour of wind and waves tearing him from his book, the narrator—he is still the narrator even now—is able to accept change, and to accept it without any fear of detriment to the total self of which thought and detachment will later again be part.

Christine M. Crow, *P. V.: Consciousness and Nature* (1972), pp. 23–24

Throughout V.'s work, one topic recurs with the regularity of a central theme. Eloquent of his constant endeavor to apprehend an elusive goal, "la belle endormie" [the sleeping beauty] is found time and again in the drawings that embellish his manuscripts, in his notebooks, his criticism, his poetry. She is the form given over to the beholder, a marvelously plastic Olympia in respect of whom he becomes both enchanted and enchanter. Yet we know that his act of contemplation is more than skin deep; that his glance seeks more than flesh; that here we must refer to the same *convoitise des secrets* [covetousness of secrets] he diagnosed in Degas, the same concern for intellectual and sensible possession he traced in Titian. . . . The woman is not asleep, but responsive to the probing eye and thought; nor is she merely a woman, but the means by which a mind will assuage its longings.

It can be no surprise that he was acutely sensitive to such a theme and that it provided ample matter for reflexion. His constant quest was to represent the quasi-physical structure of consciousness; and with an admirable feeling for line, an instinctive grasp of shape and mass, he took up his research like a voluptuary whose every moment is bound to a passion. To seize the wholeness of a complex thought, to contain a simultaneous vision of hazard and absorption, oblivion and pursuit, and the gamut of a myriad possibilities like the presence of a desirable form: this was the task of a lifetime.

James R. Lawler, *The Poet as Analyst: Essays on P. V.* (1974), pp. 149–50

VALLE-INCLÁN, Ramón del

(born Ramón María Valle Peña) Spanish poet, novelist, short-story writer, and dramatist, b. 28 Oct. 1866, Villanueva de Arosa; d. 5 Jan. 1936, Santiago de Compostela

Born in Galicia into genteel poverty, he turned it into a flamboyant bohemianism. He showed his rebelliousness against Spanish domestic custom by marrying an actress, and although the two raised a large family, he finally separated from his wife, taking the children with him, creating a scandal. Throughout his life, V.-I. was for his Spanish contemporaries an "extravagant" figure, and his literary reputation has subsequently been influenced by this fact.

V.-I. matured along with a group of contemporaries, including Miguel de UNAMUNO, later called the Generation of 1898. For this group, the traditional social, political, and religious forces had lost their power; he therefore sought inspiration in specific contemporary European and ancient sources, such as SYMBOLISM, MODERNISM, and even Gnosticism. Essentially he could find no faith in the realities of Spanish life in the early 1900s. Subsequently, after World War I, he abandoned aesthetic modernism and turned to the cult of the ugly and of the failure of the will—his *esperpento* (ugliness) period.

As a poet, V.-I. began under the influence of Rubén DARÍO and modernism, a movement in its earlier phases characterized by an emphasis upon the aesthetic and the exotic at the expense of the realistic. In his first volume of poetry, *Aromas de leyenda* (1907; legendary aromas), V.-I. focused on a motif made "exotic": a dreamy, nostalgic evocation of the religious and pastoral atmosphere of a Galicia of the legendary past. In these musical poems, often cast in song and ballad meters, both the religious and the rural become acceptable "poetically," when in fact V.-I. was an antichurch cosmopolitan. His next book of verse, bearing the surprisingly contemporary title *La pipa de kif* (1919; the hashish pipe), is written in the manner of his second period, when he followed the cult of the ugly and the turbulent. The setting is the city, Madrid, with a concentration on the outcasts of society and even the animals of the zoo. The poems are not intimate but ironically objective; emphasis is upon the stark, the dramatic, and the violent. In his final book of verse, *El pasajero* (1920; the wayfarer), he plunges into cultism in its ancient sense with the creation of a group of "rose" poems—marked by arcane symbolism having a philosophical base in Plato, Pythagoras, and the Gnostics. V.-I.'s mastery of forms and rhythm does not rescue these poems from cultist peculiarity, despite the elevated themes.

V.-I. always showed a tendency to mix genres. His early prose is "poetic" in style. More importantly, his novels are often "dramatic" in structure, while his dramas often have narrative content and extensive descriptive passages in the stage directions. His fiction began in the modernist vein, that is, with heavy emphasis upon the aesthetic aspect. After experimenting with the short story, V.-I. hit full stride in his creation of a series of four short novels called *Sonatas: Memorias del Marqués de Bradomín* (1902–5; *The Pleasant Memories of the Marquis de Bradomin: Four Sonatas*, 1924). Patterned on the four seasons, the *Sonatas* have as a protagonist Xavier de Bradomín, a marquis from Galicia. Bradomín, in the modernist vein, is a decadent hero; he has been called an "ironic Don Juan." In the epigraph to the first volume V.-I. declares Bradomín to be "ugly, feeling, and Catholic." A creature of awesome will, Bradomín is Catholic in the paradoxical Spanish way that the greater the sinner in this life, the greater the repentance for the next.

The *Sonata de primavera* (1904; "Sonata of Spring") is set in Italy, although at times the scene seems more like Galicia. Bradomín, an officer of the Pope, arrives on a mission, and soon finds himself pursuing María Rosario, a noble and innocent lass destined for the convent. Bradomín ultimately flees, leaving tragedy behind him, but María Rosario is to remain the "only love" of his life—he merely makes love to later conquests. In *Sonata de estío* (1903; "Sonata of Summer") the scene shifts to "tropical" Mexico, where the noble Bradomín has estates. In Mexico he meets La Niña Chole, daughter of an Aztec princess and a conquistador. Bradomín celebrates his feast of passion with her in a convent. He later demonstrates his masculine will in encounters with assorted ruffians, one being the girl's father-lover. The setting of *Sonata de otoño* (1902; "Sonata of Autumn") is predictably Galicia, where indeed the nobility is in "autumn." The hero returns to an old love who is dying of consumption. In the "decadent" manner, "feverish" love becomes love with fever, and the lady dies in Bradomín's arms. *Sonata de invierno* (1905; "Sonata of Winter") is set in an almost contemporary (19th-c.) Spain of troubles and war. The marquis loses a limb in battle, but he also meets in a convent his own daughter by an earlier liaison and almost seduces her. Ultimately, he awaits death without either hope or pity; the decadent hero expects no mercy. In style these *Sonatas* resemble musical compositions. As an artistic creation, the work is one of the perfect gems of Spanish literature.

In the 1920s V.-I. employed the *esperpento* manner in his fiction and dramas as well as in his poetry. In the *esperpento* the total atmosphere is one of ugliness, disharmony, failure, and morbid humor. The *esperpento* is related to the Spanish Baroque in that form and structure are tightly organized, while the substance is chaotic. A short farce, *Los cuernos de Don Friolera* (1925; Don Friolera's horns) has become the model of this form.

Perhaps V.-I.'s most successful novel is *Tirano Banderas* (1926; *The Tyrant: A Novel of Warm Lands*, 1929). The setting is a mythical Latin American country; the "tyrant" is an example of the omnipresent strongman ruler in Latin America. Three types compete in the novel: Indians, creoles (native-born whites of Spanish origin), and foreigners (including Spaniards). The tyrant Banderas is a figure somewhere between a scarecrow and a roughhewn genius for action. During the course of the narrative he gradually sees his former absolute power slipping away, and he seems neither surprised nor overwhelmed. Ultimately he stabs his feeble-minded daughter fifteen times so that his enemies cannot abuse her; he himself is shot and his body quartered. *Tirano Banderas* has become a source, a standard of comparison, for later writing on this Latin American theme.

With typical Spanish quixotism, V.-I. envisaged as his masterpiece a series of historical novels called *El ruedo ibérico* (the Iberian bullring), which would cover the years from Isabela II's downfall in 1868 to 1898. Unfortunately, he finished only two of them: *La corte de los milagros* (1927; the court of miracles) and *Viva mi dueño* (1928; hurrah for my master). In these novels the *esperpento* manner is developed extensively: against the order of a tight cyclical construction is pitted the chaos of the political situation. These novels reveal V.-I.'s intent to return directly to Spanish culture, but with his own peculiar artistry.

Among his uneven dramatic efforts, surely his most powerful work is the trilogy *Comedias bárbaras* (barbaric dramas), consisting (in thematic order) of *Cara de Plata* (1922; silver face), *Aguila de blasón* (1907; heraldic eagle), and *Romance de lobos* (1909; *Wolves! Wolves!*, 1957). These novelistic dramas trace the story of the Montenegro clan in its gradual decline. The patriarchal father is a "natural" Galician noble; that is, he rules despotically but wisely. At this level, the theme is Nietzschean; in his relations with his sons the theme becomes Freudian, in both the Oedipal and the "totem" senses. Ultimately, in the chaos attendant upon the father's death, the Christian theme is reasserted. Although almost impossible to stage, this trilogy is truly epic or archetypal in proportions.

During the years since his death V.-I.'s reputation has grown both in Spain and outside. Because of his aesthetic preoccupations and his refusal to treat Spanish life realistically, he was at first relegated to a secondary position in literary histories, but later scholars realized that his *esperpento* manner is closely related to various movements of the "absurd" of our own times. His novel *Tirano Banderas* has remained a classic about Latin America; his plays continue to be staged by various vanguard groups in both Spain and America. His *Sonatas* remain a classic for those who can appreciate pure creation. Gradually he has earned again a solid position in the Generation of 1898.

FURTHER WORKS: *Femeninas* (1895); *Epitalamio* (1897); *Cenizas* (1899); *Jardín umbrío* (1903); *Corte de amor* (1903); *Flor de santidad* (1904); *Historias perversas* (1907); *El marqués de Bradomín* (1907); *El yermo de las almas* (1908); *La guerra carlista* (3 vols., 1908–9); *Cuento de abril* (1910); *Voces de gesta* (1911); *La marquesa Rosalinda* (1913); *El embrujado* (1914); *La cabeza del dragón* (1914; *The Dragon's Head*, 1918); *La lámpara maravillosa* (1916); *Farsa de la enamorada del rey* (1920); *Divinas palabras* (1920; *Divine Words*, 1968); *Farsa y licencia de la reina castiza* (1922); *Luces de bohemia* (1924; *Lights of Bohemia*, 1967); *Las galas del difunto* (1926); *Zacarías el cruzado* (1926); *Retablo de la avaricia, la lujuria y la muerte* (1927); *Fin de un revolucionario* (1928); *Martes de carnaval* (1930); *Vísperas de la Gloriosa* (1930); *Obras completas* (2 vols., 1954)

BIBLIOGRAPHY: Zamora Vicente, A., *Las Sonatas de V.-I.* (1955); Greenfield, S., "Stylization and Deformation in V.-I.'s *La reina castiza*," BHS, 39 (1962): 78–89; Fernández Almagro, M., *Vida y literatura de V.-I.* (1966); Risco, A., *La estética de V.-I.* (1966); Umbral, F., *V.-I.* (1968); Zahareas, A., *R. del V.-I.* (1968); Smith, V., *R. del V.-I.* (1973); Spoto, R., *The Primitive Themes in Don R. del V.-I.* (1976); Greenfield, S. M., "Bradomín and the Ironies of Evil: A Reconsideration of *Sonata de primavera*," StTCL, 2 (1977): 23–32; Sinclair, A., *V.-I.'s "Ruedo ibérico": A Popular View of Revolution* (1977); Maier, C. S., "Symbolist Aesthetics in Spanish: The Concept of Language in V.-I.'s *La lámpara maravillosa*," in R. Grass and W. R. Risley, eds., *Waiting for Pegasus: Studies in the Presence of Symbolism and Decadence in Hispanic Letters* (1979): 77–87; Dougherty, D., "The Tragicomic Don Juan: V.-I.'s *Esperpento de las galas del difunto (The Dead Man's Duds)*," MD, 23 (1980): 44–57

—CARL W. COBB

VALLEJO, César

Peruvian poet, b. 16 Mar. 1892, Santiago de Chuco; d. 15 Apr. 1938, Paris, France

V., youngest born of a large mestizo family, began to study medicine in Lima in 1911 but took his degree in literary studies at the University of Trujillo, his thesis being *El romanticismo en la poesía castellana* (1915; romanticism in Spanish poetry). He returned in 1916 to Lima, where he experienced two unhappy love affairs, the second one ending in the untimely death of his mistress, who was pregnant with his child. In 1920 he was imprisoned in a provincial jail for several months, the innocent victim of political feuding in his home town.

In 1923 he left Peru permanently for Europe, settling in Paris, where he eked out a meager existence writing articles for Peruvian newspapers. In 1926 he met his future wife Georgette, a woman of strong socialist convictions, whom he married in 1929 after traveling to Russia and eastern Europe with her. Various trips to Spain as well as Russia reflected V.'s desperate attempt to find a place in European society as well as his quest for a better social order. After expulsion from France in 1930 because of his political activities, V. lived in Spain and joined the Communist Party there in 1931. He returned to Paris in 1932, and except for trips to Spain to support the Republicans during the civil war, he remained in France the rest of his life. He died in poverty at forty-six, his memory eulogized by many European intellectuals of the left of that period.

V.'s fame rests primarily on his poetic works, although he also was a journalist, dramatist, novelist, and short-story writer. His first published volume of poetry, *Los heraldos negros* (1918; the black messengers), initiates themes that were to remain constants in his work. It also records the transformation of his poetic style as it discards the opulent rhetoric of MODERNISM and moves toward indigenous themes and prosaic vignettes of daily or family life related in popular speech patterns that are transformed by the emotional intensity of the poet. In *Los heraldos negros* the Indian is seen as a universal symbol of mankind, unable to realize his potential because of injustice and oppression. Love is foredoomed by the conditions of human existence. Man is an orphan abandoned by God to seek hope in a world devoid of meaning. Childhood memories become painfully nostalgic, and the mother emerges as the primordial symbol of love.

Trilce (1922; *Trilce*, 1973) shattered all traditions in Peruvian poetry. This iconoclastic series of seventy-seven poems, bearing only numbers for titles, is independent of any particular literary school and truly avant-garde in its irrational and hermetic expression. In it V. discards traditional logic and attempts to instill a new life into words. His major themes remain those of an existential search for love and permanent values in an absurd and transient world. Bitter irony and dark humor give even the most inaccessible poems a sense of immediacy and urgency as the poet moves beyond the anecdotal to express the essence of his emotional experiences. The syntax reflects his often violent interior struggle to isolate through language the ultimate spiritual resources of the human animal.

V. published few additional poems during his lifetime, and continued to write and revise his work until his death. There are three different collections of his posthumously published poetry, all varying widely in chronological ordering and division of the poems into separate works: *Poemas humanos* (1939; human poems), *Obra poética completa* (1969; complete poetic work), and *Poesía completa* (1978; complete poetry). None has been clearly established as the definitive version, nor is one likely to be, but the last is the most convincingly based on available evidence of V.'s intentions with regard to his final poetic production. It is the work of Juan Larrea (1895–1982), the Spanish poet with whom V. founded the short-lived review *Favorables-Paris Poema* (1925).

Despite these differing versions, the posthumous poems reveal a style and unity that characterize V. at the height of his powers. From the intense self-absorption of *Trilce*, V. emerges to identify with the poor and oppressed everywhere, and through their redemption he seeks his own. As his gaze is directed outward, his language becomes more accessible, despite recurring obscurities that seem to reflect those of life itself. Echoes of biblical prophets mingle with fervent pleas for social justice and universal love. Daily objects are infused with spiritual values reflecting their significance in the poet's emotional odyssey.

In the group of fifteen poems entitled *España, aparta de mí este cáliz* (1939; *Spain, Take This Cup from Me*, 1974) V. calls for the salvation of mankind through fraternal love and mutual self-sacrifice, best exemplified in the death of the anonymous Republican partisans of the Spanish Civil War. The agony of "Mother Spain" becomes a microcosm of the human predicament.

The verse in *Poemas humanos* (published as *Poemas en prosa* [prose poems] and *Poemas humanos* in the *Obra poética completa* prepared by Georgette de Vallejo, but as *Nómina de huesos* [rollcall of bones] and *Sermón de la barbarie* [sermon of barbarism] in the *Poesía completa* prepared by Juan Larrea) achieves a stylistic balance that eliminates both the derivative aspects of *Los heraldos negros* and the often excessive difficulties of *Trilce*. As in the latter work, V. employs all of the resources of Spanish, including learned or archaic words and scientific and technical terms, but the syntactical distortions, neologisms, and typographic and orthographic peculiarities are better assimilated. Strong rhythms and irrational, often private images are successfully employed to express the most fundamental and universal of human emotions.

V.'s first collection of short stories, *Escalas melografiadas* (1923; scales set to music), published shortly before he left Peru for Paris, reflects his imprisonment in 1920, his early unhappy love affairs, and the metaphysical preoccupations also reflected in his first poetic work, but stylistically the stories echo *Trilce*. Most of them are characterized by the delineation of an emotional crisis in the protagonist's life (all are related in the first person). There is little plot development, the principal theme being the search for metaphysical or emotional significance in an absurd world. One metaphysical obsession, which is related to V.'s preoccupation with numbers in *Trilce*, is that of the double, the main theme of his short novel *Fábula salvaje* (1923; barbarous tale). V.'s interest in the Incan heritage is evident in the fragment *Hacia el reino de los Sciris* (1944; toward the kingdom of the Sciris), unpublished in his lifetime; it anticipates a similar concern in his last drama, *La piedra cansada* (1969; the tired stone), also published posthumously. V.'s novel *El tungsteno* (1931; tungsten) reflects his militant Marxism of the early 1930s, as do his journalistic works, *Russia en 1931* (1931; Russia in 1931) and *Rusia ante el segundo plan quinquenal* (1965; Russia confronting the second five-year plan), in which V. argues for the subordination of artistic individuality to the need to join in the class struggle.

V.'s four plays—*La piedra cansada, Lockout* (1979; title in English), *Colacho hermanos o presidentes de América* (1979; the Colacho brothers or presidents of America), *Entre las orillas corre el río* (1979; between two shores runs the river)—display a similar ideological orientation. Like his short stories, they are devoid of plot development for the most part, as well as other formal theatrical values, and none was ever produced. Taken together, however, they clearly demonstrate V.'s view of the drama as a revolutionary instrument that should not only reflect the reality of the theater public through the ethical values represented by the characters but also seek to change that reality.

V.'s considerable journalistic production, much of it un-published, promotes specific social and cultural reforms he deemed essential to the progress of mankind. His developing Marxism may be clearly traced in the articles published in Peruvian and Argentine newspapers and periodicals between 1924 and 1931. But his poetry, shunning dogmas, embraces the intrinsic dilemmas of the human condition and seeks their solution in a radical change in human nature itself. Within the past two decades V. has been recognized as one of the most important and original poets of Latin America.

FURTHER WORKS: *Artículos olvidados* (1960); *Literatura y arte* (1966); *Novelas y cuentos completos* (1967); *Obras completas* (3 vols., 1973); *Cartas: 114 cartas de C. V. a Pablo Abril de Vivero* (1974); *Enunciados de la guerra española* (1974); *Teatro completo* (1979). FURTHER WORKS IN ENGLISH: *Twenty Poems of C. V.* (1962, bilingual); *Neruda and V.: Selected Poems* (1971); *The Complete Posthumous Poetry* (1978, bilingual)

BIBLIOGRAPHY: Monguió, L., *C. V.: Vida y obra* (1952); Hays, H. R., "The Passion of C. V.," *New Directions 15* (1955): 22–28;

Coyné, A., *C. V. y su obra poética* (1958); Higgins, J., *Visión del hombre y de la vida en las últimas obras poéticas de C. V.* (1970); special V. issue, *RI*, 36, 71 (1970); Neale-Silva, E., "The Introductory Poem in V.'s *Trilce*," *HR*, 38 (1970): 2–16; Flores, A., *Aproximaciones a C. V.* (1971); Ferrari, A., ed., *El universo poético de C. V.* (1972); Ortega, J., *C. V.: El escritor y la crítica* (1974); Franco, J., *C. V.: The Dialectics of Poetry and Silence* (1976)

—KEITH A. MCDUFFIE

VANČURA, Vladislav

Czechoslovak novelist, dramatist, and short-story writer (writing in Czech), b. 26 June 1891, Háj; d. 1 June 1942, Prague

Scion of an old Czech Protestant family, V. retained his love for the early stages of his people's language and history throughout his active involvement in the leftist politics of his day. Although trained for a career in medicine, he practiced it for just a few years before turning wholeheartedly to writing. He is considered one of the greatest Czech stylists.

V. was the only prose writer of note associated closely with the important Czech avant-garde school of poetism. Although siding politically with the newly formed Czech Communist Party, the poetists rejected critical realism (that is, 19th–c.–style realism) as a guide for depicting the oppression of the workingman; instead, they set out to celebrate the modern world in all its variety and to teach the workingman to transcend his dreary existence by means of creativity and imagination.

Thus, while V.'s first novel, *Pekař Jan Marhoul* (1924; the baker Jan Marhoul), deals with a downtrodden member of the urban proletariat, it does so in the manner of a contemporary fairy tale; good battles evil in a rich, not always causally connected sequence of metaphors. The images re–create the downfall of an innocent, but without a trace of moralizing. V.'s next novel, *Pole orná a válečná* (1925; plowed fields, battlefields), portrays war as an apocalyptic horror devoid of logic and daringly uses chaos as a structural principle. It is a modern antiepic, turning battles and heroes into grim, grotesque parodies. In these two works V. established a distinctive voice, a language filled with previously unjuxtaposed elements from all stylistic levels and all periods of the Czech language. He made especially rich use of the lexicon and syntax of the Czech humanists of the late 16th and early 17th cs. and of the standard Czech Bible translation, the Kralice Bible of the late 16th c. His language is never far from poetry in its lyricism, rhythm, and imagery. It is a language diametrically opposed to that of his much translated contemporary, Karel ČAPEK, who aimed at approaching modern colloquial speech. Not surprisingly, Čapek followed the tradition of the psychological novel, while V. avoided psychologism as much as possible.

V. was enough of a virtuoso also to excel at lighter, more humorous works, as his bagatelle of a novel *Rozmarné léto* (1925; capricious summer) amply shows, but he constantly found inspiration in epic themes. His decision to turn medieval legend into a novel in *Markéta Lazarová* (1931; Markéta Lazarová) was motivated in part by a desire to counteract the standard, sentimental, bourgeois boy-meets-girl novel with pure straightforward passion.

It is represented here by the ill-starred love of a vassal's daughter for a robber. V. makes his story modern by giving it a contemporary narrator who challenges the reader's set ideas and puts the monumental and balladic elements of the narrative in a new perspective.

The novels preceding and following *Markéta Lazarová* all treat modern Czech life in V.'s characteristically ornamental style: *Poslední soud* (1925; the last judgment) tells the tale of a vital country boy ruined by the metropolis; *Hrdelní pře; anebo, Přísloví* (1930; criminal proceedings; or, proverbs) is a philosophical murder mystery; *Útěk do Budína* (1932; escape to Buda) is a story of contemporary love and marriage. In *Konec starých časů* (1934; *The End of the Old Time*, 1965), perhaps the most ebullient of his novels, V. lightheartedly illustrates the disintegration of class boundaries on an estate when an eccentric Russian nobleman comes to stay. In *Tři řeky* (1936; three rivers) he returns to his epic stance to narrate the adventures of a Czech peasant–turned–revolutionary at the Russian front during World War I; despite the subject matter, *Tři řeky* has the structure and elements of a fairy tale: three rivers, three sons, the trials of the youngest as he roams the world.

As the threat of a German invasion increased, many Czech authors turned to their past for sustenance. V.'s *Obrazy z dějin národa českého* (3 vols., 1939, 1940, 1948; tableaux from the history of the Czech nation) take the form of short Renaissance novellas. Although historically quite accurate, they are highly lyrical as well. Before he could complete them, he was arrested by the Gestapo for his resistance activities and executed.

Although V. wrote stories and plays in addition to novels, the novel gave him more room to experiment: to mix genres and types of language, to modernize legends and legendize modern life. The results are notably difficult to translate, but *Markéta Lazarová* and *Rozmarné léto* have been successfully adapted for the screen.

FURTHER WORKS: *Amazonský proud* (1923); *Dlouhý, Široký a Bystrozraký* (1924); *Nemocná dívka* (1928); *Kubula a Kuba Kubikula* (1931); *Alchymista* (1932); *Luk královny Dorotky* (1932); *Jezero Ukereve* (1935); *Rodina Horvatova* (1938); *Josefína* (1950); *Vědomí souvislostí* (1958); *Pražský žid* (1959); *Spisy* (16 vols., 1951–66)

BIBLIOGRAPHY: Doležel, L., *Narrative Modes in Czech Literature* (1973): 91–111; Grygar, M., "Bedeutungsinhalt und Sujetaufbau im *Pekař Jan Marhoul* von V. V.: Zur Poetik der lyrischen Prosa," *ZS*, 14 (1969): 199–223; Mihailovich, V. D., et al., eds., *Modern Slavic Literatures* (1976), Vol. II: 216–20; Novák, A., *Czech Literature* (1976): 310–12

—MICHAEL HEIM

VARGAS LLOSA, Mario

Peruvian novelist, critic, essayist, and short-story writer, b. 28 Mar. 1936, Arequipa

After completing his undergraduate studies at the University of San Marcos in Lima, V. L. attended graduate school at the University of Madrid and subsequently lived in Paris and Barcelona. In 1974 he returned to Peru, ending his long self-imposed exile. He has lectured at many American and European universities and has won several prestigious literary prizes.

Although V. L. is well known as a political leftist strongly committed to social justice, he has steadfastly refused to compromise aesthetic goals for revolutionary propaganda. In his essays on the creative process, he has set forth the theory that literary themes are an author's demons or obsessions emanating from his irrational unconscious. He sees the formal elements of style, technique, and structure, however, as products of the rational consciousness that should be conceived and organized in a logical manner to reinforce theme.

V. L.'s first novel, *La ciudad y los perros* (1962; *The Time of the Hero*, 1966), electrified readers of Spanish because of its experimental form and exciting plot. Today, in retrospect, many critics consider it the initiator of the so-called boom in Latin American fiction during the 1960s. The story takes place in the Leoncio Prado military academy in Lima where V. L. himself once studied. In the initial pages of the novel a chemistry exam is stolen, unleashing a series of events that culminate in the murder of an informer and the refusal of upper-echelon officers to conduct an investigation for fear of damaging the academy's reputation. By means of temporal dislocations, scrambled points of view, and other literary devices, the fictional dimensions are expanded in order to reveal the heterogeneous backgrounds of the cadets. Thus the academy emerges as a microcosm of Peruvian society, and the book as a scathing condemnation of the vice and violence engendered by an obsolete social system.

Whereas *La ciudad y los perros* reflects the naturalistic tenets of social determinism, *La casa verde* (1966; *The Green House*, 1966) enters the realms of myth and metaphor. Generally considered to be V. L.'s masterpiece, this vast, complicated novel has two major settings: the first, a provincial city (Piura) located in the northwestern Peruvian desert, where a series of highly dramatic events occur in a brothel (the Green House); the second, the Amazonian wilderness, where traders, government officials, military personnel, missionaries, and primitive Indians vie for livelihood and supremacy over an extremely hostile environment. Like most of V. L.'s fictional creations, the characters of *La casa verde* appear to be trapped by the immediacy of each situation, which causes them to react instinctively and propels them toward tragedy or defeat. They reveal themselves principally through their actions, dialogues, and interior monologues, usually set forth in fragmentary form on intersecting temporal and spatial planes. The complex novelistic framework conveys an ambiguous view of reality enriched by evocative motifs, mythical allusions, and veiled character identities. For its exotic appeal, ingeniously interwoven plot threads, and graphic depiction of man pitted against an environment he can neither comprehend nor control, *La casa verde* is truly an unforgettable literary experience.

Conversación en La Catedral (2 vols., 1969; *Conversation in The Cathedral*, 1975) once again demonstrates V. L.'s consummate craftsmanship, its primary focus being the political vicissitudes of Peruvian dictator Manuel Odría's regime (1948–56). The action is set in motion by the fortuitous meeting of *Santiago Zavala*, a disenchanted idealist estranged from his upper-class family, and Ambrosio Pardo, an indigent Negro who many years before worked for Santiago's father. The ensuing conversation between the two men in a Lima bar (La Catedral) provides the occasion for the meticulously arranged flashbacks dramatizing the destinies of individuals from all social classes. Like all of V. L.'s fiction, *Conversación en La Catedral* at first baffles, then ensnares, and finally thrusts its reader into a world torn by violence and threatened by moral decay.

Pantaleón y las visitadoras (1973; *Captain Pantoja and the Special Service*, 1978) is V. L.'s most popular novel to date, probably because of its rollicking humor. Pantoja is a diligent young army officer who is sent to the Peruvian tropics to organize a squadron of prostitutes and thus make life more bearable for lonely soldiers stationed in remote outposts. Because of his puritanical nature and zealously analytical approach to his assignment, Pantoja elicits the reader's guffaws from the beginning, but ultimately he comes to typify the absurd hero who continues to struggle against overwhelming odds. The theme of absurdity is underscored, moreover, by the hilarious parodies of military procedures, the clashing montage of incompatible episodes, and generous doses of irony and the grotesque.

For *La tía Julia y el escribidor* (1977; *Aunt Julia and the Scriptwriter*, 1982), V. L. draws on memories of his youth during the mid–1950s, namely his marriage to an aunt despite strong family opposition, and the action-packed soap operas penned by a mad colleague at a Lima radio station where V. L. was employed. The work's overriding irony stems from the juxtaposition of the two plot lines, the first based on fact and the second on imaginary events. The end result is a kind of metanovel in which the author sees the objective account of his courtship and marriage gradually assume the characteristics of melodrama.

Some critics consider *La guerra del fin del mundo* (1981; *The War of the End of the World*, 1984) V. L.'s masterpiece. This novel deals with a religious uprising against the Brazilian government in the late 19th c. In his more recent novels, the author continues his portraits of contemporary Peru, emphasizing the social and political divisions that have wracked the country. The most important of these works include *Historia de Mayta* (1984; *The Real Life of Alejandro Mayta*, 1986), *El hablador* (1990; *The Storyteller*, 1990), and *Lituma en los Andes* (1993; *Death in the Andes*, 1996).

V. L.'s two major critical works are *Gabriel García Márquez: Historia de un deicidio* (1971; Gabriel García Márquez: history of a decade), a lengthy study of Latin America's most famous contemporary novelist's life and work; and *La orgía perpetua: Flaubert y "Madame Bovary"* (1975; the perpetual orgy: Flaubert and *Madame Bovary*), a penetrating analysis of the French masterpiece. Although V. L. holds both authors in high esteem, in Flaubert he also encounters a kindred spirit because of his disciplined style, symmetrically structured plot, and, above all, his scrupulous objectivity. Both V. L. and Flaubert, moreover, seek to create the illusion of a total, self-contained reality inspired by real-life situations.

Because he has mobilized a wide variety of avant-garde devices to project an almost totally negative vision of conditions in his native land, V. L. has been described as a critical neorealist and a pessimistic observer of the human condition. Underlying his oeuvre, however, are the moralist's hope for reform and the sentimentalist's yearning for virtues perhaps not irredeemably lost. V. L. has been influenced by numerous writers, including Jean-Paul SARTRE, Albert CAMUS, and William FAULKNER. His art attains universality through his innovative representations of a world characterized by philosophical uncertainties and crumbling, outmoded values. He ranks not only as Peru's best living man of letters but also as one of the leading novelists writing in Spanish today.

FURTHER WORKS: *Los jefes* (1959); *Los cachorros: Pichula Cuellar* (1967; *The Cubs*, 1979); *La novela* (1968); *La novela en*

Mario Vargas Llosa

América Latina: Diálogo (1968, with Gabriel García Márquez); *Antología mínima de M. V. L.* (1969); *Literatura en la revolución y revolución en la literatura* (1970, with Oscar Collazos and Julio Cortázar); *Día domingo* (1971); *La historia secreta de una novela* (1971); *Novelas y cuentos* (1973); *Obras escogidas* (1973); *La utopía arcaica* (1978); *La señorita de Tacna* (1981); *La guerra del fin del mundo* (1981; *The War of the End of the World*, 1983); *Entre Sartre y Camus* (1981); *Kathie y el hipopótamo* (1983). **FURTHER WORKS IN ENGLISH:** *The Cubs, and Other Stories* (1979)

BIBLIOGRAPHY: Boldori de Baldussi, R., *V. L.: Un narrador y sus demonios* (1974); Martin, J. L., *La narrativa de V. L.: Acercamiento estilístico* (1974); special V. L. issue, *TSLL*, 19, 4 (1977); Rossman, C., and A. W. Friedman, eds., *M. V. L.: A Collection of Critical Essays* (1978); special V. L. issue, *WLT*, 52, 1 (1978); Davis, M. E., "William Faulkner and M. V. L.: The Election of Failure," *CLS*, 16 (1979): 332–43; Dauster, F., "*Pantaleón and Tirant:* Points of Contact," *HR*, 48 (1980): 269–85; Machen, S., "'Pornoviolence' and Point of View in M. V. L.'s *La tía Julia y el escribidor*," *LALR*, 9, 17 (1980): 9–16; McCracken, E., "V. L.'s *La tía Julia y el escribidor*: The New Novel and the Mass Media," *I&L*, 3, 13 (1980): 54–69; Moody, M., "Landscapes of the Damned: Natural Setting in *La casa verde*," *KRQ*, 27 (1980): 495–508

—GEORGE R. MCMURRAY

VARNALIS, Kostas

Greek poet, critic, and essayist, b. 27 Feb. 1884, Pyrgos, Bulgaria; d. 16 Dec. 1974, Athens

V. spent his childhood and adolescence in Bulgaria. In 1903 he came to Greece for the first time and enrolled in the School of Philosophy at the University of Athens. After receiving a degree in 1908, he taught Greek language and literature in Greek high schools in both Bulgaria and Greece, and later worked as an educational administrator and professor of secondary education. For a few years, beginning in 1919, he attended the Sorbonne in Paris, where he was converted to Marxism. His left-wing activities under the dictatorship (1925–26) of Theodoros Pangalos led to his dismissal from the Pedagogic Academy in Athens, where he was then teaching. Thereafter, V. made his living as a journalist, free-lance writer, and translator. In 1929 he married the poet Dora Moatsou (dates n.a.). In 1958 he was awarded the Lenin Peace Prize.

Although a major figure in modern Greek poetry, V. was more prolific as a critic and theorist of the literature and history of classical Greece and Rome, as in *I dhihtatores* (1956; dictators), and on modern Greek writers, as in *Anthropi* (1939; men), particularly the Greek national poet Dionysios Solomos (1798–1857), to whom *Solomika* (1923; on Solomos) is devoted. V.'s fiction includes eight short stories, collected in *Dhiighimata* (1979; short stories), and two longer works, *E alithini apologhia tou Socrati* (1933; the true apology of Socrates), which met with acclaim and is still considered a minor masterpiece of modern Greek literature, and *To imerologhio tis Penelopis* (1946; the journal of Penelope). V. also wrote a number of children's fairy tales and one play, *Attalos o tritos* (1972; Attila the third), and he translated several of the works of Aristophanes, Euripides, Molière, and Corneille into modern Greek.

V.'s poetic career began, like the careers of his contemporaries Nikos KAZANTZAKIS and Angelos SIKELIANOS, with finely wrought poetry written in a purist Greek characterized by the use of traditional stanzaic forms, meters, and rhymes, a style influenced by the French Parnassians and the SYMBOLISTS. After returning from Paris as a devout Marxist and participating in the linguistic struggle of the pre–World War I period to establish the demotic as the language of Greek literature, V. was never thereafter to write in anything but the demotic. The author of the first thoroughly left-wing poetry in Greek, in *To fos pou kei* (1922; the burning light), V. was to become known as the country's conscience and its greatest social poet. In this, his most widely known work, the poet presents the Leader, no longer the son of God or one descended from the clouds, but a force arising from the masses' angry hearts, coming to help them topple "the murderous kingdoms of foul man / founded on fraudulence and lies" and to create "the kingdom of Work / . . . the one kingdom / of Human Friendship throughout the world." In *Sklavi poliorkimeni* (1927; the slaves besieged), written after Greece's defeat by Turkey in Asia Minor in 1922, the poet extends his social criticism to express a hatred of war and to protest against those who would blind the masses into accepting slavery and fascism.

The subject matter and tone established in these works were to change little over the course of V.'s career. His poetry became increasingly polemical and satiric, at times moving from the merely biting to the savage. Nevertheless, throughout his career he continued to use traditional poetic techniques; moreover, he remained attracted to the classical past, which he evoked in many poems.

FURTHER WORKS: *Kirithes* (1905); *Ekloghes* (1954); *Piimata* (1956); *Pezos loghos* (1957); *Esthitika-kritika* (2 vols. 1958); *Eleftheros kosmos* (1965); *Orghi laou* (1975); *Filoloyika apomnimonevmata* (1980); *Philologika apomnimonevmata* (1980)

BIBLIOGRAPHY: Friar, K., Introduction to *Modern Greek Poetry: From Cavafis to Elytis* (1973): 39–43

—KOSTAS MYRSIADES

VAROUJAN, Daniel

(pseud. of Daniel Cheboukiarian) Armenian poet, b. 20 Apr. 1884, Brgnik; d. 13 Aug. 1915, between Çankiri and Ankara, Turkey

V. came from an educated but poor family. During the 1896 Turkish massacres of his people his father, who had gone to Constantinople to look for work, was jailed. When he disappeared, V. left his village home to search for him; this episode was responsible for V.'s political and social orientation.

A brilliant student, he was sent by his teachers in Constantinople to Venice to study with Mekhitarist monks. He later attended the University of Ghent in Belgium and took a degree in social studies and literature in 1908. He taught school in his native village until 1912, when he moved to Constantinople as the principal of an Armenian school. He was one of the founders of the magazine *Mehian* in 1914.

By the time he was killed (with the first two hundred Armenian intellectuals at the onset of the 1915 massacre), V. had established himself as the most powerful voice in Armenian poetry since the 11th–c. mystic Krikor Narekatsi, and he remains so to this day.

V.'s four volumes of poetry reflect the four stages of a young man reacting to his environment. His first, *Sarsoorner* (1906; shivers), expresses the experience of an adolescent, but in the powerful, sinewy phrases that became V.'s hallmark. His second collection, *Tsegheen seerduh* (1909; heart of a nation), established him, along with Siamanto (pseud. of Adom Yarjanian, 1878–1915), as one of the two major poets of that time. In this volume, although the influence of the romantic poet Ghevont Alishan (1820–1907) is still apparent, the panoramic and lush style is distinctively V.'s. Misery and death, good and evil, past and present, myth and concrete reality are postulated, presented, and examined—always with optimism.

In his third book, *Hetanos erker* (1912; pagan songs), through the re-creation of pagan myths, of stories from the heroic past, the poet gives his people a sense of magnificent history in order to raise hope for deliverance from their present miseries. V.'s poetry has become stronger, more sensuous and erotic, full of life. Even in translation the poem "Arevelian paghaneek" ("The Oriental Bath," 1978) from this collection has been called by one critic "one of the most life-filled poems in all of western literature."

V.'s stay in Ghent and his observations of working conditions in an industrial city heightened his social consciousness and inspired poetry that broadened his reputation as humanist and socialist.

After V.'s assassination his friends ransomed from the Turks an unpublished manuscript, *Hatseen erkuh* (1921; the song of bread), a sequence of poems on village life, full of sunlight and the fragrance of hayloft and harvest. The sequence is amazing, considering it was written in prison before his execution.

BIBLIOGRAPHY: Kurtikian, S., "V.: Priest of Paganism," *Ararat*, 17 (1976): 14–15; Tolegian, A., "D. V.," *Ararat*, 17 (1976): 16–26

—MARZBED MARGOISSAN

VASSANJI, M(oyez) G.

Canadian novelist and short-story writer, b. 30 May 1950, Nairobi, Kenya

V., considered an Asian-African, was born in Nairobi, Kenya, and lived there until his father died. His family subsequently moved to Tanzania, in Dar es Salaam where he lived in the Indian community speaking two Indian languages: Cutchi and Gujarati, and some Hindi. "We were brought up as Indians. We grew up speaking two Indian languages," he says. V.'s family originally came to Africa from Gujarat in western India; in Africa, they were second and third generation Indians. V. left Dar es Salaam in 1970 to study at the Massachusetts Institute of Technology in the U.S. With a Ph.D. in physics from the University of Pennsylvania, he moved to Canada in 1978, where he worked at the Chalk River power station, then as a research associate and lecturer in physics at the University of Toronto.

V.'s writing is about in-between lives and inexorable change in the context of pre and postindependence realities embracing the flux of cultures and religions in the wider context of diaspora. V.'s writing career took off when he published his first novel, *The Gunny Sack* (1989), which won the Commonwealth Writers' Prize for best first book in the African region: a work about the essence of Indianness being slowly transformed by African mores despite Indian traditions in a tightly-knit community. At this same time V. began writing short stories; he also identified with the South Asian presence in the Canadian literary scene by assisting to coordinate seminars at University of Toronto. Drawing on these experiences, he edited *A Meeting of Streams: South Asian Canadian Literature* (1985). In addition, he started the literary journal the *Toronto South Asian Review,* which later became the *Toronto Review of International Writing Abroad.*

His second novel, *No New Land* (1991), is about the immigrant community from East Africa settling in Canada: a work set in the Toronto suburb of Don Mills. Essentially, this book is about the predicament of Indians of the diaspora living lives as immigrants in a predominantly white society and absorbing Western values in the flux of time and change. *Uhuru Street* (1992), a collection of stories set in Dar es Salaam, reflects on the past ghosts of life; the title here might have derived from V. S. NAIPAUL's earlier short-story collection, *Miguel Street.* Like Naipaul's stories, this book is considered funny, yet serious. V.'s reputation was further enhanced with his *Book of Secrets* (1994), a novel of realism, yet with an unconventional technique combining a metafictional formal structure with linearity that captures images from the 1913 diary of a British colonial administrator—found in 1988 in a shopkeeper's dusty room by Pius Fernandes, a retired school teacher. Fernandes is fascinated by the diary's coded history. Through deft narration V. explores the stories and the people in the diary's pages, uncovering many generations and embracing intriguing liaisons and family secrets.

Generally, V.'s work draws on his personal experiences from his community, with a mix of traditional and contemporary aspects of narration: his seemingly formal technique assimilates the postmodern with unaffected ease as he weaves old values with contemporary nuances, sometimes giving the impression of moving away from the community towards the individual's struggle for selfhood while simultaneously longing for belonging in a wider world. "There is still a sense of self-realization in many of my stories," V. says. "There is a quest within the story of the writer trying to find answers within the story or the novel, trying to understand. . . .And partly the question is, What am I going to discover about myself?"

BIBLIOGRAPHY: Sarvan, C., "M. G. V.'s *The Gunny Sack*: A Reflection on History and the Novel, *MFS*, 37 (Autumn 1991): 511–17; Malak, A., "Ambivalent Affiliations and Post-Colonial Conditions in the Fiction of M. G. V.," *WLT*, 37 (Spring 1993): 277–82; Ball, J. C., "Interview with M. G. V.," *CFR*, 15 (Winter 1993–Spring 1994): 3–8; George, M. G., "Traveling Light: Of Immigration, Invisible Suitcases and Gunny Sacks," *JFCS*, 4, 2 (1992): 72–99; de Mer, N., "Mediating Origins: M. V. and Discursivities of Migrant Identities," in A. Gurnah, ed., *Essays on African Writing* (1995), Vol. 2: 159–77

—CYRIL DABYDEEN

VASSILIKOS, Vassilis

Greek novelist and short-story writer, b. 18 Nov. 1934, Kavalla

V. studied law at the University of Thessaloniki and film directing in New York. Although never involved in politics, he could not bear living under a military dictatorship. Consequently, during the period of the colonels' regime in Greece (1967–74) he lived in self-imposed exile in western Europe. With the establishment of a civilian government, he returned to Athens. He is now a director of the Greek National Broadcasting System.

V.'s early works can be described as the "period of innocence." The novella *He diegese tou Iasona* (1953; the narrations of Jason) is a tender tale in which the activities of the young Prince Jason are fused with V.'s own recollections of his childhood and youth. The story of the Argonauts' quest for the golden fleece has been variously used by many writers, but V. was the first to focus on the psychological development of Jason from childhood to the day of his departure for his long journey. The three short stories in *Trilogia* (1961; *The Plant; The Well; The Angel: A Trilogy*, 1964) are characterized by the same spirit of idealism as *He diegese tou Iasona.*

V.'s next works are marked by dissatisfaction with society as it is. The theme of social injustice in Greece dominates V.'s collection of short stories *Ektos ton teihon* (1965; *Outside the Walls*, 1973). The title story, the best of the collection, is a tableau of a group of elitists isolated in their ivory tower. Although they provide leadership for the nation, they are far removed from the life of the ordinary people, whom they exploit while pretending to serve.

V.'s most famous work, the novel *Z* (1966; *Z*, 1968), filmed by Costa Gavras, is a political thriller based on the assassination of a left-wing member of the Greek parliament. Published before the colonels' coup, it prophesied what was to come. Despite the novel's fame, however, its literary value is minor. Its emotionally charged political atmosphere notwithstanding, the emphasis is on the relentless plot rather than on character analysis.

During the junta period V.'s talent was directed entirely toward a single goal—the depiction of the miserable situation both of the Greeks in Greece and, more often, of exiled Greeks in western Europe. To achieve this goal he either recorded with dry realism the psychology of the self-exiles almost like a tape recorder, as in *Kafeneion Emigrek* (1968; Café Emigrek), or he narrated the activities of his anti-junta heroes with breath-taking plots and the technique of thrillers. In the novel *Ho iatrodikastes* (1976; the coroner), for example, written during the junta period but published later, a ruthless ship-owner who murders his wife escapes punishment, his crime being covered up by the corrupt government. This novel, while using techniques similar to those of *Z*, is more profound in its psychological insights.

In many of V.'s novels of this type there is an obvious anti-Americanism, which somewhat distorts the realistic depictions of his heroes; an example is *To psarotoufeko* (1971; *The Harpoon Gun*, 1973), in which V. expresses his bitterness at what he views as the collaboration of the U.S. government with the junta. This stubborn subjectivism is also found in V.'s earlier travel books, such as *He mythologia tes Amerikes* (1960; the mythology of America), in which he describes the U.S. as a devil's hole without a single bright point.

At the end of the junta period V. wrote the novel *Glaukos Thrasakes* (3 vols., 1974–75; Glaukos Thrasakes), the last two volumes of which were written after his return to Greece. In this work the seeds of his new approach to life are evident: he now discards any real hope of social reform, although he continues to offer lip service to it.

In the postdictatorship period V. has become almost a different writer. His experiences in western Europe filled him with skepticism, or rather, nihilism. Now back in Greece without his mortal enemies—the dictators and their cohorts—he has lost his perennial targets and is left in a vacuum.

FURTHER WORKS: *Thymata eirenes* (1956); *Hoi fotografies* (1964; *The Photographs*, 1971); *Pasha stous Gargalianous* (1968); *Planodios plasie* (1969); *Metokisen eis agnoston dieuthynsin* (1969); *20.20* (1971); *Fifty, fifty* (1972); *He dike ton hex* (1973); *He kathodos* (1974); *Ho monarhes* (1974; *The Monarch*, 1976); *Ta poiemata* (1979); *Ho tromeros Menas Augustos* 1978 (1979); *Autoktonia me erotematiko 1950–54* (1981); *Ta haza boutia* (1981); *Hronografemata* (1982); *K.* (1992)

BIBLIOGRAPHY: Decavalles, A., on *The Plant; The Well; The Angel: A Trilogy, Poetry*, 105 (1964), 65; Friar, K., on *The Plant; The Well; The Angel: A Trilogy*, SatR, 4 July 1964: 26; Clements, R. J., on *Z*, SatR, 16 Nov. 1968: 51; Zuckerman, A. J., on *Z*, NYTBR, 17 Nov. 1968: 81; Bailey, A., on *Outside the Walls*, NYTBR, 6 May 1973: 38; Sourian, P., on *The Harpoon Gun*, NYTBR, 6 May 1973: 39; Bouyoucas, P., "V. V.: The Writer as Chronicler," *Athenian*, July 1979: 30–32; Raizis, M. B., on *Mia istoria ayapis*, WLT, 52, 3 (Summer 1978): 503–4

—VASSILIOS CHRISTIDES

VEGA, Ana Lydia

Puerto Rican short-story writer and essayist, b. 1946, Santurce

V. is one of the most important and popular writers of the newer generation of Puerto Rican writers. Her popularity is due to her unique utilization of parody, irony, and humor, and to the fact that she has made Puerto Rican popular culture the main poetics of her work. For V., popular language, as it uniquely identifies the cultural and historical saga of Puerto Rico, is always the main character of her short stories.

In her youth V. became interested in French language and cultures, an interest that took her to France to study and later to receive a Ph.D. in French, for which she wrote a doctoral dissertation on the myth of King Christophe in Haitian literature. Currently, she is a professor of French at the University of Puerto Rico in Río Piedras and has traveled to several universities as an invited visiting professor and guest speaker. Reared in Puerto Rico, she was part of a very unique generation who lived through important transitional moments in the politics of the island, and who dreamed of becoming a nation independent of the U.S.; a generation that has produced the most important and internationally acclaimed body of literature in Puerto Rico. During her childhood and adolescence, she was also influenced by her father, from whom she learned deep appreciation and interest in popular culture and oral traditions. He improvised "décimas," or poems to be sung with a guitar in competitions with other poets, a tradition very typical to the Caribbean and to other regions of Latin America. Although her main interest in writing was not poetry, her interest for the popular, in themes, language, and traditions, is evident in her work. Inspired by her sense of resistance on the one hand, and her interest in popular culture on the other, in the late 1980s V. and Carmen Lugo Filippi (dates n.a.) plotted to write together a collection of daring short stories, unveiling many of the cultural myths and taboos of Puerto Rican society as perceived by women in a colonial society. It was a mischievous and iconoclastic enterprise. Thus, since they could not predict the reader's reaction, each chose a pseudonym to hide their true identity: Carmen Lugo Filippi took the name of Scaldada and V. of Talía Cuervo. *Vírgenes y mártires* (1988; Virgins and Martyrs) was an immediate success. The text was an open performance, an erotic dance and cultural strip tease, divided into three sections, the first two of six short stories each by each of the two writers, and a third, and last accord to that symphony of popular voices, a narrated duet between Scaldada and Talía.

The success of *Vírgenes y mártires* was partly due to its unique exploration of the many and different feminine worlds of Puerto Rican society: beauty salons, motels, tourism, weddings and divorces, soap operas, the street, office, home, married and single women, the dominated and the independent, as well as the many expectations society places on women. The erotic in popular culture is transformed in V.'s work through humor in such a way that reality is left naked, seen as it is and not as it should be, and her characters are left abandoned, alone, with their most intimate fears and desires. Humor, which characterizes V.'s short stories, often hides a critical view of Puerto Rican society as a semicolonial world in which sexual dominance is allegorical, also sociopolitical dependence. V. dismantles social myths and taboos and exposes intimate social idiosyncrasies through parody, including a unique bilingual play that is part of the colloquial speech V. has mastered in her narrative and that makes many of her short stories very difficult to translate to other languages. Through satire, humor, and parody *Vírgenes y mártires* dismantles the many faces of a modern colonial society in which the dependence and domination of women by men, and by women, are seen by V. in the perspective of a greater colonialism that has affected, and in part has defined, contemporary Puerto Rican society.

Encouraged by the success of *Vírgenes y mártires*, V. published (no longer under a pseudonym) a second collection of short stories, addressed not just to Puerto Rico, but to the larger Caribbean, as one single yet diverse cultural entity. The title she chose for this text, *Encancaranublado y otros cuentos de naufragio* (1982; Very Overcasted and Other Stories of Shipwrecks), is literally untranslatable, like many of her texts. The title is taken from a popular tongue twister, with the prefix "encancara," which could be applied to any Spanish word, and adds the meaning of intensity or embroilment. Applied to the Caribbean, the title intensifies cloudiness to imply "stormy" in an allegorical sense. It also articulates the uniqueness of language and culture as a unifying, yet separating, force in the Caribbean. The uniqueness of this simultaneous/parallel unity and diversity is the underlying theme of this collection. The Caribbean is a homogeneous region, with a very similar history and, in essence, a similar cultural experience, and yet, very diverse, separated by languages (French, Spanish, and English), and by race. In *Encancaranublado* V. explores and meditates on those differences and prejudices, most of the time constructed out of a false sense of superiority. V. dismantles, reconstructs, and reinvents stereotypes through humorous parodies that hide strong criticisms with laughter. The different short stories that make up this collection not only re-create the multiplicity and diversity of the Caribbean through humor, but also fantasy. Her stories in this text are staged in a larger and more diverse society that acts, reacts, and speaks the same cultural language, as seen in "El jueguito de la Habana" (The Little Game in Havana), "Puerto Rican Syndrome," "Jamaica Farewell," and "Contrapunto haitiano" (Haitian Counterpoint). In another one of these stories, "Otra maldad de Pateco" (Another One of Pateco's Mischievous Tricks), V. explores the world of fantasy and the fantastic in a Caribbean context through Afro-Caribbean mythology. Pateco, a popular figure in Puerto Rican folklore, causes a Plantation owner's son to be born with a white body and a black head. Disgraced and ashamed by the half colored child, the baby is sent to live with an old woman slave who raises him in her own beliefs and traditions. The half white half black child's saga into manhood—his education into African culture and lore, and his desire to be black like his true cultural mother—becomes an allegory of what, for V., is the Caribbean condition.

In her next collection of short stories, *Pasión de historia y otras historias de pasión* (1987; Passion of History and Other Histories of Passion), V. combines the themes and techniques she used in her past work—humor, satire, parody, and criticism of a colonial society to dismantle social, political, and sexual dominance and power—with her love for the detective story. The search through tales and writing for a truth that is always illusive, ultimately an imaginary construct, staged in a Puerto Rican context where gossip is portrayed as the creator and destroyer of reality, is the dominant theme of "Pasión de historia" (Passion of History), winner of the Juan Rulfo International Award in 1984.

In 1989 V. received a scholarship from the John S. Guggenheim Foundation that allowed her to spend several months in the southern coast of the island, where, much like her character in "Pasión de historia," she spent the time gathering local stories, historical information, and writing another collection of short stories, *Falsas crónicas del sur* (1991; False Chronicles of the South). Inspired by history and oral traditions, V. rediscovered and reinvented events, characters, and places, interweaving romance with action, adventure, and sociopolitical satire. In these stories her iconoclastic techniques and her irreverence for taboos are more subtle, allowing her narratives to approximate the rhetoric of the chronicles; however, events and characters of national and regional importance, of social and political prestige, are still revisited and reconstructed through humor and gossip.

V. is also an accomplished essayist. In *Esperando a Loló y otros delirios de generación* (1994; Waiting for Loló and Other Generation Delusions), a book she dedicated to her daughter, with the same humorous satire and irony that characterizes her fictional work, V. reflects upon the experiences and saga of her generation in Puerto Rico, and the experiences of being a professional woman, a mother, and a writer in a semicolonial society. Her essays, like her works of fiction, make of the popular and daily life in Puerto Rico, as seen, lived, and told by feminine voices, the poetics of her writing. V. does not write poetry or "décimas" like her father did, but she would like to think that her writing continues her father's tradition and is an ode to him as a popular poet.

FURTHER WORKS: *Scaldada y Cuervo SA presentan a Carmen Lugo Filippi* (1981); *Tramo ancla. Ensayos puertorriqueños de hoy* (2 vols., 1989, 1991); *Cuentos calientes* (1992); *Historia y literatura* (1995)

BIBLIOGRAPHY: Muñoz, E. M., "El discurso de la mujer colonizada en dos cuento de A. L. V.," *Alva de América*, 4 (July 1986): 37–47; Emmanueli-Huertas, J., "Antillanos, náufragos, míseros y trashumantes: A un siglo del toque de queda de Martí," *Confluencia*, 3 (Fall 1987): 101–4; Galván, D., "Sincretismo cultural en estructura policíaca: A. L. V. y su 'Pasión de historia y otras historias de pasión,'" *AmRev*, 21 (Fall–Winter 1993): 139–49; González Pérez, A., "A. L. Pluravega: Unidad y multiplicidad caribeña en la obra de A. L. V.," *RI*, 59 (January–June 1993): 162–63, 289–300; Captain–Hidalgo, Y., "El espíritu de la risa en el cuento de A. L. V.," *RI*, 59 (January–June 1993): 162–63, 301–08; Falcoón, R., "Aleluya a la caribeñidad: Los cuentos negristas de A. L. V.," *AHR*, 13 (Fall 1994): 41–44; Velez, D., "We Are (Not) in This Together: The Caribbean Imaginary in 'Encancaranublado' by A. L. V.," *Callaloo*, 17 (Summer 1994): 826–33; Engling, E., "Thematic and Narrative Strategies in L. V.'s 'Pollito chicken,'" *CLAJ*, 39 (March 1996): 341–56; Puleo, A., "A. L. V., the Caribbean Storyteller," *PRL*, 15 (Fall 1996): 21–25

—JULIA CUERVO HEWITT

VELOZ MAGGIOLO, Marcio

Dominican novelist and short-story writer, b. 13 Aug. 1936, Santo Domingo

V. M. is one of the most important contemporary Dominican novelists. He has also written theater, poetry, essay, and history. He studied philosophy at the University of Santo Domingo, where he received his Licenciatura in 1961, and he obtained a Ph.D. in history at the University of Madrid (1970). He has been a university professor since 1962, having also been a prominent diplomat for his country in Mexico, Italy, Peru, Bolivia, Egypt, and Romania.

V. M.'s first novel was *El buen ladrón* (1960; the good thief), which obtained a mention from the William Faulkner Foundation as the best Dominican novel written after World War II. With *La vida no tiene nombre* (1965; life has no name) and *Los ángeles de hueso* (1966; angels made of bone) V. M. broke away from the traditional Dominican novel, thus initiating a renewal in that country's narrative, which culminated in *De abril en adelante* (1975; from April onward), one of the novels selected for the Seix Barral Prize in Barcelona, Spain. The novel obtained a resounding success, and initiated V. M. in the barrio and dictatorship themes, both of which became central to his later work. In 1981, with *Biografía difusa de Sombra Castañeda* (1981; diffuse biography of Sombra Castañeda), V. M. obtained the National Prize for the Novel in the Dominican Republic, followed by the National Prize for Short Stories with *La fértil agonía del amor* (1982; love's fertile agony). With *Materia Prima* (1988; raw material) he again won the National Prize for the Novel.

His work had begun to attract attention as of the early 1970s when critics had noticed the recurrence of the theme of dictatorship, and of the figure of the dictator, as basic to V. M.'s narrative. V. M. focuses his work on experiences that, while appearing to be local on a first reading, develop universal dimensions. In his most recent novel, *Ritos de cabaret* (1991; nightclub rites), V. M. tries, as in his previous work, to transform the local Caribbean experience into material of a larger interest. He is considered a poet of prose writing, and frequently uses experimental techniques to intersperse the more traditional realist prose with the magical and hallucinatory elements characteristic of his production.

FURTHER WORKS: *El prófugo* (1962); *De donde vino la gente* (1978); *Novelas cortas* (1980); *Cuentos, recuentos y casi cuentos* (1986)

BIBLIOGRAPHY: González Cruz, L., "Desde el absurdo. La narrativa de V. M.," *ALHis*, 8 (1979): 119–25; García, J. E., "M. V. M. en el centro del cuento dominicano," *Isla abierta*, 16 (1982): 4–16; Sommer, D., *One Master for Another* (1983): 197–228; Mármol, J., "El cerco infranqueable del pasado," *Coloquio*, 4 (1989): 6–7; Amarante, H., "Materia Prima: el discurso del barrio," *Coloquio*, 4 (1989): 13–14; Tejada Holguin, R., "*Materia Prima:* una novela caótica o una representación del caos?," *Coloquio*, 4 (1989): 14–15

—NICASIO SILVERIO

VENDA LITERATURE
See under South Africa Literature

VENEZIS, Elias

(pseud. of Elias Mellos) Greek novelist, short-story writer, and dramatist, b. 4 Mar. 1904, Ayvalik, Ottoman Empire; d. 3 Aug. 1973, Athens

V.'s literary career was shaped by his experiences in Asia Minor, where he was born. The Disaster of 1922, at the close of the war with Turkey (1920–22)—which left close to a million dead, and a million and a half uprooted—left an indelible mark on him.

As a victim of this catastrophic event, he was imprisoned by the Turkish authorities for fourteen months (1922–23) and served in a labor battalion under brutal conditions. After his release he settled in Lesbos, where he worked for the National Bank of Greece. In 1957 he became a director of the Greek National Theater and a member of the Academy of Athens.

V.'s first collection of short stories, *O Manolis Lekas, kai alla diigimata* (1928; Manolis Lekas, and other short stories), was followed by the novel *To noumero 31328* (1931; number 31328), based on V.'s experiences in the labor battalion. The title refers to the number assigned to the protagonist and signifies his dehumanization—his reduction to a mere number. *To noumero 31328* is a narrative of retrospection, with the narrator also the main character. In the closing pages of the novel the narrative shifts from the simple past tense, which relates the days of his captivity, to the present, the time of his release.

V.'s next novel, *Galini* (1939; serenity), deals with the problems of ethnic Greek refugees from Asia Minor in adjusting to life in Greece proper. It was followed by a collection of short stories, *Aigaio* (1941; the Aegean), and a novel, *Aeoliki ghi* (1943; *Beyond the Aegean*, 1957), V.'s best-known work, which has been widely translated. *Aeoliki ghi*, written like *To noumero 31328* in the first person, is about the narrator's childhood in Asia Minor. Other characters bring their stories into the primary narrative and at times threaten to explode the structure by displacing the protagonist's point of view. The narrative is, however, held together by the magic of a child's perspective.

The play *Block C* (1946; block C) is also autobiographical; it focuses on the author's arrest by the Nazis and the subsequent days awaiting an execution that never takes place.

V. has made a significant contribution to the modern Greek literary tradition. Power of suggestion, sensitivity, the theme of helplessness, and the terror of individual characters in the face of brutal historical events are the most prominent features of his work.

FURTHER WORKS: *Anemoi* (1944); *Ora polemou* (1944); *Fthinoporo stin Italia* (1950); *Exodos* (1950); *O Archiepiskopos Damaskinos* (1952); *Oi nikimenoi* (1954); *Amerikaniki ghi* (1955); *To chronikon tis Trapezas tis Ellados* (1955); *Okeanos* (1956); *Argonaftes* (1962); *Emmanuel Tsouderos* (1965); *Archipelagos* (1969); *Eftalou* (1972); *Periehiseis* (1973); *Stis ellinikes thalasses* (1973); *Mikrasia, haire* (1974)

BIBLIOGRAPHY: Sahinis, A., "The Fiction of E. V.," *The Charioteer*, 1 (1960): 84–90; Karanikas, A., and H. Karanikas, *E. V.* (1969); Dimaras, C. T., *Modern Greek Literature* (1972): 492–93; Politis, L., *A History of Modern Greek Literature* (1973): 250–51; Doulis, T., *Disaster and Fiction: The Impact of the Asia Minor Disaster of 1922 on Modern Greek Fiction* (1977): passim

—CHRISTOS S. ROMANOS

VENEZUELAN LITERATURE

In 1829 Venezuela became a sovereign state, independent of Greater Colombia. The literature of the new nation was influenced by political and socioeconomic factors: the fusion of three racial groups—blacks, whites, and Indians—into Venezuelan citizens;

the establishment of order out of political and economic chaos; the forging of the diversified geography of country into a manageable entity; and later, the emergence of technology and industry.

Three distinct movements have held sway since independence. One stressed local color and the recounting of legends. The second harshly criticized corruption. The third, arising out of Spanish American MODERNISM, focused on more universal themes.

Poetry

At the beginning of the 20th c. Venezuelan poetry was under the influence of modernism. Rufino Blanco Fombona (1874–1944), the best known of the modernists, was clearly a follower of Rubén DARÍO. His *Pequeña ópera lírtica* (1904; a small lyrical opera), with a prologue by Darío, displayed many of the characteristics of modernism: pessimism, the cult of beauty, the exaltation of the senses, musicality, and elevated diction. His study *El modernism y los poetas modernistas* (1929; modernism and the modernist poets) was one of the movement's critical works. Alfredo Arvelo Larriva (1883–1934) was an even more thoroughgoing modernist. His first book of poems, *Enjambre de rimas* (1906; a hive of poems), sets forth the aesthetic principles of the movement.

The poets who rebelled against modernism are known as the Generation of 1918. Although many had been greatly influenced by modernism, these writers reacted against the overemphasis on form. They stressed content and were preoccupied with landscape and folklore. Andrés Eloy Blanco (1897–1955), the best known of this group, was romantic and modernist in his early work; but in *Barco de piedra* (1937; a stone ship) and *Baedeker 2000* (1938; Baedeker 2000) he introduced radically new themes and modes of expression. In his late work Venezuelan subjects take on universal overtones.

Many writers of this generation of political and aesthetic rebels experienced imprisonment and exile during the regime of Juan Vicente Gómez, president of Venezuela from 1908 to 1936. Leading poets were Antonio Arraiz (1903–1963), Miguel Otero Silva (b. 1908), Luis Castro (1909–1952), and Luis Fernández Alvarez (1902–1952). Arraiz, also one of Venezuela's best novelists, dominated this "vanguard" movement. The poems in *Aspero* (1924; harsh) are strong reactions against the excesses of the modernists. His poetry, often primitivist, reflects the hidden, savage world of Venezuela. Otero Silva was the most politically revolutionary, and the central theme of his poems is the struggle against the injustices suffered by the unfortunate. Fernández Alvarez was the outstanding SURREALIST of the group. The central subject of his works is death. Rodríguez Cárdenas introduced the Negro and his customs into Venezuelan poetry.

In an atmosphere of optimism following the death of the dictator Gómez, a group of young poets founded the review *Viernes*. They attempted to bring Venezuelan poetry into the mainstream of Spanish-language poetry. Vicente Gerbasi (b. 1912) was the outstanding *Viernes* poet. Otto D'Sola's (b. 1912) works moved from melancholy and elegiac romanticism to surrealism. Pascual Venegas Filardo's (b. 1911) poems are marked by a deep sense of nostalgia. Rafael Olivares Figueroa's (1893–1972) poems are intellectual, similar to those of Paul VALÉRY.

Some of today's younger poets continue to write in the vein of the *Viernes* group. Others have turned toward the classics. Many are influenced by Pablo NERUDA, and a few have returned to the landscape and native subjects for inspirations. Perhaps the finest

postwar work is *Humano destino* (1950; human destiny) by Juan Liscano (b. 1915), one of Venezuela's most distinguished literary figures—poet, scholar, critic, and biographer.

The Novel

A great influence on the 20th-c. Venezuelan novel was Manuel Vicente Romero García's (1865–1917) *Peonía* (1890; Peonía [the name of a sugar plantation]), with its elements of realism, romanticism, local color, and interest in nature. The pessimism of *Peonía*—in which backwardness triumphs over reform and modernization—was to mark Venezuelan novels for decades. Rather than well-developed individuals, characters tended to be symbols, pitted against the overwhelming forces of nature and the social order.

Rufino Blanco Fombona, while in prison, wrote his best novel, *El hombre de hierro* (1907; the man of steel), a story of adultery. His ideal was the Nietzschean superman. He never believed in the triumph of good. In *El hombre de oro* (1914; *The Man of Gold*, 1916), only the base characters are successful: the opportunist politician Chichaura, and the usurer Irurtia. Like many other of Blanco Fombona's works, *El hombre de oro* sometimes degenerates into pure invective.

Manuel Díaz Rodríguez (1871–1927) was the outstanding Venezuelan modernist in fiction. His first novel, *Ídolos rotos* (1901; broken idols), set in Caracas, portrays a maladjusted artist-intellectual who tries to enlighten his country but encounters tremendous hostility and ultimately goes into exile. The style is at times excessively refined and sophisticated, in the modernist vein. *Sangre patricia* (1902; patrician blood) is a psychological study of a neurotic young man from Caracas. In *Peregrina; o, El pozo encantado* (1922; Peregrina; or, the enchanted well), his last novel, Díaz Rodríguez turned to a rural setting.

José Rafael Pocaterra (1888–1955) and others of his generation avidly read the Russian novelists of their time and were influenced by the tragic and fatalistic worldview in those works. Pocaterra reacted violently against modernism. His novels, which portray urban life and use the Venezuelan vernacular, denounce the cruel dictatorship, political corruption, and the decadence of the ruling class.

Teresa de la Parra (pseud. of Ana Teresa Parra Sanojo, 1890–1936), Venezuela's outstanding woman novelist, in *Diario de una señorita que escribio porque se fastidia* (1924; diary of a young woman who wrote because she was bored)—later retitled *Ifigenia* (Ifigenia)—portrayed in intimate details the life of a young woman in an unstable society. Her second novel, the tender *Las memorias de Mamá Blanca* (1929; *Mama Blanca's Souvenirs*, 1959), centers around a girl's life on a plantation. Parra introduced psychological analysis into the Venezuelan novel, particularly of the feminine psyche.

Rómulo GALLEGOS's three masterpieces, *Doña Bárbara* (1929; *Doña Barbara*, 1931), *Cantaclaro* (1934; a name meaning "minstrel of the plains"), and *Canaima* (1935; a name meaning "the spirit of evil"), earned him an international reputation. He always chose specifically Venezuelan themes.

Julián Padrón's (1910–1954) *La guaricha* (1934; the Indian maid), like most Venezuelan novels, gives great attention to the landscape. Set in the state of Monagas, the novel deals with the victims of the local chief of police and the regional *caciques*. In Padrón's *Madrugada* (1939; the awakening) there is again much description of the landscape (rural Caripe), as well as the retelling of local legends.

Arturo USLAR PIETRI wrote two fine historical novels. *Las lanzas coloradas* (1931; *The Red Lances*, 1963) is set in 1814, a time of turbulence and war preceding final separation from Spain. *El camino de El Dorado* (1947; the road to El Dorado) re-creates the rebellion of the conquistador Lope de Aguirre against the Spanish king in 1560.

The poet Miguel Otero Silva's first novel, *Fiebre* (1928; fever), deals with various measures taken to overthrow the dictator Gómez. *Casas muertas* (1955; dead houses) is the story of the decline of a once flourishing Venezuelan town in the interior. *Oficina No. 1* (1961; office number 1) describes a city that developed near the Venezuelan oil fields.

Ramón Díaz Sánchez's (1903–1968) first novel, *Mene* (1936; Mene [a fictional city]), about the discovery of oil and the transformation of Zulia from a rural to a highly industrialized state, offered a new theme to Venezuelan fiction. It was continued by Rómulo Gallegos in *Sobre la misma tierra* (1943; on this very earth).

By the mid-20th c. there were great sociological, political, and economic changes in Venezuela. New attitudes were combined with new fictional techniques borrowed from Europe and the U.S. PROUST, JOYCE, DOS PASSOS, and FAULKNER became models for exploring the inner worlds of characters. With the dominance of mass man, the antihero emerged.

The writers who in 1955 formed the literary circle Sardio brought universal themes to the Venezuelan novel. Although the group was short-lived, Sardio writers continued to use language for the purpose of subverting the old order. Salvador Garmendia (b. 1928), one of the original Sardio members, dominates the contemporary novel. His characters are the universal mass men, caught up in the anonymity of city life, bored with dull routine, with little or no hope of escape except in alcohol, drugs, or sex.

The Short Story

The short story as a serious genre in Venezuela originated with the modernists. In Manuel Díaz Rodríguez's first book of stories, *Cuentos de color* (1899; color stories), each story features a different symbolic color. Style is more important here than content. His best stories all have rural settings.

Rómulo Gallegos's first book, the collection of short stories *Los aventureros* (1913; the adventurers), was technically masterful. His plots are carefully constructed; his characters, sharply defined. José Rafael Pocaterra, with *Cuentos grotescos* (1922; grotesque stories), did for the short story what Gallegos did for the novel. His stories are often cruel, often crude, pictures of his time.

Leoncio Martínez's (1888–1941) *Mis otros fantoches* (1932; my other caricatures), a collection of bitter short stories, led one critic to call him the Venezuelan Zola.

Julio Garmendia (1898-1977), in *Tienda de muñecos* (1927; the doll shop), brought a whimsical, philosophical note to short fiction. His stories have a sophisticated, cosmopolitan quality not found elsewhere.

Arturo Uslar Pietri regarded local-color writers as old-fashioned; he was preoccupied with metaphor and brought more universal themes into the short story. In Antonio Arraiz's *Tío Tigre y Tío Conejo* (1945; Uncle Tiger and Uncle Rabbit), based on Venezuelan rural folklore, each animal represents a psychological type.

After World War II Venezuelan short-story writers searched for new philosophical and aesthetic values. Like the novel, the short story focused on mass man crowded into cities. The emphasis was on the inner worlds of characters.

The Essay

The essay in Venezuela became a serious literary genre after the introduction into Spanish America of positivism, derived from the works of Auguste Comte (1798–1857) in France and Herbert Spencer (1820–1903) in England. Laureano Vallenilla Lanz (1870–1936), one of the early positivists, in his *Cesarismo democrático* (1919; democratic caesarism) attempted to justify dictatorial government for Spanish American countries.

Rómulo Gallegos's essays, later collected in *Una posición en la vida* (1954; a position in life), outline the political, social, and literary reforms he advocated for his country.

Among important essayists of more recent times is Arturo Uslar Pietri, whose *Letras y hombres de Venezuela* (1948; letters and men of Venezuela) is a succinct study of the great figures in Venezuelan history, both literary and public.

Mariano Picón-Salas (1901–1965), Venezuela's most distinguished essayist, is a fine, careful writer and a humanist of great erudition. *De la conquista a la independencia: Tres siglos de historia cultural hispano-americana* (1944; *A Cultural History of Spanish America: From Conquest to Independence*, 1962) is a book fundamental to the understanding of Spanish American life today. In *Europe-América: Preguntas a la esfinge de la culture* (1947; Europe-America: questions to the sphinx regarding culture) and *Crisis, cambio, tradición* (1952; crisis, change, tradition), two of his most mature works, he is concerned with the mechanization of the world and the alienation of modern man. He sought a synthesis of the best of Europe and America and, unlike many of his contemporaries, never lost faith in the power of reason.

Drama

Drama in Venezuela, as in most other Spanish American countries, continues to mean primarily the presentation of plays by European and American writers.

Both the *sainete*, a one-act farce, and the *apropósito*, a short interlude, were popular theatrical pieces in Venezuela during the first half of the century. These plays satirized politics and local customs, often with impromptu comments by the actors. A genre called the "theater for reading only" also flourished in the first half of the century. The poet Andrés Eloy Blanco, the novelist and poet Miguel Otero Silva, and Francisco Pimentel (pseud.: Job Pim, 1890–1942) were among the closet dramatists.

Rómulo Gallegos showed the way to a serious theater with *El milagro del año* (1915; the miracle of the year). The Society of the Friends of the Theater, formed in 1945, attempted to promote the growth of drama in Venezuela. Despite the efforts of this and other groups, drama in Venezuela has still not developed fully.

BIBLIOGRAPHY: Galletti, A. Mancera, *Quienes narran y cuentan en Venezuela* (1948); Pietri, A. Uslar, *Letras y hombres de Venezuela* (1948); Crema, E., *Interpretación crítica de la literatura venezolana* (1954?); Seijas, P. Díaz, *La antigua y la moderna literatura venezolana* (1966); Medina, J. R., *50 años de literatura venezolana, 1918–1968* (1969); Liscano, J., *Panorama de la literatura venezolana actual* (1973); Miranda, J. E., *Proceso a la narrativa venezolana* (1975); Monasterios, R., *Un enfoque crítico del teatro venezolano* (1975)

—LOWELL DUNHAM

VERCORS

(pseud. of Jean Bruller) French novelist, dramatist, and essayist, b. 26 Feb. 1902, Paris; d. 10 June 1991

Trained as an engineer, Jean Bruller was known to a relatively small circle, prior to World War II, through his several albums of satirical drawings. During the German occupation he helped found Les Éditions de Minuit; the first publication of this originally clandestine press was his novella *Le silence de la mer* (1942; *The Silence of the Sea*, 1944), which made his pseudonym, chosen from a mountain range in southeastern France, world famous.

In this novel, Werner von Ebrennac, a young German officer who sincerely believes in the benefits of Franco-German solidarity—even if it has to be achieved by force—is billeted with an elderly French landowner and his niece. He enthusiastically pours out his love of France in a long monologue, which is met with patriotic, stony silence. Yet Ebrennac admires this reaction, since he disliked obsequious flattery by French people less firm in this attitude toward the Germans. When Ebrennac realizes the true nature of his Nazi masters, he volunteers for service on the Russian front, where his death is all but certain.

La marche à l'étoile (1943; *Guiding Star, in Three Short Novels*, 1946), which was also published clandestinely, focuses on an eastern European immigrant to France and his gradual disillusionment with the country he had chosen out of love.

A strong humanitarian message pervades all V.'s books. For a number of years after 1945, V.'s novels, essays, and stories dealt with dilemmas of conscience. In *La puissance du jour* (1951; the power of daylight), he traces the eventual emotional healing of a repatriated prisoner of war who owes his survival to the involuntary killing of a fellow prisoner. The essays in *Plus ou moins homme* (1949; more or less human) probe the limit beyond which man can no longer retain his pride and dignity. The stories in *Les yeux et la lumière* (1948; light shines in your eyes) without exception are devoted to cases in which the individual must make a choice for human responsibility and freedom.

Les animaux dénaturés (1952; *You Shall Know Them*, 1953) deals with the discovery of a new human species and points up our inadequate definition of what constitutes a human being. V. adapted this, his most successful novel, for the stage as *Zoo; ou, L'assassin philanthrope* (1965; *Zoo; or, The Philanthropic Assassin*, 1968). *Sylva* (1961; *Sylva*, 1961) presents the remarkable transformation of a fox into a woman and the simultaneous degradation of a woman drug addict. The tale is imbued with wry humor, yet it is serious in its drastic illustration of what makes human beings truly human.

V.'s all-pervasive preoccupation with the workings of nature finds expression both in many novels—for example, *Sillages* (1972; ships' wakes), *Tendre naufrage* (1974; gentle shipwreck), and *Les chevaux du temps* (1977; the horses of time)—and also in his essays. The essays take such forms as a dialogue with a biologist, a conversation with a musician, and historic-philosophic musings, such as the 150-page text commissioned for the centennial of the Paris Commune, "L'humanité en marche" (1971; humanity on the march). *Sens et non-sens de l'histoire* (1978; sense and nonsense of history) is a rich cultural and artistic analysis of the main events of modern times.

The short novel *Le piège à loup* (1979; the wolf trap) demonstrates anew the fine-grained art of the storyteller; V. keeps his reader breathless while probing the depths of human conscience.

Committed to social justice, V. never belonged to any political party and has often been called on to moderate debates between opposing groups, as a is evidenced in *Morale chrétienne et morale marxiste* (1960; Christian ethics and Marxist ethics), a book he edited, based on a symposium he moderated. His wartime memoirs, *La bataille du silence* (1967; *The Battle of Silence*, 1969), were hailed as an exceptionally moving account of a tragic time, and reinforced his reputation as a calm and earnest voice in turbulent times.

FURTHER WORKS: *21 recettes pratiques de mort violente* (1926); *Le songe* (1945); *Le sable du temps* (1945); *Les armes de la nuit* (1946); *L'imprimerie de Verdun* (1947; *The Verdun Press*, 1947, in *Three Short Novels*, 1947); *Les pas dans le sable* (1954); *Portrait d'un amitié* (1954); *Colères* (1956; *The Insurgents*, 1956); *Les divagations d'un français en Chine* (1956); *Pour prendre congé* (1957; *For the Time Being*, 1957); *Goetz* (1958); *Surce rivage* (3 vols., 1958–60): *I, Le périple* (in *Freedom in December*, 1961); *II, Monsieur Prousthe* (*Monsieur Prousthe, in Paths of Love*, 1961); *III, La liberté de décembre* (*December's Freedom, in Paths of Love*, 1961); *Les chemins de l'être* (1965, with Paul Misraki); *Quoto; ou, Les Pléthoriens* (1966, with Coronel; *Quota*, 1966); *Le fer et le velours* (1969); *Le radeau de la Méduse* (1969; *The Raft of the Medusa*, 1969); *Contes des cataplasmes* (1971); *Sept sentiers du désert* (1972); *Comme un frère* (1973); *Question sur la vie à messieurs les biologistes* (1973); *Ce que je crois* (1975); *Je cuisine comme un chef* (1976); *Théâtre I* (1978); *Camille; ou, L'enfant double* (1978); *Assez mentir* (1979, with Olga Wormser-Migot); *Cent and d'historie de France* (3 vols., 1981–83); *Le Tigre d'Anvers* (1996); *Le Grenier d'Armor* (1997). FURTHER WORKS IN ENGLISH: *Three Short Novels* (1947)

BIBLIOGRAPHY: Bieber, K., *L'Allemagne vue par les écrivains de la résistance française* (1954): 122–46; Brodin, P., *Présences contemporaines* (1954): 321–31; Moeller, C., *Littérature du XXe siècle et Christianisme*, Vol. III: 321–48; Konstantinović, R., *V.: Ecrivain et dessinateur* (1969); Bruller, J., "Jean Bruller et V.," *Europe*, 543–44 (1972): 333–49; Popkin, D., and Popkin, M., eds., *Modern French Literature* (1977), Vol. II: 476–80; Lottman, H. L., *The Left Bank: Writers, Artists, and Politics from the Popular Front to the Cold War* (1982): 180–84, 220–23, and passim

—KONRAD BIEBER

VERGA, Giovanni

Italian novelist, short-story writer, and dramatist, b. 31 Aug. 1840, Catania; d. 27 Jan. 1922, Catania

Although chronologically V. is largely a 19th-c. writer, any account of 20th-c. Italian fiction must begin with him, since he gave it the most determining direction thematically and formally. Thanks to him, European realism, particularly French naturalism, which entered Italy around 1860, did not remain a superimposed voguish import but became the indigenous fertile force known as *verismo*.

The eldest son of an upper-middle-class family, V. spent his early years in his native city in Sicily, with frequent stays at his father's estate of Vizzini. The rustic environment and the ethos of those who peopled it provided material for his most enduring work.

Having decided to bend all his efforts to creative writing, he abandoned his law studies before graduation. His first novel, *Amore e patria* (love and country), completed when he was seventeen but never published, was followed by *I carbonari della montagna* (1862; the mountain carbonari), which introduced him to Catania's literary circles. In 1869 he took up residence in Florence, where traditionally Italy's aspiring writers came to deprovincialize themselves culturally and linguistically. He found influential mentors, including Luigi Capuana (1839–1915), a novelist and an enthusiastic advocate of naturalism, who became his lifelong friend.

When V. moved to Milan three years later, he was welcomed by the most prestigious literary and artistic salons. He broadened his readings of such foreign writers as Darwin, Balzac, Maupassant, Flaubert, and Zola. His twenty-two-year stay in Milan marks the pinnacle of his creativity. Among the half-dozen novels written during this time are his two acknowledged masterpieces. His five short-story collections contain some of the finest examples of the genre. His stage adaptations of some of them were artistic and financial successes. In 1894 V. returned to Catania. A three-act play, *Dal tuo al mio* (what is yours is mine), was staged in Milan in 1903 and turned into a novel in 1905. V. continued to work on a new major novel, *La Duchessa di Leyra* (the Duchess of Leyra), destined to remain incomplete, published his collected theatrical writings, *Teatro* (1912; theater), and wrote a short story, "Una capanna e il tuo cuore" (1919; a hut with your heart). Writing, however, became increasingly arduous, so that he did not complete the cycle of novels he had planned. His life, too, turned more and more private; he even refused to attend the official festivities—with Luigi PIRANDELLO as the principal speaker—in honor of his eightieth birthday. Nor did he exercise any privileges when he was named a senator.

It is no longer tenable to divide V.'s fiction into two antithetical manners, with the short story "Nedda" (1874; "Nedda," 1893) as their point of demarcation. With the possible exception of the first three pseudohistorical novels, clearly imitative of the Italian (Ugo Foscolo [1778–1827], Alessandro Manzoni [1785–1878]), and transalpine (Sir Walter Scott, Alexandre Dumas père) traditions, all his works hinge on a basically unified vision of man's ultimate defeat by uncontrollable yearning or passions. In most of his works V. relies on fashionable situations and conventional modes of narration in order to project the characters he called *vinti* (vanquished). The lure for his characters is either the passion of the heart, as in *Storia di una capinera* (1871; story of a blackcap), his first popular success, or that of the flesh, as in *Eros* (1875; eros). But in two collections of short stories and in two novels these themes are developed with particular mastery. The varied characters in *Vita dei campi* (1880; life in the field) and in *Novelle rusticane* (1883; *Little Novels of Sicily*, 1925)—D. H. Lawrence was the translator of this volume, as well as of another collection of V.'s stories, *Cavalleria Rusticana, and Other Stories* (1928)—struggle against formidable odds brought about by passions that are no longer exclusively amatory.

Memorable are the protagonists of "Cavalleria rusticana" ("Cavalleria Rusticana" [rustic chivalry], 1893; later trs., 1928, 1958), the best-known story because it is the basis of Mascagni's opera, of "La Lupa" ("The She-Wolf," 1893; later tr., 1958; also tr. as "La Lupa," 1928), and of "L'amante di Gramigna" ("Gramigna's Mistress," 1893; later tr., 1958; also tr. as "Gramigna's Lover," 1928)—all in *Vita dei campi*—who, driven by lust, take each step

resolutely even though they know that they are moving inexorably to their doom. Among those whose drives are not erotic are several whose actions, despite their cruelty, irrationality, and futility, rise in the reader's eyes because, as inspiring gestures of self-assertion, they constitute the only way to preserve their own sense of integrity, as elementary and instinctive as it may be. Such are the actions of the title character of "Rosso Malpelo" ("Red-headed Malpelo," 1893; later tr. as "Rosso Malpelo," 1928, 1958) in *Vita dei campi* and of Mazzaro in "La roba" ("Property," 1925) in *Novelle rusticane*.

The novels, both set in Sicily, deal, in V.'s own words, with the "mechanism of human passions" at two different levels. In *I Malavoglia* (1881; *The House by the Medlar Tree*, 1890; new tr., 1964) the author portrays the origin and development of the first aspirations for economic well-being in the humblest classes, while in *Mastro-Don Gesualdo* (1889; *Mastro-Don Gesualdo*, 1893; later tr., 1923 [by D. H. Lawrence], 1979) he shows how, these aspirations having been fulfilled, they are replaced by ambitions of translating wealth into power, achieving respectability, and climbing the social ladder.

Although the two collections and the two novels represent the culmination of V.'s art, it is in *I Malavoglia* that the most sustained and felicitous thematic, structural, and expressive integration are found. Never melodramatic, the progression of events about Padron 'Ntoni, a fisherman whose yearning to better his family's fortunes by a single attempt at a minor business venture sets in motion a series of events that are most deleterious to himself and those he loves, has the full dimensions of tragedy. The unending calamities that test Padron 'Ntoni's physical and ethical fiber make him appear truly worthy of pity in the tragic sense. But despite these tests, he is not a pathetic character, for like the heroes of Greek tragedies, he transcends mere pity. The protagonist and the other fifty-odd characters are never portrayed from the outside, but emerge gradually either through their own words and deeds or through those of the others. True to the canons of impersonality, V. refrains throughout from commenting, interpreting, or moralizing. Remarkably he succeeds in "eclipsing" (the term is his own) himself as a narrator by the expansion of direct dialogue, by the frequent use of free indirect speech, and by the masterful transference of the syntactical, grammatical, and lexical patterns of the villagers' Sicilian dialect into the Italian of the text.

These features and many others unprecedented in Italian fiction explain why only after his death did V. loom as the equal of Manzoni and, more importantly, as the novelist whose commitment "to be true to life" on both the thematic and expressive levels became a legacy not just to writers but to many artists who felt the need to put an end to the artificiality that pervaded most Italian art forms during the Fascist era. He is acknowledged, for example, as the inspirational force behind NEOREALISM in Italian film, and Luchino Visconti, one of its eminent practitioners, made a free adaptation of *I Malavoglia* for his *La terra trema* (1948), an early landmark in postwar Italian cinematic art.

FURTHER WORKS: *Sulle lagune* (1863); *Una peccatrice* (1866); *Eva* (1873); *Tigre reale* (1873); *Primavera, e altri racconti* (1876); *Il marito de Elena* (1882); *Per le vie* (1883); *Drammi intimi* (1884); *Vagabondaggio* (1887); *I ricordi del Capitano D'Arce* (1891); *Don Candeloro e Compagni* (1894); *Dal tuo al mio* (1906); *Rose caduche* (1928); *Lettere al suo traduttore* (1954); *Lettere d'amore* (1971); *Lettere a Luigi Capuana* (1975). **FURTHER WORKS IN**

ENGLISH: *Cavalleria Rusticana, and Other Tales of Sicilian Peasant Life* (1893); *Under the Shadow of Etna: Sicilian Stories* (1896); *The She-Wolf, and Other Stories* (1958)

BIBLIOGRAPHY: Bergin, T. G., *G. V.* (1931); Ragusa, O., *V.'s Milanese Stories* (1964); Pacifici, S., *The Modern Italian Novel from Manzoni to Svevo* (1967): 98–128; Alexander, A., *G. V.* (1972); Woolf, D., *The Art of V.: A Study in Objectivity* (1977); Cecchetti, G., "V. and Verismo: The Search for Style and Language", in J. A. Molinaro, ed., *Petrarch to Pirandello: Studies in Italian Literature in Honour of Beatrice Corrigan* (1973): 169–85; Cecchetti, G., *G. V.* (1978); Rutter, J. Gatt, "*G. V.: Mastro-Don Gesualdo*," in D. A. Williams, ed., *The Monster in the Mirror: Studies in Nineteenth-Century Realism* (1978): 204–33; Ginsburg, M. P., "*I Malavoglia* and V.'s Progress," *MLN*, 95 (1980): 82–103; Lucente, G. L., *The Narrative of Realism and Myth: V., Lawrence, Faulkner, Pavese* (1981): 54–107

—EMMANUEL HATZANTONIS

VERHAEREN, Émile

Belgian poet, dramatist, and essayist (writing in French), b. 21 May 1855, Saint-Amand; d. 27 Nov. 1916, Rouen, France

V. grew up in the old Flemish town of Saint-Amand. At home, he spoke only French, the language of instruction at the University of Louvian, where V. completed his law studies and discovered poetry. In 1881 V. joined a law firm in Brussels, but he soon became absorbed by the activities of the Belgian literary renascence of that time. In the late 1880s he suffered from severe depression and underwent a mental crisis, resolved around 1891, the year of the author's marriage. While in Brussels, V. turned to socialism and shortly thereafter abandoned law to devote himself to social activism and literature. The outbreak of World War I put to the test V.'s humanitarian ideals. He traveled to England, then France, rallying support for Belgium. He died in a railway accident while en route to Paris after a lecture.

V.'s abundant poetic production derived its continuity from the author's vigorous evocation of people seen in their natural settings. The early *Les Flamandes* (1883; the Flemish women) and *Les moines* (1886; the monks) paint broad, heavily colored frescoes of women, rustics, monks, and pilgrims in procession, blending direct perception with an abstract sensuality reminiscent of the 16th-c. Flemish kermess painters. The subsequent *Les soirs* (1887; evenings), *Les débâcles* (1888; the downfalls), and *Les flambeaux noirs* (1891; the black torches) tilt toward a SYMBOLIST inwardness and toward more flexible forms. Written during the years of crisis, they channel images through a turbulent sensibility and rely on a rhetoric of hyperbole, urgent appeals, repetitions, and interrogations, all of which suggest the poet's inner turmoil.

The transitional *Les apparus dans mes chemins* (1891; those who appeared on my paths) projects personal distress beyond the self and launched a period of preoccupation with social issues. Applying descriptive techniques to the conditions of modern life, V. created visual poetry that evidences social commitment, first in *Les campagnes hallucinées* (1893; the hallucinated countryside), where quasi-allegorical, spectral figures are used to suggest the devastation of the countryside, and, two years later, in *Les villes tentaculaires* (1895; the tentacular cities), a collection of boldly accentuated poems executed in free verse. Against the background of fiery furnaces, laboratories, and locomotives, V. presents the distress of the industrial city, with its men and women caught by gigantic forces, uprooted.

Les aubes (1998; *The Dawn*, 1989), one of V.'s more successful plays, pits the city and the countryside one against the other and in the final scene, a foreshadowing of the later, joyous register, offers a message of reconciliation imbued with the author's pacifist feelings. A note of serenity is sounded in *Les visages de la vie* (1899; the faces of life), an exceptionally harmonious work where the poet maintains an intuitive contact with nature and by rediscovering energy as a beneficent force prepares the way for a trilogy of affirmation: *Les forces tumultueuses* (1902; the tumultuous forces), *La multiple splendeur* (1906; the manifold splendor), and *Les rythmes souverains* 1910; the supreme rhythms). These jubilant collections, exploding with Dionysiac rhythms, represent the terminus of V.'s poetic reflections. Viewing civilization from the vantage point of wonder, V. undertakes to extract from history and legends symbols of man's achievements and a nearly pantheistic ethic of enthusiasm.

Parallel to these projects, V. pursued a more modest vein, composing love lyrics dedicated to his wife and descriptive poems celebrating the people of Flanders. The love poems, brought together in *Les heures claires* (1896; *The Sunlit Hours*, 1916), *Les heures d'après-midi* (1905; *Afternoon*, 1917), and *Les heures du soir* (1911; *The Evening Hours*, 1918), temper exuberance with serenity and convey moments of affectionate reverie with a subtlety rarely encountered elsewhere. Among the Flanders poems, *Les villages illusoires* (1895; the illusory villages) stands out for its interesting portraits of craftsmen, as does *Les blés mouvants* (1912; wheat in motion), an experimental volume of pastoral poems that capture the charm of the Flemish countryside. The five-part cycle called *Toute la Flandre* (all of Flanders)—*Les tenderness premières* (1904; first loves), *La guirlande des dunes* (1907; the garland of the dunes), *Les héros* (1908; the heroes), *Les villes à pignons* (1910; the towns with gables), and *Les plaines* (1911; the plains)—is an imposing sweep of reminiscences, images of nature and heroes, and epico-lyric evocation of Flanders.

A widely acclaimed poet, V. was also known for his plays, stories, and essays on art and literature. Even though in recent years his fame has dimmed considerably, his poetry retains a good measure of appeal because of its sympathy for the victims of mechanization, its sense of the brotherhood of men, its descriptive power, its unorthodox images, and its vitality.

FURTHER WORKS: *Les contes de minuit* (1884); *Joseph Heymans* (1885); *Au bord de la route* (1890); *Almanach* (1895); *E. V. 1883–1896: Pour les amis du poète* (1896); *Petites légendes* (1899); *Le cloître* (1900; *The Cloister*, 1915); *Images japonaises* (1900); *Les petits vieux* (1901); *Philippe II* (1901; *Philip II*, 1916); *Rembrandt* (1904); *James Ensor* (1908); *Les visages de la vie; Les douze mois* (1908); *Pierre-Paul Rubens* (1910); *Hélène de Sparte* (1912; *Helen of Sparta*, 1916); *Œuvres* (9 vols., 1912–33); *La Belgique sanglante* (1915; *Belgium's Agony*, 1915); *Le crime allemand* (1915); *Les ailes rouges de la guerre* (1916); *Parmi les cendres: La Belgique dévastée* (1916); *Poèmes légendaires de Flandre et de Brabant* (1916); *Villes meurtries de Belgique, Anvers, Malines et Lierre* (1916); *Les flammes hautes* (1917); *Paysages disparus* (1917); *Kato* (1918); *A ceux qui vient* (1920); *Cinq récits* (1920; *Five Tales*, 1920); *Le travailleur étrange, et autres récits* (1921); *Le Caillou-qui-bique* (1923); *À la vie qui s'éloigne* (1924); *Pages belges*

(1926); *Impressions* (3 vols., 1926–28); *Chants dialogués* (1927); *Sensations* (1927); *Paul Verlaine* (1928); *Belle chair* (1931); *À Marthe Verhaeren* (1937). **FURTHER WORKS IN ENGLISH:** *Poems of E. V.* (1899); *The Love Poems of E. V.* (1916); *The Plays of E. V.* (1916)

BIBLIOGRAPHY: Zweig, S., *É. V.* (1914); Lowell, A., *Six French Poets* (1921): 347; Jones, P. M., *É. V.: A Study in the Development of His Art and Ideas* (1926); Corell, A. F., "The Contribution of V. to Modern French Lyric Poetry," *"The University of Buffalo Studies*, 5, 2 (1927): 43–73; Estève, E., *Un grand poé de la view modern: É. V.* (1928); Hellens, F., *É. V.* (1952); Jones, P. M., *V.* (1957)

—VIKTORIA SKRUPSKELIS

VERÍSSIMO, Érico

Brazilian novelist, b. 17 Dec. 1905, Cruz Alta; d. 28 Nov. 1975, Porto Alegre

Born in the state of Rio Grande do Sul, V. spent his adolescent years working in a pharmacy in his home town. Moving to Porto Alegre in 1930, he came into contact with the local literati, who, impressed by the stories he had been writing, helped him publish his first work, the collection of stories and sketches *Fantoches* (1932; puppets). Its favorable reception encouraged V. to publish his first longer prose work, *Clarissa* (1933; Clarissa), a straightforward novelette about a country girl. The ambitious novel *Caminhos cruzados* (1935; *Crossroads*, 1943) won the prestigious Graça Aranha Prize. From that time on, V. proved to be one of Brazil's most prolific and innovative novelists. His work is well known outside his country through translations, and he traveled extensively throughout the Western world.

V. is to Brazil's far south what Jorge Amado is to the Northeast—the writer who has succeeded most in capturing the essential spirit of an entire region. Steeped in the *gaúcho* (Brazilian cowboy) traditions, his fiction has always been best understood and appreciated when read in the light of the social, political, and geographic forces that spawned it. Yet in addition to its strongly regionalistic moorings, V.'s work has always exhibited a satisfying universality, an unflagging idealism, and a steady humanitarianism.

Although some of V.'s works, such as *Caminhos cruzados*, with its interlocking planes of action and multiple perspectives, and *Noite* (1954; *Night*, 1956), with its ambience of French EXISTENTIALISM, reflect his awareness of the European trends of his time, V.'s language, always faithfully Brazilian, remains clear and easy to read. *Caminhos cruzados* portrays the interconnected destinies of characters from different backgrounds during a five-day period. Although structurally similar to Aldous HUXLEY's *Point Counter Point* and Virginia WOOLF's *Mrs. Dalloway*, V.'s thematic concern is the social fabric of his nation. *Noite* is a symbolic and occasionally oneiric story of a man, reminiscent of CAMUS's "stranger," amnesiac and guilt-ridden, wandering through a dark city. The plight of the protagonist can be interpreted as the individual's struggle against the dehumanizing aspects of modern society.

Structurally similar to *Caminhos cruzados, O resto e silencio* (1943; *The Rest Is Silence*, 1946) portrays the reactions of various people to the suicide of a shop clerk. This novel represents an advance in V.'s penetration of the different ways an event affects people's lives.

V.'s masterpiece, the epic trilogy *O tempo e o vento* (time and the wind)—consisting of *O continente* (1949; *Time and the Wind*, 1951), *O retrato* (1951; the portrait), and *O arquipélago* (3 vols., 1961–62; the archipelago)—is nothing less than a mythical evocation of the entire Rio Grande do Sul region, from its settlement by Europeans in the mid-18th c. to contemporary times. This vast historical work, widely considered one of the monuments of modern Brazilian literature, embodies all of V.'s strengths as a novelist. Especially notable is his talent for creating vivid, intensely human characters who, through their thoughts and their conversations with one another, advance the basic themes of the work.

V. is often described as a "painter with words," and his finest novels are decidedly panoramic in nature. He is at his creative best when, as in *O tempo e o vento*, he has the scope to breathe life into a variety of characters and then to immerse them in issues of sweeping social and political significance.

V.'s popularity in Brazil is second only to that of Jorge AMADO, and his position as a major 20th-c. Brazilian novelist is secure.

FURTHER WORKS: *Música ao longe* (1935); *As aventuras do avião vermelho* (1936); *Um lugar ao sol* (1936); *As aventuras de Tibicuera, que são também as aventuras do Brasil* (1937); *Rosamaria no castelo encantado* (1937); *Os três porquinhos pobres* (1937); *Olhai os lírios do campo* (1938; *Consider the Lilies of the Field*, 1947); *U urso com música na barriga* (1938); *Aventuras no mundo da higiene* (1939); *A vida da elefante Basílio* (1939); *Outra vez os três porquinhos* (1939); *Viagem à aurora do mundo* (1939); *Saga* (1940); *O gato preto em campo de neve* (1941); *As mãos de meu filho: Contos e artigos* (1942); *A vida de Joana d'Arc* (1944); *Brazilian Literature: An Outline* (1945; written in English); *A volta do gato preto* (1946); *México: História de uma viagem* (1957; *Mexico: The History of a Trip*, 1960); *O ataque* (1959); *O senhor embaixador* (1967; *His Excellency, the Ambassador*, 1967); *O prisioneiro* (1967); *Israel em abril* (1970); *Incidente em Antares* (1972); *Solo de clarineta* (2 vols., 1973–76)

BIBLIOGRAPHY: Barrett, L. L., "É. V.'s Idea of the Novel," *Hispania*, 34 (1951): 30–40; Forster, M., "Structure and Meaning in É. V.'s *Noite*," *Hispania*, 45 (1962): 712–16; Menton, S., "É. V. and John Dos Passos: Two Interpretations of the Historical Novel," *RIB*, 14 (1964): 54–59; Mazzara, R., "Structure and Verisimilitude in the Novels of É. V.," *PMLA*, 80 (1965): 451–58; Ollivier, L. L., "Universality of Yesterday: *O tempo e o vento*," *Chasqui*, 4, 1 (1974): 40–45

—EARL E. FITZ

VERMEYLEN, August

Belgian essayist, novelist, critic, and art historian (writing in Flemish), b. 12 May 1872, Brussels; d. 10 Jan. 1945, Ukkel

Born into a petit-bourgeois family, V. was introduced to intellectual circles by his school friends, especially Jacques Dwelshauvers (1872–1940), who was later to become a militant anarchist (pseud.

J. Mesnil). At the age of seventeen, together with Hubert Langerock (1869–?) and Lodewijk de Raet (1870–1914)—who later played an important role in the Flemish movement as a theorist of economic reform—V. edited a literary magazine, *Jong Vlaanderen*, which carried the mottoes "reaching for beauty" and "young and bold." This experience prepared him for his work on *Van nu en straks* (1893–1901), a periodical that brought about a renewal of Flemish literature. He was the intellectual leader of this avant-garde and provocative magazine, which rejected extreme individualism and art for art's sake in favor of an "art for the community" and visions of life as a synthesis of the spiritual and the physical, the individual and his environment.

V. studied history at Brussels Free University (1890–94) and completed his studies in Berlin and Vienna (1894–96), where he was profoundly influenced by his reading of Nietzsche and the anarchist philosopher Max Stirner (1806–1856); there he also developed an intense love of Goethe. In 1899 he received his doctorate; his dissertation was on the Flemish Renaissance poet Jonker Jan van der Noot (1539/40–c. 1595). In 1901 he was invited to teach art history at the University of Brussels (he later also taught the history of Dutch literature). From 1923 until 1940 he was a professor at Ghent State University (art history, Dutch literature, and world literature). In 1921 he was chosen by the Socialist Party to serve in the Belgian senate.

V. gave a concise history of *Van nu en straks* in his survey *De Vlaamse letteren van Gezelle tot Timmermans* (1923; Flemish literature from Gezelle to Timmermans), which was updated as *De Vlaamse letteren van Gezelle tot heden* (1938; Flemish literature from Gezelle to the present). Partly as a result of his college teaching came the monumental *De geschiedenis der Europese plastiek en schilderkunst in Middeleeuwen en nieuwere tijd* (3 vols., 1921–25; history of European plastic arts and painting in the Middle Ages and in modern times), revised as *Van de catacomben tot Greco* (1946; from the catacombs to El Greco). His art criticism is highly original, synthesizing, and densely packed.

V.'s early essays, such as the influential "Kritiek der Vlaamse beweging" (1896; critique of the Flemish movement) and its corrective sequel, "Vlaamse en Europese beweging" (1900; Flemish and European movement), in which he renounced anarchism, contributed greatly to the emancipation of Flemish culture from provincialism. The fictional essay "Ene jeugd" (1896; a youth), which shows the influence of Emerson, reflects V.'s gradual evolution from anarchistic absolutism to relativistic humanism. His novels—*De wandelende Jood* (1906; the wandering Jew), relating a search for spiritual truth and harmony in symbolic and allegorical form, and the autobiographical *Twee vrienden* (1943; two friends)—are thematically closely related to his essays.

In his writings V. himself fully answered the call he made for "more brains" (a phrase borrowed from the English writer George Meredith [1828–1909]) in Flemish literature.

FURTHER WORKS: *Verzamelde opstellen* (2 vols., 1904–5); *Beschouwingen: Een nieuwe bundel verzamelde opstellen* (1942); *Verzameld werk* (6 vols., 1951–55)

BIBLIOGRAPHY: Smaele, P., de, *A. V.* (1949); Lissens, R. F., *Flämische Literaturgeschichte des 19. und 20. Jahrhunderts* (1970): 92–97

—ANNE MARIE MUSSCHOOT

VERWEY, Albert

Dutch poet, dramatist, and critic, b. 15 May 1865, Amsterdam; d. 8 Mar. 1937, Noordwijk

At the age of seventeen, V. was one of a group of young poets in Amsterdam who founded the important literary review *De nieuwe gids*. Among them was V.'s close friend and mentor Willem Kloos (1859–1938), but V. reacted against Kloos's extreme individualism and tendency to see poetry exclusively as a matter of the poet's own feelings. Eventually, he broke with Kloos; in 1890 he married and moved to Noordwijk. He became an admirer and friend of Stefan GEORGE, with whom he shared the concept that all his work was one whole to which each poem contributed.

In 1894, with Lodewijk van DEYSSEL, he founded the *Tweemandelijksch tijdschrift*, the name of which was changed to *Twintigste eeuw* in 1902. This periodical ceased publication in 1905, when V. founded his own journal, *De beweging*, which he edited until 1919, exercising great influence and authority as a literary figure and critic. He was a professor of Dutch literature at Leiden from 1925 to 1935.

V.'s first publication, *Persephone* (1883; Persephone), was in the tradition of dream poetry influenced by the English romantics. Partly as a result of his study of Spinoza, V. worked out a theory of poetic creation, beginning from the notion of God (or the Idea) as a creative force immanent in all creation. The poet's special role arises out of the fact that he shares in a special way in this creative force, specifically through the imagination, out of which individual poems take their being. But V.'s reaction against Kloos led him to evolve a poetic mode of indirection with respect to his own feelings. In the collections of poems that followed each other at regular intervals throughout his lifetime, we hear the poet's still and isolated voice, a voice at times remote, and with the passage of the years increasingly elliptical. This movement away from a personal—at times, petulant—tone of self-absorption gives the poetry a gathering strength. The poet finds in such metaphors as the trout fisherman or the helmsman a way of expressing the sense of his relationship to the external world, and an approach that is at the same time precise and suggestive of much that is left unsaid.

Essential for V.'s poetic universe is the feeling for nature. The vast sweep of space and time that his poems express is that of the natural world, and it is the measured energy of nature that V.'s poetry attempts to embody. There is a gradually sharpening sense of movement in terms of such natural rhythms as the passage of the seasons, and the poetic voice is aware of itself as a mote in the cosmic vastness, ceaselessly interrogating an inscrutable deity—perhaps not identical with the Christian God. As the poet aged, death became a more crucial concern, but the later poems show no loss of confidence, for hand in hand with the approach of death there comes a gathering sense of immortality. Death is a solution to the problem of finding what is eternal within time, of getting out of time to where God, whatever the term may imply, is located.

V. also tried his hand at verse drama in such works as *Johan van Oldenbarneveldt* (1895; Johan van Oldenbarnevelt) and *Jacoba van Beieren* (1902; Jacoba van Beieren). He has a greater importance as a critic than as a dramatist, however, and his many studies of major Dutch poets, which occupied him throughout his career, are important and influential. He also translated Shelley, and Dante's *Divine Comedy* (1923).

V.'s commanding importance as a presence in Dutch literature in his time has given rise to an intense discussion of his extensive poetry and the value of his poetic accomplishment. His firm—at times rigid—sense of control and his command of a variety of verse forms make his work technically refined and effective. At its best his poetry expresses a sense of wonderment at the complexity of the universe the poet finds himself in, yet V. never lost his conviction about the oneness of the force that animates that universe.

FURTHER WORKS: *Persephone, en andere gedichten* (1885); *Van de liefde die vriendschap heet* (1885); *Van het leven* (1888); *Verzamelde gedichten* (1889); *Een inleiding tot Vondel* (1892); *Aarde* (1896); *De nieuwe tuin* (1898); *Het brandende braambosch* (1899); *Dagen en daden* (1901); *Stillen toernooien* (1901); *De kristaltwijg* (1903); *Luide toernooien* (1903); *Het leven van Potgieter* (1903); *Uit de lage landen bij de zee* (1904); *Inleiding tot de nieuwe Nederlandsche dichtkunst* (1905); *De oude strijd* (1905); *Droom et tucht* (1908); *Het blank heelal* (1908); *Het testament van Potgieter* (1908); *Verzamelde gedichten* (3 vols., 1911–12); *Het eigen rijk* (1912); *Het levensfeest* (1912); *Het zichtbaar geheim* (1915); *Het zwaardjaar* (1916); *Hendrik Laurensz. Spieghel* (1919); *Goden en grenzen* (1920); *Proza* (10 vols., 1921–23); *De weg van de licht* (1922); *De maker* (1924); *Random mijn werk* (1925); *Het lachende raadsel* (1925; *Songs of Ultimate Understanding*, 1927); *De legende van de ruimte* (1926); *De getilde last* (1927); *Vondels vers* (1927); *De figuren van de sarkofaag* (1930); *Ritme en metrum* (1931); *De ring van leed en geluck* (1932); *Mijn verhouding tot Stefan George* (1934); *In de koorts van het kortstondige* (1936); *De dichter in het derde rijk* (1936); *Oorspronkelijk dichtwerk* (2 vols., 1938); *Frederik van Eeden* (1939)

BIBLIOGRAPHY: Baxter, B. M., *A. V.'s Translations from Shelley's Poetical Works* (1963); "Across a Frontier," *TLS* (21 April 1966): 346; Baxter, B. M., "A. V. and Shelley: Imitation, Influence or Affinity?" in F. Jost, ed., *Proceedings of the IVth Congress of the International Comparative Literature Association* (1966), vol. II: 868–74; Weevers, T., "A. V. and Stefan George: Their Conflicting Affinities," *GL&L*, 22 (1969): 79–89; Weevers, T., "A. V.'s Portrayal of the Growth of the Poetic Imagination," in W. D. Robson-Scott, ed., *Essays in German and Dutch Literature* (1973): 89–115; Meijer, R. P., *Literature of the Low Countries*, new ed. (1978): 266–71; Wolf, M., "On the Poetry of A. V." *WLT, 54* (1980): 245–46

—FRED J. NICHOLS

VESAAS, Tarjei

Norwegian novelist, poet, and dramatist, b. 20 Aug. 1897, Vinje; d. 15 Mar. 1970, Vinje

Except for periods of travel in Scandinavia and on the European continent, V. spent his whole life in the farm community of Vinje in Telemark. He wrote about rural Norwegians, interpreting their actions by means of images from the Telemark landscape. But V. is far more than a regional writer. His travels and readings brought him into contact with modern European thought, and his works,

written in a highly polished, lyrical style, deal with general human problems. Although V. wrote in *nynorsk* ("new Norwegian," formerly known as *landsmål*, "rural language") rather than in the dominant *bokmål* ("book language"), he was well-known, admired, and beloved by all his countrymen. Translations into Swedish and Danish won him a wide Scandinavian audience. His position in Norwegian letters has been compared to that of Pär LAGERKVIST in Sweden and Martin A. HANSEN.

One of V.'s main themes is the struggle for self-knowledge combined with the necessity of finding one's place in life. The most successful solution to these problems appears in *Det store spelet* (1934; *The Great Cycle*, 1967). The protagonist of this novel is Per Bufast, the oldest son of a farm family whose duty it is to take over the farm when his father dies. From his earliest childhood, Per is told that this is his destiny, but he rebels against it, trying to excel at school so that he can escape. He dreams of the excitement and pleasures in store for him in the wide world, but gradually he finds himself being pulled into the rural cycle of work and life and death. Finally he realizes the truth of his father's words that he will live on the farm all of his days and that the farm will give him all he needs.

In contrast to Per, Mattis, the hero of the novel *Fuglane* (1957; *The Birds*, 1969), is an outsider who is doomed to loneliness. A poor Simple Simon with wonderful dreams, he is unfit for any kind of work, but he struggles vainly to understand and to solve his problems. Mattis forgives easily and is grateful for small acts of kindness, but others simply do not know what to do with him. When the sister he lives with falls in love with a lumberman he has brought home, Mattis drowns himself, "feeling he has brought happiness like the birds and, like them, must die." *Fuglane* may be interpreted as a plea for understanding and acceptance of eternal children like Mattis.

The problem of communication is central to V.'s works. Many of his characters seem to be driven by demonic forces. Sometimes they work themselves to death; sometimes they struggle under the weight of fear and guilt. Often the solution to their problems is simply the process of growing up, of learning. The basis of maturing is mutual help; a word, a look, a gesture, may be enough to save a person from disaster. Intuition is perhaps more important for V. than direct communication. Like children, his characters sense reality even when they cannot adequately express what they know. The silences between people can weigh more than their conversations.

V.'s works also reflect the tragedy of World War II and the years leading up to it. The EXPRESSIONIST play *Ultimatum* (1934; ultimatum), about five young people waiting to see whether their country will go to war, carries a clearly pacifist message. His novels of the 1930s hint at the strange and threatening world beyond the small farm communities and at impending destruction.

In *Kimen* (1940; *The Seed*, 1965) V. explores the nature of violence, the desire for revenge that it evokes, and finally the resulting self-examination and search for atonement. Violence, which is insane, self-perpetuating, and against the natural order, must be countered by calm, reflection, and an attempt to bring the communal mind back to itself.

The subject of *Huset i mørkret* (1945; *The House in the Dark*, 1976) is Norway under Nazi occupation. V. is concerned here with the decision to resist or not, and with the effects of this decision on human relationships. Loneliness and the need for friendship play no small part in one's decision to collaborate or to rebel.

When he was almost fifty, V. began to publish volumes of poetry. After a rather traditional beginning, he turned to a much more modernist style, producing several excellent poems with the Norwegian landscape as a background and using simple, terse language to express a variety of moods, from simple contentment to great fear.

Although V.'s early works were often romantic, religious, and sentimental, he gradually began to emphasize human development, acceptance of responsibility, understanding, and cooperation. After World War II his style became terser and more abstract. His late work *Båten om kvelden* (1968; *The Boat in the Evening*, 1971) contains much autobiographical material and reviews those themes that had fascinated him throughout his life. It stresses the need for self-fulfillment and right action, and suggests that when one has lived properly, one is not afraid of death.

FURTHER WORKS: *Menneskebonn* (1923); *Sendemann Huskuld* (1924); *Guds bustader* (1925); *Grindegard: Morgonen* (1925); *Grindekveld; eller, Den gode engelen* (1926); *Dei svarte hestane* (1928); *Klokka i haugen* (1929); *Fars reise* (1930); *Sigrid Stallbrokk* (1931); *Dei ukjende mennene* (1932); *Sandeltreet* (1933); *Kvinnor ropar heim* (1935); *Leiret og hjulet* (1936); *Hjarta høyrer sine heimlandstonar* (1938); *Kjeldene* (1946); *Bleikeplassen* (1946); *Morgonvinden* (1947); *Leiken og lynet* (1947); *Tårnet* (1948); *Lykka for ferdesmenn* (1949); *Signalet* (1950); *Vindane* (1952); *Løynde eldars land* (1953; *Land of Hidden Fires*, 1973); *Vårnatt* (1954; *Spring Night*, 1965); *Ver ny. vår draum* (1956); *Ein vakker dag* (1959); *Brannen* (1961); *Is-slottet* (1963; *The Ice Palace*, 1966); *Bruene* (1966; *The Bridges*, 1970); *Liv ved straumen* (1970); *Huset og fuglen: Tekster og bilete 1919–1969* (1971); *Dikt i samling* (1977); *Noveller i samling* (1977)

BIBLIOGRAPHY: Skrede, R., "T. V." *Norseman*, 11 (1953): 206–9; McFarlane, J. W., *Ibsen and the Temper of Norwegian Literature* (1960): 182–87; Beyer, E., "T. V.," *Scan*, 3, 2 (1964): 97–109; Dale, J. A., "T. V.," *ASR*, 54 (1966): 369–74; Naess, H. S., Introduction to *The Great Cycle* (1967): vii–xxi; Stendahl, B. K., "T. V., a Friend," *BA*, 42 (1968): 537–39; Chapman, K. G., *T. V.* (1969); Baumgartner, W., *T. V.: Eine ästhetische Biographie* (1976)

—WALTER D. MORRIS

VESTDIJK, Simon

Dutch novelist, short-story writer, essayist, and poet, b. 17 Oct. 1898, Harlingen; d. 23 Mar. 1971, Doorn

V.'s small-town origin provided the background for some of his best novels, in which a combination of immediate experience and distant reflection determine the narrative perspective. Before he embarked on his literary career in his mid-thirties V. had studied and practiced medicine, dabbled in philosophy, psychology, and astrology, and studied music. His encyclopedic knowledge and interests are reflected in his huge oeuvre of some fifty novels, a number of collections of short stories, and many volumes of poetry and of essays and critical prose. He made significant contributions

to the literature on such subjects as the philosophy of civilization, music, and theology.

V. was the most important member of the group around the journal *Forum* (1932–35), which exerted a lasting influence on the development of Dutch letters. He did not, however, share the polemical aggressiveness of the leading editors, Edgar du PERRON and Menno ter BRAAK, who vigorously championed an approach to literature that puts ethical considerations above aesthetic values.

Yet V. left no doubt where he stood with regard to the most important issue of the time, fascism, and its attendant evils: during the German occupation of the Netherlands he sheltered two Jews from the Nazis and was himself imprisoned as a hostage for almost a year. Otherwise his life was uneventful. He lived in strict seclusion, periodically suffering from profound depressions; he devoted himself exclusively to his writing, turning out works faster, as one critic observed, than God can read.

By the early 1930s, V. had made some well-received contributions to literary journals. In 1933, influenced by Marcel PROUST, he wrote a novel recounting his entire childhood and youth. This work, entitled *Kind tussen vier vrouwen* (child between four women), was, to his great disappointment, rejected by the publisher to whom he submitted it because of its excessive length. V. subsequently used it as the basis for a series of novels dealing with different episodes from his childhood and school years, centering on the figure of his fictitious alter ego, Anton Wachter. The first of these novels to appear, *Terug tot Ina Damman* (1934; return to Ina Damman), which with penetrating psychological insight describes the tribulations of unrequited adolescent love, immediately established V. as a major writer.

Ina Damman is the prototype of the unattainable beloved, an image that also plays an important role in a number of later works not of the Anton Wachter series. Another recurring motif involves the combination of the father figure with the concepts of force and of destructive fire. This motif occurs in *Meneer Visser's hellevaart* (Mr. Visser's descent into hell), which was written prior to *Terug tot Ina Damman* but not published until 1936 because it was feared that the disrespectful depiction of small-town life and the grotesque despotic figures it encourages would alienate the reading public—which it did. Several later novels contain the father-force-fire motif cluster, among them *De schandalen* (1953; the scandals), in which it is combined with the motifs of the unattainable beloved. Both motifs represent situations in the protagonists' lives that lead them to seek shelter for their wounded egos in existential isolation.

From this situation springs the third main motif in V.'s narrative work: that of compassion as a sentiment that lures man into becoming involved in others' lives, thereby compelling him to give up his own protective isolation. This idea is also exemplified in *De schandalen* and becomes, from *Het glinsterend pantser* (1956; the shining armor) onward, a leading theme in V.'s writing.

V.'s voluminous poetry deals with the same themes as his prose and, like the lyric work of other writers of the *Forum* circle, tends toward simplicity of language. Its relentlessly intellectual nature prevented it from catching on with the reading public. Even the official recognition that came V.'s way in the form of numerous awards was granted primarily on the basis of his narrative and expository prose. In these areas he is by common consensus a towering figure in the Netherlandic world of letters. A measure of his international stature is provided by the numerous translations of his work into all the major languages of the world and into several minor ones as well.

FURTHER WORKS: *Verzen* (1932); *De oubliette* (1933); *Berijmd palet* (1933); *Vrouwendienst* (1934); *Else Böhler, Duitsch dienstmeisje* (1935); *De dood betrapt* (1935); *De bruine vriend* (1935); *Heden ik, morgen gij* (1936, with Hendrik Marsman); *Kind van stad en land* (1936); *Het vijfde zegel* (1937); *Kunstenaar en oorlogspsychologie* (1937); *Nederlandsche litteratuur van nu* (1937, with Menno ter Braak and Anton van Duinkerken); *Rilke als barokkunstenaar* (1938); *Narcissus op vrijersvoeten* (1938); *De nadagen van Pilatus* (1938); *Fabels met kleurkrijt* (1938); *De verdwenen horlogemaker* (1939); *Sint Sebastiaan: De geschiedenis van een talent* (1939); *Lier en lancet* (1939); *Strijd en vlucht op papier* (1939); *Albert Verwey en de idee* (1940); *De zwarte ruiter* (1940); *Rumeiland* (1940; *Rum Island*, 1963); *Klimmende legenden* (1940); *Water in zicht* (1940); *De vliegende Hollander* (1941); *Simplicia* (1941); *Aktaion onder de sterren* (1941); *Muiterij tegen het etmaal I* (1942); *Het geroofde lam* (1942); *Ascensus ad inferos* (1942, with Friedrich Robert August Henkels); *De terugkomst* (1943); *De houtdiefstal* (1944, with Friedrich Robert August Henkels); *De doode zwanen* (1944); *Allegretto innocente* (1944); *De uiterste seconde* (1944); *Het schuldprobleem bij Dostojewski* (1945); *Brieven over litteratuur* (1945, with Hendrik Marsman); *Ierse nachten* (1946); *De Poolsche ruiter* (1946); *Mnemosyne in de bergen* (1946); *Stomme getuigen* (1947); *De overnachting* (1947, with Jeanne Gabrielle van Schaik-Willing); *De vuuraanbidders* (1947); *Puriteinen en piraten* (1947); *Het eeuwige telaat* (1947); *Muiterij tegen het etmaal II* (1947); *De toekomst der religie* (1947); *Thanatos aan banden* (1948); *Pastorale 1943* (1948); *De redding van Fré Bolderhey* (1948); *Surrogaten voor Murk Tuinstra: De geschiedenis van een vriendschap* (1948); *De andere school: De geschiedenis van een verraad* (1949); *Bevrijdingsfeest* (1949); *De kellner en de levenden* (1949); *Avontuur met Titia* (1949, with Henriett e Catharina Maria van Eyk); *Gestelsche liederen* (1949); *De fantasia en andere verhalen* (1949); *Astrologie en wetenschap* (1949); *De koperen tuin* (1950; *The Garden Where the Brass Band Played*, 1965); *Swordplay-Wordplay* (1950, with Adriaan Roland Holst); *De glanzende kiemcel* (1950); *Ivoren wachters* (1951); *De vijf roeiers* (1951); *De dokter en het lichte meisje* (1951); *Het "programma" in de muziek* (1951, with Herman Passchier); *De verminkte Apollo* (1952); *Op afbetaling* (1952); *Essays in duodecimo* (1952); *Rembrandt en de engelen* (1956); *Het eerste en het laaste* (1956); *Zuiverende kroniek* (1956); *Merlijn* (1957); *Marionettenspel met de dood* (1957, with Sem Dresden); *Keurtroepen van Euterpe* (1957); *De beker van de min: De geschiedenis van een eerste jaar* (1957); *Open book* (1957); *De vrije vogel en zijn kooien: De geschiedenis van een domicilie* (1958); *De arme Heinrich* (1958); *Het kastje van oma* (1958); *De rimpels van Esther Ornstein: De geschiedenis van een verzuim* (1959); *De ziener* (1959); *De laatste kans: De geschiedenis van een liefde* (1960); *Een moderne Antonius* (1960); *De dubbele weegschaal* (1960); *Gustav Mahler* (1960); *Muziek in blik* (1960); *De filosoof en de sluipmoordenaar* (1961); *Een alpenroman* (1961); *Gestalten tegenover mij* (1961); *De symfonieën van Jean Sibelius* (1962); *De held van Temesa* (1962); *Hoe schrijft men over muziek?* (1963); *Bericht uit het hiernamaals* (1964); *Het genadeschot* (1964); *De zieke mens in de romanliteratuur* (1964); *De leugen is onze moeder* (1965); *Juffrouw Lot* (1965); *Zo de ouden zongen . . .* (1965); *De onmogelijke moord* (1966); *Het spook en de schaduw* (1966); *De symfonieën van Anton Bruckner* (1966); *Een huisbewaarder* (1967); *De leeuw en zijn huid* (1967); *Gallische facetten* (1968); *De hôtelier doet niet meer mee* (1968);

Het wezen van de angst (1968); *Brieven uit de oorlogsjaren aan Theun de Vries* (1968); *Het schandaal der blauwbaarden* (1968); *Het verboden bacchanaal* (1969); *Het proces van meester Eckhart* (1970); *Verzamelde gedichten* (3 vols., 1971–72)

BIBLIOGRAPHY: Meijer, R. P., *Literature of the Low Countries*, new ed. (1978): 342–49

—EGBERT KRISPYN

VIAN, Boris

French novelist and dramatist, b. 10 Mar. 1920, Ville-d'Avray; d. 23 June 1959, Paris

Born into a well-to-do bourgeois family, V. had an overprotected childhood, due in large measure to the early diagnosis of an incurable heart condition, from which he was to die at the age of thirty-nine. He excelled in mathematics, studied engineering, and found employment at the French Association for Standardization, a bureaucracy he satirizes in the novel *Vercoquin et le plancton* (1946; Vercoquin and the plankton). At one point he acquired a patent for an elastic wheel. A talented musician, V. wrote more than four hundred songs and worked as a jazz trumpeter, cabaret singer, music reviewer, and record executive.

Under the name Vernon Sullivan, an invented American writer whose work V. claimed to have translated, he wrote *J'irai cracher sur vos tombes* (1946; *I Shall Spit on Your Graves*, 1948) in ten days to fulfill a wager that he could write a best-selling novel. It succeeded beyond anyone's expectations, selling one hundred thousand copies before being banned as "objectionable foreign literature." He wrote three more "Vernon Sullivan" novels in the same vein of American-inspired sex and violence.

Under his own name V. wrote five rather more serious novels. *Vercoquin et le plancton*, remarkable for having been written in Paris in 1943 but reflecting the Occupation in no way, is a comic feast of "surprise parties," practical jokes, and erotic activity. *L'écume des jours* (1947; *Mood Indigo*, 1969), probably V.'s best-known work, is a tragic love story set in a world in which figures of speech assume a literal reality and familiar objects fight back in surrealistic ways. *L'automne à Pékin* (1947; autumn in Peking) concerns neither autumn nor China, but the construction of a pointless railway in an imaginary Exopotamia. In *L'herbe rouge* (1950; red grass) one character is haunted by a double, while another makes repeated excursions in a time machine to his own past. *L'arrache-cœur* (1953; *Heartsnatcher*, 1968) is set in an enormously cruel village whose inhabitants pay a scapegoat to assume their shame.

Each of V.'s novels becomes more interesting when read in light of the others—which is a way of saying that none of them is entirely successful on its own. He constructs a universe that appears to have nothing to do with our own until we realize that in his fictive world we find familiar philosophical problems of love, death's inevitability, the responsibility of an individual toward himself contrasted with what, if anything, he owes the rest of society. V.'s pacifism, beautifully expressed in his song "Le déserteur" (1955; pub. 1966; the deserter), could be seen as a principled and prophetic opposition to war's insanity or as the irresponsible self-indulgence of a pampered dandy who would prefer to live in a world of his own making.

V.'s plays *Le goûter des généraux* (1962; *The Generals' Tea Party*, 1967) and *L'équarissage pour tous* (1950; *The Knacker's ABC*, 1968) are witty and effective satires on the absurdities of a culture that makes war possible. *Bâtisseurs d'empire* (1959; *The Empire Builders*, 1967) is a haunting THEATER OF THE ABSURD play in which an apartment dwelling family moves to ever higher ground to escape a mysterious, undefined Noise. They are accompanied in their futile moves by a bloodied, bandaged Schmürz, the scapegoat victim of their own mindless ability to inflict pain.

V. was not a great writer, but he is often interesting, as much for the occasional brilliance of his style as for his position in 20th-c. French literature. He can be seen as an heir to the SURREALIST tradition of André BRETON and the satirical comedy of Alfred JARRY as well as a romantic alternative to the austere philosophies of Jean-Paul SARTRE and the EXISTENTIALISTS.

FURTHER WORKS: *Les morts ont tous la même peau* (1947); *Barnum's digest* (1948); *Et on tuera tous les affreux* (1948); *Elles se rendent pas compte* (1948); *Les fourmis* (1949); *Cantilènes en gelée* (1950); *Le chevalier de neige* (1953); *En avant la Zizique . . .* (1958); *Fiesta* (1958); *Les lurettes fourrées* (1962); *Je voudrais pas crever* (1962); *Le dernier des métiers* (1965); *Textes et chansons* (1966); *Trouble dans les Andains* (1966); *Chroniques de jazz* (1967); *Chansons et poèmes* (1967); *Théâtre inédit* (1970); *Le loup-garou* (1970); *Manuel de Saint-Germain-des-Prés* (1974); *Chroniques du menteur* (1974)

BIBLIOGRAPHY: Esslin, M., *The Theatre of the Absurd* (1961): 176–79; Rybalka, M., *B. V.* (1969); Arnaud, N., *Les vies parallèles de B. V.* (1970); Cismaru, A., *B. V.* (1974); Heiney, D., "B. V., the Marx Brothers, and Jean-Sol Partre," *BA*, 49 (1975): 66–69; Bens, J., *B. V.* (1976); Arnaud, N. and H. Baudin, eds., *B. V. 1–2*, Colloque de Cerisy (1977)

—RANDOLPH RUNYON

VIDAL, Gore

American novelist, essayist, and dramatist, b. 3 Oct. 1925, West Point, N.Y.

V. grew accustomed at an early age to a life among political and social notables. Raised until the age of ten in the Washington, D. C., home of his grandfather, Senator Thomas Gore of Oklahoma, and raised thereafter on the Virginia estate of his stepfather, Hugh D. Auchincloss, he learned quickly to stylize his public self and to protect his ego under a mannered sophistication. After graduation from Phillips Exeter Academy in New Hampshire, he served three years in the U.S. Army, and upon his discharge he worked six months for the publishing firm of E. P. Dutton. Since then he has supported himself entirely by his writing and occasional lecturing. Novels are his abiding commitment, but he wrote over one hundred television scripts in the mid-1950s during the medium's Golden Age, and he has written seven stage plays, at least a

Gore Vidal

dozen film scripts, a number of short stories, and over seventy essays and reviews.

As this array of genres might suggest, V. is not a one-note writer. His first novel, *Williwaw* (1946), is a conventional seafaring story whose tight-lipped pieties owe a considerable debt to Ernest HEMINGWAY. But *The City and the Pillar* (1948; rev. ed., 1965) applied the Hemingway manner to a homosexual theme and resulted in a thoroughgoing *succès de scandale*. *Julian* (1964) strikes still another note. Purporting to be a lost memoir of Julian the Apostate, it is a work of daunting historicity, and it sounded for the first time a scholarly note that characterizes much of V.'s later work. *Creation* (1981) is a companion piece to *Julian*—the memoir of an imaginary grandson of Zoroaster who travels the world in the service of Persian kings and dallies en route with Confucius, Gautama Buddha, Anaxagoras, and a host of kindred figures. Positioned at the other end of time, *Messiah* (1954; rev. ed., 1965) and *Kalki* (1978) are apocalyptic fictions that sound a death knell for the human race.

A dynastic trilogy about American history has the same blend of scholarly detail and insouciant revisionism as V.'s novels of the ancient world but comes more brilliantly alive than they. With Aaron Burr and his imaginary descendants as a connecting motif, *Washington, D.C.* (1967), *Burr* (1973), and *1876* (1976) trace in atemporal order a saga of American politics and suggest in concert that the republic's political life is increasingly effete. *Burr* is the jewel of the sequence. Its titular hero debunks his coevals with charm and wit, and he proffers insights into the early Federalist period that make him seem the greatest of the Founding Fathers, if only because his sense of style is superior to theirs. Complex and urbane, altogether fascinating, *Burr* is generally considered V.'s most impressive achievement.

If the American trilogy is the substantial main course of V.'s oeuvre, *Myra Breckinridge* (1968) and its sequel, *Myron* (1974), are spun-sugar confections that satisfy the literary palate as completely. In tandem, the novels trace the career of the transsexual Myra/Myron as her male and female selves alternately possess the fractured Breckinridge psyche. Ebullient and irrepressible, Myra thinks of herself as a feminist femme fatale; unimaginative and plodding, Myron is her mirror image and bitter antagonist. The story of their deadlocked opposition is archly comic. A certain impatience with the connection between power and sex lurks behind the novels, as advocates of sexual minorities point out, but the charm of the novels lies with their camp inconsequence. They are arguably V.'s finest work.

V.'s greatest talent is for the small scale. Anecdotes, scenes, and sentences are the richly conceived impasto of his prose; layered with wit and clotted with intelligence, they are worked to a substantiality greater than that of his characters and plots. More than just a stylist, V. is also a stylistic farceur. The interplay in his prose between the demotic and the mannered is the play of a connoisseur turned gamesman—the touch of genius that makes V. one of the great stylists of contemporary American prose.

FURTHER WORKS: *In a Yellow Wood* (1947); *The Season of Comfort* (1949); *Dark Green, Bright Red* (1950; rev. ed. 1968); *A Search for the King: A Twelfth-Century Legend* (1950); *Death in the Fifth Position* [Edgar Box, pseud.] (1952); *The Judgment of Paris* (1952; rev. ed., 1965); *Death before Bedtime* [Edgar Box, pseud.] (1953); *Death Likes It Hot* [Edgar Box, pseud.] (1954); *A Thirsty Evil: Seven Short Stories* (1956); *Visit to a Small Planet, and Other Television Plays* (1956); *Visit to a Small Planet: A Comedy Akin to Vaudeville* (1957); *The Best Man: A Play about Politics* (1960); *Rocking the Boat* (1962); *Romulus: A New Comedy, Adapted from a Play by Friedrich Dürrenmatt* (1962); *Three Plays* (1962); *Sex, Death and Money* (1968); *Weekend: A Comedy in Two Acts* (1968); *Reflections upon a Sinking Ship* (1969); *Two Sisters: A Memoir in the Form of a Novel* (1970); *An Evening with Richard Nixon* (1972); *Homage to Daniel Shays: Collected Essays 1952–1972* (1972); *Matters of Fact and of Fiction (Essays 1973–1976)* (1977); *The Second American Revolution, and Other Essays (1976–1982)* (1982); *Duluth* (1983); *Lincoln* (1984); *Empire* (1987); *At Home: Essays 1982–1988* (1988); *Hollywood* (1990); *Live from Golgotha* (1992); *Screening History* (1992); *Palimpsest* (1995); *The Smithsonian Institution* (1998)

BIBLIOGRAPHY: Aldridge, J. W., *After the Lost Generation: A Critical Study of the Writers of the Two Wars* (1951): 170–83; White, R. L., *G. V.* (1968); Dick, B. F., *The Apostate Angel: A Critical Study of G. V.* (1974); Conrad, P., "Hall of Mirrors: The Novels of G. V.," *Sunday Times* (London), 27 March 1977: 35; Ross, M. S., *The Literary Politicians* (1978): 247–300; Stanton, R. J., *Views from a Window: Conversations with G. V.* (1980); Kiernan, R. F., *G. V.* (1982)

—ROBERT F. KIERNAN

VIEIRA, José Luandino

(pseud. of José Vieira Mateus da Graça) Angolan novelist and short-story writer (writing in Portuguese), b. 5 May 1935, Pôvoa do Varzim, Portugal

V. left rural Portugal at the age of two with his settler parents for Angola, where he grew up with black and mestiço (mixed-race) children in Luanda's *musseques* (African shanty-towns that ringed the Europeanized city). Some outsiders are surprised to learn that a white man is independent Angola's greatest writer. But V. is living testimonial to the paradoxes of Portuguese colonialism, which, by means of social and economic neglect, permitted a measure of biracial creolization to occur in Luanda.

Luuanda (1964; *Luuanda: Short Stories of Angola*, 1980), V.'s first major work, was banned a year after its publication by the Portuguese authorities while the author was serving an eleven-year prison term for his nationalist activities. Since the overthrow, in 1974, of the Portuguese dictatorship, the book has gone through twelve editions in Portugal, Angola, and Brazil. A turning point in Angolan writing, *Luuanda* simulates an African storytelling tradition while successfully combining a creolized Portuguese with an equally creolized Kimbundu (one of Angola's principal Bantu languages).

The three long tales in *Luuanda* project the language and life style of the *musseques*. And in "A estória da galinha e do ovo" ("The Tale of the Hen and the Egg"), the best of the three stories, a dispute between two *musseque* women over the ownership of an egg frames the conflict between the colonizer and the colonized in terms that aggrandize the latter and challenge the hegemony of the former. In essence, the downtrodden rise above their petty differences to mobilize against the greater threat of intrusion by the hostile European power structure.

In 1961 V. wrote *A vida verdadeira de Domingos Xavier* (1974; *The Real Life of Domingos Xavier*, 1978), a novel that explicitly treats the subject of organized opposition to the colonial regime in Angola. Although the first Portuguese-language edition of the novel would not appear until thirteen years after it was written, the manuscript was spirited out of Angola to France, where Sarah Maldoror, a Guadaloupan filmmaker, adapted the story to the screen under the title *Sambizanga* (1972), which was the name of a *musseque*. The story takes place during the first months before the outbreak of armed revolt against the Portuguese, and it dramatizes the exploits and tribulations of a working-class black Angolan who joins the struggle only to pay with his life for his convictions.

While interned in Tarrafal, the Portuguese government's infamous concentration camp for political dissenters, V. managed to write several short stories and a novel, all of which add to the prestige of Angolan literature as the most mature imaginative writing of Lusophone Africa. After Angolan independence V. returned to his beloved Luanda, where he became secretary-general of the Angolan Writers Union; and although he has found little time to ply his craft as a writer, his works have profoundly influenced a new generation of Angolan writers.

In the 1990s, along with a number of other intellectuals and writers who were frustrated and somewhat disillusioned by war and political strife, V. temporarily left Angola. A Portuguese government grant allowed him to settle in northern Portugal, where he has been diligently working on a novel. If this eagerly awaited novel materializes, it will be the first work V. has written in the postcolonial period.

FURTHER WORKS: *A cidade e a infância* (1960); *Duas histórias de pequenos burgueses* (1961); *Vidas novas* (n.d.; 2nd ed. 1976); *Velhas estórias* (1974); *No antigamente, na vida* (1974); *Nós, os do Makulusu* (1975); *João Vêncio: Os seus amores* (1979; *The Loves of João Vêncio*, 1991); *Lourentinho, Dona Antónia de Sousa Neto e eu* (1981); *Macandumba* (1982)

BIBLIOGRAPHY: Figueiredo, A., "The Children of the Rape," *NewA*, Nov. 1965: 203–7; Hamilton, R. G., "Black from White and White on Black: Contradictions of Language in the Angolan Novel," *Ideologies and Literature*, Dec. 1977: 25–58; Ngwube, A., on *The Real Life of Domingos Xavier*, *NewA*, Oct. 1978: 108; Bender, T., "Translator's Preface," in *Luuanda: Short Stories of Angola* (1980): v–x; Jacinto, T., "The Art of L. V.," in Burness, D., ed., *Critical Perspectives on Lusophone African Literature* (1981): 79–87; Stern, I., "L. V.'s Short Fiction: Decolonisation in the Third Register," in Parker, C. A., et al., eds., *When the Drumbeat Changes* (1981): 141–52

—RUSSELL G. HAMILTON

VIETNAMESE LITERATURE

Nourished by centuries of patriotic protest against Chinese rule, yet with a poetic tradition patterned after Chinese models, modern Vietnamese literature has flourished, first under some eighty years of French colonial administration, then during the war against the French (1945–54), and more recently during the period of partition and war (1954–75) and subsequent reunification. The importance of sociopolitical changes in the 20th c. cannot be overstated. But the single most important factor in the development of modern Vietnamese literature was the introduction by Catholic missionaries of the roman script, whose use began in the early 20th c., accompanied by a vigorous literacy campaign, and which gradually displaced both Chinese characters and the demotic Vietnamese characters.

After the establishment of French colonial authority in Indochina in 1862, many works in both verse and prose appeared, with the latter predominating. Although poetry, written in both Chinese and Vietnamese according to the constraints of traditional Chinese Tang prosody, had held sway in previous centuries, Western prose genres began to be cultivated, including journalism, literary criticism, the essay, drama for the formal theaters (as opposed to the traditional folk play), and the realistic novel.

The main trends at the turn of the century were romanticism and patriotism. At the same time masterpieces of French and Chinese literature became known through translations using the new alphabet, thanks to the efforts of the lexicographer Paulus Huỳnh Tịnh Của (1834–1907) and of the polyglot scholar Petrus Trương Vĩnh Ký (1837–1898), who themselves wrote delightful short stories.

Chinese and French writing influenced the movement known as the Đông-kinh (Eastern Capital, i.e., Hanoi) School of the Just Cause, founded in 1906 by such patriotic scholar-writers as Phan

Bội Châu (1867–1940) and Phan Châu Trinh (1872–1926). With the decline of classical poetry, the prose writings serialized in the reviews *Đông-dương tạp-chí* and *Nam-phong*, edited respectively by Nguyễn Văn Vĩnh (1882–1936) and Phạm Quỳnh (1892–1945), were avidly read by the urban petite bourgeoisie during the period 1913–30. Romantic and lyrical poetry, was, however, published by such writers as Tản-Đà Nguyễn Khắc Hiếu (1889–1939), Đông-hồ Lâm Tấn Phát (1906–1969), and Á-nam Trần Tuấn Khải (b. 1894).

Young intellectuals of the time admired both the moralistic stories of Nguyễn Bá Học (1857–1921) and the humorous stories with vivid dialogue by Phạm Duy Tốn (1883–1924). *Tố-tâm* (1925; Tố-tâm), a psychological novel by Hoàng Ngọc Phách (1896–1973) about an unfortunate love affair, was hugely successful and spawned many works of romantic individualism. Inspired by a traditional folktale, the novelette *Quả dưa đỏ* (1927; the watermelon) by Nguyễn Trọng Thuật (1883–1940) won an important literary prize. Notable plays of the period were *Chén thuốc độc* (1921; the cup of poison), a comedy by Vũ Đình Long (1901–1960), about a wastrel who is talked out of committing suicide, and three plays by Vi Huyền Đắc (b. 1899): *Uyên-ương* (1927; lovers), a tragedy about true love; *Kim-tiền* (1937; money), a drama about a businessman; and *Ông Ký Cóp* (1938; Mr. Clerk Cop).

Besides the development of journalism, the 1930s saw the birth—and triumph—of the so-called new poetry among both the adherents and the opponents of the Self-Reliance literary group. Members of this group rejected the style patterned after Chinese writing and advocated a clearer and more naturally Vietnamese style. They also favored the emancipation of women and the rights of the individual. One member, Thế Lữ (b. 1907), saw himself as a dreamer and nature lover caught in the web of competitive urban life, with all its cruelty, loneliness, and deprivation. Compared with those of the previous generation, "our deepest feelings are more complex," he asserted. "When we burst with joy, that joy also embraces strange colors and shades." The lyrical poetry of Xuân Diệu (b. 1917), another Self-Reliance writer, expressed his craving for love as well as his appreciation for scenic beauty and sweet music. A third member, the poet Hàn Mặc Tử (1913–1940), wrote powerful poems evincing his obsession with death. The new verse still had familiar themes, such as autumn impressions, homesickness, nostalgia, bereavement, and moon gazing. But it utilized nontraditional tones, rhymes, and rhythms, and it also affirmed the importance of the individual, the presence of the "self."

Amid political turmoil and economic crisis, the review *Phong-hoá*, launched in 1932 and renamed *Ngày nay* in 1935, contributed to the "defense and illustration" of the Vietnamese language, now fully groomed for the new genres—a language that had gained in simplicity, clarity, and elegance through the efforts of social reformers, led by NHẤT-LINH and KHÁI HƯNG. Nhất-Linh wrote editorials, novels, and short stories; Khái Hưng was a novelist and short-story writer. Hoàng Đạo (1907–1948) was the theoretician of the group, Thạch Lam (1909–1943) specialized in short stories and vignettes, and Tú Mỡ (1900–1976) wrote satirical poems.

As the Self-Reliance group declined in prestige and the literary output of its members waned, several other groups came into being, and the realistic novel made a tentative appearance, followed by revolutionary writing with Marxist tendencies in the late 1930s. *Bước đường cùng* (1938; *Impasse*, 1963), a poignant tale of misery and despondency among the oppressed peasantry, was the work of the most outstanding and prolific of the realist authors, NGUYỄN

CÔNG Hoan. Ngô Tất Tố (1894–1954), in *Tắt đèn* (1939; *When the Light Is Out*, 1960), depicted the misery of the wife of a poor peasant who is coerced into selling their eldest daughter and their dog and puppies in order to pay the couple's taxes. Two other works of note are *Chí Phèo* (1956; Chi the outcast) by Nam Cao (1917–1951), and *Bỉ vỏ* (1938; thieves and pickpockets) by Nguyên Hồng (b. 1918), both of which deal with social injustices as they describe the dregs of society. The commentary both works evoked indirectly helped bring about literary criticism as a new genre.

While works of SOCIALIST REALISM began to appear during the early days of the Democratic Republic of Vietnam, before 1954 there had been a socialist tendency among writers of the anti-French resistance and a "wait-and-see" attitude among noncommunist writers, most of whom chose to move south when the armistice with the French was signed.

Poetry in North Vietnam was essentially political: works by Tố Hữu (b. 1920), Chế Lan Viên (b. 1920), and Nguyễn Đình Thi (b. 1924), for instance, were preoccupied with the longing for territorial reunification and characterized by exalted expressions of revolutionary zeal and of concern for the masses. Prose writing, too, reflected new aspects of life: the most popular topics were land reform, rent reduction, activities of cooperatives, the collectivization of the countryside, and attacks on American involvement in the war.

Meanwhile, in South Vietnam a multitude of private publishing houses and a plethora of magazines and reviews offered outlets for poets and prose writers, many of them refugees from the north. Love, family relations, army life, and city life were some of the favorite themes of writers associated with the Saigon P.E.N. Club. Lãng Nhân (b. 1907) and Trọng Lang (b. 1906), two older writers, continued to produce essays and chronicles, while Vũ Khắc Khoan (b. 1917) and Vi Huyền Đắc concentrated on playwriting. In addition to Nhất-Linh—who committed suicide in 1963—and such "old guard" writers as Tam Lang (pseud. of Vũ Đình Chí, b. 1901) and Vũ Bằng (b. 1913), both journalists, essayists, and novelists, there were many prolific, perceptive, social-minded young novelists in South Vietnam, with either a strong anticommunist stance or an apolitical attitude bordering on pessimism and fatalism. Alongside such established poets as Vũ Hoàng Chương (1916–1976) and Đông-hồ Lâm Tấn Phát, younger poets appeared, in some of whose works the influence of French writers like Jean-Paul SARTRE and Saint-John PERSE can be detected.

After the communists took over the south in 1975, scores of writers were jailed, and their works seized and burned as "specimens of a depraved culture." In 1979 a collection of "prison songs" written between 1954 and 1978 was smuggled out to Europe. Unlike other writers who remained in the north at the time the Geneva armistice agreements partitioned Vietnam and whose works stayed close to the party line, the frail author of those poems, Nguyễn Chí Thiện (b. 1933), had spent time in various prisons, punished for daring to use poignant stanzas entitled *Hoa Ủịa-ngục* (1980; *Flowers from Hell*, 1984) to denounce communist atrocities. A worldwide movement was launched in the 1980s to demand the release of this 1985 Poetry International Prize winner as well as that of Doãn Quốc Sỹ (b. 1923), a renowned writer who moved south in 1954 and who was accused after the collapse of the Saigon government in 1975 of "ties with the U.S. and the puppet régime." After the Hanoi régime authorized some "untying" policies regarding artists and writers—one can speak of perestroika in socialist

Vietnam—a "high tide" protest movement emerged between 1986 and 1990. But Dương Thu-Hương (b. 1947), a woman novelist, was condemned for her bold exposés of communist cadres' corrupt practices and her stern denunciations of the total failures of socialist functionaries. Dương's works, for example, *Thiên-đường mù* (1988; pub. in French as *Les paradis aveugles*, 1991), caused her expulsion from the Communist Party and from the Writers' Association. These three writers were released in November 1991 thanks to international pressure.

Writers in exile since the fall of Saigon have kept up the tempo of literary output overseas, facilitated by the appearance of several publishing houses, which started with pirate editions of the most popular pre-1975 writings by South Vietnam's authors. Monthly and weekly literary magazines, published in California (for example, *Văn* and *Tạp-chí Văn-học*), Texas, Washington, and Louisiana, as well as in Canada (for example, *Làng Van*), France (for example, *Quê Mẹ*), and Germany (for example, *Độc-lập*), provide recreational readings to a large refugee audience.

The best-known authors are Võ Phiến (b. 1925), Mai Thảo (b. 1927), Duyên Anh (b. 1935), Nguyễn Mộng Giác (b. 1940), Lê Tất Điều (b. 1942), and Nguyễn Ngọc Ngạn (b. 1945). Võ Phiến's works published in the U.S. are either reprints of novels and short stories published in South Vietnam prior to 1975 or completely new creations, including delightful short stories and several volumes of excellent essays. Mai Thảo has kept up his productivity in prose and poetry besides being the publisher-editor of a monthly magazine. Văn. Nguyễn Mộng Giác has had short stories as well as two trilogies published in the U.S.: *Mùa biển động* (1986–1987; season of rough seas) and *Sông Côn Mùa lũ* (1990; Côn River at flood season). Lê Tất Điều has contributed novels, short stories, and essays as well as satirical writings with political overtones. Duyên Anh, who before his self-exile in France used to write stories about street urchins, has had two of his novels published in Paris: *Một người Nga ở Saigon* (1983; pub. in French as *Un Russe à Saigon*, 1986) and *Đồi Fanta* (1983; pub. in French as *La colline de Fanta*, 1989). The most prolific is certainly Nguyễn Ngọc Ngạn, who, besides *The Will of Heaven* (1982, with E. E. Richey), has turned out dozens of novels and short stories in Vietnamese, notably *Sân khấu cuộc đời* (1986; life as a stage), *Biến vẫn đợi chờ* (1984; the sea is still waiting), *Cõi đêm* (1982; night world), *Nước* (1986; muddy waters), and *Truyện ngắn* (2 vols., 1982, 1986; short stories). Memoirs by former political and military figures of South Vietnam are of uneven quality.

The overseas writers' ranks have also been consolidated by young faces, including some remarkable female refugees, notably Phan Thị Trọng Tuyến (b. 1951), Lê Thị Huê (b. 1953), Vũ Quỳnh-Hương (b. 1957), and Trần Diệu Hằng (b. 1952).

BIBLIOGRAPHY: Durand, M. M., and Nguyễn Trần Huân, *Introduction à la littérature vietnamienne* (1969); Hoàng Ngọc Thành, *The Social and Political Development of Vietnam as Seen through the Modern Novel* (1969); Bàng Bá Lân, "Some Remarks on Contemporary Vietnamese Poetry," *Viet-Nam Bulletin*, 5, 13 (1971): 2–13; Nguyễn Khắc Viện, et al., eds., Introduction to *Anthologie de la littérature vietnamienne, Tome III: Deuxième moitié du XIXe siècle–1945* (1975): 7–68; Nguyễn Khắc Kham, "Vietnamese National Language and Modern Vietnamese Literature," *SEACS*, 15: 1–4 (1976): 177–94; Nguyễn Khắc Viện, et al., eds., Introduction to *Anthologie de la littérature vietnamienne, Tome IV: De*

1945 à nos jours (1977): 7–72; Nguyễn Đình-Hoà, "Vietnamese Language and Literature," in Nguyễn Thị Mỹ-Hường, P., ed., *Language in Vietnamese Society* (1980): 9–26; Davidson, J. H. C. S., "To Aid the Revolution: The Short Story as Pro-liberation Literature in South Viet-Nam," in Davidson, J. H. C. S., and Cordell, H., eds., *The Short Story in South East Asia: Aspects of a Genre* (1982): 203–26; Huỳnh Sanh Thông, "Main Trends of Vietnamese Literature between the Two World Wars," *The Vietnam Forum*, 3 (1984): 99–125; Durand, M. M., and Nguyễn-Trần Huân, *An Introduction to Vietnamese Literature* (1985); Xuân-Diêu, "Apport de la poèsie française dans la poésie vietnamienne moderne," *The Vietnam Forum*, 5 (1985): 146–63; Võ-Phiến, "Writers in South Vietnam, 1954–1975," *The Vietnam Forum*, 7 (1986): 176–99

—DINH-HOA NGUYEN

VIITA, Lauri

Finnish poet and novelist, b. 17 Dec. 1916, Pirkkala; d. 22 Dec. 1965, Helsinki

The son of a construction worker, V. did not finish high school and for a time earned a living as a carpenter and construction worker. He read widely, however, and was especially interested in science. In 1948 he married the poet Aila Meriluoto (b. 1924); in 1956 they were divorced. He took part in a few literary battles, and his public readings of his own poems were appreciated by large audiences. He was killed in a car accident.

V.'s first collection of poems, *Betonimylläri* (1947; a miller of concrete), was well received, and the second, *Kukunor* (1949; Kukunor), confirmed his reputation, although its whimsical elements bewildered many critics. His success encouraged other writers in Tampere, where he lived, to form a literary club of mostly working men, except for Alex Matson (1888–1972), an older critic and essayist, who guided the discussions.

V.'s novel *Moreeni* (1950; the moraine) showed him to be a good realistic writer, but his main interest was always poetry. His next volume of verse, *Käppyräinen* (1954; crinkly), less whimsical than *Kukunor*, was again a success. About this time he developed a severe neurosis and had to be temporarily hospitalized. A new collection of poems, *Suutarikin, suuri viisas* (a shoemaker is a wise man, too) appeared in 1961, and V. was planning a novelistic trilogy, of which only the first volume, *Entäs sitten, Leevi* (1965; what then, Leevi), was published before his death.

Cognizant of his working-class background, V. assumed an aggressive social stance in parts of his first collection, but soon discarded it. *Moreeni* is set in a working-class neighborhood at the beginning of this century, and although the civil war of 1918 is briefly described, V. is obviously more interested in the personal lives of his characters than in public events.

As a poet, V. made skillful use of many verse forms: regularly rhymed poems, poems in the traditional Finnish meter (as found, for instance, in the *Kalevala* epic), and unrhymed, free-form poems. The title poem of *Betonimylläri* describes the dreams of an "average" construction worker during a lunch break, but some aspects of these dreams are convincing only if one imagines a construction worker like V. himself. The poems in this collection are often violently satirical, but V. was more concerned with moral and philosophical questions than with social and political evils: although in rebellion against the human condition, he believed in man's spiritual capacity to free himself of his limitations and to reshape the world.

Kukunor is unusual in Finnish literature. It is a playful and slightly nonsensical adult fairytale about a troll and a fairy who fall in love. Finding an old atlas, they choose for themselves the most appealing names in it: Kukunor (a lake in Central Asia) and Kalahari (a desert in South Africa). Interwoven with the delightful nonsense are serious symbolic themes, such as the possibility of making the desert—representing human life—bloom again. *Käppyräinen* is more immediately accessible. V.'s humor and satire are mellower in it, and his barbs are directed against pretentiousness. V. showed his greatest formal proficiency in this collection, which includes several love poems that indicate a new freedom in personal expression. An almost absurd kind of humor is employed to hide the poet's anguish at his recognition of evil in the world, but this humor is simultaneously a protest and an expression of ultimate hope.

V. was one of those Finnish authors who, although they broke with pre-World War II literary traditions, did not follow the young MODERNISTS of the 1950s. Difficult to classify, he was a poet whose consummate formal skill and earnestness of purpose made all fashions and trends irrelevant. Somewhat forgotten at the present moment, when poetry of this type is not much appreciated, he has nevertheless secured himself a firm place in the literature of his country.

FURTHER WORKS: *Kootut teokset* (1966)

BIBLIOGRAPHY: Ahokas, J. A., *A History of Finnish Literature* (1973): 347–49

—JAAKKO A. AHOKAS

VILHJÁLMSSON, Thor

Icelandic novelist, poet, short-story writer, and essayist, b. 12 Aug. 1925, Edinburgh, Scotland

When V. was born, his father was working for an Icelandic agency in Scotland; the family moved back to Iceland when V. was five. After secondary school he studied Icelandic philology at the University of Iceland for two years (1944–46), then literature at the University of Nottingham, England, during 1946–47. He lived in Paris from 1947 to 1952, continued his studies, and began writing; in 1950 he made his literary debut. On his return to Iceland he first worked as a sailor for a year, then as a librarian. Since 1955 he has been a full-time writer.

V. was the only prose writer who joined those poets who finally brought MODERNISM to Iceland. His first book, *Maðurinn er alltaf einn* (1950; man is always alone), consists of short lyrical prose and poetry dealing with loneliness. Most of the prose fragments briefly present a melancholy situation in which a solitary man moves through vague surroundings without being able to establish contact. Similar content persists in V.'s next two books, *Dagar mannsins* (1954; days of man) and *Andlit í spegli dropans* (1957; *Faces Reflected in a Drop*, 1966), except that the situations have moved closer to reality, the scenes are longer and have more detail, and the style is more elaborate. In these works one can see the beginning of what was to become one of V.'s main characteristics: a personal feeling obtained through objective depictions.

After these three books, which in many respects can be viewed as a connected whole, V. abandoned fiction for a time and turned to writing travel books of sorts, one of which also contains articles on cultural subjects. These books—*Undir gervitungli* (1959; under a sputnik), *Regn á rykið* (1960; rain on the dust), and *Svipir dagsins, og nótt* (1961; the faces of a day, and night)—are about trips through the Soviet Union and Europe. V. is no ordinary tourist, however, but a cultural traveler through time and space. Brief encounters, a painting in a museum, an old myth or legend can suddenly grow into a grand poetic vision. And when V. visits a place, he seems to relive intensively everything that has happened there from the beginning. This attitude toward time—an attempt to capture its merciless speed and at the same time its eternal presence—became a central theme in his novels.

V.'s most important works are three novels that form a thematic trilogy: *Fljót, fljót, sagði fuglinn* (1968; quick, quick, said the bird), *Óp björllunnar* (1970; the cry of the beetle), and *Mánasigð* (1976; crescent moon). They all are about the identity crisis of the modern, alienated European intellectual, who is driven by his own fear of an imminent catastrophe through a chaotic world of loneliness. The narration is limited only by the writer's imagination, and consequently outer and inner reality are constantly intermingled.

V.'s importance lies in his revolt against the epic tradition in Icelandic prose and his contribution to the modernist movement during the 1950s, but he stands quite alone in his writing. He seems to have had some difficulties in keeping his narrative methods fresh, as his latest works have shown some tendencies toward repetition.

FURTHER WORKS: *Kjarval* (1964); *Folda* (1972); *Hvað er San Marino* (1973); *Fiskur í sjó, fugl úr beini* (1974); *Fuglaskottís* (1975); *Skuggar af skýjum* (1977); *Turnleikhúsið* (1979); *Faldafeykir* (1979); *The Deep Sea, Pardon the Ocean* (1981, in English)

BIBLIOGRAPHY: Hallberg, P., "The One Who Sees: The Icelandic Writer T. V.," *BA*, 47 (1973): 54–59; Ingólfsson, A., on *The Deep Blue Sea, Pardon the Ocean*, *WLT*, 56 (1982): 526

—NJÖRÐUR P. NJARÐVÍK

VILLA, Jose Garcia

Philippine poet and short-story writer (writing in English), b. 5 Aug. 1908, Manila

Already alienated from his father, a physician, V. became an exile from his motherland as well when he was suspended by the University of the Philippines for writing controversial poems. His stories of rejection and self-reassertion, written while a student at the University of New Mexico and Columbia University, drew the attention of the renowned editor Edward O'Brien, who dedicated

his collection *Best American Short Stories of 1932* to him. By then V.'s drawing inward had turned him to poetry, three volumes of which eventually were published in the U.S., carrying Edith SITWELL's praise on their jackets. V. became a revered figure to his countrymen who aspired to acceptance abroad.

In all his poetry transfiguration of intimate sensations occurs. Instead of providing any identifiable cultural content, his poetic images are romantic and visionary, intended to be universal and to convey the sense of a liberated spirit ascending. Deliberately, it is selfhood that is celebrated—self either as benevolent lover of woman or as contending rival for the Godhead. Doveglion (Doveeagle-lion), a pseudonym he used, indicates his self-assigned magnitude.

In addition to influences from William Blake (and less significantly from Walt Whitman and e. e. CUMMINGS), V. has been affected by his early attachment to CUBIST painting. In extended notes to his *Selected Poems and New* (1958) he explains his two technical innovations, both apparently inspired by the geometry of faceted gems. His "comma poems" introduce a symbol shaped like a comma but attached without space to the words on either side, thus providing a weighted and dignified (if unvaried) pace to the moving line. "Reversed consonance" makes rhymes out of the last-sounded consonants in any line, those same consonants being then reversed by ingenious word choice at the end of the succeeding line. The effect on the ear is subliminal, at best; but the trained eye responds to the technique as to a mirror device promoting reflective thought. Both devices epitomize the poet's dense inward-turning.

Although his interests are peripheral to the community service traditional in the Philippines, V. received the Republic Cultural Heritage Award in 1962, and in 1973 he became the first Philippine writer in English to be declared a National Artist, with a lifetime pension.

FURTHER WORKS: *Footnote to Youth: Tales of the Philippines and Others* (1933); *Many Voices* (1939); *Poems by Doveglion* (1941); *Have Come, Am Here* (1941); *Volume Two* (1949); *Poems 55* (1962); *Selected Stories* (1962); *Appasionata: Poems in Praise of Love* (1979)

BIBLIOGRAPHY: Lopez, S. P., *Literature and Society* (1940): 152–65; Casper, L., *New Writing from the Philippines* (1966): 103–13; Tinio, R., "V.'s Values," in Manuud, A., ed., *Brown Heritage* (1967): 722–38

—LEONARD CASPER

VILLAURRUTIA, Xavier

Mexican poet, dramatist, novelist, and critic, b. 27 March 1903, Mexico City; d. 25 Dec. 1950, Mexico City

It is known that V. was the son of a well-to-do commissions agent, but his personal life remained shrouded in mystery, entirely separated from his intellectual relationships. During the 1920s and early 1930s he collaborated in various avant-garde movements to revitalize Mexican literature and make its appeal more universal. The most important of these were the Contemporaries (1928–31), a school of talented young poets; and the experimental Ulysses Theater (1928), founded by a small group of playwrights. He also contributed articles to some of the major literary journals and published his only novel, *Dama de corazones* (1928; queen of hearts), an experimental work consisting of the interior monologue of a first-person narrator as he attempts to distinguish between two identical female personalities. In 1935 V. received a Rockefeller Foundation grant to study dramatic composition at Yale University. After he returned to his native land, he taught literature at the University of Mexico and wrote some of his best-known poems and plays. His early death resulted from a heart attack.

Most critics consider V. a poet first and a dramatist second. His poetry may be divided into three phases, the first of which is represented by *Reflejos* (1926; reflections). In this collection, impressionistic glimpses of external reality are presented in precise, metaphorical language shaded by tones of melancholy and solitude.

V.'s second poetic phase is exemplified by *Nostalgia de la muerte* (1938; nostalgia of death), generally viewed as his masterpiece. Here the author denies the objective world and solipsistically seeks a deeper, more intimate reality hidden within his own consciousness. Death emerges as the central theme, melancholy and solitude turning to an obsessive fear of impending disaster. In "Décima muerte" ("Ten Stanzas of Death," 1968), V.'s most famous poem and a classic in Mexican literature, death is no longer dreaded but welcomed as an eternal mistress evoked through sensuous, baroque imagery.

V.'s last volume of verse, *Canto a la primavera, y otros poemas* (1948; song to spring, and other poems), marks an abrupt thematic shift from death to unbridled amorous passion. In spite of its technical excellence, it fails to sustain the originality and depth of *Nostalgia de la muerte*.

During the 1930s V. produced five experimental one-act plays which, published under the title *Autos profanos* (1941; worldly mysteries), constitute the most significant portion of his theater. Ironic in tone, they embody the human condition in weak, puppetlike characters torn by indecision, frustrated by their inability to communicate, and ultimately condemned to loneliness. The poetic style and subtle, philosophical nature of these works create a timeless, ivory-tower atmosphere.

In the final decade of his life V. wrote and successfully staged a number of three-act plays of wider popular appeal because of their well-constructed plots and situations bordering on the melodramatic. Generally speaking, however, they lack the literary merit of *Autos profanos*, the only exception being *Invitación a la muerte* (1944; invitation to death). A provocative adaptation of *Hamlet*, this play portrays a sensitive, tormented youth attempting to determine his role in modern Mexican society while facing a dilemma similar to that of Shakespeare's hero.

Although V. is generally regarded as an innovative, cosmopolitan writer, his work is firmly rooted in the realities of Mexico. He was the first Mexican poet to discover in the psyche of his compatriots the metaphysical anguish afflicting 20th-c. man. He and Rodolfo USIGLI were the leading Mexican playwrights of their generation. V. will be remembered above all for his literary craftsmanship and his highly original treatment of existential themes.

FURTHER WORKS: *Dos nocturnos* (1931); *Nocturnos* (1931); *Parece mentira* (1933); *¿En qué piensas?* (1934); *Ha llegado el*

Jose Garcia Villa

momento (1934); *Sea Ud. breve* (1934); *Nocturno de los ángeles* (1936); *El ausente* (1937); *Nocturno mar* (1937); *Textos y pretextos* (1940); *Décima muerte, y otros poemas no coleccionados* (1941); *La hiedra* (1941); *La mujer legítima* (1942); *El yerro candente* (1944); *El solterón* (1945); *El pobre Barba Azul* (1946); *La tragedia de las equivocaciones* (1950); *Juego peligroso* (1953); *Poesía y teatro completos de X. V.* (1953); *Páramo de sueños, seguido de Imágines desterrados* (1960); *Cartas de V. a Novo, 1935–1936* (1966); *Obras* (1966); *Crítica cinematográfica* (1970)

BIBLIOGRAPHY: Beck, V. F., "X. V., dramaturgo moderno," *RI*, 18 (1952): 27–39; Dauster, F., "La poesía de X. V.," *RI*, 18 (1953): 345–59; Lamb, R. S., "X. V. and the Modern Mexican Theater," *MLF*, 39 (1954): 108–44; Moreno, A., "X. V.: The Development of His Theater," *Hispania*, 43 (1960): 508–14; Shaw, D., "Pasión y verdad en el teatro de V.," *RI*, 28 (1962): 337–46; Dauster, F., *X. V.* (1971); Forster, M. H., *Fire and Ice: The Poetry of X. V.* (1976)

—GEORGE R. MCMURRAY

VIÑAS, David

Argentine novelist, critic, and essayist, b. 1929, Buenos Aires

V. studied philosophy and letters at the University of Buenos Aires and later at the University of Rosario, where he received a

Ph.D. in 1963. He forms part of Argentina's so-called Generation of 1950, ideologically centered around opposition to the régime of Perón. In a continental context he is linked to the well-known "boom" of the 1960s. His writings all reveal his concerns for the masses; he is an excellent example of a Latin American social realist with strong Marxist tendencies.

Two vital and related ideas unite nearly all his essays, novels, and short stories: an analysis of the political history of Argentina and, to a lesser extent, that of all Latin America; and a search of Argentina's sociopolitical identity and heritage as expressed in his creative art and literature. The first idea pervades the essays *Argentina: Ejército y oligarquía* (1967; Argentina: the military and the oligarchy), *México y Cortés* (1978: Mexico and Cortes), and *Yrigoyen entre Borges y Arlt* (1989; Yrigoyen between Borges and Arlt). The works *Literatura argentina y realidad política* (1964; Argentine literature and political reality) and *Indios, ejército y frontera* (1982; Indians, the military, and the border) represent the second theme, exploring the complexities of Argentine society and literature.

Interest in Argentine identity pervades all of V.'s novels and stories. He published his first short story, "Los desorientados" (1952; the disoriented), during the height of Peronism yet did not shrink from criticizing the social ills that then beset Argentina. His earliest novels, *Cayó sobre su rostro* (1955; he fell on his face), *Los dueños de la tierra* (1959; the lords of the land), and *Dar la cara* (1962; turn the other cheek), examine and occasionally propose Marxist-oriented political solutions for his ailing country. In *Un Dios cotidiano* (1957; an everyday god) V. explores the difficulty of adopting radically independent religious or political positions; those who do are either completely rejected or forcibly brought into line by the "establishment." V.'s essays are courageous and straightforward, never seeming to fear the censorship and possible repression that have plagued much of Argentina in the last half of the 20th c.

In 1955 V. received the esteemed Gerchunoff Prize as well as the Buenos Aires Municipal Prize for his first novel; other novels have also been honored by awards from Argentina's Kraft and Losada publishing houses in 1957 and 1958, respectively. The author's best-known work, *Los hombres de a caballo* (1967; men on horseback), received the 1967 Casa de las Américas Prize for best novel of the year, an indication that his national concerns were now appreciated and understood on a continental level. The novel's story line is rather simplistic, but the frequent flashbacks, difficult monologues, bits of conversations, and fragmented narration link the novel's complex structure to similar experiments by Julio CORTÁZAR and Carlos FUENTES during the same decade. False notions of patriotism, irrational family loyalties, and supposed continental unity all come under some fire, but the military is always the main target.

In recent years V.'s committed literature has delved into the "Dirty War" and the persecution of Argentine leftists and intellectuals. *Cuerpo a cuerpo* (1979; body to body) is an autobiographical testimonial of deep human suffering during the 1976–77 period of repression, told through the eyes of a journalist who is writing a biography of one of Argentina's famous generals. In keeping with his vital concerns for his native country, V. published *Carlos Gardel* (1979; Carlos Gardel), a type of literary homage to that national hero/singer; the book is an analysis of immigration as a basic component of the national character.

V. has also written and produced several plays and television shows, often based on his novels or short stories, but few have enjoyed the success of his novels. Argentina also knows him as a thoughtful newspaper columnist and editor. In this medium he has continued the same intellectual concerns with the relationship between the individual Argentine and society, and the conflicts between the elites in power and those with none. To date his works have not been published in English translation. His eleven novels, thirteen books of essays, one collection of short stories, *Las malas costumbres* (1963; bad habits), poetry, theatrical works, movie scripts, and numerous articles and stories make him one of the most prolific Argentine writers of the 20th c.

FURTHER WORKS: *Los años despiadados* (1956); *Laferrère: del apogeo de la oligarquía a la ciudad liberal* (1965); *En la semana trágica* (1966); *Cosas concretas* (1969); *Rebeliones populares argentinas* (1971); *Grotesco, inmigración y fracaso: Armando Discépolo* (1973); *Juaría* (1974); *Literatura argentina y realidad política. Apogeo de la oligarquía* (1975); *Quées el fascismo en Latinoamérica* (1977); *Ultramar* (1980); *Anarquistas en América Latina* (1983)

BIBLIOGRAPHY: Grossi, H. M., "Angry Young Argentine: D. V. Speaks His Mind," *Américas* (January 1960): 14–17; Dellepiane, A. B., "La novela argentina desde 1950 a 1965," *RI*, 34, 66 (December 1968): 253–59; Rasi, H., "D. V., novelista y crítico comprometido," *RI*, 42, 95 (June 1976): 259–65; Glickman, N., "V.'s *En la semana trágica:* A Novelist's Focus on Argentine Pogrom," *Yiddish* (Fall 1984): 64–71; Valverde, E., *D. V.: en busca de una síntesis de la historia argentina* (1989)

—THOMAS E. LYON

VIRZA, Edvarts

(pseud. of Edvarts Lieknis) Latvian poet, b. 27 Dec. 1883, Billites; d. 1 Mar. 1940, Riga

V. was born and grew up on the fertile plain of Zemgale in southern Latvia. The patriarchal Zemgale homestead was to be a recurring theme in his works. He studied in Moscow and Paris; influenced by Russian and French SYMBOLISM, he was one of the writers who initiated a Latvian symbolist movement. His first collection of verse, *Biķeris* (1908; the goblet), shows characteristic symbolist traits: concern with personal experience, and abundance of sensuous images.

During World War I V.'s mother was killed by a stray German bullet. This tragic event effected a close bond between V. and the fate of his people. After 1918, as an editor and cultural leader, he helped to shape the ideology of the newly founded Latvian state.

V.'s translations into Latvian— *Franču renesanses lirika* (1930; French Renaissance poetry) and *Franču lirika XIX gadu simtenī* (1921; French poetry of the 19th c.)—helped him evolve his own poetic style. He discovered a spiritual kinship with the Belgian poet Émile VERHAEREN, whose homeland, Flanders, resembles the landscape of Zemgale. V.'s translations of Verhaeren's verse were published as *Verharna dzeja* (1936; poetry of Verhaeren).

V. searched eagerly for new sources of inspiration for Latvian poetry, wishing to free it from the grip of German and Russian influences. In French poetry he found such a source, and in fact, France became his second homeland: for several years he was director of the Latvian press bureau in Paris.

V. was deeply attracted by the age-old peasant ethos and made the yearly cycle of a 19th-c. Zemgale farm the subject of his novel-length prose poem *Straumēni* (1933; the Straumēni homestead). The timeless peasant way of life, memorialized in Latvian folk songs, is intertwined in this work with Christian elements, and events are subordinate to the main protagonist—the old farmstead and its spirit—which inescapably determines the course of their lives. The narrative style is biblical and solemn. Although plot and action are minimal in *Straumēni*, the reader is swept along by its emotional power and by the directness and lucidity of the narrative.

Among the subjects of V.'s epic poems are romanticized portrayals of historical personages, as well as aspects of Latvian peasant life, as in *Dievi un zemnieki* (1939; gods and peasants). He also published essays on literature, cultural life, and politics. He employed an exalted style; conclusions are presented in the form of striking aphorisms.

V. is a major Latvian poet. His mastery of the strict classical form is especially evident in *Dievišķīgās rotaļas* (1919; divine pastimes), *Laikmets un lira* (1923; era and lyre), *Skaidrība* (1927; serenity), *Dzejas un poēmas* (1933; lyrics and poems), and *Pēdējās dzejas* (1942; last poems). The mature balance and limpidity of his love and nature poems contrast with the intense feeling of his patriotic verse.

FURTHER WORKS: *Zaļā Zemgale* (1917); *Poēmas* (1924); *La littérature lettonne depuis le reveil national* (1925); *Lauku balsis* (1927); *Laikmeta dokumenti* (1930); *Zem karoga* (1935); *Kārlis Ulmanis* (1935); *Jaunā junda* (1936); *Hercogs Jēkabs* (1937); *Kopoti raksti* (4 vols., 1939–40); *V.s sarakste ar V. Dambergu* (1954); *Kopoti raksti* (4 vols., 1956–66)

BIBLIOGRAPHY: Andrups, J., and V. Kalve, *Latvian Literature* (1954): 151–52; Matthews, W. K., ed., *A Century of Latvian Poetry* (1957): 13

—JĀNIS ANDRUPS

VITTORINI, Elio

Italian novelist, essayist, and critic, b. 23 July 1908, Syracuse; d. 12 Feb. 1966, Milan

Son of a Sicilian stationmaster, V. spent his childhood in isolated towns. His father sent him to accounting school, where he did very badly. He ran away from home three times before he was seventeen. In 1927 he went north and worked as a laborer on a road-building gang. At this time he began to publish in periodicals. In 1930 he settled in Florence, where he worked as a proofreader and reviewed books and movies. He studied English and did translating for a living. He got into trouble with the Fascists in 1936 for advocating intervention on the Republican side in the Spanish Civil War. In 1938 he moved to Milan and in 1942 joined the Communist Resistance and was forced to hide out in the mountains. After the war he worked in Milan. He left the Communist Party in 1951 but continued to be active in public life, running on a Socialist ticket in the Sicilian regional elections of 1959. In 1960 he organized a manifesto of Italian intellectuals against the war in Algeria.

V.'s influence on mid-20th-c. Italian thought was enormous. He was in the forefront of every important cultural movement from 1930 to 1965. He belonged to the European (anti-Fascist) Solaria group, and his translations (STEINBECK, SAROYAN, FAULKNER) were, under prevailing conditions, political actions: along with his introductions in the anthology *Americana* (1941; Americana)—its distribution was halted by the Fascist censors; when the book was reissued in 1943, V.'s essays were deleted—they helped to create the myth of America that became a rallying point for the Resistance. V. also founded and edited two of the most important postwar cultural periodicals, *Il politecnico* (1945–47) and *Il menabò* (1959–63), the first conceived as a meeting point for workers and intellectuals, presenting the Sino-Soviet *and* the Western points of view, the latter as a forum for stylistic breakthroughs to reflect Italy's new, industrial reality. V. also founded series such as I Gettoni (telephone tokens), which published new writers and aimed to promote "global cultural discussions."

V.'s first book, *Piccola borghesia* (1931; petite bourgeoisie), is a series of polished short stories. *Il garofano rosso* (written 1933, pub. 1948; *The Red Carnation*, 1952) is a long psychological novel about adolescence, sex, and revolution. It documents the attractions of Fascism for V.'s generation. The Spanish Civil War caused him to interrupt work on *Erica e i suoi fratelli* (pub. 1956 with *La Garibaldina; The Dark and the Light: Erica and La Garibaldina*, 1961). It is a lyrical novel that, through the poetic use of fable, fuses V.'s myth of childhood as a time of innocence and intuitive vision with his myth of the noble worker. It is the first product of his search for a new style that infuses "poetry" into the novel as music infuses "intensity and truth" into opera.

Conversazione in Sicilia (1941; *In Sicily*, 1947), his best novel, creates a new and poetic style, involving repetition, musical rhythms, and parataxis. The protagonist travels from Milan to visit his native Sicily; the rediscovery of his childhood gives him an understanding of the suffering of the poor and of the need for effective reforms on all levels. The book combines all V.'s myths into one explosive, allegorical indictment of the "sorrow of the suffering world," a crystallization precipitated by his emotional protest against Fascism. Its central hope is that the "progressive" tendency in civilization (revolution) will overcome the "reaction-ary" one (inertia).

V.'s postwar fiction continued to be experimental, from the Hemingwayesque Resistance novel *Uomini e no* (1945; men and non-men) to the short, intense, lyrical *Il sempione strizza l'occhio al Frejus* (1947; *The Twilight of the Elephant*, 1951), an allegory of the need to replace bourgeois civilization with a proletarian one, and *Le donne di Messina* (1949; rev. ed., 1964; *Women of Messina*, 1973), an epic of the struggle between the communal and the Fascist ideologies in the formation of postwar Italy.

Among V.'s essayistic works, *Diario in pubblico* (1957; public diary) is a collection of excerpts from his essays, articles, reviews, and prose pieces, chronologically divided into four "motivations": "literary" (1929–36), "antifascist" (1937–45), "cultural" (1945–47), and "civic" (1948–56). *Le due tensioni* (1967; twin tensions), edited and published after his death, contains his often brilliant thoughts on the "rational" and the "affective" thrusts underlying all facets of literature and culture.

V. ranks with Cesare PAVESE and Italo CALVINO as a master of modern Italian fiction. *Conversazione in Sicilia* has been hailed as both the manifesto and the inspiration for contemporary literature. Few intellectuals have exerted such an influence on Italian culture.

FURTHER WORKS: *Nei Morlacchi; Viaggio in Sardegna* (1936); *La tragica vicenda di Carlo III* (1939); *Guttuso* (1942); *Le città del*

Mondo (1969); *Nome e lagrime, e altri racconti* (1972); *Gli anni del Politecnico: Lettere 1945–1951* (1977)

BIBLIOGRAPHY: Fernandez, D., *Le roman italien et la crise de la conscience moderne* (1958): 183–97; Heiney, D., *Three Italian Novelists* (1968): 147–213; Schneider, M., "Circulation as Mode and Meaning in *Conversazione in Sicilia,*" MLN, 90 (1975): 93–108; Potter, J., *E. V.* (1979)

—JOY M. POTTER

VOICULESCU, Vasile

Romanian poet, dramatist, novelist, and short-story writer, b. 13 Oct. 1884, Pîrscov; d. 26 Apr. 1963, Bucharest

A physician by profession, V. first began publishing verse in *Convorbiri literare* and *Luceafărul*. His first volumes of poetry, *Poezii* (1916; poems), *Din țara zimbrului* (1918; from the land of the bison), and *Pîrgă* (1921; early ripening), revealed his talent for depicting local color and peasant life. Initially employing conventional and highly regular meter that echoes earlier Romanian poets, V. slowly developed originality and mastery of rhythms. *Din țara zimbrului* won the Romanian Academy Prize; *Pîrgă*, more polymetric and relaxed, showed the influence of French free verse.

His association in 1921 with the newly founded Cluj journal *Gândirea* (or *Gîndirea*) brought V. into contact with the distinguished literary group that looked to Romanian village life and Orthodox Christianity as the true sources of a national literature. The members drew upon colorful Romanian folk materials and Byzantine iconography.

V.'s masterpiece, *Poeme cu îngeri* (1927; poems with angels), was the work of a mature poet. Here the mystic emerged fully. The dominant image is the angel, who pervades the entire universe in various guises—as a cloud, as a bee ("frantic angel"), as an airplane ("iron archangel"). Through these "angels" man finds his identity with God. The first poems in this collection are polymetric, but others are in a free-verse form that nonetheless retains rhymes.

In *Urcus* (1937; the ascent; repub. as *Suire* [climbing]) and *Întrezăriri* (1939; glimpses) V. returned to traditional metrics and the quatrain, redisciplining his lines to the old forms but profiting from his previous experimentation with free verse to produce double rhythms and an enrichment of traditional prosody. The poems show the influence on V. of SYMBOLISM.

In line with the *Gândirea* group's stress on the complementary function of the arts, especially poetry and drama, in 1932 V. had made his first attempt at a dramatic poem, in the manner of a medieval mystery play: *La pragul minunii* (1934; on the threshold of a miracle). His first plays, *Fata ursului* (perf. 1930; daughter of the bear) and *Umbra* (perf. 1935; shadow), were published together as *Duhul pămîntului* (1943; the earth spirit). He continued writing plays until World War II; the last before the theater was closed to him by the Communist regime that came to power in 1946 was *Demiurgul* (1943; the demiurge). He left other plays in manuscript, however: the comedies *Gimnastică sentimentală* (1972; sentimental exercise) and *Trandafir agățător* (climbing rose), the historical drama *Pribeaga* (1972; the woman wanderer), and two radio plays, *Darul domnișoarei Amalia* (the gift of Miss Amalia) and *Două furtuni* (two storms). V.'s talents lay chiefly in poetry, but *Pribeaga*,

an experimental play influenced by Bernard SHAW and Luigi PIRANDELLO and anticipating elements later in Eugène IONESCO and the THEATER OF THE ABSURD, will doubtless survive as one of V.'s major works.

After 1946 V. was black-listed, although he continued to write privately. While in this literary limbo he served a five-year prison term (1958–63) as an "enemy of the state." Shortly before his death a shift in official government policy led to his rehabilitation, and he published some short stories and some new verse in the journal *Steaua*. This rehabilitation led to a revival of interest in his work and to a discovery of his talents as a prose writer.

The posthumously published verse in *Ultimele sonete închipuite ale lui Shakespeare în traducere imaginară de V. V.* (1964; last sonnets of Shakespeare as imagined and translated by V. V.) reveals the same sensuous robustness and metrical felicity as his earlier work, showing a similar mingling of free-verse cadence and traditional meter and rhyme. More than just whimsy, these poems also celebrate in the Renaissance spirit V.'s thirst for spiritual completeness.

V.'s prose tales, written between 1946 and 1958 and published in *Povestiri* (2 vols., 1966; tales), and his one novel, *Zahei orbul* (written 1949–54, pub. 1970; Zahei the blind man), once again reveal his love of peasant life, his use of folklore for its philosophical implications, and his undiminished vitality. These works established V.'s reputation as a major writer of fiction as well as a poet and playwright. They are characterized by an attention to the fantastic, to religious mysticism, and to the search for spiritual verities. These tales from a writer previously well known only as a poet and a marked and dramatic reaction to the accepted order of prose were a shock to the literary world.

Although a physician, V. believed in the limitations of exact sciences and dedicated himself to probing whatever transcended our senses, centering around the fundamental Mystery. Partly in reaction to Marxist realism, he set out to create an artistic antireality, an archaic, legendary Romania, an ageless and non-historical universe of rapidly disappearing traditions and myths and peopled by fishermen, monks, magicians, and hunters—searching for the origin of our spiritual nature. His best stories begin in contemporary life with a common event where one of the characters relates a story that takes the reader into the mythical, primeval, subterranean space of the story, where dramatic or extraordinary events happen with symbolic meaning and where ordinary laws no longer work. His skillful, innovative, and original technique is to accumulate facts which build up to an unexpected climax, nullifying any difference between the normal and the fantastic, never severing the ties between the two. V.'s stories appeared at a critical moment as young writers were turning to myth and symbol in village life and he contributed significantly to the creation of this new prose.

Collections of most of his verse—*Poezii* (2 vols., 1968; poems)—and of his four major plays—*Teatru* (1972; plays)—also appeared posthumously. Much of his work—most of it from the post–World War II period—has yet to be edited and appear in print.

V. is one of the writers of the interwar period recently rediscovered by the current generation of Romanian poets and critics. In search of a national identity and a faith for modern times, these young writers find special meaning in V.'s religious expression, which although derived from Orthodox Christianity is also mystically rooted in peasant feeling and lore—in what has been called his "autochthonous spirituality." They also admire V.'s craftsmanship: his subtle adaptations of new rhythms to old prosody and his adaptation of form to matter, as he blends the past with the future.

FURTHER WORKS: *Amintiri despre Vlahuță* (1927); *Destin* (1933); *La pragul minunii* (1934); *Poezii* (1944). FURTHER WORKS IN ENGLISH: *Vasile Voiculescu: The Last Sonnets of Shakespeare's in Imaginary Translation* (1982); *Tales of Fantasy and Magic* (1986)

BIBLIOGRAPHY: Munteano, B., *Modern Rumanian Literature* (1939): 291–93; MacGregor-Hastie, R., ed., *Anthology of Contemporary Romanian Poetry* (1969): 45; "V. V. (1884–1964)," *Classical and Contemporary Romanian Writers* (1972): 89–91; Eulert, D., S. Avădanei, and M. Drăgan, eds., *Modern Romanian Poetry* (1973): 40–41; Apetroaie, I., "Résumé," *V. V.: Studiu monografic* (1975): 265–77; Porucic, A., "The Dramatic Triangle with Shakespeare and V.," *Analele Universitate "Al. I. Cuza," Iasi: Linguistică-literatură* (1975): 71–77; Popa, M., *Geschichte der rumänischen Literatur* (1980): 199–202; Grecu, M., and A. Stănescu, "A Case of 'Luciferic' Self-Awareness—V. V.," *Journal of the American Romanian Academy of Arts and Sciences* 18 (1933): 66–79

—THOMAS AMHERST PERRY

VOJNOVIĆ, Ivo

Yugoslav dramatist and short-story writer (writing in Croatian), b. 9 Oct. 1857, Dubrovnik, Austro-Hungary (now Croatia); d. 30 Aug. 1929, Belgrade

Born into a prominent family—his father was a well-known Croatian politician and scholar, and his mother was an aristocrat—V. grew up in Split and Dubrovnik before moving in 1874 to Zagreb, where he graduated from law school in 1879. He practiced law until 1890, was a civil servant (1890–1907), the dramaturge of the Zagreb National Theater (1907–11), and a full-time writer (1911–14) before the Austro-Hungarian authorities in Dubrovnik imprisoned him in 1914 as a Yugoslav nationalist. His serious eye disease forced them to transfer him to Zagreb in 1915. From 1919 to 1922, V. lived in France, then settled in Dubrovnik. In 1928, seeking treatment for his deteriorating vision, he entered a Belgrade hospital. He died the following year.

V. began his literary career writing short fiction, and his first-published novella, *Geranium* (1880; geranium), remains his best. This "story of a spinster" focuses, in V.'s words, "on the anatomy of the heart of an unattractive woman." Having lost the man she secretly loved to her frivolous but pretty sister, Mare eventually takes into her house her gravely handicapped niece, to whom she transfers all her love. Caring for the sick child, the spinster experiences the only period of true happiness and fulfillment in her life.

V. is best remembered as an innovative playwright who was a true master of the stage; his popularity was at its peak before World War I. In his most outstanding plays V. magnificently captures the atmosphere and the moods of 19th-c. Dubrovnik, in a period during which the once wealthy and powerful city-republic experienced a steady and irreversible political, economic, and social decline.

Ekvinocij (1895; the equinox) is a four-act play in which realistic, symbolic, and lyrical elements are interlaced to create a moving drama of mother love and violent human passions against the background of rampaging equinoctial winds over the stormy Adriatic. Jela's lover, who had abandoned her and had gone to America before she gave birth to their son, returns years later as a wealthy man. His selfishness threatens to destroy the future and the

happiness of their son. The play reaches its climax when Jela murders her former lover and then commits suicide in order to enable their son and his fiancée to leave for America together and begin a new and happy life, which Jela herself never had.

Dubrovačka trilogija (1902; *A Trilogy of Dubrovnik*, 1921; later tr., 1951) is composed of three one-act plays: *Allons enfants!* (*Allons Enfants*), *Suton* (*Afterglow*; later tr., *The Twilight*), and *Na taraci* (*On the Terrace*). Varying in style and set in several different periods (1806, 1832, and 1900, respectively), the three plays complement each other and form a harmonious dramatic entity. The first focuses on the entrance of Napoleon's troops into Dubrovnik, and the other two depict the further deterioration of the old aristocratic social order and the transformation of the proud and independent republic into an ordinary coastal town and a future sea resort. Aware of the inevitability of changes brought about by modern times, V. nevertheless looks with sadness and nostalgia at the decline of Dubrovnik and at the disappearance of his own aristocratic class.

V.'s omnipresent lyricism, his sensitivity to music and color, his theatrical craftsmanship and readiness to experiment on the stage, his creation of a gallery of three-dimensional female characters, the detailed and explicit instructions for staging his plays (often longer than the actual dramatic text and an integral part of it), the local dialect saturated with Italianisms, and his nostalgic love for Dubrovnik and its patricians—these are some of the hallmarks associated with V. the playwright. And although his mediocre plays outnumber the truly outstanding ones, the latter secured for him a prominent place in Yugoslav dramatic literature.

FURTHER WORKS: *Perom i olovkom* (1884); *Ksanta* (1886; rev. ed., *Stari grijesi*, 1919); *Psyche* (1889); *Smrt Majke Jugovića* (1907); *Gospoda sa suncokretom: San mlatačke noći* (1912); *Lazarevo vaskresenje* (1913; *The Resurrection of Lazarus*, 1926); *Akordi* (1917); *Imperatrix: Misterija ostrva zaboravi* (1918); *Maškarate ispod kuplja* (1922); *Prolog nenapisane drame* (1929); *Sabrana djela* (3 vols, 1939–41); *Drame I. V.* (1962); *Pjesme; Pripovijetke; Drame* (1964)

BIBLIOGRAPHY: Venzelides, A., "The Plays of I. V.," *SEER*, 8 (1929): 368–74; Kadić, A., *Contemporary Croatian Literature* (1960): 27–30; Barac, A., *A History of Yugoslav Literature* (1973): 216–17

—BILJANA ŠLJIVIĆ-ŠIMŠIĆ

VOLPONI, Paolo

Italian novelist, poet, and essayist, b. 5 Feb. 1924, Urbino; d. Aug. 1994

V. is one of the most interesting and original writers to have emerged from the group around the experimental journal *Officina*. Both his upbringing in the small city of Urbino (with its beautiful surrounding countryside, which inspired his early lyrical and idyllic poetry) and his later experiences in the industrial areas of Ivrea and Turin (where he worked for Olivetti and later for Fiat, in the public relations department), recur as subjects in his writings. The lyrical and nostalgic feelings inspired by nature are frequently contrasted with alienating urban settings, particularly in the trilogy of novels consisting of *Memoriale* (1962; *My Troubles Began*, 1964), *La macchina mondiale* (1965; *The Worldwide Machine*, 1967), and *Corporale* (1975; corporeal).

Memoriale was widely praised as epitomizing the type of writing called "literature and industry" in the early 1960s. The novel's social and ideological dimensions received much greater attention than its more interesting and original psychological, linguistic, and structural techniques, such as its narrative in the form of a diary, which the protagonist, Saluggia, uses as self-therapy. Saluggia is the first of V.'s eccentric, at times almost pathological, rebels who provide a disturbing but lucid view of consumer society. He is afflicted by neuroses, a persecution complex, and numerous frustrations resulting from his inability to find in industry and society the "order" he seeks. Yet he struggles to prevent others from curing him of his sickness, because he feels that his real and imaginary diseases are his only private possessions. Saluggia's first-person narration reveals how he, like other of V.'s main characters, is trapped in an ambivalent relationship of love and hate, of attraction and repulsion, to industry, nature, and other people.

In *La macchina mondiale* the peasant-philosopher Crocioni ultimately rebels against a society that he had intended to improve. Because of his treatise, "The Academy of Friendship for Qualified People," based on his scientific and philosophic theories that men are "machines built by other men," Crocioni is considered insane and is rejected by his wife, fellow peasants, and society as a whole. As a result of these rebuffs, he first turns against nature, which he feels is responsible together with religion and politics, for keeping man from perfecting himself, and finally he commits suicide. V.'s unusual linguistic methods, as manifested in Crocioni's love for word associations and lists of words with particular visual and musical effects, help convey the tragedy of the protagonist, who believes in scientific progress but realizes that society is too tied to old ideas that proscribe total freedom.

Corporale is one of the most intricate Italian novels of the 1970s. Divided into four parts and written in alternating first-and third-person points of view, the work narrates the many unusual adventures of Gerolamo Aspri, who at times, in order to live—or act out—his neurotic fantasies, masquerades as the desperado Joaquín Murrieta (executed in California in 1853). Narcissism and other psychological elements—above all, the psychiatrist R. D. Laing's (b. 1927) theory of the "divided self" and Jacques Lacan's (1901–1981) treatment of the role of "desire" and of the "Other" in the formation of the "I"—are inherent in both the language and the structure of *Corporale*. In Aspri's sadomasochistic, master-slave relationship with the symbolic character Overath, Saluggia's and Crocioni's neuroses, complexes, and needs for order and freedom can be discerned. The novel ends with Aspri's almost fatal failure to build a nuclear bomb shelter near Urbino. The apocalyptic theme returns in the novel *Il pianeta irritabile* (1978; the irritable planet), in which a monkey, a midget, a duck, and an elephant are the sole survivors of a nuclear holocaust. *Il lanciatore di giavellotto* (1981; the javelin thrower), which won the Europe Prize, is a novel about a young athlete who discovers both sex and social pressure while preparing for a national track meet.

V. stimulates and often provokes his readers with his analysis of modern man torn between internal anxieties and a world that adds to the sense of alienation, making him more and more neurotic, paranoid, even schizophrenic.

FURTHER WORKS: *Il ramarro* (1948); *L'antica moneta* (1955); *Le porte dell'Appennino* (1960); *Il sipario ducale* (1975); *Poesie e poemetti 1946–1966* (1980)

BIBLIOGRAPHY: Pacifici, S., on *Memoriale, BA*, 36 (1962), 422; Pacifici, S., "Literary Trends and Books in Italy," *CBC*, 5, 1 (1962): 3–11; Rebay, L., on *La macchina mondiale, BA*, 40 (1966): 330; Capozzi, R., "The Narrator-Protagonist and the 'Divided-Self' in *Corporale*," *FI*, 10 (1976): 203–17; Capozzi, R., on *Il sipario ducale, BA*, 50 (1976): 383–84; Hutcheon, L., *Narcissistic Literature* (1980): 104–17

—ROCCO CAPOZZI

VONNEGUT, Kurt, Jr.

American novelist and short-story writer, b. 11 Nov. 1922, Indianapolis, Ind.

The youngest of three children of a second-generation Indiana architect and, on his mother's side, of a well-to-do midwestern brewing family, V. grew up in the Midwest, during the Depression era, a time that helped shape his philosophy of life and his fictional themes. Heeding his father's advice against studying architecture, V. majored in biochemistry at Cornell University from 1940 to 1943. Enlisting in the U.S. Army in 1943, he was taken prisoner in the Battle of the Bulge. Imprisoned in Dresden, Germany, he survived the Allied fire-bombing of that city. After the war, he studied for an M.A. in anthropology at the University of Chicago, but as with Cornell left without taking a degree. From 1947 to 1950 he worked in public relations for General Electric in Schenectady, N.Y. His first story was published in *Collier's* magazine in February 1950. For the next twelve years he supported a growing family by writing stories for slick magazines and science-fiction pulps, and paperback originals. In 1965, with five novels published but only one in print, and critically overlooked, V. had, for financial reasons, to take a job teaching creative writing at the University of Iowa, where he found himself for the first time in the company of other serious authors and so began to think self-consciously about the craft of writing. He received a Guggenheim Fellowship in 1967. Since 1971 he has lived in New York.

For roughly twenty years, from 1950 to 1970, V. led, much as his fictional alter ego Kilgore Trout, the anonymous life of a drug-store-rack writer of such ostensible science fiction and sociopolitical fables as *Player Piano* (1952), *The Sirens of Titan* (1959), and *Mother Night* (1962). With *Cat's Cradle* (1963) and *God Bless You, Mr. Rosewater* (1965) V. acquired an underground college following, and with the apocalyptic *Slaughterhouse-Five* (1969), given a lavish wide-screen, color filming, he surfaced to public notice, acclaim in *Time* and *Life* magazines, and television exposure. In 1970 his play *Happy Birthday, Wanda June* (1971) was produced in New York. Since then V. has become something of a guru, his utterances accorded reverent attention and his grizzled visage icon prominence. V.'s change in fortune coincided with the growth in academic respectability of the popular genres of science fiction, western tales, and detective stories; with the recognition that he is less a science fantasist restricted to space-age gimmickry than a wry commentator on mid-20th-c. man and society, who does not hesitate to use science-fiction techniques; and finally with the emergence of an important literary movement in the 1960s of

BLACK HUMOR numbering him among its principal practitioners. V. concluded this two-decade-long imaginative effort to come to terms with all aspects of life in middle America in the second half of the 20th c. with *Breakfast of Champions* (1973).

V. takes a pessimistic view of man as intransigently self-destructive. His quizzical position is that human creativity in this respect is endless, but the specters that preoccupy him are the familiar ones of this century: overpopulation, pollution, racism, commercial greed, automation, drugs, global war, and genocide. As V. tells it, man has created for himself an ersatz civilization that is electronically and chemically packaged and consumer-product oriented; and in the process he has mechanized himself into obsolescence, not unlike that planned by systems management for most products. Ecologically, humans live on a blasted and dying planet brought about by ruthless technological over-exploitation, and socially they maintain economic systems calculated to sustain unequal ownership and distribution of the earth's riches. Nor does V. believe that the future holds anything different. Given the constancy of human nature, nothing changes for better or for worse.

V.'s Ecclesiastian view of life is presented in a deceptively simple and artless manner that hides its own considerable artistry. Whimsical self-mockery is the most persistent tone; rarely is the voice allowed to be self-righteous, angry, or condemnatory. V. prefers to dilate informally on the comical absurdity of our actions rather than to lecture dogmatically point by point on our self-destructive tendencies. And his novels follow a comparable digressive ramble: they become progressively more loosely structured and inclusive and daringly heedless of maintaining the temporal and narrative conventions of fiction.

Not many readers took V. at his word when he announced at the end of *Breakfast of Champions* that, having exorcised the ghosts of his first half-century of life, he was freeing his characters from their fictional bondage to pursue lives of their own. And indeed, in his subsequent novels—*Slapstick; or, Lonesome No More* (1976), *Jailbird* (1979), and *Deadeye Dick* (1982)—V. has reneged on the promise he made his characters; if anything, he has stepped up his habit of recycling them through one fiction after another, although he may have curtailed his continuation and expansion of this practice for future stories, since he obliterated a goodly number of them in *Deadeye Dick* with the accidental explosion of a neutron bomb. Since *Breakfast of Champions*, V. has made his presence increasingly felt through his persona as author-narrator self-consciously moving the story. He has also taken to insinuating himself into the narrative directly as a full-fledged character and indirectly through projections of facets of his self into other of his fictive protagonists. This experimentation, along with what some have judged to be a falling off of V.'s creative imagination, characterized by self-parody, repetition of old themes, and hardening of narrative habits into mannerisms, has led other critics to divide V.'s novelistic career into two periods, with *Breakfast of Champions* marking both the end of the first and beginning of the second phase.

In his recent novels V. appears to be trying to find a positive view to convey of the world and of individuals. Women figure as a creative force more centrally than before. In both *Jailbird* and *Deadeye Dick* V. strives to transform the middle-class values and common experiences of ordinary life into modern fairy tales and, an equally difficult feat, to translate into fictional form the social and political course of American history in this century. At the same time, however, the loneliness—as well as the sacredness—of the human condition receives increased confirmation. V.'s commandments for a better world are quickly enumerated: honor the

Kurt Vonnegut, Jr.

Sermon on the Mount; stop exploiting and killing people; instead, be kind to everyone. In these edicts V. expresses an extreme and idealistic version of the midwestern middle-class values that nourished his Indiana boyhood. Similarly, his forthright, self-effacing, unadorned language is an implied rebuke of the double-speak that has assailed America from Joseph McCarthy to Richard Nixon.

Still, V.'s stories persist in archly refusing to confirm the efficacy of his homespun advice. They parody human faith not only in technology and capitalism but also in philanthropy, religion, social welfare, humanitarianism, and planned economy. Seemingly none of the myths, slogans, and fictions we live by are exempt from his satirical scrutiny. The smirk of his irreverence is directed at everything from the century's collective pursuit of self-destruction to the individual's modish quest for self-identity, from our national faith in firearms to his own personal hope in the regenerative and authenticating power of words. One cannot accuse V. of living the unexamined life—or of advocating it; his is clearly a genuine response to the horrors of our age. Yet after reading him, one is left with a moot question. Are his simplistic presentations of the nature of man and of the quality of 20th-c. life self-critical fables of a mind truly reflecting a universal vision of reality, or are they rather intellectually fuzzy and philosophically jejune attempts at making sense of a universe seemingly gone haywire because his response is limited to surface features? V. remains difficult to categorize: science fictionist, social satirist, fairy-tale fabulist, or slick-magazine sentimentalist? He is one or another of these at all times, without his ever quite disclosing which is the real V.

FURTHER WORKS: *Canary in a Cat House* (1961); *Welcome to the Monkey House* (1968); *Between Time and Timbuktu; or, Prometheus-5* (1972); *Wampeters, Foma & Granfallons: Opinions* (1974); *Sun Moon Star* (1980); *Palm Sunday* (1981); *Galapagos* (1985); *Bluebeard* (1987); *Hocus Pocus* (1990); *Timequake* (1997)

BIBLIOGRAPHY: special V. issue, *Crit*, 12 (1971); Tanner, T., *City of Words* (1971): 181–201; Goldsmith, D., *K. V.: Fantasist of Fire and Ice* (1972); Klinkowitz, J., and J. Somer, eds., *The V. Statement* (1973); Schulz, M. F., *Black Humor Fiction of the Sixties* (1973): 43–65; Schatt, S., *K. V., Jr.* (1976); Lundquist, J., *K. V., Jr.* (1976); Klinkowitz, J., and D. L. Lawler, eds., *V. in America: An Introduction to the Life and Work of K. V.* (1977); Scholes, R., *Fabulation and Metafiction* (1979): 156–62, 203–5; Klinkowitz, J., *K. V.* (1982)

—MAX F. SCHULZ

VOSKOVEC, Jiří (George)

Czechoslovak dramatist and song lyricist (writing in Czech), b. 19 June 1905, Sázava; d. 1 July 1981, Pearblossom, Calif., U.S.A.

WERICH, Jan

Czechoslovak dramatist and song lyricist (writing in Czech), b. 6 Feb. 1905, Prague; d. 31 Oct. 1980, Prague

V. and W. were university-educated non-professionals, still law students, when they became an overnight theatrical success in Prague with their *Vest Pocket Revue* (perf. 1927), which they wrote and performed in. Until the 1938 Munich crisis and the dismemberment of Czechoslovakia they were the extremely successful producers, playwrights, lyricists, and leading actors of their Liberated Theater in Prague. After spending the war years in the U.S. and unsuccessfully attempting to revive their theater after the war, V. and W. pursued separate acting careers in the U.S. and Prague, respectively.

Two halves of a single creative inspiration, V. and W. collaborated on over twenty-five full-length revues and plays with music, marked by zany farce and provocative sociopolitical satire.

The language of their scripts and lyrics ranged from slang and sophisticated multilingual punning to allusions drawn from classical myth, history, and international politics. Some of their most effective writing occurred in their song lyrics, which were often the equivalent of a parabasis (choral ode) in an Aristophanic comedy: witty, aggressive commentary on current issues.

The earliest works were purely revues, adaptations of existing plays, or lampoons of boulevard comedy. A subsequent group of works were called "jazz revues" because of their heavy dose of jazz music and an overall tone that caught the pulse of the post–World War I world, for example, *Sever proti jihu* (perf. 1930; north against south), *Don Juan & Comp.* (perf. 1931), and *Golem* (perf. 1931; golem). A number of significant political revues followed, chief among them being *Osel a stín* (perf. 1933; ass and shadow) and *Kat a blázen* (perf. 1934; executioner and fool), in which the growing threat of fascist dictatorship led to more tightly constructed plots and frontal attacks in dialogue and song on leading personalities and incidents of the era.

The ripest collaborations of V. and W. were comic-satiric plays with music rather than revues. The main thrust of *Balada z hadrů* (perf. 1935; rag ballad), *Rub a líc* (perf. 1936; heads or tails), and *Těžká Barbora* (perf. 1937; heavy Barbora) shifted from mockery to rallying cries for positive, cooperative action. Their final work, *Pěst na oko* (perf. 1938; a fist in the eye), recapitulated the antifascist themes of their previous productions within a matured, more complex version of the revue format.

The humanistic spirit and sophisticated wit of these two intellectual clowns, who were legends in their time, embodied the independence and adventurousness of the prewar First Republic during its brightest and also its darkest hours.

FURTHER WORKS: *Hry osvobozeného divadla* (4 vols., 1956–57); *Fata Morgana, a jiné hry* (1967)

BIBLIOGRAPHY: Burian, J. M., "The Liberated Theatre of V. and W.," *ETJ*, 29 (1977): 153–77

—JARKA M. BURIAN

VOYNOVICH, Vladimir Nikolaevich

Russian novelist, short-story writer, and dramatist, b. 26 Sept. 1932, Dushanbe, Russia (now Kazakhstan)

One of Russia's finest contemporary satirists, V. began writing during the Thaw of the 1960s. His formal education was limited to one and a half years at a pedagogical institute in Moscow. While in the Soviet army (1951–55), V. began writing poetry. In 1960 one of his songs became the unofficial "Anthem of Soviet Cosmonauts." His literary career soared after January 1961 with the publication of his novella "My zdes' zhyvem" (1961; "We Live Here," 1979) in the prestigious *Novyi Mir*. By the early 1970s, V. was recognized as a leading Soviet writer.

During the late 1960s and early 1970s V. became a fighter for human rights, gradually becoming a dissident. This process began after he signed letters defending Andrey SINYAVSKY and Yuly Daniel (1925-1988), and later Aleksandr SOLZHENITSYN; it continued when, in 1969, he published abroad the opening sections of *Zhizn i neobychainye prikliucheniia soldata Ivana Chonkina* (1975; rev. ed., 1990; *The Life and Extraordinary Adventures of Private Ivan Chonkin*, 1977), part of which had been circulating in *samizdar* since 1963. Finally, his 1973 letter satirizing the formation of the All-Union Authors' Rights Agency (VAPP) was perceived as an open challenge to the Soviet establishment. As a result, in 1974, he was expelled from the Union of Soviet Writers, officially "for actions defaming the title of Soviet Citizen." His name became anathema, his books were banned, and he was subject to constant KGB harassment. In 1980 V. was forced to leave the Soviet Union, emigrating to West Germany. The following year he was stripped of Soviet citizenship and proclaimed an "enemy of the people."

In exile V. has taught at Princeton University, been a fellow of the Kennan Institute in Washington, D.C., and lectured widely in the West. Since glasnost, all of his works have been published in Russia and his plays performed in Moscow and other cities of the former Soviet Union. In 1990 he was fully rehabilitated: his citizenship was restored, he was given an apartment in Moscow, and he received an official apology from the Writer's Union. He currently resides in both Moscow and Munich. Since returning to

Russia he has written several books and numerous articles, including a fictitious autobiography. He has become one of the most popular writers in Russia, and is a public figure, appearing frequently on Russian radio and television. His film, based on the novel *Life and Extraordinary Adventures of Private Ivan Chonkin*, has added to his fame. In 1994 V. began painting, has had a number of exhibitions of his work, and is now known as both artist and writer. In 1997 he received the much coveted "Triumph Literary Award," presented to him "for a lifetime of acheivement in Russian letters."

V.'s early works published in *Putem vzaimnoi perepiski* (1979; *In Plain Russian*, 1979) are brutally realistic portrayals of life in rural Russia, set in villages, collective farms, and provincial towns, during the 1950s and 1960s. His characters are poorly educated, rootless, isolated, and lonely peasants, town dwellers, workers, and soldiers. He exposes the moral and spiritual poverty, the atrophy of imagination and vision, and their boredom, hardships, and gray existence.

A brilliant satirist, V. uses grotesque imagery, caricature, and exaggeration to ridicule and describe an incongruous and incredible world in which all moral and ethical values are turned upside down. This talent is best revealed in his picaresque novel *Zhizn' i neobychainye prikliucheniia soldata Ivana Chonkina*. It is a hilarious attack on the sacred cows of the Soviet system: the NKVD (later KGB), the Soviet Red Army, collectivization, Lysenkovism, and even the morality of a society in which a little girl, when asked by Chonkin whom she loves better, "her mother or her father," replies: "Comrade Stalin!" V. views the world through the naive eyes of Ivan Chonkin who, like the proverbial Russian fairytale hero Ivan the fool, sees objects in their primary, unsophisticated, and defamiliarized sense. *Pretendent na prestol* (1979; rev. ed., 1990; *Pretender to the Throne*, 1981) continues Chonkin's adventures and misadventures. Set in a Soviet prison and under Nazi occupation, it is even more bitter, somber, and grotesque.

Many of V.'s works are permeated by strong autobiographical elements. This is particularly true of *Ivan'kiada* (1976; *The Ivankiad*, 1977), *Antisovetskii Sovetskii Soiuz* (1985; *The Anti-Soviet Soviet Union*, 1986), and *Moskva 2042* (1986; rev. ed., 1990; *Moscow 2042*, 1987). His works give clear insight into *homus sovieticus*. *Ivan'kiada* is an autobiographical account of V.'s trials and tribulations during his purchase of a larger apartment. In this Kafkaesque world, V. lashes out at the official Soviet writers' establishment with its system of privileges. He paints a vivid portrait of the talentless party apparatchik Ivanko, who upon becoming a diplomat uses his position to amass material goods, especially the legendary blue diamond-studded American toilet, on which, in a surreal, fantasmagoric nightmare, Ivanko charges through a brick wall into V.'s apartment. In this work, Ivanko, a concrete, living figure, is transformed into a monster threatening the individual writer. Ivanko becomes a symbol of Soviet society and a metaphor for the whole system.

Antisovetskii Sovetskii Soiuz consists of essays, stories, parables, "fairy tales," vignettes, and anecdotes presenting a composite picture of various aspects of life, especially private lives, in the Soviet Union of the 1960s, 1970s, and 1980s. In *Shapka* V. again attacks and satirizes hack writers, the Soviet literary establishment, and the Union of Soviet Writers. Like Gogol in "The Overcoat," he uses clothing as a status symbol and form of identity.

Moskva 2024 has been called a parody of George ORWELL's *1984* (1949) and has been compared to the works of Gogol and Andrey BELY. Antiutopian, it is a dystopia in which V. describes a future Soviet Union as a bankrupt, demoralized, and disintegrated country. Moscowrep (The Moscow Republic) is all that remains. The novel's protagonist, the exiled writer Kartsev (modeled on V. himself), travels through time and returns to his native Moscow in 2042, sixty years into the future, after the Great August Revolution (an eerie, clairvoyant depletion of August 1991 reality). V.'s humor and satire spares nothing and no one, including the inefficient Soviet system with its inability to make anything work. He criticizes the writers' establishment, and individual writers, both in the Soviet Union and abroad. He singles out Solzhenitsyn, whom he attacks as Karnavalov (later, Czar Serafim) for his anti-Western attitudes, reactionary views, and monarchist longings. This time, V.'s comments are not limited to the Soviet Union but include his own impressions of the West, and observations of other contemporary Soviet dissident émigré writers.

Since his rehabilitation and return to Russia V. published his *Zamysel: avtibiograficheskii roman* (1995; Inkling; An Autobiographical Novel). Popular among Russian readers, it became a best–seller. Conceived as an autobiography, it is a mixture of stories, autobiographical facts, fiction, reflections on life, and comments on some of his fictitious characters. In 1990 he published *Nulevoi reshenie* (Zero decision), in 1994 *Delo N. 34840* (Case number 34840). The latter is an autobiographical work based on his experience with the KGB in which he recounts his interrogation, both at the Lubianka prison, and later that year at the Metropole Hotel. In 1994 he also published *Russkoe bogatstvo, zhurnal odnogo avtora* (The Russian treasure: A journal by one author).

Between 1993 and 1995 V. published the first edition of his collected works, *Maloe sobranie sochinenii v 5 tomakh* (A small collection of works in 5 volumes). It includes almost all of his works written and published in the Soviet Union, as well as those in "tamizdat," in exile, and in Russia following his rehabilitation and return. This collection included V.'s major works, *Life and Extraordinary Adventures of Private Ivan Chonkin* and *Pretender to the Throne*. Since 1990 four editions have been reprinted in Russian and two in English. In 1997 he published *Skazki dlia vzroslykh* (Fairy tales for adults), and a collection of short stories, *Zapakh shokolada* (The smell of chocolate). During this period he also published a number of other short stories and articles, including several dealing with "the New Russians." V.'s works continue to be popular in Russia and other European countries, especially Germany, Italy, and France.

V. has earned his place in the canon of Russian satirical literature, alongside GOGOL, Mikhail ZOSHCHENKO, and Vladimir MAYAKOVSKY. A great satirist, he portrays an accurate picture of the world through a distorted, exaggerated, and skewed vision. He strips pretensions and verbal falsehood from words, presents things for what they really are, and makes us laugh. V.'s work is distinguished by moral integrity, honesty, and unwillingness to compromise his beliefs.

FURTHER WORKS: *My zdes' zhivem* (1963); *Povesti* (1972); *Stepen' doveriia* (1972); *Tribunal* (1986); *Shapka* (1988; *The Fur Hat*, 1989); *Khochu byt' chestnym* (1989); *Fiktivnyi brak* (1991)

BIBLIOGRAPHY: Szporluk, M., "V. V.: The Development of a New Satirical Voice," *RLT*, 14 (1976): 99–121; Hosking, G., *Beyond Socialist Realism: Soviet Fiction since Ivan Denisovich* (1980): 136–54, 243–46; Kasak, W., "V. and His Undesirable Satires," *AN*, 2 (1980): 305; Porter, R. C., "V. V. and the Comedy of Innocence,"

FMLS, 16 (1980): 97–108; Brown, E. J., *Russian Literature since the Revolution*, rev. ed. (1982): 365–70; Dunlop, J., ed., "V. V.'s Pretender to the Throne," in K. M. Brostrom, ed., *Russian Literature and American Critics* (1984); Starr, S. F., on *The Anti-Soviet Soviet Union, NYTBR*, 31 Aug. 1986: 5; Fanger, D., "Back to the Future," *PR*, 56, 3 (1989): 499–504; Baley, J., on *The Fur Hat, NYRB*, 3 (1990): 26; Ryan-Hayes, K., "Decoding the Dream in the Satirical Works of V. V.," *SEEJ*, 34, 3 (Fall 1990): 289–307; Rancour-Laferriere, D., "From Incompetence to Satire: V.'s Image of Stalin as Castrated Leader of the Soviet Union in 1941," *SlavR*, 50, 1 (Spring 1991): 36–47; Ryan-Hayes, K., "V.'s *Moskva 2042* as Literary Parody," *RCSCSPL*, 35, 4 (Nov. 1994): 453–80; Lewis, B., "Homunculi Sovetici: The Soviet Writers in V.'s *Shapka*," *ASEES*, 10, 1 (1996): 17–27; Khan, H., "Folklore and Fairy Tale Elements in V. V.'s Novel *The Life and the Extraordinary Adventures of Private Ivan Chonkin*," *SEEJ*, 40, 3 (Fall 1996): 494–518; Beraha, L., "The Fixed Fool: Raising and Resisting Picaresque Mobility in V.'s Conkin Novels," *SEEJ*, 40, 3 (Fall 1996): 475–93

—HELEN SEGALL

VOZNESENSKY, Andrey

Russian poet, b. 12 May 1933, Moscow

After spending the World War II years with his mother in the Urals, V. returned to Moscow, took up painting, and enrolled in the Moscow Institute of Architecture; he left in 1957, before graduating. That same year he met Boris PASTERNAK, whom he considers the greatest personal influence on him. Some of V.'s poems appeared the following year in *Literaturnaya gazeta* and met with instant success. His first two collections were published in 1960, the year he made his first visit to the U.S.

In the late 1950s the Soviet public came to regard poetry as the most effective medium for articulating and sorting out the moral, psychological, and social complexities of the post-Stalin era, and large crowds attended V.'s masterful readings of his modernistic, emotionally accessible verses. Yet he polarized the opinion of the Russian reading public and critics more than any other poet.

V.'s approach to poetry consistently shows a studied ambivalence of values. Metaphors with multiple connotations produce hints that may or may not be intended; jarring images negate overtly stated meanings. V.'s advocates argue that the ambivalences are consistent enough to serve as a dialectical path toward his main goal of "reaching the essence of things" and of making the reader intuit the truth among the multiple semantic layers. V. is extremely generous with startling metaphors for data that are quite trivial, but the same trivia serve as targets for his satire and as symbols of his own ordinariness, creating the effect of a folksy frankness. His thoughts are never sustained, but are fragmented, via similes, into highly vivid sensations. The disparateness of the sensations portrays the complexity of perceptions and implies an authenticity of experience. The main object is the display of the sensitivity and the mental bravado of the persona.

Underneath all the digressions, a network of rather safe values forms a small circle of recurrent themes. V. is an active participant, not an observer of life, for "man is the maker of history." The resultant moral maximalism at times strains the credibility of the lyricist, but it forms a part of his youthful will to identify both

himself and the reader with the giants of art and with humanity. V.'s moral criteria are derived from nature, motherland, compassion, and labor. Settings are used not as still-lives or as background for action but as symbols whose recall affects the moral formation of the lyrical hero. Encounters with nature yield the notion of motherland. Remaining history also helps to promote his national awareness—a criterion of his poetic conscience. The notion of Russia often merges with the image of a suffering woman. The tragic price she pays for love or for just being a woman becomes one of his major themes. In "Monolog Merilin Monro" (1964; "Monologue of Marilyn Monroe," 1966) it assumes a cosmic relevance involving also the exploiters-versus-artist motif.

The long poem "Mastera" (1960; craftsmen) finds its source in folklore. In it V. sees the creative power and joy of hard work of the people, and their revolt against the oppression of individual creativity by tyrants. It is not said whether or not the hated "barbarians of all times" include any of the current domestic officials; their system is never condemned. His collections include poems devoted to Lenin, and his own country is praised.

V.'s trips abroad inspired curiosity about new angles of vision. In his poems, Western man, on the verge of being devoured by machines and by soulless commercialism, resorts to sleazy entertainment. Hippies express a genuine if ineffective protest against dehumanization. On the other hand, space age technology, an extension of the human mind, reflects that mind in new ways.

V. designates his mixed genres as "lyrical reportage." Until the mid-1970s, his "long poems" were broken up into many sections, presenting a loosely associated series of digressions of various lengths. And the digressions themselves seldom feature a coherent discourse or a continuous line by which the colorful bits of information are strung together. But such paucity of narrative organization is compensated for by expressiveness of language. Varied rhythmic and graphic organization of verse, internal rhyming, imagery couched in unusually vivid colors, and bold metaphors distinguish his style, which resurrects that of the prerevolutionary MODERNISTS. V.'s irreverent diction and graphic displays derive from the early work of Vladimir MAYAKOVSKY, the density of metaphors from early Pasternak, the stressing of latent meanings within words and the free rhyming from Velemir KHLEBNIKOV, and the whimsical intonational lunges from Marina TSVETAEVA. V. does not surpass the older masters, but he is the only officially published Russian in recent times who seeks to combine modernist devices with current experiences.

Despite his rhythmical virtuosity and a broad metrical spectrum, V. has introduced no new meters into Russian versification. Free verse is rare, although fusing of poetry and prose is not. But when the aural and visual images seem to converge, as in the poem "Ya Goya" (1959; "I Am Goya," 1964), they evoke a deeper meaning than does the lexical denotation of the words.

Heightened expressiveness of details and lowered cohesiveness of their organization cause a major shift in levels of communication. The thematic weight switches from text to subtext. Such a shift often causes problems for official censorship, and it is on the level of subtext that V. has received most of the favorable and unfavorable attention.

V. was among the contributors to *Metropol* (1979; *Metropol*, 1983), a collection of various writings published abroad, which had been rejected by Soviet censorship. He seems, however, to have escaped any of the serious sanctions applied to the main participants. In 1981 the rock musical *Avos*—based on V.'s poem originally titled *Povest pod parusami* (1971; *Story under Full Sail*,

1974) but retitled *Avos* (1972; Avos [the name of a ship], also meaning "perchance")—was staged at the Lenin Komsomol Theater in Moscow. Set in the early 19th c., it combines rock music with Russian religious and seafaring chants.

With the collection *Soblazn* (1979; temptation), V. chose a new and a more difficult poetic course; the poems are marked by economy of metaphor, metrical and stanzaic regularity, stricter rhyming, and a restrained vocabulary. The pretense of political import is absent. It remains to be seen if V. will cultivate this more subtle distinctiveness.

FURTHER WORKS: *Mozaika* (1960); *Parabola* (1960); *Treugolnaya grusha* (1962); *Pishetsya kak lyubitsa* (1962); *Antimiry* (1964; *Antiworlds*, 1966); *Akhillesovo serdtse* (1966); *Moy lyubovny dnevik* (1966); *Ten zvuka* (1970); *Vypusti ptitsu* (1975); *Dubovy list violonchelny* (1975); *Vitraznykh del master* (1976). FURTHER WORKS IN ENGLISH: *Selected Poems of A. V.* (1964); *V.: Selected Poems* (1964); *Antiworlds and The Fifth Ace* (1967, bilingual); *Dogalypse* (1972); *Nostalgia for the Present* (1978)

BIBLIOGRAPHY: Blake, P., and M. Hayward, Introduction, *Antiworlds and The Fifth Ace* (1967): xiii–xxiii; Bailey, J., "The Verse of A. V. as an Example of Present-Day Russian Versification," *SEEJ*, 17 (1973): 155–73; Jones, W. G., "A Look Around: The Poetry of A. V.," in E. J. Brown, ed., *Major Soviet Writers* (1973): 178–92; Thomson, R. D. B., "A. V.: Between Pasternak and Mayakovsky," *SEER*, 54 (1976): 41–59; Brown, D., "'Loud' and 'Quiet' Poetry of the Nineteen Sixties," *Papers in Slavonic Philology*, No. 2 (1977): 19–26; Gladilin, A., *The Making and Unmaking of a Soviet Writer* (1979), passim; James, C., "V.'s Case," *NYRB* (16 August 1979): 14–17; Mickiewicz, D., "On the Art of Linguistic Opportunism," *RusL*, 8 (1980): 553–78

—DENIS MICKIEWICZ

VŨ HOÀNG CHƯƠNG

Vietnamese poet and dramatist, b. 5 May 1916, Nam-định; d. 7 Sept. 1976, Saigon

One of the most active and prolific poets of modern Vietnam, French-educated in Nam-định, then Hanoi, V. H. C. studied law and worked as a railroad inspector before starting to write poetry in 1939, with his first collection published as *Thơ say* (1940; drunk poetry). People have dubbed him Vietnam's Li Po since his verse revealed someone drunk with alcohol, with music and songs, with unrequited love, with opium, and with Western dancing. In his youth V. H. C. switched to science studies, but quit early to publish his second collection, *Thơ mây* (1943; cloud poetry). He also authored the play *Trương Chi* (1944: *Trương Chi*, the boatman). In the early days of the resistance war against the French, he continued his productivity with *Thơ lửa* (1947; poetry of fire), appearing in the Maquis. While being a schoolteacher between 1950 and 1953, he produced two new plays in verse, before moving to the south when the Geneva armistice agreements brought about the partition of Vietnam in 1954. The first collection of poems that appeared in South Vietnam was *Rừng phong* (1954; autumnal forest), followed by *Hoa đăng* (1959; flowered lantern). The public thinks a great deal of *Cảm-thông* (1960; communion). A man of delicate health, V. H. C. represented South Vietnam at the 4e

Biennale Internationale de Poésie in Knokke-le-Zoute, Belgium, in 1959, and at meetings of P.E.N. International in Thailand (1964), Yugoslavia (1965), and Ivory Coast (1967).

His favorite themes were romantic love, alcohol, and opium, and his writings between 1940 and 1945 showed a mixture of classicism and MODERNISM. A carefully polished style continued to characterize the later creations of this bard of the prewar period, during which his poems already expressed some degree of weariness typical of his contemporaries. In later decades, when he was also a part-time teacher of Vietnamese literature, his poetry breathed more optimism in the stabilized atmosphere of anticommunist South Vietnam, which enabled all literary talents to execute long and exacting projects. Many of the poems of this period dealt with historical events, notably *Bài ca bình Bắc* (epic of the northern pacification), a narrative poem that praised the military talent of Nguyễn Huê and his victory over the Chinese Ch'ing in 1789. V. H. C. philosophically wondered about "all the question marks that completely encircle a human life."

In the early 1970s he turned away from politics and concentrated on his childhood love, Zen, the flame of Buddhist mercy, and indulged in playfully rearranging Nguyễn Du's (1765–1820) words in *Đoạn-trường Tân-thanh* (n.d.; *The Tale of Kieu*, 1983), as well as his own melodious words into twenty-eight-word sentences. In an interview in 1970 he said he was waiting for his death, and even contemplated suicide. "I no longer write poetry, and even if I write something, there will be no reader." Nobody believed him then, as South Vietnam had been offering the refugee writers and artists freedom, security, prosperity, and hope.

Arrested on 13 May 1976, more than a year after the fall of Saigon, V. H. C. died shortly after his release from Chí-Hoà prison. Overseas Vietnamese audiences still consider him their greatest poet, one whose subjectivity and sensuality are illustrated by means of metrical coherence and musical cadence.

FURTHER WORKS: *Mây* (1943); *Tâm-sự kẻ sang Tần* (1961); *Tâm-tình ngươi đẹp* (1961), pub. in French as *Les 28 étoiles*); *Trời một Phương* (1962); *Thi-tuyển* (1963, pub. in French as *Poèmes choisis*); *Ánh trăng đạo* (1966); *Bút nở hoa đàm* (1967); *Cành mai trắng mộng* (1968); *Ta đã làm chi đời ta* (n.d.)

BIBLIOGRAPHY: Bùi Xuân-Bào, *Le roman vietnamien contemporain* (1972): 270, 312–13; Nguyễt;-Trần Huân, "The Literature of Vietnam, 1954–1973," in Tham Seong Chee, ed., *Essays on Literature and Society in Southeast Asia* (1981): 337; Durand, M. M., and Nguyễn-Trần Huân, *An Introduction to Vietnamese Literature* (1985): 171–72 and passim

—DINH-HOA NGUYEN

VURGUN, Samed

Azerbaijani poet and dramatist, b. 21 Mar. 1906, Salakhli; d. 27 May 1956, Baku

Although trained as a teacher, V. by 1930 had decided to make writing his career. Beginning in 1934 he held high positions in the Writers' Union and the Communist Party, and in 1956 the title of National Poet of Azerbaijan was bestowed upon him.

V.'s early verse deviated sharply from the civic poetry promoted by the Communist Party, as he oscillated between radical modernism and the folk tradition. By 1930, when his first volume of poems, *Shairin andy* (the poet's vow), appeared, he had abandoned his "artistic wanderings" and had decided on "timely" themes as his subject matter and realism as his primary mode of expression.

V.'s mature poetry is a summons to transform society and glorifies the common man. The drive to collectivize the countryside and build the industrial base of socialism are therefore major themes. The long poem "Mugan" (1949; Mugan) is typical. It chronicles the metamorphosis of a desolate valley into a bountiful commonwealth. Yet, the changes that occur are not merely economic. The very process of socialist construction expands the human spirit, as in the unfinished epic "Komsomol poemacy" (1930 ff.; the Komsomol [Communist youth movement] poem) and "Basti" (1937; Basti), where the new Soviet man, optimistic and master of his own fate, comes to life. Love of country is rarely absent, achieving its most sustained expression in "Azerbaijan" (1935; Azerbaijan). Here and elsewhere the reader is continually reminded that the homeland is secure only within the greater Soviet family of peoples.

After World War II V. wrote much political poetry. He also returned to the realistic epic in his long novel in verse, *Aigun* (1952; Aigun), which describes the momentous social changes of postwar Azerbaijan through a sensitive psychological portrayal of an individual family.

V. wrote several plays in verse, all on subjects drawn from the early or recent history of Azerbaijan. His poetic masterpiece is *Vagif* (1938; Vagif), which is based on the life on the 18th-c. Azerbaijani poet and statesman Molla Panah Vagif (1717–1797). In it he rearranges history to create a romantic hero who identifies himself completely with the national and social aspirations of his people. A Bolshevik worker is the hero of *Khanlar* (1939; Khanlar), which is set in the time of the Russian Revolution. Although highly praised at the time, it bears the impress of the Stalinist cult of personality.

Although most of V.'s mature poems deal with themes that were the order of the day, their clear, harmonious language, enriched by the vernacular and by folk poetry, raises him above the crowd of lesser poets who, like him, were obliged to pay their dues to a totalitarian system.

FURTHER WORKS: *Izbrannye sochinenia* (Russian tr.: 2 vols., 1958); *Eserleri* (6 vols., 1960–72)

BIBLIOGRAPHY: Brands, H. W., "Aspekte der aserbaidschanischen Gegenwartsliteratur," *WI*, 8 (1963): 178–84

—KEITH HITCHINS

VYNNYCHENKO, Volodymyr

Ukrainian dramatist, novelist, short-story writer, and philosopher, b. 27 July 1880, Velyky Kut; d. 6 Mar. 1951, Mougins, France

Born into a poor peasant family, V. had a difficult childhood. After finishing grammar school in his hometown, he attended secondary school in Elizavetgrad (now Kirovograd), a city whose cultural environment was Russian-dominated. He reacted sharply and often even violently to all forms of discrimination on the part of his teachers and fellow students who harassed him because of his origins. Despite these difficulties, V. completed his secondary education and enrolled in 1901 at the University of Kiev, where he founded a clandestine Ukrainian student organization. His repeated arrests by the tsarist regime and his continued exposure to suffering and injustice radicalized V.'s thinking, honed his socialist views, and strengthened his personal commitment to revolutionary activities. In 1902 V. joined the Revolutionary Ukrainian Party. In 1917–19 he played a leading role in the government of the short-lived Ukrainian People's Republic; following its demise he spent the rest of his life in exile, mostly in southern France.

V. is the only Ukrainian dramatist whose plays were regularly performed in the theaters of Western Europe. He began his literary career, however, as a short-story writer; his first collections, *Povisty i opovidannya* (1903; novellas and stories) and *Krasa i syla, i inshi opovidannya* (1906; beauty and strength, and other tales), whose main subject is Ukrainian village life, established his reputation as a powerful, original writer. His early fiction is often characterized by thematic contrasts, as in the short story "Chudny epizod" (1902; "A Strange Episode," 1973), in which the universal beauty of art is juxtaposed with the ugliness and depravity of prostitution.

In his major works of fiction, such as the novels *Holota* (1905; the mob) and *Chesnist z soboyu* (1906; honesty with oneself), V. advocated the right of the individual to live according to the dictates of his own intelligence and conscience. In the process of writing these works, V. formulated a theory of "inner harmony" and happiness, which culminated in a philosophical system known as "concordism." The novel *Zapysky kyrpatoho Mefistofelya* (1917; notes of the pug-nosed Mephistopheles) explores the abnormal psychology of a degenerate revolutionary; in the science-fiction novel *Sonyashna mashyna* (1928; the sun machine) he invents a panacea for the ills of mankind. In his later fiction, such as the novel *Nova zapovid* (1950; the new commandment) and the posthumously published *"Slovo za toboyu, Staline!"* (1971; "take the floor, Stalin!"), V. attempted to postulate a synthesis of communism and socialism based on voluntary collectivism without state control.

V.'s international reputation rests primarily on his plays. His first, *Dysharmonia* (1906; disharmony), is about the revolution of 1905. Here, as in *Chesnist z soboyu*, V. deals with the conflict between the individual and society and espouses a violent individualism. In *Velyky Molokh* (1907; the great Moloch) man's dependence on society is assailed. In his later plays dealing with revolutions, such as *Mizh dvokh syl* (1919; between two powers), V. analyzes the Ukraine's struggle with Russia and depicts the spiritual conflicts in the Ukrainian soul. *Chorna pantera i bily vedmid* (1918; black panther and white bear) and *Brekhnya* (1925; the lie), however, are free from ideological and political motifs and deal exclusively with human psychology and personal tragedy.

V.'s work was banned by the Soviets for his pro-Ukrainian stand and has been shunned by Ukrainian nationalists for his socialist views. Nevertheless, it is today gaining in popularity, primarily through the efforts of the literary historian Hryhory Kostiuk in the U.S.

FURTHER WORKS: *Shchabli zhyttya* (1907); *Chuzhi lyudy* (1909); *Tretya knyzhka opovidan* (1910); *Na prystani ta ynshe* (1914); *Bozhky* (1914); *Tvory* (9 vols., 1915); *Bilya mashyny: Opovidanye* (1916); *Bazar: Pyesa na chotyry rozdily* (1918); *Panna Mara* (1918); *Khochu* (1919); *Tvory* (11 vols., 1919); *Hrikh* (1920); *Vidrodzennya natsiyi* (3 vols., 1920); *Zapovit batkiv* (1922); *Zakon* (1923); *Na toy bik* (1924); *Povorot na Ukrayinu* (1926); *Tvory* (23 vols., 1926–29); *Promin sontsya* (1927); *Kuplya* (1927); *Velyky sekret* (1928); *Chad* (1929); *Pisnya Izrayilya* (1930); *Pered novym etapom: Nashi pozytsiyi* (1938); *Rozlad i pohodzennya: Vidpovid moyim prykhylnykam i neprykhylnykam* (1948); *Shchodennyk* (Vol. I, 1980); *Poklady zolota* (1988); *Sonyachna mashyna* (1989); *Zapovit bortsyam za vyzvolennya* (1991). **FURTHER WORKS IN ENGLISH:** *Selected Short Stories* (1991); *A New Commandment* (1992)

BIBLIOGRAPHY: Mihailovich, V. D., et al., eds., *Modern Slavic Literatures* (1976), Vol. II: 526–29; Czajkowskyj, M., "V. V. and His Mission to Moscow and Kharkiv," *JUkGS*, 3, 2 (1978): 3–24; Bojko-Blochyn, J., *Gegen den Strom: Ausgewählte Beiträge zur Geschichte der slavischen Literaturen* (1979): 315–26

—LEONID RUDNYTZKY

VYSOTSKY, Vladimir

Russian poet, b. 25 Jan. 1938, Moscow; d. 25 July 1980, Moscow

Adored by millions of his compatriots, V. was the closest the Soviet Union has ever come to producing a genuine superstar. His extraordinary popularity as a poet-bard cut across all class lines to encompass laborers, truck drivers, soldiers, and students as well as prominent public figures. V. was born in Moscow, the child of a career military officer and translator of German. After spending the war years in evacuation in Orenburg with his mother, in 1947 V. joined his father and stepmother in occupied Germany. Two years later, V. returned to Moscow, where he finished school and entered an engineering-construction institute. But his interests lay elsewhere, and a year later, in 1957, he left the institute and entered the Moscow Art Theater School-Studio to study acting. Upon graduation V. worked in several Moscow theaters before joining the newly reorganized Taganka Theater under the leadership of Yuri Lyubimov. V. made his formal debut at the Taganka in 1964, in Lermontov's *A Hero of Our Time*. Two years later, at twenty-eight, V. played the title role in Bertolt BRECHT's *The Life of Galileo*. Despite his coarse features and unimposing stature, V.'s bold interpretation of the great Italian astronomer established him almost overnight as one of the most promising young actors in the Soviet theater. V. Continued to perform at the Taganka until his death, always bringing to each role his unique combination of raw vigor and audacity. As the runaway convict Khlopush in the Taganka's production in 1967 of *Pugachev*, Sergey YESENIN's verse drama about the Pugachev uprising, the hard-drinking actor seemed to become one with the character. His other major roles in the 1970s included a guitar-playing hippie Hamlet, Lopakhin in *The Cherry Orchard*, and Svidrigailov in *Crime and Punishment*.

V. also worked as a film and television actor, appearing in more than thirty films and videos during his twenty-year career. He played a wide variety of roles, from mountain climber to Don Juan, frequently appearing with his guitar, singing ballads he himself had composed. V.'s first major role was as a wireless operator in *Vertical* (1967; vertical). Among his other roles were the geologist Maxim in *Kira Muratova's Korotkie vstrechy* (1967; brief encounters), a White Guard lieutenant in *Sluzhili dva tovarishcha* (1968; two comrades served), and the lead in the spy thriller *Chetvortyl* (1972; the fourth man).

But for all his popularity as an actor, it was as a poet and author of some 800 songs that V. won the hearts of his countrymen.

Begrudgingly tolerated but never officially recognized, during his lifetime V. saw the publication in his homeland of only fifteen of his songs and one of his poems. Yet in spite of the fact that his performances were never televised or heard on the radio, his fame rapidly spread to the farthest reaches of the Soviet Union. By the time of his death in 1980, he had become a national hero, a singer loved by people from all walks of life. V. traveled extensively throughout the country performing in factories and clubs, as well as at more formal concerts, none of which were ever publicly advertised. Tapes of his songs made by loyal fans were endlessly copied and circulated, so that his gravelly voice could be heard everywhere coming through open windows and sounding from the cabs of trucks and passing taxis.

V.'s success as a poet-bard rested largely on his ability to convey in his verses the reality of everyday life in the vernacular, often ironic language of the street. Saturated in metaphors, lyrics such as his "Okhota na volki" (the wolf hunt) reflected the fears and the yearnings of his fellow citizens. He sang of average people worn down by endlessly waiting in lines and mocked the privileged elite with access to special stores. He satirized phony veterans, their chests full of medals, and the mouthings of pompous bureaucrats. His songs of wartime heroes and ordinary soldiers were so vivid that his listeners were convinced he had served in the military; equally graphic were his "criminal songs," leading many to believe that he had served time in a labor camp.

V. was an individualist to the core. His extravagant life-style, particularly after his marriage to the French film actress Marina Vlady in 1969, only added to his stature as a folk hero. A hard drinker given to periodic binges and a wild driver, V. seemed to invite an early death, even prefiguring it in his many songs in which the hero rushes headlong toward his death. Worn down by alcohol, narcotics, and exhaustion, the forty-two-year-old V. died in a Moscow hospital of a heart attack on 25 July 1980.

Not since the death of Stalin did Moscow see such an outpouring of mourners as it did when word spread of V.'s death. On the day of his funeral, tens of thousands of people filled the streets around the Taganka Theater and along the highway leading to the cemetery. Since his death, thousands of ordinary citizens daily visit his grave in Bagankovskoe Cemetery to pay homage to the poet who "gave voice to his generation." Denied official recognition during his lifetime, V. has been posthumously canonized by the state, an irony he himself would have appreciated. In 1987, on the seventieth anniversary of the Revolution, V. was awarded the U.S.S.R. State Prize, the country's highest cultural honor. Currently, in addition to a steady stream of articles, books, recordings, and documentaries, plans are also under way to establish a museum in his honor.

FURTHER WORKS: *Nerv* (1981); *Pesmi i stikhi* (2 vols., 1983); *Chetyre chetverti puti* (1988); *Ya, konechno, vernus'* . . . (1988); *Chetyre vechera s V. V.: po motivarn televizionnoi peredachi* (1989)

BIBLIOGRAPHY: Smith, G. S., "V. V.," *Songs to Seven Strings* (1984): 145–79; Valdy, M., *Vladimir ou le vol arrâté* (1987); Sosin, G., and G. D. Sosin, "Moscow Coopts V.," *The New Leader*, 71 (22 February 1988): 13–24; Lazarski, C., "V. V. and His Cult," *RR*, 51 (January 1992): 58–71

—ALMA H. LAW

WAIN, John

English novelist, poet, essayist, and critic, b. 14 Mar., 1925, Stoke-on-Trent; d. 24 May 1994

Son of a dentist, W. was educated at a local grammar school and at St. John's College, Oxford. There he met two recent graduates who were aspiring writers, Kingsley AMIS and Philip LARKIN (qq.v.); the three of them became the nucleus of the "Movement" or the "Angry Young Men," a group that came to prominence in the 1950s. Seedy as their own postwar world was, they preferred confronting it with the honest realism of a George ORWELL to retreating into a private world and inventing a private language, as they thought the great modernists like James JOYCE, T. S. ELIOT, and Virginia WOOLF had done: literature should be public and accessible. Some of their ideas found expression in *Mandrake*, a little magazine that W. coedited from 1945 to 1947, the year when he became lecturer in English at the University of Reading. The Movement really came to popular notice, however, through a series of radio broadcasts W. made in 1953 called "First Reading."

In that same year he introduced a new type of unheroic hero—soon to be widely imitated—in his first novel, *Hurry on Down* (Am., *Born in Captivity*). Charles Lumley, on leaving Oxford, does not try to climb the ladder of success but goes down in the world, in Orwellian fashion. Trying to avoid being trapped in the sticky web of middle-class gentility, he begins a series of picaresque adventures, as window cleaner, dope peddler, hospital attendant, and gag writer for a radio show; eventually he has to compromise and make his peace with society. The novels that followed in quick succession—*Living in the Present* (1955), *The Contenders* (1958), and *A Travelling Woman* (1959)—similarly mingle a satiric vision with a strain of down-to-earth morality; they only made it seem, however, that W. was less the born novelist than Amis, whom he would never equal in humorous situations or memorable characterizations.

W., in fact, has admitted to his own loss of confidence in the novel as the form in which he could express his vision of the world. But he has come very close to excellence in *The Smaller Sky* (1967), a brief parable about a man trying to take refuge from the world in a London railway station; *A Winter in the Hills* (1970), about a philologist learning about the nature of human society in the Welsh mountains; and *The Pardoner's Tale* (1978), a complex mystery story. As a critic has noted, he always seems on the verge of transforming his tale from a conventionally competent novel to something rich and strange—but never quite succeeds.

In "First Readings" W. described the present as one of consolidation rather than innovation in poetry; he emphasized the need for clarity, discipline, and form. His own collections *Mixed Feelings* (1951) and *A Word Carved on a Sill* (1956) exhibited typical "Movement" characteristics in dealing lucidly and ironically with small topics and giving little sense of emotional force or intensity. Since then he has revealed that he is a poet of large ambitions: in *Wildtrack* (1965), a meditation on the theme of human interdependence written in a mixture of styles; in *Letters to Five Artists* (1969), an exploration of the creative process modeled on the poetry of Pope; and in *Feng* (1975), a retelling of the story of *Hamlet* (Feng is Claudius, and the poem examines what the lust for power does to him). Despite his virtuosity, however, he has striven to become a major poet but has not proved that he is one.

Editing *Interpretations* (1955), a collection of good critical essays, W. attacked academics who wrote only for each other and neglected ordinary readers; since then, the academics have had occasion to say that he would write better criticism if he worked more slowly and checked his facts. Nevertheless, he can write highly perceptive and interesting criticism, even if he is guilty of annoying errors and indefensible judgments. He has written workmanlike introductions to editions of Shakespeare and Samuel Johnson; he is perhaps most successful with writers with whom he has a special affinity, like Orwell and Arnold BENNETT.

In sum, W. has not developed into a major novelist, poet, or critic, but into a talented and prolific man of letters, who has done many things well.

FURTHER WORKS: *Preliminary Essays* (1957); *Gerard Manley Hopkins* (1960); *Nuncle, and Other Stories* (1960); *Weep before God* (1961); *Sprightly Running; Part of an Autobiography* (1962); *Strike the Father Dead* (1962); *Essays on Literature and Ideas* (1963); *The Living World of Shakespeare: A Playgoer's Guide* (1964); *The Young Visitors* (1965); *Death of the Hind Legs, and Other Stories* (1966); *Arnold Bennett* (1967); *Shakespeare* (1968); *Letters to Five Artists* (1969); *The Life Guard* (1971); *A House for the Truth: Critical Essays* (1972); *The Shape of Feng* (1972); *Professing Poetry* (1977); *The Pardoner's Tale* (1978); *King Caliban, and Other Stories* (1978); *Thinking about Mr. Person* (1980); *Poems, 1949–1979* (1980); *Lizzie's Floating Shop* (1981); *Young Shoulders* (1982)

BIBLIOGRAPHY: Gindin, J., *Postwar British Fiction: New Accents and Attitudes* (1962): 128–44; Karl, F. R., *A Reader's Guide to the Contemporary English Novel* (1963): 220–37; O'Connor, W. V., *The New University Wits and the End of Modernism* (1963): 30–53; Press, J., *Rule and Energy: Trends in British Poetry since the Second World War* (1963): passim; Rabinovitz, R., *The Reaction against Experiment in the English Novel, 1950–1960* (1967): passim; Morrison, B., *The Movement: English Poetry and Fiction of the 1950s* (1980): passim; Salwak, D., *J. W.* (1981)

—D. J. DOOLEY

WALCOTT, Derek

Trinidadian poet and dramatist, b. 23 Jan. 1930, Castries, St. Lucia

W. was born and raised in St. Lucia. Both his life and his work have been deeply affected by his experience as a colonial child on an isolated Caribbean island. After graduating from St. Mary's College, St. Lucia, and the University of the West Indies, Jamaica, he moved to Trinidad in 1953, working as a book reviewer, an art critic, and a playwright. In 1959 he founded the Trinidad Theater Workshop. Since then he has traveled extensively, but his commitment to the Caribbean experience, and in particular to developing an indigenous theater, has kept him essentially rooted in the West Indies. Recently, however, he has also spent a significant amount of each year in the U. S., teaching first at Harvard and subsequently at Boston University. Thus he now divides his time between Trinidad and Boston.

W.'s first major volume, *In a Green Night: Poems 1948–1960* (1962), is a landmark in Caribbean literature. With no vital Caribbean literary tradition to draw from, W. turned for formal models to the 17th-c. English metaphysical poets and to contemporary poets like Dylan THOMAS and W. H. AUDEN. Most importantly, this book skillfully embodied and defined his primary task: to create a literature faithful to the complex realities of West Indian life.

Throughout his subsequent work W. has explored the paradoxes of life as a West Indian artist. The very titles of his books—*The Castaway* (1965) and *The Gulf* (1969)—suggest the burdens of artistic isolation. So, too, he has continually returned to the story of Robinson Crusoe because it represents for him the double nature of working out one's destiny on a small island. W.'s Crusoe may despair at being alone, but he is also exhilarated by being the monarch of his island, the creative owner of a new world. In W.'s work Adam's task of giving things their names is an emblem for the artist facing his native Caribbean culture.

W.'s most sustained single work is his book-length autobiographical poem, *Another Life* (1973). The poem's first three parts treat his life from childhood through adolescence; its final part reflects back on provincial life through the lens of a later perspective. The task is to record and transfigure memory. As the story of the growth of a West Indian intelligence, it is W.'s counterpart to James JOYCE's *Portrait of the Artist as a Young Man*. This self-portrait is both complemented and deeply enhanced by plays such as *The Sea at Dauphin* (1954), *Ti-Jean and His Brothers* (1958), *Malcochon* (1959), and *Dream on Monkey Mountain* (1970), which turn outward to render, often in a Creole-inflected English, the landscape and life of West Indian foresters and fishermen. The plays represent W.'s attempt to root his individual sensibility in a communal expression and experience.

In his more recent books of poems, *The Star-Apple Kingdom* (1979) and *The Fortunate Traveller* (1982), he has continued to reexamine the West Indies through the lens of a restless traveler, lucky in his ability to move and ultimately escape, but also haunted by the fate of the underdeveloped countries of the Caribbean.

W.'s works are characterized by an intense symbolic imagination that is at once both personal and Caribbean. He is the most important West Indian poet and playwright writing in English today.

FURTHER WORKS: *Twenty-five Poems* (1948); *Epitaph for the Young* (1949); *Poems* (1952); *Henry Christophe* (1957); *Selected Poems* (1964); *Sea Grapes* (1976); *The Joker of Seville and O Babylon!: Two Plays* (1978); *Remembrance & Pantomime: Two Plays* (1980); *Midsummer* (1983)

BIBLIOGRAPHY: King, C., and James, L., "In Solitude for Company: The Poetry of D. W.," in James, L., ed., *The Islands in Between: Essays on West Indian Literature* (1968): 86–99; King, L., "D. W.: The Literary Humanist in the Caribbean," *CarQ*, 16, 4 (1970): 36–42; Lane, T., "At Home in Homelessness: The Poetry of D. W.," *DR*, 53 (1973): 325–38; Fabre, M., "Adam's Task of Giving Things Their Names: The Poetry of D. W.," *NewL*, 41, 1 (1974): 91–107; Baugh, E., *D. W. Memory as Vision: Another Life* (1978); Hirsch, E., "An Interview with D. W.," *ConL*, 20 (1979):

Derek Walcott

279–92; Hamner, R. D., *D. W.* (1981); Terada, R., *D. W.'s Poetry: American Mimicry* (1993); Hamner, R. D., ed., *Critical Perspectives on D. W.* (1993); Parker, M., and R. Starkey, eds., *Postcolonial Literatures: Achebe, Ngugi, Desai, W.* (1995)

—EDWARD HIRSCH

WALDINGER, Ernst

Austrian poet, b. 16 Oct. 1896, Vienna; d. 1 Feb. 1970, New York, N.Y., U.S.A.

W., whose parents ran a small leather factory, was seriously wounded in World War I: the right half of his face and his right hand were paralyzed as the result of a head wound. After the war he studied German literature and art history at the University of Vienna. Although he earned his Ph.D., he worked for a commercial firm. Writing poetry, however, was the core of his life. For his first published volume, *Die Kuppel* (1934; the cupola), W. received the Julius Reich Prize of the University of Vienna. He was forced to leave Austria in 1938 after the Anschluss. He emigrated to the U.S. and after some years of economic hardship, in 1947 he became a professor of German literature and language at Skidmore College in Saratoga Springs, New York, where he taught until his retirement in 1965.

Much of what the blows of fate mercilessly did to his life found expression in his lyrical writing: his youth broken because of war wounds, which left him a semiinvalid throughout his life; his narrow escape to the U.S. in 1938; his longing for his lost homeland, for Austrian speech and song, for the mellow landscape around the Danube and the Wienerwald, and for the streets and alleys of Vienna, which remained his sentimental and intellectual home.

In a time of general dissolution of form and disintegration of values W. strove for and postulated the strict observance of form. This artistic creed is professed in many of his poems, particularly in the volume *Der Gemmenschneider* (1936; the gemcutter). A virtuoso with words, W. wrote on an extraordinary variety of themes in a multiplicity of stanzaic forms, such as tercets, sonnets, and ballads. His poems are usually contemplative but nevertheless of great emotional intensity. His prosody lends itself to his dialectical way of thinking, in that it confronts thesis with antithesis to end up in a liberating synthesis of reconciled contrasts.

As is evidenced by many of his poems, W. saw himself as a guardian of the purity of the German language. He believed in the purifying power of poetry, which could healingly confront our disjointed time and our mechanized life with the concept of a better world. "It is necessary," he said, "to write poetry in order to hold against that which is most inhuman in us that which is most humane, the longing for what man should be. Poetry is not entertainment; its aim is not to create tension or to relieve it but to lead to concentration and to a deepening of our humanity, a direction that, in this time of alienation, we so badly need."

W.'s primary concern was the preservation of the humanistic tradition, which had been betrayed by barbarians in Germany and in his homeland. He never gave up his conviction that Europe's humane spirit could find its true poetic voice only through formal—perhaps classical—structure, the antithesis of chaos.

W.'s clear and pure voice was the noblest of the Austrian and German emigration. It is our own fate, poetically heightened, that we confront in his work.

FURTHER WORKS: *Die kühlen Bauernstuben* (1946); *Musik für diese Zeit* (1946); *Glück und Geduld* (1952); *Zwischen Hudson and Donau* (1958); *Gesang vor dem Abgrund* (1961); *Ich kann mit meinem Menschenbruder sprechen* (1965)

BIBLIOGRAPHY: Brunngraber, R., "E. W. zum 60. Geburtstag," *Wort in der Zeit,* 1 (Nov. 1956): 1–5; Picard, J., "E. W. at Sixty," *BA*, 31 (1957): 28–29; Kauf, R., "E. W.: An Austro-American Poet," *AGR*, 27, 6 (1961): 11–13; Kauf, R., "Stiller Dichter in lärmender Zeit: Zum 70. Geburtstag E. W.s," *Wiener Bücherbriefe,* 6 (1966): 181–85

—FREDERICK UNGAR

WALKER, Alice

American novelist, short-story writer, poet, critic, and essayist, b. 9 Feb. 1944, Eatonton, Ga.

W. grew up in the rural South, the youngest of eight children whose parents were sharecroppers. Blinded in one eye by an accident at the age of eight, W. was a shy and solitary child who found comfort and solace in reading books. She finished first in her class in high school and attended Spelman College in Atlanta (1961-1963), where she became involved in the civil rights movement. She completed her B.A. at Sarah Lawrence College in Bronxville, N.Y. (1965). In 1967 W. was named consultant on black history to the Friends of the Children of Mississippi. She was writer-in-residence and teacher of black studies at Jackson State College (1968-1969) and at Tougaloo College (1970-1971), and then became lecturer in literature at both Wellesley College and the University of Massachusetts in Boston (1972-1973). She was appointed Distinguished Writer in Afro-American Studies at the University of California, Berkeley, in the spring 1982 term, and Fannie Hurst Professor of Literature at Brandeis University in the fall of 1982. W. is a member of the board of trustees of Sarah Lawrence College and continues to lend her voice as a spokesperson for black women.

By the time W. published her first volume of poetry, *Once* (1968), she had already been a Bread Loaf Writer's Conference Scholar (1966), won first prize in an essay contest sponsored by *The American Scholar* (1967), and received both a Merrill Writing Fellowship and a McDowell Colony Fellowship (1967). The latter fellowship was awarded to W. again in 1977-1978. Among the many awards she has earned are two National Endowment for the Arts grants (1969 and 1977) and a Radcliffe Institute fellowship (1971–1973). Her poetry collection *Revolutionary Petunias and Other Poems* (1973) won the Southern Regional Council's Lillian Smith Award and was nominated for a National Book Award. In 1977-1978 W. was the recipient of a Guggenheim award.

Most of the poems in her first collection, *Once*, which the then writer-in-residence at Sarah Lawrence, Muriel RUKEYSER, read and brought to the attention of an editor, were inspired by a period in W.'s senior year of college when she had to confront an unwanted pregnancy. Desperate and suicidal, W. began writing of her fears and her concerns about how her family would respond. She surmised they would react with sorrow should she kill herself, but that they would only feel shame and outrage in regard to her pregnancy. It was her recognition of the role that family/societal forces played in her life and in the lives of so many other women that allowed W. to reject the idea of suicide, to terminate the pregnancy, and then to acknowledge publicly that she had had an abortion. The poems in *Once* reflect her delight in being alive, but also contain the seeds of her attempt to promote unity among women in an effort to change not just the ways in which society defines women, but also the ways in which women define themselves.

W.'s lifelong commitment to battling sexism and racism comes directly out of her own background and experience. Much of her work focuses on the horrors of the lives of poor, uneducated black women who are emotionally and physically abused—often murdered—by black men who are themselves victims of a racist society. But she also explores the victimization of the black woman who manages to become "accepted" by white society because she has become "raceless" through education and a desire to escape her background. By cutting herself off from her African-American heritage, by rejecting her past and her family, such a woman may escape the physical pain and abuse, but must pay a devastating price in psychological and spiritual suffering. Yet such a victim in W.'s fiction usually allows W. to introduce the subject of the possibility of change, the sense, almost unthinkable before the events of the 1960s, that there are options and choices available to such women, that their futures need not resemble their pasts. Many of W.'s characters offer the hope that black women can struggle successfully against poverty and oppression, that they can and should be politically active, and that their ultimate goals must be to reclaim, reexamine, and reestablish their roles in and their relationships to their background and their heritage. And in so doing, many of W.'s female characters institute a restructured relationship between themselves and their men. It is this freedom—the ability to carve a space for themselves within white society without rejecting their roots or selling out—that for W. makes the pain and effort of the struggle worthwhile.

W.'s novel *The Third Life of Grange Copeland* (1970) and her short-story collection *In Love and Trouble: Stories of Black Women* (1973) focus directly on the fight of black women against oppression and abuse by black men. In *Meridian* (1976) W. moves into a deeper and more complex investigation of her heroine's struggle toward selfrealization and autonomy. The protagonist's life serves as an extended metaphor for the black woman's fight to change what is blindly held to be valid just because it is traditional. Published some five years after *Meridian*, the stories in *You Can't Keep a Good Woman Down* (1981) indicate that W.'s themes are evolving, and that her characters are attempting to shape their futures from a more politically conscious and self-aware perspective. Many of the pieces move away from the traditional form of the short story as a finished product in favor of womanist prose, pieces in process-a technique meant to reflect the belief that women view life as unfolding, growing, and emerging out of personal histories and political contexts. *The Color Purple* (1982) is written in epistolary style (letters as the only acceptable form of women's writing in white-male-dominated society) and is strongly feminist in its emphasis on the importance of sisterhood in liberating women from oppression. The novel enjoyed enormous popularity, conferring best-seller status on W.'s work, and the film version was nominated for an Academy Award. But *The Color Purple* was a critical success as well. It was awarded the 1983 Pulitzer Prize and the American Book Award.

The primary focus of W.'s writing, whether fiction, poetry, or commentary, continues to be the African-American woman, but the scope and the power of W.'s work transcend easy sterotyping. She continues to evolve as a major American literary figure.

FURTHER WORKS: *Langston Hughes: American Poet* (1974); *Good Night, Willie Lee, I'll See You in the Morning* (1979); *In Search of Our Mother's Gardens: Womanist Prose* (1983); *Horses Make a Landscape Look More Beautiful: Poems* (1984); *To Hell With Dying* (1988); *The Temple of My Familiar* (1989); *Living by the Word: Selected Writings, 1973–1987* (1989); *Finding the Green Stone* (1991); *Her Blue Body, Everything We Know: Earthling Poems, 1965–1990* (1991); *Possessing the Secret of Joy* (1992); *Warrior Marks* (1993); *By the Light of My Father's Smile* (1998)

BIBLIOGRAPHY: Harris, T., "Violence in *The Third Life of Grange Copeland*," *CLAJ*, 19 (Dec. 1975): 238–47; Washington, M. H., "An Essay on A. W.," in Bell, R. P., Parker, B. J., and Sheftall, B. G., eds., *Sturdy Black Bridges: Visions of Black Women in Literature* (1979): 133–49; McDowell, D. E., "The Self in Bloom: A. W.'s Meridian," *CLAJ*, 24 (Mar. 1981): 262–75; Parker-Smith, B. J., "A. W.'s Women: In Search of Some Peace of Mind," in Evans, M., ed., *Black Women Writers* (1950–1980): *A Critical Evaluation* (1984): 478–93; Early, G., "*The Color Purple* as Everybody's Protest Art," *AR* (Summer 1986): 270–75; Bloom, H., ed., *A. W.* (1989); Banks, E. D., and Byerman, K., *A. W.: An Annotated Bibliography 1968–1986* (1989); Winchell, D. H., *A. W.* (1992)

Alice Walker

—MARGARET D. SULLIVAN

WALLANT, Edward Lewis

American novelist and short-story writer, b. 19 Oct. 1926, New Haven, Conn.; d. 5 Dec. 1962, New York, N.Y.

W. graduated from the Pratt Institute and, later, in his early thirties, while working in an advertising agency in New York, studied writing at the New School. His talent matured rapidly. In the remaining years of his short life he produced a prodigious amount of fiction; the three published short stories and the four novels (two published posthumously) on which his reputation rests represent less than half of his output during this brief time.

Vision is a key word for W. In *Teacher's Notebook in English* (1963) he wrote of the craft of fiction: "*Seeing* is my key word, seeing with the heart, with the brain, with the eye. . . . Normally we see others only as they relate to our own immediate needs, and for that, normal vision is often sufficient. Yet there are times when we have a need we cannot recognize, a sudden hunger to know what lies in the hearts of others. It is then that we turn to the artist."

An EXISTENTIALIST with a penchant for apocalypse, concerned with the psychology of human disaster and the possibilities of redemption in the claustrophobic atmosphere of modern life, W. wrote with a large, blunt pen. His themes, characters, and settings are all magnified, writ large. His usual mix of things combines Jewish suffering with Christian hope as his characters, caught in circumstances beyond their control, first face and then force their way through to some sort of personal atonement symbolically larger than they are.

If W.'s themes are often similar, so is his organizational technique in all his books. Usually, he creates a plot and a setting (a pawnshop, a hospital, a series of apartment houses) in which an isolated character is brought into contact with a series of other characters who represent the full spectrum of existence. Typically, his protagonist, deadened to life at the outset of the novel, moves toward a "threshold of pain" that is the prelude to his authentic existence before the book ends.

Sol Nazerman, the title character of W.'s best-known novel, *The Pawnbroker* (1961), is the paradigmatic W. protagonist. A Jew who survived the Nazi concentration camps, Sol has come to America to run a pawnshop in Harlem. A man suffering, mourning the murder of his family, Sol imprisons himself behind the bars of his pawnshop until he is forced back into participation in life by the self-sacrifice of his assistant, whom he has come to see as a surrogate son. This reentry to life as the result of the sacrifice of another, frequently a surrogate father or son, is a typical theme for W. In *The Tenants of Moonbloom* (1963), W.'s comic masterpiece, Norman Moonbloom moves slowly toward his "threshold" of existence as he makes the rounds of the four decaying apartment houses under his care. When he is accidentally covered with excrement when the swollen wall behind the toilet in the apartment of one of his tenants breaks, he shouts, "I'M BORN!" In *Tannenbaum's Journey*, unfinished and unpublished, the novel he was working on when he died, W. forces his obsession with fathers and sons to ultimate conclusion when he creates a real, not surrogate, father who searches through Europe for his own lost son.

In some ways W. was an old-fashioned artist, interested in the conventional themes of spiritual regeneration and personal transcendence in the midst of a world gone awry. Because of this, and because he turned to writing late, produced little, and died before he reached the height of his powers, his work could easily have been ignored or neglected. That it was not, that it continues to attract new, enthusiastic readers testifies to the authenticity of W.'s vision. If W. is not, ultimately, a major writer, surely he is one of the writers of postwar America who, because he helped define the terrors of love and death in this century, will always be part of it.

FURTHER WORKS: *The Human Season* (1960); *The Children at the Gate* (1964)

BIBLIOGRAPHY: Baumbach, J., *The Landscape of Nightmare: Studies in the Contemporary American Novel* (1965): 138–51; Rovit, E., "A Miracle of Moral Animation," *Shenandoah*, 16 (1965): 59–62; Lorch, T. M., "The Novels of E. L. W.," *ChiR*, 19 (1967): 78–91; Davis, W. V., "The Sound of Silence: E. L. W.'s *The Children at the Gate*," *Cithara*, 8 (1968): 3–25; Hoyt, C. A., *Minor American Novelists* (1971): 118–37; Davis, W. V., "Learning to Walk on Water: E. L. W's *The Pawnbroker*," *LitR*, 17 (1973): 149–65; Galloway, D., *E. L. W.* (1979)

—WILLIAM V. DAVIS

WALSCHAP, Gerard

Belgian novelist and essayist (writing in Flemish), b. 9 July 1898, Londerzeel; d. 25 Oct. 1989, Antwerp

Son of a café owner, W. studied Thomist philosophy at the University of Louvain. His contributions to various Flemish periodicals quickly established his reputation as a journalist. For twenty-three years he was employed by the government as Inspector of Public Libraries. In 1936 he was elected to the Royal Flemish Academy of Literature; he resigned his membership in 1962 to protest the domination of the group by Catholic rightists. He was made a baron by King Baudouin in 1975.

The passion-laden plots of W.'s stories revolve around cursed Flemings who suppress their violent urges and rebellious feelings until they burst forth. The stories, nevertheless, often end on an affirmative note. His fiction focuses on heightened emotion and eschews "good taste." He believes that descriptions of nature or local-color touches detract from the psychological force. He presents man and society in a semijournalistic style that is direct, functional, and sometimes sloppy.

W.'s first major novel, *Adelaïde* (1929; Adelaïde), deals with a woman's desperate struggle against inherited physical and mental flaws, which take her from indulgence of the senses to insanity. This novel, together with *Eric* (1931; Eric) and *Carla* (1933; Carla), was republished as *De familie Roothoofd* (1939; the Roothoofd family). The trilogy is marked by masterful, objective psychological analysis of the characters.

Celibaat (1934; Ordeal, in *Ordeal and Marriage*, 1963) is a tale of gothic horror whose evil protagonist is the last descendant of a Flemish noble line. Moving love scenes contrast with sickening descriptions of the antihero's pathological behavior.

Determined to expose egoism, cruelty, and hypocrisy wherever he found it, W. came into open conflict with many of his fellow Catholics, who were offended by his bold criticism of religious abuses in *Sybille* (1938; Sybille). *Bejegening van Christus* (1940; treatment of Christ) heralded his final divorce from the Church. Having shed the notion of sin, W., in what is considered his masterpiece, *Houtekiet* (1941; Houtekiet), portrays the Dionysiac pagan he himself "would like to be" and seeks a harmony between man and nature.

Denise (1942; Denise) recounts the emotional and moral crises of a tormented woman in her relationships with a wide variety of social types. W.'s distinctive, compressed writing powerfully serves a tumultuous plot full of strange coincidences. He faithfully captures Flemish folk speech as he expertly integrates dialogue with the narrative.

W. has examined contemporary historical events in several of his works. The moral conflicts generated by World War II and the Nazi occupation of Belgium are analyzed in *Zwart en wit* (1948; black and white). In *Oproer in Congo* (1952; revolt in the Congo) the mounting problems of Belgian colonialism are dissected. W.'s play *De Spaansche gebroeders* (1937; the Spanish brothers) uses sibling rivalry as a device to explore the causes of the Spanish Civil War.

In *Muziek voor twee stemmen* (1965; music for two voices), a collection of demanding essays on epistemology and teleology, W. also includes accounts of his fight against Catholic interference in the arts and education. He uses sweeping, angry prose to urge tolerance and to force the reader to face crucial problems of ethics.

W. remains focused on a strip of Flemish territory that he believes has significance for the village or city dweller, the Belgian, the foreigner, and the stateless person alike.

FURTHER WORKS: *Liederen van leed* (1923); *Flirt* (1924, with F. Delbeke); *Dies irae* (1924, with F. Delbeke); *Lente* (1924, with F. Delbeke); *De vuurproef* (1925, with F. Delbeke); *De loutering* (1925); *Waldo* (1928); *Volk* (1930); *Uitingen in de moderne wereldletterkunde* (1930); *De dood in het dorp* (1930); *Nooit meer orlog* (1931); *Jan-Frans Cantré* (1932); *Trouwen* (1933; *Marriage* in *Ordeal and Marriage*, 1963); *De vierde koning* (1935; *Een mensch van goeden wil*, 1936); *Het kind* (1939); *Vaarwel dan!* (1940); *De wereld van Soo Moereman* (1941); *Zotje Petoetje* (1941); *Ganse Kwak* (1942); *De consul* (1943); *Genezing door aspirine* (1943); *Voorpostgevechten* (1943); *Ons geluk* (1946); *Moeder* (1950); *Zuster Virgilia* (1951); *Het kleine meisje en ik* (1953); *De graaf* (1953); *Manneke maan* (1954); *Reynaert de vos* (1954); *Salut en merci* (1955); *Janneke en mieke in de oorlog* (1955); *De Française* (1957); *De verloren zoon* (1958); *De ongelooflijke avonturen van Timan Armenaas* (1960); *Nieuw Deps* (1961); *Alter ego* (1964); *Dossier W.* (1966); *Het gastmaal* (1966); *De kaartridder* (1967); *Het avondmaal* (1968); *De culturele repressie* (1969); *Het Oramproject* (1975); *De olifant die struikrover werd* (1978); *Vertelsel van de acht broers* (1978); *De heilige Jan Mus* (1979)

BIBLIOGRAPHY: de Backer, F., *Contemporary Flemish Literature* (1934): 48–49; Greshoff, J., *Belgian Literature in the Dutch Language* (1945): 299–300; Goris, J. A., *Belgian Letters* (1946): 31–32; Mallinson, V., *Modern Belgian Literature* (1966): 96–97; Meijer, R. P., *Literature of the Low Countries*, new ed. (1978): 329–31

—HENRI KOPS

WALSER, Martin

West German novelist, dramatist, and critic, b. 24 March 1927, Wasserburg/Bodensee

W. studied humanities at the University of Tübingen (1945–51), earning his Ph.D. with a dissertation on Franz KAFKA. After a few years as radio producer he became a full-time writer. He has received wide recognition at home and abroad and has won numerous literary prizes.

Ein Flugzeug über dem Haus (1955; an airplane above the house), W.'s first collection of stories, showed clearly that he had a style of his own, although there is some evidence of the influence of Kafka. They contain the themes of W.'s subsequent works. His primary concern is the struggle of the individual against the dehumanized mechanisms of society. Seldom able to escape, the protagonist gradually (often unknowingly) succumbs to them. Observing and narrating from a distance, W. holds up a mirror to West German society. With great skill and discipline, he satirizes it clearly and convincingly. He is a moralist, intending to shock people out of their complacency—a first step to change.

The novel *Ehen in Philippsburg* (1957; *Marriage in Philippsburg*, 1961) centers on the institution of marriage as it is represented by several couples. One couple, the wealthy, socially powerful Volkmanns, are unable to sustain a close marital relationship. Mrs. Volkmann betrays her husband only with "respected men." All the characters are either exploiters or victims, either in business or in love.

One of Philippsburg's inhabitants, Anselm Kristlein, is the hero of three novels: a traveling salesman in *Halbzeit* (1960; half-time), an aspiring writer in *Das Einhorn* (1966; *The Unicorn*, 1971), and a famous writer in *Der Sturz* (1973; the fall). Torn between his love of nature and a concomitant desire to withdraw from society, he nevertheless still craves social success. At the end of the third novel, he plans to drive without snow tires over a dangerous mountain pass in late fall, presumably seeking a "death that does not allow a coffin."

Other W. heroes are spiritual brothers of Kristlein. In *Die Gallistl'sche Krankheit* (1972; the Gallistl syndrome) Gallistl contemplates his life and finds that he is dissatisfied with himself, his family, and society. He, and Horn in the later *Jenseits der Liebe* (1976; *Beyond All Love*, 1983) finds no escape, because he has internalized the hostile outer world. Halm, the hero of *Ein fliehendes Pferd* (1978; a horse in flight), can only wish to "get out, out, out" and dream about a primeval jungle or a fortress perched on a steep rock, where he could hide. In *Seelenarbeit* (1979; soul work) the chauffeur Xaver Zürn loathes his monotonous and oppressed existence but is unable to act differently, like a wheel in a machine. He replaces another man, only to be replaced himself.

Not until *Das Schwanenhaus* (1980; *The Swan Villa*, 1982) does the hero fare slightly better—in spite of a gigantic professional mishap. Significantly, his name is Gottlieb, and he lives, like W., on Lake Constance, has daughters, and is the same age as the author. It seems that Kristlein's ("little Christ's") last incarnation has finally become "beloved by God," or at least he loves God.

Like the novels, W.'s plays deal with different types of warfare. They focus, like *Eiche und Angora* (1962; oak and angora), on commitment, guilt, and suffering in post-World War II Germany. German society as a whole is on trial, whether the emphasis is on ruthless business rivalry, as in *Überlebensgroß Herr Krott* (1963; Herr Krott, larger than life), or on the war between the sexes, as in *Die Zimmerschlacht* (1967; *Home Front*, 1972) and *Der Abstecher* (1967; the side trip). The past, particularly the Nazi period, is also the subject of two plays in which children reveal their fathers' guilt and demand justice: *Der schwarze Schwan* (1964; the black swan) and *Kinderspiel* (1970; child's play). This ironic social observer and critic analyzes the individual, revealing a good deal about himself and a moment in history.

In his fiction and drama W. conveys contemporary German history from the 1950s to our time, focusing on the middle class. He reacts to events during this period and creates mouthpieces for ideas that a large number of German people share with him. Fictions about Kristlein, Halm, or Zürn are (auto)biographies of a narrator-author who reiterates the same messages from behind various masks as he makes his transition from phenomenology toward Marxism. The outsider-hero, basically asocial, wishes to withdraw from society but cannot because he needs society for self-confirmation. Whenever he is about to break loose into freedom, he either falls silent or adjusts and continues to fight for survival in a society he dislikes.

FURTHER WORKS: *Beschreibung einer Form: Franz Kafka* (1961); *Lügengeschichten* (1964); *Erfahrungen und Lesserfahrungen* (1965);

Heimatkunde; Aufsätze; Reden (1968); *Fiction* (1970); *Aus dem Wortschatz unserer Kämpfe* (1971); *Wie und wovon handelt Literatur: Aufsätze und Reden* (1973); *Das Sauspiel. Szenen aus dem 16. Jahrhundert* (1975); *Was zu bezweigeln war: Aufsätze und Reden 1958–1975* (1976); *Der Grund zur Freude: 99 Sprüche zur Erbauung des Bewußtseins* (1978); *Wer ist ein Schriftsteller: Aufsätze und Reden* (1978); *Heimatlob: Ein Bodensee-Buch* (1978, with André Ficus); *Selbstbewußtsein und Ironie: Frankfurter Vorlesung* (1981); *Brief an Lord Liszt* (1982); *In Goethes Hand* (1982)

BIBLIOGRAPHY: Beckermann, T., ed., *Über M. W.* (1970); Pezold, K., *M. W.: Seine schriftstellerische Entwicklung* (1971); Schwarz, W. J., *Der Erzähler M. W.* (1971); Pickar, G. B., "Narrative Perspective in the Novels of M. W.," *GQ*, 44 (1971): 48–57; Waine, A. E., *M. W.: The Development as Dramatist 1950–1970* (1978); Waine, A. E., *M. W.* (1980); Siblewski, K., *M. W.* (1981)

—ANNA OTTEN

WALSER, Robert

Swiss novelist, short-story writer, and poet (writing in German), b. 15 April 1878, Biel; d. 25 Dec. 1956, Herisau

From 1895, when he left home at the age of seventeen, until 1929, W. led a peripatetic life devoted to literature and personal independence made difficult by limited public acceptance of his writings. During most of the decade 1896–1905 W. was in Zurich, working intermittently in mainly clerical jobs, and writing. Some of his early poems and short plays appeared in the Munich literary journal *Die Insel*. W.'s literary ambitions took him to Berlin in 1905, where—except for three months as a servant in a Silesian ducal castle—he lived until 1913. The three novels he wrote in Berlin, prose pieces in literary magazines, and a book of verse established his reputation among writers and critics. But W. became disaffected by Berlin's literary life and by cavils with his writing. (Later, W. claimed to have destroyed manuscripts of three further novels while in Berlin.) Feeling he had failed as a novelist, W. returned to his hometown in Switzerland and concentrated on shorter prose. In the last phase of his career, in Bern from 1921 on, W. surpassed the productivity of his best years in Berlin, but he began to drink heavily and experienced hallucinations. In 1929 he committed himself to a mental institution in Bern, where he was summarily diagnosed as a schizophrenic. The circumstances of the committal and the diagnosis have become subjects of critical examination. W. continued to write for publication until 1933, when he was forcibly removed to a sanatorium in eastern Switzerland; thereafter he stopped writing.

Plot lines in W.'s better-known work, the novels *Geschwister Tanner* (1907; the Tanner siblings), *Der Gehülfe* (1908; the assistant), and his masterpiece, *Jakob von Gunten* (1909; *Jakob von Gunten*, 1969) are minimal. All revolve about a young man seeking selfunderstanding and self-realization in a society undergoing decisive economic, moral, and cultural change. The encounter with this society throws into question the heroes' instinctive and ethical disposition, that is, their trust in extra rational experience and their faith that society by definition comprehends specifically individual

members. The aesthetic appeal of the novels derives from their singular balance of disparate characterological and narrative registers: the hero is intellectually and socially imprepossessing but reflectively insightful; nature and instinct are celebrated by analytic intelligence; incisive psychological characterization alternates with conciliatory tolerance; ironic, ambiguous narrative perspective elicits critical response in the reader; an increasingly dispiriting analysis of prospects for a humane society contests with resolute individual affirmation.

The distinctiveness of form, theme, and style in the novels notwithstanding, W.'s true achievement lies in his shorter prose, a form cultivated in more than a thousand works, the bulk of which were collected only posthumously. These defy easy categorization because of their variety, their refinement of characteristic themes over the years to parabolic levels, and the varying combinations in them of putative self-portraiture, narrative, and essayistic reflections that tend increasingly to aphorism. They include portraits of writers and artists in whom W. recognized aspects of his own personality, such as Kleist, Jean Paul, Hölderin, and Cézanne; ironic love letters to a departed beloved as recalcitrant muse; real and imaginary walks framing intellectual and aesthetic perambulations; glosses on popular literature; comic, adulatory descriptions of scenes from classical German plays; and stories that are oblique yet trenchant critiques of social hierarchies, mores, and culture.

W.'s solitary life, a peripheral literary career, and his institutionalization have impeded a fair assessment of him as a shaper of modern literature. Earlier, incomplete readings to the contrary notwithstanding, W.'s work is now recognized as deeply social in character and intent, and his portrayals of self seen as paradigmatic and metaphoric. His influence on very diverse present-day German authors has been extensive. The creative force of his confidence in language and a native distrust of "high" literature enabled him to extend the premises of the genres in which he wrote: novel, short prose (essay and story), dramatic dialogue, and verse. At the core of W.'s writing is an analytical irony that posits uncertainty and inevitable social and institutional change. Paradoxically, this irony is fundamentally hopeful and emancipatory, for it successfully aims to revivify love, courage, and resilience based on awareness of humankind's complexity.

FURTHER WORKS: *Fritz Kochers Aufsätze* (1904); *Gedichte* (1909); *Aufsätze* (1913); *Geschichten* (1914); *Kleine Dichtungen* (1914); *Prosastücke* (1917); *Kleine Prosa* (1917); *Der Spaziergang* (1917; *The Walk*, 1957); *Poetenleben* (1918); *Komödie* (1919); *Seeland* (1919); *Die Rose* (1925); *Dichtungen in Prosa* (5 vols., 1953–1961); *Das Gesamtwerk* (13 vols., 1966–1975). FURTHER WORKS IN ENGLISH: *The Walk, and Other Stories* (1957); *Selected Stories* (1982)

BIBLIOGRAPHY: Middleton, J. C., "The Picture of Nobody: Some Remarks on R. W., with a Note on W. and Kafka," *RLV*, 24 (1958): 404–28; Avery, G. C., *Inquiry and Testament: A Study of the Novels and Short Prose of R. W.* (1968); Herzog, U., *R. W.s Poetik: Literatur und soziale Entfremdung* (1974); Kerr, K., ed., *Über R. W.* (3 vols., 1978–1979); Wagner, K., *Herr und Knecht: R. W.s Roman "Der Gehülfe"* (1980); Walser, M., *Selbstbewußtsein und Ironie: Frankfurter Vorlesungen* (1981): 117–52 and passim; Sontag, S., Introduction to *Selected Stories* (1982): vii–ix

—GEORGE C. AVERY

WALTER, Otto F.

Swiss novelist (writing in German), b. 5 June 1928, Rickenbach

W. is one of the leading experimental authors of Switzerland. After studying the book trade, he held a series of minor jobs in the publishing business. In 1956 he became the head of the literary program for his father's publishing house, the Walter Verlag. He served in this capacity until 1966, when he accepted a similar position at Luchterhand publishers in Germany. Here he succeeded in obtaining a foothold for several Swiss authors in the West German market. He quit his job in 1972 to return to Switzerland to become a full-time writer. He now lives in Solothurn.

W.'s first five novels are set in the imaginary town of Jammers, near the Jura mountains in the canton of Solothurn. The first two in this series, *Der stumme* (1959; the mute) and *Herr tourel* (1962; Mr. Tourel) are very much like the French *nouveau roman* in that they avoid the use of plot and characterization in favor of highly subjective introspection. The narrator of the first novel tries to reconstruct the past of the silent protagonist, who lost his voice because of his father, through a series of speculations and conjectures. The second book is a mixture of recollections, associations, overheard conversations, and imaginary dialogues. W. was reacting here to a widespread literary skepticism in the German-speaking world, whereby standard language and conventional literary forms were no longer considered adequate to cope with the perversion of language under the Nazis and the demands of a new technological age.

W. outgrew his fascination with the purely subjective, and his next works show an increased concern with contemporary political and social issues. In *Die ersten unruhen* (1972; the first unrests) Jammers has become a large town dominated by capitalism, and this has split the populace into several groups alienated from each other. Lawlessness and loneliness abound and everyone seems to have lost his or her purpose in life. The alienation and inequalities that capitalism engenders are also the theme of *Die verwilderung* (1977; growing wild). A group of dropouts try to form a democratic commune in an abandoned factory outside of Jammers, but their presence cannot be tolerated by the local citizens, who violently disband them. Through his mouthpiece, the journalist Blumer, W. expresses the fear that the encroachment of the political and economic system into every aspect of our lives will result in a severe curtailment of our freedom and will ultimately lead to a return to fascism. Both of these novels have a strong documentary flavor, for they include numerous passages quoted from other sources. Stylistically they are linked to the first two novels, in that they consist of collages, but this time the collages are on a much grander scale and incorporate a wide variety of material, including fictive texts, authorial comments, and newspaper articles.

The novella *Wie wird beton zu gras: fast eine liebesgeschichte* (1979; how does concrete turn to grass: almost a love story) reverts to a more conventional style, but the thematics remain constant. Three siblings demonstrate against the construction of a nuclear power plant and thereafter become gradually alienated from Swiss society and its imposed restrictions. This familial aspect is expanded to epic proportions in *Zeit des fasans* (1988; time of the pheasant), a long novel, which chronicles the history of the industrialist family Winter, who lives in Jammers. The main question of the plot-who is responsible for the mother's murder-takes a backseat to the theme W. has been developing in his previous novels, namely capitalism and its concomitant evils. W. is

particularly interested in the family's history in the 1930s and 1940s, thus trying to show the links between capitalism and fascism. Once again the novel is a montage of fictive texts, flashbacks, comments from the author, quotations, and other materials.

Through his literature W. has developed into one of the foremost critics of Swiss society and of Western consumer culture. His works call on us to critically reflect on the dangers that our political and social systems hold for our personal development and for the environment.

FURTHER WORKS: *Elio oder eine fröhliche gesellschaft* (1965); *Das staunen der schlafwandler am ende der nacht* (1983); *Eine insel finden* (1983); *Gegenwort* (1988)

BIBLIOGRAPHY: Weber, W., *Tagebuch eines Lesers* (1965): 232–50; Bucher, W., *Schweizer Schriftsteller im Gespräch* (1971): 219–40; Mattes, M., *Das Bild des Menschen im Werk O. F. Ws* (1973); Zeltner-Neukomm, G., *Das Ich ohne Gewähr* (1980): 81–100; Acker, R., "O. F. W.'s *Die Verwilderung*: Swiss *Engagement* in the 70's," *UDR*, 16, 3 (Winter 1983–1984): 33–38

—ROBERT ACKER

WANG Anyi

Chinese novelist and short-story writer, b. 1954, Nanjing

W. Was reared in Shanghai, the native city of her mother Ru Zhijuan, also a well-known writer. She graduated from junior high school in 1969 and was dispatched with thousands of other high school graduates to the poorest areas of rural China by Mao Zedong's orders: they were the "Urban Youth" generation that was supposed to reeducate themselves by learning from the peasants. W. managed to leave her rural commune in Anhui by joining a local performing arts troupe as a cellist in 1973. After the Cultural Revolution, she returned to Shanghai in 1978 and began her literary career. Unlike many other writers of the Urban Youth generation, W. does not see any redeeming quality in the enforced "rustication" of a whole generation of young people; she considers it a terrible waste of human potential and human lives. W. spent three months at the International Writing Program in Iowa in 1984, an experience that had an impact on her development as a writer. Short trips to various parts of Asia since the mid-1980s have also been a source of inspiration for her. The most important influence on her outlook and her work, however, remains the city of Shanghai.

W.'s success at writing fiction was immediate if not spectacular. In the first phase of her career, personal experience was her mainstay. The stories in *Yu, sha sha sha* (1981; The Rain Patters On) deal primarily with the feelings of young people in situations similar to hers. Her exposure to Western culture in 1984 led to a change in creative direction: an exploration of traditional values still alive in the Chinese countryside. This resulted in the highly acclaimed and award-winning novella entitled *Xiao Baozhuang* (1985; *Baotown*, 1989).

The novella is W.'s forte, as exemplified in her "Love Trilogy": *Xiaocheng zhi lian* (1986; *Love in a Small Town*, 1988), *Huangshan zhi lian* (1986; *Love on a Barren Mountain*, 1991) and *Jinxiugu zhi lian* (1987; *Brocade Valley*, 1992). With premarital and extramarital sex in a repressive society as the main focus of her exploration into human nature and relationships, the trilogy drew immediate fire from conservative critics in China for breaking a long-held taboo. However, instead of detracting from W.'s success, the trilogy strengthened her position as one of the most dedicated and daring writers of her generation. She continued to probe the issues of relationships and marriage in her short stories of the late 1980s and early 1990s.

The 1990s saw yet another departure in W.'s creative direction. Using her personal experience and family history as a starting point, she experimented with the demarcation between versions of reality and narration, fact and fiction. "Shushu de gushi" (1993; An Uncle's Story) won unanimous critical acclaim. This was followed by "Shangxin Taipingyang" (1994; The Sad Pacific), an exploration of her paternal heritage, and the novella *Jishi yu Xugou* (1994; Fact and Fiction), a journey through over one thousand years of history that traces the real and imaginary roots of her mother's family.

Since the mid-1990s, W. has been frequently referred to as a Shanghai writer, obvious even in her early stories. Critics consider *Changhen ge* (1996; Song of Everlasting Sorrow) one of her most notable achievements in this respect. The novel follows the life of a beauty pageant winner from 1940s Shanghai through fifty years of political changes in China, but focuses unswervingly on the private trials and tribulations of its protagonist.

W. is now at the pinnacle of her creative powers. While her existing oeuvre will ensure her a prominent place in the history of Chinese literature, there is reason to believe that the imaginative scope of her work will continue to grow. If one is to find fault with her writing, it is with a slight tendency towards verbosity—a trait that would benefit from the advice of a judicious editor. Unfortunately, such help that most writers in the West take for granted is not normally available to Chinese writers.

FURTHER WORKS: *Benci lieche zhongdian* (1982; *The Destination*, 1984), *Liu shi* (1983; *Lapse of Time*, 1988), *Da Liuzhuang* (1985, Liu Village), *Mi Ni* (1992; Millie)

BIBLIOGRAPHY: Wang, Z., "Three Interviews: W. A., Zhu Lin, Dai Qing," *MCL*, 4 (1988): 99-148; Laung, L., "W. A.: Restless Explorer," in *Morning Sun: Interviews with Chinese Writers of the Lost Generation* (1994): 177-87

—EVA HUNG

WANG Meng

Chinese novelist and short-story writer, b. 15 Oct. 1934, Beijing

W. became a member of the Chinese Communist Party before his fourteenth birthday in 1948, and in 1949 began work as a party secretary in the New Democratic Youth League while studying political theory at the Central League Academy in Beijing. W. was attacked during the 1957 AntiRightist Campaign and exiled to the countryside, where he performed manual labor for five years before returning to Beijing in 1962. After teaching in the Chinese department of Beijing Normal College for one year, W. was sent to the Xinjiang Province branch of the Chinese Writers Association, and in 1965 he went to a commune to work in manual labor. In 1973 W. was transferred to the Xinjiang ministry of culture where he worked as a translator, and in 1979 he returned to Beijing as a writer. In 1986 W. was appointed minister of culture but stepped down in 1989 and was replaced by Ho Ching-chih (He Jingzhi).

W.'s writing career began in 1953 with *Ch'ing-ch'un wan-sui* (long live youth), which was not published until 1979. He gained fame with a short story, "Tsu-chih-pu lai-le ke nian-ch'ing-jen" (1956; "The Young Newcomer in the Organization Department," 1983). Foreshadowing the themes of a later novel—*Pu-li* (1979; *Bolshevik Salute*, 1989)—this story depicts a young and native office worker who rejects the corruption and sterility of party bureaucracy and attempts to make reforms. As the Anti-Rightist Movement gained momentum and many well-established literary intellectuals were criticized for individualism and antiparty ideas, W. became one of the younger victims. Like many writers forced to work in the countryside or jailed during the Cultural Revolution (1966–1976), W. published little during that period.

After the death of Mao Zedong (Mao Tse-tung) and the fall of the Gang of Four in 1976, W. and other writers from the 1950s and earlier reemerged. In 1980 W. published a series of short stories, including "Yeh te yen" ("The Eyes of Night," 1983), "Hu-tie" ("The Butterfly," 1983), and "Ch'un chih sheng" ("Voices of Spring," 1983), which utilized techniques similar to STREAM OF CONSCIOUSNESS, fragmented plot, and interior monologue to reevaluate the psychological and social damage done by the Cultural Revolution. These stories and W.'s novel *Pu-li*, the story of a young party member who retains loyalty throughout years of senseless criticism, formed part of a modernist movement that challenged the forty-year supremacy of SOCIALIST REALISM and called for new, more critical roles for the literary intellectual.

In 1980 critics attacked W.'s contemporary works as antirealist, non-Marxist, and un-Chinese. This critique of certain cultural productions as violating the emphasis on the masses that Socialist Realism had espoused culminated in the Anti-Spiritual Pollution Campaign of 1983, during which W.'s experiments with modernist techniques were branded as foreign, elitist, and politically unprogressive. Although many were afraid the campaign would develop into a second Cultural Revolution, it stopped abruptly at the end of 1983, and W. continued to write. The fact that in July of 1983, as the campaign was warming up, W. became editor in chief of *People's Literature* shows that criticism of his works as pollution had only a mild effect on his career.

Recently W. has been a prolific writer, publishing the novels *Hsiang-chien shih nan* (1982; *The Strain of Meeting*, 1989) and *Huo-tung pian-jenhsing* (1987; *The Movable Parts*, 1989), as well as numerous stories and a few essays on literary creativity. W.'s work investigates themes such as party corruption, the effect of political movements on daily life, and human relations in adverse circumstances. He remains a writer whose career has spanned the existence of the People's Republic of China and whose work stands as a testimony to the political upheavals that defined contemporary culture and from which no Chinese writer could escape.

FURTHER WORKS: *Yeh te yen chi ch'i-t'a* (1981); *W. M. Chin-tso hsüan* (1981); *W. M. hsiao-shuo pao-kao wen-hsüeh hsüan* (1981); *W. M. t'an ch'uang-tso* (1983); *W. M. chung-p'ian hsiao-shuochi* (1985); *Ch'uang-tso shih i-chung jan-shao* (1985); *Wen-hsüeh ti yu huo* (1987). **FURTHER WORKS IN ENGLISH:** *The Butterfly and Other Stories* (1983); *Selected Works of W. M. I: The Strain of Meeting* (1989); *Selected Works of W. M. II: Snowball* (1989)

BIBLIOGRAPHY: Tay, W., "W. M., Stream of Consciousness, and the Controversy over Modernism," *MCL*, 1, 1 (Sept. 1984): 7–24; Larson, W., Introduction and "*Bolshevik Salute*: The Chinese Intellectual and Negative Self-Definition," *Bolshevik Salute: A*

Modernist Chinese Novel (1989): xiii–xx, 133–54; Tay, W., "Modernism and Socialist Realism," *WLT*, 65, 3 (Summer 1991): 411–13

—WENDY LARSON

WANISSI, Zuhūr

(also spelled Zhor Ounissi) Algerian novelist, short-story writer, and journalist (writing in Arabic), b. 13 Dec. 1936, Constantine

One of the first writers of Arabic in preindependence Algeria, W. has had a varied political and literary career. Shortly before her twentieth birthday in 1956, she joined the Algerian Nationalist Party (FLN). She was awarded two medals of valor for her commitment to the nationalist cause during the Algerian war of independence (1954-62). Her political activities did not stop her from pursuing her university studies. She gained two degrees, one in arts and the other in philosophy, before proceeding to graduate studies in sociology. In 1962 W. became the first woman member of the newly formed parliament in independent Algeria. An ardent campaigner for women's rights and education for girls, she has worked as a teacher and journalist, while holding ministerial posts. She became Minister of Social Affairs before being appointed Minister of Education, a post she occupied for several years. A member of the National Association of Algerian Writers and the Association of Algerian Journalists, W. was director and editor of the women's journal, *Al-Jazaā'iriyya*, from 1970 until 1982. At the beginning of 1998 she was appointed a senator.

W. began her literary career as early as 1955, writing short stories and publishing them in the few Arabic journals that were available at the time. During the war of independence it was difficult for Algerian writers to publish long works because of the unavailability of Arabic publishing houses in the country, and the lack of communication with other Arab countries. Publishing in journals seemed to set the pattern for W. whose subsequent works appeared first in magazines and newspapers. Her novels also were first serialized in newspapers before they were published in book form. W.'s first collection of short stories, *Al-Rasīf al-Nā'im* (1967; The Sleeping Sidewalk), was published in Egypt. The collection was one of the first Arabic books from Algeria to reach readers in other parts of the Arab world. It immediately established W.'s reputation as an important Algerian writer.

W.'s second collection of short stories, *'Alā al-Shāti' al-Ākhar* (1974; On the Other Bank), was published in Algeria, by which time a national publishing house had been established. One of W.'s best known stories, "'Amaliyyat Hubūt" (1990; The Act of Going Down), was translated into French as "La Descente" (1991). Narrated in the third person, it is a moving account of a sixty-year-old woman who in her youth had shown great promise, becoming a teacher of Arabic at the age of eighteen. Here the narrator tells readers that Arabic was highly respected by a nation that had been deprived of it for well over a century, and anyone who perfected it was considered to be learned. But for some unknown reason the young woman turned to teaching dressmaking. After hearing a lot of gossip about her from those who were jealous of her success, she withdrew and lived the life of a recluse. The narrator, in an aside, questions what happened to her between the ages of twenty and sixty. The story ends with the woman taking a decision to go down from her apartment to the street. She begins by taking the first step,

and then the next slowly until the last step. This story was written at a time of political unrest in Algeria when well-known figures, who had been prominent in public life, suddenly disappeared from view. In this story W. does not dwell on the woman's experiences as a teacher, a theme she explores fully in her semiautobiographical novel, *Min Yawmiyyāt Mudarrisa* (1978; From the Diary of a Teacher), based on her own recollections. Much of W.'s work is based on her life experiences.

Besides French, some of W.'s stories have been translated into Flemish, Norwegian and Russian. She does not always introduce a female central character, and the events in several of her stories are seen through the eyes of men, as in *Al-Hilm wa al-Kābūs* (1990; The Dream and the Nightmare). Here the central character is a dedicated employee whose life revolves around his work. He has not missed a single day's work through illness and goes to the office at exactly the same time every morning, making his way through the busy streets with their crowded shop fronts that he does not notice. But despite his dedication to his work, his boss decides to dismiss him because he wants to employ someone else in his place. The man docilely accepts the boss's decision and leaves the office. He retraces his steps walking slowly back home, and, for the first time, notices the shops and their wares.

W.'s stories describe the experiences of ordinary people who quietly accept what fate has decreed for them. There is in most of them a quiet pessimism which mirrors and reflects the anxieties of national uncertainty, reminiscent of the works of the Algerian reformer Reda Houhou (1911-1956). Like Houhou, W. frequently uses an intrusive narrator to reflect on the significance of the story and to offer further comments on events and characters. This occurs also in her highly acclaimed novel *Lūnja wa al-Ghūl* (1993; Lūnja and the Giant). The title refers to the well-known Algerian fairytale about Lunja, the human daughter of a Giant who lived in a large castle with high walls so no one could reach her. W. uses the story of Lūnja as a metaphor for the central character of the novel, the daughter and widow of men who fought and died for the independence of their country.

The war of independence is vividly evoked in a number of W.'s works which also depict the mores and values of Algerian society. This aspect gives W.'s art a unity of purpose, making her the spokesperson of a generation who had to witness some of the most crucial changes in Algeria's modern history.

FURTHER WORKS: *Al-Dilāl al-Mumtadda* (1982); *'Ajā'iz al-Qamar* (1994); *Najmat al-Rā'ī* (1998)

BIBLIOGRAPHY: Déjeux, J., *La Littérature algérienne contemporaine* (1975); Al-A'raj, W., *Al-Usūl al-Tarikhiyya al-Wāqi'iyya al-Ishtirākiyya fī al-Adab al-Riwā'ī al-Jazā'irī* (1986); Hallaq, J., and Gonzalez-Quijano, *Nouvelles arabes du Maghreb* (1991)

—FARIDA ABU-HAIDAR

WANNŪS, Sa'dallāh

Syrian dramatist, producer, and drama critic, b. 1941, Syria

Trained in Syria, Egypt, and France, W. has made major contributions to the theater tradition of his homeland as well as to the development of a corpus of theoretical writing about drama, most notably that connected with performance and the relationship between actors and audience.

The turning point in his career came with the performance of his play *Haflat samr mun ajl alkhāmis min Huzayrān* (1968; evening entertainment for the 5th of June). Before that, W. had written a number of plays with clear political messages but belonging more to the category of *théâtre des idées*. In *Haflat samr* he addressed himself to the issues surrounding the June defeat of 1967 in a carefully organized theatrical event through which the audience found itself drawn into a corporate condemnation of the power structures that had failed the Arab people. Although productions of the play were soon banned, some 20,000 people are said to have attended a later series of performances in Damascus in 1972.

Haflat samr has been characterized by some critics as an ephemeral piece. It is certainly the case that the parameters that W. established in that play have been explored with greater dramatic effect in the plays that he has written since that time. W.'s basic aim, expressed in a series of articles, reviews, and retorts, has been to break down the barriers separating the actors involved in the performance on stage and the audience watching in the auditorium; it is not surprising that, in his discussions of drama theory, the names of Erwin Piscator (1893–1966) and Bertolt BRECHT are among those cited. He regards this development as a necessity for Arabic drama, not least because a lively interchange between actors and audience was a prominent feature of drama performances in the 19th c. He has written at length on what he terms *masrah al-tasyīs* (theater of politicization) and has provided copious directions and suggestions regarding the means of performing his works.

W. explored these ideas in two plays of the early 1970s: *Mughāmarat ra's al-mamlūk Jābir* (1972; the adventures of Mamlūk Jābir's head), based on a tale of treachery from the Abbasid era of Islamic history; and *Sahra ma'a Abī Khalīl al-Qabbānī* (1972; an evening entertainment with Abū Khalīl al-Qabbānī). The first of these plays makes use of an "audience" of actors of the stage and the manipulative figure of the *hakawātī* (the traditional storyteller) to orchestrate the reactions and, W. even hopes in an introduction, the participation, of the audience. In *Sahra* we encounter the "play within a play" format, through which W. attempts to explore some of the issues associated with modern Arabic drama through an illustration of the trials of al-Qabbānī (1833–1902) in producing and performing a play culled from the tales of *A Thousand and One Nights* in Ottoman-controlled Syria in the 19th c.

Later in the decade W. published *Al-Malik huwa al-malik* (1977; the king's the king), a play inspired by tales from the Hārūn al-Rashīd cycle in *A Thousand and One Nights*, in which a henpecked husband is spirited away to the Caliph's palace and made ruler for the night. The modern twist to the plot is that no one seems to notice the difference; at the end of the play the ruler who decided to have some fun at someone else's expense has come to regret the game he has initiated. In this play, too, W. makes use of a number of theatrical devices, puppets, and the manipulating orchestrators of the action, Zāhid and 'Ubyd.

Besides his obvious desire to experiment with the dynamics of drama in the Arab world context, W. has made a radical and interesting decision regarding the problem of dramatic language in Arabic (the language of speech, the various colloquial dialects, not being considered a "literary" language by many critics). In the introduction to *Mughāmarat ra's al-mamlūk Jābir* he suggests that the published text of the play should be regarded as merely a blueprint, and that producers in the various regions of the Arab world should feel free to adapt the dialogue to conform with the local dialect and indeed choose props and music appropriate to the local audience's taste.

Accounts of performances of W.'s plays make it clear that theater directors and audiences have had considerable difficulty carrying out his agenda for Arabic drama; critics report audience discomfort over the confusion as to who were the real actors and who were the audience. It is also clear that the import of almost all W.'s plays has not been to the taste of governmental authorities who use various means of censorship to keep a very close watch on dramatic productions. This will probably account for W.'s extended silence throughout the 1980s. Even so, the corpus of plays that he has published thus far remains a significant contribution to the development of an indigenous tradition of modern Arabic drama.

FURTHER WORKS: *Al-Fīl, yā Malik al-Zamān* (1970); *Ma'sāt bā'i' al-dibs al-faqīr* (1977); *Fasad al-dam* (1978); *al-Ightisāb* (1990); *Munamnamah tārīkhiyyah* (1994); *Tuqūs al-ishārāt wa-al-tahawwulāt* (1994); *Yawm min zamāninā wa-Ahlām shaqiyyah* (1995)

BIBLIOGRAPHY: Allen, R., "Arabic Drama in Theory and Practice: The Writings of S. W.," *JarabL*, 15 (1984): 94–113; Ceccato, R. D., "Il teatro contemporaneo in Siria: L'impegno di S. W.," *Quaderni di studi arabi*, 1 (1983): 53–65; Gouryh, A., "Recent Trends in Syrian Drama," *WLT*, 60, 2 (Spring 1986): 216–21

—ROGER ALLEN

WARNER, Sylvia Townsend

English short-story writer, novelist, poet, and biographer, b. 6 Dec. 1893, Harrow; d. 1 May 1978, Maiden Newton

Although her father served as housemaster and teacher at Harrow School, W. received no formal education. This lack proved no handicap to one who through a wide range of activities, coupled with a powerful intellect and sensibility, found ample means to sustain a life devoted to letters. She worked, for example, in a munitions factory during World War I; later she spent ten years as one of the four editors of a ten-volume work entitled *Tudor Church Music* (1922–29). In 1927 she came to New York, where she was a guest critic for the *Herald Tribune*. For some forty years she published her fiction in *The New Yorker*, and through this publication she developed a large and devoted following. In 1929 she moved to Dorset, the region that was to enrich so much of her writing. In the 1930s she was active against Franco and witnessed the Spanish Civil War at first hand.

W. produced a body of writing marked equally by its range as by its quality. Her poetry—*The Espalier* (1925); *Time Importuned* (1928); *Opus 7* (1931), a novel in verse; *Whether a Dove or Seagull* (1934, with Valentine Ackland)—constitutes an early and somewhat separate phase of her literary career. While critics commended her poetry and even compared it to that of Thomas HARDY, Edith SITWELL, W. H. DAVIES, and Gerard Manley Hopkins, it was in prose, a more natural literary medium for her, that she made a permanent contribution to English literature.

With the publication of the novels *Lolly Willowes* (1926) and *Mr. Fortune's Maggot* (1927), W. established a reputation that was further enhanced by *The True Heart* (1929), *Summer Will Show* (1936), *After the Death of Don Juan* (1938), and *The Corner That Held Them* (1948). The themes of these novels are as varied as their subjects: the first two involve astringent and compassionately satiric clarifications of the relationship of self to society and religion, and are among the more distinctly autobiographical works in the W. canon; the four later ones reflect her devotion to historical fiction, not as an end in itself but as a mode of illuminating timeless human issues.

It must be acknowledged, though, that W.'s short stories, more than her poetry or novels or even her acclaimed biography *T. H. White* (1967), earned her a place among the masters of English prose. Her stories appeared in numerous collections, such as *The Cat's Cradle Book* (1940), *The Museum of Cheats* (1947), *Winter in the Air* (1956), *The Innocent and the Guilty* (1971), and *Kingdoms of Elfin* (1977). While critics were undiluted in their praise for these volumes, they were not equally enthusiastic about an earlier collection entitled *The Salutation* (1932), but in the title story, a haunting exploration of the meaning of exile, one can see a powerful demonstration of W.'s mind and style. Like so much of her best short fiction, it ends not so much on a point that is quickly forgotten but on an impression that continues to grow upon recollection.

The essence of W.'s art, whether in poetry or in fiction, lies not in its philosophical depth—she tells us nothing new—but in her extraordinary capacity to depict with an engaging, ironic style those mundane areas of life in which we struggle daily. Her writing is concerned less with actions and events and more with states of mind, malaises of soul. Her best stories never have the polemical urgency of a D. H. LAWRENCE, nor do they end with the sense of point and completion that seem to characterize much of Somerset MAUGHAM. In their lyricism and controlled emotion they may remind some readers of Richard Church (1893–1972). In many, one can say, as Sir Kenneth Clark did of Edith Sitwell's later poems, that they give one the sense of being on the brink of understanding some deep mystery. Through the power of style and a judicious choice of theme, W. seems consistently attuned to those truths that hover just over the horizon. In seizing these evanescent moods, which probably define life more than those events we tend to judge as definitive, W. has succeeded as few other writers have.

FURTHER WORKS: *Some World Far from Ours and "Stay Corydon, Thou Swain"* (1929); *Elinor Barley* (1930); *Rainbow* (1931); *A Moral Ending, and Other Stories* (1931); *More Joy in Heaven* (1935); *A Garland of Straw* (1943); *Somerset* (1949); *The Flint Anchor* (1954); *A Spirit Rises* (1962); *A Stranger with a Bag* (1966 Am., *Swans on an Autumn River*); *Twelve Poems* (1980); *Scenes of Childhood, and Other Stories* (1981); *Collected Poems* (1983); *Letters* (1983)

BIBLIOGRAPHY: Fadiman, C., on *Mr. Fortune's Maggot, Nation* (25 Jan. 1927): 588; Allen, W., on *T. H. White: A Biography, NYTBR* (21 Apr. 1968): 1; Abbott, J., on *The Innocent and the Guilty, SSF*, 10 (1973): 111–12; Annan, G., on *Kingdoms of Elfin, TLS* (14 Jan. 1977): 25; Feaver, V., on *Twelve Poems, TLS* (23 May 1980): 586; Cantwell, M., *Scenes of Childhood, and Other Stories, NYT* (30 Dec. 1981): C16

—JOHN LAWRENCE ABBOTT

Robert Penn Warren

WARREN, Robert Penn

American poet, novelist, and critic, b. 24 April 1905, Guthrie, Ky.; d. 15 Sept. 1989, Stratton, Vt.

During boyhood and adolescence W. generally spent summers on the farm of his grandfather and the school months in a small Kentucky town where his father worked as a banker—an upbringing that provided a rich store of landscapes, characters, and anecdotes for his later career as a creative writer. At fifteen he obtained an appointment to Annapolis but an eye injury disqualified him from the naval service, and he resolved instead to study electrical engineering at Vanderbilt University. Here, however, a freshman English course with John Crowe RANSOM turned his interest to literature, and his lifetime commitment to the profession of letters soon took shape under the influence of Ransom, Allen TATE, and other members of the Vanderbilt literary elite who came to be known as the Fugitives, after the magazine they published in the mid-1920s. Following graduation in 1925, W. pursued graduate study at Berkeley, Yale, and (as a Rhodes Scholar) Oxford, where he earned his B.Litt. in 1930. As a professor of literature, W. cofounded *The Southern Review* at Louisiana State University in the 1930s, taught at the University of Minnesota in the 1940s, and worked from 1950 until retirement at Yale University. Divorced from Emma Brescia in 1951, he married the writer Eleanor Clark (b. 1913) in 1952, making his residences thereafter in Connecticut and in rural Vermont, a recurring site for his poetry.

W. may well be the most versatile American man of letters of the century. His literary criticism includes brilliant studies of major writers like Joseph CONRAD, Theodore DREISER, Ernest HEMINGWAY, William FAULKNER, Coleridge and Melville. Textbooks like *Understanding Poetry* (1938, with Cleanth BROOKS; rev. eds., 1950, 1960) helped revolutionize the teaching of literature by bringing the New Criticism into general practice in America's college classrooms. His *The Legacy of the Civil War* (1961) was perhaps the most original meditation on regional ideologies to appear during that war's centennial, and his two studies in race relations, *Segregation: The Inner Conflict in the South* (1956) and *Who Speaks for the Negro?* (1965), gain extra resonance when juxtaposed against two other works separated by half a century: *John Brown: The Making of a Martyr* (1929) and *Jefferson Davis Gets His Citizenship Back* (1980).

Substantial as they are, these achievements are secondary to W.'s prolific output as a creative writer. Author of ten novels, numerous volumes of poetry, a short-story collection, and a play, W. is the only writer ever to win Pulitzer Prizes in both fiction—for *All the King's Men* (1946)—and poetry—for *Promises: Poems, 1954–1956* (1957), which also won a National Book Award. He received numerous other awards for various collections of poetry, including another Pulitzer for *Now and Then: Poems 1976–1978* (1978). Other honors include the National Medal for Literature in 1970, the Presidential Medal of Freedom in 1980, and the Prize Fellowship of the John D. and Catherine T. MacArthur Foundation in 1981.

W.'s early career as a poet attracted little public attention, and for many years his fame as a writer rested chiefly upon his carefully crafted philosophical novels. *Night Rider* (1939), the first of these, drew upon a historical episode of strife among Kentucky's tobacco farmers for its nightmare vision of flux, violence, and alienation relating to ideological delusion and betrayal. The need for a valid connection to a larger community dawns too late upon the book's protagonist. *At Heaven's Gate* (1943), showing something of a Fugitive/Agrarian bias in its revulsion against a business magnate's "hollow man" condition, was constructed (W. has said) along the lines of Dante's treatment of the Violators of Nature. W.'s fictional master-piece, in the view of many, is *All the King's Men*, a novel that—as its title implies—subjects all its major characters to a fall of some sort from innocence into a shattering awareness of evil or corruption. Famous partly for its fictionalized portrait of Louisiana governor Huey Long, this novel ranges beyond its political interest to develop themes like naturalistic determinism, the search for self-knowledge, and the pragmatic necessity of accepting one's self and the world in their fallen condition. Originally conceived as a play and first performed in 1939 (pub. 1960), *All the King's Men* has been made into a movie and an opera. W.'s own favorites among his other novels are *World Enough and Time* (1950), a Gothic romance set in 19th-c. Kentucky, and *Flood: A Romance of Our Time* (1964). His most recent novel, *A Place to Come To* (1977), displays among other features an admirably zestful erotic sensibility in its septuagenarian author.

W.'s fictional themes—especially the theme of a fall from innocence—recur in his poetry, but here his continuously evolving technique marks a sharp departure from his practice in fiction. His early work in *Thirty-six Poems* (1935) displays the formal discipline of mentors like Ransom, Thomas HARDY, and the 17th-c. metaphysical poets whom he specialized in teaching, but he was already employing as well the radical, loosening effects exemplified in a favorite modern poet of his, T. S. ELIOT. This experimental

tendency continued in his next volume, *Eleven Poems on the Same Theme* (1942), and culminated in one of his very finest poems, "The Ballad of Billie Potts," in *Selected Poems, 1923–1943* (1944), which alternates lyric and narrative voices. W.'s most ambitious poetic opus, *Brother to Dragons* (1953), a book-length "Tale in Verse and Voices," centers upon the historical incident of a savage murder committed by Thomas Jefferson's nephew. The volumes of poetry that have appeared since then—including a rewritten *Brother to Dragons* in 1979—feature a virtually unlimited range of forms and styles: sonnets, nursery rhymes, terza rima, blank verse, free verse, poems designed as visual objects or organized like movie shots, and numerous anecdotal/meditative sequences. The poems also range, more so than the fiction, through almost unlimited subject matter, from intensely personal griefs, joys, and memories to imaginative constructions based on W.'s reading.

W.'s governing theme of self-definition develops with fuguelike complexity through three broad phases of the artist's work. In his early writing, W.'s version of "original sin" predominates, typically involving the discovery of unexpected weakness or depravity close to and ultimately within oneself. Exacerbated by nihilistic impressions of the outer world, this lapsarian trauma precipitates feelings of alienation, shame, and meaninglessness tantamount to a loss of identity, from which the W. character is prone to seek a false refuge in various forms of worldly success or ideological passion. Rescue from this bankrupt condition occurs, in W.'s middle period, through development of a "sacramental view of life," which promotes various modes of reconciliation: between the ideal self and the beastly within the psyche; between past and present (often portrayed in terms of father and son); between the death-foreseeing individual and the whole of time and nature. The end of "The Ballad of Billie Potts" may be W.'s most moving instance of this reconciling vision, which W. elsewhere describes as "a mystic osmosis of being" producing "such a sublimation that the world which once provoked . . . fear and disgust may now be totally loved"; other instances, in the later work, occur in the cosmic consciousness of *Promises* ("all Time is a dream, and we're all one Flesh, at last"), the theme of life's "blessedness" in *Flood*, and the love of the world in *Audubon*. The philosophical depth and coherence of W.'s life work, in tandem with its exceptional variety, excellence, and abundance, assures him a place of high distinction among American men of letters.

FURTHER WORKS: *Understanding Fiction* (1943; rev. ed., 1959, with Cleanth Brooks); *Blackberry Winter* (1946); *The Circus in the Attic, and Other Stories* (1947); *Proud Flesh* (prod. 1947, rev. version, 1948); *Modern Rhetoric* (1949; rev. ed. 1958, with Cleanth Brooks); *Fundamentals of Good Writing* (1950; rev. ed., 1956, with Cleanth Brooks); *Band of Angels* (1955); *Selected Essays* (1958); *The Cave* (1959); *You, Emperor, and Others: Poems, 1957–1960* (1960); *Wilderness: A Tale of the Civil War* (1961); *Selected Poems, New and Old, 1923–1966* (1966); *A Plea in Mitigation: Modern Poetry and the End of an Era* (1966); *Incarnations: Poems 1966–1968* (1968); *Audubon: A Vision* (1969); *Meet Me in the Green Glen* (1971); *Homage to Theodore Dreiser* (1971); *John Greenleaf Whittier's Poetry: An Appraisal and a Selection* (1971); *Or Else: Poem/Poems 1968–1974* (1974); *Democracy and Poetry* (1975); *Selected Poems, 1923–1975* (1976); *Being Here: Poems 1977–1980* (1980); *R. P. W. Talking: Interviews* (1980); *Rumor Verified: Poems 1979–1980* (1981); *Chief Joseph of the Nez Perce* (1983)

BIBLIOGRAPHY: Bradbury, J. A., *The Fugitives: A Critical Account* (1958); Casper, L., *R. P. W.: The Dark and Bloody Ground* (1960); Longley, J. L., Jr., ed., *R. P. W.: A Collection of Critical Essays* (1965); Stewart, J. L., *The Burden of Time: The Fugitives and Agrarians* (1965); Guttenberg, B., *Web of Being: The Novels of R. P. W.* (1975); Strandberg, V., *The Poetic Vision of R. P. W.* (1977); Gray, R., ed., *R. P. W.: A Collection of Critical Essays* (1980); Bohner, C. H., *R. P. W.*, rev. ed. (1981); Clark, W. B., ed., *Critical Essays on R. P. W.* (1981); Justus, J. H., *The Achievement of R. P. W.* (1981); Nakadate, N., ed., *R. P. W.: Critical Perspectives* (1981); Watkins, F., *Then & Now: The Personal Past in the Poetry of R. P. W.* (1982); Watkins, F., *Then and Now: The Personal Past in the Poetry of R. P. W.* (1982); Millichap, J. R., *R. P. W.: A Study of the Short Fiction* (1992); Koppelman, R. S., *R. P. W.'s Modernist Spirituality* (1995); Blotner, J. L., *R. P. W.: A Biography* (1997)

—VICTOR STRANDBERG

WASSERMANN, Jakob

German short-story writer and novelist, b. 10 March 1873, Fürth; d. 1 Jan. 1934, Alt-Aussee, Austria

W., the son of a poor Jewish merchant, was born just a few years after the establishment of the German Reich, while his death coincided roughly with the passing of democracy in Germany. Thus, his life spanned two major epochs, the Wilhelminian Empire and the Weimar Republic. These periods and their political and social developments provided the background for W.'s works.

W. was secretary to Ernst von Wolzogen (1855–1934), a novelist and founder of the cabaret Überbrettl. Through Wolzogen's intercession W. was invited to join the staff of the literary journal *Simplicissimus*.

The concept of justice is a significant and recurring one in W.'s work. His experiences with a cruel stepmother and his first encounters with anti-Semitism as a soldier contributed to W.'s sensitivity to injustice. *Caspar Hauser; oder, Die Trägheit des Herzens* (1909; *Caspar Hauser*, 1928), whose alternate title means "indolence of the heart," is based on the life of the curious foundling who appeared in the 19th c. in Nuremberg. His innocence allows him to become the victim of the self-serving interests of society. The question of injustice is dealt with again in *Christian Wahnschaffe* (2 vols., 1919; expanded ed., 1932; *The World's Illusion*, 1920). The novel's eponymous hero, son of a wealthy industrialist, abandons his family and affluence in order to experience the penury and suffering of the masses, hoping to uncover the source of societal injustice.

W.'s ultimate credo, his most mature statement on injustice, is the Andergast trilogy, comprising *Der Fall Maurizius* (1928; *The Maurizius Case*, 1929), *Etzel Andergast* (1930; *Doctor Kerkhoven*, 1932), and *Joseph Kerkhovens dritte Existenz* (1934; *Kerkhoven's Third Existence*, 1934). Legal injustice is the theme of the first volume. The labyrinth of courtrooms and penal institutions, their deficiencies, and the nature of crime and punishment are the main concerns of W. in this novel based on an actual miscarriage of justice. Secondary themes include the rebellion of sons against

Jakob Wassermann

fathers and the collapse of the traditional family structure. Etzel Andergast, the hero of *Der Fall Maurizius*, is also the main character in the next volume. But he is no longer the champion of freedom he was earlier. Rather, W. locates him within the orbit of lost generation. Here Etzel wanders aimlessly and becomes involved with radical youth groups, who represent the political extremism of the 1920s. *Joseph Kerkhovens dritte Existenz* appeared posthumously; it is marred by stylistic flaws that no doubt would have been corrected had W. lived. This last work treats the spiritual dimension of the justice motif. As W. neared the end of his life and saw his once-monolithic world crumble with the onslaught of Nazism, he focused his attention on the realm of divine and metaphysical justice.

W.'s works are set in a bourgeois milieu. In this stratum injustice originates within the family unit and spreads to society at large. Indifference and the lack of love in the home were, for W., the root of injustice.

Heinrich MANN said of W. that had the novel not existed, W. would have been the one to invent it. He was a talented weaver of tales who wrote in the style of the 19th c., with often a tinge of melodrama. He shied away from politics even though his major themes were essentially political in nature. Thus, he was widely read between the wars but virtually forgotten after World War II.

FURTHER WORKS: *Melusine* (1896); *Die Juden von Zirndorf* (1897; *The Dark Pilgrimage*, 1953); *Schläfst du, Mutter?* (1897);

Die Schaffnerin (1897); *Hockenjos; oder, Die Lügenkomödie* (1898); *Die Geschichte der jungen Renate Fuchs* (1901); *Der Moloch* (1903); *Der nie geküßte Mund* (1903); *Die Kunst der Erzählung* (1904); *Alexander in Babylon* (1905; *Alexander in Babylon*, 1949); *Die Schwestern* (1906; *Clarissa Mirabel*, 1915); *Die Masken Erwin Reiners* (1910); *Der Literat* (1910); *Der goldene Spiegel* (1911); *Die ungleichen Schalen* (1912); *Faustina: Ein Gespräch über die Liebe* (1912); *Der Mann von vierzig Jahren* (1913); *Deutsche Charaktere und Begebenheiten* (2 vols., 1915); *Das Gänsemännchen* (1915; *The Goose Man*, 1922); *Der Wendekreis* (4 vols., 1920–1924: I, *Der unbekannte Gast, Adam Urbas* [*Adam Urbas*, 1927], *Golowin* [*Golovin*, 1927], *Lukardis* [*Lukardis*, 1927], *Erasmus Ungnad* [*Erasmus*, 1927], *Jost* [*Jost*, 1927]; II, *Oberlins drei Stufen* [*Oberlin's Three Stages*, 1926], *Sturreganz*; III, *Ulrike Woytich* [*Gold*, 1924]; IV, *Faber; oder, Die verlorenen Jahre* [*Faber; or, The Lost Years*, 1925]); *Mein Weg als Deutscher und Jude* (1921; *My Life as German and Jew*, 1933); *Das Gold von Caxamalca* (1923); *Der Geist des Pilgers* (1923); *Laudin und die Seinen* (1925; *Wedlock*, 1926); *Der Aufruhr um den Junker Ernst* (1926; *The Triumph of Youth*, 1927); *Lebensdienst* (1928); *Christoph Columbus, Der Don Quichotte des Ozeans* (1929; *Christopher Columbus, Don Quixote of the Seas*, 1930); *Hofmannsthal, der Freund* (1930); *Bula Matari: Das Leben Stanleys erzählt* (1932; *Bula Matari: Stanley, Conqueror of a Continent*, 1933); *Selbstbetrachtungen* (1933); *Tagebuch aus dem Winkel* (1935); *Olivia* (1937); *Briefe an seine Braut und Gattin Julie, 1900–1929* (1940; *The Letters of J. W. to Frau Julie Wassermann*, 1935); *Gesammelte Werke* (7 vols., 1944–48); *Geliebtes Herz: Briefe an eine Unbekannte* (1949); *Bekenntnisse und Begegnungen* (1950). FURTHER WORKS IN ENGLISH: *World's Ends: Five Stories by J. W.* (1927)

BIBLIOGRAPHY: Goldstein, W., *J. W.: Sein Kampf um Wahrheit* (1928); Bing, S., *J. W.*, 2nd ed. (1933); Karlweis, M., *J. W.* (1935); Blankenagel, J. C., *The Writings of J. W.* (1942); Garrin, S., *J. W.'s Andergast Trilogy and the Concept of Justice* (1979)

—STEPHEN H. GARRIN

WASSERSTEIN, Wendy

American dramatist and essayist, b. 18 October 1950, Brooklyn, New York

Taking a summer playwriting course at Smith College and earning an M.A. in creative writing at City College of New York led W. to opt for the M.F.A. program at Yale University School of Drama instead of an M.B.A. at Columbia. Her first professional production, *Any Woman Can't*, at Playwrights Horizons forged a long association with that group and particularly with its one-time artistic director, Andre Bishop. Her plays have won numerous awards, including the Tony Award, the Pulitzer Prize, the New York Drama Critics Circle, the Drama Desk, the Susan Smith Blackburn Prize, the Hull-Warriner Award—all for *The Heidi Chronicles* (1990), as well as the Outer Critics Circle Award for both *The Heidi Chronicles* and *The Sisters Rosensweig* (1993). She has also won a Guggenheim Fellowship, serves on the artistic

boards of Playwrights Horizons and the 52nd Street Project, and is a contributing editor of *NY Woman* magazine.

W.'s works have been described as "serious plays that are funny." She is noted for her one-liners, although the overall content is often a penetrating look at issues that she feels are ignored in theater—the pain contemporary women suffer with their new-found ability to choose coupled with the paradoxes these choices create. The pain, and the humor, emerges from her own experiences as an upper-middle-class Jewish woman trying to establish herself in a difficult career in spite of family pressures to marry and have a family. Her answer is her common theme of creating families out of one's associates. In *Uncommon Women and Others* (1978), for example, the characters form familial-style relationships with individuals, with their group, with all the residents of their hall, and with the others attending their college. Just the fact that the characters attend a Seven Sisters college implies such a relationship. Similarly, in *The Heidi Chronicles* Heidi forms ties that go beyond mere friendship in an attempt to create the family she ultimately chooses.

While feminist issues have had significant place in W.'s plays, the outcomes she presents are not generally supported by this group as the focus shifts from general ideology to the individual frame of reference of the character. The ending of *The Heidi Chronicles* caused a stir with its apparent suggestion that women could not be happy without succumbing to the maternal instinct. However, W. would argue that the choice was right for this character in this instance though maybe not right for all.

W.'s learning curve as a dramatist is clear, as she moves from episodic structures in early works to the more difficult narrative cohesiveness of recent plays. In *An American Daughter* (1998) W. confronts again the issue of choice, only to reveal that as her generation matures, women's choices are again restricted because of the doors these choices have locked in front of them or the doors that have now closed behind them. In this, her first play to go directly to Broadway, W. tackles women's choices in a significantly more overt political and serious style.

In both her writing and in her private life, W. expounds the relevance of theater as a means to draw attention to those elements of our society that tend to oppress. Theater is a means of listening to individual voices, she believes, while telling stories, resolving conflicts, and uplifting souls.

FURTHER WORKS: *The Sorrows of Gin* (1979); *Isn't It Romantic* (1984); *The Girl from Fargo* (1987, with Terrence McNally); *Bachelor Girls* (1990); *Pamela's First Musical* (1996)

BIBLIOGRAPHY: Betsko, K., and R. Koenig, *Interviews with Contemporary Women Playwrights* (1987); Shapiro, W., "Chronicler of Frayed Feminism," *Time* (7 Mar. 1989): 90-92; Simon, J., "The Best So Far," *New York* (Nov. 1992): 100-01; Magill, F., ed., "W. W.," *Great Women Writers* (1994): 571-75; Alter, I., "W. W.," in Shapiro, A. R., ed., *Jewish Women Writers* (1994): 448-57; Bryer, J. R., ed., *The Playwright's Art: Conversations with Contemporary American Dramatists* (1995); Balakian, J., "W. W.," in Kolin, P. C., and C. H. Kullman, eds., *Speaking on Stage: Interviews with Contemporary American Playwrights* (1996): 379-91; Franklin, N., "The Time of Her Life," *New Yorker* (4 Apr. 1997): 62-71

—BEVERLY BRONSON SMITH

WÄSTBERG, Per

Swedish novelist, essayist, poet, and editor, b. 20 Nov. 1933, Stockholm

Born into an upper-middle-class family, W. enjoyed many social advantages, including a good education. He earned his B.A. from Harvard and a graduate degree from the University of Uppsala. He made his formal literary debut at fifteen with *Pojke med såpbubblor* (1949; boy blowing soap bubbles), a novel showing remarkable maturity and linguistic control. In the late 1950s he was awarded a Rotary grant for travel to Africa, where he was deeply struck by the injustice and suffering that resulted from white supremacy. W. became an articulate exponent of basic human rights in the region and a mediator of black African culture. He has remained in the public eye as cultural editor and then editor-in-chief of the Stockholm newspaper *Dagens nyheter* and an active member of the International PEN club.

Many of W.'s most important beliefs and perceptions emerge with arresting power from his accounts of the impact of his visits to Africa. The suffering and abuse that black Africans throughout much of the continent have had to endure are chronicled in chilling detail in *Förbjudet område* (1960; forbidden territory), *På svarta listan* (1960; on the blacklist), and *Angola-Moçambique* (1962, with Anders Ehnmark; *Angola and Mozambique: The Case against Portugal*, 1963). The force of W.'s ringing call for justice and respect in place of exploitation and denigration is heightened by his own work as an editor, anthologizer, and interpreter of African literature.

W.'s most accomplished fiction is at once the converse and extension of his interest in Africa. The trilogy *Vattenslottet* (1968; the water castle), *Luftburen* (1969; *The Air Cage*, 1973), and *Jordmånen* (1972; *Love's Gravity*, 1977) examines passion, abundance, and human potential and seems to suggest that the enlightened liberalism that abhors political repression demands complete sexual and personal freedom. The love scenes abound in joyous sensuality; but more significantly, W. endeavors throughout to portray modern and enlightened love as a fulfilling interaction of individuals and society unfettered by norms or conventions.

Many of W.'s other works have a more directly personal tone. His poetry collected in *Tio atmosfärer* (1963; ten atmospheres) and *Enkel resa* (1964; one-way trip) expresses his awareness of the fragility and transitoriness of life in contrast to its rich abundance of varied experience. In articles, pamphlets, and books, W. also provides a highly personal and appreciative view of Stockholm and its surroundings indicative of his keen sense of place and his ability to portray varying locales with charm, grace, or force as the situation may demand.

W. is a many-faceted but highly disciplined writer. He enjoys broad appeal even though his liberalism, intellectualism, and romanticism tend to distinguish him from the majority of his contemporaries for whom political commitment is singularly important. His social engagement is to broad issues concerning fundamental human rights and values and can be evoked with great power but also with considerable sophistication and subtlety.

FURTHER WORKS: *Enskilt arbete* (1952); *Ett gammalt skuggspel* (1952); *Halva kungariket* (1955); *Klara* (1957); *Arvtagaren* (1958); *Östermalm* (1962); *Ernst och Mimmi* (1964); *En dag på världsmarknaden* (1967); *Afrikas moderna litteratur* (1969); *Röda huset: Ett spel i Stockholm* (1970, with Anna-Lena Wästberg); *Sommaröarna: En bok om stockholmarnas skärgård* (1973); *Afrika,*

ett uppdrag: Reflexioner, beskrivninger, gissningar (1976); *Berättarens öganblick* (1977); *Ett hörntorn vid Riddargatan, och andra Stockholmsskildringar* (1980); *Obestämda artiklar* (1981); *Bestämda artiklar* (1982)

BIBLIOGRAPHY: Lask, T., on *The Air Cage*, *NYT* (24 June 1972): 29

—STEVEN P. SONDRUP

WATKINS, Vernon

Welsh poet (writing in English), b. 27 June 1906, Maesteg; d. 8 Oct. 1967, Seattle, Wash., U.S.A.

When W. was six, his Welsh-speaking parents moved to Gower Peninsula, where he spent most of the rest of his life. At Magdalene College, Cambridge, he studied modern foreign languages and developed a love for European poetry. From twenty-six to sixty, he was employed by Lloyd's Bank, except for service in the Royal Air Force during World War II. In 1951 he was elected Fellow of the Royal Society of Literature and in 1966 was appointed the first Calouste Gulbenkian Fellow in Poetry at University College, Swansea. W. called himself "a Welsh poet writing in English" and professed the belief that his verse "is characteristically Welsh in the same way that the verse of Yeats is characteristically Irish." He died in Seattle during his second appointment as Visiting Lecturer in Modern Poetry at the University of Washington.

Eight volumes of W.'s poetry were published during his lifetime, and several more appeared posthumously. In all of them one finds poems about Wales. His first, *The Ballad of Mari Lwyd, and Other Poems* (1941), is based on an ancient Welsh New Year's custom, the carrying of a mare's skull by singers and poets from house to house in anticipation of receiving food and drink. T. S. ELIOT spoke highly of the poetic skill it exhibited. In addition to Wales, its landscape, and the locale of Gower in particular, W.'s favorite themes were suggested by W. B. YEATS, whom he self-consciously imitated, and Dylan THOMAS, whose close friend and poetic mentor W. was. In the 1930s Thomas called W. probably the finest poet then writing in Britain. Four years after Thomas's death, W. edited the volume *Dylan Thomas: Letters to V. W.* (1957). Few poets of the 20th c. have devoted so much attention in their writing to the meaning of the poet's vocation and function.

In addition to the continuing influence upon W. of the work and approaches of Yeats, most evident perhaps in the posthumous *The Influences* (1977), William Blake's mysticism also affected W.'s metaphysical vision. Like other poets who have chosen tradition as their lodestone—W. wrote of "defending ancient springs"—W.'s poetry is both hieratic and hermetic.

A romantic concerned with the elemental tides that provide the rhythm of man's universe, W. was fascinated by Welsh mythology, to which he returned repeatedly, developing and ornamenting the motifs. Curiously, the Welsh meters do not seem to come easily to him. On the other hand, he employs a great variety of English meters, especially lyric and ballad forms, with the Sapphic meter one of his favorites.

Although W. claimed to believe that his finest poetry would come to him in old age, there are anticipations in some of his poems that death was imminent. Addressing his own aesthetic, he wrote,

"Far from believing that an artist should not repeat himself, I believe that he should make what cannot be repeated by others. Repetition may be a reinforcement of the individual will, even a statement of faith, and that is sacred. Unless there is a constant and a recurrence, there is no depth in the matrix."

FURTHER WORKS: *The Lamp and the Veil* (1945); *Selected Poems* (1948); *The Lady with the Unicorn* (1948); *The North Sea* (1951; tr. of Heine); *The Death Bell: Poems and Ballads* (1954); *Cypress and Acacia* (1959); *Affinities* (1962); *Selected Poems 1930–1960* (1967); *Arrival in East Shelby* (1968); *Uncollected Poems* (1969); *I That Was Born in Wales: Selected Poems* (1976); *Influences* (1977); *Selected Verse Translations* (1977); *Unity of the Stream: A New Selection of Poems* (1978); *The Ballad of the Outer Dark, and Other Poems* (1979); *The Breaking of the Wave* (1979)

BIBLIOGRAPHY: Heath-Stubbs, J., "Pity and the Fixed Stars: An Approach to V. W.," *Poetry Quarterly*, 12, 1 (1950): 18–23; Raine, K., *Defending Ancient Springs* (1967): 17–34; McCormick, J., ed., *V. W.: A Bibliography* (1968); Norris, L., ed., *V. W., 1906–1967* (1970); Mathias, R., *V. W.* (1974)

—THOMAS E. BIRD

WATTĀR, al-Tāhir

Algerian novelist and short-story writer, b. 15 Aug. 1936, near Sedrata

W. received most of his education in Tunisia while his country was fighting for its independence. He worked for many years as a journalist in Algeria and was later appointed as political adviser in the National Liberation Front. He became the director of Algerian radio and television in 1990. W. is the editor of the journal *At-Tabyine*, a publication of the literary association al-Jāhiz, while the name of the journal is the second half of the title of his book *al-Bayān wat-Tabyīne*. W. is Algeria's most prominent fiction writer and the most outspoken defender of the country's socialist policy adopted after its independence in 1962. He published one play, *Al-Hārib* (1969; the fugitive), as well as novels and short stories. W.'s approach is both explicit and daring even while discussing topics traditionally considered taboo in his society. His short stories in particular raised the question of suppressed feelings among the Algerian youth and compared life to a barren desert. Such a complaint was strongly voiced by the hero of "Sahrā' Abadan" (desert forever) and other stories in his collection *Dukhkhān min qalbī* (n.d.; smoke from my heart). In spite of W.'s early concern for the absence of love in his society he gave it very little attention in his novels. Love themes are practically nonexistent in his books, where the relation between men and women is reduced to a sexual adventure, serving more as an escape from life's enduring problems of poverty and repression. It is significant that his two novels relating to love, *Al-'ishq wa al-Mawt fi al-Zaman al-Harrāshī* (1974; Passion and death in the Harrashi time) and *Tajribatun fi al-'Ishq* (1978; An experience in passion), carry in their title the term "passion" and not love.

Women do not play a significant role in W.'s early novels, particularly those dealing with the war of independence. Whenever he portrays feminine characters, they are generally singled out in

unusual situations and do not represent the Algerian woman in real life. Thus, while the heroine of his short story "Nawwāh" (n.d.; Nawwāh) reveals a panicking mother trying to save her children during an air raid on her village, *Rummānah* (1981; Rummanah), on the other hand, is the image of the woman as sex symbol, the way men in her society conceive her. She serves to point out men's vices rather than women's virtues. This tendency to use women as symbols characterizes. W.'s novels; used as such, they are stiff and even artificial, with the possible exception of the prostitutes in his novel *'Urs baghl* (1978; marriage of a mule). In fact, W. does not do justice to the women of his country. So far, the most successful portrayal of a feminine character has been Fajriyyah in *Tajribah fi al-'Ishq*. She is undoubtedly the most human of his feminine characters, though manifestly symbolic, and even endowed with magical powers.

W.'s novels present an assessment of Algeria's long march through history, old and new, and the various pitfalls on the way from the days of French colonialism to the postindependence period. This concern with history takes precedence over the fiction side of W.'s works. Both the novels and most of the short stories relate the political realities in Algeria, depending in most cases on symbols to convey the author's message. In *Al-zilzāl* (1974; the earthquake), for example, the choice of the geographical setting of the city of Constantine and the reference to a natural disaster to denote the huge changes that took place in Algeria as a result of the war of independence, mark a successful approach. A more direct use of history and political reality is apparent in *Al-lāz* (1974; al-Laz), *Al-'ishq wa-al mawt fi-al-zaman al-harrāshī*, and *Tajribah fi al-'Ishq*. Recent and contemporary political figures and events dominate the scene in the three novels. Facts are mentioned bluntly without any effort to camouflage names or incidents or even the author's feelings and emotions toward them. Some of the situations described here were prefigured in the short stories of *Al-Shuhadā' ya' ūdūn hādhā al-usbū‘* (1974; the martyrs are coming back this week). Phony communists and the opportunists of the war of independence are particularly highlighted. The optimistic tone of *Al-'ishq wa-al mawt fi-al-zaman al-harrāshī* gives way to a melancholic despair and a moral nonchalance.

It is difficult to foresee the future trend of W.'s literary path, especially with the recent political changes in Algeria. So far he has proved to be a prolific writer, whose in-depth study of the social and the political Algerian scene as well as juggle of history and fiction brought him universal renown. W. is the best-known Algerian writer in the Arab world.

FURTHER WORKS: *Al-hawwāt wa-al-qasr* (1980); *Al-Ta'anāt* (1981); *Ash-Sham‘a wa al-Dahālīz* (1997)

BIBLIOGRAPHY: Makarius, R., and Makarius, L., *Anthologie de la littérature arabe contemporaine* (1964): 404–8; Déjeux, J., *La littérature algérienne contemporaine* (1975): 116; Bamia, A. A., "La littérature algérienne de langue arabe," *Europe*: 567–68 (July–Aug. 1976): 38–48; Bamia, A. A., "Le roman algérien de langue arabe depuis l'indépendance," *Annuaire de l'Afrique du Nörd*, 19 (1980): 1127–33; Allen, R., *The Arabic Novel* (1982): 74–75; Bamia, A. A., "L'homme dans l'œuvre de T. W.," *Littératures da Maghreb* 4–5 (1984): 339–49; Allen, R., ed., *Modern Arabic Literature* (1987): 340–42; Bonn, C., *Anthologie de la littérature algérienne* (1990): 107–8, 151–54, 223–34

—AIDA A. BAMIA

WAUGH, Evelyn

English novelist, b. 28 Oct. 1903, London; d. 10 April 1966, Taunton

Son of the publisher Arthur and younger brother of the popular novelist Alec Waugh (1898–1981), W. was educated at Lancing School and Oxford. Following his years at Oxford (1922–24) W., who had hoped for a career as an illustrator, had a brief, checkered career as a schoolmaster and an even briefer, and not very successful one as a journalist. By 1929 he had found his way to a literary career and had published his first two works, the critical biography *Rossetti: His Life and Works* (1928) and the satirical romance *Decline and Fall* (1928).

In 1930 W. converted to Roman Catholicism. During the 1930s W. moved in aristocratic and fashionable circles; like his Oxford experiences, these associations provided him with materials for his fiction. His second marriage, to Laura Herbert, in 1937, proved to be a fortunate one; six children were the issue of the union, the eldest son being the writer Auberon Waugh (b. 1939). During World War II W. served in the Royal Marines, in the Commandos, and, with his friend Randolph Churchill, in the British Military Mission to Yugoslavia; but he was, in fact, ill-suited to military service and grew increasingly disillusioned with the conduct of the war, in particular with his nation's policy in Yugoslavia. His disillusionment with English policy and political life continued into the postwar period.

In his later years W.'s conduct, in public appearances and controversies, was often outrageous; his eccentric conservatism was, in part, the romantic aesthete's impulse to bait the bourgeoisie, but it was also the satirist's need to shock all holders of accepted contemporary opinions. In these years, too, the insomnia, ennui, and melancholia to which W. was always subject grew more acute; he was profoundly distressed by changes within the Roman Catholic Church, especially by the abandonment of the Latin Mass.

W.'s first novel, *Decline and Fall*, which recounts the adventures of Paul Pennyfeather after his expulsion from Oxford, is picaresque and episodic; it is also a hilarious satiric assault on Oxford, public schools, the smart set, modern architecture, and prison reformers. W.'s most significant technical indebtedness in this satire, and in others, was to Ronald FIRBANK, whose kaleidoscopic shifting of scene and objective manner inspired W.'s counterpoint technique and pose of ironic detachment.

Vile Bodies (1930) revealed that he could create a world, that of the Bright Young People, and give brilliant expression to his sense of the futility of modern experience. The "happy ending," which leaves his antihero on "the biggest battlefield in the history of the world," raised fantasy to the level of prophecy. Another wasteland satire, *A Handful of Dust* (1934), is a masterpiece of poised irony; in this account of adultery W. revealed the baseness underlying the surface gloss of the fashionable world and also the spiritual inadequacy of Tony Last's devotion to the past. Fleeing the present and seeking an illusory "Gothic" city in the Brazilian jungle, Tony is imprisoned by a halfbreed and forced to read Dickens aloud, over and over. The appalling irony is that Tony is treated no worse by the half-savage than he was by the near-savages in England. In the perspective of time, this economical novel has come to be regarded as a major work of its period.

Constantly on the move during the 1930s but responsive to political developments, W. produced, among other travel books, *Remote People* (1931; Am., *They Were Still Dancing*) and *W. in*

Evelyn Waugh

Abyssinia (1936), which leaned so far to the right that they obscured his actual allegiance to an ideal of the aristocratic life. W.'s travels in Africa inspired the novel *Black Mischief* (1932), a devastating burlesque of the attempted modernization of an African kingdom; and *Scoop* (1938), a spoof on varieties of imperialism and the excesses of the press. Both satires ridiculed the "civilizing" of the barbaric and the barbarism of "modernism." In *Black Mischief*, for instance, natives devour the boots distributed to them, and the amoral Basil Seal unwittingly eats his mistress at a cannibal feast. In the light of the events that have taken place in Africa since W.'s death, the shocking images of these works have lost none of their satiric edge.

Following on the destructive satires W. produced during the 1930s, *Put Out More Flags* (1942) seemed to move toward affirmation, for in it Basil Seal and other 1930s types are caught up in the spirit of the "Churchillian renaissance." But this mood of political euphoria was not to survive for long. After World War II fiction of a mordant character appeared. *Scott-King's Modern Europe* (1947) exposed a seedy Balkan dictatorship. *The Loved One* (1948) exploited the decadence of mortuary customs in California. Less original than these, *Love among the Ruins* (1953) followed Aldous HUXLEY and George ORWELL into the totalitarian future, protesting things as they are by predicting things to come.

Brideshead Revisited (1945), W.'s greatest popular success, indicated that W. was moving ambitiously toward a more realistic mode. Brilliant in its depiction of the Oxford world of the late 1920s, the novel is flawed in certain other respects. Although

Brideshead Revisited was the first W. novel to make explicit his Catholicism, its narrator, Charles Ryder, so mingles social and religious values in his nostalgic memories of Brideshead and its aristocrats that the intended religious theme is overwhelmed. On the other hand, in *Helena* (1950) W. imbued a saint's legend with rationalistic Catholicism and satire, making it a vehicle for Catholic apologetics.

The distinguished trilogy *Men at Arms* (1952), *Officers and Gentlemen* (1955), and *Unconditional Surrender* (1961; Am., *The End of the Battle*) revealed the adjustment of W.'s religious vision, his political commitments, his comic sense, and his satiric impulse to the conventions of the novel. (In 1965, W. issued a one-volume "recension" of these novels under the title *Sword of Honour*.) Tracing the World War II career of his first true hero, artfully modulating from burlesque to irony, W. portrayed Guy Crouchback's discovery that his crusade against the modern age was an illusion, that in an ambiguous world good never comes from public causes, but that it may result from individual acts of charity. Disillusioned the story of Guy Crouchback may be, but in it, W. struck the deepest notes of his career and produced England's finest novel of the war.

In the autobiographical *The Ordeal of Gilbert Pinfold* (1957), a self-mocking short novel based upon a bout of hallucinations caused by his over-indulgence in both alcohol and sleeping potions, W. suggested that although the major writers of the century were gone, a "generation notable for elegance and variety and contrivance" had survived. His statement suggested the graces of such impeccable biographies as *Edmund Campion* (1935) and *The Life of the Right Reverend Ronald Knox* (1959; Am., *Monsignor Ronald Knox*) and the wit, urbanity, and discretion of *A Little Learning* (1964), the first volume of an unfinished autobiography, but it did not quite suggest the seriousness of W.'s finest work nor his right to be spoken of as the most accomplished English satirist of his time.

The posthumously published *Diaries of E. W.* (1976) have been described by Auberon Waugh as showing "that the world of E. W. did, in fact exist." It would be more accurate to say of them that, like his novels, they demonstrate his unique perception of his world.

FURTHER WORKS: *Labels: A Mediterranean Journal* (1930; Am., *A Bachelor Abroad*); *Ninety-two Days: The Account of a Tropical Journey through British Guiana and Part of Brazil* (1934); *Mr. Loveday's Little Outing, and Other Sad Stories* (1936); *Robbery under Law: The Mexican Object Lesson* (1939; Am., *Mexico: An Object Lesson*); *Work Suspended: Two Chapters of an Unfinished Novel* (1942); *When the Going Was Good* (abridged reprint of *Labels, Remote People, Ninety-two Days*, and *W. in Abyssinia*, 1946); *Wine in Peace and War* (1947); *Work Suspended, and Other Stories* (1949); *The Holy Places* (1952); *Tactical Exercise* (1954); *Tourist in Africa* (1960); *Basil Seal Rides Again* (1963); *The Diaries of E. W.* (1976); *A Little Order: A Selection from His Journalism* (1977); *The Letters of E. W.* (1980); *Charles Ryder's Schooldays, and Other Stories* (1982)

BIBLIOGRAPHY: DeVitis, A. A., *Roman Holiday: The Catholic Novels of E. W.* (1956); Bradbury, M., *E. W.* (1964); Carens, J. F., *The Satiric Art of E. W.* (1966); Waugh, A., *My Brother Evelyn, and Other Profiles* (1967): 162–98; Doyle, P., *E. W.* (1969); Lodge, D., *E. W.* (1971); Pryce-Jones, D., ed., *E. W. and His World* (1973); Sykes, C., *E. W.: A Biography* (1975); Davis, R. M., *E. W., Writer* (1981); Lane, C. W., *E. W.* (1981); Heath, J., *The Picturesque Prison: E. W. and His Writing* (1982)

—JAMES F. CARENS

WAŻYK, Adam

Polish poet, short-story writer, novelist, dramatist, literary critic, and translator, b. 17 Nov. 1905, Warsaw; d. 13 Aug. 1982, Warsaw

W. was born into a middle-class Jewish family and had an apparently unexceptional upbringing. He made his literary debut as a poet; his first two volumes of verse, *Semafory* (1924; semaphores) and *Oczy i usta* (1926; eyes and lips) can, perhaps, best be labeled CUBIST in inspiration. In this early poetry W. sought to achieve a fresh vision of "what is" without having recourse to the symbolic and magical functions of poetic language. He often posed as the static or passive observer, recording a stream of oddly juxtaposed impressions received from external reality.

In the 1930s W. virtually abandoned poetry for prose. His major work from this decade is the novel *Mity rodzinne* (1938; family myths), a psychological study of a Warsaw doctor's family. During World War II he served with the Polish forces attached to the Red Army. His war poems are collected in *Serce granatu* (1944; the heart of the grenade) and are, predictably, passionate expressions of love for Poland and of a determination to rebuild the war-ravaged nation. One of the most interesting poems of this collection is "Szkic pamiętnika" ("Sketch for a Memoir," 1965)—an essay in verse that traces the moral disintegration of the Polish intelligentsia during the 1930s.

After the war W. served as editor of two important literary periodicals: *Kuźnica*, from 1946 to 1950; and *Twórczość*, from 1950 through 1954. These were the years of Polish Stalinism, and W. acted as a severe taskmaster for the Party, goading other writers to produce work consonant with the political demands of the time. It came as something of a shock, then, when in 1955 W. published another essay in verse, "Poemat dla dorosłych" ("A Poem for Adults," 1955), a harsh denunciation of the terrorism and hypocrisy of the Stalinist order. The poems that followed this public confession of his own complicity in the creation of a vile myth are reminiscent of his earliest associative poetry and are often marked by an ironic detachment. The most notable collections of the late poems are *Wagon* (1963; carriage) and *Zdarzenia* (1977; events).

In the 1960s and 1970s W. also published a number of critical works on Polish poetics and on SURREALISM and cubism. Some of these contain implicit explorations of the sources of his own work. He was a distinguished translator, most notably of Pushkin, Guillaume APOLLINAIRE, and Horace.

Although W. is not a major figure in Polish literature, he played an important public role, for better and worse, during much of this century.

FURTHER WORKS: *Człowiek w burym ubraniu* (1930); *Latarnie świecą w Karpowie* (1933); *Wiersze zebrane* (1934); *Stary dworek* (1945); *Wiersze wybrane* (1947); *Piosenka na rok 1949* (1949); *W stronę humanizmu* (1949); *Nowy wybór wierszy* (1950); *Mickiewicz i wersyfikacja narodowa* (1951; rev. ed., 1954); *Widziałem Krainę Środka* (1953); *Przemiany Słowackiego: Esej* (1955); *Poemat dla dorosłych i inne wiersze* (1956); *Planetarium: Komedia współczesna* (1956); *Wiersze i poematy* (1957); *Epizod* (1961); *Labirynt* (1961);

Esej o wierszu (1964); *Od Rimbauda do Éluarda* (1964); *Kwestia gustu* (1966); *Wybór poezji* (1967); *Surrealizm: Teoria i praktyka literacka* (1973); *Wiersze* (1973); *Gra i doświadczenie* (1974); *Dziwna historia awangardy* (1976); *Wiersze wybrane* (1978)

BIBLIOGRAPHY: Miłosz, C., *The History of Polish Literature* (1969): 405–8; Mihailovich, V. D., et al, eds. *Modern Slavic Literatures* (1976), Vol. II: 412–17

—MADELINE G. LEVINE

WEDDE, Ian

New Zealand poet, essayist, novelist, and short-story writer, b. 17 Oct. 1946, Blenheim

W. spent his first years in a provincial farming center, but in later childhood traveled extensively with his globe-trotting parents. Returning to New Zealand to finish secondary school, he completed an M.A. in English literature at the University of Auckland. More travel followed, including two years in Jordan, which led to W.'s translation of the *Selected Poems* of Mahmud DARWISH (1973, with Fawwaz Tuqan). He returned to New Zealand in 1972 to take up the Burns Fellowship at the University of Otago, Dunedin. In 1975 he relocated to Wellington where he lives today. An increasingly busy involvement as an art critic and curator led in 1993 to a high-profile appointment at the Museum of New Zealand Te Papa Tongarewa, whose controversial opening in 1998 has kept W. in the forefront of national cultural debates.

W. began his career as a poet and soon gained a reputation as the outstanding figure among a new wave of poets often referred to as the *Freed* generation (after the journal that signaled their arrival). This first phase of W.'s output is exemplified by the volumes that date from his time in Dunedin. *Earthly: Sonnets for Carlos* (1975) is a tightly connected sequence addressed to the poet's infant son—named after William Carlos WILLIAMS. These sonnets, whose apparently fragmentary surfaces are in tension with an intricate formal patterning, celebrate parenthood and other complex orders of relation and intrication against the backdrop of a harbor landscape. The agenda is lyrical, local, and upbeat, but this mood is constantly encroached upon by broader horizons of anxiety and violence: memories of Jordan, the news from Southeast Asia, or more personal reflections. In *Spells for Coming Out* (1977) these intimations of personal trauma gather towards a full-dress confessional narrative, albeit with a teasingly shadowy plot. W.'s deployment of this intimate biography is driven, at least in part, by a sense of local poetic history—a desire to get beyond a kind of sexless austerity perceived by the *Freed* writers in the cultural nationalist endeavors of the preceding half-century. Thus, while never less than dense and intellectually demanding, above all W.'s early poems dramatize connectedness and intimacy.

The buoyancy informing even the most troubled of the Dunedin poems gives way in *Castaly* (1980) to a tone that is more cynical and chastened, and yet in places more politically combative. Poems like "Don't Listen" and the ecological protest narrative "Pathway to the Sea" anticipate an invective against the corporate "flesh-eaters" that will animate much of W.'s writing through the later 1980s. Meanwhile, other equally scathing pieces appear to be self-interrogative. In an eloquent chip-on-the-shoulder style that results in some of W.'s most memorable performances, the confident

assumptions of the poems of the 1970s are subjected to trenchant epistemological and gender-political critique. Similar combinations of self-directed ironies and tough-talking politics inform the twin volumes of the mid-1980s, *Georgicon* (1984) and *Tales of Gotham City* (1984).

But increasingly during the 1980s the emphasis of W.'s output begins to shift towards fiction. *Dick Seddon's Great Dive* (1976) and *The Shirt Factory and Other Stories* (1981) were read with respect, but to some extent as the by-products of a career in poetry. With *Symmes* [sic] *Hole* (1986) W.'s work as a novelist emerges in its own right. *Symmes Hole* consists of two parallel plots that mirror one another across 150 years of colonial history. In the 1830s the whaler James Heberley is attempting to make a home among the Maori of the South Island's Marlborough Sounds. In the Wellington of the 1980s a nameless "researcher" surveys the wreckage of his own household through a dense fog of alcohol, drugs, and paranoia. The researcher's W.-like obsessions—Herman Melville, McDonald's hamburgers, the shore whaling industry, and the historical figure of Heberley himself—achieve a riveting alignment in one of the novel's climactic images: the calf of a pigmy sperm whale entombed in the freezer of a small-town takeaway bar. The novel, then, is an ongoing history of Pacific exploitation. It is also a kind of postcolonial family romance: a search among the earliest Pakeha settlers, themselves soon displaced by the official "planned settlement" of the New Zealand Company, for legitimate Pakeha antecedents who can speak to the problems of settler identity in the context of a nascent biculturalism.

This investigation of the postcolonial context continues in a second major project of the 1980s, *The Penguin Book of New Zealand Verse* (1985), which W. edited with Harvey McQueen (b. 1934). The decision, which was hotly contested at the time, to include a substantial amount of material in Maori produced a landmark publication, as notable in its own terms as Allen CURNOW's famous predecessor of 1960. W.'s long and sometimes difficult introduction is also part of an increasingly fluent output as an essayist. *How to Be Nowhere* (1995) collects critical writings, chiefly from about 1983, and predominantly focused on the visual arts. Although W. as critic is sometimes opaque, he can also be highly stimulating, and this thick book of essays is his weightiest publication from a decade in which, although he has continued to publish poetry, the center of his work has once again appeared to shift: this time in the direction of curatorship and commentary. Running through all these recent undertakings, from the Penguin anthology to his work at Te Papa, is a consistent determination to contextualize high culture within a broad range of practices and for as inclusive an audience as possible.

While his status as the foremost New Zealand poet of his generation is now challenged by the growing reputation of Bill MANHIRE, W. has recorded definitively the moods of the 1970s, while continuing, with his volumes of the mid-1980s, to galvanize critical discussion like no one else around him. But poetry is only one part of the story, and perhaps as much as anything he is to be valued for the sureness of his self-reinventions. Through each of his three successive "careers"—as poet, as novelist, as critic and cultural interpreter—W.'s work is marked by a quality of alertness that makes it an exemplary indicator of the state of New Zealand culture.

FURTHER WORKS: *Homage to Matisse* (1971); *Made Over* (1974); *Driving into the Storm: Selected Poems* (1987); *Survival Arts* (1988); *The Drummer* (1993)

BIBLIOGRAPHY: Crisp, P., "I. W.'s Poetry: 1971-1975," *Islands*, 17 (1976): 293-301; Leggott, M., "Certainties & Aches," *Islands*, 31-32 (1980): 167-70; special W. section, *And*, 4 (1985): 82-149; Williams, M., "Hungry Generations: I. W. at 39," *Landfall*, 153 (1985): 66-74; McLaren, J., "Beyond All Law: I. W.'s New Zealand Settlers," *ANZSC*, 7 (1992): 119-25

—JOHN NEWTON

WEDEKIND, Frank

German dramatist, poet, short-story writer, and novelist, b. 24 July 1864, Hannover; d. 9 March 1918, Munich

The son of a politically liberal German-American physician (W.'s given names were Benjamin Franklin) and a German-born opera singer, W. was raised near Aarau, Switzerland, in a cosmopolitan atmosphere conducive to his later critical outlook on prewar German society. He studied literature and law at Lausanne and Münster, at the same time dabbling in drama and poetry. After an interlude as an advertising manager in Zurich, financial independence attained in 1888 enabled him to pursue his literary career. Subsequently traveling to Berlin, Munich, Paris, and London, W. was associated with various artistic circles. A brief friendship with August STRINDBERG had a lasting impact on his development. In 1896 he cofounded the satirical journal *Simplizissimus* in Munich and later spent six months in prison on the grounds of lese majesty

Frank Wedekind

for a satire published in it. After 1898 he worked as a stage director and actor in Leipzig, Berlin, and Munich, often collaborating with the actress Tilly Newes, who became his wife in 1906. W. was a prominent figure in bohemian circles, a celebrated cabaret singer, and one of the spiritual fathers of DADAISM.

In his early comedies up to *Kinder und Narren* (1891; children and fools; repub. as *Junge Welt*, 1898) W. attempted to break away from contemporary naturalism. While still grappling with his own concept of a new morality founded on Nietzsche's contempt for the bourgeoisie and the deterministic philosophy of Eduard von Hartmann (1842–1906), he tentatively evolved his playwriting techniques. He created a stark, provocative dialogue that often provides a countercurrent to the action on stage. His plays, episodic in structure, stress the impact of the individual scene rather than the coherence of the whole. W.'s modernism, his drive for the essential and his penchant for grotesque and fantastic effects made him an important precursor of EXPRESSIONISM.

His first major success, *Frühlings Erwachen* (1891; *The Awakening of Spring*, 1909; later tr., *Spring's Awakening*, 1923), heralded the revolution of 20th-c. theater. Through rapid mood change and strident contrasts, the tragedy juxtaposes the anguish of adolescent sexuality and a brutally stultifying moral code. Society crushes all but one of the young protagonists. The sole survivor chooses life and vitality over desperation and death, thus capturing the play's essence: the appeal for a new, liberated social structure. Although it owes its theme—the clash of human nature with the strictures of civilization—to naturalism, the drama otherwise breaks with all convention. Not only are the characters highly stylized and often distorted to the point of travesty, but the lack of communication inherent in the dialogue presages Dadaism as well as the THEATER OF THE ABSURD.

W.'s intention was to shock his audience into awareness of the oppression of human vitality by prewar capitalism. This theme is even more pronounced in the two-part drama *Der Erdgeist* (1895; repub. as *Lulu*, 1903; *Earth-Spirit*, 1914) and in *Die Büchse der Pandora* (1904; *Pandora's Box*, 1914). The three-part tragedy centers around Lulu, a "wild, beautiful beast," cruelly immoral by all conventional standards, but for W. the incarnation of ultimate, earthy morality. Leaving a trail of victims behind her, Lulu in the end herself becomes a victim of Jack the Ripper, thus demonstrating the inexorable proximity of death and sexual lust, one of W.'s principal themes. Supported by a poignant, often paradoxical dialogue reminiscent of Oscar Wilde, the play uses highly unorthodox circus technique and dazzles its audience with vividly contrasting emotions, ranging from the ostensibly tragic to the bizarre and farcical. Based on the play, Alban Berg's (1885–1935) opera *Lulu* (1934) became a classic of modern musical drama.

In a series of "confessional plays" W. explored the situation of the artist in an often hostile, indifferent society. *Der Kammersänger* (1897; *The Court Singer*, 1915; later tr., *The Tenor*, 1921) is a supercharged, cynical one-act lesson on the dichotomy of the artist's life: deadening drudgery versus boundless idealism. Similarly, *Der Marquis von Keith* (1900; *The Marquis of Keith*, 1952) measures the invariably foiled efforts of a moralist against the ultimate triumph of a reckless, amoral swindler. The play, regarded by many critics as W.'s masterpiece, abounds with grotesque effects and testifies to an extremely agnostic, near-absurdist view of human existence. The theme of the nonconformist who, although ostracized by society, must carry on his struggle, is continued in the tragicomedy *König Nicolo; oder, So ist das Leben* (1901; *Such Is Life*, 1912). The weakest play of the set, it nevertheless left its imprint on the expressionist generation. In *Hidalla; oder, Karl Hetmann der Zwergriese* (1903; Hidalla; or, Karl Hetmann the dwarf giant), W. resumed his attack on the bourgeoisie with unrelenting fervor. The tragic clown Hetmann, pitted against a venal society, remains, next to Lulu, his most impressive character.

The later plays have met with considerably less acclaim. The somber *Totentanz* (1905; repub. as *Tod und Teufel*, 1909; *Damnation*, 1923), a one-act tragedy set in a bordello, further develops the theme of sexuality. For the first time, this is seen as a destructive force. *Musik* (1906; music), a documentary farce on inhuman abortion laws, prefigures the "epic" theater of Bertolt BRECHT. *Schloß Wetterstein* (1910; *Castle Wetterstein*, 1952), his most controversial piece, is a fireworks display of erotic sensationalism and violence that, although skillfully crafted, fails to sustain its attack on capitalism convincingly. Late in his life, W. rescinded his position on free morality in *Franziska* (1911; Franziska), a somewhat incoherent "modern mysterium" based on Goethe's *Faust*. His heroine, not unlike Faust, achieves altruistic fulfillment within the boundaries of conventional society.

W.'s poems, collected in *Die vier Jahreszeiten* (1905; the four seasons) and *Lautenlieder* (1920; songs for the lute), contain starkly evocative, often brutally cynical images of big-city life, poverty, violence, and death. They spearheaded the development of modern lyrical aesthetics and influenced expressionism as well as the young Brecht. W.'s prose is less distinctive. Some of the short stories, published in part in *Die Fürstin Russalka* (1897; *Princess Russalka*, 1919), provide an atmospherically dense counterpart to the plays. In his fragmentary only novel, *Mine-Haha; oder, Über die körperliche Erziehung der jungen Mädchen* (1903; Mine-Haha; or, regarding the physical education of young girls), W. expounds on the importance of physical fitness in a utopian childhood paradise.

W. was a rebel and a determined egocentric, driven by the often single-minded desire to proclaim the power of unleashed sexuality. Justifiably, he was hailed by Brecht at the time of his death as the foremost educator of the 20th c. Through his almost single-handed attack against a stifling milieu and its passive acceptance in naturalist art, he tilled the ground for the large-scale cultural revolution brought by expressionism and international modernism. His formal and stylistic innovations were absorbed by a multitude of authors, including such diverse talents as Antonin ARTAUD—whose Theater of Cruelty is an extension of W.'s dramaturgy—Friedrich DÜRRENMATT, Erich KÄSTNER, Carl STERNHEIM, and Kurt TUCHOLSKY. During the 1920s and 1930s he became a cult figure for many writers, symbolizing the integrity and loneliness of the artist spurned by society.

FURTHER WORKS: *Der Schnellmaler; oder, Kunst und Mammon* (1889); *Fritz Schwigerling* (1892; repub. as *Der Liebestrank*, 1899; *The Solar Spectrum*, 1958); *Feuerwerk* (1906); *Die Zensur* (1908); *Oaha* (1908); *Der Stein der Weisen* (1909); *Simson; oder, Scham und Eifersucht* (1914); *Bismarck* (1916); *Herakles* (1917); *Gesammelte Werke* (9 vols., 1919–1920); *Gesammelte Briefe* (2 vols., 1924); *Prosa, Dramen, Verse* (2 vols., 1954, 1964). FURTHER WORKS IN ENGLISH: *Rabbi Ezra, The Victim* (1911); *Tragedies of Sex* (1923); *Five Tragedies of Sex* (1952); *The Lulu Plays* (1967)

BIBLIOGRAPHY: Kutscher, A., *F. W.* (3 vols., 1922, 1927, 1931; rev., abridged ed., 1964); Faesi, R., "F. W.," in Friedmann, H. and O. Mann, eds., *Expressionismus* (1956): 241–63; Hill, C., "W. in Retrospect," *MD*, 3 (1960): 82–92; Völker, K., *F. W.* (1965); Sokel,

W., "The Changing Role of Eros in W.'s Drama," *GQ*, 39 (1966): 201–7; Maclean, H., "W.'s *Der Marquis von Keith*: An Interpretation Based on the Faust and Circus Motifs," *GR*, 43 (1968): 163–87; Rothe, F., *F. W.s Dramen* (1968); Gittleman, S., *F. W.* (1969); Best, A., *F. W.* (1975); Michelsen, P., "F. W.," in von Wiese, B., ed., *Deutsche Dichter der Moderne*, 3rd ed. (1975): 51–69; Jelavich, P., "W.'s *Spring's Awakening*: The Path to Expressionist Drama," in Brouner, S., and D. Kellner, eds., *Passion and Rebellion* (1983): 129–50

—GERHARD P. KNAPP

WEIL, Simone

French essayist and philosopher, b. 3 Feb. 1909, Paris; d. 24 Aug. 1943, Ashford, England

The child of agnostic Jewish parents, from an early age W. showed a strong commitment to the ideals of social justice. She was a student of ALAIN in the lycée before attending the École Normale Supérieure. She passed the *agrégation* in 1931 and during the next several years taught philosophy in various girls' lycées. In addition to teaching, she was also active in the trade-union movement, wrote voluminously on social and political problems, worked as a machine operator in Paris factories, and served briefly as a volunteer during the Spanish Civil War.

The idea of man as worker—a being who both thinks and acts upon the world—has a central place in W.'s philosophy and in her vision of a just society. She was attracted by the revolutionary syndicalist (trade-union) movement because of its belief in the ethical value of work and the dignity of the worker. She was also attracted to much of Marx's thought (especially his attempt to develop a scientific method of social analysis), but she was critical of his prediction that capitalism would inevitably give way to socialism; she observed in the early 1930s that modern methods of industrial production were giving rise to conditions that favored the development not of socialism but of the totalitarian state. Oppression would not end, she thought, without transformations in technology to eliminate dehumanizing conditions in the workplace and a reversal of the trends toward centralization of power and specialization of worker tasks.

After the fall of France in June 1940 W. and her parents lived for two years in Marseille and then emigrated to the U.S. Unwilling to remain safe in New York, W. got a job at the headquarters of the Free French movement in London, vainly hoping that she would be sent on a mission into occupied France. After a few months in London, years of overwork and increasing malnutrition (she refused to eat more than the ration allowed in France) took their toll; in April of 1943 she collapsed and was found to have tuberculosis. She was hospitalized, but, unable to eat enough to sustain her life, she died a few months later.

The moral idealism that characterized all of W.'s life took on a religious dimension in the late 1930s when she began to have mystical experiences. She subsequently developed a mystical theology that was profoundly Christian and yet, in some respects, distinctly heterodox. Very close to Catholicism, she considered herself a Catholic "by right but not in fact," but she was never baptized. Although not all of her writing in the last two years of her life is on religious subjects, all of it is informed with a religious vision.

W.'s writings, collected and published posthumously, fill twenty volumes in French. She is perhaps best known to English-speaking readers for *Attente de Dieu* (1950; *Waiting for God*, 1951), a collection of letters and essays on religious subjects; *L'enracinement* (1949; *The Need for Roots*, 1952), which sums up her social and political theories in the context of her vision of the spiritual needs of man; and *Oppression et liberté* (1955; *Oppression and Liberty*, 1958), a collection of essays on political and philosophical topics.

FURTHER WORKS: *La pesanteur et la gâce* (1947; *Gravity and Grace*, 1952); *La connaissance surnaturelle* (1950); *Cahiers* (3 vols., 1951–1956; *The Notebooks of S. W.*, 2 vols., 1956); *La condition ouvrière* (1951); *Intuitions pre-chrétiennes* (1951); *Lettre à un religieux* (1951; *Letter to a Priest*, 1953); *La source grecque* (1953); *Venise sauvée* (1955); *Écrits de Londres et dernières lettres* (1957); *Leçons de philosophie* (1959; *Lectures on Philosophy*, 1978); *Écrits historiques et politiques* (1960); *Pensées sans ordre concernant l'amour de Dieu* (1962); *Sur la science* (1966); *Poèmes, suivis de Venise sauvée* (1968); *Cahiers* (new enlarged ed., 3 vols., 1970–1974). FURTHER WORKS IN ENGLISH: *Intimations of Christianity among the Ancient Greeks* (1957); *Selected Essays: 1934–1943* (1962); *Seventy Letters* (1965); *On Science, Necessity, and the Love of God* (1968); *First and Last Notebooks* (1970); *Gateway to God* (1974); *The S. W. Reader* (1977)

BIBLIOGRAPHY: Tomlin, E. W. F., *S. W.* (1954); Perrin, J. -M., and G. Thibon, *S. W. as We Knew Her* (1953); Cabaud, J., *S. W.: A Fellowship in Love* (1964); Rees, R., *S. W.: A Sketch for a Portrait* (1966); Pétrement, S., *S. W.: A Life* (1976); White, G. A., ed. *S. W.: Interpretations of a Life* (1981); McFarland, D. T., *S. W.* (1983)

—DOROTHY TUCK MCFARLAND

WEISS, Ernst

Austrian novelist, dramatist, essayist, and poet, b. 28 Aug. 1882, Brünn, Austro-Hungarian Empire (now Brno, Czechoslovakia); d. 14 June 1940, Paris, France

W., the son of a Jewish textile merchant in Moravia, studied medicine in Vienna, where he attended lectures by Sigmund FREUD, and acquired a lasting interest in psychoanalysis; later he practiced surgery in Bern, Switzerland, and in Vienna. After contracting tuberculosis, he had to give up surgery and became a ship's doctor on voyages to China, Japan, and India. In 1913 he formed a friendship with Franz KAFKA that left an unmistakable imprint on his work. During World War I he served on the eastern front as doctor of a regiment in the Austrian army. In 1920 he moved to Berlin and thenceforth devoted himself entirely to writing. Forced to flee from the Nazis, he emigrated to France in 1933. When the Germans occupied Paris, he committed suicide.

Although best known as a novelist, W. also wrote plays, stories, poems, essays, and reviews, and also translated from the French and English.

W.'s first two novels, *Die Galeere* (1913; the slave ship), in which the human condition is equated with that of a galley slave, and *Der Kampf* (1916; the struggle; rev. ed., *Franziska*, 1919), about the conflicts in the relationship between a man and a woman, and, according to Kafka "even more beautiful" than the first, follow

the tradition of Viennese impressionism. His subsequent works until about 1924—most pronouncedly perhaps the revolutionary tragic drama *Tanja* (1919; Tanja)—are generally regarded as EXPRESSIONIST in theme and style. The later novels are studies of inner development in the realistic mode, with strong psychological interest.

Many of W.'s subjects are drawn from his own experiences. Thus, the first-person narrator, typical of his work, is often a doctor, as in the two novels sometimes cited as his best: *Georg Letham, Arzt und Mörder* (1931; Georg Letham, physician and murderer) and *Der arme Verschwender* (1936; the poor spendthrift). In the former W. utilizes his medical knowledge and his familiarity with the tropics to tell a powerful story of guilt and atonement, a theme that occurs with some regularity in his work. The latter novel treats another characteristic subject—the complex relationship between father and son.

The posthumously published *Ich—der Augenzeuge* (1963; *The Eyewitness*, 1977), written in 1939, was W.'s last work. In it, the story of the hysterical blindness of "A. H." and his cure at "P." is a barely fictionalized account of a corresponding episode in Hitler's life, based on information W. had received from the attending psychiatrist.

Although W.'s work had some success during his lifetime, after his death it was all but forgotten until the mid-1960s. The current revival is well deserved: W.'s novels reflect his time authentically and critically, while portraying individual conflicts with impressive insight into the human psyche.

FURTHER WORKS: *Tiere in Ketten* (1918; rev. eds., 1922, 1930); *Mensch gegen Mensch* (1919); *Das Versöhnungsfest* (1920); *Stern der Dämonen* (1921); *Nahar* (1922); *Die Feuerprobe* (1923); *Atua* (1923); *Olympia* (1923); *Hodin* (1923); *Daniel* (1924); *Der Fall Vukobrancovics* (1924); *Männer in der Nacht* (1925); *Boëtius von Orlamünde* (1928); *Dämonenzug* (1928); *Das Unverlierbare* (1928); *Der Gefängnisarzt; oder, Die Vaterlosen* (1934); *Der Verführer* (1938); *Gesammelte Werke* (16 vols., 1982)

BIBLIOGRAPHY: Fröhlich, H. J., "Arzt und Dichter: E. W.," *LuK*, 4 (1966): 50–53; Taylor, H. U., "E. W.: Fortune's Stepchild," *WVUPP*, 15 (1966): 43–48; Rochelt, H., "Die Ohnmacht des Augenzeugen: Über den Schriftsteller des Augenzeugen," *LuK*, 39 (1969): 552–56; Lattmann, D., "E. W.," in Ungar, F., ed. *Handbook of Austrian Literature* (1973): 270–72; Hinze, K.-P, *E. W.: Bibliographie der Primär und Sekundärliteratur* (1977); Pazi, M., *Fünf Autoren des Prager Kreises* (1978): 71–127; Längle, U., *E. W.: Vatermythos und Zeitkritik* (1981)

—STELLA P. ROSENFELD

WEISS, Peter

German dramatist, novelist, and essayist (also writing in Swedish), b. 8 Nov. 1916, Nowawes (now Babelsberg, East Germany); d. 10 May 1982, Stockholm, Sweden

W., the son of a Hungarian-born Jewish textile manufacturer with Czech citizenship, emigrated from Germany to England in 1934; he then moved to Czechoslovakia in 1936 and, after a sojourn in Switzerland, to Sweden in 1939, acquiring Swedish citizenship in 1945. W. began his artistic career as a painter and graphic artist; he also worked in experimental and documentary cinema, translated several of August STRINDBERG'S plays into German, and adapted Franz KAFKA's *The Trial* for the stage. He received numerous literary awards, including the Lessing Prize (1965), the Heinrich Mann Prize (1966), and the Büchner Prize (1982).

Although W. had been writing in both Swedish and German since the mid-1940s, he only achieved recognition after the publication of his "micronovel" *Der Schatten des Körpers des Kutschers* (1960; *The Shadow of the Coachman's Body,* in *Bodies and Shadows,* 1970). The idiosyncratic title refers to a cohabitation scene during which the narrator observes the participants' silhouettes. Minute observation and faithful recording of the everyday occurrences in a dilapidated country boardinghouse as well as the lack of psychological probing are—somewhat in the fashion of the NEW NOVEL—the distinguishing features of the narrative, which is presented in unemotional language.

In two autobiographical accounts, the prose narrative *Abschied von den Eltern* (1961; *The Leavetaking,* 1962) and the novel *Fluchtpunkt* (1962; *Vanishing Point,* 1968), W. relates his gradual breaking away from the stolidly respectable and solidly bourgeois world of his parents—an experience far more crucial to him than that of having become an exile—and the search for his identity as an artist. His severing of the filial bond resulted in freedom but at the same time in rootlessness, extreme individualism, and, in contrast to his later stance, a noncommittal political attitude.

After writing unsuccessful plays in a surrealistic and Kafkaesque vein such as *Der Turm* (1963; *The Tower,* 1965) and *Die Versicherung* (1967; the insurance policy), W. achieved world renown with *Die Verfolgung und Ermordung Jean Paul Marats dargestellt durch die Schauspielgruppe des Hospizes zu Charenton unter Anleitung des Herrn de Sade* (1964; *The Persecution and Assassination of Jean-Paul Marat as Performed by the Inmates of the Asylum of Charenton under the Direction of the Marquis de Sade,* 1965). In this drama about the French Revolution, written somewhat in the manner of Georg Büchner (1813–1837), W. fused elements of Bertolt BRECHT's epic theater with those of Antonin ARTAUD's Theater of Cruelty by pitting the revolutionary Marat, a Marxist-Leninist before his time, against the pre-Freudian nihilistic aesthete and individualist de Sade. The dialectics inherent in the presentation of antithetical views through the device of a play within a play tend to counteract the emergence of a clear political message. Actually, as the author and director of, as well as participant in, the play about Marat's assassination, de Sade is in the privileged position of retaining control over the performance. But since the actors of the play within the play, the inmates of an insane asylum in post-revolutionary France who are performing before an audience of Napoleonic dignitaries, are given to either forgetting their lines or naïvely identifying with the revolutionary figures they represent, the play ends in pandemonium and offers no solution to the problem of how to change the world for the better. Its inconclusive ending notwithstanding, the play was almost universally praised for its eminent theatricality.

In the "oratorio" *Die Ermittlung* (1965; *The Investigation,* 1966) W. abandoned the concept of "total theater" in favor of a documentary approach. The play is based on the transcripts of the Auschwitz trials, held in Frankfurt from 1963 to 1965, which W. condensed and transposed into sparse, rhythmic language. Although he confined his account to the operations within the Dantesque inferno of the death camp, the trial situation on stage enabled the playwright to indict not only the unrepentant accused officers and guards but the capitalist system itself, which, in W.'s

Peter Weiss

view, contributed to creating Auschwitz and benefited from it. Yet he avoids unadulterated communist propaganda by reminding readers and audiences of their collective guilt in the face of continuing injustices.

W.'s commitment to socialism is, occasionally to the detriment of artistic merit, quite pronounced in his later plays. The political revue *Gesang vom Lusitanischen Popanz* (1967; *Song of the Lusitanian Bogey,* 1970) attacks Portuguese colonialism in Angola; *Diskurs über die Vorgeschichte und den Verlauf des lang andauernden Befreiungskrieges in Viet Nam* (1968; *Discourse on the Progress of the Prolonged War of Liberation in Viet Nam,* 1970) protests American imperialism in Vietnam. Both the rarely staged *Trotzki im Exil* (1970; *Trotsky in Exile,* 1972) and the acclaimed *Hölderlin* (1971; Hölderlin) feature historical figures who challenge the established order. Whereas Trotsky is an acknowledged revolutionary, the German poet Friedrich Höderlin (1770–1843) is portrayed by W. in a new light, that is, as the last German Jacobin, who feigned madness to escape imprisonment. In presenting Hölderlin's subjective poetic vision and Marx's concrete analysis of social conditions as equally valid, W. indicated the major theme of his last work.

Die Ästhetik des Widerstands (3 vols., 1975–81; the aesthetics of resistance) may be considered W.'s political and aesthetic summa. Although subtitled "novel," the work does not, strictly speaking, conform to the norms of the genre. W. depicts both the artistic and political development of a nameless first-person narrator from 1937 to 1945 in terms of his own "wishful autobiography."

Owing to the narrator's proletarian roots (versus W.'s bourgeois origins), he never wavers in his fight against both Nazism and capitalist exploitation—in Berlin, in Spain during the civil war, in Paris, and in Stockholm, in the last of which he engages in underground activities for the exiled German Communist Party. A kind of proletarian *Bildungsroman*, the work deemphasizes plot in favor of long, essayistic passages in which the narrator reflects on its main theme: the postulated connection between art and politics in resisting Nazism. W. imparted a high degree of authenticity to his fictionalized autobiography by introducing a host of historical figures—among them Willy Brandt and Bertolt Brecht.

In *Notizbücher 1971–1980* (2 vols., 1981; notebooks, 1971–1980) W. offered documentation attesting to the impressive scope of his research for the novel. With its emphasis on the social and political responsibility of the artist and writer, *Die Ästhetik des Widerstands* clearly runs counter to the "new subjectivism" in West German literature of the 1970s. Precisely because of its uncompromising—but by no means simplistic—insistence on the fusion of political liberation and cultural emancipation, the complex novel is likely to endure as a major literary work.

FURTHER WORKS: *Från ö till ö* (1947); *De besegrade* (1948); *Dokument I* (1949); *Duellen* (1953; Ger. tr., *Das Duell*, 1971); *Das Gespräch der drei Gehenden* (1963; *Conversation of the Three Wayfarers*, in *Bodies and Shadows*, 1971); *Nacht mit Gästen* (1963; *Night with Guests*, 1968); *Vietnam* (1967); *Wie dem Herrn Mockinpott das Leiden ausgetrieben wird* (1968; *How Mister Mockinpott Was Cured of His Suffering*, 1971); *Dramen* (2 vols., 1968); *Bericht über die Angriffe der US-Luftwaffe und -Marine gegen die Demokratische Republik Viet Nam* (1968, with Gunilla Palmstierna-Weiss); *Notizen zum kulturellen Leben der Demokratischen Republik Viet Nam* (1968); *Rapporte* (2 vols., 1968–1971); *Stücke* (2 vols., 1977)

BIBLIOGRAPHY: Sontag, S., "Marat/Sade/Artaud," *PR*, 32 (1965): 210–19; Roloff, M., "An Interview with P. W.," *PR*, 32 (1965): 220–32; Freed, D., "P. W. and the Theatre of the Future," *Drama Survey*, 12 (1967): 119–71; White, J. J., "History and Cruelty in P. W.'s *Marat/Sade*," *MLR*, 63 (1968): 437–48; Hilton, I., *P. W.: A Search for Affinities* (1970); Best, O. F., *P. W.* (1976); Haiduk, M., *Der Dramatiker P. W.* (1977); Bosmajian, H., *Metaphors of Evil: Contemporary German Literature and the Shadow of Nazism* (1979): 147–82; Vormweg, H., *P. W.* (1981); Arnold, H. L., ed., special W. issue, *TuK*, No. 37, rev. ed. (1982)

—SIEGFRIED MEWS

WELDON, Fay

British novelist, dramatist, and critic, b. 22 Sept. 1933, Alvechurch, Worcestershire

W. grew up in an all-female household in London after her parents' divorce when she was ten. She was educated at Hampstead Girls' High School and St. Andrews University, Fife, where she gained an M. A. in economics and psychology in 1954.

W. has written many novels, most of which tend to have a married or unmarried mother at their center. Her work takes up some of the issues that are of concern to the women's movement, such as friendship and rivalry between women, motherhood, women and work, the oppressive nature of heterosexual relationships, patriarchal attitudes toward women, etc., but suggests that, while women can do something to alter their situation, such activity will ultimately tend toward greater accommodation within existent expectations of how women are to fulfill their patriarchally determined roles. There seems little hope for attitudinal changes toward women in society at large in W.'s work. In her novels, many of her female characters experience lack of control, the "blindness" of having children, the no-win situation that society places them in. W.'s second novel, *Down among the Women* (1971), follows the lives and explores the survival instincts of a group of women of whom W. says, "Men are irrelevant. Women are happy or unhappy, fulfilled or unfulfilled, and it has nothing to do with men." Alternating between blaming women and blaming men for women's lot, W. is clear-sighted enough to see the shortcomings of both sexes and exploit these for her comic representations of life in 20th-c. Britain.

Female Friends (1975) gives an account of the enduring friendship of Marjorie, Chloe, and Grace through the various stages of their lives. Stylistically this novel is interesting because much of the dialogue is set apart from the rest of the text by being written in play form with the name of the speaking character appearing before each bit of speech. The result is a curious sense of stagedness of the conversations, which points to the artificiality of individuals' preoccupations. In *Remember Me* (1976) the same stylistic device is employed; not only is dialogue set out as if in a play, the reader is also offered a second version of the conversations in which what people "really mean" is revealed.

Little Sisters (1978) changes the scenario from "ordinary" people to the ultrarich. Elsa and her lover spend a weekend with his wealthy friends Hamish and Gemma, who is wheelchair-bound. Embedded in the story of that weekend, which turns into a disaster, is Gemma's story. This story-within-story device, used also in *Praxis* (1978), allows W. to present different time sequences within one work, thus giving the impression of the repetition of women's experience through time.

Puffball (1980) describes the interactions of Liffey, a pregnant woman, with the rural community in Somerset where she stays while her husband continues to work in London, and where he joins her for weekends. Liffey finds herself at the mercy of various members of the community. W. in this novel invokes the supernatural and witchcraft to express Liffey's uneasiness at her situation. She suggests similar forces in the title of *The Life and Loves of a She-Devil* (1983). Here a large woman uses her abilities, supernatural or otherwise, to revenge herself upon her unfaithful accountant husband by gradually breaking down the popular woman novelist with whom he has been having an affair. In the end the "she-devil," through a number of means such as ensuring that her husband is in prison for a prolonged period of time during which she undergoes extensive plastic surgery, manages to change her exterior to match that of her husband's ex-lover, and, in effect, takes over completely that lover's role and life, including her home and her professional career. She becomes that other woman. Other novels include *The President's Child* (1982) and *The Shrapnel Academy* (1986), which uses an intrusive narrator to distance the reader from the awful and violent events; and most recently W. has consolidated her reputation with the novels *Darcy's Utopia* (1990) and *Life Force* (1992).

W. has become known to a wider audience, both through the publication of short stories in magazines such as *Cosmopolitan*,

Company, and *Woman's Own*, and through numerous adaptations and plays she has written both for radio and television. Her first original television serial, *The Heart of the Country* (1987), is a black comedy that probes marital relationships and the myth of rural living through the experiences of a middle-class wife who lives through the destruction of her cozy, affluent world. W.'s stories were collected in two volumes, *Watching Me, Watching You* (1981) and *Polaris and Other Stories* (1985). She won the SFTA Award for the Best Series for Episode 1 of *Upstairs, Downstairs* (1971), and the Giles Cooper Award for Best Radio Play for *Polaris* (1978). W. was chairwoman of the Booker Prize in 1983, and of the Sinclair Prize in 1986. She is on the Video Censorship Appeals Committee, and was a member of the Arts Council literary panel.

(Adapted from *British Women Writers*, 1989, edited by Janet Todd)

FURTHER WORKS: *The Fat Woman's Joke* (1967); *Permanence* (1969); *Time Hurries On* (1972); *Words of Advice* (1974); *Moving House* (1976); *Friends* (1978); *Mr. Director* (1978); *Action Replay* (1978); *I Love My Love* (1981); *Woodworm* (1981); *After the Prize* (1983); *Letters to Alice* (1984); *Rebecca West* (1985); *The Hearts and Lives of Men* (1987); *The Rules of Life* (1987); *Leader of the Band* (1988); *The Cloning of Joanna May* (1989); *Moon over Minneapolis, or, Why She Couldn't Stay* (1991)

BIBLIOGRAPHY: Zeman, A., *Presumptuous Girls: Women and Their World in the Serious Woman's Novel* (1977): 64–65; Krouse, A. N., "Feminism and Art in F. W.'s Novels," *Crit*, 20, 2 (1978): 5–20; Wilde, A., "'Bold, But Not Too Bold': F. W. and the Limits of Poststructuralist Criticism," *ConL*, 29, 3 (Fall 1988): 403–19

—GABRIELE GRIFFIN

Fay Weldon

WELLEK, René

American critic (writing in English and Czech), b. 22 Aug. 1903, Vienna, Austria

W.'s father, a lawyer in Vienna, was Czech; in 1918 the family moved to Prague, where W. studied at Charles University. He later did graduate work at Princeton, subsequently teaching at Charles University and the University of London. In 1939 he emigrated to the U.S., where he first taught at the University of Iowa, and, from 1946 to 1972, at Yale University. He is now widely acknowledged as one of the most distinguished, wide-ranging, and productive theoreticians and historians of literary criticism in this century.

In his youth W. grounded himself in various modes of literary study; historical scholarship in English, German, and Czech literature; philosophical and aesthetic speculation from Kant and Hegel to Edmund Husserl (1859–1938) and Benedetto CROCE; linguistics and stylistics then being reexamined by the Russian formalists and later the Prague linguistic circle; German *Geistesgeschichte* (intellectual history); and the transnational conception of literature as a general human phenomenon. While the roots of these schools may be traced to German romanticism and German historicism, W.'s formation and achievement is an explicit critique of the irrational elements of the one (romanticism) and the scientific pretensions of the other (historicism).

In his earliest works concerned with German-English literary and intellectual relations, W. followed the general method of influence studies and *Geistesgeschichte* but worked in this vein with finesse and inventiveness. For instance, *Immanuel Kant in England 1793–1838* (1931) presents a full and still valid account of the early impact of Kantian philosophy upon English romantic thought. One chapter began W.'s lifelong concern with the multifarious mind of Coleridge, whose borrowings and occasionally concealed plagiarism from German sources are the subject of continuing debate.

Another early interest that has continued to occupy W. is the nature and feasibility of literary history. In *The Rise of English Literary History* (1941) and in articles and reviews, he has dealt with the problems of writing literary history—the inadequacies of handbooks that supply little more than biography and potted history and evade sensitive evaluation; the inadequacies of single-minded deterministic theories of literary history or of revolt against convention; the inadequacies of national literary histories that ignore crucial developments outside the given language.

Recently W. has reconsidered the complex of problems inherent in composing literary history and has come to a somewhat skeptical conclusion. He is convinced that at the core of literary study are the individual works of art, the value of which lies in attributes quite free of historical causality or concatenation. Similarly, the history of literary criticism can hardly be seen as an evolutionary development that will eventuate in an acceptable body of critical universals.

Such skepticism modifies the bouyant program for literary study propounded in *Theory of Literature* (1949, with Austin Warren), and indeed if the book were to be rewritten it would need to be couched quite differently for the very reason that its great success (translation into eighteen languages) has brought about wide-ranging clarification and reform in theory and methodology of literary study in many parts of the world. The skepticism of W.'s more recent views about the writing of literary history and of criticism in no way precludes his faith in the possibility of refinement of those imperfect and hybrid enterprises, nor does it suggest inevitable failure in less comprehensive works (such as histories of a genre, theme, technique, mode, or period style).

The prime concern of *Theory of Literature* is to keep in proper focus the central subject matter of study: literary works of art. Hence, the stress on the "intrinsic study of literature"; on the discussion of the "mode of existence" of a literary work of art; on the central importance of structure, style, imagery, versification, modes of fiction, genres; and on the inescapable but often avoided question of value and evaluation. Fundamental here is the Kantian conception of art as a relatively autonomous realm in human activity; of the "purposeless purposiveness," or nonutilitarian nature, of the aesthetic object; and the aesthetic emotion of disinterested pleasure. The immediate dangers on either hand are the misuse of art for didactic or hedonistic purposes. Yet because literature is expressed through the medium of language and because of its close and complex relation to other human activities, it can properly be studied also in relation to society, psychology, intellectual history, and the other arts—what W. and Warren call "the extrinsic *approach* to the study of literature." To some readers this division between intrinsic and extrinsic has seemed a division into sheep and goats, the right way and the wrong way; but a proper reading of the book reveals no such invidious distinction.

Aside from its remarkable achievement in range, compression, and the ordering of aesthetic argument and factual information, the most effective contribution to literary *theory* of *Theory of Literature* is W.'s chapter on the "mode of existence of a literary work of art," which persuasively elaborates and extends insights of the Polish phenomenologist Roman Ingarden (1893–1970).

W.'s most sustained, massive work is *History of Modern Criticism: 1750–1950* (Vols. I–II, 1955; Vols. III–IV, 1965; Vols. V–VI, in progress). The four volumes so far published not only constitute expositions of the doctrines of individual critics and the main lines of development, grouping, and transition but also offer an exhaustive scholarly apparatus and ample quotations in the original and in translation. The work of individual critics is expounded and evaluated in comprehensive detail. The method of exposition allows for sympathetic understanding of the critic's position in its own terms and in its proper historical setting, for a selection of significant arguments and judgments concerning literary texts (often evaluated in turn), and for the providing of a balanced evaluation. Of signal merit is W.'s ability to explicate subtly a critic's system or manner of thought.

W. has been taken to task for pronouncing on the validity of past ideas and formulations in terms of the present. His defense for his approach (formulated in the "Postscript" to Volume IV) is that literary history "cannot be written without a sense of direction, a feeling for the future. We must know where it is tending; we require some ideal, some standard and some hindsight." He concludes that "the past survives within the present; the present is comprehensible in terms of the past, and the past only in terms of the present."

Generally, within literary criticism the great issues for W. are the danger of positivism (that is, the reductive method of approaching literary study as if it were the natural sciences) and the danger of relativism (the denial of any standard other than personal whim and unsubstantiated assertion). Such a position is not easy to maintain in the strong crosscurrents of the present. The task is to hold fast to specifically *aesthetic* value against the onslaught of simplistic solutions, such as impressionism, Marxism, Freudianism (see Freud), biographical determinism, psychologism, displaced religiosity or ethics, covert philosophizing, cultural anthropology, linguistic or semiotic reductionism, idiosyncratic assertion, vague high-mindedness, and "apocalyptic" propheticism.

In turn, W. posits the possibility of truly comprehending the essence of a literary work of art through a synthesis of perspectives in which the critic takes all the approaches to the work that serve to explicate it, to illuminate it, to set off in its integrity and particularity, and at the same time to allot it its place in a *class* of works. Centering on its aesthetic value, not denying the delicate and complex relations of the work to external reality, to history, and to the mind's life, W. has written a number of essays on period concepts such as baroque, classicism, romanticism, and SYMBOLISM, on the general concepts of literature and criticism, on contemporary criticism, and on the idea of comparative literature. Many of these are collected in *Concepts of Criticism* (1963) and *Discriminations: Further Concepts of Criticism* (1970).

Nothing in his career has been more constantly and clearly expounded than the concept of comparative literature as essentially being the study of literature in all its aspects as a free human activity. The epithet "comparative" thus becomes the distinguishing label of a view of literature and literary study that recognizes no artificial or arbitrary limits, whether linguistic or national, while at the same time giving its due to the richness of linguistic and national traditions. It is a concept that remains conscious of the realities of the past and that is alert to the summons of the present and future, maintaining the freedom of the artistic imagination and of literary forms and ideas. W.'s position as critic is tolerant and balanced, inclusive and keen in exposing fallacy and pretense.

FURTHER WORKS: *Essays on Czech Literature* (1963); *Confrontations: Studies in the Intellectual and Literary Relations between Germany, England, and the United States during the Nineteenth Century* (1965); *Four Critics: Croce, Valéry, Lukács, Ingarden* (1981); *The Attack on Literature, and Other Essays* (1982)

BIBLIOGRAPHY: Auerbach, E., on *History of Modern Criticism*, Vols. I–II (1955), *Gesammelte Aufsätze zur romanischen Philologie* (1967): 354–63; Holthusen, H. E., *Kritisches Verstehen* (1961): 197–215; Demetz, P., Introduction to R. W., *Essays on Czech Literature* (1963): 7–10; Bucco, M., *R. W.* (1981)

—NELSON LOWRY

WELLS, H(erbert) G(eorge)

English novelist and essayist, b. 21 Sept. 1866, Bromley; d. 13 Aug. 1946, London

W.'s mother was the head housekeeper in a declining Great House and his father, once a professional cricket player, was notable mainly for his inability to adjust to Victorian commerce. As important as W.'s marginally middle-class background was his religious one. His mother, the dominant force in his childhood, was a fundamentalist Protestant, with an affinity for the apocalyptic tradition. From her, W. absorbed visions of the Last Judgment and the New Jerusalem.

W.'s formal education was irregular until 1884, when he won a scholarship to T. H. Huxley's Normal School of Science at South Kensington. W. left before his final year and began working as a schoolteacher and a science journalist. He made little money and his personal life was chaotic until 1895, when he published his first extended work of fiction, *The Time Machine*. The novella was an immediate sensation, and in the next ten years, W. wrote twenty-four books, including his best science fiction works.

W. articulated the pessimism of turn-of-the-century England in his early science fiction: in *The Time Machine* the aristocracy have become the decadent and uncomprehending Eloi, and the proletari-at, the mole-like, cannibal Morlocks; in *The Invisible Man* (1897) a gifted individual is swallowed by mass society; in *The Island of Doctor Moreau* (1898) humans are turned into beasts and in the end are indistinguishable from them; and in *The War of the Worlds* (1898) complacent, smug Victorian England is attacked by unfeel-ing aliens. In these first novels, W. contributed many new themes to the genre of science fiction. He was particularly adept at taking ordinary, realistic settings and turning them into landscapes filled with futuristic horrors.

In all of W.'s science fiction, catastrophe and persecution are present—for example, planetary collision and the green vapor of *In the Days of the Comet* (1906), nuclear war and devastation in *The World Set Free* (1914), plague and fire in *The Food of the Gods* (1906), aerial bombardment and world chaos in *The War in the Air* (1908). But utopia is often at hand—the reawakening to rebuild the world in *In the Days of the Comet*, world assembly and reconstruc-tion in *The World Set Free*, the arrival of the Rule of the Saints (W. uses the exact term), in *The Shape of Things to Come* (1933), the samurai technocrats of *A Modern Utopia* (1905), and the benign airmen in *The Sleeper Awakes* (1910). In his writing W. used traditional apocalyptic ideas, but probably his most important contribution to the genre of science fiction is his articulation of the apocalypse in 20th-c. terms, especially scientific ones.

W. did not confine his apocalyptic imagination to science fiction and prophesying essays. His realistic fiction also pivots on conditions becoming worse until they are intolerable, followed by a smash, escape, and rebirth. In *Kipps* (1906) and *The History of Mr. Polly* (1910) the heroes, who resemble the young W., cannot tolerate working in drapery shops; suddenly they overturn their lives and are reborn into new ones. Most of W.'s realistic fiction contains a version of this plot, but, to his credit as a writer, his realistic characters and settings control the apocalyptic dramas. When his heroes try to escape from their oppressive situations, they act in appropriate ways and their utopias are usually 19th-c. British pastoral dreams.

W.'s picaresque fictions have similar structures, and even those like *Tono-Bungay* (1909), with variations on the plot, pivot on actions of destruction and regeneration. In his formal essays and books, especially the prophesying ones like *Anticipations* (1901), W. repeated his apocalyptic themes for almost fifty years.

When, in August 1914, the war that W. had long predicted broke out, he immediately wrote the essay "The War That Will End War." His title became the slogan of the Allies. When the crusade

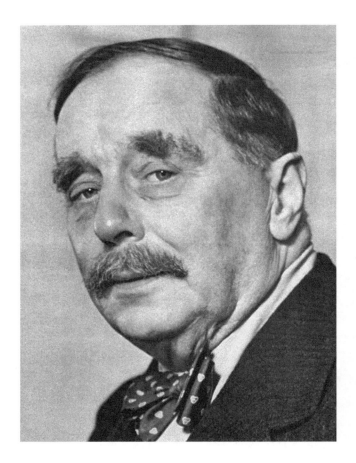

H. G. Wells

turned to mud, when the British War Ministry would not consider seriously his proposals for tanks, missiles, and atomic bombs, he wrote *Mr. Britling Sees It Through* (1916). The immense success of this book extended W.'s already huge following. The Great War marked the height of his popularity, for it was the crisis that he could respond to and articulate for the largest audience.

In the early 1920s W.'s audience began to fragment. Many readers welcomed *The Outline of History* (1920) because, like its author, after the war they searched for answers to massive and basic questions. Many younger readers, however, saw him as a symbol of the wartime and prewar eras. H. L. MENCKEN called him a "false Messiah" and titled his attack "The Late Mr. Wells."

In the 1930s, the combination of new political problems and W.'s increasing wealth and isolation separated him permanently from the reading public's concerns. His writing became sloppy and repetitious, and was badly received. W. did not understand and fought against his decline, and in so doing—in producing windier and less appropriate statements and books—he accelerated it.

Until his death W. continued to turn out books. His most noteworthy later work was his *Experiment in Autobiography* (1934). W. never understood the reasons for his original success as a writer. He wrote quickly and, to use his analogy, as if in a dream or trance. W.'s ability was not based on a supernatural gift, as he and his followers often believed. His education in science and his passion for technology gave him an advantage over almost all contemporary English writers, with their narrow training in the classics. W. was alert to scientific achievements and possibilities:

when he placed them within his apocalyptic framework and projected them into the future, he could appear prophetic. Significantly, his most accurate predictions concern warfare and catastrophe. As long as these problems plague humankind, W. will find readers.

FURTHER WORKS: *A Textbook of Biology* (1893); *Select Conversations with an Uncle* (1895); *The Wonderful Visit* (1895); *The Stolen Bacillus and Other Incidents* (1895); *The Wheels of Chance: A Holiday Adventure* (1896); *The Plattner Story, and Others* (1897); *Certain Personal Matters* (1897); *Thirty Strange Stories* (1897); *Tales of Space and Time* (1899); *Love and Mr. Lewisham* (1899); *The First Men in the Moon* (1901); *The Sea Lady: A Tissue of Moonshine* (1902); *The Discovery of the Future* (1902); *Twelve Stories and a Dream* (1903); *Mankind in the Making* (1903); *Socialism and the Family* (1906); *The Future in America: A Search after Realities* (1906); *New Worlds for Old* (1908); *First and Last Things* (1908); *This Misery of Boots* (1908); *Ann Veronica: A Modern Love Story* (1909); *The New Machiavelli* (1910); *The Country of the Blind, and Other Stories* (1911); *The Door in the Wall, and Other Stories* (1911); *Marriage* (1912); *The Passionate Friends* (1913); *The Wife of Sir Isaac Harman* (1914); *An Englishman Looks at the World* (1914); *Boon* (1915); *Bealby* (1915); *The Research Magnificent* (1915); *The Elements of Reconstruction* (1916); *What Is Coming?: A European Forecast* (1916); *God the Invisible King* (1917); *The Soul of a Bishop* (1917); *Joan and Peter* (1918); *In the Fourth Year: Anticipations of a World Peace* (1918); *The Undying Fire* (1919); *History Is One* (1919); *Russia in the Shadows* (1921); *The Salvaging of Civilisation* (1921); *Washington and the Hope of Peace* (1922); *The Secret Places of the Heart* (1922); *A Short History of the World* (1922); *Men Like Gods* (1923); *The Dream* (1924); *A Year of Prophesying* (1924); *Christina Alberta's Father* (1925); *The World of William Clissold: A Novel at a New Angle* (1926); *Meanwhile* (1927); *Democracy under Revision* (1927); *The Open Conspiracy: Blue Prints for a World Revolution* (1928); *Mr. Blettsworthy on Rampole Island* (1928); *The King Who Was a King* (1929); *The Adventures of Tommy* (1929); *The Common Sense of World Peace* (1929); *The Way the World Is Going* (1929); *The Autocracy of Mr. Parham* (1930); *What Are We to Do with Our Lives?* (1931); *The Science of Life* (1931, with Julian Huxley and G. Wells); *The Work, Wealth and Happiness of Mankind* (1931); *After Democracy* (1932); *The Bulpington of Blup* (1933); *Stalin-Wells Talk* (1934); *The New America: The New World* (1935); *The Anatomy of Frustration: A Modern Synthesis* (1936); *The Croquet Player: A Story* (1937); *Star Begotten: A Biological Fantasia* (1937); *The Man Who Could Work Miracles* (1937); *Brynhild* (1937); *The Camford Visitation* (1937); *The Brothers: A Story* (1938); *Apropos of Dolores* (1938); *World Brain* (1938); *The Fate of Homo Sapiens* (1939); *The Holy Terror* (1939); *Travels of a Republican Radical in Search of Hot Water* (1939); *The Common Sense of War and Peace* (1940); *Babes in the Darkling Wood* (1940); *The New World Order* (1940); *The Rights of Man* (1940); *Guide to the New World* (1941); *All Aboard for Ararat* (1941); *Science and the World-Mind* (1942); *Phoenix: A Summary of the Inescapable Conditions of World Organization* (1942); *The Conquest of Time* (1942); *You Can't Be Too Careful: A Sample of Life 1901–51* (1942); *'42 to '44: A Contemporary Memoir* (1944); *Crux Ansata: An Indictment of the Roman Catholic Church* (1944); *The Happy Turning* (1945); *Mind at the End of Its Tether* (1945); *[The Letters of] Henry James and H. G. W.* (1958); *[The Letters of] George Gissing and H. G. W.* (1958); *[The Letters of] Arnold Bennett and H. G. W.* (1960); *[The Letters of]*

George Gissing and H. G. W. (1961); *H. G. W.: Journalism and Prophecy 1893–1946* (1965); *Complete Short Stories* (1966); *The Wealth of Mr. Waddy* (1969); *H. G. W.: Early Writings in Science and Science Fiction* (1975); *H. G. W.'s Literary Criticism* (1980)

BIBLIOGRAPHY: Wagar, W. W., *H. G. W. and the World State* (1961); Bergonzi, B., *The Early H. G. W.* (1961); Hillegas, M. R., *The Future as Nightmare: H. G. W. and the Anti-Utopians* (1967); Dickson, L., *H. G. W.: His Turbulent Life and Times* (1967); Parrinder, P., *H. G. W.* (1970); MacKenzie, N., and MacKenzie, J. *H. G. W.: A Biography* (1973); Williamson, J., *H. G. W.: Critic of Progress* (1973); Bergonzi, B., ed. *H. G. W.: A Collection of Critical Essays* (1976); Suvin, D., and R. Philmus, *H. G. W. and Modern Science Fiction* (1977); McConnell, F., *The Science Fiction of H. G. W.* (1981); Kemp, P., *H. G. W. and the Culminating Ape* (1982)

—MURRAY A. SPERBER

WELSH LITERATURE

In Welsh

Poetry

At the beginning of the century, four men dominated Welsh poetry: T. Gwynn Jones (1871–1949), W. J. Gruffydd (1881–1954), Robert Williams Parry (1884–1956), and Sir John Morris-Jones (1864–1929). Gwynn Jones, the most prolific modern Welsh author, excelled in all genres, his forte perhaps being "classical" meters (intricate alliteration and internal rhyme, in a system called *cynghanedd*, sometimes translated as "chiming"). "Ymadawiad Arthur" (1902; the passing of Arthur), an *awdl* (Welsh ode), differed from pretentious odes of earlier days treating ancient Celtic lore, in that it offered straight-forward narration, nonpedantic diction, and poetic elegance. Subsequently revised, it became a classic. W. J. Gruffydd preferred the "free" meters (although not free in the English sense). After publishing jointly with R. Silyn Roberts (1871–1930) a derivative volume, *Telynegion* (1900; lyrics), he produced progressively more mature volumes of his own. A poem on the Tristan and Isolde theme, wrongly regarded as glorifying infidelity, shocked many. Sometimes he purposely offended the puritanically pious, only later realizing that they had a nobility of their own. R. Williams Parry wrote a memorable *awdl*, "I'r Haf" (1910; to summer). Its message, taken from the *Rubaiyat*, shocked puritans again, but the poem, although later parodied by its author, remained a favorite. Later themes of his were nature, war, death, love, and nostalgia—the peculiar Welsh variety called *hiraeth*, allegedly untranslatable, but not far in meaning from "longing."

T. H. Parry-Williams (1887–1975) couched sophisticated, subtle thoughts in a deceptively simple style. He was also a master of the sonnet, as in *Ugain o gerddi* (1949; twenty poems). Often singing in fascination even of life's trifles, he also proclaims the utter indifference of the universe to man's activity.

The short lyric early became quite popular. Morris-Jones had shown its potential even before the turn of the century. His lyrics treated love, nostalgia, Wales and its language, death. The lyric soon achieved an outstanding melodiousness, as Wales begot a host of poets, probably more per capita than any other country.

Eliseus Williams (1867–1926; bardic name, Eifion Wyn) was successful in nature poems, somewhat naïve in singing of love, and brilliant in a poem on the Gypsies, who always fascinate the Welsh. William Crwys Williams (1875–197?) employed subjects ranging from ancient Egypt to a figure as commonplace as an old man sweeping the autumn leaves. William Evans (1883–19??); bardic name, Wil Ifan) excelled in poems of nature and *hiraeth*. I. D. Hooson (1880–1848) wrought with such care that a superficial reading might make him seem artificial. His subjects included Gypsies, an ancient cemetery, the dawn, lost love, and a striking Welsh variant of the Pied Piper. Iorwerth C. Peate (1901–1982), learned and versatile yet inspired withal, dealt with historical, political, social, religious, and regional subjects. Albert Evans Jones (1895–1970; bardic name, Cynan) shows the influence of English poetry of the style and period of John MASEFIELD. Occasionally frivolous, he is also sometimes searingly critical. James Morgan Edwards (b. 1903) uses medieval and modern motifs with equal skill. John Gwyn Griffiths (b. 1911) deplores the deterioration of life and nature in the Welsh valleys but does not despair.

The foremost bard of the midcentury was probably D. Gwenallt Jones (1899–1968; bardic name, Gwenallt). With an ethical base and great poetic power, he sees Wales as sacred territory, ravaged by industrialism and economic exploitation. Viewing himself and his fellow-Welshmen as partly guilty, he longs for a past that probably never was. Another fine poet, but a far more versatile author, is Saunders LEWIS, who has written in other genres, excelling in all. He writes of nature, religion, love, nationalism, the Celtic past and present.

Bobi Jones (b. 1929) learned Welsh as a second language and became a master of all forms of Welsh poetry. He transforms common subjects and everyday occurrences into entities of a higher order. Euros Bowen (b. 1904), standing somewhat apart from his fellow poets, conspicuously reflects French SYMBOLISM, despite his denials. E. Prosser Rhys (1901–1945), after iconoclastic attacks on the faith of his fathers, matured during World War II, realizing that his youthful discoveries had been made by many writers before him. His brilliant style and deepening philosophy gave promise that was, however, thwarted by his premature death. T. Glynne Davies (b. 1926) wrote a scathing poem on the investiture of Prince Charles, echoing the sentiments of many Welshmen. Rhydwen Williams (b. 1916) is often naturalistic in his expression, as he berates and deflates mankind. Pennar Davies (b. 1911), on beholding the supposed bones of the three Wise Men in the Cologne Cathedral, asks embarrassing questions about their journeying. The remarkable T. E. Nicholas (1879–1970)—Congregational minister, pacifist, communist, dentist, incarcerated war resister, and prolific poet—wrote poems of social and political criticism, but also pure lyrics, with more than a hint of Walt Whitman.

The Essay

Brilliant essayists hark back to O. M. Edwards (1858–1920), who provided the stylistic model. T. H. Parry-Williams, in *Ysgrifau* (1928; essays) and *Myfyrdodau* (1957; meditations), wrote essays using as their starting point mundane things, from which he develops ideas of startling revelation and insight. Saunders Lewis has used the essay for literary, social, and political comment, as in the collection *Canlyn Arthur* (1938; following Arthur). Iorwerth C. Peate, a prolific essayist as well as a poet, wrote about anthropology and its duties, war and peace, religion, colorful personalities (including the above-mentioned T. E. Nichols), and Welsh culture

past and present. The collection *Ym mhob pen* (1948; in every head) contains twenty representative essays: An independent, taking a dim view of all political parties, he reaped resentment from all. Among many other fine essayists, Eluned Morgan (1870–1938), of the Welsh settlement in Patagonia (Argentina), wrote cogently on the Middle East, Wales, and the Indians of the Andes.

Fiction

The short story achieved its highest point in the work of Kate Roberts (b. 1891). She is concerned with both the universal and the microcosmic in depicting North Wales quarrymen and their families: the agony of lasting illness, the tyranny of the sick themselves, the desperate effort to maintain the native culture and the individual household, the problems of the sexes, the specter of poverty and the greater deprivation of spiritual life. While the truths she presents are usually grim, despair is not her reaction.

E. Tegla Davies (1880–1967) also wrote fine stories, more optimistic than Kate Roberts, while Idwal Jones (1895–1937) excelled in humor and parody. Amy Parry-Williams (dates n.a.), the wife of T. H. Parry-Williams, wrote an excellent collection of short stories, *Deg o storïau* (1950; ten stories), with a keen understanding of the lives of humble people and true empathy. The stories of D. J. Williams (1885–1970), set in South Wales, treat people and problems like those in Kate Roberts's stories, yet at times approach the idyllic.

Kate Roberts is also the outstanding Welsh novelist. Her settings in such works as *Traed mewn cyffion* (1936; *Feet in Chains*, 1978) and *Y byw sy'n cysgu* (1956; *The Living Sleep*, 1978) are the same as in the short stories, but the longer form affords her extended character development. Elena Puw Morgan (b. 1900) sets her novels, for example, *Y wisg sidan* (1939; the silk dress) and *Y graith* (1943; the scar) in rural Wales and deals with complex family relationships. She differs from Roberts in her interest in villains (of both sexes). T. Rowland Hughes (1903–1941) wrote five outstanding novels. Four of them deal with the same area and themes as Roberts's works. But Hughes's novels are softened somewhat by optimism and even romanticism. Islwyn Ffowc Elis (b. 1924), a sensitive modern novelist, eschews sentimentality and shows a firm grasp of psychology. *Cysgod y Cryman* (1953; the shadow of the sickle) has a futuristic Orwellian twist to it. John Rowlands (b. 1938) treats the erotic daringly in *Ienctid yw 'mhechod* (1965; *A Taste of Apples*, 1966), whose title translates literally as "youth is my sin," but his figure of a fallen clergyman is exceedingly trite. Geraint Vaughan Jones (dates n.a.) just completed a trilogy of novels: *Y fro dirion* (1973; the pleasant country), *Eira llynedd* (1979; snow of yesteryear), and *Yr hen a'r ifainc* (1983; the old and the young). This family saga incorporates the all too familiar motif of drowning Welsh valleys to provide water for England; but here the motif takes on cultural symbolism.

Drama

The Welsh drama has been developing slowly, although opportunities for having plays produced have expanded. Saunders Lewis's plays deal with ancient tradition, love and its complications, religion, and war. D. T. Davies (dates n.a.) in *Branwen ferch Llyr* (1921; Branwen, daughter of Llyr) modernizes an ancient motif from the *Mabinogi*. J. Gwilym Jones (b. 1904), perhaps the leading dramatist today, uses a sanatorium for the setting of one tragedy, *Diofal yw dim* (1942; nothing is secure)—not exactly a miniature *Magic Mountain*, but not without similarities to that work. There are echoes of FREUD in other plays by Jones. His dialogue is genuine, and the plays perform well.

Although it is still true that no writer in Welsh can make a living from his works alone, and although the number of Welsh speakers is only half a million, there are reasons to be optimistic about both the literature and the language, for there has been a burst of enthusiasm on the part of the young, including both speakers and writers. More writing in Welsh is produced now than fifty years ago, and the quality is higher. The new fourth channel of Welsh television has also been a positive factor, especially for drama.

BIBLIOGRAPHY: Lewis, S., *An Introduction to Contemporary Welsh Literature* (1926); Bell, H. I., *The Development of Welsh Poetry* (1936); Bell, H. I., *The Welsh Literary Renascence of the Twentieth Century* (1953); Parry, T., *A History of Welsh Literature* (1955, with supplement by H. Bell); Jones, R. M., *Highlights in Welsh Literature* (1969); Adams, S., *Triskel One: Essays on Welsh and Anglo-Welsh Literature* (1971); Williams, G., *An Introduction to Welsh Literature* (1978); Jones, G. and J. Rowlands, *Profiles* (1981)

—ROBERT A. FOWKES

In English

Although there is a strong literary tradition in Welsh, the large majority of the population now speaks only English, and 90 percent of the Welsh-speaking minority is bilingual. Paradoxically, although the number of people who can understand Welsh has declined considerably in this century, the influence of the language, together with specific economic, social, and geographical factors, gives what is often called Anglo-Welsh literature its distinctive qualities.

A typical early 20th-c. writer was Arthur Machen (1863–1947), known for his numerous tales of horror and the supernatural. One of his most successful books was *The Bowmen, and Other Legends of the War* (1915), whose title story tells the legend of the Angels of Mons, phantom Welsh archers who come to the relief of a company of Welsh infantry during World War I.

Onto an Anglo-Welsh literary scene dominated by Machen and, on a lower plane, such writers as Allen Raine (pseud. of Ann A. Puddicombe, 1836–1908), whose style was one of bland and quaint regionalism, and Sir Lewis Morris (1833–1907), who wrote restrained and formal verse, burst Caradoc Evans (1878–1945), a native of Cardiganshire who had moved to London. In *My People* (1915) he wrote, in a dialect that imitated Welsh syntax, short satiric tales about the stingy antics of his fellow Cardies, while his *My Neighbours* (1919) presents acidic portraits of the London Welsh, with oblique references to the then Prime Minister, David Lloyd George. "Cant and hypocrisy belong to Wales," wrote Evans, and his distorting mirror was held up to demonstrate this view with depictions that have made some of his countrymen wince, at the same time delighting others who felt such criticisms were long overdue. A typical tale is "Be This Her Memorial" in *My People*, in which Nanni, a peasant woman, starves herself to be able to contribute to the Chapel. Welsh Calvinistic Methodism was a chief target of Evans, and it remains a sticking point for his fellow Anglo-Welsh writers today. In a manner reminiscent of the reaction in Ireland to J. M. SYNGE's *The Playboy of the Western World*, the performance in London of Evans's play *Taffy* (1923), because of its astringent portraiture of parsimony, greed, hypocrisy, and meanness among the rural Welsh, set off riots, which were the secret delight of Evans and his well-wishers.

Jack Jones (1884–1970) is more typical of the older generation of Anglo-Welsh writers. He wrote realistic novels about the mining valleys of his native South Wales. Another close contemporary of Evans's, W. H. DAVIES, first became known as a poet but established his literary reputation with the prose work *Autobiography of a Super Tramp* (1907). He wrote of country, seafaring, and bohemian life. Davies settled in England, and his work does not, on the whole, have a specifically Welsh content. Also of this generation was Huw Menai (1888–1961), whose verse dealt with the natural beauty of South Wales and also of the suffering and death of that region.

In the 1930s and 1940s the Anglo-Welsh movement was heralded and supported by such literary journals as *Wales*, edited by Keidrych Rhys (b. 1915) and *The Welsh Review*, edited by Gwyn Jones (b. 1907), a professor of English and an influential critic as well as an important short-story writer, novelist, and translator.

Like other Anglo-Welsh writers of the period, Dylan THOMAS depended for much of his subject matter on the countryside, as in the elegiac "In Memory of Ann Jones" (1939), a clear and resonant lament for his aunt. As in other poems, Thomas here demonstrates his familiarity with the ancient Welsh device of alliteration and internal rhyme known as *cynghanedd*. Thomas was accused at this time of obscurantism. His close friendship with the poet Vernon WATKINS, begun in 1936, probably contributed significantly to the trend toward greater clarity in Thomas's later works. There are a handful of later poems—including "Fern Hill" (1946) and "Poem in October" (1946)—and stories that are wonderful achievements. They all owe much of their success to Wales and the Welsh-language literary tradition.

Watkins, like Thomas, was a careful craftsman. Some of his work derived from Welsh folklore. "The Ballad of the Mari Lwyd" (1941), for example, is a long poem concerned with the continuity of Welsh traditions—in this case, the custom of mummers going from door to door at New Year's with a horse's skull on a staff, trading rhymes with residents. Watkins's work evolved until it entered the mainstream of modern European awareness, but his roots in Wales remained firm. Another poet active in the interwar period was Idris Davies (1905–1953), a radical idealist whose simple verse dealt mainly with Welsh miners.

Anglo-Welsh writers frequently draw on Celtic myths and the Arthurian legend. David JONES's *In Parenthesis* (1937) is a masterful rendering of the experiences of a modern soldier—like Jones, of Welsh extraction—who during one particular crisis in World War I discovers his Christian heritage and the importance of roots in the Welsh myths, especially those of the *Mabinogion* and the Arthurian stories. Although his later works—*Epoch and Artist* (1959), a collection of critical essays, and *Anathemata* (1952), a long poem whose theme is the search for identity and meaning—have less affinity with Wales, Jones always insisted on the importance of his Welshness.

Rhys Davies (1903–1978), a close friend of D. H. LAWRENCE's, began writing in the 1920s. He produced masterful short stories and novels set in his native coal-mining valley in South Wales and demonstrated his keen insight into the Welsh character in the nonfiction work *My Wales* (1937). Hilda Vaughan's (b. 1892) novels deal with rural life in the Welsh border counties.

Perhaps the most widely read novel about Wales has been Richard Llewellyn's (1906–1983) *How Green Was My Valley*

(1939), about a young man leaving the family home in a Welsh village and all the turmoil that this move entails. It has had a lot of imitators in what has become known as the "Welsh etceteras." Emlyn Williams (b. 1905) had a huge success during this same period with his perennially popular drama *The Corn Is Green* (1938), a touching story of a Welsh-speaking farmboy who is urged by a sympathetic English schoolteacher to go on to a university education.

World War II created a hiatus in literary activities and meant loss of lives. A promising career cut short was that of Alun Lewis (1915–1944), a poet and short-story writer who wrote of the war and army life and who was killed in action.

Dylan Thomas's postwar volume *Deaths and Entrances* (1946) contains "Poem in October," the most significant of his "birthday poems" and a reconciliation of birth, love, and death. His *Under Milk Wood* (1945) is a verse play with a bucolic Welsh setting and a roistering set of Welsh reprobates.

Glyn Jones (b. 1907), a schoolteacher who began writing short stories and poetry before the war, has since written humorous novels on Welsh subjects—*The Valley, the City, the Village* (1956) and *The Learning Lark* (1960)—as well as criticism. Gwyn Thomas (1913–1981), an essayist, novelist, short-story writer, and playwright, employed a brilliant comic style in writing about life in his native coal-mining region of South Wales.

There is no dearth of recent Welsh writing in English. Neither is there a shortage of novels rehashing such subjects as flooded valleys, degenerate ministers, and the Free Wales Army. A contemporary who stands apart is the poet R. S. THOMAS, a parson in a Welsh country parish. His melancholy over the decline of the ancient rural ways of Wales is equaled by his gloom over man's spiritual poverty. Gillian Clarke (b. 1937) is a sensitive poet whose works seem redolent of the confessional strain so common in American writing. Another commanding poet is John Ormond (b. 1923), whose inspiration comes from his own Welsh childhood and not from other writers such as Dylan Thomas.

The Anglo-Welsh movement that began with Caradoc Evans and developed through the journals *Wales* and *The Welsh Review*, and later in *Dock Leaves* (now called *The Anglo-Welsh Review*) seems to have completed a major phase. Still, there is continuing vitality in the work of Gillian Clarke, the poet John Tripp (b. 1927), the "concrete" poet Peter Finch (dates n.a.), and Danny Abse (b. 1923), whose Welshness, Jewishness, and medical profession are all reflected in his verse. Much current writing is Cardiff-centered and appears in *The Anglo-Welsh Review* and *Poetry Wales*; it bears few traces of the influence of rural Wales, the Chapel, the *eisteddfod* (poetry festival), or bardic strictures. Some might applaud this modernity. It remains to be seen, however, whether the political rumblings of the Welsh-language sector will give renewed vigor to writing in English and whether those writing in English will find a new, distinctively Welsh vision.

BIBLIOGRAPHY: Lewis, S., *Is There an Anglo-Welsh Literature?* (1939); Adam, G. F., *Three Contemporary Anglo-Welsh Novelists* (1948); Jones, Gwyn, *The First Forty Years: Some Notes on Anglo-Welsh Literature* (1957); Griffith, W., "Welsh Writers in English," *The Welsh* (1964): 103–116; Jones, Glyn, *The Dragon Has Two Tongues: Essays on Anglo-Welsh Writers and Writing* (1968); Garlick, R., *An Introduction to Anglo-Welsh Literature* (1970); Jones, B., *A Bibliography of Anglo-Welsh Literature, 1900–1965* (1970); Jones, Gwyn, ed., Introduction to *Twenty-five Welsh Short Stories* (1971): ix–xvi; Dale-Jones, D. and R. Jenkins, eds., Introduction to *Twelve Modern Anglo-Welsh Poets* (1975): 13–16

—DAVID C. JENKINS

WELTY, Eudora

American short-story writer, novelist, essayist, and autobiographer, b. 13 Apr. 1909, Jackson, Miss.

Reared in a family fond of reading, W. early on developed voracious reading habits and a love of writing, publishing several pieces in children's magazines as a preteen. W. studied for two years (1925-27) at the Mississippi State College for Women, but transferred to the University of Wisconsin—Madison to finish her education, taking her B.A. in English there in 1929. W. then briefly studied advertising at the Columbia University Business School in New York before returning to Jackson, Mississippi in 1931. Back home in Jackson, W. first worked for a local radio station, and then wrote society news for the popular northwest Mississippi newspaper, *Commercial Appeal*. During the Great Depression, W. took a position as a "junior publicity agent" with the Works Progress Administration. This job called for W. to travel across Mississippi promoting economic development in remote, rural areas of the state. In 1936 W. caught the attention of the editors of the *Southern Review*, Robert Penn WARREN and Cleanth BROOKS, when she published a short story entitled "Death of a Traveling Salesman" in

Eudora Welty

Manuscript. W. subsequently published short stories in several prominent periodicals, including the *Atlantic Monthly*, the *New Yorker*, and the *Sewanee Review*. W. fully established her reputation as a major regionalist writer in 1941 with the publication of her first short-story collection, *A Curtain of Green and Other Stories*. Since then, W. has remained an incredibly prolific and highly acclaimed writer, garnering many awards and honors, including four O. Henry Awards (1941, 1942, 1943, and 1968), the Gold Medal for Fiction of the National Institute of Arts and Letters (1972), the Pulitzer Prize in fiction (1973), the National Medal of Literature and Medal of Freedom (1981), and the National Medal of Arts (1986).

It has often been noted that W.'s writing does not lend itself easily to categorization, for her flexible, versatile talent and wide-ranging interests in terms of both subject and narrative technique has produced a substantially varied body of work. However, it is possible to identify dominant characteristics and themes that often recur in her writing. For instance, from the beginning of her literary career, critics have observed W.'s exceptional abilities with language, including her remarkable awareness of, and talent for accurately reproducing, regional dialect. Often cited examples of W.'s masterful use of dialect include her short story "Why I Live at the P.O.," and the novels *The Ponder Heart* (1954), *Losing Battles* (1970), and *The Optimist's Daughter* (1972). W. is also well known for her acute and precise observations of people and place—observations that have produced in her work amazingly varied arrays of thoroughly believable characters, and lush, realistic landscapes. W. has been quite consistent about setting in her writing, for the vast majority of her tales take place in her native Mississippi. Her preference for region and for focusing on South-ern folk culture has often resulted in W. being termed a Southern regionalist writer, yet most critics who know her work well insist that in both appeal and significance, her work is much more universal than that label implies.

Thematically, W.'s attention is often fixed on examining the nature of family and community ties as well as the essential isolation of the individual. W. does not regularly approach matters of family and community in a completely celebratory fashion, but rather insists on looking at both sides of family and community life, as dark as that may turn out to be at times. *Losing Battles*, a novel that observes, or rather listens to, a reunion of an extended family over the course of a day and a half, is a particularly noteworthy example of W.'s treatment of this subject. The reader is presented with the Renfro family chatter, which reveals a tightly-knitted clan, but also betrays the sometimes oppressive nature of such closely wrought family ties. Also noteworthy here is the short story "Why I live at the P.O.," a comic study in familial fracture: the narrator, Sister, becomes so isolated from the rest of the family that she moves her personal possessions out of the family home and into the local post office.

While much of her work has been sharply realistic, W. is also well known for crafting what critics have variously termed fairy tale, mythic, or fabular stories. Such work has often been lauded as some of her most compelling. In works like her first novel *The Robber Bridegroom* (1942), or short stories like "The Wide Net" and "Livvie," W. weaves folk legend, myth, fantasy, and regional history together to produce narratives of astonishing depth and exquisite complexity.

FURTHER WORKS: *Selected Stories* (1954); *Three Papers on Fiction* (1962); *The Shoe Bird* (1964); *Thirteen Stories* (1965); *One Time, One Place: Mississippi in the Depression—A Snapshot Album* (1971); *Twenty Photographs* (1980); *Moon Lake, and Other Stories* (1980); *One Writer's Beginnings* (1984); *Morgana* (1988); *Stories, Essays, and Memoirs* (1998)

BIBLIOGRAPHY: Vande Keift, R., *E. W.* (1962); Appel, A., *A Season of Dreams: The Fiction of E. W.* (1965); Prenshaw, P., ed., *E. W.: Critical Essays* (1979); Westling, L., *Sacred Groves and Ravaged Gardens: The Fiction of E. W., Carson McCullers, and Flannery O'Connor* (1985); Devlin, A., ed., *W.: A Life in Litera-ture* (1987); Trouard, D., *E. W.: Eye of the Storyteller* (1989); Polk, N., *W.: A Bibliography of Her Work* (1994)

—MARSHA WATSON

WEN I-to

Chinese poet, scholar, and critic, b. 24 Nov. 1899, Hsi-shui, Hupeh Province; d. 15 July 1946, Kunming, Yunnan Province

Born into a traditional scholar's family, W. nonetheless re-ceived a modern, Western-style education at the Tsing Hua School in Peking (1913–21). There he came under the spell of English romantic poetry, especially the works of John Keats, his spiritual mentor. During the May Fourth (1919) Movement, he played only a minor role in the student attacks on China's feudal past and demands for the use of the vernacular language as a medium for serious literature.

In 1922 W. came to study in the U.S., where he remained for three years, enrolling first at the Art Institute of Chicago and later at Colorado College. After returning to China, W. taught Western literature at the Wusung Political Academy near Shanghai and at the Central University in Nanking. From 1928 to 1937 he taught Chinese literature at several universities, including his alma mater, Tsing Hua, For three years (1926–29) he was closely associated with Hsü CHIH-MO, with whom he founded the Crescent Moon Society, which published an influential monthly literary magazine. This society, which included Hu SHIH and Liang Shih-ch'iu (b. 1901), served to check the growth of realism among writers; it fiercely championed the supremacy of form and technique for writing *pai-hua*, or vernacular, poetry.

Although W. published only two slim volumes of poetry during his life—*Hung-chu* (1923; *Red Candle*, 1972) and *Szu-shui* (1928; dead water)—he had an enormous influence on modern Chinese poetry. The first volume consists mostly of poems on nature and reflections on art, literature, and life. They are characterized by rich symbolism, by W.'s heavy reliance on synesthesia, and by his unrelenting concern with form through his invention of a predomi-nantly ten-syllable, end-stopped verse line. The influence of classi-cal Chinese poets such as Wang Wei (701–761), Li Po (701–762), and Li Shang-yin (813?–858) is strongly evident in W.'s verse.

Szu-shui offers a greater variety of stanzaic patterns, as well as a shift of emphasis in the subject matter. As indicated in the title poem, the poems in this volume focus on the uglier aspects of life and attest to the poet's frustration over the fate of a disunited China. Subjects include the tragedy of student demonstrations, the gloom of a war-torn village, death, and the sense of the futility of intellectuals.

Finding the Crescent Society's commitment to pure beauty unsatisfying, W. turned to the study of classical Chinese literature and published many volumes of critical studies, which are still held in high repute. Among them are annotated chronologies of Tu Fu (712–770) and Ts'en Shen (715–770); several commentaries on two classics of Chinese poetry, the *Shih ching* (book of songs), the earliest anthology of Chinese poetry, compiled by Confucius, and the *Ch'u tz'u* (song of Ch'u), the second oldest anthology in Chinese, originally ascribed to Ch'ü Yuan (d. 278 B.C.); two anthologies of early Chinese verse; a compendium of T'ang poetry; and an anthology of modern Chinese verse.

W. was always open to the appreciation of new forms of poetry. As late as 1943, in the famous essay "Shih-tai te ku-shou" ("The Drummer of the Age," 1947), he hailed the poetry of T'ien Chien (b. 1914), whose declamatory verse, usually in short staccato lines, was inspired by the poetry of Vladimir MAYAKOVSKY. Although this poetry is very different from the poetry of Keats, whom W. so much admired, the drum, W. points out, is a more fitting expression of a war-torn China than the delicate sound of a lute, which belonged to another era.

Although up to the last moment of his life W. dedicated his energy and talents to his twin passions for beauty and truth, he never retreated into a poet's ivory tower or denied the responsibility of an artist in society. The long trek during the Sino-Japanese War, in which he walked more than a thousand miles from Changsha to Kunming with colleagues and students who were being evacuated from coastal cities; the plight of refugees and conscripted soldiers he saw on the road; and the general living conditions during the Sino-Japanese War rekindled in him a sense of political mission. In 1945 he joined the Democratic League, then a third force trying to negotiate between the Kuomintang, dominated by Chiang Kai-shek, and the Chinese Communist Party, led by Mao Tse-tung. W. refused to flee Kunming when a prominent member of the Democratic League was assassinated; instead he stayed and, at the memorial service on 15 July 1946, delivered a ringing speech denouncing political killings. A few hours later, in front of his house, W. himself was felled by the bullets of assassins.

FURTHER WORKS: *W. I. ch'üan-chi* (4 vols., 1948)

BIBLIOGRAPHY: Lin, J. C., ed., *Modern Chinese Poetry: An Introduction* (1972): 75–100; Hsü, K., *W. I.* (1980)

—IRVING YUCHENG LO

WENDIAN LITERATURE

See Lusatian Literature

WENDT, Albert

Samoan poet, b. 27 Oct. 1939, Western Samoa

W. is the leading figure of modern Pacific literature. He is an educator, social activist, and creative writer, having three books of poetry, *Inside Us the Dead* (1976), *Shaman of Visions* (1984), and *Photographs* (1995), two collections of short stories, *Flying Fox in a Freedom Tree* (1974) and *The Birth and Death of the Miracle Man* (1986), and five novels, *Sons for the Return Home* (1973), *Pouliuli* (1977), *Leaves of the Banyan Tree* (1979), *Ola* (1992), and *Black Rainbow* (1992), to his credit. Two of his fictional works—

Sons for the Return Home and *Flying Fox in a Freedom Tree*— have been made into feature films. W. has also promoted creative writing across the Pacific, leading workshops and editing the two key anthologies of English-language work: *Lali*, 1980 and *Nuanua*, 1995.

W. grew up in Western Samoa nourished by his grandmother Mele's storytelling—a mix of traditional tales and localized versions of Bible stories, and Aesop's fables. He went to New Zealand on a scholarship to New Plymouth Boys High, and encountered print literature—notably George ORWELL's *Animal Farm* (1945)— and began writing for himself. He studied history at Victoria University, Wellington (on indigenous anticolonial movements), and trained as a teacher, mixing with literary figures like poet-prophet James K. BAXTER and Maori poet Hone TUWHARE. In 1965 W. returned to Samoa to teach, becoming head of Samoa College and extending the curriculum to include creative arts drawing on local traditions. While teaching, he produced *Sons for the Return Home*, a cross-racial romance that critiques both white New Zealand prejudice against Maori and Islanders, and Samoan myths of perfect traditions and superior morality. The unnamed male protagonist is the first of a number of figures drawing on CAMUS's EXISTENTIALISM, caught between sacred and secular worlds. *Flying Fox in a Freedom Tree*, written over the same period as the novel, depicts a lively but degraded world of street Samoan English and colorful unscrupulous characters. *Inside Us the Dead* brought together W.'s light lyrics, social satire of "vampire" local elites, and ironic self-examination as someone imbued with the colonial privilege he works to reject. The novella *Pouliuli*, regarded by many as his best work, creates a symbolically powerful image of an old Lear-like chieftain, sickened by materialist greed and haunted by his past. He tries to opt out, but is tragically trapped into madness.

W. left Samoa in 1974 to become a lecturer at the University of the South Pacific in Fiji, where he coordinated distance education and taught writing and literature classes and as well edited anthologies of verse. In this period he began to articulate his view of his own role as writer and of the project of Pacific literature in essays such as "Towards a New Oceania" and "In a Stone Castle in the South Seas." Isolated from communal oral tradition, one that was irremediably mixed with modern ways, the writer had, nonetheless to speak on behalf of tradition and local identity to correct the absences and distortions generated by colonialist literary views of the Pacific. His outlook is reflected in the epic saga of social change in Samoa, *Leaves of the Banyan Tree*, a blend of social realism and personal metaphysics with powerful mythic symbols arising from Samoa's landscape and Polynesian traditions.

W. was awarded the first chair in Pacific literature at University of the South Pacific in Suva, and in 1988 he moved to Auckland to take up a chair in New Zealand and Pacific literature. He continues to articulate the role of the Pacific writer as asserting a dynamic viable cultural identity, to work for relevant schooling and access to education for Pacific Islanders and Maori, and to oppose racism and colonialist practices. *Black Rainbow*, an attack on French nuclear testing in the Pacific, is also a mocking political fable about the Thatcherization of New Zealand, and employs metafictional references to local literary and academic figures. It builds on his love of popular culture to create the first Pacific science fiction/ detective story. His other recent novel, *Ola*, features a woman protagonist as a counter to accusations of sexism in his work and shows Samoan cultural identity to be interacting with globalization. *Photographs* takes W.'s poetry into a more intensely personal and mythic phase, incorporating his response to contemporary free-form verse, his Yeatsian reconstruction of self through art and his Blakean visionary intensity.

BIBLIOGRAPHY: Martin, M. S., "Order, Disorder, and Rage in the Islands: The Novels of V. S. Naipaul and A. W.," *PCL*, 10 (1984): 33-39; Ellerman, E., "Intertextuality in the Fiction of Camus and W.," in Moore, C., ed., *Comparative Literature East and West: Traditions and Trends* (1989): 43-50; Guiart, J., "A. W.'s Anthropological Truth," *CE&S*, 16, 2 (1993): 38-43

—PAUL SHARRAD

WEÖRES, Sándor

Hungarian poet and translator, b. 22 June 1913, Szombathely; d. 22 Jan. 1989, Budapest

Son of a former army officer and an educated woman, W. received an excellent education and published his first poem at the age of fourteen. At the University of Pécs he studied philosophy and aesthetics; he earned a doctorate with the dissertation *A vers születése* (1939; the birth of the poem). While still in his teens, W. had published in the literary journal *Nyugat*, and some of his poems were set to music by the great composer Zoltán Kodály. In 1947 he married the poet Amy Károlyi (b. 1909). Unable to publish during the postwar Stalinist regime, he had to support himself by doing translations until the 1956 "thaw." Since then he has been recognized as one of the most original contemporary Hungarian poets, and in 1970 he was awarded the Kossuth Prize.

W.'s first collection of poems, *Hideg van* (1934; it's cold), was characterized by a philosophical bent and technical virtuosity, also evident in *A kő és az ember* (1935; stone and man). A greater maturity and depth marks the poetry of *A teremtés dicsérete* (1938; in praise of creation), perhaps traceable to his travels to India and Malaya and his immersion in Oriental religion and philosophy. His continuing work on a translation of the Sumerian *Epic of Gilgamesh* and his studies in mythology bore fruit in the long dramatic poem *Theomachia* (1941; theomachy [battle among the gods]).

Throughout his career, mythical, religious, and mystical elements have dominated W.'s poetry. These interests explain the often hysterical rejection of W. by doctrinaire Marxist critics, who have accused him of escapism and nihilism. Yet W.'s religion is far from orthodox; he stresses man's alienation from God as well as the futility of man's claims to political and scientific progress. Instead, he advocates individual efforts at self-improvement.

A fogak tornáca (1947; the vestibule of teeth) was hailed as a major literary event during the short-lived postwar democratic regime; except for his translations and the still popular book of poems for children, *Bóbita* (1955; crest), no work of his appeared until the gigantic *A hallgatás tornya* (1956; tower of silence), which contains "Az elveszített napernyő," a succinct statement of W.'s cosmology, and "Le journal" (French: the newspaper), a devastating indictment of Stalinism. Since then W. has been very prolific. His later volumes, including *Ének a határtalanról* (1980; song of the limitless), indicate a more hopeful view of the future than he had earlier expressed.

FURTHER WORKS: *Bolond Istók* (1943); *Medúza* (1943); *A teljesség felé* (1945); *Elysium* (1946); *Szerelem ábécéje* (1946); *Gyümölcskosár* (1946); *Testtelen nyáj* (1947); *Tarka forgó* (1958, with Amy Károlyi); *Tűzkút* (1964); *Hold és sárkány* (1967); *Merülő Saturnus* (1968); *Zimzizim*(1969); *Egybegyüjtött irások* (2 vols., 1970); *Psyché* (1972); *Áthallások* (1976); *Válogatott versek* (1976); *Egybegyüjtött műforditások* (1976); *Három veréb hat szemmel* (1977); *Harmincöt vers* (1978); *Ének a határtalanról* (1980). **FURTHER WORKS IN ENGLISH:** *S. W./Ferenc Juhász: Selected Poems* (1970)

BIBLIOGRAPHY: Reményi, J., "S. W.: Contemporary Hungarian Poet," *MLJ*, 33 (1949): 302–8; Szabó, L. Cs., "Conversation with W.," in Gömöri, G., and Newman, C., eds., *New Writing of East Europe* (1968): 63–67; Gömöri, G., "S. W.: Unity in Diversity," *BA*, 43 (1969): 36–41

—DALMA H. BRUNAUER

WEREWERE LIKING

Cameroonian playwright, b. 1 May 1950, Bondè, Makak

Living from an early age with her paternal grandparents in a small African village, W. had the typical upbringing of a child raised in a large and an extended family. Aged sixteen, she left her village with the hope of becoming a famous singer. Two years later she experimented with painting, but success only came a few years later when she turned her energy towards theater and literature and became engrossed with the Ki-Yi initiation ritual, which she inherited from an aunt. In 1978 she arrived in Côte d'Ivoire. Her association with the University of Abidjan from 1979 to 1985 gave her an opportunity to explore further the traditional literary forms, especially rituals that have been the cornerstone of her theatrical activities and that of fellow writer, friend, and often coauthor Marie-José Hourantier (dates n.a.).

The Ki-Yi M'Bock theater troupe created in 1985 by W. has been the focal point of the author's cultural activities and achievements over the last fifteen years. Artists from a large variety of cultural backgrounds have come to the Villa Ki-Yi, a small estate located on the outskirts of Abidjan. Actors and their families live together and put to work W.'s ideals of a new panafricanism rooted in tradition and yet open to plurality and modernity. This microcosm of African diversity has led W. to shift from a theater dominated by idiosyncratic and esoteric symbolism towards live performances dealing with contemporary issues and incorporating arts in all its shapes and forms such as traditional music, song, dance, body painting, puppetry, and a variety of African and non-African languages.

Self-taught and very interested in many African and artistic art forms, W. remains best known for her literary achievement as a playwright and a theater director. Her first play *La queue du diable* (1979; The Devil's Tail) received an award from Radio France International and many plays written in the 1980s are notable for their high literary standards: *La puissance de Um* (1979; The Power of Um); *Une nouvelle terre* (1980; A New Earth, 1996); *Dieu-Chose* (1987; God-object); *Les cloches* (1988; The Bells); *Les mains veulent dire* (1987; The Hands Want to Speak); *La rougeole arc en ciel* (1987; The Spotty Rainbow). They have all contributed to a rejuvenation of African theatrical tradition and contributed in a significant fashion to critical debate surrounding African theater's form and purpose after Independence. W.'s writing has become one of the yardsticks by which African contemporary literature and theater is being measured.

Plays produced in the 1990s at the rate of a new production every year have been increasingly geared towards action packed entertainment rather then pure literary achievements. Nonetheless, a very perceptive feel for Africa's past, present, and future is always at the center of the spectacle. *Singue Mura* (1990; Singue Mura) deals with the suicide of a young women whose academic achievements count for nothing in the eyes of her in laws because she cannot bear a child. *Percus percues ou esquisse pour un opéra de percussion* (1991; "Struck" or Some Elements of Operatic Tymphany) brings on stage twenty actors and thirty beating drums to tell of contemporary issues confronting Africa. *La Veuve dilemme* (1992; *The Widow Dilemma*, 1994) comes back to women's issues. *Un Touareg s'est marié à une pygmée* (1992; *A Touareg Married a Pygmy*) is structured around eleven stopovers in a musical journey through Africa's past, present and future. *Y'a match* (1992; *There's a Match*) deals with society split between the haves and the have-nots; *Danse révolte* (1995; Dance Revolt) addresses sickness and heath and the last production to date, *Quelque chose Afrique* (1996; Something Africa) is an examination of the role of the arts in contemporary African society in fostering a positive outlook for the future. As the troupe grows, its demand in material increases and spectacle becomes more sophisticated but W. remains flexible enough to perform in small ill equipped venues. The Ki-Yi M'bock is also performing regularly in the Villa Ki-Yi's theater but it has taken the ample opportunities to travel in Africa and around the world to places such as Europe, Japan, and the U.S.

While W.'s contribution to the stage has been of major proportion, it could be argued that her writing in relation to other genres is quite substantial as well. Novels such as *Elle sera de jaspe et de corail* (1983; She Will Be Made of Jasper and Coral) or *L'amour cent vies* (1988; One Hundred Love Lives) which deal with African societies from a strong and powerful feminist point of view are amongst the best novels written by African women writers. Furthermore, a large number of essays, tales, books on African Arts, scenario and adaptations for the cinema make W. one of the most prolific and entrepreneurial minds of her generation. This capability has been recognized by the many prizes she has been awarded for her work over the last ten years.

FURTHER WORKS: *Du rituel à la scène chez les Bassa du cameroun* (1979; with Jacques Sherer and Marie-José Hourantier); *A la rencontre de . . .* (1980; with Marie-José Hourantier); *Du sommeil d'injuste* (1980); *Orphée Dafric—Orphée d'Afrique* (1981; with Marie-José Hourantier); *Liboy li Nkundung* (1982); *Contes d'initiations féminines* (1983); *La Vision de Kaydara d'Hamadou Hampaté Bâ* (1984); *La Femme mêle* (1985); *Statuettes peintes d'Afrique de l'Ouest* (1987); *Héros d'eau* (1993); *Dans la lumière* (1994); *Ma Tignan* (1995; with Josette Abondio-Desclercs)

BIBLIOGRAPHY: Mamari, "W.," *Amina*, 130 (1983): 26-27; Borgomano, M., *Voix de femmes* (1989): 75-78; Pillot, C., "Le vivre vrai de W.," *Notre Librairie*, 102 (1990): 54-60; Adams, A., "To Write a New Language: W.'s Adaptation of Ritual to the Novel," *Callaloo*, 16, 1 (1993): 153-86; Volet, J.-M. *La parole aux Africaines* (1993): 215-44; d'Almeida, I. A., *Francophone African Women Writers: Destroying the Empiness of Silence* (1994): 125-40

—JEAN-MARIE VOLET

WERFEL, Franz

Austrian novelist, short-story writer, poet, dramatist, and essayist, b. 10 Sept. 1890, Prague, Austro-Hungarian Empire; d. 26 Aug. 1945, Beverly Hills, Cal., U.S.A.

W. was born into a wealthy Jewish merchant family. While a student at the German University of Prague he became friends with Max BROD and Franz KAFKA. In 1912 he took a job as a reader for a publisher in Leipzig. With Walter Hasenclever (1890–1940) and Kurt Pinthus (1886–1975) he edited the EXPRESSIONIST series *Der jüngste Tag* (judgment day). During World War I W. served in the Austrian army. After the war he settled in Vienna, where he met Alma Mahler-Gropius, wife of the architect Walter Gropius and widow of the composer Gustav Mahler. After she divorced Gropius, she and W. lived together and were married in 1929. With Hitler's annexation of Austria in 1938, he went into exile, living in Switzerland and France before coming in 1940 to the U.S., where he remained until his death.

W. began his career as a lyric poet. His early poems in *Der Weltfreund* (1911; the world's friend) created a sensation and became a crucial document in the history of expressionism. Eschewing sophisticated refinements of diction and form, W. embarks upon a passionate celebration of human brotherhood on a cosmic scale, the world appearing as a glowing vision of the poet's euphoric identification with all existence. Yet in *Wir sind* (1913; we are) and *Einander* (1915; together), the painful tension between his effusion and the resistance of a world divided against itself comes more and more to the fore. Love now assumes the proportions of an ethical imperative—sacrificial self-denial, born of a spirit of personal responsibility for all creation.

From 1920 on, W. turned more and more to the drama and the novel, although he continued to write poetry until his death. Yet the ecstatic fervor of the poet with a mission, the often jarring tension between pessimistic *Weltfeindschaft* (enmity of the world) and optimistic faith in the redeeming force of divine grace and love, give way to a less rhetorical stance and a more sober tone. W. no longer feels that human love is enough to regenerate the world; indeed, altruistic action, especially in the realm of politics, is suspected of being a disguised form of spiritual self-aggrandizement.

Man's temptation to self-deification, his fall and salvation form the dramatic core of W.'s *Spiegelmensch* (1920; *Mirror Man*, n.d.), a mystery play set in a fantastic Orient. In contrast to *Spiegelmensch*, which ends with the hopeful vision of loving cosmic awareness, extolling the moral perfectibility of Faustian man, the play *Bocksgesang* (1922; *Goat Song*, 1926), with its pervasive idea of the unredeemed animal in man, reflects W.'s equally deep concern over the ineradicable presence of evil, lurking to break forth unexpectedly in an attempt to impose its chaotic reign. In retrospect, one is struck by the play's prophetic vision of the Nazi era and World War II.

In his later dramas W. turned to history and the relation of the individual to the state to make his points about good and evil. Although plays such as *Juarez und Maximilian* (1925; *Juarez and Maximilian*, 1926) and *Das Reich Gottes in Böhmen* (1930; the kingdom of God in Bohemia) can be said to deal with the question of historical pragmatism versus political idealism, the dramatic conflict is not limited to this aspect. For at issue is not so much the historical dimension of the protagonists' actions but rather the defective nature of their visions and their inner conflicts.

The tension between man's "two souls," his metaphysical import and his basically flawed worldly nature, is also at the heart of W.'s fiction. The problem of political action in its relation to the significance of religiousness is at the center of *Barbara; oder, Die Frömmigkeit* (1929; *The Pure in Heart*, 1931). W.'s experiences in the war and in revolutionary Vienna are the backdrop for an exploration of the nature and meaning of political activism, and its definite rejection in favor of the individual's inner life and devotion to God, the absolute reality of faith taking precedence over the relativity of a flawed worldly reality. Social and political changes are seen to be hollow and futile, since they do not really affect the basic character of man or that of the material world.

While the theme of religious devotion and affirmation of faith is further elaborated in *Der veruntreute Himmel* (1939; *Embezzled Heaven*, 1940) and *Das Lied von Bernadette* (1941; *The Song of Bernadette*, 1942), W. once more returned to the theme of political activism in *Die vierzig Tage des Musa Dagh* (1933; *The Forty Days of Musa Dagh*, 1934), the powerful story of the persecution of the Armenians by the Turks. With Daniel Bagradian, who succeeds in reconciling political action with spiritual integrity, W. arrives at an attitude of qualified approval of political activism. W.'s awareness of the threat posed by the rabid anti-Semitism of the Nazis certainly was a factor in his reassessment.

In his last work, the posthumously published *Der Stern der Ungeborenen* (1946; *The Star of the Unborn*, 1946), W. transports the reader into the distant future, a fantasy reflecting the ultimate development of 20th-c. man's spiritual and technological tendencies and possibilities. This philosophical sciencefiction novel represents the summa of W.'s views on God, man, and the universe. The narrative device of fusing the author as the historical Californian exile of the 1940s with his mysteriously resurrected self summoned to the "astromental age," one hundred thousand years in the future, allows W. to practice his novelistic craft with a shrewd sense of romantic irony; the work of art itself, the vehicle for spiritually transcending the limitations of historicity, appears as an exercise in "astromentalism" par excellence, "as the art of giving body to the infinitely mobile mental images of our psyche and setting them in space and time."

W.'s entire work reflects its author's profound conviction that he was a man with a mission: to sing the divine mysteries and the sanctity of man created in God's image, and to arouse modern man from the antimetaphysical stupor of his this-worldly satisfaction. At the same time, his often-voiced criticism of himself as a writer reflects an acute awareness of the precarious position that was his as a religiously inclined moralist aspiring to be a public figure in communion with mankind, desirous of capturing the imagination of the people.

FURTHER WORKS: *Die Versuchung* (1913); *Die Troërinnen* (1915); *Gesänge aus den drei Reichen* (1917); *Der Gerichtstag* (1919); *Der Besuch aus dem Elysium* (1920); *Spielhof* (1920); *Nicht der Mörder, der Ermordete ist schuldig* (1920; *Not the Murderer*, 1937); *Schweiger* (1922; *Schweiger*, 1926); *Arien* (1922); *Die Mittagsgöttin* (1923); *Beschwörungen* (1923); *Verdi: Roman der Oper* (1924; *Verdi: A Novel of the Opera*, 1925); *Paulus unter den Juden* (1926; *Paul among the Jews*, 1928); *Gesammelte Gedichte* (1927); *Der Snobismus als geistige Weltmacht* (1927); *Der Tod des Kleinbürgers* (1927; *The Man Who Conquered Death*, 1927); *Geheimnis eines Menschen* (1927; *Saverio's Secret*, 1937); *Gesammelte Werke* (8 vols., 1927–1936); *Der Abituriententag* (1928; *The Class Reunion*, 1929); *Dramatische Dichtungen* (1929);

Realismus und Innerlichkeit (1931); *Kleine Verhältnisse* (1931; *Poor People*, 1937); *Die Geschwister von Neapel* (1931; *The Pascarella Family*, 1932); *Können wir ohne Gottesglauben leben* (1932); *Die Kämpfe der Schwachen* (1933); *Schlaf und Erwachen* (1935); *Der Weg der Verheißung* (1935; *The Eternal Road*, 1936); *In einer Nacht* (1937); *Höret die Stimme* (1937; repub. as *Jeremias*, 1956; *Hearken unto the Voice*, 1938); *Von der reinsten Glückseligkeit des Menschen* (1938); *Gedichte aus dreißig Jahren* (1939); *Eine blaßblaue Frauenschrift* (1941); *Zwischen Gestern und Morgen* (1942); *Die wahre Geschichte vom wiederhergestellten Kreuz* (1942); *Jacobowsky und der Oberst* (1944; *Jacobowsky and the Colonel*, 1944); *Gedichte aus den Jahren 1908–1945* (1945; *Poems from the Years 1908–1945*, 1945); *Zwischen Oben und Unten* (1946; *Between Heaven and Earth*, 1944); *Die arge Geschichte vom gerissenen Galgenstrick* (1948); *Gesammelte Werke* (16 vols., 1948–75). FURTHER WORKS IN ENGLISH: *Twilight of a World* (1937); *Poems by F. W.* (1945)

BIBLIOGRAPHY: Schumann, D. W., "The Development of W.'s 'Lebensgefühl' as Reflected in His Poetry," *GR*, 6 (1931): 27–53; Kohn-Brahmstedt, E., "F. W. as a Novelist," *ContempR*, 146 (1934): 66–73; Klarmann, A. D., "F. W.'s Eschatology and Cosmogony," *MLQ*, 7 (1946): 385–410; Foltin, L. B., ed., *F. W.: 1890–1945* (1961); Fox, W. H., "F. W.," in Natan, A., ed., *German Men of Letters* (1964), Vol. III: 107–25; Foltin, L. B., *F. W.* (1972); Williams, C. E., *The Broken Eagle: The Politics of Austrian Literature from Empire to Anschluss* (1974): 60–90; Rolleston, J. L., "The Usable Future: F. W.'s *Star of the Unborn* as Exile Literature," in Strelka, J. P., Bell, F. R., and Dobson, E., eds., *Protest-Form-Tradition: Essays on German Exile Literature* (1979): 57–80; Moeller, H.-B, "America as a Counterimage in the Works of F. W.," in Jennings, B. L., and Schulz-Behrend, G., eds., *Vistas and Vectors: Essays Honoring the Memory of Helmut Rehder* (1979): 164–69; Nehring, W., and H. Wagener, eds., *F. W. im Exil* (1992); Michaelis, J. E., *F. W. and the Critics* (1994); Rosenthal, R., "Reinscribing the Other: Transformations of the Wandering Jew in Heym, Kafka, and W.," *Carleton Germanic Papers*, 24 (1996): 127–53

—FRIEDHELM RICKERT

WERICH, Jan

See under Voskovec, Jiří

WESKER, Arnold

English dramatist, short-story writer, and essayist, b. 24 May 1932, London

W.'s personal experiences are the basic material for his plays. He was born into a working-class Jewish family during the Great Depression, and the hard times of his childhood became the basis for his early dramas. His apprenticeship to a furniture maker became part of *I'm Talking about Jerusalem* (perf. 1960). His brief stint in the Royal Air Force, during which he refused to take part in bayonet practice, became the basis of *Chips with Everything*

(1962). And his work with Centre 42, a project for carrying the arts to the common people, was the core of *Their Very Own and Golden City* (1966). But perhaps most important to his dramas was W.'s three-year experience as a pastry cook in London and Paris, a profession used in a number of plays.

Chicken Soup with Barley (perf. 1958), *Roots* (perf. 1959), and *I'm Talking about Jerusalem* together make up *The W. Trilogy* (pub. 1960). All three plays are centered on a Jewish working-class family, which, W. says, corresponds to his own family. Sarah, the strong mother, keeps the communist faith and the family together from the 1930s through the 1950s. The son Ronnie, a frank characterization of W. himself, is the pastry cook whose affair with Beatie Bryant is the basis for the best play of the three, *Roots*.

Roots illustrates the potential in the common man, or in Beatie's case, the common woman. Throughout the play Beatie, an uneducated girl from the country, docilely quotes her fiancé Ronnie, the urban, former communist intellectual, to provoke her family to think and to question. But at the end, on finding herself jilted, she discovers she has begun to think for herself. There is no stronger statement of W.'s faith in the common laborer than the words he has Beatie say: "Did you listen to me? I'm talking. . . . I'm not quoting no more. . . . I'm beginning, on my own two feet— I'm beginning."

Although Beatie triumphs, all three plays end in stoic failure. At the end of *Chicken Soup with Barley* Ronnie loses faith in communism and falls into despair. In the final play, *I'm Talking about Jerusalem*, Dave, Ronnie's brother-in-law, is revealed as a liar and petty thief who fails at a sort of utopian social experiment. Again, Ronnie despairs. Unanswered for Ronnie is the question "What has worth?"

In *The Kitchen* (perf. 1959, pub. 1960), written before the trilogy, W. again raises the question of what is worthwhile. It appears in *The Kitchen* after the main character, Peter, has run amok, broken the gas line to the ovens, and smashed a table of plates. The restaurant owner, who says he pays a good wage and the help can work *and* eat, asks in despair at the wreckage, "What more do you want? What is there more, tell me?. . . What is there more?"

W. moved to the milieu of RAF barracks life in *Chips with Everything*. One recruit, Pip, from the upper class, avoids his own class and leads the other men in minor revolts against the regulations, refusing to take part in bayonet practice. But when confronted by one of the officers who accuses him of becoming a leader of men from the lower classes because he cannot secure recognition in his own class, he wilts. Here W. again depicts the failure of one weak man who has lost faith in the worth of his cause.

The recurrent theme of the questionable worth of ideals reappears in *The Old Ones* (perf. 1972, pub. 1973), when one of the main characters asks, "Capital versus labor? Computer versus individual? Rich world versus third world? Affluence versus spiritual poverty? Which is it? One or all or something else?"

W. was catapulted to success in the wake of the "angry young men" of the 1950s. When *Chicken Soup with Barley* opened, W. was immediately hailed as one of the most promising of these angry new voices from the working class. But in a movement born of anger, W., without anger, depicted the defeat of his lower-class characters. He dramatized them constantly eating without really living. Cooking and eating were so predominant in his early plays that they became a dramatic image for the earthbound, brutish part of man that keeps him from realizing his potential.

In his more recent works, however, W. has turned to other themes: the significance of death in *The Friends* (1970), *The Old*

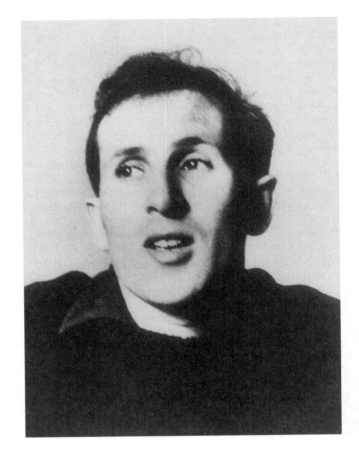

Arnold Wesker

Ones, and several short stories; the necessity for expressing joy in life (again in *The Old Ones*); and the need to love fully rather than restrictively, in *The Four Seasons* (perf. 1965, pub. 1966). Also, W. has moved away from sociopolitical milieus and in the process has accomplished some technical triumphs—notably with poetic language in *The Four Seasons* and with characterization in *The Journalists* (pub. 1973, perf. 1977).

W. is also a perceptive short-story writer. The stories in *Love Letters on Blue Paper* (1974), like several of his plays, deal sympathetically with East End Jews and other working-class people. Those in *Said the Old Man to the Young Man* (1978) analyze age-old questions of life and death and reflect the more universal themes of his later dramatic works.

Although most critics have seen W. as a social dramatist, he has no real political message. He has great doubts about the validity of communism, socialism, or any of the ideologies of his century. Instead, W. has turned to the expression and experiencing of art as a partial solution to man's attempt to understand the meaning of life and death. In the essay collection *Fears of Fragmentation* (1970) he noted, "In this life some things must remain sacred . . . and one . . . is the nerve-racking sight of a vulnerable man exposing his confusions, wounds or despair, or simply singing hymns of praise at being alive." And in *The Old Ones*, in the character of Emanuel, the exponent of Hasidic Judaism, he offers the expression of joy in life as a means of confronting life's confusions. While it is perhaps still too early to weigh the value of W.'s work as a whole, he seems to be groping toward a partial solution for the complexities of life, namely, that one may find joy in experiences if not answers in ideologies.

FURTHER WORKS: *Six Sundays in January* (1971); *The Wedding Feast* (perf. 1974, pub. 1977); *Words* (1976); *The Merchant* (1977); *Journalism: A Triptych* (1978); *Fatlips* (1978); *Caritas* (1981)

BIBLIOGRAPHY: Ribalow, H. V., *A. W.* (1965); Kitchin, L., "Drama with a Message: A. W.," in Brown, J. R., ed., *Modern British Dramatists: A Collection of Critical Essays* (1968): 71–82; Page, M., "Whatever Happened to A. W.: His Recent Plays," *MD*, 11 (1968): 317–25; Leeming, G., and Trussler, S., *The Plays of A. W.: An Assessment* (1971); Wellwarth, G., *The Theater of Protest and Paradox*, rev. ed. (1971): 271–82; Hayman, R., *A. W.* (1973); Leeming, G., *W.: The Playwright* (1983)

—HONORA M. LYNCH

WEST, Nathanael

(pseud. of Nathan Weinstein) American novelist and screenwriter, b. 17 Oct. 1903, New York, N.Y.; d. 22 Dec. 1940, El Centro, Cal.

W., whose parents were Russian Jewish immigrants, entered Brown University in 1922, where some of his first work appeared in college publications. His cartoons, essays, and poetry were marked by a sardonic style that owed something to the influence of a fellow student who became a lifelong friend, the humorist S. J. Perelman (1904–1979).

W. left Brown in 1924, determined to be a successful writer. Unfortunately, before he could complete his first book, the Depression began. Until his death in an automobile accident in 1940, W. worked at various low-paying jobs, failed at various money-making schemes, and produced four short novels, which only after his death established his reputation.

The Dream Life of Balso Snell (1931) loosely strings together a number of satirical episodes, including comic "turns" that go back to W.'s college days. W. tried here and, with greater success, in his other books for a delicate balance between BLACK HUMOR and compassion, surrealistic imagery and a search for order, nihilism and spiritual values. In his later fiction he developed protagonists who struggle to reconcile these seeming contradictions. The "Westian hero," through his quest, confronts the great mass of humanity, depicted both as a number of strikingly individual types and as a faceless and dangerous mob.

What many feel was W.'s finest expression of this conflict came in *Miss Lonelyhearts* (1933), inspired both by W.'s encounters as a night manager of a New York hotel and by his visit to a newspaper columnist who showed him letters from readers asking for help. W. saw in these experiences the subject for his novel—a newspaper-man who needs to find answers to the problems of suffering posed by the down and out. He revised tirelessly, publishing excerpts in *Contact*, a magazine he started with William Carlos WILLIAMS in 1932.

His original idea was for a novel "in the form of a comic strip." This visual quality is reflected in the style, which has the spareness of etched steel engravings and the violence of nightmare. The reporter, known only as Miss Lonelyhearts, struggles, amid the cynicism and escapism of his colleagues, for an answer to the cries of help that haunt him. Interspersed are the contrasting voices of the letters themselves—some directly quoting those W. had read. Reviewers praised the book, and W. felt his success was assured. But in one of the ironies that plagued his fiction and his life, the book was withdrawn from sale when the publisher went bankrupt; when it finally did appear, it was remaindered and, for a time, forgotten.

This bitter dashing of his hopes helped shape *A Cool Million* (1934), a satire that depicts an America that had, in the Depression, changed from a land of opportunity to a land of opportunists. The hero is an idealist who clings to the shattered dream as he is physically dismembered. Ultimately, he finds his calling—as a martyr whose death enables fascism to take over America.

A minor work, *A Cool Million* lacks the craft and depth of W.'s other novels, although it displays a savage wit that ridicules the Horatio Alger myth while warning of the more dangerous fantasies that threaten to supplant it.

W.'s own search for success led him in the mid-1930s to Hollywood, where he worked as a screenwriter on various "B" pictures. These years of poverty and hackwork gave him the setting and inspiration for his last novel, *The Day of the Locust* (1939). Here, Hollywood becomes a place where individuals pursue the dream of success by manufacturing synthetic dreams for others, where the American rainbow ends not in a pot of gold but in disillusionment, despair, and the threat of mass destruction. The dreamers are both the mass, who "come to California to die," and a collection of strange and affecting individuals whose paths cross with that of the hero. Tod Hackett is another version of the Westian seeker, a painter pursuing meaning and order in the human chaos that over-whelms him. He chases his own dream, a tawdry would-be actress turned prostitute, while portraying himself and everyone he meets as figures on a giant canvas, a painting in progress called "The Burning of Los Angeles." W.'s longest work, this novel is itself a complex picture. It orchestrates a cast of characters toward a climax that turns awareness of the gulf between cheap dreams and grim reality into an opportunity for mindless violence.

After W.'s death in 1940, he was recognized not only as one of the best chroniclers of the Depression, taken to be the betrayal of the American Dream, but also as a forerunner of the Black Humorists of the post-World War II era. Although disillusion and despair are leitmotifs in his art, W. wrote with humor, compassion, and a genuine respect for the hopes and aspirations of humanity.

W. did not feel that the artist must spell out solutions to the problems he depicts. Instead he sought to fix on his canvas the world as it is. His distinctive satirical style put his vision in bold relief, although throughout are subtle shadings that suggest unrealized possibilities and human complexities. Like the artist-hero of *The Day of the Locust*, W. was both victim and observer of the failure of the American Dream in the 1930s; he saw his art as ironic commentary and shouted warning. Thus, in the last line of this last novel, Tod Hackett, rescued from the violence of the mob, re-sponds as W. did in all his work. He imitates the sound of a siren and, at the same time, laughs.

FURTHER WORKS: *The Complete Works of N. W.* (1957)

BIBLIOGRAPHY: Light, F., *N. W.: An Interpretive Study* (1961); Volpe, E. L., "The Waste Land of N. W.," *Renascence*, 13 (1961): 69–77; Hyman, S. E., *N. W.* (1962); Comerchero, W., *N. W., the Ironic Prophet* (1964); Martin, J., *N. W.: The Art of His Life* (1970);

Martin, J., ed., *N. W.: A Collection of Critical Essays* (1972); White, W., *N. W.: A Comprehensive Bibliography* (1975); Tropp, M., "N. W. and the Persistence of Hope," *Renascence*, 31 (1979): 205–14

—MARTIN TROPP

WEST, Rebecca

(pseud. of Cicily Isabel Fairfield) English novelist, journalist, critic, historian, b. 21 Dec. 1892, County Kerry, Ireland; d. 15 March 1983, London

Third daughter of gifted but not wealthy parents, W. was educated in Edinburgh; drama study in London provided only her pen name (from Ibsen's spirited heroine). In 1911 she began writing for London publications, first in *The Freewoman*. A turbulent ten-year love affair with H. G. WELLS began in 1913, a son (the writer Anthony West) being born in 1914. Years later, in 1930, she married a banker, Henry Maxwell Andrews; the marriage, a stable and happy one, lasted until his death in 1968. All along, W. wrote constantly—novels, journalism, criticism. Traveling and lecturing widely, she pursued an influential literary career into her late eighties. She received numerous honors, including Dame Commander of the British Empire.

W. herself regretted that she was not able to devote more of her prodigious output to belles—lettres, but her greatest influence was as an interpretive writer. One powerful work, *Black Lamb and Grey Falcon* (1941), the record of a journey through Yugoslavia in 1937, synthesizes the history of eastern Europe that culminated in the world wars. *The Meaning of Treason* (1947), *A Train of Powder* (1955), and *The New Meaning of Treason* (1964) interpret major intellectual, judicial, or political events, as does the more recent *1900* (1982). These books show her to be a sympathetic but hard—thinking observer of modern life.

Her list of distinguished literary criticism and biography begins with her first book, *Henry James* (1916). *The Strange Necessity* (1928) explores early 20th-c. writing and theories of creativity and cognition. *St. Augustine* (1933), in many ways her most meaningful book, examines the impact of the saint and thinker on the Western psyche. *The Court and the Castle* (1957) is an analysis of power and politics by means of Shakespeare criticism. Collection of the important but not easily available newspaper and magazine criticism has begun with *The Young Rebecca: Writings of R. W. 1911–1917* (1982).

The six important novels are so different in tone and approach as to seem the work of several authors. *The Return of the Soldier* (1918) is a brief, well—crafted story about a shell—shocked soldier. Far more ambitious but not entirely effective is *The Judge* (1922), a Hardyesque chronicle of illegitimacy and feminine suffering. *Harriet Hume* (1929) is a fantasy, mainly celebrating the city of London. Most enduringly successful of the four novels written before World War II is *The Thinking Reed* (1936), a witty comedy of manners about the very rich. The two big novels written since the war were well received both critically and popularly. *The Fountain Overflows* (1956), about an Edwardian family, is at least partly autobiographical. Projected as the first volume of a trilogy, it was not followed up except by a fragment of a succeeding novel published in *R. W.: A Celebration* (1977), a compendium of much preceding work. The last full novel, *The Birds Fall Down* (1966),

views political and marital intrigue through the shrewd, innocent eyes of a young girl.

All of the novels are written from an intensely feminine, sometimes feminist, point of view, one by no means sheltered or limited. All reflect the feminine need, and personal search, for order and peace, as opposed to masculine force and chaos. Usually the outcome of this mismatch is destructive to women, although occasionally a blending of the two can produce energized harmony.

In a long, rich, and varied literary career, W. wrote more than twenty major books and many stories, articles, and essays; as a literary personality, she knew everyone of consequence in the world of European, British, and American letters, and many of consequence in the worlds of politics and power. A reporter of genius, perhaps the best public writer of her age, she was a thinker as well as a writer. Her fiction processed her public concerns—history, women's rights, literature—into art. Her literary career is impressive not so much for its length—more than seventy years—as for its unbroken level of excellence. So much work could not all be of equal value, but most of her writing shows a diamond—hard brilliance of intellect, of realized thought, and a pure lucidity of style that few writers can match.

Her eclecticism as an artist precludes categorizing, and her work has not yet been the subject of much adequate critical analysis. Her position is clear, however; at the end of her life she was unquestionably England's foremost woman of letters.

FURTHER WORKS: *Lions and Lambs* (1928); *D. H. Lawrence* (1930); *Arnold Bennett Himself* (1931); *Ending in Earnest* (1931); *A Letter to a Grandfather* (1933); *The Modern "Rake's Progress"* (1934); *The Harsh Voice* (1935); *The Vassall Affair* (1963)

BIBLIOGRAPHY: Hutchinson, G., *The Itinerant Ivory Tower* (1953): 241–55; Orlich, M., *The Novels of R. W.* (1967); Kobler, T., "The Eclecticism of R. W.," *Crit*, 13 (1971): 30–49; Wolfe, P., *R. W.: Artist and Thinker* (1971); Ray, G., *H. G. Wells and R. W.* (1974); Hynes, S., "Introduction: In Communion with Reality," in *R. W.: A Celebration* (1977): ix–xviii; Deakin, M., *R. W.* (1980); Warner, M., "R. W.: The Art of Fiction," *Paris Review*, 23 (1981): 116–64

—TURNER S. KOBLER

WEST INDIAN LITERATURE

See English-Caribbean Literature

WESTERN SAMOAN LITERATURE

See Pacific Islands Literature

WHARTON, Edith

(née Edith Newbold Jones) American novelist and short-story writer, b. 24 Jan. 1862, New York, N.Y.; d. 11 Aug. 1937, Saint-Brice-sous-Forêt, France

W. was born into patrician New York City society. A precocious child, she was educated by European governesses, whether at home in New York and Newport, Rhode Island, or in Europe. At

Edith Wharton

eleven she made her first attempt to write a novel. At twenty-three she married Edward W., presumably thereafter to fulfill her destiny as a wife with social graces. The tension between this limited role and that of an aspiring writer resulted in nervous collapse, punctuated by sporadic story writing in the early 1890s. A decade later she was writing more consistently. The Whartons based themselves increasingly in Paris. After divorcing her husband in 1913, W. continued to live in France. Her last visits to the U.S. were in 1913 and 1923.

W. established her reputation as a novelist with *The House of Mirth* (1905). In it she turned to her own contemporary New York City society for the background as well as the theme: the destruction of the heroine Lily Bart by the pitiless society on whose fringes she lives, doubly vulnerable by virtue of being a woman. This society is not the patrician society of W.'s childhood but its more ambitious hybrid successor, a society devoted excessively to outer forms, lacking human substance.

W. translated this society, perhaps now slightly less parochial, to Europe in *The Reef* (1912). It is the only one of her novels to show any considerable influence of her friend Henry JAMES, who, however, despite his admiration, felt moved to point out the "unreferred" relationship between the scene and the characters. The same might be said of most of the relationships between the characters themselves. They—especially but not exclusively the men—prefer social form to the risks of genuine human relationships. Anna Leath, the heroine, at once exemplifies and suffers from the struggle between the two modes.

In *The Custom of the Country* (1913) society has become more materialistic, and not less chauvinistic. Undine Spragg, unlike W.'s previous heroines, knows how to play the game of social—not to speak of material—advancement, even though as a woman her avenues are severely restricted. In the course of her dubious achievement she comes close to being a dehumanized abstraction, as W. in her disdain of this society steers an uncertain line between satire and mere caricature. To the old, "better" society she accords one contrapuntal "book" of the lengthy novel, an affectionate, ironic evocation of the past, whose anachronistic characters are no match for Undine Spragg.

W.'s best-known novel, *Ethan Frome* (1911), lies outside the mold of those more typical novels dealing with patrician society and its materialistic and mercantile descendants. Set in impoverished rural New England, *Ethan Frome* is a more direct transmutation of W.'s emotions as well as a reflection of her earlier, if patrician, sympathy for the lower classes as chief victims of an industrial, material culture. Her characterizations are complex and thoroughly believable. Her realism, typically suggested by leitmotif, is gripping. The theme is starkly simple: some people are fated for suffering.

The Age of Innocence (1920) is an extensive reaching back, both loving and critical, to the vanished and vanquished society of W.'s childhood. The banishment of Ellen Olenska for breaking society's taboo—divorcing her husband—strikes us as vindictive, possibly because of that society's extremely unequal treatment of women. Having sown no wild oats, as do the men commonly, Ellen is nonetheless thrown overboard for rocking the boat of social convention, and none of the men, not even the one who loves her—in his fashion (and the fashion of most W. heroes)—will in the long run go to her rescue.

During the decade after *The Age of Innocence*, W. wrote ten much less distinguished novels essentially for serialization in slick magazines. They are marked on the whole by superficial characterization and a failure of verisimilitude, both probably owing to W.'s growing unfamiliarity with contemporaneous America. The moving quality of her last, uncompleted, posthumously published novel, *The Buccaneers* (1938), which harks back to her own New York City generation, suggests, however, that her novelistic powers had not waned but had only lain idle.

Both early and late, W. devoted herself to writing short stories (including ghost stories) as well as novels. Cleverly plotted, most of them dwell on the foibles of the New York City societies—and their European extensions—dwelt on in her longer fiction. In addition to early poetry, to critical essays and reviews, and to travel literature, W. also wrote an autobiography, *A Backward Glance* (1934). It is highly eclectic, omitting much and eschewing introspection.

While W. cultivated the form of the traditional 19th-c. novel, she was original in the brilliant depiction of her particular social topos. Indeed, as a consequence of this very virtuosity, some critics have averred that she treats the trivial doings of trivial people. These doings and these people, however, typified a society in crisis, about which there were things to be said. W. said them, with consummate irony. Alert at first hand to the special disadvantages to which her society subjected women, above all brilliant women, still, W. was only partly a feminist. Social class was even more important to her than sexual equality. It would perhaps have struck her as the crowning irony that the former, at least in her sense, has become an anachronism while the latter now has wide support.

FURTHER WORKS: *Verses* (1878); *The Decoration of Houses* (1897, with Ogden Codman, Jr.); *The Greater Inclination* (1899); *The Touchstone* (1900); *Crucial Instances* (1901); *The Valley of Decision* (1902); *Sanctuary* (1903); *The Descent of Man* (1904); *Italian Villas and Their Gardens* (1904); *Italian Backgrounds* (1905); *Madame de Treymes* (1907); *The Fruit of the Tree* (1907); *A Motor-Flight through France* (1908); *The Hermit and the Wild Woman* (1908); *Artemis to Actaeon* (1909); *Tales of Men and Ghosts* (1910); *Fighting France, from Dunkerque to Belfort* (1915); *Xingu* (1916); *Summer* (1917); *The Marne* (1918); *French Ways and Their Meaning* (1919); *In Morocco* (1920); *The Glimpses of the Moon* (1922); *A Son at the Front* (1923); *Old New York: False Dawn, The Old Maid, The Spark, New Year's Day* (1924); *The Mother's Recompense* (1925); *The Writing of Fiction* (1925); *Here and Beyond* (1926); *Twelve Poems* (1926); *Twilight Sleep* (1927); *The Children* (1928); *Hudson River Bracketed* (1929); *Certain People* (1930); *The Gods Arrive* (1932); *Human Nature* (1933); *The World Over* (1936); *Ghosts* (1937); *An E. W. Treasury* (1950); *The Best Short Stories of E. W.* (1958); *The E. W. Reader* (1965); *The Collected Short Stories of E. W.* (1968); *Fast and Loose* (1977)

BIBLIOGRAPHY: Lubbock, P., *Portrait of E. W.* (1947); Nevius, B., *E. W.: A Study of Her Fiction* (1953); Coolidge, O., *E. W.: 1862–1937* (1964); Kellogg, G., *The Two Lives of E. W.* (1965); Walton, G., *E. W.: A Critical Interpretation* (1970); Auchincloss, L., *E. W.* (1971); Lewis, R. W. B., *E. W.* (1975); Lindberg, G. H., *E. W. and the Novel of Manners* (1975); McDowell, M. B., *E. W.* (1976); Lawson, R. H., *E. W.* (1977); Wolff, C. G., *A Feast of Words: The Triumph of E. W.* (1977); Wershoven, C., *The Female Intruder in the Novels of E. W.* (1982)

—RICHARD H. LAWSON

E. B. White

WHITE, E(lwyn) B(rooks)

American essayist, journalist, editor, poet, short-story writer, and children's-book author; b. 11 July 1899, Mount Vernon, N.Y.; d. 1 Oct. 1985, North Brooklin, Maine

W. served as a private in the U.S. Army during World War I and received his A.B. from Cornell University in 1921. After his graduation he became a reporter for United Press and American Legion News Service and then joined the *Seattle Times*. In 1924 he returned to New York to work as a production assistant and copywriter at an advertising agency. W. began submitting pieces to the *New Yorker* soon after the magazine started publishing in 1925. Editor Harold Ross was impressed with W.'s work and invited him to join the staff of the magazine. For the next eleven years, W. wrote and edited the "Talk of the Town" section of the *New Yorker* which is comprised of topical expository pieces ranging in subject matter from the often serious political commentary in "Notes and Comment" to the two or three light, amusing, and sometimes frivolous reports that present slices of New York life. In 1929 W. married the literary editor of the *New Yorker*, Katherine Sargeant Angell (1892–1977), with whom he edited *A Subtreasury of American Humor* (1941). In 1936 W. and his family moved to Maine, and W. commuted to New York only when necessary. From 1938 to 1943 he wrote and edited a column called "One Man's Meat" for *Harper's*. He continued to be a regular contributor to the

New Yorker for the rest of his working life. W. was awarded the Presidential Medal of Freedom (1963) and the National Medal for Literature (1971). He died in Maine of Alzheimer's disease at the age of eighty-five.

W.'s first books were published in 1929, *The Lady Is Cold*, a collection of light poems, and the humorous *Is Sex Necessary? or Why You Feel the Way You Do*, which he wrote in collaboration with his friend and colleague at the *New Yorker*, James THURBER. W. later published a second volume of poetry, *The Fox of Peapack* (1938). His short stories and entertaining commentaries are collected in *Alice through the Cellophane* (1933), *Quo Vadimus?* (1939), and *The Second Tree from the Corner* (1954).

It is W.'s clear and graceful prose style, sometimes amusing but more often satirical, that makes him one of America's finest essayists. A master of the informal personal essay, W.'s writing has the ability to convey a sense of whimsy while maintaining a tone that remains modest though ironical. He is often credited with establishing the crisp, light, and slightly playful style that has long been associated with the *New Yorker*.

In 1957 the *New Yorker* published W.'s sketch of his late professor at Cornell, "Will Strunk," which describes parts of the short rhetoric Strunk had published privately called *The Elements of Style*. The piece caught the attention of editors at the publishing house of Macmillan, and W. was asked to revise and expand Strunk's book. Since its republication in 1959, *The Elements of Style* has become a mainstay of high-school and college English courses in the U.S. It is the rare American student who has not used what Strunk had called "the *little* book," now often referred to simply as "the Strunk and White."

Although W. was a shy, introverted man, the strength of his ethical, moral and intellectual convictions is always evident, even if just below the surface of his writing. His children's books, *Stuart Little* (1945), *Charlotte's Web* (1952), and *The Trumpet of the Swan* (1970), show his empathy for, and understanding of, the pain, the loss, and the fears connected with the child's emotional struggles in moving toward maturity.

W. was always a humane and sensitive spokesman for the freedom of the individual and a keen advocate of the right to privacy. While he often wrote from the perspective of slightly ironic onlooker, there was never anything of the merely superficial about his crisp, direct, and engaging prose.

FURTHER WORKS: *Ho-Hum: Newsbreaks from The New Yorker* (1931); *Another Ho-Hum* (1932); *Every Day Is Saturday* (1934); *Farewell to the Model T* (1936); *One Man's Meat* (1942); *The Wild Flag: Editorials from The New Yorker on Federal World Government and Other Matters* (1946); *Here Is New York* (1949); *The Points of My Compass* (1962); *An E. B. W. Reader* (1966); *Letters of E. B. W.* (1976); *Essays of E. B. W.* (1977); *Poems and Sketches of E. B. W.* (1981); *Writings from The New Yorker, 1927–1976* (1991)

BIBLIOGRAPHY: Thurber, J., "E. B. W.," *Saturday Review of Literature*, 18 (15 Oct. 1938): 8–9; Hasley, L., and W. R. Steinhoff, "'The Door,' 'The Professor,' 'My Friend the Poet (Deceased),' 'The Washable House,' and 'The Man Out in Jersey,'" *CE*, 23 (Dec. 1961): 229–32; "The Talk of the Town and the County: E.B.W.," *Connecticut Review*, 5 (Oct. 1971): 37–45; Sampson, E. C., *E. B. W.* (1974); Updike, J., *Hugging the Shore* (1983): 187–95; Elledge, S., *E. B. W.: A Biography* (1984)

—MARGARET D. SULLIVAN

WHITE, Patrick

Australian novelist, short-story writer, and dramatist, b. 28 May 1912, London, England; d. 30 Sept. 1990, Sydney

W. was born to Australian parents, well-established landowners, who were visiting England at the time; he was taken back to Australia when he was six months old. He was educated in Australia until he was thirteen, then sent to Cheltenham College, a public school in England. After finishing school he returned to Australia and worked for three years as a jackeroo (ranch hand) on sheep stations in New South Wales before going back to England in 1932 to complete his education at Cambridge. In his youth he traveled in Europe and the U.S. His early writings—stories, poems, dramatic sketches—belong to the London of the 1930s and have no Australian reference. He served in the R.A.F. during World War II and after the war settled on a farm near Sydney.

Happy Valley (1939), W.'s first published novel, marks his confrontation with Australia as a subject. It has a documentary interest as a "country town" novel, as precise in recording the Race Week Ball among the potted palms at the School of Arts as in tracing the jealousies and frustrations of a small community isolated in the snow country of New South Wales. *Happy Valley*

indicates W.'s preoccupation with the solitariness of human beings, the epigraph (from Gandhi) presenting the "law of suffering" as the "indispensable condition of our being."

The concern for unfulfilled lives extends to *The Living and the Dead* (1941), set in London's Bloomsbury in the 1930s and focusing on Elyot Standish as a "Prufrock" figure, an outcast from life's feast. Eden, his dark, intense sister, tries to throw off the malaise by compulsively entering into love affairs and going off to Spain during the civil war, but this is no more a solution than the life of desperately brittle elegance pursued by Catherine Standish, her mother. No one achieves the "intenser form of living."

These perplexities disappear in *The Aunt's Story* (1948). Theodora Goodman, a sallow spinster, is the first of W.'s characters to attain a visionary awareness. She resists the pressures of conformity and lives in the moments of insight she shares with others, or in the rare states when she feels her personality dissolving in the created world. The novel presents a character advancing toward the extinction of self—"that desirable state . . . which resembles nothing more than air or water." When Theodora is taken off to the asylum at the end, her integrity unimpaired, it is the values of the sane that are in question.

The theme of alienation persists through the series of major novels that followed W.'s return to Australia after World War II. *The Tree of Man* (1955) seemed to revive the Australian pioneering saga, tracing the life of one man and one woman who establish a holding in the wilderness and endure flood, drought, and bushfire as their shack becomes part of a wider settlement. The deeper theme is the struggle of Stan and Amy Parker for some fulfillment, some enlightenment that seems always withheld. Although there is an insistence, reminiscent of D. H. LAWRENCE, on Stan's absorption in his peasantlike activities, he achieves his "illumination" finally in transcending this workaday world, and is then isolated as never before.

The way of transcendence is examined in *Voss* (1957). A German explorer leads an expedition across the Australian continent in order to mortify and exalt himself by suffering, as though in rivalry with Christ, to prove that man may become God. Voss's tortures in trying to sustain his selfhood—scourging himself for momentarily yielding to human relationships or to the beauty of the natural world—make this the most compelling of W.'s novels. The defeat of Voss's aspiration—the simplicity and humility to which he comes—reveals the underlying values that would be developed in W.'s later work.

These themes are further explored, by means of the personalities, in the four visionaries of *Riders in the Chariot* (1961). Miss Hare, Himmelfarb, Mrs. Godbold, and Alf Dubbo are all studies in alienation, inasmuch as they are people whom a bourgeois society would despise or ignore. Although the chariot of which they have differing visions is a symbol of transcendence, the emphasis falls more strongly on the concept of "loving kindness" shown in human terms in the later chapters—flawed as it is by the aversion shown to those outside the visionary circle, and by the sometimes suffocating quality of "loving kindness" in Mrs. Godbold.

The Solid Mandala (1966) deals with the twins Waldo and Arthur Brown. Waldo belongs to the world of "tidiness and quick answers, of punctuality and unbreakable rules." Arthur is an abnormal child who peers into the fathomless depths of four marbles that are his cherished possessions, his solid mandalas. Although the mandala, like the chariot, is a symbol of perfection, the idea of transcendence is now diminished further. Arthur eventually manages painfully to articulate his vision in the uncertain world of human relationships, and dies as a failed visionary, while communicating to others their need to find "somebody to worship," to find liberation from the self in love.

In *The Vivisector* (1970) the theme of the artist, which had engaged W. previously in characters like Mr. Gage in *The Tree of Man* and Alf Dubbo in *Riders in the Chariot*, is singled out for special treatment. Hurtle Duffield's compulsion to express the truth as he sees it is destructive of human relationships—with his adoptive mother, Alfreda Courtney, or with the prostitute Nance Lightfoot, or with representatives of the fashionable or exotic world like Boo Hollingrake and Hero Pavloussis. While to others it seems that Duffield is practicing cruelty with his vivisecting eye, to him it seems that he is being practiced upon by the "Divine Vivisector," who torments his creation. "Yes, I believe in Him," he declares. "Otherwise, how would men come by their cruelty—and their brilliance?" The discovery to which Duffield is brought is that his art is a mode of worship, a celebration of the world in its ugliness and cruelty as much as in its beauty and innocence.

Whereas W.'s earlier protagonists had been seekers of the transcendent, Duffield has it thrust upon him. This is also the experience of Elizabeth Hunter in *The Eye of the Storm* (1973). She does not qualify as a visionary by being humble, indigent, homely, or rejected. Elizabeth Hunter is wealthy, elegant, self-centered and covetous of the life of others, and yet she is chosen—in the language of the second epigraph to the novel—to be pursued by "heaven's own perverse love." She may have spent her life seducing men and exposing the pretensions of women, but even when she is on her deathbed everyone else in the novel is measured against her standard: not only her son, who is the famous actor Sir Basil Hunter, and her daughter, who is the Princesse de Lascabanes, but also the nurses who attend her in shifts and Mrs. Lippmann the housekeeper. She possesses the vision without having deserved it.

The process by which enlightenment is imposed rather than achieved, almost as though independent of any human wishes in the matter, recurs in *A Fringe of Leaves* (1976). Ellen Roxburgh is a fictional counterpart of Mrs. Eliza Fraser, shipwrecked on the Queensland coast in 1836, taken captive by aborigines, and eventually led to safety by an Irish convict. She is curiously passive amid the privations and humiliations she endures, like earlier W. characters who are unable to interpret their experience to themselves, so that her spiritual progress is signaled rather by external events in the narrative and by the changed responses of others. If Ellen Roxburgh is a redeemed figure at the end, her redemption seems to have happened almost irrespective of her own volition.

The novels from *The Solid Mandala* to *A Fringe of Leaves* show a shift of emphasis in W.'s work. They are like the earlier books in being pledged to a scale of values set quite apart from those of bourgeois society, but unlike them in seeing that limited and materialist bourgeois world not with a fastidious aversion but with a redeeming vision. Elizabeth Hunter is chosen from the world of the idle and the fashionable; Ellen Roxburgh goes back to her existence there after her sufferings; and Duffield's last paintings are done amid the sour milk and rat pellets in the house in Flint Street, where he sees himself "looking for a god—a *God*—in every heap of rusty tins amongst the wormeaten furniture out the window in the dunny of brown blowies and unfinished inscriptions."

The Twyborn Affair (1979) extends the pattern. It is the study of a transsexual, Eddie Twyborn, who makes three successive attempts at fulfillment—in a woman's role in Europe before World War I, as an army officer during the war and a jackeroo in Australia after, and as a madam in a select brothel in London's Chelsea after

Patrick White

that—but fails in them all. *The Twyborn Affair* combines elements of the detective novel with the comedy of manners, and is a brilliant demonstration of W.'s belief that what is commonly seen as bizarre or abnormal is as "real" as anything else. It is consistent with the novels before it, however, in the value now conferred on the ordinary satisfactions of life—through the hero's tragic inability to share them.

During the 1960s W. turned to the theater, and four plays of his were produced: *The Ham Funeral* (perf. 1961), *The Season at Sarsaparilla* (1962), *A Cheery Soul* (1963), and *Night on Bald Mountain* (1964), published together in *Four Plays* (1965). Dealing with themes similar to those of the novels, they are EXPRESSIONIST in structure and style.

The audacity of conception in W.'s work is matched by a daring in style and method, and is joined to a perceptiveness and compassion that make him the leading contemporary Australian novelist. He was awarded the Nobel Prize for literature in 1973.

FURTHER WORKS: *The Ploughman, and Other Poems* (1935); *The Burnt Ones* (1964); *The Cockatoos: Shorter Novels and Stories* (1974); *Big Toys* (1978); *The Night the Prowler* (1978); *Flaws in the Glass: A Self-Portrait* (1981)

BIBLIOGRAPHY: Dutton, G., *P. W.* (1961 rev. ed. 1971); Brissenden, R. F., *P. W.* (1966); Argyle, B., *P. W.* (1967); Morley, P. A., *The Mystery of Unity: Theme and Technique in the Novels of P. W.* (1972); Wilkes, G. A., ed., *Ten Essays on P. W.* (1970); Dyce, J. R.,

P. W. as Playwright (1974); Lawson, A., *P. W.: A Bibliography* (1974); McLeod, A. L., "P. W.: Nobel Prize for Literature 1973," *BA*, 48 (1974): 439–45; Beatson, P., *The Eye in the Mandala—P. W.: A Vision of Man and God* (1976); Björksten, I., *P. W.: A General Introduction* (1976); Walsh, W., *P. W.'s Fiction* (1977); Meyers, D., *The Peacocks and the Bourgeoisie: Ironic Vision in P. W.'s Shorter Fiction* (1978); Shepherd, R. E., and Singh, K., eds., *P. W.: A Critical Symposium* (1978); special W. issue, *TSLL*, 21, 2 (1979); Kiernan, B., *P. W.* (1980); *Laden Choirs: The Fiction of P. W.* (1983); Marr, D., *P. W.: A Life* (1992)

—G. A. WILKES

The tradition to which [W.'s] fiction belongs is in the broadest sense European—but only in the broadest sense. Although he may seem atypical, P. W. is inescapably Australian. Indeed it was not until he returned, both in fact and in imagination, to his own country that he began to produce work of any real power and distinction. His talents are such that he would almost certainly have become an unusually good novelist no matter where he chose to write. But Australia has clearly presented him with just that challenge and that stimulus which were necessary to develop his powers to the full. If he did not in some sense belong to Australia he could not feel such an urgent necessity to come to terms with it. He brings to the encounter, however, a sensibility at once more complex and more cosmopolitan than that possessed by most Australian writers.

Everything he has produced bears the impress of an authentically creative imagination; and nowhere is this creative power more apparent than in his treatment of the Australian scene. Indeed it could be argued that Australia has supplied him with the only medium, the only terminology, through which he could make fully meaningful his own intensely personal view of the world. As a result he has achieved in his later novels and plays a vision of life which is both distinctively individual and generally relevant, a vision which illuminates in a fresh, sometimes strange, but always revealing manner the familiar universe, and which at the same time adds a quickening and transforming element to our experience of it.

Robert F. Brissenden, *P. W.* (1966), p. 8

To stress either W.'s Australianness or his Englishness . . . would be to fall into the trap set by primitive nationalism that holds so many of his occasional critics. His work sports no favours, and asks for none. It is modern not only in its idiom and concern, but also in its denial of boundaries and coast-lines. This is one reason why so many of his novels involve a journey. Another reason is that the journey, extended into a metaphor of the mind, is an exploration of the past in order that the present should be in a fit state to have a future. It is evident from his work that W. has also undertaken this journey more frequently than most. He moves easily in literatures of the past and in

languages other than English, taking from them what is useful to his own work. To this extent, he can be called a traditional writer. For a body of work to be modern and at the same time acknowledge an inherited tradition is enough to establish any writer's claim to the grateful attention of his contemporaries.

Barry Argyle, *P. W.* (1967), p. 4

The view of man and his world which underlies W.'s novels is religious in its basic orientation. His heroes are seeking the true permanence or unchanging structure beneath the illusory flux, the true freedom which is valid even beyond physical death. All his novels testify to the reality of another world, not outside this one but inside, "wholly within," as stated in the first two epigraphs to *The Solid Mandala*. And essential to W.'s vision is the affirmation that this other or spiritual world is immanent in our natural one, *as well as* transcendent to it. William Blake found God in a grain of sand; W. finds him in a gobbet of spit, or a table. Like Pierre Teilhard de Chardin, W. views matter as something good, something inherently spiritual, not opposed to spirit as the ancient Greeks conceived it to be. . . .

Although his novels *are* novels, not mystical essays as one critic suggests, the vision from which they spring belongs to the tradition of mysticism, which seeks direct experience or immediate awareness of God, and sees the soul as something wholly distinct from the reasoning mind with its powers.

Patricia A. Morley, *The Mystery of Unity: Theme and Technique in the Novels of P. W.* (1972), pp. 1–2

The use of expressionistic devices [in his plays] gives P. W. an opportunity to strike at deeper levels of response from his audiences than did Ibsen, for example, in *A Doll's House*. In *The Ham Funeral* there are the stylized dance-like movements of the animal, and the chorus of relatives at the funeral supper. In *The Season at Sarsaparilla* the soliloquies, and the visual effect of the razzle-dazzle of time; and in *A Cheery Soul* the music-hall gags of the first act, and the imaginary journey by car to the crematorium in the second. The last play, *Night on Bald Mountain*, is more naturalistic in style than the others, but here the imaginary goats, and the multiple set which makes it possible to overhear the Professor at prayers in the third act, are conventional devices of the same order. There are few playwrights from Miller to Pinter who do not employ similar kinds of non-naturalistic contrivances. The justification of their use is that a more vivid impression of reality is conveyed.

In some of the critical articles written locally about the performances, there has been a reaction against the convention used by W. To my mind, after close analysis of the plays, this is not to be supported. The playwright's dramatic methods do not detract from the vitality of his work, in fact, they enhance it. If reservations are to be held, the reason is to be found in

W.'s strength as a novelist proving a handicap to him as a dramatist.

    J. R. Dyce, *P. W. as Playwright* (1974), pp. 5–6

The subject matter of P. W.'s novels is at the same time most familiar and most strange to the average reader. It is familiar because W. records the private thoughts, secret trials and intimate emotions of the inner life with almost frightening understanding and accuracy. His observations on the nature and processes of the emotional life are universally recognizable and applicable. It is strange because these observations are often attached to the lives of the outsider, the afflicted, the genius or the elect—characters who have their being in a world that is beyond the compass of what we are pleased to call "normality." Equally, his creation or evocation of external Australian reality in both its natural and its social modes is familiar to the antipodean who is acquainted with the forms of its landscape and the cadences of its social voice, but is strange, alluring and possibly alarming to the overseas reader. But even inside the zone where W.'s writing is, or should be, familiar, there is a further element of strangeness or mystery that makes his work stand apart from the secular tradition of psychological, natural or social realism. P. W. has taken the language of the familiar and injected into it a sense of the arcane and the esoteric that transforms his words into the hieroglyphs of a vision that may be disquieting to those reared in a predominantly secular society. The familiar is fused with the strange to transform the map of Australia and the topography of the inner life into a real of myth. That which is known and rational is used in the service of the unknown and the non-rational.

    Peter Beatson, *The Eye in the Mandala—P. W.: A Vision of Man and God* (1976), p. 1

P. W. does not make things easy for his readers. His work is select, like all writing that deals with non-superficial knowledge, experiences, and problems. But it is not impenetrable; it is not art for art's sake, but art for people's sake. He does not sheer away from the unpleasant and frightening. He never becomes ingratiating or palliative in his criticism of society and people. He knows that people, perhaps mostly through thoughtlessness, often do more harm than good and that they recklessly try to dominate over others, particularly when they fail in the difficult art of making something of their own lives and of giving life a satisfactory meaning.

As a result of his not closing his ears to the voices of evil and cruelty, his vision has been called malicious, destructive. But the evil W. describes is not something of his own making. Apart from evil being an unavoidable ingredient of the human psyche, it is included as an empirical entity in our scales of reference. Only the reader who understands nothing of history can refuse to see how this evil is intermingled with the type of life that W. criticizes, and how

primitively such a type of life gives voice to its feelings. "It is not usual for a human being to resist an opportunity to destroy," writes W. in *The Tree of Man*.

The basic theme in P. W. is mankind's search for a meaning for, and a value in, existence. The mystery of the human psyche offers him a challenge which has shown itself to be fruitful. He does not make claims for a life after this one. Nothing in his works would suggest any doubts that this earthly existence is the only one mankind has been granted, and that we are dependent on our fellows for its perfection. That W. is aware of forces beyond apparent reality does not mean that he believes in a life after death. It is in order to make the only existence of his "elect" meaningful that he sends them out on the paths of suffering.

    Ingmar Björksten, *P. W.: A General Introduction* (1976), pp. 116–17

In [W.'s] work generally there are shifts in emphasis, qualifications to and developments of earlier attitudes. There are recurrent themes, situations, character types, images, motifs and verbal patterns throughout (as has been pointed out often enough; and would be true of most writers anyway), but more remarkable is the protean, creative redevelopment of these in successive novels. The struggle between experience and the desire to transcend it involves all his major characters, and redefines itself in each work. All might arrive at the realisation that the meaning of life lies in its totality, but the totality of each life is individual, the experience of struggle and joy is different, and the meaning cannot be abstracted from the life. Reading some attempts at such abstractions can induce a numbing sense that if the novels are only, or simply, about such theosophical concerns, the reader would be much better served by going directly to their presumed esoteric sources without being distracted by "the bags and iron of Australian life" and the attendant comedy and satire. P. W.'s struggle with "the sticks and stones of words" to discover, and communicate, a sense of (in a recurring phrase) "the whole of life," to reconcile poetically the dualities seen as intrinsic to the experience of life—not least the irony that "pure being" should manifest itself within quotidian actuality—is the larger drama in his work which reconciles the consistency of his preoccupations over forty years to his imaginative reengagement with them in such very different works.

    Brian Kiernan, *P. W.* (1980), p. 139

WIECHERT, Ernst

German novelist and short-story writer, b. 18 May 1887, Forsthaus Kleinort; d. 24 Aug. 1950, Uerikon, Switzerland

The son of a chief forester, W. was raised in the remote Masurian marshlands of East Prussia, whose natural beauty had a lasting influence on his writings. After attending the University of Königsberg, he taught German at secondary schools in Königsberg and Berlin, except for the period of World War I, when he served as an army officer. After 1933 he retired to rural Bavaria and devoted himself solely to his writing.

In the 1930s W. spoke out against the Nazi regime in public readings from the manuscript of *Der weiße Büffel* (the white buffalo), a parabolic narrative that was not published until 1946. In those years he was an active supporter of Pastor Martin Niemöller (b. 1892), the outspoken anti-Nazi theologian. In 1938, after he lectured at the University of Munich on "Der Dichter und die Zeit" (pub. 1945; "The Poet and His Time," 1948), W. was imprisoned for several months in the concentration camp at Buchenwald. This experience is described in *Der Totenwald* (1946; *The Forest of the Dead*, 1947). After his release and until the end of the war he maintained a political silence.

W. was generally expected to become the moral and literary spokesman for Germany after World War II. His attempts to fulfill this expectation led to embitterment on all sides, and the final years of his life were spent in self-imposed exile. In *Jahre und Zeiten* (1949; *Tidings*, 1959) W. gives his version of the events of this period.

W.'s narratives have an extremely conservative tinge. They could almost be considered as belonging to the "blood and soil" school favored by the Nazis. He preaches a chthonic religion, which he sometimes loosely terms "primitive Christianity," and he idealizes the primitive, feudal east European world of his childhood, opposing it to corrupt Western urban civilization, the organized Christian church, and the Western rational tradition.

W.'s style shows little variety or development after 1928. His frequent landscape descriptions are laden with emotional mysticism and obvious symbolism. His morally good characters are at one with nature; his villains are alienated from it, as in the stories collected under the title *Die Flöte des Pan* (1930; the pipe of Pan). Allegedly aiming to edify and console the common man, W. writes with a mannered, equivocal simplicity.

Das einfache Leben (1939; *The Simple Life*, 1954), W.'s best-known novel, is typical of his work. Its hero, Captain von Orla, flees from city, family, and himself to an island on a Masurian lake. At the expense of surface action, the book describes at length Orla's inconclusive struggle to find spiritual rest through manual labor and agnostic resignation. His broodings are reflected in stock secondary characters: clergymen, Prussian aristocrats, an ancient and wise fisherman, and a woman who hates God for having let her son die. His next novel, *Die Jerominkinder* (2 vols., 1945–47; *The Earth Is Our Heritage*, 1950), seeks to justify Orla's escapism as a positive ethic not unlike Albert Schweitzer's reverence for life. But W.'s last work, *Missa sine nomine* (1950; *Missa sine Nomine*, 1953), is a fictional expression of the death wish.

W.'s most balanced works appeared in the period 1928–35. Two short novels—*Die Magd des Jürgen Doskocil* (1932; *The Girl and the Ferryman*, 1947) and *Die Majorin* (1934; *The Baroness*, 1936)—established his reputation throughout Europe. The themes are no different, but W. does less preaching. The same holds for several tales from this time, of which *Hirtennovelle* (1935; the herdsman's story) is the finest. It tells of the growth, temptation, resignation, and heroic—but all too allegorical—death of a young village herdsman. Other well-made narratives are the title stories in the collections *Der silberne Wagen* (1928; the Big Dipper) and *Der Todeskandidat* (1934; the candidate for death), as well as "Tobias" in *Atli der Best mann* (1938; Atli the first mate).

FURTHER WORKS: *Die Flucht* (1916); *Der Wald* (1922); *Der Totenwolf* (1924); *Die blauen Schwingen* (1925); *Der Knecht Gottes Andreas Nyland* (1926); *Die Kleine Passion* (1929); *Jedermann* (1931); *Das Spiel vom deutschen Bettelmann* (1933); *Der verlorene Sohn* (1935); *Wälder und Menschen* (1936); *Das heilige Jahr* (1936); *Totenmesse* (1945); *Demetrius* (1945); *Märchen* (2 vols. 1946–1949); *Okay; oder, Die Unsterblichen* (1946); *Der Richter* (1948); *Der Exote* (1951); *Sämtliche Werke* (1957); *Häftling Nr. 7188* (1966). FURTHER WORKS IN ENGLISH: *The Poet and His Time: Three Addresses* (1948)

BIBLIOGRAPHY: Workman, J. D., "E. W.'s Escapism," *Monatshefte*, 35 (1943): 22–33; Ebeling, H., *E. W.* (1947); Hollmann, W., "Ethical Responsibility and Personal Freedom in the Works of E. W.," *GR*, 25 (1950): 37–49; Puknat, S. B., "God, Man, and Society in the Recent Fiction of E. W.," *GL&L*, 3 (1950): 221–30; Chick, E. M., "E. W.'s Flight to the Circle of Eternity," *GR*, 30 (1955): 282–93; Kirschner, S., "A Bibliography of Critical Writing about E. W.," *Librarium*, 7 (1964): 3–11; Sommer, H. W., "Das Menschenbild im Romanwerk E. W.s," *Monatshefte*, 57 (1965): 343–54

—EDSON M. CHICK

WIERZYŃSKI, Kazimierz

Polish poet and biographer, b. 27 Aug. 1894, Drohobychz (then in Austro-Hungarian Empire); d. 14 Feb. 1969, London, England

Son of a railway clerk, W. studied literature at the universities of Cracow, Lvov, and Vienna. During World War I he fought on the Austrian side in Marshal Pilsudski's Legion and was taken prisoner by the Russians. He escaped from the Soviet Union in 1921. In Warsaw he joined the Skamander group of poets. W.'s interest in athletics was reflected in his editorship of *Przegląd sportowy* in 1926–27 and in his poems about athletic events in *Laur Olimpijski* (1927; Olympic laurel), for which he received first prize in a contest held at the Ninth Olympic Games in Amsterdam in 1928. In 1938 he was elected a member of the Polish Academy of Literature. He escaped from Nazi-occupied Poland in 1939 and spent most of his exile years in New York. He never returned to Poland and was living in London at the time of his death.

W.'s early poetry is a youthful celebration of the joys of life. The fitness of his own body, good food and wine, good weather, or even a bird's song occasioned many poems in *Wiosna i wino* (1919; spring and wine) and *Wróble na dachu* (1921; sparrows on the roof). Such themes were characteristic of the Skamander group, whose members believed in poetry free from excessive formal experimentation and unburdened by programmatic patriotism.

The three years W. spent in Russian captivity and his other war experiences received belated attention in *Wielka Niedźwiedzica* (1923; the Great Bear [constellation]) and *Pamiętnik miłości* (1925; love diary), two volumes permeated with a "bitterness that gradually accumulates in the depths of the human heart."

The poems in *Laur Olimpijski* on discus throwers, soccer matches, and pole vaulting capture the communal excitement accompanying the efforts of the athletes, as well as the exultation of winning. This volume best exemplifies what may be called W.'s realism—the down-to-earth quality of his poetry.

In the volumes published between 1930 and 1939 romantic and patriotic attitudes (quite different from W.'s earlier poetry) prevail. These poems reflect the romantic view that Poland was the "Christ of nations," by virtue of the repeated invasions and sufferings it had endured. This mood carried on into W.'s exile poetry. *Ziemia—wilczyca* (1941; earth—the she-wolf) reflects the conviction that, as was the case many times in the past, Poland in World War II again fought for European civilization.

In the postwar years W.'s continuing interest in the physical world assumed the form of empathy for animals, birds, and plants. In *Korzec maku* (1951; a bushel of poppyseeds) and *Siedem podków* (1954; seven horseshoes) he speaks with the voice of a Francis of Assisi rather than of an Olympic athlete. Another transformation of the same interest occurs in *Tkanka ziemi* (1960; tissue of earth), in which poems about illness and hospitals abound.

Of W.'s prose works the most successful is *Życie Chopina* (1953; *The Life and Death of Chopin*, 1949). Highly praised by the pianist Arthur Rubinstein, who wrote a foreword to it, this detailed biography of Chopin interprets the composer's mature life through the events of his childhood.

W. was a poet of moderate talent but of extraordinary poetic and personal vitality. In his verse about sports and athletes, animals, plants, and physical decay, he comes close to the tradition of ancient Greek poetry of celebrating communal events rather than personal problems. His neoclassical style is well suited to his subject matter, although he is a bit academic in his topics and forms. In spite of his lifelong interest in the workings of nature, he is clearly a poet of urban civilization.

FURTHER WORKS: *Rozmowa z puszczą* (1929); *Pieśni fanatyczne* (1929); *Utwory zebrane* (1929); *Granice świata* (1933); *Gorzki urodzaj* (1933); *Wolość tragiczna* (1936); *W garderobie duchów* (1938); *Wiersze wybrane* (1938); *Kurhany* (1938); *O Bolesławie Leśmianie* (1939); *Barbakan warszawski* (1940); *Róża wiatrów* (1942); *Współczesna literatura polska na emigracji* (1943); *Ballada o Churchillu* (1944); *Pobojowisko* (1945); *Podzwonne za kaprala Szczapę* (1945); *Krzyże i miecze* (1946); *Comrade October* (1955 [not pub. in Polish]); *Poezje zebrane* (1959); *Kufer na plecach* (1964); *Cygańskim wozem* (1966); *Moja prywatna Ameryka* (1966); *Czarny polonez* (1968); *Poezje zebrane* (1968); *Sen mara* (1969); *Wybór wierszy powojennych* (1969); *Poezje wybrane*: 1951–1964 (1972); *Poezje* (1975). FURTHER WORKS IN ENGLISH: *The Forgotten Battlefield* (1944); *Selected Poems* (1957); *Selected Poems* (1959)

BIBLIOGRAPHY: Mills, C., et al., "K. W.: A Symposium," *LitR*, 3 (1960): 401–15; Folejewski, Z., "K. W.: Forty Years of Poetry," *PolR*, 6 (1961): 3–10; Miłosz, C., *The History of Polish Literature* (1969): 395–96

—EWA THOMPSON

WIESEL, Elie

(born Eliezer Wiesel) French-language novelist, essayist, and short-story writer, b. 30 Sept. 1928, Sighet, Hungary (now Romania)

A survivor of the horrors of the German concentration camps and of the Holocaust (characterized by W. as "The Event"), W.

Elie Wiesel

represents the conscience if not the voice of the Jewish people throughout the world. He does nearly all of his most serious writing in French and must be considered as a member of the tradition of contemporary French literature. Among the authors who played a meaningful part in his intellectual and literary formation are Albert CAMUS, André MALRAUX, François MAURIAC, and Jean-Paul SARTRE. His hometown of Sighet was a center for Hasidic Jewish learning, a fact that has colored much of his writing. From his father and mother he learned Yiddish; in Hebrew School he studied biblical Hebrew; and after being liberated from Auschwitz and Buchenwald, he went to Paris, received a French university education, and mastered French. Later on, as a journalist, he went to the U.S. and learned English. Dodye Feig, his maternal grandfather, played a critical role in imbuing in W.'s boyhood soul the love for Hasidic culture, customs, and storytelling. After a happy childhood in a tightly united, traditional Jewish family, the sixteen-year-old adolescent was arrested by the Germans with his parents and sisters as well as with the 15,000 other Jews of Sighet and deported to Auschwitz. His earliest writings relate the inhumane and nightmarish existence of the concentration camps, where his parents and a sister as well as most of his relatives and closest friends perished from starvation or in the gas chambers. In April 1945, having miraculously survived, he was liberated by the U.S. Third Army. Thanks to the intervention of General Charles de Gaulle, he and many of the survivors of his group were sent to France, where he remained until 1951. After studying philosophy, psychology, and literature at the Sorbonne in Paris, he found a job as journalist for the Franco-Jewish newspaper *L'Arche*, and eventually was assigned to cover the fledgling state of Israel. In 1952 he became a reporter for the Tel Aviv newspaper *Yediot Ahronot*, and eventually was sent to New York to cover the United Nations in 1956. Naturalized in 1963, he has since resided in New York and, in 1969, married Marion Erster Rose, herself a survivor of the German concentration camps. She became his principal translator into English. In 1972 the couple had their only child, a son, Shlomo Elisha. W. travels frequently to France and to Israel, and in many respects these countries are second homes to him. An inspiring speaker, he has given thousands of lectures at college campuses, synagogues, and at other public forums around the world. Since 1976 W. has been Andrew Mellon Professor of the Humanities at Boston University, and he commutes to Boston weekly during the academic year to give courses in several humanistic disciplines. Enjoying an immense international reading public, W. received in 1986 the Nobel Peace Prize.

Most recently W. has devoted much of his time to the redaction and publication of his memoirs and also to organizing and participating in a number of prestigious international conferences and events. Especially noteworthy was his willingness in 1988 to preside over a conference attended by seventy-five Nobel laureates at the Elysée Palace, the official residence of the French presidency, hosted by the late President François Mitterrand. In 1992, invited by presidents Izetbegovic of Bosnia and Milosevic of Servia, W. visited the former Yugoslavia to observe the war-ravaged cities and countrysides of that beleaguered area and to see with his own eyes the tragic consequences of genocidal atrocities. Profoundly affected by what he saw there, W. reinvigorated his ongoing campaign against hatred and persecution.

In July of 1995, in commemoration of the fiftieth anniversary of the liberation of the relatively few remaining survivors (among whom was W. himself) of Germany's concentration camps, a major colloquium, held under the auspices of the French Ministry of Culture, took place at the International Cultural Center at the Chateau de Cerisy-La-Salle and at the General Council building of nearby Saint-Lô in Normandy. Organized by Michael de Saint Cheron, an important W. authority, the colloquium featured significant presentations by W. himself and by a number of eminent panelists including religious and political leaders, literary critics, and academic scholars from Europe and North America. The proceedings were published the following year.

Rededicating himself to his tireless campaign in behalf of human rights and the elimination of hatred and intolerance, W. the writer became an increasingly committed spokesperson for the oppressed, the downtrodden. Undoubtedly his literary productivity has been slightly reduced by his indefatigable efforts to improve the human condition around the world and by his ceaseless travels to almost every corner of the globe. In a word, W. stands out as *the* engaged writer par excellence of our times.

The experiences of the concentration camp were such a cataclysmic event in W.'s life that although he yearned to be a writer, he could not gather the courage to recount what he had witnessed there. Nor could he find words adequate to recapture the agony of the nightmare. For ten years he anguished over this dilemma: Should he try to share with a reading public what he had seen or should he forever remain silent? Finally, he could no longer contain himself, and he published an 800–page tome in Buenos Aires, writing in Yiddish, the only language he felt comfortable with at the time, the detailed account of his concentration-camp experience: *Und di Velt hot Geschvign* (1956; and the world was silent).

The principal theme dealt with the silence of the entire world while Hitler and his forces exterminated six million Jewish adults and children. Relatively few readers could appreciate this initial publication, and in 1958, encouraged by François Mauriac, the Nobel Prize laureate and celebrated French Catholic writer, he reduced the dimensions of his first book from 800 to only 127 pages; but this more concise version he wrote in French, and it appeared in 1958 under the title of *La nuit* (*Night*, 1960).

La nuit became an instantaneous best-seller around the world and was immediately translated into every major language. A genuine modern classic, it recaptures with terrifying precision the excruciating barbarism of life in the camps: the torture, suffering, brutalities, as well as the personal poignancy of W.'s loss of his parents and sister.

Not only did W. gain international notoriety from the publication of *La nuit*, but he realized that he could verbalize in French, one of the great languages of Western civilization, the memories stirring within his soul. Once he gained confidence in himself, almost one book per year has since flowed from his prolific pen. Instead of retelling repeatedly the agonies of the Holocaust, he turned immediately to the aftermath of "The Event" and began to concentrate on the adventures lived by the generations surviving the gas chambers, notably in *L'aube* (1960; *Dawn*, 1961) and *Le jour* (1961; *The Accident*, 1962). In the first work a survivor of the camps seeks to kill the enemies of the nascent Jewish state of Israel; in the second book, another survivor unconsciously lets himself have a serious automobile accident in New York because he really does not desire to live any longer—he feels a sense of guilt at having survived while his dearest friends and family had perished at Auschwitz.

In *La ville de la chance* (1962; *The Town beyond the Wall*, 1964), the author depicts the silence of a non-Jewish spectator who remains passive as his Jewish neighbors and lifelong friends pass through the streets of Sighet, moving toward the cattle cars where they will be sent to the camps of death. W. cannot comprehend the silence of the non-Jews, most of whom did nothing to save their fellow Jews from destruction. This theme of a silent, immobile, and passionless gentile world reasserts itself obsessively throughout W.'s literature.

In 1968 W. wrote one of his most exuberant novels, *Le mendiant de Jerusalem* (*Beggar of Jerusalem*, 1970), the subject of which is the triumphant victory of the state of Israel during the Six-Day War over the overwhelming odds of the entire Arab world. Recipient of the coveted Prix Médicis in Paris (1968), it was an enormously successful work on both sides of the Atlantic.

One of his finest works of fiction is *Le crépuscule au loin* (1987; *Twilight*, 1988). This complicated work deals with a question that ceaselessly fascinates W.: the nature of sanity and insanity. Often, according to W., the insane have a clearer understanding of reality than those who are regarded as sane. Were the highly educated, refined, and cultured henchmen of the Nazi era truly sane people? Where are the frontiers that divide madness from sanity?

In his most recent novel, *L'oublié* (1989; *The Forgotten*, 1992) W. constructs his text with multitudinous elements drawn form the tapestry of his own biography. The central theme in the novel is based on the close relationship between Elhanon Rosenbaum, a survivor badly scarred by the Holocaust, and his intellectually curious son, Malkiel, a young man raised in the urban landscape of Manhattan. So keenly affected was the widower-father in the novel by his tribulations in the death-camps and by the aftermath of liberation that his health has begun to deteriorate severely: he gives evidence of losing his ability to speak; his memory has begun to fade rapidly. Before his father becomes totally forgetful and mute, the son struggles throughout much of the novel to penetrate into his father's past, eventually learning about his family roots and about how his mother had died during his birth. The discovery of his past generates in Malkiel a new passion for life, and he faces the future with increasing hope. Memory triumphs over forgetfulness, words win over silence, and hope replaces despair.

But W. has published much more during his prodigious career than novels, most of which are based on his Holocaust memories. He has written collections of Hasidic tales like *Célébration hassidique* (1972; *Souls on Fire*, 1972) and biblical stories like *Célébration biblique: Portraits et Légendes* (1975; *Messengers of God*, 1976) and *Silences et mémoire d'hommes* (1989; *Sages and Dreamers*, 1991), anthologies of varied essays dealing with W.'s usual subjects, including the six million victims of the Holocaust, the question of collective or individual guilt, post-World-War-II Germany, the Klaus Barbie trial in France, the evils of racism, indifference to evil, and the Jewish faith. He has written collections of essays on the scandalous situation of the Soviet Jews, essays and thoughts on contemporary human problems, interreligious relations, war and peace. Noteworthy is a three volume collection edited by Irving Abrahamson in 1985 entitled *Against Silence; The Voice and Vision of E. W.*; it is a vast compendium of his public lectures, scattered essays and thoughts, maxims and aphorisms, and informal speeches delivered for decades around the world.

W.'s style is that of a minimalist; he compares writing to the work of the sculptor who must chisel away all the excess marble, leaving only the absolute essentials. His principal themes deal with "man's inhumanity toward man," not only during the Holocaust but throughout the world wherever human suffering, discrimination, and racial genocide have taken place. Despite seemingly hopeless circumstances, W. never despairs and pleads for the human race to come to its senses by realizing that the most precious commodity on earth is human life itself. Another recurrent theme is that of silence versus verboseness. Sometimes words are simply too feeble to convey with authenticity the depth of human suffering and joy. Indifference for him is the most terrible sin; his life's motto is "Indifference to evil is evil." This motto is engraved on the gold surface of the Congressional Medal of Achievement he received from President Ronald Reagan in 1984.

One of the world's most honored men of letters, in addition to the Nobel Peace Prize, he holds honorary doctorates from dozens of prestigious universities around the globe and is Commander of the French Legion of Honor. The chairman of the Nobel Prize committee called him a "Messenger to Mankind."

FURTHER WORKS: *Les portes de la forêt* (1964; *The Gates of the Forest*, 1966); *Les Juifs du silence* (1966; *The Jews of Silence: A Personal Report on Soviet Jewry*, 1966); *Les chants des morts* (1966; *Legends of Our Time*, 1968); *Zalmen ou la folie de Dieu* (1968); *Entre deux soleils* (1970; *One Generation After*, 1970); *Le serment de Kolvillag* (1973; *The Oath*, 1973); *Ani Maamin: Un chant perdu et retrouvé* (1973); *Un Juif aujourd'hui* (1977; *A Jew Today*, 1978); *Le procès de Shamgorod (tel gu'il se déroula le 25 février 1649)* (1979; *The Trial of God*, 1979); *Le testament d'un poète juif assassiné* (1980; *The Testament: Five Biblical Portraits*, 1981); *Contre la mélancolie: Célébration hassidique II* (1981; *Somewhere a Master: Further Hasidic Portraits and Legends*, 1982); *Paroles d'étranger* (1982); *Le cinquième fils* (1983, *The Fifth Son*, 1985); *Signes d'exode* (1985); *Job ou Dieu dans la*

tempête (1986); *Silences et mémoire d'hommes* (1989); *L'oublie* (1989). FURTHER WORKS IN ENGLISH: *Dimensions of the Holocaust: Lectures at Northwestern University* (1977); *Four Hasidic Masters and Their Struggle against Melancholy* (1978); *The Golem: The Story of a Legend As Told by E. W.* (1983); *The Six Days of Destruction* (1988, with Albert H. Friedlander); *From the Kingdom of Memory* (1990)

BIBLIOGRAPHY: Halperin, I., *Messengers from the Dead* (1970): 65–106; Abramowitz, M., comp., *E. W.: A Bibliography* (1974); Joseloff, S. H., "Link and Promise: The Works of E. W.," *SHR*, 8 (Spring 1974): 163–70; Langer, L., *The Holocaust and the Literary Imagination* (1975): 75–89; Green, M. J., "Witness to the Absurd: E. W. and the French Existentialist," *Renascence*, 29 (Summer 1977): 170–84; Rosenfeld, A. H., and Greenberg, I., eds., *Confronting the Holocaust: The Impact of E. W.* (1978); Berenbaum, M., *The Vision of the Void: Theological Reflections on the Works of E. W.* (1979); Estess, T. L., *E. W.* (1980); Rabi, W., "E. W.: Un homme, une œuvre, un public," *Esprit*, 9 (1980): 79–92; Fine, E. S., *Legacy of Night: The Literary Universe of E. W.* (1982); Friedman, J., *Le rire dans l'univers tragique* (1982); Stern, E. N., *E. W.: Witness for Life* (1982); Brown, R. M., *E. W.: Messenger to All Humanity: Critical Essays by Major Jewish and Christian Scholars* (1983); Diamond, D., "E. W.: Reconciling the Irreconcilable," *WLT*, 57, 2 (Spring 1983): 228–33; Freedman, S. G., "Bearing Witness: The Life and Work of E. W.," *NYTMag* (23 Oct. 1983): 32–36; McCain, N., "E. W.: The Struggle To Reconcile the Reality of Evil with Faith in God," *The Chronicle of Higher Education* (13 Apr. 1983): 21–22; Friedman, J. S., "The Art of Fiction LXXIX: E. W.," *Paris Review*, 26 (Spring 1984): 130–78; Cohen, B.-F, *E. W.—Qui êtes-vous?* (1987); Rittner, C., ed., *E. W.: Between Memory and Hope* (1990); Davis, C., *E. W.'s Secretive Texts* (1994); Saint Cheron, P. M.de, *E. W.* (1994); Sibelman, S. P., *Silence in the Novels of E. W.* (1995); Saint Cheron, P. M.de, *Autour de E. W.: Une Parole pour l'avenir* (1996)

—JACK KOLBERT

Night is an account of a young boy's divorce from life, a drama of recognition whose scenes record the impotence of the familiar in the face of modern atrocity; at its heart lies the profoundest symbolic confrontation of our century, the meeting of man and Auschwitz (a meeting reenacted by Rolf Hochhuth in the culminating episode of *The Deputy*)—and this confrontation in turn confirms (as in Anthony Hecht's "More Light! More Light!") the defeat of man's tragic potentiality in our time, and the triumph of death in its most nihilistic guise. . .

Throughout *Night*, W. displays a remarkable talent for investing the "items" of reality, and of the fantastic "irreality" that replaces it, with an animistic quality, and then setting both on a pathway leading to an identical destination: death.

Lawrence L. Langer, "The Dominion of Death," in
Henry James Cargas, ed., *Responses to E. W.*
(1978), pp. 34–35

All of W.'s writings are concerned with the ramifications of the Holocaust for man, God, and Israel.

Peter Berger has argued that death is the marginal experience *par excellence* which threatens to reveal the innate precariousness of all socially constructed universes. If death is the marginal experience *par excellence*, then the death of six million Jews in the Holocaust is the marginal experience *extraordinaire* which has undermined the socially constructed universe of normative Judaism. W.'s writings are an attempt to come to terms with that marginal experience and to construct a new universe to replace the one that was shattered.

The progression in W.'s first three novels, *Night, Dawn,* and *Le Jour (The Accident)*, from night to dawn to day, is not merely a positive progression from a world of darkness to a world of light, but also a progression from a world in which God is present (at the beginning of *Night*), to a world in which God is killed so that man can live (in *Dawn*), and finally to a world in which God is absent (in *Le Jour*). In *Le Jour* God's presence is no longer felt, and the individual lives without meaning and without God. It is ironic that W.'s titles become brighter as the presence of God becomes dimmer, but this irony reflects W.'s reliance upon man in a world devoid of God. Nonetheless, the transition from a God-filled world to a Godless world is not easy for W. He continually emphasizes not only the initial suffering that brought him to his view of a Godless world, but also the internal pain that accompanies this new consciousness. He yearns to return to the God-filled world and to the shtetl in the Carpathian Mountains from which he was prematurely snatched and taken into the kingdom of night.

Michael Berenbaum, *The Vision of the Void* (1979), pp. 9–10

"In truth," states Elie Wiesel, "I think I have never spoken about the Holocaust except in one book, *Night*,—the very first—where I tried to tell a tale directly, as though face to face with the experience." Correct . . . but only to a degree. Wiesel has stated, "*Night* was the foundation; all the rest is commentary." All events are linked, and thus Wiesel's writings are rarely more than once-removed from the flames and smoke of Auschwitz. Indeed his continuing accomplishment is that of having the courage to remember and interrogate the Holocaust—forecast, real, and aftermath—in ways that honor the victims and teach the living.

This man does not see himself primarily as a philosopher, theologian, or political theorist. Instead he is a storyteller. Storytellers can explore questions without answering them straight out, and that possibility attracts Wiesel as a way of confronting what can now be called a Holocaust Universe. Its reality and significance elude words, at least those that are direct. Thus, the prospects afforded by theory-building disciplines seem less fruitful to Wiesel than those offered by the indirect approach of telling tales. And yet, in the midst of recounting stories linked to—if

not of—the Holocaust, philosophy, theology, politics come to life in ways that theory alone never yields.

Writing mainly in French, Wiesel employs varied forms of prose and poetry, fact and fiction, as he draws heavily on Jewish legend and tradition. Echoes of modern thinkers such as Kierkegaard, Kafka, Buber, and Camus can be heard in his writings, too. He is transforming all of these resources into a literature of lasting power and moral authority. In spite of and at the same time because of this success, the gift of Elie Wiesel—born in suffering and silence—remains mysterious. Perhaps more than anyone, he is troubled by the meanings of his own survival and achievement, and by the duties that both lay upon him: "Man is responsible not only for what he says, but also for what he does not say."

John K. Roth, *Consuming Fire: Encounters with E. W. and the Holocaust* (1979), pp. 25–26

In W.'s novels there is a general progression from witnessing to bearing witness. The survivor-protagonist, whose voice has been silenced by nocturnal flames, struggles to express himself and to recover the faculty of speech. He slowly learns to reach out to others and to reaffirm his identity as a member of the human community. The assertion of the voice is linked to the vocation of witness and is at the core of the thematic development. In their quest for a voice, the Wieselean characters pass through various stages, reflecting the author's own spiritual-intellectual itinerary. Their story is basically his, for his is very much a part of many of his protagonists. Yet, transposed into a fictional mode, W.'s story exposes the reader to the intensely problematic nature of the witness. The contradictions inherent in the act of testifying are revealed in both conscious and unconscious forms. A close study of the texts discloses an underlying tension between the compulsion to tell the tale and the fear of betraying the sanctity of the subject. The author has created characters who allow him to confront himself, and a new kind of protagonist— emblem of our times—issues forth from the literary mind after Auschwitz: *the protagonist as witness.*

W.'s novels lend themselves to a chronological investigation. They follow a logical sequence, each exploring a particular option open to the survivor after the journey to the end of night: killing, suicide, madness, faith and friendship, return from exile, silence, and involvement in revolutionary movements, in history itself. "The books came one after the other to answer the questions I was asking myself," W. tells us. "Each time a gate closed, the possibilities diminished, and one hope after another was stripped away." But if each text shuts a door, it also points the way to the volume that follows. The continuity and cumulative force of his oeuvre are sustained by the repetition of themes and the reappearance of characters who resemble one another.

Ellen S. Fine, *Legacy of Night: The Literary Universe of E. W.* (1982), p. 3

How is contact made between E. W.'s world, *l'univers concentrationnaire*, and our world?

The connecting link is story.

E. W. is not a historian (though he deals with the stuff of history), nor is he a collector of data (though every line he writes provides data for a new geography of the soul and of hell), nor a systematician (though systematic reflection can follow from his words). No, he is a teller of tales. You want to know about the kingdom of night? There is no way to describe the kingdom of night. But let me tell you a story . . . You want to know about the condition of the human heart? But let me tell you a story . . . You want a description of the indescribable? There is no way to describe the indescribable. But let me tell you a story. . . .

If we are to learn from E. W., we must listen to stories. His stories. They challenge our stories. They open horizons we had never seen before. They smash barriers we had thought were impregnable. They leave us desolate. They also bind us in new and deeper relationships.

Robert McAfee Brown, *E. W.: Messenger to All Humanity* (1983), pp. 6–7

As a storyteller, E. [W.] speaks with a quiet intensity that holds the audience totally attentive. No one can adequately or fully appreciate W. the writer who has not heard him tell a story; for his writing, in the end, is nothing other than a mosaic of tales, a written embodiment of the living voice. But what I have appreciated equally as much as W.'s gifts as a storyteller is his wonderful, genuine, and subtle sense of humor. Although his present life is a happy and full one—an all too full one—he bears the unimaginable burden of his memoirs of the Holocaust as a touchstone of reality for our time. That precisely he should live and speak with such a rich interweaving of humor is a grace for which those of us who know him can only be grateful in the fullest and most religious sense of that term. If it were not for his humor, he would not be thoroughly genuine, and his witness would not be as compelling as it is. Humor is the milk brother of faith, Martin Buber said when speaking of his friend Franz Rosenzweig. This is equally true for E. W.

Maurice Friedman, *Abraham Joshua Heschel and E. W., You Are My Witnesses* (1987), p. 110

W. is the voice of the Jew in the Western world. When he speaks to the President in the White House, he is also the conscience of our society. When he teaches and publishes, when he lectures and dreams, he breaks the conspiracy of silence which has become the malady of our time. . . .

Indifference leads to silence. There must be words for those who care. Ignorance leads to silence. There must be records of past and present cruelties done in the world, so that each generation can remember— not only the evil of the past, but also the glowing goodness, the courage and the decency, which existed in the darkest days. In this test, W. brings us words to destroy indifference and to awaken remembrance. The words are small, glowing embers of despair. And hope. They are history. And they are prayers.

Albert H. Friedlander (and E. W.), *The Six Days of Destruction* (1988), pp. 8–9

WILBUR, Richard

American poet and translator, b. 1 March 1921, New York, N.Y.

Born in Manhattan, W. grew up on a farm in New Jersey. After college he served in the infantry during World War II and began publishing his poetry shortly afterward. Along with contemporaries such as Karl SHAPIRO and Howard NEMEROV, W. came to prominence in the 1950s and taught English at several colleges, most notably at Wesleyan University in Connecticut. His collection *Things of This World* (1956) won the Pulitzer Prize and the National Book Award; he has also won a Guggenheim Fellowship and a Prix de Rome, among numerous other awards. He is a member of the National Institute of Arts and Letters.

By temperament W. is allied to a New England sensibility, and his poetry reflects this by its avoidance of extreme claims or excessive energies. Yet this sense of tact and control is never flawed by cynicism or corrosive irony. It is in his marvelous control and love of words and rhythms that W. complements his sensibility

Richard Wilbur

with an elegance that is almost French in its poise. Born in a skeptical age, and heir in part to the irony of poetry after T. S. ELIOT, W. nevertheless has used his work to express a wide and humane response to experience. He knows about fanaticism and madness, but he has steadfastly harbored a belief in the saving forces of rationality.

In his first two volumes of poetry, *The Beautiful Changes* (1947) and *Ceremony, and Other Poems* (1950), W. demonstrated a mastery of form and manner that was perhaps most indebted to the models of W. H. AUDEN and Marianne MOORE. Using a subject matter that was often pastoral and a nearly Augustan purity of diction, W. pleased more readers than he startled. But with his third book, *Things of This World*, he showed that facility was well on the way to becoming mastery. The theme of balancing opposites was present in the treatment of such diverse subjects as appetite, history, evolution, and religious longing. Some critics, however, complained that his gentle pastoral irony was close to becoming a static suburban complacency. In the late 1950s and early 1960s some people faulted him for not addressing himself to pressing social and political issues. Others, however, staunchly defended his apparent quietism and praised his superb technique. The question was sometimes framed as to whether his technical skill, generally conceded to be among the greatest of the poets of his generation, was the effect or the cause of his avoidance of committed writing.

As if in response to these questions, W. turned to social subjects in *Advice to a Prophet, and Other Poems* (1961). In poems such as "Junk" and "Shame" the wit and elegance that were his trademarks are employed on seemingly unpoetic material. In the title poem of this volume the poet imagines a nuclear catastrophe and "the death of the race." Throughout the other poems, however, and even in those mentioned here, the dominant feeling is one of dispassionate, although not unemotional, reflection on mankind's limitations and destructiveness. All this is done with a habit of mind that insists on seeing as many sides to the question as press for our attention. This openness to experience, or rather the consideration of experience and the hope of wisdom, is W.'s greatest strength. Readers who realize that his precise control is gained only after an exposure to extremes will most value his accomplishments. Those others who still demand a transforming or extravagant vision may know that W.'s true genius has been fully developed in its own terms. In his subsequent volumes he returns to a more pastoral mode, often dealing with the New England landscape.

Perhaps the essence of W.'s talent lies in his translations of Molière's plays—since it is as an almost classical satirist that W. achieves his truest expression. Combining European sagacity and tolerance with New England skepticism and bluntness, W. has firmly continued in the native strain perfected by Robert FROST, while with equal success he has drawn on the verbal dexterity exemplified by Wallace STEVENS. Finally, W. has maintained for himself a most difficult balance, tempering the multiple awareness of irony with the saving grace of optimism.

FURTHER WORKS: *Candide* (1957, lyrics for comic opera); *The Poems of R. W.* (1963); *Walking to Sleep: New Poems and Translations* (1969); *Opposites* (1973); *Responses: Prose Pieces, 1948–1976* (1976); *The Whale, and Other Uncollected Translations* (1982)

BIBLIOGRAPHY: Hill, D., *R. W.* (1967); Weatherhead, A. K., "R. W.'s Poetry of Things," *ELH*, 35 (1968): 606–17; Cummins, P. F., *R. W.: A Critical Essay* (1971); Farrell, J. P., "The Beautiful Changes in R. W.'s Poetry," *ConL*, 12 (1971): 74–87; Heyen, W., "On R. W.," *SoR*, 9 (1973): 617–34; Woodward, C., "R. W.'s Critical Condition," *CP*, 2 (1977): 16–24; Michelson, B., "R. W.: The Quarrel with Poe," *SoR*, 14 (1978): 245–61

—CHARLES MOLESWORTH

WILDER, Thornton

American novelist and dramatist, b. 17 April 1897, Madison, Wis.; d. 7 Dec. 1975, Hamden, Conn.

In 1905 W.'s family moved to China, where his father served as American Consul General of Hong Kong and later of Shanghai. Mrs. W. and the children returned to the U.S. after only six months and settled in Berkeley, California, where W. attended public schools until 1910. He returned to China for a while with his family, then went back to California, where he finished high school. In 1915 W. enrolled in Oberlin College, where he studied the Greek and Roman classics in translation and found a sympathetic atmosphere for his blossoming writing abilities, publishing several pieces in the *Oberlin Literary Magazine*. The W. family moved to New Haven, Connecticut, in 1917, and W. fulfilled his ambition of enrolling at Yale University. His senior year saw the serial publication of his first full-length play, *The Trumpet Shall Sound* (1920), in the *Yale Literary Magazine*. W. spent a number of months sitting in on archaeology courses at the American Academy in Rome, the setting for his first novel, *The Cabala* (1926). While teaching French at the Lawrenceville School in New Jersey, he continued to write and earned an M.A. from Princeton University in 1926. That same year the American Laboratory Theater produced *The Trumpet Shall Sound*, the first important staging of W.'s work, and formally launched his career in the theater. It was not, however, until the publication of his second novel, *The Bridge of San Luis Rey* (1927), that W. began to receive popular and critical acclaim—earning him the first of three Pulitzer Prizes. He resigned his position at Lawrenceville in 1928 and embarked on a full-time career as a writer.

Although not among his best novels, *The Cabala* reflects the charm and grace so characteristic of W.'s best prose and also points toward the Christian humanism that thematically dominates his later work. *The Bridge of San Luis Rey* is, typically for W., set in the long ago and far away—1714 in Peru—and through its episodic construction focuses on several different types of love for its main theme. In both of these early novels W. demonstrates his cosmopolitan education as he attacks those obsessed with scientific, external proof while he emphasizes the importance of the internal qualities of faith, hope, and love.

The Woman of Andros (1930), based partly on Terence's *Andria*, reflects W.'s love for and understanding of the classics primarily through the character of Chrysis, a courtesan who captivates all around her with her humanistic spirit. But she also points toward the Christian era in her quest for eternal religious truth as she becomes W.'s archetype of the virtue of hope. *Heaven's My Destination* (1935), W.'s first novel set in America, perhaps best demonstrates his talents for subtlety and irony in its satire on the evangelical fundamentalist traveling salesman George Brush. A thoroughgoing idealist, Brush proves to be a stubborn prig on the one hand and a charming, sincere seeker on the other—W.'s embodiment of the worst and the best of American Christianity. W. returned to classical and historical sources for his fictional portrayal of Julius Caesar, *The Ides of March* (1948). In this most experimental of W.'s novels, he imaginatively presents fiction as if it were source material for a real biography—letters, diaries, reports, proclamations—in seeking the essence of Caesar's soul, not explanations for actions surrounding the emperor's final days. And this, perhaps, is W.'s most characteristic focus—on people, not ideas or events.

W.'s last two novels, *The Eighth Day* (1967) and *Theophilus North* (1973), reflect his tendencies toward bookishness and didacticism. His themes of faith, hope, and love are stressed as ideas in the mystery of John Ashley, but *The Eighth Day* is also a novel that insists upon the reality and the value of suffering in the world. Ted North's story, based on W.'s own experiences, demonstrates the necessity for individual action as an outgrowth of love, while emphasizing the theme of individual freedom.

W. established himself as one of America's leading dramatists with *Our Town* (1938), for which he earned his second Pulitzer Prize. His best-known work, it is set in Grover's Corners, New Hampshire, and in three acts traces the childhood, courtship, marriage, and death of Emily Webb and George Gibbs. While the subject matter is for W. unusually provincial, his dramatic and theatrical techniques are highly sophisticated, even innovative: his telescoping of time, his use of the folksy Stage Manager as a godlike chorus, and the absence of elaborate sets and stage properties. More typically, W.'s theme is humanistic, optimistic, and universal as he asserts the supreme value of daily events in the most ordinary lives imaginable.

The Skin of Our Teeth (1942), indebted to James Joyce's *Finnegans Wake*, won for W. his third Pulitzer Prize and successfully extended his EXPRESSIONIST dramatic techniques. He again telescopes time, but does so here by deliberately scrambling history into a mélange of anachronisms centered in George Antrobus, archetypal man. Sabina, the character who opens and closes the play with the same speech, at times steps out of the dramatic world of the play and directly addresses the audience as W. seeks to merge art and reality in this remarkable tour de force. Thematically, he presents mankind's successes and failures, its glory and its shame, in a kind of dramatized fable of man's ability to endure and prevail, thereby reasserting the importance of basic everyday life. *The Matchmaker* (1954), a reworking of his *The Merchant of Yonkers* (1938), is theatrically W.'s most conventional full-length play, although he parodies familiar stage comedy in the process.

At his best, W. writes in a highly polished, subtle, classical style characterized by irony and objectivity—much as W. himself was an educated, intellectual, witty, somewhat detached man; at his worst, he becomes a bit bookish, sentimental, and didactic. As novelist he is a lively storyteller, a classic prose stylist, and an optimistic moralist; as dramatist he is an entertaining observer of life, a theatrical innovator, and a penetrating analyst of the eternal verities. Above all, W.'s Christian humanism portrays a suffering universe in which people—individuals—can achieve qualified happiness through everyday living. *Our Town* and *The Skin of Our Teeth* have earned him a permanent place in American dramatic literature, while his graceful prose, his entertaining stories, and his universal themes have prompted a modest, but growing, critical appreciation of W.'s novels.

FURTHER WORKS: *The Angel That Troubled the Waters, and Other Plays* (1928); *The Long Christmas Dinner, and Other Plays*

Thornton Wilder

in One Act (1931); *Our Century* (1947); *The Drunken Sisters* (1957); *Plays for Bleecker Street* (1962); *The Alcestiad; or, A Life in the Sun, with a Satyr Play, The Drunken Sisters* (1977); *American Characteristics, and Other Essays* (1979)

BIBLIOGRAPHY: Cowley, M., Introduction to *A T.W. Trio* (1956): 1–19; Burbank, R. J., *T. W.* (1961; 2nd ed., 1978); Goldstein, M., *The Art of T. W.* (1965); Haberman, D., *The Plays of T. W.* (1967); Papajewski, H., *T. W.* (1968); Stresau, H., *T. W.* (1971); Kuner, M. C., *T. W.: The Bright and the Dark* (1972); Goldstone, R. H., *T. W.: An Intimate Portrait* (1975); Simon, L., *T. W.: His World* (1979); Wilder, A. N., *T. W. and His Public* (1980)

—W. CRAIG TURNER

WILLIAMS, John A.

American novelist, biographer, and essayist, b. 5 Dec. 1925, Jackson, Miss.

W. is a remarkably prolific writer who has published ten novels, along with biography, other nonfiction books and articles, and two anthologies. His fiction occupies an uneasy place between art, popular genres, and polemic, and he himself falls between two African-American literary generations. The result of these multiple ambiguities—none of which has anything to do with the uniformly high quality of his writing—has assured that W. has so far attracted a less wide audience than his work deserves.

There is a sense in which W.'s early work shows the influence of the Beat writers and belongs in any consideration of that movement. To situate it there, however, would entail a redefinition of the Beat Generation that could encompass the directly racial anger of a young black, as well as W.'s insider's view of jazz music and its culture. The alienation that characterizes the white authors usually identified with the beat scene, their relation to masculinity, even their devotion to black music, all take on different meanings when seen through the lens of the black author's alienation, struggle for manhood, and involvement with jazz.

As the black movement in society and in the arts took on new energy through the 1960s and 1970s, W.'s work became clearly identified with that struggle. He compiled two anthologies of African-American writing. *The Angry Black* (1962) and *Beyond the Angry Black* (1967), wrote articles and reviews calling attention to the new black writers, and produced biographies of Richard WRIGHT—*The Most Native of Sons* (1970)—and of Martin Luther King, Jr.—*The King God Didn't Save* (1970). At the same time, his fiction reflects the major themes of race and the search for a viable identity that are salient in much black literature.

In a number of his novels, W. brings both the rhetoric of political struggle and the diction of sensational popular fiction to bear on the questions of individual identity and race relations. He places his characters within the history of American (and, to some extent, international) racism, and he illuminates that history. At the same time, he attributes an intentionality to that history that gives a number of his novels the tonality of thrillers or spy fiction. Given what has happened to black people in the past several hundred years, he seems to be saying, we should consider whether there is an intentional conspiracy. This is the polemicist's hypothesis. The novelist's contribution is to imagine what such a conspiracy would look and sound like, to people it, and give it a voice.

Thus, *Sons of Darkness, Sons of Light* (1969), takes place in a proximate Mafia-run future. *The Man Who Cried I Am* (1967), W.'s best-known novel, introduces the discovery of a final solution type plot for the extermination of the black population of the U.S. And *Captain Blackman* (1972), a fictionalized survey of black military history from the American Revolution through Vietnam, posits actual meetings of the ruling white elite throughout that history, in which decisions are made about how best to exploit the blacks without granting them the material or civic benefits of their service.

W.'s work is sometimes reminiscent of Ralph ELLISON's, in the combination of hyperrealism and SURREALISM with which social themes are treated. The rapid pace of his novels, however, and their dependency on plotting brings them much closer to the world of fiction for the mass audience, an audience that W. has only rarely been able to reach.

FURTHER WORKS: *The Angry Ones* (1960); *Night Song* (1961); *Sissie* (1963); *The Protectors* (1964); *This Is My Country, Too* (1965); *Africa: Her Lands and People* (1969); *Flashbacks: A Twenty-Year Diary of Article Writing* (1973); *Mothersill and the Foxes* (1975); *One for New York* (1975); *Minorities in New York* (1975); *The Junior Bachelor Society* (1976); *!Click Song* (1982); *The Berhama Account* (1985); *Jacob's Ladder* (1987); *If I Stop I'll Die: The Comedy and Tragedy of Richard Pryor* (1991, with D. A. Williams)

BIBLIOGRAPHY: Karrer, W., "Multiperspectives and the Hazards of Integration: J. W.'s *Night Song* (1961)," in Bruck, P., and Karrer, W., eds., *The Afro-American Novel since 1960* (1982): 75–101; Muller, G. H., *J. A. W.* (1984); Nadel, A., "My Country Too: Time, Place and Afro-American Identity in the Work of J. A. W.," *Obsidian II*, 2 (1987): 25–41; Reilly, J. M., "Thinking History in *The Man Who Cried I Am*," *BALF*, 21 (1987): 25–42; Salaman, F., "To Be or Not To Be a Part of the United States: Itinéraire de l'écrivain noir dans *The Man Who Cried I Am* de J. A. W.," in Martin, J.-P., ed., *Les États-Unis: Conformismes et dissidences* (1987): 33–57; Ramsey, P. R., "J. A. W., The Black American Narrative and the City," in Hakutani, Y. and D. Butler, eds., *The City in African-American Literature* (1995)

—LILLIAN S. ROBINSON

WILLIAMS, Tennessee

(born Thomas Lanier Williams) American dramatist, short-story writer, novelist, and poet, b. 26 March 1911, Columbus, Miss.; d. 25 Feb. 1983, New York, N.Y.

W. grew up in Mississippi and in St. Louis, Missouri, where the family moved when W. was seven. He attended the University of Missouri at Columbia for two years, worked for several years for the shoe company where his father was a sales manager, then attended Washington University, St. Louis (1936–37), and finally received a B. A. from the University of Iowa in 1938. During this time he had a number of plays produced by amateur and regional theater groups. In 1938 he went to New Orleans; at this time he first used the name "Tennessee" on a story he published in *Story* magazine. After travels to California and Mexico, he returned to St. Louis. After winning a Rockefeller Foundation grant in 1939, he came to New York, where the theatrical agent Audrey Wood put him in touch with the director Elia Kazan. During the 1940s and early 1950s he was associated with some of the major figures in the arts in America: the stage designer Jo Mielziner, the director Lee Strasberg, and Carson MCCULLERS. An inveterate peripatetic, W. often drew on his wide-ranging travels for the settings of his works: languorous Mississippi delta towns, New Orleans, Key West, Manhattan, the California coast, Mexico City, and Rome.

Although critics treated W.'s later efforts harshly, he was unquestionably one of the most important playwrights in America. Moreover, more people throughout the world have seen his plays than those of any other American dramatist. He won the New York Drama Critics' Circle Award in 1945, 1947, 1955, and 1961 and the Pulitzer Prize in 1947 and 1955, became a member of the National Institute of Arts and Letters in 1952, was made an honorary member of the American Academy of Arts and Letters in 1977, and was awarded the Medal of Freedom by President Carter in 1980.

The condition of his sister Rose, with her delicate mental health, plus a family with a heavy-drinking, frequently absent father and an oppressed, self-pitying mother, were significant factors in W.'s poignant early life in St. Louis. He deftly dramatized these circumstances in his first triumph, *The Glass Menagerie* (1945). The play, furthermore, serves to disclose the artist's palette. This gentle drama of lonely people cherishing vain illusions is rooted in theatrical characteristics, which become, with varying degrees of intensity, his typical creative mode. That his dramas play better than they read is not surprising, because of his resolve to fuse the various means at a dramatist's disposal into what he called "plastic theater." Thus, as early as 1945, he was drawing upon symbolic imagery, often religious in nature, and resorting to cinematic devices to evoke a lambent wistfulness that he highlights both with images projected on the scrim and with appropriate mood music. Even while the action is ostensibly realistic, it in fact is being unobtrusively distilled by the narrator's memory. All this subtle detail is strategically deployed in elaborate stage directions and notes for the director. These innovative techniques resulted in a poetic naturalism that only in his last works gave way to overt criticism of society in plays with more stylized characterization and greater freedom in their construction.

A Streetcar Named Desire (1947) solidified W.'s reputation as a major American dramatist. It is a lyrical play that traces the decline and fall of Blanche Du Bois, who plays into the hands of her brother-in-law Stanley Kowalski. Audiences are fascinated, impressed (and sometimes a bit shocked) at the playwright's ability to convey delicate shades of highly nuanced emotions even in the context of an impending violence that constantly threatens to nullify those feelings. But Stanley, who personifies this turbulent force, possesses the unique ability not only to attract an audience through his sexuality but simultaneously to repel it through his brutality. An added source of audience involvement in the play stems from their awareness that their vacillation about the hero finds a counterpart in an ambivalence on the author's part. The audience can never be sure of W.'s attitude toward the struggle between illusion and reality, which he hints is also a conflict between innocence and corruption, represented in the clash between Blanche and Stanley. W. creates a highly charged, energized vision of a world continually offering titillations on which it can never deliver. Thus, *A Streetcar Named Desire* is a potent illustration of the power of desire to drive and to destroy.

W.'s next two plays, *Summer and Smoke* (1948) and *The Rose Tattoo* (1951), continue to mirror this basic conflict between his characters' physical and spiritual needs—the first play through blatant symbolism, the latter through bantering humor. *Camino Real* (1953), a commercial failure, is an expressionistic version of W.'s own world view; its combination of allegory and archetypes into a formal structure prefigures his most recent plays.

Cat on a Hot Tin Roof (1955) had the longest run of any of W.'s plays and was made into an extremely successful movie in 1958. Typical of the ironies plaguing W.'s life, the prize-winning, performed version, rewritten at the behest of W.'s favorite director, Elia Kazan, betrays the play's initial intention: to arouse the audience's admiration for Brick's refusal to lie in order to bolster the false vision of reality held by Maggie, Big Daddy, and Big Mama. To understand the power of the sense of loss at the heart of W.'s plays is to recognize the discrepancy between the version he originally wrote—now readily accessible in the edition of his collected plays—and what has been available for audiences to see.

For the next five years W.'s career alternated between short-run or off-Broadway plays like *Orpheus Descending* (1957), *Garden District* (1958)—comprising *Something Unspoken* and *Suddenly Last Summer*—and *Period of Adjustment* (1960) and Hollywood successes: his screenplays not only for the Kazan film *Baby Doll* (1956) but also for his own haunting *Suddenly Last Summer* (1959) as well as *The Fugitive Kind* (1960), adapted from *Orpheus*

Tennessee Williams

Descending. His only real Broadway hit during this period was *Sweet Bird of Youth* (1959), in which an artist figure, here an aging actress, seeks to retrieve an evanescent purity despite a tainted past and the ravages of time.

Then in 1961, as W. entered what he calls his "Stoned Age," he wrote *The Night of the Iguana*, a play that marks a watershed in his development. On the one hand, its content harks back to some of his basic tenets; for example, a character, echoing Terence, remarks that "nothing human disgusts me unless it's unkind, violent." On the other hand, its formal technique adumbrates the increased stylization present in the plays of the last period. Moreover, Shannon, the male protagonist, embodies a dilemma that W. confronted at that point in his own life. Both men are anxious to live in the realm of fantasy, but, as Shannon laments, mankind is compelled to "operate on the realistic level."

W., however, decided to opt for the less mundane. Most of his plays after 1961 eschew "operating" and give free rein to his desire to create fantasy and to write brilliant comedy. The very titles give some indication of the playful, exotic range of his imagination: *The Eccentricities of a Nightingale* (1964)—a new version of *Summer and Smoke*—*In the Bar of a Tokyo Hotel* (1969), *The Red Devil Battery Sign* (1975), and *This Is (An Entertainment)* (1976). One of the earliest of these works, a two-part play comprising The Mutilated and *The Gnädiges Fräulein*, bears the paradoxical title *Slapstick Tragedy* (1966). The *Gnädiges Fräulein* is an outrageously satiric melodrama held together by the grotesque "cocaloony birds," W.'s whimsical invention to make concrete the forces victimizing the

Fräulein. They pluck out her eyes and scalp her during her battle to survive. Typical of W.'s later plays, the horror story persistently invades the domain of farce. W. himself expressed his fondness for some of the less fanciful of these plays: the Chekhovian *Small Craft Warnings* (1972) and especially the one variously known as *The Two-Character Play* or, in its revisions, *Out Cry* (1973). Innovatively and searchingly, *The Two-Character Play* delves into the age-old dramatic crux of illusion and reality through the device of the play within a play.

W.'s exploration of this theme, however, was not limited solely to the stage. One can turn to his novels, short stories, and poems to study how he transformed his themes into drama. The story "The Portrait of a Girl in Glass" (1948) was turned into *The Glass Menagerie*, and "Man Bring This Up Road" (1959) became *The Milk Train Doesn't Stop Here Anymore* (1963); the story "The Night of the Iguana" (1948) became the play of the same title. On stage or off, W. was a consummate storyteller who delighted in plying his narrative craft. The care W. lavished on the stage directions of his plays was intimately related to his attention to vivid detail; thus he enabled the reader of his novels *The Roman Spring of Mrs. Stone* (1950) and *Moise and the World of Reason* (1975) to experience his settings and locales sensorily. His short stories focus on the chiseled, well-defined incident, whether their tone be bawdy, evocative, tortured, nostalgic, passionate, or lyric. A poet manqué in one of his early stories says "words are a net to catch beauty." It is as if W. sought to practice this definition in his poems. While they run the gamut from free-verse poems with a leisurely paced line to taut, ironic constructions in a metaphysical vein, they read as though W. felt liberated by poetry to transmute his experiences into statements of conviction.

W. was excoriated by his detractors for rubbing his audiences' faces in superfluous sex, be it heterosexual or homosexual, and in needless violence. Hovering on the edge of pornography, W. pandered shamelessly to our basest instincts, these critics asserted. But such a position ignores W.'s exaltation of love and companionship and his compassion for human vulnerability. Within the context both of mankind's fears of death, solitude, and loss and of mankind's perennial quest for innocence, purity, and commitment, W. steadfastly asserted his admiration and respect for the fundamental need to hold fast to its dignity and maintain its integrity against the onslaughts of compromise and falsehood.

Just as Flaubert said that he was Emma Bovary, so W. often claimed that "I am Blanche Du Bois." This was his way of underlining his identification with the alienated outcasts of society. Thus, at the end of what otherwise is a series of rather self-indulgent *Memoirs* (1975), he composed the following as a tribute to his mad sister Rose: "High station in life is earned by the gallantry with which appalling experiences are survived with grace." Actually, this sentence—both in its style and its content—epitomizes the struggling lives of his most memorable characters and the values W. defended. It also succinctly defines the achievement of his own career.

FURTHER WORKS: *Battle of Angels* (1940); *I Rise in Flame, Cried the Phoenix* (1941); *You Touched Me!* (1945, with Donald Windham); *Wagons Full of Cotton, and Other One-Act Plays* (1946; expanded ed., 1953); *American Blues: Five Short Plays* (1948); *One Arm, and Other Stories* (1948); *Hard Candy: A Book of Stories* (1954; new ed., 1959); *Three Players of a Summer Game* (1960); *In the Winter of Cities* (1964); *The Knightly Quest: A Novella and Four Short Stories* (1966); *Dragon Country: Eight Plays* (1970); *The Theatre of T. W.* (7 vols., 1971–1981); *Eight Mortal Ladies Possessed* (1974); *Kingdom of Earth* (1975 [rev. version of unpub. *The Seven Descents of Myrtle*]); *T. W.'s Letters to Donald Windham, 1940–1965* (1977); *Androgyne, Mon Amour* (1977); *Vieux Carré* (1977); *Where I Live: Selected Essays* (1978); *Tiger Tail* (1978); *Creve Coeur* (1978; retitled *A Lovely Sunday for Creve Coeur*); *Clothes for a Summer Hotel* (1980); *Will Mr. Merriweather Return from Memphis?* (1980); *Something Cloudy, Something Clear* (1981); *The Bag People* (1982); *It Happened the Day the Sun Rose* (1982); *Clothes for a Summer Hotel* (1983)

BIBLIOGRAPHY: Nelson, B., *T. W.: The Man and His Work* (1961); Tischler, N. M., *T. W.: Rebellious Puritan* (1961); Donahue, F., *The Dramatic World of T. W.* (1964); Weales, G., *T. W.* (1965); Jackson, E. M., *The Broken World of T. W.* (1966); Steen, M., *A Look at T. W.* (1969); Tischler, N. M., *T. W.* (1969); Stanton, S. S., *T. W.: A Collection of Critical Essays* (1977); Tharpe, J., ed., *T. W.: A Tribute* (1977); Yacowar, M., *T. W. and Film* (1977); Falk, S., *T. W.* (1978); Leavitt, R. F., *The World of T. W.* (1978); Londré, F. H., *T. W.* (1979); Gunn, D., *T. W.: A Bibliography* (1980)

—JAMES B. ATKINSON

You would be struck by the . . . liveliness of the dialogue [in *A Streetcar Named Desire*], a liveliness that the American theater has heard from only two or three native playwrights. It is a dialogue caught from actual life and then submitted to only the gentlest treatment at the playwright's hand. . . . Its subtle and changing contours are suggested by the melody and rhythm and passion of active speech. [It] seems to me on the borderline of really good drama . . . because . . . the sentimental patterns are at work which cramp most honest effort in the theater today. . . . How deep does the play go? The episode of the black-coated couple from the madhouse compels the answer: not very. . . . Williams writes plays that our actors can perform and that our directors can direct. That's the advantage of being conventional. . . . This play . . . uses conventional patterns very expertly: working within the clichés, W. has contrived (in some measure) to transcend them. . . . For *Streetcar* is a . . . well-composed play of American life, rather realistic, and seeming more realistic than it is, in which the actors are handled in the "Stanislavsky" manner, and the action is domestic drama with lots of punch and personal emotion. [1948]

Eric Bentley, *In Search of Theater* (1953), p. 33

W.'s work has been popularly called "poetic realism." It edges over into *theatricalist realism* because he tends toward the symbolist school of writing. . . . Had he devoted himself solely to poetry he would have been a "symbolist." Fortunately he did not, for he would have been a distinctly minor, perhaps only barely tolerable, lyric poet. The theatre has compelled him to objectify experience, which he can do very well. . . . He has a theatrical imagination and likes to use it. W., moreover, has been suspicious of realism. . . . Probably, too, he has confused realism with naturalism to such a degree that he would have been pleased to do without the realistic technique and style entirely if he had been less strongly ruled by his talent for observation and his emotional closeness to his early environment in the South. He has himself edged over into naturalism from time to time. . . . Naturalism pushes realism over the edge of moderation and good taste and becomes a sensational exploitation of sordid behavior and circumstances. . . . In his best scenes and plays, however, W. has managed realism without excess and with considerable insight, sympathy, and accurate observation.

John Gassner, *The Theatre in Our Time* (1954), p. 351

T. W. is the protagonist of the romantic quest, and yet it is precisely his inability to carry this quest through to fruition which gives his work its particular defining characteristic.

No one in W.'s universe can triumph because there is nothing to which the individual can appeal. The sins of the earth are its incompletions, W. tells us; the universe is fragmented and man born into it is born into incompletion. Everything that governs human action emanates from the broken condition which is the root condition of the universe. Man's life is a constant attempt to compensate for this lack of wholeness which he feels in himself. In the work of T. W., human action is defined by universal incompletion. Not only can the individual not appeal to forces beyond himself, but because his life is defined in terms of his universe and is thus marked by guilt and atonement, he cannot rely even upon personal responsibility. There is no sense of individual responsibility in this deterministic view of existence, and without this responsibility no one can attain tragic fulfillment. If there is tragedy in W.'s work it is the tragedy of circumstance rather than character: Blanche trapped by her past and her dreams and fighting heroically for survival; Amanda struggling to hold a disintegrating family together; and Big Daddy Pollitt desperately attempting to save his son. With the exception of Big Daddy the characters are not large enough spiritually or morally to triumph even in their destruction. Their universe will not allow for tragic exaltation. Only Big Daddy possesses this possibility, but characteristically Williams is unable to sustain him.

Benjamin Nelson, *T. W.: The Man and His Work* (1961), p. 290

He seems not quite ready to admit that what he has been doing the last few years, sometimes accidentally, is communicating the violence and horror that he finds in the world not by its poetic representation, but by its comic transmutation into grotesquerie. Now that he seems to have passed beyond the pathos of the early plays, his best vein other than the comic, he has

depended more and more on melodramatic climax and decadent *frisson* for his effects. It is here that the unconscious comedy begins to take over. The line between the farcical and the melodramatic, between the parodic and the decadent, is so thin that only the most delicate performer can walk it, and a romanticist like W. is too fond of grand gestures to retain his balance. . . . W. would better serve himself and his audience by following the lead of Archie Lee [in *Baby Doll*] and Alexandra [in *Sweet Bird of Youth*]; the kind of frightening comedy that they represent is not only a valid reaction to the world as he sees it, but a more viable dramatic presentation of that reaction.

Gerald Weales, *American Drama since World War II* (1962), pp. 37–38

The drama of the American playwright T. W. represents a significant level of achievement in the total movement of Western theatre toward a distinctively contemporary form. There has developed around this playwright a highly articulate dramaturgy. A whole art of writing, staging, acting, and design has resulted which has synthesized elements drawn from European drama with pure native forms. W.'s form retains characteristic aspects of American cinema, dance, painting, and sculpture, as well as features drawn from the tradition of American poetry and fiction. W. describes his theatric form as "plastic," as a kind of drama in which he has rewoven the complete fabric of the performing arts. Despite its debt to the theories and practices of earlier epochs, the theatre of W. may be described as the image of a "new sensibility"; that is, its idea of form represents a major adjustment in the concept of dramatic imitation. Like other contemporary playwrights, W. has transposed into the fabric of his drama a new perception of reality. The image of experience which appears in works such as *A Streetcar Named Desire* is not, however, entirely the creation of the dramatist. On the contrary, it is a symbol that owes its existence, in part, to the cultural history of the late nineteenth and twentieth centuries, especially to those explorations in thought which are given explication in the work of Hegel, Nietzsche, Darwin, Jung, Freud, Bergson, and others. W., like these thinkers, seeks to engage modern man in a search for new dimensions of truth, to develop within our time a "will-to-meaning."

Esther Merle Jackson, *The Broken World of T. W.* (1965), pp. 156–57

[W.'s] work has already taken a significant place, richer perhaps, more allusive, fluid, personal, and suggestive than the plays of any other American dramatist, O'Neill's included. . . . The ambitious nature of later work is never a way of insuring a success equal to the more modest claims of the early plays. The fact remains, even the best of the later plays— and here I place *Cat on a Hot Tin Roof, Suddenly Last Summer*, and *The Night of the Iguana*—miss the cohesion, force, and above all, the formal inevitability of *[The Glass] Menagerie* and *[A] Streetcar [Named Desire]*. . . . In *Menagerie*, scenes followed one another, fading in and out behind the filmy scrim, almost before there was a chance to feel their presence. Similarly, the eleven scenes of *Streetcar*, though never arbitrary in their endings, seemed almost more compact and complete individually than the entire play itself. W., in short, was never so much an expert *playwright* as he was a superlative *scenewright*. . . . W. is never less at home than when he is trying to be large, grand, and cohesive. For him, the great arching curve of epic or romantic drama is an alien line, whereas a tight succession of full stops represents a natural language for dramatic action.

> Gordon Rogoff, "The Restless Intelligence of T. W.," *TDR*, 10, 4 (1966), pp. 89–90

The dramatis personae [of W.'s last plays] may be transients or permanent residents, but . . . their existence has much of the uprooted, the peripheral, the hanging on. Various people are on the edge of death, or hold out poorly against it, or are done in, or endure a sort of death-in-life. Against the nonsurvivors or the marginal survivors are ranged a few tougher types—crass or ruthless or simply gifted with more vitality. . . . There is a familiar melodramatic contrast of the weak and the strong . . . and of the allegorical shaping of experience toward which W.'s imagination occasionally turns (in addition to the life-versus-death presence in various plays there is . . . a generalized rendering of the fate of "the artist"). None of these materials looks naturally toward the tragic. . . . [There is] an absence of the individuality and human stature essential to tragic quality. Yet W. has used the word *tragedy* of two of the plays, and in two others he conceives of a character in terms that could lead to a tragic structure. True, when he does use the word *tragedy* he is being suggestive rather than literal, and ironic rather than solemn.

> Robert B. Heilman, *The Iceman, the Arsonist, and the Troubled Agent: Tragedy and Melodrama on the Modern Stage* (1973), pp. 135–36

W.'s understanding of and compassion for the illusions of the Wingfields [in *The Glass Menagerie*] are based upon an implicit recognition that work in America is alienating drudgery. . . . They are indeed victims of a larger social failure, for humane democratic values have been . . . inverted . . . as a use of knowledge to gain power and money. . . . W.'s religious language in the play becomes—however unconsciously—a strategic mode for evading the implications of his social analysis, about which . . . he is finally muddled. If his sense of cosmic catastrophe and of the metaphysical abandonment of his characters in the universe is . . . a great dramatic and linguistic strength of the play, it is . . . a typical weakness of W. and American writers in general.

Failing in their art to explore humankind adequately in society, they shift responsibility for the human condition to the divine and write metaphysical romances rather than trenchant social drama. . . . This weakness is especially apparent in W.'s later plays, which frequently exploit . . . the romance of violence. The greatness of *The Glass Menagerie*, as art and as human statement . . . lies in W.'s ability . . . to sustain a sense of the individual, the social, and the religious dimensions of our experience poised in delicate poetic balance.

> Roger B. Stein, 1976 postscript to "*The Glass Menagerie* Revisited: Catastrophe without Violence," in Stephen Stanton, ed., *T. W.: A Collection of Critical Essays* (1977), pp. 43–44

WILLIAMS, William Carlos

American poet, b. 17 Sept. 1883, Rutherford, N. J.; d. 4 March 1963, Rutherford, N.J.

The son of an English father and a Puerto Rican mother who settled in the U. S. after their marriage, W. lived virtually his entire life in northern New Jersey, on the outskirts of New York City, and made this locality the primary source of his art. He attended the University of Pennsylvania Medical School, where he divided his time between his studies and writing poetry and began his friendship with Ezra POUND. W. received his M.D. in 1906, interned for three years in New York, and shortly thereafter became a general practitioner in Rutherford with a special interest in obstetrics and pediatrics. At about the same time, he launched his writing career. During World War I W. was in touch with avant-garde poets and painters in New York, including Marianne MOORE and Wallace STEVENS. He was represented in Pound's anthology *Des Imagistes* (1914). He joined the group that gathered around the little magazine *Others*, and his work appeared as well in *Poetry*, *The Egotist*, and *The Little Review*. From 1920 to 1923 he edited *Contact* with the poet and fiction writer Robert McAlmon (1895–1956). He was briefly associated in the 1930s with the Objectivists, a group of younger poets spearheaded by Louis ZUKOFSKY. W. assiduously carried on the tasks of doctor and writer for over forty years, and the two activities functioned symbiotically for him, each providing its own kind of stimulation and bringing relief from the frustrations of the other. A stroke forced his retirement from medical practice in 1951, but he continued to write profusely until his death. W.'s achievements as a poet earned him several honors, beginning with the award of *The Dial* magazine in 1926 and culminating with the Pulitzer Prize and the Gold Medal of the National Institute of Arts and Letters in 1963.

W.'s poetry celebrates the struggle for new beginnings and the perpetual rediscovery of the present moment. The early long poem "The Wanderer" (1914), in which he sloughed off his youthful absorption with the romanticism of Keats, first revealed the recurrent mythic pattern in his work: the descent to the elemental, unformed ground of being or consciousness that is continually necessary to the creative act and the renewal of the self and the world. The poem dramatized W.'s commitment to his immediate place and time in the ritual action of immersion in "the filthy

Passaic" River of his native region. That commitment set the direction of his mature poetry, which comprises twelve collections of poems published between 1913 and 1949, the bulk of which are now contained in *Collected Earlier Poems* (1951) and *Collected Later Poems* (1950; rev. ed., 1963); his major long poem, *Paterson* (5 vols., 1946–58); and verse gathered in *Pictures from Breughel: Collected Poems 1950–1962* (1962).

W.'s development cohered around his career-long adherence to a few key principles: a primary respect for objective, material reality; the belief that poetry springs from one's familiar surroundings; and the conviction that the modern poet's chief obligation is the renewal of language. Early on, he was identified with the IMAGIST movement, although his work was more strongly influenced by the revolutionary theories and techniques of modern painting, particularly CUBISM. The imagist tenet of direct treatment of the thing evolved in his poetics into his personal dictum, "no ideas but in things." This means not that the imagination simply transcribes the real world but that it lifts the objects of its attention to a fresh realization in the form of a new-made object that is the poem. The result is poetry that transmits sharply etched observations of everyday things and captures moments of vivid perception in all their immediacy and sensory particularity. Such well-known poems as "The Great Figure" (1921) and "The Red Wheelbarrow" (1923) render these vibrant instants in a concentrated, intense form; but other poems, like "January Morning" (1917) or "Perpetuum Mobile: The City" (1936), present them through a more elaborate montage of juxtaposed images and responses. By such means, W. strove to expose the hidden beauty in the commonplace particulars of his natural and human environment—a field of Queen Anne's lace in bloom, a woman pausing to locate a nail in her shoe, bits of green glass in a cinder-strewn hospital yard—and thus to bring to expression his American locale.

His insistence that poetry must have a local center led also to his concern with the American language. Like Walt Whitman, whose democratic sympathies he deeply shared, W. wanted a poetic idiom close to the life and speech of ordinary people. Yet he saw the failure of the common language as a root cause of the deformity of present-day American society and culture, and believed that the poet must redeem the tawdriness of modern life by restoring words to their pristine power. In seeking a style and form commensurate to this purpose, W. became a leading shaper of modern free verse. His ongoing search for a poetic line that conformed closely to the patterns and rhythms of the vernacular produced his plain style, with its hard, clean verbal surface, and his characteristically short line, which highlights the distinctive qualities of individual words and phrases apart from their larger syntactic and ideational contexts.

The struggle of the poetic self to invent its language and its world anew is the subject of W.'s masterwork, *Paterson*. The generative principle of the poem is the identification of a man with his city. W. found in Paterson, New Jersey, and its environs the quintessential particularization of his own urban milieu and an analogue for the whole of modern industrial America; its topography, history, and present-day life provide the substance of the poem and the primary symbols, the Passaic River and its Falls. The city's human counterpart and the poem's dramatic center is Dr. Paterson, the poet-doctor within whose consciousness unfolds the quest to release the "beautiful thing" immured in his quotidian world. In its attempt to articulate the total culture, *Paterson* shares a quasi-epical purport with Whitman's *Song of Myself*, Pound's *Cantos*, and Hart CRANE's *The Bridge*. Like these poets also, W. eschewed

a traditional narrative or autobiographical structure, and invented a unique form for the long poem in which heterogeneous verse sections are interspersed with prose extracts from various documentary sources. The design reflects W.'s conviction that the poem must embody the unfinished nature of the poetic act. The absence of fixed sequence, the multiple perspectives, and the abrupt shifts in style and tone create the protean quality W. aesthetically valued. Yet the poem achieves its own dynamic order, arising from the tension between the poetic urge toward a visionary synthesis and the recalcitrance of the unmediated prosaic materials. W. originally composed the poem in four parts, but in keeping with its open form, he later added *Paterson, Book V*, which, while it extends the same essential themes, tempers the insistent localism of the earlier books through its governing motif of the medieval Unicorn Tapestries and carries the poem into W.'s late mode.

W.'s late verse constitutes a reflorescence of his sensibility. His continued preoccupation with the poetic line led him to develop a more regular and more expansive line divided into three parts, each of relatively equal weight and duration but having a different syllable count (what W. termed a "variable foot"). His discovery of this "new measure" coincided with the appearance in his poetry of a more reflective and serene stance. The late poems relax the rigorous submission of mind to the immediate material world, and display a greater reliance on memory and imagination that modifies the tense objectivity of his earlier verse, allowing now for more expression of subjective feeling and a fuller play of figurative and allusive language. W.'s late phase produced several exceptional poems, most notably, his glowing celebrations of the renewal of the imagination in "The Desert Music" (1951) and of the renewal of love in "Asphodel, That Greeny Flower" (1955).

W. also wrote several works of fiction. His short stories, collected in *The Farmers' Daughters* (1961), generally depict encounters with his townspeople, especially the poor, presented through straightforward narrative and conversational dialogue, with little or no plot development. Very often they involve the relationship between doctor and patient, and typically, W. looks at his characters with the mingled sympathy and probing curiosity of a physician examining another person's ills. At their finest, as in "Old Doc Rivers" (1932) or "Jean Beicke" (1933), his stories pierce through unseeing social attitudes and stereotypes to perceive the elemental mystery and worth of individual personality and human survival amid stunted conditions. W.'s effort to replicate fictionally the texture of everyday American living also marks his best-known novels: *White Mule* (1937), *In the Money* (1940), and *The Build-up* (1952). Based on his wife's family history, this Stecher trilogy counterpoises the account of young Flossie's personal growth and the story of her immigrant parents' successful social rise and their submission to middle-class mores and values. The vivid and detailed evocation of Flossie's infancy is a remarkable achievement.

Two other prose works deserve special note. The STREAM-OF-CONSCIOUSNESS improvisations in *Kora in Hell* (1920) were a significant early experiment for W. at breaking free from customary patterns of thought and language, and the "Prologue" is the first important formulation of his aesthetic ideas. *In the American Grain* (1925) propounds W.'s personal myth of America, with Columbus as its archetypal hero. In a series of highly individualized portraits of historical figures from Eric the Red to Lincoln, W. appropriates materials from primary sources to shape, through an array of forms and styles, his vision of the dialectic of American history: the voluptuous opening up of the self to vital contact with the New World versus the "Puritanical" inhibition that holds back from it and exploits it.

Although W.'s prolific outpouring of poetry and other writings over almost half a century inevitably yielded its share of unexceptional work, his best things are charged with rare originality and authenticity. Recognition as a major modern American poet came late to him. His beliefs put him squarely at odds with the poetry and the literary doctrines of T. S. ELIOT, prompting him to make his fellow poet his personal bête noire, and during the long period of Eliot's ascendancy in literary and academic circles, W. tenaciously cultivated his own ground. His reputation is now secure, however, crowned by *Paterson* and the other accomplishments of his later career. His emergence from Eliot's shadow is due in no small part to his impact on recent poets as diverse as Robert LOWELL, Charles OLSON, Denise LEVERTOV, and Allen GINSBERG, and his influence on the contemporary American poetry of open forms.

FURTHER WORKS: *Poems* (1909); *The Tempers* (1913); *Al Que Quiere!* (1917); *Sour Grapes* (1921); *The Great American Novel* (1923); *Spring and All* (1923); *Go Go* (1923); *A Voyage to Pagany* (1928); *A Novelette, and Other Prose* (1932); *The Knife of the Times* (1932); *Collected Poems 1921–1931* (1934); *An Early Martyr* (1935); *Adam and Eve and the City* (1936); *Life along the Passaic River* (1938); *Complete Collected Poems 1906–1938* (1938); *The Broken Span* (1941); *The Wedge* (1944); *A Dream of Love* (1948); *The Clouds* (1948); *The Pink Church* (1949); *Selected Poems* (1949); *Make Light of It: Collected Stories* (1950); *The Autobiography of W. C. W.* (1951); *Selected Essays* (1954); *The Desert Music* (1954); *Journey to Love* (1955); *Selected Letters* (1957); *I Wanted to Write a Poem* (1958); *Yes, Mrs. Williams* (1959); *Many Loves, and Other Plays* (1961); *Embodiment of Knowledge* (1974)

BIBLIOGRAPHY: Pearce, R. H., *The Continuity of American Poetry* (1961): 111–30, 335–48, and passim; Wagner, L. W., *The Poems of W. C. W.* (1964); Miller, J. H., *Poets of Reality* (1965): 285–359; Weatherhead, A. K., *The Edge of the Image* (1967): 96–169 and passim; Guimond, J., *The Art of W. C. W.: A Discovery and Possession of America* (1968); Paul, S., *The Music of Survival: A Biography of a Poem by W. C. W.* (1968); Whitaker, T., *W. C. W.* (1968); Dijkstra, B., *The Hieroglyphics of a New Speech: Cubism, Stieglitz, and the Early Poetry of W. C. W.* (1969); Breslin, J. E., *W. C. W.: An American Artist* (1970); Connaroe, J., *W. C. W.'s "Paterson": Language and Landscape* (1970); Wagner, L. W., *The Prose of W. C. W.* (1970); Weaver, M., *W. C. W.: The American Background* (1971); Mazzaro, J., *W. C. W.: The Later Poems* (1973); Riddle, J., *The Inverted Bell: Modernism and the Counterpoetics of W. C. W.* (1974); Coles, R., *W. C. W.: The Knack of Survival in America* (1975); Mariani, P., *W. C. W.: The Poet and His Critics* (1975); Whittemore, R., *W. C. W.: Poet from Jersey* (1975); Mariani, P., *W. C. W.: A New World Naked* (1981); Doyle, C., *W. C. W. and the American Poem* (1982)

—PETER W. DOWELL

The process [of W.'s poetry] is simply this: There is the eye, and there is the thing upon which that eye alights; while the relationship existing between the two is a poem. . . .

Seen from this angle, Contact might be said to resolve into the counterpart of Culture, and W. becomes thereby one of our most distinguished Neanderthal men. His poetry deals with the coercions of nature—and by nature I mean iron rails as well as iron ore—rather than with the laborious structure of ideas man has erected above nature. His hatred of the idea in art is consequently pronounced, and very rightly brings in its train a complete disinterest in form. . . . The Contact writer deals with his desires; the Culture writer must erect his desires into principles and deal with those principles rather than with the desires; the *urphenomen*, in other words, becomes with the man of Culture of less importance than the delicate and subtle instruments with which he studies it.

W., however, must go back to the source. And the process undeniably has its beauties.

Kenneth Burke, "Heaven's First Law," *The Dial*, 72 (1922), pp. 197, 199–200

What W. gives, on the whole, is not sentiment but the reaction from sentiment, or, rather, a little sentiment, very little, together with acute reaction.

His passion for the anti-poetic is a blood-passion and not a passion of the inkpot. The antipoetic is his spirit's cure. He needs it as a naked man needs shelter or as an animal needs salt. To a man with a sentimental side the anti-poetic is that truth, that reality to which all of us are forever fleeing.

The anti-poetic has many aspects. The aspect to which a poet is addicted is a test of his validity. Its merely rhetorical aspect is valueless. As an affectation it is a commonplace. As a scourge it has a little more meaning. But as a phase of a man's spirit, as a source of salvation, now, in the midst of a baffled generation, as one looks out of the window at Rutherford or Passaic, or as one walks the streets of New York, the anti-poetic acquires an extraordinary potency, especially if one's nature possesses that side so attractive to the Furies.

Wallace Stevens, Preface to W. C. W., *Collected Poems: 1921–1931* (1934), p. 2

The romantic principles which have governed Dr. W.'s work [his belief in "the surrender to feeling and to instinct as the only way to wisdom and to art"] have limited his scope in the ways which I have mentioned. The combination of purity and of richly human feeling to be found in his language at times reminds one of [Thomas] Hardy or of [Robert] Bridges, and in beauty of execution he is their equal, though in so different a mode; but his understanding is narrower than theirs, and his best poems are less great. On the other hand, when poems are so nearly unexceptionable in their execution, one regards the question of scope regretfully: [Robert] Herrick is less great than Shakespeare, but he is probably as fine, and, God willing, should last as long. If I may venture, like [Matthew] Arnold, to make a prediction, it is this: that the end of the present century will see him securely established, along with [Wallace] Stevens, as one of the two best poets of his generation.

Yvor Winters, "Poetry of Feeling," *KR*, 1 (1939), p. 106

[W.] is historian, geographer, reporter, critic, medical practitioner, Peeping Tom—all that he needs to be to put down what Paterson, the place, actually is. Moreover, he is poet; so that putting down what Paterson actually is, he puts down himself. He has a right to call himself Dr. Paterson, because he invents himself, having discovered himself *in* Paterson. Yet the structure of the poem will oblige him to acknowledge in all piety that there is much he cannot understand. Thus the synthesis and the balance: on the one hand Paterson, any man's world, sufficient unto itself; on the other hand Dr. Paterson, any man, caught up at once in his knowledge of that sufficiency and a sense (which sometimes reaches the height of knowledge) of his own insufficiency. He longs to transcend his own insufficiency, yet in the very longing, knows that he cannot. The form and function of the poem initiate that infinite series of discoveries of self through discoveries of the other. The series ends, the poem ends, only when the fact of spiralling infinity (which is a sign of man's infinitude) is confronted, and he who confronts it (turning, somersaulting, within himself) becomes something of a hero.

Roy Harvey Pearce, *The Continuity of American Poetry* (1961), p. 114

The problems which gave rise to action in earlier literature have disappeared [from W.'s poetry]: no difficulty in knowing other people; no uncertain approach to external objects by the subjective mind; no pathos of a distant and unattainable God. Poetry in such a world seems to be limited to variations on a first instant which contains everything and appeases every desire.

There is, however, much drama in W.'s work, but it lies in a dimension appropriate to the realm of immanence which he has entered. Three elements are always present in that realm, and these must be brought into the proper relation or life will fall back to some form of inauthenticity. Yet they are mutually incompatible. When one is present the others tend to disappear or to be occulted. Like matter and anti-matter they destroy one another. Only with great difficulty can they be brought into balance. All W.'s work is an attempt to discover ways to do this.

The three elements are the formless ground, origin of all things; the formed thing, defined and limited; a nameless presence, the "beautiful thing," there in every form but hidden by it.

J. Hillis Miller, *Poets of Reality* (1965), p. 328

Paterson has much in common with [Thoreau's] *Walden*. Each has at its core the specific American place from which its title derives, and each examines ideas that radiate from this place and that are inextricably related to it. . . . In each the narrator examines in painstaking detail his particular locale, describing its natural features, documenting its history, relating its myths, and analyzing the morbid poverty of the mass of men who are divorced from its life-giving richness. Each writer focuses on the familiar landscape with the illuminating vision of that rare man who is awake, and causes the reader to notice, for the first time, what he has often looked at but has never actually seen. Moreover, each book represents a conscious attempt by an American sensibility to create an intrinsically American book—to reawaken a local consciousness and thereby reunite man with those sources from which he is so disastrously separated. . . .

For to W., as to Thoreau, home is not, as T. S. Eliot has said, "where one starts from" ("East Coker"), nor is place "always and only place" ("Ash Wednesday"). Home is, rather, where man has his experience, thereby shaping his life and thus contributing to the source of any creative act, of any writing that is good.

Joel Connaroe, *W. C. W.'s "Paterson": Language and Landscape* (1970), pp. 11–12

But if W., like all the moderns, assumes an initial separation between himself and his reader, his work attempts to dissolve that distance. . . . The tension between author and audience, a gap to be spanned, becomes a source of energy for the poet; their relation is finally one of mutual dependence. What begins in alienation ends in a comradely embrace.

The important point is that while W. did see himself as a man apart, his perspective on society was from a point below rather than above. This does not mean that he was more humble than Pound or Eliot, only that he had a different kind of pretension. For the difference between adopting tradition or place as the creative source is that the ground is available to anyone who will look under his bootsoles. W. speaks from a crude locus—in the earth and in the body— that is potentially, if not actually, common. It is by adopting this physical perspective that W. deals with the modern breakdown of belief; he can now claim to be articulating a kind of consciousness that is buried in all of us.

James E. Breslin, *W. C. W.: An American Artist* (1970), pp. 47–48

Those stories and novels [*Life along the Passaic River* (1938) and the Stecher trilogy] are not the inadequate but pretentious offspring of a poet who didn't always know where his genius lay. . . . The trilogy, in particular, haunted him; it is, in many respects, a fictional counterpart to *Paterson*—long, wide-ranging, closely connected to this nation's history, especially the social forces unleashed by the industrialism of our Northeast. It can be said that fiction was for this particular writer a means of reconciliation—it was not in vain, the time spent in hospitals, in his office, on the road, going up the stairs of tenement houses to visit (so often) near penniless immigrants who were in pain, but who, often as not, distrusted fiercely the doctor they also knew they required. Rather, lives healed could become lives presented to others—and always, with W., made an occasion for moral instruction or ethical inquiry. The man who in 1925 published *In the American Grain*, with its brilliant evocations and interpretations of Cotton Mather, Abraham Lincoln, and the beginning of slavery in this country, was not one for "distance" from either his "subjects" or the implications their lives might have for those of us right now living ours.

Robert Coles, *W. C. W.: The Knack of Survival in America* (1975), pp. 19–20

WILSON, Angus

English novelist and short-story writer, b. 11 Aug., 1913, Bexhill; d. 31 May 1991, Bury St. Edmund's

Son of a Scottish father and a South African mother, W. attended Westminster School in London and Merton College, Oxford, where he studied history. Except during World War II, when he did secret work under the direction of the Foreign Office, he was employed until 1955 in the library of the British Museum, eventually as Deputy Superintendent of the Reading Room. In 1963 he joined the faculty of the University of East Anglia; he has given lectures in universities in many countries, especially on the state of the novel. He was knighted in 1980.

W.'s first two collections of short stories, *The Wrong Set* (1949) and *Such Darling Dodos* (1950), gave him a considerable literary reputation. Besides capturing the speech and manners of people from middle-class backgrounds like his own, he showed them as involved in inhibiting sets of relationships, and betraying in their actions the liberal, progressive values they espoused.

The same broadly satirical emphasis informed his early novels; against a background of broad tolerance but lack of vision, he depicted characters forced to look deeply within themselves and see the need for change. *Hemlock and After* (1952) deals with a successful novelist who realizes that he has not been a successful human being; *Anglo-Saxon Attitudes* (1956), with a sixty-year-old historian facing up to the fact that he has been involved in an archaeological hoax; and *The Middle Age of Mrs. Eliot* (1958), with a woman undergoing a metamorphosis following the death of her husband. *Late Call* (1964) was a somewhat surprising departure for him, since it is a sympathetic study of a very ordinary old woman, rather than an intellectual, coming to the New Town of Carshall and finding herself an outsider in a supposedly enlightened community in which people bustle about but life is not truly lived.

W.'s later novels show a tendency to express his vision of human life in parable form. In *The Old Men at the Zoo* (1961) he looks into a future not very different from the present, "a world where public events move increasingly faster than private conscience," and issues a warning against men themselves becoming zoological specimens. *As If by Magic* (1973) sends Hamo Langmuir,

inventor of a strain of "Magic Rice," on a world tour to inspect the results. Although sex, power, and money turn out to be the fundamental determinants of our existence, the novel implies a search for spiritual coherence and the desire to attain that state through magic or mystery. *Setting the World on Fire* (1980) plays with the ambiguities suggested by the title. It is about the fire that inspires human beings to the arts of civilization and also about self-destructiveness and the possibility of the whole world being set on fire.

W.'s approach to the writing and criticism of novels is made clear in *The Wild Garden; or, Speaking of Writing* (1963), *The World of Charles Dickens* (1970), and many other essays and reviews. Emphasizing the continuity of literary tradition, he objects to a facile dismissal of great novelists from the past, like Richardson, Scott, and Dickens. He sees their excellence as lying not in a realistic portrayal of life but rather in the power of the human imagination to transform experience. At a time when the New Criticism was concentrating on the text itself, he kept insisting that information about a writer's life and times and literary antecedents, when brought into relationship with his main themes and moral emphases, could provide valuable insights into his work. With his strong sense of the personal and social roots of literature, he views his own novels as set firmly in the English tradition of the portrayal of human manners. Not an abstract thinker but a dramatizer and a person with strong emotional responses, he warns English writers that they should beware of "blowing some great Tolstoyan note with too much wind."

Although many critics regard W. as a major novelist, his stature remains uncertain. His longer novels bring out his weaknesses, especially his tendency to reduce characters to types, caricatures, or mental constructs. While he admires Evelyn WAUGH, he does not follow him in economy, sharpness of focus, or incisiveness of style; his style is sometimes loose and self-indulgent, his focus often shifts, and his novels are Dickensian in length, scope, and detail. He is full of paradoxes: a liberal humanist, he is preoccupied with the paradoxes of liberal humanism; an exposer of hypocrisy and self-deception, he makes life with truth appear no more bearable than life without it; a social satirist, he is impelled by psychological curiosity to find explanations for his characters' failures and therefore to weaken his satire. He is a clever and ingenious novelist, with great powers of comic invention, who suffers from not being wholly convincing.

FURTHER WORKS: *Émile Zola* (1952; rev. ed., 1965); *For Whom the Cloche Tolls: A Scrapbook of the Twenties* (1953, with Philippe Jullian); *The Mulberry Bush* (1956); *A Bit Off the Map, and Other Stories* (1957); *Tempo: The Impact of Television on the Arts* (1964); *No Laughing Matter* (1967); *Death Dance: 25 Stories* (1969); *The Return of Sherlock Holmes* (1974); *The Naughty Nineties* (1976); *The Strange Ride of Rudyard Kipling: His Life and Works* (1977)

BIBLIOGRAPHY: Gindin, J., *Postwar British Fiction: New Accents and Attitudes* (1963): 145–64; Halio, J., *A. W.* (1964); Bradbury, M., "The Short Stories of A. W.," *SSF*, 3 (1966): 117–25; Rabinovitz, R., *The Reaction against Experiment in the English Novel, 1950–1960* (1967): 64–96; Gransden, K. W., *A. W.* (1969); Bergonzi, B., *The Situation of the Novel* (1970): 149–61; Shaw, V., "The Middle Age of Mrs. Eliot and Late Call*: A. W.'s Traditionalism," *CritQ*, 12 (1970): 9–27; Faulkner, P., *A. W.: Mimic and Moralist* (1980);

Drabble, M., "'No Idle Rentier': A. W. and the Nourished Literary Imagination," *SLitI*, 13, 1 (1980): 119–29; McEwan, N., *The Survival of the Novel: British Fiction in the Later Twentieth Century* (1981): 60–77

—D. J. DOOLEY

WILSON, August

American dramatist and poet, b. 27 Apr. 1945, Pittsburgh, Pa.

The most honored American dramatist to emerge in the 1980s, W. grew up in poverty in a slum community in Pittsburgh, Pennsylvania. Raised by his mother, he never knew his biological father and had an often troubled relationship with his stepfather; the relationship of father and son is one of the recurrent concerns of W.'s plays. A high-school dropout at the age of fifteen, W. educated himself at the public library, where he discovered the writings of black American authors; this first acquaintance with writers like Langston HUGHES, Richard WRIGHT, and Ralph ELLISON gave to the disaffected adolescent a sense of possibilities that his formal education had somehow excluded. He began to think of himself as a writer.

W. has published poetry that is by no means without interest, but he has in recent years established himself as primarily a dramatist, and it is certainly his work in the theater that has brought him the attention and acclaim of a growing audience. His association with the theater began in Pittsburgh, where he was the cofounder of the Black Horizon Theatre, a black activist company that produced several of his earliest plays. By the late 1960s, W. had become involved with the Black Power movement, and these early plays reflected a belief that a function of theater is to raise the political consciousness of the audience. W. still regards himself as a Black Nationalist, but his mature work has not been overtly political.

In 1978 W.'s *Black Bart and the Sacred Hills* was staged at the Penumbra Theatre in St. Paul. Minnesota, where W. had moved earlier in the year. But it was when he received a Jerome fellowship in 1980 for his play *Jitney*, which would have its first full-scale production in Pittsburgh in 1982, that W. began to think of himself as a playwright rather than as a poet who happened to be writing plays. As a reflection of this new seriousness of purpose, in 1980 W. submitted three plays to the Eugene O'Neill Conference: *Black Bart, Fullerton Street*, and *Why I Learned to Read*. The plays were rejected, but W.'s commitment remained firm; he began work on the play that would become *Ma Rainey's Black Bottom*, which he submitted to the O'Neill Conference in 1982. This time his play was selected for workshops and readings, bringing W. into contact with Lloyd Richards, who would eventually direct this and all of W.'s later works as they made their way to Broadway.

Ma Rainey's Black Bottom (1985) is the first of four outstanding plays that have established W. as a major force in the contemporary American theater, winner of two Pulitzer Prizes, three New York Drama Critics Circle awards, and a number of other honors. The play, set in Chicago in the 1920s, is meant to be one of what is ultimately to be a series of ten plays, the series as a whole to constitute a depiction of the struggles of African-Americans during each decade of the 20th c. *Fullerton Street*, set in the 1940s, fits the

August Wilson

general pattern, but it is not clear whether that play, not one of W.'s successes, will, at least in its present form, remain W.'s last word on that decade. The other three plays that W. has completed in the series are all set in Pittsburgh: *Fences* (1986) in the 1950s, *Joe Turner's Come and Gone* (1988) in 1911, and *The Piano Lesson* (1990) in the 1930s. W.'s most recent play, *Two Trains Running*, set in the 1960s, opened on Broadway in 1992. Whatever the specific geographical setting of the individual play, the South is a felt presence, as is the history of black America before the 20th c., including the experience of slavery and its aftermath. Further, W. is concerned, especially in the two more recent plays, with exploring the continuing African dimension in the African-American experience. That black Americans are an African people is for W. a given, and to bring his audience, especially his black audience, to a shared awareness of this perception is one of his goals.

Ma Rainey's Black Bottom and *Fences* are both written in the mode of social realism verging on naturalism. Both explore tensions among black characters: musicians in the first play, the family group in the second. In both, these tensions arise ultimately out of situations created by racism: the exploitation of black musicians, the exclusion in the first half of this century of black athletes from major-league professional sports. Yet the tensions also arise from the specific traits and frustrations of the individual characters. W.'s ability to sustain this sort of dual vision is an important source of the plays' emotional power and complexity, as well as a tribute to his honesty.

The most recent plays reflect both thematic and structural developments in W.'s art. Thematically, *Joe Turner's Come and Gone* and *The Piano Lesson* give greater emphasis than the earlier work to the affirmation of the healing power of African-American folk culture; essentially, the characters' chance of survival is closely related to their willingness to accept that cultural tradition. Structurally, W. moves toward more imaginatively open forms, less bound by the conventions of social realism, that are able to accommodate without condescension or apology elements of magic and the supernatural; the plays thus formally enact the very acceptance of folk cultural traditions that they thematically affirm.

Although W. regards himself as a Black Nationalist, the recognition he has enjoyed, as reflected in awards, critical acclaim, and at least some measure of commercial success, attests to the general appeal of his work. There is not the slightest reason to doubt the genuineness of W.'s nationalism, but, at least as reflected in his plays, it is a nationalism that is neither narrow nor negative. W. is committed to exploring the life of black Americans. His work provides us with compelling images of that life as black, as American, as human.

BIBLIOGRAPHY: Smith, P., "*Ma Rainey's Black Bottom:* Playing the Blues as Equipment for Living," in Hartigan, K. V., ed., *Within the Dramatic Spectrum* (1986): 177–86; Freedman, S., "A Voice from the Streets," *NYTMag* (10 June 1987): 36ff; Staples, B., "A. W.," *Essence* (Aug. 1987): 51, 111, 113; Poinsett, A., "A. W.: Hottest New Playwright," *Ebony* (Nov. 1987): 68ff; Ching, M. C., "Wrestling against History," *Theater*, 19, 3 (1988): 70–71; Glover, M., "Two Notes on A. W.: The Songs of a Marked Man," *Theater*, 19, 3 (1988): 69–70; Reed, I., *Writin' Is Fightin': Thirty-Seven Years of Boxing on Paper* (1988): 161–81; Brown, C., "The Light in August," *Esquire* (Apr. 1989): 116ff

—W. P. KENNEY

WILSON, Edmund

American critic, journalist, dramatist, and novelist, b. 8 May 1895, Red Bank, N.J.; d. 12 June 1972, Talcottville, N.Y.

The son of a prominent attorney, W. was educated at the prestigious Hill School in Pottstown, Pennsylvania, and at Princeton University. After his graduation in 1916 he began his career as a reporter for the New York *Evening Sun*, which he left in 1917 to enlist in the U.S. Army, serving in France with a hospital unit and then with the Intelligence Corps. In 1920 he joined *Vanity Fair* as managing editor (until 1921); thereafter he wrote for other magazines as well, notably *The New Republic* (1926–31) and *The New Yorker*, for which he was book reviewer from 1944 to 1948 and to which he contributed essays for the rest of his life. He was married four times; his third wife was Mary MCCARTHY.

W.'s work covers over forty volumes, several posthumously published. An indefatigable keeper of notebooks and diaries, he was always a journalist of the first rank. But his reputation as the foremost American man of letters in our time was founded on his literary criticism; he usually approached literature with an eye for its historical, sociological, biographical, or psychological context. As he wrote to his Princeton mentor Christian Gauss (1878–1951) in the preface to his first book of criticism, *Axel's Castle* (1931): "It was principally from you that I acquired then my idea of what literary criticism ought to be—a history of man's ideas and imaginings in the setting of the conditions which have shaped them." Subtitled *A Study in the Imaginative Literature of 1870–1930*, this book was one of the first examinations of the SYMBOLIST movement and its influence on W. B. YEATS, Paul VALÉRY, T. S. ELIOT, Marcel PROUST, James JOYCE, and Gertrude STEIN. It is closer to pure criticism than most of W.'s later writings. Explication, analysis, and evaluation did not content him, however; and as for literary theory, W. said late in his career that he did "not believe in such things."

By the time he published *The Triple Thinkers* (1938; rev., enl. ed., 1948), his interest in literature was as a revelation of its author's personalities. The two most ambitious pieces offer psychobiographical portraits of Henry JAMES and Ben Jonson. But the most significant essay is "The Historical Interpretation of Literature," which emphasizes literature's "attempt to give a meaning to our experience—that is, to make life more practicable." Although W. derided both the politicosocial formulas of the Marxists and the moral proscriptions of the neohumanists, he shared their concern with the value of literature in human reform, in the articulation of actual problems, just as in *Axel's Castle* he had deplored the artist's isolation. The foreword to the 1948 edition of *The Triple Thinkers* gives a clue to W.'s critical function: "My purpose has always been to try to contribute something new: I have aimed either to present some writer who was not well enough known or, in the case of a familiar writer, to call attention to some neglected aspect of his work or his career."

In this next and perhaps most controversial collection of essays, *The Wound and the Bow* (1941), W. adopted the theory that artistic ability may be a kind of compensation for a psychological wound and that, therefore, the literary work can be adequately understood only through knowing its author's emotional disability. Unfortunately, this approach detracts from W.'s genuine criticism, particularly in "Dickens: The Two Scrooges" and "The KIPLING That Nobody Read." But certainly there is nothing dull about the seven essays, all of which reveal W.'s strengths as a critic: summary, paraphrase, comparison, survey, taste, excellent prose style.

W.'s most impressive book, *Patriotic Gore: Studies in the Literature of the Civil War* (1964), is his most historical and biographical work, a kind of counterpart in criticism to his celebrated history of European revolutionists, *To the Finland Station* (1940); more closely than any of his other writings it approximates the task of criticism he had learned from Gauss. Here W. considers over thirty authors of the Civil War era and shows what they reveal of the moral and political confusion of the times. Few are major or even "creative" literary figures, but rather are memoirists, polemicists, orators, and letter writers. W.'s primary contribution to criticism, or perhaps American literary history, appears in two chapters. "The Myth of the Old South" establishes the *literary* origin of Southern chivalry and shows how it developed, to culminate in the poetry of Sidney Lanier (1842–1881). "The Chastening of American Prose Style" explains the transformation from the turgid writing earlier in the 19th c. to a plain, economical style deriving from the "plain" man (Lincoln), journalism, military writing, and the machine age.

One of the interesting aspects of *Patriotic Gore* is the way it turns into polemic, which evoked criticism among its reviewers. W. wished to define the issues provoking the war in order to suggest how their resolution had lain in the rise of a powerful, centralized government at the expense of an older republicanism.

Thus, the states-rights question had become one of exercising power, through force if necessary, and in the 20th c. became directly related to the "exactions of centralized bureaucracies of both the state and federal authorities."

The individual citizen's bewildered response to an increasingly authoritarian government occupied W. througout his career and appeared as the central theme in his reporting, of which the best example is *The American Earthquake: A Documentary of the Jazz Age, the Great Depression and the New Deal* (1958). This is a collection of excellent on-the-scene articles about America during its least attractive domestic phase. From New York and the "follies" of the 1920s, W. moved across the country during the "earthquake" years of 1930–31, depicting day-to-day situations which exemplified the racial, social, economic, and moral contradictions and stresses in stunned nation. In the foreword W. wrote: "How difficult it is for persons who were born too late to have memories of the depression to believe that it really occurred, that between 1929 and 1933 the whole structure of American society seemed actually to be going to pieces." The book concludes with the early New Deal years and W.'s dissatisfaction with its uneasy politics; for example, the first inaugural address of President Roosevelt suggested to W. a dictatorship. He observed unflinchingly yet uncomfortably, alienated from the new America. His later "protest," *The Cold War and the Income Tax* (1963), is a far more personal, much less detached view of what seemed to him a still more exploitative big government.

W.'s susceptibility to diatribe marks his plays, whose major failing as drama is not in characterization or plot but in their tendency to exhort. Of his eight published plays only two were produced during his lifetime. *The Crime in the Whistler Room* (1924), like several of his early stories, attacks pre-World War I morality as stifling and cruel. *The Little Blue Light* (1950) is a jeremiad against selfishness, political apathy, and materialism. W.'s best play, *Cyprian's Prayer* (1954), not produced professionally, is the account of a 15th-c. youth who learns back magic so that he may elevate peasant life. But Cyprian discovers that self-reliance and intellectual power are superior to any force outside oneself and that reform cannot be hurried.

W.'s most interesting imaginative writing is his fiction, which overlaps much of his other work in its theme of the intellectual's efforts to accept and even contribute to the world of actuality. Although he published only two novels and fourteen stories, several of the latter and superior, and his loosely constructed *Memoirs of Hecate County* (1946), viewed by some readers as a collection of stories, ranks among the better novels of our time. An account of a young scholar's struggles to love, work, and keep his sanity in an environment of despair, it was suppressed when first published because of some graphic sexuality. With *To the Finland Station, The American Earthquake,* and *Patriotic Gore, Memoirs of Hecate County* is one of W.'s finest books.

But W. is most valued finally as a very special reporter, and it seems significant that of his writings published since he died, the most impressive are selections from his notebooks and diaries: *The Twenties* (1975), *The Thirties* (1980), and *The Forties* (1983), all finely edited and introduced by Leon Edel. Considered together, W.'s writings form a record of 20th-c. America's inner and outer life, sympathetically scrutinized, scrupulously judged.

FURTHER WORKS: *The Undertaker's Garland* (1922, with John Peale Bishop); *Discordant Encounters: Plays and Dialogues* (1926);

I Thought of Daisy (1929; repub. with "Galahad" [1927], 1967); *Poets, Farewell!* (1929); *The American Jitters: A Year of the Slump* (1932); *Travels in Two Democracies* (1936); *This Room and This Gin and These Sandwiches: Three Plays* (1937); *The Boys in the Back Room: Notes on California Novelists* (1941); *Note-Books of Night* (1942); *The Shock of Recognition: The Development of Literature in the United States Recorded by the Men Who Made It* (1943); *Europe without Baedeker: Sketches among the Ruins of Italy, Greece and England* (1947; repub. with *Notes from a European Diary: 1963–64,* 1966); *Classics and Commercials: A Literary Chronicle of the Twenties and Thirties* (1952); *Eight Essays* (1954); *Five Plays* (1954); *The Scrolls from the Dead Sea* (1955); *A Piece of My Mind: Reflections at Sixty* (1956); *Red, Black, Blond and Olive: Studies in Four Civilizations: Zuñi, Haiti, Soviet Russia, Israel* (1956); *A Literary Chronicle: 1920–1950* (1956); *Apologies to the Iroquois* (1959, with Joseph Mitchell's "The Mohawks in High Steel" [1949]); *Night Thoughts* (1961); *O Canada: An American's Notes on Canadian Culture* (1965); *The Bit between My Teeth: A Literary Chronicle of 1950–1965* (1965); *A Prelude: Landscapes, Characters and Conversations from the Earlier Years of My Life* (1967); *The Fruits of the MLA* (1969); *The Duke of Palermo, and Other Plays* (1969); *The Dead Sea Scrolls: 1947–1969* (1969); *Upstate: Records and Recollections of Northern New York* (1971); *Homage of Henry James* (1971, with Marianne Moore); *A Window on Russia for the Use of Foreign Readers* (1972); *The Devils and Canon Barham: Ten Essays on Poets, Novelists and Monsters* (1973); *Letters on Literature and Politics, 1912–1972* (1977); *The Nabokov-W. Letters 1940–1971* (1979)

BIBLIOGRAPHY: Rubin, L. D., Jr., "E. W. and the Despot's Heel," *SR,* 71 (1963): 109–15; Paul, S., *E. W.: A Study of the Literary Vocation in Our Time* (1965); Berthoff, W., *E. W.* (1968); Frank, C. P., *E. W.* (1970); Kriegel, L., *E. W.* (1971); Douglas, G. H., "E. W.: The Critic as Artist," *TQ* 17 (1974): 58–72; Josephson, M., "Encounters with E. W.," *SoR,* 11 (1975): 731–65; Bell, P. K., "E. W.'s *Axel's Castle,*" *Daedalus,* 105 (1976): 115–25; Wellek, R., "E. W.," *CLS,* 15 (1978): 97–123; Thwaite, A., "Literary Life," *Encounter,* Fall 1978: 58–63; Wain, J., ed., *E. W.: The Man and His Work* (1978); French, P., *Three Honest Men: E. W., F. R. Leavis, Lionel Trilling: A Critical Mosaic* (1980): 17–43

—CHARLES FRANK

WILSON, Lanford

American dramatist, b. 13 Apr. 1937, Lebanon, Mo.

W. is considered one of the most influential contemporary American playwrights. Raised in a small town and on a farm, he presents a Midwestern perspective in many of his important works. After working in factories and studying art briefly at Southwest Missouri State College and San Diego State College (1955–1957), he moved to Chicago to work as a commercial artist. In 1959 he discovered a talent for playwriting and gave up art and short-story writing. W. moved to Greenwich Village, New York City, in 1962 and became acquainted with the THEATER OF THE ABSURD at Caffe

Cino. Joe Cino produced his *So Long at the Fair* in 1963, a work inspired by the madcap but serious plays of Eugène IONESCO. During the next few years, W.'s plays became the mainstay of Caffe Cino. In 1965 his full-length plays were produced successfully on the larger stage of Ellen Stewart's La Mama Experimental Theatre. W. and friends organized the nonprofit Circle Repertory Theatre in 1969, which proved the most successful locus for his playwriting. The ensemble policies and varied repertoire of this institution allowed W. to create certain roles for known actors and to envision locales in familiar acting spaces. His three most significant plays won box-office approval and critical acclaim at the Circle Repertory Theatre. Among these were *The Hot-L Baltimore* (1973), which received the New York Drama Critics Circle Award, the Outer Circle Award, and the Obie Award; *The Mound Builders* (1975), the Obie Award; and *Talley's Folly* (1980), the Pulitzer Prize.

The Hot-L Baltimore shows life among the remnants of a vanishing era, a theme that W. would return to, particularly in *The Mound Builders*. A portrait of a marginalized and down-and-out community, the play follows the dramatic traditions of Maxim GORKY's *The Lower Depths* (1912), Eugene O'NEILL's *The Iceman Cometh* (wr. 1939, pub. 1946), and most especially William SAROYAN's *The Time of Your Life* (1939), whose wayward but somewhat sentimentalized characters W. at times redraws. The play is set in the early 1970s in a soon-to-be demolished railway hotel built during the Gilded Age; everything is allowed to deteriorate without repair. The characters are prostitutes, homosexual partners, the dispossessed, the put-upon, and the despairing. A golden age of travel (and of personal dreams) has given way to a hard reality, which has left the characters little sense of hope or fulfillment. W. reveals a spectrum of individual responses to this condition: Some of the characters, especially The Girl, a street prostitute, show an awareness of what has been lost. As a child, W. was fascinated by the American railroads, and this vanishing transportation system functions as a symbol in the play of life's elusive goals.

In *The Mound Builders*, W. returns to the American Midwest, and to a strong Middle-American presence, for his inspiration. Two archaeologists and their wives live in a farmhouse, itself fast becoming an artifact and locus for nostalgic reflection on a more ideal time in American life. Structurally the play follows a pattern of parallel-and-contrast between the vanished society for which the archaeologists are digging and the vacuities of their own lives. During periodic flashback scenes, photographic slides are projected by August, the senior archaeologist, which depict alternately the significant people in his life—the other characters in the play— with shots of the decaying glory in the dig site. W.'s humor is based on the wit of the characters, their self-deprecating commentary and their ironic perception of the futility of all attempts at meaning in civilization, including above all their own. *The Mound Builders* seems to expose our general complicity in the destruction of meaning in American life, even as we pursue such ideals as a greater understanding of past history.

With *Talley's Folly* W. began what was planned as a five-play cycle dealing with the history of the Talley family of Lebanon, Missouri, from the Civil War era to the present. Only two other plays of the cycle have been completed: *War in Lebanon* (1980) and *Talley and Son* (1986). *Talley's Folly* garnered critical and popular acclaim for its unusual performance structure—the main character both opens and closes the stage action in a framing device spoken directly to the audience—as well as for the effective simplicities of plot and character. Using only two characters, one setting, and a very restricted time frame—the ninety-six-minute running time of the performance—the play focuses on the developing relationship of the two characters and their tensive dialogue. Set in 1944, the plot is an episode in the history of the Talleys, a respected Missouri family. Matt, a Jewish-American, successfully courts Sally Talley, who rejects his love overtures until she is convinced of his sincerity.

Burn This (1987) presents the ills of urban living with dialogue and characterization somewhat more acerbic than W.'s earlier plays, although, as in *Talley's Folly*, it reveals a continued interest in the dynamic chemistry between a romantic odd couple. Anna is invaded late at night in her downtown Manhattan loft by Pale, her deceased roommate's brother. They are immediately drawn to each other, but soon digress into frenetic musings brought about by the pressures of their modern life-styles and their complex psychologies.

As a dramatist, W. follows the traditions of Tennessee WILLIAMS, Lillian HELLMAN, and William INGE in presenting character and conflict from America's heartland. His straightforward realism is enhanced by elements of lyricism and nostalgia for a bygone era when ideals were still believed in. His people strive for meaning in life, often failing, but at times achieving some sort of perception. In the tradition of Anton CHEKHOV, the characters often express through humor and reflection an earnest desire for fulfillment and an end to aimlessness and spiritual vacuity. Although W.'s plays have been criticized for insufficient character motivation and occasional sentimentality, his sense of human speech patterns, his sympathy for a wide range of characters, and his experiments with play structure, particularly with layered dialogue and choric commentary, have been exemplary.

FURTHER WORKS: *Balm in Gilead* (1965); *Days Ahead* (1965); *Home Free!* (1965); *This Is the Rill Speaking* (1967); *Days Ahead* (1967); *The Madness of Lady Bright* (1967); *The Rimers of Eldritch* (1967); *Wandering* (1967); *The Gingham Dog* (1969); *Lemon Sky* (1970); *The Sand Castle* (1970); *Sextet (Yes)* (1970); *Stop: A Turn* (1970); *Summer and Smoke* (1972, libretto adaptation, with Lee Hoiby); *The Family Continues* (1973); *The Great Nebula in Orion* (1973); *Ikke, Ikke, Nye, Nye, Nye* (1973); *Victory on Mrs. Dandywine's Island* (1973); *Serenading Louie* (1976); *Brontosaurus* (1978); *5th of July* (1979); *A Tale Told* (1981); *Angels Fall* (1982); *Thymus Vulgaris* (1982); *Halls of North American Forests* (1988); *The Moonshot Tape* (1988); *Redwood Curtain* (1992); *By the Sea* (1996)

BIBLIOGRAPHY: Barnett, G. A., *L. W.* (1987); Barnett, G. A., "Recreating the Magic: An Interview with L. W.," *BSUF*, 25 (Spring 1984): 57–74; Dasgupta, G., "L. W.," in Marranca, B., and Dasgupta, G., eds., *American Playwrights: A Critical Survey* (1981): 27–39; Dreher, A., "L. W.," in MacNicholas, J., ed., *DLB: Twentieth-Century American Dramatists*, Part 2 (1981): 350–68; Harriet, E., "L. W.: To Vanish without a Trace," *American Voices* (1989): 19–35; Jacobi, M. J., "The Comic Vision of L. W.," *SLitI*, 21 (1988): 119–34; Kellman, B., "The American Playwright in the Seventies: Some Problems and Perspectives," *Theatre Quarterly*, 8, 29 (1978): 45–58; Schvez, H. I., "Images of the Past in the Plays of L. W.," in Bock, H., ed., *Essays in Contemporary American*

Drama (1981): 225–40; B., Witham. B., "Images of America: W., Weller and Horovitz," *TJ*, 21 (Fall 1988): 119–34

—WILLIAM OVER

WINTERS, Yvor

American poet and critic, b. 17 Oct. 1900, Chicago, Ill.; d. 26 Jan. 1968, Palo Alto, Cal.

Having spent his childhood in California and Oregon, W. returned to Chicago to attend high school. When it was discovered during his freshman year at the University of Chicago (1917–18) that he had tuberculosis, he moved to Santa Fe, New Mexico. From the University of Colorado, he earned an A.B. and an A.M. in Romance languages. Stanford University granted him a Ph.D. in 1934. After teaching French and Spanish at the University of Idaho (1925–27), W. accepted a position in 1928 at Stanford, and he remained there until his retirement in 1966. Among his most significant awards are the Brandeis University Creative Arts Award (1960); the Harriet Monroe Poetry Award (1960–61); the Bollingen Prize for his *Collected Poems* (rev. ed., 1960) in 1961; and a Guggenheim grant (1961–62).

W.'s early poetry of the 1920s was experimental free verse, influenced by William Carlos WILLIAMS and the IMAGIST movement, in which he aimed at intensity of individual images and lines, and rarely attempted to deal with ideas, which he called "anti-images." By 1928 he had moved from free verse to regular meters in poems that began to emphasize abstractions while depending primarily on sensory detail. With the publication of *Before Disaster* (1934), however, it was evident that W. had acquired an abstract style and a moral absolutist stance, both of which he maintained throughout the balance of his career. Severe and somber in theme and language, W.'s best poems are strictly disciplined and rational efforts to perfect a moral attitude toward a particular experience; hence, they are frequently topical and epigrammatic. For models he turned to the Elizabethans Sir Fulke Greville and Sir Walter Raleigh.

W.'s iconoclastic views, his insistence on rigorous discrimination, and his unrelenting emphasis on moral judgments made him the American counterpart to F. R. LEAVIS. Like the neohumanist Irving Babbitt (1865–1933), the American critic he most closely resembles (although he did not regard himself a neohumanist), W. identified romanticism as a distorting force in modern literature, and he rejected the concept of the aesthetic autonomy of a work. W.'s most influential critical views, which were developed in the 1930s and finally spelled out in *Primitivism and Decadence: A Study of American Experimental Poetry* (1937), contrasted sharply with those of the New Critics, who came into prominence during the same period and long dominated American criticism. W. concentrated on the relationship between form and content in a poem and examined the paraphrasable rational content of a poem and the emotion appropriate to it, as well as the language and formal devices in which the content is presented. Because of these views, W. took exception to T. S. ELIOT's concepts of the "objective correlative" and of "dissociation of sensibility," for the claimed they excluded precise judgment of emotion from Eliot's view of art.

W. made many critical pronouncements, which have been variously received as brilliant, perverse, or outrageous, for few writers merited his praise, many his censure. For example, W. raised Edith WHARTON above Henry JAMES, and he ranked the English poet Robert Bridges's (1844–1930) verse superior to that of W. B. YEATS, Hart CRANE, Marianne MOORE, William Carlos Williams, and Eliot, "incomparably" superior to that of Ezra POUND, and more original than the Gerard Manley Hopkins (1844–1889) in every respect. Moreover, W. held that T. Sturge Moore (1870–1944) was the "nearest rival to Bridges," and that the "finest British poet since. . . Moore" was Elizabeth Daryush (1887–?), Bridges's daughter. Nevertheless, W.'s *Maule's Curse: Seven Studies in the History of American Obscurantism* (1938) includes some perceptive and challenging assessments of Hawthorne, Melville, Poe, Emerson, Dickens, Henry James, and others.

The author of a small body of what was once prize-winning poetry, W. will be remembered longer for his provocative evaluative criticism, however idiosyncratic it was, and for his intensely argued interrogation of the function of literature, which any comprehensive assessment of modernism must consider.

FURTHER WORKS: *The Immobile Wind* (1921); *The Magpie's Shadow* (1922); *The Testament of a Stone: Notes on the Mechanics of the Poetic Image* (1924); *The Bare Hills* (1927); *The Proof* (1930); *The Journey, and Other Poems* (1931); *Brink of Darkness* (1932); *Edgar Allan Poe: A Crisis in the History of American Obscurantism* (1937); *Poems* (1940); *The Anatomy of Nonsense* (1943); *The Giant Weapon* (1943); *Edwin Arlington Robinson* (1946; rev. ed., 1971); *In Defense of Reason* (1947); *Three Poems* (1950); *Collected Poems* (1952; rev. and enlarged, 1960; rev. 1963); *The Function of Criticism* (1957); *On Modern Poets* (1957); *The Poetry of W. B. Yeats* (1960); *The Poetry of J. V. Cunningham* (1961); *Early Poems of Y. W., 1920–1928* (1966); *Forms of Discovery* (1967); *Uncollected Essays and Reviews* (1973); *The Collected Poems of Y. W.* (1978); *Hart Crane and Y. W.: Their Literary Correspondence* (1978); *The Poetry of Y. W.* (1979)

BIBLIOGRAPHY: Hyman, S. E., *The Armed Vision: A Study in the Methods of Modern Literary Criticism*, rev. ed. (1955): 22–53; Alvarez, A., *Beyond All This Fiddle: Essays 1955–1967* (1968): 255–59; Fraser, J., "Leavis, W. and 'Tradition,'" *SoR*, 7 (1971): 963–85; Sexton, D. E., *The Complex of Y. W.'s Criticism* (1973); Powell, G. E., *Language as Being in the Poetry of Y. W.* (1980); Isaacs, E., *An Introduction to the Poetry of Y. W.* (1981); Davis, D., *Wisdom and Wilderness: The Achievement of Y. W.* (1983)

—ARTHUR B. COFFIN

WITKIEWICZ, Stanisław Ignacy

(pseud.: Witkacy) Polish dramatist, novelist, and essayist, b. 24 Feb. 1885, Warsaw; d. 18 Sept. 1939, Jeziory

Son of the well-known art critic and painter Stanisław W. (1851–1915), W. spent his early years in Zakopane, where he was exposed to the cultural and intellectual life flourishing in that mountain resort at the turn of the century. Between 1904, when he began his studies at the Cracow Academy of Fine Arts, and 1911 he traveled extensively in Western Europe. In 1914 he joined his friend, the anthropologist Bronisław Malinowski (1884–1942), in a scientific expedition to Australia. As a Russian subject, he served in the Russian army during World War I and witnessed the Bolshevik revolution while in its ranks. After the war he returned to Zakopane, where he began to write extensively. For twenty-one years he devoted himself to his writing, studies of theater, and art. In September 1939, when Poland was overrun by Germany, he fled eastward. Upon hearing the news of the Soviet occupation of eastern Poland, he committed suicide.

W. came under the influence of the formalists after World War I and developed his own theory of pure form, based on painting. Carrying it over to drama, he continued to make use of examples of painting in his arguments. His essays on aesthetics—the book-length *Nowe formy w malarstwie i wynikające stąd nieporozumienia* (1919; new forms in painting and misunderstandings resulting therefrom) and the collection *Szkice estetyczne* (1922; aesthetic sketches)—were accompanied by a series of abstract portraits. *Teatr: Wstęp do teorii czystej formy w teatrze* (1923; theater: introduction to the theory of pure form in theater) is a collection of essays in which W. formulates the aesthetic theory that underlies his dramas.

To demonstrate his theory of pure form and to communicate to the public his view that the individual is destined to obliteration, W. wrote approximately thirty plays between 1918 and 1934, each of which is meant to shock the audience into a new consciousness. They were highly controversial and mostly misunderstood in his lifetime. If produced at all, they appeared only in small, experimental theaters; those that were not produced were circulated in manuscript.

Most of W.'s plays are set in a nightmarish world where characters die and come to life and die again. The surrealistic action foreshadows the THEATER OF THE ABSURD. In *Kurka wodna* (perf. 1922, pub. 1962; *The Water Hen*, 1968) the world collapses in revolution while financiers wallow in luxury. At the center of *Szalona lokomotywa* (written 1923, pub. 1962, perf. 1964; *The Crazy Locomotive*, 1968) are two criminals, one disguised as a railway engineer, the other as his fireman. To determine who will have the woman they both love, they decide to run the train, full of passengers, at breakneck speed until they crash; the survivor will be the winner. With the play W. created a grim metaphor—that the fate of the world depends entirely on insane criminals.

Wariat i zakonnica; czyli, Nie ma złego, co by na jeszcze gorsze nie wyszło (1925; *The Madman and the Nun: or, There Is Nothing Bad Which Could Not Turn Into Something Worse*, 1968) is set in an insane asylum in which the doctors seem to need psychiatric treatment more than the patients. As in most of W.'s plays, the action and the characters' emotions transcend reality. After the protagonist has killed himself, his corpse walks and talks—a symbol of modern, mechanized man.

Szewcy (written 1934, pub. 1948, perf. 1957; *The Shoemakers*, 1968), perhaps the most important of W.'s dramas, contains all the characteristic elements of his theater—presentation of the absurdity of human relationships, grotesqueries, BLACK HUMOR—and the violent social criticism that pervades all his works. A deeply pessimistic play, it dramatizes W.'s belief that individual man is doomed, and that mass man, a machine like being programmed to exist in a technological society, will reign absolutely.

Permeated with strong satirical overtones and erotic imagery, W.'s novels complement the grotesque and catastrophic vision of modern times revealed in his essays and forming the core of his theater and his painting. In *Pożegnanie jesieni* (1927; farewell to autumn) and *Nienasycenie* (1930; *Insatiability*, 1976), two antiutopian novels, he presents his theory that European culture and modern society are in a state of apocalyptic crisis. Both novels are set in the future in an imaginary country, which nevertheless suggests the Poland of W.'s time. The protagonist of *Pożegnanie jesieni*, Atanazy Bazakbal, an artist and intellectual, flees to the border to escape the "universal grayness" that has followed the revolution in his country. At the moment of escape, however, he turns back in the hope that, if people can be roused to the threat hanging over them, the trend toward depersonalization can be reversed. Caught by the guards, he is executed.

In the world of *Nienasaycenie* Russia is no longer communist. Poland, ruled by the dictator Kocmoluchowicz, is looked to by communist Europe to save them from the "yellow peril" of the threatening Chinese army. Central to the outcome are the Chinese-made pills that are distributed; when taken, they cure the insatiability of metaphysical craving, ridding the individual of anxiety and the will to resist.

In recent years, W.'s work has received long-delayed recognition. He is now considered one of the most original 20th-c. European playwrights, one whose contribution helped to shape the modern Theater of the Absurd. In the mid-1950s he was "rediscovered" in Poland, and since the 1960s his dramas have been translated and staged in many western European countries, as well as in the U.S.

FURTHER WORKS: *Pragmatyści* (1920; *The Pragmatists*, 1972); *Mister Price; czyli, Bzik tropikalny* (1920; *Mr. Price; or, Tropical Madness*, 1972); *Oni* (1920; *They*, 1968); *Tumor Mózgowicz* (1921; *Tumor Brainiowicz*, 1980); *Gyubal Wahazar; czyli, Na przełęczach bezsensu* (1921; *Gyubal Wahazar; or, Along the Cliffs of the Absurd*, 1972); *Metafizyka dwugłowego cielęcia* (1921; *Metaphysics of a Two-Headed Calf*, 1972); *Nowe wyzwolenie* (1922); *Nadobnisie i koczkodany; czyli, Zielona pigułka* (1922; *Dainty Shapes and Hairy Apes*, 1980); *Matka* (1924; *The Mother*, 1968); *Nikotyna, alkohol, kokaina, peyotl, morfina, eter* (1932); *Szewcy* (1934; *The Shoemakers*, 1968); *Pojęcia i twierdzenia implikowane przez pojęcie istnienia, 1917–32* (1935); *Straszliwy wychowawca* (1935); *Sonata Belzebuba; czyli, Prawdziwe zdarzenie w Mordowarze* (1938; *Beelzebub Sonata; or, What Really Happened in Mordowar*, 1980); *W małym dworku* (1948); *Nowe formy w malarstwie i inne pisma estetyczne* (1959); *Jedyne wyjście* (1968); *Dramaty* (2 vols., 1962; enlarged ed., 1972); *622 upadki Bunga; czyli, Demoniczna kobieta* (1972); *Listy do Bronisława Malinowskiego* (1981). **FURTHER WORKS IN ENGLISH:** *The Madman and the Nun, and Other Plays* (1968); *Tropical Madness: Four Plays* (1972); *Beelzebub Sonata: Plays, Essays, and Documents* (1980)

BIBLIOGRAPHY: Puzyna, K., "The Prism of Absurd," *PolP*, 6 (1963): 34–44; Miłosz, C., "S. I. W.: A Polish Writer for Today," *TriQ*, 9 (1967): 143–54; Grabowski, Z., "S. I. W.: A Polish Prophet of Doom," *PolR*, 12, 1 (1967): 39–49; Krzyżanowski, J. R., "W.'s Anthroponomy," *CompD*, 3 (1969): 193–98; special W. issue *The Theatre in Poland, No. 3* (1970); special W. issue *PolR*, 18: 1–2 (1973); Dukore, B. F., "Spherical Tragedies and Comedies with Corpses: Witkacian Tragicomedy," *MD*, 18 (1975): 291–315;

special W. issue *The Theatre in Poland*, Nos. 6–7 (1978); Gerould, D., *Witkacy: S. I. W. as an Imaginative Writer* (1981)

—JERZY R. KRZYŻANOWSKI

WITTIG, Monique

French feminist writer, b. 1935, Belgium

W. has been secretive about her life. Allegedly the daughter of the Belgian poet Henri Dubois, she earned a degree in modern literature at the Sorbonne; studied oriental languages; and then worked first in the Bibliothèque Nationale and later as a proofreader. Her first novel, *L'opoponax* (1964; *The Opoponax*, 1966), was hailed by Marguerite DURAS, Mary MCCARTHY, and Claude Simon (qq.v.). It won the prestigious Médicis Prize. In 1970 W. contributed to writing the official anthem of the Mouvement de Libération des Femmes; she also became the leader of the Féministes Révolutionnaires; and she created a well-publicized scandal by trying to place a wreath under the Arc de Triomphe to honor the wife of the Unknown Soldier. In 1976 she emigrated to the U.S. She moves frequently, by choice, among the colleges and universities where she teaches. She has contributed important articles on the lesbian identity to *Questions féministes* and to *Feminist Issues*.

L'opoponax forcefully depicts the oppressive atmosphere of a convent school and its indoctrination of girls into partriarchal culture. The impressionistic style and focus on group interactions recalls Nathalie SARRAUTE. Over the years, the class gradually achieves a limited autonomy and critical detachment, while the heroine discovers herself through her love for a classmate. The gender-neutral pronoun *on* is used throughout. *Les guérillères* (1969; *The Guérillères*, 1971), a utopian epic, shows an independent society of warrior women who learn to create their own traditions without being bound by them; to appreciate their bodies without worshiping them; to fight, win, and to dismiss with laughter derogatory clichés about women. They then conquer men, and rehabilitate a few men of good will as they pursue a worldwide revolution. *Le corps lesbien* (1973; *The Lesbian Body*, 1975) evokes the Song of Songs with a cycle of prose poems that praise the lover's body, including the internal organs and the secretions. Lesbian love, at times violent, is glorified as complete and democratic. *The Brouillon pour un dictionnaire des amantes* (1976, with Sande Zeig; *Lesbian Peoples: Material for a Dictionary*, 1979) depicts a utopian future society and offers sample articles for a feminist revision of all knowledge. All references to males are erased; "lesbian" is redefined as "companion lover." "History," the long central entry, rejects *l'écriture féminine* (femininitude). *Virgile, non* (1985; *Across the Acheron*, 1987) parodies Dante's *Divine Comedy* and is set in San Francisco. Hell is filled with horrific processions of women enslaved, battered, and mutilated by men; Limbo is occupied by cruising lesbians, isolated in their hedonism; and Paradise is emotional and sensual fulfillment. "Wittig" and her angelic guide try mostly in vain to persuade the women in Hell to take up their arms and escape. *Le voyage sans fin* (1985; pointless [or endless] voyage), an experimental playscript and video, recreates *Don Quixote* by Miguel de Cervantes (1547–1616) with female characters. Quichotte (the French spelling of Quixote) is

opposed by her own conventional mother and sister. Independent series of words and of pantomime are interwoven.

W. is the leader of the militant French feminists who seek to attack and subvert the concept of the difference between the sexes, a concept they denounce as the foundation of the patriarchal hierarchy, male domination, and the enslavement of women. She has called for a worldwide revolution in which writing would constitute only an initial call to arms. Thus she opposes the countervailing French feminist movement led by Hélène CIXOUS advocating the glorification of woman's difference in *l'écriture féminine*. The accessible *L'opoponax* remains highly regarded as a narrative of childhood. In academic circles, *Les guérillères* is considered a model of feminist fiction. The *Brouillon* has greatly influenced the "Women's Language" debate and Cheris Kramarae (b. 1938) and Paula Treichler's (b. 1943) monumental *Feminist Dictionary* (1985). W.'s experiments with rejecting plot, and her consistent, idealistic attempts to replace the cult of personality with a collectivist ethic have made her works less appealing to conventional readers than to those familiar with the NEW NOVEL and with poststructuralist theories of language. Her major thrust has been to reappropriate language and culture for women.

BIBLIOGRAPHY: McCarthy, M., "Everybody's Childhood," *The Writing on the Wall and Other Literary Essays* (1970): 102–11; Higgins, L., "Nouvelle, nouvelle autobiographie: M. W.'s *Le corps lesbien*," *SubStance*, 14 (1976): 160–66; Wenzel, H. V., "The Text as Body/Politics: An Appreciation of M. W.'s Writing in Context," *FSt*, 7 (1981): 264–87; Shaktini, N., "Displacing the Phallic Subject: W.'s Lesbian Writings," *Signs*, 8 (1982): 29–44; Crowder, D., "Amazons and Mothers? M. W., Hélène Cixous, and Theories of Women's Writing," *ConL*, 24 (1983): 117–44; special W. issue, *Vlasta*, 4 (1985); Duffy, J., "M. W.," in Brosman, C. S., ed. *DLB: French Novelists since 1960* (1989): 330–44; Porter, L. M., "Writing Feminism: Myth, Epic and Utopia in M. W.'s *Les guérillères*," *ECr*, 29 (1989): 92–100

—LAURENCE M. PORTER

WITTLIN, Józef

Polish poet, novelist, essayist, and translator, b. 17 Aug. 1896, Dmytrów (then Austro-Hungarian Empire); d. 19 Feb. 1976, New York, N.Y., U.S.A.

Born in northeastern Galicia, and of Jewish extraction, W. was educated in Lvov and Vienna, and during World War I he served in the Austrian army. In 1921 he moved to Łódź and became literary director of the Municipal Theater there, also lecturing at the School of Drama, of which he was a cofounder. His novel *Sól ziemi* (1935; *Salt of the Earth*, 1939), which revealed the absurdity and cruelty of war, was translated into thirteen languages, achieved international recognition, and earned W. awards in Poland and the U.S., to which he emigrated in 1941. He was the first Polish author to receive a prize from the American Academy of Arts and Letters and from the National Institute of Arts and Letters. He lived in New York City until his death.

W.'s creative output centered around his "settling accounts with war." In his first collection of poems, *Hymny* (1920; hymns), published by the Poznań group of Polish EXPRESSIONISTS, with whom he was affiliated, he used powerful rhythms and free verse to express deep emotions: fear of death, love of God, and concern for the soul of modern man.

W. wrote and translated poetry throughout his life. The volume *Poezje* (1978; poems), posthumously published in Warsaw, contains, in addition to *Hymny*, occasional verse written in the interwar period and during World War II, as well as some poetry from the 1960s. The later poetry is different from the early, somewhat metaphysical verse of *Hymny*; it is more "earthly," marked by specific images and colors rather than by allegory and abstraction. The more recent work in *Poezje* is ironic and aphoristic, and its philosophical mainly existential tinge has endeared W. to postwar Polish poets.

W. was also of great importance as a translator. He published a Polish paraphrase of the Babylonian epic *Gilgamesh* in 1922. In his rendering in verse of Homer's *Odyssey* (1924) he tried to impress upon Polish readers the metaphysical qualities of the Greek epic. By 1939 W. had translated and adapted over twenty works from Italian and German, and later he translated contemporary American, English, German, Italian, and Spanish poetry into Polish.

As an essayist, W. displayed enormous imagination and erudition. He defendant humanistic values, arousing lofty longings in man to return to the paradise he was exiled from. In the collection of essays *Wojna, pokój i dusza poety* (1925; war, peace, and the poet's soul) he present the viewpoint of a pacifist and a utopian who believes that literature should assume the function of religion. His keen powers of perception and the originality of his style are especially evident in a book of travel sketches, *Etapy* (1933; stages), in which he plumbs existential depths, finding philosophical meaning in concrete details. *Mój Lwów* (1946; my Lvov), published in New York, is a powerful evocation of W.'s favorite city; it was later incorporated into a large collection of his essays and journalistic writings, *Orfeusz w piekle XX wieku* (1963; Orpheus in the inferno of the twentieth century), published in Paris.

W.'s most important work, *Sól ziemi*, is a modernized epic that can be read on many levels. It was conceived as the first part of a projected trilogy entitled "Powieść o cierpliwym piechurze" (saga of the patient foot soldier), and is a literary monument to the "unknown soldier," an intense and spirited depiction of a simple human conscience and its workings during the crises of war. The recruit Piotr Niewiadomski (whose last name means "unknown"), a humble railway worker, reacts to everything he witnesses and in which he is involved in a fresh and innocent way, thus exposing false war myths and bureaucratic and military absurdities, no matter how rational they seem on the surface. The lyrical, symbolic, and satirical components of this poetic novel blend into a great and highly distinctive work of art. Thomas MANN said that *Sól ziemi* "extends into the sphere of the typical and thus the mythical and epical."

W. considered himself primarily a poet. His fiction is that of a poet who has a deep understanding and mastery of the epic genre. W.'s vision was timeless, its expression poignant and enduring.

BIBLIOGRAPHY: Coleman, A. P., "Recent Novels by Polish Writers," *NYTBR* (5 July 1936): 4–5; Marcel, G., on *Le sel de la terre* [French tr. of *Sól ziemi*], *Le jour* (16 June 1939): 3; Kazin, A., on *Salt of the Earth*, *NYHT* (25 Oct. 1941): 2; Hymann, S., "The Patient Foot-Soldier", *New Republic* (27 Oct. 1941): 559–60; Folejewski, Z., "The Creative Path of J. W.," *PolR*, 9 (1964): 67–72; Härtling, P., "J. W.: *Das Salz der Erde*" [German tr. of *Sól ziemi*], *Die Welt der Literatur* (20 Jan. 1966): 7; Yurieff, Z., *J. W.* (1973)

—ZOYA YURIEFF

WODEHOUSE, P(elham) G(renville)

English short-story writer, novelist, dramatist, and screenwriter, b. 15 Oct. 1881, Guildford; d. 14 Feb. 1975, Remsenburg, N.Y., U.S.A.

The third son of a member of the Hong Kong civil service, W. was raised by various relatives in England. After graduating from Dulwich College, he worked first for a London bank and then for *The Globe*, a London evening paper, and also began to write short stories and novels. In 1909 W. moved to Greenwich Village, New York, and spent the remainder of his life in several homes in the U.S. and Europe. Interned in France in 1940 by the Germans, he naïvely recorded five interviews, which, when broadcast by German radio, were widely considered treasonous and led to his being arrested by the French after the liberation of Paris. Released through the intervention of British officials in 1945, he moved permanently to the U.S. in 1947 and spent most of the rest of his life in Remsenburg, Long Island.

W.'s early stories and novels, written usually for serial publication in magazines, deal with life in the English public school. Unlike the work of numerous British authors, they ignore serious issues and instead stress the value of the "public school spirit," the now nearly discredited code of conduct that theoretically was to build character and civilized behavior in those who were to rule the British Empire.

W.'s later, and more mature, works are gently satiric, offering playful caricatures of British institutions such as gentlemen's clubs, stately homes, law courts, and universities, and of national character types such as peers, baronets, bishops, millionaires, headmasters, judges, and policemen. Influenced by wide reading, W. frequently parodies Shakespeare, sentimental novels, juvenile literature, and melodramas.

W.'s most popular stories resemble Restoration comedies in treating wealthy and titled gallants and their shrewd and calculating servants and they present a gallery of characters who have endeared themselves to readers, for example, Stanley Featherstonehaugh Ukridge, an engaging but unscrupulous rogue totally innocent of principles, and his opposite, Rupert Psmith, the calm fastidious man with a social conscience. W.'s most famous creations are Bertie Wooster, a type of village idiot in an English upper-class setting, and his intelligent, ingenious, and morally sound butler, Jeeves. In these characters, W. skillfully uses Jeeves's reason to balance Wooster's emotion, and the result is a wonderful comic duo.

W. wrote over a hundred books in a career that spanned over seventy years, and he attracted an enormous and loyal reading public who enjoy the timeless Edwardian world of his stories. It is a world where the real problems of the human condition are absent or dismissed by laughter, where life is gentle and simple and frequently silly. It is uniquely W.'s milieu, and it is one to which readers will return for many years.

FURTHER WORKS: *The Pothunters* (1902); *A Prefect's Uncle* (1903); *Tales of St. Austin's* (1903); *The Gold Bat* (1904); *William Tell Told Again* (1904); *The Head of Kay's* (1905); *Love among the Chickens* (1906); *The White Feather* (1907); *Not George Washington* (1907); *The Globe by the Way Book* (1908); *The Swoop* (1909); *Mike* (1909); *The Intrusion of Jimmy* (1910); *A Gentleman of Leisure* (1910); *Psmith in the City* (1910); *The Prince and Betty* (1912); *The Little Nugget* (1913); *The Man Upstairs* (1914); *Something New* (1915); *Something Fresh* (1915); *Uneasy Money* (1916); *Piccadily Jim* (1917); *The Man with Two Left Feet* (1917); *Psmith Journalis* (1919); *My Man Jeeves* (1919); *Their Mutual Child* (1919); *A Damsel in Distress* (1919); *The Coming of Bill* (1920); *The Little Warrior* (1920); *Jill the Reckless* (1921); *Indiscretions of Archie* (1921); *The Clicking of Cuthbert* (1922); *Three Men and a Maid* (1922); *The Girl on the Boat* (1922); *The Adventures of Sally* (1922); *Mostly Sally* (1923); *Jeeves* (1923); *Leave It to Psmith* (1923); *The Inimitable Jeeves* (1924); *Ukridge* (1924); *Bill the Conqueror* (1924); *Golf without Tears* (1924); *Sam the Sudden* (1925); *Sam in the Suburs* (1925); *He Rather Enjoyed It* (1926); *The Heart of a Goof* (1926); *Hearts and Diamons* (1926); *Carry On Jeeves* (1927); *Divots* (1927); *The Play's the Thing* (1927); *The Small Bachelor* (1927); *Meet Mr. Mulliner* (1927); *Good Morning Bill* (1928); *Money for Nothing* (1928); *Mr. Mulliner Speaking* (1929); *Fish Preferred* (1929); *Summer Lightning* (1929); *Baa, Baa, Black Sheep* (1930); *Very Good, Jeeves* (1930); *Big Money* (1931); *If I Were You* (1931); *Jeeves Omnibus* (1931); *Louder and Funnier* (1932); *Doctor Sally* (1932); *Hot Water* (1932); *Nothing but W.* (1932); *Mulliner Nights* (1933); *Heavy Weather* (1933); *Candlelight* (1934); *Methuen's Library of Humour: P. G. W.* (1934); *Thank You, Jeeves* (1934); *Right Ho, Jeeves* (1934); *Brinkley Manor* (1934); *Mulliner Omnibus* (1935); *Blandings Castle* (1935); *The Luck of the Bodkins* (1935); *Anything Goes* (1936, with Cole Porter); *Young Men in Spats* (1936); *Laughing Gas* (1936); *Lord Emsworth and Others* (1937); *Crime Wave at Blandings* (1937); *Summer Moonshine* (1937); *The Code of the Woosters* (1938); *The Three Musketeers* (1939, with Clifford Grey and George Grossmith); *Week-End W.* (1939); *Uncle Fred in the Springtime* (1939); *W. on Golf* (1940); *Eggs, Beans and Crumpets* (1940); *Quick Service* (1940); *Money in the Bank* (1940); *Quick Service* (1940); *Money in the Bank* (1942); *Joy in the Morning* (1946); *Full Moon* (1947); *Spring Fever* (1948); *Uncle Dynamite* (1948); *The Best of W.* (1949); *The Mating Season* (1949); *Nothing Serious* (1950); *The Old Reliable* (1951); *Barmy in Wonderland* (1952); *Angel Cake* (1952); *Pigs Have Wings* (1952); *Mike at Wrykyn* (1953); *Mike and Psmith* (1953); *Ring for Jeeves* (1953); *Bring On the Girls* (1953); *Performing Flea* (1953); *Jeeves and the Feudal Spirit* (1954); *Carry On Jeeves* (1956); *French Leave* (1956); *America, I Like you* (1956); *Over Seventy* (1957); *Something Fishy* (1957); *The Butler Did It* (1957); *Selected Stories by P. G. W.* (1958); *Cocktail Time* (1958); *A Few Quick Ones* (1959); *The Most of P. G. W.* (1960); *How Right You Are, Jeeves* (1960); *The Ice in the Bedroom* (1961); *Service with a Smile* (1961); *Stiff Upper Lip, Jeeves* (1963); *Biffen's Millions* (1964); *The Brinksmanship of Galahad Threepwood* (1965); *Plum Pie* (1966); *The World of Jeeves* (1967); *The Purloined Paperweight* (1967); *Do Butler Burgle Banks?* (1968); *A Pelican at Blandigns* (1969); *No Nudes Is Good Nudes* (1970); *The Girl in Blue* (1970); *Much Obliged, Jeeves* (1971); *Jeeves and the Tie That Binds* (1971); *Pearls, Girls, and Monty Bodkin* (1972); *The Golf Omnibus* (1973); *Bachelors*

P. G. Wodehouse

Anonymous (1973); *The World of Psmith* (1974); *Aunts Aren't Gentlemen* (1974); *The World of Blandings* (1976); *The Uncollected W.* (1976); *Vintage W.* (1977); *Sunset at Hundings* (1977); *W. on Crime: A Dozen Tales of Fiendish Cunning* (1981); *Fore!: The Best of W. on Golf* (1983)

BIBLIOGRAPHY: Wind, H. W., *The World of P. G. W.* (1972); Cazalet-Keir, T., ed., *Homage to P. G. W.* (1973); Usborne, R., *W. at Work to the End* (1977); Green, G., *P. G. W.: A Literary Biography* (1981); Jasen, D. A., *P. G. W. A Portrait of a Master* (1981); Donaldson, F., *P. G. W.: A Biography* (1982); Shama, M. N., *W., the Fictionist* (1982)

—ROBERT L. CALDER

WOESTIJNE, Karel van de

Belgian poet, short-story writer, and essayist (writing in Flemish), b. 10 March 1878, Ghent; d. 23 Aug. 1929, Zwijnaarde

Son of a prosperous coppersmith, W. received a Jesuit secondary education and then studied for a time at the University of Ghent, also teaching Dutch in high schools. He lived in Brussels from 1906 until 1921, working as correspondent for the leading Dutch paper *De Nieuwe Rotterdamse Courant*, covering social and political events and the arts; at the same time he worked as a civil servant at the ministry of fine arts (1911–21) and also published poetry. In 1921 he was appointed to the chair of Netherlands Literature at the University of Ghent, a post he held until his death from tuberculosis.

W.'s first volumes of poetry were in the SYMBOLIST vein of Jules Laforgue (1860–1887) and RILKE. His work, however, is not derivative but is a complex synthesis of narcissism and fin-de-siècle melancholy. Yet his lyricism was also nourished by his love for his wife and son, and by a keen sense of nature. He was preoccupied with sensory perceptions and the transitory pleasure that lust produces. The poems have a somber melody and adhere to strict hexameters or alexandrines, including internal rhymes.

W. greatly admired the sober neo-Hellenism of the Greco-French poet Jean Moréas (1856–1910). *Interludiën* (2 vols., 1912–14; interludes) contains epic poems that tend to metamorphose mythological personages like Hercules, Helen, and Orpheus into heroes and heroines of his own equivocal generation, who are torn between heaven and earth. W.'s poetic trilogy, *De modderen man* (1920; the muddled man), *God an zee* (1926; God at the seaside), and *Het bergmeer* (1928; the mountain lake)—brought together under the title *Wiekslag om de kim* (1928; winging over the horizon)—contains extraordinary descriptions of the tension between surrender and refusal, enjoyment and sorrow. His transmutation of carnal rhythms to spiritual revelations and resigned asceticism recall Saint Augustine or Saint John of the Cross in quest of God. W.'s language in his late poetry is compressed and wry but retains the balance of abstraction and concrete imagery.

There is nothing in Flemish literature so sincere and durable, so wide-ranging in its register of poignant feelings and of problems of moral responsibility, as W.'s poetry. His leitmotifs of love and death are comparable to those of Wagnar and Baudelaire. Poetry was central to his life. His musical verse flows seemingly without effort, inspired by almost any feeling or thing. There is great variety of form. The meaning is sometimes obscure, as with Paul VALÉRY. W. would coin words rather than hamper his verse with an inadequate word.

Subtle turns of phrase or strange epithets make his prose writings hermetic at times. His fiction reflects the same preoccupations as in his poetry and is charged with a like anguish. His stories are marked by a richness and subtlety of tone new in Flemish writing. Many of his prose works, like *Janus met het dubbele voorhoofd* (1908; two-faced Janus), are legends, biblical stories, or lives of saints transformed by the author's imagination; they are quite self-revelatory. His best short stories reveal a profound familiarity with peasant life. The style is highly descriptive; while slow-moving at times, it serves to record a dense wealth of sensory perceptions.

W., who had a keen understanding of mathematical philosophers, from Pythagoras through Pascal to Alfred North Whitehead (1861–1947), was a gifted, introspective thinker as well as an observer of physical details. His critical essays on numerous topics are collected in *De schroeflijn* (2 vols., 1928; the spiral).

Thirsting for the absolute, W. brought a universal resonance to Flemish poetry, previously smugly provincial. He combined spontaneous confessions of inadequacy with analytical thought and refined craft. His poems convey the combat between angel and beast. W. still ranks among the foremost modern European poets, continuing to cast the spell of his tormented magic on new writers and readers.

FURTHER WORKS: *De vlaamse primitieven* (1903); *Het vaderhuis* (1903); *Laethemsche brieven over de lente* (1904); *Verzen* (1905); *De boomgaard der vogelen en der vruchten* (1905); *De vrouw van Kandaules* (1908); *De gulden schaduw* (1910); *Afwijkingen* (1910); *Kunst en geest in Vlaanderen* (1911); *Goddelijke verbeeldingen* (1918); *De bestendige aanwezigheid* (1918); *Zon in den rug* (1924); *Substrata* (1924); *Beginselen der chemie* (1925); *De heilige van het getal; De boer die sterft; Het zatte hart* (1926); *Christophorus* (1926); *De leemen torens* (2 vols., with Teirlinc k Herman); *De nieuwe Esopet* (1933); *Over schrijvers en boeken* (2 vols., 1933); *Nagelaten gedichten* (1942); *Verzameld werk* (8 vols., 1948–1950); *Verzamelde gedichten* (1953). FURTHER WORKS IN ENGLISH: *Lyra Belgica I* (1950)

BIBLIOGRAPHY: de Backer, F., *Contemporary Flemish Literature* (1934): 29–30; Greshoff, J., *Belgian Literature in the Dutch Language* (1945): 292–93; Mallinson, V., *Modern Belgian Literaure* (1966): 48–50; Meijer, R. P., *Literature of the Low Countries*, new ed. (1978): 270–74

—HENRI KOPS

WOHMANN, Gabriele

(née Guyot) West German short-story writer, novelist, radio and television dramatist, poet, and essayist, b. 21 May 1932, Darmstadt

Born at the dawn of the Third Reich, daughter of a Protestant clergyman, W. spent a protected childhood within a close-knit, anti-Nazi family. The resultant allegiance to the private sphere and a deep mistrust of political realities were formative in her development. After two years of study at the University of Frankfurt (literature, music, and philosophy) she was briefly employed as a language teacher, but since 1957 she has devoted herself exclusively to writing. She joined Group 47, the influential circle of West German writers, in 1960.

Following the publication of her first short story, "Ein unwiderstehlicher Mann" (1957; an irresistible man), W. rapidly became known for her terse prose sketches. These show the stylistic and structural influence of Conrad AIKEN, William FAULKNER, Ernest HEMINGWAY, James JOYCE, and William Carlos WILLIAMS. The stories written between 1956 and 1966, especially those in the collections *Trinken ist das Herrlichste* (1963; drinking is the greatest), *Ländliches Fest* (1968; garden party), and *Sonntag bei den Kreisands* (1970; Sunday with the Kreisands), established W.'s literary reputation and are still among her most widely read works. They focus on the sufferings of a vulnerable, often abnormal individual repressed by a callously superficial milieu. W.'s subtle and psychologically compelling stories defend the nonconformist outsider and at the same time drive home a biting attack on bourgeois hypocrisy, complacency, and greed.

W.'s insistent denunciation, prior to 1975, of genteel society earned her the epithet "evil eye," a term that refers both to her keen observation, which deliberately magnifies deficient behavior, and to an incisive and rancorous style. Equally important, however, is her empathy for children, adolescents, and social misfits. W.'s alliance with the underdogs counterbalances the "evil eye" focused on their oppressors. But after a major turning point in her writing around 1975, caused by the death of her father, she repudiated her previous antagonistic stance altogether.

W. has often stated her preference for the humdrum and seemingly trite details of everyday life as her major source of inspiration. She has refrained from comment on sociopolitical issues, asserting that personal relationships reflect the greater social framework and are essential as such. Thus, her works invariably portray the laborious search for meaningful human contact in a hostile world and are often cited as examples of "new sensibility," a recent trend in German literature stressing subjectivism.

W.'s reputation as virtuoso of the short story has overshadowed her extensive work in other genres. A first novel, *Jetzt und nie* (1958; now and never), was virtually ignored; a second one, *Abschied für länger* (1965; farewell for a long time), received moderate acclaim. Since 1970 she has written, in addition to dozens of poems, essays, and scripts for the media, several more novels. All reaffirm her interest in the minutiae of domestic strife and in identity crises. In contrast to W.'s earlier focus on the rejects of an affluent society, the more recent novels deal with well-fed, solipsistic intellectuals whose reflections on their own happiness tend to eclipse all social and political issues. Although *Schönes Gehege* (1975; pleasant enclosure), *Frühherbst in Badenweiler* (1978; early fall in Badenweiler), and *Das Glücksspiel* (1981; the gamble) raise questions of social conscience, the private emotional sphere is clearly predominant. W.'s works present contemporary ideologies, particularly feminism, as a threat to individual sensitivity. *Paulinchen war allein zu Haus* (1974; Paulinchen was at home alone) is a satirical attack on antiauthoritarian, pseudoprogressive childrearing. It is W.'s only novel to grant the heroine, an adopted child, a solution to her dilemma and the hope for a better future.

Throughout her career, W. has worked with the media as author of radio and television scripts, twice acting roles herself. In 1980 she adapted her radio play *Wanda Lords Gespenster* (1979; Wanda Lord's ghosts) as her first stage work. Her poems, appreciations of private daily life, have been published in four collections to date. The lengthy prose pieces in *Paarlauf* (1979; running in pairs) represent a hybrid of novel and short story.

W. was one of the first and most outspoken critics of the development of postwar German society at the beginning of the "economic miracle." The late 1950s and early 1960s in Germany were characterized by pressure to conform to society's norms as well as by the collective fervor of economic recovery. Within this context, W.'s poignant short stories aptly diagnose the inverse proportionality of increasing wealth and of the declining worth of the individual. Her more recent works continue to support the individual's claim to happiness and, equally, the urgent need for sensitivity in a materialistic and ideology-ridden society.

FURTHER WORKS: *Mit einem Messer* (1958); *Sieg über die Dämmerung* (1960); *Erzählungen* (1963); *Erzählunge* (1966); *Theater von innen: Protokoll einer Inszenierung* (1966); *Die Bütos* (1967); *In Darmstadt leben die Künste* (1967); *Ernste Absicht* (1970); *Treibjagd* (1970); *Der Fall Rufus* (1971); *Die Gäste* (1971); *Große Liebe* (1971); *Selbstverteidigung* (1971); *Alles für die Galerie* (1972); *Gegenangriff* (1972); *Die Witwen; oder, Eine vollkommene Lösung* (1972); *Habgier* (1973); *Entziehung* (1974); *So ist die Lage* (1974); *Dorothea Wörth* (1975); *Ein unwiderstehlicher Mann: Erzählungen* (1975); *Alles zu seiner Zeit* (1976); *Ausflug mit der Mutter* (1976); *Böse Streiche* (1977); *Das dicke Wilhelmchen* (1978); *Der Nachtigall fällt auch nichts Neues ein* (1978); *Grund zur Aufregung* (1978); *Heiratskandidaten* (1978); *Nachrichtensperre* (1978); *Streit* (1978); *Ausgewählte Erzählungen aus zwanzig Jahren*

(2 vols., 1979); *Der Nachtigall fällt auch nichts Neues ein: Vier Hörspiele* (1979); *Ach wie gut, daß niemand weiß* (1980); *Ich weiß das auch nicht besser* (1980); *Meine Lektüre: Aufsätze über Bücher* (1980); *Vor der Hochzeit* (1980); *Wir sind eine Familie* (1980); *Ein günstiger Tag* (1981); *Komm lieber Mai* (1981); *Nachkommenschaften* (1981); *Einsamkeit* (1982); *Der kürzeste Tag des Jahres* (1983)

BIBLIOGRAPHY: Hughes, K., "The Short Fiction of G. W.," *SSF*, 13 (1976): 61–70; Wellner, K., *Leidan an der Familie: Zur sozialpathologischen Rollenanalyse im Werk G.W.s* (1976); Scheuffelen, T., ed., *G. W. Materialienbuch* (1977); Holbeche, Y., "The Early Novels of G. W.," *AUMLA*, 52 (1979): 241–52; Ferchl, I., *Die Rolle des Alltäglichen in der Kurzprosa von G. W.* (1980); Knapp, G., and M. Knapp, *G. W.* (1981); Häntzschel, G., *G. W.* (1982)

—MONA KNAPP

WOLF, Christa

German novelist and short-story writer, b. 18 March 1929, Landsberg

W. studied Germanic philology in Leipzig and Jena. In 1953 she began various activities that exposed her to the mainstream of East German literature: by 1959 she had worked as a technical assistant for the East German Writers' Union and as an editor for *Neue Deutsche Literatur* and an East Berlin publishing house. She then moved to Halle, where she was employed as an editor for the Mitteldeutscher Verlag until 1962. After leaving Halle, she lived in Kleinmachow near Berlin and devoted her time to her writing. As her works became more widely known, she spent time as a visiting lecturer and scholar at universities in Frankfurt am Main, Zurich, and the U.S. She is a member of several literary and cultural organizations and has received numerous awards for her creative writing, among them the Georg Büchner Prize (1980), the Schiller Prize (1983), the Austrian National Prize for European Literature (1985), the Premio Mondello (1990), and the Rahel Varnhagen von Ense Medal (1994, with Gerhard Wolf).

W. belongs to the generation of East German writers that first began to publish after the initial turbulent years of postwar reconstruction. As a group, these authors accepted the challenge to document in literature the growth, development, and problems of the infant German Democratic Republic. Because of this focus, World War II itself is of little concern in W.'s early works. Hers is a personal prose, imbued with a subjectivity reflecting both the autobiographical bent of her writing and her critical examination of specific kinds of experience. By contrasting action with reflection, she not only gives her own style a greater degree of sophistication but also more easily meets the political demand for self-analysis and self-criticism. At the same time, her writings are not without indictment of her own society and have therefore caused significant controversy.

Moskauer Novelle (1961; Moscow novella), W.'s first attempt at narrative fiction, is weak and unconvincing. It is not so much the style that causes the work to fail as its ambition. W. endeavors to turn a relatively uncomplicated love story into an allegory of national guilt in the wartime relations between Germany and Russia. The attempted treatment of great social problems and happenings, in all their complexity and paradox, simply does not fit within the framework of the novella. For that reason alone it lacks the impact of her more mature works.

In 1963 Christa W. received the Heinrich Mann Prize for her first novel, *Der geteilte Himmel* (1963; *Divided Heaven*, 1976). This work is particularly significant as one of the few noteworthy pieces of literature generated by the Bitterfeld Movement. (This movement, ultimately unsuccessful and later abandoned, was a formal program designed to make literature more representative of life in the workers' state: workers were urged to write, while writers were challenged to participate in industry.) In response to the Bitterfeld demand, W. sought out a workers' brigade in a Halle railroad-car factory. Her experiences there provided both material and a strong element of realism for the novel. The narrative strength of *Der geteilte Himmel* derives in part from the successful balance W. created between action and reflection. As the protagonist comes to grips with her own life, she is projected against the more general happenings of the times. The choices with which she is confronted are those that must be faced by Western civilization as a whole. Her actions reveal the complexity of forces that govern decision making. Because her course is the product of human rather than dogmatic considerations, her search for personal identity is relevant outside her own geographical and temporal milieu. For that reason, *Der geteilte Himmel* is one of the most important literary documents written in postwar East Germany.

Nachdenken über Christa T. (1969; *The Quest for Christa T.*, 1970) is a more complex if less satisfying work than *Der geteilte Himmel*. Plot and action are subordinated entirely to the analytical process, a technique that causes a recurring loss of momentum. Although the narration is at times traditional, the protagonist is also presented through letters, other personal writings, and the narrator's memories and reflections. The method employed here is similar to that of Uwe JOHNSON in his *Mutmaßungen über Jakob*. The novel is concerned not so much with the story of Christa T. as with the revelation of her nature as a representative of her generation. She is a child of the German Democratic Republic and a product of its problems and its inheritance from the past. Through the narrator's analysis, Christa T. speaks for herself about her own life and ours.

W.'s writings of the 1970s reveal a broadening of focus and an intensification of her attempt to master through experimentation the problems of her times and those of literary expression. The three "improbable" stories in the collection *Unter den Linden* (1974; the street in Berlin) achieve their effect through elements foreign to dogmatic SOCIALIST REALISM: the fantastic, the grotesque, the absurd. The novel *Kindheitsmuster* (1976; *A Model Childhood*, 1980) is a grand experiment involving new and peculiar variations of form, language, and style. An ambitiously complex work, *Kindheitsmuster* is a combination of fiction, reflected autobiography, and theoretical essay. It examines possibilities and conditions of meaningful individual life in modern society. Interwoven with elements of the protagonist's childhood are potent reflections concerning the author-narrator's grapplings with reality on two other levels: impressions of a visit to a Polish town and the three-year process of creating the novel itself. The result is an effective summary of W.'s thought and writings.

In various ways, W.'s writings of the 1980s reflect a more intimate grappling with the problems of her own society as well as those of the world at large. Her penetrating exploration of questions surrounding the Soviet nuclear disaster at Chernobyl in *Störfall. Nachrichten eines Tages* (1987; *Accident: A Day's News*, 1989) and the poignant reflections about a final, happy, harmonious

period before the collapse of her political illusions, found in the rurally idyllic portrayal of the life enjoyed by a group of East German artists and intellectuals in *Sommerstück* (1989; Summer Piece), demonstrate her deep sensitivity to the immediate real-world issues of her time.

The most significant and far-reaching development in her writing in recent years, beginning with the novel *Kassandra* (1983; *Cassandra*, 1984), and even more forcibly present in *Medea. Stimmen* (1996; *Medea*, 1998), is the embedding of personal experience in portrayals of female figures selected from classical Greek literature, whom she employs as foils for the effective examination of a variety of problems relating to the role and situation of women in contemporary society.

By her own admission, W. is a literary disciple of Anna SEGHERS. Although her work has not yet achieved the lasting significance of Segher's writings, it has made her one of the most important and interesting writers to emerge from East Germany.

FURTHER WORKS: *Lesen und Schreiben: Aufsätze und Betrachtungen* (1972; *The Reader and the Writer*, 1977); *Till Eulenspiegel* (1973, with Gerhard Wolf); *Fortgesetzter Versuch* (1979); *Kein Ort. Nirgends* (1979; *No Place on Earth*, 1982); *Gesammelte Erzählunge* (1980); *Lesen und Schreiben: Neue Sammlung* (1980); *Geschlechtertausch* (1980, with Sarah Kirsch and Irmtraud Morgner); *Neue Lebensansichten eines Katers* (1981); *Neue Lebensansichten eines Katers* (1981); *Historischer Verein für Hessen 1934-1983* (1983); *Die Dimension des Autors* (2 vols., 1987; *The Fourth Dimension: Interviews with C. W.*, 1983); *Ansprachen* (1988); *Im Dialog* (1990); *Was bleibt* (1990; *What Remains*, 1993); *Reden im Herbst* (1990); *Auf dem Weg nach Tabou* (1994; *Parting from Phantoms*, 1997); *Das erzählerische Werk* (6 vols., 1994); *Unsere Freunde die Maler* (1995, with Gerhard Wolf); *Was nicht in den Tagebüchern steht* (1995, with Franz Fühlmann); *Im Stein* (1998); *Mitleidend bleibt das ewige Herz noch fest* (1998). FURTHER WORKS IN ENGLISH: *What Remains and Other Stories* (1993); *The Author's Dimension* (1993)

BIBLIOGRAPHY: Huebener, T., *The Literature of East Germany* (1970): 112–15; Pawel, E., on *The Quest for Christa T.*, *NYTBR* (31 Jan. 1971): 7; Willet, J., "The Quest for East Germany," *NYRB* (2 Sept. 1971): 21–23; Stephan, A., *C. W.* (1976); Kane, B. M., "In Search of the Past: C. W.'s *Kindheitsmuster*," ML, 59 (1978): 19–23; Frieden, S., "'In eigener Sache': C. W.'s *Kindheitsmuster*," GQ, 54 (1981): 473–87; McPherson, K., "In Search of the New Prose: C. W.'s Reflections on Writing and the Writer in the 1960s and 1970s," *NGS*, 9, 1 (1981): 1–13; Fries, M. S., ed., *Responses to C. W.* (1989); Krogman, W., *C. W.* (1989); Wallace, I., ed., *C. W. in Perspective* (1994); Resch, M., *Understanding C. W.* (1997); Kuhn, A. K., *C. W.'s Utopian Vision* (1998)

—LOWELL A. BANGERTER

WOLF, Friedrich

German dramatist and novelist, b. 23 Dec. 1888, Neuwied; d. 5 Oct. 1953, Lehnitz

Of liberal middle-class Jewish origin, W. briefly studied art before turning to medicine. His World War I experiences—the young doctor served on both western and eastern fronts—turned W. into a convinced pacifist. He became a member of the Independent Socialist Party in 1918 and was elected to the Dresden Workers' and Soldiers' Council. In 1920 he accepted a position as municipal doctor in Remscheid, where he was actively involved in the suppression of the Kapp Putsch, an attempted military coup by reactionary elements of the officers' corps. For a short time he worked as a doctor and peat cutter in a colony of disabled veterans near Worpswede and then practiced medicine from 1921 to 1933. He joined the Communist Party in 1928 and became a member of the League of Proletarian Revolutionary Writers. In 1933 he had to flee from Germany; he went to Russia, from where he traveled to the U.S., Scandinavia, and France. When World War II broke out, he was interned in France until 1941, when the Russians effected his release. In the former U.S.S.R. he served as a propagandist and lecturer in the camps for German prisoners of war. W. returned to what is now East Germany in 1945 and became very active in cultural politics. From 1949 to 1951 he served as the first ambassador to Poland from the newly founded German Democratic Republic.

Although he wrote in most modern literary genres, including radio plays and film scripts, W. is best known as a playwright who made his impact with topical dramas and problem plays. His fiction is of somewhat uneven literary quality, the novel *Zwei an der Grenze* (1938; two at the border) representing his best achievement.

W.'s beginnings clearly class him, both thematically and stylistically, with EXPRESSIONISM. The focus of his early plays is quite unmistakably on man's spiritual renewal. A good example is *Das bist du* (1919; that is you). Even when a play has all the makings of a social drama, as with *Mohammed* (written 1917–18, pub. 1922; Mohammed) and *Tamar* (1922; Tamar) the protagonist decides against political activism, choosing instead the subjective solution of personal regeneration.

With *Der arme Konrad* (1924; poor Konrad), W. found the material and style appropriate to him: a well-defined setting, concrete action, lifelike individualized characters reflecting the social conditions and ideological forces that helped shape them. This social drama about the abortive German Peasant revolt of 1514 examines the factors that turned it into a tragic failure. At the same time, it provides an oblique commentary, in historical guise, on the frustrated revolutionary aspirations of 1918.

With *Cyankali* (1929; cyanide), W. became well known outside Germany. Aiming to provoke and to establish a dialogue between stage and audience, he struck a responsive chord with the tragedy of a young girl who, because she cannot afford the illegal but nevertheless available services of professionals, dies from a botched abortion. The drama is a stinging attack on both the socioeconomic injustices of the Weimar Republic and the moral corruption hidden under a mask of social respectability. W.'s revolutionary social criticism eschews the ardent proclamations and passionate slogans of the run-of-the-mill agit-prop plays; rather, it is implicit in the realistically presented slice of life depicting characters of flesh and blood caught in human conflicts resulting from economic hardships and social inequities.

The political failure of many liberal democrats, their misjudgment of the true nature of Nazism, and their touching faith in legality provide the backdrop for *Professor Mamlock* (1934; *Professor Mamlock*, 1935), a drama that achieved worldwide fame, especially through its Russian film version (1938). The stirring tragedy of a Jewish doctor, whose apolitical humanism and self-deluding detachment from public affairs bring about his own destruction by the forces whose ascendancy he tolerated, is a remarkable example of political dramatic art.

For all his commitment, W. in *Beaumarchais; oder. Die Geburt des "Figaro"* (1946; Beaumarchais; or the birth of *Figaro*) shows that he was well aware of the dilemma confronting the artist who finds himself caught between the claims of art and politics. He himself was not always able to reconcile the two, although in his best works the validity of his ethical concern and his humanistic outlook transcend the narrow confines of the immediate social context and the political ideology of a purely militant theater.

FURTHER WORKS: *Der Löwe Gottes* (1921); *Der Unbedingte* (1921); *Die schwarze Sonne* (1921); *Fahrt* (1922); *Elemente* (1922); *Die Schrankkomödie* (written 1922, perf. 1976); *Der Sprung durch den Tod* (1925); *Das Heldenepos des Alten Bundes* (1925); *Kreatur* (1925); *Der Mann im Dunkel* (1927); *Koritke* (1927); *Kolonne Hund* (1927); *Kunst its Waffe* (1928); *Kampf im Kohlenpott* (1928); *SOS. . . RAO. . . RAO. . . Foyn—"Krassin" rettet "Italia"* (1929); *Die Matrosen von Cattaro* (1930; *Sailors of Cattaro*, 1935); *John D. erobert die Welt* (1930); *Tai Yang erwacht* (1931); *Die Jungens von Mons* (1931); *Von New York bis Shanghai* (1932); *Wie stehn die Fronten* (1932); *Bauer Baetz* (1932); *Florids dorf* (1936; *Flordisdorf: The Vienna Workers in Revolt*, 1935); *Die Nacht vor Bèthinville* (1936); *Das trojanische Pferd* (1937); *Peter kehrt heim* (1937); *Das Schiff auf der Donau* (written in 1938, perf. 1955); *Gefährlicher Beifall* (1941); *KZ Vernet* (1941); *Sieben Kämpfer vor Moskau* (1942); *Der Russenpelz* (1942); *Der Kirschbaum* (1942); *Heimkehr der Söhne* (1944); *Doktor Wanner* (1944); *Was der Mensch säet . . .* (1945); *Märchen für große und kleine Kinder* (1946); *Patrioten* (1946); *Die letzte Probe* (1946); *Dramen* (2 vols., 1946); *Die Nachtschwalbe* (1947); *Zeitprobleme des deutschen Theaters* (1947); *Dramen* (5 vols., 1947–1955); *Wie Tiere des Waldes* (1948); *Bitte der Nächste: Dr. Isegrimms Rezeptfolgen* (1948); *Goethe* (1949); *Bürgermeister Anna* (1950); *Lilo Herrmann: Ein biographisches Poem* (1951); *Die Unverlorenen* (1951); *So fing es an* (1951); *Ausgewählte Werke in Einzelausgaben* (14 vols., 1951–1960); *Tiergeschichten für große und kleine Kinder* (1952); *Menetekel; oder. Die fliegenden Untertassen* (1952); *Erzählungen, Kurzgeschichten, Sketche* (1952); *Maxim Gorki* (1953); *Thomas Münzer: Der Mann mit der Regenbogenfahne* (1953); *Ausgewählte Gedichte* (1954); *Fabeln* (1957); *Die lebendige Mauer* (1957); *Aufsaätze über Theater* (1957); *Filmerzählungen* (1958); *Briefe* (1958); *Gesammelte Werke* (16 vols., 1960–1967); *F. W.: Ein Lesebuch für unsere Zeit* (1961); *F. W. und Wsewolod Wischnewskij: Eine Auswahl aus ihrem Briefwechsel* (1965); *Der verschenkte Leutnant* (1967); *Briefwechsel* (1968); *Briefe* (1969); *W. in 2 Bänden* (1973)

BIBLIOGRAPHY: Thomas, R. H., "F. W.: His Development as Dramatist," *GL&L*, 5 (1951): 30–41; Pollatscheck, W., *Das Bühnenwerk F. W.s* (1958); Pollatscheck, W., *F. W.: Eine Biographie* (1963); Zalubska, C., *Der literaturtheoretische Werdegang F. W.s im Spiegel seiner Dichtung* (1968); Grimm, R., "The Play within a Play in Revolutionary Theatre," *Mosaic*, 9 (1975): 41–52; Winkler, M., "F. W.'s *Beaumarchais*—A Propaganda Play Nonetheless?," in Elfe, W., et al., eds., *Deutsches Exildrama und Exiltheater* (1977): 133–38; Jehser, W., *F. W.: Leben und Werk* (1977); Heizer, D. K., *Jewish-German Identity in the Orientalist Literature of Else Lasker-Schüler, F. W., and Franz Werfel* (1996)

—FRIEDHELM RICKERT

Thomas Wolfe

WOLFE, Thomas

American novelist, b. 3 Oct. 1900, Asheville, N.C.; d. 15 Sept. 1938, Baltimore, Md.

Youngest of eight children of a stonecutter and a boardinghouse keeper, W. grew up in the small mountain city of Asheville. After graduating from private school there, he attended the University of North Carolina (1916–20), where he became interested in writing folk plays for Professor F. H. Koch's newly formed Carolina Playmakers. At Harvard (1920–23) W. attended the famous playwriting course of George Pierce Baker while pursuing an M.A. in English. In 1924, after several of his plays were rejected by professional producers, he accepted a position teaching freshman composition at New York University and continued to do so intermittently until 1930. On board ship in 1925 returning from the first of seven trips to Europe, W. met the prominent stage and costume designer Aline Bernstein, a married woman eighteen years his senior. Thereafter, during a love affair often tempestuous, she supported W. when he took leaves of absence from the university to work on a novel. After the publication of *Look Homeward, Angel* (1929) and his being awarded a Guggenheim Fellowship, W. terminated the affair and settled in Brooklyn. For several years he struggled to discover a formula for his second book, meeting almost daily with his editor, Maxwell Perkins, of Charles Scribner's Sons, to shape the materials he had on hand. Although *Of Time and the River* (1935) was an immediate success,

W. decided to displace his youthful romanticism with a mature realism. He left Scribner for Harper & Brothers, whose editor Edward Aswell was primarily responsible for the pattern of the two posthumously published novels. W. died at Johns Hopkins Hospital following surgery for a brain infection.

W.'s separate novels and short stories are mere parts of a single book narrating the continuing experiences of their semiautobiographical hero. W. was a large man, and his novels are big books, often peopled with outsized characters similar to himself. Throughout his fiction, the hero is a wanderer, an exile, hungry for sensations and knowledge. "I am at home only when I am homeless," W. wrote in 1926; two years later he wrote, "Faust's problem touches me more than Hamlet's—his problem is mine. . . He wants to know everything, to be a God—and he is caught in the terrible net of human incapacity." The wanderings of W.'s hero become a symbolic search for the romantic ideal ("the apple tree, the singing, and the gold"), for the father ("wisdom . . . belief . . . power"), and for the "unfound door" beyond which lie perfection and art. He was "lost in America"; his search prompted him to attempt identifying himself in terms of his huge, chaotic, beloved country. This he could do only by defining America, by understanding the American experience. In trying to do so, W. mirrored Walt Whitman's descriptions and catalogues, but W.'s novels are not so much Whitman's poetic glorification of America as a step–by–step quest to find America in himself. This examination of the greatness of America gives W.'s fiction an epic quality. Although he deplored the waste, he believed in the promise of the fabled American Dream of abundance, liberty, and opportunity.

The pursuit of these themes did not allow for traditional well–made novels. Not only was the nature of the search episodic, but W.'s custom was to write clearly defined segments of narrative, rarely in chronological order, trusting they would later fit somehow into the whole. With noticeable echoes of his favorites—the Preacher of Ecclesiastes, Coleridge, Wordsworth, Whitman, and James JOYCE—the novels developed a sort of sprawl like those of Herman Melville that many critics found as unsatisfactory as W.'s apparent dependence on autobiography.

W. permitted himself a number of styles and moved easily from the most sensuously lyric to the most starkly realistic. He was an expert at caricature, parody, and satire. He had an ear for dialect, a gift for mimicry. He could present an incident with the simplest reporting or with the extravagance of Southern rhetoric.

Most of these styles are apparent in *Look Homeward, Angel*, which takes Eugene Gant, a persona for W. himself, from his birth in Altamont (Asheville) through his college years at Pulpit Hill (Chapel Hill). Subtitled "A Story of the Buried Life," the novel operates on two levels: beneath the surface events lies Eugene's secret life whereby he attempts to escape his eccentric family, the restrictions of hometown and region, and the "prison" of his loneliness. In the sequel, *Of Time and the River*, Eugene studies at Harvard, then returns to the South briefly when his father dies. He begins teaching at a university in New York City and takes a lengthy trip to Europe. Termed variously a "novel on wheels" or a "fictional thesaurus" of units in prose and verse, the book continues Eugene's Faustian search and is supplied with a loose shape by evoking such figures from Greek mythology as Orestes, Telemachus, and Jason. Representative of America's strength and creativity is Eugene's father W. O. Gant (W. O. Wolfe), while his dilettante friend Francis Starwick (Kenneth Raisbeck) exemplifies the destructive antithesis of creativity.

In *The Web and the Rock* (1939), prefaced by the novelist's declared intention to observe a rigid objectivity to replace his former lyrical subjectivity, the hero George Webber, still similar to Eugene Gant, grows up in the Southern mountain town of Libya Hill (Asheville), attends a small college, moves to New York to be a writer, and has a stormy love affair with Esther Jack (Aline Bernstein), the talented middle–aged Jewish wife of a Wall Street broker. Emphasized in the latter portion of the novel are a number of contrasts: town/city, Gentile/Jew, youth/maturity, innocence/sophistication. George's story is continued in *You Can't Go Home Again* (1940). Depressed by the boosterism in his hometown, by the display of his mistress's wealth, and by his hometown's repudiation of his first novel, well received elsewhere, George gives up his job at the School of Utility Cultures (New York University) and retreats to Brooklyn. On trips to Europe he is further disillusioned by the famous but decadent Lloyd McHarg (Sinclair LEWIS) and the growing Nazi threat. In the aftermath of each of these experiences, George is aware he can never "go home again" to blind family allegiance, to privilege and love, to success, to fame, and to a fatalistic attitude toward life. He breaks with his loyal editor Foxhall Edwards (Maxwell Perkins), and the novel ends with the transcendent statement: "I believe that we are lost here in America, but I believe we shall be found. . . I think the true discovery of America is before us."

Among additional symbols, often shifting in their intent but always heightening the significance of Eugene–George's experiences, are the angel and the ghost (the source and permanence of art), the stone and leaf (the unchanging and the transient), the train (the voyage out to new lands and new knowledge), the river (the ceaseless flow of time), and the web and the rock (entaglements and certainties).

The total of W.'s fiction is constant progression from youthful rebellion to responsibility, from romanticism to realism, from indecision to resoluteness, from rebellion to maturity, and from self to all mankind.

FURTHER WORKS: *From Death to Morning* (1935); *The Story of a Novel* (1936); *The Face of a Nation* (1939); *The Hills Beyond* (1941); *T. W.'s Letters to His Mother* (1943); *A Stone, a Leaf, a Door* (1946); *The Portable T. W.* (1946); *Mannerhouse* (1948); *A Western Journal* (1951); *The Letters of T. W.* (1956); *The Short Novels of T. W.* (1961); *The T. W. Reader* (1962); *T. W.'s Purdue Speech* (1964); *The Letters of T. W. to His Mother* (1968); *The Notebooks of T. W.* (1970); *The Mountains* (1970); *Welcome to Our City: A Play in Ten Scenes* (1983); *The Autobiography of an American Novelist* (1983); *My Other Loneliness: Letters of T. W. to Aline Bernstein* (1983); *Beyond Love and Loyalty: The Letters of T. W. and Elizabeth Nowell* (1983)

BIBLIOGRAPHY: Rubin, L. D., Jr., *T. W.: The Weather of His Youth* (1955); Watkins, F. C., *T. W.'s Characters* (1957); Nowell, E., *T. W.* (1960); Kennedy, R. S., *The Window of Memory: The Literary Career of T. W.* (1962); special W. issue, *MFS*, 11, 3 (1965); Turnbull, A., *T. W.* (1967); Reeves, P., ed., *T. W.: The Critical Reception* (1974); Holman, C. H., *The Loneliness at the Core: Studies in T. W.* (1975); Phillipson, J. S., *T. W.: A Reference Guide* (1977); Walser, R., *T. W. Undergraduate* (1977)

—RICHARD WALSER

Tom Wolfe

WOLFE, Tom

(born Thomas Kennerly Wolfe, Jr.) American essayist, journalist, and novelist, b. 2 Mar. 1930, Richmond, Va.

W. is one the most original and influential American prose writers of the 20th c. He played a major role in helping create a more experimental style of nonfiction writing that came to be widely called "the New Journalism." In 1957, W. earned a doctorate in American studies from Yale. After working as a reporter and feature writer for the *Washington Post* and the *New York Herald Tribune*, he gained national attention in 1963 with a lengthy feature story on customized cars published in *Esquire* magazine.

In this piece, "There Goes (Varoom! Varoom!) The Kandy-Kolored Tangerine-Flake Streamline Baby," W. employs the slangy, hyperbolic, and highly descriptive style that he would continue to refine in the years to come. In two early collections of essays. *The Kandy-Kolored Tangerine-Flake Streamline Baby* (1965) and *The Pump House Gang* (1968), W. also first showed his interest in examining closely a variety of subcultural groups—among them surfers, gamblers, and stock-car drivers—who were then still largely ignored by mainstream journalism.

W.'s *The Electric Kool-Aid Acid Test* (1968) focuses on novelist Ken KESEY and his band of "Merry Pranksters" as they travel the country shooting a movie, ingesting hallucinogens, and, eventually, finding themselves in conflict with the law. This book, a major best-seller, demonstrates not only W.'s capacity for exhaustive research, but his ability to use artfully the novelist's techniques in the writing of nonfictional prose. Here, for example, W. seeks to narrow the mental and verbal distance between himself and the Pranksters, in part by carefully recording—and often imitating—the distinctive flair and rhythm of their highly colloquial speech. Morever, he shifts points of view, and builds drama through the careful pacing of precisely detailed scenes. W.'s especially creative use of such strategies encouraged their wide adoption; in fact, by the mid-1970s, a more subdued form of this "New Journalism" could be found in a wide variety of books, newspapers, and magazines.

Although some critics complained that W. looked too sympathetically at the drug-promoting Pranksters, a more careful reading of the book show's that his interest in the group and their various mystical and social pursuits was less personal than intellectual, and that his own cultural biases were fairly conservative—a fact that became clearer during the 1970s, a period W. indelibly dubbed "the Me Decade."

Indeed, in *Radical Chic & Mau-Mauing the Flak Catchers* (1970), his most acid book, W. savages what he believed to be a growing trend among affluent white liberals (such as the composer Leonard Bernstein) to court and support far-left groups, many of whom were calling for the revolutionary transformation of American society, and thus, ironically, of the very system that made both affluence and liberalism possible.

In another controversial work, *The Painted Word* (1975), W. remained on the attack, this time seeking to debunk many of the more celebraned practitioners and promoters of modern art. Essentially, W. argues that modern art, particularly in America, has been characterized chiefly not by an explosion of unique and innovative talent, but by a widespread and rather slavish adherence to fashionable aesthetic theories. Although many critics found *The Painted Word* to be a witty and valuable exposé of hype and pretentiousness in the arts, others found it inaccurate and simplistic, revealing primarily the large gaps in W.'s knowledge of the painters and theoreticians he was attempting to analyze.

In *The Right Stuff* (1979), W. strikes a more celebratory tone as he describes the lives of the elite group of astronauts involved in the American space program during its earliest—and most dangerous—phase. There would seem to be little in common between a clean-cut corps of fighter pilots and the many eccentrics, outsiders, and outlaws who had previously appeared in W.'s writing. But the themes and concerns of *The Right Stuff* can also be found in such works as *The Electric Kool-Aid Acid Test*. Once again, W. is interested in examining the rhetoric—and thus the belief system—of a group who not only live well outside the mainstream of American society, but who continually seek escape from the predictability of daily life.

W.'s first novel, *The Bonfire of the Vanities* (1987), was widely hailed as one of the decade's most significant fictions. In this large, lively bestseller, W.'s principal target is the American legal system, but he also looks satirically at the world of journalism, and at the spirit of greed and social climbing that often seemed to prevail in the 1980s. Although the book contains no sympathetic characters, many critics praised its bold sweep and linguistic vitality. In various essays and interviews, W. indicated that he wrote the novel to illustrate the qualities of fiction writing he most admires and associates with a tradition of "realism," which includes Dickens, Balzac, and Zola. Moreover, W. has condemned the trend toward fantasy, self-obsession, and "minimalism" that he finds dominant in much recent American fiction.

These observations provoked an often heated discussion on the aims of fiction that raged for months in various journals and magazines. W.'s own writings—as well as his famously dapper, white-suited persona—came under severe attack. Once again, W. was accused of being old-fashioned and elitist, and of simplifying complex aesthetic and cultural issues.

But even many of the harshest of these critics have been forced to admit that, over the years, W. has expressed his beliefs with a force and verve that few of his literary contemporaries have been able to match. Indeed, in many respects, W. can be likened to H. L. MENCKEN, who played a similarly provocative role in the 1920s and 1930s. Like Mencken, W. is an erudite, articulate, and wide-ranging author whose distinctive and seriously playful style will ensure that many of his works are likely to endure for years to come.

FURTHER WORKS: *Mauve Gloves & Madmen, Clutter & Vine, and Other Short Stories* (1976); *In Our Time* (1980); *From Bauhaus to Our House* (1981); *The Purple Decades: A Reader* (1982); *A Man in Full* (1998)

BIBLIOGRAPHY: Hersey, J., "The Legend on the License," *YR*, 75, 2 (Winter 1986): 289–314; Anderson, C., *Style As Argument: Contemporary American Nonfiction* (1987): 8–47; Epstein, J., "T. W.'s Vanities," *NewC*, 6, 6 (Feb. 1988): 5–16; Crawford, S., "T. W.: Outlaw Gentleman," *Journal of American Culture*, 13, 2 (1990): 39–50; Grunwald, L., "T. W. Aloft in the Statussphere," *Esquire* (Oct. 1990): 146–60

—BRIAN MURRAY

WOLFF, Egon

Chilean dramatist, b. 13 Apr. 1926, Santiago

W. was born of German immigrant parents and grew up in an atmosphere of solid social values and a strong work ethic. He graduated from the Catholic University in Santiago with a degree in chemical engineering. Although he studied science and worked in the development of chemicals, he was always interested in literature, the classics, and the humanities in general.

W. began writing his plays at a time when there was a great deal of theatrical creativity in his country, especially at the University of Chile and the Catholic University in Santiago. Almost every play he wrote earned him a first prize in one competition or another. While he is perhaps not the most radically innovative of recent Latin American playwrights, he is one of the most powerful and most widely performed. He himself has been invited to premieres of his plays throughout the world. A recurring theme in his work concerns the threat of some kind of Other, a chaotic, anarchic force from the "outside" on a comfortable but fragile order built on illusion.

W.'s first plays are in the tradition of the social realism begun in Latin America in the first decade of the 20th c. by Florencio SÁNCHEZ. *Mansión de lechuzas* (1956; mansion of owls), depicts the struggle of two sons to resist their fearful mother's efforts to protect them from the dangers of the outside world. *Discípulos del miedo* (1957; disciples of fear) reverses this image of the mother figure; the character Matilde is almost pathologically concerned with her quest for psychological security through the acquisition of material things and her dreamed-of entry into the entrepreneurial class. A third play, *Niñamadre* (1962; childmother), portrays a variety of characters from the lower class. It deals primarily, however, with a good-hearted, sentimental prostitute who wants to have her baby in spite of the psychological insecurity her desire precipitates in her macho lover. These early plays are strongly mimetic, involve the audience emotionally with the characters and the conflicts, and are well constructed with rising tension in each of the three acts and an unambiguously resolved conflict with a clear social message. Objects and lighting are used in effectively, albeit rather conventionally, symbolic ways.

Los invasores (1963; the invaders) marks a change in W.'s dramatic method if not in his worldview. While it may not be his best work, it remains his most popular and most critically discussed. The social message remains clear—the "secure" world of the middle class is falsely constructed on the sands of their indifference to the plight of the poor. It is the latter, under the leadership of the enigmatic character China who invade, insidiously take over, and eventually destroy the home of the industrialist Lucas Meyer. The play is charged with ambiguities that allude to terrifying psychological and metaphysical insecurities beyond the mere social order. China is a fascinatingly ambivalent character—reassuring, threatening, constructive, sinister, priestly, revolutionary—Christ, Lucifer, Lenin, Che Guevara, and Robespierre all rolled into one. The play's resolution, too, is openended. Although it has all been Lucas's dream, it is a dream that threatens to repeat itself in reality. Numerous defamiliarization devices are used in the play to create an unreal atmosphere. The result is an artistic blending of social realism, surrealism, and the THEATER OF THE ABSURD.

Most experts would agree that *Flores de papel* (1970; *Paper Flowers*, 1971), is probably W.'s masterpiece. It is similar in theme to *Los invasores* but more intense in that it is restricted to two characters and has a more claustrophobic atmosphere with its strict limitation of scene. Here the elegant, middle-class apartment of Eva, a refined middle-aged woman who lives alone, is gradually destroyed by the derelict known as The Hake, who intrudes into her world, unobtrusively at first, by offering to carry home her groceries. The play goes beyond *Los invasores* also in the devastating nature of the destruction that takes place, for here the very structure of Eva's psyche is undermined as she is utterly stripped by The Hake of her individuality, her femininity, and her identity. This play has had a wide variety of interpretations—social, psychological, metaphysical, even aesthetic—but continues to resist closure. In the almost allegorical reductionism of the portrayal of character and scene, in the emotional detachment of the dialogue, in its dependence on language for dramatic effect, and in the strange unreality of the atmosphere, one is reminded of the plays of Harold PINTER.

W. is not only a craftsman of the first order. He is a dramatist of profound vision as well. Although he deals locally with Chilean social reality, he has at the same time great universal appeal. He fascinates because he gives dramatic form to our most fundamental human fears and forces us to face the fragility of the structures on which we build our society, our psyches, and our views of reality. For these reasons he is one of the outstanding dramatists of Latin America today.

FURTHER WORKS: *Parejas de trapo* (1959); *El signo de Caín* (1969); *Kindergarten* (1977); *Espejismos* (1978); *José* (1980); *Alamos en la azotea* (1981); *La balsa de la Medusa* (1984); *Parejas de trapo* (1988); *Invitación* (1995); *Cicatrices* (1995)

BIBLIOGRAPHY: Peden, M. S., "Three Plays of E. G., *LATR*, 3 (1969): 29–35; Lyday, L. F., "E. W.'s *Los invasores*: A Play within a Dream," *LATR*, 6, 1 (1972): 19–26; Peden, M. S., "The Theater of E. W.," in Woodyard, L. F., ed., *Dramatists in Revolt* (1976): 190–201; Peden, M. S., "*Kindergarten*: A New Play by E. W.," *LATR*, 10 (Spring 1977): 5–10; Chrzanowski, J., "Theme, Characterization, and Structure in *Los invasores*," *LATR*, 11, 2 (Spring 1978): 5–10; López, D., "Ambiguity in *Flores de pape*," *LATR*, 12 (1978): 43–50; Lyday, L. F., "Whence W.'s Canary: A Conjecture on Commonality," *LATR*, 16, 2 (Spring 1983): 23–29; Taylor, D., "Art and Antiart in E. W.'s *Flores de papel*," *LATR*, 18, 1 (Fall 1984): 65–68; Elizondo, P. B., *La dramaturgia de E. W.* (1985)

—ROBERT SCOTT

WOLFF, Tobias

American memoirist and short-story writer, b. 19 June 1956, Birmingham, Alabama

W. dropped out of high school and eventually enlisted in the military where he became a member of the U.S. Army Special Forces in Vietnam. Following his military service, he enrolled at Oxford University; he earned a B.A. in 1972 and an M.A. in 1975. He also holds a M.A. from Stanford University. W. has held teaching positions at Stanford, Goddard College, Arizona State University, Temple University, and Syracuse University. He currently teaches English and creative writing at Stanford University.

In his critically acclaimed memoirs, *This Boy's Life: A Memoir* (1989) and *In Pharaoh's Army: Memories of a Lost War* (1994), W. writes his life like a well-wrought novel. Less concerned with the simple retelling of events, W. tells his story by dramatizing select scenes and using re-created dialogue to chronicle his experiences. In both memoirs W. presents himself as a picaresque figure who uses a native intelligence to take advantage of other people's misfortunes and plays pranks on unsuspecting victims. *This Boy's Life* chronicles his American childhood and, in the process, provides a literary document of what it was like to grow up between World War II and the Vietnam War. The tightly woven structure of the memoirs includes an unforgettable cast of characters including an absent father, a loving, but overwhelmed mother, an evil stepfather, inept school teachers, high school bullies, and adolescent hoodlums. Similarly, *In Pharaoh's Army*, W.'s account of his service as an inept lieutenant in the Vietnam War, is organized around vividly drawn characters and well-chosen scenes. One scene in particular serves as an example of W.'s ability to dramatize a personal experience and pack it with national significance. During his tour in Vietnam W. comes across a group of Vietnamese soldiers who are ready to slaughter a puppy and use if for their evening meal. W. saves and then adopts the puppy. Later, the puppy is recaptured by the South Vietnamese and served to W. in the form of a stew. W. employs his ironic imagination here to use this scene as an illustration of the American presence in Vietnam: the well-meaning, sentiment-driven Americans' attempt to heroically save the innocents.

In addition to his memoirs, W. has written a novella, *The Barracks Thief* (1985), and three collections of short stories: *In the Garden of the North American Martyrs* (1981), *Back in the World* (1985), and *The Night in Question* (1996). All have been critically acclaimed, and *The Barracks Thief* won the PEN/Faulkner Award in fiction in 1985. In his short fiction W. is a humane, tender narrator of characters who are overwhelmed by the complexities of their lives, but usually find a way to manage their predicaments and challenges. In all of his stories W. is a clever, learned writer who is never pretentious. Written in a realistic and minimalistic style, W.'s stories tend to focus on an American middle-class experience, but W. is also at home writing about soldiers in the Vietnam War, as in "Soldier's Story" and "Casualty," priests who find themselves in compromising situations, as in "The Missing Person," and downwardly mobile families hopelessly looking for the American Dream, as in "Face to Face" and "Firelight." In two of his early stories, "Hunters in the Snow" and "Smokers," W. shows that he is a moralist who refuses to moralize. Throughout his fiction W. examines the issue of shifting identifies, notably in "Passengers" and "The Episode in the Life of Professor Burke." "The Life of the Body" and "Migraine," published in his third collection of stories, are examples of W.'s interest in exploring complex human motivations and desires that lay below the surface of reality. W.'s fiction is indebted to but not reliant upon the influence of CHEKHOV, Ernest HEMINGWAY, John CHEEVER, Flannery O'CONNOR, and especially Raymond CARVER, a friend and colleague of W.'s before his untimely death.

W. has edited several collections of short stories, including *Matters of Life and Death* (1983) and *The Vintage Book of Contemporary Short Stories* (1994). He has also written numerous articles and stories that have appeared major American magazines such as *Esquire* and the *Atlantic Monthly*.

W. is an important literary figure in the late 20th c. because he has been able to find both a popular and a more critical audience. His memoirs are highly readable and widely read, and his short fiction has been heralded by some of the finest contemporary writers and critics of the day.

BIBLIOGRAPHY: Bailey, P. J., "Why Not Tell the Truth? The Autobiographies of Three Fiction Writers," *Critique*, 32 (Summer 1991): 211-23; Hannah, J., *T. W.: A Study of the Short Fiction* (1996); Oliver, B., "An Interview with T. W.," *ConL*, 31 (1990): 1-16

—ERIC FRETZ

WOLKER, Jiři

Czechoslovak poet, dramatist, and short-story writer (writing in Czech), b. 29 March 1900, Prostějov; d. 3 Jan. 1924, Prostějov

Son of a bank clerk, W. acquired a sound education in classical and modern languages. In his early youth he was attracted to painting and music. While studying law at the University of Prague, he attended lectures given in the faculty of arts, mainly those of the famous critic F. X. ŠALDA. W. contracted tuberculosis during the course of his studies and died before his twenty–fourth birthday.

Inspired by Victor Hugo, at fourteen W. wrote a poetic drama (never published) entitled *Zrádce* (traitor). His early adult works were strongly influenced by Fráňa Šrámek (1887–1952) and, to a lesser extent, by S. K. Neumann (1875–1947) and Josef HORA, but he soon found an individual poetic voice that combined his gentleness with revolt against social injustice. W. had a powerful poetic vision that, according to Šalda, was comparable to that of Shelley and Whitman.

W.'s first collection of poems, *Host do domu* (1921; a guest in the house), expressed his love of life and his sense of fraternity with the downtrodden, poor, sick, hurt, and oppressed. These poems carried on the tradition of pre–World War I Czech poets who wanted to introduce everyday events into poetry. Drawing their strength from childhood reminiscences, W.'s poems show the dawning of a social conscience. Their realism and sincerity immediately established him as a popular poet. W.'s long poem "Svatý Kopeček" (Holy Mount), originally published separately in 1921 and later added to *Host do domu*, is a semi–epic that shows W.'s increasing attraction to the social themes, an interest more fully developed in the collection *Těžká hodina* (1922; difficult hour).

While *Host do domu* is the work of a youthful poet, *Těžká hodina* marks the transition from adolescence to maturity; the artist wishes to take an active part in the creation of a better world. The humanitarian compassion for the exploited evident in the poems of this volume established W. as the chief representative of postwar "proletarian poetry." It contains some of W.'s most powerful poems—"Tvář za sklem" (the face behind the glass), "Jaro" (the spring), "Moře" (the sea), "Mirogoj" (Mirogoj)—and ballads. The best known of the latter, "Balada o očích topičových" ("The Eyes of the Stoker," 1958), most aptly expresses W.'s celebration of the exploited working class and his dramatization of the struggle for social justice, which would remove poverty completely from the world. The form of the ballad, particularly its narrative strength, was perhaps the most suitable mode for W. Influenced by K. J. Erben (1811–1870), whose balladic heroes were like toys in the hands of some supernatural power and unchanging world order, W. went beyond Erben and demanded the liberation of men from the fallible established laws of society. The ballad form also lent itself well to W.'s preoccupation with the moral problems of his heroes, especially in "Balada o námořníku" (ballad of a sailor) and "Balada z nemocnice" ("Ballad from a Hospital," 1945). It is a great pity that he died before he could carry out his plan to write a separate collection of ballads.

In his posthumously published poems W.'s eroticism and personal joys are increasingly overshadowed by his awareness of social inequality and his presentiment of death. These themes are developed most powerfully in "U roentgenu" (1923; the X ray).

Although primarily a poet, W. also wrote three one–act plays, collected in *Tři hry* (1923; three plays): *Nemocnice* (the hospital), *Hrob* (the grave), and *Nejvyšší oběť* (the greatest sacrifice). They are, however, of documentary rather than artistic significance. Nevertheless, W. had a keen interest in the theater. He also wrote short fiction: his posthumously published *Povídky a pohádky* (1925; stories and fairy tales), in which he focuses on social and moral themes, is one of the few important attempts in Czech literature to modernize fairy tales.

W. is sometimes described as the poet of the young because his verse is permeated by strong, vibrant emotions. The powerful imagery and moving expression of social compassion, which influenced many poets of the interwar period, give his work a lasting appeal.

FURTHER WORKS: *Listy příteli* (1950); *Korespondence s rodiči* (1952); *Listy dvou básníků* (1953); *Spisy* (4 vols., 1953–54)

BIBLIOGRAPHY: Thumin, J. H., *Das Problem von Form und Gattung bei J. W.* (1966); French, A., *The Poets of Prague: Czech Poetry between the Wars* (1969): 14–17, 21–28, 40–41; Drews, P., *Devětsil und Poetismus: Künstlerische Theorie und Praxis der tschechischen Avantgarde am Beispiel V. Nezvals, J. Seiferts und J. W.s* (1975); Novák, A., *Czech Literature* (1976): 318

—B. R. BRADBROOK

WOLOF LITERATURE
See Senegalese Literature

WOOLF, Virginia

English novelist, critic, and essayist, b. 25 Jan. 1882, London; d. 28 March 1941, Rodmell

From a family that represented the late–19th–c. intellectual aristocracy, W. even as a child was preparing herself to be a writer. She had access to the well–stocked library of her father, Leslie Stephen (1832–1904), who had been a tutor at Cambridge before establishing his name as an essayist and biographer. W. learned how to work from watching his steady application that produced several articles a week. Her mother, Julia Duckworth Stephen, was a striking personality in her own right—intelligent, beautiful, and managerial.

Under the demands and restrictions of her parents' discipline, W. began early to acquire the education that exclusion from the man's world of the universities denied her. During the early years when she was writing about literature and beginning her first novel, she was fortunate in being surrounded by some of the most stimulating minds of her generation. Her brother Thoby had introduced several of his Cambridge friends to her in the Bloomsbury house where she had moved after her father's death. There the nucleus of what was later called the Bloomsbury Group met to talk about art and ideas: W.'s sister Vanessa, the novelist E. M. FORSTER, the economist John Maynard Keynes (1883–1946), the poet and biographer Lytton STRACHEY, the painter Duncan Grant (1885–1978), and the art critic Clive Bell (1881–1964), Vanessa's husband.

Bloomsbury had a double influence on W., reflected in the social gatherings so important in her novels. The coterie's play of wit and ideas stimulated her intellect, and their laughter and high spirits helped to alleviate the intermittent despair brought on periodically by illness and a morbid family situation. One of the group, her brother Thoby's friend, the writer Leonard Woolf (1880–1969), became her husband in 1912. Whether Leonard's companionship was helpful to Virginia or detrimental and whether her periodic malaise was a form of madness or neurasthenia aggravated by medical incompetence became the center of critical attention in the 1970s and 1980s.

Temperamentally right for her or not, Leonard certainly made contributions to her stock of ideas and to her values. He influenced her musical taste, and her diary makes frequent reference to her reliance on his literary judgment. The founding of the Hogarth Press in 1917 resulted directly from his concern for Virginia's health. He hoped that the manual work of setting type and binding books would calm her mental hyperactivity. Unfortunately for this objective, the very success of the enterprise necessitated having the work done by others. One advantage ensued—that she was kept

Virginia Woolf

abreast of contemporary writing through reading manuscripts submitted for publication.

The fact remains that despite almost constant ill health W. produced an impressive amount of writing. Beginning in 1904, when her first review was published, W.'s long, regular work schedule resulted in six volumes of collected essays and reviews, two biographies, two libertarian books, several volumes of letters and diaries, nine novels, and two collections of short stories.

The first of her novels, *The Voyage Out* (1915), presents nearly all the major subjects that form the basis for imaginative speculation in her subsequent work: the misunderstanding between parents and children, the inadequate preparation of women for life, male arrogance, the marriage relationship, the state as a machine, militarism as an instrument of the mechanical state, revulsion against the hypocrisy of organized religion, the incompetence of medical practitioners, the enigma of time, and the significance of art. Because her way of writing about such matters had yet to be thought out and refined by practice, *The Voyage Out* is occasionally ponderous, as is the next novel, *Night and Day* (1919), which takes as its thesis woman's place in society, intellectual life, and marriage. Although the style in this novel is more discursive than any until *The Years* (1937), there are intermittent passages in which the "fever pitch" described in *Jacob's Room* (1922) as the sign of intellectual fervor creates the visionary intensity that characterizes W.'s most effective writing.

The "visionary" quality of W.'s writing originates in her tireless search for ways to represent ideas and emotions, beyond action, as the true objects of interest in fiction. Part of that search resulted in the reviews and essays that recorded her debt to predecessors in literature. But the full account of her explorations is found in the last seven novels, in which as far as possible through words she made an approach to the "silent land" of inner personal life—which she describes in *Walter Sickert: A Conversion* (1934)—without sacrificing the movement, light, and sounds of physical reality.

The Edwardian novelists she had attacked in *Mr. Bennett and Mrs. Brown* (1924) were, W. believed, preoccupied with externals. In her view they attributed more importance to the paraphernalia of society than to the spark of vital incandescence in each individual. As W., in "An Unwritten Novel" (from *Monday or Tuesday*, 1921), imagines the life of the unattractive, lonely woman sitting in the railway compartment opposite her, the imagined existence becomes more credible than the physical reality presented only by external appearance. To "love life," and to describe that life as physical, yet to insist that the life "increasingly real to us" dwells in personality, not in acts, is to establish and maintain a paradox that creates the tension in W.'s writing.

Jacob's Room dramatizes the primary value of the inner life by making intensity of experience the true measure of time. When one speaks of intellectual fervor, it is not just knowledge of Greek or Latin or a certain place like Cambridge but a particular writer saying a particular thing, and the fever pitch when "mind prints upon mind indelibly." Jacob's "room" is the human collective mind—concretely, all the rooms in which Jacob reads or talks, his imagination on fire to resist the darkness pressing in on all sides. The sections about the contending impulses of civilization and barbarism are memorable, those dealing with male dominance and militarism striking but overly formalized and rigidly satiric. The "new form for a new novel," here marvelous though imperfect, showed itself in the next novel as a masterwork.

Millions of Jacobs died during World War I because of insanity in high places. In *Mrs. Dalloway* (1925) this theme, shaped to congruence with W.'s own experience with doctors, is developed in the story of a combat veteran, Septimus Smith, who falls into the hands of medical practitioners. They dominate their patient instead of healing him, and he kills himself. His story is intertwined with that of Clarissa Dalloway, who is also passing through a mental crisis, although they never meet. Clarissa moves away from isolation toward an acceptance of life. In *Mrs. Dalloway*, the first of her accomplished novels following the apprentice work at experimental writing in *Jacob's Room*, W. perfected several techniques for connecting inner with outer life. The special atmosphere of this novel depends on her having extended that connection of private self with public persona to the world of nature. The extremes of this organic connection are manifest in the earthy association of mothers suckling their babes with the lush fertility of nature on this June day and in the psychotic delusions of Septimus Smith. W.'s own term for this technique was tunneling, digging "caves" behind the characters into the past in order to bring them out into the light of day, to connect the past with the present. The result is a complex interrelation of thought, act, and feeling conveyed in a narrative rich in a striking combination of sensory data and ethical considerations.

W.'s success in using her own neurasthenia as a subject for fiction provided the necessary confidence for attempting the equally delicate material of her next novel, *To the Lighthouse* (1927), which is concerned with W.'s unhappy childhood and the dominant personalities of her parents. In this novel W. introduces several varieties of three—part structures. The form of the novel itself is a triad: "The Window," "Time Passes," "The Lighthouse." In "Time Passes" W. employs a narrative triptych that is a miniature of the novel's form, here used for ironic inflection of what goes before and comes after the short, bracketed middle parts that are concerned with death. The triptychs, which distance personal loss and inexplicable catastrophes of nature, enabled W. to adopt a new attitude toward the persisting influence (malign, as she saw it) of her parents, and provide the reader with an aesthetic equivalent of her personal accommodation to mutability and death. Yet there is comedy, too, in this account of family life in a summer house by the sea (like the Stephen place at St. Ives, where W. spent the summers of her childhood), derived from the conflict between egos of one generation and another, the different treatment accorded to boys and girls, and the uneasy relationship of man and woman in marriage.

W.'s sense of humor, often observed in her social life, is not just an occasional intrusion into the otherwise serious fabric of her work. From one of her earliest pieces, written when she was ten, "The Experiences of a Pater-familias" (pub. 1972), to her last, *Between the Acts* (1941), a novel where in the opening sentence she balances "summer night" with "cesspool," her comic effects range from the self–dramatization of Mr. Ramsey in *To the Lighthouse* through the manipulation of historical time in *Orlando* (1928). W.'s comedy originates in an awareness of the contradictions, opposition, and absurdities of life.

These qualities characterize the thematic sexual ambivalences of *Orlando*, which is the "grand historical picture" of her friends, sketched in the character of *Orlando*, who changes from one sex to the other between the 16th c. and the "present."

In her teens, W. admired women like the novelist *Madge Vaughan* (1869–1925), who is pictured as the extroverted Sally Seton in *Mrs. Dalloway*. In middle life, W. was much attracted to the writer Victoria (Vita) Sackville–West (1892–1962), as a strong independent spirit and as a lover. W. was also interested in a quite different kind of woman, Katherine MANSFIELD, although W.'s interest in her was professional, a mixture of admiration and envy. She and Vita were both worked into *Orlando* in a vicarious display of all that W. was not, and envied: worldly assurance, spontaneity, promiscuousness, and exoticism.

Despite its capriciousness, *Orlando* is a substantial work of fiction. If it suffers in comparison with her next novel, *The Waves* (1931), W. at least recognized both works as necessary expressions of her creative energy—*Orlando* of her need to "play on the surface" and *The Waves* of her compulsion to "dive" and explore the depths. *The Waves* is not a novel in which one event clarifies what preceded it, the object being not clarification but enrichment of correspondences between nature and human nature. It is W.'s most complex attempt to say how we can know what we do not know—about human destiny, love, and creativity. The nine stages in the daily course of the sun are associated with nine stages in the fifty–year span of human life in the soliloquies, beginning with drawn in nature and with children in the nursery. W.'s governing "new concept" was to exclude everything that did not belong to the moment: "why admit anything to literature that is not poetry?"—and by poetry she seems to mean a verbal intensity that expresses momentarily vivid states of being.

In *The Years*, however, W. admitted a good deal that was not poetry, but not as much as the plan for the novel provided originally, which was to show life "whole" by introducing "ideas" in the form of essays into the narrative. These were omitted and later published as *Three Guineas* (1938). In the novel as published, the concerns of the essays remain in Rosie's rebelliousness against the established order, Sally's independence, and Eleanor's deepening insights into sexual relations, regular and irregular. The novel is about children and their difficult lives, adults as children, and humanity as the childhood of the race. The long party section at the end of *The Years* is a triumph of sustained narration that moves away from the foregoing rancor, ugliness, confusion, and bickering to conclude on a moment of transcendent beauty and wholeness, which is functional, both in style and theme, as the possibility of human advance beyond the stage of childhood is offered tentatively but without open skepticism.

W.'s last work of fiction, posthumously published as *Between the Acts*, makes a trilogy with the two preceding novels in its shared concern with reaches of time, the darkness of human history, and the creative association of powers in nature and human nature. Concern with the vastness of time is represented through one character's preoccupation with H. G. Wells's *Outline of History* and through the village pageant's panorama of four hundred years; concern with the darkness of history through a backdrop of human prehistory against which the passions of a single day at Pointz Hall are acted out; and concern with creativity through the struggles of the director to create and produce the pageant. All these matters are treated with irony of situation and character in an economy and directness of style that W. was mastering in this novel at the time she committed suicide by drowning herself in the River Ouse near her home in Sussex.

During nearly two decades after the publication of W.'s first libertarian book, *A Room of One's Own* (1929), more copies of her non-fiction than of fiction were sold. Since the end of World War II, more readers have purchased the novels. As to the relative merit of her two kinds of writing, enough opinion has been offered by both common readers and critics to suggest that division of preference will continue. *A Writer's Diary* (1953), with entries from 1918 to 1941 selected by Leonard Woolf, exemplifies W.'s search for the best way to express her vision of life in literature. The diary is an account of works in progress, and a record of what she learned from her predecessors in the art of storytelling. It also logs the private explorations of her personal life—frequently expressing her chagrin at not being on a par with men, but also the uncertainty of what that parity should be.

A Room of One's Own, the more effective of her two book-length works about the suppression of women, develops the thesis that a woman of genius will not appear until she can be independent, have enough to live on, and possess "a room of her own." Ways of obtaining these goals is the subject of *Three Guineas* (1938), her other book on this theme and her final book of social protest, in which the subject of male domination and its heavily ironic treatment are carried over from *Jacob's Room* and developed with extensive documentation, which, with the polemic essay, were the portions excluded from the final version of *The Years*.

In her writings about art W. turned from the public world of disorder and catastrophe to the private satisfactions of painting and music. Despite her belief that the public and the private worlds are one, she was clearly more at home in the private. Her dutiful biography of artist and critic *Roger Fry* (1940) quotes with approval his view that in painting, in music, and in literature lay the enduring reality.

Critical attention, which at first concentrated largely on the merits of W.'s idiosyncratic style and on textual exegesis, advanced in the 1970s and 1980s to serious investigations into her contributions to narrative technique and into the relationships

between aspects of her life and the imaginative transcriptions of those aspects. By the 1980s her reputation was firmly established as one of the century's authentic major voices.

FURTHER WORKS: *The Common Reader* (1925); *Street Haunting* (1930); *On Being III* (1930); *Beau Brummell* (1930); *A Letter to a Young Poet* (1932); *The Common Reader: Second Series* (1932); *Flush: A Biography* (1933); *Reviewing* (1939); *The Death of the Moth, and Other Essays* (1942); *A Haunted House, and Other Short Stories* (1943); *The Moment, and Other Essays* (1948); *The Captain's Death Bed, and Other Essays* (1950); *V. W. and Lytton Strachey: Letters* (1956); *Hours in a Library* (1958); *Granite and Rainbow: Essays* (1958); *Contemporary Writers* (1965); *Nurse Lugton's Golden Thimble* (1966); *Collected Essays* (4 vols., 1966–1967); *Mrs. Dalloway's Party A Short Story Sequence* (1973); *The Letters of V. W.* (6 vols., 1975–1980); *The Waves: The Two Holograph Drafts* (1976); *Freshwater* (1976); *Moments of Being: Unpublished Autobiographical Writings* (1976); *Books and Portraits* (1977); *The Diary of V. W.* (4 vols., 1977–1982); *Melymbrosia: An Early Version of "The Voyage Out"* (1982); *The London Scene* (1982)

BIBLIOGRAPHY: Johnston, J. K., *The Bloomsbury Group: A Study of E. M. Forster, Lytton Strachey, V. W., and Their Circle* (1954); Woolf, L., *An Autobiography of the Years 1880–1969* (4 vols., 1960–1969); Daiches, D., *V. W.* (1963); Guiget, J., *V. W. and Her Works* (1965); Schaefer, J., O'B. *The Three-Fold Nature of Reality in the Novels of V. W.* (1965); Richter, H., *V. W.: The Inward Voyage* (1970); Sprague, C., ed., *V. W.: A Collection of Critical Essays* (1971); Bell, Q., *V. W.: A Biography* (2 vols., 1972); special W. issue, *MFS*, 18, 3 (1972); Noble, J. R., *Recollections of V. W.* (1972); Bazin, N. T., *V. W. and the Androgynous Vision* (1973); Johnson, M., *V. W.* (1973); Kelley, A. v. B., *The Novels of V. W.* (1973); McLaurin, A., *V. W.: The Echoes Enslaved* (1973); Nareman, J., *The World without a Self: V. W. and the Novel* (1973); Alexander, J., *The Venture of Form in the Novels of V. W.* (1974); Fleishman, A., *V. W.: A Critical Reading* (1975); Majumdar, R., and McLaurin, A., eds., *V. W.: The Critical Heritage* (1975); Novak, J., *The Razor Edge of Balance* (1975); Leaska, M., *The Novels of V. W.* (1977); DeSalvo, L. A., *V. W.'s First Voyage: A Novel in the Making* (1980); Spilka, M., *V. W.'s Quarrel with Grieving* (1980); Harper, H., *Between Language and Silence: The Novels of V. W.* (1982); Radin, G., *V. W.'s "The Years": The Evolution of a Novel* (1982)

—MANLY JOHNSON

Vividness alone, of course, is not art: it is only the material of art. But Mrs. W. has, I think, a finer sense of form than any but the oldest living English novelist. As well as the power of brilliant evocation she has that creative faculty of form which differs from what is ordinarily called construction in the same way that life differs from mechanism: the same quality as Cézanne. In the case of the painter, of course, this "form" is purely visual; the synthesis—relation—rhythm—whatever you call it, is created on this side of the eye; while in the case of the poet the pattern is a mental one, created behind the eye of the reader, composed directly of mental processes, ideas, sensory evocation—not of external agents (not of the words used, I mean). So, in the case of Mrs. W., and of the present novel [*Mrs. Dalloway*], it is not by its vividness that her writing ultimately stays in the mind, but by the coherent and processional form which is composed of, and transcends, that vividness.

Richard Hughes, "A Day in London Life," *Saturday Review of Literature*, 16 May 1925, p. 755

In *The Waves* [her] prose has put away all hesitation, and cuts out images and thoughts in one sweep. It is impatiently, almost violently immediate. What it recalls most strongly is Rilke's superb prose, which was a sort of inspired shorthand. And one imagines that it has changed in this astonishing way because Mrs. W. is dealing directly now with immediate and essential truths of experience. The result is an authentic and unique masterpiece, which is bound to have an influence on the mind of this generation.

Edwin Muir, on *The Waves*, *Bookman* (New York), Dec. 1931, p. 367

Her books . . . are not written for this new age. If one rereads several of them in succession, as I did recently, one is more likely to be impressed by their narrow range of characters and emotions than by their cool wit and their warm imagination. The outside world has made itself real to us as it never was to the people in her novels. But it would be wrong to treat the judgment of our moment in time as if it were that of history. The days will come again when people have leisure to appreciate her picture of the inner world and her sense of the living past. The spirit if not the body of Georgian England survives in her novels.

Malcolm Cowley, on *Between the Acts*, *New Republic*, 6 Oct. 1941, p. 440

In certain of Mrs. W.'s novels, an archetypal pattern of feeling appears to serve as the emotional form for the entire work. The elaborate fairy—tale phantasy of the awakening of the feminine instinct in *Orlando*, as well as the realization of its potentialities, may touch a hidden area of response in women readers. The seeking of parental love and approbation in *To the Lighthouse* (in psychological terms, a search for the father and motherimago), and the myth of the "night journey" in *The Voyage Out* (with its descent into the self, its repeating motifs of frustration and suffocation), are patterns of feeling which, evoking universal aspects of experience, seem to possess the power to touch deep reservoirs of energy. The reader is led to feel a catharsis of relief when Rachel dies, after her duplicate journeys into the jungles of love and fever. A similar resolution of conflict is achieved in *To the Lighthouse* when the related principles of father and mother, of *Logos* and *Eros*, are reached as the children finally land at the lighthouse and Lily has her glimpse of Mrs. Ramsay. However complex the

patterns of feeling, in each of Mrs. W.'s novels a sequence of tensions is built up which, when the climax occurs, is suddenly resolved, and the reader seems to be bathed in a flood of peace.

Harvena Richter, *V. W.: The Inward Voyage* (1970), p. 243

In this vision [of spontaneity in nature and in people], as in [Miss La Trobe's] pageant [in *Between the Acts*], the pattern is not stable as in a painting but constantly changing as in a film. The emphasis in either case is the same; it falls not upon the representational but upon the nonrepresentational aspect of reality, that is, upon pattern, rhythm, and color. Certainly, in order to reconstruct Miss La Trobe's vision of what she wanted the pageant to be, the reader must see the pageant in these terms. In short, he does not merely hear about the pageant as he heard about Rachel Vinrace's music [in *The Voyage Out*] or Lily Briscoe's painting [in *To the Lighthouse*]. Rather he is asked to see it, and to interpret it. In this sense, V. W. is silent while the reader is constantly reacting to and contributing to the content of the novel.

Nancy Topping Bazin, *V. W. and the Androgynous Vision* (1973), pp. 220–21

V. W. was . . . a repetitive writer, both in her thematic concerns and in her means of expression. It is scarcely necessary to cite childhood trauma—the series of deaths in her family, the explosive father, or the "interfering" stepbrother—to see that W. was inordinately burdened with her past. Nor is it greatly enlightening to posit a neurotic (or psychotic) compulsion to repeat, to return to the same psychic cruxes, when we consider the satisfying formal order she made of her preoccupations in *Jacob's Room*, *Mrs. Dalloway*, *The Waves*, *The Years*, and most of all in *To the Lighthouse*. We know that W. dwelt on the past, on the scenes and persons of her childhood and later years; we have also seen that in doing so she used certain images, phrases, and words over and over again. Can we say that the peculiar mixture of eeriness and pleasure which emanates from W.'s fiction is related to that feeling of the uncanny which we have in the presence of the past? W.'s reworking of persons and places is, of course, different from Wordsworth's return to remembered scenes; her repetition of words and themes is distinct from the reverberations of "*temps*" in the closing pages of Proust's *Recherche* Nevertheless, these writers are her proper company: she takes her place in the tradition—still alive, although Romantic art has passed—that tells us not only how it feels to be but also how it feels *to have been*. At the same time, there is no avoiding the implication that so powerful an impulse toward the past, now dead, is in line with the temptation to return to a prior state of being that has become known as the "death—instinct."

Avrom Fleishman, *V. W.: A Critical Reading* (1975), p. 226

V. W. once described *The Voyage Out* as a harlequinade and at another time spoke of her fiction as if it were a masquerade for autobiography. One can conceptualize her creation of *The Voyage Out* in the terms with which she herself described it. In the earliest stages, W. established the emotional center of her story—the necessity of a young woman's death before her marriage because she has been both unfaithful and overardently attached to a man identified with her father. Then W. rewrote [the early ms.] *Melymbrosia* by reatiring it: it became *The Voyage Out*. She kept the novel's core but it became less visible, less accessible, not because it had been obliterated, but because she had dressed it differently, with so many other and distracting accessories, that it became very difficult to see. More importantly, its emotional strength and artistic integrity became disguised. The result was a draft which now was a modification of that early design, but a modification which amounted to a masquerade.

Louise A. DeSalvo, *V. W.'s First Voyage* (1980),
p. 156

By 1922, when she began writing *Mrs. Dalloway*, she had finally read *Ulysses* in full and had begun to assimilate its subjective possibilities for her fiction. In her previous novel, *Jacob's Room* (1922), she had employed an experimental method closer to Katherine Mansfield's than to Joyce's. What she offered, in effect, was a brief life history of a young war—victim, Jacob Flanders, as conveyed by the random impressions of other characters, and from time to time through his own impressions. Her method was lyric, poetic, oblique; it afforded a great deal of tantalizing mystery about Jacob's inner nature, and very little inner substance. Joyce's stream–of–consciousness method brought her closer, however, to "the quick of the mind," or to her own touchstone for reality, the "luminous halo" of "life itself," as she began her new novel.

Mark Spilka, *V. W.'s Quarrel with Grieving*
(1980), p. 48

WRIGHT, Charles

American poet, b. 25 Aug. 1935, Pickwick Dam, Tennessee

Reared and educated in the American South, W. did not become a poet until he served in Italy with the U.S. Army in the late 1950s. There, discovering the language of Dante and the work of modernists such as Ezra POUND, he began to explore the imagistic, meditative style he has continued to develop throughout his career. As a graduate student under Donald JUSTICE at the University of Iowa, W. received formal training in metered and syllabic forms, but his published work consists almost entirely of free verse.

W.'s poetry often is described as luminous or lapidary. A typical W. poem is condensed, contemplative, and tightly crafted; he is original and often witty in creating metaphors, but rarely surreal. His diction, though broad and richly musical, characteristically is more sober than manic or street-savvy. He situates most of his writing in specific landscape and places (often Italy or the terrains of childhood, and also Southern California). Even when at its least narratively explicit, the poem still arises out of a particular physical moment, then transcends that environment to invoke the possibility of other worlds. His technique can be compared to Pound's, but his sensibility more closely parallels the late poems by T. S. ELIOT.

W.'s publications divide into three groups. *The Grave of the Right Hand* (1970), *Hard Freight* (1973), *Bloodlines* (1975), and *China Trace* (1977) comprise the first period, collected in *Country Music* (1982), which won a National Book Award. One achievement of his earlier work is extreme compression. All elements—diction, persona, tone, title, stanza length—receive scrupulous distillation, resulting in poems of crystalline intensity. In *China Trace*, for example, poems range from one to twelve lines (none are longer); in *Bloodlines* the two central sequences, "Tattoos" and "Skins," each require a page of explanatory notes. In interviews W. has said that the fifty poems of *China Trace* can be read as chapters of one story, an account of a lifetime's pilgrimage; just as true is the observation that they sound like the collective voices of a congregation singing hymns in a language we almost (but not quite) have forgotten.

Southern Cross (1981) marks the second period, as W. develops a more relaxed poetic line and allows a wider range of diction. In that book and *The Other Side of the River* (1984) earlier thematic concerns remain—the first book's title refers simultaneously to a constellation, to nostalgia for the South, and to the central icon of Christianity, while the "Other Side" alludes to crossing the frontiers of memory and death. Although still visionary, still dense, and still highly imagistic, poems in these books are longer than his previous work. They also reveal more of W.'s subtle sense of humor. Along with longer lines and longer overall length, the poems display more varied spatial compositions as well.

Zone Journals (1988) furthers W.'s maturation into a more discursive line. Using ten journal entries, the book investigates sacred places and haunted (and haunting) language, often via long, two-part lines. To W., the dropped "low rider" is still part of the first line; using it allows him to extend thought and image without overburdening cadence. *Xionia* (1990) also relies on journal forms and includes "Language Journal," W.'s rebuttal to the Language Poetry movement. He is unimpressed with their claims of priority and focus; as W. has said, "all poets are language poets." *The World of The Ten Thousand Things* (1990) collects work from 1980 to 1990.

W.'s third period is identified thus far by two publications, *Chickamauga* (1995), which won the Lenore Marshall Prize, and *Black Zodiac* (1997), winner of the Pulitzer Prize. The humor is still there as is the celestial longing, but individual poems now can be shorter, less journey-filled, nearly conversational. As before, noun fragments accrete incrementally, but the content is more frequently aphoristic, as if W. were finally comfortable with meeting both the demands of readability and the pressure of describing the indescribable. In both books, when he is at his most first-personal, he seems his most self-effaced. As a poet concerned with "language, landscape, and the idea of God," the specific particulars of his own life serve only as conduits to more general concerns.

This is not decorum so much as a willingness to discard the inessential. In effect, W. becomes the poetic equivalent of a Christian ascetic, albeit a highly articulate one, someone who tries again and again to describe "the passageways of Paradise."

FURTHER WORKS: *Halflife: Improvisations and Interviews, 1977-1987* (1988); *Quarter Notes: Improvisations and Interviews* (1995)

BIBLIOGRAPHY: Andrews, T., *The Point Where All Things Meet* (1995); St. John, D., *Where the Angels Come toward Us* (1995); Vendler, H., "The Nothing That Is," *NewR* (7 Aug. 1995): 42-45; Logenbach, J., "Between Soil and Stars," *The Nation* (14 Apr. 1997): 27-30; Muske, C., "Guided By Dark Stars," *NYTBR* (31 Aug. 1997): 11-12

—CHARLES HOOD

WRIGHT, James

American poet, b. 13 Dec. 1927, Martins Ferry, Ohio; d. 25 Mar. 1980, New York, N.Y.

W. grew up the son of a factory worker in Martins Ferry, Ohio, which is both a literal and a ghostly presence in his poetry, life there the apparent source of his trademark identification with the lonely,

James Wright

the derelict, and the damned. The rich literary tradition of Kenyon College, where he was a student from 1948 to 1952, is another ghostly presence in his work. It stands clearly behind the closed-form poetry of his first collections, and it survived in a continued reverence for Horatian craft, restraint, distance, and elegance even as he shifted from closed to open forms under the influence of the poet Robert BLY and under the stimulus of translating such surrealistic Spanish American poets as Pablo NERUDA, César VALLEJO, and Juan Ramón JIMÉNEZ. After earning a Ph.D. at the University of Seattle (1959), where he studied with Theodore ROETHKE, W. taught at the University of Minnesota, at Macalester College in St. Paul, and from 1966 until his death in 1980 at Hunter College in New York City.

W.'s first collection, *The Green Wall* (1957), was selected for publication in the Yale Series of Younger Poets by W. H. AUDEN. Most of its poems are neo-Georgian in style, written in rhyme and meter, as are a substantial number of the poems in *Saint Judas* (1959). Especially striking in these volumes at the time because of their unexpected sympathies, striking now because they symptomize a darkening tone and an increasing pressure of personality, are a trio of poems about men condemned to death; "A Poem about George Doty in the Death House," "American Twilights, 1957," and "At the Executed Murderer's Grave." Other poems have as their subjects mad girls, black prostitutes, deaf children, and the poet Sappho. Traditional form seems to be proffered in these early poems as aesthetic compensation for the way things are.

W. remarked upon the publication of *Saint Judas* that whatever he wrote thereafter would be completely different, and so it is generally thought to have been. The early poems only hint at the spare, colloquial, raggedly personal style of *The Branch Will Not Break* (1963), and they have few glimmers of the natural beauty that is allowed in the latter volume to transform the act of perception into something deeply affecting. Indeed, the new poems of *The Branch Will Not Break*, *Shall We Gather at the River* (1968), and the *Collected Poems* (1971) possess an alertness to the particulars and to the particular moments of experience that is extraordinarily resonant, for the logically discursive progression and elaborate closure of the earlier poetry give way in those collections to anecdotal non sequiturs and a flatness of statement that reach downward to the emotional gestalt of what has come to be termed "the deep image." Poems like "Lying in a Hammock at William Duffy's Farm in Pine Island, Minnesota" and "A Blessing" became instantly famous for sudden shifts of feeling that are responses to such deeply buried figures of understanding. Like other Deep Imagists—Robert BLY, Robert Kelly (b. 1935), James DICKEY, Jerome Rothenberg (b. 1931), Diane Wakoski (b. 1937)—W. was reacting in part against the tendency of the so-called New York Poets to fragment perception into an apparently discontinuous stream of images. Famously, he rebuked the New York Poets in the poem "Many of Our Waters: Variations on a Poem by a Black Child" for their disdain of the "pure clear word."

In the wake of his *Collected Poems* and the Pulitzer Prize that it earned him, W. experimented unsuccessfully with prose poems in *Two Citizens* (1973), a collection he later regretted, and in *Moments of the Italian Summer* (1976), a collection of fourteen prose poems published in limited edition. A number of such poems, some of them recycled from the latter volume, also appear in W.'s last collections, *To a Blossoming Pear Tree* (1977) and the posthumously published *This Journey* (1982). The late poems are colloquial in their diction, loose in their rhythms, and elliptical in their structures, but a firm technique of lineation, a talismanic sense of the word, and an unmannered fluidity lend them classical grace. Even when their anecdotes are riven suddenly by auctorial intrusions, the poems tend to be shapely psychological wholes—the poems in particular that are inspired by the landscape of Italy and that speak of irredeemable loneliness opened inexplicably to joy even under the shadow of W.'s approaching death.

Above the River: The Complete Poems (1990) makes clear that loneliness was W.'s abiding subject, with death looming large as the final loneliness. His is a particularly American strain of loneliness because it is permeated with both a Jamesian sense that the inner life has no home in the Martin Ferries of America and a Whitmanesque recognition that loneliness admits one to the fraternity of outsiders. It is also a loneliness particularly W.'s own in his turning to the place within, only to discover Martin Ferry there, too, even in Italy. One of the most appealing strategies of his poetry, because it sets off chiaroscurically this preoccupation with loneliness, is the irradiating shaft of joy that tends to emanate in the early poems from communication with the natural world; in the later poems, from love of his wife. At its best, the interplay of the two lends extraordinary psychological drama to lyrics of high technical achievement and establishes W. in the first rank of American poets in his generation.

FURTHER WORKS: *The Lion's Tale and Eyes: Poems Written Out of Laziness and Silence* (1962); *Salt Mines and Such* (1971); *I See the Wind* (1974); *Old Booksellers and Other Poems* (1976); *The Summer of James and Annie Wright: Sketches and Mosaics* (1981, with Ann Wright); *In Defense against This Exile: Letters to Wayne Burns/J. W.* (1985); *The Delicacy and Strength of Lace: Letters between Leslie Marmon Silko and J. W.* (1986)

BIBLIOGRAPHY: Saunders, W. S., *J. W.: An Introduction* (1979); Smith, D., ed., *The Pure Clear Word: Essays on the Poetry of J. W.* (1982); Mazzaro, J., "Dark Water: J. W.'s Early Poetry," *CentR*, 27 (1983): 135–55; Graves, M., "Crisis in the Career of J. W.," *HC*, 22, 5 (1985): 1–9; Blakely, R., "Form and Meaning in the Poetry of J. W.," *SDR*, 25, 2 (1987): 20–30; Dougherty, D. C., *J. W.* (1987); Lammon, M. D., "Making Acquaintance: Second Hand Notes on J. W.," *IowaR*, 17, 1 (1987): 55–71; Bly, R., "J. W. and the Slender Woman," *APR*, 17, 3 (1988): 29–33; Stein, K., *J. W.: The Poetry of a Grown Man: Constancy and Transition in the Work of J. W.* (1989); Stitt, P. and, and F. Graziano, eds., *J. W.: The Heart of the Light* (1990)

—ROBERT F. KIERNAN

WRIGHT, Judith

Australian poet, critic, short-story writer, environmentalist and autobiographer, b. 31 May 1915, Armidale

Daughter of pastoralists (ranchers), W. was educated at home by correspondence until, after the death of her mother, she went to boarding school in early adolescence. She studied literature at the University of Sydney but preferred her own self-directed, broadly-based reading program and did not graduate. Before marrying the

philosopher J. P. McKinney, she worked at a variety of clerical and administrative jobs. Her poetry is firmly rooted in the various regions in which she has lived: the New England, New South Wales, plateaux of her youth, the subtropical rain forests of Mount Tamborine, Queensland, after her marriage, and later the plains of the southern highlands near Braidwood, New South Wales. In recent years she has increasingly devoted her energies to the politics of conservation. She has seven times been awarded honary Doctors of Letters from Australian universities; has won many prestigious poetry awards in Australia and abroad, including the Queen's Gold Medal for Poetry in 1992, and been appointed a foundation fellow of the Australian Academy of the Humanities and an emeritus professorship of the Literature Board of the Arts Council of Australia, the premier Arts organization in the nation.

During the 1940s W., as a poet and critic in association with the nationalist literary journal *Meanjin Papers*, was in the vanguard of the movement that resulted in an upsurge of nationalist consciousness and self-confidence in Australian literature. Her critical work *Preoccupations in Australian Poetry* (1965) was a pioneering effort, its most important contribution to Australian letters being its intelligent and sensitive scrutiny of poets who at the time of publication were underrated, if not forgotten.

W.'s chief significance is as a philosophical poet. Her poetry, and the aesthetic informing it, owes much to the romantics and to T. S. ELIOT, but she departs from romantic aesthetics by disputing the primacy of the imagination. She is concerned to acknowledge that man is part of the natural process, its procreative rhythms, and so must inevitably die. However, she criticizes contemporary man for having alienated himself from nature, from his subconscious self, and also from his history. This awareness of a discrepancy between what man ideally is—a being who is an integral part of nature—and what he actually is—a fractured, disinherited soul—leads her to focus on her own emotional ambivalence, and, intellectually, into exploring paradoxes. She is aware of the ways in which, through words, the mind creates inner and outer realities, but in the process interposes linguistic structures between the mind and nature. In part, she attributes the fact that Australians are alienated from the land to the inadequacy of the language and art available to depict it, and sets herself the mission to find words and poetic forms to assist the reconciliation between art and nature, man and earth.

In her early poetry, notably *The Moving Image* (1946) and *Woman to Man* (1949), although she is aware of darker aspects of the paradoxes outlined above, she focuses on the unity existing between the mind and nature, and the exhilaration arising from it, seeing love as an essentially creative and procreative force that can do much to alleviate the pain of living. In later work, however, especially *The Two Fires* (1955), about Hiroshima, she reassesses her attitude toward love and takes up a more pessimistic stance about man's power to destroy the race, and even the cycles of nature. At this point, the solutions she had offered earlier—the ideal of renouncing self and immersing oneself in the cycles of nature—no longer seem applicable. The death of her husband in 1966 reinforced her sense of the vulnerability of love and the impersonal cruelty of the natural process. Hence, one finds a development in her poetry of a more realistic appraisal of the costs of existing within time. As she has become more despairing about man's impact on the environment, her poetry has become more direct and prosaic; occasionally, she expressed doubts and reservations about the failure of poetry to deal with pressing ecological problems.

W. is conscious of writing as a woman, and some of her most anthologized lyrics concern motherhood, seeing it as analogous to the creative forces within nature. However, her views do not substantially question traditional male and female roles. In later collections, such as *The Other Half* (1966) and *Alive: Poems 1971-72* (1973), her poems often take ordinary domestic incidents as the starting point for philosophical analysis, though on occasion, the subject matter is inflated and carries its import uneasily.

Consistent with her concern for the welfare of the environment and its original inhabitants in Australia, she has for many decades been a political activist and thinker. Her revision of an earlier colonialist history of her family, *The Generations of Men* (1959), from a postcolonial perspective and in the light of further research, was published as *The Cry for the Dead* (1981).

W.'s contribution to Australian Literature is incontestable: she celebrated and documented the land at a time when it was unfashionable to do so; she was concerned to marry the indigenous with the mainstream English literary tradition; finally, her poetry, at its best, is technically expressive and demonstrates a high degree of craftsmanship.

FURTHER WORKS: *Australian Bird Poems* (1940); *The Gateway* (1953); *William Baylebridge and the Modern Problem* (1955); *Kings of the Dingoes* (1958); *The Generations of Men* (1959); *The Day the Mountains Played* (1960); *Australian Bird Poems* (1961); *Birds: Poems by J. W.* (1962); *Range the Mountains High* (1962); *Charles Harpur* (1963, rev. ed., 1977); *Country Towns* (1963); *Five Senses* (1963); *J. W.: Selection and Introduction by the Author* (1963); *Shaw Neilson* (1963); *City Sunrise* (1964); *The Nature of Love* (1966); *The Other Half* (1966); *The River and the Road* (1966); *Henry Lawson* (1967); *Birds* (1967 with Annette Macarthur-Onslow); *Poetry from Australia* (1969); *Witnesses of Spring: Unpublished Poems by Shaw Neilson* (1970); *Collected Poems, 1942-1970* (1971); *Because I Was Invited: Literary Criticism, Conservation and Education* (1975); *Half Dream* (1975); *Conservation: Choice or Compulsion?* (1975); *Fourth Quarter, and Other Poems* (1976); *Boundaries* (1976); *The Coral Battleground* (1977); *The Double Tree: Selected Poems, 1942-1976* (1978); *Reef, Rainforest, Mangroves, Man* (1980); *Journeys* (1982); *Phantom Dwelling* (1985); *Many Roads Meet Here: Qui Incontrano Molte Strad* (1985, trans. Marina Pelizzer); *Phantom Dwelling* (1985); *We Call for a Treaty* (1985); *Rainforest* (1987); *New Zealand After Nuclear War* (1987, with Wren Green and Tony Cairns); *A Human Pattern: Selected Poems* (1990); *Born of the Conquerers* (1991); *Magpie Summer* (1991); *Going on Talking* (1992); *J. W.: Collected Poems 1942-1985* (1994); *The Flame Tree* (1994)

BIBLIOGRAPHY: Thomson, A. K., ed., *Critical Essays on J. W.* (1968); Hope, A. D., *J. W.* (1975); Sturm, T., "Continuity and Development in J. W.," *Southerly*, 35, 2 (1975), 183-91; Walker, S., *The Poetry of J. W.: A Search for Unity* (1980); Dowling, D., "J. W.'s Delicate Balance," *ALS*, 9 (1980), 488-96; Walker, S., *The Poetry of J. W.: A Search for Unity* (1980); *Vanishing Edens: Responses to Australia in the Works of Mary Gilmore, J. W. and Dorothy Hewett* (1992); *Flame and Shadow: A Study of J.W.'s Poetry* (1996); Lucas, R., and McCredden, L., *Bridgings: Readings in Australian Women's Poetry* (1996); Brady, V., *South of My Days: A Biography of J. W.* (1998)

—FRANCES DEVLIN GLASS

WRIGHT, Richard

American novelist, essayist, poet, dramatist, and short–story writer, b. 4 Sept. 1908, near Natchez, Miss.; d. 28 Nov. 1960, Paris, France

W. was the son of an illiterate sharecropper father and a schoolteacher mother. His father abandoned the family, and his mother fell ill, so W. was raised by his maternal grandmother, a strict Seventh Day Adventist. Although a bright student, he dropped out of school after the ninth grade, moving to Memphis and then to Chicago. W. educated himself, especially in sociology, psychology, and literature. In Chicago, WPA projects and the Communist–affiliated John Reed Club encouraged his literary development. In 1932 he joined the Communist Party and wrote his early poetry, essays, and stories for several leftist publications, among them *New Masses*. His WPA project became *12 Million Black Voices* (1941), a Marxist analysis of the American class struggle.

The first of three breakthroughs to a large mainstream American audience came with the publication of a collection of four short stories, *Uncle Tom's Children* (1938), which contained "Big Boy Leaves Home," "Down by the Riverside," "Long Black Song," and "Fire and Cloud." A second edition (1940) added a fifth story, "Bright and Morning Star," and as a preface, the autobiographical essay "The Ethics of Living Jim Crow." All these stories have as their theme the maturation of a black man or woman struggling to move from childlike naïveté to ripened militancy in the segregationist South. The writing is tightly controlled, poetic, and effective in eliciting audience sympathy for the children victimized by racist terror.

W.'s second breakthrough was *Native Son* (1940), the most widely read of his novels. The book received wide critical acclaim and was compared with John STEINBECK's *The Grapes of Wrath* and Theodore DREISER's *An American Tragedy* for its impressive naturalistic power. Bigger Thomas, the protagonist, is a black youth living in a slum on the South Side of Chicago. He awakens to the sight of a large rat. With fear, disgust, and hatred, he crushes that symbol of his continuing enslavement. The same emotions make it impossible for him to function as a rational human being. In prison awaiting execution for murder, he himself is a rat to be crushed as a menace to the society that produced him. Two thirds of *Native Son* is excellent narrative; but from the point at which Bigger Thomas is captured, the novel bogs down in long, undramatic passages of cause-and-effect analysis preparatory to and including a courtroom trial.

Native Son was made into a play, opening on Broadway on March 25, 1941, with Canada Lee as Bigger Thomas (the play, coauthored by W. and Paul Green [1894–1981], was published in 1941). In 1951 a poorly financed film version of *Native Son* appeared, with W. himself playing the lead.

The third breakthrough came with the autobiography *Black Boy, A Record of Childhood and Youth* (1945), which captures the pain and fear, pleasures and hopes, innocence and growth of W. toward an uncertain adulthood. Like the stories in *Uncle Tom's Children*, especially "Big Boy Leaves Home," *Black Boy* shows the forces at work to cut short the pleasures of childhood.

Another work of the early 1940s, the novella "The Man Who Lived Underground" (first published in the anthology *Cross Section 1944* [1944], edited by Edwin Seaver, and later included in W.'s *Eight Men* [1961]), may well be his best work. The narrative is swift and compelling, uninterrupted by polemics. Its theme of invisibility and self-discovery are provocatively presented.

Although W. had moved to New York in 1937 and had become the Harlem editor for the *The Daily Worker*, his patience with Communist Party discipline wore thin, especially after reviews in the Communist press of *Native Son* took it to task for ideological "faults." He broke with the Party in 1942, going public in 1944 in a widely publicized essay, "I Tried to Be a Communist" (published in *Atlantic Monthly* and later included in Richard Crossman's *The God That Failed*, 1949), but he continued to write from a Marxist perspective the rest of his life.

W. visited France in 1946 at the invitation of Gertrude STEIN and others. There he saw the opportunity for working as an artist free from American racial prejudice. In 1947 he moved his family to Paris, where he developed friendships with Jean-Paul Sartre and Simone de Beauvoir, among others. He manifested increasing interest in the problems of poor African and Asian countries emerging from colonial rule.

Until his death W. lived and wrote mainly in Paris. His next published novel, *The Outsider* (1953), reveals a weakening of his narrative power; excessive EXISTENTIALIST intellectualizing and polemics overwhelm the story. With the novel *The Long Dream* (1958), W. partially recovered the power and eloquence of *Uncle Tom's Children* and *Black Boy*. The subject is the growth and psychology of a black youth (Fishbelly) in racist Mississippi. W. suggests that Fishbelly's emotional maturation would ultimately depend on his leaving America.

W. regarded himself as an elder statesman for a younger generation for American blacks: writers, artists, community leaders, and students. He established close relationships with black African and West Indian intellectuals, some of whom wrote for *Présence africaine*, the influential African journal published in Paris. Among his contacts were the African statesmen Kwame Nkrumah of Ghana and Léopold Sédar SENGHOR of Senegal. They in turn influenced his writing such journalistic works as *Black Power* (1954), a product of his 1953 trip to Ghana, then the British colony Gold Coast. W. warned of the dangers of tribalism and—following the thinking of his West Indian historian friend George Padmore (1903–1959), author of *Pan-Africanism or Communism?* (1956), and the American W. E. B. DUBOIS (1868–1963)—envisioned a Union of African States, a form of pan–Africanism.

Because of his activities, American intelligence agents followed his movements and periodically harassed him. Much of this experience is described in an unpublished novel, *Island of Hallucination*, a sequel to *The Long Dream*.

W. traveled more and more to lecture, observe, and report. *The Color Curtain* (1956), which was first published in French in 1955, reported from Indonesia the results of the Bandung Conference, a 1955 meeting of Third World nations to discuss racism and colonialism. *White Man, Listen!* (1957), four essays delivered as lectures in many western European cities, warns of the catastrophe that could result from the economic deprivation and continued denial of human rights of colonial and Third World peoples.

One of W.'s best travel books is *Pagan Spain* (1957), the result of trips in 1954 and 1955. Here he quotes from a fascist catechism, comments upon religious rituals that remind him of the Ku Klux Klan, and notes the oppression that makes Franco's Spain seem like Jim Crow Mississippi.

W.'s reputation is firmly established. He is now remembered as a prophet of racial turbulence, a master at describing individuals

Richard Wright

psychologically struggling against authority, and a skillful blender of poetic beauty with harsh reality.

FURTHER WORKS: *Savage Holiday* (1954); *Lawd Today* (1963); *American Hunger* (1977)

BIBLIOGRAPHY: Webb, C., *R. W.: A Biography* (1968); Margolies, E., *The Art of R. W.* (1969); McCall, D., *The Example of R. W.* (1969); Kinnamon, K., *The Emergence of R. W.: A Study in Literature and Society* (1972); Ray, D., and Farnsworth, R. M., eds., *R. W.: Impressions and Perspectives* (1973); Bakish, D., *R. W.* (1973); Fabre, M., *The Unfinished Quest of R. W.* (1973); Reilly, J. M., ed., *R. W.: The Critical Reception* (1978); Gayle, A., *R. W.: Ordeal of a Native Son* (1980); Hakutani, Y., ed., *Critical Essays on R. W.* (1982)

—DAVID BAKISH

WYSPIAŃSKI, Stanisław

Polish dramatist and poet, b. 15 Jan. 1869, Cracow; d. 28 Nov. 1907, Cracow

W.'s childhood was spent in the ambience of the workshop of his sculptor father. The living statues with which he peopled his plays may well have been born of these early impressions. Another powerful influence on W.'s talent was Cracow, the museum city, the repository of Polish history and its "New Athens," center of Polish arts and literature of the period. W. received his secondary education there, and later attended the Cracow School of Arts. In 1890 he went abroad; he traveled in Italy and Germany, visiting art galleries, and spent several years painting in Paris.

W. was an artist par excellence, a man of exceptional versatility. A professional painter—his stained-glass windows in the church of the Franciscan Fathers in Cracow and his portraits are famous—a lyric poet of renown, a connoisseur of music (he was a great admirer of Richard Wagner) and graphic arts, he put all these talents to the service of his greatest among them—playwriting. For W., theater was not a place of entertainment but a temple of art where, as its priest, he served as set designer, stage director, and, of course, playwright.

Well versed in the classics, widely traveled and well read in world literature, very active in the intellectual and artistic circles of Cracow, W. was one of the most distinguished representatives of Young Poland, the Polish SYMBOLIST movement, and a precursor of the contemporary theater. His theatrical art presents a rare blend of elements of classicism, romanticism, and symbolism. His theatrical style shows an affinity to that of Maurice MAETERLINCK, foreshadows that of Bertolt BRECHT, and was a harbinger of EXPRESSIONISM. While W.'s originality in his interpretation of and attitudes toward these various trends is unquestionable, he shared the common concern of Polish artists and writers of all periods in the theme of Poland: her past, present, and future. All the numerous works he produced during his short creative life (barely nine years) are in some way connected with that theme.

Thus, in *Wyzwolenie* (1903; deliverance) W. attacks Polish romanticism in the person of its bard, Adam Mickiewicz (1798–1855), accusing him of adversely influencing, through the mystique of a glorious past, the nation's present-day participation in its own political future. Nevertheless, two of W.'s best-known dramas, *Warszawianka* (1898; battle song of insurgent Warsaw) and *Noc listopadowa* (1904; November night) deal with an important event of the past, the fateful uprising of 1830–31; and several, notably *Bolesław Śmiały* (1903; Boleslav the Bold), are set in medieval Poland.

The world of antiquity is represented in W.'s works by the frequent appearances of pagan deities among mortals even in his plays with modern settings, and by a cycle of Greek dramas. Of these, *Powrót Odyssa* (1904; *The Return of Odysseus*, 1966) is especially distinguished by the artistry of its construction, the somber intensity of atmosphere, and by its message: humans are helpless toys of a blind fate. W. does not strictly adhere to the Homeric version of the story. His Odysseus is a killer, a restless, aimless wanderer, a link in the chain of a dynastic curse of violence and crime, between his father, whom he longs and fears to murder, and his son, whom he dares not love. Yet Odysseus is only the man he is fated to be, and he accepts himself, while loathing his deeds, and his destiny, with bitter and dignified courage.

The tragic and heroic spirit permeates W.'s entire theatrical oeuvre. His protagonists are kings, warriors, achievers of heroic

deeds—unless, as in W.'s most famous play, *Wesele* (1901; the wedding), they are shown instead to be mired in empty talk and political apathy, and thus serve as the poet's bitter indictment of his contemporaries' present. *Wesele*, justifying W.'s claim to fame as the founder of modern Polish theater, combines the technique of a medieval allegorical play with both the European theater of marionettes and the *szopka*, the Polish nativity puppet show, performed in villages at Christmastime. It is a mixture of political satire and fantasy, introducing side by side with fictional personages a group of symbolic characters, listed as "dramatis personae," who are materialized dreams of the "real" members of the wedding—an actual event W. himself had attended. Realistic settings (a peasant hut) and language (deliberately crude but powerful verse), a musical background, and skillful stage lighting create a pervasively weird atmosphere. This atmosphere and the accompanying sense of tragedy became W.'s trademark. They are heightened by the absence of plots, which are replaced by separate scenes loosely connected by the presence of the protagonists. In *Noc listopadowa* and *Akropolis* (1904; Acropolis) there is no real action at all, only an ambience of unreality and dread created by background music and the presence of statues, or figures in tapestries, come to life. Like Maeterlinck, W. tended to let events take place offstage, as in *Warszawianka*, where the onstage "action" consists of anxious waiting for and finally grieving at the news of the outcome of the insurrection's decisive battle.

True to the spirit of Young Poland's "decadence," W. was a pessimist, and death hovers over all his plays as it did over his own span of life, shortened by incurable disease. The struggle against inexorable fate by his heroes—be they mighty kings, valiant insurgents, or humble villagers—end in the spirit of the classical tragedy, in defeat. Yet in spite of its macabre aspects, his theater is not depressing. It derives vigor from the same faith in the final triumph of human will and genius that led the dying W. to assert in a poem that on his bier lies only a body, while the spirit is rising in a pillar of flames.

FURTHER WORKS: *Legenda* (1898); *Meleager* (1889; *Meleager*, 1933); *Protesilaus i Laodamia* (1899; *Protesilaus and Laodamia*, 1933); *Klątwa* (1899); *Kazimierz Wielki* (1899); *Lelewel* (1899); *Legion* (1900); *Achilleis* (1903); *Skałka* (1907); *Sędziowie* (1907); *Dzieła zebrane* (16 vols., 1958–1969)

BIBLIOGRAPHY: Srebrny, S., "S.W.," *SlavonicR*, 2 (1923): 359–80; Borowy, W., "S.W." *SlavonicR*, 11 (1933): 617–30; Rosenthal, B., *Heinrich von Kleist and S. W.* (1938); Backvis, C., *Le dramaturge S. W.* (1952); Clarke, H., Introduction to *The Return of Odysseus* (1966): vii–xxviii; Miłosz, C., *The History of Polish Literature* (1969): 351–58; Pruska-Munk, M., "W.'s *The Wedding* and Witkiewicz's *The Shoemakers*: From Polish to Universal Question," *PolR*, 22, 4 (1977): 40–44; Krzyżanowski, J., *A History of Polish Literature* (1978): 501–12

—XENIA GASIOROWSKA

X

XENOPOULOS, Ghrighorios

Greek short-story writer, novelist, dramatist, journalist, critic, and editor, b. 9 Dec. 1867, Constantinople, Ottoman Empire (now Istanbul, Turkey); d. 14 Jan. 1951, Athens

X.'s family came from the Ionian island of Zakinthos (Zante); he grew up there and learned the Italianate islanders' dialect and manners, with which he colored many of his stories and novels, including the two sentimental best sellers, *Stella Violandi* (1901; Stella Violandi) and *O kokkinos vrahos* (1905; *Red Rock*, 1955). In 1883 X. moved to Athens, studied mathematics at the university, began publishing fiction, belonged briefly, in 1890, to the Socialist Party, but eventually established himself as a successful professional man of letters.

Many of X.'s novels first appeared as serials in newspapers. Later, X. wrote a fictionalized reminiscence of his early years in his best novel, the semiautobiographical *Plousii ke ftohi* (1919; rich and poor). Unlike X., however, the naïve but lovable hero, Popos Dhaghatoras, dies in poverty, a political martyr. X. himself was politically moderate, and his literary ambitions were tempered by the simpler, more conservative tastes of the wide readership on whom he depended for a living. Many of these readers had developed an affection for X. by reading, when young his exhortations to patriotism, honesty, and hard work in the children's magazine *I dhiaplasis ton pedhon*, which he edited from 1894 until his death. X. capped his career as a leading prose writer by founding, in 1927, the literary magazine *Nea estia*, which is still published today. He was elected to the Academy of Athens in 1931.

As a novelist, X. was the Green Zola; as a dramatist, the Greek Ibsen. Like the works of Zola and Ibsen, X.'s fiction and drama were naturalistic. But unlike Zola, X. excelled at describing bourgeois life, particularly that of rapidly expanding Athens. And unlike Ibsen, X. skimmed the surface of his characters' psyches, satisfied often with pure genre pictures of, say, genteel girls, austere fathers, or womanizing tycoons. Unlike Zola, he did not propound elaborate social theories; unlike Ibsen, he softened the hardships of his characters through familial affection and human kindness.

The most frequently revived of X.'s plays is *To mistiko tis knotessas Valerenas* (1904; the secret of Countess Valerena). In this well-crafted drama about an elderly, strong-well-crafted drama about an elderly, strongwilled noblewoman, X. illustrated his favorite theme of the conflict between traditional social ideals and the practical compromises of modern life.

X. should also be remembered as the first important critic to recognize the merits of C. P. CAVAFY, whose work he analyzed in the essay "Enas piitis" (1903; a poet), at a time when Cavafy's genius was quite unknown.

X. was a writer always of technical proficiency, frequently of social insight, and sometimes of literary greatness. He helped shape modern Greek literature by breaking from the old, provincial themes and turning to new, urban ones. By writing, in his mature works, a literate demotic Greek, he helped legitimize *kathomiloumeni*, the mixture of purist and demotic Greek that has become the living language of contemporary Greece.

FURTHER WORKS: *Anthropos tou kosmou* (1886); *Nikolas Sigalos* (1890); *Margharita Stefa* (1893); *I mitryia* (1897); *Dhiiyimata* (3 vols., 1901–1907); *O kakos dhromos* (1908); *Fotini Sandri* (1908); *I Afrodhiti* (1913–1914); *I timi tou adhelfou* (1915); *Mistiki arravones* (1915–1916); *I trimorfi yineka* (1917); *Laoura* (1917); *O kosmos ki' o Kosmas* (1919); *Petries ston Ilio* (1919); *O polemos* (1919); *Timii ke atimi* (1921–1922); *Anadhiomeni* (1923); *Tiheri ke atihi* (1924); *O katiforos* (1926); *Teresa Varma-Dhakosta* (1926); *Anamesa se tris yinekes* (1930); *Righina Leza* (1935–1936); *Athanasia* (1945); *Thion oniron* (1951; "Divine Dream," 1969); *Apanda: Theatron* (4 vols., 1945); *Apanda: Pezografia* (11 vols., 1958–1971). FURTHER WORKS IN ENGLISH: *The Downfall: A Novel* (1992); *The Three-Sight Woman: A Novel* (1992)

BIBLIOGRAPHY: Dimaras, K., *A History of Modern Greek Literature* (1972): 438–41; Politis, L., *A History of Modern Greek Literature* (1973): 175–78

—EDWARD PHINNEY

XHOSA LITERATURE
See under South African Literature

XI XI

(also romanized as Hsi Hsi; pseud of Zhang Yan) Chinese novelist, short-story writer, and essayist, b. 7 Oct. 1938, Shanghai

X., of Cantonese extraction, moved with her family from Shanghai to Hong Kong in 1950, shortly after the Chinese Communist Party took over mainland China. In 1958 she qualified as a primary school teacher and embarked on a twenty-year teaching career, during which she gave expression to her creativity. Besides poetry, fiction, and essays, she wrote film scripts in the 1960s, and was a film and art critic and newspaper columnist. She was editor of two of Hong Kong's most important literary magazines: *Damuzhi zhoubao* in 1975-77 and *Suye wenxue* in 1981-84. X. took early retirement from teaching in 1979 to pursue a full-time literary career. She was diagnosed with breast cancer in 1989, for which she underwent surgery, chemotherapy, and radiotherapy. Her detailed account of this experience, *Aidao rufang* (1992; Elegy for a Breast), was the first Chinese work that dealt with cancer in a literary manner.

The work that first won X. recognition locally was "Ma-li-ya" (1965; "Maria," 1986). This story of a Catholic nun and a young Corsican mercenary captured by the revolutionary soldiers in 1960s Congo in many ways typifies X.'s short stories: unusual—sometimes exotic—subject matter, an innovative mode of narration, and a pervasive but unobtrusive sense of compassion. One of her central concerns is the exploration of identity and sense of belonging, with many of the protagonists in her fiction being culturally and/or geographically displaced or marginalized people.

Wo cheng (1974; *My City: A Hong Kong Story*, 1993) was X.'s first full-length novel and arguably the one most representative of her innovative spirit. Her interest in MAGIC REALISM and SURRE-ALIST art plays an important part in the conception of many of the scenes in this novel. However, the most important innovation is linguistic: in this work she breaks the taboo that excludes Canton-ese vocabulary and syntax from standard written Chinese, and weaves different linguistic registers to form a deceptively childlike narrative rich in local Hong Kong colors. In this sense *Wo cheng* is a landmark not only in X.'s literary career, but also in the history of Hong Kong literature.

The work of short fiction that brought X. fame and a growing readership outside of Hong Kong was "Xiang wo zheyang de yige nuzi" (1982; "A Girl like Me," 1986), which won Taiwan's prestigious *United Daily* award. "Ganmao" (1982; "The Cold," 1986), written with a lyricism evocative of classical Chinese literature, is equally well known. Although she does not care for linguistic purity or refinement for its own sake, X. demonstrates in these stories that she has a surer grasp of the refined and lyrical style than the average Chinese writer.

Between 1982 and 1996 X. wrote three short stories and one novel known collectively as the "Feitu zhen" (Fertile Town) series: "Feitu zhen de gushi" (1982; "The Story of Fertile Town," 1997), "Zhen zhou" (1885; "Town Curse"), "Fei tu zhen huilan ji" (1986; "The Fertile Town Chalk Circle," 1997), and *Fei zhan* (1996; Flying Carpet). Three other stories thematically related to the series were also written in the same period: "Fucheng zhiyi" (1986; "Marvels of a Floating City," 1997), "Mali gean" (1986; "The Case of Mary," 1998), and "Yuzhou qiqu lu buyi" (1988; "Delights of the Universe: a Supplement"). Conceived and written during the prolonged Sino-British negotiations over the return of Hong Kong to Chinese sovereignty, this fiction series can be described as the literary chronicle of the mood of Hong Kong during those years of uncertainty. Through fantastic and fablelike narratives, the short stories explore issues of identity, cultural roots and self-determina-tion, while the novel *Fei zhan* is a bold attempt to trace Hong Kong's rich and diverse cultural heritage from early colonial days to the present.

X. is commonly recognized as Hong Kong's leading writer. Although she is remarkably versatile and covers most genres, she will be best remembered for her works of fiction. One of her major contributions is the sense of humor and fun that she brings to contemporary Chinese literature.

FURTHER WORKS: *Meili dasha* (1990); *Houniao* (1991). FUR-THER WORKS IN ENGLISH: *A Girl Like Me and Other Stories* (1986); *Marvels of a Floating City* (1997)

BIBLIOGRAPHY: Ling Chung, "Perspectives and Spatiality in the Fiction of Three Hong Kong Writers," in Duke, M. S., ed., *Chinese Women Writers* (1989): 217-35

—EVA HUNG

Y

YACINE, Kateb

See Kateb Yacine

YAKUT LITERATURE

The Yakuts are a Siberian Turkic people of the Soviet Union. The structure of the Yakut language is unmistakably Turkic, but its phonology and vocabulary differ considerably from the mainstream of Turkic languages, since they were subject to the influence of Mongolian and Tungusic languages as well. Russians early came in contact with Yakuts as they extended their trade and missions across northern Siberia; thus, the city of Yakutsk dates from 1639. In the 19th and early 20th cs., when Russian intellectuals were exiled to Siberia, some of them came to Yakut territory, where Lenin spent time (he took his pseudonym from the Lena River, which flows through the region). Some of these people investigated ethnography and linguistics; we owe to these early researchers much information about Yakut language and literature.

Before the introduction of writing around the turn of the century, when scholars adapted the Cyrillic alphabet to the language, there was only oral literature. In addition to the usual sort of tales, stories, fables, riddles, and proverbs, Yakut literature has epics and sagas peopled by heroes, monsters, fair damsels, and fairy goddesses. Many of these elements are shared with other Turkic and Siberian epics. After the advent of literacy, some of these were written down in Yakut, as were biblical translations. Consequently, a certain amount of native material was available at the time of the revolution in 1917. Because of policies current at that time, Yakut began to be written in the Latin alphabet, but in 1930, during the general changeover for most Soviet peoples, the Cyrillic alphabet was reintroduced.

Nonfolkloric literature in Yakut began around the time of the 1905 revolution. The works of Alexey Yeliseevich Kulakovsky (1877–1926), Anempodist Ivanovich Sofronov (1886–1935), and Nikolay Denisovich Neustroev (1895–1929) are important. Kulakovsky was the earliest literary figure; he was an ethnographer of Yakut culture as well as a poet. Sofronov, one of the founders of Yakut literature, was a poet, prose writer, and dramatist; after the revolution he became an adherent of socialism and founded the Yakut national theater. Neustroev wrote tales, sketches, and dramas. All three showed the prerevolutionary way of life of the Yakuts, the harshness of their customs, the conditions of tsarist colonialism, and the dominance of feudal-patriarchal relations. Before 1917, however, their social criticism was limited.

In the Soviet period, after the development of an educational system and the extension of literacy, there began a literature of SOCIALIST REALISM, embracing poetry, fiction, drama, and the essay. The founder of Soviet Yakut literature was Bylatan Ölöksüöyebis (Platon Alexeevich) Oyunsky (pseud. of P. A. Sleptsov, 1893–1939), a poet, dramatist, and writer of tales and stories; he was a social activist. His most important work, *Kyhyl oyuun* (1917–25; the red shaman), a long dramatic poem in praise of the revolution, drew on symbols derived from folklore. Oyunsky nonetheless was the first poet to depict the new life of the people and thus one of the prime movers behind modern Yakut literature. Ellyay (pseud. of Serafim Aramaanabys Kulaaskar [Serafim Romanovich Kulachikov], b. 1904) is the most important Yakut poet; prolific and wide-ranging, he has strongly influenced the development of Yakut verse.

Künde (pseud. of Alexey Andreevich Ivanov, 1898–1934) depicted the early years of the revolution in one of his plays. His collection of verse *Kyyhar tungat* (1926; the scarlet glow) praised the collectivization of agriculture. Kün Jiribine (pseud. of S. Savin, 1903–1970) wrote "fables" satirizing "class enemies." In the prewar years of the Five-Year Plans, some plays and poems described the mass entry of the Yakut peasantry into the collective farms. *Revolyutsia uolattara* (1936; sons of the revolution) by Erilik Eristin (pseud. of Semyon Stepanovich Yakovlev, 1892–1942) is typical of the long tales of the period glorifying the Soviet people.

A number of works focused on the events of World War II: Eristin's novel *Markychaan ychchattara* (1942; the youth of Marykchaan) is an outstanding example. One of the most important novels in Yakut literature is *Saasky kem* (1944; springtime) by Amma Achchygyya (pseud. of Nyukulay Jögyörebis Muordinap [Nikolay Yegorovich Mordinov], b. 1906), which deals with Yakut life from 1910 to the 1930s.

In the postwar period many poetic works appeared. Prominent poets have been Leonid Andreevich Popov (b. 1919), Sergey Stepanovich Vasiliev-Borogonsky (b. 1907), and the older Mikhail Nikolaevich Timofeev-Tery-oshkin (1883–1957).

BIBLIOGRAPHY: Krueger, J. R., *Yakut Manual* (1962); Okladnikov, A. P. and H. Michael, ed., *Yakutia before Its Incorporation into the Russian State*, (1970); Shoolbraid, G. M. H., *The Oral Epic of Siberia and Central Asia*, (1975)

—JOHN R. KRUEGER

YÁÑEZ, Agustín

Mexican novelist, short-story writer, biographer, and critic, b. 4 May 1904, Guadalajara, d. 17 Jan. 1980, Mexico City

Y. combined an intense political career with prolific literary activity. Born into a middle-class family, he began his career as an educator while still a student. He earned the Master of Philosophy degree from the National University of Mexico in 1935 and eventually became one of the most prestigious professors there. In 1952 he became one of the sixteen Mexicans who constitute the National College, the highest honor the Mexican Republic bestows. Also impressive are his journalistic undertakings: he served as director of three literary magazines and for various journals wrote numerous articles on literature, history, philosophy, ethics, psychology, politics, and economics. Y. also held prominent political and cultural posts that gave him the opportunity to observe and judge the economic, political, social, educational, governmental, and religious problems of Mexico.

A thorough study of leading European and American philosophers, writers, and social theoreticians imbued Y. with a forceful and ethical concept of society, which gave his works a pervading moral tone, with an underlying didactic purpose. More than any other writer he understood his native state of Jalisco and succeeded in creating characters who are singular types—profoundly human and therefore universal. His novels, like those of Balzac and PROUST, are not only literary works but also social and political documents.

Critics unanimously consider Y.'s masterpiece to be the ethnographic, psychologically realistic novel *Al filo del agua* (1947; *The Edge of the Storm*, 1963). The book inaugurated a new trend in Mexican fiction by utilizing techniques previously rarely encountered in Mexican fiction, such as interior monologue, flashback, double perspective, fragmentation of time and action, juxtaposition of the natural and supernatural, surrealism, and cinematic imagery. It depicts life in a hermetically closed village, presumably Yahualica, Jalisco, during the years 1909 and 1910, immediately preceding and after the outbreak of the Mexican Revolution. The inhabitants, mostly mestizos, are dominated by a rigid, Spanish-type Roman Catholic Church. Against a background of Spanish traditions mixed with indigenous influences, Y. paints a passionate and pessimistic picture of governmental and theocratic oppression and captures an atmosphere of fear, superstition, and sexual repression. A sustained musical and verbal rhythm, intense lyricism, a copious vocabulary, religious motifs, and a baroque quality distinguish Y.'s prose.

In *La creación* (1960; the creation), a novel that fuses the real and the fantastic, the protagonist devotes his life to raising national music to the level of universality. This novel suffers somewhat from Y.'s allowing his theories of artistic creation to interfere with the vividness of his characterization.

Ojerosa y pintada (1960; hollow-eyed and painted) is an incisive novel, reminiscent of Zola and Balzac, portraying the people of Mexico City—the ethical and unethical, the wealthy and destitute, the patriots and snobs. By having representatives from many segments of society ride in the same taxicab, Y. reveals the complex social structure of the city.

The luxuriant jungle, rich in natural resources, stretching along the Pacific coastline of Jalisco, is the setting of *La tierra pródiga* (1960; the lush land). Tensions and bloody conflicts erupt among the seven ruthless caciques struggling for control of the land. The powerful and charismatic Ricardo Guerra Victoria outmaneuvers the rival caciques and devises a scheme to exploit the area as a tourist paradise like Acapulco. His plans are quashed by the engineer Medellín, who symbolizes modern technology placed at the service of the government bureaucracy.

Las tierras flacas (1962; *The Lean Lands*, 1968) realistically depicts the persistence of myth, sorcery, witchcraft, and religion as organic aspects of a patriarchal society in the early 1920s, despite the impact of a complex industrial economy promoted by the centralized government. An ailing cacique rules tyrannically over a collection of ranches ironically named Tierra Santa (holy land). An illegitimate son of this cacique brings electricity, irrigation, and armed henchmen to the lean lands; the result is a conflict that ends apocalyptically. An ironic use of biblical and religious motifs and a dynamic use of animal imagery serve as major devices of characterization, and a remarkable profusion of proverbs enlivens and lends authenticity to the speech of the *rancheros* by introducing a poetic and aphoristic element into the dialogue.

Y. used modern fictional techniques to create a vast panorama essential to an interpretation of the Mexican ethos. He ranks among the foremost Spanish American writers.

FURTHER WORKS: *Espejismo de Juchitán* (1940); *Fray Bartolomé de las Casas: El conquistador conquistado* (1942); *Flor de juegos antiguos* (1942); *Genio y figuras de Guadalajara* (1942); *Pasión y convalescencia* (1943); *Don Juan va a tener un hijo* (1943); *Archipiélago de mujeres* (1943); *El contenido social de la literatura ibero-americana* (1944); *Fichas mexicanas* (1945); *Esta es mala suerte* (1945); *Alfonso Gutiérrez Hermosillo y algunos amigos* (1945); *El clima espiritual de Jalisco* (1945); *Melibea, Isolda y Alda en tierras cálidas* (1946); *Informes del estado de la Administración Púlica en Jalisco* (6 vols., 1954–1959); *Discursos por Jalisco* (1958); *Discursos por la Reforma* (1958); *Don Justo Sierra: Su vida, sus ideas y su obra* (1962); *La formación política* (1962); *Los sentidos del aire* (1964); *Tres cuentos* (1964); *Conciencia de la revolución* (1964); *Días de Bali* (1964); *Discursos al servicio de la educación pública* (6 vols., 1964–1970); *Obras escogidas* (1970); *Las vueltas del tiempo* (1973); *Por tierras de Nueva Galicia* (1975); *Santa Anna: Espectro de una sociedad* (1982)

BIBLIOGRAPHY: Schade, G. D., "Augury in *Al filo del agua*," *TSLL*, 2, 1 (1960): 78–87; Brushwood, J. S., *Mexico in Its Novel* (1966): 7–12, 45–48; Sommers, J., *After the Storm* (1968): 37–68, 184–92; Flasher, J., *México contemporáneo en las novelas de A. Y.* (1969); Van Conant, L. M., *A. Y.: Intérprete de la novela mexicana moderna* (1969); Langford, W. M., *The Mexican Novel Comes of Age*, (1971): 71–87; García, L., "El tema religioso en *Al filo del agua de A. Y.*," in Brown, L. C., ed., *Religion in Latin American Life and Literature* (1980): 233–40

—JOHN FLASHER

YANG Chiang

(also romanized as Yang Jiang; pseud. of Yang Chi-k'ang) Chinese dramatist, essayist, translator, and novelist, b. 17 July 1911, Beijing

Born to a father who worked for the early and unstable Republican (1911-49) government, Y. spent most of her childhood moving among major cities in eastern China before her family finally settled in Soochow (Suzhou), Kiangsu (Jiangsu) Province, during her teenage years. She attended Chen-hua (Zhenhua) Girls' Middle School in Soochow and graduated from Soochow University in 1932 with a B.A. in politics. After three years of graduate study in the Department of Foreign Languages at Tsinghua University in Peking (Beijing, then Pei-p'ing), Y. studied at Oxford University for two years, earning an M. Phil. in literature in 1937, and for one year at the University of Paris. Y. returned to China in 1938 and lived in Shanghai until 1949, when she moved to Peking to teach Spanish at Tsinghua University. In 1953 Y. became a research fellow at the Institute of Foreign Literature, first at the Chinese Academy of Sciences, and later of the Chinese Academy of Social Sciences, a position she retains to this day. She has lived in Peking continuously since 1949, with the exception of two years (1970-72) during the Cultural Revolution, when she was labeled a "bourgeois scholar" and transferred to a cadre school in Honan (Henan) Province for "reeducation."

Y. first achieved literary notoriety for four modern stage plays written between 1942 and 1946, three of which were performed in Japanese-occupied Shanghai. Her two "comedies," *Ch'en-hsin ju-i* (1942; As You Desire) and *Nong-chen ch'eng-chia* (1943; The Cheat), are provocative meditations on the grim choices facing urban youth, especially women, during the middle years of the Republic. Her third play, a farce, was performed but never published, while her fourth, *Feng-hsu* (1946; *Windwept Blossoms*, 1983), is a tragedy focusing on the disillusionment of progressive urban youth caught in a love triangle in rural China. Her plays are all characterized by their focus on the psychological profiles of the main characters.

Y. has been best known as a scholar for her translations and literary criticism. Her most important translation, *T'ang Chi-ke-the* (1978), of Miguel de Cervantes's *Don Quixote*, occupied her for more than a decade, and in 1985 her efforts were recognized by Juan Carlos, King of Spain, who awarded her the Alfonso X "The Wise" Award for her contribution to the spread of Spanish culture. The second printing includes as its preface a sustained, diagrammatic discussion of the art of translation, "Shih-pai ti ching-yan: shih-t'an fan-i" (1979; The Experience of Defeat: An Essay on Translation). One of China's leading scholars of European literature, Y. has also written a number of widely read works of comparative literature. Her two main volumes of literary criticism, *Ch'un-ni chi* (1979; Spring Soil) and *Kuan-yü hsiao-shuo* (1986; In Regards to Fiction), include treatments of Cervantes, Jane Austin, Henry Fielding, Li Yu (1611-1680?), and Ts'ao Chan (d. 1763), focusing largely on literary aesthetics and form.

Y.'s most widely read works are a series of memoirs she began writing in the early 1980s. *Kan-hsiao liu-chi* (1981; *Six Chapters of My Life "Downunder,"* 1984), a work loosely modeled on Shen Fu's (1763?-1808) well-known *Six Chapters from a Floating Life* (1960), focuses on her and her husband's cadre school life during the Cultural Revolution. It stands out among memoirs of this period for its refined use of allegory and its sustained attention to matters generally not considered political in nature. Unlike most Cultural Revolution memoirs, which give center stage to political struggle, violence, and personal betrayal, *Kan-hsiao liu-chi* focuses in great detail on such seemingly mundane tasks as digging a well, tending a vegetable plot, and befriending a stray dog. A second memoir written several years later similarly devotes considerable space to a detailed description of cleaning a women's lavatory. By highlighting the author's separation from her husband and the efforts and risks they took to see each other during these years, Y. also succeeds in turning *Kan-hsiao liu-chi* into a love story. Themes of love and friendship recur in many subsequent autobiographical and biographical essays on friends and family, which she has continued to publish into the 1990s. One of these works, *Chi Ch'ien Chung-shu yü Wei-ch'eng* (1987; Remembering Ch'ien Chung-shu and Fortress Besieged), a one-volume work containing two short accounts of her husband and the writing of his famous novel, was one of the most popular prose essay collections published in Chinese during the 1980s.

Hsi-tsao (1988; Taking a Bath), Y.'s only novel, returns to many of the themes treated earlier in her drama (and in a handful of short stories written before 1949), but also builds on the author's insights into the history of political campaigns during the People's Republic. The work is part love story and part fictionalization of how intellectuals responded to thought-reform and learned to perform public self-criticisms during the Three-Antis Campaign of 1951. As in her Cultural Revolution memoirs, Y. meticulously details the mundane context in which the political campaign unfolds, giving special attention to marital strife, extramarital affairs, and thwarted romance, while the campaign itself occupies less than a third of the novel. Though clearly a farce, *Taking a Bath* nonetheless offers an unflattering portrait of intellectuals, whom it depicts more often as perverts and hoarders of intellectual resources, than as virtuous scholars devoted to research. Ultimately, the novel seems less concerned with indicting the state and its use of political campaigns for destroying the lives of individual scholars than it is with suggesting how intellectuals destroy their own lives and the lives of their colleagues through personal politics.

Although most of Y.'s own creative work could be called "realist" in style, she nonetheless ranks among the most versatile of China's 20th-c. writers, having made important contributions to the development of modern Chinese drama, fiction, and prose. Through her translations and literary criticism, she has also been highly influential in shaping Chinese understandings of European literature. Her prose style stands out in particular for its precision and high degree of restraint (some no doubt find it too subtle), and it has won her an unusually wide readership for an academic writer. Y.'s fiction and drama are important for their sustained, serious treatment of romance, domestic life, and marital strife, and for suggesting how political events of a national magnitude are shaped by these more mundane aspects of daily life.

FURTHER WORKS: *Tao-ying chi* (1982); *Hui-i liang-p'ian* (1986); *Chiang-yin-ch'a* (1987); *Tsa-i yü tsa-kan* (1992); *Y. C. tsuo-p'in chi*, (3 vols., 1993)

BIBLIOGRAPHY: Gunn, E. M., Jr., *Unwelcome Muse: Chinese Literature in Shanghai and Peking, 1937-1945* (1980): 231-43; T'ian H. L., K. H. Ma, and K. Y. Ch'en, eds., *Ch'ien Chung-shu Y. C. yen-chiu tzu-liao chi* (1990): 511-672; *Y. C. tsuo-p'in chi*, (3 vols., 1993); Dooling, A. D., "In Search of Laughter: Y. J.'s [C.'s] Feminist Comedy," *MCL*, 8 (1994): 41-67

—MARK SWISLOCKI

YAVOROV, Peyo

(pseud. of Peyo Totev Kracholov) Bulgarian poet and dramatist, b. 13 Jan. 1878, Chirpan; d. 29 Oct. 1914, Sofia

In 1899 a provincial telegrapher submitted a poem about parted lovers, "Kaliopa" (Calliope), to the literary monthly *Misul*. Its editors Pencho SLAVEYKOV and Krustyo Krustev (1866–1919) christened him Y. and arranged for his transfer to Sofia. Y. espoused socialist-agrarian causes and supported the Macedonian independence movement. He fought with the Macedonian rebel Gotse Delchev against the Turks in the Pirin Mountains, but he became disillusioned after disputes with leaders of the rebellion and the death of Delchev in 1903.

Appointed head librarian of the National Library in 1904, with a leave of absence in 1906–7 to study poetry in France. Y. helped edit *Misul* from 1905 to 1907. He was dramaturge of the National Theater in Sofia from 1908 to 1913. Two tragedies then fatally scarred his life: the death first of his adored Mina, sister of fellow-writer Petko Todorov (1879–1916) in 1910, and then, in 1913, of Lora (Karavelova) the year after his marriage to her. Lora, upset by Y.'s alleged flirtations, shot and killed herself before his eyes. He then tried to take his own life but only partially blinded himself. A year later, however, broken and ostracized, he committed suicide.

In his early verse, in *Stikhotvorenia* (1901; 2nd ed., 1904; verses), Y. recorded the plight of Macedonian and Armenian refugees and of the peasantry in newly liberated Bulgaria. He writes, for instance, of the cataclysmic shattering of harvest hopes in "Gradushka" ("Hailstorm," 1951), while in "Chudak" (freak) he portrays himself as the alienated poet, a Bulgarian Lermontov. Only rarely, as in "Prolet" (spring), does he yield to pure lyrical delight in nature. Much more typical are the "Esenni motivi" (autumn motifs), with their haunting melancholy and mounting sense of despair.

Y. recorded the Macedonian conflict in his guerrilla diaries, *Khaydushki kopnenia* (1909; guerilla yearnings) and his short biography, *Gotse Delchev* (1904; Gotse Delchev). The Macedonian struggle also inspired "Khaydushki pesni" (1903; guerilla songs) in the folk style at which his revolutionary predecessor Khristo Botev (1848–1876) had excelled.

The poem "Nosht" (1901; night) marked the onset of the soul–searching crises of Y.'s last period. Supported by Slaveykov's preface to the second edition of his *Stikhotvorenia*, Y. in "Pesen na pesenta mi" (1906; my song's song) explicitly forsook his "causes" to concentrate on his own personal anguish and alienation. The fruits of this introspection, enriched by his special interest in French SYMBOLISM, are the poems in *Bezsunitsi* (1907; sleepless nights). The volume includes evocations of Sappho, Cleopatra, and Messalina as tragic heroines of antiquity and confirms Y. as a remarkable innovator in Bulgarian poetry, to which he brought great tragic content with a new flexibility and range of verse forms.

Y.'s two plays, *V polite na Vitosha* (1911; on the edges of Vitosha) and *Kogato grum udari* (1912; when thunder rolls), both somewhat autobiographical, were the first plays to depict the social life of Sofia. But drama was not his forte, perhaps because he could not detach himself from his own somewhat theatrical life. His fame rests on his poems, for their bitter, brilliant rendering of his concern for the pain of others and for their evocation of his own suffering and all-engulfing despair.

FURTHER WORKS: *Podir senkite na oblatsite* (1910); *Subrani suchineniya* (5 vols., 1959–1960)

BIBLIOGRAPHY: Pinto, V., ed., Introduction to *Bulgarian Prose and Verse* (1957): xxix–xxx; Moser, C. A., *A History of Bulgarian Literature 867–1944* (1972): 137–44

—VIVIAN PINTO

YEATS, William Butler

Irish poet, dramatist, and essayist, b. 13 June 1865, Dublin; d. 28 Jan. 1939, Cap Martin, France

Y. was the oldest of five children born into a middle-class Anglo-Irish Protestant family. His paternal grandfather, the Reverend William Butler Yeats (1806–1862) was a rector of the Church of Ireland, but a firm religious skepticism kept his father, the portrait painter John Butler Yeats (1839–1922), from entering the clergy. Y.'s later involvement with unorthodox spiritualism of all types steered a course between his grandfather's orthodoxy and his father's agnosticism. On his mother's side, Y. was descended from the Pollexfens and Middletons of Sligo, a family of merchants and shipowners whom he considered aristocratic. Because the elemental beauty of Sligo came to figure so prominently in Y.'s poetry, John Butler Yeats would later claim that by marrying Susan Pollexfen he "had given a tongue to the sea cliffs."

William Butler Yeats

Y.'s difficult childhood was divided between London, Dublin, and Sligo. In later years he associated London—where he spent much of his adult life—with all that was spiritually moribund in the modern world. Throughout his life, Sligo remained his favorite landscape, associated with a deep pastoral beauty. A solitary, moody child, he loved to wander the countryside, and to hear the traditional stories of the country people. His early formal education was irregular, although he later attended Erasmus Smith High School (1881–83) and the Metropolitan School of Art in Dublin (1884–86). He originally intended to become a painter, but soon recognized a deeper commitment to poetry.

Y. began in the 1880s and 1890s with three primary and wholly separate interests: a belief in cultural nationalism, an abiding interest in occult philosophy, and a devotion to a postromantic, SYMBOLIST aesthetic of literature. He spent much of his life trying to bring these diverse interests together.

John O'Leary (1830–1907), the old Fenian and guiding spirit of the Irish Renaissance, first directed Y. to the untapped resources of Irish folklore and saga literature. Thereafter, Y. vehemently retained his belief that art should be national, and he worked tirelessly toward establishing and renewing a national culture for Ireland. The movement gained momentum after the controversial political fall of the Irish leader Charles Stuart Parnell in 1891, and Y. placed himself at the center of the new cultural revival. He edited several collections of Irish folklore (*Fairy and Folk Tales of the Irish Peasantry*, 1888; *Irish Folk Tales*, 1892) and of earlier Irish fiction (*Stories from Carleton*, 1889; *Representative Irish*

Tales, 1891), published his own literary sketches of folk tradition (*The Celtic Twilight*, 1893), wrote a series of articles for American newspapers (later collected as *Letters to the New Island*, 1934), and helped found nationalist literary societies in London (1891) and Dublin (1892), all the while writing poems, stories, and plays based on traditional Irish materials. All of this work was meant to signal a new spiritual force coming into Irish culture.

Y. had a lifelong preoccupation with the occult, although it was tinged with a certain reluctant skepticism. Unable to believe in Christianity, but refusing to accept his father's philosophy of rationalism, he became deeply involved with heterodox religious movements, founding the Dublin Hermetic Society in 1885 and joining Madame Blavatsky's (1831–1891) Theosophical Society in 1887 and the Order of the Golden Dawn in 1890. He was intent on refuting Victorian materialism, and studied the antiscientific creeds of Theosophy, Rosicrucianism, Platonism, and Neoplatonism, as well as the mystical writings of Jakob Boehme (1575–1624) and Emanuel Swedenborg (1688–1772). These reenforced his belief in the supernatural and contributed to his own evolving symbolic system.

Y.'s interest in the occult conjoined with his symbolist aesthetics. He was personally influenced by William Morris (1834–1896) and Oscar Wilde (1854–1900) during a period when he was also helping to organize a group of young English writers—including Arthur Symons (1865–1945), Lionel Johnson (1867–1902), and Ernest Dowson (1867–1900)—into the Rhymers' Club. The group met regularly to discuss poetry, and Y. shared their fin-de-siècle belief in the sacred role of the artist and in "art for art's sake," ideas that derived from a blend of Walter Pater's (1839–1894) aestheticism and French symbolism. But Y. was also powerfully influenced by Shelley's poetics, Nietzsche's philosophy, and Blake's symbolism, collaborating on a three-volume edition of Blake's work with Edwin Ellis (1848–1918) in 1893. Y.'s fascination with dramatic theories of personality and philosophy, his boundless energy and enthusiasm, and his desire to write more directly out of his own people eventually led him to break away from a group he later named the "tragic generation."

In 1889 Y. fell in love with the beautiful, passionate nationalist, Maud Gonne, and the trouble of his life began. Under her influence he flirted with revolutionary politics, but ultimately his political ideas were aristocratic and authoritarian. Most importantly, he repeatedly and vainly proposed marriage, and a violent "barren passion" for her sweeps through his work until the end of his life. The crisis of his unrequited love affair came in 1903, when Maud Gonne abruptly married John MacBride. After MacBride was executed by the British for his role in the 1916 Easter Rebellion, Y. proposed—and was refused—one final time. Soon afterward, in 1917, he married Georgie Hyde-Lees, a young Englishwoman who shared his interest in the occult.

In 1897 Y. spent the first of many summers at Lady Gregory's (1852–1932) house at Coole Park. Together with Edward Martyn (1859–1923) and George MOORE they began a national theater movement that slowly evolved into the world-famous Abbey Theatre, founded in 1904 with the patronage of Annie Horniman (1860–1937). For many years Y. was deeply involved with the theater, writing and collaborating on his own verse plays, helping to produce the dramas of writers such as Sean O'CASEY and John Millington SYNGE, and steering a course between those political nationalists who wanted a strictly patriotic literature and those antinationalists who were against a specifically Irish theater. The many controversies, such as the riots over Synge's *The Playboy of the Western World* in 1907, eventually left Y. estranged from the popular theater, although he was again reconciled to his country after the abortive, heroic Easter Rebellion.

After 1917 the Yeatses divided their time between Dublin and an old Norman tower in western Ireland, Thoor Ballylee, which became one of his most substantial later symbols. Soon after they were married, Mrs. Yeats tried "automatic" writing; the messages they received from the "unknown instructors" so excited Y. that he began constructing a symbology, systematizing his philosophy into a cyclical theory of history and an antithetical theory of personality, and defining in detail the stages of the soul after death. This work resulted in the two versions of *A Vision* (1925, 1937). He became a senator when the Irish Free State was founded in 1922 and a year later was awarded the Nobel Prize for literature. But despite the happiness of his marriage and the birth of his two children, Y.'s last years were marked by a series of violent physical, emotional, and intellectual efforts at renewal. He railed against old age, espoused an aristocratic theory of Irish history and politics, and was tormented by the impending chaos of the modern world. Y.'s work continued to grow in power, energy, and stature until the end of his life.

Y. was first and foremost a poet. His first book, *The Wanderings of Oisin, and Other Poems* (1889), shows him combining a romantic, Pre-Raphaelite style with a self-consciously Irish subject matter. The ambitious title poem, which tells the story of Oisin's journey to three different Elysium worlds, represents Y.'s first extended use of Irish legendary materials. The poem also suggests a major theme of Y.'s early work: the continual desire to escape from the constraints of the real, time-bound world into a transcendental realm outside of time. The same theme animates his popular early works, "The Lake Isle of Innisfree" (1890) and the play *The Land of Heart's Desire* (1894). Similarly, Oisin's fairy-mistress Niamh—akin to the nameless fairy woman who appears in the short story "Dhoya" (1891)—is the archetype of the many dream goddesses who appear in Y.'s work.

Y.'s next book, *The Countess Kathleen. and Various Legends and Lyrics* (1892) shows him heightening the dramatic intensity of his work. *The Countess Cathleen* (the spelling was later changed), a poetic drama Y. began shortly after meeting Maud Gonne, tells the story of a countess who heroically sells her soul to demon-merchants in order to save her countrymen from starvation. Whereas Oisin's story is pre-Christian, *The Countess Cathleen* is a vaguely medieval retelling of the Faust legend and reflects Y.'s ambition to mingle his own ideas with the beliefs of Christian Ireland. In the lyric poems of the book, Y. establishes the primary symbol of the rose. In Irish poetry the rose had traditionally stood for Ireland itself, but Y. also uses it as a symbol of incorruptible spiritual beauty. In terms borrowed from the Order of the Golden Dawn, Y. established a "mystic marriage" between the rose, a female principle of eternal beauty, and the cross, a male principle of sacrifice. In his symbolist stories "The Adoration of the Magi" (1897) and "The Secret Rose" (1897) Y. also presented the rose as a symbol of a new change coming into the world.

Y.'s early work culminates in the stately, tapestry-like verse of *The Wind among the Reeds* (1899). The poems are evanescent and hermetic, and their highly cadenced, wavering rhythms create an incantatory tone of mystery. The book is animated by the symbolist doctrine of correspondences, the idea that all material things correspond to concepts in the disembodied, spiritual world. It is poetry of moods and distilled essences, whose indistinct images and evasive, shadowy symbols in a way represent a culmination of the aestheticism of the 1890s.

A new robustness entered Y.'s work in the 20th c. The deliberate reshaping of his style first began to manifest itself in *In the Seven Woods* (1904), was developed further in *The Green Helmet, and Other Poems* (1910), and was fully realized in *Responsibilities* (1914). In these works Y. developed a more passionate, earthy idiom and syntax. He was encouraged to seek a more direct language by writing prose and verse plays for the Abbey Theatre, and he tirelessly revised his work to bring it closer to actual speech. Further encouraged by Ezra POUND to become a *modern* poet, he wrote bitterly satirical poems about the Parnell controversy, the dispute over *The Playboy of the Western World*, and the fierce debates about a gallery for Hugh Lane's collection of French paintings. He was now a poet who could deal bitingly with contemporary events.

Y.'s poetry reached new heights in the four major volumes that constitute his central achievement: *The Wild Swans at Coole* (1919), *Michael Robartes and the Dancer* (1921), *The Tower* (1928), and *The Winding Stair, and Other Poems* (1933). The poems show an enormous growth both in scale and range, taking up Y.'s memorable themes of old age, the destruction of the Anglo-Irish Great Houses (and consequently of an aristocratic, 18th-c. world that he valued highly), and, beyond that, the rise and fall of entire civilizations. He was now a master elegist mourning the loss of a "soldier, scholar, horseman" in "In Memory of Major Robert Gregory" (1918); a powerful public poet commemorating the heroic, tragic sacrifice of the victims of the Easter Rebellion in "Easter, 1916" (1916); and a meditative poet reflecting on the natural transitoriness of life in "The Wild Swans at Coole" (1917). In these books Y. apprehended that all was approaching decay and ruin, both on a national scale ("Nineteen Hundred and Nineteen," 1919) and on an international one. "The Second Coming" (1920) tells of a world "whose centre cannot hold"; its final image of a "rough beast" that "slouches towards Bethlehem to be born" prophesies the destruction of our own civilization and the violent birth of a new god. In "Sailing to Byzantium" (1928) and "Byzantium" (1929) Y. also contrasted the approaching conflagration to the idealized, visionary world of Byzantium.

During this period Y. also used a series of poems—"Ego Dominus Tuus" (1915), "The Phases of the Moon" (1918), and "The Double Vision of Michael Robartes" (1919)—to expound the symbolic system he later described in *A Vision* (1925; rev. ed., 1937). These "texts for exposition," as Y. called this series of poems, establish his cyclical theory of history, which defines historical epochs in two-thousand-year cycles corresponding to the twenty-eight phases of the moon, reaffirm his dramatic concept of the Mask, and postulate an oppositional theory of personality, the idea that the self ("primary" man) always seeks to accommodate its opposite, an antiself ("antithetical" man) and thus discover its own true nature. Both Blake and Nietzsche influenced his belief that "contraries are positive" and that "consciousness is conflict."

In the face of what he believed was a universal destruction, Y. continued to celebrate a tragic gaiety and joy. His exemplary hero was Cuchulain, a reckless, passionate man questing for immortality. Over the years Y. wrote five plays in a variety of dramatic forms that show the Irish hero's character in action at five different points in his life: *On Baile's Strand* (1904), modeled on Jacobean drama; *The Green Helmet* (1910), written in the mode of epic farce; and *At the Hawk's Well* (1917), *The Only Jealousy of Emer* (1919), and *The Death of Cuchulain* (1939), all of which accommodate Irish mythology to the Japanese Nō drama of spirits. What binds these plays into a sequence is Cuchulain's tragic and joyous epic character.

Y.'s posthumously published *Last Poems and Plays* (1941) demonstrate his continued belief in the imperishable imagination. His last work has a reckless, exuberant quality—what "Lapis Lazuli" (1936) calls "gaiety transfiguring all that dread"—taking up old themes with renewed energy, forcefulness, and candor. In some of the volume's ballads and epigrams Y. continues to decry the degradation of the modern age, although perhaps the book's most important themes are love and death, love rejoicing in the face of death. In one of Y.'s greatest retrospective poems, "The Circus Animals' Desertion" (1938), he rejects his earlier "masterful images" and asks to lie down "in the foul ragand—bone shop of the heart." This is his last heroic quest to write a poetry behind the Mask that reveals the naked heart. The book's final poem, "Under Ben Bulben" (1938), is a last testament, a kind of elegy for himself reaffirming his visionary principles and setting out the fierce words to be carved on his gravestone: "Cast a cold eye/On life, on death;/ Horseman pass by."

Y. had the ability to remake continually both himself and his poetry. His work stands at the center of the romantic and modernist traditions, and he is arguably the most important poet writing in English in the 20th c. T. S. ELIOT called him "the greatest poet of our time—certainly the greatest in this language, and so far as I am able to judge, in any language."

FURTHER WORKS: *Mosada* (1886); *Poems* (1895); *The Shadowy Waters* (1900); *Cathleen ni Houlihan* (1902); *Where There Is Nothing* (1902); *The Hour-Glass, and Other Plays* (1903); *Ideas of Good and Evil* (1903); *The King's Threshold, and On Baile's Strand* (1904); *The Pot of Broth* (1904); *Stories of Red Hanrahan* (1904); *Poems, 1899–1905* (1906); *The Poetical Works* (2 vols., 1906–1907); *Deirdre* (1907); *Discoveries* (1907); *The Golden Helmet* (1908); *The Unicorn from the Stars* (1908, with Lady Gregory); *Poetry and Ireland* (1908, with Lionel Johnson); *Synge and the Ireland of His Time* (1911); *Plays for an Irish Theatre* (1911); *The Cutting of an Agate* (1912); *Poems Written in Discouragement* (1913); *Reveries over Childhood and Youth* (1915); *Per Amica Silentia Lunae* (1918); *Two Plays for Dancers* (1919); *Four Plays for Dancers* (1921); *Later Poems* (1922); *The Trembling of the Veil* (1922); *Plays and Controversies* (1923); *The Cat and the Moon, and Certain Poems* (1924); *Essays* (1924); *The Bounty of Sweden* (1925); *Early Poems and Stories* (1925); *Autobiographies* (1926); *October Blast* (1927); *The Death of Synge* (1928); *Fighting the Waves* (1929); *A Packet for Ezra Pound* (1929); *St. Patrick's Breast-Plate* (1929); *Stories of Michael Robartes and His Friends* (with *The Resurrection*, 1931); *Words for Music Perhaps* (1932); *Collected Poems* (1933); *The King of the Great Clocktower* (1934); *Wheels and Butterflies* (1934); *Collected Plays* (1934 enl. ed., 1952); *A Full Moon in March* (1935); *Dramatis Personae* (1935); *Modern Poetry* (1936); *Essays, 1931–1936* (1937); *The Home's Egg* (1938); *New Poems* (1938); *The Autobiography* (1938); *Last Poems and Two Plays* (1939); *On the Boiler* (1939); *Letters on Poetry to Dorothy Wellesley* (1940); *If I Were Four-and-Twenty* (1940); *Pages from a Diary* (1944); *Tribute to Thomas Davis* (1947); *The Poems* (2 vols., 1949); *The Collected Poems* (1950); *Diarmuid and Grania* (1951, with George Moore); *The Collected Plays* (1952); *W. B. Y. and T. S. Moore: Their Correspondence* (1953); *Letters to Katharine Tynan* (1953); *Letters* (1954); *The Variorum Edition of the Poems of W. B. Y.* (1957); *Mythologies* (1959); *Essays and Introductions* (1960); *Senate Speeches* (1960); *Explorations* (1962); *Selected Criticism* (1964); *The Variorum Edition of the Plays of W. B. Y.* (1966); *Autobiographies* (1966);

Uncollected Prose (2 vols., 1970, 1975); *Memoirs* (1972); *The Correspondence of Robert Bridges and W. B. Y.* (1977); *The Secret Rose: Stories by W. B. Y.—A Variorum Edition* (1981); *The Death of Cuchulain: Manuscript Materials Including the Author's Final Text* (1982)

BIBLIOGRAPHY: Ellis-Fermor, U., *The Irish Dramatic Movement* (1939); MacNeice, L., *The Poetry of W. B. Y.* (1941); Ure, P., *Towards a Mythology: Studies in the Poetry of W. B. Y.* (1946); Ellmann, R., *Y.: The Man and the Masks* (1948); Jeffares, N. A., *W. B. Y.: Man and Poet* (1949); Hall, J., and Steinmann, M., eds., *The Permanence of Y.* (1950); Henn, T. R., *The Lonely Tower: Studies in the Poetry of W. B. Y.* (1950; rev. and enl. ed., 1965); Ellmann, R., *The Identity of Y.* (1954; 2nd ed., 1964); Adams, H., *Blake and Y.* (1955); Unterecker, J., *A Reader's Guide to W. B. Y.* (1959); Stock, A. G., *W. B. Y.: His Poetry and Thought* (1961); Ure, P., *Y. the Playwright* (1963); Vendler, H., *Y.'s "Vision" and the Later Plays* (1963); Whitaker, T., *Swan and Shadow: Y.'s Dialogue with History* (1964); Donoghue, D., and J. Mulryne, eds., *An Honoured Guest: New Essays on W. B. Y.* (1965); Jeffares, A. N., and Cross, K. G. W., eds., *In Excited Reverie: A Centenary Tribute to W. B. Y.* (1965); Skelton, R., and A. Saddlemeyer, eds., *The World of W. B. Y.: Essays in Perspective* (1965; rev. ed., 1967); Maxwell, D. E. S., and R. Bushrui, eds., *W. B. Y., 1865–1965: Centenary Essays on the Art of W. B. Y.* (1965); Miller, J. H., *Poets of Reality: Six Twentieth Century Writers* (1965): 68–130; Zwerdling, A., *Y. and the Heroic Ideal* (1965); Ellmann, R., *Eminent Domain: Y. among Wilde, Joyce, Pound, Eliot and Auden* (1967); Hoffman, D., *Barbarous Knowledge: Myth in the Poetry of Y., Graves and Muir* (1967): 3–125; Bloom, H., *Y.* (1970); Marcus, P., *Y. and the Beginning of the Irish Renaissance* (1971); Moore, J. R., *Masks of Love and Death: Y. as Dramatist* (1971); Parkinson, T., *W. B. Y., Self Critic: A Study of His Early Verse and the Later Poetry* (1971); Meir, C., *The Ballads and songs of W. B. Y.: The Anglo-Irish Heritage in Subject and Style* (1974); Langbaum, R., *The Mysteries of Identity: A Theme in Modern Literature* (1977): 147–247; Jochum, K., *P. S. W. B. Y.: A Classified Bibliography of Criticism* (1978); Worth, K., *The Irish Drama of Europe from Y. to Beckett* (1978): 140–219; Bradley, A., *W. B. Y.* (1979); Lynch, D., *Y.: The Poetics of the Self* (1979); Freyer, G., *W. B. Y. and the Anti-Democratic Tradition* (1981)

—EDWARD HIRSCH

Mr. Y. is the only one among the younger English poets who has the whole poetical temperament, and nothing but the poetical temperament. He lives on one plane, and you will find in the whole of his work, with its varying degrees of artistic achievement, no unworthy or trivial mood, no occasional concession to the fatigue of high thinking. It is this continuously poetical quality of mind that seems to me to distinguish Mr. Y. from the many men of talent, and to place him among the few men of genius. . . . And that, certainly, is the impression which remains with one after a careful reading of the revised edition of Mr. Y.'s collected poems and of his later volume of lyrics, *The Wind among the Reeds* . . .

Arthur Symons, *Studies in Prose and Verse*
(1900), pp. 230, 234–35

When Y., at the crucial period of his life, attempted to leave fairyland behind, when he became aware of the unsatisfying character of the life of iridescent revery, when he completely recreated his style so as to make it solid, homely, and exact where it had formerly been shimmering or florid—the need for dwelling with part of his mind—or with his mind for part of the time—in a world of pure imagination, where the necessities of the real world do not hold, had, none the less, not been conjured away by the new artistic and intellectual habits he was cultivating. Where the early Y. had studied Irish folk-lore, collected and sorted Irish fairy tales, invented fairy tales for himself, the later Y. worked out from the mediumistic communications to his wife the twenty-eight phases of the human personality and the transformations of the soul after death. Y.'s sense of reality today is inferior to that of no man alive—indeed, his greatness is partly due precisely to the vividness of that sense.

Edmund Wilson, *Axel's Castle: A Study in the Imaginative Literature of 1870–1930* (1931), pp. 57–58

The Public Prosecutor: . . . In 1900 he believed in fairies; that was bad enough: but in 1930 we are confronted with the pitiful, the deplorable spectacle of a grown man occupied with the mumbo-jumbo magic and the nonsense of India. Whether he seriously believed such stuff to be true, or merely thought it pretty, or imagined it would impress the public, is immaterial. The plain fact remains that he made it the center of his work. Gentlemen, I need say no more.

The Counsel for the Defense: . . . From first to last [the poems] express a sustained protest against the social atomization caused by industrialism, and both in their ideas and their language a constant struggle to overcome it. The fairies and heroes of the early work were an attempt to find through folk tradition a binding force of society, and the doctrine of Anima Mundi found in the later poems is the same thing, in a more developed form, which has left purely local peculiarities behind, in favour of something that the deceased hoped was universal; in other words, he was working for a world religion.

W. H. Auden, "The Public against the Late Mr. W. B. Y.," *PR*, 6, 3 (1939), pp. 48, 51

Y. commonly hovered between myth and philosophy, except for transcending flashes, which is why he is not of the greatest poets. His ambition was too difficult for accomplishment; or his gift too small to content him. His curse was not that he rebelled against the mind of his age, which was an advantage for poetry, considering that mind, but that he could not create, except in fragments, the actuality of his age, as we can see Joyce and Mann and it may be Eliot, in equal rebellion, nevertheless doing. Y., to use one of his own lines, had "to wither into the truth." That he made himself into the greatest poet in

English since the seventeenth century was only possible because in that withering he learned how to create fragments of the actual, not of his own time to which he was unequal, but of all time of which he was a product.

To create greatly is to compass great disorder. Y. suffered from a predominant survival in him of that primitive intellect which insists on asserting absolute order at the expense of the rational imagination; hence his system, made absolute by the resort to magic and astrology, which produced the tragic poetry appropriate to it.

> R. P. Blackmur, "Between Myth and Philosophy, "
> *SoR*, 7 (1941–42), p. 424

The Y. of the Celtic Twilight—who seems to me to have been more the Y. of the Pre-Raphaelite twilight—uses Celtic folklore almost as William Morris uses Scandinavian folklore. His longer narrative poems bear the mark of Morris. Indeed, in his Pre-Raphaelite phase, Y. is by no means the least of the Pre-Raphaelites . . .

I think the phase in which he treated Irish legend in the manner of Rossetti or Morris is a phase of confusion. He did not master this legend until he made it a vehicle for his own creation of character—not, really, until he began to write the *Plays for Dancers*. The point is, that in becoming more Irish, not in subject-matter but in expression, he became at the same time universal.

> T. S. Eliot, "The Poetry of W. B. Y.," *SoR*, 7
> (1941–42), pp. 447–48

Usually the poems take one or two directions: either they are visionary, concerned with matters of prophecy, of the relations of the time-world and daimonic timelessness, or they are concerned with human enterprise, the relations of people with each other or with their own secret hopes and ambitions. In the visionary poems such as "Leda and the Swan" or "The Second Coming," Y. is concerned to intermesh the divine world with the animal, to show the world of time as centaurlike, beautiful and monstrous, aspiring and deformed. In the poems which deal with artists or with heroes or with other men, he wishes also to show how brute fact may be transmogrified, how we can sacrifice ourselves, in the only form of religion he sanctions, to our imagined selves, which offer far higher standards than anything offered by social convention. If we must suffer, it is better to create the world in which we suffer, and this is what heroes do spontaneously, artists do consciously, and all men do in their degree.

> Richard Ellmann, *The Identity of Yeats*, 2nd ed.
> (1964), pp. xxiii–xxiv

The received opinion among readers of Y. is that the classic poems are in *The Tower*. And yet by comparison with *The Wild Swans at Coole* the human image in that spectacular book is curiously incomplete; remarkably intense, but marginal; a little off-centre. Does this matter? Yes, it does; intensity is not enough. It matters greatly that *The Wild Swans at Coole* is at the very heart of the human predicament, groping for values through which man may define himself without frenzy or servility.

This book is concerned with the behavior of men in the cold light of age and approaching death. The ideal stance involves passion, self-conquest, courtesy, and moral responsibility. Y. pays the tribute of wild tears to many people and to the moral beauty which they embody; the entire book is crammed with moral life. Most of the poems were written between 1915 and 1919, and it is significant that those were the years in which Y. was perfecting his dance-drama; because the dancer was the culmination of the efforts which Y. made in *The Wild Swans at Coole* to represent the fullness of being as a dynamic action.

> Denis Donoghue, *The Ordinary Universe:
> Soundings in Modern Literature* (1968),
> pp. 117–18

[The] late poems speak most movingly about the paradox of being a poet: how a heightened capacity for the imaginative entertaining of images, dreams, "presences," seems to involve waverings, dissatisfactions, guilt about matters of the heart. . . . Out of this discovery, and out of his own poems about the heart as victim and torturer, came the heroic stock-taking of what has good imaginative reason to be thought of as Y.'s final poem, "The Circus Animals' Desertion." It is a bona fide modernist poem in that, like so much of Eliot or Stevens or Williams, it is about itself and about Poetry, extraordinarily self-absorbed even as it mounts a criticism of certain aggrandizing and inhuman tendencies in the poet's omnivorous self. It also managed to be . . . boldly though not crassly unrepentant, and it ends in exultation not prayer. . . This poetry says, when all the poetry is taken away from it, that with the circus animals, the ladders gone, the poet will settle at last for his heart in all its sordidness and poverty. . . .

> William H. Pritchard, "The Uses of Y.'s Poetry,"
> in Reuben A. Brower, ed., *Twentieth-Century
> Literature in Retrospect*, Harvard English Studies,
> No. 2 (1971), pp. 129–31

YEHOSHUA, A(braham) B.

Israeli novelist, dramatist, and essayist, b. 19 Dec. 1936, Jerusalem

Y. started publishing stories in 1957, and his first collection, *Mot hazaqen* (death of the old man) appeared in 1962. Characteristic stylistic features are already discernible in his early work, although they underwent conscious modification, change, and transformation in his subsequent fiction. These early stories are distinguished by the starkness of the sentences, the shocking transitions, the surprising shifts in plot, the blankness of the narrator, the symbolism of the action and names, and overall allegorization. These features were continued and refined in his second work, a volume of novellas, *Mul hayearot* (1968; facing the forests), still considered by many the author's major achievement. On the whole, allegorization gives way to metaphor, and the metaphor works both on the abstract level in the particular narrative circumstances and in the transforming suggestion.

Y. is adept at setting up extreme and ambivalent situations indicating mixed and contrasting motives within the characters. In the novella *Bithilat qayits 1970* (1972; *Early in the Summer of 1970*, 1973) a father tells of the death of his own son, victim of the ongoing war. Only it transpires that there has been a case of mistaken identity; it is not his son. We then see that he, the narrator, the "bereaved" father, is in love with his role and cannot exist without it. The features noticeable then are role reversal, shock, surprise, psychological attack, and national implications. In all his work, Y. has displayed a preoccupation with form. *Bithilat qayits 1970* is constructed in a circular pattern, where the final chapter repeats the first, with variations, as though time could be played with. When Y. started to write novels, this preoccupation was dominant. His first novel, *Hameahev* (1977; *The Lover*, 1978), consists of a series of monologues uttered by separate voices, where each successive section takes up the story from the previous. Again we have a mystery, a mystery of motivation and impulse. Even clearer in its national and radical connotations is *Gerushim meaharim* (1982; *A Late Divorce*, 1984), where the divorce that is projected by the old man, living in America, coming to finalize matters in Israel, is paralleled by the national situation. The two are inextricably linked, and the reader will have difficulty in disentangling the surface narrative elements from the metaphorical and allegorical leads.

In a later novel, *Molkho* (1987; *Five Seasons*, 1989), Y. attempted to return to a more traditional form, writing a third-person narrative of the eponymous hero, recently widowed, who attempts to make a new life for himself in late middle-age. Absent here are the typical elements of Y.'s prose—the odd images, the shock reverses, the surprising developments, the allegorical leads. Here we have a tale of a very average, not to say boring, man, in his routine ambition and attempted reengagement. Molcho is a man removed from history. This is not the same sort of story as is told in *Mar maniy* (1990; *Mr. Mani*, 1992), where both the obsessional pursuit after the meaning of Israeli Jewish history and the interest in technique return. Here, the manner of telling adopted is of the telephone conversation. We only hear one side of a dialogue, and have to infer the other. An even greater surprise is the direction of the narrative. Spaced over 200 years or so, in five episodes, the story begins almost in the present, in the early 1980s, and goes back through key episodes in Jewish history to the accompaniment of a "Mani" representative. Mani, unlike Molcho (so unrelated to history) is always by the side of great events, although he himself does not forge them. The first of the Manis to appear (in the final chapter) wonders whether he is to be the last of the line. Here, technique, in pursuit of meaning, has shunned meaning aside, and displayed itself on the stage as exclusive exhibit.

FURTHER WORKS: *Hashivah mehodu* (1994); *Masa el tom haelef* (1997). FURTHER WORKS IN ENGLISH: *Three Days and a Child* (1971); *The Continuous Silence of a Poet* (1988); *Open Heart* (1996)

BIBLIOGRAPHY: Yudkin, L. I., *Escape into Siege: A Survey of Israeli Literature Today* (1974): 108–11; Yudkin, L. I., *1948 and After: Aspects of Israeli Fiction* (1984): 35–36, 116–19, 154–55, 167–73; Fisch, H., *A Remembered Future: A Study in Literary Mythology* (1984): 56–57, 96–97, 126; Fuchs, E., "The Sleepy Wife; a Feminist Consideration of A. B. Y.'s Fiction," *HAR* 8 (1984): 71–81

—LEON I. YUDKIN

YEROFEEV, Venedikt

Russian novelist, dramatist, and essayist, b. 28 Oct. 1938, Poyakonda, Murmansk Oblast; d. 11 May 1990, Moscow

Y. was Russia's preeminent prose-poet of the 1970s and 1980s whose art and perception of the world were dominated by alcohol. Unpublished in his homeland until late 1988, his *samizdat* writings were nonetheless widely known. After his father was arrested and he was abandoned by his impoverished mother, Y. was raised in a state orphanage in the Murmansk region north of the arctic circle. Dropping out of Moscow University at the end of his first year (1956), Y., a chronic alcoholic, wandered the country as a menial laborer. A brief stay at the Vladimir Pedagogical Institute led to his expulsion as ringleader of a Christian student group (1962). In spite of his sketchy formal education, Y. had a wide knowledge of history, literature, and music. His writing, mostly done in spurts at long intervals, was circulated by friends who also sent it abroad where it garnered critical acclaim. Only with the advent of glasnost did Y., by now stricken with fatal throat cancer, become a public figure in the U.S.S.R. Y.'s long existence on the fringe of Soviet society and, more recently, his own irascibility, heavy irony, and whimsy make much of his life, his views, and his work difficult to assess.

Y.'s fame with both public and critics derives from *Moskva-Petushki* (1973; *Moscow to the End of the Line*, 1980), which has now appeared in more than a dozen languages. It was written in 1969 or 1970 while Y. (like his eponymous hero, Venichka) was working as a cable layer, the title referring to an interurban train line to a village some seventy miles from Moscow. In the mind of the drunken narrator, Petushki is heaven on earth. Awaiting him there are his beloved mistress and, a bit further on, his three-year-old son. Having spent the night drunk in a stairwell, Venichka makes his way to the train station, stopping to fill his suitcase with bottles on the way. During the drunken journey, he reflects on events from his sad life and talks with angels, the devil, and the Sphinx, as well as with fellow passengers who join him in drinking. The train arrives at the village, which mysteriously contains wide streets and high buildings. The hero is pursued by four hooligans who kill him in the Moscow stairwell, which he has apparently never left. It has been suggested that the murderous villains are Marx and Engels, Lenin and Stalin.

Moskva-Petushki, subtitled an epic poem but more accurately a mock epic, has little plot. Punctuated by the numerous station stops on the journey, the hero's rambling monologue is a series of wry anecdotes, witty aphorisms, and paradoxes, ranging from the personal to the cosmic. The novel, whose exuberant language and action is thoroughly uninhibited, abounds in playful humor such as cocktail recipes containing cologne, foot antiperspirant, and furniture polish, and bearing names like "Tears of a Komsomol Girl."

Much of the humor is, however, of the blackest hue. All of European cultural history and a grandiose, meretricious, Soviet pseudoculture are hilariously reassessed in terms of alcohol, that universal solvent of Soviet society. Alcohol plays a dual role in *Moskva-Petushki*, as it does in Russian culture. It serves as both a release from a harsh external reality and as a mechanism for the expression of mystical transcendence. The former role provides a playing field for Y.'s ribald humor; the latter, for his religious pathos. The novel draws upon an extraordinary range of historical and cultural figures for its allusions, but the single most important source is the Bible. Venichka sees himself as a Christ figure, and, significantly, his last journey falls on Friday, the day of the crucifixion. The tale's most frequent motif is a series of variants on *talipha cumi*, " . . . I say unto thee, arise," Christ's words to a resurrected girl.

Y. has proclaimed the arch conservative Russian journalist and philosopher Vasilii Rozanov (1856–1919) as his forebear. Y., whose iconoclastic outlook and aphoristic style evoke Rozanov's, expressed his admiration in a curious story-essay *Vasilii Rozanov glazami ekstsentrika* (wr. 1973, pub. 1982; Vasilii Rozanov through the eyes of an eccentric). The alcoholic narrator, deserted, attempts to kill himself with three pistols. Missing, and in hope of obtaining poison, he goes to see a pharmacist friend who gives him a dose of hemlock and three volumes of Rozanov, an author forbidden in enlightened Soviet society. Rozanov's iconoclastic condemnation of conventional pieties and his rejection of rationalism in favor of "a tender idea," revives the despondent hero.

During the 1980s Y. devoted himself to drama. *Valpurgieva noch; ili, 'shagi komandora'* (1985; Walpurgis Night, or the commandant's steps) is set in a Soviet psychiatric hospital on May Day eve. The hero, an alcoholic, involves the other patients in a drinking bout that ends fatally for all of the participants. The grim setting and even grimmer denouement provide a framework for the same sort of riotous language play and debunking of official reality found in *Moskva-Petushki*. Again the theme is the clash between the joys of an irrational humanity and a repressive "rational" social order. *Valpurgieva noch* was to be the second part of a trilogy collectively called *Drei Nächte* (three nights)—the first night, being Saint John's eve and the third night, Christmas eve. Y. whimsically, but accurately, noted that the outrageous—only partly published—trilogy observes Boileau's classical unities of time, place, and action. Not long before his death, Y. also spoke of a play called *Fanny Kaplan*, the antibolshevik radical who attempted to assassinate Lenin in 1919, as being almost ready for publication.

Although Y. was apolitical in any strict sense, he produced one curious piece that might be described as political, *Moia malenkaia Leniniana* (1990; my little Leniniana). The common view is that Lenin was a great and decent man whose ideas were perverted into the nightmare created by Stalin. In 1988 Y. gathered a selection of quotes from Lenin's correspondence showing him to have been scarcely less bloodthirsty than his notorious successor. The quotes are framed by Y.'s wry introductory remarks and tongue-in-cheek commentary. On the occasion of Y.'s death, *Literaturnaia gazeta*, the organ of the Writer's Union, published a short selection of aphorisms gathered from his writer's notebook "Ot pravoslavnogo novogo goda 1981" (from the orthodox new year 1981). The selection was entitled "Mne khorosho, ia zhivu v stabilnoi sverkhderzhave" (1990; I am glad that I live in a stable superpower). Since Y.'s death, publication of some of the early writings and late notebooks has been promised. Among the works unpublished at the time of his death are *Zapiski psikhopata* (wr. 1955–1956; notes of a

psychopath), *Blagaia vest* (wr. 1963; glad tidings), and essays on the Norwegian writers Henrik Ibsen (1828–1906), Bjørnstjerne Bjørnson (1832–1910), and Knut HAMSUN. The only manuscript copy of his novel *Dmitrii Shostakovich* (wr. 1972; Dimitry Shostakovich) was stolen during a drunken train journey.

Y. was an enormously gifted writer—part holy fool, part social and aesthetic provocateur. His wit, linguistic exuberance, and almost perverse delight in shattering idols made him unique in the "stagnation" of the 1970s and 1980s. In his dark view of the human condition (Soviet and otherwise) and in the religious yearnings he expressed in his art, he is akin to both Gogol and Dostoevsky and, more immediately, to the masters of the Silver Age, that last flare-up of artistic and intellectual creativity before the Soviet period. Y.'s oeuvre is small, and his style laconic, but as the author of *Moskva-Petushki* he is assured a place in the pantheon of 20th-c. Russian literature.

BIBLIOGRAPHY: Paperno, I. A., and B. Gasparow, "Vstan' i idi," *Slavica Hierosolymitana*: 5–6 (1981): 387–400; Hosking, G., "Drinking Mystically, Traveling Sentimentally," *TLS* (15 Jan. 1982): 63; Brown, E. J., *Russian Literature since the Revolution*, rev. ed. (1982): 376–79; Lowe, D. A., *Russian Writing since 1953: A Critical Survey* (1987): 104–5, 190–92; Yerofeyev, V., "I'll Die before I Understand It," interview, *Moscow News*, 50 (1989), 13

—D. BARTON JOHNSON

YESENIN, Sergey

(also transliterated Esenin) Russian poet, b. 2 Oct. 1895, Konstantinovo, now Yesenino; d. 27 Dec. 1925, Leningrad

Born into a religious family, Y. was educated at a village school and then at a teachers' seminary. He soon discovered his gift for poetry and at seventeen left home to seek recognition in the literary worlds of Moscow and St. Petersburg. Y.'s fresh and original talent almost immediately captured attention. Attired in expensive imitations of peasant clothing, he gave flamboyant recitals. His first collection of poems, *Radunitsa* (1916; mourning for the dead), brought him the success he craved, but with success came also the enticements of bohemian life, which perhaps more than other factors were to determine his destiny.

In 1918 Y. helped found the IMAGIST school, modeled after the movement in English poetry headed by Ezra POUND. In their efforts to attract attention, the imagists wrote shocking and blasphemous verses, often meager in content, and soon gained notoriety with their offensive self-aggrandizement and disreputable conduct.

Undiscouraged by two unsuccessful marriages, in 1922 Y. married the famous American dancer Isadora Duncan. He followed her on tour to Europe and America, naïvely hoping that his poetry would receive due recognition abroad. He returned to Russia a year later, alone, disappointed in his expectations, and suffering from a severe depression. Some of the verses he wrote while abroad appeared in *Moskva kabatskaya* (1924; Moscow tavern life), but, as the title indicates, the majority of the poems in this collection reflect the grim and decadent aspects of Moscow's bohemia. Y. was censored, accused of glorifying drunkenness and debauchery. His poems on historical and revolutionary themes, written in 1924, were favorably received but did not obliterate his reputation for drinking and his antiestablishment pronouncements.

In June 1925 Y. married a granddaughter of Lev Tolstoy, but this marriage failed, too, and in December of the same year, in a state of severe depression, he took his own life. So great was his popularity and the appeal of his poetry that his death led to a rash of suicides across the nation. His books were banned and publication was not resumed until after World War II.

Y.'s output is relatively small and limited in theme. His peasant origins left an imprint on all his works. Y.'s lack of classical education and his limited knowledge of Western languages and literatures kept his poetry free from influences that might have affected his spontaneity and originality. Whether his poems reveal intimate feelings or glorify the revolution, express a nostalgic longing for his native village or an abhorrence of and bewilderment before the new forces of industrialization, they have a distinct quality of lyricism and simplicity reminiscent of the traditional Russian folk song.

In his early verses Y. contemplates the peaceful, modest countryside of his native region. A pantheistic perception of it animates his lines: the sky, rivers, sunsets, dawns, trees, and animals are invested with human characteristics and become protagonists in a world without hardships or daily toil. Yet there is also a graphic realism in Y.'s depictions. Many of the poems have religious themes, but the Christian idea is mainly borne by the terminology and has no philosophical depth. Christ and the saints are endowed with a folklike humanity and familiarity more reminiscent of the ancient folktales than of their biblical source. The language is interspersed with regional colloquialisms, Church Slavonicisms, intonations of folk songs, and prayers.

Y.'s colorful, idiosyncratic vision of the Russia of his childhood can also be found in his second book of poems, *Goluben* (1918; blueness). The mood of the poetry of this early period is serene but tinged with melancholy and often wistful. Here and there notes of doom enter unobtrusively. Yearning for the country and the ancestral village life grows more intense for this uprooted peasant as he watches the old world disappear and dreaded modernity spread its tentacles even into the remotest parts of the Russian countryside.

Y. greeted the revolution with enthusiasm, for he saw in it the promise of a new role and a better life for the peasantry. He presented his allegorical vision of the future in "Inonia" (1918; otherland), an irreverent poem in which, casting himself in the messianic role of prophet and spiritual leader of a new Russia, he urges his countrymen to forsake religion and denounce industrialization as evils, and in return promises them happiness and prosperity. Enthusiasm for the new regime began to wane after he witnessed the sufferings and violence that the revolution and the civil war left in their wake and after he realized how little his mystic view of the event had to do with Soviet reality.

Y.'s poems written between 1919 and 1921 are consciously imagistic—highly ornamental and full of elaborate and often contrived conceits—and are not his best. Imagism did, however, open new artistic vistas beyond the narrow peasant and religious imagery with which he had become associated. Outstanding among the works of this period are: the lyrical drama *Pugachyov* (1922; Pugachyov), a romanticized portrayal of the 18th-c. peasant leader; and the poem "Sorokoust" (1920; prayer for the dead), a requiem to the patriarchal rural world of his youth.

The poems written after Y.'s return to Russia reflect his need to find in poetry a haven from the storms of his personal life and from the haunting nightmares of his troubled conscience. The poet wrote superb verses filled with gentle melancholy and joyous acceptance, while the man lived a defiantly rebellious and self-destructive life.

In his lyrics Y. is concealed behind seemingly artless masks: he is the simple peasant, the superfluous individual, the victim vilified and hounded, the hooligan, the repentant son.

Despondency and hopelessness became the dominant notes of the poetry of Y.'s last years. Some of his most celebrated lyrics belong to this period. Especially moving are those addressed to his village and his family still living there. The language of these poems is simple and straightforward, without any trace of mysticism or affectation. Nowhere does Y.'s despair with life and with himself stand out more starkly than in "Chyorny chelovek" (1925; "The Black Man," 1973). It is an account of a hallucination: a man dressed in black evening clothes appears before the poet and mockingly recounts the story of his sinful life. Y. refuses to see a connection between himself and the black man's tale and angrily hurls his cane at him. When he recovers from this hallucination, he finds himself, still dressed in formal clothes, standing before a shattered mirror. Two weeks later, in a hotel room in Leningrad, Y., having slashed his wrists, wrote in his own blood his farewell to life—and also to poetry, the only love to which he had remained true to the end: "In this life it is not new to die, but neither it is new to be alive."

FURTHER WORKS: *Selsky chasoslov* (1918); *Preobrazhenie* (1918); *Treryadnitsa* (1920); *Triptikh* (1921); *Ispoved khuligana* (1921); *Stikhi 1920–1924* (1924); *Rus Sovetskaya* (1925); *Persidskie motivy* (1925); *Strana sovetskaya* (1926); *Sobranie sochineny* (4 vols., 1926–1927); *Sobranie sochineny* (5 vols., 1966–1968). FURTHER WORKS IN ENGLISH: *Confessions of a Hooligan: Fifty Poems* (1973)

BIBLIOGRAPHY: Zavalishin, V., *Early Soviet Writers* (1958): 118–39; Lafitte, S., *S. E.: Une étude* (1959); Poggioli, R., *The Poets of Russia* (1960): 264–75; Slonim, M., *Soviet Russian Literature: Writers and Problems* (1964): 11–18; de Graff, F., *S. E.: A Biographical Sketch* (1966); McVay, G., *E.: A Life* (1976); Ponomareff, C. V., *S. E.* (1978); Prokushev, Y., *S. Y.: The Man, the Verse, the Age* (1979); Visson, L., *S. E.: Poet of the Crossroads* (1980); Davies, J., ed., *E.: A Biography in Memoirs, Letters, and Documents* (1982)

—LUCY VOGEL

YEVTUSHENKO, Yevgeny Alexandrovich

Russian poet, b. 18 July 1933, Zima

Y. was born in Siberia. His father, a geologist, and his mother, a professional singer, were divorced when he was eleven. Y. began to write poetry while a boy. He was accepted in 1952 as a student at the prestigious Gorky Literary Institute in Moscow but was expelled in 1957, ostensibly for "irregular attendance at lectures." The real reason was his outspoken defense of Vladimir Dudintsev's (b. 1918) controversial book attacking the Soviet bureaucracy, *Ne khlebom yedinym* (1956; *Not by Bread Alone*, 1957).

Y. has become the most famous and popular Soviet poet of the post-Stalin era, both at home and abroad. He is also the most widely traveled and is even permitted to live part of each year in England with his third wife, a British subject.

The scope and originality of Y.'s talent were evident in the poems of his first collections, published in the 1950s. These poems were loud, oratorical, and obviously intended for public recitation. They were also somewhat naïve and overloaded with slogans. But readers were immediately impressed by the poet's fresh voice, optimism, daring, and open-minded search for new roads in life and literature.

The long poem *Stantsia Zima* (1956; *Winter Station*, 1964) made Y. the favorite poet of the younger generation almost immediately, although it also provoked furious attacks from the guardians of Party orthodoxy. In it he reminisces about his home town. He sees the past and its values with a critical eye, across a gulf of time and experience. But his doubts, dissatisfactions, and searching questions also apply to the present. The poem has lyrical and patriotic overtones and solemn passages about the people. Another of its notable features is the use of techniques derived from Vladimir MAYAKOVSKY, such as lines printed in unconventional "steps of stairs" format, unusual rhyme schemes, bold metaphors, and "folk" and slang expressions.

Y.'s international reputation and popularity increased after the publication of *Baby Yar* (1961; *Babi Yar*, 1968). In this poem he deplored the fact that no monument had been built to mark the site of Baby Ravine, near Kiev, where the Nazis had murdered thousands of Jews during World War II. He attributed this deliberate oversight to the endemic anti-Semitism of the Soviet government. Public reaction to the poem at home was intense and divided.

His next poem, "Nasledniki Stalina" (1963; "The Heirs of Stalin," 1966) equaled *Baby Yar* in scope and political impact. The poet fears that the dark forces of Stalinism still remain under the surface of Soviet society. Like *Baby Yar*, "Nasledniki Stalina" denounces evil and injustice with solemn pathos and in a highly emotional tone. Unlike *Baby Yar*, it met with approval at the Kremlin, since it conformed with the Party's current de-Stalinization policy.

Buoyed by all this success and adulation, Y. dreamed of becoming the voice of an entire generation who would use poetry as a weapon in the fight for truth in society. In 1962, while he was in Paris, *L'express* published a French translation of his autobiography under the title *Autobiographic précoce*. Never published in the Soviet Union, it subsequently appeared in Russian in London as *Avtobiografia* (1964; *A Precocious Autobiography*, 1973). The artistic value of this work is not high, but it is an important account of Y.'s thoughts and feelings, search for truth, growing awareness of injustice, and decision to fight against it. Because of the unauthorized foreign publication of this work, he was hastily summoned to Moscow, officially censured by Khrushchev, and deprived of his privileged position and right to travel abroad for about two years.

A long epic poem, *Bratskaya GES* (1965; "Bratsk Station," 1967), continued Y.'s autobiographical project. The poet is still searching for the right relationship with his fellow-countrymen. The wealth and variety of its subject matter and the verbal dynamism and mastery of verse forms helped to ensure the success of this collection. *Bratskaya GES* also has weaknesses, including some rather shoddy effusions of patriotic rhetoric, evidence of his new desire to mollify the Party ideologists.

In recent years Y. has experimented in prose, including film writing, and has published critical essays. But he is a poet first. His output remains enormous, but since the 1960s there has been an increase in more lyrical works, as opposed to political or purely topical poems. His ease at moving from topical to lyrical subjects, and from social to personal themes, is one of his greatest strengths and sources of popularity. The salient feature of his lyric poetry is a compassionate concern for suffering and oppressed human beings, particularly women and children.

Many commentators consider Y. to be a genuine world citizen, because of his compassion for ordinary people, opposition to all forms of evil, and struggle against corruption. Some other poets among Y.'s contemporaries, for example, Andrey VOZNESENSKY, may surpass him in intellectual verve and sophistication, but Y. was the first of his generation to integrate what he had learned from the early 20th-c. Russian masters into the new Soviet poetry.

FURTHER WORKS: *Razvedchiki gryadushchego* (1952); *Trety sneg* (1955); *Shosse entuziastov* (1956); *Obeshchanie* (1957); *Luk i lira* (1959); *Stikhi raznykh let* (1959); *Yabloko* (1960); *Vzmakh ruki* (1961); *Nezhnost* (1962); *Kachka* (1966); *Kater svyazi* (1966); *Idut belye snegi* (1969); *Kazansky universitet* (1971 "Kazan University," (1973); *Ya sibirsky porody* (1971); *Doroga nomer odin* (1972); *Intimnaya lirika* (1973); *Poet v. Rossii bolshe chem poet* (1973); *Izbrannye proizvedenia* (1975); *Ottsovsky slukh* (1975); *Proseka* (1977); *V polny rost* (1977); *Utrenny narod* (1978); *Talant yest chudo nesluchaynoe: Kniga statey* (1980). FURTHER WORKS IN ENGLISH: *Selected Poems* (1962); *Y. Y.: Selected Poetry* (1963); *Y. Poems* (1966, bilingual); *The Poetry of Y. Y., 1953–1965*, rev. and enl. ed. (1967, bilingual); *Bratsk Station, and Other Poems* (1967); *Flowers and Bullets, and Freedom to Kill* (1970); *Stolen Apples: Poetry by Y. Y.* (1971); *Y.'s Reader: The Spirit of Elbe: A Precocious Autobiography; Poems* (1973); *Kazan University, and Other New Poems* (1973); *From Desire to Desire* (1976); *The Face behind the Face: Poems* (1979); *Ivan the Terrible and Ivan the Fool* (1980); *Invisible Threads* (1981); *A Dove in Santiago* (1983)

BIBLIOGRAPHY: Milner-Gulland, R. R., Introduction to *Y. Y.: Selected Poetry* (1963): vii–xix; Reeve, F. D., "The Work of Russian Poetry Today," *KR*, 26 (1964): 533–53; Ireland, R., Introduction to *Bratsk Station, and Other New Poems* (1967): ix–xxii; Reavey, G., Introduction to *The Poetry of Y. Y., 1953–1965*, rev. and enl. ed. (1967): vii–xxxviii; Conquest, R., "The Politics of Poetry: The Sad Case of Y. Y.," *NYTMag* (30 Sept. 1972): 16–17, 56–70; Slonim, M., *Soviet Russian Literature: Writers and Problems, 1917–1967* (1967): 324–28; McVay, G., "An Interview with Y. Y.," *JRS*, 33 (1977): 13–18; Babenko, V. A., "Women in Y.'s Poetry," *RusR*, 36 (1977): 320–33; Brown, D., "'Loud' and 'Quiet' Poets of the Nineteen Sixties," in Stolz, B. A., ed., *Papers in Slavic Philology I* (1977): 18–26

—VICTORIA A. BABENKO-WOODBURY

YIDDISH LITERATURE

The Yiddish language has been the basic means of communication among the Ashkenazic Jews (those living in northern, central, and eastern Europe) since its origins in the 10th c. in the Jewish settlement of Loter, in the middle Rhine-Moselle region. For over two hundred years before the present century, Yiddish served as the lingua franca of east European Jewry. It has been spoken by a larger number of Jews for a longer period of time than any other Jewish vernacular.

Modern Yiddish literature was born in the Pale of Settlement (Byelorussia, parts of Lithuania, eastern Poland, and the Ukraine) and passed rapidly through a period of modernization, accomplishing in decades what other literatures took generations to achieve.

Three interpreters of *yidishkayt*, the totality of eastern European Jewish culture, provided the foundations for a modern literature: Mendele Mokher Sforim ("Mendele the Bookseller," pseud. of Sholem Jacob Abramovitsch, 1836–1917), Sholem Aleichem (pseud. of Sholem Rabinovitsh, 1859–1916), and Yitskhok Leybush Peretz (1851–1915). Mendele, social critic and storyteller, belongs to the social realism of the 19th c. The humorist Sholem Aleichem, most popular of the three, is the bard of the average man. Peretz, in his Hasidic and folkloristic tales, explored the underpinnings of Jewish life; his poetry captures the life of east European Jewry. Taking as their sources Yiddish medieval epics with their stylized biblical language, the 18th- and 19th-c. classics, and the comedies and satires of the Haskalah (Enlightenment), this trio forged an instrument for literary expression. Their work and example nourished an intellectual class of writers, many of whom were also profoundly influenced by other European literatures.

Three important events around the turn of the century gave rise to modern Jewish nationalism: (1) the Yidishe Arbeterbund (Jewish Workers' Union) was founded in Vilna (Russian Empire) in 1897; (2) the First Zionist Congress was convened in Basel, Switzerland, in 1897; (3) the First Yiddish Language Conference was held in Czernowitz, Bukovina (Austro-Hungarian Empire) in 1908. Proclaiming Yiddish to be a national language of the Jewish people, the delegates to the language conference provided the impetus for Yiddish to be viewed as a medium of refined and significant literary activity.

During this same period, a very popular and important Yiddish literature was taking shape in the U.S. Its creators were the proletarian poets Yoysef Bovshover (1873–1915), Dovid Edelshtat (1866–1892), Morris Rosenfeld (1862–1923), and Morris Vinchevsky (1856–1932), protest writers who were the intellectual leaders of the first generation of east European Jewish immigrants. (The critic N. B. Minkoff said that there had not been a Yiddish literature of such impact since the *tkhines*, the moralistic penny booklets, of the 16th and 17th cs.)

A group of New York-based poets, calling themselves the Young Ones, rebelled against the tenets of that earlier generation. Parnassians, they expanded the boundaries of poetic subject matter, emphasizing form over content. Major motifs for them were the fear of urbanization, a sense of loss and alienation, and the values of the ivory tower. Important members of this group were Moyshe Leyb HALPERN, Mani Leyb (1883–1953), Zisha Landau (1889–1937), Reuben Iceland (1884–1955), Moyshe Nadir (1885–1943), I. J. Schwartz (1885–1971), Leyb Naydus (1890–1918), Menachem Boraisho (1888–1949), and Isaac Raboy (1882–1944).

The attitudes and thematics of the Young Ones provoked a counter-response in the writings of several major poets who called themselves Introspectivists. Americanized and urbanized, they moved away from the attitudes and mood of the Young Ones. Exploring FREUDIAN notions and appealing to personal experience as the touchstone of authentic creativity, they found inspiration in the work of Yehoyesh (pseud. of Solomon Bloomgarden, 1870–1927). The leading Introspectivists were Aron Glants-Leyeles

(1889–1966), Yankev Glatshteyn (Jacob GLATSTEIN), and Nokhum Borekh Minkoff (1893–1958).

Before World War I Warsaw was the major European center of Yiddish literature, with Vilna second. After the February 1917 revolution the Russian Provisional Government revoked the prohibition against Yiddish publishing, which had been issued by the tsarist government in July 1915. Major publishing houses soon opened, and in Kiev there appeared two volumes of an anthology, *Eygns* (1918, 1920; our own), containing poems and stories by such writers as Dovid BERGELSON, Peretz MARKISH, Der NISTER, Yekhezkil Dobrushin (1882–1953), Dovid Hofshteyn (1889–1952), Nakhman Mayzel (1887–1966), and Osher Shvartsman (1889–1919). During the 1920s, under the influence of Alexandr BLOK, Sergey YESENIN, and Vladimir MAYAKOVSKY, Yiddish writers turned to the revolution and the new way of life, the tragedy of the civil war and of the pogroms in the Ukraine, the challenge of adapting to the new society, and the struggle to evolve from the narrowness of the *shtetl*.

In Łódź, Poland, in 1919 the poet Yankev Adler (1895–1949) and the poet and theater director Moyshe Broderzon (1890–1956) founded the Young Yiddish group, which had its own journal. The group attempted to renovate Jewish traditions by using an EXPRESSIONIST-MODERNIST vision, giving them a secular guise that would satisfy the need for new links. Bohemians, they employed nocturnal settings, erotica, and themes of madness and despair.

Other major Yiddish avant-garde literary groups of the post-World War I period were Our Own (Kiev, 1918–20), the Introspectivists (New York, 1919–39), the Stream group (Moscow, 1922–24), the Pomegranate group (Berlin, 1922–24), and the Gang (Poland, 1922–25). Similar in some ways to the Our Own group, the Gang reflected the general expressionist tendencies prevalent throughout post-World War I Europe. The two anthologies published by the Gang—*Khalyastre* (1922, 1924; gang)—are characterized by hyperbole, pessimism, and chiliasm. The most important members of the Gang were the poets Uri Zvi GREENBERG, Melekh Ravitsh (1893–1976), and later Peretz Markish.

A group called Young Vilna was formed in that city not long before the start of World War II. More homogeneous when seen in retrospect than was apparent at the time, these writers strove to wrest the hegemony of literary leadership from Warsaw, whose outstanding writers included Israel RABON, Alter-Sholem Katsizne (1885–1941), and Yitskhok Katsenelson (1886–1944). Major representatives of the self-assertive and idiosyncratic Young Vilna group were Chaim GRADE, Avrom SUTSKEVER, and Elkhanon Vogler (1907–1969).

Czernowitz (Cernăuţi, Romania, after World War I, and later Chernovtsy, Ukrainian S.S.R.) was another center of Yiddish culture. One of its foremost writers was Eliezer SHTEYNBARG, author of innovative fables and children's stories.

Beginning in the mid-1920s and continuing for a decade, a group of writers centered in the Byelorussian capital of Minsk played an important role in Soviet Yiddish letters. Most prominent were the poets Zelik Akselrod (1904–1941), Izzi Kharik (1898–1937), and Moyshe Kulbak (1896–1940), and the critic and historian of Yiddish literature Maks Erik (1898–1937). The 1930s were remarkable for the high quality of belles-lettres and the strongly national note in much that was published. In 1934 the Minsk leaders and several others were arrested, accused of chauvinism or terrorism, and subsequently imprisoned or executed. Other victims of this first organized campaign against Yiddish literati were the critic Khatskl Duniets (?-after 1935), the critic and newspaper editor Moyshe Litvakov (1875–1937), and Yisroel Tsinberg (1873–1939), author of the monumental *Geshikhte fun literatur bay Yidn* (10 vols., 1927–37; *History of Jewish Literature*, 12 vols., 1972–75).

During World War II there was an upsurge in literary activity in the Soviet Union, triggered by the Nazi cataclysm. After several more years of relative freedom following the war's end, in January 1948 the world-renowned actor-director Shloyme Mikhoels was murdered on Stalin's order, his successor was shot, and by November the signal had been given by the government to suppress Yiddish literature and annihilate Yiddish culture. Schools were closed, interrogations took place, followed by arrests and exile, culminating in the tragedy of 12 August, 1952, when twenty-four cultural leaders and writers were executed. Among the victims was the popular children's poet Leyb Kvitko (1893–1952). The philosophical poet Shmuel Halkin (1899–1960) was one of the few to survive imprisonment, returning from Siberian exile in 1954.

Following Stalin's death in 1953 there was a halfhearted attempt—for the most part private and unpublicized—to "rehabilitate" some of these writers, to publish some of their works, mostly in Russian translation rather than in the original Yiddish. In 1961 the journal *Sovetish heymland* began to appear. Some very talented writers were published, for example, Note Lurye (b. 1905), Elye Shekhtman (b. 1908), and Natan Zabare (1908–1975). With the emigration of many of the leading writers to the West, only a trickle of Yiddish writing continues in the Soviet Union, and it is of no major consequence.

Even more horrendous than the losses to Soviet Yiddish literature brought about by war and persecution was the total disappearance, as a result of the Holocaust, of Yiddish literature in Poland, where it had flourished during the interwar period. Itskhok Meyer Vaysenberg (1881–1938) was the leader of a group of naturalists, including Oyzer Vatshavski (1898–1944), whose novel *Shmugler* (1920; the smugglers) describes the demoralization of a *shtetl*; and Shimen Horonchik (1889–1939), whose *Farplonterte vegn* (1924; confused ways) analyzes a *shtetl* under German occupation during World War I and whose *In roysh fun mashinen* (1928; in the whir of machines) and *Zump* (1931; swamp) deal with the lower middle class. Writing out of their rabbinical and Hasidic backgrounds, I. J. SINGER and Yekhiel Yeshaya Trunk (1887–1961), both of whom immigrated to America, described Hasidic courts and their complex lifestyle: Singer in *Yoshe Kalb* (1932; *The Sinner*, 1933; repub. as *Yoshe Kalb*, 1965), Trunk in *Simkhe Plakhte* (pub. 1951; Simkhe Plakhte). Israel Rabon wrote moving descriptions of Jewish poverty in *Digas* (1928; the street) and *Balut: Roman fun a forshtot* (1934; Balut: a novel about a suburb). Efrayim Kaganovski (1893–1958), an important writer of fiction and memoirs, created perceptive short prose works about his native Warsaw.

As in Europe, so in America there was a pleiad of writers who had taken Y. L. Peretz as their mentor, among them Hirsch Dovid Nomberg (1874–1927), known as the first aesthete in Yiddish literature, and the poet Avrom Reyzen (Abraham Reisen, 1876–1953). Sholem ASCH, who had emigrated from Poland in 1910, gained an international readership with his trilogy *Farn mabul* (1929–31; *Three Cities*, 1933) and with *Der tehilim Yid* (1934; *Salvation*, 1934; rev. ed., 1951).

Among the Young Ones in the U.S., Dovid Ignatov (1885–1954) was capable of writing in a Hasidic mode, as in *Vunder mayses fun altn Prag* (1920; tales of wonder from old Prague), and with a labor leader as his narrator, as in the novel *Oyf vayte vegn* (3 vols., 1932; on distant roads). The erudite Isaac Raboy longed for a rural life; his two autobiographical novels reflect this yearning: *Der*

pas fun yam (1918; the seaside) and *Der yidisher kouboy* (1942; the Jewish cowboy). Borekh Glazman (1893–1945), an individualist who wrote in both Yiddish and English, was not comfortable in his adopted home, although he graduated from an American university and served in the U.S. Army. His *Lender un lebn* (1935; lands and lives) is the epic of a family who immigrates to America from Russia; *In goldenem zump* (1940; in the golden swamp) is an attack on the Yiddish American literary establishment. Yoysef (Joseph) Opatoshu (1886–1954) was an imaginative romantic novelist and short-story writer who moved with ease from 16th-c. German Jewry, in *A tog in Regensburg* (1933; *A Day in Regensburg*, 1968), through 19th-c. Polish Jewry in *In poylishe velder* (1921; *In Polish Woods*, 1938), to his own time in *A roman fun a ferd-ganev* (1917; a novel about a horse thief).

In addition to those who came to the U. S. and settled chiefly in New York, there was also a contingent of Yiddish writers who immigrated to Canada and resided mainly in Montreal, including the poets Moyshe Mordkhe Shafir (b. 1909), J. I. Segal (1896–1954), and Sholom Shtern (b. 1907), and, of a younger generation, Chava Rosenfarb (b. 1923), a poet, playwright, and novelist who came to Canada after surviving the Holocaust.

Following World War II, Jacob Glatstein, Chaim Grade, and the poet Itsik MANGER enjoyed the broadest readership among cognoscenti in the West. Manger, born in Bukovina, reached America in 1951 and spent his last years in Israel. His poetry, SURREALISTIC and mythic, stands apart from the Yiddish mainstream. Glatstein, like so many other Yiddish writers after 1945, memorialized those who perished in the Holocaust. Grade wrote poetry and fiction about the life of east European Jews now gone forever. Isaac Bashevis SINGER, brother of I. J. Singer, had come to the U.S. in the 1930s. His worldwide fame dates to the 1950s, when English translations of his short stories and novels began to appear.

After World War II the American-Yiddish public also eagerly sought after the works of leading Soviet Yiddish writers. Although Itsik Kipnis (1896–1974) wrote forthrightly about Jewish nationalism and pride, he managed to escape the horror of 12 August, 1952, and died a natural death. He was the first to write about the massacre of the Jewish population of Kiev at Babi Yar. An outstanding short-story writer, he also wrote the popular novel *Khadoshim un teg* (1926; months and days), about a worker caught up in the wave of revolutionary enthusiasm. Note Lurye's fiction is marked by a nuanced psychological approach; his best-known novels are *Der step ruft* (2 vols., 1932, 1948; the steppe calls) and *Himl un erd* (1965; heaven and earth). Peretz Markish wrote epic verse and epic-length novels. He was one of a number of Yiddish writers who left the U.S.S.R. during the civil-war years, only to return in the late 1920s or early 1930s. Loyal to his Jewish origins and traditions, Markish was also an enthusiast for the new order. In 1939 he received the Order of Lenin from Stalin, on whose command he was executed in 1952. Der Nister's *Di mishpokhe Mashber* (2 vols., 1939, 1948; the Mashber family) ranks among the finest works in the Yiddish language. Elye Shekhtman's novel *Erev* (1962; *Erev*, 1967) deals with the fortunes of a family from the turn of the century onward. Shekhtman now lives in Israel. Natan Zabare was a master of medieval Jewish history and the arcane lexicon of the period, as evidenced in his posthumously published novel *Galgal hakhoyzer* (1979; and still it turns), about Jewish life in 13th-c. Provence, and *'S iz nokh groys der tog* (1975; the day is yet young), a novel that, while set in medieval Europe, in fact refers to contemporary issues.

Drama in Yiddish is closely linked to developments in theater history and therefore evolved along somewhat different lines from the other genres. Although amateur traveling Yiddish theater troupes existed in eastern Europe at the close of the 19th c., the greater part of their stage productions were on the level of what was called *shund* (trash).

Modern Yiddish theater began in Iaşi, Romania, during the Russo-Turkish war, in 1876, when Avrom (Abraham) Goldfaden (1840–1908) saw the possibilities of upgrading the light entertainment then available. His contributions as writer (of some forty plays and sketches), composer, director, and producer earned him the title of "father of the Yiddish theater."

The second important figure in the history of the Yiddish drama was Jacob Gordin (1853–1909), who came to the U.S. from Russia in 1891. A pioneer in the realistic theater, he broke with what existed at the time: the *purimshpil* (religious plays recounting biblical stories) and the stock characters of this early period of improvisation. Moving beyond the broad *commedia dell'arte* of Goldfaden and the *border zinger* (itinerant folk singers), Gordin wrote to and for the intelligentsia, although his plays appealed equally to sweatshop workers. In addition to adapting or translating major European dramatists, he composed Jewish versions of, for example, Shakespeare—the memorable *Mirele Efros* (1898; Mirele Efros), a female King Lear tragedy; and Goethe—*Got, mentsh, un tayvl* (1903; God, man, and the devil), a Faust drama.

Another early attempt at serious theater was the troupe that gathered around Peretz Hirshbein (1880–1948), beginning in Odessa in 1908. This troupe toured Russia, Byelorussia, and the Ukraine, presenting Hirshbein's own plays together with those of Asch, Gordin, and Dovid (David) Pinski (1872–1959). Hirshbein's efforts were largely responsible for improving the quality of plays on the Yiddish stage in Russia.

The Warsaw Yiddish Theater opened in 1921, achieving world acclaim under the artistic leadership of Esther Rokhl Kaminska (1870–1925) and later her daughter Ida Kaminska (1899–1980). In the late 1920s the experimental Young Theater, under the direction of Mikhl Vaykhert (1890–1967), introduced new techniques in stage design and set building.

In the wake of the Russian Revolution, the Yiddish State Theater was formed in Moscow, under the direction of Alexandr Granovsky (pseud. of Avrom Azarkh, 1890–1937), and included Marc Chagall in the company. It enjoyed three decades of popularity and success before being peremptorily closed in 1948.

In the U.S. the Yiddish theater matured intellectually while at the same time it reached out to ordinary workers and new immigrants, for whom—with no Yiddish school system and no regular book market—the daily press and the stage served as the chief vehicles for education and acculturation. The Yiddish Art Theater began under the direction of Maurice Schwartz (1890–1960), the leading figure in the New York Yiddish theater between 1918 and 1950. It engaged fine actors, staged plays of good quality, and became an enduring influence. Another important force in Yiddish (and American) drama was the Arbeter Teater Farband, or Artef, the Workers' Theater League, founded in 1926. It served as a platform for the ideas of the left-wing sector of the community until the late 1930s. Benno Schneider (1902–1977), its stage director and a disciple of the Russian director Yevgeny Vakhtangov, came to Artef after working with the Habima Theater in Moscow.

In recent years four Yiddish theater companies, with the Folksbine the most prominent, have staged performances in New York each season. A State Yiddish Theater also continues to function on a regular basis in Romania.

Dovid Pinski, a novelist as well as a dramatist, was a disciple of Y. L. Peretz. He wrote problem plays for half a century, becoming one of the best-known and most widely translated Yiddish writers in any genre. *Dovid hamelekh un zayne vayber* (1919; *King David and His Wives*, 1966), one of his best plays, depicts several stages in the life of the biblical king.

Peretz Hirshbein, who arrived in America in 1911, produced his *Di puste kretshme* (1913; *The Haunted Inn*, 1921) on Broadway in 1922. His *Farvorfn vinkl* (1913; a distant corner) is a rustic Romeo and Juliet folk play with a joyful ending.

H. Leivick (pseud. of Leyvik Halper, 1888–1962), who settled in New York in 1913, has a high reputation as a poet because of his verse play *Der Golem* (1921; *The Golem*, 1966). He also wrote some twenty fine prose plays, the best of which is *Shmates* (1921; rags), a tragedy about a scholar alienated from his new American environment. *Hirsh Lekert* (1927; Hirsh Lekert) treats the struggle of an idealist with a frustrating bureaucracy.

S. Anski (pseud. of Shloyme Zanvl Rapoport, 1863–1920) wrote the most famous play in the Yiddish canon, *Der dibuk* (1919; *The Dybbuk*, 1925), about the spirit of a dead person who enters another's body. It is set in the world of Hasidic pietism and mysticism. Sholem Asch, better known for his novels to the non-Yiddish reader, wrote some twenty plays that remain in the repertory of the Yiddish theater.

Moyshe Kulbak, an expressionist poet and author of the novel *Zelmenyaner* (2 vols., 1931–35; *Zelmenyaner*, 1977) also wrote several important plays, including *Yakov Frank* (1923; Yakov Frank), about a false messiah in 18th-c. Poland; *Boytre* (1936; Boytre), a drama about a Robin Hood figure set in an early-19th-c. *shtetl*; and *Binyumin Magidov* (1936; Binyumin Magidov), a historical play about the leader of a partisan band in Byelorussia.

Alter-Sholem Katsizne, who lived in Vilna, Kiev, and Warsaw, was an intriguing and gifted playwright of refined skill and exceptional dramatic power, as well as a novelist and essayist. His major plays are *Dukus* (1926; the duke), based on a legend about a righteous convert; *Herodus* (1926; Herod), a historical tragedy about the King of Judea; *Dem yidns opere* (pub. 1967; the Jews' opera), about Portuguese Marranos in the 18th c.; and *Shvartsbard* (pub. 1972; *Schwartzbard*, 1980), about the Ukrainian hetman Semyon Petliura.

Since the founding of the State of Israel in May 1948, Yiddish has been viewed as a functional rival of the nation's official language, Hebrew. Despised as the jargon of the *shtetl* and associated with Diaspora powerlessness and entrepreneurial "nonproductivity," it was further scorned as the everyday language of two anti-Zionist groups, the Labor Bund and the ultra-Orthodox religious community. Some twenty years after the declaration of Israel's statehood, President Zalman Shazar declared that the struggle against Yiddish did not belong to the present but to the distant past.

Although research has documented a Yiddish-speaking settlement in Palestine since at least as early as the mid-15th c., acceptance of Yiddish has not yet been achieved in Israel. Radio programing is extremely limited, and there is virtually no Yiddish television broadcasting. There is, however, evidence of a growing mood of toleration, as Yiddish comes to be viewed as the "martyrs' tongue" (President Chaim Weizmann's phrase), the speech of the six million who died in the Holocaust and of the unnumbered victims of Stalin's purges. Among the more encouraging signs: a chair of Yiddish has been established at the Hebrew University; an annual prize for Yiddish writing has been awarded since 1973, under the patronage of the Prime Minister's office; and Peretz-Farlag and Yisroel-Bukh have become two of the leading publishers of writing in Yiddish from around the world.

Three groups can be distinguished among Israeli Yiddish writers: (1) those who were born in or settled in Palestine during the early part of the century: the poets Uri Zvi Greenberg, Avrom Lev (b. 1911), Yoysef Papiernikov (b. 1897), and Arye Shamri (b. 1907); (2) those who came in the late 1940s: the poets Rivke Basman (b. 1925), Rokhl Fishman (b. 1935), Yankev Fridman (1906–1972), the fiction writer Mendl Man (1916–1974), Moyshe Yungman (1922–1983), a poet and founder of the Young Israel group, and Avrom Sutskever, Israel's premier Yiddish poet and editor of the literary journal *Di goldene keyt*; (3) those who have come from the U.S.S.R. in the past dozen years, some of the most vibrant and productive Yiddish writers now publishing: Rokhl Boymvol (b. 1914), Meyer Kharats (b. 1912), Hirsh Osherovitsh (b. 1908), Shloyme Roytman (b. 1913), Elye Shekhtman, and Ziame Telesin (b. 1907). This last group focuses largely on the contemporary period and publishes frequently in the periodicals *Yerushalayimer almanakh*, originally edited by Dovid Sfard (1905–1981) and then by Yoysef Kerler (b. 1918), and *Bay zikh*, edited by Itskhak Janosowicz (b. 1909).

The number of people for whom Yiddish is a first language diminishes every day, and for a time it was considered a dying language. A recent renewal of interest in Yiddish, especially among young people in America, and its use among immigrants from the Soviet Union in Israel are indications that it survives, and older Yiddish works are being rediscovered through numerous translations.

BIBLIOGRAPHY: Roback, A. A., *The Story of Yiddish Literature* (1940); Roback, A. A., *Contemporary Yiddish Literature* (1957); Liptzin, S., *The Flowering of Yiddish Literature* (1963); Madison, C., *Yiddish Literature: Its Scope and Major Writers* (1968); Biletzky, I. C., *Essays on Yiddish Poetry and Prose Writers of the Twentieth Century* (1969); Howe, I. and E. Greenberg, eds., Introduction to *A Treasury of Yiddish Poetry* (1969): 1–66; Liptzin, S., *The Maturing of Yiddish Literature* (1970); Dobzynski, C., Introduction to *Le miroir d'un peuple: Anthologie de la poésie yidich 1870–1970* (1971): 5–19; Howe, I. and E. Greenberg, eds., Introduction to *Voices from the Yiddish* (1972): 1–15; Landis, J. C., ed., Introduction to *The Great Jewish Plays* (1972): 1–14; Liptzin, S., *The History of Yiddish Literature* (1972); Shmeruk, C., "Yiddish Literature in the U.S.S.R.," in L. Kochan, ed., *The Jews in Soviet Russia*, 2nd ed. (1972): 232–68; Telesin, Z., "Contemporary Yiddish Prose in the Soviet Union," in A. Tartakower and Z. Kolitz, eds., *Jewish Culture in the Soviet Union* (1973): 76–90; Goldsmith, E. S., *Architects of Yiddishism at the Beginning of the Twentieth Century* (1976); Fishman, J. A. and D. E. Fishman, "Yiddish in Israel," in J. Fishman, ed., *Advances in the Study of Societal Multilingualism* (1977): 232–68; Singer, I. B., *Nobel Lecture* (1979); Jewish theater issue, *TDR*, 24, 3 (1980); Fishman, J. A., ed., *Never Say Die: A Thousand Years of Yiddish in Jewish Life and Letters* (1981); Schulman, E., *The Holocaust in Yiddish Literature* (1983)

—THOMAS E. BIRD

YOKOMITSU Riichi

Japanese novelist and short-story writer, b. 17 March 1898, Fukushima; d. 30 Dec. 1947, Tokyo

Y. grew up in a family with no intellectual or cultural pretensions. From the age of twelve he was obliged to spend much of his time away from home: his father worked in Korea for a number of years and Y.'s mother went with him, leaving the youth with relatives or in lodging houses. These lonely adolescent years perhaps account for the desperate tone of much of his work. He had no other career except that of a professional writer. He was married twice, his first wife dying when she was only twenty, an event of great impact on his writing: it seems to have put an end to his literary experimentalism.

Y. made his literary debut with a stylistically experimental novella, *Nichirin* (1923; the sun in heaven), at a time when European modernism was being introduced into Japan. In 1924, with Kawabata YASUNARI and others, he founded the magazine *Bungei jidai*, which during its two-and-a-half-year existence published the writings of the Shinkankakuha (New Sense-Impression Group), whose theoretical aim was to describe the world in terms of the sense impressions as they are directly received, rather than as mediated by the mind or the emotions. This group, in fact, represented the one significant attempt in Japanese literature in the 1920s to write a modernist prose, and Y. was the only member of it who did so with any real vigor.

This modernism was only short-lived, since proletarian writing soon came to dominate the literary scene, but Y.'s second collection of short stories, *Haru wa basha ni notte* (1927; spring riding in a carriage), reestablished his reputation. When he came to write his first long novel in 1927–28, *Shanghai* (1932; Shanghai), he was already famous. This novel shows a gradual abandoning of the impressionistic, brisk sentences of his earlier experimental work, a stylistic change completed in his most famous short story, "Kikai" (1930; "Machine," 1962), in which Y. uses long, convoluted sentences in an attempt to reveal the devious and obscure inner workings of the mind. "Kikai" is also typical of his writing in that it has a hero whose habit of self-reflection reveals little about himself. Y. thus creates a nightmarish image of man's inability to grasp the truth of existence—that human life is dominated by a deterministic "machine" beyond human control. This theme is the keynote of his serious writing.

The result of Y.'s experiments with psychological fiction was a series of long novels written during the 1930s in which he shows a growing concern with the division between "pure" and "popular" literature, attempting to create an amalgam of the two, although these works look, at least at first, more popular than serious.

A six-month stay in Europe in 1936 produced (or intensified) a sense of alienation from the spiritual Westernization that he presumed Japan had undergone, and he devoted much of the next ten years to the long, uncompleted, serially published novel, *Ryoshū* (1937–48; travel sadness), an attempt to debate this question in terms of the story of two men, one representing the Japanese, the other the Westernized spirit, and the women they love. After the 1945 defeat, Y. refused to swing with the reversal of the intellectual current, which now favored democracy and criticized the emperor worship and anti-Western views of the war years. Thus, he fell totally out of favor with the literary world, and so he remained until his death.

Y. was perhaps the leading Japanese novelist during the 1930s, but since his death he has been mainly ignored, his work overshadowed by that of his contemporary and close friend Kawabata. There are now signs, however, that some kind of reappraisal of his writings is about to take place. Even if his only truly accomplished work is seen as a handful of short stories, his central importance in the history of the Japanese novel during the experimental interwar years is beyond question.

FURTHER WORKS: *Onmi* (1924); *Hanabana* (1931); *Shin'en* (1932); *Monsho* (1934); *Tokei* (1934); *Seisō* (1935); *Tenshi* (1935); *Kazoku kaigi* (1935); *Haruzono* (1937); *Mi imada juku sezu* (1938); *Keien* (1941); *Yoru no kutsu* (1947). **FURTHER WORKS IN ENGLISH:** *Time, and Others* (1965, bilingual); *Love, and Other Stories of Y. R.* (1974)

BIBLIOGRAPHY: Keene, D., Introduction to *Love, and Other Stories* (1974): ix–xxii; Keene, D., *Y. R.: Modernist* (1980)

—DENNIS KEENE

YORUBA LITERATURE
See Nigerian Literature

YOSANO Akiko

(formerly Hō Shō) Japanese poet, essayist, translator, and short-story writer, b. 7 Dec. 1878, Sakai; d. 29 May 1942, Tokyo

The third daughter of a confectionery shop owner in Sakai in western Japan, Y. was drawn as a girl to the Japanese classics and the new romantic literature of the Meiji period (1868–1912). After publishing her first poems in the local Kansai literary journals in the late 1890s, she joined the progressive New Poetry Society founded by Yosano Hiroshi (pseud. of Yosano Tekkan, 1873–1935) in Tokyo and began to publish her poems in its literary journal, *Myōjō*. Soon her passionate love for Hiroshi compelled her to leave her family in 1901 for Tokyo to be with him. The five years after their marriage in that same year witnessed a remarkable surge of creative energy in Y., resulting in the publications of some of the poetry collections for which Y. was best known, namely *Midaregami* (1901; *Tangled Hair*, 1935), *Koōgi* (1904; little fan), *Koigoromo* (1905; intimate love, with Yamakawa Tomiko [1879–1909] and Masuda Masako [1880–1946]), and *Maihime* (1906; the dancing girl). Having established herself as a noteworthy and innovative romantic poet before she turned thirty, she continued to publish an extraordinary number of poems throughout the late Meiji and into the Taishō era (1912–1926). Her love for her eleven children provided the impetus for a series of poetic works and children's tales such as *Yatsu no yoru* (1914; eight nights) and *Uneunekawa* (1915; meandering river).

In 1912 Y. went to France, her first experience abroad, to join Hiroshi, and stayed in Europe for about half a year. While the trip partly inspired another one of Y.'s poetry collections, entitled *Natsu yori aki e* (1914; from summer to fall), more importantly it further stimulated Y.'s already burgeoning interest in feminist

issues. After returning to Japan, she began to publish social commentaries on a wide range of topics related to women and education, including such collections as *Hito oyobi onna to shite* (1916; as a human being and a woman), *Warera nani o motomuru ka* (1917; what are we seeking?), *Ai, risei oyobi yūki* (1917; love, reason, and courage), and *Gekidō no naka o yuku* (1919; walking into the midst of upheaval). To practice what she preached about women's education, she became in 1921 the school superintendent of the Academy of Culture, a school that advocated a liberal educational philosophy.

Among Y.'s extensive publications were fifteen collections of essays and three volumes of critical writings on the art of poetry. She was also an indefatigable translator of some of the major works of classical Japanese literature into modern Japanese, the most noteworthy of which was her unprecedented four-volume translation of the 11th-c. romance *Genji monogatari* (*The Tale of Genji*) entitled *Shin'yaku Genji monogatari* (1912–1913; a modern translation of *The Tale of Genji*). Toward the end of her life, she even renewed her efforts in producing yet another eight-volume translation of the same work called *Shin shin'yaku Genji monogatari* (1938–1939; the newest translation of *The Tale of Genji*).

Y. continued to publish collections of her poetry and essays in the early part of the Shōwa period (1926–1989) such as *Kokoro no enkei* (1928; the distant scene in the heart), *Hikaru kumo* (1928; the glistening clouds), and *Man-mō yūki* (1930; travels in Manchuria and Mongolia). But among her later works, the most notable was probably her collection *Hakuōshū* (1942; a collection of white cherry blossoms). Published posthumously, many of the poems imparted Y.'s feelings of melancholy and loneliness after the death of Hiroshi as well as her reflections on her own illness. She died at the age of sixty-three (sixty-five by Japanese count).

The most prolific and well-known of modern Japanese women poets, Y. has been best remembered for the sensual quality of her poems and their innovative imagery enlivened by a vibrant, imaginative diction. This was especially true of her romantic love poems collected in her most widely read and most thoroughly studied collection, *Midaregami*. Her long poem "Kimi shi ni tamōkoto nakare" (1904; "Heaven Forbid That You Shall Die!" 1951), published in the midst of the Russo-Japanese War and harshly criticized by the contemporary poet Ōmachi Keigetsu (1869–1925) as unpatriotic, has been cherished by some critics after 1945 as one of the most celebrated antiwar poems in prewar Japan, while others have noted its limitations. All her other poetry collections and her writings in other genres are much lesser known and are awaiting scholarly attention both in Japan and abroad.

FURTHER WORKS: *Dokugusa* (1904); *Yume no hana* (1906); *Kurokami* (1907); *Eihon otogibanashi* (1908); *Byakkō* (1908); *Jōka* (1908); *Saohime* (1909); *Hana* (1910, with Enami Bunzō); *Joshi no fumi* (1910); *Shōnen shōjo* (1910); *Shundeishū* (1911); *Ichigū yori* (1911); *Seikaiba* (1912); *Kumo no iroiro* (1912); *Pari yori* (1914, with Yosano Hiroshi); *Sakurasō* (1915); *Yosano Akiko shū* (1915); *Zakkichō* (1915); *Uta no tsukuriyō* (1915); *Shuyōshū* (1916); *Akarumi e* (1916); *Tanka sanbyakukō* (1916); *Maigoromo* (1916); *Akiko shinshū* (1917); *Myōjōshō* (1918); *Wakaki tomo e* (1918); *Shintō zassō* (1919); *Itte mairimasu* (1919); *Hi no tori* (1919); *Akiko kawa* (1919); *Akiko tanka zenzhū* (1919–1920); *Nyonin sōzō* (1920); *Taiyō to bara* (1921); *Ningen reihai* (1921); *Tabi no uta* (1921); *Kusa no yume* (1922); *Akiko renkashō* (1923); *Ai no sōsaku* (1923); *Ryūsei no michi* (1924); *Rurikō* (1925); *Deido jizō* (1925); *Suna ni kaku* (1925); *Ningen ōrai* (1925); *Fujitarō no* *tabi* (1925); *Akiko shihen zenshū* (1929); *Kirishima no uta* (1929); *Gaitō ni okuru* (1931); *Yosano Akiko zenshū* (13 vols., 1933–1934); *Yūshōsha to nare* (1934); *Tanka bungaku zenshū. Yosano Akiko hen* (1936); *Gendai tanka sōsho. Yosano Akiko hen* (1940); *Rakkashō* (1942); *Yosano Akiko shokanshū* (1948); *Teihon Yosano Akiko zenshū* (20 vols., 1979–1981)

BIBLIOGRAPHY: Honda, H., *The Poetry of Y.A.* (1957); Shinoda, S., and S. Goldstein, Introduction to *Tangled Hair* (1971): 1–23; Ueda, M., *Modern Japanese Poets and the Nature of Literature* (1983): 53–94; special Y. issue, *JATJ*, 25, 1 (Apr. 1991)

—CHIA-NING CHANG

YOURCENAR, Marguerite

(pseud. of Marguerite de Crayencour) French novelist, short-story writer, essayist, autobiographer, dramatist, poet, and translator, b. 8 June 1903, Brussels, Belgium; d. 17 Dec. 1987, Maine, USA

Y. was the only child of a French father and a Belgian mother, who died shortly after her daughter's birth. Y. was educated privately under the guidance of her father, a man of broad literary culture, and later traveled extensively in Europe and Asia Minor, studying and writing. In 1939 she left Europe for the U.S., where she taught from 1942 to 1953. She lived on Mount Desert Island off the coast of Maine. In 1980 she became the first woman ever elected to the French Academy.

At the center of Y.'s writings is a meditation on mortality, with its corollary themes that involve a questioning of humanism and of the meaning of the solitary first person singular "I." Her texts blend the cultural and spiritual with the sensual, and the past with the present, thereby suggesting a coherence and a continuity. Her major characters, haunted by an ideal of beauty and lucidity, are caught in the historical dramas of their age. The ambience may be Mussolini's Rome in *Denier du rêve* (1934; *A Coin in Nine Hands*, 1982); the aftermath of World War I and the Russian Revolution in *Le coup de Grâce* (1939; *Coup de Grâce*, 1957); Hadrian's Rome in *Mémoires d'Hadrien* (1951; *Memoirs of Hadrian*, 1954); the upheavals of 16th-c. Europe in *L'œuvre au noir* (1968; *The Abyss*, 1976); the social history of Y.'s family from prehistoric times to the 20th c. in *Souvenirs pieux* (1974; in memoriam) and *Archives du nord* (1977; archives of the north). Y.'s passion for precise knowledge concerning all manifestation of the human presence contributes to the perfection and scope of her writing. Her extraordinary erudition and audacious clarity, her persistent reworking of the same material, her notes that contain scholarly comment and critical appraisal, place her at a significant distance from many of her less patient and more dogmatic contemporaries.

Because certain periods of the past are an integral part of Y.'s consciousness, her effort as a writer is directed toward interweaving what was once and what is now. The past imposes a distance; the distance imposes a discipline in method and sensibility. To retell the story of Theseus, to rewrite many of her own texts, to translate into French Virginia WOOLF, Henry JAMES, Constantine CAVAFY, American Negro spirituals (*Fleuve profond, sombre rivière* [1964; deep dark river]), and ancient Greek lyric poetry (*La couronne et la lyre* [1979; the crown and the lyre], to tell the story of her family in Flanders, are related activities.

Marguerite Yourcenar

Mémoires d'Hadrien has been acclaimed as the product of a singularly learned and sensitive mind. Hadrian's essential quality is his acute attention to all aspects of his experience: hunting, loving, learning, traveling, governing, and dying. He is a man of strong passions, but is also a man of stern discipline, capable of both action and meditation. Hadrian belongs to a small group of philosophers aware of their intellectual superiority, but aware, too, of the limits imposed on all human endeavors by death, and even more by the tragedies of living. Between Hadrian's 2nd c. A.D. and our 20th c. there are some analogies: a similar eclecticism, a similar skepticism, the heavy weight of a rich, ancient culture, the curiosity for new modes of life and new religious experience. The analogies with our disturbed times are even greater in *L'œuvre au noir*, in which Zeno, a lucid and courageous man, lives and dies, caught between conflicting forms of fanaticism in a world torn by war, and is threatened to the end by the ignorance and suspicion of mankind.

Several of Y.'s plays, such as *Electre; ou, La chute des masques* (1954; Electra; or, the fall of the masks), *Le mystère d'Alceste* (1963; the mystery of Alcestis), and *Qui n'a pas son Minotaure?* (1963; who does not have his Minotaur?), are based on Greek legends. As she indicates in her preface to *Electre*, Y. does not attempt modern interpretations of Greek myths such as those by Eugene O'NEILL, Jean GIRAUDOUX, and Jean-Paul SARTRE, but rather proposes her own version of Greek consciousness and conscience.

In Y.'s texts defeat and death are always accompanied by a triumph of the individual who heroically retains, until the very end, his or her particular integrity and, in so doing, learns before dying some truths about life and about the self. Y.'s compelling voice is one of the richest of the 20th c.

FURTHER WORKS: *Le jardin des chimères* (1921); *Les dieux ne sont pas morts* (1922); *Alexis; ou, Le traité du vain combat* (1929); *La nouvelle Eurydice* (1931); *Pindare* (1932); *La mort conduit l'attelage* (1934); *Feux* (1936; *Fires*, 1981); *Nouvelles orientales* (1938); *Les songes et les sorts* (1938); *Les charités d'Alcippe* (1956); *Présentation de Constantin Cavafy* (1958); *Sous bénéfice d'inventaire* (1962); *Présentation critique d'Hortense Flexner* (1969); *Discours de réception de M. Y. à l'Académie Royale Belge de Langue et de Littérature Françaises* (1971); *Théâtre* (2 vols., 1971); *La couronne et la lyre* (1979); *Mishima; ou, La vision du vide* (1980); *Discours de réception de M. Y. à l'Académie Française* (1981); *Œuvres romanesques* (1982)

BIBLIOGRAPHY: Aubrion, M., "M. Y.; ou, La mesure de l'homme," *RG*, No. 1 (1970): 15–29; Blot, J., *M. Y.* (1971; rev. ed., 1980); Rosbo, P. de, *Entretiens radiophoniques avec M. Y.* (1972); Crosland, M., *Women of Iron and Velvet: French Women Writers after George Sand* (1976): 116–27; Farrell, C. F., Jr., Farrell, E. R., "M. Y.: The Art of Re-writing," *ECr*, 19, 2 (1979): 36–46; special Y. issue, *ELit*, 12, 1 (1979); Peyre, H., "M. Y.: Independent, Imaginative and 'Immortal,'" *WLT*, 57 (1983): 191–95

—ELAINE MARKS

YOVKOV, Yordan

Bulgarian short-story writer and dramatist, b. 9 Nov. 1880, Zheravna; d. 15 Oct. 1937, Plovdiv

After working as a teacher in Dobrudzha, a region later ceded by Bulgaria to Romania, Y. served in the Balkan Wars and World War I as soldier and journalist. In the 1920s Y. was employed for seven years at the Bulgarian legation in Bucharest, and thereafter until his death as a minor official of the Ministry of Foreign Affairs in Sofia.

After making his debut as a poet in 1905, Y. eventually turned to the shorter prose genres; it was in these that he left his mark in Bulgarian literature. His prose works based upon his war experiences are remarkable for the spirit of reconciliation in which they treat that most horrendous of human conflicts. His major collections of short stories—*Staroplaninski legendi* (1927; Balkan legends), *Vecheri v Antimovskiya khan* (1928; evenings at the Antimovo inn), and *Zhenski surtse* (1935; a woman's heart)—chronicle the life and legends of the Bulgarian peasant village. Y. is never blind to the cruelties of life, but he is always persuaded that even its apparent catastrophes in the end work for the good. Among his most characteristic protagonists is the good-hearted dreamer entranced by beauty who does not quite fit into a world not made by dreamers. In the short-story collection *Ako mozhekha da govoryat* (1936; if they could speak) Y. investigated the psychological world of animals.

Y. also wrote several short novels, of which the most important, *Chiflikut kray granitsata* (1934; the farmstead at the frontier), is set among the violent events of a domestic insurrection in 1923. In the 1930s he turned to the theater, publishing four plays. In the earliest of these, *Albena* (1930; Albena), he described the destructive

potential of that very beauty and harmony to which he himself had consistently been devoted.

In a literature that has always been strongest in the shorter genres, Y. stands as the supreme master of the short story. His stories are finely wrought and require close attention, lest some crucial plot detail escape the reader. By the power of his literary art Y. creates a world of the imagination which, although firmly grounded in the reality of the Bulgarian countryside and its folklore traditions, is both uniquely his own and universal.

FURTHER WORKS: *Razkazi* (2 vols., 1917–1918); *Zhetvaryat* (1920); *Posledna radost* (1926); *Milionerut* (1930); *Boryana* (1932); *Obiknoven chovek* (1936); *Priklyucheniyata na Gorolomov* (1938). **FURTHER WORKS IN ENGLISH:** *The White Swallow, and Other Short Stories* (1947); *Short Stories* (1965)

BIBLIOGRAPHY: Moser, C., "The Visionary Realism of Jordan Jovkov," *SEEJ*, 11 (1967): 44–58; Moser, C., "Jovkov's Place in Modern Bulgarian Literature," in Butler, T., ed., *Bulgaria Past and Present* (1976): 267–72

—CHARLES A. MOSER

YÜ Kwang-chung

(also romanized as Yu Guangzhong) Chinese poet and essayist, b. 9 Sept. 1928, Nanking

Y. is a leading poet, essayist, critic, and translator, well known to readers in Taiwan, Hong Kong, and, recently, mainland China. A graduate of the Foreign Languages and Literature Department, National Taiwan University, Y. received his M.F.A. from the University of Iowa. He has been a professor of English literature at universities in Taiwan, Hong Kong, and the U.S. Since 1985 he has been dean of the Liberal Arts College, National Sun Yat-sen University in Kaohsiung.

He has written some forty books, fifteen of which are in verse, and has received half a dozen major literary awards in Taiwan. Though he is regarded by some as a Taiwan writer, both his life experience and the scope of his writings prove that he is a veritable Chinese writer. A native of Fukien, before he came to Taiwan at twenty-two, he had resided and traveled in many cities in China, including Hang-chou, Kun-ming, Chungking, Nanking, and Amoy. Not only is China his obsession, his beloved motherland, but Chinese classical literature and history furnish rich vision and imagery to his imaginary world.

Y. is a great master of the Chinese language. His early poetry and lyrical prose abound in newly coined phrases and ingeniously rearranged syntactical structures. He forges a new style that fuses classical language, modern Chinese vernacular, and English syntactical structure into one. The following subject matters are his main concerns: fervent patriotism, passion for natural beauty, especially that of Hong Kong and southern Taiwan, conservationism, friendship, and romantic love, which is the major theme in his poetry collection *Lien ti lien-hsiang* (1964; associations of the lotus). W. B. YEATS and the Chinese poet Tu Fu (712–770) are the two writers who have had greatest impact on him. His tone is sometimes serious and passionate, sometimes witty and intellectual, but always conveys an imposing tension. His poetry is well-structured and often enriched with well-wrought conceits.

His early poetic style shows a heavy imprint of Chinese poetry written in the 1930s and 1940s. Then, influenced by EXISTENTIALISM and MODERNISM, his poetry collection *Wan-sheng-chieh* (1960; Halloween) deals with his experiences in the U.S. and shows ingenuity in both form and technique. Using an outspoken, audacious voice, his poetry collections *Wu-ling shao-nien* (1967; a youth of T'ang) and *Tien-lang-hsing* (1976; Sirius) are permeated with modern images, strong moods such as anger, despair, and anxiety, and an acute sense of contention. On the other hand, *Lien ti lien-hsiang* marks a return to Chinese classicism, to the graceful poetic world of ancient China. The poetry collections *Chiao-ta hsüeh* (1969; music percussive) and *Pai-yü k'u-kua* (1974; white jade bitter gourd) unravel his profound love for his ailing mother and motherhood. Poems like "Tang wo szu shih" (when I die) and "Pai-yü k'u-kua" (white jade bitter gourd) are so touching that they have become classics extolled by Chinese readers all over the world. Contemplating the Vietnam War, *Tsai leng-chan ti nien-tai* (1959; in years of cold war) uncovers the poet's conscientiousness. The style of his later poetry such as *Tzu-ching-fu* (1986; bauhinia) and *Meng yü ti-li* (1990; dream and geography) has become more temperate, smooth, and mature.

Some consider that his achievements in prose writing exceed those in poetry. His lyrical essays in *Tso-shou ti miu-szu* (1963; the left-handed muse), *Hsiao-yau-yu* (1963; the untrammeled traveler), and *Ting-t'ing na leng-yü* (1974; listen to the cold rain) are highly experimental and innovative. Forging an elaborate style unrivaled by any modern Chinese writer, he presents new combinations or new correlations in his diction, phrase, syntax, tone, and metaphor. Meanwhile, his consciousness expands to the classical literary world of thousands of years. His recent essays, such as those dealing with natural beauty in *Ko-shui hu-tu* (1990; calling for the ferry), are fraught with keen observation, wit, and warmth. Some of his Chinese translations are very popular. *Fan-ku chuan* (1957), his translation of *Lust for Life: The Story of Vincent van Gogh* by Irving Stone (1903–1989) is itself a classic, and his rendering of Oscar Wilde's *The Importance of Being Earnest* has been a stage success in Taiwan, Hong Kong, and mainland China. Y. also participated actively in compaigning for the modern poetry movement in the 1960s and in protesting against pollution in the 1980s. In the past three decades he has sponsored and intermittently edited the poetry journal *Lan Hsing*.

The quality and quantity of Y.'s poetry and prose, as well as his mastery of the Chinese language, secure him a position of a major Chinese writer of this century.

FURTHER WORKS: *Chou-tzu ti bei-ke* (1952); *Lanse ti yü-mau* (1954); *Chung-ju shih* (1960); *Changshang yü* (1964); *Wang-hsiang ti mu-shen* (1968); *Tien-kuo ti yeh-shih* (1969); *Fen-ho-jen* (1972); *Yü Kuang-chung san-wen hsüan* (1975); *Ch'ingch'ing pien-chou* (1977); *Yü Yung-heng pa-ho* (1979); *Wen-hsüeh ti sha-tien* (1981); *Fen-shuiling shang* (1981); *Yü Kuang-chung shih-hsüan* (1981); *Ko-shui kuan-yin* (1983); *Chi-i hsiang Piethkuei i-yang chang* (1987); *Yü Kuang-chung shihhsüan* (1988); *Yü Kuang-chung i-pai-shou* (1988; rev. ed., 1989). FURTHER WORKS IN ENGLISH: *Acres of Barbed Wire* (1971)

BIBLIOGRAPHY: Hsia, C. T., "The Continuing Obsession with China: Three Contemporary Writers," *RNL*, 6, 1 (1975): 76–99; Donath, A., "Ein Langgedicht von Y.," *China: Kultur, Polish und Wirtschaft* (1976): 51–56; Hou, S. S., "*The Phoenix Bathing in Fire: Y. tso-p'in p'ing-lun chi*, by Wong Wai-leung," *CLEAR* 7, 1–2 (1987): 201–9; Chien, C. C., "Y.: Writing As the Phenomenal World of Exile," *Chung-hsing ta-hsüeh wen-shih hsüeh-pao*, 21 (1991): 1–28

—CHUNG LING

YUGOSLAV LITERATURE

When in the 7th c. A.D. the migrating southern Slavs settled in the regions of present day Yugoslavia, they were already divided into ethnically distinct groups. During the next thirteen centuries they drifted even further apart, through religious fragmentation, foreign cultural influences, the divergence of their respective languages (Serbo-Croatian, Slovene, Macedonian), the growth of distinctly regional dialects, and the adoption of two different alphabets (Latin and Cyrillic). The precarious political unity since 1918 has not been enough to erase deep social, cultural, and linguistic differences. The Slavic literatures of Yugoslavia remain related but distinct. (There is writing as well by non-Slavic peoples living in the country; see separate sections following main article.-Ed.)

The literatures of the Serbs and the Croats are both quantitatively and qualitatively the most prominent. They are written in the same language (although not in the same alphabet) but differ in their historical development, cultural orientation, and dialectal shadings. Next comes the literature of the Slovenes, whose language forms a bridge between those of the western and southern Slavs, and that of the Macedonians, whose language provides a link between Serbo-Croatian and Bulgarian. The literature of Montenegro is historically and linguistically within the Serbian literary tradition, while that of Bosnia and Herzegovina is oriented toward either Serbian or Croatian, depending upon the family background, linguistic heritage, and cultural bent of each writer.

Serbian Literature

Serbian literature in the 20th c. can be divided into three periods, separated and influenced by significant historical events: (1) from the overthrow of the Obrenović dynasty in 1903 to the end of World War I; (2) from the unification of the Yugoslavs to the end of World War II; (3) from the emergence of socialist Yugoslavia until the present.

After 1900 the traditional Russian influence on Serbian literature yielded to the French, primarily because of the increasing number of Serbs who went to France and Switzerland for higher education. The new trend affected poetry strongly. Fiction continued to be dominated by regionalism and nostalgia for the simple patriarchal past.

The leading Serbian poet at the turn of the century was the Herzegovinian Jovan DUČIĆ. A preoccupation with form and verbal elegance dominates his work. His favorite subjects are the vanished worlds of the frivolous Dubrovnik aristocracy and the mystical and austere Serbian medieval nobility. Of poets from Serbia proper, the most prominent was Milan Rakić (1876–1938) who, like Dučić, had studied in Paris. The sixty poems, most of them somber and pessimistic, that constitute his lifelong poetic effort show that he possessed an exceptional sense of verse rhythm and sonority. The poems of Milutin Bojić (1892–1917)—who died during World War I, his talent not yet fully developed—are full of buoyant optimism, vigorous sensuality, and poignant patriotic fervor. But since he wrote hastily, they also occasionally display traces of declamatory rhetoric and verbosity.

The most notable writer of fiction of this period was Borislav Stanković (1876–1927). His several volumes of stories, the novel *Nečista krv* (1911; tainted blood), and also his play *Koštana* (1902; Koštana) capture the colorful ambience of his native Vranje, in which the human spirit was perenially torn between Oriental sensuality and rigid patriarchalism. An equally significant regionalist was Petar Kočić (1877–1916), who championed the hardy Bosnian peasant, oppressed by poverty and foreign domination, but sly and full of resilience and earthy wit.

The leading dramatist of both this and the next period was Branislav NUŠIĆ. Despite his keen wit and a sharp eye for the ludicrous, however, he was not a profound social satirist.

The chief literary critics of this time were Bogdan Popović (1863–1944) and Jovan Skerlić (1877–1914). Popović founded the most important Serbian literary journal, *Srpski knjizevni glasnik*. In his criticism he emphasized form and seldom discussed content. His disciple, Skerlić, was much more sociologically oriented. He became the champion of ethical positivism in art and dismissed some of the more radical trends in Serbian literature as worthless.

In the interwar period Serbian poetry continued to develop under a strong French influence. Its previous distance from fiction became less pronounced because of new writers who distinguished themselves in both genres. Fiction, however, still retained much of its regionalist flavor, despite a noticeable growth in sophistication.

The most outstanding poet of this era was Rastko Petrović (1898–1949). Educated in France, he early fell under the spell of Guillaume APOLLINAIRE, Paul ÉLUARD, and Jean COCTEAU. His best collection of poems, *Otkrovenje* (1922; revelations), was considered sensationalist and blasphemous by conservatives and the clergy. Petrović favored spontaneous poetic outbursts, unhampered by contemplation and polishing touches.

Although Desanka MAKSIMOVIĆ produced a score of prose works, poetry remained her forte. Her verse—rich in rhythmic melodiousness, freshness of imagery, and fluidity of thought—slips at times into mawkish sentimentality and generalization. Some of her earlier poems about her illusions and disappointments in love are among her best.

Miloš CRNJANSKI, in the poetic collections *Lirika Itake* (1919; lyrics of Ithaca) and *Odabrani stihovi* (1954; selected verse), presented a distinctly personal, emotionally intense, and often elegiac view of contemporary man. His greatest prose work is *Seobe* (Part I, 1929; Part II, 1962; the migrations), a historical novel that depicts the 18th-c. Serbian exodus into Austrian lands. A profoundly pessimistic work, it underscores the futility of the human quest for peace, a better life, and domestic tranquillity.

Another writer of this era who excelled in more than one genre was Stanislav Vinaver (1891–1955). Educated in France and influenced by Paul VALÉRY, he produced ethereal poetry, rich in rhythmic melodiousness, but often rendered difficult by his ceaseless stylistic experimenting. Vinaver's numerous essays and his critical study of the 19th-c. Serbian poet Laza Kostić (1841–1910), *Zanosi i prkosi Laze Kostića* (1964; ravings and rancors of Lara Kostić), display his immense linguistic versatility as well as his love of polemics and literary ridicule.

Among the writers of fiction of the interwar years, the most distinguished was Ivo ANDRĆ. The three volumes of his short

stories published in this period introduced a distinctively Bosnian milieu that dominated Andrić's later major works, *Na Drini ćuprija* (1945; *The Bridge on the Drina*, 1959) and *Travnička hronika* (1945; *Bosnian Chronicle*, 1963). Although rooted in regionalism and realism. Andrić was an acute observer of inner life and a subtle psychologist and stylist.

A Bosnian of Jewish origin and Viennese education, Isak Samokovlija (1899–1955) excelled in short fiction. His best stories are distinguished by a constant mixture of the heroic and ludicrous, the tragic and humorous, the lyrical and naturalistic. Samokovlija showed a great affinity for impoverished but picturesque characters and used an archaic language of biblical flavor, with many Yiddish and obscure expressions.

Isidora Sekulić (1877–1958) devoted herself primarily to the short story and literary criticism. Her best story collections, *Iz prošlosti* (1919; from the past) and *Hronika palanačkog groblja* (1940; chronicle of a small-town cemetery), reveal her strong romantic affinities and a frequent preoccupation with the dichotomy of human nature. Her long essay *Njegošu: Knjiga duboke odanosti* (1951; to Njegoš: a book of deep devotion) is imaginative, albeit subjective and occasionally inaccurate.

Branimir Ćosić (1903–1934) is remembered chiefly for his last novel, *Pokošeno polje* (1934; the mowed field), a largely autobiographical work and the only one of this period to depict successfully the contemporary Serbian urban milieu.

The leading literary critic of his time, whose career continued well into the postwar years, was Milan Bogdanović (1892–1964). Influenced by the French critic Jules Lemaître (1853–1914) and by Skerlić, he stressed that literature should be relevant and committed. His style is marked by fluidity and polish, and his critical judgment is notable for its harmonious blend of ethical and aesthetic considerations.

In the first postwar decade an attempt was made to replace the traditional Western influence with Soviet-patterned SOCIALIST REALISM. Later, because of the growing independence of Yugoslavia from the Eastern bloc and because of fewer restrictions on artistic expression, the modernists gradually regained lost ground.

At the outset of the socialist period the Belgrade literary scene was dominated by a group who, after championing a largely unsuccessful movement toward SURREALISM in the 1930s, joined the communist cause. The most notable among them are Milan Dedinac (1902–1966), Dušan Matić (1898–19??), Aleksandar Vučo (b. 1897), and Oskar DAVIČO, all from Serbia proper, all educated in Belgrade and Paris, and all involved in their formative years primarily with poetry. Dedinac shifted from the dream world of abstractions, striking metaphors, and symbolic visions of his early poetry to socially relevant expressions, although he continued to over intellectualize his subject matter. As a writer of fiction and essays Matić is urbane and erudite but seldom gripping; as a poet he has been hailed as one of the most vibrant and influential figures of the postwar era. Vučo's poetry is characterized by its black humor, his novels by erudite complexity.

Davičo is both the most prolific and the most modernist author of this group. In his poetry he frequently resorts to irrational constructions, exaggerated metaphors, and vague verbosity. His best novel, *Pesma* (1952; rev. ed., 1953; *The Poem*, 1959), depicts the actions and dilemmas of a young and overimpulsive Resistance fighter in occupied Belgrade.

Another prominent writer of this group is the satirist Erih Koš (b. 1913). His novel *Veliki Mak* (1956; *The Strange Story of the Great Whale, also Known as Big Mac*, 1962), ridicules the human proclivity for idolatry and exposes the futility of an individual's quixotic struggle to oppose it. A similar tone pervades his novel *Vrapci Van Pea* (1961; Van Pe's sparrows).

The social realists in the postwar period largely adhered to subject matter from the liberation struggle and the communist reconstruction of the country. Branko ĆOPIĆ's career started in the prewar era with stories that deplored the plight of the poor in his native Bosnia. While serving as a partisan fighter in the war, he turned out a number of patriotic and propagandistic poems of great popular appeal; after the liberation he returned to fiction, producing short stories and novels that depict both humorously and solemnly events and characters from the war.

The Montenegrin Mihailo LALIĆ also matured during the war while fighting with the partisans. In his numerous stories and novels he concentrates on his dark memories of the fratricidal encounters of the two main anti-Nazi groups. His characters are well drawn, their conflicts authentic. Still, the singularity of his preoccupation with war, suffering, and destruction often gives his fiction a certain monotony.

Similar to Lalić in background and experiences but of greater talent is Dobrica ĆOSIĆ. His first novel, *Daleko je sunce* (1951; *Far Away Is the Sun*, 1963), about the partisan struggle, was acclaimed for its objectivity and artistic vigor; Ćosić then produced an even better one, *Koreni* (1954; the roots), a penetrating portrayal of life in a rich Serbian peasant family at the turn of the century. *Deobe* (3 vols., 1961; the divisions) follows a descendant of the same family through the ordeals of World War II. *Vreme smrti* (4 vols., 1972–79; *A Time of Death*, 1978; *Reach to Eternity*, 1980; *South to Destiny*, 1981), through a blend of psychological and historical detail, depicts the epic struggle of the Serbian nation for its survival during World War I.

A special place among the war-inspired writers of fiction belongs to the Montenegrin novelist Miodrag BULATOVIĆ. In his major works, *Heroj na magarcu* (1967; *Hero on a Donkey*, 1966), *Rat je bio bolji* (1969; *The War Was Better* 1972), and *Ljudi sa četiri prsta* (1975; the people with four fingers), he uses a highly unusual mixture of realistic and grotesque, EXPRESSIONIST touches. Usually obsessed by war and carnage, his fantastic and bizarre heroes perennially oscillate between horrible and ludicrous experiences in a world bereft of order and meaning.

Chronologically in this group but thematically closer to the preceding generation of prose writers is a late-blooming Bosnian novelist and story writer, Meša SELIMOVIĆ. He won great acclaim for the novel *Derviš i smrt* (1966; the dervish and death), a meandering memoir of bygone Bosnian Muslim life, rich in semi-Oriental, fantastic atmosphere and imbued with an overpowering sense of fatalism. Selimović's subsequent novels are in the same vein.

Of the generation that came into prominence in the 1960s, the most notable poet is Vasko POPA. A connoisseur of French and German surrealist and expressionist poetry, Popa made his debut with the collection *Kora* (1953; tree bark), composed of several cycles of thematically related poems, an arrangement that has reappeared in all his subsequent works. The most translated of all contemporary Serbian writers, Popa is a poet of striking metaphors, superb verbal virtuosity, and rare depth of imagination.

Equally profound, although much less known abroad, is Miodrag PAVLOVIĆ, whose volumes of verse testify to his intellectual preoccupation with the mind. Free of surrealist influence, his poetry often has images and themes from classical mythology and is at times highly abstract. Less cerebral, but very rich in intimate lyricism, is the poetry of Stevan Raičković (b. 1928). A particularly

keen observer of nature, Raičković frequently uses it as a background and catalyst for his visions of the tragic limits of our physical and spiritual existence.

Among writers born after 1930 the most notable poets are Ivan Lalić (b. 1931) and Matija Bećković. Lalić's verse is rich in delicate moods and subtle imagery and deals with the eternal themes of love, death, happiness, national traditions, and the land's Byzantine heritage, while that of Bećković, with its resplendent verbal polyphony and epic strength, evokes the tone of folk laments.

The best novelists of this group are Danilo KIŠ and Slobodan Selenić (b. 1933). Kiš's *Psalm 44* (1963; *psalm 44*), *Bašta, pepeo* (1965; *Garden, Ashes*, 1975), and *Peščanik* (1972; the hourglass) show that he is one of the boldest stylistic experimenters in Serbian prose today. Selenić's acclaimed novel *Memoari Pere bogalja* (1968; the memoirs of Pera the cripple) offers a sardonic view of the country's postwar social changes in which the lower-class victors are gradually corrupted by newly won privileges and petit-bourgeois materialist comfort.

The most representative postwar Serbian literary critics are Marko Ristić (b. 1902) and Velibor Gligorić (b. 1899). In the 1960s Ristić became one of the leading supporters of modernism in Serbian literature. His work is difficult to interpret, since his pronouncements often oscillate between aestheticism and political pamphleteering. Gligorić has consistently been a champion of social realism. He denied any literary merit to the interwar modernists and encouraged those postwar authors who defended the social aims of literature. His polemicism mellowed considerably in the postwar years, especially in his works of literary history.

BIBLIOGRAPHY: Barac, A., *History of Yugoslav Literature* (1955); Kadić, A., *Contemporary Croatian Literature* (1960); Kadić, A., *Contemporary Serbian Literature* (1964); Vaupotić, M., *Contemporary Croatian Literature* (1966); Luckić, S., *Contemporary Yugoslav Literature: A Sociological Approach* (1972); Mihailovich, V. D., "Yugoslav Literature," in Ivask, I., and G. von Wilpert, eds., *World Literature since 1945* (1973): 682–700; Eekman, T., *Thirty Years of Yugoslav Literature (1945–1975)* (1978); Lencek, R. L., "On the Options of the Poetry of a Small Nation," *SlovS*, 1 (1979): 4–13; Eekman, T., "Modernist Trends in Contemporary Serbo-Croatian and Slovene Prose," in Birnbaum, H., and T. Eekman, *Fiction and Drama in Eastern and Southeastern Europe: Evolution and Experiment in the Postwar Period* (1980): 121–35; Beker, M., ed., *Comparative Studies in Croatian Literature* (1981)

—NICHOLAS MORAVČEVICH

Albanian Literature

Yugoslavia has a population of one and three-quarter million Albanian speakers, residing principally in the Autonomous Province of Kosova and in neighboring parts of Macedonia and Montenegro. Although before World War II illiteracy was extremely high, by 1943 publication in Albanian was beginning. The quick growth in literacy since World War II has often meant that some of the most gifted people became simultaneously teachers, literary critics, editors, journalists, and creative writers, much of their output appearing in literary magazines published in Prishtina (Priština), Shkup (Skopje), and Titograd.

Of the prewar generation, Esad Mekul (b. 1916) was a notable lyric poet and founder of the newspaper *Rilindja*. The work of Mark Krasniqi (dates n.a.) and Hivzi Sylejmani (1912–1972) also began to appear before World War II. Both have written novels, but Krasniqi has come to be known chiefly for his poems for children. Sylejmani has written poetry and drama as well as fiction, his main themes being drawn from the War for National Liberation (World War II) and the radical changes of the early postwar years.

The first novel by a Yugoslav Albanian was *Rrushi ka nis me u pjekë* (1953; the grape has begun to ripen) by Sinan Hasani (b. 1922); it portrays the establishment of Communism after World War II, concentrating on social changes and the role of women in Albanian society. Nazmi Rrahmani's (b. 1941) novels manifest a deep commitment to the problems of the Kosovar people, depicting in particular the difficulties faced by women in their struggle against traditional Muslim restrictions. Other novelists include Anton Pashku (b. 1939), Maksut Shehu (b. 1930), and Rexhai Surroi (b. 1929).

Poetry is written very extensively. Llazar Siliqi (b. 1925) has extolled local patriotism and wartime bravery in such volumes as *Prishtina* (1949; Prishtina) and *Kujtimi i Leninit* (1959; the remembrance of Lenin). The poems of Martin Camaj (b. 1927) convey an almost physical identity with his native Dukagjin, an affection heightened by his years of living abroad, mostly in Italy and Germany. His *Diella* (1958; Diella) is a novel, interspersed with poems, about a school-teacher's unhappy love affair. Enver Gjerku (b. 1927), chiefly a lyrical poet, is a master of the sonnet. Azem Shkreli's (b. 1938) *Engjujt e rrugëve* (1963; the angels on the roads), containing evocations of his native village and the time when he was a shepherd there, is among the most powerful of the many treatments of such themes. His concern is to reconcile his socialist faith with his attachment to ancient customs. Ali Podrimja's (dates n.a.) early work is mostly lyrical. His later poetry is rich in irony, while his most recent poems deal with universal concerns.

One of the most effective dramatists, Josip Real (1895–1964), wrote in the archaic northern Albanian dialect and dealt with peasant problems.

Albanian literature in Yugoslavia has developed rapidly but unevenly, with poetry being the most distinguished genre. Pride in his language, and therefore also in his literature, is central to the Albanian's awareness of his distinctiveness in Yugoslavia.

BIBLIOGRAPHY: Pipa, A., *Albanian Literature: Social Perspectives*, Albanische Forschungen 19 (1978)

—HOWARD J. GREEN

Hungarian Literature

Many prominent Hungarian writers, such as Dezső KOSZTOLÁNYI and Ferenc Herczez (1863–1954), came from the southern area known as the Vajdaság (Vojvodina), which became part of the newly created kingdom of Yugoslavia after World War I. Because of earlier Turkish occupation, which had lasted for centuries, and its agrarian socioeconomic structure, the region lacked cultural centers comparable to those of Transylvania and western Hungary. Before 1918 Hungarian literature in the Vajdaság was almost exclusively Budapest-oriented. But after the collapse of the Austro-Hungarian Empire there emerged a local Hungarian literature designed to preserve the minority's ethnic and cultural traditions.

The initiator and later leader of the Hungarian literary revival in Yugoslavia was Kornél Szenteleky (1893–1933). Aesthete, literary critic, and novelist, Szenteleky had an eclectic philosophy in which the French critic Hippolyte Taine's (1828–1893) theories on the

importance of the social milieu to the writer were blended with the French essayist Julien Benda's (1867–1956) concept of the writer's social responsibility. Szenteleky's highly praised novel *Isola Bella* (1931; Isola Bella) is representative of his philosophy. In 1932 Szenteleky, together with the poet and short-story writer Zoltán Csuka (b. 1901), founded *Kalangya*, a literary periodical that soon became the focal point of Hungarian literary activities in Yugoslavia. Among the most prominent members of the *Kalangya* circle were the poets József Debreczeni (b. 1905) and Kálmán Dudás (b. 1912), who sought formal perfection in the best tradition of Mihály BABITS and Árpád TOTH. The novelist and short-story writer János Herceg (b. 1909) excelled in treating psychological problems in the context of the region's social and cultural life.

Preoccupation with social and political issues characterized the activities of another group, formed around the literary periodical *Hid*. While members of the *Kalangya* circle professed a pacifist humanism and followed the middle of the road, the *Hid* group was committed to militant socialism. Its most important member was Ervin Sinkó (b. 1898), whose novels explore the impact of great historical unheavals on the individual consciousness. István Laták (b. 1910) has described in a realistic style and with great compassion the wretched existence of the working classes. The poets László Gál (b. 1902) and Lajos Thurzó (1915–1950) adopted Vladimir MAYAKOVSKY's tumultuous style to project their revolutionary world view.

After the long period of stagnation into which the cultural life of all of eastern Europe had fallen during the period following World War II, Hungarian literature in Yugoslavia began to show new vigor. In the last two decades the works of the lyric poets Károly Ács (b. 1928) and Ference Fehér (b. 1928), along with the prose writings of Nándor Major (b. 1931), have attracted well-deserved attention.

—ANN DEMAITRE

Romanian Literature

In the 18th and 19th cs. the Romanian ethnic minority of the Vojvodina province of the Austro-Hungarian Empire had developed its own cultural traditions. After World War I, when the Vojvodina became part of the new state of Yugoslavia, folklore collections and essays about the traditions of this largely agrarian population were published. Romanian publications appeared in the city of Vršac, where a newspaper, *Nădejdea* (1927–44), played an important cultural role.

Genuine literary work, however, developed only after World War II: the review *Libertatea literară* began publication in 1945, and the remarkable *Lumina*, a monthly devoted to literature and the arts, was founded at Pančevo in 1947. The first generation of Romanian writers in Yugoslavia after World War II was faced with the painful situation of writing for a small public, one that moreover was limited by tradition. Thus, the best talents gave up writing in their mother tongue: the poet Vasko POPA, the first editor of *Lumina*, switched to Serbian very early; and the poet Florica Ştefan (b. 1929), after her first two volumes, *Cîntecul tinereţii* (1949; the song of youth) and *Lacrimi şi raze* (1953; tears and rays), also began writing in Serbian.

Gradually, however, the situation improved. The Lumina publishing house began bringing out from four to six original volumes in Romanian annually. Among the younger generation, there are two distinguished poets: Slavco Almăjan (b. 1940) and Ioan Flora

(b. 1950). Almăjan, who is bilingual (he made his debut in 1968 with a volume in Serbian), is a complex writer—a poet of cerebral, metaphsical eroticism in *Bărbatul în stare lichidă* (1970; the man in liquid condition) and *Casa deşertului* (1971; the desert house), and a writer of fiction remarkable for his psychological insight in the novel *Noaptea de hîrtie* (1971; paper night). Flora, who studied in Bucharest, is a poet who records immediate experiences, with a very direct, sometimes rough, but sensitive perception of the world; his volumes include *Valsuri* (1970; waltzes), *Iedera* (1975; ivy), *Fişe poetice* (1977; poetic index cards), and *Lumea fizică* (1977; the physical world). Among the older generation, the short-story writer Ion Bălan (1925–1976) and the literary historian Radu Flora (b. 1922) made notable contributions.

Although not quantitatively large, Romanian writing in Yugoslavia is full of vitality. It has had a favorable reception in Yugoslavia—much has been translated into Serbo-Croatian—and in Romania itself. Thus it serves as an intermediary between two cultures.

—MIRCEA ANGHELESCU

Turkish Literature

The written literature of the Turkish minority of former Yugoslavia (a population of about 120,000 living mainly in Macedonia) has evolved only since the late 1940s. Its beginnings can be traced to the literary section of the newspaper *Birlik*, established in Skopje in 1944. In Macedonia, since 1950, the major literary periodical *Sesler* has encouraged the development of poetry and short fiction. The journals *Tan* and *Çevren*, published in the Kosovo region, have also made a significant contribution. Still in its formative period, it was influenced by other literatures of former Yugoslavia as well as by Balkan writing in general. Its strongest ties, however, are with Turkey.

Necati Zekeriya (b. 1928), who has published many collections of his own poems and has edited numerous anthologies published in both Yugoslavia and Turkey, is essentially a romantic poet, as shown in his *Nerde olsam* (1954; wherever I am) and *Sevgi* (1965; love). *Lorka'dan olmak* (1975; being from Lorca), invoking a spiritual link with Federico GARCÍA LORCA, contains many poems of universal humanism. Zekeriya's style and diction are akin to the vernacular of Turkey, whereas the work of most of his colleagues has a "Yugoslav" flavor.

Ilhami Emin (b. 1931) writes poetry of intellectual complexity and daring stylistic experimentation. His *Gülçiçek* (1972; rosebud)—coming in the wake of *Gülkiliç* (1971; rose sword), a cycle of poems that intriguingly blends the rose and the sword as fertility symbols—has established him as an original voice. In *Gülçiçekhane* (1971; rosebud house) Emin attempts to come to terms with the tradition of Turkish poetry by quoting from major and minor Ottoman poets of the 13th through 19th cs.

Nusret Diş Ülkü (b. 1938) and Hasan Mercan (b. 1944) are notable for the lyric flow and the sensuousness of their verse. Mercan's short poems, as well as some of the cycles in *Aynam* (1967; my mirror) and *Sari Yusuf* (1972; blond Yusuf), are among the best of the Turkish poetry of former Yugoslavia. The many young poets who have been developing original styles will probably give the Turkish poetry of Macedonia an even more distinctive voice. This voice is becoming noteworthy in the quintessential verse of Fahri Ali (b. 1948) and intellectually challenging poems of Suat Engüllü (b. 1950).

Fiction is virtually confined to short stories, heavily influenced by Yugoslav and Turkish masters. Fahri Kaya (b. 1930), Şükrü Ramo (1918-1987), and Mustafa Karahasan (dates n.a.) are among the leading narrative writers. Şecaettin Koka's (dates n.a.) novella *Karadüzen* (1979; black order) is an action-filled story of passion, collapse of morality, and blood feud in the early 20th c.

The People's Theater in Skopje has produced numerous plays in Turkish, such as Süreyya Yusef's (?–1977) *Ömrümün tek rüyasi* (1971; the only dream of my life), Yusef's dramatic recital featuring the writings of Nazim HIKMET, and several dramatic works by Ilhami Emin.

—TALAT SAIT HALMAN

Z

ZABOLOTSKY, Nikolay Alekseevich

Russian poet, b. 7 May 1903, Kazan; d. 14 Oct. 1958, Moscow

The son of an agronomist, Z. grew up in a village not far from Kazan. In 1920 he went to Moscow and enrolled in the university. Within a year he transferred to the Herzen Pedagogical Institute in Leningrad, where he studied literature. After graduating from the Institute in 1925, he supported himself by writing books for children and contributing to children's journals. In 1938 Z. was arrested and exiled to the Far East, where he worked as a construction laborer and draftsman. He was released in 1946 and allowed to return to Moscow. He then worked as a translator of the verse of Georgian and foreign poets, and resumed writing poetry of his own.

In Z.'s first collection of verse, *Stolbtsy* (1929; *Scrolls*, 1971), can be felt the SURREALIST influence of the avant-grade literary circle OBERIU (an acronym for a Russian name meaning "Association of Real Creativity"), to which Z. belonged in the late 1920s. *Stolbsty* portrays life in Leningrad during the period of the New Economic Policy as a monstrous phantasmagoria. The poems are characterized by bold and bizarre imagery, an incongruous mixing of "high" and "low" styles, and constant wordplay. The fantastic element is strong; ghosts and talking animals mingle with fishmongers, thieves, and clowns. Unexpected metamorphoses abound: the city becomes a sea, a streetcar becomes a steamship, prostitutes turn into Sirens. The collection met with severe criticism.

Z.'s long poem *Torzhestvo zemledelia* (1933; the triumph of agriculture) was also strongly criticized. An idiosyncratic celebration of the collectivization of Soviet agriculture, it was inspired by the pantheistic ideas of the Russian FUTURIST poet Velemir KHLEBNIKOV and envisions a utopian world where humans and animals will live in harmony.

Z.'s postexile poetry is much more traditional. Gone is the grotesque imagery, the element of fantasy, the cosmic dimension. Z.'s models became the classical 19th-c. Russian poets: Alexandr Pushkin, Fyodor Tyutchev (1803–73), and Yevgeny Baratynsky (1800–44). Z.'s late poetry is marked by great beauty and philosophical profundity. Z. is now regarded as one of the most important and original Russian poets to emerge in the Soviet period.

FURTHER WORKS: *Vtoraya kniga* (1937); *Stikhotvorenia* (1948); *Stikhotvorenia* (1957); *Izbrannoe* (1960); *Izbrannoe* (1972)

BIBLIOGRAPHY: Karlinsky, S., "Surrealism in Twentieth-Century Russian Poetry: Churilin, Z., Poplavski," *SlavR*, 26 (1967): 605–17; Muchnic, H., "There Inner Émigrés: Anna Akhmatova, Osip Mandelstam, N. Z.," *RusR*, 26 (1967): 13–25; Milner-Gulland, R. R., "Z.: Philosopher Poet," *Soviet Studies*, 22 (1971): 598–608; Milner-Gulland, R. R., "Grandsons of Kozma Prutkov: Reflections on Z., Oleynikov, and Their Circle," in R. Freeborn, et al., eds., *Russian and Slavic Literature* (1976): 313–27; Masing-Delić, I., "Z.'s Occult Poem 'Carica Mux,'" *Svantevit*, 3, 2 (1977): 21–38

—SONA STEPHAN HOISINGTON

ZAFZAF, Mohammed

Moroccan novelist and short-story writer, b. 1945, near Rabat

Z., who has lived most of his life in Morocco, was born in the north of the country and moved to Casablanca where he now lives. He studied philosophy at Rabat University, and after graduation, became a teacher at secondary school. His literary career started much earlier, when he was still in his teens. A short story, "Thalāthat Asābī'" (1962; Three Weeks), which he wrote as a schoolboy, was published in the Moroccan journal *Al-Atlasī*. This gave the young Z. the incentive to take up writing. He joined the Union of Moroccan Writers in 1968. Despite his success as a writer, Z. has not given up teaching. He is currently working at a secondary school in Casablanca.

Z.'s vast output, comprising numerous novels and collections of short stories, has made him one of the best-known and widely read Moroccan writers in the Arab world. His books are not only published in Morocco, but also in Tunisia and parts of the Middle East where they have proved to be extremely popular. Z. does not try to imitate a Middle Eastern style of writing but produces work that is Maghrebi in essence. He is considered to be one of a small group of writers who have made a lasting contribution to the development of fictional writing in Morocco. Z. recognizes the multicultural and plurilingual heritage of his country. Although he himself has chosen to write in Arabic, he has often repeated, in interviews, that Arabic literature alone cannot give a full picture of Moroccan reality that owes a great debt to Berber oral folklore and Francophone literature. Z. does not write poetry, but is appreciative of the poetic output of his compatriots. In 1977 he coedited an issue of the periodical *Traces*, dedicating it to French translations of selections of poems by thirteen Moroccan poets of Arabic expression.

Z.'s first three books—a collection of short stories, *Hiwār fī Layl Muta'akhkhir* (1970; Conversation Late at Night), and two novels, *Al-Mar'a wa al-Warda* (1972; The Woman and the Rose) and *Arsifa wa Judrān* (1974; Sidewalks and Walls)—depict a world where men seem to be obsessed with sex and alcohol. The central character of *Al-Mar'a wa al-Warda*, for example, is given to womanizing and frequenting bars. He eventually smuggles hashish to Spain where he spends his days in a haze of drugs and debauchery. This novel was the cause of much heated debate in the Arab press, with critics condemning it as pornographic literature.

Despite his reputation as a writer who deals openly with "taboo" subjects, Z. has become a popular and respected writer. He has to date published more than twenty volumes of short stories and novels. Z.'s mastery lies in his portrayal of Moroccan society with all its good and bad points that he re-creates with verbal ingenuity. Most of his fictional works deal with pressing issues concerning Moroccans, both at home and abroad. In a short story entitled "'Alā Shāti' Janawa" (By the Sea in Genoa), which appeared in his collection *Bā'i'at al-Ward* (1996; The Flower Seller), he focusses on Moroccan immigrants in Italy, who traffic in drugs and sex. But far from condemning them for their actions, Z. believes that they are driven to such measures in order to survive. His novel *Muhawalat 'Aysh* (1985, An Attempt to Live) describes the efforts of a young newspaper-seller in Casablanca to eke out a living amid hardship and poverty. He spends his days at the harbor where the big ocean liners dock, and his nights in taverns, finding warmth in drink and the company of an aged prostitute. In "Sārdīn wa Burtuqāl" (Sardines and Oranges), which appeared in the collection Al-'Araba (1993, The Carriage), groups of hungry youth go scavenging for food in the garbage tips of a sardine factory and an orange-packing warehouse. Here the narrator says with dismay that independence may have given Moroccans self-rule, but that it did not provide them with the basic necessities for survival.

Statements condemning the conditions Moroccans have to endure recur as a motif throughout Z.'s works. In "Kayfa Nahlam bi Mōsko" (How We Dream in Moscow), one of the stories in Bā'i'at al-Ward, the central character describes the wretchedness he sees around him in Moscow and compares it with conditions in Morocco. He concludes that people are of two kinds: those who trample over a rose without any feeling, and those who pick a rose and give it to someone they love. The rose in Z.'s fiction is used as a symbol of love and life. In the title story the central character used to sell roses in her little shop before she fell to her death from the balcony of her apartment. No one knew where she came from. Some said she was of Senegalese origin. Throughout her life, nobody visited her, except her customers. After her death the authorities sealed her shop and the roses inside were left to wither and die.

The elderly flower seller is yet another example of the marginal characters one finds in Z.'s works. They are practically all antiheroes, opposed to the status quo, their sole aim being to survive in a world they seem unable to put right. Two courses are usually open to them: either to leave, or to remain in the country and continue to criticize and condemn those who wheedle their way to the top and become merciless tyrants over them.

FURTHER WORKS: Buyūt Wāti'a (1977); Qubūr fī al-Mā' (1978); Al-Aqwā (1978); Al-Af'ā wa al-Bahr (1979); Al-Shajara al-Muqaddasa (1980); Ghajar fī al-Ghāba (1982); Baydat al-Dīk (1984); Malik al-Jinn (1988); Malāk Abyad (1988); Al-Tha'lab alladhī Yadhar wa Yakhtafī (1989); Al-Hayy al-Khalfī (1992)

BIBLIOGRAPHY: Al-Khatib, I., "Al-Mar'a wa al-Warda," Aqlām, 4 (1972): 67-77; Farhāt, A., Aswāt Thaqāfiyya min al-Maghrib (1984); Hallaq, J., and T. Gonzalez-Quijano, Nouvelles arabes du Maghreb (1991); Al-Wazzani, H., Dalīl al-Kuttāb al-Maghāriba (1993); El Outmani, I., "Prolegomena to the Study of the 'Other' Moroccan Literature," RAL, 28, 3 (1997): 110-21

—FARIDA ABU-HAIDAR

ZAGAJEWSKI, Adam

Polish poet, novelist, and essayist, b. 21 June 1945, Lwów (Lvov), U.S.S.R. (now Russia)

Z. appeared on the Polish literary stage at the threshold of the 1970s as one of a group of Cracow poets calling themselves "Now," and from the beginning was considered one of the leaders of the literary New Wave. A graduate in philosophy from the Jagiellonian University in Cracow, he introduced many philosophical motifs into his writing and was an advocate of "plain speaking" in poetry. This term did not mean a rejection of devices considered poetic. In fact, Z., like other poets of the so-called "Generation of 68," extensively used metaphors, syntactic and lexical repetitions, and adopted irony. In his view, "plain speaking" was a matter of representing reality as openly as possible and directly communicating human experiences in their richness and complexity.

Most of Z.'s programmatic ideas were directed against the dominating tendencies of the 1960s, especially against a concept of poetry devoid of the specific "here and now," and exclusively using allusion and abstract symbols. His motifs were explained in a series of articles published in the student literary press and subsequently included—along with Julian Kornhauser's manifestos—in the collection of essays Świat nie przedstawiony (1974; unrepresented world). Z.'s first two volumes of poetry, Komunikat (1972; the communiqueé) and Sklepy miçsne (1975; meat shops), were both an attempt at representing reality and, at the same time, a document of the poet's struggle with communist censorship. This attempt to represent the human condition under existing socialism was also characteristic of Z.'s first novel, Cieplo, zimno (1975; warm and cold). However, the idea of "truth" connected with "plain speaking" could hardly be implemented under the circumstances prevailing in the mid-1970s. In 1975 Z. became involved in political protests and, like several other poets of the New Wave, started publishing beyond the pale of censorship. Along with Stanislaw BARAŃCZAK and Ryszard KRYNICKI, he published the underground quarterly Zapis. He also issued a new collection of poems, List (1981; a letter) outside official channels.

Since the late 1970s, Z. has been residing in the West, chiefly in Paris. When visiting Poland in 1981, he became an eyewitness of the imposition of martial law. In his collection List—Oda do wielości (1982; a letter—ode to plurality) the thematic layer of the new poems has been penetrated by the spirit of solidarity with those remaining in Poland. The more recent books by Z. reflect a different sensitivity. According to his articles contained in the volumes Solidarność i Samotność (1986; Solidarity, Solitude, 1990), and Dwa miasta (1991; Two Cities: On Exile, History, and the Imagination, 1995), the artistic production of the 1970s and the 1980s was, in the case of many Polish writers publishing underground, a negative reflection of "official" literature. Its vision of the world was often reduced to two colors, black and white, symbolizing good and evil. Its predominant tone was negation. For Z. the important question became whether it was possible to accept a world that, from the moral point of view, was quite unacceptable. In the place of an ethical attitude he proposed one that he termed "ecstatic." This category was to designate a spontaneous perception of the world in all its richness and variety.

In his volumes of poetry Jechać do Lwowa (1985; to go to Lwów) and Płótno (1990; Canvas, 1991), and Ziemia ognista (1994; Fiery land) moral issues are pushed into the background by ontological and epistemological questions. Also, a tone of affirmation is predominant. Instances from general history take the place of events connected with contemporary Polish affairs. More and more often Z. focuses on ecumenical questions, while the history depicted in his poems contends with objects that release wonder and a sense of mystery of existence.

Z. is the winner of several Polish and international literary prizes, among others the Kościelskis Prize (1975), the Tucholsky Prize (1985), the Kijowski Prize (1986), the Malrieu Prize (1990), and the Vilenica Prize (1996).

FURTHER WORKS: *Drugi oddech* (1978); *Cienka kreska* (1983); *Dzikie czeriśnie* (1992); *Trzej aniołowie* (1997, biling. ed.); *Późne święknie* (1998). **FURTHER WORKS IN ENGLISH:** *Tremor: Selected Poems* (1985); *Mysticism for Beginners* (1997)

BIBLIOGRAPHY: Levine, M. G., "A. Z., *Jechać do Lwowa i inne wiersze. Tremor: Selected Poems*," *PolR*, 32, 1 (1987): 113–15; Witkowski, T., "The Poets of the New Wave in Exile," *SEEJ* 33, 2 (Summer 1989): 204–16; Barańczak, S., "Alone But Not Lonely," *Breathing under Water and Other East European Essays* (1990): 214–18; Witkowski, T., "A. Z.: In Praise of Multiplicity," *Studium Papers*, 14, 3–4 (1990): 168–69; Carpenter, B., "A. Z., *Two Cities*," *WLT*, 69, 3 (Summer 1995); Witkowski, T., "Between Poetry and Politics: Two Generations," *Periphery: Journal of Polish Affairs*, 2, 1/2 (1996): 38–43; Witkowski, T., "Politics for Art's Sake," *Periphery: Journal of Polish Affairs*, 3, 1/2 (1997): 62–68

—TADEUSZ WITKOWSKI

ZAMBIAN LITERATURE

Zambia became independent in 1964 after the collapse of the Central African Federation, which consisted of Northern and Southern Rhodesia and Nyasaland. A one-party state was established in 1973 under Kenneth Kaunda (b. 1924), but in the multiparty election of 1991 his United National Independence Party was defeated by Frederick Chiluba's Movement for Multiparty Democracy, which increased its majority in the 1996 election. This was also a discursive shift: the Christian humanism of Kaunda's own political autobiography *Zambia Shall Be Free* (1962) may be contrasted with the cosmopolitan egoism of opposition businessman Vernon Mwaanga's (b. 1939) autobiography *An Extraordinary Life* (1985).

During the colonial period, literature in Bemba, Lozi, Tonga, and Nyanja was encouraged by the African Literature Committee and the Northern Rhodesia Publications Bureau, whose adaptations of traditional tales intended for primary schools omitted indigenous military and epic elements. Writing in Bemba, Stephen Mpashi's (b. 1920) novels written in the 1950s, notably *Uwakwensho bushiku* (1955; He Who Leads You through the Night), adapt genres such as the romance and the detective story to an urban Zambian setting, making use of "town Bemba," with its loan words and code-switching. Other works of the period include M. M. Sakubita's (b. 1930) *Liswanelo za luna kwa li lu siile* (1954; How Not to Treat Animals), written in Lozi; M. C. Mainza's (b. ca. 1930) *Kabuca uleta tunji* (1956; Every Day Brings Something New), written in Tonga; and Stephen Luwisha's (b. ca. 1930) *Mukulilacoolwe* (1962; You Have Survived by Luck), written in Lenje.

The English Medium Scheme for schools was introduced in 1966. A year later the National Educational Company of Zambia (Neczam) replaced the Publications Bureau. However, the aim of constructing a Zambian national literature in English was only partly realized in the works published between 1967 and 1980. Fwanyanga Mulikita's (b. 1928) collection of short stories, *A Point of No Return* (1968), gives tales and anecdotes of rural life a

philosophical and psychological dimension. Andreya Masiye's (b. 1922) novel *Before Dawn* (1971), about a young man's failure to adapt to colonial urban life, rejects modernity, as do some of the stories in Mufalo Liswaniso's (dates n.a.) edition entitled *Voices of Zambia* (1971), but the plot of Dominic Mulaisho's (b. 1933) novel *The Tongue of the Dumb* (1971), influenced by the style of Nigerian novelist Chinua ACHEBE, vindicates Western education, medicine, and religion rather than "African ways."

Since Zambia is one of the most urbanized countries in Africa, the experience of town life has been a dominant theme in Zambian novels. The independence struggle, merely a backdrop in Gideon Phiri's (b. 1942) *Ticklish Sensation* (1973), where sex and politics climax together, is the subject matter of Mulaisho's *The Smoke That Thunders* (1979), which champions Kaunda's leadership, and William Saidi's (b. 1937) *Day of the Baboons* (1988). Town life, the colonial legacy, and the failure of young men to adapt are the main concerns in Phiri's *Victims of Fate* (1971); in Grieve Sibale's (b. 1952) *Between Two Worlds* (1979), where the abandonment of the colonized antihero by his white shift boss gives a hint of Zambia's own failure to become economically independent of South Africa; in Storm Banjamoyo's (b. 1956) *Sofiya* (1979), a sensationalized yet observant account of urban mores; and in Smokey Haangala's (1959-1988) semiautobiographical *The Black Eye* (1988), where the son's failure to mature thwarts the wishes of the father. Other Zambian novels include William Simukwasa's (b. 1948) *Coup* (1979), a derivative spy thriller, Lazarus Miti's (b. 1948) *The Father* (1985), Susan Chitabanta's (b. 1953) *Behind the Closed Door* (1988), an indictment of patriarchal law and religion, and John Luangala's (b. 1940) *The Chosen Bud* (1991), set in a village in modern times. The satire of pseudonymous newspaper columnist Kapelwa Musonda (b. 1940) in *The Kapelwa Musonda File* (1972) and *The Best of Kapelwa Musonda* (1979) is arguably more "Zambian" than most Zambian fiction.

Zambia has a thriving theatrical culture, though this is not well represented in published work. The University of Zambia's Chikwakwa Theater specialized in popular, unscripted plays, and its traveling theater helped to generate numerous popular traveling theater groups throughout the country. Published Zambian plays include Kabwe Kasoma's (b. 1935) *Black Mamba* trilogy (1973), which traces Kaunda's rise to power; Masautso Phiri's (b. 1945) *Soweto Flowers Will Grow* (1978), a response to the Soweto uprising, and works by Andreya Masiye, Steve Moyo (b. 1945), Graig Lungu (1963-1994), and Dickson Mwansa (b. 1952).

In contrast to neighboring Malawi, Zambia has few poets of any distinction. Lyson Tembo's (b. 1943) *Poems* (1976) shows modernist influences; A. M. Mbikusita-Lewanika's (dates n.a.) *For the Seeds in Our Blood* (1981) has a fiery Pan-Africanism, and Parnwell Munatamba's (b. 1942) *My Battle Cry* (1985) is modeled after the Senegalese poet Léopold Sédor SENGHOR.

Although hopes of constructing an "authentic" Zambian literature have grown fainter in harsh economic times, locally published writing and popular theater are still much in evidence.

BIBLIOGRAPHY: Gérard, A. S., *African Language Literature* (1981): 226-32; Crehan, A. S., "Zambian Fiction: Its Role in Zambia's Development," *Ngoma*, 2, 1 (1987): 1-12; Mulengela, B., "Zambian Poetry in English," *Ngoma*, 3, 1 (1988): 1-29; Moody, J. A., "Kapelwa Musonda and the Development of a Zambian National Literary Tradition," *Ngoma*, 3, 2 (1988): 1-40; Sumaili, F. K. M., *Zambian Writers Talking* (1991); Crehan, A. S., "Patronage, the

State and Ideology in Zambian Theatre," in L. Gunner, ed., *Politics and Performance: Theatre, Poetry and Song in Southern Africa* (1994): 253-72; Kerr, D., *African Popular Theatre* (1996)

—A. S. CREHAN

ZAMBRANO, María

Spanish essayist, b. 25 Apr. 1904, Vélez-Málaga; d. Aug. 1991, Madrid

The first woman and first philosopher to receive the Spanish language's premier award, the Cervantes Prize (1988), Z. was essentially unknown when so distinguished. Gender, genre, and prolonged exile all contributed to her relative obscurity, as did the densely intellectual quality of her work. Despite teaching mostly in provincial towns, Z.'s parents provided a cultured, philosophically-oriented, and enlightened home in which poet Antonio MACHADO and other intellectuals frequently visited. Following a near-fatal illness at age four, she decided precociously to become a thinker (philosopher). After the family moved to Madrid in 1926, Z. completed her degree in philosophy and letters amid the pre-Republic political and intellectual ferment. She studied with Spain's major philosophers—José ORTEGA Y GASSET, Xavier Zubiri (1898-1983), and Manuel García Morente (1886-1942)—moving in literary circles with Rosa CHACEL, Rafael ALBERTI, Pedro SALINAS, and other poets of the "Generation of 1927."

Like most disciples of Ortega, Z. belonged to the *Revista de Occidente* group. While doing doctoral work and participating in such political initiatives as Ortega's "League of Social Education," she began lecturing in philosophy in 1930. Z. joined the Republic's Cultural Missions with intellectuals and artists including Luis CERNUDA, Rafael Dieste (1899-1981), José Antonio Maravall (b. 1911), and painter Ramón Gaya; she befriended Miguel HERNÁNDEZ, and future Nobel laureate Camilo José CELA, all figures evoked in her memoir, *Los intelectuales en el drama de España* (1937; Intellectuals in the Drama of Spain). Her incipient thought appeared in *Hacia un saber sobre el alma* (1937; Toward a Knowledge of the Soul).

Republican involvement impelled Z. into exile following the Civil War (1936-39), and she taught in Mexico, Cuba, and Puerto Rico. She spent eleven years in Rome (1952-63), resided briefly in Switzerland, then moved to France, living on a small farm near Geneva from 1964 to 1980. In 1981 the national Prince of Asturias literary prize initiated significant official and critical recognition in Spain, and in her eightieth year (1984) Z. returned to Madrid, among the last exiles repatriated. The scarcity of women essayists and philosophers undoubtedly slowed reception of Z., who left over two hundred articles and some thirty books. Gender and culture barriers, plus Republican affiliation, prolonged Z.'s obscurity during the Franco dictatorship, but conditions had changed radically when she returned, and numerous honors gladdened her final years.

Z.'s earliest volume, *Nuevo liberalismo* (1930; New Liberalism), builds upon the utopian socialist thought of her father, an enduring influence, second only to Ortega. While working on her doctoral dissertation (treating individual salvation in Spinoza), she began publishing the first of some fifteen commentaries on Ortega's

work. Her apprenticeship teaching in metaphysics soon moved her beyond the master's thought, enunciating lifelong interest in the human soul, although lacking mystico-religious aspects acquired later. Z. drew upon other philosophers, with Henri BERGSON influencing her concepts of time, intuition, history, and her blending of the poetic, personal and philosophical, while Martin Heidegger (1889-1976) contributed to her rejection of philosophical rationalism and scientific reason, her fusion of style and thinking, and progressive divergence from Ortega. She approaches many problems of modern philosophy synthetically, within the framework of Hegelian dialectic, being less concerned than Ortega with epistemological dichotomies between abstract reason or absolute truth and extreme relativism (perhaps convinced that Ortega had solved this problem). Philosopher-poet Antonio Machado models her vision of poetry as philosophy and vice-versa, expounded in *Filosofía y poesía* (1939; Philosophy and Poetry) and *Pensamiento y poesía en la vida española* (1939; Thought and Poetry in Spanish Life). Both present the philosopher's initiation via intuitive "poetic reason"—quite unrelated to prior rationalism and closer to revelation.

Z.'s youthful verse appeared in Republican periodicals, and she wrote critical essays on contemporary poets, anticipating later theoretical plumbing of poetry's role in epistemological epiphanies. She also published *Delirio y destino* (1989; Delirium and Destiny), a quasi-novelesque autobiographical memoir with bildungsroman attributes, set in 1929-30, reflecting her philosophical and personal relationship with teacher-mentor Ortega y Gasset. Other critico-literary exegeses include *La España de Galdós* (1959; Galdós's Spain), *El freudismo, testimonio del homber actual* (1940; Freudianism, Testimony to Contemporary Man), and *El pensamiento vivo de Séneca* (1944; Seneca's Living Thought). Several wartime works attest her anguish over the conflict in Europe, notably *Isla de Puerto Rico (Nostalgia y esperanza de un mundo mejor)* (1940; Puerto Rico [Nostalgia and Hope of a Better World]) and *La agonía de Europa* (1945; Europe's Agony).

Like Ortega, Z. often published her works first in the popular press, an implied readership dictating clarity, without philosophical jargon or complexity, although not necessarily without substance and density. *El hombre y lo divino* (1955; Man and Divinity), deemed her masterpiece, employs poetic reason in elucidating religious experience, the sacred, sacrifice, and human attitudes toward the unknown. Her most characteristic philosophical formulations concern intimate, subjective dream-states, explorations of time's role in human life, with dream-time and dreaming approaching atemporal passivity, revelatory of time's origination. Her dream-theories synthesize relationships between dreams and the creative word, tragedy, religion, poetry, the novel, and philosophy, as seen in *El sueño creador* (1965; Creative Dreaming). Rather than existential self-awareness, Z. promulgates "creative sleep." *Los sueños y el tiempo* (1992; Dreams and Time), ostensibly literary, as is *España, sueño y verdad* (1965; Spain, Dream and Truth), reveals intertextual indebtedness to Calderón's vision of life as dream, waking as death. *Claros del bosque* (1977; Forest Clearings) explores being, presence and reality, concealment and revelation, presenting ontological concerns and the concept of passive epiphany. Other pivotal concepts include the creative word (*logos*) and dawn, presented in *De la aurora* (1986; Concerning Dawn). Z.'s subjective privileging of intuition places her within a mystical or gnostic tradition and she advocates reform of understanding via the irrational. Interested by things neither objective nor intelligible to abstract reason, she views man as enigma or project to be deciphered or realized (vocation). She sees (traditional) philosophy as yielding to revelation of life, to history, then poetry: new understanding results from transcendent revelation of knowledge immanent in the soul.

FURTHER WORKS: *Horizonte del liberalismo* (1930); *La tumba de Antígona* (1967); *Obras reunidas. Primera entrega* (1971); *Ensayos y notas (1939-1969)* (1977); *Dos escritos autobiográficos (El nacimiento)* (1981); *Dos fragmentos sobre el amor* (1982); *Andalucía, sueño y realidad* (1984); *Senderos* (1986); *Persona y democracia. La historia sacrificial* (1988); *La confesión: Género literario* (1989); *Notas de un método* (1989); *Los bienaventurados* (1990); *El parpadeo de la luz* (1991); *Los sueños y el tiempo* (1992); *Para una historia de la piedad* (1993)

BIBLIOGRAPHY: Muñoz Victoria, F., *M. Z. o la metafísica recuperada* (1982); Donahue, D., "National History as Autobiography: M. Z.'s *Delirio y destino*," *MRRM*, 9 (1993): 116-24; Moreno Sanz, J., *La razón en la sombra. Antología del pensamiento de M. Z.* (1993); Summerhill, S., "Toward the Postmodern Sublime: The Late Essays of M. Z.," in Galvan, D. V., et al., eds., *Studies in Honor of Donald W. Bleznick* (1995): 185-202; Johnson, R., "M. Z.'s Theory of Literature as Knowledge and Contingency," *Hispania*, 79 (May 1996): 215-21; Pérez, J., "Razón Vital y Razón Poética: La Solución Meta-racional de M. Z.," *Letras Femeninas*, 23, 1-2 (1997): 9-25; Pérez, J., *Public Forums—Private Views: Women Essayists of Spain* (1998)

—JANET PÉREZ

ZAMYATIN, Yevgeny Ivanovich

Russian novelist, short-story writer, dramatist, essayist, literary critic, and editor, b. 1 Feb. 1884, Lebedyan; d. 10 March 1937, Paris, France

The son of an Orthodox priest, Z. was raised in provincial central Russia. While a student at the Polytechnic Institute in St. Petersburg, he joined the Bolshevik Party; he was imprisoned and exiled in 1905 for revolutionary activity. Graduating as a naval engineer in 1908, Z. taught in the department of naval architecture and began publishing fiction and technical articles. Exiled again in 1911, Z. began writing in earnest and completed the first work that was to gain him recognition: the *povest* (long story) "Uezdnoe" (1913; "A Provincial Tale," 1967). Given amnesty in 1913, he continued his dual career, supervising the construction of Russian icebreakers in England for two years during World War I.

Returning to Russia on the eve of the October Revolution, Z. played a critical role in the subsequent cultural revival. He served on the executive councils of the Union of Practitioners of Imaginative Literature, the House of Arts, and the All-Russian Union of Writers. He edited Russian translations of Jack LONDON, H. G. WELLS, Anatole FRANCE, Romain ROLLAND, and O. Henry for the World Literature Publishing House; he was also on the editorial boards of several journals. Frequently attacked throughout the 1920s by Communist Party-line critics, Z. became the object of intensive vilification in 1929: he was denied access to publication, his plays were banned from production, and his books were

removed from libraries. A direct appeal to Stalin with Maxim GORKY's intercession enabled Z. to travel abroad in 1931. He settled in Paris, where he remained until his death.

Inspired by an ardent humanism, Z.'s prerevolutionary fiction attacks brutality, ignorance, and inhumanity. The square-jawed hero of "Uezdnoe" is likened to an absurd heathen Russian stone idol embodying a cruel, stagnant, provincial Russia devoid of human compassion. Z.'s second *povest*, "Nakulichkakh" (1914; out in the sticks), depicts the destruction of several sensitive souls amid the drunken debauchery of a Siberian military garrison on the Pacific. The journal in which it appeared was confiscated by the authorities, and Z. was tried for maligning the Russian military. In the long story "Alatyr" (1915; Alatyr) the daily tedium of the provinces is humorously enlivened by a host of ridiculous dreamers, but the final note again is one of spiritual doom. The most distinctive aspect of these works, however, is their ornamental prose style.

During the turbulent years of revolution and civil war Z. achieved mastery of the craft of fiction, elaborating a philosophical system based on humanism, infinite revolution, impassioned heresy, and flaming love, all disrupting philistine stagnation. Stimulated by his sojourn in Newcastle-on-Tyne, Z. first developed these new themes in "Ostrovityane" (1918; "The Islanders," 1972) and "Lovets chelovekov" (1922; the fisher of men), using an elliptical style characterized by impressionistic urban metaphors, color symbolism, and intensification of acoustical and rhythmical qualities. The same themes and style were transplanted to Russia's White Sea in the balladlike "Sever" (1922; repub. as "Fonar" 1926; "The North," 1967) and liberally laced with an earthy primitivism inspired by Knut HAMSUN and D. H. LAWRENCE. The apogee of Z.'s formal mastery of the extended metaphor was represented by the often-anthologized gems "Peshchera" (1922; "The Cave," 1923) and "Mamay" (1921; "Mamai," 1934), where the integrating images of a cave and a ship, respectively, each spawn an entire system of derivative images in depicting deprivation and dehumanization in war-torn Petrograd.

Although Z. did experiment with a multiplanar, philosophical, fantastic narrative format in "Rasskaz o samom glavnom" (1924; "A Story about the Most Important Thing," 1967), most of his later stories, like "Iks" (1926; "X," 1967) and "Mucheniki nauki" (written 1931, pub. 1962; "Another Turning of the Worm," 1931), are finely wrought anecdotal works in which gentle irony is joined with literary parody to depict the frailties of people trying to adapt to the new Soviet environment. In his last decade Z. developed a simple, unobtrusive style with infrequent but audacious metaphors, which he used in creating two masterpieces of tragic passion: "Yola" (1928; the yawl), echoing Gogol's "The Overcoat," and "Navodnenie" (1929; "The Flood," 1967), inspired by Dostoevsky's *Crime and Punishment*. Z. spent his last years working on the unfinished novel *Bich Bozhy* (1939; the scourge of God), viewing the struggle between Attila and Rome as a historic parallel to the 20th-c. conflict between Russian and the West.

The originality and stylistic mastery of Z.'s fiction has ensconced him in the pantheon of 20th-c. Russian literature, but his renown in world literature rests on one work—the dystopian novel *My* (corrupt text, 1927; complete text, 1952; *We*, 1924), which anticipated Aldous HUXLEY's *Brave New World* and influenced George ORWELL's *1984*, has been translated into a dozen languages and was recently made into a film in West Germany, yet has never been published in Russia. Rooted in the Dostoevskian critique of collectivist ideals, *My* was the first novel of literary importance that provided a prophetic vision of the realization of utopia, forewarning the modern reader of the hypertrophy of the state and the machine.

From the contemporary perspective, Z.'s achievements as essayist and literary critic stand equal to his achievements in fiction. Beginning as a reviewer in the early 1910s, Z. later wrote polemical articles under the pseudonym of M. Platonov in 1917–18 in Socialist Revolutionary newspapers. Although Z. welcomed the revolution, he criticized subsequent repression and sycophancy in literary essays that extolled integrity and personal freedom—"Ya boyus" (1921; "I Am Afraid," 1970) and "O segodnyashnem i sovremennom" (1924; "The Day and the Age," 1970)—and in political fables—*Bolshim detyam skazki* (1922; fables for grownup children). Fortunately, most of the carefully crafted, original, and frequently witty essays have been preserved in the posthumous collection *Litsa* (1955; faces).

Z. significantly influenced many young writers through his lectures and workshops. Much of this material, including the seminal "Sovremennaya russkaya proza" (1956; "Contemporary Russian Literature," 1970) and the revealing "Psikhologia tvorchestva" (1956; "The Psychology of Creative Work," 1970), was published only posthumously in Russian émigré journals.

Z.'s eight plays remain the least known aspect of his literary legacy. Of the three original plays, *Ogni svyatogo Dominika* (1922; the fires of Saint Dominic) deals with personal freedom, censorship, and the fallibility of monolithic truth; *Atilla* (1950; Attila), a tragedy in verse, focuses on themes of love, hate, vengeance, and betrayal; while *Afrikansky gost* (1963; the African guest) satirizes superficial accommodation to Soviet ways. Of five dramatic adaptations, the most famous and successful is *Blokha* (1926; the flea), a lively folk play in the *commedia dell'arte* tradition based on Nikolay Leskov's (1831–95) story "Levsha" (1881; "The Left-Handed Craftsman," 1961).

A master stylist and one of the most original and gifted literary minds of 20th-c. Russia, Z. remains virtually unknown there. Highly valued in the West for his exciting and prophetic novel *My*, Z. has only recently begun to receive just recognition as an influential craftsman in Russian fiction and as an astute literary critic.

FURTHER WORKS: *Uezdnoe: Povesti i rasskazy* (1916); *Vereshki* (1918); *Pismenno; Kryazhi* (1918); *Gerbert Uells* (1922; "H. G. Wells," 1970); *Chrevo; Zemlemer* (1922); *Ostrovityane: Povesti i rasskazy* (1922); *Robert Mayer* (1922); *Tri dnya* (1922); "O tom kak istselen byl inok Erazm"(1922; "The Healing of the Novice Erasmus," 1967); "Rus" (1923; "In Old Russia," 1967); *Na kulichkakh: Povesti i rasskazy* (1923); *Obshchestvo pochetnykh zvonarey* (1926); *Nechestivye rasskazy* (1927); *Sobranie sochineny* (4 vols., 1929); *Zhitie Blokhi to dnya chudesnogo ee rozhdenia i do dnya priskorbnoy konchiny* (1929); *Povesti i rasskazy* (1963); *Sochinenia* (Vol. I, 1970). FURTHER WORKS IN ENGLISH: *The Dragon: Fifteen Stories* (1967); *A Soviet Heretic: Essays* (1970)

BIBLIOGRAPHY: Woodcock, G., "Utopias in Negative," *SR*, 64 (1956): 81–97; Richards, D. J., *Z.: A Soviet Heretic* (1962); Shane, A. M., *The Life and Works of E. Z.* (1968); Struve, G., *Russian Literature under Lenin and Stalin, 1917–1953* (1971): 43–50; Voronsky, A., "E. Z.," *RLT*, 3 (1972): 153–75; Collins, C., *E. Z.: An Interpretive Study* (1973); Mihailovich, V. D., "Critics on E. Z.," *PLL*, 10 (1974): 317–34; Brown, E. J., *"Brave New World,"* *"1984," and "We": An Essay on Anti-Utopia: Z. and English Literature* (1976); Rhodes, C. H., "Frederick Winslow Taylor's System of Scientific Management in Z.'s *We*," *JGE*, 28, 1 (1976): 31–42; Edwards, T. R. N., *Three Russian Writers and the Irrational: Z., Pilnyak, and Bulgakov* (1982): 36–86 and passim

—ALEX M. SHANE

ZANZOTTO, Andrea

Italian poet, essayist, and short-story writer, b. 10 Oct. 1921, Pieve di Soligo

Born into a family in which for generations the men had been artists, Z. broke with precedent by taking a degree in literature at the University of Padua, graduating in 1942. After being involved with the Resistance during World War II, he spent several years traveling and working at menial jobs in Switzerland and France. Upon returning to Italy in the late 1940s, he settled in his home town, where he began a career of teaching and administration in elementary and secondary schools throughout the Veneto region and where he has remained since his retirement in 1975.

In 1950 Z. received the prestigious San Babila Prize for unpublished authors from a jury including Giuseppe UNGARETTI and Eugenio MONTALE. His first book of poems, *Dietro il paesaggio* (1951; behind the landscape), appeared the following year, eliciting some critical attention. In this volume Z. uses the landscape as metaphor for, among other things, the systems of signs that determine and circumscribe the existential situation of the individual who perceives them. As its title indicates, this book also presents a subjective desire to go beyond the limits imposed by this landscape of signs.

Two subsequent volumes, which gained increasing attention for Z., follow this subjective struggle further. *Vocativo* (1957; vocative) presents it in emblematic grammatical terms: the perceiving subject is reduced to a pronoun, the desire to a grammatical case (the vocative). *IX ecloghe* (1962; nine eclogues) shows the conflict as a contest in which both poet and poetry strive for an unattainable linguistic authenticity. The central importance of the notions of subjectivity, perception, and language in these volumes is an indication of the appeal for Z. of both modern linguistic theory and contemporary French psychoanalytic theory, with its insistence on the role of language in the formation of the psyche.

It is perhaps an acceptance of both the arbitrary and the formative, or determinant, aspects of language that leads to the unique style of Z.'s later poetry. Beginning with *Labeltá* (1968; beauty) and *Pasque* (1973; Easters), Z.'s texts demonstrate an extreme awareness of signifying procedures, not only in language and meters traditionally considered poetic but also in the slogans of mass media, the words of popular songs, and the phonic similarities that suggest unconscious connections between words. Z.'s work is directly influenced, moreover, by his particular historical linguistic situation. Pievan dialect appears in his texts as an intimate and maternal, although fast-disappearing, alternative to the modern, standardized Italian of the schools and the media. Latin words function as skeletal remains of an already mute tongue. German carries not only associations with the occupation but also signals of a literary and philosophical tradition of great importance to Z., as does French. By contrast, English stands as the language of the future, a potentially universal sign system fast making others obsolete. Thus, although Z. is not the only contemporary Italian poet to speak both dialect and Italian, to know Latin, or to be conversant in foreign tongues, his poetic use of these various sign systems is uniquely symbolic.

Z.'s most recent major work, *Il galateo in bosco* (1978; a woodland book of manners), takes the awareness of signifying procedures even further, placing poems that contain cartoons, for example, around a central cycle of perfectly constructed sonnets. The preeminence of such simultaneous, combinatory stylistics is integral to the book's thematic suggestions of an opposition of poetic to historical discourse, an accusation of the oppressions of history, a revelation of poetry as an enduring protest and an essential alternative to those oppressions.

Z. is considered by many to be the most important Italian poet born in our century. His poems have been translated into several languages. His prose writings include short stories depicting events and people in a regional context and dozens of articles that have established him as one of Italy's foremost contemporary literary critics. A prize-winning poet who continues to lead a simple village life, Z. is now widely read for the intricate and highly intelligent way his books speak of being and meaning in our time.

FURTHER WORKS: *Elegia, e altri versi* (1954); *Sull'altopiano (prose 1942–54)* (1964); *Gli sguardi i fatti e senhal* (1969); *A che valse?* (1970); *Poesie (1938–1972)* (1973; 2nd ed., 1980); *Filò* (1976); *Circhi e cene/Circuses and Suppers* (1979, bilingual); *Mistieroi* (1980); *Fosfeni* (1983). FURTHER WORKS IN ENGLISH: *Selected Poetry of A. Z.* (1979)

BIBLIOGRAPHY: Feldman, R., and B. Swann, "A Presentation of the Italian Poet A. Z.," *BA* 48 (1974): 462–68; Cambon, G., Foreword to *Selected Poetry of A. Z.* (1975): xii–xxii; Rizzo, G., Afterword to *Selected Poetry of A. Z.* (1975): 307–23; Allen, B., "On Translating Z.," in A. Z., *Circhi e cene/Circuses and Suppers* (1979): 13; Kilmer, N., "Enigmas Coloring," *Parnassus*, 7, 2 (1979): 178–85; Hainsworth, P. R. J., "The Poetry of A. Z.," *IS*, 37 (1982): 101–21

—BEVERLY ALLEN

ZAPATA OLIVELLA, Manuel

Colombian novelist, short-story writer, dramatist, and anthropological essayist, b. 17 Mar. 1920, Lorica

Z. O. is by profession a physician, who has spent his life working and writing on behalf of the lower economic classes and Afro-Colombian people. His work, always directed toward social problems and racial prejudice, includes fiction and anthropological essays on the condition, history, and cultures of Afro-Colombians. He has been very active fomenting the organization of folkloric groups, conferences, and other educational activities in his country, is the director of the Colombian journal *Letras nacionales* and currently the Columbian Cultural Ataché in Martinique. Born in a poor community of Lorica, Z. O. has had firsthand knowledge of the plight of poor Afro-Colombians and the violence to which the

lower economic classes are subjected to in his country. His literary work has been a monumental effort to give voice to this silent majority and to unveil the psychological complexities of social, economic, and racial discrimination. His sense of curiosity and his urgent desire to learn about the world, influenced by his readings of Maxim GORKY and other writers and thinkers, inspired him at age twenty-two to travel north in spite of his difficult economic circumstances. In 1942 he started out by boat through the Amazon on his way to Panama, where he was arrested for "looking suspicious." After a series of similar experiences, and bold experimentations, he reached first Mexico City, where he earned his living writing for the Mexican journals *Sucesos, Así*, and *Tiempo*. Later, in New York City, he met Langston HUGHES, who became a decisive influence in Z. O.'s life and career. Z. O.'s experiences in Harlem were later recaptured in *He visto la noche* (1954; I have seen the night), a testimonial autobiography of his trip to the U.S. during the 1940s, and his testimony of the prejudice he experienced and witnessed in the U.S. toward African-Americans and Latinos.

When Z. O. reached New York he was carrying with him a rough draft of what was going to be his first novel, *Tierra mojada* (1947; wet land). The famous Spanish American novelist Ciro ALEGRÍA, who was also at this time in New York and read the manuscript on Z. O.'s request, writes in his prologue to Z. O.'s first novel that, in spite of its awkwardness and exuberant rhetoric, while reading it he felt that with *Tierra mojada* the black Spanish American novel was about to be born. This text, as well as all of Z. O.'s work since then, communicates, with the same direct and simple style that characterizes Z. O.'s writing, a deep sense of injustice and a deep feeling of compassion toward the oppressed.

In 1948 Z. O. published his second book, *Passion vagabunda* (roaming passion), an account of personal experiences. It was a few years later, however, with the publication of *Cuentos de muerte y libertad* (1956; stories of death and freedom), *El galeón sumergido* (1963; the sunken galleon), and *¿Quién le dio el fusil a Oswald?* (1967; who gave Oswald the rifle?) that Z. O. finally showed his true talent as a writer with a mature style, in narratives where the fantastic, the marvelous, and the crude reality he lived and witnessed are intertwined. In all of these stories, the poor, the black, the oppressed are always victims of a system that robs humans of dignity and hope. Z. O.'s fictional world is a world of deep-rooted political, economic, and psychological violence, in which the victim's attempt to revolt and to cry for justice is always destroyed, as can be seen in his short stories "La ciénaga cercada" (sieged swamp), "Siembra nocturna" (night crop), and "La tinaja en la sombra" (the clay pot in the shadow). Violence, in Z. O.'s work, not only targets the powerless, it is also a psychological phenomenon that accompanies the many manifestations of vengeance, because for Z. O. violence, in Colombia, like anywhere where there is discrimination and class struggle, becomes a state of mind, and, ultimately, a self-devouring way of life.

In some of Z. O.'s short stories there are surrealistic and fantastic elements characteristic of postwar vanguard movements and of what later came to be called in Latin America MAGIC REALISM. The interpolation of these elements in Z. O.'s work shows the writer's interest in blending social realism with innovative techniques, for example, in his short stories "La telaraña (the spiderweb), "El ausente" (the absent man), and "Un extraño bajo mi piel" (another under my skin), a fantastic account of a black man who turns white at a moment of racial danger only to turn black again when threatened with violent discrimination. In this excellent short story the main character lives at the edge of two different racial worlds, experiencing prejudice on both barriers of colors, like, allegorically, the experience of mulattos and of educated African-Americans.

The theme of violence, reiterated in various forms throughout Z. O.'s work, is also the theme of *La calle 10* (1960; 10th street), for which he received the Colombian National Award for the Novel. Different modalities of the same theme of violence can also be found in *En Chimá nace un santo* (1974; *A Saint Is Born in Chimá*, 1991), a gripping story of superstition, where a fetish religion of hope is born out of poverty and despair, and in *Chambacú: Corral de negros* (1963; *Chambacú. Black Slum*, 1989), the story of a destituted community that attempts to voice its demands for justice and is crushed for it. With the publication of *Detrás del rostro* (1969; behind the face), for which Z. O. received the Colombian National Novel Award given by the Colombian Language Academy, Z. O. shifts toward a more innovative and experimental style. This complex text is narrated by several voices from different perspectives, all of which serve as windows to many different individual interests that are all equally oppressive in Colombian society.

In a more recent book, *Changó, el gran putas* (1983; Changó, the great whore/devil), Z. O.'s research on the history and mythologies of Afro-Colombian lore, his mature style, and his simple and direct narrative techniques come together to produce a complex text that blends poetry and prose, investigation and fiction, concrete reality and myths. This text is a monumental invocation in the style of an African *oriki*, as a chant of praise in which indigenous beliefs and the mythologies brought by African slaves to America come together in a majestic cry for freedom and justice. The text is a dance and an embrace between humans and *orishas*, in the memory of Changó, the Yoruba deity of thunder, lightning, and justice.

Although Z. O.'s themes and motifs have changed little since his first writings, his shift away from social realism to a mythological text that interpolates in its pages the memory of ancient African traditions in America, is also a shift in Afro-Colombian literature toward a new demarginalized zone of racial, ethnic, and historical awareness—and a shift that brings Z. O.'s work closer to the poetic sensitivity of other Afro-Caribbean writers like the Cuban poet Nicolás Guillén and the Puerto Rican poet Luis Palés Matos (1899–1959).

FURTHER WORKS: *China 6 a.m.* (1955); *El cirujano de la selva* (1962); *Teatro por Manuel y Juan Zapata Olivella* (1972); *El hombre colombiano* (1974); *El fusilamiento del diablo* (1986); *Nuestra voz; aportes del habla popular latinoamericano al idioma español* (1987); *Las claves mágicas de América* (1989); *Levántate mulato (por mi raza hablará el espíritu)* (1990); *Fábulas de Tamalameque* (1990); *Hemingway el cazador de muerte* (1993)

BIBLIOGRAPHY: Jackson, R., "Myth, History and Narrative Structure in M. Z. O.'s *Chango, el gran putas*," *Revl*, 13, 1–4 (1983): 108–19; Clemons, B. F., "M. Z. O.'s 'Un extraño bajo mi piel': A Study of Repression," *AHR*, 2, 3 (Sept. 1983): 5–7; Carullo, S., "La dialéctica hambre-agresión en *Chambacú: Corral de negros*," *AHR*, 2, 3 (Sept. 1983): 19–22; Captain Hidalgo, Y., "El espacio del tiempo en *Chango, el gran putas*," in R. L. Williams, ed., *Ensayos de literatura colombiana* (1985): 157–66; Kooreman, T., "Integración artística de la protesta social en las novelas de M. Z. O.," *AHR*, 6, 1 (Jan. 1987): 27–30; Heredia, A., "Figuras arquetípicas y la armonía racial en *Chambacú: Corral de negros* de M. Z. O.," *AHR*, 6, 2 (May 1987): 3–8; Mose, K., "*Changó, el gran putas* y el negro en la novelística del colombiano Z. O.," *AHR*, 7, 1–3 (Jan.–Sept. 1988): 45–48; Kooreman, T., "*Pasión vagabunda*, comienzo de una creación ficcionesca," *AHR*, 8, 3 (Sept. 1989): 3–6

—JULIA CUERVO HEWITT

ZARDOYA, Concha

(pseud. of María Concepcíon Zardoya González) Spanish poet and essayist, b. 14 November 1914, Valparaíso, Chile; d. 1995, Madrid

After twenty years in Chile, Z.,'s working-class parents returned to Spain (1932) following proclamation of the Second Republic. She attended university in Madrid (1934-36) while teaching, tutoring, and doing secretarial work for Nobel prize-winning poet, Gabriela MISTRAL (then Chilean consul). During the Spanish Civil War (1936-39), Z. performed cultural tasks for the Republic's Ministry of Public Instruction, supervising wartime library installations. Her younger brother and best friend was killed in the war, and grief for his death and loss of other friends imbues her earliest poems, published in the Loyalist periodical, *Hoar de España* (1938). Five wartime collections remain unpublished. Working as a seamstress, typist, and teacher at a private school, Z. completed her modern philology degree by examination in 1947; with advancement blocked by Francoist hostility to former Republicans, she moved to the University of Illinois, where she completed her doctorate in Spanish Literature (1951). She taught at Tulane University until 1963, and briefly at other U.S. institutions, alternating poetry with teaching and criticism for twenty-two years, and returned to Spain (1976) after Franco's death. She remained active culturally, lecturing and publishing another dozen poetry collections before her death.

Z. published no works written before *Pájaros del nuevo mundo* (1946; New World Birds), which treats neither the new World nor birds but employs symbolic, larger-than-life Chilean settings to project the poet's vision of war's terrors in Spain. Principal themes are liberty and death; birds represent the fallen. *Dominio del llanto* (1947; Domain of Weeping) continues personal and collective portrayals of pain and death, while introducing a mystical love of creation. Surreal landscapes littered with dead children and disinterred bodies provide the background for enunciation of the theme of life's beauty, darkened by the shadow of Franco. Beauty and vitality persist in *La hermosura sencilla* (1953; Simple Beauty) and *Los signos* (1954; Signs), in which lyric intuitions and mysterious symbolism introduce Z.'s metaphysical and ontological concerns, a positive emphasis partially concealing war's psychic scars and attempting to transcend its trauma. Z. employs visual and sonorous evocations of nature's beauty, painting landscapes, animals, and simple objects with love of detail and a Franciscan respect for life. Death of the poet's father while working on her next collection moved her to dedicate *Desterrado ensueño* (1955; Expatriate Daydream) to Spanish political refugees. Autobiographical and emotional resonances, nostalgia, and grief abound as she invokes the homelands—cities, rivers, buildings, flora, fauna, artists, teachers, and humble people—amid allusions to injustice, suffering, and alienation. Death is an obsessive theme here and in *Elegías* (1961; Elegies), *Corral de vivos y muertos* (1965; Corral of the Living and Dead), and *El corazón y la sombra* (1977; Heart and Shadow).

Debajo de la luz (1959; Beneath the Light) introduces another repetitive theme, probing beneath appearances in search of essence, seeking the spirit of things beneath the material surface. As in numerous subsequent works, Z. crosses boundaries between dream and reality, past and present, life and death.

The poet's exile inspired several works, such as *La casa deshabitada* (1959; The Abandoned House), which presents the poet as half alive, with her body in America and her soul in Spain, an "empty house" symbolizing solitude and loneliness. In *Hondo Sur* (1968; Deep South) the poet paints critical vignettes of social problems against the background of New Orleans and southern plantations, swamps, bayous, and cotton fields, alluding to contemporary history via mentions of civil rights leaders and their antagonists, inserting bits of African-American spirituals, music, and oral traditions. *Los engaños de Tremont* (1971; Deceits of Tremont) juxtaposes the poet's residence, Tremont-on-the-Green (Boston) and Spain, with "deceits" ranging from the Franco regime to a portrait of the poet's (deceased) mother, civic and literary deceits, and the descriptions of art and mistaken perspectives on reality, contrasting these with internal realities—love, authenticity, immortality—buried beneath superficial appearances. *Las hiedras del tiempo* (1972; Ivy of Time) also paints landscapes where the poet has lived, and roads traveled from Chartres to Manhattan, Fiésole to Canada. *Manhattan y otras latitudes* (1983; Manhattan and Other Latitudes) likewise recreates former places of residence.

Even more significant thematically is art, one form of salvation visualized by Z. (dreams, love, and memories also allow humanity to transcend daily existence and daily life). *Mirar al cielo es tu condena* (1957; Your Sentence Is Looking at the Sky) includes twelve compositions inspired by Michelangelo's painting and sculpture, emphasizing human insignificance in the cosmos. *Corral de vivos y muertos,* expressing grief provoked by reburial of her brother's remains, also abounds in homages to El Greco, Velázquez, Goya, Solana, and Picasso; indeed, Goya is a special favorite, inspiring poems in several collections, and Z.'s admiration for Miró produced *Poemas a Joan Miró* (1984; Poems to Joan Miró). *Los perplejos hallazgos* (1986; Perplexed Discoveries) celebrates contemporary masterpieces discovered in Madrid museums, including a thirty-three poem homage to Paul Cézanne, and twenty-seven dedicated to Juan Gris. Other poets' masterpieces inspire *Los ríos caudales* (1982; Mighty Rivers), portraying bards of the Generation of 1927 as seers who reveal eternal truths, emphasizing creativity and the poet's mission. Z.'s books typically revolve around specific themes, as explained in the prologue to *Retorno a Magerit* (1983; Return to Magerit [Madrid]). She visualizes an entire work with its unifying theme(s), sentiment or dominant philosophy, conceiving each poem as part of the whole. Major themes include death, Spain's Civil War, nature, love, time, exile, and salvation. Spain, memory, solitude, travel, dreams, art, poetry, and music also constitute obsessive concerns. Death, grief, and time appear with variations in numerous works. Z. published some thirty volumes of poetry, and ten volumes of criticism, and is belatedly receiving recognition as one of Spain's most significant wartime and postwar women poets. Her having been born in Chile, combined with the Franco regime's censorship of works by pro-Republican writers and silencing of critical works about them, kept her writing largely unknown in Spain until her repatriation following the dictator's death.

FURTHER WORKS: *Miguel Hernández 1910-1942* (1955); *Donde el tiempo resbala* (1966); *Ritos, cifras y evasiones* (197?); *Diotima*

y sus edades (1981); *Forma de esperanza* (1985); *No llega a ser ceniza lo que arde* (1985); *Altamor* (1986); *Grádiva y un extraño héroe* (1987); *Estación del silencio* (1989); *Patrimonio de ciegos* (1992); *El don de la simiente* (1993)

—JANET PÉREZ

ZAYTSEV, Boris Konstantinovich

Russian short-story writer, novelist, essayist, translator, and dramatist, b. 29 Jan. 1881, Orel; d. 28 Jan. 1972, Paris, France

Z. came from a family of landed gentry. In 1898, after completing secondary school, he entered the Moscow Technological School, from which he was expelled because of participation in student disorders. In 1902 he matriculated at the law school of Moscow University, but he left to go to Italy to study art. His first short story, the impressionistic "Noch" (the night), was published in the newspaper *Kurier* in 1901. He was not in sympathy with the 1917 October Revolution, and in 1922 he emigrated to Germany, then moved to Italy, and finally settled in Paris.

God and His relation to mankind became a major theme for Z. early in his career. From the agnosticism of his early youth evident in *Rasskazy: Kniga pervaya* (1906; stories: first book), Z. passed through a period of pantheism seen in *Rasskazy: Kniga vtoraya* (1909; stories: second book), before his religious ideas finally crystallized in the mold provided by Orthodox Christianity, which permeates the stories in *Sny: Kniga tretia* (1911; dreams: third book), the novel *Dalny kray* (1915; distant land), and the collection of stories *Putniki* (1919; travelers).

Later, in exile, Z. dealt with religious themes in descriptive works containing philosophical and religious meditations: *Prepodobny Sergy Radonezhsky* (1925; Saint Sergius of Radonezh), *Afon* (1929; Mount Athos), and *Valaam* (1936; Valaam [an island, site of a famous monastery]). The novel *Zolotoy uzor* (1926; golden pattern) is concerned with the October Revolution and also has a clear religious and philosophical foundation: a judgment on certain segments of the prerevolution intelligentsia who had not led a "righteous" life, who had, perhaps inadvertently, inflicted suffering on others and who had themselves suffered after the revolution. It is both a condemnation and a penance—a confession of guilt.

Z.'s writings on Italy are *sui generis*—in his own words, there is almost nothing "Russian" in them. Most representative are *Rafael* (1924; Raphael) and *Italia* (1951; Italy). He referred to Florence as the "mysterious home" of his soul. And he was inspired by the city to translate Dante's *Inferno* into Russian (*Ad*, 1961).

Z.'s tetralogy of autobiographical novels—*Puteshestvie Gleba* (1937; Gleb's journey), *Tishina* (1948; silence), *Yunost* (1950; youth), and *Drevo zhizni* (1953; the tree of life)—set against the background of the Russian countryside, have a graceful lyrical quality and engagingly relate the author's life in Russia. Z. also wrote fictionalized biographies of his favorite writers: *Zhizn Turgeneva* (1932; the life of Turgenev), *Zhukovsky* (1951; Zhukovsky), and *Chekhov* (1954; Chekhov).

Z.'s important short novel *Anna* (1929; Anna, 1937) has been widely translated. It is a finely etched picture of a fragment of a woman's life during the early days of Soviet rule in Russia, a story of her tragic love for the ruined landowner Arkady. The major and minor characters might have stepped from pages of TURGENEV or CHEKHOV, so richly are they drawn. *Anna* is refreshingly free from propaganda: the author's abhorrence of murder as a method of attaining one's goals is merely human, not inspired by any political bias.

Z. has often been called by Russian critics a *"tishayshy"* ("most unassuming") writer. His works, however—full of "moods," descriptions of nature, and expressions of religious feeling—have a wonderfully soothing effect on the reader. Z.'s world is dominated by God, Who is both loving and just, although not in any anthropomorphic sense. Love and understanding imply accepting human faults and shortcomings, and Z.'s chief claim to greatness as a man and importance as a writer lies in this understanding and acceptance.

FURTHER WORKS: *Sobranie sochineny* (7 vols., 1922–23); *Ulitsa Svyatogo Nikolaya* (1923); *Grekh* (1927); *Strannoe puteshestvie* (1927); *Izbrannye rasskazy* (1929); *Dom v Passi* (1935); *Moskva* (1939); *V puti* (1951); *Reka vremyon* (1964); *Dalyokoe* (1965)

BIBLIOGRAPHY: V., Weidlé V., "Un maître du roman lyrique: M. B. Z. et la 'Guirlande dorée,'" *Le mois* (1 October 1933): 194–200; Cournos, J., on *Anna*, *NYTBR* (10 October 1937): 8; Struve, G., "Current Russian Literature, VII: B. Z.," *SlavonicR*, 17 (1938–1939): 445–51; Strakhovsky, L. I., "B. Z.—the Humanist," *RusR*, 12, 2 (1953): 95–99; Lo Gatto, E., *Histoire de la littérature russe des origines á nos jours* (1965): 569–72; Guerra, R., *Bibliographie des œuvres de B. Z.* (1982)

—SERGE KRYZYTSKI

ŻEROMSKI, Stefan

Polish novelist, b. 14 Oct. 1864, Strawiczyn; d. 20 Nov. 1925, Warsaw

Born into a family of impoverished gentry, Ż. studied in a veterinary school in Warsaw, then worked as a private tutor and as librarian in the Polish Museum in Rapperswil, Switzerland. Throughout his life he was socially and politically active. In 1922 he received the first State Literary Award.

Ż.'s early writing is dominated by short narrative forms: short stories, novellas, poetic prose, and essays. Uncompromising in their realism, these works reveal a mastery of style surprising for so young was writer. His preference for the cruel and the ugly brought him close to naturalism. Ż.'s first novel, *Syzyfowe prace* (1897; Sisyphean labors), is a thinly disguised autobiography based on his experiences in high school: the book depicts the ability of the Polish students to resist efforts at Russification by the school authorities. A detached tone and gentle humor distinguish this novel from Ż.'s other works.

Ludzie bezdomni (1899; homeless people) brought Ż. recognition and contains all the key motifs of his writings: passion, suffering, and sensitivity to social injustice. The only goal of the protagonist, Dr. Judym, is to improve the living conditions of the poor; he rejects the love of a woman to devote his life to social service. The behavioral pattern proposed as a model by Ż.—that personal happiness should be sacrificed for a higher, here social, cause—derives from the romantic tradition.

Popioły (1903; *Ashes*, 1928) is an epic novel about life in Poland during the Napoleonic era. It alternates between scenes from everyday life and descriptions of battles, between passionate love affairs and profound philosophical meditations; and the action

extends all the way from the Polish provinces to Venice, Saragossa in Spain, and Paris. The novel is loosely constructed, consisting of fragments and tableaux rather than a well-articulated sequence of events. The three protagonists unify the novel by providing a focus for its three major aspects. The violent, passionate Rafał Olbromski is the incarnation of primordial instincts; the sensitive Krzysztof Cedro is an upholder of the national cause and the moral barometer of the novel; while Prince Gintułt—who has a reflective and critical mind—provides a metaphysical perspective. *Popioły* reveals a philosophy that is Manichaean: the glory of war is overshadowed by its cruelty, the beauty of life by its misery, the exaltation of love by its destructiveness. This philosophical duality is reflected in a style that alternates between realism and impressionistic, intensely lyrical passages. In his meditations on the origin of good and evil, Ż. adopts a skeptical view of history and of Polish social reality. Through this moral prism Ż. discredits the idealized image of the Polish nobility, confronting it with the reality of social injustice. He also questions the Napoleonic myth, reexamining the role of the Polish legions in the Napoleonic army. Ostensibly a historical novel, *Popioły* touches on issues that were subjects of controversy among Ż.'s contemporaries: national liberation through military action versus the program of peaceful cooperation with the occupying powers, and the priority of national versus social struggle. A partisan of military action, Ż. saw at the same time that social reforms were a prerequisite in the struggle for national independence.

Wierna rzeka (1912; *The Faithful River*, 1943) is artistically one of Ż.'s most accomplished novels. Thematically and stylistically it recalls his earlier realistic pieces. Against the grim backdrop of national tragedy—the 1863 uprising—a depressing love story with prominent social underpinnings is narrated in a masterly, contained tone.

Uroda życia (1912; the beauty of life) introduces a strong utopian element, which became characteristic of Ż's later writings; in his last novel, *Przedwiośnie* (1924; before spring), however, the confrontation of utopia with reality leads to disillusionment. The ending of *Przedwiośnie* has been a source of controversy. The protagonist joins a communist worker's demonstration; meant as a warning against communism, the novel has been frequently misinterpreted both by communist critics and by anticommunist readers as procommunist propaganda.

Ż's writing is stamped by a duality reflecting his own personality, torn between passion and conscience, exaltation and reflection, realism and idealism. His contemporaries gave him the two labels "conscience of the nation" and "insatiable heart." Extreme emotionality, combined with strong eroticism and at the same time intellectuality and stern morality verging on didacticism, produce a tension in Ż's writings that is the source of both his strength and his weakness. At his worst sentimental and exalted, at his best Ż. wrote some of the most intense and poetic pages of Polish prose. Of undisputed moral authority among his contemporaries, Ż. is an eminently Polish author. His Polishness is manifest both in the themes of his works and in his extreme sensitivity to national and social issues. All of his writings communicate a sense of mission that makes him an heir of the great romantics. This characteristic accounts for his relative unpopularity among non-Polish readers, but at the same time assures him a special place not only in Polish literature but, even more, in the history of the Polish national consciousness.

FURTHER WORKS: *Dzienniki, 1882–1891* (3 vols., 1953–1956); *Opowiadania* (1895); *"Rozdzióbią nas kruki, wrony": Obrazki z ziemi mogił i krzyżów* (1896); *Utwory powieściowe* (1898); *Aryman* *mści się; Godzina* (1904); *Echa leśne* (1905); *Powieść o Udałym Walgierzu* (1906); *Duma o Hetmanie* (1908); *Dzieje grzechu* (1908); *Słowo o bandosie* (1908); *Róża* (1909); *Sułkowski* (1910); *Sen o szpadzie* (1915); *Nawracanie Judasza* (1916); *Sen o szpadzie i sen o chlebie* (1916); *Zamieć* (1916); *Wisła* (1918); *Charitas* (1919); *Ponad śnieg bielszym się stanę* (1921); *Biała rękawiczka* (1921); *Wiatr od morza* (1922); *Pomyłki* (1923); *Turoń* (1923); *Międzymorze* (1924); *Uciekła mi przepióreczka . . .* (1924); *Pisma* (23 vols., 1922–1930); *Pisma* (32 vols., 1928–1929); *Pisma* (26 vols., 1947–1956); *Dzieła* (32 vols., 1956–1957, 1963–1970)

BIBLIOGRAPHY: Topass, J., *Visages d'écrivains polonais: Les aspects du roman polonais* (1930): 59–75; Zaleski, Z. L., *Attitudes et destinées: Faces et profils d'écrivains polonais* (1932): 197–226; Borowy, W., "*Ż.*," *SlavonicR, No. 41* (1936): 403–20; Kridl, M., *A Survey of Polish Literature and Culture* (1956): 421–35; Kwiatkowska-Siemieńska, I., *S. Ż.: La nature dans son expérience et sa pensée* (1964); Milosz, C., *The History of Polish Literature* (1969): 365–69; Krzyżanowski, J., *A History of Polish Literature* (1978): 522–31

—BOGDANA CARPENTER

ZIEDONIS, Imants

Latvian poet, essayist, and screenwriter, b. 3 May 1933, Ragaciems

The principal theme of Z.'s first collection of poems, *Zemes un sapņu smilts* (1961; The Sand of Earth and Dreams), is the beauty and importance of physical work. The description of a harsh nature, of the ordinary working people—the fishermen and women of his native village—created an appreciation of everydayness that was new in postwar Latvian literature. Z. also considers the work ethic in the context of an older tradition—of a sense of pride and responsibility to be achieved by the individual who refuses to be a simple cog in a vast mechanism. The collection *Motocikls* (1965; Motorcycle) marks a break with the poet's earlier idealism. The enthusiastic striving is now counterbalanced by a thematic pattern of stillness and peace, by a dialectical interplay that allows the poet to develop a more penetrating analysis of the relations tying the individual to his or her world.

The period of the late 1960s and early 1970s was marked by sociocultural processes whose effect was to undermine all notions of the self-determination and autonomy in Latvia and other Soviet Republics. For Z., the resulting feelings of dread, solitude, and alienation could only be resisted by means of a counterstrategy that valorizes the profound meaning of an individual's ethnic and cultural being. He thus undertakes an intensive study of Latvian folklore, especially of the *dainas*, of Eastern philosophy, and of the writings of Jānis RAINIS and Aleksandrs ČAKS. The collection *Kā svece deg* (1971; How the Candle Burns) brings out the poet's maturing insights in the form of an alienation aggravated by a sense of loss of ethical bearings as well as the realization of a looming ecological crisis. At the same time, it is a pessimism that is thwarted by an assertion of the individual's right to be different, the will to resist, and to search for new values.

The sense of new poetic and philosophical possibilities drawn from folklore and mythology is evoked powerfully in the book-length poem *Poēma par pienu* (1977; A Poem about Milk), and the collection *Man labvēlīgā tumsā* (1979; In Darkness That Wishes Me Well). In "Poēma par pienu," Z. turns to the fundamental values inherent in love of mother, family, homeland, nation, and work. Woman is the central figure of the poem; she becomes, in effect, the thematic point of intersection for all the important ethical problems concerning the present situation as well as the historical past. By contrast, in the unfinished poem "Viddivvārpā" (In Middoubleearofwheat) included in *Maize* (1982; Bread), the stress is on the necessary role of the masculine, represented by the figure of the man who tends the earth and makes bread—thus ensuring the survival of humanity. The poetry written at this time reveals a profound change in the poet's representation of the individual: the ideals of a strong will or purposeful resolve have been replaced by a trusting acceptance of the world's order, as well as an opening to the thought of a divine purpose made manifest by the symbolism of light and the sun. The poems in *Taureņu uzbrukums* (1988; Attack of the Butterflies) present the world in terms of a dynamic, pulsating rhythm in which highs alternate with lows, the noble with the base.

In 1970 Z. published *Kurzemīte* (Little Courland), a work that achieved immense popularity. In it, the author writes about his beloved native province of Courland, describing its people, their customs and traditions, and narrating its history. What interests Z. above all is the inner character and strength of its people, traits that become manifest in certain colorful personalities. He also considers the ties that link individuals to their land, to its nature and history. In describing the contemporary situation, his narrative points out the contradictions between what has been inherited and what has been imposed, thus invalidating, in effect, the rhetoric of progress and accomplishment that constituted the official party line.

Over the course of his career, Z. has contributed much to the development of children's literature. In the 1970s he began writing literary flares and in the 1980s he began to write regularly for children—poetry, fairy tales, and educational works. Lastly, Z. has always manifested an interest in other forms of artistic expression and has been involved in cinematic arts in particular. He has written screenplays for four films, two based on classics in Latvian literature and two documentaries. He has also been involved with theater and opera, dramatizing his own work as well as that of Aleksandrs Čaks. In addition, Z. is well known for his travel journals in which records reflections on the uniqueness of a people's ethnic and cultural characteristics, on their importance in the context of civilization's achievements, and on the need to preserve them.

The literary productions, journalistic writings, and political activism of Z. have made him one of the most important personalities within the contemporary Latvian cultural scene. Z. effectively blends his love of Latvian folklore and his appreciation for values fortified by centuries of history with an experimental search for new forms and modes of poetic expression. He remains one of the more influential creative minds in Latvia today and still contributes in important ways to the ongoing process that is shaping his country's new cultural and political identity.

FURTHER WORKS: *Sirds dinamīts* (1965); *Dzejnieka dienasgrāmata* (1965); *Pa putnu ceļu* (1968): *Es ieeju sevī* (1968); *Epifānijas 1* (1971); *Perpendikulārā karote* (1972); *Krāsainas pasakas* (1973); *Pūt vējiņi!* (1973); *Epifānijas 2* (1974); *Kurzemīte 2* (1974); *Caurvējš* (1975); *Garainis, kas veicina vārīšanos* (1976); *Lāču pasaka* (1976); *Puika* (1977); *Zaļā pasaka* (1977); *Suns funs un vējš* (1978); *Ar tikko grieztu ķeizarkroni rokā* (1979); *Izlase* (1980);

Blēņas un pasakas (1980); *Re, kā* (1980); *Kas ir kolhozs?* (1981); *tas ir—kolhozs?* (1983); *Visādas pasakas* (1983); *Ceļmallapas* (1983); *Man vienai māsiņai* (1984); *Māte* (1984); *Pasāžas* (1985); *Tik un tā* (1985); *Sākamgrāmata* (1985); *Mūžības temperaments* (1991); *Tutepatās* (1992); *Es, cilvēks, pasaulē* (1993); *Mirkļi. Foreles* (1993); *Viegli* (1993); *Epifānijas 3* (1994); *Raksti* (6 vols., 1995-1997); *Es skaitīju un noncācu pie Viena* (1997)

BIBLIOGRAPHY: Peters, J., "Piena gaismā, sev labvēlīgā tumsā," *Liesma*, 4 (1979): 5-6; Ķikāns, V., "I. Z. dzejas trīs valzivis," *Kritikas gadagrāmata*, 11 (1983): 167-78; Kravalis, O., *Mūsdienu latviešu padomju literatūra: 1960-1980* (1985): 144-59; Bērziņš, U., and A. Huzangajs, "Es jūtu, jūtu, jūtu šo zemi . . ." *Kritikas gadagrāmata*, 16 (1988): 145-59; Cimdiņa, A., "Šķi Svēto Rakstu vai gurķu lapas," in Z., *Raksti*, 1 (1995-1997): 362-67; Cakla, I., "Brīvības nolūks," in Z., *Raksti* (1995), Vol. 1: 530-39

—KARLIS RACEVSKIS

ZILAHY, Lajos

Hungarian novelist, dramatist, and short-story writer, b. 27 March 1891, Nagyszalonta; d. 1 Dec. 1974, Novi Sad, Yugoslavia

Z. earned a degree in jurisprudence from the University of Budapest and for a time practiced law. He was wounded in World War I, during which he gained renown for some poems. Subsequently he was a journalist in Budapest, Paris, and London. Between the two world wars his plays and novels were very successful. After World War II he was elected president of the Hungarian-Soviet Cultural Society, but he soon became disillusioned with the Communist regime and emigrated to the U.S. in 1947. After this date many of his works were published first (or only) in English.

Z. was a popular novelist in the best sense of the phrase: he appealed to a large public without compromising his literary standards. His plots have clarity, and his characterizations are realistic. A humanist, he affirmed the values of peace, love, family, and country. *Halálos tavasz* (1922; deadly spring) is about a young man who shoots himself over an unhappy affair with a frivolous girl. *Két fogoly* (1927; *Two Prisoner*, 1931) is the moving story of a young couple, prisoners of fate, who are torn apart by World War I. In *A lélek kialszik* (1932; the soul is extinguished) a young immigrant in American observes the memories of his homeland fading away until his soul "goes out like a candle."

Z.'s most ambitious—and most controversial—fictional work is the Dukay saga. Somewhat resembling John GALSWORTHY's *The Forsyte Saga*, it is a chronicle of the heyday and subsequent decline of an aristocratic family spanning more than a century, from 1814 to after World War II. It comprises *Ararát* (1947; *The Dukays*, 1949), *The Angry Angel* (1953), *Krisztina és a király* (1954; Krisztina and the king), and *Century in Scarlet* (1965). The saga was eventually published in three volumes in Novi Sad as *A Dukay család* (1968; the Dukay family).

As with his novels, in his plays the recognizable characters and situations—sometimes comic, sometimes tragic—made them popular. *Szibéria* (1928; Siberia) is about Hungartan prisoners of war during World War I. In *A szőz és a gödölye* (1927; Virgin with Kid) a wealthy family is torn apart by their own conflicts, symbolized by their varied attitudes toward a priceless heirloom, the Renaissance

painting of the play's title. Different in tone is *Szépanyám* (1943; my great-great-grandmother), a poignant and at times zany family chronicle.

Z.'s most controversial play, *Fatornyok* (1943; rewritten 1945 and 1947; wooden steeples), is an allegory of true patriotism, defined as devotion to the cherished memories of one's childhood home. The play was banned first by the Nazis because of its antifascist implications and then by the Communists because of Z.'s defense of what were considered outdated bourgeois values. In 1982, however, the authorities permitted a production in Budapest.

Z. eschewed ideologies, although he was an idealist. He was frequently attacked and misinterpreted by doctrinaire critics and derogated by highbrow reviewers. Yet he is too good a writer to be dismissed. Several film versions of his novels made him even more popular, and his works have been translated into many languages.

FURTHER WORKS: *Versei* (1916); *Az ökör és más komédiák* (1920); *Hazaháró lélek* (1923); *A jégcsap* (1923); *Szépapám szerelme* (1923); *Az ezüstszárnyü szélmalom* (1924); *Süt a nap* (1924); *Csillagok* (1925); *Zenebohócok* (1925); *A fehér szarvas* (1927); *A világbajnok* (1927); *Házasságszédelgö Birtokpolitika* (1928); *A tábornok* (1928); *Valamit visz a víz* (1929); *A szökevény* (1930; *The Deserter*, 1932); *A kizasszony* (1931); *Leona* (1932); *Tuzmadar* (1932); *A tizenkettedik óra* (1933); *Az utolsó szerep* (1935); *Fehér hajó* (1935); *A fegyverek visszanéznek* (1936; *The Guns Look Back*, 1938); *A földönfutó város* (1939); *Gyümülcs a fán* (1939); *Csöndes élet és egyéb elbeszélések* (1941)

BIBLIOGRAPHY: Reményi, J., *Hungarian Writers and Literature* (1964): 414–23

—DALMA H. BRUNAUER

ZIMBABWEAN LITERATURE

In English

The first writings about the part of Africa that was to become Zimbabwe were reminiscences of hunting, travel, and missionary work. F. C. Selous's (1851-1917) *A Hunter's Wanderings in South Africa* (1881), Edward Mohr's (1828-1876) account of his travels, translated as *To The Victoria Falls of the Zambesi* (1876) and the missionary T. M. Thomas's (1828-1884) *Eleven Years in Central South Africa* (1873) are representative accounts of these different ways of engaging with the interior. The earliest novels are often plotted as romances of hunting and exploration, a form that Henry Rider Haggard (1856-1925) used in *King Soloman's Mines* (1885) whose inspiration is partly the ruins of Great Zimbabwe. Haggard's influence can be seen in numerous Rhodesian novels in which the ruins of earlier colonies are discovered. After Rhodes's occupation of the country, wars with the Ndebele and the Shona become a frequent preoccupation of the fiction. With the Ndebele and the Shona conquered by 1897 and an increase in the number of white settlers, the country was no longer written as savage and exotic. Writers such as Gertrude Page (d. 1922), the author of *Love in the Wilderness* (1907), *The Rhodesian* (1912), and *The Pathway* (1914) and Cynthia Stockley (d. 1936), the author of *Virginia of the Rhodesians* (1903), and *The Claw* (1911) wrote best-selling novels that contributed to the idea of a discrete white Rhodesian identity and helped to lay the foundations of white Rhodesian nationalism. Another fictional tradition was critical of Rhodesian attitudes and behavior. Arthur Shearly Cripp's (1869-1952) *The Brooding Earth* (1911) and *Bay-Tree Country* (1913) are important early examples. Doris LESSING's *The Grass is Singing* (1950) and the first four volumes of *Children of Violence: Martha Quest* (1952), *A Proper Marriage* (1954), *A Ripple from the Storm* (1958), and *Landlocked* (1965) are scathing accounts of white Rhodesia observed from within. The final fictional expressions of white nationalism are novels about the Liberation War out of which Zimbabwe was born in 1980, notably John Gordon Davis's *Hold My Hand I'm Dying* (1967) and Robert Early's (dates n.a.) *A Time of Madness* (1977).

Fiction in English by black writers has from its beginnings experimented with formal innovations. Stanlake Samkange's (1922-1988) novels quote extensively from historical documents and *On Trial for My Country* (1966), *The Mournned One* (1975), and *The Year of the Uprising* (1978) show how white intransigence in the last years of Rhodesia transformed Samkange from liberal to nationalist militant. Charles MUNGOSHI's *Waiting for the Rain* (1975) conveys a sense of a people without a collective memory and like Stanley Nyamfukudza's (1951) *The Non-Believer's Journey* (1980) implicitly refuses the certainties of nationalist polemics with open-ended narratives. Dambudzo MARECHERA is the most original writer Zimbabwe has so far produced. His Guardian Prize-winning *The House of Hunger* (1979) and his masterpiece, *Black Sunlight* (1980), confront his complex cultural heritage with constantly shifting perspectives and fragmented narratives that look skeptically at both British imperialist and Pan-Africanist ideologies. A different sort of experiment can be seen in Chenjerai Hove's (b.1924) novels. His Noma Award-winning *Bones* (1988) shows the war of independence from the perspectives of both the ancestors and the most marginal of Zimbabwe's people and *Shadows* (1991) shows the rural people as perpetual victims. Shimmer CHINODYA has produced more conventionally realist narratives. *Harvest of Thorns* (1989), which won a Commonwealth African Prize, explores the war but concentrates on the complex private motives of his guerilla protagonist. John Eppel (dates n.a.) has developed the range of Zimbabwe writing with satirical novels and his *D G G Berry's The Great North Road* (1922) won the M-Net Book prize.

A new generation of women writers has appeared since independence. Tsitsi Dangarembga's (b. 1959) *Nervous Conditions* (1988) shows women trying to take command of their own lives in Rhodesia. Yvonne Vera (dates n.a.) has brought another distinct voice to Zimbabwean writing. Her novels—including *Nehanda* (1993), yet another Commonwealth Prize-winner, and *Under the Tongue* (1996)—use complex imagistic patterns to order their narratives. Rhodesia and Zimbabwe have produced short-story writers of ability, notably Arthur Shearly Cripps, Doris Lessing and Charles Mungoshi with his *Coming of the Dry Season* (1972) and *Some Kinds of Wounds* (1980), as well as Alexander Kanengoni (b. 1951), whose *Effortless Tears* (1993) was short-listed for the Commonwealth Writers Prize, and Musaemura Zimunya (b. 1949) with *Nightshift* (1993). Cripps and Noel Brettel (1908-1989) were the most important white Rhodesian poets. Zimunya is Zimbabwe's leading poet and his poetry celebrates the nation and the vitality and the plight of the rural and urban poor. His publications include the Noma Award-winning *Kingfisher, Jikinya and Other Poems* (1982). Anthologies include Kizito Mechemwa's (dates n.a.) *Zimbabwean Poetry in English* (1977), which was the first anthology devoted to black writing. After Zimbabwean independence, Zimunya and

Mudereri Kadhani (dates n.a.) published their important anthology *And Now the Poets Speak* (1981). The most historically complete anthology is Colin Style (b. 1937) and O-lan Style's (b. 1943) *Mambo Book of Zimbabwean Verse in English* (1988).

BIBLIOGRAPHY: Pichanick, J., A. Chennells, and L. Rix, comps., *Rhodesian Literature in English: A Bibliography* (1890-1975) (1977); Zimunya, M., *Those Years of Drought and Hunger: The Birth of African Fiction in Zimbabwe* (1982); McLoughlin, T. O., "Black Writing in English from Zimbabwe," in G. D. Killam, ed., *The Writing of East and Central Africa* (1983): 100-19; Zinyemba, R., *Zimbabwe Drama: A Study of English and Shona Plays* (1986); Veit Wild, F., *Teachers, Preachers, Non-Believers: A Social History of Zimbabwean Literature* (1993); Chennells, A., "Rhodesian Discourse, Rhodesian Novels and the Zimbabwean Liberation War," in N. Bhebhe, and T. Ranger, eds., *Society in Zimbabwe's Liberation War* (1995), vol. 2: 102-29; Ngara, E., ed., *New Writing from Southern Africa* (1996)

—ANTHONY CHENNELLS

In Ndebele

Long before the Ndebele language was given a written form, European scholars were collecting and analyzing the oral literature. This traditional literary art served as a model for Ndebele writers, especially the early ones, in creating a modern fiction.

The first Ndebele novel was *AmaNdebele kaMzilikazi* (1956; the Ndebele of Mzilikazi) by Ndabaningi Sithole (b. 1920). He used a historical situation but made no pretenses about his political objectives; it was not surprising that the Ian Smith regime banned the novel in the 1960s. The historical novel *Umthwakazi* (1957; the owner of the state), by Peter S. Mahlangu (b. 1923), is on the surface an account of the Ndebeles, tracing their struggles from pre-colonial times up until their defeat by white settlers under Cecil Rhodes in the uprising of 1896–97. His true aim is to show the greatness of his people.

The period 1958–62 saw the emergence of works resembling European novels. The narration and characterization, however, were greatly influenced by traditional folktales. These novels are marked by a concern for social values in changing times. Isaac N. Mpofu (b. 1932), in *Akusoka lingenasici* (1958; no one is perfect) and *Wangithembisa lami* (1960; you also promised me), exposes human vanity and shows how modernization has brought out personality flaws.

Social themes were taken up by other writers, who yearned for the bygone days and condemned the new social order. This particular theme was pioneered by David Ndoda (b. 1925) in *Vusezindala* (1958; in days gone by), which was followed by Elkana M. Ndlovu's (b. 1913) *Inhlamvu zaseNgodlweni* (1959; the offspring of Ngodlweni). Ndoda's characterization was based on folktales, while Ndlovu's was inspired by modern Western models.

Although women played a leading role in narrating oral folktales, written creative work by women was slow to develop. A breakthrough came with Lassie Ndondo's (b. c. 1930) novel *Qaphela ingane* (1962; take care of the boy); the chief concern of the book is the proper upbringing of children. A similar theme had been used by Amos Mzilethi (b. 1914) in his *Uyokhula umfana* (1961; the boy grows up). The major weakness of such novels, and of most Ndebele fiction to date, is their didacticism; the reason for this is that publishers wanted novels with clear messages geared to young students, who formed the bulk of the readership.

The early 1970s saw an upsurge in novel writing. The themes were still social, dwelling on such issues as industrialization and its attendant problems, unemployment, squalor, and prostitution. Older writers tended to offer their criticism straightforwardly, for example, Sithembile O. Mlilo (b. 1924) in *Lifile* (1975; it has passed away) and *Bantu beHadlana* (1977; people of Hadlana). Younger writers, influenced by European literature, often found more subtle forms for these themes; examples are Ndabezinhle Sigogo's (b. 1932) *Akula zulu emhlabeni* (1971; there is no heaven on earth) and Barbara Makhalisa's (b. 1949) *Umendo* (1977; marriage).

Poetry and drama have lagged behind fiction. Several anthologies have been published, but no outstanding poet has emerged. The subjects have ranged from love, death, and nature to social and political problems. The styles and techniques have been based sometimes on English poetry, sometimes on traditional praise poetry, and sometimes on a combination of the two.

Only two plays have been written so far. *Indlalifa ngubani?* (1976; who is the heir?) by Ndabezinhle Sigogo is concerned with social problems related to traditional life, while *Umhlaba lo* (1977; what a world) by Barbara Makhalisa relates the plight of young women in the modern city. Both plays are constructed along the lines of realistic European drama, with Sigogo making use of traditional local humor.

BIBLIOGRAPHY: Krog, W., ed., *African Literature in Rhodesia* (1966): 211–36; Gérard, A. S., *African Language Literatures* (1981): 232–41

—T. M. NDLOVU

In Shona

Shona is the term coined by missionary scholars to describe mutually intelligible dialects spoken by Karanga, Korekore, Manyika, and Zezuru people who comprise three quarters of the current eleven million population of Zimbabwe. All have rich oral traditions that—through language, myths, legends, and folktales—have shaped, to some degree, the texture of written Shona literature, which emerged in the late 1950s. The literarture itself can be divided into three broad categories—those texts set in the precolonial era (before 1890), those dealing with the colonial situation (1890-1980), and those exploring the issues of the postindependence period.

The writing of Shona novels starts in the 1950s with the publication of Solomon Mutsvairo's (b. 1924) *Feso* (1956; Devil Thorns) and Patrick Chakaipa's (b. 1932) *Karikoga Gumi Remiseve* (1958; The Lonely One of the Ten Arrows), among others. Noticeable is the yearning for a once glorious Shona past characterized by communal values and a common identity. The novels themselves are a result of the blending of elements of Shona legends and folktales with aspects of the Western novel. As for the majority of the novels dealing with the colonial situation and that, at present, constitute the bulk of Shona literature, they are largely about the disintegration of Shona cultural values. Of interest is the way most of these eschew the political, hardly question the political system, and tend to see social and political problems in terms of weaknesses of individual characters; hence, they become didactic and moralistic. This trend is evident in Bernard Chidzero's (b. 1927) *Nzvenga Mutsvairo* (1957; Dodge the Broom) and Chakaipas's (b. 1932)

Dzasukwa Mwana Asina Hembe (1967; The Pots Have Been Cleaned for Beer Brewing). Those that tend to be more critical of the colonial situation are exemplified by Thompson Tzodzo's (b. 1947) *Pafunge* (1970; Think about It) and Aaron Moyo's (b. 1950) *Ziva Kwawakabva* (1976; Know Where You Came From).

The state-controlled Literature Bureau established in 1953 as well as the influence of missionary teaching affected the nature and orientation of the Shona novel. It is only after the attainment of independence in 1980 that the Shona novel becomes explicit on the suffering caused by oppression and the Zimbabwean war of independence. Mordecai Hamutyinei's (b. 1934) *Zvakanga Zvaoma Muzimbabwe* (1984; Life Had Become Difficult in Zimbabwe) and Mutsvairo's *Mweya Wanehanda* (1988; The Spirit of Nehanda) are fine examples. Since then, vibrant creativity has taken place with more novels coming out almost every year. However, the vibrancy is not always matched by experimentation with form and style except in Charles Mungoshi's *Ndiko Kupindana Kwamazuva* (1978; That Is How Time Passes) and *Kunyarara Hakusi Kutaura?* (1983; Is Silence Not Communicating?). In these novels psychological realism and the stream of consciousness techniques are used to explore the inner lives of characters and the philosophical implications of human existence. In all over one hundred and twenty novels had been published by the mid-1990s and there is no doubt that the novel as a genre has been the dominant one in Shona literature.

The first published Shona book in verse, Herbert Chitep's (1923-1975) *Soko Risina Musoro* (1958; A Tale without a Head), is a long poem of epic proportions and the only one to date that, like the Shona colonial novel, bemoans the passing away of an idyllic pastoral life while underlining the cultural confusion and vulnerability that characterize African life with the onset of colonialism. This epic has been followed up with the publication of twelve substantive poetry anthologies. The issue of identity and the relentless erosion of Shona values brought about by the coming of Westernization are the dominant concerns that preoccupy poets such as Solomon Mutsvairo and Nathan Shamuyarira (b. 1929) in *Madetembedzo Makare Na Matsva* (1959; Tradition and Modern Poetry). Ironically some of their poems are heavily dependent on English romantic poetry for their themes, style, and form and sometimes sound contrived. The imitative aspects are also discernible in other anthologies such as *Mabvumira Enhetembo* (1969; Rhythm of Poetry), *Nhetembo* (1972; Poetry), and *Gwenyambira* (1979; The Mbira Player) although some of the more prominent poets such as Mordecai Hamutyinei (b. 1934) and Joseph Kumbirai (b. 1922) were more innovative in style and form but heavily influenced by the Christian gospel. Alongside the muffled poetic tradition of the colonial period there also developed a body of poetry specifically aimed at preserving Shona customs and traditions, and at the forefront are Aaron Hodza (b. 1924) and George Fortune (b. 1915), notably with his *Shona Praise Poetry* (1976) But again all these writers avoid the political until the anthology edited by Musaemura Zimunya (b. 1949), *Chakarira Chindunduma* (1985; The Uprising Resounded). In it dense metaphorical writing of the earlier anthologies designed to evade Rhodesian censorship gives way to lucid writing influenced by Shona and African history. The increased creativity of the 1980s is also evident in the publication of individual poetry collections, notably *Rukuvhute* (1990; Umbilical Cord) by Chirikure Chirikure (b. 1962) and *Dama Rekutanga* (1990; The First Promise) by Samuel Chimsoro (b. 1949). Both are mindful of the enormous sacrifices made by the freedom fighters during the liberation war and are critical of the betrayal of the aspirations of the majority in post-colonial Zimbabwe.

On the surface Shona plays seem to be much fewer than novels and for a long time much less than published poetry. However, much more staging of plays than is reflected in the list of publications has been taking place in village settings, schools, churches, and township theaters. The first Shona play, Paul Chidyausiku's (b. 1927) *Ndakambokuyambira* (1968; I Warned You Before), looks at domestic scene and how women fail to keep family secrets. Other plays by Julien Lwanda, Davison Mugabe, Pearson Mashiri (dates n.a.), and Mordecai Hamutyinei have since been published. Most of them are mainly exploring the rather worn out theme of cultural conflict in a society that is in transition. There is a general failure to explore issues in depth and at length in a complex and sophisticated way, even after the attainment of independence. One of the most promising is Charles Mungoshi's *Inongova Njake Njake* (1980) where retrospective reporting, cinematic presentation and the stream of consciousness techniques are used to portray characters in a society that is morally anarchic and directionless. Thompson Tsodzo's *Babamunini Francis* (1977) and *Shanduko* (1983) dwell on similar themes but in a didactic manner that has bedeviled Shona writing for a long time. By 1996 over twenty plays had been published and some of them have been broadcast on radio and screened on television. Playwrights such as Aaron Moyo and Agness Gwatiringa seem to be more inclined to write specifically for television rather than for the stage.

Now that the censorship of the colonial period is gone and writers are relatively more free to write on any area of their interest there has been some vibrant literary fermentation taking place in Zimbabwe since 1980. A less servile literary tradition in Shona than the colonial one is likely to emerge soon if only Shona writers could experiment more with form, style, and writing techniques.

BIBLIOGRAPHY: Chiwome, E. M., *A Critical History of Shona Poetry* (1996); Chiwome, E. M., *A Social History of the Shona Novel* (1996); Kahari, G., *The Novels of Patrick Chakaipa* (1972); Kahari, G., *The Imaginative Writings of Paul Chidyausiku* (1980); Kahari, G., *Aspects of the Shona Novel* (1986); Kahari, G., *Soko Risina Musoro: The Tale Without a Head—A Critique* (1988); Veit Wild, F., *Teachers, Preachers and Non-Believers: A Social History of Zimbabwean Literature* (1993); Zinyemba, R., *Zimbabwean Drama: A Study of Shona and English Plays* (1986)

—RINO ZHUWARARA

ZĪVERTS, Martiņš

Latvian dramatist, b. 5 Jan. 1903, Mežmuiža parish; d. 4 Oct. 1990, Sweden

Z. studied philosophy at the University of Latvia. Later he was the dramaturge at the National and Daile theaters in Riga, for which he also wrote plays. After 1944 he lived in Sweden and had frequently been invited to direct stage productions in Denmark, England, West Germany, and Australia.

Z. began his writing career by attacking the formless stage productions in vogue during the 1930s; questions of form are of central importance in his work. But even after one of his plays, *Nafta* (1931; oil), was produced at the National Theater, Z. found little support for his attempt to renew serious drama. In *Tīreļpurvs* (1936; the bog) he stripped the form of the play down to its bare essentials, using a single set and limiting himself to three characters. External effects and peripheral plots were avoided, and the focus was on the inner experiences of the characters.

In his early period Z. also wrote some more conventional plays: *Āksts* (1938; the jester), whose protagonist is Shakespeare; *Trakais Juris* (1938; mad Juris); and *Minchauzena precības* (1941; Münchausen's wedding). In them, the central conflicts are developed before the eyes of the audience and lead to traditional climax and dénouement. But although this form had the advantage of holding audience interest by means of colorful action, Z. felt that it lacked the discipline necessary to probe his characters in depth. He therefore turned to writing analytic chamber plays, in which the audience is presented with a dramatic conflict that has begun before the curtain goes up. In this tightly disciplined form, the main lines of the dénouement are contained in the exposition, and the action of the play concentrates on the unraveling of the threads tangled by life.

Ķīnas vāze (1940; the Chinese vase), a comedy, is an effective realization of the chamber play. Because of its universal character, it has held the Latvian stage, unaffected by political changes. After *Tīreļpurvs* Z. returned to the episodic play infrequently, only when the subject matter demanded it, as in *Rūda* (1954; The Ore, 1968; later tr., *Mad Christopher*, 1977).

But even the analytic chamber play failed to satisfy Z., who felt that its psychologically and logically determined dénouement was still dependent on stock theatrical devices, whereas it should be determined by the very nature of the dramatic genre. He has worked at developing an ideal form in which the uninterrupted action would continuously rise in intensity. Constructing his plays in a one-act form, he specified that when their length requires an intermission the curtain can be dropped at any point—even in the middle of a sentence.

An example of this ideal form is *Vara* (1944; power), which focuses on the nature of political power. In line with Z.'s belief that every play is built around a so-called grand scene, the heart of this play is a monologue in which King Mindaugas of Lithuania justifies his ruthlessness as being in the best interests of the state.

The most important present-day Latvian playwright, Z. has written some fifty plays, many of which have been staged but never published. It may seem that technique in his work takes the upper hand over content. But he felt that the task of the dramatist is not to provide a finished literary work but only the "raw material" for a theatrical experience.

FURTHER WORKS: *Katakombas* (1926); *Lietuvēns* (1927); *Hasana harems* (1927); *Cilvēks bez galvas* (1931); *Kropļi* (1933); *Zelta zeme* (1933); *Jaunā demokratija* (1934); *Pavēste* (1934); *Galvu augšā* (1935); *Kolka* (1937); *Melngalvji* (1938); *Partizāni* (1939); *Nauda* (1943); *Karatavu komēdija* (1945); *Rakte* (1945); *Kaklatiesa* (1945); *Trīs skeči* (1946); *Kāds, kura nav* (1947); *Cilvēks grib dzīvot* (1948); *Zaļā krūze* (1949); *Tvans* (1950); *Cenzūra* (1951); *Meli meklē meli* (1952); *Lielo Grēcinieku iela* (1953); *Smilšu tornis* (1954); *Pēdējā laiva* (1956); *Rakete* (1958); *Fiasko* (1959); *Fiksā ideja* (1960); *Kāzaglis naktī* (1961); *Kurpurru* (1962); *Nekā nav tumšāka par gaismu* (1964); *Kaļostro Vilcē* (1965); *Durnā merga* (1965); *Rīga dimd* (1966); *Totems* (1968); *Pēdējā laiva* (1970); *Kopenhagenas dialogs* (1979)

BIBLIOGRAPHY: Andrups, J., and V. Kalve, *Latvian Literature* (1954): 188; Silenieks, J., "Introduction to *Mad Christopher*," in A. Straumanis, ed., *Confrontations with Tyranny: Six Baltic Plays*

(1977): 157–61; Straumanis, A., ed., *Baltic Drama: A Handbook and Bibliography* (1981): 119–20

—ANDRUPS JĀNIS

ZOHRAB, Krikor

Armenian novelist, short-story writer, essayist, critic, and editor, b. 26 June 1861, Constantinople, Ottoman Empire (now Istanbul, Turkey); d. 1915, on the road to Tigranakert, Turkey

Z. was an engineer and lawyer as well as a writer. At the start of his literary career his progressive views were not welcomed by the conservative Armenian dailies, and his essays began appearing in *Lraber*, a liberal publication. In the 1880s, during the height of the Armenian realist movement, Z.'s first novel *Anhedatsads seroont muh* (1887; a disappearing generation) began appearing in serial form in *Erkrakoond*. But *Massis*, the leading conservative daily, took over the final chapters. By 1892 Z. was its editor-in-chief. During the Turkish purges and massacres of 1905 he left Constantinople and lived in Western Europe until 1908. His experiences of the period are recorded in *Etcher oughevorie muh orakren* (1922; pages from a traveler's diary). He returned to Turkey after the Declaration of Constitutional Reforms (1908) and was elected a member of parliament.

Z.'s career as writer was firmly established after the publication of three volumes of short stories: *Kheghjmedankee tsayner* (1900; voices of conscience), *Loor tsaver* (1911; silent griefs), and *Gyankuh inchbes vor eh* (1911; life as it is). He delighted in exposing the hypocrisy of the clergy, the snobbishness of the wealthy, and the frailty of all people. He wrote more with love than anger, and with an acute awareness of order, disorder, and human connection. Hence, although set in a very specific time and place, his stories, with their deft characterizations, remain timeless.

Z. depicted the daily social life of the Armenian people of Constantinople. He introduced sex into Armenian fiction and was the first to show the effect of the libido on human action. For example, in the novel *Magdalena* (1902; Magdalen), a dying woman is denied her last wish for holy communion because she was forced into prostitution to support her family. In this work, as in several others, Z.'s thrusts at pomposity, mediocrity, manners, and mannerisms are somewhat softened by his quiet humor.

Although he has been accused of avoiding political involvement and ignoring the plight of his people, Z. had written, under an assumed name, a pamphlet during his 1908 stay in Paris, *La question arménienne à la lumière des documents* (1908; the Armenian question in light of documents), depicting the evolution of the Armenian situation, the nature of the Turkish occupation of the land, and the persecutions of his people.

In spite of opportunities to leave the country, Z. stayed in Constantinople in 1915 after the arrest of other Armenian leaders. A month later, he was arrested and assassinated by a band of Turkish irregulars on the road to Tigranakert, where he was to have been tried. His life, like one of his short stories, was rich, filled with irony and humor, but finally tragic.

FURTHER WORKS: *Nartik* (1891); *Jeedeen bardkuh* (1892); *Dsanot temker* (1932); *Oughevorie etcher* (1932)

BIBLIOGRAPHY: Gertmenian, H., "K. Z.," *Ararat*, 17 (1976): 27–30; Kelikian, H., "K. Z., the Complete Armenian," *Ararat*, 17 (1976): 31–36

—MARZBED MARGOSSIAN

ZOSHCHENKO, Mikhail Mikhailovich

Russian short-story writer and novelist, b. 10 Aug. 1895, Poltava; d. 22 July 1958, Leningrad

Z. was born into an intellectual family. His father, a nobleman, was an artist of the Peredvizhniki movement (the Society of Circulating Artists), a civic-oriented, realistic trend in art that dominated Russian painting during the last three decades of the 19th c. His mother had been an actress. In 1904 Z. moved to St. Petersburg and in 1913 began to study law at the university there. The outbreak of World War I interrupted his studies, and his ensuing service as an army officer marked the beginning of a long chain of different positions he held (postmaster, cobbler, poultry breeder, border patrolman, detective, Red Army volunteer, office manager) before becoming a full-time writer in 1921.

In 1921 Z. joined the Serapion Brothers, a literary group that included many outstanding talents who were able to uphold, throughout much of the 1920s, the value of individual artistic independence in the face of Communist-inspired pressures toward literary conformity. In 1922 Z. gained overnight fame with the publication of *Rasskazy Nazara Ilicha, gospodina Sinebryukhova* (the tales of Mr. Nazar Ilich Bluebelly). War and revolution form the backdrop for Bluebelly's narratives, wherein what happens is, artistically, minor in comparison to the way it is narrated. As was to be typical for Z. during much of the 1920s, the narrator is a semiliterate loser, whose speech is an inimitably humorous stylistic salad—in this case, a combination of military jargon, pretentious belletristic phrasings, bureaucratese, and journalese—all ill-digested and misused. This "oral" form of narration is characteristic of Z.'s best works of the 1920s and 1930s.

Besides its oral orientation, Z.'s *skaz* (narrative leaning toward the spoken tale) is noted for its comic exploitation of the discrepancy between deformed speech and the canons of the standard literary language. The deformations make a dolt of the narrator, at the same time illustrating Z.'s own verbal inventiveness. The *skaz* was an excellent vehicle for satirizing the Soviet man-on-the-street and the shortcomings of the new order, for example, the housing crisis in the tale "Pushkin" (1927; "Pushkin," 1942), in which the homeless hero exclaims, "It's an absolute utopia." Here, the concept of a utopia is turned on its head by associating it with a Russian word meaning drowning (*utopit*).

Z. published hundreds of short *skaz* miniatures in the 1920s. Many appeared in twenty different cycles published between 1922 and 1926. Sales of his works could be counted in the millions, and he was almost certainly the most popular of Soviet authors. Toward the end of the 1920s, with the end of NEP and the start of the Five Year Plans, the Soviet Union began to take itself very seriously. This new attitude had a devastating effect on satire. Z. correctly stated: "My genre, that is, the genre of a humorist, is incompatible with the description of achievements." Like many other Soviet authors of the time, Z. was unable to sing paeans to Soviet accomplishments, for his talent was fundamentally satirical. During the 1930s he was still able to write satire, but its edge had been blunted, it often bordered on the openly didactic, and the style was nowhere near as racy as in the 1920s, because now a new improved Soviet man was allegedly emerging to replace the confused oaf of the still semicapitalist 1920s. Z.'s major satirical achievement of the 1930s was *Golubaya kniga* (1935; a sky-blue book), a "short history of human relations," which Z. divided into sections devoted to money, love, perfidy, failures, and amazing events. The world Z. depicts here, as elsewhere, has been aptly described as reflecting the priority of coarseness over refinement, matter over form, material over spirit, the collective over the individual, chaos over order.

Paradoxically, for a man who could evoke howls of laughter from his readers and listeners, Z. the man was morose and suffered increasingly from pathological depression. An attempt to exorcise his psychic demons can be found in the semiserious novella *Vozvrash-chennaya molodost* (1933; *Youth Restored*, 1935) and ultimately in the altogether serious autobiography *Pered voskhodom solntsa* (written 1937–43; partial text pub. 1943; full text pub. 1973; *Before Sunrise*, 1974), an extensive and fascinating attempt at self-psychoanalysis wherein Z. moves progressively back in time, even into infancy, in an attempt to cure his depression.

These three longer works of the 1930s figure among a number of otherwise undistinguished efforts by Z. to go beyond the very short form that had made him so popular. *Pered voskhodom solntsa* began to be published serially in the journal *Oktyabr* during a 1943 wartime thaw period in Soviet literature. Its self-centered theme and overall gloominess, however, were too far removed from Soviet literary norms, and Z. was accused of "mucking about in his nasty little soul in the midst of the national holocaust." The work's publication was suspended after two issues by an apologetic editorship. The remainder of the text would appear in the U.S.S.R. only in 1972. Z. became the focal point for further scandal as a result of his short story "Priklyuchenia obezyany" (1946; "The Adventures of a Monkey," 1963), allegedly a satire of Soviet man.

In 1946 Andrey Zhdanov (1888–1948), a secretary of the Party Central Committee, publicly and viciously took Z. to task for being a "brainless scribbler" and a "toadyish cosmopolitan." Z., who had been decorated for his service during the war, was now expelled from the Soviet Writers' Union, although he was reinstated shortly after Stalin's death. Just before his own death he was "rehabilitated" through the publication of some of his early works. Since the 1960s his writings have reappeared with relative frequency, and his place as one of the greats of Soviet literature seems secure. He will be especially remembered for the colorful style of his humorous works, which often set an embarrassingly high standard by which to judge those who have ventured after him to write in the same mode. The playfulness, absurdity, and satire of his stories can be captured in translation, but their style, the guarantor of Z.'s immortality, has so far eluded his translators.

FURTHER WORKS: *Koza* (1923); *Mudrost* (1925); *O chem pel solovyey* (1925); *Strashnaya noch* (1925); *Uvazhaemie grazhdane* (2 vols., 1926, 1940); *Vesyoloe priklyuchenie* (1927); *Nervnye lyudi* (1927); *Dni nashey zhizni* (1929); *Siren tsvetyot* (1930); *Mikhail Sinyagin* (1930); *Istoria odnoi zhizni* (1934); *Lichnaya zhizn* (1934); *Fedot da ne tot* (1939); *Taras Shevchenko* (1939); *Rasskazy i povesti 1923–1956* (1959); *Rasskazy, feletony, komedii* (1963); *Neizdanny Z.* (1975); *Izbrannaya* (2 vols., 1978). FURTHER WORKS IN ENGLISH: *Russia Laughs* (1935); *The Woman*

Who Could Not Read, and Other Tales (1940); *The Wonderful Dog, and Other Tales* (1940); *Scenes from the Bathhouse, and Other Stories* (1961); *Nervous People, and Other Satires* (1963)

BIBLIOGRAPHY: Fen, E., Preface to *The Wonderful Dog, and Other Tales* (1942): v–ix; Domar, R. A., "The Tragedy of a Soviet Satirist; or, The Case of Z.," in E. J. Simmons, ed., *Through the Glass of Soviet Literature* (1953): 201–43; Monas, S., Introduction to *Scenes from the Bathhouse, and Other Stories* (1961): v–xvii; Mihailovich, V., "Z.'s 'Adventures of a Monkey' as an Allegory," *Satire Newsletter*, 4 (1967): 84–89; Wiren-Garczynski, V. von, "Z.'s Psychological Interests," *SEEJ*, 11 (1967): 3–22; Struve, G., *Russian Literature under Lenin and Stalin, 1917–1953* (1971): 155–60, 350–55; Kern, G., "After the Afterword," in M. Z., *Before Sunrise* (1974): 345–64; McLean, H., "Belated Sunrise: A Review Article," *SEEJ*, 18 (1974): 406–10; Slonim, M., *Soviet Russian Literature: Writers and Problems, 1917–1977*, 2nd ed. (1977): 92–98; Brown, E. J., *Russian Literature since the Revolution*, rev. ed. (1982): 184–89

—ROBERT L. BUSCH

ZUCKMAYER, Carl

German dramatist, novelist, and short-story writer, b. 23 Dec. 1896, Nackenheim; d. 18 Jan. 1977, Visp, Switzerland

Z., son of a small industrialist, attended school at Mainz before serving in the army during World War I. After several years of study and stage directing in various German cities he settled in Henndorf near Salzburg, Austria, in 1926. Forced to leave Europe in 1939—he had a Jewish grandfather, and his writing was considered "degenerate" by the Nazis—he emigrated to the U.S. and lived in Vermont until 1958, when he returned permanently to Europe, making his home in Saas-Fee, Switzerland.

Z. was generally considered the "other" major German playwright after Gerhart HAUPTMANN well into the 1950s. The remarkable reputation of his plays was based not so much on their intrinsic literary merit as on the fact that they happened to appear at historical moments that ensured their willing reception by the German public. Like Bertolt BRECHT, Z. had turned to writing after some training in the natural sciences and was, again like Brecht, soon caught up for some time in the breathless activism of the EXPRESSIONISTS. His first play, *Kreuzweg* (1920; crossroads), with its heavy symbolism and its aura of violence and revolt, parallels Brecht's *Baal*. Yet whereas Brecht turned to intellectual analysis and political instruction, Z. showed an increasing concern with regional folklore and individual human passion. His first successful play, *Der fröhliche Weinberg* (1925; the joyful vineyard), with its vernacular dialogue, its frank treatment of rural manners in the author's home region, and the raucous hilarity of its scenes of daily business and tavern brawls, achieved a *succès de scandale*.

Schinderhannes (1927; Schinderhannes) and *Katharina Knie* (1928; Katharina Knie) are plays that reflect the misery of social and economic conditions in Swabia, although at different historical periods. Both were sufficiently different from the prevailing theatrical fare, which was marked by the vague pathos and the political agitation of the 1920s, to maintain Z.'s hold on the public until his next big success, *Der Hauptmann von Köpenick* (1931; *The Captain of Köpenick*, 1932). This play is a satire on the military culture shaping public life in imperial Germany. As in Z.'s earlier plays, the paucity of plot is disguised by a number of convincing and entertaining extraneous scenes loosely strung together by following the protagonist's life to his glorious although in the end abortive coup.

The Nazis' rise to power drastically reduced Z.'s readership and audience, the author being branded as Jewish and decadent. His subsequent plays—*Der Schelm von Bergen* (1933; the knave of Bergen), a historical romance about love between an empress and an executioner's son, and *Bellman* (1938; Bellman), a series of scenes from the life of the Swedish poet Carl Michael Bellman (1740–1795), centered on his love for the pretty serving maid Ulla Winblad—could no longer be produced in Germany.

The loss of his German-speaking audience forced Z. to return to the writing of fiction, which he had little practiced after having abandoned a projected novel on the Sioux chieftain Sitting Bull in the mid-1920s. *Salwäre; oder, die Magdalena von Bozen* (1936; *The Moons Ride Over*, 1937), a novel about an artist with a contemporary setting, revealed a sensitivity and reflectiveness in Z. that had previously been overshadowed by the simplicity and directness of his dramatic work, while the straight chronological progression of its plot and its essentially scenic conception still bespoke the playwright.

When Z. returned to fiction in the 1950s, his narrative style had matured: it was less personal and more economical. The novellas *Engele von Löwen* (1955; Little Angel of Leuven) and *Die Fastnachtsbeichte* (1959; *Carnival Confession*, 1961), both inspired by experiences before and during World War I, deal with the themes of guilt and innocence, love and renunciation, clothed in narrative of an almost classic nobility.

It seems significant that Z. was the only German émigré writer in the U.S. to settle in the isolation of the countryside, leasing a Vermont farm, which he tried to cultivate in order to escape the irrelevancies of modern culture as much as to make a living. In this light, the play *Des Teufels General* (1946; *The Devil's General*, 1962), written at a time when the return to his native country began to appear possible, takes on a special significance. The play's ostensible concern with recent political events is but the vehicle for a more fundamental preoccupation with the ethical and philosophical problem of personal guilt in the context of history.

The play was a huge success on the postwar German stage and reestablished Z.'s reputation as a popular author, but none of his subsequent dramatic works, with the possible exception of *Der Gesang im Feuerofen* (1950; the song in the fiery furnace), which deals with an incident involving the Resistance in France, ever again found such wide acclaim. As is also the case with the play *Barbara Blomberg* (1949; Barbara Blomberg), set in the Spanish Netherlands of the late 16th c., history in *Der Gesang im Feuerofen* is dissolved, reduced to ever-present elementary human passions and conflicts.

By the time his last play appeared, *Das Leben des Horace A. W. Tabor* (1964; the life of Horace A. W. Tabor), which represented a return to Z.'s early theme of the untrammeled life of adventure with its majesty and its squalor, he had become a living legend. He came to the public's attention once more when he published a volume of memoirs, *Als wär's ein Stück von mir* (1969; *A Part of Myself*, 1970).

FURTHER WORKS: *Pankraz erwacht* (1925); *Der Baum* (1926); *Kakadu-Kakada* (1930); *Die Affenhochzeit* (1932); *Herr über Leben und Tod* (1938); *Second Wind* (1940); *Der Seelenbräu* (1945); *Die deutschen Dramen* (1947); *Die Brüder Grimm* (1947); *Gedichte 1916–1948* (1948); *Die Erzählungen* (1952); *Herbert Engelmann* (1952; completion of drama by Gerhart Hauptmann); *Ulla Winblad* (1953; rev. version of Bellman); *Das Kalte Licht* (1955); *Der trunkene Herkules* (1958); *Gesammelte Werke* (4 vols., 1960); *Die Uhr schlägt eins* (1961); *Mainzer Umzug* (1962; libretto, music by Paul Hindemith); *Geschichten aus 40 Jahren* (1963); *Der Kranichtanz* (1966); *Auf einem Weg im Frühling* (1970); *Henndorfer Pastorale* (1972); *Der Rattenfänger* (1975); *Einmal, wenn alles vorüber ist: Briefe an Kurt Grell; Gedichte; Dramen; Prosa aus den Jahren 1914–1920* (1981)

BIBLIOGRAPHY: Engelsing-Malek, I., *Amor fati in Z.s Dramen* (1960); Glade, H., "C. Z.'s *The Devil's General* as Autobiography," *MD*, 9 (1966): 54–61; Speidel, E., "The Stage as Metaphysical Institution: Z.'s Dramas *Schinderhannes* and *Der Hauptmann von Köpenick*," *MLR*, 62 (1968): 425–37; Jacobius, A. J., *C. Z.: Eline Bibliographie* (1971); Bauer, A., *C. Z.* (1976); Mews, S., *C. Z.* (1981)

—KURT OPITZ

ZUKOFSKY, Louis

American poet and critic, b. 23 Jan. 1904, New York, N.Y.; d. 12 May 1978, New York, N.Y.

Z. Was born of Russian immigrant parents, and until entering public school spoke only Yiddish. He received the M.A. degree from Columbia University in 1924 and taught English at the University of Wisconsin and Queens College during the 1930s. He spent the bulk of his academic career at the Polytechnic Institute of Brooklyn (1947–66). In 1939 Z. married the composer and poet Celia Thaew, with whom he collaborated on literary-musical projects. Z. received many literary awards.

As editor of a special "objectivists" issue of *Poetry* magazine in 1931, Z. early articulated a philosophy of poetry, abstracted from the theories and practice of Ezra POUND and William Carlos WILLIAMS, among others, to which he adhered throughout his life. "The objectivist," he says, "is interested in living with things as they exist." Z. distrusts poets who romanticize nature by forcing it into shapes or meanings it does not intrinsically possess.

For nearly fifty years (1928–77) Z. worked on a long poem titled "A," which demonstrated his critical theory in action. Like Walt Whitman's *Leaves of Grass* or William's *Patterson* or Pound's *Cantos*, "A" was a life-poem, constantly in progress, appearing in bits and pieces, endlessly subject to revision; it was not available in a single volume until after his death. Z. claims to have begun "A" with a fairly precise notion of the poem's final form—" a silent structural eloquence"—before writing any of the words to be fitted into that form. His poem perceives and records particularities—images—which achieve poetic syntax by being carefully ordered the way words in a sentence acquire meaning through context.

Because Z.'s practice of objectivism approaches poetic gnosticism—cryptic, orphic, tremendously difficult of access—even a friendly commentator such as William Carlos Williams could say of *"A" 1–12* (1959): "I often did not know what he was driving at."

Similar difficulties persist with his shorter poems, his critical essays, and his translations of Catullus. All of Z.'s productions are spectacularly erudite collages, punctuated with classical allusions in a half-dozen languages, with digressions that seek to tie together immense disparities. Yet he consistently refuses to gratify the reader's desire to know what he is driving at. Frequently critics reach totally different conclusions about the meaning and quality of his work.

Z.'s "objectivism" often seems utterly subjective. Few of his poems are *about* any external object: they are highly self-conscious demonstrations of his own mind at work. Their driving force is a relentlessly subjective egoism.

Despite the variety of responses to Z.'s work, most critics recognize in him the perceptive skills and linguistic talents of a true poet. His connections with Pound and Williams place him in the midst of American poetic ferment of the 1930s and 1940s; his rediscovery in the 1960s by the Black Mountain poets (Robert CREELEY, Charles OLSON, Robert DUNCAN, and others) ensure him a continuing position of influence in the American poetic consciousness.

FURTHER WORKS: *Le Style Apollinaire* (1934); *Arise, Arise* (1936); *A Test of Poetry* (1948); *Five Statements for Poetry* (1958); *It Was* (1961); *Bottom: On Shakespeare* (1963); *All the Collected Short Poems, 1923–1958* (1965); *All the Collected Short Poems, 1956–1964* (1966); *Prepositions: The Collected Critical Essays of L. Z.* (1967; expanded ed. 1981); *Ferdinand* (1968); *"A" 13–21* (1969); *The Gas Age* (1969); *Catullus: Gai Valeri Catulli Veronensis* (1969; translation with Celia Zukofsky); *Autobiography* (1970, with music by Celia Zukofsky); *"A" 24* (1972); *"A" 22–23* (1975); *"A" 1–24* (1978); *80 Flowers* (1978)

BIBLIOGRAPHY: Dembo, L. S., "L. Z.: Objectivist Poetics and the Quest for Form," *AL*, 44 (1972): 74–96; special Z. issue, *MAPS*, No. 5 (1973); special Z. issue, *Paideuma*, 7, 3 (1978); Terrell, C. F., ed., *L. Z.: Man and Poet* (1979); Zukofsky, C., *A Bibliography of L. Z.* (1980); Ahearn, B., *Z.'s "A": An Introduction* (1983)

—LARRY TEN HARMSEL

ZULU LITERATURE

See under South African Literature

ŽUPANČIČ, Oton

Yugoslav poet, dramatist, translator, and critic (writing in Slovene), b. 23 Jan. 1878, Vinica; d. 11 June 1949, Ljubljana

Born in Bela Krajina, that part of Slovenia bordering on Croatia, Ž. enjoyed a serene childhood in a comfortable and loving home. Although his parents moved with him to Ljubljana in 1891 in pursuit of further educational opportunities for their son, Ž. preserved strong ties to his native region all his life; many folk motifs and regional expressions from there appear frequently in his poetry. As early as 1893 he began to publish his verse in the major journals of the day. And when, in 1896, he moved to Vienna to enter the university, he still kept active in Slovene poetic circles through his extensive writing and his friendships with the other

principal Slovene MODERNIST poets, Josip Murn-Alexandrov (1879–1901), Dragotin Kette (1876–1899), and Ivan CANKAR. On graduation in 1902, Ž. traveled widely in France, Austria, and Germany. Only in 1910 did he return to Ljubljana to take up permanent residence.

Translating, editing, and raising a family, with fewer forays into original verse composition, occupied Ž. for the next decade and a half. His earliest positions involved him with the stage (as director of the National Theater, 1912) and archival research. He was particularly active in translating: he put into Slovene most of Shakespeare's major plays as well as works by other English writers, and masterpieces of French, German, Italian, and Spanish literature. In 1917 he became editor of the *Ljubljanski zvon*, the principal Slovene cultural journal. After 1924 Ž. fell silent for a variety of personal and professional reasons, emerging only a decade later at the center of a literary-cultural polemic he himself provoked with an article praising the Slovene emigrant Louis Adamic (1899–1951), who wrote only in English: "Adamič in slovenstvo" (1934; Adamic and the Slovenes). Thereafter Ž. resumed his poetry writing, continued translating, and became increasingly active in the cultural politics of the day. During World War II he supported the Yugoslav resistance movement of the partisans, and afterward placed himself at the service of the new regime for all matters cultural and poetic.

Ž.'s most important poems were written before 1910 and collected in the volumes *Čaša opojnosti* (1899; the cup of intoxication), *Čez plan* (1904; over the plain), and *Samogovori* (1908; soliloquies). Many of these early poems display an interest in the erotic bordering occasionally on the decadent. Some deal thoughtfully with national issues, particularly independence for Slovenia. All are characterized by linguistic vigor and freshness of expression (Ž. introduced free verse into Slovene poetry), as well as powerful imagery, often drawn from the realm of religion.

Ž.'s poetry for children— *Pisanice* (1900; Easter eggs), *Lahkih nog naokrog* (1913; leaping lightly), *Ciciban in še kaj* (1915; Ciciban and other things), and *Sto ugank* (1915; one hundred riddles)—is less provocative than his serious poetry, but popular for the same reasons: Ž. was an absolute master of the sounds of Slovene.

His historical tragedy *Veronika Deseniška* (1924; Veronika of Desenice), which portrays the sacrifice of an innocent girl as a result of the political intrigues of the House of Celje, early rivals of the Hapsburgs for power in central Europe, reveals Ž.'s fine sense of the dramatic, as do the play *Noč na verne duše* (1904; All Soul's Eve) and an early unfinished epic, *Jerala* (1908; Jerala). In Ž.'s last poetic collection, *Žimželen pod snegom* (1945; evergreen under the snow), where he sought to rally his people from the miseries of the war in order to construct a revived Slovenia in a politically and socially new Yugoslavia, the poet assumes the mantle of spokesman of the nation—some say propagandist. Yet even at its most programmatic, his later verse retains the verbal richness and vigor evident in all his writing from the very start.

Thanks to a long life, Ž. felt the impact of every major literary trend of the first half of the 20th c.; neoromanticism, Decadence, impressionism, EXPRESSIONISM, even SOCIALIST REALISM. As a result his work is rich in different tones. But at base it is remarkably consistent: occasionally pensive, but more often optimistic and life-affirming, structurally flexible, unwaveringly attentive to patterns of sound and rhythm, and uncompromisingly involved with the exploration of Slovenia's destiny as perceived by the devoted native son.

FURTHER WORKS: *Naša beseda* (1918); *Mlada pota* (1920); *V zarje Vidove* (1920); *Ostrnice* (1935); *Veš, poet, svoj dolg* (1948); *Zbrano delo* (6 vols., 1956–1972); *Pesmi za Berto* (1978). FURTHER WORKS IN ENGLISH: *O. Ž.: A Selection of Poems* (1967)

BIBLIOGRAPHY: Slodnjak, A., *Geschichte der slowenischen Literatur* (1958): passim; Barac, A., *History of Yugoslov Literature* (1976): 233–35; Cooper, H. R., Jr., "Ž. and Whitman," *Southeastern Europe*, 9 (1982): 7–59

—HENRY R. COOPER, JR.

ZWEIG, Arnold

German novelist, poet, dramatist, and journalist, b. 10 Nov. 1887, Glogau (now Glogów, Poland); d. 26 Nov. 1968, East Berlin (now Berlin)

Z. was born into a Jewish family in the former Prussian province of Silesia. He studied literature, modern languages, philosophy, and history at various universities. After serving in the German army during World War I, he was a writer in Munich (1918–23) before moving to Berlin to edit the *Jüdische Rundschau*. A Zionist and a pacifist, Z. emigrated to Palestine in 1933 via Czechoslovakia, England, and France, and he contributed to various émigré journals. From 1942 to 1943 he was coeditor of the Haifa journal *Orient*, and in 1948 he returned to settle in East Berlin, in the German Democratic Republic. A member of the Volkskammer (parliament), Z. participated in the 1949 World Peace Congress in Paris, and he served as president of the East German Academy of Arts (1950–53). He received several major literary awards, including the Lenin Peace Prize (1958).

A prolific writer, Z. is perhaps best known for a group of novels known collectively as *Der große Krieg der weißen Männer* (the great war of the white men), an epic united by the recurring and somewhat autobiographical figure of Werner Berlin, a middle-class Jewish writer whose experiences are representative of those of many German intellectuals of the time. Taking World War I as the focal point, Z. analyzes the psychological effects of war and traces the social developments leading from imperialism to socialism. *Die Zeit ist reif* (1959; the time is ripe) was written retrospectively to chronicle the years 1913–15. Through the example of the intellectual and indigent Berlin, who meets with social disapproval while courting Leonore Wahl, the daughter of a rich banking family, Z. indicates his opposition to middle-class stratification. *Junge Frau von 1914* (1931; *Young Woman of 1914*, 1932), a warm love story, shows Leonore's many disappointments (she aborts her illegitimate pregnancy) and problems before marrying Berlin. In stirring passages, Z. traces her maturation from a complacent, middle-class young woman into a vigorous opponent of war. In *Erziehung vor Verdun* (1935; *Education before Verdun*, 1936). Bertin, as a soldier, observes and experiences the effects of rampant militarism and is converted to pacifism.

The breakdown of justice is the theme of Z.'s best-known novel, *Der Streit un den Sergeanten Grischa* (1927; *The Case of Sergeant Grischa*, 1928), a novelization of a play Z. had written in 1921. In violation of all legal principles, the high command of the German army has a Russian war prisoner executed as an example to those German soldiers who are drawn to Russian revolutionary ideology. Z. appealed to the conscience of the world in this indictment of militarism. The novel's controversial theme, the author's skill in building a dramatic situation and in clearly characterizing both major and minor figures, and the meticulous analysis of various social points of view contributed to the book's international success. The dramatic version was first performed in 1930.

Die Feuerpause (1954; the ceasefire), one of Z.'s weakest novels, is an example of Z.'s work under the influence of editors who urged him toward SOCIALIST REALISM. After the armistice and the Treaty of Brest Litovsk, Berlin unconvincingly changes from a liberal idealist to a militant socialist. *Einsetzung eines Königs* (1937; *The Crowning of a King*, 1938) focuses on a German officer who is eventually drawn into the social, economic, political, and military intrigues surrounding the Lithuanian throne in 1918. Z. meant to round out the novelistic series with a work entitled *Das Eis bricht* (the ice breaks), which was to describe the dilemma of a country whose social basis is built on militaristic ideals and war industry.

Z.'s novellas and short stories prove him to be a skillful writer who is able to depict the fate of middle-class intellectuals, and who is both sympathetic to their plight and sensitively ironic in dealing with their foibles. As a follower of FREUD, in his early works Z. was able to convey psychological dilemmas successfully, but the books of his later years failed because they tended to be the ideological products of a Marxist social scientist.

In a Germany deeply divided by politics and ideologies, Z. stood out as a pacifist whose works emphasize harmony, optimism, and a deep appreciation of human nature. He must increasingly be regarded as the conscience of a disinherited majority.

FURTHER WORKS: *Der englische Garten* (1910); *Aufzeichnungen über eine Familie Klopfer* (1911); *Die Novellen um Claudia* (1912; *Claudia*, 1930); *Abigail und Nabal* (1913; rev. ed., 1920); *Die Bestie* (1914); *Ritualmord in Ungarn* (1914; rev. ed., *Die Sendung Semaels*, (1918); *Geschichtenbuch* (1916); *Benarône* (1918); *Drei Erzählungen* (1920); *Entrückung und Aufruhr* (1920); *Söhone: Das zweite Geschichtenbuch* (1923); *Gerufene Schatten* (1923); *Frühe Fährten* (1925); *Regenbogen* (1925); *Lessing, Kleist, Büchner: Drei Versuche* (1925); *Die Umkehr des Abtrünnigen* (1925; repub. as *Die Umkehr*, 1927); *Der Spiegel des großen Kaisers* (1926; rev. ed., 1949); *Caliban; oder, Politik und Leidenschaft* (1927); *Juden auf der deutschen Bühne* (1927); *Pont und Anna* (1928); *Herkunft und Zukunft: Zwei Essays zum Schincksals eines Volkes* (1929); *Laubheu und keine Bleibe* (1930); *Die Aufrichtung der Menorah* (1930); *Knaben und Männer* (1931); *Mädchen und Frauen* (1931); *De Vriendt Kehrt heim* (1932; *De Vriendt Goes Home*, 1933); *Spielzeug der Zeit* (1933; *Playthings of Time*, 1935); *Bilanz der deutschen Judenheit 1933* (1934; *Insulted and Exiled: The Truth about German Jews*, 1937); *Versunkene Tage* (1938 repub. as *Verklungene Tage*, 1950); *Bonaparte in Jaffa* (1939); *Das Beil von Wandsbek* (1948; first pub. in Hebrew, 1943; *The Axe of Wandsbek*, 1948); *Ein starker Esser* (1947); *Allerleirauh* (1949); *Stufen: Fünf Erzählungen* (1949); *Über den Nebeln* (1950); *Der Elfenbeinfächer* (1952); *Westlandsaga* (1952); *Der Regenbogen* (1955); *Soldatenspiele* (1956); *Der Früchtekorb; Jüngste Ernte: Aufsätze* (1956); *Ausgewählte Werke* (16 vols., 1957–1967); *Fünf Romanzen* (1958); *Novellen 1907–1955* (1961); *Traum ist teuer* (1962); *Jahresinge* (1964); *Über Schriftsteller* (1967); *Briefwechsel mit Sigmund Freud* (1968; *The Letters of Sigmund Freud and A. Z.*, 1970); *A. Z. 1887–1968: Werk und Leben in Dokumenten und Bildern, mit unveröffentlichen Manuskripten und Briefen aus dem Nachlaß* (1978); *Briefwechsel zwischen Louis Fürnberg und A. Z.: Dokumente einer Freundschaft*

(1978). **FURTHER WORKS IN ENGLISH:** *A Bit of Blood, and Other Stories* (1959)

BIBLIOGRAPHY: Rudolph, J., *Der Humanist A. Z.* (1955); Kamnitzer, H., *Erkenntnis und Bekenntnis: A. Z. 70 Jahre* (1958); Kaufmann, E. A., *Z.s Weg zum Roman: Vorgeschichte und Analyse des Grischaromans* (1967); Hilscher, E., *A. Z.: Leben und Werk* (1968); Kahn, L., "A. Z.: From Zionism to Marxism," *Mirrors of the Jewish Mind* (1968): 194–209; Salamon, G., *A. Z.* (1975); Midgley, D. R., *A. Z.: Zu Werk und Wandlung 1927–1948* (1980); Wetzel, H., "War and Destruction of Moral Principles in A. Z.'s *Der Streit um den Sergeanten Grischa and Erziehung vor Verhun,*" in C. N. Genno and H. Wetzel, eds., *The First World War in German Narrative Prose*, (1980): 50–70

—STEFAN GRUNWALD

ZWEIG, Stefan

Austrian biographer, novelist, dramatist, essayist, and poet, b. 28 Nov. 1881, Vienna; d. 22 Feb. 1942, Petrópolis, Brazil

Z. was born to a wealthy Jewish industrialist and grew up in what he later described as the "world of security." He studied German and Romance literatures at the University of Vienna, and by the time he took his degree there in 1904 he was well launched on a literary career, having had a feuilleton accepted by the prestigious daily *Neue Freie Presse* and being the author of a volume of verse, *Silberne Saiten* (1901; silver strings). Early trips to Germany, France, Belgium, Holland, England, Italy, Spain, India, and North America served to broaden the horizon of the lifelong world traveler. But what most decisively shaped Z.'s evolution from an aesthetically oriented member of the Young Vienna group of writers to a "great European" was his encounter with the Belgian poet Émile VERHAEREN, whose intense, vibrantly contemporary, life–affirming poetry Z. regarded as a lyrical encyclopedia of his age and whom he tirelessly served as a translator, biographer, and promoter. Z.'s European education was continued through his friendship with the French writer Romain ROLLAND, whose exemplary pacifism and humanistic activities in wartime were a great inspiration to Z. While working at the Austrian War Archives in Vienna, Z. was able to go to Zurich in 1917 for the premiere of his pacifist play *Jeremias* (1917; *Jeremiah*, 1922). As his letters to Martin BUBER from that period indicate, Z. regarded his Jewishness as a tool for surviving those difficult years as a citizen of the world. Rejecting any kind of nationalism, Z. affirmed the value of the Jewish spirit in the Diaspora and spurned the Zionist movement.

In 1919 Z. moved to Salzburg and soon was able to solemnize his union with the writer Friderike Maria Burger von Winternitz (1882–1971). The couple's impressive home on the picturesque Kapuzinerberg became a shrine to Z.'s central idea, the intellectual unification of Europe, and the mecca of a cultural elite, many of whom Z. numbered among his friends. His bibliophile pursuits, particularly his legendary collection of manuscripts, promoted this most fecund period of his creativity. But after 1933 Salzburg became a dangerously exposed and inhospitable place, and an almost paranoid uneasiness took hold of the apolitical Z. His move to England in 1934 marked the beginning of years of insecurity, restless globe–trotting, and mounting despair. His first marriage

had broken up and he married Elisabeth Charlotte Altmann in Bath, England, in 1939. Profoundly depressed by the fate of Europe, his spiritual homeland, and fearing that the humanistic spirit was crushed forever, Z. committed suicide together with his second wife while they were in Brazil.

The work of Z. was that of a mediator. He strove "to understand even what is most alien to us, always to evaluate peoples and periods, figures and works only in their positive and creative sense, and to let this desire to understand and share this understanding with others serve humbly and faithfully our indestructible ideal: humane communication among persons, mentalities, cultures, and nations." Z. the storyteller is noted for his vivid, virtuosic style and his skillful psychological (or psychoanalytical) penetration of his characters. His work in the novella form ranges from *Die Liebe der Erika Ewald* (1904; the love of Erika Ewald) to his last completed work, *Schachnovelle* (1942; *The Royal Game*, 1944), which poignantly foreshadows a time of increasing specialization, mechanization, and dehumanization in which men of mind are doomed to be checkmated by brutish technocrats. The collection *Erstes Erlebnis* (1911; first experience) contains sensitive studies of childhood and adolescence; the stories in *Verwirrung der Gefühle* (1927; *Conflicts*, 1927) and *Amok* (1922; *Amok*, 1931) deal with adult passions and problems. Z.'s only completed full–length novel, *Ungeduld des Herzens* (1939; *Beware of Pity*, 1939), is a haunting portrayal of a crippled girl and her love. The legend *Der begrabene Leuchter* (1937; *The Buried Candelabrum*, 1937) has been called (by S. Liptzin) "as sad an affirmation of Jewishness as ever was penned in our century."

Another literary form in which Z. achieved great success and an international readership in thirty languages was the *vie romancée*. As a biographer Z. favored the cyclical form, attempting to present a "typology of the spirit." *Drei Meister* (1920; *Three Masters*, 1930) contains biographical studies of Balzac, Dickens, and Dostoevsky; *Der Kampf mit dem Dämon* (1925; the struggle with the demon) examines Hölderlin, Kleist, and Nietzsche; and *Drei Dichter ihres Lebens* (1928; *Adepts in Self–Portraiture*, 1928) presents the great autobiographers Casanova, Stendhal, and Tolstoy. These biographical studies appeared in one volume as *Baumeister der Welt* (1935; *Master Builders*, 1939). Another biographical triptych, *Die Heilung durch den Geist* (1931; *Mental Healers*, 1932), is devoted to Franz Anton Mesmer, Mary Baker Eddy (who is debunked), and Sigmund FREUD, to whom Z. felt close. *Triumph und Tragik des Erasmus von Rotterdam* (1934; *Erasmus of Rotterdam*, 1934) is a very personal book, for Z. regarded the Dutch humanist, who also disdained political action in a turbulent age, as his spiritual ancestor and mentor.

Z.'s collaboration with Richard Strauss on the comic opera *Die schweigsame Frau* (1935; the silent woman), based on a play by Ben Jonson, became a *cause célèbre*: Strauss was unwilling to abandon his Jewish librettist but had to resign as president of the Reichsmusikkammer after only a few performances of the opera had been permitted. In his universally admired autobiography *Die Welt von gestern* (1944; *The World of Yesterday*, 1943) Z. modestly keeps his own life and work in the background as he presents a brilliant, poignant panorama of European life and culture in the first half of the 20th c. Z. was one of the most prolific and most distinguished men of letters of his time.

FURTHER WORKS: *Verlaine* (1905); *Die frühen Kränze* (1906); *Tersites* (1907); *Émile Verhaeren* (1910; *Émile Verhaeren*, 1914); *Das Haus am Meer* (1912); *Der verwandelte Komödiant* (1913);

Erinnerungen an Émile Verhaeren (1917); *Das Herz Europas* (1918); *Fahrten* (1919); *Legende eines Lebens* (1919); *Marceline Desbordes–Valmore* (1920); *Angst* (1920); *Der Zwang* (1920); *Romain Rolland* (1921); *Die Augen des ewigen Bruders* (1922); *Brief einer Unbekannten* (1922); *Frans Masereel* (1923); *Die gesammelten Gedichte* (1924); *Volpone* (1926; adaptation of play by Ben Jonson; *Volpone*, 1928; *Die unsichtbare Sammlung* (1926; *The Invisible Collection*, 1926); *Der Flüchtling: Episode am Genfer See* (1926); *Die Flucht zu Gott* (1927); *Abschied von Rilke* (1927; *Farewell to Rilke*, 1975); *Sternstunden der Menschheit* (1927; enlarged ed., 1945; *The Tide of Fortune*, 1940); *Quiproquo* (1928, with Alexander Lernet-Holenia under pseud. Clemens Neydisser); *Joseph Fouché: Bildnis eines politischen Menschen* (1929; *Joseph Fouché*, 1930); *Kleine Chronik* (1929); *Das Lamm des Armen* (1929); *Marie Antoinette: Bildnis eines mittleren Charakters* (1932; *Marie Antoinette: The Portrait of an Average Woman*. 1933); *Kaleidoskop* (1934); *Maria Stuart* (1935; *Mary, The Queen of Scots*, (1935); *Sinn und Schönheit der Autographen* (1935); *Gesammelte Erzählungen* (1936); *Castellio gegen Calvin* (1936; *The Right to Heresy*, 1936); *Arturo Toscanini* (1936); *Begegnungen mit Menschen, Büchern, Städten* (1937); *Magellan: Der Mann und seine Tat* (1938; *Conqueror of the Seas: The Story of Magellan*, 1938); *Worte am Grabe Sigmund Freuds* (1939); *Brasilien, ein Land der Zukunft* (1941; *Brazil, a Land of the Future*, 1941); *Zeit und Welt* (1943); *Amerigo: Die Geschichte eines historischen Irrtums* (1944; *Amerigo: A Comedy of Errors in History*, 1942); *Legenden* (1945); *Balzac: Der Roman Seines Leben* (1946; *Balzac*, 1946); *S. und Friderike Z.: Ein Briefwechsel 1912–1942* (1954; new ed., *Unrast der Liebe*, (1981); *S. and Friderike Z.: Their Correspondence*, 1954); *Richard Strauss und S. Z.: Briefwechsel* (1957; *A Confidential Matter: The Letters of Richard Strauss and S. Z., 1931–1935*, 1977); *Europäisches Erbe* (1960); *Durch Zeiten und Welten* (1961); *Fragment einer Novelle* (1961); *Im Schnee* (1963); *Die Dramen* (1964); *Unbekannte Briefe aus der Emigration an eine Freundin* (1964); *Der Turm zu Babel* (1964); *Frühlingsfahrt durch die Provence* (1965); *Silberne Saiten: Gedichte und Nachdichtungen* (1966); *Die Monotonisierung der Welt* (1976); *Briefe an Freunde* (1978); *Rausch der Verwandlung* (1982); *Tagebücher* (1984); *Briefwechsel* (1987); *S. Z.-Joseph Gregor Correspondence 1921-1938* (1991); *Briefe 1897-1914* (1995). FURTHER WORKS IN ENGLISH: *Passion and Pain* (1925); *Letter from an Unknown Woman* (1932); *Kaleidoscope* (1934); *The Old Book Peddler, and Other Tales for Bibliophiles* (1937); *Stories and Legends* (1955); *The Royal Game, and Other Stories* (1981); *Jewish Legends* (1987)

BIBLIOGRAPHY: Rieger, E., *S. Z.: Der Mann und das Werk* (1928); Zweig, F. M., *S. Z.* (1946); Arens, H., ed., *S. Z.: A Tribute to His Life and Work* (1950); Zohn, H., "S. Z. and Contemporary European Literature," *GL & L*, 5 (1952): 202–12; Leftwich, J., "S. Z. and the World of Yesterday," *Leo Baeck Institute Year Book III* (1958): 81–99; Fitzbauer, E., ed., *S. Z.: Spiegelungen einer schöpferischen Persönlichkeit* (1959); Zweig, F. M., *S. Z.: Eine Bibliographie* (1961); Klawiter, R. J., *S. Z.: A Bibliography* (1965); Prater, D. A., *European of Yesterday: A Biography of S. Z.* (1972); Strelka, J. P., *S. Z.* (1981); special Z. issue, *MAL*, 14, 3–4 (1981); Müller, H., *S. Z.* (1988); Zohn, H., "S. Z.," in *DLB*, 118 (1992): 270–81; Renoldner, K., et al., eds., *S. Z. Bilder, Texte, Dokumente* (1993); special Z. issue, *Europe* (June–July 1995)

—HARRY ZOHN

ZWILLINGER, Frank Gerhard

Austrian dramatist, poet, and essayist, b. 29 Nov. 1909, Vienna; d. 11 Nov. 1989, Garches (near Paris), France

Z., who began to write when very young, took a doctoral degree in German language and literature at the University of Vienna. Immediately after the Anschluss Z. emigrated to Italy, and in 1939 he reached Indochina via Singapore. After working for an export firm in Saigon for a few months, he served in the French Foreign Legion for a year and a half. He then founded and operated the first cosmetics factory in the country. In March 1945 Z. took part in the resistance to the Japanese attack on the European population of Saigon and lost a leg. In 1946 he went to France, where he lived for the rest of his life. Until the early 1970s he led the dual life of an industrialist and a man of letters, achieving increasing recognition as a dramatist and poet. Despite several Austrian and French prizes, decorations, titles, and other distinctions, he did not escape the multifarious frustrations of an exiled writer.

Reflecting the conflicts between faith and science, human nature and the scientific revolution, humanism and politics, reason and emotion, Z.'s plays are truly tracts for our time. His four major dramatic works appeared in one volume, *Geist und Macht* (1973; mind and might). The five–act play *Maharal* (written 1951; *Maharal*, 1979) deals with the legend of the Golem, who is said to have been created by Grand Rabbi Loew for the protection of the Jews in the ghetto of medieval Prague. *Galileo Galilei* (written 1953, pub. 1962; *Galileo Galilei*, 1980) highlights the clash between science and faith, scholarship and political-religious power. The conflict in *Archimedes* (ten scenes written in several versions between 1957 and 1965) is between science and ethics; Archimedes is presented as a spiritual ancestor of Albert Einstein whose benign theories are tragically converted into malign practices. In *Kettenreaktion* (written 1972; *Chain Reaction*, 1981) the emphasis shifts from gifted individuals to teams of researchers and the dilemmas of brilliant but powerless nuclear physicists in unstable times. Exemplifying Z.'s concept of a "planetary theater," this multimedia play strives for a new kind of worldwide unity of time, place, and action.

Z.'s rustic comedy *Der Streik Gottes* (1965; God's strike) was performed on several stages in Germany and telecast in 1968 as *Der Glockenstreik* (the strike of the bells). Foremost among Z.'s unperformed and unpublished plays is *Wiener Welttheater* (written 1965; Vienna world theater), set in the 17th c., at the time of the Plague (1679), the Turkish siege (1683), and the expulsion of the Jews from the city in 1670.

Z.'s poetry reflects a great variety of themes and forms. *Wandel und Wiederkehr: Gedichte des Lebens* (1950; change and return: poems of life) contains poems about places and moods of the old and new worlds and some autobiographical poems. The ballads of *Der magische Tanz* (1960; the magic dance), about great figures of history and legend, and written with great verve and wit, were followed by a comprehensive collection called *Gedichte* (3 vols., 1963; poems). Z.'s more recent poetry—often cyclical in form and in free verse—is more visionary and introspective than his earlier verse, presenting manifestations of the cosmic pulse of life in imagery drawn from nature, history, and the sciences. A new kind of concision is evident in the collections *Entzifferung* (1976; decipherment), *ortung: kosmische texte* (1976; position finding: cosmic texts), and the lyrical triptych *durch blick* (1980; perspective), *einsicht* (1980; insight), and *ideogramme* (1980; ideograms).

FURTHER WORKS: *Dalmatinisches Bilderbuch* (1938); *Zwischen Tod und Leben* (written 1967; *Between Death and Life*, 1979); *Dobratsch* (1981)

BIBLIOGRAPHY: Zohn, H., "Geist und Macht," *MAL*, 7 (1974): 257–60; McManus, J., "F. Z.: A Poet's Odyssey," *Brandeis Bulletin*, 13 Dec. 1974: 11; Berendsohn, W. A., *Vom Lebensweg und Lebenswerk F. Z.s* (1975); Bortenschlager, W., *Geschichte der spirituellen Poesie* (1976): 213–22; Fitzell, J., *"Entzifferung and ortung,"* *GN*, 8: 1–4 (1977): 51–52; Frey, E., "Modernes Weltbild in der modernen Lyrik: F. Z.'s Naturgedichte," *GN*, 14, 3 (1983): 33–35; Blumenthal, B., "F. Z.'s Writings," *MAL*, 19, 1 (1986): 85–102: Zohn, H., "Aspects of F. Z.'s Theater," in Gelber, M. H., ed., *Von Franzos zu Canetti* (1996): 357–67

—HARRY ZOHN

NATIONALITY INDEX

ALBANIAN
Agolli, Dritëro
Camaj, Martin
Fishta, Gjergj
Kadaré, Ismail

ALGERIAN
al-A'raj, Wāsīnī
Belamri, Rabah
Boudjedra, Rachid
Dib, Mohammed
Djaout, Tahar
Djebar, Assia
Feraoun, Mouloud
Ibn Hadūqa, 'Abd al-Hamīd
Kateb Yacine
Mammeri, Mouloud
Mimouni, Rachid
Mustaghānmī, Ahlām
Sebbar, Leïla
Sénac, Jean
Wanissi, Zuhūr
Wattār, al-Tāhir

AMERICAN
Adams, Henry
Agee, James
Aiken, Conrad
Albee, Edward
Algren, Nelson
Ammons, A(rchibald) R(andolph)
Anderson, Sherwood
Angelou, Maya
Ashbery, John
Auchincloss, Louis
Auden, W(ystan) H(ugh)
Baldwin, James
Banks, Russell
Baraka, Amiri
Barnes, Djuna
Barth, John
Barthelme, Donald
Barthelme, Frederick
Beattie, Ann
Bellow, Saul
Benét, Stephen Vincent
Berger, Thomas
Berryman, John
Bierce, Ambrose
Bishop, Elizabeth
Blackmur, R(ichard) P(almer)
Bloom, Harold
Bly, Robert
Bogan, Louise
Bowles, Jane Auer
Bowles, Paul
Boyle, Kay
Boyle, T(homas) Coraghessan
Brooks, Cleanth
Brooks, Gwendolyn
Buck, Pearl S(ydenstricker)
Bukowski, Charles
Bullins, Ed
Burke, Kenneth
Burroughs, William S.
Cain, James M.
Caldwell, Erskine
Capote, Truman
Carver, Raymond
Cather, Willa
Chandler, Raymond
Cheever, John
Chesnutt, Charles W.
Cisneros, Sandra
Coover, Robert
Cortez, Jayne
Cowley, Malcolm
Cozzens, James Gould
Crane, Hart
Creeley, Robert
Cullen, Countee
cummings, e(dward) e(stlin)
DeLillo, Don
Dickey, James
Didion, Joan
Doctorow, E(dgar) L(awrence)
Doolittle, Hilda
Dos Passos, John
Dove, Rita
Dreiser, Theodore
Du Bois, W(illiam) E(dward) B(urghardt)
Duncan, Robert
Eliot, T(homas) S(tearns)
Elkin, Stanley
Ellison, Ralph
Erdrich, Louise
Farrell, James T.
Faulkner, William
Fiedler, Leslie A.
Fitzgerald, F(rancis) Scott
Foote, Horton
Ford, Richard
Frost, Robert
Fuller, Charles H., Jr.
Gaddis, William
Gaines, Ernest J.
García, Cristina
Gardner, John
Gass, William H.
Gates, Henry Louis, Jr.
Ghose, Zulfikar
Gilchrist, Ellen

Ginsberg, Allen
Giovanni, Nikki
Gordon, Caroline
Goyen, William
Graham, Jorie
Green, Julien
Guare, John
Gurney, A(lbert) R(amsdell)
Hammett, Dashiell
Hansberry, Lorraine
Harjo, Joy
Hass, Robert
Hawkes, John
Hayden, Robert
Hecht, Anthony
Heller, Joseph
Hellman, Lillian
Hemingway, Ernest
Himes, Chester
Hinojosa-Smith, Rolando
Hongo, Garrett Kaoru
Howe, Irving
Hughes, Langston
Hugo, Richard
Hurston, Zora Neale
Ignatow, David
Inge, William Motter
Irving, John
Isherwood, Christopher
James, Henry
Jarrell, Randall
Jeffers, Robinson
Johnson, James Weldon
Jones, James
Justice, Donald R(odney)
Kazin, Alfred
Keillor, Garrison
Kelley, William Melvin
Kennedy, William
Kerouac, Jack
Kesey, Ken
Killens, John Oliver
Kingston, Maxine Hong
Kinnell, Galway
Kizer, Carolyn
Komunyakaa, Yusef
Kosinski, Jerzy
Kumin, Maxine
Kushner, Tony
Levertov, Denise
Levine, Philip
Lewis, Sinclair
Lindsay, Vachel
London, Jack
Lord, Audre
Lowell, Amy
Lowell, Robert
MacLeish, Archibald
Madhubuti, Haki R.
Mailer, Norman

Major, Clarence
Malamud, Bernard
Mamet, David
Marquand, J(ohn) P(hillips)
Marshall, Paule
Mason, Bobbie Ann
Masters, Edgar Lee
McCarthy, Cormac
McCarthy, Mary
McCullers, Carson
McGuane, Thomas
McKay, Claude
McMurtry, Larry
McNally, Terrence
McPherson, James Alan
Mencken, H(enry) L(ouis)
Merrill, James
Merwin, W(illiam) S(tanley)
Millay, Edna St. Vincent
Miller, Arthur
Miller, Henry
Momaday, N(atachee) Scott
Moore, Marianne
Morris, Wright
Morrison, Toni
Naylor, Gloria
Nemerov, Howard
Nin, Anaïs
Oates, Joyce Carol
O'Connor, Flannery
Odets, Clifford
O'Hara, Frank
O'Hara, John
Oliver, Mary
Olsen, Tillie
Olson, Charles
O'Neill, Eugene
Ozick, Cynthia
Paley, Grace
Patchen, Kenneth
Percy, Walker
Petry, Ann
Plath, Sylvia
Porter, Katherine Anne
Pound, Ezra
Price, Reynolds
Purdy, James
Pynchon, Thomas
Rabe, David
Ransom, John Crowe
Reed, Ishmael
Rexroth, Kenneth
Rice, Elmer
Rich, Adrienne
Robinson, Edwin Arlington
Roethke, Theodore
Roth, Henry
Roth, Philip
Rukeyser, Muriel
Salinger, J(erome) D(avid)

Salter, Mary Jo
Sanchez, Sonia
Sandburg, Carl
Santayana, George
Saroyan, William
Sarton, May
Schuyler, James
Schwartz, Delmore
Sexton, Anne
Shapiro, Karl
Shepard, Sam
Silko, Leslie Marmon
Simpson, Mona
Sinclair, Upton
Singer, Isaac Bashevis
Smiley, Jane
Smith, Lee
Snyder, Gary
Sontag, Susan
Soto, Gary
Spencer, Elizabeth
Stegner, Wallace
Stein, Gertrude
Steinbeck, John
Steiner, George
Stevens, Wallace
Stone, Robert
Strand, Mark
Styron, William
Tate, Allen
Tate, James
Taylor, Peter
Theroux, Paul
Thurber, James
Toomer, Jean
Trilling, Lionel
Tyler, Anne
Updike, John
Valdez, Luis
Vidal, Gore
Vonnegut, Kurt, Jr.
Walker, Alice
Wallant, Edward Lewis
Warren, Robert Penn
Wasserstein, Wendy
Wellek, René
Welty, Eudora
West, Nathanael
Wharton, Edith
White, E(lwyn) B(rooks)
Wilbur, Richard
Wilder, Thornton
Williams, John A.
Williams, Tennessee
Williams, William Carlos
Wilson, August
Wilson, Edmund
Wilson, Lanford
Winters, Yvor
Wolfe, Thomas

Wolfe, Tom
Wolff, Tobias
Wright, Charles
Wright, James
Wright, Richard
Zukofsky, Louis

ANGOLAN
Pepetela
Soromenho, Fernando Monteiro de Castro
Vieira, José Luandino

ANTIGUAN
Kincaid, Jamaica

ARGENTINE
Arlt, Roberto
Bioy Casares, Adolfo
Borges, Jorge Luis
Cortázar, Julio
Costantini, Humberto
Denevi, Marco
Dragún, Osvaldo
Gálvez, Manuel
Gambaro, Griselda
Giardinelli, Mempo
Girri, Alberto
Guido, Beatriz
Güiraldes, Ricardo
Lugones, Leopoldo
Lynch, Marta
Mallea, Eduardo
Marechal, Leopoldo
Martínez Estrada, Ezequiel
Mujica Láinez, Manuel
Payró, Roberto Jorge
Piglia, Ricardo
Puig, Manuel
Sábato, Ernesto
Shua, Ana María
Soriano, Osvaldo
Szichman, Mario
Valenzuela, Luisa
Viñas, David

ARMENIAN
Charents, Eghishe
Matevossian, Hrant
Oshagan, Hagop
Sevag, Barouyr
Varoujan, Daniel
Zohrab, Krikor

AUSTRALIAN
Astley, Thea
Brennan, Christopher John
Carey, Peter
Furphy, Joseph

Herbert, Xavier
Hope, A(lec) D(erwent)
Jolley, Elizabeth
Keneally, Thomas
Malouf, David
Murray, Les
Noonuccal, Oodgeroo
Richardson, Henry Handel
Stead, Christina
White, Patrick
Wright, Judith

AUSTRIAN

Aichinger, Ilse
Artmann, H(ans) C(arl)
Bachmann, Ingeborg
Bahr, Hermann
Bauer, Wolfgang
Beer-Hofmann, Richard
Bernhard, Thomas
Broch, Hermann
Brod, Max
Bruckner, Ferdinand
Buber, Martin
Canetti, Elias
Celan, Paul
Csokor, Franz Theodor
Doderer, Heimito von
Freud, Sigmund
Friedell, Egon
Gütersloh, Albert Paris
Handke, Peter
Hochwälder, Fritz
Hofmannsthal, Hugo von
Horváth, Ödön von
Jandl, Ernst
Kafka, Franz
Kramer, Theodor
Kraus, Karl
Lind, Jakov
Mayröcker, Friederike
Meyrink, Gustav
Musil, Robert
Polgar, Alfred
Preradović, Paula von
Rilke, Rainer Maria
Rosei, Peter
Roth, Joseph
Schnitzler, Arthur
Soyfer, Jura
Sperber, Manès
Stoessl, Otto
Szyszkowitz, Gerald
Torberg, Friedrich
Trakl, Georg
Waldinger, Ernst
Weiss, Ernst
Werfel, Franz
Zweig, Stefan
Zwillinger, Frank Gerhard

AZERBAIJANI

Mamedkulizade, Djalil
Vurgun, Samed

BARBADIAN

Brathwaite, Edward Kamau
Lamming, George

BELGIAN

Boon, Louis Paul
Brulez, Raymond
Claes, Ernest
Claus, Hugo
Crommelynck, Fernand
Daisne, Johan
Elsschot, Willem
Ghelderode, Michel de
Gijsen, Marnix
Maeterlinck, Maurice
Mallet-Joris, Françoise
Michaux, Henri
Ostaijen, Paul van
Pillecijn, Filip de
Roelants, Maurice
Simenon, Georges
Streuvels, Stijn
Teirlinck, Herman
Timmermans, Felix
Verhaeren, Émile
Vermeylen, August
Walschap, Gerard
Woestijne, Karel van de

BELIZEAN

Edgell, Zee

BOLIVIAN

Arguedas, Alcides
Jaimes Freyre, Ricardo

BRAZILIAN

Amado, Jorge
Andrade, Carlos Drummond de
Andrade, Mário de
Andrade, Oswald de
Aranha, José da Graça
Bandeira, Manuel
Boal, Augusto
Buarque, Chico
Callado, Antônio
Fonseca, Rubem
Freyre, Gilberto
Lispector, Clarice
Lobato, Monteiro
Meireles, Cecília
Melo Neto, João Cabral de
Piñon, Nélida
Queiroz, Rachel de
Ramos, Graciliano

Rego, José Lins do
Ribeiro, Darcy
Ribeiro, João Ubaldo
Ricardo, Cassiano
Rodrigues, Nelson
Rosa, João Guimarães
Scliar, Moacyr
Telles, Lygia Fagundes
Veríssimo, Érico

BUKHARAN
Fitrat, Abdalrauf (Abdurauf)

BULGARIAN
Bagryana, Elisaveta
Dalchev, Atanas
Dimitrova, Blaga
Elin Pelin
Kristeva, Julia
Slaveykov, Pencho
Talev, Dimitur
Yavorov, Peyo
Yovkov, Yordan

BURMESE
Thahkin Ko-Daw Hmaing
Thaw-Da Hswei
Thein Hpei Myint

BYELORUSSIAN
Arsiennieva, Natalla
Bykaw, Vasil

CAMEROONIAN
Beti, Mongo
Beyala, Calixthe
Oyono, Ferdinand
Werewere Liking

CANADIAN
Aquin, Hubert
Atwood, Margaret
Bessette, Gerard
Blais, Marie-Claire
Brossard, Nicole
Callaghan, Morley
Cohen, Leonard
Davies, Robertson
Ferron, Jacques
Frye, Northrop
Gallant, Mavis
Godbout, Jacques
Hébert, Anne
Klein, A(braham) M(oses)
Langevin, André
Laurence, Margaret
Layton, Irving
Leacock, Stephen
MacLennan, Hugh
Munro, Alice

Nelligan, Émile
Ondaatje, Michael
Pratt, E(dwin) J(ohn)
Richler, Mordecai
Ringuet
Roy, Gabrielle
Theriault, Yves
Tremblay, Michel
Vassanji, M(oyez) G.

CATALAN
Calders, Pere

CHILEAN
Alegría, Fernando
Allende, Isabel
Barrios, Eduardo
Bombal, Maria Luisa
Donoso, José
Dorfman, Ariel
Edwards, Jorge
Guzmán, Nicomedes
Huidobro, Vicente
Lafourcade, Enrique
Lihn, Enrique
Mistral, Gabriela
Neruda, Pablo
Parra, Nicanor
Rojas, Manuel
Skármeta, Antonio
Teillier, Jorge
Wolff, Egon

CHINESE
Ai Ch'ing
Bei Dao
Chang Ai-ling
Chao Shu-li
Chou Li-po
Ho Ch'i-fang
Hsü Chih-mo
Hu Shih
Kao Hsiao-sheng
Kuo Mo-jo
Lao She
Li Ang
Li Jui
Liu Ya-tzu
Lu Hsün
Mao Tun
Mo Yen
Pa Chin
Pai Hsien-yung
Su Man-shu
Ting Ling
Ts'ao Yü
Wang Anyi
Wang Meng
Wen I-to
Xi Xi

Yang Chiang
Yü Kwang-chung

COLOMBIAN
Álvarez Gardeazábal, Gustavo
Buenaventura, Enrique
Caballero Calderón, Eduardo
Carranza, Eduardo
Carrasquilla, Tomás
Cepeda Samudio, Alvaro
Gaitán Durán, Jorge
García Márquez, Gabriel
Mejía Vallejo, Manuel
Moreno-Duran, Rafael Humberto
Mujica, Elisa
Mutis, Alvaro
Niño, Jairo Aníbal
Rivera, José Eustasio
Zapata Olivella, Manuel

CONGOLESE
Bemba, Sylvain
Lopes, Henri
Mudimbe, V(alentin) Y(ves)
Tansi, Sony Labou
Tchicaya U Tam'si

COSTA RICAN
Marín Cañas, José
Naranjo, Carmen
Odio, Eunice
Oreamuno, Yolanda
Rovinski, Samuel

CROATIAN
Aralica, Ivan
Marinković, Ranko
Šegedin, Petar

CUBAN
Arenas, Reinaldo
Ballagas, Emilio
Cabrera, Lydia
Cabrera Infante, Guillermo
Carpentier, Alejo
Guillén, Nicolás
Lezama Lima, José
Montes-Huidobro, Matías
Novás Calvo, Lino
Padilla, Heberto
Piñera, Virgilio
Rojo, Antonio Benítez
Sarduy, Severo
Triana, José

CZECHOSLOVAK
Bezruč, Petr
Březina, Otokar
Čapek, Karel

Durych, Jaroslav
Fuks, Ladislav
Halas, František
Hašek, Jaroslav
Havel, Václav
Holan, Vladimir
Holub, Miroslav
Hora, Josef
Hostovský, Egon
Hrabal, Bohumil
Jilemnický, Peter
Jirásek, Alois
Karvaš, Peter
Klíma, Ivan
Krasko, Ivan
Kukučín, Martin
Kundera, Milan
Lustig, Arnošt
Machar, Josef Svatopluk
Majerová, Marie
Mňačko, Ladislav
Nezval, Vítězslav
Novomeský, Laco (Ladislav)
Olbracht, Ivan
Páral, Vladimír
Šalda, František Xaver
Seifert, Jaroslav
Škvorecký, Josef
Vaculík, Ludvík
Vančura, Vladislav
Voskovec, Jiří (George)
Werich, Jan
Wolker, Jiři

DANISH
Abell, Kjeld
Alpar, Murat
Andersen, Benny
Bjørnvig, Thorkild
Bodelsen, Anders
Brandt, Jørgen Gustava
Branner, Hans Christian
Christensen, Inger
Dinesen, Isak
Hansen, Martin A.
Hansen, Thorkild
Høeck, Klaus
Høeg, Peter
Højholt, Per
Hultberg, Peer
Jæger, Frank
Jensen, Johannes Vilhelm
Kampmann, Christian
Kirk, Hans Rudolf
Kristensen, Tom
Larsen, Marianne
Laugesen, Peter
Madsen, Svend Åge
Malinovski, Ivan
Munk, Kaj

Nexø, Martin Andersen
Nordbrandt, Henrik
Paludan, Jacob
Panduro, Leif
Petersen, Nis
Reich, Ebbe Kløvedal
Rifbjerg, Klaus
Sarvig, Ole
Schade, Jens August
Seeberg, Peter
Sørensen, Villy
Stangerup, Henrik
Strunge, Michael
Tafdrup, Pia
Turèll, Dan

DOMINICAN
Veloz Maggiolo, Marcio

DUTCH
Achterberg, Gerrit
Berge, H(ans) C(ornelius) Ten
Blaman, Anna
Bordewijk, Ferdinand
Boutens, Pieter Cornelis
Braak, Menno ter
Brouwers, Jeroen
Couperus, Louis
Deyssel, Lodewijk van
Eeden, Frederik Willem van
Haasse, Hella
Heijermans, Herman
Hermans, W(illem) F(rederik)
Leopold, Jan Hendrik
Lucebert
Marsman, Hendrik
Mulisch, Harry
Nijhoff, Martinus
Nooteboom, Cees
Perron, Edgar du
Roland Holst, Adriaan
Roland Holst-Van der Schalk, Henriëtte
Schendel, Arthur van
Slauerhoff, Jan Jacob
Verwey, Albert
Vestdijk, Simon

ECUADOREAN
Aguilera Malta, Demetrio
Carrera Andrade, Jorge
Gallegos Lara, Joaquín
Icaza, Jorge
Pareja Diezcanseco, Alfredo

EGYPTIAN
'Abd Al-Sabūr, Salāh
Chedid, Andrée
Dunqul, Amal
Faraj, Alfred

al-Ghītānī, Jamāl
al-Hakīm, Tawfīq
Haqqī, Yahyā
Hijazi, Ahmad 'Abd al-Mu'tī
Husayn, Tāhā
Idrīs, Yūsuf
al-Kharrāt, Edwar
Mahfūz, Najīb
al-Sa'dāwī, Nawāl
Taymūr, Mahmūd

ENGLISH
Amis, Kingsley
Amis, Martin
Arden, John
Armah, Ayi Kwei
Auden, W(ystan) H(ugh)
Ayckbourn, Alan
Bainbridge, Beryl
Ballard, J(ames) G(raham)
Barker, George
Barnes, Julian
Bates, H(erbert) E(rnest)
Belloc, Hilaire
Bennett, Arnold
Betjeman, Sir John
Bolt, Robert
Bond, Edward
Bowen, Elizabeth
Bradbury, Malcolm
Braine, John
Brooke-Rose, Christine
Brookner, Anita
Brophy, Brigid
Bunting, Basil
Burgess, Anthony
Byatt, A(ntonia) S(usan)
Cary, Joyce
Chatwin, Bruce
Chesterton, G(ilbert) K(eith)
Churchill, Caryl
Compton-Burnett, Ivy
Conrad, Joseph
Coppard, A(lfred) E(dgar)
Coward, Noel
Day Lewis, C(ecil)
de la Mare, Walter
Dennis, Nigel
Douglas, Keith
Drabble, Margaret
Durrell, Lawrence
Eliot, T(homas) S(tearns)
Empson, William
Enright, D(ennis) J(oseph)
Firbank, Ronald
Fitzgerald, Penelope
Ford, Ford Madox
Forster, E(dward) M(organ)
Fowles, John
Fry, Christopher

Fuller, Roy
Galsworthy, John
Golding, William
Graves, Robert
Gray, Simon
Green, Henry
Greene, Graham
Gurnah, Abdulrazak
Hanley, James
Hardy, Thomas
Hartley, L(eslie) P(oles)
Heppenstall, Rayner
Hill, Geoffrey
Hinde, Thomas
Housman, A(lfred) E(dward)
Hughes, Richard
Hughes, Ted
Huxley, Aldous
Isherwood, Christopher
Jennings, Elizabeth
Jhabvala, Ruth Prawer
Johnson, B(ryan) S(tanley)
Jones, David (Michael)
Kipling, Rudyard
Koestler, Arthur
Larkin, Philip
Lawrence, D(avid) H(erbert)
Leavis, F(rank) R(aymond)
le Carré, John
Lessing, Doris
Lewis, C(live) S(taples)
Lewis, Wyndham
Lodge, David
Lowry, (Clarence) Malcolm
Macaulay, Rose
MacNeice, Louis
Manning, Olivia
Mansfield, Katherine
Masefield, John
Moore, George
Morrison, Blake
Murdoch, Iris
Myers, L(eopold) H(amilton)
Orwell, George
Osborne, John
Owen, Wilfred
Phillips, Caryl
Pinter, Harold
Pitter, Ruth
Powell, Anthony
Powys, John Cowper
Powys, T(heodore) F(rancis)
Priestley, J(ohn) B(oynton)
Pritchett, V(ictor) S(awdon)
Pym, Barbara
Raine, Kathleen
Read, Herbert
Reid, Christopher
Renault, Mary
Rhys, Jean

Richards, I(vor) A(rmstrong)
Richardson, Dorothy Miller
Rosenberg, Isaac
Sansom, William
Sassoon, Siegfried
Scott, Paul
Shaffer, Peter
Shaw, George Bernard
Sillitoe, Alan
Sinclair, May
Sitwell, Edith
Smith, Stevie
Snow, C(harles) P(ercy)
Spender, Stephen
Stoppard, Tom
Storey, David
Strachey, Lytton
Tennant, Emma
Thomas, Edward
Tolkien, J(ohn) R(onald) R(euel)
Wain, John
Warner, Sylvia Townsend
Waugh, Evelyn
Weldon, Fay
Wells, H(erbert) G(eorge)
Wesker, Arnold
West, Rebecca
Wilson, Angus
Wodehouse, P(elham) G(renville)
Woolf, Virginia

ESTONIAN
Alver, Betti
Liiv, Juhan
Masing, Uku
Rannit, Aleksis
Ristikivi, Karl
Talvik, Heiti
Tammsaare, A. H.
Under, Marie

ETHIOPIAN
Deressa, Solomon

FINNISH
Bargum, Johan
Björling, Gunnar
Carpelan, Bo
Chorell, Walentin
Diktonius, Elmer
Donner, Jörn
Enckell, Rabbe
Haanpää, Pentti
Haavikko, Paavo
Huldén, Lars
Jansson, Tove
Joenpelto, Eeva
Kallas, Aino
Kihlman, Christer Alfred
Kilpi, Eeva

Kilpi, Volter
Lehtonen, Joel
Leino, Eino
Linna, Väinö
Manner, Eeva-Liisa
Meri, Veijo
Saarikoski, Pentti
Salama, Hannu
Sillanpää, Frans Eemil
Södergran, Edith
Talvio, Maila
Tikkanen, Märta
Tuuri, Antti
Viita, Lauri

FRENCH
Adamov, Arthur
Alain
Alain-Fournier
Anouilh, Jean
Apollinaire, Guillaume
Aragon, Louis
Artaud, Antonin
Audiberti, Jacques
Aymé, Marcel
Barbusse, Henri
Barthes, Roland
Bataille, Georges
Beauvoir, Simone de
Bergson, Henri
Bernanos, Georges
Blanchot, Maurice
Bonnefoy, Yves
Breton, André
Butor, Michel
Camus, Albert
Cayrol, Jean
Céline, Louis-Ferdinand
Char, René
Chraïbi, Driss
Cixous, Hélène
Claudel, Paul
Cocteau, Jean
Colette, Sidonie-Gabrielle
Damas, Léon-Gontran
Daumal, René
Derrida, Jacques
Desnos, Robert
Drieu la Rochelle, Pierre
Duhamel, Georges
Duras, Marguerite
Éluard, Paul
Emmanuel, Pierre
Fargue, Léon-Paul
Faye, Jean-Pierre
Feydeau, Georges
Foucault, Michel
France, Anatole
Gascar, Pierre
Genet, Jean

Gide, André
Giono, Jean
Giraudoux, Jean
Gracq, Julien
Guilloux, Louis
Humbert, Marie-Thérèse
Ionesco, Eugène
Jabès, Edmond
Jacob, Max
Jammes, Francis
Jarry, Alfred
Jouhandeau, Marcel
Jouve, Pierre Jean
Kristeva, Julia
Labro, Philippe
Lacan, Jacques
Larbaud, Valery
La Tour du Pin, Patrice de
Le Clézio, J(ean) M(arie) G(ustave)
Leduc, Violette
Leiris, Michel
Lévi-Strauss, Claude
Lyotard, Jean-François
Malraux, André
Marcel, Gabriel
Martin du Gard, Roger
Maugham, W(illiam) Somerset
Mauriac, Claude
Mauriac, François
Maurois, André
Modiano, Patrick
Montherlant, Henry de
Morand, Paul
Nizan, Paul
Ollier, Claude
Pagnol, Marcel
Paulhan, Jean
Péguy, Charles
Perec, Georges
Pieyre de Mandiargues, André
Pinget, Robert
Ponge, Francis
Prévert, Jacques
Proust, Marcel
Queneau, Raymond
Rachilde
Radiguet, Raymond
Reverdy, Pierre
Ricardou, Jean
Robbe-Grillet, Alain
Roblès, Emmanuel
Rolland, Romain
Romains, Jules
Roussel, Raymond
Roy, Claude
Sagan, Françoise
Saint-Exupéry, Antoine de
Saint-John Perse
Salacrou, Armand
Sarraute, Nathalie

Sartre, Jean-Paul
Sénac, Jean
Simon, Claude
Sollers, Philippe
Soupault, Philippe
Supervielle, Jules
Tardieu, Jean
Tournier, Michel
Tzara, Tristan
Vailland, Roger
Valéry, Paul
Vercors
Vian, Boris
Weil, Simone
Wiesel, Elie
Wittig, Monique
Yourcenar, Marguerite

GAMBIAN
Peters, Lenrie
Sallah, Tijan M.

GEORGIAN
Chkheidze, Otar
Djavakhishvili, Mikheil
Gamsakhurdia, Konstantine
Robakidse, Grigol
Tabidze, Galaktion

GERMAN
Adorno, Theodor W(iesengrund)
Andersch, Alfred
Andres, Stefan Paul
Auerbach, Erich
Barlach, Ernst
Bauer, Walter
Becker, Jurek
Benjamin, Walter
Benn, Gottfried
Biermann, Wolf
Bobrowski, Johannes
Böll, Heinrich
Borchert, Wolfgang
Braun, Volker
Brecht, Bertolt
Brinkmann, Rolf Dieter
Carossa, Hans
Curtius, Ernst Robert
Döblin, Alfred
Domin, Hilde
Eich, Günter
Enzensberger, Hans Magnus
Feuchtwanger, Lion
Fleisser, Marieluise
Frank, Bruno
George, Stefan
Goes, Albrecht
Graf, Oskar Maria
Grass, Günter
Hacks, Peter

Hauptmann, Gerhart
Heissenbüttel, Helmut
Hermlin, Stephan
Hesse, Hermann
Heym, Stefan
Hildesheimer, Wolfgang
Hochhuth, Rolf
Hofmann, Gert
Höllerer, Walter
Huch, Ricarda
Huchel, Peter
Jahnn, Hans Henny
Johnson, Uwe
Jünger, Ernst
Kaiser, Georg
Kant, Hermann
Kaschnitz, Marie Luise
Kästner, Erich
Kipphardt, Heinar
Kirsch, Sarah
Koeppen, Wolfgang
Kolb, Annette
Kolmar, Gertrud
Kroetz, Franz Xaver
Krolow, Karl
Kunert, Günter
Kunze, Reiner
Lasker-Schüler, Else
Lenz, Siegfried
Mann, Heinrich
Mann, Thomas
Meckel, Christoph
Mehring, Walter
Mon, Franz
Morgenstern, Christian
Müller, Heiner
Nossack, Hans Erich
Piontek, Heinz
Regler, Gustav
Remarque, Erich Maria
Rinser, Luise
Sachs, Nelly
Schallück, Paul
Schmidt, Arno
Seghers, Anna
Sternheim, Carl
Stramm, August
Strittmatter, Erwin
Toller, Ernst
Tucholsky, Kurt
Walser, Martin
Wassermann, Jakob
Wedekind, Frank
Weiss, Peter
Wiechert, Ernst
Wohmann, Gabriele
Wolf, Christa
Wolf, Friedrich
Zuckmayer, Carl
Zweig, Arnold

GHANAIAN
Aidoo, Ama Ata
Anyidoho, Kofi
Awoonor, Kofi
Laing, Kojo
Sutherland, Efua Theodora Morgue

GREEK
Cavafy, C(onstantine) P.
Elytis, Odysseus
Haris, Petros
Kambanellis, Iakovos
Karyotakis, Kostas
Kazantzakis, Nikos
Myrivilis, Stratis
Palamas, Kostis
Panayotopoulos, I(oannis) M(ichael)
Papadiamantis, Alexandros
Plaskovitis, Spyros
Prevelakis, Pandelis
Ritsos, Yannis
Samarakis, Andonis
Seferis, George
Sikelianos, Angelos
Taktsis, Costas
Terzakis, Anghelos
Theotokas, Yorghos (George)
Tsirkas, Stratis
Varnalis, Kostas
Vassilikos, Vassilis
Venezis, Elias
Xenopoulos, Ghrighorios

GUADELOUPEAN
Condé, Maryse
Manicom, Jacqueline
Maximin, Daniel
Pineau, Gisèle
Schwarz-Bart, Simone

GUATEMALAN
Asturias, Miguel Ángel
Solórzano, Carlos

GUINEAN
Cabral, Amílcar
Camara Laye
Monenembo, Tierno

GUYANESE
Carew, Jan
Carter, Martin
D'Aguiar, Fred
Gilroy, Beryl A.
Harris, Wilson
Mittelholzer, Edgar
Nichols, Grace

HAITIAN
Chauvet, Marie Vieux

Depestre, René
Marcelin, Pierre
Métellus, Jean
Phelps, Anthony
Roumain, Jacques
Thoby-Marcelin, Philippe

HEBREW
Tchernichowsky, Saul

HONDURAN
Sosa, Roberto
Suarez, Clementina

HUNGARIAN
Ady, Endre
Ambrus, Zoltán
Babits, Mihály
Benjámin, László
Bródy, Sándor
Csoóri, Sándor
Déry, Tibor
Esterházy, Pèter
Illyés, Gyula
József, Attila
Juhász, Gyula
Kaffka, Margit
Karinthy, Frigyes
Kassák, Lajos
Konrád, George (György)
Kosztolányi, Dezső
Krúdy, Gyula
Lukács, György
Mészöly, Miklós
Molnár, Ferenc
Móricz, Zsigmond
Nádas, Péter
Nagy, Lajos
Németh, László
Pilinszky, János
Radnóti, Miklós
Szabó, Lörinc
Tóth, Árpád
Weöres, Sándor
Zilahy, Lajos

ICELANDIC
Bergsson, Guðbergur
Grímsson, Stefán Hördur
Guðmundsson, Tómas
Gunnarsson, Gunnar
Hjartarson, Snorri
Jóhannes úr Kötlum (Jónasson)
Laxness, Halldór
Sigurdsson, Ólafur Jóhann
Sigurjónsson, Jóhann
Steinarr, Steinn
Thórdarson, Thórbergur
Vilhjálmsson, Thor

INDIAN

Anand, Mulk Raj
Banerji, Bibhuti-Bhusan
Bharati, Subramania
Chatterji, Saratchandra
Das, Jibanananda
Desai, Anita
Desani, G(ovindas) V(ishnoodas)
Deshpande, Shashi
Ezekiel, Nissim
Ghose, Aurobindo
Ghose, Zulfikar
Hyder, Qurratulain
Iqbal, Muhammad
Jhabvala, Ruth Prawer
Karanth, Kota Shivaram
Khandekar, Vishnu Sakharam
Malgonkar, Manohar Dattatray
Markandaya, Kamala
Menon, Vallathol Narayana
Mohanty, Gopinath
Mukherjee, Bharati
Naidu, Sarojini
Narayan, R(asipuram) K(rishnaswamy)
Nazrul, Islam
Premchand
Rakesh, Mohan
Rao, Raja
Roy, Arundhati
Rushdie, Salman
Seth, Vikram
Singh, Khushwant
Tagore, Rabindranath

INDONESIAN

Achdiat Karta Mihardja
Chairil Anwar
Pramoedya Ananta Toer
Takdir Alisjahbana, Sutan

IRANIAN

Alavi, Buzurg
Al-e Ahmad, Jalal
Chubak, Sadeq
Faqiri, Amin
Farrokhzad, Forugh
Hedayat, Sadeq
Hoveyda, Fereydoun
Sa'edi, Gholam-Hossein

IRAQI

al-Bayyātī, 'Abd al-Wahhāb
Farmān, Ghā'ib Tu'ma
al-Malā'ika, Nāzik
al-Sayyāb, Badr Shākir

IRISH

Beckett, Samuel
Behan, Brendan

Bowen, Elizabeth
Brophy, Brigid
Carroll, Paul Vincent
Cary, Joyce
Clarke, Austin
Durcan, Paul
Friel, Brian
Hanley, James
Heaney, Seamus
Johnston, Denis
Joyce, James
Kavanagh, Patrick
Kinsella, Thomas
MacNeice, Louis
Mahon, Derek
Montague, John
Moore, Brian
Moore, George
Murphy, Richard
Ní Dhomhnaill, Nuala
O'Brien, Edna
O'Brien, Flann
O'Casey, Sean
O'Connor, Frank
Russell, George William
Shaw, George Bernard
Stephens, James
Synge, John Millington
Trevor, William
Yeats, William Butler

ISRAELI

Agnon, S(hmuel) Y.
Aloni, Nissim
Alterman, Natan
Amichai, Yehudah
Appelfeld, Aharon
Greenberg, Uri Zvi
Grossman, David
Kahana-Carmon, Amalia
Kenaz, Yehoshua
Megged, Aharon
Oz, Amos
Schutz, David
Shabtai, Yaakov
Tammuz, Benjamin
Yehoshua, A(braham) B.

ITALIAN

Alvaro, Corrado
Bacchelli, Riccardo
Bassani, Giorgio
Bernari, Carlo
Berto, Giuseppe
Betocchi, Carlo
Betti, Ugo
Bigongiari, Piero
Bontempelli, Massimo
Brancati, Vitaliano
Calvino, Italo

Campana, Dino
Cardarelli, Vincenzo
Cassola, Carlo
Croce, Benedetto
D'Annunzio, Gabriele
De Filippo, Eduardo
Deledda, Grazia
Di Giacomo, Salvatore
Duranti, Francesca
Eco, Umberto
Fenoglio, Beppe
Fo, Dario
Gadda, Carlo Emilio
Gatto, Alfonso
Ginzburg, Natalia
Gozzano, Guido
Jovine, Francesco
Landolfi, Tommaso
Levi, Carlo
Levi, Primo
Luzi, Mario
Malerba, Luigi
Maraini, Dacia
Marinetti, Filippo Tommaso
Mastronardi, Lucio
Montale, Eugenio
Morante, Elsa
Moravia, Alberto
Ortese, Anna Maria
Ottieri, Ottiero
Palazzeschi, Aldo
Parise, Goffredo
Pascoli, Giovanni
Pasolini, Pier Paolo
Pavese, Cesare
Pazzi, Roberto
Piccolo, Lucio
Piovene, Guido
Pirandello, Luigi
Porta, Antonio
Pratolini, Vasco
Prisco, Michele
Quasimodo, Salvatore
Rea, Domenico
Rèbora, Clemente
Saba, Umberto
Sanguineti, Edoardo
Sbarbaro, Camillo
Sciascia, Leonardo
Sereni, Vittorio
Silone, Ignazio
Soldati, Mario
Svevo, Italo
Tabucchi, Antonio
Tobino, Mario
Tomasi di Lampedusa, Giuseppe
Tozzi, Federigo
Ungaretti, Giuseppe
Verga, Giovanni
Vittorini, Elio

Volponi, Paolo
Zanzotto, Andrea

IVOIRIAN
Boni, Tanella S(usane)
Dadié, Bernard Binlin
Kourouma, Ahmadou
Tadjo, Véronique

JAMAICAN
Bennett, Louise (Simone)
Goodison, Lorna
Hearne, John
Johnson, Linton Kwesi
Mais, Roger
McKay, Claude
Morris, Mervyn
Rhone, Trevor
Salkey, Andrew
Scott, Dennis
Senior, Olive

JAPANESE
Abe Kōbō
Akutagawa Ryūnosuke
Ariyoshi Sawako
Dazai Osamu
Enchi Fumiko
Endō Shūsaku
Furui Yoshikichi
Futabatei Shimei
Hagiwara Sakutarō
Hayashi Fumiko
Ibuse Masuji
Inoue Yasushi
Ishiguro, Kazuo
Ishikawa Jun
Ishikawa Takuboku
Izumi Kyōka
Kawabata Yasunari
Kinoshita Junji
Kishida Kunio
Kobayashi Hideo
Kunikida Doppo
Masaoka Shiki
Mishima Yukio
Miyazawa Kenji
Mori Ōgai
Murakami Haruki
Nagai Kafū
Natsume Sōseki
Nishiwaki Junzaburō
Ōba Minako
Ōe Kenzaburō
Shiga Naoya
Shimazaki Tōson
Taneda Santōka
Tanizaki Jun'ichirō
Tsushima Yūko
Yokomitsu Riichi

Yosano Akiko

KAZAKH
Auezov, Mukhtar Omarkhan-ŭlï
Duwlat-ŭlï, Mir Jaqib
Kunanbaev, Abai

KENYAN
Imbuga, Francis
Macgoye, Marjorie Oludhe
Ngugi wa Thiong'o
Ogot, Grace

KIRGIZ
Aytmatov, Chïngïz

KURDISH
Goran, Abdulla

KUWAITI
Ismāʻīl, Ismāʻīl Fahd

LATVIAN
Bels, Alberts
Brigadere, Anna
Čaks, Aleksandrs
Ezera, Regīna
Rainis, Jānis
Skalbe, Kārlis
Vācietis, Ojārs
Virza, Edvarts
Ziedonis, Imants
Zīverts, Martiņš

LEBANESE
Abū Mādī, Īliyyā
Accad, Evelyne
ʻAql, Saʻīd
ʻAwwād, Tawfīq Yūsuf
Barakat, Hoda
al-Hājj, Unsī Lūwīs
Hāwī, Khalīl
al-Khāl, Yūsuf
Nuʻayma, Mīkhāʼīl
al-Shaykh, Hanān

LEBANESE-AMERICAN
Gibran, Kahlil

LESOTHO
Mofolo, Thomas

LIBYAN
al-Kūnī, Ibrāhīm

LITHUANIAN
Aistis, Jonas
Grušas, Juozas
Krėvė, Vincas
Mykolaitis, Vincas

Radauskas, Henrikas
Vaičiulaitis, Antanas

MALAGASY
Rabearivelo, Jean-Joseph
Rabemananjara, Jacques
Rakotoson, Michèle

MALAYSIAN
Shahnon Ahmad
Usman Awang

MALTESE
Ebejer, Francis
Friggieri, Oliver
Psaila, Carmelo

MARTINICAN
Capécia, Mayotte
Césaire, Aimé
Chamoiseau, Patrick
Glissant, Edouard
Maran, René

MEXICAN
Agustín, José
Arreola, Juan José
Azuela, Arturo
Azuela, Mariano
Carballido, Emilio
Castellanos, Rosario
Elizondo, Salvador
Fuentes, Carlos
Garro, Elena
González Martínez, Enrique
Gorostiza, José
Guzmán, Martín Luis
Hernández, Luisa Josefina
Ibargüengoitia, Jorge
Leñero, Vicente
López y Fuentes, Gregorio
Magdaleno, Mauricio
Nervo, Amado
Novo, Salvador
Pacheco, José Emilio
Paz, Octavio
Pellicer, Carlos
Poniatowska, Elena
Revueltas, José
Reyes, Alfonso
Romero, José Rubén
Rulfo, Juan
Sabines, Jaime
Sainz, Gustavo
Solares, Ignacio
Spota, Luis
Traven, B.
Usigli, Rodolfo
Villaurrutia, Xavier
Yáñez, Agustín

MOROCCAN
Ben Jelloun, Tahar
Berrada, Mohamed
Chraïbi, Driss
Ghallāb, Abd al-Karim
Khatibi, Abdelkebir
Zafzaf, Mohammed

MOZAMBICAN
Craveirinha, José

NEW ZEALAND
Baxter, James K(eir)
Curnow, Allen
Duff, Alan
Frame, Janet
Gee, Maurice
Grace, Patricia
Hulme, Keri
Manhire, Bill
O'Sullivan, Vincent
Sargeson, Frank
Smithyman, Kendrick
Tuwhare, Hone
Wedde, Ian

NICARAGUAN
Alegría, Claribel
Belli, Gioconda
Cardenal, Ernesto
Darío, Rubén
Ramírez, Sergio

NIGERIAN
Achebe, Chinua
Amadi, Elechi
Clark-Bekederemo, J(ohn) P(epper)
Ekwensi, Cyprian
Emecheta, Buchi
Iyayi, Festus
Nwapa, Flora (Nwanzuruaha)
Ojaide, Tanure
Okafor, Chinyere Grace
Okara, Gabriel
Okigbo, Christopher
Okri, Ben
Onwueme, (Osonye) Tess
Osofisan, Femi
Rotimi, Ola
Soyinka, Wole
Tutuola, Amos

NORWEGIAN
Bjerke, André
Bjørneboe, Jens
Bojer, Johan
Borgen, Johan
Bull, Olaf
Carling, Finn
Christov, Solveig

Duun, Olav
Eidem, Odd
Falkberget, Johan
Fangen, Ronald
Fløgstad, Kjartan
Grieg, Nordahl
Hamsun, Knut
Hauge, Olav H.
Hoel, Sigurd
Holt, Kåre
Jacobsen, Rolf
Mehren, Stein
Øverland, Arnulf
Sandel, Cora
Sandemose, Aksel
Solstad, Dag
Undset, Sigrid
Uppdal, Kristofer
Vesaas, Tarjei

PAKISTANI
Ali, Ahmed
Faiz, Faiz Ahmed
Ghose, Zulfikar

PALESTINIAN
Darwīsh, Mahmūd
Habībī, Emile
Jabrā, Jabrā Ibrāhīm
Kanafānī, Ghassān
Sāyigh, Tawfīq

PARAGUAYAN
Roa Bastos, Augusto

PERSIAN
Lahuti, Abulqasim

PERUVIAN
Alegría, Ciro
Arguedas, José María
Belli, Carlos Germán
Bryce Echenique, Alfredo (Marcelo)
Chocano, José Santos
Goldemberg, Isaac
González Prada, Manuel
Ribeyro, Julio Ramón
Salazar Bondy, Sebastián
Vallejo, César
Vargas Llosa, Mario

PHILIPPINE
Gonzalez, N(estor) V(icente) M(adali)
Joaquin, Nick
Santos, Bienvenido N.
Ty-Casper, Linda
Villa, Jose Garcia

POLISH
Andrzejewski, Jerzy

Barańczak, Stanislaw
Białoszewski, Miron
Borowski, Tadeusz
Brandys, Kazimierz
Broniewski, Władysław
Czechowicz, Józef
Dabrowska, Maria
Dygat, Stanisław
Gałczyński, Konstanty Ildefons
Goetel, Ferdynand
Gombrowicz, Witold
Herbert, Zbigniew
Hłasko, Marek
Iwaniuk, Wacław
Iwaszkiewicz, Jarosław
Jastrun, Mieczysław
Kaden-Bandrowski, Juliusz
Konwicki, Tadeusz
Kossak, Zofia
Kruczkowski, Leon
Krynicki, Ryszard
Lechoń, Jan
Leśmian, Bolesław
Miłosz, Czesław
Mrożek, Sławomir
Nałkowska, Zofia
Parandowski, Jan
Parnicki, Teodor
Przyboś, Julian
Przybyszewski, Stanisław
Reymont, Władysław Stanisław
Rostworowski, Karol Hubert
Różewicz, Tadeusz
Schulz, Bruno
Sienkiewicz, Henryk
Słonimski, Antoni
Szymborska, Wisława
Tuwim, Julian
Ważyk, Adam
Wierzyński, Kazimierz
Witkiewicz, Stanisław Ignacy
Wittlin, Józef
Wyspiański, Stanisław
Zagajewski, Adam
Żeromski, Stefan

PORTUGUESE
Andrade, Eugénio de
Andresen, Sophia de Mello Breyner
Brandão, Fiama Hasse Pais
Brandão, Raúl
Castro, José Maria Ferreira de
Faria, Almeida
Gonçalves, Olga
Jorge, Lidia
Namora, Fernando Gonçalves
O'Neill, Alexandre
Pessoa, Fernando
Pires, José Cardoso
Redol, António Alves

Régio, José
Ribeiro, Aquilino
Sá-Carneiro, Mário de
Saramago, José
Sena, Jorge de
Soromenho, Fernando Monteiro de Castro
Teixeira de Pascoaes
Torga, Miguel

PUERTO RICAN
Ferré, Rosario
Laguerre, Enrique
Marqués, René
Sánchez, Luis Rafael
Soto, Pedro Juan
Vega, Ana Lydia

ROMANIAN
Arghezi, Tudor
Bacovia, George
Barbu, Ion
Blaga, Lucian
Blandiana, Ana
Blecher, M(arcel)
Călinescu, George
Caragiale, Mateiu
Caraion, Ion
Cioran, E(mil) M.
Doinas, Stefan Augustin
Dumbrăveanu, Anghel
Eliade, Mircea
Goga, Octavian
Lovinescu, Eugen
Maniu, Adrian
Negoiţescu, Ion
Papadat-Bengescu, Hortensia
Petrescu, Camil
Philippide, Alexandru
Pillat, Ion
Popescu, Dumitru Radu
Preda, Marin
Rebreanu, Liviu
Sadoveanu, Mihail
Sorescu, Marin
Stănescu, Nichita
Urmuz
Voiculescu, Vasile

RUSSIAN
Abramov, Fyodor
Akhmadulina, Bella
Akhmatova, Anna
Aksyonov, Vasily Pavlovich
Andreev, Leonid
Annensky, Innokenty
Babel, Isaak Emanuilovich
Bagritsky, Edvard
Bahdanovich, Maksim
Bakhtin, Mikhail Mikhailovich
Balmont, Konstantin Dmitrievich

Bely, Andrey
Bialik, Chayim Nachman
Blok, Alexandr
Brodsky, Joseph
Bryusov, Valery
Bulgakov, Mikhail Afanasievich
Bunin, Ivan
Chekhov, Anton Pavlovich
Dovlatov, Sergey (Donatovich)
Ehrenburg, Ilya Grigorevich
Fadeev, Alexandr Alexandrovich
Fedin, Konstantin Alexandrovich
Gladkov, Fyodor Vasilievich
Gorky, Maxim
Gumilyov, Nikolay Stepanovich
Hippius, Zinaida
Ilf, Ilya
Iskander, Fazil Abdulovich
Ivanov, Vyacheslav Ivanovich
Kataev, Valentin Petrovich
Kaverin, Veniamin
Kazakov, Yury
Khlebnikov, Velemir Vladimirovich
Khodasevich, Vladislav Felitsianovich
Klyuev, Nikolay Alexeevich
Kuprin, Alexandr Ivanovich
Kuzmin, Mikhail Alexeevich
Leonov, Leonid Maximovich
Lipkin, Semyon Izrailevich
Lisnyanskaya, Inna
Mandelshtam, Osip Emilevich
Markish, Peretz
Mayakovsky, Vladimir Vladimirovich
Merezhkovsky, Dmitry Sergeevich
Nabokov, Vladimir
Nagibin, Yury Markovich
Narbikova, Valeria
Okudzhava, Bulat Shalvovich
Olesha, Yury Karlovich
Osorgin, M. A.
Ostrovsky, Nikolay Alexeevich
Panova, Vera Fyodorovna
Pasternak, Boris
Paustovsky, Konstantin Georgievich
Petrov, Yevgeny
Petrushevskaya, Ludmila
Pilnyak, Boris
Platonov, Andrey Platonovich
Prishvin, Mikhail Mikhailovich
Radzinsky, Edvard
Rasputin, Valentin
Remizov, Alexey Mikhaylovich
Rozanov, Vasily Vasilyevich
Sholokhov, Mikhail
Shukshin, Vasily Makarovich
Simonov, Konstantin Mikhaylovich
Sinyavsky, Andrey Donatovich
Sokolov, Sasha
Sologub, Fyodor
Soloukhin, Vladimir Alexeevich

Solzhenitsyn, Aleksandr Isaevich
Tendryakov, Vladimir Fyodorovich
Tolstaya, Tatyana
Tolstoy, Alexey Nikolaevich
Trifonov, Yury Valentinovich
Tsvetaeva, Marina Ivanova
Tursunzoda, Mirzo
Tvardovsky, Alexandr Trifonovich
Voynovich, Vladimir Nikolaevich
Voznesensky, Andrey
Vysotsky, Vladimir
Yerofeev, Venedikt
Yesenin, Sergey
Yevtushenko, Yevgeny Alexandrovich
Zabolotsky, Nikolay Alekseevich
Zamyatin, Yevgeny Ivanovich
Zaytsev, Boris Konstantinovich
Zoshchenko, Mikhail Mikhailovich

SALVADORAN
Alegría, Claribel
Argueta, Manlio
Salarrué

SAMOAN
Wendt, Albert

SAUDI
Munīf, 'Abd al-Rahman

SCOTTISH
Banks, Iain (Menzies)
Barrie, James M.
Bridie, James
MacCaig, Norman
MacDiarmid, Hugh
Muir, Edwin
Smith, Sydney Goodsir
Soutar, William
Spark, Muriel

SENEGALESE
Bugul, Ken
Diallo, Nafissatou
Diop, Birago
Ndao, Cheikh Aliou
Sembène Ousmane
Senghor, Léopold Sédar
Sow Fall, Aminata

SERBIAN
Kiš, Danilo
Nastasijević, Momčilo
Pavić, Milorad

SIERRA LEONEAN
Cheney-Coker, Syl

SLOVAK
Bednár, Alfonz

Figuli, Margita
Haľamová, Maša
Hronský, Jozef Cíger
Johanides, Ján
Tatarka, Dominik
Timrava

SLOVENE
Debeljak, Aleš
Hieng, Andrej
Šalamun, Tomaž

SOMALI
Farah, Nuruddin

SOUTH AFRICAN
Abrahams, Peter
Breytenbach, Breyten
Brink, Andreé P(hilippus)
Brutus, Dennis
Campbell, Roy
Coetzee, J(ohn) M.
Fugard, Athol
Gordimer, Nadine
Head, Bessie
Jacobson, Dan
Joubert, Elsa
La Guma, Alex
Millin, Sarah Gertrude
Mphahlele, Ezekiel (Es'kia)
Ndebele, Njabulo S.
Paton, Alan
Plomer, William
Rive, Richard
Schreiner, Olive
Smith, Pauline
Stockenström, Wilma
Tlali, Miriam Mesoli

SOUTH KOREAN
Pak Tu-jin
Sŏ Chŏng-ju

SPANISH
Alberti, Rafael
Aleixandre, Vicente
Alonso, Dámaso
Álvarez Quintero, Serafín and Joaquín
Arniches, Carlos
Arrabal, Fernando
Atencia, María Victoria
Aub, Max
Ayala, Francisco
Azorín
Baroja, Pío
Benavente, Jacinto
Benet, Juan
Blasco Ibáñez, Vicente
Buero Vallejo, Antonio

Casona, Alejandro
Cela, Camilo José
Celaya, Gabriel
Cernuda, Luis
Chacel, Rosa
Champourcin, Ernestina de
Conde, Alfredo
Conde (Abellán), Carmen
Cunqueiro, Álvaro
Delibes, Miguel
Echegaray, José
Espriu, Salvador
Fernández Cubas, Cristina
Foix, J(osep) V(icenç)
García Lorca, Federico
Gironella, José María
Gomez de la Serna, Ramón
Goytisolo, Juan
Grau (Delgado), Jacinto
Guillén, Jorge
Hernández, Miguel
Jarnés, Benjamín
Jiménez, Juan Ramón
Laforet, Carmen
Machado, Antonio
Martín Gaite, Carmen
Martínez Sierra, Gregorio and María
Martín-Santos, Luis
Matute, Ana María
Miró, Gabriel
Oliveri I Cabrer, Maria-Antònia
Ortega y Gasset, José
Otero, Blas de
Palacio Valdés, Armando
Pardo Bazan, Emilia
Pedrolo, Manuel de
Pérez de Ayala, Ramón
Pérez Galdós, Benito
Riba, Carles
Riera, Carme
Rodoreda, Mercè
Salinas, Pedro
Sánchez Ferlosio, Rafael
Sastre, Alfonso
Sender, Ramón J.
Torrente Ballester, Gonzalo
Unamuno, Miguel de
Valle-Inclán, Ramón del
Zambrano, María
Zardoya, Concha

SURINAMESE
Roemer, Astrid H.

SWEDISH
Ahlin, Lars
Åkesson, Sonja
Arnér, Sivar
Aspenström, Werner
Aurell, Tage

Bengtsson, Frans G(unnar)
Bergman, Hjalmar
Bichsel, Peter
Boye, Karin
Dagerman, Stig
Delblanc, Sven
Ekelöf, Gunnar
Ekelund, Vilhelm
Ekman, Kerstin
Enquist, Per Olov
Ferlin, Nils
Forssell, Lars
Gullberg, Hjalmar
Gustafsson, Lars
Gyllensten, Lars
Jersild, P(er) C(hristian)
Johnson, Eyvind
Lagerkvist, Pär
Lidman, Sara
Lindegren, Erik
Lindgren, Torgny
Lo-Johansson, Ivar
Lundkvist, Artur
Martinson, Harry
Moberg, Vilhelm
Norén, Lars
Söderberg, Hjalmar
Strindberg, August
Sundman, Per Olof
Tranströmer, Tomas
Trotzig, Birgitta
Wästberg, Per

SWISS
Blatter, Silvio
Böni, Franz
Cendrars, Blaise
Dürrenmatt, Friedrich
Frisch, Max
Gomringer, Eugen
Jung, Carl Gustav
Leutenegger, Gertrud
Meyer, E. Y.
Muschg, Adolf
Ramuz, Charles-Ferdinand
Spitteler, Carl
Walser, Robert
Walter, Otto F.

SYRIAN
Adūnīs
al-Māghūt, Muhammad
Mīna, Hannā
Qabbānī, Nizār
Tāmir, Zakariyyā
al-'Ujaylī, 'Abd al-Salām
Wannūs, Sa'dallāh

TAIWANESE
Huang Chun-ming

TAJIK
Aini, Sadriddin
Muhammadiev, Fazluddin Aminovich
Qanoat, Mu'min
Sobir, Bozor
Ulughzoda, Sotim

TANZANIAN
Gurnah, Abdulrazak
Robert, Shaaban

THAI
Chart Korbjitti
Dokmai Sot
Kukrit Pramoj
Lao Khamhom
Siburapha
Sidaoru̇ang

TRINIDADIAN
Anthony, Michael
Hodge, Merle
Jones, Marion Patrick
Khan, Ismith
Lovelace, Earl
Naipaul, Shiva
Naipaul, V(idiadhar) S(urajprasad)
Selvon, Samuel
Walcott, Derek

TUNISIAN
Mas'adī, Mahmūd
Memmi, Albert
al-Shābbī, Abū al-Qāsim

TURKISH
Adivar, Halide Edib
Ağaoğlu, Adalet
Alpar, Murat
Anday, Melih Cevdet
Cansever, Edip
Cumali, Necati
Dağlarca, Fazıl Hüsnü
Dilmen, Gűngőr
Hikmet, Nazım
İlhan, Attilâ
Karaosmanoğlu, Yakup Kadri
Kemal, Yaşar
Necatigil, Behçet
Nesin, Aziz

UGANDAN
Nazareth, Peter
p'Bitek, Okot

UKRAINIAN
Drach, Ivan
Franko, Ivan
Honchar, Oles
Kostenko, Lina

Kotsyubynsky, Mykhaylo
Rudenko, Mykola
Rylsky, Maxym
Shevchuk, Valery
Stefanyk, Vasyl
Stus, Vasyl
Ukrayinka, Lesya
Vynnychenko, Volodymyr

URUGUAYAN
Amorim, Enrique
Benedetti, Mario
Butazzoni, Fernando
Hernández, Felisberto
Herrera y Reissig, Julio
Onetti, Juan Carlos
Peri Rossi, Cristina
Porzecanski, Teresa
Quiroga, Horacio
Reyles, Carlos
Rodó, José Enrique
Sánchez, Florencio

UZBEK
Aybek
Behbudiy, Mahmud Khoja
Qadiriy, Abdullah

VENEZUELAN
Gallegos, Rómulo
Uslar Pietri, Arturo

VIETNAMESE
Khái-Hưng
Nguyễn Công Hoan
Nguyễn Tuân
Nhất-Linh
Vũ Hoàng Chương

WELSH
Davies, W(illiam) H(enry)
Hughes, Richard
Jones, David (Michael)
Lewis, Saunders

Thomas, Dylan
Thomas, R(onald) S(tuart)
Watkins, Vernon

YIDDISH
Asch, Sholem
Bergelson, Dovid
Glatstein, Jacob
Grade, Chaim
Halpern, Moyshe Leyb
Manger, Itsik
Der Nister
Rabon, Israel
Shteynbarg, Eliezer
Singer, I(srael) J(oshua)
Sutskever, Avrom

YUGOSLAV
Andrić, Ivo
Bećković, Matija
Begović, Milan
Bulatović, Miodrag
Cankar, Ivan
Ćopić, Branko
Ćosić, Dobrica
Crnjanski, Miloš
Davičo, Oskar
Desnica, Vladan
Dučić, Jovan
Krleža, Miroslav
Lalić, Mihailo
Maksimović, Desanka
Nušić, Branislav
Pavlović, Miodrag
Popa, Vasko
Selimović, Meša
Ujević, Tin (Augustin)
Vojnović, Ivo
Župančič, Oton

ZIMBABWEAN
Chinodya, Shimmer
Marechera, Dambudzo
Mungoshi, Charles

GENERAL INDEX